June 4–8, 2011
San Jose, California, USA

Association for
Computing Machinery

Advancing Computing as a Science & Profession

PLDI'11

Proceedings of the 2011 ACM Conference on

Programming Language Design and Implementation

Sponsored by:

ACM SIGPLAN

Supported by:

National Science Foundation, Google, Microsoft Research, Intel, HP, IBM, Sun/Oracle, and Qualcomm

Association for
Computing Machinery

Advancing Computing as a Science & Profession

The Association for Computing Machinery
2 Penn Plaza, Suite 701
New York, New York 10121-0701

ISBN: 978-1-4503-0663-8

Additional copies may be ordered prepaid from:

ACM Order Department
PO Box 30777
New York, NY 10087-0777, USA

Phone: 1-800-342-6626 (USA and Canada)
+1-212-626-0500 (Global)
Fax: +1-212-944-1318
E-mail: acmhelp@acm.org
Hours of Operation: 8:30 am – 4:30 pm ET

ACM Order Number: 548110

Printed in the USA

Message from the General Chair and Program Chair

Together with the program committee, it is our great pleasure to welcome you to the 32nd *ACM SIGPLAN Conference on Programming Language Design and Implementation – PLDI'11*. This year's conference continues its tradition of being the premier forum for the exchange of ideas on programming languages and their implementations.

This year's conference exhibits the growth of importance of programming language research and practice. We received a record 236 submissions, almost 15% more than last year's previous record. The program committee accepted a record 55 papers, and as a consequence, PLDI'11 will for the first-time have a dual-track program.

These 55 papers were selected after a careful evaluation which involved almost 1000 reviews. Most of these reviews (62%) came from the 31 member Program Committee (PC). The fifty-five member External Review Committee (ERC) contributed with most of the other evaluations. One hundred twelve other reviewers also participated in the evaluation process helping with their expertise in some highly specialized areas. Papers submitted by Program Committee members were evaluated by the External Review Committee and the decision on these papers was made by consensus. The acceptance rate for PC papers was the same as the overall acceptance rate.

Authors were given the opportunity to comment on the first evaluations during the January 15-19 rebuttal period. The identity of the authors was withheld from the reviewers until the evaluations from the PC and ERC were submitted. Unveiling the identity of the authors facilitated the rebuttal process and gave reviewers access to information on impact and research history that would not have been available otherwise. The Program Committee met on January 29 and 30 in Chicago and made the final decision on each of the submissions except for those authored by PC members. Thanks to the introduction of the dual track schedule which removed constraints in the number of slots, acceptance was based exclusively on the quality of the submissions. No paper was rejected due to lack of space.

In addition to the papers, PLDI'11 also includes several other key program components. New this year is a panel on education organized by Laurie Hendren, in light of the broadening of computer science curricula and the simultaneous broadening reach of programming language research. We also continue two traditions of recent PLDI conferences, a Fun and Interesting Thoughts session for discussing new ideas, and an ACM Student Research Competition. Prior to the conference, a program of five workshops and six tutorials informed our attendees on diverse topics ranging from parallel computing, memory systems, program analysis, security, experimental evaluation and adaptive self tuning.

Putting together *PLDI 2011* was a team effort. First of all, we would like to thank the authors, and workshop and tutorial organizers for providing the content of the program. We would like to express our gratitude to the tireless efforts of the program committee, external review committee and external reviewers for their direct contributions to this program. We owe a debt of gratitude to he chairs of our special sessions, Student Research Competition chair Armando Solar-Lezama, and Fun and Interesting Thoughts co-chairs Keshav Pingali and Milind Kulkarni. We are enormously grateful to Publicity and Website Chair Matt Might for his significant efforts and the expanded use of social networking technology for conveying information to participants. Lastly, our sponsor the ACM, and our supporters the National Science Foundation, Microsoft Research, Google, Intel, HP

Labs, IBM, Oracle and Qualcomm have expanded PLDI's reach to students through supporting travel and the Student Research Competition, and our attendees through support of special events.

We hope that you will find this program interesting and thought-provoking and that the symposium will provide you with a valuable opportunity to share ideas with other researchers and practitioners from institutions around the world.

Mary Hall
PLDI'11 General Chair
University of Utah

David Padua
PLDI'11 Program Chair
University of Illinois at Urbana-Champaign

Table of Contents

Session 5b: Transforming and Editing by Example

Session Chair: Amer Diwan *(Google and University of Colorado)*

Session 6a: Security

Session Chair: Ben Livshits *(Microsoft Research)*

Session 6b: Concurrency Defects

Session Chair: Armando Solar-Lezama *(Massachusetts Institute of Technology)*

Session 7a: Singular Topics

Session Chair: Vikram Adve (*University of Illinois at Urbana-Champaign)*

Session 7b: Debugging II

Session Chair: Michael Burke *(Rice University)*

Session 8a: Program Parallelization

Session Chair: Thomas Gross *(ETH Zurich)*

PLDI 2011 Conference Organization

General Chair: Mary Hall, *University of Utah*

Program Chair: David Padua, *University of Illinois at Urbana-Champaign*

Student Research Competition Chair: Armando Solar-Lezama, *Massachusetts Institute of Technology*

Fun and Interesting Thoughts Session Co-Chairs: Keshav Pingali, *The University of Texas at Austin*
Milind Kulkarni, *Purdue University*

Web and Publicity Chair: Matt Might, *University of Utah*

Steering Committee Chair: Jack Davidson, *University of Virginia*

Steering Committee:
Alex Aiken, *Stanford University*
Jack Davidson, *University of Virginia*
Amer Diwan, *Google and University of Colorado*
Kathleen Fisher, *Tufts University*
Mary Hall, *University of Utah*
Michael Hind, *IBM Research*
Graham Hutton, *University of Nottingham*
Chandra Krintz, *University of California, Santa Barbara*
David Padua, *University of Illinois at Urbana-Champaign*
Philip Walder, *University of Edinburgh*
Ben Zorn, *Microsoft Research*

Program Committee:
Saman Amarasinghe, *Massachusetts Institute of Technology*
Andrew W. Appel, *Princeton University*
Michael Burke, *Rice University*
John Cavazos, *University of Delaware*
Albert Cohen, *INRIA*
Amer Diwan, *Google and University of Colorado*
Evelyn Duesterwald, *IBM Research*
Michael Franz, *University of California, Irvine*
David Gregg, *Trinity College Dublin*
Thomas Gross, *ETH Zurich*
Manuel Hermenegildo, *IMDEA Software Inst. and T.U. Madrid*
Suresh Jagannathan, *Purdue University*
Mahmut Kandemir, *Pennsylvania State University*
Ulrich Kremer, *Rutgers*
Viktor Kuncak, *EPFL*
James Larus, *Microsoft Research*
Ben Livshits, *Microsoft Research*
Kathryn S. McKinley, *The University of Texas at Austin*
Greg Morrisett, *Harvard University*

External Review Committee (continued):

Samuel Midkiff, *Purdue University*
Nick Mitchell, *IBM Research*
Anders Møller, *Aarhus University*
J. Eliot B. Moss, *University of Massachusetts, Amherst*
Hanspeter Mössenböck, *Johannes Kepler University Linz*
Alan Mycroft, *University of Cambridge*
Yunheung Paek, *Seoul National University*
Sanjay Rajopadhye, *Colorado State University*
Lakshminarayanan Renganarayana, *IBM Research*
Martin Rinard, *Massachusetts Institute of Technology*
Anne Rogers, *The University of Chicago*
Grigore Rosu, *University of Illinois at Urbana-Champaign*
Andrey Rybalchenko, *Technische Universität München*
P. Sadayappan, *The Ohio State University*
Michael L. Scott, *University of Rochester*
William Thies, *Microsoft Research, India*
Mahesh Viswanathan, *University of Illinois at Urbana-Champaign*
David S. Warren, *Stony Brook University*
Stephanie Weirich, *University of Pennsylvania*
Chengyong Wu, *Chinese Academy of Sciences*
Youfeng Wu, *Intel Labs*
Greta Yorsh, *IBM Research*

Student Research Competition Committee:

Shaz Qadeer, *Microsoft Research*
Vivek Sarkar, *Rice University*
Mary Lou Soffa, *University of Virginia*
Armando Solar-Lezama, *Massachusetts Institute of Technology*

Additional reviewers:

Christophe Alias
Jason Ansel
Matthew Arnold
Aurangzeb
Hansang Bae
Xiaoying Bai
Michael Bebenita
Lars Bergstrom
Frederic Boussinot
Edwin Brady
Magnus Carlsson
Manuel Carro
Corky Cartwright
Mason Chang
Philippe Charles
Tian Chen
Weiyu Chen
Adam Chlipala
Alain Darte
Joseph Devietti
Sophia Drossopoulou
Chucky Ellison
John Field
Stephen Fink
Robert France
Codruța Girlea
Michael Gordon
Alexey Gotsman
Jungwoo Ha
Sean Halle
William Harrison
Mohammed Amber Hassaan
Christian Häubl
Chris Hawblitzel
Ming-Yu Hung
Todd Jackson
Choonki Jang
Predrag Janicic
Vladimir Janjic
Dongyun Jin
Gangwon Jo
Barbara Jobstmann
Fahed Jubair
Hongjune Kim
Jungwon Kim
Etienne Kneuss
Christopher Krieger
Cesar Kunz
Okwan Kwon
Byeong Lee
Jun Lee
Yong-Fong Lee
Sangik Lee

Additional reviewers (continued):

Seyong Lee
Jack Liu
Pedro Lopez-Garcia
Brandon Lucia
David MacQueen
Geoffrey Mainland
Zoltan Majo
Mark Marron
Daniel Massey
Isabella Mastroeni
Nicholas Matsakis
Laurent Mauborgne
Mario Mendez-Lojo
Na Meng
Patrick O'Neil Meredith
Maged Michael
Jose F. Morales
Jorge Navas
Donald Nguyen
Yang Ni
Durica Nikolic
Pablo Nogueira
Marek Olszewski
Mathias Payer
Ruzica Piskac
Marco Pistoia
Antoniu Pop
Louis-Noel Pouchet
Michael Pradel
Herbert Prähofer
Susanne Cech Previtali
Dimitris Prountzos
Shaz Qadeer
Anand Raghunathan
Jonathan Regan-Kelley
Cesar Sanchez
Sangmin Seo
Traian Florin Şerbănuţă
Avraham Shinnar
Yannis Smaragdakis
Fausto Spoto
Andrei Ştefănescu
Philippe Suter
Gang Tan
Gabriel Tanase
Oliver Trachsel
Jean-Baptiste Tristan
Gregor Wagner
Cheng Wang
Shao-Chung Wang
Ben Wiedermann
Christian Wimmer
Ryan Wisnesky
Benjamin Wood
Guoqing Xu
Karen Zee
Qin Zhao
Ben Zorn

PLDI 2011 Sponsor & Supporters

Sponsor:

Supporters:

Commutative Set: A Language Extension for Implicit Parallel Programming

Prakash Prabhu Soumyadeep Ghosh Yun Zhang Nick P. Johnson David I. August

Princeton University
Princeton, NJ
{pprabhu, soumyade, yunzhang, npjohnso, august}@princeton.edu

Abstract

Sequential programming models express a total program order, of which a partial order must be respected. This inhibits parallelizing tools from extracting scalable performance. Programmer written semantic commutativity assertions provide a natural way of relaxing this partial order, thereby exposing parallelism implicitly in a program. Existing implicit parallel programming models based on semantic commutativity either require additional programming extensions, or have limited expressiveness. This paper presents a generalized semantic commutativity based programming extension, called Commutative Set (COMMSET), and associated compiler technology that enables multiple forms of parallelism. COMMSET expressions are syntactically succinct and enable the programmer to specify commutativity relations between groups of arbitrary structured code blocks. Using only this construct, serializing constraints that inhibit parallelization can be relaxed, independent of any particular parallelization strategy or concurrency control mechanism. COMMSET enables well performing parallelizations in cases where they were inapplicable or non-performing before. By extending eight sequential programs with only 8 annotations per program on average, COMMSET and the associated compiler technology produced a geomean speedup of 5.7x on eight cores compared to 1.5x for the best non-COMMSET parallelization.

Categories and Subject Descriptors D.1.3 [*Programming Techniques*]: Concurrent Programming—Parallel Programming; D.3.4 [*Programming Languages*]: Processors—Compilers, Optimization

General Terms Languages, Performance, Design, Experimentation

Keywords Implicit parallelism, semantic commutativity, programming model, automatic parallelization, static analysis

1. Introduction

The dominant parallel programming models for multicores today are explicit [8, 10, 33]. These models require programmers to expend enormous effort reasoning about complex thread interleavings, low-level concurrency control mechanisms, and parallel programming pitfalls such as races, deadlocks, and livelocks. Despite this effort, manual concurrency control and a fixed choice of parallelization strategy often result in parallel programs with poor performance portability. Consequently, parallel programs often have to be extensively modified when the underlying parallel substrates evolve, thus breaking abstraction boundaries between software and hardware.

Recent advances in automatic thread extraction [26, 30, 34] provide a promising alternative. They avoid pitfalls associated with explicit parallel programming models, but retain the ease of reasoning of a sequential programming model. However, sequential languages express a total order, of which a partial order of program execution must be respected by parallelizing tools. This prohibits some execution orders that are often permitted by high-level algorithm specifications. As a result, automatic parallelizing tools, overly constrained by the need to respect the sequential semantics of programs written in languages like C/C++, are unable to extract scalable performance.

Implicit parallel programming models (IPP) [4, 13, 15, 31] offer the best of both approaches. In such models, programmers implicitly expose parallelism inherent in their program without the explicit use of low-level parallelization constructs. An interesting subclass of models within this space includes those that are based on top of sequential programming models [15]. In such models, programmer insights about high-level semantic properties of the program are expressed via the use of extensions to the sequential model. These language extensions are then exploited by transformation tools to automatically synthesize a correct parallel program. This approach not only frees the programmer from the burden of having to worry about the low-level details related to parallelization, but also promotes retargetability of such programs when presented with newer parallel substrates.

Recent work has shown the importance of programmer specified semantic commutativity assertions in exposing parallelism implicitly in code [5, 7, 18, 27, 30]. The programmer relaxes the order of execution of certain functions that read and modify mutable state, by specifying that they legally *commute* with each other, despite violating existing partial orders. Parallelization tools exploit this relaxation to extract performance by permitting behaviors prohibited under a sequential programming model. However, existing solutions based on semantic commutativity either have limited expressiveness or require programmers to use additional parallelism constructs. This paper proposes an implicit parallel programming model based on semantic commutativity, called Commutative Set (COMMSET), that generalizes existing semantic commutativity

PLDI'11, June 4–8, 2011, San Jose, California, USA.

IPP System	Concept					Specific Parallel Implementation					
	Expressiveness of Commutativity Specification				Requires Additional Extensions	Parallelism Forms Supported			Concurrency Control Mechanism	Parallelization Driver	Optimistic or Speculative Parallelism[1]
	Predication		Commuting Blocks	Group Commutativity		Task[1]	Pipelined	Data			
	Interface	Client									
Jade [27]	×	×	×	×	Yes	✓	✓	×	Automatic	Runtime	×
Galois [18]	✓	×	×	×	Yes	×	×	✓	Manual	Runtime	✓
DPJ [5]	×	×	×	×	Yes	✓	×	✓	Manual	Programmer	×
Paralax [30]	×	×	×	×	No	×	✓	×	Automatic	Compiler	×
VELOCITY [7]	×	×	×	×	No	×	✓	×	Automatic	Compiler	✓
COMMSET	✓	✓	✓	✓	No	×	✓	✓	Automatic	Compiler	×

Table 1: Comparison between COMMSET and other parallel models based on semantic commutativity

constructs and enables multiple forms of parallelism from the same specification.

Table 1 compares COMMSET with existing parallel programming models based on semantic commutativity. The main advantages of COMMSET over existing approaches are: (a) COMMSET's commutativity construct is more general than others. Prior approaches allow commutativity assertions only on interface declarations. However, commutativity can be a property of client code as well as code behind a library interface. COMMSET allows the commutativity assertions between arbitrary structured code blocks in client code as well as on interfaces, much like the `synchronized` keyword in Java. It also allows commutativity to be predicated on variables in a client's program state, rather than just function arguments as in earlier approaches. (b) COMMSET specifications between a group of functions are syntactically succinct, having linear specification complexity rather than quadratic as required by existing approaches. (c) COMMSET presents an implicit parallel programming solution that enables both pipeline and data parallelism without requiring any additional parallelism constructs. Existing approaches use parallelism constructs that tightly couple parallelization strategy with concrete program semantics, in contravention of the principle of "separation of concerns." In contrast, using only COMMSET primitives in our model, parallelism can be implicitly specified at a semantic level and is independent of a specific form or concurrency control mechanism.

The contributions of this work are:

1. The design, syntax, and semantics of COMMSET, a novel programming extension that generalizes, in a syntactically succinct form, various existing notions of semantic commutativity.
2. An end-to-end implementation of COMMSET within a parallelizing compiler that includes the front-end, static analysis to enhance the program dependence graph with commutativity properties, passes to enable data and pipeline parallelizations, and automatic concurrency control.
3. A demonstration of COMMSET's applicability in expressing implicit parallelism by extending eight real world sequential programs with commutativity assertions, and an evaluation of the performance on real hardware.

The features of COMMSET are first motivated by a running example. A description of its syntax and semantics follows. An implementation of COMMSET within a parallelizing compiler is explained step by step, followed by an evaluation and a discussion of related work.

2. Motivating Example

Figure 1 shows a code snippet from a sequential implementation of md5sum (plus highlighted `pragma` directives introduced for COMMSET that are discussed later). The main loop iterates through a set of input files, computing and printing a message digest for each file. Each iteration opens a file using a call to `fopen`, then calls the `mdfile` function which, in turn, reads the file's contents via calls to `fread` and then computes the digest. The main loop prints the digest to the console and closes the file by calling `fclose` on the file pointer. Although it is clear that digests of individual files can be safely computed out of order, a parallelizing tool cannot infer this automatically without knowing the client specific semantics of I/O calls due to its externally visible side effects. However, the loop can be parallelized if the commuting behaviors of `fopen`, `fread`, `fclose`, and `print_digest` on *distinct* files are conveyed to the parallelizing tool.

One way to specify commuting behavior is at the interface declarations of file operations. Galois [18] extracts optimistic parallelism by exploiting semantic commutativity assertions specified between pairs of library methods at their interface declarations. These assertions can optionally be predicated on their arguments. To indicate the commuting behaviors of the calls on distinct files, one would ideally like to predicate commutativity on the filename. Since only `fopen` takes in the filename as an argument, this is not possible. Another approach is to predicate commutativity on the file pointer `fp` that is returned by `fopen`. Apart from the fact that expensive runtime checks are required to validate the assertions *before* executing the I/O calls (which are now on the critical path), this approach may prevent certain valid commuting orders due to recycling of file pointers. Operations on two distinct files at different points in time that happen to use the same file pointer value are now not allowed to commute. This solution is also not valid for all clients. Consider the following sequence of calls by a client that writes to a file (`fp1`) and subsequently reads from it (`fp2`) in the next iteration: `fwrite(fp1)`, `fclose(fp1)`, `fopen(fp2)`, `fread(fp2)`. Here, even though `fp1` and `fp2` may have different runtime values, they still may be pointing to the same file. Commuting `fopen(fp2)`, `fread(fp2)` with `fclose(fp1)` may cause a read from the file before the write file stream has been completed. Approaches that annotate data (file pointer `fp` in this case) to implicitly assert commutativity between all pairs of operations on that file pointer [27], run into the same problem.

Allowing predication on the client's program state can solve the above problem for md5sum. Since the input files naturally map to different values of the induction variable, predicating commutativity on the induction variable (in the client) solves the problems associated with interface based predication. First, no legal commuting behavior is prohibited since induction variables are definitely different on each iteration. Second, runtime checks for commutativity assertions are avoided since the compiler can use static analysis to symbolically interpret predicates that are functions of the induction variable to prove commutativity on separate iterations.

In order to continue using commutativity specifications on function declarations while still predicating on variables in client state, programmers either have to change existing interfaces or create new wrapper functions to take in those variables as arguments. Changing the interface breaks modularity since other clients which do not want commutative semantics are now forced to pass in ad-

[1] The commutativity specifications languages of Galois, Paralax, VELOCITY and COMMSET are conceptually amenable to task and speculative parallelism

Main Loop

```
#pragma CommSetDecl(FSET, Group)                                    1
#pragma CommSetDecl(SSET, Self)                                     2
#pragma CommSetPredicate(FSET, (i1), (i2), (i1 != i2))              3
#pragma CommSetPredicate(SSET, (i1), (i2), (i1 != i2))              4

for (i=0 ; i < argc; ++i) { // Main Loop                            A
  FILE *fp; unsigned char digest[16];

  #pragma CommSet(SELF, FSET(i))                                    5
  {
    fp = fopen(argv[i], FOPRBIN);
  }                                                                 B

  #pragma CommSetNamedArgAdd(READB(SSET(i), FSET(i)))               6
  mdfile(fp, digest);

  #pragma CommSet(SELF, FSET(i))                                    7
  {
    print_digest(digest);
  }                                                                 H
  #pragma CommSet(SELF, FSET(i))                                    8
  {
    fclose(fp);
  }                                                                 I
}
```

Message Digest Computation Function

```
#pragma CommSetNamedArg(READB)                                      9
int mdfile(FILE *fp, unsigned char *digest);

int mdfile(FILE *fp, unsigned char *digest)
{
  unsigned char buf[1024]; MD5_CTX ctx; int n;
  MD5Init(&ctx);                                                    C
  do {
    #pragma CommSetNamedBlock(READB)                                10
    {
      n = fread(buf, 1, sizeof(buf), fp);
    }                                                               D
    if (n == 0) break;
    MD5Update(&ctx, buf, n);                                        E
  } while (1);                                                      F

  MD5Final(digest, &ctx);
  return 0;                                                         G
}
```

Figure 1: Sequential version of md5sum extended with CommSet

ditional dummy arguments to prevent commuting behaviors. Creating wrapper functions involves additional programmer effort, especially while replicating functions along entire call paths. In the running example, the `mdfile` interface has to be changed to take in the induction variable as an argument, to allow for predicated commutativity of `fread` calls with other file operations (`fopen` and `fclose`) in the main loop.

The additional programmer effort in creating wrappers can be avoided by allowing structured code blocks enclosing the call sites to commute with each other. This is easily achieved in md5sum by enclosing the call sites of `fopen`, `fread`, `print_digest`, and `fclose` within anonymous commutative code blocks. Commutativity between multiple anonymous code blocks can be specified easily by adding the code blocks to a named set, at the beginning of their lexical scope. Grouping commutative code blocks or functions into a set, as presented here, has linear specification complexity. In contrast, existing approaches [5, 18] require specifying commutativity between pairs of functions individually leading to quadratic specification complexity. The modularity problem (mentioned above) can be solved by allowing optionally commuting code blocks and exporting the option at the interface, without changing interface arguments. Clients can then enable the commutativity of the code blocks if it is in line with their intended semantics, otherwise default sequential behavior is preserved. In the case of md5sum, the `fread` call can be made a part of an optionally commuting block. The option is exported at the interface declaration of `mdfile` and is enabled by the main loop, while other clients that require sequential semantics can ignore the option.

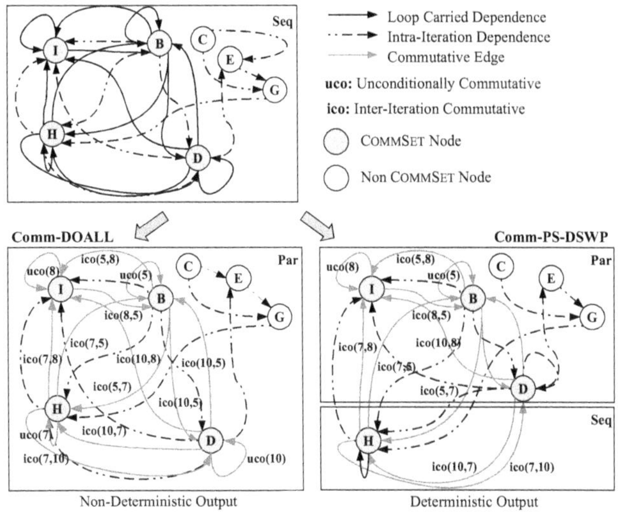

Figure 2: PDG for md5sum with CommSet extensions

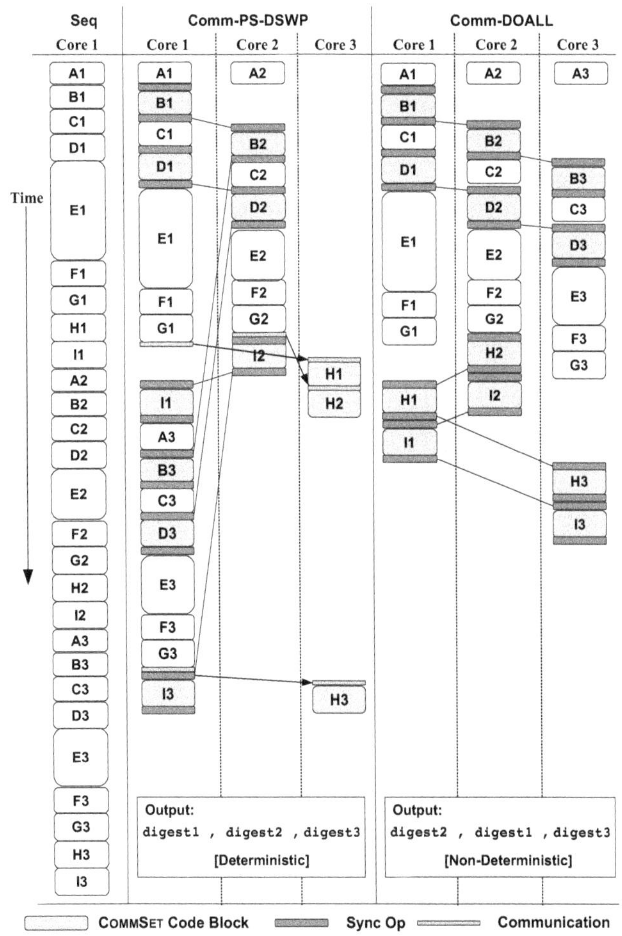

Figure 3: Timeline for md5sum Parallelizations

A commuting code block gives the programmer the flexibility to choose the extent to which partial orders can be relaxed in a program. This, in turn, determines the amount of freedom a parallelizing tool has, to extract parallelism. For instance, enclosing `fread` calls inside `mdfile` within a commuting block gives more freedom to a parallelizing tool to extract performance, as opposed to the outer call to `mdfile`. Depending on the intended semantics, the programmer can choose the right granularity for the commuting blocks which a parallelizing system should automatically guarantee to be atomic. Commuting blocks allow for a declarative specification of concurrency which a parallelizing tool can exploit to automatically select the concurrency mechanism that performs best for a given application. Automatic concurrency control has the advantage of not requiring invasive changes to application code when newer mechanisms become available on a particular hardware substrate.

Parallelizing tools should be able to leverage the partial orders specified via commutativity assertions without requiring the programmer to specify parallelization strategies. Existing runtime approaches require the use of additional programming extensions that couple parallelization strategies to program semantics. Galois [18] requires the use of set iterators that constrain parallelization to data parallelism. Jade [27] requires the use of task parallel constructs. DPJ [5] uses explicitly parallel constructs for task and data parallelism. COMMSET does not require such additional extensions. For instance, in md5sum, a programmer requiring deterministic output for the digests, should be able to express the intended semantics without being concerned about parallelization. The implementation should be able to automatically change to the best parallelization strategy given the new semantics. Returning to md5sum, specifying that `print_digest` commutes with the other I/O operations, but not with itself constrains output to be deterministic. Given the new semantics, the compiler automatically switches from a better performing data parallel execution of the loop to a slightly less performing (in this case) pipelined execution. In the data parallel execution, each iteration of the loop executes in parallel with other iterations. In a pipeline execution, an iteration is split into stages, with the message digests computed in parallel in earlier stages of the pipeline being communicated to a sequential stage that prints the digest in order to the console.

Parallelization within the compiler is based on the Program Dependence Graph (PDG) structure [12]. Figure 2 shows the simplified PDG for sequential md5sum. Each labeled code block is represented by a node in the PDG and a directed edge from a node n_1 to n_2 indicates that n_2 is dependent on n_1. Parallelizing transforms (e.g. DOALL [16] and PS-DSWP [26]) partition the PDG and schedule nodes onto different threads, with dependences spanning threads automatically respected by insertion of communication and/or synchronization operations. With the original PDG, DOALL and PS-DSWP cannot be directly applied due to a cycle with loop carried dependences: $B \rightarrow D \rightarrow H \rightarrow I \rightarrow B$ and self loops around each node in the cycle. The COMMSET extensions help the compiler to relax these parallelism-inhibiting dependences, thereby enabling wider application of existing parallelizing transforms.

Figure 3 shows three schedules with different performance characteristics for md5sum execution. The first corresponds to sequential execution and the other two parallel schedules are enabled by COMMSET. Each of these schedules correspond to three different semantics specified by the programmer. The sequential execution corresponds to the in-order execution of all I/O operations, as implied by the unannotated program. The PS-DSWP schedule corresponds to parallel computation of message digests overlapped with the sequential in-order execution of `print_digest` calls. Finally, the DOALL schedule corresponds to out-of-order execution of digest computation as well `print_digests`. Every COMMSET block in both the DOALL and PS-DSWP schedules is synchronized by the use of locks (provided by libc), while PS-DSWP has additional communication operations. The DOALL schedule achieves a speedup of 7.6x on eight threads over sequential execution while PS-DSWP schedule gives a speedup of 5.8x. The PS-DSWP schedule is the result of one less COMMSET annotation than the DOALL schedule. The timeline in Figure 3 illustrates the impact of the semantic choices a programmer makes on the freedom provided to a parallelizing tool to enable well performing parallelizations. In essence, the COMMSET model allows a programmer to concentrate on high-level program semantics while leaving the task of determining the best parallelization strategy and synchronization mechanism to the compiler. In doing so, it opens up an parallel performance optimization space which can be systematically explored by automatic tools.

3. Syntax and Semantics

This section describes the semantics of various COMMSET features and the syntax of the COMMSET primitives.

3.1 CommSet Semantics

Self and Group Commutative Sets. The simplest form of semantic commutativity is a function commuting with itself. A *Self* COMMSET is defined as a singleton set with a code block that is self-commutative. An instantiation of this COMMSET allows for reordering dynamic invocation sequences of the code block. A straightforward extension of self-commutativity that allows commutativity between pairs of functions has quadratic specification complexity. Grouping a set of commuting functions under a name can reduce the specification burden. However, it needs to account for the case when a function commutes with other functions, but not with itself. For instance, the `insert()` method in a STL `vector` implementation does not commute with itself, but commutes with `search()` on different arguments. A *Group* COMMSET is a set of code blocks where pairs of blocks commute with each other, but each block does not commute with itself. These two concepts together achieve the goal of completeness and conciseness of commutativity specification.

Domain of Concurrency. A COMMSET aggregates a set of code blocks that read and modify shared program state. The members are executed concurrently in a larger parallelization scope, with atomicity of each member of the COMMSET guaranteed by automatic insertion of appropriate synchronization primitives. In this sense, COMMSET plays the role of a "concurrency domain," with updates to the shared mutable state being done in arbitrary order. However, the execution orders of members of a COMMSET with respect to the rest of code (sequential or other COMMSETs) are determined by flow dependences present in sequential code.

Non-transitivity and Multiple Memberships. Semantic commutativity is intransitive. Given three functions `f`, `g`, and `h` where two pairs (`f`, `g`), (`f`, `h`) semantically commute, the commuting behavior of (`g`, `h`) cannot be automatically inferred without knowing the semantics of state shared exclusively between `g` and `h`. Allowing code blocks to be members of multiple COMMSETs enables expression of either behavior. Programmers may create a single COMMSET with three members or create two COMMSETs with two members each, depending on the intended semantics. Two code blocks commute if they are both members of *at least* one COMMSET .

Commutative Blocks and Context Sensitivity. In many programs that access generic libraries, commutativity depends on the client code's context. The COMMSET construct is flexible enough to allow for commutativity assertions at either interface level or in client code. It also allows arbitrary structured code blocks to commute with other COMMSET members, which can either be functions or structured code blocks themselves. Functions belonging to a module can export optional commuting behaviors of code blocks in their body by using named block arguments at their interface, without requiring any code refactoring. The client code can choose to enable the commuting behavior of the named code blocks at its call site, based on its context. For instance, the `mdfile` function in Figure 1 that has a code block containing calls to `fread` may expose the commuting behavior of this block at its interface via the use of a named block argument *READB*. A client which does not care about the order of `fread` calls can add *READB* to a COMMSET optionally at its call site, while clients requiring sequential order can ignore the named block argument. Optional COMMSET specifications do not require any changes to the existing interface arguments or its implementation.

Predicated Commutative Set. The COMMSET primitive can be predicated on either interface arguments or on variables in a client's program state. A predicate is a C expression associated with the COMMSET and evaluates to a Boolean value when given arguments corresponding to any two members of the COMMSET . The predicated expression is expected to be pure, i.e. it should return the same value when invoked with the same arguments. A pure predicate expression always gives a deterministic answer for deciding commutativity relations between two functions. The two members commute if the predicate evaluates to true when its arguments are bound to values of actual arguments supplied at the point where the members are invoked in sequential code.

Orthogonality to Parallelism Form. Semantic commutativity relations expressed using COMMSET are independent of the specific form of parallelism (data/pipeline/task) that are exploited by the associated compiler technology. Once COMMSET annotations are added to sections of a sequential program, the same program is amenable to different styles of parallelization. In other words, a single COMMSET application can express commutativity relations between (static) lexical blocks of code and dynamic instances of a single code block. The former implicitly enables pipeline parallelism while the latter enables data and pipeline parallelism.

Well-defined CommSet members. The structure of COMMSET members has to obey certain conditions to ensure well-defined semantics in a parallel setting, especially when used in C/C++ programs that allow for various unstructured and non-local control flows. The conditions for ensuring well-defined commutative semantics between members of a COMMSET are: (a) The control flow constructs within each code block member should be local or structured, i.e. the block does not include operations like `longjmp`, `setjmp`, etc. Statements like `break` and `continue` should have their respective parent structures within the commutative block. (b) There should not be a transitive call from one code block to another in the same COMMSET . Removing such call paths between COMMSET members not only avoids the ambiguity in commutativity relation defined between a caller and a callee, but also simplifies reasoning about deadlock freedom in the parallelized code. Both these conditions are checked by the compiler.

Well-formedness of CommSets. The concept of well-definedness can be extended from code blocks in a single COMMSET to multiple COMMSETs by defining a COMMSET graph as follows: A COMMSET *graph* is defined as a graph where there is a unique node for each COMMSET in the program, and there exists an edge from a node S_1 to another node S_2, if there is a transitive call in the program from a member in COMMSET S_1 to a member in COMMSET S_2. A set of COMMSETs is defined to be *well-formed* if each COMMSET has well-defined members and there is no cycle in the COMMSET graph. Our parallelization system guarantees deadlock freedom in the parallelized program if the only form of parallelism in the input program is implicit and is expressed through a well-formed set of COMMSETs. This guarantee holds when either

CommSet Global Declarations	`#pragma` **`CommSetDecl`**`(CSet,` **`SELF`**|**`Group`**`)`
	
	`#pragma` **`CommSetPredicate`**`(CSet,`
	`(x_1, ..., x_n), (y_1, ..., y_n),`
	`Pred(x_1, ..., x_n, y_1, ..., y_n))`
	
	`#pragma` **`CommSetNoSync`**`(CSet)`

CommSet Instance Declarations	`#pragma` **`CommSet`**`(CSets)`
	|**`CommSetNamedArg`**`(Blocks)`
	`type_return function-name(t_1 x_1, ..., t_n x_n);`
	
	`#pragma` **`CommSet`**`(CSets)`
	|**`CommSetNamedBlock`**`(B_name)`
	`{`
	`Structured code region`
	`}`
	
	`#pragma` **`CommSetNamedArgAdd`**`(BPairs)`
	`retval = function-name(x_1, ...,x_n);`

CommSet List	`CSets ::= PredCSet` | `PredCSet, CSets`
	`PredCSet ::= CSet` | `CSet(CVars)`
	`CVars ::= C_var` | `C_var, Cvars`
	`CSet ::=` **`SELF`** | `Set_id`
	`BPairs ::= B_id(CSets)` |`B_id(CSets), BPairs`
	`Blocks ::= B_id` | `B_id, Blocks`

Figure 4: COMMSET Syntax

pipeline or data parallelism is extracted and for both pessimistic and optimistic synchronization mechanisms (see Section 4.6).

3.2 CommSet Syntax

The COMMSET extensions are expressed using `pragma` directives in the sequential program. `pragma` directives were chosen because a program with well-defined sequential semantics is obtained when they are elided. Programs with COMMSET annotations can also be compiled without any change by a standard C/C++ compiler that does not understand COMMSET semantics.

Global Declarations. The name of a COMMSET is indicative of its type. By default, the SELF keyword refers to a Self COMMSET, while COMMSETs with other names are Group COMMSETs. To allow for predication of Self COMMSETs, explicit type declaration can be used. The COMMSETDECL primitive allows for declaration of COMMSETs with arbitrary names at global scope. The COMMSETPREDICATE primitive is used to associate a predicate with a COMMSET and is declared at global scope. The primitive takes as arguments: (a) the name of the COMMSET that is predicated, (b) a pair of parameter lists, and (c) a C expression that represents the predicate. Each parameter list represents the subset of program state that decides the commuting behavior of a pair of COMMSET members, when they are executed in two different parallel execution contexts. The parameters in the lists are bound to either a commutative function's arguments, or to variables in the client's program state that are live at the beginning of a structured commutative code block. The C expression computes a Boolean value using the variables in the parameter list and returns true if a pair of COMMSET members commute when invoked with the appropriate arguments. By default, COMMSET members are automatically synchronized when their source code is available to the parallelizing compiler. A programmer can optionally specify that a COMMSET does not need compiler inserted synchronization using COMMSETNOSYNC. The primitive is applied to COMMSETs whose members belong to a thread-safe library which has been separately compiled and whose source is unavailable.

Instance Declarations and CommSet List. A code block can be declared a member of a list of COMMSETs by using the COMMSET directive. Such instance declarations can be applied either at a function interface, or at any point in a loop or a function for adding an arbitrary structured code block (a compound statement in C/C++) to a COMMSET. Both compound statements and functions are treated in the same way as far as reasoning about commutativity is concerned. In the case of predicated COMMSETs in the COMMSET list, the actual arguments for the COMMSETPREDICATE are supplied at the instance declaration. For function members of a COMMSET, the actual arguments are a list of parameter declarations, while for compound statements, the actual arguments are a set of variables with primitive type that have a well-defined value at the beginning of the compound statement. Optionally commuting compound statements can be given a name by enclosing the statements within COMMSETNAMEDBLOCK directive. A function containing such a named block can expose the commuting option to client code using COMMSETNAMEDARG at its interface declaration. The client code that invokes the function can enable the commuting behavior of the named block by adding it to a COMMSET using the COMMSETNAMEDARGADD directive at its call site.

3.3 Example

Figure 1 shows the implicitly parallel program obtained by extending md5sum with COMMSET primitives. The code blocks *B*, *H*, *I* enclosing the file operations are added to a *Group* COMMSET *FSET* using annotations *5*, *7*, and *8*. Each code block is also added to its own *Self* COMMSET. *FSET* is predicated on the loop induction variable's value, using a COMMSETPREDICATE expression (*3*) to indicate that each of the file operations commute with each other on separate iterations. The block containing `fread` call is named *READB* (*10*) and exported by `mdfile` using the COMMSETNAMEDARG directive at its interface (*9*). The client code adds the named block to its own *Self* set (declared as *SSET* in *2*) using the COMMSETNAMEDARGADD directive at *6*. *SSET* is predicated on the outer loop induction variable to prevent commuting across inner loop invocations (*4*). A deterministic output can be obtained by omitting *SELF* from annotation *7*.

4. Commutative Set Implementation

We built an end-to-end implementation of COMMSET within a parallelizing compiler. The compiler is an extension of the clang/LLVM framework [19]. Figure 5 shows the parallelization workflow. The parallelization focuses on hot loops in the program identified via runtime profiling. The PDG for the hottest loop is constructed over the LLVM IR, with each node representing an instruction in the IR. The memory flow dependences in the PDG that inhibit parallelization are displayed at source level to the programmer, who inserts COMMSET primitives and presents the program back to the compiler. The subsequent compiler passes analyze and transform this program to generate different versions of parallelized code.

4.1 Frontend

The COMMSET parser in the frontend parses and checks the syntax of all COMMSET directives, and synthesizes a C function for every COMMSETPREDICATE. The predicate function computes the value of the C expression specified in the directive. The argument types for the function are automatically inferred by binding the parameters in COMMSETPREDICATE to the COMMSET instances. Type mismatch errors between arguments of different COMMSET instances are also detected. Commutative blocks are checked for enclosing non-local control flow by a top-down traversal of the abstract syntax tree (AST) starting at the node corresponding to the particular commutative block. Finally, global COMMSET meta-data is annotated at the module level, while COMMSET instance data is annotated on individual compound statement or function AST nodes. This meta-data is automatically conveyed to the backend during the lowering phase.

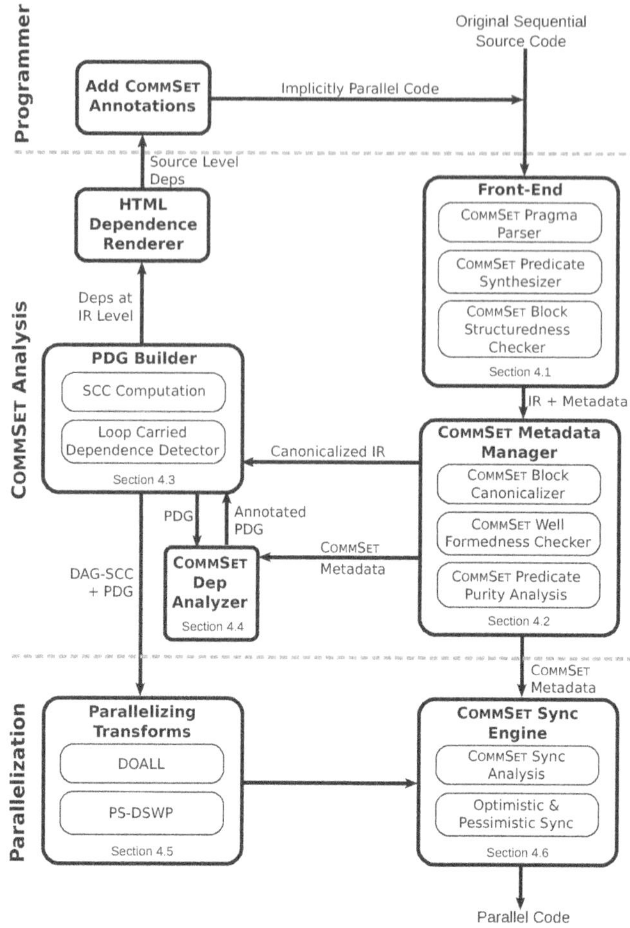

Figure 5: COMMSET Parallelization Workflow

4.2 CommSet Metadata Manager

In the backend, the COMMSET meta-data is an abstraction over the low-level IR constructs, instead of the AST nodes. The COMMSET Metadata Manager processes and maintains a meta-data store for all COMMSET instances and declarations, and answers queries posed by subsequent compiler passes. The first pass of the manager canonicalizes each commutative compound statement, now a structured region (set of basic blocks) within the control flow graph, by extracting the region into its own function. Nested commutative regions are extracted correctly by a post-order traversal on the control flow graph (CFG). The extraction process ensures that arguments specified at a COMMSET instance declaration are parameters to the newly created function. At the end of this pass, all the members of a COMMSET are functions. Call sites enabling optionally commutative named code blocks are inlined to clone the call path from the enabling function call to the COMMSETNAMEDBLOCK declaration. A robust implementation can avoid potential code explosion by automatically extending the interface signature to take in additional arguments for optional commuting blocks. Next, each COMMSET is checked for well-formedness using reachability and cycle detection algorithms on the call graph and the COMMSET graph respectively. The COMMSETPREDICATE functions are tested for purity by inspection of its body.

4.3 PDG Builder

The PDG builder constructs the PDG over the LLVM IR instructions for the target loop using well-known algorithms [12]. A loop carried dependence detector module annotates dependence edges

Algorithm 1: *CommSetDepAnalysis*

```
1  foreach edge e ∈ PDG do
2      let n1 = src(e); let n2 = dst(e);
3      if typeOf(n1) ≠ Call ∨ typeOf(n2) ≠ Call then
4          continue
5      end
6      let Fn(n1) = f(x1, ..., xn) and Fn(n2) = g(y1, ..., yn);;
7      let S_in = CommSets(f) ∩ CommSets(g);
8      foreach C_s ∈ S_in do
9          if not Predicated(C_s) then
10             Annotate(e, PDG, uco);
11         end
12         else
13             let f_p = PredicateFn(C_s);
14             let args1 = CommSetArgs(C_s, f);
15             let args2 = CommSetArgs(C_s, g);
16             let fargs = FormalArgs(f_p);
17             for i = 0 to | args1 − 1 | do
18                 let x1 = args1(i) ; let x2 = args2(i);
19                 let y1 = fargs(2 * i) ; let y2 = fargs(2 * i + 1);
20                 Assert(x1 = y1); Assert(x2 = y2);
21             end
22             if LoopCarried(e) then
23                 Assert(i1 ≠ i2); // induction variable;
24                 r = SymInterpret(Body(f_p), true);
25                 if (r = true) and (Dom(n2, n1)) then
26                     Annotate(e, PDG, uco);
27                 end
28                 else if (r = true) then
29                     Annotate(e, PDG, ico);
30                 end
31             end
32             else
33                 r = SymInterpret(Body(f_p), true);
34                 if (r = true) then
35                     Annotate(e, PDG, uco);
36                 end
37             end
38         end
39     end
40 end
```

as being loop carried whenever the source and/or destination nodes read and update shared memory state.

4.4 CommSet Dependence Analyzer

The COMMSET Dependence Analyzer (Algorithm 1) uses the COMMSET metadata to annotate memory dependence edges as being either unconditionally commutative (*uco*) or inter-iteration commutative (*ico*). Figure 2 shows the PDG edges for md5sum annotated with commutativity properties along with the corresponding source annotations. For every memory dependence edge in the PDG, if there exists an unpredicated COMMSET of which both the source and destination's target functions are members, the edge is annotated as *uco* (Lines 9-11). For a predicated COMMSET, the actual arguments of the target functions at their call sites are bound to corresponding formal parameters of the COMMSETPREDICATE function (Lines 17-19). The body of the predicate function is then symbolically interpreted to prove that it always returns *true*, given the inequality assertions about induction variable values on separate iterations (Lines 21-22). If the interpreter returns true for the current pair of COMMSET instances, the edge is annotated with a commutativity property as follows: A loop carried dependence is annotated as *uco* if the destination node of the PDG edge dominates the source node in the CFG (Lines 23-34), otherwise it is annotated as *ico* (Lines 26-27). An intra-iteration dependence edge is always annotated as *uco* if the predicate is proven to be true (Lines 32-34). Once the commutative annotations are added to the PDG, the PDG builder is invoked again to identify strongly connected components (SCC) [16]. The directed acyclic graph of SCCs (DAG-SCC) thus obtained forms the basis of DSWP family of algorithms [24].

4.5 Parallelizing Transforms

The next step runs the DOALL and PS-DSWP parallelizing transforms, which automatically partition the PDG onto multiple threads for extracting maximal data and pipelined parallelism respectively. For all the parallelizing transforms, the *ico* edges are treated as intra-iteration dependence edges, while *uco* edges are treated as non-existent edges in the PDG. The DOALL transform tests the PDG for absence of inter-iteration dependencies, and statically schedules a set of iterations to run in parallel on multiple threads. The DSWP family of transforms partition the DAG-SCC into a sequence of pipeline stages, using profile data to obtain a balanced pipeline. The DSWP algorithm [25] only generates sequential stages, while the PS-DSWP algorithm [26] can replicate a stage with no loop carried SCCs to run in parallel on multiple threads. Dependences between stages are communicated via lock-free queues in software. Together, the *uco* and *ico* annotations on the PDG enable DOALL, DSWP, and PS-DSWP transforms when previously they were not applicable. Currently, the compiler generates one of each (DSWP, PS-DSWP, and DOALL) schedule whenever applicable, with a corresponding performance estimate. A production quality compiler would typically use heuristics to select the optimal across all parallelization schemes.

4.6 CommSet Synchronization Engine

This step automatically inserts synchronization primitives to ensure atomicity of COMMSET members with respect to each other, taking multiple COMMSET memberships into account. The compiler generates a separate parallel version for every synchronization method used. Currently three synchronization modes are supported: optimistic (via Intel's transactional memory (TM) runtime [33]), pessimistic (mutex and spin locks) and lib (well known thread safe libraries or programmer specified synchronization safety for a COMMSET). Initially, the algorithm assigns a unique rank to each COMMSET which determines the global order of lock acquires and releases. The next step determines the set of potential synchronization mechanisms that apply to a COMMSET. Synchronization primitives are inserted for each member of a COMMSET by taking into account the other COMMSETs it is a part of. In the case of TM, a new version of the member wrapped around transactional constructs is generated. For the lock based synchronizations, lock acquires and releases are inserted according to the assigned global rank order. The global ordering along with the acyclic communication primitives that use the lock free queues preserve the invariants required to ensure deadlock freedom [20].

5. Evaluation

The COMMSET programming model was evaluated on a set of eight programs shown in Table 2. The programs were selected from a repository sourced from a variety of benchmark suites. Seventeen randomly selected programs with potential parallelism-inhibiting memory flow dependencies were examined. Out of these, programs whose hottest loops did not require any semantic changes for parallelization were omitted. For the remaining programs, COMMSET primitives were applied to relax certain execution orders after a careful examination of the intended program semantics. Apart from evaluating parallelization schemes enabled by COMMSET primitives in these programs, alternative parallelization schemes without using COMMSET primitives were also evaluated whenever applicable. Figure 6 shows the speedup of the parallelized programs running on a 1.6GHz Intel Xeon 64-bit dual-socket quad core machine with 8GB RAM running Linux 2.6.24.

Program	Origin	Main loop	Exec. Time	Lines of Code		CommSet Attributes	Parallelizing Transforms	Best Speedup	Best Scheme
				# CommSet Annotations	Total SLOC				
md5sum	Open Src [2]	`main`	100%	10	399	PC, C, S&G	DOALL, PS-DSWP	7.6x	DOALL + Lib
456.hmmer	SPEC2006 [14]	`main_loop_serial`	99%	9	20658	PC, C&I, S&G	DOALL, PS-DSWP	5.8x	DOALL + Spin
geti	MineBench [23]	`FindSomeETIs`	98%	11	889	PI&PC, C&I, S&G	DOALL, PS-DSWP	3.6x	PS-DSWP + Lib
ECLAT	MineBench [23]	`newApriori`	97%	11	3271	PC, C&I, S&G	DOALL, DSWP	7.5x	DOALL + Mutex
em3d	Olden [9]	`initialize_graph`	97%	8	464	I, S&G	DSWP, PS-DSWP	5.8x	PS-DSWP + Lib
potrace	Open Src [29]	`main`	100%	10	8292	PC, C, S&G	DOALL, PS-DSWP	5.5x	DOALL + Lib
kmeans	STAMP [22]	`work`	99%	1	516	C, S	DOALL, PS-DSWP	5.2x	PS-DSWP
url	NetBench [21]	`main`	100%	2	629	I, S	DOALL, PS-DSWP	7.7x	DOALL + Spin

Table 2: Sequential Programs evaluated, their origin, execution time spent in target loop, number of CommSet annotations over sequential code, total number of lines of source code, CommSet features applied (PI: Predication at Interface, PC: Predication at Client, C: Commuting Blocks, I: Interface Commutativity, S: Self Commutativity, G: Group Commutativity), Parallelizing Transforms, Best Speedup Obtained on eight threads, and corresponding Parallelization Scheme with synchronization mechanism (Mutex: Mutex locks, Spin: Spin locks, Lib: Thread-safe Libraries).

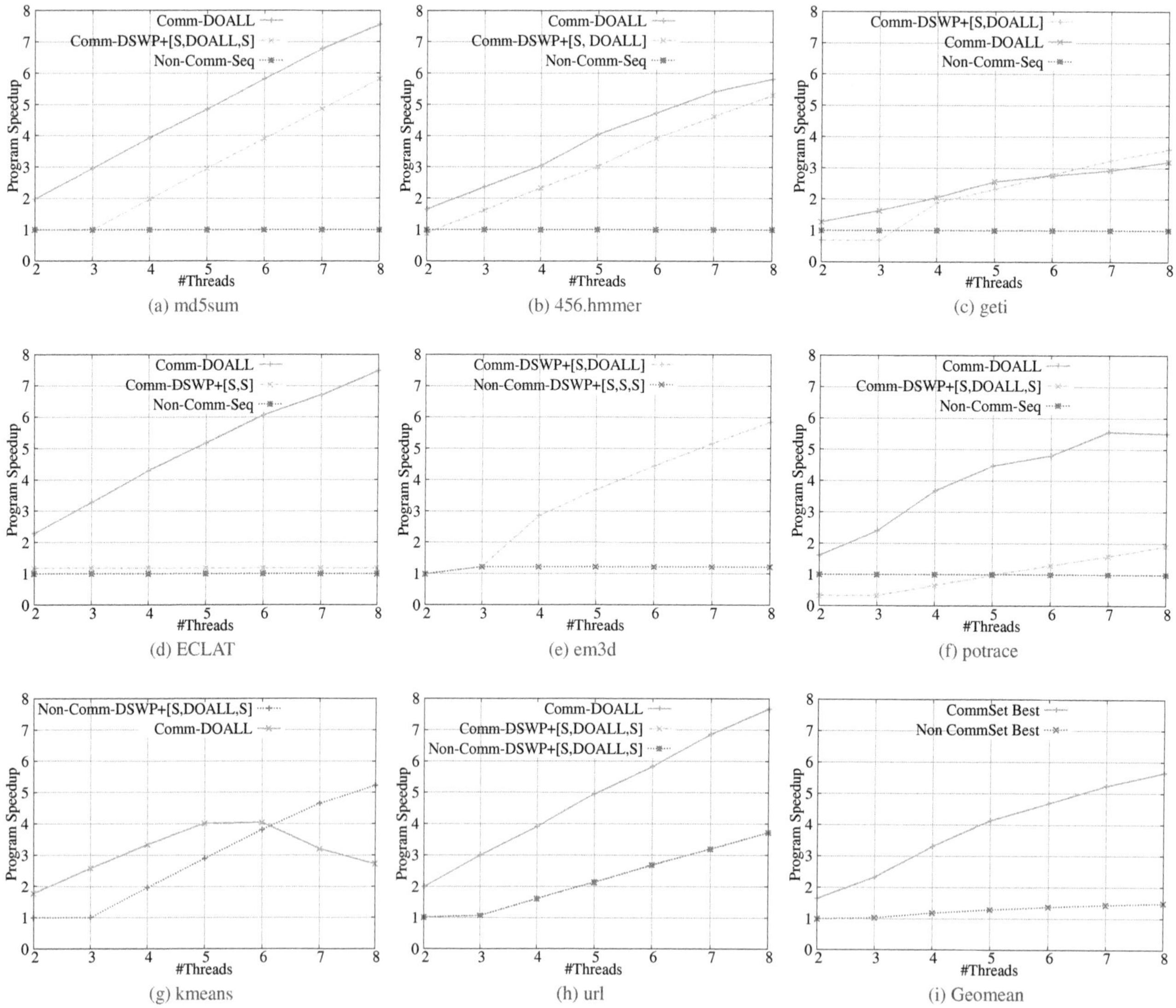

(a) md5sum (b) 456.hmmer (c) geti
(d) ECLAT (e) em3d (f) potrace
(g) kmeans (h) url (i) Geomean

Figure 6: Performance of DOALL and PS-DSWP schemes using CommSet extensions. Parallelization schemes in each graph's legend are sorted in decreasing order of speedup on eight threads, from top to bottom. The DSWP + [. . .] notation indicates the DSWP technique with stage details within [. . .] (where *S* denotes a sequential stage and *DOALL* denotes a parallel stage). Schemes with *Comm-* prefix were enabled only by the use of CommSet . For each program, the best Non-CommSet parallelization scheme, obtained by ignoring the CommSet extensions is also shown. In some cases, this was sequential execution.

5.1 456.hmmer: Biological Sequence Analysis

456.hmmer performs biosequence analysis using Hidden Markov Models. Every iteration of the main loop generates a new protein sequence via calls to a random number generator (RNG). It then computes a score for the sequence using a dynamically allocated matrix data structure, which is used to update a histogram structure. Finally the matrix is deallocated at the end of the iteration. By applying COMMSET annotations at three sites, all loop carried dependences were broken: (a) The RNG was added to a SELF COMMSET, since any permutation of a random number sequence still preserves the properties of the distribution. (b) The histogram update operation was also marked self commuting, as it performs an abstract SUM operation even though the low-level statements involve floating point additions and subtractions. (c) The matrix allocation and deallocation functions were marked as commuting with themselves on separate iterations. Overall, the DOALL parallelization using spin locks performs best for eight threads, with a program speedup of about 5.82x. A spin lock works better than mutex since it does not suffer from sleep/wakeup overheads in the midst of highly contended operations on the RNG seed variable. The three stage PS-DSWP pipeline, gives a speedup of 5.3x (doing better than the mutex and TM versions of DOALL) by moving the RNG to a sequential stage, off the critical path.

5.2 GETI: Greedy Error Tolerant Itemsets

GETI is a C++ data mining program that determines a set of frequent items that are bought together frequently in customer transactions (*itemsets*). *Itemsets* are implemented as `Bitmap` objects, with items acting as keys. Items are queried and inserted into the `Bitmap` by calls to `SetBit()` and `GetBit()`. Each *itemset* is inserted into an STL vector and then printed to the console. By adding COMMSET annotations at three sites, the main loop was completely parallelizable with DOALL and PS-DSWP: (a) Itemset constructors and destructors are added to a COMMSET and allowed to commute on separate iterations. (b) `SetBit()` and `GetBit()` interfaces were put in a COMMSET predicated on the input key values, to allow for insertions of multiple items to occur out of order. (c) The code block with `vector::push_back()` and prints was context sensitively marked as self commutative in client code. The correctness of this application follows from the set semantics associated with the output. The inter-iteration commutativity properties for constructor/destructor pairs enabled a well performing three-stage PS-DSWP schedule. Transactions were not applicable due to use of external libraries and I/O. Although DOALL schemes initially did better than PS-DSWP, the effects of buffering output indirectly via lock-free queues for PS-DSWP and the increasing number of acquire/release operations for DOALL led to a better performing schedule for PS-DSWP on eight threads. PS-DSWP achieved a limited speedup of 3.6x due to the sequential time taken for console prints but maintained deterministic behavior of the program.

5.3 ECLAT: Association Rule Mining

ECLAT is a C++ program that computes a list of frequent itemsets using a vertical database. The main loop updates objects of two classes `Itemset` and `Lists<Itemset*>`. Both are internally implemented as lists, the former as a client defined class, and the latter as an instantiation of a generic class. Insertions into `Itemset` have to preserve the sequential order, since the `Itemset` intersection code depends on a deterministic prefix. Insertions into the `Lists<Itemset*>` can be done out of order, due to set semantics attached with the output. COMMSET extensions were applied at four sites: (a) Database read calls (that mutate shared file descriptors internally) were marked as self commutative. (b) Insertions into `Lists<Itemset*>` are context-sensitively tagged as self commuting inside the loop. Note that it would be incorrect to tag `Itemset` insertions as self-commuting as it would break the intersection code. (c) Object construction and destruction operations were marked as commuting on separate iterations. (d) Methods belonging to `Stats` class that computes statistics were added to a unpredicated Group COMMSET. A speedup of 7.4x with DOALL was obtained, despite pessimistic synchronization, due to a larger fraction of time spent in computation outside critical sections. Transactions are not applicable due to use of I/O operations. The PS-DSWP transform, using all the COMMSET properties generates a schedule (not shown) similar to DOALL. The next best schedule is from DSWP, that does not leverage COMMSET properties on database read. The resulting DAG-SCC has a single SCC corresponding to the entire inner `for` loop, preventing stage replication.

5.4 em3d: Electro-magnetic Wave propagation

em3d simulates electromagnetic wave propagation using a bipartite graph. The outer loop of the graph construction iterates through a linked list of nodes in a partition, while the inner loop uses a RNG to select a new neighbor for the current node. Allowing the RNG routine to execute out of order enabled PS-DSWP. The program uses a common RNG library, with routines for returning random numbers of different data types, all of which update a shared seed variable. All these routines were added to a common Group COMMSET and also to their own SELF COMMSET . COMMSET specifications to indicate commutativity between the RNG routines required only eight annotations, while specifying pair-wise commutativity would have required 16 annotations. Since the loop does a linked list traversal, DOALL was not applicable. Without commutativity, DSWP extracts a two-stage pipeline at the outer loop level, yielding a speedup of 1.2x. The PS-DSWP scheme enabled by COMMSET directives achieves a speedup of 5.9x on eight threads. A linear speedup was not obtained due to the short execution time of the original instructions in the main loop, which made the overhead of inter-thread communication slightly more pronounced.

5.5 potrace: Bitmap tracing

potrace vectorizes a set of bitmaps into smooth, scalable images. The code pattern is similar to md5sum, with an additional option of writing multiple output images into a single file. In the code section with the option enabled, the SELF COMMSET annotation was omitted on file output calls to ensure sequential output semantics. The DOALL parallelization yielded a speedup of 5.5x, peaking at 7 threads, after which I/O costs dominate the runtime. For the PS-DSWP parallelization, the sequentiality of image writes limited speedup to 2.2x on eight threads.

5.6 kmeans: K means clustering algorithm

kmeans clusters high dimensional objects into similar featured groups. The main loop computes the nearest cluster center for each object and updates the center's features using the current object. The updates to a cluster center can be re-ordered, with each such order resulting in a different but valid cluster assignment. Adding the code block that performs the update to a SELF COMMSET breaks the only loop carried dependence in the loop. The DOALL scheme with pessimistic synchronization showed promising speedup until five threads (4x), beyond which frequent cache misses due to failed lock/unlock operations resulted in performance degradation. Transactions (not shown) do not help either, with speedup limited to 2.7x on eight threads. The three-stage PS-DSWP scheme was best performing beyond six threads, showing an almost linear performance increase by executing the cluster update operation in a third sequential stage. It achieved a speedup of 5.2x on eight threads. This highlights the performance gains achieved by moving highly contended dependence cycles onto a sequential stage, an important insight behind the DSWP family of transforms.

5.7 URL: url based switching

The main loop in the program switches a set of incoming packets based on its URL and logs some of the packet's fields into a file. The underlying protocol semantics allows out-of-order packet switching. Adding the function to dequeue a packet from the packet pool and the logging function to SELF COMMSETs broke all the loop carried flow dependences. No synchronization was necessary for the logging function while locks were automatically inserted to synchronize multiple calls to the packet dequeuing function. A two stage PS-DSWP pipeline was also formed by ignoring the SELF COMMSET annotation on the packet dequeue function. The DOALL parallelization (7.7x speedup on eight threads) outperforms the PS-DSWP version (3.7x on eight threads) because of low lock contention on the dequeue function and the overlapped parallel execution of the packet matching computation.

5.8 Discussion

The application of COMMSET achieved a geomean speedup of 5.7x on eight threads for the programs listed in Table 2, while the geomean speedup for Non-COMMSET parallelizations is 1.49x (Figure 6i). For four out of the eight programs, the main loop was not parallelizable at all without the use of COMMSET primitives. With the application of COMMSET, DOALL parallelization performs better than PS-DSWP on 5 benchmarks, although PS-DSWP has the advantage of preserving deterministic output in two of them. For two of the remaining programs, PS-DSWP yields better speedup since its sequential last stage performs better than concurrently executing COMMSET blocks in the high lock contention scenarios. DOALL was not applicable for em3d, due to pointer chasing code. In terms of programmer effort, an average of 8 lines of COMMSET annotations were added to each program to enable the various parallelization schemes. Predication based on the client state, as a function of the induction variable enabled well performing parallelizations without the need for runtime checks. The use of commuting blocks avoided the need for major code refactoring. The applicability of COMMSET compared favorably to the applicability of other compiler based techniques like Paralax and VELOCITY. VELOCITY and Paralax cannot be used to parallelize four benchmarks: geti, eclat, md5sum and potrace since they do not support predicated commutativity. For 456.hmmer, VELOCITY would require a modification of 45 lines of code (addition of 43 lines and removal of 2 lines) in addition to the commutativity annotations. COMMSET did not require those changes due to the use of named commuting blocks.

6. Related Work

Semantic Commutativity based Parallelizing Systems. Jade [27] supports object-level commuting assertions to specify commutativity between every pair of operations on an object. Additionally, Jade exploits programmer written read/write specifications for exploiting task and pipeline parallelism. The COMMSET solution relies on static analysis to avoid read/write specifications and runtime profiles to select loops for parallelization. Galois [18], a runtime system for optimistic parallelism, leverages commutativity assertions on method interfaces. It requires programmers to use special set abstractions with non-standard semantics to enable data parallelism. The COMMSET compiler currently does not implement runtime checking of COMMSETPREDICATEs required for optimistic parallelism. However, the COMMSET model is able to extract both data and pipelined parallelism without requiring any additional programming extensions. DPJ [5], an explicitly parallel extension of Java uses commutativity annotations at function interfaces to override restrictions placed by the type and effect system of Java. Several researchers have also applied commutativity properties for semantic concurrency control in explicitly parallel settings [10, 17]. Paralax [30] and VELOCITY [6, 7] exploit self-commutativity at the interface level to enable pipelined parallelization. VELOCITY also provides special semantics for commutativity between pairs of memory allocation routines for use in speculative parallelization. Compared to these approaches, the COMMSET language extension provides richer commutativity expressions. Extending the compiler with a speculative system to support all COMMSET features at runtime is part of future work. Table 1 summarizes the relationship between COMMSET and the above programming models.

Implicit Parallel Programming. OpenMP [3] extensions require programmers to explicitly specify parallelization strategy and concurrency control using additional primitives (“`#pragma omp for`”, “`#pragma omp task`”, “`critical`”, “`barrier`”, etc.). In the COMMSET model, the choice of parallelization strategy and concurrency control is left to the compiler. This not only frees the programmer from having to worry about low-level parallelization details, but also promotes performance portability. Implicit parallelism in functional languages have been studied recently [13]. IPOT [31] exploits semantic annotations on data to enable parallelization. Hwu et al. [15] also propose annotations on data to enable implicit parallelism. COMMSET extensions are applied to code rather than data, and some annotations like `reduction` proposed in IPOT can be easily integrated with COMMSET.

Compiler Parallelization. Research on parallelizing FORTRAN loops with regular memory accesses [11, 16] in the past has been complemented by more recent work on irregular programs. The container-aware [32] compiler transformations parallelize loops with repeated patterns of collections usage. Existing versions of these transforms preserve sequential semantics. The COMMSET compiler can be extended to support these and other parallelizing transforms without changes to the language extension.

Commutativity Analysis. Rinard et al. [28] proposed a static analysis that determines if commuting two method calls preserves concrete memory state. Aleen et al. [1] apply random interpretation to probabilistically determine function calls that commute subject to preservation of sequential I/O semantics. Programmer written commutativity assertions are more general since they allow multiple legal outcomes and give a programmer more flexibility to express intended semantics within a sequential setting.

7. Conclusion

This paper presented an implicit parallel programming solution based on a unified, syntactically succinct and generalized semantic commutativity construct called COMMSET. The model provides programmers the flexibility to specify commutativity relations between arbitrary structured blocks of code and does not require the use of any additional parallel constructs. Parallelism exposed implicitly using COMMSET is independent of any particular parallelization strategy or concurrency control mechanism. A complete end-to-end implementation of COMMSET exists in a parallelizing compiler. Evaluation of eight real world programs indicates that the use of COMMSET extensions and the associated compiler technology enables scalable parallelization of programs hitherto not amenable to automatic parallelization. This demonstrates the effectiveness of the COMMSET construct in exposing different parallelization opportunities to the compiler.

Acknowledgments

We thank the entire Liberty Research Group for their support and feedback during this work. We also thank the anonymous reviewers for their insightful comments. This material is based on work supported by National Science Foundation Grants 1047879, 0964328, and 0627650, and United States Air Force Contract FA8650-09-C-7918.

References

[1] F. Aleen and N. Clark. Commutativity analysis for software parallelization: Letting program transformations see the big picture. In *Proceedings of the 14th International Conference on Architectural Support for Programming Languages and Operating Systems (ASPLOS)*, 2009.

[2] Apple Open Source. md5sum: Message Digest 5 computation. `http://www.opensource.apple.com/darwinsource/`.

[3] E. Ayguadé, N. Copty, A. Duran, J. Hoeflinger, Y. Lin, F. Massaioli, X. Teruel, P. Unnikrishnan, and G. Zhang. The design of OpenMP tasks. *IEEE Transactions on Parallel and Distributed Systems*, 2009.

[4] G. E. Blelloch and J. Greiner. A provable time and space efficient implementation of NESL. In *Proceedings of the First ACM SIGPLAN International Conference on Functional Programming (ICFP)*, 1996.

[5] R. L. Bocchino, Jr., V. S. Adve, D. Dig, S. V. Adve, S. Heumann, R. Komuravelli, J. Overbey, P. Simmons, H. Sung, and M. Vakilian. A type and effect system for Deterministic Parallel Java. In *Proceedings of the 24th ACM SIGPLAN Conference on Object Oriented Programming Systems, Languages, and Applications (OOPSLA)*, 2009.

[6] M. Bridges, N. Vachharajani, Y. Zhang, T. Jablin, and D. August. Revisiting the sequential programming model for multicore. In *Proceedings of the 40th Annual IEEE/ACM International Symposium on Microarchitecture (MICRO)*, 2007.

[7] M. J. Bridges. *The VELOCITY compiler: Extracting efficient multicore execution from legacy sequential codes*. PhD thesis, 2008.

[8] D. R. Butenhof. *Programming with POSIX threads*. Addison-Wesley Longman Publishing Co., Inc., 1997.

[9] M. C. Carlisle. *Olden: Parallelizing programs with dynamic data structures on distributed-memory machines*. PhD thesis, 1996.

[10] B. D. Carlstrom, A. McDonald, M. Carbin, C. Kozyrakis, and K. Olukotun. Transactional collection classes. In *Proceedings of the 12th ACM SIGPLAN Symposium on Principles and Practice of Parallel Programming (PPoPP)*, 2007.

[11] R. Eigenmann, J. Hoeflinger, Z. Li, and D. A. Padua. Experience in the automatic parallelization of four Perfect-benchmark programs. In *Proceedings of the Fourth International Workshop on Languages and Compilers for Parallel Computing (LCPC), 1992.*

[12] J. Ferrante, K. J. Ottenstein, and J. D. Warren. The program dependence graph and its use in optimization. *ACM Trans. Program. Lang. Syst.*, 9(3), 1987.

[13] T. Harris and S. Singh. Feedback directed implicit parallelism. In *Proceedings of the 12th ACM SIGPLAN International Conference on Functional Programming (ICFP)*, 2007.

[14] J. L. Henning. SPEC CPU2006 benchmark descriptions. *SIGARCH Comput. Archit. News*, 2006.

[15] W.-m. Hwu, S. Ryoo, S.-Z. Ueng, J. Kelm, I. Gelado, S. Stone, R. Kidd, S. Baghsorkhi, A. Mahesri, S. Tsao, N. Navarro, S. Lumetta, M. Frank, and S. Patel. Implicitly parallel programming models for thousand-core microprocessors. In *Proceedings of the 44th annual Design Automation Conference (DAC)*, 2007.

[16] K. Kennedy and J. R. Allen. *Optimizing Compilers for Modern Architectures: a Dependence-based Approach*. Morgan Kaufmann Publishers Inc., 2002.

[17] E. Koskinen, M. Parkinson, and M. Herlihy. Coarse-grained transactions. In *Proceedings of the 37th Annual ACM SIGPLAN-SIGACT Symposium on Principles of Programming Languages (POPL), 2010.*

[18] M. Kulkarni, K. Pingali, B. Walter, G. Ramanarayanan, K. Bala, and L. P. Chew. Optimistic parallelism requires abstractions. In *Proceedings of the 2007 ACM SIGPLAN Conference on Programming Language Design and Implementation (PLDI)*.

[19] C. Lattner and V. Adve. LLVM: A compilation framework for lifelong program analysis and transformation. In *Proceedings of 2nd International Symposium on Code Generation and Optimization (CGO)*, 2004.

[20] R. Leino, P. Müller, and J. Smans. Deadlock-free channels and locks. In *Proceedings of the 19th European Symposium on Programming (ESOP)*, 2010.

[21] G. Memik, W. H. Mangione-Smith, and W. Hu. NetBench: a benchmarking suite for network processors. In *Proceedings of the 2001 IEEE/ACM International Conference on Computer-Aided Design (ICCAD)*, 2001.

[22] C. C. Minh, J. Chung, C. Kozyrakis, and K. Olukotun. STAMP: Stanford Transactional Applications for Multi-Processing. In *IEEE International Symposium on Workload Characterization (IISWC)*, 2008.

[23] R. Narayanan, B. Ozisikyilmaz, J. Zambreno, G. Memik, and A. Choudhary. MineBench: A benchmark suite for data mining workloads. In *IEEE International Symposium on Workload Characterization (IIWSC)*, 2006.

[24] G. Ottoni. *Global Instruction Scheduling for Multi-Threaded Architectures.* PhD thesis, 2008.

[25] G. Ottoni, R. Rangan, A. Stoler, and D. I. August. Automatic thread extraction with decoupled software pipelining. *Proceedings of the 38th annual IEEE/ACM International Symposium on Microarchitecture (MICRO)*, 2005.

[26] E. Raman, G. Ottoni, A. Raman, M. J. Bridges, and D. I. August. Parallel-stage decoupled software pipelining. In *Proceedings of the 6th annual IEEE/ACM International Symposium on Code Generation and Optimization (CGO)*, 2008.

[27] M. C. Rinard. *The design, implementation and evaluation of Jade, a portable, implicitly parallel programming language.* PhD thesis, 1994.

[28] M. C. Rinard and P. Diniz. Commutativity analysis: A new analysis framework for parallelizing compilers. In *Proceedings of the ACM SIGPLAN 1996 Conference on Programming Language Design and Implementation (PLDI).*

[29] P. Selinger. potrace: Transforming bitmaps into vector graphics. `http://potrace.sourceforge.net`.

[30] H. Vandierendonck, S. Rul, and K. De Bosschere. The Paralax infrastructure: Automatic parallelization with a helping hand. In *Proceedings of the 19th International Conference on Parallel Architectures and Compilation Techniques (PACT)*, 2010.

[31] C. von Praun, L. Ceze, and C. Caşcaval. Implicit parallelism with ordered transactions. In *Proceedings of the 12th ACM SIGPLAN Symposium on Principles and Practice of Parallel Programming (PPoPP)*, 2007.

[32] P. Wu and D. A. Padua. Beyond arrays - a container-centric approach for parallelization of real-world symbolic applications. In *Proceedings of the 11th International Workshop on Languages and Compilers for Parallel Computing (LCPC), 1999.*

[33] R. M. Yoo, Y. Ni, A. Welc, B. Saha, A.-R. Adl-Tabatabai, and H.-H. S. Lee. Kicking the tires of software transactional memory: Why the going gets tough. In *Proceedings of the Twentieth Annual Symposium on Parallelism in Algorithms and Architectures (SPAA)*, 2008.

[34] H. Zhong, M. Mehrara, S. Lieberman, and S. Mahlke. Uncovering hidden loop level parallelism in sequential applications. In *Proceedings of 14th International Conference on High-Performance Computer Architecture (HPCA)*, 2008.

The Tao of Parallelism in Algorithms *

Keshav Pingali[1,3], Donald Nguyen[1], Milind Kulkarni[5],
Martin Burtscher[4], M. Amber Hassaan[2], Rashid Kaleem[1], Tsung-Hsien Lee[2], Andrew Lenharth[3],
Roman Manevich[3], Mario Méndez-Lojo[3], Dimitrios Prountzos[1], Xin Sui[1]

[1]Department of Computer Science, [2]Electrical and Computer Engineering and [3]Institute for Computational Engineering and Sciences
The University of Texas at Austin
[4]Department of Computer Science, Texas State University–San Marcos
[5]School of Electrical and Computer Engineering, Purdue University

Abstract

For more than thirty years, the parallel programming community has used the *dependence graph* as the main abstraction for reasoning about and exploiting parallelism in "regular" algorithms that use dense arrays, such as finite-differences and FFTs. In this paper, we argue that the dependence graph is not a suitable abstraction for algorithms in new application areas like machine learning and network analysis in which the key data structures are "irregular" data structures like graphs, trees, and sets.

To address the need for better abstractions, we introduce a data-centric formulation of algorithms called the *operator formulation* in which an algorithm is expressed in terms of its action on data structures. This formulation is the basis for a structural analysis of algorithms that we call *tao-analysis*. Tao-analysis can be viewed as an abstraction of algorithms that distills out algorithmic properties important for parallelization. It reveals that a generalized form of data-parallelism called *amorphous data-parallelism* is ubiquitous in algorithms, and that, depending on the tao-structure of the algorithm, this parallelism may be exploited by compile-time, inspector-executor or optimistic parallelization, thereby unifying these seemingly unrelated parallelization techniques. Regular algorithms emerge as a special case of irregular algorithms, and many application-specific optimization techniques can be generalized to a broader context.

These results suggest that the operator formulation and tao-analysis of algorithms can be the foundation of a systematic approach to parallel programming.

Categories and Subject Descriptors D.1.3 [*Programming Techniques*]: Concurrent Programming—Parallel Programming; D.3.3 [*Programming Languages*]: Language Constructs and Features—Frameworks

General Terms: Algorithms, Languages, Performance

Keywords: amorphous data-parallelism, Galois system, irregular programs, operator formulation, tao-analysis.

* This work is supported in part by NSF grants 0923907, 0833162, 0719966, and 0702353 and by grants from IBM, NEC and Intel.

PLDI'11, June 4–8, 2011, San Jose, California, USA.

1. Introduction

道 n. /tau/, /dau/: **1. a.** the source and guiding principle of all reality as conceived by Taoists; **b.** process which is to be followed for a life of harmony. Origin: Chinese *dào*, literally, way. (adapted from Merriam-Webster)

Dense matrix computations arise naturally in high-performance implementations of important computational science methods like finite-differences and multigrid. Therefore, over the years, the parallel programming community has acquired a deep understanding of the patterns of parallelism and locality in these kinds of "regular" algorithms. In contrast, "irregular" data structures such as sparse graphs, trees and sets are the norm in most emerging problem domains such as the following.

- In social network analysis, the key data structures are extremely sparse graphs in which nodes represent people and edges represent relationships. Algorithms for betweenness-centrality, maxflow, etc. are used to extract network properties [10].
- Machine-learning algorithms like belief propagation and survey propagation are based on message-passing in a factor graph, a sparse bipartite graph [44].
- Data-mining algorithms like k-means and agglomerative clustering operate on sets and multisets [59].
- Simulations of electrical circuits and battlefields often use event-driven (discrete-event) simulation [49] over networks of nodes.
- Optimizing compilers perform iterative and elimination-based dataflow analysis on structures like inter-procedural control-flow graphs [1].
- Even in computational science, n-body methods use spatial decomposition trees [6], and finite-element methods use 2D and 3D meshes produced using algorithms like Delaunay mesh generation and refinement [11].

Unfortunately, we currently have few insights into the structure of parallelism and locality in irregular algorithms, and this has stunted the development of techniques and tools that make it easier to produce parallel implementations. Domain specialists have written parallel programs for some of the algorithms discussed above (see [5, 20, 31, 33] among others). There are also parallel graph libraries such as Boost [22] and STAPL [2]. However, it is difficult to extract broadly applicable abstractions, principles, and mechanisms from these implementations. Another approach is to use points-to and shape analysis [19, 27, 30] to find data structure invariants that might be used to prove independence of computations. This approach has been successful in parallelizing n-body methods like Barnes-Hut that are organized around trees [17], but most of the applications discussed above use sparse graphs with no particular structure, so shape analysis techniques fail to find any parallelism. These difficulties have seemed insurmountable, so irregular algorithms remain the Cinderellas of parallel programming in spite of their central role in emerging applications.

In this paper, we argue that these problems can be solved only by changing the abstractions that we currently use to reason about parallelism in algorithms. The most widely used abstraction is the *dependence graph* in which nodes represent computations, and edges represent dependences between computations; for programs with loops, dependence edges are often labeled with additional information such as dependence distances and directions. Computations that are not ordered by the transitive closure of the dependence relation can be executed in parallel. Dependence graphs produced either by studying the algorithm or by compiler analysis are referred to as *static* dependence graphs. Although static dependence graphs are used extensively for implementing regular algorithms, they are not adequate for modeling parallelism in irregular algorithms. As we explain in Section 2, the most important reason for this is that dependences between computations in irregular algorithms are functions of runtime data values, so they cannot be represented usefully by a static dependence graph.

To address the need for better abstractions, Section 3 introduces a *data-centric* formulation of algorithms, called the *operator formulation* of algorithms. In the spirit of Niklaus Wirth's aphorism "Program = Algorithm + Data Structure" [63], we express algorithms in terms of operations on abstract data types (ADTs), independently of the concrete data structures used to implement the abstract data types. This formulation is the basis of a structural analysis of algorithms that we call *tao-analysis* after the three key dimensions of the analysis. In the literature on parallel programming, there are many abstractions of parallel machines, such as a variety of PRAM models [32]. Tao-analysis can be viewed as an abstraction of algorithms that distills out properties important for parallelization, hiding unnecessary detail.

Tao-analysis reveals that a generalized data-parallelism called *amorphous data-parallelism* is ubiquitous in algorithms, as we discuss in Section 4. We also show that depending on the tao-structure of the algorithm, this parallelism may be exploited by compile-time, inspector-executor or optimistic parallelization, thereby unifying these seemingly unrelated techniques by consideration of the binding time of scheduling decisions. In addition, regular algorithms emerge as special cases of irregular algorithms.

In Section 5, we show how these concepts can be applied to the parallelization of many important algorithms from the literature. Some of the techniques discussed in this paper have been incorporated into the Galois system[1]. In Section 6, we give experimental results for three full applications that demonstrate the practical utility of these ideas. Extensions to the amorphous data-parallelism model are discussed in Section 7. We summarize the main contributions in Section 8.

2. Inadequacy of static dependence graphs

The need for new algorithmic abstractions can be appreciated by considering Delaunay Mesh Refinement (DMR) [11], an irregular algorithm used extensively in finite-element meshing and graphics. The Delaunay triangulation for a set of points in a plane is the triangulation in which each triangle satisfies a certain geometric constraint called the Delaunay condition [14]. In many applications, triangles are required to satisfy additional quality constraints, and this is accomplished by a process of iterative refinement that re-

[1] Available from http://iss.ices.utexas.edu/galois

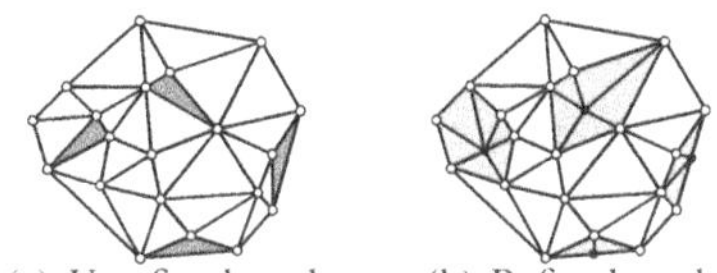

(a) Unrefined mesh (b) Refined mesh

Figure 1. Fixing bad triangles

```
Mesh mesh = // read in initial mesh
Worklist<Triangle> wl;
wl.add(mesh.badTriangles());
while (wl.size() != 0) {
  Triangle t = wl.poll(); // get bad triangle
  if (t no longer in mesh) continue;
  Cavity c = new Cavity(t);
  c.expand();
  c.retriangulate();
  mesh.update(c);
  wl.add(c.badTriangles());
}
```

Figure 2. Pseudocode of the mesh refinement algorithm

peatedly fixes "bad" triangles (those that do not satisfy the quality constraints) by adding new points to the mesh and re-triangulating. Refining a bad triangle by itself may violate the Delaunay property of triangles around it, so it is necessary to compute a region of the mesh called the *cavity* of the bad triangle and replace all the triangles in the cavity with new triangles. Figure 1 illustrates this process; the darker-shaded triangles are "bad" triangles, and the cavities are the lighter shaded regions around the bad triangles. Re-triangulating a cavity may generate new bad triangles, but it can be shown that, at least in 2D, this iterative refinement process will ultimately terminate and produce a guaranteed-quality mesh. Different orders of processing bad triangles lead to different meshes, although all such meshes satisfy the quality constraints and are acceptable outcomes of the refinement process [11]. This is an example of Dijkstra's *don't-care non-determinism* (also known as *committed-choice non-determinism*) [16]. Figure 2 shows the pseudocode for mesh refinement. Each iteration of the while-loop refines one bad triangle; we call this computation an *activity*.

DMR can be performed in parallel since bad triangles whose cavities do not overlap can be refined in parallel. Note that two triangles whose cavities overlap can be refined in either order but not concurrently. Unfortunately, static dependence graphs are inadequate for exposing this parallelism. In Delaunay mesh refinement, as in most irregular algorithms, dependences between loop iterations (activities) are functions of runtime values: whether or not two iterations of the while-loop in Figure 2 can be executed concurrently depends on whether the cavities of the relevant triangles overlap, and this depends on the input mesh and how it has been modified by previous refinements. Since this information is known only during program execution, a static dependence graph for Delaunay mesh refinement must conservatively assume that every loop iteration might interfere with every prior iteration, serializing the execution.

A second problem with dependence graphs is that they do not model don't-care non-determinism. In dependence graphs, computations can be executed in parallel if they are not ordered by the dependence relation. In irregular algorithms like Delaunay mesh refinement, it is often the case that two activities can be done in either order but cannot be done concurrently, so they are not ordered by dependence and yet cannot be executed concurrently. Exploiting don't-care non-determinism can lead to more efficient parallel implementations, as we discuss in Section 4.

Event-driven simulation [49], which is used in circuit simulations and system modeling, illustrates a different kind of complex-

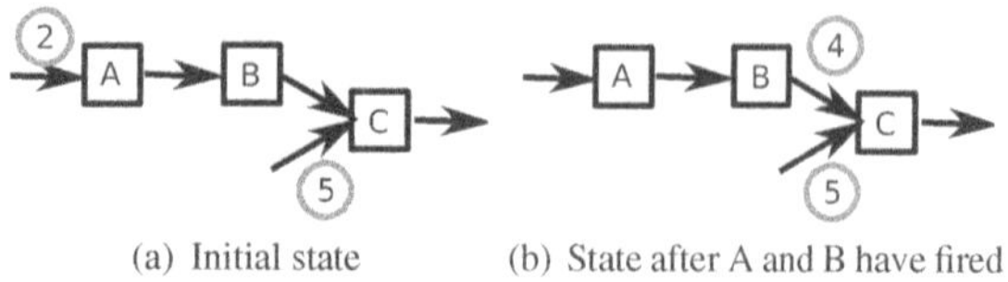

Figure 3. Conflicts in event-driven simulation

ity exhibited by some irregular algorithms. This application simulates a network of processing stations that communicate by sending messages along FIFO links. When a station processes a message, its internal state may be updated, and it may produce zero or more messages on its outgoing links. Sequential event-driven simulation is implemented by maintaining a global priority queue of events called the event list and processing the earliest event at each step. In this irregular algorithm, activities correspond to the processing of events.

In principle, event-driven simulation can be performed in parallel by processing multiple events from the event list simultaneously, rather than one event at a time. However, unlike in Delaunay mesh refinement, in which it was legal to process bad triangles concurrently provided they were well-separated in the mesh, it may not be legal to process two events in parallel even if their stations are far apart in the network. Figure 3 demonstrates this. Suppose that in a sequential implementation, node A fires and produces a message time-stamped 3, and then node B fires and produces a message time-stamped 4. Notice that node C must consume this message *before* it consumes the message time-stamped 5. Therefore, in Figure 3(a), the events at A and C cannot be processed in parallel even though the stations are far apart in the network. However, notice that if the message from B to C had a time-stamp greater than 5, it would have been legal to process in parallel the events at nodes A and C. To determine if two activities can be performed in parallel at a given point in the execution of this algorithm, we need a crystal ball to look into the future!

In short, static dependence graphs are inadequate abstractions for irregular algorithms for the following reasons.

1. Dependences between activities in irregular algorithms are usually complex functions of runtime data values, so they cannot be usefully captured by a static dependence graph.
2. Many irregular algorithms exhibit don't-care non-determinism, but this is hard to model with dependence graphs.
3. Whether or not it is safe to execute two activities in parallel at a given point in the computation may depend on activities created later in the computation. It is not clear how one models this with dependence graphs.

3. Operator formulation of algorithms

These problems can be addressed by a data-centric formulation of algorithms, called the *operator formulation*, in which an algorithm is viewed in terms of its action on data structures. The operator formulation can be defined for any abstract data type, and we will use the *graph* ADT to illustrate the key ideas. As is standard, a graph is (i) a set of nodes V, and (ii) a set of edges $E \subseteq V \times V$ between these nodes. Graphs can be directed or undirected, and nodes and edges may be labeled with values.

We will not discuss a particular *concrete representation* for the graph ADT. The implementation is free to choose the concrete representation that is best suited for a particular algorithm and machine: for example, cliques may be represented using dense arrays, while sparse graphs may be represented using adjacency lists. This is similar to the approach taken in relational databases: SQL programmers use the relation ADT in writing programs, and the underlying DBMS system is free to implement the ADT using B-trees, hash tables, and other concrete data structures.

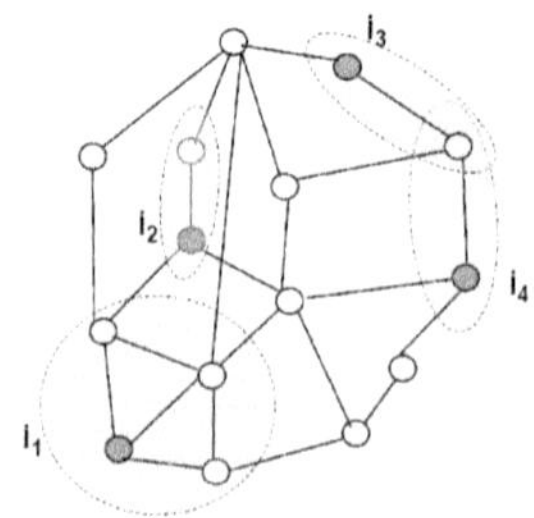

Figure 4. Active elements and neighborhoods

3.1 Active elements, neighborhoods and ordering

Active elements: At each point during the execution of a graph algorithm, there are certain nodes or edges in the graph where computation might be performed. These nodes and edges are called *active elements*; to keep the discussion simple, we assume from here on that active elements are nodes. To process an active node, an *operator* is applied to it, and the resulting computation is called an *activity*.

Neighborhoods: Performing an activity may require reading or writing other nodes and edges in the graph. Borrowing terminology from the literature on cellular automata, we refer to the set of nodes and edges that are read or written while performing an activity as the *neighborhood* of that activity. Figure 4 shows an undirected sparse graph in which the filled nodes represent active nodes, and shaded regions represent the neighborhoods of those active nodes. Note that in general, the neighborhood of an active node is distinct from its neighbors in the graph.

Ordering: In general, there are many active nodes in a graph, so a sequential implementation must pick one of them and perform the appropriate activity. In some algorithms such as Delaunay mesh refinement, the implementation is allowed to pick *any* active node for execution. We call these *unordered* algorithms. In contrast, some algorithms dictate an order in which active nodes must be processed by a sequential implementation; we call these *ordered* algorithms. Event-driven simulation is an example: the sequential algorithm for event-driven simulation processes messages in global time order. The order on active nodes may be a partial order.

We illustrate these concepts using the algorithms from Section 2. In DMR, the mesh is usually represented by a graph in which nodes represent triangles and edges represent adjacency of triangles. The active nodes in this algorithm are the nodes representing bad triangles, and the neighborhood of an active node is the cavity of that bad triangle. In event-driven simulation, active nodes are stations that have messages on their input channels, and neighborhoods contain only the active node.

3.2 From algorithms to programs

A natural way to write these algorithms is to use worklists to keep track of active nodes. However, programs written directly in terms of worklists, such as the one in Figure 2, encode a particular order of processing worklist items and do not express the don't-care nondeterminism in unordered algorithms. To address this problem, we can use the Galois programming model, which is a *sequential*, object-oriented programming model (such as sequential Java), augmented with two *Galois set iterators* [40]:

DEFINITION 1. *Galois set iterators:*

- **Unordered-set iterator: foreach (e in Set S) {B(e)}**
The loop body B(e) is executed for each element e of set S. The order in which iterations execute is indeterminate and can be chosen by the implementation. There may be dependences

between the iterations. When an iteration executes, it may add elements to S.

- **Ordered-set iterator: foreach (e in OrderedSet S) {B(e)}** *This construct iterates over an ordered set S. It is similar to the unordered set iterator above, except that a sequential implementation must choose a minimal element from S at every iteration. When an iteration executes, it may add elements to S.*

```
Mesh mesh = // read in initial mesh
Workset<Triangle> ws;
ws.add(mesh.badTriangles());
foreach (Triangle t in Set ws) {
  if (t no longer in mesh) continue;
  Cavity c = new Cavity(t);
  c.expand();
  c.retriangulate();
  mesh.update(c);
  ws.add(c.badTriangles());
}
```

Figure 5. DMR using an unordered Galois set iterator

Iterators over multi-sets can be defined similarly. In principle, unordered iterators are a special case of ordered iterators, but they are sufficiently important in applications that we give them special treatment. Allowing break statements in the body of a Galois iterator permits early exits out of iterators. This can be useful for search problems. Some unordered algorithms can also be written using divide-and-conquer, as discussed in Section 7.

Set iterators were first introduced in the SETL programming language [57] and can now be found in most object-oriented languages such as Java and C++. However, *new elements cannot be added to sets while iterating over them, which is possible with Galois set iterators*. Note that the iterators have a well-defined sequential semantics. The unordered-set iterator specifies the don't-care nondeterminism of unordered algorithms.

The Galois system provides a (concurrent) data structure library, similar in spirit to the Java collections library, containing implementations of key ADTs such as graphs, trees, grids, work-sets, etc. Application programmers write algorithms in sequential Java, using the appropriate library classes and Galois set iterators. Figure 5 shows pseudocode for Delaunay mesh refinement, written using the unordered Galois set iterator. The body of the Galois set iterator is the implementation of the operator. Note that neighborhoods are defined *implicitly* by the calls to the graph ADT; for example, if the body of the iterator invokes a graph API method to get the outgoing edges from an active node, these edges become part of the neighborhood for that activity. Therefore, in general, the neighborhood of an activity is known only when that activity is completed. This has important implications for parallelization, as we discuss in Section 4.

3.3 Tao-analysis of algorithms

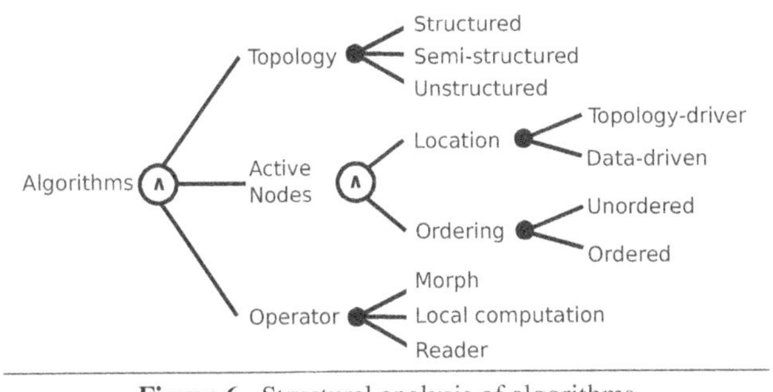

Figure 6. Structural analysis of algorithms

The operator formulation permits a natural structural analysis of algorithms along three dimensions (shown in Figure 6): Topology, Active nodes and Operator. The topology describes the data structure on which computation occurs. The active nodes dimension describes how nodes become active and how active nodes should be ordered, providing a global view of an algorithm. Finally, the operator describes the action of the operator on an active node, providing a local view of an algorithm. We call this *tao-analysis*. Exploiting this structure is key to efficient parallel implementations as we discuss in Section 4.

1. *Topology:* We classify graph topologies according to the (Kolmogorov) complexity of their descriptions. Highly structured topologies can be described concisely with a small number of parameters, while unstructured topologies require verbose descriptions. The topology of a graph is an important indicator of the kinds of optimizations available to algorithm implementations; for example, algorithms in which graphs have highly structured topologies may be amenable to static analysis and optimization.
   - *Structured:* An example of a structured topology is a graph consisting of labeled nodes and *no* edges: this is isomorphic to a set or multiset. Its topology can be described by a single number, which is the number of elements in the set/multiset. If the nodes are totally ordered, the graph is isomorphic to a sequence or stream. Cliques (graphs in which every pair of nodes is connected by a labeled edge) are isomorphic to square dense matrices (row/column numbers are derived from a total ordering of the nodes). Their topology is completely specified by a single number, which is the number of nodes in the clique. The final example we will consider in this paper is the rectangular grid; its topology is determined completely by two numbers, its height and width.
   - *Semi-structured:* We classify trees as semi-structured topologies. Although trees have useful structural invariants, there are many trees with the same number of nodes and edges.
   - *Unstructured:* General graphs fall in this category.
2. *Active nodes:* This dimension describes how nodes become active and the order in which they must be processed.
   - *Location:* Nodes can become active in a *topology-driven* or *data-driven* manner. In topology-driven algorithms, the active nodes are determined by the graph, so the execution of the operator at some active node does not cause other nodes to become active. Common examples are algorithms that iterate over all the nodes or edges of a graph. In data-driven algorithms, an activity at one node may cause other nodes to become active, so nodes become active in a data-dependent and unpredictable manner. Some examples are the preflow-push algorithm for maxflow computation in graphs and algorithms for event-driven simulation.
   - *Ordering:* As discussed above, active nodes in some algorithms are ordered whereas others are unordered.
3. *Operator:* We classify operators based on how they modify the graph.
   - *Morph:* A morph operator may modify its neighborhood by adding or deleting nodes and edges, and it may also update values on nodes and edges. The Delaunay mesh refinement operator is an example; other examples are discussed in Section 5.1.
   - *Local computation:* A local computation operator may update values stored on nodes and edges in its neighborhood, but it does not change the graph connectivity. Finite-difference computations are the classic example; other examples are discussed in Section 5.2.

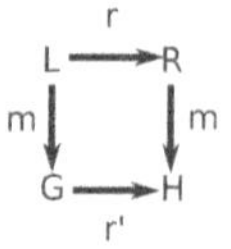

Figure 7. Graph rewriting: single-pushout approach

- *Reader:* An operator is a reader for a data structure if it does not modify it in any way. For example, the ray-tracing operator is a reader for the scene being rendered; other examples are discussed in Section 5.3.

These definitions can be generalized in the obvious way for algorithms that deal with multiple data structures. In that case, neighborhoods span multiple data structures, and the classification of an operator is with respect to a particular data structure. For example, in matrix multiplication $C = AB$, the operator is a local computation operator for C and a reader for matrices A and B.

3.4 Discussion

As mentioned above, under-specification of the order of processing active nodes in unordered algorithms is an instance of don't-care non-determinism. In some unordered algorithms, the output is independent of the order in which active nodes are processed, a property that is referred to as the *Church-Rosser property* since the most famous example of this behavior is β-reduction in λ-calculus. Dataflow graph execution [4, 15] and the preflow-push algorithm for computing maxflow [12] also exhibit this behavior. In other algorithms, the output may be different for different choices of active nodes, but all such outputs are acceptable, so the implementation can still pick any active node for execution. Delaunay mesh refinement and Petri net simulation are examples. The preflow-push algorithm also exhibits this behavior if the algorithm outputs both the min-cut and the max-flow. Even for unordered algorithms, iteration execution order may affect cache performance and the number of executed iterations, so control of iteration order is useful for efficiency. Nguyen and Pingali describe a notation and an implementation for doing this [50].

The metaphor of operators acting on neighborhoods is reminiscent of notions in term-rewriting systems, such as graph grammars in particular [18, 42]. The semantics of functional language programs are usually specified using term rewriting systems that describe how expressions can be replaced by other expressions within the context of the functional program. The process of applying rewrite rules repeatedly to a functional language program is known as string or tree reduction.

Tree reduction can be generalized in a natural way to graph reduction by using graph grammars as rewrite rules [18, 42]. A graph rewrite rule is defined as a morphism in the category $\mathbf{C}$ of labeled graphs with partial graph morphisms as arrows: $r : L \rightarrow R$, and a rewriting step is defined by a single pushout diagram [42] as shown in Figure 7. In this diagram, G is a graph, and the total morphism $m : L \rightarrow G$, which is called a *redex*, identifies the portion of G that matches L, the left-hand side of the rewrite rule. The application of a rule r at a redex m leads to a direct derivation $(r, m) : G \Rightarrow H$ given by the pushout in Figure 7.

In graph reduction, rewrite rules are applied repeatedly to the text of the *program* until a normal or head-normal form is reached; in the operator formulation on the other hand, the operator is applied to the *data structure* until there are no more active nodes. In addition, we do not require operators to be expressible as a finite set of "syntactic" rewrite rule schemas (it is not clear that Delaunay mesh refinement, for example, can be specified using graph grammars, although some progress along these lines is reported by Panangaden and Verbrugge [60]). Nevertheless, the terminology of graph grammars may be useful for providing a theoretical foundation for the operator formulation of algorithms. For example, in the context of Figure 7, the graph structure of L and R are identical for local computation operators, while for reader operators, the rewrite rule r is the identity morphism. We also note that whether operators make imperative-style in-place updates to graphs or create modified copies of the graph in a functional style can be viewed as a matter of implementation.

4. Amorphous data-parallelism

The operator formulation of an algorithm is not explicitly parallel, but Figure 4 shows intuitively how opportunities for exploiting parallelism arise in an algorithm: if there are many active nodes at some point in the computation, each one is a site where a processor can perform computation, subject to neighborhood and ordering constraints. When active nodes are unordered, the neighborhood constraints must ensure that the output produced by executing the activities in parallel is the same as the output produced by executing the activities one at a time in some order. For ordered active elements, this order must be the same as the ordering on active elements.

DEFINITION 2. *Given a set of active nodes and an ordering on active nodes,* amorphous data-parallelism *is the parallelism that arises from simultaneously processing active nodes, subject to neighborhood and ordering constraints.*

Amorphous data-parallelism is a generalization of conventional data-parallelism in which (i) concurrent operations may conflict with each other, (ii) activities can be created dynamically, and (iii) activities may modify the underlying data structure. Not surprisingly, the exploitation of amorphous data-parallelism is more complex than the exploitation of conventional data-parallelism. In this section, we present a baseline implementation that uses optimistic or speculative execution.

4.1 Baseline: speculative parallel execution

In the baseline execution model, the graph is stored in shared-memory, and active nodes are processed by some number of threads. A thread picks an active node from the work-set and speculatively applies the operator to that node, making calls to the graph API to perform operations on the graph as needed. The neighborhood of an activity can be visualized as a blue ink-blot that begins at the active node and spreads incrementally whenever a graph API call is made that touches new nodes or edges in the graph. To ensure that neighborhoods are disjoint, the concurrent graph class can use exclusive logical locks: each graph element has an exclusive lock that must be acquired by a thread before it can access that element. Locks are held until the activity terminates. If a lock cannot be acquired because it is already owned by another thread, a conflict is reported to the runtime system, which rolls back one of the conflicting activities. Lock manipulation is performed entirely by the methods in the graph class; in addition, to enable rollback, each graph API method that modifies the graph makes a copy of the data before modification, as is done in other systems that use speculation such as transactional memory and thread-level speculation [25, 29, 55, 61].

If active elements are not ordered, the activity commits when the application of the operator is complete, and all acquired locks are then released. If active elements are ordered, active nodes can still be processed in any order, but they must commit in serial order. This can be implemented using a data structure similar to a reorder buffer in out-of-order processors [40]. In this case, locks are released only when the activity commits (or is aborted). Exclusive logical locks can be implemented by using a compare-and-set instruction to mark a graph element with the id of the activity that touches it.

Neighborhoods of concurrent activities can be permitted to overlap if these activities do not modify nodes and edges in the intersection of these neighborhoods (consider activities i_3 and i_4 in Figure 4). Therefore, additional concurrency is possible if we recognize read-only data structures and do not lock their elements; reader/writer locks are another solution. The most general solution is to use commutativity conditions; this allows iterations to execute in parallel even if they perform reduction operations on shared variables, for example. To keep the discussion simple, we do not describe these alternatives here but refer the interested reader to Kulkarni *et al.* [39]. The literature on PRAM algorithms has explored similar variations such as the EREW and combining CRCW models [32, 62].

4.1.1 Parallelism profiles

For an algorithm like matrix multiplication for which a static dependence graph can be generated, it is possible to give closed-form estimates of the critical path length and the amount of parallelism at each point of execution (these estimates are usually parameterized by the size of the input). For example, in multiplying two $N \times N$ matrices using the standard algorithm, there are N^3 multiplications that can be performed in parallel. In contrast, amorphous data-parallelism in irregular algorithms is usually a function of runtime values, and closed-form estimates are not generally possible.

One measure of amorphous parallelism in irregular algorithms is the number of active nodes that can be processed in parallel at each step of the algorithm for a given input, assuming that (i) there is an unbounded number of processors, (ii) an activity takes one time step to execute, (iii) the system has perfect knowledge of neighborhood and ordering constraints so it only executes activities that can complete successfully, and (iv) a maximal set of non-conflicting activities is executed at each step. This is called the *available parallelism* at each step, and a graph showing the available parallelism at each step of execution of an irregular algorithm for a given input is called a *parallelism profile*. For algorithms for which a static dependence graph can be generated, the available parallelism at any step corresponds to the width of the dependence graph at that step. In this paper, we will present parallelism profiles produced by the ParaMeter tool [38].

Figure 8 shows the parallelism profiles of Boruvka's and Prim's minimal spanning tree (MST) algorithms; the input is a random graph. As explained in Section 5.1, Boruvka's algorithm is unordered while Prim's algorithm is ordered. At first sight, it is surprising that an ordered algorithm like Prim has any parallelism, but an intuitive explanation is that processing active nodes in the specified order is sufficient but not necessary to produce correct results. A parallel implementation can process active nodes out of order, and as long as no conflicts are detected before the activity commits, the output produced by the parallel execution will be correct. This is similar to how out-of-order execution processors find parallelism in sequential machine language programs. In our experience, many problems can be solved by both ordered and unordered algorithms, but the critical path is shorter for the unordered algorithm although it may perform more work than its ordered counterpart (see Hassaan *et al.* [26] for more details).

4.2 Exploiting structure to reduce overheads

The overheads of the baseline system can be reduced by exploiting structure when it is present. The following structure is very important in applications.

DEFINITION 3. *An implementation of an operator is said to be* cautious *if it reads* all *the elements of its neighborhood before it modifies* any *of them.*

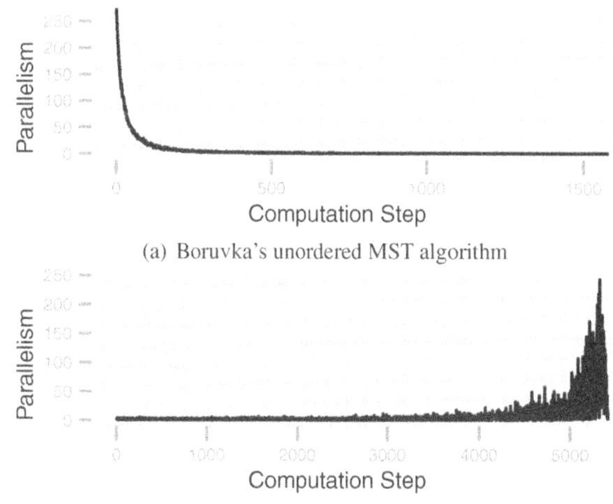

(a) Boruvka's unordered MST algorithm

(b) Prim's ordered MST algorithm

Figure 8. MST parallelism profiles of a random graph with 10,000 nodes and 35,605 edges; the edges have random, uniformly distributed weights between 1 and 1,000.

Operators can usually be implemented in different ways: for example, one implementation might read node A, write to node A, read node B, and write to node B, in that order, whereas a different implementation might perform the two reads before the writes. By Definition 3, the second implementation is cautious, but the first one is not. In our experience, the natural implementations of most operators such as Delaunay mesh refinement are cautious[2]. In contrast, the operator for the well-known Delaunay triangulation algorithm of Guibas, Knuth and Sharir [23] does not have a naturally cautious implementation. It performs graph mutations called edge flips, which are done incrementally.

Unordered algorithms with cautious operator implementations can be executed speculatively without buffering updates or making backup copies of modified data because all conflicts are detected during the read-only phase of the operator execution. Blandford *et al.* [7] exploit this optimization in their DMR implementation; phrasing this optimization in terms of algorithmic structure permits a general-purpose system like Galois to use it for other algorithms (see Méndez-Lojo *et al.* [47]). Prountzos *et al.* [54] present a shape analysis for determining cautiousness using static analysis.

4.3 Exploiting structure for coordinated scheduling

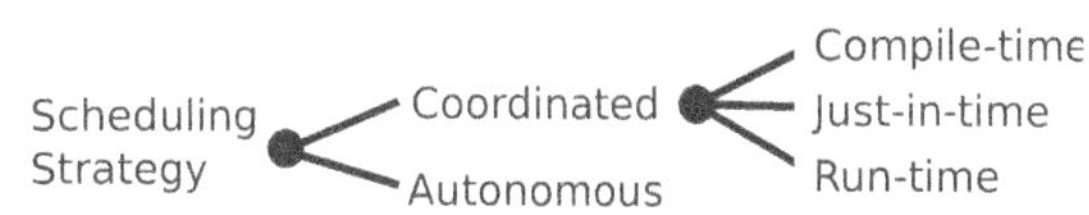

Figure 9. Scheduling strategies

The scheduling strategy implemented in the baseline system can be called *autonomous scheduling* because activities are executed in an uncoordinated way, requiring online conflict detection and rollback for correct execution. Speculative overheads are eliminated if we ensure that only non-conflicting iterations are scheduled for simultaneous execution, a strategy that we call *coordinated scheduling*. Figure 9 shows a number of coordinated scheduling strategies. All of these strategies are based on constructing a dependence graph either explicitly or implicitly, but they do so at different points during program compilation and execution.

[2] In principle, every operator has a trivial cautious implementation that touches all graph elements before beginning the computation (equivalently, it locks the whole graph). The obvious disadvantage is that this approach eliminates all parallelism.

In terms of the operator formulation, construction of the dependence graph involves the following steps: (i) determine all active nodes, (ii) determine neighborhoods and ordering of the corresponding activities, and (iii) create a partial order of activities that respects neighborhood and ordering constraints. Activities can then be executed in parallel without speculation but with proper synchronization to ensure that the partial order of activities is respected. Although this approach seems obvious, ordered, data-driven algorithms like event-driven simulation cannot in general be parallelized using this approach: the execution of one activity may cause a new node to become active, and this new activity may have higher priority than and conflict with existing activities. It is likely that optimistic parallelization is the only general-purpose approach for parallelizing ordered, data-driven algorithms, even if they are expressed in a functional language. All other classes of algorithms can be executed without speculation as described below.

4.3.1 Runtime coordination

Unordered data-driven algorithms: These algorithms can be parallelized without speculation by interleaving the construction of the dependence graph with execution of activities. The execution of the algorithm proceeds in rounds. In each round, a set of non-conflicting activities is selected and executed in parallel without synchronization. Any newly created activities are postponed to the next round at which point they are considered for execution together with unprocessed activities from the current round. Implementing this strategy requires solving two problems: (i) how do we compute the neighborhoods of activities, and (ii) given a set of activities and their neighborhoods, how do we find a set of non-conflicting activities?

In general, we must execute the operator completely to find the neighborhood of an activity, and this may cause side-effects to global data structures. If an activity is not chosen for execution in the current round (because of conflicts), these side-effects must be undone for correct execution. One solution is to privatize these updates as is done in some versions of transactional memory. In effect, activities are executed twice in each round: once with privatization to determine neighborhoods, and then again for real if they are chosen for execution in the current round. Implemented literally, this strategy is not very efficient; fortunately, most algorithms have structure that can be exploited to eliminate the need for repeated execution. In all data-driven local computation algorithms we have studied (see Section 5.2.2), the neighborhood of an activity is just the active node and its immediate neighbors in the graph. In morph algorithms, most operator implementations are cautious, so the neighborhood of an activity can be determined by executing it partially up to the point where it starts to make modifications to its neighborhood. If the activity is chosen for execution in that round, execution simply continues from that point.

Once the neighborhoods of all activities have been determined, we can build a *conflict graph* in which nodes represent the active nodes from the algorithm, and edges represent conflicts between activities. Luby's randomized parallel algorithm can be used to find a *maximal independent set* of activities [43], and this set of activities can be executed in parallel without synchronization. This approach can be viewed as building and exploiting the dependence graph level by level, with barrier synchronization between levels. The DMR implementation of Hudson *et al.* uses this approach [31].

Topology-driven algorithms: In these algorithms, activities do not create new active nodes, so both unordered and ordered algorithms can be executed using runtime coordination. Unordered topology-driven algorithms can be executed in rounds as described above. A variation of this approach can be used for ordered topology-driven algorithms. In this case, we find a maximal prefix of the sequence of active nodes (rather than a maximal independent set of the set of active nodes) such that all active nodes in the prefix have non-interfering neighborhoods, and execute these nodes in parallel. This process can then repeated with the remaining suffix of active nodes.

Notice that runtime coordination can be used for all irregular algorithms other than ordered, data-driven algorithms.

4.3.2 Just-in-time coordination

For some topology-driven algorithms, the dependence graph is independent of the labels on nodes and edges of the graph and it is a function purely of the graph topology. Therefore, a dependence graph can be generated at runtime after the input graph is given but before the program is executed. We call this strategy *just-in-time coordination*, and it is a generalization of the *inspector-executor method* of Saltz *et al.* [64].

For topology-driven algorithms, active nodes are known once the input is given, so the remaining problems are the determination of neighborhoods and ordering. In local computation algorithms amenable to just-in-time scheduling, these can usually be determined from an inspection of the graph and the resulting code is called the *inspector*. A well-known example is the implementation of sparse iterative solvers on distributed-memory computers. The distribution of the graph between processors is known only at runtime, so inspection of the graph is required to determine input dependences for use in communication schedules, as advocated by Saltz *et al.* [64]. Other examples are parallel top-down and bottom-up walks of trees. In a bottom-up walk, a recursive descent from the root sets up the dependences, and the bottom-up computations can then be done in parallel with appropriate synchronization; an example is the center-of-mass computation in n-body methods.

For topology-driven *morph* algorithms amenable to just-in-time scheduling, inspection of the graph may be insufficient since the structure of the graph can be modified during the execution of the algorithms, changing neighborhoods and dependences. For these algorithms, neighborhoods and ordering can be determined by a symbolic execution of the algorithm. Parallel sparse Cholesky factorization is the most famous example of this approach [20]. The algorithms is unordered but heuristics like minimal degree ordering are used to order the active nodes for efficiency. The algorithm is executed symbolically to compute the dependence graph (this phase is called *symbolic factorization* and the dependence graph is called the *elimination tree*). The elimination tree is then used to perform the actual factorization in parallel (this phase is known as *numerical factorization*). Symbolic factorization is done efficiently using Boolean operations, and for large matrices, it takes little time relative to numerical factorization. Just-in-time coordination cannot be used for sparse LU factorization with pivoting since its dependence graph is affected by pivoting, which depends on the data values in the matrix.

4.3.3 Compile-time coordination

Some algorithms amenable to just-in-time coordination have structured input graphs. In that case, the dependence graph, suitably parameterized by the unknown parameters of the input graph, can be produced at compile-time. For example, if the graph is a grid as it is in finite-difference methods, the dependence graph is parameterized by the dimensions of the grid. Other important examples are dense Cholesky and LU factorization (the input graph is a clique), the dense Basic Linear Algebra Subroutines (the input graph is a clique), and FFTs (sequences or sequences of sequences).

Given the importance of these algorithms in high-performance computing, it is not surprising that *automatic* generation of dependence graphs for this class of algorithms has received a lot of attention. These techniques are known as *dependence analysis* in the literature, and methods based on integer linear programming are successful for regular, dense array programs in which array subscripts are affine functions of loop indices [35]; LU with pivoting requires fractal symbol analysis [48].

Compile-time coordination is also possible regardless of the topology if the algorithm is a topology-driven local computation and the neighborhood of an activity is just the active node itself, ignoring read-only data structures. In this case, activities are trivially independent (subject to ordering constraints) because each one modifies a disjoint portion of the graph. A typical example is computing some result for each node in a graph. The output is a vector indexed by node. Each activity reads some portion of the graph but only writes to the node-specific portion of the output vector. In the literature, most PRAM algorithms and algorithms written using DO-ALL loops fall in this category.

4.4 Discussion

To the best of our knowledge, the first use of optimistic parallelization was in Jefferson's Timewarp system for event-driven simulation [33]. However, Timewarp was not a general-purpose parallel programming system. Thread-level speculation (TLS) was proposed by Rauchwerger and Padua [55] for parallelizing array programs in which subscripts could not be analyzed by the compiler. This work was very influential, and it inspired a lot of work on architectural support for speculative execution [61]. TLS systems were designed for languages like FORTRAN and C, so there was no support for don't-care non-determinism or unordered algorithms. Moreover, data abstractions do not play a role in the implementation of TLS. Another influential line of work is the transactional memory (TM) work of Herlihy, Moss, Harris and others [25, 29]. In contrast to our approach, the application programming model is *explicitly parallel*; threads synchronize using transactions, and the overheads of executing this synchronization construct are reduced using optimistic synchronization. In addition, most TM systems other than boosted systems [28] perform memory-level conflict checking rather than ADT-level conflict checking. This results in spurious conflicts that prevent efficient parallel execution. For example, if an iteration of an unordered iterator is rolled back, the concrete state of the work-set must also be restored to its original state, and all other iterations that were executed since that iteration must also be rolled back [40].

Relatively little is known about automatic generation of dependence graphs for runtime and just-in-time coordination. The discussion in this section shows that there is no sharp dichotomy between regular and irregular algorithms: instead, regular algorithms are a special case of irregular algorithms in the same way that metric spaces are a special case of general topologies in mathematics. Note that although coordinated scheduling seems attractive because there is no wasted work from mis-speculation, the overhead of generating a dependence graph may limit its usefulness even when it is possible to produce one.

5. Case studies of algorithms

In this section, we discuss how the tao-analysis described in Section 3 and the implementation strategies described in Section 4 can be applied to important algorithms. The discussion is organized by the type of the operator.

5.1 Morph algorithms

Morphs are the most complex variety of operators. Although they can be viewed abstractly as replacing sub-graphs with other graphs, it is more intuitive to classify them as follows.

- *Refinement:* A refinement operator makes the graph bigger by adding new nodes and edges, possibly removing a few nodes and edges in the process.

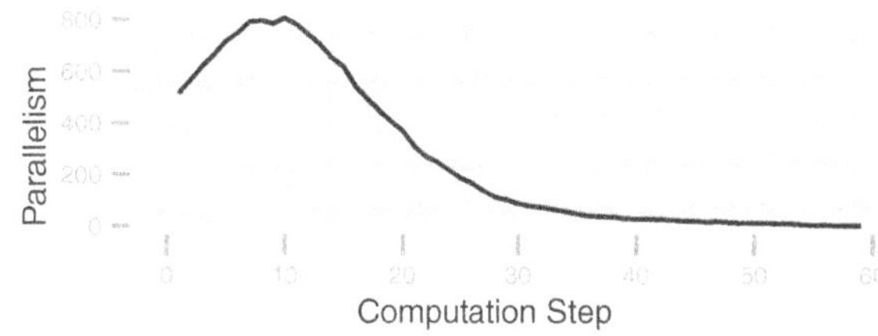

Figure 10. Available parallelism in Delaunay mesh refinement

- *Coarsening:* A coarsening operator clusters nodes or sub-graphs together, replacing them with a smaller sub-graph that represents the cluster.
- *General morph:* All other operations that modify the graph structure fall in this category.

5.1.1 Refinement

Data-driven refinement algorithms usually operate on a single graph. Most topology-driven refinement operators operate on two data structures G_i and G_o; G_i is read-only and its topology determines the active nodes in the algorithm, while G_o is morphed by each activity.

Map-reduce: In the map-reduce programming model [13], a map operation applies a function "point-wise" to each element of a set or multi-set S_i to produce another set or multi-set S_o. The active nodes are the elements of S_i, and they can be processed in any order. This is a topology-driven, unordered algorithm, which is a refinement morph for S_o since elements are added incrementally to S_o during execution.

Streams: A stream operator in languages like StreamIt [21] is a refinement morph from its input streams to its output streams (streams are non-strict sequences [53]). Stateless and stateful stream operators can be expressed using unordered and ordered iteration on sequences.

Prim's MST algorithm: Most algorithms that build trees in a top-down fashion use refinement morphs. Figure 11 shows one implementation of Prim's algorithm for computing MSTs; it is a topology-driven, ordered algorithm in which the operator is a reader for the graph g and a refinement morph for tree mst. Initially, one node is chosen as the root of the tree and added to the MST, and all of its edges are added to the ordered work-set, ordered by weight. In each iteration, the smallest edge (s, t) is removed from the work-set. Note that node s is guaranteed to be in the tree. If t is not in the MST, (s, t) is added to the tree, and all edges (t, u) are added to the work-set, provided u is not in the MST. When the algorithm terminates, all nodes are in the MST. This algorithm has the same asymptotic complexity as the standard algorithm in textbooks [12], but the work-set contains edges rather than nodes. The standard algorithm requires a priority queue in which node priorities can be decreased dynamically. It is unclear whether it is worth generalizing the implementation of ordered-set iterators in a general-purpose system like Galois to permit dynamic updates to the ordering.

N-body tree-building: Top-down tree construction is also used in n-body methods like Barnes-Hut [6] and fast multipole. The tree is a recursive spatial partitioning in which each leaf contains a single particle. Initially, the tree is a single node, representing the entire space. Particles are then inserted into the tree, splitting leaf nodes so that each leaf node contains only a single particle. The work-set in this case is the set of particles. In contrast to Prim's algorithm, this algorithm is unordered because particles can be inserted into the tree in any order.

Andersen-style inclusion-based points-to analysis: This compiler algorithm [3] is an example of a refinement morph on general graphs. It builds a *points-to graph* in which nodes represent pro-

```
Graph g = // read in input graph
Tree mst; // create empty tree
mst.setRoot(r); // r is an arbitrary vertex in g
OrderedWorkset<Edge> ows; // ordered by edge weight
ows.add(g.getEdges(r));
foreach (Edge (s,t) in OrderedSet ows) {
  if (mst.contains(t)) continue;
  mst.addEdge(s,t); // s becomes parent of t
  foreach (Edge (t,u) in Set g.getEdges(t)) {
    if (!mst.contains(u)) ows.add((t,u));
  }
}
```

Figure 11. Top-down tree construction: Prim's MST algorithm

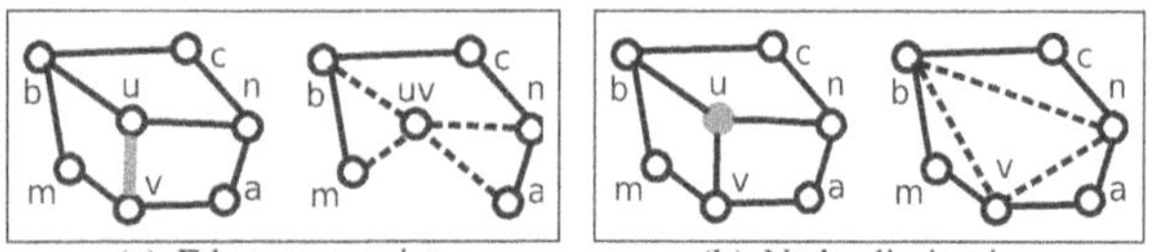

(a) Edge contraction (b) Node elimination

Figure 12. Two kinds of coarsening operators

gram variables, and an edge (a, b) asserts that variable a may point to b at some point in the program. Each iteration of the algorithm may discover new points-to facts, and if it does, it adds new edges to the points-to graph. This is an unordered, data-driven algorithm that uses a refinement morph on the graph.

Delaunay mesh refinement: This is an unordered, data-driven morph algorithm on an unstructured graph (see Section 2).

Discussion: Refinement algorithms in which graph elements are only added and never removed are called *strong* refinement algorithms. All the algorithms listed above other than DMR are strong refinement algorithms. Section 6.3 describes how this property can be exploited to produce efficient implementations.

Although parallelism in most irregular algorithms is very input dependent, algorithms that use refinement morphs have a characteristic profile when executed with randomized input data. Figure 10 shows the parallelism profile for DMR for an input of 100,000 triangles. Available parallelism starts at some level, increases as the data structure gets larger (because there is less likelihood of conflicts), and then ramps down as work is completed. The parallelism profile for Prim's algorithm, shown in Figure 8(b), has a similar pattern—in this algorithm, the available parallelism is very small initially since only one activity succeeds in growing the tree from the root. As the MST gets larger, there are more sites where the tree can grow, so parallelism ramps up and then ramps down as the MST is completed. Tree-building in Barnes-Hut exhibits a similar parallelism profile, as can be seen in Figure 13(a).

5.1.2 Coarsening

There are three main ways of doing coarsening: edge contraction, node elimination and sub-graph contraction.

Edge contraction An edge is eliminated from the graph by fusing the two nodes at its end points and removing redundant edges from the resulting graph, as shown in Figure 12(a). When redundant edges are eliminated, the weight on the remaining edge is adjusted in application-specific ways. In sparse graphs, each edge contraction affects a relatively small neighborhood, so in sufficiently large graphs, many edge contraction operations can happen in parallel.

Boruvka's MST algorithm: Boruvka's algorithm [12] computes MSTs bottom-up by performing edge contraction on the input graph until there is only one node left. A separate graph represents the MST as it is built bottom-up. The MST is initialized with every node in the input graph forming its own single-node tree, i.e., a forest. The active nodes are the nodes remaining in the input graph. In each iteration, an active node n finds the minimum weight edge (n, m) incident on it and performs edge contraction along this edge. This edge is added to the MST where it connects two previously disjoint trees. A new node nm is created in the input graph to represent the merged nodes n and m. If there are redundant edges during edge contraction, only the least weight edge is kept. Finally, nm is added back to the work-set. When the input graph has been contracted to one node, the MST graph will be the correct minimal spanning tree of the input graph.

Figure 8(a) shows a parallelism profile for Boruvka's algorithm. Interestingly, Kruskal's algorithm [12] also finds MSTs by performing edge contraction, but it iterates over an ordered work-set of edges, sorted by edge weight.

Metis graph partitioner: Graph coarsening by edge contraction is a key step in the Metis graph partitioner [34]. This algorithm builds a sequence of successively coarser graphs until a coarse-enough graph is obtained; this graph is then partitioned, and the partitioning is interpolated back to the original graph. Each of the coarsening steps is performed by an unordered, topology-driven morph (the nodes of the finer graph are the active nodes).

The parallel implementation of Metis uses runtime coordinated scheduling. The problem of finding a maximal independent set of edges that can be contracted in parallel can be solved by finding *maximal matchings* [12]. Efficient heuristics are known for computing maximal cardinality matchings and maximal weighted matchings in graphs of various kinds. Metis uses randomized matching since that seems to perform well in practice; this strategy is well-suited for autonomous scheduling as well.

Agglomerative clustering and map/reduce: Agglomerative clustering, a well-known data-mining algorithm, also uses a coarsening morph. The input is (i) a data-set, and (ii) a measure of the distance between items in the data-set. At each step, the two closest points in the data-set are clustered together and replaced by a single new point that represents the new cluster. The location of this new point may be determined heuristically [59]. The greedy strict consensus merger (SCM) algorithm for phylogeny reconstruction implements this algorithm for a set of trees. These algorithms can be expressed using an ordered set iterator. The *reduce* operation in the map-reduce model [13] can be implemented in many ways; an in-place reduction can be implemented by an unordered iterator in which the operator replaces randomly chosen pairs of elements from the set with the result of applying the reduction operation to these elements.

Node elimination Graph coarsening can also be based on *node elimination*. Each step removes a node from the graph and inserts edges as needed between its erstwhile neighbors to make a clique, adjusting weights on the remaining nodes and edges appropriately. In Figure 12(b), node u is eliminated, and edges (b, v), (v, n) and (n, b) are inserted to make $\{b, v, n\}$ a clique. Node elimination is the graph-theoretic foundation of matrix factorization algorithms such as Cholesky and LU factorizations.

Sparse Cholesky factorization in particular has received a lot of attention in the numerical linear algebra community. The new edges inserted by node elimination are called *fill* since they correspond to zeroes in the original matrix that become non-zeros as a result of the elimination process. Different node elimination orders result in different amounts of fill in general; therefore, although the basic algorithm is unordered, practical implementations of sparse Cholesky factorization use heuristic orderings for node elimination to minimize fill. One heuristic is *minimal-degree ordering*, which greedily picks the node with minimal degree at each elimination step. Just-in-time coordination is used to schedule computations [20].

Sub-graph contraction Graphs can be coarsened by contracting entire sub-graphs at a time (edge contraction is a special but important sub-case). In the compiler literature, *elimination-based al-*

gorithms perform dataflow analysis on control-flow graphs by contracting "structured" sub-graphs whose dataflow behaviors have a concise description. Dataflow analysis is performed on the reduced graph, and within contracted sub-graphs, interpolation is used to determine dataflow values. This idea can be used recursively on the reduced graph. Sub-graph contraction can be performed in parallel. This approach to parallel dataflow analysis has been studied by Ryder [41] and Soffa [37].

5.1.3 General morph

Some applications make structural updates that are neither refinements nor coarsenings, but many of these updates may nevertheless be performed in parallel.

Some algorithms build trees using complicated structural manipulations that cannot be classified neatly as top-down or bottom-up construction. For example, when values are inserted into a heap or a red-black tree, the final data structure is a tree, but each insertion may perform complex manipulations [12]. The structure of the final heap or red-black tree depends on the order of insertions, but for most applications, any of these final structures is adequate, so this is an example of don't-care non-determinism, and it can be expressed with an unordered set iterator.

Algorithms that perform general morph operations on trees usually require optimistic parallelization. The simple conflict detection policy described in Section 4.1, which ensures disjointness of neighborhoods, is not adequate for these applications since every neighborhood contains the root of the tree. This class of algorithms may benefit from mechanisms like transactional memory that use more sophisticated conflict detection policies [29]; in fact, the parallelization of red-black tree operations is a standard microbenchmark in the literature on transactional memory.

Graph reduction of functional language programs and social network maintenance [10] are general morphs on graphs.

5.2 Local computation algorithms

We divide our discussion of local computation algorithms based on whether their active nodes are topology-driven or data-driven.

5.2.1 Topology-driven local computation algorithms

Cellular automata: Cellular automata operate on grids of one or two dimensions. Grid nodes represent cells of the automaton, and the state of a cell c at time t is a function of the states at time $t-1$ of cells in some neighborhood around c. This iterative scheme can be written using unordered iterators. A large variety of neighborhoods (stencils) are used in cellular automata.

Finite-differences: A similar state update scheme is used in finite-difference methods for the numerical solution of partial differential equations (PDEs) where it is known as Jacobi iteration. In this case, the grid arises from spatial discretization of the domain of the PDE, and nodes hold values of the dependent variable of the PDE. A disadvantage of Jacobi iteration is that it requires two arrays for its implementation to hold the states at the current and previous time steps. More complex update schemes have been designed to get around this problem. Intuitively, all these schemes blur the sharp distinction between old and new states, so nodes are updated using both old and new values. For example, *red-black ordering*, or more generally *multi-color ordering*, assigns a minimal number of colors to nodes in such a way that no node has the same color as the nodes in its neighborhood. Nodes of a given color therefore form an independent set that can be updated concurrently. These algorithms can be expressed using unordered set iterators with one loop for each color. Methods like Gauss-Seidel can be expressed using ordered set iterators.

In all these algorithms, active nodes and neighborhoods can be determined from the grid structure, which is known at compile-time. As a result, compile-time scheduling can be very effective for coordinating the computations. Most parallel implementations of Jacobi iteration partition the grid into blocks, and each processor is responsible for updating the nodes in one block. This data distribution requires less inter-processor communication than other distributions such as row or column cyclic distributions.

Tree traversals: Top-down and bottom-up are classic examples of tree traversals. The center-of-mass computation for cells in Barnes-Hut and other n-body methods are performed using a bottom-up walk over the spatial decomposition tree. This traversal can be expressed using an ordered iterator. For a tree, the amount of parallelism decreases as the computation advances up the tree, as can be seen in Figure 13(a).

Sparse MVM: The key operation in iterative linear system solvers like the conjugate-gradient method and GMRES is sparse matrix-vector multiplication (MVM), $y = Ax$, in which the matrix A is an $N \times N$ sparse matrix and x and y are dense vectors. Such a matrix can be viewed as a graph with N nodes in which there is a directed edge from node i to node j with weight A_{ij} if A_{ij} is non-zero. This algorithm can be expressed using unordered iteration over the nodes of the graph. The inspector-executor method is used to produce efficient communication schedules on distributed-memory machines, as discussed in Section 4.3. Compile-time coordination is possible on shared-memory machines since the operator is a reader for A and x, and it is trivial to determine that each iteration writes into a different element of y.

5.2.2 Data-driven local computation algorithms

In these algorithms, there is an initial set of active nodes, and performing an activity may cause other nodes to become active, so nodes become active in an unpredictable, data-driven fashion. Examples include the preflow-push algorithm [12] for the maxflow problem, AI message-passing algorithms such as belief propagation and survey propagation [44], Petri nets, and discrete-event simulation [33, 49]. In other algorithms, such as some approaches to solving spin Ising models [56], the pattern of node updates is determined by externally-generated data such as random numbers.

Although graph topology is typically less important for data-driven algorithms than it is in topology-driven ones, it can nevertheless be useful for reasoning about certain algorithms. For example, belief propagation is an exact inference algorithm on trees, but it is an approximate algorithm when used on general graphs because of the *loopy propagation problem* [44]. Grid structure is exploited in spin Ising solvers as well to reduce synchronization [56].

Preflow-push algorithm: This maxflow algorithm is the archetypal example of a data-driven local computation operator. Active nodes are nodes that have excess in-flow at intermediate stages of the algorithm. The algorithm also maintains at each node a value called *height*, which is a lower bound on the distance of that node to the sink. Two operations, *push* and *relabel*, are performed at active nodes to update the flow and height values respectively until termination. The algorithm is unordered.

Event-driven simulation: In the literature, there are two approaches to parallel event-driven simulation, called conservative and optimistic event-driven simulation [49]. Conservative event-driven simulation reformulates the algorithm so that in addition to sending data messages, processing stations also send out-of-band messages to update time at their neighbors. Each processing station can operate autonomously without fear of deadlock, and there is no need to maintain an ordered event list. This is an example of algorithm reformulation that replaces an ordered work-set with an unordered work-set. In contrast, Timewarp [33] is an optimistic parallel implementation of event-driven simulation. It can be viewed as an application-specific implementation of ordered set iterators as described in Section 4.1, with two key differences. First, threads are allowed to work on new events created by speculative activities that have not yet committed. This increases parallelism but opens up the possibility of cascading roll-backs. Second, instead of the global commit queue in the implementation of Section 4.1, there are periodic sweeps through the network to update "global virtual time" [33]. Both of these features can be implemented in a general-purpose way in a system like Galois, but more study is needed to determine if this is worthwhile.

5.2.3 Discussion

Solving fixpoint equations: Iterative methods for computing solutions to systems of equations can usually be formulated in both topology-driven and data-driven ways. A classic example is iterative dataflow analysis in compilers. Systems of dataflow equations can be solved by iterating over all the equations using a Jacobi or Gauss-Seidel formulation until a fixed point is reached; these are topology-driven approaches. Alternately, the classic worklist algorithm processes an equation only if its inputs have changed; this is a data-driven approach [1]. The underlying graph in this application is the control-flow graph, and for flow-sensitive problems, the dataflow values are implemented as labels on nodes or edges.

Speeding up local computation algorithms: Local computation algorithms can often be made more efficient by a preprocessing step that coarsens the graph, since this speeds up the flow of information across the graph. The multigrid method for solving linear systems is a classic example. This idea is also used in dataflow analysis of programs [1]. An elimination-based dataflow algorithm is used first to coarsen the graph. If the resulting graph is a single node, the solution to the dataflow problem is read off by inspection; otherwise, iterative dataflow analysis is applied to the coarse graph. In either case, the solution for the coarse graph is interpolated back into the original graph. One of the first hybrid dataflow algorithms along these lines was Allen and Cocke's *interval-based algorithm* for dataflow analysis. This algorithm finds and collapses intervals, which are single-entry, multiple-exit loop structures in the control-flow graph of the program.

Some local computation algorithms can be sped up by periodically computing and exploiting global information. The *global-relabel* heuristic in preflow-push is an example of such an operation. Preflow-push can be sped up by periodically performing a breadth-first search from the sink to update the height values [12]. In the extreme, global information can be used in every iteration. For example, iterative linear solvers often *precondition* the matrix iterations with another matrix that is obtained by a graph coarsening computation such as incomplete LU or Cholesky factorization.

5.3 Reader algorithms

An operator that reads a graph without modifying it in any way is a reader operator for that graph. Operators that perform *multiple* traversals over a fixed graph are a particularly important category. Each traversal maintains its own state, which is updated during the traversal, so the traversals can be performed concurrently. Force computation in n-body algorithms like Barnes-Hut [6] is an example. The force calculation is an unordered iteration over particles that computes the force on each particle by making a top-down traversal of a prefix of the tree. This step is completely parallel since each particle can be processed independently. The only shared data structure in this phase is the octree, which is not modified.

Another classic example is ray-tracing. Each ray is traced through the scene. If the ray hits an object, new rays may be spawned to account for reflections and refraction; these rays must also be processed. After the rays have been traced, they are used to construct the rendered image.

The key concern in implementing such algorithms is exploiting locality. One approach to enhancing locality in algorithms such as ray-tracing is to "chunk" similar work together. Rays that will propagate through the same portion of the scene are bundled together and processed simultaneously by a given processor. Because each ray requires the same scene data, this approach can enhance cache locality. A similar approach can be taken in Barnes-Hut: particles in the same region of space are likely to traverse similar parts of the octree during the force computation and thus can be processed together to improve locality [58].

In some cases, reader algorithms can be more substantially transformed to further enhance locality. In ray-tracing, bundled rays begin propagating through the scene in the same direction but may eventually diverge. Rather than using an *a priori* grouping of rays, groups can be dynamically updated as rays propagate through a scene, maintaining locality throughout execution [52].

5.4 Discussion

Some irregular applications have multiple phases, and each phase may use a different operator. N-body methods like Barnes-Hut are good examples; the tree-building phase uses a refinement morph whereas the force computation phase uses a reader operator since it does not modify the spatial decomposition tree. This is discussed in more detail in Section 6.1.

The structural analysis of algorithms presented in this section is different from the many efforts in the literature to identify *parallelism patterns*, such as the work of Mattson *et al.* [45], Snir's Parallel Processing Patterns [36] and the Berkeley motifs [51]. These approaches place related algorithms into categories (dense linear algebra, n-body methods, etc.), whereas this paper proposes structural decompositions of irregular algorithms. For example, n-body methods fall into a single category in the Berkeley motifs whereas we distinguish between the operators in the different phases of n-body methods. To use a biological metaphor, existing approaches produce classifications like the Linnaean taxonomy in biology, whereas the approach in this paper is more like molecular biology, producing "genetic profiles" of algorithms. On the other hand, existing classifications are broader in scope than ours since they seek to categorize implementation mechanisms such as whether task-queues or the master-worker approach is used to distribute work.

6. Case studies of applications

In this section, we present experimental results for three algorithms introduced previously: Barnes-Hut n-body simulation, Delaunay mesh refinement and inclusion-based points-to analysis. These algorithms were implemented using the Galois system, and illustrate how the principles of tao-analysis (in particular, Section 4.3) can be used to optimize performance.

We used two machines for our experimental results. The first contains two quad-core Intel Xeon X5570 processors for a total of eight cores. The second contains four six-core Intel Xeon X7540 processors for a total of 24 cores. Both run Linux 2.6.32.

6.1 Barnes-Hut n-body simulation

Barnes-Hut shows how tao-analysis can be used to leverage compile-time optimizations even though the Galois system uses optimistic parallelization as its baseline. Figure 13(a) shows the parallelism profile for one time-step of the algorithm. There are four phases, each with a different structural classification.

1. *Tree build:* The first phase builds the spatial decomposition tree top-down by inserting particles into the tree and splitting nodes as needed so there is one particle per leaf node (topology: tree, operator: refinement morph, active nodes: topology-driven and unordered). Note that the parallelism profile is similar to the parallelism profiles of other refinement morphs shown in Figure 10.

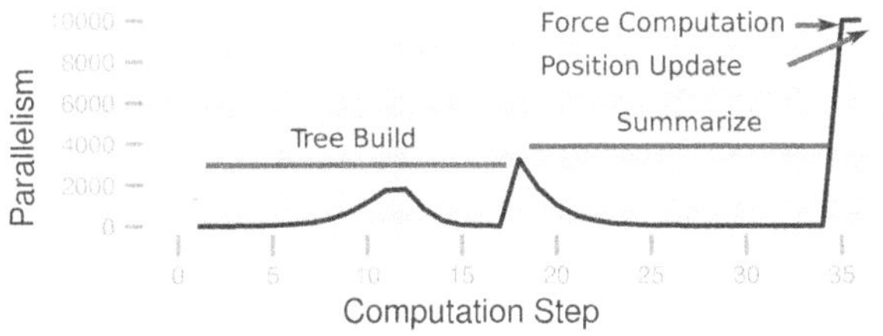

(a) Parallelism profile for 10,000 bodies

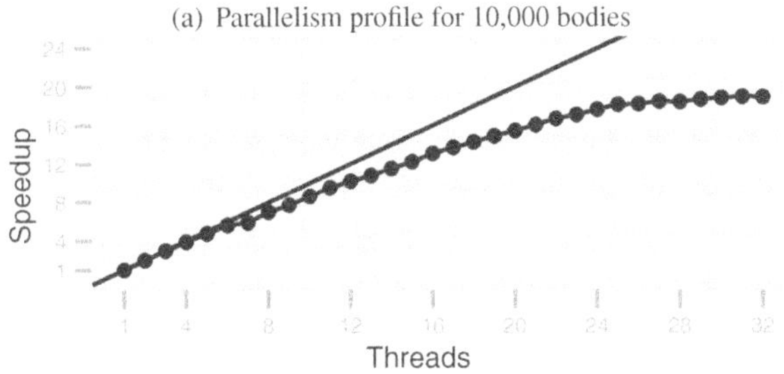

(b) Speedup for 1,000,000 bodies; sequential runtime is 122.2 s.

Figure 13. Parallelism profile and speedup for Barnes-Hut. All inputs initialized using the Plummer model.

2. *Summarize:* The second phase computes the center-of-mass and total mass of each internal node using a bottom-up walk of the octree (tree, local computation, topology-driven and ordered).
3. *Force computation:* The third phase computes the force acting upon each particle by traversing parts of the octree (tree, reader, unordered).
4. *Force update:* The last phase moves each particle to a new position (set, local computation, topology-driven and unordered).

Figure 13(b) shows the speedup on the 24 core machine. Most of the execution time is spent in the force computation phase. By default, the Galois system would use speculative execution for this phase, but tao-analysis reveals that it is possible to use compile-time coordinated scheduling. Using this information, we can execute activities non-speculatively, taking advantage of reduced runtime overheads. The machine supports simultaneous multithreading (SMT), and we show a few data points with more than 24 threads, which correspond to adding SMT threads. Performance scales well up to 24 threads. After that point, each additional SMT thread improves performance slightly, which suggests that there is room for locality improvements.

6.2 Delaunay mesh refinement

Figure 14 shows results for Delaunay mesh refinement on the 24 core machine. We take advantage of the cautious property of the operator implementation to reduce some overheads of speculative execution. As before, we show data points for additional SMT threads as well. This application is floating-point intensive. Performance scales well up to 24 threads, but after that point, SMT threads share floating-point resources, which limits continued scalability.

6.3 Inclusion-based points-to analysis

Inclusion-based points-to analysis is an example of how properties of operators can be used to reduce synchronization overheads. The algorithm performs a context-insensitive, flow-insensitive analysis that determines the variables that a pointer variable might point to during the execution of a program. A pass through the program generates a system of set constraints that implicitly defines the points-to set for each variable in the program. These constraints can be represented as a graph in which nodes represent variables, and edges represent constraints. The process of solving these set

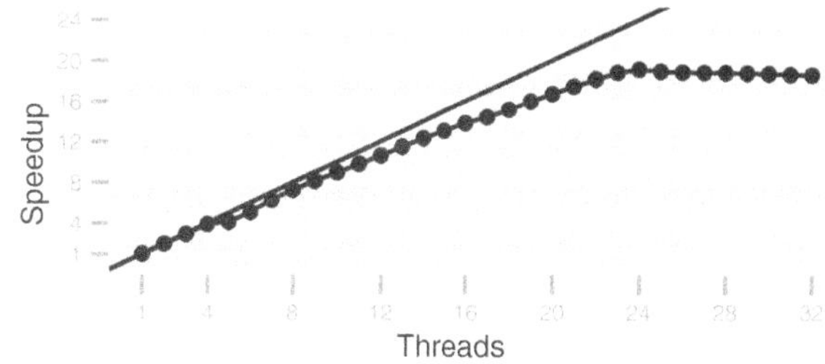

Figure 14. Speedup for Delaunay mesh refinement. The input is randomly generated. Initially, there are 1,999,998 triangles (951,964 bad triangles). Sequential runtime is 22.2 s.

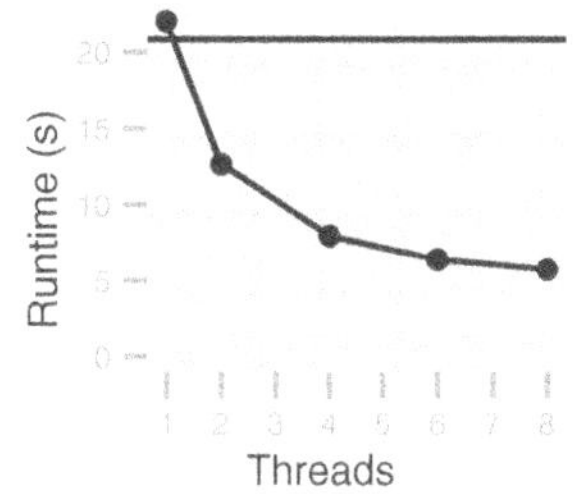

(a) Gimp input

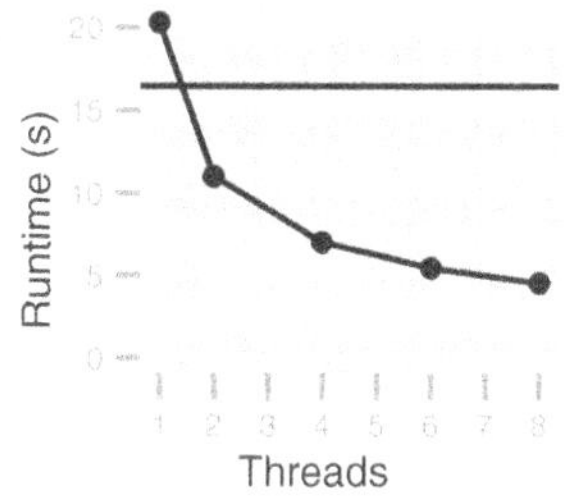

(b) Mplayer input

Figure 15. Points-to analysis times. Horizontal line is performance of the reference implementation. Best speedup over reference for gimp and mplayer are 3.63 and 3.62 respectively.

constraints can be viewed in terms of the application of three graph rewrite rules to the constraint graph [46].

Each rewrite rule adds edges to the graph but does not remove existing nodes or edges, so the operator is a strong refinement morph. The baseline implementation described in Section 4.1 would acquire abstract locks on all the nodes participating in the rewrite rule. However, because the operator is a strong refinement morph, it is only necessary to acquire a lock on the node at which the new edge is added, reducing synchronization costs.

Figure 15 shows the performance of this approach on the eight core machine compared to a highly optimized sequential reference implementation written by Hardekopf [24]. The results are for two of the benchmarks from Hardekopf's suite. This is the first successful parallelization of Andersen-style points-to analysis.

7. Extensions to the amorphous data-parallelism model

In this section, we discuss two kinds of parallelism that are not exploited by the basic amorphous data-parallel execution model described in Section 4.1: nested amorphous data-parallelism and pipeline parallelism. We also discuss how the task-parallel execution model fits into our framework.

7.1 Nested amorphous data-parallelism

The pattern of parallelism described in this paper arises from applying an operator at multiple active nodes in a graph as shown in Figure 4. Since the neighborhood of each activity is some region of the graph, an activity can itself be executed in parallel; we call this parallelism *intra-operator parallelism* to distinguish it from the first variety of parallelism that we can call *inter-operator parallelism*. Inter-operator parallelism is the dominant parallelism pattern in problems for which neighborhoods are small compared to the overall graph since it is likely that most activities do not conflict; in these problems, intra-operator parallelism is usually fine-grain, instruction-level parallelism. Conversely, when each neighborhood is a large part of the graph, activities are likely to conflict and intra-operator parallelism may be more important. Inter/intra-operator parallelism is an example of *nested data-parallelism* [8].

The sparsity of the graph usually plays a major role in this balance between inter- and intra-operator parallelism. For many operators, neighborhoods include all the neighbors of the active node, so if the graph is very densely connected, a single neighborhood may encompass most of the graph and intra-operator parallelism is dominant. An extreme case is the factorization of dense matrices: the underlying graph is a clique, and each factorization step updates the entire graph, as explained in Section 5.1.2, so the only parallelism is intra-operator parallelism. In factorizing sparse matrices, inter-operator parallelism dominates for the first few steps; after some number of coarsening steps, the residual graph becomes dense enough that most high-performance sparse matrix codes switch to dense matrix techniques to exploit intra-operator parallelism [20].

7.2 Pipeline parallelism

In some applications, a data structure is produced incrementally by a computation called the *producer* and read incrementally by another computation called the *consumer*. If it is possible to overlap the executions of the producer and consumer, the resulting parallelism is called pipeline parallelism. The key problem in exploiting pipeline parallelism is determining when the producer has completed all the modifications it will ever make to an element the consumer wants to read. This problem is undecidable in general, so one approach to exploiting pipeline parallelism is to execute the consumer speculatively in parallel with the producer, rolling the consumer back if the producer overwrites data read by the consumer. This approach is unlikely to be practical since the consumer cannot commit any work until the producer has finished execution.

Pipeline parallelism becomes practical if the producer is a strong refinement morph since in that case, each iteration of the producer may add new elements to the graph but it does not modify elements that have already been produced. As long as the consumer does not test for the absence of an element, the producer and consumer can be executed safely in parallel. This amorphous data-parallel view of pipeline parallelism generalizes the standard view of pipeline parallelism in which the shared data structure is restricted to be a stream (sequence), as in StreamIt [21]; for example, we can pipeline the execution of a client of points-to analysis information with the execution of the points-to analysis algorithm described in Section 6.3 since the operator is a refinement morph.

7.3 Task parallel execution

Task parallel execution can be used to exploit amorphous data-parallelism by using a divide-and-conquer formulation of algorithms rather than an iterative formulation. Divide-and-conquer algorithms are naturally data-centric since they partition the data structure and execute the algorithm recursively on each partition; intuitively, the division step is a way of clustering active nodes based on their location in the data structure. If all data dependences are subsumed by call/return control dependences, the recursive calls can be executed safely in parallel. The Cilk project has explored this approach to exploiting parallelism [9].

This approach obviously requires an efficient partitioner for the data structure. Partitioning is straightforward for structured and semi-structured topologies, so most task-parallelism studies have focused on algorithms that deal with sets, sequences (arrays), cliques (dense matrices), grids and trees. Partitioning general graphs is more difficult, and for many algorithms, the partitioning step can be more expensive than the algorithm itself. Furthermore, ordered algorithms like event-driven simulation do not lend themselves to a natural divide-and-conquer formulation. Therefore, our view of task parallel execution is that it is a way of exploiting amorphous data-parallelism in unordered algorithms that deal with structured and semi-structured topologies: at each stage of the division process, activities whose neighborhoods lie entirely within a partition are executed during the processing of that partition while activities whose neighborhoods span partitions at that level can be executed when returning from the recursive calls.

8. Conclusions

Dependence graphs have been used for more than thirty years by the parallel programming community to reason about parallelism in algorithms. In this paper, we argued that this program-centric abstraction is inadequate for most irregular algorithms. To address this problem, we proposed a data-centric formulation of algorithms called the operator formulation, which led to a structural analysis of algorithms called tao-analysis. Tao-analysis reveals that a generalized form of data-parallelism called amorphous data-parallelism is ubiquitous in algorithms, and that depending on the tao-structure of the algorithm, this parallelism may be exploited by compile-time, inspector-executor or optimistic parallelization, thereby unifying these seemingly unrelated parallelization techniques. Parallelization of regular algorithms is just one special case, and tao-analysis allows many application-specific optimizations to be generalized. An extensive survey of key algorithms and experimental results from three applications provided evidence for these claims.

Parallel programming today is burdened by abstractions like dependence graphs that are inadequate for many algorithms and by a plethora of application-specific optimizations and isolated mechanisms. In many ways, this state of the art resembles alchemy rather than a science like chemistry. To move forward, we need a systematic way of understanding parallelism and locality—a way to generalize from specific cases and a way to apply generalizations to specific cases. In short, we need a science of parallel programming. We believe that the operator formulation and tao-analysis of algorithms are key elements of such a science.

साकारमनृतं विद्धि निराकारं तु निश्चलं ।
एतत्तत्त्वोपदेशेन न पुनर्भवसंभव: ॥

That which has form is not real; only the amorphous endures.
When you understand this, you will not return to illusion.

— Ashtavakra Gita(1:18)

References

[1] A. Aho, R. Sethi, , and J. Ullman. *Compilers: principles, techniques, and tools*. Addison Wesley, 1986.

[2] P. An, A. Jula, S. Rus, S. Saunders, T. Smith, G. Tanase, N. Thomas, N. Amato, and L. Rauchwerger. STAPL: An adaptive, generic parallel C++ library. In *LCPC*, 2003.

[3] L. O. Andersen. *Program Analysis and Specialization for the C Programming Language*. PhD thesis, DIKU, University of Copenhagen, 1994.

[4] Arvind and R.S.Nikhil. Executing a program on the MIT tagged-token dataflow architecture. *IEEE Trans. on Computers*, 39(3), 1990.

[5] D. Bader and G. Cong. Fast shared-memory algorithms for computing the minimum spanning forest of sparse graphs. *Journal of Parallel and Distributed Computing*, 66(11):1366–1378, 2006.

[6] J. Barnes and P. Hut. A hierarchical o(n log n) force-calculation algorithm. *Nature*, 324(4), December 1986.

[7] D. K. Blandford, G. E. Blelloch, and C. Kadow. Engineering a compact parallel Delaunay algorithm in 3D. In *Symposium on Computational Geometry*, pages 292–300, 2006.

[8] G. Blelloch. Programming parallel algorithms. *Communications of the ACM*, 39(3), March 1996.

[9] R. D. Blumofe, C. F. Joerg, B. C. Kuszmaul, C. E. Leiserson, K. H. Randall, and Y. Zhou. Cilk: an efficient multithreaded runtime system. *SIGPLAN Not.*, 30(8):207–216, 1995.

[10] U. Brandes and T. Erlebach, editors. *Network Analysis: Methodological Foundations*. Springer-Verlag, 2005.

[11] L. P. Chew. Guaranteed-quality mesh generation for curved surfaces. In *SCG*, 1993.

[12] T. Cormen, C. Leiserson, R. Rivest, and C. Stein, editors. *Introduction to Algorithms*. MIT Press, 2001.

[13] J. Dean and S. Ghemawat. Mapreduce: Simplified data processing on large clusters. In *OSDI*, 2004.

[14] B. Delaunay. Sur la sphere vide. *Izvestia Akademii Nauk SSSR, Otdelenie Matematicheskikh i Estestvennykh Nauk,*, 7:793–800, 1934.

[15] J. Dennis. Dataflow ideas for supercomputers. In *CompCon*, 1984.

[16] E. Dijkstra. *A Discipline of Programming*. Prentice Hall, 1976.

[17] P. Diniz and M. Rinard. Commutativity analysis: a new analysis technique for parallelizing compilers. *ACM TOPLAS*, 19(6), 1997.

[18] H. Ehrig and M. Löwe. Parallel and distributed derivations in the single-pushout approach. *Theoretical Computer Science*, 109:123–143, 1993.

[19] R. Ghiya and L. Hendren. Is it a tree, a dag, or a cyclic graph? a shape analysis for heap-directed pointers in C. In *POPL*, 1996.

[20] J. R. Gilbert and R. Schreiber. Highly parallel sparse Cholesky factorization. *SIAM Journal on Scientific and Statistical Computing*, 13:1151–1172, 1992.

[21] M. I. Gordon, W. Thies, and S. Amarasinghe. Exploiting coarse-grained task, data, and pipeline parallelism in stream programs. In *ASPLOS*, 2006.

[22] D. Gregor and A. Lumsdaine. Lifting sequential graph algorithms for distributed-memory parallel computation. In *OOPSLA*, 2005.

[23] L. J. Guibas, D. E. Knuth, and M. Sharir. Randomized incremental construction of delaunay and voronoi diagrams. *Algorithmica*, 7(1):381–413, December 1992.

[24] B. Hardekopf and C. Lin. The ant and the grasshopper: fast and accurate pointer analysis for millions of lines of code. In *PLDI*, 2007.

[25] T. Harris and K. Fraser. Language support for lightweight transactions. In *OOPSLA*, pages 388–402, 2003.

[26] M. A. Hassaan, M. Burtscher, and K. Pingali. Ordered vs. unordered: a comparison of parallelism and work-efficiency in irregular algorithms. In *PPoPP*, 2011.

[27] L. Hendren and A. Nicolau. Parallelizing programs with recursive data structures. *IEEE TPDS*, 1(1):35–47, January 1990.

[28] M. Herlihy and E. Koskinen. Transactional boosting: a methodology for highly-concurrent transactional objects. In *PPoPP*, 2008.

[29] M. Herlihy and J. E. B. Moss. Transactional memory: architectural support for lock-free data structures. In *ISCA*, 1993.

[30] S. Horwitz, P. Pfieffer, and T. Reps. Dependence analysis for pointer variables. In *PLDI*, 1989.

[31] B. Hudson, G. L. Miller, and T. Phillips. Sparse parallel Delaunay mesh refinement. In *SPAA*, 2007.

[32] J. JaJa. *An Introduction to Parallel Algorithms*. Addison-Wesley, 1992.

[33] D. R. Jefferson. Virtual time. *ACM TOPLAS*, 7(3), 1985.

[34] G. Karypis and V. Kumar. Multilevel k-way partitioning scheme for irregular graphs. *JPDC*, 48(1):96–129, 1998.

[35] K. Kennedy and J. Allen, editors. *Optimizing compilers for modern architectures*. Morgan Kaufmann, 2001.

[36] F. Kjolstad and M. Snir. Ghost cell pattern. In *Workshop on Parallel Programming Patterns*, 2010.

[37] R. Kramer, R. Gupta, and M. L. Soffa. The combining DAG: A technique for parallel data flow analysis. *IEEE Transactions on Parallel and Distributed Systems*, 5(8), August 1994.

[38] M. Kulkarni, M. Burtscher, R. Inkulu, K. Pingali, and C. Cascaval. How much parallelism is there in irregular applications? In *PPoPP*, 2009.

[39] M. Kulkarni, D. Nguyen, D. Prountzos, X. Sui, and K. Pingali. Exploiting the commutativity lattice. In *PLDI*, 2011.

[40] M. Kulkarni, K. Pingali, B. Walter, G. Ramanarayanan, K. Bala, and L. Chew. Optimistic parallelism requires abstractions. In *PLDI*, 2007.

[41] Y. Lee and B. G. Ryder. A comprehensive approach to parallel data flow analysis. In *Supercomputing*, pages 236–247, 1992.

[42] M. Lowe and H. Ehrig. Algebraic approach to graph transformation based on single pushout derivations. In *Workshop on Graph-theoretic concepts in computer science*, 1991.

[43] M. Luby. A simple parallel algorithm for the maximal independent set problem. *SIAM J. Comput.*, 15, 1986.

[44] D. Mackay. *Information Theory, Inference and Learning Algorithms*. Cambridge University Press, 2003.

[45] T. Mattson, B. Sanders, and B. Massingill. *Patterns for Parallel Programming*. Addison-Wesley Publishers, 2004.

[46] M. Méndez-Lojo, A. Mathew, and K. Pingali. Parallel Anderson-style points-to analysis. In *OOPSLA*, 2010.

[47] M. Méndez-Lojo, D. Nguyen, D. Prountzos, X. Sui, M. A. Hassaan, M. Kulkarni, M. Burtscher, and K. Pingali. Structure-driven optimizations for amorphous data-parallel programs. In *PPoPP*, 2010.

[48] V. Menon, K. Pingali, and N. Mateev. Fractal symbolic analysis. *ACM TOPLAS*, March 2003.

[49] J. Misra. Distributed discrete-event simulation. *ACM Comput. Surv.*, 18(1):39–65, 1986.

[50] D. Nguyen and K. Pingali. Synthesizing concurrent schedulers for irregular algorithms. In *ASPLOS*, 2011.

[51] D. Patterson, K. Keutzer, K. Asanovica, K. Yelick, and R. Bodik. Berkeley dwarfs. `http://view.eecs.berkeley.edu/`.

[52] M. Pharr, C. Kolb, R. Gershbein, and P. Hanrahan. Rendering complex scenes with memory-coherent ray tracing. In *SIGGRAPH*, 1997.

[53] K. Pingali and Arvind. Efficient demand-driven evaluation. part 1. *ACM Trans. Program. Lang. Syst.*, 7, April 1985.

[54] D. Prountzos, R. Manevich, K. Pingali, and K. McKinley. A shape analysis for optimizing parallel graph programs. In *POPL*, 2011.

[55] L. Rauchwerger and D. A. Padua. The LRPD test: Speculative run-time parallelization of loops with privatization and reduction parallelization. *IEEE Trans. Parallel Distrib. Syst.*, 10(2):160–180, 1999.

[56] E. E. Santos, S. Feng, and J. M. Rickman. Efficient parallel algorithms for 2-dimensional Ising spin models. In *IPDPS*, 2002.

[57] J. T. Schwartz, R. B. K. Dewar, E. Dubinsky, and E. Schonberg. *Programming with sets: An introduction to SETL*. Springer-Verlag, 1986.

[58] J. P. Singh, C. Holt, T. Totsuka, A. Gupta, and J. L. Hennessy. Load balancing and data locality in adaptive hierarchical n-body methods: Barnes-hut, fast multipole, and radiosity. *Journal Of Parallel and Distributed Computing*, 27, 1995.

[59] P.-N. Tan, M. Steinbach, and V. Kumar, editors. *Introduction to Data Mining*. Pearson Addison Wesley, 2005.

[60] C. Verbrugge. *A Parallel Solution Strategy for Irregular, Dynamic Problems*. PhD thesis, McGill University, 2006.

[61] T. N. Vijaykumar, S. Gopal, J. E. Smith, and G. Sohi. Speculative versioning cache. *IEEE Trans. Parallel Distrib. Syst.*, 12(12):1305–1317, 2001.

[62] U. Vishkin *et al.* Explicit multi-threading (xmt) bridging models for instruction parallelism. In *SPAA*, 1998.

[63] N. Wirth. *Algorithms + Data Structures = Programs*. Prentice-Hall, 1976.

[64] J. Wu, R. Das, J. Saltz, H. Berryman, and S. Hiranandani. Distributed memory compiler design for sparse problems. *IEEE Transactions on Computers*, 44, 1995.

Parallelism Orchestration using DoPE: the Degree of Parallelism Executive

Arun Raman Hanjun Kim Taewook Oh Jae W. Lee† David I. August

Princeton University
Princeton, NJ
{rarun, hanjunk, twoh, august}@princeton.edu

† Parakinetics Inc.
Princeton, NJ
leejw@parakinetics.com

Abstract

In writing parallel programs, programmers expose parallelism and optimize it to meet a particular performance goal on a single platform under an assumed set of workload characteristics. In the field, changing workload characteristics, new parallel platforms, and deployments with different performance goals make the programmer's development-time choices suboptimal. To address this problem, this paper presents the Degree of Parallelism Executive (DoPE), an API and run-time system that separates the concern of exposing parallelism from that of optimizing it. Using the DoPE API, the application developer expresses parallelism options. During program execution, DoPE's run-time system uses this information to dynamically optimize the parallelism options in response to the facts on the ground. We easily port several emerging parallel applications to DoPE's API and demonstrate the DoPE run-time system's effectiveness in dynamically optimizing the parallelism for a variety of performance goals.

Categories and Subject Descriptors D.1.3 [*Programming Techniques*]: Concurrent Programming—Parallel Programming; D.3.4 [*Programming Languages*]: Processors—Run-time environments

General Terms Design, Languages, Performance

Keywords parallelization, parallelism, dynamic, run-time, scheduling, task, loop-level, nested, loop nest, pipeline, parametric, optimization

1. Introduction

As multicore processors become ubiquitous, application developers and compilers must extract thread level parallelism (TLP) in order to exploit the execution resources afforded by the hardware. Parallelism of multiple types may exist in an application, such as task parallelism, data parallelism, and pipeline parallelism. Much progress has been made in methodologies and systems to extract parallelism, even from seemingly sequential code [6, 7, 24, 25, 34, 40]. Tools such as POSIX threads (Pthreads) [33], Intel Threading Building Blocks (TBB) [26], Cilk [5], OpenMP [22], and Galois [14] allow application developers to express TLP.

Many applications have parallelism in multiple loops in a loop nest. Each loop may be parallelized by exploiting different types of parallelism to varying extents by allocating a different number of parallel resources (hardware threads) to each loop. The type and extent of each loop parallelization is called the *degree of parallelism* (DoP). Simultaneously parallelizing multiple loops can provide both scalability and latency-throughput benefits.

Unfortunately, determining the right degree of parallelism for even a single loop, let alone multiple loops in a nest, is a complicated task. Application developers or parallel run-times typically fix the degree of parallelism of each loop statically at development-time or run-time. This is often suboptimal in the face of several *run-time* sources of performance variability that could potentially result in leaving hardware resources idle or over-subscribed. The application workload characteristics may vary as in the case of web services such as search and video. The parallel platform characteristics (number of cores, memory bandwidth, etc.) may vary [18, 30]. Furthermore, the performance goals may not be fixed and could be some complex time-varying functions of energy, throughput, etc. Together, these three sources of variability—workload characteristics, platform characteristics, and performance goals—are referred to as the execution environment of an application.

To solve the above problem, the application developer could statically produce multiple versions of code and dynamically select a version that best fits each execution environment. Unfortunately, the number of scenarios resulting from a myriad of platforms, workloads, and performance goals is so large as to preclude the possibility of incorporating all of them into statically-compiled codes. To address the limitations of the static approach, run-time systems have been proposed to map parallel applications to their execution environments. Low-level substrates enable parallel library composition but do not leverage application-specific run-time information [15, 23]. Prior work that performs adaptation by monitoring application features has typically focused on a specific type of parallelism (such as pipeline parallelism or task parallelism) and fixed dynamic adaptation mechanisms that are tightly coupled to the target parallelism type [4, 5, 26, 29, 30, 35, 38]. More importantly, in all known prior work, the adaptation mechanisms are restricted to a single loop in a loop nest.

This paper proposes DoPE, a novel API and run-time system that enables the separation of the concern of developing a functionally correct parallel program from the concern of optimizing the parallelism for different execution environments. The separation of concerns enables a mechanism developer to specify *mechanisms* that encode the logic to adapt an application's parallelism

PLDI'11, June 4–8, 2011, San Jose, California, USA.

Library	Multiple Performance Goals	Parallelism in Loop Nest	Multiple Parallelism Types	Application Feature Monitoring	Multiple Optimization Mechanisms
Pthreads [33]	×	✓	✓	×	×
Intel TBB [26]	×	×	✓	×	×
FDP [29]	×	×	×	✓	×
DoPE [This paper]	✓	✓	✓	✓	✓

Table 1. Comparison of various software-only parallelization libraries for general-purpose applications

configuration to meet the performance goals that are set by the *administrator*. Table 1 highlights DoPE's advantages over other parallelism management libraries. With DoPE, the application developer can expose all the parallelism in an application and express it in a unified manner just once. Then, a run-time system adapts the application's parallelism configuration by monitoring key application features and responding to changes in the application's execution environment. Specifically, the run-time system automatically and continuously determines:

- which tasks to execute in parallel (e.g. what are the stages of a pipeline)
- how many hardware threads to use (e.g. how many threads to allocate to each stage of the pipeline)
- how to schedule tasks on to hardware threads (e.g. on which hardware thread should each stage be placed to maximize locality of communication)

We ported several emerging parallel applications to use the DoPE interface. Different performance goals included response time minimization, throughput maximization, and throughput maximization under power constraint. DoPE automatically adapted the application to meet the goals, without necessitating a change in the application code by the developer. To adapt the parallelism, it used new mechanisms proposed in this paper and also mechanisms proposed in prior work [29, 38], demonstrating the robustness of DoPE's interface and the ability for a mechanism developer to implement better mechanisms in the future in a non-disruptive way.

On a 24-core Intel Xeon machine, DoPE improved the response time characteristics of four web service type applications to dominate the characteristics of the best static parallelizations. The throughputs of two batch-oriented applications were improved by 136% (geomean) over their original implementations. For one application (an image search engine), three different goals—involving response time, throughput, and power—were independently specified. DoPE automatically determined a stable and well performing parallelism configuration operating point in all cases.

The primary contributions of this work are:

- An API that separates the concern of correct specification of an application's parallelism from the concern of optimization of the application's execution in a variety of environments
- A smart run-time system that enables the interface and monitors application execution to dynamically adapt the parallelism in program loop nests by means of suitable mechanisms in order to meet specified performance goals

The rest of this paper is organized as follows. The need for dynamic adaptation and separation of concerns is first motivated, followed by a description of DoPE's interfaces for the application developer, mechanism developer, and administrator. Various mechanisms that were implemented are described, followed by an evaluation of the DoPE system and a discussion of related work.

2. Motivation

A parallel application's execution environment consists of the application workload characteristics, platform characteristics, and performance goals. Variability in any of these parameters can necessitate dynamic adaptation of parallelism in order to meet the specified performance goal. The following video transcoding example concretely demonstrates the impact of workload characteristic variability.

Example: Video Transcoding Video sharing websites such as YouTube, Google Video, and Dailymotion transcode user submitted videos on their servers. Figure 1 shows the parallelism in video transcoding using `x264`, an implementation of the popular H.264 standard [39]. Each video may be transcoded in parallel with others. Furthermore, a single video may itself be transcoded in parallel by exploiting parallelism across the frames in the video in a pipelined fashion. $<DoP_{outer}, DoP_{inner}>$ represents the type of parallelism of, and number of threads assigned to, the outer (inter-video) and inner (intra-video) loops in the loop nest. Examples of types of parallelism are DOALL and pipeline (PIPE) [1]. Statically fixing the DoP assigned to each loop may not be optimal for a given performance goal in all execution environments. To demonstrate this, we measured throughput and execution time on a 24-core machine with Intel Xeon X7460 processors. User requests were simulated by a task queueing thread with arrivals distributed according to a Poisson distribution. The average system load factor is defined as the average arrival rate of tasks (videos to be transcoded) divided by the maximum throughput sustainable by the system.

Figure 2(a) shows that exploiting intra-video parallelism provides much lower per-video transcoding execution time than when only the outer loop is parallelized. T_{exec} is improved up to a maximum of 6.3× on the evaluation platform. This speedup is achieved when 8 threads are used to transcode each video. Figure 2(b), however, shows the dependency of throughput on the application load. At heavy load (load factor 0.9 and above), turning on intra-video parallelism actually degrades throughput. This is due to the inefficiency of parallel execution (a speedup of only about 6× on 8 threads at load factor 1.0) caused by overheads such as thread creation, communication, and synchronization.

This experiment shows that the usual static choices of parallelism configuration are not ideal across all load factors for *both* execution time and throughput. In other words, there is a tradeoff between the two. This tradeoff impacts end user response time which is the primary performance metric of service oriented applications. Equation 1 is helpful to understand the impact of the execution time/throughput tradeoff on response time. The time to transcode a video is the execution time, T_{exec}. The number of videos transcoded per second is the throughput of the system,

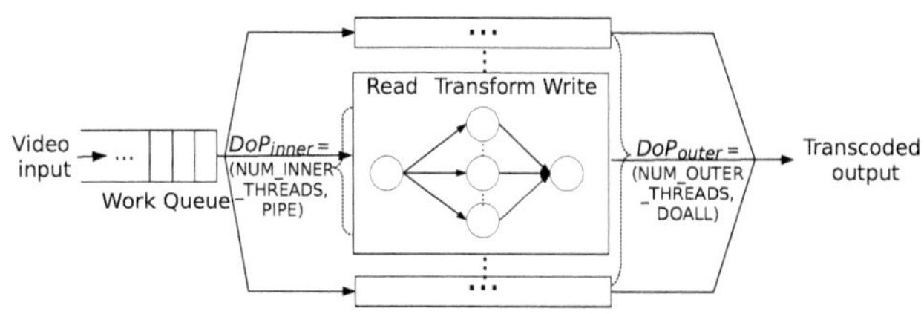

Figure 1. Two-level loop nest in video transcoding: Across videos submitted for transcoding and across frames within each video

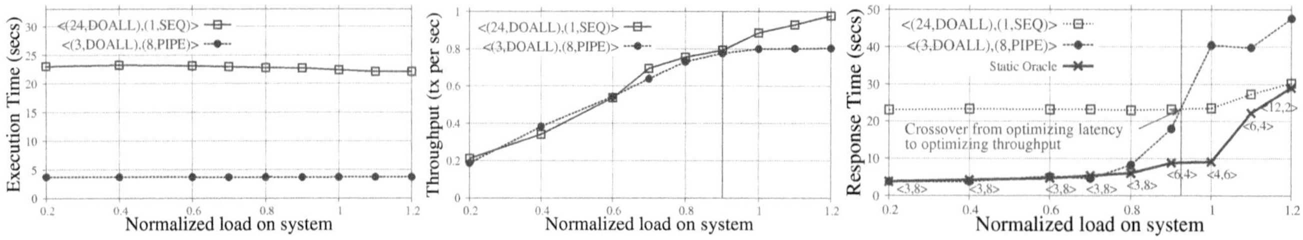

(a) Execution Time (b) Throughput (c) Response Time

Figure 2. Variation of (a) execution time and (b) throughput with load factor and parallelism configuration in a video transcoding application on a 24-core Intel Xeon machine; (c) impact of throughput and execution time on end user response time; an oracle achieves the best response time characteristic by continuously varying DoP with load (ideal parallelism configuration for each load factor is shown)

Throughput. The number of outstanding requests in the system's work queue is the instantaneous load on the system, $q(t)$.

$$T_{response}(t) = T_{exec}(DoP) + \frac{q(t)}{Throughput(DoP)} \quad (1)$$

The response time of a user request, $T_{response}$, is the time interval from the instant the video was submitted for transcoding (at time t) to the instant the transcoded video is output. $T_{response}$ has two components: wait time in the work queue until the request reaches the head of the queue, and execution time, T_{exec}. At light to moderate load, the average arrival rate is lower than the system throughput. Consequently, the wait time will tend to zero, and $T_{response}$ will be determined by T_{exec}. Assuming reasonably efficient intra-video parallelism, increasing the DoP extent of the inner loop reduces T_{exec} and in turn $T_{response}$. In other words, in this region of operation, $<DoP_{outer}, DoP_{inner}>$ must be optimized for execution time ($\text{DoP}_{inner} = (8, PIPE)$). At heavy load, $T_{response}$ is dominated by the wait time in the work queue which is determined by the system throughput. In this region of operation, DoP_{inner} must be set to a value that optimizes throughput ($\text{DoP}_{inner} = (1, SEQ)$). Figure 2(c) presents experimental validation of the described response time characteristic. The same figure also shows that a mere "turn inner parallelism on/off" approach is suboptimal; an oracle that can predict load and change DoP continuously achieves significantly better response time.

In addition to workload characteristics, platform characteristics including number of hardware contexts, memory space, etc. may vary. Further, the same system (application+platform) may be called upon to maximize system utility with a variety of performance goals involving energy, throughput, etc. If the application developer were tasked with matching application code to the variety of dynamic execution environments that might arise, there would be a combinatorial explosion in the number of versions of application code. Each version would remain *ad hoc* as the application is deployed on newer platforms and is used in the context of different performance goals.

Separation of Concerns To address the explosion of developer effort and code versions, the task of expressing application parallelism must be separated from the task of adapting that parallelism to specific execution environments. Further, an administrator must be able to specify the current performance goal, and the application must adapt itself to meet the goal. Such a separation of concerns would enable:

- application developers to focus on functional correctness of the parallel application
- administrators to specify arbitrary performance goals involving performance, power, etc.
- mechanism developers to implement parallelism adaptation mechanisms that meet the specified performance goals

Table 1 evaluates existing choices for enabling such a separation of concerns. Using Pthreads, a developer specifies a concrete, unchanging parallelism configuration, or codes an ad hoc adaptation mechanism for every new execution environment. Intel TBB [26] and similar libraries [5, 22] support task parallelism for independent tasks and their schedulers optimize only for throughput. Feedback Directed Pipelining (FDP) implements an adaptation mechanism tied to throughput maximization for a single loop in the application [29]. In summary, these libraries support only a single performance goal, and closely couple the goal with a specific mechanism to adapt parallelism in order to meet the goal.

DoPE enables an application developer to express common paradigms of nested parallelism in a unified fashion. DoPE enables an administrator to specify different performance goals for the same application. DoPE enables a mechanism developer to implement multiple mechanisms that reconfigure application parallelism to meet a specified performance goal. The application developer needs to write the application just once, and the application executes robustly across multiple scenarios of use, platforms, and workloads.

3. DoPE for the Application Developer

3.1 DoPE API

DoPE presents a task-oriented interface to the application developer. A task consists of a template function that abstracts the control for creating dynamic instances of each task, function objects (functors) that encapsulate the task's functionality and expose application level information, and a descriptor that describes the parallelism structure of the task. Figure 3 defines the `Task` type and the types from which it is composed.

```
Task = {control: TaskExecutor, function: Functor,
        load: LoadCB, desc: TaskDescriptor,
        init: InitCB, fini: FiniCB}
TaskDescriptor = {type: TaskType, pd: ParDescriptor[]}
TaskType = SEQ | PAR
ParDescriptor = {tasks: Task[]}
TaskStatus = EXECUTING | SUSPENDED | FINISHED
```

Figure 3. DoPE type definitions

`TaskExecutor` DoPE provides the control flow abstraction shown in Figure 4(a). Loop exit is determined by `status` (line 7 in Figure 4(a)). The abstraction is templated on the `Functor` type that encapsulates a task's functionality.

Method	Description
`TaskStatus Task::begin()`	Signal DoPE that the CPU intensive part of the task has begun; DoPE returns task status
`TaskStatus Task::end()`	Signal DoPE that the CPU intensive part of the task has ended; DoPE returns task status
`TaskStatus Task::wait()`	Wait until child tasks complete; DoPE returns status of master child task
`DoPE* DoPE::create(ParDescriptor* pd)`	Launch parallel application described by specified parallelism descriptor under the DoPE run-time system
`void DoPE::destroy(DoPE* dope)`	Finalize and destroy the DoPE run-time system; wait for registered tasks to end

Table 2. DoPE API

```
template<Functor>
void TaskExecutor(Functor
                  Function){
  ...
  while(true) {
    ...
    TaskStatus status =
              Function();
    ...
  }
}
```

(a) Control flow abstraction

```
1 class Functor{
2   ... //Capture local variables
3
4   ... //Constructor
5
6   TaskStatus operator()(){
7     ... //Task function body
8     return taskstatus;
9   }
10 };
11
```

(b) Functor for task functionality

Figure 4. Separation of task's control and functionality in DoPE

`Functor` The developer must implement a functor that encapsulates the desired functionality of a task. The functor binds the local variables of the original method containing the parallelized loop as member fields (line 2 in Figure 4(b)). At run-time, a task could be either executing, suspended, or finished. The functor must return the status of the task after each instance of the task (line 8 in Figure 4(b)). In particular, when a loop exit branch is to be taken, the functor must return `FINISHED`; otherwise, the functor must return `EXECUTING`. Combined with the control flow abstraction in Figure 4(a), the control flow structure of the original loop is duplicated. The functor can also return `SUSPENDED`—its discussion is deferred until Section 3.2.

`LoadCB` Section 2 described the importance of application features such as workload to determine the optimal parallelism configuration for a given performance goal. To capture the workload on each task, the developer implements a callback functor that when invoked returns the current load on the task.

`InitCB` and `FiniCB` To restart parallel execution from a globally consistent program state after DoPE reconfigures parallelism, DoPE requires the programmer to implement the `InitCB` (`FiniCB`) functor that is invoked exactly once before (after) the task is executed.

`TaskDescriptor` A task can be sequential (`SEQ`) or parallel (`PAR`). A parallel task's functionality can be executed by one or more threads. In other words, the `Functor()` method (lines 6–9 in Figure 4(b)) can be invoked concurrently by multiple threads. To enable description of nested parallelism, a task can specify one or more parallelism descriptors (`ParDescriptor`). Specifying more than one descriptor exposes a choice to DoPE which at run-time chooses the optimal parallelism configuration (described by the corresponding `ParDescriptor`).

`ParDescriptor` A parallelism descriptor is defined recursively in terms of `Tasks`. A `ParDescriptor` is an array of one or more tasks that execute in parallel and potentially interact with each other (line 6 in Figure 3).

```
void Transcode(){
  Q* inq, outq;
  Video* input, *output;
  while(true){
    *input = inq→deque();
    output = transcode(input);
    outq→enqueue(*output);
  }
}
```

Figure 5. Outer loop in x264 video transcoding

Putting it all together Figure 5 shows the outer loop code in x264 video transcoding. Figure 6 shows the transformation of the loop by instantiation of the DoPE types discussed above. In Figure 6(a), duplicated code from the original loop in Figure 5 is shown in bold. Referring to Figure 1, the outer loop task can itself be executed

```
class TranscodeFunctor{
  //Capture local variables
  Queue*& inq;
  Queue*& outq;
  ... //Constructor
  TaskStatus operator()(){
    Video* input, *output;
    *input = inq→deque();
    output = transcode(input);
    outq→enqueue(*output);
    return EXECUTING;
  }
};
```

(a) Functionality

```
class TranscodeLoadCB{
  //Capture local variables
  Queue*& inq;
  Queue*& outq;
  ... //Constructor
  float operator()(){
    //Return occupancy
    return inq→size();
  }
};
```

(b) Workload

```
TaskDescriptor
  *readTD(SEQ, NULL),
  *transformTD(PAR, NULL),
  *writeTD(SEQ, NULL);
  ...//Create tasks
    //using descriptors
ParDescriptor
  *innerPD({readTask,
            transformTask,
            writeTask});
TaskDescriptor
  *outerTD(PAR, {innerPD});
```

(c) Descriptor

```
void Transcode(){
  Queue* inq, *outq;
  Task* task
    (TranscodeFunctor(inq, outq),
     TranscodeLoadCB(inq, outq),
     outerTD);
  //TaskExecutor<OuterLoopFunctor>
  //is used automatically by DoPE
}
```

(d) Task

Figure 6. Task definition using DoPE

in a pipeline parallel fashion. Figure 6(c) shows the definition of the outer loop task descriptor in terms of the inner loop parallelism descriptor. Note that the process of defining the functors is mechanical—it can be simplified with compiler support.

3.2 Using the API: A Video Transcoding Example

A developer uses the types in Figure 3 and associated methods in Table 2 to enhance a parallel application using DoPE. Figure 7 describes the port of a Pthreads based parallelization (column 1) of the video transcoding example from before to the DoPE API (column 2). Code that is common between the Pthreads version and the DoPE version is shown in bold.

Step 1: Parallelism Description In the Pthreads parallelization, lines 4–7 create `NUM_OUTER` threads that execute the `Transcode` method. In the `Transcode` method, a thread dequeues work items (videos) from the work queue (line 14), transcodes them (lines 15–25), and enqueues the transcoded items to the output queue (line 26). Each video transcoding can itself be done in parallel in a pipelined fashion. For this, the `Transcode` method spawns `NUM_INNER` threads to execute the pipeline. One thread each executes `Read` and `Write`, and one or more threads execute `Transform`. A common practice is to set both `NUM_OUTER` and `NUM_INNER` statically based on profile information [21]. Section 2 already presented the shortcomings of this approach—to operate optimally, an application must dynamically change its parallelism configuration as the execution environment changes.

In the DoPE parallelization, the application's parallelism is described in a modular and bottom-up fashion. Line 4 gets the task definition of the outer loop by invoking `Transcode_getTask`. To encode nested parallelism, the `Transcode_getTask` method specifies that `Transcode` can be executed in parallel using the parallelism descriptor `pd` (lines 12–17 in `Transcode_getTask`). Line 5 in `transcodeVideos` creates a parallelism descriptor for the outer loop.

Step 2: Parallelism Registration Line 6 in `transcodeVideos` registers the parallelism descriptor for execution by DoPE by invoking `DoPE::create`. Line 7 waits for the parallel phase of the application to finish before freeing up execution resources by invoking `DoPE::destroy`.

Step 3: Application Monitoring Each task marks the begin and end of its CPU intensive section by invoking `Task::begin` and `Task::end`, respectively. DoPE records application features such as task execution time in between invocations of these methods. To monitor per-task workload, the developer implements `LoadCB` for each task to indicate the current workload on the task. The callback returns the current occupancy of the work queue in the case of the outer task (line 26), and the input queue occupancies in the case of `Transform` (line 62) and `Write` (line 75). The callbacks are registered during task creation time.

Step 4: Task Execution Control If a task returns `EXECUTING`, DoPE continues the execution of the loop. If a task returns `FINISHED`, DoPE waits for other tasks that are at the same level in the loop nest to also return `FINISHED`. A task can explicitly wait on its children by invoking `Task::wait`. Exactly one task in each parallelized loop is assigned the role of the *master task* (the first task in the array of tasks registered in the parallelism descriptor). In the running example, the task corresponding to `Transcode` is the master task for the outer loop and the task corresponding to `Read` is the master task for the inner loop. Invoking `Task::wait` on `task` (line 17) returns the status of the master child task.

Step 5: Task Yielding for Reconfiguration By default, DoPE returns `EXECUTING` when either `Task::begin` or `Task::end`

(a) Parallelization using POSIX threads	**(b) Parallelization using DoPE**	

(1) Run-time initialization

(a)
```
1 #include <pthread.h>
2 void transcodeVideos() {
3   Q* inq, *outq;
4   pthread_t threads[NUM_OUTER];
5   for (i = 0 ; i < NUM_OUTER ; i++) {
6     pthread_create(threads[i], attr, Transcode,
7                    new ArgT(inq, outq));
8   }
9 }
```

(b)
```
1 #include <dope>
2 void transcodeVideos() {
3   Q* inq, *outq;
4   Task* outerTask = Transcode_getTask(inq, outq);
5   ParDescriptor* outerPD = new ParDescriptor({outerTask});
6   DoPE* dope = DoPE::create(outerPD);
7   DoPE::destroy(dope); // Wait for tasks to finish
8 }
9
```

(2) Transcoding of an individual video clip

(a)
```
10 void* Transcode(void* arg) {
11   Q* inq = (ArgT*)arg->inq;
12   Q* outq = (ArgT*)arg->outq;
13   for(;;) {
14     *input = inq->dequeue();
15     ... //Initialize q1 and q2
16     pthread_t threads[NUM_INNER];
17     pthread_create(threads[0], attr, Read,
18                    new ArgR(input, q1));
19     for (i = 1 ; i < NUM_INNER - 1 ; i++) {
20       pthread_create(threads[i], attr,
21             Transform, new ArgTr(q1, q2));
22     }
23     pthread_create(threads[NUM_INNER-1],
24       attr, Write, new ArgW(q2, output));
25     ... // Join threads
26     outq->enqueue(*output);
27   }
28 }
```

(b)
```
10 class TranscodeFunctor {
11   Task* task; //This functor's task
12   ... //Capture local variables
13   ... //Constructor
14   TaskStatus operator()() {
15     *input = inq->dequeue();
16     ... //Initialize q1 and q2
17     status = task->wait();
18     if (status == SUSPENDED)
19       return SUSPENDED;
20     outq->enqueue(*output);
21     return EXECUTING;
22   }
23   friend Task* Transcode_getTask(...);
24 };
25
26
27
28
```

```
10 Task* Transcode_getTask(Q* inq, Q* outq) {
11   TranscodeFunctor* func = new TranscodeFunctor(inq,outq);
12   ParDescriptor* pd = new ParDescriptor
13     ({Read_getTask(func->q1),
14       Transform_getTask(func->q1, func->q2),
15       Write_getTask(func->q2)});
16   // Note hierarchical description of parallelism
17   TaskDescriptor* td = new TaskDescriptor(PAR, {pd});
18   Task* task = new Task(func, new TranscodeLoadCB(inq),
19                         td, NULL, NULL);
20   func->task = task;
21   return task;
22 }
23 class TranscodeLoadCB {
24   Q* inq;
25   TranscodeLoadCB(Q* inq) : inq(inq) {}
26   double operator()() {return inq.size();}
27 };
28
```

Figure 7. Comparison of parallelization using POSIX threads and DoPE—continued on next page

(3) Stages of pipeline to transcode an individual video clip

```
29 void* Read(void* arg) {
30   ... //Get input and q1 from arg
31   for(;;) {
32     frame = readFrame(*input);
33     if (frame == NULL) break;
34       q1->enqueue(frame);
35   }
36   q1->enqueue(NULL);
37 }
38
39
40
41
42
43
44
45
46 void* Transform(void* arg) {
47   ... //Get q1 from arg
48   for(;;) {
49     frame = q1->dequeue();
50     if (frame == NULL) break;
51     frame = encodeFrame(frame);
52     q2->enqueue(frame);
53   }
54   q2->enqueue(NULL);
55 }
56
57
58
59
60
61
62
63
64 void* Write(void* arg) {
65   ... //Get q2 and output from arg
66   for(;;) {
67     frame = dequeue(q2);
68     if (frame == NULL) break;
69     writeFrame(output, frame);
70   }
71 }
72
73
74
75
76
77
78
```

```
29 class ReadFunctor {
30   Task* task; //This functor's task
31   ... //Capture local variables
32   ... //Constructor
33   TaskStatus operator()() {
34     status = task->begin();
35     if (status == SUSPENDED)
36       return SUSPENDED;
37     frame = readFrame(*input);
38     if (frame == NULL)
39       return FINISHED;
40     task->end();
41     q1->enqueue(frame);
42     return EXECUTING;
43   }
44   friend Task* Read_getTask(...);
45 };
46 class TransformFunctor {
47   Task* task; //This functor's task
48   ... //Capture local variables
49   ... //Constructor
50   TaskStatus operator()() {
51     frame = q1->dequeue();
52     if (frame == null)
53       return FINISHED;
54     status = task->begin();
55     frame = encodeFrame(frame);
56     status = task->end();
57     q2->enqueue(frame);
58     return EXECUTING;
59   }
60   friend Task* Transform_getTask(...);
61 };
62
63
64 class WriteFunctor {
65   Task* task; //This functor's task
66   ... //Capture local variables
67   ... //Constructor
68   TaskStatus operator()() {
69     frame = q2->dequeue();
70     if (frame == null)
71       return FINISHED;
72     status = task->begin();
73     writeFrame(output, frame);
74     status = task->end();
75     return EXECUTING;
76   }
77   friend Task* Write_getTask(...);
78 };
```

```
29 Task* Read_getTask(Q* q1) {
30   ReadFunctor* func = new ReadFunctor(q1);
31   TaskDescriptor* td = new TaskDescriptor(SEQ, NULL);
32   Task* task = new Task(func, NULL, td, NULL,
33                         new ReadFiniCB(q1));
34   func->task = task;
35   return task;
36 }
37
38 class ReadFiniCB {
39   Q* q1;
40   ReadFiniCB(Q* q1) : q1(q1) {}
41   void operator()() {q1->enqueue(NULL);};
42 };
43
44
45
46 Task* Transform_getTask(Q* q1, Q* q2) {
47   TransformFunctor* func = new TransformFunctor(q2);
48   TaskDescriptor* td = new TaskDescriptor(PAR, NULL);
49   Task* task = new Task(func, new TransformLoadCB(q1),
50                 td, NULL, new TransformFiniCB(q2));
51   func->task = task;
52   return task;
53 }
54 class TransformFiniCB {
55   Q* q2;
56   TransformFiniCB(Q* q2) : q2(q2) {}
57   void operator()() {q2->enqueue(NULL);}
58 };
59 class TransformLoadCB {
60   Q* q1;
61   TransformLoadCB(Q* q1) : q1(q1) {}
62   double operator()() {return q1.size();}
63 };
64 Task* Write_getTask(Q* q2) {
65   WriteFunctor* func = new WriteFunctor(q1);
66   TaskDescriptor* td = new TaskDescriptor(SEQ, NULL);
67   Task* task = new Task(func, new WriteLoadCB(q2), td,
68                         NULL, NULL);
69   func->task = task;
70   return task;
71 }
72 class WriteLoadCB {
73   Q* q2;
74   WriteLoadCB(Q* q2) : q2(q2) {}
75   double operator()() {return q2.size();}
76 };
77
78
```

Figure 7. Comparison of parallelization using POSIX threads and DoPE

is invoked. When DoPE decides to reconfigure, it returns `SUSPENDED`. The application should check this condition (lines 35–36 in `ReadFunctor`), and then enter a globally consistent state prior to reconfiguration. The `FiniCB` callbacks are used for this purpose. In this particular example, `Read` notifies `Transform` (via the `ReadFiniCB` callback) which in turn notifies `Write` (via the `TransformFiniCB` callback). The notifications are by means of enqueuing a sentinel `NULL` token to the in-queue of the next task. Note by comparing the Pthreads (lines 36 and 54) and DoPE versions (lines 41 and 57) that the developer was able to reuse the thread termination mechanism from the Pthreads parallelization to implement the `FiniCB`s. `InitCB` callbacks are used symmetrically for ensuring consistency before the parallel region is re-entered after reconfiguration. The video transcoding example does not require any `InitCB` callbacks to be defined.

3.3 Summary

In the Pthreads based parallelization, the developer is forced to implement a concrete, unchanging configuration of parallelism. In the DoPE based parallelization, the developer declares the parallelism structure of the program, while deliberately not specifying the exact parallelism configuration. This underspecification allows DoPE to adapt parallelism to determine the optimal configuration at runtime. While the API has been described for use by a developer, a parallelizing compiler could also target the API in the same way as it targets Pthreads.

4. DoPE for the Administrator

The administrator specifies a performance goal that includes an objective and a set of resource constraints under which the objective must be met. Examples of performance goals are "minimize response time" and "maximize throughput under a peak power constraint". The administrator may also invent more complex performance goals such as minimizing the energy-delay product [9], or minimizing electricity bills while meeting minimum performance requirements [19]. DoPE aims to meet the performance goals by dynamically adapting the configuration of program parallelism.

A mechanism is an optimization routine that takes an objective function such as response time or throughput, a set of constraints including number of hardware threads and power consumption, and determines the optimal parallelism configuration. The administrator provides values to a mechanism's constraints. An example specification by the administrator to a mechanism that maximizes throughput could be "24 threads, 600 Watts" thereby instructing the mechanism to optimize under those constraints. In the absence of a suitable mechanism, the administrator can play the role of a mechanism developer and add a new mechanism to the library.

5. DoPE for the Mechanism Developer

Figure 8 shows the DoPE system architecture. The DoPE-*Executive* is responsible for directing the interactions between the various system components. DoPE maintains a *Thread Pool* with as many threads as constrained by the performance goals. DoPE uses *mechanisms* to adapt parallelism in order to meet the specified goals.

There are two main information flows when an application is launched. First, the application registers its parallelism descriptors (expressed by the application developer). Second, the administrator specifies the performance goals. The DoPE run-time system then starts application execution. During execution, it monitors and adapts the parallelism configuration to meet those goals.

Referring to Figure 8, DoPE monitors both the application (A) and platform (B). Section 3.2 already described the methods that enable DoPE to monitor application features such as task execution time and task load. DoPE uses per thread timers (updated using calls to `clock_gettime`) to obtain task execution time. To enable DoPE to monitor platform features such as number of hardware contexts, power, temperature, etc., the mechanism developer registers a feature with an associated callback that DoPE can invoke to get a current value of the feature. Figure 9 shows the registration API. For example, the developer could register "`SystemPower`" with a callback that queries the power distribution unit to obtain the current system power draw [2].

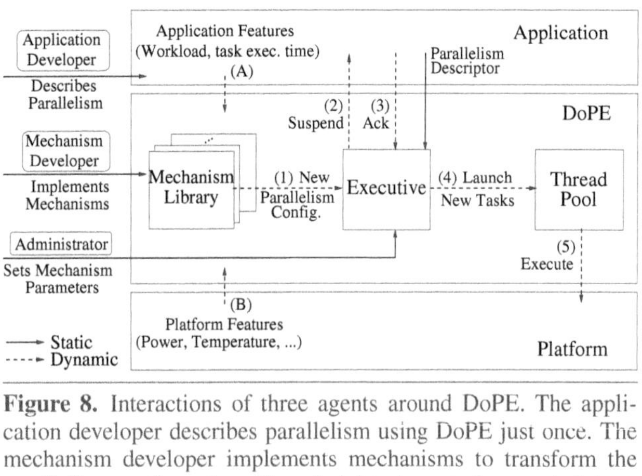

Figure 8. Interactions of three agents around DoPE. The application developer describes parallelism using DoPE just once. The mechanism developer implements mechanisms to transform the parallelism configuration. The administrator sets the constraint parameter values of the mechanism. (A) and (B) represent continuous monitoring of application and platform features. (1)–(5) denote the sequence of events that occurs when parallelism reconfiguration is triggered.

```
//Application features
double DoPE::getExecTime(Task* task);
double DoPE::getLoad(Task* task);
//Platform features
void DoPE::registerCB(string feature, Functor* getValueOfFeatureCB);
void* DoPE::getValue(string feature);
```

Figure 9. DoPE Mechanism Developer API

The primary role of the mechanism developer is to implement the logic to adapt a parallelism configuration to meet a performance goal by using the information obtained via monitoring. For this, DoPE exposes the query API shown in Figure 9 to the mechanism developer. Figure 10 shows a mechanism that can enable a "Maximize Throughput with N threads" performance goal. Every mechanism must implement the `reconfigureParallelism` method. The method's arguments are the descriptor of the current parallelism configuration and the maximum number of threads that can be used to construct a new configuration. The new configuration is returned to the caller (DoPE-Executive).

```
1  ParDescriptor* Mechanism::reconfigureParallelism
2                          (ParDescriptor* pd, int nthreads){
3    float total_time = 0.0;
4    // 1. Compute total time
5    foreach (Task* task: pd→tasks) {
6      total_time += DoPE::getExecTime(task);
7    }
8    // 2. Assign DoP proportional to execution time;
9    // recurse if needed
10   foreach (Task* task: pd→tasks) {
11     task→dop = nthreads * (DoPE::getExecTime(task)/total_time);
12     ParDescriptor* innerPD = task→pd;
13     if (innerPD) {
14       task→pd = reconfigureParallelism(innerPD, task→dop);
15     }
16   }
17   ... // 3. Construct new configuration – Omitted
18   return newPD;
19 }
```

Figure 10. Mechanism to maximize throughput—Assigns DoP to each task proportional to task's execution time

The intuition encoded by the mechanism in Figure 10 is that tasks that take longer to execute should be assigned more resources. In step 1, the mechanism computes total execution time (lines 4–7) so that each task's execution time can be normalized. In step 2, the mechanism assigns a DoP that is proportional to the normalized execution time of each task (line 11). `reconfigureParallelism` is recursively invoked to assign DoPs to the inner loops in the loop nest. For each loop, a new configuration is constructed with the new task descriptors and returned to the parent descriptor. For brevity, this last step is omitted.

6. DoPE Operation Walk-through

Once a mechanism is selected, DoPE uses it to reconfigure parallelism. The Executive triggers a parallelism reconfiguration in response to changes in the execution environment such as increase in workload. When reconfiguration is triggered, the following sequence of events occurs (refer to Figure 8):

1. The Mechanism determines the optimal parallelism configuration, which it conveys to the Executive.
2. The Executive returns `SUSPENDED` to invocations of `Task::begin` and `Task::end` in order to convey to the application DoPE's intent of reconfiguration.

3. In response, the application and DoPE steer execution into a suspended state by invoking the `FiniCB` callbacks of all the tasks.
4. The Executive then schedules a new set of tasks for execution by the Thread Pool—the task set is defined by the new parallelism configuration specified by the Mechanism.
5. The Thread Pool executes the new tasks on the Platform.

7. Performance Goals and Mechanisms Tested

One advantage of the separation of concerns enabled by the DoPE interface is that a mechanism developer can implement new mechanisms and add them to the library in order to better support existing performance goals or to enable new ones, without changing the application code. The separation of concerns also enables reuse of mechanisms across many parallel applications. This separation allowed us to implement and test three different goals of system use, with multiple mechanisms to achieve them. *For each performance goal, there is a best mechanism that DoPE uses by default. In other words, a human need not select a particular mechanism to use from among many.* Multiple mechanisms are described for each performance goal in order to demonstrate the power of DoPE's API. Table 3 lists the implemented mechanisms and the number of lines of code for implementing each. Two of the mechanisms are proposed in prior work for a fixed goal-mechanism combination.

Mechanism					
WQT-H	WQ-Linear	TBF	FDP [29]	SEDA [38]	TPC
28	9	89	94	30	154

Table 3. Lines of code to implement tested mechanisms

7.1 Goal: "Min Response time with N threads"

For systems serving online applications, the system utility is often maximized by minimizing the average response time experienced by the users, thereby maximizing user satisfaction. In the video transcoding example of Section 2, the programmer used an observation to minimize response time: If load on the system is light, a configuration that minimizes execution time is better, whereas if load is heavy, a configuration that maximizes throughput is better. This observation informs the following mechanisms:

Mechanism: Work Queue Threshold with Hysteresis (WQT-H) WQT-H captures the notion of "latency mode" and "throughput mode" in the form of a 2-state machine that transitions from one state to the other based on occupancy of the work queue. Initially, WQT-H is in the SEQ state in which it returns a DoP extent of 1 (sequential execution) to each task. When the occupancy of the work queue remains under a threshold T for more than N_{off} consecutive tasks, WQT-H transitions to the PAR state in which it returns a DoP extent of M_{max} (DoP extent above which parallel efficiency drops below 0.5) to each task. WQT-H stays in the PAR state until the work queue threshold increases above T and stays like that for more than N_{on} tasks. The hysteresis allows the system to infer a load pattern and avoid toggling states frequently. The hysteresis lengths (N_{on} and N_{off}) can be weighted in favor of one state over another. For example, one extreme could be to switch to the PAR state only under the lightest of loads ($N_{off} \gg N_{on}$).

Mechanism: Work Queue Linear (WQ-Linear) A more graceful degradation of response time with increasing load may be achieved by varying the DoP extent continuously in the range $[M_{min}, M_{max}]$, rather than just toggling between two DoP extent values. WQ-Linear assigns a DoP extent according to Equation 2.

$$DoP_{extent} = max(M_{min}, M_{max} - k \times WQo) \quad (2)$$

WQo is the instantaneous work queue occupancy. k is the rate of DoP extent reduction ($k > 0$). k is set according to Equation 3.

$$k = \frac{M_{max} - M_{min}}{Q_{max}} \quad (3)$$

Q_{max} in Equation 3 is derived from the maximum response time degradation acceptable to the end user and is set by the system administrator taking into account the service level agreement (SLA), if any. The degradation is with respect to the minimum response time achievable by the system at a load factor of 1.0. The threshold value T in the WQT-H mechanism is obtained similarly by a back-calculation from the acceptable response time degradation. A variant of WQ-Linear could be a mechanism that incorporates the hysteresis component of WQT-H into WQ-Linear.

7.2 Goal: "Max Throughput with N threads"

Many applications can be classified as throughput-oriented batch applications. The overall application throughput is limited by the throughput of the slowest parallel task. By observing the in-queue occupancies of each task and task execution time, throughput limiting tasks can be identified and resources can be allocated accordingly. This informs the following mechanisms:

Mechanism: Throughput Balance with Fusion (TBF) TBF records a moving average of the throughput (inverse of execution time) of each task. When reconfiguration is triggered, TBF assigns each task a DoP extent that is inversely proportional to the average throughput of the task. If the imbalance in the throughputs of different tasks is greater than a threshold (set to 0.5), TBF fuses the parallel tasks to create a bigger parallel task. The rationale for fusion is that if a parallel loop execution is heavily unbalanced, then it might be better to avoid the inefficiency of pipeline parallelism. Our current implementation requires the application developer to implement and register the desired fused task via the `TaskDescriptor` API that allows expression of choice of `ParDescriptors` (see lines 4 and 6 in Figure 3). Creating fused tasks is easy and systematic: Unidirectional inter-task communication should be changed to method argument communication via the stack. Some of the applications that we studied already had pre-existing code for fusing tasks in the original Pthreads-parallelized source code. These were originally included to improve sequential execution in case of cache locality issues. Once registered, DoPE will automatically spawn the fused task if task fusion is triggered by the mechanism. Other mechanisms for throughput maximization that we tested are:

Mechanism: Feedback Directed Pipelining (FDP) FDP uses task execution times to inform a hill climbing algorithm to identify parallelism configurations with better throughput [29].

Mechanism: Stage Event-Driven Architecture (SEDA) SEDA assigns a DoP extent proportional to load on a task [38].

7.3 Goal: "Max Throughput with N threads, P Watts"

Mechanism: Throughput Power Controller (TPC) The administrator might want to maximize application performance under a system level constraint such as power consumption. DoPE enables the administrator to specify a power target, and uses a closed-loop controller to maximize throughput while maintaining power consumption at the specified target. The controller initializes each task with a DoP extent equal to 1. It then identifies the task with the least throughput and increments the DoP extent of the task if throughput improves and the power budget is not exceeded. If the power budget is exceeded, the controller tries alternative parallelism configurations with the same DoP extent as the configuration prior to power overshoot. The controller tries both new configurations

Application	Description	Lines of Code					Number of Loop Nesting Levels	Inner DoP_{min} extent for speedup
		Added	Modified	Deleted	Fused	Total		
x264	Transcoding of yuv4mpeg videos [3]	72	10	8	-	39617	2	2
swaptions	Option pricing via Monte Carlo simulations [3]	85	11	8	-	1428	2	2
bzip	Data compression of SPEC `ref` input [6, 28]	63	10	8	-	4652	2	4
gimp	Image editing using oilify plugin [10]	35	12	4	-	1989	2	2
ferret	Image search engine [3, 17]	97	15	22	59	14781	1	-
dedup	Deduplication of PARSEC `native` input [3]	124	10	16	113	7546	1	-

Table 4. Applications enhanced using DoPE. Columns 3–7 indicate the effort required to port the original Pthreads based parallel code to the DoPE interface. Where applicable, column 6 indicates the number of lines of code in tasks created by fusing other tasks. Column 8 indicates the number of loop nesting levels in each application that were exposed for this study. Where applicable, the last column indicates the minimum DoP extent of the inner loop at which the execution time of a transaction is improved.

and configurations from recorded history in order to determine the configuration with best throughput. The controller monitors power and throughput continuously in order to trigger reconfiguration if needed.

8. Evaluation

Table 4 provides a brief description of the applications that have been enhanced using DoPE. All are computationally intensive parallel applications.

8.1 The DoPE Interface

Columns 3–7 in Table 4 are indicative of the effort required to port existing Pthreads based parallel applications to the proposed DoPE API. The nature of the changes has already been illustrated in Section 3. The number of additional lines of code written by the application developer could be significantly reduced with compiler support for functor creation and variable capture in C++ and task fusion.

8.2 The DoPE Run-time System

The DoPE run-time system is implemented as a user-land shared library built on top of Pthreads. The performance overhead (compared to the Pthreads parallelizations) of run-time monitoring of workload and platform characteristics is less than 1%, even for monitoring each and every instance of all the parallel tasks. While we have explored more combinations, for all but one benchmark in Table 4, we present results on one performance goal. For one benchmark—an image search engine (`ferret`)—we present results on all the tested performance goals.

All improvements reported are over the baseline Pthreads based parallelizations. All evaluations were done natively on an Intel Xeon X7460 machine composed of 4 sockets, each with a 6-core Intel Core Architecture 64-bit processor running at 2.66GHz. The total number of cores (and hardware contexts) is 24. The system is equipped with 24GB of RAM and runs the 2.6.31-20-server Linux kernel. Applications were compiled using *gcc* 4.4.1 with the `-O3` optimization flag. Reported numbers are average values over three runs. In the case of applications with online server behavior, the arrival of tasks was simulated using a task queuing thread that enqueues tasks to a work queue according to a Poisson distribution. The average arrival rate determines the load factor on the system. A load factor of 1.0 corresponds to an average arrival rate equal to the maximum throughput sustainable by the system. The maximum throughput is determined as N/T where N is the number of tasks and T is the time taken by the system to execute the tasks in parallel (but executing each task itself sequentially). To determine the maximum throughput for each application, N was set to 500.

8.2.1 Goal: "Min Response time with N threads"

The applications studied for this goal are video transcoding, option pricing, data compression, image editing, and image search. All applications studied for this goal have online service behavior. Minimizing response time is most interesting in the case of applications with nested loops due to the potential latency-throughput tradeoff described in Section 2. The outermost loop in all cases iterates over user transactions. The amount of parallelism available in this loop nesting level varies with the load on the servers.

Figure 11 shows the performance of the WQT-H and WQ-Linear mechanisms compared to the static $<DoP_{outer}, DoP_{inner}>$ configurations of DoP = $<(24, DOALL), (1, SEQ)>$ and DoP = $<(N/M_{max}, DOALL), (M_{max}, PIPE \mid DOALL)>$. Here, M_{max} refers to the extent of DoP_{inner} above which parallel efficiency drops below 0.5.

Interestingly, WQT-H outperforms both static mechanisms at certain load factors. For example, consider the response times at load factor 0.8 in Figure 11(b). Analysis of the work queue occupancy and DoP assignment to tasks reveals that even though the load factor is on average equal to 0.8, there are periods of heavier and lighter load. DoPE's dynamic adaptation of the DoP between DoP = $<(24, DOALL), (1, SEQ)>$ and DoP = $<(N/M_{max}, DOALL), (M_{max}, PIPE \mid DOALL)>$ results in an average DoP somewhere in between the two, and this average DoP is better than either for minimizing response time. This provides experimental validation of the intuitive rationale behind WQ-Linear, which provides the best response time characteristic across the load factor range. In the case of data compression (Figure 11(c)), the minimum extent of DoP_{inner} at which speedup is obtained over sequential execution is 4 (see Table 4). This results in two problems for WQ-Linear. First, WQ-Linear may give unhelpful configurations such as $<(8, DOALL), (3, PIPE)>$. Second, the number of configurations at WQ-Linear's disposal is too few to provide any improvement over WQT-H.

Figure 12 shows the response time characteristic of `ferret`. The figure shows the static distribution of threads to each pipeline stage. For example, $(<1, 6, 6, 6, 6, 1>, PIPE)$ indicates a single loop parallelized in a pipelined fashion with 6 threads allocated to each parallel stage and 1 thread allocated to each sequential stage. Oversubscribing the hardware resources by allocating 24 threads to each parallel task results in much improved response time compared to a static even distribution of the 24 hardware threads. DoPE achieves a much better characteristic by allocating threads proportional to load on each task.

8.2.2 Goal: "Max Throughput with N threads"

For batch processing applications, a desirable performance goal is throughput maximization. DoPE uses the mechanisms described in Section 7.2 to improve the throughput of an image search engine and a file deduplication application.

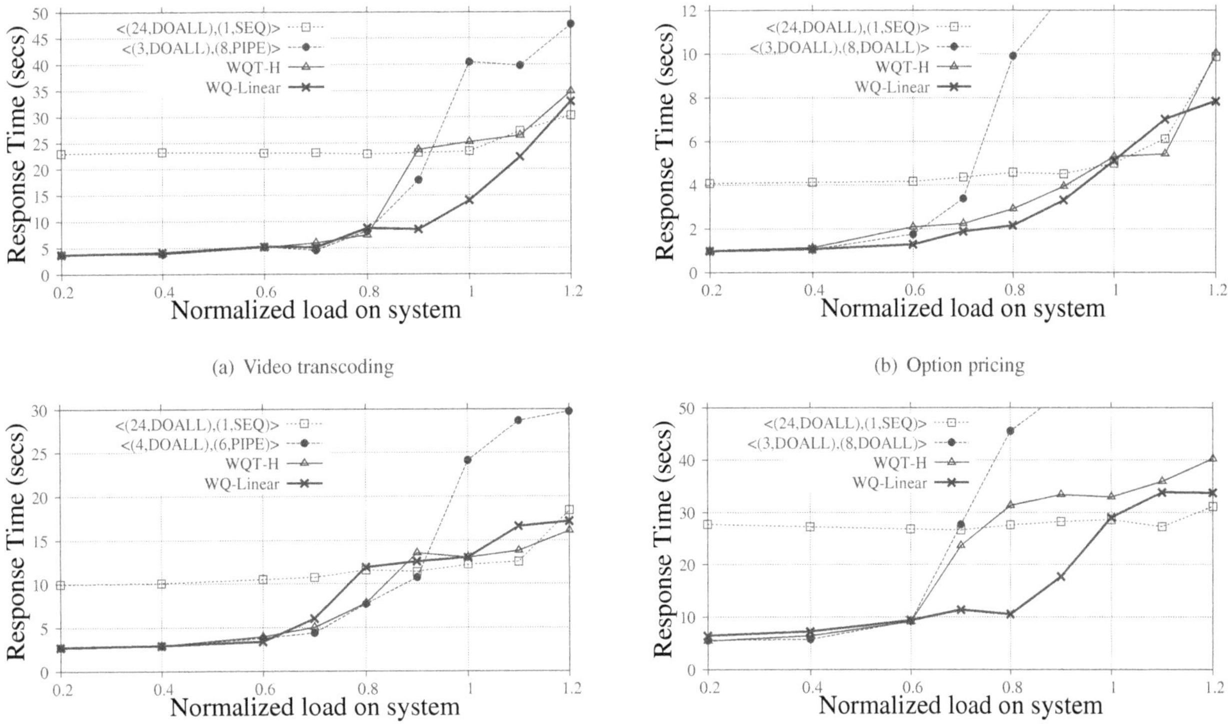

(a) Video transcoding

(b) Option pricing

(c) Data compression

(d) Image editing

Figure 11. Response time variation with load using Static, WQT-H, and WQ-Linear mechanisms

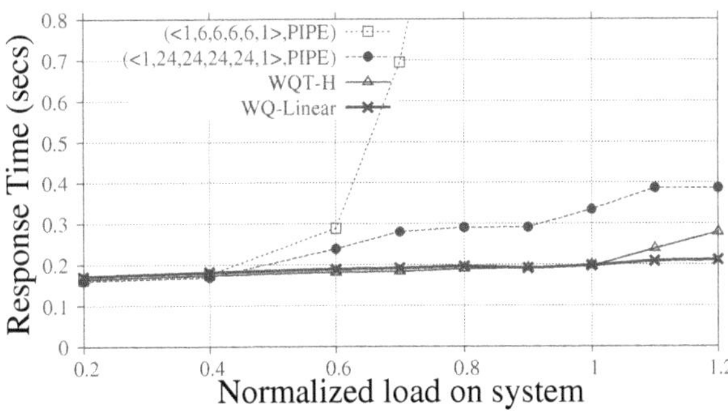

Figure 12. `ferret` Response Time

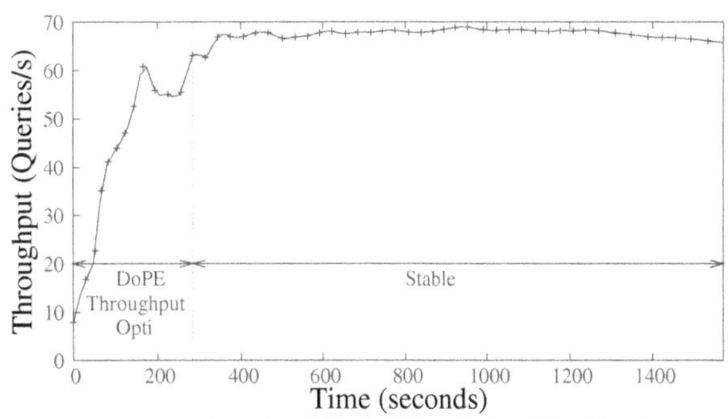

Figure 13. `ferret` Throughput

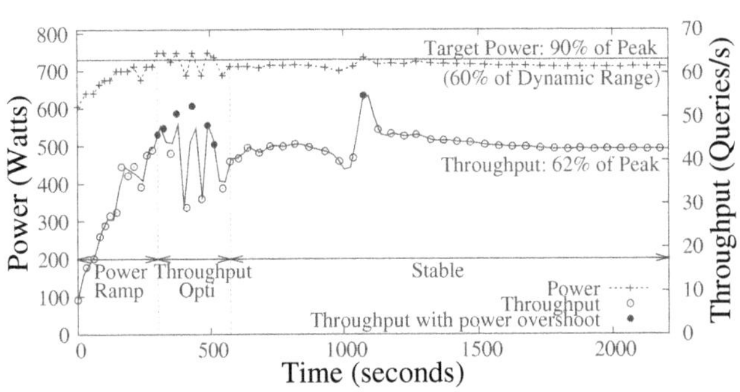

Figure 14. `ferret` Power-Throughput

Apps.		ferret	dedup
Pthreads	Baseline	1.00×	1.00×
	OS	2.12×	0.89×
DoPE	SEDA [38]	1.64×	1.16×
	FDP [29]	2.14×	2.08×
	TB	1.96×	1.75×
	TBF	2.35×	2.36×

Figure 15. Throughput improvement over static even thread distribution

Table 15 shows the throughput improvements for `ferret` and `dedup` using different mechanisms. Pthreads-Baseline is the original Pthreads parallelization with a static even distribution of available hardware threads across all the parallel tasks after assigning a single thread to each sequential task. (This is a common practice [21].) The Pthreads-OS number shows the performance when each parallel task is initialized with a thread pool containing as many threads as the number of available hardware threads in the platform, and the operating-system's scheduler is called upon to do load balancing. The remaining numbers represent the performance of the DoPEd applications using the mechanisms described in Section 7.2. DoPE-TB is the same as DoPE-TBF but with task fusion turned off, in order to demonstrate the benefit of task fusion.

DoPE-TBF outperforms all other mechanisms. OS scheduling causes more context-switching, cache pollution, and memory consumption. In the case of `dedup`, these overheads result in virtually no improvement over the baseline. The overheads may become prominent even in the case of `ferret` on a machine with a larger number of cores. In addition, this mechanism is still a static scheme that cannot adapt to run-time events such as more cores becoming available to the application. Each task in SEDA resizes its thread pool locally without coordinating resource allocation with other tasks. By contrast, both FDP and TBF have a global view of resource allocation and are able to redistribute the hardware threads according to the throughput of each task. Additionally, FDP and TBF are able to either fuse or combine tasks in the event of very uneven load across stages. Compared to FDP which simulates task fusion via time-multiplexed execution of tasks on the same thread, TBF has the additional benefit of avoiding the overheads of forwarding data between tasks by enabling the developer to explicitly expose the appropriate fused task.

Figure 13 shows the dynamic throughput characteristic of `ferret`. DoPE searches the parallelism configuration space before stabilizing on the one with the maximum throughput under the constraint of 24 hardware threads.

8.2.3 Goal: "Max Throughput with N threads, P Watts"

Figure 14 shows the operation of DoPE's power-throughput controller (TPC) on `ferret`. For a peak power target specified by the administrator, DoPE first ramps up the DoP extent until the power budget is fully used. DoPE then explores different parallelism configurations and stabilizes on the one with the best throughput without exceeding the power budget. Note that 90% of peak total power corresponds to 60% of peak power in the dynamic CPU range (all cores idle to all cores active). DoPE achieves the maximum throughput possible at this setting. Fine-grained per core power control can result in a wider dynamic range and greater power savings [27]. Full system power was measured at the maximum sampling rate (13 samples per minute) supported by the power distribution unit (AP7892 [2]). This limited the speed with which the controller responds to fluctuations in power consumption. Newer chips have power monitoring units with higher sampling rates and clock gating per core. They could be used to design faster and higher performance controllers for throttling power and parallelism. The transient in the Stable region of the figure shows how constant monitoring enables DoPE to respond to system events.

9. Related Work

Parallelization Libraries Several interfaces and associated run-time systems have been proposed to adapt parallel program execution to run-time variability [4, 8, 9, 13, 20, 26, 29, 35, 37, 38]. However, each interface is tied to a specific performance goal, specific mechanism of adaptation, or a specific application/platform domain. OpenMP [22], Cilk [5], and Intel TBB [26] support task parallelism for independent tasks and their schedulers optimize only for throughput. DoPE enables the developer to express parallelism in loop nests involving interacting tasks, and enables administrators to specify different performance goals. Navarro et al. developed an analytical model for pipeline parallelism to characterize performance and efficiency of pipeline parallel implementations [21]. Suleman et al. proposed Feedback Directed Pipelining (FDP) [29]. Moreno et al. proposed a technique similar to FDP called Dynamic Pipeline Mapping (DPM) [20]. We implemented FDP as a throughput maximization mechanism.

Domain-specific Programming Models Traditionally, multiple levels of parallelism across tasks and within each task has been investigated in the database research community for SQL queries [7, 12, 31, 32]. DoPE extends these works by providing dynamic adaptation to general-purpose applications that typically involve other forms of parallelism like pipeline parallelism, task parallelism, etc. DoPE also allows the administrator to specify different performance goals, and optimizes accordingly. For network service codes, programming models such as the Stage Event-Driven Architecture (SEDA) [38] and Aspen [35] have been proposed. We implemented the SEDA controller as a throughput maximization mechanism. Compared to these models, DoPE is applicable to programs with loop nests, and supports multiple performance goals. The mechanisms proposed for different performance goals in the context of DoPE could form a valuable part of the respective run-time schedulers of SEDA and Aspen. Blagojevic et al. propose user-level schedulers that dynamically "rightsize" the loop nesting level and degree of parallelism on a Cell Broadband Engine system [4]. Unlike DoPE, they exploit only one form of intra-task parallelism—loop-level DOALL parallelism.

Auto-tuning Wang et al. use machine learning to predict the best number of threads for a given program on a particular hardware platform [37]. They apply their technique on programs with a single loop. Luk et al. use a dynamic compilation approach and curve fitting to find the optimal distribution of work between a CPU and GPU [16]. Hall and Martonosi propose to increase or decrease threads allocated to compiler parallelized DOALL loops at run-time as the measured speedup exceeds or falls short of the expected speedup [11]. The ADAPT dynamic optimizer applies loop optimizations at run-time to create new variants of code [36]. Some of these sophisticated machine learning techniques could be used to improve DoPE's mechanisms.

10. Conclusion

Parallel applications must execute robustly across a variety of execution environments arising out of variability in workload characteristics, platform characteristics, and performance goals. For this, a separation of concerns of parallel application development, its optimization, and use, is required. The Degree of Parallelism Executive (DoPE) enables such a separation. Using DoPE, the application developer can specify all of the potential parallelism in loop nests just once; the mechanism developer can implement mechanisms for parallelism adaptation; and the administrator can select a suitable mechanism that implements a performance goal of system use. As a result of DoPE, they can be confident that the specified performance goals are met in a variety of application execution environments.

Acknowledgments

We thank the entire Liberty Research Group for their support and feedback during this work. We thank Alexander Wauck for help with the data compression application. We also thank the anonymous reviewers for their valuable feedback. This material is based on work supported by National Science Foundation Grants

0964328 and 1047879, and by United States Air Force Contract FA8650-09-C-7918. Arun Raman is supported by an Intel Foundation Ph.D. Fellowship.

References

[1] R. Allen and K. Kennedy. *Optimizing compilers for modern architectures: A dependence-based approach.* Morgan Kaufmann Publishers Inc., 2002.

[2] APC metered rack PDU user's guide. `http://www.apc.com`.

[3] C. Bienia, S. Kumar, J. P. Singh, and K. Li. The PARSEC benchmark suite: characterization and architectural implications. In *Proceedings of the Seventeenth International Conference on Parallel Architecture and Compilation Techniques (PACT)*, 2008.

[4] F. Blagojevic, D. S. Nikolopoulos, A. Stamatakis, C. D. Antonopoulos, and M. Curtis-Maury. Runtime scheduling of dynamic parallelism on accelerator-based multi-core systems. *Parallel Computing*, 2007.

[5] R. D. Blumofe, C. F. Joerg, B. C. Kuszmaul, C. E. Leiserson, K. H. Randall, and Y. Zhou. Cilk: An efficient multithreaded runtime system. In *Proceedings of the 5th ACM SIGPLAN Symposium on Principles and Practice of Parallel Programming (PPoPP)*, 1995.

[6] M. Bridges, N. Vachharajani, Y. Zhang, T. Jablin, and D. August. Revisiting the sequential programming model for multi-core. In *Proceedings of the 40th Annual IEEE/ACM International Symposium on Microarchitecture (MICRO)*, 2007.

[7] C. B. Colohan, A. Ailamaki, J. G. Steffan, and T. C. Mowry. Optimistic intra-transaction parallelism on chip multiprocessors. In *Proceedings of the 31st International Conference on Very Large Data Bases (VLDB)*, 2005.

[8] M. Curtis-Maury, J. Dzierwa, C. D. Antonopoulos, and D. S. Nikolopoulos. Online power-performance adaptation of multithreaded programs using hardware event-based prediction. In *Proceedings of the 20th International Conference on Supercomputing (ICS)*, 2006.

[9] Y. Ding, M. Kandemir, P. Raghavan, and M. J. Irwin. Adapting application execution in CMPs using helper threads. *Journal of Parallel and Distributed Computing*, 2009.

[10] GNU Image Manipulation Program. `http://www.gimp.org`.

[11] M. W. Hall and M. Martonosi. Adaptive parallelism in compiler-parallelized code. In *Proceedings of the 2nd SUIF Compiler Workshop*, 1997.

[12] N. Hardavellas, I. Pandis, R. Johnson, N. Mancheril, A. Ailamaki, and B. Falsafi. Database servers on chip multiprocessors: Limitations and opportunities. In *Proceedings of the Third Biennial Conference on Innovative Data Systems Research (CIDR)*, 2007.

[13] W. Ko, M. N. Yankelevsky, D. S. Nikolopoulos, and C. D. Polychronopoulos. Effective cross-platform, multilevel parallelism via dynamic adaptive execution. In *Proceedings of the International Parallel and Distributed Processing Symposium (IPDPS)*, 2002.

[14] M. Kulkarni, K. Pingali, B. Walter, G. Ramanarayanan, K. Bala, and L. P. Chew. Optimistic parallelism requires abstractions. In *Proceedings of the ACM SIGPLAN 2007 Conference on Programming Language Design and Implementation (PLDI)*, 2007.

[15] R. Liu, K. Klues, S. Bird, S. Hofmeyr, K. Asanovi, and J. Kubiatowicz. Tessellation: Space-time partitioning in a manycore client OS. In *Proceedings of the First USENIX Workshop on Hot Topics in Parallelism (HotPar)*, 2009.

[16] C.-K. Luk, S. Hong, and H. Kim. Qilin: Exploiting parallelism on heterogeneous multiprocessors with adaptive mapping. In *Proceedings of the 42nd Annual IEEE/ACM International Symposium on Microarchitecture (MICRO)*, 2009.

[17] Q. Lv, W. Josephson, Z. Wang, M. Charikar, and K. Li. Ferret: A toolkit for content-based similarity search of feature-rich data. *ACM SIGOPS Operating Systems Review*, 2006.

[18] J. Mars, N. Vachharajani, M. L. Soffa, and R. Hundt. Contention aware execution: Online contention detection and response. In *Proceedings of the Eighth Annual International Symposium on Code Generation and Optimization (CGO)*, 2010.

[19] D. Meisner, B. T. Gold, and T. F. Wenisch. PowerNap: Eliminating server idle power. In *Proceedings of the Fourteenth International Symposium on Architectural Support for Programming Languages and Operating Systems (ASPLOS)*, 2009.

[20] A. Moreno, E. César, A. Guevara, J. Sorribes, T. Margalef, and E. Luque. Dynamic Pipeline Mapping (DPM). In *Proceedings of the International Euro-Par Conference on Parallel Processing (Euro-Par)*, 2008.

[21] A. Navarro, R. Asenjo, S. Tabik, and C. Cascaval. Analytical modeling of pipeline parallelism. In *Proceedings of the Eighteenth International Conference on Parallel Architecture and Compilation Techniques (PACT)*, 2009.

[22] The OpenMP API specification for parallel programming. `http://www.openmp.org`.

[23] H. Pan, B. Hindman, and K. Asanović. Composing parallel software efficiently with Lithe. In *Proceedings of the ACM SIGPLAN 2010 Conference on Programming Language Design and Implementation (PLDI)*, 2010.

[24] M. K. Prabhu and K. Olukotun. Exposing speculative thread parallelism in SPEC2000. In *Proceedings of the 10th ACM SIGPLAN Symposium on Principles and Practice of Parallel Programming (PPoPP)*, 2005.

[25] A. Raman, H. Kim, T. R. Mason, T. B. Jablin, and D. I. August. Speculative parallelization using software multi-threaded transactions. In *Proceedings of the Fifteenth International Symposium on Architectural Support for Programming Languages and Operating Systems (ASPLOS)*, 2010.

[26] J. Reinders. *Intel Threading Building Blocks*. O'Reilly & Associates, Inc., Sebastopol, CA, USA, 2007.

[27] G. Semeraro, G. Magklis, R. Balasubramonian, D. H. Albonesi, S. Dwarkadas, and M. L. Scott. Energy-efficient processor design using multiple clock domains with dynamic voltage and frequency scaling. In *Proceedings of the Eighth International Symposium on High-Performance Computer Architecture (HPCA)*, 2002.

[28] Standard Performance Evaluation Corporation (SPEC). `http://www.spec.org`.

[29] M. A. Suleman, M. K. Qureshi, Khubaib, and Y. N. Patt. Feedback-directed pipeline parallelism. In *Proceedings of the Nineteenth International Conference on Parallel Architecture and Compilation Techniques (PACT)*, 2010.

[30] M. A. Suleman, M. K. Qureshi, and Y. N. Patt. Feedback-driven threading: Power-efficient and high-performance execution of multithreaded workloads on CMPs. In *Proceedings of the Thirteenth International Symposium on Architectural Support for Programming Languages and Operating Systems (ASPLOS)*, 2008.

[31] Sybase adaptive server. http://sybooks.sybase.com/nav/base.do.

[32] J. Tellez and B. Dageville. *Method for computing the degree of parallelism in a multi-user environment*. United States Patent No. 6,820,262. Oracle International Corporation, 2004.

[33] The IEEE and The Open Group. *The Open Group Base Specifications Issue 6 IEEE Std 1003.1, 2004 Edition*. 2004.

[34] C. Tian, M. Feng, V. Nagarajan, and R. Gupta. Copy or discard execution model for speculative parallelization on multicores. In *Proceedings of the 41st Annual IEEE/ACM International Symposium on Microarchitecture (MICRO)*, 2008.

[35] G. Upadhyaya, V. S. Pai, and S. P. Midkiff. Expressing and exploiting concurrency in networked applications with Aspen. In *Proceedings of the 12th ACM SIGPLAN Symposium on Principles and Practice of Parallel Programming (PPoPP)*, 2007.

[36] M. J. Voss and R. Eigenmann. ADAPT: Automated De-Coupled Adaptive Program Transformation. In *Proceedings of the 28th International Conference on Parallel Processing (ICPP)*, 1999.

[37] Z. Wang and M. F. O'Boyle. Mapping parallelism to multi-cores: A machine learning based approach. In *Proceedings of the 14th ACM SIGPLAN Symposium on Principles and Practice of Parallel Programming (PPoPP)*, 2009.

[38] M. Welsh, D. Culler, and E. Brewer. SEDA: An architecture for well-conditioned, scalable internet services. *ACM SIGOPS Operating Systems Review*, 2001.

[39] T. Wiegand, G. J. Sullivan, G. Bjontegaard, and A. Luthra. Overview of the H.264/AVC video coding standard. *IEEE Transactions on Circuits and Systems for Video Technology*, 2003.

[40] H. Zhong, M. Mehrara, S. Lieberman, and S. Mahlke. Uncovering hidden loop level parallelism in sequential applications. In *Proceedings of the 14th International Symposium on High-Performance Computer Architecture (HPCA)*, 2008.

Data Representation Synthesis *

Peter Hawkins
Computer Science Department, Stanford University
hawkinsp@cs.stanford.edu

Alex Aiken
Computer Science Department, Stanford University
aiken@cs.stanford.edu

Kathleen Fisher
Computer Science Department, Tufts University †
kfisher@eecs.tufts.edu

Martin Rinard
MIT Computer Science and Artificial Intelligence Laboratory
rinard@csail.mit.edu

Mooly Sagiv
Tel-Aviv University
msagiv@post.tau.ac.li

Abstract

We consider the problem of specifying combinations of data structures with complex sharing in a manner that is both declarative and results in provably correct code. In our approach, abstract data types are specified using relational algebra and functional dependencies. We describe a language of decompositions that permit the user to specify different concrete representations for relations, and show that operations on concrete representations soundly implement their relational specification. It is easy to incorporate data representations synthesized by our compiler into existing systems, leading to code that is simpler, correct by construction, and comparable in performance to the code it replaces.

Categories and Subject Descriptors D.3.3 [*Programming Languages*]: Language Constructs and Features—Abstract data types, Data types and structures; E.2 [*Data Storage Representations*]

General Terms Languages, Design, Algorithms, Performance, Verification

Keywords Synthesis, Composite Data Structures

1. Introduction

One of the first things a programmer must do when implementing a system is commit to particular choices of data structures. For example, consider a simple operating system process scheduler. Each process has an ID pid, a $state$ (running or sleeping), and a variety of statistics such as the cpu time consumed. Since we need to find and update processes by ID, we store processes in a hash table indexed by pid; as we also need to enumerate processes in each state, we simultaneously maintain a linked list of running processes and a separate list of sleeping processes.

* This work was supported by NSF grants CCF-0702681 and CNS-050955.

† Kathleen was at AT&T Labs Research when this research was done.

PLDI'11, June 4–8, 2011, San Jose, California, USA.

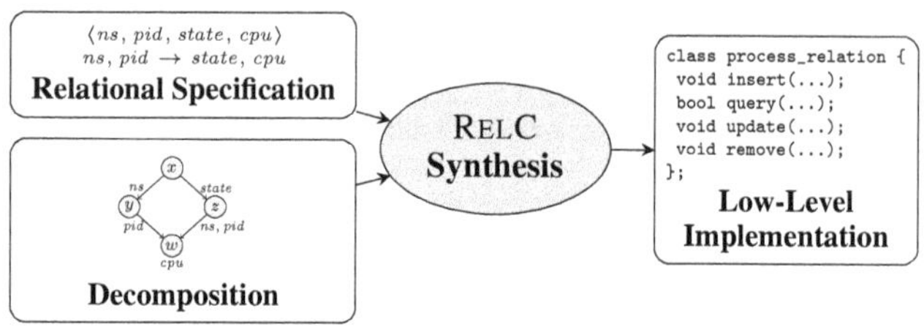

Figure 1. Schematic of Data Representation Synthesis.

Whatever our choice of data structures, it has a pervasive influence on the subsequent code, and as requirements evolve it is difficult and tedious to change the data structures to match. For example, suppose we add virtualization support by allowing processes with the same pid number to exist in different namespaces ns, together with the ability to enumerate processes in a namespace. Extending the existing data structures to support the new requirement may require many changes throughout the code.

Furthermore, invariants on multiple, overlapping data structures that represent different views of the same data are hard to state, difficult to enforce, and easy to get wrong. For the scheduler, we require that each process appears in both the hash-table indexed by process ID and exactly one of the running or sleeping lists. Such invariants must be enforced by every piece of code that manipulates the scheduler's data structures. It is easy to forget a case, say by failing to add a process to the appropriate list when it changes state or by failing to delete a hash table entry when a process terminates. Invariants of this nature require deep knowledge about the heap's structure, and are difficult to enforce through existing static analysis or verification techniques.

We propose a new method termed *data representation synthesis*, depicted in Figure 1. In our approach, a data structure client writes code that describes and manipulates data at a high-level as *relations*; a data structure designer then provides *decompositions* which describe how those relations should be represented in memory as a combination of primitive data structures. Our compiler RELC takes a relation and its decomposition and synthesizes efficient and correct low-level code that implements the relational interface.

Synthesis allows programmers to describe and manipulate data at a high level as relations, while giving control of how relations are represented physically in memory. By abstracting data from its representation, programmers no longer prematurely commit to a particular representation of data. If programmers want to change or extend their choice of data structures, they need only change the decomposition; the code that uses the relation need not change at all. Synthesized representations are correct by construction; so long as the programmer conforms to the relational specification, invariants on the synthesized data structures are automatically maintained.

We build on our previous work [12], which introduced the idea of synthesizing shared low-level data structures from a high-level relational description. Our theoretical framework is substantially simpler and more flexible. In particular, we can handle destructive updates to relations while still preserving all relation invariants. We have also implemented a compiler for relational specifications and an autotuner that finds the best decomposition for a relation automatically. Finally, we have integrated synthesized data representations into existing C++ code as a proof of concept.

Each section of this paper highlights a contribution of our work:

- We describe a new scheme for synthesizing efficient low-level data representations from abstract relational descriptions of data (Section 2). We describe a relational interface that abstracts data from its concrete representation.
- The decomposition language (Section 3) specifies how relations should be mapped to low-level physical implementations, which are assembled from a library of primitive data structures. The decomposition language provides a new way to specify high-level heap invariants that are difficult or impossible to express using standard data abstraction or heap-analysis techniques. We describe adequacy conditions that ensure a decomposition faithfully represents a relation.
- We synthesize efficient implementations of queries and updates to relations, tailored to the specified decomposition (Section 4). Key to our approach is a query planner that chooses an efficient strategy for each query or update. We show queries and updates are sound, that is, each query or update implementation faithfully implements its relational specification.
- A programmer may not know the best decomposition for a particular relation. We describe an autotuner (Section 5), which given a relational specification and a performance metric finds the best decomposition up to a user-specified bound.
- The compiler RELC (Section 6) takes as input a relation and its decomposition, and generates C++ code implementing the relation, which is easily incorporated into existing systems. We show different decompositions lead to very different performance characteristics. We incorporate synthesis into three real systems, namely a web server, a network accounting daemon and a map viewer, in each case leading to code that is simpler, correct by construction, and comparable in performance.

2. Relational Abstraction

We first introduce the relation abstraction via which data structure clients manipulate synthesized data representations. Representing and manipulating data as relations is familiar from databases, and our interface is largely standard. We use relations to abstract a program's data from its representation. Describing particular representations is the task of the decomposition language of Section 3.

A *relational specification* is a set of column names C and functional dependencies Δ. In the scheduler example from Section 1 a natural way to model the processes is as a relation with columns $\{ns, pid, state, cpu\}$, where the values of $state$ are drawn from the set $\{S, R\}$, representing sleeping and running processes respectively, and the other columns have integer values. Not every relation represents a valid set of processes; all meaningful sets of processes satisfy a functional dependency $ns, pid \rightarrow state, cpu$, which allows at most one $state$ or cpu value for any given process.

To formally define relational specifications, we need to fix notation for values, tuples, and relations:

Values, Tuples, Relations We assume a set of untyped values v drawn from a universe $\mathbb{V}$ that includes the integers ($\mathbb{Z} \subseteq \mathbb{V}$). A *tuple* $t = \langle c_1 \colon v_1, c_2 \colon v_2, \dots \rangle$ maps a set of *columns* $\{c_1, c_2, \dots\}$ to values drawn from $\mathbb{V}$. We write $\operatorname{dom} t$ for the columns of t. A tuple t is a *valuation* for a set of columns C if $\operatorname{dom} t = C$. A *relation* r is a set of tuples $\{t_1, t_2, \dots\}$ over identical columns C. We write $t(c)$ for the value of column c in tuple t. We write $t \supseteq s$ if the tuple t *extends* tuple s, that is $t(c) = s(c)$ for all c in $\operatorname{dom} s$. We say tuple t *matches* tuple s, written $t \sim s$, if the tuples are equal on all common columns. Tuple t matches a relation r, written $t \sim r$, if t matches every tuple in r. We write $s \lhd t$ for the merge of tuples s and t, taking values from t wherever the two disagree on a column's value. For example, the scheduler might represent three processes as the relation:

$$r_s = \{ \langle ns\colon 1, pid\colon 1, state\colon S, cpu\colon 7\rangle, \langle ns\colon 1, pid\colon 2, state\colon R, cpu\colon 4\rangle, \langle ns\colon 2, pid\colon 1, state\colon S, cpu\colon 5\rangle\} \quad (1)$$

Functional Dependencies A relation r has a *functional dependency* (FD) $C_1 \rightarrow C_2$ if any pair of tuples in r that are equal on columns C_1 are also equal on columns C_2. We write $r \models_{\text{fd}} \Delta$ if the set of FDs Δ hold on relation r. If a FD $C_1 \rightarrow C_2$ is a consequence of FDs Δ we write $\Delta \vdash_{\text{fd}} C_1 \rightarrow C_2$. Sound and complete inference rules for functional dependencies are well-known.

Relational Algebra We use the standard notation of relational algebra. Union ($\cup$), intersection ($\cap$), set difference ($\setminus$), and symmetric difference ($\ominus$) have their usual meanings. The operator $\pi_C\, r$ projects relation r onto a set of columns C, and $r_1 \bowtie r_2$ is the natural join of relation r_1 and relation r_2.

Relational Operations We provide five operations for creating and manipulating relations. Here we represent relations as ML-like references to a set of tuples; $\mathsf{ref}\ x$ denotes creating a new reference to x, $!r$ fetches the current value of r and $r \leftarrow v$ sets the current value of r to v:

$$\begin{aligned} \mathsf{empty}\ () &= \mathsf{ref}\ \emptyset \\ \mathsf{insert}\ r\ t &= r \leftarrow\ !r \cup \{t\} \\ \mathsf{remove}\ r\ s &= r \leftarrow\ !r \setminus \{t \in\ !r \mid t \supseteq s\} \\ \mathsf{update}\ r\ s\ u &= r \leftarrow \{\mathsf{if}\ t \supseteq s\ \mathsf{then}\ t \lhd u\ \mathsf{else}\ t \mid t \in\ !r\} \\ \mathsf{query}\ r\ s\ C &= \pi_C\{t \in\ !r \mid t \supseteq s\} \end{aligned}$$

Informally, $\mathsf{empty}\ ()$ creates a new empty relation. The operation $\mathsf{insert}\ r\ t$ inserts tuple t into relation r, $\mathsf{remove}\ r\ s$ removes tuples matching tuple s from relation r, and $\mathsf{update}\ r\ s\ u$ applies the updates in tuple u to each tuple matching s in relation r. Finally $\mathsf{query}\ r\ s\ C$ returns the columns C of all tuples in r matching tuple s. The tuples s and u given as arguments to the remove, update and query operations may be partial tuples, that is, they need not contain every column of relation r. Extending the query operator to handle comparisons other than equality or to support ordering is straightforward; however, for clarity of exposition we restrict ourselves to queries based on equalities.

For the scheduler example, we call $\mathsf{empty}\ ()$ to obtain an empty relation r. To insert a new running process into r, we invoke:

$$\mathsf{insert}\ r\ \langle ns\colon 7, pid\colon 42, state\colon R, cpu\colon 0\rangle$$

The operation

$$\mathsf{query}\ r\ \langle state\colon R\rangle\ \{ns, pid\}$$

returns the namespace and ID of each running process in r, whereas

$$\mathsf{query}\ r\ \langle ns\colon 7, pid\colon 42\rangle\ \{state, cpu\}$$

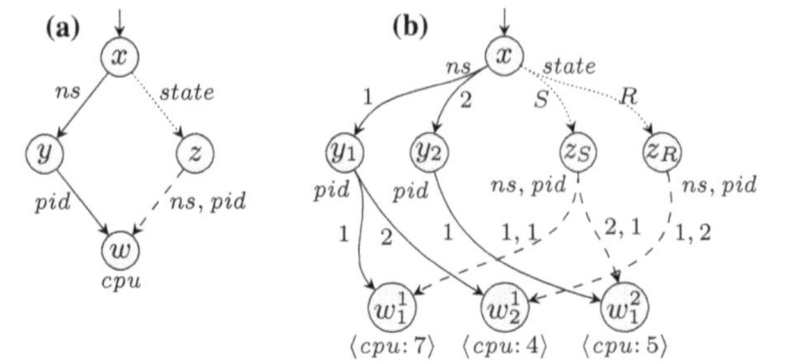

Figure 2. Data representation for a process scheduler: **(a)** a decomposition, **(b)** an instance of that decomposition. Solid edges represent hash tables, dotted edges represent vectors, and dashed edges represent doubly-linked lists.

returns the state and cpu of process 42 in namespace 7. By invoking

$$\mathsf{update}\ r\ \langle ns{:}\,7, pid{:}\,42\rangle\ \langle state{:}\,S\rangle$$

we can mark process 42 as sleeping, and finally by calling

$$\mathsf{remove}\ r\ \langle ns{:}\,7, pid{:}\,42\rangle$$

we can remove the process from the relation.

The RELC compiler emits C++ classes that implement the relational interface, which client code can then call. For the scheduler relation example the compiler generates the class:

```
class scheduler_relation {
  void insert(tuple_cpu_ns_pid_state const &r);
  void remove(tuple_ns_pid const &pattern);
  void update(tuple_ns_pid const &pattern,
              tuple_cpu_state const &changes);
  void query(tuple_state const &input,
             iterator_state__ns_pid &output);
  ...
};
```

Each method of the class instantiates a relational operation. We could generate instantiations of each operation for all possible kinds of tuples passed as arguments, however in practice we allow the programmer to specify the needed instantiations.

3. Decompositions and Decomposition Instances

Decompositions describe how to represent relations as a combination of primitive data structures. Our goal is to prove that the low-level representation of a relation faithfully implements its high-level specification. In this section, we develop the technical machinery to reason about the correspondence between relations and their decompositions.

A decomposition is a static description of the structure of data, akin to a type. Its run-time (dynamic) counterpart is the *decomposition instance*, which describes the representation of a particular relation using the decomposition. We define an *abstraction function* that computes the relation represented by a given decomposition instance, and *well-formedness criteria* that check that a decomposition instance is a well-formed instance of a particular decomposition. Finally, we define *adequacy conditions* which are sufficient conditions for a decomposition to faithfully represent a relation.

3.1 Decompositions

A *decomposition* is a rooted, directed acyclic graph that describes how to represent a relational specification. The subgraph rooted at each node of the decomposition describes how to represent part of the original relation; each edge of the decomposition describes a way of breaking up a relation into a set of smaller relations.

$$\begin{array}{lr}
\hat{p} ::= C \mid C \overset{\psi}{\mapsto} v \mid \hat{p}_1 \bowtie \hat{p}_2 & \text{decomposition primitives} \\
\hat{d} ::= \mathsf{let}\ v{:}\ C_1 \triangleright C_2 = \hat{p}\ \mathsf{in}\ \hat{d} \mid v & \text{decompositions} \\
\psi ::= \mathsf{dlist} \mid \mathsf{htable} \mid \mathsf{vector} \mid \cdots & \text{data structures}
\end{array}$$

Figure 3. The decomposition language.

$$\begin{array}{lr}
p ::= t \mid \{t \mapsto v_{t'}, \dots\} \mid p_1 \bowtie p_2 & \text{instance primitives} \\
d ::= \mathsf{let}\ \{v_t = p, \dots\}\ \mathsf{in}\ d \mid v_{\langle\rangle} & \text{instances}
\end{array}$$

Figure 4. Decomposition instances.

We use the scheduler example to explain the features of the decomposition language. Figure 2(a) shows one possible decomposition for the scheduler relation. Informally, this decomposition reads as follows. From the root (node x), we can follow the left-hand edge, which uses a hash table to map each value n of the ns field to a sub-relation (node y) with the $\{pid, cpu\}$ values for n. From one such sub-relation, the outgoing edge of node y maps a pid (using another hashtable) to a sub-relation consisting of a single tuple with one column, the corresponding cpu time. The $state$ field is not represented on the left-hand path. Alternatively, from the root we can follow the right-hand edge, which maps a process $state$ (running or sleeping) to a sub-relation of the $\{ns, pid, cpu\}$ values of the processes in that state. Each such sub-relation (rooted at node z) maps a $\{ns, pid\}$ pair to the corresponding cpu time. While the left path from x to w is implemented using a hash table of hash tables, the right path is a vector with two entries, one pointing to a list of running processes, the other to a list of sleeping processes. Because node w is shared, there is only one physical copy of each cpu value, shared by the two access paths.

A *decomposition instance*, or *instance* for short, is a rooted, directed acyclic graph representing a particular relation. Each node of a decomposition corresponds to a set of nodes in an instance of that decomposition. Figure 2(b) shows an instance of the decomposition representing the relation r_s defined in Equation (1). The structure of an instance corresponds to a low-level memory state; nodes are objects in memory and edges are data structures navigating between objects. Note, for example, node $z_{\langle state:\, S\rangle}$ has two outgoing edges, one for each sleeping process; the dashed edge indicates that the collection of sleeping processes is implemented as a doubly-linked list.

To reason formally about decompositions and decomposition instances we encode graphs in a let-binding notation, using the language shown in Figure 3 for decompositions and Figure 4 for instances. We stress that this notation is isomorphic to the graph notation and only exists to aid formal reasoning.

The decomposition of Figure 2(a) written in let-notation is:

$$\begin{array}{l}
\mathsf{let}\ w{:}\ \{ns, pid, state\} \triangleright \{cpu\} = \{cpu\}\ \mathsf{in} \\
\mathsf{let}\ y{:}\ \{ns\} \triangleright \{pid, cpu\} = \{pid\} \overset{\mathsf{htable}}{\longmapsto} w\ \mathsf{in} \\
\mathsf{let}\ z{:}\ \{state\} \triangleright \{ns, pid, cpu\} = \{ns, pid\} \overset{\mathsf{dlist}}{\longmapsto} w\ \mathsf{in} \\
\mathsf{let}\ x{:}\ \emptyset \triangleright \{ns, pid, cpu, state\} = \\
\qquad (\{ns\} \overset{\mathsf{htable}}{\longmapsto} y) \bowtie (\{state\} \overset{\mathsf{vector}}{\longmapsto} z)\ \mathsf{in}\ x
\end{array} \tag{2}$$

In a decomposition a let-binding $\mathsf{let}\ v{:}\ B \triangleright C = \hat{p}\ \mathsf{in}\ \hat{d}$ allows us to share instances of the sub-relation v with decomposition $\hat{p}$ between multiple parts of a decomposition $\hat{d}$. Let-bound variables must be distinct (to avoid name conflicts) and in $\mathsf{let}\ v{:}\ B \triangleright C =$

$\hat{p}$ in $\hat{d}$, variable v must appear in $\hat{d}$ (to ensure the decomposition graph is connected). Each decomposition variable is annotated with a "type," consisting of a pair of column sets $B \rhd C$; every instance of variable v in a decomposition instance has a distinct valuation of columns B, and each such instance represents a relation with columns C. Figure 2(b) written in the let-notation of instances is:

$$
\begin{aligned}
&\mathsf{let}\ \{w_{\langle ns:1, pid:1, state:S\rangle} = \langle cpu: 7\rangle\,,\\
&\quad w_{\langle ns:1, pid:2, state:R\rangle} = \langle cpu: 4\rangle\,,\\
&\quad w_{\langle ns:2, pid:1, state:S\rangle} = \langle cpu: 5\rangle\}\ \mathsf{in}\\
&\mathsf{let}\ \{y_{\langle ns:1\rangle} = \{\langle pid: 1\rangle \mapsto w_{\langle ns:1, pid:1, state:S\rangle},\\
&\qquad\qquad \langle pid: 2\rangle \mapsto w_{\langle ns:1, pid:2, state:R\rangle}\},\\
&\quad y_{\langle ns:2\rangle} = \{\langle pid: 1\rangle \mapsto w_{\langle ns:2, pid:1, state:S\rangle}\}\}\ \mathsf{in}\\
&\mathsf{let}\ \{z_{\langle state:S\rangle} = \{\langle ns: 1, pid: 1\rangle \mapsto w_{\langle ns:1, pid:1, state:S\rangle},\\
&\qquad\qquad \langle ns: 2, pid: 1\rangle \mapsto w_{\langle ns:2, pid:1, state:S\rangle}\},\\
&\quad z_{\langle state:R\rangle} = \{\langle ns: 1, pid: 2\rangle \mapsto w_{\langle ns:1, pid:2, state:R\rangle}\}\}\ \mathsf{in}\\
&\mathsf{let}\ \{x_{\langle\rangle} = \{\langle ns: 1\rangle \mapsto y_{\langle ns:1\rangle}, \langle ns: 2\rangle \mapsto y_{\langle ns:2\rangle}\}\\
&\quad \bowtie \{\langle state: S\rangle \mapsto z_{\langle state:S\rangle}, \langle state: R\rangle \mapsto z_{\langle state:R\rangle}\}\}\ \mathsf{in}\ x_{\langle\rangle}
\end{aligned}
$$

Each let-binding in the instance parallels a binding of $v \colon B \rhd C$ in the decomposition; the instance binds a set of variable instances $\{v_t, v_{t'}, \dots\}$, each for different valuations of columns B. For example, decomposition node z has two different instances $z_{\langle state:S\rangle}$ and $z_{\langle state:R\rangle}$, one for each *state* value in the relation.

We now describe the three decomposition primitives and their corresponding decomposition instance primitives.

- A *unit* C represents a single tuple t with columns C. Unit decompositions in diagrams are nodes labeled with columns C. For example, in Figure 2(a) node w is a unit decomposition containing a single *cpu* value.
- A *map* $C \overset{\psi}{\mapsto} v$ represents a relation as a mapping $\{t \mapsto v_{t'}, \dots\}$ from a set of columns C, called *key columns*, to a set of *residual relations* $r_{t'}$, one for each valuation t of the key columns. Each residual relation $r_{t'}$ is in turn represented by the decomposition v. The data structure used to implement the map is ψ, which can be any data structure that implements a key-value associative map interface. In the example ψ is one of dlist (an unordered doubly-linked list of key-value pairs), htable (a hash table), or vector (an array mapping keys to values). The set of data structures is extensible; any data structure implementing a common interface may be used. The choice of ψ only affects the computational complexity of operations on a data structure; where the complexity is irrelevant we omit ψ and simply write $C \mapsto v$. In diagrams we depict map decompositions as edges labeled with the set of columns C. For example, in Figure 2(a) the edge from y to w labeled *pid* indicates that for each instance of vertex y in a decomposition instance there is a data structure that maps each value of *pid* to a different residual relation, represented using the decomposition rooted at w.
- A *join* $\hat{p}_1 \bowtie \hat{p}_2$ represents a relation as the natural join of two different sub-relations r_1 and r_2, where $\hat{p}_1$ describes how to decompose r_1 and $\hat{p}_2$ describes how to decompose r_2. In diagrams, join decompositions exist wherever multiple map edges exit the same node. For example, in Figure 2(a) node x has two outgoing map edges and hence is the join of two map decompositions.

3.2 Abstraction Function

The abstraction functions $\alpha(d, \Gamma)$ and $\alpha(p, \Gamma)$ map instances d and instance primitives p, respectively, to the relation they represent. Argument Γ is an environment that maps instance variables to definitions. We write $\cdot$ to denote the initial empty environment.

$$
\begin{aligned}
\alpha(t, \Gamma) &= \{t\}\\
\alpha(\{t \mapsto v_{t'}\}_{t \in T}, \Gamma) &= \bigcup_{t \in T} (\{t\} \bowtie \alpha(v_{t'}, \Gamma))\\
\alpha(p_1 \bowtie p_2, \Gamma) &= \alpha(p_1, \Gamma) \bowtie \alpha(p_2, \Gamma)\\
\alpha(\mathsf{let}\ \{v_t = p_t\}_{t \in T}\ \mathsf{in}\ d, \Gamma) &= \alpha(d, \Gamma \cup \{v_t \mapsto p_t \mid t \in T\})\\
\alpha(v_t, \Gamma) &= \{\alpha(\Gamma(v_t), \Gamma)\}
\end{aligned}
$$

$$
\text{(WFUNIT)}\ \frac{\operatorname{dom} t = C}{\Gamma, t \models \hat{\Gamma}, C}
\qquad
\text{(WFMAP)}\ \frac{\forall t \in T.\ \operatorname{dom} t = C \quad t \sim \alpha(v_{t'}, \Gamma) \quad \Gamma, v_{t'} \models \hat{\Gamma}, v}{\Gamma, \{t \mapsto v_{t'}\}_{t \in T} \models \hat{\Gamma}, C \mapsto v}
$$

$$
\text{(WFJOIN)}\ \frac{\Gamma, p_1 \models \hat{\Gamma}, \hat{p}_1 \quad \Gamma, p_2 \models \hat{\Gamma}, \hat{p}_2 \quad r_1 = \alpha(p_1, \Gamma) \quad r_2 = \alpha(p_2, \Gamma) \quad \pi_{\operatorname{dom} r_2} r_1 = \pi_{\operatorname{dom} r_1} r_2}{\Gamma, p_1 \bowtie p_2 \models \hat{\Gamma}, \hat{p}_1 \bowtie \hat{p}_2}
\qquad
\text{(WFVAR)}\ \frac{\Gamma, \Gamma(v_t) \models \hat{\Gamma}, \hat{\Gamma}(v)}{\Gamma, v_t \models \hat{\Gamma}, v}
$$

$$
\text{(WFLET)}\ \frac{\forall t \in T.\ \operatorname{dom} t = B \quad \Gamma \cup \{v_t \mapsto p_t\}_{t \in T}, d \models \hat{\Gamma} \cup \{v \mapsto \hat{p}\}, \hat{d}}{\Gamma, \mathsf{let}\ \{v_t = p_t\}_{t \in T}\ \mathsf{in}\ d \models \hat{\Gamma}, \mathsf{let}\ v \colon B \rhd C = \hat{p}\ \mathsf{in}\ \hat{d}}
$$

Figure 5. Well-formed instances: $\Gamma, d \models \hat{\Gamma}, \hat{d}$ and $\Gamma, p \models \hat{\Gamma}, \hat{p}$

3.3 Well-formed Decomposition Instances

Next we introduce a well-formedness invariant ensuring that the structure of an instance d corresponds to that of a decomposition $\hat{d}$. We say that a decomposition instance d is a *well-formed instance* of a decomposition $\hat{d}$ if $\cdot, d \models \cdot, \hat{d}$ follows from the rules given in Figure 5. The first argument to the judgment is an environment Γ mapping instance variables to definitions; similarly the third argument $\hat{\Gamma}$ is an environment mapping decomposition variables to definitions. Rule (WFUNIT) checks that a unit node is a tuple with the correct columns. Rule (WFMAP) checks that each key tuple t has the correct columns, that t matches all tuples in the associated residual relation, and that variable instance $v_{t'}$ is well-formed. Rule (WFJOIN) checks that we do not have "dangling" tuples on one side of a join without a matching tuple on the other side. Rule (WFLET) introduces variables into environments Γ and $\hat{\Gamma}$ and checks variable instantiations have the correct columns. Finally rule (WFVAR) checks the definition of a variable is well-formed.

3.4 Adequacy of Decompositions

Not every relation can be represented by every decomposition. In general a decomposition can only represent relations with specific columns satisfying certain functional dependencies. For example the decomposition $\hat{d}$ in Figure 2(a) cannot represent the relation

$$
\begin{aligned}
r' = \{\, &\langle ns: 1, pid: 2, state: S, cpu: 42\rangle\,,\\
&\langle ns: 1, pid: 2, state: R, cpu: 34\rangle\},
\end{aligned}
$$

since for each pair of *ns* and *pid* values the decomposition $\hat{d}$ can only represent a single value for the *state* and *cpu* fields. However r' does not correspond to a meaningful set of processes—the relational specification in Section 2 requires that all well-formed sets of processes satisfy the functional dependency $ns, pid \rightarrow state, cpu$, which allows at most one *state* or *cpu* value for any given process.

We say that a decomposition $\hat{d}$ is *adequate* for relations with columns C satisfying FDs Δ if $\cdot; \emptyset \vdash_{a,\Delta} \hat{d}; C$ follows from the rules in Figure 6. The first argument to the judgement is an environment Σ that maps a variable v bound in the context to a pair $B \rhd C$, where

$$(\text{AVAR})\ \frac{(v\colon \emptyset \rhd C) \in \Sigma}{\Sigma; \emptyset \vdash_{a,\Delta} v; C} \qquad (\text{AUNIT})\ \frac{A \neq \emptyset \qquad \Delta \vdash_{\text{fd}} A \to C}{\Sigma; A \vdash_{a,\Delta} C; C}$$

$$(\text{AMAP})\ \frac{\begin{array}{c}(v\colon A \rhd D) \in \Sigma \\ \Delta \vdash_{\text{fd}} B \cup C \to A \qquad A \supseteq B \cup C\end{array}}{\Sigma; B \vdash_{a,\Delta} C \mapsto v; C \cup D}$$

$$(\text{AJOIN})\ \frac{\begin{array}{c}\Delta \vdash_{\text{fd}} A \cup (B \cap C) \to B \ominus C \\ \Sigma; A \vdash_{a,\Delta} \hat{p}_1; B \qquad \Sigma; A \vdash_{a,\Delta} \hat{p}_2; C\end{array}}{\Sigma; A \vdash_{a,\Delta} \hat{p}_1 \bowtie \hat{p}_2; B \cup C}$$

$$(\text{ALET})\ \frac{\Sigma; B \vdash_{a,\Delta} \hat{p}; C \qquad \Sigma, v\colon B \rhd C; A \vdash_{a,\Delta} \hat{d}; D}{\Sigma; A \vdash_{a,\Delta} \text{let } v\colon B \rhd C = \hat{p} \text{ in } \hat{d}; D}$$

Figure 6. Adequacy rules: $\Sigma; A \vdash_{a,\Delta} \hat{d}; B$ and $\Sigma; A \vdash_{a,\Delta} \hat{p}; B$

B is the set of columns bound on any path to node v from the root of the decomposition, and C is the set of columns bound within the subgraph rooted at v. The second argument A is a set of columns fixed by the context. If a decomposition $\hat{d}$ is adequate, then it can represent every possible relation with columns C satisfying FDs Δ:

Lemma 1 (Soundness of Adequacy)**.** If $\cdot; \emptyset \vdash_{a,\Delta} \hat{d}; C$ then for each relation r with columns C such that $r \models_{\text{fd}} \Delta$ there is some d such that $\cdot, d \models \cdot, \hat{d}$ and $\alpha(d, \cdot) = r$.

The adequacy rules enforce several properties, most of which are boundary conditions. Rule (AVAR) ensures the root vertex has exactly one instance (since $\emptyset$ has only one valuation). Rules (AUNIT) and (AMAP) record the columns they contain, and the top-level rule (AVAR) then ensures the decomposition represents all columns of the relation. Rule (AUNIT) also ensures that unit decompositions are not part of the graph root. Since a unit decomposition represents exactly one tuple, a unit decomposition at the root ($A = \emptyset$) would prevent us from representing the empty relation.

Rule (AMAP) is the most involved and consequential rule. Sharing occurs when the same variable is the target of two or more maps (see the uses of variable w in (2) for an example). Rule (AMAP) checks in two steps that decomposition instances are shared only when the corresponding relations are equal. First, note that $B \cup C$ are columns bound from the root to v, and the functional dependency $B \cup C \to A$ guarantees there is a unique valuation of A per valuation of $B \cup C$. Second, the requirement that $A \supseteq B \cup C$ guarantees that A includes all the columns bound on all paths reaching v (since this same requirement is also applied to other map edges that share v). Because $B \cup C \to A$, and A includes any other key columns used in other maps reaching v, the sub-relation reached via any of these alternative paths is the same.

To split a relation into two parts using a join decomposition, rule (AJOIN) requires a functional dependency that ensures that we can match tuples from each side without anomalies, such as missing or spurious tuples; recall $\ominus$ denotes symmetric difference. Finally rule (ALET) introduces variable typings from let bindings into the variable binding environment Σ.

4. Querying and Updating Decomposed Relations

In Section 3 we introduced decompositions, which describe how to represent a relation in memory as a collection of data structures. In this section we show how to compile the relational operations described in Section 2 into code tailored to a particular decomposition. There are two basic kinds of relational operation, namely queries and mutations. Since we use queries when implementing mutations, we describe queries first.

$$q ::= \mathsf{qunit} \mid \mathsf{qscan}(q) \mid \mathsf{qlookup}(q) \mid \mathsf{qlr}(q, lr) \mid \mathsf{qjoin}(q_1, q_2, lr)$$
$$lr ::= \mathsf{left} \mid \mathsf{right}$$

Figure 7. Query Plan Operators

4.1 Queries and Query Plans

Recall that the *query* operation retrieves data from a relation; given a relation r, a tuple t, and a set of columns C, a query returns the projection onto columns C of the tuples of r that match tuple t. We implement queries in two stages: *query planning*, which attempts to find the most efficient execution plan q for a query, and *query execution*, which evaluates a particular query plan over a decomposition instance. This approach is well-known in the database literature, although our formulation is novel.

In the RELC compiler, query planning is performed at compile time; the compiler generates specialized code to evaluate the chosen plan q with no run-time planning or evaluation overhead. The compiler is free to use any method it likes to chose a query plan, as long as the resulting query satisfies the *query validity* criteria described in Section 4.2. We describe the query planner implementation of the RELC compiler in Section 4.3.

As a motivating example, suppose we want to find the set of pid values of processes that match the tuple $\langle ns\colon 7, state\colon R\rangle$ using the decomposition of Figure 2. That is, we want to find the running processes in namespace 7. One possible strategy would be to look up $\langle state\colon R\rangle$ on the right-hand side, and then to iterate over all ns, pid pairs associated with the state, checking to see whether they are in the correct namespace. Another strategy would be to look up namespace 7 on the left-hand side, and to iterate over the set of pid values associated with the namespace. For each pid we then check to see whether the ns and pid pair is in the set of processes associated with $\langle state\colon R\rangle$ on the right-hand side. Each strategy has a different computational complexity; the query planner enumerates the alternatives and chooses the "best" strategy.

We describe the semantics of query execution using a function $\mathsf{dqexec}\ q\ d\ t$ which takes a query plan q, a decomposition instance d, an input tuple t, and evaluates the plan over the decomposition, and produces a set of tuples in the denotation of d that match tuple t. We do not implement dqexec directly; instead the compiler emits instances of dqexec specialized to particular queries q.

A *query plan* is a tree of query plan operators, shown in Figure 7. The query plan tree is superimposed on a decomposition and rooted at the decomposition's root. A query plan prescribes an ordered sequence of nodes and edges of the decomposition instance to visit. There are five query plan operators:

Unit The qunit operator returns the unique tuple represented by a unit decomposition instance if that tuple matches t. It returns the empty set otherwise.

Scan The operator $\mathsf{qscan}(q)$ invokes operator q for each child node v_s where s matches t. Recall a map primitive is a mapping from a set of key columns C to a set of child nodes $\{v_t\}_{t \in T}$. Since operator qscan iterates over the contents of a map data structure, it typically takes time linear in the number of entries.

Lookup The $\mathsf{qlookup}(q)$ operator looks up a particular set of key values in a map decomposition; each of the key columns of the map must be bound in the tuple t given as input to the operator. Query operator q is invoked on the resulting sub-decomposition, if any. The complexity of the $\mathsf{qlookup}$ depends on the particular choice of data structure ψ. In general, we expect $\mathsf{qlookup}$ to have better time complexity than qscan.

Left/Right The $\mathsf{qlr}(q, lr)$ operator performs query q on either the left-hand or right-hand side of a join specified by the argument lr. The other side of the join is ignored.

Join The $\mathsf{qjoin}(q_1, q_2, lr)$ operator performs a join across both sides of a join decomposition. The computational complexity of the join may depend on the order of evaluation. If lr is the value left, then first query q_1 is executed on the left side of the join decomposition, then query q_2 is executed on the right side of the join for each tuple returned by tuple q_1; the result of the join operator is the natural join of the two subqueries. If lr is the value right, the two queries are executed in the opposite order.

In the scheduler example, the query

$$\mathsf{query}\ r\ \langle ns\colon 7, pid\colon 42\rangle\ \{cpu\}$$

returns the cpu values associated with the process with pid 42 in namespace 7. One possible query plan is:

$$q_{cpu} = \mathsf{qlr}(\mathsf{qlookup}(\mathsf{qlookup}(\mathsf{qunit})), \mathsf{left}).$$

To perform query q_{cpu} on an instance d we evaluate

$$\mathsf{dqexec}\ q_{cpu}\ d\ \langle ns\colon 7, pid\colon 42\rangle$$

which first looks up namespace 7 in the data structure corresponding to decomposition edge from x to y, returning an instance of node y. We lookup pid 42 in the data structure corresponding to the edge from y to w, obtaining an instance of node w. We then use the qunit operator to retrieve the cpu value associated with node w.

Recall our motivating example, namely the query

$$\mathsf{query}\ r\ \langle ns\colon 7, state\colon R\rangle\ \{pid\}$$

that returns the set of running processes in namespace 7. Two plans that implement the query are

$$q_1 = \mathsf{qjoin}\big(\mathsf{qlookup}(\mathsf{qscan}(\mathsf{qunit})),\ \mathsf{qlookup}(\mathsf{qlookup}(\mathsf{qunit})), \mathsf{left}\big)$$
$$q_2 = \mathsf{qlr}\big(\mathsf{qlookup}(\mathsf{qscan}(\mathsf{qunit})), \mathsf{right}\big).$$

Plan q_1 first enumerates the set of processes with ns 7 (the left-hand side of the join), and then checks whether each process is associated with the running state (the right-hand side of the join). Plan q_2 iterates over all processes in the running state, checking to see whether they are in the appropriate namespace.

An important property of the query operators is that they all require only constant space; there is no need to construct intermediate data structures to execute a query. Having a predictable space overhead for queries ensures that query execution does not need to allocate memory. Constant-space queries can also be a disadvantage; for example, the current restrictions would not allow a "hash-join" strategy for implementing the join operator, nor is it possible to perform duplicate-elimination. It would be straightforward to extend the query language with non-constant-space operators.

4.2 Query Validity

Not every query plan is a correct strategy for evaluating a query. We must check three properties: first that queries produce all of the columns requested as output, second that when performing a lookup we already have all of the necessary key columns, and third that enough columns are computed on each side of a join so that tuples from each side can be accurately matched with one another. Figure 8 gives inference rules for a validity judgment that is a sufficient condition for query plan correctness. We say a query plan is *valid*, written $\hat{\Gamma}, \hat{d}, A \vdash_{q,\Delta} q, B$ if q correctly answers queries over decomposition $\hat{d}$, where A is the set of columns bound in the input tuple pattern t and B is the set of columns bound in the output tuples; $\hat{\Gamma}$ is an environment that maps variables in the decomposition to their definitions, whereas Δ is a set of FDs.

$$\text{(QUNIT)}\ \frac{}{\hat{\Gamma}, C, A \vdash_{q,\Delta} \mathsf{qunit}, C} \qquad \text{(QSCAN)}\ \frac{\hat{\Gamma}, \hat{\Gamma}(v), (A \cup C) \vdash_{q,\Delta} q, B}{\hat{\Gamma}, C \mapsto v, A \vdash_{q,\Delta} \mathsf{qscan}(q), B \cup C}$$

$$\text{(QLOOKUP)}\ \frac{C \subseteq A \qquad \hat{\Gamma}, \hat{\Gamma}(v), A \vdash_{q,\Delta} q, B}{\hat{\Gamma}, C \mapsto v, A \vdash_{q,\Delta} \mathsf{qlookup}(q), B \cup C}$$

$$\text{(QJOIN)}\ \frac{\begin{array}{cc}\hat{\Gamma}, \hat{p}_1, A \vdash_{q,\Delta} q_1, B_1 & \hat{\Gamma}, \hat{p}_2, A \cup B_1 \vdash_{q,\Delta} q_2, B_2 \\ \Delta \vdash_{\mathrm{fd}} A \cup B_1 \to B_2 & \Delta \vdash_{\mathrm{fd}} A \cup B_2 \to B_1\end{array}}{\begin{array}{c}\hat{\Gamma}, \hat{p}_1 \bowtie \hat{p}_2, A \vdash_{q,\Delta} \mathsf{qjoin}(q_1, q_2, \mathsf{left}), B_1 \cup B_2 \\ \text{or } \hat{\Gamma}, \hat{p}_2 \bowtie \hat{p}_1, A \vdash_{q,\Delta} \mathsf{qjoin}(q_2, q_1, \mathsf{right}), B_1 \cup B_2\end{array}}$$

$$\text{(QLR)}\ \frac{\hat{\Gamma}, \hat{p}_1, A \vdash_{q,\Delta} q, B}{\begin{array}{c}\hat{\Gamma}, \hat{p}_1 \bowtie \hat{p}_2, A \vdash_{q,\Delta} \mathsf{qlr}(q, \mathsf{left}), B \\ \text{or } \hat{\Gamma}, \hat{p}_2 \bowtie \hat{p}_1, A \vdash_{q,\Delta} \mathsf{qlr}(q, \mathsf{right}), B\end{array}}$$

$$\text{(QVAR)}\ \frac{\hat{\Gamma}, \hat{\Gamma}(v), A \vdash_{q,\Delta} q, B}{\hat{\Gamma}, v, A \vdash_{q,\Delta} q, B} \qquad \text{(QLET)}\ \frac{\hat{\Gamma} \cup \{v \mapsto \hat{p}\}, \hat{d}, A \vdash_{q,\Delta} q, B}{\hat{\Gamma}, \mathsf{let}\ v\colon \cdots = \hat{p}\ \mathsf{in}\ \hat{d}, A \vdash_{q,\Delta} q, B}$$

Figure 8. Validity of query plans: $\hat{\Gamma}, \hat{d}, A \vdash_{q,\Delta} q, B$

Rule (QUNIT) states that querying a unit decomposition binds its fields. Rule (QSCAN) states when scanning over a map decomposition we bind the keys of the map both as input to the sub-query and in the output. Rule (QLOOKUP) is similar, however lookups require that the key columns already be bound in the input. Rule (QJOIN) requires that each subquery of a join must bind enough columns so that we can match the results of the two subqueries without any ambiguity. As a special case, rule (QLR) allows arbitrary queries that only inspect one side of a join. Finally rules (QVAR) and (QLET) handle introduction and elimination of decomposition variables into the variable binding environment $\hat{\Gamma}$.

Lemma 2 (Decomposition Query Soundness)**.** Suppose we have $\hat{d}$, C, Δ, d, and r such that decomposition $\hat{d}$ is adequate (i.e., $\cdot;\emptyset \vdash_{a,\Delta} \hat{d}; C$), instance d is well-formed (i.e., $\cdot, d \models \cdot, \hat{d}$), and d represents a relation r (i.e., $\alpha(d, \cdot) = r$) satisfying the FDs Δ (i.e., $\Delta \models_{\mathrm{fd}} r$). If a query plan q is valid for input tuples with columns A and produces columns B (i.e., $\cdot, \hat{d}, A \vdash_{q,\Delta} q, B$), then for any tuple s with $\operatorname{dom} s = A$ we have

$$\pi_B(\mathsf{dqexec}\ q\ d\ s) = \pi_B\{t \in r \mid t \supseteq s\}.$$

4.3 Query Planner

To pick good implementations for each query, the compiler uses a query planner that finds the query plan with the lowest cost as measured by a heuristic cost estimation function. The query planner enumerates the set of valid query plans for a particular decomposition d, input columns B, and output columns C, and it returns the plan with the lowest cost. It is straightforward to enumerate query plans, although there may be exponentially many possible plans for a query.

The RELC compiler uses a simple query cost estimator $E_{\hat{\Gamma}}$ that has performed well in our experiments. Many extensions to our cost model are possible, inspired by the large literature on database query planning. For every edge from node v_1 to node v_2 in a decomposition $\hat{d}$ we require a count $c(v_1, v_2)$ of the expected number of instances of the edge outgoing from any given instance of node v_1. The count can be provided by the user, or recorded as part of a profiling run. Each data structure ψ must provide a function $m_\psi(n)$ that estimates the number of memory accesses to lookup a key in a data structure ψ containing n elements. For

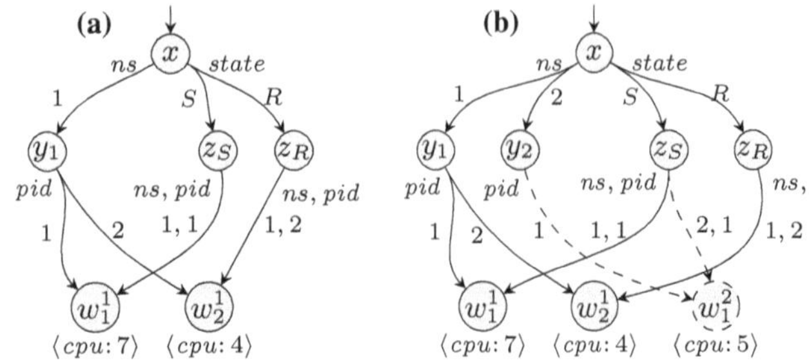

Figure 9. Example of insertion and removal. Inserting the tuple $t = \langle ns\colon 2, pid\colon 1, state\colon S, cpu\colon 5\rangle$ into instance (a) produces instance (b); conversely removing tuple t from (b) produces (a). Differences between the instances are shown using dashed lines.

a binary tree we might set $m_{\mathsf{btree}}(n) = \log_2 n$, whereas for a linked list we might set $m_{\mathsf{dlist}}(n) = n$. Let $\hat{\Gamma}$ be the environment mapping each let-bound variable in $\hat{d}$ to its definition. We compute $E_{\hat{\Gamma}}(q, v, \hat{d})$, where v is the decomposition root:

$$E_{\hat{\Gamma}}(\mathsf{qunit}, v, C) = 1$$
$$E_{\hat{\Gamma}}(\mathsf{qscan}(q), v_1, C \overset{\psi}{\mapsto} v_2) = c(v_1, v_2) \times E_{\hat{\Gamma}}(q, v_2, \hat{\Gamma}(v_2))$$
$$E_{\hat{\Gamma}}(\mathsf{qlookup}(q), v_1, C \overset{\psi}{\mapsto} v_2) = m_\psi(c(v_1, v_2)) \times E_{\hat{\Gamma}}(q, v_2, \hat{\Gamma}(v_2))$$
$$E_{\hat{\Gamma}}(\mathsf{qjoin}(q_1, q_2, \_), v, \hat{p}_1 \bowtie \hat{p}_2) = E_{\hat{\Gamma}}(q_1, v, \hat{p}_1) + E_{\hat{\Gamma}}(q_2, v, \hat{p}_2)$$
$$E_{\hat{\Gamma}}(\mathsf{qlr}(q, \mathsf{left}), v, \hat{p}_1 \bowtie \hat{p}_2) = E_{\hat{\Gamma}}(q, v, \hat{p}_1)$$
$$E_{\hat{\Gamma}}(\mathsf{qlr}(q, \mathsf{right}), v, \hat{p}_1 \bowtie \hat{p}_2) = E_{\hat{\Gamma}}(q, v, \hat{p}_2)$$

The cost estimate for joins is optimistic since it assumes that queries on each side of the join need only be performed once each, whereas in general one side of a join is executed once for each tuple yielded by the other side. We could extend the heuristic to estimate how many tuples are returned by a query, however this has not proved necessary so far.

4.4 Mutation: Empty and Insert Operations

Next we turn our attention to compiling the empty and insert operations. The empty operation is implemented using a function dempty $\hat{d}$ which creates an empty instance of a decomposition $\hat{d}$. The insert operation is implemented by a function dinsert $\hat{d}$ t d, which inserts a tuple t into a decomposition instance d.

To create an empty instance of a decomposition, the dempty operation simply creates a single instance of the root node of the decomposition graph; since the relation does not contain any tuples, we do not need to create instances of any map edges. The adequacy conditions for decompositions ensure that the root node does not contain any unit decompositions, so it is always possible to represent the empty relation.

To insert a tuple t into an instance d of a decomposition $\hat{d}$, for each node $v{:}B \triangleright C$ in the decomposition we need to find or create an instance v_s where $s = \pi_B\, t$ in the decomposition instance. For each edge in the decomposition we also need to find or create an instance of the edge connecting the corresponding pair of node instances.

We perform insertion over the nodes of a decomposition in topologically-sorted order. For each node v we locate the existing node instance v_s corresponding to tuple t, if any. If no such v_s exists, we create one, inserting v_s into any data structures that link it to its ancestors. For example, suppose we want to insert the tuple

$$t = \langle ns\colon 2, pid\colon 1, state\colon S, cpu\colon 5\rangle$$

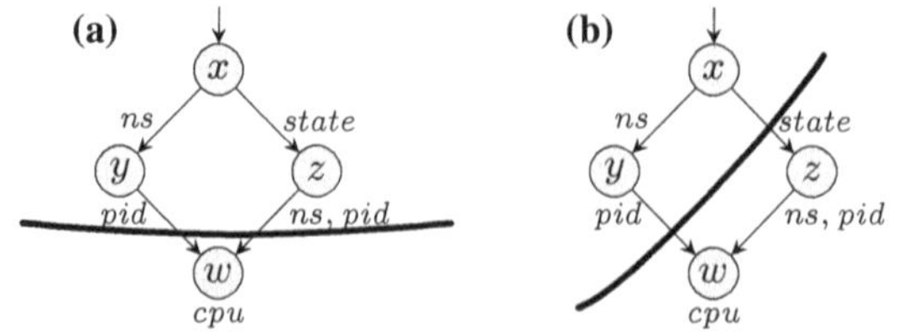

Figure 10. Two cuts of a decomposition: (a) the cut for columns $\{ns, pid\}$, and (b) the cut for columns $\{state\}$.

into the decomposition instance shown in Figure 9(a). We need to find or create the node instances $x_{\langle\rangle}$, $y_{\langle ns\colon 2\rangle}$, $z_{\langle state\colon S\rangle}$, and $w_{\langle ns\colon 2, pid\colon 1, state\colon S, cpu\colon 5\rangle}$. We consider each in topologically-sorted order. Node $x_{\langle\rangle}$ is the root of the decomposition instance, so we know its location already. Next we lookup the tuple $\langle ns\colon 2\rangle$ in the instance of the map from x to y associated with $x_{\langle\rangle}$; no such tuple exists so we create a new node $y_{\langle ns\colon 2\rangle}$ and insert it into the map. Similarly we look up the tuple $\langle state\colon S\rangle$ in the instance of the map from x to z associated with node $x_{\langle\rangle}$ to discover the existing node instance $z_{\langle state\colon S\rangle}$. Finally, we have a choice; we can either look up tuple $\langle pid\colon 1\rangle$ in the map from y to w or look up the tuple $\langle ns\colon 2, pid\colon 1\rangle$ in the map from z to w; in either case we find that no such tuple exists, hence we must create a new instance of vertex w and insert it into both maps. If tuple t was a duplicate of a tuple already present in the relation then vertex w would have already been present and we would not need to do any further work.

4.5 Mutation: Removal and Update Operations

We next consider the remove and update operations. We implement remove using a function dremove $\hat{d}$ s d, which removes tuples matching tuple s from an instance d of decomposition $\hat{d}$. The operation works by removing any nodes and edges from d that form part of the representation of tuples that only match s.

To implement removal and update we need the notion of a *cut* of a decomposition. Given a tuple t with domain C, a cut of a decomposition $\hat{d}$ is a partition (X, Y) of the nodes of $\hat{d}$ into nodes $y_A \in Y$ that can only be part of the representation of tuples matching t, that is, $\Delta \vdash_{\mathsf{fd}} A \rightarrow C$, and nodes $x_B \in X$ that may form part of the representation of tuples that do not match t, that is $\Delta \vdash_{\mathsf{fd}} B \nrightarrow C$. Figure 10 shows two possible cuts of the scheduler decomposition for different sets of columns C.

Edges in a decomposition cut (X, Y) may point from X to Y but not vice-versa. This result follows from the adequacy judgment, which ensures that the columns bound in the child of a map edge must functionally determine the columns bound in its parent. The adequacy judgement also guarantees that the cut for a particular decomposition $\hat{d}$ and set of columns C always exists and is unique.

To remove tuples matching a tuple t using a cut (X, Y), we simply break any edges crossing the cut. That is, we remove any references from data structures linking instances of nodes in X to instances of nodes in Y that form part of the representation of tuples that match t. Once all such references are removed, the instances of nodes in Y are unreachable from the root of the decomposition instance and can be deallocated. We can also clean up any map nodes in X that are now devoid of children.

For example, suppose we want to remove all tuples matching the tuple $t = \langle ns\colon 2, pid\colon 1\rangle$ from the decomposition instance shown in Figure 9(b). Tuple t has the domain $C = \{ns, pid\}$; Figure 10(a) shows the corresponding decomposition cut. Nodes x, y, and z lie above the cut; an instance of node x is always present in every possible relation, instances of node y are specific to a particular namespace but not to any particular process id, and instances of node z are specific to a particular process state but not to any particular process. Node w lies below the cut; each instance of node w forms part of exactly one valuation for the columns C. To perform removal, we break any instances of the edges from instances of nodes y and z to instances of node w which match tuple t; these edges are drawn as dashed lines in Figure 9(b). Once the dashed edges/nodes in Figure 9 are removed, we have the option to deallocate the map at node y_2 as well. Our implementation deallocates empty maps to minimize space consumption.

To find the edge instances to break we can reuse the query planner. Any query that takes columns C as input and visits each of the edges we want to cut will work. One such plan is

$$\mathsf{qjoin}\big(\mathsf{qlookup}(\mathsf{qlookup}(\mathsf{qunit})), \mathsf{qlookup}(\mathsf{qlookup}(\mathsf{qunit})), \mathsf{left}\big).$$

For some data structures, such as intrusive doubly-linked lists, we can remove edges given the destination node alone. If the edge from z to w uses such a data structure we could use the cheaper plan:

$$\mathsf{qlr}\big(\mathsf{qlookup}(\mathsf{qlookup}(\mathsf{qunit})), \mathsf{left}\big).$$

We implement update using a function dupdate $\hat{d}\ s\ u\ d$, which updates tuples matching s using values from u in an instance d of decomposition $\hat{d}$. Semantically, updates are a removal followed by an insertion. In the implementation we can reuse the nodes and edges discarded in the removal in the subsequent insertion—i.e., we can perform the update in place.

We provide only the common case for updates of tuples t matching a tuple pattern s, namely when s is a key for the relation and u does not alter columns appearing in s. Non-key patterns or key-modifying tuple updates may merge multiple tuples, and hence require the implementation to merge nodes. Our restriction guarantees no merging can occur. We can reuse nodes and edges below the cut, and any changes in u that apply to nodes below the cut can be performed in-place.

4.6 Soundness of Relational Operations

Next we show that the operations on decompositions faithfully implement the corresponding relational specifications. We show that sequences of relational operations on graph decompositions are sound with respect to their logical counterparts (Theorem 5) by induction using initialization and preservation lemmas.

Lemma 3 (Decomposition Initialization). For any decomposition $\hat{d}$, if $d = \mathsf{dempty}\ \hat{d}$ then $\cdot, d \models \cdot, \hat{d}$ and $\alpha(d, \cdot) = \emptyset$.

Lemma 4 (Decomposition Preservation). For all $\hat{d}$, Δ, t, d, C, and r where decomposition $\hat{d}$ is adequate ($\cdot; \emptyset \vdash_{\mathrm{a},\Delta} \hat{d}; C$), decomposition instance d is well-formed ($\cdot, d \models \cdot, \hat{d}$), and d represents relation r ($\alpha(d, \cdot) = r$) satisfying FDs Δ ($\Delta \models_{\mathrm{fd}} r$), we have:

(a) If $\operatorname{dom} t = C$, $d' = \mathsf{dinsert}\ \hat{d}\ t\ d$, and $\Delta \models_{\mathrm{fd}} r \cup \{t\}$ then $\cdot, d' \models \cdot, \hat{d}$ and $\alpha(d', \cdot) = r \cup \{t\}$.

(b) If $\operatorname{dom} t \subseteq C$ and $d' = \mathsf{dremove}\ \hat{d}\ s\ d$ then $\cdot, d' \models \cdot, \hat{d}$ and $\alpha(d', \cdot) = r'$ where $r' = r \setminus \{t \in r \mid t \supseteq s\}$ and $r' \models_{\mathrm{fd}} \Delta$.

(c) Suppose s is a key for r ($\Delta \vdash_{\mathrm{fd}} \operatorname{dom} s \to \operatorname{dom} C$), the domains of s and u do not intersect ($\operatorname{dom} s \cap \operatorname{dom} u = \emptyset$), and we have $d' = \mathsf{dupdate}\ \hat{d}\ s\ u\ d$ and $r' = \{\mathsf{if}\ t \supseteq s\ \mathsf{then}\ t \lhd u\ \mathsf{else}\ t \mid t \in r\}$. If $r' \models_{\mathrm{fd}} \Delta$ then $\cdot, d' \models \cdot, \hat{d}$ and $\alpha(d', \cdot) = r'$.

Theorem 5 (Decomposition Soundness). Let C be a set of columns, Δ a set of FDs, and $\hat{d}$ a decomposition adequate for C and Δ. Suppose a sequence of insert, update and remove operators starting from the empty relation produce a relation r, and that each operation satisfies the conditions of Lemma 4. Then the corresponding sequence of dinsert, dupdate, and dremove operators given dempty $\hat{d}$ as input produce d such that $\cdot, d \models \cdot, \hat{d}$ and $\alpha(d, \cdot) = r$.

5. Autotuner

Thus far we have concentrated on the problem of compiling relational operations for a particular decomposition of a relation. However, a programmer may not know, or may not want to invest time in finding the best possible decomposition for a relation. We have therefore constructed an *autotuner* that, given a program written to the relational interface, attempts to infer the best possible decomposition for that program.

The autotuner takes as input a benchmark program that produces as output a cost value (e.g., execution time), together with the name of a relation to optimize. The autotuner then exhaustively constructs all decompositions for that relation up to a given bound on the number of edges, recompiles and runs the benchmark program for each decomposition, and returns a list of decompositions sorted by increasing cost. We do not make any assumptions about the cost metric—any value of interest such as execution time or memory consumption may be used.

6. Experiments

We have implemented a compiler, named RELC, that takes as input a relational specification and a decomposition, and emits C++ code implementing the relation. We evaluate our compiler using micro-benchmarks and three real-world systems. The micro-benchmarks (Section 6.1) show that different decompositions have dramatically different performance characteristics. Since our compiler generates C++ code, it is easy to incorporate synthesized data representations into existing systems. We apply synthesis to three existing systems (Section 6.2), namely a web server, a network flow accounting daemon, and a map viewer, and show that synthesis leads to code that is simultaneously simpler, correct by construction, and comparable in performance to the code it replaces.

We chose C++ because it allows low-level control over memory-layout, has a powerful template system, and has widely-used libraries of data structures from which we can draw. Data structure primitives are implemented as C++ template classes that implement a common associative container API. The set of data structures can easily be extended by writing additional templates and providing the compiler some basic information about the data structure's capabilities. We have implemented a library of data structures that wrap code from the C++ Standard Template Library and the Boost Library [4], namely both non-intrusive and intrusive doubly-linked lists (`std::list`, `boost::intrusive::list`), non-intrusive and intrusive binary trees (`std::map`, `boost::intrusive::set`), hash-tables (`boost::unordered_map`), and vectors (`std::vector`). Since the C++ compiler expands templates, the time and space overheads introduced by the wrappers is minimal.

6.1 Microbenchmarks

We implemented a selection of small benchmarks: a benchmark based on our running example of a process scheduler, a cache benchmark based on the real systems discussed in the next section, and a graph benchmark. For space reasons, we focus just on the graph benchmark.

The graph benchmark reads in a directed weighted graph from a text file and measures the times to construct the edge relation, to perform forwards and backwards depth-first searches over the whole graph, and to remove each edge one-by-one. We represent the edges of a directed graph as a relation `edges` with columns $\{src, dst, weight\}$ and a functional dependency $src, dst \to weight$. We represent the set of the graph nodes as a relation `nodes` consisting of a single *id* column. The RELC compiler emits a C++ module that implements classes `nodes::relation` and `edges::relation` with methods corresponding to each rela-

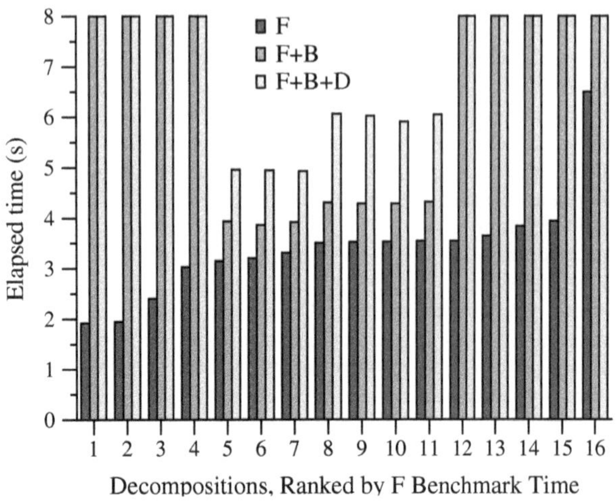

Figure 11. Elapsed times for directed graph benchmarks for decompositions up to size 4 with identical input. For each decomposition we show the times to traverse the graph forwards (F), to traverse both forwards and backwards (F+B), and to traverse forwards, backwards and delete each edge (F+B+D). We elide 68 decompositions which did not finish a benchmark within 8 seconds.

tional operation. A typical client of the relational interface is the algorithm to perform a depth-first search:

```
edges::relation graph_edges;
nodes::relation visited;

// Code to populate graph_edges elided.

stack<int> stk;
stk.push(v0);
while (!stk.empty()) {
  int v = stk.top();
  stk.pop();
  if (!visited.query(nodes::tuple_id(v))) {
    visited.insert(nodes::tuple_id(v));
    edges::query_iterator_src__dst_weight it;
    graph_edges.query(edges::tuple_src(v), it);
    while (!it.finished()) {
      stk.push(it.output.f_dst());
      it.next();
    }
  }
}
```

The code makes use of the standard STL `stack` class in addition to an instance of the nodes relation `visited` and an instance of the edges relation `graph_edges`.

To demonstrate the tradeoffs involved in the choice of decomposition, we used the autotuner framework to evaluate three variants of the graph benchmark under different decompositions. We used a single input graph representing the road network of the northwestern USA, containing 1207945 nodes and 2840208 edges. We used three variants of the graph benchmark: a forward depth-first search (DFS); a forward DFS and a backward DFS; and finally a forward DFS, a backward DFS, and deletion of all edges one at a time. We measured the elapsed time for each benchmark variant for the 84 decompositions that contain at most 4 map edges (as generated by the autotuner).

Timing results for decompositions that completed within an 8 second time limit are shown in Figure 11. Decompositions that

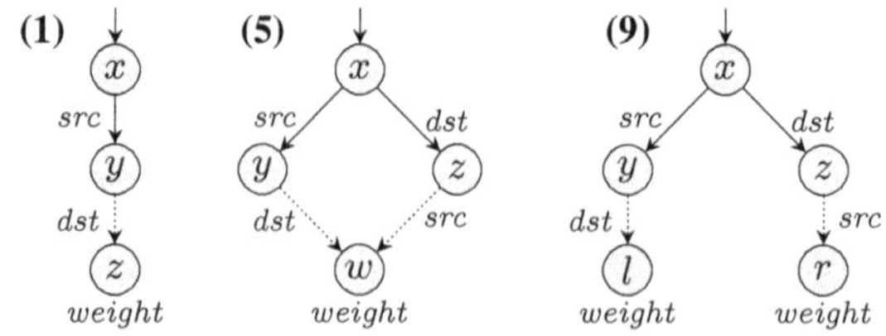

Figure 12. Decompositions 1, 5 and 9 from Figure 11. Solid edges represent instances of `boost::intrusive::map`, dotted edges represent instances of `boost::intrusive::list`.

are isomorphic up to the choice of data structures for the map edges are counted as a single decomposition; only the best timing result is shown for each set of isomorphic decompositions. There are 68 decompositions not shown that did not complete any of the benchmarks within the time limit. Since the autotuner exhaustively enumerates all possible decompositions, naturally only a few of the resulting decompositions are suitable for the access patterns of this particular benchmark; for example, a decomposition that indexes edges by their weights performs poorly.

Figure 12 shows three representative decompositions from those shown in Figure 11 with different performance characteristics. Decomposition 1 is the most efficient for forward traversal, however it performs terribly for backward traversal since it takes quadratic time to compute predecessors. Decompositions 5 and 9 are slightly less efficient for forward traversal, but are also efficient for backward traversal, differing only in the sharing of objects between the two halves of the decomposition. The node sharing in decomposition 5 is advantageous for all benchmarks since it requires fewer memory allocations and allows more efficient implementations of insertion and removal; in particular because the lists are intrusive the compiler can find node w using either path and remove it from both paths without requiring any additional lookups.

6.2 Data Representation Synthesis in Existing Systems

To demonstrate the practicality of our approach, we took three existing open-source systems—thttpd, Ipcap, and ZTopo—and replaced core data structures with relations synthesized by RELC. All are publicly-available programs with real-world users.

The thttpd web server is a small and efficient web server implemented in C. We reimplemented the module of thttpd that caches the results of the `mmap()` system call. When thttpd receives a request for a file, it checks the cache to see whether the same file has previously been mapped into memory. If a cache entry exists, it reuses the existing mapping; otherwise it creates a new mapping. If the cache is full then the code traverses through the mappings removing those older than a certain threshold. Other researchers have used thttpd's cache module as a program analysis target [21].

The IpCap daemon is a TCP/IP network flow accounting system implemented in C. IpCap runs on a network gateway, and counts the number of bytes incoming and outgoing from hosts on the local network, producing a list of network flows for accounting purposes. For each network packet, the daemon looks up the flow in a table, and either creates a new entry or increments the byte counts for an existing entry. The daemon periodically iterates over the collection of flows and outputs the accumulated flow statistics to a log file; flows that have been written to disk are removed from memory. We replaced the core packet statistics data structures with relations implemented using RELC.

ZTopo is a topographic map viewer implemented in C++. A map consists of millions of small image tiles, retrieved using HTTP over the internet and reassembled into a seamless image. To minimize network traffic, the viewer maintains memory and disk caches

	Original		Synthesis	
System	Everything	Module	Decomposition	Module
thttpd	7050	402	42	239
Ipcap	2138	899	55	794
ZTopo	5113	1083	39	1048

Table 1. Non-comment lines of code for existing system experiments. For each system, we report the size of entire original system and just the source module we altered, together with the size of the altered source module and the mapping file when using synthesis.

of recently viewed map tiles. When retrieving a tile, ZTopo first attempts to locate it in memory, then on disk, and as a last resort over the network. The tile cache was originally implemented as a hash table, together with a series of linked lists of tiles for each state to enable cache eviction. We replaced the tile cache data structure with a relation implemented using RELC.

Table 1 shows non-comment lines of code for each test-case. In each case the synthesized code is comparable to or shorter than the original code in size. Both the thttpd and ipcap benchmarks originally used open-coded C data structures, accounting for a large fraction of the decrease in line count. ZTopo originally used C++ STL and Boost data structures, so the synthesized abstraction does not greatly alter the line count. The ZTopo benchmark originally contained a series of fairly subtle dynamic assertions that verified that the two different representations of a tile's state were in agreement; in the synthesized version the compiler automatically guarantees these invariants, so the assertions were removed.

For each system, the relational and non-relational versions had equivalent performance. If the choice of data representation is good enough, data structure manipulations are not the limiting factor for these particular systems. The assumption that the implementations are good enough is important, however; the auto-tuner considered plausible data representations that would have resulted in significant slow-downs, but found alternatives where the data manipulation was no longer the bottleneck. For example we used the auto-tuner on the Ipcap benchmark to generate all decompositions up to size 4; Figure 13 shows the elapsed time for each decomposition on an identical random distribution of input packets. The best decomposition is a binary-tree mapping local hosts to hash-tables of foreign hosts, which performs approximately $5\times$ faster than the decomposition ranked 18th, in which the data structures are identical but local and foreign hosts are transposed. For this input distribution the best decomposition performs identically to the original hand-coded implementation to within the margin of measurement error.

Our experiments show that different choices of decomposition lead to significant changes in performance (Section 6.1), and that the best performance is comparable to existing hand-written implementations (Section 6.2). The resulting code is concise (Sections 6.1 and 6.2), and the soundness of the compiler (Theorem 5) guarantees that the resulting data structures are correct by construction.

7. Discussion and Related Work

We build on our previous work [12], which introduced the idea of synthesizing shared low-level data structures from a high-level relational description. We decompose relations directly using graphs, rather than first decomposing relations into trees that are then fused into graphs. As a consequence our theoretical framework is much simpler. We describe a complete query planning implementation, and we show how to reuse the query planning infrastructure to perform efficient destructive updates using graph cuts. We present a compiler that can synthesize efficient C++ implementations of relational operations; previous work only described a proof-of-concept simulator. We present an autotuner that automatically infers the best decomposition for a relation. Finally, using three real examples we show that synthesis leads to code that is simpler, guaranteed to be correct, and comparable in performance to the code it replaces.

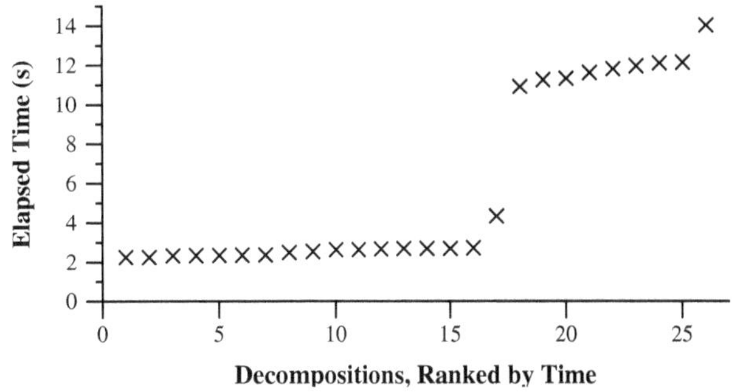

Figure 13. Elapsed time for IpCap to log 3×10^5 random packets for 26 decompositions up to size 4 generated by the auto-tuner, ranked by elapsed time. The 58 decompositions not shown did not complete within 30 seconds.

Relational Representations Many authors propose adding relations to both general- and special-purpose programming languages (e.g., [3, 22, 23, 26, 30]). We focus on the orthogonal problem of specifying and implementing the underlying representations for relational data. Relational representations are well-known from the database community; however, databases typically treat the relations as a black box. Many extensions of our system are possible, motivated by the extensive database literature. Data models such as E/R diagrams and UML rely heavily on relations. One application of our technique is to close the gap between modeling languages and implementations.

The autotuner framework has a similar goal to AutoAdmin [6]. AutoAdmin takes a set of tables, together with a distribution of input queries, and identifies a set of indices that are predicted to produce the best overall performance under the query optimizer's cost model. The details differ because our decomposition and query languages are unlike those of a conventional database.

Synthesizing Data Representations The problem of automatic data structure selection was explored in SETL [5, 24, 27] and has also been pursued for Java collection implementations [28]. The SETL representation sublanguage [9] maps abstract SETL set and map objects to implementations, although the details are quite different from our work. Unlike SETL, we handle relations of arbitrary arity, using functional dependencies to enforce complex sharing invariants. In SETL, set representations are dynamically embedded into carrier sets under the control of the runtime system, while by contrast our compiler synthesizes low-level representations for a specific decomposition with no runtime overhead.

Previous work has proposed using a programming model based on relations which is implemented in the backend using container data structures [8, 29]. A novel aspect of our approach is that our relations can have specified restrictions (specifically, functional dependencies) which enable a much wider range of possible implementations, including complex patterns of sharing. We also present the first formal results, including the notion of adequate decompositions and a proof that operations on adequate decompositions are sound with respect to their relational specifications. Unlike previous work, we propose a dynamic autotuner that can automatically synthesize the best decomposition for a particular relation, and we present our experience with a full implementation of these techniques in practice.

Synthesizing specialized data representations has previously been considered in other domains. Ahmed et al. [1, 15] proposed transforming dense matrix computations into implementations tailored to specific sparse representations as a technique for handling the proliferation of complicated sparse representations.

Synthesis Versus Verification Approaches A key advantage of data representation synthesis over hand-written implementations is the synthesized operations are correct by construction, subject to the correctness of the compiler. We assume the existence of a library of data structures; the data structures themselves can be proved correct using existing techniques [31]. Our system provides a modular way to assemble individually correct data structures into a complete and correct representation of a program's data.

The Hob system uses abstract sets of objects to specify and verify end-to-end properties of systems using multiple data structures that share objects [17, 19]. Monotonic typestates enable aliased objects to monotonically change their typestates in the presence of sharing without violating type safety [11]. Researchers have developed systems that have mechanically verified data structures (for example, hash tables) that implement binary relational interfaces [7, 31, 32]. The relation implementation presented in this paper is more general (it can implement relations of arbitrary arity) and solves problems orthogonal to those addressed in previous research.

Specifying And Inferring Shared Representations The decomposition language provides a "functional" description of the heap that separates the problem of modeling individual data structures from the problem of modeling the heap as a whole. Unlike previous work, decompositions allow us to state and reason about complex sharing invariants that are difficult to state and impossible to verify using previous techniques. Previous work investigated modular reasoning about data structures shared between different modules [13]. Graph types [14] extend tree-structured types with extra pointers that are functionally determined by the structure of the tree backbone, but cannot reason about overlapping structures. Separation logic allows elegant specifications of disjoint data structures [25], and mechanisms have been added to separation logic to express some types of sharing [2, 10]. Some static analysis algorithms infer some sharing between data structures in low level code [16, 18, 20, 21]; however verifying overlapping shared data structures in general remains an open problem for such approaches. The combination of relations and functional dependencies allows us to reason about sharing that is beyond current static analysis techniques.

8. Conclusion

We have presented a system for specifying and operating on data at a high level as relations while correctly compiling those relations into a composition of low-level data structures. Most unusual is our ability to express, and prove correct, the use of complex sharing in the low-level representation. We show using three real-world systems that data representation synthesis leads to code that is simpler, correct by construction, and comparable in performance to existing hand-written code.

Acknowledgments

The fourth author thanks Viktor Kuncak, Patrick Lam, Darko Marinov, Alex Sălcianu, and Karen Zee for discussions in 2001–2 on programming with relations, with the relations implemented by automatically-generated linked data structures. The second author thanks Daniel S. Wilkerson and Simon F. Goldsmith for discussions in 2005 on Wilkerson's language proposal Orth, which includes relational specifications of data structures, the generation of functions for querying and maintaining them, and was further envisioned by Goldsmith to perform automatic data structure selection via profiling.

References

[1] Nawaaz Ahmed, Nikolay Mateev, Keshav Pingali, and Paul Stodghill. A framework for sparse matrix code synthesis from high-level specifications. In *Supercomputing*, page 58. IEEE Computer Society, November 2000. doi: 10.1109/SC.2000.10033.

[2] Josh Berdine, Cristiano Calgano, Byron Cook, Dino Distefano, Peter W. O'Hearn, Thomas Wies, and Hongseok Yang. Shape analysis for composite data structures. In *CAV*, volume 4590 of *LNCS*, pages 178–192. Springer Berlin / Heidelberg, 2007. doi: 10.1007/978-3-540-73368-3_22.

[3] Gavin Bierman and Alisdair Wren. First-class relationships in an object-oriented language. In *ECOOP*, volume 3586 of *LNCS*, pages 262–286. Springer Berlin / Heidelberg, 2005. doi: 10.1007/11531142_12.

[4] Boost. Boost C++ libraries, 2010. URL `http://www.boost.org/`.

[5] Jiazhen Cai and Robert A. Paige. "Look ma, no hashing, and no arrays neither". In *POPL*, pages 143–154, New York, NY, USA, 1991. ACM. ISBN 0-89791-419-8. doi: 10.1145/99583.99605.

[6] Surajit Chaudhuri and Vivek R. Narasayya. An efficient cost-driven index selection tool for Microsoft SQL Server. In *VLDB*, pages 146–155, San Francisco, CA, USA, 1997. Morgan Kaufmann Publishers. ISBN 1-55860-470-7.

[7] Adam Chlipala, Gregory Malecha, Greg Morrisett, Avraham Shinnar, and Ryan Wisnesky. Effective interactive proofs for higher-order imperative programs. In *ICFP*, pages 79–90, New York, NY, USA, 2009. ACM. ISBN 978-1-60558-332-7. doi: 10.1145/1596550.1596565.

[8] Donald Cohen and Neil Campbell. Automating relational operations on data structures. *IEEE Software*, 10(3):53–60, May 1993. ISSN 0740-7459. doi: 10.1109/52.210604.

[9] Robert B. K. Dewar, Arthur Grand, Ssu-Cheng Liu, Jacob T. Schwartz, and Edmond Schonberg. Programming by refinement, as exemplified by the SETL representation sublanguage. *ACM Trans. Program. Lang. Syst.*, 1(1):27–49, January 1979. ISSN 0164-0925. doi: 10.1145/357062.357064.

[10] Dino Distefano and Matthew J. Parkinson. jStar: towards practical verification for Java. In *OOPSLA*, pages 213–226, New York, NY, USA, 2008. ACM. ISBN 978-1-60558-215-3. doi: 10.1145/1449764.1449782.

[11] Manuel Fähndrich and K. Rustan M. Leino. Heap monotonic typestates. In *International Workshop on Alias Confinement and Ownership*, July 2003.

[12] Peter Hawkins, Alex Aiken, Kathleen Fisher, Martin Rinard, and Mooly Sagiv. Data structure fusion. In *APLAS*, volume 6461 of *LNCS*, pages 204–221. Springer Berlin / Heidelberg, 2010. doi: 10.1007/978-3-642-17164-2_15.

[13] Uri Juhasz, Noam Rinetzk, Arnd Poetzsch-Heffter, Mooly Sagiv, and Eran Yahav. Modular verification with shared abstractions. In *International Workshop on Foundations of Object-Oriented Languages (FOOL)*, 2009.

[14] Nils Klarlund and Michael I. Schwartzbach. Graph types. In *POPL*, pages 196–205, New York, NY, USA, 1993. ACM. ISBN 0-89791-560-7. doi: 10.1145/158511.158628.

[15] Vladimir Kotlyar, Keshav Pingali, and Paul Stodghill. A relational approach to the compilation of sparse matrix programs. In *Euro-Par'97 Parallel Processing*, volume 1300 of *LNCS*, pages 318–327. Springer Berlin / Heidelberg, 1997. doi: 10.1007/BFb0002751.

[16] Jörg Kreiker, Helmut Seidl, and Vesal Vojdani. Shape analysis of low-level C with overlapping structures. In *VMCAI*, volume 5044 of *LNCS*, pages 214–230. Springer Berlin / Heidelberg, 2010. doi: 10.1007/978-3-642-11319-2_17.

[17] Victor Kuncak, Patrick Lam, Karen Zee, and Martin Rinard. Modular pluggable analyses for data structure consistency. *IEEE Transactions*

on Software Engineering, 32(12):988–1005, 2006. ISSN 0098-5589. doi: 10.1109/TSE.2006.125.

[18] Viktor Kuncak, Patrick Lam, and Martin Rinard. Role analysis. In *POPL*, pages 17–32, New York, NY, USA, 2002. ACM. ISBN 1-58113-450-9. doi: 10.1145/503272.503276.

[19] Patrick Lam, Viktor Kuncak, and Martin Rinard. Generalized typestate checking for data structure consistency. In *VMCAI*, volume 3385 of *LNCS*, pages 430–447. Springer Berlin / Heidelberg, 2005. doi: 10.1007/978-3-540-30579-8_28.

[20] Oukseh Lee, Hongseok Yang, and Rasmus Petersen. Program analysis for overlaid data structures. In *CAV*, LNCS, 2011. To appear.

[21] Bill McCloskey, Thomas Reps, and Mooly Sagiv. Statically inferring complex heap, array, and numeric invariants. In *Static Analysis*, volume 6337 of *LNCS*, pages 71–99. Springer Berlin / Heidelberg, 2011. doi: 10.1007/978-3-642-15769-1_6.

[22] Eric Meijer, Brian Beckman, and Gavin Bierman. LINQ: Reconciling objects, relations and XML in the .NET framework. In *SIGMOD*, pages 706–706, New York, NY, USA, 2006. ACM. ISBN 1-59593-434-0. doi: 10.1145/1142473.1142552.

[23] Christopher Olston, Benjamin Reed, Utkarsh Srivastava, Ravi Kumar, and Andrew Tomkins. Pig Latin: a not-so-foreign language for data processing. In *SIGMOD*, pages 1099–1110, New York, NY, USA, 2008. ACM. ISBN 978-1-60558-102-6. doi: 10.1145/1376616.1376726.

[24] Robert Paige and Fritz Henglein. Mechanical translation of set theoretic problem specifications into efficient RAM code — a case study. *Journal of Symbolic Computation*, 4(2):207–232, 1987. ISSN 0747-7171. doi: 10.1016/S0747-7171(87)80066-4.

[25] John C. Reynolds. Separation logic: A logic for shared mutable data structures. In *LICS*, pages 55–74, 2002. doi: 10.1109/LICS.2002.1029817. Invited paper.

[26] Tom Rothamel and Yanhong A. Liu. Efficient implementation of tuple pattern based retrieval. In *PEPM*, pages 81–90, New York, NY, USA, 2007. ACM. ISBN 978-1-59593-620-2. doi: 10.1145/1244381.1244394.

[27] Edmond Schonberg, Jacob T. Schwartz, and Micha Sharir. Automatic data structure selection in SETL. In *POPL*, pages 197–210, New York, NY, USA, 1979. ACM. doi: 10.1145/567752.567771.

[28] Ohad Shacham, Martin Vechev, and Eran Yahav. Chameleon: adaptive selection of collections. In *PLDI*, pages 408–418, New York, NY, USA, 2009. ACM. ISBN 978-1-60558-392-1. doi: 10.1145/1542476.1542522.

[29] Yannis Smaragdakis and Don Batory. DiSTiL: a transformation library for data structures. In *Conference on Domain-Specific Languages (DSL '97)*, pages 257–271. USENIX, October 1997.

[30] Mandana Vaziri, Frank Tip, Stephen Fink, and Julian Dolby. Declarative object identity using relation types. In *ECOOP*, volume 4609 of *LNCS*, pages 54–78. Springer Berlin / Heidelberg, 2007. doi: 10.1007/978-3-540-73589-2_4.

[31] Karen Zee, Viktor Kuncak, and Martin Rinard. Full functional verification of linked data structures. In *PLDI*, pages 349–361, New York, NY, USA, 2008. ACM. ISBN 978-1-59593-860-2. doi: 10.1145/1375581.1375624.

[32] Karen Zee, Viktor Kuncak, and Martin Rinard. An integrated proof language for imperative programs. In *PLDI*, pages 338–351, New York, NY, USA, 2009. ACM. ISBN 978-1-60558-392-1. doi: 10.1145/1542476.1542514.

Synthesizing Geometry Constructions

Sumit Gulwani
Microsoft Research
Redmond, WA, USA
sumitg@microsoft.com

Vijay Anand Korthikanti *
UIUC
Urbana Champaign, IL, USA
vkortho2@uiuc.edu

Ashish Tiwari †
SRI International
Menlo Park, CA, USA
tiwari@csl.sri.com

Abstract

In this paper, we study the problem of automatically solving ruler/compass based geometry construction problems. We first introduce a logic and a programming language for describing such constructions and then phrase the automation problem as a program synthesis problem. We then describe a new program synthesis technique based on three key insights: (i) reduction of symbolic reasoning to concrete reasoning (based on a deep theoretical result that reduces verification to random testing), (ii) extending the instruction set of the programming language with higher level primitives (representing basic constructions found in textbook chapters, inspired by how humans use their experience and knowledge gained from chapters to perform complicated constructions), and (iii) pruning the forward exhaustive search using a goal-directed heuristic (simulating backward reasoning performed by humans). Our tool can successfully synthesize constructions for various geometry problems picked up from high-school textbooks and examination papers in a reasonable amount of time. This opens up an amazing set of possibilities in the context of making classroom teaching interactive.

Categories and Subject Descriptors D.1.2 [*Programming Techniques*]: Automatic Programming; I.2.2 [*Artificial Intelligence*]: Program Synthesis; K.3.1 [*Computers and Education*]: Computer uses in Education

General Terms Algorithms, Theory

Keywords Program synthesis, Ruler-Compass geometry constructions, Abstraction, Forward and Backward Analysis

1. Introduction

Program Synthesis is the task of automatically synthesizing a program in some *underlying language* from a given *specification* using some *search technique* [12]. It has been used for a wide variety of applications targeted towards various classes of users.

- Discovery of new algorithms for *Algorithm Designers*: Bit-vector algorithms [14], Mutual exclusion algorithms [3, 21], Concurrent algorithms [34, 39], parameters of embedded systems [6, 37].
- General purpose programming assistance for *Software Developers*: Partial programming [4, 23, 33], Template based programming [35, 36], Automated debugging [40], Program understanding [18].
- Automating repetitive tasks for *End-users*: Programming by Demonstration systems [9, 26], Programming by Example systems [13, 15], shell scripts [25].

However, we feel that the most revolutionary application of program synthesis technology can be in K-12 education. The potential impact size of target population is simply mind boggling: *billion* students and teachers (compared to say *ten thousand* algorithmic designers, *million* software developers, and *hundred million* end-users).

Program synthesis technology can be applied to *automating constructions* for various domains in *high-school curriculum*. Examples of such constructions include (i) ruler/compass based geometric constructions in mathematics (ii) constructions of chemical compounds or biological proteins using (bio)chemical reactions under appropriate conditions governed by catalysts, temperature and pressure in chemistry and biology, (iii) constructions of electrical circuits using series and parallel composition of resistances and capacitances in physics, and so on.

One might wonder what is the connection between program synthesis and automating constructions. Programming languages allow us to formally describe these constructions. Take the example of geometric constructions that involve constructing a set of objects O with desired properties ϕ_2 from an initial set of objects I with certain properties ϕ_1 using a series of steps S, where each step involves using ruler or compass to create new objects. The objects I and O are like program variables and S is the program whose instruction set includes ruler/compass operations.[1] The formulas ϕ_1 and ϕ_2 play the role of precondition and postcondition respectively. Checking the correctness of a given geometric construction is like checking the validity of the Hoare triple $\langle \phi_1, S, \phi_2 \rangle$, which is a program verification problem. In fact, this verification problem has been studied intensively in the context of geometric constructions. Synthesizing the geometric construction S, given ϕ_1 and ϕ_2, is the program synthesis problem, which is what we address in this paper in the context of geometric constructions.

We focus on automating geometry constructions because geometry is regarded to be one of the most difficult as well as important subjects in high-school curriculum. Geometry education is supposed to help exercise logical abilities of the left-brain, visualization abilities of the right-brain, and hence enables students to make the two connect and work together as one. Geometric con-

* Work done while visiting SRI International.

† Research supported in part by NSF grants CSR-EHCS-0834810, CSR-0917398 and SHF:CSR-1017483.

PLDI'11, June 4–8, 2011, San Jose, California, USA.

[1] In fact, a programming language for drawing such geometric objects is used to motivate freshman and non-major students to take up programming lang. course at UCSD [29].

structions have a close connection to axiomatic logic. The skills needed to figure out how to construct, say, a square without a protractor, are closely related to the thinking skills needed to prove theorems about squares [1]. The visual nature of geometry makes it initially more accessible than other parts of mathematics, such as algebra or number theory. "Construction can reinforce proof and lend visual clarity to many geometric relationships." [30] "They give the secondary school student, starved for a Piagetian concrete-operational experience, something tangible." [28].

One might also wonder why we insist on high-school curriculum as opposed to undergraduate/graduate curriculum for our success metric. We want to build tools that are scalable, predictive in their power and can have a real practical impact. Given scalability limitations of program synthesis techniques in terms of being able to automatically synthesize only relatively small snippets of code in a reasonable amount of time, high-school problem solving (where solution size is relatively small enough and are less involved compared to undergraduate/graduate problems) is an excellent fit.

We present a new program synthesis technique for automating geometry constructions. Our program synthesis technique is based on exhaustive search, but exploits three key ideas, inspired by human experience and intelligence, to make it scalable.

Idea 1: Reducing symbolic reasoning to concrete First, we reduce the problem of symbolic reasoning to concrete reasoning. We reduce the problem of "obtaining a construction that can transform input objects I with precondition ϕ_1 to output objects O with postcondition ϕ_2" to that of "obtaining a construction that can perform the transformation on a randomly chosen concrete model for I and O that satisfies constraints ϕ_1 and ϕ_2". In our implementation, we generate such a random model using a numerical (multivariate) function minimization procedure. The probabilistic soundness of this reduction relies on a deep theoretical result that is an extension of randomized polynomial identity testing theorem. (This result is analogous to reducing verification of a straight-line program to testing on a random input.) This reduction is critically important because symbolic reasoning would not scale - it would make our technique multiple orders of magnitude slower, and hence useless in an interactive setting. This reduction is inspired by how humans also work out geometric constructions by visually working out the construction on a randomly chosen configuration.

Idea 2: Using extended set of common constructions When humans typically solve a construction problem, they don't attempt to construct everything from first principles. They think in terms of some key higher level abstractions, where they exploit their knowledge of how to perform some key multi-step constructions. Our technique, which is based on exhaustive search, exploits this observation by working with an extended set of common constructions found in textbook chapters (Table 2) as opposed to simply working with a basic minimal set of constructions (Table 1). This can also be thought of as giving preference to certain combinations of basic construction steps, which is related to the notion of using priors in the machine learning community. This allows for transforming the search process with small width and large depth to one with large width and small depth.

Idea 3: Performing goal-directed search We prune our forward exhaustive search by applying a construction (from the extended set of constructions) only when the *goodness measure* function suggests that it may be useful to apply that construction. For example, the goodness measure function might suggest that if a construction results in a line L_1 that passes through a given output point P, then it may be useful to apply that construction (since we might be able to construct another line L_2 in the future that also passes through P, and hence intersection of L_1 and L_2 can yield desired point P). This is inspired by backward reasoning performed by humans in doing such constructions. This can also be thought of as pruning the forward search by integrating it with backward search.

Based on these ideas, we built a tool for automating geometry constructions. Our tool could solve most standard geometry construction problems in less than a second. Surprisingly, it could also solve some nontrivial problems whose solution is not immediately clear, such as, constructing a square whose (extended) sides pass through four given points. While our focus is on synthesizing geometry constructions, the basic concepts used here could be applicable in other domains as well.[2]

Another interesting application of our algorithm is in the context of dynamic geometry, or creating animations. Suppose we can find a model for declarative constraints using numerical methods in 1 second, and it takes 5 seconds to synthesize an equivalent construction for the declarative problem specification. The importance of having the construction (besides education purposes) is that running that construction will take micro-seconds. So, if the goal is to quickly re-compute coordinates of various points after assigning a new value to the free variables, running the construction will be faster by orders of magnitude compared to using numerical methods.

This paper makes the following key contributions.

- Using the specific example of geometry constructions, the paper points out the role that programming languages, logic, and program synthesis can play in the area of building automated tutoring systems, which is traditionally considered to be a subfield of AI.
- We present a novel search algorithm that combines three key ideas picked up from different research areas: property testing (theoretical computer science), higher-level abstractions (programming languages), and goal-directed reasoning (AI). We believe that the principles underlying our search algorithm are general enough to be applicable to other automated problem solving domains, and other program synthesis applications.
- We report on a successful experimental prototype thereby establishing the feasibility of building automated tutoring systems around the important high-school subject of ruler-compass based geometry constructions.

2. Overview of our Approach

Consider the problem: *Construct a triangle, given its base, a base angle and sum of the other two sides.* We wish to synthesize a program S that performs the above construction using ruler and compass instructions. Before we can discover S, we first need to formally state its inputs $\vec{I}$, output $\vec{O}$, its precondition $\phi_{\texttt{pre}}$ and its postcondition $\phi_{\texttt{post}}$.

The inputs $\vec{I}$ consist of a line segment (points p_1, p_2, and a line $L = \texttt{Line}(p_1, p_2)$) that defines the base of the desired triangle, a length r and an angle a.[3] The desired output $\vec{O}$ consists of a single point p.

The precondition $\phi_{\texttt{pre}}$ arises from the triangle inequality as

$$r > \texttt{Length}(p_1, p_2) \quad (1)$$

[2] The idea of representing knowledge as a library and then constructing new structures by composing elements of the library can be viewed as one way of interpreting (Turing award winner) Ed Feigenbaum's recent remarks in an interview in ACM Communications, where he calls out for having a way for computer to read books and learn to solve problems after that, as opposed to building domain specific tools [32].

[3] In our formalization of geometry constructions, we distinguish between the cases when we have just two points on a plane versus when we also have the line segment connecting those two points explicitly drawn on the plane.

The postcondition $\phi_{\texttt{post}}$ can be stated as,

$$\texttt{Angle}(p, p_1, p_2) = a \ \wedge \ \texttt{Length}(p, p_1) + \texttt{Length}(p, p_2) = r \quad (2)$$

After we have a formal description of the inputs $\vec{I}$, outputs $\vec{O}$, precondition $\phi_{\texttt{pre}}$ and postcondition $\phi_{\texttt{post}}$, we next find a (random) concrete input-output pair that is consistent with the pre/post specification (Idea 1). In other words, we need to find coordinates of the input points p_1, p_2, the distance r, the angle a, and the coordinates of the output point p such that the conditions in Equation 1 and Equation 2 are satisfied. These conditions are (multivariate) nonlinear constraints over the reals. We translate these nonlinear constraints into a multivariate nonlinear optimization problem (as described in Section 6.2) and then use a (numerical) multivariate nonlinear optimization routine to find a concrete input-output pair. During this process, we ensure that the concrete input-output pair is picked sufficiently randomly. Let us say that we find the following concrete input-output pair:

$$L = \texttt{Line}(\langle 81.62, 99.62\rangle, \langle 99.62, 83.62\rangle)$$
$$r = 88.07 \qquad a = 0.81 \text{ radians}$$
$$p = \langle 131.72, 103.59\rangle$$

Let $(\vec{I}_c, \vec{O}_c)$ denote these concrete input-output objects. (Here all numerals are truncated to 2 digits after decimal, but the implementation uses a much higher precision).

Now we have a concrete input-output pair, $(\vec{I}_c, \vec{O}_c)$, for the problem. The geometry synthesis problem is also given an executable library of functions that should be used to synthesize S. For example, assume we have a library that implements the "ruler-compass" functions in Table 1 (the functions take concrete inputs and output concrete objects).

Our tool now searches for a program S *that works correctly on this one input-output pair* $(\vec{I}_c, \vec{O}_c)$. It searches for S by enumerating programs up to a certain length. However, to reduce the size of the search space, rather than using the basic library in Table 1, we use an extended library that additionally implements functions in Table 2 (Idea 2). Furthermore, we use a heuristic goodness metric to make the search for S goal-directed (Idea 3).

When searching for S, we generate several partial programs. These partial programs will, when given the input $\vec{I}_c$, generate different geometric objects like points, lines and circles - all of which are represented using points. Figure 1 shows all these intermediate points in two different settings. On the left, we show the points generated when we use the goodness metric to prune the search space, and on the right, we show the points generated when we do not use the goodness metric. It is clearly evident that when we do not use a goodness metric to prune the search space, then the approach does not scale.

Once we find a program S that works on input $\vec{I}_c$, we return it if it also works correctly on a second randomly sampled concrete input. The program synthesized by our tool for the above problem (using the extended library in Table 2) is:

```
Test10(p1,p2,L,r,a):
  L1 := ConstructLineGivenAngleLinePoint(L,a,p1);
  C1 := ConstructCircleGivenPointLength(p1,r);
  (p3,p4) := LineCircleIntersection(L1,C1);
  L2 := PerpendicularBisector2Points(p2,p3);
  p5 := LineLineIntersection(L1,L2);
  return p5;
```

The line `L1` is good because the output point p lies on it. The circle `C1` is good because it intersects an existing object (namely, line `L1`) at a good point `p3`: `p3` is good because it is equidistant from the output point p and the input point p_2. Similarly, we can establish goodness of all the other intermediate objects. Without using goodness, the search for S fails to terminate in allocated time. Fig. 1(right) shows the points constructed during a truncated search.

The above program was synthesized in 3.5 seconds. When rewritten in terms of the basic library, the above program expands to a program with 17 instructions. We remark that our implementation distinguishes between lines and rays, but we do not show this distinction here for simplicity.

3. Geometry Programming Language

We describe a programming language for geometric constructions. We will later synthesize programs in this programming language starting from a given specification.

Traditional (imperative) programming languages manipulate *values* of *variables*. These *values* are typically integers, floats, Booleans, or addresses (pointers). The entities that our programming language for geometry manipulates are *objects*, such as *points*, *lines* and *circles*. Specifically, our programming language for geometry has the following set of object types:

Point. A point is a primitive object in our language. It is represented using Cartesian coordinates. In this paper, we restrict ourselves to 2-dimensional geometry and a point is represented using its x- and y-coordinates that remain hidden.

Line. A line is represented by a pair of two distinct points that lie on it. The constructor $\texttt{Line}(p_1, p_2)$ returns a line object that is defined by the points p_1 and p_2.

Angle. An angle is a number in the range $[0, 2 * \pi)$. An angle is represented using three points. The function ExplodeAngle returns these three points.

Length. A length is a number in the range $[0, \infty)$. The constructor $\texttt{Length}(\texttt{p}_1, \texttt{p}_2)$ returns a length object denoting the distance between points p_1 and p_2.

Circle. A circle is represented as a pair of a point and a length. For a point p and length l, the constructor $\texttt{Circle}(p, l)$ returns the circle with center p and radius l. The radius of a circle is always a nonzero positive number.

Program variables are typed and are given one of the five types defined above. A *program* takes some objects as inputs, and using a predefined library `Lib` of functions $F_1, \ldots, F_k$, it constructs new objects and outputs one or more of these objects. Thus, a program takes as input $\vec{I}$ and uses (tuples of) temporary variables $\vec{\texttt{t}}_i$ to compute the output $\vec{O}$ as follows:

$$\begin{array}{l} \underline{\texttt{geoProgram}(\vec{I}):} \\ \quad \vec{\texttt{t}}_1 := F_{\pi_1}(\vec{V}_1); \\ \quad \quad \vdots \\ \quad \vec{\texttt{t}}_n := F_{\pi_n}(\vec{V}_n); \\ \quad \vec{O} := \vec{V}_{n+1}; \\ \quad \texttt{return } \vec{O}; \end{array}$$

where

- each variable in $\vec{V}_i$ is either an input variable from $\vec{I}$, or a temporary variable from $\vec{\texttt{t}}_j$ such that $j < i$, and
- $1 \leq \pi_i \leq k$.

3.1 The Expression Language

There is only one kind of expression in our geometry programming language, namely a function call $F_i(\vec{V})$, where F_i is a function from a given library. The library for "ruler-and-compass" constructions is shown in Table 1. It consists of functions for constructing lines, circles, and lengths from points, and functions for constructing points from line-line intersection, line-circle intersection, and

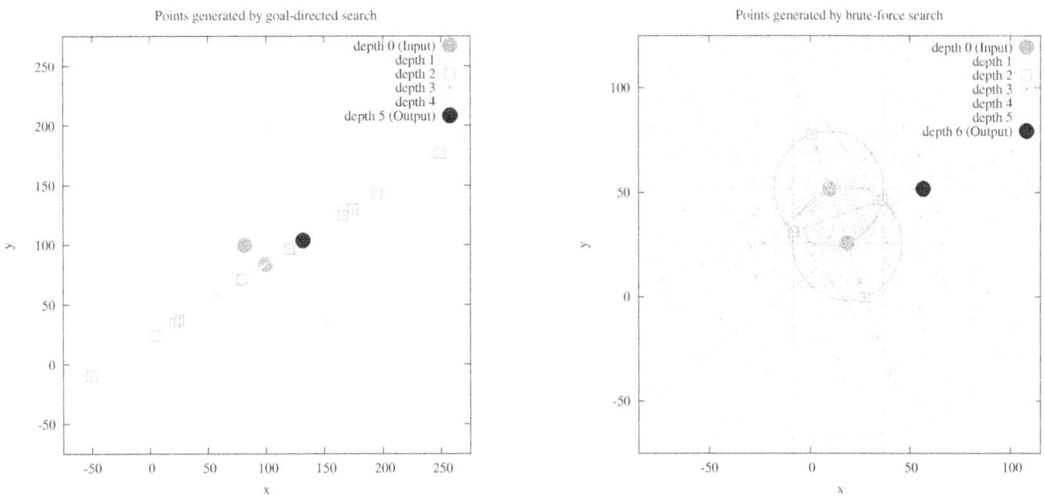

Figure 1. Points visited in a goal-directed search (left) and a brute-force search (right). The concrete inputs and output were picked independently in the two runs. The output point was not reached in the brute-force search and the search had to be truncated.

Function	Description
`L = Line(p1,p2)`	L is the line joining p1 and p2 (provided p1 $\neq$ p2).
`C = Circle(p,r)`	C is the circle with center p and radius r.
`r = Length(p1,p2)`	r is the length of the segment from p1 to p2 (provided p1 $\neq$ p2).
`p = LineLineXn(L1,L2)`	p is the point that lies at the intersection of L1 and L2 (provided L1, L2 are not parallel).
$\vec{p}$ `= LineCircleXn(L1,C1)`	$\vec{p}$ is the vector containing (1 or 2) points that lie on both L1, C1 (provided they intersect).
$\vec{p}$ `= CircleCircleXn(C1,C2)`	$\vec{p}$ is the vector containing (1 or 2) points that lie on both C1, C2 (provided they intersect).
$\vec{p}$ `= ExplodeAngle(a)`	$\vec{p}$ is the vector of (three) points that define angle a.

Table 1. Library functions in the geometry programming language: the type of $p1, p2, \ldots$ is Point, $\vec{p}$ is a vector of points, L is a line, C a circle, a an angle, and r a length.

circle-circle intersection. It also consists of a function to expose points that define a given angle. It is not difficult to observe that programs in our geometry programming language correspond directly to "ruler-and-compass" constructions on paper.

However, the library shown in Table 1 contains only the primitive "ruler-and-compass" operations. It can be extended by including new (derived) functions such as those in Table 2. We later show that such an extension enables synthesis of nontrivial geometry programs.

3.2 The Specification Language

The specification language is used to write the precondition and the postcondition of a geometry program.

A specification is given as a *conjunction* of atomic facts. An *atomic fact* is an equality or inequality between two arithmetic expressions. An arithmetic expression is built using the standard arithmetic operations, $+, -, *$, applied on numeral objects, the `Length` and `Angle` functions, and the functions:

- `distL(p,L)` returns distance between point p and line L.
- `slope(L)` returns the slope of line L.

We found that these functions were sufficient to describe almost all high-school geometry problems. For example, note that we can specify that "point p lies on line joining points p_1 and p_2" as an equality between two slopes,

$$\texttt{slope}(p, p_1) = \texttt{slope}(p_1, p_2),$$

and we can specify that $\texttt{Line}(p_1, p_2)$ and $\texttt{Line}(p_3, p_4)$ are perpendicular as an equality between arithmetic expressions:

$$\texttt{slope}(p_1, p_2) * \texttt{slope}(p_3, p_4) = -1$$

4. Problem Definition

Our goal is to synthesize programs in our geometry programming language given their specification in the form of precondition and postcondition. Here we will formally define the synthesis problem for the geometry domain.

The synthesis problem is given the specification of the desired program and also the executable code implementing a given library. The goal of the geometry synthesis problem is to discover a program in the geometry programming language that correctly implements the specification.

Formally, the geometry synthesis problem requires the user to provide the following:

- A *specification* $\langle \vec{I}, \vec{O}, \phi_{\texttt{pre}}(\vec{I}), \phi_{\texttt{post}}(\vec{I}, \vec{O}) \rangle$ of the desired program, which includes
  - a tuple of typed input variables $\vec{I}$ and output variables $\vec{O}$.
  - a formula $\phi_{\texttt{pre}}(\vec{I})$ that specifies the precondition and a formula $\phi_{\texttt{post}}(\vec{I}, \vec{O})$ that specifies the postcondition.
- A *library* of executable specifications

$$\texttt{Lib} := \{\langle \vec{I}_i, \vec{O}_i, F_i(\vec{I}_i) \rangle \mid i = 1, \ldots, k\},$$

where F_i is an executable implementation of the i-th library function.

The *geometry program synthesis problem* seeks to synthesize a geometry program S – a composition of the primitive operations from Lib – that implements the given specification; that is, the following correctness criterion holds:

$$\forall \vec{I}, \vec{O} : (\phi_{\texttt{pre}}(\vec{I}) \wedge \vec{O} = f_S(\vec{I})) \Rightarrow \phi_{\texttt{post}}(\vec{I}, \vec{O}) \quad (3)$$

where f_S is the function computed by the program S.

We note here that the problem definition above does not require a formal specification of the library functions, but only an executable specification. This is one important point that distinguishes our work from other work on synthesis; see also Section 7.

The synthesis procedure needs to find a program from the huge space of all possible programs that works correctly *for all* concrete inputs.

5. The Synthesis Procedure

In this section, we present our synthesis approach for automatically discovering geometry programs that meet some given specification.

As a first approach, one can perform an exhaustive search on the space of all possible programs (of some fixed length). In other words, one could enumerate all possible compositions of library functions and then verify if any one implements the given specification. This is, however, not feasible for two reasons. First, the number of possible programs (even of a fixed depth) is huge, and expensive to exhaustively enumerate. Second, verifying whether a program implements a given specification is a hard "geometry theorem proving" problem. Specifically, it involves checking the validity of a nonlinear formula in the theory of reals. While this theory is decidable [38], decision procedures are not practical in our setting since solving a single synthesis problem will involve making a large number of verification queries.

We use a new and different approach for synthesis that completely avoids all symbolic reasoning and significantly prunes the search space of all programs. Figure 2 presents the pseudocode of our synthesis procedure. The program GeoSynth takes two inputs: a specification ($\phi_{\texttt{pre}}, \phi_{\texttt{post}}$) of the desired program and a library Lib of available functions. It first generates a concrete input-output pair ($\vec{I}_c, \vec{O}_c$) that satisfies the given specification. It then calls the recursive function GeoSynthRec with the arguments $\vec{I}_c, \vec{O}_c$, Lib and an empty program P. If the concrete output objects $\vec{O}_c$ are already contained in the available objects $\vec{I}_c$, then there is nothing to synthesize and the function GeoSynthRec returns the program P (after checking that it works on a second concrete input-output pair). If not, then the synthesis procedure generates new objects from the available objects and adds them to the set of available objects if they are new and *good*, and recursively calls itself.

The procedure in Figure 2 for synthesis completely avoids all symbolic reasoning and significantly prunes the search space of all programs. It achieves this using three key ideas:

Concretization: From Symbolic to Numeric We discover the program by finding a program that works for a concrete input-output pair. By using a concrete input-output pair, we avoid doing any symbolic reasoning on nonlinear constraints. However, we still need to solve symbolic nonlinear constraints to generate a concrete input-output pair. This we do by using numerical techniques for nonlinear optimization.

Acceleration: Using Extended Library While searching for the correct program, we use a library of *high-level functions*. Each high-level function can be implemented using the basic functions in the given library. A high-level function performs a frequently-used subtask. A few calls to high-level functions often suffice to achieve what many calls to basic functions can achieve. This helps in reducing the search space of programs.

```
GeoSynth(φspec, Lib):
// Input φspec := (φpre, φpost) is the specification
// Input Lib:= ⟨(F_i)_{i=1,2,...}⟩, where F_i implements
              the i-th library function
// Output: A program or "Failure"
I_c := Random concrete objects s.t. φpre(I_c) holds
O_c := Concrete objects s.t. φpost(I_c, O_c) holds
return GeoSynthRec(I_c, O_c, Lib, ε, φspec);

GeoSynthRec(I_c, O_c, Lib, P, φspec):
// Input I_c, concrete objects we have constructed
// Input O_c, concrete objects we wish to construct
// Input P, the program (so far)
if (O_c are contained in I_c) return(Verify(P,φspec));
forall functions F_i ∈ Lib {
  forall possible choices of arguments args for F_i
         picked from I_c {
    newObj := F_i(args);
    if (newObj is Good and
        newObj is not already present in I_c) {
      newP := (P; t := F_i(args));
      newI := I_c ∪ {newObj};
      result := GeoSynthRec(newI,O_c,Lib,newP,φspec);
      if (result ≠ "Failure") return(result);
    }
  }
}
return "Failure"

Verify(P, φspec):
// Check if P works correctly on a second input
I_c := Random concrete objects s.t. φpre(I_c) holds
O_c := f_P(I_c);
if (φpost(I_c,O_c) == true) return(P);
else return "Failure";
```

Figure 2. GeoSynthesizer's Synthesis procedure.

Goal-Directed Search: Goodness Measure A naive search for the correct program based on enumerating all programs is blind to the goal. We can make the search goal-directed by developing a measure for the progress toward the goal. For any newly created object (using the basic/high-level library), the goodness function returns a measure of its goodness with respect to (achieving) the goal.

We provide more details on these three techniques below.

5.1 Concretization: Symbolic to Numeric

Recall that the goal is to *synthesize* a program P that works for all inputs; that is, it meets the given correctness criterion in Formula 3. The problem of even *verifying* that a given program satisfies the given correctness criterion is not easy. First, the set of all possible inputs is unbounded. The traditional solution is to reason about one arbitrary *symbolic* input. Formula 3 is a nonlinear formula in the theory of reals. For example, the atomic formula Length(p1,p2)=Length(p1,p3), when expanded using coordinates (x_i, y_i) for pi, takes the form

$$(x_2 - x_1)^2 + (y_2 - y_1)^2 = (x_3 - x_1)^2 + (y_3 - y_1)^2$$

which is a quadratic formula over 6 real variables. Nonlinear formulas are hard to decide symbolically. There are some symbolic geometry theorem proving tools that can automatically prove Formula 3, but in a synthesis procedure, one requires to check Formula 3 not once, but several times, while searching for the correct P. Hence, symbolic techniques are unlikely to scale for synthesis.

`GeoSynth` avoids all symbolic manipulation by synthesizing programs that work for some *concrete* input-output pairs. `GeoSynth` assumes that the library functions are provided as executable code that compute the concrete output objects given concrete input objects. From the descriptions of the functions in Table 1, the implementation should be immediately clear. For example, the function $\texttt{LineLineXn}(L1, L2)$ computes the x- and y-coordinates of the unique point, if any, that lies on the intersection of concrete lines $L1 = \texttt{Line}(p1, p2)$ and $L2 = \texttt{Line}(p3, p4)$ as follows:

$$\begin{aligned} x &= [(x_1y_2 - y_1x_2)(x_3 - x_4) - (x_1 - x_2)(x_3y_4 - y_3x_4)]/D \\ y &= [(x_1y_2 - y_1x_2)(y_3 - y_4) - (y_1 - y_2)(x_3y_4 - y_3x_4)]/D \end{aligned}$$

where $D = (x_1-x_2)(y_3-y_4)-(y_1-y_2)(x_3-x_4)$, $p1 = (x_1, y_1)$, $p2 = (x_2, y_2)$, $p3 = (x_3, y_3)$, and $p4 = (x_4, y_4)$. Similarly, we can get algebraic expression that implement the other functions. The functions are implemented using floating point representation for the reals.

By using executable code for the library functions, `GeoSynth` synthesizes a program that works for one concrete input. How do we argue that the synthesized program also works for all other inputs? The key observation here is that if a geometry construction is correct for a concrete input that is randomly chosen from the space of all valid inputs (inputs that satisfy the precondition), then, with very high probability, it is correct for all valid inputs. The only assumption required is that the postcondition $\phi_{\texttt{post}}(\vec{I}, \vec{O})$ be such that for any concrete input $\vec{I_c}$, there is at most one (more generally, a constant fraction of the input space) output $\vec{O_c}$ such that $\phi_{\texttt{post}}(\vec{I_c}, \vec{O_c})$ holds.

THEOREM 1. *Let P be a geometry program constructed using the library* `Lib` *from Table 1 and let f_P denote the function P computes. Let $(\phi_{\texttt{pre}}(\vec{I}), \phi_{\texttt{post}}(\vec{I}, \vec{O}))$ be a specification, where the number of inputs, $|\vec{I}|$, is n. Let $\vec{I_c}$ be a concrete input point obtained by sampling uniformly at random the subspace $\{\vec{c} \in \mathbb{R}^n \mid \phi_{\texttt{pre}}(\vec{c})\}$ that represents all non-degenerate inputs. If $\vec{O_c} = f_P(\vec{I_c})$ and if $\phi_{\texttt{post}}(\vec{I_c}, \vec{O_c})$ also holds, then with probability one it is the case that*

$$\forall \vec{I}, \vec{O} : (\phi_{\texttt{pre}}(\vec{I}) \wedge \vec{O} = f_P(\vec{I})) \quad \Rightarrow \quad \phi_{\texttt{post}}(\vec{I}, \vec{O})$$

PROOF: (Sketch) Assume the specification is deterministic so that there is a function f_{spec} that computes, for any given valid (non-degenerate) input, the output that is consistent with the specification $\phi_{\texttt{post}}$; that is, f_{spec} has the property that

$$\forall \vec{I_c} : \phi_{\texttt{pre}}(\vec{I_c}) \Rightarrow \phi_{\texttt{post}}(\vec{I_c}, f_{spec}(\vec{I_c}))$$

Consider the functions f_P and f_{spec}. It is well-known property of ruler-and-compass constructions that these two functions can be described using compositions of the arithmetic $+, -, *, /$ operations and the square-root operation, and hence we can argue that they are analytic over the domain of valid (non-degenerate) inputs (analytic with respect to each variable). Now consider the function $f_P - f_{spec}$. It is analytic too. Hence, unless it is identically zero, the space of zeros of this function has measure zero in the space of all inputs. Hence, for a random (valid non-degenerate) input $\vec{I_c}$, since we have $f_P(\vec{I_c}) - f_{spec}(\vec{I_c}) = 0$, it follows that, with probability one, $f_P - f_{spec}$ is identically zero and hence, the claim holds. □

The theorem is a generalization of a similar result for polynomial identity testing [31]. Similar results have been folklore in geometry theorem proving where it has been noted that geometry theorems can be proved by testing them on one random concrete instance [43]. The "probability one" claim in Theorem 1 assumes that exact computation on the reals is performed and we sample the real space. However, this is not possible and the implementation only uses finite precision floating point representation and samples over floating point numbers. These issues will slightly increase the probability of our procedure giving wrong answers, but, as one would expect, the probability will continue to remain very low.

Theorem 1 states that the probability of returning a specific wrong program P is very low. But the space of programs is large, and these probabilities could add up so that the probability of returning *some* wrong program from the space of all programs could become substantial. Hence, `GeoSynth` uses one concrete input-output pair to synthesize the program, and then another randomly sampled input-output pair to check it again (see the `Verify` function in the pseudocode). Therefore, `GeoSynth` can return a wrong answer only if the specific program P (that is synthesized using one concrete input-output pair) does not match the specification on a randomly sampled input. By Theorem 1, we know this is very low, and this establishes the probabilistic soundness of `GeoSynth`. In fact, in our experiments (reported in Section 6), the `Verify` function never returned "`Failure`". If `Verify` fails, note that the pseudocode continues its search for the correct program.

5.2 Acceleration: Extended Library

Discovering a geometry program that works correctly on even a single concrete input is not easy. This is because the search space of all possible programs is huge. We need ways to efficiently search this large state space. We use ideas from program analysis – forward and backward analysis – to significantly prune the search space. We argue that this is also the way that humans perform the search.

Consider the size of the search space of all programs. If the library has M functions that take, say, two arguments each, then the state space of all programs of length N that can be constructed using the library functions is $O((M(N + |\vec{I}|)^2)^N)$. This is super-exponential in N. This shows that we can not search for very long programs. Unfortunately, even for performing simple tasks, geometry programs P that are built using the library shown in Table 1 can be very long.

`GeoSynth` works on an extended library. Apart from the primitive functions listed in Table 1, the extended library also contains the functions listed in Table 2. Each new library function can be implemented using the primitive functions. Using the extended library, however, we can find much shorter programs P that meet the given specification. Hence, we can discover the correct P by searching for *shorter programs using the extended library*, rather than searching for *long programs using the primitive library*.

Table 2 lists the new functions in the extended library. For example, consider the function `PerpendicularBisector2Points`. Constructing the perpendicular bisector of two points will require at least three steps using the functions provided in the primitive library in Table 1. However, it is a commonly used "subroutine" when performing geometry constructions and it is useful to add such a function in the extended library, as it will likely reduce the length of the program P we are trying to discover by at least three.

The use of extended library for discovering the correct program matches the way humans synthesize programs. Rather than working with low-level primitives, complex systems are built by composing higher-level components. In geometry programs, the extended library contains high-level constructions that encode the *knowledge* the student is taught to solve more complex geometry

Function Name	Description
L = PerpendicularBisector2Points(p1,p2)	L is the perpendicular bisector of line joining p1 and p2.
p = MirrorPointLine(p1,L)	p is the reflection of p1 about line L.
$\vec{C}$ = CircleGivenChordAngle(L,a)	$\vec{C}$ is a vector of (1 or 2) circles C s.t. L is a chord of C subtending angle a.
L = ConstructLineGivenAngleLinePoint(L1,a,p)	L is at an angle a with L1 at point p (on L1).
C = ConcentricCircle(C1,r)	C is concentric to C1 and at distance r away from it.
L = PerpendicularToLineThruPoint(p,L1)	L is perpendicular to L1 and passes through p.
$\vec{L}$ = AngularBisectorLines(L1,L2)	$\vec{L}$ is the tuple of (two) lines that are angular bisectors of L1 and L2.
p = MidpointGiven2points(p1,p2)	p is the midpoint between p1 and p2.
$\vec{L}$ = TangentPointToCircle(p,C)	$\vec{L}$ is the vector of (two) lines that are tangent to C and pass through p.
L = ParallelLine(p,L1)	L is the line parallel to L1 and passing through p.
$\vec{L}$ = ParallelLineGivenLength(L1,r)	$\vec{L}$ is the vector of (two) lines that are parallel to L1 and distance r away from it.

Table 2. Extended Library

construction exercises. In fact, `GeoSynth` takes the library as an input, and hence, as the student learns more concepts, the library can be extended too, which will then enable `GeoSynth` to synthesize more complex geometry constructions.

In the experimental results in Section 6, we show the impact of using extended library by comparing it against the use of primitive library.

The use of extended library also has its analogue in the field of program analysis. It corresponds to using forward search (forward propagation) to see what search space is reachable in a few steps. The technique of *acceleration* in program analysis [5] explicitly computes high-level (multi-step transition) functions that are compositions of low-level (one-step transition) functions.

Besides efficiency, the idea of using library functions may provide another important benefit. By changing the library functions, the tool can be forced to be find constructions that use a particular primitive construction step. It is fairly common that exercises at the end of textbook chapters are framed so that their solution requires students to use the concepts introduced in that chapter. Using our tool, the same effect can be achieved. Teachers could re-inforce the learning of constructions taught in a certain chapter by just manipulating the library.

5.3 Goal-Directed Search: Goodness Measure

Introduction of an extended library reduces the depth of the programs that we need to search for finding the correct program. Despite this reduction, exhaustive enumeration of all possible programs remains infeasible. We use the third key idea – using backward analysis – to enable a more goal-directed search for the correct program.

`GeoSynth` performs a goal-directed search for the correct program by using a heuristic *goodness measure* that determines if an intermediate object could be useful in finally constructing the output objects. How to compute the goodness measure? Ideally, an intermediate object is good if an output object can be constructed using the intermediate object and the other existing objects. How can we efficiently check an intermediate object is good without continuing with the forward search? We can do so by performing some backward analysis starting from the output objects.

Performing exact backward analysis is challenging. Consider, for example, the case when the output object is a point p. Now consider one of the library functions, for example, the function $\texttt{CircleCircleXn}(C_1, C_2)$. There are infinitely many circles (C_1, C_2) whose intersection could give p, so backward analysis would involve representing all these cases. However, if we fix C_1 to be an existing circle and we also fix the center of C_2 to be an existing point, then this fixes the circle C_2. This way of performing *partial backward analysis* can make backward analysis feasible.

Rather than explicitly performing partial backward analysis, `GeoSynth` directly tests if an intermediate object is backward reachable from the goal using multiple partial backward steps. These tests are coded using a goodness function. Specifically, the `Good` function takes as argument the set `currObjs` of objects we have already constructed, the set $\vec{O}$ of objects we need to construct, the object $\vec{\texttt{t}}$ whose goodness we are trying to evaluate, and the library `Lib` of available functions. `Good` returns a Boolean answer – indicating if $\vec{\texttt{t}}$ is possibly useful for eventually constructing $\vec{O}$. Depending on the type of the object $\vec{\texttt{t}}$, `Good` performs different checks.

- A point $\vec{\texttt{t}}$ is good if either
  - $\vec{\texttt{t}}$ is an output point in $\vec{O}$.
  - $\vec{\texttt{t}}$ is on an output line or circle.
  - $\vec{\texttt{t}}$ lies on a line joining an existing point in `currObjs` with an output point in $\vec{O}$.
  - $\vec{\texttt{t}}$ lies on a circle defined by a combination of some existing point(s) and output point(s).
- A line $\vec{\texttt{t}} := \texttt{Line}(p_1, p_2)$ is good if either
  - $\vec{\texttt{t}}$ is an output line in $\vec{O}$.
  - an output point in $\vec{O}$ lies on $\vec{\texttt{t}}$.
  - $\vec{\texttt{t}}$ is parallel or perpendicular to a line defined by output objects $\vec{O}$ and existing objects `currObjs`.
  - the intersection of the line $\vec{\texttt{t}}$ with an existing line or circle object in `currObjs` gives a good point.
- A circle $\vec{\texttt{t}} := \texttt{Circle}(p, r)$ is good if either
  - $\vec{\texttt{t}}$ is an output circle in $\vec{O}$.
  - some output point in $\vec{O}$ lies on $\vec{\texttt{t}}$ or is the center of $\vec{\texttt{t}}$.
  - the intersection of the circle $\vec{\texttt{t}}$ with an existing line or circle object in `currObjs` gives a good point.

These rules for goodness clearly measure the progress $\vec{\texttt{t}}$ makes toward the goal $\vec{O}$. The rules essentially test if $\vec{\texttt{t}}$ lies in the set of objects obtained from the goal $\vec{O}$ objects using a few selected partial backward steps.

The extended library encodes the facts a student is taught in a chapter, and the goodness function attempts to encode the intuition (search strategy) the student is expected to apply (in conjunction with the facts in the extended library) to solve the exercises at the end of the chapter.

`GeoSynth` uses the function `Good` to prune its search space. In the pseudocode in Figure 2, `Good` is used in the condition guarding the recursive call. A newly created object $\vec{\texttt{t}}$ is added to the set of currently available objects only if it is `Good`. `GeoSynth` allows the user to turn-off goodness checking. In Section 6 we will compare

1. Find the circumcenter of a triangle.
2. Find the incenter of a triangle.
3. Find the orthocenter of a triangle.
4. Construct a regular hexagon inside a circle.
5. Construct length a+b given lengths a and b.
6. Construct a triangle given length of its 3 sides.
7. Construct a triangle given two sides and an included angle.
8. Construct a triangle given two angles and an included side.
9. Construct a △ given two sides and the angle opposite one.
10. Construct a triangle, given its base, a base angle and sum of other two sides.
11. Construct a triangle, given its base, a base angle and difference of other two sides.
12. Construct a △, given its perimeter and its two base angles.
13. Draw a pair of tangents to a circle that make an angle of 60° with each other.
14. Construct a triangle given a side and two altitudes.
15. Construct a triangle given one angle, the side opposite this angle, and the length of altitude to that side.
16. Construct a ◯ that is inscribed in a given quadrant of a ◯.
17. Given point A, line L not passing through A, and point B on L, construct a ◯ passing through A that is tangent to L at B.
18. Given points A and B on the same side of a line L, find point C on L such that AC and BC make the same angle with L
19. Find the centroid of a triangle.
20. Given non-parallel lines L1 and L2 and a radius r, construct a circle of radius r that is tangent to both L1 and L2.
21. Draw arcs of radius r that are tangent to a given line and to a given circle.
22. Draw arcs of radius r that are tangent to two given circles.
23. Construct a square whose extended sides pass through 4 given points.
24. Construct a right △ given one acute angle and sum of legs.
25. Given a circle and points D and E in its interior, construct an inscribed right triangle such that one leg contains D and other leg contains E.

Table 3. Informal description (in English) of the 25 benchmarks used to report results in this paper.

the effect of turning on-and-off the goodness check when synthesizing geometry programs.

6. Experimental Results

We implemented `GeoSynth` and tested it on a variety of high-school geometry construction exercises obtained from books and examination papers. Table 4 reports details of the runs of `GeoSynth` on selected 25 examples. As Column 4 indicates, `GeoSynth` successfully solved all the problems in a few seconds: 18 problems were solved in less than a second and only 3 problems required more than 10 seconds. We experimentally evaluated the efficacy of our two key ideas – using an extended library (E vs B) and using goal-directed search (G vs N) – by varying the inputs and command-line flags of `GeoSynth`. Specifically, Table 4 provides values of the following functions for the 25 examples:

T_EG: time when using **E**xtended library and **G**oodness
T_EN: time when using **E**xtended library and **N**o goodness
T_BG: time when using **B**asic library and **G**oodness
T_BN: time when using **B**asic library and **N**o goodness

6.1 Benchmarks

`GeoSynth` works off a fairly intuitive front-end language for writing the specification formulas describing the desired geometry construction:

GIVEN ⟨ list of input objects $\vec{I}$ ⟩
that satisfy $\phi_{\texttt{pre}}(\vec{I})$
CONSTRUCT ⟨ list of output objects $\vec{O}$ ⟩
that satisfy $\phi_{\texttt{post}}(\vec{I},\vec{O})$

The formula $\phi_{\texttt{pre}}(\vec{I})$ specifies the constraints on the input objects, and the formula $\phi_{\texttt{post}}(\vec{I},\vec{O})$ specifies the relationship between the input and output objects. The language of the formulas was described in Section 3.2.

In the selected benchmarks used for experimental study, Test1–Test9 and Test19 are standard problems in geometry, Test10–Test13 were taken from a Mathematics textbook for high-school students[4], and the rest were taken from course webpages and other websites devoted to such problems[5]. An informal description of the 25 examples is given in Table 3.

As an example of the specification of a benchmark in the above front-end language, consider our running example: *Construct a triangle given its base, base angle, and the sum of its other two sides.* This is presented to `GeoSynth` as:

```
GIVEN  Segment(p1,p2), Length(p3,p4), Angle(p5,p6,p7)
that satisfy Length(p3,p4) > Length(p1,p2)
CONSTRUCT   Point(p)
that satisfy
      Length(p,p1) + Length(p,p2) = Length(p3,p4) and
      Angle(p,p1,p2) = Angle(p5,p6,p7)
```

We note that the English text specification of a geometry construction problem is often ambiguous. In the example above, the English specification does not tell us how the sum of the two side is given or how the angle is given. The formal specification needs to eliminate this ambiguity. In the example above, the formal specification has assumed that the sum of the two sides is given as the distance between two new points $p3$ and $p4$, as opposed to, say, by point(s) that lies on the line extending the triangle's base.

6.2 Multivariate Optimizers

`GeoSynth` finds a (random) concrete input-output pair that satisfies the given precondition and postcondition using a numerical multivariate optimizer. `GeoSynth` currently uses an off-the-shelf implementation of such a function.

Recall that the precondition and the postcondition is a conjunction of nonlinear constraints. These constraints are difficult to solve symbolically. We instead use numerical techniques to get a feasible solution. First, we transform all inequalities, say $p > 0$, where p is a multivariate polynomial, to an equality constraint, namely $p - u^2 = 0$, where u is a new real-valued variable. Next, we transform a conjunction of equality constraints, say $p = 0 \wedge q = 0$, into a function minimization problem: $\texttt{minimize}\ (p^2 + q^2)$. The minimum value is zero iff the nonlinear constraints have a solution. Thus, using a multivariate function minimizer, `GeoSynth` finds a concrete input-output $(\vec{I_c}, \vec{O_c})$ that satisfies the given specification.

Recall that we also have to ensure that the concrete input-output pair is chosen at random. We achieve this by using heuristics to partition the set of unknowns into independent and dependent variables. Then, we randomly pick concrete values for the independent variables and fix them. We use the multivariate optimizer to find

[4] `http://ncertbooks.prashanthellina.com/class_9.Mathematics.Mathematics/chap-11\%20(02-12-2005).pdf`

[5] Test14–Test15 from `http://www-math.cudenver.edu/~wcherowi/courses/m3210/lecchap5.pdf`, Test16–Test18, Test20–Test22 from `www.geometer.org/mathcircles/construct.pdf`, Test23 from `http://puhep1.princeton.edu/~mcdonald/examples/4point.pdf` and Test24–Test25 from `http://www.misterhoffman.com/downloads/SpringProblemSets.pdf`

Test	Extended Library				Basic Library				Numerical Solving	
	LoCE	d,w	Time(T_EG)	T_EN	LoCB	#Makes	T_BG	T_BN	Mean	Min.
(1)	(2)	(3)	(4)	(5)	(6)	(7)	(8)	(9)	(10)	(11)
Test1	3	2,2	0.131	0.147	7	6	NoSol	0.146	0.24	0.004
Test2	3	2,2	0.194	3.290	21	8	NoSol	Timeout	0.61	0.003
Test3	3	2,2	0.331	2.569	13	8	NoSol	Timeout	0.75	0.009
Test4	2	2,1	0.095	0.078	4	3	0.114	1.010	0.04	0.005
Test5	3	3,1	0.123	0.180	3	1	0.101	0.960	0.04	0.009
Test6	4	3,2	0.132	3.018	4	2	0.122	0.134	0.04	0.003
Test7	4	3,2	0.179	3.074	13	5	NoSol	Timeout	0.03	0.004
Test8	3	2,2	0.144	0.193	21	8	NoSol	Timeout	0.03	0.004
Test9	4	3,2	0.176	3.357	13	5	NoSol	Timeout	0.15	0.006
Test10	6	6,1	3.149	Timeout	17	8	NoSol	Timeout	0.28	0.006
Test11	6	6,1	3.550	Timeout	17	8	NoSol	Timeout	0.06	0.019
Test12	7	5,2	63.028	Timeout	45	19	NoSol	Timeout	3.91	0.555
Test13	3	3,1	0.121	0.093	4	2	0.118	0.100	1.84	0.157
Test14	5	4,2	13.684	44.198	22	14	NoSol	Timeout	0.11	0.019
Test15	4	3,2	0.150	4.185	32	20	NoSol	Timeout	1.54	0.030
Test16	6	6,1	82.613	Timeout	26	11	NoSol	Timeout	0.06	0.011
Test17	3	2,1	0.128	0.390	10	7	NoSol	Timeout	0.07	0.010
Test18	3	3,1	0.139	1.966	8	5	NoSol	Timeout	1.35	0.021
Test19	5	3,2	0.203	1.902	13	10	NoSol	Timeout	0.16	0.029
Test20	3	2,2	0.189	2.528	25	13	NoSol	Timeout	0.90	0.002
Test21	4	3,2	0.148	570.550	23	12	NoSol	Timeout	0.03	0.004
Test22	4	3,2	0.130	211.220	14	6	NoSol	Timeout	0.04	0.004
Test23	13	8,2	1.929	Timeout	25	17	NoSol	Timeout	20.35	2.616
Test24	6	6,1	2.301	Timeout	29	13	NoSol	Timeout	0.33	0.086
Test25	4	4,1	0.125	212.359	8	5	NoSol	Timeout	0.27	0.044

Table 4. Experimental results for 25 construction exercises. Column 2–5 report results when using the extended library: Column 2 is the length of program constructed; Column 3 gives the depth(d) and width(w) of this program; Column 4-5 give the time (in sec.) taken to synthesize the program when using goodness (Col. 4) and when not using goodness (Col. 5). Column 6–9 report results when using the basic library: Column 6 is the length of program; Column 7 is the number of *constructor calls* in this program; Column 8-9 give the time (in sec.) for synthesizing the program with (Col. 8) and without (Col. 9) using goodness. Column 10–11 report time taken for finding one concrete input-output pair using nonlinear optimization: Column 10 is the mean and Column 11 is the minimum (both in sec.) of 15 runs. NoSol indicates 'procedure terminated but failed to find a solution'. Timeout indicates 'procedure did not terminate in 10 min.'.

values only for the dependent variables, *having randomly fixed the values for the independent variables.*

To illustrate the approach, consider the precondition and post-condition from the example in Section 2.

$$r > \texttt{Length}(p_1, p_2)$$
$$\texttt{Angle}(p, p_1, p_2) = a$$
$$\texttt{Length}(p, p_1) + \texttt{Length}(p, p_2) = r$$

Let x_1, y_1 (respectively x_2, y_2 and x, y) denote the coordinates of point p_1 (respectively point p_2 and point p). Thus, the above constraint has 8 variables. We identify x_1, y_1, x_2, y_2, a as the independent variables and we pick values for them randomly. We determine the values for the other three variables, x, y and r, by solving the above constraint. We find x, y, r by minimizing the following non-linear function over these three variables and the auxiliary variable u:

$$(r - \texttt{Length}(p_1, p_2) - u^2)^2 + (\texttt{Angle}(p, p_1, p_2) - a)^2 + (\texttt{Length}(p, p_1) + \texttt{Length}(p, p_2) - r)^2$$

The time taken by the minimization routine varies across different runs, and hence, in Table 4, we report the average (Column 10) and minimum (Column 11) time spent on finding a concrete input-output pair for each benchmark. (We performed 15 different runs for this purpose.) The time spent is proportional to the complexity of the postcondition constraint; in particular, the number of output objects. (Test23 seeks to construct a square, and hence the output has 4 points, which is 8 variables.)

6.3 Extended Library vs. Basic Library

We compared the performance of `GeoSynth` when it was given the basic library with its performance when it was given the extended library. There are two cases to consider depending on whether or not we use the "goodness" heuristic.

First, consider the case when we do not use the "goodness" heuristic for pruning the search space. When using the basic library, `GeoSynth` fails to find the correct program in 10 minutes of allocated time (Col. 9). In contrast, when using the extended library, `GeoSynth` successfully finds the correct solution in 19 out of the 25 examples (Col. 5).

Second, consider the case when we do use the "goodness" heuristic. When it is given the basic library, `GeoSynth` terminates without finding the solution in 21 examples (Col. 8). This is because the "goodness" measure (incorrectly) pruned the branches that had solutions. Note that "goodness" heuristic performs only a few backward steps, and the objects created by the basic library functions fail to be "good". In contrast, the extended library can quickly (in a few steps) create "good" objects. As shown in Col. 4, when using extended library, all examples were successfully solved.

Why is using the extended library better? The reason is that when we use the extended library, we find small correct solutions.

Comparing Column 2 with Column 6, we note program lengths (lines of code) varied between 2 and 13 for the 25 benchmarks when using the extended library (Col. 2), whereas its range was 3–45 for basic library (Col. 6). Smaller programs translated to smaller search space and hence, better timing, for synthesizing the programs.

6.4 Goodness vs. No Goodness

Let us now compare the effect of using goodness. Without goodness, `GeoSynth` performs a brute-force search, whereas with goodness, it performs a goal-directed search.

There are two cases depending on whether we use the basic library or the extended library. The case when we use the basic library is uninteresting: with goodness, the search is pruned too aggressively (Col 8), without goodness, the search explodes and seldom terminates (Col 9). When we use the extended library, the use of goodness (Col. 4) significantly improves the runtime of `GeoSynth` over the case when we do not use goodness (Col. 5). The reason is clear: goal-directed search explores much fewer paths than an exhaustive search (see Figure 1).

6.5 Variations in T_EG

Looking at Column 4 of Table 4, we notice that `GeoSynth` solves 18 of the examples in less than a second, and takes more than 10 seconds on only 3 examples. Without goodness (Col. 5), `GeoSynth` fails to terminate on 6 examples. To understand the reason for this variation, we also provide the depth (d) and width (w) of the solution in Column 3. (Intuitively, whereas lines of code (LoC) is the sequential complexity, depth (d) is the parallel complexity, and width (w) is the number of parallel processors required.) The ability to find the correct solution when performing exhaustive search (Col. 5) is directly correlated with the depth of the solution. Exhaustive search fails when depth of the solution is 5 or higher. However, the depth does not explain the variation in Column 4. Certain property of Test12, Test14 and Test16 interferes with the goodness measure making it less effective in pruning the search space.

7. Related Work

Program Synthesis using Brute-force Search [12] provides a good survey of various program synthesis techniques: brute-force search, logical reasoning, probabilistic inference, and version-space algebras. Our algorithm is closely related to the brute-force search strategy. There have been few success stories of using brute-force search for program synthesis. It has been used to discover new algorithms (mutual-exclusion algorithms [3] and bitvector algorithms [11]). It has been used to search for desired small functional programs by generating a sequence of type-correct programs in a systematic and exhaustive manner and evaluating them against given specifications [20]. In comparison, our algorithm leverages some sophisticated novel concepts, essential for it to scale: obviating need for symbolic reasoning, performing a goal-directed search, and transforming the search space to one with larger width but smaller depth.

Program Synthesis using Input-Output Examples There is a lot of work on inductive program synthesis where the specification from the user comes in the form of multiple input-output examples: string manipulation macros [13], table manipulation programs [15], bit-vector algorithms [18], graph algorithms [16]. In contrast, our system accepts logical specifications, but for scalability reasons, internally transforms the logical specification into a (probabilistically equivalent) input-output example based specification.

Existing inductive program synthesis techniques are based on version space algebras [13, 15] or combinatorial search using SAT/SMT solvers [16, 18]. In case of geometry, the mathematical semantics of the operators involves higher order algebraic equations: any symbolic reasoning (including reduction to SAT using bit-vector blasting) would be prohibitively expensive, and it is noto clear how to use version space algebras in this context.

Interactive Geometry Systems There are several dynamic geometry systems such as Geometer's sketchpad [17] and Cabri Geometer [24] that allow users/students to create geometric constructions, invent conjectures, and check facts. Recent systems also permit one to build proofs (e.g., [2]), or to check facts using an automated theorem prover (e.g., Geometry Expert [10], Cinderella [22], and Geometry Explorer [41]). Automated geometry theorem proving (consisting of several techniques such as Wu's method [42], Grobner basis method [19], and angle method [7]) is one of the most successful areas of automated reasoning. In contrast, we address a technically harder problem of synthesizing constructions, as opposed to the problem of producing correctness proof of a given construction. Our scalable solution relies on a novel approach of using randomness to avoid performing symbolic reasoning. Also, another useful advantage of our framework is that teachers can configure the extended library to ensure that the tool generates small solutions that emphasize use of certain concepts (e.g., ones taught in an earlier chapter). Existing automated geometry theorem proving systems tend to produce arbitrary proofs in the underlying logical domain that may not be readable and may be beyond the vocabulary taught in the class.

GRAMY [27] is an interesting system for proving theorems that in its search for a proof, performs some constructions to enable the application of certain postulates. All computations in GRAMY are symbolic, whereas our search is completely numeric. Our tool discovers a construction, but does not output any symbolic proof of its correctness. GRAMY can only discover proofs that do not involve arithmetic operations. For example, it can not find proofs that involve inequalities, ratios, and coincident intersections. Our tool can generate constructions whose correctness relies on arithmetic reasoning; several of our benchmark examples have this feature. GRAMY uses an exhaustive forward symbolic search, followed by a symbolic backward step to suggest a construction. The backward step enables new forward steps, and the process repeats. Unlike GRAMY, in our case, forward search is non-terminating and numeric. Our backward goal-directed strategy is also numeric, and it is used to prune, and not expand, the forward search.

Chou et. al. [8] also consider the problem of discovering geometry constructions. However, there are several differences: (i) A necessary condition for their approach to work is that the locus of every intermediate point should be a point, line or circle. We do not require this condition. For example, given points A,B, the loci of point C s.t. AC+CB=1 is an ellipse, and hence this paper can not handle such constraints (which we can handle). This severely limits the kind of examples (from highschool textbooks) that their approach can handle. (ii) Their approach does not use any backward goal-directed strategy. As we have demonstrated, forward search needs to be pruned by backward reasoning both for handling large examples, and also to make the tool more useful for pedagogical purposes. (iii) Their approach uses symbolic reasoning (theorem proving), and not numeric computation, to solve the problem. This can affect scalability by orders of magnitude. (iv) Our system is better suited for pedagogical purposes, as we can generate specific kinds of solutions that involve using certain concepts taught in a certain chapter of a certain textbook for a certain grade (by simply changing the library used by our synthesizer). This is in line with the kind of solution that the teacher expects the students to produce. Our system can also extend a partial solution of a student to produce the nearest correct solution as opposed to producing an arbitrary solution.

8. Conclusion and Future Work

We presented a novel synthesis algorithm based on combining numerical methods with symbolic methods, and apply it to synthesizing ruler-compass based geometry constructions.

It may be tempting to question the relevance of plane geometry constructions. Here one should note that plane geometry provides a good platform for teaching logical reasoning abilities while keeping it simple, visual, and fun. "They are just the rules of a game mathematicians play. There are many other ways to do constructions, but the compass and straightedge were chosen as one set of tools that make a construction challenging, by limiting what you are allowed to do, just as sports restrict what you can do (e.g. touching but not tackling, or tackling but no nuclear weapons) in order to keep a game interesting. Other tools could have been chosen instead; for example, geometric constructions can be done using origami." [1]

This paper is the first in the planned series of works on automating high-school education, and in particular, high-school geometry education. We have taken the first step towards this goal and we are in the process of building an end-to-end system that can interact with users in natural language. There is ongoing work on building a natural language front-end for our system that will translate English description of geometry problems to the logical problem representation described in this paper. There is also ongoing work on building a *paraphrasing* back-end for our system that will translate the construction in the programming language described in this paper to natural language.

The technology proposed in this paper forms the foundation for the following technical problems that we plan to tackle next, which will help take this technology to classrooms. The work done in software engineering community can play a big role in addressing some of these problems.

- Provide hints to students instead of the entire solution.
- Point out bugs in an incorrect solution of a student (taking inspiration from the work on bug localization techniques in the programming languages and software engineering community), and suggest fixes to an incorrect solution of student (perhaps using ideas from automated bug fixing techniques [40]),
- Quantify difficulty level of a given problem (by correlating various metrics of a problem, its solution, and scores of students, using ideas from work on software metrics)
- Generate problems of a measured difficulty level.

Solutions to these problems would help in realizing the goal of personalized learning or making teaching *interactive*. However, this is just a short-term goal. The real prize for investing into synthesizers for such domains lies in enabling building of an ultra-intelligent computer, and also a complete model of how the human mind works [32].

References

[1] http://mathforum.org/library/drmath/view/61335.html.

[2] J. R. Anderson, C. F. Boyle, and G. Yost. The geometry tutor. In *IJCAI*, pages 1–7, 1985.

[3] Y. Bar-David and G. Taubenfeld. Automatic discovery of mutual exclusion algorithms. In *DISC*, 2003.

[4] S. Barmany, R. Bodik, S. Chandra, J. Galensony, D. Kimelman, C. Rodarmory, and N. Tungy. Programming with angelic nondeterm. In *POPL*, 2010.

[5] B. Boigelot. On iterating linear transformations over recognizable sets of integers. *TCS*, 309(2), 2003.

[6] S. Chaudhuri and A. Solar-Lezama. Smooth interpretation. In *PLDI*, pages 279–291, 2010.

[7] S. Chou, X. Gao, and J. Zhang. *Machine Proofs in Geometry–Automated Production of Readable Proofs for Geometric Theorems*. World Scientific, 1994.

[8] S.-C. Chou, X.-S. Gao, and J.-Z. Zhang. Automated generation of construction steps for geometric constraint problems. In *Automated reasoning and its applications: Essays in honor of Larry Wos*, pages 49–69. 1997.

[9] A. Cypher, D. C. Halbert, D. Kurlander, H. Lieberman, D. Maulsby, B. A. Myers, and A. Turransky. *Watch what I do: programming by demonstration*. MIT Press, 1993.

[10] X.-S. Gao and Q. Lin. Mmp/geometer: A software package for auto. geometric reasoning. In *Automated Deduction in Geometry*, volume 2930 of *LNCS*. 2004.

[11] T. Granlund and R. Kenner. Eliminating branches using a superoptimizer and the gnu c compiler. In *PLDI*, 1992.

[12] S. Gulwani. Dimensions in program synthesis (invited talk paper). In *ACM Symposium on PPDP*, 2010.

[13] S. Gulwani. Automating string processing in spreadsheets using input-output examples. In *POPL*, 2011.

[14] S. Gulwani, S. K. Jha, A. Tiwari, and R. Venkatesan. Synthesis of loop-free programs. In *PLDI*, 2011.

[15] B. Harris and S. Gulwani. Spreadsheet table transformations from examples. In *PLDI*, 2011.

[16] S. Itzhaky, S. Gulwani, N. Immerman, and M. Sagiv. A simple inductive synthesis methodology and its applications. In *OOPSLA*, pages 36–46, 2010.

[17] N. Jackiw. The geometer's sketchpad. Key Curriculum Press, Berkeley, 1991-1995, http://www.keypress.com.

[18] S. Jha, S. Gulwani, S. Seshia, and A. Tiwari. Oracle-guided component-based program synthesis. In *ICSE*, 2010.

[19] D. Kapur. Using Gröbner bases to reason about geometry problems. *J. Symb. Comput.*, 2(4), 1986.

[20] S. Katayama. Systematic search for lambda expressions. In *Trends in Func. Programming*, 2005.

[21] G. Katz and D. Peled. Genetic programming and model checking: Synthesizing new mutual exclusion algorithms. In *ATVA*, pages 33–47, 2008.

[22] U. Kortenkamp and J. Richter-gebert. Using auto. theorem proving to improve the usability of geometry software. In *Mathematical User Interfaces*, 2004.

[23] V. Kuncak, M. Mayer, R. Piskac, and P. Suter. Complete functional synthesis. In *PLDI*, 2010.

[24] J.-M. Laborde and F. Bellemain. Cabri-geometry ii. `http://www.cabri.net` (1993-1998).

[25] T. Lau, L. Bergman, V. Castelli, and D. Oblinger. Programming shell scripts by demonstration. In *Workshop on Supervisory Control of Learning and Adaptive Systems, AAAI*, 2004.

[26] T. A. Lau, P. Domingos, and D. S. Weld. Version space algebra and its application to programming by demonstration. In *ICML*, pages 527–534, 2000.

[27] N. Matsuda and K. Vanlehn. Gramy: A geometry theorem prover capable of construction. *J. Autom. Reason.*, 32:3–33, January 2004.

[28] J. M. Robertson. *Geometric Constructions Using Hinged Mirrors*, pages 380–386. May 1996.

[29] P. Rondon. Programming lang. or how to sweet talk a computer, 2010. cseweb.ucsd.edu/~prondon/talks/plintro.pdf.

[30] C. V. Sanders. *Sharing Teaching Ideas: Geometric Constructions: Visualizing and Understanding Geometry*, pages 554–556. October 1998.

[31] J. T. Schwartz. Fast probabilistic algorithms for verification of polynomial identities. *J. ACM*, 27(4):701–717, 1980.

[32] L. Shustek. An interview with Ed Feigenbaum. *Commun. ACM*, 53(6):41–45, 2010.

[33] A. Solar-Lezama. *Program Synthesis by Sketching*. PhD thesis, University of California, Berkeley, 2008.

[34] A. Solar-Lezama, C. G. Jones, and R. Bodík. Sketching concurrent data structures. In *PLDI*, 2008.

[35] S. Srivastava, S. Gulwani, S. Chaudhuri, and J. Foster. Path-based inductive synthesis for program inversion. In *PLDI*, 2011.

[36] S. Srivastava, S. Gulwani, and J. S. Foster. From program verification to program synthesis. In *POPL*, pages 313–326, 2010.

[37] A. Taly, S. Gulwani, and A. Tiwari. Synthesizing switching logic using constraint solving. In *VMCAI*, pages 305–319, 2009.

[38] A. Tarski. *A Decision Method for Elementary Algebra and Geometry*. University of California Press, 1948.

[39] M. T. Vechev and E. Yahav. Deriving linearizable fine-grained concurrent objects. In *PLDI*, 2008.

[40] W. Weimer, T. Nguyen, C. L. Goues, and S. Forrest. Automatically finding patches using genetic programming. In *ICSE*, pages 364–374, 2009.

[41] S. Wilson and J. D. Fleuriot. Combining dynamic geometry, automated geometry theorem proving and diagrammatic proofs. In *UITP*, 2005.

[42] W.-T. Wu. Basic principles of mechanical theorem proving in elementary geometrics. *J. Autom. Reason.*, 2(3), 1987.

[43] J. Zhang, L. Yang, and M. Deng. The parallel numerical method of mechanical theorem proving. *Theor. Comp. Sci.*, 74:253–271, 1990.

Synthesis of Loop-free Programs

Sumit Gulwani
Microsoft Research, Redmond
sumitg@microsoft.com

Susmit Jha *
University of California, Berkeley
jha@eecs.berkeley.edu

Ashish Tiwari †
SRI International, Menlo Park
tiwari@csl.sri.com

Ramarathnam Venkatesan
Microsoft Research, Redmond
venkie@microsoft.com

Abstract

We consider the problem of synthesizing loop-free programs that implement a desired functionality using components from a given library. Specifications of the desired functionality and the library components are provided as logical relations between their respective input and output variables. The library components can be used at most once, and hence the library is required to contain a reasonable overapproximation of the multiset of the components required.

We solve the above *component-based synthesis problem* using a constraint-based approach that involves first generating a *synthesis constraint*, and then solving the constraint. The synthesis constraint is a first-order $\exists\forall$ logic formula whose size is quadratic in the number of components. We present a novel algorithm for solving such constraints. Our algorithm is based on counterexample guided iterative synthesis paradigm and uses off-the-shelf SMT solvers.

We present experimental results that show that our tool `Brahma` can efficiently synthesize highly nontrivial 10-20 line loop-free bitvector programs. These programs represent a state space of approximately 20^{10} programs, and are beyond the reach of the other tools based on sketching and superoptimization.

Categories and Subject Descriptors D.1.2 [*Programming Techniques*]: Automatic Programming; I.2.2 [*Artificial Intelligence*]: Program Synthesis

General Terms Algorithms, Theory, Verification

Keywords Program Synthesis, Component-based Synthesis, SMT

1. Introduction

Composition has played a key role in enabling configurable and scalable *design and development* of efficient hardware as well as software systems. Hardware developers find it useful to design specialized hardware using some base components, such as adders and multiplexers, rather than having to design everything using universal gates at bit-level. Similarly, software developers prefer to use library features and frameworks. Composition has also played a key role in enabling scalable *verification* of systems that have been designed in a modular fashion. This involves verifying specifications of the base/constituent components in isolation, and then assuming these specifications to verify specification of the higher-level system made up of these components.

In this paper, we push the above-mentioned applications of composition to another dimension, that of synthesis. We focus on the *component-based synthesis* problem where the goal is to build a system by composing base components. Automating component-based synthesis is attractive for many reasons. First, the designed system is correct by construction, which obviates the need for verification. Second, the designed system can be guaranteed to be optimal in terms of using the fewest possible number of components. Third, automation improves developer's productivity, since finding the exact set of components and their correct composition can be a daunting task, especially when the base component library is huge.

We present a synthesis procedure that takes as input a specification for the desired program and specifications of the base components, and synthesizes a circuit-style composition – a straight-line program – using these base components. Our procedure is semi-automated as it relies on the user to provide one additional piece of information: an over-approximation of the number of times each base component is used in the desired program. Our synthesis procedure views the base component library as a multiset whose elements are treated as resources that can be used at most once. Hence, our procedure can be seen as solving a *resource-bounded component-based synthesis* problem. Our procedure is also restricted to discovering only straight-line programs. Note that loop-free control-flow can be encoded as a straight-line program by providing the ite (if-then-else) operator as a base component, but synthesizing loops is left for future work. The reliance on the user for making copies of the base components and for discovering loops is indicative that the true success of program synthesis may lie in an interactive process that combines higher-level insights of humans with computational capabilities of computers.

While our focus on synthesizing loop-free programs may appear narrow, it is nevertheless a significant goal in itself [12]. Techniques for synthesizing loop-free code will be needed when synthesizing more complex code patterns. Synthesis of loops requires techniques that are mostly orthogonal to the techniques for synthesizing straight-line code, and hence it is fruitful to study them separately [13]. Loop-free program synthesis has several independent applications too that have been pursued in different com-

* Work done while visiting SRI International.

† Research supported in part by NSF grants CNS-0720721, CSR-EHCS-0834810 and CSR-0917398.

PLDI'11, June 4–8, 2011, San Jose, California, USA.

munities recently; such as, optimizing the core of many compute intensive loops (superoptimizers) [28], synthesizing API call sequence (e.g., Jungloid [26]), bitvector algorithms, geometry constructions [14, 18], text-editing [24, 38] and table-manipulation programs [16]. Finally, despite its appearance, loop-free program synthesis is challenging as the search space of loop-free programs is still huge.

While we foresee several applications of component-based program synthesis, most of the examples in this paper relate to discovering intricate bitvector programs, which combine arithmetic and bitwise operations. Bitvector programs can be quite unintuitive and extremely difficult for average, or sometimes even expert, programmers to discover methodically. Consider, for example, the problem of turning-off the rightmost 1-bit in a bitvector x. This can be achieved by computing $x \& (x-1)$, which involves composing the bitwise & operator and the arithmetic subtraction operator in an unintuitive manner. In fact, the upcoming 4th volume of the classic series *art of computer programming* by Knuth has a special chapter on bitwise tricks and techniques [23]. In this paper, we demonstrate how to semi-automate the discovery of small, but intricate, bitvector programs using the currently available formal verification technology. This semi-automation can be exposed to users in at least two different ways. First, software development environments can provide this capability to help programmers write correct and efficient code. Alternatively, compilers can use the synthesis procedure to optimize implementations or make them more secure. Superoptimizers, for example, perform automatic translation of a given sequence of instructions into an optimal sequence of instructions for performing aggressive peephole optimizations [5] or binary translation [6]. Rather than achieve efficiency, the goal of such translation can also be to reduce vulnerability in software. For example, any piece of code that computes the average of two numbers, x and y, by evaluating $(x+y)/2$ is inherently flawed and vulnerable since it can overflow. However, using some bitwise tricks, the average can be computed without overflowing (e.g., $(x|y) - ((x \oplus y) >> 1)$). Compilers can replace vulnerable snippets of code by the discovered equivalent secure code.

The number of straight-line programs that can be constructed using a given set of base library components is exponential in the number of base components. Rather than performing a naive exponential search for finding the correct program, our synthesis algorithm relegates all exponential reasoning to tools that have been engineered for efficiently performing exponential search, namely the Satisfiability (SAT) and Satisfiability Modulo Theory (SMT) solvers[1]. SMT solvers use intelligent backtracking and learning to overcome the complexity barrier. SMT solvers can be used to verify that a given (loop-free) system meets a given specification. In this paper, we show how to use the same SMT solving technology to synthesize systems that meet a given specification.

Existing synthesis techniques based on superoptimizers [11, 22, 28] and sketching [32, 33] can also be used to solve the component-based synthesis problem. Superoptimizers explicitly perform an exponential search. Sketching solves a more general program synthesis problem, and is not designed for solving the component-based synthesis problem. When they are used to solve the component-based synthesis problem, both superoptimizers and sketching were empirically found to not scale. In contrast, our technique leaves the inherent exponential nature of the problem to the underlying SMT solver, whose engineering advances over the years have made them effective at solving the "usually-not-so-hard" instances that arise in practice, and hence end up not requiring exponential reasoning.

Our assumption that we are given (by developers) logical specifications of the desired program may appear to be unrealistic. It is not. The logical specification can be given in the form of an (unoptimized) program, which are easy to write. In fact, we did exactly this in our experiments. In many domains, writing such logical specifications is much less time-consuming than discovering optimized straight-line code.

Our synthesis algorithm is based on a *constraint-based* approach that involves reducing the synthesis problem to that of solving a constraint. This involves the two key steps of constraint generation and constraint solving.

In the constraint generation phase, the synthesis problem is encoded as a constraint, referred to as *synthesis constraint*. Our synthesis constraint has two interesting aspects.

- The synthesis constraint is a first-order logic formula.
  The synthesis problem can be viewed as a generalization of the verification problem. It is well known that verification of a straight-line program can be reduced to proving validity of a first-order logic formula, and hence the synthesis problem can be reduced to finding satisfiability of a second-order logic formula. But, the non-trivial aspect of our encoding is that it generates a first-order logic formula. This is significant because off-the-shelf constraint solvers cannot effectively solve second-order formulas.
- The size of the synthesis constraint is quadratic in the number of components.
  One way to generate a first-order logic constraint would be to use the constraint generation methodology used inside the sketching technique, which is also a constraint-based technique. However, the size of the constraint generated by the sketching technique could potentially be exponential in the number of components. In contrast, our encoding yields a constraint that is guaranteed quadratic in the number of components.

In the constraint solving phase, we use a refined form of the classic counterexample guided iterative synthesis technique [10, 30] built on top of off-the-shelf SMT solvers. The synthesis constraint obtained from our encoding is an $\exists\forall$ formula, which cannot be effectively solved using off-the-shelf SMT solvers directly. The counterexample guided iterative synthesis technique involves choosing some initial set of test values for the ($\forall$) universally quantified variables and then solving for the ($\exists$) existentially quantified variables in the resulting constraint using SMT solvers. If the solution for the existentially quantified variables works for all choices of universally quantified variables, then a solution has been found. Else, a counterexample is discovered and the process is repeated after adding the counterexample to the set of test values for the universally quantified variables. We use this method, suitably adapted to handle *definitions* correctly, to solve our synthesis constraint.

We have implemented our constraint generation and constraint solving technique in a tool called `Brahma`. We have applied `Brahma` to several different examples. Majority of the examples come from the domain of bitvector program synthesis using a set of components that implement basic bitvector operations. These programs typically involve unintuitive composition of the bitvector operations, and are quite challenging to synthesize manually. `Brahma` is able to synthesize (equivalent variants of) a variety of bitvector programs picked up from a classic book [37] in time ranging from 1.0 to 2778.7 seconds. In contrast, the Sketch and AHA tools, based respectively on sketching and super-optimization, time-out on 9 and 12 of the 25 examples respectively where timeout was set to 3600 seconds. Sketch is slower by an average factor of 20 on the remaining examples.

[1] SMT solving is an extension of SAT solving technology to work with theory facts, rather than just propositional facts. In fact, there is a SMT solving competition that is now held every year, and it has stimulated improvement in solver implementations [1].

Contributions and Organization

- We define the problem of component-based synthesis using a set of base components (Section 3).
- We present an encoding that reduces the synthesis problem to that of finding a satisfying assignment to a first-order logic constraint with quantifier alternation, whose size is at most quadratic in the number of base components. (Section 5).
- We present a novel technique for solving first-order logic constraints with quantifier alternation using off-the-shelf SMT solvers (Section 6).
- We apply our constraint generation and solving technique to a set of benchmark examples. We also experimentally compare our technique with other existing techniques, namely sketching and superoptimization, that can be used to synthesize bitvector programs (Section 7). Tools based on other techniques either perform order of magnitude slower or timeout and fail to yield a solution.

2. Running Example

First, we introduce a small example to give a high-level overview of our technique. We also use this example as a running example to illustrate several details of our technique in following sections.

Consider the task of designing a bitvector program that masks off the right-most significant 1-bit in an input bitvector. More formally, the bitvector program takes as input one bitvector I and outputs a bitvector O such that O is obtained from I by setting the right-most significant 1-bit in I to 0. For example, the bitvector program should transform the bitvector 01100 into 01000.

A simple method to accomplish this would be to iterate over the input bitvector starting from the rightmost end until a 1 bit is found and then set it to 0. However, this algorithm is worst-case linear in the number of bits in the input bitvector. Furthermore, it uses undesirable branching code inside a loop.

There is a non-intuitive, but elegant, way to achieving the desired functionality in constant time by using a tricky composition of the standard subtraction operator and the bitwise logical & operator, which are supported by almost every architecture. The desired functionality can be achieved using the following composition:

$$I \;\&\; (I - 1)$$

The reason why we can do this seemingly worst-case linear task in unit time using the subtraction operator and the logical bitwise-and operator is because the hardware implementations of these operators manipulate the constituent bits of the bitvectors in parallel in constant time.

One way to discover the above tricky composition would be exhaustive enumeration. Let f_1 denote a unary component that implements the subtract-one operation, and let f_2 denote a binary component that implements a binary bitwise-and operation. Suppose we knew that the desired functionality can be achieved by some unknown composition of these two components f_1 and f_2. We can then simply enumerate all different ways of composing a unary operator and a binary operator, and then verify which one of them meets the functional specification with the help of an SMT solver (using the process described in Section 4). Figure 1 shows the six different straight-line-programs that can be obtained from composition of one unary and one binary operator. Of these the programs shown in 1(e) and 1(f) provide the desired functionality. There is a major problem with this explicit enumeration approach; it is too expensive. In fact, superoptimizers [28] do such an exhaustive enumeration, and hence fail to scale beyond composition of 4 components.

In contrast, our technique encodes (instead of explicitly enumerating) the space of all (six) possible straight-line programs for composing the two operations f_1 and f_2 using a logical formula $\psi_{\mathtt{wfp}}$. The formula $\psi_{\mathtt{wfp}}$ uses (five) integer variables, each corresponding to an input or output of some component. Intuitively, the integer variable corresponding to the output of some component denotes the line number at which the component is positioned. The integer variable corresponding to an input of some component denotes the line number where the actual parameter corresponding to that input is defined. The formula $\psi_{\mathtt{wfp}}$ is such that the satisfying assignments to the integer variables have a one-to-one correspondence with the different straight-line programs that can be obtained from composition of these operators. In conjunction with some other constraints that encode the functional specifications of the base component programs and the desired program, our technique generates a formula that we refer to as the *synthesis constraint*. A satisfying assignment to the integer variables that satisfies the synthesis constraint corresponds to the desired straight-line program. The synthesis constraint is a first-order logic constraint with quantifier alternation, and is not amenable to solving directly using off-the-shelf constraint solvers. One of the key technical contributions of the paper is an algorithm to find satisfying assignments to such synthesis constraints by using an off-the-shelf SMT solver.

Even though there is no provable polynomial time guarantee associated with our technique, there is a crucial difference between the exponential exhaustive enumeration technique and our technique based on synthesis-constraint generation and solving. The number of variables in the synthesis constraint is linear in the number of components and the size of the synthesis constraint is quadratic in the number of components. The winning advantage comes from the fact that we ride upon the recent engineering advances made in SMT solving technology to solve a constraint with a linear number of unknowns as opposed to explicitly performing an exhaustive enumeration over an exponential search space.

3. Problem Definition

The goal of this paper is to synthesize a program by using a given set of base software components. The program as well as the base components are specified using their functional description. This description is given in the form of a logical formula that relates the inputs and the outputs.

For simplicity of presentation, we assume that all components have exactly one output. We also assume that all inputs and the output have the same *type*. These restrictions can be easily removed.

Formally, the synthesis problem requires the user to provide:

- A specification $\langle \vec{I}, O, \phi_{\mathtt{spec}}(\vec{I}, O)\rangle$ of the program, which includes
  - a tuple of input variables $\vec{I}$ and an output variable O.
  - an expression $\phi_{\mathtt{spec}}(\vec{I}, O)$ over the variables $\vec{I}$ and O that specifies the desired input-output relationship.
- A set of specifications $\{\langle \vec{I_i}, O_i, \phi_i(\vec{I_i}, O_i)\rangle \mid i = 1, \ldots, N\}$, called a *library*, where $\phi_i(\vec{I_i}, O_i)$ is a specification for base component f_i. All variables $\vec{I_i}, O_i$ are assumed distinct.

The goal of the synthesis problem is to discover a program `f_impl` that correctly implements the specification $\phi_{\mathtt{spec}}$ using only the components provided in the library. The program `f_impl` is essentially a straight-line program that takes as input $\vec{I}$ and uses the set $\{O_1, \ldots, O_N\}$ as temporary variables in the following form:

$\underline{\mathtt{f\_impl}(\vec{I})\mathtt{:}}$
$\quad O_{\pi_1} := f_{\pi_1}(\vec{V}_{\pi_1});\quad \ldots;\quad O_{\pi_N} := f_{\pi_N}(\vec{V}_{\pi_N});$
$\quad \mathtt{return}\ O_{\pi_N};$

$f_{\phi_{\texttt{impl}}}(I)$: $O_2 := f_2(I, I)$; $O_1 := f_1(O_2)$; `return` O_1;	$f_{\phi_{\texttt{impl}}}(I)$: $O_2 := f_2(I, I)$; $O_1 := f_1(I)$; `return` O_1;	$f_{\phi_{\texttt{impl}}}(I)$: $O_1 := f_1(I)$; $O_2 := f_2(I, I)$; `return` O_2;	$f_{\phi_{\texttt{impl}}}(I)$: $O_1 := f_1(I)$; $O_2 := f_2(O_1, O_1)$; `return` O_2;	$f_{\phi_{\texttt{impl}}}(I)$: $O_1 := f_1(I)$; $O_2 := f_2(O_1, I)$; `return` O_2;	$f_{\phi_{\texttt{impl}}}(I)$: $O_1 := f_1(I)$; $O_2 := f_2(I, O_1)$; `return` O_2;
$l_{I_1} = 1$ $l_{O_1} = 2$ $l_{I_2} = 0$ $l_{O_2} = 1$ $l_{I'_2} = 0$	$l_{I_1} = 0$ $l_{O_1} = 2$ $l_{I_2} = 0$ $l_{O_2} = 1$ $l_{I'_2} = 0$	$l_{I_1} = 0$ $l_{O_1} = 1$ $l_{I_2} = 0$ $l_{O_2} = 2$ $l_{I'_2} = 0$	$l_{I_1} = 0$ $l_{O_1} = 1$ $l_{I_2} = 1$ $l_{O_2} = 2$ $l_{I'_2} = 1$	$l_{I_1} = 0$ $l_{O_1} = 1$ $l_{I_2} = 1$ $l_{O_2} = 2$ $l_{I'_2} = 0$	$l_{I_1} = 0$ $l_{O_1} = 1$ $l_{I_2} = 0$ $l_{O_2} = 2$ $l_{I'_2} = 1$
(a)	(b)	(c)	(d)	(e)	(f)

Figure 1. The first row shows six different ways of composing a unary component f_1 and a binary component f_2 to synthesize a straight-line program $f_{\phi_{\texttt{impl}}}$ with one input I. Second row shows an integer encoding of the corresponding program using *location variables*.

where

- each variable in $\vec{V}_{\pi_i}$ is either an input variable from $\vec{I}$, or a temporary variable O_{π_j} such that $j < i$,
- $\pi_1, \ldots, \pi_N$ is a permutation of $1, \ldots, N$, and
- the following correctness criteria holds:

$$\forall \vec{I}, O_1, \ldots, O_N : \left(\phi_{\pi_1}(\vec{V}_{\pi_1}, O_{\pi_1}) \wedge \cdots \wedge \phi_{\pi_N}(\vec{V}_{\pi_N}, O_{\pi_N})\right) \Rightarrow \phi_{\texttt{spec}}(\vec{I}, O_{\pi_N}) \quad (1)$$

The last formula above is called the *verification constraint*. It states the correctness criterion for the output program: for all inputs $\vec{I}$, if O_{π_N} is the output of the implementation on $\vec{I}$, then O_{π_N} should also be the output of the specification on $\vec{I}$; that is, the implementation should imply the specification.

We note that the implementation above is using *all* components from the library. We can assume this without any loss of generality. Even when there is a correct implementation using fewer components, that implementation can always be extended to an implementation that uses all components by adding dead code. Dead code can be easily identified and removed in a post-processing step.

We also note that the implementation above is using each base component only once. If there is an implementation using *multiple* copies of the same base component, we assume that the user provides multiple copies explicitly in the library (discussed further in Section 7.3). Such a restriction of using each base component only once is interesting in two regards: It can be used to enforce efficient or minimal designs. This restriction also prunes down the search space of possible designs making the problem finite and tractable.

Informally, the synthesis problem seeks to come up with an implementation – using only the base components in the given library – that implies the given specification.

EXAMPLE 1 (Problem Definition). *The problem definition for the running example in Sec. 2 can be stated as:*

- *The formal specification of the desired program to be synthesized is given by the following relationship $\phi_{\texttt{spec}}$ between the input bitvector I and the output bitvector O. We use b to denote the total number of bits in the bitvectors, and $I[j]$ to denote the bit at j^{th} position in bitvector I, when viewed as an array of bits.*

$$\phi_{\texttt{spec}}(I, O) \quad := \quad \bigwedge_{t=1}^{b} \left(\left(I[t] = 1 \wedge \bigwedge_{j=t+1}^{b} I[j] = 0 \right) \Rightarrow \left(O[t] = 0 \wedge \bigwedge_{j \neq t} O[j] = I[j] \right) \right)$$

- *The number of base components in the library is $N = 2$. One of them is a unary component f_1 that implements the subtract-one operation, and its formal specification is given by the following relationship ϕ_1 between its input parameter I_1 and output O_1.*

$$\phi_1(I_1, O_1) \quad := \quad O_1 = (I_1 - 1)$$

The other component is a binary component that implements the bitwise-and operation, and its formal specification is given by the following relationship ϕ_2 between its input parameters I_2, I'_2 and output O_2.

$$\phi_2(I_2, I'_2, O_2) \quad := \quad O_2 = (I_2 \,\&\, I'_2)$$

4. Revisiting Verification Constraint

Before we describe our approach for solving the synthesis problem – consisting of the synthesis constraint generation phase and the constraint solving phase – we will perform two steps in this section to support the transition to these two phases. First, we will rewrite the verification constraint in Eq. 1 so that it resembles the synthesis constraint. Second, we discuss solving of the verification constraint, which is a small part of the process of solving the synthesis constraint.

Consider the verification constraint in Eq. 1. We can replace each atomic fact $\phi_{\pi_i}(\vec{V}_{\pi_i}, O_{\pi_i})$ in the antecedent by $\phi_{\pi_i}(\vec{I}_{\pi_i}, O_{\pi_i}) \wedge \vec{I}_{\pi_i} = \vec{V}_{\pi_i}$. We can also replace the fact $\phi_{\texttt{spec}}(\vec{I}, O_{\pi_N})$ in the consequent by $\phi_{\texttt{spec}}(\vec{I}, O)$ provided we add $O = O_{\pi_N}$ in the antecedent. Hence, the verification constraint can be rewritten as:

$$\forall \vec{I}, O, \vec{I}_1, \ldots, \vec{I}_n, O_1, \ldots, O_N : \left((O = O_{\pi_N}) \wedge \bigwedge_{i=1}^{N} (\phi_i(\vec{I}_i, O_i) \wedge \vec{I}_i = \vec{V}_i) \right) \Rightarrow \phi_{\texttt{spec}}(\vec{I}, O)$$

We now split the antecedent in the above formula into two parts $\phi_{\texttt{lib}}$ and $\phi_{\texttt{conn}}$. We also group together the formal inputs and outputs of the base components into two sets $\mathbf{P}$ and $\mathbf{R}$ to rewrite the above verification constraint as:

$$\forall \vec{I}, O, \mathbf{P}, \mathbf{R} : (\phi_{\texttt{lib}}(\mathbf{P}, \mathbf{R}) \wedge \phi_{\texttt{conn}}(\vec{I}, O, \mathbf{P}, \mathbf{R})) \Rightarrow \phi_{\texttt{spec}}(\vec{I}, O) \quad (2)$$

where

$$\phi_{\texttt{lib}} := \left(\bigwedge_{i=1}^{N} \phi_i(\vec{I}_i, O_i)\right), \quad \phi_{\texttt{conn}} := (O = O_{\pi_N}) \wedge \left(\bigwedge_{i=1}^{N} \vec{I}_i = \vec{V}_i\right),$$

Here $\mathbf{P}$ and $\mathbf{R}$ denote the union of all formal inputs (Parameters) and formal outputs (Return variables) of the components:

$$\mathbf{P} := \bigcup_{i=1}^{N} \vec{I}_i \qquad \mathbf{R} := \bigcup_{i=1}^{N} \{O_i\} = \{O_1, \ldots, O_N\}$$

Note that $\phi_{\texttt{lib}}$ represents the specifications of the base components, and $\phi_{\texttt{conn}}$ represents the interconnections that includes the *mappings from formals to actuals* and from the return variable of some component to the output of the program. Observe that $\phi_{\texttt{conn}}$ is a conjunction of equalities between a variable in $\mathbf{P} \cup \{O\}$ and a variable in $\mathbf{R} \cup \vec{I}$. The connectivity constraint $\phi_{\texttt{conn}}$ determines:

- the order in which base components occur in the program.
- the value of each input parameter of each base component.

EXAMPLE 2 (Verification Constraint). *The verification constraint for the program in Figure 1(e) when regarded as a solution to the running example formally described in Example 1 is the following formula.*

$$\forall I, O, I_1, I_2, I_2', O_1, O_2\, (\phi_{\texttt{lib}} \wedge \phi_{\texttt{conn}} \Rightarrow \phi_{\texttt{spec}})$$

$$\begin{array}{lll} \textit{where} \quad \phi_{\texttt{lib}} & := & \phi_1(I_1, O_1) \ \wedge \ \phi_2(I_2, I_2', O_2) \\ \textit{and} \quad \phi_{\texttt{conn}} & := & I_1 = I \ \wedge \ I_2 = O_1 \ \wedge \ I_2' = I \ \wedge \ O = O_2 \end{array}$$

and $\phi_1, \phi_2, \phi_{\texttt{spec}}$ are as defined in Example 1.

We now briefly discuss the process of solving the verification constraint, which is a universally quantified formula. The complexity of deciding the validity of the formula in Eq. 2 depends on the expression language used for defining $\phi_{\texttt{spec}}$ and ϕ_i's. If this expression language is a subset of the language that can be handled by Satisfiability Modulo Theory (SMT) solvers, then we can use off-the-shelf SMT solvers to decide the formula in Eq. 2 and thus solve the verification problem. Specifically, we can check validity of a (universal) formula by asking an SMT solver for checking satisfiability of the negation of that formula.

5. Synthesis Constraint

In this section, we show how to reduce the problem of straight-line-program synthesis to that of finding a satisfying assignment to a first order logic constraint. Given a library of base components, and a specification for the desired program, we show how to generate a formula that encodes the existence of a program that is constructed using the base components and that meets the given specification.

Consider the verification constraint in Eq. 2. We are given $\phi_{\texttt{spec}}$ and $\phi_{\texttt{lib}}$ as part of the synthesis problem. However, we do not know the interconnections $\phi_{\texttt{conn}}$ between the inputs and outputs of the base components. Hence, the synthesis problem is equivalent to solving the following constraint:

$$\exists \phi_{\texttt{conn}} : \forall \vec{I}, O, \mathbf{P}, \mathbf{R} : \\ (\phi_{\texttt{lib}}(\mathbf{P}, \mathbf{R}) \wedge \phi_{\texttt{conn}}(\vec{I}, O', \mathbf{P}, \mathbf{R})) \Rightarrow \phi_{\texttt{spec}}(\vec{I}, O)$$

where we have a second-order existential quantifier over the set of all possible interconnections.

In the remaining part of this section, we show how to convert the second-order existential quantifier into a first-order existential quantifier. The basic idea is to introduce new first-order integer-valued variables, referred to as *location variables*, whose values decide the interconnections between the various components. To describe a program, we have to determine *which component goes on which location (line-number), and from which location (line-number or program input) does it get its input arguments*. This information can be described by a set of *location variables* L

$$L := \{l_x \mid x \in \mathbf{P} \cup \mathbf{R}\}$$

that contains one new variable l_x for each variable x in $\mathbf{P} \cup \mathbf{R}$ with the following interpretation associated with each of these variables.

- If x is the output variable O_i of component f_i, then l_x represents the line in the program where the component f_i is positioned.
- If x is the jth input parameter of component f_i, then l_x represents the *location* "from where component f_i gets its jth input".

A *location* above refers to either a line of the program, or to some program input. To represent different possible locations, we use integers in the set $\{0, .., M-1\}$, where M is the sum of the number N of components in the library and the number $|\vec{I}|$ of program inputs, i.e., $M = N + |\vec{I}|$, with the following interpretation.

- The jth input is identified with the location $j-1$.
- The jth line or the assignment statement in the program is identified with the location $j + |\vec{I}| - 1$.

EXAMPLE 3 (Location Variables). *For our running example formally described in Example 1, the set L of location variables consists of 5 integer variables. $L = \{l_{O_1}, l_{O_2}, l_{I_1}, l_{I_2}, l_{I_2'}\}$. The variables l_{O_1} and l_{O_2} denote the location at which the components f_1 and f_2 are positioned respectively. The variable l_{I_1} denotes the location of the definition of the input to the unary component f_1. The variables l_{I_2} and $l_{I_2'}$ denote the locations of the definitions of the first and the second input respectively of the binary component f_2. Since there are two components and one input, we have $N = 2$ and $M = 3$. The variables l_{O_1}, l_{O_2} take values from the set $\{1, 2\}$, while the variables $l_{I_1}, l_{I_2}, l_{I_2'}$ take values from the set $\{0, 1, 2\}$.*

The synthesis constraint, which uses the location variables L, is given in Eq. 4 in Section 5.3. We next discuss the key constituents of the synthesis constraint. For notational convenience (for the discussion below), we also define l_x for the global inputs $\vec{I}$ and output O. We define l_O to be equal to $M-1$, denoting that the output O of the program is defined on the last line of the program. For the jth input x to the program, we define l_x to be $j-1$, which is the integer location that we associated with the jth program input.

5.1 Encoding Well-formed Programs: $\psi_{\texttt{wfp}}$

We noted above that every straight-line program can be encoded by assigning appropriate values from the set $\{0, .., M-1\}$ to variables in L. On the other hand, any possible assignment to variables in L from the set $\{0, .., M-1\}$ does not necessarily correspond to a well-formed straight-line program. We require the variables in L to satisfy certain constraints to guarantee that they define well-formed programs. The following two constraints guarantee this.

Consistency Constraint : Every line in the program has at most one component. In our encoding, l_{O_i} encodes the line number where component f_i is positioned. Hence for different i, l_{O_i} should be different. Thus we get the following *consistency constraint*.

$$\psi_{\texttt{cons}} := \bigwedge_{x,y \in \mathbf{R}, x \not\equiv y} (l_x \neq l_y)$$

Acyclicity Constraint : In a well-formed program, every variable is initialized *before* it is used. In our encoding, component f_i is positioned at location l_{O_i} and its inputs are coming from locations $\{l_x \mid x \in \vec{I_i}\}$. Thus, we get the following *acyclicity constraint*.

$$\psi_{\texttt{acyc}} := \bigwedge_{i=1}^{N} (\bigwedge_{x \in \vec{I_i}, y \equiv O_i} l_x < l_y)$$

The acyclicity constraint says that, for every component, if x is an input of that component and y is an output of that component, then the location l_x where the input is defined, should be earlier than the location l_y where the component is positioned and its output is defined.

We now define $\psi_{\texttt{wfp}}(L)$ to be following constraint that encodes the interpretation of the location variables l_x along with the consistency and acyclicity constraints.

$$\psi_{\texttt{wfp}}(L) \ := \ \bigwedge_{x \in \mathbf{P}} (0 \leq l_x \leq M-1) \ \wedge \ \bigwedge_{x \in \mathbf{R}} (|\vec{I}| \leq l_x \leq M-1) \ \wedge$$

$$\psi_{\text{cons}}(L) \ \wedge \ \psi_{\text{acyc}}(L)$$

We note that if the location variables L satisfy $\psi_{\texttt{wfp}}$, then L defines a well-formed straight-line program in static single assignment (SSA) form [7], whose assignments make calls to the components in the library. Specifically, the function `Lval2Prog` returns the program corresponding to a given valuation L as follows: in the ith line of `Lval2Prog`(L), we have the assignment $O_j := f_j(O_{\sigma(1)}, .., O_{\sigma(t)})$ if $l_{O_j} = i, l_{I_j^k} = l_{\sigma(k)}$ for $k = 1, .., t$, where t is the arity of component f_j, and $(I_j^1, .., I_j^t)$ is the tuple of input variables $\vec{I_j}$ of f_j.

Our encoding has the following natural property.

THEOREM 1. *Let* $\mathbf{L}$ *be the set of all valuations of* L *that satisfy the well-formedness constraint* $\psi_{\texttt{wfp}}$. *Let* $\mathbf{\Pi}$ *be the set of all straight-line programs in SSA form that take input* $\vec{I}$ *and contain the* N *assignments,* $O_i := f(\vec{V_i})$, *such that every variable is defined before it is used. Then, the mapping* `Lval2Prog` *goes from* $\mathbf{L}$ *to* $\mathbf{\Pi}$ *and it is bijective.*

EXAMPLE 4 (Well-formedness Constraint). *For our running example formally described in Example 1, the constraint* $\psi_{\texttt{wfp}}$ *is:*

$$\psi_{\texttt{wfp}} := \psi_{\text{cons}} \wedge \psi_{\text{acyc}} \wedge \bigwedge_{x \in \mathbf{P}} (0 \leq l_x \leq 2) \ \wedge \ \bigwedge_{x \in \mathbf{R}} (1 \leq l_x \leq 2)$$

$$\textit{where} \ \ \psi_{\text{cons}} := (l_{O_1} \neq l_{O_2})$$
$$\textit{and} \ \ \psi_{\text{acyc}} := (l_{I_1} < l_{O_1}) \ \wedge \ (l_{I_2} < l_{O_2}) \ \wedge \ (l_{I_2'} < l_{O_2})$$

Here $\mathbf{P} = \{\vec{I_1}, \vec{I_2}, \vec{I_2'}\}$ *and* $\mathbf{R} = \{O_1, O_2\}$. *There are 6 solutions for* $l_{I_1}, l_{I_2}, l_{I_2'}, l_{O_1}, l_{O_2}$ *that satisfy the constraint* $\psi_{\texttt{wfp}}$. *Each of these solutions correspond to a syntactically distinct and well-formed straight-line program obtained by composition of unary component* f_1 *and binary component* f_2. *These 6 solutions and the corresponding straight-line-programs are shown in Figure 1.*

5.2 Encoding Dataflow in Programs: ψ_{conn}

Given an interconnection among components specified by values of location variables L, we can relate the input/output variables of the components and the program by the following *connectivity constraint*:

$$\psi_{\text{conn}} := \bigwedge_{x,y \in \mathbf{P} \cup \mathbf{R} \cup \vec{I} \cup \{O\}} (l_x = l_y \Rightarrow x = y)$$

The constraint ψ_{conn} will play the role of ϕ_{conn} later.

5.3 Putting it all together

We are now ready to present the (first-order) *synthesis constraint* that encodes the synthesis problem.

We showed how the set of all valid programs can be described by valuations of the location variables L. Hence, the synthesis problem reduces to finding a value for the variables L such that
(1) this valuation corresponds to a well-formed program and
(2) the corresponding well-formed program is correct, as described by the verification constraint (Eq. 2).
In other words, we get the following *synthesis constraint*:

$$\exists L : (\psi_{\texttt{wfp}}(L) \wedge \forall \vec{I}, O, \mathbf{P}, \mathbf{R} : \phi_{\texttt{lib}}(\mathbf{P}, \mathbf{R}) \ \wedge \ \psi_{\text{conn}}(\vec{I}, O, \mathbf{P}, \mathbf{R}, L) \Rightarrow \phi_{\texttt{spec}}(\vec{I}, O)) \quad (3)$$

We merge the (temporary) variables $\mathbf{P}$ and $\mathbf{R}$ and call it the set T. We rewrite the formula in Eq. 3 by pulling out the universal quantifier to get the following *synthesis constraint*.

$$\exists L \forall \vec{I}, O, T : \psi_{\texttt{wfp}}(L) \wedge (\phi_{\texttt{lib}}(T) \wedge \psi_{\text{conn}}(\vec{I}, O, T, L) \Rightarrow \phi_{\texttt{spec}}(\vec{I}, O)) \quad (4)$$

EXAMPLE 5 (Synthesis Constraint). *Of the 6 solutions to the location variables L described in Example 4, there are 2 solutions that satisfy the entire synthesis constraint. These two solutions are shown in Figure 1(e) and Figure 1(f).*

The following theorem states that the synthesis constraint in Eq. 4 is quadratic in size and it exactly encodes our synthesis problem. Hence, solving the synthesis problem is equivalent to solving the synthesis constraint. The proof of the theorem follows from the definition of `Lval2Prog`, Theorem 1, and the definitions of the verification and synthesis constraints.

THEOREM 2 (Synthesis Constraint). *Let* $(\phi_{\texttt{spec}}, \phi_{\texttt{lib}})$ *be the given specifications. Let* ψ *be the corresponding synthesis constraint, defined in Eq. 4, that is derived from the given specifications. The size of* ψ *is* $O(n + m^2)$ *where* n *is the size of* $(\phi_{\texttt{spec}}, \phi_{\texttt{lib}})$ *and* m *is the number of base components in the library. Furthermore,* ψ *is valid if and only if there is a straight-line program that implements the specification* $\phi_{\texttt{spec}}$ *using only the components in* $\phi_{\texttt{lib}}$.

PROOF: The number of variables in L is $O(m)$ and hence the size of ψ is seen to be $O(n + m^2)$.

($\Rightarrow$): Suppose ψ is valid. This implies that there exists a value for L, say L_0, such that $\psi_{\texttt{wfp}}(L_0)$ holds and the formula $\forall \vec{I}, O, \mathbf{P}, \mathbf{R} : \phi_{\texttt{lib}}(\mathbf{P}, \mathbf{R}) \wedge \psi_{\text{conn}}(\vec{I}, O, \mathbf{P}, \mathbf{R}, L_0) \Rightarrow \phi_{\texttt{spec}}(\vec{I}, O)$ is valid. Since $\psi_{\texttt{wfp}}(L_0)$ holds, we can use Theorem 1 to get a Program `Lval2Prog`(L), call it P. Now, the definition of `Lval2Prog` and the constraint ψ_{conn} together guarantee that the connectivity constraint ϕ_{conn} defined by P and the connectivity constraint $\psi_{\text{conn}}(L_0)$ are equivalent. Since we know $\forall \vec{I}, O, \mathbf{P}, \mathbf{R} : \phi_{\texttt{lib}} \wedge \psi_{\text{conn}} \Rightarrow \phi_{\texttt{spec}}$ is valid, it follows that the formula $\forall \vec{I}, O, \mathbf{P}, \mathbf{R} : \phi_{\texttt{lib}} \wedge \phi_{\text{conn}} \Rightarrow \phi_{\texttt{spec}}$ is also valid. This shows that the verification constraint for correctness of P is valid.

($\Leftarrow$): Suppose there is a straight-line program, say P, that correctly implements the given specification $\phi_{\texttt{spec}}$ using only the components in $\phi_{\texttt{lib}}$. Given a program P, we can immediately define values for the location variables L such that ϕ_{conn} is equivalent to $\psi_{\text{conn}}(L)$. Since the program P is assumed to be well-formed, this valuation of L will satisfy $\psi_{\texttt{wfp}}$. Furthermore, since P is correct, the verification constraint is valid. Replacing ϕ_{conn} in the verification constraint by ψ_{conn} shows that the synthesis constraint is also valid. □

6. Synthesis Constraint Solving

In this section, we show how to solve the synthesis constraint (Eq. 4 in Section 5.3). In particular, we show how to find an assignment to the decision variables L that would witness the validity of the synthesis constraint.

Our procedure is built over the standard counterexample-guided iterative refinement paradigm [10, 30]. It solves $\exists L \forall \vec{I} : \phi(L, \vec{I})$ by iteratively finding values for L that work for more and more values of $\vec{I}$. Let $\mathcal{S}$ denote a finite set of valuations of $\vec{I}$. In each iteration, our procedure first finds a valuation for L that works for the choices in $\mathcal{S}$. It then tests if the discovered valuation for L works *for all* $\vec{I}$. If it does not, then a valuation of $\vec{I}$ for which *it does not work* is added to the set $\mathcal{S}$ and the process is repeated.

The Procedure `ExAllSolver` shown in Figure 2 is a high-level description of our solver for the synthesis constraint. It alternates

```
   ExAllSolver(ψ_wfp, φ_lib, ψ_conn, φ_spec):
1    // ∃L∀I⃗,O,T : ψ_wfp ∧ (φ_lib ∧ ψ_conn ⇒ φ_spec)
     //        is a synthesis constraint
2    // Output: synthesis failed or values for L
3    S := {I⃗_0} // I⃗_0 is an arbitrary input
4    while (1) {
5       model := T-SAT(∃L,O_1,...,O_n,T_1,...,T_n : ψ_wfp(L)∧
                       ⋀_{I⃗_i∈S}(φ_lib(T_i) ∧ ψ_conn(I⃗_i,O_i,T_i,L)
                                              ∧φ_spec(I⃗_i,O_i)));
        if (model ≠ ⊥) {
6          currL := model|_L
        } else {
7          return("synthesis failed");
        }
8       model := T-SAT(∃I⃗,O,T :ψ_conn(I⃗,O,T,currL)∧
                                  φ_lib(T) ∧ ¬φ_spec(I⃗,O));
        if (model ≠ ⊥) {
9          I⃗_1 := model|_I⃗; S := S ∪ {I⃗_1};
        } else {
10         return(currL);
        }
11   }
```

Figure 2. Counterexample guided $\exists\forall$ solver for solving the synthesis constraint. Note that Line 5 and Line 8 use different formulas. If successful, the procedure outputs values for L that can be used to extract the desired straight-line program (Theorem 1).

between *finite synthesis* – finding a valuation for L that works some finite choices of $\vec{I}$ – and *verification* – checking that the valuation works for all $\vec{I}$ – and, in each iteration, the two steps learn from each other. The new value for L is always guided by a set of inputs on which the previous choice for L failed.

A technical issue worth pointing out in Procedure `ExAllSolver` is that it handles variables O, T differently from the variables $\vec{I}$ even though they are all universally quantified in the synthesis constraint. Intuitively, this is because O, T are not "independent" variables, but their values depend on $\vec{I}$ and L. Specifically, Procedure `ExAllSolver` uses the following two *different* variants of the synthesis constraint in its two steps. The formula $(\mathtt{F_{ver}})$ is same as the synthesis constraint, while the formula $(\mathtt{F_{syn}})$ is a weaker version of the synthesis constraint.

$$(\mathtt{F_{ver}}) \qquad \exists L\, \forall \vec{I}, O, T : (\psi_{\mathtt{wfp}} \wedge (\phi_{\mathtt{lib}} \wedge \psi_{\mathtt{conn}} \Rightarrow \phi_{\mathtt{spec}}))$$
$$(\mathtt{F_{syn}}) \qquad \exists L\, \forall \vec{I}\, \exists O, T : (\psi_{\mathtt{wfp}} \wedge (\phi_{\mathtt{lib}} \wedge \psi_{\mathtt{conn}} \wedge \phi_{\mathtt{spec}}))$$

The two phases of the procedure can now be described as follows.

Finite Synthesis (Lines 5-7): In this step, we synthesize a design that works for finitely many inputs. Specifically, the procedure finds values for L that work for all the inputs in $\mathcal{S}$ (Line 5,6). If no such values are found, we terminate and declare that no design could be found (Line 7). Line 5 is effectively solving for Formula $(\mathtt{F_{syn}})$, which is different from the synthesis constraint.

Verification (Lines 8-10): In this step, we verify if the synthesized design – that we know works for the inputs in $\mathcal{S}$ – also works for all inputs. Specifically, if the generated value curr$L$ for L work for all inputs, then we terminate with success. If not, then we find an input $\vec{I}_1$ on which it does not work and add $\vec{I}_1$ to $\mathcal{S}$ (Line 9). Line 8 is verifying Formula $(\mathtt{F_{ver}})$, which is the synthesis constraint.

The function `T-SAT` checks for satisfiability modulo theory of an existentially quantified formula. If the formula is satisfiable, then it returns a model, i.e., values for the existential variables that make the formula true. Note that the function `T-SAT` is essentially a call to the SMT solver.

We need to argue that Procedure `ExAllSolver` always returns the correct answer on termination. This is stated in Theorem 3. But, before that, we need a lemma that relates the two formula $(\mathtt{F_{syn}})$ and $(\mathtt{F_{ver}})$. Under the assumption that the implementations f_i's of the base components in the library are all *terminating*, we can prove that $(\mathtt{F_{ver}})$ logically implies $(\mathtt{F_{syn}})$.

LEMMA 1. *Suppose the implementation of each base component f_i in the library is terminating. Then, $(\mathtt{F_{ver}})$ logically implies $(\mathtt{F_{syn}})$.*

PROOF: Suppose $(\mathtt{F_{ver}})$ holds. Let L_0 be the values of L that show validity of $(\mathtt{F_{ver}})$. We need to prove that $(\mathtt{F_{syn}})$ also holds. We will show that the values L_0 will also make the formula $(\mathtt{F_{syn}})$ valid. Let $\vec{I}$ be an arbitrary input. We need to show that there are values for $\mathbf{P}, \mathbf{R}$ and O such that $\phi_{\mathtt{lib}}(\mathbf{P}, O) \wedge \psi_{\mathtt{conn}}(\vec{I}, O, \mathbf{P}, \mathbf{R}, L_0)$ holds. Since $\psi_{\mathtt{wfp}}(L_0)$ is true, it follows from Theorem 1 that there is a well-formed program P. Since all components in the library are assumed to be terminating, the program P on input $\vec{I}$ will compute at least one value for each variable in the program. These values will make the formula $\phi_{\mathtt{lib}}(\mathbf{P}, O) \wedge \psi_{\mathtt{conn}}(\vec{I}, O, \mathbf{P}, \mathbf{R}, L_0)$ true. □

The following theorem states the correctness of our constraint solving procedure, and its proof follows from Lemma 1.

THEOREM 3. *Suppose that Procedure* `ExAllSolver` *is called with the input $\psi_{\mathtt{wfp}}(L)$, $\phi_{\mathtt{lib}}(T)$, $\psi_{\mathtt{conn}}(\vec{I}, O, T, L)$, and $\phi_{\mathtt{spec}}(\vec{I}, O)$, where $T := (\mathbf{P} \cup \mathbf{R})$. Then,*

(a) If the procedure terminates with answer `synthesis successful`*, then the synthesis constraint is valid.*

(b) If the procedure terminates with answer `synthesis failed`*, then the synthesis constraint is not valid.*

PROOF: Proof of Part (a): First, since `curr`L is (a part of) a model for the formula in Line 6, the value of `curr`L in the program always satisfies the constraint $\psi_{\mathtt{wfp}}(L)$. Second, the procedure returns `synthesis successful` only when the constraint $\exists \vec{I}, O, T : \phi_{\mathtt{lib}} \wedge \psi_{\mathtt{conn}} \wedge \neg\phi_{\mathtt{spec}}$ is unsatisfiable. This means that the verification constraint, $\forall \vec{I}, O, T : \phi_{\mathtt{lib}} \wedge \psi_{\mathtt{conn}} \Rightarrow \phi_{\mathtt{spec}}$, is valid. This completes the proof of Part (a).

Proof of Part (b): The procedure returns `synthesis failed` only when the constraint $\exists L, O_1, \ldots, O_n, T_1, \ldots, T_n : \psi_{\mathtt{wfp}}(L) \wedge \bigwedge_{\mathbf{P}_i \in \mathcal{S}} (\phi_{\mathtt{lib}}(T_i) \wedge \psi_{\mathtt{conn}}(\vec{I}_i, O_i, T_i, L) \wedge \phi_{\mathtt{spec}}(\vec{I}_i, O_i))$ is unsatisfiable. By Lemma 1, this implies that the verification constraint is unsatisfiable. □

Now we have all the components – synthesis constraint generation (Eq. 4), synthesis constraint solving (Figure 2), and the mapping from values of L to programs (`Lval2Prog`) – to describe our overall approach. Our complete synthesis procedure is described in Figure 3, and its correctness follows from the correctness of the three steps, namely Theorem 1, Theorem 2 and Theorem 3.

7. Experimental Results

In this section, we present an experimental evaluation of our synthesis technique. We also experimentally compare our technique with other existing techniques.

Benchmarks We selected 25 examples, numbered P1-P25, from the book *Hacker's Delight*, commonly referred to as the Bible of

P1(x) : Turn-off rightmost 1 bit. This is the running example in the paper.

o_1:=bvsub (x,1)
res:=bvand (x,o_1)

P2(x) : Test whether an unsigned integer is of the form 2^{n-1}

o_1:=bvadd (x,1)
res:=bvand (x,o_1)

P3(x) : Isolate the rightmost 1-bit

o_1:=bvneg (x)
res:=bvand (x,o_1)

P4(x) : Form a mask that identifies the rightmost 1 bit and trailing 0s

o_1:=bvsub (x,1)
res:=bvxor (x,o_1)

P5(x) : Right propagate rightmost 1-bit

o_1:=bvsub (x,1)
res:=bvor (x,o_1)

P6(x) : Turn on the rightmost 0-bit in a word

o_1:=bvadd (x,1)
res:=bvor (x,o_1)

P7(x) : Isolate the rightmost 0-bit

o_1:=bvnot (x)
o_2:=bvadd (x,1)
res:=bvand (o_1,o_2)

P8(x) : Form a mask that identifies the trailing 0's

o_1:=bvsub (x,1)
o_2:=bvnot (x)
res:=bvand (o_1,o_2)

P9(x) : Absolute Value Function

o_1:=bvshr (x,31)
o_2:=bvxor (x,o_1)
res:=bvsub (o_2,o_1)

P10(x, y) : Test if nlz(x) == nlz(y) where nlz is number of leading zeroes

o_1:=bvand (x,y)
o_2:=bvxor (x,y)
res:=bvule (o_2,o_1)

P11(x, y) : Test if nlz(x) $<$ nlz(y) where nlz is number of leading zeroes

o_1:=bvnot (y)
o_2:=bvand (x,o_1)
res:=bvugt (o_2,y)

P12(x, y) : Test if nlz(x) $<=$ nlz(y) where nlz is number of leading zeroes

o_1:=bvnot (y)
o_2:=bvand (x,o_1)
res:=bvule (o_2,y)

P13(x) : Sign Function

o_1:=bvshr (x,31)
o_2:=bvneg (x)
o_3:=bvshr (o_2,31)
res:=bvor (o_1,o_3)

P14 (x, y) : Floor of average of two integers without over-flowing

o_1:=bvand (x,y)
o_2:=bvxor (x,y)
o_3:=bvshr (o_2,1)
res:=bvadd (o_1,o_3)

P15 (x, y) : Ceil of average of two integers without over-flowing

o_1:=bvor (x,y)
o_2:=bvxor (x,y)
o_3:=bvshr (o_2,1)
res:=bvsub (o_1,o_3)

P16 (x, y) : Compute max of two integers

o_1:=bvxor (x,y)
o_2:=bvneg (bvuge (x,y))
o_3:=bvand (o_1,o_2)
res:=bvxor (o_3,y)

P17(x) : Turn-off the rightmost contiguous string of 1 bits

o_1:=bvsub (x,1)
o_2:=bvor (x,o_1)
o_3:=bvadd (o_2,1)
res:=bvand (o_3,x)

P18(x) : Determine if an integer is a power of 2 or not

o_1:=bvsub (x,1)
o_2:=bvand (o_1,x)
o_3:=bvredor (x)
o_4:=bvredor (o_2)
o_5:=!(o_4)
res:=(o_5 && o_3)

P19(x, m, k) : Exchanging 2 fields A and B of the same register x where m is mask which identifies field B and k is number of bits from end of A to start of B

o_1:=bvshr (x,k)
o_2:=bvxor (x,o_1)
o_3:=bvand (o_2,m)
o_4:=bvshl (o_3,k)
o_5:=bvxor (o_4,o_3)
res:=bvxor (o_5,x)

P20(x) : Next higher unsigned number with same number of 1 bits

o_1:=bvneg (x)
o_2:=bvand (x,o_1)
o_3:=bvadd (x,o_2)
o_4:=bvxor (x,o_2)
o_5:=bvshr (o_4,2)
o_6:=bvdiv (o_5,o_2)
res:=bvor (o_6,o_3)

P21(x, a, b, c) : Cycling through 3 values a,b,c

o_1:=bvneg (bveq (x,c))
o_2:=bvxor (a,c)
o_3:=bvneg (bveq (x,a))
o_4:=bvxor (b,c)
o_5:=bvand (o_1,o_2)
o_6:=bvand (o_3,o_4)
o_7:=bvxor (o_5,o_6)
res:=bvxor (o_7,c)

P22(x) : Compute Parity

o_1:=bvshr (x,1)
o_2:=bvxor (o_1,x)
o_3:=bvshr (o_2,2)
o_4:=bvxor (o_2,o_3)
o_5:=bvand (o_4,0x11111111)
o_6:=bvmul (o_5,0x11111111)
o_7:=bvshr (o_6,28)
res:=bvand (o_7,0x1)

P23(x) : Counting number of bits

o_1:=bvshr (x,1)
o_2:=bvand (o_1,0x55555555)
o_3:=bvsub (x,o_2)
o_4:=bvand (o_3,0x33333333)
o_5:=bvshr (o_3,2)
o_6:=bvand (o_3,0x33333333)
o_7:=bvadd (o_4,o_6)
o_8:=bvshr (o_7,4)
o_9:=bvadd (o_8,o_7)
res:=bvand (o_9,0x0F0F0F0F)

P24(x) : Round up to the next highest power of 2

o_1:=bvsub (x,1)
o_2:=bvshr (o_1,1)
o_3:=bvor (o_1,o_2)
o_4:=bvshr (o_3,2)
o_5:=bvor (o_3,o_4)
o_6:=bvshr (o_5,4)
o_7:=bvor (o_5,o_6)
o_8:=bvshr (o_7,8)
o_9:=bvor (o_7,o_8)
o_{10}:=bvshr (o_9,16)
o_{11}:=bvor (o_9,o_{10})
res:=bvadd (o_{10},1)

P25(x, y) : Compute higher order half of product of x and y

o_1:=bvand (x,0xFFFF)
o_2:=bvshr (x,16)
o_3:=bvand (y,0xFFFF)
o_4:=bvshr (y,16)
o_5:=bvmul (o_1,o_3)
o_6:=bvmul (o_2,o_3)
o_7:=bvmul (o_1,o_4)
o_8:=bvmul (o_2,o_4)
o_9:=bvshr (o_5,16)
o_{10}:=bvadd (o_6,o_9)
o_{11}:=bvand (o_{10},0xFFFF)
o_{12}:=bvshr (o_{10},16)
o_{13}:=bvadd (o_7,o_{11})
o_{14}:=bvshr (o_{13},16)
o_{15}:=bvadd (o_{14},o_{12})
res:=bvadd (o_{15},o_8)

Figure 4. Benchmark Examples. The functions used in the examples have the usual semantics defined in SMTLIB QF_BV logic [2].

```
CompositionSynthesis(φspec, {φi | i = 1,...,N}):
    // Input: φspec: component specification
    //        {φi | i = 1,...,N}: library specification
    // Output: Failure/Program implementing φspec
    Let ∃L∀I⃗,O,P,R : ψwfp ∧ (φlib ∧ ψconn ⇒ φspec)
       be the synthesis constraint.
    L := ExAllSolver(ψwfp, φlib, ψconn, φspec);
    if (L ≠ "synthesis failed") {
       return(Lval2Prog(L));
    } else {
       return("synthesis failed")};
    }
```

Figure 3. Algorithm for the component-based synthesis problem.

Q1(a, b, c): Evaluate $a * h^2 + b * h + c$

```
o1:=a * h
o2:=o1+ b
o3:=o2* h
res:=o3+ c
```

Q2(x): Compute x^{31}

```
o1:=x * x
o2:=o1* o1
o3:=x * o2
o4:=o2* o3
o5:=o4* o2
o6:=o5* o4
res:=o6* o4
```

Figure 5. Representative Arithmetic Benchmark Examples. The arithmetic functions used in the examples have the usual semantics.

bit twiddling hacks [37]. We picked 2 non-bitvector benchmarks Q1-Q2.

The bitvector examples are described in Figure 4. The examples, P1-P25, are numbered in increasing order of complexity: P1 is a 2-line program and P25 is a 16-line program. Example Q1-Q2 in Figure 5 involve arithmetic. For each example, we provided the specification of the desired circuit by specifying the functional relationship between the inputs and output of the circuit. We also provided the set of base components (in the form of their functional specifications) used in these examples.

We chose 25 bitvector programs because they use ingenious little programming tricks that can "sometimes stall programmers for hours or days" and their correctness is "not at all obvious until explained or fathomed" [37]. Furthermore, it allows us to use existing tools based on superoptimization [4, 28] and sketching [32, 33] as a baseline for experimentally evaluating our work. We chose the 2 additional benchmarks to illustrate the need for SMT solvers.

Some programs in our benchmarks require us to also discover constants, such as `0xffff`, that may occur in the program. Our synthesis framework can be easily extended to discovering such constants by introducing a generic base component f_c that simply outputs an arbitrary constant c. Then, in the final synthesis constraint (Equation 4), we existentially quantify over c too.

Implementation and Experimental Setup We implemented our technique in a tool called `Brahma`. It uses Yices 1.0.21 [3] as the underlying SMT solver, which supports reasoning for quantifier-free bitvectors and rational linear arithmetic. For bitvector examples, we synthesized programs to work on bit-vectors of size 32 bits. We used the optimization of synthesizing for increasingly large bitvector lengths until verification succeeded on bitvectors of size 32 bits. We ran our experiments on 8x Intel(R) Xeon(R) CPU 1.86GHz with 4GB of RAM. `Brahma` was able to synthesize the desired programs for each of the benchmark examples. We now present various statistics below.

Benchmark Id	#lines	Brahma Iter.	runtime sec	Sketch runtime sec	ratio Sketch/Brahma	AHA time(sec) [#cand]
1	2	3	4	5	6	7
P1	2	2	3.2	69.8	22	0.1[1]
P2	2	3	3.6	28.9	8	0.1[1]
P3	2	3	1.4	91.8	63	0.1[1]
P4	2	2	3.3	68.4	21	0.1[1]
P5	2	3	2.2	67.9	31	0.1[1]
P6	2	2	2.4	87.0	36	0.1[1]
P7	3	2	1.0	69.6	68	1.7[9]
P8	3	2	1.4	70.0	51	1.4[9]
P9	3	2	5.8	85.1	15	6.5[5]
P10	3	14	76.1	timeout	NA	10.4[1]
P11	3	7	57.1	timeout	NA	9.3[1]
P12	3	9	67.8	timeout	NA	9.5[1]
P13	4	4	6.2	193.7	31	timeout
P14	4	4	59.6	935.3	16	timeout
P15	4	8	118.9	726.5	6	timeout
P16	4	5	62.3	820.8	13	timeout
P17	4	6	78.1	626.1	8	108.6[9]
P18	6	5	45.9	117.2	2	timeout
P19	6	5	34.7	472.8	14	timeout
P20	7	6	108.4	timeout	NA	timeout
P21	8	5	28.3	timeout	NA	timeout
P22	8	8	279.0	timeout	NA	timeout
P23	10	8	1668.0	timeout	NA	timeout
P24	12	9	224.9	timeout	NA	timeout
P25	16	11	2778.7	timeout	NA	timeout
Q1	4	2	0.2	timeout	NA	–
Q2	7	4	295.8	timeout	NA	–

Table 1. Comparing our tool Brahma with Sketch and AHA. Timeout was 1 hour. NA denotes not applicable. The table shows the runtime for `Brahma` (Col. 4), Sketch (Col. 5) and AHA (Col. 7) on 25 benchmarks sorted by lines of code (Col. 2). We also report the number of iterations needed by `Brahma` (Col. 3), ratio of runtimes of `Brahma` and Sketch (Col. 6) and the number of candidate solutions found by AHA (within brackets in Col. 7).

7.1 Performance of Synthesis Algorithm

Table 1 reports some interesting statistics about the synthesis algorithm (presented in Fig. 3). The total time taken by the algorithm (col. 4) on the various examples varies between 1.0 to 2778.7 seconds. We also report the number of iterations taken by the loop (col. 3) inside our constraint solving algorithm in Fig. 2 while performing the refined counterexample guided iterative synthesis. The small number of these iterations (which varies between 2 to 14) illustrates the effectiveness of our technique in using counterexamples for iterative synthesis.

There has been a huge investment in building formal reasoning technology for performing verification of hardware or software systems. In this paper, we show that this verification technology can be lifted to perform synthesis. In that context, the number of iterations required by our technique points out the extra factor of computational resources required to go from verification to synthesis. The largest example in our experimental evaluation took over 45 minutes but it involved only 11 iterations. Hence, the largest SAT problem solved during synthesis is roughly 11 times the size of the SAT problem for verification. Any improvement in satisfiability solvers for verification would also directly increase the scalability of our technique.

No. of	Runtime		Ratio of Runtime	Normalized Constraint Size	
Comps.	Brahma	Sketch	Sketch/Brahma	Brahma	Sketch
1	2	3	4	5	6
2	0.11	0.27	2.45	1	1
3	0.14	0.83	5.93	1.52	5.00
4	0.20	2.09	10.45	1.91	19.85
5	0.25	6.78	27.12	2.36	48.01
6	0.36	19.69	54.70	3.18	129.26
7	0.33	164.80	499.39	3.76	242.04

Table 2. Comparing Brahma and Sketch on running example by increasing the number of components. Constraint size is normalized with respect to the size for 2 components.

7.2 Comparison with Sketch and AHA

We experimentally compared the implementation of our synthesis technique `Brahma` with two other existing tools for synthesis, namely Sketch and AHA.

Sketch The Sketch tool [32, 33] takes as input a *sketch* – a program with holes – and synthesizes programs by correctly filling the holes. Hence, for comparing Sketch with `Brahma`, we expressed the component based design problem as a sketch. There are many different ways of achieving this, and after consultation with the Sketch team, we picked one encoding that produces a sketch that has size linear in the size of the component based synthesis problem. We note that implicit in the sketch is an upper bound on how many times a component can be used. The Sketch tool can not solve the *unbounded* component based synthesis problem. We used version v1.3.0 of Sketch for comparison with our technique.

At a high level, the approach used in Sketch for synthesis is similar to the approach used by `Brahma` – both generate constraints in the first step and then use off-the-shelf solvers to solve these constraints in the second step. However, there are fundamental differences in the constraints generated by the two techniques as well as the algorithms used for solving the constraints.

Sketch internally generates Boolean constraints, which are solved using Boolean satisfiability solvers. `Brahma` generates formulas in a richer logic, which are solved using Satisfiability Modulo Theory (SMT) solvers. As a result, Sketch performs poorly when there is reasoning in a theory, such as linear arithmetic, involved. Sketch times out on the arithmetic examples, Q1 and Q2, whereas `Brahma` easily synthesizes them. (The description of Q1-Q2 may appear to involve nonlinear expressions, but nonlinear reasoning can be eliminated easily and SMT solvers can be used).

Since Sketch is a generic tool, and not tailored for component based synthesis, it uses a suitably general translation of the synthesis problem into a Boolean constraint. Consequently, while the size of the (SMT) constraints generated by `Brahma` is provably quadratic in the number of components, experimental evidence indicates that the size of the constraints generated by Sketch is either exponential or a high degree polynomial in the number of holes or components. To highlight this difference, we used `Brahma` and Sketch to synthesize the running example, but we successively increased the number of components in the library. The time taken by Sketch, reported in Col. 3 of Table 2, appears to scale exponentially, whereas the time taken by `Brahma`, reported in Col. 2 of Table 2, appears to scale non-exponentially as the number of components in the library increases from 2 to 7. The ratio of Sketch runtime to `Brahma` runtime, shown in col. 4 of Table 2, increases from 2 to nearly 500. In Table 2, we also show the normalized size of the constraints generated by both techniques against the number of components (Col. 5 and Col. 6 for `Brahma` and Sketch respectively). We normalize the size of the constraints with respect to the

Benchmark	Verification Runtime(ms)		
	Brahma	Sketch	Ratio
P1	35	18	1.94
P2	11	16	0.69
P3	98	57	1.72
P4	58	31	1.87
P5	59	45	1.31
P6	78	32	2.43
P7	03	11	0.27
P8	78	66	1.18
P9	14	08	1.75
P10	48	NA	NA
P11	29	NA	NA
P12	29	NA	NA
P13	12	16	0.75
P14	69	38	1.82
P15	108	56	1.93
P16	77	41	1.88
P17	109	78	1.40
P18	72	47	1.53
P19	64	52	1.23
P20	96	NA	NA
P21	42	NA	NA
P22	127	NA	NA
P23	103	NA	NA
P24	62	NA	NA
P25	184	NA	NA

Table 3. Comparing the verification times of Brahma and Sketch. Timeout was 1 hour. For the *similar* verification step, Sketch is slower only by an average factor of 1.4 (maximum factor is 2.43) on all examples. NA denotes that Sketch timeouts on that example and hence there is no verification time. For the algorithmically-different synthesis step, as shown in Table 1, Sketch was slower by a factor of 20 on examples on which it terminates – so, even if we normalize for use of different constraint solvers, sketch continues to be an order-of-magnitude slower.

constraint size for 2 components. This ensures a fair comparison of the rate of increase in constraint size with increase in number of components for the two tools irrespective of the absolute size of the generated constraints which may depend on optimizations and preprocessing. Clearly, for both tools, the runtime is correlated with the size of the constraint, but constraints generated by `Brahma` are much more succinct and scale better than Sketch.

The total runtime of Sketch on the bitvector examples is presented in col. 5 in Table 1. Sketch times out on 6 examples and is slower by an average factor of over 20 on other examples (col. 6). One might speculate that the runtime gains of `Brahma` over Sketch arise because `Brahma` uses a different SMT solver. However, this is not true, since `Brahma` and Sketch are experimentally observed to take comparable time for performing the verification step; see Table 3. It follows that the differences are entirely due to the algorithmic improvements in `Brahma`.

AHA The AHA tool [4] is a superoptimizer, endorsed by our benchmark book [37] as *A Hacker's Assistant*. It is based on an idea by Henry Massalin [28], and was made widely available by Granlund and Kenner as the GNU superoptimizer [11]. For experimental comparison, we provided the set of base components as a set of library functions. AHA enumerates all possible composition of these functions to generate candidate programs (in a way described in Figure 1), but it tests the correctness of the candidate programs only on some inputs, and often outputs a number of potential solutions. The solutions produced by AHA must be verified in order to select the right solution. Table 1 lists the total number of solutions generated by AHA (col. 7 within [brackets]) and the total time (col. 7) taken for generation and verification of these solutions. AHA times out on 12 examples. The better performance of Brahma is explained by the fact that Brahma does not perform an exhaustive enumeration of the exponential state space, but relies on a non-trivial strategy of candidate selection and elimination though SMT solving. Thus, we exploit the engineering advances in the underlying SMT solving technology for an efficient search.

7.3 Choice of Multi-set of Base Components

We now discuss the strategy that we used for choosing the multi-set of base components for our benchmark examples. Picking the multi-set of base components is the only step in our approach that currently requires human guidance.

In our experiments, we started with a common multi-set of base components, referred to as *the standard library*, for all benchmarks. The standard library included 12 components, one each for performing standard operations, such as bitwise-and, bitwise-or, bitwise-not, add-one, bitwise-xor, shift-right, comparison, add, and subtract operations. The standard library was sufficient for synthesizing the first 17 benchmark examples. For other examples, the library was augmented with a set of new components suggested by the user. We call this set *the extended library*. (Giving user the option to extend libraries can facilitate hierarchical synthesis – the user can specify a synthesized program as a new component in the extended library.)

For the above-mentioned incremental design technique to be successful, it is pertinent that the synthesis engine not only synthesize correct designs quickly but also report infeasibility of the synthesis problem quickly. In our experiments, we noted that Brahma reports infeasibility of design rather quickly. More specifically, when the standard library was insufficient, Brahma terminated in less than 100 seconds on almost all examples. Hence, *reliance on human guidance can be reduced using a strategy where components are successively added to the library until synthesis is successful.*

Regarding the issue of synthesis of optimal designs – designs that use the minimal number of components – we observed that in experiments, we always got minimal designs. However, this is not a guarantee. Minimality can, however, be ensured by iteratively removing each component as long as a design exists.

8. Related Work

The component-based synthesis problem was recently independently formulated for the case when the components were finite-state machines with outputs (transducers) [25]. Our formulation allows for high-level components whose specifications are given using logical formulas in rich theories. More recently, linear-time programs were synthesized from specification automata recognizing the input/output relation [15].

Counterexample Guided Inductive Synthesis Inductive synthesis refers to the process of generating a system from input-output examples. This process involves using each new input-output example to refine the hypothesis about the system until convergence is reached. Inductive synthesis had its origin in the pioneering work by Gold on language learning [10] and by Shapiro on algorithmic debugging and its application to automated program construction [30]. The inductive approach [9, 29] for synthesizing a program involves *debugging* the program with respect to positive and negative examples until the correct program is synthesized. The negative examples can be counterexamples discovered while trying to prove a program's correctness. Counterexamples have been used in incremental synthesis of programs [17, 33] and switching logic for hybrid systems [20].

We have recently extended the ideas described in this paper to provide an alternative to writing formal specifications for synthesis [19], wherein logical specification of the desired program is replaced by an input-output oracle. This is especially important for the application of software deobfuscation. Quite interestingly, this also obviates the need for having a verifier, albeit at the cost of introducing potential unsoundness in the process. In contrast, the approach in this paper makes use of a verifier and we show how to transform a verifier into a synthesizer. This theme of transforming a verifier into a synthesizer is also present in recent work [34, 36], where the focus is on synthesizing code fragements along with inductive invariants as first-order instantiations of user-provided templates. In contrast, our focus in this paper is restricted to straight-line code fragments, but with the benefit of requiring the user to only provide a multi-set of required components.

Automated API Composition The Jungloid mining tool [26] synthesizes code-fragments (over a given set of API methods annotated with their type signatures) given a simple query that describes the desired code in terms of input and output types. We push this work forward to synthesizing code-fragments that meet a functional specification as opposed to simply type specifications. Typing constraints can also be easily incorporated in our synthesis constraints.

DIPACS [21] compiler incorporates an AI planner to replace a call of a programmer-defined abstract algorithm with a sequence of library calls. It uses programmer-compiler interaction to prune undesirable compositions. DIPACS requires the library (or application) programmer to specify behavior of the library procedures (or, desired effect of the abstract algorithm) using high-level *abstractions*, such as predicates *sorted* and *permutation*. Furthermore, it then needs axioms for these predicates. This is similar to some early work on automatic program synthesis [27, 35], where a theorem prover was used instead of an AI planner. This early work was later extended [8] to perform schema-guided deductive synthesis. Our approach does not use abstract predicates and axioms and relies on the predicates provided by the SMT solver. Our approach can only solve synthesis problems whose formalization can be done in SMT-supported theories, whereas the work on deductive synthesis uses more general-purpose deductive engines, but at the price of requiring axiomatization and performing incomplete reasoning. In our approach, the SMT solver reasons about the implicit theories using decision procedures.

Sketching *Sketching* [31–33] relies on the developer to come up with the algorithmic insight and uses the sketch compiler to fill in missing details using counterexample guided inductive synthesis. In contrast, our tool seeks to discover algorithmic insights, albeit at cost of being more suited for a special class of programs. We chose bitvector programs as our main application domain since coming up with algorithmic insight is the hard part here.

Super-optimizers Superoptimization is the task of finding an optimal code sequence for a straight-line target sequence of instructions, and it is used in optimizing performance-critical inner loops. One approach to superoptimization has been to simply enumerate sequences of increasing length or cost, testing each for equality with the target specification [28]. Another approach has been to constrain the search space to a set of equality-preserving transformations expressed by the system designer [22] and then select the one with the lowest cost. Recent work has used superoptimization [5, 6] to automatically generate general purpose peephole optimizers by optimizing a small set of instructions in the code. In these approaches, the exhaustive state space search is quite expensive making them amenable to only discovering optimal instructions of length four or less in reasonable amount of time.

Use of satisfiability solving for synthesis SAT solvers have been used for synthesis previously: Massalin [28] used them for verification of candidate synthesized programs and Sketching [33] used them to implement the inductive program synthesis technique. We use SMT solving to implement our algorithm for solving synthesis constraints. This makes our synthesis approach more efficient as well as more general.

9. Conclusion and Future Work

Program synthesis has the potential to revolutionize the process of system development. Up until recently, automating synthesis of non-trivial programs has mostly been impractical. However, huge engineering advances in logical reasoning have significantly changed the landscape. These advances have enabled verification of large systems, and in this paper, we show that they can also be used to synthesize 10-20 line programs with some help from the user and using computational resources that are within one order of magnitude of the resources required for verification.

We have applied our component-based synthesis methodology to synthesis of bit-vector circuits. However, our solution applies more generally to other naturally resource-constrained domains, such as loop-free assembly of physical components (e.g., FPGA circuits, or even some physical/chemical/biological systems). In such situations, the user naturally starts out with resource constraints that provide a good over-approximation of the multi-set of available components.

We also foresee generalizations of our formulation of the component-based synthesis problem. This includes synthesizing programs with richer control structure, such as loops and recursion, and synthesizing from partial specifications. There is also potential for using richer theories, and limited first-order reasoning that is supported by modern SMT solvers, to synthesize from components whose specifications use richer logical formulas. A followup problem worth investigating is to approximate some functionality using a given multi-set of components. We believe that our paper lays down the foundation for investigating such a line of work.

Acknowledgment We thank Viktor Kuncak, Rishabh Singh and other members of the Sketch team, and the anonymous reviewers for their help and valuable feedback.

References

[1] Satisfiability modulo theories competition (smt-comp). `http://www.smtcomp.org/2009/index.shtml`.

[2] SMTLIB: Satisfiability modulo theories lib. `http://smtlib.org`.

[3] Yices: An SMT solver. `http://yices.csl.sri.com`.

[4] The AHA! (A Hacker's Assistant) Superoptimizer, 2008. Download: `http://www.hackersdelight.org/aha.zip`, Documentation: `http://www.hackersdelight.org/aha/aha.pdf`.

[5] S. Bansal and A. Aiken. Automatic generation of peephole superoptimizers. In *ASPLOS*, 2006.

[6] S. Bansal and A. Aiken. Binary translation using peephole superoptimizers. In *OSDI*, 2008.

[7] R. Cytron, J. Ferrante, B. K. Rosen, M. N. Wegman, and F. K. Zadeck. An efficient method of computing static single assignment form. In *POPL*, 1989.

[8] B. Fischer and J. Schumann. Autobayes: A system for generating data analysis programs from statistical models. *J. Funct. Program.*, 13(3):483–508, 2003.

[9] P. Flener and L. Popelmnsky. On the use of inductive reasoning in program synthesis: Prejudice and prospects. In *LOBSTR*. 1994.

[10] E. M. Gold. Language identification in the limit. *Information and Control*, 10(5):447–474, 1967.

[11] T. Granlund and R. Kenner. Eliminating branches using a superoptimizer and In *PLDI*, 1992.

[12] S. Gulwani. Dimensions in program synthesis. In *PPDP*, pages 13–24. ACM, 2010.

[13] S. Gulwani. Automating string processing in spreadsheets using input-output examples. In *POPL*, 2011.

[14] S. Gulwani, V. Korthikanti, and A. Tiwari. Synthesizing geometry constructions. In *PLDI*, 2011.

[15] J. Hamza, B. Jobstmann, and V. Kuncak. Synthesis for regular specifications over unbounded domains. In *FMCAD*, 2010.

[16] B. Harris and S. Gulwani. Spreadsheet table transformations from examples. In *PLDI*, 2011.

[17] S. Itzhaky, S. Gulwani, N. Immerman, and M. Sagiv. A simple inductive synthesis methodology and its applications. In *OOPSLA*, pages 36–46, 2010.

[18] R. N. Jackiw and W. F. Finzer. The geometer's sketchpad: programming by geometry. In *Watch what I do: programming by demonstration*, pages 293–307. MIT Press, 1993.

[19] S. Jha, S. Gulwani, S. Seshia, and A. Tiwari. Oracle-guided component-based program synthesis. In *ICSE*, pages 215–224, 2010.

[20] S. Jha, S. Gulwani, S. Seshia, and A. Tiwari. Synthesizing switching logic for safety and dwell-time requirements. In *Proc. 1st ACM/IEEE Intl. Conf. on Cyber-Physical Systems, ICCPS*, pages 22–31, 2010.

[21] T. A. Johnson and R. Eigenmann. Context-sensitive domain-independent algorithm composition and selection. In *PLDI*, 2006.

[22] R. Joshi, G. Nelson, and K. H. Randall. Denali: A goal-directed superoptimizer. In *PLDI*, 2002.

[23] D. E. Knuth. The art of computer programming. `http://www-cs-faculty.stanford.edu/~knuth/taocp.html`.

[24] T. A. Lau, P. Domingos, and D. S. Weld. Version space algebra and its application to programming by demonstration. In *ICML*, 2000.

[25] Y. Lustig and M. Vardi. Synthesis from component libraries. In *Proc. FoSSaCS*, pages 395–409, 2009.

[26] D. Mandelin, L. Xu, R. Bodík, and D. Kimelman. Jungloid mining: helping to navigate the API jungle. In *PLDI*, pages 48–61, 2005.

[27] Z. Manna and R. Waldinger. A deductive approach to program synthesis. *ACM TOPLAS*, 2(1):90–121, 1980.

[28] H. Massalin. Superoptimizer - a look at the smallest program. In *ASPLOS*, pages 122–126, 1987.

[29] S. Muggleton, editor. *Inductive Logic Programming*, volume 38 of *The APIC Series*. Academic Press, 1992.

[30] E. Y. Shapiro. *Algorithmic Program DeBugging*. MIT Press, Cambridge, MA, USA, 1983.

[31] A. Solar-Lezama, G. Arnold, L. Tancau, R. Bodík, V. A. Saraswat, and S. A. Seshia. Sketching stencils. In *PLDI*, pages 167–178, 2007.

[32] A. Solar-Lezama, R. Rabbah, R. Bodík, and K. Ebcioglu. Programming by sketching for bit-streaming programs. In *PLDI*, 2005.

[33] A. Solar-Lezama, L. Tancau, R. Bodík, S. Seshia, and V. Saraswat. Combinatorial sketching for finite programs. In *ASPLOS*, 2006.

[34] S. Srivastava, S. Gulwani, and J. S. Foster. From program verification to program synthesis. In *POPL*, pages 313–326, 2010.

[35] M. Stickel, R. Waldinger, M. Lowry, T. Pressburger, and I. Underwood. Deductive composition of astro. software from subroutine libraries. In *CADE*, '94.

[36] A. Taly, S. Gulwani, and A. Tiwari. Synthesizing switching logic using constraint solving. In *VMCAI*, pages 305–319. Springer, 2009.

[37] H. S. Warren. *Hacker's Delight*. Addison-Wesley, '02.

[38] I. H. Witten and D. Mo. TELS: learning text editing tasks from examples. In *Watch what I do: programming by demonstration*, pages 293–307. MIT Press, Cambridge, MA, USA, 1993.

Generalized Just-In-Time Trace Compilation using a Parallel Task Farm in a Dynamic Binary Translator

Igor Böhm Tobias J.K. Edler von Koch Stephen Kyle Björn Franke Nigel Topham

Institute for Computing Systems Architecture
School of Informatics, University of Edinburgh
Informatics Forum, 10 Crichton Street, Edinburgh, EH8 9AB, United Kingdom

I.Bohm@sms.ed.ac.uk, T.J.K.Edler-Von-Koch@sms.ed.ac.uk, S.C.Kyle@sms.ed.ac.uk, bfranke@inf.ed.ac.uk, npt@inf.ed.ac.uk

Abstract

Dynamic Binary Translation (DBT) is the key technology behind cross-platform virtualization and allows software compiled for one Instruction Set Architecture (ISA) to be executed on a processor supporting a different ISA. Under the hood, DBT is typically implemented using Just-In-Time (JIT) compilation of frequently executed program regions, also called *traces*. The main challenge is translating frequently executed program regions as fast as possible into highly efficient native code. As time for JIT compilation adds to the overall execution time, the JIT compiler is often decoupled and operates in a separate thread independent from the main simulation loop to reduce the overhead of JIT compilation. In this paper we present *two* innovative contributions. The first contribution is a *generalized* trace compilation approach that considers *all* frequently executed paths in a program for JIT compilation, as opposed to previous approaches where trace compilation is restricted to paths through loops. The second contribution reduces JIT compilation cost by compiling several hot traces in a concurrent task farm. Altogether we combine generalized light-weight tracing, large translation units, parallel JIT compilation and dynamic work scheduling to ensure timely and efficient processing of hot traces. We have evaluated our industry-strength, LLVM-based parallel DBT implementing the ARCompact ISA against three benchmark suites (EEMBC, BIOPERF and SPEC CPU2006) and demonstrate speedups of up to 2.08 on a standard quad-core Intel Xeon machine. Across short- and long-running benchmarks our scheme is robust and never results in a slowdown. In fact, using four processors total execution time can be reduced by on average 11.5% over state-of-the-art decoupled, parallel (or *asynchronous*) JIT compilation.

Categories and Subject Descriptors D.3.4 [*Programming Languages*]: Processors—Incremental Compilers

General Terms Design, experimentation, measurement, performance

Keywords Dynamic binary translation, just-in-time compilation, parallelization, task farm, dynamic work scheduling

1. Introduction

DBT is a widely used technology that makes it possible to run code compiled for a target platform on a host platform with a different ISA. With DBT, machine instructions of a program for the target platform are translated to machine instructions for the host platform during the execution of the program. Among the main uses of DBT are *cross-platform virtualization* for the migration of legacy applications to different hardware platforms (e.g. DEC FX!32 [9], Apple Rosetta and IBM POWERVM LX86 [32] both based on Transitive's QuickTransit, or HP ARIES [44]) and the provision of *virtual platforms* for convenient software development for embedded systems (e.g. Virtual Prototype by Synopsys). Other current and emerging uses of DBT include, but are not limited to, generation of cycle-accurate architecture simulators [6, 12], dynamic instrumentation [17], program analysis, cache modeling, and workload characterization [23], software security [42], and transparent software support for heterogeneous embedded platforms [11].

Efficient DBT heavily relies on Just-in-Time (JIT) compilation for the translation of target machine instructions to host machine instructions. Although JIT compiled code generally runs much faster than interpreted code, JIT compilation incurs an additional overhead. For this reason, only the most frequently executed code regions are translated to native code whereas less frequently executed code is still interpreted. Using a single-threaded execution model, the interpreter pauses until the JIT compiler has translated its assigned code block and the generated native code is executed directly. However, it has been noted earlier [1, 16, 20] that program execution does not need to be paused to permit compilation, as a JIT compiler can operate in a separate thread while the program executes concurrently. This *decoupled* or *asynchronous* execution of the JIT compiler increases complexity of the DBT, but is very effective in hiding the compilation latency – especially if the JIT compiler can run on a separate processor.

Our main contribution is to demonstrate how to effectively reduce dynamic compilation overhead and speedup execution by doing *parallel* JIT compilation, exploiting the broad proliferation of multi-core processors. The key idea is to detect *independent*, large translation units in execution traces and to *farm out* work to *multiple, concurrent* JIT compilation workers. To ensure that the latest and most frequently executed code traces are compiled first, we apply a priority queue based dynamic work scheduling strategy where the most recent, hottest traces are given highest priority.

We have integrated this novel, concurrent JIT compilation methodology into our LLVM-based state-of-the-art ARCSIM [19, 38] DBT implementing the ARCompact ISA and evaluated its performance using three benchmark suites: EEMBC, BIOPERF and

SPEC CPU2006. We demonstrate that our parallel approach yields an average speedup of 1.17 across all 61 benchmarks – and up to 2.08 for individual benchmarks – over decoupled JIT compilation using only a single compilation worker thread on a standard quad-core Intel Xeon host platform. At the same time our scheme is robust and never results in a slowdown even for very short- and long-running applications.

1.1 Trace-based JIT Compilation

Before we take a more detailed look at our approach to generalization of JIT trace compilation using a parallel task farm, we provide a comparison of state-of-the-art trace-based JIT compilation approaches to highlight our key concepts (see Figure 1).

Trace-based JIT compilation systems start executing in interpreted mode until a special structure (e.g. loop header, method entry) is detected. This causes the system to switch from interpreted mode to trace mode. In trace mode executed paths within that particular structure are recorded to form a trace data structure. Once the traced code region's execution count reaches a threshold, the recorded trace is compiled just-in-time and control flow is diverted from the interpreter to the faster, native code. In general, trace-based JIT compilation approaches can be categorized based on the following criteria:

- *Trace Boundaries* - One popular [14–16, 26, 27, 29, 37] approach is to only consider paths within natural loops (①②③ in Figure 1). However, there are also paths outside of loops (e.g. paths crossing method or function boundaries, IRQ handlers, irreducible loops) which are executed frequently enough to justify their compilation to machine code. In this work we propose a *generalized* approach to tracing based on traced control-flow-graphs (CFG) of basic blocks, that can start and end almost anywhere in the program (④ in Figure 1). As a result we can discover more hot traces and capture larger regions of frequently executed code than just loop bodies.
- JIT *Compilation Strategy* - Some state-of-the-art JIT trace compilers [26, 27, 37] are sequential and wait for JIT compilation of a trace to finish before continuing execution (① in Figure 1). An early approach to parallel JIT compilation [14] proposed to split trace compilation into multiple, parallel pipeline stages operating at instruction granularity (② in Figure 1). While the compiler pipeline can – in principle – be parallelized, this approach is fundamentally flawed as execution is stopped until compilation of a complete trace is finished. This results in consistent slowdowns over all benchmarks in [14]. Synchronization of up to 19 pipeline stages for every compiled instruction adds significantly to the overall compilation time while no new translation units are discovered. The HOTSPOT JVM [29] and [16] implement a concurrent JIT compilation strategy by running the JIT compiler in *one* separate helper thread whilst the master thread continues to interpret code (③ in Figure 1). We build on this approach and extend it to run *several* JIT compilers in a parallel task farm whilst execution continues. We do this to further hide JIT compilation cost and switch to native execution of hot traces even sooner and for longer (④ in Figure 1) than previous approaches.

The objective of our trace-based JIT compilation strategy ④ outlined in Figure 1 is translating frequently executed program regions into native code faster when compared to e.g. ①②③ [14–16, 26, 27, 29, 37]. Figure 1 also illustrates that task parallel JIT compilation ④ reduces the time until native code execution starts in comparison to current approaches ①②③.

Our generalized approach to tracing enables us to start tracing right from the first instruction, avoiding a period of interpretation until specific structures (e.g. loop headers) are encountered. Consequently we can find more opportunities for JIT compilation (i.e. hot traces) earlier. Being able to discover more hot traces that can be compiled independently, we take the idea of decoupled JIT compilation a step further, and propose a truly parallel and scalable JIT compilation scheme based on the parallel task farm design pattern.

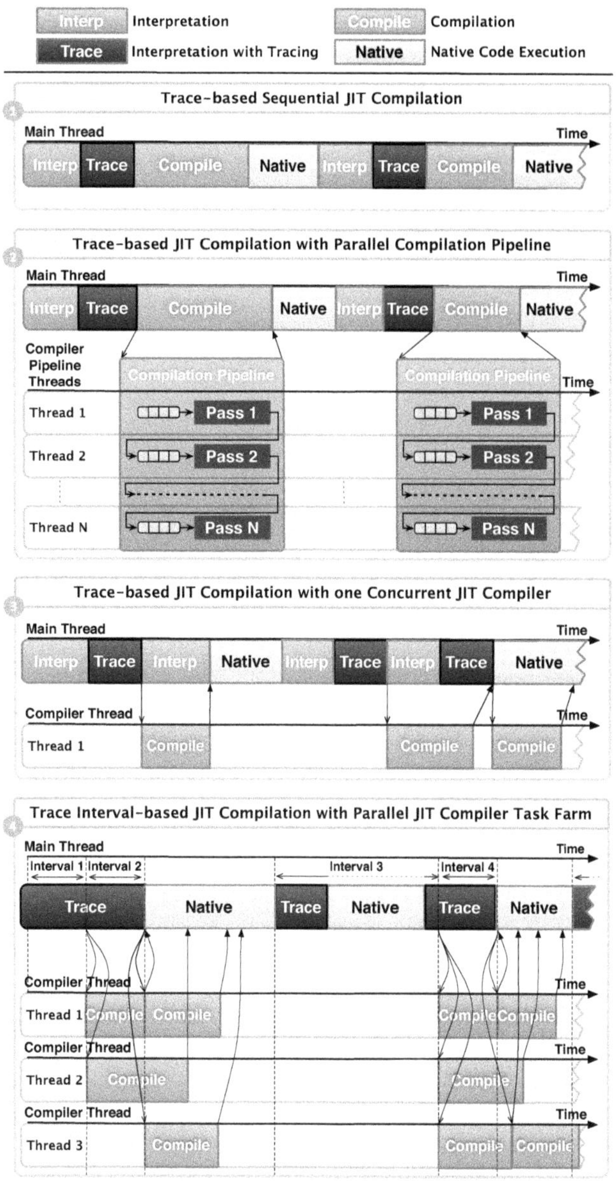

Figure 1. Comparison of trace-based JIT compilation approaches: ① sequential approach [15, 26, 27, 37], ② parallel compilation pipeline [14], ③ decoupled JIT compilation using *one* thread [16, 29]. Finally, ④ depicts our parallel JIT compilation task farm.

1.2 Motivating Example

Consider the full-system simulation of a Linux OS configured and built for the ARC 700 processor family (RISC ISA). On a standard quad-core Intel Xeon machine we simulate the complete boot-up sequence, the automated execution of a set of commands simulating interactive user input at the console, followed by the full shut-down sequence. This example includes rare events such as boot-up and shut-down comparable to the initialization phase in an application,

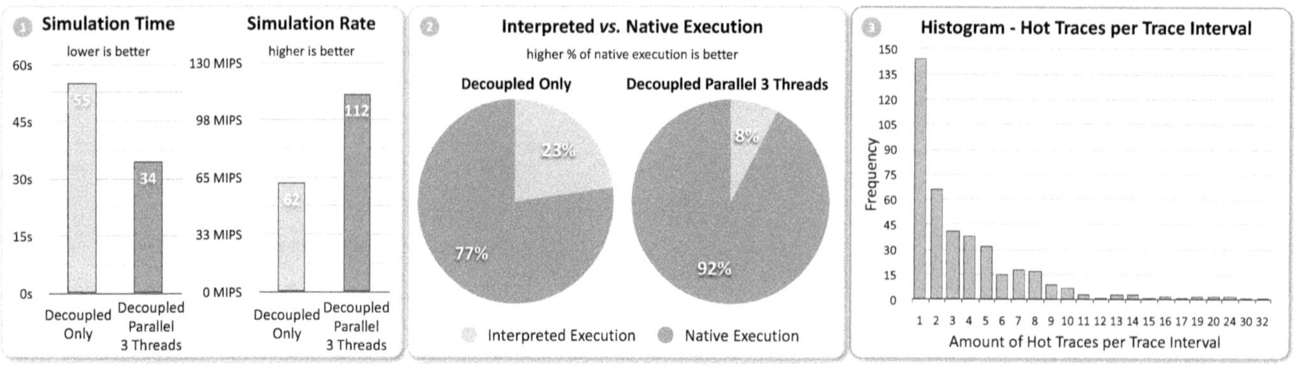

Figure 2. Full-system Linux simulation benchmark - comparison of ① simulation *time* in seconds, *rate* in MIPS, and ② interpreted *vs.* natively executed instructions in %, between *decoupled only* and *decoupled parallel* JIT compilation using three JIT compilation worker threads. Histogram ③ demonstrates how often more than one *hot* trace per trace interval is found.

but it also includes very frequent events occurring after the boot-up sequence during interactive user mode. In a full-system OS simulation there are frequent calls to interrupt service routines that must be simulated. Our generalized tracing approach can easily identify frequent traces including interrupt service routines that would otherwise be missed if we would restrict tracing to loop or function boundaries.

Our dynamic binary translator speeds up the simulation by identifying and translating hot traces to native `x86` code during simulation using the sequence of steps illustrated in Figure 3. As simulation runs in parallel to JIT compilation we continue to discover and dispatch more hot traces to the JIT compiler. In fact, it is possible that JIT compilation of the previous trace has not yet been completed by the time new traces are discovered. In this case, work is distributed over several JIT compilation threads. To ensure that the most *profitable* traces are compiled first, we have implemented a dynamic work scheduling strategy that dynamically prioritizes compilation tasks according to their *heat* and *recency*.

For the purpose of this motivating example we compare a simulation using only one decoupled JIT compiler thread (current state-of-the-art) with a simulation using multiple decoupled JIT compiler threads in parallel (see ④ in Figure 1). In Chart ① of Figure 2 we compare the overall simulation time in seconds and the simulation rate in MIPS for both approaches. Our new approach using three decoupled JIT compilers in parallel completes the previously outlined sample application 21 seconds earlier. This results in an improvement of 38% and, thus, achieves a speedup of **1.6** when compared to using only one decoupled JIT compiler. The overall simulation rate (in MIPS) improves from 62 to 112 MIPS by using our new approach. As several JIT compilers work on hot traces in parallel, native translations are available much earlier than using a single decoupled JIT compiler (see ③ in Figure 1), leading to a substantial increase from 77% to 92% of natively executed target instructions (see Chart ② of Figure 2).

The obvious question to ask is where does the speedup come from? Histogram ③ in Figure 2 shows how often a certain amount of frequently executed traces is found per trace interval. The fact that 65% of the time there are at least two or more hot traces discovered per interval clearly demonstrates the benefits of having more than one JIT compiler available on today's multicore machines. Even if only one hot trace per interval is discovered, the JIT compilation of the previous hot trace might not have finished. Having several JIT compilers that can already start working on the newly discovered hot traces before others have finished helps to effectively hide most of the JIT compilation latency (see Box ① in Figure 5).

1.3 Contributions

Among the contributions of this paper are:

1. The introduction of a light-weight and generalized JIT trace compilation approach considering frequently executed paths (i.e. hot traces) that can start and end almost anywhere in a program and are not restricted to loop or function boundaries,
2. the introduction of an innovative *parallel task farming* strategy for truly concurrent JIT compilation of hot traces,
3. the development of *dynamic work scheduling* and *adaptive hotspot threshold selection* approaches that give priority to the most recent, hottest traces in order to reduce time spent in interpreted simulation mode, and
4. an extensive evaluation of our LLVM-based DBT targeting the ARCompact ISA using three full benchmark suites, EEMBC, BIOPERF and SPEC CPU2006.

1.4 Overview

The remainder of this paper is structured as follows. In section 2 we give an overview of the LLVM-based ARCSIM dynamic binary translator. This is followed by a presentation of our tracing approach and parallel JIT compilation scheme in section 3. We then explain the evaluation methodology and show our empirical results in section 4. Related work is discussed in section 5 and, finally, we summarize and conclude in section 6.

2. Background

In our work we extended our DBT ARCSIM, a target adaptable simulator with extensive support of the ARCompact ISA. It is a full-system simulator, implementing the processor, its memory sub-system (including MMU), and sufficient interrupt-driven peripherals to simulate the boot-up and interactive operation of a complete Linux-based system. The DBT has a very fast and highly-optimized interpreted simulation mode [38]. By using a trace-based JIT compiler to translate frequently interpreted instructions into native code, our DBT is capable of simulating applications at speeds approaching or even exceeding that of a silicon ASIP whilst faithfully modeling the processor's architectural state [38].

The JIT compiler is based on release 2.7 of the LLVM compiler infrastructure [22] and executes in a concurrent thread to the main interpretation loop, reducing the overhead caused by JIT compilation [16, 29]. The LLVM JIT compilation engine implementation provides a mature and competitive JIT compilation environment

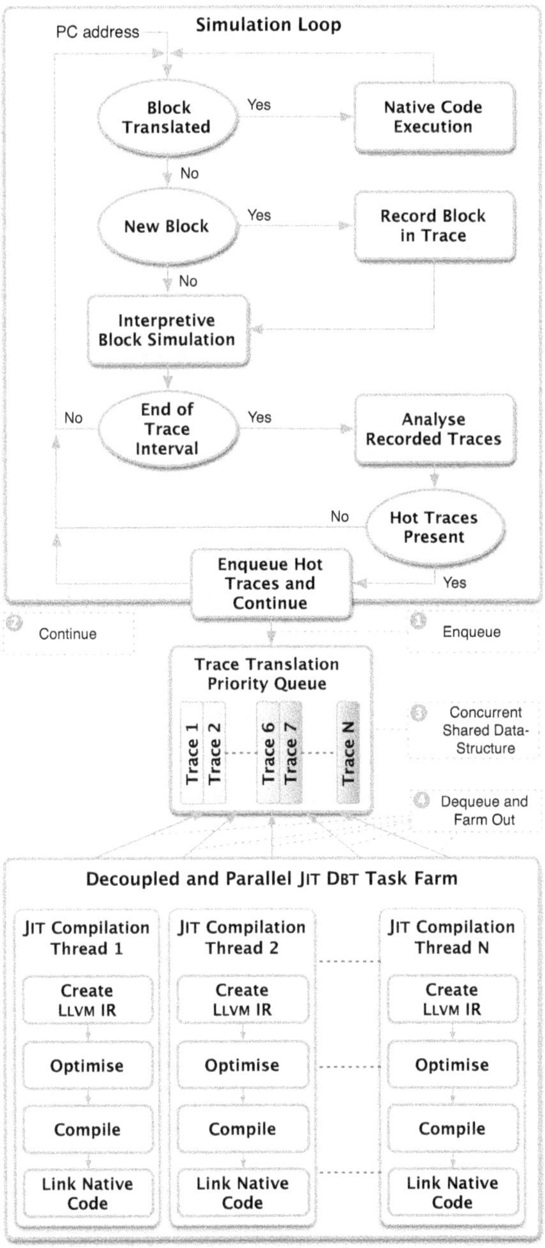

Figure 3. Trace-based JIT DBT flow showing main simulation loop at the top, priority queue scheduling in the middle, and parallel task farm at the bottom.

used in many major products by companies such as Apple, Adobe, Nvidia, and Sony, to name just a few [36].

State-of-the-art trace-based JIT compilers typically use natural loops as boundaries for traces, resulting in relatively small units of translation [14–16, 26, 27, 29, 37]. Our DBT deliberately considers larger traces by allowing traces to start and end almost anywhere in a program. This approach is comparable to the techniques evaluated in [3, 19] and has the benefit of providing greater scope for optimizations to the JIT compiler as it can operate on larger traces. Furthermore our DBT includes various software caches [3, 38] (e.g. decode cache to avoid re-decoding recently decoded instructions, translation cache to improve lookup times for locations of native code) to improve simulation speed.

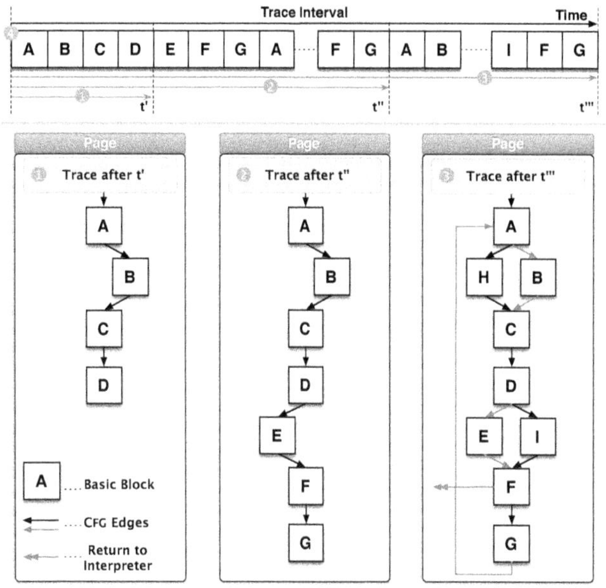

Figure 4. Incremental ①②③ trace construction from sequence of interpreted basic blocks ④ during one trace interval.

3. Methodology

Our approach to parallel and decoupled JIT compilation in a dynamic binary translator significantly speeds up execution whilst maintaining full architectural observability of the target architecture. We use a light-weight approach to discover and construct traces eligible for JIT compilation. A trace reflects the control flow exhibited by the source program at run-time. Newly discovered hot traces are then translated using multiple decoupled JIT compiler threads in parallel. Decoupling the simulation (i.e. interpretation) loop from JIT compilation prevents any slowdown incurred by JIT compilation as the simulation continues while hot traces are being translated [16, 34]. By adding more JIT compilation threads, working on independent hot traces, JIT compilation time is further reduced resulting in increased simulation speed as native code becomes available earlier.

In the following sections we outline our trace generation and hotspot detection technique and explain why this technique discovers more relevant hot traces for JIT compilation than previous approaches [14–16, 26, 27, 29, 37]. We also discuss the decoupling and parallelization of JIT compilation and demonstrate the importance of scheduling hot traces for JIT compilation. The key idea behind our scheduling scheme is to consider heat and recency of traces in order to prioritize hot traces that are being simulated right now and to JIT compile them first.

3.1 Trace Construction and Hotspot Detection

Interpreted simulation time is partitioned into *trace intervals* (see Figures 3, 4 and 5) whose *length* is determined by a user-defined number of interpreted instructions. After each trace interval, the hottest recorded traces are dispatched to a priority queue for JIT compilation before the simulation loop continues. Decoupled from this simulation loop, JIT compilation workers dequeue and compile the dispatched traces. The *heat* of a trace is defined as the sum of the execution frequencies of its constituent basic blocks.

Our DBT must maintain an accurate memory model (see Section 2) to preserve full architectural observability. This means that traces generated during a trace interval are separated at page boundaries, where a page can contain up to 8 KB of target instructions. For

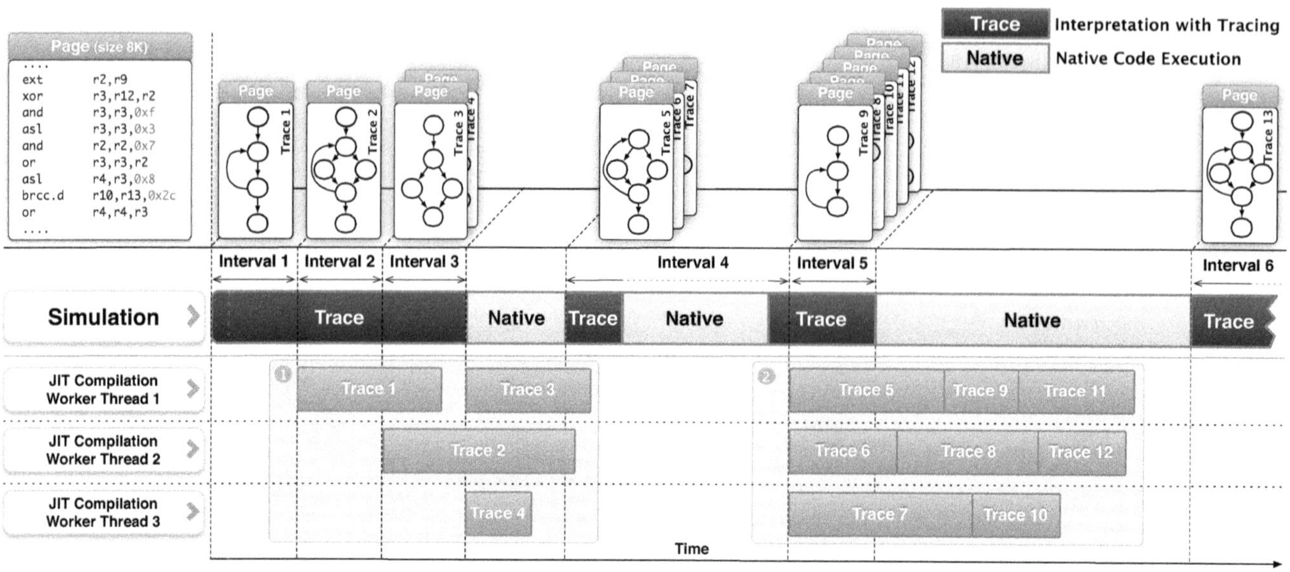

Figure 5. Concurrent JIT compilation of hot traces - Box ② demonstrates how we exploit *task parallelism* by JIT compiling independent hot traces in parallel. Box ① shows how several concurrent JIT compilation threads can effectively hide most of the JIT compilation latency by overlapping compilation of hot traces.

each page a trace recording interpreted basic blocks contained in that page is maintained (see Figure 5). Tracing is light-weight because we only record basic block entry points (i.e. memory addresses) as nodes, and pairs of source and target entry points as edges in the per-page CFG traces. Figure 4 shows the incremental trace construction for interpreted basic blocks within one page during one trace interval and highlights our trace boundary or unit of compilation, namely a trace within a page of target memory instructions.

Typically JIT compilation schemes [14–16, 26, 27, 29, 37] are based on compilation units reaching threshold frequencies of execution to determine when to trigger compilation. Our approach is based around the concept of trace intervals during which traces are recorded and execution frequencies are maintained. At the end of a trace interval we analyze generated traces for each page that has been touched during that interval and dispatch frequently executed traces to a trace translation priority queue (see ①②③ in Figure 3). We decided to use an interval based scheme because we found it generates more uniformly sized compilation units, resulting in better and more predictable load balance between compilation and execution. Our trace intervals are somewhat related to the concept of bounded history buffers in DYNAMO [3] but impose fewer restrictions on their use.

3.2 Parallel JIT Compilation

Our main contribution is the demonstration, through practical implementation, of the effectiveness of a parallel multi-threaded JIT compilation task farm based on release 2.7 of the LLVM [22] compiler infrastructure. By parallelizing JIT compilation we effectively hide JIT compilation latency and exploit the available parallelism exposed by our generalized trace construction scheme.

A concurrent trace translation priority queue acts as the main interface between the simulation loop and multiple JIT compilation workers (see ③ and ④ in Figure 3). Each JIT compilation worker thread dequeues a trace and generates a corresponding LLVM intermediate representation (IR). Subsequently, a sequence of standard LLVM optimization passes is applied to optimize the generated LLVM-IR. We use LLVM's `ExecutionEngine` to JIT-compile and link the generated LLVM-IR code. Each JIT compilation worker thread receives its own private `ExecutionEngine` instance upon thread creation.

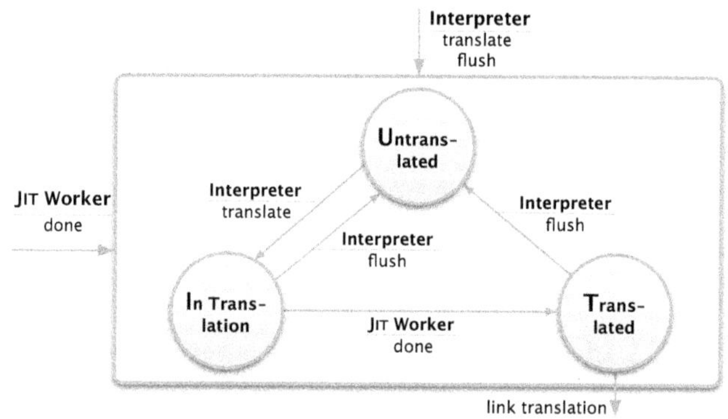

Figure 6. Trace translation state variable transitions.

In our parallel trace-based JIT compiler the interpreter uses a *translation state variable* to mark unseen traces for JIT compilation and to determine if a native translation for a trace already exists. While traces are JIT compiled, the interpreter continues to execute the program. As soon as JIT compilation of a trace is finished, the JIT compilation worker immediately modifies its translation state variable such that the interpreter is notified about its availability. Thus, a trace can be in one of the following three states:

- UNTRANSLATED - When a trace is seen for the first time, its state is set to *untranslated* by the interpreter.
- IN TRANSLATION - When a trace is dispatched for JIT compilation the interpreter changes its state from *untranslated* to *in translation*.
- TRANSLATED - When a JIT compilation worker is finished with the translation of a trace it changes its state from *in translation* to *translated*.

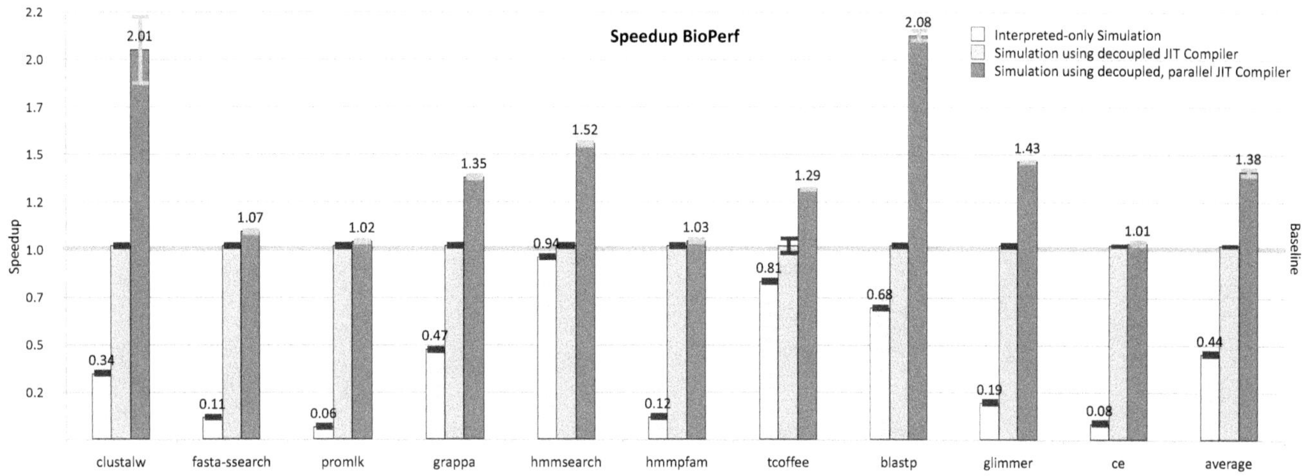

Figure 7. Speedups using the BioPerf benchmark suite comparing (a) interpreted-only simulation, (b) simulation using a decoupled JIT compiler, and (c) simulation using our novel, parallel JIT compiler with three JIT compilation worker threads including dynamic work scheduling.

This particular use of a state variable indicating the translation state of a trace allows for *lock-free* synchronization between JIT compilation threads and the simulation loop (see Figure 6). This approach is somewhat similar to the compiled state variable concept implemented in [16].

3.3 Dynamic Work Scheduling

In any kind of JIT compilation environment it is paramount to translate hot code regions as fast as possible into highly efficient native code. Thus having discovered multiple traces across several trace intervals we would like to JIT compile the most recently and frequently executed traces first.

To efficiently implement a dynamic work scheduling scheme based on both recency and frequency of interpreted traces, we have chosen a priority queue as an abstract data type using a binary heap as the backbone data-structure. We chose a binary heap because of its worst case complexity of $O(log(n))$ for inserts and removals. Our sorting criteria insert the most frequently executed trace from the most recent trace interval at the front of the priority queue.

3.4 Adaptive Hotspot Threshold Selection

It is possible that our trace-selection and dispatch system can produce more tasks than the JIT workers can reasonably handle. The aforementioned dynamic work scheduling mitigates this problem by ensuring that the hottest and most recent traces are serviced first, leaving relatively colder and older tasks waiting until the important work has been completed. However, it would also be beneficial to reduce the number of tasks actually being dispatched to the trace translation queue in the event of an overloaded JIT compilation task farm.

In order to avoid large amounts of waiting trace translation tasks, we implemented an adaptive hotspot threshold scheme. Initially, the hotspot threshold is set to a constant value based on the number of JIT workers available – as the number of workers increases, the threshold can be set more aggressively. This threshold is then adjusted based on the priority queue's current length, where a longer queue raises the threshold at which new potential traces are considered to be hot enough. The threshold can either be tied directly to the length of the queue, or a certain queue length can trigger an increase in the hotspot threshold.

4. Empirical Evaluation

We have evaluated our parallel trace-based just-in-time compilation and dynamic work scheduling approach across more than 60 industry standard benchmarks, including BioPerf, Spec, EEMBC, and CoreMark, from various domains. In this section we describe our experimental setup and methodology before we present and discuss our results.

4.1 Evaluation Methodology

We have evaluated our parallel trace-based JIT compilation approach using the BioPerf benchmark suite that comprises a comprehensive set of computationally-intensive life science applications [2]. It is well suited for evaluating our parallel trace-based JIT compiler as it exhibits many different potential hotspots per application for most of its benchmarks. We also used the industry standard EEMBC 1.1, and CoreMark [35] embedded benchmark suites. These benchmarks represent small and relatively short running applications with complex algorithmic kernels. An evaluation using Spec Cpu 2006 benchmarks [18] is included as they are widely used and considered to be representative of a broad spectrum of application domains.

The BioPerf benchmarks were run with "class-A" input datasets available from the BioPerf web site. The EEMBC 1.1 benchmarks were run for the default number of iterations and CoreMark was run for 1000 iterations. For practical reasons we used the largest possible data set for each of the Spec Cpu 2006 benchmarks such that simulation time does not become excessive.

Our main focus has been on simulation speedup by reducing the overall simulation time. Therefore we have measured the elapsed real time between invocation and termination of our simulator using the Unix `time` command. We used the average elapsed wall clock time across 10 runs for each benchmark and configuration (i.e. interpreted-only, decoupled, decoupled parallel) in order to calculate speedups. Additionally, we provide error bars for each benchmark result denoting the standard deviation to show how much variation there is between different program runs.

We use a strong and competitive baseline for our comparisons, namely a decoupled trace-based JIT compiler using one asynchronous thread for JIT compilation [16]. Relative to that baseline we plot the speedups achieved by our parallel trace-based JIT compiler using three asynchronous JIT compilation threads. Fur-

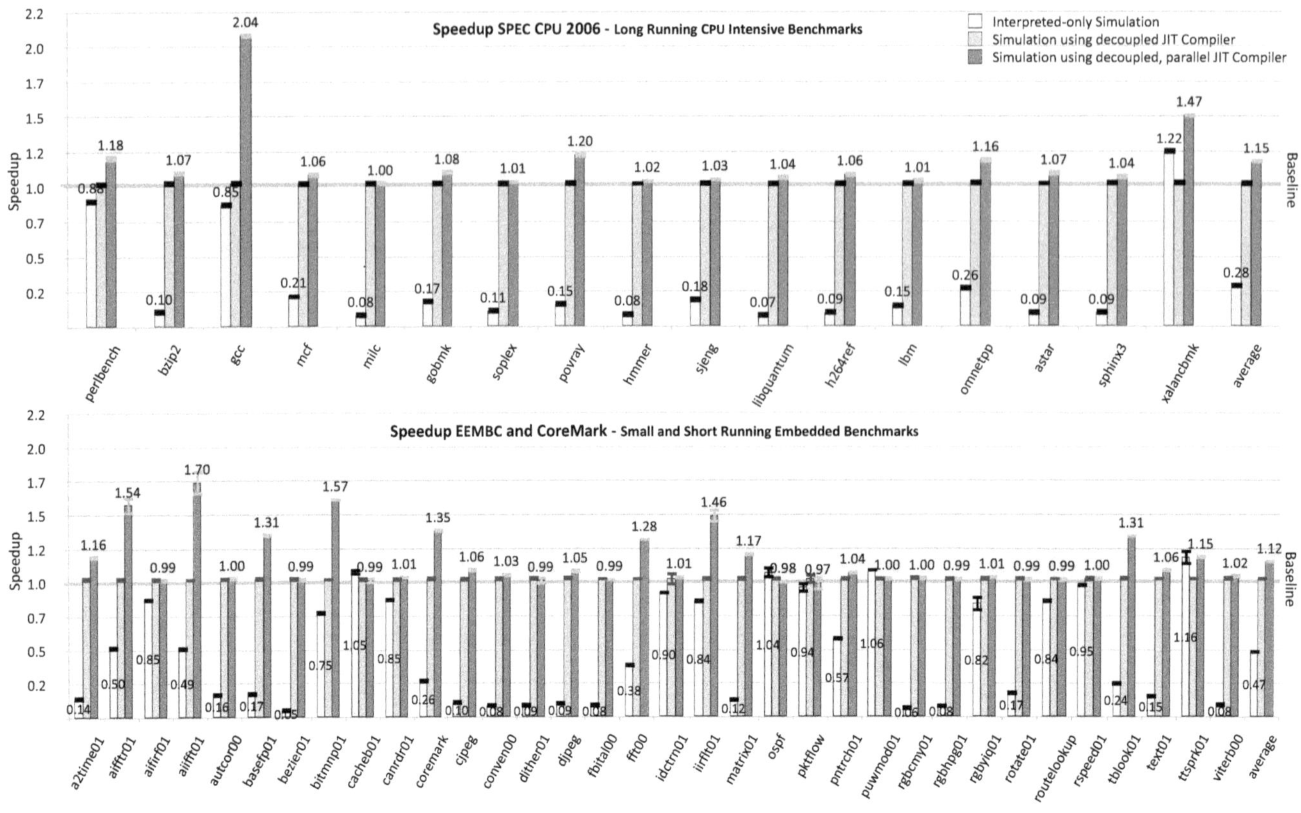

Figure 8. Speedups using SPEC CPU 2006, EEMBC and COREMARK benchmark suites comparing (a) interpreted-only simulation, (b) simulation using a decoupled JIT compiler, and (c) simulation using our novel, parallel JIT compiler with three JIT compilation worker threads including dynamic work scheduling.

thermore, we also present speedups (i.e. slowdowns) relative to our baseline when using interpreted simulation only (i.e. disabling trace-based JIT compilation).

All measurements were performed on a standard x86 DELL™ POWEREDGE™ quad-core outlined in Table 1 under conditions of low system load. To evaluate the scalability of our approach, when adding more cores, we performed additional measurements on a parallel symmetric multiprocessing machine with 16 2.6 GHz AMD Opteron™ (AMD64e) processors running Scientific Linux 5.0 (see Section 4.4).

4.2 Summary of Key Results

Our novel parallel trace-based JIT compilation approach is *always* faster than the baseline decoupled JIT compiler and achieves an average speedup of **1.38** equivalent to an average execution time reduction of **22.8%** for the BIOPERF benchmark suite. This corresponds directly to an average increase of **14.7%** in the number of natively executed instructions compared to the baseline.

For some benchmarks (e.g. `blastp`, `clustalw`) our proposed scheme is more than *twice* as fast as the baseline. This can be explained by the fact that 59% of the time we find more than one hot trace per trace interval for `blastp`. From this it follows that `blastp` exhibits a large amount of task parallelism (see Box ② in Figure 5). `Clustalw` mainly benefits from hiding compilation latency by using several JIT compilation worker threads (see Box ① in Figure 5).

Shorter running BIOPERF benchmarks perform particularly well with our scheme (e.g. `tcoffee`, `hmmsearch`, `clustalw`) because more JIT compilation workers can deliver translations much quicker as they can split the workload (i.e. hide compilation latency). Especially for `hmmsearch` where the baseline decoupled JIT compiler performs worse than the interpreted-only version, our scheme can significantly boost execution speed and reduce overall simulation time by 34.4%. Even for very long running BIOPERF benchmarks (e.g. `fasta-ssearch`, `promlk`, `hmmer-hmmpfam`, `ce`), where JIT compilation time typically represents only a small fraction of the overall execution time, our scheme achieves a reduction of execution times of up to 6.8%.

4.3 Worst-Case Scenarios

The BIOPERF benchmark suite is well suited to show the efficacy of our parallel trace-based JIT compiler. Additionally we also demonstrate its favorable impact on benchmarks where we would not expect to see significant speedups from our technique - so called *worst-case scenarios*.

For this analysis we have considered short running embedded benchmarks (EEMBC, COREMARK) containing few application hotspots (i.e. algorithmic kernels). Some of these benchmarks are so short that interpreted only execution takes less than two seconds, leaving very little scope for improvement by a JIT compiler. At the other end of the scale are very long running and CPU intensive benchmarks (SPEC CPU 2006) where JIT compilation time contributes only a marginal fraction to the overall execution time.

Across the SPEC CPU 2006 benchmarks our parallel trace-based JIT compiler is *never* slower than the baseline and achieves an average speedup of **1.15**, corresponding to an average increase of **4.2%** in the number of natively executed instructions. The best speedups are achieved for `gcc` (2.04x), `xalancbmk` (1.47x),

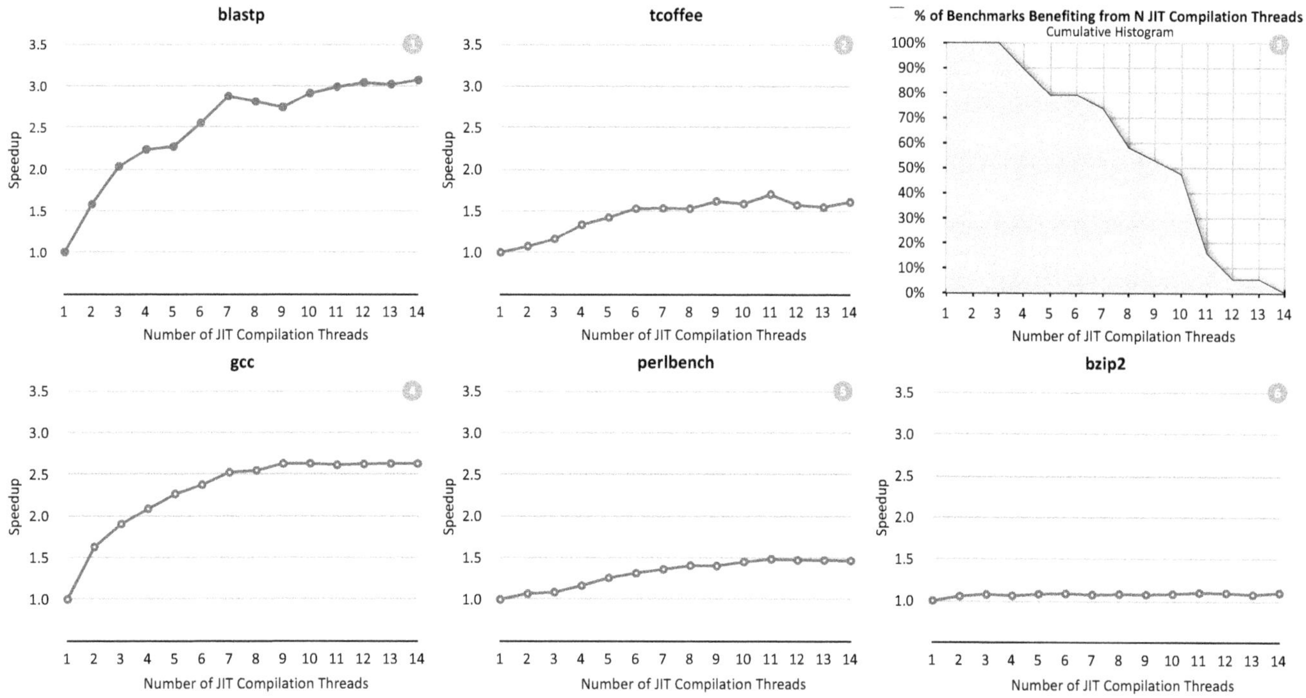

Figure 9. Scalability charts for selected benchmarks from BIOPERF ①② and SPEC CPU 2006 ④⑤⑥ demonstrating the effect of additional JIT compilation workers on speedup. Top right cumulative histogram ③ shows % of benchmarks benefiting from given number of JIT compilation threads.

Vendor & Model	DELL™ POWEREDGE™ 1950
Number CPUs	4 (quad-core)
Processor Type	Intel© Xeon™ processor E5430
Clock/FSB Frequency	2.66/1.33 GHz
L1-Cache	32K Instruction/Data caches
L2-Cache	12 MB
Operating System	Scientific Linux 5.5 (64-bit)

Table 1. Simulation Host Configuration.

povray (1.2x), and perlbench (1.18x). For perlbench and gcc the number of natively executed instructions improves by 19.5% and 38.0%, respectively, when using our parallel trace-based JIT compiler. The gcc benchmark greatly benefits from our approach as it runs a compiler with many optimization flags enabled resulting in a multitude of application hotspots representing compilation phases.

Xalancbmk is one of the shorter running SPEC CPU benchmarks performing XML transformations. Due to its short runtime and abundance of application hotspots the tracing overhead causes the baseline decoupled JIT compiler to be slower than the interpreted-only version. Our parallel trace-based JIT can easily recover this overhead resulting in a speedup of 1.47 when compared to the baseline, and a speedup of 1.21 when compared to interpreted-only simulation. Povray represents a long running benchmark where we achieve a speedup of 1.2. This is again due to an abundance of application hotspots across the runtime of the povray benchmark.

For the EEMBC and COREMARK benchmark suites our approach achieves an average speedup of 1.12 over the baseline, and an average improvement of 3.8% in the number of natively executed instructions. Small embedded benchmarks do not often benefit from task parallelism because they rarely exhibit more than one hot trace per trace interval. The speedups are mostly due to the fact that JIT compilation workers can already start working on newly discovered traces while previous traces are being translated by other workers. Also tracing must be light-weight, causing only very little overhead, to enable speedups for small benchmarks like EEMBC and COREMARK.

For all benchmarks performing Fast Fourier Transforms (i.e. aifftr01, aiifft01, fft00) speedups ranging from 1.46 to 1.7 are achieved by our parallel trace-based JIT compiler. The bit manipulation (bitmnp01) and infinite impulse response filter (iirflt01) benchmarks also show speedups of 1.57 and 1.46 using our scheme. Three EEMBC benchmarks (cacheb01, puwmod01, ospf) yield very short runtimes using interpreted-only mode (i.e. below one second) causing a small slowdown of the baseline decoupled JIT compiler and our parallel JIT compiler. This is entirely due to the fact that for very short benchmarks a JIT compiler has almost no chance to speed up execution, actually causing a slight slowdown due to the overheads caused by tracing and JIT compiler thread creation.

4.4 Available Parallelism and Scalability

According to Amdahl's law we expected only marginal improvements with increasing numbers of JIT compilation worker threads, so it is remarkable how well some benchmarks scale (see Figure 9) on a 16-core system. For blastp ① from BIOPERF the maximum speedup of 3.1 is reached with 14 JIT compilation workers. The gcc ④ and perlbench ⑤ benchmarks from SPEC CPU reach their maximum speedup of 2.6 and 1.5 with 10 and 11 JIT compilation workers, respectively. Not all benchmarks show benefits from adding more JIT compilation threads. For bzip2 ⑥ from SPEC CPU the peak speedup is reached with 3 JIT compilation threads, thus adding more threads does not improve execution time.

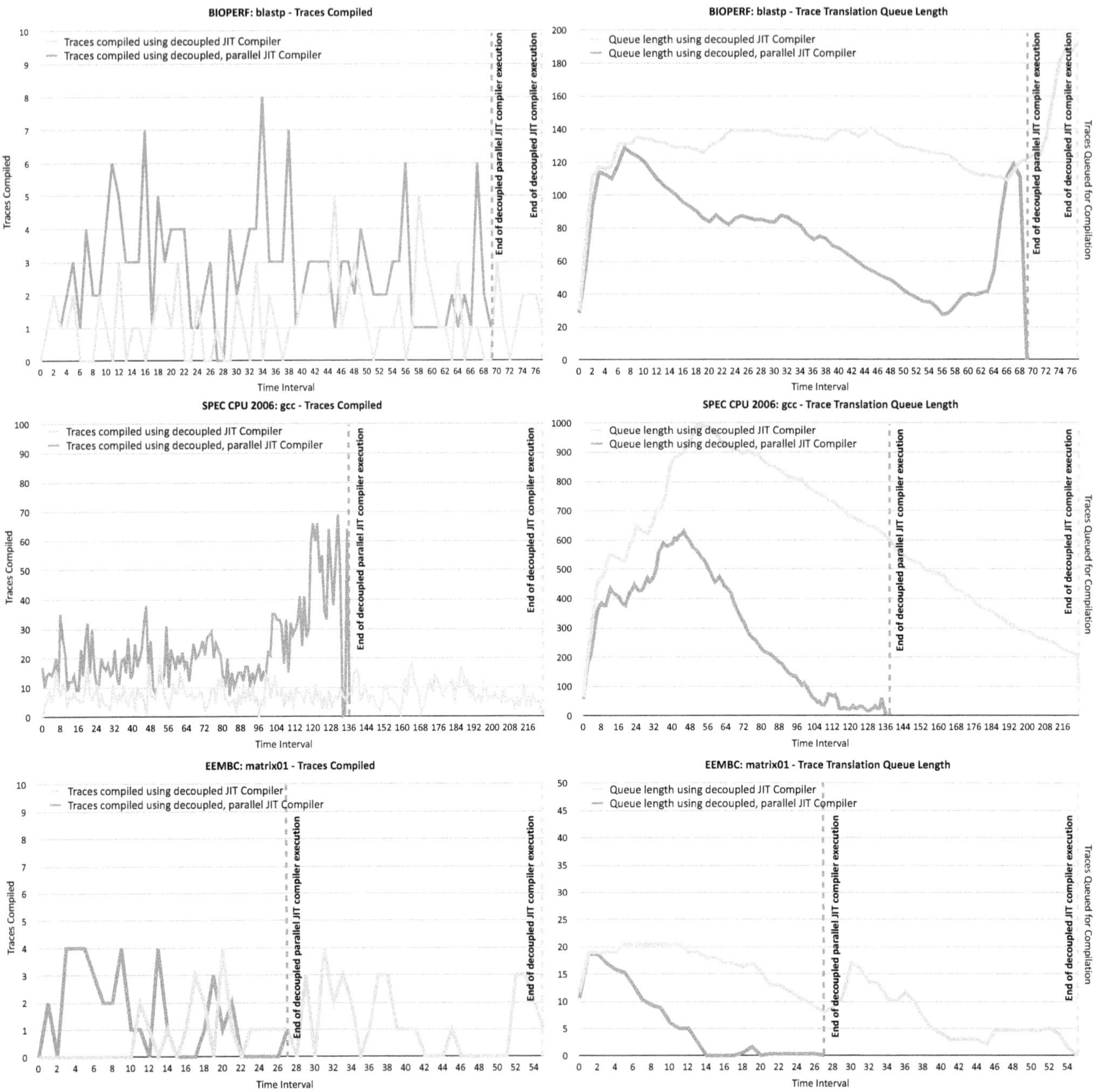

Figure 10. Comparing compiled traces per time interval and trace translation queue length per time interval using an *aggressive* threshold for hot trace selection for (a) simulation using a decoupled JIT compiler, and (b) simulation using our novel, parallel JIT compiler with three JIT compilation worker threads.

As shown in the scalability charts in Figure 9, the peak speedup is reached with different numbers of JIT compilation worker threads. So what is the maximum number of JIT compilation threads such that 100% of all benchmarks show speedup, i.e. how far does it scale? The cumulative histogram ③ in Figure 9 answers this question by depicting the number of benchmarks (in %) that show an improvement by adding more JIT compilation threads. From the histogram we can see *all* benchmarks show speedups with 3 JIT compilation worker threads and 50% of all benchmarks benefit from 9 or more JIT compilation threads.

4.5 Dynamic Work Scheduling

We have also evaluated the impact of our novel dynamic work scheduling scheme in comparison to a simpler approach that schedules traces based on their order of creation for JIT compilation. For BIOPERF, we measured an average improvement of 8.9%, which is equivalent to an average speedup of 1.13. For the SPEC CPU 2006 benchmarks, the average improvement and speedup are 3.5% and 1.04, respectively.

4.6 Compiled Traces and Trace Translation Queue Length over Time

The key performance indicator of our parallel trace compilation scheme is the reduction of overall simulation time. In this section we give a more detailed overview of two additional performance indicators, namely (1) the number of compiled traces per time interval (i.e. rate at which work is completed), and (2) the resulting trace translation queue lengths over the runtime of three selected benchmarks (see Figure 10). We chose one benchmark from each benchmark suite exhibiting a variety of application hotspots over time, and used a rather aggressive threshold for hot trace selection to highlight some of the main advantages of using more than one JIT compilation thread.

A comparison of the number of compiled traces and trace translation queue lengths over time indicates that our parallel JIT compilation task farm is able to translate traces significantly faster than the decoupled scheme which relies on a single JIT compilation thread. On average, three parallel JIT compilation threads can translate 2.1, 3.1 and 1.5 times as many traces per time interval than the decoupled JIT compiler for `blastp`, `gcc` and `matrix01`, respectively. Consequently, the *average* trace translation queue length is 43%, 52% and 51% shorter, and the *maximum* observed queue sizes are 33%, 37%, and 9% shorter for the same three benchmarks, respectively. At the same time, the queue length grows at a noticeably slower rate.

Using a very aggressive initial hotspot threshold, the amount of hot traces identified per trace interval and the resulting translation queue lengths quickly exceed the number of available JIT translation workers, even for a short benchmark such as `matrix01`. This demonstrates the need for our dynamic work scheduling and adaptive hotspot threshold selection schemes. Dynamic work scheduling ensures that the most recent and hottest traces are scheduled for translation first, whereas adapting the hotspot threshold based on the translation queue length aims at improving the utilisation of available resources.

4.7 Memory Overhead of Parallel JIT Compilation

The use of multiple LLVM JIT compiler threads incurs a memory overhead. However, we found this overhead to be modest compared to the baseline. Internal memory consumption (i.e. memory which is not application data or target binary code) never exceeds 150 MB for any of the benchmarks.

5. Related Work

5.1 Dynamic Binary Translation

Dynamic translation techniques are used to overcome the lack of flexibility inherent in statically-compiled simulators. The MIMIC simulator [24] simulates IBM SYSTEM/370 instructions on the IBM RT PC and translates groups of target basic blocks into host instructions. SHADE [10] and EMBRA [21] use DBT with translation caching techniques in order to increase simulation speeds. The Ultra-fast Instruction Set Simulator [45] improves the performance of statically-compiled simulation by using low-level binary translation techniques to take full advantage of the host architecture.

Just-In-Time Cache Compiled Simulation (JIT-CCS) [28] executes and caches pre-compiled instruction-operation functions for each function fetched. The Instruction Set Compiled Simulation (IC-CS) simulator [31] was designed to be a high performance and flexible functional simulator. To achieve this the time-consuming instruction decode process is performed during the compile stage, whilst interpretation is enabled at simulation time. The SIMICS [31] full system simulator translates the target machine-code instructions into an intermediate format before interpretation. During simulation the intermediate instructions are processed by the interpreter which calls the corresponding service routines. QEMU [5] is a fast simulator using an original dynamic translator. Each target instruction is divided into a simple sequence of micro-operations, the set of micro-operations having been pre-compiled offline into an object file. During simulation the code generator accesses the object file and concatenates micro-operations to form a host function that emulates the target instructions within a block. More recent approaches to JIT DBT ISS are presented in [7, 19, 30, 38]. Apart from different target platforms these approaches differ in the granularity of translation units (basic blocks *vs.* pages or CFG regions) and their JIT code generation target language (ANSI-C *vs.* LLVM IR).

Parallel simulation of multi-core target platforms on multi-core host platforms has been demonstrated in [21, 25, 40]. These approaches, however, are mainly concerned with the mapping of target to host processors and do not consider the parallelization of the embedded JIT compiler.

5.2 Trace-based JIT Optimization/Compilation

Tracing is a well established technique for dynamic profile guided optimization of native binaries. Bala et al. [3] introduced tracing as a method for runtime optimization of native program binaries in their DYNAMO system. They used backward branch targets as candidates for the start of a trace, but did not attempt to capture traces of loops. Zaleski et al. [43] used DYNAMO-like tracing in order to achieve inlining, indirect jump elimination, and other optimizations for Java. Their primary goal was to build an interpreter that could be extended to a tracing VM.

Whaley [41] uses partial method compilation to reduce the granularity of compilation to the sub-method level. His system uses profile information to detect never or rarely executed parts of a method and to ignore them during compilation. If such a part gets executed later, execution continues in the interpreter. Compilation still starts at the beginning of a method. Similarly, Suganuma et al. [33] propose region-based compilation to overcome the limitations of method-based compilation. They use heuristics and profiles to identify and eliminate rarely executed sections of code, but rely on expensive runtime code instrumentation for trace identification.

Gal et al. [13, 15] proposed an approach to building dynamic compilers in which no CFG is ever constructed, and no source code level compilation units such as methods are used. Instead, they use runtime profiling to detect frequently executed cyclic code paths in the program. The compiler then records and generates code from dynamically recorded code traces along these paths. It assembles these traces dynamically into a trace tree, a tree-like data-structure, that covers frequently executed (and thus compilation worthy) code paths through hot code regions. Trace trees suffer from the problem of code explosion when many control-flow paths are present in a loop, causing them to grow to very large sizes due to excessive tail duplication as outlined in [4]. To solve this problem Bebenita et al. [4] propose to use trace-regions as a data-structure for tracing in their implementation of Hotpath, a trace-based Java JIT compiler in the Maxine VM. Trace-regions are an extension to trace trees as they can include join nodes instead of using tail duplication. Locations where trace recording can be enabled, so called *anchors*, are determined statically during byte-code verification, and trace regions are restricted to method boundaries. In contrast, our approach does not rely on statically determined anchors for tracing and trace regions are not confined to method boundaries.

5.3 Parallel JIT Compilation

JIT compilation has a long history [1] dating back to the 1960s. The possibility of reducing the overhead of dynamic compilation by decoupling the JIT compiler from the main simulation loop and executing it in a separate thread has been suggested by several researchers, e.g. [16, 20, 39].

Parallel JIT compilation is not an entirely new concept. Some approaches [8, 14] have attempted to exploit *pipeline parallelism* in the JIT compiler. However, pipelining of the JIT compiler has significant drawbacks. First, compiler stages are typically not well balanced and the overall throughput is limited by the slowest pipeline stage – this is often the front-end or IR generation stage. Second, unlike method based compilers, trace-based JIT compilers operate on relatively small translation units in order to reduce the compilation overhead to a bare minimum [15]. Small translation units and long compilation pipelines, however, increase the relative synchronization costs between pipeline stages and, again, limit the achievable compiler throughput. Third, compilation pipelines are static and do not scale with the available *task parallelism* in inherently independent translation units.

Most relevant to our work is the approach presented in [30]. This paper pioneered the concept of concurrent JIT compilation workers to speed up DBT, but suffers from a number of flaws. First, rather than taking a trace-based compilation approach entire pages are translated – this is unnecessarily wasteful in a time-critical JIT environment. Second, there are no provisions for a dynamic work scheduling scheme that prioritizes compilation of hot traces – this may defer compilation of critical traces and lower overall efficiency. Third, JIT compilers reside in separate processes on remote machines – this significantly increases the communication overhead and limits scalability. This last point is critical, as results shown in [30] are based solely on CPU time of the main simulation process rather than the more relevant wall clock time that includes CPU time, I/O time and communication channel delay.

6. Summary and Conclusions

In this paper we have presented a generalized trace construction scheme enabling parallel JIT compilation based on a task farm design pattern. By combining parallel JIT compilation with lightweight tracing, large translation units and dynamic work scheduling, we not only minimize and hide JIT compilation overhead, but fully exploit the available hardware parallelism in standard multicore desktop PCs. Across three full benchmark suites comprising non-trivial and long-running applications from various domains we achieve an average reduction in total execution time of 11.5% – and up to 51.9% – for four processors. Our innovative, parallel JIT scheme is robust and never results in a slowdown. Given that only a small fraction of the overall execution time is spent on JIT compilation, and the majority of time is spent executing natively-compiled code, these results are more than remarkable.

While primarily developed for DBT, the concept of concurrent JIT compilation may also be exploited elsewhere to effectively reduce dynamic compilation overheads and speedup execution. Prime examples are JIT-compiled Java Virtual Machines (JVM) or JavaScript engines. In our future work, we plan to extend our DBT for the simulation of multi-core architectures, and explore alternative dynamic work scheduling strategies.

References

[1] J. Aycock. A brief history of just-in-time. *ACM Comput. Surv.*, 35: 97–113, June 2003.

[2] D. Bader, Y. Li, T. Li, and V. Sachdeva. Bioperf: a benchmark suite to evaluate high-performance computer architecture on bioinformatics applications. In *Proceedings of the IEEE International Workload Characterization Symposium*, IISWC'05, pages 163–173, 2005.

[3] V. Bala, E. Duesterwald, and S. Banerjia. Dynamo: a transparent dynamic optimization system. In *Proceedings of the ACM SIGPLAN 2000 Conference on Programming Language Design and Implementation*, PLDI '00, pages 1–12, New York, NY, USA, 2000. ACM.

[4] M. Bebenita, M. Chang, G. Wagner, A. Gal, C. Wimmer, and M. Franz. Trace-based compilation in execution environments without interpreters. In *Proceedings of the 8th International Conference on the Principles and Practice of Programming in Java*, PPPJ '10, pages 59–68, New York, NY, USA, 2010. ACM.

[5] F. Bellard. QEMU, a fast and portable dynamic translator. In *Proceedings of the USENIX Annual Technical Conference*, ATEC '05, page 41, Berkeley, CA, USA, 2005. USENIX Association.

[6] I. Böhm, B. Franke, and N. Topham. Cycle-accurate performance modelling in an ultra-fast just-in-time dynamic binary translation instruction set simulator. In *Proceedings of the International Conference on Embedded Computer Systems*, IC-SAMOS'10, pages 1 – 10, 2010.

[7] F. Brandner, A. Fellnhofer, A. Krall, and D. Riegler. Fast and accurate simulation using the llvm compiler framework. In *Proceedings of the 1st Workshop on Rapid Simulation and Performance Evaluation: Methods and Tools*, RAPIDO'09, pages 1–6, 2009.

[8] S. Campanoni, G. Agosta, and S. C. Reghizzi. A parallel dynamic compiler for CIL bytecode. *SIGPLAN Not.*, 43:11–20, April 2008.

[9] A. Chernoff, M. Herdeg, R. Hookway, C. Reeve, N. Rubin, T. Tye, S. Bharadwaj Yadavalli, and J. Yates. FX!32: a profile-directed binary translator. *Micro, IEEE*, 18(2):56–64, 1998.

[10] B. Cmelik and D. Keppel. Shade: a fast instruction-set simulator for execution profiling. In *Proceedings of the 1994 ACM SIGMETRICS Conference on Measurement and Modeling of Computer Systems*, SIGMETRICS '94, pages 128–137, New York, NY, USA, 1994. ACM.

[11] A. Cohen and E. Rohou. Processor virtualization and split compilation for heterogeneous multicore embedded systems. In *Proceedings of the 47th Design Automation Conference*, DAC '10, pages 102–107, New York, NY, USA, 2010. ACM.

[12] S. Farfeleder, A. Krall, and N. Horspool. Ultra fast cycle-accurate compiled emulation of inorder pipelined architectures. *J. Syst. Archit.*, 53:501–510, August 2007.

[13] A. Gal, C. W. Probst, and M. Franz. HotpathVM: an effective JIT compiler for resource-constrained devices. In *Proceedings of the 2nd International Conference on Virtual Execution Environments*, VEE '06, pages 144–153, New York, NY, USA, 2006. ACM.

[14] A. Gal, M. Bebenita, M. Chang, and M. Franz. Making the compilation "pipeline" explicit: Dynamic compilation using trace tree serialization. Technical Report 07-12, University of California, Irvine, 2007.

[15] A. Gal, B. Eich, M. Shaver, D. Anderson, D. Mandelin, M. R. Haghighat, B. Kaplan, G. Hoare, B. Zbarsky, J. Orendorff, J. Ruderman, E. W. Smith, R. Reitmaier, M. Bebenita, M. Chang, and M. Franz. Trace-based just-in-time type specialization for dynamic languages. In *Proceedings of the 2009 ACM SIGPLAN Conference on Programming Language Design and Implementation*, PLDI '09, pages 465–478, New York, NY, USA, 2009. ACM.

[16] J. Ha, M. Haghighat, S. Cong, and K. McKinley. A concurrent trace-based just-in-time compiler for single-threaded JavaScript. In *Proceedings of the Workshop on Parallel Execution of Sequential Programs on Multicore Architectures*, PESPMA'09, 2009.

[17] M. Hauswirth, P. F. Sweeney, A. Diwan, and M. Hind. Vertical profiling: understanding the behavior of object-priented applications. In *Proceedings of the 19th annual ACM SIGPLAN Conference on Object-oriented Programming, Systems, Languages, and Applications*, OOPSLA '04, pages 251–269, New York, NY, USA, 2004. ACM.

[18] J. L. Henning. SPEC CPU2006 benchmark descriptions. *SIGARCH Comput. Archit. News*, 34:1–17, September 2006.

[19] D. Jones and N. Topham. High speed CPU simulation using LTU dynamic binary translation. In *High Performance Embedded Architectures and Compilers*, volume 5409 of *Lecture Notes in Computer Science*, pages 50–64. Springer Berlin Heidelberg, 2009.

[20] C. J. Krintz, D. Grove, V. Sarkar, and B. Calder. Reducing the overhead of dynamic compilation. *Software: Practice and Experience*, 31(8):717–738, July 2001.

[21] R. Lantz. Fast functional simulation with parallel Embra. In *Proceedings of the 4th Annual Workshop on Modeling, Benchmarking and Simulation*, MOBS'08, 2008.

[22] C. Lattner and V. Adve. LLVM: A compilation framework for lifelong program analysis & transformation. In *Proceedings of the International Symposium on Code Generation and Optimization*, CGO '04, page 75, Washington, DC, USA, 2004. IEEE Computer Society.

[23] C.-K. Luk, R. Cohn, R. Muth, H. Patil, A. Klauser, G. Lowney, S. Wallace, V. J. Reddi, and K. Hazelwood. PIN: building customized program analysis tools with dynamic instrumentation. In *Proceedings of the 2005 ACM SIGPLAN Conference on Programming Language Design and Implementation*, PLDI '05, pages 190–200, New York, NY, USA, 2005. ACM.

[24] C. May. MIMIC: a fast System/370 simulator. In *Papers of the Symposium on Interpreters and Interpretive Techniques*, SIGPLAN '87, pages 1–13, New York, NY, USA, 1987. ACM.

[25] J. Miller, H. Kasture, G. Kurian, C. Gruenwald, N. Beckmann, C. Celio, J. Eastep, and A. Agarwal. Graphite: A distributed parallel simulator for multicores. In *Proceedings of the IEEE 16th International Symposium on High Performance Computer Architecture*, HPCA'10, pages 1–12, 2010.

[26] Mozilla Foundation. Tamarin project, 17 November 2010. URL `http://www.mozilla.org/projects/tamarin/`.

[27] Mozilla Foundation. Tracemonkey, 17 November 2010. URL `https://wiki.mozilla.org/JavaScript:TraceMonkey`.

[28] A. Nohl, G. Braun, O. Schliebusch, R. Leupers, H. Meyr, and A. Hoffmann. A universal technique for fast and flexible instruction-set architecture simulation. In *Proceedings of the 39th annual Design Automation Conference*, DAC '02, pages 22–27, New York, NY, USA, 2002. ACM.

[29] Oracle Corporation. HotSpot VM, 17 November 2010. URL `http://java.sun.com/performance/reference/whitepapers/`.

[30] W. Qin, J. D'Errico, and X. Zhu. A multiprocessing approach to accelerate retargetable and portable dynamic-compiled instruction-set simulation. In *Proceedings of the 4th International Conference on Hardware/Software Codesign and System Synthesis*, CODES+ISSS '06, pages 193–198, New York, NY, USA, 2006. ACM.

[31] M. Reshadi, P. Mishra, and N. Dutt. Instruction set compiled simulation: a technique for fast and flexible instruction set simulation. In *Proceedings of the 40th annual Design Automation Conference*, DAC '03, pages 758–763, New York, NY, USA, 2003. ACM.

[32] E. Stahl and M. Anand. A comparison of PowerVM and x86-based virtualization performance. Technical Report WP101574, IBM Techdocs White Papers, 2010.

[33] T. Suganuma, T. Yasue, and T. Nakatani. A region-based compilation technique for dynamic compilers. *ACM Trans. Program. Lang. Syst.*, 28:134–174, January 2006.

[34] V. Tan. Asynchronous just-in-time compilation. *United States Patent Application*, WO/2007/055883, 2007.

[35] The Embedded Microprocessor Benchmark Consortium. EEMBC benchmark suite, 12 August 2009. URL `http://www.eembc.org`.

[36] The LLVM Compiler Infrastructure. Users of LLVM JIT compilation engine, 17 November 2010. URL `http://llvm.org/Users.html`.

[37] The WebKit Open Source Project. SquirrelFish, 17 November 2010. URL `http://trac.webkit.org/wiki/SquirrelFish`.

[38] N. Topham and D. Jones. High speed CPU simulation using JIT binary translation. In *Proceedings of the Annual Workshop on Modelling, Benchmarking and Simulation*, MOBS '07, 2007.

[39] P. Unnikrishnan, M. Kandemir, and F. Li. Reducing dynamic compilation overhead by overlapping compilation and execution. In *Proceedings of the 2006 Asia and South Pacific Design Automation Conference*, ASP-DAC '06, pages 929–934, Piscataway, NJ, USA, 2006. IEEE Press.

[40] K. Wang, Y. Zhang, H. Wang, and X. Shen. Parallelization of IBM Mambo system simulator in functional modes. *SIGOPS Oper. Syst. Rev.*, 42:71–76, January 2008.

[41] J. Whaley. Partial method compilation using dynamic profile information. In *Proceedings of the 16th ACM SIGPLAN Conference on Object-oriented Programming, Systems, Languages, and Applications*, OOPSLA '01, pages 166–179, New York, NY, USA, 2001. ACM.

[42] B. Yee, D. Sehr, G. Dardyk, J. Chen, R. Muth, T. Ormandy, S. Okasaka, N. Narula, and N. Fullagar. Native Client: A sandbox for portable, untrusted x86 native code. In *30th IEEE Symposium on Security and Privacy*, pages 79–93, May 2009.

[43] M. Zaleski, A. D. Brown, and K. Stoodley. YETI: a gradually extensible trace interpreter. In *Proceedings of the 3rd International Conference on Virtual Execution Environments*, VEE '07, pages 83–93, New York, NY, USA, 2007. ACM.

[44] C. Zheng and C. Thompson. PA-RISC to IA-64: transparent execution, no recompilation. *Computer*, 33(3):47 –52, Mar. 2000.

[45] J. Zhu and D. D. Gajski. A retargetable, ultra-fast instruction set simulator. In *Proceedings of the Conference on Design, Automation and Test in Europe*, DATE '99, New York, NY, USA, 1999. ACM.

Brainy: Effective Selection of Data Structures

Changhee Jung [1] Silvius Rus [2] Brian P. Railing [1] Nathan Clark [3] Santosh Pande [1]

[1]Georgia Institute of Technology
{cjung9, brailing, santosh}@cc.gatech.edu

[2]Google Inc.
rus@google.com

[3]Virtu Financial
nclark@virtufinancial.com

Abstract

Data structure selection and their tuning are one of the most critical aspects of developing effective applications. By analyzing data structures' behavior and their interaction with the rest of the application, tools can make suggestions for alternative data structures. Such a process is quite dependent on the execution efficiency of the data structure on a given architecture. Consequently, developers can optimize their data structure usage to make the application conscious of an underlying architecture and a particular program input.

This paper presents the design and evaluation of Brainy, a new program analysis tool that automatically selects the best data structure for a given program on a specific microarchitecture. The data structures' interface functions are instrumented to dynamically monitor how the data structure interacts with the application for a given input. The instrumentation records traces of various runtime characteristics including underlying architecture-specific events. These generated traces are analyzed and fed into an offline model constructed using machine learning; this model then selects the best data structure. That is, Brainy exploits runtime feedback of data structures to understand the situation an application runs on, and selects the best data structure for a given application/input/architecture combination based on the constructed model. The empirical evaluation shows that this technique is highly accurate across several real-world applications with various program input sets on two different state-of-the-art microarchitectures. Consequently, Brainy achieved an average performance improvement of 27% and 33% on both microarchitectures, respectively.

Categories and Subject Descriptors D.2.3 [*Software Engineering*]: Coding Tools and Techniques; D.2.5 [*Testing and Debugging*]: Diagnostics; D.3.3 [*Language Constructs and Features*]: Data types and structures

General Terms Languages, Algorithms, Performance

Keywords Data Structure Selection, Application Generator, Training Framework, Performance Counters

1. Introduction

Niklaus Wirth famously noted, "Algorithms + Data Structures = Programs" [35], and it follows that one of the most critical aspects of creating effective applications is data structure selection.

PLDI'11, June 4–8, 2011, San Jose, California, USA.

Data organization is one of the defining characteristics in determining how effectively applications can leverage hardware resources such as memory and parallelism. Indeed, it is not uncommon to find situations where simply changing the data structures can result in orders of magnitude improvement in application performance for many important domains. For example, scientific applications leveraging matrix inversion [3] and matrix multiplication [34], information mining from large databases [2], and analyzing genetic data for patterns [10], are instances of criticality of data structure selection in an application tuning process. According to [3], proper data structure selection can make the 2-D table implementation used in that study 20 times faster.

In one recent study, researchers at Google analyzed the use of the C++ Standard Template Library (STL) [30] on several of their internal applications, and found many instances where expert developers made suboptimal decisions on which data structures to use [17]. Simply changing a single data structure in one application resulted in a 17% speedup in that study. When applying this type of speedup to data-center-sized computations, poor data structure selection can result in millions of dollars in unnecessary costs. Thus, selecting the appropriate data structures in applications is an important problem.

However, the reality is that most often developers do not select data structure implementations at all; they simply rely on a data structure library and assume that the library designer made a good decision for them. Data structure libraries were designed to be effective in the common case, and often leave considerable room for improvement in application-specific scenarios.

When developers do manually select a data structure implementation, they most frequently utilize asymptotic analysis to guide their decision. Asymptotic analysis is an excellent mathematical tool for understanding data structure properties; however, it often leads to incorrect conclusions in real systems. For example, comparing the STL `set` (implemented as a red-black tree) with `unordered_set` (implemented as a hash table), the `set` has worse asymptotic behavior but almost always has faster lookup times on modern architectures when holding fewer than 200 data elements. In other situations data structures have identical asymptotic behavior but very different real-world behavior. For example, splay trees [29] almost always perform better than red-black trees on real-world data though they have the same asymptotic complexity. Asymptotic complexity measures were designed as a unified basis for comparing and choosing an algorithm and not data structures. To a large extent, once an algorithm is chosen, attention is rarely paid to the choice of data structures. This can leave substantial inefficiencies on the table. In short, traditional solutions leave much to be desired.

Unfortunately, selecting the best data structure for a given situation is a very difficult problem. This requires thorough understanding both of how a program uses a data structure, and of the underlying architecture. Even further, input changes can lead to different optimal data structures. Thus, a tool that ignores inputs could not possibly make a high-quality decision for selecting the best data structure. To ameliorate the data structure selection problem, this paper presents Brainy, an automated tool to develop a repeatable process for creating accurate *cost models* that predict the best data structure implementation for a given application/input/architecture combination.

In order to construct an input- and architecture-aware cost model, the model must be trained to understand the effect of architectural behaviors while taking into account input changes. This is accomplished by first constructing a set of synthetic programs that exercise different behaviors of a given data structure under consideration. For example, the test programs will stress all of the data structures' interface functions with modeling different inputs by varying data type sizes and various numbers of elements stored in the data structure. Then several measurements are collected through hardware performance counters and code instrumentation in order to understand how each data structure behaves. These measurements are then summarized into statistics which are then fed into a machine learning model. The machine learning model creates a function to accurately determine the optimal data structure choice for each static program variable. Machine learning characterization has been shown repeatedly to be more effective than human designed models because machine learning picks up on subtle interactions human experts often miss [7, 16, 22, 31, 33]. This paper demonstrates that leveraging machine learning to generate cost models, which leverage architectural events and dynamic software behavior, is significantly more accurate than asymptotic analysis or human designed models for data structure selection. This paper also demonstrates that using these models can result in significant performance improvements in real-world applications. Moreover such techniques are shown to be repeatable empirically on two different architectures across a variety of data structures.

The vision of this work is that the synthetic program generation tool we have developed can be used to tune a cost model once for each target system at install-time. These models can then be used either by a developer manually (e.g., as part of a performance debugging tool similar to Intel's VTune), or built into data structure libraries so that the compiler or runtime can automatically select the best implementations for many users of the libraries. Utilizing machine learning to automatically generate cost models for data structure selection is a fundamentally new way to analyze data structure behavior; this method is significantly more effective than the traditional asymptotic analysis.

The contributions of this work include:

- A repeatable methodology for characterizing the performance of data structures using architectural events and runtime software properties of the application.
- An analysis on what program and hardware properties are most important to consider when selecting data structure implementations on modern architectures. This paper presents several non-intuitive discoveries. For example, branch misprediction rate is a very useful predictive feature.
- An empirical demonstration of the machine learning model, compared with traditional hand-constructed and asymptotic methods. This paper demonstrates that considering performance counters and dynamic properties can provide significant improvements in application performance.

2. Motivation

Effective data structure selection requires thorough understanding of how a data structure interacts with the application. Apart from the asymptotic behavior of data structures, a number of factors should be considered, such as what types of functions interact with the data, how many times the interface functions are invoked, how big each data element is, and so on. It is also important to take into account hardware behavior to understand the effect of the underlying architecture on data structure related code. Given all this, identifying a function that accurately predicts the best data structure implementation is very challenging.

As an example, assume that a developer is deciding between a `vector` and `list` data structure from the C++ Standard Template Library (STL) [30]. The former is a dynamically-sized array stored contiguously in memory and the latter is a doubly-linked list. The developer might think that `vector` is almost always better than `list` because its contiguous data layout better leverages spatial locality in memory hierarchies, and the dynamically adjusting size will make tail insertions require fewer memory allocations than with a linked list. In reality, `vector` is preferable in situations with frequent search or iteration over data elements. However, data insertion into (or removal from) the middle of the structure is extremely expensive for `vector`, since all data elements located after the insertion point must be moved backwards (or forwards) to maintain contiguity. The challenging issue is how to quantify the pros and cons of each data structure to accurately compare them. For example, how many `find` or iteration operations are enough to overcome poor insertion and deletion times for `vector` to perform better than `list`? In some sense, we are looking at performing amortized analysis of different operations that are associated with a given data structure. Purely basing such an analysis on the frequency of operations would be a naive simplification of the problem, since the operations and their costs are linked to the program state and are continuously varying throughout the execution. It is a challenge about how to come up with such an amortized cost model without worrying about the deeper notions of the program state; a challenge partially solved by this paper. We first delve on this issue of generating an appropriate cost model.

Without worrying the issues of program state, one could limit oneself to the interface functions and their order of executions, and try to approximate the model of behaviors exercised. In general, constructing a cost function is much more difficult than illustrated by the above example, since there are many functions that interact with each data structure. The best data structure implementation changes as each interface function is invoked more or less frequently relative to the others. Beyond just interface functions, any changes in data element size, the number of data elements, data search pattern, and so on, which can be affected by program inputs, can have a significant impact on the most appropriate data structure implementation. For example, STL's `find` searches for the first instance of a data element located in the structure without iterating over all the elements. This means the data being stored affects how important iteration is to the performance of the application. These and other input-dependent factors make it very difficult to hand-construct accurate data structure cost models.

A final challenge is that underlying hardware can have a considerable effect on data structure selection results. Even if a programmer chooses the best data structure, that data structure will not always be the best when it runs on different microarchitectures. That is, architectural changes can make the data structure, which was the best, suboptimal as input changes. For instance, in the previous example of data structure selection, a developer might choose a `vector` over a `list` for fewer cache misses during iteration, although hardware systems with larger cache sizes might execute `list` faster than `vector`. The reason is that `list` nodes will typically remain cached after a cold start; however, whenever `vector` is resized the cold start penalty will have to be paid anew. Thus, architectural events have a very important role in data structure selection.

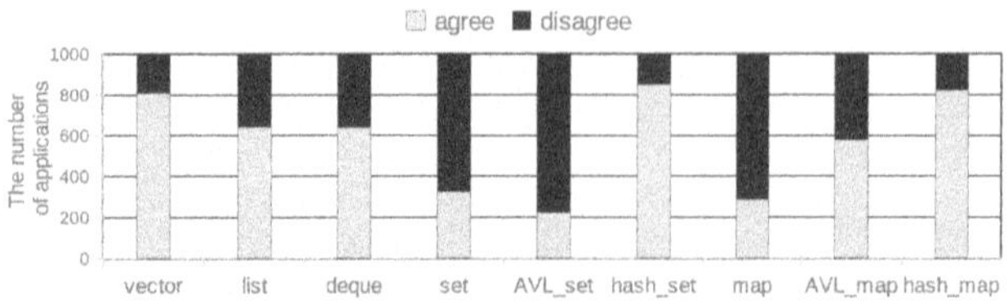

Figure 1. Different data structure selection results on two microarchitectures: Intel Core2 Q6600 and Intel Atom N270. Each bar represents 1000 applications whose best data structure on the Core2 is shown in the x-axis. For each application, if the data structure remains the same on the Atom, the application is classified as "agree". Otherwise, the application is classified as "disagree".

To further motivate the importance of microarchitectural differences for effective data structure selection, this work analyzed several thousand randomly generated applications that exercise different behaviors of C++ STL data structures (further details on the application generator will be discussed in Section 4.1). Each application was run on both an Intel Core2 Q6600 and an Intel Atom N270 to see what the best data structure implementation for each architecture is. Figure 1 shows how differently two distinct microarchitectures can behave. Each bar in the figure represents 1000 randomly-generated applications whose best data structure implementation on the Core2 is shown on the x-axis. For example, the left-most bar in the figure represents 1000 applications whose best data structure on the Core2 was a `vector`. The dark gray, top portion of the bar represents how many of those exact same applications the best data structure was not a `vector` on the Atom architecture. So in $\approx$200 applications where `vector` performed best on the Core2, another data structure would perform better on the Atom.

This experiment demonstrates that the best data structure choice for each application significantly differs on the two different microarchitectures. The degree of such an inconsistency varies across data structures. On average, 43% of the randomly generated applications have different optimal data structures. Thus, all efforts to construct a data structure cost model *without* considering architectural properties will necessarily be lacking. The complexity of modern architectures further motivates the need for an automated tool to construct these models, as human-constructed models will be tedious and likely inaccurate. Section 7 shows that it is inherently difficult and sometimes impossible for hand-constructed models to capture the architectural events of an alternative data structure. E.g., the number of branch mispredictions in the original data structure has no causal relation to that in the alternative data structure.

3. Overview

The purpose of this work is to provide a tool that can report the best data structures for different situations due to specific input sets and underlying hardware architecture changes. To keep up with the various behaviors of an application, this work exploits dynamic profiling that utilizes runtime instrumentation. Every interface function of each data structure is instrumented to model how that data structure interacts with the application. The instrumentation code observes how the data structure is used by the application (i.e, software features), and at the same time monitors a set of performance counters (i.e., hardware features) from the underlying architecture. The runtime system maintains the trace information in a context-sensitive manner, i.e., the calling sequences are considered at the data structure's construction time. This helps developers know the location in the source code of the data structures to be replaced. Once program execution finishes, the trace files are fed into a machine learning tool. Finally, the machine learning tool reports what data structures should be replaced with which alternatives.

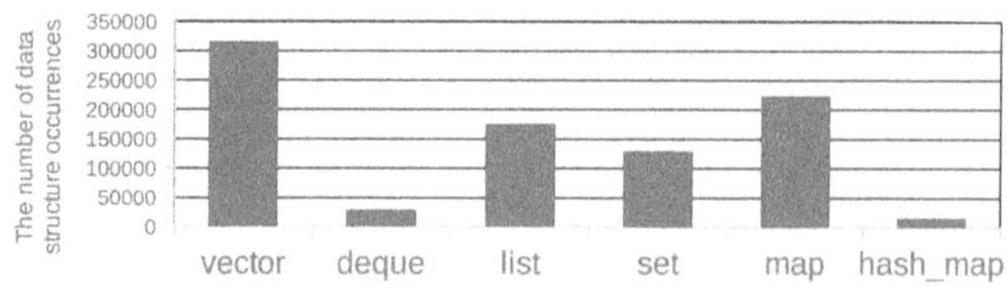

Figure 2. The number of data structure occurrences in all the code registered in Google Code Search.

Due to a significant amount of effort involved, to train and build machine learning models for the data structures, this paper limits its focus to C++ programs using a subset of the STL. It may be noted that as the tool is not fundamentally limited, the approach should be applicable to other data structures expressed in other contexts. To determine the target data structure replacements, we surveyed programs using Google Code Search (GCS) [9]. GCS indexes many open-source projects on the Internet. Figure 2 shows the number of static references to each data structure type across the entire index. This figure shows that `vector`, `list`, `set`, and `map` are the most common STL data structures used, thus this paper will focus on various implementations of these structures. Simply counting the number of static references to each data structure ignores the importance of data structure's impact to the application performance at runtime. However, this gives a rough estimate for which data structure needs to be targeted initially.

Given this set of target data structures, it is also necessary to define a set of implementations, and delineate what implementations can be replaced by what. Table 1 shows the possible data structure replacements considered, along with the benefits and limitations of each. For example, `vector` can be replaced with `list` for faster insertion, and with `set` for faster search. Similarly, if `vector` is frequently searched with a key for a match, e.g., using *std::find_if*, then it can be replaced with `map`. However, `vector` cannot always be replaced by `set` or `map` because they are oblivious to the data insertion order (i.e., order-oblivious); Since they internally sort data elements, iteration over them leads to the sorted sequence of the elements. Therefore, iterating over the `vector` precludes these replacement candidates. Those particular implementations in Table 1 were chosen because they are already implemented within the STL, and other implementations could easily be added to the cost model construction system.

DS	Alternate DS	Benefit	Limitation
vector	list	Fast insertion	None
	deque	Fast insertion	None
	set (map)	Fast search	Order-oblivious
	avl_set (avl_map)	Fast search	Order-oblivious
	hash_set (hash_map)	Fast insertion & search	Order-oblivious
list	vector	Fast iteration	None
	deque	Fast iteration	None
	set (map)	Fast search	Order-oblivious
	avl_set (avl_map)	Fast search	Order-oblivious
	hash_set (hash_map)	Fast search	Order-oblivious
set	avl_set	Fast search	None
	vector	Fast iteration	Order-oblivious
	list	Fast insertion & deletion	Order-oblivious
	hash_set	Fast insertion & search	Order-oblivious
map	avl_map	Fast search	None
	hash_map	Fast insertion & search	Order-oblivious

Table 1. Data structure replacements considered for each target data structure.

With this set of target implementations in mind, Figure 3 shows a high-level diagram of the proposed usage model. At compile time, an application is linked with a modified C++ Standard Template Li-

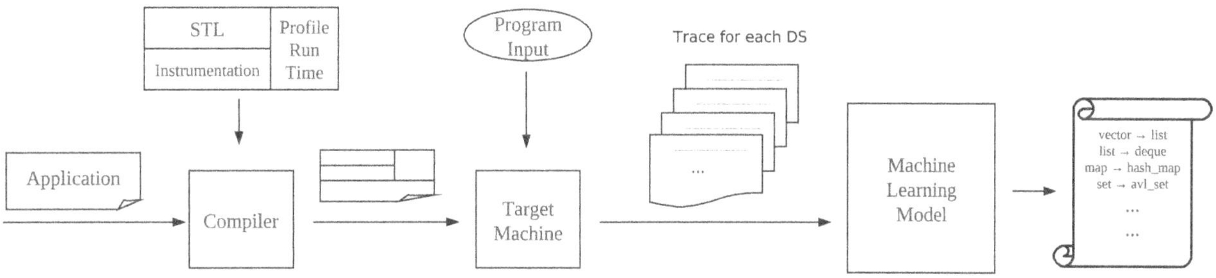

Figure 3. The framework of the data structure selection.

brary (STL) so that profiling data structures are used instead of the original ones. The profiling data structures are inherited from the original STL data structure, and their interface functions contain code which records the behaviors including hardware performance counters, and then calls the original interfaces. All the profiling features are recorded in trace files, which are post-processed and sorted by data structure. This sorting takes both relative execution time and calling context into consideration, in order to provide developers with a prioritized list of which data structures are most important to change. Once the data is sorted, the machine-learning-based cost model provides a suggestion of what data structures should be replaced with alternate implementations. Optionally, this output could be fed into a code refactoring tool [18], which could automate the implementation replacements. This type of optimization tool can have a significant impact on the performance of real-world applications.

4. Model Construction

Accurate model construction is essential for effective data structure selection. Brainy leverages machine learning to construct the model for predicting the best data structure implementations. The model must satisfy three properties to be successful. First, the model should be accurate across many different data structure behaviors and usage patterns. Second, the model should be aware of microarchitectural characteristics of the underlying system. Third, the methodology for characterizing the performance of data structures should be automated and repeatable so that it is easy to construct new models for new microarchitectures.

If these properties are not satisfied by the model, architectural variations would easily make the predicting performance of the model inaccurate. In this case, improving the accuracy of the model requires re-training the model on the new microarchitecture. A more serious problem is that the training applications/examples[1] painfully-collected to cover the huge design space on the original microarchitecture might not provide abundant learning capabilities any longer on the new microarchitecture (See Figure 1). That is, due to the architectural change, the original training applications could not produce the broad spectrum of the best data structures as before, thus failing to model various data structure behaviors. Therefore, new training applications should be collected again to cover the missing portion of the design space. This is extremely time-consuming and requires enormous effort without the help of the automated and repeatable methodology. This section describes how these issues are addressed. It must be noted that just using machine learning itself cannot satisfy the issues. These issues are rather the prerequisites for the success of machine learning.

Formally, the description of the data structure selection model is as follows: given a set of input features X and a set of data structure implementations Y as output, the model is to find a function $f: X \rightarrow Y$ such that the predicted result $y = f(x)$, where $y \in Y$ and x is a set of features for a data structure in an application, matches the best data structure (*BestDS*) of the application. The training set of the model is comprised of many pairs of the feature set and the best data structure, i.e., $(x^1, BestDS^1)$, $(x^2, BestDS^2)$, ..., etc. The features include both software features such as the number of interface invocations and hardware features such as cache misses (Section 5.1 discusses the both features in more detail). Thus, features capture various aspects of the data structure usage when an application is running. In collecting the training set, Brainy uses an application generator to prepare a significant quantity of applications and executes each application through two phases of data collection: first to measure the runtime and second to record the detailed performance metrics. This section describes why so many applications are required, the details of the application generator, and how it is used in the two phases of data collection.

[1] This paper uses the terms "training applications" and "training examples" interchangeably.

4.1 Training Set and Overfitting

Creating an accurate model using machine learning that represents a vast array of different data structure behaviors requires having a large and thorough set of training examples. If the training examples are not representative of the many varied behaviors of real world applications, then the resulting model cannot yield accurate predictions. Therefore, training should provide the machine learning algorithm with all critical patterns of data structures' behaviors in which one implementation performs much better than another. Unfortunately, constructing such a training set is a very difficult problem.

The main difficulty of constructing effective training example sets is the very large design space. For example, an application may use only a subset of interface functions, or use them with a consistent frequency distribution (e.g., always performing twice as many lookups as insertions). On top of that, there are many hardware-specific characteristics, such as the size of data elements in relation to cache-block size, that make the training example sets constructed for one architecture potentially irrelevant for another.

Compounding the problem, each portion of the design space must be fully represented in order to avoid *overfitting* the model. *Overfitting* is a well-documented problem where machine learning algorithms adjust to random features (i.e., noise) of the training examples. Since such random features have no causal relation to the prediction function, the resulting prediction performance on unseen data becomes poorer while the performance on the training examples improves [5]. Thus, *overfitting* misleads the resulting model away from the optimum. This is most likely to become a severe problem for insufficient amount of training examples, since the noises are much more outstanding in that case, i.e., the model is inevitably inaccurate.

Because of the immense search space and the problems from *overfitting*, sample benchmarks cannot effectively train a machine learning model for data structure selection.

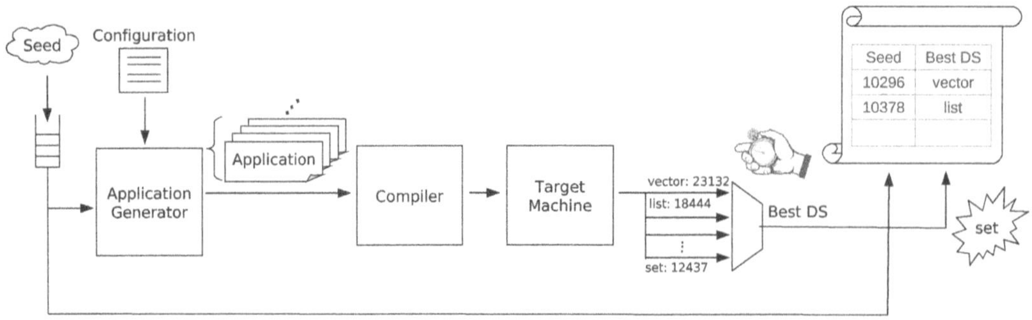

Figure 4. Training Framework Phase-I; Generating Applications and Measuring Execution Times

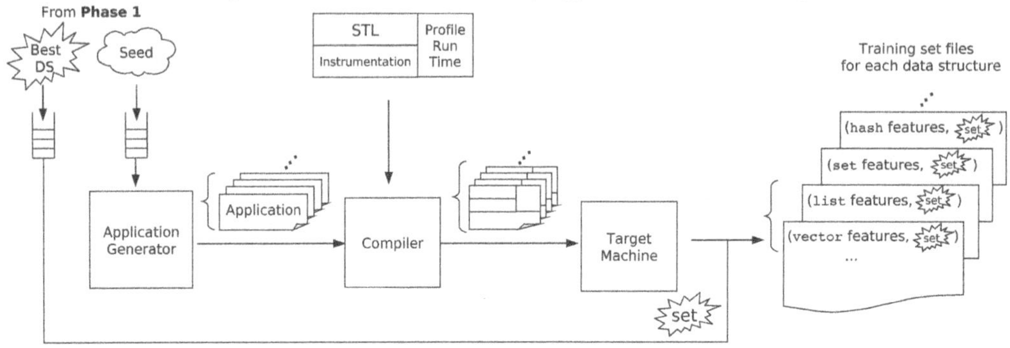

Figure 5. Training Framework Phase-II; Collecting Software and Hardware Features

4.2 Application Generator

Instead, this work proposes using an *application generator* to cover the design space sufficiently with synthetic applications. That is, a tool (the application generator) creates a variety of applications that test different parts of the overall space. Each application models particular behaviors of a single data structure which are randomly determined, i.e., a probability distribution determines how the interface functions should be invoked. Using the application generator, Brainy can easily have as many training examples as needed, thereby avoiding the *overfitting*. Note that if there are a sufficient number of training examples, then the noise would play a vanishingly small role in the learning process. The vision is that the application generator and the configuration file can be distributed with the data structure library, and can be used to train the machine learning model at install-time for the specific hardware of the system.

The application generator first prepares a synthetic application with an abstract data type (ADT) implemented by a C++ template that can take each data structure. The modeling is achieved via randomization. To illustrate, the synthetic application runs a function-dispatch loop. A random number determines which interface function is invoked every iteration of the loop. Thus, the order of interface invocations and their invocation frequencies are random. Randomization also controls how the dispatched interface is invoked, e.g., what data element is searched for `find`. Table 2 represents what property is randomly determined, and how it is specified in a configuration file. In particular, this configuration only specifies the total number of all the interface invocations. In each generated application, the number of invocations of each interface may vary, but the total number of invocations is constant across the applications.

To cover the different behaviors of interface invocations, the number of invocations for a given interface should be able to vary between zero and the total number. To achieve this goal, Brainy exploits a random number distribution to choose the number of invocations for each interface, such that the sum of the invocations is the configured total.

After determining how the application interacts with the ADT, the application generator finally creates a set of applications with interchangeable data structures, based on the replacement limitations described in Table 1. This is achieved by simply specifying an actual data structure in the ADT, which is a C++ template. Thus, the behavior of the synthetic applications is exactly same, i.e., the only difference is that they have a different data structure.

Since the random numbers completely determine every behavior of a data structure, a different sequence of random numbers leads to different interactions with the ADT, and thus different sets of applications. With that in mind, the application generator must use a randomization method that has a sufficiently low probability of generating equivalent random sequences.

4.3 Training Framework

Figure 4 and Figure 5 show how the training framework of Brainy functions based on the application generator. The training consists of two phases, each of which are iterative processes. As detailed in Algorithm 1, the first phase (Phase-I) consists of iterations of generating sets of synthetic applications with the same behavior but different data structures using the application generator. The applications are compiled, run on the target machine, and the execution time is measured to determine which data structure is the best for each application. Then in $seed\_ds\_pairs$, the best data structure is recorded together with the seed value used to generate the set of the applications [2].

Updating $need\_more\_sets$ is complex as there is no intervention or effort to generate applications that are best for a specific data structure; so after many iterations some data structures will

[2] Brainy records the best data structure only if it is 5% or more faster than any another. This prevents a data structure, which is barely the best, from being selected as an alternative.

Data structure behavior determined randomly	Specification example	Description
Total number of invocations for all interface functions	$TotalInterfCalls = 1000$	Randomly divide 1000 invocations and assign them to each interface
Size of data element	$DataElemSize = \{4, 8, 64, ...\}$	Randomly pick one from the specified set
Maximum value of data to be inserted	$MaxInsertVal = 65536$	Insert a random number between 0 and 65536 on `insert`
Maximum value of data to be removed	$MaxRemoveVal = 65536$	Remove a random number between 0 and 65536 on `erase`
Maximum value of data to be searched	$MaxSearchVal = 65536$	Search a random number between 0 and 65536 on `find`
Maximum number of data elements to be iterated	$MaxIterCount = 65536$	Iterate data elements a random number of times under 65536 on ++/--

Table 2. The behaviors of a data structure which are randomly decided, and the specification example in a configuration file.

input : $data\_structures$ from config
input : $need\_more\_sets$ from config
output: $seed\_ds\_pairs$ - pairs of seeds and data structures

Map<seed, DS> $seed\_ds\_pairs \leftarrow \emptyset$
Map<DS, time> $runtime \leftarrow \emptyset$
while $need\_more\_sets$ **do**
    $seed \leftarrow Time()$
    forall the $DS \in data\_structures$ **do**
        $A \leftarrow Compiler(AppGen(seed, DS))$
        $A()$ // run
        $runtime[DS] \leftarrow GetRuntime()$
    end
    $seed\_ds\_pairs \leftarrow$
    $seed\_ds\_pairs \cup (seed, FastestDS(runtime))$
    $runtime[DS] \leftarrow \emptyset$
    update $need\_more\_sets$
end

Algorithm 1: Training Framework Phase-I

have more "best" applications than others. Brainy stops Phase-I when a certain number of applications, e.g., ten thousand, is best for each data structure and switches to the next step (Phase-II). This threshold number is adjustable, and it is possible to use a different threshold for each data structure through the configuration file. It is important to note that the Phase-I is very fast since it does not perform any expensive profiling to extract features. Thus, measuring the applications' execution time to determine the best data structure has minimal overhead.

input : $data\_structures$ from config
input : $seed\_ds\_pairs$ from Phase-I
output: $train\_set$ - training data for model

Map<DS, Map<features,DS>> $train\_set \leftarrow \emptyset$
forall the $seed \in seed\_ds\_pairs$ **do**
    forall the $DS \in data\_structures$ **do**
        $A \leftarrow$
        $Compiler(AppGen(seed, DS), Instrumentation)$

        $A()$ // run
        $features \leftarrow GetFeatures()$
        $train\_set[DS] \leftarrow$
        $train\_set[DS] \cup (features, seed\_ds\_pairs[seed])$
    end
end

Algorithm 2: Training Framework Phase-II

In Phase-II, the application generator replays the executions of the applications in Phase-I by taking the seed value recorded in Phase-I (as using the same seed guarantees producing the same sequence of random numbers in most pseudo-random number generators). Note, using seeds is but one way of retaining the applications between phases. That is, the applications are regenerated, and therefore Brainy can execute millions of training applications without an explosion in disk space. As shown in Algorithm 2, this phase iterates through the recorded seed values ($seed\_ds\_pairs$), regenerates the applications, and compiles them with additional instrumentation, specifically a modified STL library that has profiling for data structures. With this profiling, all of the software and hardware features can be collected during program execution. The profiling data structures record the features in a designated training set file according to the type of the data structure. $train\_set$ is updated with the collected features and the best data structure as observed in Phase-I. Again, the applications generated in each iteration have the exact same behavior, and the only difference between them is the data structure implementation. This iterative process stops when all the seeds are consumed. At the end, each data structure's training set file is fed into the machine learning tool to train the corresponding model.

In addition, Brainy's training framework is flexible. When long training time is unacceptable, users can specify that training occur for only a small number of training applications for each data structure, e.g., train only 1000 applications for each data structure. The two-phase training framework can prevent extra applications generated in Phase-I from being fed into Phase-II which performs a time-consuming feature profiling. E.g., if Phase-I generates 1500 and 1000 applications for `vector` and `list`, respectively, Phase-II does not accept the rest 500 `vector` applications. In this way, the framework can dramatically reduce the training time.

One might suggest simply using real applications to train the machine learning algorithm. However, this approach is neither practical nor plausible. Assume that there is a good real application which clearly shows `list` is better than `vector`. Nevertheless, this real application just shows one particular case among millions of situations where `list` outperforms `vector`. For effective data structure selection, the training process must cover as many cases as possible, so that the machine learning model will yield accurate prediction results for unseen applications, which are practically infinite. That is, if the model just learns a few cases where one data structure is better than another, the resulting data structure selection is very likely to be inaccurate for real applications that were unseen in the training process.

The application generator is a reasonable approach for modeling the myriad cases required for accurate machine learning predictions. Furthermore, this framework for modeling has further advantages over real applications (or hand constructed benchmarks) by not being tied to current implementations / architectures. Otherwise, every variation to any part of the system would potentially require constructing a new set of applications. Therefore, it is desirable that the framework can automatically produce training examples tuned to the specific architecture within a reasonable time.

5. Artificial Neural Network (ANN)

Several machine learning techniques have been proposed over the last few decades, and it remains a question of great debate as to which machine learning technique is optimal for a given classification problem. The accuracy of the machine learning technique is inherently dependent on the characteristics of the data set. For example, Artificial Neural Network and Support Vector Machine generally perform better when the features are continuous and multicollinearity is present. They can both deal with a case where relationship between input and output features is non-linear[3], i.e., data are not linearly separable. [15, 21].

The features generated by instrumentation code show both linear and non-linear characteristics. Brainy exploits Artificial Neural Network (ANN), since it is robust to noise as well as effective for linear and non-linear statistical data modeling [11]. This seems an appropriate approach in that data structure selection is a highly complex problem domain and its training examples may have considerable noise and model-bias, thereby hurting the prediction accuracy. The training of the ANN model in this work leverages a back-propagation algorithm [24].

The ANN model predicts the alternative data structure that achieves the best performance in replacing the original data structure in an application. The target data structures, determined in Section 3, have their own ANN model as shown in Figure 3. That is because the list of features necessary for predicting the best data structure type is different between data structures. For example, `vector` suffers from `resizing` when its capacity is full, but `list` does not. In particular, there is another model for `vector` and `list` to address the situation when they are used in an order-oblivious manner (where insertion order has nothing to do with data organization in the data structure). When they are used in this manner, `vector` and `list` can be replaced with `hash_set` or `set`. When the underlying hardware system is changed, the ANN models for data structures should be trained and learned again for the new microarchitecture, possibly with a new set of training examples. This is achieved with the help of the application generator.

5.1 Feature Selection

It is important to determine which subset of features to collect for the training examples. By selecting only the most relevant features, the machine learning model will be more accurate and the learning process will converge faster. Initially, most of interface functions of a data structure and, if available, how much work is done on their invocation are collected through instrumentation code. This work calls the latter a cost of each interface invocation. For example, `find` has a cost to model how many data elements are accessed until the search operation is finished. Similarly, for `erase` and `insert`, their costs represent how many data elements, located after the insertion and removal point, are moved backwards or forwards. Along with these software features, hardware features are also considered to make the model aware of underlying hardware architecture.

Initially, we collected the numbers on L1 and L2 caches, TLB, retired instruction, page faults and processor clock cycles, and so on. Especially, this work omits some features such as L2 cache misses, TLB misses, OS page faults, and bus utilization, since manual feature selection empirically shows that these features rarely affect the prediction of the best data structure. Since all the code to be executed becomes entirely different after data structure replacements, Brainy uses hardware features just to capture how the original data structures show certain behaviors useful for data structure selection.

To perform the feature selection, this work leverages the evolutionary approach based on genetic algorithm due to its success especially for large dimensions of features [28]. This approach represents a given subset of features as a *chromosome*, a binary string with the length of the total number of features. In the *chromosome*, each binary value represents the presence of a corresponding feature. The population of chromosomes (different feature selection candidates), evolves toward better solutions. Meanwhile, *mutation* in the genetic algorithm prevents the evolution from getting stuck in local optima, helping to approach the global optimum. In particular, this work constitutes the *chromosome* as real-valued weights, instead of binary value, that show which feature has more impact on the resulting model instead of binary values [12, 13].

[3] Support Vector Machines can also address this case with the help of transformed feature space. A linear separation in the transformed feature space corresponds to a non-linear separation in the original space [15].

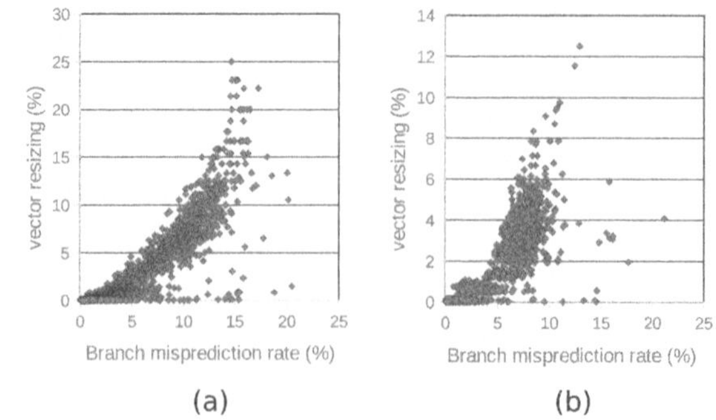

Figure 6. Correlation between conditional branch misprediction and vector `resizing` when the data structure is order-aware (a) and order-oblivious (b)

Table 3 shows the top five features with the highest weight for each ANN model. For each data structure, the order of features shown in the table follows the decreasing order of the weights, e.g., the first low corresponds to the features with the highest weight.

The most important features to decide whether `vector` should be replaced, no matter if it is order-aware or order-oblivious, contain the number of `resizes`, that is performed on data insertion when the size of `vector` is full. It is interesting that a misprediction rate of conditional branches belongs to the important features. This results from the fact that such a branch misprediction can model exceptional behaviors of data structures, e.g. invoking `resize` on `insert` operations of `vector` and `hash table`. In other words, data insertion to the data structures does not suffer from performing `resize` for most of time if the capacity of the dynamic array is not full. Note that once `resize` is invoked due to insufficient capacity, it takes a while to see the recurrence of another `resize`. The reason is that `resize` extends the capacity, in case there are many more data insertions to again fill the array. In the `insert` function, a conditional branch instruction determines whether `resize` is invoked. The branch predictor could fail to correctly predict the branch instruction for this uncommon path, which is a taken branch to call `resize`. This is justified in Figure 6 where the X-axis corresponds to the branch misprediction rate while the Y-axis to the `resize` ratio (%) among the total interface invocations.

It turns out that `insert` and `insert_cost` are relevant features for `vectors`. This makes sense since these features capture how much `vector` suffers from shifting data after the insertion point. The same goes for why `erase_cost` is relevant for the order-oblivious `vector`. In particular, when `vector` is used in the order-oblivious manner, `find` is a relevant feature. Note that in this case, there is no explicit iteration operation, thus every data access is performed by `find`.

For order-aware and order-oblivious `lists`, L1 cache miss rate is a relevant feature. It can be thought that the miss rate would capture how the nodes of the linked list fit into a cache block. Again, for the order-oblivious `list`, `find`-related features are relevant. In particular, `push_front` is relevant when `list` is used in the order-aware manner. This is understandable given how

vector	order-oblivious vector	list	order-oblivious list	set	map
resizing	br_miss	iterate	find_cost	find_cost	L1_miss
insert	find_cost	push_front	find	L1_miss	data-size / cache block-size
br_miss	L1_miss	L1_miss	L1_miss	data-size / cache block-size	br_miss
insert_cost	resizing	insert	erase	find	insert_cost
iterate	erase_cost	erase_cost	data-size / cache block-size	insert_cost	find_cost

Table 3. Selected features for each data structure

frequently data insertion occurs at the beginning of data structures, which can guide whether vector or deque is an appropriate alternative.

For set and map, find-related features are most relevant, as their data structure selection highly depends on how frequently find is performed and how many data elements a find operation accesses. Again, the insert_cost and find_cost represent the number of data elements accessed while the corresponding operations reach the insertion point and the search location, respectively. In addition, L1 cache miss rates and data element size per cache block size can capture how long the latency of each data element is on the find operation. Thus, they can quantify the cost of data accesses involved in find operations.

5.2 Limitation

While Brainy captures many useful properties with synthetic applications created by the application generator, it also has a limitation that leaves room for future improvement. The synthetic applications might not accurately model the impact of other parts of a real application on the microarchitectural state, e.g., the L1 is polluted by data in intervening instructions. However, it should be noted that Brainy is aware of such a microarchitectural behavior, and possibly another synthetic application can capture the polluted L1 cache behavior.

Even with these drawbacks, it turns out that the training with the synthetic applications can "cover" real applications. That is it is conjectured that the behaviors exhibited in actual execution would be a subset of training behaviors therefore hoping that the actual execution model would be subset of the constructed one. Section 6 demonstrates that for real-world applications, Brainy can consistently select optimal data structures across input and architectural changes.

6. Evaluation

In order to evaluate the effectiveness of Brainy, we implemented it as a part of C++ Standard Template Library (STL) for GCC 4.5 [8]. To access hardware performance counters, we used PAPI [6]. Especially, to show Brainy's accuracy across different inputs, we selected a set of C++ applications where the best data structure varies on input changes. The data structure selection experiments were performed on two different systems that have Intel Core2 and Intel Atom microarchitectures, respectively. The detailed system configurations are described in Table 7.

In the next sections, we first validate Brainy's data structure selection models. Then, we show four case studies with real-world applications. In the first two applications, the optimal data structures vary across inputs and even microarchitectures (Section 6.3). Thus, they show the difficulty of accurate data structure selection. In the next two applications, the optimal data structures are rarely affected by input and microarchitecture changes. Thus, we show their results briefly compared to the first two applications.

Figure 8 summarizes the performance improvement of each application obtained from Brainy's data structure replacement. In cases where the optimal data structure varies across inputs, only the best performance result Brainy achieved appears in the figure.

Desktop	
CPU	Intel Core2 Quad Q6600 2.4 GHz
Caches	4 X 32 KB L1 data, 2 X 4 MB L2 unified
Memory / DISK	2 GB SDRAM, 200 GB HDD
Operating System	64-bit Ubuntu Desktop 8.04
Compiler	GCC 4.5 with libstdc++ 4.5.0
Laptop	
CPU	Intel Atom N270 1.6 GHz with HyperThreading
Caches	32 KB L1 data, 512 KB L2 unified
Memory / DISK	512 MB SDRAM, 8 GB solid state disk (SSD)
Operating System	32-bit Ubuntu Netbook Remix 9.10
Compiler	GCC 4.5 with libstdc++ 4.5.0

Figure 7. Target systems configurations

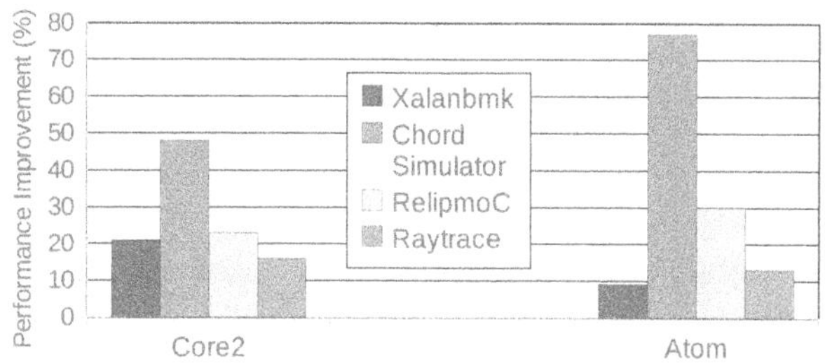

Figure 8. Performance improvement Brainy achieved

Brainy achieved an average performance improvement of 27% and 33% on Core2 and Atom microarchitectures, and up to 77% for some case (Section 6.3).

6.1 Model Validation with an Application Generator

Validating Brainy's data structure selection models leverages the application generator. For an accurate and fair evaluation, the application generator newly produces 1000 random applications for each data structure model. Note that all these random applications have never been seen by the models, i.e., the model validation is performed with completely new applications. Thus, the applications here are not the ones used to train the models. The accuracy is calculated as follows;

$$accuracy(\%) = 1 - \frac{The\ number\ of\ mispredictions}{1000} \quad (1)$$

Figure 9 shows how accurate the prediction results of each data structure model are for the 1000 applications on the Core2 and Atom microarchitectures. Overall, for Core2 microarchitecture, the accuracies of models are between 80% and 90%. This is impressive in that the 1000 applications for each model capture a variety of behaviors of data structure usages, thus the best data structure is quite different across the applications. It needs to be noted that each data structure model attempts to select the best data structure among many replaceable data structures as described in Table 1. For instance, the model for vector selects the best data structure among possible six candidates, when it is used in the order-oblivious manner. For Atom microarchitecture, the accuracies of models are between 70% and 80%. This is enough to effectively

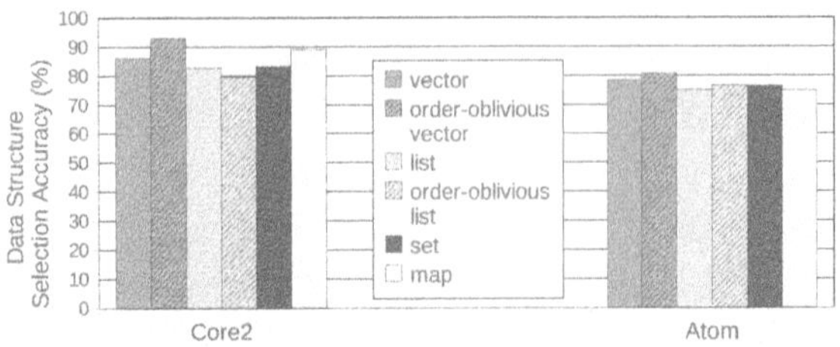

Figure 9. Accuracy of data structure selection models; for the same data structure, there are two different models for Core2 and Atom microarchitectures, respectively.

predict the best data structure of a real application as described in the next section.

6.2 Xalancbmk

Xalancbmk is an open source XSLT processor that performs XML to HTML transformations. It takes as inputs an XML document and an XSLT style sheet with detailed instructions for the transformation. The program maintains a string cache comprised of two levels, *m_busyList* and *m_availableList*, `vector`s. When a string is freed in *XalanDOMStringCache::release*, it moves the string to the *m_availableList*, provided it is found in the *m_busyList*. To determine whether the string is found in the latter list, the data structure, `vector`, performs `find` operations. In general, these operations are often recurring, but the frequency of performing them is varying across program inputs. In addition, each input brings about different search patterns.

To define the accuracy of Brainy for data structure selection, the evaluation process leverages comparison with the Oracle scheme which is empirically determined across program inputs on each microarchitecture. If the resulting data structure selection agrees with the Oracle's, the result are considered accurate.

In addition, the evaluation compares Brainy with Perflint, the state-of-the-art data structure advisor that relies on hand-constructed models [17]. On each interface invocation, Perflint assigns the cost taking into account traditional asymptotic analysis. As an example, for the cost of a `find` operation among N data elements, `vector` leverages average case for linear search, i.e., '3/4N', while `set` uses 'log$N$' for binary search[4]. Each cost is multiplied with a coefficient value, which is determined by linear regression analysis for execution time, and accumulated whenever the interface function is called. In particular, Perflint provides the hand-constructed model for `vector-to-set` replacement while `vector-to-hash_set` is not supported. Each interface invocation of the original data structure (`vector`) updates the costs of both `vector` and `set`. Based on comparing the accumulated costs at the end of program execution, Perflint selectively reports the alternative data structure.

Figure 10 shows execution times of three selected data structures, `vector`, `set`, and `hash_set` with those schemes. The ideal data structure selection (Oracle), i.e., `vector` is the best for a train input while `hash_set` for test and reference inputs, are identical on both microarchitectures. Especially, `set` performs differently on the two microarchitectures. That is, for test and reference inputs, `set` outperforms `vector` on Core2 microarchitecture while the data structure replacement to `set` does not achieve significant performance improvement on Atom microarchitecture.

Figure 11 shows the results of each data structure selection scheme for the two different microarchitectures. Baseline represents the original data structure in the figure. According to the Oracle, for test and reference inputs, the original data structure, which

[4] For binary search, the average and worst cases are exactly the same.

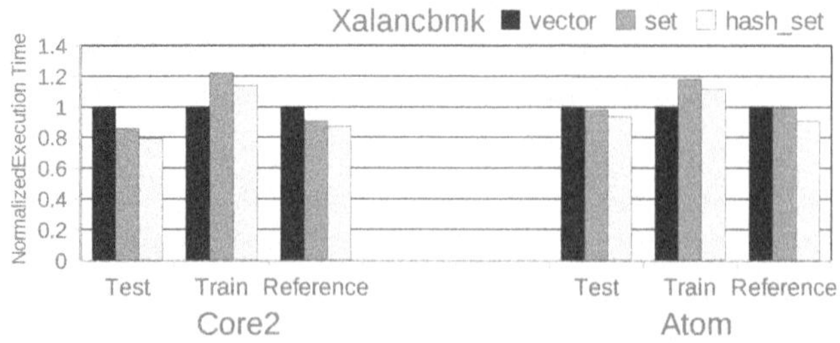

Figure 10. Normalized execution time across different data structures; The baseline execution times (in second) are on Core are 3s, 74s, and 234s for test, train, and reference, respectively. On Atom, the baseline execution times for these inputs are 18s, 611s, and 1345s, respectively. Brainy selects the best data structure for each input of Xalancbmk

Input Size	Selection Schemes	Reported Best DS	
		Core2	Atom
Test	Baseline	`vector`	`vector`
	Perflint	`set`	`set`
	Brainy	`hash_set`	`hash_set`
	Oracle	`hash_set`	`hash_set`
Train	Baseline	`vector`	`vector`
	Perflint	`set`	`set`
	Brainy	`vector`	`vector`
	Oracle	`vector`	`vector`
Reference	Baseline	`vector`	`vector`
	Perflint	`set`	`set`
	Brainy	`hash_set`	`hash_set`
	Oracle	`hash_set`	`hash_set`

Figure 11. Xalancbmk's data selection results on Core2 and Atom microarchitectures.

is `vector`, is desired to be replaced with `hash_set` for better performance. The reason is that the data structure executes many search operations. However, for a train input where `hash_set` is suboptimal, `vector` is the best data structure. This is not easily understandable and rather surprising. According to the profiled features with instrumentation code of Brainy, the application invokes the `find` function more than 60 millions times for a train input as well as for a reference input. On top of that, the train input causes the application to `erase` the first data element from the head of the dynamic array almost 30 times more frequently than the reference input does, which is pretty problematic for `vector`. On the other hand, for the test input, the application achieves the best performance with `hash_set` in spite of a relatively small number of `find` function invocations, which is about thirty-seven thousand. Thus, accurate data structure selection is very difficult for this application.

With the help of the profiled feature results, it turns out that `find` operation is much more dominant compared to the problematic `erase` operation. What happened behind the scenes related to the `find` operation is that the number of data elements the operation touched is varying across program inputs. This is mainly due to the change of search patterns across inputs. Table 4 presents more detailed information about this situation. This implies that building an accurate hand-constructed model would be much more difficult.

Input Size	`find` invocations	Touched data elements
Test	37,594	32,804,644
Train	62,438,422	2,569,120,180
Reference	67,720,063	89,454,229,684

Table 4. The number of `find` invocations and the total number of touched data elements for all the invocations across program inputs.

For the training input, a majority of `find` operations succeed in searching the designated data element in the very beginning of the dynamic array of the original data structure, `vector`. In this case, `hash_set` just causes extra memory consumption compared to `vector`. It is desirable to force the application not to pay for complex operations such as maintaining hash buckets which is not really necessary, thus `vector` is preferable to `hash_set`. Brainy can recognize the search pattern based on `find`-related features as described in Section 5.1. Together with considering other software and hardware features profiled, Brainy correctly reported the same results as the Oracle across different inputs for the both microarchitectures.

Meanwhile, Perflint failed to consistently report accurate prediction results for the best data structure, even if it only needs to perform a binary decision between `vector` and `set`. For the train input, Perflint incorrectly reported that `set` is preferable to `vector`. This is problematic because the resulting data structure replacement to `set` causes performance degradation on both microarchitectures as shown in Figure 10. For the reference input, Perflint reported that `set` is preferable, which only works on Core2 microarchitecture, i.e., replacing `vector` with `set` achieves little performance improvement on Atom microarchitecture. Again, Brainy selected the optimal data structures consistently across all the program inputs on both microarchitectures.

6.3 Chord Simulator

This application is an open source simulator for Chord, a distributed lookup protocol to locate Internet resources. The main work of the simulation is to send query requests for a certain resource over the network and to record if the lookup fails by checking the response to the query. Whenever the response is received, the simulator drops the message, which corresponds to the resource of the response, in a pending list of routing messages. The search performance thus translates to the simulation time reduction. In particular, determining the message to be dropped performs *std::find_if* on the pending list, which is implemented using `vector`, checking an ID field of each message structure. Thus, the vector can be replaced with map-like data structures using the ID field as its key.

Brainy suggested to replace the original `vector` with `map` or `hash_map`, according to different inputs. In the application, the optimal data structure varies across different inputs on both microarchitectures, as shown Figure 13. It is important to note that for the Large input, the optimal data structures on both microarchitectures do not agree with each other, i.e., `vector` is optimal on Core2 whereas `map` performs the best on Atom. This shows the difficulties of the data structure selection in the application. Overall, Brainy correctly reported the same results as the Oracle across different inputs and microarchitectures. It needs to be noted that when `vector`, the original data structure, is optimal, Brainy correctly selected this data structure. Figure 12 shows the performance results of different data structures across different inputs and microarchitectures. The configuration of the graph and the table follows the one in the previous section.

Again, we compared Brainy with Perflint[5]. Perflint selected `map` for all combinations of inputs and mircroarchitectures. However, for the Large input on Core2, `map` performs worse than the original data structure, `vector`. Perflint's suggestion causes performance degradation in this case. In contrast, Brainy consistently selected the optimal data structures for all combinations of inputs and microarchitectures.

[5] Since Perflint does not support `vector-to-map` replacement explicitly, this work considers its suggestion of `set` as the replacement to `map`. We believe that the implementation of the replacement should exactly follow the manner that `vector-to-set` is implemented.

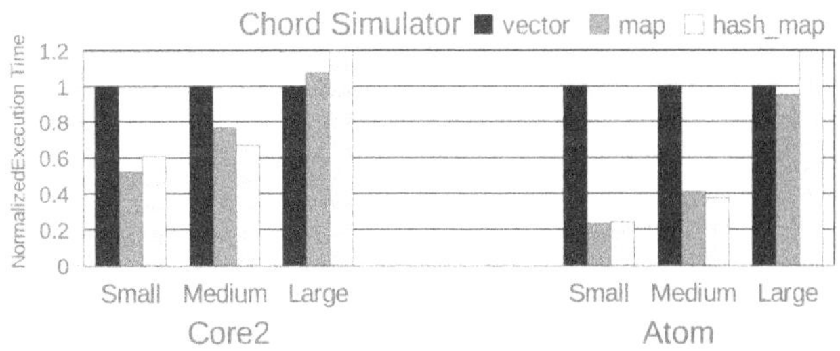

Figure 12. Normalized execution times across different data structures: the baseline execution times (in second) on Core2 are 9s, 19s, and 306s for test, train, and reference, respectively. On Atom, the baseline execution times for these inputs are 47s, 203s, and 2952s, respectively. Brainy selects the best data structure for each input of Chord Simulator.

Input Size	Selection Schemes	Reported Best DS	
		Core2	Atom
Small	Baseline	vector	vector
	Perflint	map	map
	Brainy	map	map
	Oracle	map	map
Medium	Baseline	vector	vector
	Perflint	map	map
	Brainy	hash_map	hash_map
	Oracle	hash_map	hash_map
Large	Baseline	vector	vector
	Perflint	map	map
	Brainy	vector	map
	Oracle	vector	map

Figure 13. Chord simulator's data selection results on Core2 and Atom microarchitectures.

6.4 RelipmoC

RelipmoC is an open source translator that converts i386 assembly code to C code, i.e., a decompiler for i386 assembly. It analyzes the input assembly code and builds a list of basic blocks implemented using STL `set`, thus a red-black tree. On the `set` data structure, it performs data flow and control flow analyses to extract high level expressions, and to recover program constructs, e.g., loops and conditional statements, along with the information about their nesting level. It frequently checks if a basic block belongs to the program constructs which are normally a list of basic blocks. In the meantime, `find` and iteration operations are executed many times for short lists and long lists of basic blocks, respectively. Brainy suggested replacing `set` with `avl_set`, the implementation of which is an AVL tree. By conducting the suggested replacement, we improved the execution time of the application on Core2 and Atom microarchitectures by 23% and 30% on both microarchitectures, respectively. The baseline execution times (in seconds) of this application on Core2 and Atom are 41s and 120s. We could not compare Brainy with Perflint since it does not support any replacement for `set`.

6.5 Raytrace

This application draws a 3D image of groups of spheres using a ray tracing algorithm implemented in C++ STL. The spheres are divided into groups that use `list` to store them. The main computation of the program occurs in a loop on *intersect* of each group object. First, the intersection calculation is performed for each group of spheres. If a ray hits the group, it is subsequently performed for its spheres (scenes). Thus the `list` is heavily accessed and iterated during the ray tracing, i.e., `vector` is much preferable. Brainy correctly suggested to replace the `list` with `vector`. By taking Brainy's suggestion, we replaced the original data structure with `vector` thereby reducing the execution time of the application on Core2 and Atom microarchitectures by 16% and 13%, respectively. The baseline execution times (in seconds) of this application on Core2 and Atom are 79s and 347s. This time Perflint selected the optimal data structure just as Brainy did.

7. Related Work

Selecting the best data structure implementation is often a problem ignored by developers; they simply rely on library developers to choose a good implementation for the average case and accept the results. This leaves significant room for improvement. When developers do select specific implementations, they typically rely on asymptotic analysis, even though it can often lead to incorrect decisions in real-world applications. As pointed out, asymptotic analysis was always intended to be used in algorithmic selection and not in data structure selection/tuning.

Several researchers have previously investigated the problem of data structure selection in various contexts [14, 17, 25–27]. Jung and Clark propose a dynamic analysis that can automatically identify data structures and their interface functions. They showed that the resulting information, e.g., how the functions interact with the data structures, is very useful for data structure selection [14]. Other researchers suggests language level supports for data structure selection. For example, in high-level programming languages, such as SETL, it is impossible to select data structure implementations; all data structures are specified as abstract data types, and the compiler must determine the implementation [25]. Work in this area focused on using only static analysis for data structure selection [26]. While the raised abstraction level of these languages did help productivity, the performance of these tools was generally worse than hand-selected implementations.

The Chameleon [27] and Perflint [17] projects are the most similar to Brainy. Chameleon and Perflint instrument Java and C++ applications, respectively, to collect runtime statistics on behaviors such as interface function calls. Additionally, Chameleon collects heap-related information from the garbage collector. These statistics are then fed into hand-constructed diagnostics to determine if the data structures should be changed. Both Chameleon and Perflint showed impressive space and performance improvements for real-world benchmarks. In particular, Brainy considers memory bloat as Chameleon does. Recall that the application generator varies the number of data elements in a data structure as well as the size of each element, thus the generator can create applications suffering from memory bloat. Brainy extends those prior works by 1) using machine learning to automatically construct more accurate models, instead of relying on hand-construction, and 2) incorporating hardware performance counters into the analysis, thus providing greater accuracy. In particular, unlike Chameleon, Brainy is not restricted to languages that have managed runtime features such as garbage collection.

The prior works have three problems. First, they require many models for each data structure replacement. For example, if M data structures can be replaced with N alternative data structures, the prior works require total M x N models. Note that modeling the execution of alternative data structures depends on the original data structure. On the contrary, Brainy needs only M models, thus the instrumentation overhead can be greatly reduced.

Second, modeling the accurate execution of the alternative data structure is inherently difficult and sometimes impossible. For example, in a `vector-to-set` data structure replacement, it is very difficult to know how many data elements are accessed for a `find` operation in the alternative data structure (`set`) just by instrumenting the code of the original data structure (`vector`); that requires exactly tracking data insertion and deletion, operation order, orderedness of data values, search patterns, and so on. This subtlety of modeling the execution behavior of the alternative data structure forces the prior works to rely on asymptotic analysis and average case. However, such approximation is likely to generate inaccurate models. Thus we conclude that if the resulting models are inaccurate, why pay the cost of heavy instrumentation code for M x N models?

In this work, rather than modeling the execution of the alternative data structure, Brainy's machine learning-based model tries to answer the question, *'what alternative data structure is desirable when the original data structure behaves in a certain way?'* That is, Brainy focuses on modeling how the original data structure is executed to identify the relation between the execution location and the alternative data structures suited for the role. Consequently, Brainy reduces the number of models required compared to the prior works.

The last problem is about using hardware features, which are important as shown in Section 5.1. Unlike software features such as the number of function calls and their costs, it is almost impossible to model hardware features of the alternative data structure. For example, the number of mispredictions of conditional branches in the original data structure has no causal relation to the number of mispredictions in the alternative data structure. Thus, the prior works cannot effectively exploit hardware features while Brainy's machine learning-based model can. Again, the hardware features are critical for effective data structure selection.

In a different perspective, a body of work has been done to address inefficient use of data structures in terms of memory bloat [19, 20, 36, 37]. In [19], Mitchell and Sevitsky suggest a systematic approach to detect those data structures that end up with unnecessary memory (bloat). They introduces a new notion, *Health*, that analyzes how the memory space of a data structure is organized and used; and they present judgement schemes based on the notion to determine the inefficiency of the data structure use [36]. Xu and Rountev also present static and dynamic tools that detect inefficiently used data structures to avoid. They first identify interface functions (e.g, ADD/GET) of a data structure using static analysis. Then the static or dynamic tools analyze how these interface functions are called during the data structure execution.

There are key differences between these prior works and Brainy. First, they target Java and rely on virtual machine support. Again, Brainy is not restricted to languages that have managed runtime features. Second, they can deal with only case of the bloat-caused inefficiency of data structures. In C/C++, bloat is less of a concern than in Java where garbage collection is very important. Brainy can deal with many more cases of data structure inefficiency. Finally, they do not select a data structure, i.e., they just show if a data structure is inefficient in terms of bloat. In contrast, Brainy does provide a solution for inefficient usage of a data structure by selecting an alternative data structure.

Looking beyond data structures, the use of machine learning has become quite popular in the design of program optimizers [7, 16, 22, 31–33]. This paper applies many of the same techniques to a new domain, and provides insight on what needs to be considered for the success of machine learning in this particular problem. Coons et al. showed that careful feature selections can be helpful in reducing the dimensions of the search space, as well as achieving better solutions for finding good distributed instruction placements for an EDGE architecture [4]. This paper also considers careful feature selections.

Many researchers have also investigated hardware effects for high performance computing. Especially, in computational science domain, the awareness of underlying architecture is essential for extracting the best performance [23]. One promising approach is ATLAS (Automatically Tuned Linear Algebra Software) library. The philosophy of ATLAS exactly follows Brainy's. ATLAS fine-tunes its computational kernel by considering underlying hardware architecture during its install-time and adapts the various parameters of the library internals accordingly [1]. Since many developers of the system can keep using the optimized library, the tuning time is not a problem in general. Similarly, data structure library is one of the most frequently used libraries in many systems; Brainy's training time is not a problem in that sense.

8. Summary

Data structure selection is one of the most critical aspects in determining program efficiency. This paper presents Brainy, a novel and repeatable methodology for generating machine-learning based models to predict what the best data structure implementation is given a program, a set of inputs, and a target architecture. The work introduces a random program generator that is used to train the machine learning models, and demonstrates that these models are more accurate and more effective than previously proposed hand-constructed models based on traditional asymptotic analysis for real-world applications. The experimental results show that Brainy achieved an average performance improvement of 27% and 33% on two real machines with different processors.

Acknowledgments

Many thanks to Hyojun Kim, Sangho Lee, Hyunshik Shin, Jonathan C. Kim, Phillip Wright, Haicheng Wu, Nishad Kothari who helped edit initial versions of this draft, as well as Ahmad Sharif, Robert Hundt, and the anonymous referees who provided excellent feedback to help shape this work. Portions of this work were made possible with support from Google. The authors gratefully acknowledge the support of NSF grants CCF-1018544 and CCF-0916962.

References

[1] C. W. Antoine, A. Petitet, and J. J. Dongarra. Automated empirical optimization of software and the atlas project. *Parallel Computing*, 27:2001, 2000.

[2] M. Aref. Discussions on the LogicBlox Datalog Optimization Engine, 2009. personal communication.

[3] I.-H. Chung. *Towards Automatic Performance Tuning*. PhD thesis, University of Maryland, College Park, 2004.

[4] K. E. Coons, B. Robatmili, M. E. Taylor, A. Maher, D. Burger, and K. S. Mckinley. Feature selection and policy optimization for distributed instruction placement using reinforcement learning. In *PACT'08 : Proceddings of the 17th International Conference on Parallel Architectures and Compilation Techniques*, 2008.

[5] S. Q. Ding and C. Xiang. Overfitting problem: a new perspective from the geometrical interpretation of mlp. pages 50–57, 2003.

[6] J. Dongarra, K. London, S. Moore, P. Mucci, and D. Terpstra. Using papi for hardware performance monitoring on linux systems. In *Proceedings of the 2nd International Conference on Linux Clusters: The HPC Revolution, Linux Clusters Institute*, 2001.

[7] C. Dubach, J. Cavazos, B. Franke, G. Fursin, M. F. P. O'Boyle, and O. Temam. Fast compiler optimisation evaluation using code-feature based performance prediction. In *ACM International Conference on Computing Frontiers*, 2007.

[8] GCC, the GNU Compiler Collection. the gcc team, 2010. http://gcc.gnu.org.

[9] Google. Google code search, 2009. http://www.google.com/codesearh.

[10] D. Gusfield. *Algorithms on Strings, Trees, and Sequences: Computer Science and Computational Biology*. Cambridge University Press, 1997.

[11] M. H. Hassoun. *Fundamentals of Artificial Neural Networks*. MIT Press, Cambridge, MA, USA, 1995.

[12] F. Hussein. Genetic algorithms for feature selection and weighting, a review and study. In *ICDAR '01: Proceedings of the Sixth International Conference on Document Analysis and Recognition*, page 1240, Washington, DC, USA, 2001.

[13] J. Jarmulak and S. Craw. S.: Genetic algorithms for feature selection and weighting. in. In *Proceedings of the IJCAI'99 workshop on Automating the Construction of Case Based Reasoners*, pages 28–33, 1999.

[14] C. Jung and N. Clark. Ddt: design and evaluation of a dynamic program analysis for optimizing data structure usage. In *MICRO 42: Proceedings of the 42nd Annual IEEE/ACM International Symposium on Microarchitecture*, pages 56–66, New York, NY, USA, 2009. ACM.

[15] S. B. Kotsiantis. Supervised machine learning: A review of classification techniques. *Informatica (Slovenia)*, 31(3):249–268, 2007.

[16] H. Leather, E. Bonilla, and M. O'Boyle. Automatic Feature Generation for Machine Learning Based Optimizing Compilation. In *Proc. of the 2009 International Symposium on Code Generation and Optimization*, Mar. 2009.

[17] L. Liu and S. Rus. perflint: A Context Sensitive Performance Advisor for C++ Programs. In *Proc. of the 2009 International Symposium on Code Generation and Optimization*, Mar. 2009.

[18] T. Mens and T. Tourwe. A survey of software refactoring. *IEEE Transactions on Software Engineering*, 30(2):126–139, 2004.

[19] N. Mitchell and G. Sevitsky. The causes of bloat, the limits of health. In *Proceedings of the 22nd annual ACM SIGPLAN conference on Object-oriented programming systems and applications*, OOPSLA '07, pages 245–260, New York, NY, USA, 2007.

[20] N. Mitchell, E. Schonberg, and G. Sevitsky. Four trends leading to java runtime bloat. *IEEE Software*, 27:56–63, 2010.

[21] T. M. Mitchell. *Machine Learning*. McGraw-Hill, New York, 1997.

[22] A. Monsifrot, F. Bodin, and R. Quiniou. A machine learning approach to automatic production of compiler heuristics. In *AIMSA '02: Proceedings of the 10th International Conference on Artificial Intelligence: Methodology, Systems, and Applications*, pages 41–50, 2002.

[23] M. Muller-Hannemann and S. Schirra, editors. *Algorithm engineering: bridging the gap between algorithm theory and practice*. Springer-Verlag, Berlin, Heidelberg, 2010. ISBN 3-642-14865-4, 978-3-642-14865-1.

[24] D. E. Rumelhart, G. E. Hinton, and R. J. Williams. Learning internal representations by error propagation. pages 673–695, 1988.

[25] E. Schonberg, J. T. Schwartz, and M. Sharir. An automatic technique for selection of data representations in setl programs. *ACM Trans. Program. Lang. Syst.*, 3:126–143, April 1981.

[26] J. T. Schwartz. Automatic data structure choice in a language of very high level. In *POPL '75: Proceedings of the 2nd ACM SIGACT-SIGPLAN symposium on Principles of programming languages*, pages 36–40, 1975.

[27] O. Shacham, M. Vechev, and E. Yahav. Chameleon: adaptive selection of collections. In *PLDI '09: Proceedings of the 2009 ACM SIGPLAN conference on Programming language design and implementation*, pages 408–418, 2009.

[28] W. Siedlecki and J. Sklansky. A note on genetic algorithms for large-scale feature selection. *Pattern Recogn. Lett.*, 10(5):335–347, 1989.

[29] D. D. Sleator and R. E. Tarjan. Self-adjusting binary search trees. *J. ACM*, 32(3):652–686, 1985.

[30] A. Stepanov and M. Lee. The standard template library. Technical report, WG21/N0482, ISO Programming Language C++ Project, 1994.

[31] M. W. Stephenson. *Automating the Construction of Compiler Heuristics Using Machine Learning*. PhD thesis, Massachusetts Institute of Technology, 2006.

[32] G. Tournavitis, Z. Wang, B. Franke, and M. F. O'Boyle. Towards a holistic approach to auto-parallelization: integrating profile-driven parallelism detection and machine-learning based mapping. In *Proceedings of the 2009 ACM SIGPLAN conference on Programming language design and implementation*, PLDI '09, pages 177–187, New York, NY, USA, 2009. ACM.

[33] Z. Wang and M. F. O'Boyle. Mapping parallelism to multi-cores: a machine learning based approach. In *PPoPP '09: Proceedings of the 14th ACM SIGPLAN symposium on Principles and practice of parallel programming*, pages 75–84, 2009.

[34] S. Williams, L. Oliker, R. Vuduc, J. Shalf, K. Yelick, and J. Demmel. Optimization of Sparse Matrix-Vector Multiplication on Emerging Multicore Platforms. In *Proc. Supercomputing '07*, 2007.

[35] N. Wirth. *Algorithms + Data Structures = Programs*. Prentice Hall, 1978.

[36] G. Xu and A. Rountev. Detecting inefficiently-used containers to avoid bloat. In *ACM SIGPLAN 2010 Conference on Programming Language Design and Implementation*. ACM, 2010.

[37] G. Xu, N. Mitchell, M. Arnold, A. Rountev, and G. Sevitsky. Software bloat analysis: finding, removing, and preventing performance problems in modern large-scale object-oriented applications. In *Proceedings of the FSE/SDP workshop on Future of software engineering research*, FoSER '10, pages 421–426, New York, NY, USA, 2010. ACM.

An SSA-based Algorithm for Optimal Speculative Code Motion under an Execution Profile

Hucheng Zhou
Tsinghua University
zhou-hc07@mails.tsinghua.edu.cn

Wenguang Chen
Tsinghua University
cwg@tsinghua.edu.cn

Fred Chow
ICube Technology Corp.
frdchow@gmail.com

Abstract

To derive maximum optimization benefits from partial redundancy elimination (PRE), it is necessary to go beyond its safety constraint. Algorithms for optimal speculative code motion have been developed based on the application of minimum cut to flow networks formed out of the control flow graph. These previous techniques did not take advantage of the SSA form, which is a popular program representation widely used in modern-day compilers. We have developed the MC-SSAPRE algorithm that enables an SSA-based compiler to take full advantage of SSA to perform optimal speculative code motion efficiently when an execution profile is available. Our work shows that it is possible to form flow networks out of SSA graphs, and the min-cut technique can be applied equally well on these flow networks to find the optimal code placement. We provide proofs of the correctness and computational and lifetime optimality of MC-SSAPRE. We analyze its time complexity to show its efficiency advantage. We have implemented MC-SSAPRE in the open-sourced Path64 compiler. Our experimental data based on the full SPEC CPU2006 Benchmark Suite show that MC-SSAPRE can further improve program performance over traditional SSAPRE, and that our sparse approach to the problem does result in smaller problem sizes.

Categories and Subject Descriptors D.3.4 [*Programming Language*]: Processors—Compilers, Optimization

General Terms Algorithms, Design, Experimentation, Measurement, Performance, Theory

Keywords Code motion, Flow network, Minimum cut, Partial redundancy elimination, Profiling, Speculation, Static single assignment

1. Introduction

Partial redundancy elimination (PRE) is a powerful and indispensable optimization in modern optimizing compilers. It recognizes computations that are redundant in some or all paths of execution and eliminate them. PRE has been modeled as a code placement problem, in which the best set of insertion points for the computation is to be determined [19]. The insertions render some original computations to be fully redundant, so they can be trivially deleted. Since global common subexpression elimination and loop-invariant code motion are special cases of PRE, they are subsumed by PRE.

Knoop *et al.* developed the code placement strategy called lazy code motion (LCM) that guarantees that the code placement performed is both computationally and lifetime optimal [15][16]. A code placement is computationally optimal if the number of computations cannot be further reduced by *safe* code motion [13]. A code placement is lifetime optimal if it is computationally optimal and the lifetimes of the temporaries introduced for storing the computed values are minimized.

In safe code motion, a computation is not allowed to be inserted at a point in the program where the computation is not down-safe (i.e. fully anticipated). This safety attribute guarantees that the transformed code will never run slower than the original program, but it limits the extents to which PRE can speed up the program. Speculation refers to inserting the computation at points in the program where the computation is not down-safe. It suppresses redundancy in some path at the expense of another path along which it is computed but unused. Speculation may or may not be beneficial to program performance, because it depends on which execution paths are taken more frequently. But when execution profile data are available, it is possible to perform speculative PRE to further improve the run-time performance for program executions that match the given profile. Xue and Cai developed an algorithm that performs computationally optimal speculative PRE based on an execution profile [3]. They later improved their algorithm to make it also lifetime-optimal [22].

LCM is based on a bit-vector formulation of the PRE problem and on the iterative solution of the data flow equations. Chow *et al.* developed the SSAPRE algorithm that adapts LCM to SSA form [5][14]. SSA is a popular program representation used in modern optimizing compilers [6]. Optimizations based on SSA all take advantage of the *sparse* representation of SSA that also encodes use-def information. Data flow attributes can be propagated through SSA form in a smaller number of steps and in linear time, compared to $O(n^2)$ in iterative data flow analysis. The lower computational complexities in SSA-based algorithms is also attributed to their operating on one candidate at a time, instead of an entire population encoded in bit vector data structures. Another advantage of an SSA-based algorithm is that we do not have to implement the local and global versions of the optimization separately, as SSA-based algorithms are insensitive to basic block boundaries. Thus, a compiler that uses SSA as its program representation will always prefer to use SSA-based optimization algorithms.

Like LCM, Xue and Cai's computational and lifetime optimal algorithm for speculative PRE, called MC-PRE, uses bit-vector-based data flow analysis. No SSA-based algorithm for optimal speculative code motion exists today. In this paper, we present the algorithm we developed, called MC-SSAPRE, that performs opti-

PLDI'11, June 4–8, 2011, San Jose, California, USA.

mal speculative code motion in the SSA framework. The contributions of this paper are as follows:

First, we show that a flow network can be formed out of a SSA graph to solve for a minimum cut. We prove that the code placement according to the minimum cut is both computationally and lifetime optimal. A compiler that uses SSA as its program representation can now continue to use the SSA form to perform optimal speculative profile-based PRE, thus reaping all the benefits of SSA-based algorithms outlined above.

Second, MC-SSAPRE computes the optimal code placement more efficiently compared with other min-cut approaches based on the control flow graph and non-SSA program representation. Among the many reasons for the improved efficiency are the smaller sizes of SSA graphs and their resulting narrower solution space.

Third, MC-SSAPRE requires only node frequencies to do its job, whereas MC-PRE requires edge frequencies. Thus, MC-SSAPRE exerts less demand on instrumentation and the profile data collection process, which is an important consideration in just-in-time compilers. Using edge frequencies would not have been as straightforward as node frequencies for MC-SSAPRE, because each edge in the SSA graph can correspond to multiple edges in the control flow graph.

Lastly, we provide experimental data that confirm that MC-SSAPRE can further improve program performance over traditional PRE. We also provide statistical data about the problem size distribution to confirm the advantage of our sparse approach to the problem.

The rest of this paper is organized as follows: Section two discusses prior work in speculative code motion. Section three presents the MC-SSAPRE algorithm, proves its correctness and optimality and analyzes its time complexity. Section four compares MC-SSAPRE with MC-PRE. Section five presents experimental results collected using our implementation of MC-SSAPRE. Section six concludes the paper and points out promising areas for further investigation.

2. Prior Related Work

There are three main classes of techniques to overcome the conservativeness of safe PRE: control speculation, data speculation and control flow restructuring.

Control speculation refers to the introduction of a computation to a program path that does not need to perform that computation. The term speculation by itself refers to control speculation, since this is the most common form of speculation. Data speculation makes the assumption that certain values have not changed, so that more redundancies can be eliminated among the computations that use those values. Lin *et al* incorporated data speculation into the SSAPRE framework [17]. The technique requires hardware support in the form of special check instructions inserted in place of the eliminated computations so that, in the event the speculation fails, recovery code will be executed to correct the computation. Since such hardware support is not common, we only address control speculation in this paper.

The most fundamental example of control flow restructuring is the restructuring of a while loop to a do-while loop, as shown in Figure 1. Because a while loop may iterate zero times, moving a computation out of the loop may make the program run slower or alter the behavior of the program if the hoisted computation generates exceptions. By introducing an entry test that duplicates the termination condition, the main loop can be converted to a do-while loop, which iterates at least one time. This loop restructuring has been performed by the earliest optimizing compilers. Though it causes a small increase in code size, it makes it unnecessary to incur speculation while performing loop-invariant code motion.

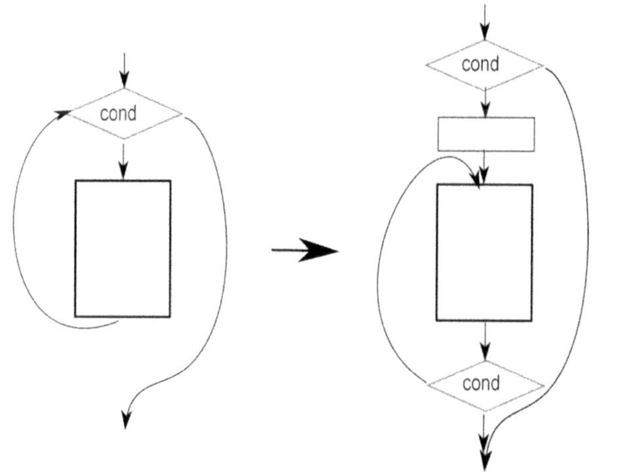

Figure 1. Traditional control flow restructuring of while loops

Bodik *et al.* applied more general control flow restructuring so as to enable more partial redundancies to be eliminated without speculation [2]. To avoid code size explosion, their control flow restructuring is only applied conservatively in a framework that also involves speculation with profile data.

Speculation improves performance only when the path that is burdened with more computations is executed less frequently than the path where the computations are avoided. Computations that can cause runtime exceptions or faults cannot be speculated, as they would alter the external behavior of the program. Murphy *et al.* proposed techniques that enable such computations to be more freely speculated under specific situations in the program [20]. They implemented their techniques in the SSAPRE framework.

In the absence of profile data, speculative PRE can be conservatively performed by restricting it to loops. Such speculative loop-invariant code motion is generally profitable because the benefit of suppressing a computation inside the loop outweighs the cost of computing it once at the loop header. Lo *et al.* has implemented this conservative form of speculative PRE in the SSAPRE framework [18].

When execution profile data are available, it is possible to tailor the use of speculation to maximize run-time performance for executions of the program that match the profile. Gupta *et al.* [9] and Lo *et al.* [18] introduced different algorithms for performing PRE guided by profile data. But because their algorithms do not compare frequencies in the global scope, they are not computationally optimal. Horspool and Ho [10] were the first to relate this problem to network flow and proposed the use of a min-cut algorithm, but their formulation of the algorithm did not always produce optimal solutions. The algorithm developed in Bodik's Ph.D. thesis [1] also involves the technique of solving the min-cut in a flow network. Because his framework includes control flow restructuring under his Code-Motion-Preventing (CMP) Region abstraction in addition to speculation, the computational optimality of his algorithm cannot be clearly defined.

To avoid the computational intensiveness of min-cut algorithms, Horspool *et al.* developed a heuristics-based algorithm to perform speculative PRE [11]. Their algorithm, called Isothermal Speculative PRE (ISPRE), relies only on bit-vector-based data flow analyses that are faster and simpler than those used in PRE, making it suitable for deployment in just-in-time compilers. But in this process, they sacrificed the optimality of their results.

Cai and Xue were the first to provide an algorithm for speculative PRE that is provably computationally optimal under an edge profile [3]. The key to their algorithm lies in the removal of the non-essential edges from the control flow graph (CFG) so that the problem of finding the optimal code placement is reduced to one of finding a minimum cut in the reduced flow graph. They subsequently enhanced their algorithm to produce a code placement that is also lifetime optimal [22]. In this paper, MC-PRE will refer to the enhanced version of their algorithm.

Scholz *et al.* came up with their own formulation for performing computationally optimal speculative code motion [21]. Though their algorithm is driven by local data flow attributes, it does not involve any global data flow analysis. Their final solution also involves finding a minimum cut in the flow graph formed out of the CFG. They regard the entry and exit of each basic block as two separate nodes, so they only need node frequencies for their solution. Finding the min-cut corresponds to minimizing the objective function formed out of totaling the costs of the local transformations in the basic blocks. Their formulation also enables their algorithm to consider placements that minimize the number of static occurrences. Their objective function can be chosen to optimize for speed or code size or a trade-off between the two.

Despite the greater adaptability of the algorithm of Scholz *et al.*, we consider MC-PRE to be more practical for the following reasons. First, Scholz's flow graphs are substantially larger not only because each basic block yields two nodes, but also because they do not use global data flow properties to remove edges that will not contribute to the final solution. Scholz *et al.* did employ a different technique that uses their correctness constraints to merge multiple adjacent nodes into one. Second, because the objective function in Scholz's algorithm requires summing over many basic blocks, finding their min-cut is more computationally intensive. Third, Scholz's algorithm does not optimize the lifetimes of the temporaries introduced for storing computation results for re-use. This issue is especially important when optimizing only for code size, because speculative code hoisting to reduce the number of static occurrences often increases the lifetimes of the temporaries. Such opportunities are also much more widespread than the opportunities for redundancy elimination. The increased register pressure can cause indiscriminate register spilling that negates the effect of code size reduction. The experimental data given in their paper [21] only contain statistics collected during their optimization phase. There is no measured data to show how the timing or code size of the final executables improve.

In this paper, we present a new algorithm, MC-SSAPRE, for performing computational and lifetime optimal speculative PRE based on applying min-cut to flow networks formed out of SSA graphs.

3. The MC-SSAPRE Algorithm

As in all literature related to PRE, we present our algorithm by focusing on the optimization of an expression *a+b* that appears in the program. The PRE phase in the compiler will apply the algorithm to each lexically identified expression[1] in the program one after another.

Figure 2 shows the running example we use to illustrate our algorithm. Each rectangle denotes a basic block, with its execution frequency below the block number to the left of each block. As shown in the example, the program input to MC-SSAPRE is already in SSA form.

[1] Two expressions are lexically identified to be the same expression if they apply the same operation to the same variables or constants before being represented in SSA form.

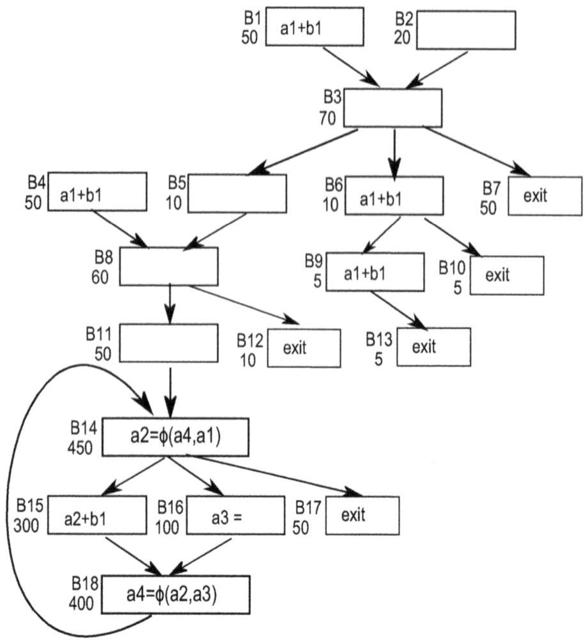

Figure 2. The Running Example

3.1 The Algorithm

We first give an overview of how SSAPRE computes safe optimal PRE. Then we describe how we modify SSAPRE to make it perform optimal speculative PRE for an execution profile. The main focus is to determine the best positions to perform insertions. Once the insertions have been performed, the computations rendered fully redundant can be trivially deleted. The overall code motion can be regarded as insertions followed by deletions.

3.1.1 SSAPRE Overview

As described by Kennedy *et al.*, the SSAPRE algorithm consists of six steps [14]. The first two steps, *Φ-Insertion* and *Rename*, applies the SSA construction algorithm to each occurrence of *a+b* in the program. The *Φ-Insertion* step inserts Φ's at the dominance frontiers of all the occurrences of *a+b*. These Φ's capture all the possible insertion points for the purpose of PRE. The *Rename* step assigns versions to the occurrences of *a+b* such that two occurrences with the same version will compute to the same value. The renaming is done via a pre-order traversal of the dominator tree. A renaming stack is maintained for *a+b* during the traversal such that the top of the stack gives the current version of the expression.

The resulting SSA form for *a+b* is a representation of redundancy relationships among the occurrences of *a+b* in the program. A less abstract view is to think of it as the SSA representation of the hypothetical temporary *h* that will be introduced to store its computed values for re-uses in the optimized output. The graph inherent in this expression SSA form is called the *factored redundancy graph* (FRG). In this paper, the term *SSA graph* will refer exclusively to the FRG, though it could also be used to refer to the graph inherent in the SSA form for variables. We use the term *real occurrences* to refer to the occurrences of *a+b* that exist before the SSA construction. Thus, Φ's and Φ operands are not real occurrences.

One characteristic of FRG that is absent from the ordinary SSA form for variables is that a Φ operand can be ⊥, which means that there is no computation of *a+b* available at the incoming edge corresponding to that Φ operand. In addition, each edge in the FRG

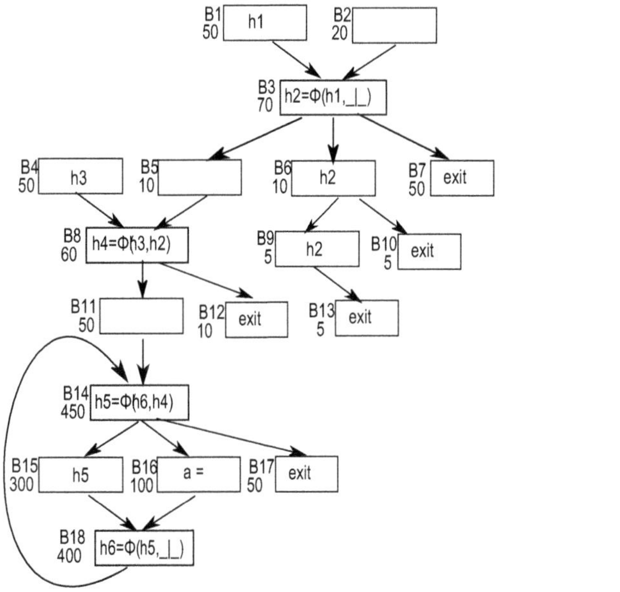

Figure 3. After SSA construction where h refers to $a+b$

that ends at a Φ operand is marked with a *has_real_use* flag. This flag is set to $true$ if the Φ operand is defined by a real occurrence of $a+b$ or if the path leading to its definition by a Φ crosses a real occurrence of $a+b$.

The third and fourth steps of SSAPRE, *DownSafety* and *WillBeAvail*, perform data flow analysis on the SSA graph to solve for the Φ's where insertions are to be performed for safe PRE. After the fourth step, the insertion points for $a+b$ have been completely determined. For each Φ operand, it sets the predicate $insert$ to denote whether insertion will be performed there. A Φ operand's $insert$ is set to $true$ if and only if the following hold:

- the Φ's *will_be_avail* attribute is $true$; and
- the operand is $\perp$; or *has_real_use* is false for the operand and the operand is defined by a Φ whose *will_be_avail* attribute is $false$.

The fifth step of SSAPRE, *Finalize*, determines the form of the optimized code by introducing the real temporary t for storing the computed values of $a+b$. For each occurrence of $a+b$, it determines if its computation should be deleted and replaced by a use of t, and if not, if its computed value should be saved to t for re-use later. The uses of t are linked to their defs and extraneous ϕ's for t are removed so that t is put in its minimal SSA form.

The sixth and last step of SSAPRE, *CodeMotion*, effects the PRE of $a+b$ by updating the native SSA representation of the program.

3.1.2 MC-SSAPRE Preview

MC-SSAPRE makes the same assumption as in SSAPRE that all *critical edges* in the CFG have been removed by inserting empty basic blocks at such edges[2]. SSAPRE's code placement for $a+b$ is guaranteed to be beneficial regardless of the execution profile. MC-SSAPRE will compute a different set of insertion points for $a+b$ to effect code motion that goes beyond that of SSAPRE so as to minimize the number of dynamic computations according to the execution profile. From this point of view, MC-SSAPRE

[2] A critical edge is one where both its head and tail blocks have multiple successors and predecessors respectively.

1. *Φ-Insertion* — Same as in SSAPRE.
2. *Rename* — Same as in SSAPRE; in addition, mark use nodes dominated by its own non-Φ SSA versions as *rg_excluded*.
3. *Data Flow* — Solve for full availability and partial anticipability
4. *Graph Reduction* — Form the reduced SSA graph by including only the following:
   - Φ nodes that are not fully available and also partially anticipated, and
   - their use nodes that are not marked *rg_excluded*, and
   - the def-use edges between the above two types of nodes.
5. *Single Source* — Create an artificial source node for the reduced SSA graph; for at each $\perp$ Φ operand in the SSA graph, create an edge that leads from the source node to the Φ node, annotating its frequency with the frequency of the predecessor basic block corresponding to that $\perp$ Φ operand.
6. *Single Sink* — Create an artificial sink node for the reduced SSA graph; for each real occurrence in the reduced SSA graph, create an edge that leads from the real occurrence node to the sink, annotating its frequency as infinity.
7. *Min-Cut* — Find the optimal insertion points as a minimum cut on the formed single-source single-sink graph. Pick later cuts in case of ties.
8. *WillBeAvail* — Compute the *insert* and *will_be_avail* attributes for each Φ based on the determined insertion points.
9. *Finalize* — Same as in SSAPRE.
10. *CodeMotion* — Same as in SSAPRE.

Figure 4. Steps of the MC-SSAPRE algorithm

only needs to differ from SSAPRE in how the insertion points are computed. In fact, we have designed MC-SSAPRE so that it differs from SSAPRE only in the latter's steps 3 and 4, apart from making step 2 compute an additional attribute. MC-SSAPRE consists of the ten steps summarized in Figure 4. We have replaced SSAPRE's steps 3 and 4 by MC-SSAPRE's steps 3 to 8. Steps 9 and 10 of MC-SSAPRE are the same as SSAPRE's steps 5 and 6.

3.1.3 MC-SSAPRE Steps 1 and 2

Figure 3 shows our running example after the first two steps. The constructed SSA graph is identical to that from SSAPRE. As in SSAPRE, the Φ nodes in this SSA graph capture all the possible insertion points for performing optimal speculative code motion.

Because in step 4, we want to exclude occurrences at points in the graph where the computation is fully available, we use the preorder traversal of the dominator tree during step 2 to easily identify occurrences made fully redundant by single real occurrences. This requires us to push initially encountered real occurrences on the expression stack, regardless of whether it defines a new version or not. Any subsequent encounter of an occurrence of the same operands' versions as the real occurrence on the top of the expression stack will cause that occurrence to be marked with the attribute *rg_excluded*, which means "excluded from reduced graph". Such *rg_excluded* occurrences do not need to be pushed on the stack. In Figure 3, h_2 at B9 and h_5 at B18 are marked *rg_excluded* after step 2.

3.1.4 MC-SSAPRE Step 3

Next, we want to identify nodes and edges in the SSA graph that will never be useful insertion points even under speculative code

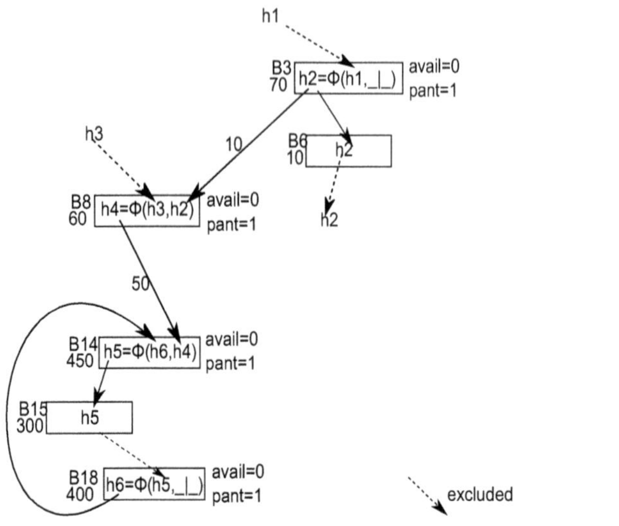

Figure 5. SSA graph after data flow analysis and excluding useless nodes and edges (steps 3 and 4 of MC-SSAPRE)

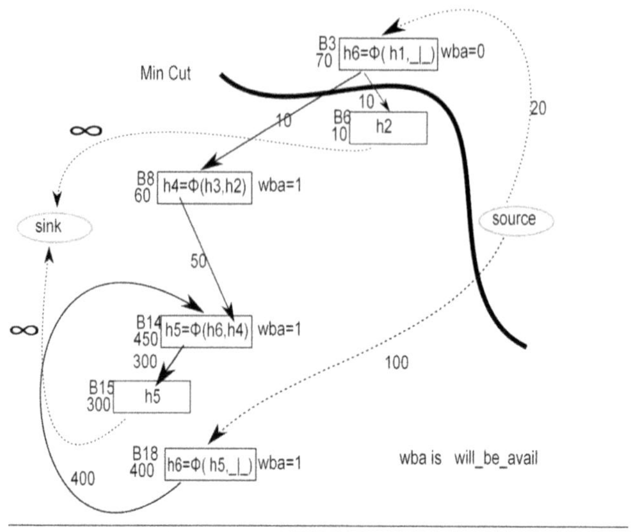

Figure 6. Completed flow network (EFG) after adding the artificial source and sink, performing min-cut and computing *will_be_avail* (step 5, 6, 7 and 8 of MC-SSAPRE)

motion. For this purpose, we solve for the following two data flow attributes:

- Full availability — Any insertion at a point in the graph where the computation is fully available would be a redundant computation, so such insertions can be precluded.
- Partial anticipability — Any insertion at a point in the graph where the computation is *not* partially anticipated would be a useless computation, so such insertions can be precluded.

Each of the above two data flow attributes can be efficiently computed via the typical one-pass data flow propagation algorithm for SSA graphs [14].

3.1.5 MC-SSAPRE Step 4

After computing the above two data flow attributes in step 3, step 4 starts with an empty graph and construct the *reduced SSA graph* as described in step 4 of Figure 4 using the data flow attributes computed in step 3. Figure 5 shows the reduced SSA graph of our running example after steps 3 and 4. Note the excluded edges. For our running examples, none of the Φ's can be excluded.

In MC-SSAPRE, the execution profile only needs to provide node frequencies. But min-cut on the flow graph relies on edge frequencies. We now describe how to derive the edge frequencies in the reduced SSA graph from node frequencies in the CFG based on how we perform insertions on edges in the SSA graph.

In our reduced SSA graph, there are only two types of edges, which we refer to as follows:

Type 1 edge — an edge that leads from Φ to Φ operands.

Type 2 edge — an edge that leads from Φ to a real occurrence.

In Figure 5, the edge ending at B8 and the two edges ending at B14 are type 1 edges. In performing an insertion at a type 1 edge, the absence of critical edges allows us to insert at the exit of the predecessor block corresponding to the Φ operand. For this reason, we annotate each type 1 edge with the node frequency of the predecessor block that corresponds to the Φ operand. In our example, the edge ending at B8 is annotated with the node frequency of B5, which is 10; the edge from B8 to B14 is annotated with the node frequency of B11, which is 50; the backward edge from B18 to B14 is annotated with the node frequency of B18, which is 400.

In Figure 5, the edges ending at B6 and B15 are type 2 edges. A cut at a type 2 edge does not require an insertion. Instead, we can just postpone the computation until the real occurrence, at which it will be computed *in place*. For this reason, we annotate a type 2 edge with the node frequency of the block of the real occurrence. In our example, the edge from B3 to B6 is annotated with the frequency of B6, which is 10; the edge from B14 to B15 is annotated with the frequency of B15, which is 300.

3.1.6 MC-SSAPRE Step 5

Using the edge insertion model, the edges in the CFG leading to ⊥ Φ operands represent the earliest useful insertion points for speculative code motion. As we'll prove in Section 3.2, any insertion before them would not be more computationally optimal and would increase the live range of the temporary. Step 5 introduces an artificial source node as the common head of these edges. Since each of these edges from the source node ends at a ⊥ Φ operand, they are type 1 edges. As a result, each of them is annotated with the node frequency of the corresponding predecessor block of its ⊥ Φ operand.

3.1.7 MC-SSAPRE Step 6

The sinks of the flow network are represented by all the real occurrences in the reduced SSA graph. To complete the flow network, step 6 introduces an artificial sink node and adds edges that lead to it from all the real occurrences in the graph. These edges are marked with the largest possible frequency (infinite in our illustration) to prevent any of them from becoming part of the min-cut. As a result, the minimum cut will always split the flow network such that all the real occurrences are located downstream from the cut. This in turn guarantees that the computation will have been performed before reaching any of the real occurrences.

Figure 6 shows the single-source single-sink flow network formed out of our running example. We call it the *essential flow graph* (EFG), since it is the basis for performing the minimum cut.

3.1.8 MC-SSAPRE Step 7

Minimum cut is defined as a cut that separates the source from the sink such that the sum of the weights across the cut edges is minimized. Step 7 performs this task in the flow network. To ensure

```
procedure Reset_will_be_avail(g)
    will_be_avail(g) ← false
    for each f ∈ set of Φ's in the SSA graph with operand ω
        such that g = def(ω)
        if (not has_real_use(ω) and not insert(ω)
            Reset_will_be_avail(f)
end Reset_will_be_avail

procedure Compute_will_be_avail()
    for each f ∈ set of Φ's in the SSA graph
        will_be_avail(f) ← true
    for each f ∈ set of Φ's in the SSA graph
        if (will_be_avail(f) and
            ∃ an operand ω of f that is ⊥ and not insert(ω))
                Reset_will_be_avail(f)
end Compute_will_be_avail
```

Figure 7. MC-SSAPRE's algorithm used in step 8 to compute *will_be_avail*

that we find the unique solution that minimizes the lifetime of the temporary, we use the Reverse Labeling Procedure of Ford and Fulkerson [7]. Referring to our running example, there are actually two possible min-cuts: $\{(\text{source, B3}), (\text{source, B18})\}$ or $\{(\text{B3,B8}), (\text{B3, B6}), (\text{source, B18})\}$[3]. The min-cut algorithm we apply will pick the second one, shown in Figure 6, since it yields a smaller live range for the temporary.

3.1.9 MC-SSAPRE Step 8

This step computes the *insert* attribute for each Φ operand and the *will_be_avail* attribute for each Φ. The purpose of this step is to enable our implementation to use the algorithms in Step 5 of SSAPRE without modification. An implementation may choose to skip this step, in which case the *Finalize* step will need to be modified to take the min-cut result as input.

In SSAPRE, the *will_be_avail* attribute tells whether the computation will be fully available at each Φ after PRE. This will then be used to compute the *insert* attribute. In MC-SSAPRE, we can easily determine the *insert* attribute from the result of the min-cut by setting a Φ operand's *insert* to *true* if a cut is at its incoming edge. The *will_be_avail* attribute is computed by forward propagation in the SSA graph based on the settings of the *insert* attribute. Figure 7 gives the pseudo-code for *Compute_will_be_avail*. The forward propagation is performed in the recursive procedure *Reset_will_be_avail*. The final values for *will_be_avail* in our running example is shown via the *wba* annotations in Figure 6.

3.1.10 MC-SSAPRE Steps 9 and 10

By computing the *insert* and *will_be_avail* attributes in step 8, the algorithms in SSAPRE's steps 5 and 6 can be re-used for these last two steps. Figure 8 shows the final output after applying MC-SSAPRE to our running example.

3.2 Correctness and Optimality

We now cover the theoretical aspects of the MC-SSAPRE algorithm. We refer to the expression being optimized as X and begin by stating MC-SSAPRE's job.

[3] The basic blocks are not part of the SSA graph structure; we use the block numbers in our discussion purely for easy reference to the various parts of the SSA graph.

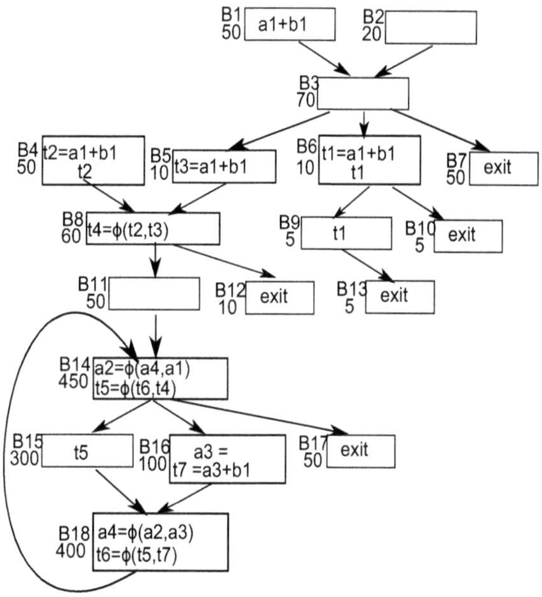

Figure 8. Running example after MC-SSAPRE

3.2.1 Problem Statement

Definition 1 *Original computation points* are the points in the input program where X's computations take place.

MC-SSAPRE will find a new set of computation points for X that satisfies all of the following criteria:

1. Correctness — The new set of computation points for X makes X fully available at its original computation points so they can be deleted.
2. Computational optimality — The set of new computation points minimizes the dynamic number of computations of X under the given execution profile.
3. Lifetime optimality — Subject to the computational optimality, the life range of the temporary introduced to store X is minimized.

3.2.2 Proof of Correctness

We call a partial redundancy *strictly partial* if it is not redundant along some path. Strictly partial redundancies can only be eliminated by performing insertions.

Observe that the each occurrence of X at their original computation points can be qualified by exactly one of the following:

- fully redundant,
- strictly partially redundant (SPR), or
- non-redundant.

LEMMA 1. *The fully redundant occurrences of X at the original computation points can be excluded from consideration in determining the new computation points without affecting the correctness and optimality requirements for MC-SSAPRE's output.*

Proof The fully redundant occurrences of X are made fully redundant by the SPR and non-redundant occurrences in the input program. In the output program, X will continue to be available at the SPR and non-redundant original computation points. Thus, X will continue to be fully redundant at the fully redundant original computation points. ∎

MC-SSAPRE's step 2 starts looking for those occurrences made fully redundant by single real occurrences and marks them *rg_excluded*. The remaining fully redundant occurrences are identified based on the fully available attribute computed in step 3 and excluded in step 4.

Next, we use Lemma 3 from Kennedy *et al.* [14] and re-word it as the following:

LEMMA 2. *The factored redundancy graph (FRG) constructed in steps 1 and 2 captures all redundancies in X in the program.*

Any edge in the FRG represents a redundancy relationship between two occurrences of X. Between any two mutually redundant occurrences of X, there must be a path in the FRG between them. An occurrence with no predecessor in the FRG is non-redundant. For such occurrences, the best strategy is to compute *in place*, since inserting earlier would only lengthen the temporary's live range unnecessarily. Based on this, we can also conclude that the best set of final computation points will always include these non-redundant occurrences. In Figure 3, h_1 in B1 and h_3 in B4 are non-redundant occurrences. Thus, for the rest of our proofs, we only need to attend to the SPR occurrences. We refer to the new computation points found by MC-SSAPRE for X as *insertion points*. We use I to refer to any set of insertion points found by MC-SSAPRE and $\mathcal{I}_{corr}$ to refer to all the I's that satisfy the correctness criterion. $\overline{\mathcal{I}_{corr}}$ designates the complement of $\mathcal{I}_{corr}$.

Definition 2 *Useless insertion points* are the points in the input program where X is either fully available or not partially anticipated.

This was explained earlier in 3.1.4. We can infer that any part of the CFG that cannot reach the FRG, including the part downstream from the FRG, are useless insertion points because X is not partially anticipated. Thus, all useful insertion points lie in the part of the CFG covered by the FRG plus the region of the CFG preceding it starting from the entry point.

We now prove that the best insertion points can be located based on the FRG. For this, we need the following two lemmas that enable us to model insertions on the FRG instead of the CFG:

LEMMA 3. *The best insertion point on an edge in the FRG that ends at a Φ operand (the type 1 edge of Section 3.1.5) is at the exit of the predecessor block P corresponding to that Φ operand.*

Proof Because of the absence of critical edges, block P must not have any successor other than the block containing the Φ. Thus, each traversal along that edge in the FRG will visit block P exactly once. The exit of block P is also the latest insertion point, resulting in the shortest life range for the temporary. ∎

LEMMA 4. *The best insertion point on an edge from A to B in the FRG where B is a real occurrence (the type 2 edge of Section 3.1.5) is not to insert at any edge, but to compute X in place at B.*

Proof If A is a real occurrence, any insertion on the edge is unnecessary. Thus, A must be a Φ. Since A dominates B, the only way for B to be executed more often than A is for B to be part of a loop inside the mini-CFG from A to B. Such a loop is not possible due to the absence of any Φ from A to B. Thus, it is best to compute X as late as possible at its original point in B, which yields the shortest life range for the temporary if the value needs to be saved. ∎

We have now proven that all useful insertion points can be located on the reduced FRG, formed at the end of step 4, plus the region of the CFG preceding it starting from the entry point.

LEMMA 5. *In the reduced FRG formed at the end of step 4, $I \in \overline{\mathcal{I}_{corr}}$ if and only if there exists a path from a $\perp$ Φ operand to any SPR occurrences with no insertion of X.*

Proof Assume we are to solve for the full availability attribute after performing the insertions represented by I. We would start by initializing all Φ's to fully available except any Φ with any $\perp$ operand that has no insertion will be initialized to not fully available, which represent the boundary condition for the forward propagation. In the subsequent forward propagation, since X is partially anticipated at all the Φ's, some Φ that has an SPR occurrence among its uses will be made not fully available. $I \in \overline{\mathcal{I}_{corr}}$ because X is not fully available at some SPR occurrence.

For the converse, suppose $I \in \overline{\mathcal{I}_{corr}}$. That means some SPR occurrence is defined by a Φ that is not fully available. Such a Φ must either have a $\perp$ Φ operand that has no insertion, or has an operand defined by another Φ that is not fully available. By induction, at least one Φ in the reduced FRG has a $\perp$ Φ operand that has no insertion. ∎

Lemma 5 implies that for each $I \in \mathcal{I}_{corr}$, there is at least one insertion along any path that leads from a $\perp$ Φ operand to a SPR occurrence. Along each such path, we want to perform one and only one insertion since that is sufficient to achieve the correctness criteria. We refer to such I's as belonging to $\mathcal{I}_{cut} \subset \mathcal{I}_{corr}$. We view the $\perp$ Φ operands as sources, the SPR occurrences as sinks, and each insertion as a cut along a path.

Next we make Lemma 3 applicable to insertions at $\perp$ Φ operands by performing step 5, which introduces an artificial source node with edges that lead from it to all the $\perp$ Φ operands. The implication is that any potential insertion point in the region of the CFG preceding the FRG does not need to be considered, because it will not be as good as insertion at the exits of the predecessor blocks corresponding to the $\perp$ Φ operands that it will reach. With the artificial source node, the reduced FRG also becomes one connected flow network. In order to apply the classical min-cut algorithm, we perform step 6 to introduce a single artificial sink. By annotating edges leading from the multiple SPR occurrences to the single sink with infinite weight, we ensure insertion will not be performed on these artificial edges.

THEOREM 6. *MC-SSAPRE is correct.*

Proof This is the result of combining Lemmas 1 to 5, and the fact that the set of insertion points found by MC-SSAPRE satisfies $I \in \mathcal{I}_{cut} \subset \mathcal{I}_{corr}$. ∎

3.2.3 Proof of Computational Optimality

We use $\mathcal{I}_{comp}$ to refer to the subset of $\mathcal{I}_{corr}$ in which the dynamic number of computations of X is at the smallest possible value.

THEOREM 7. *MC-SSAPRE is computationally optimal.*

Proof In the EFG formed at the end of step 6, the weight of each edge represents the additional number of times X would be computed during program execution if there is an insertion of X at that edge. In step 7, by finding the minimum cut, the total number of computations of X arising from the insertions across all the edges of the cut is minimized. Thus, the insertions at and only at all the edges of the minimum cut is the computationally optimal set of insertions. ∎

3.2.4 Proof of Lifetime Optimality

We now show that MC-SSAPRE yields minimum live range for the temporary t introduced to store X subject to the computational optimality criterion. We first prove the correctness of step 8:

LEMMA 8. *Given a set of insertions of X at Φ operands, the WillBeAvail algorithm of Figure 7 causes a Φ to be marked will_be_avail if and only if X is fully available at the Φ.*

Proof The algorithm to compute *will_be_avail* shown in Figure 7 computes the fully available attribute via forward propagation in the FRG. The algorithm is correct since it applies the standard depth-first search propagation technique on SSA graphs. ∎

THEOREM 9. *MC-SSAPRE is lifetime optimal.*

Proof There are two factors in MC-SSAPRE that contribute to lifetime optimality. The first factor is that the insertions performed need to be as late as possible on the FRG. The fact that the minimum cut may not be unique means that among the candidates of $\mathcal{I}_{comp}$, we need to find I_{opt} in which the cut along each path is as close to the sink as possible. This has been achieved by applying the Reverse Labeling Procedure of Ford and Fulkerson [7] while performing min-cut in step 7.

The second factor is for ensuring that the temporary t for storing X is not unnecessarily stored into or loaded. Lemma 8 assures that we feed the correct information to the *Finalize* step of Step 9. Since steps 9 and 10 are the same as SSAPRE's steps 5 and 6, we cite the lifetime optimality of SSAPRE established by Kennedy *et al.* [14] to claim this second factor for MC-SSAPRE. ∎

3.3 Time Complexity

Using the same analysis as Kennedy *et al.* [14], we can establish the complexities of steps 1, 2, 3, 8, 9 and 10 as being linear with respect to the sum of the number of nodes and number of edges in the FRG. The same linearity applies to step 4. Steps 5 and 6 can be done simultaneously in one pass throught the nodes of the FRG, so is also linear. That leaves step 7, finding the minimum cut, as being the only step not linear in complexity.

Chekuri *et al.* studied the performance of several minimum cut algorithms and found that they are all of polynomial time complexities [4]. The algorithm we use is $O(V^2\sqrt{E})$, where V and E are the number of nodes and edges in the ERG respectively. Since the EFG is a subset of the FRG, and the FRG is usually much smaller than the CFG, MC-SSAPRE is much less affected by the polynomial time complexity of the min-cut step.

4. Comparison with MC-PRE

Xue and Cai's MC-PRE algorithm [22] finds the optimal insertion points for profile-driven speculative code motion by determining the minimum cut in the flow network formed by removing non-essential edges from the CFG. Our work on MC-SSAPRE has shown that this min-cut approach can be applied equally well in the FRG context to yield similarly optimal results. But there are many intrinsic differences between the two algorithms.

MC-PRE eliminates only strictly global redundancies. A separate technique like local common subexpression elimination has to be applied to each basic block to cover locally redundant computations. In contrast, MC-SSAPRE covers both global and local redundancies uniformly.

MC-PRE uses classical bit-vector-based data flow analysis to solve for full availability and partial anticipability. Thus, it can solve for all the expressions in the program at the same time. MS-SSAPRE solves for these data flow attributes one expression at a time, but its representation is sparse and the propagation algorithm is linear. Both approaches handle one expression at a time in the remaining parts of their algorithms.

MC-PRE's flow networks are always based on the CFG[4]. All the nodes in each reduced flow graph that have no predecessor have to be connected to the single source node. The edges coming out of the single source node cannot be insertion points, and they are annotated with infinite frequency. For MC-SSAPRE, the flow graphs are formed from the SSA graphs. They are sparse, because the number of nodes depends only on how many times the expression occurs and the Φ nodes instantiated by them. MC-SSAPRE has fewer edges emanating from the single source node, because only Φ nodes with $\perp$ operands need to be connected to the single source. These edges coming out of the single source can themselves be insertion points. The reduced search space in MC-SSAPRE's flow networks enables its min-cut solution to incur much less overhead relative to MC-PRE. MC-SSAPRE's running time for each expression depends more on the problem size and less on the size of the program. Since the min-cut parts of both algorithms work on one expression at a time, flow graph size is the overriding factor affecting efficiency.

Since MC-PRE uses edge placement for performing insertions, it uses edge frequencies to model the costs of insertions. Though MC-SSAPRE also models insertions as edge placements, it only inserts at the ends of the predecessor blocks. This requires all critical edges to have been removed by inserting empty blocks at such edges. In Section 3.1.5, we have described how the frequencies of the edges of the flow network are determined based on the blocks where the computation will be inserted. This in effect enables us to derive edge frequencies in the SSA graph from node frequencies in the CFG. In profiling, collecting node frequencies incurs less run-time overhead than edge frequencies.

To ensure that a computation that has no redundancy is not unnecessarily stored to its temporary, and to ensure that any inserted computation post-dominated by its first use is not computed earlier than needed, MC-PRE conducts a third data flow analysis phase to identify such isolated computations to prevent unnecessary code motion. The latter situation corresponds somewhat to MC-SSAPRE's type 2 edge discussed in Section 3.1.5. MC-SSAPRE's *WillBeAvail* and *Finalize* steps can be regarded as corresponding to MC-PRE's live range analysis for the temporary. But MC-SSAPRE's final output is in SSA form. MC-PRE would not meet the need of a compiler that uses SSA as its program representation unless it incurs the additional cost to construct SSA from its output.

5. Experimental Results

We have implemented MC-SSAPRE in the open-sourced Path64 compiler [8]. This compiler is a descendant of the SGI MIPSpro compiler in which the SSAPRE algorithm was originally developed [5][14]. This allows us to make use of its SSAPRE infrastructure in our implementation of MC-SSAPRE. The current compiler is targeted to x86/x86-64, which is the most widely used processor in servers, desktops and notebook computers nowadays.

We implemented MC-SSAPRE as we have described in Section 3.1, replacing steps 3 and 4 of SSAPRE by steps 3 to 8 of MC-SSAPRE. The compiler always restructures while loops in the way depicted in Figure 1 so that loop-invariant code motion can occur without involving speculation in these loops.

We first provide experimental data based on benchmark running times. Then we provide statistical data on the sizes of the EFGs formed by MC-SSAPRE during the compilation of the same benchmarks.

5.1 Run-time Performance Improvements

Our benchmarking machine is a Linux system based on the Intel Core™ i7-970 Processor running at 2.67GHz with 8MB on-chip cache. The operating system is Ubuntu 9.10 and the system has 6GB on-board memory.

We use the popular SPEC CPU2006 Benchmark Suite [12] in performing our experiments. The SPEC benchmarks facilitate feedback-directed optimizations (FDO) by providing training input

[4] Some basic blocks in MC-PRE's CFG have to be split to allow the top part to function as a source and the bottom part to function as a sink.

Benchmark	A. SSAPRE	B. SSAPRE$_{sp}$	C. MC-SSAPRE	$\frac{A-C}{A}$	$\frac{B-C}{B}$
perlbench	455 sec	452 sec	442 sec	2.86%	2.21%
bzip2	599 sec	598 sec	583 sec	2.67%	2.51%
gcc	406 sec	402 sec	397 sec	2.22%	1.24%
mcf	414 sec	415 sec	409 sec	1.21%	1.45%
gobmk	539 sec	540 sec	526 sec	2.41%	2.59%
hmmer	528 sec	526 sec	521 sec	1.33%	0.95%
sjeng	600 sec	601 sec	593 sec	1.17%	1.33%
libquantum	602 sec	610 sec	565 sec	6.15%	7.38%
h264ref	1696 sec	1720 sec	1682 sec	0.83%	2.21%
omnetpp	538 sec	525 sec	516 sec	4.09%	1.71%
astar	611 sec	621 sec	609 sec	0.33%	1.93%
xalancbmk	1472 sec	1489 sec	1467 sec	0.34%	1.48%
Average				2.13%	2.25%

Table 1. CINT2006 execution times and speedup ratios of MC-SSAPRE relative to SSAPRE and SSAPRE$_{sp}$

data that are separate from the input data for the reference runs. Compilation with FDO uses the execution profiles generated by the training runs.

We compare the benchmark running times, measured in seconds, between PRE performed via SSAPRE and MC-SSAPRE. All benchmarks were compiled at -O3 and with FDO. The original SSAPRE implementation in our compiler does not use profile data even when the compilation is with FDO. It by default performs speculation for invariant computations inside loops. In our experiment, we perform the following three separate compiles and runs:

A. SSAPRE — PRE via SSAPRE with speculation turned off, with no use of profile data

B. SSAPRE$_{sp}$ — PRE via SSAPRE with loop-based speculation, with no use of profile data

C. MC-SSAPRE — PRE via MC-SSAPRE (with speculation), with use of profile data

All other optimization phases in the three compiles are unchanged.

The SPEC CPU2006 Benchmark Suite is divided into the CINT2006 suite, made up of 12 integer benchmarks, and the CFP2006 suite, made up of 17 floating-point benchmarks. We show the running times of the full set of CINT2006 benchmarks in Table 1, and the running times of the full set of CFP2006 benchmarks in Table 2. The running times displayed in the second to fourth columns of the tables correspond to A, B and C described above. Each running time shown is the average of three runs. We found very little variation among the three runs of each benchmark, which means any observed difference in performance is real and reproducible.

The fifth column of each table gives the speedup of MC-SSAPRE over safe SSAPRE. For CINT2006, the speedup ranges from 0.33% to 6.15%, with an average of 2.13%. For CFP2006, the speedup ranges from 0.87% to 8.78%, with an average of 2.76%. The last column of each table gives the speedup of MC-SSAPRE over SSAPRE with loop-based speculation. For CINT2006, this speedup ranges from 0.95% to 7.38%, with an average of 2.25%. For CFP2006, this speedup ranges from 0.29% to 8.61%, with an average of 1.96%.

The data show that the loop-based speculation in the original compiler is not always beneficial relative to safe SSAPRE. But it is more beneficial in the floating-point benchmarks than the integer benchmarks, since floating-point benchmarks in general are more loop-oriented than integer benchmarks. This explains why, out of the four averages, MC-SSAPRE gives the highest average speedup when compared with safe SSAPRE in CFP2006, and the lowest

Benchmark	A. SSAPRE	B. SSAPRE$_{sp}$	C. MC-SSAPRE	$\frac{A-C}{A}$	$\frac{B-C}{B}$
bwaves	386 sec	382 sec	375 sec	2.85%	1.83%
gamess	1034 sec	1030 sec	997 sec	3.58%	3.20%
milc	450 sec	452 sec	443 sec	1.56%	1.99%
zeusmp	407 sec	403 sec	400 sec	1.72%	0.74%
gromacs	578 sec	576 sec	570 sec	1.38%	1.04%
cactusADM	547 sec	546 sec	499 sec	8.78%	8.61%
leslie3d	598 sec	588 sec	584 sec	2.34%	0.68%
namd	506 sec	505 sec	500 sec	1.19%	0.99%
dealII	476 sec	465 sec	459 sec	3.57%	1.29%
soplex	654 sec	641 sec	616 sec	5.81%	3.90%
povray	324 sec	326 sec	315 sec	2.78%	3.37%
calculix	825 sec	823 sec	811 sec	1.70%	1.46%
GemsFDTD	505 sec	502 sec	493 sec	2.38%	1.79%
tonto	552 sec	541 sec	535 sec	3.08%	1.11%
lbm	344 sec	342 sec	341 sec	0.87%	0.29%
wrf	593 sec	588 sec	586 sec	1.18%	0.34%
sphinx3	701 sec	691 sec	686 sec	2.14%	0.72%
Average				2.76%	1.96%

Table 2. CFP2006 execution times and speedup ratios of MC-SSAPRE relative to SSAPRE and SSAPRE$_{sp}$

average speedup when compared with SSAPRE with loop-based speculation in CFP2006.

In general, the usefulness of FDO depends on how well the training runs correlate with the reference runs. Any non-correlation could be the cause of the smaller improvements of MC-SSAPRE observed in some of the benchmarks.

Figure 9 and Figure 10 display the data of Table 1 and Table 2 respectively in bar chart form after normalizing the running times under safe SSAPRE to 1. These running time data verify that the optimal speculative code motion performed by MC-SSAPRE is effective in improving program performance beyond traditional SSAPRE. The positive across-the-board improvements are a good indication of the optimality of MC-SSAPRE.

5.2 Sizes of EFGs

To verify the advantages of our sparse approach to speculative code motion, we collected data on the sizes of the EFGs formed by MC-SSAPRE during the course of compiling the 29 SPEC CPU2006 benchmarks. We exclude empty EFGs in our statistics, and measure graph sizes according to the number of nodes in the graph. The results are shown in the bar chart of Figure 11, where each bar gives the number of EFGs of the size(s) given in the horizontal axis.

The most noteworthy observation is that 50% of the EFGs have only 4 nodes. A non-empty EFG cannot be smaller than 4 nodes because there must be at least the artificial source node, the artificial sink node, a Φ node and a strictly partially redundant real occurrence node for it to require a minimum cut. As the sizes of EFGs increase, their numbers taper off very quickly. Among the 183,152 EFGs formed in the compilation of the 29 benchmarks, there are only 24 EFGs larger than 300 nodes, and the largest EFG has 805 nodes.

Figure 11 also plots the cumulative percentages of EFGs with sizes less than the given number of nodes. We found that 86.5% of the EFGs are less than or equal to 10 nodes, 99.0% of the EFGs are less than or equal to 50 nodes, and 99.67% of the EFGs are less than or equal to 100 nodes. This verifies that our SSA-based approach does result in mostly small and trivial EFGs, which helps to ensure that the polynomial time complexity of the min-cut step would only have very limited impact on the optimization efficiency.

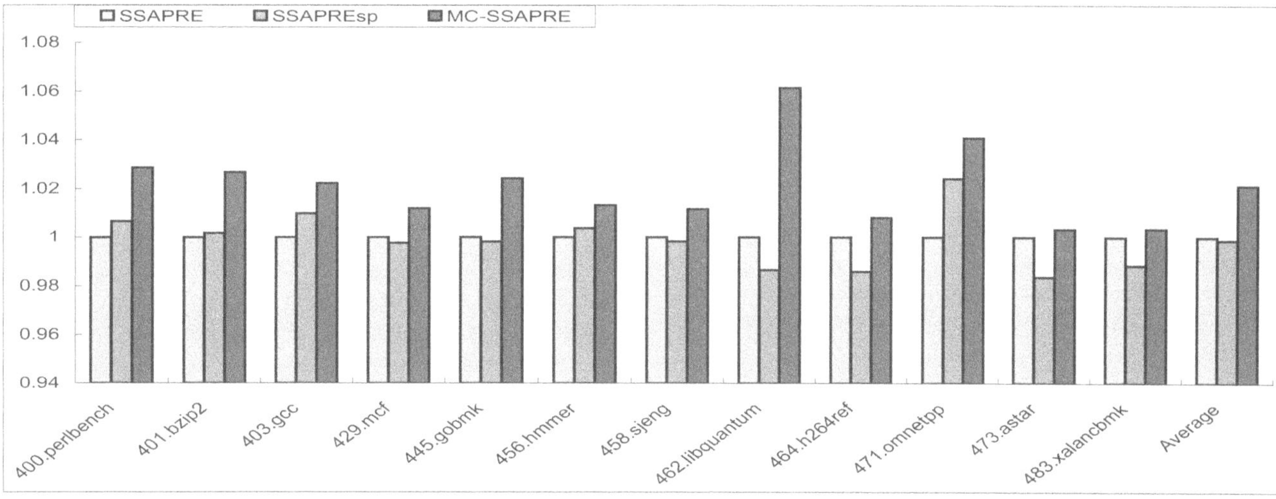

Figure 9. Performance comparison between SSAPRE, $SSAPRE_{sp}$ and MC-SSAPRE based on the CINT2006 benchmarks

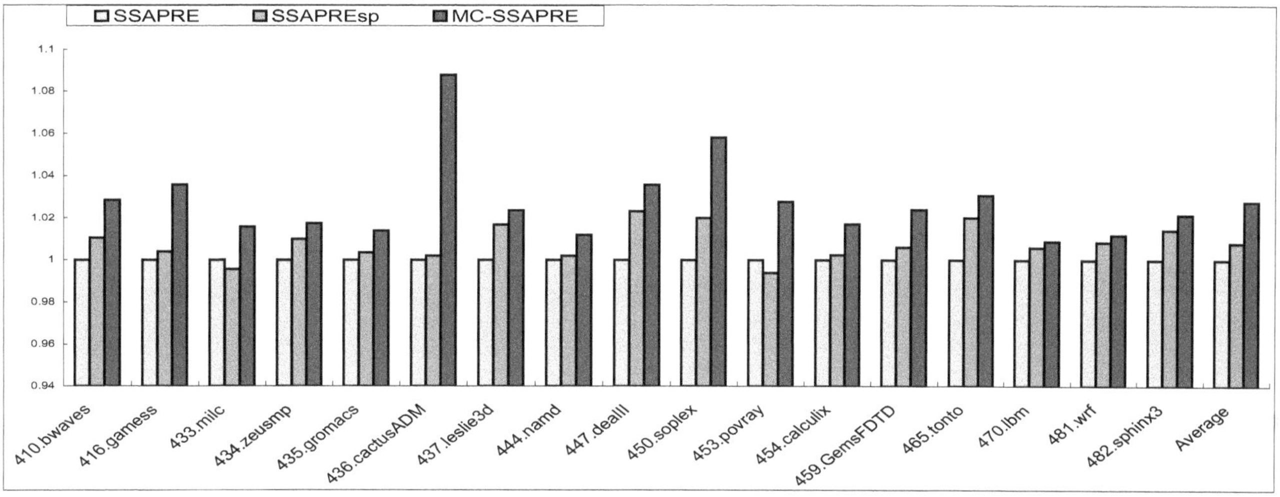

Figure 10. Performance comparison between SSAPRE, $SSAPRE_{sp}$ and MC-SSAPRE based on the CFP2006 benchmarks

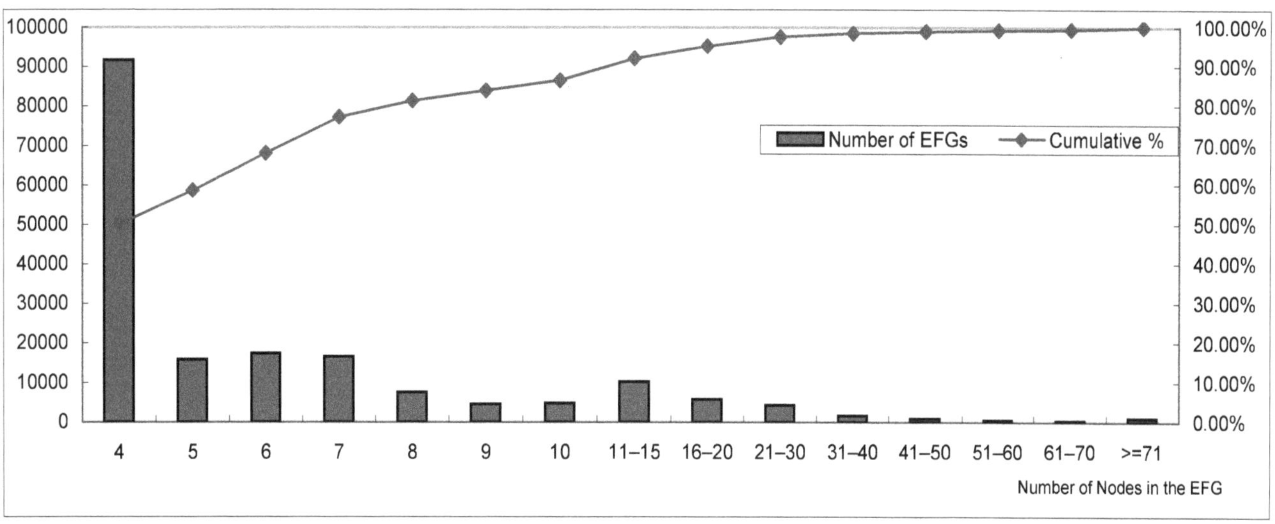

Figure 11. EFG size distribution based on number of nodes

6. Conclusion and Further Work

Speculative code motion under an execution profile can be modeled as a flow network problem. Previous works have solved this problem optimally by applying min-cut to flow networks formed out of the control flow graphs of the programs. In this paper, we have shown that the min-cut technique can be applied equally well to flow networks formed out of SSA graphs. Since SSA is a sparse program representation, this SSA-based approach to solve for optimal speculative code motion substantially reduces the problem size, thus enabling the optimization to be performed much more efficiently. The techniques described in this paper enables a compiler that uses SSA as its internal program representation to perform optimal speculative code motion with very low compile-time overhead. This in turn opens the way for this optimization to be deployed in just-in-time compilers, where it can put the collected dynamic profile data to good use and with low re-compilation time penalty.

This paper has only addressed computational and lifetime optimality in speculative code motion. Performing speculative code motion has already benefited code size by making it unnecessary for the compiler to do traditional control flow restructuring of the kind depicted in Figure 1. There is potential for using speculative code motion to further decrease code size, as shown by the work of Scholz *et al.* [21]. It may also be possible to use our framework to optimize other program properties sensitive to code positioning, like power consumption. We are currently investigating these other possibilities for our SSA-based min-cut technique, and will report on any interesting finding.

Acknowledgments

We would like to thank the anonymous reviewers for their constructive feedback regarding the contents of this paper. We would also like to thank the PathScale team, especially Christopher Bergström, for their support of the compiler during the experimental phase of this project. This work was funded by the National Core Scientific and Technological Development Project of China under Grant 2009ZX01036-001-002.

References

[1] R. Bodik. *Path-Sensitive Value-Flow Optimizations of Programs*. PhD thesis, University of Pittsburgh, 1999.

[2] R. Bodik, R. Gupta, and M. L. Soffa. Complete removal of redundant expressions. In *Proceedings of the ACM SIGPLAN '98 Conference on Programming Language Design and Implementation*, pages 1–14, 1998.

[3] Q. Cai and J. Xue. Optimal and efficient speculation-based partial redundancy elimination. In *Proceedings of the 2th annual IEEE/ACM international symposium on Code generation and optimization*, pages 91–102, 2003.

[4] C. S. Chekuri, A. V. Goldberg, D. R. Karger, M. S. Levine, and C. Stein. Experimental study of minimum cut algorithms. In *Proceedings of the Eighth Annual ACM-SIAM Symposium on Discrete Algorithms (SODA)*, pages 324–333, 1997.

[5] F. Chow, S. Chan, R. Kennedy, S. Liu, R. Lo, and P. Tu. A new algorithm for partial redundancy elimination based on ssa form. In *Proceedings of the ACM SIGPLAN '97 Conference on Programming Language Design and Implementation*, pages 273–286, 1997.

[6] R. Cytron, J. Ferrante, B. K. Rosen, M. N. Wegman, and F. K. Zadeck. Efficiently computing static single assignment form and the control dependence graph. *ACM Trans. Program. Lang. Syst.*, 13(4):451–490, 1991. ISSN 0164-0925. doi: http://doi.acm.org/10.1145/115372.115320.

[7] L. Ford and D. Fulkerson. *Flows in Networks*. Princeton University Press, 1962.

[8] git://github.org/path64/compiler.git.

[9] R. Gupta, D. A. Berson, and J. Z. Fang. Path profile guided partial redundancy elimination using speculation, 1997.

[10] R. N. Horspool and H. Ho. Partial redundancy elimination driven by a cost-benefit analysis, 1997.

[11] R. N. Horspool, D. J. Pereira, and B. Scholz. Fast profile-based partial redundancy elimination. In *Proceedings of the 7th Joint Modular Languages Conference*, pages 362–376, September 2006.

[12] http://www.spec.org/cpu2006.

[13] K. Kennedy. Safety of code motion. *International Journal of Computer Mathematics*, 3(2 and 3):117–130, 1972.

[14] R. Kennedy, S. Chan, S. Liu, R. Lo, P. Tu, and F. Chow. Partial redundancy elimination in ssa form. *ACM Trans. Program. Lang. Syst.*, 21(3):627–676, 1999.

[15] J. Knoop, O. Rüthing, and B. Steffen. Lazy code motion. In *Proceedings of the ACM SIGPLAN '92 Conference on Programming Language Design and Implementation*, pages 224–234, 1992.

[16] J. Knoop, O. Rüthing, and B. Steffen. Optimal code motion: theory and practice. *ACM Trans. Program. Lang. Syst.*, 16(4):1117–1155, 1994.

[17] J. Lin, T. Chen, W. chung Hsu, and P. chung Yew. A compiler framework for speculative analysis and optimizations. In *Proceedings of the ACM SIGPLAN 03 Conference on Programming Language Design and Implementation*, pages 289–299, 2003.

[18] R. Lo, F. Chow, R. Kennedy, S. Liu, and P. Tu. Register promotion by sparse partial redundancy elimination of loads and stores. In *Proceedings of the ACM SIGPLAN '98 Conference on Programming Language Design and Implementation*, pages 26–37, 1998.

[19] E. Morel and C. Renvoise. Global optimization by suppression of partial redundancies. *Communications of the ACM*, 22(2):96–103, 1979.

[20] B. Murphy, V. Menon, F. Schneider, T. Shpeisman, and A. Adl-Tabatabai. Fault-safe code motion for type-safe languages. In *Proceedings of the 6th annual IEEE/ACM international symposium on Code generation and optimization*, pages 144–154, 2008.

[21] B. Scholz, N. Horspool, and J. Knoop. Optimizing for space and time usage with speculative partial redundancy elimination. In *Proceedings of the 2004 ACM SIGPLAN/SIGBED Conference on Languages, Compilers, and Tools for Embedded Systems*, pages 221–230, 2004.

[22] J. Xue and Q. Cai. A lifetime optimal algorithm for speculative pre. *ACM Transactions on Architecture and Code Optimization*, 3(2):115–155, 2006.

Caisson: A Hardware Description Language for Secure Information Flow

Xun Li Mohit Tiwari Jason K. Oberg* Vineeth Kashyap
Frederic T. Chong Timothy Sherwood Ben Hardekopf

Department of Computer Science
University of California, Santa Barbara
Santa Barbara, CA
{xun,tiwari,vineeth,chong,sherwood,benh}@cs.ucsb.edu

*Department of Computer Science and Engineering
University of California, San Diego
San Diego, CA
jkoberg@cs.ucsd.edu

Abstract

Information flow is an important security property that must be incorporated from the ground up, including at hardware design time, to provide a formal basis for a system's root of trust. We incorporate insights and techniques from designing information-flow secure programming languages to provide a new perspective on designing secure hardware. We describe a new hardware description language, Caisson, that combines domain-specific abstractions common to hardware design with insights from type-based techniques used in secure programming languages. The proper combination of these elements allows for an expressive, provably-secure HDL that operates at a familiar level of abstraction to the target audience of the language, hardware architects.

We have implemented a compiler for Caisson that translates designs into Verilog and then synthesizes the designs using existing tools. As an example of Caisson's usefulness we have addressed an open problem in secure hardware by creating the first-ever provably information-flow secure processor with micro-architectural features including pipelining and cache. We synthesize the secure processor and empirically compare it in terms of chip area, power consumption, and clock frequency with both a standard (insecure) commercial processor and also a processor augmented at the gate level to dynamically track information flow. Our processor is competitive with the insecure processor and significantly better than dynamic tracking.

Categories and Subject Descriptors B.6.3 [*Design Aids*]: Hardware Description Languages

General Terms Security, Verification, Languages

Keywords Hardware Description Language, Non-interference, State Machine

1. Introduction

High-assurance embedded systems such as those used in banks, aircraft and cryptographic devices all demand strong guarantees on information flow. Policies may target confidentiality, so that secret information never leaks to unclassified outputs, or they may target integrity, so that untrusted data can never affect critical system data. The high cost of a policy violation ensures that these systems are evaluated extensively before being deployed; for instance, certifying systems using Common Criteria [2] or FIPS [3] requires a painstaking process at a cost of millions of dollars over multiple years [4].

Information flow policies are expressed using a lattice of security levels [14] such that higher elements in the lattice correspond to information with more restricted flow (i.e., secret information for confidentiality or untrusted information for integrity). A simple example of a security lattice would be the typical military classification levels: `Unclassified` $\sqsubseteq$ `Secret` $\sqsubseteq$ `Top Secret`. An important information flow policy based on such lattices is *non-interference* [18], which requires that no information at a given level in the lattice can flow anywhere except to higher elements in the lattice (e.g., `Secret` information can flow to `Top Secret`, but not vice-versa). High-assurance systems require a static guarantee of non-interference and depend on a *hardware-based root of trust* to enforce this policy. We present a new hardware description language named Caisson that meets this need by extending HDLs like Verilog with language abstractions that enable precise static verification of secure synchronous hardware designs.

1.1 Secure Hardware Design

While ciphers provide a sound theoretical primitive for building secure systems, their actual *implementations* have been shown to be a rich source of vulnerabilities. Numerous attacks exploit hardware structures such as shared data caches [35], instruction caches [6], and branch predictors [5, 7] to leak information about private keys. Other studies have found vulnerabilities lurking in obscure and even undocumented corners of hardware designs [41], e.g., when the floating point registers are persistent across context switches. Complete information flow security must begin with a principled approach to designing hardware that accounts for the intricate interaction among different hardware components, analyzes the hardware design in its entirety, and does so efficiently enough to be useful in practice. Note that non-digital side channels such as power analysis [25] are not within the scope of this paper.

Existing work has explored using hardware assistance to dynamically track information flow and prohibit leaks [12, 13, 38, 43]. However, most such systems only track information flow at the ISA level or above, ignoring micro-architectural features such as caches and branch predictors that can leak information. These systems cannot protect against the attacks outlined above.

One existing system, GLIFT [46], dynamically tracks information flow at the gate-level and does take micro-architectural fea-

PLDI'11, June 4–8, 2011, San Jose, California, USA.

tures into account; however, this technique requires the information tracking logic to be physically instantiated in the synthesized circuit, greatly increasing chip area and power consumption. Also, GLIFT only detects policy violations at runtime; it cannot guarantee statically that no violations will occur. GLIFT is currently the only alternative for enforcing information flow for an entire processor below the ISA level of abstraction, and we use GLIFT as our main comparison point in our evaluation.

1.2 Our Approach

In contrast to existing approaches, we take language-level techniques for secure information flow and apply them to domain-specific abstractions for hardware design (specifically, finite state machines) to create a new Hardware Description Language (HDL) named Caisson. Our goal is to enable the creation of synchronous hardware designs that are statically-verifiable as secure. Additional benefits of Caisson are that it allows hardware designers to operate at familiar level of abstraction, enables architects to quickly and easily iterate through potential designs without having to wait for synthesis and simulation to test security properties, and the resulting designs do not suffer from the crippling overhead that comes with dynamic tracking in terms of additional chip area and power consumption

While there are existing HDLs based on finite state machines, none target security as a first-class concern. Caisson employs two novel features on top of finite state machines, *nested states* and *parameterized states* (described in §2) to enable precise and expressive enforcement of security policies. To demonstrate the utility of these features and of Caisson in general, we design an information-flow secure processor in Caisson. Designing secure hardware controllers is an active research area, and specifying a statically-verifiable secure general-purpose processor is an open problem. Such processors have an important application in high-assurance embedded systems such as those found in aircraft and automobiles [27]. Current tools and methodologies for secure hardware design are laborious and expensive (taking millions of dollars and multiple years to complete even simple designs); a general-purpose processor with microarchitectural features such as pipelining and cache is notorious in the hardware community for being too complicated to design in a verifiably secure manner.

Caisson is based on key insights into secure hardware design, and it provides language-level support for these design patterns. We believe, and have found in our own experience, that Caisson promotes *thinking* about secure hardware design in new, useful ways that don't naturally arise in existing languages.

1.3 Contributions

This paper makes the following specific contributions:

- We describe Caisson, a hardware description language targeting statically-verifiable information-flow secure hardware design.
- We formally prove that Caisson enforces timing-sensitive non-interference.
- We design and implement a verifiably information-flow secure processor with complex micro-architectural features including pipelining and cache.
- We synthesize our design and empirically compare it with an insecure commercial CPU design as well as a GLIFT CPU design that dynamically tracks information flow. We find that Caisson introduces much less overhead than GLIFT over the baseline processor in terms of chip area (1.35× vs. 3.34×), clock frequency (1.46× vs. 2.63×) and power (1.09× vs. 2.82×).

The rest of the paper is organized as follows. We begin in §2 by informally describing the Caisson language and motivating its features. In §3 we formalize the language description and provide a proof sketch of its security properties. In §4 we describe the design of a secure processor in Caisson and empirically evaluate the characteristics of the synthesized design against a comparable GLIFT hardware design. §5 discusses related work, and §6 concludes.

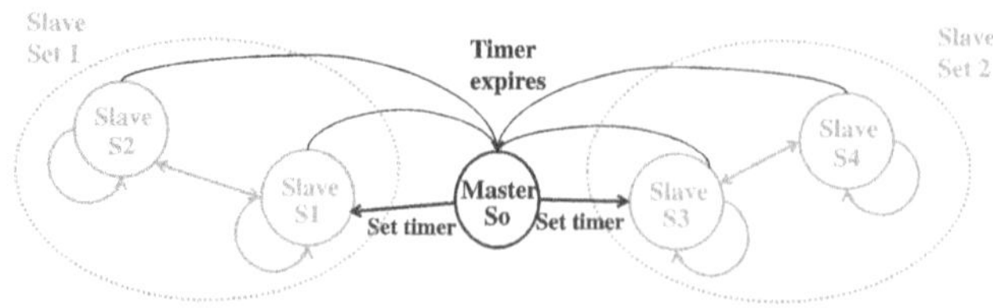

Figure 1. State Machine Diagram of Execution Lease Controller

2. Overview of Caisson

In this section we provide an overview of the Caisson language and motivate its design via a simple hardware example. For concreteness, we specifically address the issue of integrity using a 2-level lattice `Trusted` $\sqsubseteq$ `Untrusted`[1] (though Caisson can be used for arbitrary lattices). We demonstrate the Caisson language using an Execution Lease secure hardware controller [45]. We first review the concept of execution leases, then demonstrate how Caisson can create a statically-verifiable instantiation of an execution lease controller.

Execution Leases An execution lease is an architectural mechanism used to allow trusted code to grant untrusted code limited access to machine resources. One use-case is to allow a trusted separation kernel [24] to securely multiplex multiple untrusted processes on a CPU. One can think of a lease as a space-time sandbox that allows an untrusted process to take over the CPU and execute code using only a limited range of memory and a limited amount of time; the lease mechanism forces untrusted code to relinguish control back to the trusted code when its time allotment expires. Figure 1 gives a state-machine diagram of the execution lease controller. The trusted master state sets a timer and transfers control to either the untrusted set of slave states (S1 and S2) or the trusted set of slave states (S3 and S4). Each set of slave states can transition among themselves arbitrarily during the lease, but once the timer expires, control is relinguished back to the trusted master state.

Caisson Language Finite-state representations of hardware control systems, such as in Figure 1, are popular in hardware design. Existing tools such as Altera Quartus, Xilinx ISE, Statecharts [20], and Esterel [44] are widely used to model systems explicitly as state machines. In designing Caisson we wish to capitalize on this trend and allow hardware designers to operate at a familiar level of abstraction, allowing hardware designs to be easily and transparently modeled using Caisson. For this reason, we base the Caisson language on *finite-state machines*. To illustrate this concept, Figure 2**(a)** shows a Caisson implementation of the lease controller. This implementation is secure (i.e., does not leak `Untrusted` information), but it is *not* typable in the Caisson type system we introduce in Section 3. We will use this version of the implementation to motivate and introduce two features of Caisson: *nested states* and *parameterized states*. First, though, we give a quick illustration of the Caisson language using Figure 2**(a)**.

The name of the entire program is `lease`, and it uses four hardware registers: `timer`, `data1`, `data2`, and `mode`. Each register has

[1] This ordering can be confusing, but is correct: `Untrusted` is *high* in the lattice because the flow of untrusted information should be more restricted than the flow of trusted information.

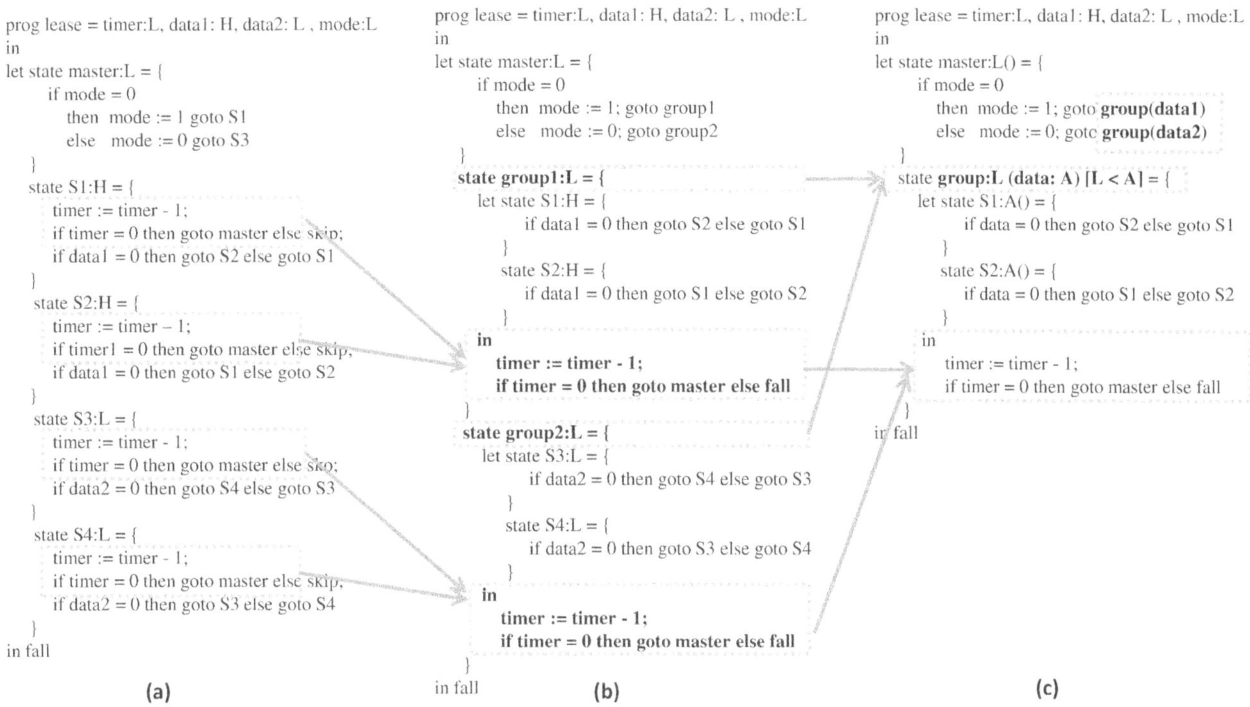

Figure 2. Implementation of the Lease Controller in Caisson language. (a) Implementation only with the ability to explicitly define each individual state (b) Implementation with nested states (c) Implementation with parameterized states.

type L (*low*, i.e. `Trusted`) except for `data1`, which is H (*high*, i.e. `Untrusted`). There are five states corresponding to the five states in Figure 1; `master`, `S3`, and `S4` are `Trusted`, while `S1` and `S2` are `Untrusted`. The `master` state uses `mode` to alternately transfer control (using the **goto** command) to either `S1` or `S3`. Each of `S1`—`S4` are similar: they decrement `timer`, check whether `timer` is 0, and if so transition back to the `master` state. Otherwise, depending on the value of `data1` (`data2`), they transition to themselves or their fellow slave state. Each state corresponds to a combinational hardware logic circuit and takes exactly one cycle to execute.

The reason that Figure 2(**a**) is not typable is that `timer` is decremented in states `S1` and `S2`. These states are `Untrusted`, yet they manipulate `Trusted` information (i.e., `timer`). This manipulation can create an implicit information leak from the high security level (`Untrusted`) to the low security level (`Trusted`)—if the `Untrusted` states modify the `Trusted` register `timer` in different ways, then the value of `timer` would depend on which `Untrusted` states are executed. Intuitively, however, we can see that the design actually *is* secure: since *every* state is guaranteed to decrement `timer` in exactly the same way, in reality there is no information leakage—nothing about the `Untrusted` states or transitions between those states can be inferred from the value of `timer`.

Nested States This observation motivates the first Caisson language feature, *nested states*. Nested states allow the designer to factor out shared code among states to identify exactly such situations. Figure 2(**b**) gives a valid (i.e., typable) Caisson implementation of the same design but using nested states. This design nests states `S1` and `S2` into the same *group state* `group1`, and similarly nests `S3` and `S4` into `group2`. In each group, the code common to the nested (or *child*) states has been factored out and associated with the group state containing those child states. The semantics of nested states effectively treats the command of a group state as if it were inlined into the command of each child state, so the code in Figure 2(**b**) has the same behavior as the code in Figure 2(**a**). For example, each time the code transitions from `S1` to `S2` using **goto**, the command for `group1` that decrements and checks `timer` executes before the command for `S2`. The **fall** command signals that the group state's command is complete and to begin executing the appropriate child state's command. When transitioning to a group state (as in the `master` state's command "**goto** group1" in Figure 2(**b**)), the default fall-through state is the first listed state (e.g., `S1` for group state `group1`).

The benefit of nested states is that Caisson is allowed to type a group state separately from the its child states. In Figure 2(**b**) state `group1` is typed L (*low*, or `Trusted`) while its child states `S1` and `S2` are typed H (*high*, or `Untrusted`). As explained above, this is safe because the semantics of Caisson guarantees that `group1`'s command executes identically in each child state, and so no information is leaked even though `group1`'s command modifies `Trusted` information.

Note that nested states are distinct from the related concept of *hierarchical states* in languages like Statecharts [20]. In Statecharts, child states *specialize* parent states. If an event is not handled by a child state, then the parent states are checked to determine if they can handle the event (somewhat like OOP virtual methods). Caisson's nested states have different semantics, as explained informally above and formally in §3. Nested states can also be seen as a concept dual to the notion of *linear continuations* [16, 55]. Whereas linear continuations identify code that is guaranteed to be executed *afterwards* by factoring the code out into a continuation, nested states identify code that is guaranteed to be executed *beforehand* by factoring it out into a group state.

Parameterized States While Figure 2(**b**) is a valid Caisson program, it is not as efficient as it could be. Note that `group1` and `group2` have identical logic; the only difference is that `group1` operates on `Untrusted` data (`data1`) while `group2` operates on `Trusted` data (`data2`). Therefore the two groups must be kept separate. When synthesizing this design, each group would be compiled down to its own separate logic circuit. It would be more efficient in terms of chip area to synthesize the *same* logic circuit for the two groups and reuse that circuit by securely multiplexing the different data (`data1` vs `data2`) onto that circuit. This observation motivates the second Caisson language feature, *parameterized states*. Figure 2**(c)** shows the same program as Figure 2**(b)** except using parameterized states.

This new implementation has a single `group` state that now has a *parameter*: a variable that represents some register on which the state will operate. Since the exact register that the state will operate on can vary each time the state executes, Caisson uses a type variable A to represent the parameter's type and specifies a set of type constraints that the type variable must obey in order to guarantee security (in this example, the only requirement is that A must be no less than L). The Caisson implementation assumes the given type constraints are valid when it type-checks `group`.

When transitioning to a parameterized state, the **goto** command must specify a particular register to pass as the target state's parameter. In Figure 2**(b)**, the `master` state transitions to `group` with two different arguments depending on `mode`: either `data1`, replicating the behavior of the original `group1`, or `data2`, replicating the behavior of the original `group2`. The Caisson implementation statically verifies that any arguments given to a parameterized state must necessarily satisfy the given type constraints, thereby statically guaranteeing the security of the design.

The benefit of parameterized states is that Caisson can synthesize a single logic circuit that can safely be used at multiple security levels. In other words, the data being operated on (the Caisson registers) must have distinct types, but the logic operating on the data (the Caisson states) can be parameterized over the types of the data, making the synthesized circuit much more efficient.

3. Formal Description of Caisson

In this section we formally describe a core subset of Caisson and its type system and prove that Caisson enforces timing-sensitive non-interference. The actual implementation of Caisson incorporates a large subset of Verilog, allowing existing Verilog designs to be easily refactored into Caisson programs. This subset of Verilog does not add anything of interest to the formal presentation and so we omit the full details from this section.

Figure 3 describes Caisson's abstract syntax (which uses types as described in Figure 5—we defer discussion of types to §3.2). Registers in the language correspond to registers in hardware and hold integer values. Variables range over registers rather than values (i.e., a variable maps to a register) and act as state parameters to abstract a state's behavior from specific registers.

A Caisson program consists of a list of registers followed by a list of nested state definitions. The nested state definitions form a hierarchy of states with a single *root* state. We define a *leaf state* as a state at the bottom of the state hierarchy; these states each specify a single command. A *group state* is any non-leaf state and specifies both (1) a nested list of states and (2) a command. The **goto** command triggers a state transition. Caisson describes synchronous hardware designs, hence the language implementation enforces that the length of time between any two state transitions (i.e., **goto**s) is exactly one cycle. Within each cycle, Caisson enforces the following invariant: before executing the command of any state S, Caisson executes the commands of all of S's ancestor states (the intended semantics of nested states).

The **fall** command forces execution to fall-through from the current state to one of its child states: it ends evaluation of the current state's command and begins the evaluation of the child state's command. Falling from a state to its child does not count as a state transition (i.e., a **fall** command does not end a cycle, only a **goto** command can do that). By default the target child state of

$$r \in \mathit{Register} \quad v \in \mathit{Variable} \quad x \in \mathit{Register} \cup \mathit{Variable}$$
$$n \in \mathbb{Z} \quad \oplus \in \mathit{Operator} \quad l \in \mathit{Program\ Label}$$

$$\begin{aligned}
prog \in \mathit{Prog} &::= \textbf{prog}\ l = \vec{r_\ell}\ \textbf{in}\ d \\
d \in \mathit{Def} &::= \textbf{let}\ \vec{s}\ \textbf{in}\ c \mid c \\
s \in \mathit{State} &::= \textbf{state}\ l_\tau\ (\vec{v_\alpha})\,\kappa = d \\
e \in \mathit{Exp} &::= n \mid x \mid e \oplus e \\
c \in \mathit{Cmd} &::= \textbf{skip} \mid x := e \mid c\ ;\ c \mid \textbf{fall}_l \\
&\quad\mid \textbf{goto}\ l(\vec{x}) \mid \textbf{if}\ e\ \textbf{then}\ c\ \textbf{else}\ c \\
p \in \mathit{Phrase} &::= prog \mid d \mid s \mid e \mid c
\end{aligned}$$

Figure 3. Abstract syntax. Type annotations ℓ, α, τ, and κ are described in Figure 5

a **fall** command is the first child state in the list of nested state definitions; this state is called the *default child state* of that group state. The target child state for a **fall** may change during program execution as described in the next subsection.

To simplify the formal presentation of the language we make the following assumptions without explicitly enforcing them (though it is simple to do so in practice):

- All the variables and type variables have distinct names.
- A default child state can not take any parameters.
- Every **goto** targets a defined label and can only target a state in the same group and at the same nested depth[2].
- For each $\textbf{fall}_l$, the subscript label l must be the label of the state containing that **fall** command (the label is a syntactic convenience for the semantics and type system; it can be left out of the concrete syntax). A leaf state can not contain a **fall**.
- Either both branches of an **if** command must execute a **goto** or **fall** or neither of them do. All paths through a state end in either a **goto** or a **fall**.

The structure of a program defines a tree of state definitions (the state hierarchy) with **prog** being at the root. From this structure we derive different versions of a function $\mathcal{F} : l \mapsto (\vec{v} \cup p \cup l)$ that for each program label l gives the following mappings:

- $\mathcal{F}_{pnt}(l)$ maps to the label of state l's parent state.
- $\mathcal{F}_{def}(l)$ maps to the label of state l's default child state.
- $\mathcal{F}_{cmd}(l)$ maps to state l's command.
- $\mathcal{F}_{prm}(l)$ maps to state l's parameters.

In addition, $\mathcal{F}_{root}$ maps to the root command of the **prog** program phrase.

3.1 Semantics

Figure 4 shows the small-step operational semantics of Caisson. This figure gives the abstract machine configuration, defines the evaluation context, and gives the small-step transition rules.

[2] This requirement is due to the semantics of nested states: the target of a **goto** influences which ancestor states' commands execute, which could leak information without this restriction. This restriction does not greatly impact expressiveness: we can still get from any state to any other state by constructing a sequence of **goto**s, though we won't necessarily get there in a single cycle.

$$\gamma \in Env : (v \mapsto r) \cup (l \mapsto l) \qquad \sigma \in Store : r \mapsto n$$
$$\delta \in Time : \mathbb{N} \qquad \mathbb{C} \in Config : \langle p, \gamma, \sigma, \delta \rangle$$

$$E ::= \square \mid E \oplus e \mid n \oplus E \mid x := E \mid E \,;\, c$$
$$\mid \textbf{prog}\ l = \vec{r_\ell}\ \textbf{in}\ E \mid \textbf{let}\ \vec{s}\ \textbf{in}\ E$$

$$\langle E[r], \gamma, \sigma, \delta \rangle \rightsquigarrow \langle E[\sigma(r)], \gamma, \sigma, \delta \rangle \qquad \text{(REG)}$$

$$\langle E[v], \gamma, \sigma, \delta \rangle \rightsquigarrow \langle E[\sigma(\gamma(v))], \gamma, \sigma, \delta \rangle \qquad \text{(VAR)}$$

$$\langle E[n_1 \oplus n_2], \gamma, \sigma, \delta \rangle \rightsquigarrow \langle E[n_1 [\![\oplus]\!] n_2], \gamma, \sigma, \delta \rangle \qquad \text{(OP)}$$

$$\frac{\langle e, \gamma, \sigma, \delta \rangle \rightsquigarrow^* \langle n, \gamma, \sigma, \delta \rangle}{\langle E[r := e], \gamma, \sigma, \delta \rangle \rightsquigarrow \langle E[\textbf{skip}], \gamma, \sigma[r \mapsto n], \delta \rangle} \ \text{(ASSIGN-R)}$$

$$\frac{\langle e, \gamma, \sigma, \delta \rangle \rightsquigarrow^* \langle n, \gamma, \sigma, \delta \rangle}{\langle E[v := e], \gamma, \sigma, \delta \rangle \rightsquigarrow \langle E[\textbf{skip}], \gamma, \sigma[\gamma(v) \mapsto n], \delta \rangle} \ \text{(ASSIGN-V)}$$

$$\frac{\langle e, \gamma, \sigma, \delta \rangle \rightsquigarrow^* \langle n, \gamma, \sigma, \delta \rangle \qquad c' = \begin{cases} c_1 & : n = 0 \\ c_2 & : n \neq 0 \end{cases}}{\langle E[\textbf{if}\ e\ \textbf{then}\ c_1\ \textbf{else}\ c_2], \gamma, \sigma, \delta \rangle \rightsquigarrow \langle E[c'], \gamma, \sigma, \delta \rangle} \ \text{(IF)}$$

$$\langle E[\textbf{skip}\ ;\ c], \gamma, \sigma, \delta \rangle \rightsquigarrow \langle E[c], \gamma, \sigma, \delta \rangle \qquad \text{(SEQ)}$$

$$\langle E[\textbf{fall}_l], \gamma, \sigma, \delta \rangle \rightsquigarrow \langle \mathcal{F}_{cmd}(\gamma(l)), \gamma, \sigma, \delta \rangle \qquad \text{(FALL)}$$

$$\frac{\begin{array}{c} \gamma_1 = Reset(\gamma, l) \\ \gamma_2 = \gamma_1[\mathcal{F}_{pnt}(l) \mapsto l] \\ \gamma_3 = \gamma_2[\mathcal{F}_{prm}(l) \mapsto \gamma(\vec{x})] \end{array}}{\langle E[\textbf{goto}\ l(\vec{x})], \gamma, \sigma, \delta \rangle \rightsquigarrow \langle \mathcal{F}_{root}, \gamma_3, \sigma, \delta{+}1 \rangle} \ \text{(GOTO)}$$

Figure 4. Small-step semantic rules for Caisson ($\rightsquigarrow^*$is the reflexive transitive closure of $\rightsquigarrow$).

The abstract machine configuration consists of the current program phrase p, an environment γ, a store σ, and a time value δ. The environment γ maps variables (state parameters) to registers and maps state labels to other state labels; the store σ maps registers to values; and δ is the current time measured in cycles. The mapping from labels to labels in γ records for each state l its target child state (i.e., the command to begin evaluating if l executes a **fall** command—we initialize the mapping to the default child states). The rules are fairly standard except for **fall** and **goto**, which we now describe in detail.

The FALL rule applies when executing a $\textbf{fall}_l$ command. The rule looks up in γ the target child state for the current state l (recall that we require l for a command $\textbf{fall}_l$ to be the label of the current state) and begins executing that target child state's command.

The GOTO rule applies when executing a **goto** command. The rule does three things: (1) creates a new environment γ as described below; (2) increments the time δ, since a state transition marks the beginning of a new cycle; and (3) begins evaluating the root command at the top of the state hierarchy.

The most complex part of the GOTO rule is the set of premises that create the new environment γ_3 with which we evaluate the root command. The key is to understand the intended semantics of nested states: upon each state transition to a state l, we must maintain the invariant that all of l's ancestor states' commands execute before executing l's command. Hence, the **goto** sets the next command to $\mathcal{F}_{root}$ rather than the command of the target state. When evaluating a state's command it will eventually execute either another **goto** (restarting this whose process) or a **fall**. The environment must map each state's target child state such that a sequence of **fall**s will follow the correct path down the state hierarchy to eventually reach l, the original target of the **goto** that began the current cycle.

The first premise uses a helper function *Reset*, which we define here: *Reset* takes an environment γ and a state label l and returns a new environment γ' identical to γ except that label l and the labels of all states that are descendents of l in the state hierarchy are mapped to their default child states (the same as their initial values). This ensures that each time the program transitions to a state group, any prior evaluations of that state group do not affect the current evaluation.

The second premise looks up l's parent state ($\mathcal{F}_{pnt}(l)$) and sets the parent state's target child state to be l. This ensures that when evaluating the parent state's command and executing a **fall**, execution will fall-through to the correct child state (i.e., l). The last premise maps the target state l's parameters to the arguments of the **goto** command.

3.1.1 Example

Consider the code in Figure 2**(b)** and assume `mode` is initialized to 0 and `timer` is initialized to 3. Note that $\mathcal{F}_{root}$ is the outermost **fall** command (at the bottom of the code). Execution will proceed in the following manner,where C⟨X⟩ represents cycle X in the execution:

C0 The outermost **fall** command is executed, which by default falls through to state `master`. Since the **if** guard is true, `mode` is set to 1 and the command `goto group1` is executed. The GOTO rule changes the environment so that the fall-through state is now `group1` instead of `master` and resets the next command to be $\mathcal{F}_{root}$.

C1 The outermost **fall** command is executed. Because of the changed environment, control falls through to state `group1`. `timer` is decremented to 2; since `timer` is not 0 the else branch is taken and the **fall** command is executed. By default, control falls through to state `S1`. Assume that `data1` = 0; then the command `goto S2` is executed. This changes the environment so that the fall-through state for `group1` is now `S2` instead of `S1` and resets the next command to be $\mathcal{F}_{root}$.

C2 The outermost **fall** command is executed. As previously, control falls through to state `group1` and `timer` is decremented to 1. Since `timer` is not 0 the else branch is taken and the **fall** command is executed. Because of the changed environment control falls through to state `S2`. Assume `data1` is now 1; then the command `goto S2` is executed, which leaves the environment unchanged and resets the next command to be $\mathcal{F}_{root}$.

C3 The outermost **fall** command is executed. As previously, control falls through to state `group1` and `timer` is decremented to 0. Since `timer` is now 0, the true branch is taken and the command `goto master` is executed; this changes the environment so `group1`'s fall-through state goes back to its default (i.e., `S1`) and the root fall-through state is now `master` instead of `group1`, and resets the next command to be $\mathcal{F}_{root}$.

C4 The logic from cycle C0 is repeated, except that `mode` = 1 and so the program will transition to `group2` instead of `group1`.

$\ell \in \mathcal{L}$	security labels
$\tau ::= \ell \mid \alpha$	base types, type variables
$\kappa ::= \{\tau <: \tau\} \mid \kappa_1 \cup \kappa_2$	type constraints
$\rho ::= \tau \mid \mathtt{cmd}_\tau \mid \mathtt{st}_\tau(\vec{\alpha}, \kappa)$	phrase types

Figure 5. Types

3.2 Type System

Figure 5 gives the types used by our language. The base types are elements of the security lattice $\mathcal{L}$. Type variables range over base types and are implicitly universally quantified. We assume each state uses a disjoint set of type variables. The type variables are bounded by the type constraints κ which specify required subtype relations among the type variables and base types. The type system statically checks that all **goto** commands satisfy these constraints.

Expressions have type τ, commands have type $\mathtt{cmd}_\tau$, and states have type $\mathtt{st}_\tau(\vec{\alpha}, \kappa)$. We omit the standard subtyping rules: expression types are covariant ($e : \tau$ means that e contains no variables or registers greater than τ); command types are contravariant ($c : \mathtt{cmd}_\tau$ means that c does not change the state of any variable or register less than τ); and state types are invariant ($s : \mathtt{st}_\tau(\vec{\alpha}, \kappa)$ means that, assuming the state parameters have types $\vec{\alpha}$ that satisfy the constraints in κ, the state's command is type $\mathtt{cmd}_\tau$).

The program syntax explicitly notes the types of each register and state; we use this information to initialize the type environment $\Gamma : (r \mapsto \ell) \cup (v \mapsto \alpha) \cup (l \mapsto \mathtt{st}_\tau(\vec{\alpha}, \kappa)) \cup \kappa$. Γ maps all registers to a base type, all state parameters to a type variable, and all state labels to a state type, and also records the type constraints in all κ. The whole program (i.e. the *root* state) is always mapped to $\mathtt{st}_\perp(\_, \_)$. Γ also records the subtype relations between base types (i.e., security labels) as given in the security lattice. Since Γ remains constant, we factor it out of the individual type rules.

Most of the rules are standard (see, e.g., Volpano et al [51]) except for rules T-FALL and T-GOTO which we now explain in detail. Rule T-FALL states that if the type of the default child state's command is $\mathtt{cmd}_\tau$ then so must be the type of the current state's command. This requirement is due to the differing semantics of **fall** and **goto** commands: a **fall** command immediately begins executing the child state's command, whereas a **goto** begins executing the root command $\mathcal{F}_{root}$. Without this rule, if a conditional with a *high* guard has a **goto** in one branch and a **fall** in the other then a *low* observer might be able to observe the outcome of the conditional based on whether execution proceeds from $\mathcal{F}_{root}$ or not. The rule only needs to check the type of the default child state's command ($\mathcal{F}_{cmd}(\mathcal{F}_{def}(l))$) even though at runtime a state can fall-through to any child state. Since we require transitions must be to neighbor states in the state hierarchy, other child states can only be reached via the default child state. Thus, typing consistency between the parent state and all its child states is enforced indirectly by a combination of the T-FALL and T-GOTO rules.

The most complicated type rule is T-GOTO. The **goto** command has a target state l and a list of arguments $\vec{x}$. The type rule must accomplish two things:

- It must verify that the arguments $\vec{x}$ given to the **goto** satisfy the type constraints κ of the target state l. This requirement is checked by the first premise on the second line of the type rule. State l's type constraints κ are modified to map the type of each state parameter to the type of its corresponding argument (via $\kappa[\vec{\alpha} \mapsto \Gamma(\vec{x})]$); then the resulting type constraints are verified to be valid assertions (i.e., that the constraints can be derived using the sub-typing rules and the information in Γ).

$$n : \perp \qquad \text{(T-CONST)}$$

$$\frac{\Gamma(x) = \tau}{x : \tau} \qquad \text{(T-REG/VAR)}$$

$$\frac{e_1 : \tau \qquad e_2 : \tau}{e_1 \oplus e_2 : \tau} \qquad \text{(T-OP)}$$

$$\frac{\Gamma(x) = \tau \qquad e : \tau}{x := e : \mathtt{cmd}_\tau} \qquad \text{(T-ASSIGN)}$$

$$\frac{e : \tau \qquad c_1 : \mathtt{cmd}_\tau \qquad c_2 : \mathtt{cmd}_\tau}{\textbf{if } e \textbf{ then } c_1 \textbf{ else } c_2 : \mathtt{cmd}_\tau} \qquad \text{(T-IF)}$$

$$\frac{c_1 : \mathtt{cmd}_\tau \qquad c_2 : \mathtt{cmd}_\tau}{c_1 \; ; \; c_2 : \mathtt{cmd}_\tau} \qquad \text{(T-SEQ)}$$

$$\textbf{skip} : \mathtt{cmd}_\top \qquad \text{(T-SKIP)}$$

$$\frac{\Gamma(l) = \mathtt{st}_\tau(\vec{\alpha}, \kappa) \qquad \mathcal{F}_{cmd}(\mathcal{F}_{def}(l)) : \mathtt{cmd}_\tau}{\textbf{fall}_l : \mathtt{cmd}_\tau} \qquad \text{(T-FALL)}$$

$$\frac{\begin{array}{c}\Gamma(l) = \mathtt{st}_\tau(\vec{\alpha}, \kappa) \\ \vdash \kappa[\vec{\alpha} \mapsto \Gamma(\vec{x})] \quad \tau' = \tau[\vec{\alpha} \mapsto \Gamma(\vec{x})]\end{array}}{\textbf{goto } l(\vec{x}) : \mathtt{cmd}_{\tau'}} \qquad \text{(T-GOTO)}$$

$$\frac{\Gamma(l) = \mathtt{st}_\tau(\vec{\alpha}, \kappa) \qquad d : \mathtt{cmd}_\tau}{\textbf{state } l_\tau \; (\vec{v_\alpha}) \, \kappa = d : \mathtt{st}_\tau(\vec{\alpha}, \kappa)} \qquad \text{(T-STATE)}$$

$$\frac{s_i : \mathtt{st}_{\tau_i}(\vec{\alpha_i}, \kappa_i) \qquad c : \mathtt{cmd}_\tau}{\textbf{let } \vec{s} \textbf{ in } c : \mathtt{cmd}_\tau} \qquad \text{(T-DEF)}$$

$$\frac{d : \mathtt{cmd}_\tau}{\textbf{prog } l = \vec{r_\ell} \textbf{ in } d : \mathtt{cmd}_\tau} \qquad \text{(T-PROG)}$$

Figure 6. Caisson type rules

- It must also confirm the type of the **goto** command in the conclusion of the rule. This is confirmed by the last premise on the second line of the rule. The target state has type $\mathtt{st}_\tau(\vec{\alpha}, \kappa)$, meaning that its command has type $\mathtt{cmd}_\tau$. However, we cannot simply make the type of the **goto** command be type $\mathtt{cmd}_\tau$—τ may be a type variable, and we assume that the sets of type variables used in any two states are disjoint. Therefore, the rule must translate type τ, valid for the target state, into an appropriate type τ', valid for the source state. The rule uses the same substitution operator as used earlier to perform this translation.

We sketch a proof that the Caisson type system enforces timing-sensitive noninterference in Appendix A.

3.2.1 Example

Here we use the type rules to show that specific parts of the example program in the previous section are well-typed. We don't show the entire type derivation, but we do show how both the T-GOTO and T-FALL rules are used.

Consider the code in Figure 2(c), and specifically the command `goto group(data1)`. The rule T-GOTO first confirms that the type of the argument (i.e., `data1`, which is type H) satisfies the type constraints of the target `group`, i.e., that L <: H—this is true. The rule then finds a suitable type for the `goto` command based on the type of the target state (`group`, which is type L); hence the type of the `goto` command is $\mathtt{cmd}_L$.

Now consider the command `goto group(data2)`. By the same logic this command is also typed $\texttt{cmd}_L$, except that when checking that the argument (i.e., `data2`, which is type L) satisfies the type constraints, the rules confirms that L <: L, which is also true. Since `mode` is type L, the type of the **if** statement is $\texttt{cmd}_L$ which matches the declared type of state `master`.

From the above we can confirm that all transitions to `group` satisfy the type constraints. When typing `group` itself, we assume that the type constraints are met, i.e., that L <: A. Hence, when typing the false branch of the **if** command in `group` the **fall** command, using rule T-FALL, is initially typed as $\texttt{cmd}_A$. However, by contravariance and since L <: A, it can also be typed as $\texttt{cmd}_L$. Since the true branch is typed $\texttt{cmd}_L$ (by the T-GOTO rule), the **if** command is well-typed as $\texttt{cmd}_L$, which matches the declared type of state `group`.

When checking state `S1`, the declared type (i.e., $\texttt{st}_A$(L <: A)) forces the **if** command to be type $\texttt{cmd}_A$; the T-GOTO rules confirms that is true for both branches of the **if** command. The same holds true for state S2.

Therefore each state of the program, and the entire program itself, is well-typed.

4. Information-Flow Secure Processor

In this section we concretely demonstrate the utility of Caisson by designing and evaluating an information-flow secure processor that safely muliplexes execution of *trusted* and *untrusted* code. Securely executing mixed-trust programs has historically been difficult to get right. For instance, all known cache attacks stem from the basic problem that cache controllers must use both trusted and untrusted information to decide which lines to evict from a cache [35, 54]. Information has been also shown to leak through branch predictor history table [5] or through the instruction cache lines [6]. More generally, any perturbation in the execution of a trusted program based on untrusted data is a vulnerability, and we must prevent all possible sources of such information leaks.

We begin the section with a description of a complete four-stage processor pipeline that securely implements a RISC ISA. We then extend the processor to include a cache hierarchy that is verifiably secure against all known attacks [35, 54]. These designs demonstrate that Caisson's language abstractions allow the CPU to be cleanly specified in a natural fashion and enable a statically-verifiable, efficient design. For this processor design we employ the same two-level lattice `Trusted` $\sqsubseteq$ `Untrusted` as used in §2.

4.1 Secure CPU Design

The public interface of a CPU is its Instruction Set Architecture (ISA). Table 1 describes the ISA of our processor; this is a standard ISA (derived from the commercial Altera Nios processor). The ISA is implemented using a combination of hardware data- and control-flow controlled by the execution pipeline. Figure 7 shows the four-stage pipeline of our processor, with stages Fetch, Decode, Execute, and Commit. Additional microarchitectural features such as caches, prefetchers, and branch predictors can be attached to the pipeline to improve processor performance. Our processor implements a cache to illustrate how these microarchitectural features can be designed for security; the other features can be implemented using similar strategies.

The easiest method to ensure that `Untrusted` data can never affect `Trusted` computation is to physically isolate them, i.e., have two separate instances of the CPU, one for `Trusted` computation and one for `Untrusted` computation. While simple and easy to verify, economic reality means that this is not a practical solution. Even in high assurance systems the hardware components are often shared, e.g., the Boeing 787 trusted aircraft control network shares the physical bus with the untrusted passenger network [15].

Instruction	Description
jump If RegZero	If the value of a register is zero then jump to the target.
jump To RegValue	Jump to the address which is stored in specified register.
load Immediate	Load an immediate value to a register.
load/store Direct	Load/store data from/into an immediate memory address to a register.
load PC To Reg	Load the value of PC into a register (for store/restore context purpose).
load/store Indirect –global load/store Indirect –local	Load/store data from/into a memory address specified by a based address in register and an offset. The global version operates on data outside the current lease which is a range setup by the leaser while the local version operates on local data inside current memory bound.
directJump	Directly jump to a target address.
and, or, not, xor, shl, shr, add, sub, cmpeq, cmpl	Arithmetic instructions.

Table 1. The ISA of our RISC processor

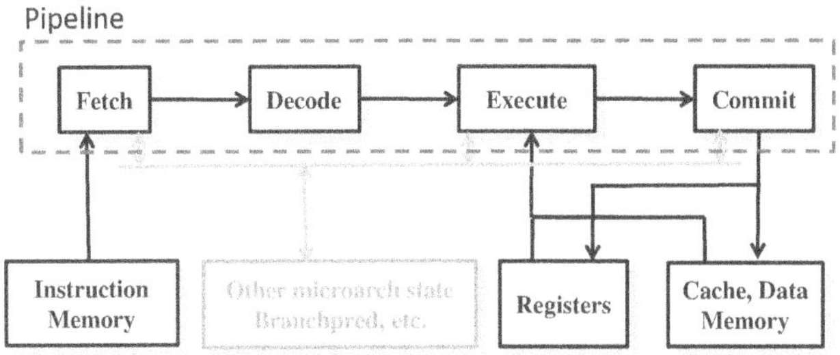

Figure 7. A typical CPU pipeline and its interaction with memories, registers and other components. Our CPU design implements all parts in **bold**.

The only alternative solution is to *time multiplex* the `Trusted` and `Untrusted` computation on the same physical hardware. The key to secure hardware design is to guarantee that any state changes due to `Untrusted` computation never affect any `Trusted` computation even when the computations share the same pipeline stages, cache, and other processor features. Caisson's language abstractions and type system collaborate to provide the hardware designer with the tools needed to easily encode and verify a secure design. In the remainder of the section we describe in detail the Caisson implementation of our processor.

4.2 Secure Execution Pipeline

The execution pipeline is the backbone of the processor and the foundation of a secure design. Our goal is to take a *trusted context* (i.e., registers and memory) and a separate *untrusted context* and use the same physical processor logic circuits to safely operate on both. The resulting processor is a 32-bit RISC processor with 128KB each of Instruction and Data memory (64KB for the trusted context and 64KB for the untrusted context), two program counters, and 16 general purpose registers (split evenly between the trusted and untrusted contexts). There is a *single* four-stage pipeline shared between the trusted and untrusted contexts (as well as a 2K shared data cache, described in the next subsection). Figure 8 shows a state-machine diagram of the pipeline design.

This design interweaves the `Trusted` and `Untrusted` computation at a coarse granularity. There is a Reset state that resets the hardware state to its initial conditions and a Master state that controls the pipeline logic. The Master state sets a timer and allows the pipeline to be used in alternate time intervals by the `Trusted` and `Untrusted` computation. In this design, every stage of the pipeline contains data from the same execution context (`Trusted` or `Untrusted`). Figure 9 shows the hardware diagram of the cor-

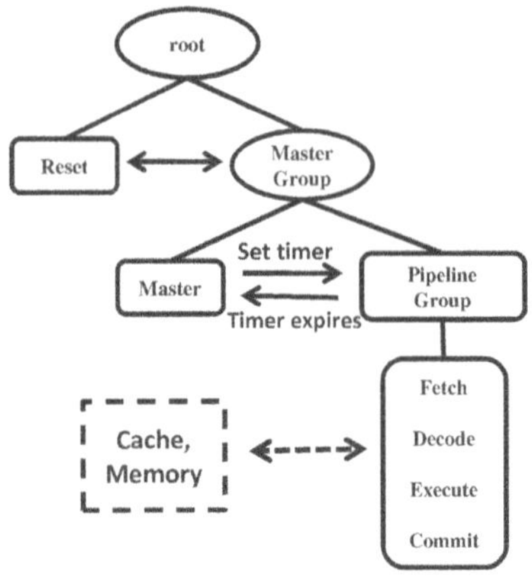

Figure 8. State Machine Diagram of the Coarse-Grained Time-multiplexed Pipeline. The memory hierarchy shown in the dash box does not represent any concrete state in the state machine, but it is included in our CPU and accessed by the pipeline.

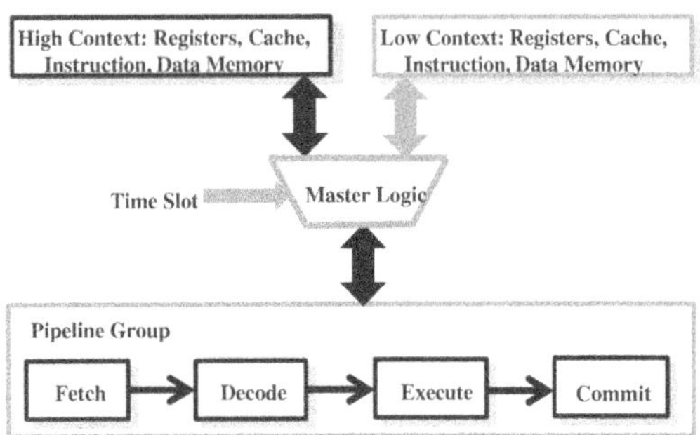

(b)

Figure 9. Synthesized hardware implementation of the Coarse-Grained Time-multiplexed Pipeline CPU logic when the entire pipeline is multiplexed between *high* and *low* code.

responding synthesized circuit. Figure 10 gives a skeleton of the Caisson code that implements the pipeline design (where 'HighContext' and 'LowContext' stand for the untrusted and trusted contexts, respectively). Note that the design uses nested states to allow verification of the design and parameterized states to share the physical logic. In fact, this design is similar to the Execution Lease controller design in §2.

4.2.1 Fine-Grained Sharing of Execution Pipeline

One possible drawback of the previous pipeline design is that the sharing between `Trusted` and `Untrusted` computation is coarse-grained; the time intervals during which they each have control of the pipeline must be sufficiently large to counteract the cost of stalling the pipeline each time the context is switched between them. An alternative design can share the pipeline at a much finer granularity, so that *each pipeline stage* continuously alternates between `Trusted` and `Untrusted` computation at each cycle. This design may be an attractive option when the computation at each security level requires a low latency response.

Figure 12 shows the intuition behind this design, along with a state-machine diagram illustrating the design. Figure 11 gives a skeleton of the Caisson code that implements the design. Each pipeline stage is initialized at a particular security level, so that Fetch is `Trusted`, Decode is `Untrusted`, Execute is `Trusted`, and Commit is `Untrusted`. In each cycle (i.e., at each state transition

```
prog CPU = HighContext: H, LowContext:L, timer:L, mode:L
in let state reset:L() = {
        mode := 0;
        goto mastergroup()
    }
    state mastergroup:L() = {
      let state master:L() = {
          timer = ...
          if mode then mode:=1;  goto pipegroup(HighContext)
                  else mode:=0;  goto pipegroup(LowContext)
        }
        state pipegroup:L(context:A) [L<A] = {
          let state pipe:L() = {
              //Fetch, Decode, Execute, Commit
              goto pipe()
            }
          in
            if (timer==0) then goto master()
                          else timer := timer - 1; fall
        }
      in
        fall
    }
```

Figure 10. Implementation of the coarse-grained multiplexing pipeline. The timer can be initialized to any number hence we omit the concrete value here.

```
prog CPU = F_init: L, D_init: H, E_init: L, C_init : H
in let state reset:L() = {
            goto pipe(F_init, D_init, E_init, C_init)
    }

    state pipe:L(F_ctxt:A, D_ctxt: B, E_ctxt: A, C_ctxt: B) = {
            //Fetch, Decode, Execute, Commit
            // New context with security level B is obtained for Fetch
            // Each stage calculates and updates their context
            goto pipe(newF_ctxt, F_ctxt, D_ctxt, E_ctxt)
    }
```

Figure 11. Implementation of the fine-grained multiplexing pipeline using Caisson

goto), the security context at one stage is passed on to the next stage in turn.

4.3 Secure Cache Design

A secure execution pipeline prevents information leaks via hardware data- and control-flow, but information can still be leaked via microarchitectural features such as cache memory. For example, there are well-known security attacks that exploit a shared memory to covertly communicate between two supposedly isolated processes by selectively causing page faults and/or cache misses [5, 35]. We implement a secure cache for our processor design to illustrate how to secure microarchitectural features; other features, such as branch predictors, can be securely implemented using similar strategies.

As with the execution pipeline, there are two basic approaches to securing the cache: physical isolation (statically partitioning the cache between `Trusted` and `Untrusted data`) or time multiplexing (sharing the cache, but flushing it each time the processor switches between the `Trusted` and `Untrusted` contexts). In this case, unlike the pipeline, the extreme cost of flushing the cache at each context switch means that partitioning the cache is the pre-

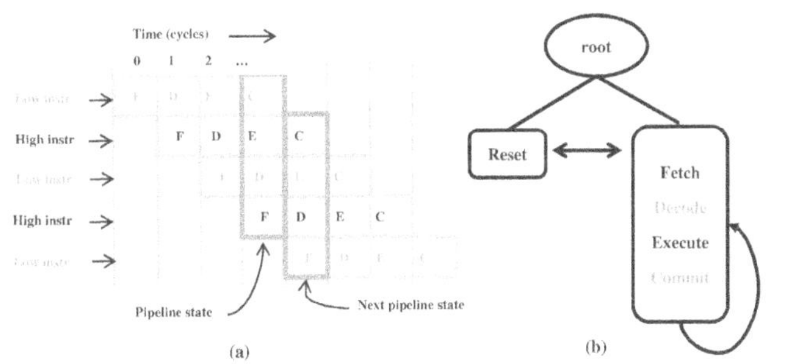

Figure 12. Fine-Grained Pipeline Multiplexing. (a) Intuition behind the design (b) State Machine Diagram

ferred solution. Other existing work has come to the same conclusion [54]. Our contribution is not the design of a secure cache itself, but the fact that a secure cache can be easily implemented and statically verified using Caisson, as well as securely integrated into a larger secure system (i.e., our processor). Static verification is important—previous work on secure cache design [54] has been shown to possess subtle flaws that violate security [26].

In Caisson, the implementation of a partitioned cache is simple: the design passes the particular cache partition each context should use as part of the context information for the parameterized states. In Figure 10, the cache partitions would be part of 'HighContext' and 'LowContext'. Equally as important as the cache memory itself is the cache controller—the logic that processes cache hits and misses. Unlike the cache memory, the cache controller can be shared among the different security levels in the same manner as the execution pipeline.

4.4 Evaluation

We have proven that Caisson gaurantees the security of our processor design, but an interesting question is how the resulting design performs in comparison to existing processor designs, both traditional insecure processors and other processors designed for security. The relevant performance metrics are: synthesis time (how long it takes to transform a high-level design into an actual circuit); chip area (how large the resulting circuit is); delay (inversely proportional to clock frequency); and power (the power consumption of the circuit).

4.4.1 Synthesis Methodology

To quantify the hardware design overhead introduced by our approach we compare our processor design (**Caisson**) with a non-secured, simplified version of the commercial Nios Processor (**Base**) and the same Nios processor augmented to dynamically track information flow using GLIFT (**GLIFT**) [46]. GLIFT implements full system information flow tracking at the logic gate level: it associates each bit in the system with a taint bit indicating its security level, and augments each gate in the hardware design with additional gates that compute taint propagation.

All CPUs have identical functionality and configuration. However both **Caisson** and **GLIFT** can only utilize half of the cache and memory capacity effectively although they have identical configuration as the **Base** processor. The reason is that in our Caisson design the memory and cache have to be partitioned into two parts with different security levels, while **GLIFT** needs to associate a one-bit tag for each bit in the memory and cache. Increasing the cache and memory utilization efficiency for **Caisson** is part of our future work.

We implemented the **Base** processor (from the Nios design) in Verilog with no additional security features. To get the Caisson implementation we remodeled the **Base** implementation using

	Base	GLIFT		Caisson	
Synthesis Time (min)	1:50	153:56	**83.96X**	4:04	**2.22X**
Area (μm²)	38462.86	128506.89	**3.34X**	52088.78	**1.35X**
CPU delay (ns)	2.96	7.79	**2.63X**	4.32	**1.46X**
Power (μW)	614.148	1730	**2.82X**	666.912	**1.09X**

Table 2. Synthesized results of the different CPU designs: the simplified Nios Processor (Base), the GLIFT-based CPU, and the Caisson-based CPU.

security widgets provided by the Caisson language and statically partitioned all registers, caches, and memories into `Trusted` and `Untrusted`. To get the **GLIFT** implementation, we first synthesized the **Base** design into a gate level netlist and then augmented the netlist with shadow logic to track information flow. We passed the **Base** and **Caisson** designs through Altera's QuartusII v8.0 tool to synthesize the designs onto a Stratix II FPGA for functional testing and verification. We then obtain the area, timing and power results using the Synopsis Design Compiler and the SAED 90nm technology library [1] assuming a switching activity factor of 50% for the circuit.

4.4.2 Results

Almost as important as the quantitative performance results are the *qualitative* results of how easy each design was to implement—this is an important test for the usability of a language. We find anecdotally that Caisson is easily usable by a programmer trained in Verilog. The original **Base** design required 709 lines of Verilog—the corresponding **Caisson** design required only 724 lines and took little additional time to implement. By contrast, **GLIFT** required us to make a hard choice: we could either (1) manually design the gate-level netlist at a structural level (i.e., manually place the logic gates to create the design), which in our experience is infeasible for such a complex design; or (2) generate a gate-level netlist from the behavioral Verilog design using an existing tool, then automatically generate the GLIFT shadow logic using the resulting netlist. We used the latter option, and while it simplifies the process for the programmer the resulting design is intractably difficult to debug and optimize.

Table 2 gives the performance figures for each design. We give the concrete numbers for all three designs as well as normalized numbers for **Caisson** and **GLIFT** (using **Base** as a baseline). The area numbers do not include the memory hierarchy since all three designs use an identical memory configuration. The power numbers include both dynamic and leakage power. The **GLIFT** design comes with a large overhead in all four performance categories due to the shadow logic that GLIFT introduces to the processor. This shadow logic takes a long time to synthesize, requires a large chip area, consumes a great deal of power, and drastically slows the processor cycle frequency.

Caisson, in contrast, has a much lower overhead, though it is certainly not free. This overhead mainly comes from two sources: the duplicated state (i.e., registers) and the additional encoders and decoders used to multiplex the partitioned state onto the same logic circuits. We note that the overhead generated by the **Caisson** design does not grow with CPU complexity (e.g., number of functional units)—a more powerful and complex CPU would not require any additional overhead, while the **GLIFT** design's overhead *would* proportionately with the CPU complexity. For perhaps the most important performance metric, power, **Caisson**'s overhead is almost negligible. The synthesis time for the Caisson design includes type-checking, which is sufficient to verify the design's security. The GLIFT synthesis time does *not* include verification—GLIFT only detect security violations at runtime.

These results show that designing a secure processor using Caisson not only provides a strong static guarantee about information flow security, but also (1) allows a more straightforward and natural way of designing a secure processor, and (2) introduces much less area, timing and power overhead than dynamic tracking techniques such as GLIFT.

5. Related Work

Secure information flow has been widely studied; a survey by Sabelfeld and Myers [39] gives a comprehensive summary of this work. Here we concentrate on (1) hardware-assisted secure information flow, and (2) analyzing hardware designs for secure information flow, for both secrecy and integrity. Although the concept of integrity has sometimes been generalized to include other properties such as program correctness [17, 30], we deal only with information integrity in this paper.

A number of papers deal with timing-sensitive secure information flow for programming languages [8–10, 21, 37, 42, 52, 56]. These papers enforce timing-sensitivity by restricting computation, e.g., by not allowing any branches or loops on high information. These restrictions wouldn't allow for any useful hardware designs and so these works can't be used in Caisson; instead, we take advantage of the characteristics of sychronous hardware to enforce timing sensitivity (as explained in Appendix A).

5.1 Hardware-Assisted Secure Information Flow

Secure information flow has been enforced at a variety of levels of abstraction in computer systems. At the programming language level information flow can be enforced statically (e.g., via a type system [33, 53]) or dynamically [29, 36]. At lower levels of abstraction dynamic enforcement is the norm. Projects such as LoStar [59], HiStar [58] and Flume [28] apply distributed information flow control (DIFC) [57] through general-purpose operating system abstractions. Tag-based tracking at the virtual machine, architecture, or ISA levels is a popular dynamic solution that tracks information flows through all registers and memory [12, 13, 34, 38, 43, 49, 50].

However, even hardware-assisted secure-information flow tracking does not go below the ISA abstraction level to account for microarchitectural features such as pipelining and cache. There are existing dedicated secure cache [54] and memory controller [32] designs, however these designs only enforce information flow policies for specific components in the computer architecture; this existing work does not address the entire processor design, nor does it provide a general methodology for designing secure hardware.

5.2 Information Flow Analysis for Hardware Design

The traditional method for checking the security of a hardware design is to simulate and extensively test the design, a laborious and expensive process. While static analysis [19, 22, 23, 40] and model checking [11] are often used for *functional* verification, they are not often used to check security. Tolstrup et al [47, 48] describe a type-system based information flow analysis to verify hardware security policies for VHDL designs. Their work is limited to analyzing simple cryptographic hardware designs, and as pointed out by Li et al [31], directly applying conventional information flow analysis to existing hardware description languages often leads to imprecise results.

Unlike the existing work, Caisson extends HDLs like VHDL and Verilog with language abstractions that specifically target precise static verification of hardware designs.

6. Conclusion

Hardware mechanisms for information flow control often form the root of trust in high assurance systems and are used to enforce policies such as non-interference. While programming language techniques have been used extensively for creating secure software, languages to create information-flow secure hardware have not received much attention. We combine insights from traditional type-based secure languages with domain-specfic design patterns used for hardware design and present a new hardware description language, Caisson, for constructing statically-verifiable secure hardware designs. By formalizing certain security design patterns and providing direct language support for enforcing their correct use, Caisson promotes *thinking* about secure hardware design in new, useful ways that don't naturally arise in existing languages. Using Caisson, we are able to express information flow control mechanisms in a natural manner and quickly verify a variety of novel secure hardware designs. In particular, we show how the insights gained from developing Caisson allow us to design the first ever implementation of a pipelined processor that verifiably enforces noninterference.

A. Proof of Noninterference

We sketch a proof that Caisson enforces timing-sensitive noninterference between security levels. The invariant that we wish to enforce is that an observer at security level ℓ cannot distinguish between two runs of the same program that differ only in the information at security levels $\ell' \not\sqsubseteq \ell$. Because Caisson models synchronous hardware designs there are two important implications that we leverage: (1) observers can see the stores only at the end of each cycle, i.e., they cannot see changes to the store that happen during a cycle until that cycle ends; and (2) the length of time between two sequential **goto** commands is *always* exactly one cycle, regardless of the number of semantic steps taken. These two facts are justified by the synchronous nature of the hardware: the flip-flops only read in new values on a clock edge, and the clock frequency is set so that each state (corresponding to a combinational circuit) is guaranteed to have completed within one cycle.

We define "distinguishability" using the *L-equivalence* relation defined below. We then give a set of lemmas and our main noninterference theorem.

A.1 L-equivalence

First we define the set of security types L that an observer at security level ℓ can observe. This includes base types that are subtypes of ℓ as well as type variables of state parameters that the current environment γ maps to registers whose base types are subtypes of ℓ. Formally, for a given security level ℓ and environment γ let $L =$ the minimum fixpoint of $\{\ell' \mid \ell' \sqsubseteq \ell\} \cup \{\alpha \mid \exists v \in dom(\gamma).v : \alpha \wedge \gamma(v) \in L\}$. Then let $H = \{\tau \mid \tau \notin L\}$, i.e., the security types that an observer at level ℓ can't distinguish. Types L and H are always with respect to some environment γ.

We lift the type constructors and typing relation to operate on L and H in the obvious way. We now use L and H to define the *L-equivalence* relation $\sim_L$ on stores, environments, commands, and configurations such that L-equivalent items are indistinguishable from each other for an L-observer.

- **Environment:** Two environments are equivalent ($\gamma_1 \sim_L \gamma_2$) if they cannot be used to create effects distinguishable by an L-observer. This means that (1) any writable L-typed state parameter (i.e., not from an H-typed state) must be mapped to the same register in both environments; and (2) if γ_1 maps a label l to an L-typed state then so must γ_2 and vice-versa:

- For all parameters v of any state $l : \mathtt{st}_L(\vec{\alpha}, \kappa)$, $v : L$ w.r.t. either γ_1 or $\gamma_2 \Rightarrow \gamma_1(v) = \gamma_2(v)$, **and**
- $\forall l \,.\, \gamma_1(l) : \mathtt{st}_L(\vec{\alpha}, \kappa) \vee \gamma_2(l) : \mathtt{st}_L(\vec{\alpha}, \kappa) \Rightarrow \gamma_1(l) = \gamma_2(l)$

- **Store:** Two stores are equivalent if they agree on all values that can be seen by an L-observer. Let the $\downarrow_L$ operator project out all registers with type H from a store (since registers always have a base type we don't need γ to determine H); then $\sigma_1 \sim_L \sigma_2$ if $(\sigma_1 \downarrow_L) = (\sigma_2 \downarrow_L)$
- **Command:** Two commands are equivalent w.r.t. an environment γ ($c_1 \sim_L^\gamma c_2$) if (1) they are the same command and both typed $\mathtt{cmd}_L$ w.r.t. γ, hence will modify state in the same way; or (2) both commands are typed $\mathtt{cmd}_H$ w.r.t γ, hence cannot modify state that is L-observable:
  - $c_1 = c_2 \wedge c_1 : \mathtt{cmd}_L \wedge c_2 : \mathtt{cmd}_L$, **or**
  - $(c_1 : \mathtt{cmd}_H \wedge c_2 : \mathtt{cmd}_H)$
- **Configuration:** Two configurations are equivalent ($\mathbb{C}_1 \sim_L \mathbb{C}_2$) if their stores, environments, and commands are equivalent *and* they have the same time: $\exists\gamma$ s.t. $\gamma_1 \sim_L \gamma \wedge \gamma_2 \sim_L \gamma \wedge c_1 \sim_L^\gamma c_2 \wedge \sigma_1 \sim_L \sigma_2 \wedge \delta_1 = \delta_2$

A.2 Lemmas

This section introduces a set of lemmas that we use for the noninterference proof. Simple security states that an expression $e : L$ contains only low sub-expressions, while confinement states that $c : \mathtt{cmd}_H$ cannot create any effects involving L-typed variables. The types L and H are with respect to a well-formed environment γ.

Lemma 1 (Simple Security). *$e : L \Rightarrow$ no sub-expression of e has type H.*

Proof. By induction on the structure of e. □

Lemma 2 (Confinement). *$c : \mathtt{cmd}_H \Rightarrow$ evaluating c using environment γ and some store σ does not modify the value of any variable or register with type L.*

Proof. By induction on the structure of c. □

Lemma 3 (Subject Reduction). *$\langle c, \gamma, \sigma, \delta \rangle \rightsquigarrow \langle c', \gamma', \sigma', \delta \rangle$ and $c : \mathtt{cmd}_H$ w.r.t. $\gamma \Rightarrow c' : \mathtt{cmd}_H$ w.r.t. γ'*

Proof. By induction on the structure of c. □

A.3 Noninterference

We now come to the noninterference theorem itself, which holds for all well-typed Caisson programs. Recall that because the language models synchronous hardware, we assume that changes to the store are only visible upon a state transition and that time only increments at state transitions (regardless of the number of semantic steps taken). With that in mind, we give the noninterference theorem below. It states that given two configurations $\mathbb{C}_A$ and $\mathbb{C}_B$, both of which are L-equivalent and start at the root command, when the resulting evaluations each reach a state transition (i.e., a **goto**) the resulting new configurations must also be L-equivalent.

Theorem 1 (Noninterference).
Let

- $\mathbb{C}_A = \langle \mathcal{F}_{root}, \gamma_A, \sigma_A, \delta_A \rangle$
- $\mathbb{C}'_A = \langle \mathcal{F}_{root}, \gamma'_A, \sigma'_A, \delta_A + 1 \rangle$
- $\mathbb{C}_B = \langle \mathcal{F}_{root}, \gamma_B, \sigma_B, \delta_B \rangle$
- $\mathbb{C}'_B = \langle \mathcal{F}_{root}, \gamma'_B, \sigma'_B, \delta_B + 1 \rangle$

Then

$$\mathbb{C}_A \rightsquigarrow^* \mathbb{C}'_A \wedge \mathbb{C}_B \rightsquigarrow^* \mathbb{C}'_B \wedge \mathbb{C}_A \sim_L \mathbb{C}_B \Rightarrow \mathbb{C}'_A \sim_L \mathbb{C}'_B$$

Proof. By induction on the steps of the computation and Lemmas 1, 2, and 3. □

The proof itself is straightfoward and omitted for space. Note that the noninterference theorem is timing-sensitive: it guarantees that given two L-equivalent configurations, a Caisson program must make identical L-observable changes *at the same times* under both configurations (where time is measured as number of cycles).

Acknowledgments

This research was supported by the US Department of Defense under AFOSR MURI grant FA9550-07-1-0532.
The views and conclusions contained herein are those of the authors and should not be interpreted as necessarily representing the official policies or endorsements, either expressed or implied, of the sponsoring agencies.

References

[1] 90nm generic CMOS library, Synopsys University program, Synopsys Inc.

[2] Common critera evaluation and validation scheme. http://www.niap-ccevs.org/cc-scheme/cc_docs/.

[3] Validated FIPS 140-1 and FIPS 140-2 cryptographic modules. http://csrc.nist.gov/groups/STM/cmvp/documents/140-1/140val-all.htm.

[4] What does CC EAL6+ mean? http://www.ok-labs.com/blog/entry/what-does-cc-eal6-mean/.

[5] O. Accigmez, J. pierre Seifert, and C. K. Koc. Predicting secret keys via branch prediction. In *The Cryptographers' Track at the RSA Conference*, pages 225–242. Springer-Verlag, 2007.

[6] O. Aciiçmez. Yet another microarchitectural attack: Exploiting i-cache. In *CCS Computer Security Architecture Workshop*, 2007.

[7] O. Aciiçmez, J.-P. Seifert, and C. K. Koc. Micro-architectural cryptanalysis. *IEEE Security and Privacy*, 5:62–64, July 2007.

[8] J. Agat. Transforming out timing leaks. In *Proceedings of the 27th ACM SIGPLAN-SIGACT symposium on Principles of programming languages*, POPL '00, pages 40–53, New York, NY, USA, 2000. ACM.

[9] G. Barthe, T. Rezk, and M. Warnier. Preventing Timing Leaks Through Transactional Branching Instructions. *Electronic Notes Theoretical Computer Science*, 153:33–55, May 2006.

[10] G. Boudol and I. Castellani. Noninterference for concurrent programs. pages 382–395, 2001.

[11] E. M. Clarke, O. Grumberg, and D.Peled. *Model Checking*. MIT Press, 2000.

[12] J. R. Crandall and F. T. Chong. Minos: Control data attack prevention orthogonal to memory model. In *Micro*, pages 221 – 232, 2004.

[13] M. Dalton, H. Kannan, and C. Kozyrakis. Raksha: A flexible information flow architecture for software security. In *ISCA*, pages 482–493, 2007.

[14] D. E. Denning and P. J. Denning. Certification of programs for secure information flow. *Communications of the ACM*, 20(7):504–513, 1977.

[15] F. A. A. (FAA). Boeing model 787-8 airplane; systems and data networks security-isolation or protection from unauthorized passenger domain systems access. http://cryptome.info/faa010208.htm.

[16] A. Filinski. Linear continuations. In *Proceedings of the 19th ACM SIGPLAN-SIGACT symposium on Principles of programming languages*, POPL '92, pages 27–38, New York, NY, USA, 1992. ACM.

[17] C. Fournet and T. Rezk. Cryptographically sound implementations for typed information-flow security. In *POPL*, pages 323–335, 2008.

[18] J. A. Goguen and J. Meseguer. Security policies and security models. In *IEEE Symposium on Security and Privacy*, 1982.

[19] C. Hankin. Program analysis tools. *International Journal on Software Tools for Technology Transfer*, 2(1), 1998.

[20] D. Harel. Statecharts: A visual formalism for complex systems. *Science of Computer Programming 8*, 1987.

[21] D. Hedin and D. Sands. Timing aware information flow security for a javacard-like bytecode. 141(1):163–182, 2005.

[22] C. Hymans. Checking safety properties of behavioral VHDL descriptions by abstract interpretation. In *International Static Analysis Symposium*, pages 444–460. Springer, 2002.

[23] C. Hymans. Design and implementation of an abstract interpreter for VHDL. *D.Geist and E.Tronci, editors, CHARME*, 2860 of LNCS, 2003.

[24] G. Klein, K. Elphinstone, G. Heiser, J. Andronick, D. Cock, P. Derrin, D. Elkaduwe, K. Engelhardt, R. Kolanski, M. Norrish, T. Sewell, H. Tuch, and S. Winwood. seL4: formal verification of an OS kernel. In *SOSP*, pages 207–220, 2009.

[25] P. C. Kocher, J. Jaffe, and B. Jun. Differential power analysis. In *Proceedings of the 19th Annual International Cryptology Conference on Advances in Cryptology*, pages 388–397, 1999.

[26] J. Kong, O. Aciiçmez, J.-P. Seifert, and H. Zhou. Deconstructing new cache designs for thwarting software cache-based side channel attacks. In *Proc. of the 2nd ACM workshop on Computer security architectures*, pages 25–34, 2008.

[27] K. Koscher, A. Czeskis, F. Roesner, S. Patel, T. Kohno, S. Checkoway, D. McCoy, B. Kantor, D. Anderson, H. Shacham, and S. Savage. Experimental security analysis of a modern automobile. *IEEE Symposium on Security and Privacy*, pages 447–462, 2010.

[28] M. Krohn, A. Yip, M. Brodsky, N. Cliffer, M. Frans, K. Eddie, and K. R. Morris. Information flow control for standard OS abstractions. In *SOSP*, 2007.

[29] L. C. Lam and T.-c. Chiueh. A general dynamic information flow tracking framework for security applications. In *Proceedings of the 22nd Annual Computer Security Applications Conference*, pages 463–472, 2006.

[30] P. Li, Y. Mao, and S. Zdancewic. Information integrity policies. In *Proceedings of the Workshop on Formal Aspects in Security and Trust*, 2003.

[31] X. Li, M. Tiwari, B. Hardekopf, T. Sherwood, and F. T. Chong. Secure information flow analysis for hardware design: Using the right abstraction for the job. *The Fifth ACM SIGPLAN Workshop on Programming Languages and Analysis for Security(PLAS)*, June 2010.

[32] O. Mutlu and T. Moscibroda. Stall-time fair memory access scheduling for chip multiprocessors. In *Micro*, pages 146–160, 2007.

[33] A. C. Myers, N. Nystrom, L. Zheng, and S. Zdancewic. Jif: Java information flow. Software release. http://www.cs.cornell.edu/jif, July 2001.

[34] J. Newsome and D. Song. Dynamic taint analysis for automatic detection, analysis, and signature generation of exploits on commodity software. In *NDSS*, 2005.

[35] C. Percival. Cache missing for fun and profit. In *Proc. of BSDCan*, 2005.

[36] F. Qin, C. Wang, Z. Li, H.-s. Kim, Y. Zhou, and Y. Wu. Lift: A low-overhead practical information flow tracking system for detecting security attacks. In *Micro*, pages 135–148, 2006.

[37] A. Russo, J. Hughes, D. Naumann, and A. Sabelfeld. Closing internal timing channels by transformation. pages 120–135, 2007.

[38] O. Ruwase, P. B. Gibbons, T. C. Mowry, V. Ramachandran, S. Chen, M. Kozuch, and M. Ryan. Parallelizing dynamic information flow tracking. In *SPAA*, pages 35–45, 2008.

[39] A. Sabelfeld and A. C. Myers. Language-based information-flow security. *IEEE Journal on Selected Areas in Communications*, 21(1), Jan. 2003.

[40] M. Schlickling and M. Pister. A framework for static analysis of VHDL code. *7th International Workshop on Worst-Case Execution Time (WCET) Analysis*, 2007.

[41] O. Sibert, P. A. Porras, and R. Lindell. An analysis of the intel 80x86 security architecture and implement ations. *IEEE Transactions on Software Engineering*, 22(5):283–293, 1996.

[42] G. Smith and D. Volpano. Secure information flow in a multi-threaded imperative language. pages 355–364, 1998.

[43] G. E. Suh, J. W. Lee, D. Zhang, and S. Devadas. Secure program execution via dynamic information flow tracking. In *ASPLOS*, pages 85–96, 2004.

[44] E. Technologies. *The Esterel v7 Reference Manual, version v7.30 - initial IEEE standardization proposal edition*. 2005.

[45] M. Tiwari, X. Li, H. Wassel, F. Chong, and T. Sherwood. Execution leases: A hardware-supported mechanism for enforcing strong non-interference. In *Micro*, 2009.

[46] M. Tiwari, H. Wassel, B. Mazloom, S. Mysore, F. Chong, and T. Sherwood. Complete information flow tracking from the gates up. In *ASPLOS*, March 2009.

[47] T. K. Tolstrup. *Language-based Security for VHDL*. PhD thesis, Technical University of Denmark, 2006.

[48] T. K. Tolstrup, F. Nielson, and H. R. Nielson. Information flow analysis for VHDL. volume 3606 of LNCS, 2005.

[49] N. Vachharajani, M. J. Bridges, J. Chang, R. Rangan, G. Ottoni, J. A. Blome, G. A. Reis, M. Vachharajani, and D. I. August. Rifle: An architectural framework for user-centric information-flow security. In *Micro*, pages 243–254, 2004.

[50] G. Venkataramani, I. Doudalis, Y. Solihin, and M. Prvulovic. Flexi-Taint: A programmable accelerator for dynamic taint propagation. In *HPCA*, pages 196–206, 2008.

[51] D. Volpano, C. Irvine, and G. Smith. A sound type system for secure flow analysis. *J. Comput. Secur.*, 4:167–187, January 1996.

[52] D. Volpano and G. Smith. Eliminating covert flows with minimum typings. page 156, 1997.

[53] D. Volpano and G. Smith. A type-based approach to program security. In *In Proceedings of the 7th International Joint Conference on the Theory and Practice of Software Devel-opment*, pages 607–621. Springer, 1997.

[54] Z. Wang and R. B. Lee. New cache designs for thwarting software cache-based side channel attacks. In *ISCA*, pages 494–505, New York, NY, USA, 2007. ACM.

[55] S. Zdancewic and A. C. Myers. Secure information flow via linear continuations. 15(2-3):209–234, 2002.

[56] S. Zdancewic and A. C. Myers. Observational determinism for concurrent program security. pages 29–43, 2003.

[57] N. Zeldovich, S. Boyd-Wickizer, and D.Mazieres. Security distributed systems with information flow control. In *NSDI*, pages 293–308, Apr. 2008.

[58] N. Zeldovich, S. Boyd-Wickizer, E. Kohler, and D. Mazières. Making information flow explicit in HiStar. In *OSDI*, 2006.

[59] N. Zeldovich, H. Kannan, M. Dalton, and C. Kozyrakis. Hardware enforcement of application security policies using tagged memory. In *OSDI*, Dec. 2008.

Steno: Automatic Optimization of Declarative Queries

Derek G. Murray
University of Cambridge Computer Laboratory
Derek.Murray@cl.cam.ac.uk

Michael Isard Yuan Yu
Microsoft Research Silicon Valley
{misard, yuanbyu}@microsoft.com

Abstract

Declarative queries enable programmers to write data manipulation code without being aware of the underlying data structure implementation. By increasing the level of abstraction over imperative code, they improve program readability and, crucially, create opportunities for automatic parallelization and optimization. For example, the Language Integrated Query (LINQ) extensions to C# allow the same declarative query to process in-memory collections, and datasets that are distributed across a compute cluster. However, our experiments show that the *serial* performance of declarative code is several times slower than the equivalent hand-optimized code, because it is implemented using run-time abstractions—such as iterators—that incur overhead due to virtual function calls and superfluous instructions.

To address this problem, we have developed Steno, which uses a combination of novel and well-known techniques to generate code for declarative queries that is almost as efficient as hand-optimized code. Steno translates a declarative LINQ query into type-specialized, inlined and loop-based imperative code. It eliminates chains of iterators from query execution, and optimizes nested queries. We have implemented Steno for uniprocessor, multiprocessor and distributed computing platforms, and show that, for a real-world distributed job, it can almost double the speed of end-to-end execution.

Categories and Subject Descriptors D.3.4 [*Programming Languages*]: Processors—Code generation, Optimization

General Terms Design, Performance

Keywords query optimization, abstract machines

1. Introduction

The declarative style of programming has long been proposed as a superior alternative to imperative programming. Recently, declarative programming has found an important application in data-center programming: systems such as MapReduce [10], DryadLINQ [32] and FlumeJava [7] allow users to compose a declarative specification of an application's logic, and execute it across hundreds or thousands of machines. However, these systems are implemented in common imperative languages (C++, C# and Java), and simulating the declarative style results in code that is less efficient than the equivalent imperative code. In this paper, we focus on one of these systems—DryadLINQ—and describe a technique for code generation that significantly improves the end-to-end execution time of distributed jobs.

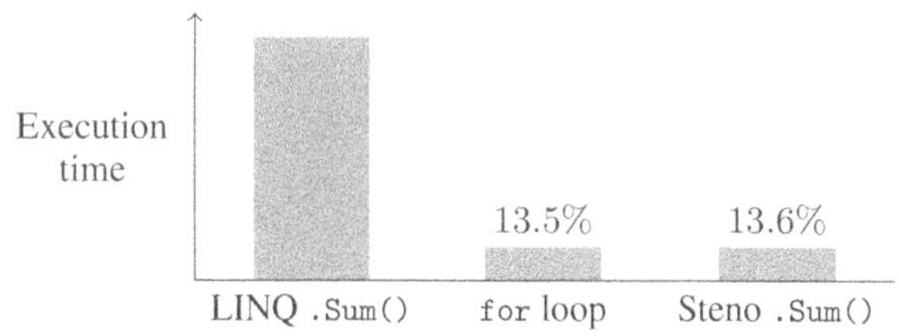

Figure 1. Relative execution time for computing the sum of squares of 10^7 `doubles` using LINQ, an imperative loop, and a Steno-optimized query. Steno achieves a 7.4× speedup over LINQ.

DryadLINQ is a system that takes a query written in .NET Language Integrated Query (LINQ) syntax, and generates a distributed query plan for executing the query across compute nodes in a data center [32]. The main advantage of DryadLINQ is that queries can include user-defined types and functions, which allows the developer to use the full .NET type system and class library. DryadLINQ divides the query into *vertices* in a Dryad [19] task dependency graph: each vertex executes a portion of the query on a partition of the overall data. The generated code itself uses LINQ queries to achieve multiprocessor parallelism within a single machine. However, our experiments have shown that LINQ queries are far slower than the equivalent imperative code (Figure 1), for four reasons:

1. LINQ queries are lazily evaluated, and use *iterators* to communicate elements between stages of the query [2]. An iterator imposes the overhead of two virtual function calls per element per query operator.
2. LINQ queries may be nested, which involves each element flowing through multiple iterators. The iterator overhead is therefore multiplied by the number of nesting levels.
3. The lazy iterator implementation includes state machine logic to simulate coroutine behavior [22], which adds further per-element overhead.
4. An operator's behavior—such as a predicate or transformation function—is specified as a function object, which incurs a further virtual call per element per operator.

To address these overheads, we have implemented Steno: an optimizer for LINQ queries that generates the equivalent loop-based imperative code. Steno performs two optimizations: *iterator fusion* (Section 4), and *nested loop generation* (Section 5). Similar optimizers have been developed for functional languages [9, 31] and relational database query languages [15, 23]. However, Steno makes several contributions beyond existing work:

PLDI'11, June 4–8, San Jose, California, USA.

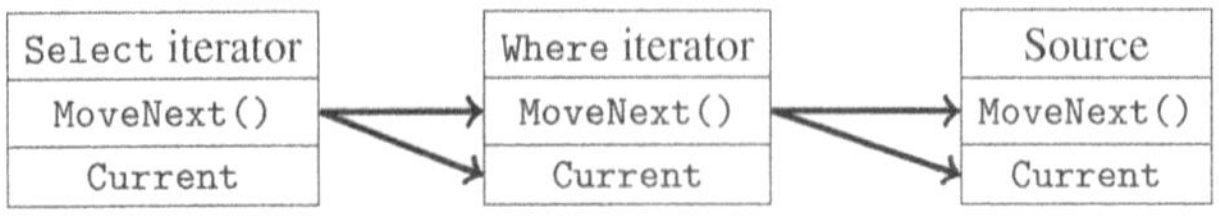

Figure 2. Call graph in a chain of query operators. Virtual function calls are represented by bold arrows.

- Steno integrates with an existing object-oriented language (C#), and does not require changes to the compiler or standard libraries (Section 3).
- Steno uses a novel automaton-based code generator to transform a sequence of query operators into loop-based code (Sections 4 and 5).
- Steno may be combined with DryadLINQ to generate code that runs in parallel across a data center, and across multiple processors on each machine (Section 6).
- We evaluate the performance of Steno-optimized queries running on a single machine and on a distributed compute cluster (Section 7).

Steno generates loop-based code, which is simple for a compiler to optimize and would be simple for a moderately-experienced programmer to write. The principal advantage of writing queries in a declarative style is that it is also possible to apply higher-level optimizations. In particular, DryadLINQ [32, 33], FlumeJava [7] and Pig [26] optimize many operations, including aggregation, joins and sorting, by applying high-level transformations on the query operator graph. The guiding principle in this work is that code should be written at the highest possible level, so that it can benefit from multiple levels of optimization. Steno provides further incentive to write at a high level, because the resulting code is almost as efficient as low-level imperative code. Our evaluation shows that, even in a distributed setting, our optimizations can significantly improve end-to-end execution times (Section 7).

Though this paper focuses on query optimization for LINQ and DryadLINQ, the techniques can be applied to any system that uses iterators to process streaming data or simulate lazy evaluation. However, to motivate our specific implementation, we begin with a brief description of how LINQ is currently implemented.

2. From queries to iterators

In this paper, we focus on the LINQ extensions that were added to .NET 3.5. LINQ extends C# with SQL-like *query comprehension* syntax, first-class *lambda expressions*, and a set of generic *query operators* that can be applied to any object implementing the enumerable interface (`IEnumerable<T>`) [2].

The following is an example of a simple LINQ query:

```
IEnumerable<int> xs = ...;

var evenSquares = from x in xs
                  where x % 2 == 0
                  select x * x;
```

The compiler desugars that query into the following C# expression:

```
IEnumerable<int> evenSquares = xs.Where(x => x % 2 == 0)
                                 .Select(x => x * x);
```

The `where` and `select` clauses in the query comprehension are transformed into calls to the `Where()` and `Select()` methods, which—in this case—operate on and return an `IEnumerable<int>`. LINQ defines many other query operators, as we will describe in Sections 4 and 5.

Enumerable objects expose a single method, `GetEnumerator()`, which returns an object of type `IEnumerator<T>`, with the following (simplified) interface:

```
interface IEnumerator<T> {

    // Return the element at the current position.
    T Current { get; }

    // Advance to next element, returning false if no
    // more elements remain.
    bool MoveNext();

    // [Reset() and Dispose() methods not shown.]
}
```

In this interface, `Current` is a read-only *property*, which is syntactic sugar that allows accessor methods to be written in the same form as instance field accesses.

An enumerable object can be traversed using the `foreach(var x in xs)` statement. Again, this statement is syntactic sugar for operations on an `IEnumerable<T>` object (`xs`), and it translates to:

```
IEnumerator<T> enum = xs.GetEnumerator();
while (enum.MoveNext()) {
  T x = enum.Current;
  // foreach loop body...
}
enum.Dispose();
```

Note that since `MoveNext()` and `Current` are defined in an interface, they are virtual functions, so each iteration of the `while` loop involves at least two virtual calls.

LINQ uses iterators to implement lazy query evaluation. An iterator (`IEnumerator<T>`) object is typically implemented as a state machine that advances through the collection upon calls to `MoveNext()`, which update the `Current` property. Composable LINQ operators (such as `Select()`, `Where()` and `GroupBy()`) are implemented as iterators that consume elements from an upstream iterator, and *yield* (possibly-transformed) elements to downstream operators (Figure 2). Aggregate operators—which return a scalar (such as `Sum()`, `Min()` and `Average()`)—are eagerly evaluated and contain a `foreach` loop that consumes the upstream iterator.

Due to the use of iterators, each LINQ operator makes at least two virtual calls for each element that it processes[1]. A further virtual call per element is incurred when evaluating the predicate or transformation function. As Krikellas *et al.* explain, virtual calls impose a severe overhead on query execution because they are difficult to inline automatically [23]. As a result, each call causes an indirect branch, which inhibits instruction pipelining. Furthermore, iterators contain state machine logic in the `MoveNext()` function, which adds more instructions to the per-element overhead.

Writing the equivalent "hand-optimized" C# code for this query would be straightforward for most programmers:

```
foreach (int x in xs) {
    if (x % 2 == 0) {
        yield return x * x;
    }
}
```

The iterators for the `Where` and `Select` operators are *fused*, by storing the current element in the loop variable, `x`, and the predicate and transformation expressions are inlined. Steno automatically performs these optimizations on chains of query operators.

[1] An alternative approach, as used in Java, combines the `MoveNext()` and `Current` operations into a single virtual call. However, this precludes the use of non-reference types or null elements in collections, because the combined method returns `null` to indicate that there are no more elements.

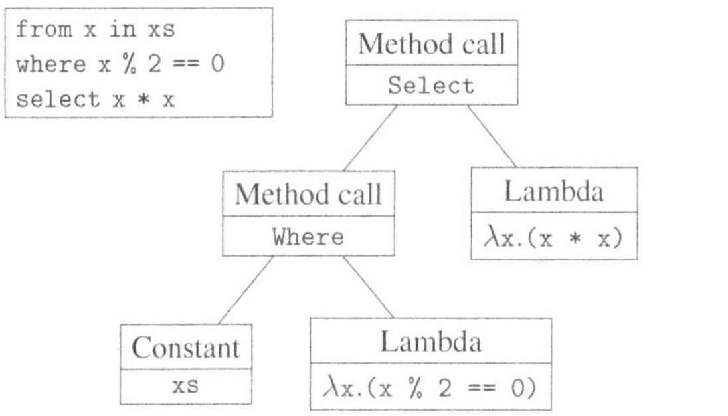

Figure 3. Translation from LINQ query syntax into AST form.

3. Outline of approach

At a high level, Steno converts queries into efficient, loop-based imperative code. Our main contribution is a novel technique for generating the imperative code. In this section, however, we first put this technique in context, by describing the main steps that comprise Steno optimization:

1. The query is transformed into an intermediate representation (QUIL) (§3.1).
2. The query AST is transformed into an equivalent C# AST (§3.2; see also §4 and §5).
3. The C# AST is compiled, loaded and invoked (§3.3).

Note that our implementation of Steno is a .NET library: it does not modify the compiler or the .NET core library. To apply Steno to a query, the `WithSteno()` extension method is applied to the source collection, as follows:

```
var evenSquares = from x in xs.WithSteno()
                  where x % 2 == 0
                  select x * x;
```

Since the C# compiler already performs source-to-source transformations on LINQ queries [2], Steno's optimizations could also be applied at compile-time. We speculate about how this approach could be taken further in Section 9.

3.1 Query extraction

The optimization process begins with a query expression, which can be written in query comprehension syntax or as a sequence of LINQ method invocations. To gain a usable representation of the query, we use the LINQ *query provider* facility, which reconstructs the query AST at run-time. A similar technique is used in DryadLINQ, which uses the information to build a distributed query graph [32]; and in LINQ-to-SQL, which turns a LINQ query into the equivalent SQL database query [25].

The query AST represents each LINQ operator as a method-call expression, and the operator arguments as lambda expressions (Figure 3). To simplify the code generation process, Steno translates this AST into a chain of operators, by post-order traversing the tree, and yielding a canonical[2] *operator* for each method-call expression. Steno also traverses the AST of the lambda expressions to identify nested queries, as we discuss further in Section 5.

3.2 Optimized code generation

The code generation process takes a (possibly nested) chain of operators and transforms it into optimized imperative code. To achieve this, Steno uses an automaton-based approach. Steno traverses the chain of operators (and any nested chains), and emits one or more symbols of *Query Intermediate Language* (QUIL) per operator. The code generator automaton recognizes any valid string of QUIL, and generates the appropriate C# code for each symbol. We introduce QUIL in Subsection 4.1.

The code generator automaton performs two principal optimizations. First, it eliminates the iterators from chains of operators (§4). It also identifies nested queries, and transforms these into nested loops (§5). As it parses a sequence of QUIL symbols, the code generator builds a new C# class with a single method that implements the optimized query. It builds the class using the .NET CodeDOM library, which provides an object model for the C# (and other .NET languages') AST. The automaton builds up the AST from loops, conditional statements, declarations and assignments, according to the QUIL symbols that it receives.

3.3 Final steps

Once the query class has been generated, it must be compiled and loaded in order to execute the query. This step invokes the C# compiler to build a dynamic link library (DLL) from the CodeDOM AST. Steno dynamically loads the resulting DLL, and instantiates a compiled query object using the reflection API.

Before the query is invoked, Steno must resolve any object references that were captured in the query. As a pre-processing step, Steno replaces all captured object references in the query with placeholder instance variables. Once the generated code has been loaded, Steno uses the reflection API to set the relevant fields of the compiled query object appropriately. Since using the dynamic loading and reflection APIs incurs a relatively high constant cost (§7.1), the query object may be cached between invocations. However, by integrating Steno with DryadLINQ, this cost can be eliminated by performing Steno code generation in the initial DryadLINQ code generation process (§6), and generating static code that sets the captured variables.

4. Iterator fusion

Iterator fusion replaces a chain of iterators with a sequence of imperative statements in a loop body. To achieve this, Steno generates type-specialized iteration code for the source collection, and inline element-processing code for each operator in the query.

Table 1 classifies the LINQ operators according to their type, and maps each to a symbol in our intermediate language, QUIL. In Subsection 4.1, we describe QUIL, and specify a finite state machine that can parse QUIL sentences. Then, in Subsection 4.2, we show how Steno uses the state machine to generate optimized code without iterators. Finally, in Subsection 4.3, we show how Steno can use additional information from the operator graph to generate more-efficient specialized code.

4.1 Query Intermediate Language

The Query Intermediate Language (QUIL) serves three main purposes:

- It simplifies query optimization by reducing the large number of LINQ operators to six fundamental QUIL operators.
- It simplifies the code generator by allowing it to be structured as an automaton that recognizes the language.
- It enables extensibility, by specifying the interface that each operator must provide.

As Table 1 shows, we have defined six symbols, which comprise the QUIL alphabet and correspond to LINQ operators. In this subsection, we define the behavior of each operator, and show how operators may be combined to represent a LINQ query.

[2] For example, there are three overloaded versions of the `Aggregate` method, and eight overloaded versions of the `GroupBy` method.

Operator class	QUIL symbol	LINQ operators	Haskell equivalent	Input type	Output type
Source	Src	Range, Repeat	List constructor	—	IEnumerable<T>
Transform	Trans	Select	map	IEnumerable<T>	IEnumerable<U>
Predicate	Pred	Where, Take, Skip, etc.	filter	IEnumerable<T>	IEnumerable<T>
Sink	Sink	GroupBy, OrderBy, etc.	foldl	IEnumerable<T>	IEnumerable<U>
Aggregate	Agg	Aggregate, Min, Sum, etc.	foldl	IEnumerable<T>	U
Nested	—	SelectMany, Join	concatMap	IEnumerable<T>	IEnumerable<U>
Return	Ret	—	—	IEnumerable<T> or T	—

Table 1. The LINQ operator classes map on to QUIL symbols (§4.1). T and U are generic type variables. Nested operators map to multiple QUIL symbols, as explained in Section 5.

A QUIL expression begins with a Src symbol, and ends with a Ret symbol. The Src symbol represents an enumerable source collection, and may be annotated with the collection's run-time type, which enables Steno to produce efficient iteration code for the collection. LINQ collection generators, such as Range(start, count) are also represented by Src. The Ret symbol denotes the end of a query, and may appear after any other QUIL symbol. Therefore, a query may return either a collection or a scalar value.

The other QUIL operators are analogous to LINQ operators:

- The Trans operator applies an element-wise transformation to each element in the input collection, yielding a new collection. Trans is parameterized with a function, $f : \mathtt{T} \rightarrow \mathtt{U}$, that transforms a single input element into an output element.
- The Pred operator applies a predicate to each element in the input collection, and yields an output collection containing only elements that match the predicate. Pred is parameterized with a function, $f : \mathtt{T} \rightarrow \mathbb{B}$, that performs the predicate test on a single input element.
- The Sink operator transforms the input collection into an intermediate collection that may be enumerated subsequently. Typically, Sink builds up the intermediate collection in memory. Sink is parameterized with two functions. The first function, $f : () \rightarrow$ IEnumerable<U>, constructs an empty intermediate collection; and the second function, g : IEnumerable<U> $\times$ T $\rightarrow$ IEnumerable<U>, updates a collection with a new input element. Sink may also provide type-specialized iteration code for the intermediate collection.
- The Agg operator reduces elements into a single, scalar value. Agg is parameterized with two functions. The first function, $f : () \rightarrow \mathtt{U}$, returns the identity scalar value; and the second function, $g : \mathtt{U} \times \mathtt{T} \rightarrow \mathtt{U}$, creates a new scalar value of type U from the current scalar value and a single input element.

For each operator, the function parameters may be specified as an appropriately-typed lambda expression, delegate function or functor object. Note that we can assume that the C# compiler has already type-checked the query expression, so Steno does not perform additional type-checking.

We now define QUIL by considering what constitutes a valid query. Every query begins with Src and ends with Ret. The Trans, Pred and Sink symbols transform one enumerable collection into another collection. Therefore, it is possible to chain together an unbounded number of these operators in an arbitrary order. As we will discuss in Section 5, a nested query may substitute for a Trans or Pred symbol. Finally, since Agg returns a scalar value, its result can only be consumed by Ret, and Agg may only appear as the penultimate symbol. These rules may be stated concisely using the following grammar:

$$\langle query \rangle \;::=\; \mathsf{Src}\ (\ \mathsf{Trans} \mid \mathsf{Pred} \mid \mathsf{Sink} \mid \langle query \rangle)^{*}\ \mathsf{Agg}^{?}\ \mathsf{Ret}$$

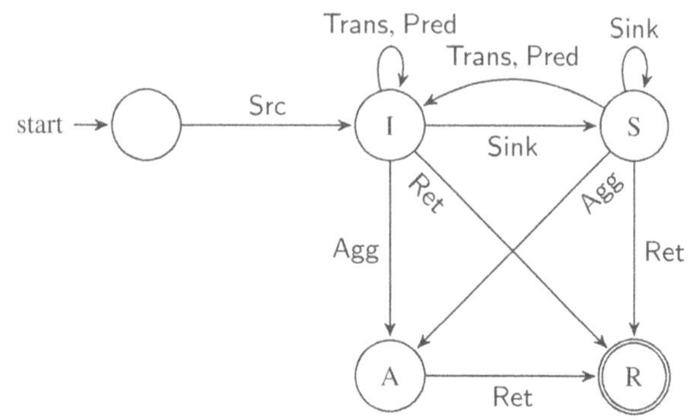

Figure 4. State machine used to perform iterator fusion in Steno.

To simplify the explanation, we will defer the discussion of nested queries to Section 5.

If we ignore the possibility of nested queries, QUIL is a regular language and can therefore be recognized by a finite state machine (FSM). Steno uses the FSM shown in Figure 4 to perform iterator fusion on QUIL expressions.

The QUIL FSM has five states. The initial Src symbol, and the element-wise Trans and Pred symbols cause a transition to the ITERATING state. The Agg symbol causes a transition to the AGGREGATING state, and the Sink symbol causes a transition to the SINKING state. Note that the SINKING and ITERATING states are separate, because the code generated on a transition from those states will differ (§4.2). Finally, the Ret symbol causes a transition to the terminal RETURNING state. In the following subsection, we show how these transitions can generate optimized code without iterators.

4.2 Code generation

Code generation is driven by transitions of the FSM shown in Figure 4. In this subsection, we describe the overall structure of the generated code, and explain the code that is emitted by each transition.

All QUIL queries begin with a Src operator, which corresponds to an enumerable collection, and therefore intuitively causes a new loop to be generated. Figure 5 shows the structure of the generated loop code: it contains a linked list of C# statements, with three internal pointers to positions where statements may be inserted. Insertion point α is the *loop prelude* (i.e. the list of statements immediately preceding the loop); μ is the *loop body*; and ω is the *loop postlude*. The loop prelude contains aggregation and sink variable declarations, the loop body contains element-wise operations, and the loop postlude may contain return statements.

The generated loop code depends on the run-time type of the source collection. For example, if the source is an array or array-backed collection, it is more efficient to use indexed element access than an iterator to access an element. The generated code is a loop

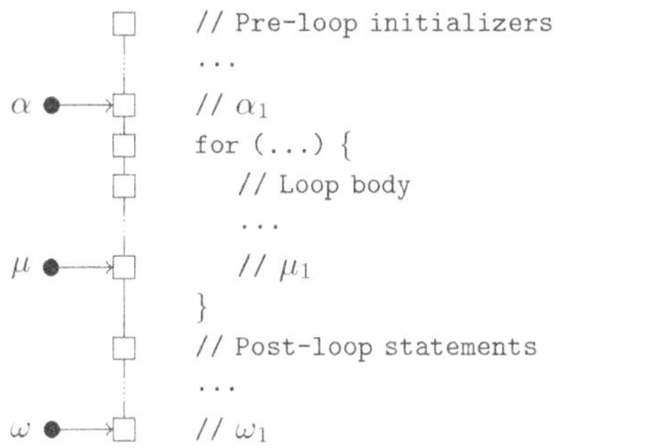

Figure 5. The generated code is maintained as a linked list of statements. Steno maintains three insertion points: the loop prelude (α), the loop body (μ), and the loop postlude (ω).

```
Select(x => f(x))
↪μ var elem_{i+1} = f(elem_i);
```
(a) Trans(f)

```
Where(x => f(x))
↪μ if (!f(elem_i)) continue;
```
(b) Pred(f)

Figure 6. Generated code fragments for element-wise operators. **N.B.** The $\hookrightarrow_\mu$ symbol denotes that code is inserted at the μ pointer.

through the indices of the array, which also enables the compiler to hoist the array bounds check. Steno also provides Src implementations for the `Range` and `Repeat` operators, which generate new collections based on their parameters.

The code generator uses local variables to store intermediate values, such as the result of a transformation. There are three kinds of variable in the generated code:

$\texttt{elem}_i$	A (possibly-transformed) element in a collection
$\texttt{agg}_j$	The current scalar value of the jth Agg operator
$\texttt{sink}_k$	The current sink collection of the kth Sink operator

The code generator maintains the current names for each kind of variable as an integer index, which some transitions may increment. In the remainder of the paper, $\texttt{varname}_i$ is the current variable name, and $\texttt{varname}_{i+1}$ is the next variable name.

When the FSM is in the ITERATING state, the Trans and Pred element-wise operators insert code in the current loop body at the μ pointer. Figure 6 shows the code that is inserted in each case. Both operators operate on the current element ($\texttt{elem}_i$), and Trans creates a new element variable ($\texttt{elem}_{i+1}$). In addition, Steno inlines the transformation or predicate function, which eliminates the overhead of a virtual call on a function object per element.

The Agg and Sink operators reduce the current element into a scalar aggregate value or a sink collection, respectively. Therefore the code generator must insert code both for declaring and updating the reduction variable. Figure 7 shows the code that is inserted for the `Aggregate` and `GroupBy` operators. In both cases, the declaration is inserted at the α pointer before the loop, and the update statement is inserted at the μ pointer.

Following a Sink operator, the FSM is in the SINKING state, which behaves like the ITERATING state with one main exception: the following operator is applied to the sink collection. For example, a common pattern is to follow a `GroupBy` Sink operator with a `Where` Pred operator to filter the groups (cf. the `GROUP BY ...HAVING` pattern in SQL). To handle this, the code generator must insert a new loop that iterates through the sink collection. The loop

```
Aggregate(seed, (agg, elem) => g(agg, elem))
↪α var agg_{j+1} = seed;
↪μ agg_{j+1} = g(agg_{j+1}, elem_i);
```
(a) Agg(f)

```
GroupBy(x => Key(x))
↪α Lookup<K, T> sink_{k+1} = new Lookup<K, T>();
↪μ sink_{k+1} = sink_{k+1}.Put(Key(elem_i), elem_i);
```
(b) Sink

Figure 7. Generated code fragments for aggregating and sinking operators. In (b), `Lookup<K, T>` is a utility class that maintains a key-value multi-map, implements the `IEnumerable<IGrouping<K, T>>` interface, and provides a `Put` method that returns the updated collection.

```
↪ω return agg_j;
```
(a) AGGREGATING

```
↪ω return sink_k;
```
(b) SINKING

```
↪μ yield return elem_i;
```
(c) ITERATING

Figure 8. Generated code fragments for the Ret operator, which depend on the current state.

is inserted at the current ω insertion point, and the insertion pointers are reset relative to the new loop.

Finally, the Ret symbol causes a transition to the terminal RETURNING state, which generates code that returns one or more values to the caller (Figure 8). If the FSM is in the SINKING or AGGREGATING states, this inserts a `return` statement (with the $\texttt{sink}_k$ or $\texttt{agg}_j$ variable respectively) at the ω insertion point. If it is in the ITERATING state, the transition inserts a `yield return` statement at the μ pointer: this turns the optimized query into an iterator, which enables the query to be lazily evaluated[3].

4.3 Operator specialization

By analysing the intermediate query representation, Steno can make high-level optimizations that are not possible when dealing with abstract iterators. In this subsection, we consider one concrete example: the `GroupBy-Aggregate` optimization.

The `GroupBy` operator (Figure 7(b)) is a Sink operator that builds a mapping from keys to bags of values, and is analogous to the `GROUP BY` clause in a SQL statement. LINQ provides several implementations of `GroupBy`, including some that allow the caller to specify a *result selector*, which applies a function to each key and the collection of values associated with that key.

The result selector is often used to aggregate—or *reduce*—the set of values associated with a key into a single scalar. Indeed, the `reduce()` function in MapReduce [10] has the same signature as the `GroupBy` result selector, and performs the equivalent operation [33]. If the result selector is an Agg operator (such as `Aggregate`, `Sum` or `Min`), we can save memory by storing per-key partial aggregates instead of the group of values.

To implement this optimization, Steno identifies `GroupBy` operators with an aggregating result selector when building the operator chain (§3.1), and inserts a specialized `GroupByAggregate` Sink operator in place of a conventional `GroupBy`. The `GroupByAggregate` operator performs the aggregation as each element is processed, and updates an intermediate hashtable-based sink object.

[3] It is often more efficient to store the elements in an array and return this to the caller, but it is unsafe to do this for some queries where the collection may be very large (or unbounded). Therefore, the caller can use the explicit `ToArray` Sink operator to enable this optimization.

The memory requirements can be decreased further (to $O(1)$ keys and reduction variables) if it is known that the collection is ordered by the same key as the grouping. DryadLINQ implements this optimization in order to aggregate key sets that are too large to fit in memory [33].

5. Nested loop generation

We now consider the case where a QUIL expression may contain a nested query. As defined in Subsection 4.1, a nested query may substitute for the transformation and predicate functions of Trans and Pred operators, respectively. In this section, we explain how Steno generates efficient nested loops for nested queries.

At first, it might seem that nested queries can be trivially supported by running a second instance of the optimizer on the nested query, and inserting a call to the optimized subquery in the parent. In fact, this is an appropriate solution if the nested query has a scalar result (i.e. if it contains an Agg operator). However, if the nested query returns an enumerable collection, this solution is inefficient, because the outer query obtains an opaque collection, and can only access the result elements through the iterator interface, which incurs two virtual calls per element (§2). The `SelectMany` operator illustrates this point:

```
int[] xs = ..., ys = ..., zs = ...;

int result = xs.SelectMany(x =>
                 ys.SelectMany(y =>
                     zs.Select(z => F(x, y, z)))
             .Sum();
```

This query computes the Cartesian product of three arrays—`xs`, `ys` and `zs`—applies `F` to each resulting element, and sums the results. The equivalent loop-based code is simple to write:

```
int total = 0;

for (int i = 0; i < xs.Length; ++i) {
    for (int j = 0; j < ys.Length; ++j) {
        for (int k = 0; k < zs.Length; ++k) {
            total += F(xs[i], ys[j], zs[k]);
        }
    }
}
```

However, a naïve implementation using nested FSM-based optimizers would not generate this code, because the `Sum` operator is part of the outermost query, yet it must inject code into the loop body of the innermost query. Without this ability, the `Sum` and nested `SelectMany` operators must consume from iterators, which limits the potential performance improvement.

The `SelectMany` operator *flattens* a collection of collections (one per original element) into a single collection. It is a fundamental operator in MapReduce, in which the `map()` function transforms a single element into zero or more key-value pairs [10]. DryadLINQ implements this functionality using `SelectMany` [32], and similar operators exist in FlumeJava [7] and Pig Latin [26], both of which execute on a MapReduce cluster. Furthermore, since it can implement the Cartesian product, `SelectMany` can also be used to implement joins across multiple collections:

```
int[] xs = ..., ys = ...;

var zs = xs.SelectMany(x => ys.Where(y => x == y)....);
```

The above example shows an equi-join on two arrays of integers. However, in practice, this is an inefficient way to implement joins on two large data sets, and partitioning or sorting is used to reduce the necessary amount of processing, I/O and/or memory [13, 32].

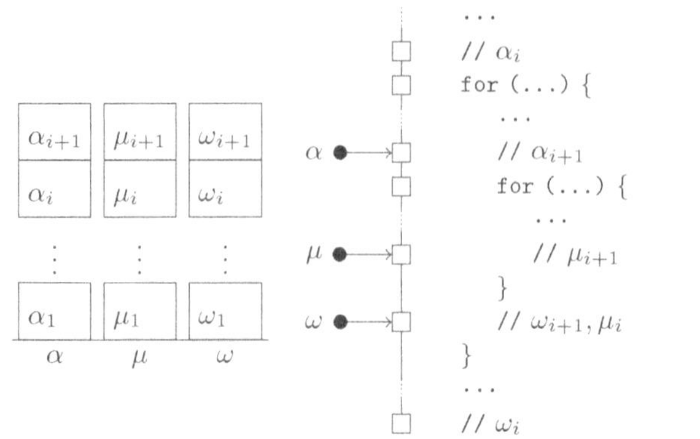

Figure 9. In the nested case, insertion pointers are arranged in a stack, with the innermost nesting level at the top. The current (α, μ, ω) pointers are read from the top of the stack.

Having motivated the need for nested query support, we now discuss how Steno uses QUIL to support nested queries (§5.1), and their effect on code generation (§5.2).

5.1 Adding a stack

Since a QUIL query can recursively contain another query, the language is context-free. Therefore, the FSM in Figure 4 is not powerful enough to recognize all valid QUIL queries. To recognize the full context-free language, we must add a *stack* to the code generator, making it a (deterministic) pushdown automaton. In order to reuse the iterator fusion optimization, the pushdown automaton is exactly equivalent to the FSM in the non-nested case. Therefore, in this subsection, we reintroduce the nested query transitions and how these manipulate the stack.

Recall that the code generator has α, μ and ω insertion pointers, which correspond to the current loop's prelude, body and postlude, respectively (Figure 5). Since all queries—nested or otherwise—involve iterating through a collection, a nested query will create a new loop, with a different prelude, body and postlude. After exiting a nested query, it may be necessary to recover the outer query's insertion points, so that code for subsequent operators may be inserted. Therefore, we define the stack, S, as containing $(\alpha_i, \mu_j, \omega_k)$ triples, where $i, j, k \geq 1$ are the nesting levels of each insertion point. The code generator uses the topmost triple as the current values for α, μ and ω.

S is initially empty. When a Src operator is encountered at nesting level $i = length(S)$, a new loop is inserted at position μ_i, and insertion points $(\alpha_{i+1}, \mu_{i+1}, \omega_{i+1})$ are pushed onto the stack. Figure 9 shows the state of the stack and the generated AST after entering nesting level $i + 1$.

5.2 Code generation

Following a nested Src operator, the automaton is in the ITERATING state. Subsequent Trans, Pred, Sink and Agg operators behave as in the non-nested case, though code is inserted at the nested insertion points. In addition, the nested query may refer to the current element in the outer query, as in this example:

```
xs.SelectMany(x => ys.Select(G(x, y)));
```

Therefore, before generating any code for the nested query, all occurrences of `x` in the nested query are rewritten with the current $\texttt{elem}_i$ variable name in the outer query.

The behavior on encountering a nested Ret operator depends on the current state of the automaton. The SINKING and AGGREGATING cases are simpler. If the code generator is in either of these

$\hookrightarrow_\omega$ `var elem`$_{i+1}$ `= agg`$_j$`;` (a) AGGREGATING

$\hookrightarrow_\omega$ `var elem`$_{i+1}$ `= sink`$_k$`;` (b) SINKING

Figure 10. Generated code fragments for the nested Ret operator, in the AGGREGATING and SINKING states.

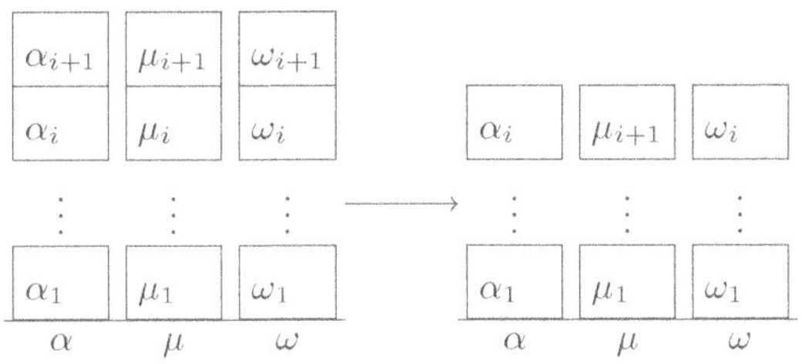

Figure 11. Code generator stack contents before and after encountering a nested Ret operator in the ITERATING state. After the transition, the α and ω pointers point to positions in the outer query, and the μ pointer is unchanged.

states, it assigns the current aggregation or sink variable to a new element variable in the nested loop postlude (Figure 10), then pops the current insertion pointer triplet from the stack.

If the code generator encounters a nested Ret operator while in the ITERATING state, the stack management is slightly more complicated. Recall that, in the non-nested case (§4.2), encountering Ret while ITERATING causes a `yield return` statement to be emitted. In this case, we want the code for subsequent operators to be inserted in the current nested loop body. Therefore we pop two insertion pointer triples from the stack, and push back the triple $(\alpha_{\text{outer}}, \mu_{\text{nested}}, \omega_{\text{outer}})$ (Figure 11). This ensures that the element-wise code for each operator (transformation, predicate testing and reduction variable updating) will be inserted in the nested loop, while any declarations or return statements will be placed in the outer scope.

This formulation means that *nested* `Select` and `SelectMany` have the same representation in QUIL. In a `Select` operator, the nested query will typically end with an Agg operator and return a scalar value; by definition, a `SelectMany` operator will yield many values. However, instead of creating an iterator using a `yield return` statement, the Ret in a nested query moves the insertion pointers so that subsequent operators consume the results of the nested query directly.

6. Optimizing parallel queries

A principal advantage of expressing a computation as a LINQ query is that it may be executed in parallel across multiple processors [29] or multiple machines in a data center [32]. However, the optimizations described above generate sequential code. In this section, we explain how Steno can be combined with DryadLINQ in order to improve the performance of distributed queries.

To execute a query on a large data set, a common strategy is to divide the data set into *partitions*, and execute the query in parallel on each partition [12]. If the query operators are *homomorphic* (i.e. apply to each element independently), the query may be applied to each partition in parallel, to yield a new set of partitions. Trans, Pred and nested queries are homomorphic. However, if a query operator performs an aggregation (Agg) or builds a sink collection (Sink), this requires coordination between the partitions.

To optimize a query that can execute in parallel, Steno traverses the QUIL representation of the query and identifies the homomorphic operators. Contiguous subsequences of homomorphic operators are combined into subqueries, and the subqueries are optimized

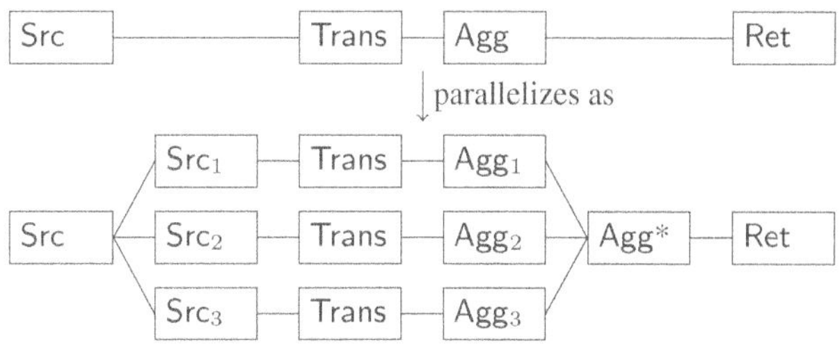

Figure 12. Parallel optimization of a `Select-Aggregate` query. Steno applies optimization to the Src$_i$-Trans-Agg$_i$ subquery, which executes in parallel on the partitions of the data.

separately. Note that, if an *associative* Sink or Agg operator follows a subquery, a *partial* Sink$_i$ or Agg$_i$ operator can be appended to the ith subquery, which reduces the amount of coordination between partitions. For example, if the Agg operator represents `Sum`, the corresponding Agg$_i$ operator computes a partial sum for each partition. Figure 12 shows how a simple query is parallelized. In that example, a special Agg* operator collects the partially-aggregated results from each partition.

We have integrated Steno with DryadLINQ, which executes queries in parallel across a compute cluster. DryadLINQ also identifies homomorphic query operators, and transforms a LINQ query into a directed acyclic graph of query operators, which Dryad executes as a collection of parallel tasks [19]. In addition, DryadLINQ performs various static and dynamic optimizations on the query before generating the code for each task: for example, it transforms a `OrderBy` Sink operator into a distributed sort, which samples the data to estimate an appropriate partitioning, range-partitions the data based on that estimate, and sorts each resulting partition in parallel [32]. DryadLINQ also optimizes distributed aggregation where the aggregation function is commutative and associative [33]. After optimization, an individual task may contain a sequence of query operators: our modified version of DryadLINQ applies Steno-optimization to the subsequences of homomorphic operators in each task.

DryadLINQ can also execute subqueries in parallel within a single task. Previously, it used Parallel LINQ (PLINQ) to execute homomorphic subqueries using a thread-pool [29]. PLINQ provides the same operators as LINQ, but operates on a `ParallelEnumerable` collection, which uses a `Partitioner` object to assign elements to each thread. PLINQ uses iterators to compose query operators, and therefore suffers from similar virtual call overheads to sequential LINQ. To ameliorate this, we created a new PLINQ operator, called `HomomorphicApply`, which maps a function across partitions in parallel (as opposed to each element), and returns a new set of partitions. Our modified version of DryadLINQ invokes this operator with the compiled query method, which allows the optimized code to execute in parallel.

7. Evaluation

We now evaluate the performance improvement that Steno can achieve. We first evaluate a collection of single-machine microbenchmarks, which operate on in-memory data (§7.1). We then evaluate the impact of applying Steno to a real-world application that uses DryadLINQ on a distributed compute cluster (§7.2).

All experiments described in this paper were performed on our research cluster, from which we use up to 100 nodes. Each computer has two dual-core AMD Opteron 2218 HE processors running at 2.6 GHz, 16 GB of DDR2 RAM, and four 750 GB SATA hard drives in a RAID 0 (striped) configuration. The computers are connected using gigabit Ethernet, in a three-level tree topology.

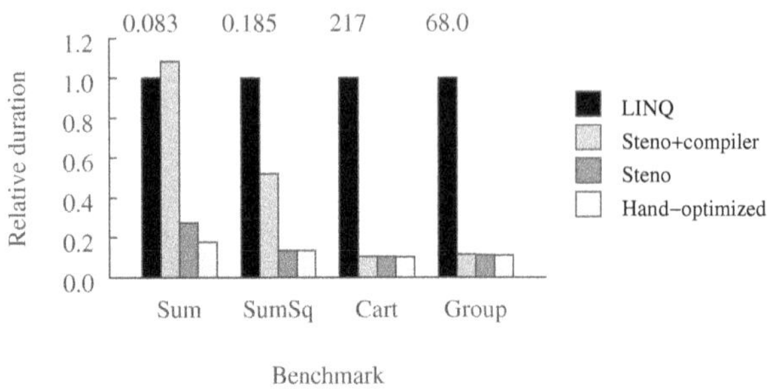

Figure 13. Relative performance of LINQ, Steno-optimized and hand-optimized queries for sequential microbenchmarks. Lower values are better. Each query is annotated with the absolute LINQ execution time, in seconds.

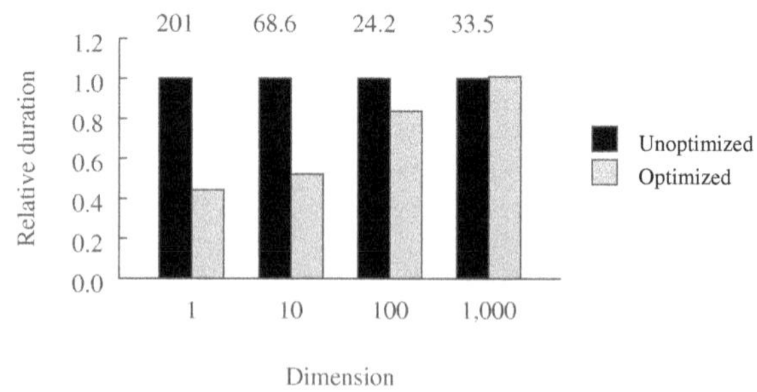

Figure 14. Relative performance of unoptimized and Steno-optimized k-means algorithm, running on DryadLINQ. Each query is annotated with the absolute unoptimized execution time for one iteration, in seconds.

All computers run the 64-bit version of Microsoft Windows Server 2003, and the 64-bit version of Microsoft .NET Framework 3.5[4].

7.1 Sequential microbenchmarks

We evaluated the performance of sequential Steno optimization using the following four queries on in-memory arrays:

Sum Calculate the sum of 10 million `double` values.

SumSq Calculate the sum of squares of 10 million `double` values.

Cart Calculate the Cartesian product of 10 million and 1000 `double` values, multiply together each pair, and sum.

Group Randomly generate 10 million `double` values according to a one-dimensional mixture-of-Gaussians distribution, and compute a binned histogram of the data.

Figure 13 shows four quantities for each benchmark: LINQ, Steno including compilation, Steno excluding compilation, and hand-optimized. In order to allow comparison of different benchmarks, the results are normalized to the LINQ execution time.

For all of the microbenchmarks, the Steno-optimized query is faster than the equivalent LINQ query. The speedup ranges from 3.32× for Sum to 14.1× for Group. As expected, the nested queries (Cart and Group) yield a bigger speedup due to the LINQ code using nested iterators. Compared to the hand-optimized, loop-based code, the worst overhead is 53%—for Sum, the simplest query—due to the .NET JIT compiler missing a possible temporary variable elimination in the Steno-generated code, which leads to two extraneous `movsd` instructions in the loop body. For the other queries, the overhead (compared to hand-optimized) is less than 3%.

However, Steno optimization carries a one-off cost per query, which is dominated by invoking the C# compiler and dynamically loading the optimized query class. The compiled query object can then be cached by the application. In our experiments, this cost was 69 milliseconds on average. Therefore, if an application contains mostly short, infrequently-executed queries, it is not worth invoking Steno at run-time. Summing 10 million `doubles` with LINQ takes approximately 83 ms, whereas with Steno it takes 25 ms plus 69 ms for compilation. The break-even point is approximately 12 million `doubles`. Note that, if the optimization were added to the C# compiler, this cost would be paid at compile-time. In addition, the optimized query object may be stored and reused in order to amortize the cost of compilation. In the current implementation, the user must explicitly instruct Steno to compile a given expression, but a query caching approach (based on Nectar [18]) could be added.

[4] The current version of DryadLINQ is not compatible with .NET 4.0. Steno is compatible with .NET 3.5 and 4.0. We confirmed that microbenchmark performance is the same using both versions.

7.2 Distributed k-means

We now evaluate the performance of Steno-optimized code for a representative distributed query: k-means clustering. A distributed cluster is a more challenging environment for Steno: since data sets are often too large to fit in memory, they must be read from disk, and network communication is required to coordinate between partitions. By contrast, the microbenchmarks use in-memory arrays.

The k-means algorithm groups a set of data points into k clusters by estimating the centroid of each cluster, and iteratively updating the centroids by averaging the points in each cluster. The main computational step involves computing the (e.g. Euclidean) distance from each point to each centroid, and assigning each point to the cluster whose centroid is closest. We implemented the algorithm in DryadLINQ, and each iteration comprises two steps:

1. In parallel, for each data point (nested `Select`), compute the distance to each centroid (`Select`), and choose the cluster with the closest centroid (`Aggregate`). Then group these results by cluster ID (`GroupBy`) and compute partial sums of the points in each cluster (`Aggregate`).
2. Group the partial sums from each partition by cluster ID (`GroupBy`), add them together (`Aggregate`), and compute the new cluster centroids by taking the mean (`Select`).

This query exploits iterator fusion (§4), `GroupBy-Aggregate` specialization (§4.3) and nested loop generation (§5).

The benefits from Steno-optimization are greatest when (i) a large number of elements are processed, and (ii) the amount of work that each operator performs is small. The k-means algorithm offers us the opportunity to vary both quantities, but (since k-means has $O(n)$ complexity for n data points) it is more meaningful to vary to amount of work per element. We achieve this by varying the number of dimensions in each point, which is directly proportional to the number of floating-point operations in the Euclidean distance calculation. Figure 14 shows the effect of varying the dimension on the performance of unoptimized and Steno-optimized k-means. The overall size of the input data (number of points × dimension) is held constant at 10^9 `doubles` ($\approx$ 8 GB).

The most notable result is that Steno achieves substantial speedup over LINQ for dimensions less than 1000, which demonstrates that iterator overheads can have a large effect on the performance of distributed query execution. Larger speedups are achieved for smaller dimensions: for example, 1.9× for 10-dimensional points. However, as the dimension increases, Steno manages to speed up execution, and it achieves a 19% improvement for 100-dimensional data. Eventually, however, the execution converges with the unoptimized case, as the fraction of time spent in the distance computation becomes closer to 100%.

8. Related work

There is a large volume of related work on the optimization of declarative programs. Steno combines ideas from database systems, functional programming, XML processing and object-oriented programming to optimize the execution of declarative data-parallel programs. In this section, we survey the related work in each of these fields, and compare it to Steno.

8.1 Relational databases

The stated aim of Codd's relational algebra was to hide details of "how the data is organized in the machine (the internal representation)." [8] This set the precedent for database access using SQL, a declarative query language, which in turn influenced the design of LINQ [2]. Query evaluation can be implemented using iterators [3], which motivates use of `IEnumerator` objects to compose LINQ operators. Because relational databases are designed to hold large volumes of data, research into query efficiency has been carried out since the earliest implementations of the relational model.

IBM's System R implemented SEQUEL (a precursor of SQL) query evaluation by assembling fragments of System/370 machine code in a query-specific subroutine [6]. System R used a preprocessor to extract SEQUEL queries from COBOL or PL/1 source code, and replace them with calls to the generated machine code. However, the use of pre-defined code fragments led to overhead from procedure calls, and poor portability [15].

Freytag and Goodman refined this method by transforming a query into iterative C or Pascal code, which is then compiled by an existing compiler [15, 16]. Their system compiles queries written in a dialect of SQL—comprising operators for projection, filtering, left-join and aggregation—into iterative code, using rule-based transformations.

Most recently, Krikellas *et al.* revisited the problem of efficient query execution, and analysed the costs of the iterator model at the computer-architectural level [23]. They propose "holistic query evaluation" (HQE), which uses a code generator to turn SQL queries into C code, and then compiles it using an existing optimizing compiler. Like System R, HQE relies on a library of templates to provide the generated code. It offers a restricted form of nested loop generation for table joins, but does not support arbitrarily-nested query expressions such as those described in Section 5.

The techniques for optimizing query execution are similar to Steno, in that they propose generating lower-level code, which can be compiled or executed directly. However, all of these techniques target SQL, which is less general than LINQ (it lacks a `SelectMany` operator), and does not—at least, in the database systems described above—integrate with user-defined code in a general-purpose language. Furthermore, none of these techniques are shown to apply to nested queries. The automaton-based approach that we describe in this paper could be applied to SQL query optimization and may be useful in extending these systems with nested query support.

8.2 Functional programming

The LINQ execution framework shares several features with lazily-evaluated functional languages: in particular, the `Select`, `Where`, `Aggregate` and `SelectMany` operators correspond to Haskell's `map`, `filter`, `foldl` and `concatMap` functions [25]. Therefore, techniques for efficiently compiling a lazy functional program are related to (and can inform) our technique for efficiently compiling a LINQ expression.

Lazy evaluation can reduce the storage cost of some programs by only evaluating the values in a collection when they are needed by a consumer. However accessing the not-yet-evaluated portions of intermediate collections imposes a hidden cost that is analogous to the iterator overhead in LINQ. Wadler developed the "deforestation" algorithm to eliminate intermediate lists (and trees) from programs written in a restrictive, first-order, lazy functional language [31]. However, deforestation is considered impractical because it restricts programs to a "treeless" form that prohibits, amongst other things, intermediate data structures [17].

Practical versions of deforestation include "`build/foldr`" [17], "`destroy/unfoldr`" [28] and stream fusion [9]. These techniques use equational transformations in Haskell to transform functions that produce and consume lists into fused code that does not use intermediate lazy lists. Of the three techniques, stream fusion is the most powerful, and can optimize the nested `concatMap` function, which is analogous to `SelectMany` in LINQ. However, stream fusion is not well-suited to deeply-nested list computations because the Glasgow Haskell Compiler's optimizer cannot always generate efficient code from the fused intermediate form [9]. By contrast, Steno generates simple nested `for` loops that the C# compiler can easily optimize.

8.3 XML processing

The growing popularity of XML as a data interchange format has prompted research into efficient processing of XML documents and streams. XML query languages such as XQuery and XPath provide declarative syntax for computations over XML documents, and early query processing systems used an iterator-based approach for query evaluation [14].

Li and Agarwal developed a code generation technique called "Generalized Nested Loops" (GNLs), which can be used to optimize the evaluation of XQuery expressions on large data sets [24]. Although superficially similar to nested queries in QUIL (§5), GNLs can only represent nested loops that perform an associative aggregation function. Therefore, the GNL code generation technique could not be applied to nested queries that flatten a collection, such as `SelectMany` and `Join`.

Reichenbach *et al.* have studied the optimization of XML-processing computations that are embedded in the XJ imperative language, which is based on Java [27]. They developed a program analysis that identifies potential XPath queries that are latent in imperative code, and exploits opportunities for sharing results between queries. By contrast, Steno attempts to optimize the execution of explicit queries. However, since XJ supports LINQ-like query syntax, it may be possible to apply this analysis to C# programs, and identify opportunities for common subexpression evaluation between Steno-optimized queries.

8.4 Object-oriented programming

In an object-oriented programming language, virtual calls are expensive because the compiler does not have enough information to generate inline code at the call site: the receiver method is only known at run-time. To solve this problem, various devirtualization techniques have been proposed.

Calder and Grunwald proposed a simple transformation for C++ code that inlines the code for the most likely receiver of a virtual call, guarded by a run-time type check [5]. Since the guard code contains a simple branch instruction, hardware branch prediction can ameliorate the overhead of the type check. However, a LINQ operator may be used to consume from different iterator implementations at different points in the same program (or even in the same query), so the receiver for a particular call site is not usually predictable.

Dean *et al.* developed static class hierarchy analysis, which performs static analysis on the inheritance hierarchy and intraprocedural data-flow analysis to identify the precise type of an object (and hence potentially eliminate a virtual call) [11]. This technique is less useful for C#, which allows dynamic classloading, though a just-in-time approach that "revirtualizes" methods as appropriate has been developed [20]. Furthermore, since the `IEnumerator<T>`

interface has many implementing classes, it is rarely possible to make a precise static judgement about the run-time type of an iterator, without expensive interprocedural analysis.

Although devirtualization could improve the performance of LINQ queries, it is not implemented in the current version of the .NET Common Language Runtime (CLR). Furthermore, even if perfect devirtualization were achieved, the resulting inlined code would include the state machine logic from each iterator, which would be less efficient than the simple for loops generated by Steno. We are not aware of a compiler that could eliminate this semantically redundant logic and yield code that is as efficient as a Steno-optimized query.

8.5 Data-parallel computing

Steno was originally developed to optimize the performance of DryadLINQ programs, which run in parallel on a distributed compute cluster. The restrictions imposed by the declarative style of programming make it simple to parallelize a program written as a declarative query (§6), and several systems use this approach to exploit the computational resources of large compute clusters.

Dean and Ghemawat's MapReduce is an influential system for data-parallel programming [10]. In MapReduce, developers specify their computations by providing two functions: a *mapper*, which transforms input records into lists of key-value pairs (cf. `SelectMany`, §5), and a *reducer*, which aggregates all of the values corresponding to a single key (cf. `GroupBy-Aggregate`, §4.3). MapReduce uses an iterator in the reducer to provide access to the values corresponding to a single key; the open-source Hadoop implementation of MapReduce uses iterators extensively in the processing of records [1]. We expect that generating specialized code to eliminate iterators would yield a performance improvement similar to what Steno achieves.

Chambers *et al.* described FlumeJava, which (like DryadLINQ) uses lazy evaluation to build a distributed execution plan from a graph of operators [7]. In FlumeJava, however, the execution engine is Google's MapReduce implementation. We note the similarity of FlumeJava's `parallelDo()`, `groupByKey()`, `combineValues()` and `flatten()` functions to LINQ's `Select`, `GroupBy`, `Aggregate` and `SelectMany` operators, respectively. The optimizations that we have developed in Steno apply equally to FlumeJava programs. However, whereas LINQ uses `Expression` objects with an in-memory AST, FlumeJava uses classes that implement a functor interface to encapsulate operator behavior. This is less amenable to run-time optimization, and bytecode rewriting techniques would be necessary to eliminate virtual function calls from the optimized code.

Two contemporary projects have performed static analysis on (Hadoop) MapReduce programs in order to derive an optimized program. Manimal [4] and HadoopToSQL [21] analyse the Java bytecode of MapReduce programs in order to generate an equivalent relational algebra expression. The expression is then converted to SQL, and passed to a cluster of SQL databases. The intermediate representation bears some similarity to the LINQ expression tree that Steno uses. Therefore, the analyses that these systems perform could be combined with Steno-style code generation in order to generate optimized query execution code.

Since Steno integrates into DryadLINQ, it can take advantage of higher-level optimizations. For example, Yu *et al.* added a transformation to DryadLINQ that optimizes distributed aggregation (`GroupBy-Aggregate`) by partially performing associative and commutative aggregation functions before the communication step [33]. Gunda *et al.* developed a system called Nectar, which caches the results of previous DryadLINQ jobs, and uses the cached data to achieve common subexpression elimination across multiple DryadLINQ jobs [18]. Steno is applied after these transformations, which further improves the performance of DryadLINQ queries.

9. Conclusions

In this paper, we have presented Steno: an automatic optimizer for declarative queries that generates efficient, loop-based, imperative code. Our automaton-based approach provides a useful abstraction for structuring the code generator, and made it straightforward to implement support for our two key optimizations: iterator fusion and nested loop generation. Though these optimizations generate sequential code, we have integrated Steno with DryadLINQ, which extends the optimization to code running in parallel on a distributed compute cluster. Our evaluation showed that, even in the challenging distributed case, Steno can almost double the performance of real-world DryadLINQ jobs.

Our approach in developing Steno has been conservative. We did not modify the C# compiler or the .NET core libraries, and we faithfully reproduced the semantics of unoptimized LINQ. This leaves scope for further optimization. First, we can apply such optimizations as common subexpression elimination only if it is possible to prove that the subexpression has no side effects, and that materializing the subexpression does not exhaust memory. The difficulty of this problem suggests that there are opportunities for developer-guided optimization. Also, we have hitherto only considered C# as the target language, but it may be possible to gain more efficiency by directly generating bytecode, C or even native machine code. We note that many operators could benefit from vectorization, so SIMD execution using instruction-set extensions or GPGPUs would achieve greater efficiency [30].

The implementation of Steno as a library is a mixed blessing. The main advantage is that Steno works with a standard .NET toolchain, but as we have shown in Section 7, invoking the C# compiler at run-time introduces a one-off overhead of tens of milliseconds. As a result, the developer must be judicious in deciding when to optimize a query, by identifying frequently-executed or long-running queries. This problem could be addressed by modifying the C# compiler to perform Steno optimizations at compile-time. The compiler already desugars LINQ queries that are written in query comprehension syntax [2], and it would be conceptually straightforward to extend this compiler pass to use Steno.

The current implementation of Steno can only optimize the standard LINQ queries. Steno cannot optimize user-defined iterators that are created with the `yield return` statement, because this statement is syntactic sugar that is transformed into an iterator state machine at compile-time [22]. A typical user-defined iterator contains a loop over some internal data structure that `yield`s one or more elements. If Steno were able to access the original syntax tree for the iterator method, it could perform more-aggressive iterator fusion and nested loop generation, which would further improve the performance of iterator-based programs.

The overall lesson that we draw from this work is that it is advantageous to write in the declarative style wherever possible. The main benefit is simpler code, which is easier to develop, and which systems like PLINQ and DryadLINQ can automatically transform and optimize for parallel or distributed execution. Previously, developers were forced to choose between efficient serial execution and access to these transformations. Steno demonstrates that this is a false dichotomy, by making the performance of declarative queries competitive with hand-optimized code, while still exploiting higher-level transformations.

Acknowledgments

We wish to thank Frank McSherry, Mihai Budiu and the PLINQ team for helpful discussions during the development of Steno. We would also like to thank Steve Hand and the anonymous reviewers, whose comments on earlier drafts of this paper have been invaluable for improving the presentation of this work.

References

[1] Apache Hadoop. `http://hadoop.apache.org/`, accessed 18th March, 2011.

[2] G. M. Bierman, E. Meijer, and M. Torgersen. Lost in translation: Formalizing proposed extensions to C♯. In *Proceedings of OOPSLA*, 2007.

[3] P. Buneman, R. E. Frankel, and R. Nikhil. An implementation technique for database query languages. *ACM Trans. Database Syst.*, 7(2), 1982.

[4] M. J. Cafarella and C. Ré. Manimal: Relational optimization for data-intensive programs. In *Proceedings of WebDB*, 2010.

[5] B. Calder and D. Grunwald. Reducing indirect function call overhead in C++ programs. In *Proceedings of POPL*, 1994.

[6] D. D. Chamberlin, M. M. Astrahan, M. W. Blasgen, J. N. Gray, W. F. King, B. G. Lindsay, R. Lorie, J. W. Mehl, T. G. Price, F. Putzolu, P. G. Selinger, M. Schkolnick, D. R. Slutz, I. L. Traiger, B. W. Wade, and R. A. Yost. A history and evaluation of System R. *Commun. ACM*, 24 (10), 1981.

[7] C. Chambers, A. Raniwala, F. Perry, S. Adams, R. R. Henry, R. Bradshaw, and N. Weizenbaum. FlumeJava: easy, efficient data-parallel pipelines. In *Proceedings of PLDI*, 2010.

[8] E. F. Codd. A relational model of data for large shared data banks. *Commun. ACM*, 13(6), 1970.

[9] D. Coutts, R. Leshchinskiy, and D. Stewart. Stream fusion: from lists to streams to nothing at all. In *Proceedings of ICFP*, 2007.

[10] J. Dean and S. Ghemawat. MapReduce: simplified data processing on large clusters. In *Proceedings of OSDI*, 2004.

[11] J. Dean, D. Grove, and C. Chambers. Optimization of object-oriented programs using static class hierarchy analysis. In *Proceedings of ECOOP*, 1995.

[12] D. J. DeWitt and J. Gray. Parallel database systems: the future of high performance database systems. *Commun. ACM*, 35(6), 1992.

[13] D. J. DeWitt, R. H. Katz, F. Olken, L. D. Shapiro, M. R. Stonebraker, and D. A. Wood. Implementation techniques for main memory database systems. In *Proceedings of SIGMOD*, 1984.

[14] D. Florescu, C. Hillery, D. Kossmann, P. Lucas, F. Riccardi, T. Westmann, M. J. Carey, A. Sundararajan, and G. Agrawal. The BEA/XQRL streaming XQuery processor. In *Proceedings of VLDB*, 2003.

[15] J. C. Freytag and N. Goodman. On the translation of relational queries into iterative programs. *ACM Trans. Database Syst.*, 14(1), 1989.

[16] J. C. Freytag and N. Goodman. Translating aggregate queries into iterative programs. In *Proceedings of VLDB*, 1986.

[17] A. Gill, J. Launchbury, and S. L. Peyton Jones. A short cut to deforestation. In *Proceedings of FPCA*, 1993.

[18] P. K. Gunda, L. Ravindranath, C. A. Thekkath, Y. Yu, and L. Zhuang. Nectar: Automatic Management of Data and Computation in Data Centers. In *Proceedings of OSDI*, 2010.

[19] M. Isard, M. Budiu, Y. Yu, A. Birrell, and D. Fetterly. Dryad: Distributed data-parallel programs from sequential building blocks. In *Proceedings of EuroSys*, 2007.

[20] K. Ishizaki, M. Kawahito, T. Yasue, H. Komatsu, and T. Nakatani. A study of devirtualization techniques for a Java Just-In-Time compiler. In *Proceedings of OOPSLA*, 2000.

[21] M.-Y. Iu and W. Zwaenepoel. HadoopToSQL: a MapReduce query optimizer. In *Proceedings of EuroSys*, 2010.

[22] B. Jacobs, E. Meijer, F. Piessens, and W. Schulte. Iterators revisited: proof rules and implementation, 2005.

[23] K. Krikellas, S. D. Viglas, and M. Cintra. Generating code for holistic query evaluation. In *Proceedings of ICDE*, 2010.

[24] X. Li and G. Agrawal. Efficient evaluation of XQuery over streaming data. In *Proceedings of VLDB*, 2005.

[25] E. Meijer. Confessions of a used programming language salesman. *SIGPLAN Not.*, 42(10), 2007.

[26] C. Olston, B. Reed, U. Srivastava, R. Kumar, and A. Tomkins. Pig Latin: a not-so-foreign language for data processing. In *Proceedings of SIGMOD*, 2008.

[27] C. Reichenbach, M. G. Burke, I. Peshansky, and M. Raghavachari. Analysis of imperative XML programs. *Information Systems*, 34(7), 2009.

[28] J. Svenningsson. Shortcut fusion for accumulating parameters & zip-like functions. In *Proceedings of ICFP*, 2002.

[29] R. Tan, P. Nagpal, and S. Miller. Automated black box testing tool for a parallel programming library. In *Proceedings of ICST*, 2009.

[30] D. Tarditi, S. Puri, and J. Oglesby. Accelerator: using data parallelism to program GPUs for general-purpose uses. In *Proceedings of ASPLOS*, 2006.

[31] P. Wadler. Deforestation: transforming programs to eliminate trees. In *Proceedings of ESOP*, 1988.

[32] Y. Yu, M. Isard, D. Fetterly, M. Budiu, Ú. Erlingsson, P. K. Gunda, and J. Currey. DryadLINQ: a system for general-purpose distributed data-parallel computing using a high-level language. In *Proceedings of OSDI*, 2008.

[33] Y. Yu, P. K. Gunda, and M. Isard. Distributed aggregation for data-parallel computing: interfaces and implementations. In *Proceedings of SOSP*, 2009.

Languages as Libraries *

Sam Tobin-Hochstadt
Northeastern University

Vincent St-Amour
Northeastern University

Ryan Culpepper
University of Utah

Matthew Flatt
University of Utah

Matthias Felleisen
Northeastern University

Abstract

Programming language design benefits from constructs for extending the syntax and semantics of a host language. While C's string-based macros empower programmers to introduce notational shorthands, the parser-level macros of Lisp encourage experimentation with domain-specific languages. The Scheme programming language improves on Lisp with macros that respect lexical scope.

The design of Racket—a descendant of Scheme—goes even further with the introduction of a full-fledged interface to the static semantics of the language. A Racket extension programmer can thus add constructs that are indistinguishable from "native" notation, large and complex embedded domain-specific languages, and even optimizing transformations for the compiler backend. This power to experiment with language design has been used to create a series of sub-languages for programming with first-class classes and modules, numerous languages for implementing the Racket system, and the creation of a complete and fully integrated typed sister language to Racket's untyped base language.

This paper explains Racket's language extension API via an implementation of a small typed sister language. The new language provides a rich type system that accommodates the idioms of untyped Racket. Furthermore, modules in this typed language can safely exchange values with untyped modules. Last but not least, the implementation includes a type-based optimizer that achieves promising speedups. Although these extensions are complex, their Racket implementation is just a library, like any other library, requiring no changes to the Racket implementation.

Categories and Subject Descriptors D.3.3 [*Programming Languages*]: Language Constructs and Features

General Terms Languages, Design

1. Growing Many Languages

I need to design a language that can grow. — Guy Steele, 1998

Virtual machines inspire language experimentation. For example, the Java Virtual Machine and the .NET CLR attracted many implementors to port existing languages. Their goal was to benefit from the rich set of libraries and runtime facilities, such as garbage collectors and thread abstractions, that these platforms offer. Both platforms also inspired language design projects that wanted to experiment with new paradigms and to exploit existing frameworks; thus Clojure, a parallelism-oriented descendant of Lisp, and Scala, a multi-paradigm relative of Java, target the JVM, while F# is built atop .NET. In all of these cases, however, the platform is only a target, not a tool for growing languages. As a result, design experiments on these platforms remain costly, labor-intensive projects.

To follow Steele's advice on *growing a language* (1998) requires more than a reusable virtual machine and its libraries; it demands an extensible *host language* that supports *linguistic reuse* (Krishnamurthi 2001). Thus, a derived language should be able to reuse the scoping mechanisms of the host language. Similarly, if the host language offers namespace management for identifiers, a language designer should have the freedom to lift that management into an experimental language.

Providing such freedoms to designers demands a range of extension mechanisms. A programmer may wish to manipulate the surface syntax and the AST, interpose a new context-sensitive static semantics, and communicate the results of the static semantics to the backend. Best of all, this kind of work can proceed without any changes to the host language, so that the resulting design is essentially a library that supplements the existing compiler.

In this paper, we present the Racket[1] (Flatt and PLT 2010) platform, which combines a virtual machine and JIT compiler with a programming language that supports extension mechanisms for all phases of language implementation. With Racket's arsenal of extension mechanisms, a programmer may change all aspects of a language: lexicographic and parsed notation, the static semantics, module linking, and optimizations. The Racket development team has exploited this extensibility for the construction of two dozen frequently used languages, e.g., language extensions for classes (Flatt et al. 2006) and ML-style functors (Flatt and Felleisen 1998; Culpepper et al. 2005), another for creating interactive web server applications (Krishnamurthi et al. 2007), two languages implementing logic programming[2] and a lazy variant of Racket (Barzilay and Clements 2005). This paper is itself a program in Racket's documentation language (Flatt et al. 2009).

Racket derives its power from a carefully designed revision of a Scheme-style macro systems. The key is to make language choice specific to each module. That is, individual modules of a program can be implemented in different languages, where the language implementation has complete control over the syntax and semantics of the module. The language implementation can reuse as much of the base language as desired, and it can export as much of the module's internals as desired. In particular, languages can reuse Racket's macro facilities, which is supported with a mechanism for locally expanding macros into attributed ASTs.

* A preliminary version of this work appeared at the Workshop on Scheme and Functional Programming (Culpepper et al. 2007). This work has been supported by the DARPA, Mozilla Foundation, NSERC, and NSF.

PLDI'11, June 4–8, 2011, San Jose, California, USA.

[1] Formerly known as PLT Scheme.

[2] Schelog (1993) `http://docs.racket-lang.org/racklog`
Datalog (2010) `http://docs.racket-lang.org/datalog`

For simplicity, we demonstrate the idea of true language extensibility via a single example: the Typed Racket implementation. Typed Racket (Tobin-Hochstadt and Felleisen 2008) is a statically typed sister language of Racket that is designed to support the gradual porting of untyped programs. Its type system accommodates the idioms of Racket, its modules can exchange values with untyped modules, and it has a type-driven optimizer—all implemented as plain Racket libraries.

The remainder of this paper starts with a description of Racket's language extension facilities and the challenges posed by the Typed Racket extension. Following these background sections, the paper shows how we use syntactic extension to introduce Typed Racket notation; how we splice the type checker into the tool chain; how we enable inter-language linking; and how we add realistic optimizing transformations via a library. Finally, we relate our approach to existing facilities for meta-programming with static semantics as well as extensible compiler projects.

2. Language Extension in Racket

Racket provides a range of facilities for language extension. In this section, we outline the most relevant background as well as extension mechanisms provided with Racket.

2.1 Macros

From Lisp (Steele Jr. 1994) and Scheme (Sperber et al. 2009), Racket takes hygienic macros as the basis of its syntactic extension mechanisms. In Racket, macros are functions from syntax to syntax, which are executed at compile time. During compilation, Racket's macro expander recursively traverses the input syntax. When it reaches the use of a macro, it runs the associated function, the *transformer*, and continues by traversing the result.

Macros may use arbitrary Racket libraries and primitives to compute the result syntax. The following macro queries the system clock at compile time:

```
(define-syntax (when-compiled stx)
  (with-syntax ([ct (current-seconds)])
    #'ct))
```

This macro computes, at compile time, the current time in seconds, and uses the `with-syntax` form to bind the identifier `ct` to a *syntax object* representing this number. Syntax objects are the ASTs of Racket, and contain syntactic data as well as metadata such as source location information. The `#'` form (analogous to `'` for lists) constructs syntax objects and can refer to identifiers bound by `with-syntax` in its context. In the following function, we use the `when-compiled` macro:

```
(define (how-long-ago?)
  (- (current-seconds) (when-compiled)))
```

Since the `when-compiled` form expands into the current date in seconds *at the time the form is compiled* and since the value of `(current-seconds)` continues to change, the value produced by `how-long-ago?` continually increases

```
> (how-long-ago?)
0
> (sleep 1)
> (how-long-ago?)
1
```

Most macros generate new expressions based on their input:

```
(define-syntax (do-10-times stx)
  (syntax-parse stx
    [(do-10-times body:expr ...)
     #'(for ([i (in-range 10)])
         body ...)]))
> (do-10-times (display "*") (display "#"))
*#*#*#*#*#*#*#*#*#*#
```

The `do-10-times` macro consumes a sequence of expressions and produces code that runs these expressions 10 times. To this end, it first decomposes its input, `stx`, with the `syntax-parse` form (Culpepper and Felleisen 2010), a pattern matcher designed for implementing macros. The pattern requires a sequence of subexpressions, indicated with `...`, named `body`, each of which is constrained to be an `expr`. The resulting syntax is a `for` loop that contains the `body` expressions. Thanks to macro hygiene, if the `body`s use the variable `i`, it is *not* interfered with by the use of `i` in the `for` loop.

2.2 Manipulating Syntax Objects

Since syntax objects are Racket's primary compile-time data structure, roughly analagous to the ASTs of conventional languages, syntax objects come with a rich API.

Constructors and Accessors Besides `with-syntax` and `#'` for constructing and manipulating syntax objects, the remainder of the paper also uses the following forms and functions:

- `syntax->list` converts a non-atomic syntax object to a list;
- `free-identifier=?` compares two identifiers to determine if they refer to the same binding;
- the `` #` `` and `#,` forms implement Lisp's quasiquote and unquote for syntax object construction.

Syntax properties Racket macros can add out-of-band information to syntax objects, e.g., source locations, dubbed *syntax properties*. The `syntax-property-put` and `syntax-property-get` procedures attach and retrieve arbitrary key-value pairs on syntax objects, which are preserved by the macro expander. Thus syntactic extensions may communicate with each other without interfering with each other.

Local Expansion The `local-expand` procedure expands a syntax object to *core Racket*. This explicitly specified core language consists of approximately 20 primitive syntactic forms that implement Racket; see figure 1 for a subset of this grammar. Using `local-expand`, a language extension may analyze an arbitrary expression, even if that expression uses macros. For example, the following macro requires that its argument be a λ expression:

```
(define-syntax (only-λ stx)
  (syntax-parse stx
    [(_ arg:expr)
     (define c
       (local-expand #'arg 'expression '()))
     (define k (first (syntax->list c)))
     (if (free-identifier=? #'#%plain-lambda k)
         c
         (error "not λ"))]))
```

The `only-λ` macro uses `local-expand` on the `arg` subexpression to fully expand it:

```
> (only-λ (λ (x) x))
#<procedure>
> (only-λ 7)
```

not λ

If we add a definition that makes `function` the same as λ, we still get the correct behavior.

```
> (only-λ (function (x) x))
#<procedure>
```

The `only-λ` macro can see through the use of `function` because of the use of `local-expand`.

2.3 Modules and Languages

Racket provides a first-order module system that supports import and export of language extensions (Flatt 2002). For the purposes

```
mod-form = expr
         | (#%provide provide-spec)
         | (define-values (id) expr)
         | ...

    expr = id
         | (#%plain-lambda (id ...)
             expr ...+)
         | (if expr expr expr)
         | (quote datum)
         | (#%plain-app expr ...+)
         | ...
```

Figure 1: Racket's core forms (abbreviated)

of this paper, two aspects of the module system are crucial. First, modules can export static bindings, such as macros, as well as value bindings, such as procedures, without requiring clients to distinguish between them. Thus, value bindings can be replaced with static bindings without breaking clients. Second, each module is compiled with a *fresh store*. That is, mutations to state created during one compilation do not affect the results of other compilations.

Every module specifies—in the first line of the module—the language it is written in. For example,

```
#lang racket
```

specifies `racket` as the module's language, and

```
#lang datalog
```

specifies `datalog` instead, a language extension with different lexical syntax, static and dynamic semantics from plain Racket.

For the purposes of this paper, a *language* `L` is a library that provides two linguistic features:

- a set of bindings for `L`, including both syntactic forms such as `define` and values such as `+`, which constitute the base environment of modules written in the language, and
- a binding named `#%module-begin`, which is used to implement the whole-module semantics of `L`.

The `#%module-begin` form is applied to the entire module before the macro expander takes over. For example, here is the `#%module-begin` form for the `count` language:

```
(define-syntax (#%module-begin stx)
  (syntax-parse stx
    [(#%module-begin body ...)
     #`(#%plain-module-begin
         (printf "Found ~a expressions."
                 #,(length
                     (syntax->list
                       #'(body ...))))
         body ...)]))
```

The `#%plain-module-begin` form is the base module wrapper, adding no new static semantics.

When this language is used, it prints the number of top-level expressions in the program, then runs the program as usual. For example, consider the following module written in `count`:

```
#lang count
(printf "*~a" (+ 1 2))
(printf "*~a" (- 4 3))
```

When run, this module prints:

```
Found 2 expressions.*3*1.
```

The `#%module-begin` language mechanism allows a language author to implement arbitrary new whole-module static semantics using macro rewriting.

3. Typed Racket as a Library

Typed Racket combines a type system for enriching Racket modules with sound type information and a mechanism for linking typed and untyped modules. Its implementation not only benefits from, but demands, as much linguistic reuse as possible. After all, Typed Racket must implement the same semantics as Racket plus purely syntactic type checking; there is no other way to provide a smooth migration path that turns Racket programs into Typed Racket programs on a module-by-module basis. And the best way to implement the same semantics is to share the compiler.

At the same time, linguistic reuse poses novel challenges in addition to those faced by every implementer of a typed language. In this section, we explain these challenges with examples; in the remainder of the paper we explain our solutions. As for the particular challenges, we show how to:

1. annotate bindings with type specifications;
2. check type correctness in a context-sensitive fashion;
3. type check programs written in an extensible language;
4. integrate type checking with separate compilation of modules;
5. provide safe interaction with untyped modules; and
6. optimize programs based on type information.

3.1 Layering Types on an Untyped Language

Consider this trivial Typed Racket program:

```
#lang typed/racket
(define: x : Number 3)
```

It specifies that `x` has type `Number`. To implement `define:`, Typed Racket *reuses* the plain `define` provided by Racket. Thus we must associate the type declaration for `x` out-of-band.

Further, although modern languages come with a wide variety of syntactic forms, most can be reduced to simpler forms via rewrite rules implemented as macros, e.g.:

```
(define-syntax (let: stx)
  (syntax-parse stx
    [(let ([x:id : T rhs:expr]) body:expr)
     #'((λ: ([x : T]) body) rhs)]))
```

For Typed Racket, these rewriting rules must preserve the specified type information without interfering with the implementation of the typechecker.

These are two instances of Typed Racket's linguistic reuse. This linguistic reuse is comprehensive through all layers of Typed Racket. Modules in Typed Racket are simply Racket modules. The same is true of functions and variables, which map directly to their Racket equivalents. At the intermediate level, Typed Racket reuses Racket's binding forms, such as `define` and λ, with additions for the specification of types as described above. At the lowest level, runtime values are shared between Racket and Typed Racket.

Returning to our example, the plain Racket definition form is:

```
(define x 3)
```

There is no place in such a definition for a type annotation. Hence, the macro must store the type information out-of-band. Fortunately, syntax properties allow for `define:` to record precisely such additional information:

```
(define-syntax (define: stx)
  (syntax-parse stx
    [(define: name:id : ty rhs:expr)
     (with-syntax
         ([ann-name
           (syntax-property-put
             #'name 'type-annotation #'ty)])
       #'(define ann-name rhs))]))
```

Here, `ann-name` is the original name, but with a syntax property indicating that it is annotated with the type `ty`. With this implementation, later stages of processing can read the type annotation from the binding, but the type annotation does not affect the behavior of Racket's `define`, allowing reuse as desired.

3.2 Challenges

Next we turn to the challenges of other processing phases.

Context-sensitive Checking Type checking is inherently context-sensitive. For example, this Typed Racket program:

```
#lang typed/racket
(: f (Number -> Number))
(define (f z) (sqrt (* 2 z)))
(f 7)
```

relies on contextual information about the type of `f` when checking the function application `(f 7)`. Tracking this information demands an implementation that typechecks the entire module, rather than just the syntax available at a particular program point; in other words, it is a whole-module analysis.

Checking an Extended Language Typed Racket programmers expect to use the numerous libraries provided by Racket, many of which provide syntactic abstractions. For example, this module uses `match`, a syntactic form implemented in a library written in plain Racket, rather than a primitive form as in ML or Haskell, but nonetheless indistinguishable from a language primitive:

```
#lang racket
(match (list 1 2 3)
  [(list x y z)
   (+ x y z)])
```

Naturally, Typed Racket programmers want to reuse such convenient libraries, ideally without modifications, so that the above becomes a valid Typed Racket module by using `typed/racket`.

Therefore, we must either extend our typechecker to handle `match`, or translate `match` into a simpler form that the typechecker understands. The former solution works for existing language extensions, but in Racket, programmers can write new language extensions at any time, meaning that Typed Racket cannot possibly contain a catalog of all of them.

Supporting Modular Programs Racket programs consist of multiple modules; Typed Racket therefore supports modules as well. The types of bindings defined in one module must be accessible in other typed modules without the need to repeat type declarations. For example:

```
#lang typed/racket ;; module server
(: add-5 : Integer -> Integer)
(define (add-5 x) (+ x 5))
;; export 'add-5' from the module
(provide add-5)

#lang typed/racket ;; module client
(require server)
(add-5 7) ;; type checks correctly
```

Because modules are compiled separately, the `server` module is compiled before the `client` module, but must communicate the static information about the type of `add-5` to `client`. Therefore, compiling a Typed Racket module must produce a *persistent* record of the types of exported bindings.

Integrating with Untyped Modules Racket comes with hundreds of thousands of lines of libraries, almost all of which are written without types. Effective use of Typed Racket, therefore, requires interoperation with untyped modules. Typed Racket supports such interoperation in both directions. First, typed modules can import untyped bindings by specifying their types:

```
#lang typed/racket
(require/typed racket/file
  [file->lines (Path -> (Listof String))])
(file->lines "/etc/passwd")
```

Second, untyped modules can import typed bindings:

```
#lang racket ;; client
(require server)
(add-5 12) ;; safe use
(add-5 "bad") ;; unsafe use
```

Typed Racket must protect its soundness invariants and check value flow across the boundary between typed and untyped programs. It must also avoid, however, imposing unnecessary dynamic checks between typed modules.

Optimizing with Type Information Type information enables a wide variety of optimizations. Tag checking, ubiquitous in untyped Racket programs, is unnecessary in typed programs. For example, this program need not check that the argument to `first` is a pair:

```
#lang typed/racket
(: p : (List Number Number Number))
(define p (list 1 2 3))
(first p)
```

Of course, with type information, more significant optimizations are also possible. The following loop is transformed into one that performs only machine-level floating-point computation:

```
#lang typed/racket
(: count : Float-Complex -> Integer)
(define (count f)
  (let loop ([f f])
    (if (< (magnitude f) 0.001)
        0
        (add1 (loop (/ f 2.0+2.0i))))))
```

In particular, the type information should assist the compiler backend with the treatment of complex and floating-point numbers.

4. A Single-Module Typechecker

This section presents the single-module core of a simply-typed version of Typed Racket. It concludes with an explanation of how to scale the system to the full typechecker of Typed Racket.

4.1 An Example

Assume our language is available from the `simple-type` library. Thus, we can write modules like the following:

```
#lang simple-type
(define x : Integer 1)
(define y : Integer 2)
(define (f [z : Integer]) : Integer
  (* x (+ y z)))
```

Such a module is first fully expanded to the appropriate core forms and then typechecked. Thus, type-incorrect definitions and expressions signal compile-time errors.

```
(define w : Integer 3.7)
```

typecheck: wrong type in: 3.7

Modules with type errors are not executable.

4.2 Wiring Up the Typechecker

Typechecking a module is a context-sensitive process and therefore demands a whole-module analysis via `#%module-begin`.

Since Racket provides a rich mechanism for syntactic extension, many important language features are implemented as language extensions. Major examples are pattern matching, keyword arguments, and even simple conditional forms such as `case` and `cond`. Providing appropriate type rules for every syntactic extension, however, is clearly impossible, because programmers can invent new extensions at any time. Instead, we consider only the

```
(define-syntax (#%module-begin stx)
  (syntax-parse stx
    [(_ forms ...)
     (with-syntax ([(_ core-forms ...)
                    (local-expand #'(#%plain-module-begin forms ...) 'module-begin '())])
       (for-each typecheck (syntax->list #'(core-forms ...)))
       #'(#%plain-module-begin core-forms ...))]))
```

Figure 2: The Top-level Driver

```
(define (typecheck t [check #f])
  (define the-type
    (syntax-parse t
      [v:identifier (lookup-type #'v)]
      [(quote n:number) (cond [(exact-integer? (syntax-e #'n)) IntT]
                              [(flonum? (syntax-e #'n)) FloatT]
                              [else NumberT])]
      [(if e1 e2 e3)
       (typecheck #'e1 BooleanT)
       (unless (equal? (typecheck #'e2) (typecheck #'e3))
         (type-error "if branches must agree"))
       (typecheck #'e3)]
      [(#%plain-lambda formals body:expr)
       (define formal-types (map type-of (syntax->list #'formals)))
       (for-each add-type! (syntax->list #'formals) formal-types)
       (make-fun-type formal-types (typecheck #'body))]
      [(#%plain-app op . args)
       (define argtys (map typecheck (syntax->list #'args)))
       (match (typecheck #'op)
         [(struct fun-type (formals ret))
          (unless (and (= (length argtys) (length formals)) (andmap subtype argtys formals))
            (type-error "wrong argument types" t))
          ret]
         [t (type-error "not a function type" #'op)])]
      [(define-values (id) rhs)
       (add-type! #'id (type-of #'id)) (typecheck #'rhs (type-of #'id))]))
  (when (and check (not (subtype the-type check))) (type-error "wrong type" t))
  the-type)
;; get the type of a binding
(define (type-of id)
  (unless (syntax-property-get id 'type) (type-error "untyped variable" id))
  (parse-type (syntax-property-get id 'type)))
```

Figure 3: The Typechecker

small fixed set of core forms of figure 1, and reduce all other forms to these *before* type checking.

Given an implementation of the typechecker, we must connect it to the program so that it receives appropriate fully-expanded syntax objects as input. The basic driver is given in figure 2. The driver is straightforward, performing only two functions. Once we have fully expanded the body of the module, we typecheck each form in turn. The typechecker raises an error if it encounters an untypable form. Finally, we construct the output module from new core forms, thus avoiding a re-expansion of the input.

The strategy of reducing syntactic sugar to core forms is common in many other languages, and even specified in the standards for ML (Milner et al. 1997) and Haskell (Marlow 2010). In a language with syntactic extension, we need more sophisticated support from the system to implement this strategy, and that support is provided in Racket by `local-expand`.

For successful typechecking, we must also provide an initial environment. The initial environment specifies types for any identifiers that the language provides, such as +, as well as the initial type names. Finally, we provide the `define` and λ binding forms that attach the appropriate syntax properties for type annotations to the bound variables, as described in section 2.1.

4.3 Typechecking Syntax

Figure 1 displays the grammar for our simple language. It is a subset of the core forms of full Racket. Modules consist of a sequence of *mod-forms*, which are either expressions or definitions.

Figure 3 specifies the typechecker for this core language. The `typecheck` function takes a term and an optional result type. Each clause in the `syntax-parse` expression considers one of the core forms described in figure 1.

Two aspects of the typechecker are distinctive. First, the type environment uses a mutable table mapping identifiers to types based on their binding; the table is accessed with `lookup-type` and updated with `add-type!`. Shadowing is impossible because identifiers in fully-expanded Racket programs are unique with respect to the entire program. We update the type environment in the clauses for both `#%plain-lambda` and `define-values`. Using an identifier-keyed table allows reuse of the Racket binding structure without having to reimplement variable renaming or environments.

The second distinctive feature of the typechecker is the `type-of` function. It reads the syntax properties attached by forms such as `define:` in section 3.1 with a known key to determine the type the user has added to each binding position.

4.4 Scaling to Typed Racket

While this module-level typechecker is simple, the full implementation for Typed Racket employs the same strategy. The important differences concern mutual recursion and complex definition forms. Mutual recursion is implemented with a two-pass typechecker: the first pass collects definitions with their types, and the second pass checks individual expressions in this type context. Complex declarations, such as the definition of new types, are also handled in the first pass. They are recognized by the typechecker, and the appropriate bindings and types are added to the relevant environments.

Of course, the Typed Racket type system is much more complex (Strickland et al. 2009; Tobin-Hochstadt and Felleisen 2010) than the one we have implemented here, but that complexity does not require modifications to the structure of the implementation—it is encapsulated in the behavior of `typecheck` on the core forms.

5. Modular Typed Programs

The typechecker in section 4 deals only with individual modules. To deal with multiple modules, we must both propagate type information between typed modules, and also persist type information in compiled code to support separate compilation.

For the first point, we reuse some Racket infrastruture. Namespace management in a modular language is a complex problem, and one that Racket already solves. In particular, identifiers in Racket are given globally fresh names that are stable across modules during the expansion process. Since our type environment is keyed by identifiers, type environment lookup reuses and respects Racket's scoping. An identifier imported from one module maintains its identity in the importing module, and therefore the typechecker is able to look up the appropriate type for the binding.

The second step is to maintain the type environment across compilations. Since each module is compiled in a separate and fresh store, mutations to the type environment do not persist between compilations. Therefore, Typed Racket must incorporate the type environment into the residual program, because that is the only persistent result of compilation. Our strategy — due to Flatt (2002) — is to include code in the resulting module that populates the type environment every time the module is required.

In our example system, we implement this by adding a single rewriting pass to the `#%module-begin` form for Typed Racket. Expressions and definitions are left alone; an appropriate compile-time declaration is added for each export:

```
(provide n) ; The original export
; ==> (is rewritten into)
(with-syntax ([t (serialize (type-of #'n))])
 #'(begin
     (#%provide n) ; The core export form
     (begin-for-syntax
       (add-type! #'n t))))
```

The resulting code uses `#%provide` to maintain the original export. The type declaration is wrapped in `begin-for-syntax`, meaning that it is executed at compile time to declare that `n` is mapped to the serialization of its type in the type environment.

```
(define-syntax (require/typed stx)
  (syntax-parse stx
    [(_ module [id ty])
     #'(begin-ignored
        ; Stage 1
        (require (only-in module
                   [id unsafe-id]))
        ; Stage 2
        (begin-for-syntax
         (add-type! #'id (parse-type #'ty)))
        ; Stage 3
        (define id
          (contract
           #,(type->contract
              (parse-type #'ty))
           unsafe-id
           (quote module)
           'typed-module)))]))
```

Figure 4: Import of Untyped Code

6. Safe Cross-Module Integration

A module in Typed Racket should have access to the large collection of untyped libraries in Racket. Conversely, our intention to support gradual refactoring of untyped into typed systems demands that typed modules can export bindings to untyped modules. However, untyped programs are potentially dangerous to the invariants of typed modules. To protect these invariants, we automatically generate run-time contracts from the types of imported and exported bindings (Tobin-Hochstadt and Felleisen 2006).

However, a large library of untyped modules is useless if each must be modified to work with typed modules. Therefore, our implementation must automatically wrap imports from untyped code, and protect exports to untyped code, *without* requiring changes to untyped modules. Further, communication between typed modules should not involve extra contract checks, since these invariants are enforced statically.

6.1 Imports from Untyped Modules

Typed Racket requires the programmer to specify the types of imports from untyped modules:

```
(require/typed file/md5
  [md5 (Bytes -> Bytes)])
```

This specification imports the `md5` procedure, which computes the MD5 hash of a byte sequence. The procedure can be used in typed code with the specified type, and the type is converted to a contract and attached to the procedure on import. This translation and interposition is implemented in the `require/typed` form; see figure 4 for an implementation for our `simple-type` language.

The implementation of `require/typed` works in three stages. Stage 1 imports the specified identifier, `id` from `module` under the new name `unsafe-id`. Stage 2 parses and adds the specified type to the table of types with `add-type!`. Finally, stage 3 defines the identifier `id` as a wrapper around `unsafe-id`. The wrapper is a generated contract and establishes a dynamically enforced agreement between the original module (named `module`) and the typed module (with the placeholder name).[3] The entire output is wrapped in `begin-ignored` so that the type checker does not process this meta-information.

In our example, we would now be able to use the `md5` function in typed code according to the specified type, getting a static type error if `md5` is applied to a number, for example. Conversely, if the

[3] In practice, type checking renders the domain contract superfluous.

`file/md5` library fails to return a byte string value, a dynamic contract error is produced, avoiding the possibility that the typed module might end up with a value that it did not expect.

6.2 Exports to Untyped Modules

Unlike imports into a typed module, exports from such a module pose a serious problem because the Typed Racket language implementation is not necessarily in control of the use site. After all, an exported identifier may be used in both typed *and* untyped contexts. Since typed modules statically verify that uses of typed identifiers accord with their types, no contracts are necessary for exports to such modules. In contrast, exports from typed to untyped modules require the insertion of dynamic checks to ensure type safety.

To implement this behavior without cloning every module, we adopt a novel two-stage module compilation strategy. First, each export is replaced with an indirection that chooses whether to reference the contracted or plain version of the exported binding. Second, the compilation of *typed* modules sets a flag inside the `#%module-begin` transformer before expansion of the module's contents; the exported indirections choose which version to reference based on this flag. Since each module is compiled with a fresh state, this flag is only set during the compilation of typed modules—untyped modules have no way to access it. Therefore, during the compilation of untyped modules, the export indirections correctly choose the contract-protected version of bindings. The compilation of typed modules, in contrast, see the set version of the flag and are able to use the uncontracted versions of bindings.

Implementation Exported identifiers are rewritten in the same stages as imported identifiers. Since this rewriting occurs *after* typechecking, however, it is performed by the `#%module-begin` form, just as declarations are added to exports:

```
(#%provide n) ; An export of n
; ==> (is rewritten to)
#'(begin
    ... the declaration from section 5 ...
    ; Stage 1
    (define defensive-n
      (contract
       #,(type->contract (typecheck #'n))
       n 'typed-module 'untyped-module))
    ; Stage 2
    (define-syntax (export-n stx)
      (if (unbox typed-context?)
          #'n #'defensive-n))
    ; Stage 3
    (provide (rename-out [export-n n])))
```

First, we define a `defensive` version of the identifier `n`, which uses a contract generated from the type of `n`. Second, we define an `export-n` version of the identifier `n`, which selects between `n` and `defensive-n` depenending on the value of `typed-context?`. Third, we provide `export-n` under the name `n`, making the indirection transparent to clients of the typed module.

The second part comes in the definition of the language:

```
(define-syntax (#%module-begin stx)
  (set-box! typed-context? #t)
  ... check and transform stx, as in figure 2 ...
  ... rewrite provides, as above ...)
```

The initial flag setting means that the expansion of the module, and in particular the expansion of the indirections imported from other typed modules, see the `typed-context?` flag as set to `#t`.

Finally, because the `typed-context?` flag is accessible only from the implementation of the `simple-type` language, it is simple to verify that the flag is only set to `#t` in the `#%module-begin` form. Therefore, the implementation can rely on this flag as an indicator, without the possibility that untyped code might be able to deceive the typechecker.

6.3 Scaling to Typed Racket

The full implementation of module integration in Typed Racket follows the strategy outlined. The major complication is the export of macros and other static information from typed modules. Since macros from typed modules can refer to internal identifiers not protected by contracts, expanding such macros in untyped modules could potentially allow untyped modules to violate the invariants of typed modules. Therefore, Typed Racket currently prevents macros defined in typed modules from escaping into untyped modules.

7. Optimization via Rewriting

Source-to-source transformations can express large classes of optimizations, which makes it possible to apply them in the front end of the compiler. With the right language extension mechanisms, we can express these transformations as libraries and use them to build competitive optimizers.

7.1 Compiler architecture

Since Typed Racket is built as a language extension of Racket and the Racket compiler is for an untyped language, Typed Racket has to apply typed optimizations before handing programs to the Racket compiler. In contrast, compilers for typed languages can keep track of types across all phases in the compiler and use them to guide optimizations. Hence, Typed Racket features a type-driven optimization pass after typechecking. This optimization pass transforms the code that the front end of Typed Racket generates, using the validated and still accessible type information.

To support realistic optimizers as libraries, the host language must provide ways for language extensions to communicate their results to the compiler's backend. As part of its language extension features, Racket exposes unsafe type-specialized primitives.[4] For instance, the `unsafe-fl+` primitive adds two floating-point numbers, but has undefined behavior when applied to anything else. These type-specialized primitives are more efficient than their generic equivalents; not only do these primitives avoid the run-time dispatch of generic operations, they also serve as signals to the Racket code generator to guide its unboxing optimizations.

Typed Racket's optimizer generates code that uses these primitives. In figure 5, we show an excerpt from the optimizer that specializes floating-point operations using rewrite rules; the optimizer rewrites uses of generic arithmetic operations on floating-point numbers to specialized operations.

7.2 Scaling to Typed Racket

Typed Racket uses the same techniques as the simple optimizer presented here, but applies a wider range of optimizations. It supports a number of floating-point specialization transformations, eliminates tag-checking made redundant by the typechecker and performs arity raising on functions with complex number arguments.

7.3 Results

Untyped Racket is already competitive among optimizing Scheme compilers. The addition of a type-driven optimizer makes a noticeable difference and makes it an even more serious contender.

We show the impact of our optimizer on micro-benchmarks taken from the Gabriel (1985) and Larceny (Clinger and Hansen 1994) benchmark suites and the Computer Language Benchmark Game,[5] as well as on large benchmarks: the pseudoknot (Hartel

[4] Initially these primitives were provided because some programmers wanted to hand-optimize code.

[5] `http://shootout.alioth.debian.org`

```
(define (optimize t)
  (syntax-parse t
    [(#%plain-app op:id e1:expr e2:expr)
     (with-syntax ([new-op (if (and (equal? FloatT (type-of #'e1))
                                    (equal? FloatT (type-of #'e2)))
                               (cond [(free-identifier=? #'op #'+) #'unsafe-fl+]
                                     [(free-identifier=? #'op #'-) #'unsafe-fl-]
                                     [else #'op])
                               #'op)])
       #`(#%plain-app new-op #,(optimize #'e1) #,(optimize #'e2)))]
    ... structurally recur on the other forms ...) )
```

Figure 5: The Optimizer

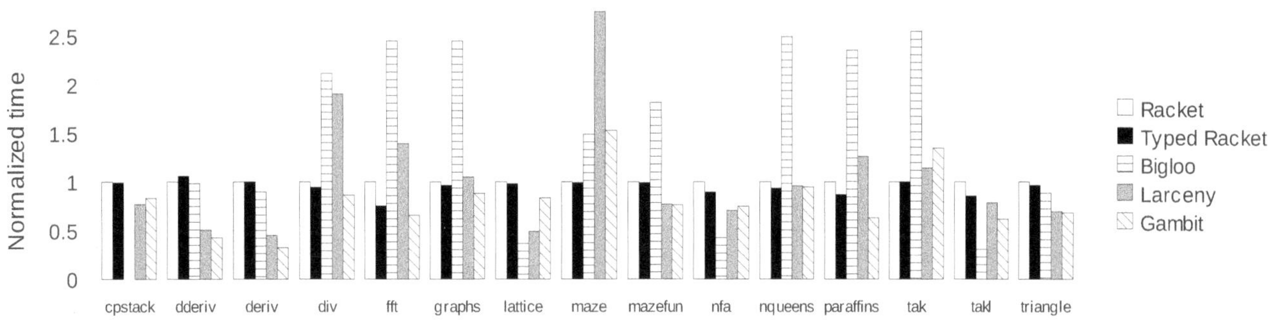

Figure 6: Results on the Gabriel and Larceny benchmarks (smaller is better)

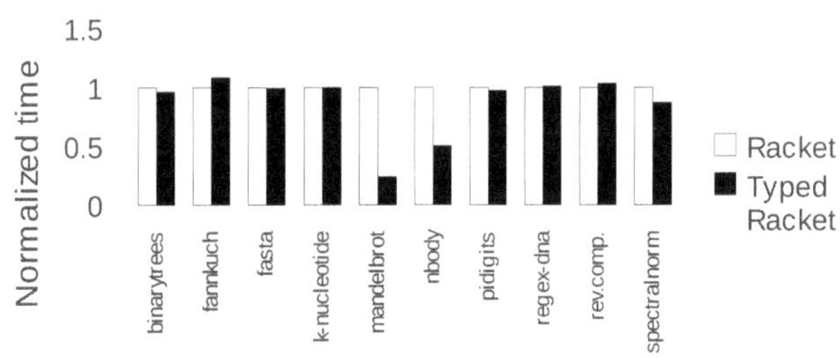

Figure 7: Results on the Computer Language Benchmark Game (smaller is better)

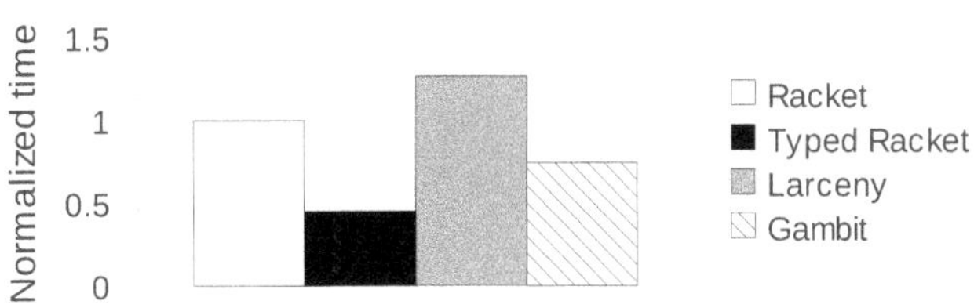

Figure 8: Results on pseudoknot (smaller is better)

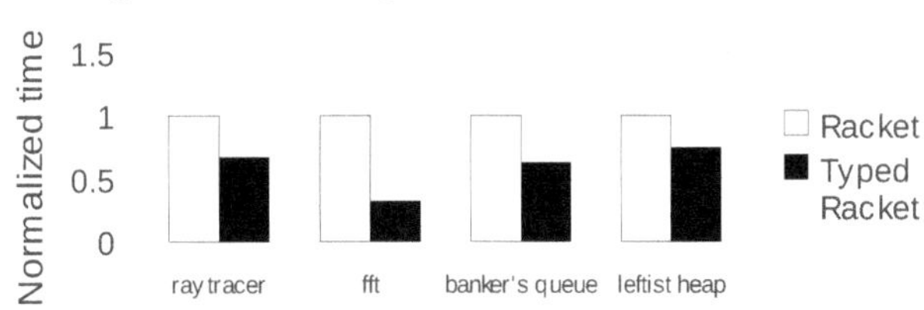

Figure 9: Results on large benchmarks (smaller is better)

et al. 1996) floating-point benchmark, a ray tracer, an industrial strength FFT and the implementation of two purely functional data structures (Prashanth and Tobin-Hochstadt 2010). Each benchmark comes in two versions: the original version and a translation to Typed Racket. The typed versions have type annotations and extra predicates where required to typecheck the program.

The typed version runs in Racket 5.0.2 using our type-driven optimizer and the untyped version in Racket 5.0.2, Gambit 4.6.0 (Feeley and Miller 1990), Larceny 0.97 (Clinger and Hansen 1994) and Bigloo 3.5a (Serrano and Weis 1995), using the highest safe optimization settings in each case. Benchmarks from the Computer Language Benchmarks Game and our sample applications use Racket-specific features and cannot be measured with other Scheme compilers. Bigloo fails to compile the `cpstack` and pseudoknot benchmarks. All our results are the average of 20 runs on a Dell Optiplex GX270 running GNU/Linux with 1GB of memory.

These benchmarks fall into two categories: benchmarks where Racket is already competitive with other well-known optimizing Scheme compilers, and benchmarks where Racket does not perform as well. In some cases where Racket is slower than the competition, Typed Racket's optimizer helps bridge the gap. For instance, it is responsible for a 33% speedup on the `fft` benchmark and a 123% speedup on pseudoknot. The large applications benefit even more from our optimizer than the microbenchmarks.

The results presented in this section demonstrate (a) that the Racket compiler and runtime are already competitive with leading compilers for Scheme, and (b) that Typed Racket's optimizer, written entirely as a library, nonetheless provides noticeable speedups on both widely-used benchmarks and existing Racket programs.

8. Related Work

While many individual aspects of our extensible language have long histories, some are novel and so is the combination as a whole. In this section, we sketch the history of each of these aspects.

8.1 Extensible Static Semantics

Macros have a long history in Lisp and Scheme (Kohlbecker 1986; Steele Jr. and Gabriel 1993; Dybvig et al. 1992). Several aspects of Racket's macro system improve on prior techniques.

First, the `#%module-begin` macro offers control over the entire module. Many Lisp programmers have approximated it with explicit wrappers. Second, many Lisp systems provide analogues of `local-expand` under the names `expand` or `macroexpand`. These features are more limited, however. Most importantly, they do not compose with other macros (Culpepper and Felleisen 2010). Third, Chez Scheme (Dybvig 2009) provides a `define-property` form, which simulates identifier-keyed tables for the same purposes described in section 5. Chez Scheme's form is less general than Racket's: while `define-property` would support Typed Racket's maintenance of type environments, it would not work for the interoperability mechanism described in section 6.2.

Fisher and Shivers (2006; 2008) present a system for handling analysis of programs written in an extensible language. Specifically, their system can implement static analyses, such as type systems, on top of extensible languages, without requiring the analysis to know about every possible language extension. The system employs a dispatch mechanism so that each extension can answer the static analysis question about its own use. This approach is extensible and expressive, but inherently unsound, because language extensions may provide analysis results that disagree with their runtime behavior. Our solution using `local-expand` relies on the inference of high-level properties from core forms and respects soundness, though it imposes limits on some macro uses in language extensions.

In the functional-logic programming world, the Ciao Prolog system (Hermenegildo et al. 2008) comes close to Racket. It also allows programmers to annotate their programs with new static assertions and to control when these assertions are checked. This strategy accommodates customizable static semantics and enabling new optimizations. In contrast to our system, Ciao builds the assertion language into the compiler, which furthers tight integration with its existing static analyzers and compiler, but prevents users from developing truly new semantics and whole program checking.

The ArBB and Rapidmind (Ghuloum et al. 2010) tools take the approach of embedding languages for novel execution models within C++. In contrast with the approach we present, their embedding demands the use of the C++ type system and necessitates the creation of ad-hoc replacements for fundamental language features such as 'if' and 'for' statements, thus limiting linguistic reuse. Additionally, because individual constructs see only a portion of the program, the scope for an analysis is necessarily local, in contrast to Typed Racket which can check an entire module.

8.2 Extensible Compilers

Since compilers are valuable and complex pieces of software, many projects have designed extensible compilers. Extensibility means that programmers can add front-ends, backends, optimizations, analyses, or other plug-ins (Bravenboer and Visser 2004; Cox et al. 2008; Nystrom et al. 2003; Bachrach and Playford 2001). All of these systems differ significantly from our implementation of a language as a library. First, they require interoperation at the level of the compiler rather than the language. Language extensions in Racket are implemented as Racket programs, operate on Racket programs, and produce Racket programs; they operate without any reliance on the details of the underlying compiler or runtime. This higher level of abstraction means that the compiler can be modified without breaking existing extensions, and extensions need not depend on the specialized representations and analyses in the compiler implementation.

Second, extensible compilers are not libraries in the same sense as ordinary libraries. Instead, they are plug-ins to a different application—the compiler, which may be written in a different language using a different architecture. This means compiler plugins cannot take advantage of the same library distribution mechanisms, debugging mechanisms, tools, and the rest of the software infrastructure around the language. This difference makes them both more difficult to develop and to use for programmers, thus limiting language experimentation.

8.3 Rewriting-based Optimization

The specific optimization techniques described in section 7 are not new to Typed Racket. Kelsey (1989) presents a transformational compiler that expresses optimizations as rewritings from the source language, an extended continuation-passing style lambda calculus, to itself. These transformations are encoded inside the compiler, however, which places them off-limits for programmers.

The Glasgow Haskell Compiler (Peyton Jones 1996) also expresses optimizations as rewrite rules. Unlike Kelsey's work, GHC makes it possible for programmers to supplement these rules with their own. To preserve safety, the compiler enforces that all rewrite rules must preserve types; that is the result of applying a rewrite rule must be of the same type as the original term. In contrast to Racket, the GHC rewrite rules are expressed in a limited domain-specific language.

It would be impossible to implement the arity-raising transformation mentioned in section 7.2 in the GHC rewriting framework; such optimizations are instead built in to GHC.

9. Conclusion

In *Growing a Language*, Steele writes "if we grow the language in these few ways, then we will not need to grow it in a hundred other ways; the users can take on the rest of the task." In this paper, we have explained how Racket's small number of language extensibility mechanisms empower the application programmer to grow even a highly sophisticated language. While these mechanisms continue the long tradition of Lisp and Scheme macros, they also go far beyond macros. Most importantly, Racket programmers can use `#%module-begin` to create libraries that process modules in a context-sensitive manner—without interfering with macros. Further, the syntax system can use attributed ASTs to communicate out-of-band information. As a result, programmers can interpolate context-sensitive analyses and source-based optimizations where the latter may exploit the result of the former.

One running example, Typed Racket, illustrates the range of Racket's extensibility mechanism. Specifically, the implementation of Typed Racket covers almost all aspects of language experimentation, from the front end to the back end. As our benchmarks demonstrate, the current backend of Typed Racket delivers competitive performance. What reduces the performance from "highly competitive" to just "competitive" is the lack of Racket APIs for processing intermediate representations and/or JIT compiler information. Until such APIs are available, compiler optimizations for language extensions remain limited to source-level transformations.

Acknowledgments

Robby Findler and Shriram Krishnamurthi have contributed to this design over many years. Numerous members of the Northeastern PRL provided feedback on earlier drafts of this paper. Mitch Wand suggested the title.

Bibliography

Jonathan Bachrach and Keith Playford. The Java syntactic extender. In *Proc. Conf. Object-Oriented Programming Systems, Languages, and Applications*, pp. 31–42, 2001.

Eli Barzilay and John Clements. Laziness Without All the Hard Work. In *Proc. Works. Functional and Declarative Programming in Education*, pp. 9–13, 2005.

Martin Bravenboer and Eelco Visser. Concrete syntax for objects: domain-specific language embedding and assimilation without restrictions. In *Proc. Conf. Object-Oriented Programming Systems, Languages, and Applications*, pp. 365–383, 2004.

John Clements, Matthias Felleisen, Robert Bruce Findler, Matthew Flatt, and Shriram Krishnamurthi. Fostering Little Languages. *Dr. Dobb's Journal*, pp. 16–24, 2004.

William D. Clinger and Lars Thomas Hansen. Lambda, the ultimate label or a simple optimizing compiler for Scheme. In *Proc. Conf. on LISP and functional programming*, pp. 128–139, 1994.

Russ Cox, Tom Bergan, Austin T. Clements, Frans Kaashoek, and Eddie Kohler. Xoc, an extension-oriented compiler for systems programming. In *Proc. Conf. Architectural Support for Programming Languages and Operating Systems*, pp. 244–254, 2008.

Ryan Culpepper and Matthias Felleisen. Debugging hygienic macros. *Science of Computer Programming* 75(7), pp. 496–515, 2010.

Ryan Culpepper and Matthias Felleisen. Fortifying macros. In *Proc. International Conf. on Functional Programming*, pp. 235–246, 2010.

Ryan Culpepper, Scott Owens, and Matthew Flatt. Syntactic abstraction in component interfaces. In *Proc. Conf. Generative Programming and Component Engineering*, pp. 373–388, 2005.

Ryan Culpepper, Sam Tobin-Hochstadt, and Matthias Felleisen. Advanced Macrology and the Implementation of Typed Scheme. In *Proc. Scheme and Functional Programming*, 2007.

R. Kent Dybvig. *Chez Scheme Version 8 User's Guide*. Cadence Research Systems, 2009.

R. Kent Dybvig, Robert Hieb, and Carl Bruggeman. Syntactic abstraction in Scheme. *Lisp and Symbolic Computation* 5(4), pp. 295–326, 1992.

Marc Feeley and James S. Miller. A parallel virtual machine for efficient Scheme compilation. In *Proc. Conf. on LISP and Functional Programming*, pp. 119–130, 1990.

Matthias Felleisen, Robert Bruce Findler, Matthew Flatt, and Shriram Krishnamurthi. Building Little Languages With Macros. *Dr. Dobb's Journal*, pp. 45–49, 2004.

David Fisher and Olin Shivers. Static semantics for syntax objects. In *Proc. International Conf. on Functional Programming*, pp. 111–121, 2006.

David Fisher and Olin Shivers. Building language towers with Ziggurat. *J. of Functional Programming* 18(5-6), pp. 707–780, 2008.

Matthew Flatt. Composable and compilable macros: you want it when? In *Proc. International Conf. on Functional Programming*, pp. 72–83, 2002.

Matthew Flatt, Eli Barzilay, and Robert Bruce Findler. Scribble: closing the book on ad-hoc documentation tools. In *Proc. International Conf. on Functional Programming*, pp. 109–120, 2009.

Matthew Flatt and Matthias Felleisen. Units: Cool modules for HOT languages. In *Proc. Conf. on Programming Language Design and Implementation*, pp. 236–248, 1998.

Matthew Flatt, Robert Bruce Findler, and Matthias Felleisen. Scheme with classes, mixins, and traits. In *Proc. Asian Symp. on Programming Languages and Systems*, pp. 270–289, 2006.

Matthew Flatt and PLT. Reference: Racket. PLT Inc., PLT-TR-2010-1, 2010. `http://racket-lang.org/tr1/`

Richard P. Gabriel. *Performance and Evaluation of LISP Systems*. MIT Press, 1985.

Anwar Ghuloum, Amanda Sharp, Noah Clemons, Stefanus Du Toit, Rama Malladi, Mukesh Gangadhar, Michael McCool, and Hans Pabst. Array Building Blocks: A Flexible Parallel Programming Model for Multicore and Many-Core Architectures. *Dr. Dobb's Journal*, 2010.

Pieter H. Hartel, Marc Feeley, Martin Alt, Lennart Augustsson, Peter Baumann, Marcel Beemster, Emmanuel Chailloux, Christine H. Flood, Wolfgang Grieskamp, John H. G. van Groningen, Kevin Hammond, Bogumił Hausman, Melody Y. Ivory, Richard E. Jones, Jasper Kamperman, Peter Lee, Xavier Leroy, Rafael D. Lins, Sandra Loosemore, Niklas Röjemo, Manuel Serrano, Jean-Pierre Talpin, Jon Thackray, Stephen Thomas, Pum Walters, Pierre Weis, and E.P. Wentworth. Benchmarking implementations of functional languages with "pseudoknot" a float-intensive benchmark. *J. of Functional Programming* 6(4), pp. 621–655, 1996.

Manuel V. Hermenegildo, Francisco Bueno, Manuel Carro, Pedro Lopez, José F. Morales, and German Puebla. An overview of the Ciao multiparadigm language and program development environment and its design philosophy. In *Concurrency, Graphs and Models*. Springer-Verlag, pp. 209–237, 2008.

Richard Andrew Kelsey. *Compilation by Program Transformation*. PhD dissertation, Yale University, 1989.

Eugene Kohlbecker. *Syntactic Extensions in the Programming Language Lisp*. PhD dissertation, Indiana University, 1986.

Shriram Krishnamurthi. *Linguistic Reuse*. PhD dissertation, Rice University, 2001.

Shriram Krishnamurthi, Peter Walton Hopkins, Jay McCarthy, Paul T. Graunke, Greg Pettyjohn, and Matthias Felleisen. Implementation and use of the PLT Scheme web server. *Higher-Order and Symbolic Computing* 20(4), pp. 431–460, 2007.

Simon Marlow. Haskell 2010 Language Report. 2010.

Robin Milner, Mads Tofte, Robert Harper, and David MacQueen. *The Definition of Standard ML, Revised Edition*. MIT Press, 1997.

Nathaniel Nystrom, Michael Clarkson, and Andrew Myers. Polyglot: an extensible compiler framework for Java. In *Proc. International Conf. on Compiler Construction*, pp. 138–152, 2003.

Simon L Peyton Jones. Compiling Haskell by program transformation a report from the trenches. In *Proc. European Symp. on Programming*, pp. 18–44, 1996.

Hari Prashanth K R and Sam Tobin-Hochstadt. Functional data structures for Typed Racket. In *Proc. Works. Scheme and Functional Programming*, pp. 1–7, 2010.

Manuel Serrano and Pierre Weis. Bigloo: a portable and optimizing compiler for strict functional languages. In *Proc. Static Analysis Symp.*, pp. 366–381, 1995.

Michael Sperber, Matthew Flatt, Anton Van Straaten, R. Kent Dybvig, Robert Bruce Findler, and Jacob Matthews. Revised^6 report on the algorithmic language Scheme. *J. of Functional Programming* 19(S1), pp. 1–301, 2009.

Guy L. Steele Jr. *Common Lisp: The Language*. Second edition. Digital Press, 1994.

Guy L. Steele Jr. Growing a language, Keynote at OOPSLA 1998. *Higher-Order and Symbolic Computation* 12(3), pp. 221–236, 1999.

Guy L. Steele Jr. and Richard P. Gabriel. The evolution of Lisp. In *Proc. Conf. on History of Programming Languages*, pp. 231–270, 1993.

T. Stephen Strickland, Sam Tobin-Hochstadt, and Matthias Felleisen. Practical Variable-Arity Polymorphism. In *Proc. European Symp. on Programming*, 2009.

Sam Tobin-Hochstadt and Matthias Felleisen. Interlanguage refactoring: from scripts to programs. In *Proc. Dynamic Languages Symp.*, pp. 964–974, 2006.

Sam Tobin-Hochstadt and Matthias Felleisen. The design and implementation of Typed Scheme. In *Proc. Symp. on Principles of Programming Languages*, pp. 395–406, 2008.

Sam Tobin-Hochstadt and Matthias Felleisen. Logical types for untyped languages. In *Proc. International Conf. on Functional Programming*, pp. 117–128, 2010.

Automatic CPU-GPU Communication Management and Optimization

Thomas B. Jablin Prakash Prabhu James A. Jablin †
Nick P. Johnson Stephen R. Beard David I. August

Princeton University, Princeton, NJ
{tjablin, pprabhu, npjohnso, sbeard, august}@cs.princeton.edu

†Brown University, Providence, RI
jjablin@cs.brown.edu

Abstract

The performance benefits of GPU parallelism can be enormous, but unlocking this performance potential is challenging. The applicability and performance of GPU parallelizations is limited by the complexities of CPU-GPU communication. To address these communications problems, this paper presents the first fully automatic system for managing and optimizing CPU-GPU communcation. This system, called the CPU-GPU Communication Manager (CGCM), consists of a run-time library and a set of compiler transformations that work together to manage and optimize CPU-GPU communication without depending on the strength of static compile-time analyses or on programmer-supplied annotations. CGCM eases manual GPU parallelizations and improves the applicability and performance of automatic GPU parallelizations. For 24 programs, CGCM-enabled automatic GPU parallelization yields a whole program geomean speedup of 5.36x over the best sequential CPU-only execution.

Categories and Subject Descriptors D.1.3 [*Programming Techniques*]: Concurrent Programming—Parallel Programming

General Terms Algorithms, Experimentation, Performance

Keywords GPU, communication, management, optimization

1. Introduction

Currently, even entry-level PCs are equipped with GPUs capable of hundreds of GFLOPS. Real applications, parallelized to take advantage of GPUs, regularly achieve speedups between 4x and 100x [8, 10, 20]. Unfortunately, parallelizing code for GPUs is difficult due to the typical CPU-GPU memory architecture. The GPU and CPU have separate memories, and each processing unit may efficiently access only its own memory. When programs running on the CPU or GPU need data-structures outside their memory, they must explicitly copy data between the divided CPU and GPU memories.

The process of copying data between these memories for correct execution is called *Managing Communication*. Generally, programmers manage CPU-GPU communication with `memcpy`-style functions. Manually managing CPU-GPU communication is tedious and error-prone. Aliasing pointers, variable sized arrays, jagged arrays, global pointers, and subversive typecasting make it difficult for programmers to copy the right data between CPU and GPU memories. Unfortunately, not all communication management is efficient; cyclic communication patterns are frequently orders of magnitude slower than acyclic patterns [15]. Transforming cyclic communication patterns to acyclic patterns is called *Optimizing Communication*. Naïvely copying data to GPU memory, spawning a GPU function, and copying the results back to CPU memory yields cyclic communication patterns. Copying data to the GPU in the preheader, spawning many GPU functions, and copying the result back to CPU memory in the loop exit yields an acyclic communication pattern. Incorrect communication optimization causes programs to access stale or inconsistent data.

This paper presents CPU-GPU Communication Manager (CGCM), the first fully automatic system for managing and optimizing CPU-GPU communication. Automatically managing and optimizing communication increases programmer efficiency and program correctness. It also improves the applicability and performance of automatic GPU parallelization.

CGCM manages and optimizes communication using two parts, a run-time library and a set of compiler passes. To manage communication, CGCM's run-time library tracks GPU memory allocations and transfers data between the CPU memory and GPU memory. The compiler uses the run-time library to manage and optimize CPU-GPU communication without strong analysis. By relying on the run-time library, the compiler postpones, until run-time, questions that are difficult or impossible to answer statically. Three novel compiler passes for communication optimization leverage the CGCM run-time: map promotion, alloca promotion, and glue kernels. Map promotion transforms cyclic CPU-GPU communication patterns into acyclic communication patterns. Alloca promotion and glue kernels improve the applicability of map promotion.

The contributions of CGCM over prior work are:

- The first fully automatic CPU-GPU communication *management* system.
- The first fully automatic CPU-GPU communication *optimization* system.

Figure 1 shows a taxonomy of CPU-GPU communication management techniques. No prior work fully automates CPU-GPU communication, but several semi-automatic techniques can manage communication if programmers supply annotations [12, 24, 26]. Some of these communication management techniques are strongly coupled with automatic parallelization systems [12, 24]; others are not [26]. None of the semi-automatic communication systems optimize CPU-GPU communications. Some prior automatic parallelization techniques require manual communication [3, 13, 25]. The earliest GPU parallelization systems feature manual parallelization and manual communication [6, 11, 16]. These systems remain the most popular. CGCM enables fully-automatic communication management for manual and automatic parallelizations.

Communication management is also a problem for distributed memory systems. Inspector-executor techniques automatically manage communication for distributed memory systems [4, 14, 22]

PLDI'11, June 4–8, 2011, San Jose, California, USA.

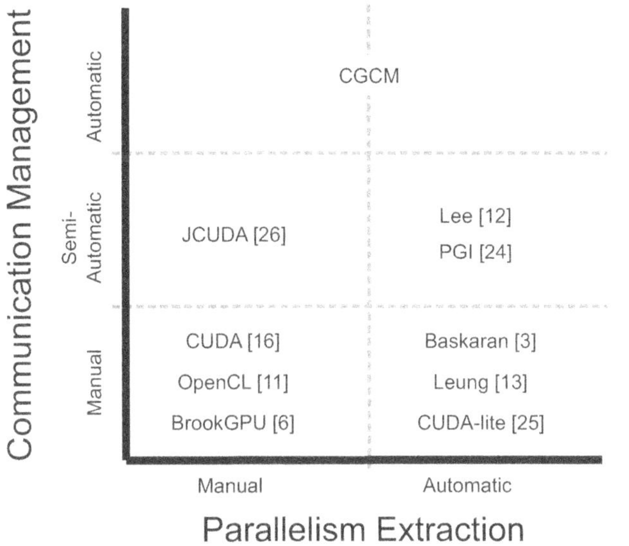

Figure 1. A taxonomy of related work showing automatic and manual communication and parallelization as independent axes.

but have not been used for CPU-GPU systems. Inspector-executor techniques can reduce the number of bytes transferred, but the overall communication pattern remains cyclic.

We have coupled CGCM with an automatic parallelizing compiler to produce a fully automatic GPU parallelization system. To compare a strong cyclic communication system against CGCM's acyclic communication, we adapted inspector-executor to GPUs. Across 24 programs, CGCM coupled with automatic parallelization shows a geomean whole program speedup of 5.36x over sequential CPU-only execution versus 0.92x for inspector-executor.

This paper provides a detailed description of the design and implementation of CGCM and presents an evaluation of the system. Section 2 describes background information about the challenges of CPU-GPU communications and limitations of related work. Section 3 describes the run-time support library. Section 4 explains how the compiler automatically inserts calls to the CGCM library. The map promotion, alloca promotion, and glue kernel techniques for optimizing CPU-GPU communication appear in Section 5. Section 6 interprets the performance results for 24 programs taken from the PARSEC [5], StreamIt [23], Rodinia [7], and PolyBench [17] benchmark suites. This section also compares CGCM to an idealized inspector-executor system. Section 7 discusses related work, and Section 8 concludes.

2. Motivation

The divided CPU-GPU memories create communication management and optimization difficulties that motivate CGCM. Managing communication means copying data between CPU and GPU memories to ensure each processing unit has the data it needs. Manual communication management is time-consuming and error-prone, and semi-automatic communication management in prior work has limited applicability. Optimizing communication means transforming communication patterns to remove cyclic dependencies. Optimizing communication is vital for program performance, but increases the difficulty of communication management. Lack of optimized communication limits the performance of prior semi-automatic communication management frameworks. CGCM is the first fully-automatic communication management and optimization system.

Listing 1: Manual explicit CPU-GPU memory management

```
char *h_h_array[M] = {
  "What so proudly we hailed at the twilight's last gleaming,",
  ...
};

__global__ void kernel(unsigned i, char **d_array);

void foo(unsigned N) {
  /* Copy elements from array to the GPU */
  char *h_d_array[M];
  for(unsigned i = 0; i < M; ++i) {
    size_t size = strlen(h_h_array[i]) + 1;
    cudaMalloc(h_d_array + i, size);
    cudaMemcpy(h_d_array[i], h_h_array[i], size,
               cudaMemcpyHostToDevice);
  }

  /* Copy array to the GPU */
  char **d_d_array;
  cudaMalloc(&d_d_array, sizeof(h_d_array));
  cudaMemcpy(d_d_array, h_d_array, sizeof(h_d_array),
             cudaMemcpyHostToDevice);

  for(unsigned i = 0; i < N; ++i)
    kernel<<<30, 128>>>(i, d_d_array);

  /* Free the array */
  cudaFree(d_d_array);

  /* Copy the elements back, and free the GPU copies */
  for(unsigned i = 0; i < M; ++i) {
    size_t size = strlen(h_h_array[i]) + 1;
    cudaMemcpy(h_h_array[i], h_d_array[i], size,
               cudaMemcpyDeviceToHost);
    cudaFree(h_d_array[i]);
  }
}
```

□ Useful work ▒ Communication ■ Kernel spawn

Listing 2: Automatic implicit CPU-GPU memory management

```
char *h_h_array[M] = {
  "What so proudly we hailed at the twilight's last gleaming,",
  ...
};

__global__ void kernel(unsigned i, char **d_array);

void foo(unsigned N) {
  for(unsigned i = 0; i < N; ++i) {
    kernel<<<30, 128>>>(i, h_h_array);
  }
}
```

□ Useful work ▒ Communication ■ Kernel spawn

2.1 Communication Management

Communication management presents a major difficulty for manual and automatic GPU parallelizations. Current GPU programming languages, such as CUDA and OpenCL, require manual communication management using primitive `memcpy`-style functions.

Framework	Comm. Opti.	Requires Annotations	Applicability						Acyclic Communication
			CPU-GPU	Aliasing Pointers	Irregular Accesses	Weak Type Systems	Pointer Arithmetic	Max Indirection	
JCUDA [26]	×	Yes	✓	✓	✓	×	×	∞	No
Named Regions [12]	×	Yes	✓	✓	×	✓	×	1	No
Affine [24]	×	Yes	✓	×	×	✓	×	1	With Annotation
Inspector-Executor [4, 14, 22]	×	Yes	×	×	✓	✓	×	1	No
CGCM	✓	No	✓	✓	✓	✓	✓	2	After Optimization

Table 1. Comparison between communication systems

Manually copying complex data-types from CPU memory to GPU memory is tedious and error-prone. Listing 1 shows how a CUDA programmer might copy an array of strings to and from the GPU, allocating and freeing memory as necessary. Almost every line of code in the listing involves communication management and not useful computation. Furthermore, the programmer must manage buffers and manipulate pointers. Buffer management and pointer manipulation are well-known sources of bugs.

Automatic communication management avoids the difficulties of buffer management and pointer manipulation, improving program correctness and programmer efficiency. However, automatically managing communication based on compile-time static analysis is impossible for general C and C++ programs. In C and C++, any argument to a GPU function could be cast to a pointer, and an opaque pointer could point to the middle of data-structures of arbitrary size. Prior work restricts its applicability to avoid these difficulties [12, 24, 26].

Table 1 compares the applicability of prior communication management techniques. Prior GPU techniques [12, 24, 26] require programmer annotations, do not handle the full generality of pointer arithmetic and aliasing, create cyclic CPU-GPU communication patterns by default, and do not optimize communication. Consequently, prior automatic communication management techniques have limited applicability and frequently yield poor performance. To gain acceptance in the GPU programming community, automatic communication management techniques must overcome these limitations.

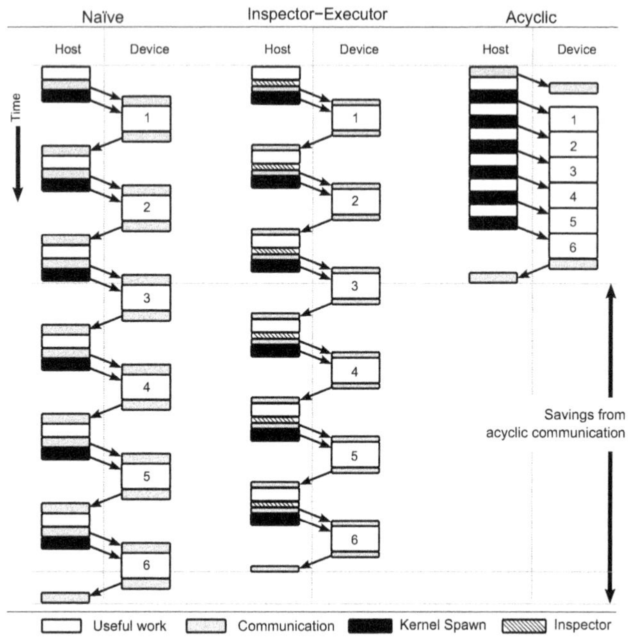

Figure 2. Execution schedules for naïve cyclic, inspector-executor, and acyclic communication patterns

2.2 Communication Optimization

Figure 2 shows execution schedules for three communication patterns: a naïve cyclic pattern, an inspector-executor pattern, and an acyclic pattern. In the naïve schedule, data transfers to and from GPU memory create cyclic dependencies, forcing the CPU and GPU to wait for each other. GPU programmers understand cyclic dependencies dramatically increase execution time. Nevertheless, all prior automatic GPU communication systems generate cyclic communication [12, 24, 26]. Cyclic communication patterns prevent these systems from efficiently parallelizing complex programs that launch many GPU functions.

Inspector-executor systems manage communication in clusters with distributed memory [4, 14, 22]. The inspector-executor approach breaks loops into an inspector, a scheduler, and an executor. The inspector simulates the loop to determine which array offsets the program reads or writes during each iteration. After the inspection, a scheduler assigns loop iterations to cluster nodes and transfers the appropriate data. Executors on each cluster node compute loop iterations in parallel. The inspector-executor schedule in Figure 2 outperforms the naïve communication schedule because the benefit of communicating only the needed array elements exceeds the cost of the inspection. However, in real programs the cost of sequential inspection may exceed the benefits of parallel execution. Generally, inspector-executor is cyclic since it transfers only the needed bytes for a single iteration at a time. Acyclic inspector-executor variants require annotations or strong static analysis [18, 21].

Figure 2 shows the execution schedule for acyclic CPU-GPU communications. Removing cyclic communication avoids the latency of back-and-forth communication and allows the CPU and GPU to work in parallel. The performance benefit of acyclic communication is significant.

2.3 Overview

CGCM avoids the limitations of prior work by employing a run-time support library and an optimizing compiler to automatically manage and optimize CPU-GPU communication, respectively. The run-time library determines the size and shape of data-structures during execution. The compiler uses the run-time library to manage memory without strong analysis and then optimizes communications to produce acyclic patterns. CGCM has two restrictions:

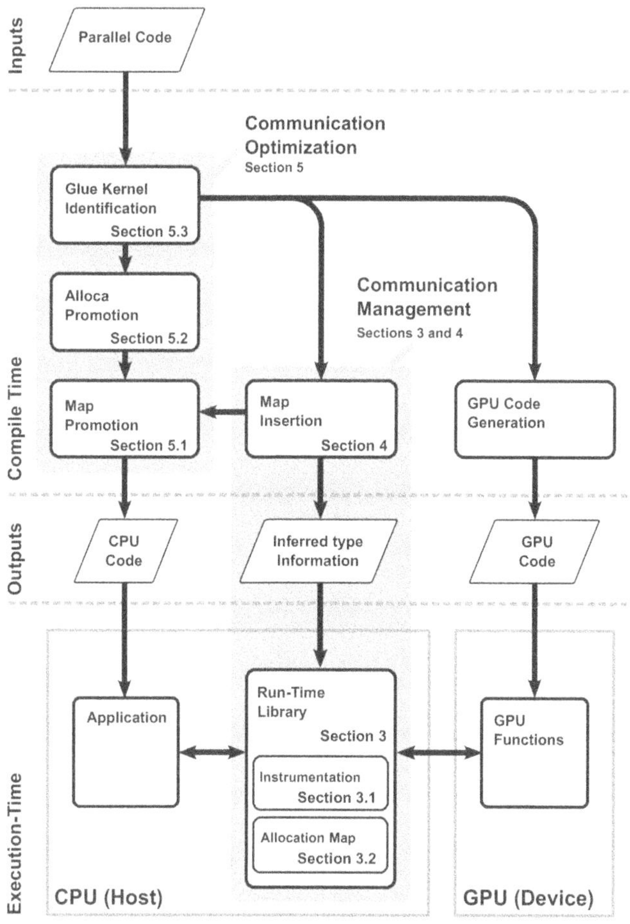

Figure 3. High-level overview of CGCM

CGCM does not support pointers with three or more degrees of indirection, and it does not allow pointers to be stored in GPU functions. Using CGCM, programmers can write the example code in Listing 1 as Listing 2. Replacing explicit CPU-GPU communication with CGCM yields dramatically shorter, simpler, clearer code and prevents several classes of programmer error.

Figure 3 shows a high-level overview of CGCM's transformation and run-time system. The run-time library provides *mapping* functions which translate CPU pointers to equivalent GPU pointers (Section 3). The compiler inserts mapping functions to manage CPU-GPU communication (Section 4). Map promotion optimizes CPU-GPU communication by transferring data to the GPU early and keeping it there as long as possible (Section 5). Two enabling transformations, glue kernels and allocation promotion, improve map promotion's applicability.

3. Run-Time Library

The CGCM run-time library enables automatic CPU-GPU communication management and optimization for programs with complex patterns of memory allocation and unreliable typing. To accomplish this feat, the run-time library correctly and efficiently determines which bytes to transfer. For correctness, the run-time library copies data to the GPU at *allocation unit* granularity. A pointer's allocation unit comprises all bytes reachable from a pointer by valid pointer arithmetic. Using the concept of allocation units, the run-time library can support the full semantics of pointer arithmetic without strong static analysis. A one-to-one mapping between allocation units in CPU memory and allocation units in GPU memory allows the run-time library to translate pointers.

3.1 Tracking Allocation Units

Unlike inspector-executor systems which manage memory on a per-byte or per-word granularity, CGCM manages memory at the granularity of *allocation units*. CGCM determines which bytes to transfer by finding allocation information for opaque pointers to the stack, heap, and globals. In C and C++, an allocation unit is a contiguous region of memory allocated as a single unit. Blocks of memory returned from `malloc` or `calloc`, local variables, and global variables are all examples of allocation units. All bytes in an array of structures are considered part of the same allocation unit, but two structures defined consecutively are different allocation units. Transferring entire allocation units between CPU and GPU memories ensures that valid pointer arithmetic yields the same results on the CPU and GPU, because the C99 programming standard [1] stipulates that pointer arithmetic outside the bounds of a single allocation unit is undefined.

Copying an allocation unit between CPU and GPU memories requires information about the allocation unit's base and size. The run-time library stores the base and size of each allocation unit in a self-balancing binary tree map indexed by the base address of each allocation unit. To determine the base and size of a pointer's allocation unit, the run-time library finds the greatest key in the *allocation map* less than or equal to the pointer. Although allocation information for global variables is known at compile-time, stack and heap allocations change dynamically at run-time. The run-time library uses different techniques to track the allocation information for global, stack, and heap memory.

- To track global variables, the compiler inserts calls to the run-time library's `declareGlobal` function before `main`. Declaring addresses at run-time rather than at compile-time or link-time avoids the problems caused by position independent code and address space layout randomization.
- To track heap allocations, the run-time library wraps around `malloc`, `calloc`, `realloc`, and `free`. These wrappers modify the allocation map to reflect the dynamic state of the heap at run-time.
- To track escaping stack variables, the compiler inserts calls to `declareAlloca`. The registration expires when the stack variable leaves scope.

3.2 CPU-GPU Mapping Semantics

Table 2 lists each function in the run-time library and its arguments. The run-time library contains functions that translate between CPU and GPU pointers. The three basic functions are `map`, `release`, and `unmap`. Each of these functions operates on opaque pointers to CPU memory.

- *Mapping* a pointer from CPU to GPU memory copies the corresponding allocation unit to GPU memory, allocating memory if necessary. The run-time library employs reference counting to deallocate GPU memory when necessary. Mapping a pointer from CPU to GPU memory increases the GPU allocation unit's reference count.
- *Unmapping* a CPU pointer updates the CPU allocation unit with the corresponding GPU allocation unit. To avoid redundant communication, the run-time library will not copy data if the CPU allocation unit is already up-to-date. Since only a GPU function can modify GPU memory, `unmap` updates each allocation unit at most once after each GPU function invocation.
- *Releasing* a CPU pointer decreases the corresponding GPU allocation unit's reference count, freeing it if necessary.

Function prototype	Description
`map(ptr)`	Maps from host to device pointer, allocating and copying memory if necessary. Increases the allocation unit's reference count.
`unmap(ptr)`	Maps to host memory if the allocation unit's epoch is not current. Updates the allocation unit's epoch.
`release(ptr)`	Decreases the reference count of the allocation unit. If the reference count is zero, frees resources.
`mapArray(ptr)`	Maps from host to device pointer, allocating and copying memory if necessary. Increases the allocation unit's reference count.
`unmapArray(ptr)`	Maps to host memory if the allocation unit's epoch is not current. Updates the allocation unit's epoch.
`releaseArray(ptr)`	Decreases the reference count of the allocation unit. If the reference count is zero, frees resources.
`declareAlloca(size)`	Allocates memory on the stack and registers it with the run-time library.
`declareGlobal(name,ptr,size,isReadOnly)`	Registers a global with the run-time library.

Table 2. CGCM's run-time library interface

Listing 3: Listing 2 after the compiler inserts run-time functions (unoptimized CGCM).

```
  char *h_h_array[M] = {
    "What so proudly we hailed at the twilight's last gleaming,",
    ...
  };

□ __global__ void kernel(unsigned i, char **d_array);

  void foo(unsigned N) {
□   for(unsigned i = 0; i < N; ++i) {
▒     char **d_d_array = mapArray(h_h_array);
■     kernel<<<30, 128>>>(i, d_d_array);
▒     unmapArray(h_h_array);
▒     releaseArray(h_h_array);
    }
  }
```

□ Useful work ▒ Communication ■ Kernel spawn

Each of the primary run-time library functions has an array variant. The array variants of the run-time library functions have the same semantics as their non-array counterparts but operate on doubly indirect pointers. The array mapping function translates each CPU memory pointer in the original array into a GPU memory pointer in a new array. It then maps the new array to GPU memory. Using run-time library calls, Listing 2 can be rewritten as Listing 3.

3.3 Implementation

The `map`, `unmap`, and `release` functions provide the basic functionality of the run-time library. The array variations follow the same patterns as the scalar versions.

Algorithm 1 is the pseudo-code for the `map` function. Given a pointer to CPU memory, `map` returns the corresponding pointer to GPU memory. The `allocaInfoMap` contains information about the pointer's allocation unit. If the reference count of the allocation unit is non-zero, then the allocation unit is already on the GPU.

Algorithm 1: Pseudo-code for `map`

Require: ptr is a CPU pointer
Ensure: Returns an equivalent GPU pointer
info ← greatestLTE(allocInfoMap, ptr)
if info.refCount = 0 **then**
  if ¬info.isGlobal **then**
    info.devptr ← cuMemAlloc(info.size)
  else
    info.devptr ← cuModuleGetGlobal(info.name)
  cuMemcpyHtoD(info.devptr, info.base, info.size)
info.refCount ← info.refCount + 1
return info.devptr + (ptr − info.base)

Algorithm 2: Pseudo-code for `unmap`

Require: ptr is a CPU pointer
Ensure: Update ptr with GPU memory
info ← greatestLTE(allocInfoMap, ptr)
if info.epoch ≠ globalEpoch ∧ ¬info.isReadOnly **then**
  cuMemcpyDtoH(base, info.devptr, info.size)
info.epoch ← globalEpoch

When copying heap or stack allocation units to the GPU, `map` dynamically allocates GPU memory, but global variables must be copied into their associated named regions. The `map` function calls `cuModuleGetGlobal` with the global variable's name to get the variable's address in GPU memory. After increasing the reference count, the function returns the equivalent pointer to GPU memory.

The `map` function preserves aliasing relations in GPU memory, since multiple calls to `map` for the same allocation unit yield pointers to a single corresponding GPU allocation unit. Aliases are common in C and C++ code and alias analysis is undecidable. By handling pointer aliases in the run-time library, the compiler avoids static analysis, simplifying implementation and improving applicability.

Algorithm 3: Pseudo-code for `release`

```
Require: ptr is a CPU pointer
Ensure: Release GPU resources when no longer used
info ← greatestLTE(allocInfoMap, ptr)
info.refCount ← info.refCount − 1
if info.refCount = 0 ∧ ¬info.isGlobal then
    cuMemFree(info.devptr)
```

The pseudo-code for the `unmap` function is presented in Algorithm 2. Given a pointer to CPU memory, `unmap` updates CPU memory with the latest state of GPU memory. If the run-time library has not updated the allocation unit since the last GPU function call and the allocation unit is not in read only memory, `unmap` copies the GPU's version of the allocation unit to CPU memory. To determine if the CPU allocation unit is up-to-date, `unmap` maintains an epoch count which increases every time the program launches a GPU function. It is sufficient to update CPU memory from the GPU just once per epoch, since only GPU functions alter GPU memory.

Algorithm 3 is the pseudo-code for the `release` function. Given a pointer to CPU memory, `release` decrements the GPU allocation's reference count and frees the allocation if the reference count reaches zero. The `release` function does not free global variables when their reference count reaches zero. Just as in CPU codes, it is not legal to free a global variable.

4. Communication Management

CPU-GPU communication is a common source of errors for manual parallelization and limits the applicability of automatic parallelization. A CGCM compiler pass uses the run-time library to automatically manage CPU-GPU communications. For each GPU function spawn, the compiler determines which values to transfer to the GPU using a liveness analysis. When copying values to the GPU, the compiler must differentiate between integers and floating point values, pointers, and indirect pointers. The C and C++ type systems are fundamentally unreliable, so the compiler uses simple type-inference instead.

The communication management compiler pass starts with sequential CPU codes calling parallel GPU codes without any CPU-GPU communication. All global variables share a single common namespace with no distinction between GPU and CPU memory spaces. For each GPU function, the compiler creates a list of live-in values. A value is live-in if it is passed to the GPU function directly or is a global variable used by the GPU.

The C and C++ type systems are insufficient to determine which live-in values are pointers or to determine the indirection level of a pointer. The compiler ignores these types and instead infers type based on usage within the GPU function, ignoring usage in CPU code. If a value "flows" to the address operand of a load or store, potentially through additions, casts, sign extensions, or other operations, the compiler labels the value a pointer. Similarly, if the result of a load operation "flows" to another memory operation, the compiler labels the pointer operand of the load a double pointer. Since types flow through pointer arithmetic, the inference algorithm is field insensitive. Determining a value's type based on use allows the compiler to circumvent the problems of the C and C++ type systems. The compiler correctly determined unambiguous types for all of the live-in values to GPU functions in the 24 programs measured.

For each live-in pointer to each GPU function, the compiler transfers data to the GPU by inserting calls to `map` or `mapArray`. After the GPU function call, the compiler inserts a call for each live-out pointer to `unmap` or `unmapArray` to transfer data back to the CPU. Finally, for each live-in pointer, the compiler inserts a call to `release` or `releaseArray` to release GPU resources.

Algorithm 4: Pseudo-code for map promotion

```
forall region ∈ Functions ∪ Loops do
    forall candidate ∈ findCandidates(region) do
        if ¬pointsToChanges(candidate, region) then
            if ¬modOrRef(candidate, region) then
                copy(above(region), candidate.map)
                copy(below(region), candidate.unmap)
                copy(below(region), candidate.release)
                deleteAll(candidate.DtoH)
```

Listing 4: Listing 3 after map promotion

```
   char *h_h_array[M] = {
     "What so proudly we hailed at the twilight's last gleaming,",
     ...
   };

□  __global__ void kernel(unsigned i, char **d_array);

   void foo(unsigned N) {
▒    mapArray(h_h_array);
□    for(unsigned i = 0; i < N; ++i) {
▒      char **d_d_array = mapArray(h_h_array);
■      kernel<<<30, 128>>>(i, d_d_array);
▒      releaseArray(h_h_array);
     }
▒    mapArray(h_h_array);
▒    releaseArray(h_h_array);
   }
```

□ Useful work ▒ Communication ■ Kernel spawn

5. Optimizing CPU-GPU Communication

Optimizing CPU-GPU communication has a profound impact on program performance. The overall optimization goal is to avoid cyclic communication. Cyclic communication causes the CPU to wait for the GPU to transfer memory and the GPU to wait for the CPU to send more work. The map promotion compiler pass manipulates calls to the run-time library to remove cyclic communication patterns. After map promotion, programs transfer memory to the GPU, then spawn many GPU functions. For most of the program, Communication flows one way, from CPU to GPU. The results of GPU computations return to CPU memory only when absolutely necessary. The alloca promotion and glue kernels compiler passes improve the applicability of map promotion.

5.1 Map Promotion

The overall goal of map promotion is to hoist run-time library calls out of loop bodies and up the call graph. Algorithm 4 shows the pseudo-code for the map promotion algorithm.

First, the compiler scans the region for promotion candidates. A region is either a function or a loop body. Each promotion candidate captures all calls to the CGCM run-time library featuring the same pointer. Map promotion attempts to prove that these pointers point to the same allocation unit throughout the region, and that the allocation unit is not referenced or modified in the region. If successful, map promotion hoists the mapping operations out of the target region. The specific implementation varies slightly depending on whether the region is a loop or a function.

For a loop, map promotion copies `map` calls before the loop, moves `unmap` after the loop, and copies `release` calls after the loop. Map promotion copies the `map` calls rather than moving them since these calls provide CPU to GPU pointer translation. Copying `release` calls preserves the balance of map and release operations. Inserting `map` calls before the loop may require copying some code from the loop body before the loop.

For a function, the compiler finds all the function's parents in the call graph and inserts the necessary calls before and after the call instructions in the parent functions. Some code from the original function may be copied to its parent in order to calculate the pointer earlier.

The compiler iterates to convergence on the map promotion optimization. In this way, map operations can gradually climb up the call graph. Recursive functions are not eligible for map promotion in the present implementation.

CGCM optimizes Listing 3 to Listing 4. Promoting the initial `mapArray` call above the loop causes the run-time library to transfer `h_h_array`'s allocation units to the GPU exactly once. The subsequent calls to `mapArray` inside the loop do not cause additional communication since the GPU version of the allocation units is already active. Moving the `unmapArray` call below the loop allows the run-time to avoid copying allocation units back to CPU memory each iteration. The optimized code avoids all GPU to CPU communication inside the loop. Spawning GPU functions from the CPU is the only remaining communication inside the loop. The final result is an acyclic communication pattern with information only flowing from CPU to GPU during the loop.

5.2 Alloca Promotion

Map promotion cannot hoist a local variable above its parent function. Alloca promotion hoists local allocation up the call graph to improve map promotions applicability. Alloca promotion preallocates local variables in their parents' stack frames, allowing the map operations to climb higher in the call graph. The alloca promotion pass uses similar logic to map promotion, potentially copying code from child to parent to calculate the size of the local variable earlier. Like map promotion, alloca promotion iterates to convergence.

5.3 Glue Kernels

Sometimes small CPU code regions between two GPU functions prevent map promotion. The performance of this code is inconsequential, but transforming it into a single-threaded GPU function obviates the need to copy the allocation units between GPU and CPU memories and allows the map operations to rise higher in the call graph. The glue kernel optimization detects small regions of code that prevent map promotion using alias analysis and lowers this code to the GPU.

Interrelationships between communication optimization passes imply a specific compilation schedule. Since alloca promotion and glue kernels improve the applicability of map promotion, the compiler schedules these passes before map promotion. The glue kernel pass can force some virtual registers into memory, creating new opportunities for alloca promotion. Therefore, the glue kernel optimization runs before alloca promotion, and map promotion runs last.

6. Evaluation

CGCM is applicable to all 101 DOALL loops found by a simple automatic DOALL parallelizer across a selection of 24 programs drawn from the PolyBench [17], Rodinia [7], StreamIt [23], and PARSEC [5] benchmark suites. The named region technique [12] and inspector-executor [4, 14, 22] were only applicable to 80. Without communication optimizations, many programs show limited speedup or even dramatic slowdown with automatic communication management. By optimizing communication, CGCM enables a whole program geomean speedup of 5.36x over best sequential CPU-only execution.

6.1 Experimental Platform

The performance baseline is an Intel Core 2 Quad clocked at 2.40 GHz with 4MB of L2 cache. The Core 2 Quad is also the host CPU for the GPU. All GPU parallelizations were executed on an NVIDIA GeForce GTX 480 video card, a CUDA 2.0 device with 1,536 MB of global memory and clocked at 1.40 GHz. The GTX 480 has 15 streaming multiprocessors with 32 CUDA cores each, for a total of 480 cores. The CUDA driver version is 3.2 release candidate 2.

The parallel GPU version is always compared with the original single threaded C or C++ implementation running on the CPU, even when multithreaded CPU implementations are available. All figures show whole program speedups, not kernel or loop speedups. All program codes are compiled without any alterations.

The sequential baseline compilations are performed by the clang compiler version 2.9 (trunk 118020) at optimization level three. The clang compiler produced SSE vectorized code for the sequential CPU-only compilation. The clang compiler at optimization level three does not use automatic parallelization techniques beyond simple vectorization.

The nvcc compiler release 3.2, V0.2.1221 compiled all CUDA C and C++ programs using optimization level three.

CGCM uses the same performance flags to manage and optimize communication for all programs. The optimizer runs the same passes with the same parameters in the same order for every program. A simple DOALL GPU parallelization system coupled with CGCM and an open source PTX backend [19] performed all automatic parallelizations.

6.2 Benchmark Suites

PolyBench [2, 9] is a suite composed of programs designed to evaluate implementations of the polyhedral model of DOALL parallelism in automatic parallelizing compilers. Prior work on automatic GPU parallelization reports impressive performance on kernel-type micro-benchmarks without communication optimization. The `jacobi-2d-imper`, `gemm`, and `seidel` programs have been popular targets for evaluating automatic GPU parallelization systems [3, 12]. The simple DOALL parallelizer found opportunities in all of the PolyBench programs, and CGCM managed communication for all GPU functions. Figure 4 shows performance results for the entire PolyBench suite.

The Rodinia suite consists of 12 programs with CPU and GPU implementations. The CPU implementations contain OpenMP pragmas, but CGCM and the DOALL parallelizer ignore them. The simple DOALL parallelizer found opportunities in six of the 12 Rodinia programs and from one selected program from the PARSEC and StreamIt benchmark suites. CGCM managed communications for all functions generated by the DOALL parallelizer. The StreamIt benchmark suite features pairs of applications written in C and the StreamIt parallel programming language. PARSEC consists of OpenMP parallelized programs for shared memory systems. The eight applications from Rodinia, StreamIt, and PARSEC are larger and more realistic than the PolyBench programs.

6.3 Results

Figure 4 shows whole program speedup over sequential CPU-only execution for inspector-executor, unoptimized CGCM, opti-

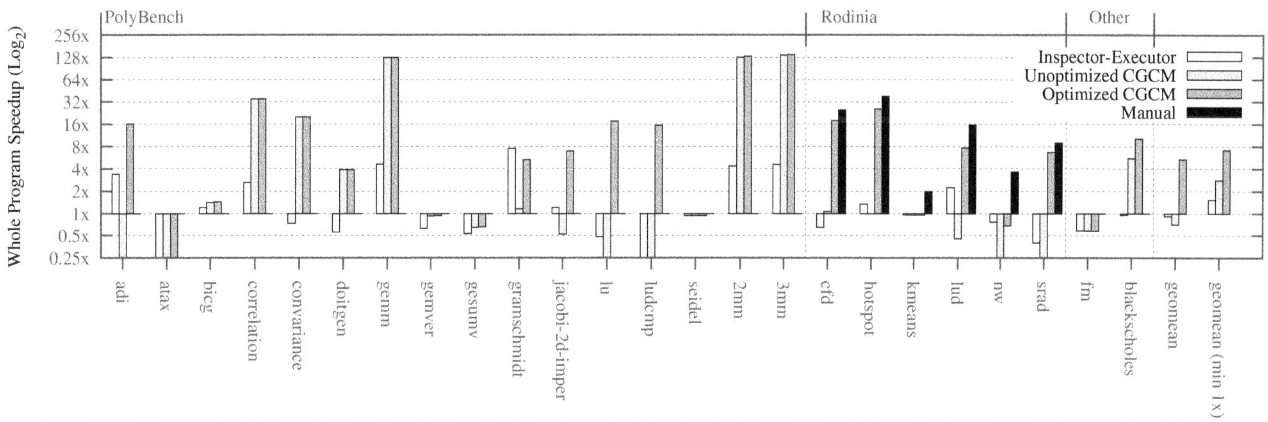

Figure 4. Whole program speedup of inspector-executor, unoptimized CGCM, optimized CGCM, and manual parallelizations over sequential CPU-only execution.

Program	Suite	Limiting Factor	Performance Study				Applicability Study				Manual Prior Work
			GPU		Communication		Total Kernels	CGCM	Inspector-Executor	Named Regions	
			UnOpti.	Opti.	UnOpti.	Opti.					
adi	PolyBench	GPU	0.02%	100.00%	99.98%	0.00%	7	7	7	7	
atax	PolyBench	Comm.	0.28%	0.28%	98.20	98.44%	3	3	3	3	
bicg	PolyBench	Comm.	4.36%	4.46%	72.38%	74.15%	2	2	2	2	
correlation	PolyBench	GPU	87.49%	87.39%	10.17%	10.12%	5	5	5	5	
covariance	PolyBench	GPU	77.12%	77.28%	18.61%	18.43%	4	4	4	4	
doitgen	PolyBench	GPU	87.48%	87.52%	11.29%	11.20%	3	3	3	3	
gemm	PolyBench	GPU	73.49%	73.76%	19.69%	19.49%	4	4	4	4	
gemver	PolyBench	Comm.	4.06%	4.10%	88.21%	89.36%	5	5	5	5	
gesummv	PolyBench	Comm.	6.17%	6.29%	86.17%	86.74%	2	2	2	2	
gramschmidt	PolyBench	Comm.	1.82%	8.37%	98.18%	90.91%	3	3	3	3	
jacobi-2d-imper	PolyBench	GPU	7.20%	95.97%	92.82%	3.32%	3	3	3	3	
seidel	PolyBench	Other	0.01%	0.01%	0.59%	0.59%	1	1	1	1	
lu	PolyBench	GPU	0.41%	88.05%	99.59%	7.02%	3	3	2	2	
ludcmp	PolyBench	GPU	1.23%	87.38%	98.10%	4.13%	5	5	3	3	
2mm	PolyBench	GPU	75.53%	77.25%	17.96%	18.25%	7	7	7	7	
3mm	PolyBench	GPU	78.75%	79.29%	17.86%	17.85%	10	10	10	10	
cfd	Rodinia	GPU	4.65%	77.96%	85.90%	0.16%	9	9	3	3	[7]
hotspot	Rodinia	GPU	2.78%	71.57%	92.60%	0.89%	2	2	1	1	[7]
kmeans	Rodinia	Other	0.65%	0.00%	10.84%	0.05%	2	2	2	2	[7]
lud	Rodinia	GPU	3.77%	63.57%	91.56%	0.39%	6	6	1	1	[7]
nw	Rodinia	Other	0.00%	2.44%	100.00%	24.19%	4	4	2	2	[7]
srad	Rodinia	Other	0.00%	27.08%	100.00%	6.20%	6	6	1	1	[7]
fm	StreamIt	Other	0.00%	0.00%	0.00%	0.00%	4	4	4	4	
blackscholes	PARSEC	Other	1.74%	3.23%	45.84%	0.96%	1	1	0	0	

Table 3. Summary of program characteristics including: program suite, limiting factor for performance, the contributions of GPU and communication time to total execution time as a percentage, the number of applicable kernels for the CGCM, Inspector-Executor, and Named Region management techniques, and a citation for prior manual parallelizations.

mized CGCM, and a manual parallelization if one exists. The figure's y-axis starts at 0.25x, although some programs have lower speedups. Table 3 shows additional details for each program. The geomean whole program speedups over sequential CPU only execution across all 24 applications are 0.92x for inspector-executor, 0.71x for unoptimized CGCM, and 5.36x for optimized CGCM. Taking the greater of 1.0x or the performance of each application yields geomeans of 1.53x for inspector-executor, 2.81x for unoptimized CGCM, and 7.18x for optimized CGCM.

Before optimization, most programs show substantial slowdown. The `srad` program has a slowdown of 4,437x and `nw` has a slowdown of 1,126x. By contrast, `ludcmp`'s slowdown is only 4.54x. After optimization, most programs show performance improvements and none have worse performance. However, several fail to surpass the CPU-only sequential versions. For comparison, we simulate an idealized inspector-executor system. The inspector-executor system has an oracle for scheduling and transfers exactly one byte between CPU and GPU for each accessed allocation unit. A compiler creates the inspector from the original loop [4]. To measure performance ignoring applicability constraints, the inspector-executor simulation ignores its applicability guard. CGCM outperforms this idealized inspector-executor system. The disadvantages of sequential inspection and frequent synchronization were not overcome by transferring dramatically fewer bytes.

Figure 4 shows performance results for automatic parallelization coupled with automatic communication management. Across all 24 applications, communication optimizations never reduce performance. This is a surprising result since the glue kernel optimization has the potential to lower performance, and CGCM's implementation lacks a performance guard. Communication optimization improves the performance for five of the sixteen PolyBench programs and six of the eight other programs. For many PolyBench programs, the outermost loop executes on the GPU, so there are no loops left on the CPU for map promotion to target. Therefore, optimization only improve performance for six of the 16 PolyBench programs.

Table 3 shows the number of GPU kernels created by the DOALL parallelizer. For each DOALL candidate, CGCM automatically managed communication correctly without programmer intervention. Unlike CGCM, the parallelizer requires static alias analysis. In practice, CGCM is more applicable than the simple DOALL transformation pass.

The table also shows the applicability of named regions [12] and inspector-executor management systems [4, 14, 22]. Affine communication management [24] has the same applicability as named regions, but a different implementation. The named region and inspector-executor techniques require that each of the live-ins is a distinct named allocation unit. The named regions technique also requires induction-variable based array indexes. The named region and inspector-executor systems are applicable to 66 of 67 kernels in the PolyBench applications. However, they are applicable to only 14 of 34 kernels from the more complex non-PolyBench applications. Although inspector-executor and named region based techniques have different applicability guards, they both fail to transfer memory for the same set of kernels.

Table 3 shows the GPU execution and communication time as a percent of total execution time. The contributions of CPU execution and IO are not shown. This data indicates the performance limiting factor for each program: either GPU execution, communication, or some other factor (CPU or IO). GPU execution time dominates total execution time for 13 programs, ten from PolyBench and three from other applications. The simpler PolyBench programs are much more likely to be GPU performance bound than the other more complex programs. GPU-bound programs would benefit from more efficient parallelizations, perhaps using the polyhedral model. Communication limits the performance of five programs, all from PolyBench. The only application where inspector-executor outperforms CGCM, `gramschmidt`, falls in this category. Finally, six programs, one from PolyBench and five from elsewhere, are neither communication nor GPU performance bound. Improving the performance of these applications would require parallelizing more loops. Two of the applications that are neither GPU nor communication-bound, `srad` and `blackscholes`, outperform sequential CPU-only execution. These applications have reached the limit of Amdahl's Law for the current parallelization.

The manual Rodinia parallelizations involved complex algorithmic improvements. For example, in `hotspot` the authors replace the original grid-based simulation with a simulation based on the pyramid method. Surprisingly, the simple automatic parallelization coupled with CGCM is competitive with expert programmers using algorithmic transformations. Table 3 explains why. Programmers tend to optimize a program's hottest loops, but ignore the second and third tier loops which become important once the hottest loops scale to thousands of threads. Automatic GPU parallelizations substitutes quantity for quality, profiting from Amdahl's Law.

7. Related Work

Although there has been prior work on automatic parallelization and semi-automatic communication management for GPUs, these implementations have not addressed the problems of fully-automatic communication management and optimization.

CUDA-lite [25] translates low-performance, naïve CUDA functions into high performance code by coalescing and exploiting GPU shared memory. However, the programmer must insert transfers to the GPU manually.

"C-to-CUDA for Affine Programs" [3] and "A mapping path for GPGPU" [13] automatically transform programs similar to the PolyBench programs into high performance CUDA C using the polyhedral model. Like CUDA-lite, they require the programmer to manage memory.

"OpenMP to GPGPU" [12] proposes an automatic compiler for the source-to-source translation of OpenMP applications into CUDA C. Most programs do not have OpenMP annotations. Furthermore, these annotations are time consuming to add and not performance portable. Their system automatically transfers *named regions* between CPU and GPU using two passes. The first pass copies all named annotated regions to the GPU for each GPU function, and the second cleanup pass removes all the copies that are not live-in. The two passes acting together produce a communication pattern equivalent to unoptimized CGCM communication.

JCUDA [26] uses the Java type system to automatically transfer GPU function arguments between CPU and GPU memories. JCUDA requires an annotation indicating whether each parameter is live-in, live-out, or both. Java implements multidimensional arrays as arrays of references. JCUDA uses type information to flatten these arrays to Fortran-style multidimensional arrays but does not support recursive data-types.

The PGI Fortran and C compiler [24] features a mode for semi-automatic parallelization for GPUs. Users target loops manually with a special keyword. The PGI compiler can automatically transfer *named regions* declared with C99's `restrict` keyword to the GPU and back by determining the range of *affine* array indices. The `restrict` keyword marks a pointer as not aliasing with other pointers. By contrast, CGCM is tolerant of aliasing and does not require programmer annotations. The PGI compiler cannot parallelize loops containing general pointer arithmetic, while CGCM preserves the semantics of pointer arithmetic. Unlike CGCM, the PGI compiler does not automatically optimize communication across GPU function invocations. However, programmers can use an optional annotation to promote communication out of loops. Incorrectly using this annotation will cause the program to access stale or inconsistent data.

Inspector-executor systems [18, 21] create specialized *inspectors* to identify precise dependence information among loop iterations. Some inspector-executor systems achieve acyclic communication when dynamic dependence information is reusable. This condition is rare in practice. Salz et al. assume a program annotation to prevent unsound reuse [21]. Rauchwerger et al. dynamically check relevant program state to determine if dependence information is reusable [18]. The dynamic check requires expensive sequential computation for each outermost loop iteration. If the check fails, the technique defaults to cyclic communication.

8. Conclusion

CGCM is the first fully automatic system for managing and optimizing CPU-GPU communication. CPU-GPU communication is a crucial problem for manual and automatic parallelizations. Manually transferring complex data-types between CPU and GPU memories is tedious and error-prone. Cyclic communication constrains the performance of automatic GPU parallelizations. By managing and optimizing CPU-GPU communication, CGCM eases manual GPU parallelizations and improves the performance and applicability of automatic GPU parallelizations.

CGCM has two parts, a run-time library and an optimizing compiler. The run-time library's semantics allow the compiler to manage and optimize CPU-GPU communication without programmer annotations or heroic static analysis. The compiler breaks cyclic communication patterns by transferring data to the GPU early in the program and retrieving it only when necessary. CGCM outperforms inspector-executor systems on 24 programs and enables a whole program geomean speedup of 5.36x over best sequential CPU-only execution.

Acknowledgments

We thank the entire Liberty Research Group for their support and feedback during this work. We also thank Helge Rhodin for generously contributing his PTX backend. Additionally, we thank the anonymous reviewers for their insightful comments.

This material is based on work supported by National Science Foundation Grants 0964328 and 1047879, and by United States Air Force Contract FA8650-09-C-7918. James A. Jablin is supported by a Department of Energy Office of Science Graduate Fellowship (DOE SCGF).

References

[1] ISO/IEC 9899-1999 Programming Languages – C, Second Edition, 1999.

[2] C. Ancourt and F. Irigoin. Scanning polyhedra with DO loops. In *Proceedings of the Third ACM SIGPLAN Symposium on Principles and Practice of Parallel Programming (PPoPP)*, 1991.

[3] M. M. Baskaran, J. Ramanujam, and P. Sadayappan. Automatic C-to-CUDA code generation for affine programs. In *Compiler Construction (CC)*, 2010.

[4] A. Basumallik and R. Eigenmann. Optimizing irregular shared-memory applications for distributed-memory systems. In *Proceedings of the Eleventh ACM SIGPLAN Symposium on Principles and Practice of Parallel Programming (PPoPP)*, 2006.

[5] C. Bienia, S. Kumar, J. P. Singh, and K. Li. The PARSEC benchmark suite: characterization and architectural implications. In *Proceedings of the 17th International Conference on Parallel Architectures and Compilation Techniques (PACT)*, 2008.

[6] I. Buck, T. Foley, D. Horn, J. Sugerman, K. Fatahalian, M. Houston, and P. Hanrahan. Brook for GPUs: Stream computing on graphics hardware. *ACM Transactions on Graphics*, 23, 2004.

[7] S. Che, M. Boyer, J. Meng, D. Tarjan, J. W. Sheaffer, S.-H. Lee, and K. Skadron. Rodinia: A benchmark suite for heterogeneous computing. 2009.

[8] D. M. Dang, C. Christara, and K. Jackson. GPU pricing of exotic cross-currency interest rate derivatives with a foreign exchange volatility skew model. *SSRN eLibrary*, 2010.

[9] P. Feautrier. Some efficient solutions to the affine scheduling problem: I. one-dimensional time. *International Journal of Parallel Programming (IJPP)*, 1992.

[10] D. R. Horn, M. Houston, and P. Hanrahan. Clawhmmer: A streaming HMMer-Search implementation. *Proceedings of the Conference on Supercomputing (SC)*, 2005.

[11] Khronos Group. *The OpenCL Specification*, September 2010.

[12] S. Lee, S.-J. Min, and R. Eigenmann. OpenMP to GPGPU: a compiler framework for automatic translation and optimization. In *Proceedings of the Fourteenth ACM SIGPLAN Symposium on Principles and Practice of Parallel Programming (PPoPP)*, 2009.

[13] A. Leung, N. Vasilache, B. Meister, M. M. Baskaran, D. Wohlford, C. Bastoul, and R. Lethin. A mapping path for multi-GPGPU accelerated computers from a portable high level programming abstraction. In *Proceedings of the 3rd Workshop on General-Purpose Computation on Graphics Processing Units (GPGPU)*, pages 51–61, 2010.

[14] S.-J. Min and R. Eigenmann. Optimizing irregular shared-memory applications for clusters. In *Proceedings of the 22nd Annual International Conference on Supercomputing (SC)*. ACM, 2008.

[15] NVIDIA Corporation. *CUDA C Best Practices Guide 3.2*, 2010.

[16] NVIDIA Corporation. *NVIDIA CUDA Programming Guide 3.0*, February 2010.

[17] L.-N. Pouchet. PolyBench: The Polyhedral Benchmark suite. http://www-roc.inria.fr/ pouchet/software/polybench/download.

[18] L. Rauchwerger, N. M. Amato, and D. A. Padua. A scalable method for run-time loop parallelization. *International Journal of Parallel Programming (IJPP)*, 26:537–576, 1995.

[19] H. Rhodin. LLVM PTX Backend. http://sourceforge.net/projects/llvmptxbackend.

[20] S. Ryoo, C. I. Rodrigues, S. S. Baghsorkhi, S. S. Stone, D. B. Kirk, and W.-m. W. Hwu. Optimization principles and application performance evaluation of a multithreaded GPU using CUDA. In *Proceedings of the Thirteenth ACM SIGPLAN Symposium on Principles and Practice of Parallel Programming (PPoPP)*, 2008.

[21] J. Saltz, R. Mirchandaney, and R. Crowley. Run-time parallelization and scheduling of loops. *IEEE Transactions on Computers*, 40, 1991.

[22] S. D. Sharma, R. Ponnusamy, B. Moon, Y.-S. Hwang, R. Das, and J. Saltz. Run-time and compile-time support for adaptive irregular problems. In *Proceedings of the Conference on Supercomputing (SC)*. IEEE Computer Society Press, 1994.

[23] StreamIt benchmarks. http://compiler.lcs.mit.edu/streamit.

[24] The Portland Group. PGI Fortran & C Accelator Programming Model. White Paper, 2010.

[25] S.-Z. Ueng, M. Lathara, S. S. Baghsorkhi, and W.-m. W. Hwu. CUDA-Lite: Reducing GPU Programming Complexity. In *Proceeding of the 21st International Workshop on Languages and Compilers for Parallel Computing (LCPC)*, 2008.

[26] Y. Yan, M. Grossman, and V. Sarkar. JCUDA: A programmer-friendly interface for accelerating Java programs with CUDA. In *Proceedings of the 15th International Euro-Par Conference on Parallel Processing*. Springer-Verlag, 2009.

Automatic Compilation of MATLAB Programs for Synergistic Execution on Heterogeneous Processors

Ashwin Prasad Jayvant Anantpur R. Govindarajan

Supercomputer Education and Research Centre,
Indian Institute of Science, Bangalore, India

ashwin@hpc.serc.iisc.ernet.in jayvant@hpc.serc.iisc.ernet.in govind@serc.iisc.ernet.in

Abstract

MATLAB is an array language, initially popular for rapid prototyping, but is now being increasingly used to develop production code for numerical and scientific applications. Typical MATLAB programs have abundant data parallelism. These programs also have control flow dominated scalar regions that have an impact on the program's execution time. Today's computer systems have tremendous computing power in the form of traditional CPU cores and throughput oriented accelerators such as graphics processing units(GPUs). Thus, an approach that maps the control flow dominated regions to the CPU and the data parallel regions to the GPU can significantly improve program performance.

In this paper, we present the design and implementation of MEGHA, a compiler that automatically compiles MATLAB programs to enable synergistic execution on heterogeneous processors. Our solution is fully automated and does not require programmer input for identifying data parallel regions. We propose a set of compiler optimizations tailored for MATLAB. Our compiler identifies data parallel regions of the program and composes them into kernels. The problem of combining statements into kernels is formulated as a constrained graph clustering problem. Heuristics are presented to map identified kernels to either the CPU or GPU so that kernel execution on the CPU and the GPU happens synergistically and the amount of data transfer needed is minimized. In order to ensure required data movement for dependencies across basic blocks, we propose a data flow analysis and edge splitting strategy. Thus our compiler automatically handles composition of kernels, mapping of kernels to CPU and GPU, scheduling and insertion of required data transfer. The proposed compiler was implemented and experimental evaluation using a set of MATLAB benchmarks shows that our approach achieves a geometric mean speedup of 19.8X for data parallel benchmarks over native execution of MATLAB.

Categories and Subject Descriptors D.3.2 [*Programming Languages*]: Language Classifications—Very high-level languages; D.3.4 [*Programming Languages*]: Processors—Compilers

General Terms Algorithms, Languages, Performance

1. Introduction

Recent advances in the design of Graphics Processing Units (GPUs) [3][20][23] have significantly increased the compute capabilities of these processors. Today's desktops and servers, in addition to having multiple CPU cores, have graphics processing units with hundreds of SIMD cores. GPUs, due to their ability to accelerate data-parallel applications, are well suited for numerical and scientific computation. However, programming in these platforms remains a challenge as the programmer needs to manually coordinate tasks across the CPU cores and the GPU and manage data transfer. This requires him to have a detailed understanding of the machine architecture.

MATLAB [21], an array language, is popular for implementing numerical and scientific applications. MATLAB programs naturally express data-level parallelism and are therefore ideal candidates for acceleration using throughput-oriented processors like GPUs. Frequently, MATLAB programs are hand translated into compiled languages like C to improve performance. Manually translating MATLAB programs to use available accelerators requires the programmer to manage details such as data transfer and scheduling. This makes the translation a painstaking and error prone process. Therefore, a tool to automatically transform MATLAB programs so that accelerators are used to speedup the data-parallel parts of the program and the CPU is used to efficiently execute the rest of the program would be very useful.

In this paper, we present MEGHA[1], a compiler that automatically compiles MATLAB programs for execution on machines that contain both CPU and GPU cores. Prior work on compiling MATLAB has focussed on compiling it to languages such as FORTRAN [10] or C [17]. Just-in-time compilation techniques for execution of MATLAB programs on CPUs were implemented in MaJIC [2] and McVM [8]. However, these efforts on automatic translation are limited to CPUs and do not consider GPUs. Currently, Jacket [14] and GPUmat [12] provide the user with the ability to run MATLAB code on GPUs. These require users to specify arrays whose operations are to be performed on the GPU by declaring them to be of a special type. Further, the user needs to identify which operations are well suited for acceleration on the GPU, and is required to manually insert calls to move the data to and from the GPU memory.

Our compiler automatically identifies regions of MATLAB programs that can be executed efficiently on the GPU and tries to schedule computations on the CPU and GPU in parallel to further increase performance. There are several associated challenges. First, the CPU and GPU operate on separate address spaces requiring explicit memory transfer commands for transferring data from

[1] **M**ATLAB **E**xecution on **G**PU based **H**eterogeneous **A**rchitectures. *Megha* also means cloud.

and to the GPU memory. Second, sets of statements (kernels) in the input program that can be run together on the GPU need to be identified. This is required to minimize data transfers between host and device memory and also to reduce kernel call overheads. Third, program tasks [2] need to be mapped to either GPU cores or CPU cores and scheduled so that the program execution time is minimized. Required data transfers also need to be taken into account while mapping and scheduling tasks. Lastly, efficient code needs to be generated for each task depending on which processor it is assigned to.

The following are the main contributions of this work.

- We present a compiler framework, MEGHA, that translates MATLAB programs for synergistic parallel execution on machines with GPU and CPU cores.
- We formulate the identification of data parallel regions of a MATLAB program as a constrained graph clustering problem and propose an efficient heuristic algorithm to solve the problem.
- We propose an efficient heuristic algorithm to map kernels to either the CPU or GPU and schedule them so that memory transfer requirements are minimized. Techniques for generating efficient code for kernels mapped to either the CPU or GPU are also described.
- Experimental evaluation on a set of MATLAB benchmarks shows a geometric mean speedup of 19.8X for data parallel benchmarks over native MATLAB execution. Compared to manually tuned GPUmat versions of the benchmarks, our approach yields speedups up to 10X.

To the best of our knowledge, MEGHA is the first effort to *automatically* compile MATLAB programs for parallel execution across CPU and GPU cores. The rest of this paper is organized as follows: Section 2 briefly reviews the necessary background. Section 3 provides an overview of the compiler and briefly describes various stages in the frontend. Section 4 describes the details of our proposed compilation methodology. In Section 5, we present our experimental methodology and report performance results. Section 6 discusses related work and Section 7 concludes.

2. Background

2.1 NVIDIA GPUs and CUDA

This section describes the architecture of NVIDIA GPUs in general. While models might differ in the amount of resources available, the basic architecture stays roughly the same [22][20]. The architecture of NVIDIA GPUs is hierarchical. They consist of a set streaming multiprocessors (SMs) each of which consists of several scalar units (SUs). For example, the 8800 series GPUs have 16 SMs each having 8 SUs. The basic schedulable entity for GPUs is a *warp* which currently consists of 32 contiguous threads. SMs have support for the time interleaved execution of several warps. They periodically switch between warps to hide latency. Within an SM, all SUs execute instructions in lock-step. Additionally, any divergence in the execution path of threads within a warp results in a performance penalty. Each SM has a partitioned register file and a *shared memory* which is accessible by all SUs in the SM. The shared memory is similar to a software managed cache or a scratch pad memory. The 8800 series GPUs have register banks containing 8192 32-bit registers and 16KB of shared memory.

All SMs are connected to the *device memory* by a very wide bus. This bus is 256-512 bits wide for 8800 series GPUs depending on the model. The memory bus is capable of providing very high bandwidth, provided all threads in a warp access consecutive memory locations. Such accesses are said to be *coalesced*. Essentially the address accessed by thread n of a warp must be of the form $BaseAddress + n$.

Programs to be run on NVIDIA GPUs are typically written using the CUDA(Compute Unified Device Architecture) programming language which is an extension of C++ [22]. The CUDA programming model provides a higher level view of the GPU architecture to application programmers. From the programmer's point of view, threads are divided into *thread blocks*, and several thread blocks form a *grid*. A GPU *kernel* call, which is executed on the GPU, in general consists of multiple thread blocks organized as a grid. Each thread block is executed on a single SM and can contain up to 512 threads. However, a single SM can execute multiple thread blocks simultaneously depending on the register and shared memory requirement per block. Kernel calls are asynchronous in the sense that control is returned to the calling CPU thread before the kernel execution on the GPU completes. Data transfers between GPU and CPU memory must be initiated by the CPU thread.

2.2 Supported MATLAB Subset

MATLAB is a dynamically typed array based programming language which is very popular for developing scientific and numerical applications. As MATLAB has grown into a diverse and vast language over the years, the compiler described in this paper supports only a representative subset of MATLAB. A brief description of the subset of MATLAB supported and a set of other assumptions made by our compiler implementation are presented below.

1. MATLAB supports variables of several primitive types like `logical`, `int`, `real`, `complex` and `string`. It is also possible to construct arrays of these types with any number of dimensions. Currently, our compiler does not support variables of type `complex` and `string`. Arrays are also restricted to a maximum of three dimensions.
2. MATLAB supports indexing with multi-dimensional arrays. However, our implementation currently only supports indexing with single dimensional arrays.
3. In MATLAB, it is possible to change the size of arrays by assigning to elements past their end. We currently do not support indexing past the end of arrays. Further, in this paper, we refer to assignments to arrays through indexed expressions (Eg: `a(i)`) as indexed assignments or *partial assignments*.
4. We assume that the MATLAB program to be compiled is a single script without any calls to user-defined functions. Support for user defined functions can be added by extending the frontend of the compiler. Also, anonymous functions and function handles are not currently supported.
5. In general, types and shapes (array sizes) of MATLAB variables are not known until run-time. The compiler currently relies on a simple data flow analysis to extract sizes and types of program variables. It also relies on programmer input when types cannot be determined. We intend to extend our type system to support symbolic type inferencing in future [16]. Ultimately, we envision that the techniques described in this paper will be used in both compile time and run-time systems.

3. Compiler Overview

A high level overview of the proposed compiler is shown in Figure 1. The input to the compiler is a MATLAB script and the output is a combination of C++ and CUDA code. This section briefly describes the frontend of the compiler. A detailed explanation of the stages in the backend is given in Section 4.

[2] Statements that can only run on the CPU and kernels (which can be run on CPU or GPU) are collectively called tasks.

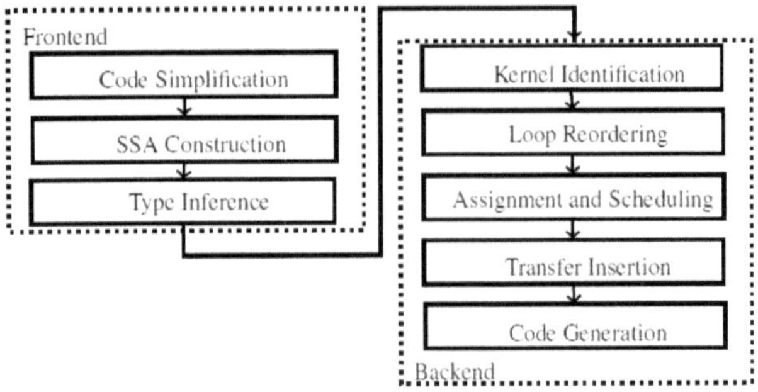

Figure 1: Compiler Overview

3.1 Code Simplification

The compiler first simplifies the input source code by breaking complex expressions into simpler ones. The output of this pass is a single operator intermediate form; i.e., each statement in the resulting IR has at most one operator on the right hand side of assignments. Expressions are broken into single operator form by introducing temporaries. For example,

```
x = (a + b) - c;
```

is converted to

```
tempVar1 = a + b;
x = tempVar1 - c;
```

Array indexing is also treated as an operator. First each indexing expression is simplified if needed. Then a simplified array reference is emitted. For example,

```
x = a(2*i);
```

is converted to

```
tempVar1 = 2*i;
x = a(tempVar1);
```

However, it is not always possible to completely simplify indexing expressions. This is the case when indexing expressions contain *magic ends* (e.g., `a(2:end)` refers to all elements of `a` starting from the second element) and *magic colons* (e.g., `a(:)` refers to all elements of `a`). These are handled using a set of semantics preserving transformations described below.

3.2 Semantics Preserving Transformations

Transformation of the MATLAB code is necessary to simplify subsequent analysis, enable conversion to single assignment form and ultimately enable CUDA code generation. Hence, our compiler makes the following changes to the simplified IR before converting it to SSA form.

MATLAB supports "context-sensitive" indexing of arrays. Users can specify all elements along a dimension by simply using a ":" in the index corresponding to that dimension. For example, to set all elements of a vector "a" to 42, one could write:

```
a( : ) = 42
```

One can also use the keyword `end` inside an array index expression in MATLAB to refer to the last element of the array along that dimension. For example, if "a" is a vector,

```
a(4:end) = 42;
```

assigns 42 to all elements of "a" starting from element 4. The compiler removes these context-sensitive operators by replacing them by the indices they imply : e.g., `a(:)` is replaced by `a(1:length(a))` and `a(2:end)` is replaced by `a(2:length(a))`.

Some transformations are also needed on for-loops in user code to preserve MATLAB semantics. In MATLAB, assignments to the loop index variable or to the loop bounds inside the loop body do not have any effect on the iteration count of the loop. For example, the loop in the following program runs for ten iterations.

```
n = 10;
for i=1:n
  % ....
  i = i + 10;
endfor
```

Our compiler preserves these semantics by renaming the loop index (and bounds). A statement to copy the new loop index into the old loop index is inserted at the head of the loop. Therefore, the above code would be transformed to the following equivalent code.

```
n = 10;
for tempIndex=1:n
  i = tempIndex;
  % ....
  i = i + 10;
endfor
```

3.3 Static Single Assignment Construction

Since static single assignment form (SSA) is a well established IR for performing optimizations, we choose it as our intermediate form. The SSA form is constructed using the method described by Cytron et al [9]. However, since the variables in the program are possibly arrays, it is important to optimize the insertion of ϕ nodes. One optimization we make is that we insert ϕ nodes for a variable at a point only if it is live at that point. Further, assignments to array variables through indexed expressions are not renamed; in other words, values are assigned in-place. However, all total assignments are renamed.

3.4 Type and Shape Inference

Since MATLAB is a dynamically typed language, type and shape information needs to be inferred before a MATLAB script can be compiled to a statically typed language like C. Our definition of the type of a variable is based on the definition used by De Rose et al [10]. The type of a variable is a tuple consisting of the following elements

1. *Intrinsic Type* which can be `boolean`, `integer` or `real`,
2. *Shape* which can be `scalar`, `vector`, `matrix` or `3D-array`, and
3. *Size* which indicates the size of each dimension of the variable.

Our compiler currently tries to infer base types of variables and shapes of arrays based on program constants and the semantics of built-in MATLAB functions and operators by performing a forward data flow analysis that is similar to what was used in FALCON [10] and MaJIC [2]. It is also possible for the user to specify types of variables in the input MATLAB script via annotations. The compiler does not currently implement symbolic type inference and symbolic type equality checking [16]. We leave this for future work.

4. Backend

The backend of the compiler performs kernel identification, mapping, scheduling and data transfer insertion. Kernel identification identifies sets of statements, called *kernels*[3], which can be treated as a single entity by the mapping and scheduling phase. It also transforms kernels into loop nests from which the code generator can generate efficient lower level code. The mapping and scheduling phase assigns a processor to each identified kernel and also decides when it should be executed. Kernel identification and mapping are performed per basic block. Global transfer insertion then performs a global data flow analysis and inserts the required inter basic block transfers.

4.1 Kernel Identification

The purpose of the kernel identification process is to identify the entities on which mapping and scheduling decisions can be made. We call these entities *kernels* or tasks[4]. They are sets of IR statements that, when combined, can be efficiently run on the GPU. The kernel identification process consists of the following steps.

1. Identify IR statements that are data parallel as "GPU friendly" statements.
2. *Kernel Composition* identifies sets of statements that can be grouped together in a common kernel.
3. *Scalarization* and *Index Array elimination* eliminate arrays that are not needed because of the way statements were grouped together.
4. *Surrounding Loop Insertion* transforms kernels into loop nests consisting of parallel loops.

Our compiler currently tags statements that perform element-wise operations or other data parallel operations like matrix multiplication as "GPU friendly" statements. It should be noted that this step just identifies statements that *could* run on the GPU and does not make any decisions on what should actually be run on the GPU.

```
1: A = (B + C) + (A + C);
2: C = A * C;
```

(a) MATLAB Statements

```
1: tempVar0 = B + C;
2: tempVar1 = A + C;
3: A_1 = tempVar0 + tempVar1;
4: tempVar2 = A_1 * C;
5: C_1 = tempVar2;
```

(b) IR Representation

Figure 2: A simple MATLAB program and its IR representation. A, B and C are 100x100 matrices.

Once GPU friendly statements have been identified, the kernel composition step decides the granularity at which mapping decisions are to be made. It does this by grouping IR statements together. It is inefficient to make these decisions at the level of IR statements as there may be too many of them. Kernel composition reduces the number of entities that need to be mapped and could also lead to a significant decrease in the memory requirement of the compiled program. To understand why, consider the example in Figure 2(a). Code simplification generates a considerable number of temporaries that are used only once after they are defined as can be seen in Figure 2(b). If mapping decisions are made per IR statement, the definition and use of these temporaries could be mapped to different processors necessitating the storage of these temporaries, which may be arrays, in memory. In the example in Figure 2(b), three temporaries, each of which is a matrix have been generated by the simplification process. In the worst case, when all these temporaries need to be stored in memory, the memory requirement of the program increases significantly. However, if statements 1, 2 and 3 are grouped into the same kernel, it is possible to replace the arrays `tempVar0` and `tempVar1` with scalars. When this kernel is rewritten as a loop nest, these variables are only live within one iteration of the loop nest. Hence they can be replaced by scalars as in the following code.

```
for i=1:100
  for j=1:100
    tempVar0_s = B(i, j) + C(i, j);
    tempVar1_s = A(i, j) + C(i, j);
    A_1(i, j) = tempVar0_s + tempVar1_s;
  endfor
endfor
```

The above problem is even more exaggerated in real benchmarks. To give a specific example, in the benchmark fdtd [15], we observed that worst case memory requirement increase can be as high as 30X. Combining statements into kernels is also important because the mapping and scheduling phase would then be able to solve a scheduling problem with a fewer number of nodes.

We refer to this process of reducing arrays to scalar variables as *Scalarization*. However, the newly created scalars are likely to be saved in registers thereby increasing the register utilization.

Two statements can be combined into a kernel only if the following conditions hold for the statements to be combined.

1. Both statements perform element-wise operations.
2. Both statements have identical iteration spaces. (By iteration space of a statement, we mean the iteration space of the parallel loops surrounding the statement.)
3. Combining the statements will not result in cyclic dependencies among kernels.
4. The loops surrounding the kernel created by combining the two statements should be parallel[5].

In the example in Figure 2(b), it is legal to group the first three statements, in the simplified IR, into the same kernel. However, it is illegal to put statement 4 into the same group as matrix multiplication is not an element-wise operation and requires elements at other points in the iteration space to have been computed. Thus, combining the addition and the multiplication statements introduces cross iteration dependencies and therefore the surrounding loops of the resulting group are no longer parallel. Even though condition 1 is subsumed by condition 4, it is specified separately as it is easier to check for violations of condition 1.

Condition 4 is similar to the condition for legal loop fusion [18] but is stricter. For loop fusion to be legal, it is only required that directions of dependencies between statements in the loops being fused are not reversed because of the fusion. However, for kernel composition to be legal, we require that the surrounding loops still be parallel loops after the statements are combined as our objective is to map identified kernels to the GPU.

Combining statements into kernels has many benefits. Compiler generated temporary arrays and user arrays can be converted to scalars. Locality between the combined statements can be exploited. Lastly, combining statements into kernels also results in a reduction in the CUDA kernel invocation overhead at run-time. However, forming larger kernels can also increase register usage and the memory footprints of kernels. These factors are extremely

[3] We use "kernel" to refer to either the smallest unit of data-parallel work in a set of IR statements or a set of GPU friendly IR statements. Which is meant will be clear from context.

[4] The term kernel or task is used depending on whether they are mapped to the GPU or CPU respectively. We use both terms interchangeably when the mapping is not known.

[5] Parallel loops are loops whose iterations can all be run in parallel.

important if the kernel is to be run on the GPU. Larger kernels may also require more variables to be transferred to and from the GPU. This may lead to decreased opportunities for overlapping computation and data transfer. Thus there are trade offs in kernel composition.

We model the kernel composition problem as a constrained clustering problem modelling the costs and benefits described above. It is loosely related to the parameterized model for loop fusion [24]. However, compared to the model for loop fusion, our formulation additionally models memory utilization of kernels. Register utilization is also more accurately modelled. The details of the construction and a heuristic algorithm to compute a solution are described in the following sub-sections.

4.1.1 Graph Formulation

The problem of composing statements into kernels is that of clustering the nodes of an augmented data flow graph $G = (V, E)$ into clusters. A cluster is a set of nodes of the graph G. The graph G is defined as follows.

1. Each node $n \in V$ represents an IR statement in the basic block under consideration. The statement represented by $n \in V$ is denoted by $stm(n)$.
2. The set of edges, E has two types of edges.
    - *Dependence edges* are directed edges between nodes whose statements are data dependent. An edge (n_1, n_2) implies that n_2 must run after n_1. All types of dependences (true, anti and output) are represented uniformly.
    - A *Fusion preventing edge* connects a pair of nodes that cannot be merged. For example, such an edge would exist between the vertices for statements 3 and 4 in Figure 2(b). There are also fusion preventing edges between nodes representing GPU friendly statements and others representing non GPU friendly statements.

The kernel composition problem is that of clustering the set of nodes V into a set of clusters $\{C_1, C_2, ...C_n\}$. All the C_i's are disjoint and their union is V. An edge $e = (n_1, n_2)$ is said to be in a cluster C_i if n_1 and n_2 are in C_i.

To accurately model register utilization, we consider the original register usage of each statement in the basic block and the increase in register usage due to scalarization of arrays. First, the register utilization of each statement $stm(n)$, for each $n \in V$, denoted by reg_n, is estimated as the number of scalars used in $stm(n)$. Secondly, we need to differentiate between variables that can be scalarized (scalarizable variables) and those that cannot be scalarized by combining two statements. To model the increase in register utilization when two statements are combined, we define the weight reg_e on each edge $e = (n_1, n_2) \in E$. The value of this quantity is the number of variables that can be scalarized by combining $stm(n_1)$ and $stm(n_2)$. For example, it is 1 for the edge between the nodes for statements 1 and 3 in the above example since `tempVar0` can be eliminated by combining these statements. Now, when a cluster is formed, the register utilization of the kernel represented by the cluster is the sum of the reg values of all nodes and edges in the cluster. Therefore, to limit the register utilization of each cluster, we introduce the following constraint for each cluster C_i.

$$\sum_{e \in C_i} reg_e + \sum_{n \in C_i} reg_n \leq R_{max} \quad (1)$$

To model memory utilization, the distinction between scalarizable variables and non-scalarizable variables is needed again. For scalarizable variables, such as `tempVar0`, the memory utilization becomes zero when its defining node and use node are combined (statements 1 and 3 in this case). However, for non-scalarizable variables, the memory usage is the sum of the sizes of all such variables used by statements in the cluster.

To model the memory utilization due to scalarizable variables, we use weights on both edges and nodes. For a node n, we define mem_n as the sum of sizes of all scalarizable variables in $stm(n)$. Therefore mem_n, for the node representing statement 1 is $size(tempVar0)$. For an edge e between n_1 and n_2, if there is a variable $scal\_var$ that can be scalarized by combining $stm(n_1)$ and $stm(n_2)$, we define $mem_e = -2.size(scal\_var)$. Therefore, the memory utilization of a scalarizable variable reduces to zero if both its definition and use are in the same cluster as the weights on the nodes are cancelled out by the weight of the edge between them. The total memory usage of the kernel represented by the cluster C_i, due to scalarizable variables is therefore given by:

$$\sum_{n \in C_i} mem_n + \sum_{e \in C_i} mem_e = M_{scal,i} \quad (2)$$

For non-scalarizable variables, we use a bit vector to model the memory utilization. For each node $n \in V$, and each non-scalarizable variable var, we define $used_n(var)$ to be 1 if n uses var. For example, the node m, representing statement 1 in the above example, has $used_m(B) = 1$ and $used_m(C) = 1$. A variable var is used in a cluster if any of the nodes in the cluster has $used(var)$ as 1. The memory utilization of a cluster due to non-scalarizable variables is the sum of sizes of all such variables used in the cluster. The memory utilization due to non-scalarizable variables is given by:

$$\sum_{var \in Vars} (\bigvee_{n \in C_i} used_n(var)).size(var) = M_{nonscal,i} \quad (3)$$

where $Vars$ is the set of all non-scalarizable variables in the program.

To limit the total memory utilization of each kernel, we introduce the following constraint.

$$M_{scal,i} + M_{nonscal,i} \leq M_{max} \quad (4)$$

Additionally, for all fusion preventing edges $e \in E$, e must not be in any cluster C_i. Also, when nodes are grouped together as kernels, the graph must remain acyclic.

For each edge $e = (n_1, n_2) \in E$, $benefit_e$, quantifies the benefit of combining the statements $stm(n_1)$ and $stm(n_2)$ into the same kernel. The benefit of collapsing an edge is defined as

$$benefit_e = \alpha Mem(n_1, n_2) + \beta Loc(n_1, n_2) + \gamma$$

where, $Mem(n_1, n_2)$ is the sum of sizes of array variables that can be eliminated by combining $stm(n_1)$ and $stm(n_2)$, $Loc(n_1, n_2)$ quantifies the locality between the two statements. It is currently estimated as the number of pairs of overlapping array references in the two statements. If two statements being considered for composition have a common array reference, then this can be read into shared memory and reused. The term $Loc(n_1, n_2)$ is meant to model this. γ represents the reduction in the kernel call overhead. α and β are parameters.

The objective of kernel composition is to maximize the total $benefit$:

$$benefit = \sum_{C_i} \sum_{e \in C_i} benefit_e$$

subject to the above constraints. The above problem can be shown to be NP-hard by a reduction from the loop fusion problem defined by Singhai and McKinley [24]. We therefore use a heuristic algorithm to solve the kernel composition problem.

4.1.2 Kernel Composition Heuristic

Our heuristic kernel clustering method uses a k-level look ahead to merge nodes of the graph G into clusters. It computes the benefits and memory requirement for collapsing all possible legal sets of k edges starting at node n by exhaustively searching through all possibilities. (By collapsing an edge, we mean combining its source and destination nodes). It then collapses the set of k edges that results in the maximum benefit. For small values of $k (k = 3$ or $k = 4)$, this achieves reasonably good results without a significant increase in compile time. The details of the clustering algorithm are listed in Algorithm 1. The function $legalKDepthMerges$ returns multiple sets of (up to) k edges that can be *legally* collapsed. This function makes sure that clusters that have fusion preventing edges are not formed and that no cycles are formed in the graph. It also ensures that the constraints listed earlier are not violated. The function $maxBenefit$ returns the set of edges with the maximum benefit and $collapseEdges$ collapses all edges in a set of edges and adds all combined nodes to C_i.

Algorithm 1 Kernel Composition Heuristic

procedure KernelComposition($G = (V, E)$)
  $nodes \leftarrow V$
  $clusters \leftarrow \phi$
  while $nodes \neq \phi$ **do**
    $n \leftarrow$ node in $nodes$ that uses minimum memory
    $C_i \leftarrow n$
    $nodes \leftarrow nodes - \{n\}$
    while $true$ **do**
      $T \leftarrow legalKDepthMerges(C_i, k)$
      if $T \neq \phi$ **then**
        $bestSet \leftarrow maxBenefit(T)$
        $collapseEdges(C_i, bestSet)$
        for all $e = (n_1, n_2) \in bestSet$ **do**
          $nodes \leftarrow nodes - \{n_1\}$
          $nodes \leftarrow nodes - \{n_2\}$
        end for
      else
        break
      end if
    end while
    $clusters \leftarrow clusters \cup C_i$
  end while
end procedure

4.1.3 Identifying In and Out Variables

Once kernels have been identified, we need to compute the set of variables that are required for the execution of the kernel and the set of variables that are modified by the kernel and are needed by future computations. To do this we first perform a live-variable analysis [1] on the SSA IR. A variable is an "in-variable" of a given kernel if it is live on entry to the kernel and is accessed (either read or partially written) within the kernel. We define a variable as an "out-variable" if the variable is modified inside the kernel and is live at the exit of the kernel. Data transfer from CPU memory or GPU memory may be required for in-variables and out-variables depending on the processors kernels are ultimately mapped to.

4.1.4 Array Elimination

As discussed in Section 4.1, arrays that become unnecessary after kernel composition need to be eliminated. Replacing these arrays with scalar variables not only reduces memory requirements but also eliminates memory accesses that are expensive, especially if they are serviced out of GPU device memory. To remove array variables, we use the two transformations, scalarization and index array elimination, described below.

Scalarization

After in-variables and out-variables of each kernel have been identified it is possible to replace an array that is neither an in-variable nor an out-variable by a scalar as shown in the earlier example. This is possible because it is guaranteed that no subsequent statement depends on writes to the array within this kernel and that this kernel does not depend on the prior value of this array. We refer to this process as *scalarization*.

Index Array Elimination

In MATLAB programs, arrays (especially those defined using the colon operator) are frequently defined and used either for indexing or in element-wise computations. It is possible to replace some references to these arrays with scalars that are computed inside the kernel in which the original array was used. Any array representable as a function $f : \mathbb{Z}^+ \rightarrow \mathbb{Z}^+$ that maps the index of an array element to the element value and used to index one or more dimensions of another array is called an *index array*. A total reference to such an array in a kernel can be replaced by a scalar that takes the value $f(i)$ in the ith iteration of the surrounding loop. Consider the following example, in which a subset of the 3D array `Ey` is copied into `tempVar1`.

```
tempVar0 = Nz + 1;
tempVar1 = 2:tempVar0;
tempVar2 = Ey(:, :, tempVar1);
```

Here, `tempVar1` is an index array with the function f given by $f(i) = 2 + (i - 1)$. It can be eliminated by replacing it with a scalar while adding surrounding loops as shown below (details in Section 4.1.5).

```
tempVar0 = Nz + 1;
for i = 1:Sx
  for j = 1:Sy
    for k = 1:Sz
      indexVar1 = 2 + (k-1);
      tempVar2(i, j, k) = Ey(i, j, indexVar1);
    end
  end
end
```

`Sx`,`Sy` and `Sz` represent the size of the iteration space of the original assignment in the first, second and third dimension respectively. We refer to this transformation as *index array elimination*.

Currently, our compiler identifies arrays defined using the colon operator as index arrays. However, arrays defined using functions like `linspace` [6] and in user loops could also be identified as index arrays. We intend to implement these extensions in the future.

4.1.5 Surrounding Loop Insertion

Before code can be generated, identified kernels need to be transformed into a form more suitable for code generation. The compiler achieves this by adding loops around kernels and introducing the necessary indexing.

For kernels that contain element-wise operations, the required number of surrounding loops are inserted and array references are changed as described next. Consider the example in Section 4.1.4. Introducing indexing is simple for originally unindexed references like `tempVar2`. The indices are just the loop variables of the surrounding loops. However, the case for indexed references is slightly more complicated. The nth *non-scalar* index in the indexed reference is transformed according to the following rules.

[6] `linspace` is a MATLAB function that generates linearly spaced vectors. `linspace(x, y, n)` generates `n` linearly spaced numbers from `x` to `y`. For example, `linspace(1, 9, 3)` returns the array `[1 5 9]`.

1. If it is a magic colon, replace it by i_n that is the loop variable of the nth surrounding loop. For example, the first and second indexing expressions in the reference to `Ey` in the above example are changed to `i` and `j`.
2. If the indexer is an index array, replace the array by a scalar variable initialized with the value $f(i_n)$, where f is the function described in Section 4.1.4. This rule is used to change the third indexing expression in the reference to `Ey` from `tempVar2` to `indexVar1`.
3. Otherwise, if the nth non-scalar indexer is x, then replace it by $x(i_n)$.

Once surrounding loops are inserted, the body of the loop nest represents exactly the CUDA code that would need to be generated if the kernel under consideration gets mapped to the GPU.

Kernels that contain more complex operators such as matrix multiplication are treated as special cases when they are transformed into loop nests. The compiler also keeps the original high-level IR as this is useful during code generation (for example to map a matrix multiplication kernel to a BLAS library call).

4.2 Parallel Loop Reordering

After the steps described in the previous section have been performed, the IR contains a set of kernels and their surrounding parallel loops. The in-variables and out-variables of each kernel are also known. When these kernels are ultimately executed, the way in which the iteration space of the surrounding loops is traversed can have a significant impact on performance irrespective of whether the kernel is mapped to the CPU or the GPU. Further, the iteration space may need to be traversed differently depending on whether the kernel is mapped to the CPU or the GPU. Since the surrounding loops are parallel, the iteration space of these loops can be traversed in any order. The loop reordering transform decides how the iteration space must be traversed to maximize performance.

For a kernel that is executed on the CPU, locality in the inner most loop is important from a cache performance viewpoint. For example, consider the code listed in Section 4.1.4. There are three surrounding loops with indices `i`, `j` and `k`. Therefore, the two indexed references to `tempVar2` and `Ey` will access consecutive memory locations for consecutive values[7] of `j`. This implies that having the `j` loop as the innermost loop will maximize locality.

GPU memory optimizations are however very different from memory optimizations implemented by the CPU. When all threads in a warp access a contiguous region of memory, the GPU is able to coalesce [22] these multiple memory requests into a single memory request thereby saving memory bandwidth and reducing the overall latency of the memory access. If a kernel is assigned to the GPU, the code generator maps the index of the outer most loop to the x dimension of the thread block. The GPU groups neighboring threads in the x dimension into the same warp. Therefore, in the GPU case, the loop with the maximum locality needs to be the outermost loop (which in the above example is the `j` loop).

At this stage, since it is not known which processor, CPU or GPU, a kernel is mapped to, the compiler computes loop orders for both of them. Also, both versions are needed during the profiling stage. Currently, a simple heuristic is used to compute the loop ordering. The number of consecutive memory references in successive iterations of each loop (with all other loop indices staying constant) is computed. The loops are then sorted based on this number. The loop that causes accesses to consecutive memory locations for the most references in the kernel is treated as the loop with the maximum locality.

For the CPU loop order, the loops are sorted in increasing order of locality. (The first loop in the sorted sequence is the outermost loop and the last loop is the inner most loop.) For the example above, the `j` loop has the most locality since both indexed references access successive memory locations for successive values of `j`. The other loops have no locality. Therefore, the `j` loop becomes the innermost loop when the above kernel is executed on the CPU.

For the GPU, the loop with the maximum locality becomes the outer-most loop since this enables coalescing for the greatest number of accesses. If a particular kernel is mapped to the GPU, final code generation maps the iteration number in the outermost loop in the GPU order to the thread ID in the X direction. It generates thread blocks of size (32, 1, 1). Since CUDA supports only 2 dimensional grids, the iteration space of the next two loops (if they exist) is flattened into the block ID in the y direction. In the above example, `j` becomes the outer most loop and the `i` and `k` loop get flattened into a single loop as shown below.

```
tempVar0 = Nz + 1;
for tidx = 1:Sy
  for tidy = 1:Sx*Sz
    j = tidx;
    i = floor(tidy/Sz);
    k = tidy % Sz;
    indexVar1 = 2 + (k-1);
    tempVar2(i, j, k) = Ey(i, j, indexVar1);
  end
end
```

It is possible that changing the layout of certain arrays depending on the surrounding loops may improve performance by either improving locality on CPUs or increasing the number of coalesced accesses on the GPU. We leave this problem for future work.

4.3 Mapping and Scheduling

Once kernels have been identified by the preceding steps of the compiler, each basic block can be viewed as a directed acyclic graph (DAG) whose nodes represent kernels. Edges represent data dependencies. It is now required to assign a processor and a start time to each node in the DAG such that the total execution time of the basic block under consideration is minimized. This problem is similar to the traditional resource constrained task/instruction scheduling problem except that some tasks can be scheduled either on the CPU or GPU. Therefore, when dependent tasks are mapped to different types of processors, required data transfers also need to be inserted. This makes the above problem harder than the scheduling problem. It is therefore NP-hard. Thus, we propose a heuristic approach for the integrated mapping and scheduling problem.

The compiler uses a variant of list scheduling to assign nodes to processors. The heuristic is based on the observation that a node whose performance is very good on one processor and very bad on the other needs to be given maximum chance to be assigned to the processor on which it performs best. We define $skew(n)$ where n is a node in the DAG as

$$skew(n) = max\left(\frac{T_{GPU}(n)}{T_{CPU}(n)}, \frac{T_{CPU}(n)}{T_{GPU}(n)}\right)$$

where T_{GPU} and T_{CPU} are functions that give the execution time of n on the GPU and CPU respectively. To obtain estimates for the execution time for each node, we currently use profiling information.

The algorithm maintains resource vectors for the GPU, CPU and the bus. In every iteration, it gets the node from the ready queue with the highest skew and tries to schedule it so that the finish time is minimized. While scheduling a node, transfers required to

[7] Currently, in our implementation, three dimensional arrays are stored as stacked row major matrices in the spirit of MATLAB. Therefore, `tempVar2(i, j, k)` and `tempVar2(i, j+1, k)` are in successive memory locations.

```
1:   n = 100;          (CPU)
2:   A = rand(n, n);(CPU)
3:   for i=1:n
4:       A = A * A;   (GPU)
5:   end
6:   print(A);         (CPU)
```

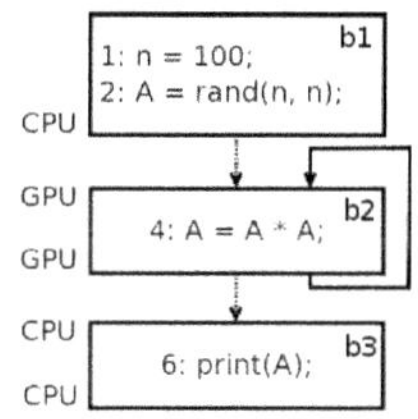

Figure 3: Motivating Example for Edge Splitting. Processor name in brackets indicates mapping. The control flow graph shows split edges as dotted lines and the location of A at each program point.

start the node need to be considered. The algorithm computes the earliest time at which the node can start on the GPU and the CPU considering the data transfers that need to be performed so that all required data is available. The finish time of the node is computed for both the CPU and the GPU and the node is then scheduled on the processor on which it has the lower finish time. The details are given in Algorithm 2.

In the algorithm, $readyQueue$ is a priority queue that is prioritized based on $skew$. The function $computeMinimumStartTime$ computes the minimum time at which a node can start on a given processor considering the data transfers that are needed due to prior processor assignments and the resource availability. The functions $scheduleOnGPU$ and $scheduleOnCPU$ schedule a node onto the GPU and CPU respectively. They also insert and schedule the required data transfers and update the resource vectors.

Algorithm 2 Processor Assignment

procedure Assignment (DataFlowGraph $G = (V, E)$)
  $readyQueue \leftarrow \phi$
  $\forall v \in V$ with no *in edges* : $readyQueue.insert(v)$
  while $readyQueue \neq \phi$ **do**
    $v \leftarrow readyQueue.remove()$
    $start_{GPU} \leftarrow computeMinimumStartTime(v, GPU)$
    $start_{CPU} \leftarrow computeMinimumStartTime(v, CPU)$
    $finish_{GPU} \leftarrow start_{GPU} + T_{GPU}(v)$
    $finish_{CPU} \leftarrow start_{CPU} + T_{CPU}(v)$
    if $finish_{GPU} \leq finish_{CPU}$ **then**
      $scheduleOnGPU(v, start_{GPU})$
    else
      $scheduleOnCPU(v, start_{CPU})$
    end if
    $V = V - v$
    for all $v_1 \in V$ with all preds scheduled **do**
      $readyQueue.insert(v_1)$
    end for
  end while
end procedure

4.4 Global Data Transfer Insertion

All the previously described optimizations are performed per basic block. The mapping heuristic assumes that data which is read before it is written in a basic block is available on both the GPU and CPU. However, where the data actually is when the basic block begins executing depends on the program path that was taken to get to the basic block.

Consider the code segment in Figure 3. When execution reaches statement 4, matrix A may either be in the CPU memory or GPU memory depending on the path the program took to get to statement 4. If the path taken was 1→2→4, then A is in CPU memory since statement 2 runs on the CPU. However, if the path taken to reach statement 4 was 1→2→4→4, then A is in GPU memory since statement 4 runs on the GPU. Additionally, statement 4 assumes that A is available on the GPU.

To remove this dependence of a variable's location on the program path taken, we use a two step process. We first use a data flow analysis to compute the locations of all program variables at the entry and exit of each basic block in the program. Then, we split control flow edges whose source and destination have variables in different locations.

4.4.1 Variable Location Analysis

The aim of the data flow analysis is to compute the locations of all program variables at the beginning and end of each basic block. The location of a variable is an element from the lattice $\mathcal{L}$, defined over the set

$$\mathcal{T} = \{Unknown, CPUAndGPU, GPU, CPU\}$$

with the partial order $\prec$ and the join operator $\wedge$ where,

$$\bot = Unknown, \top = CPU$$

$$Unknown \prec CPUAndGPU \prec GPU \prec CPU$$

The reason CPU dominates GPU in the lattice is that the CPU is the coordinating processor. At a program point where a variable is on the GPU along one reaching path, and on the CPU on another, it is probably better to move the variable to the CPU. Also, $CPUAndGPU$ is dominated by both CPU and GPU to avoid extra transfers. Consider the case when GPU is dominated by $CPUandGPU$. Then, at a program point where a variable is on the GPU on one reaching path, and on both along another, a transfer would have been needed for the GPU path to make the variable available on both. It is faster to just say that the variable is no longer available on the CPU. Similar reasoning applies for the CPU case.

If $Vars$ is the set of all variables in the program and B is the set of all basic blocks, for each basic block $b \in B$ and each $v \in Vars$, the following values are defined.

1. $in(v, b) \in \mathcal{T}$ is the location of v at the start of b.
2. $out(v, b) \in \mathcal{T}$ is the location of v at the exit of b.
3. $asmp(v, b) \in \mathcal{T}$ is the mapping of all statements in b that read v before it is written in b. It is $\bot$ if v is not accessed in b.
4. $grnt(v, b) \in \mathcal{T}$ indicates where v will be after the execution of b. If v is not used in b it is defined to be $\bot$.

The data flow analysis is defined by the following equations.

$$in(v,b) = \begin{cases} asmp(v,b) & \text{if } asmp(v,b) \neq \bot; \\ \bigwedge_{b' \in preds(b)} out(v,b') & \text{Otherwise.} \end{cases} \tag{5}$$

$$out(v,b) = \begin{cases} grnt(v,b) & \text{if } grnt(v,b) \neq \bot; \\ in(v,b) & \text{Otherwise.} \end{cases} \tag{6}$$

A standard forward data flow analysis algorithm [1] is used to find a fixed point for $in(v, b)$ and $out(v, b)$ using the data flow equations defined in equations 5 and 6. When a fixed point is reached for in and out, the values of $in(v, b)$ and $out(v, b)$ signify where v needs to be at the start of basic block b and where v will be at the end of basic block b.

The motivating example has three basic blocks as shown in Figure 3. The values of in and out for the variable A are: $in(A, b_1) = Unknown$; $out(A, b_1) = CPU$; $in(A, b_2) = GPU$; $out(A, b_2) = GPU$; $in(A, b_3) = CPU$ and $out(A, b_3) = CPU$.

4.4.2 Edge Splitting

Once the data flow analysis is performed, the location of every variable at the entry and exit of every basic block is known. When a variable changes locations across a control flow edge, a transfer needs to be inserted. More precisely, a transfer for a variable v needs to be inserted on a control flow edge $e = (b_1, b_2)$, when $out(v, b_1) \neq in(v, b_2)$.

MEGHA does not have the ability to explicitly split a control flow edge as it emits structured C++ code[8]. We therefore split edges by dynamically determining which control flow edge was taken to reach the current basic block. This is done by assigning ID numbers to each basic block and inserting code to set the value of a variable, _prevBasicBlock, to the ID at the end of the basic block. Then, at the entry of basic blocks, _prevBasicBlock can be checked to determine which control flow edge was taken and the required transfers can be performed. For the example in Figure 3, the edges (b_1, b_2) and (b_2, b_3) need to be split. This results in the following code.

```
n = 100;
A = rand(n, n);
_prevBasicBlock = 1;
for i=1:n
   if (_prevBasicBlock == 1)
      transferToGPU(A);
   A = A * A;
   _prevBasicBlock = 2;
end
if (_prevBasicBlock == 2)
   transferToCPU(A);
print(A);
```

4.5 Code Generation

Currently our code generator generates C++ code for parts of the input program mapped to the CPU and CUDA kernels for all kernels mapped to the GPU. For kernels that are assigned to the CPU, the loop nests are generated with the computed CPU loop order.

For a kernel mapped to the GPU, each thread of the generated CUDA kernel performs the computation for a single iteration of the surrounding loop nest. Assignment of threads to points in the iteration space is performed as described in Section 4.2. For the example in Section 4.2, the following CUDA kernel would be generated (Some details related to indexing have been simplified. Sizes of Ey and tempVar2 need to be passed to the kernel to correctly index them on line 13).

```
1: __global__ void
2: gpuKernel(float *Ey, float *tempVar2,
3:           int Sx, int Sy, int Sz)
4: {
5:  int tidx = (blockIdx.x*blockDim.x)+threadIdx.x;
6:  int tidy = (blockIdx.y*blockDim.y)+threadIdx.y;
7:  j = tidx;
8:  i = floor(tidy/Sz);
9:  k = tidy % Sz;
10: if (i>Sx || j>Sy || k>Sz)
11:   return;
12: indexVar1 = 2 + (k-1);
13: tempVar2(i, j, k) = Ey(i, j, indexVar1);
14:}
```

The above kernel would be called as follows.

```
dim3 grid(ceil(Sx/32), Sy*Sz, 1);
dim3 block(32, 1, 1);
gpuKernel<<< grid, block >>>(Ey, tempVar2,
                             Sx, Sy, Sz);
```

[8] This decision was made so that the optimizations of the C++ compiler would be more effective.

We chose to generate GPU kernels in this form since it is suitable for further automatic optimization [29]. For kernels that perform matrix multiplication, the code generator emits calls to the matrix multiply in CUBLAS rather than trying to generate an optimized matrix multiply kernel. This is possible because a matrix multiply kernel cannot be composed with other kernels (Section 4.1).

To perform memory transfers, the code generator uses the blocking cudaMemcpy routine. Therefore, the generated code does not overlap memory transfers with computation. However, it is possible to implement a code generation scheme that achieves this. Such a scheme would further improve the performance of the generated code. We leave this to future work.

5. Experimental Evaluation

We implemented MEGHA using the GNU Octave [11] system and used the benchmarks listed in Table 1 to evaluate it. These benchmarks are from several previous projects[9] with the exception of bscholes, which was developed in-house. For each benchmark the table shows the number of tasks identified by our compiler, e.g. clos has a total of 37 tasks out of which 27 are GPU friendly kernels and 10 are CPU only tasks. The number of kernels can be larger than the number of MATLAB statements as the compiler frontend generates many IR statements for each statement in the MATLAB code. We had to make minor modifications to capr as our compiler does not support *auto-growing arrays*. We modified the loop counts to increase the amount of computation in clos and fiff. As our compiler does not support user functions, we manually inlined calls to user-defined functions in all these benchmarks. The code generated by our compiler was compiled using nvcc (version 2.3) with the optimization level -O3. The generated executables were run on a machine with an Intel Xeon 2.83GHz quad-core processor[10] and a GeForce 8800 GTS 512 graphics processor. We also ran these on a machine with the same CPU but with a Tesla S1070 [20]. Both machines run Linux with kernel version 2.6.26. We used the time system utility to measure the runtimes of the executables generated by MEGHA and used the MATLAB function clock to measure the runtime for MATLAB programs run in the MATLAB environment.

For each benchmark, we report the runtime in the MATLAB environment, execution time of CPU only C++ code generated by our compiler and the execution time of C++ plus CUDA code generated by our compiler and the speedups achieved by these two versions over MATLAB execution. Each benchmark was run multiple times. The reported runtime is the average execution time per run. Also, all experiments were performed in single precision since the GeForce 8800 does not have support for double precision arithmetic.

Table 2 shows the runtimes for benchmarks with data parallel regions. In benchmark bscholes we get a speedup of 191X over MATLAB for large problem sizes. In this benchmark our compiler was able to identify the entire computation as one kernel and execute it on the GPU. MATLAB performs better than our CPU only code in bscholes as it handles full array operations better than our C++ code. Speedups for fdtd are higher on Tesla (63X-94X) as memory accesses are coalesced better on the Tesla than on the 8800. We did not report runtimes for the benchmark clos with C++ code as it uses matrix multiplication and our C++ code generator at present generates naïve code for matrix multiplication. However, these routines can easily be replaced by

[9] http://www.ece.northwestern.edu/cpdc/pjoisha/MAT2C/

[10] Although our experimental system contained two quad-core Xeon processors (8 cores), in our experiments, we use only a single core as the present compiler schedules tasks to a single GPU and a single CPU core. The compiler can easily be extended to use multiple CPU cores.

Benchmark	Size	Execution Time (in Seconds)				Speedup over MATLAB		
		MATLAB	CPU	CPU+8800	CPU+Tesla	CPU	CPU+8800	CPU+Tesla
bscholes	51200 Options, 100 Iters	0.9	1.99	0.03	0.02	0.45	30	45
	102400 Options, 500 Iters	8.9	19.7	0.07	0.05	0.45	127	178
	204800 Options, 500 Iters	17.2	39.5	0.1	0.09	0.43	172	191
clos	1024 vertices	0.5	-	0.18	0.11	-	2.8	4.5
	2048 vertices	4.1	-	1.13	0.73	-	3.6	5.6
	4096 vertices	30.8	-	mem-exc	5.82	-	-	5.3
fdtd	512 x 512 x 15	187	13.5	10.1	2.94	13.8	18.5	63.6
	512 x 512 x 32	408	30.5	22.69	5.48	13.4	18.0	74.4
	1024 x 512 x 32	806	62.7	mem-exc	9.8	12.8	-	82.2
	1024 x 1024 x 32	1623	121.6	mem-exc	17.2	13.3	-	94.4
nb1d	4096 bodies	14.8	7.6	5.4	5.4	1.95	2.7	2.7
	8192 bodies	50.1	29.2	13.7	15	1.7	3.6	3.3
	16384 bodies	513	323	119	128	1.6	4.3	4.0
nb3d	512 bodies	42.3	12.4	4.82	3.64	3.4	8.8	11.6
	1024 bodies	224.8	47.5	17.8	16.7	4.7	12.6	13.5
	1536 bodies	508	101.5	38.6	37.15	5.0	13.2	13.7

Table 2: Runtimes and speedups for data parallel benchmarks

Benchmark	Description	# of Lines	Tasks
`bscholes`(dp)	Stock Option Pricing	50	35/7
`capr`	Line Capacitance	60	69/23
`clos`(dp)	Transitive Closure	30	27/10
`crni`	Heat Equation Solver	60	55/14
`dich`	Laplace Equation Solver	55	68/15
`edit`	Edit Distance	60	35/15
`fdtd`(dp)	EM Field Computation	70	74/12
`fiff`	Wave Equation Solver	40	45/11
`nb1d`(dp)	1D N-Body Simulation	80	63/18
`nb3d`(dp)	3D N-Body Simulation	75	69/26

Table 1: Description of the benchmark suite. (dp) indicates benchmarks with data parallel regions. Number of kernels/number of CPU only statements are reported under the column Tasks.

calls to optimized BLAS libraries. The GPU versions for `clos`, which use the CUBLAS library, achieve a speedup[11] of 2.8X-5.6X on 8800 and Tesla. For `nb1d` and `nb3d` the GPU versions achieve speedups of 2.7X-4.0X and 8.8X-13.7X respectively. Lastly, even the CPU only version gives considerable speedups of 1.6X-13.4X for `fdtd`, `nb1d` and `nb3d` on a single CPU core.

Table 3 shows the runtimes for benchmarks with no or very few data parallel regions. The performance benefits over MATLAB are mainly due to compiling the MATLAB code to C++. Even here, we observe an improvement in execution time by factors of 2X-10X.

Table 4 compares performance of code generated by our compiler with that of GPUmat. GPUmat requires the user to explicitly mark variables as GPU variables before an operation on them can be performed on the GPU. The user has to manually identify data parallel regions and insert code to move data to the GPU only in these regions. Incorrect use of GPU variables can have an adverse impact on performance. We used some information from the code generated by our compiler to mark the GPU variables. GPUmat performs considerably better than MATLAB. However, because our compiler can automatically identify GPU kernels and reduce the amount of data transfer by intelligent kernel composition, we were able to get better performance (1.5X-10X) than GPUmat.

[11] Benchmarks `clos` (with 4096 vertices) and `fdtd` (problem size of 1024x512x32 or 1024x1024x32) could not be run on the 8800 as the kernel memory requirement exceeded the available memory (512MB) in the GPU.

Benchmark	Size	Execution Time (in Seconds)		
		MATLAB	CPU	CPU+8800
capr	256 x 512	9.15	1.43	1.43
	500 x 1000	17.3	2.65	2.66
	1000 x 2000	34.7	5.37	5.38
crni	2000 x 1000	16.05	6.33	6.39
	4000 x 2000	64.1	24.7	23
	8000 x 4000	254.8	104	103
dich	300 x 300	1.24	0.3	0.3
	2000 x 2000	55.7	8.01	8.15
	4000 x 4000	249.2	31.95	31.89
edit	512	0.35	0.11	0.11
	4096	22.1	0.45	0.45
	8192	88.1	1.47	1.48
fiff	450 x 450	0.51	0.22	0.21
	2000 x 2000	2.04	0.41	0.41
	4096 x 4096	8.17	2.5	2.51

Table 3: Runtimes for non data parallel benchmarks

Benchmark	Size	Execution Time (in Seconds)		
		MATLAB	GPUmat	CPU+Tesla
`bscholes`	102400, 500	8.9	7.2	0.08
`clos`	2048	4.1	1.13	0.73
`fdtd`	512 x 512 x 15	187	30	2.94
`nb1d`	4096	14.8	12.03	5.44
`nb3d`	1024	224.8	172	16.67

Table 4: Comparison with GPUmat

Our compiler reorders loops to improve cache locality on CPUs and coalesced accesses on GPUs. Table 5 shows the performance gains obtained by reordering loop nests. The benchmark `fdtd` has 3 dimensional arrays and benefits a lot on both the CPU and GPU with this optimization. Loop reordering improved the performance of `fdtd` CPU+GPU code by a factor of 16 and CPU only code by a factor of 5.1. Whereas for `nb3d` this optimization results in an improvement of 3X for CPU+GPU code and 1.05X for CPU only code.

Benchmark	Execution Time (in Seconds)				
	MATLAB	CPU Only		CPU + GPU	
		No Opt	Opt	No Opt	Opt
fdtd	187	82.05	15.82	48.14	2.94
nb3d	224.8	50.1	47.5	47.6	16.7

Table 5: Performance gains with parallel loop reordering. Problem sizes are 512 x 512 x 15(fdtd) and 1024(nb3d).

6. Related Work

Several previous projects have studied the problem of compiling MATLAB. The first of these was the FALCON project that compiled MATLAB programs to FORTRAN [10]. Most of our frontend is based on work done in the FALCON project. MaJIC [2] is a just-in-time MATLAB compiler that compiled and executed MATLAB programs with a mixture of compile time and run-time techniques. The MAGICA project [16] focussed on statically inferring symbolic types for variables in a MATLAB program and establishing relationships between shapes of various variables. Mat2C [17] is a MATLAB to C compiler based on MAGICA. MATCH [13] is a virtual machine that executes MATLAB programs in parallel by mimicking superscalar processors. The possibility of using expensive compile time analysis for generating high performance libraries from MATLAB routines was studied by Chauhan et al [7]. More recently, McVM [8], a virtual machine for the execution of MATLAB programs, that performs specialization based on types has been developed. However, none of these projects studied automatically compiling MATLAB to machines with distributed memory or heterogeneous processors.

Jacket [14] and GPUMat [12] are systems that enable users to execute parts of MATLAB programs on GPUs. However, these require users to specify what is to be run on the GPU by annotating the source code. Arrays whose operations are to be performed on the GPU are declared with a special type. This is similar to the concept of data parallel arrays in Accelerator [25]. Similarly, Khoury et al extend Octave to target the Cell BE processor [19]. However, their system still requires users to cast matrices to a specific type so that operations on these matrices can be performed on the SPEs. It also uses a virtual machine based approach to perform matrix operations on the SPEs as opposed to generating custom code.

Several previous works have studied problems related to compilation for GPUs. Techniques for optimizing naïve CUDA kernels were studied by Yang et al [29]. The use of the polyhedral model to optimize code for accelerator architectures was studied by Baskaran et al [4][5]. These techniques are complementary to those discussed in this paper as they can be used to optimize kernels and low level code generated by our compiler.

Previous works have also explored compiling programs in other high level languages to GPUs. For example, compilation of stream programs to GPUs and heterogeneous machines was studied by Udupa et al [26][27]. To the best of our knowledge, our paper is the first to study the problem of automatically compiling MATLAB programs for execution on systems with heterogeneous processors.

7. Conclusions and Future Work

In this paper, we presented a compiler framework, MEGHA, for the automatic compilation of MATLAB programs for execution on systems with heterogeneous processors. We presented a technique for identifying and composing kernels in the input MATLAB program while taking several costs and benefits into account. An efficient heuristic for automatically mapping and scheduling identified kernels on CPU and GPU has also been proposed. The heuristic takes into account data transfer while mapping kernels to processors. Then, a data flow analysis based edge splitting strategy to handle dependencies across basic blocks was proposed. The proposed framework was implemented and initial performance results indicate that our approach is promising with performance gains up to 191X over native MATLAB execution being obtained.

There are also several interesting directions for future work. One interesting direction is to implement the techniques described in this paper as a mixture of static and dynamic optimizations. Also, in this paper, we did not consider GPU memory constraints while mapping and scheduling kernels. This needs to be considered for larger programs to be correctly run. Optimizing the generated kernels using shared memory and performing other optimizations on them also needs to be studied.

Acknowledgments

We thank R. Manikantan and other members of the Lab for High Performance Computing, IISc for several helpful discussions regarding the work described in this paper. We would also like to thank the anonymous reviewers for several valuable suggestions that helped improve our paper. We would also like to acknowledge funding received from Microsoft and NVIDIA.

References

[1] A. V. Aho, Ravi Sethi, J. D. Ullman, M. S. Lam. *Compilers: Principles, Techniques, & Tools*. Pearson Education, 2009.

[2] G. Almasi, D. Padua. *MaJIC: Compiling MATLAB for Speed and Responsiveness*. In the ACM SIGPLAN 2002 Conference on Programming Language Design and Implementation (PLDI '02).

[3] ATI Technologies, *http://ati.amd.com/products/index.html*

[4] M. Baskaran, U. Bondhugula, S. Krishnamoorthy, J. Ramanujam, A. Rountev, P. Sadayappan. *A Compiler Framework for Optimization of Affine Loop Nests for GPGPUs*. In the 22nd Annual International Conference on Supercomputing (ICS '08).

[5] M. Baskaran, U. Bondhugula, S. Krishnamoorthy, J. Ramanujam, A. Rountev, P. Sadayappan. *Automatic Data Movement and Computation Mapping for Multi-level Parallel Architectures with Explicitly Managed Memories*. In the 13th ACM SIGPLAN Symposium on Principles and Practice of Parallel Programming (PPoPP '08).

[6] U. Bondhugula, A. Hartono, J. Ramanujam, P. Sadayappan. *A Practical Automatic Polyhedral Parallelizer and Locality Optimizer*. In the 2008 ACM SIGPLAN conference on Programming language design and implementation (PLDI '08).

[7] A. Chauhan, C. McCosh, K. Kennedy, and R. Hanson. *Automatic Type-Driven Library Generation for Telescoping Languages*. In the 2003 ACM/IEEE Conference on Supercomputing (SC '03).

[8] M. Chevalier-Boisvert, L. Hendren, C. Verbrugge. *Optimizing MATLAB Through Just-In-Time Specialization*. In the 2010 International Conference on Compiler Construction (CC '10).

[9] R. Cytron, J. Ferrante, B. K. Rosen, M. N. Wegman, F. K. Zadeck. *Efficiently Computing Static Single Assignment Form and the Control Dependence Graph*. In the ACM Transactions on Programming Languages and Systems, 13(4):451–490, Oct. 1991.

[10] L. De Rose, D. Padua. *Techniques for the translation of MATLAB programs into Fortran 90*. In the ACM Transactions on Programming Languages and Systems, 21(2):286–323, Mar. 1999.

[11] J. W. Eaton. *GNU Octave Manual*, Network Theory Limited, 2002.

[12] GPUMat Home Page. *http://gp-you.org/*

[13] M. Haldar et. al. *MATCH Virtual Machine: An Adaptive Run-Time System to Execute MATLAB in Parallel*. In the 2000 International Conference on Parallel Processing (ICPP '00).

[14] Jacket Home Page. *http://www.accelereyes.com/*

[15] P. Joisha, P. Banerjee. *Static Array Storage Optimization in MATLAB*. In the ACM SIGPLAN 2003 conference on Programming language design and implementation (PLDI '03).

[16] P. Joisha, P. Banerjee. *An Algebraic Array Shape Inference System for MATLAB.* ACM Transactions on Programming Languages and Systems, 28(5):848–907, September 2006.

[17] P. Joisha, P. Banerjee. *A Translator System for the MATLAB Language*, Research Articles on Software Practices and Experience '07.

[18] K. Kennedy, K. S. McKinley. *Maximizing Loop Parallelism and Improving Data Locality via Loop Fusion and Distribution.* In the 6th International Workshop on Languages and Compilers for Parallel Computing (LCPC '93).

[19] R. Khoury, B. Burgstaller, B. Scholz, *Accelerating the Execution of Matrix Languages on the Cell Broadband Engine Architecture.* IEEE Transactions on Parallel and Distributed Systems, 22(1):7–21, Jan. 2011.

[20] E. Lindholm, J. Nickolls, S. Oberman, J. Montrym. *NVIDIA Tesla: A Unified Graphics and Computing Architecture.* IEEE Micro, March 2008.

[21] Mathworks Home Page. *http://www.mathworks.com/*

[22] NVIDIA Corp, *NVIDIA CUDA: Compute Unified Device Architecture: Programming Guide*, Version 3.0, 2010.

[23] NVIDIA Corp, Fermi Home Page, *http://www.nvidia.com/object/fermi_architecture.html*

[24] S. K. Singhai, K. S. Mckinley. *A Parametrized Loop Fusion Algorithm for Improving Parallelism and Cache Locality*, Computer Journal, 1997.

[25] D. Tarditi, S. Puri, J. Oglesby. *Accelerator: Using Data Parallelism to Program GPUs for General-Purpose Uses.* In the 12th International Conference on Architectural Support for Programming Languages and Operating Systems (ASPLOS-XII).

[26] A. Udupa, R. Govindarajan, M. J. Thazhuthaveetil. *Software Pipelined Execution of Stream Programs on GPUs.* In the 7th annual IEEE/ACM International Symposium on Code Generation and Optimization (CGO '09).

[27] A. Udupa, R. Govindarajan, M. J. Thazhuthaveetil. *Synergistic Execution of Stream Programs on Multicores with Accelerators.* In the 2009 ACM SIGPLAN/SIGBED Conference on Languages, Compilers, and Tools for Embedded Systems (LCTES '09).

[28] V. Volkov, J. W. Demmel. *Benchmarking GPUs to Tune Dense Linear Algebra.* In the 2008 ACM/IEEE Conference on Supercomputing (SC '08).

[29] Y. Yang, P. Xiang, J. Kong, H. Zhou. *A GPGPU Compiler for Memory Optimization and Parallelism Management.* In the 2010 ACM SIGPLAN conference on Programming Language Design and Implementation (PLDI '10).

EnerJ: Approximate Data Types for Safe and General Low-Power Computation

Adrian Sampson Werner Dietl Emily Fortuna Danushen Gnanapragasam
Luis Ceze Dan Grossman
University of Washington, Department of Computer Science & Engineering
http://sampa.cs.washington.edu/

Abstract

Energy is increasingly a first-order concern in computer systems. Exploiting energy-accuracy trade-offs is an attractive choice in applications that can tolerate inaccuracies. Recent work has explored exposing this trade-off in programming models. A key challenge, though, is how to *isolate parts of the program that must be precise from those that can be approximated* so that a program functions correctly even as quality of service degrades.

We propose using type qualifiers to declare data that may be subject to approximate computation. Using these types, the system automatically maps approximate variables to low-power storage, uses low-power operations, and even applies more energy-efficient algorithms provided by the programmer. In addition, the system can statically guarantee isolation of the precise program component from the approximate component. This allows a programmer to control explicitly how information flows from approximate data to precise data. Importantly, employing static analysis eliminates the need for dynamic checks, further improving energy savings. As a proof of concept, we develop EnerJ, an extension to Java that adds approximate data types. We also propose a hardware architecture that offers explicit approximate storage and computation. We port several applications to EnerJ and show that our extensions are expressive and effective; a small number of annotations lead to significant potential energy savings (10%–50%) at very little accuracy cost.

Categories and Subject Descriptors C.0 [*Computer Systems Organization*]: General—Hardware/software interfaces; D.3.3 [*Programming Languages*]: Language Constructs and Features—Data types and structures

General Terms Languages, Performance, Design

Keywords Accuracy-aware computing, power-aware computing, energy, soft errors, critical data

1. Introduction

Energy consumption is an increasing concern in many computer systems. Battery life is a first-order constraint in mobile systems, and power/cooling costs largely dominate the cost of equipment in data-centers. More fundamentally, current trends point toward a "utilization wall," in which the amount of active die area is limited by how much power can be fed to a chip.

Much of the focus in reducing energy consumption has been on low-power architectures, performance/power trade-offs, and resource management. While those techniques are effective and can be applied without software knowledge, exposing energy considerations at the programming language level can enable a whole new set of energy optimizations. This work is a step in that direction.

Recent research has begun to explore energy-accuracy trade-offs in general-purpose programs. A key observation is that systems spend a significant amount of energy guaranteeing correctness. Consequently, a system can save energy by exposing faults to the application. Many studies have shown that a variety of applications are resilient to hardware and software errors during execution [1, 8, 9, 19, 21–23, 25, 31, 35]. Importantly, these studies universally show that applications have portions that are more resilient and portions that are "critical" and must be protected from error. For example, an image renderer can tolerate errors in the pixel data it outputs—a small number of erroneous pixels may be acceptable or even undetectable. However, an error in a jump table could lead to a crash, and even small errors in the image file format might make the output unreadable.

While approximate computation can save a significant amount of energy, distinguishing between the critical and non-critical portions of a program is difficult. Prior proposals have used annotations on code blocks (e.g., [9]) and data allocation sites (e.g., [23]). These annotations, however, do not offer any guarantee that the fundamental operation of the program is not compromised. In other words, these annotations are either *unsafe* and may lead to unacceptable program behavior or *need dynamic checks* that end up consuming energy. We need a way to allow programmers to compose programs from approximate and precise components safely. Moreover, we need to guarantee safety statically to avoid spending energy checking properties at runtime. The key insight in this paper is the application of type-based information-flow tracking [32] ideas to address these problems.

Contributions. This paper proposes a model for approximate programming that is both *safe* and *general*. We use a type system that isolates the precise portion of the program from the approximate portion. The programmer must explicitly delineate flow from approximate data to precise data. The model is thus *safe* in that it guarantees precise computation unless given explicit programmer permission. Safety is statically enforced and no dynamic checks are required, minimizing the overheads imposed by the language.

We present EnerJ, a language for principled approximate computing. EnerJ extends Java with type qualifiers that distinguish between *approximate* and *precise* data types. Data annotated with the "ap-

PLDI'11, June 4–8, 2011, San Jose, California, USA.

proximate" qualifier can be stored approximately and computations involving it can be performed approximately. EnerJ also provides *endorsements*, which are programmer-specified points at which approximate-to-precise data flow may occur. The language supports programming constructs for algorithmic approximation, in which the programmer produces different implementations of functionality for approximate and precise data. We formalize a core of EnerJ and prove a non-interference property in the absence of endorsements.

Our programming model is *general* in that it unifies approximate data storage, approximate computation, and approximate algorithms. Programmers use a single abstraction to apply all three forms of approximation. The model is also *high-level and portable:* the implementation (compiler, runtime system, hardware) is entirely responsible for choosing the energy-saving mechanisms to employ and when to do so, guaranteeing correctness for precise data and "best effort" for the rest.

While EnerJ is designed to support general approximation strategies and therefore ensure full portability and backward-compatibility, we demonstrate its effectiveness using a proposed approximation-aware architecture with approximate memory and imprecise functional units. We have ported several applications to EnerJ to demonstrate that a small amount of annotation can allow a program to save a large amount of energy while not compromising quality of service significantly.

Outline. We first detail the EnerJ language extensions in Section 2. Section 3 formalizes a core of the language, allowing us to prove a non-interference property. The full formalism and proof are presented in an accompanying technical report [33]. Next, Section 4 describes hypothetical hardware for executing EnerJ programs. While other execution substrates are possible, this proposed model provides a basis for the evaluation in Sections 5 and 6; there, we assess EnerJ's expressiveness and potential energy savings. The type checker and simulation infrastructure used in our evaluation are available at `http://sampa.cs.washington.edu/`. Section 7 presents related work and Section 8 concludes.

2. A Type System for Approximate Computation

This section describes EnerJ's extensions to Java, which are based on a system of type qualifiers. We first describe the qualifiers themselves. We next explain how programmers precisely control when approximate data can affect precise state. We describe the implementation of approximate operations using overloading. We then discuss conditional statements and the prevention of implicit flows. Finally, we describe the type system's extension to object-oriented programming constructs and its interaction with Java arrays.

EnerJ implements these language constructs as backwards-compatible additions to Java extended with type annotations [11]. Table 1 summarizes our extensions and their concrete syntax.

2.1 Type Annotations

Every value in the program has an approximate or precise type. The programmer annotates types with the @Approx and @Precise qualifiers. Precise types are the default, so typically only @Approx is made explicit. It is illegal to assign an approximate-typed value into a precise-typed variable. Intuitively, this prevents direct flow of data from approximate to precise variables. For instance, the following assignment is illegal:

```
@Approx int a = ...;
int p; // precise by default
p = a; // illegal
```

Approximate-to-precise data flow is clearly undesirable, but it seems natural to allow flow in the opposite direction. For primitive Java types, we allow precise-to-approximate data flow via subtyping. Specifically, we make each precise primitive Java type a subtype of its approximate counterpart. This choice permits, for instance, the assignment a = p; in the above example.

For Java's reference (class) types, this subtyping relationship is unsound. The qualifier of a reference can influence the qualifiers of its fields (see Section 2.5), so subtyping on mutable references is unsound for standard reasons. We find that this limitation is not cumbersome in practice.

We also introduce a @Top qualifier to denote the common supertype of @Approx and @Precise types.

Semantics of approximation. EnerJ takes an all-or-nothing approach to approximation. Precise values carry traditional guarantees of correctness; approximate values have no guarantees. A more complex system could provide multiple levels of approximation and guaranteed error bounds, but we find that this simple system is sufficiently expressive for a wide range of applications.

The language achieves generality by leaving approximation patterns unspecified, but programmers can informally expect approximate data to be "mostly correct" and adhere to normal execution semantics except for occasional errors. The degree of precision is an orthogonal concern; a separate system could tune the frequency and intensity of errors in approximate data.

2.2 Endorsement

Fully isolating approximate and precise parts of a program would likely not be very useful. Eventually a program needs to store data, transmit it, or present it to the programmer—at which point the program should begin behaving precisely. As a general pattern, programs we examined frequently had a phase of fault-tolerant computation followed by a phase of fault-sensitive reduction or output. For instance, one application consists of a resilient image manipulation phase followed by a critical checksum over the result (see Section 6.3). It is essential that data be occasionally allowed to break the strict separation enforced by the type system.

We require the programmer to control explicitly when approximate data can affect precise state. To this end, we borrow the concept (and term) of *endorsement* from past work on information-flow control [2]. An explicit static function endorse allows the programmer to use approximate data as if it were precise. The function acts as a cast from any approximate type to its precise equivalent. Endorsements may have implicit runtime effects; they might, for example, copy values from approximate to precise memory.

The previous example can be made legal with an endorsement:

```
@Approx int a = ...;
int p; // precise by default
p = endorse(a); // legal
```

By inserting an endorsement, the programmer certifies that the approximate data is handled intelligently and will not cause undesired results in the precise part of the program.

2.3 Approximate Operations

The type system thus far provides a mechanism for approximating *storage*. Clearly, variables with approximate type may be located in unreliable memory modules. However, approximate *computation* requires additional features.

We introduce approximate computation by overloading operators and methods based on the type qualifiers. For instance, our language provides two signatures for the + operator on integers: one taking two precise integers and producing a precise integer and the other taking two approximate integers and producing an approximate integer. The latter may compute its result approximately and thus may run on low-power hardware. Programmers can extend this concept by overloading methods with qualified parameter types.

Bidirectional typing. The above approach occasionally applies precise operations where approximate operations would suffice.

Construct	Purpose	Section
@Approx, @Precise, @Top	Type annotations: qualify any type in the program. (Default is @Precise.)	2.1
endorse(*e*)	Cast an approximate value to its precise equivalent.	2.2
@Approximable	Class annotation: allow a class to have both precise and approximate instances.	2.5
@Context	Type annotation: in approximable class definitions, the precision of the type depends on the precision of the enclosing object.	2.5.1
_APPROX	Method naming convention: this implementation of the method may be invoked when the receiver has approximate type.	2.5.2

Table 1. Summary of EnerJ's language extensions.

Consider the expression a = b + c where a is approximate but b and c are precise. Overloading selects precise addition even though the result will only be used approximately. It is possible to force an approximate operation by upcasting either operand to an approximate type, but we provide a slight optimization that avoids the need for additional annotation. EnerJ implements an extremely simple form of bidirectional type checking [7] that applies approximate arithmetic operators when the result type is approximate: on the right-hand side of assignment operators and in method arguments. We find that this small optimization makes it simpler to write approximate arithmetic expressions that include precise data.

2.4 Control Flow

To provide the desired property that information never flows from approximate to precise data, we must disallow *implicit flows* that occur via control flow. For example, the following program violates the desired isolation property:

```
@Approx int val = ...;
boolean flag; // precise
if (val == 5) { flag = true; } else { flag = false; }
```

Even though flag is precise and no endorsement is present, its value is affected by the approximate variable val.

EnerJ avoids this situation by prohibiting approximate values in conditions that affect control flow (such as if and while statements). In the above example, val == 5 has approximate type because the approximate version of == must be used. Our language disallows this expression in the condition, though the programmer can work around this restriction using if(endorse(val == 5)).

This restriction is conservative: it prohibits approximate conditions even when the result can affect only approximate data. A more sophisticated approach would allow only approximate values to be produced in statements conditioned on approximate data. We find that our simpler approach is sufficient; endorsements allow the programmer to work around the restriction when needed.

2.5 Objects

EnerJ's type qualifiers are not limited to primitive types. Classes also support approximation. Clients of an *approximable* class can create precise and approximate instances of the class. The author of the class defines the meaning of approximation for the class. Approximable classes are distinguished by the @Approximable class annotation. Such a class exhibits qualifier polymorphism [14]: types within the class definition may depend on the qualifier of the instance.

Note that precise class types are not subtypes of their approximate counterparts, as is the case with primitive types (Section 2.1); such a subtyping relationship would be fundamentally unsound for the standard reasons related to mutable references.

2.5.1 Contextual Data Types

The @Context qualifier is available in definitions of non-static members of approximable classes. The meaning of the qualifier depends on the precision of the instance of the enclosing class. (In terms of qualifier polymorphism, @Context refers to the class' qualifier parameter, which is determined by the qualifier placed on the instance.) Consider the following class definition:

```
@Approximable class IntPair {
  @Context int x;
  @Context int y;
  @Approx int numAdditions = 0;
  void addToBoth(@Context int amount) {
    x += amount;
    y += amount;
    numAdditions++;
  }
}
```

If a is an approximate instance of IntPair, then the fields a.x, a.y, and a.numAdditions are all of approximate integer type. However, if p is a precise instance of the class, then p.x and p.y are precise but p.numAdditions is still approximate. Furthermore, the argument to the invocation p.addToBoth() must be precise; the argument to a.addToBoth() may be approximate.

2.5.2 Algorithmic Approximation

Approximable classes may also specialize method definitions based on their qualifier. That is, the programmer can write two implementations: one to be called when the receiver has precise type and another that can be called when the receiver is approximate. Consider the following implementations of a mean calculation over a list of floats:

```
@Approximable class FloatSet {
  @Context float[] nums = ...;
  float mean() {
    float total = 0.0f;
    for (int i = 0; i < nums.length; ++i)
      total += nums[i];
    return total / nums.length;
  }
  @Approx float mean_APPROX() {
    @Approx float total = 0.0f;
    for (int i = 0; i < nums.length; i += 2)
      total += nums[i];
    return 2 * total / nums.length;
  }
}
```

EnerJ uses a naming convention, consisting of the _APPROX suffix, to distinguish methods overloaded on precision. The first implementation of mean is called when the receiver is precise. The second implementation calculates an approximation of the mean: it averages only half the numbers in the set. This implementation will be used for the invocation s.mean() where s is an approximate instance of FloatSet. Note that the compiler automatically decides which implementation of the method to invoke depending on the receiver type; the same invocation is used in either case.

It is the programmer's responsibility to ensure that the two implementations are similar enough that they can be safely substituted. This is important for backwards compatibility (a plain Java compiler will ignore the naming convention and always use the precise

$$
\begin{array}{rcl}
Prg & ::= & \overline{Cls},\ C,\ e \\
Cls & ::= & \texttt{class}\ Cid\ \texttt{extends}\ C\ \{\ \overline{fd}\ \overline{md}\ \} \\
C & ::= & Cid \mid \texttt{Object} \\
P & ::= & \texttt{int} \mid \texttt{float} \\
q & ::= & \texttt{precise} \mid \texttt{approx} \mid \texttt{top} \mid \texttt{context} \mid \texttt{lost} \\
T & ::= & q\ C \mid q\ P \\
fd & ::= & T\ f; \\
md & ::= & T\ m(\overline{T\ pid})\ q\ \{\ e\ \} \\
x & ::= & pid \mid \texttt{this} \\
e & ::= & \texttt{null} \mid \mathcal{L} \mid x \mid \texttt{new}\ q\ C() \mid e.f \mid e_0.f{:=}e_1 \mid e_0.m(\overline{e}) \\
 & & \mid (q\ C)\ e \mid e_0 \oplus e_1 \mid \texttt{if}(e_0)\ \{e_1\}\ \texttt{else}\ \{e_2\}
\end{array}
$$

f	field identifier	pid	parameter identifier
m	method identifier	Cid	class identifier

Figure 1. The syntax of the FEnerJ programming language. The symbol $\overline{A}$ denotes a sequence of elements A.

version) and "best effort" (the implementation may use the precise version if energy is not constrained).

This facility makes it simple to couple algorithmic approximation with data approximation—a single annotation makes an instance use both approximate data (via @Context) and approximate code (via overloading).

2.6 Arrays

The programmer can declare arrays with approximate element types, but the array's length is always kept precise for memory safety. We find that programs often use large arrays of approximate primitive elements; in this case, the elements themselves are all approximated and only the length requires precise guarantees.

EnerJ prohibits approximate integers from being used as array subscripts. That is, in the expression a[i], the value i must be precise. This makes it easier for the programmer to prevent out-of-bounds errors due to approximation.

3. Formal Semantics

To study the formal semantics of EnerJ, we define the minimal language FEnerJ. The language is based on Featherweight Java [16] and adds precision qualifiers and state. The formal language omits EnerJ's endorsements and thus can guarantee isolation of approximate and precise program components. This isolation property suggests that, *in the absence of endorsement*, approximate data in an EnerJ program cannot affect precise state.

The accompanying technical report [33] formalizes this language and proves type soundness as well as a non-interference property that demonstrates the desired isolation of approximate and precise data.

3.1 Programming Language

Figure 1 presents the syntax of FEnerJ. Programs consist of a sequence of classes, a main class, and a main expression. Execution is modeled by instantiating the main class and then evaluating the main expression.

A class definition consists of a name, the name of the superclass, and field and method definitions. The @Approximable annotation is not modeled in FEnerJ; all classes in the formal language can have approximate and precise instances and this has @Context type. The annotation is required only in order to provide backward-compatibility with Java so that this in a non-approximable class has @Precise type.

We use C to range over class names and P for the names of primitive types. We define the precision qualifiers q as discussed in Section 2.1, but with the additional qualifier `lost`; this qualifier is used to express situations when context information is not expressible (i.e., lost). Types T include qualifiers.

Field declarations consist of the field type and name. Method declarations consist of the return type, method name, a sequence of parameter types and identifiers, the method precision, and the method body. We use the method precision qualifier to denote overloading of the method based on the precision of the receiver as introduced in Section 2.5.2. Variables are either a parameter identifier or the special variable `this`, signifying the current object.

The language has the following expressions: the null literal, literals of the primitive types, reads of local variables, instantiation, field reads and writes, method calls, casts, binary primitive operations, and conditionals. For brevity, the discussion below presents only the rules for field reads, field writes, and conditionals.

Subtyping. Subtyping is defined using an ordering of the precision qualifiers and subclassing.

The following rules define the ordering of precision qualifiers:

$\boxed{q <:_{\text{q}} q'}$ ordering of precision qualifiers

$$
\frac{q \neq \texttt{top}}{q <:_{\text{q}} \texttt{lost}} \qquad \frac{}{q <:_{\text{q}} \texttt{top}} \qquad \frac{}{q <:_{\text{q}} q}
$$

Recall that `top` qualifies the common supertype of `precise` and `approx` types. Every qualifier other than `top` is below `lost`; every qualifier is below `top`; and the relation is reflexive. Note that the `precise` and `approx` qualifiers are not related.

Subclassing is the reflexive and transitive closure of the relation induced by the class declarations. Subtyping takes both ordering of precision qualifiers and subclassing into account. For primitive types, we additionally have that a precise type is a subtype of the approximate type as described in Section 2.1.

Context adaptation. We use *context adaptation* to replace the `context` qualifier when it appears in a field access or method invocation. Here the left-hand side of $\triangleright$ denotes the qualifier of the receiver expression; the right-hand side is the precision qualifier of the field or in the method signature.

$\boxed{q \triangleright q' = q''}$ combining two precision qualifiers

$$
\frac{q'{=}\texttt{context} \ \wedge\ (q \in \{\texttt{approx}, \texttt{precise}, \texttt{context}\})}{q \triangleright q' = q}
$$

$$
\frac{q'{=}\texttt{context} \ \wedge\ (q \in \{\texttt{top}, \texttt{lost}\})}{q \triangleright q' = \texttt{lost}} \qquad \frac{q' {\neq} \texttt{context}}{q \triangleright q' = q'}
$$

Note that `context` adapts to `lost` when the left-hand-side qualifier is `top` because the appropriate qualifier cannot be determined.

We additionally define $\triangleright$ to take a type as the right-hand side; this adapts the precision qualifier of the type.

We define partial look-up functions FType and MSig that determine the field type and method signature for a given field/method in an access or invocation. Note that these use the adaptation rules described above.

Type rules. The static type environment ${}^{s}\Gamma$ maps local variables to their declared types.

Given a static environment, expressions are typed as follows:

$\boxed{{}^{s}\Gamma \vdash e : T}$ expression typing

$$
\frac{{}^{s}\Gamma \vdash e_0 : q\ C \qquad \text{FType}(q\ C, f) = T}{{}^{s}\Gamma \vdash e_0.f : T}
$$

$$
\frac{\begin{array}{ll} {}^{s}\Gamma \vdash e_0 : q\ C & \text{FType}(q\ C, f) = T \\ \texttt{lost} \notin T & {}^{s}\Gamma \vdash e_1 : T \end{array}}{{}^{s}\Gamma \vdash e_0.f := e_1 : T}
$$

$$\frac{{}^{s}\Gamma \vdash e_0 : \texttt{precise}\ P \qquad {}^{s}\Gamma \vdash e_1 : T \qquad {}^{s}\Gamma \vdash e_2 : T}{{}^{s}\Gamma \vdash \texttt{if}(e_0)\ \{e_1\}\ \texttt{else}\ \{e_2\}\ : T}$$

A field read determines the type of the receiver expression and then uses FType to determine the adapted type of the field.

A field write similarly determines the adapted type of the field and checks that the right-hand side has an appropriate type. In addition, we ensure that the adaptation of the declared field type did not lose precision information. Notice that we can read a field with lost precision information, but that it would be unsound to allow the update of such a field.

Finally, for the conditional expression, we ensure that the condition is of a precise primitive type and that there is a common type T that can be assigned to both subexpressions.

3.2 Operational Semantics

The runtime system of FEnerJ models the heap h as a mapping from addresses ι to objects, where objects are a pair of the runtime type T and the field values v of the object. The runtime environment ${}^{r}\Gamma$ maps local variables x to values v.

The runtime system of FEnerJ defines a standard big-step operational semantics:

$\boxed{{}^{r}\Gamma \vdash h, e \rightsquigarrow h', v}$ big-step operational semantics

$$\frac{{}^{r}\Gamma \vdash h, e_0 \rightsquigarrow h', \iota_0 \qquad h'(\iota_0.f) = v}{{}^{r}\Gamma \vdash h, e_0.f \rightsquigarrow h', v}$$

$$\frac{\begin{array}{l}{}^{r}\Gamma \vdash h, e_0 \rightsquigarrow h_0, \iota_0 \qquad {}^{r}\Gamma \vdash h_0, e_1 \rightsquigarrow h_1, v \\ h_1[\iota_0.f := v] = h'\end{array}}{{}^{r}\Gamma \vdash h, e_0.f := e_1 \rightsquigarrow h', v}$$

$$\frac{\begin{array}{l}{}^{r}\Gamma \vdash h, e_0 \rightsquigarrow h_0, (q, {}^{r}\mathcal{L}) \qquad {}^{r}\mathcal{L} \neq 0 \\ {}^{r}\Gamma \vdash h_0, e_1 \rightsquigarrow h', v\end{array}}{{}^{r}\Gamma \vdash h, \texttt{if}(e_0)\ \{e_1\}\ \texttt{else}\ \{e_2\} \rightsquigarrow h', v}$$

$$\frac{{}^{r}\Gamma \vdash h, e_0 \rightsquigarrow h_0, (q, 0) \qquad {}^{r}\Gamma \vdash h_0, e_2 \rightsquigarrow h', v}{{}^{r}\Gamma \vdash h, \texttt{if}(e_0)\ \{e_1\}\ \texttt{else}\ \{e_2\} \rightsquigarrow h', v}$$

These rules reflect precise execution with conventional precision guarantees. To model computation on an execution substrate that supports approximation, the following rule could be introduced:

$$\frac{{}^{r}\Gamma \vdash h, e \rightsquigarrow h', v \qquad h' \cong \tilde{h}' \qquad v \cong \tilde{v}}{{}^{r}\Gamma \vdash h, e \rightsquigarrow \tilde{h}', \tilde{v}}$$

We use $\cong$ to denote an equality that disregards approximate values for comparing heaps and values with identical types. The rule permits any approximate value in the heap to be replaced with any other value of the same type and any expression producing a value of an approximate type to produce any other value of that type instead. This rule reflects EnerJ's lack of guarantees for approximate values.

3.3 Properties

We prove two properties about FEnerJ: type soundness and non-interference. The full proofs are listed in the accompanying technical report [33].

The usual type soundness property expresses that, for a well-typed program and corresponding static and runtime environments, we know that (1) the runtime environment after evaluating the expression is still well formed, and (2) a static type that can be assigned to the expression can also be assigned to the value that is the result of evaluating the expression. Formally:

$$\left.\begin{array}{l}\vdash Prg\ \texttt{OK} \land \vdash h, {}^{r}\Gamma : {}^{s}\Gamma \\ {}^{s}\Gamma \vdash e : T \\ {}^{r}\Gamma \vdash h, e \rightsquigarrow h', v\end{array}\right\} \Longrightarrow \left\{\begin{array}{l}\vdash h', {}^{r}\Gamma : {}^{s}\Gamma \\ h', {}^{r}\Gamma(\texttt{this}) \vdash v : T\end{array}\right.$$

The proof is by rule induction over the operational semantics; in separate lemmas we formalize that the context adaptation operation $\triangleright$ is sound.

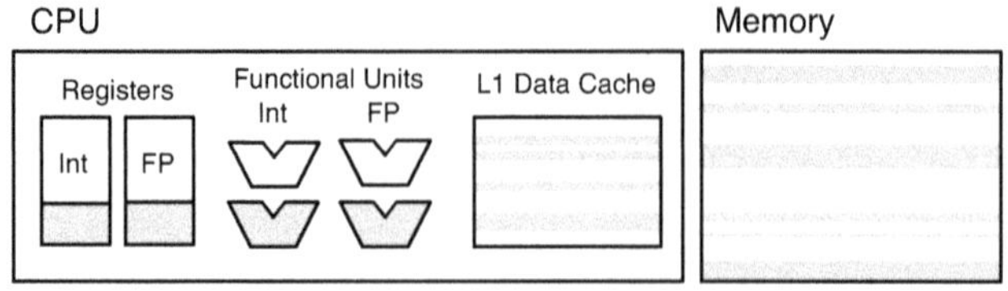

Figure 2. Hardware model assumed in our system. Shaded areas indicate components that support approximation. Registers and the data cache have SRAM storage cells that can be made approximate by decreasing supply voltage. Functional units support approximation via supply voltage reduction. Floating point functional units also support approximation via smaller mantissas. Main memory (DRAM) supports approximation by reducing refresh rate.

The non-interference property of FEnerJ guarantees that approximate computations do not influence precise values. Specifically, changing approximate values in the heap or runtime environment does not change the precise parts of the heap or the result of the computation. More formally, we show:

$$\left.\begin{array}{l}\vdash Prg\ \texttt{OK} \land \vdash h, {}^{r}\Gamma : {}^{s}\Gamma \\ {}^{s}\Gamma \vdash e : T \\ {}^{r}\Gamma \vdash h, e \rightsquigarrow h', v \\ h \cong \tilde{h} \land {}^{r}\Gamma \cong {}^{r}\tilde{\Gamma} \\ \vdash \tilde{h}, {}^{r}\tilde{\Gamma} : {}^{s}\Gamma\end{array}\right\} \Longrightarrow \left\{\begin{array}{l}{}^{r}\tilde{\Gamma} \vdash \tilde{h}, e \rightarrow \tilde{h}', \tilde{v} \\ h' \cong \tilde{h}' \\ v \cong \tilde{v}\end{array}\right.$$

For the proof of this property we introduced a *checked* operational semantics that ensures in every evaluation step that the precise and approximate parts are separated. We can then show that the evaluation of a well-typed expression always passes the checked semantics of the programming language.

4. Execution Model

While an EnerJ program distinguishes abstractly between approximate and precise data, it does not define the particular approximation strategies that are applied to the program. (In fact, one valid execution is to ignore all annotations and execute the code as plain Java.) An approximation-aware execution substrate is needed to take advantage of EnerJ's annotations. We choose to examine approximation at the architecture level. Alternatively, a runtime system on top of commodity hardware can also offer approximate execution features (e.g., lower floating point precision, elision of memory operations, etc.). Also, note that algorithmic approximation (see Section 2.5) is independent of the execution substrate. This section describes our hardware model, the ISA extensions used for approximation, and how the extensions enable energy savings.

4.1 Approximation-Aware ISA Extensions

We want to leverage both approximate *storage* and approximate *operations*. Our hardware model offers approximate storage in the form of unreliable registers, data caches, and main memory. Approximate and precise registers are distinguished based on the register number. Approximate data stored in memory is distinguished from precise data based on address; regions of physical memory are marked as approximate and, when accessed, are stored in approximate portions of the data cache. For approximate operations, we assume specific instructions for approximate integer ALU operations as well as approximate floating point operations. Approximate instructions can use special functional units that perform approximate operations. Figure 2 summarizes our assumed hardware model.

An instruction stream may have a mix of approximate and precise instructions. Precise instructions have the same guarantees as instructions in today's ISAs. Note that an approximate instruction is simply a "hint" to the architecture that it may apply a variety of energy-saving approximations when executing the given instruction. The particular approximations employed by a given architecture are not exposed to the program; a processor supporting no approximations just executes approximate instructions precisely and saves no energy. An approximation-aware ISA thus allows a single binary to benefit from new approximations as they are implemented in future microarchitectures.

Layout of approximate data. Our hardware model supports approximate memory data at a cache line granularity, in which software can configure any line as approximate. This can be supported by having a bit per line in each page that indicates whether the corresponding line is approximate. Based on that bit, a cache controller determines the supply voltage of a line (lower for approximate lines), and the refresh rate for regions of DRAM. This bitmap needs to be kept precise. With a typical cache line size of 64 bytes, this is less than 0.2% overhead. Note that both selective supply voltage for caches [13] and selective refresh rate for DRAM [15] are hardware techniques that have been proposed in the past.

Setting approximation on a cache line basis requires the runtime system to segregate approximate and precise data in different cache lines. We propose the following simple technique for laying out objects with both approximate and precise fields. First, lay out the precise portion of the object (including the `vtable` pointer) contiguously. Each cache line containing at least one precise field is marked as precise. Then, lay out the approximate fields after the end of the precise data. Some of this data may be placed in a precise line (that is, a line containing some precise data already); in this case, the approximate data stays precise and saves no memory energy. (Note that wasting space in the precise line in order to place the data in an approximate line would use more memory and thus more energy.) The remaining approximate fields that do not fit in the last precise line can be placed in approximate lines.

Fields in superclasses may not be reordered in subclasses. Thus, a subclass of a class with approximate data may waste space in an approximate line in order to place precise fields of the subclass in a precise line.

While we simulate the artifacts of this layout scheme for our evaluation, a finer granularity of approximate memory storage would mitigate or eliminate the resulting loss of approximation. More sophisticated layout algorithms could also improve energy savings; this is a target for compile-time optimization. Note that even if an approximate field ends up stored in precise memory, it will still be loaded into approximate registers and be subject to approximate operations and algorithms.

The layout problem is much simpler for arrays of approximate primitive types. The first line, which contains the length and type information, must be precise, with all remaining lines approximate.

4.2 Hardware Techniques for Saving Energy

There are many strategies for saving energy with approximate storage and data operations. This section discusses some of the techniques explored in prior research. We assume these techniques in our simulations, which we describe later. The techniques are summarized in Table 2.

Voltage scaling in logic circuits. Aggressive voltage scaling can result in over 30% energy reduction with $\sim 1\%$ error rate [10] and 22% reduction with $\sim 0.01\%$ error rate. Recent work [9, 17] proposed to expose the errors to applications that can tolerate it and saw similar results. In our model, we assume aggressive voltage scaling for the processor units executing approximate instructions, including integer and floating-point operations. As for an error model, the choices are single bit flip, last value, and random value. We consider all three but our evaluation mainly depicts the random-value assumption, which is the most realistic.

	Mild	Medium	Aggressive
DRAM refresh: per-second bit flip probability	10^{-9}	10^{-5}	10^{-3}
Memory power saved	17%	22%	24%
SRAM read upset probability	$10^{-16.7}$	$10^{-7.4}$	10^{-3}
SRAM write failure probability	$10^{-5.59}$	$10^{-4.94}$	10^{-3}
Supply power saved	70%	80%	90%*
`float` mantissa bits	16	8	4
`double` mantissa bits	32	16	8
Energy saved per operation	32%	78%	85%*
Arithmetic timing error probability	10^{-6}	10^{-4}	10^{-2}
Energy saved per operation	12%*	22%	30%

Table 2. Approximation strategies simulated in our evaluation. Numbers marked with * are educated guesses by the authors; the others are taken from the sources described in Section 4.2. Note that all values for the Medium level are taken from the literature.

Width reduction in floating point operations. A direct approach to approximate arithmetic operations on floating point values is to ignore part of the mantissa in the operands. As observed in [34], many applications do not need the full mantissa. According to their model, a floating-point multiplier using 8-bit mantissas uses 78% less energy per operation than a full 24-bit multiplier.

DRAM refresh rate. Reducing the refresh rate of dynamic RAM leads to potential data decay but can substantially reduce power consumption with a low error rate. As proposed by Liu et al. [23], an approximation-aware DRAM system might reduce the refresh rate on lines containing approximate data. As in that work, we assume that reducing the refresh rate to 1 Hz reduces power by about 20%. In a study performed by Bhalodia [4], a DRAM cell not refreshed for 10 seconds experiences a failure with per-bit probability approximately 10^{-5}. We conservatively assume this error rate for the reduced refresh rate of 1 Hz.

SRAM supply voltage. Registers and data caches consist of static RAM (SRAM) cells. Reducing the supply voltage to SRAM cells lowers the leakage current of the cells but decreases the data integrity [13]. As examined by Kumar [18], these errors are dominated by *read upsets* and *write failures*, which occur when a bit is read or written. A read upset occurs when the stored bit is flipped while it is read; a write failure occurs when the wrong bit is written. Reducing SRAM supply voltage by 80% results in read upset and write failure probabilities of $10^{-7.4}$ and $10^{-4.94}$ respectively. *Soft failures*, bit flips in stored data due to cosmic rays and other events, are comparatively rare and depend less on the supply voltage.

Section 5.4 describes the model we use to combine these various potential energy savings into an overall CPU/memory system energy reduction. To put the potential energy savings in perspective, according to recent studies [12, 24], the CPU and memory together account for well over 50% of the overall system power in servers as well as notebooks. In a smartphone, CPU and memory account for about 20% and the radio typically close to 50% of the overall power [6].

5. Implementation

We implement EnerJ as an extension to the Java programming language based on the pluggable type mechanism proposed by Papi et al. [28]. EnerJ is implemented using the Checker Framework[1]

[1] `http://types.cs.washington.edu/checker-framework/`

infrastructure, which builds on the JSR 308[2] extension to Java's annotation facility. JSR 308 permits annotations on any explicit type in the program. The EnerJ type checker extends the rules from Section 3 to all of Java, including arrays and generics. We also implement a simulation infrastructure that emulates an approximate computing architecture as described in Section 4. [3]

5.1 Type Checker

EnerJ provides the type qualifiers listed in Table 1—@Approx, @Precise, @Top, and @Context—as JSR 308 type annotations. The default type qualifier for unannotated types is @Precise, meaning that any Java program may be compiled as an EnerJ program with no change in semantics. The programmer can add approximations to the program incrementally.

While reference types may be annotated as @Approx, this only affects the meaning of @Context annotations in the class definition and method binding on the receiver. Our implementation never approximates pointers.

5.2 Simulator

To evaluate our system, we implement a compiler and runtime system that executes EnerJ code as if it were running on an approximation-aware architecture as described in Section 4. We instrument method calls, object creation and destruction, arithmetic operators, and memory accesses to collect statistics and inject faults. The runtime system is implemented as a Java library and is invoked by the instrumentation calls. It records memory-footprint and arithmetic-operation statistics while simultaneously injecting transient faults to emulate approximate execution.

To avoid spurious errors due to approximation, our simulated approximate functional units never raise divide-by-zero exceptions. Approximate floating-point division by zero returns the NaN value; approximate integer divide-by-zero returns zero.

5.3 Approximations

Our simulator implements the approximation strategies described in Section 4.2. Table 2 summarizes the approximations used, their associated error probabilities, and their estimated energy savings.

Floating-point bit-width reduction is performed when executing Java's arithmetic operators on operands that are approximate float and double values. SRAM read upsets and write failures are simulated by flipping each bit read or written with a constant probability. For DRAM refresh reduction, every bit also has an independent probability of inversion; here, the probability is proportional to the amount of time since the last access to the bit.

For the purposes of our evaluation, we distinguish SRAM and DRAM data using the following rough approximation: data on the heap is considered to be stored in DRAM; stack data is considered SRAM. Future evaluations not constrained by the abstraction of the JVM could explore a more nuanced model.

5.4 Energy Model

To summarize the effectiveness of EnerJ's energy-saving properties, we estimate the potential overall savings of the processor/memory system when executing each benchmark approximately. To do so, we consider a simplified model with three components to the system's energy consumption: instruction execution, SRAM storage (registers and cache), and DRAM storage. Our model omits overheads of implementing or switching to approximate hardware. For example, we do not model any latency in scaling the voltage on the logic units. For this reason, our results can be considered optimistic; future work should model approximate hardware in more detail.

To estimate the savings for instruction execution, we assign abstract energy units to arithmetic operations. Integer operations take 37 units and floating point operations take 40 units; of each of these, 22 units are consumed by the instruction fetch and decode stage and may not be reduced by approximation strategies. These estimations are based on three studies of architectural power consumption [5, 20, 27]. We calculate energy savings in instruction execution by scaling the non-fetch, non-decode component of integer and floating-point instructions.

We assume that SRAM storage and instructions that access it account for approximately 35% of the microarchitecture's power consumption; instruction execution logic consumes the remainder. To compute the total CPU power savings, then, we scale the savings from SRAM storage by 0.35 and the instruction power savings, described above, by 0.65.

Finally, we add the savings from DRAM storage to get an energy number for the entire processor/memory system. For this, we consider a server-like setting, where DRAM accounts for 45% of the power and CPU 55% [12]. Note that in a mobile setting, memory consumes only 25% of power so power savings in the CPU will be more important [6].

6. Results

We evaluate EnerJ by annotating a variety of existing Java programs. Table 3 describes the applications we used; they have been selected to be relevant in both mobile and server settings.

Applications. We evaluate the FPU-heavy kernels of the SciMark2 benchmark suite to reflect scientific workloads.[4] ZXing is a bar code reader library targeted for mobile devices based on the Android operating system.[5] Our workload decodes QR Code two-dimensional bar code images. jMonkeyEngine is a 2D and 3D game engine for both desktop and mobile environments.[6] We run a workload that consists of many 3D triangle intersection problems, an algorithm frequently used for collision detection in games.

ImageJ is an image-manipulation program; our workload executes a flood fill operation.[7] This workload was selected as representative of error-resilient algorithms with primarily integer—rather than floating point—data. Because the code already includes extensive safety precautions such as bounds checking, our annotation for ImageJ is extremely aggressive: even pixel coordinates are marked as approximate. Raytracer is a simple 3D renderer; our workload executes ray plane intersection on a simple scene.[8]

Annotation approach. We annotated each application manually. While many possible annotations exist for a given program, we attempted to strike a balance between reliability and energy savings. As a rule, however, we attempted to annotate the programs in a way that never causes them to crash (or throw an unhandled exception); it is important to show that EnerJ allows programmers to write approximate programs that never fail catastrophically. In our experiments, each benchmark produces an output on every run. This is in contrast to approximation techniques that do not attempt to prevent crashes [22, 23, 35]. Naturally, we focused our effort on code where most of the time is spent.

[2] `http://types.cs.washington.edu/jsr308/`

[3] The EnerJ type checker and simulator are available from our website: `http://sampa.cs.washington.edu/sampa/EnerJ`

[4] SciMark2: `http://math.nist.gov/scimark2/`

[5] ZXing: `http://code.google.com/p/zxing/`

[6] jMonkeyEngine: `http://www.jmonkeyengine.com/`

[7] ImageJ: `http://rsbweb.nih.gov/ij/`

[8] Raytracer: `http://www.planet-source-code.com/vb/scripts/ShowCode.asp?txtCodeId=5590&lngWId=2`

Application	Description	Error metric	Lines of code	Proportion FP	Total decls.	Annotated decls.	Endorse-ments
FFT	Scientific kernels from the SciMark2 benchmark	Mean entry difference	168	38.2%	85	33%	2
SOR		Mean entry difference	36	55.2%	28	25%	0
MonteCarlo		Normalized difference	59	22.9%	15	20%	1
SparseMatMult		Mean normalized difference	38	39.7%	29	14%	0
LU		Mean entry difference	283	31.4%	150	23%	3
ZXing	Smartphone bar code decoder	1 if incorrect, 0 if correct	26171	1.7%	11506	4%	247
jMonkeyEngine	Mobile/desktop game engine	Fraction of correct decisions normalized to 0.5	5962	44.3%	2104	19%	63
ImageJ	Raster image manipulation	Mean pixel difference	156	0.0%	118	34%	18
Raytracer	3D image renderer	Mean pixel difference	174	68.4%	92	33%	10

Table 3. Applications used in our evaluation, application-specific metrics for quality of service, and metrics of annotation density. "Proportion FP" indicates the percentage of dynamic arithmetic instructions observed that were floating-point (as opposed to integer) operations.

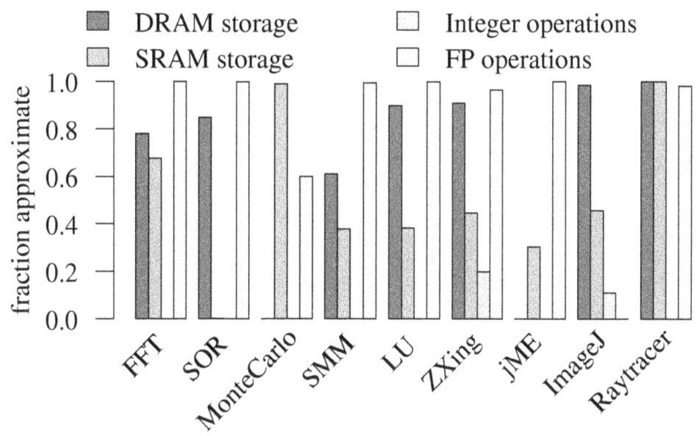

Figure 3. Proportion of approximate storage and computation in each benchmark. For storage (SRAM and DRAM) measurements, the bars show the fraction of byte-seconds used in storing approximate data. For functional unit operations, we show the fraction of dynamic operations that were executed approximately.

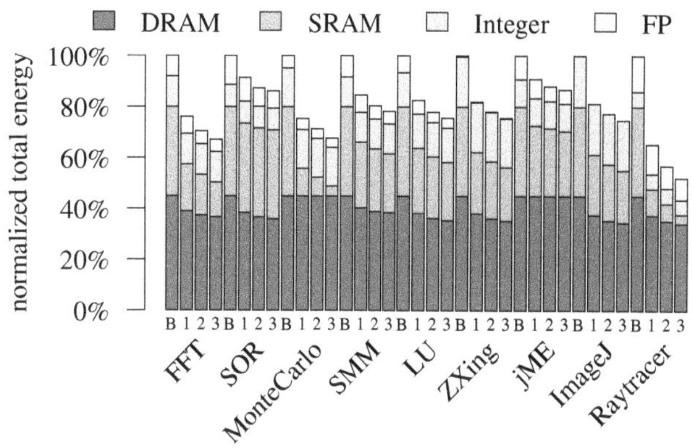

Figure 4. Estimated CPU/memory system energy consumed for each benchmark. The bar labeled "B" represents the baseline value: the energy consumption for the program running without approximation. The numbered bars correspond to the Mild, Medium, and Aggressive configurations in Table 2.

Three of the authors ported the applications used in our evaluation. In every case, we were unfamiliar with the codebase beforehand, so our annotations did not depend on extensive domain knowledge. The annotations were not labor intensive.

QoS metrics. For each application, we measure the degradation in output quality of approximate executions with respect to the precise executions. To do so, we define application-specific quality of service (QoS) metrics. Defining our own ad-hoc QoS metrics is necessary to compare output degradation across applications. A number of similar studies of application-level tolerance to transient faults have also taken this approach [3, 8, 19, 21, 25, 35]. The third column in Table 3 shows our metric for each application.

Output error ranges from 0 (indicating output identical to the precise version) to 1 (indicating completely meaningless output). For applications that produce lists of numbers (e.g., SparseMatMult's output matrix), we compute the error as the mean entry-wise difference between the pristine output and the degraded output. Each numerical difference is limited by 1, so if an entry in the output is NaN, that entry contributes an error of 1. For benchmarks where the output is not numeric (i.e., ZXing, which outputs a string), the error is 0 when the output is correct and 1 otherwise.

6.1 Energy Savings

Figure 3 divides the execution of each benchmark into DRAM storage, SRAM storage, integer operations, and FP operations and shows what fraction of each was approximated. For many of the FP-centric applications we simulated, including the jMonkeyEngine and Raytracer as well as most of the SciMark applications, nearly all of the floating point operations were approximate. This reflects the inherent imprecision of FP representations; many FP-dominated algorithms are inherently resilient to rounding effects. The same applications typically exhibit very little or no approximate integer operations. The frequency of loop induction variable increments and other precise control-flow code limits our ability to approximate integer computation. ImageJ is the only exception with a significant fraction of integer approximation; this is because it uses integers to represent pixel values, which are amenable to approximation.

DRAM and SRAM approximation is measured in byte-seconds. The data shows that both storage types are frequently used in approximate mode. Many applications have DRAM approximation rates of 80% or higher; it is common to store large data structures (often arrays) that can tolerate approximation. MonteCarlo and jMonkeyEngine, in contrast, have very little approximate DRAM data; this is because both applications keep their principal data in local variables (i.e., on the stack).

The results depicted assume approximation at the granularity of a 64-byte cache line. As Section 4.1 discusses, this reduces the number of object fields that can be stored approximately. The impact of this constraint on our results is small, in part because much of the approximate data is in large arrays. Finer-grain approximate memory could yield a higher proportion of approximate storage.

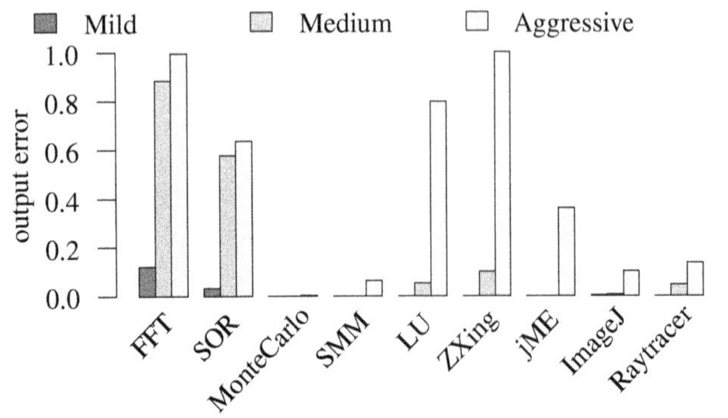

Figure 5. Output error for three different levels of approximation varied together. Each bar represents the mean error over 20 runs.

To give a sense of the energy savings afforded by our proposed approximation strategies, we translate the rates of approximation depicted above into an estimated energy consumption. Figure 4 shows the estimated energy consumption for each benchmark running on approximate hardware relative to fully precise execution. The energy calculation is based on the model described in Section 5.4. These simulations apply all of the approximation strategies described in Section 4.2 simultaneously at their three levels of aggressiveness. As expected, the total energy saved increases both with the amount of approximation in the application (depicted in Figure 3) and with the aggressiveness of approximation used.

Overall, we observe energy savings from 9% (SOR in the Mild configuration) to 48% (Raytracer in the Aggressive configuration). The three levels of approximation do not vary greatly in the amount of energy saved—the three configurations yield average energy savings of 19%, 24%, and 26% respectively. The majority of the energy savings come from the transition from zero approximation to mild approximation. As discussed in the next section, the least aggressive configuration results in very small losses in output fidelity across all applications studied.

The fifth column of Table 3 shows the proportion of floating point arithmetic in each application. In general, applications with principally integer computation (e.g., ZXing and ImageJ) exhibit less opportunity for approximation than do floating-point applications (e.g., Raytracer). Not only do floating-point instructions offer more energy savings potential in our model, but applications that use them are typically resilient to their inherent imprecision.

6.2 Quality-of-Service Tradeoff

Figure 5 presents the sensitivity of each annotated application to the full suite of approximations explored. This quality-of-service reduction is the tradeoff for the energy savings shown in Figure 4.

While most applications show negligible error for the Mild level of approximation, applications' sensitivity to error varies greatly for the Medium and Aggressive configurations. Notably, MonteCarlo, SparseMatMult, ImageJ, and Raytracer exhibit very little output degradation under any configuration whereas FFT and SOR lose significant output fidelity even under the Medium configuration. This variation suggests that an approximate execution substrate for EnerJ could benefit from tuning to the characteristics of each application, either offline via profiling or online via continuous QoS measurement as in Green [3]. However, even the conservative Mild configuration offers significant energy savings.

Qualitatively, the approximated applications exhibit gradual degradation of perceptible output quality. For instance, Raytracer always outputs an image resembling its precise output, but the amount of random pixel "noise" increases with the aggressiveness of approximation. Under the Mild configuration, it is difficult to distinguish the approximated image from the precise one.

We also measured the relative impact of various approximation strategies by running our benchmark suite with each optimization enabled in isolation. DRAM errors have a nearly negligible impact on application output; floating-point bit width reduction similarly results in at most 12% QoS loss in the Aggressive configuration. SRAM write errors are much more detrimental to output quality than read upsets. Functional unit voltage reduction had the greatest impact on correctness. We considered three possibilities for error modes in functional units: the output has a single bit flip; the last value computed is returned; or a random value is returned. The former two models resulted in significantly less QoS loss than the random-value model (25% vs. 40%). However, we consider the random-value model to be the most realistic, so we use it for the results shown in Figure 5.

6.3 Annotation Effort

Table 3 lists the number of qualifiers and endorsements used in our annotations. Only a fraction of the types in each program must be annotated: at most 34% of the possible annotation sites are used. Note that most of the applications are short programs implementing a single algorithm (the table shows the lines of code in each program). Our largest application, ZXing, has about 26,000 lines of code and only 4% of its declarations are annotated. These rates suggest that the principal data amenable to approximation is concentrated in a small portion of the code, even though approximate data typically dominates the program's dynamic behavior.

Endorsements are also rare, even though our system requires one for every approximate condition value. The outlier is ZXing, which exhibits a higher number of endorsements due to its frequency of approximate conditions. This is because ZXing's control flow frequently depends on whether a particular pixel is black.

Qualitatively, we found EnerJ's annotations easy to insert. The programmer can typically select a small set of data to approximate and then, guided by type checking errors, ascertain associated data that must also be marked as approximate. The requirements that conditions and array indices be precise helped quickly distinguish data that was likely to be sensitive to error. In some cases, such as jMonkeyEngine and Raytracer, annotation was so straightforward that it could have been largely automated: for certain methods, every `float` declaration was replaced indiscriminately with an `@Approx float` declaration.

Classes that closely represent data are perfect candidates for `@Approximable` annotations. For instance, ZXing contains `BitArray` and `BitMatrix` classes that are thin wrappers over binary data. It is useful to have approximate bit matrices in some settings (e.g., during image processing) but precise matrices in other settings (e.g., in checksum calculation). Similarly, the jMonkeyEngine benchmark uses a `Vector3f` class for much of its computation, which we marked as approximable. In this setting, approximate vector declarations (`@Approx Vector3f v`) are syntactically identical to approximate primitive-value declarations (`@Approx int i`).

We found that the `@Context` annotation helped us to approach program annotation incrementally. A commonly-used class that is a target for approximation can be marked with `@Context` members instead of `@Approx` members. This way, all the clients of the class continue to see precise members and no additional annotation on them is immediately necessary. The programmer can then update the clients individually to use the approximate version of the class rather than addressing the whole program at once.

An opportunity for algorithmic approximation also arose in ZXing. The `BitArray` approximable class contains a method `isRange` that takes two indices and determines whether all the bits between the two indices are set. We implemented an approximate version of the method that checks only some of the bits in the range by skipping some loop iterations. We believe that application domain experts would use algorithmic approximation more frequently.

In one case, we found it convenient to introduce a slight change to increase the fault tolerance of code dealing with approximate data. ZXing has a principally floating-point phase that performs an image perspective transform. If the transform tried to access a coordinate outside of the image bounds, ZXing would catch the ArrayIndexOutOfBoundsException and print a message saying that the image transform failed. We modified the algorithm to silently return a white pixel in this case. The result was that the image transform became more resilient to transient faults in the transformation coordinates. We marked these coordinates as approximate and then endorsed them at the point they are used as array indices. In no case, however, does an application as we annotated it do *more* computation than the pristine version.

7. Related Work

Space constraints preclude a discussion of the vast body of compiler or hybrid hardware/software work to improve energy efficiency. Instead, we focus on work we are aware of that exploits approximate computing to improve energy.

Many studies have shown that a variety of applications have a high tolerance to transient faults [8, 19, 21, 22, 25, 35]. However, certain parts of programs are typically more fault-tolerant than others. Our work exploits this property by allowing the programmer to distinguish critical from non-critical computation.

Our work at the language level was influenced by previous work on techniques for trading off correctness for power savings. Flikker [23] proposes a programming model for reducing the DRAM refresh rate on certain heap data via low-level program annotations. Besides being limited to heap storage, Flikker does not provide any safety guarantees. Relax [9] is an architecture that exposes timing faults to software as opposed to providing error recovery automatically in hardware; its goal is to improve error tolerance with lower power by exploiting portions of code that are tolerant to error. While Relax focuses on error recovery and hardware design simplicity, EnerJ emphasizes energy-efficiency over error detectability and supports a wider range of power-saving approximations. Moreover, Relax explores a *code-centric* approach, in which blocks of code are marked for failure and recovery while EnerJ employs *data-centric* type annotations.

Work by Rinard et al. proposes approximate code transformations in the compiler [1, 25, 31]. Relatedly, EnerJ's support for algorithmic approximation, the ability to write an approximate implementation and a precise implementation of the same functionality, bears some similarity to the Green programming model [3]. However, Green primarily concerns itself with online monitoring of application QoS; EnerJ's guarantees are entirely static. Overall, EnerJ's type system makes approximation-based approaches to energy savings general (it supports approximate operations, storage, and algorithms) and safe (it provides static isolation guarantees).

Using types to achieve fine-grained isolation of program components is inspired by work on information flow types for secure programming [26, 32]. That body of work also influenced the *endorsement* construct for explicitly violating non-interference.

Work by Perry et al. also focuses on static verification of fault tolerance [29, 30]. That work focuses on detection and recovery rather than exposing transient faults.

8. Conclusion

Approximate computing is a very promising way of saving energy in large classes of applications running on a wide range of systems, from embedded systems to mobile phones to servers. We propose to use a type system based on information-flow tracking ideas: variables and objects can be declared as approximate or precise; approximate data can be processed more cheaply and less reliably; and we can statically prove that approximate data does not unexpectedly affect the precise state of a program. Our type system provides a general way of using approximation: we can use approximate storage by mapping data to cheaper memory, cache, and registers; we can use approximate operations by generating code with cheaper, approximate instructions; and we can use method overloading and class parameterization to enable algorithmic approximation.

We implement our type system on top of Java and experiment with several applications, from scientific computing to image processing to games. Our results show that annotations are easy to insert: only a fraction of declarations must be annotated and endorsements are rare. Once a program is annotated for approximation, the runtime system or architecture can choose several approximate execution techniques. Our hardware-based model shows potential energy savings in the 10% to 50% range.

Acknowledgments

We would like to thank the anonymous reviewers for their valuable comments. We also thank the members of the Sampa group for their feedback on the manuscript. This work was supported in part by NSF grant CCF-1016495, NSF CAREER REU grant CCF-0846004, an NSF Graduate Fellowship and a Microsoft Research Faculty Fellowship.

References

[1] A. Agarwal, M. Rinard, S. Sidiroglou, S. Misailovic, and H. Hoffmann. Using code perforation to improve performance, reduce energy consumption, and respond to failures. Technical report, MIT, 2009.

[2] A. Askarov and A. C. Myers. A semantic framework for declassification and endorsement. In *ESOP*, 2010.

[3] W. Baek and T. M. Chilimbi. Green: a framework for supporting energy-conscious programming using controlled approximation. In *PLDI*, 2010.

[4] V. Bhalodia. SCALE DRAM subsystem power analysis. Master's thesis, MIT, 2005.

[5] D. Brooks, V. Tiwari, and M. Martonosi. Wattch: a framework for architectural-level power analysis and optimizations. In *ISCA*, 2000.

[6] A. Carroll and G. Heiser. An analysis of power consumption in a smartphone. In *USENIX*, 2010.

[7] A. Chlipala, L. Petersen, and R. Harper. Strict bidirectional type checking. In *TLDI*, 2005.

[8] M. de Kruijf and K. Sankaralingam. Exploring the synergy of emerging workloads and silicon reliability trends. In *SELSE*, 2009.

[9] M. de Kruijf, S. Nomura, and K. Sankaralingam. Relax: an architectural framework for software recovery of hardware faults. In *ISCA*, 2010.

[10] D. Ernst, N. S. Kim, S. Das, S. Pant, R. Rao, T. Pham, C. Ziesler, D. Blaauw, T. Austin, K. Flautner, and T. Mudge. Razor: a low-power pipeline based on circuit-level timing speculation. In *MICRO*, 2003.

[11] M. D. Ernst. Type Annotations specification (JSR 308). `http://types.cs.washington.edu/jsr308/`, 2008.

[12] X. Fan, W.-D. Weber, and L. A. Barroso. Power provisioning for a warehouse-sized computer. In *ISCA*, 2007.

[13] K. Flautner, N. S. Kim, S. Martin, D. Blaauw, and T. Mudge. Drowsy caches: simple techniques for reducing leakage power. In *ISCA*, 2002.

[14] J. S. Foster, M. Fähndrich, and A. Aiken. A theory of type qualifiers. In *PLDI*, 1999.

[15] M. Ghosh and H.-H. S. Lee. Smart refresh: An enhanced memory controller design for reducing energy in conventional and 3D die-stacked DRAMs. In *MICRO*, 2007.

[16] A. Igarashi, B. C. Pierce, and P. Wadler. Featherweight Java: a minimal core calculus for Java and GJ. *TOPLAS*, 23(3), 2001.

[17] A. Kahng, S. Kang, R. Kumar, and J. Sartori. Designing a processor from the ground up to allow voltage/reliability tradeoffs. In *HPCA*, 2010.

[18] A. Kumar. *SRAM Leakage-Power Optimization Framework: a System Level Approach*. PhD thesis, University of California at Berkeley, 2008.

[19] L. Leem, H. Cho, J. Bau, Q. A. Jacobson, and S. Mitra. ERSA: error resilient system architecture for probabilistic applications. In *DATE*, 2010.

[20] S. Li, J. H. Ahn, R. Strong, J. Brockman, D. Tullsen, and N. Jouppi. McPAT: An integrated power, area, and timing modeling framework for multicore and manycore architectures. In *MICRO*, 2009.

[21] X. Li and D. Yeung. Exploiting soft computing for increased fault tolerance. In *ASGI*, 2006.

[22] X. Li and D. Yeung. Application-level correctness and its impact on fault tolerance. In *HPCA*, 2007.

[23] S. Liu, K. Pattabiraman, T. Moscibroda, and B. G. Zorn. Flikker: Saving refresh-power in mobile devices through critical data partitioning. In *ASPLOS*, 2011.

[24] A. Mahesri and V. Vardhan. Power consumption breakdown on a modern laptop. In *PACS*, 2004.

[25] S. Misailovic, S. Sidiroglou, H. Hoffman, and M. Rinard. Quality of service profiling. In *ICSE*, 2010.

[26] A. C. Myers. JFlow: practical mostly-static information flow control. In *POPL*, 1999.

[27] K. Natarajan, H. Hanson, S. W. Keckler, C. R. Moore, and D. Burger. Microprocessor pipeline energy analysis. In *ISLPED*, 2003.

[28] M. M. Papi, M. Ali, T. L. Correa Jr., J. H. Perkins, and M. D. Ernst. Practical pluggable types for Java. In *ISSTA*, 2008.

[29] F. Perry and D. Walker. Reasoning about control flow in the presence of transient faults. In *SAS*, 2008.

[30] F. Perry, L. Mackey, G. A. Reis, J. Ligatti, D. I. August, and D. Walker. Fault-tolerant typed assembly language. In *PLDI*, 2007.

[31] M. Rinard, H. Hoffmann, S. Misailovic, and S. Sidiroglou. Patterns and statistical analysis for understanding reduced resource computing. In *Onward!*, 2010.

[32] A. Sabelfeld and A. C. Myers. Language-based information-flow security. *IEEE Journal on Selected Areas in Communications, special issue on Formal Methods for Security*, 21(1), 2003.

[33] A. Sampson, W. Dietl, E. Fortuna, D. Gnanapragasam, L. Ceze, and D. Grossman. EnerJ: Approximate Data Types for Safe and General Low-Power Computation — Full Proofs. Technical Report UW-CSE-10-12-01, University of Washington, 2011.

[34] J. Y. F. Tong, D. Nagle, and R. A. Rutenbar. Reducing power by optimizing the necessary precision/range of floating-point arithmetic. *IEEE Trans. VLSI Syst.*, 8(3), 2000.

[35] V. Wong and M. Horowitz. Soft error resilience of probabilistic inference applications. In *SELSE*, 2006.

Understanding POWER Multiprocessors

Susmit Sarkar[1] Peter Sewell[1] Jade Alglave[2,3] Luc Maranget[3] Derek Williams[4]
[1]University of Cambridge [2]Oxford University [3]INRIA [4]IBM Austin

Abstract

Exploiting today's multiprocessors requires high-performance and correct concurrent systems code (optimising compilers, language runtimes, OS kernels, etc.), which in turn requires a good understanding of the observable processor behaviour that can be relied on. Unfortunately this critical hardware/software interface is not at all clear for several current multiprocessors.

In this paper we characterise the behaviour of IBM POWER multiprocessors, which have a subtle and highly relaxed memory model (ARM multiprocessors have a very similar architecture in this respect). We have conducted extensive experiments on several generations of processors: POWER G5, 5, 6, and 7. Based on these, on published details of the microarchitectures, and on discussions with IBM staff, we give an abstract-machine semantics that abstracts from most of the implementation detail but explains the behaviour of a range of subtle examples. Our semantics is explained in prose but defined in rigorous machine-processed mathematics; we also confirm that it captures the observable processor behaviour, or the architectural intent, for our examples with an executable checker. While not officially sanctioned by the vendor, we believe that this model gives a reasonable basis for reasoning about current POWER multiprocessors.

Our work should bring new clarity to concurrent systems programming for these architectures, and is a necessary precondition for any analysis or verification. It should also inform the design of languages such as C and C++, where the language memory model is constrained by what can be efficiently compiled to such multiprocessors.

Categories and Subject Descriptors C.1.2 [*Multiple Data Stream Architectures (Multiprocessors)*]: Parallel processors; D.1.3 [*Concurrent Programming*]: Parallel programming; F.3.1 [*Specifying and Verifying and Reasoning about Programs*]

General Terms Documentation, Languages, Reliability, Standardization, Theory, Verification

Keywords Relaxed Memory Models, Semantics

1. Introduction

Power multiprocessors (including the IBM POWER 5, 6, and 7, and various PowerPC implementations) have for many years had aggressive implementations, providing high performance but exposing a very relaxed memory model, one that requires careful use of dependencies and memory barriers to enforce ordering in concurrent code. A priori, one might expect the behaviour of a multiprocessor to be sufficiently well-defined by the vendor architecture documentation, here the Power ISA v2.06 specification [Pow09]. For the sequential behaviour of instructions, that is very often true. For concurrent code, however, the observable behaviour of Power multiprocessors is extremely subtle, as we shall see, and the guarantees given by the vendor specification are not always clear. We therefore set out to discover the actual processor behaviour and to define a rigorous and usable semantics, as a foundation for future system building and research.

The programmer-observable relaxed-memory behaviour of these multiprocessors emerges as a whole-system property from a complex microarchitecture [SKT+05, LSF+07, KSSF10]. This can change significantly between generations, e.g. from POWER 6 to POWER 7, but includes: cores that perform out-of-order and speculative execution, with many shadow registers; hierarchical store buffering, with some buffering shared between threads of a symmetric multithreading (SMT) core, and with multiple levels of cache; store buffering partitioned by address; and a cache protocol with many cache-line states and a complex interconnection topology, and in which cache-line invalidate messages are buffered. The implementation of coherent memory and of the memory barriers involves many of these, working together. To make a useful model, it is essential to abstract from as much as possible of this complexity, both to make it simple enough to be comprehensible and because the detailed hardware designs are proprietary (the published literature does not describe the microarchitecture in enough detail to confidently predict all the observable behaviour). Of course, the model also has to be *sound*, allowing all behaviour that the hardware actually exhibits, and sufficiently *strong*, capturing any guarantees provided by the hardware that systems programmers rely on. It does not have to be tight: it may be desirable to make a loose specification, permitting some behaviour that current hardware does not exhibit, but which programmers do not rely on the absence of, for simplicity or to admit different implementations in future. The model does not have to correspond in detail to the internal structure of the hardware: we are capturing the external behaviour of reasonable implementations, not the implementations themselves. But it should have a clear abstraction relationship to implementation microarchitecture, so that the model truly *explains* the behaviour of examples.

To develop our model, and to establish confidence that it is sound, we have conducted extensive experiments, running several thousand tests, both hand-written and automatically generated, on several generations of processors, for up to 10^{11} iterations each. We present some simple tests in §2, to introduce the relaxed behaviour allowed by Power

PLDI'11, June 4–8, 2011, San Jose, California, USA.

processors, and some more subtle examples in §6, with representative experimental data in §7. To ensure that our model explains the behaviour of tests in a way that faithfully abstracts from the actual hardware, using appropriate concepts, we depend on extensive discussions with IBM staff. To validate the model against experiment, we built a checker, based on code automatically generated from the mathematical definition, to calculate the allowed outcomes of tests (§8); this confirms that the model gives the correct results for all tests we describe and for a systematically generated family of around 300 others.

Relaxed memory models are typically expressed either in an axiomatic or an operational style. Here we adopt the latter, defining an abstract machine in §3 and §4. We expect that this will be more intuitive than typical axiomatic models, as it has a straightforward notion of global time (in traces of abstract machine transitions), and the abstraction from the actual hardware is more direct. More particularly, to explain some of the examples, it seems to be necessary to model out-of-order and speculative reads explicitly, which is easier to do in an abstract-machine setting. This work is an exercise in making a model that is as simple as possible but no simpler: the model is considerably more complex than some (e.g. for TSO processors such as Sparc and x86), but does capture the processor behaviour or architectural intent for a range of subtle examples. Moreover, while the definition is mathematically rigorous, it can be explained in only a few pages of prose, so it should be accessible to the expert systems programmers (of concurrency libraries, language runtimes, optimising compilers, etc.) who have to be concerned with these issues. We end with discussion of related work (§9) and a brief summary of future directions (§10), returning at last to the vendor architecture.

2. Simple Examples

We begin with an informal introduction to Power multiprocessor behaviour by example, introducing some key concepts but leaving explanation in terms of the model to later.

2.1 Relaxed behaviour

In the absence of memory barriers or dependencies, Power multiprocessors exhibit a very relaxed memory model, as shown by their behaviour for the following four classic tests.

SB: Store Buffering Here two threads write to shared-memory locations and then each reads from the other location — an idiom at the heart of Dekker's mutual-exclusion algorithm, for example. In pseudocode:

Thread 0	Thread 1
x=1 r1=y	y=1 r2=x
Initial shared state: x=0 and y=0	
Allowed final state: r1=0 and r2=0	

In the specified execution both threads read the value from the initial state (in later examples, this is zero unless otherwise stated). To eliminate any ambiguity about exactly what machine instructions are executed, either from source-language semantics or compilation concerns, we take the definitive version of our examples to be in PowerPC assembly (available online [SSA+11]), rather than pseudocode. The assembly code is not easy to read, however, so here we present examples as diagrams of the memory read and write events involved in the execution specified by the initial and final state constraints. In this example, the pseudocode r1 and r2 represent machine registers, so accesses to those are not memory events; with the final state as specified, the only conceivable execution has two writes, labelled a and c, and two reads, labelled b and d, with values as below. They are related by program order po (later we elide implied po edges), and the fact that the two reads both read from the initial state (0) is indicated by the incoming reads-from (rf) edges (from writes to reads that read from them); the dots indicate the initial-state writes.

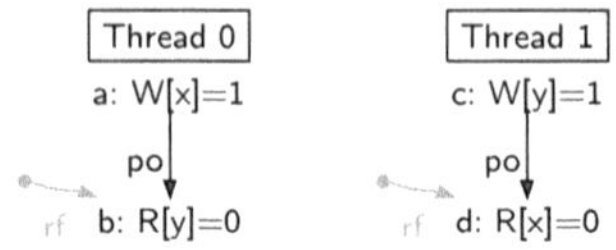

Test SB : Allowed

This example illustrates the key relaxation allowed in Sparc or x86 TSO models [Spa92, SSO+10]. The next three show some ways in which Power gives a weaker model.

MP: Message passing Here Thread 0 writes data x and then sets a flag y, while Thread 1 reads y from that flag write and then reads x. On Power that read is not guaranteeed to see the Thread 0 write of x; it might instead read from 'before' that write, despite the chain of po and rf edges:

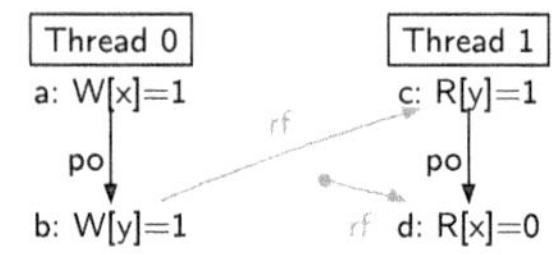

Test MP : Allowed

In real code, the read c of y might be in a loop, repeated until the value read is 1. Here, to simplify experimental testing, we do not have a loop but instead consider only executions in which the value read is 1, expressed with a constraint on the final register values in the test source.

WRC: Write-to-Read Causality Here Thread 0 communicates to Thread 1 by writing x=1. Thread 1 reads that, and then later (in program order) sends a message to Thread 2 by writing into y. Having read that write of y at Thread 2, the question is whether a program-order-subsequent read of x at Thread 2 is guaranteed to see the value written by the Thread 0 write, or might read from 'before' that, as shown, again despite the rf and po chain. On Power that is possible.

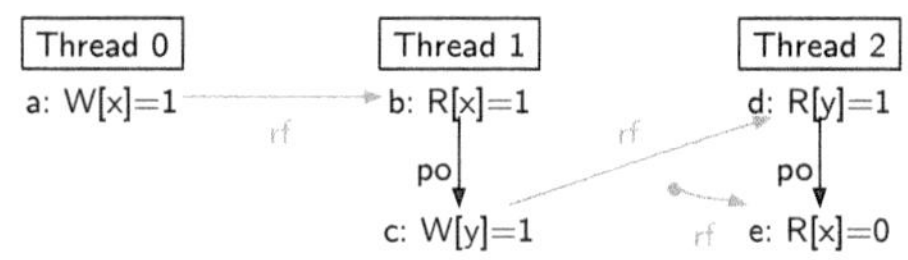

Test WRC : Allowed

IRIW: Independent Reads of Independent Writes Here two threads (0 and 2) write to distinct locations while two others (1 and 3) each read from both locations. In the specified allowed execution, they see the two writes in different orders (Thread 1's first read sees the write to x but the program-order-subsequent read does not see the write of y, whereas Thread 3 sees the write to y but not that to x).

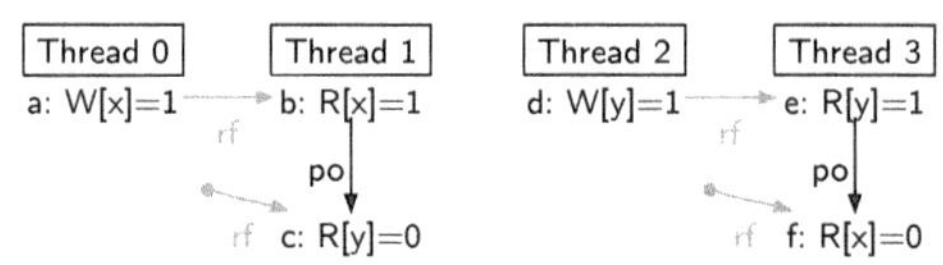

Test IRIW : Allowed

Coherence Despite all the above, one does get a guarantee of *coherence*: in any execution, for each location, there is a single linear order (co) of all writes (by any processor) to that location, which must be respected by all threads. The four cases below illustrate this: a pair of reads by a thread cannot read contrary to the coherence order (CoRR1); the coherence order must respect program order for a pair of writes by a thread (CoWW); a read cannot read from a write that is coherence-hidden by another write program-order-preceding the read (CoWR), and a write cannot coherence-order-precede a write that a program-order-preceding read read from. We can now clarify the 'before' in the MP and WRC discussion above, which was with respect to the coherence order for x.

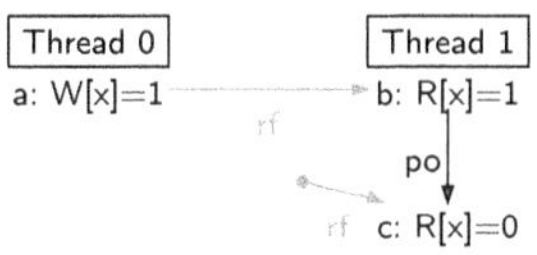

Test CoRR1 : Forbidden

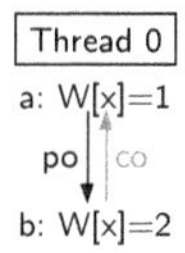

Test CoWW : Forbidden

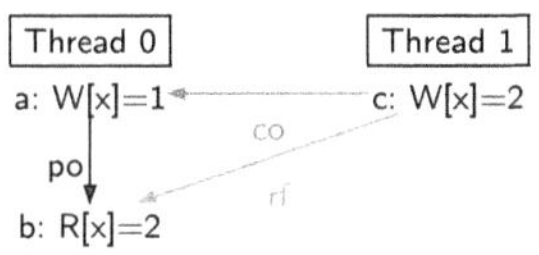

Test CoWR : Forbidden

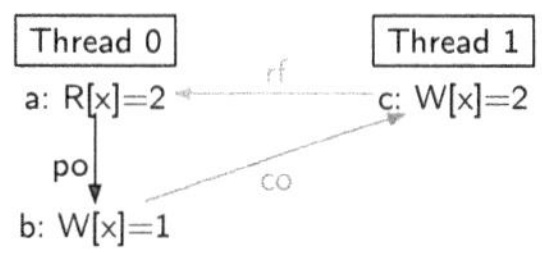

Test CoRW : Forbidden

2.2 Enforcing ordering

The Power ISA provides several ways to enforce stronger ordering. Here we deal with the sync (heavyweight sync, or hwsync) and lwsync (lightweight sync) barrier instructions, and with dependencies and the isync instruction, leaving load-reserve/store-conditional pairs and eieio to future work.

Regaining sequential consistency (SC) using sync If one adds a sync between every program-order pair of instructions (creating tests SB+syncs, MP+syncs, WRC+syncs, and IRIW+syncs), then all the non-SC results above are forbidden, e.g.

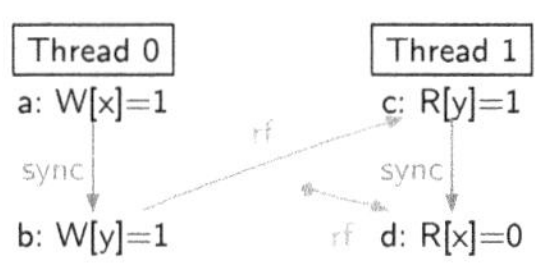

Test MP+syncs : Forbidden

Using dependencies Barriers can incur a significant runtime cost, and in some cases enough ordering is guaranteed simply by the existence of a dependency from a memory read to another memory access. There are various kinds:

- There is an *address dependency* (addr) from a read to a program-order-later memory read or write if there is a data flow path from the read, through registers and arithmetic/logical operations (but not through other memory accesses), to the address of the second read or write.
- There is a *data dependency* (data) from a read to a memory write if there is such a path to the value written. Address and data dependencies behave similarly.
- There is a *control dependency* (ctrl) from a read to a memory write if there is such a dataflow path to the test of a conditional branch that is a program-order-predecessor of the write. We also refer to control dependencies from a read to a read, but ordering of the reads in that case is *not* respected in general.
- There is a *control+isync dependency* (ctrlisync) from a read to another memory read if there is such a dataflow path from the first read to the test of a conditional branch that program-order-precedes an isync instruction before the second read.

Sometimes one can use dependencies that are naturally present in an algorithm, but it can be desirable to introduce one artificially, for its ordering properties, e.g. by XOR'ing a value with itself and adding that to an address calculation.

Dependencies alone are usually not enough. For example, adding dependencies between read/read and read/write pairs, giving tests WRC+data+addr (with a data dependency on Thread 1 and an address dependency on Thread 2), and IRIW+addrs (with address dependencies on Threads 1 and 3), leaves the non-SC behaviour allowed. One cannot add dependencies to SB, as that only has write/read pairs, and one can only add a dependency to the read/read side of MP, leaving the writes unconstrained and the non-SC behaviour still allowed.

In combination with a barrier, however, dependencies can be very useful. For example, MP+sync+addr is SC:

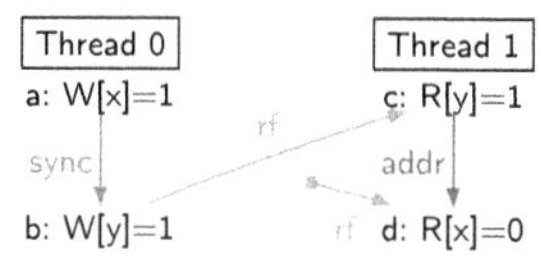

Test MP+sync+addr : Forbidden

Here the barrier keeps the writes in order, as seen by any thread, and the address dependency keeps the reads in order.

Contrary to what one might expect, the combination of a thread-local reads-from edge and a dependency does *not* guarantee ordering of a write-write pair, as seen by another thread; the two writes can propagate in either order (here [x]=z initially):

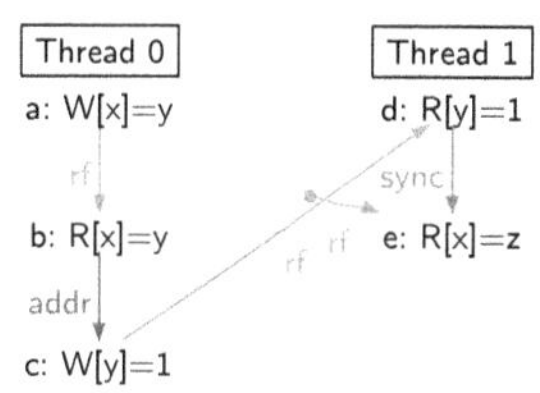

Test MP+nondep+sync : Allowed

Control dependencies, observable speculative reads, and isync Recall that control dependencies (without isync) are only respected from reads to writes, not from reads to reads. If one replaces the address dependency in MP+sync+addr by a dataflow path to a conditional branch before the second read (giving the test named MP+sync+ctrl below), that does not ensure that the reads on Thread 1 bind their values in program order.

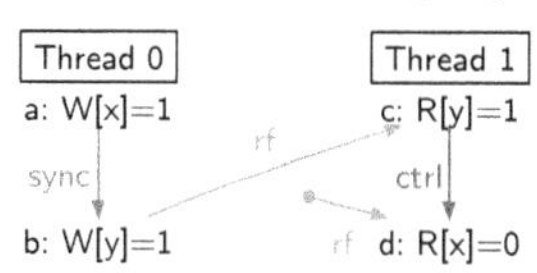

Test MP+sync+ctrl : Allowed

Adding an isync instruction between the branch and the second read (giving test MP+sync+ctrlisync) suffices.

The fact that data/address dependencies to both reads and writes are respected while control dependencies are only respected to writes is important in the design of C++0x low-level atomics [BA08, BOS+11], where release/consume atomics let one take advantage of data dependencies without requiring barriers (and limiting optimisation) to ensure that all source-language control dependencies are respected.

Cumulativity For WRC it suffices to have a sync on Thread 1 with a dependency on Thread 2; the non-SC behaviour is then forbidden:

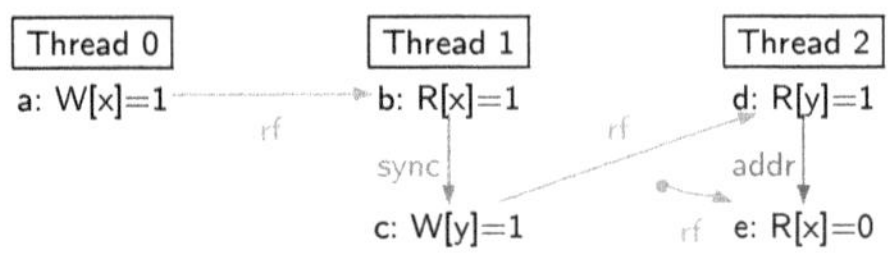

Test WRC+sync+addr : Forbidden

This illustrates what we call *A-cumulativity* of Power barriers: a chain of edges before the barrier that is respected. In this case Thread 1 reads from the Thread 0 write before (in program order) executing a sync, and then Thread 1 writes to another location; any other thread (here 2) is guaranteed to see the Thread 0 write before the Thread 1 write. However, swapping the sync and dependency, e.g. with just an rf and data edge between writes a and c, does not guarantee ordering of those two writes as seen by another thread:

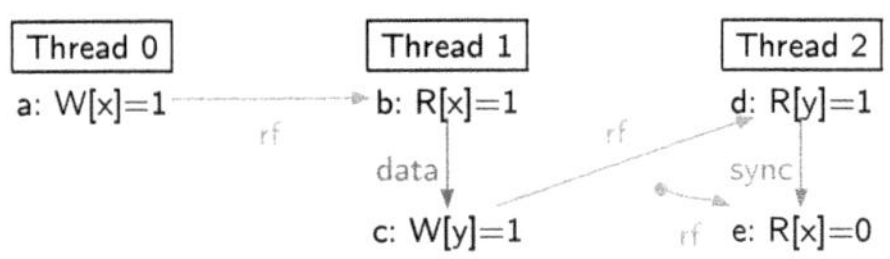

Test WRC+data+sync : Allowed

In contrast to that WRC+data+sync, a chain of reads-from edges and dependencies *after* a sync does ensure that ordering between a write before the sync and a write after the sync is respected, as below. Here the reads e and f of z and x cannot see the writes a and d out of order. We call this a *B-cumulativity* property.

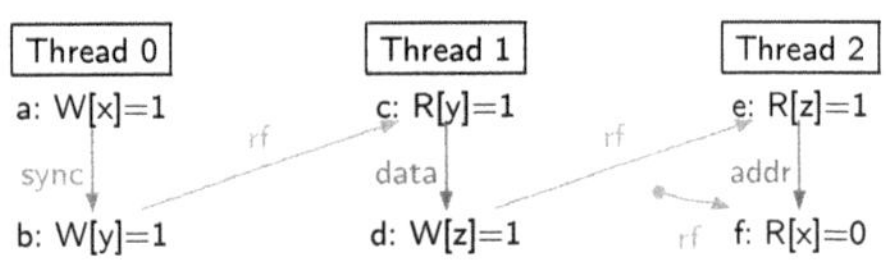

Test ISA2+sync+data+addr : Forbidden

Using lwsync The lwsync barrier is broadly similar to sync, including cumulativity properties, except that does not order store/load pairs and it is cheaper to execute; it suffices to guarantee SC behaviour in MP+lwsyncs (MP with lwsync in each thread), WRC+lwsync+addr (WRC with lwsync on Thread 1 and an address dependency on Thread 2), and ISA2+lwsync+data+addr, while SB+lwsyncs and IRIW+lwsyncs are still allowed. We return later to other differences between sync and lwsync.

3. The Model Design

We describe the high-level design of our model in this section, giving the details in the next. We build our model as a composition of a set of *(hardware) threads* and a single *storage subsystem*, synchronising on various *messages*:

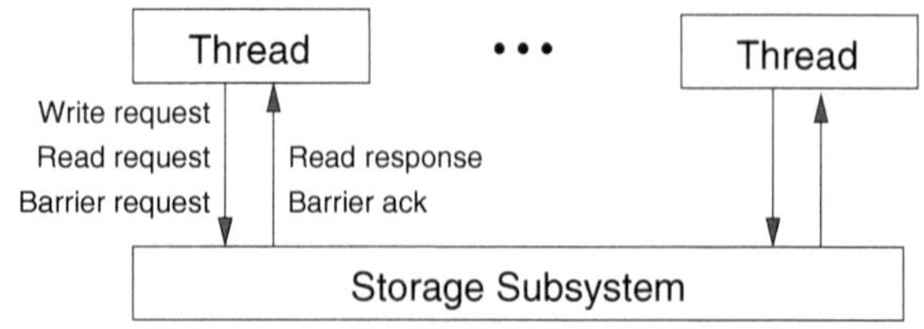

Read-request/read-response pairs are tightly coupled, while the others are single unidirectional messages. There is no buffering between the two parts.

Coherence-by-fiat Our storage subsystem abstracts completely from the processor implementation store-buffering and cache hierarchy, and from the cache protocol: our model has no explicit memory, either of the system as a whole, or of any cache or store queue (the fact that one can abstract from all these is itself interesting). Instead, we work in terms of the write events that a read can read from. Our storage subsystem maintains, for each address, the current constraint on the coherence order among the writes it has seen to that address, as a strict partial order (transitive but irreflexive). For example, suppose the storage subsystem has seen four writes, w_0, w_1, w_2 and w_3, all to the same address. It might have built up the coherence constraint on the left below, with w_0 known to be before w_1, w_2 and w_3, and w_1 known to be before w_2, but with as-yet-undetermined relationships between w_1 and w_3, and between w_2 and w_3.

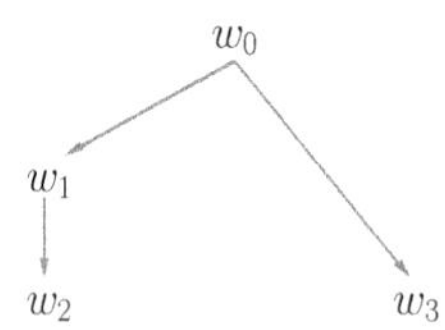

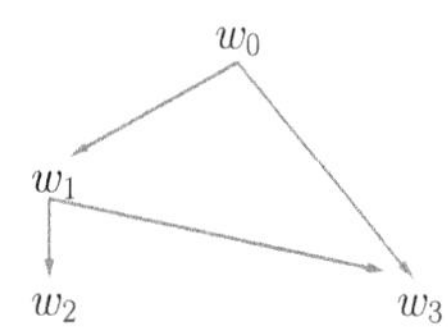

The storage subsystem also records the list of writes that it has *propagated* to each thread: those sent in response to read-requests, those done by the thread itself, and those propagated to that thread in the process of propagating a barrier to that thread. These are interleaved with records of barriers propagated to that thread. Note that this is a storage-subsystem-model concept: the writes propagated to a thread have not necessarily been sent to the thread model in a read-response.

Now, given a read request by a thread *tid*, what writes could be sent in response? From the state on the left above, if the writes propagated to thread *tid* are just $[w_1]$, perhaps because *tid* has read from w_1, then:

- it cannot be sent w_0, as w_0 is coherence-before the w_1 write that (because it is in the writes-propagated list) it might have read from;
- it could re-read from w_1, leaving the coherence constraint unchanged;
- it could be sent w_2, again leaving the coherence constraint unchanged, in which case w_2 must be appended to the events propagated to *tid*; or
- it could be sent w_3, again appending this to the events propagated to *tid*, which moreover entails committing to w_3 being coherence-after w_1, as in the coherence constraint on the right above. Note that this still leaves the relative order of w_2 and w_3 unconstrained, so another

thread could be sent w_2 then w_3 or (in a different run) the other way around (or indeed just one, or neither).

In the model this behaviour is split up into separate storage-subsystem transitions: there is one rule for making a new coherence commitment between two hitherto-unrelated writes to the same address, one rule for propagating a write to a new thread (which can only fire after sufficient coherence commitments have been made), and one rule for returning a read value to a thread in response to a read-request. The last always returns the most recent write (to the read address) in the list of events propagated to the reading thread, which therefore serves essentially as a per-thread memory (though it records more information than just an array of bytes). We adopt these separate transitions (in what we term a *partial coherence commitment* style) to make it easy to relate model transitions to actual hardware implementation events: coherence commitments correspond to writes flowing through join points in a hierarchical-store-buffer implementation.

Out-of-order and Speculative Execution As we shall see in §6, many of the observable subtleties of Power behaviour arise from the fact that the threads can perform read instructions out-of-order and speculatively, subject to an instruction being restarted if a conflicting write comes in before the instruction is committed, or being aborted if a branch turns out to be mispredicted. However, writes are not sent to the storage subsystem before their instructions are committed, and we do not see observable value speculation. Accordingly, our thread model permits very liberal out-of-order execution, with unbounded speculative execution past as-yet-unresolved branches and past some barriers, while our storage subsystem model need not be concerned with speculation, retry, or aborts. On the other hand, the storage subsystem maintains the current coherence constraint, as above, while the thread model does not need to have access to this; the thread model plays its part in maintaining coherence by issuing requests in reasonable orders, and in aborting/retrying as necessary.

For each thread we have a tree of the *committed* and *in-flight* instruction instances. Newly fetched instructions become in-flight, and later, subject to appropriate preconditions, can be committed. For example, below we show a set of instruction instances $\{i_1, \ldots, i_{13}\}$ with the program-order-successor relation among them. Three of those ($\{i_1, i_3, i_4\}$, boxed) have been committed; the remainder are in-flight.

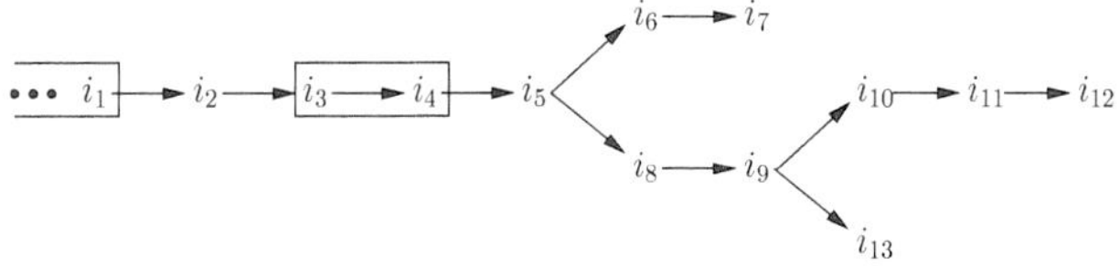

Instruction instances i_5 and i_9 are branches for which the thread has fetched multiple possible successors; here just two, but for a branch with a computed address it might fetch many possible successors. Note that the committed instances are not necessarily contiguous: here i_3 and i_4 have been committed even though i_2 has not, which can only happen if they are sufficiently independent. When a branch is committed then any un-taken alternative paths are discarded, and instructions that follow (in program order) an uncommitted branch cannot be committed until that branch is, so the tree must be linear before any committed (boxed) instructions.

In implementations, reads are retried when cache-line invalidates are processed. In the model, to abstract from exactly when this happens (and from whatever tracking the core does of which instructions must be retried when it does), we adopt a *late invalidate* semantics, retrying appropriate reads (and their dependencies) when a read or write is committed. For example, consider two reads r_1 and r_2 in program order that have been satisfied from two different writes to the same address, with r_2 satisfied first (out-of-order), from w_1, and r_1 satisfied later from the coherence-later w_2. When r_1 is committed, r_2 must be restarted, otherwise there would be a coherence violation. (This relies on the fact that writes are never provided by the storage subsystem out of coherence order; the thread model does not need to record the coherence order explicitly.)

Dependencies are dealt with entirely by the thread model, in terms of the registers read and written by each instruction instance (the register footprints of instructions are known statically). Memory reads cannot be satisfied until their addresses are determined (though perhaps still subject to change on retry), and memory writes cannot be committed until their addresses and values are fully determined. We do not model register renaming and shadow registers explicitly, but our out-of-order execution model includes their effect, as register reads take values from program-order-preceding register writes.

Barriers (sync and lwsync) and cumulativity-by-fiat The semantics of barriers involves both parts of the model, as follows.

When the storage subsystem receives a barrier request, it records the barrier as *propagated to* its own thread, marking a point in the sequence of writes that have been propagated to that thread. Those writes are the *Group A* writes for this barrier. When all the Group A writes (or some coherence-successors thereof) of a barrier have been propagated to another thread, the storage subsystem can record that fact also, propagating the barrier to that thread (thereby marking a point in the sequence of writes that have been propagated to that thread). A write cannot be propagated to a thread *tid* until all relevant barriers are propagated to *tid*, where the relevant barriers are those that were propagated to the writing thread before the write itself. In turn (by the above), that means that the Group A writes of those barriers (or some coherence successors) must already have been propagated to *tid*. This models the effect of cumulativity while abstracting from the details of how it is implemented.

Moreover, a sync barrier can be *acknowledged* back to the originating thread when all of its Group A writes have been propagated to all threads.

In the thread model, barriers constrain the commit order. For example, no memory load or store instruction can be committed until all previous sync barriers are committed and acknowledged; and sync and lwsync barriers cannot be committed until all previous memory reads and writes have been. Moreover, memory reads cannot be satisfied until previous sync barriers are committed and acknowledged. There are various possible modelling choices here which should not make any observable difference — the above corresponds to a moderately aggressive implementation.

4. The Model in Detail

We now detail the interface between the storage subsystem and thread models, and the states and transitions of each. The transitions are described in §4.3 and §4.5 in terms of their precondition, their effect on the relevant state, and the messages sent or received. Transitions are atomic, and synchronise as shown in Fig. 1; messages are not buffered. This is a prose description of our mathematical definitions, available on-line [SSA+11].

4.1 The Storage Subsystem/Thread Interface

The storage subsystem and threads exchange messages:

- a *write request* (or *write*) w specifies the writing thread tid, unique request id eid, address a, and value v.
- a *read request* specifies the originating thread tid, request id eid, and address a.
- a *read response* specifies the originating thread tid, request id eid, and a write w (itself specifying the thread tid' that did the write, its id eid', address a, and value v). This is sent when the value read is bound.
- a *barrier request* specifies the originating thread tid, request id eid, and barrier type b (sync or lwsync).
- a *barrier ack* specifies the originating thread tid and request id eid (a barrier ack is only sent for sync barriers, after the barrier is propagated to all threads.

4.2 Storage Subsystem States

A storage subsystem state s has the following components.

- $s.threads$ is the set of thread ids that exist in the system.
- $s.writes\_seen$ is the set of all writes that the storage subsystem has seen.
- $s.coherence$ is the current constraint on the coherence order, among the writes that the storage subsystem has seen. It is a binary relation: $s.coherence$ contains the pair (w_1, w_2) if the storage subsystem has committed to write w_1 being before write w_2 in the coherence order. This relation grows over time, with new pairs being added, as the storage subsystem makes additional commitments. For each address, $s.coherence$ is a strict partial order over the write requests seen to that address. It does not relate writes to different addresses, or relate any write that has not been seen by the storage subsystem to any write.
- $s.events\_propagated\_to$ gives, for each thread, a list of:
  1. all writes done by that thread itself,
  2. all writes by other threads that have been propagated to this thread, and
  3. all barriers that have been propagated to this thread.

  We refer to those writes as the writes that have been propagated to that thread. The Group A writes for a barrier are all the writes that have been propagated to the barrier's thread before the barrier is.
- $s.unacknowledged\_sync\_requests$ is the set of sync barrier requests that the storage subsystem has not yet acknowedged.

An initial state for the storage subsystem has the set of thread ids that exist in the system, exactly one write for each memory address, all of which have been propagated to all threads (this ensures that they will be coherence-before any other write to that address), an empty coherence order, and no unacknowledged sync requests.

4.3 Storage Subsystem Transitions

Accept write request A write request by a thread tid can always be accepted. Action:

1. add the new write to $s.writes\_seen$, to record the new write as seen by the storage subsystem;
2. append the new write to $s.events\_propagated\_to\ (tid)$, to record the new write as propagated to its own thread; and
3. update $s.coherence$ to note that the new write is coherence-after all writes (to the same address) that have previously propagated to this thread.

Partial coherence commitment The storage subsystem can internally commit to a more constrained coherence order for a particular address, adding an arbitrary edge (between a pair of writes to that address that have been seen already that are not yet related by coherence) to $s.coherence$, together with any edges implied by transitivity, if there is no cycle in the union of the resulting coherence order and the set of all pairs of writes (w_1, w_2), to any address, for which w_1 and w_2 are separated by a barrier in the list of events propagated to the thread of w_2.
Action: Add the new edges to $s.coherence$.

Propagate write to another thread The storage subsystem can propagate a write w (by thread tid) that it has seen to another thread tid', if:

1. the write has not yet been propagated to tid';
2. w is coherence-after any write to the same address that has already been propagated to tid'; and
3. all barriers that were propagated to tid before w (in $s.events\_propagated\_to\ (tid)$) have already been propagated to tid'.

Action: append w to $s.events\_propagated\_to\ (tid')$.

Send a read response to a thread The storage subsystem can accept a read-request by a thread tid at any time, and reply with the most recent write w to the same address that has been propagated to tid. The request and response are tightly coupled into one atomic transition. Action: send a read-response message containing w to tid.

Accept barrier request A barrier request from a thread tid can always be accepted. Action:

1. append it to $s.events\_propagated\_to\ (tid)$, to record the barrier as propagated to its own thread (and thereby fix the set of Group A writes for this barrier); and
2. (for sync) add it to $s.unacknowledged\_sync\_requests$.

Propagate barrier to another thread The storage subsystem can propagate a barrier it has seen to another thread if:

1. the barrier has not yet been propagated to that thread; and
2. for each Group A write, that write (or some coherence successor) has already been propagated to that thread

Action: append the barrier to $s.events\_propagated\_to\ (tid)$.

Acknowledge sync barrier A sync barrier b can be acknowledged if it has been propagated to all threads. Action:

1. send a barrier-ack message to the originating thread; and
2. remove b from $s.unacknowledged\_sync\_requests$.

Storage Subsystem Rule	Message(s)	Thread Rule
Accept write request	write request	Commit in-flight instruction
Partial coherence commitment		
Propagate write to another thread		
Send a read response to a thread	read request/read response	Satisfy memory read from storage subsystem
		Satisfy memory read by forwarding an in-flight write
Accept barrier request	barrier request	Commit in-flight instruction
Propagate barrier to another thread		
Acknowledge sync barrier	barrier ack	Accept sync barrier acknowledgement
		Fetch instruction
		Register read from previous register write
		Register read from initial register state
		Internal computation step

Figure 1. Storage Subsystem and Thread Synchronisation

4.4 Thread States

The state t of a single hardware thread consists of:

- its thread id.
- the initial values for all registers, *t.initial_register_state*.
- a set *t.committed_instructions* of committed instruction instances. All their operations have been executed and they are not subject to restart or abort.
- a set *t.in_flight_instructions* of in-flight instruction instances. These have been fetched and some of the associated instruction-semantics micro-operations may have been executed. However, none of the associated writes or barriers have been sent to the storage subsystem, and any in-flight instruction is subject to being aborted (together with all of its dependents).
- a set *t.unacknowledged_syncs* of sync barriers that have not been acknowledged by the storage subsystem.

An initial state for a thread has no committed or in-flight instructions and no unacknowledged sync barriers.

Each instruction instance i consists of a unique id, a representation of the current state of its instruction semantics, the names of its input and output registers, the set of writes that it has read from, the instruction address, the program-order-previous instruction instance id, and any value constraint required to reach this instruction instance from the previous instance. The instruction semantics executes in steps, doing internal computation, register reads and writes, memory reads, and, finally, memory writes or barriers.

4.5 Thread Transitions

Fetch instruction An instruction *inst* can be fetched, following its program-order predecessor *iprev* and from address a, if

1. a is a possible next fetch address for *iprev*; and
2. *inst* is the instruction of the program at a.

The possible next fetch addresses allow speculation past calculated jumps and conditional branches; they are defined as:

1. for a non-branch/jump instruction, the successor instruction address;
2. for a jump to a constant address, that address;
3. for a jump to an address which is not yet fully determined (i.e., where there is an uncommitted instruction with a dataflow path to the address), any address; and
4. for a conditional branch, the possible addresses for a jump together with the successor.

Action: construct an initialized instruction instance and add it to the set of in-flight instructions. This is an internal action of the thread, not involving the storage subsystem, as we assume a fixed program rather than modelling fetches with reads; we do not model self-modifying code.

Commit in-flight instruction An in-flight instruction can be committed if:

1. its instruction semantics has no pending reads (memory or register) or internal computation (data or address arithmetic);
2. all instructions with a dataflow dependency to this instruction (instructions with register outputs feeding to this instruction's register inputs) are committed;
3. all program-order-previous branches are committed;
4. if a memory load or store is involved, all program-order-previous instructions which might access its address (i.e., which have an as-yet-undetermined address or which have a determined address which equals that one) are committed;
5. if a memory load or store is involved, or this instruction is a sync, lwsync, or isync, then
   (a) all previous sync, lwsync and isync instructions are committed, and
   (b) there is no unacknowledged sync barrier by this thread;
6. if a sync or lwsync instruction, all previous memory access instructions are committed;
7. if an isync, then all program-order-previous instructions which access memory have their addresses fully determined, where by 'fully determined' we mean that all instructions that are the source of incoming dataflow dependencies to the relevant address are committed and any internal address computation is done.

Action: note that the instruction is now committed, and:

1. if a write instruction, restart any in-flight memory reads (and their dataflow dependents) that have read from the same address, but from a different write (and where the read could not have been by forwarding an in-flight write);
2. if a read instruction, find all in-flight program-order successors that have read from a different write to the same address, or which follow a lwsync barrier program-order after this instruction, and restart them and their dataflow dependents;

3. if this is a branch, abort any untaken speculative paths of execution, i.e., any instruction instances that are not reachable by the branch taken; and
4. send any write requests or barrier requests as required by the instruction semantics.

Accept sync barrier acknowledgement A sync barrier acknowledgement can always be accepted (there will always be a committed sync whose barrier has a matching *eid*). Action: remove the corresponding barrier from *t.unacknowledged_syncs*.

Satisfy memory read from storage subsystem A pending read request in the instruction semantics of an in-flight instruction can be satisfied by making a read-request and getting a read-response containing a write from the storage subsystem if:

1. the address to read is determined (i.e., any other reads with a dataflow path to the address have been satisfied, though not necessarily committed, and any arithmetic on such a path completed);
2. all program-order-previous syncs are committed and acknowledged; and
3. all program-order-previous isyncs are committed.

Action:

1. update the internal state of the reading instruction; and
2. note that the write has been read from by that instruction.

The remaining transitions are all thread-internal steps.

Satisfy memory read by forwarding an in-flight write directly to reading instruction A pending memory write w from an in-flight (uncommitted) instruction can be forwarded directly to a read of an instruction i if

1. w is an uncommitted write to the same address that is program-order before the read, and there is no program-order-intervening memory write that might be to the same address;
2. all i's program-order-previous syncs are committed and acknowledged; and
3. all i's program-order-previous isyncs are committed.

Action: as in the *satisfy memory read from storage subsystem* rule above.

Register read from previous register write A register read can read from a program-order-previous register write if the latter is the last write to the same register program-order before it. Action: update the internal state of the in-flight reading instruction.

Register read from initial register state A register read can read from the initial register state if there is no write to the same register program-order before it. Action: update the internal state of the in-flight reading instruction.

Internal computation step An in-flight instruction can perform an internal computation step if its semantics has a pending internal transition, e.g. for an arithmetic operation. Action: update the internal state of the in-flight instruction.

4.6 Final states

The final states are those with no transitions. It should be the case that for all such, all instruction instances are committed.

5. Explaining the simple examples

The abstract machine explains the allowed and forbidden behaviour for all the simple tests we saw before. For example, in outline:

MP The Thread 0 write-requests for x and y could be in-order or not, but either way, because they are to different addresses, they can be propagated to Thread 1 in either order. Moreover, even if they are propagated in program order, the Thread 1 read of x can be satisfied first (seeing the initial state), then the read of y, and they could be committed in either order.

MP+sync+ctrl (control dependency) Here the sync keeps the propagation of the writes to Thread 1 in order, but the Thread 1 read of x can be satisfied speculatively, before the conditional branch of the control dependency is resolved and before the program-order-preceding Thread 1 read of y is satisfied; then the two reads can be committed in program order.

MP+sync+ctrlisync (isync) Adding isync between the conditional branch and the Thread 1 read of x prevents that read being satisfied until the isync is committed, which cannot happen until the program-order-previous branch is committed, which cannot happen until the first read is satisfied and committed.

WRC+sync+addr (A-cumulativity) The Thread 0 write-request for a:W[x]=1 must be made, and the write propagated to Thread 1, for b to read 1 from it. Thread 1 then makes a barrier request for its sync, and that is propagated to Thread 1 after a (so the write a is in the Group A set for this barrier), before making the write-request for c:W[y]=1. That write must be propagated to Thread 2 for d to read from it, but before that is possible the sync must be propagated to Thread 2, and before that is possible a must be propagated to Thread 2. Meanwhile, the dependency on Thread 2 means that the address of the read e is not known, and so e cannot be satisfied, until read d has been satisfied (from c). As that cannot be until after a is propagated to Thread 2, read e must read 1 from a, not 0 from the initial state.

WRC+data+sync Here, in contrast, while the Thread 0/Thread 1 reads-from relationship and the Thread 1 dependency ensure that the write-requests for a:W[x]=1 and c:W[y]=1 are made in that order, and the Thread 2 sync keeps its reads in order, the order that the writes are propagated to Thread 2 is unconstrained.

ISA2 (B-cumulativity) In the ISA2+sync+data+addr B-cumulativity example, the Thread 0 write requests and barrier request must reach the storage subsystem in program order, so Group A for the sync is {a} and the sync is propagated to Thread 0 before the b write request reaches the storage subsystem. For c to read from b, the latter must have been propagated to Thread 1, which requires the sync to be propagated to Thread 1, which in turn requires the Group A write a to have been propagated to Thread 1. Now, the Thread 1 dependency means that d cannot be committed before the read c is satisfied (and committed), and hence d must be after the sync is propagated to Thread 1. Finally, for e to read from d, the latter must have been propagated to Thread 2, for which the sync must be propagated to Thread 2, and hence the Group A write a propagated to Thread 2. The Thread 2 dependency means that f cannot be satisfied until e is, so it must read from a, not from the initial state.

The same result and reasoning hold for the lwsync variant of this test (note that the reasoning did not involve sync acks or any memory reads program-order-after the sync).

IRIW+syncs Here the two syncs (on Threads 1 and 3) have the corresponding writes (a and d) in their Group A sets, and hence those writes must be propagated to all threads before the respective syncs are acknowledged, which must happen before the program-order-subsequent reads c and f can be be satisfied. But for those to read 0, from coherence-predecessors of a and d, the latter must not have been propagated to all threads (in particular, they must not have been propagated to Threads 3 and 1 respectively). In other words, for this to happen there would have to be a cycle in abstract-machine execution time:

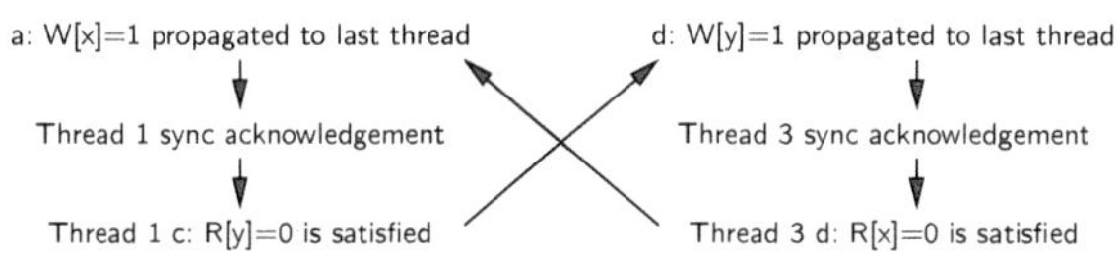

With lwsyncs instead of syncs, the behaviour is allowed, because lwsyncs do not have an analogous acknowledgement when their Group A writes have been propagated to all threads, and memory reads do not wait for previous lwsyncs to reach that point.

6. Not-so-simple examples

We now discuss some more subtle behaviours, explaining each in terms of our model.

Write forwarding In the PPOCA variant of MP below, f is address-dependent on e, which reads from the write d, which is control-dependent on c. One might expect that chain to prevent read f binding its value (with the *satisfy memory read from storage subsystem* rule) before c does, but in fact in some implementations f can bind out-of-order, as shown — the write d can be forwarded directly to e within the thread, before the write is committed to the storage subsystem. The *satisfy memory read by forwarding an in-flight write* rule models this. Replacing the control dependency with a data dependency (test PPOAA, not shown) removes that possibility, forbidding the given result on current hardware, as far as our experimental results show, and in our model. The current architecture text [Pow09] leaves the PPOAA outcome unspecified, but we anticipate that future versions will explicitly forbid it.

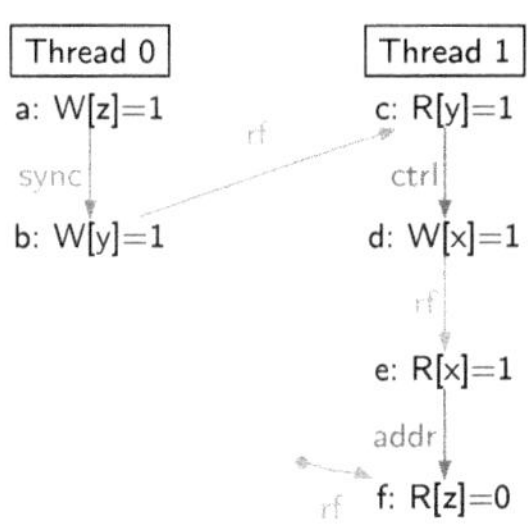

Test PPOCA : Allowed

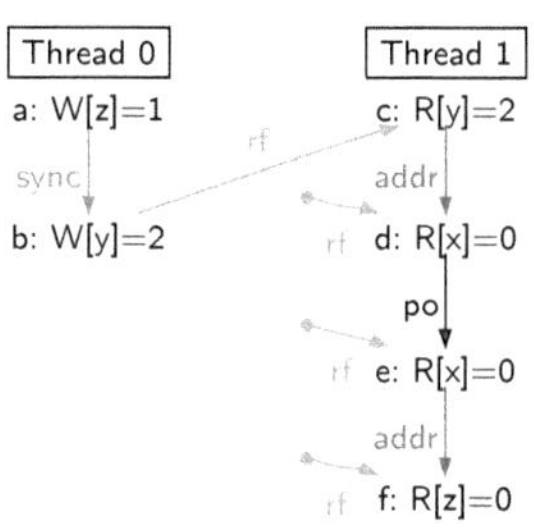

Test RSW : Allowed

Aggressively out-of-order reads In the reads-from-same-writes (RSW) variant of MP above, the two reads of x, d and e, happen to read from the same write (the initial state). In this case, despite the fact that d and e are reading from the same address, the e/f pair can satisfy their reads out-of-order, before the c/d pair, permitting the outcome shown. The address of e is known, so it can be satisfied early, while the address of d is not known until its address dependency on c is resolved. In contrast, in an execution in which d and e read from different writes to x (test RDW, not shown), with another write to x by another thread), that is forbidden — in the model, the commit of the first read (d) would force a restart of the second (e), together with its dependencies (including f), if e had initially read from a different write to d. In actual implementations the restart might be earlier, when an invalidate is processed, but will have the same observable effect.

Coherence and lwsync: blw-w-006 This example shows that one cannot assume that the transitive closure of lwsync and coherence edges guarantees ordering of write pairs, which is a challenge for over-simplified models. In our abstract machine, the fact that the storage subsystem commits to b being before c in the coherence order has no effect on the order in which writes a and d propagate to Thread 2. Thread 1 does not read from either Thread 0 write, so they need not be sent to Thread 1, so no cumulativity is in play.

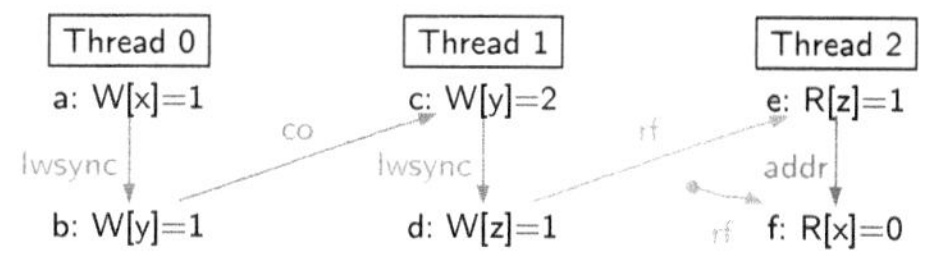

Test blw-w-006 : Allowed

In some implementations, and in the model, replacing both lwsyncs by syncs (bsync-w-006) forbids this behaviour. In the model, it would require a cycle in abstract-machine execution time, from the point at which a propagates to its last thread, to the Thread 0 sync ack, to the b write accept, to c propagating to Thread 0, to c propagating to its last thread, to the Thread 1 sync ack, to the d write accept, to d propagating to Thread 2, to e being satisfied, to f being satisfied, to a propagating to Thread 2, to a propagating to its last thread. The current architecture text again leaves this unspecified, but one would expect that adding sync everywhere (or, in this case, an address dependency between two reads) should regain SC.

Coherence and lwsync: 2+2W and R01 The 2+2W+lwsyncs example below is a case where the interaction of coherence and lwsyncs *does* forbid some behaviour. Without the lwsyncs (2+2W), the given execution is allowed. With them, the writes must be committed in program order, but after one partial coherence commitment (say d before a) is done, the other (b before c) is no longer permitted. (As this test has only writes, it may be helpful to note that the coherence order edges here could be observed either by reading the final state or with additional threads reading x twice and y twice. Testing both versions gives the same result.) This example is a challenge for axiomatic models with a view order per thread, as something is needed to break the symmetry. The given behaviour is also forbidden for the version with syncs (2+2W+syncs).

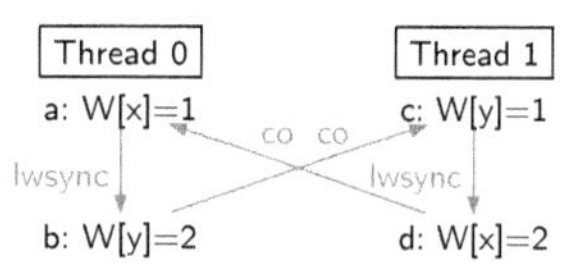

Test 2+2W+lwsyncs : Forbidden

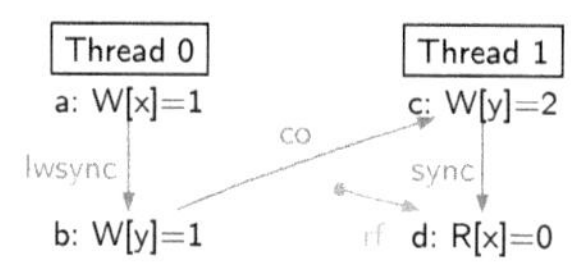

Test R01 : Allowed

The R01 test on the right above is a related case where we have not observed the given allowed behaviour in practice, but it is not currently forbidden by the architecture, and our model permits it. In the model, the writes can all reach the storage subsystem, the b/c partial coherence commitment be made, c be propagated to Thread 0, the sync be committed and acknowledged, and d be satisfied, all before a and the lwsync propagate to Thread 1.

LB and (no) thin-air reads This LB dual of the SB example is another case where we have not observed the given allowed behaviour in practice, but it is clearly architecturally intended, so programmers should assume that future processors might permit it, and our model does. Adding data or address dependencies (e.g. in LB+datas) should forbid the given behaviour (the data dependency case could involve out-of-thin-air reads), but experimental testing here is vacuous, as LB itself is not observed.

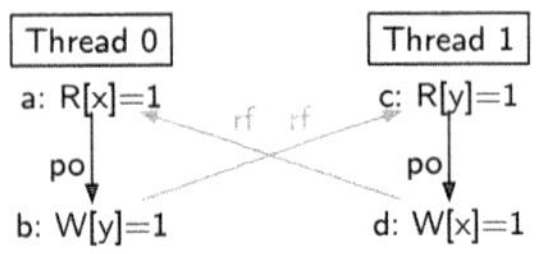

Test LB : Allowed

Register shadowing Adir et al. [AAS03] give another variant of LB (which we call LB+rs, for Register Shadowing), with a dependency on Thread 1 but re-using the same register on Thread 0, to demonstrate the observability of shadow registers. That is also allowed in our model but not observable in our tests — unsurprisingly, given that we have not observed LB itself. However, the following variant of MP does exhibit observable register shadowing: the two uses of r3 on Thread 1 do not prevent the second read being satisfied out-of-order, if the reads are into shadow registers. The reuse of a register is not represented in our diagrams, so for this example we have to give the underlying PowerPC assembly code.

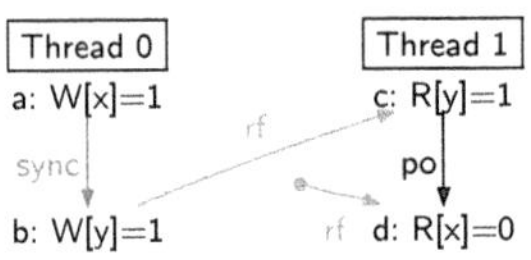

Test MP+sync+rs : Allowed

Thread 0	Thread 1

li r1,1
stw r1,0(r2)
sync
li r3,1
stw r3,0(r4)
	lwz r3,0(r2)
	mr r1,r3
	lwz r3,0(r4)

Initial state: 0:r2=x ∧ 0:r4=y ∧ 1:r2=y ∧ 1:r4=x	
Allowed: 1:r1=1 ∧ 1:r3=0	

7. Experiments on hardware

The use of small *litmus-test* programs for discussing the behaviour of relaxed memory models is well-established, but most previous work (with notable exceptions) does not empirically investigate how tests behave on actual hardware. We use our `litmus` tool [AMSS11] to run tests on machines with various Power processors: Power G5 (aka PowerPC 970MP, based on a POWER4 core), POWER 5, POWER 6, and POWER 7. The tool takes tests in PowerPC assembly and runs them in a test harness designed to stress the processor, to increase the likelihood of interesting results. This is black-box testing, and one cannot make any definite conclusions from the absence of some observation, but our experience is that the tool is rather discriminating, identifying many issues with previous models (and [AMSS10] report the discovery of a processor erratum using it).

Our work is also unusual in the range and number of tests used. For this paper we have established a library based on tests from the literature [Pow09, BA08, AAS03, ARM08], new hand-written tests (e.g. the PPOCA, PPOAA, RSW, RDW, and 2+2W in §6, and many others), and systematic variations of several tests (SB, MP, WRC, IRIW, ISA2, LB, and two others, RWC and WWC) with all possible combinations of barriers or dependencies; we call this the "VAR3" family, of 314 tests. We ran all of these on Power G5, 6, and 7. In addition, we use the `diy` tool [AMSS10] to systematically generate several thousand interesting tests with cycles of edges (dependencies, reads-from, coherence, etc.) of increasing size, and tested some of these. As an important style point, we use tests with constraints on the final values (and hence on the values read) rather than loops, to make them easily testable. We give an excerpt of our experimental results below, to give the flavour; more are available online [SSA+11]. For example, PPOCA was observable on POWER G5 (1.0k/3.1G), not observable on POWER 6, and then observable again on POWER 7 — consistent with the less aggressively out-of-order microarchitecture of POWER 6.

Test	Model	POWER 6		POWER 7	
WRC	Allow	ok	970k / 12G	ok	23M / 93G
WRC+data+addr	Allow	ok	562k / 12G	ok	94k / 93G
WRC+syncs	Forbid	ok	0 / 16G	ok	0 / 110G
WRC+sync+addr	Forbid	ok	0 / 16G	ok	0 / 110G
WRC+lwsync+addr	Forbid	ok	0 / 16G	ok	0 / 110G
WRC+data+sync	Allow	ok	150k / 12G	ok	56k / 94G
PPOCA	Allow	unseen	0 / 39G	ok	62k / 141G
PPOAA	Forbid	ok	0 / 39G	ok	0 / 157G
LB	Allow	unseen	0 / 31G	unseen	0 / 176G

The interplay between manual testing, systematic testing, and discussion with IBM staff has been essential to the development of our model. For example: the PPOCA/PPOAA behaviour was discovered in manual testing, leading us to conjecture that it should be explained by write-forwarding, which was later confirmed by discussion; the blw-w-006 test, found in systematic testing, highlighted difficulties with coherence and lwsync in an earlier model; and the role of coherence and sync acknowledgements in the current implementations arose from discussion.

8. Executing the model

The intricacy of relaxed memory models (and the number of tests we consider) make it essential also to have tool support for exploring the model, to automatically calculate the outcomes that the model permits for a litmus test, and to compare them against those observed in practice. To ease model development, and also to retain confidence in the tool, its kernel should be automatically generated from the model definition, not hand-coded. Our abstract machine is defined in Lem, a new lightweight language for machine-formalised mathematical definitions, of types, functions and inductive relations [OBZNS]. From this we generate HOL4 prover code (and thence an automatically typeset version of the machine) and executable OCaml code, using a finite set library, for the precondition and action of each transition rule. We also formalised a symbolic operational semantics for the tiny fragment of the instruction set needed for our tests. Using those, we build an exhaustive memoised search procedure that finds all possible abstract-machine executions for litmus tests.

This has confirmed that the model has the expected behaviour for the 41 tests we mention by name in this paper, for the rest of the VAR3 family of 314 systematic tests, and for various other tests. In most cases the model exactly matches the Power7 experimental results, with the exception of a few where it includes the experimental outcomes but is intentionally looser; this applies to 60 tests out of our batch of 333. Specifically: the model allows instructions to commit out of program order, which permits the LB and LB+rs test outcomes (not observed in practice); the model also allows an isync to commit even in the presence of previously uncommitted memory accesses, whereas the specified outcomes of tests such as WRC with an lwsync and isync have not been observed; and the R01 test outcome is not observed. In all these cases the model follows the architectural intent, as confirmed with IBM staff.

Our experimental results also confirm that Power G5 and 6 are strictly stronger than Power 7 (though in different ways): we have not seen any test outcome on those which is not also observable on Power 7. The model is thus also sound for those, to the best of our knowledge.

9. Related Work

There has been extensive previous work on relaxed memory models. We focus on models for the major current processor families that do not have sequentially consistent behaviour: Sparc, x86, Itanium, ARM, and Power. Early work by Collier [Col92] developed models based on empirical testing for the multiprocessors of the day. For Sparc, the vendor documentation has a clear Total Store Ordering (TSO) model [SFC91, Spa92]. It also introduces PSO and RMO models, but these are not used in practice. For x86, the vendor intentions were until recently quite unclear, as was the behaviour of processor implementations. The work by Sarkar, Owens, et al. [SSZN+09, OSS09, SSO+10] suggests that for normal user- or system-code they are also TSO. Their work is in a similar spirit to our own, with a mechanised semantics that is tested against empirical observation. Itanium provides a much weaker model than TSO, but one which is more precisely defined by the vendor than x86 [Int02]; it has also been formalised in TLA [JLM+03] and in higher-order logic [YGLS03].

For Power, there have been several previous models, but none are satisfactory for reasoning about realistic concurrent code. In part this is because the architecture has changed over time: the lwsync barrier has been added, and barriers are now cumulative. Corella, Stone and Barton [CSB93] gave an early axiomatic model for PowerPC, but, as Adir et al. note [AAS03], this model is flawed (it permits the non-SC final state of the MP+syncs example we show in §2). Stone and Fitzgerald later gave a prose description of PowerPC memory order, largely in terms of the microarchitecture of the time [SF95]. Gharachorloo [Gha95] gives a variety of models for different architectures in a general framework, but the model for the PowerPC is described as *"approximate"*; it is apparently based on Corella et al. [CSB93] and on May et al. [MSSW94]. Adve and Gharachorloo [AG96] make clear that PowerPC is very relaxed, but do not discuss the intricacies of dependency-induced ordering, or the more modern barriers. Adir, Attiya, and Shurek give a detailed axiomatic model [AAS03], in terms of a view order for each thread. The model was *"developed through an iterative process of successive refinements, numerous discussions with the PowerPC architects, and analysis of examples and counterexamples"*, and its consequences for a number of litmus tests (some of which we use here) are described in detail. These facts inspire some confidence, but it is not easy to understand the force of the axioms, and it describes *non-cumulative* barriers, following the pre-PPC 1.09 PowerPC architecture; current processors appear to be quite different. More recently, Chong and Ishtiaq give a preliminary model for ARM [CI08], which has a very similar architected memory model to Power. In our initial work in this area [AFI+09], we gave an axiomatic model based on a reading of the Power ISA 2.05 and ARM ARM specifications, with experimental results for a few tests (described as work in progress); this seems to be correct for some aspects but to give an unusably weak semantics to barriers.

More recently, we gave a rather different axiomatic model [AMSS10], further developed in Alglave's thesis [Alg10] as an instance of a general framework; it models the non-multi-copy-atomic nature of Power (with examples such as IRIW+addrs correctly allowed) in a simple global-time setting. The axiomatic model is sound with respect to our experimental tests, and on that basis can be used for reasoning, but it is weaker than the observed behaviour or architectural intent for some important examples. Moreover, it was based principally on black-box testing and its relationship to the actual processor implementations is less clear than that for the operational model we present here, which is more firmly grounded on microarchitectural and architectural discussion. In more detail, the axiomatic model is weaker than one might want for lwsync and for cumulativity: it allows MP+lwsync+addr and ISA2+sync+data+addr, which are not observed and which are intended to be architecturally forbidden. It also forbids R01, which is not observed but architecturally intended to be allowed, and which is allowed by the model given here. The two models are thus incomparable.

We mention also Lea's *JSR-133 Cookbook for Compiler Writers* [Lea], which gives informal (and approximate) models for several multiprocessors, and which highlights the need for clear models.

10. Conclusion

To summarise our contribution, we have characterised the actual behaviour of Power multiprocessors, by example and by giving a semantic model. Our examples include new tests illustrating several previously undescribed phenomena, together with variations of classic tests and a large suite of automatically generated tests; we have experimentally investigated their behaviour on a range of processors. Our model is: *rigorous* (in machine-typechecked mathematics); *experimentally validated*; *accessible* (in an abstract machine style, and detailed here in a few pages of prose); *usable* (as witnessed by the explanations of examples); *supported by a tool*, for calculating the possible outcomes of tests; and sufficient to *explain* the subtle behaviour exposed by our examples and testing. It is a new abstraction, maintaining coherence and cumulativity properties by fiat but modelling out-of-order and speculative execution explicitly.

The model should provide a good intuition for developers of concurrent systems code for Power multiprocessors, e.g. of concurrency libraries, language runtimes, OS kernels, and optimising compilers. Moreover, as the ARM architecture memory model is very similar, it may well be applicable (with minor adaptation) to ARM.

The model also opens up many directions for future research in verification theory and tools. For example, it is now possible to state results about the correct compilation of the C++0x concurrency primitives to Power processors, and to consider barrier- and dependency-aware optimisations in that context. We have focussed here primarily on the actual behaviour of implementations, but there is also work required to identify the guarantees that programmers actually rely on, which may be somewhat weaker — some of our more exotic examples are not natural use-cases, to the best of our knowledge. There is also future work required to broaden the scope of the model, which here covers only cacheable memory without mixed-size accesses.

We described our model principally in its own terms and in terms of the observed behaviour, without going into details of the relationship between the model and the underlying microarchitecture, or with the vendor architecture specification [Pow09]; this remains future work. A central notion of the memory model text in the latter is that of when a memory read or write by one thread is *performed* with respect to another, which has a hypothetical (or subjunctive) definition, e.g. for loads: *"A load by a processor P1 is performed with respect to a processor P2 when the value to be returned can no longer be changed by a store by P2"*, where that P2 store may not even be present in the program under consideration (again, ARM is similar). This definition made perfect sense in the original white-box setting [DSB86], where the internal structure of the system was known and one can imagine the hypothetical store by P2 appearing at some internal interface, but in the black-box setting of a commercial multiprocessor, it is hard or impossible to make it precise, especially with examples such as PPOCA. Our abstract-machine model may provide a stepping stone towards improved architectural definitions, perhaps via new axiomatic characterisations.

Acknowledgements We acknowledge funding from EPSRC grants EP/F036345, EP/H005633, and EP/H027351, from ANR project ParSec (ANR-06-SETIN-010), and from INRIA associated team MM.

References

[AAS03] A. Adir, H. Attiya, and G. Shurek. Information-flow models for shared memory with an application to the PowerPC architecture. *IEEE Trans. Parallel Distrib. Syst.*, 14(5):502–515, 2003.

[AFI+09] J. Alglave, A. Fox, S. Ishtiaq, M. O. Myreen, S. Sarkar, P. Sewell, and F. Zappa Nardelli. The semantics of Power and ARM multiprocessor machine code. In *Proc. DAMP 2009*, January 2009.

[AG96] S. V. Adve and K. Gharachorloo. Shared memory consistency models: A tutorial. *IEEE Computer*, 29(12):66–76, 1996.

[Alg10] Jade Alglave. *A Shared Memory Poetics.* PhD thesis, Université Paris 7 – Denis Diderot, November 2010.

[AMSS10] J. Alglave, L. Maranget, S. Sarkar, and P. Sewell. Fences in weak memory models. In *Proc. CAV*, 2010.

[AMSS11] J. Alglave, L. Maranget, S. Sarkar, and P. Sewell. Litmus: Running tests against hardware. In *Proc. TACAS*, 2011.

[ARM08] ARM. ARM Barrier Litmus Tests and Cookbook, October 2008. PRD03-GENC-007826 2.0.

[BA08] H.-J. Boehm and S. Adve. Foundations of the C++ concurrency memory model. In *Proc. PLDI*, 2008.

[BOS+11] M. Batty, S. Owens, S. Sarkar, P. Sewell, and T. Weber. Mathematizing C++ concurrency. In *Proc. POPL*, 2011.

[CI08] N. Chong and S. Ishtiaq. Reasoning about the ARM weakly consistent memory model. In *MSPC*, 2008.

[Col92] W.W. Collier. *Reasoning about parallel architectures.* Prentice-Hall, Inc., 1992.

[CSB93] F. Corella, J. M. Stone, and C. M. Barton. A formal specification of the PowerPC shared memory architecture. Technical Report RC18638, IBM, 1993.

[DSB86] M. Dubois, C. Scheurich, and F. Briggs. Memory access buffering in multiprocessors. In *ISCA*, 1986.

[Gha95] K. Gharachorloo. Memory consistency models for shared-memory multiprocessors. *WRL Research Report*, 95(9), 1995.

[Int02] Intel. A formal specification of Intel Itanium processor family memory ordering, 2002. `developer.intel.com/design/itanium/downloads/251429.htm`.

[JLM+03] R. Joshi, L. Lamport, J. Matthews, S. Tasiran, M. Tuttle, and Y. Yu. Checking cache-coherence protocols with TLA+. *Form. Methods Syst. Des.*, 22:125–131, March 2003.

[KSSF10] R. Kalla, B. Sinharoy, W. J. Starke, and M. Floyd. Power7: IBM's next-generation server processor. *IEEE Micro*, 30:7–15, March 2010.

[Lea] D. Lea. The JSR-133 cookbook for compiler writers. `http://gee.cs.oswego.edu/dl/jmm/cookbook.html`.

[LSF+07] H. Q. Le, W. J. Starke, J. S. Fields, F. P. O'Connell, D. Q. Nguyen, B. J. Ronchetti, W. Sauer, E. M. Schwarz, and M. T. Vaden. IBM POWER6 microarchitecture. *IBM Journal of Research and Development*, 51(6):639–662, 2007.

[MSSW94] C. May, E. Silha, R. Simpson, and H. Warren, editors. *The PowerPC architecture: a specification for a new family of RISC processors.* Morgan Kaufmann Publishers Inc., San Francisco, CA, USA, 1994.

[OBZNS] S. Owens, P. Böhm, F. Zappa Nardelli, and P. Sewell. Lightweight tools for heavyweight semantics. Submitted for publication `http://www.cl.cam.ac.uk/~so294/lem/`.

[OSS09] S. Owens, S. Sarkar, and P. Sewell. A better x86 memory model: x86-TSO. In *Proc. TPHOLs*, pages 391–407, 2009.

[Pow09] *Power ISA*^{TM} *Version 2.06.* IBM, 2009.

[SF95] J. M. Stone and R. P. Fitzgerald. Storage in the PowerPC. *IEEE Micro*, 15:50–58, April 1995.

[SFC91] P. S. Sindhu, J.-M. Frailong, and M. Cekleov. Formal specification of memory models. In *Scalable Shared Memory Multiprocessors*, pages 25–42. Kluwer, 1991.

[SKT+05] B. Sinharoy, R. N. Kalla, J. M. Tendler, R. J. Eickemeyer, and J. B. Joyner. POWER5 system microarchitecture. *IBM Journal of Research and Development*, 49(4-5):505–522, 2005.

[Spa92] *The SPARC Architecture Manual, V. 8.* SPARC International, Inc., 1992. Revision SAV080SI9308. `http://www.sparc.org/standards/V8.pdf`.

[SSA+11] S. Sarkar, P. Sewell, J. Alglave, L. Maranget, and D. Williams. Understanding POWER multiprocessors. `www.cl.cam.ac.uk/users/pes20/ppc-supplemental`, 2011.

[SSO+10] P. Sewell, S. Sarkar, S. Owens, F. Zappa Nardelli, and M. O. Myreen. x86-TSO: A rigorous and usable programmer's model for x86 multiprocessors. *Communications of the ACM*, 53(7):89–97, July 2010.

[SSZN+09] S. Sarkar, P. Sewell, F. Zappa Nardelli, S. Owens, T. Ridge, T. Braibant, M. Myreen, and J. Alglave. The semantics of x86-CC multiprocessor machine code. In *Proc. POPL 2009*, January 2009.

[YGLS03] Y. Yang, G. Gopalakrishnan, G. Lindstrom, and K. Slind. Analyzing the Intel Itanium memory ordering rules using logic programming and SAT. In *Proc. CHARME, LNCS 2860*, 2003.

Partial-Coherence Abstractions for Relaxed Memory Models

Michael Kuperstein
Technion, Haifa, Israel
mkuper@cs.technion.ac.il

Martin Vechev
IBM T.J. Watson Research Center
mtvechev@us.ibm.com

Eran Yahav *
Technion, Haifa, Israel
yahave@cs.technion.ac.il

Abstract

We present an approach for automatic verification and fence inference in concurrent programs running under relaxed memory models. Verification under relaxed memory models is a hard problem. Given a finite state program and a safety specification, verifying that the program satisfies the specification under a sufficiently relaxed memory model is undecidable. For stronger models, the problem is decidable but has non-primitive recursive complexity.

In this paper, we focus on models that have store-buffer based semantics, e.g., SPARC TSO and PSO. We use abstract interpretation to provide an effective verification procedure for programs running under this type of models. Our main contribution is a family of novel *partial-coherence* abstractions, specialized for relaxed memory models, which partially preserve information required for memory coherence and consistency. We use our abstractions to automatically verify programs under relaxed memory models. In addition, when a program violates its specification but can be fixed by adding fences, our approach can automatically infer a correct fence placement that is optimal under the abstraction. We implemented our approach in a tool called BLENDER and applied it to verify and infer fences in several concurrent algorithms.

Categories and Subject Descriptors D.1.3 [*Concurrent Programming*]; D.2.4 [*Program Verification*]

General Terms Algorithms, Verification

Keywords Concurrency, Synthesis, Abstract Interpretation, Relaxed Memory Models, Weak Memory Models

1. Introduction

In the early 1990s, features like out-of-order execution and multi-level caches became common in commodity CPU architectures. These features drastically improved performance in a programmer-transparent fashion: their introduction did not change the semantics of existing (sequential) programs. With the advent of symmetric multiprocessing and multi-core CPUs, preserving the illusion of in-order memory operations became more difficult. One possible approach is to keep the illusion—known as *sequential consistency* [20] in a multi-processor setting—and sacrifice performance. The other is to define architectural *relaxed memory models* (RMMs) that allow improved performance at the cost of weaker semantics.

A relaxed memory model allows observable executions that cannot occur if instructions running on different processors are simply interleaved. As a result, a program that runs correctly on the sequentially-consistent model may violate its specification when running on a relaxed memory model. In practice, relaxed memory models are used by all major CPU designs, among them Intel x86 [33], SPARC [36] and PowerPC [16]. To enforce order between memory operations, these architectures provide special *memory fence* instructions. Informally, inserting a fence instruction prohibits certain re-orderings, thus restricting the set of relaxed executions. For example, a fence inserted between two store instructions will force these two stores to appear to execute in-order. It is the programmer's (or the compiler's) responsibility to correctly place fences.

Program Verification and Fence Inference To place fences, the programmer must first be able to know whether the program is correct given a fence placement - in other words, she needs to be able to verify the program. However, verification of concurrent programs is not an easy task even under the sequentially consistent memory model. Relaxed memory models make reasoning about program correctness, both manually and automatically, even harder, as they require reasoning about non sequentially-consistent executions. Even for finite-state programs, automatic verification under relaxed memory models is a hard problem. Given a finite state program and a safety specification, verifying that the program satisfies a specification under a sufficiently relaxed memory model (e.g., SPARC RMO) is undecidable. For somewhat stronger memory models (e.g., SPARC TSO, PSO), the problem is decidable but has non-primitive recursive complexity [2].

Even given a verification procedure, inserting fences is still non-trivial. On the one hand, since each fence incurs a heavy performance penalty, the programmer should not insert fences unless they are strictly required for correctness. On the other hand, missing a fence may lead to subtle concurrency bugs.

Store Buffers Relaxed memory models allow two basic relaxations of sequential consistency: memory operations may be reordered with respect to each other, and stores may be executed non-atomically across processors [1]. Some relaxations can be naturally modeled using store buffers [25], emulating the actual hardware implementation. In store-buffer based semantics, one or more FIFO queues ("store buffers") are associated with each processor. Memory writes are split into two phases: a "store" phase and a "flush" phase. The store phase adds a value into a local store buffer, and the flush phase propagates the stored value to main memory (or directly to other processors).

The basic hurdle for automatic verification under those models is that store buffers can grow without a bound, even for programs that are otherwise finite state. To enable automatic program verification and fence inference on relaxed memory models, we need a technique that can represent those buffers in a bounded way.

* Deloro Fellow

PLDI'11, June 4–8, 2011, San Jose, California, USA.

Existing Approaches Existing approaches either employ under-approximations such as bounded checking [5] and testing [8], or side-step the problem by focusing on a restricted class of programs. For instance, [32] considers data-race free programs, and [28] focuses on programs free from a particular ("triangular") type of data races. Bounded checking and testing are valuable, but cannot establish that the program satisfies its specification on all executions. When used for automatic fence inference, bounded techniques (e.g., [5, 18]) might miss required fences. Targeting only race-free programs simplifies the problem by allowing consideration of only sequentially-consistent executions. However, it is often unrealistic, as many concurrent programs contain "benign data races" [27]. For example, some mutual exclusion algorithms, such as Dekker's algorithm, contain benign triangular data races. Thus we cannot apply the results of [28], even if we restrict attention only to the TSO model.

In contrast to these approaches, our technique *over-approximates* possible program behaviors and is able to *verify* programs executing under RMMs. When used for fence inference, our technique is guaranteed to produce all required fences.

Our Approach We present a technique for automatic verification and fence inference in finite-state programs running on relaxed memory models. Based on abstract interpretation [9], we introduce a family of *partial-coherence* abstractions for store buffers. Our abstractions provide a bounded representation for (potentially) unbounded store buffers. We use the term *abstract memory model* to refer to a memory model that uses an abstract structure to represent store buffers. Our approach provides a range of abstractions with varying precision, enabling successive abstraction refinements of a given abstract memory model M_A.

Given a program P, a specification S and an abstract memory model M_A, the question we are trying to answer is whether $P \models_{M_A} S$, that is, whether the program satisfies the specification under the given abstract memory model. When $P \not\models_{M_A} S$, it is possible to:

- *Refine the abstraction*: refine M_A and try to find a more precise memory model $M_{A'}$ under which $P \models_{M_{A'}} S$.
- *Restrict the program*: find a program P' obtained from P by adding memory fences that restrict the permitted re-orderings during execution, such that $P' \models_{M_A} S$.

In this work, we focus on restricting the program by inserting fences, and show how using different abstract memory models affects the precision of the resulting fence placement. We focus on a family of abstractions for the TSO and PSO memory models, as those models are implemented in common hardware (e.g., Intel x86 [29], SPARC) and have simple concrete operational semantics.

Partial-Coherence Abstractions The challenge for abstractions of store buffers is to provide a bounded representation that (partially) preserves the following three key properties (described in more detail in Section 2):

- Intra-process memory coherence: a process should only see its own most recently written value to a variable.
- Inter-process memory coherence: a process should observe values written by another process in the order they were written.
- Fence semantics: a fence executed by a process writes to memory the most recent value written by the process.

The main idea behind our abstractions is to preserve only a limited amount of order inherent in a store buffer. In particular, our abstract buffer representation preserves information about: i) the most recent store to a buffer, and ii) the order between a bounded number of the oldest stores in the buffer. While inter-process coherence is only partially preserved, we show this choice is particularly effective for verifying concurrent algorithms running on relaxed memory models (see Section 4 for details).

Process 0:

```
while(true)
{
 store ent0 = true;
 store turn = 1;
 do
 {
  load e = ent1;
  load t = turn;
 }
 while(e==true && t==1);
 //Critical Section
 store ent0 = false;
}
```

Process 1:

```
while(true)
{
 store ent1 = true;
 store turn = 0;
 do
 {
  load e = ent0;
  load t = turn;
 }
 while(e==true && t==0);
 //Critical Section
 store ent1 = false;
}
```

Figure 1. Peterson's Algorithm with explicit memory operations

Process 0:

```
while(true)
{
 store ent0 = true;
 fence;
 store turn = 1;
 fence;
 do
 {
  load e = ent1;
  load t = turn;
 }
 while(e==true && t==1);
 //Critical Section
 store ent0 = false;
}
```

Process 1:

```
while(true)
{
 store ent1 = true;
 fence;
 store turn = 0;
 fence;
 do
 {
  load e = ent0;
  load t = turn;
 }
 while(e==true && t==0);
 //Critical Section
 store ent1 = false;
}
```

Figure 2. Peterson's Algorithm with fences that guarantee mutual exclusion under the PSO memory model. Fences were automatically inferred by our approach.

1.1 Main Contributions

The main contributions of this paper are as follows:

- We describe a family of parametric abstractions that enable automatic verification of safety properties for programs under relaxed memory models.
- When a program violates its specification but can be fixed by adding fences, our approach can automatically infer a correct fence placement that is optimal under the given abstraction.
- We have implemented our approach in a tool called BLENDER and applied it for verification and fence inference of several challenging concurrent algorithms.

2. Overview

2.1 Motivating Example - Peterson's Algorithm

Fig. 1 shows the code of Peterson's mutual exclusion algorithm [31]. In this algorithm, two processes repeatedly enter and exit a critical section. We would like to show that the algorithm satisfies the *mutual exclusion* property: it is impossible for both processes to be in the critical section simultaneously. Indeed, Peterson's algorithm satisfies mutual exclusion under a sequentially-consistent (SC) memory model. Unfortunately, under relaxed memory models, such as "Partial Store Order" (PSO), the algorithm *does not* satisfy the property. To see why, we first give a brief explanation of the PSO memory model.

The Partial Store Order (PSO) Memory Model PSO is one of three memory consistency models defined for the SPARC architecture [36]. In PSO, a store to some memory location l may become

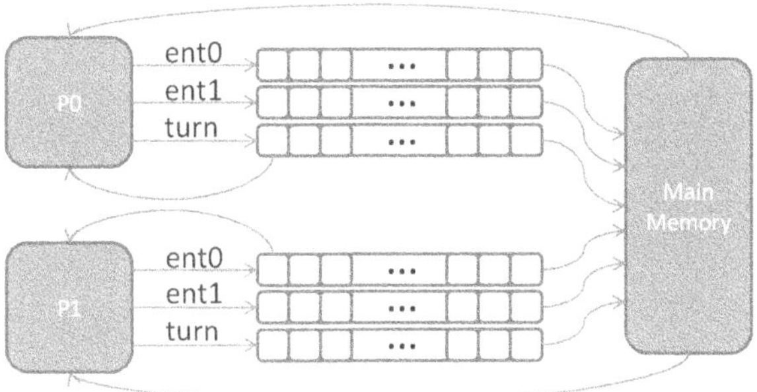

Figure 3. Store buffers for Peterson's algorithm of Fig. 1 under the PSO memory model. Note that buffers can grow without a bound.

visible to other processes only after the storing process executes later loads and stores to different memory locations.

The PSO model can be formalized operationally by associating with each processor a set of FIFO queues (store buffers), one for each variable, as shown in Fig. 3. The informal semantics of store buffers for PSO can be summarized as follows:

- Store buffering: A store issued by process p_i to variable x is written into the store buffer associated with (p_i, x).
- Store forwarding: A load by p_j from y is performed from its local store buffer (associated with (p_j, y)) if it is not empty, or from the global memory otherwise.
- Flushing: The oldest value stored in the buffer may be written to the global memory and removed from the buffer at non-deterministic points in the execution.

The Problem: Delayed Stores Under the PSO model, the following execution of Peterson's algorithm is possible:

- p_0 runs alone until line 11, however the store to `ent0` in line 3 is written only to the buffer but not flushed.
- p_1 runs. Since the store to `ent0` is delayed, it is not visible to p_1. p_1 enters the critical section, and mutual exclusion is violated.

Peterson's algorithm relies on *ordering* of loads and stores for synchronization. It requires p_0's store to `ent0` to be visible to p_1 before p_0 loads `ent1`, and symmetrically on p_1's store to `ent1` to be visible to p_0 before p_1 loads `ent0`. When the underlying memory model does not preserve this order, Peterson's algorithm, as it appears in Fig. 1, does not satisfy mutual exclusion.

Restoring Order with Fences To allow programmer control over ordering in relaxed memory models, processors provide special memory fence instructions. Intuitively, the semantics of a fence are that memory operations issued before the fence must take global effect before memory operations after the fence may execute. In general, there are different kinds of fences (e.g., store-load, store-store) that impose order between different types of operations. A store-load fence executed by a processor forces all stores issued by that processor to complete before any new loads by the same processor start. In this paper we assume the model provides the strongest type of fence (a "full memory barrier") that restricts reordering of any memory operations. In Fig. 2 the fences in lines 4 and 6 prevent the erroneous execution above (and other possible related bugs) by forcing the stores in lines 3 and 5 to take global effect before the storing process can advance. Unfortunately, fence instructions are very costly in terms of CPU cycles. Thus, we wish to place fences only when they are required for correctness.

Efficient Fence Placement The programmer's challenge is, then, in finding a fence placement that permits as much re-ordering as possible but does not allow the specification to be violated. To find an efficient placement of fences, we need to observe what re-orderings lead to violation of the specification, and find a minimal placement (often, there are multiple non-comparable solutions) that prevents these re-orderings. When the program is finite-state, we can enumerate all reachable program states, identify error states and find fences that prevent execution from reaching those states (c.f [18]). Unfortunately, Peterson's algorithm without fences running on PSO has an infinite state-space. The length of the store buffers generated by the program is not bounded: running p_0 alone for t iterations of the outer loop without flushing will generate a buffer of length $2t$ for the `ent0` variable.

2.2 Abstraction

To handle programs that have an unbounded state-space, we introduce a family of parametric abstractions that provide a conservative bounded representation. Our abstractions induce a hierarchy of (abstract) memory models with varying degrees of consistency. Before describing the abstraction, we note that concrete PSO semantics preserve the following 3 properties.

1. Intra-process coherence: If a process stores several values to shared variable x, and then performs a load from x, it should not see any value it has itself stored except the most recent one.
2. Inter-process coherence: A process p_i should not observe values written to shared variable x by process p_j in an order different from the order in which they were written.
3. Fence semantics: If a process p_i executes a fence when its buffer for variable x is non-empty, the value of x visible to other processes immediately after the fence should be the most recent value p_i wrote.

The properties above are phrased in terms of PSO semantics (store buffer per variable), but it is easy to formulate similar properties for other memory models. For example, for TSO, the only change is that inter-process coherence is global and not per variable. In that case, the desired property may be called inter-process *consistency*.

Partial-Coherence Abstraction The challenge in designing an abstraction for store-buffer based memory models lies in preserving properties 1-3 (to the greatest possible extent) using a bounded representation of each buffer. To preserve intra-process coherence, our abstractions maintain recency information per variable. To preserve inter-process coherence, our abstractions preserve order between stores up to some constant bound (a parameter of our abstraction), and treat the remaining stores as an unordered set. While property 2 is not fully preserved, this *partial coherence* is often sufficient in practice. The intuition is that if a process stores many (possibly different) values to the same shared variable without an intervening fence, the order in which they become visible is not important for the correctness of the algorithm.

Fig. 4 shows a schematic view of a partial-coherence abstraction of PSO store buffers for the Peterson algorithm of Fig. 1. In this abstraction, a store buffer is represented by treating items after a bounded head (of length k) of the buffer as a set, and additionally recording the most recently stored value for each buffer.

In Section 3, we give a formal concrete semantics for the PSO memory model and in Section 4 present our abstract semantics. Using this abstraction with the fence inference algorithm of Section 5, our approach automatically infers the fences shown in Fig. 2. In Section 6, we show that we can use different parameters to achieve more scalable abstractions and still get reasonable results. We also show that there is a tradeoff between the precision of the abstraction and the quality of the inferred fences. Finer abstractions lead to successful inference with fewer fences, while restricting the program by adding fences enables verification with a coarser abstraction. In particular, our partially disjunctive abstraction (see Section 4.3) produces non-trivial fence placements for programs for which the fully disjunctive abstraction leads to state-space explosion.

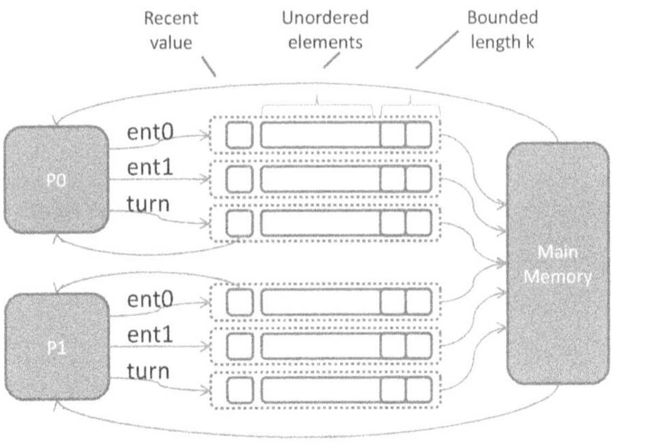

Figure 4. A partial-coherence abstraction of PSO store buffers for the Peterson algorithm of Fig. 1. In this abstraction, a store buffer is given a bounded representation by representing items after a bounded head of the buffer as a set, and recording the recently stored value for each buffer.

3. Operational Semantics for Relaxed Memory Models

In this section, we present an operational semantics for the PSO memory model. It is easy to give similar semantics for other conceptually close models such as TSO, NTSO and NPSO [24].

3.1 Preliminaries

Sequence Notation Given a finite domain D, we use $Seq_n(D)$ to denote the set of all sequences of length n over D, $Seq_{\leq n}(D)$ to denote the set of all sequences shorter than or equal in length to n over D, $Seq(D)$ to denote the set of all finite sequences over D, $|w|$ to denote the length of a sequence w and ϵ to denote an empty sequence. We denote the concatenation of two sequences w_1, w_2 by $w_1 \cdot w_2$. For $k > |w|$, we define $head(w, k)$ as the subsequence consisting of the first k items in w and $tail(w, k)$ as the subsequence consisting of the last k items in w. For $0 < k \leq |w|$ we define $head(w, k) = tail(w, k) = w$ and for $k \leq 0$, $head(w, k) = tail(w, k) = \epsilon$. We define $last(w)$ to be the only element in $tail(w, 1)$, or $\perp$ if $tail(w, 1) = \epsilon$. We define $Set(w)$ to be the set of elements in the sequence w. Finally, we define $UTail(w, k)$ as $Set(tail(w, |w| - k))$ — the set of all but the first k elements of w.

Program Syntax We consider programs written in a simple assembly-like programming language with the operations load, store, branch, CAS (compare and swap) and sequential and parallel composition. Our language also contains a full fence operation. We assume that instructions in our programs are labeled, and the labels used in the code of process are unique. We denote the set of program labels by *Labs*.

Program Semantics A transition system for a program P under a memory model M is a tuple $\langle \sigma_0, \Sigma, T \rangle$, where Σ is a set of states, $\sigma_0 \in \Sigma$ is the initial state of P, and T is a set of transitions $\sigma \xrightarrow{t} \sigma'$. A transition $\sigma \xrightarrow{t} \sigma'$ is in T if $\sigma, \sigma' \in \Sigma$, and execution from state σ according to the semantics of M can result in state σ'. A trace π of the program is a (possibly infinite) sequence of transitions $\sigma_0 \rightarrow \sigma_1 \rightarrow \sigma_2 \rightarrow ...$, where for all i, $\sigma_i \longrightarrow \sigma_{i+1} \in T$. In all of our semantics, a single transition will correspond to action taken by a single process. Thus we will associate a transition t with that process, and denote the associated process $proc(t)$. A transition t_p is *enabled* for process p in state σ if $p = proc(t_p)$ and there exists some σ_2 such that $\sigma \xrightarrow{t_p} \sigma_2 \in T$.

Throughout the paper we present the semantics in a standard operational style as a set of inference rules. To simplify presentation, when updating mappings, we use $M'(x) = v$ as a shorthand for $M' = M[x \mapsto v]$. Components not updated in the inference rule are assumed to be left unchanged.

3.2 Store Buffers

In our memory model semantics we follow [2, 7, 25] and assume that processes execute their programs sequentially, and any violations of sequential consistency happen within the memory subsystem. This is in contrast to other formulations that combine the memory and processor effects (e.g., [30, 35, 41]).

Our formulation is based on store-buffers, and our concrete semantics uses the following semantic domains:

- $G^\natural \in SVar$ where $SVar = Shared \rightarrow D$. Valuation of shared variables from the domain D.
- $L^\natural \in Env$ where $Env = PID \rightarrow (Local \rightarrow D)$. Valuation of local variables for each process.
- $pc^\natural \in PC$ where $PC = PID \rightarrow Labs$. Program counters.
- $B^\natural \in SB$ where SB differs between different memory models, and is intentionally left unspecified at this stage. A representation of the store buffers.

Here D represents the domain from which the variables in the program take values.

A state $\sigma = \langle G^\natural_\sigma, L^\natural_\sigma, pc^\natural_\sigma, B^\natural_\sigma \rangle \in C^\natural$ is a tuple where $C^\natural = SVar \times Env \times PC \times SB$. We use $next(pc(p))$ to mean the instruction following $pc(p)$ in the program code. Furthermore, we will omit the p when the referenced process is clear from the context.

3.3 Partial Store Order (PSO) Model

Concrete Semantics For PSO, a separate FIFO store buffer is maintained for every (process, variable) pair. That is, formally, $SB = PID \rightarrow (Shared \rightarrow Seq(D))$

Semantics 1 Operational semantics defining transition from $\langle G, L, pc, B \rangle$ to $\langle G', L', pc', B' \rangle$ under PSO.

$$\frac{stmt(pc) = load\ x, r \quad B(x) = \epsilon \quad G(x) = v}{L'(r) = v \quad pc' = next(pc)} \ \text{(LOAD-G)}$$

$$\frac{stmt(pc) = load\ x, r \quad B(x) = b \cdot v}{L'(r) = v \quad pc' = next(pc)} \ \text{(LOAD-B)}$$

$$\frac{stmt(pc) = store\ r, x \quad B(x) = b \quad L(r) = v}{B'(x) = b \cdot v \quad pc' = next(pc)} \ \text{(STORE)}$$

$$\frac{B(x) = v \cdot b}{B'(x) = b \quad G'(x) = v} \ \text{(FLUSH)}$$

$$\frac{stmt(pc) = fence \quad \forall x. B(x) = \epsilon}{pc' = next(pc)} \ \text{(FENCE)}$$

$$\frac{\begin{array}{c} stmt(pc) = cas\ x, r, s, q \\ G(x) = L(r) \quad L(s) = v \quad B(x) = \epsilon \end{array}}{G'(x) = v \quad L'(q) = true \quad pc' = next(pc)} \ \text{(CAS-T)}$$

$$\frac{stmt(pc) = cas\ x, r, s, q \quad G(x) \neq L(r) \quad B(x) = \epsilon}{L'(q) = false \quad pc' = next(pc)} \ \text{(CAS-F)}$$

Sem. 1 shows the concrete operational semantics of the PSO model. Each inference rule applies only to a single process. Thus, the p parameter is consistently omitted in all inference rules presented. However it is always implicitly existentially quantified. For example, the premise of the LOAD-G rule should be read as

$$\exists p.stmt(pc(p)) = load\ x, r \wedge B(p)(x) = \epsilon \wedge G(x) = v$$

The semantics show the role played by the store buffer for storing and loading values to/from main memory (STORE, LOAD-G, LOAD-B, FLUSH). The FENCE and CAS rules have memory fence semantics. These two rules are enabled only when the buffer of the executing process is empty. This means that when a process encounters, e.g., a fence instruction, it cannot continue execution until all of the buffers are flushed. For simplicity we omit the semantics of instructions that do not access shared memory (register operations, branches) and leave expression evaluation implicit. That is, $L(r)$ is extended to the evaluation of complex expressions r. Such a complex expression may only depend on local variables — expression evaluation may not cause a memory access.

The premise of all rules except FLUSH depends on the program counter of the process. They are enabled only if $pc(p)$ points to an instruction of a specific type. The FLUSH rule, on the other hand, is always enabled for a given buffer $B(p)(x)$ if that buffer is not empty. This captures the fact that flushes can be performed non-deterministically at any stage of program execution.

3.4 Total Store Order (TSO) Model

The TSO concrete state differs from the PSO concrete state only in the definition of the store buffer. For TSO, there is only a single, buffer for all variables of a process. That is, $SB = PID \rightarrow Seq(Shared \times D)$. The semantics must also be updated to take the difference into account. The flavor of the required changes can be seen in the TSO version of the LOAD-G rule in Sem. 2. Note that as the difference between PSO and TSO lies purely in the grouping of shared variables into store buffers, we can treat them as special cases of the same general model.

Semantics 2 LOAD-G rule for concrete TSO

$$\frac{stmt(pc) = load\ x, r \quad \forall (y, d) \in B. y \neq x \quad G(x) = v}{L'(r) = v \quad pc' = next(pc)} \text{(LOAD-G)}$$

4. Partial-Coherence Abstractions

In this section, we present a family of abstract memory models that abstract the concrete semantics of Section 3. The presentation focuses on abstractions of the SPARC PSO model, but the adaptation to TSO is straight-forward. The main idea behind our *partial-coherence* abstractions is to vary how much of the order between memory operations we preserve. The ability to vary the precision is useful as different algorithms can be verified with different levels of precision and cost. When the abstraction is used for fence inference, Section 6 shows that there exists a trade-off between the precision of the analysis (which affects the state-space size) and the quality of inferred fences.

4.1 Abstract Domain

The abstract domain is designed to represent store buffers in a bounded way by losing order information between items past a certain bound. To achieve this goal, we represent a concrete buffer $B^\natural$ by a tuple $\langle l, S, H\rangle$. The $l \in D$ element records the latest (most recent) value that was written into the buffer. $H \in Seq_{\leq k}(D)$ records the k oldest values in the buffer (in the original order) if those are known. $S \subseteq D$ records a set of values that were written into the buffer, abstracting away the order between them, as well as the number of times each elements appears in the buffer. Formally, we define, for a buffer $B^\natural$:

$$\beta_B(B^\natural) = \langle last(B^\natural), UTail(B^\natural, k), head(B^\natural, k)\rangle$$

An abstract state σ is a tuple $\langle G, L, pc, B\rangle$ where G, L and pc are defined as in the concrete semantics. B maps a (process, shared variable) pair to the tuple $\langle l, S, H\rangle$ defined earlier. To simplify notation, we will use short-hands such as $l_p(x)$ to represent the l element of $B(p)(x)$. As in the concrete semantics, we will often omit the p. We denote by A the set of all abstract states.

To define the abstract domain, we define several order relations. The order $\sqsubseteq_b$ is defined on $\langle l, S, H\rangle$ tuples:

$$\langle l_1, S_1, H_1\rangle \sqsubseteq_b \langle l_2, S_2, H_2\rangle$$

if $l_1 = l_2$ and:

$$\exists t. H_2 = head(H_1, t) \wedge S_2 = S_1 \cup UTail(H_1, t)$$

Intuitively, $\langle l_2, S_2, H_2\rangle$ is produced from $\langle l_1, S_1, H_1\rangle$ by removing part of the tail end of H_1 and adding all the removed elements into the set. We then use $\sqsubseteq_b$ to define a partial order $\sqsubseteq_s$ on abstract states $\sigma_1 = \langle G_1, L_1, pc_1, B_1\rangle, \sigma_2 = \langle G_2, L_2, pc_2, B_2\rangle$: $\sigma_1 \sqsubseteq_s \sigma_2$ if the two states coincide on G, L, pc and:

$$\forall p, x. B_1(p)(x) \sqsubseteq_b B_2(p)(x)$$

Finally, we define our abstract domain $\mathbb{A} \subseteq 2^A$ as the set of all antichains of A. That is:

$$\mathbb{A} = \{\Sigma \subseteq A \mid \forall \sigma, \rho \in \Sigma. \sigma \neq \rho \Rightarrow \sigma \not\sqsubseteq_s \rho\}$$

The order relation $\sqsubseteq: \mathbb{A} \times \mathbb{A}$ is defined as:

$$\Sigma_1 \sqsubseteq \Sigma_2 \ \texttt{iff}\ \forall \sigma_1 \in \Sigma_1. \exists \sigma_2 \in \Sigma_2. \sigma_1 \sqsubseteq_s \sigma_2$$

The join operator over $\mathbb{A}$, implied by the above order, is:

$$\Sigma_1 \sqcup \Sigma_2 = \{\sigma \in \Sigma_1 \cup \Sigma_2 \mid \forall \rho \in (\Sigma_1 \cup \Sigma_2). \sigma \neq \rho \Rightarrow \sigma \not\sqsubseteq \rho\}$$

We define the abstraction function $\alpha: 2^{C^\natural} \rightarrow \mathbb{A}$ using an extraction function $\beta: C^\natural \rightarrow A$:

$$\alpha(\Sigma) = \bigsqcup_{\sigma \in \Sigma} \{\beta(\sigma)\}$$

$$\beta(\sigma) = \langle G^\natural_\sigma, L^\natural_\sigma, pc^\natural_\sigma, \hat{\beta_B}\rangle$$

$$\hat{\beta_B} = \lambda p, x. \beta_B(B^\natural_\sigma(p)(x))$$

The intuition behind this abstraction is shown in Fig. 3. That figure can, however, be slightly misleading: it is important to note the entire concrete buffer is covered by the concatenation of values from S to H. Specifically, l does not need to be concatenated to the end. Thus if $S = \emptyset$, then l is always equal to the last element of H and is in fact redundant. If $S \neq \emptyset$, then $l \in S$ is an invariant. A more precise representation of the abstraction is given in Fig. 5. Fig. 5(a) shows the case in which the concrete buffer is longer than k and Fig. 5(b) shows the case in which the concrete buffer is of length at most k.

The Importance of Recency Our abstraction uses l to record the most recent value stored for a variable. This is motivated by the need to preserve the *intra-process coherence* requirement that a process storing several values to a shared variable x, and then performing a load from x, should not see any value it has itself stored except the most recent one. This is a very basic property and abstractions that do not preserve this information will fail to verify many reasonable programs.

Partial Inter-Process Coherence The abstract domain only partially preserves the *inter-process coherence* requirement. For example, suppose processor p stores the values a and then b to the variable x. The resulting concrete buffer $B^\natural_p(x)$ is "ab". Taking $k = 0$, the abstract buffer is $B = \beta_B("ab") = \langle a, \{a, b\}, \epsilon\rangle$. Note that, for example, $\beta_B("ab") = \beta_B("aba")$. So given the abstract buffer B we must allow a different process q to observe the values being written in the opposite order. Worse, since, for example,

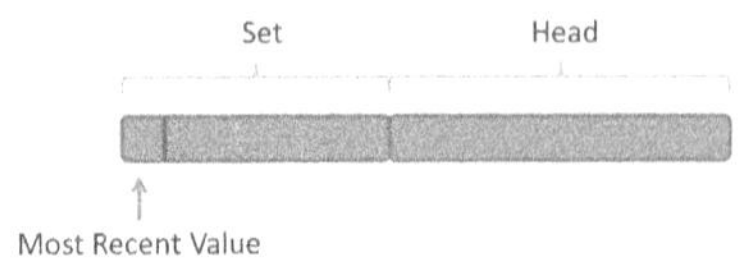

(a) The length of the buffer is higher than k

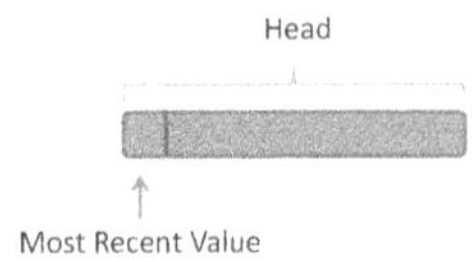

(b) The length of the buffer is at most k

Figure 5. Abstraction of a single buffer

$\beta_B(\text{"}ab\text{"}) = \beta_B(\text{"}abab\text{"})$ it is possible for process q to observe the stores in the opposite order, and for a third process r to observe them in the original order.

This behavior occurs only if a process performs more than k stores to the same memory location without an intervening fence or CAS. As long as at most k stores to a memory location are performed without an intervening fence, the abstract domain is fully precise.

Abstract Domain Design One of our observations is that in a correct program a process rarely performs an unbounded number of stores to a memory location without a fence. When a process does perform a large number of stores to a memory location without a fence, it means that the order in which these stores are performed is not important for program correctness. Following this observation, our abstraction is designed to: (i) preserve the order between a small number of stores to the same memory location; (ii) abstract away the order in long sequences of stores but preserve the stored values, such that values cannot appear "out of thin air".

Given that programmers do not normally think in terms of unordered stores, we expect many correct programs to only utilize very short buffers. This is validated by our results (c.f Section 6) — correct versions of the benchmark algorithms could be verified using $k = 1$. However, there are examples of correct programs where buffers may become very long. One such example is the Sieve of Eratosthenes implementation in [3], which only requires that values do not appear out of thin air.

Furthermore, we wish our verification procedure to remain sound for arbitrary programs. This is impossible using bounded buffers, as it is trivial to construct an incorrect program which would appear to be correct using bounded buffers of some given length k. Similarly, when the abstraction is used for fence inference, we wish to always infer a correct placement. This is impossible if we simply bound the buffer length.

Domain of Variables Throughout this paper we do not specify the domain D from which local and shared variables take values. However, the domain is in fact critically important to the effectiveness of the abstraction. Let d be the number of values a shared variable may potentially take during the execution of a program. Then the number of possible H values for that variable is d^k, and the number of possible S values is 2^d. Since in the worst case, $d = |D|$, we may expect an increase in state-space size (w.r.t state-space under SC) that is exponential in $|D|$. The examples we used for our experiments do not suffer from this problem, as the variables only take a small number of values in any given execution. However, for different programs this may become a real issue. Note, however, that our abstraction can be trivially composed with value abstractions (e.g., sign abstraction, parity abstraction, interval abstraction [10]). Instead of using the concrete domain D, we can replace it with an abstract value domain $D^\sharp$. We can then store those abstract values in the buffer and perform local operations on values according to the semantics dictated by $D^\sharp$, retaining a sound abstraction.

4.2 Abstract Semantics

Sem. 3 shows the abstract semantics with partial coherence parameterized by k. In the figure, we use the shorthand $emp(x) \stackrel{\text{def}}{=} H(x) = \epsilon \wedge S(x) = \emptyset$.

Loading Values and Recency In the concrete semantics, a process may load the latest value it wrote by reading its own store buffer. Correspondingly, in the abstract semantics, the rule LOAD-B reads the most recent value recorded in l. Had we not recorded the most recent value l that a process wrote, a process p that performs a load when $S_p(x) \neq \emptyset$ would have to conservatively explore all possible values in the set $S_p(x)$. The rule LOAD-G is similar to the concrete semantics: when the buffer is known to be empty, the value is loaded from global store.

Storing Values In the abstract semantics, `store` is split into two cases STORE-H and STORE-S, based on whether the size of the buffer $H(x)$ has reached the bound k. As long as $|H(x)| < k$ and $S(x) = \emptyset$, the contents of the buffer are known precisely. Thus, similarly to the concrete semantics, the effect of a store follows STORE-H, adding the value to the tail of the buffer $H(x)$ and updating the most recent value $l(x)$. When $|H(x)| = k$, the size of the buffer H has been exceeded and no more values can be stored in H. Therefore, the new value is stored in the (unordered) set of values $S(x)$ (as shown in the rule STORE-S) and the most recent value $l(x)$ is updated accordingly. When $S(x) \neq \emptyset$ we have lost the information on the precise number of elements on the buffer, and thus are also forced to keep updating the set.

Flushing Values In the abstract semantics, `flush` is split into three cases: FLUSH-H, FLUSH-SN and FLUSH-SD. When we have $H(x) \neq \epsilon$ then FLUSH-H behaves as the FLUSH rule in the concrete semantics: it selects the oldest element in $H(x)$, writes it to $G(x)$ and updates $H(x)$. However, when $H(x) = \epsilon$ and $S(x) \neq \emptyset$, any of the values in $S(x)$ become possible candidates for flushing (since $S(x)$ is unordered, we do not know which value is the oldest one). The rules FLUSH-SD (*flush from set, destructive*) and FLUSH-SN (*flush from set, non-destructive*) then only differ on whether the value selected to be flushed is removed from $S(x)$ or kept in it. This is required since we do not know how many times every value appears in the buffer. Thus, in the concrete domain, FLUSH-SD of a value v represents a flush of the last occurrence of v in the buffer. In contrast, FLUSH-SN represents the situation in which more instances of v remain.

We improve the precision of the analysis by disabling the FLUSH-SD rule when we know that the resulting abstract states do not represent any possible concrete states and will only introduce imprecision. In particular, if $v = l(x)$ and $S(x) \neq \{v\}$, FLUSH-SD need not fire. If we apply the concrete FLUSH rule to any concretization of such a state, the value v will stay in the (concrete) buffer, while if we flush v from the abstract state using FLUSH-SD, it will remove v from the abstract buffer, leading to abstract states that could not arise in the concrete semantics.

Example: Motivating Recency and Order Next, we illustrate via an example why maintaining recency and order is important for verification and inference. Consider a naive set abstraction for the store buffers, and a version of Peterson's algorithm with fences shown in Fig. 2 (in Section 2). Under standard concrete semantics of PSO,

Semantics 3 Abstract operational semantics defining transition from $\langle G, L, pc, B\rangle$ to $\langle G', L', pc', B\rangle$

$$\frac{stmt(pc) = load\ x, r \quad emp(x) \quad v = G(x)}{L'(r) = v \quad pc' = next(pc)} \ (\text{LOAD-G})$$

$$\frac{stmt(pc) = load\ x, r \quad \neg emp(x) \quad v = l(x)}{L'(r) = v \quad pc' = next(pc)} \ (\text{LOAD-B})$$

$$\frac{\begin{array}{c} stmt(pc) = store\ r, x \\ S(x) = \emptyset \quad H(x) = h \quad |h| < k \quad L(r) = v \end{array}}{H'(x) = h \cdot v \quad l'(x) = v \quad pc' = next(pc)} \ (\text{STORE-H})$$

$$\frac{\begin{array}{c} stmt(pc) = store\ r, x \\ S(x) = s \quad s \neq \emptyset \vee |H(x)| = k \quad L(r) = v \end{array}}{S'(x) = s \cup \{v\} \quad l'(x) = v \quad pc' = next(pc)} \ (\text{STORE-S})$$

$$\frac{H(x) = v \cdot h}{H'(x) = h \quad G'(x) = v} \ (\text{FLUSH-H})$$

$$\frac{H(x) = \epsilon \quad v \in S(x)}{G'(x) = v} \ (\text{FLUSH-SN})$$

$$\frac{H(x) = \epsilon \quad v \in S(x) \quad \neg(v = l(x) \wedge S(x) \neq \{v\})}{G'(x) = v \quad S'(x) = S(x) \setminus v} \ (\text{FLUSH-SD})$$

$$\frac{stmt(pc) = fence \quad \forall x. emp(x)}{pc' = next(pc)} \ (\text{FENCE})$$

$$\frac{\begin{array}{c} stmt(pc) = cas\ x, r, s, q \\ emp(x) \quad L(r) = G(x) \quad L(s) = v \end{array}}{G'(x) = v \quad L'(q) = true \quad pc' = next(pc)} \ (\text{CAS-T})$$

$$\frac{stmt(pc) = cas\ x, r, s, q \quad emp(x) \quad L(r) \neq G(x)}{L'(q) = false \quad pc' = next(pc)} \ (\text{CAS-F})$$

those fences guarantee that it is impossible for both processes to be concurrently executing line 13. Let us consider an abstract memory model where order and recency are not maintained, that is, we only maintain $S_p(x)$ but without maintaining $l_p(x)$ and $H_p(x)$. Then, we cannot show that the algorithm is correct. Consider the following execution:

1. Initially both processes start with empty buffers, and $ent0 = ent1 = turn = 0$.
2. Process 0 runs through one iteration of the outer loop (executes lines 1-14 inclusively), without performing a flush after line 14.
3. Process 0 then tries to enter the critical section again and executes lines 1-3 inclusively. At this stage, $S_{p_0}(ent0) = \{true, false\}$.
4. Two flush actions are performed on $S_{p_0}(ent0)$, first flushing $true$ and then $false$. At this point $G(ent0) = false$.
5. Process 0 completes entering the critical section.
6. Process 1 loads ent0 from global store and since ent0 is $false$ process 1 also enters the critical section.

The above example would not have been possible had we kept either: i) ordering information via $H_p(ent0)$ for at least two values (i.e., $k = 2$) or ii) recency information via $l_p(ent0)$. In the first case, the order in which $\{true, false\}$ are flushed would have been consistent with the order in which the values were written: we would have first flushed $false$ and then $true$. In the second case, the fence in line 4 would have forced fully flushing $S_{p_0}(ent0)$, resulting in writing out the most recent value (i.e., $G(ent0) = true$). While in this case we could have used either $l_p(ent0)$ or $H_p(ent0)$ with $k = 2$, in other examples both of these refinements with respect to a set are required.

4.3 A Partially Disjunctive Abstraction for Store Buffers

The abstraction of Section 4.1 distinguishes two abstract buffers $B_1 = \langle l_1, S_1, H_1\rangle, B_2 = \langle l_2, S_2, H_2\rangle$ even when they differ only on the contents of their unordered sets $S_1 \neq S_2$. This leads to distinctions between abstract states that are often more precise than necessary. We observe that a more efficient abstraction can be obtained without a significant sacrifice in precision by merging such states. In Section 6, we show that combining such states leads to a more scalable abstraction, while keeping a sufficient level of precision. The one distinction that we do wish to preserve regarding the S component is the difference between an empty set and a non-empty set, as many of the rules in Sem. 3 distinguish between these two cases. To capture this, we change the definition of $\sqsubseteq_b$ as follows: The order $\sqsubseteq_b^\tau$ is defined on $\langle l, S, H\rangle$ tuples.

$$\langle l_1, S_1, H_1\rangle \sqsubseteq_b^\tau \langle l_2, S_2, H_2\rangle$$

if $l_1 = l_2$ and one of the two following conditions holds:

$$(1)\ H_1 = H_2 = \epsilon \wedge S_1 = S_2 = \emptyset$$

$$(2)\ S_1 \neq \emptyset \wedge \exists t. H_2 = head(H_1, t) \wedge S_2 \supseteq S_1 \cup UTail(H_1, t)$$

The orders $\sqsubseteq_s^\tau$ and $\sqsubseteq^\tau$ are then defined exactly as before but with respect to $\sqsubseteq_b^\tau$ instead of $\sqsubseteq_b$. α^τ is also defined as before, but using $\bigsqcup^\tau$ instead of $\bigsqcup$. Note that this small change in the formalism drastically changes the intuitive meaning of the set S. Let $B = \langle l, S, \epsilon\rangle$ be an abstract buffer, and $B^\natural$ a concrete buffer such that $\beta_B(B^\natural) \sqsubseteq_b^\tau B$. In the fully-disjunctive abstraction, this implies that $Set(B^\natural) = S$. This means that a value v was in S if and only if it appeared at least once in $B^\natural$. In the partially-disjunctive abstraction, this is no longer true. Consider the concrete buffer "a". Assuming $k = 0$, $\beta_B(\text{"}a\text{"}) = \langle a, \{a\}, \epsilon\rangle \sqsubseteq_b \langle a, \{a, b\}, \epsilon\rangle$. If a value appears at least once in $B^\natural$ then it is necessarily in S, but the converse does not hold.

The new abstraction also implies a change to the abstract transformer. In the fully disjunctive abstraction, flushes from S were split into two cases: `FLUSH-SD` to represent flushing the last instance of a value from the buffer, and `FLUSH-SN` to represent an instance that is not the last one. The case split for the partially disjunctive abstraction is slightly different. The new flush semantics are shown in Sem. 4. The rule `FLUSH-NE` covers the case in which a flush leaves S non-empty, while `FLUSH-E` represents flushing the only remaining element of the concretization of the abstract buffer. Note that it's possible for both types of flush rules to be enabled for the same buffer.

Semantics 4 Partially-disjunctive flush semantics

$$\frac{H(x) = \epsilon \quad v \in S(x)}{G'(x) = v} \ (\text{FLUSH-NE})$$

$$\frac{H(x) = \epsilon \quad S(x) \neq \emptyset}{G'(x) = l(x) \quad S'(x) = \emptyset} \ (\text{FLUSH-E})$$

5. Fence Inference

In this section, we introduce a new technique for inferring memory fences under store-buffer based abstract memory models. For our algorithm, we follow the same general recipe as outlined in [40]: (i) Construct (a possibly abstract) transition system and find the reachable error states. (ii) Construct a boolean formula that describes how traces leading to those error states can be avoided. (iii) Implement satisfying assignments of the formula using syntactic constructs.

The main challenge in implementing this general recipe is in defining which transitions may be avoided, and how they can be avoided syntactically. Next, we present the definitions that are appropriate for each of our semantics: concrete, fully-disjunctive and partially-disjunctive. We also show an example demonstrating the interplay between the precision of the abstraction and the quality of inferred fences.

5.1 Recoverability of Sequential Consistency

Before we introduce the details of the inference algorithm, we note that the problem always has a trivial (inefficient) solution under concrete memory models. However, for some abstract memory models, the problem no longer has a solution. We would like to restrict attention to abstractions in which the existence of a solution is guaranteed. Consider a program P that satisfies its specification S under the sequentially consistent memory model, $P \models_{SC} S$, but violates it under a weaker memory model M, $P \not\models_M S$. We say that M is *SC-Recoverable (SCR)* when for any such P there exists a program P' obtained from P by adding fences such that $P' \models_M S$. For SC-Recoverable memory models, when $P \models_{SC} S$, the trivial solution in which fences are added after every memory store in P always exists. This property might seem trivial, however it is easy to design seemingly reasonable abstract models for which it does not hold. For instance, as demonstrated in Section 6, a partial-coherence abstraction with recency and $k = 0$ does not satisfy the SCR property.

For the partial coherence abstractions of Section 4, $k \geq 1$ guarantees SC-Recoverability. If we place a fence immediately after every store instruction, then i) $|H|$ can never grow above 1 so stores cannot become visible out of order and ii) the store cannot be observed by the process itself before it is flushed. In effect this makes the store and flush operations atomic, reducing the program's behaviors to those possible under sequential consistency.

5.2 Fence Inference under Concrete Semantics

Buffers of Labeled Stores The semantics given in Section 3 do not preserve enough information about program execution to enable fence inference. Using those semantics, it is not possible to determine that a given memory operation was delayed by examining only the source state and the transition associated with the operation. Therefore, we instrument the concrete semantics with additional information about the instruction that stored each value. To achieve this, for a process p and variable x, we extend the store buffer $B_p(x) \in Seq(Labs \times D)$ to be a sequence of pairs $\langle l, v\rangle$. For every value stored we also record the label of the program instruction that stored the value.

Avoiding Error States Let P be a program, and $\langle \sigma_0, \Sigma, T\rangle$ be the program's transition system. Every transition $t \in T$ that is not a flush transition is associated with a instruction in the code that caused the transition. We denote by l_t the label of this instruction. Our goal is to construct a program P' by inserting fences into P such that the state-space of P' does not contain any error states. To "remove" a state from the state-space, we must prohibit all program traces that contain it. The question then becomes "how can a program trace be prohibited?"

The intuition behind the recipe of [40] is that program traces can be classified as either *avoidable* and *unavoidable*. The classification is performed according to the syntactic device we have to eliminate traces. In our setting, the syntactic device used to prohibit traces is a memory fence. If a trace π contains a store transition $\sigma_i \xrightarrow{t_p} \sigma_{i+1}$ by process p which is not immediately followed by a flush of the stored value, we can prohibit π by placing a fence immediately after the store. This means a trace is unavoidable if and only if every store is immediately followed by a flush.We can refine the concept of an avoidable trace and talk about *avoidable transitions*. A transition t_p performed by process p is avoidable if it is a memory operation (store, load or CAS), and some store buffer associated with p is non-empty.

Formally, let t be the transition $\sigma \xrightarrow{t} \tau$. Let v be a value written by the instruction at label l_v such that $\langle l, v\rangle$ appears in some buffer $B_{\sigma,p}(x)$. Then t is avoidable, and can be avoided by placing fences on all program paths between l_v and l_t, forcing the value v to be flushed before l_t is reached. We formalize this by defining *ordering constraints*: we say an ordering constraint $[l_v \prec l_t]$ is *enforced* if a fence is placed on all program paths between l_v and l_t. We say the constraint is *violated* by a transition if l_t is executed while a value stored by l_v is in the buffer. A constraint is violated by a trace if it is violated by one of its transition. Note that if a constraint is enforced by a fence, it cannot be violated by any transition. This implies a trace π of P cannot appear in P' if at least one of the constraints it violates is enforced in P'. This fact gives us a complete characterization of how a state can be removed from the state-space: by enforcing at least one constraint that is violated by each trace leading to that state. We call this characterization the *avoid formula* of a state.

A direct implementation of the method described above to compute the avoid formulae would be very inefficient, as it requires enumerating all program traces. Below we give a brief description of a more efficient algorithm. A fuller description, albeit in a different setting, is given in [18].

As a first stage in the algorithm we construct the transition system $\langle \sigma_0, \Sigma, T\rangle$. We then label every state $\sigma \in \Sigma$ with a propositional formula that captures how σ can be made unreachable (avoided) through the use of ordering constraints. Intuitively, a state σ can be avoided by avoiding *all* incoming transitions to σ in the program's transition system. In turn, a single transition $\mu \rightarrow \sigma$ can be avoided by either avoiding its source state μ or by prohibiting the transition itself. We associate with each transition $t \in T$ a formula:

$$prevent(t) = \bigvee\{[l \prec l_t] \mid \exists x, v.\langle l, v\rangle \in Set(B_{src(t),proc(t)}(x))\}$$

Here, we use $proc(t)$ to denote the process that executes the transition t and $src(t)$ to denote the source state of the transition. This formula captures all possible ordering constraints that would prohibit execution of t. Formally, it is a disjunction because it is enough to enforce one of the constraints to make t unreachable.

To compute how a state $\sigma \in \Sigma$ can be avoided, we define a labeling function L and:

$$avoid(L, \sigma) = \bigwedge\{(L(\mu) \vee prevent(t)) \mid t = (\mu \rightarrow \sigma) \in T\}$$

We then define a transformer that updates the labeling function:

$$infer(L) = L[\sigma \mapsto (L(\sigma) \wedge avoid(L, \sigma))]$$

Given an initial mapping L_0 that maps all unavoidable states to $false$ and the rest to $true$, the greatest fixed point of $infer(L_0)$ describes all the possible ways in which any state σ can be avoided. The greatest fixed point is computed with respect to implication partial order $L_1 \sqsubseteq L_2 \equiv \forall\sigma \in \Sigma.L_1(\sigma) \Rightarrow L_2(\sigma)$. Using the provided specification, we identify a set $E \subseteq \Sigma$ of reachable error states. We then compute the overall constraint formula ψ by taking the conjunction of avoid constraints for all error states: $\psi = \bigwedge\{L(\sigma) \mid \sigma \in E\}$. A satisfying assignment to this formula is guaranteed to represent a correct fence placement.

5.3 Inference under Abstract Semantics

We can extend the abstract model in the same way we extended the concrete model. That is, $H_p(x)$ and $S_p(x)$ will contain $\langle label, value\rangle$ pairs.

5.3.1 Inference under Disjunctive Abstraction

Using the abstract semantics of Sec. 4.2, we can construct an abstract transition system for the program, and apply the same reasoning as in the concrete semantics, except that we adjust $prevent(t)$:

$$Q_{\sigma,p}(x) = S_{\sigma,p}(x) \cup Set(H_{\sigma,p}(x))$$

$$prevent(t) = \bigvee\{[l \prec l_t] \mid \exists x, v.\langle l, v\rangle \in Q_{src(t),proc(t)}(x)\}$$

This adjustment is safe because we know that if $\langle l_v, v\rangle \in Q_p(x)$, then for any concretization $\sigma^\natural$ of σ, $B_{\sigma^\natural,p}(x)$ must contain $\langle l_v, v\rangle$ at least once. This means that placing a fence between any such l_v and l_t is sufficient to avoid t from $\sigma^\natural$.

Note that it is possible to infer more fences than necessary due to the imprecision of the abstraction. Consider the simple example in Fig. 6, with the specification that in a final state $r1 \leq r2$. If we attempt to execute this program under partial-coherence semantics with $k = 0$, we may get a trace where in the final state we have $r1 = 2$, $r2 = 1$: *(a)* Process 1 performs both stores. *(b)* Process 1 flushes the value 2. *(c)* Process 2 performs the load at line 1. *(d)* Process 1 flushes the value 1. *(e)* Process 2 performs the load at line 2. The single avoidable transition in this trace is the execution of the second store by process 1. The only way to avoid this transition is by placing a fence between the two stores. However, if we increase the precision of the abstraction and use $k = 1$, we will not produce this (spurious) trace and will not infer the redundant fence.

Process 1:	Process 2:
`store x = 1;`	`load r1 = x;`
`store x = 2;`	`load r2 = x;`

Figure 6. Fully disjunctive partial-coherence abstraction with k = 0 leads to a redundant fence between the stores in Process 1, while with k = 1 the inference algorithm determines that no fences are necessary.

5.3.2 Inference under Partially Disjunctive Abstraction

For the abstract semantics of Sec. 4.3, we need to adjust $prevent(t)$:

$$prevent(t) = \bigwedge\{[l \prec l_t] \mid \exists x, v.\langle l, v\rangle \in Q_{src(t),proc(t)}(x)\}$$

The only change from the fully disjunctive abstraction is in replacing $\bigvee$ with $\bigwedge$. The reason for this change becomes clear once we examine the concretization function for the partially disjunctive abstraction. As pointed out in the previous section, given an abstract state σ and a non-empty $S_{\sigma,p}(x)$, there exist concretized states which do *not* contain all values in $S_{\sigma,p}(x)$. Since prohibiting a transition from σ requires prohibiting that transition from all concrete states represented by σ, $prevent(t)$ must be a *conjunction* over the possible prevent formulas in the concrete domain. For many transitions, this formula will be stronger than the optimal one, potentially leading to a fence placement worse than the one produced by the fully disjunctive abstraction with the same k value.

5.4 Fine-grained fence inference

The inference algorithm described above generates sets of constraints that must be enforced so that the specification is satisfied. One simple way to enforce a constraint $[l_1 \prec l_2]$ is by placing a full fence on every path between l_1 and l_2 on the control-flow graph of the program. If finer-grained fences are available on the architecture we can use information encoded in the constraint to implement it more efficiently. For example if the architecture provides separate *store-store* and *store-load* fences we can place the appropriate fence based on whether the instruction at l_2 is a store or a load. If the architecture provides fences that enforce flushing only one variable (e.g., CAS in our concrete PSO semantics) then we can place the correct fence type based on the variable written to by l_1. For simplicity, in Section 6 we assume the only fence available is a full fence. However, whenever inference succeeds we could trivially place finer-grained fences.

6. Experience

We implemented our abstractions together with the verification and inference algorithms in a tool called BLENDER. Using BLENDER, we demonstrate the effectiveness of our abstractions by successfully verifying and inferring the required fences in a number of challenging algorithms. None of these algorithms could be handled by existing approaches. Further, we illustrate an inherent trade-off between the optimality of fence inference and the state-space size dictated by the abstraction.

BLENDER is implemented in Java and uses the JavaBDD library to represent avoid formulae as BDDs. All experiments were conducted on an 8-CPU Xeon 1.6GHz with 16GB memory running a 64-bit Sun JVM on Red Hat Linux.

Abstractions In our experiments, we consider a range of abstract memory models, all of which are abstractions of the concrete PSO memory model:

- *Set*: an abstraction of the store buffer to a set, without any additional information such as recency.
- *FD*: the partial coherence abstraction shown in Sem. 3, with varying k.
- *PD*: the partially disjunctive abstraction described in Sec. 4.3.

Note that the *Set* abstraction and *FD/PD* with $k = 0$ are generally not SC-Recoverable. Thus, it is possible that during fence inference, BLENDER will report the program as impossible to fix.

6.1 Benchmarks

To evaluate our tool, we chose various classic concurrent algorithms such as well-known mutual exclusion algorithms (mutex) and synchronization barrier algorithms. All algorithms were exercised in a loop by two concurrent processes ("repeated entry"):

- *Dekker's Algorithm* [11]. To evaluate both inference and verification we used two versions:
  - *Dek0*: has no added fences and is incorrect under the PSO memory model.
  - *Dek2*: has two added fences and is known to be correct.
- *Peterson's Algorithm* [31], using two versions, *Pet0* and *Pet2*.
- A variation of *Lamport's Bakery* [19] using two versions, *Lam0* and *Lam2*. To make this algorithm finite-space we manually bounded the maximum ticket number at 2.
- *Lamport's Fast Mutex* [21] using two versions, *Fast0* and *Fast3*.
- *CLH queue lock* [26] using two versions, *CLH0* and *CLH2*
- Centralized sense-reversing synchronization barrier [14] using two versions *Sense0* and *Sense1*.

For the mutual exclusion, the specification is that there cannot be more than one process inside the critical section. "Release semantics" for operations within the critical section are not enforced. The benchmarks were selected based on two criteria:

Novelty The benchmarks could not be handled by any of the previous approaches. For instance, as mutual exclusion algorithms inherently contain benign data races, using techniques like delay set analysis [34] would result in a gross over-estimation of the required fences. Furthermore, some of the benchmarks — for instance *Dek* and *Fast* — contain benign *triangular* data races (as defined in [28]). Thus, even if we focus squarely on the TSO memory model, we could not use the results of [28] to establish the correctness of the algorithms by focusing only on sequentially consistent executions. Finally, all of the benchmarks contain unbounded spin-loops, and as such, they cannot be handled directly using the bounded techniques of [18] or [5].

Simplicity Our focus in this work has been abstracting the effect of the relaxed memory model in isolation from other sources of unboundedness. Hence, we chose our algorithms to be finite-state when executed under the SC model. We defer the problem of verifying infinite-state programs using abstract memory models (e.g., by composing our abstractions with heap or predicate abstractions) to future work.

6.2 Verification

Tab. 1 shows the verification results produced by BLENDER with three abstractions. The programs we used here are the ones we know to be correct under the *concrete* PSO semantics, that is, appropriate fences have been placed in advance. All verification runs completed within 30 seconds. Each entry in the table contains the total number of states explored (in thousands). A ● mark is placed if verification succeeded and a ○ mark if a spurious (abstract) counter-example was found. In some of the runs of *CLH2*, BLENDER exhausted the available memory, and thus we do not report the state-space size. However, in both those cases an (abstract) counter-example was found before BLENDER ran out of memory.

Prog.	*Set*		$FD_{k=0}$		$FD_{k=1}$	
Sense1	●	0.6	●	1.7	●	0.8
Pet2	○	7.7	●	2.4	●	1.8
Dek2	○	9.7	●	4.5	●	3.1
Lam2	○	41.2	●	22.2	●	9
Fast3	○	22.2	○	16.4	●	11.1
CLH2	○	M	○	M	●	68.8

Table 1. Verification results and number of states (in thousands).

6.2.1 Discussion

As Tab. 1 shows, none of the correct examples could be verified using the naive set abstraction, however all of them could be verified using *FD* with $k = 1$. Since verification of all examples successfully completed with *FD*, there was no need to use the *PD* abstraction. The table also shows $FD_{k=0}$ generated spurious counter-examples for *CLH2* and *Fast3* but not the other algorithms. When $k = 0$, the partial-coherence abstraction ($FD_{k=0}$) reduces to the set abstraction with recency information. This is enough to verify the simpler algorithms, however it fails on the more complex ones.

The example of Lamport's fast mutex is particularly interesting, as it demonstrates the type of executions possible with non SC-recoverable abstractions. Consider the code in Fig. 7. In this implementation a process can enter the critical section either along the fast path (the `if` condition in line 15 is false) or along the slow path (the conditions is true). Under an abstract model with $k = 0$, the following execution is possible:

- Process 1 enters the critical section along the fast path, executes it, and runs until line 29.
- Process 1 executes line 29. At this point $S_1(y) = \{0\}$.
- Process 1 flushes y non-destructively, using the FLUSH-SN rule. Now $G(y) = 0$.
- Process 2 enters the critical section. Since $G(y) = 0$ it enters along the fast-path setting $y = 2$ in the process. This is flushed destructively using the FLUSH-SD rule. At this point $G(y) = 2$, $S_1(y) = \{0\}$, $S_2(y) = \emptyset$.
- Process 1 resumes. It first performs a flush of y, setting $G(y) = 0$. Then it proceeds to enter the critical section again, using the fast path.

This execution relies on the fact p_1 only stored the value 0 to y once, but this store is flushed twice. In effect, p_2 observed this store as if it happened *before* its own, and p_1 observed it as if it happened *after* the store of p_2. This coherence violation would have been prevented if we kept more information in the content of the buffer, by using $k > 0$. Indeed, with $k = 1$, *Fast3* passes verification.

```
1   while(true)
2   {
3     start:
4     store b[i] = true;
5     store x = i;
6     load local_y = y;
7     if (local_y ≠ 0) {
8       store b[i] = false;
9       while(local_y ≠ 0)
10        load local_y = y;
11      goto start;
12    }
13    store y = i;
14    load local_x = x;
15    if (x ≠ i) {
16     store b[1] = false;
17     do {
18      load other_b = b[3-i];
19     } while (other_b ≠ 0);
20     load local_y = y;
21     if (local_y ≠ i)
22     {
23       while(local_y ≠ 0)
24         load local_y = y;
25       goto start;
26     }
27    }
28    //Critical Section
29    store y = 0;
30    store b[i] = false;
31  }
```

Figure 7. A version of Lamport's fast mutex algorithm for 2 processors. The code given is for process i.

6.3 Inference

In Tab. 2 we show the state-space size and inference results for 5 of the under-fenced implementations. A mark of ● means the optimal fences were inferred, ◐ means that sub-optimal fences were inferred, and ○ means that BLENDER was unable to infer fences as according to the analysis any fence placement would leave the program incorrect. M appears if BLENDER ran out of memory.

Prog.	$FD_{k=0}$		$FD_{k=1}$		$PD_{k=0}$		$PD_{k=1}$		$PD_{k=2}$	
Sense0	◐	57.6	●	58.6	◐	31.9	●	44.3	●	6.1
Pet0	●	69.2	●	524.5	◐	25.3	◐	244.7	●	1124.2
Dek0	●	424.2	●	3238.1	◐	16.5	◐	358.1	●	2350.0
Lam0	M	-	M	-	◐	421.0	◐	4045.9	M	-
Fast0	M	-	M	-	○	220.6	M	-	M	-
Fast1a	◐	139.0	●	105.2	○	33.0	●	88.1	●	41.9
Fast1b	◐	832.9	●	972.3	○	78.6	◐	501.6	●	878.4
Fast1c	M	-	M	-	○	110.4	◐	1173.4	●	1858.1
CLH0	M	-	M	-	M	-	M	-	M	-

Table 2. Inference results and number of states (in thousands).

6.3.1 Discussion

Initially, we used BLENDER to perform fence inference with abstractions $FD_{k=0}$ and $FD_{k=1}$. However, BLENDER ran out of memory for *Lam0*, *Fast0*, and *Fast1c*. Using the partially disjunctive abstraction $PD_{k=0}$ enabled us to run the inference algorithm for both *Lam0* and *Fast1c* and obtain a sound fence placement for both. Furthermore, despite the loss of precision in the PD abstraction, in both cases the inferred fences are not trivial.

6.3.2 Peterson's Algorithm

Our results for Peterson's algorithm demonstrate the inherent trade-offs between inference optimality and abstraction precision:

- With the FD abstraction BLENDER was able to infer the optimal fence placement with $k = 0$. With the PD abstraction it required $k = 2$ and a much larger state-space.
- With the $PD_{k=0}$ abstraction we can produce a smaller state space but the result is suboptimal: 3 fences are required instead of 2. In addition to the two fences shown in Fig. 2, another fence, immediately after the store in line 14, is inferred.

The same trade-off can also be observed when using a similar partial-coherence abstraction of the *TSO* model. For $k = 0$ and $k = 1$ suboptimal fence placement is generated, while with $k = 2$ the result is optimal (for TSO).

6.3.3 Lamport's Fast Mutex

For both *Fast0* and *Sense0*, we experienced a loss of precision when using a k value that is too small. In the case of *Fast0*, the inference algorithm reported the program as unfixable when using $PD_{k=0}$. This is due to the fact the counter-example presented for *Fast3* under this abstract model cannot be fixed with any number of fences. Unfortunately, BLENDER was unable to build the state-space of *Fast0* under $PD_{k=1}$. Thus, we've run a complementary set of experiments in which 1 of the 3 required fences was placed. The 3 versions of Lamport's fast mutex (Fig. 7) we have ran had a single fence inserted: (i) between lines 5 and 6 (*Fast1a*), (ii) between lines 13 and 14 (*Fast1b*), (iii) between lines 29 and 30 (*Fast1c*). As expected, for all 3 programs, when running under $PD_{k=0}$ the program was unfixable. However, in all 3 cases we were able to infer a correct fence placement using $PD_{k=1}$. Furthermore, for *Fast1a* and *Fast1b* the optimal placement of the two other fences was found when using $PD_{k=2}$. For *Fast1c* even with $k = 2$ the placement was still suboptimal. This demonstrates another example of the interplay between the placed fences and the precision of the required abstraction. Even though for *Fast1c* we could not infer the optimal fence placement using $PD_{k=1}$, had we placed them manually, this abstraction could be used to verify them.

7. Related Work

Data-Race Freedom Guarantee A common technique to reduce the complexity of analyzing programs under relaxed memory models is to focus only on programs that have no data-races under sequentially consistent executions. For such programs the "fundamental property of memory models" [32] (also known as the DRF theorem) ensures that there can be no sequentially inconsistent executions. Owens (in [28]) studies a generalization of this theorem for the x86-TSO model. To guarantee correctness under this model one needs only to prove sequentially consistent executions satisfy "triangular race-freedom", a property weaker than general data race-freedom. In our work, we focus on abstractions of arbitrary programs and unlike these methods, we can handle programs that contain data-races, such as common lock-free algorithms and mutual exclusion primitives.

Checking Equivalence To Sequential Consistency In [6] and [7] algorithms are presented that can, based only on sequentially consistent executions, find violations of sequential consistency under the TSO and PSO memory models. Similarly, it is possible to place fences to preserve only SC executions using *Delay Set Analysis* ([34]), for instance as implemented in the Pensieve compiler ([12, 22]). However, a violation of SC does not necessarily cause a violation of any high-level properties. Thus those algorithms are often needlessly conservative. Our approach, on the other hand, uses a high-level specification and allows a trade-off between precision and optimality of the solution.

Explicit Model Checking for Relaxed Memory Models [17, 18, 30] describe explicit-state model checking under the Sparc RMO model. Among those, [18] focuses on fence inference. [15] also describes an explicit-state model checking and inference technique for the .NET memory model, but it suffers from significant technical drawbacks (c.f. [18]). However, the techniques presented in [18] are not applicable in our setting. (i) The FENDER algorithm described in [18] can only infer fences for programs that are finite-state *under the relaxed memory model*, and not under the sequentially consistent model. While this distinction might seem subtle, it is in fact significant. For example, FENDER relies on finite clients of lock-free data structures being finite-state. Unfortunately, there is no guarantee that a data structure that is lock-free under SC will stay lock-free under a relaxed model. More generally, any code that uses a spin-loop with a store in the loop body will always be infinite-state under a relaxed model, unless the store is followed by a fence. Since classical implementations of synchronization primitives use this code pattern, it is not possible to use FENDER to infer fences in those implementations. In contrast, the technique we present in this paper requires the input to be finite-state *only under SC*. (ii) More technically, the algorithm is phrased in terms of execution buffer semantics. Adapting it to store-buffer semantics is challenging, especially in the abstract case.

In [5], Burckhardt et. al take a different approach to verification under RMM. Instead of working with operational memory models and explicit model-checking, they convert programs into a form that can be checked against an axiomatic model specification. This technique still suffers from the same limitation — it must unroll loops at a preprocessing stage. Thus it cannot verify programs that contain unbounded spinning. In contrast, our verification approach is based on abstract interpretation and is sound for any input program and any values of the abstraction parameters. An alternative approach, in the spirit of [5, 18], is to assume a bound on the size of buffers or the number of loop iterations. Combined with iterative increase of the bound, this may work for some examples — but not in the general case. In addition, using an abstraction is beneficial not only when the buffers are unbounded. Even if the buffer is bounded, the concrete state-space may simply be too large — while in fact representing the buffers with full precision is not important to the correctness of the algorithm.

Synchronization Inference In [38, 40], the authors propose algorithms that automatically infer synchronization constructs such as atomic sections and conditional critical regions. These works assume sequential consistency and do not support weak memory models. The approach of [38] is close to our work in spirit, and deals with inferring synchronization under abstraction, but it enumerates traces explicitly, which does not scale to our setting.

In [37, 39], inference of synchronization is performed by syntactic exploration of placements of atomic sections to create candidate algorithms, and using a backing verifier to attempt verification of each candidate. In principle, a similar approach can be employed for fence inference by exploring candidate algorithms with all possible fence placements. In contrast, our constraint-based approach lays the ground for inference of more advanced fences, such as fence per variable, and conditional fences, for which syntactic exploration will yield a non-feasible number of candidates.

Alternative Buffer Abstractions In [23] the authors use automata as symbolic representation of store buffers in the TSO memory model. Their approach uses an acceleration technique that does not guarantee termination. Furthermore, their automata-based representation preserves redundant information, and as noted by the authors themselves, ends up being too expensive to be of practical interest. Since store buffers are similar to FIFO channels in communicating FSMs (CFSMs), it is tempting to employ techniques from CFSMs in our context as well. These techniques include algorithms based on symbolic representation of channel content (e.g., [4]), and conservative abstractions for FIFO channels (e.g., [13]). Abstraction of FIFO channels, as presented in [13], is similar in spirit to our approach in that it guarantees termination by using approximation. However, their abstraction preserves a slightly different kind of information than the information required for reasoning about store buffers. They use a regular abstraction of queue content and an expensive widening operation to establish correct usage of protocols. This is more than what is required in our setting in terms of characterization of buffer content, and often less than needed in terms of recency information. In contrast to these, our technique guarantees termination by using conservative approximation, and our abstractions are tailored to relaxed memory models.

8. Conclusions and Future Work

We present an approach for automatic verification and fence inference for concurrent programs running under relaxed memory models. Our approach is based on abstract interpretation, and its technical core is a family of partial-coherence abstractions that provide a (parametric) bounded representation for potentially unbounded store buffers. Our abstractions enable us to automatically verify concurrent algorithms without worrying about the size of the underlying store buffers. Because partial coherence abstractions are designed to be SC-Recoverable, they can be used for automatic inference of memory fences. We have implemented our approach in a tool called BLENDER and applied it to verify several correctly-fenced concurrent algorithms and automatically infer fences in under-fenced versions of these algorithms. In the future, we plan to combine our abstractions with heap abstractions to enable verification of heap-manipulating programs under RMMs.

Acknowledgments

The authors wish to thank Noam Rinetzky and Greta Yorsh for their comments on earlier drafts of this paper. This research was partially supported by *The Israeli Science Foundation* (grant no. 965/10).

References

[1] ADVE, S. V., AND GHARACHORLOO, K. Shared memory consistency models: A tutorial. *IEEE Computer 29* (1995), 66–76.

[2] ATIG, M. F., BOUAJJANI, A., BURCKHARDT, S., AND MUSUVATHI, M. On the verification problem for weak memory models. In *POPL* (2010), pp. 7–18.

[3] BOEHM, H.-J. Threads cannot be implemented as a library. *SIGPLAN Not. 40*, 6 (2005), 261–268.

[4] BOIGELOT, B., GODEFROID, P., WILLEMS, B., AND WOLPER, P. The power of QDDs. In *SAS* (1997), Springer, pp. 172–186.

[5] BURCKHARDT, S., ALUR, R., AND MARTIN, M. M. K. CheckFence: checking consistency of concurrent data types on relaxed memory models. In *PLDI* (2007), pp. 12–21.

[6] BURCKHARDT, S., AND MUSUVATHI, M. Effective program verification for relaxed memory models. In *CAV* (2008), pp. 107–120.

[7] BURNIM, J., SEN, K., AND STERGIOU, C. Sound and complete monitoring of sequential consistency in relaxed memory models. Tech. Rep. UCB/EECS-2010-31.

[8] BURNIM, J., SEN, K., AND STERGIOU, C. Testing concurrent programs on relaxed memory models. Tech. Rep. UCB/EECS-2010-32.

[9] COUSOT, P., AND COUSOT, R. Abstract interpretation: A unified lattice model for static analysis of programs by construction of approximation of fixed points. In *POPL* (1977), pp. 238–252.

[10] COUSOT, P., AND COUSOT, R. Systematic design of program analysis frameworks. In *POPL* (1979), pp. 269–282.

[11] DIJKSTRA, E. Cooperating sequential processes, TR EWD-123. Tech. rep., Technological University, Eindhoven, 1965.

[12] FANG, X., LEE, J., AND MIDKIFF, S. P. Automatic fence insertion for shared memory multiprocessing. In *ICS* (2003), pp. 285–294.

[13] GALL, T. L., JEANNET, B., AND JRON, T. Verification of communication protocols using abstract interpretation of FIFO queues. In *AMAST* (2006), pp. 204–219.

[14] HENSGEN, D., FINKEL, R., AND MANBER, U. Two algorithms for barrier synchronization. *Int. J. Parallel Program. 17*, 1 (1988), 1–17.

[15] HUYNH, T. Q., AND ROYCHOUDHURY, A. Memory model sensitive bytecode verification. *Form. Methods Syst. Des. 31*, 3 (2007).

[16] IBM. *Power ISA v.2.05*. 2007.

[17] JONSSON, B. State-space exploration for concurrent algorithms under weak memory orderings: (preliminary version). *SIGARCH Comput. Archit. News 36*, 5 (2008), 65–71.

[18] KUPERSTEIN, M., VECHEV, M., AND YAHAV, E. Automatic inference of memory fences. In *FMCAD* (2010), pp. 111–119.

[19] LAMPORT, L. A new solution of Dijkstra's concurrent programming problem. *Commun. ACM 17*, 8 (1974), 453–455.

[20] LAMPORT, L. How to make a multiprocessor computer that correctly executes multiprocess program. *IEEE Trans. Comput. 28*, 9 (1979), 690–691.

[21] LAMPORT, L. A fast mutual exclusion algorithm. *ACM Trans. Comput. Syst. 5*, 1 (1987), 1–11.

[22] LEE, J., AND PADUA, D. A. Hiding relaxed memory consistency with a compiler. *IEEE Trans. Comput. 50*, 8 (2001), 824–833.

[23] LINDEN, A., AND WOLPER, P. An automata-based symbolic approach for verifying programs on relaxed memory models. In *SPIN* (2010), pp. 212–226.

[24] MADOR-HAIM, S., ALUR, R., AND MARTIN, M. M. K. Generating litmus tests for contrasting memory consistency models. In *CAV* (2010), pp. 273–287.

[25] MADOR-HAIM, S., ALUR, R., AND MILO, M. Plug and Play Components for the Exploration of Memory Consistency Models. Tech. Rep. MS-CIS-10-02, University of Pennsylvania, 2010.

[26] MAGNUSSON, P. S., LANDIN, A., AND HAGERSTEN, E. Queue locks on cache coherent multiprocessors. In *Proceedings of the Int. Symp. on Parallel Processing* (1994), IEEE, pp. 165–171.

[27] NARAYANASAMY, S., WANG, Z., TIGANI, J., EDWARDS, A., AND CALDER, B. Automatically classifying benign and harmful data races using replay analysis. In *PLDI* (2007), pp. 22–31.

[28] OWENS, S. Reasoning about the implementation of concurrency abstractions on x86-TSO. In *ECOOP* (2010).

[29] OWENS, S., SARKAR, S., AND SEWELL, P. A better x86 memory model: x86-TSO. In *TPHOLs* (2009), pp. 391–407.

[30] PARK, S., AND DILL, D. L. An executable specification and verifier for relaxed memory order. *IEEE Trans. on Computers 48* (1999).

[31] PETERSON, G. L. Myths about the mutual exclusion problem. *Inf. Process. Lett. 12*, 3 (1981), 115–116.

[32] SARASWAT, V. A., JAGADEESAN, R., MICHAEL, M., AND VON PRAUN, C. A theory of memory models. In *PPoPP* (2007), ACM, pp. 161–172.

[33] SARKAR, S., SEWELL, P., NARDELLI, F. Z., OWENS, S., RIDGE, T., BRAIBANT, T., MYREEN, M. O., AND ALGLAVE, J. The semantics of x86-cc multiprocessor machine code. In *POPL* (2009), pp. 379–391.

[34] SHASHA, D., AND SNIR, M. Efficient and correct execution of parallel programs that share memory. *ACM Trans. Program. Lang. Syst. 10*, 2 (1988), 282–312.

[35] SHEN, X., ARVIND, AND RUDOLPH, L. Commit-reconcile & fences (CRF): a new memory model for architects and compiler writers. *SIGARCH Comput. Archit. News 27*, 2 (1999), 150–161.

[36] SPARC INTERNATIONAL, INC. *The SPARC architecture manual (version 9)*. Prentice-Hall, Inc., Upper Saddle River, NJ, USA, 1994.

[37] VECHEV, M., AND YAHAV, E. Deriving linearizable fine-grained concurrent objects. In *PLDI* (2008), pp. 125–135.

[38] VECHEV, M., YAHAV, E., AND YORSH, G. Abstraction-guided synthesis of synchronization. In *POPL* (2010), pp. 327–338.

[39] VECHEV, M. T., YAHAV, E., BACON, D. F., AND RINETZKY, N. CGCExplorer: a semi-automated search procedure for provably correct concurrent collectors. In *PLDI* (2007), pp. 456–467.

[40] VECHEV, M. T., YAHAV, E., AND YORSH, G. Inferring synchronization under limited observability. In *TACAS* (2009), pp. 139–154.

[41] YANG, Y., GOPALAKRISHNAN, G., AND LINDSTROM, G. UMM: an operational memory model specification framework with integrated model checking capability. *Concurr. Comput. : Pract. Exper. 17*, 5-6 (2005), 465–487.

A Case for an SC-Preserving Compiler

Daniel Marino[†] Abhayendra Singh[*] Todd Millstein[†] Madanlal Musuvathi[‡] Satish Narayanasamy[*]

[†]University of California, Los Angeles [*]University of Michigan, Ann Arbor [‡]Microsoft Research, Redmond

Abstract

The most intuitive memory consistency model for shared-memory multi-threaded programming is *sequential consistency* (SC). However, current concurrent programming languages support a relaxed model, as such relaxations are deemed necessary for enabling important optimizations. This paper demonstrates that an SC-preserving compiler, one that ensures that every SC behavior of a compiler-generated binary is an SC behavior of the source program, retains most of the performance benefits of an optimizing compiler. The key observation is that a large class of optimizations crucial for performance are either already SC-preserving or can be modified to preserve SC while retaining much of their effectiveness. An SC-preserving compiler, obtained by restricting the optimization phases in LLVM, a state-of-the-art C/C++ compiler, incurs an average slowdown of 3.8% and a maximum slowdown of 34% on a set of 30 programs from the SPLASH-2, PARSEC, and SPEC CINT2006 benchmark suites.

While the performance overhead of preserving SC in the compiler is much less than previously assumed, it might still be unacceptable for certain applications. We believe there are several avenues for improving performance without giving up SC-preservation. In this vein, we observe that the overhead of our SC-preserving compiler arises mainly from its inability to aggressively perform a class of optimizations we identify as *eager-load* optimizations. This class includes common-subexpression elimination, constant propagation, global value numbering, and common cases of loop-invariant code motion. We propose a notion of *interference checks* in order to enable eager-load optimizations while preserving SC. Interference checks expose to the compiler a commonly used hardware speculation mechanism that can efficiently detect whether a particular variable has changed its value since last read.

Categories and Subject Descriptors D.3.2 [*Programming Languages*]: Language Classifications—Concurrent, distributed, and parallel languages; D.3.4 [*Programming Languages*]: Processors—Optimization

General Terms Languages, Performance

Keywords memory consistency models, sequential consistency, SC preservation, interference checks

1. Introduction

A memory consistency model (or simply *memory model*) defines the semantics of a concurrent programming language by specifying the order in which memory operations performed by one thread become visible to other threads in the program. The most natural memory model is sequential consistency (SC) [31]. Under SC, the individual operations of the program appear to have executed in a global sequential order consistent with the per-thread program order. This semantics matches the intuition of a concurrent program's behavior as a set of possible thread interleavings.

It is commonly accepted that programming languages must relax the SC semantics of programs in order to allow effective compiler optimizations. This paper challenges that assumption by demonstrating an optimizing compiler that retains most of the performance of the generated code while preserving the SC semantics. A compiler is said to be *SC-preserving* if every SC behavior of a generated binary is guaranteed to be an SC behavior of the source program.

Starting from LLVM [32], a state-of-the-art C/C++ compiler, we obtain an SC-preserving compiler by modifying each of the optimization passes to conservatively disallow transformations that might violate SC.[1] Our experimental evaluation (Section 3) indicates that the resulting SC-preserving compiler incurs only 3.8% performance overhead on average over the original LLVM compiler with all optimizations enabled on a set of 30 programs from the SPLASH-2 [49], PARSEC [7], and SPEC CINT2006 (integer component of SPEC CPU2006 [26]) benchmark suites. Moreover, the maximum overhead incurred by any of these benchmarks is just over 34%.

1.1 An Optimizing SC-Preserving Compiler

The empirical observation of this paper is that a large class of optimizations crucial for performance are either already SC-preserving or can be modified to preserve SC while retaining much of their effectiveness. Several common optimizations, including procedure inlining, loop unrolling, and control-flow simplification, do not change the order of memory operations and are therefore naturally SC-preserving. Other common optimizations, such as common subexpression elimination (CSE) and loop-invariant code motion, can have the effect of reordering memory operations. However, these optimizations can still be performed on accesses to thread-local variables and compiler-generated temporary variables. The analysis required to distinguish such variables is simple, modular, and is already implemented by modern compilers such as LLVM. Furthermore, transformations involving a single shared variable are also SC-preserving under special cases (Section 2).

Consider the instance of CSE in Figure 1, where the compiler eliminates the subexpression `X*2`. By reusing the value of `X` read at `L1` in `L3`, this transformation effectively reorders the second access to `X` with the access to `Y` at `L2`. While invisible to sequential

[1] The SC-preserving version of LLVM is available at `http://www.cs.ucla.edu/~todd/research/memmodels.html`.

Original		Transformed	Concurrent Context

`L1: t = X*2;`
`L2: u = Y;`
`L3: v = X*2;`
	⇒	`L1: t = X*2;`
		`L2: u = Y;`
		`M3: v = t;`
			`N1: X = 1;`
			`N2: Y = 1;`

(a)		(b)	(c)

Figure 1: A compiler transformation from program (a) into (b) that eliminates the common subexpression `X*2`. In the presence of a concurrently running thread (c) and an initial state where all variables are zero, (b) can observe a state `u == 1 && v == 0`, which is not visible in (a). Lowercase variables denote local temporaries, while uppercase variables are potentially shared.

`L1: t = X*2;`
`L2: u = Y;`
`L3: v = X*2;`
	⇒	`L1: t = X*2;`
		`L2: u = Y;`
		`M3: v = t;`
		`C3: if(X modified since L1)`
		`L3:    v = X*2;`

(a)		(b)

Figure 2: Performing common subexpression elimination while guaranteeing SC. The interference check at `C3` ensures that the value of `X` has not changed since last read at `L1`. This allows the compiler to reuse the value of `X*2` computed in `L1` without violating SC.

programs, this reordering can introduce non-SC behaviors in a concurrent program, as shown in Figure 1. However, an SC-preserving compiler can still perform this transformation as long as at least one of `X` and `Y` is known to be thread-local. If `X` is thread-local, then its value does not change between `L1` and `L3` and so the transformation is SC-preserving. On the other hand, if `Y` is thread-local then any SC execution of the transformed program can be shown to be equivalent to an SC execution of the original program in which instructions `L1` to `L3` execute without being interleaved with instructions from other threads. By carefully enabling transformations only when they are SC-preserving, our compiler is able to achieve performance comparable to a traditional optimizing compiler while retaining the strong SC semantics.

1.2 Providing End-to-End Programmer Guarantees

Providing end-to-end SC semantics to the programmer requires executing the output of an SC-preserving compiler on SC hardware. The empirical results in this paper complement recent architecture research [8, 15, 23, 24, 28, 44] that demonstrates the feasibility of efficient SC hardware. The basic idea behind these proposals is to speculatively reorder memory operations and recover in the rare case that these reorderings can become visible to other processors. While such speculation support necessarily increases hardware complexity, we hope that our work on an SC-preserving compiler increases the incentives for building SC hardware, since in combination they enable end-to-end SC semantics for programmers at a reasonable cost.

Even in the absence of SC hardware, the techniques described in this paper can be used to provide strong semantics to the programmer. For instance, when compiling to x86 hardware, which supports the relatively-strong total store order (TSO) memory model [40], a compiler that preserves TSO behavior (Section 7.2) provides TSO semantics at the programming language level. The result is a language-level memory model that is stronger and simpler than the current memory-model proposals for C++ [6, 11] and Java [36].

1.3 Speculative Optimization For SC-Preservation

While the cost of an SC-preserving compiler is much less than previously assumed, one possible concern is that some applications might be unwilling to pay this cost, however small. We argue that one should exhaust possible avenues for improving the performance of SC-preservation, such as more sophisticated static and dynamic analyses, before exposing a relaxed program semantics to the programmer.

In this vein, we observe that a number of disabled optimizations responsible for lost performance in our SC-preserving compiler involve an *eager load*. For instance, the elimination of the expression `X*2` in Figure 1 can be considered as performing the load of variable `X` eagerly at line `L1` instead of at `L3`. Other eager-load optimizations include constant propagation, copy propagation, partial-redundancy elimination, global value numbering, and common cases of loop-invariant code motion. Our experiments show that fully enabling these eager-load optimizations in our compiler reduces the maximum slowdown of any benchmark from 34% to 6.5%.

To enable eager-load optimizations without violating SC, we propose the use of compiler-inserted *interference checks* to dynamically ensure the correctness of optimizations that cannot be statically validated as SC-preserving (Section 4). Figure 2 demonstrates this idea. The figure shows the code from Figure 1(a) and its transformation with an interference check. For the CSE optimization to be sequentially valid, the compiler already ensures that the variable `X` is not modified by instructions between `L1` and `L3`. The interference check lifts this correctness requirement to concurrent programs by ensuring that no other thread has modified `X` since last read at `L1`. If the check succeeds, the program can safely reuse the earlier computation of `X*2`; if not, the program reverts to the unoptimized code.

Our interference checks are inspired by a common hardware speculation mechanism [23] that is used to safely strengthen hardware memory models. This mechanism allows a processor to track cache-coherence messages to conservatively detect when a particular memory location may have been modified by another processor. We observe that this speculation mechanism can be used to discharge our interference checks efficiently. We describe a simple interface for exposing this capability to the compiler, based on the Itanium architecture's design of a similar feature [29] (Section 5). We have built a hardware simulator supporting our speculation mechanism and have performed a simulation study on 15 parallel programs from the SPLASH-2 and PARSEC benchmarks. By incorporating interference checks into a single optimization pass, we reduce the average performance overhead of our SC-preserving compiler on simulated TSO hardware from 3.4% to 2.2% and reduce the maximum overhead from 23% to 17% (Section 6).

2. Compiler Optimizations as Memory Reorderings

In this section, we classify compiler optimizations based on how they affect the memory reorderings of the program [2, 47].

2.1 SC-Preserving Transformations

Informally, we represent the (SC) behaviors of a program as a set of interleavings of the individual memory operations of program threads that respect the per-thread program order. A compiler transformation is SC-preserving if every behavior of the transformed program is a behavior of the original program. Note that it is acceptable for a compiler transformation to reduce the set of behaviors.

Transformations involving thread-local variables and compiler-generated temporaries are always SC-preserving. Furthermore, some transformations involving a single shared variable are SC-preserving [47]. For example, if a program performs two consecutive loads of the same variable, as in Figure 3(a), the compiler can remove the second load. This transformation preserves SC as any execution of the transformed program can be emulated by an interleaving of the original program where no other thread executes

a) redundant load:	`t=X; u=X;`	⇒	`t=X; u=t;`
b) forwarded load:	`X=t; u=X;`	⇒	`X=t; u=t;`
c) dead store:	`X=t; X=u;`	⇒	`X=u;`
d) redundant store:	`t=X; X=t;`	⇒	`t=X;`

Figure 3: SC-preserving transformations

```
L1: X = 1;        L1: X = 1;
L2: P = Q;   ⇒    L2: P = Q;
L3: t = X;        L3: t = 1;
```

(a)

```
                     u = X*X;
for(...){            for(...){
  ...                  ...
  P = Q;       ⇒       P = Q;
  t = X*X;             t = u;
  ...                  ...
}                    }
```

(b)

Figure 4: Examples of eager-load optimizations include constant/copy propagation (a) and loop-invariant code motion (b). Both involve relaxing the L → L and S → L ordering constraints.

between the two loads. On the other hand, this transformation reduces the set of behaviors, as the behavior in which the two loads see different values is not possible after the transformation.

Similar reasoning can show that the other transformations shown in Figure 3 are also SC-preserving. Further, a compiler can perform these transformations even when the two accesses on the left-hand side in Figure 3 are separated by local accesses, since those accesses are invisible to other threads.

2.2 Ordering Relaxations

Optimizations that are not SC-preserving change the order of memory accesses performed by one thread in a manner that can become visible to other threads. We characterize these optimizations based on relaxations of the following ordering constraints among loads and stores that they induce: L → L, S → L, S → S, and L → S.

Consider the CSE example in Figure 1(a). This optimization involves relaxing the L → L constraint between the loads at L2 and L3, moving the latter to be performed right after the first load of X at L1, and eliminating it using the transformation in Figure 3(a). If the example contained a store, instead of a load, at L2, then performing CSE would have involved an S → L relaxation. We classify an optimization as an *eager load* if it only involves L → L and S → L relaxations, as these optimizations involves performing a load earlier than it would have been performed before the transformation.

Another example of an eager load optimization is constant/copy propagation as shown in Figure 4(a). In this example, the transformation involves moving the load of X to immediately after the store of X (which requires L → L and S → L relaxation with respect to the P and Q accesses) and then applying the transformation in Figure 3(b). The loop-invariant code motion example in Figure 4(b) involves eagerly performing the (possibly unbounded number of) loads of X within the loop once before the loop. This also requires relaxing L → L and S → L ordering constraints due to the store and load to shared variables P and Q respectively.

Figure 5 shows examples of optimizations that are *not* eager loads. The dead-store elimination example in Figure 5(a) involves relaxing the S → S and S → L constraints by delaying the first store and then applying the SC-preserving step of combining the adjacent stores as in Figure 3(c). Figure 5(b) shows an example of a redundant store elimination that involves eagerly performing the store of X by relaxing the L → S and S → S ordering constraints and then applying the transformation in Figure 3(d).

```
X = 1;        ;
P = Q;   ⇒    P = Q;
X = 2;        X = 2;
```

(a)

```
t = X;        t = X;
P = Q;   ⇒    P = Q;
X = t;        ;
```

(b)

Figure 5: (a) Dead store elimination involves relaxing the S → S and S → L constraints. (b) Redundant store elimination involves relaxing the L → S and S → S constraints.

3. An SC-Preserving Modification to LLVM

This section describes the design and implementation of our optimizing SC-preserving compiler on top of LLVM and evaluates the compiler's effectiveness in terms of performance of the generated code versus that of the baseline LLVM compiler.

3.1 Design

As described in the previous section, we can characterize each compiler optimization's potential for SC violations in terms of how it reorders memory accesses. In order to build our SC-preserving compiler, we examined each transformation pass performed by LLVM and determined whether or not it could potentially reorder accesses to shared memory. We further classified these passes based on what types of accesses might be reordered.

Perhaps surprisingly, many of LLVM's passes do not relax the order of memory operations at all and these SC-preserving passes can be left unmodified. These passes include sparse conditional constant propagation, dead argument elimination, control-flow graph simplification, procedure inlining, scalar replication, allocation of function-local variables to virtual registers, correlated value propagation, tail-call elimination, arithmetic re-association, loop simplification, loop rotation, loop unswitching, loop unrolling, unreachable code elimination, virtual-to-physical register allocation, and stack slot coloring.

Other LLVM optimizations can relax the order of memory operations. Table 1 lists these optimization passes and classifies the kinds of relaxations that are possible in each. To ensure that the compiler would be SC-preserving, we disabled a few of these passes and modified the remaining passes to avoid reordering accesses to potentially shared memory.

3.2 Implementation

Our compiler does not perform any heavyweight and/or whole-program analyses to establish whether or not a location is shared (e.g., thread-escape analysis). Rather we use simple, conservative, local information to decide if a location is potentially shared. During an early phase of compilation, LLVM converts loads and stores of non-escaping function-local variables into reads and writes of virtual registers. Operations on these virtual registers can be freely reordered. In certain situations, structures that are passed by value to a function are accessed using load and store operations. Our compiler recognizes these situations and allows these memory operations to be reordered in any sequentially valid manner. In addition, shared memory operations may be reordered with local operations. Thus, for instance, we can safely allow the "instcombine" pass to transform `t=X; t+=u; t+=X;` into `t=X << 1; t+=u;` when both `t` and `u` are local variables.

Incorporating our modifications to LLVM was a fairly natural and noninvasive change to the compiler code. LLVM already avoids reordering and removing loads and stores marked as being *volatile*. Therefore, in the IR optimization passes we were often able to use existing code written to handle volatiles in order to restrict optimizations on other accesses to shared memory. The primary mechanism by which we avoided reordering during the x86 code generation passes was by "chaining" memory operations to one

Table 1: This table lists the passes performed by a standard LLVM compilation for an x86 target that have the potential to reorder accesses to shared memory. The table indicates which memory orderings may be relaxed and whether our SC compiler disables the pass entirely or modifies it to avoid reordering.

Short Name	Description	L → L	L → S	S → L	S → S	SC Version
LLVM IR Optimization Passes						
instcombine	Performs many simplifications including algebraic simplification, simple constant folding and dead code elimination, code sinking, reordering of operands to expose CSE opportunities, limited forms of store-to-load forwarding, limited forms of dead store elimination, and more.	yes	no	yes	no	modified
argpromotion	Promotes by-reference parameters that are only read into by-value parameters; by-value struct types may be changed to pass component scalars instead.	yes	no	yes	no	disabled
jump-threading	Recognizes correlated branch conditions and threads code directly from one block to the correlated successor rather than executing a conditional branch. While this threading in itself would not reorder memory accesses, this pass performs some partially redundant load elimination to enable further jump threading, and that may have the effect of performing an eager load.	yes	no	yes	no	modified
licm	Performs loop-invariant code motion and register promotion.	yes	yes	yes	yes	modified
gvn	The global value numbering pass performs transformations akin to common subexpression elimination, redundant and partially redundant load elimination, and store-to-load forwarding.	yes	no	yes	no	modified
memcopyopt	Performs several optimizations related to memset, memcpy, and memmov calls. Individual stores may be replaced by a single memset. This can cause observable reordering of store operations (e.g. `A[0]=-1; A[2]=-1; A[1]=-1` becomes `memset(A,-1,sizeof(*A)*3)`. This pass can also introduce additional loads not present in the original program through a form of copy propagation.	no	yes	no	yes	disabled
dse	Performs dead store elimination and redundant store elimination as described in Figure 5	no	yes	yes	yes	disabled
x86 Code Generation Passes						
seldag	Builds the initial instruction selection DAG. Performs some CSE during construction.	yes	no	no	no	modified
nodecombine	Performs forms of CSE, constant folding, strength reduction, store-to-load forwarding, and dead store elimination on the selection DAG. Can reduce atomicity of certain operations; for instance a store of a 64-bit float that can be done atomically on some architectures may be changed to two 32-bit integer stores. Also, bit-masking code may be recognized and changed to smaller operations without masking. This can have the effect of reordering a store with prior loads.	yes	yes	no	no	modified
scheduling	Schedules machine instructions.	yes	no	no	no	modified
machinesinking	Sinks load instructions and dependent computation to successor blocks when possible to avoid execution on code paths where they are not used.	yes	no	no	no	modified

another in program order in the instruction selection DAG. This indicates to the scheduler and other passes that there is a dependence from each memory operation to the next and prevents them from being reordered.

3.3 Example

The example in Figure 6 helps illustrate why an SC-preserving compiler can still optimize programs effectively. The source code shown in part (a) of the figure is a simplifed version of a performance-intensive function in one of our benchmarks. The function calculates the distance between two n-dimensional points represented as (possibly shared) arrays of floating point values. In addition to performing the floating point operations that actually calculate the distance, directly translating this function into x86 assembly would allocate space on the stack for the locally declared variables and perform four address calculations during each iteration of the loop. Each address calculation involves an integer multiply and an integer add operation as hinted by the comments in Figure 6 (a). Our SC-preserving compiler is able to perform a variety of important optimizations on this code:

- Since the locally declared variables (including the parameters) do not escape the function, they can be stored in registers rather than on the stack.
- CSE can be used to remove two of the address calculations since they are redundant and only involve locals.
- Loop-induction-variable strength reduction allows us to avoid the multiplication involved in the two remaining address calculations by replacing the loop variable representing the array index with a loop variable representing an address offset that starts at zero and is incremented by 4 each iteration.
- Using loop-invariant code motion (and associativity of addition), we can increment the array addresses directly during each iteration rather than incrementing an offset and later adding it to the base addresses.

The final result of applying the above SC-preserving optimizations is shown in part (b) of the figure (using C syntax rather than x86 assembly). The fully optimizing compiler that does not preserve SC is able to perform one additional optimization: it can use CSE to eliminate the redundant floating point loads and subtraction in each iteration of the loop. The resulting code is shown in part (c) of the figure.

```
float Distance(
    float* x, float*y, int n){
  float sum = 0;
  int i=0;

  for(i=0; i<n; i++){
     sum += (x[i]-y[i])
          *(x[i]-y[i]);
     // Note: x[i] is *(x+i*4)
     //  and  y[i] is *(y+i*4)
  }

  return sqrt(sum);
}
```

(a)

```
float Distance(
    float* x, float* y, int n){
  register float sum = 0;
  register px = x;
  register py = y;
  register rn = n;

  for(; rn-->0; px+=4,py+=4){
    sum += (*px-*py)
          *(*px-*py);
  }

  return sqrt(sum);
}
```

(b)

```
float Distance(
    float* x, float* y, int n){
  register float sum = 0;
  register px = x;
  register py = y;
  register rn = n;

  for(; rn-->0; px+=4,py+=4){
    register t = (*px-*py);
    sum += t*t;
  }

  return sqrt(sum);
}
```

(c)

Figure 6: Example demonstrating the allowed optimizations in an SC-preserving compiler. The function in (a) computes the distance between two n-dimensional points x and y represented as arrays. An SC-preserving compiler is able to safely perform a variety of optimizations, leading to the version in (b). However, it cannot eliminate the common-subexpression `*px - *py` involving possibly-shared accesses to the array elements. A traditional optimizing compiler does not have this restriction and is able to generate the version in (c).

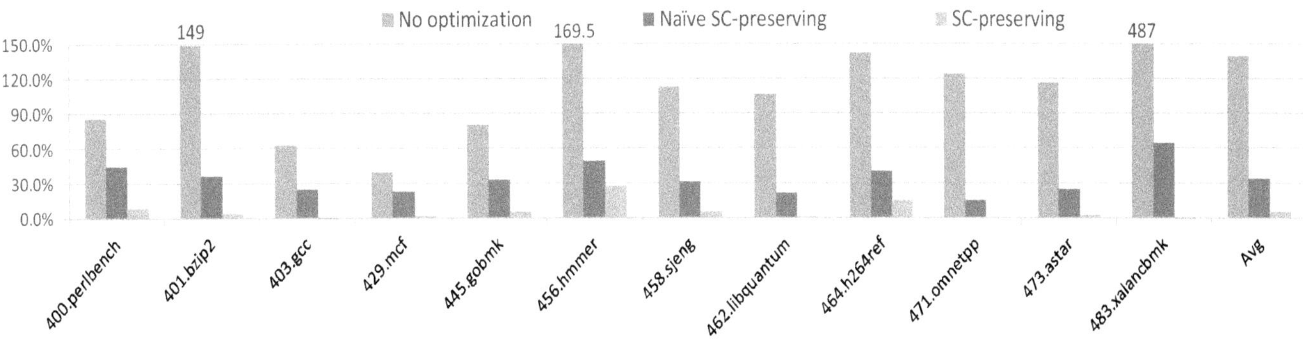

Figure 7: Performance overhead incurred by various compiler configurations compared to the stock LLVM compiler with -O3 optimization for SPEC CINT2006 benchmarks.

3.4 Evaluation

We evaluated our SC-preserving compiler on a variety of sequential and parallel benchmarks. Even though the topic of this paper only concerns multi-threaded programs, we included the sequential benchmarks in our evaluation as optimizing compilers are tuned to perform well for these benchmarks. Our experimental results indicate that the vast majority of the optimizations in LLVM responsible for good performance are in fact SC-preserving.

We executed all programs on an Intel Xeon machine with eight cores, each of which supports two hardware threads and 6 GB of RAM. We evaluated each program under three compiler configurations. The configuration "No optimization" is the stock LLVM compiler with all optimizations disabled; "Naïve SC-preserving" enables only those LLVM passes that are already SC-preserving, because they never reorder accesses to shared memory; and "SC-preserving" is our full SC-preserving compiler, which includes modified versions of some LLVM passes.

Figure 7 shows the results for the SPEC CINT2006 benchmarks. The figure shows the performance overhead of each benchmark under the three compiler configurations, normalized to the benchmark's performance after being compiled with the stock LLVM compiler and all optimizations enabled (-O3). With no optimizations, the benchmarks incur an average 140% slowdown. Re-enabling just the optimizations guaranteed to preserve SC reduces this overhead all the way to 34%. Our full SC-preserving compiler reduces the average overhead to only 5.5%, with a maximum overhead for any benchmark of 28%.

The results for parallel applications from the SPLASH-2 and PARSEC benchmark suites are shown in Figure 10 from Section 6 (the last two compiler configurations shown in the figure pertain to the notion of interference checks that we introduce in the next section). The results agree with those of the sequential benchmarks. Without optimizations the benchmarks incur an average 153% slowdown. Re-enabling "naïvely SC" optimizations reduces the overhead to 22%, and our full SC-preserving compiler incurs an average overhead of only 2.7%, with a maximum overhead for any benchmark of 34%.

4. Speculation for SC-Preservation

As shown in Table 1, most of the optimization passes that reorder shared memory accesses only relax the L $\rightarrow$ L and S $\rightarrow$ L orderings. In other words, these optimizations have the potential to perform eager loads but no other memory reorderings. In order to evaluate how important these eager-load optimizations are for performance, we fully enabled the four (SC-violating) eager-load IR optimization passes in our SC-preserving compiler and re-ran our parallel benchmarks. The "Only-Eager-Loads" configuration in Figure 10 illustrates the results. The benchmark with the largest overhead in our SC-preserving compiler, `facesim`, rebounded from a 34% slowdown to only a 6.5% slowdown, and many other benchmarks regained of all of their lost performance.

This experiment motivates our desire to *speculatively* perform eager-load optimizations and then dynamically recover upon a possible SC violation in order to preserve SC. This section describes how our compiler performs such speculation via a notion of *inter-*

```
                    DOM'
                    ORIG'
DOM                 i.chk monitoredAccesses, rcvr
ORIG      =>        jump cont
CONTINUE
              rcvr: RECOVER
              cont: CONTINUE'
```

Figure 8: Introducing interference checks when performing eager-load transformations in ORIG, a single-entry, single-exit region of code with no stores. Either or both of DOM' and ORIG' contain the definitions for monitoredAccesses for the eager loads involved in the transformation.

ference checks, which conservatively determine whether a memory location's value has been modified since it was last read by the current thread. First we specify the instruction set architecture (ISA) extensions in the hardware that support interference checks. Then we show how a compiler can use these new instructions to speculatively perform eager-load optimizations, and we argue for the correctness of the approach.

4.1 ISA Extensions

Interference checks rely on three new instructions to be provided by the architecture: `m.load` (monitored load), `m.store` (monitored store), and `i.check` (interference check). The `m.load` and `m.store` instructions behave as regular loads and stores but additionally instruct the processor to start monitoring possible writes to the memory location being accessed. We assume that the processor can monitor up to a maximum of N locations simultaneously. These instructions therefore take as an additional parameter a tag from 0 to $N-1$, which is used as an identifier for the memory location being monitored.

The `i.check` instruction provides a mechanism to query the hardware as to whether or not writes could have occurred to a set of memory locations. It accepts an N-bit mask and a recovery branch target as a parameter. The instruction conditionally branches to the recovery target based on whether or not writes may have occurred for any of the monitored memory addresses indicated by the mask. If the instruction does not branch, it is guaranteed that no thread has written to any of the locations indicated by the mask since the instructions that initiated their monitoring were executed. When using an `i.check` in the examples below, we will list the tags explicitly for clarity rather than using a bit mask.

Note that our use of tags to identify accesses, rather than simply identifying them with the address they access, allows the compiler to safely use interference checks in the face of potential aliasing. The compiler may end up monitoring two accesses to the same location using separate tags due to unknown aliasing. The hardware will correctly report interference between the time when the monitored access for each tag was executed and the time of the `i.check` for that tag. This design places the burden on the compiler to manage the resources available for monitoring. It must ensure that when it reuses a tag, the access that was previously assigned to that tag no longer needs to be monitored.

4.2 Interference Check Algorithm

Figure 8 illustrates how our compiler performs eager load optimizations with interference checks. Informally, the algorithm works on code in Static Single Assignment form (SSA) in the following steps:

1. Find a contiguous, single-entry, single-exit block of code without stores. Call this block `ORIG`.
2. Create a branch target at the first instruction after `ORIG`. Call the following instructions, starting at this new target, `CONTINUE`.
3. Make a copy of `ORIG` in its entirety and call it `RECOVER`. Note that, since we are manipulating SSA code, all local and temporary values will be given a new SSA name in the copied code.
4. Apply eager-load transformations in `ORIG` and call the resulting block of code `ORIG'`. The transformations may include any combination of the following:
   (a) Eliminate a load and replace its uses with a value from a previous load or store to that address that dominates the current load. This prior memory access may or may not be in `ORIG`. Convert this previous memory access to an `m.load` or `m.store` if it is not already one. If multiple definitions reach the load to be removed, all of them have to be converted.
   (b) Hoist a load from `ORIG` to a position dominating all of its uses, potentially reordering with previous load and/or store operations. Its new position may or may not be in `ORIG`. Convert the hoisted load to an `m.load`.

   We'll call the code that dominated `ORIG` and may now contain monitored instructions `DOM'`. Each access that is converted to a monitored instruction must use a distinct tag, so the compiler is limited to at most N eager-load conversions in this step.
5. Perform any desired SC-preserving optimizations on the code remaining in `ORIG'`.
6. Insert an `i.check` instruction after `ORIG'` that checks for interference on all accesses that were marked as monitored by step 4 and branches to the recovery code on failure.
7. For all values that are live-out of `ORIG`, transform `CONTINUE` by inserting an SSA phi instruction at the beginning choosing the appropriate value based on whether code flowed from `ORIG'` or `RECOVER`. Call the transformed block `CONTINUE'`.

4.3 Implementation and Example

We modified LLVM's global value numbering (GVN) pass to make use of interference checks in order to allow more aggressive optimization while maintaining SC. The GVN pass performs a variety of eager-load optimizations, including CSE, partial redundancy elimination, and copy/constant propagation. Due to time limitations, we have not implemented the algorithm on other passes.

Figure 9 shows some LLVM IR code that calculates $X^2 + Y + X^2$, along with the transformations that take place on it during the GVN pass in order to eliminate the redundant computation of X^2. Virtual registers, or temporaries, are prefixed by the % symbol and are in SSA form. First, the GVN pass removes the second load of memory location X (which defines %5) and replaces all of its uses with the first load of X. After this load elimination, we are left with the code in (b), where it is clear that the second `mul` instruction is unnecessary, so it is removed and its use is replaced with the previously calculated value in virtual register %2. The final code with the load and multiply eliminated is shown in (c). Figure 9(d) shows how our algorithm adds interference checks to make this transformation SC-preserving.

4.4 Correctness of the Algorithm

We now argue that our algorithm for inserting interference checks is SC-preserving. First consider the case when the interference check fails. Neither `ORIG` nor `ORIG'` contains any stores. Thus, the state of non-local memory does not change during the execution of `ORIG'`. As the code is in SSA form, all the effects of `ORIG'` on local state become dead once the code switches to `RECOVER`, which is a copy of `ORIG`. Hence, other than needlessly executing `ORIG'`, the transformed program has the same behavior as the original program when the interference check fails.

Now consider the case when the interference check succeeds. This means that each monitored memory location is guaranteed to

Original

```
// DOM
%1 = load X
%2 = mul %1, %1
%3 = load Y
%4 = add %2, %3

//ORIG
%5 = load X
%6 = mul %5, %5

//CONTINUE
%7 = add %4, %6
```

(a)

⇒

Load Eliminated

```
// DOM
%1 = load X
%2 = mul %1, %1
%3 = load Y
%4 = add %2, %3

// ORIG'
%6 = mul %1, %1

// CONTINUE
%7 = add %4, %6
```

(b)

⇒

CSE

```
// DOM
%1 = load X
%2 = mul %1, %1
%3 = load Y
%4 = add %2, %3

// ORIG'

// CONTINUE
%7 = add %4, %2
```

(c)

SC with `i.check`

```
// DOM'
%1 = m.load X, 0
%2 = mul %1, %1
%3 = load Y
%4 = add %2, %3

// ORIG'
i.check 0, rcvr
jump cont

// RECOVER
rcvr:
%5 = load X
%6 = mul %5, %5

// CONTINUE
cont:
%merge = phi (orig, %2, rcvr, %6)
%7 = add %4, %merge
```

(d)

Figure 9: GVN first transforms program (a) into (b) by eliminating the "available load" from X, then notices that the result of the second multiplication has already been computed and performs common subexpression elimination to arrive at (c). This transformation is not SC since it reorders the second load of X with the load of Y.

be unmodified from the start of monitoring through the execution of ORIG'. The key property of our algorithm is that every memory location involved in an eager load is monitored from the point where the eager load occurs until at least the point at which the load would have occurred in the original program (since it would have occurred somewhere within ORIG). Thus the value loaded in the optimized code is the value that would have been read by the original program, thereby preserving SC.

5. Hardware Support for Interference Checks

In this section we describe hardware support for efficiently implementing the `m.load`, `m.store`, and `i.check` instructions described in the previous section. The hardware changes required are simple and efficient, and therefore practical. In fact, the new instructions we propose are similar to the data speculation support in the Itanium's ISA [29], which was designed to enable speculative optimizations in a single thread in the face of possible memory aliasing. Our design safely supports both our goal (to ensure sequential consistency) as well as Itanium's speculative load optimizations. Our required hardware support is simple: a structure to store N addresses (32 in our implementation), each with an associated bit indicating whether the address was possibly written.

5.1 Hardware Design

We propose a hardware structure called the Speculative Memory Address Table (SMAT) which is similar to the Advanced Load Address Table (ALAT) used in Itanium processors [29]. SMAT is a Content-Addressable-Memory (CAM). It has N entries, enabling the compiler to monitor interference on N addresses at any instant of time. Each entry in the SMAT contains an address field and an interference bit.

We collectively refer to `m.load` and `m.store` instructions as *monitor* instructions. As described in the previous section, each monitor instruction contains a tag between 0 and $N-1$. When executing a monitor instruction, the hardware stores the address accessed by that instruction in the SMAT entry specified by the tag, resets that entry's interference bit, starts to monitor writes to the address, and executes the memory operation requested by the instruction.

A processor core can easily detect when another processor core wants to write an address by monitoring invalidation coherence requests. When a processor core receives an invalidation to a cache block, the interference bit of each SMAT entry holding an address from that block is set. The interference bit of an entry is also set when a store to the associated address commits from the current processor. While the latter behavior is not necessary to preserve SC, it enables Itanium-style speculative load optimizations [29].

The compiler generates an `i.check` instruction with an N-bit `mask` to check for interference on a maximum of N different addresses. Each bit in the `mask` corresponds to an entry in the SMAT. The hardware executes the `i.check` instruction by checking the interference bits of the SMAT entries specified in its `mask`. If any of the checked interference bits is set, the hardware branches to the recovery code whose target is specified in the `i.check` instruction.

The hardware updates the SMAT for a monitor instruction and executes `i.check` instructions only when they are ready to commit from a processor core's instruction window. This ensures that the hardware does not update SMAT entries speculatively while executing instructions on an incorrect path taken due to branch misprediction. The next section explains a subtlety in implementing the monitor instructions in out-of-order processors.

5.2 Relation To In-Window Hardware Speculation

Our approach of monitoring invalidation coherence requests to detect interference for a set of addresses is similar to what many processors already implement for efficiently supporting TSO at the hardware level [23]. TSO does not allow a load to be executed before another load in program order even if they are accessing different addresses. To achieve good performance, Gharachorloo et al. [23] proposed to speculatively execute loads out-of-order. However, instructions are still committed in order from a FIFO queue called the reorder buffer (ROB). Therefore, to detect misspeculation the hardware simply needs to detect when another processor tries to write to an address that has been read by a load that is yet to commit from the ROB. This is achieved by monitoring the address of invalidation coherence requests from other processor cores. On detecting a misspeculation, the hardware flushes the misspeculated load and its following instructions from the pipeline and restarts execution.

Our proposed hardware design essentially extends the above hardware mechanism to detect interference for addresses of certain memory operations (specified by the compiler) even after they are committed from the ROB. This allows our compiler to eagerly execute loads and later check for interference at the original location of the load in the source code. On a `m.load`, the monitoring needs to start logically when the processor receives the value of the load. However, the SMAT entry is updated only when the instruction is committed. In between the two events, when the load instruction is in flight in the ROB, we rely on the monitoring performed above to provide the required semantics of the `i.check`.

5.3 Conservative Interference Checks

While an implementation of interference checks must detect interference whenever it occurs, it is legal to signal interference when none actually exists. Such false positives are acceptable in our design because they simply result in execution of the unoptimized code, losing some performance but maintaining SC. The ability to tolerate false positives allows us to avoid a number of potentially complex issues and keep the hardware simple.

First, our hardware monitors interference at the cache block granularity as coherence invalidation messages operate at cache block level. This may result in false positives when compared to a detector that monitors byte-level access. But the probability that a cache block gets invalidated between a monitor instruction and an `i.check` is very low. Moreover, frequent invalidations or "false sharing" of hot cache lines result in performance degradations and thus can expected to be rare in well-tuned applications.

Second, we conservatively invalidate SMAT entries for a cache block that gets evicted due to capacity constraints. Monitoring interference for uncached blocks would require significant system support (similar in complexity to unbounded transactional memory systems [17]), but we believe it is not necessary for performance.

Third, in ISAs like `x86` one memory instruction could potentially access two or more cache lines, but our SMAT entry can monitor only one cache block address. To address this problem, if a monitor instruction accesses more than one cache block we immediately set the interference bit for the SMAT entry that monitors the associated address, which could cause a future `i.check` to fail forcing execution down an unoptimized path. Fortunately, such unaligned cache accesses are rare.

Finally, a context switch may occur while multiple addresses are monitored in the hardware SMAT. Instead of virtualizing this structure, we propose to set the interference bit in all SMAT entries after a context switch. This may cause future `i.check` instructions from the same thread to fail unnecessarily when it is context switched back in, but we expect this overhead to be negligible as context switches are relatively rare when compared to the frequency of memory accesses.

6. Results

The experimental results relating to the performance of our SC-preserving compiler were discussed in Section 3.4. In this section we discuss additional experiments which evaluate the potential effectiveness of our interference checks. In addition, we compare the performance of our SC-preserving compilers to a fully optimizing compiler running on simulated hardware that uses a DRF0 memory model which is more relaxed (allows more hardware reorderings) than TSO. This gives a sense of the performance burden of providing a strong, end-to-end memory model across hardware and software.

6.1 Compiler Configurations

As described in Section 3.4, our baseline compiler is the out-of-the-box LLVM compiler with all optimizations (`-O3`). For our experiments on parallel benchmarks, we used the three compiler configurations discussed in that section ("No optimization", "Naïve SC-preserving", and "SC-preserving"), as well as two additional configurations. The "Only Eager Loads" configuration includes all the optimizations from the SC-preserving compiler plus the unmodified (SC-violating) version of all IR passes that perform only eager load optimizations (GVN, instcombine, argpromotion, and jump-threading). This configuration is intended to give a sense of the opportunity for improvement available to optimizations based on our interference check technique and is only used for experiments on native hardware and not on simulated machines. Finally, the "SC-preserving+GVN w/ ICheck" configuration includes all of the optimizations from the SC-preserving compiler plus a modified GVN pass that is made SC-preserving using our interference checks and recovery code. When this configuration targets a simulated machine with appropriate support, it emits `m.load`, `m.store`, and `i.check` instructions. But when it targets native hardware, the configuration emits `m.load` and `m.store` instructions as regular loads and stores and emulates a never-failing `i.check` using a logical comparison of constant values followed by a conditional branch. Thus, when running on the native machine, the overhead caused by increased code size and the additional branch is captured, but the effect of actual or false conflicts on monitored accesses is not. In a real implementation, however, we expect the `i.check` instruction to be more efficient than a branch.

Table 2: Baseline IPC for simulated DRF0 hardware running binaries from the stock LLVM compiler.

Application	Avg. IPC	Application	Avg. IPC
blackscholes	1.94	bodytrack	1.61
fluidanimate	1.28	swaptions	1.67
streamcluster	1.42	barnes	1.57
water(nsquared)	1.66	water(spatial)	1.66
cholesky	1.78	fft	1.39
lu(contiguous blocks)	1.64	radix	0.99

6.2 Benchmarks

We evaluated the performance of the various compiler configurations on the PARSEC [7] and SPLASH-2 [49] parallel benchmark suites. Table 2 lists the average instructions executed per cycle (IPC) for each of these benchmarks when compiled with the stock LLVM compiler at `-O3` optimization and run on our simulated DRF0 hardware which implements weak consistency and is described below. All of these benchmarks are run to completion. For our experiments on actual hardware, we used the `native` input for PARSEC benchmarks, while for the simulated machines we used the `sim-medium` input set to keep the simulation time reasonable. (Since `streamcluster` was especially slow to simulate, we used the `sim-small` input.) For SPLASH-2 applications, we used the default inputs for simulation. We modified the inputs to increase the problem size for experiments on native hardware. We verified the correct behavior of the benchmarks under all compiler configurations by using a self-testing option when available, or by comparing results with those produced when compiling the benchmark using gcc.

6.3 Experiments on Native Hardware

We evaluated all six compiler configurations (including the baseline) on an Intel Xeon machine with eight cores each of which supports two hardware threads and 6 GB of RAM. Each benchmark was run five times for each compiler configuration and the execution time was measured. (The results given here are for CPU user time, though the results for total time elapsed were very similar.) The overheads given are relative to the baseline, fully-optimizing compiler and are shown in Figure 10. Let's consider the base SC-preserving compiler

Table 3: Processor Configuration

Processor	4 core CMP. Each core operating at 2Ghz.
Fetch/Exec/ Commit width	4 instructions(maximum 2 loads or 1 store) per cycle in each core.
Store Buffer	TSO: 64 entry FIFO buffer with 8 byte granularity. DRF0, DRFx: 8 entry unordered coalescing buffer with 64 byte granularity.
L1 Cache	64 KB per-core (private), 4-way set associative, 64B block size, 1-cycle hit latency, write-back.
L2 Cache	1MB private, 4-way set associative, 64B block size, 10-cycle hit latency.
Coherence	MOESI directory protocol
Interconnection	Hierarchical switch, 10 cycle hop latency.
Memory	80 cycle DRAM lookup latency.
SMAT	32 entries CAM structure, 1 cycle associative lookup

first. Notice that for many of our benchmarks, restricting the compiler to perform only SC-preserving optimizations has little or no effect. In fact, in some cases, disabling these transformations appears to speed the code up, indicating that the compiler ought not to have performed them in the first place. There are several benchmarks, however, for which the SC-preserving compiler incurs a noticeable performance penalty, 34% in the case of `facesim`.[2] On average, we see a 2.7% slowdown. Consider now the compiler configuration which re-enables various eager load optimizations. Several of the applications which suffered a significant slowdown under the SC-preserving compiler regain much of this performance in this configuration. Most notably, `facesim` vastly improves to 6.5% and `bodytrack`, `streamcluster`, and `x264` recover all (or nearly all) of their lost performance. On average, the compiler with eager load relaxations enabled is as fast as the stock compiler, indicating that our technique of using interference checks to safely allow eager load optimizations holds significant promise. Finally, the rightmost bar in the graph shows the slowdown of the aggressive SC-preserving compiler that includes the modified GVN pass with interference checks. (Remember, we are running on a native machine in this set of experiments, so a never-fail load check is emulated.) We see that this technique regains a good portion of the performance lost by the base SC-preserving compiler for `facesim`, reducing the overhead from 34% to under 20%, with `streamcluster` and `x264` showing a more modest improvement.

6.4 Experiments on Simulated Machines

To study the performance of interference checks in hardware, we used a cycle-accurate, execution driven, Simics [35] based x86_64 simulator called FeS2 [19]. We simulated TSO hardware with and without support for interference checks and compared it to DRF0 hardware that supports weak consistency. The processor configuration that we modelled is shown in Table 3. For the TSO simulation, we modelled a FIFO store buffer that holds pending stores and retires them in-order. We also modelled speculative load execution support [23]. The weakly consistent DRF0 simulation allowed stores and loads to retire out-of-order.

Figure 11 shows the results of our simulation study. When compared to the fully optimizing compiler configuration running on the simulated DRF0 machine, the performance overhead of using our SC-preserving compiler on simulated TSO hardware is 3.4% on average. This cost is reduced to 2.2% when the GVN pass with interference checks is used. For several programs that incur significant overhead, such as `bodytrack` and `facesim`, our interference check optimizations reduce the overhead to almost zero. For `streamcluster`, the overhead is reduced from about 23% to 17%. We also found that the frequency of load-check failures is, on average, only about one in ten million instructions. This indicates that the performance overhead due to false positives arising from several hardware simplifications described in Section 5.3 is negligible.

7. Discussion and Related Work

7.1 Relationship to Data-Race-Free Memory Models

Today's mainstream concurrent programming languages including C++ and Java use variants of the *data-race-free* memory model known as DRF0 [2, 3]. These memory models are rooted in the observation that good programming discipline requires programmers to protect shared accesses to data with appropriate synchronization (such as locks). For such data-race-free programs, these models guarantee SC. For programs with data races, however, these models guarantee either no semantics [11] or a weak and complex semantics [36]. The compiler and hardware are restricted in the optimizations allowed across synchronization accesses, but they can safely perform most sequentially-valid optimizations on regular memory accesses.

Our work is primarily motivated by the need to provide understandable semantics to racy programs [1] both for debugging ease of large software systems that are likely to have data races and for guaranteeing security properties in safe languages such as Java [36].

In the context of a DRF0-compliant compiler (such as LLVM), our interference checks can be seen as a specialized form of data race detection. Our approach allows the compiler to speculatively perform the eager-load optimizations which would be allowed in the DRF0 model. However, rather than silently providing undefined or weak semantics upon a data race, our interference checks dynamically detect the race and recover in order to preserve SC. In this way, data-race-free programs can be aggressively optimized and incur just the additional cost of the interference check itself and the rare false interference check that may occur (Section 5.3). Furthermore, even racy programs benefit from our approach, because the interference check captures exactly the requirement necessary to justify an optimization's SC-preservation. For instance, data races on variables that are not eagerly loaded, as well as data races on eagerly-loaded variables that occur outside of the scope of that reordering, cannot violate SC preservation and so need not be detected.

While this paper focuses on eager-load optimizations, we hope to explore in future work speculation mechanisms that enable other DRF0-compliant optimizations while preserving SC.

7.2 A TSO-Preserving Compiler

Providing SC semantics to the programmer requires that the output of an SC-preserving compiler be executed on SC hardware. While most hardware platforms today support a relaxed memory model, popular platforms such as Intel's x86 and Sun's SPARC platforms provide a relatively-strong memory model known as total store ordering (TSO). Conceptually, TSO can be seen as a relaxation of SC that allows $\mathsf{S} \rightarrow \mathsf{L}$ reorderings [2] and has a precise understandable operational semantics [40].

Our approach to developing an SC-preserving compiler can be naturally adapted to instead preserve TSO, thereby providing end-to-end TSO semantics on existing TSO hardware. Transformations

[2] Additional profiling and investigation revealed that the slowdown in `facesim` was largely caused by a commonly invoked 3x3 matrix multiply routine. The SC-preserving compiler was unable to eliminate the two redundant loads of each of the 18 shared, floating point matrix entries involved in the calculation. This resulted in 36 additional load instructions for each matrix multiplication performed by the SC-preserving version of `facesim`. Our GVN pass with interference checks is able to relegate the 36 additional loads to the recovery code, eliminating them on the fast path. A straightforward rewrite of the source code to first read the 18 shared values into local variables would have allowed the base SC-preserving compiler to generate the fully optimized code.

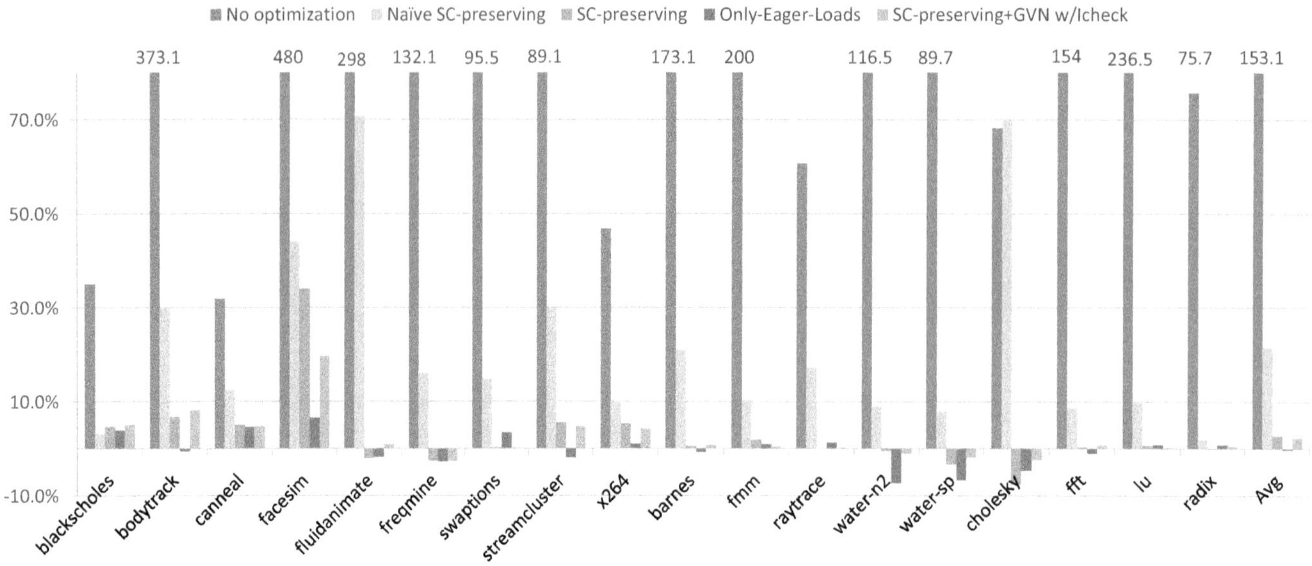

Figure 10: Performance overhead incurred by the various compiler configurations compared to stock LLVM compiler with -O3 optimization running on native Xeon hardware for PARSEC and SPLASH-2 benchmarks.

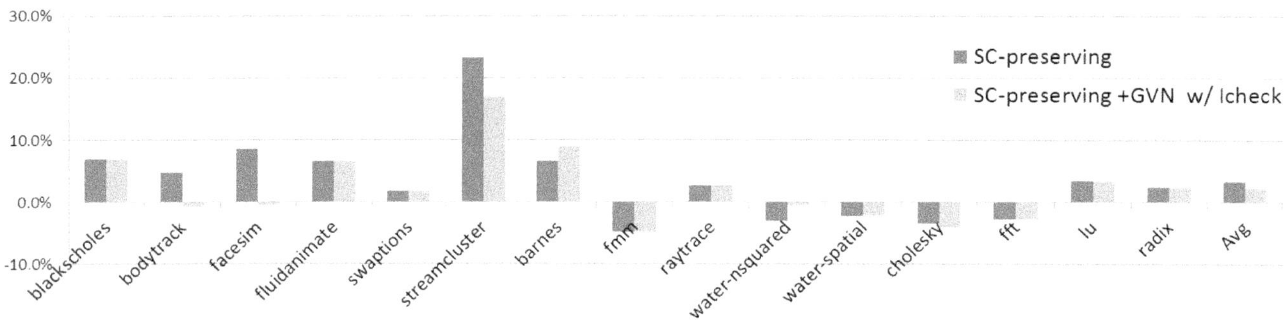

Figure 11: Performance overhead of SC-preserving compiler on simulated TSO hardware with and without using interference checks relative to fully optimizing SC-violating compiler on simulated DRF0 hardware.

that do not reorder memory accesses and those that only reorder thread-local variables are TSO-preserving [48]. In addition, all of the SC-preserving transformations shown in Figure 3 also preserve TSO except for redundant store elimination [14].

In the context of a DRF0-compliant compiler, the result of this approach would be a language-level memory model that provides SC semantics for data-race-free programs and TSO semantics for racy programs. This variation on DRF0 is significantly stronger and much simpler than both the C++0x [6, 11] and Java [36] memory models.

In recent work, Ševčík et al. describe a concurrency extension to a small C-like programming language that provides end-to-end TSO semantics [48]. They modify an existing compiler for the language and mechanically prove that the optimizations are TSO-preserving, thereby providing an end-to-end guarantee when the resulting binaries are executed on x86 hardware. Our performance measurements complement their work by indicating that a TSO-preserving compiler could be practical to use in a full-fledged programming language.

7.3 Dynamic Detection of Data Races and SC Violations

Others have argued for the use of dynamic race detection to improve the DRF0 memory model [10, 16, 18], in order to halt an execution when its semantics becomes undefined, analogous with Java's fail-stop approach to preventing array-bounds violations and null-pointer dereferences. However, detecting data races either incurs 8x or more performance overhead in software [20] or incurs significant hardware complexity [4, 38, 43] despite many proposed optimizations to the basic technique.

Recently, Marino et al. [37] and Lucia et al. [34] observed that it suffices to dynamically detect SC violations rather than races, and that this can be done much more efficiently. In their approaches, the compiler partitions a program into regions and may perform most sequentially valid optimizations within a region but cannot optimize across regions. Region boundaries are communicated to the hardware as memory fences, thereby also preventing hardware optimizations across regions. Given these requirements, the hardware can conservatively identify data races that potentially cause SC violations by detecting conflicting accesses in concurrently executing regions, similar to the conflict detection performed by transactional memory (TM) systems [27].

Our interference checks are a form of dynamic data-race detection that is sufficient to ensure SC-preservation of compiler transformations. Such detection provides a weaker guarantee than the above approaches, which additionally detect SC violations due to hardware reorderings. However, our approach has a number of advantages. First, our detection scheme is fine-grained, requiring only data race detection for variables that are involved in a compiler optimization and only during the dynamic lifetime of that optimization's effect. Second, we can perform this detection with relatively minimal hardware support based on existing hardware speculation mechanisms [50], rather than requiring the complexity of TM-style conflict detection. Finally, we show how to safely recover from interference for common compiler optimizations based on eager loads, thereby allowing the execution to safely continue while maintaining SC.

7.4 Optimistic Optimization via Hardware Speculation

Our interference checks are inspired by a common hardware mechanism for enabling out-of-order execution in the presence of strong memory models [23]. This mechanism [50] allows a memory load to be executed out-of-order speculatively, before earlier instructions have completed. Once those instructions have completed, the load need not be re-executed if the value has not changed in the meanwhile, and this can be conservatively detected by checking if the associated cache line has been invalidated. We illustrate how this technique can be adapted to the compiler by viewing common compiler optimizations as performing eager (i.e., speculative) reads, and we describe a simple way for the hardware to expose this mechanism to the compiler.

Others have proposed hardware support for dynamically detecting memory aliasing between local loads and stores in a single thread and expose that feature to the compiler so that it can perform optimistic optimizations [22, 41]. The Itanium processor implemented this feature using an Advanced Load Address Table (ALAT) to enable aggressive load optimizations [29]. Recently, Nagarajan and Gupta [39] extended Itanium's ALAT mechanism to detect memory aliasing with remote writes, enabling the compiler to speculatively reorder memory operations across memory barriers. While our hardware mechanism to detect memory aliasing is similar to these proposals, we apply it to solve a different problem: preserving SC in the face of common compiler transformations.

7.5 Guaranteeing End-to-End Sequential Consistency

Our approach ensures that the compiler is SC-preserving but does not prevent the hardware from exposing non-SC behavior. We could augment our compiler to address this problem by inserting memory fences to prevent hardware reorderings that potentially violate SC. Such fences cause a significant performance penalty, so there has been research in minimizing the number of fences required. Shasha and Snir proposed the *delay sets* algorithm for determining the set of fences to insert [45]. Recent research has further reduced the number of fences required by incorporating analyses that detect which memory locations are possibly accessed by multiple threads [30, 46]. Finally, recent work describes a new hardware mechanism called a *conditional fence* [33], which uses the results of a compiler analysis to dynamically decide whether a given fence in the instruction stream can be safely ignored while still ensuring SC. All of these approaches rely critically on whole-program analyses to obtain sufficient precision.

A different way to ensure SC at the language level is by statically rejecting possibly racy programs. Several static type systems have been proposed that prevent races (e.g., [12, 13, 21]) and ensure stronger properties such as determinism [9]. By rejecting potentially racy programs, these type systems ensure that all program executions have SC semantics. However, these type systems enforce a restricted programming style that is necessarily conservative. For example, many static type systems for race detection only account for lock-based synchronization and will reject race-free programs that use other synchronization mechanisms. Further, even correct programs that employ locks can be rejected due to imprecise information about pointer aliasing. More precision in static race detection can be achieved through whole-program analysis [42].

Hammond et al. [25] proposed the transactional coherency and consistency (TCC) memory model. The programmer and the compiler ensure that every instruction is part of some transaction. The runtime uses transactional memory [27] to ensure serializability of transactions, which in turn guarantees SC at the language level. The Bulk compiler [5] and the BulkSC hardware [15] together also guarantee SC at the language level. The bulk compiler partitions a program into "chunks" and the BulkSC hardware employs speculation and recovery to ensure serializable execution of chunks. Conflicts are resolved through rollback and re-execution of chunks. These techniques obtain a strong guarantee of SC, but at the cost of significant hardware extensions that are similar to transactional memory support.

8. Conclusions

A memory model forms the foundation of shared-memory multithreaded programming languages. This paper empirically demonstrates that the performance incentive for relaxing the intuitive SC semantics in the compiler is much less than previously assumed. In particular, this paper describes how to engineer an SC-preserving compiler through simple modifications to LLVM, a state-of-the-art C/C++ compiler. For a wide range of programs from the SPLASH-2, PARSEC, and SPEC CINT2006 benchmark suites, our SC-preserving compiler results in a performance overhead of only 3.8% on average with a maximum of 34% overhead.

While the overheads, however small, might be unacceptable for certain applications, this paper argues that other avenues for improving the performance of SC-preserving compilers should be explored before resorting to relaxing the program semantics. We proposed a novel hardware-software cooperation mechanism in the form of interference checks, which enabled us to regain much of the performance lost due to restrictions imposed on compiler optimizations to preserve SC.

9. Acknowledgements

The authors would like to thank Sarita Adve, Vikram Adve, Hans Boehm, Sebastian Burckhardt, Mark Hill, Suresh Jagannathan, Milo Martin, Todd Mytkowicz, and Jaroslav Ševčík for insightful discussions regarding this work. We also like to thank the anonymous reviewers for valuable feedback on this paper. This work is supported by the National Science Foundation under awards CNS-0725354, CNS-0905149, and CCF-0916770 as well as by the Defense Advanced Research Projects Agency under award HR0011-09-1-0037.

References

[1] S. V. Adve and H.-J. Boehm. Memory models: A case for rethinking parallel languages and hardware. *Commun. ACM*, 53(8):90–101, 2010.

[2] S. V. Adve and K. Gharachorloo. Shared memory consistency models: a tutorial. *Computer*, 29(12):66–76, 1996.

[3] S. V. Adve and M. D. Hill. Weak ordering—a new definition. In *Proceedings of ISCA*, pages 2–14. ACM, 1990.

[4] S. V. Adve, M. D. Hill, B. P. Miller, and R. H. B. Netzer. Detecting data races on weak memory systems. In *ISCA*, pages 234–243, 1991.

[5] W. Ahn, S. Qi, J.-W. Lee, M. Nicolaides, X. Fang, J. Torrellas, D. Wong, and S. Midkiff. BulkCompiler: High-performance sequential consistency through cooperative compiler and hardware support. In *42nd International Symposium on Microarchitecture*, 2009.

[6] M. Batty, S. Owens, S. Sarkar, P. Sewell, and T. Weber. Mathematizing C++ concurrency. In *Proceedings of the 38th annual ACM SIGPLAN-SIGACT symposium on Principles of programming languages*, POPL '11, pages 55–66. ACM, 2011.

[7] C. Bienia, S. Kumar, J. P. Singh, and K. Li. The PARSEC benchmark suite: Characterization and architectural implications. In *Proceedings of the 17th International Conference on Parallel Architectures and Compilation Techniques*, October 2008.

[8] C. Blundell, M. M. Martin, and T. F. Wenisch. InvisiFence: Performance-transparent memory ordering in conventional multiprocessors. In *Proceedings of the 36th annual International Symposium on Computer architecture*, ISCA '09, pages 233–244. ACM, 2009.

[9] R. Bocchino, V. Adve, D. Dig, S. Adve, S. Heumann, R. Komuravelli, J. Overbey, P. Simmons, H. Sung, and M. Vakilian. A type and effect system for Deterministic Parallel Java. In *OOPSLA*, 2009.

[10] H. J. Boehm. Simple thread semantics require race detection. In *FIT session at PLDI*, 2009.

[11] H. J. Boehm and S. V. Adve. Foundations of the C++ concurrency memory model. In *Proceedings of PLDI*, pages 68–78. ACM, 2008.

[12] C. Boyapati and M. Rinard. A parameterized type system for race-free Java programs. In *Proceedings of OOPSLA*, pages 56–69. ACM Press, 2001.

[13] C. Boyapati, R. Lee, and M. Rinard. Ownership types for safe programming: Preventing data races and deadlocks. In *Proceedings of OOPSLA*, 2002.

[14] S. Burckhardt, M. Musuvathi, and V. Singh. Verifying local transformations on relaxed memory models. In *Compiler Construction*, volume 6011 of *Lecture Notes in Computer Science*, pages 104–123. Springer Berlin / Heidelberg, 2010.

[15] L. Ceze, J. Tuck, P. Montesinos, and J. Torrellas. BulkSC: Bulk enforcement of sequential consistency. In *ISCA*, pages 278–289, 2007.

[16] L. Ceze, J. Devietti, B. Lucia, and S. Qadeer. The case for system support for concurrency exceptions. In *USENIX HotPar*, 2009.

[17] W. Chuang, S. Narayanasamy, G. Venkatesh, J. Sampson, M. V. Biesbrouck, G. Pokam, B. Calder, and O. Colavin. Unbounded page-based transactional memory. *International Conference on Architectural Support for Programming Languages and Operating Systems*, 2006.

[18] T. Elmas, S. Qadeer, and S. Tasiran. Goldilocks: A race and transaction-aware Java runtime. In *PLDI*, pages 245–255, 2007.

[19] FeS2. The FeS2 simulator. URL `http://fes2.cs.uiuc.edu/`.

[20] C. Flanagan and S. Freund. FastTrack: Efficient and precise dynamic race detection. In *Proceedings of PLDI*, 2009.

[21] C. Flanagan and S. N. Freund. Type-based race detection for Java. In *Proceedings of PLDI*, pages 219–232, 2000.

[22] D. M. Gallagher, W. Y. Chen, S. A. Mahlke, J. C. Gyllenhaal, and W. mei W. Hwu. Dynamic memory disambiguation using the memory conflict buffer. In *ASPLOS*, pages 183–193, 1994.

[23] K. Gharachorloo, A. Gupta, and J. Hennessy. Two techniques to enhance the performance of memory consistency models. In *Proceedings of the 1991 International Conference on Parallel Processing*, volume 1, pages 355–364, 1991.

[24] C. Gniady and B. Falsafi. Speculative sequential consistency with little custom storage. In *IEEE PACT*, pages 179–188, 2002.

[25] L. Hammond, V. Wong, M. K. Chen, B. D. Carlstrom, J. D. Davis, B. Hertzberg, M. K. Prabhu, H. Wijaya, C. Kozyrakis, and K. Olukotun. Transactional memory coherence and consistency. In *ISCA*, pages 102–113, 2004.

[26] J. L. Henning. SPEC CPU2006 benchmark descriptions. *SIGARCH Computer Architecture News*, 34:1–17, September 2006. ISSN 0163-5964.

[27] M. Herlihy and J. E. B. Moss. Transactional memory: architectural support for lock-free data structures. In *Proceedings of ISCA*, pages 289–300. ACM, 1993.

[28] M. D. Hill. Multiprocessors should support simple memory-consistency models. *IEEE Computer*, 31:28–34, 1998. ISSN 0018-9162.

[29] Itanium. Inside the Intel Itanium 2 processor. *Hewlett Packard Technical White Paper*, 2002.

[30] A. Kamil, J. Su, and K. Yelick. Making sequential consistency practical in Titanium. In *Proceedings of the 2005 ACM/IEEE conference on Supercomputing*, page 15. IEEE Computer Society, 2005.

[31] L. Lamport. How to make a multiprocessor computer that correctly executes multiprocess programs. *IEEE Transactions on Computers*, 100(28):690–691, 1979.

[32] C. Lattner and V. Adve. LLVM: A compilation framework for lifelong program analysis & transformation. In *Proceedings of the International Symposium on Code Generation and Optimization: Feedback-Directed and Runtime Optimization*. IEEE Computer Society, 2004.

[33] C. Lin, V. Nagarajan, and R. Gupta. Efficient sequential consistency using conditional fences. In *International Conference on Parallel Architectres and Compilation Techniques*, 2010.

[34] B. Lucia, L. Ceze, K. Strauss, S. Qadeer, and H. Boehm. Conflict Exceptions: Providing simple parallel language semantics with precise hardware exceptions. In *37th Annual International Symposium on Computer Architecture*, June 2010.

[35] S. Magnusson, M. Christensson, J. Eskilson, D. Forsgren, G. Hållberg, J. Högberg, F. Larsson, A. Moestedt, and B. Werner. Simics: A full system simulation platform. *IEEE Computer*, 35(2):50–58, 2002.

[36] J. Manson, W. Pugh, and S. V. Adve. The java memory model. In *Proceedings of POPL*, pages 378–391. ACM, 2005.

[37] D. Marino, A. Singh, T. Millstein, M. Musuvathi, and S. Narayanasamy. DRFx: A simple and efficient memory model for concurrent programming languages. In *PLDI '10*, pages 351–362. ACM, 2010.

[38] A. Muzahid, D. Suarez, S. Qi, and J. Torrellas. SigRace: Signature-based data race detection. In *ISCA*, 2009.

[39] V. Nagarajan and R. Gupta. Speculative optimizations for parallel programs on multicores. In *LCPC*, pages 323–337, 2009.

[40] S. Owens, S. Sarkar, and P. Sewell. A better x86 memory model: x86-TSO. In *In TPHOLs '09: Conference on Theorem Proving in Higher Order Logics, volume 5674 of LNCS*, pages 391–407. Springer, 2009.

[41] M. Postiff, D. Greene, and T. N. Mudge. The store-load address table and speculative register promotion. In *MICRO*, pages 235–244, 2000.

[42] P. Pratikakis, J. S. Foster, and M. Hicks. LOCKSMITH: Context-sensitive correlation analysis for race detection. In *Proceedings of PLDI*, pages 320–331, 2006.

[43] M. Prvulovic and J. Torrelas. Reenact: Using thread-level speculation mechanisms to debug data races in multithreaded codes. In *Proceedings of ISCA*, San Diego, CA, June 2003.

[44] P. Ranganathan, V. Pai, and S. Adve. Using speculative retirement and larger instruction windows to narrow the performance gap between memory consistency models. In *SPAA '97*, pages 199–210, 1997.

[45] D. Shasha and M. Snir. Efficient and correct execution of parallel programs that share memory. *ACM Transactions on Programming Languages and Systems (TOPLAS)*, 10(2):282–312, 1988.

[46] Z. Sura, X. Fang, C. Wong, S. Midkiff, J. Lee, and D. Padua. Compiler techniques for high performance sequentially consistent java programs. In *Proceedings of PPoPP*, pages 2–13, 2005.

[47] J. Ševčík and D. Aspinall. On validity of program transformations in the Java memory model. In *ECOOP*, pages 27–51, 2008.

[48] J. Ševčík, V. Vafeiadis, F. Zappa Nardelli, S. Jagannathan, and P. Sewell. Relaxed-memory concurrency and verified compilation. In *Proceedings of the 38th annual ACM SIGPLAN-SIGACT symposium on Principles of programming languages*, POPL '11, pages 43–54. ACM, 2011.

[49] S. C. Woo, M. Ohara, E. Torrie, J. P. Singh, and A. Gupta. The SPLASH-2 programs: characterization and methodological considerations. In *ISCA*, pages 24–36, New York, NY, USA, 1995. ACM.

[50] K. Yeager. The MIPS R10000 superscalar microprocessor. *Micro, IEEE*, 16(2):28–41, 2002. ISSN 0272-1732.

Probabilistic, Modular and Scalable Inference of Typestate Specifications

Nels E. Beckman
Carnegie Mellon University
nbeckman@cs.cmu.edu

Aditya V. Nori
Microsoft Research India
adityan@microsoft.com

Abstract

Static analysis tools aim to find bugs in software that correspond to violations of specifications. Unfortunately, for large and complex software, these specifications are usually either unavailable or sophisticated, and hard to write.

This paper presents ANEK, a tool and accompanying methodology for inferring specifications useful for modular typestate checking of programs. In particular, these specifications consist of pre and postconditions along with aliasing annotations known as access permissions. A novel feature of ANEK is that it can generate program specifications even when the code under analysis gives rise to conflicting constraints, a situation that typically occurs when there are bugs. The design of ANEK also makes it easy to add heuristic constraints that encode intuitions gleaned from several years of experience writing such specifications, and this allows it to infer specifications that are better in a subjective sense. The ANEK algorithm is based on a modular analysis that makes it fast and scalable, while producing reliable specifications. All of these features are enabled by its underlying probabilistic analysis that produces specifications that are very *likely*.

Our implementation of ANEK infers access permissions specifications used by the PLURAL [5] modular typestate checker for Java programs. We have run ANEK on a number of Java benchmark programs, including one large open-source program (approximately 38K lines of code), to infer specifications that were then checked using PLURAL. The results for the large benchmark show that ANEK can quickly infer specifications that are both accurate and qualitatively similar to those written by hand, and at 5% of the time taken to manually discover and hand-code the specifications.

Categories and Subject Descriptors D.2.4 [*Software/Program Verification*]: Statistical methods

General Terms Algorithms, Verification

Keywords aliasing, inference, object protocol, ownership, permission, typestate, specification

1. Introduction

Developing correct and reliable software is a hard problem, one that is supported by various analysis tools for improving software quality and reliability. Even though these tools are largely automated, many require user-provided specifications that describe the property or protocol that the code under analysis is required to satisfy [2, 5, 8, 11] and this greatly limits their application in practice. However, writing good specifications is a hard and laborious task that also requires some degree of expertise on the codebase under analysis.

In this paper we present ANEK[1], a tool and an accompanying methodology for inferring specifications necessary for modular typestate [18] checking. Given an API annotated with typestate specifications by its developers, ANEK allows users of that API to quickly infer the specifications needed in their code in order to modularly check API conformance.

Specifically, ANEK infers access permission specifications [5], specifications which, in addition to encoding abstract states of objects, also encode aliasing information, which allows for sound modular checking. Our inference algorithm is novel because it combines both the logical facts relating to permission creation and destruction as well as heuristics describing likely specifications, and does so using a scheme of *probabilistic* constraints. The result is an inference that is faster, generates better specifications and scales better than more traditional approaches.

To illustrate our point, consider an example. A programmer wants to ensure correct use of Java's iterator API, modeled in Figure 1 and annotated by its developers with access permission specifications in Figure 2. Its specification says that in order to call the `next` method, the receiver object must be known to be in the "HASNEXT" abstract state, which a client can be sure the object is in if the `hasNext` method returns true. The `Collection` interface is also specified. It says that when the `iterator` method is called, a unique (unaliased) iterator will be returned in the "ALIVE" state.[2]

Our hypothetical programmer wants to ensure that her simple spreadsheet application, partially given in Figure 3, is always using

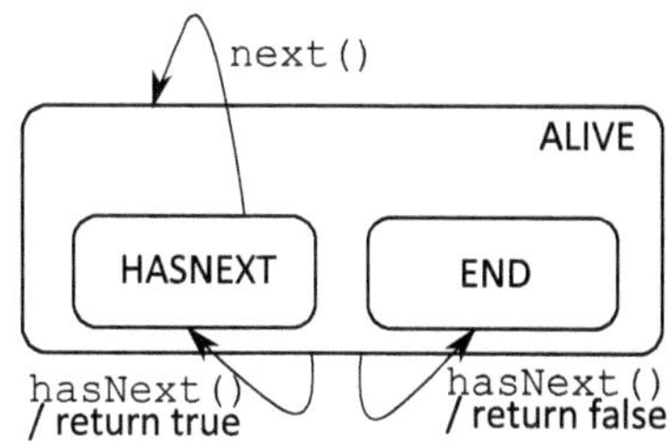

Figure 1. The iterator protocol.

[1] *Anek* is the Hindi word meaning *plural*.

[2] The "ALIVE" state in the PLURAL methodology is the root of the state hierarchy, so this statement is equivalent to saying the iterator is not in any state of interest.

PLDI'11, June 4–8, 2011, San Jose, California, USA.

```
interface Iterator<T> {
  @Spec(requires="full(this) in HASNEXT",
        ensures="full(this) in ALIVE")
  T next();

  @Spec(requires="pure(this) in ALIVE",
        ensures="pure(this)")
  @TrueIndicates("HASNEXT")
  @FalseIndicates("END")
  boolean hasNext();
}

interface Collection<T> extends Iterable<T> {
  @Spec(ensures="unique(result) in ALIVE")
  Iterator<T> iterator();
  // Continues...
}
```

Figure 2. Iterator and collection interfaces annotated with access permission specifications.

the iterator API correctly, and wants to use the PLURAL modular typestate checker [5] to do so, but does not want to spend time writing specifications. In this program, a `Row` class acts as an abstraction of a spreadsheet row, and wraps an instance of the `Collection` class. Notably, the `createColIter` method on line 4 simply returns the result of the collection's `iterator` method. A number of uses of the column iterator in this program are similar to its use in the `copy` method, line 12, where the iterator's `next` method is called in a loop, and only when calls to the `hasNext` method return true. However, one use of the column iterator occurs in a test method, `testParseCSV` on line 22, which tests the ability to input data in CSV format. In this use, the `next` method is immediately called on iterator returned by the `createColIter` method (line 25). The reasoning is that, assuming the program is implemented correctly, the `parseCSVRow` method will return a non-empty row for the given inputs.

Here, let us concentrate on the specification to be inferred for the return value of the `createColIter` method (line 4). Traditional approaches would have difficulty inferring specifications here because different uses of the `createColIter` method give rise to conflicting constraints. The use of the method on line 25 implies that the returned value must be in the "HASNEXT" state. At the same time, the existing specification of the `iterator` method indicates that the iterator is returned in the "ALIVE" state, and this is consistent with its use in `copy` and all of the similar uses not shown. A traditional analysis would generate two constraints containing conflicting information, satisfaction of these constraints with a Boolean constraint solver would be impossible, and no specification would be produced.

In contrast, our approach builds logical constraints on top of probabilities, so that conflicting facts can coexist. ANEK will generate a constraint at line 25 saying that the return value of `createColIter` must be in the "HASNEXT" state *with high probability*, and will generate constraints at line 5, line 16 and all similar sites saying that the return value must be in the "ALIVE" state *with high probability*. The evidence for the "HASNEXT" state is outweighed by the evidence against it, and the "ALIVE" abstract state will be chosen for the return value. Such an inferred specification may cause a typestate checker to issue a warning on line 25.

While it may seem somewhat strange to infer specifications that are only mostly correct, and may indeed lead to analysis warnings, in practice [6] some number of false positives are inevitable when analyzing any large program, and practically-motivated programmers still desire to verify as much of their code as is possible. Note

```
1  class Row {
2    Collection<Integer> entries;
3
4    Iterator<Integer> createColIter() {
5      return entries.iterator();
6    }
7    void add(int val){...}
8    // Continues...
9  }
10
11 // Many similar uses of iterator exist
12 Row copy(Row original) {
13   Iterator<Integer> iter =
14     original.createColIter();
15   Row result = new Row();
16   while( iter.hasNext() ) {
17     result.add(iter.next());
18   }
19 }
20
21 @Test
22 void testParseCSV() {
23   Row r1 = parseCSVRow("1,2,3,4");
24   Row r2 = parseCSVRow("4,6,7,8");
25   int sum = r1.createColIter().next() +
26             r2.createColIter().next();
27   assert(sum,5);
28 }
```

Figure 3. An application using the iterator API for which specifications are needed.

also that the PLURAL static analysis is sound, so there are no safety concerns due to the approximative nature of the inference.

As a further benefit, ANEK's system of probabilistic constraints allows us to easily incorporate heuristic information from a variety of sources, heuristics which can be used to guide the inference process. This issue is relevant for inferring the specification on the returned value of the `createColIter` method. Each call to the `next` method of the iterator requires a full aliasing permission, as indicated by the specification in Figure 2. In the access permissions methodology, this indicates an exclusive modifying permission that can coexist with other read-only permissions. However, another permission, unique, which indicates an absence of any other references and is returned by the `iterator` method of the collection, is stronger than full, and can be used to satisfy the precondition of the `next` method as well. The question becomes, should the `createColIter` method be inferred to return a permission of type full or unique, in the absence of any other constraints? ANEK includes the heuristic that all method names beginning with "create" return unique permissions with higher probability, since they are, in practice, often wrappers for constructors. As returned permissions go, unique is the best choice whenever possible because it gives the strongest guarantees to callers. This heuristic applies to the `createColIter` method, and therefore is used to determine that the return permission specification should be unique.

In addition to encoding heuristics and allowing the generation of specifications in the face of conflicting constraints, probabilistic constraints also enable ANEK to perform inference in a modular fashion. One problem with many existing inference algorithms is that they lack scalability, since the entire program must be analyzed at once. ANEK, in contrast, is a modular algorithm that generates method summaries in the form of probabilities representing likely method specifications, which can then be refined as methods are analyzed and reanalyzed in an iterative fashion. Since the analysis is approximate, it suffices to run the inference algorithm for a fixed number of iterations without reaching a fixpoint (as is usually required by traditional iterative algorithms). Varying the number of iterations allows for a trade-off between specification accuracy and scalability.

ANEK infers specifications required by the PLURAL modular static typestate checker [3, 5]; these are method pre and postconditions that describe both the abstract states parameters must inhabit and aliasing permissions. The probabilistic constraints encode: (a) logical rules which determine how permissions can be used, and (b) heuristic rules which encode the most common or "best" specifications in various scenarios. These constraints form a model that represents a probabilistic view of the space of all possible specifications. A solution to this model results in specifications that are very likely. This paper makes the following contributions:

- We have developed a probabilistic specification inference algorithm that combines logical rules (that encode program invariants) with heuristic rules (that encode program intuitions) for generating typestate specifications that in practice is fast and generates good specifications.
- The algorithm generates probabilistic method summaries which enable a modular analysis that can scale the inference to large programs.
- We have evaluated ANEK on a number of small benchmark programs and one large open-source program containing 38,483 lines of code. The results for this large benchmark show that ANEK can quickly infer specifications that are both accurate and qualitatively similar to those written by hand, and at 5% of the time taken to manually discover and hand-code the specification. As a consequence, these programs can be verified by PLURAL automatically, with no user provided specifications.

This paper is organized as follows. Section 2 gives an overview of the problem and also some background on the PLURAL system. Section 3 defines the abstraction and constraint system in ANEK together with the inference algorithms. Section 4 describes our empirical evaluation of ANEK. And finally, Sections 5 and 6 describe the related work and conclusion respectively.

2. Background and Goals

The purpose of ANEK is to infer typestate specifications, which are then fed to PLURAL [3, 5], a static modular typestate checker for Java programs. With PLURAL, programs can be checked for correct protocol usage by examining one method at a time without ever having to reconsider methods previously analyzed (in a manner analogous to type-checking in most languages). In PLURAL, reference types are supplemented with specifications that act as type refinements. These refinements are flow-sensitive, so that they can change at each step of the program as objects change state (for example, as a file might change from open to closed). These refinements are called *access permissions*. An access permission includes information about the abstract state of an object and a succinct description of which operations any existing aliases to that object are permitted to perform. The need for tracking the abstract state of the reference is mostly straightforward. As a program reference transitions through the body of the method, PLURAL keeps track of the abstract state of the object as methods are called and as fields are read and assigned. When a method is called in the method currently under analysis, PLURAL will check the abstract states of each of the arguments and make sure they match the required states for each of the parameters to the method, as indicated by the method's specification.

But a modular checker also needs to know something about how objects might be aliased if it is to perform a sound static analysis. In the absence of any aliasing information, a sound modular checker would be forced to conservatively assume that just about every method call may modify the abstract states of all of the objects in the static context through other program references. The aliasing summary contained in each access permission informs the analysis when it can be sure an object is not being modified through other aliases, and when it must assume the object is. Because the aliasing summaries are checked for consistency, the entire process is sound.

The aliasing summaries used by PLURAL are called *permission kinds*, and there are five of them. Each permission kind associated with a reference determines whether or not modification can be performed through that reference, and whether or not other aliases, if they exist, can read or modify. The five permission kinds are summarized in Figure 4.

	Other aliases		
This Ref.	N/A	Can Read	Can Write
Can Read	Unique	Immutable	Pure
Can Write	Unique	Full	Share

Figure 4. The five permission kinds.

At the point in code where an object is constructed, the new reference is associated with a unique permission. From that point forward, new aliases can be introduced through a process known as *splitting*. For example, from a reference with unique permission, a new modifying alias can be introduced by destroying the original unique permission and creating two new share permissions, one for the original reference and one for the new reference. Alternatively, a single unique permission could be exchanged for one full permission and multiple pure permissions. PLURAL makes sure that these splits are done soundly, in a manner that respects the meaning of each permission introduced. Additionally, permissions are associated with fractional values which allow multiple weaker permissions to be combined into stronger ones in a process known as *merging*. This feature comes from existing work on fractional permissions [7].

The most common way to use PLURAL is for framework and library designers to annotate their APIs with access permission specifications. API clients can run PLURAL on their code to ensure that they are using the APIs correctly. If API objects are passed as method parameters or stored as fields in a client's program, then she may need to add a specification to her own program in order to inform the analysis what permissions are available.

Figure 2 shows a specification for the Iterator interface using access permissions. The `next` method requires an exclusive modifying permission (full) to the receiver which it returns to the caller. Before the call, the receiver must be in the "HASNEXT" state. The `hasNext` method, which does not need to modify the iterator object, takes a pure permission, which it returns to the caller.

2.1 Goals for ANEK

While the PLURAL approach is quite powerful, it has one major drawback; it requires programmers to write specifications at method boundaries. This has the nice benefit of enabling modular checking, but places an additional burden on the programmer who merely wants to ensure correct protocol usage. Therefore, ANEK has been designed to eliminate this burden by statically inferring the access permission specifications.

We envision programmers using ANEK and PLURAL in the following manner: First, developers of libraries and frameworks would continue to provide PLURAL annotations along with their APIs. This allows the most knowledgeable developers to build the abstractions specific to their APIs, and formally define the ways in which they must be used. Since an API is typically used by many client programs, this effort is amortized over all the users of the API. When a client wishes to use an API (annotated with specifications), however, they start by running the ANEK inference tool over their code. ANEK will see which API methods are being used and will infer appropriate PLURAL specifications in the client's code. With the new specifications, the programmer will then run PLURAL. Since PLURAL is a sound checker, if PLURAL passes the resulting program with the newly inferred annotations, it constitutes a guarantee that the programmer is using the API correctly, with little additional burden on the programmer's part.

ANEK's inference algorithm is probabilistic. In other words, it solves a number of probabilistic constraints in order to determine what specifications are *likely* to be used (rather than what specifications *must* be used). We have chosen to develop a probabilistic inference, as opposed to a more traditional, logical inference, for a number of reasons. Probabilistic constraints allow us to easily include heuristics, encoding intuitions gleaned from several years of experience writing such specifications. The specifications output by ANEK are therefore idiomatic, and in some sense are the most desirable specifications, rather than being just one of many satisfying specifications. But additionally, even the logical constraints, which encode basic invariants of access permissions that should always hold true, are encoded probabilistically. This allows ANEK to determine a solution even in the face of conflicting constraints, such as when a bug exists in the program under inference. Because PLURAL is a sound checker and will be run on the resulting specifications, there is no danger due to the approximation.

On the performance side, there are very real benefits to using an approximate approach. First, it can perform better than an exact approach. But more interestingly, such an approach allows us to infer specifications in a modular way. This is an important goal for ANEK since it allows inference to scale to larger programs. In the approach, probabilistic specification summaries describing the current most likely specification are placed at method boundaries. These summaries are refined and made more accurate over time, while still presenting an interface against which method bodies are locally inferred. The details of this algorithm are discussed in Section 3.4.

```
Row copy(Row original) {
  Iterator<Integer> iter =
    original.createColIter();
  Row result = new Row();
  while( iter.hasNext() ) {
    result.add( iter.next() );
  }
}
```

Figure 5. The copy method from Figure 3 whose representation is given in Figure 6

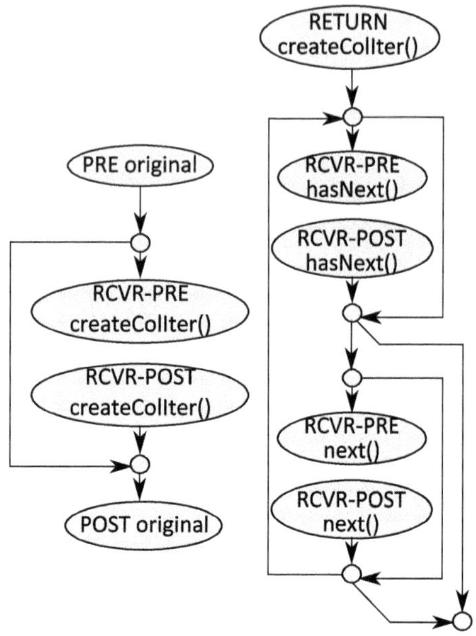

Figure 6. The PFG G_{copy} generated for the method copy in Figure 5.

3. The ANEK system

ANEK constructs a probabilistic constraint system that is based on logical and heuristic rules from an abstraction of the program under analysis. These constraints are solved in a modular fashion in order to compute the desired specifications.

3.1 Permissions Flow Graph

The inference algorithm performs inference over an abstraction of the program called the *Permissions Flow Graph* (PFG). A PFG is a directed graph of the flow of permissions in each method of a program. Permission flow itself is identical to a data flow except for two differences. First, at method call sites and field assignments, some amount of permission is retained in the calling or assigning context. Second, permission can flow *out* of the arguments at a method call site after the called method returns, representing the manner in which permission is returned to a calling argument at a call site. These are the only two differences.

A PFG G_m for a method m is constructed as follows: For each method parameter, including the receiver for instance methods, two nodes are created. One represents the permission required at the precondition and the other represents the permission returned at the postcondition. The flow of permission that originates at a parameter precondition and is transformed as it passes through a method body is represented using nodes and edges. A control flow graph is constructed in order to determine the flow of the permission. Additionally, a local must-alias analysis helps us track permission (which fundamentally are related to *objects*) even if those objects are reassigned to other local variables. If a variable is passed as an argument to a method, then the graph will contain a directed edge from the previous node in the graph to a node representing the precondition of the corresponding method argument and call site. The entire process is best explained with an example.

Consider the method `copy` shown in Figure 5. This method gives rise to the PFG G_{copy} shown in Figure 6. This figure ignores portions of the graph related to the `result` variable for simplicity. There are several interesting features worth pointing out.

First, note the path of the permission relating to the `original` variable, which appears on the left-hand side of the figure. This shows how methods calls are represented when there is no interesting control flow. The node "PRE original" is generated, which corresponds to the permission available to the `original` variable at the precondition of the `copy` method. This node is connected to a split node which itself has two successor nodes. The first successor is a node representing the precondition permission to the receiver of the `createColIter` method. The second successor is a permission merge node. The first edge represents the permission that is passed to the `createColIter` method, while the second edge represents the permission to the object that is retained by the `copy` method for the duration of the call. If a permission split is going to occur before the call, where a strong permission is converted to multiple weaker permissions, such as the case when a `unique` permission is available but only a `full` permission is needed for a call, it will be manifest at this split node. Next, a node representing the permission to the receiver node returned from the `createColIter` method is generated. It is important to note that this node has nothing to do with the return value of the `createColIter` method. It merely represents permission to the receiver that is no longer used by the method. The next node, the merge node, combines permission that was held at the call site with any permission returned by the method. Finally, the node "POST original" represents the permission available to the `original` object at the end of the method body.

The right-hand side of Figure 6, which represents the permission returned to the return value of the `createColIter` method, is quite similar. It contains two method calls whose structure is similar to the call to the `createColIter` method. However, because this method call occurs in a loop, there are additional edges to account for the possible control flow paths. For example, an edge connecting the receiver postcondition of the `hasNext` method and the end of the method body exists, and represents the flow of permission to the iterator when the `hasNext` method returns false.

```
Object accessFields(C o) {
  o.f = new Object();
  return o.f;
}
```

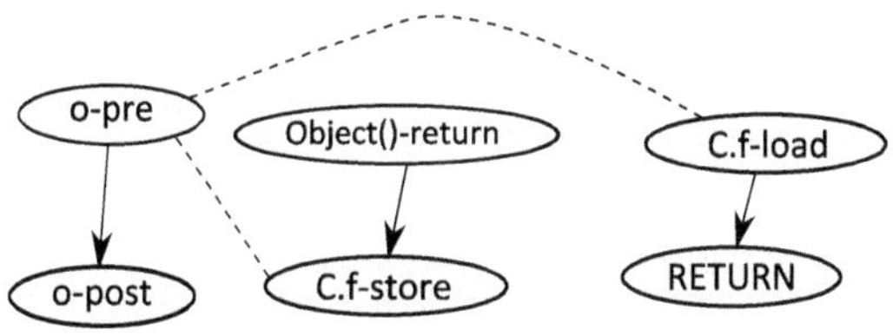

Figure 7. A permission graph containing field accesses and the program from which it was generated. The dotted line represents the reference a field access node maintains to its receiver.

For each field read and each field assignment in a program, a corresponding node is generated in the permission flow graph. Field read nodes will be connected via edges to the variables to which they are assigned, and act as permission sources. Field assignments act as permission sinks. They never contain outgoing edges, but will have incoming edges leading from the nodes from which they are assigned. All instance field read and assignment nodes will separately keep track of the receiver node from which they were accessed. In Figure 7, which illustrates a graph generated from field accesses, the relationship with the receiver node is represented as a dotted line.

3.2 Random variables and prior probabilities

Let $G_m = (V_m, E_m)$ be a PFG for a method m with node set V_m and edge set E_m. We associate each node $n \in V_m$ with five Bernoulli random variables X^n_{unique}, X^n_{full}, $X^n_{immutable}$, X^n_{share} and X^n_{pure}, one for each permission kind. Each variable models the probability that such a permission is available at the associated node. The variables are distributed according to $\mathcal{B}(p)$, a Bernoulli distribution with mean p. If, for instance, X^n_{unique} is distributed according to $\mathcal{B}(0.1)$, this means that node n has permission unique with probability 0.1.

Additionally, for each abstract state in the hierarchy of the type with which the node is associated, we have a random variable associated with that state. For instance, for a node associated with a parameter i where the parameter is an iterator, that node would have three random variables $X^i_{HASNEXT}$, X^i_{END}, X^i_{ALIVE}, one for each of its abstract states.

Each random variable is given a *prior distribution*. This prior distribution models our initial belief of how likely a given variable is to be $true$. For most of the variables ANEK creates, we have no information on their respective values (that is, $true$ or $false$), since we are trying to infer the specifications. For that reason, most variables are given a prior distribution equal to $\mathcal{B}(0.5)$ representing this lack of information. However, if a specification already exists in the source program, this strengthens our prior beliefs on how the variables are distributed. For example, consider the specification for the receiver parameter shown in Figure 8. Based on this specification,

```
@Perm(requires="full(this) in HASNEXT",
      ensures="full(this) in ALIVE")
T next() {...}
```

Figure 8. PLURAL specification for the receiver parameter.

ANEK will set the prior distributions for the variables associated with the receiver pre and postcondition nodes. For the precondition node, it will set the prior distributions for both the full permission kind and the "HASNEXT" abstract state to the distribution $\mathcal{B}(0.9)$ denoting the fact that both the full permission and "HASNEXT" abstract state are high probability events. The remaining variables will be given a low prior distribution of $\mathcal{B}(0.1)$. Therefore, the prior distributions for each of the random variables associated with the precondition node are as follows.

Random Variable	Prior Distribution
X_{unique}	$\mathcal{B}(0.1)$
X_{full}	$\mathcal{B}(0.9)$
$X_{immutable}$	$\mathcal{B}(0.1)$
X_{share}	$\mathcal{B}(0.1)$
X_{pure}	$\mathcal{B}(0.1)$
$X_{HASNEXT}$	$\mathcal{B}(0.9)$
X_{END}	$\mathcal{B}(0.1)$
X_{ALIVE}	$\mathcal{B}(0.1)$

It is important to note that even though the specification is given, we still say that the specification permission is only very likely to be $true$ (i.e., $true$ with a probability of 0.9). This allows for the possibility that the original specification was incorrect if the evidence against it (as inferred from the analysis) is overwhelming. Analogous to the nodes, each edge $e \in E_m$ in the PFG is also associated with a similar set of random variables $\{X^e_k\}$, where k is either a permission kind or an abstract state. This allows the distribution of one node to influence the distributions of adjacent nodes via the corresponding edge, as discussed in the next section.

3.3 The probabilistic constraint system

Setting the prior probabilities for the random variables in the PFG models our initial beliefs based on known specifications. Subsequently, we add probabilistic constraints over these random variables that are based on the features of the program itself. These constraints model dependencies that hold among the random variables. A solution to the constraints tells us for each node in PFG, which permission kind and which abstract state are most likely to be true.

We broadly classify all of the constraints that are added as being of one of two types, *logical* constraints or *heuristic* constraints. Logical constraints encode basic permission rules which must always hold, such as those governing sound permission splitting [5]. Heuristic constraints, on the other hand, encode features that are *generally* true of good PLURAL specifications. Importantly, even though the logical rules must always be true in a program verified by PLURAL, ANEK only dictates that they be true with some high probability. It is precisely this feature which allows ANEK to infer specifications even in the face of buggy programs. In the next two sections, we will present each of the constraint generation rules in turn. Each constraint generation rule is parametrized by some probability $h_n \in [0, 1]$ that represents high probability, and is given as input to the algorithm. Parametrization of these high probabilities allows us to tune the performance of inference.

3.3.1 Logical constraints

ANEK encodes the basic logic of access permissions through a series of logical constraints. The logical constraints labeled $L_1, \ldots, L_3$ are described below.

L_1: ***Outgoing Permissions*** At every node in the graph, the permission at the node must be related somehow to the permissions on its outgoing edges. If the node only has one outgoing edge, this is pretty easy. The edge and the node must have the exact same permission. So the following constraint is applied on the permission and state random variables associated with that node (n) and edge (e), with high probability:

$$\bigwedge_{k \in \{\mathsf{unique},\mathsf{full},\mathsf{immutable},\mathsf{share},\mathsf{pure}\} \cup \mathsf{states}(n)} X_k^n = X_k^e \,|_{h_1} \tag{1}$$

However, if there are multiple outgoing edges, the story is a little more complicated. Nodes can have multiple outgoing edges for one of two reasons. In some cases, it is because the permission at the node is being split into multiple permissions as new aliases are introduced. In other cases, the multiple edges are due to control flow branches in the original program. Since permission splits can only occur before method calls and field reads, we can mark these nodes as such, and apply different rules for splitting and control flow branches. At branches, we apply constraint 1 for each outgoing edge, mandating that the permission available at the node is equal to the permission available at each outgoing edge. For permission splits, however, the permission on the outgoing edges generally cannot be identical.

There are certain ways in which an access permission can be soundly split. For example, a unique permission can be split into two share permissions, two immutable permissions or two pure permissions. It cannot, however, be split into two full permissions or two unique permissions, as those two newly created permissions would violate the assumptions made by one another. Therefore, at each node, constraints are placed on the corresponding random variables that will enforce sound permission splitting. The (long) series of constraints is as follows:

$$\begin{aligned}
&((X_{unique}^n \wedge \textstyle\bigwedge_{e \in \mathsf{outgoing}(n)} \bigvee_{k \in \{\mathsf{unique},\mathsf{full},\mathsf{imm},\mathsf{share},\mathsf{pure}\}} X_k^e) \vee \\
&(X_{full}^n \wedge \textstyle\bigwedge_{e \in \mathsf{outgoing}(n)} \bigvee_{k \in \{\mathsf{full},\mathsf{imm},\mathsf{share},\mathsf{pure}\}} X_k^e) \vee \\
&(X_{imm}^n \wedge \textstyle\bigwedge_{e \in \mathsf{outgoing}(n)} \bigvee_{k \in \{\mathsf{imm},\mathsf{share},\mathsf{pure}\}} X_k^e) \vee \\
&(X_{share}^n \wedge \textstyle\bigwedge_{e \in \mathsf{outgoing}(n)} \bigvee_{k \in \{\mathsf{share},\mathsf{pure}\}} X_k^e) \vee \\
&(X_{pure}^n \wedge \textstyle\bigwedge_{e \in \mathsf{outgoing}(n)} X_{pure}^e)) \wedge \\
&\textstyle\bigwedge_{e \in \mathsf{outgoing}(n)} X_{unique}^e \Rightarrow \bigwedge_{e_2 \in \mathsf{outgoing}(n) - e} \neg(X_{unique}^{e_2} \vee X_{full}^{e_2}) \\
&\textstyle\bigwedge_{e \in \mathsf{outgoing}(n)} \bigwedge_{s \in \mathsf{states}(n)} X_s^e = X_s^n \,|_{h_2}
\end{aligned} \tag{2}$$

L_2: ***Incoming Permissions*** When a node has incoming edges, ANEK also adds constraints on the relationship between the incoming edge permissions and the node permission. Specifically, ANEK says that the permission associated with a node is equal to one of the permissions on the incoming edges with high probability. The following constraints are generated for a node n with incoming edges:

$$\bigvee_{e \in \mathsf{incoming}(n)} \bigwedge_{k \in \{\mathsf{unique},\mathsf{share},\mathsf{imm},\mathsf{share},\mathsf{pure}\} \cup \mathsf{states}(n)} X_k^n = X_k^e \,|_{h_3} \tag{3}$$

L_3: ***Field Write*** For any field store node (i.e., field assignment), the associated receiver node cannot be associated with one of the read-only permissions, immutable or pure. This constraint then sets the receiver to be immutable or pure with a very low probability. A field cannot be modified without writing permission to its receiver, so whenever we see a field store we know that we have writing permission to the receiver object.

3.3.2 Heuristic Constraints

For the random variables generated from a PFG, a series of additional "heuristic" constraints are also added. These constraints correspond to our intuitions about what makes a good PLURAL specification.

H_1: ***Constructors*** Constructors generally return unique permission, so for the specification for the object created by a constructor, we say that the variable X_{unique} is likely to be true with elevated probability. This is merely a heuristic since constructors do not have to return unique permission. Aliases can be introduced and stored in various data structures before the constructor returns.

H_2: ***Pre and Post*** For a given parameter of a method, the permission kind, but not the state, of the pre and postcondition nodes are the same with high probability. This is again a heuristic as it is possible for methods to retain an input permission and return a different permission.

H_3: ***Factory Methods*** Methods whose names begin with the word "create" usually return a unique permission, much like a constructor. These methods in practice are often static factory methods. Therefore, in our analysis, the return variable from such methods, X_{unique}, is true with elevated probability.

H_4: ***Setter Methods*** Methods whose names begin with the word "set" generally require a writing permission (i.e., unique, full or share) to their receiver, since they are often used to write to receiver fields. Therefore, when encountering such a method in the PFG, the variables $X_{immutable}$ and X_{pure} for the receiver pre and postcondition are constrained to be true with low probability.

H_5: ***Thread-Shared*** Targets of synchronized blocks are of full, share or pure permission with high probability. This heuristic is based on ideas developed in the concurrent version of the PLURAL analysis [3]. The permissions full, share and pure are the three permission kinds that may indicate possible thread-shared objects.

3.4 Probabilistic model and inference

In the previous section, we described how logical constraints L_1, L_2, L_3 and heuristic constraints H_1, H_2, H_3, H_4, H_5 can be derived from a PFG representation. We will now show how these constraints can be looked upon as a probabilistic model, in particular, a joint probability distribution describing the whole space of specifications.

Let $X_1, \ldots, X_n$ be n Bernoulli random variables where for each $1 \le i \le n$, X_i takes values from the domain $\{0, 1\}$. Let $p(X_1, \ldots, X_n)$ be a joint probability distribution function over these variables. Associated with $p(X_1, \ldots, X_N)$ are n *marginal functions* $p_i(X_i), 1 \le i \le n$ defined as:

$$p_i(X_i) = \sum_{X_1 \in \{0,1\}} \cdots \sum_{X_{i-1} \in \{0,1\}} \sum_{X_{i+1} \in \{0,1\}} \cdots \sum_{X_n \in \{0,1\}} p(X_1, \ldots, X_n) \tag{4}$$

where the sum is over all variables except X_i. Intuitively, the marginal function $p_i(X_i = a)$ corresponds to the probability of the variable X_i taking the value $a \in \{0, 1\}$. Since there are an exponential number of terms in the above equation, a naïve algorithm for computing $p_i(X_i)$ is not tractable. Suppose that $p(X_1, \ldots, X_n)$ can be written as a product of functions, where each function has some subset of $\{X_1, \ldots, X_n\}$ as its arguments, that is:

$$p(X_1, \ldots, X_n) = \prod_{j \in J} f_j(\mathcal{Z}_j) \tag{5}$$

where J is a discrete index set, $\mathcal{Z}_j \subseteq \{X_1, \ldots, X_n\}$ and $f_j(\mathcal{Z}_j)$ is a function having the elements of $\mathcal{Z}_j$ as arguments, with the interval $(0, 1]$ as its range, and the product is the usual pointwise product of functions. Given this factorization, there are a number of machine learning techniques that efficiently estimate the marginal functions by exploiting the fact that every factor is a function of small number of variables [14].

In our setting, each of the functions $f_j(\mathcal{Z}_j)$ in Equation 5 is a probabilistic constraint that describes either a logical constraint or a heuristic constraint as defined in Section 3.3. For instance, consider the conjunct $X^n_{share} = X^e_{share}\ |_{h_1}$ in Equation 1 (logical constraint L_1). This can be encoded as a probabilistic constraint as follows.

$$f(X^n_{share}, X^e_{share}) = \begin{cases} h_1 & \text{if } (X^n_{share} = X^e_{share}) \\ 1 - h_1 & \text{otherwise} \end{cases} \tag{6}$$

The pointwise product of such probabilistic constraints represents the probability space over specifications. The specifications are computed by sampling the marginal functions (defined by Equation 4) for the joint probability distribution. The problem of inferring specifications can be formally defined as follows:

Definition 1. *Let P be a program defined by a set of methods M, and let Π_m be the probabilistic model for a method $m \in M$ defined as follows.*

$$\Pi_m = \Gamma_m \cdot \left(\prod_{c \in \text{CALLSITES}(m)} \text{PARAMARG}(c) \right)$$

where Γ_m denotes the pointwise product of the logical and heuristic constraints associated with method m, and PARAMARG(c) *defines a set of equality constraints that bind the method m's parameters to their respective arguments at a call site c. The probabilistic model Π_P for the program P is the product of the probabilistic models for all its methods and defined as.*

$$\Pi_P = \prod_{m \in M} \Pi_m$$

Then, we are interested in computing marginal functions for the probabilistic model Π_P.

It is important to note that the specifications for the program can be easily derived from the marginal functions of Π_P via sampling. These marginal functions can be computed by using an off-the-shelf machine learning algorithm. However, a serious drawback of such an approach is that it would not be modular, thus severely limiting scalability.

We propose an inference procedure ANEK-INFER that is a modular analysis (shown in Figure 9). The set of all methods M in the program under analysis is the input to this procedure. $\mathcal{X}_m$ is the set of all random variables for a method m as defined in Section 3.2. We denote the PFG for method m by G_m. The probabilistic constraints system Γ_m is as defined in Definition 1.

In line 1, a worklist W of probabilistic models is initialized to the empty list. Next, in lines 2–6, for every method m:

(a) The random variables in $\mathcal{X}_m$ are initialized (described in Section 3.2).

(b) A probabilistic constraint system Γ_m is created by the procedure Model(G_m).

procedure ANEK-INFER

input:
  M: Set of all methods in the program

vars:
  $\mathcal{X}_m$: Set of all random variables for method m
  G_m: PFG for method m
  Γ_m: Probabilistic constraints for method m
  W: Worklist of probabilistic models
  π_m: Probabilistic summary for method m
  σ_m: A deterministic summary for method m

output:
  σ: Specification that maps every method to its deterministic summary

1: $W := \emptyset$
2: for each $m \in M$ do
3:   INIT($\mathcal{X}_m$)
4:   $\Gamma_m :=$ MODEL(G_m)
5:   $W := W \cup \{\Gamma_m\}$
6: end for
7: $count := 0$
8: while $count \leq MaxIters$ do
9:   $count := count + 1$
10:   $\Gamma_m :=$ CHOOSE(W)
11:   $W := W \setminus \{\Gamma_m\}$
12:   for each $c \in$ CALLSITES(m) do
13:     APPLYSUMMARY(Γ_m, π_c))
14:   end for
15:   $\mathcal{X}^{old}_m := \mathcal{X}_m$
16:   $\mathcal{X}_m :=$ SOLVE(Γ_m)
17:   if $\mathcal{X}_m \neq \mathcal{X}^{old}_m$ then
18:     UPDATESUMMARY($\pi_m, \mathcal{X}_m$)
19:     $W := W \cup \{\Gamma_m\}$
20:   end if
21: end while
22: for each $m \in M$ do
23:   for each $X \in \pi_m$ do
24:     if $p(X = true) > t$ then
25:       $\sigma_m(X) := true$
26:     end if
27:   end for
28:   $\sigma(m) := \sigma_m$
29: end for
30: return σ

Figure 9. The annotation inference algorithm ANEK-INFER.

(c) The worklist W is initialized to a list of probabilistic models for methods.

ANEK-INFER is an iterative algorithm (lines 8–21). In lines 10 and 11, a model Γ_m for method m is picked from the worklist W by the choice function CHOOSE(W) and removed from W. In lines 12–14, for every call site corresponding to a method c, a probabilistic summary π_c for that method is applied to the model Γ_m (where method m calls method c). A *probabilistic summary* π_c for method c is the set of all random variables associated with the precondition and postcondition nodes in its PFG G_c. Due to the initialization in line 3, all probabilistic summaries for methods are also appropriately initialized. A probabilistic summary maintains the current values of the random variables corresponding to the precondition and postcondition nodes for a method. The procedure Solve called in line 16 takes Γ_m as input and computes approximate

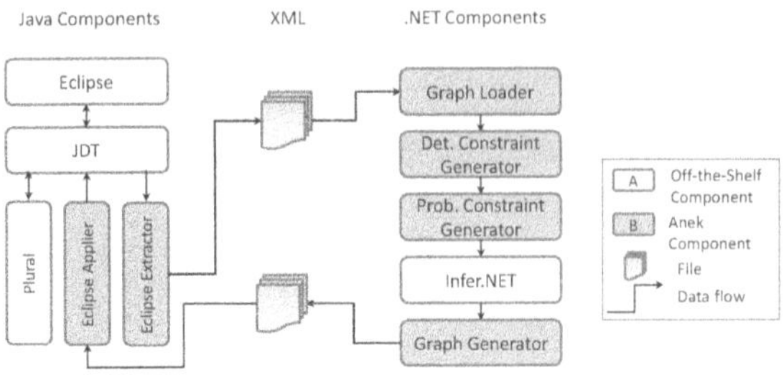

Figure 10. The architecture diagram for ANEK.

marginal functions[3] for the variables $\mathcal{X}_m$. We use an off-the-shelf machine learning algorithm to efficiently implement Solve. If the distributions associated with the random variables in $\mathcal{X}_m$ have changed, then the summary π_m for method m is updated via the procedure UPDATESUMMARY (line 18) and the model Γ_m is added to the worklist W (line 19). It is important to note that summaries are computed by analyzing each method once at a time and it is via these summaries that analysis information is disseminated across methods. This makes the ANEK-INFER algorithm a modular analysis.

The loop (8–21) is run $MaxIters$ number of times (as opposed to computing a fixpoint) which is another source of approximation. Lines 22–27 compute the specification from the probabilistic summaries for each procedure. If for each random variable X in the probabilistic summary π_m for a method m, the probability $p(X = true)$ is greater than a user-defined threshold $t \in [0.5, 1)$, then the deterministic value of that variable is set to $true$ and this information is stored in a map σ_m. This deterministic summary σ for all methods forms the specification that is returned by ANEK-INFER. It is interesting to note that the result computed by ANEK-INFER(M) at a fixpoint (corresponding to an exact computation) is identical to the result computed by SOLVE(Π_P).

4. Evaluation

In this section, we describe our implementation and report the empirical results of running the combination of ANEK and PLURAL on a number of Java benchmark programs. All experiments were performed on a system with a 3.19 GHz Intel Pentium 4 processor and 2 GB RAM running Microsoft Windows XP.

4.1 The ANEK Implementation

The architecture of ANEK is shown in Figure 10. Each component of ANEK is organized into a pipeline. The first component, the Eclipse Extractor, is a plugin to the Eclipse Java Development Tools (JDT), the Java IDE in Eclipse. Its job is to visit the Java AST generated by JDT for the program under inference and generate the abstract representation. This representation is stored to disk in an intermediate, XML-based format. This component is also responsible for the user interface, the menus and action items in Eclipse that allow users of PLURAL to run inference without ever leaving their IDE.

Once ANEK has generated an XML representation of the program, this representation is handed off to an F# program[4]. It begins by generating a number of constraints based on the shape of the program (Deterministic Constraint Generator). These are the constraints described in Section 3.3. However, at this phase each of the constraints is deterministic; there are no probabilities involved.

It is in the next component, the Probabilistic Constraint Generator, that the deterministic constraints are transformed into probabilistic ones and the ANEK-INFER algorithm is invoked. ANEK-INFER is implemented using INFER.NET [16], a library that exposes a number of abstractions, in the form of types and methods, which allow networks of probabilistic variables and constraints to be assembled and solved. If the most likely permission kind and abstract state, as determined by ANEK-INFER, is greater than some threshold value, then a generated graph representation will contain this newly inferred specification.

Finally, in the last component, the newly generated representation is applied to the original Java program inside another Eclipse plugin called the Eclipse Applier. This program walks through the AST of the original Java program and applies the new specification.

4.2 Experiments

In order to evaluate the utility of ANEK, we performed a number of small experiments and one main experiment. The goal was to see if ANEK would infer annotations that were correct and would not lead to a large number of false warnings when running the PLURAL tool.

First, we developed a number of test benchmarks. Each of these benchmarks consisted of one or more classes, with one or more methods, some of which were annotated by us before running the ANEK tool. Each experiment was designed to test some particular ANEK constraint or feature. During the experiments we would run ANEK on the test suite, and ensure that correct annotations were inferred, and that after inference PLURAL would report no warnings. At issue is the evolution of ANEK in response to newly perceived problems. One of the great benefits of ANEK's architecture is that it is so easy to evolve it by adding new constraints. Over the course of its implementation we added new constraints or modified existing constraints numerous times. However, we wanted to ensure that the new constraints, which may fix one particular problem, did not come at the expense of any previously-correct behavior. Therefore, our small experiment suite formed a regression suite of sorts and also as a training set to fine-tune the parameters of the inference engine.

Our primary experiment, though, was to use ANEK to infer annotations for the PMD static analysis framework (Table 1). In this experiment, the Java Iterator API was annotated and then ANEK was used to infer annotations within the PMD application, which makes extensive use of the API.

PMD	
Lines of Source:	38,483
Number of Classes:	463
Number of Methods:	3,120
Calls to Iterator.next():	170

Table 1. Simple statistics for the PMD application.

Specifically, PMD was used as the client-side case study in Kevin Bierhoff's doctoral thesis [4]. In his experiment, Bierhoff took an annotated Iterator API, ran PLURAL on PMD, and added

[3] Since we are only interested in estimating the likely values of the random variables and not their exact distributions, computing approximate marginal functions suffices for our purpose.

[4] http://research.microsoft.com/fsharp/fsharp.aspx

appropriate annotations **by hand** to the program until there were as few remaining warnings as possible. Our goal was essentially to replicate this experiment by using ANEK instead of doing any specification by hand.

Method	Annotations	Warnings	Time Taken
Original	0	45	0
Bierhoff	26	3	75min [4]
Anek	31	4	3min 47sec
Anek Logical	N/A	N/A	DNF

Table 2. The results of running ANEK on PMD.

Table 1 contains a number of basic statistics for the PMD application. Of particular note is the number of calls to the method, `java.util.Iterator.next`. This is important because the `next` method is the most important for verification purposes. It is the only method on the `Iterator` interface that requires the iterator instance to be in a particular state when called.

Table 2 shows the results of our experiments. We ran several experiments and recorded three statistics for each one. The first configuration is Original, where we ran PLURAL on PMD with no annotations at all, in its original form. The point of this experiment is just to show that *some* annotations must be inferred in the application in order to verify correct use of the Iterator API. To that end, PLURAL reported 45 warnings when run on the unannotated program. The next configuration, Bierhoff, is PMD as annotated by Bierhoff for his thesis work. Manual annotation took 75 minutes as reported in [4]. PLURAL reported three warnings, all of which were false positives. In these three cases, the `next` is called on an iterator without first calling the `hasNext` method to establish dynamically that the iterator has subsequent elements. In all three cases, other program invariants not expressed in PLURAL guarantee that the call to `next` will not fail at run-time because the underlying collection is known to be non-empty. In fact, these cases were quite similar to, and the insipration for the `testParseCSV` method from Figure 3.

The next experiment uses ANEK to infer annotations on PMD. The Anek configuration is the standard configuration. When running PLURAL on PMD with the annotations inferred by ANEK, four warnings are generated, and the inference process takes 3 minutes and 47 seconds. Of the four warnings, three are exactly the same warnings issued by PLURAL as in the Bierhoff configuration. The fourth warning, which is also a false-positive, can be attributed to a lack of branch-sensitivity. While the PLURAL static analysis takes the result of conditional expressions into account, ANEK currently does not, and therefore cannot infer the correct specification for a method that is only called in *true* branches of a conditional. As is evident from the experiments, ANEK performs as well as with hand-coded annotations, and at approximately 5% of the elapsed time and with no human involvement.

Finally, in addition to comparing ANEK to manual annotation, we wanted to compare it to a more traditional specification inference approach, specifically, approaches that are built on top of logical constraint solvers. While such an inference tool currently does not exist for PLURAL, two experiments were performed in an attempt to understand how such tools might perform.

First, we modified ANEK to add an additional Logical mode. In this configuration only logical constraints are considered and solved deterministically, while all heuristic constraints are turned off. In this experiment, Anek Logical was run on PMD in an attempt to infer specifications. When this was done, the inference procedure ran out of memory before a fixed point was reached, and therefore no results could be presented.

Our second attempt to compare ANEK to a traditional inference algorithm relies on PLURAL's own local permission inference.

Inference Tool	Time Taken	Warnings
ANEK	22 sec	0
Plural Local Inference	181 sec	0

Table 3. The results of running ANEK on a test program to compare performance again Plural's local inference

While PLURAL requires annotations on method boundaries it uses a local permission inference so that programmers do not have to write annotations on local variables. This analysis is responsible for determining which fractions of permissions are consumed and returned by different parts of a method body, for finding a satisfying assignment for all of the various permission constraints imposed by all of the called methods and returned permissions. The underlying algorithm relies upon Gaussian Elimination to find satisfying fractional permission assignments [4, ch. 5]. The overall approach is comparable to other similar fractional inference algorithms [19]. In order to use PLURAL's local inference as a point of comparison, we took a small test program crafted for this experiment which contained numerous short methods and ran ANEK on it to infer method specifications. Then, in a second run, we inlined each method so that the resulting program consists of one single large method and ran PLURAL on this program. Both inference tools end up doing the same work, since by solving permission constraints for the entire large method body, PLURAL is essentially inferring which permissions must be available at the same points as ANEK. Table 3 shows the results for this experiment. The program under inference is small (400 lines) but contains numerous control flow branches. ANEK performed well, doing the same inference task in roughly one ninth of the time.

4.3 Discussion

In this section, we will discuss the results of our experiment and their ramifications. Overall, we were quite pleased with the results of the experiment. In approximately 5% of the time it took to annotate the program by hand, ANEK was able to infer specifications that were almost as good, and with no human involvement. Specifically, the specifications inferred by ANEK lead to four warnings when the PLURAL tool was subsequently run on the result, versus three warnings from hand-written specifications. This difference of one warning is entirely due to ANEK's lack of path-sensitivity in its inference scheme, a feature PLURAL itself supports. Precision-wise, ANEK does a very good job with the annotations it infers. Moreover, when compared with other PLURAL case studies where annotations were applied manually [6], the PMD case study went very quickly. Often it takes several hours to manually annotate a code base, so we expect to see even bigger time savings on future experiments.

While our experiments comparing ANEK to logical inference tools were somewhat rough, they suggest that ANEK can outperform traditional-style inference tools. We largely attribute this to the use of approximation algorithms for probabilistic constraint solving.

We also claimed that our approach is a good idea because probabilistic permissions enable reasoning in the face of conflicting constraints. This feature was needed for our PMD experiment because of the three locations in which the `next` method was called without a proceeding call to `hasNext`. Just as in the example presented in the introduction, the conflicting constraints introduced by such calls were tolerated, and satisfactory specifications were still inferred rather than ANEK giving up. Given that the remaining 167 calls to the `next()` method were correctly verified by PLURAL, the resulting specifications are still quite useful to programmers.

Description	Count
Same	14
ANEK Added Helpful Spec.	6
ANEK Added Constraining Spec.	1
ANEK Removed Spec.	3
ANEK Changed Spec., More Restrictive	6
ANEK Changed Spec., Wrong	3

Table 4. Comparison of by-hand annotations with Anek

The quality of the specifications inferred by ANEK is generally good. Table 4 summarizes the annotations inferred. Specifically, these numbers are for the specifications inferred by ANEK with respect to the hand-specified version (Bierhoff). 14 of the specifications were exactly the same. ANEK inferred 6 specifications that were correct, potentially useful in future versions of the application and imposed no additional proof burden. In one case ANEK added a specification that was not necessary and may, in the future, cause additional proof burdens. In 3 cases, ANEK did not infer a specification that was present in the hand-specified version. All three of these were related to dynamic state test methods, which ANEK currently does not attempt to infer. The removed specifications were immaterial because at all use sites, a super-type specification took precedence. In 6 places, ANEK changed an existing specification to make it more restrictive, which, while not causing any additional errors now, may lead to additional proof burdens in future versions of the application. Finally, 3 specifications were wrong outright. One of these incorrect specifications led to the additional warning. The other two did not affect verification at all.

One nice benefit of creating an analysis based on probabilistic constraints is the ease of design. It turned out to be quite easy to add new constraints. As we went through our design iterations, we started with a basic suite of probabilistic constraints that we thought would yield good results. However, on some of our small benchmarks, we found that for one reason or another these constraints were not quite yielding the expected results. Fortunately, it is quite easy to add new constraints. So, as we realized that one constraint was overly specific, or that another, say, did not work in all situations, it was trivial to add a new constraint so that the results would be more to our liking.

5. Related work

Our work is related to MERLIN [15], a tool based on probabilistic analysis for inferring security annotations useful for detecting information flow vulnerabilities. In general, the specifications ANEK infers are much more detailed and intricate behavioral properties than those inferred by MERLIN. Furthermore, ANEK introduces a general framework that is based on the philosophy of combining logical rules with heuristic rules. As such, ANEK must know much more about the details of each function's behavior. In contrast, MERLIN's annotation inference is based on how functions are used in the implementation and does not rely on the function's actual behavior. Moreover, the inference in MERLIN is not modular and this limits its scalability. Additionally, with ANEK, we have the nice feature that after specifications are inferred, a sound static analysis can be run, verifying the results of the inference and acting as a safety net. For MERLIN, such a tool was unavailable.

Kremenek et al. [13] propose a technique for inferring ownership annotations that is also based on a probabilistic analysis. Like MERLIN, this analysis also infers less expressive specification and is not modular.

Dietl [9] developed a global analysis for inferring Universe Type annotations using a SAT solver. Besides the fact that we are inferring typestate annotations, the primary difference between this work and ours is that it requires satisfiability. If a program has bugs and therefore has no valid ownership type, the inference will fail with unsatisfiable constraints. On the other hand, ANEK will always produce the best possible specification.

Terauchi [19] proposed a global analysis for inferring fractional permissions in order to verify a lack of race conditions. While the methodology itself solves a problem that might be useful in our work, their underlying methodology is much different, since they do not use probabilistic constraints. Presumably such an analysis would have to give up when confronted with false positives of the sort we encountered in our case study.

Houdini [10] is an annotation inference engine for the ESC/Java tool [12]. It first heuristically generates a number of candidate annotations or invariants and subsequently, incorrect annotations are pruned away by invoking ESC/Java. This is similar to the manner in which the specifications inferred by ANEK are checked by PLURAL in order to ensure soundness of verification.

An important line of work has addressed the related but different problem of *protocol inference*. Such approaches have used static [1, 17, 20] and dynamic [21, 22] analysis to determine which classes in a program place restrictions on the ordering of their method calls, and attempt to infer a specification for their correct usage. The dynamic approaches generally use statistical methods to determine which sequences of method calls represent protocols, and which are merely due to coincidence. While the problem of inferring protocols is different from the problem of inferring aliasing annotations, these approaches clearly complement our own, and in the future we plan to investigate their combination.

6. Conclusion

In this paper we presented ANEK, a probabilistic specification inference tool that can be used to infer access permissions for use in modular typestate checking. ANEK is novel in that it is modular and is built using probabilistic constraints. These constraints allow us as developers to easily encode into the analysis our understanding of what makes a good specification. Probabilistic constraints also make ANEK robust to bugs in the program under inference and enable a modular analysis. In order to evaluate our approach, we used ANEK to infer specifications for PMD, mimicking a case study that was performed by Bierhoff [4] by hand as part of his Ph.D. thesis. The results were good – in fact, the specifications inferred by ANEK were nearly as good as those written by hand and were obtained in approximately 5% of the time it took to manually discover them.

Acknowledgments

We thank G. Ramalingam for suggesting the idea of classifying ANEK's constraints as logical and heuristic constraints. We also thank Jonathan Aldrich, Akash Lal and Sriram Rajamani for their invaluable comments. Thanks are also due to John Winn for help with using the INFER.NET API. The first author was supported by several grants including DARPA grant #HR0011-0710019, NSF grant CCF-0811592, R&D Project Aeminium CMU-PT/SE/0038/2008 in the CMUPortugal program, Army Research Office grant #DAAD19-02-1-0389 entitled "Perpetually Available and Secure Information Systems," the Department of Defense, the Software Industry Center at CMU and its sponsors, especially the Alfred P. Sloan Foundation and a National Science Foundation Graduate Research Fellowship (DGE-0234630).

References

[1] R. Alur, P. Černý, P. Madhusudan, and W. Nam. Synthesis of interface specifications for java classes. In *POPL '05: Principles of Programming Languages*, pages 98–109, 2005.

[2] M. Barnett and K. R. M. Leino. Weakest-precondition of unstructured programs. In *PASTE '05: Program Analysis For Software Tools and Engineering*, pages 82–87, 2005.

[3] N. E. Beckman, K. Bierhoff, and J. Aldrich. Verifying correct usage of atomic blocks and typestate. In *OOPSLA '08: Object Oriented Programming Systems, Languages, and Applications*, pages 227–244, 2007.

[4] K. Bierhoff. *API Protocol Compliance in Object-Oriented Software*. PhD thesis, Carnegie Mellon University, April 2009.

[5] K. Bierhoff and J. Aldrich. Modular typestate checking of aliased objects. In *OOPSLA '07: Object Oriented Programming Systems, Languages and Applications*, pages 301–320, 2007.

[6] K. Bierhoff, N. E. Beckman, and J. Aldrich. Practical API protocol checking with access permissions. In *ECOOP '09: European Conference on Object-Oriented Programming*, pages 195–219, July 2009.

[7] J. Boyland. Checking interference with fractional permissions. In *SAS '03: Static Analysis Symposium*, pages 55–72. Springer, 2003.

[8] J. Condit, B. Hackett, S. K. Lahiri, and S. Qadeer. Unifying type checking and property checking for low-level code. In *POPL '09: Principles of Programming Languages*, pages 302–314, 2009.

[9] W. Dietl. *Universe Types: Topology, Encapsulation, Genericity, and Tools*. PhD thesis, ETH Zurich, December 2009.

[10] C. Flanagan and K. R. M. Leino. Houdini, an annotation assistant for ESC/Java. In *FME '01: International Symposium of Formal Methods Europe*, pages 500–517, 2001.

[11] C. Flanagan, K. R. M. Leino, M. Lillibridge, G. Nelson, J. B. Saxe, and R. Stata. Extended static checking for java. In *PLDI '02: Programming Language Design and Implementation*, pages 234–245, 2002.

[12] C. Flanagan, K. R. M. Leino, M. Lillibridge, G. Nelson, J. B. Saxe, and R. Stata. Extended static checking for Java. In *PLDI '02: Programming Language Design and Implementation*, pages 234–245, 2002.

[13] T. Kremenek, P. Twohey, G. Back, A. Ng, and D. Engler. From uncertainty to belief: Inferring the specification within. In *OSDI '06: Operating Systems Design and Implementation*, pages 161–176, 2006.

[14] F. R. Kschischang, B. J. Frey, and H. A. Loeliger. Factor graphs and the sum-product algorithm. *IEEE Transactions on Information Theory*, 2(47):498–519, 2001.

[15] B. Livshits, A. V. Nori, S. K. Rajamani, and A. Banerjee. Merlin: specification inference for explicit information flow problems. In *PLDI '09: Programming Language Design and Implementation*, pages 75–86, 2009.

[16] T. Minka, J. Winn, J. Guiver, and D. Knowles. Infer.NET 2.4, 2010. Microsoft Research Cambridge. http://research.microsoft.com/infernet.

[17] M. K. Ramanathan, A. Grama, and S. Jagannathan. Static specification inference using predicate mining. In *PLDI '07: Programming Language Design and Implementation*, pages 123–134, 2007.

[18] R. E. Strom and S. Yemini. Typestate: A programming language concept for enhancing software reliability. *IEEE Trans. Softw. Eng.*, 12(1):157–171, 1986.

[19] T. Terauchi. Checking race freedom via linear programming. In *PLDI '08: Programming Language Design and Implementation*, pages 1–10, 2008.

[20] J. Whaley, , M. C. Martin, , and M. S. Lam. Automatic extraction of object-oriented component interfaces. In *ISSTA '02: International Symposium on Software Testing and Analysis*, pages 218–228, 2002.

[21] J. Yang, D. Evans, D. Bhardwaj, T. Bhat, and M. Das. Perracotta: Mining temporal API rules from imperfect traces. In *ICSE '06: International Conference on Software engineering*, pages 282–291, 2006.

[22] H. Zhong, T. Xie, L. Zhang, J. Pei, and H. Mei. MAPO: Mining and recommending API usage patterns. In *ECOOP '09: European Conference on Object-Oriented Programming*, pages 318–343, 2009.

Predicate Abstraction and CEGAR for Higher-Order Model Checking

Naoki Kobayashi
Tohoku University
koba@ecei.tohoku.ac.jp

Ryosuke Sato
Tohoku University
ryosuke@kb.ecei.tohoku.ac.jp

Hiroshi Unno
Tohoku University
uhiro@kb.ecei.tohoku.ac.jp

Abstract

Higher-order model checking (more precisely, the model checking of higher-order recursion schemes) has been extensively studied recently, which can automatically decide properties of programs written in the simply-typed λ-calculus with recursion and *finite* data domains. This paper formalizes predicate abstraction and counterexample-guided abstraction refinement (CEGAR) for higher-order model checking, enabling automatic verification of programs that use *infinite* data domains such as integers. A prototype verifier for higher-order functional programs based on the formalization has been implemented and tested for several programs.

Categories and Subject Descriptors D.2.4 [*Software Engineering*]: Software/Program Verification; F.3.1 [*Logics and Meanings of Programs*]: Specifying and Verifying and Reasoning about Programs

General Terms Languages, Reliability, Verification

Keywords Predicate Abstraction, CEGAR, Higher-Order Model Checking, Dependent Types

1. Introduction

The model checking of higher-order recursion schemes (*recursion schemes*, for short) has been extensively studied [19, 24, 28], and recently applied to verification of functional programs [20, 22, 26]. Recursion schemes are grammars for describing infinite trees [19, 28], and the recursion scheme model checking is concerned about whether the tree generated by a recursion scheme satisfies a given property. It can be considered an extension of finite state and pushdown model checking, where the model checking of order-0 and order-1 recursion schemes respectively correspond to finite state and pushdown model checking. From a programming language point of view, a recursion scheme is a term of the simply-typed, call-by-name λ-calculus with recursion and tree constructors, which generates a single, possibly infinite tree. Various verification problems for functional programs can be easily reduced to recursion scheme model checking problems [20, 22, 26]. Thanks to the decidability of recursion scheme model checking [28], the reduction yields a sound, complete, and automatic verification method for programs written in the simply-typed λ-calculus with recursion and *finite* data domains (such as booleans).

There is, however, still a large gap between the programs handled by the above-mentioned method and real functional programs. One of the main limitations is that infinite data domains such as integers and lists cannot be handled by the recursion scheme model checking. To overcome that limitation, this paper extends the techniques of predicate abstraction [12] and counterexample-guided abstraction refinement (CEGAR) [4, 8] for higher-order model checking (i.e., recursion scheme model checking).

The overall structure of our method is shown in Figure 1. Given a higher-order functional program, predicate abstraction is first applied to obtain a higher-order boolean program (Step 1 in Figure 1). For example, consider the following program M_1:

```
let f x g = g(x+1) in let h y = assert(y>0) in
let k n = if n>0 then f n h else () in k(randi())
```

Here, `assert` takes a boolean as an argument and is reduced to `fail` if the argument is false. The function `randi` returns a non-deterministic integer value. Using a predicate $\lambda x.x > 0$, we obtain the following higher-order boolean program e_1:

```
let f b g = if b then g(true) else g(randb()) in
let h c = assert(c) in
let k () = if randb() then f true h else () in k()
```

Here, `randb` returns a non-deterministic boolean value. Note that the integer variables `x` and `y` have been replaced by the boolean variable `b` and `c` respectively, which represents whether the values of `x` and `y` are greater than 0. In the abstract version of `f`, `b` being true means that `x>0`, which implies `x+1>0`, so that `true` is passed to `g` in the then-part. In the else-part, `x<=0`, hence `x+1>0` may or may not hold, so that a non-deterministic boolean value is passed to `g`. The higher-order boolean program thus obtained is an abstraction of the source program; for any reduction sequence of the source program, there is a corresponding reduction sequence of the higher-order boolean program (but not vice versa). Thus, for example, if the abstract program does not cause an assertion failure, neither does the source program.

The higher-order boolean program is then represented as a recursion scheme and model-checked by using an existing recursion scheme model checker [21, 22] (Step 2 in Figure 1). If the higher-order boolean program satisfies a given safety property,[1] the source program is also safe. Otherwise, an error path of the boolean program is inspected (Step 3 in Figure 1). If it is also an error path of the source program, then it is reported that the program is unsafe. Otherwise, new predicates are extracted from the error path, in order to refine predicate abstraction (Step 4 in Figure 1).

PLDI'11, June 4–8, 2011, San Jose, California, USA.

[1] For the sake of simplicity, throughout the paper, we only consider the reachability property.

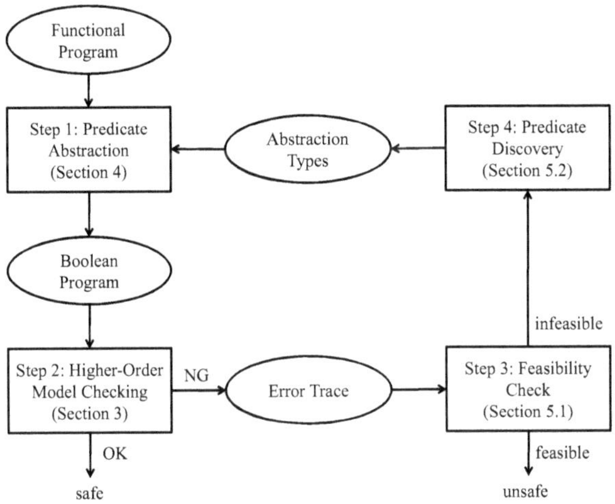

Figure 1. Higher-Order Model Checking with Predicate Abstraction and CEGAR

In the example above, we actually start predicate abstraction with the empty set of predicates, and obtain the following abstract program e_0:

```
let f g = g() in let h () = assert(randb()) in
let k () = if randb() then f h else () in k()
```

The model checking of this program yields the following reduction sequence, leading to an assertion failure:

```
k() ⟶ if randb() then f h else ()
⟶ if true then f h else () ⟶ f h
⟶ h() ⟶ assert (randb())
⟶ assert (false) ⟶ fail                ···(1)
```

The corresponding reduction sequence in the source program M_1 is:

```
k n ⟶ if n>0 then f n h else () ⟶n>0 f n h
⟶ h(n+1) ⟶ assert (n+1>0) ⟶n+1<=0 fail   ···(2)
```

Here, n is some integer, and we have annotated the sequence with the conditions that should hold at each step. As n>0 $\wedge$ n+1<=0 is unsatisfiable, we know that the reduction sequence above is actually infeasible, so that the source program may not cause an assertion failure. From the unsatisfiable constraint above, we can learn that information about whether an integer is positive is useful. By using it, we get the refined abstract program shown earlier. As the new abstract program is safe (i.e. does not cause an assertion failure), we can conclude that the source program is also safe.

The idea sketched above is basically the same as the techniques for predicate abstraction and CEGAR used already in finite state and pushdown model checking [4, 8], except that models have been replaced by higher-order boolean programs (or recursion schemes). As discussed below, however, it turned out that there are many challenging problems in developing effective methods for predicate abstraction and CEGAR for higher-order model checking.

First, for predicate abstraction, it is unreasonable to use the same set of predicates for all the integer variables. For example, let us modify the program above into the following program M_2:

```
let f x g = g(x+1) in let h y = assert(y>0) in
let k n = if n>=0 then f n h else () in k(randi())
```

Then, the predicate $\lambda\nu.\nu \geq 0$ should be used for x, while $\lambda\nu.\nu > 0$ should be used for y. We should consistently use predicates; for example, with the choice of the predicates above, g's argument should be abstracted by using $\lambda\nu.\nu > 0$, rather than $\lambda\nu.\nu \geq 0$. We use *types* (called *abstraction types*) to express which predicate should be used for each variable. For example, for the above program, the following abstraction types are assigned to f, h, and k:

$$f : \mathtt{int}[\lambda\nu.\nu \geq 0] \to (\mathtt{int}[\lambda\nu.\nu > 0] \to \star) \to \star$$
$$h : \mathtt{int}[\lambda\nu.\nu > 0] \to \star \qquad k : \mathtt{int}[\,] \to \star$$

The type of f means that the first argument of f should be an integer abstracted by the predicate $\lambda\nu.\nu \geq 0$, and the second argument be a function that takes an integer abstracted by the predicate $\lambda\nu.\nu > 0$ as an argument and returns a unit value.[2] By using these abstraction types, the problem of checking that predicates are consistently used boils down to a type checking problem. For example, the standard rule for application:

$$\frac{\Gamma \vdash M : \tau_1 \to \tau_2 \qquad \Gamma \vdash N : \tau_1}{\Gamma \vdash MN : \tau_2}$$

ensures that N is abstracted using the predicates expected by the function M; there is no such case that an abstraction of function M expects a value abstracted by using the predicate $\lambda\nu.\nu > 0$ but the actual argument N is abstracted by using $\lambda\nu.\nu \geq 0$.

A further twist is necessary to deal with multi-ary predicates. For example, consider the following modified version M_3:

```
let f x g = g(x+1) in let h z y = assert(y>z) in
let k n = if n>=0 then f n (h n) else () in
  k(randi())
```

The variable y should now be abstracted by using $\lambda\nu.\nu >$ z, which depends on the value of z. Thus, the above program should be abstracted by using the following *dependent* abstraction types:

$$f : (x : \mathtt{int}[\,] \to (w : \mathtt{int}[\lambda\nu.\nu > x] \to \star) \to \star)$$
$$h : (z : \mathtt{int}[\,] \to y : \mathtt{int}[\lambda\nu.\nu > z] \to \star) \qquad k : \mathtt{int}[\,] \to \star$$

Here, please note that the types of the second arguments of f and h refer to the values of the first arguments. Thus, our type system for ensuring the consistency of predicates is actually a *dependent* one. A predicate abstraction algorithm is then formalized as a type-directed transformation relation $\Gamma \vdash M : \tau \Rightarrow e$ based on the dependent abstraction type system, where M is a source program and e is an abstract program.[3]

The predicate abstraction mentioned above is sound in the sense that if an abstract program is safe (i.e., does not reach **fail**), so is the source program. Further, we can show that it is relatively complete with respect to a dependent (refinement) intersection type system [32]: If a source program is typable in the dependent intersection type system, our predicate abstraction can generate a safe abstract boolean program by using certain abstraction types. This means that, as long as suitable predicates are provided (by a user or an automated method like the CEGAR discussed below), the combination of our predicate abstraction and higher-order model checking has at least the same verification power as (and actually strictly more expressive than, as discussed later: see Remark 1 in Section 4) the dependent intersection type system. Here, note that we need only atomic predicates used in the dependent types; higher-order model checking can look for arbitrary boolean combinations of the atomic predicates as candidates of dependent types. Thus, this part alone provides a good alternative to Liquid types [31], which also asks users to provide templates of predicates, and infers dependent

[2] Here, abstraction types should not be confused with refinement types [35]; the abstraction type of a term only tells how the term should be abstracted, not what are possible values of the term. For example, integer 3 can have type $\mathtt{int}[\lambda\nu.\nu < 0]$ (and it will be abstracted to the boolean value *false*).

[3] To avoid the confusion, we call dependent abstraction types just *abstraction types* below. We use the term "dependent types" to refer to ordinary dependent types used for expressing refinement of simple types.

types. Thanks to the power of higher-order model checking, however, our technique can infer dependent, *intersection* types unlike Liquid types.

We now discuss the CEGAR part. Given an error path of an abstract boolean program, we can find a corresponding (possibly infeasible) error path of the source program. Whether the error path is feasible in the source program can be easily decided by symbolically executing the source program along the error path, and checking whether all the branching conditions in the path are satisfiable (recall the example given earlier). The main question is, if the error path turns out to be infeasible, how to find a suitable refinement of abstraction types, so that the new abstraction types yield an abstract boolean program that does not contain the infeasible error path. This has been well studied for first-order programs [2–4, 8, 13–15], but it is not clear how to lift those techniques to deal with higher-order programs.

Our approach to finding suitable abstraction types is as follows. From a source program and its infeasible error path, we first construct a *straightline higher-order program* (abbreviated to SHP) that exactly corresponds to the infeasible path, and contains neither recursion nor conditional branches. In the case of the program M_3 above, this is easily obtained, as follows:

```
let f1 x g = g(x+1) in let h1 z y = assert(y>z) in
let k1 n = assume(n>=0); f1 n (h1 n) in k1(c)
```

Here, `c` is a constant, and `assume`(b) evaluates b, and proceeds to the next instruction only if b is true. (But unlike `assert`, it is not reduced to `fail` even if b is false.) For general programs that contain recursions, the construction is more involved: see Section 5.

For SHP, a standard dependent (refinement) type system is sound and *complete*, in the sense that a program does not reach `fail` if and only if the program is typable in the type system. Further, (a sub-procedure of) previous algorithms for inferring dependent types based on interpolants [32, 33] is actually complete (modulo the assumption that the underlying logic is decidable and interpolants can always be computed) for SHP. Thus, we can automatically infer the dependent type of each function in the straightline program. For example, for the program above, we obtain:

$$\begin{aligned}&\texttt{f1} : (x : \texttt{int} \to (y : \{\nu : \texttt{int} \mid \nu > x\} \to \star) \to \star)\\ &\texttt{h1} : (z : \texttt{int} \to y : \{\nu : \texttt{int} \mid \nu > z\} \to \star)\\ &\texttt{k1} : (z : \texttt{int} \to \star)\end{aligned}$$

Here, the type of `h1` means that given integers z and y such that $y > z$, $\texttt{h1}\, z\, y$ returns a unit value without reaching `fail`. (These dependent types should not be confused with abstraction types: the latter only provides information about how the source program should be abstracted.)

We then refine the abstraction type of each function in the source program with predicates occurring in the dependent types of the corresponding functions in the SHP. For example, given the above dependent types, we get the following abstraction types:

$$\begin{aligned}&\texttt{f} : (x : \texttt{int}[\,] \to (y : \texttt{int}[\lambda\nu.\nu > x] \to \star) \to \star)\\ &\texttt{h} : (z : \texttt{int}[\,] \to y : \texttt{int}[\lambda\nu.\nu > z] \to \star) \qquad \texttt{k} : \texttt{int}[\,] \to \star\end{aligned}$$

We can show that the abstraction types inferred in this manner are precise enough, in that the abstract program obtained by using the new abstraction types no longer has the infeasible error path. (Thus, the so-called "progress" property is guaranteed as in CEGAR methods for finite-state or pushdown model checking.)

Based on the predicate abstraction and CEGAR techniques mentioned above, we have implemented a prototype verifier for (simply-typed) higher-order functional programs with recursion and integer base types, and tested it for several programs.

Our contributions include: (i) the formalization of predicate abstraction for higher-order programs, based on the novel notion of abstraction types, (ii) the formalization of CEGAR for higher-order programs, based on the novel notion of SHP and reduction of the predicate discovery problem to dependent type inference, (iii) theoretical properties like the relative completeness of our method with respect to a dependent intersection type, the progress property, etc., and (iv) the implementation and preliminary experiments.

The rest of this paper is structured as follows. Section 2 introduces the source language, and Section 3 introduces a language of higher-order boolean programs, and reviews the result on higher-order model checking. Sections 4 and 5 respectively formalize predicate abstraction and CEGAR for higher-order programs. Section 6 reports our prototype implementation and preliminary experiments. Section 7 discusses related work, and Section 8 concludes. For the space restriction, proofs are omitted, which are available in a full version [25].

2. Language

This section introduces a simply-typed, higher-order functional language, which is used as the target of our verification method.

We assume a set $\mathbf{B} = \{b_1, \ldots, b_n\}$ of data types, and a set $[\![b_i]\!]$ of constants, ranged over by c, for each data type b_i. We also assume that there are operators $\mathrm{op} : b_{i_1}, \ldots, b_{i_k} \to b_j$; we write $[\![\mathrm{op}]\!]$ for the function denoted by op. We assume that the set of data types includes $\star$ with $[\![\star]\!] = \langle\rangle$, and `bool` with $[\![\texttt{bool}]\!] = \{\texttt{true}, \texttt{false}\}$, and that the set of operators includes $= : b, b \to \texttt{bool}$ for every $b \in \mathbf{B}$, and boolean connectives such as $\wedge : \texttt{bool}, \texttt{bool} \to \texttt{bool}$.

The syntax of the language is given by:

$$\begin{aligned}D\ (\text{program}) \quad &::= \quad \{f_1\, \widetilde{x}_1 = e_1, \ldots, f_m\, \widetilde{x}_m = e_m\}\\ e\ (\text{expressions}) \quad &::= \quad c \mid x\, \widetilde{v} \mid f\, \widetilde{v} \mid \texttt{let}\ x = e_1\ \texttt{in}\ e_2 \mid \mathrm{op}(\widetilde{v})\\ &\quad\ \mid \quad \texttt{fail} \mid \texttt{assume}\ v; e \mid e_1 \,\Box\, e_2\\ v\ (\text{values}) \quad &::= \quad c \mid x \mid f\, \widetilde{v}\end{aligned}$$

Here, $\widetilde{x}$ abbreviates a (possibly empty) sequence $x_1, \ldots, x_n$. In the definition $f\, \widetilde{x} = e$, we call the length of $\widetilde{x}$ the *arity* of f. In the definition of values, the length of $\widetilde{v}$ in $f\, \widetilde{v}$ must be smaller than the arity of f. (In other words, $f\, \widetilde{v}$ must be a partial application.) We assume that every function in D has a non-zero arity, and that D contains a distinguished function symbol $\mathit{main} \in \{f_1, \ldots, f_m\}$ whose simple type is $\star \to \star$.

Most of the expressions are standard, except the following ones. The expression `fail` aborts the program and reports a failure. The expression `assume` $v; e$ evaluates e if v is true; otherwise it stops the program (without a failure). The expression $e_1 \,\Box\, e_2$ evaluates e_1 or e_2 in a non-deterministic manner. Note that a standard conditional expression `if` v `then` e_1 `else` e_2 can be expressed as:

$$(\texttt{assume}\ v; e_1) \,\Box\, (\texttt{let}\ x = \neg v\ \texttt{in}\ \texttt{assume}\ x; e_2).$$

We can express the assertion `assert` v as `if` v `then` $\langle\rangle$ `else fail`. The random number generator *randi* used in Section 1 is defined by:

$$\begin{aligned}\mathit{randi}\,\langle\rangle &= (\mathit{randiFrom}\ 1)\Box(\mathit{randiTo}\ 0)\\ \mathit{randiFrom}\ n &= n\Box(\mathit{randiFrom}\ (n+1))\\ \mathit{randiTo}\ n &= n\Box(\mathit{randiTo}\ (n-1))\end{aligned}$$

We assume that a program is well-typed in the standard simple type system, where the set of types is given by:

$$\tau ::= b_1 \mid \cdots \mid b_n \mid \tau_1 \to \tau_2.$$

Furthermore, we assume that the body of each definition has a data type b_i, not a function type. This is not a limitation, as we can always use the continuation-passing-style (CPS) transformation to transform a higher-order program to an equivalent one that satisfies the restriction.

We define the set of *evaluation contexts* by: $E ::= [\,] \mid \texttt{let}\ x = E\ \texttt{in}\ e$. The reduction relation is given in Figure 2. We label the

$$\frac{f\,\widetilde{x} = e \in D}{E[f\,\widetilde{v}] \xrightarrow{\epsilon}_D E[[\widetilde{v}/\widetilde{x}]e]} \quad \text{(E-APP)}$$

$$E[\mathtt{let}\ x = v\ \mathtt{in}\ e] \xrightarrow{\epsilon}_D E[[v/x]e] \quad \text{(E-LET)}$$

$$E[\mathrm{op}(\widetilde{c})] \xrightarrow{\epsilon}_D E[[\![\mathrm{op}]\!](\widetilde{c})] \quad \text{(E-OP)}$$

$$E[e_0 \,\Box\, e_1] \xrightarrow{i}_D E[e_i] \quad \text{(E-PAR)}$$

$$E[\mathtt{assume\ true}; e] \xrightarrow{\epsilon}_D E[e] \quad \text{(E-ASSUME)}$$

$$E[\mathtt{fail}] \xrightarrow{\epsilon}_D \mathtt{fail} \quad \text{(E-FAIL)}$$

Figure 2. Call-by-Value Operational Semantics

reduction relation with $0, 1, \epsilon$ to record which branch has been chosen by a non-deterministic expression $e_1 \,\Box\, e_2$; it will be used to relate reductions of a source program and an abstract program later in Sections 4 and 5. We write $e_1 \stackrel{l_1 \cdots l_n}{\Longrightarrow}_D e_2$ if

$$e_1 (\xrightarrow{\epsilon}_D)^* \xrightarrow{l_1}_D (\xrightarrow{\epsilon}_D)^* \cdots (\xrightarrow{\epsilon}_D)^* \xrightarrow{l_n}_D (\xrightarrow{\epsilon}_D)^* e_2.$$

We often omit the subscript D when it is clear from the context. The goal of our verification method is to check whether $\mathit{main}\,\langle\rangle \stackrel{s}{\Longrightarrow}_D \mathtt{fail}$.[4]

3. Higher-Order Boolean Programs and Model Checking

A source program is translated to a higher-order boolean program (abbreviated to HBP) by the predicate abstraction discussed in Section 4. The language of HBP is essentially the same as the source language in the previous section, except:

- The set of data types consists only of types of the form $\underbrace{\mathtt{bool} \times \cdots \times \mathtt{bool}}_{m}$ (which is identified with $\star$ when $m = 0$, and $\mathtt{bool}$ when $m = 1$). We assume there are the following operators to construct or deconstruct tuples:

$$\begin{array}{rcl} \langle \cdot, \ldots, \cdot \rangle & : & \mathtt{bool}, \ldots, \mathtt{bool} \rightarrow \mathtt{bool} \times \cdots \times \mathtt{bool} \\ \sharp_i & : & \mathtt{bool} \times \cdots \times \mathtt{bool} \rightarrow \mathtt{bool} \end{array}$$

- The set of expressions is extended with $e_1 \blacksquare e_2$ and unnamed functions $\lambda x.e$. The former is used for expressing the non-determinism introduced by abstractions; it is the same as $e_1 \,\Box\, e_2$, which is used to express the non-determinism present in a source program, except that the reduction is labelled with ϵ. This distinction is convenient for the CEGAR procedure discussed in Section 5 to find a corresponding execution path of the source program from an execution path of the abstract program. Unnamed functions are used just for technical convenience for defining predicate abstraction; with λ-lifting, we can easily get rid of λ-abstractions. (The evaluation rules and evaluation contexts are accordingly extended with $E[(\lambda x.e)v] \longrightarrow E[[v/x]e]$ and $E ::= \cdots \mid E\,e \mid v\,E$.)

The following theorem is the basis of our verification method. It follows immediately from the decidability of the model checking of higher-order recursion schemes [28].

Theorem 3.1. *Let D be an HBP. The property $\exists s.(\mathit{main}\langle\rangle \stackrel{s}{\Longrightarrow}_D$ $\mathtt{fail})$ is decidable.*

[4] Thus, we consider the reachability problem for a closed program. Note, however, that we can express unknown values by using non-determinism (recall *randi*). It is also easy to extend our method to deal with more general verification problems, such as resource usage verification [22].

$$\frac{\mathtt{A2S}(\Gamma), x : b \vdash_{\mathtt{ST}} \psi_i : \mathtt{bool} \text{ for each } i \in \{1, \ldots, n\}}{\Gamma \vdash_{\mathtt{wf}} b[\lambda x.\psi_1, \ldots, \lambda x.\psi_n]}$$

$$\frac{\Gamma \vdash_{\mathtt{wf}} \sigma_1 \qquad \Gamma, x : \sigma_1 \vdash_{\mathtt{wf}} \sigma_2}{\Gamma \vdash_{\mathtt{wf}} x : \sigma_1 \rightarrow \sigma_2} \qquad \frac{}{\vdash_{\mathtt{wf}} \emptyset} \qquad \frac{\vdash_{\mathtt{wf}} \Gamma \qquad \Gamma \vdash_{\mathtt{wf}} \sigma}{\vdash_{\mathtt{wf}} \Gamma, x : \sigma}$$

Figure 3. Well-formed types and type environments

We can use a recursion scheme model checker TRECS [21, 22] to decide the above property.[5] If $\exists s.(\mathit{main}\langle\rangle \stackrel{s}{\Longrightarrow}_D \mathtt{fail})$ holds, the model checker generates an error path s. The knowledge about recursion schemes is unnecessary for understanding the rest of this paper, but an interested reader may wish to consult [20, 22, 28].

4. Predicate Abstraction

This section formalizes predicate abstraction for higher-order programs. As explained in Section 1, we use *abstraction types* to express which predicates should be used for abstracting each subexpression. The syntax of abstraction types is given by:

$$\begin{array}{rcl} \sigma \text{ (abstraction types)} & ::= & b_1[\widetilde{P}] \mid \cdots \mid b_n[\widetilde{P}] \mid x : \sigma_1 \rightarrow \sigma_2 \\ P, Q \text{ (predicates)} & ::= & \lambda x.\psi \\ \Gamma \text{ (type environments)} & ::= & \emptyset \mid \Gamma, f : \sigma \mid \Gamma, x : \sigma \end{array}$$

Here, the meta-variable ψ represents an expression of type $\mathtt{bool}$ (which is called *a formula*) that is constructed only from variables of base types, constants, and primitive operations; we do not allow formulas that contain function applications, like $y > f(x)$. The base type $b_i[\widetilde{P}]$ describes values v of type b_i that should be abstracted to a tuple of booleans $\langle P_1(v), \ldots, P_n(v)\rangle$. For example, the integer 3 with the abstraction type $\mathtt{int}[\lambda\nu.\nu > 0, \lambda\nu.\nu < 2]$ is abstracted to $\langle \mathtt{true}, \mathtt{false}\rangle$. We often abbreviate $b[\,]$ to b. The dependent function type $x : \sigma_1 \rightarrow \sigma_2$ describes functions that take a value v of type σ_1, and return a value of type $[v/x]\sigma_2$. The scope of x in the type $x : \sigma_1 \rightarrow \sigma_2$ is σ_2. When x does not occur in σ_2, we often write $\sigma_1 \rightarrow \sigma_2$ for $x : \sigma_1 \rightarrow \sigma_2$. As mentioned already, abstraction types only describe how each expression should be abstracted, not the actual value. For example, 3 can have type $\mathtt{int}[\lambda\nu.\nu < 0]$, and $\lambda x.x$ can have type $x : \mathtt{int}[\,] \rightarrow \mathtt{int}[\lambda\nu.\nu = x + 1]$ (and abstracted to $\lambda x : \star.\mathtt{false}$).

We do not consider types whose predicates are ill-typed or violate a variable's scope, such as $x : \mathtt{bool}[\,] \rightarrow \mathtt{int}[\lambda y.x + 1 = y]$ and $x : \mathtt{int}[\lambda x.y > x] \rightarrow y : \mathtt{int}[\,] \rightarrow \mathtt{bool}[\,]$. (The former uses a boolean variable as an integer, and the latter refers to the variable y outside its scope.) Figure 3 defines the well-formedness conditions for types and type environments. In the figure, $\Delta \vdash_{\mathtt{ST}} e : \tau$ denotes the type judgment of the standard simple type system. We write $\mathtt{A2S}(\sigma)$ and $\mathtt{A2S}(\Gamma)$ respectively for the simple type and the simple type environment obtained by removing predicates. For example, $\mathtt{A2S}(f : (x : \mathtt{int}[\,] \rightarrow \mathtt{int}[\lambda y.y > x]), z : \mathtt{int}[\lambda z.z > 0]) = f : \mathtt{int} \rightarrow \mathtt{int}, z : \mathtt{int}$.

Figure 4 defines the predicate abstraction relation $\Gamma \vdash e_1 : \sigma \rightsquigarrow e_2$, which reads that an expression e_1 (of the source language in Section 2) can be abstracted to an expression e_2 (of the HBP language given in Section 3) by using the abstraction type σ, under the assumption that each free variable x of e_1 has been abstracted using the abstraction type $\Gamma(x)$. In the rules, it is implicitly assumed that all the type environments and types are well-formed. We do not distinguish between function vari-

[5] The gap between the operational semantics of our language and that of recursion schemes can be filled by the CPS transformation. Note also that finite state or pushdown model checkers cannot be used, as higher-order programs are in general strictly more expressive [10].

$$\frac{e \text{ is a constant, a variable or an expression of the form } \mathrm{op}(\widetilde{v}) \quad \mathtt{A2S}(\Gamma) \vdash_{\mathrm{ST}} e : b}{\Gamma \vdash e : b[\lambda\nu.\nu = e] \rightsquigarrow \mathtt{true}} \text{(A-BASE)}$$

$$\frac{\Gamma \vdash e : b[\widetilde{Q}] \rightsquigarrow e' \quad \beta(\Gamma, x : b[\widetilde{Q}]) \vdash_{\mathrm{ST}} \psi : \mathtt{bool} \quad \beta(\Gamma, x : b[\widetilde{Q}]) \vdash_{\mathrm{ST}} \psi' : \mathtt{bool} \quad \models P(x) \Rightarrow \theta_{\Gamma, x:b[\widetilde{Q}]}(\psi) \quad \models \neg P(x) \Rightarrow \theta_{\Gamma, x:b[\widetilde{Q}]}(\psi') \quad e'' = (\mathtt{assume}\ \psi; \mathtt{true}) \blacksquare (\mathtt{assume}\ \psi'; \mathtt{false})}{\Gamma \vdash e : b[\widetilde{Q}, P] \rightsquigarrow \mathtt{let}\ x = e'\ \mathtt{in}\ \langle x, e'' \rangle} \text{(A-CADD)}$$

$$\frac{\Gamma \vdash e : b[\widetilde{Q}, \widetilde{P}] \rightsquigarrow e'}{\Gamma \vdash e : b[\widetilde{P}] \rightsquigarrow \mathtt{let}\ \langle \widetilde{x}, \widetilde{y} \rangle = e'\ \mathtt{in}\ \langle \widetilde{y} \rangle} \text{(A-CREM)}$$

$$\frac{\Gamma(x) = (y_1 : \sigma_1 \to \cdots \to y_k : \sigma_k \to \sigma) \quad \Gamma, y_1 : \sigma_1, \ldots, y_{i-1} : \sigma_{i-1} \vdash v_i : [v_1/y_1, \ldots, v_{i-1}/y_{i-1}]\sigma_i \rightsquigarrow e_i \ \text{(for each } i \in \{1, \ldots, k\})}{\Gamma \vdash x\,\widetilde{v} : [\widetilde{v}/\widetilde{y}]\sigma \rightsquigarrow \mathtt{let}\ y_1 = e_1\ \mathtt{in} \cdots \mathtt{let}\ y_k = e_k\ \mathtt{in}\ x\,\widetilde{y}} \text{(A-APP)}$$

$$\frac{\Gamma \vdash e_1 : \sigma' \rightsquigarrow e_1' \quad \Gamma, x : \sigma' \vdash e_2 : \sigma \rightsquigarrow e_2'}{\Gamma \vdash \mathtt{let}\ x = e_1\ \mathtt{in}\ e_2 : \sigma \rightsquigarrow \mathtt{let}\ x = e_1'\ \mathtt{in}\ e_2'} \text{(A-LET)}$$

$$\frac{\beta(\Gamma) \vdash_{\mathrm{ST}} \psi : \mathtt{bool} \quad \models \theta_\Gamma(\psi)}{\Gamma \vdash \mathtt{fail} : \sigma \rightsquigarrow \mathtt{assume}\ \psi; \mathtt{fail}} \text{(A-FAIL)}$$

$$\frac{\Gamma \vdash v : \mathtt{bool}[\lambda x.x] \rightsquigarrow e_1 \quad \Gamma, x : \mathtt{bool}[\lambda x.v] \vdash e : \sigma \rightsquigarrow e_2}{\Gamma \vdash \mathtt{assume}\ v; e : \sigma \rightsquigarrow \mathtt{let}\ x = e_1\ \mathtt{in}\ \mathtt{assume}\ x; e_2} \text{(A-ASM)}$$

$$\frac{\Gamma \vdash e_1 : \sigma \rightsquigarrow e_1' \quad \Gamma \vdash e_2 : \sigma \rightsquigarrow e_2'}{\Gamma \vdash e_1 \Box e_2 : \sigma \rightsquigarrow e_1' \Box e_2'} \text{(A-PAR)}$$

$$\frac{\Gamma \vdash e : (x : \sigma_1' \to \sigma_2') \rightsquigarrow e' \quad \Gamma, x : \sigma_1 \vdash x : \sigma_1' \rightsquigarrow e_1' \quad \Gamma, x : \sigma_1, x' : \sigma_1', y : \sigma_2' \vdash y : \sigma_2 \rightsquigarrow e_2'}{\Gamma \vdash e : (x : \sigma_1 \to \sigma_2) \rightsquigarrow \mathtt{let}\ f = e'\ \mathtt{in}\ \lambda x.\mathtt{let}\ x' = e_1'\ \mathtt{in}\ \mathtt{let}\ y = f\ x'\ \mathtt{in}\ e_2'} \text{(A-CFUN)}$$

$$\frac{f_i : (\widetilde{x}_i : \widetilde{\sigma}_i \to \sigma_i) \in \Gamma \quad \Gamma, \widetilde{x}_i : \widetilde{\sigma}_i \vdash e_i : \sigma_i \rightsquigarrow e_i' \ \text{(for each } i \in \{1, \ldots, m\}) \quad \Gamma(\mathit{main}) = \star[\,] \to \star[\,]}{\vdash \{f_1\,\widetilde{x}_1 = e_1, \ldots, f_m\,\widetilde{x}_m = e_m\} : \Gamma \rightsquigarrow \{f_1\,\widetilde{x}_1 = e_1', \ldots, f_m\,\widetilde{x}_m = e_m'\}} \text{(A-PROG)}$$

Figure 4. Predicate Abstraction Rules

ables and other variables (hence, A-APP applies also to a function variable f). In A-CADD, $\mathtt{assume}\ e_1; e_2$ is a syntax sugar for $\mathtt{let}\ x_1 = e_1\ \mathtt{in}\ \mathtt{assume}\ x_1; e_2$.

In A-CADD and A-FAIL, $\beta(\sigma)$ ($\beta(\Gamma)$, resp.) represent the simple type (simple type environment, resp.) obtained by replacing each occurrence of a base abstraction type $b[P_1, \ldots, P_m]$ with $\underbrace{\mathtt{bool} \times \cdots \times \mathtt{bool}}_{m}$. Intuitively, $\beta(\Gamma)$ represents the type environment for the output program of the transformation.

We explain the main rules. Base values are abstracted by using three rules A-BASE, A-CADD, and A-CREM. Before explaining those rules, let us discuss the following simplified version, specialized for a single predicate:

$$\frac{\models P(e) \Rightarrow \theta_\Gamma(\psi) \quad \models \neg P(e) \Rightarrow \theta_\Gamma(\psi')}{\Gamma \vdash e : b[P] \rightsquigarrow (\mathtt{assume}\ \psi; \mathtt{true}) \blacksquare (\mathtt{assume}\ \psi'; \mathtt{false})} \text{(A-BSIMP)}$$

Here, we assume that e is a constant, a variable, or an expression of the form $\mathrm{op}(\widetilde{v})$ and has a base type b. ψ and ψ' are boolean formulas that may contain variables in Γ. As e may contain variables, we need to take into account information about the values of the variables, which is obtained by using the substitution θ_Γ, defined as: $\{x \mapsto \langle P_1(x), \ldots, P_m(x) \rangle \mid \Gamma(x) = b[P_1, \ldots, P_m]\}$. For example, let Γ be $x : \mathtt{int}[\lambda x.x > 0, \lambda x.x < 0]$ and ψ be $\sharp_1(x) \wedge \sharp_2(x)$. Then, $\theta_\Gamma(\psi) = x > 0 \wedge x < 0$. As in this example, the substitution θ_Γ maps a boolean expression of an abstract program to the corresponding condition in the source program. In rule A-BSIMP above, $\models P(e) \Rightarrow \theta_\Gamma(\psi)$ means that $P(e)$ is true only if $\theta_\Gamma(\psi)$ is true, i.e. the value of ψ in the abstract program is true. Thus, the abstract value of e may be $\mathtt{true}$ only if the value of ψ is $\mathtt{true}$, hence the part $\mathtt{assume}\ \psi; \mathtt{true}$ in the abstract program. Similarly, the abstract value of e may be $\mathtt{false}$ only if the value of ψ' is $\mathtt{true}$, hence the part $\mathtt{assume}\ \psi'; \mathtt{false}$.

For example, let $e \equiv x + 1$, $P \equiv \lambda x \geq 0$, and $\Gamma \equiv x : \mathtt{int}[P]$. Then, $\models P(x+1) \Rightarrow \mathtt{true}$ and $\models \neg P(x+1) \Rightarrow \neg P(x)$, so that e is abstracted to $(\mathtt{assume}\ \mathtt{true}; \mathtt{true}) \blacksquare (\mathtt{assume}\ \neg x; \mathtt{false})$. Note that $\theta_\Gamma(\neg x) = [P(x)/x]\neg x = \neg P(x)$.

We need to generalize the above rule to the case for multiple predicates. The following is a naive rule.

$$\frac{\Gamma \vdash e : b[P_i] \rightsquigarrow e_i}{\Gamma \vdash e : b[P_1, \ldots, P_n] \rightsquigarrow \langle e_1, \ldots, e_n \rangle} \text{(A-BCARTESIAN)}$$

This produces a well-known cartesian abstraction, which is often too imprecise. The problem is that each boolean value of the abstraction is computed separately, ignoring the correlation. For example, let $P_1 \equiv \lambda x.x > 0$ and $P_2 \equiv \lambda x.x \leq 0$ with $n = 2$. Then, a possible abstraction of an unknown integer should be $\langle \mathtt{true}, \mathtt{false} \rangle$ and $\langle \mathtt{false}, \mathtt{true} \rangle$, but the above rule would generate $\langle (\mathtt{true} \blacksquare \mathtt{false}), (\mathtt{true} \blacksquare \mathtt{false}) \rangle$, which also contains $\langle \mathtt{true}, \mathtt{true} \rangle$ and $\langle \mathtt{false}, \mathtt{false} \rangle$.

The discussion above motivated us to introduce the three rules A-BASE, A-CADD, and A-CREM. In order to abstract an expression e with $b[P_1, \ldots, P_n]$, we first use A-BASE to abstract e to $\mathtt{true}$ by using the abstraction type $b[\lambda\nu.\nu = e]$; this is necessary to keep the exact information about e during the computation of abstractions. A-CADD is then used to add predicates $P_1, \ldots, P_n$ one by one, taking into account the correlation between the predicates. Note that in A-CADD, the result of abstraction by the other predicates is taken into account by the substitution $\theta_{\Gamma, x:b[\widetilde{Q}]}$. Finally, A-CREM is used to remove the unnecessary predicate $\lambda\nu.\nu = e$. See Example 4.1 for an application of these rules.

Note that rule A-CADD is non-deterministic in the choice of conditions ψ and ψ', so that how to compute the conditions is left unspecified. We have intentionally made so, because depending on base data types, the most precise conditions (the strongest conditions entailed by $P(x)$ and $\neg P(x)$) may not be computable or are too expensive to compute. For linear arithmetics, however, we can use off-the-shelf automated theorem provers to obtain such conditions.

In rule A-APP, each argument v_i is abstracted by using the abstraction type σ_i with $y_1, \ldots, y_{i-1}$ being replaced by the actual arguments. Note that this rule applies also to the case where the sequence $\widetilde{v}$ is empty (i.e. $k = 0$). Thus, we can derive $\Gamma \vdash y : \sigma \rightsquigarrow y$ if $\Gamma(y) = \sigma$. Note also that the boolean expression e_i in A-APP can depend on $y_1, \ldots, y_{i-1}$.

In A-FAIL, the assume statement is inserted for filtering out an invalid combination of abstract values. For example, let Γ be

$x : \texttt{int}[\lambda x.x > 0, \lambda x.x < 0]$. Then, $\texttt{assume}\ (\sharp_1(x) \wedge \sharp_2(x))$; is inserted since $x > 0$ and $x < 0$ cannot be true simultaneously. In A-ASM, we can use the fact that v is $\texttt{true}$ in e for abstracting e.

Rule A-CFUN is used for changing the abstraction type of a function from $x : \sigma_1 \to \sigma_2$ to $x : \sigma_1' \to \sigma_2'$, which is analogous to the usual rule for subtyping-based coercion. If a function f is used in different contexts which require different abstraction types of f, A-CFUN can be used to adjust the abstraction type of f to that required for each context.

We can read the predicate abstraction rules for $\Gamma \vdash e : \sigma \rightsquigarrow e'$ as an algorithm that takes Γ, e and σ as input, and outputs e' as an abstraction of e, by (1) restricting applications of the rules for coercion (of names A-CXYZ) to the actual arguments of function applications, and (2) fixing an algorithm to find the boolean formulas ψ and ψ' in A-CADD. (Note that in A-LET, the type σ' can be obtained from Γ and e_1.) The rule for $\vdash D : \Gamma \rightsquigarrow D'$ can then be interpreted as an algorithm that takes D and Γ as input, and outputs an HBP D' as an abstraction of D.

Example 4.1. Recall the program M_2 in Section 1. Let Γ be:

$$x : \texttt{int}[\lambda\nu.\nu \geq 0], g : \texttt{int}[\lambda\nu.\nu > 0] \to \star$$

The body of f is transformed as follows. $x + 1$ is transformed by:

$$\dfrac{\dfrac{}{\Gamma \vdash x + 1 : \texttt{int}[\lambda\nu.\nu = x + 1] \rightsquigarrow \texttt{true}}\ \text{A-BASE}}{\dfrac{\Gamma \vdash x + 1 : \texttt{int}[\lambda\nu.\nu = x + 1, \lambda\nu.\nu > 0] \rightsquigarrow e_1}{\Gamma \vdash x + 1 : \texttt{int}[\lambda\nu.\nu > 0] \rightsquigarrow e_2}\ \text{A-CREM}}\ \text{A-CADD}$$

Here, $e_1 \equiv \texttt{let}\ y_1 = \texttt{true}\ \texttt{in}\ \langle y_1, e_3\rangle$ and $e_2 \equiv \texttt{let}\ \langle y_1, y_2\rangle = e_1\ \texttt{in}\ y_2$, with $e_3 \equiv (\texttt{assume}\ \texttt{true}; \texttt{true}) \blacksquare (\texttt{assume}\ \neg(x \wedge y_1); \texttt{false})$. Here, we used $\texttt{true}$ and $\neg(x \wedge y_1)$ as ψ and ψ' respectively, in A-CADD. (Note that $P(y_1) \Rightarrow \theta_{\Gamma, y_1:\texttt{int}[\lambda\nu.\nu = x+1]}(\psi_1)$, i.e., $y_1 \leq 0 \Rightarrow \neg(x \geq 0 \wedge y_1 = x + 1)$ holds.) By simplifying e_2, we get $\texttt{if}\ x\ \texttt{then}\ \texttt{true}\ \texttt{else}\ \texttt{true} \blacksquare \texttt{false}$. Thus, the body $g(x + 1)$ of function f is transformed by using A-APP as follows:

$$\dfrac{\Gamma(g) = \texttt{int}[\lambda\nu.\nu > 0] \to \star \qquad \dfrac{\vdots}{\Gamma \vdash x + 1 : \texttt{int}[\lambda\nu.\nu > 0] \rightsquigarrow e_2}}{\Gamma \vdash g(x + 1) : \star \rightsquigarrow \begin{array}{l}\texttt{let}\ y = \texttt{if}\ x\ \texttt{then}\ \texttt{true} \\ \qquad\qquad \texttt{else}\ (\texttt{true} \blacksquare \texttt{false})\ \texttt{in}\ g(y)\end{array}}$$

Our predicate abstraction rules are applicable to programs that use infinite data domain other than integers. See [25] for an example of abstracting a list-processing program.

We discuss properties of the predicate abstraction relation below. First, we show that if abstraction types are consistent, there is always a valid transformation. We write $\Gamma \vdash_{\texttt{AT}} e : \sigma$ for the type judgment relation obtained from the predicate abstraction rules by removing all the conditions on outputs: see [25].

Theorem 4.1. *Suppose* $\Gamma \vdash_{\texttt{AT}} e : \sigma$. *Then,* $\texttt{A2S}(\Gamma) \vdash_{\texttt{ST}} e : \texttt{A2S}(\sigma)$. *Furthermore, there exists* e' *such that* $\Gamma \vdash e : \sigma \rightsquigarrow e'$.

Proof. Straightforward induction on the derivation of $\Gamma \vdash_{\texttt{AT}} e : \sigma$. Note that in the rule for A-CADD, we can choose $\texttt{true}$ as ψ and ψ'. □

The following lemma guarantees that the output of the transformation is well-typed.

Lemma 4.2. *If* $\Gamma \vdash e_1 : \sigma \rightsquigarrow e_2$, *then* $\beta(\Gamma) \vdash_{\texttt{ST}} e_2 : \beta(\sigma)$.

Proof. Straightforward induction on the derivation of $\Gamma \vdash e_1 : \sigma \rightsquigarrow e_2$. □

The theorem below states that our predicate abstraction is sound in the sense that if a source program fails, so does its abstraction (see [25] for the proof). Thus, the safety of the abstract program (which is decidable by Theorem 3.1) is a sufficient condition for the safety of the source program.

Theorem 4.3 (soundness). *If* $\vdash D_1 : \Gamma \rightsquigarrow D_2$ *and* $main\langle\rangle \stackrel{s}{\Longrightarrow}_{D_1} \texttt{fail}$, *then* $main\langle\rangle \stackrel{s}{\Longrightarrow}_{D_2} \texttt{fail}$.

The theorem above says that the abstraction is sound but not how good the abstraction is. We compare below the verification power of the combination of predicate abstraction and higher-order model checking with the dependent intersection type system given in [25], which is essentially equivalent to the one in [32].

We write $\mathcal{B}[\psi_1, \ldots, \psi_k]$ for the set of formulas constructed from $\psi_1, \ldots, \psi_k$ and boolean operators $(\texttt{true}, \texttt{false}, \wedge, \vee, \neg)$. For an abstraction type σ, the set $DepTy(\sigma)$ of dependent types is:

$$\begin{array}{l} DepTy(b[P_1, \ldots, P_n]) = \{\{\nu : b \mid \psi\} \mid \psi \in \mathcal{B}[P_1(\nu), \ldots, P_n(\nu)]\} \\ DepTy(x : \sigma_1 \to \sigma_2) = \{(x : \delta_{11} \to \delta_{21}) \wedge \cdots \wedge (x : \delta_{1m} \to \delta_{2m}) \\ \qquad \mid \delta_{11}, \ldots, \delta_{1m} \in DepTy(\sigma_1), \delta_{21}, \ldots, \delta_{2m} \in DepTy(\sigma_2)\} \end{array}$$

We extend $DepTy$ to a map from abstraction type environments to the powerset of dependent type environments by:

$$\begin{array}{l} DepTy(\{x_1 : \sigma_1, \ldots, x_n : \sigma_n\}) = \\ \{\{x_1 : \delta_1, \ldots, x_n : \delta_n\} \mid \delta_i \in DepTy(\sigma_i) \text{ for each } i \in \{1, \ldots, n\}\} \end{array}$$

The following theorem says that our predicate abstraction (with higher-order model checking) has at least the same verification power as the dependent intersection type system.

Theorem 4.4 (relative completeness). *Suppose* $\vdash_{DIT} D : \Delta$. *If* $\Delta \in DepTy(\Gamma)$, *then there exists* D' *such that* $\vdash D : \Gamma \rightsquigarrow D'$ *and* $main\langle\rangle \not\Longrightarrow_{D'} \texttt{fail}$.

Remark 1. The converse of the above theorem does not hold: see [25]. Together with Theorem 4.4, this implies that our combination of predicate abstraction and higher-order model checking is strictly more powerful than the dependent intersection type system.

Remark 2. The well-formedness condition for abstraction types is sometimes too restrictive to express a necessary predicate. For example, consider the following program.

```
let apply f x = f x in let g y z = assert(y=z) in
let k n = apply (g n) n; k(n+1) in  k(0)
```

In order to verify that the assertion failure does not occur, we need a correlation between the argument of f and x, which cannot be expressed by abstraction types. The problem can be avoided either by adding a dummy parameter to `apply` (as `let apply n f x = ...`) and using the abstraction type $n : \texttt{int}[\,] \to (\texttt{int}[\lambda\nu.\nu = n] \to \star) \to \texttt{int}[\lambda\nu.\nu = n] \to \star$, or by swapping the parameters f and x. A more fundamental solution (which is left for future work) would be to introduce *polymorphic* abstraction types, like $\forall m : \texttt{int}.(\texttt{int}[\lambda\nu.\nu = m] \to \star) \to \texttt{int}[\lambda\nu.\nu = m] \to \star$, and extend the predicate abstraction rules accordingly.

5. Counterexample-Guided Abstraction Refinement (CEGAR)

This section describes a CEGAR procedure to discover new predicates used for predicate abstraction when the higher-order model checker TRECS has reported an error path s of a boolean program.

5.1 Feasibility checking

Given an error path s of an abstract program, we first check whether s is feasible in the source program D, i.e. whether $main\langle\rangle \stackrel{s}{\Longrightarrow}_D \texttt{fail}$. This can be easily checked by actually executing the source program along the path s, and checking whether all the branching conditions are true. (Here, we assume that the program is closed. If we allow free variables for storing base values, we can just symbolically execute the source program along the path, and check whether all the conditions are satisfiable.) If the source program indeed has the error path (i.e. $\mathit{main}\langle\rangle \overset{s}{\Longrightarrow}_D \texttt{fail}$), then we report the error path as a counterexample.

5.2 Predicate discovery and refinement of abstraction types

If the error path is infeasible (i.e. $\mathit{main}\langle\rangle \overset{s}{\not\Longrightarrow}_D \texttt{fail}$), we find new predicates to refine predicate abstractions.

In the case of the model checking of first-order programs, this is usually performed by, for each program point ℓ in the error path, (i) computing the strongest condition C_1 at ℓ, (ii) computing the weakest condition C_2 for reaching from ℓ to the failure node, and (iii) using a theorem prover to find a condition C such that $C_1 \Rightarrow C$ and $C \Rightarrow \neg C_2$. Then the predicates in C can be used for abstracting the state at the program point. For example, in the reduction sequence (2) of M_1 in Section 1, the condition C_1 on the local variable x is $n>0 \wedge x=n$, and the condition C_2 is $x+1 \geq 0$. From them, we obtain $C \equiv x > 0$ as a predicate for abstracting x.

It is unclear, however, how to extend it to deal with higher-order functions. For example, in the example above, how can we find a suitable abstraction type for functions f and g? To address this issue, as mentioned in Section 1, we use the following type-based approach. From an infeasible error path, we first construct a *straightline higher-order program* (abbreviated to SHP, which is straightline in the sense that it contains neither branches nor recursion and that each function is called at most once) that has exactly one execution path, corresponding to the path s of the source program. We then infer the dependent types of functions in the straightline program, and use the predicates occurring in the dependent types for refining abstraction types of the source program. We describe each step in more detail below.

5.2.1 Constructing SHP

Given a source program and a path s, the corresponding SHP is obtained by (i) making a copy of each function for each call in the execution path, and (ii) for each copy, removing the branches not taken in s.

Example 5.1. Recall the program M_3 in Section 1.

$$\begin{array}{l}
\mathit{main}\langle\rangle = k\ m \qquad f\ x\ g = g(x+1) \\
h\ z\ y = (\texttt{assume}\ y > z; \langle\rangle) \,\square\, (\texttt{assume}\ \neg(y > z); \texttt{fail}) \\
k\ n = (\texttt{assume}\ n \geq 0; f\ n\ (h\ n)) \square (\texttt{assume}\ \neg(n \geq 0); \langle\rangle)
\end{array}$$

Here, we have represented conditionals and assert expressions in our language.[6] Given the spurious error path $0 \cdot 1$, we obtain the following SHP.

$$\begin{array}{ll}
\mathit{main}\langle\rangle = k\ m & h\ z\ y = \texttt{assume}\ \neg(y > z); \texttt{fail} \\
f\ x\ g = g(x+1) & k\ n = \texttt{assume}\ n \geq 0; f\ n\ (h\ n)
\end{array}$$

It has been obtained by removing irrelevant non-deterministic branches in h and k.

The construction of an SHP generally requires duplication of function definitions and function parameters. For example, consider the following program:

$$\begin{array}{l}
\mathit{main}\langle\rangle = k\ m \qquad \mathit{twice}\ f\ x = f(f\ x) \\
g\ x = \texttt{if}\ x \leq 0\ \texttt{then}\ 1\ \texttt{else}\ 2 + g(x-1) \\
k\ n = \texttt{let}\ x = \mathit{twice}\ g\ n\ \texttt{in}\ \texttt{assert}\ (x > 0)
\end{array}$$

(where m is some integer constant). The program calls the function g twice, and asserts that the result x is positive. Suppose that an infeasible path 0101 has been given, which represents the following (infeasible) execution path:

$$\begin{array}{l}
\mathit{main}\langle\rangle \longrightarrow k\ m \Longrightarrow \texttt{let}\ x = g(g\ m)\ \texttt{in} \cdots \\
\quad \underset{0}{\Longrightarrow} \texttt{let}\ x = g(1)\ \texttt{in} \cdots \underset{1}{\Longrightarrow} \texttt{let}\ x = 2 + g(0)\ \texttt{in} \cdots \\
\quad \underset{0}{\Longrightarrow} \texttt{let}\ x = 2 + 1\ \texttt{in} \cdots \underset{1}{\Longrightarrow} \texttt{assert}\ 3 > 0 \Longrightarrow \texttt{fail}
\end{array}$$

The path is infeasible because the final transition is invalid.

From the source program and the path above, we construct the following straightline program:[7]

$$\begin{array}{ll}
\mathit{main}\langle\rangle = k\ m & \mathit{twice}\ \langle f^{(1)}, f^{(2)}\rangle\ x = f^{(2)}(f^{(1)}\ x) \\
g^{(1)}\ x = \texttt{assume}\ x \leq 0; 1 & g^{(3)}\ x = \texttt{assume}\ x \leq 0; 1 \\
\multicolumn{2}{l}{g^{(2)}\ x = \texttt{assume}\ \neg(x \leq 0); 2 + g^{(3)}(x-1)} \\
\multicolumn{2}{l}{k\ n = \texttt{let}\ x = \mathit{twice}\ \langle g^{(1)}, g^{(2)}\rangle\ n\ \texttt{in}\ \texttt{assume}\ \neg(x > 0); \texttt{fail}}
\end{array}$$

As g is called three times, we have prepared three copies $g^{(1)}$, $g^{(2)}$, $g^{(3)}$ of g, and eliminated unused non-deterministic branches. Note that the function parameter f of *twice* has been replaced by a function pair $\langle f^{(1)}, f^{(2)}\rangle$ accordingly.

The general construction is given below. Consider a program normalized to the following form:

$$\begin{array}{lcl}
D & ::= & \{f_1\ \widetilde{x}_1 = e_{10} \square e_{11}, \ldots, f_m\ \widetilde{x}_m = e_{m0} \square e_{m1}\} \\
e & ::= & \texttt{assume}\ v; a \mid \texttt{let}\ x = \mathrm{op}(\widetilde{v})\ \texttt{in}\ a \\
a & ::= & \langle\rangle \mid x\ \widetilde{v} \mid f\ \widetilde{v} \mid \texttt{fail} \\
v & ::= & c \mid x\ \widetilde{v} \mid f\ \widetilde{v}
\end{array}$$

Here, for the sake of simplicity, we have assumed that every function definition has at most one (tail) function call, and the return value is $\langle\rangle$; this does not lose generality as the normal form can be obtained by applying CPS transformation and λ-lifting. Given a path $s = b_1 \cdots b_\ell$ of D (which means that the branch b_i has been chosen at ith function call), the corresponding SHP $D' = \mathbf{SHP}(D, s)$ is given by:

$$\begin{array}{l}
D' = \{f_i^{(j)}\ \widetilde{x}_i = [e_{ib_j}]_{j+1} \mid i \in \{1, \ldots, m\}, j \in \{1, \ldots, \ell\}, \\
\qquad \text{the target of the } j\text{th function call is } f_i\} \\
\quad \cup \{f_i^{(j)}\ \widetilde{x}_i = \langle\rangle \mid i \in \{1, \ldots, m\}, j \in \{1, \ldots, \ell\}, \\
\qquad \text{the target of the } j\text{th function call is not } f_i\} \\
\quad \cup \{\mathit{main}\langle\rangle = \mathit{main}^{(1)}\langle\rangle\}
\end{array}$$

Here, $[e]_j$ is given by:

$$\begin{array}{l}
[\texttt{assume}\ v; a]_j = \texttt{assume}\ v; [a]_j \\
[\texttt{let}\ x = \mathrm{op}(\widetilde{v})\ \texttt{in}\ a]_j = \texttt{let}\ x = \mathrm{op}(\widetilde{v})\ \texttt{in}\ [a]_j \\
[\langle\rangle]_j = \langle\rangle \qquad [\texttt{fail}]_j = \texttt{fail} \qquad [x]_j = x \\
[x\ v_1 \cdots v_k]_j = \sharp_j(x)\ {v_1}^{\flat_{j+1}} \cdots {v_k}^{\flat_{j+1}} \qquad (k \geq 1) \\
[f\ v_1 \cdots v_k]_j = f^{(j)}\ {v_1}^{\flat_{j+1}} \cdots {v_k}^{\flat_{j+1}} \\
c^{\flat_j} = c \qquad x^{\flat_j} = x \quad (\text{if } x \text{ is a base variable}) \\
(x\ \widetilde{v})^{\flat_j} = \langle\underbrace{\lambda\widetilde{y}.\langle\rangle, \ldots, \lambda\widetilde{y}.\langle\rangle}_{j-1}, \sharp_j(x)(\widetilde{v}^{\flat_j}), \ldots, \sharp_\ell(x)(\widetilde{v}^{\flat_j})\rangle \\
\quad (\text{if } x \text{ is a function variable}) \\
(f\ \widetilde{v})^{\flat_j} = \langle\underbrace{\lambda\widetilde{y}.\langle\rangle, \ldots, \lambda\widetilde{y}.\langle\rangle}_{j-1}, f^{(j)}(\widetilde{v}^{\flat_j}), \ldots, f^{(\ell)}(\widetilde{v}^{\flat_j})\rangle
\end{array}$$

Here, each function parameter has been replaced by a ℓ-tuple of functions.

The SHP $\mathbf{SHP}(D, s)$, constructed from a source program D and a spurious error path s, contains neither recursion nor non-deterministic branch, and is reduced to $\texttt{fail}$ if and only if $\mathit{main}\langle\rangle \overset{s}{\Longrightarrow}_D \texttt{fail}$. Furthermore, each function in the SHP is called at most once.

[6] Here, for the sake of simplicity, we assume that m is some integer constant. As already mentioned, the random number generator *randi* can actually be encoded in our language.

[7] For clarity, we have extended our language with tuples of functions. If necessary, they can be removed by the currying transformation.

The generated straightline program satisfies the following properties.

Lemma 5.1. *Suppose $D' = \textbf{\textit{SHP}}(D, s)$. Then:*

1. *D' contains neither recursions nor non-deterministic branches $e_1 \Box e_2$.*
2. *$main\langle\rangle \stackrel{s}{\Longrightarrow}_D$ `fail` if and only if $main\langle\rangle \Longrightarrow_{D'}$ `fail`.*
3. *Each function $f_i^{(j)}$ in D' is called at most once.*

5.2.2 Typing SHP

The next step is to infer dependent types for functions in SHP. Thanks to the properties that SHP contains neither recursion nor non-deterministic branch and that every function is linear, the standard dependent type system is sound and complete for the safety of the program. Let us write $\vdash_{\rm DT} D$ if D is typable in the fragment of the dependent type system presented in Section 4 without intersection types (but extended with (non-dependent) tuple types).

Lemma 5.2. *Let $D' = \textbf{\textit{SHP}}(D, s)$. Then, $\vdash_{DT} D' : \Delta$ for some Δ if and only if $main\langle\rangle \not\Longrightarrow_{D'}$ `fail`.*

Proof sketch The "only if" part follows immediately from the soundness of the dependent type system. For the "if" part, it suffices to observe that, as every function in D' is linear, each variable x of base type can be assigned a type $\{\nu : b \mid \nu = v\}$, where v is the value that x is bound to. □

We can use existing algorithms [32, 33] to infer dependent types: we first prepare a template of a dependent type for each function, generate constraints on predicate variables, and solve the constraints. We give below an overview of the dependent type inference procedure through an example; an interested reader may wish to consult [32, 33].

Example 5.2. Recall the straightline program in Example 5.1. We prepare the following templates of the types of functions f, h, k:

$$\begin{array}{l} f : (x : \{\nu : \texttt{int} \mid P_1(\nu)\} \rightarrow (y : \{\nu : \texttt{int} \mid P_2(\nu, x)\} \rightarrow \star) \rightarrow \star) \\ h : (z : \{\nu : \texttt{int} \mid P_3(\nu)\} \rightarrow y : \{\nu : \texttt{int} \mid P_4(\nu, z)\} \rightarrow \star) \\ k : (x : \{\nu : \texttt{int} \mid P_0(\nu)\} \rightarrow \star) \end{array}$$

From the program, we obtain the following constraints on $P_0, \ldots, P_4$:

$$\begin{array}{l} P_0(m) \qquad \forall x.(P_1(x) \Rightarrow P_2(x+1, x)) \\ \forall z, y.(P_3(z) \wedge P_4(y, z) \Rightarrow y > z) \\ \forall n, y.P_0(n) \Rightarrow \\ \qquad (n \geq 0 \Rightarrow (P_1(n) \wedge P_3(n) \wedge (P_2(y, n) \Rightarrow P_4(y, n)))) \end{array}$$

Each constraint has been obtained from the definitions of *main*, f, g, and k. They can be normalized to:

$$\begin{array}{l} \forall \nu.(\nu = m \Rightarrow P_0(\nu)) \\ \forall n, \nu.(P_0(n) \wedge n \geq 0 \wedge \nu = n \Rightarrow P_1(\nu)) \\ \forall x, \nu.(P_1(x) \wedge \nu = x + 1 \Rightarrow P_2(\nu, x)) \\ \forall n, \nu.(P_0(n) \wedge n \geq 0 \wedge \nu = n \Rightarrow P_3(\nu)) \\ \forall n, z, \nu.(P_0(n) \wedge n \geq 0 \wedge z = n \wedge P_2(\nu, n) \Rightarrow P_4(\nu, z)) \\ \forall z, y.(P_3(z) \wedge P_4(y, z) \Rightarrow y > z) \end{array}$$

These constraints are "acyclic" in the sense that for each constraint of the form $C_i \Rightarrow P_i(\widetilde{x})$, C_i contains only (positive) occurrences of predicates P_j's such that $j < i$ occur. Such constraints can be solved by using a sub-procedure of existing methods for dependent type inference based on interpolants [32, 33], and the following predicates can be obtained. (The inferred predicates depend on the underlying interpolating theorem prover.)

$$\begin{array}{c} P_0(\nu) \equiv P_1(\nu) \equiv P_3(\nu) \equiv \texttt{true} \\ P_2(\nu, x) \equiv P_4(\nu, x) \equiv \nu > x \end{array}$$

Thus, we obtain the following types for f and h:

$$\begin{array}{l} f : (x : \{\nu : \texttt{int} \mid \texttt{true}\} \rightarrow (y : \{\nu : \texttt{int} \mid \nu > x\} \rightarrow \star) \rightarrow \star) \\ h : (z : \{\nu : \texttt{int} \mid \texttt{true}\} \rightarrow y : \{\nu : \texttt{int} \mid \nu > z\} \rightarrow \star) \end{array}$$

5.2.3 Refining abstraction types

The final step is to refine the abstraction types of the source program, based on the dependent types inferred for the straightline program. Let $\delta_{f,j}$ be the inferred dependent type of $f^{(j)}$. Then, we can obtain an abstraction type $\sigma_{f,j}$ such that $\textbf{undup}(\delta_{f,j}) \in$ *DepTy*$(\sigma_{f,j})$ (the choice of such $\sigma_{f,j}$ depends on what predicates are considered atomic), where $\textbf{undup}(\delta)$ is defined by:

$$\begin{array}{rcl} \textbf{undup}(\{\nu : b \mid \psi\}) & = & \{\nu : b \mid \psi\} \\ \textbf{undup}(x : \delta_1 \rightarrow \delta_2) & = & x : \textbf{undup}(\delta_1) \rightarrow \textbf{undup}(\delta_2) \\ \textbf{undup}(\delta_1 \times \cdots \times \delta_n) & = & \bigwedge_{i \in \{1, \ldots, n\}} \textbf{undup}(\delta_i) \end{array}$$

The new abstraction type σ'_f of f is given by:

$$\sigma'_f = \sigma_f \sqcup \sigma_{f,1} \sqcup \cdots \sqcup \sigma_{f,\ell},$$

where σ_f is the previous abstraction type of f and $\sigma_1 \sqcup \sigma_2$ is obtained by just merging the corresponding predicates:

$$\begin{array}{l} b[\widetilde{P}] \sqcup b[\widetilde{Q}] = b[\widetilde{P}, \widetilde{Q}] \\ (x : \sigma_1 \rightarrow \sigma_2) \sqcup (x : \sigma'_1 \rightarrow \sigma'_2) = x : (\sigma_1 \sqcup \sigma'_1) \rightarrow (\sigma_2 \sqcup \sigma'_2) \end{array}$$

We write *Refine*(Γ, Δ) for the refined abstraction type environment $f_1 : \sigma'_{f_1}, \ldots, f_n : \sigma'_{f_n}$. (There is a non-determinism coming from the choice of $\sigma_{f,j}$, but that does not matter below.)

Example 5.3. Recall Example 5.3. From the dependent types of f and g, we obtain the following abstraction types:

$$\begin{array}{l} f : (x : \texttt{int}[\,] \rightarrow (y : \texttt{int}[\lambda\nu.\nu > x] \rightarrow \star) \rightarrow \star) \\ h : (z : \texttt{int}[\,] \rightarrow y : \texttt{int}[\lambda\nu.\nu > z] \rightarrow \star) \end{array}$$

Suppose that the previous abstraction types were

$$\begin{array}{l} f : (x : \texttt{int}[\,] \rightarrow (y : \texttt{int}[\,] \rightarrow \star) \rightarrow \star) \\ h : (z : \texttt{int}[\lambda\nu.\nu = 0] \rightarrow y : \texttt{int}[\lambda\nu.\nu > 0] \rightarrow \star) \end{array}$$

Then, the refined abstraction types are:

$$\begin{array}{l} f : (x : \texttt{int}[\,] \rightarrow (y : \texttt{int}[\lambda\nu.\nu > x] \rightarrow \star) \rightarrow \star) \\ h : (z : \texttt{int}[\lambda\nu.\nu = 0] \rightarrow y : \texttt{int}[\lambda\nu.\nu > 0, \lambda\nu.\nu > z] \rightarrow \star) \end{array}$$

5.3 Properties of the CEGAR algorithm

We now discuss properties of the overall CEGAR algorithm. If the refined abstraction type is obtained from an infeasible error path s, the new abstract boolean program no longer has the path s. This is the so called "progress property" known in the literature on CEGAR for the usual (i.e. finite state or pushdown) model checking. Formally, we can prove the following property (see [25] for the proof):

Theorem 5.3 (progress). *Let D_1 be a well-typed program and s be an infeasible path of D_1. Suppose $D_2 = \textbf{\textit{SHP}}(D_1, s)$ and $\vdash_{DIT} D_2 : \Delta$ with $\Gamma = Refine(\Gamma', \Delta)$ for some Γ'. Then, there exists D_3 such that $\vdash D_1 : \Gamma \rightsquigarrow D_3$, and $main\langle\rangle \stackrel{s}{\not\Longrightarrow}_{D_3}$ `fail`.*

The progress property above does not guarantee that the verification will eventually terminate: There is a case where the entire CEGAR loop does not terminate, finding new spurious error paths forever (see Section 6). Indeed, we cannot expect to obtain a sound and complete verification algorithm, as the reachability is undecidable in general even if programs are restricted to those using only linear arithmetics.

We can however modify our algorithm so that it is *relatively complete* with respect to the dependent intersection type system, in the sense that all the programs typable in the dependent intersection type system can be verified by our method. Let *genP* be a total map from the set of integers to the set of predicates. (Such a total map exists, as the set of predicates is recursively enumerable.) Upon the i-th iteration of the CEGAR loop, add the predicate *genP*(i)

to each position of abstraction type, in addition to the predicates inferred from counterexamples. Then, if a program is well-typed under Δ in the dependent intersection type system, an abstraction type environment Γ such that $\Delta \in \mathit{DepTy}(\Gamma)$ is eventually found, so that by Theorem 4.4, our verification succeeds. Of course, this is impractical, but we may be able to adapt the technique of [18] to get a practical algorithm.

6. Implementation and Preliminary Experiments

Based on our method described so far, we have implemented a prototype verifier for a tiny subset of Objective Caml, having only booleans and integers as base types. Instead of the non-deterministic choice ($e_1 \Box e_2$), the system allows conditionals and free variables (representing unknown integers). Our verifier uses TRECS [21, 22] as the underlying higher-order model checker (for Step 2 in Figure 1), and uses CSIsat [6] for computing interpolants to solve constraints (for Step 4). CVC3 [5] is used for feasibility checking (for Step 3) and computing abstract transitions (i.e., to compute formulas ψ and ψ' in rule A-CADD of Figure 4 for Step 1). As computing the precise abstract transitions (i.e. the strongest formulas ψ and ψ' in rule A-CADD) is expensive, we have adapted several optimizations described in Section 5.2 of [2] such as bounding the maximum number of predicates taken into account for computing abstraction with a sacrifice of the precision. The implementation can be tested at `http://www.kb.ecei.tohoku.ac.jp/~ryosuke/cegar/`. The full version [25] contains more details about the experiments.

The results of preliminary experiments are shown in Table 1. The column "S" shows the size of programs, measured in word counts. The column "O" shows the largest order of functions in the program (an order-1 function takes only base values as arguments, while an order-2 function takes order-1 functions as arguments).[8] The column "C" shows the number of CEGAR cycles. The remaining columns show running times, measured in seconds. The column "abst" shows the time spent for computing abstract programs (from given programs and abstraction types). The column "mc" shows the time spent (by TRECS) for higher-order model checking. The column "cegar" shows the time spent for finding new predicates (Step 4 in Figure 1). The column "total" shows the total running time (machine spec.: 3GHz CPU with 8GB memory).

The programs used in the experiment are as follows. Free variables denote unknown integers.

- `intro1`, `intro2`, and `intro3` are the three examples in Section 1.
- `sum` and `mult` compute $1 + \cdots + n$ and $\underbrace{n + \cdots + n}_{n}$ respectively, and asserts that the result is greater than or equal to n. Here is the code of `sum`.

```
let rec sum n =
  if n <= 0 then 0 else n + sum (n - 1)
in assert (n <= sum n)
```

- `max` defines a higher-order function that takes a function that computes the maximum of two integers, and three integers as input, and returns the maximum of the three integers:

```
let max max2 x y z = max2 (max2 x y) z in
let f x y = if x >= y then x else y in
let m = max f x y z in assert (f x m = m)
```

The last line asserts that the return value of `max` is greater than or equal to `x` (with respect to the function f).

[8] Because of the restriction of the model checker TRECS, all the source programs are actually verified after the CPS transformation. Thus, all the tested programs are actually higher-order, taking continuation functions.

- `mc91` is McCarthy 91 function.

```
let rec mc91 x =
  if x > 100 then x - 10 else mc91(mc91(x + 11))
in if n <= 101 then assert (mc91 n = 91)
```

The last line asserts that the result is 91 if the argument is less than or equal to 101.

- `ack` defines Ackermann function ack and asserts $ack(n) \geq n$.
- `repeat` defines a higher-order function that takes a function f and integers n, s, then returns $f^n(s)$.

```
let rec repeat f n s =
  if n = 0 then s else f (repeat f (n - 1) s) in
let succ x = x + 1 in
  assert (repeat succ n 0 = n)
```

- `fhnhn` is a program not typable in the dependent intersection type system but verifiable in our method (c.f. Remark 1):

```
let f x y = assert (not (x() > 0 && y() < 0)) in
let h x y = x in let g n = f (h n) (h n) in g m
```

- `hrec` is a program that creates infinitely many function closures:

```
let rec f g x =
  if x >= 0 then g x else f (f g) (g x) in
let succ x = x + 1 in assert(f succ n >= 0)
```

- `neg` is an example that needs nested intersection types:

```
let g x y = x in
let twice f x y = f (f x) y in
let neg x y = -x() in
  if n >= 0 then assert(twice neg (g n) () >= 0)
  else ()
```

- `apply` is the program discussed in Remark 2.
- `a-prod`, `a-cppr`, and `a-init` are programs manipulating arrays. A (functional) array has been encoded as a pair of the size and a function from indices to array contents. For example, the functions for creating and updating arrays are defined as follows.

```
let mk_array n i = assert(0<=i && i<n); 0
let update i n a x =
  a(i); let a' j = if i=j then x else a(i) in a'
```

For `a-prod` and `a-cppr`, it has been verified that there is no array boundary error. Program `a-init` initializes an array, and asserts the correctness of initialization. and `a-max` creates an array of size n whose i-th element is $n-i$, computes the maximum element m, and asserts that $m \geq n$. These examples show an advantage of higher-order model checking; various data structures can be encoded as higher-order functions, and their properties can be verified in a uniform manner.

- `l-zipunzip` and `l-zipmap` are taken from list-processing programs. We have manually abstracted lists to integers (representing the list length), and then verified the size properties of list functions. For example, the code for l-zipunizp is:

```
let f g x y = g (x+1) (y+1) in
let rec unzip x k =
  if x=0 then k 0 0 else unzip (x-1) (f k) in
let rec zip x y =
  if x=0 then if y=0 then 0 else fail()
  else if y=0 then fail() else 1+zip(x-1)(y-1)
in unzip n zip
```

- `hors` encodes a model checking problem for higher-order recursion schemes *extended with integers* (which cannot be handled by recursion scheme model checkers).
- `e-simpl` and `e-fact` model programs that use exceptions, where an exception handler is expressed as a continuation, and assert that there are no uncaught exceptions. The idea of the encoding of exceptions is similar to [20], but unlike [20], exceptions can carry integer values.
- `r-lock` and `r-file` model programs that use locks and files, and assert that they are accessed in a correct manner. The encoding

is similar to [22], but (unlike [22]) the programs' control behaviors depend on integer values.

- A program of name "xxx-e" is a buggy version of the program "xxx".

The above programs have been verified (or rejected, for wrong programs) correctly, except `apply`. As discussed in Remark 2, `apply` cannot be verified because of the fundamental limitation of abstraction types. Our system continues to infer new (but too specific) abstraction types $(\mathtt{int}[\lambda\nu.\nu = i] \to \star) \to \mathtt{int}[\lambda\nu.\nu = i] \to \star$ for $i = 0, 1, 2, \ldots$ forever and (necessarily) does not terminate. The program can however be verified if the arguments of `apply` are swapped. The same problem has been observed for variations of some of the programs above: sometimes we had to add or swap arguments of functions.

Another limitation revealed by the experiments is that for some variations of the programs, the system infers too specific predicates and does not terminate. For example, the verification for `a-max` fails if we assert $m \geq a(j)$ instead of $m \geq n$ (where m is the maximal element computed, a is the array, and j is some index). Relaxing these limitations seems necessary for verification of larger programs, and we plan to do so by adding heuristics to generalize inferred abstraction types (e.g. by using widening techniques [9]).

Apart from the limitations above, our system is reasonably fast. This indicates that, although higher-order model checking has the extremely high worst-case complexity (n-EXPTIME complete [28]), our overall approach works at least for small programs as long as suitable predicates are found. See further discussions on the scalability in Section 8.

7. Related Work

7.1 Model Checking of Higher-Order Programs

The model checking of higher-order recursion schemes has been extensively studied [19, 24, 28]. Ong [28] proved the decidability of the modal μ-calculus model checking of recursion schemes. Kobayashi [22] then proposed a new framework of higher-order program verification based on the model checking of recursion schemes, already suggesting a use of predicate abstraction and CEGAR to deal with programs manipulating infinite data domain. There were two missing pieces in his framework, however. One was a practical model checking algorithm for recursion schemes (note that the model checking of recursion schemes is in general n-EXPTIME-complete), and the other was a method to apply predicate abstraction and CEGAR to higher-order programs. The former piece has been supplied later by Kobayashi [20], and supplying the latter piece was the goal of the present paper.

In parallel to the present work, Unno et al. [26, 34] and Ong and Ramsay [29] proposed applications of higher-order model checking to verification of tree-processing programs. Their approaches are radically different from ours. First, they use different abstraction techniques: tree data are abstracted using either tree automata [26, 34] or patterns [29], which cannot abstract values using binary predicates (such as $2 \times x \geq y$). Secondly, The method of [26] applies only to programs that can be expressed in the form of (higher-order) tree transducers, and the extension in [34] requires user annotations. Ong and Ramsay's method [29] applies to general functional programs and includes a CEGAR mechanism, but the precision of their method is heavily affected by that of a variable binding analysis, and their CEGAR is completely different from ours. Their technique does not satisfy relative completeness like Theorem 4.4.

7.2 Dependent Type Inference

There have been studies on automatic or semi-automatic inference of dependent types [7, 11, 16, 31–33]. There are similarities between the goals of those studies and that of our work. First, one of the goals of dependent type inference is to prove the lack of assertion failures, as in the present work. Secondly, our technique can actually be used for inferring dependent types. Recursion scheme model checker TRecS [20] is type-based, and produces type information as a certificate of successful verification. For example, for the abstraction of the last example in Section 1, it infers the type $\star \to (\mathtt{true} \to \star) \to \star$ for (the abstract version of) f. Combined with the abstraction type of f, we can recover the following dependent type for $f : (x : \mathtt{int} \to (y : \{\nu : \mathtt{int} \mid \nu > x\} \to \star) \to \star)$.

Though the goals are similar, the techniques are different. Rondon et al.'s liquid types [31] requires users to specify predicates (or more precisely, shapes of predicates, called *qualifiers*) used in dependent types. Jhala et al. [16] proposed an automatic method for inferring qualifiers for liquid types. Their method extracts qualifiers from a proof that a finite unfolding of a source program does not get stuck, and has some similarity to our method to infer abstraction types from an error path. Unno and Kobayashi [33] proposed an automatic method for inferring dependent types. They first prepare templates of dependent types (that contain predicate variables) and generate (possibly recursive) constraints on predicate variables. They then solve the constraints by using an interpolating theorem prover. Jhala et al. [17] also propose a similar method, where they reduce the constraint solving in the last phase to model checking of imperative programs. These approaches [16, 17, 31, 33] do support higher-order functions, but in a limited manner, in the sense that nested intersection types are not allowed. The difference between dependent types with/without intersections is like the one between context (or flow) sensitive/insensitive analyses. The former is more precise though it can be costly.[9] In general, nested intersection types are necessary to verify a program when function parameters are used more than once in different contexts. Indeed, as discussed in [25], several of the programs in Section 6 (e.g. `neg`, where the first argument of `twice` is used in two different contexts) require nested intersection types, and almost all the examples given by Kobayashi [20, 22] call for nested intersection types.

The limitation of our current prototype implementation is that the supported language features are limited. We believe that it is possible to extend our implementation to deal with data structures. In fact, the predicate abstraction introduced in Section 4 applies to data structures given an appropriate theorem prover. We expect the CEGAR part can also be extended, e.g. by restricting the properties on data structures to size properties, by treating data constructors as uninterpreted function symbols, etc.

Technically, most closest to ours is Terauchi's work [32]. In his method, candidates for dependent types are inferred from a finite unfolding of a source program, and then a fixedpoint computation algorithm is used to filter out invalid types. If the source program is not typable with the candidates for dependent types, the program is further unfolded and more candidates are collected. This cycle (which may diverge) is repeated until the source program is found to be well-typed or ill-typed. This is somewhat similar to the way our verification method works: abstraction types are inferred from an error trace (instead of an unfolding of a program), and then higher-order model checking (which also involves a fixedpoint computation) is applied to verify the abstract program. If the verification fails and an infeasible error path is found, the error path is used to infer more predicates, and this cycle is repeated. Thus, roughly speaking, our CEGAR phase corresponds to that of Terauchi to find candidates for dependent types, and our phases for predicate abstraction and higher-order model checking corresponds to Terauchi's fixedpoint computation phase. Advantages of

[9] Our method is an extreme case of context/flow sensitive analysis, which is sound and complete for programs with finite data domains.

program	S	O	C	abst	mc	cegar	total	program	S	O	C	abst	mc	cegar	total
intro1	27	2	1	0.00	0.00	0.00	0.01	a-init	96	2	5	0.16	0.18	0.38	0.73
intro2	29	2	1	0.00	0.00	0.00	0.00	a-max	70	2	5	2.34	2.01	0.43	4.78
intro3	30	2	1	0.00	0.00	0.00	0.00	l-zipunzip	81	2	3	0.03	0.08	0.02	0.12
sum	24	1	2	0.00	0.00	0.01	0.02	l-zipmap	65	2	4	0.07	0.09	0.03	0.20
mult	31	1	2	0.01	0.00	0.02	0.03	hors	64	2	2	0.00	0.00	0.00	0.01
max	42	2	1	0.00	0.00	0.03	0.03	e-simple	27	2	1	0.00	0.00	0.00	0.00
mc91	32	1	2	0.01	0.04	0.02	0.07	e-fact	55	2	2	0.00	0.01	0.00	0.01
ack	53	1	3	0.02	0.09	0.03	0.15	r-lock	54	1	5	0.01	0.02	0.02	0.04
repeat	37	2	3	0.01	0.02	0.12	0.15	r-file	168	1	12	0.30	4.78	0.16	5.23
fhnhn	37	2	1	0.01	0.01	0.02	0.04	sum-e	26	1	0	0.00	0.00	0.00	0.00
hrec	34	2	2	0.00	0.01	0.02	0.03	mult-e	33	1	0	0.00	0.00	0.00	0.00
neg	47	2	1	0.01	0.01	0.01	0.03	mc91-e	32	1	0	0.00	0.00	0.00	0.00
apply	34	2	-	-	-	-	-	repeat-e	35	2	0	0.00	0.00	0.00	0.00
a-prod	70	2	4	0.07	0.06	0.08	0.22	a-max-e	70	2	2	0.01	0.06	0.06	0.13
a-cppr	149	2	6	0.32	2.82	0.26	3.40	r-lock-e	54	1	0	0.00	0.00	0.00	0.00

Table 1. Results of preliminary experiments

ours are: (i) our method can generate an error path as a counterexample; there is no false alarm. On the other hand, a counterexample of Terauchi's method is an unfolding of a program, which may actually be safe. (ii) We infer predicates from an error trace, rather than from an unfolding of a program; From the latter, too many constraints are generated, especially for programs containing non-linear recursions. (iii) Our method can find dependent types constructed from arbitrary boolean combinations of the inferred predicates, while Terauchi's method only looks for dependent types constructed from the formulas directly generated by an interpolating theorem prover; thus, the success of the latter more heavily relies on the quality or heuristics of the underlying interpolating theorem prover. (iv) Because of the point (iii) above, our method (predicate abstraction + higher-order model checking) can also be used in a liquid type-like setting [31] where atomic predicates are given by a user. (v) Because of the point discussed in Remark 1, the combination of our predicate abstraction and higher-order model checking is strictly more powerful than Terauchi's approach (as long as suitable predicates are found). (vi) Our method can be extended to verify more general properties (expressed by the modal μ-calculus), by appealing to the results on higher-order model checking [24, 28].

7.3 Traditional Model Checking

Predicate abstraction and CEGAR have been extensively studied in the context of finite state or pushdown model checking [2–4, 8, 12–15]. Predicate abstraction has also been applied to the game-semantics-based model checking [1]. We are not, however, aware of previous work that applies predicate abstraction and CEGAR to higher-order model checking. As discussed in Section 1, the extension of predicate abstraction and CEGAR to higher-order model checking is non-trivial. One may think that defunctionalization [30] can be used to eliminate higher-order functions and apply conventional model checking. The defunctionalization however uses recursive data structures to represent closures, so that the resulting verification method is too imprecise, unless a clever abstraction technique for recursive data structures is available.

The three components of our verification method, predicate abstraction, higher-order model checking (TRecS), and CEGAR, may be seen as higher-order counterparts of the three components of SLAM [2–4]: C2BP, BEBOP, and NEWTON. Our use of dependency in abstraction types appears to subsume Ball et al.'s polymorphic predicate abstraction [3]. For example, the `id` function in [3] can be abstracted by using the abstraction type x : $\texttt{int}[\,] \rightarrow \texttt{int}[\lambda y.y = x]$.

There are a lot of studies to optimize predicate abstraction (especially for optimizing or avoiding the costly computation of abstract transition functions) in the context of conventional model checking [2, 27]. We have already borrowed some of the optimization techniques as mentioned in Section 6, and plan to adapt more techniques.

7.4 Abstract Interpretation

The combination of predicate abstraction and higher-order model checking may be viewed as a kind of abstract interpretation [9]. The abstract domain used for each functional value is defined by abstraction types, and predicate abstraction transforms a source program into an HBP whose semantics corresponds to the abstract semantics of the source program. Higher-order model checking then computes the abstract semantics. An advantage here is that thanks to the model checking algorithm [20] for higher-order recursion schemes, the computation of the abstract semantics is often much faster than a naive fixed-point computation (which is extremely costly for higher-order function values).

8. Conclusion

We have proposed predicate abstraction and CEGAR techniques for higher-order model checking, and implemented a prototype verifier. We believe that this is a new promising approach to automatic verification of higher-order functional programs. Optimization of the implementation and larger experiments are left for future work.

We conclude the paper with discussions on the scalability of our method. The current implementation is not scalable for large programs, but we expect that (after several years of efforts) we can eventually obtain a much more scalable verifier based on our method, for several reasons. First, the complexity of the model checking of higher-order recursion schemes is n-EXPTIME complete [28], but with certain parameters being fixed, the complexity is actually polynomial (linear, if restricted to safety properties) time in the size of a recursion scheme (or, the size of HBP). Furthermore, n-EXPTIME completeness is the *worst-case* complexity, and recent model checking algorithms [20, 23] do not immediately suffer from the n-EXPTIME bottleneck. Secondly, the implementation of the underlying higher-order model checker TRecS is premature, and there is a good chance for improvement. Thirdly, the current implementation of predicate abstraction and CEGAR is also quite naive. For example, the current implementation computes abstract programs eagerly. We expect that a good speed-up is obtained by computing abstract programs lazily.

Acknowledgment

We would like to thank members of our research group for discussion and comments. We would also like to thank anonymous referees for useful comments. This work was partially supported by Kakenhi 20240001.

References

[1] A. Bakewell and D. R. Ghica. Compositional predicate abstraction from game semantics. In *TACAS '09*, pages 62–76. Springer, 2009.

[2] T. Ball, R. Majumdar, T. Millstein, and S. K. Rajamani. Automatic predicate abstraction of C programs. In *PLDI '01*, pages 203–213. ACM, 2001.

[3] T. Ball, T. Millstein, and S. K. Rajamani. Polymorphic predicate abstraction. *ACM Transactions on Programming Languages and Systems*, 27(2):314–343, 2005.

[4] T. Ball and S. K. Rajamani. The SLAM project: debugging system software via static analysis. In *POPL '02*, pages 1–3. ACM, 2002.

[5] C. Barrett and C. Tinelli. CVC3. In *CAV '07*, volume 4590 of *LNCS*, pages 298–302. Springer, July 2007.

[6] D. Beyer, D. Zufferey, and R. Majumdar. CSIsat : Interpolation for LA+EUF (tool paper). In *CAV '08*, volume 5123 of *LNCS*, pages 304–308, July 2008.

[7] W.-N. Chin and S.-C. Khoo. Calculating sized types. *Higher-Order and Symbolic Computation*, 14(2-3):261–300, September 2001.

[8] E. Clarke, O. Grumberg, S. Jha, Y. Lu, and H. Veith. Counterexample-guided abstraction refinement for symbolic model checking. *Journal of the ACM*, 50(5):752–794, 2003.

[9] P. Cousot and N. Halbwachs. Automatic discovery of linear restraints among variables of a program. In *POPL '78*, pages 84–96. ACM, 1978.

[10] W. Damm. The IO- and OI-hierarchies. *Theoretical Computer Science*, 20(2):95 – 207, 1982.

[11] C. Flanagan. Hybrid type checking. In *POPL '06*, pages 245–256. ACM, 2006.

[12] S. Graf and H. Saïdi. Construction of abstract state graphs with PVS. In *CAV '97*, volume 1254 of *LNCS*, pages 72–83. Springer, June 1997.

[13] M. Heizmann, J. Hoenicke, and A. Podelski. Nested interpolants. In *POPL '10*, pages 471–482. ACM, 2010.

[14] T. A. Henzinger, R. Jhala, R. Majumdar, and K. L. McMillan. Abstractions from proofs. In *POPL '04*, pages 232–244. ACM, 2004.

[15] T. A. Henzinger, R. Jhala, R. Majumdar, and G. Sutre. Lazy abstraction. In *POPL '02*, pages 58–70. ACM, 2002.

[16] R. Jhala and R. Majumdar. Counterexample refinement for functional programs. Manuscript, available from `http://www.cs.ucla.edu/~rupak/Papers/CEGARFunctional.ps`, 2009.

[17] R. Jhala, R. Majumdar, and A. Rybalchenko. Refinement type inference via abstract interpretation. arXiv:1004.2884v1, 2010.

[18] R. Jhala and K. L. McMillan. A practical and complete approach to predicate refinement. In *TACAS '06*, volume 3920 of *LNCS*, pages 459–473. Springer, 2006.

[19] T. Knapik, D. Niwinski, and P. Urzyczyn. Higher-order pushdown trees are easy. In *FoSSaCS '02*, volume 2303 of *LNCS*, pages 205–222. Springer, 2002.

[20] N. Kobayashi. Model-checking higher-order functions. In *PPDP '09*, pages 25–36. ACM, 2009.

[21] N. Kobayashi. TRecS. `http://www.kb.ecei.tohoku.ac.jp/~koba/trecs/`, 2009.

[22] N. Kobayashi. Types and higher-order recursion schemes for verification of higher-order programs. In *POPL '09*, pages 416–428. ACM, 2009.

[23] N. Kobayashi. A practical linear time algorithm for trivial automata model checking of higher-order recursion schemes. In *FoSSaCS '11*. Springer, 2011.

[24] N. Kobayashi and C.-H. L. Ong. A type system equivalent to the modal mu-calculus model checking of higher-order recursion schemes. In *LICS '09*, pages 179–188. IEEE, 2009.

[25] N. Kobayashi, R. Sato, and H. Unno. Predicate abstraction and CEGAR for higher-order model checking. An extended version, available from `http://www.kb.ecei.tohoku.ac.jp/~uhiro/`, 2011.

[26] N. Kobayashi, N. Tabuchi, and H. Unno. Higher-order multi-parameter tree transducers and recursion schemes for program verification. In *POPL '10*, pages 495–508. ACM, 2010.

[27] K. L. McMillan. An interpolating theorem prover. *Theoretical Computer Science*, 345(1):101–121, 2005.

[28] C.-H. L. Ong. On model-checking trees generated by higher-order recursion schemes. In *LICS '06*, pages 81–90. IEEE, 2006.

[29] C.-H. L. Ong and S. J. Ramsay. Verifying higher-order functional programs with pattern-matching algebraic data types. In *POPL '11*, pages 587–598. ACM, 2011.

[30] J. C. Reynolds. Definitional interpreters for higher-order programming languages. In *Proceedings of the ACM annual conference - Volume 2*, pages 717–740. ACM, 1972.

[31] P. Rondon, M. Kawaguchi, and R. Jhala. Liquid types. In *PLDI '08*. ACM, 2008.

[32] T. Terauchi. Dependent types from counterexamples. In *POPL '10*, pages 119–130. ACM, 2010.

[33] H. Unno and N. Kobayashi. Dependent type inference with interpolants. In *PPDP '09*, pages 277–288. ACM, 2009.

[34] H. Unno, N. Tabuchi, and N. Kobayashi. Verification of tree-processing programs via higher-order model checking. In *APLAS '10*, volume 6461 of *LNCS*, pages 312–327. Springer, October/December 2010.

[35] H. Xi and F. Pfenning. Dependent types in practical programming. In *POPL '99*, pages 214–227. ACM, 1999.

Mostly-Automated Verification of Low-Level Programs in Computational Separation Logic

Adam Chlipala

Harvard University
Cambridge, MA, USA
adamc@cs.harvard.edu

Abstract

Several recent projects have shown the feasibility of verifying low-level systems software. Verifications based on automated theorem-proving have omitted reasoning about *first-class code pointers*, which is critical for tasks like certifying implementations of threads and processes. Conversely, verifications that deal with first-class code pointers have featured long, complex, manual proofs. In this paper, we introduce the Bedrock framework, which supports mostly-automated proofs about programs with the full range of features needed to implement, e.g., language runtime systems.

The heart of our approach is in mostly-automated discharge of verification conditions inspired by separation logic. Our take on separation logic is *computational*, in the sense that function specifications are usually written in terms of *reference implementations in a purely functional language*. Logical quantifiers are the most challenging feature for most automated verifiers; by relying on functional programs (written in the expressive language of the Coq proof assistant), we are able to avoid quantifiers almost entirely. This leads to some dramatic improvements compared to both past work in classical verification, which we compare against with implementations of data structures like binary search trees and hash tables; and past work in verified programming with code pointers, which we compare against with examples like function memoization and a cooperative threading library.

Categories and Subject Descriptors F.3.1 [*Logics and meanings of programs*]: Mechanical verification; D.2.4 [*Software Engineering*]: Correctness proofs, formal methods

General Terms Languages, Verification

Keywords interactive proof assistants, separation logic, low-level programming languages, functional programming

1. Introduction

The desirability of verifying systems infrastructure software has long been recognized. If our operating systems and runtime systems are not correct, then we can hope for little guarantee about the behavior of our applications. Thus, the pay-off of formal correctness verification of systems software is large, but the human cost of verification has been considered to be so great as to offset the benefit. Several recent projects have given reason to reconsider that position. The L4.verified project [18] has finished a complete functional correctness verification for a realistic operating system microkernel, based on a quite non-trivial amount of proof code for the Isabelle/HOL proof assistant [27]. The Verve project [30] has completed a mostly-automated Boogie [1] verification of the core of an operating system which is designed to serve as a kind of runtime system for code written in C#.

The productivity advantage of mostly-automated verification over manual tactic-based proving seems clear. Unfortunately, the well-known automated verification systems restrict specifications to first-order logic, which creates a dramatic restriction on which specifications may be expressed compactly, or even expressed at all. For instance, it seems unlikely that these first-order systems will ever be able to handle a proof of type safety for a non-trivial programming language, but exactly that kind of proof is required to complete the Verve project. It is possible to use different tools for different parts of a verification, but the programmer's task is certainly made simpler by sticking to a single environment. This choice should also help to minimize the trusted code base, which seems quite relevant, given the security consequences of operating system bugs.

There has been a significant amount of work on low-level verification systems that are higher-order in at least two distinct senses: they allow higher-order logic in specifications, and they allow reasoning about code pointers as data. For instance, the Certified Assembly Programming project has suggested several such program logics, including XCAP [24] and SCAP [13]. These systems have been used to complete complex verifications of threading libraries and other examples involving first-class code pointers. Unfortunately, the Coq [8] proofs involved are very long, complex, detailed, and brittle to changes of specification.

In this paper, we introduce Bedrock, a Coq library in which we have attempted to reconcile the above concerns. In particular, Bedrock is:

- **Low-level**: The framework supports verification of programs that, for performance reasons or otherwise, cannot tolerate any abstraction beyond that associated with assembly language.
- **Foundational**: The output of a Bedrock verification is a theorem whose statement depends only on the predicates chosen for the key specifications and on the operational semantics of some machine language. That is, there is no need to trust that the verification framework is bug-free; rather, one need only trust the usual Coq proof-checker and the formalization of the machine language semantics.
- **Higher-order**: Bedrock facilitates quite pleasant reasoning about code pointers as data.

PLDI'11, June 4–8, 2011, San Jose, California, USA.

- **Computational**: Many useful functions are specified most effectively by comparing with "reference implementations" in a pure functional language. Bedrock supports that model, backed by the full expressive power of Coq's usual programming language.
- **Structured**: Bedrock is an *extensible programming language*: any client program may add new control flow constructs by providing their (sound) proof rules. For example, adding high-level syntax for your own calling convention or exception handling construct is relatively straightforward and does not require tweaking the core library code. Unfortunately, for reasons of space, we will not discuss this aspect of Bedrock more in the present paper.
- **Mostly-automated**: Tactics (proof procedures) automate verification condition generation (in a form inspired by separation logic [28]) and most of the process of discharging those conditions. Manual proof effort is generally confined to, first, annotations specifying which simplification rules for abstract impure predicates should be applied at which program points; and, second, hint lemmas about mathematical objects like sets, maps, and lists. Crucially, neither kind of manual work deals explicitly with program syntax, memories, or program states.

The next section of the paper introduces Bedrock with the complete code for two simple examples: swapping two values in memory and incrementing the integer value in every node of a linked list. After walking through the examples, we explain how the reasoning we applied may be generalized into a mechanical procedure for reducing verification conditions in separation logic to simpler conditions that deal only with normal mathematical objects. This forms the basis of a very effective verification framework. To back up that claim, we perform two main sorts of comparison.

First, we compare against some examples implemented with Jahob [32], a representative of recent developments in mostly-automated functional correctness verification of data structure implementations. While Jahob deals with high-level Java programs, in Bedrock we must implement a `malloc` and `free` library before getting started, and all programs must contain explicit memory management code for both the heap and the stack. Despite that handicap, our annotation burden is comparable to that documented for Jahob, and we even achieve much more compact proofs for some examples, including hash tables, thanks to the *computational* specification approach we adopt.

Second, we implement a set of interesting programs that use code pointers in ways beyond usual function calling conventions. These examples cannot even be specified, let alone verified, in classical verifiers. In Bedrock, each of our higher-order examples requires only about a page of annotation, compared to thousands of lines in related work. The examples are an abstract memoization module, operating on imperative functions that compute pure functions over machine words, using arbitrary persistent local state; destructive concatenation of linked lists, written in continuation-passing style using explicit closures, which is the largest example from the first XCAP paper [24]; and a simple cooperative threading library, similar to an earlier XCAP implementation [25, 26]. For the examples where we compare against past XCAP implementations, we reduce annotation overhead by a factor of about 100, and we also pass the qualitative threshold of giving mostly-automated proofs that often adapt automatically to specification changes.

The complete code for the framework and the examples is available online at:

`http://adam.chlipala.net/bedrock/`

2. Bedrock by Example

The C programming language is often described as a "macro assembly language." Bedrock fits that description taken literally. The Bedrock Coq library is parametrized over a machine language with some concept of a basic block. In this paper, we deal with the framework instantiated to a simple idealized machine language. The language is idealized in that it has infinite-sized words and an infinite memory. In other respects, it is a realistic machine language, with a finite supply of global registers, a memory that can be modeled as an infinite array of words, and so on. Further details of this language will not be critical for what follows, and our code examples will provide further demonstrations. We expect that the Bedrock framework is applicable both to more realistic machine languages and, for slightly higher-level programs that do not need to manipulate machine contexts, to common compiler intermediate languages.

Bedrock generalizes the XCAP program logic [24], in the sense that, in place of deduction rules for particular instructions of a fixed machine language, Bedrock can be thought of as having a single rule that operates a basic block at a time. The rule (and the other deductive parts of Bedrock) is parametrized over a standard operational semantics for the machine language in use. Every basic block is assigned a logical precondition, and the basic block rule requires that, if execution enters a block in a state satisfying its precondition, then execution must proceed safely and reach a jump to some block whose precondition is then satisfied. In our idealized language, execution only "goes wrong" when a jump is made to a label that does not exist in the (unverified) program. Therefore, the block preconditions are the main component of program correctness theorems.

XCAP is based on an assertion logic (the language in which preconditions are written) whose design involves some subtleties which we will mostly ignore in this presentation, referring the reader to the first XCAP paper [24] for further details. It is a reasonable approximation to say that the assertion language is mostly a standard second-order logic, in the sense that quantification is allowed over both normal mathematical objects and over specifications themselves, but not over some more exotic domains like functions over specifications. So far, this summary describes a sub-language of the logic built into Coq. All of the differences stem from an unusual connective of the form $i@@p$, which says that there is a basic block at program counter i whose precondition is implied by specification p. This connective is the source of support for reasoning about sophisticated uses of code pointers, based on the possibility for quantified variables to appear inside p. We may even use second-order variables that stand for other specifications.

Prior work with XCAP has involved coding assembly programs directly. Bedrock makes the programmer's job easier by supporting a structured programming notation, such that programs look much like C code where atomic statements are literal assembly instructions. The details of Bedrock's low-level deductive system do not appear in verifications based on structured programming. Rather, we apply the standard technique of verification condition generation, so that the conditions to be proved do not refer to program syntax. As is usual, verification condition generation depends on invariant annotations in the program code. Structured syntax and its associated proofs are automatically "compiled" to proofs about normal machine code programs.

The rest of the details of Bedrock verification are best introduced through examples that demonstrate the core of our proof methodology, a procedure for simplifying verification conditions that are based on separation logic [28]. Figure 1 provides a quick informal reference for the programming and specification features that we will use.

Program syntax

R_i	Register
`$[E]`	Memory dereference
`L <- E`	Assignment command
`C;; C`	Command sequencing
`Goto E`	Computed jump
`[p] While (E) { C }`	Loop (with invariant)
`Use [lemmaName]`	Proof hint

Program states `st`

`st#`R_i	Project value of register
`st.[E]`	Project value stored at memory address
`st[L <- E]`	Update based on assignment command

Assertions `p`

`st ~> p`	State predicate (`st` bound in `p`)
`p /\ p`	Conjunction
`Ex x. p`	Existential quantification
`Ex x : T. p`	Existential with type annotation
`i @@ A`	Assertion about precondition of a code pointer
`![ P ] st`	Separation logic assertion

Separation logic assertions `P`

`[< p >]`	Lift normal assertion
`u ==> v`	"Pointer `u` points to value `v`"
`P * P`	Separating conjunction
`Ex x. P`	Existential quantification
`Ex x : T. P`	Existential with type annotation
`![ x ]`	Second-order specification variable
`!{ f` $v_1 \ldots v_n$ `}`	Abstract predicate

Figure 1. Bedrock syntax reference

```
Definition swap := bmodule {{
  bfunction "swap" [st ~> Ex fr : hprop,
    Ex a : nat, Ex b : nat,
    ![ st#R0 ==> a * st#R1 ==> b * ![fr] ] st
    /\ st#Rret @@ (st' ~>
      ![ st#R1 ==> a * st#R0 ==> b
        * ![fr] ] st') ] {
    R2 <- $[R0];;
    $[R0] <- $[R1];;
    $[R1] <- R2;;
    Goto Rret
  }
}}.

Theorem swapOk : moduleOk swap.
  structured; sep.
Qed.
```

Figure 2. A Bedrock function implementing pointer swapping

2.1 Swapping the Values at Two Memory Locations

Figure 2 gives the complete code to implement and verify a Bedrock function for swapping the values at two memory addresses. This code is processed by the normal, unmodified Coq interpreter, thanks to the use of Coq's syntax extension mechanism (or "macro system"). We start by defining a code module with the `bmodule` keyword. Inside the module is a single function `"swap"`, introduced with the `bfunction` keyword. After the function name appears the function precondition, which we will turn to shortly. First, we note that the function body here is a list of assembly instructions. The function inputs are in registers `R0` and `R1`, and the first three instructions use register `R2` as a temporary in swapping the contents of the memory cells pointed to by the inputs. The notation `<-` is for assignment, while `$[E]` stands for the memory cell pointed to by expression `E`. The last instruction returns from the function by jumping to the return pointer stored in register `Rret`.

The function precondition may appear daunting at first. It uses a few standard concepts with perhaps unusual ASCII syntax, along with a few less usual concepts. First, the notation `st ~> p` is a special "lambda" form that triggers the use of a special parsing nonterminal for `p`, so that `p` is parsed as an XCAP-style assertion. The variable `st` is bound in `p`; it is the function argument, standing for a machine state.

The body of `swap`'s precondition begins with three existential quantifiers, written `Ex`. The simplest two of the three bound variables are `a` and `b`, which stand for the initial contents of the memory cells pointed to by `R0` and `R1`, respectively. In this idealized machine language, memory cells contain natural numbers, so we annotate `a` and `b` with the Coq type `nat`. We will return shortly to the remaining variable `fr`.

After the quantifiers, we have an assertion of the form `![ P ] st`, where `P` is an assertion of separation logic that we are requiring must hold in machine state `st`. Within these brackets, we may write `u ==> v` to assert that the memory cell at address `u` holds word `v`. The separating conjunction `P * Q`, which has lower parsing precedence than `==>`, asserts that the machine memory may be broken into two disjoint pieces, such that `P` satisfies one and `Q` the other. In our example, we calculate two memory cell addresses for "points-to" facts using the `#` operator, which projects a particular register value out of a machine state.

A third assertion is added to this memory precondition with the separating conjunction: we see the variable `fr` used with the syntax `![fr]`. Inside a separation logic assertion, the `![_]` notation indicates a *specification variable*. That is, in this example, we are quantifying over a memory specification `fr` and then using it to describe one part of the initial memory. Concretely, `fr` has type `hprop`, the type of predicates over partial heaps. The name `fr` is meant to be suggestive of *frame condition*, a condition that describes all parts of memory that are irrelevant to the present function. Standard separation logic contains the *frame rule* for the statement partial correctness judgment $\{P\}s\{Q\}$:

$$\frac{\{P\}s\{Q\}}{\{P * R\}s\{Q * R\}}$$

That is, when a statement satisfies a particular precondition and postcondition pair, the statement is also correct with respect to the conjunction of an arbitrary specification R to both precondition and postcondition. R stands for some additional part of the memory that s will not be allowed to touch. It is more natural to describe assembly programs with preconditions alone, especially to facilitate unusual control patterns that do not fit the stack-based function convention that normal separation logic assumes. One consequence is that the usual frame rule is inapplicable. Instead, we may represent frame conditions explicitly with second-order quantification, as we do in this example.

To give us the usual flexibility of the frame rule for function calls, we must refer to the frame condition in one more place. This is part of a use of the $i@@p$ connective that we introduced earlier. We state that register `Rret` points to a code block that is safe to jump to if a particular condition holds. We have a nested use of the `~>` notation, this time defining a specification over a new state `st'`, which effectively stands for the state upon *returning from* the function, while `st` stands for the state upon *calling* the function.

The return-time invariant is identical to the initial separation logic assertion, except that we have swapped the values found at the two distinguished memory locations, as one would expect from this function's informal specification. Crucially, the same frame variable appears in the two snapshots of memory. Since we impose no further conditions on fr, it will be impossible to prove that any memory slice satisfies fr, with the sole exception of the memory on entry to the function. Therefore, if the function manages to satisfy the condition attached to the return pointer, all memory but the two distinguished cells will have been preserved.

One further subtle point in this specification style deserves some explanation. Most classical verification tools support *ghost variables*, which are additional program variables used solely for specification and verification. In more standard specifications for our swap example, we would probably see ghost variables used in place of existential quantification for the initial values a and b of the two distinguished memory cells. In classical first-order tools, ghost variables increase expressiveness beyond simple existential quantification, but only because *function return pointers are not made explicit*. Ghost variables provide the ability to share variables between function preconditions and postconditions. When we are able to talk about return pointers in a first-class way, as we have in this example, we need only preconditions, and so there is no further need for sharing of variables between specs.

Once the function has a specification, we can prove that the specification is met. A Coq Theorem command begins our proof of that fact. The proof is given with a Coq *proof script*, a program in a domain-specific language for proof search. In this case, our script says that the proof proceeds in two steps. First, we call the Bedrock tactic structured to reduce the theorem to the truth of a set of automatically-generated verification conditions. We use the semicolon operator to chain on a second tactic, which should be run on every verification condition. This second tactic is the Bedrock tactic sep, a generic simplifier for conditions involving separation logic.

In our particular example, there is one condition to prove, which amounts to showing the following implication, where we use the notation st[i] to denote the effect of executing instruction i in state st:

```
State 1: st
Pred. 1: R0 ==> a * R1 ==> b * ![fr]
State 2: st[R2 <- R0][$[R0] <- $[R1]][$[R1] <- R2]
Pred. 2: R1 ==> a * R0 ==> b * ![fr]
```

We want to show that the truth of Predicate 1 in State 1 implies the truth of Predicate 2 in State 2. A good first step is to inline the state information into the two predicates, so that both are expressed in terms of the same variable st. We write st.[E] for the value found at memory cell E in state st.

```
Pred. 1: st#R0 ==> a * st#R1 ==> b * ![fr]
Changes: R0 <- st.[st#R1]; R1 <- st.[st#R0]
Pred. 2: st#R1 ==> a * st#R0 ==> b * ![fr]
```

Next, we can use Predicate 1 to simplify the list of changes. Any read st.[u] may be replaced by v, whenever Predicate 1 contains a conjunct u ==> v. Our new implication is:

```
Pred. 1: st#R0 ==> a * st#R1 ==> b * ![fr]
Changes: R0 <- b; R1 <- a
Pred. 2: st#R1 ==> a * st#R0 ==> b * ![fr]
```

To finish the proof, we want to eliminate the need to take into account the set of memory changes. Our strategy to do so is to *execute the changes symbolically in Predicate 1*. That is, for each write of value v to memory at address u, we find a fact u ==> v' in Predicate 1 and replace v' with v. That algorithm reduces the implication to:

```
Pred. 1: st#R0 ==> b * st#R1 ==> a * ![fr]
Pred. 2: st#R1 ==> a * st#R0 ==> b * ![fr]
```

This implication is *almost* trivially true, modulo the fact of *'s commutativity. Applying such facts manually can be quite a hassle. Our separation logic tactic takes commutativity and associativity into account and automatically finishes proofs like this by *cancellation*. That is, we iterate through finding a conjunct that appears on both sides of the implication and "crossing it out." If the verification has been set up properly, cancellation eventually gives us an implication between identical formulas, which we can dispatch trivially.

We have completed our first Bedrock verification, and we would like now to stress one key property of our approach that distinguishes it from the mostly-automated verification methods embodied in tools like ESC [14], Boogie [1], and Jahob [32]. Solvers for boolean satisfiability (SAT) and satisfiability modulo theories (SMT) have become increasingly practical in program verification, and more and more projects work by reducing verification conditions to domains that such solvers understand. The solver works by a mechanical process with too many steps for humans to follow closely. Completeness guarantees for decision procedures sometimes make this loss of simplicity acceptable. Unfortunately, the constraint-solver approach to verification tends to lead to relatively inexpressive specification languages, as these solvers do not support techniques like local universal quantification over specification variables.

Bedrock relies on a very different approach. Users of SMT-based verification tools often describe separation logic as too hard to automate, but we think of that statement as only true in the context of normal SMT solvers. A simple *syntactic* algorithm can be very effective at discharging separation logic implications. The informal procedure we just demonstrated for swap scales up to much more interesting verifications, as we will demonstrate with our next example and in our further case studies.

When the proof state is set up properly beforehand, our sep tactic reduces separation implications to facts about normal mathematical objects like numbers, sets, maps, and lists. These simpler facts are usually straightforward to discharge with traditional solvers, ideally those giving completeness guarantees. The key win is that the reduction removes all need to reason about machine states or memories. We manage to handle that part of the reasoning in a *quantifier-free* way, avoiding one of the biggest headaches for SMT solvers. The syntactic simplification procedure is much simpler for a programmer to keep track of than the usual SMT-based alternatives, which have to do with predicting the action of quantifier-instantiation triggers or adding manual instantiation annotations.

At this point, the reader may be willing to believe that such a syntactic approach works for trivial examples like swap, while maintaining skepticism that we can scale to more complex examples like typical imperative data structures. Our next example shows how to accomplish that scaling, based on *computational abstract predicates* and modest use of *unfolding hints* that simplify uses of those predicates.

2.2 Incrementing All of a Linked List

Figure 3 shows our next example, which walks a singly-linked list of words, incrementing the value of every word. A list node is a pair of adjacent bytes, the first storing the data value and the second storing the next pointer, which is 0 in the final node of a list. The definition of the function linc introduces some structured programming constructs. We have a standard "while" loop, which, as usual, must be prefaced by a loop invariant (here placed inside square brackets). For this example, the loop invariant is the same as the function precondition, so we assigned that shared condition the name lincS. There are also a few Use statements here; we will explain shortly how they are used to guide automated proving.

The specification lincS follows the basic form of our previous example's precondition. The variables a and b have been replaced

```
Definition lincS : state -> PropX pc state := st ~>
  Ex fr, Ex ls, ![ !{llist ls st#R0} * ![fr] ] st
  /\ st#Rret @@ (st' ~>
    ![ !{llist (map S ls) st#R0} * ![fr] ] st').

Definition linkedList := bmodule {{
  bfunction "linc" [lincS] {
    [lincS]
    While (R0 != 0) {
      Use [llist_nonempty_fwd];;
      Use [llist_nonempty_bwd];;
      $[R0] <- $[R0] + 1;;
      R0 <- $[R0+1]
    };;
    Use [llist_empty_fwd];;
    Use [llist_empty_bwd];;
    Goto Rret
  }
}}.

Theorem linkedListOk : moduleOk linkedList.
  structured; sep.
Qed.
```

Figure 3. A Bedrock function to increment all of a linked list

by `ls`, which is a normal, purely-functional Coq list. This list serves as a *functional model* of the imperative list that is to be manipulated, and the action of the `linc` function can be modeled with a *purely functional reference implementation*. In particular, the pre-state contains the assertion `!{llist ls st#R0}`, where the notation `!{_}` denotes the use of an abstract predicate. In this case, we are requiring that a linked list is present in memory, rooted at `st#R0` and containing data elements matching those in `ls`. We model the action of the function in our choice of alternate arguments to `llist` in the post state. We write `!{llist (map S ls) st#R0}`, applying the usual higher-order function `map` to replace every element of `ls` with the result of applying `S` (the increment-by-one function) to it.

We should emphasize that, while we try to aid intuition about the computational specification approach by writing that it relies on "purely functional reference implementations," we are not literally writing a library in both functional and imperative versions and proving equivalence between them. Non-trivial functional programs may still deserve quite non-trivial verifications of their own, as ample research on the subject can attest to. Instead, we rely only locally on functional programs as alternatives to traditional mathematical notation. For example, the specification discussed in the previous paragraph is structured mostly as normal second-order logic, with one localized use of a functional program that applies `map` to express how the function should mutate a list.

Contrast this with an approach that might be used with SMT solvers, where a list is modeled as an array, and we might characterize `linc`'s behavior like this in terms of pre- and post- versions a and a' of an array:

$$\forall i.\ a'[i] = a[i] + 1$$

By using a quantifier, we forfeit completeness guarantees, as most first-order theories with quantifiers are undecidable. With the computational approach in Coq, we usually avoid the need to consider decidability questions. We know that any Coq term has a single well-defined answer which may be determined by normalization under appropriate conditions. As Coq executes terms automatically throughout its proof infrastructure, a well-chosen computational abstraction can give us many proof steps for free.

Some verification tools such as Jahob [32] allow the use of sets and set theory in specifications, which removes some need for quantifiers. However, universally-quantified invariants still appear in most data structure implementations. In all of our case studies so far, there have been only four functions that we verified with invariants that use quantifiers in any way besides strings of existential quantifiers at the beginnings of preconditions, as seen in our examples so far. All of our data structure invariants stick to this restricted use of quantifiers, too. This pattern is much closer to the well-understood *ghost variables* of classical verification than to the more involved use of quantifiers that causes trouble for SMT solvers. Quantifiers are hard to reason about, and our encoding approach allows us to delegate almost all reasoning work to the simple syntactic procedure that we began describing with the last example.

In our proof of correctness for the **`linkedList`** module, the **`structured`** tactic will hand us three verification conditions: we must show that the function precondition implies the loop invariant (which is trivial for this example), that the loop body preserves the loop invariant when we assume that the loop test succeeded, and that the loop invariant implies the postcondition when we assume that the loop test failed.

We focus on the first of the non-trivial implications, dealing with the effect of going once through the loop. Skipping to the second stage of the procedure we used for the last example, we have the following implication goal, which includes a pure fact implied by the success of the loop test. Since we are not returning from the function immediately, the existential variables of the post-state are up to us to instantiate. In effect, the loop body contains an "assignment" for each of these "ghost variables," and we will choose the righthand side of each such assignment as we complete the proof. We will write the new variable values as `ls'` and `fr'` until we determine what we want them to be; these are *unification variables*, part of Coq's standard proof search support.

```
   Pure: st#R0 <> 0
Pred. 1: !{llist st#R0 ls} * ![fr]
Changes: R0 <- st.[st#R0]+1
Pred. 2: !{llist (st.[st#R0+1]) ls'} * ![fr']
```

We would like to simplify the memory projection from the changes list, but clearly our previous simple procedure is inadequate. That procedure involves consulting the set of points-to facts in Predicate 1, and we have no such facts here. However, given our knowledge of how linked lists are represented, we know that the list must not be empty because `R0` is nonzero, so Predicate 1 is *equivalent to* some predicate with a points-to fact for `R0`. To make this more formal, we should start with the formal definition of the abstract predicate `llist`. We use Coq's standard facilities for recursive definitions and pattern-matching, along with a new separation assertion notation `[< p >]`, which lifts the pure predicate `p` into an impure predicate that asserts the truth of `p` and applies only to empty heaps.

```
Fixpoint llist (ls : list nat) (hd : nat) : sprop :=
  match ls with
    | nil => [< hd = 0 >]
    | x :: ls' => Ex u, [< hd <> 0 >]
      * hd ==> x * (hd+1) ==> u * !{llist ls' u}
  end.
```

This definition says: An empty list is represented by an empty memory and a head pointer with value 0. A nonempty list is represented based on a local existentially-quantified "ghost variable" `u`, standing for the next pointer. We assert that the head pointer is nonzero, that it points to the head `x` of `ls`, that the next memory cell contains u, and that u is the root of a linked list representing the tail ls' of ls.

From this definition, it is clear intuitively that we can "materialize" a points-to fact for the beginning of a nonempty list. The following *unfolding lemma* makes that fact explicit, in terms of a separation logic implication operator ===>, which uses three = characters, in contrast to the points-to operator which uses two.

```
Theorem llist_nonempty_fwd : forall ls hd, hd <> 0
  -> llist ls hd ===> Ex x, Ex ls', Ex u,
     [< ls = x :: ls' >] * hd ==> x * (hd+1) ==> u
     * !{llist ls' u}.
  destruct ls; sepLemma.
Qed.
```

The theorem is proved trivially, using destruct to ask for a case analysis on the list ls, and then calling a variant of our separation logic simplifier to do the rest of the work. We are now ready to learn the purpose of the Use statements in the program code. The first such statement references our new unfolding lemma. By including this annotation statement, we are asking the separation simplifier to use our new lemma to replace an instance of the ===> lefthand side with the corresponding righthand side. Coq uses unification to discover the values of the lemma variables ls and hd, and Coq uses its extensible proof hint mechanism to discharge any extra hypotheses. In this example, that hypothesis is hd <> 0, which is discharged using the pure fact from the proof state. Coq introduces new variables to stand for the values x, ls', and u that we assert to exist. This brings our state to:

```
   Pure: st#R0 <> 0 /\ ls = x :: ls''
Pred. 1: st#R0 ==> x * (st#R0+1) ==> u
         * !{llist ls'' u} * ![fr]
Changes: R0 <- st.[st#R0]+1
Pred. 2: !{llist ls' (st.[st#R0+1])} * ![fr']
```

Now that a points-to fact for R0 is exposed, we can simplify our explicit memory accesses.

```
   Pure: st#R0 <> 0 /\ ls = x :: ls''
Pred. 1: st#R0 ==> x * (st#R0+1) ==> u
         * !{llist ls'' u} * ![fr]
Changes: R0 <- x+1
Pred. 2: !{llist ls' u} * ![fr']
```

It is now easy to run symbolic evaluation of the memory changes in Predicate 1.

```
   Pure: st#R0 <> 0 /\ ls = x :: ls''
Pred. 1: st#R0 ==> x+1 * (st#R0+1) ==> u
         * !{llist ls'' u} * ![fr]
Pred. 2: !{llist ls' u} * ![fr']
```

At this point, cancellation will allow us to finish this case of the proof, in a subtle method of *automatic application of a frame rule*. The two abstract predicates may be canceled if we set unification variable ls' to ls''. That leaves the frame condition unification variable fr' for us to determine. By setting it equal to all of Predicate 1 that remains, we can finish the case by reflexivity. The part of Predicate 1 that has been absorbed into fr' constitutes *the parameter R to the standard frame rule*, and it has been determined using a very generic unification technique that applies just as well to non-standard control structures that need not follow a usual function call convention.

The loop invariant is a conjunction, and we have finished with the first conjunct. The second conjunct is an assertion about the conditions under which it is safe to jump to the function return pointer. In particular, we need to show:

```
Pred. 1: st#Rret @@ (st' ~>
  ![ !{llist (map S ls) st#R0} * ![fr] ] st')
Pred. 2: st#Rret @@ (st' ~>
  ![ !{llist (map S ls') st#R0} * ![fr'] ] st')
```

It turns out that one @@ assertion about a code pointer implies another about the same pointer if their predicate operands imply each other in the reverse order. We apply that rule and also substitute the values of ls' and fr' that we learned in proving the last conjunct.

```
Pred. 1: !{llist (map S ls'') u}
         * st#R0 ==> x+1 * (st#R0+1) ==> u * ![fr]
Pred. 2: !{llist (map S (x :: ls'')) st#R0} * ![fr]
```

Coq automatically uses computation to replace map S (x :: ls'') by S x :: map S ls''. To make further progress, we would like to unfold the abstract predicate in Predicate 2, similarly to the way we did for Predicate 1 in an earlier step. It is easy to prove another lemma that is like llist_nonempty_fwd but runs the implication in the other direction. This is exactly the lemma that we suggest with the second Use statement within the loop body. Based on that hint, our sep tactic will first introduce new unification variables x', ls''', and u', standing for the existential quantifiers in the theorem statement. Then, the pure goals st#R0 <> 0 and map S (x :: ls'') = x' :: ls''' are queued for solving by normal mathematical means. By stating the first of these facts outside of the separation implication in the theorem statement, we ask that it be proved before proceeding, and this is easily done, based on the first pure hypothesis in the proof state. The second pure fact is queued to be reconsidered after we finish the impure part of the proof. Hopefully the unification variables will have been determined by then, simplifying the job of our pure solvers, many of which are unable to handle unification variables.

Before we can get there, we must finish with this new modified proof state based on the lemma statement:

```
Pred. 1: !{llist (map S ls'') u}
         * st#R0 ==> x+1 * (st#R0+1) ==> u * ![fr]
Pred. 2: st#R0 ==> x' * (st#R0+1) ==> u'
         * !{llist ls''' u'} * ![fr]
```

The canceler finishes this proof by unifying x' with x+1, u' with u, and ls''' with map S ls''. Notice that this is very simple, eager syntactic unification that occurs as we try to cross predicates off from both sides of the implication. We need none of the complexity of "E-graph matching" as pioneered in solvers like Simplify [10]. The particular unification that we discover leaves the earlier queued fact map S (x :: ls'') = x' :: ls''' solvable trivially by computational normalization, and we have finished proving the correctness of this verification condition.

The final verification condition has a similar but simpler proof, based on analogous unfolding lemmas for empty lists that are invoked in the last two Use statements of the program. Each of our unfolding lemmas has a trivial one-line proof. The Use statement also supports partial instantiation of a lemma's quantifiers, when unification is not sufficient to discover instantiations correctly; and there is a further form to allow references to the current machine state in computing the instantiations. We find this kind of quantifier instantiation to be easier to keep track of than in the case of universally-quantified program invariants, as the quantifier reasoning may be kept local and is also completed solely by unification in a majority of cases.

3. A Simplification Procedure for Separation Assertions

Our walk-throughs of examples have demonstrated the basic five-step procedure that we use in discharging all Bedrock verification conditions. The procedure is easily formalized as an algorithm, broken into discrete steps that are reasonably easy for humans to keep track of. Here is the procedure, including three "extra" steps that are not specific to separation logic.

1. **Standard first-order logic simplification**: Before beginning, it is useful to put standard Coq simplification to work. For instance, our last example involved proving an implication between two conjunctions. This can be reduced to separate proofs of the two conclusion conjuncts, in each case assuming the truth of both hypothesis conjuncts. This stage also involves using each hypothesis disjunction to split the proof into two cases, replacing each existentially-quantified hypothesis with a version of its body that refers to a freshly-introduced variable, and so on.
2. **Forward unfolding of abstract predicates**: We apply the hints suggested with `Use` statements, along with some hints that have been registered globally, so that they should be used wherever they apply. The separation logic hypothesis ("Predicate 1" in our examples) is easily normalized to an iterated separating conjunction of impure facts. We walk through the conjuncts, looking for a hint proving an implication whose lefthand side unifies with the current conjunct. When we find a match, we first check that the premises of the lemma can be proved immediately, by calling all solvers that have been registered as hints. If this process succeeds, we introduce new variables for any existential quantifiers in the implication conclusion, new pure hypotheses for any pure conclusions, and replace the original conjunct with the new impure conclusions from the lemma. This process is iterated until no more hints match.
3. **Simplification of memory accesses**: For every points-to fact `u ==> v` in the separation hypothesis (referring to state `st`), we replace every occurrence of the memory access `st.[u]` with `v`, anywhere the former appears in the proof state.
4. **Symbolic execution of memory writes**: For every write of value `v` to address `u` implied by the current basic block's straightline instructions, find a fact `u ==> v'` in the separation hypothesis and replace `v'` with `v`.
5. **Backward unfolding of abstract predicates**: This phase is very similar to the forward unfolding phase, but with consideration of hints that apply to the separation conclusion ("Predicate 2" in our examples). We replace the conclusion of a lemma with its premises. New existential variables are instantiated as *unification variables*, whose values should be determined later through syntactic unification. Rather than adding pure premises to our proof state, we queue them as proof obligations to return to later. These obligations often contain some of our new unification variables. With proper foresight in `Use` annotations, the cancellation step will determine the values of almost all of these unification variables, so that, when we return to the obligations, they are in forms not so different from what SMT solvers are designed to handle.
6. **More aggressive first-order logic simplification**: Here we repeat all the simplifications of the first step, with one addition: When the goal begins with an existential quantifier, we generate a fresh unification variable, substitute it for the quantifier's variable, and make this substitution result the new goal. This quickly reduces our goal to a set of goals, some using separation logic and some using more standard mathematical theories. We will try to finish with the separation goals before proceeding, in hopes of determining most unification variable values.
7. **Cancellation**: We iterate through all conjuncts in the separation hypothesis, trying to find a unifiable conjunct in the conclusion. Every matching pair is eliminated. By reflexivity of implication, we are finished when the full hypothesis and conclusion may be unified.
8. **Proof of remaining pure facts**: If cancellation worked properly, we should now be faced only with a collection of pure goals that deal only with standard mathematical theories. These can be discharged by various solvers that are registered as hints. For instance, we have used congruence closure, a solver for linear arithmetic, brute force search via Prolog-style logic programming, and other techniques.

We also allow the programmer to register *rewrite rules*, designed to simplify proof states by simple syntactic replacement of one pattern by another. We apply these rules wherever possible, between every pair of steps above.

The whole process is implemented in Coq's Ltac language [9], which is a Turing-complete domain-specific language for proof search. By construction, every Ltac program generates a *proof term* to explain why it concluded that a fact is true. These proof terms use a relatively simple, generic logical language that relies on a small number of axioms. Thus, it is possible to implement a small, trustworthy standalone checker for these proof terms. To trust a proof, one need only trust the checker, not the more heuristic process by which proof terms are found. Therefore, since we implement our procedure as the Ltac program `sep`, we arrive at correctness by construction: whenever the procedure succeeds, it has made only valid deductions.

The `sep` procedure is the workhorse for Bedrock verification, but it is important that programmers can build on it with further problem-specific Ltac code. For instance, most reasoning about code pointers must be done through Ltac, rather than through traditional solvers, which are unable to cope with the second-order quantification that is usually involved. Each variety of control transfer generally demands its own modest piece of Ltac code. For instance, our last example program involved reasoning about the way the `@@` operator is used to model return pointers. Our case studies use about 10 lines of Ltac code to guide the automatic application of the appropriate reasoning principle. Other constructs like computed function calls, exception handling, and so on will generally require similar up-front investments. Once this support code is written, no extra work is required in the verification of individual programs.

Though `sep` is designed to automate most of the proof process, we often break it into its individual steps while verifying a program, so that we can watch to make sure that each step goes the way we expect. Compared to SMT solvers and related techniques, we think it is an advantage of our high-level approach that humans can keep track of the steps of the algorithm and glean useful information from watching its progress. That is, at each stage of the proof, the human user is shown intermediate states that look much like those given for the examples in Section 2. Even the full `sep` tactic is not an all-or-nothing solver; when it fails to prove a goal, it returns the unproved obligations in the same human-understandable format, with the possibility for exploratory proving to determine what went wrong.

For each domain of uses of code pointers, we usually write a single automation tactic, but we also break the proof process into a series of calls to simpler named tactics. On approaching a new verification condition, we step through these sub-stages to get a sense for which `Use` annotations and hints will be needed. Any step may be traced in more detail, using Coq's usual proof debugging commands. When the user figures out that a particular `Use` annotation is useful, a tactic may be called to add it from within the exploratory proving process; these hints can later be migrated into the program source, once all of the cases work. At that point, we switch to the mostly-automated approach. We want to stress that these lower-level tactics are still more like states in a small, fixed finite state machine than like the more common, very manual Coq proof scripts. Also, in switching to mostly-automated proofs, we often find that our proofs continue working even after making modest changes to a program's specification. The human prover need only find the key reasons why a program is correct, and then the automation can take care of the details.

4. Evaluation

The Bedrock framework implementation consists of about 5000 lines of Coq code. We have also implemented a suite of case study programs, chosen to exercise both traditional first-order reasoning and the more unusual higher-order reasoning about code pointers. None of the case studies require manual proof about specific program states, despite the fact that we are always proving full functional correctness of our libraries, not just more shallow properties like memory safety. Figure 4 gives some statistics about the case study programs.

We explain the column meanings in left-to-right order: First, we give each module's total lines-of-code count (including both implementation and proof), followed by its number of structured assembly functions and the number of lines of code devoted to these functions, minus proof-related annotations. After that, we have, respectively, lines-of-code counts for data structure representation invariants, pure lemmas (which do not deal with memories or machine states), impure lemmas (which are phrased as implications in separation logic), invariants included in programs (e.g., loop invariants), `Use` annotations, proof hints (which guide automatic solving of pure goals), and the main correctness proof scripts for modules. In the cases of impure and pure lemmas, we differentiate between the lines devoted to theorem statements and the lines devoted to their proofs (with the latter inside parentheses).

The last column of the table shows the time needed to compile each module, proofs included, on a 3.16 GHz Intel Core 2 Duo processor running Linux. Among the examples with the most code, two take about a half and a quarter hour, with the rest finishing in 6 minutes or less. To suggest a fair comparison with other verification tools, we note that our case studies spend over half their time in generation and checking of proof terms, which is a kind of "bonus" on which most other tools spend no time. Bedrock is also implemented on top of the normal Coq engine, which uses naive interpretation to execute proof search programs; we would expect to see a constant-factor speedup of at least several times with a custom implementation in a general-purpose language. Ideally, a future Coq version will include an improved optimizing engine that brings these benefits to our existing code. Even as the framework stands today, we find that the programmer experience is quite reasonable, with just a few seconds wait time required when focusing on and stepping through the proof of a single verification condition. As is usual, the different conditions may be tackled in parallel; though Coq does not support this kind of parallelism yet, we expect that simple optimizations in Coq to enable multi-core execution would also bring large speed-ups.

To give a more qualitative account of the verification experience, we turn to descriptions of the case studies.

First, we have the `Malloc` module, a heap memory management library that all of the other modules rely on. Its interface is independent of the implementation strategy; for now, we are using a simple unsorted free list with no coalescing. This data structure is an interesting take on the familiar linked list: we have variable-sized free list nodes that must store both their own sizes and their "next" pointers, rather than uniformly-sized list nodes that point to data allocated elsewhere. Verifying `Malloc` requires proving impure lemmas covering maneuvers like splitting a free list block into one piece to return to client code and another to keep in the list, based on the size of the memory chunk requested by the client.

The remaining case studies fall into two categories. First, we compare against recent developments in data structure verification by implementing our own versions of five case studies used with the Jahob tool [32]. Second, we demonstrate Bedrock's support for reasoning about code pointers, via examples mostly inspired by past work with the XCAP logic [24].

4.1 Data Structures

Our data structure examples can be split into three groups, based on the mathematical domain used to model the data structures. Each of our implementations provides the same functionality as the "public methods" in a particular example from a recent paper on Jahob [32]. We prove full functional correctness of each method, showing that the imperative code realizes the same behavior as with the "obvious" implementation of each operation via a small functional program. Our job is inherently harder than in Java-specific Jahob, since every module is at the assembly level of abstraction and must do explicit management of heap and stack memory, but our results show that the effective burden is not so great.

First, we have arrays, modeled using functional lists. One module develops the program-independent aspects of this theory, including impure lemmas covering different ways of isolating cells within arrays. For instance, here is a theorem for unfolding an array in a way that exposes a points-to fact for the cell at index `n`.

```
Theorem array_mid_fwd : forall n a ls,
  n < length ls
  -> array ls a ===> !{array (firstn n ls) a}
    * (a+n) ==> nth n ls 0
    * !{array (skipn (n+1) ls) (a+n+1)}.
```

Notice the key use of the *computational* approach we have mentioned a few times already. Usual mostly-automated program verification deals with array cell isolation mostly through universally-quantified invariants. Instead, we take advantage of the rich possibilities for computation with lists in Coq, describing a three-way split of an array in terms of recursive functions for keeping only the first `n` elements of a list, extracting the `n`th element, or dropping the first `n` elements, respectively. A few rewriting hints about the interactions of these recursive functions enable very effective proof automation about array operations, after we add a few `Use` statements that suggest lemmas like `array_mid_fwd`. We, in effect, reduce quantifier-heavy reasoning about arrays to quantifier-free reasoning about functional lists. The `ArrayList` module applies this approach in the implementation of 19 common operations on an abstract datatype of growable arrays. As, compared to linked data structures, arrays offer relatively little opportunity for simple computational abstraction, our Bedrock `ArrayList` involves about 40% more annotation than the Jahob version.

Next, we have a theory of sets, modeled as Coq values of type `nat -> bool`. That is, a set is a mathematical function from machine words (natural numbers) to booleans, telling us whether each word belongs to the set. We also define a common interface for assembly implementations of imperative finite sets, providing operations for membership checking and addition and removal from a set. We give two implementations of this interface, with unsorted singly-linked lists and with binary search trees. The latter module additionally provides functions for extracting the minimum or maximum element from a nonempty set. The computational approach helps us give dramatically simpler binary search tree invariants than in the Jahob code, where even the basic data structure invariants include 10 universal quantifiers. We rely instead on the ability to filter sets by computable predicates; for instance, in considering an internal node of the tree, to come up with the set that its left child

Module	Total	#Funcs.	Impl.	Data	Pure (pfs)	Imp. (pfs)	Inv.	Use	Hints	Main	Build (min)
`Malloc`	267	3	71	8	3(1)	50(14)	16	24	2	1	5
Theory of arrays/lists	111	-	-	5	2(2)	35(32)	-	-	7	-	<1
`ArrayList`	771	19	272	3	79(37)	29(15)	168	83	20	1	35
Theory of sets	159	-	-	-	61(43)	-	15	-	7	-	<1
`SinglyLinkedList`	157	4	54	6	-	14(6)	20	14	2	6	2
`BinarySearchTree`	355	6	127	10	-	32(7)	43	40	2	28	13
Theory of maps	69	-	-	-	7(23)	-	20	-	1	-	<1
`AssociationList`	200	6	85	6	-	12(6)	28	27	2	1	3
`Hashtable`	374	6	90	6	36(13)	38(13)	56	39	18	1	4
`Memoize`	191	2	45	7	21(6)	6(3)	36	5	5	18	2
`AppendCPS`	155	2	56	5	-	9(3)	44	12	-	1	4
`ThreadLib`	225	4	67	9	6(2)	22(7)	34	20	1	7	6

Figure 4. Statistics on case studies, mostly in terms of number of lines of code of each kind

represents, we filter the original set by a function that keeps only those elements less than the current data value.

Finally, we define a similar theory of maps, modeled with the Coq type `nat -> option nat`, where an "`option nat`" is either `None` or `Some n`, for number `n`. Our two finite map implementations use unsorted singly-linked lists and hash tables. Unlike its Jahob counterpart, our hash table implementation uses the linked list implementation, treated abstractly through its interface, within hash buckets. The computational approach again brings some significant simplifications for hash tables. A crucial function is "`only`", which restricts a map to just those keys that hash to a particular value, implemented using the natural number equality test `eq_nat_dec`.

```
Definition only (m : map) (hmax n : nat) : map :=
  fun k => if eq_nat_dec (hash hmax k) n
           then m k else None.
```

We use `only` to state impure lemmas like the following, which isolates a particular bucket within a hash table.

```
Theorem htableOk_mid_fwd : forall n m hmax
  curHash len a,
  n < len -> htableOk m hmax curHash len a
  ===> Ex a', !{htableOk m hmax curHash n a}
  * (a+n) ==> a'
  * !{alist (only m hmax (curHash+n)) a'}
  * !{htableOk m hmax (curHash+n+1)
      (len-n-1) (a+n+1)}.
```

Without focusing on the details, we point out that a single case of the hash table representation predicate `htableOk` is expanded to two other uses that together skip one bucket, where the missing bucket is described in terms of a points-to fact to a pointer `a'`. This pointer itself represents an association list, which we express using the abstract predicate `alist` exported by the `AssociationList` module. We say that the association list represents the restriction of the overall map to just those keys that belong in the bucket we have isolated.

Summing up all of the different kinds of proof and annotation from Figure 4, we arrive at a total of about 200 for `Hashtable`. The Jahob version uses over 250 lines of annotation just within the methods used to implement the remove-from-map operation. The bulk of these annotations are qualitatively different from those required in Bedrock, as they involve explicitly nested proofs based on the quantifier structure of invariants. Our removal function is self-contained, including one 5-line invariant and 5 `Use` statements. The remaining lines are normal executable code.

Our data structure case studies deal only with keys and values that are uninterpreted machine words. However, since we are working with low-level programs, machine words are sufficient as a representation of arbitrary data structures. These words may be treated as pointers by client code, and we may write invariants about the layout of such nested data structures solely in terms of the functional model of a set or map, avoiding any coupling to the details of the data structure implementation. It is still true that our implementations of sets and maps may not have the intended semantics when used to store nested data structures via pointers, since our fixed comparison and hashing operations compare pointers and ignore further structure. Variations on the case studies from this section should support the use of user-provided comparison and hashing functions, when accompanied by proofs of key facts about them (e.g., a comparator implements a total order in terms of some functional model of the nested data structure).

4.2 Code Pointers as Data

Our remaining case studies go beyond the domain of most previous mostly-automated verification tools, where most assertions about callable code pointers may not even be expressed, let alone verified. Here we are still proving full functional correctness, though it is often less obvious what precisely that means for libraries that work with code pointers. We choose our specifications to formalize the intuitive notion of the abstraction that the library is meant to provide. For instance, our threads library will include a yield function whose specification guarantees that, when the yielding thread is rescheduled, its private memory has not been changed.

Our first example is a generic function memoizer, backed by hash tables, which are themselves backed by association lists, creating a non-trivial tower of uses of abstract datatypes. Any function may be memoized into values of a particular abstract datatype of memo tables. Each function is associated with a pure specification, a mathematical relation between input and output words. Additionally, a memoized function may use *local state*, represented by a completely unconstrained separation logic predicate, which might stand for, e.g., a local cache data structure. Memo tables use hash tables internally, along with an extra invariant that refers only to the functional map that models the hash table contents. We require that every mapping is consistent with the pure specification. This allows us to expose the memo table as a function with almost the same specification as the original. (We must expand the specification to require that the memo table is loaded in memory before the call and guarantee it is loaded afterward.)

Our final two case studies are based on examples from papers about the XCAP program logic. First, we reimplemented and reverified the main example from the original XCAP paper [24]. This is an implementation of in-place concatenation of two linked lists, written in a form that might be output by an ML compiler. Rather than following a C-style calling convention, the "append" function's return pointer is represented as an explicit closure, which pairs a function pointer with an "environment" argument that the function expects to be passed when called. The old version of this example was coded in an assembly language even more idealized than the one we use in this paper, where `malloc` and `free` are instructions, rather than library functions that must be implemented. Nonetheless, despite this disadvantage, our Bedrock version is substantially simpler. The XCAP version involves about 1500 lines of very manual proof. Our new version relies on just three of the four unfolding lemmas used for lists in Section 2.2, 12 `Use` statements, and a one-line main proof. Our invariants correspond to code that already appeared explicitly as basic block preconditions in the XCAP version, so it seems fair to say that we have reduced the proof burden by two orders of magnitude.

We also verified a cooperative threads library, similar to one implemented in XCAP [25, 26]. That is, the library relies on threads to yield to other threads, in place of the more common interrupt-based approach of preemptive threading. Here, the setting of past work is more challenging, as they verified real x86 code, but the basic approach is similar. We implement a fair round-robin thread scheduler, supporting dynamic thread creation, yielding, and exiting. There is a shared global invariant, characterizing the part of memory that threads may use to communicate with each other. Each blocked thread also has its own local invariant, which is indexed by the thread's saved stack pointer. Here is an example specification that uses the abstract data type of thread schedulers; in particular, this is the precondition for the yield function.

```
Definition yieldS := st ~> Ex fr, Ex ginv,
  Ex invs, Ex root,
  susp ginv (fun sp => sep ([< sp = st#Rsp >]
                    * ![fr])%Sep) st#Rret
  /\ codesOk ginv invs
  /\ ![ !{mallocHeap 0} * st#Rsp ==> root
      * !{threads invs root} * ![ginv] * ![fr] ] st.
```

We see explicit quantification over a global invariant `ginv`. The `susp` predicate characterizes when a code pointer (the return pointer, in this invariant) is safe to *susp*end, in terms of the global and local invariants. The local invariant we choose here combines the frame condition with the requirement that the stack pointer upon resumption equals the original. The `codesOk` invariant asserts similar properties for all of the suspended threads, as represented by the functional model `invs`. Both `susp` and `codesOk` are implemented using second-order quantification. The precondition ends with a more normal separation logic formula, requiring a valid `malloc` heap, a pointer to the scheduler data structure in the first local stack slot (found at an address based on stack pointer `Rsp`), the scheduler data structure itself, the global invariant, and the frame condition.

The old XCAP implementation used about 8000 lines of code just for the proofs of correctness for three basic blocks that implement key operations on saved thread contexts [26]. A comparable amount of additional complexity was associated with the thread scheduler and its data structure. The complete Bedrock implementation, including assembly code and verification, totals just 250 lines. We again see a reduction of about two orders of magnitude in the amount of program-state-specific proof.

Of course, counting lines of annotation and proof gives only an approximation of the human cost of verifying a program. We would rather know the time spent by a programmer in coming up with these lines, since some shorter proofs may be harder to find in practice. Unfortunately, we have not found much data of this kind in the literature. We can give one piece of anecdotal evidence for the effectiveness of the Bedrock approach: The authors of the XCAP cooperative thread scheduling library mention that they spent six person-months completing it [25]. This figure includes time spent building and tweaking the verification framework, but we hope it still gives a good sense of the scale of this sort of effort. In contrast, starting from no prior code dealing with threads, we coded and verified our threads library in the course of two days of work.

5. Related Work

We have already discussed the CAP project [15] extensively. That line of work has been very successful at designing program logics suitable for foundational verification of low-level code, leading to successful case studies in dynamic thread creation [11], embedded code pointers [24], garbage collection [21], self-modifying code [3], and hardware interrupts [12]. The Bedrock project takes these results as its base and adds infrastructure for higher-level coding and automated verification, demonstrating that foundational guarantees can be had, for code that manipulates code pointers as data, without giving up the signature benefits of classical verification tools.

Classical verification tools like ESC [14], Boogie [1], and Jahob [31, 32] have been shown to be effective in a variety of verification tasks that can be completed using first-order solvers (or additionally, in the case of Jahob, using an integrated proof language for a higher-order logic). Hawblitzel and collaborators have done automated classical verification of garbage collectors [16] and the core of an operating system kernel [30] with Boogie. Bedrock aims to take this style of highly productive verification and add three main benefits. First, we apply the *computational* approach to specification to reduce the need for logical quantifiers and simplify proofs. Second, we support callable code pointers with polymorphic specifications. Third, we reduce the trusted code base to a foundational level, where only the standard Coq proof checker must be trusted to believe a verification. Foundational verification also opens the door for integration with proofs that would be hard to write in a classical verifier but are tractable in general-purpose proof assistants. For example, the Verve project [30] aims to integrate a soundness proof for a typed assembly language; with such a proof and a Bedrock verification both carried out in Coq, the combined system can have a simple foundational correctness theorem.

Separation logic has been applied successfully in program analysis tools, including Smallfoot [2]. Follow-on work on abductive inference [4] infers procedure specifications that can be used to prove memory safety, without requiring whole-program analysis. Alternative shape analysis techniques have been applied automatically in tools like TVLA [29] and XISA [5]. Compared to Bedrock, these tools have applied to languages at higher levels of abstraction than assembly, they have not been verified formally, and they do not support reasoning about code pointers. All of these features contribute to some desirable properties of these other tools: superior performance and greater applicability to mainstream programming languages.

McCreight's Coq tactics for separation logic [20] address similar concerns to the tactic support presented in this paper, raising the level of abstraction in proof about imperative low-level programs. This alternate verification framework satisfies all of our desiderata from the introduction, with the exception that it is not "mostly-automated." Proofs using McCreight's tactics still involve a significant number of manual proof steps, applying such operations as explicit rearrangement of separating conjunctions using associativity and commutativity. For example, a useful comparison comes from a simple in-place linked list reversal function implemented with both systems. McCreight's proof includes about 80 atomic tactic calls, while the Bedrock proof includes about 10 atomic tactic calls and 4 Use statements. About half of McCreight's atomic tactic calls mention variable or hypothesis names that are bound within the proof; none of the tactics in the Bedrock proof do.

The computational approach to data structure specification has been adopted by many projects working within higher-order logics. Mehta and Nipkow [22] used computational specification without separation logic, and the combination with separation logic has appeared in work on XCAP [24], Ynot [23], CFML [6], and VeriFast [17].

The Ynot library [7] for Coq supports automated verification of monadically impure Haskell-like programs annotated with specifications, using separation logic. Every Coq program is also a valid Ynot program, so implicit memory management is baked into the system. Bedrock is designed to apply to languages that are more realistic for low-level infrastructure. While the Ynot language and its verification rules are specified with Coq axioms, Bedrock supports languages defined foundationally with operational semantics. Bedrock has a few more high-level advantages over Ynot: it applies frame rules automatically, supports the inlining of quantifier instantiation hints (`Use` statements) in programs, and deals with the compilation of more convenient, higher-level code into lower-level formats.

The VeriFast [17] verifier has been under development in parallel with Ynot and Bedrock and involves many similar design decisions. Program verification is mostly-automatic, based on computational separation logic specifications with support for higher-order reasoning. VeriFast is a standalone tool, with no formal proof of correctness, which enables better performance and easier integration of convenience features for programmers. VeriFast also targets C and Java rather than assembly-level programs. Lack of integration with a traditional proof assistant may make it harder to carry out some verifications that rely on reasoning outside the domain of the standard automation.

The Bedrock approach usually reduces goal facts about program behavior into sets of quantifier-free facts about normal mathematical objects like numbers, sets, maps, lists, and trees. So far, we have proved many of these facts with some amount of manual proof, since this total burden is not significant compared to the costs of reasoning concretely about data structures and pointer aliasing. We might also try taking advantage of recent progress on complete decision procedures [19] for very rich theories that encompass much of our pure proof obligations. Any such decision procedure should be relatively straightforward to integrate with Coq, if it can be made to generate proof witnesses.

6. Conclusion

We have introduced Bedrock, a framework for implementation and verification of low-level programs in Coq. Bedrock's key productivity features center on automatic proof of invariants expressed with the concepts of separation logic. Unlike other systems providing similar levels of automation, Bedrock supports reasoning about first-class code pointers in terms of second-order variables that stand for unknown invariants. This facility is critical for handling of runtime and operating systems. To the best of our knowledge, ours is the first verified thread library with less than a few thousand lines of proof. Our implementation fits well within that mark, with a total of 250 lines, including program code and proofs.

The framework is parametrized over machine languages and their operational semantics. To date, we have only experimented with Bedrock instantiated to an idealized language with infinite-width words. We expect that the approach will continue to work well for the machine languages of today's common microarchitectures, though future work is needed to be sure. Effective decision procedures for bitvector arithmetic are likely to be the main new requirement.

Bedrock follows a very *computational* approach to separation logic, where most imperative functions are specified in terms of purely-functional "reference implementations." This allows us to replace much formal reasoning with execution of programs in the specification language. Quantified invariants are one of the greatest challenges for automated verification, and the computational approach allows us to replace almost all uses of quantifiers with calls to recursive functions in a functional language.

Most program verification today is done by direct reduction to domains with effective decision procedures. Even complete procedures for complex theories like (restricted forms of) transitive closure can have poor enough performance that the human verifier must do extra work to guide the procedures. With Bedrock, we follow an alternate approach, where the heart of verification condition proving is a *symbolic* procedure for separation logic simplification. This procedure has a few simple steps that humans can follow without much trouble, and our Coq library provides good support for stepping through the procedure and animating the moves it makes. Understanding this process requires no reasoning about "semantic" theories, just about the syntactic form of separation assertions.

When a program is annotated with some relatively simple invariants and invocations of simplification lemmas for abstract predicates, the simplification procedure reduces program correctness to the truth of quantifier-free facts that refer only to very basic mathematical theories. These facts are much easier to reason about than the original program, and we can hope that most will eventually be automatable with a few decision procedures. Thus, Bedrock helps programmers do the "hard parts" of verification with the familiar activity of programming and solve the remaining problems with traditional mathematical methods.

Acknowledgments

We would like to thank Gregory Malecha and Ryan Wisnesky for helpful comments on drafts of this paper. This work was funded within the DHOSA project through AFOSR MURI grant FA9550-09-01-0539.

References

[1] Mike Barnett, Bor-Yuh Evan Chang, Robert Deline, Bart Jacobs, and K. Rustan M. Leino. Boogie: A modular reusable verifier for object-oriented programs. In *Proc. FMCO*, 2006.

[2] Josh Berdine, Cristiano Calcagno, and Peter W. O'Hearn. Smallfoot: Modular automatic assertion checking with separation logic. In *Proc. FMCO*, 2005.

[3] Hongxu Cai, Zhong Shao, and Alexander Vaynberg. Certified self-modifying code. In *Proc. PLDI*, 2007.

[4] Cristiano Calcagno, Dino Distefano, Peter O'Hearn, and Hongseok Yang. Compositional shape analysis by means of bi-abduction. In *Proc. POPL*, 2009.

[5] Bor-Yuh Evan Chang and Xavier Rival. Relational inductive shape analysis. In *Proc. POPL*, 2008.

[6] Arthur Charguéraud. Program verification through characteristic formulae. In *Proc. ICFP*, 2010.

[7] Adam Chlipala, Gregory Malecha, Greg Morrisett, Avraham Shinnar, and Ryan Wisnesky. Effective interactive proofs for higher-order imperative programs. In *Proc. ICFP*, 2009.

[8] Coq Development Team. The Coq proof assistant reference manual, version 8.3. 2010.

[9] David Delahaye. A tactic language for the system Coq. In *Proc. LPAR*, 2000.

[10] David Detlefs, Greg Nelson, and James B. Saxe. Simplify: a theorem prover for program checking. *J. ACM*, 52(3):365–473, 2005.

[11] Xinyu Feng and Zhong Shao. Modular verification of concurrent assembly code with dynamic thread creation and termination. In *Proc. ICFP*, 2005.

[12] Xinyu Feng, Zhong Shao, Yuan Dong, and Yu Guo. Certifying low-level programs with hardware interrupts and preemptive threads. In *Proc. PLDI*, 2008.

[13] Xinyu Feng, Zhong Shao, Alexander Vaynberg, Sen Xiang, and Zhaozhong Ni. Modular verification of assembly code with stack-based control abstractions. In *Proc. PLDI*, 2006.

[14] Cormac Flanagan, K. Rustan M. Leino, Mark Lillibridge, Greg Nelson, James B. Saxe, and Raymie Stata. Extended static checking for Java. In *Proc. PLDI*, 2002.

[15] Nadeem Abdul Hamid and Zhong Shao. Interfacing Hoare logic and type systems for foundational proof-carrying code. In *Proc. TPHOLs*, 2004.

[16] Chris Hawblitzel and Erez Petrank. Automated verification of practical garbage collectors. In *Proc. POPL*, 2009.

[17] Bart Jacobs, Jan Smans, and Frank Piessens. A quick tour of the VeriFast program verifier. In *Proc. APLAS*, 2010.

[18] Gerwin Klein, Kevin Elphinstone, Gernot Heiser, June Andronick, David Cock, Philip Derrin, Dhammika Elkaduwe, Kai Engelhardt, Rafal Kolanski, Michael Norrish, Thomas Sewell, Harvey Tuch, and Simon Winwood. seL4: Formal verification of an OS kernel. In *Proc. SOSP*, 2009.

[19] Viktor Kuncak, Ruzica Piskac, Philippe Suter, and Thomas Wies. Building a calculus of data structures (invited paper). In *Proc. VMCAI*, 2010.

[20] Andrew McCreight. Practical tactics for separation logic. In *Proc. TPHOLs*, 2009.

[21] Andrew McCreight, Zhong Shao, Chunxiao Lin, and Long Li. A general framework for certifying garbage collectors and their mutators. In *Proc. PLDI*, 2007.

[22] Farhad Mehta and Tobias Nipkow. Proving pointer programs in higher-order logic. In *Proc. CADE*, 2003.

[23] Aleksandar Nanevski, Greg Morrisett, Avraham Shinnar, Paul Govereau, and Lars Birkedal. Ynot: Reasoning with the awkward squad. In *Proc. ICFP*, 2008.

[24] Zhaozhong Ni and Zhong Shao. Certified assembly programming with embedded code pointers. In *Proc. POPL*, 2006.

[25] Zhaozhong Ni, Dachuan Yu, and Zhong Shao. Modular verification of machine-level thread implementation. Technical report, 2006.

[26] Zhaozhong Ni, Dachuan Yu, and Zhong Shao. Using XCAP to certify realistic system code: Machine context management. In *Proc. TPHOLs*, 2007.

[27] Lawrence C. Paulson. Isabelle: A generic theorem prover. *Journal of Automated Reasoning*, 5, 1994.

[28] John C. Reynolds. Separation logic: A logic for shared mutable data structures. In *Proc. LICS*, 2002.

[29] Mooly Sagiv, Thomas Reps, and Reinhard Wilhelm. Parametric shape analysis via 3-valued logic. *TOPLAS*, 24, 2002.

[30] Jean Yang and Chris Hawblitzel. Safe to the last instruction: automated verification of a type-safe operating system. In *Proc. PLDI*, 2010.

[31] Karen Zee, Viktor Kuncak, and Martin Rinard. Full functional verification of linked data structures. In *Proc. PLDI*, 2008.

[32] Karen Zee, Viktor Kuncak, and Martin Rinard. An integrated proof language for imperative programs. In *Proc. PLDI*, 2009.

Toward Generating Reducible Replay Logs

Kyu Hyung Lee   Yunhui Zheng   Nick Sumner   Xiangyu Zhang

Department of Computer Science, Purdue University, West Lafayette, IN, 47907, USA

{kyuhlee,zheng16,wnsumner,xyzhang}@cs.purdue.edu

Abstract

Logging and replay is important to reproducing software failures and recovering from failures. Replaying a long execution is time consuming, especially when replay is further integrated with runtime techniques that require expensive instrumentation, such as dependence detection. In this paper, we propose a technique to reduce a replay log while retaining its ability to reproduce a failure. While traditional logging records only system calls and signals, our technique leverages the compiler to selectively collect additional information on the fly. Upon a failure, the log can be reduced by analyzing itself. The collection is highly optimized. The additional runtime overhead of our technique, compared to a plain logging tool, is trivial (2.61% average) and the size of additional log is comparable to the original log. Substantial reduction can be cost-effectively achieved through a search based algorithm. The reduced log is guaranteed to reproduce the failure.

Categories and Subject Descriptors D.2.5 [*Software Engineering*]: Testing and Debugging—Debugging aids, Tracing

General Terms Reliability, Performance

Keywords Software reliability, Log reduction, debugging, replay, instrumentation

1. Introduction

Logging and replay is an important technique for software dependability [6, 11, 20]. It records the interactions between a program and its environment during execution by logging system calls and signals. The execution can be replayed as many times as necessary for various purposes, such as diagnosis of software failures and state recovery from failures. The state of the art logging techniques have low overhead, usually less than 10% [6, 18], support concurrent programs [1, 5, 16], and are even provided as part of the operating system. These features make the techniques highly desirable when intensive on-the-fly human attention is infeasible during execution, such as in the emerging cloud computing scenario.

For long running programs such as server programs and user interactive (UI) programs, replay logs may correspond to executions as long as a few hours or even days. Large logs entail long replay times. The programmer may have to wait for hours before a failure is reproduced. Sending such large log files over network could also be problematic. Checkpoints [4] are often created to mitigate the problem. However, as checkpointing often entails taking snapshots of the entire address space of the application, its frequent use cannot be afforded. We aim to develop a practical technique that reduces an execution by reducing its replay log. Given a reduction criterion, such as a program failure, the technique removes events from the log in a way that the reduced log can still properly drive the execution to the criterion. Such a technique is particularly desirable when replay is integrated with debugging techniques that require expensive instrumentation easily causing an order of magnitude slow down [25]. There are also iterative debugging techniques that require repeated replay [24]. In such a context, even a log for a few minutes of execution is hardly affordable. Furthermore, if a failure occurs in remote execution, the large replay log can be reduced on the remote site before it is sent back to the developer.

Challenges of Replayable Log Reduction.

During replay, events from the log are retrieved in order to drive the execution. *The first challenge is that reduction may induce a different control flow path such that the reduced log cannot properly align with the replayed execution.* An event in the reduced log may no longer be encountered during replay due to the different path. Or, replay may take a new path such that an event is expected but not present in the log.

The second challenge is that reduction may change variable values, leading to inconsistency. For example, it may change the number of bytes that are supposed to be read at a system call. That is, the log indicates x bytes were read but the replayed execution expects $x+c$ bytes. Solving such inconsistency demands substantial effort. Existing work tries to achieve replayable reduction by retaining the events that are in the transitive closure of dependences for the criterion [19, 25]. However, it demands replaying the full execution at least once to detect dependences. Tracking all instruction level dependences often incurs 5-10 times slow down [19]. Since reduction is mainly needed for long executions, the resulting cost could be very high. Furthermore, we observe that for complex programs, dependences between events are so pervasive that the transitive closure may involve all events, so reduction can hardly be achieved.

(a) Program		(b) Sample log
1 read(&x);	1	R(10)
2 print("x="+x);	2	W(x=10)
3 read(&y);	3	R(20)
4 print("y="+y);	4	W(y=20)
5 read(&z);	5	R(30)
6 print("z="+z);	6	W(z=30)

Figure 1. Structural constraints. `R()` stands for an input event. `W()` stands for an output event. The numbers to the left of the log are where events happened.

Dependences are not the only factor needing consideration in reduction. Events independent to the reduction criteria may need to be included due to *structural constraints*. Specifically, *an event is needed if the control flow structure demands its presence even*

PLDI'11, June 4–8, 2011, San Jose, California, USA.

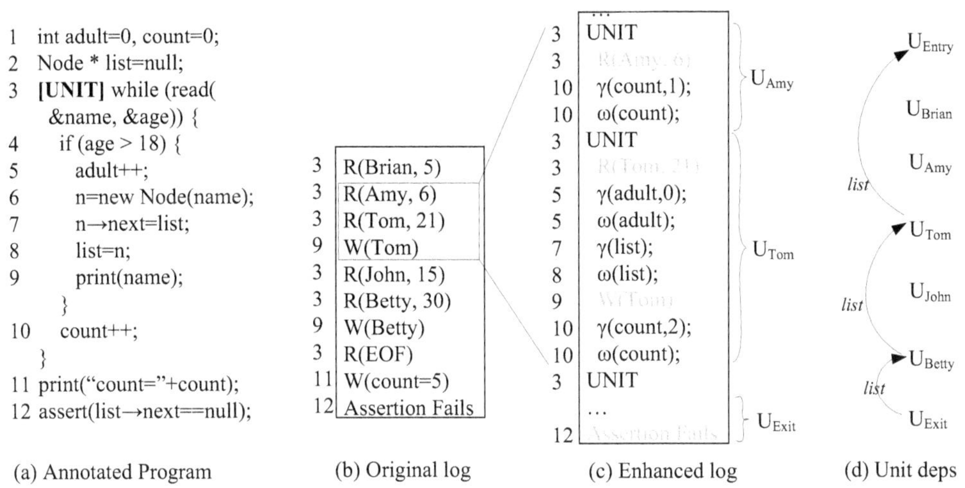

Figure 2. An example of our design. Events not shaded in (c) are those generated by our technique. γ() and ω() are memory accesses. For readability, we use the name being read in the iteration as the subscript of a unit.

though there is no (transitive) dependence between the criterion and the event. This is the third challenge.

Consider the example in Fig. 1. Ideally, if we want to replay the output of `z` at 6, we only need to replay the read at 5. However, none of the events can be reduced because all of them are expected during replay due to the straight line structure.

Our Design. Our goal is to address the above challenges and develop a practical log reduction technique. The basic idea of this paper is to *selectively record extra information such that reduction can be achieved by analyzing the log.* The approach is *efficient*: it introduces negligible overhead; the additional information needed to be logged is typically not substantial compared to the original log size. It is *effective* in achieving reduction.

In particular, our technique divides an execution into units such that reduction is only carried out at the unit level. In this paper, a unit is an iteration of an event processing loop. For a program driven by external events, its execution is dominated by these iterations. To distinguish the term event from that used in a replay log, we call external events *requests*, and an event loop is hence called a request handling loop. There are many log entries generated inside a unit. They are either reduced entirely or retained for awhile. Such a design allows us easily handle structural constraints. Moreover, there are few dependences crossing unit boundaries because a unit is often supposed to carry out a relatively independent task.

On the other hand, units are not completely independent, so replaying individual units is seldom possible. For example, in the `apache` server program, a unit receives a request from a user, pushes the request to a queue, and then terminates. Another unit pops the request, establishes the connection, and handles the request. It is easy to tell that replaying either unit alone will not succeed. Hence, we need to detect inter-unit dependences. We observe that considering all dependences likely makes the log irreducible as all units are inter-dependent in some way. We propose weaving two kinds of replay. For variables or data structure fields of primitive types, their values are restored at unit boundaries so that we can avoid replaying their dependences. For variables of pointer types or other complex types, we replay their dependences (the units where the variables were defined) because directly restoring their values is either too expensive or problematic. Our compile time analysis instruments the program to collect sufficient runtime information to support such replay. Reduction is done offline by analyzing the enhanced log. Driven by the reduced log, the replay ensures two properties: (1) *the replay control flow must be identical to the corresponding part of the original execution*; (2) *variables must have identical values at identical control flow points*. These properties promise the reproduction of the criterion.

Overview Example. Consider the example in Fig. 2 (a). The program reads personal information and stores the adult information to a linked list. At the end, it asserts the linked list has precisely one element. The user annotates the main request handling loop using keyword "**[UNIT]**", meaning each iteration of the loop is considered a unit. Figure (b) shows the original replay log of an example execution in which the information for two adults is provided. Calls to `read()` and `print()` are logged as input/output events.

The data structures that may cause inter-unit dependences are then identified. They are `adult`, `count`, and `list`. The statements relevant to these variables are instrumented. Part of the enhanced log is presented in Fig. 2 (c). In particular, `UNIT` events delimit execution units. Reads and writes of the relevant data structures are logged. As `count` and `adult` have primitive types, their reads are logged with values. In comparison, the reads of `list` are logged without the pointer values. In Figure (d), the inter-unit dependences regarding variable `list` are presented. Each node denotes a unit. The variable causing a dependence is labeled on the dependence edge. Note that non-pointer dependences are usually not considered. In order to replay the assertion failure, unit U_{exit} needs to be replayed. Transitively, U_{betty}, U_{tom} and U_{entry} are included in the reduced log due to the pointer dependences. Replaying the four events faithfully reconstructs the linked list. When replaying a unit, the values of `count` and `adult` are retrieved from the log instead of being recomputed. Note that `count` causes inter-unit dependences between each pair of consecutive units. Hence, if we consider its dependences, we have to replay all units.

The contributions of the paper are highlighted as follows.

- We propose a novel logging technique that generates reducible logs. It selectively logs memory access information with very little runtime overhead. Reduction is achieved by analyzing the log. In particular, we consider unit level reduction so that less runtime information needs to be logged. We consider primitive and pointer variables separately, which allows us to reach a balance in the logging overhead and the achievable reduction.
- We formally introduce the logging semantics, the replay semantics and the reduction algorithm. The logging semantics is designed such that it avoids redundancy. We develop an aggressive reduction algorithm that saves us from reconstructing the whole memory state while still reproducing the criterion (failure).

- We prove that our reduction scheme can faithfully reproduce the criterion.
- We evaluate our technique on a set of real world programs. Results show the runtime overhead is 2.6% on average and the additional space consumption is comparable to traditional techniques. We can reduce executions with tens of thousands of units to just a few units, and still reproduce the bugs.

2. Language

KERNEL-LANGUAGE $\mathcal{L}$

$$
\begin{array}{rcl}
P \in \mathcal{L} & ::= & s \\
x \in Var & ::= & \{x_1, x_2, \ldots\} \\
c \in Const & ::= & \{\texttt{true}, \texttt{false}, \ldots, -1, 0, 1, \ldots\} \\
a \in Addr & ::= & \{0, 1, 2, \ldots\} \\
d \in Dev & ::= & \{\texttt{stdin}, \texttt{stdout}, \texttt{file}_1, \texttt{file}_2, \ldots\} \\
e \in Expr & ::= & x^\ell \mid c \mid \&x \mid *x^\ell \mid e_1 \ \texttt{binop} \ e_2 \\
s \in Stmt & ::= & x :=^\ell e \mid *x :=^\ell e \mid \texttt{if} \ x^\ell \ \texttt{then} \ s_1 \ \texttt{else} \ s_2 \mid \\
 & & \textbf{[UNIT]} \ \texttt{while} \ x^\ell \ \{s\} \mid \texttt{while} \ x^\ell \ \{s\} \mid s_1 ; s_2 \mid \\
 & & x := \texttt{read}^\ell(d) \mid \texttt{write}^\ell(d, x) \mid x_1 := \texttt{alloc}^\ell(x_2) \\
 & & \mid \texttt{skip} \mid \texttt{assert}^\ell(x) \mid \texttt{exit}
\end{array}
$$

Figure 3. Language Syntax

To facilitate discussion, we introduce a kernel language. The syntax of the language is presented in Fig. 3. We explicitly model memory addresses. We allow the *address-of* and *pointer-dereference* operations, pointer manipulation, and dynamic memory allocation through the `alloc()` statement. We explicitly model devices and I/O with `read()` and `write()` statements. Failures are modeled as assertion violations. The `while` loop with the **[UNIT]** annotation denotes that it is a request handling loop. Supporting concurrent programs is discussed in Section 9.

$$
\begin{array}{rcl@{\qquad}rcl}
v \in Val & ::= & a \mid c & \sigma \in Store & ::= & Addr \rightarrow Val \\
\alpha \in VarAddr & ::= & Var \rightarrow Addr & \iota \in IOStore & ::= & Dev \rightarrow \overline{Val} \\
e_r \in RefExpr & ::= & x \mid *x & & &
\end{array}
$$

$$
addrOf(e_r) = \begin{cases} \alpha(x) & e_r = x \\ \sigma(\alpha(x)) & e_r = *x \end{cases}
$$

Figure 4. Definitions

Fig. 4 presents definitions for the semantics. In particular, the variable address mapping α maps a variable to its address. The mapping is static. The device store ι denotes the state of device, which is a mapping from a device to a sequence of values. A reference expression e_r is the shorthand for a variable or a dereference of a pointer variable. Method $addrOf()$ identifies the address of the given reference expression.

The semantics are presented in Fig. 5. We have two sets of rules. The first set evaluates an expression to a value, provided the store and the variable address mapping. The second set evaluates statements. Statement evaluation has the configuration $\langle s, \sigma, \iota \rangle$ with s the statement, σ the store and ι the device store (defined in Fig. 4). Most evaluations are standard. The evaluation of the annotated `while` statement is the same as the regular `while` statement. Evaluation terminates normally at $\langle \texttt{skip}, \sigma, \iota \rangle$ or abnormally at $\langle \texttt{exit}, \sigma, \iota \rangle$.

We model simple stream devices through rules [Read] and [Write]. In particular, one value is read at a time from the head of a stream device; and a value can be written to the tail of the stream. More I/O complexity is omitted to simplify our formal discussion. Our system supports most system calls and signals. Rule [Alloc] describes dynamic allocation behavior. Symbol $\perp$ means undefined. Initially, the addresses of static variables are mapped to value 0 in the store. The remaining addresses are not defined. We assume infinite memory and do not model deallocation. Note that

EXPRESSION RULES

$\boxed{e \xrightarrow{e} v}$ parameterized on α and σ

$$
\frac{}{e_r^\ell \xrightarrow{e} \sigma(addrOf(e_r))}\ [\text{Ref}] \qquad \frac{}{\&x \xrightarrow{e} \alpha(x)}\ [\text{Addr-Of}]
$$

$$
\frac{}{c \xrightarrow{e} c}\ [\text{Const}] \qquad \frac{e_1 \xrightarrow{e} v_1 \quad e_2 \xrightarrow{e} v_2}{e_1 \ binop \ e_2 \xrightarrow{e} v_1 \ binop \ v_2}\ [\text{Binop}]
$$

STATEMENT RULES

$\boxed{\langle s, \sigma, \iota \rangle \xrightarrow{s} \langle s', \sigma', \iota' \rangle}$ parameterized on α

$$
\frac{addrOf(e_r) = a \quad e \xrightarrow{e} v \quad \sigma' = \sigma[a \mapsto v]}{\langle e_r :=^\ell e, \sigma, \iota \rangle \xrightarrow{s} \langle \texttt{skip}, \sigma', \iota \rangle}\ [\text{Assign}]
$$

$$
\frac{x \xrightarrow{e} \texttt{true}}{\langle \texttt{if} \ x^l \ \texttt{then} \ s_1 \ \texttt{else} \ s_2, \ \sigma, \iota \rangle \xrightarrow{s} \langle s_1, \ \sigma, \iota \rangle}\ [\text{If-True}]
$$

$$
\frac{r = \texttt{if} \ x^\ell \ \texttt{then skip else exit}}{\langle \texttt{assert}^\ell(x), \sigma, \iota \rangle \xrightarrow{s} \langle r, \sigma, \iota \rangle}\ [\text{Assert}]
$$

$$
\frac{}{\langle \texttt{skip}; s, \ \sigma, \iota \rangle \xrightarrow{s} \langle s, \ \sigma, \iota \rangle}\ [\text{Skip}] \qquad \frac{}{\langle \texttt{exit}; s, \ \sigma, \iota \rangle \xrightarrow{s} \langle \texttt{exit}, \ \sigma, \iota \rangle}\ [\text{Exit}]
$$

$$
\frac{\iota(d) = v \cdot S \quad a = \alpha(x) \quad \sigma' = \sigma[a \mapsto v] \quad \iota' = \iota[d \mapsto S]}{\langle x := \texttt{read}^\ell(d), \sigma, \iota \rangle \xrightarrow{s} \langle \texttt{skip}, \sigma', \iota' \rangle}\ [\text{Read}]
$$

$$
\frac{\iota(d) = S \quad x \xrightarrow{e} v \quad \iota' = \iota[d \mapsto S \cdot v]}{\langle \texttt{write}^\ell(d, x), \sigma, \iota \rangle \xrightarrow{s} \langle \texttt{skip}, \sigma, \iota' \rangle}\ [\text{Write}]
$$

$$
\frac{\begin{array}{c} x_2 \xrightarrow{e} size \quad \sigma(a, \ldots, a + size - 1) = \perp \\ \sigma' = \sigma[a, \ldots, a + size - 1 \mapsto 0, \alpha(x_1) \mapsto a] \end{array}}{\langle x_1 := \texttt{alloc}^\ell(x_2), \sigma, \iota \rangle \xrightarrow{s} \langle \texttt{skip}, \sigma', \iota \rangle}\ [\text{Alloc}]
$$

Figure 5. Operational Semantics

it does not mean our system cannot handle finite memory and deallocation. Such complexity is just not needed for our discussion. The evaluation rule specifies that with an allocation request of a certain size, a consecutive sequence of undefined addresses of the size is allocated. These addresses are then associated with value 0. The base address is associated with variable x_1. Note that multiple valuations of a could satisfy the rule, which models the nondeterminism of dynamic allocation. We do not explicitly model memory errors, which can be modeled by assertion failures if necessary.

3. Logging Semantics

In the logging phase, besides recording the I/O behavior of the execution, our technique divides the execution into units and logs memory reads and writes. The goal of logging memory accesses is twofold. First, it identifies dependences between units. Particularly, pointer dependences allow us to reconstruct relevant memory state. Second, it allows restoring values when we choose not to replay through dependences.

One naïve way logs all accesses. To discover cross-unit dependences, given a read access in unit U_B from address x, the post-processing algorithm traverses backward in the log file to find the latest write to x that precedes the read. If the write is in a different unit U_A, there is a cross-unit dependence between U_A and U_B, denoted as $U_B \xrightarrow{x} U_A$.

However, this simple logging strategy introduces a lot of redundancy. In particular, if an address is written inside a unit, the values of the following reads from the address in the same unit are deter-

$$
\begin{array}{lcl}
\mu_r \in ReadMask & ::= & Addr \rightarrow UnitId \\
\mu_w \in WriteMask & ::= & Addr \rightarrow UnitId \\
\mathcal{L} \in Log & ::= & \overline{U} \qquad\qquad id \in UnitId \ ::= \ Z^+ \\
U \in LogUnit & ::= & \texttt{UNIT}(id,\ell)\cdot\overline{E} \\
E \in LogEntry & ::= & \texttt{R}(id,d,\ell,v) \mid \texttt{W}(id,d,\ell,v) \mid \\
 & & \texttt{FAIL}(id,\ell) \mid \gamma(id,\ell,a,v) \mid \omega(id,\ell,a) \\
 & & \\
e_{nr} \in NoRefExpr & ::= & c \mid \&x \mid \texttt{nil} \\
s_o \in RegularStmt & ::= & \texttt{skip} \mid \texttt{exit} \mid \texttt{while}\ x^\ell\ \{s\} \mid s_1;s_2 \\
 & & \texttt{if}\ x^\ell\ \texttt{then}\ s_1\ \texttt{else}\ s_2 \mid x :=^\ell e \mid \\
 & & *x :=^\ell e \mid x_1 := \texttt{alloc}^\ell(x_2)
\end{array}
$$

$$
expr(s_o) = \begin{cases} e & s_o = x :=^\ell e \\ e, x^\ell & s_o = *x :=^\ell e \\ x_2^\ell & s_o = x_1 := \texttt{alloc}^\ell(x_2) \\ x^\ell & s_o = \texttt{if}\ x^\ell\ \texttt{then}\ s_1\ \texttt{else}\ s_2 \\ \texttt{nil} & others \end{cases}
$$

$$
def(s_o) = \begin{cases} x & s_o = x :=^\ell e \\ *x & s_o = *x :=^\ell e \\ x_1 & s_o = x_1 := \texttt{alloc}^\ell(x_2) \\ \texttt{nil} & others \end{cases}
$$

$$
\begin{array}{lcl}
need2logwrite(s_o) & = & \texttt{let}\ x = def(s_o)\ \texttt{in}\ x \neq \texttt{nil} \\
 & & \wedge\ \mu_w(addrOf(x)) \neq uid \\
accessed(a) & = & \mu_w(a) = uid \ \vee\ \mu_r(a) = uid
\end{array}
$$

uid: the shorthand for $\sigma(\alpha(\texttt{unit\_id}))$;
$uid \uparrow$: the shorthand for $\alpha(\texttt{unit\_id}) \mapsto \sigma(\alpha(\texttt{unit\_id})) + 1$.

Figure 6. Definitions for Logging Semantics

	Execution	Log
1_1	$x = \ldots;$	$\omega(\&x)$
2_1	**[UNIT]** `while` {	
3_1	$\ldots = x;$	$\gamma(\&x)$
4_1	$x = x+1;$	$\omega(\&x)$
5_1	$\ldots = x;$	
6_1	x=...;	
2_2	**[UNIT]** `while` {	
3_2	$\ldots = x;$	$\gamma(\&x)$
	...	

Figure 7. The accesses at 5_1 (that is, the 1st instance of line 5) and 6_1 are redundant and not logged. Symbols $\gamma()$ and $\omega()$ represent memory read and write logs.

ministic and such reads cannot cause any cross-unit dependence[1]. Hence, logging them is unnecessary. Similarly, the following writes in the same unit do not need to be logged. When a cross-unit dependence involves one of these writes, keeping the first write in the log is sufficient for disclosing the same unit level dependence. Furthermore, if a read from an address has been logged, the following reads in the same unit don't need to be logged because they must have the same value and they only reveal the same cross-unit dependence that the first read reveals.

Consider the example in Fig. 7. It shows a trace of two iterations of an annotated loop. The read in 4_1 is not logged because of the read at 3_1. The read at 5_1 is not logged because of the definition at 4_1. The write at 6_1 is not logged because of the write at 4_1.

The rules are presented in Fig. 8 and the relevant definitions can be found in Fig. 6. We compute a few relations during evaluation. According to the definitions in Fig. 6, relation μ_r maps an address to the id of a unit that most recently reads the address. It is used to avoid logging redundant reads. Similarly, μ_w identifies the most recent unit that writes to an address. Symbol $\mathcal{L}$ denotes the generated log. A log comprises a sequence of log units. A log unit U

[1] This assumes sequential semantics and Section 9 discusses handling threads.

EXPRESSION LOGGING RULES

$\boxed{\langle e,\mu_r,\mathcal{L}\rangle \overset{e}{\Rightarrow} \langle \mu_r',\mathcal{L}'\rangle}$ parameterized on α, σ, and μ_w.

$$
\frac{addrOf(e_r) = a \quad \neg accessed(a) \quad v = \sigma(a)}{\langle e_r^\ell,\mu_r,\mathcal{L}\rangle \overset{e}{\Rightarrow} \langle \mu_r[a \mapsto uid],\ \mathcal{L}\cdot\gamma(uid,\ell,a,v)\rangle} \quad \text{[LE-Log]}
$$

$$
\frac{addrOf(e_r) = a \quad accessed(a)}{\langle e_r^\ell,\mu_r,\mathcal{L}\rangle \overset{e}{\Rightarrow} \langle \mu_r,\mathcal{L}\rangle} \quad \text{[LE-NoLog]}
$$

$$
\frac{}{\langle e_{nr},\mu_r,\mathcal{L}\rangle \overset{e}{\Rightarrow} \langle \mu_r,\mathcal{L}\rangle} \quad \text{[LE-NoRef]}
$$

$$
\frac{\langle e_1,\mu_r,\mathcal{L}\rangle \overset{e}{\Rightarrow} \langle \mu_r',\mathcal{L}'\rangle \quad \langle e_2,\mu_r',\mathcal{L}'\rangle \overset{e}{\Rightarrow} \langle \mu_r'',\mathcal{L}''\rangle}{\langle e_1\ binop\ e_2,\mu_r,\mathcal{L}\rangle \overset{e}{\Rightarrow} \langle \mu_r'',\mathcal{L}''\rangle} \quad \text{[LE-Binop]}
$$

STATEMENT LOGGING RULES

$\boxed{\langle s,\sigma,\iota,\mu_r,\mu_w,\mathcal{L}\rangle \overset{s}{\Rightarrow} \langle s',\sigma',\iota',\mu_r',\mu_w',\mathcal{L}'\rangle}$ parameterized on α

$$
\frac{s_T = s;\ \texttt{while}\ x^\ell\ \{s\} \quad \sigma' = \sigma[uid\uparrow] \quad \mathcal{L}' = \mathcal{L}\cdot\texttt{UNIT}(uid,\ell)}{\begin{array}{c}\langle \textbf{[UNIT]}\texttt{while}\ x^\ell\ \{s\},\ \sigma,\iota,\mu_r,\mu_w,\mathcal{L}\rangle \overset{s}{\Rightarrow} \\ \langle \texttt{if}\ x^\ell\ \texttt{then}\ s_T\ \texttt{else}\ \texttt{skip},\ \sigma',\iota,\mu_r,\mu_w,\mathcal{L}'\rangle\end{array}} \quad \text{[LS-Unit-While]}
$$

$$
\frac{\begin{array}{c}\langle x = \texttt{read}^\ell(d),\sigma,\iota\rangle \overset{s}{\rightarrow} \langle \texttt{skip},\sigma',\iota'\rangle \quad a = \alpha(x) \\ \mu_w' = \mu_w[a \mapsto uid] \quad \mathcal{L}' = \mathcal{L}\cdot\texttt{R}(uid,d,\ell,\sigma'(a))\end{array}}{\langle x = \texttt{read}^\ell(d),\sigma,\iota,\mu_r,\mu_w,\mathcal{L}\rangle \overset{s}{\Rightarrow} \langle \texttt{skip},\sigma',\iota',\mu_r,\mu_w',\mathcal{L}')\rangle} \quad \text{[LS-Input]}
$$

$$
\frac{\begin{array}{c}\langle \texttt{write}^\ell(d,x),\sigma,\iota\rangle \overset{s}{\rightarrow} \langle \texttt{Skip},\sigma,\iota'\rangle \quad x \overset{e}{\rightarrow} v \\ \langle x^\ell,\mu_r,\mathcal{L}\rangle \overset{e}{\Rightarrow} \langle \mu_r',\mathcal{L}'\rangle \quad \mathcal{L}'' = \mathcal{L}'\cdot\texttt{W}(uid,d,\ell,v)\end{array}}{\langle \texttt{write}^\ell(d,x),\sigma,\iota,\mu_r,\mu_w,\mathcal{L}\rangle \overset{s}{\Rightarrow} \langle \texttt{skip},\sigma,\iota',\mu_r',\mu_w,\mathcal{L}''\rangle} \quad \text{[LS-Output]}
$$

$$
\frac{\langle x^\ell,\mu_r,\mathcal{L}\rangle \overset{e}{\Rightarrow} \langle \mu_r',\mathcal{L}'\rangle \quad x \overset{e}{\rightarrow} \texttt{false} \quad \mathcal{L}'' = \mathcal{L}'\cdot\texttt{FAIL}(uid,\ell)}{\langle \texttt{assert}(x^\ell),\sigma,\iota,\mu_r,\mu_w,\mathcal{L}\rangle \overset{s}{\Rightarrow} \langle \texttt{exit},\sigma,\iota,\mu_r',\mu_w,\mathcal{L}''\rangle} \quad \text{[LS-Assert-Fail]}
$$

$$
\frac{\langle x^\ell,\mu_r,\mathcal{L}\rangle \overset{e}{\Rightarrow} \langle \mu_r',\mathcal{L}'\rangle \quad x \overset{e}{\rightarrow} \texttt{true}}{\langle \texttt{assert}(x^\ell),\sigma,\iota,\mu_r,\mu_w,\mathcal{L}\rangle \overset{s}{\Rightarrow} \langle \texttt{skip},\sigma,\iota,\mu_r',\mu_w,\mathcal{L}'\rangle} \quad \text{[LS-Assert-Pass]}
$$

$$
\frac{\begin{array}{c}\langle expr(s_o),\mu_r,\mathcal{L}\rangle \overset{e}{\Rightarrow} \langle \mu_r',\mathcal{L}'\rangle \quad need2logwrite(s_o) \\ \langle s_o^\ell,\sigma,\iota\rangle \overset{s}{\rightarrow} \langle r,\sigma',\iota\rangle \quad a = addrOf(def(s_o))\end{array}}{\langle s_o^\ell,\ \sigma,\iota,\mu_r,\mu_w,\mathcal{L}\rangle \overset{s}{\Rightarrow} \langle r,\sigma',\iota,\mu_r',\mu_w[a \mapsto uid],\mathcal{L}'\cdot\omega(uid,\ell,a)\rangle} \quad \text{[LS-Log-Wrt]}
$$

$$
\frac{\begin{array}{c}\langle expr(s_o),\mu_r,\mathcal{L}\rangle \overset{e}{\Rightarrow} \langle \mu_r',\mathcal{L}'\rangle \quad \neg need2logwrite(s_o) \\ \langle s_o^\ell,\sigma,\iota\rangle \overset{s}{\rightarrow} \langle r,\sigma',\iota\rangle\end{array}}{\langle s_o^\ell,\ \sigma,\iota,\mu_r,\mu_w,\mathcal{L}\rangle \overset{s}{\Rightarrow} \langle r,\sigma',\iota,\mu_r',\mu_w,\mathcal{L}'\rangle} \quad \text{[LS-NoLog-Wrt]}
$$

Figure 8. Logging Semantics

corresponds to an execution unit, containing a `UNIT()` event followed by a sequence of other events. The `UNIT()` event contains the id of the unit and the program location ℓ of the loop that generates the unit. Besides the `UNIT()` event, we model other 5 kinds of events, described by symbol E. In particular, `R()` and `W()` are the input and output events, in which we log the unit id, the device id, the program location of the event, and the input/output value. The `FAIL()` event records an assertion failure. Events $\gamma()$ and $\omega()$ represent memory reads and writes. The remaining definitions in Fig. 6 are auxiliary to the rules.

The expression rules are of the format $\langle e,\mu_r,\mathcal{L}\rangle \overset{e}{\Rightarrow} \langle \mu_r',\mathcal{L}'\rangle$, provided α, σ, and μ_w. Rules [LE-Log] and [LE-NoLog] evaluate reference expression e_r, which is either x or $*x$ (Fig. 4). A reference expression involves a memory read. It tests whether the address being referred to has been accessed in the same unit (through method *accessed*() defined in Fig. 6). If so, we don't need to log the read. Otherwise, we attach a γ event to the log and update the most recent read unit of the address. Note that we introduce a program variable *unit_id* to denote the dynamic unit id. Symbol *uid* is shorthand for its value. Rule [LE-NoRef] handles expressions not involving memory reads.

Statement evaluation has the configuration of $\langle s, \sigma, \iota, \mu_r, \mu_w, \mathcal{L}\rangle$. Rule [LS-Unit-While] specifies that *uid* is incremented and a UNIT() event is logged when an annotated while statement is evaluated. Note that the UNIT() event leads the unit corresponding to the iteration if the loop predicate evaluates true, otherwise, it leads the unit corresponding to the execution from the end of the loop to the beginning of the next annotated loop. Rules [LS-Input] and [LS-Output] attach R() and W() entries, respectively, to the log. In [LS-Input], the most recent write unit to the left hand side variable x is updated. In [LS-Output], the read of x may be logged by the expression evaluation. When an assertion fails (rule [LS-Assertion-Fail]), a FAIL() event is logged. It is then the last event in the log as the `exit` statement leads to the termination of the evaluation.

Rules [LS-Log-Wrt] and [LS-NoLog-Wrt] describe evaluation of the other statements, denoted as s_o, whose definitions are in Fig. 6. Two auxiliary functions $expr(s_o)$ and $def(s_o)$ are used. The former function returns the expressions that need to be evaluated for a s_o statement. Such expressions lead to memory reads. For instance, $expr(*x :=^{\ell} e) = e, x^{\ell}$, with e, x being the concatenation of the two expressions. When the concatenated expression is evaluated under rule [LE-Binop], e is evaluated first and then x, ensuring the reads are logged in the proper order. Function $def(s_o)$ returns the target of a memory write if s_o involves one, or `nil` otherwise. In rules [LS-Log-Wrt] and [LS-NoLog-Wrt], the expressions s_o are first evaluated. If the write target has not been written previously in the same unit, a $\omega()$ event is logged (rule [LS-Log-Wrt]). Evaluation starts with $\mathcal{L} = \texttt{UNIT}(0,0)$ such that the execution from the beginning to the start of the first annotated loop belongs to U_0.

4. Reduction Algorithm

$$pointerdep(U, X) = \exists\omega(id, \ell, a) \in U \text{ and } \gamma(id', \ell', a, v) \in X\, s.t.\ ispointer(\ell) \wedge \nexists\omega(id'', \ell'', a) \in S \text{ with } \omega(id, \ell, a)\cdot S \cdot \gamma(id', \ell', a, v) \subset \mathcal{L}$$

$$isloopexit(U) = U = \texttt{UNIT}(uid, \ell)\cdot S \wedge U \cdot U' \subset \mathcal{L} \wedge U' = \texttt{UNIT}(uid+1, \ell')\cdot S' \wedge \ell \neq \ell'$$

$$X \in ReducedLog ::= \overline{U}$$

LOG REDUCTION $\boxed{\langle \mathcal{L}, X\rangle \rightsquigarrow \langle \mathcal{L}', X'\rangle}$

$$\frac{\texttt{FAIL}(id, \ell) \in U_c}{\langle \mathcal{L}_h \cdot U_c, \texttt{nil}\rangle \rightsquigarrow \langle \mathcal{L}_h, U_c\rangle}\ \text{[X-Crit]} \qquad \frac{pointerdep(U, X)}{\langle \mathcal{L}_h \cdot U, X\rangle \rightsquigarrow \langle \mathcal{L}_h, U \cdot X\rangle}\ \text{[X-PointerDep]}$$

$$\frac{isloopexit(U)}{\langle \mathcal{L}_h \cdot U, X\rangle \rightsquigarrow \langle \mathcal{L}_h, U \cdot X\rangle}\ \text{[X-LoopExit]} \qquad \frac{}{\langle U, X\rangle \rightsquigarrow \langle \texttt{nil}, U \cdot X\rangle}\ \text{[X-FirstUnit]}$$

$$\frac{\neg pointerdep(U, X) \quad \neg isloopexit(U)}{\langle \mathcal{L}_h \cdot U, X\rangle \rightsquigarrow \langle \mathcal{L}_h, X\rangle}\ \text{[X-Reduce]}$$

Figure 9. Log Reduction.

Given a replay criterion, e.g. a failure, our reduction algorithm identifies a small subset of units that are replayable and produce the criterion. The approach includes units that are relevant to the criterion through cross-unit pointer dependences or other complex dependences such as those through buffers and complex fields in data structures. We call this *replay by dependence*. For uses of variable having primitive types and defined in other units, we retrieve

```
1 s0;
2 [UNIT] while (...)
3     s1;
4 s2;
5 [UNIT] while (...)
6     s3;
```

(a) Code

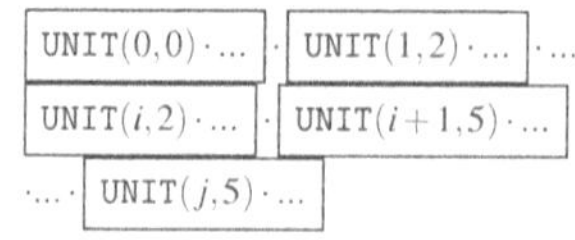

(b) Original Log

Figure 10. Ex. for reduction with structural constraints. Variables i and j are ids and the 2nd numbers in UNIT() are line numbers.

the values from the log, avoiding replay of their dependence precedence. We call this *replay by value*. For example, if a pointer x is defined in unit U_B and then used in U_A, we need to replay U_B if we replay U_A. Assume x has a primitive field f, and $x \rightarrow f$ is defined in U_C and used in U_A. We don't need to replay U_C when replaying U_A as we acquire its value directly from the log.

The reason for this design is that restoring pointer values from the log is problematic due to dynamic allocation. Furthermore, for dependences on buffers and complex fields, restoring values implies logging their values, which is much more expensive than logging primitive variables/fields.

Note that our technique nonetheless allows the developer to replay primitive variables/fields by dependences if needed. All the necessary information is available in the log. One can imagine cases in which the root cause resides in a unit different than the criterion and affects the criterion through primitive dependences, the developer can choose to replay the dependence of a primitive value if she/he decides the value is suspicious and wants to inspect the computation leading to the value.

Fig. 9 presents the log reduction algorithm. The evaluation starts with the original log $\mathcal{L}$ and an empty reduced log $X = \texttt{nil}$. The units in $\mathcal{L}$ are evaluated in a backward fashion. The evaluation terminates with all units processed, and X is the reduced log. Rule [X-Crit] adds the unit containing the criterion event to X. In this paper, we assume the criterion is a failure. Rule [X-PointerDep] mandates that the last unit in $\mathcal{L}$ is added to X if some unit in X has a pointer dependence on the unit. Method $pointerdep(U, X)$ tests if there is a memory write in U and a read in X with the same address, and there is not other writes to the address in-between. If so, the unit is added to X.

Rule [X-LoopExit] tests whether a unit under consideration denotes a loop exit, meaning the unit encompasses the execution between the exit of an annotated loop and the beginning of the next annotated loop. If so, we need to add the unit to X to respect the structural constraint. If we did not, and the unit were not replayed, the execution wouldn't be able to get out of the annotated loop. Method $isloopexit(U)$ decides whether U is a loop exit by testing whether the label of the leading UNIT() event of the unit is different from that of the next unit. A unit is reduced if there are no pointer dependences between the unit and the previously computed X and it is not a loop exit (rule [X-Reduce]). Finally, the first unit, which corresponds to the execution from the beginning to the first annotated loop, is always included (rule [X-FirstUnit]). This is for the consideration of structural constraints.

Consider the example in Fig. 10. There are two annotated loops. Figure (b) shows a sample log. Each box represents a unit. Assume the replay criterion is U_j, the shorthand for the unit starting with $\texttt{UNIT}(j,5)$, and it has no cross-unit pointer dependences with any other units. According to the rules, units U_0 and U_i are included in the reduced log. U_0 drives the execution to the loop at 2 and U_i forces the execution get out of loop 2 and reach loop 5.

EXPRESSION REPLAY RULES

$\boxed{\langle e, \sigma, \mu_r, X\rangle \twoheadrightarrow^e \langle \sigma', \mu_r', X'\rangle}$ parameterized on α, σ, and μ_w.

$$\frac{addrOf(e_r) = a \quad \neg accessed(a) \quad \neg ispointer(\ell) \quad \boxed{X = \gamma(id, \ell, a', v)\cdot X'} \quad \sigma' = \sigma[a \mapsto v]}{\langle e_r^{\ell}, \sigma, \mu_r, X\rangle \twoheadrightarrow^e \langle \sigma', \mu_r[a \mapsto uid], X'\rangle} \text{[RE-ByValue]}$$

$$\frac{addrOf(e_r) = a \quad \neg accessed(a) \quad ispointer(\ell) \quad \boxed{X = \gamma(id, \ell, a', v)\cdot X'}}{\langle e_r^{\ell}, \sigma, \mu_r, X\rangle \twoheadrightarrow^e \langle \sigma, \mu_r[a \mapsto uid], X'\rangle} \text{[RE-ByDep]}$$

$$\frac{addrOf(e_r) = a \quad accessed(a)}{\langle e_r^{\ell}, \sigma, \mu_r, X\rangle \twoheadrightarrow^e \langle \sigma, \mu_r, X\rangle} \text{[RE-NoLog]}$$

$$\frac{}{\langle e_{nr}, \sigma, \mu_r, X\rangle \twoheadrightarrow^e \langle \sigma, \mu_r, X\rangle} \text{[RE-NoRef]}$$

$$\frac{\langle e_1, \sigma, \mu_r, X\rangle \twoheadrightarrow^e \langle \sigma', \mu_r', X'\rangle \quad \langle e_2, \sigma', \mu_r', X'\rangle \twoheadrightarrow^e \langle \sigma'', \mu_r'', X''\rangle}{\langle e_1 \; binop \; e_2, \sigma, \mu_r, X\rangle \twoheadrightarrow^e \langle \sigma'', \mu_r'', X''\rangle} \text{[RE-Binop]}$$

STATEMENT REPLAY RULES

$\boxed{\langle s, \sigma, \mu_r, \mu_w, X\rangle \twoheadrightarrow^s \langle s', \sigma', \mu_r', \mu_w', X'\rangle}$ parameterized on α

$$\frac{\boxed{X = \texttt{UNIT}(id, \ell)\cdot X'} \quad \sigma' = \sigma[uid \uparrow] \quad s_T = s; \texttt{while}\ x^{\ell}\ \{s\}}{\langle \textbf{[UNIT]}\texttt{while}\ x^{\ell}\ \{s\}, \sigma, \mu_r, \mu_w, X\rangle \twoheadrightarrow^s \langle \texttt{if}\ x^{\ell}\ \texttt{then}\ s_T\ \texttt{else skip}, \sigma', \mu_r, \mu_w, X'\rangle} \text{[RS-Unit-While]}$$

$$\frac{\boxed{X = \texttt{R}(id, d, \ell, v)\cdot X'} \quad a = \alpha(x) \quad \sigma' = \sigma[a \mapsto v]}{\langle x = \texttt{read}^{\ell}(d), \sigma, \mu_r, \mu_w, X\rangle \twoheadrightarrow^s \langle \texttt{skip}, \sigma', \mu_r, \mu_w[a \mapsto uid], X'\rangle} \text{[RS-Input]}$$

$$\frac{\langle x^{\ell}, \sigma, \mu_r, X\rangle \twoheadrightarrow^e \langle \sigma', \mu_r', X'\rangle \quad x \xrightarrow{e}_{\sigma'} v \quad \boxed{X' = \texttt{W}(id, d, \ell, v)\cdot X''}}{\langle \texttt{write}^{\ell}(d, x), \sigma, \mu_r, \mu_w, X\rangle \twoheadrightarrow^s \langle \texttt{skip}, \sigma', \mu_r', \mu_w, X''\rangle} \text{[RS-Output]}$$

$$\frac{\langle x^{\ell}, \sigma, \mu_r, X\rangle \twoheadrightarrow^e \langle \sigma', \mu_r', X'\rangle \quad x \xrightarrow{e}_{\sigma'} \texttt{false} \quad \boxed{X' = \texttt{FAIL}(id, \ell)}}{\langle \texttt{assert}^{\ell}(x), \sigma, \mu_r, \mu_w, X\rangle \twoheadrightarrow^s \langle \texttt{exit}, \sigma', \mu_r', \mu_w, \texttt{nil}\rangle} \text{[RS-Assert-F]}$$

$$\frac{\langle x^{\ell}, \sigma, \mu_r, X\rangle \twoheadrightarrow^e \langle \sigma', \mu_r', X'\rangle \quad x \xrightarrow{e}_{\sigma'} \texttt{true}}{\langle \texttt{assert}^{\ell}(x), \sigma, \mu_r, \mu_w, X\rangle \twoheadrightarrow^s \langle \texttt{skip}, \sigma', \mu_r', \mu_w, X'\rangle} \text{[RS-Assert-T]}$$

$$\frac{\langle expr(s_o), \sigma, \mu_r, X\rangle \twoheadrightarrow^e \langle \sigma', \mu_r', X'\rangle \quad need2logwrite(s_o) \quad \langle s_o^{\ell}, \sigma', \texttt{nil}\rangle \xrightarrow{s} \langle r, \sigma'', \texttt{nil}\rangle \quad a = addrOf(def(s_o)) \quad \mu_w' = \mu_w[a \mapsto uid] \quad \boxed{X' = \omega(id, \ell, a')\cdot X''}}{\langle s_o^{\ell}, \sigma, \mu_r, \mu_w, X\rangle \twoheadrightarrow^s \langle r, \sigma'', \mu_r', \mu_w', X''\rangle} \text{[RS-Log-Wrt]}$$

$$\frac{\langle expr(s_o), \sigma, \mu_r, X\rangle \twoheadrightarrow^e \langle \sigma', \mu_r', X'\rangle \quad \neg need2logwrite(s_o) \quad \langle s_o^{\ell}, \sigma', \texttt{nil}\rangle \xrightarrow{s} \langle r, \sigma'', \texttt{nil}\rangle}{\langle s_o^{\ell}, \sigma, \mu_r, \mu_w, X\rangle \twoheadrightarrow^s \langle r, \sigma'', \mu_r', \mu_w, X'\rangle} \text{[RS-NoLog-Wrt]}$$

Figure 11. Replay Semantics.

Note that dividing an execution into units simplifies the structural constraints. We do not support nested annotated loops. In such cases, the outer annotations are ignored.

5. Replay

Replay is driven by the reduced log. It can be considered a dual process of logging. The rules are presented in Fig. 11. Lets first consider the expression rules. If a memory read is not on a pointer value, we replay by restoring the value from the log (rule [RE-ByValue]). The store is updated with the logged value. Note, the rule dictates that the logged label and the current label match, ensuring the read happens in the same program point as before. During replay, the masks μ_r and μ_w are maintained in the same way as in the logging phase so that the replay algorithm can avoid restoring values that were found to be redundant during logging. This is important to the synchronization of the replay and the reduced log. Hence, in rule [RE-ByValue], μ_r is updated to reflect that the address has been read in the current unit. If the memory read is on a pointer value (rule [RE-ByDep]), we don't restore the value. Instead, the value is presently available due to earlier replay operations. Hence, the algorithm simply removes the current log entry. The other expression rules are similar to the logging rules.

The statement rules are similar to those in the logging phase. We summarize the key features of the replay rules as follows.

- In order for replay to progress, the reduced log has to perfectly align with the evaluation, indicated by the label of the current evaluation must be identical to that in the current log entry. This is highlighted in the boxed premises.
- The rules do not require that the current unit id *uid* matches the logged id (e.g. rule [RS-Unit-While]), because the current id could be different due to reduction.
- Replay does not concern devices. The I/O rules only interact with the log file.
- Many rules involve evaluating expressions to values. Such evaluation is conducted after the proper values are restored from the log. For instance, in rule [RS-Output], evaluation $x \xrightarrow{e}_{\sigma'} v$ is parameterized on the updated store.
- In rule [RS-Output], the output value v is constrained. It serves as a validation rule. Intuitively, we demand that the observable outputs match those recorded in the reduced log.

6. Replayability

We say a reduced log is *replayable* if it successfully drives the replay to the criterion. It is equivalent to the *progress* property for the rules in Fig. 11. Intuitively, the replay control flow has to perfectly align with the reduced log such that proper events can be retrieved. The replay outputs have to match the logged values. Otherwise, the replay evaluation will get stuck.

$T \in Trace ::= \bar{t} \qquad t \in TraceEntry ::= \texttt{trace}(s^{\ell}, v, p)$
$p \in Pointer ::= \texttt{pnt}(b, z, f)$
$b \in BaseAddr ::= Addr \qquad z \in Size ::= Z^+ \qquad f \in Offset ::= Z^+$

We leverage traces to formally discuss replayability. As presented above, a trace is a sequence of entries. A trace entry is a triple that records the evaluated statement s, the right hand side value v and the canonical pointer value if it is a pointer. Canonical pointer values allow us to reason about pointer equivalence between the original run and the replay. It is a triple tracking the base address, the size of the allocated region, and the offset in the region. A pointer obtains its canonical base address and region size at the address-of operation or the `alloc()` statement, with initial offset 0. The region size for an address-of operation is 1, indicating it is pointing to a variable. Offsets are updated by pointer manipulations. The semantics for tracing is omitted.

Definition 1. (REPLAYABILITY)
Let X be a reduction of $\mathcal{L}$ for a given criterion. Let the subtrace corresponding to X in the original run be T, the replay trace be $\tilde{T}$. We say X is a replayable reduction if $T \doteq_T \tilde{T}$.

Note that T corresponds to the executions of all the units that are in the reduced log. The trace equivalence operator $\doteq_T$ is defined in Fig. 12. It demands the two traces have the same number of entries and the corresponding entries are equivalent. If the corresponding

$$\frac{\ell_1 = \ell_2 \quad \mathit{ispointer}(\ell_1) \quad p_1 = \mathtt{pnt}(b_1, z_1, f_1) \quad p_2 = \mathtt{pnt}(b_2, z_2, f_2) \quad \exists x,\ b_1 = b_2 = \alpha(x) \quad f_1 = f_2 = 0 \quad z_1 = z_2 = 1}{\mathtt{trace}(s_1^{\ell_1}, v_1, p_1) \doteq_t \widetilde{\mathtt{trace}}(s_2^{\ell_2}, v_2, p_2)} \quad \text{[TEQ-P1]}$$

$$\frac{\begin{array}{c}\ell_1 = \ell_2 \quad \mathit{ispointer}(\ell_1) \quad p_1 = \mathtt{pnt}(b_1, z_1, f_1) \\ p_2 = \mathtt{pnt}(b_2, z_2, f_2) \quad z_1 = z_2 \quad f_1 = f_2 \\ \boxed{\begin{array}{c}\exists\, i,\ t_i = \mathtt{trace}(x_1^{\ell} := \mathtt{alloc}(x_2),\ b_1,\ \mathtt{pnt}(b_1, z_1, 0)\ ) \text{ and} \\ \tilde{t}_i = \widetilde{\mathtt{trace}}(x_1^{\ell} := \mathtt{alloc}(x_2),\ b_2,\ \mathtt{pnt}(b_2, z_2, 0)\ )\end{array}}\end{array}}{\mathtt{trace}(s_1^{\ell_1}, v_1, p_1) \doteq_t \widetilde{\mathtt{trace}}(s_2^{\ell_2}, v_2, p_2)} \quad \text{[TEQ-P2]}$$

$$\frac{\ell_1 = \ell_2 \quad \neg \mathit{ispointer}(\ell) \quad v_1 = v_2}{\mathtt{trace}(s_1^{\ell_1}, v_1, p_1) \doteq_t \widetilde{\mathtt{trace}}(s_2^{\ell_2}, v_2, p_2)} \quad \text{[TEQ-Val]}$$

$$\frac{|T| = |\tilde{T}| \quad \forall 0 \le i < |T|,\ t_i \doteq_t \tilde{t}_i}{T \doteq_T \tilde{T}} \quad \text{[TEQ]}$$

Figure 12. Trace Equivalence.

entries involve non-pointer values, their equivalence is determined by the equivalence of the statements and the values (rule [TEQ-Val]). If the entries involve pointers, the pointer values must be identical if they point to some variable (rule [TEQ-P1])[2]. If they point to dynamically allocated regions (rule [TEQ-P2]), the regions must be allocated at corresponding execution points and have the same size and the same offset (t_i and $\tilde{t}_i$ are the ith entries in the two traces). Note that the base addresses of t_i and $\tilde{t}_i$ might be different as less memory is allocated in the reduced replay.

Theorem 1. *If the program only allows comparisons and subtractions between two pointers, the reduction scheme in Fig. 9 is replayable in the absence of overflow.*

Overflow is defined as follows.

$$\frac{\mathit{ispointer}(\ell) \quad p = \mathtt{pnt}(b, z, f) \quad f \ge z}{\mathit{overflow}(\mathtt{trace}(s^{\ell}, v, p))}$$

For example, in the following program snippets "`1. b=&x; 2. p=b+1;`" and "`1. b=alloc(10); 2. p=b+12;`", overflows occur in statement 2s.

Proof Sketch of the Theorem 1 To prove replayability, we want to prove trace equivalence. According to rule [X-FirstUnit], we always replay the first unit. As a result, the theorem holds for the trace entries corresponding to the first unit.

Next, we prove by induction. We assume the theorem holds for the first k entries, and prove that it holds for the $(k+1)$th entry, that is, $t_{k+1} \doteq_t \tilde{t}_{k+1}$.

First, the statement under evaluation for the $(k+1)$th entry must be the same as the result of the equivalence of the previous entries. In particular, any predicate guarding the statement must have been evaluated previously in equivalent entries. Also, it must have been evaluated to the same result according to the assumption, leading to the execution of the same statement in the $k+1$ entry. Hence, we only need to prove all the uses (references) in the entry have equivalent values. Without loss of generality, let's consider a reference of variable x.

In case (1), x has a non-pointer value. Assume in the original run, the value is defined by a previous evaluation, denoted by trace entry t_j. If t_j and t_{k+1} are within the same unit, an equivalent evaluation must have occurred in $\tilde{t}_j$. In the absence of overflow, there are no other assignments to the same address during replay. Hence, x must have an equivalent value in $\tilde{t}_{k+1}$ during replay. If t_j and t_{k+1} are in different units, the value of x is retrieved from the log according to the replay semantics, and x is equivalent across runs.

Note that execution reduction causes `alloc()` to return different values during replay because many allocations may be reduced away. An overflow pointer may cause different variables to be overwritten. For instance, assume dynamically allocated buffers A and B are next to each other in the original run, A and C are adjacent in the replay. Assume an overflow pointer based on A overwrites B, the equivalent pointer overwrites C during replay. In other words, in the presence of overflows, writes though pointers with equivalent values at equivalent points may write to different variables (regions).

In case (2), x is a pointer. Assume it is defined at t_j. When t_j and t_{k+1} are in the same unit, the equivalence can be derived as in case (1). If they are in different units, denoted as U_m and U_n respectively, U_m is replayed according to our reduction rules. In the absence of overflow, it can be inferred that x is not redefined in-between $\tilde{t}_j$ and $\tilde{t}_{k+1}$. Otherwise, the same redefinition must have occurred in the original run. The value equivalence at the $(k+1)$th entries can be derived from the equivalence at the jth entries.

Similarly, we can prove the equivalence when the reference is through a pointer, i.e. $*x$.

Finally, it can be inferred that the same expression must yield an equivalent value if all references in it have equivalent values, assuming only the supported operations. □

According to the theorem, replayability is not guaranteed in our model in the presence of overflow. In real-world scenarios, however, if the overflow is a stack overflow, due to the determinism of variable layouts, we can always replay. For heap overflows, although we may not encounter the original failure, we very likely encounter a memory failure in a different place due to the non-determinism of heap allocations. We can attach the replay to a memory error detection tool, such as valgrind's *memcheck*, to identify heap overflows.

Note that traces and canonical pointer values just facilitate our definitions and proofs. The technique does not need to trace executions or compute canonical pointer values.

7. Aggressive Reduction

Although we divide executions into relatively independent units, non-trivial pointer dependences may limit the possible reduction. The reduction scheme in Fig. 9 is sometimes too rigid. Namely, the scheme requires that pointers used in equivalent evaluation points are defined at equivalent points with equivalent canonical values. However, as long as the pointer is pointing to the same variable or to the same offset of a region with the same size, the places they are defined are irrelevant because the value stored at the pointed-to address can be either restored from the log (if defined external to the unit) or recomputed (if defined internally). Moreover, we need to ensure that pointers to the same variable or to the same region in the original run retain such aliasing relations during replay. Otherwise, undesirable overwriting and different results in pointer comparison may occur so that the replay fails to make progress.

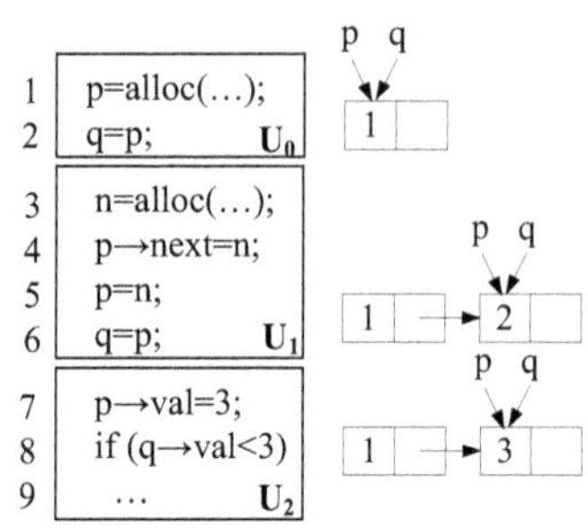

Figure 13. According to the reduction rules in Fig. 9, the log is not reducible. However, U_0 and U_2 are a replayable reduction assuming the criterion is in U_2.

[2] We assume the variable-address mapping α is static.

Consider Fig. 13. Three units are presented on the left. The execution maintains a linked list, the state of which is presented on the right at the end of each unit. Pointers p and q always point to the tail of the list. Assume the criterion is in U_2. Because $U_2 \xrightarrow{p,q} U_1 \xrightarrow{p} U_0$, we cannot achieve reduction by rules in Fig. 9. However, U_0 and U_2 compose a replayable reduction because the region pointed to by p at the end of U_0 is compatible with that at the end of U_1, and the aliasing relation of p and q is the same at the end of the two units. In other words, the state of the list at the end of U_0 is sufficient to drive the execution in U_2. Note that if after U_0 p and q were pointing to different regions, the predicate at line 8 would take a different branch, making the reduction not replayable.

In the following, we formally define compatibility.

Definition 2. [COMPATIBILITY]
Let X be a reduction and T be the sub-trace corresponding to X in the original run. X is compatible if and only if for each $U \in X$, the following conditions are satisfied.

1. *for each read to an address a logged in U (hence its definition must be external to the unit) for a pointer value* $\texttt{pnt}(b,z,f)$, *there must be a closest preceding write to a in T with the canonical value* $\texttt{pnt}(b',z,f)$.
2. *for each pair of reads from addresses a_1 and a_2 in U with pointer values* $\texttt{pnt}(b,z,f_i)$ *and* $\texttt{pnt}(b,z,f_j)$, *respectively, the closest preceding writes to a_1 and a_2 in T must have the values* $\texttt{pnt}(b',z,f_i)$ *and* $\texttt{pnt}(b',z,f_j)$.

In condition 1, the read would receive its value from the closest preceding write in T instead of the original write during replay. This dictates the two writes have the same size and offset. Condition 2 dictates the region level aliasing be retained. Note that the pointer offsets f_i and f_j may be different. Consider the code snippet within a unit "1. `x=p+2;` 2. `*x=9;` 3. `...=*q;`". Assume p and q are defined externally to the unit, pointing to the same region and with offsets 0 and 2, respectively, so they do not alias. Variable x is defined internally. After line 1, x and q point to the same address and hence the dereference at line 3 has the value 9. To ensure faithful replay, we must ensure p and q point to the same region.

Theorem 2. *A compatible reduction is replayable.*

The proof is omitted for brevity.

Search for Compatible Reduction. Given a criterion, there may be multiple compatible reductions. We use a BFS algorithm to find a compatible reduction. In particular, given a criterion, the algorithm first includes only the units dictated by structural constraints (the first unit and all loop exit units) and tries to replay with such a log. If replay fails (gets stuck), the algorithm further includes units that are 1 pointer dependence edge away, then 2 dependence edges away, and so on, until a compatible reduction is found.

8. Optimizing Instrumentation

To reduce logging overhead, we limit instrumentation to the data structures and variables that may cause inter-unit dependences. We further remove unnecessary instrumentation through static analysis. The analysis is similar in spirit to *definite assignment* analysis that decides if a local variable must have been initialized. The analysis computes the set of data structure fields and variables that must have been either read or written before a program point within a unit. Such information can be used to discover redundancy. For instance, instrumenting an object field read is not needed if the field must have been read or written before. Details are elided.

9. Handling Concurrent Programs

Our technique supports concurrent programs. The system currently supports only a single core due to limitations of the underlying *jockey* infrastructure [18]. More discussion resides in Section 10. We leave supporting multiple cores to future work. Presently, we discuss the extensions to support concurrent programs.

Maintaining Unit Id. The rules in Fig. 8 assume sequential semantics. Since units do not interleave, we can use a unit id variable across the entire program, which is not sufficient for concurrent programs. We consider two possible threading models. In the first one, an annotated loop does not spawn any thread but rather resides in a thread. We use a thread local unit id for the loop. In the other model, threads may be spawned inside an annotated loop. We need to properly attribute thread execution with the unit id of the loop. We use a thread local unit id, which is inherited from the parent when a thread is spawned.

Remote Definitions. With sequential semantics, we identify redundant reads and writes by comparing the current unit id and that stored in μ_r and μ_w. In the presence of thread interleaving, the value of a memory read may be defined remotely by a unit in a different thread. In such a case, the read should be logged even if it has a local definition in the same unit. To handle such cases, we use a pair comprising a thread id and a thread local unit id to denote a unit globally in the masks μ_r and μ_w. Upon a shared variable write, both masks are updated. If the remotely defined value is read for the first time, the difference between the global id in the masks and the current id would entail logging the read. This allows us replay by value. Replay by dependence is supported by recovering the total order of memory reads and writes for the same variable, which is easily achievable by inspecting the log. Note that the logging rules in Fig. 8 don't need to change except the above extensions.

T$_1$	**T**$_2$	$\mu_r(x)$	$\mu_w(x)$
1. **[UNIT]** `while {`			
2. [`...=x`];		$\langle T_1,0\rangle$	
	10. **[UNIT]** `while {`	$\langle T_1,0\rangle$	
	11. [`x=...`];	$\langle T_2,0\rangle$	$\langle T_2,0\rangle$
3. [`...=x`];		$\langle T_1,0\rangle$	$\langle T_2,0\rangle$
4. `...=x;`		$\langle T_1,0\rangle$	$\langle T_2,0\rangle$
	12. `...=x;`	$\langle T_1,0\rangle$	$\langle T_2,0\rangle$

Figure 14. The accesses to x are interleaved in two threads. The $\mu_r(x)$ and $\mu_w(x)$ columns show the state of the masks **after** each statement execution.The boxed executions are logged.

Consider the example in Fig. 14. Two threads interleave. Statement 2 is logged according to rule [LE-Log]. Statement 11 is logged according to rule [LS-Log-Wrt]. Note, it updates both $\mu_r(x)$ and $\mu_w(x)$. Statement 3 is logged according to rule [LE-Log] even though there is a unit-local write earlier in the same thread. The remotely defined value is hence logged. Statements 4 is not logged because $\mu_r(x)$ is equivalent to the current id (by [LE-NoLog]). Statement 12 is not logged because $\mu_w(x)$ is equivalent to the current id (by [LE-NoLog]). Intuitively, the remote reads in-between 11 and 12 do not modify the value of x and there is no need to log.

10. Evaluation

Our system makes use of LLVM, *jockey*, and *pin*. We use LLVM to analyze and instrument programs. The logging runtime works through *jockey*, an application level logging and replay tool [18]. It works directly on binaries by rewriting the instruction sequences that make syscalls to intercept the calls. This design makes it very efficient; HP used it for debugging distributed systems. Previously, *jockey* logged only syscalls and signals. We extend it to log memory accesses, directed by instrumentation inserted by the LLVM pass. *Jockey* currently only supports one core. The *jockey* replay component is insufficient to support our technique as it cannot intercept memory accesses. We implement our replay component in *pin*, a dynamic instrumentation tool. Using *pin* provides flexibility for integrating reduction with future dynamic analysis. Reduction is implemented in C++. The overall implementation is 10k LOC.

Applications	LOC	threads	Bug description
Apache-2.0.48	157K	16	#1: Atomicity violation (21287)
			#2: Unprotected buffer
			#3: Cache size problem (21285)
BerkeleyDB-4.7.25	172K	5	#1:Failure in leader election
			#2:Panic caused by out-dated msgs
Squid-2.3.4	62K	1	Buffer overflow (4148)
MC-4.5.55	106K	1	Buffer overflow (8658)
W3M-0.5.2	51K	1	Out of memory (492290)
VIM-7.0	230K	1	Hangs (100%CPU usage)
DC-1.3	9.5K	1	Segmentation fault (135029)
YAFC-1.1.1	40.6K	1	Segmentation fault

Table 1. Application and bug description

Applications	annotated loops	data structure	func.	instrumen-. tation	instrmt. after opt.
Apache	2	32	227	2,333	1,775
BerkeleyDB	3	47	1,371	24,338	15,319
Squid	1	21	401	2,877	2,232
MC	1	18	372	1,967	1,460
W3M	1	12	408	5,506	3,609
VIM	1	25	1,319	12,040	8,375
DC	1	2	44	641	521
YAFC	1	8	287	1,785	1,337

Table 2. Static instrumentation.

All experiments were conducted on an Intel L2400 1.66GHz CPU with 3GB of RAM running Linux-2.6.11. We evaluate our technique on a number of real world programs and real bugs from them as the reduction criteria. Table 1 presents the programs and the bugs. `BerkeleyDB` is a distributed database. `Squid` is a proxy server. `MC` is a user interactive file explorer. `W3M` is a text-based web browser. `Vim` is an advanced text editor and `Dc` is a calculator. `Yafc` is a FTP client.

The instrumentation results are presented in Table 2. It presents the number of annotated loops, the data structures and functions that may cause inter-unit dependences, and the instrumentations before and after the static optimization (Section 8). Observe that only a few loops need to be annotated. These loops further call other functions to carry out computation. Some of the functions may cause interesting dependences. Although our technique only instruments access points of certain data structures in certain functions, the number of such points is large due to the program size. The static optimization effectively reduces many of them (1/3 for the `BerkeleyDB` and `VIM`). It is worth mentioning that the large number of static instrumentation points do not induce high runtime overhead because we also avoid redundant logging at runtime. Figure 15 shows an annotation example from the `Apache web server`. `Apache` is a multi-threaded application and two loops were annotated. It is easy to figure out these loops because they are in the main body of each thread.

App	time (sec)	w/o opt	stat	dyn	stat+ dyn	rednt. access	jockey
Apache	210.0	2.8%	1.77%	0.97%	0.17%	87.01%	3.46%
DB	48.3	9.55%	8.47%	5.92%	4.20%	95.61%	2.94%
Squid	79.04	30.6%	12.1%	2.23%	1.1%	88.62%	2.53%
MC	58.1	29.7%	27.5%	3.35%	2.26%	93.13%	3.25%
W3M	N/A	N/A	N/A	N/A	N/A	87.13%	N/A
VIM	55.26	42.15%	34.0%	5.3%	3.93%	92.05%	0.94%
DC	35.63	85.32%	43.93%	13.62%	4.8%	96.8%	7.11%
YAFC	63.03	23.75%	17.25%	4.02%	1.82%	97.17%	3.48%

Table 3. Logging overhead

Table 3 presents the runtime overhead. In this experiment and the next space overhead experiment, we use test inputs provided with the programs if available or randomly generated inputs otherwise. We will also show results on real world workloads later. The 2nd column shows the native execution time. Columns 3-6 present the overhead of our technique over the plain jockey logging with different configurations: without any optimizations (i.e. log all accesses of the relevant data structures), static optimization only, i.e. removing instrumentation through static analysis (Section 8), dynamic optimization only, i.e. avoiding redundant logging during execution via μ_r and μ_w, and both optimizations. The 7th column presents the accesses identified as redundant by the dynamic optimization. The last column presents the *jockey* overhead (without our technique) for reference. The overhead of our technique is very small after both static and dynamic optimizations, but dynamic optimization is the more effective of the two. Its effectiveness is supported by the number of accesses that are found to be redundant. If an access is redundant, we only pay the cost of a few (usually 2) extra memory accesses and one comparison. Otherwise, we have to update μ_r and/or μ_w, store the access information into a buffer, which will be flushed to the log file later. Note that `W3M` is a user-interactive application without a batch mode, thus we could not measure its run time.

App	jockey log		our log w/o opt.		our log with opt.	
	entry	size(MB)	entry	size(MB)	entry	size(MB)
Apache	29k	8.79	58,826k	379.82	7,644k	47.24
DB	539k	6.3	11,447k	85.86	502k	3.43
Squid	734k	22.18	44,838k	265.46	5,101k	30.35
MC	255k	12.9	10,499k	67.94	715k	4.34
W3M	14K	4.42	6,483K	42.34	834K	5.09
VIM	151k	4.14	49,970k	123.48	3,974k	23.27
DC	1,035K	12.45	24,970K	160.55	846K	5.04
YAFC	1,324K	49.11	10,428K	63.95	295K	1.78

Table 4. Recording space overhead

Space overhead is presented in Table 4. We present both the number of log entries and the log size. For comparison purposes, we separate a log file into the *jockey* log and our log. Observe that our log size is comparable to the *jockey* log size for most cases except `apache` and `VIM`, which have a lot of memory accesses with effects crossing unit boundaries. Our log has more entries, but each entry has a smaller size as it only records a memory access.

Table 5 presents reduction effectiveness. In the experiment, we weave inputs used in the previous experiment with failure inducing inputs. For UI programs, the failures are induced by a sequence of user actions. We interleave the sequence with the (much longer) original inputs. For example in `MC`, the bug is triggered by following a directory path to a specific file and opening the file. We interleave the failing sequence with the original normal actions such as browsing different directories and opening other files. For server programs, failures are triggered by setting specific configurations at the beginning and providing specific requests at the end. Note that playing the last few events in the *jockey* log does not work due to dependences. More discussion can be found in the Vim case study.

Columns 2-4 present logs before reduction including the number of units (not event entries), *jockey* and our log sizes. Columns 5-7 present the reduction result if all dependences are considered. Columns 8-10 present the result if only pointer dependences are considered. Columns 11-15 present the result of compatible reduction. That is, we conduct breadth first search along pointer dependences, looking for compatible reduction. Column 14 shows the depth of the BFS search. Observe that pointer dependence reduction sometimes can achieve good reduction. The last column shows the log reduction time including the replay time needed during re-

```
697  static void *listener_thread(apr_thread_t *thd, void * dummy) {
..
729  [UNIT] while(1) {
730             if (requests_this_child <= 0) {

..
896        } // while end
..
910  } // listener_thread function end

[server/mpm/worker/worker.c]
```

(a) Listener thread annotation

```
923  static void *worker_thread(apr_thread_t *thd, void * dummy) {
..
946  [UNIT] while(!workers_may_exit) {
947             if(!is_idle) {

..
1003       } // while end
..
1015 } // worker_thread function end

[server/mpm/worker/worker.c]
```

(b) Worker thread annotation

Figure 15. Loop annotation example (Apache)

Bugs	log b/f reduction			reduced log w. all deps			reduced log w/o search			reduced log with search				
	units	jockey (MB)	ours (MB)	units	jockey (MB)	ours (MB)	units	jockey (MB)	ours MB	units	jockey (MB)	ours (MB)	BFS level	Reduction time(sec)
Apache#1	14,989	8.55	47.1	14,989	8,55	47.1	14,975	8.53	47.1	16	0.14	0.51	1	5.9
Apache#2	14,991	8.54	47.4	14,991	8.54	47.4	14,989	8.53	47.4	40	0.29	1.34	1	6.4
Apache#3	15,005	8.54	47.3	15,005	8.54	47.3	15,004	8.54	47.3	20	0.17	0.69	1	6.1
DB#1	2,033k	144.9	25.7	832	5.85	0.122	10	0.07	0.0015	2	0.06	0.0007	1	5.6
DB#2	459k	37.6	8.36	54	3.52	0.047	8	0.44	0.005	4	0.42	0.0018	1	5.2
Squid	8,000	22.2	30.4	8,000	22.2	30.4	8,000	22.2	30.4	91	0.34	0.35	6	24.8
MC	5,348	13.4	4.35	5,348	13.4	4.35	14	1.25	1.12	5	0.69	0.93	1	5.4
W3M	961	1.67	3.98	961	1.67	3.98	961	1.67	3.98	2	0.03	0.021	1	4.9
VIM	2,544	4.14	23.27	2,544	4.14	23.27	2,369	4.02	22.66	12	0.035	0.279	1	5.8
DC	6,580	12.45	5.04	6,580	12.45	5.04	6,580	12.45	5.04	14	0.94	0.65	1	1.4
YAFC	196	49.11	63.95	196	49.11	1.78	196	49.11	1.78	4	0.11	0.001	1	3.5

Table 5. Log reduction results

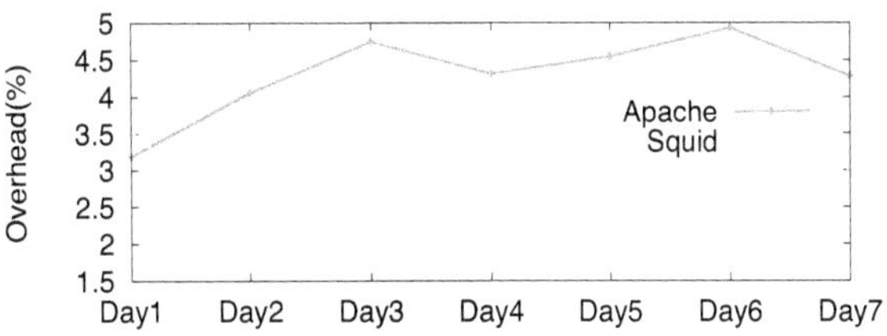

(a) Runtime overhead

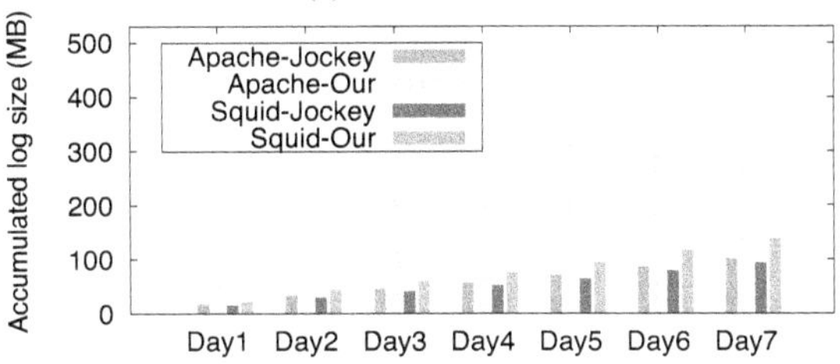

(b) Space overhead

Figure 16. Runtime and space overhead with real-world workload.

duction. The replay time of the reduced log is similar to the reduction time and elided. The dominant factor of replay time is the infrastructure overhead of Pin. The search algorithm (compatible reduction) can always achieve good results. The reduced logs are very small, leading to very short replay times. Furthermore, we want to point out that by paying the one time reduction cost, the programmer has a much smaller run to analyze for arbitrary number of times. Hence, the benefit may go beyond the savings compared to the original run. Moreover, the level of search tends to be small. We suspect that many memory states are compatible, allowing us to find one quickly. Note that small search depths do not mean our technique only acquires units towards the end of execution. Recall that our algorithm (Section 7) starts with a skeleton of units

Unit 1: first unit, need to include
Unit 2 : turn on syntax highlights
Unit 3 : open file1
Unit 44 : open file2 **(bug triggering file)**
Unit 508 : *unnecessary unit*
Unit 1066 : open file3
Unit 1187-1188 : *unnecessary units*
Unit 2489 : open file4
Unit 2541 : go back to file2 (from memory buffer)
Unit 2542 : *unnecessary unit*
Unit 2544 : goto the bug triggering line in file 2. **Failure!**

Figure 17. Reduced log of Vim

based on structural constraints. More units (and their skeletons) are added through search. Even the initial skeleton may contain units distributed along the whole execution. Furthermore, traversing one dependence edge can reach distant units. For instance, a unit close to the end may likely depend on a unit near the beginning.

Practicality Study With Real Workload. In order to evaluate the practicality of our technique, we study its efficiency and effectiveness on the two server programs `apache` and `squid` with real-world workloads. Specifically, we acquired the high level web request log for our institution's web-site for one week. We wrote a script to regenerate the workloads for 1-7 days and fed them to the two server programs. At the end of each workload, we also supplied the failure inducing requests to trigger the failure. The average runtime overhead and aggregated space overhead are presented in Figure 16. Observe that the runtime overhead is more or less consistent. The space overhead is reasonable for a few days' execution. The replayable, reduced logs (not shown) are consistently small. These results show the practicality of our technique.

Case Study. We present the `VIM` case in detail. Fig. 17 shows the reduced version of a large log. The failure occurs as follows. Unit 1 (U1) is the first unit, containing execution from the beginning to before the first request loop iteration. At U2, the user enables syntax highlighting, a precondition of the bug. Next, four files are opened with file editing actions in-between the openings (note that the unit ids of open units are not contiguous). `VIM` allocates a memory buffer for each file, so after U2489, there are four buffers. Here, the user switches back to file2, which is loaded from the buffer. At U2544, the user scrolls down to a specific line. When the syntax highlighter tries to parse the line, the bug is triggered (`VIM` hangs).

The reduced log includes 12 units. The skeleton contains the failing unit U2544 and the first unit U1. The skeleton is not replayable. With one step pointer dependence edge traversal, the 12 units are included. In particular, the dependences between file open units are through the memory buffer data structure `xfilemark`. These units construct a compatible memory state for the execution of U2544, and hence leads to successful failure replay. In particular, the failure demands the four files be loaded otherwise the memory buffer state would be different, leading to control flow difference and hence mis-alignment between the control flow and the replay log. Furthermore, it demands U2 to activate syntax highlighting. We also manually inspect the reduced log and find that 4 units are unnecessary. In other words, the ideal minimal reduced log contains 8 units. The 4 units are included because they are also reachable in one dependence edge and they do not change compatibility.

From their ids, observe that the units are sparsely distributed along the entire execution. A naive idea of replaying the last a few units would not work. We further inspect all the reduced logs and find that the second unit of the reduced log (the first unit is always included in the reduced log) is indeed in the early stage of the original executions except the `W3M` bug and `BerkeleyDB` bug #1.

11. Related Work

Execution fast forwarding (EFF) [19, 25] also has the goal of reducing logs. EFF does not instrument the program during the logging phase. Instead, it analyzes dependences between event entries offline, either through static analysis or by replaying the whole execution once to detect dependences, which is too expensive (usually 10X slowdown). EFF does not guarantee replayability. In this paper, we show that with small cost, we can acquire a reducible log on the fly. Reduction can be achieved by analyzing the log, without static analysis or replaying the full execution. We also observe that EFF is too conservative in considering all dependences, often leading to very little reduction. In contrast, we weave value and dependence based replay to a novel and highly effective scheme.

Language based replay [21] allows users to replay a program component (module). It uses profiling to find a replay cut to minimize logging efforts. Whereas the technique can be considered a reduction on the program dimension, our reduction is on the temporal dimension, and we believe the two dimensions are orthogonal. Moreover, to use their technique, the user has to know about where a bug might be to do selectively logging. In comparison, our logging is general. We also handle failures that cross components. SCARPE [10] is a similar component based technique for Java. Subgroup replay [23] groups processes and records only intergroup messages.

Checkpointing [4] is a standard approach to avoid replaying a whole execution. Incremental checkpointing [3, 15] avoids overhead from capturing memory snapshots. Language based checkpointing [22] allows users to checkpoint at arbitrary program points with contexts. Our technique is complementary to checkpointing, e.g., our technique can further reduce an execution between checkpoints. Furthermore, we allow fine-grained reduction at the unit (loop iteration) level.

There are software based replay systems that record individual memory accesses and their happens-before relations [5]. Such systems induce substantial runtime overhead. There has been substantial work on software based record and replay for parallel and distributed systems [2, 6, 11, 17, 18]. These systems only perform coarse-grained logging at the level of system calls or control flow and hence are not sufficient for reduction. Hardware based logging and replay [7, 8, 12, 14] can faithfully replay executions. While such techniques are effective, they demand special hardware.

In recent years, significant progress has been made in testing and debugging concurrent programs [1, 9, 13, 16]. These techniques search for a failure inducing schedule given certain inputs. In the future, we plan to leverage these techniques to generate reducible logs on multiple cores.

Delta debugging [24] reduces a failure inducing input by repeatedly running the program on subsets of the input. The process could be expensive for long execution.

12. Conclusion

We propose a compiler based technique that generates a reducible replay log. The technique divides an execution into units, mainly iterations of event processing loops. We instrument programs instrument to collect minimal additional information like memory accesses into the replay log. Given a criterion, reduction can be achieved through analyzing just the log. Our technique is automated, only requiring annotating the event processing loops. It is highly efficient: the average runtime overhead is 2.6% and the additional space consumption is comparable to logs containing only syscalls and signals. Our reduction and replay scheme is also novel. It seamlessly weaves value based replay and dependence based replay to achieve both great reduction and faithful reconstruction of memory state. Our results show that we can reduce executions with up to 2,033K units to less than 91 units.

13. Acknowledgment

We would like to thank the anonymous reviewers for their insightful comments. This research is supported in part by the National Science Foundation (NSF) under grants 0917007, 0845870 and 0834529. Any opinions, findings, and conclusions or recommendations in this paper are those of the authors and do not necessarily reflect the views of NSF.

References

[1] G. Altekar and I. Stoica. Odr: output-deterministic replay for multicore debugging. In *SOSP'09*.

[2] A. Ayers, R. Schooler, C. Metcalf, A. Agarwal, J. Rhee, and E. Witchel. Traceback: first fault diagnosis by reconstruction of distributed control flow. In *PLDI'05*.

[3] G. Bronevetsky, D. Marques, K. Pingali, and R. Rugina. Compiler-enhanced incremental checkpointing. In *LCPC'07*.

[4] K. M. Chandy and L. Lamport. Distributed snapshots: Determining global states of distributed systems. *ACM Trans. Comput. Syst.*, 3(1):63–75, 1985.

[5] G. W. Dunlap, D. G. Lucchetti, M. A. Fetterman, and P. M. Chen. Execution replay of multiprocessor virtual machines. In *VEE'08*.

[6] Z. Guo, X. Wang, J. Tang, X. Liu, Z. Xu, M. Wu, M. F. Kaashoek, and Z. Zhang. R2: An application-level kernel for record and replay. In *OSDI'08*.

[7] D. Hower, P. Montesinos, L. Ceze, M. D. Hill, and J. Torrellas. Two hardware-based approaches for deterministic multiprocessor replay. *Communications of the ACM*, 52(6):93–100, 2009.

[8] D. R. Hower and M. D. Hill. Rerun: Exploiting episodes for lightweight memory race recording. In *ISCA'08*.

[9] P. Joshi, C. S. Park, K. Sen, and M. Naik. A randomized dynamic program analysis technique for detecting real deadlocks. In *PLDI'09*.

[10] S. Joshi and A. Orso. Scarpe: A technique and tool for selective capture and replay of program executions. In *ICSM'07*.

[11] S. T. King, G. W. Dunlap, and P. M. Chen. Debugging operating systems with time-traveling virtual machines. In *USENIX ATEC'05*.

[12] P. Montesinos, M. Hicks, S. T. King, and J. Torrellas. Capo: a software-hardware interface for practical deterministic multiprocessor replay. In *ASPLOS'09*.

[13] M. Musuvathi and S. Qadeer. Iterative context bounding for systematic testing of multithreaded programs. In *PLDI'07*.

[14] S. Narayanasamy, C. Pereira, and B. Calder. Recording shared memory dependencies using strata. In *ASPLOS'06*.

[15] R. H. B. Netzer and M. H. Weaver. Optimal tracing and incremental reexecution for debugging long-running programs. In *PLDI'94*.

[16] S. Park, W. Xiong, Z. Yin, R. Kaushik, K. Lee, S. Lu, and Y. Zhou. Pres: Probabilistic replay with execution sketching on multiprocessors. In *SOSP'09*.

[17] M. Ronsse, K. D. Bosschere, M. Christiaens, J. C. d. Kergommeaux, and D. Kranzlmüller. Record/replay for nondeterministic program executions. *Communications of the ACM*, 46(9):62–67, 2003.

[18] Y. Saito. Jockey: a user-space library for record-replay debugging. In *AADEBUG'05*.

[19] S. Tallam, C. Tian, X. Zhang, and R. Gupta. Enabling tracing of long-running multithreaded programs via dynamic execution reduction. In *ISSTA'07*.

[20] L. D. Wittie. Debugging distributed c programs by real time reply. In *PADD'88*.

[21] M. Wu, F. Long, X. Wang, Z. Xu, H. Lin, X. Liu, Z. Guo, H. Guo, L. Zhou, and Z. Zhang. Language-based replay via data flow cut. In *FSE'10*.

[22] G. Xu, A. Rountev, Y. Tang, and F. Qin. Efficient checkpointing of java software using context-sensitive capture and replay. In *FSE'07*.

[23] R. Xue, X. Liu, M. Wu, Z. Guo, W. Chen, W. Zheng, Z. Zhang, and G. M. Voelker. Mpiwiz: subgroup reproducible replay of mpi applications. In *PPOPP'09*.

[24] A. Zeller. Isolating cause-effect chains from computer programs. In *FSE'02*.

[25] X. Zhang, S. Tallam, and R. Gupta. Dynamic slicing long running programs through execution fast forwarding. In *FSE'06*.

Higher-Order Test Generation

Patrice Godefroid
Microsoft Research
pg@microsoft.com

Abstract

Symbolic reasoning about large programs is bound to be imprecise. How to deal with this imprecision is a fundamental problem in program analysis. Imprecision forces approximation. Traditional static program verification builds "may" over-approximations of the program behaviors to check universal "for-all-paths" properties, while automatic test generation requires "must" under-approximations to check existential "for-some-path" properties.

In this paper, we introduce a new approach to test generation where tests are derived from *validity proofs* of first-order logic formulas, rather than *satisfying assignments* of quantifier-free first-order logic formulas as usual. Two key ingredients of this *higher-order test generation* are to (1) represent complex/unknown program functions/instructions causing imprecision in symbolic execution by *uninterpreted functions*, and (2) record *uninterpreted function samples* capturing input-output pairs observed at execution time for those functions. We show that higher-order test generation generalizes and is more precise than simplifying complex symbolic expressions using their concrete runtime values. We present several program examples where our approach can exercise program paths and find bugs missed by previous techniques. We discuss the implementability and applications of this approach. We also explain in what sense dynamic test generation is more powerful than static test generation.

Categories and Subject Descriptors D.2.4 [*Software Engineering*]: Software/Program Verification; D.2.5 [*Software Engineering*]: Testing and Debugging; F.3.1 [*Logics and Meanings of Programs*]: Specifying and Verifying and Reasoning about Programs

General Terms Testing, Verification

Keywords Automatic Test Generation, Software Model Checking, Uninterpreted Functions

1. Introduction

Automatic code-driven test generation aims at proving existential properties of programs: does there exist a test input that can exercise a specific program branch or statement, or follow a specific program path, or trigger a bug? Test generation dualizes traditional program verification and static program analysis aimed at proving universal properties which holds for all program paths, such as "there are no bugs of type X in this program".

PLDI'11, June 4–8, 2011, San Jose, California, USA.

Symbolic reasoning about large programs is bound to be imprecise. If perfect bit-precise symbolic reasoning was possible, static program analysis would detect standard programming errors without reporting false alarms. How to deal with this imprecision is a fundamental problem in program analysis. Traditional static program verification builds "may" over-approximations of the program behaviors in order to prove correctness, but at the cost of reporting false alarms. Dually, automatic test generation requires "must" under-approximations in order to drive program executions and find bugs without reporting false alarms, but at the cost of possibly missing bugs.

Most of the program analysis literature discusses program verification for universal properties. Yet, except for static type systems, the biggest practical impact of program analysis so far has been bug finding, not proving the absence of bugs. The study of effective program verification techniques for existential properties (i.e., "sound bug finding") has recently experienced quite a resurgence. A catalyst is arguably recent work on systematic dynamic test generation [15], and related extensions and tools (e.g., [2, 6, 17, 23, 24]). Over the last few years, these techniques have been made more scalable [16], and have been used to find many new security vulnerabilities in Windows [12] and Linux [22] applications.

Work on automatic code-driven test generation can roughly be partitioned into two groups: *static* versus *dynamic* test generation. Static test generation [20] consists of analyzing a program P *statically*, by reading the program code and using symbolic execution techniques to simulate abstract program executions in order to attempt to compute inputs to drive P along specific execution paths or branches, *without ever executing the program*. On the other hand, *dynamic test generation* [21] consists of executing the program P starting with some given or random concrete inputs, gathering symbolic constraints on inputs at conditional statements along the execution, and then using a constraint solver to infer variants of the previous inputs in order to steer the next execution of the program towards an alternative program branch; this process can be repeated with the goal of *systematically* executing all (or as many as possible) feasible program paths, while checking each execution using run-time checking tools (like Purify, Valgrind or AppVerifier) for detecting various types of errors [15].

It is argued in [15] that dynamic test generation is more powerful than static test generation because imprecision in symbolic execution can be alleviated using concrete values and randomization: whenever symbolic execution does not know how to generate a constraint for a program statement depending on some inputs, one can always simplify this constraint using the concrete runtime values of those inputs. To illustrate this point, consider the following program example [11]:

```
int obscure(int x, int y) {
  if (x == hash(y)) return -1;     // error
  return 0;                        // ok
}
```

Assume the constraint solver cannot "symbolically reason" about the function `hash` (perhaps because it is too complex or simply because its code is not available). This means that the constraint solver cannot generate two values for inputs `x` and `y` that are guaranteed to satisfy (or violate) the constraint `x == hash(y)`. In this case, static test generation cannot generate test inputs to drive the execution of the program `obscure` through either branch of the conditional statement: static test generation is *helpless* for a program like this. Note that, for test generation, it is not sufficient to know that the constraint `x == hash(y)` is satisfiable for *some* values of `x` and `y`, it is also necessary to generate *specific values* for `x` and `y` that satisfy or violate this constraint.

In contrast, dynamic test generation can easily generate, for a fixed value of `y`, a value of `x` that is equal to `hash(y)` since the latter concrete value is known at runtime. By picking randomly and then fixing the value of `y`, we can, in the next test execution, set the value of the other input `x` either to `hash(y)` or to something else in order to force the execution of the then or else branches, respectively, of the test in the function `obscure`.

In summary, static test generation is unable to generate test inputs to control the execution of the program `obscure`, while dynamic test generation can *easily* drive the executions of that same program through all its feasible program paths. In realistic programs, imprecision in symbolic execution typically creeps in in many places, and dynamic test generation allows test generation to recover from that imprecision. Dynamic test generation can be viewed as extending static test generation with additional runtime information, and is therefore more general and powerful.

But how much more powerful? How often can this concretization trick be used? It would not work in the case of a constraint like `hash(x)==hash(y)+1`. Does there exist an algorithm to determine in which cases concretization "works" and when it does not? Can concretization be modeled symbolically and therefore simulated by static symbolic execution and test generation? If so, what is the fundamental difference between static and dynamic test generation? Can one formalize both and *prove* (and clarify how and why) they are different? Is it possible to deal with imprecision in symbolic reasoning differently, in order to enable even more powerful test generation?

The purpose of this paper is to answer all these questions, which are central to test generation and program analysis. We start by carefully formalizing "concretization" as introduced in [15], and show that it may or may not generate sound path constraints (Section 3). We then introduce (Section 4) a new more general form of test generation, which we call *higher-order* because it uses a higher-order logic representation of program paths. Higher-order test generation uses *uninterpreted functions* to represent unknown functions or instructions during symbolic execution, records *uninterpreted function samples* capturing concrete input-output pairs observed at execution time for those functions, and generates new test inputs from *validity proofs* of first-order logic formulas with uninterpreted functions. We then show (in Section 5) that higher-order test generation can not only fully "simulate" concretization when the latter is done in a sound manner, but that it is also more general and powerful. We discuss how to implement this approach in practice in Section 6, and present an application (in Section 7) which requires the power of higher-order test generation: parsers with input lexers using hash functions for fast keyword recognition. We conclude (in Section 9) by clarifying in what sense dynamic test generation is more powerful than static test generation.

2. Background: Systematic Dynamic Test Generation

Dynamic test generation (see [15] for further details) consists of running the program P under test both concretely, executing the actual program, and symbolically, calculating constraints on values stored in program variables v and expressed in terms of input parameters. Side-by-side concrete and symbolic executions are performed using a concrete store M and a symbolic store S, which are mappings from *memory addresses* (where program variables are stored) to concrete and symbolic values respectively. A *symbolic value* is any expression e in some theory $\mathcal{T}$ where all free variables are exclusively input parameters. For any program variable v, $M(v)$ denotes the *concrete value* of v in M, while $S(v)$ denotes the *symbolic value* of v in S. For notational convenience, we assume that $S(v)$ is always defined and is simply $M(v)$ by default if no symbolic expression in terms of inputs is associated with v in S. When $S(v)$ is different from $M(v)$, we say that that program variable v is "symbolic", meaning that the value of program variable v is a function of some input(s) which is represented by the symbolic expression $S(v)$ associated with v in the symbolic store. We also extend this notation to allow $M(e)$ to denote the concrete value of symbolic expression e when evaluated with the concrete store M. The notation $+$ for mappings denotes updating; for example, $M' = M + [m \mapsto e]$ is the same map as M, except that $M'(m) = e$.

The program P manipulates the memory (concrete and symbolic stores) through statements, or *commands*, that are abstractions of the machine instructions actually executed. We assume a command can be an *assignment* of the form $v := e$ (where v is a program variable and e is an expression), a *conditional statement* of the form `if` e `then` C' `else` C'' where e denotes a boolean expression, and C' and C'' denote the unique[1] next command to be evaluated when e holds or does not hold, respectively, or `stop` corresponding to a program error or normal termination.

Given an input vector I assigning a concrete value I_i to the i-th input parameter, the evaluation of a program defines a unique finite[2] *program execution* $s_0 \xrightarrow{C_1} s_1 \ldots \xrightarrow{C_n} s_n$ that executes the finite sequence $C_1 \ldots C_n$ of commands and goes through the finite sequence $s_1 \ldots s_n$ of program states. Each *program state* is a tuple $\langle C, M, S, pc \rangle$ where C is the next command to be evaluated, and pc is a special meta-variable that represents the current path constraint. For a finite sequence w of commands (i.e., a control path w), a *path constraint* pc_w is a quantifier-free first-order logic formula over theory $\mathcal{T}$ that is meant to characterize the input assignments for which the program executes along w. The path constraint is *sound and complete* when this characterization is exact, i.e., when the two following conditions are satisfied.

DEFINITION 1. A path constraint pc_w is *sound* if every input assignment satisfying pc_w defines a program execution following path w. ■

DEFINITION 2. A path constraint pc_w is *complete* if every input assignment following path w is a satisfying assignment, or *model*, of pc_w. ■

Path constraints are generated during dynamic symbolic execution by collecting input constraints at conditional statements, as illustrated in Figure 2. Figure 1 illustrates how to symbolically evaluate expressions e occurring in individual program instructions (line 14 should be ignored for now). The notation $\&v$ denotes the

[1] We assume program executions are sequential and deterministic.

[2] We assume program executions terminate. In practice, a timeout prevents non-terminating program executions and issues a runtime error.

```
1  evalSymbolic(e) =
2    match (e):
3      case v: // Program variable v
4        return S(&v)
5      case +(e1, e2): // Addition
6        f1 = evalSymbolic(e1)
7        f2 = evalSymbolic(e2)
8        if f1 and f2 are constants
9            return evalConcrete(e)
10       else
11           return createExpression('+', f1, f2)
12     etc.
13     default: // default for unhandled expression
14       // pc = pc ∧ ⋀_{x_i ∈ e}(x_i = I_i)
15       return evalConcrete(e)
```

Figure 1. Symbolic expression evaluation.

```
Procedure executeSymbolic(P, I) =
  initialize M0 and S0
  path constraint pc = true
  C = getNextCommand()
  while (C ≠ stop)
    match (C):
      case (v := e):
        M = M + [&v ↦ evalConcrete(e)]
        S = S + [&v ↦ evalSymbolic(e)]
      case (if e then C' else C''):
        b = evalConcrete(e)
        c = evalSymbolic(e)
        if b then pc = pc ∧ c
        else pc = pc ∧ ¬c
    C = getNextCommand() // end of while loop
```

Figure 2. Symbolic execution.

address at which the value of program variable v is stored. To simplify the presentation, we assume that all program variables have some unique initial concrete value in the initial concrete store M_0, and that the initial symbolic store S_0 identifies the program variables v whose values are program inputs (for all those, we have $S_0(v) = x_i$ where x_i is the symbolic variable corresponding to the input parameter I_i). Initially, pc is defined to `true`. By construction, all symbolic variables appearing in pc are variables x_i corresponding to program inputs I_i.

Systematic dynamic test generation [15] consists of systematically exploring all (or in practice many) feasible control-flow paths of the program under test by using path constraints and a constraint solver. Given a program state $s = \langle C, M, S, pc \rangle$ and a constraint solver for theory $\mathcal{T}$, if C is a conditional statement of the form **if** e **then** C' **else** C'', any satisfying assignment of the formula $pc \wedge c$ (respectively $pc \wedge \neg c$) where $c =$ evalSymbolic(e) in state s, defines program inputs that will lead the program to execute the **then** (resp. **else**) branch of the conditional statement. By systematically repeating this process, such a *directed search* can enumerate (in theory) all possible path constraints and eventually execute all feasible program paths.

The search is exhaustive provided that the generation of the path constraint (including the underlying symbolic execution) and the constraint solver for the given theory $\mathcal{T}$ are both *sound and complete*, that is, for all program paths w, the constraint solver returns a satisfying assignment for the path constraint pc_w *if and only if* the path is feasible (i.e., there exists some input assignment leading to its execution). If those conditions hold, in addition to finding errors such as the reachability of bad program statements (like `assert(false)`), a directed search can also prove their absence, and therefore obtain a form of program *verification*.

THEOREM 1. *(adapted from [15]) Given a program P as defined above, a directed search using a path constraint generation and a constraint solver that are both sound and complete exercises all feasible program paths exactly once.*

Thus, if a program statement has not been executed when the search is over, this statement is not executable in any context. In practice, path constraint generation and constraint solving are usually not sound and complete.

Note that the above formalization and theorem do apply to programs containing loops or recursion, as long as all program executions terminate. However, in the presence of a single loop whose number of iterations depends on some unbounded input, the number of feasible program paths becomes infinite. In practice, search termination can always be forced by bounding input values, loop iterations or recursion, at the cost of potentially missing bugs.

3. Sound and Unsound Concretization

3.1 Concretization and Must Abstraction

When a program expression cannot be expressed in the given theory $\mathcal{T}$ decided by the constraint solver, it can be simplified using concrete values of sub-expressions, or replaced by the concrete value of the entire expression. This case corresponds to line 13 of Figure 1. Let us call *concretization* the process of replacing a symbolic expression by its current concrete value during dynamic symbolic execution.

In the presence of concretizations, path constraint generation is in general no longer "sound and complete" since constraints become approximate and path constraints no longer capture accurately program path feasibility. (In the original DART algorithm of [15], some completeness flag would then be set off and the outer loop in Figure 2 of [15] would run forever.) Moreover, Theorem 1 no longer holds since its assumptions are no longer satisfied.

Loosely speaking, concretizing a symbolic expression under-approximates its set of possible values by a singleton set containing its unique current runtime value. In that sense, concretization can be viewed as a *"must abstraction"* which is *sound for bug-finding*. Must abstractions capture existential reachability properties that hold on *some* but not all program executions.

A sound path constraint (see Definition 1) is an example of must abstraction [17]. Note that, if a sound path constraint pc_w is satisfiable, *then* the corresponding program path w is feasible. But the converse does not necessarily hold: an algorithm for generating sound path constraints may fail to generate path constraints for some feasible program paths, and hence may fail to exercise some code and may miss bugs.

3.2 Unsound Concretization

Strictly speaking, however, concretization alone does not guarantee a sound path constraint generation. Consider the following program example.

```
int foo(int x, int y) {
  if (x == hash(y)) {
    ...
    if (y == 10) return -1; // error
  }
  ...
}
```

Assume that the function `hash` is "unknown", that the program is run with the input values `x=567` and `y=42`, that `hash(42)` is 567, and hence that the execution takes the **then** branch of the first conditional statement. The path constraint generated by the DART algorithm of Figures 1 and 2 (i.e., *without* line 14 of Figure 1) is

$$x = 567 \wedge y \neq 10$$

Indeed, the expression `hash(y)` which (we assume) is outside $\mathcal{T}$ is replaced by its concrete value 567 by line 15 of Figure 1. But the algorithm does not "record" this concretization at the first conditional statement, and allows a symbolic constraint $y \neq 10$ to be generated on y later on. This path constraint correctly captures the current concrete execution (since x is indeed 567 and y is indeed different from 10 for this run), but it is *not sound*: for x equal to 567 and some value of y different from 10, the input assignment satisfies the path constraint but does not define a program execution following the same execution path if `hash(y)` is not 567.

By negating the last constraint of this unsound path constraint and solving the new path constraint

$$x = 567 \wedge y = 10$$

one gets a new test input that should drive the program towards the error, but results instead in a *divergence* [15], i.e., an unexpected program path being taken if `hash(10)` is different from 567.

The risk of divergences in the presence of unsound path constraints is not a new observation: it is discussed in [15] and motivates the need for comparing the actual path taken by the program under test with the expected path w derived from each path constraint pc_w. When additional constraints are automatically injected in path constraints for checking additional program properties such as the absence of buffer overflows, every new test input generated violating such injected constraints should be executed to confirm the bug before reporting it to the user, in order to avoid reporting false alarms due to divergences from unsound path constraints.

3.3 Sound Concretization

To generate sound path constraints, we propose the following new variant of the DART algorithm: whenever a symbolic expression e is concretized during symbolic execution, for all symbolic variables x_i occurring in e, a new *concretization constraint* $x_i = I_i$ is added to the path constraint, as illustrated in line 14 of Figure 1, which we now assume is un-commented. This implies that the value of each such symbolic variable x_i is fixed to a constant equal to the corresponding current input value I_i *below* in the path constraint. Let us call this procedure *sound concretization*.

Indeed, we now show that sound concretization results in sound path constraints.

THEOREM 2. *The algorithm of Figures 1 and 2* with *sound concretization, i.e., including line 14 of Figure 1, generates sound path constraints.*

Proof: The proof relies on the assumption that all sources of imprecision in symbolic execution are detected and trigger the `default` case in the procedure `evalSymbolic` shown in Figure 1. In every such case, line 14 is executed and a concretization constraint is injected in the path constraint. Otherwise, in all other cases, symbolic execution of individual instructions (assignments or conditional statements) is assumed to be precise, i.e., both sound and complete.

Consider a path constraint pc_w generated by this algorithm during the execution of a program path w with an input vector $I = \langle I_i | \forall i \rangle$. For every symbolic variable x_i (generalizing program input I_i) occurring in pc_w, two cases are possible. Either there is a concretization constraint forcing x_i to be equal to I_i. Or all constraints on x_i in pc_w are both sound and complete (symbolic execution is precise so far for all individual instructions involving x_i). Either way, all values of x_i satisfying pc_w satisfy all the tests on inputs along w and hence lead to a program execution following the same path w. Since the same argument holds for all symbolic variables x_i, pc_w is sound. ■

Unlike ordinary constraints derived from conditional statements executed by the program under test, concretization constraints should not be negated later in the directed search, because negating these constraints will not define alternate path constraints corresponding to new program paths. The only purpose of concretization constraints is to guarantee soundness of path constraints.

EXAMPLE 1. Consider again the example of function `foo` shown in Section 3.2. Assume again we run with program with inputs `x=567` and `y=42`, and that `hash(42)` is 567. With sound concretization, a concretization constraint $y = 42$ is generated when symbolically evaluating `hash(y)` in the first conditional statement, and dynamic symbolic execution generates the sound path constraint

$$y = 42 \wedge x = 567 \wedge y \neq 10$$

After negating the last constraint, the resulting constraint

$$y = 42 \wedge x = 567 \wedge y = 10$$

is not satisfiable, and no new test is generated to try to cover the `then` branch of the second conditional statement. ■

Sound concretization generates sound path constraints and eliminates divergences. But in practice, sound concretization is not necessarily "better" than DART's default unsound concretization, for two reasons.

First, a drawback of sound concretization is that it reduces the ability to generate new tests.

EXAMPLE 2. Consider the following program using the same `hash` function:

```
int foo-bis(int x, int y) {
  if (x != hash(y)) {
    ...
    if (y == 10) return -1; // error
  }
  ...
}
```

Assume the program is run with inputs `x=33` and `y=42`, and that `hash(42)` is 567. Sound concretization generates the sound path constraint

$$y = 42 \wedge x \neq 567 \wedge y \neq 10$$

After negating the last constraint, the resulting constraint

$$y = 42 \wedge x \neq 567 \wedge y = 10$$

is not satisfiable, no new test is generated to try to cover the `then` branch of the second conditional statement, and the error is missed. In contrast, unsound concretization would generate the path constraint

$$x \neq 567 \wedge y \neq 10$$

After negating the last constraint, a constraint solver would easily solve the (unsound) path constraint

$$x \neq 567 \wedge y = 10$$

and generate a new test that is *likely* (but not guaranteed) to hit the error, assuming `hash(10)` is likely different from the value of `x` whatever its value is. This is an example of a *"good divergence"*. ■

Second, and perhaps most importantly, sound concretization is *much harder to implement* than unsound concretization, since it requires detecting explicitly *all* sources of imprecision in symbolic execution — including conservatively estimating all possible inputs and outputs of all individual instructions and all unknown/library/operating-system functions used by the program under test —, while unsound concretization can simply be implemented by handling some program instructions and ignoring the others.

Finally, note that adding line 14 of Figure 1 is just one way to inject concretization constraints and that other variants are possible. For instance, the injection of concretization constraints for symbolic variables x_i occurring in a concretized expression e could be delayed during symbolic execution until e is actually being used in some constraint (if any) in the path constraint pc_w. This way, examples such as

```
...
x := hash(y);
if (y == 10) return -1; // error
...
```

could be handled with sound concretization by postponing injecting a concretization constraint for y from when hash(y) is computed to when program variable x is being tested (if at all), and a constraint to cover the other branch of the test (y == 10) could be generated and solved.

4. Higher-Order test Generation

We now introduce a more general form of test generation, which we call *higher-order* because it uses a higher-order logic representation of path constraints. Higher-order test generation requires three steps:

1. uninterpreted functions are used to represent unknown functions or instructions during symbolic execution;
2. new test inputs are derived from validity proofs of first-order logic formulas with uninterpreted functions;
3. concrete input-output value pairs need be recorded as uninterpreted function samples that are used when generating new concrete test inputs.

We now discuss these three steps in detail one by one.

4.1 Symbolic Execution with Uninterpreted Functions

Another well-known approach for reasoning about unknown functions is to represent those using *uninterpreted functions*. Figure 3 presents a more general algorithm for dynamic symbolic execution where unknown functions or instructions are represented *explicitly* using uninterpreted function symbols. This algorithm extends the standard symbolic execution procedure of Figure 2 with the new lines marked with *. Whenever an unknown function or instruction f is encountered during symbolic execution (line 10 of Figure 3), an uninterpreted function symbol f uniquely representing the function/instruction is used to represent the symbolic return value of the function call, which is defined as the application of the function to its symbolic input arguments (line 12). Symbolic execution resumes after the function returns.

By unknown function, we mean any function whose code is not available or not precisely representable by a symbolic expression of the theory $\mathcal{T}$ handled by the constraint solver for whatever reason (such as hash or crypto functions, operating-system functions, environment/library functions outside of the main scope of analysis, etc.). Similarly, by unknown instruction, we mean any atomic program instruction not handled by the symbolic evaluation procedure, i.e., involving some symbolic expression previously concretized in line 13 of Figure 1. For simplicity, we represent such unknown instructions by uninterpreted functions as well; line 13 of Figure 1 is thus no longer reachable, by construction, with the new algorithm.[3]

In Figure 3, args denotes a list of arguments. Each argument is a variable v whose value is an input to the function call (we consider a call-by-value function model here, for simplicity).

[3] Any symbolic expression e including an unknown function/instruction application $f(args)$ as sub-expression is equivalent to $v_{f(args)} := f(args)$ followed by e where $f(args)$ is replaced by $v_{f(args)}$.

Consider again the example of function foo shown in Section 3.2. When symbolically executing the first conditional statement (x == hash(y)), a fresh uninterpreted function symbol h is introduced to represent the unknown function hash. If the then branch of the first conditional statement is taken, the path constraint generated is then

$$x = h(y)$$

The new symbolic execution performed by the algorithm of Figure 3 typically generates more symbolic values than the standard symbolic execution procedure of Figure 2, since it represents unknown functions with "symbolic" uninterpreted functions instead of using concretization and falling back on concrete values. Therefore, the new algorithm typically generates more symbolic constraints in the path constraint pc (lines 17 and 18). We can prove that those path constraints are always sound.

THEOREM 3. *The algorithm of Figure 3 generates sound path constraints.*

Proof: The proof relies on the assumption that all sources of imprecision in symbolic execution are detected in line 10 of the procedure executeSymbolic in Figure 3 and are representable by uninterpreted functions (line 12), which implies that every unknown function/instruction is deterministic and with a known input-output signature. For all other cases, symbolic execution of individual instructions (assignments or conditional statements) is assumed to be precise, i.e., both sound and complete.

Consider a path constraint pc_w generated by this algorithm during the execution of a program path w with an input vector $I = \langle I_i | \forall i \rangle$. At any time during the symbolic execution along w, all direct dependencies on inputs are tracked precisely via the symbolic store, either in sound and complete manner via the procedure evalSymbolic of Figure 1, or using uninterpreted function applications. Therefore, at every conditional statement C executed along w, if a constraint c involving some symbolic variable x_i is added in C to the path constraint pc_w, all input values of x_i satisfying c take the same branch as the current concrete value I_i of x_i. Since the same argument holds for all symbolic variables x_i and all symbolic constraints in pc_w, every input assignment I' satisfying the path constraint pc_w defines a program execution following the given path w, which means that pc_w is sound. ■

The previous theorem states that, *if* an input assignment satisfies a path constraint pc_w generated by the algorithm of Figure 3, *then* the corresponding program execution will follow path w. For instance, considering again our running example, any input assignment to the variables x and y that satisfies the path constraint $x = h(y)$ will take the then branch of the conditional statement in function foo. But this result alone does not prescribe *how* to compute such values and generate tests from path constraints with uninterpreted function symbols. This problem is discussed next.

4.2 Generating Tests from Validity Proofs

When uninterpreted functions are used in path constraints to model imprecision in symbolic execution, test generation from such path constraints *must* be performed from *validity proofs*, instead of satisfiability proofs, as will be shown shortly. This requires path constraints to be *post-processed* before calling the validity checker: every ordinary symbolic variable representing a program input is *existentially quantified*, resulting in a first-order logic formula of the form

$$\exists x : \phi(f, x)$$

while every uninterpreted function symbol f is implicitly left *universally quantified* in the validity check. Remember that first-order logic does not allow explicit quantification over functions: universal function quantification is implicit when checking validity, while

```
  Procedure executeSymbolic(P, I) =
    initialize M_0 and S_0
    path constraint pc = true
    C = getNextCommand()
    while (C ≠ stop)
      match (C):
        case (v := e):
          M = M + [&v ↦ evalConcrete(e)]
          S = S + [&v ↦ evalSymbolic(e)]
*       case (v := f(args)): // f is an unknown function or instruction
*         M = M + [&v ↦ evalConcrete(f(args))]
*         S = S + [&v ↦ createExpression('f', evalSymbolic(args))]
*         Add (M(&v), createExpression('f', evalConcrete(args))) to IO_F;
        case (if e then C' else C''):
          b = evalConcrete(e)
          c = evalSymbolic(e)
          if b then pc = pc ∧ c
          else pc = pc ∧ ¬c
      C = getNextCommand() // end of while loop
```

Figure 3. Symbolic execution with uninterpreted functions.

existential function quantification is implicit when checking satisfiability.[4]

We emphasize that representing unknown functions by uninterpreted function symbols in validity queries is *not* new in program verification. Indeed, for *verification*, the set of possible behaviors of unknown functions needs to be *over-approximated* to guarantee a *may* abstraction that can be used to prove *correctness*, hence the use of (implicit) *universal quantification*. However, what is new here (to the best of our knowledge) is our use of (implicit) *universal quantification* for uninterpreted function symbols for *test generation*, instead of (implicit) *existential quantification* with satisfiability queries as usual in the context of test input generation. We discuss this further in Section 8.

We now illustrate this important difference, and why we need it. Consider again the example of the `obscure` function used in the introduction:

```
int obscure(int x, int y) {
  if (x == hash(y)) return -1;    // error
  return 0;                       // ok
}
```

Let us assume again that the function `hash` is "unknown", that the program is run first with the input values `x=33` and `y=42`, and that `hash(42)` is 567 and hence that the first execution takes the `else` branch of the conditional statement. With the standard symbolic execution of Figure 2, the single constraint appearing in the path constraint pc is

$$x \neq 567$$

Next, the *satisfiability* of the negation of this constraint, namely

$$x = 567$$

is checked by the constraint solver. Since it is satisfiable, the satisfying assignment returned by the constraint solver is transformed into a new input vector, namely `x=567` and `y=42`, that will drive the next execution of the program along the `then` branch of the conditional statement. Note how input variable x is existentially quantified in the *satisfiability check* performed by the constraint solver.

In contrast, with the new symbolic execution procedure of Figure 3, the single constraint appearing in the path constraint is now

$$x \neq h(y)$$

[4] A logic formula is *satisfiable* if there exists a variable assignment that makes the formula true, and it is *valid* if all variable assignments make the formula true.

where h denotes the uninterpreted function symbol representing the unknown function `hash`. After post-processing, the *validity* of the formula

$$\exists x, y : x = h(y)$$

is checked by the constraint solver (i.e., for all h). If the formula is valid, a *test-generation strategy* is derived from the *validity proof* of the formula, viewed as a strategy for making the formula always true. In this case, the formula is valid and the strategy is

"fix y, then set x to the value $h(y)$".

In other words, with the new algorithm, new tests are derived from *validity proofs*, instead of *satisfying assignments* as usual.

Indeed, we have no choice: if uninterpreted functions are used to model imprecision in symbolic execution, test generation can no longer be performed from satisfiability checks. In the above example, checking the satisfiability of the formula

$$x = h(y)$$

(where h, x and y are thus all implicitly quantified existentially) may return satisfying assignments that are unusable for test generation since the existential quantifier over h allows the constraint solver to *invent* some specific arbitrary function h that helps it prove satisfiability. For instance, the constraint solver may define function h such that $h(0) = 0$ and then return `x=0` and `y=0` as satisfying assignments. Since such a function h may differ from the specific unknown function `hash` called in the program under test, sound test generation is not possible when existentially quantifying h.

4.3 The Need for Uninterpreted Function Samples

Test strategies derived from validity proofs are *necessary but not sufficient* to compute concrete input vectors, which is required in test generation. For instance, with the above test strategy, the "value $h(y)$" is not derived from the validity proof: a concrete value for x can be obtained only when some values for y and $h(y)$ are known. In general, the value of $h(y)$ for a given y can only be known at runtime. (Unless the function h is completely known and not too complex to be represented as a logic formula; then a constraint solver using constant propagation starting from some concrete input value y could simulate the execution of h with value y as argument and compute the value $h(y)$; however, even in this case, constant propagation is orders of magnitude slower and less scalable than simply running the actual code implementing the function h with value y as argument.)

In the above example, we need to know that if y is set to 42, then $h(y)$ is 567 in order to set x to that value following the test-generation strategy derived from the validity proof.

In other words, the new symbolic execution algorithm using uninterpreted functions also needs to *record runtime concrete values* to allow for test generation of specific concrete input values. Let us call this step *uninterpreted function sampling*.

Specifically, we can record the concrete value of any function application such as $h(y)$ during dynamic symbolic execution as well as the concrete value of each of its arguments, as shown in line 13 of Figure 3: a pair $(c, f(\text{evalConcrete}(args)))$ is recorded for each function application where evalConcrete($args$) denotes the list of concrete values of each function argument and c denotes the concrete return value of the function applied to those concrete argument values. In the above example, the record pair is thus $(567, h(42))$, meaning that $567 = h(42)$.

These pairs $(c, f(\text{evalConcrete}(args)))$ of recorded values have two purposes.

- They are used to *interpret* a test generation strategy derived from a validity proof in order to assign concrete values to function applications (such as $h(y)$) appearing in the strategy and generate concrete values to new input tests.
- They can also be used to generate additional constraints of the form $c = f(\text{evalConcrete}(args))$ as an *antecedent* to the path constraint that is passed to the constraint solver. Such constraints restrict the possible interpretations for uninterpreted function symbol f, and increases the chance of validity.

The latter can be more powerful and is necessary for higher-order test generation to always subsume sound concretization, as will be shown in the next section. Therefore, we adopt this second option in what follows.

To sum up, given a path constraint pc using a set X of symbolic variables, a set F of uninterpreted functions and a set IO_F of recorded input-output function samples, the post-processed formula $POST(pc)$ obtained by post-processing pc in high-order test generation is the first-order logic formula defined by

$$POST(pc) = \exists X : A \Rightarrow pc$$

where $\exists X$ denotes that all symbolic variables $x_i \in X$ are existentially quantified, $\Rightarrow$ denotes logical implication, and A is the conjunction of equality constraints $c = f(\text{evalConcrete}(args))$ for all $(c, f(\text{evalConcrete}(args))) \in IO_F$. In what follows, we call A the *antecedent* of $POST(pc)$.

For instance, consider again our running example with a path constraint pc containing a single constraint $x = h(y)$ and a single recorded pair $(567, h(42))$. Then $POST(pc)$ is

$$\exists x, y : (567 = h(42)) \Rightarrow (x = h(y))$$

Sometimes, the antecedent does not help the validity proof itself, as in the previous example, and only helps for generating actual concrete test values. But sometimes, the antecedent is necessary to prove validity, as shown in Section 5.3.

In practice, recording *all* concrete arguments and return values of *all* uninterpreted function applications used in a path constraint can be prohibitively expensive for long program executions. Moreover, it is unfortunately hard to predict which concrete values will be needed later in the path constraint, i.e., which concrete values are concretizations of symbolic expressions with uninterpreted functions on which there are tests *below* in the path constraint. However, it is possible to track only *some* sources of imprecision and only represent those using uninterpreted functions, and to track and represent only *some* input-output pairs for tracked functions. Implementability issues will be discussed further in Section 6.

5. Comparison

In this section, we compare the test-generation power of higher-order test generation (Section 4) with sound and unsound concretization (Section 3).

5.1 Higher-Order Test Generation and Unsound Concretization are Incomparable

As discussed at the end of Section 3.3, sound and unsound concretization are incomparable in general, since unsound concretization can lead to (bad or good) divergences that will not occur with sound concretization. Similarly, by Theorem 3, higher-order test generation generates sound path constraints and is thus incomparable to unsound concretization in general, for the same reasons.

EXAMPLE 3. Consider the function

```
int bar(int x, int y) {  // x,y are inputs
  if ((x == hash(y)) AND (y == hash(x))) {
    ... // error
  }
  . ..
}
```

Given random inputs $x = 33$ and $y = 42$ and assuming `hash(42)=567` and `hash(33)=123`, unsound concretization will generate an unsound path constraint

$$x \neq 567 \vee y \neq 123$$

whose negation $x = 567 \wedge y = 123$ is satisfiable and generates a new test input pair $\langle x = 567, y = 123\rangle$ which will likely lead to a divergence. In contrast, higher-order test generation will generate a sound path constraint

$$x \neq h(y) \vee y \neq h(x)$$

After post-processing, the validity of the formula $\exists x, y : x = h(y) \wedge y = h(x)$ will be checked. But no new test will be generated since this formula is invalid (in general, unless we learn some additional property of h such as there exists an x such as $x = h(h(x))$, for instance). ■

5.2 Higher-Order Test Generation is as Powerful as Sound Concretization

In the remainder of this section, we will therefore restrict the comparison of higher-order test generation to sound concretization. Both algorithms generate sound path constraints (see Theorems 2 and 3). We now show that high-order test generation is at least as powerful as test generation with sound concretization.

Given a path constraint $pc = \bigwedge_{1 \leq i \leq n} c_i$, let $ALT(pc)$ denote the new *alternate* path constraint defined by the conjunction of the negation of the last constraint c_n of pc with all previous constraints c_j with $j < i$ in pc. We thus have

$$ALT(pc) = \neg c_n \wedge \bigwedge_{1 \leq i \leq (n-1)} c_i$$

Remember that, as explained in Section 2, all nonempty prefixes of a path constraint are also path constraints (except those ending with a concretization constraint).

Let pc_w^{SC} denote a path constraint generated for a program path w with sound concretization (Section 3.3) and whose last constraint is not a concretization constraint. Let pc_w^{UF} be the path constraint generated with higher-order test generation (Section 4.1) for the same program path w. Given any theory $\mathcal{T}$, let $\mathcal{T} \cup \mathcal{T}_{EUF}$ denote the theory combining $\mathcal{T}$ with the theory of equality with uninterpreted functions (EUF). If pc_w^{SC} and $ALT(pc_w^{SC})$ are quantifier-free formulas over $\mathcal{T}$, then pc_w^{UF} and $ALT(pc_w^{UF})$ are quantifier-free formulas over $\mathcal{T} \cup \mathcal{T}_{EUF}$, while $POST(ALT(pc_w^{UF}))$ is a first-order logic formula over $\mathcal{T} \cup \mathcal{T}_{EUF}$, by construction.

THEOREM 4. *(Simulation Theorem)*
If $ALT(pc_w^{SC})$ *is satisfiable, then* $POST(ALT(pc_w^{UF}))$ *is valid.*

Proof:
We show how to derive a validity proof for $POST(ALT(pc_w^{UF}))$ from any satisfying assignment for $ALT(pc_w^{SC})$.

Whenever a complex/unknown expression $e(x_i) \notin \mathcal{T}$ occurs during symbolic execution with sound concretization, a concretization constraint $x_i = I_i$ is introduced in pc_w^{SC}, $e(x_i)$ becomes $e(I_i)$, and all future expressions $e'(x_i)$ depending on x_i become $e'(I_i)$. In contrast, in higher-order test generation, every occurrence of a complex/unknown expression $e(x_i) \notin \mathcal{T}$ becomes $f_e(x_i)$ where f_e is an uninterpreted function symbol representing e, and the pair (evalConcrete($e(I_i)$), $f_e(I_i)$) is being recorded.

Consider any symbolic variable $x_i \in X$ for which there is a concretization constraint $x_i = I_i$ in $ALT(pc_w^{SC})$. Consider any expression $e(x_i) \notin \mathcal{T}$ concretized into $e(I_i)$ and occurring in $ALT(pc_w^{SC})$. In $POST(ALT(pc_w^{UF}))$, $e(x_i)$ is represented by $f_e(x_i)$ and evalConcrete($e(I_i)$) $= f_e(I_i)$ is in the antecedent.

In $POST(ALT(pc_w^{UF}))$, repeat the following process for all the symbolic variables x_i with a concretization constraint in $ALT(pc_w^{SC})$ and for all the functions f_e using those variables as arguments: substitute all the occurrences of x_i by I_i and then all the occurrences of any function $f_e(I_i)$ by evalConcrete($e(I_i)$). (Note that this last step would not be possible if evalConcrete($e(I_i)$) $=$ $f_e(I_i)$ was not present, i.e., known and recorded, in the antecedent of POST(ALT(pc^{UF})).)

At the end, we are left with a formula $\phi(X')$ where X' denotes the set of all remaining symbolic variables $x'_i \in X$ for which there are no concretization constraints in $ALT(pc_w^{SC})$. Therefore, we know that all expressions of the form $e(x'_i)$ in $\phi(X')$ are in $\mathcal{T}$, that they did not introduce imprecision in symbolic execution, and that they are represented in the exact same way in $ALT(pc_w^{SC})$.

Thus, by construction, the consequent of $\phi(X')$ is syntactically equivalent to $ALT(pc_w^{SC})$ when all its concretization constraints are removed. Since all occurrences of all uninterpreted function symbols f_e have been eliminated from the consequent of $\phi(X')$, the universal quantification over those functions in $\phi(X')$ becomes void intuitively. The same holds for the existential quantification for all symbolic variables $x_i \notin X'$ that no longer appear in $\phi(X')$. Since the consequent of $\phi(X')$ is logically equivalent to $ALT(pc_w^{SC})$, if the latter is satisfiable, then $\exists X' : A \Rightarrow ALT(pc_w^{SC})$ is valid. This implies that $\exists X : A \Rightarrow ALT(pc_w^{UF})$ is valid (by setting the value of each variable $x_i \in X \setminus X'$ to I_i). ■

We emphasize that the previous theorem holds *only if* uninterpreted function samples are used. Otherwise, higher-order test generation may not be able to simulate sound concretization, as illustrated by the following example.

EXAMPLE 4. Consider the function

```
int pub(int x, int y) {  // x,y are inputs
  if ((hash(x) > 0) AND (y == 10)) return -1 // error
  ...
}
```

Given random inputs $x = 1$ and $y = 2$ and assuming `hash(1)=5`, sound concretization will generate a sound path constraint

$$x = 1 \wedge y \neq 10$$

(after simplifying $5 > 0$ to `true`). The alternate path constraint $x = 1 \wedge y = 10$ is satisfiable and generates a new test input pair $\langle x = 1, y = 10\rangle$ to cover the `then` branch of the conditional statement. In contrast, higher-order test generation *without* uninterpreted function samples will generate a sound path constraint

$$h(x) > 0 \wedge y \neq 10$$

However, after post-processing of the alternate path constraint attempting to cover the `then` branch, the validity of the formula

$$\exists x, y : h(x) > 0 \wedge y = 10$$

will be checked. But no new test will be generated since this formula is invalid (to see this, consider the function h such that $h(x) = 0$ for all x, for instance). If instead we consider higher-order test generation *with* uninterpreted function samples, we then obtain after post-processing the formula

$$\exists x, y : (h(1) = 5) \Rightarrow (h(x) > 0 \wedge y = 10)$$

which is valid (by setting $\langle x = 1, y = 10\rangle$). ■

An important remark is that Theorem 4 only compares the path-constraint generation capabilities of higher-order test generation and sound concretization. But it does *not* state that if there exists a constraint solver that can prove the satisfiability of $ALT(pc_w^{SC})$, then there exists a constraint solver that can prove the validity of $POST(ALT(pc_w^{UF}))$. Thus, when we say that "higher-order test generation is as powerful as sound concretization", we assume we are given *perfect* constraint solvers for both satisfiability and validity checking.

5.3 Higher-Order Test Generation is More Powerful Than Sound Concretization

The previous theorem states that higher-order test generation is at least as powerful as sound concretization. Is it more powerful? The answer is yes, for three reasons.

First, since higher-order test generation uses $\mathcal{T} \cup \mathcal{T}_{EUF}$, it can infer test strategies thanks to axioms included in the theory of equality with uninterpreted functions (EUF), which are not available to sound concretization, which only uses $\mathcal{T}$.

EXAMPLE 5. Higher-order test generation can generate tests from validity proofs of post-processed path constraints such as

$$\exists x, y : f(x) = f(y)$$

thanks to the theory of equality with uninterpreted functions. (Solution strategy: set $x = y$). In contrast, sound concretization would force the concretization of $x, y, f(x)$ and $f(y)$, and would not be able to generate a test to cover a path with such a path constraint. ■

Second, higher-order test generation can sometimes leverage concrete input-output pairs that are part of the antecedent of a post-processed path constraint in order to prove the validity of formulas that would otherwise be invalid.

EXAMPLE 6. Consider the post-processed path constraint

$$\exists x, y : f(x) = f(y) + 1$$

This formula is in general invalid (to see this, consider a function f that always returns 0). However, assume that it is dynamically observed that $f(0) = 0$ and $f(1) = 1$. Then these recorded pairs can be part of the antecedent of the post-processed path constraint, which becomes

$$\exists x, y : (f(0) = 0 \wedge f(1) = 1) \Rightarrow f(x) = f(y) + 1$$

This formula is valid (solution strategy: set $x = 1$ and $y = 0$). In either case, sound concretization would force the concretization of $x, y, f(x)$ and $f(y)$ and would not be able to generate new tests. ■

Third, higher-order test generation can sometimes generate test strategies that involves a *sequence of new tests*, whose purpose is to collect *additional function samples* in a targeted manner, instead of a single new test as usual. Let us call this new type of test generation *multi-step test generation*.

EXAMPLE 7. Consider again the example of function `foo` of Section 3.2, reproduced here for convenience:

```
int foo(int x, int y) {
  if (x == hash(y)) {
    ...
    if (y == 10) return -1; // error
  }
  ...
}
```

Starting with $x = 33$ and $y = 42$ and assuming `hash(42)=567`, this first test takes the else branch of the first conditional statement. After negating the last constraint, we obtain the post-processed alternate path constraint

$$\exists x, y : (h(42) = 567) \Rightarrow x = h(y)$$

This formula is valid and we generate a new input vector $\langle x = 567, y = 42 \rangle$. We run this new test and we now take the then branch of the first conditional statement followed by the else branch of the second conditional statement. After negating the last constraint, we obtain the post-processed alternate path constraint

$$\exists x, y : (h(42) = 567) \Rightarrow (x = h(y) \wedge y = 10)$$

This formula is valid, and a test strategy derived from the validity proof is "set $y = 10$, set $x = h(10)$". However, since the value of $h(10)$ has never been sampled, it is currently unknown!

A new *intermediate* test with, say, $\langle x = 567, y = 10 \rangle$ is necessary to learn the value of $h(10)$, say 66. Only then can a second input vector $\langle x = 66, y = 10 \rangle$ be generated to finish interpreting the previous test strategy, to exercise the `then` branch of the second conditional statement and hit the `error`. ■

This is an example of two-step test generation. Of course, such examples can easily be generalized to k-step test generation for any k bounded by the number of program inputs.

Another related yet orthogonal suggestion would be to include in the antecedent of post-processed alternate path constraints generated with higher-order test generation, not only all the input-output value pairs observed for the current run, but also all value pairs observed during *all previous* runs.

6. Discussion: Implementability

As explained in the introduction, the main purpose of this paper is to carefully study the power of recent test generation techniques such as DART which are quickly gaining popularity. It is also to understand the fundamental difference between static and dynamic test generation. In the process, we proposed higher-order test generation as a powerful test generation technique generalizing sound concretization. How practical is higher-order test generation?

For large applications such as those targeted by whitebox fuzzing [16], exhaustively tracking *all* sources of imprecision during symbolic execution is problematic. Such imprecision can be due to unhandled individual instructions (for instance, the complete x86 instruction set contains hundreds of instructions described in a 1,000+ pages manual with exotic bit-manipulations, floating-point/SSE instructions, etc.), operating-system calls (should kernel execution be symbolic and if so up to what depth?), complex functions (for hashing, encrypting, compressing, encoding, CRC-ing data), etc. For instance, a single symbolic execution of Excel with 45K input bytes executes nearly a billion x86 instructions (see Figure 6 of [16]), including many input-tainted unhandled ones and many system calls. Moreover, some of this imprecision is hard to capture using uninterpreted functions because the real functions may look nondeterministic and/or with complex or unknown input-output signatures (such as malloc, rand, fork, etc. which take as inputs large/unknown parts of the operating-system state and may have many hidden side effects). Finally, capturing at execution time *all* observed input-output value pairs is problematic as well. For large applications, all this would slow down an already slow symbolic execution and generate gigantic path constraints that would overwhelm even the best engineered constraint solvers.

Therefore, we envision a more *focused role* for higher-order test generation in practice, targeted at reasoning about specific user-identified complex or unknown functions that must be dealt with in order to properly test an application. One such application is presented in the next section.

Another obstacle to the implementability of higher-order test generation is the relative lack of support for generating validity proofs by existing constraint solvers such as SMT solvers. Indeed, a first-order logic formula $\exists X : \phi(F, X)$ can be proved valid by checking whether its negation $\forall X : \neg\phi(F, X)$ is unsatisfiable with a *Satisfiability*-Modulo-Theories solver. For first-order logic formulas like those considered here, validity (equivalently unsatisfiability) is usually proved using saturation techniques [3]. Better tool support for generating saturation-based proofs (not just models for satisfiable instances) that are parsable by other tools would help extracting a test generation strategy from such proofs. More work is needed in this area. In fact, our paper can be viewed as a "requirement specification" for next-generation SMT solvers for test generation, a growing application area for those, by presenting higher-order test generation as a new possible application for those tools.

7. Application

In this section, we present an application which requires the power of high-order test generation: test generation for parsers with input lexers using hash functions for fast keyword recognition.

As observed in [14], dynamic test generation can be ineffective when testing applications with highly-structured inputs. Examples of such applications are compilers and interpreters. These applications process their inputs in stages, such as lexing, parsing and evaluation. Unfortunately, lexers often detect language keywords by comparing their pre-computed hash values with the hash values of strings read from the input. This effectively prevents symbolic execution and constraint solving from ever generating input strings that match those keywords since hash functions cannot be inversed (i.e., given a constraint `x == hash(y)` and a value for `x`, one cannot compute a value for `y` that satisfies this constraint). In those cases, test generation is defeated already in the first processing stages.

A typical code pattern is shown in Figure 4 in the appendix. This C code is an excerpt from the open-source flex lexer. Initially, the function `addsym` is called with every input-language keyword so that each of those are hashed (with function `hashfunct`) and stored in a hash table `table`. Once the hash table is populated, the parsing of the input starts. The input is being divided into chunks delimited by blank-spaces/tabs/etc. Each of those chunks are then parsed and the function `findsym` is called to check whether a chunk matches a keyword.

Because of the presence of function `hashfunct`, dynamic test generation may not be able to generate input strings ("chunks") matching specific keywords. In [14], it is shown how such a problematic lexer can be bypassed altogether for test generation of the subsequent input-processing stages by (1) instrumenting the lexer so that its return `symbol` values become symbolic inputs during symbolic execution, and (2) lifting the input space from character strings to sequences of symbols (token ids) using a grammar specification of the input language being parsed. Unfortunately, instrumenting a lexer this way can be problematic for complex lexers, and this approach requires a user-supplied input-grammar specification.

In contrast, higher-order test generation provides a more automated approach to test generation through such lexers. The key but only thing the user is required to specify is the name of the function `hash` (like `hashfunct` or possibly a hash-function wrapper like `findsym` in the example of Figure 4) whose calls are then tracked during symbolic execution and represented using an uninterpreted function exactly as described in Section 4. During initialization, all the pairs ⟨`hashvalue, hash(keyword)`⟩ are being recorded to be included in the antecedent of post-processed path constraints. Whenever test generation needs a specific symbol to drive the parser through a new specific program branch, the theory of equality with uninterpreted functions combined with all the input-output value pairs recorded for `hash` makes it possible to effectively "inverse" this hash function for the finitely many keywords of the input language, which is sufficient for test generation for such applications. For instance, when an assignment statement of the form `symbol = hash(inputChunk)` is followed by a conditional statement of the form `if (symbol == 52) ...`, observing that `hash('while') = 52` is sufficient for higher-order test generation to generate an `inputChunk` equal to `while` in order to exercise the `then` branch of the conditional statement.

Note that, in some lexers, hash values are pre-computed and hard-coded in the source code. Then, it is not possible to observe at execution time all relevant input-output value pairs for such hash functions at the beginning of each execution. However, such input-output pairs could still be "learned" over time by starting the testing session with a representative set of well-formed inputs, observing the hash values of all the language keywords those inputs contain, and then using all pairs recorded in all previous executions in subsequent symbolic executions.

We have performed preliminary experiments with higher-order test generation in such a targeted manner in conjunction with the whitebox fuzzer SAGE [16] and using the Z3 SMT solver [9]. Since Z3 does not support the generation of saturation-based proofs, these experiments were conducted with an ad-hoc pre-processing step to eliminate uninterpreted functions in path constraints before calling Z3 for a satisfiability check as usual: (1) all uninterpreted function samples $h(c_1) = c_2$ are collected in a table IO_F (where c_1 and c_2 denote constants), and then (2) whenever a constraint of the form $h(x) = c_2$ occurs in a path constraint, it is replaced by a disjunction of constraints $x = c_1$ for all c_1 such that $h(c_1) = c_2$ (to handle hash collisions). This procedure is simple to implement but handles only limited cases and is far from simulating the full reasoning power of $\mathcal{T} \cup \mathcal{T}_{EUF}$. Nevertheless, experiments with a simple parser including a lexer similar to Figure 4 show that this partial implementation of higher-order test generation is sufficient to accurately drive program executions through the lexer. In contrast, regular dynamic test generation is no better than blackbox random testing because it is not able to drive executions through tests involving the hash function in the lexer.

8. Other Related Work

Abstracting program functions using uninterpreted functions is a well-known technique in verification-condition generation for program verification of universal properties (e.g., [4]). In that context, the set of all program behaviors is over-approximated in presence of program-analysis imprecision, and verification is established by checking the validity of a logic formula representing the entire program (or module). Uninterpreted function symbols in the formula are therefore implicitly universally quantified as in our work.

In the context of test generation, uninterpreted functions have been used for representing symbolic test summaries in compositional symbolic execution [1, 17]. There, a function summary is represented by a first-order logic formula using an uninterpreted function symbol representing the function. A function summary is defined as a disjunction (i.e., a set) of intraprocedural path constraints expressed in terms of the function inputs and outputs. Function summaries can be computed incrementally, to include more and more intraprocedural path constraints as they are discovered during a directed search. Test generation with function summaries is performed as usual by a satisfiability check, where all uninterpreted functions are therefore implicitly existentially quantified. This use of uninterpreted functions for function summaries is thus different from their use in higher-order test generation where uninterpreted functions represent imprecision in symbolic execution in *individual* path constraints. Both types of uninterpreted functions could actually be used simultaneously, as they are orthogonal, for "higher-order compositional test generation". Note that function summaries do not have to be represented using uninterpreted functions, and can be encoded directly in propositional logic instead [11].

We do not know of any other work where tests are derived from validity proofs, or where uninterpreted functions are used to model imprecision in symbolic execution *for test generation*.

The (implicit) alternation of universal function quantifiers and existential variable quantifiers in our post-processed path constraints can be viewed as a game between an unknown environment (controlling the unknown functions) and a test generator (controlling test inputs). To view test generation as a game is not new [5, 25]. Model-driven test generation for conformance testing, i.e., checking whether a blackbox implementation conforms to a whitebox specification, can be viewed as a game and, under specific assumptions, can be encoded logically using quantifier alternation, for instance using Quantified Boolean Formulas. However, we are not aware of any work on model-based test generation using uninterpreted functions or validity proofs of first-order logic formulas as in our work.

Given a program and a set of input parameters, test generation refers to the problem of generating input tests in order to exercise a specific program path, branch or statement. In contrast, static, dynamic and higher-order test generation denote specific approaches to solving the test generation problem. Test generation is only one way of proving existential reachability properties of programs, where specific concrete input values are generated to exercise specific program paths. More generally, such properties can be proved using so-called *must abstractions* of programs, without necessarily generating concrete tests. A must abstraction is defined as a program abstraction that preserves existential reachability properties of the program. For instance, in predicate abstraction [13, 17], a *must transition* from an abstract state A_1 to an abstract state A_2 implies that

$$\forall c_1 \in A_1 : \exists c_2 \in A_2 : c_1 \rightarrow c_2$$

that is, for every concrete state c_1 abstracted by A_1, there exists a program execution from c_1 to a concrete state c_2 such that c_2 is abstracted by A_2. Must transitions can be chained together to prove existential reachability properties of programs, i.e., *find bugs in a sound manner*. Sound path constraints are particular cases of must abstractions [17]. Note the analogy between the alternation of universal and existential quantifiers in the definition of must transition and in our post-processed path constraints.

Other related work includes [8, 18] where must abstractions are built backwards from error states using static program analysis. This approach can detect program locations and states provably leading to error states (no false alarms), but may fail to prove reachability of those error states back from whole-program initial states, and hence may miss bugs or report unreachable error states. Imprecision in symbolic reasoning, e.g., due to system calls or unknown functions, is modeled by assigning nondeterministic values to all possible modified (output) variables, which is less precise than using uninterpreted functions yet still assumes all unknown functions have known sets of possible outputs/side-effects. Building must abstractions statically can be fast but requires symbolic reasoning about the whole program. On the other hand, dynamic test generation is slower but more precise by allowing symbolic execution to degrade gracefully using concrete runtime values whenever symbolic reasoning is difficult.

Static test generation can be extended to concretize symbolic values whenever static symbolic execution becomes imprecise [19]. This approach not only requires to detect all sources of imprecision, but also one call to the constraint solver for each concretization to ensure that every synthesized concrete value satisfies prior symbolic constraints along the current program path. For the reasons discussed in Section 6, such requirements are not practical for large applications. In contrast, dynamic test generation avoids these two limitations by leveraging a specific concrete execution as an automatic fall back for symbolic execution [15].

Dynamic test generation is currently an active area of research and many other extensions and applications have been proposed, such as [2, 6, 10, 23, 24] to name just a few (see [7] for a recent survey). This other related work does not specifically focus on how to deal with imprecision in symbolic execution and could benefit from the techniques introduced in our work.

9. Conclusion

We presented higher-order test generation, a powerful new form of test generation, which can also be expensive as it requires tracking explicitly sources of imprecision in symbolic execution, using uninterpreted functions, recording input-output function samples, and checking validity of first-order logic formulas. We showed how this approach can perform novel forms of test generation, such as multi-step test generation, and drive the executions of input parsers with lexers using hash functions for fast keyword recognition.

We also showed that the key property of dynamic test generation that makes it more powerful than static test generation is *only* its ability to observe concrete values and to record those in path constraints. In contrast, the process of simplifying complex symbolic expressions using concrete runtime values can be accurately simulated using uninterpreted functions. However, those concrete values are necessary to effectively compute new input vectors, a fundamental requirement in test generation.

Acknowledgments. I thank Leonardo de Moura for several insightful discussions related to this work. I also thank Nikolaj Bjorner, Yuri Gurevich and Mihalis Yannakakis for helpful comments, and Andreas Podelski and the anonymous reviewers for their constructive comments to improve the presentation.

References

[1] S. Anand, P. Godefroid, and N. Tillmann. Demand-Driven Compositional Symbolic Execution. In *Proceedings of TACAS'2008*, volume 4963 of *Lecture Notes in Computer Science*, pages 367–381, Budapest, April 2008. Springer-Verlag.

[2] S. Artzi, A. Kiezun, J. Dolby, F. Tip, D. Dig, A. M. Paradkar, and M. D. Ernst. Finding Bugs in Web Applications Using Dynamic Test Generation and Explicit-State Model Checking. *IEEE Trans. Software Eng.*, 36(4):474–494, 2010.

[3] L. Bachmair and H. Ganzinger. Resolution Theorem Proving. In *Handbook of Automated Reasoning*, pages 19–99. 2001.

[4] M. Barnett, B. E. Chang, R. DeLine, B. Jacobs, and K. R. M. Leino. Boogie: A modular reusable verifier for object-oriented programs. In *Proceedings of FMCO'2005*, volume 4111 of *Lecture Notes in Computer Science*, pages 364–387. Springer-Verlag, September 2006.

[5] A. Blass, Y. Gurevich, L. Nachmanson, and M. Veanes. Play to Test. In *Proceedings of FATES'2005*, Edinburgh, July 2005.

[6] C. Cadar, V. Ganesh, P. M. Pawlowski, D. L. Dill, and D. R. Engler. EXE: Automatically Generating Inputs of Death. In *ACM CCS*, 2006.

[7] C. Cadar, P. Godefroid, S. Khurshid, C.S. Pasareanu, K. Sen, N. Tillmann, and W. Visser. Symbolic Execution for Software Testing in Practice – Preliminary Assessment. In *Proceedings of ICSE'2011*, Honolulu, May 2011.

[8] S. Chandra, S. J. Fink, and M. Sridharan. Snugglebug: A Powerful Approach to Weakest Preconditions. In *Proceedings of PLDI'2009*, Dublin, June 2009.

[9] L. de Moura and N. Bjorner. Z3: An Efficient SMT Solver. In *Proceedings of TACAS'2008*, volume 4963 of *Lecture Notes in Computer Science*, pages 337–340, Budapest, April 2008. Springer-Verlag.

[10] M. Emmi, R. Majumdar, and K. Sen. Dynamic Test Input Generation for Database Applications. In *Proceedings of ISSTA'2007*, pages 151–162, 2007.

[11] P. Godefroid. Compositional Dynamic Test Generation. In *Proceedings of POPL'2007*, pages 47–54, Nice, January 2007.

[12] P. Godefroid. Software Model Checking Improving Security of a Billion Computers. In *Proceedings of SPIN'2009*, volume 5578 of *Lecture Notes in Computer Science*, page 1, Grenoble, June 2009. Springer-Verlag.

[13] P. Godefroid, M. Huth, and R. Jagadeesan. Abstraction-based Model Checking using Modal Transition Systems. In *Proceedings of CONCUR'2001*, volume 2154 of *Lecture Notes in Computer Science*, pages 426–440, Aalborg, August 2001. Springer-Verlag.

[14] P. Godefroid, A. Kiezun, and M. Y. Levin. Grammar-based Whitebox Fuzzing. In *Proceedings of PLDI'2008*, pages 206–215, Tucson, June 2008.

[15] P. Godefroid, N. Klarlund, and K. Sen. DART: Directed Automated Random Testing. In *Proceedings of PLDI'2005*, pages 213–223, Chicago, June 2005.

[16] P. Godefroid, M.Y. Levin, and D. Molnar. Automated Whitebox Fuzz Testing. In *Proceedings of NDSS'2008*, pages 151–166, San Diego, February 2008.

[17] P. Godefroid, A.V. Nori, S.K. Rajamani, and S.D. Tetali. Compositional May-Must Program Analysis: Unleashing The Power of Alternation. In *Proceedings of POPL'2010*, pages 43–55, Madrid, January 2010.

[18] J. Hoenicke, K. R. M. Leino, A. Podelski, M. Schaf, and Th. Wies. It's doomed; we can prove it. In *Proceedings of 2009 World Congress on Formal Methods*, 2009.

[19] Sarfraz Khurshid, Corina S. Păsăreanu, and Willem Visser. Generalized Symbolic Execution for Model Checking and Testing. In *Proceeding of TACAS'2003*, April 2003.

[20] J. C. King. Symbolic Execution and Program Testing. *Journal of the ACM*, 19(7):385–394, 1976.

[21] B. Korel. A Dynamic Approach of Test Data Generation. In *IEEE Conference on Software Maintenance*, pages 311–317, San Diego, November 1990.

[22] D. Molnar, X. C. Li, and D. Wagner. Dynamic test generation to find integer bugs in x86 binary linux programs. In *Proc. of the 18th Usenix Security Symposium*, Aug 2009.

[23] P. Saxena, D. Akhawe, S. Hanna, F. Mao, S. McCamant, and D. Song. A Symbolic Execution Framework for JavaScript. In *IEEE Symposium on Security and Privacy*, pages 513–528, 2010.

[24] N. Tillmann and J. de Halleux. Pex - White Box Test Generation for .NET. In *Proceedings of TAP'2008*, volume 4966 of *Lecture Notes in Computer Science*, pages 134–153. Springer-Verlag, April 2008.

[25] M. Yannakakis. Testing, Optimization, and Games. In *Proceedings of LICS'2004*, pages 78–88, Turku, July 2004.

```
/* addsym - add symbol and definitions to symbol table
 *
 * -1 is returned if the symbol already exists, and the change not made.
 */

static int addsym (sym, str_def, int_def, table, table_size)
     register char sym[];
     char    *str_def;
     int      int_def;
     hash_table table;
     int      table_size;
{
        int      hash_val = hashfunct (sym, table_size);
        register struct hash_entry *sym_entry = table[hash_val];
        register struct hash_entry *new_entry;
        register struct hash_entry *successor;

        while (sym_entry) {
                if (!strcmp (sym, sym_entry->name)) {   /* entry already exists */
                        return -1;
                }

                sym_entry = sym_entry->next;
        }

        /* create new entry */
        new_entry = (struct hash_entry *)
                flex_alloc (sizeof (struct hash_entry));

        if (new_entry == NULL)
                flexfatal (_("symbol table memory allocation failed"));

        if ((successor = table[hash_val]) != 0) {
                new_entry->next = successor;
                successor->prev = new_entry;
        }
        else
                new_entry->next = NULL;

        new_entry->prev = NULL;
        new_entry->name = sym;
        new_entry->str_val = str_def;
        new_entry->int_val = int_def;

        table[hash_val] = new_entry;

        return 0;
}

/* findsym - find symbol in symbol table */

static struct hash_entry *findsym (sym, table, table_size)
     register const char *sym;
     hash_table table;
     int      table_size;
{
        static struct hash_entry empty_entry = {
                (struct hash_entry *) 0, (struct hash_entry *) 0,
                (char *) 0, (char *) 0, 0,
        };
        register struct hash_entry *sym_entry = table[hashfunct (sym, table_size)];

        while (sym_entry) {
                if (!strcmp (sym, sym_entry->name))
                        return sym_entry;
                sym_entry = sym_entry->next;
        }

        return &empty_entry;
}
```

Figure 4. Code excerpt from the flex lexer (file sym.c, flex-2.5.35, February 2008).

LeakChaser: Helping Programmers Narrow Down Causes of Memory Leaks

Guoqing Xu Michael D. Bond Feng Qin Atanas Rountev
Department of Computer Science and Engineering
Ohio State University
{xug,mikebond,qin,rountev}@cse.ohio-state.edu

Abstract

In large programs written in managed languages such as Java and C#, holding unnecessary references often results in memory leaks and bloat, degrading significantly their run-time performance and scalability. Despite the existence of many leak detectors for such languages, these detectors often target low-level objects; as a result, their reports contain many false warnings and lack sufficient semantic information to help diagnose problems. This paper introduces a specification-based technique called LeakChaser that can not only capture precisely the unnecessary references leading to leaks, but also explain, with high-level semantics, why these references become unnecessary.

At the heart of LeakChaser is a three-tier approach that uses varying levels of abstraction to assist programmers with different skill levels and code familiarity to find leaks. At the highest tier of the approach, the programmer only needs to specify the boundaries of coarse-grained activities, referred to as transactions. The tool automatically infers liveness properties of these transactions, by monitoring the execution, in order to find unnecessary references. Diagnosis at this tier can be performed by any programmer after inspecting the APIs and basic modules of a program, without understanding of the detailed implementation of these APIs. At the middle tier, the programmer can introduce application-specific semantic information by specifying properties for the transactions. At the lowest tier of the approach is a liveness checker that does not rely on higher-level semantic information, but rather allows a programmer to assert lifetime relationships for pairs of objects. This task could only be performed by skillful programmers who have a clear understanding of data structures and algorithms in the program.

We have implemented LeakChaser in Jikes RVM and used it to help us diagnose several real-world leaks. The implementation incurs a reasonable overhead for debugging and tuning. Our case studies indicate that the implementation is powerful in guiding programmers with varying code familiarity to find the root causes of several memory leaks—even someone who had not studied a leaking program can quickly find the cause after using LeakChaser's iterative process that infers and checks properties with different levels of semantic information.

PLDI'11, June 4–8, 2011, San Jose, California, USA.

Categories and Subject Descriptors D.3.4 [*Programming Languages*]: Processors—Memory management, optimization, run-time environments; F.3.2 [*Logics and Meaning of Programs*]: Semantics of Programming Languages—Program analysis; D.2.5 [*Software Engineering*]: Testing and Debugging—Debugging aids

General Terms Language, Measurements, Performance

Keywords LeakChaser, memory leak detection, object lifetime assertions

1. Introduction

A memory leak in a managed language such as Java or C# occurs when references to some unused objects are unnecessarily held so that these objects cannot be garbage collected. Memory leaks crash programs when they exhaust the heap, and can frequently cause performance issues due to increased garbage collection (GC) runs and execution redundancies.

Problem: lack of semantics in leak detection Memory leak detection in Java software has recently gained much interest in the programming language and systems communities [8, 9, 10, 18, 20, 23, 29, 33, 36]. All existing detectors except one [36] track behaviors of arbitrary objects and report problems when tracked objects become *suspicious*. One major category of work [8, 9, 10, 18, 33] considers objects' staleness (i.e., time elapsed since the program last used these objects) as an indicator of problematic behavior, while another category [20, 23] treats objects as suspicious if instances of their types exhibit sustained growth. While both heuristics are reasonable in many cases, they are not *definitive evidence* of leaking objects because many normal objects can also exhibit such behaviors. For example, growing numbers of instances are not leaks if they are reclaimed later. And some GUI widgets may never be used after they are initialized, i.e., they become very stale—but they are not necessarily leaks. In addition, these leak detectors attempt to find root causes by starting from the suspicious objects (i.e., the leak symptom) and traversing the object graph. Due to the complexity of the graph, this attempt is often a heuristics-based process that ends up reporting a sea of likely problems with the true causes being buried among them. Because a memory leak often occurs due to the inappropriate handling of certain events and these tools profile the whole program execution without any focus, there is little hope that a completely automated tool can precisely pinpoint the problematic area(s) for large-scale Java applications. While prior work avoids heuristics by focusing on containers [36], the root causes of many memory leaks are not containers, but instead cached references that the programmer forgot to invalidate, as represented by the leak cases in SPECjbb2000 and Eclipse bug #115789 (Section 5).

For a more focused leak detector, it is necessary to take advantage of human insights and use programmer specifications to guide leak detection. While prior work proposes heap assertions that can be checked during GC [3, 5, 30, 35], these low-level assertions may only be employed by programmers who have deep understanding of an application (e.g., algorithms, data structures, etc.). This requirement limits significantly their usefulness in leak detection for existing Java applications (i.e., because no prior assertions were written during development), as very few performance experts have sufficient program knowledge to use these assertions during post-mortem tuning.

Insight Almost all memory leaks we have studied are in regularly occurring program events: unnecessary references can quickly accumulate and cause the memory footprint to grow if each such event forgets to clean up a small number of references.

The techniques proposed in this paper are based on the following two observations about these frequently occurring code regions. First, in these regions there usually exist implicit invariants among lifetimes of objects (e.g., "objects a and b must die together," or "the old configuration object must die before the new configuration object is created"). When such invariants are violated, memory leaks result. It is often not easy to use reachability-based heap assertions from prior work to express these lifetime relationships. Second, for each such region, there often exist objects that are strongly correlated with the liveness of the entire region. For example, consider a (web or database) transaction in an enterprise Java application. A typical lifecycle consists of a sequence of events such as the creation of the transaction object, the creation of all other objects used in this transaction, the deallocation of these (other) objects, and the deallocation of the transaction object. For this lifecycle, the transaction object is the first one that is created and the last one that is reclaimed, and it is thus the object that controls the liveness of this entire transaction region.

Our proposal We propose a three-tier approach that exploits these insights to help a programmer quickly identify unnecessary references leading to a memory leak. This approach can be used by both novices and experts to diagnose memory problems. The key idea is to introduce high-level semantics by explicitly considering coarse-grained events where leaks are observed. We refer to these events as *transactions*. As extensions of—and inspired by—enterprise transaction models (e.g., EJB transactions), our transactions describe frequently executed code regions with user-defined boundaries. Objects associated with a transaction fall into three categories: (1) transaction identifier object, (2) transaction-local objects, and (3) objects shared among transactions.

The identifier object of a transaction controls the lifetime of the transaction: all transaction-local objects should be created after this object is created and should die before it dies. Only shared objects are allowed to live after the identifier object dies. Next, we introduce the three tiers of our approach in descending order of their levels of abstraction, which is often the order in which a programmer uses our tool to solve a real-world problem.

Tier H (the high-level approach): At this highest level of the approach, our framework attempts to automatically *infer* transaction-local and shared objects from the execution, while the programmer only needs to specify transaction boundaries and identifier objects. The tool starts to work in the inference mode, and once objects shared among transactions are identified, it switches to check whether the (inferred) shared objects can actually be used in other transactions. Violations are reported if these shared objects are not used for a certain period of time. The programmer's task at this level is the easiest to perform: we found that even when we had not studied a program before, we could quickly identify these (coarse-grained) events in order to perform the diagnosis.

Tier M (the medium-level approach): In this tier, the user needs to specify not only the boundary of a transaction and the transaction identifier object, but also the objects shared across transactions, which the user does not specify in tier H.

LeakChaser *checks* the given specifications, and reports violations if the specified transaction-local objects in one instance of the transaction escape to another instance. While employing this tier of the tool requires the user to have a deeper understanding of the program and the likely cause of the problem, it can generate a more precise report.

Tier L (the low-level approach): This lowest level is essentially an assertion framework that allows the user to specify lifetime invariants for focused memory leak detection. The framework contains binary assertions that directly express object lifetime relationships. For instance, one important assertion is to specify that object a must die before object b. This assertion fails only when LeakChaser observes definitive evidence, e.g., b is dead while a is still live.

Compared to reachability-based assertions [3, 5, 30, 35], our framework has three advantages. First, passing/failing of our assertions does not depend on where GC runs are triggered and thus, assertion checking does not produce false positives. Second, program locations where our assertions are placed have no influence on the evaluation of these assertions. For example, we can assert that object a dies before object b immediately after they are created, while a reachability-based assertion such as *assertDead* in prior work has to be placed in a location where the asserted object is about to become unreachable [3]. Third, our framework can be used to assert arbitrary objects whose lifetimes are correlated due to some high-level semantics (e.g., events), while a reachability-based assertion can work only on objects that have low-level structural relationships (e.g., reachability in the object graph).

Of course, using this assertion framework requires one to understand considerable design and implementation details of the program such as how a data structure is constructed. However, performing this level of diagnosis can give the user a very precise report. Hence, these assertions can be added by developers during coding, which may ease significantly the diagnosis of memory problems when performance degradation is observed. In fact, the transaction-based properties described in the other two tiers are translated by our framework into these low-level assertions at run time. Section 3 presents details about this translation.

As the level of abstraction decreases (from tier H to tier L), the diagnosis becomes more focused. Figure 1 illustrates the process of memory leak detection using this framework. In our experience, LeakChaser is especially useful to a performance expert who is unfamiliar with the program code, since he or she can follow an iterative process that involves all these levels of diagnosis (i.e., from tier H down to tier L). The programmer starts with the tier H analysis with little program knowledge and insight. By repeating a higher-level analysis a few times (with refined specifications) and inspecting its reports, the programmer gains a deeper understanding of the program as well as more insight into the problem, and then will be able to move on to a lower-level analysis for a more focused diagnosis. Very often, this process ends up narrowing down the information to the exact cause of the leak.

For large-scale applications, LeakChaser allows programmers to specify transactions at *clients* of these applications, without digging into application implementation details. For example, to diagnose problems in a large database system, the programmer only needs to create transactions at client programs that perform database queries. We found that this feature of the tool is quite useful in simplifying the diagnostic task: all previous techniques require a programmer to understand a fair amount of low-level details of the system before she can start the diagnosis. This burden is reduced significantly by LeakChaser.

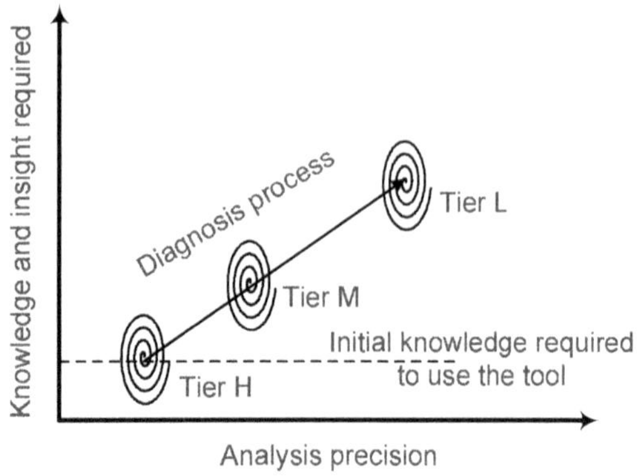

Figure 1. Illustration of the diagnosis process. Spirals at each level indicate that a user may need to run each tier multiple times with refined specifications (e.g., smaller transaction regions, more precise shared object specifications, etc.) to gain sufficient knowledge to proceed to a lower tier.

Implementation and experiments We implemented our approach in Jikes RVM 3.1.0 (`http://jikesrvm.org`), a high-performance Java-in-Java virtual machine, and successfully applied it to real leaks in large-scale applications such as Eclipse and MySQL. The implementation techniques are discussed in detail in Section 4. Section 6 evaluates analysis expenses. We add one extra word in the header of each run-time object and this space is used to store the assertion information for the object. The overall space overhead of the tool is less than 10%, including both extra header space and memory used to store the metadata of our analysis. Using the optimizing compiler and the Immix garbage collector [6], the current implementation imposes an average slowdown of 2.3× for GC only and 1.1× for overall executions for the framework infrastructure (i.e., no assertions added). Additional overhead is incurred for checking and inferring specifications. For example, after adding assertions to SPECjbb2000, 256,236 assertions were executed, and overall slowdown was 5.5×. While the overhead is probably high for production runs, we found it acceptable for performance tuning and memory leak diagnosis.

Section 5 presents six case studies on real-world memory leak problems. Among these problems, four are true leaks and for the remaining two, programmers experienced high memory footprints but were not sure whether or not there were leaks. Using our tool, we have quickly identified root causes for the true leaks, and found reasons that could explain the high memory consumption for the other two cases. In SPECjbb2000, in addition to the already-known leak, we found memory issues that have not been reported previously and actually cause more severe performance degradation than the already-known leak.

We observed significant performance improvements after fixing these problems. The experimental results strongly indicate that the proposed three-tier diagnosis methodology can be adopted in real-world development and tuning to find and prevent memory leaks, and LeakChaser is useful in helping a programmer quickly identify unnecessary references that lead to leaks and other memory issues.

The contributions of this work are:

- A three-layer methodology that introduces different levels of abstraction to help both experts and novices understand and diagnose memory leak problems.
- A new heap assertion framework that allows programmers to assert object liveness properties instead of using reachability to approximate liveness.
- An implementation of LeakChaser in Jikes RVM that piggybacks on garbage collection to check assertions.
- Six case studies demonstrating that LeakChaser can help a programmer unfamiliar with the program source code to quickly find root causes of memory leaks.

2. Overview

We illustrate our technique using a simplified version of a real-world memory leak (Eclipse bug #115789). Figure 2(a) shows the code that contains the leak. This bug can be easily reproduced on Eclipse 3.1.2 when comparing the structures of two large JAR files multiple times using an Eclipse built-in comparison option. Method `runCompare` implements a comparison operation (in plugin `org.eclipse.compare`). It is invoked every time the comparison option is chosen, and this information can be easily obtained from the Eclipse plugin APIs. The method takes a parameter of type `ISelection` that contains information about the two selected files to be compared. A `ResourceCompareInput` object is first created using this parameter (line 3). This object is fairly heavyweight as it caches the complete structures of the two files. The names of these files are then recorded in a list `visitedFiles` (lines 4 and 5), and this list may be used by the workspace GUI upon receiving a user request to view the history.

Next, `openCompareEditorOnPage` is invoked to open a compare editor in the workspace GUI that shows the differences between the two files. The (simplified) method body is shown at lines 11–17. In this method, the newly created `ResourceCompareInput` object is cached in a `NavigationHistoryInfo` object retrieved from the current workbench page for future save or restore operations (lines 14–16). Caching this heavyweight input object is actually the cause of the leak: the structures of the two files keep being created and referenced. As a result, the memory footprint grows quickly, and Eclipse runs out of memory. Note that in the real Eclipse code, this cache operation (at line 16) and the `runCompare` method are in two different plugins, which makes it particularly hard to diagnose the problem as these plugins are written by different groups of programmers. The two plugins communicate only through public interfaces and it is unclear to programmers of one plugin what side effects the other plugin can have. It is interesting to see that despite the fact that the developers of plugin `org.eclipse.compare` are aware that the input must be cleared after the comparison (e.g., in fact, the comment at line 8 is from the real code), these references are still unnecessarily kept somewhere out of their scope.

While these plugins have been studied in previous work [8, 20], we start with the tier H approach to simulate what a programmer would do at the beginning of a diagnostic task. Hence, our experience with this case, to a large degree, reflects how a programmer unfamiliar with a program can use the tool to diagnose memory leaks. We first need to identify a transaction and let the tool infer unnecessary references for the transaction. This is easy: as the comparison is the regularly occurring event leading to the leak, it is a natural idea to let the transaction cross the entire body of method `runCompare`, as shown in Figure 2(a). A transaction creation (at line 2) takes two parameters: a transaction identifier object and a mode in which the transaction works. The identifier object must be unique per transaction and must be created before the transaction starts. Here we choose *s* to be the identifier object, because *s* refers to an `ISelection` object that is created per comparison operation before `runCompare` runs. Constant *INFER* informs the tool to run in the inference mode. We found that the identifier object is usually easy to find for a transaction: a transaction body often crosses a method that is invoked on an existing object. In many cases, either the receiver object or a parameter object of the method can be se-

```
1 void runCompare(ISelection s) {
2 transaction(s, INFER){
3   fInput = new ResourceCompareInput (s);
4   visitedFiles.add(new String(s.left));
5.  visitedFiles.add(new String(s.right));
      ...
6   openCompareEditorOnPage
7                (fInput, fWorkbenchPage);
8   fInput= null; // don't reuse this input!
9 }
10}

11 static void openCompareEditorOnPage
12  (CompareEditorInput input,
13                IWorkbenchPage page){
      ...
14   NavigationHistoryInfo info =
15         page.getNavInfo();
16   info.add(input); ...
17 }
```

(a) Tier H: inferring unnecessary references

```
1 void runCompare(ISelection s) {
2  transaction(s, CHECK){
3   fInput = new ResourceCompareInput (s);
4   share {
5     visitedFiles.add(new String(s.left));
6     visitedFiles.add(new String(s.right));
7   }
      ...
8   openCompareEditorOnPage
9                (fInput, fWorkbenchPage);
10  fInput= null; // don't reuse this input!
11 }
12 }
```

(b) Tier M: checking transaction properties

```
1 void runCompare(ISelection s) {
2   fInput = new ResourceCompareInput (
3   assertDB(fInput, s);
      ...
4   openCompareEditorOnPage
5                (fInput, fWorkbenchPage);
6   fInput = null; // don't reuse.. }
```

(c) Tier L: specific lifetime assert

Figure 2. Overview of the technique, illustrated using a simplified version of Eclipse bug #115789.

lected as the transaction identifier object (as long as it is created per transaction and does not cross multiple transaction invocations).

For each transaction, its *spatial boundary* is specified by a pair of curly brackets (i.e., {...}) and its *temporal boundary* is defined by the lifetime of its identifier object. To find unnecessary references, we focus on objects created within its spatial boundary, and check their lifetimes against its temporal boundary. Informally, the semantics of a transaction is such that each *transaction-local* object must die[1] before the identifier object, and only *shared* objects can live after the identifier object dies. In the inference mode where a programmer does not explicitly specify local and shared objects, our tool infers shared objects automatically: objects created within the spatial boundary are treated as shared objects if they are still live at the time the identifier object dies. Once an object is marked as shared, the tool starts tracking its *staleness* and records a violation if it is not used for a given period of time, based on the intuition that objects that one transaction intends to share with other transactions should be used outside their creating transaction. Violations are aggregated and eventually reported in the order of their frequencies.

The following example shows a typical violation report that includes information about the transaction where the violating object is created, its creation site, violation type, the number of times this violation occurs, and the (heap) reference paths that lead to this object at the time of the violation. Each line in a reference path shows the information of an object on the path. While only one reference path is shown here (for illustration) for this violation, multiple paths were actually reported by the tool.

```
Transaction specified at:
   CompareAction:runCompare(ISelection), ln 2
Violating objects created at:
   CompareEditorInput:createOutlineContents
                 (widgets.Composite), ln 439
Violation type:
   Objects shared among transactions are not used
Frequency: 4
Reference paths:
    Type: ArrayList, created at: NavigationHistory:
                             <init>(WorkbenchPage), ln 44
--> Type: Object[], created at: ArrayList: <init>(I), ln 119
--> Type: NavigationHistoryEditorInfo, created at:
                  NavigationHistory: createEntry(...), ln 553
--> Type: ResourceCompareInput, created at: CompareAction:
                                 runCompare(ISelection), ln 3
```

[1] In this paper, an object is considered to die immediately after it becomes unreachable in the object graph.

This reference path makes it easy to explain why this `ResourceCompareInput` object is shared: the reference path exists because the object is cached (transitively) by a `NavigationHistory` object. However, this is not the only violation in the tier H report. The two strings created at lines 4 and 5 (together with many other objects) are also in the report as they are not used at all if there is no user request to perform history-related operations. It takes some time to inspect this report, as it contains a total of 36 violations. By ranking violations (based on frequencies and other factors), it is not hard for us to eliminate many of them that are lower on the list and that are obviously not leaks. For example, after inspecting the warnings, we determine that these small strings (and other similar objects) are not the major cause of the leak, because the growth of used memory is so significant that it is unlikely to be due to small objects (especially because their frequencies are not significantly higher).

As we obtain this knowledge (regarding these strings and other irrelevant violating objects), we move down to tier M for a more focused analysis. In Figure 2(b), we explicitly mark these strings (and others created by the two `add` calls) as shared (with a *share* region) and let our tool run in checking mode. Objects created in the transaction but not in the share region are marked (implicitly) as transaction-local objects. Our tool then ignores objects marked as shared and reports violations only when transaction-local objects are found live after the transaction identifier object dies. This gives us a much cleaner report (with 4 violations), and of course, the violation shown earlier appears in the report, indicating the `ResourceCompareInput` object is referenced from somewhere else.

After these two rounds of diagnosis, we have gained implementation knowledge (e.g., the general procedure of performing a comparison operation) and some insights into the problem (e.g., this leak might be caused by an unnecessary reference somewhere in `NavigationHistory`). During code inspection, we become interested in the comments in line 8 of the code: this statement has a clear purpose of releasing the input object, but why did we see it is still reachable in both tier M and tier H reports? Having this question in mind, we decide to perform a detailed (tier L) diagnosis using a lifetime assertion (e.g., `assertDB` asserts a "dies-before" relationship), as shown in Figure 2(c). This single assertion fails, which confirms our suspicions.

After some code inspection (with the help of the reference path associated with the violation), we found that `NavigationHistory` allows a user to step backward and forward through browsed editor windows. It keeps a list of `NavigationHistoryEntry` objects, each of which points to an `EditorInfo` object that, in turn, points to a `CompareEditorInput` object, the root of a data structure that holds the diff results. `NavigationHistory` uses a count to control the number of `EditorInfo` objects it caches, and removes an `EditorInfo` if the count drops to zero. However, `NavigationHistory` does not correctly decrement this count in some cases, leading to unnecessary references.objects.

This example clearly shows the difficulty of diagnosing real-world memory problems. The root cause of this bug is that the `NavigationHistory` entries are cached and not getting removed due to reference-counting problems. This occurs entirely on the UI side. The developers of the `compare` plugin may have never thought that calling a general interface to open an UI editor can cause a big chunk of memory to be cached. The complexity of the large-scale code base and the limited knowledge of each individual developer strongly call for LeakChaser's step-by-step approach. Such tool support can help a programmer who starts without insights into the program or its leak, to systematically explore the leaky behavior in order to pinpoint its cause.

3. Assertions and Transactions

This section presents a formalism to describe our analysis of unnecessary references. The presentation proceeds in three steps. First, we define a simple garbage-collected language `assert` and its abstract syntax. We next give a semantics of this language by focusing on its *traces*. Each trace is a sequence of basic events (e.g., alloc, dealloc, and use) on objects, transaction events (e.g., start and end), and assertions. Finally, we formulate assertion checking and inference of unnecessary references as judgments on traces (i.e., trace validation). Note that in our implementation (discussed in Section 4), checking and inference are performed during GC runs. Here the trace collection phase and the trace validation phase are separated for ease of presentation and formal development.

Language `assert` The abstract syntax and the semantic domains for language `assert` are defined in Figure 3. The program has a fixed set of global reference-typed variables. An allocation site has the form a = new ref^o, where o stands for an allocation site ID defined at compile time.

There are two types of assertions: `assertDB` and `assertDBA`. `assertDB`(a, b) asserts that object (pointed to by) a must die before (or together with) object (pointed to by) b. object a must die before a new object is created by object b's allocation site (i.e., it is short for "Dies Before Allocation"). This assertion is useful to enforce a "replaces" relationship between two objects. For example, it can be used to enforce that an old (invalid) screen configuration is appropriately released before a new screen configuration is created upon repainting of an interface in a GUI program. As another example, in Figure 2(c), instead of using `assertDB`, we can also write `assertDBA(fInput, fInput)` to assert that the current `ResourceCompareInput` object must die before the next `ResourceCompareInput` object (created by the same allocation site) is allocated. While our framework includes a few other assertions, they are not discussed because they can be implemented using these two basic assertions.

Variables	a, b		$\in$ V
Allocation sites	o		$\in$ O
Instance fields	f		$\in$ F
Labels	l		$\in$ N
Assertions	e	::=	assertDB(a, b) | assertDBA(a, b)
Transactions	t	::=	transaction(a, m){ tb }
Trans bodies	tb	::=	s ; tb | share { s } tb | ϵ
Trans modes	m	::=	CHECK | INFER
Statements	s	::=	$a = b$ | a = new ref^o | a = null | while ...
			| $a = b.f$ | $a.f = b$ | e | gc | if ... | s ; s
Program	p	::=	s ; p | t ; p | ϵ

(a)

Labeled object	$\hat{o}$	::=	$o^l \in \Phi$
Environment	ρ	$\in$	$\mathsf{V} \to \Phi \cup \{\bot\}$
Heap	σ	$\in$	$\Phi \times \mathsf{F} \to \Phi \cup \{\bot\}$
Operation	τ	::=	$\langle \hat{o}, \mathrm{A} \mid \mathrm{D} \mid \mathrm{U} \rangle^o \mid \langle \hat{o}, m, \mathrm{S} \mid \mathrm{E} \rangle^t$
			$\mid \langle \mathrm{S} \mid \mathrm{E} \rangle^s \mid \langle \hat{o}_a, \hat{o}_b, \mathrm{DBA} \mid \mathrm{DB} \rangle^a$
Traces	α	::=	$\tau , \alpha \mid \epsilon$

(b)

Figure 3. A simple `assert` language: (a) abstract syntax (b) semantic domains.

To ease the formal development, a GC run can only be triggered by a `gc` statement, which traverses the object graph to reclaim unreachable objects. Note that we do not allow the nesting of transactions. While this is easy to implement in our framework, we have not found it helpful for pinpointing memory leak causes.

Each run-time object is labeled with its allocation site (e.g., o) and an integer (e.g., l), denoting the index of this object among all created by the allocation site. Environment and heap are defined in standard ways. A trace is a sequence of operations. There are four types of operations, each of which is a tuple annotated with a type symbol: o for object operation, t for transaction operation, s for share region operation, and a for assert operation. Each *object operation* is an object and event pair, where an event can be either A (i.e., Alloc), D (i.e., Dealloc), or U (i.e., Use). Each *transaction operation* is a triple containing its identifier object, the mode (i.e., CHECK or INFER), and whether this operation corresponds to the start of the transaction (S) or its end (E). A *share region operation* has only a type that indicates whether it is the start or the end of the region. Each *assert operation* contains two input objects and an assertion type (DBA for `assertDBA` and DB for `assertDB`). While the language does not explicitly consider threads, our analysis is thread-safe as each transaction creation is a thread-local event. Different transaction instances created by different threads can exist simultaneously for the same transaction declaration. Trace collection and validation are also performed on a per-thread basis. A special symbol $\bot$ is added to the heap and the environment to represent a `null` value.

Language semantics An operational semantics is given in Figure 4. A judgment of the form $s, \rho, \sigma, \alpha \Downarrow \rho', \sigma', \alpha'$ starts with a statement s, which is followed by environment ρ, heap σ, and trace α. The execution of s terminates with a final environment ρ', heap σ', and trace α'. Trace concatenation is denoted by $\circ$. Rules NEW, ASSERTDB, ASSERTDBA, and COMP are defined as expected. In rules LOAD and STORE, trace α is augmented with an object use event. In rule TRAN, for each transaction, the two transaction events (i.e., S and E) are added in the beginning and at the end of the trace for the execution of the sequence of statements in the transaction. The share region events are handled in a similar way (in rule SHAREREG). Rule GC removes unreachable objects from the heap, and records deallocation events for them in the trace α.

$$\frac{\alpha' = \alpha \circ \langle \hat{o}, \mathrm{A}\rangle^{o} \qquad \hat{o}.allocsite = o \qquad \hat{o}.l = \mathrm{newObjIndex}(o)}{a = \mathrm{new\ ref}^{o}, \rho, \sigma, \alpha \Downarrow \rho[a \mapsto \hat{o}], \sigma, \alpha'} \quad (\textsc{New})$$

$$a = b.f, \rho, \sigma, \alpha \Downarrow \rho[a \mapsto \sigma(\rho(b).f)], \sigma, \alpha \circ \langle \rho(b), \mathrm{U}\rangle^{o} \quad (\textsc{Load})$$

$$a.f = b, \rho, \sigma, \alpha \Downarrow \rho, \sigma[\rho(a).f \mapsto \rho(b)], \alpha \circ \langle \rho(a), \mathrm{U}\rangle^{o} \quad (\textsc{Store})$$

$$\frac{s, \rho, \sigma, \alpha \circ \langle \rho(a), m, \mathrm{S}\rangle^{t} \Downarrow \rho', \sigma', \alpha' \qquad \alpha'' = \alpha' \circ \langle \rho(a), m, \mathrm{E}\rangle^{t}}{\mathrm{transaction}(a, m)\{s\}, \rho, \sigma, \alpha \Downarrow \rho', \sigma', \alpha''} \quad (\textsc{Tran})$$

$$\frac{s, \rho, \sigma, \alpha \circ \langle \mathrm{S}\rangle^{s} \Downarrow \rho', \sigma', \alpha' \qquad \alpha'' = \alpha' \circ \langle \mathrm{E}\rangle^{s}}{\mathrm{share}\{s\}, \rho, \sigma, \alpha \Downarrow \rho', \sigma', \alpha''} \quad (\textsc{ShareReg})$$

$$\mathrm{assertDB}(a, b), \rho, \sigma, \alpha \Downarrow \rho, \sigma, \alpha \circ \langle \rho(a), \rho(b), \mathrm{DB}\rangle^{a} \quad (\textsc{AssertDB})$$

$$\mathrm{assertDBA}(a, b), \rho, \sigma, \alpha \Downarrow \rho, \sigma, \alpha \circ \langle \rho(a), \rho(b), \mathrm{DBA}\rangle^{a} \quad (\textsc{AssertDBA})$$

$$\frac{tr = \circ\{\langle \hat{o}, \mathrm{D}\rangle^{o} \mid \hat{o} \in \sigma \wedge \hat{o} \notin \mathrm{reachable}(\rho, \sigma)\} \qquad \forall \langle \hat{o}, \mathrm{D}\rangle^{o} \in tr : \hat{o} \notin \sigma' \qquad \alpha' = \alpha \circ tr}{\mathrm{gc}, \rho, \sigma, \alpha \Downarrow \rho, \sigma', \alpha'} \quad (\textsc{GC})$$

$$\frac{s_1, \rho, \sigma, \alpha \Downarrow \rho', \sigma', \alpha' \qquad s_2, \rho', \sigma', \alpha' \Downarrow \rho'', \sigma'', \alpha''}{s_1; s_2, \rho, \sigma, \alpha \Downarrow \rho'', \sigma'', \alpha''} \quad (\textsc{Comp})$$

Figure 4. Operational semantics.

$$\frac{\underline{\nexists \hat{o}_1 : (\hat{o}_1, \hat{o}.allocsite) \in \pi} \qquad \gamma' = \gamma \cup (\hat{o}, \mathrm{top}(\omega)), \text{ if } \omega \neq \emptyset \wedge \mathrm{top}(\omega) \neq \bot \qquad \gamma' = \gamma, \text{ otherwise}}{\omega, \gamma, \pi, \iota \vdash \langle \hat{o}, \mathrm{A}\rangle^{o} \rightsquigarrow \omega, \gamma', \pi, \iota} \quad (\textsc{VAlloc})$$

$$\frac{\gamma' = \gamma \backslash \{(\hat{o}, *)\} \qquad \pi' = \pi \backslash \{(\hat{o}, *)\} \qquad \underline{\nexists \hat{o}_1 : (\hat{o}_1, \hat{o}) \in \gamma} \wedge \iota' = \iota \backslash \{(\hat{o}, *)\}, \text{ if } \omega = \emptyset \vee \mathrm{MODE} = \mathrm{CHECK} \qquad \iota' = (\iota \backslash \{(\hat{o}, *)\}) \cup \{(\hat{o}_1, 0) \mid (\hat{o}_1, \hat{o}) \in \gamma\}, \text{ otherwise}}{\omega, \gamma, \pi, \iota \vdash \langle \hat{o}, \mathrm{D}\rangle^{o} \rightsquigarrow \omega, \gamma', \pi', \iota'} \quad (\textsc{VDealloc})$$

$$\frac{\omega' = \omega \circ \hat{o} \qquad \mathrm{MODE} = m \qquad \pi' = \pi \cup (\hat{o}, \hat{o}.allocsite) \qquad \iota' = \iota[\forall \hat{p} : \hat{p} \mapsto \iota(\hat{p}) + 1]}{\omega, \gamma, \pi, \iota \vdash \langle \hat{o}, m, \mathrm{S}\rangle^{t} \rightsquigarrow \omega', \gamma, \pi, \iota'} \quad (\textsc{VTransS})$$

$$\frac{\omega = \omega' \circ \hat{o} \qquad \underline{\forall \hat{p} \in \mathrm{dom}(\iota) : \iota(\hat{p}) < \mathrm{T}}}{\omega, \gamma, \pi, \iota \vdash \langle \hat{o}, m, \mathrm{E}\rangle^{t} \rightsquigarrow \omega', \gamma, \pi, \iota} \quad (\textsc{VTranE})$$

$$\frac{\iota' = \iota \backslash \{(\hat{o}, *)\}}{\omega, \gamma, \pi, \iota \vdash \langle \hat{o}, \mathrm{U}\rangle^{o} \rightsquigarrow \omega, \gamma, \pi, \iota'} \quad (\textsc{VUse})$$

$$\omega, \gamma, \pi, \iota \vdash \langle \mathrm{S}\rangle^{s} \rightsquigarrow \omega \circ \bot, \gamma, \pi, \iota \quad (\textsc{VShareS})$$

$$\frac{\omega = \omega' \circ \bot}{\omega, \gamma, \pi, \iota \vdash \langle \mathrm{E}\rangle^{s} \rightsquigarrow \omega', \gamma, \pi, \iota} \quad (\textsc{VShareE})$$

$$\omega, \gamma, \pi, \iota \vdash \langle \hat{o}_1, \hat{o}_2, \mathrm{DB}\rangle^{a} \rightsquigarrow \omega, \gamma \cup \{(\hat{o}_1, \hat{o}_2)\}, \pi, \iota \quad (\textsc{VDB})$$

$$\omega, \gamma, \pi, \iota \vdash \langle \hat{o}_1, \hat{o}_2, \mathrm{DBA}\rangle^{a} \rightsquigarrow \omega, \gamma, \pi \cup \{(\hat{o}_1, \hat{o}_2.allocsite)\}, \iota \quad (\textsc{VDBA})$$

$$\frac{\omega, \gamma, \pi, \iota \vdash \tau \rightsquigarrow \omega', \gamma', \pi', \iota' \qquad \omega', \gamma', \pi', \iota' \vdash \alpha \rightsquigarrow \omega'', \gamma'', \pi'', \iota''}{\omega, \gamma, \pi, \iota \vdash \tau, \alpha \rightsquigarrow \omega'', \gamma'', \pi'', \iota''} \quad (\textsc{VTrace})$$

where

$\omega \in$	*Transaction stack*:	$\mathsf{N} \rightarrow \Phi \cup \{\bot\}$
$\gamma \in$	*"diesBefore" map*:	$\Phi \rightarrow \Phi$
$\pi \in$	*"diesBeforeAlloc" map*:	$\Phi \rightarrow \mathsf{O}$
$\iota \in$	*Staleness map for shared objects*:	$\Phi \rightarrow \mathsf{N}$
MODE:	Mode of transaction (CHECK or INFER)	
T:	Threshold staleness value	

Figure 5. Checking and inferring of unnecessary references.

Trace validation Checking and inference of unnecessary references are formulated as judgments $\omega, \gamma, \pi, \iota \vdash \alpha \rightsquigarrow \omega', \gamma', \pi', \iota'$ on traces. Here α is an execution trace, ω is a stack of transactions and share regions, γ is a "diesBefore" map in which each pair ($\hat{o}_a$, $\hat{o}_b$) has been asserted to have a "diesBefore" relationship (i.e., $\hat{o}_a$ must die before $\hat{o}_b$), π is a "diesBeforeAlloc" map which contains pairs ($\hat{o}_a$, o) where object $\hat{o}_a$ has been asserted to die before allocation site o creates a new object, and ι maps each object that has been marked shared (i.e., in inference mode) to its staleness value (measured in terms of the number of transactions). As we currently do not support nested transactions, ω can contain at most one transaction identifier object (and one $\bot$ symbol indicating the execution is in a share region). Transaction nesting can be implemented easily by allowing ω to contain multiple identifier objects.

The validation rules are given in Figure 5. Validity checks are underlined, and the remaining clauses (without underlines) are for environment updates. Rule VALLOC first ensures that if an object $\hat{o}_1$ has been asserted to die before this allocation site creates a new object (i.e., due to an `assertDBA` assertion), $\hat{o}_1$ is not live anymore. A violation is recorded if there is such an object. If ω is not empty (meaning the execution is currently in a transaction) and `top`(ω) is not $\bot$ (meaning we are not in a share region), a pair ($\hat{o}$, top(ω)) is added to map γ because, as mentioned earlier, all transaction-local objects are asserted to die before the transaction identifier object, and top(ω) returns the identifier object of the current transaction.

VDEALLOC removes all entries $\langle \hat{o}, * \rangle$ in the three maps upon the deallocation of $\hat{o}$. If there is no running transaction, or the running transaction is in CHECK mode, this rule checks if there exists $\langle \hat{o}_1, \hat{o} \rangle \in \gamma$. If this is the case, a violation is reported, because $\hat{o}_1$ is still live at the time $\hat{o}$ dies. If the running transaction is in INFER mode, such $\hat{o}_1$ is marked as a shared object and the tool starts to track its staleness: a pair $(\hat{o}_1, 0)$ is added to map ι.

Rule VTRANS first pushes the transaction identifier object onto stack ω. It then adds a "diesBeforeAlloc" assertion on the identifier object itself: adding a pair $(\hat{o}, \hat{o}.allocsite)$ indicates that this current instance $\hat{o}$ is asserted to die before allocation site $\hat{o}.allocsite$ creates a new object. As the lifetimes of transaction identifier objects are used to specify temporal boundaries of transactions, they are not allowed to overlap. Lifetime overlapping can lead to ambiguity of transaction behaviors. For each object inferred to be a shared object (i.e., $\hat{p} \in \mathrm{dom}(\iota)$), its staleness value is incremented. An object's staleness is defined as the number of transactions since it has been marked as shared. At the end of each transaction (rule VTRANE), this staleness value is checked against a user-defined threshold T. A violation is reported if a shared object's staleness exceeds this threshold. This rule also pops stack ω. This stack becomes empty after this rule, indicating that no transaction is currently running.

VUSE removes from ι an object marked as shared: its staleness is no longer tracked because the object is used. Rules VSHARES/VSHAREE push/pop $\bot$ onto/from stack ω. Having $\bot$ on top of ω means the execution is in a share region of a transaction. Rule VTRACE specifies the composition of two different traces.

Our system allows one to specify transactions and assertions simultaneously in a program. Transaction properties are translated into basic assertions, which are checked together with assertions specified by programmers. For example, upon the allocation of each object $\hat{o}$ in a transaction (shown in VALLOC), $\hat{o}$ and the transaction identifier object (i.e., top(ω)) are added into map γ, and

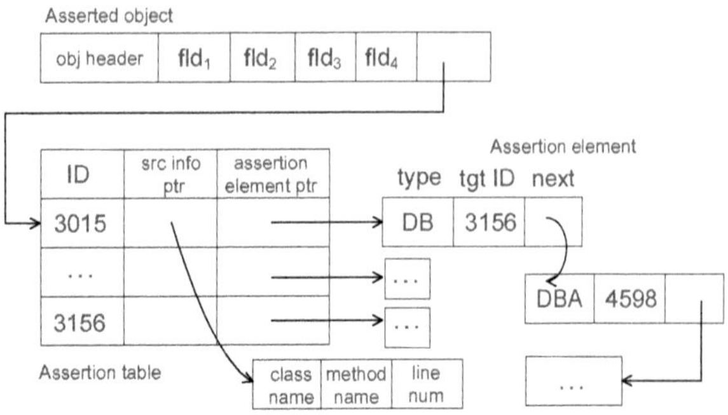

Figure 6. Assertion table implementation that allows quick assertion checks.

this relationship is checked in exactly the same way as a normal `assertDB` assertion (shown in VDB).

4. Implementation

We have implemented LeakChaser in Jikes RVM 3.1.0, a high-performance Java virtual machine [1]. LeakChaser is publicly available on the Jikes RVM Research Archive.[2]

Metadata and instrumentation LeakChaser adds one word to the header of each object that tracks the allocation site information of the object. There are two dynamic compilers in Jikes that transform Java bytecode into native code. The baseline compiler compiles each method when it first executes. When a method becomes hot (i.e., executed frequently), the optimizing compiler recompiles it at increasing levels of optimizations. LeakChaser adds instrumentation to both compilers. LeakChaser adds instrumentation at each allocation site that stores an identifier for the source code location (class, method, and line number) into the allocated object's extra header word.

Garbage collection LeakChaser performs assertion checks during garbage collection runs. It uses a table structure (discussed shortly) to represent the assertions, and scans this table to perform checks at the end of each GC run.

To implement quick assertion checks, we create an assertion table, shown in Figure 6, to record asserted "diesBefore" and "diesBeforeAlloc" relationships during the execution. Once a pair of objects is asserted, we create an assertion table entry for each of them, and then update the LeakChaser-reserved header word in each object with the address of the object's corresponding assertion table entry. The pointer to the source code information of the object initially stored in this space is moved to a field of this table entry.

For each table entry, we let its "assertion element pointer" field point to a linked list of assertion elements, each of which represents an object that has been asserted together with this object. For example, for an assertion `assertDB`(a, b), we create an assertion element (`DB`, id_b, null) and store its address in a's assertion table entry. Once a new assertion `assertDBA`(a, c) is executed, a new assertion element (`DBA`, id_c, null) is created and appended to the list (i.e., now the previous element's next field points to this new element). In this way, all objects that have been asserted through `assert...`(a,...) are in an assertion chain that is going to be checked when a's entry is traversed. We do not need to create an assertion element representing a and associate it with b and c's table entries, as this unnecessarily duplicates information.

The current implementation of LeakChaser supports all non-generational garbage collectors (e.g., MarkSweep, MarkCompact, and Immix). At the end of each GC run, the assertion table is scanned twice: the first scan marks entries that correspond to objects that are unreachable in this GC (i.e., dead objects), and the second scan performs violation detection. Hence, in the second scan, all table entries represent live objects. In order to slow down the growth of the assertion table, table entries corresponding to unreachable objects are reclaimed and reassigned later to newly asserted objects. Our current implementation does not work correctly in a generational garbage collector, as a nursery GC scans only part of the heap and thus may cause LeakChaser to report either false positives or false negatives.

For each entry, its assertion element chain is traversed. For an element whose type is `DB`, if the object represented by this element has been reclaimed, we report a violation. It is much more difficult to check a `DBA` assertion. We create a global array (per thread) and each entry in this array records the status of an allocation site. Once an `assertDBA`(a, b) assertion is executed, the array entry corresponding to b's allocation site is marked as "ASSERTED". When this allocation site creates a new object, the status of its array entry is changed to "ALLOCATED". During the scanning of the assertion table, for an assertion element (`DBA`, i, *), a violation is reported if the entry of this global array corresponding to the allocation site of the object whose assertion table entry id is i is "ALLOCATED", because it creates a new object before the asserted object dies. No false information can result from assertion failures reported by the tool because the assertions directly specify the liveness of objects (instead of reachability on the object graph) and report violations only when definitive evidence is observed.

In this paper, we focus on the real-world utility of LeakChaser, rather than its performance. Hence, this assertion table is scanned during every GC. Future work coul incorporate sampling to reduce overhead (i.e., scan the assertion table less frequently). To report the reference paths that lead to a violating object, we modify the worklist-based algorithm used by the tracing collector in a way so that when a reachable object is added into the worklist, its reference path (from which it is reached) is also added (to another worklist). The length of this path can be determined by the user. We develop a technique that aggregates violations of objects that are created by the same allocation sites and whose reference paths match, so that a violation is reported only after its (aggregated) frequency exceeds a user-defined threshold value. LeakChaser filters out violations that are associated with VM objects. Future work could consider more powerful aggregation and ranking functions, such as a combination of frequency, staleness, and the amount of memory leaked. In order to make LeakChaser work for a generational GC, future work could perform the two assertion table scans separately: the first scan (that marks dead objects) would be performed at the end of every GC, while the second scan (that checks assertions and detects violations) would be performed only at the end of each full-heap GC.

5. Case Studies

We have evaluated LeakChaser on six real, reported memory leaks. While our ultimate goal is to evaluate with enterprise-level applications such as application servers and programs running on top of them, Jikes RVM fails to run some larger server applications (such as `trade` in the latest DaCapo benchmark set [7]).

For these six cases, we also applied Sleigh [8], a publicly available research memory leak detector for Java. Sleigh finds leaks by tracking the staleness of arbitrary objects and reporting allocation and last-use sites for stale objects.

For each case, we compared our report with the report generated by Sleigh, and found that first, for the same amount of running time, information reported by our (even tier H) approach is much more relevant than that reported by Sleigh. Sleigh requires much more time to collect information and generate relatively precise re-

[2] `http://www.jikesrvm.org/Research+Archive`

Case	*#Tran*	*#TO*	*#LO*	*#SO*	*#V*	*#F*
Diff	8	2048148	1707244	340904	36	14
Jbb	4346	256236	186752	69484	14	4
Editor	12	512471	506620	5851	2	13
WTP	20	2774556	2767237	7319	27	39
MySQL	10000	319529	170902	148627	11	0
Mckoi	100	2689366	2243888	445478	10	193

Table 1. Tier H statistics for transactions for the case studies. Shown are the number of transaction runs (#Tran), the total number of objects tracked (#TO), the number of transaction-local objects (#LO), the number of shared objects inferred (#SO), the number of violations reported after filtering (#V), and the number of violations filtered by our filtering system (#F).

ports because it is designed for production runs and uses only one bit per object to encode information statistically, whereas LeakChaser tracks much more information for debugging and tuning (at a higher cost). We did not run Sleigh for as much time as in the prior work [8], and thus Sleigh results are different from those reported earlier. Second, our iterative technique produces more precise information at each tier, which eventually guides us to the root causes of leaks.

Experience summary We found that it is quite easy to specify transactions in large programs even for users who have never studied the programs before. From our experience using LeakChaser, we generalize an approach that can be employed by performance experts to select transactions. All large-scale applications we have studied can be classified into two major categories: event-based systems (e.g., web servers and GUI applications) and transaction-based systems (e.g., enterprise Java applications and databases). An event-based system often uses a loop to deal with different events received and dispatch them to their corresponding handlers. For such a system, our transaction can cross the body of the loop; that is, the handling of each event is treated as a transaction. Each event object can be used as the identifier object for the transaction. It is much easier to determine a transaction for a transaction-based system, as each "system transaction" in the original program can be naturally treated as a transaction in LeakChaser.

A particularly useful feature of LeakChaser is that it allows programmers to quickly specify transactions at a *client* that interacts with a complex system, without digging into the system to understand its implementation details. For example, we diagnose Eclipse framework bugs by specifying transactions in plugins (i.e., clients) that trigger these bugs. Likewise, for databases such as `MySQL` and `Mckoi`, we only need to create transactions at client programs that perform database queries. This feature allows performance experts like us (who are unfamiliar with these databases) to quickly get started with LeakChaser. If we could not put transactions around clients, it would be hard to even find a starting point in these systems that have thousands of classes and millions of lines of code.

Table 1 shows transaction and assertion statistics for all six cases. Despite the large number of assertions checked for each benchmark, LeakChaser reports a small number of warnings. We show statistics for tier H only, as it is the coarsest-grained approach and thus runs the most assertions and reports the most violations.

Diff *(Eclipse bug #115789)* We quickly found this bug using our three-tier approach and the detailed diagnosis process discussed in Section 2.

We have tried Sleigh on this program and the top four last-use sites (i.e., where objects are last used) reported by Sleigh are in class `java.util.HashMap` (e.g., in methods `put` and `addEntry`).

In this case, the sites leading to these `HashMap` operations point back to method `createContainer` in class `org.eclipse.compare.ZipFileStructureCreator`, which indicates that the structures of input files are cached but not used. At this point, it is completely up to the programmer to find out why these structures become stale and which objects reference them. Recall that even a violation reported by our tier H approach shows the violating object is referenced by a `NavigationHistory` object, which is actually the root cause of the leak (shown in in Section 2). According to [8], Sleigh could have reported much more precise information if the program was run for significantly more time. For example, LeakChaser reported the root cause after only 8 structure diffs were performed, while Sleigh may need more than 1000 diffs to report relatively precise information regarding where the stale objects are created. In addition, as we observed in our experiments, reporting reference paths can be more helpful for finding leak root causes than reporting program locations, which are usually far from where the true problem occurs.

Jbb SPECjbb2000 simulates an online trading system. It contains a known memory leak that has been studied many times [3, 8, 20, 36]. This bug is caused by unnecessary caching of `Order` objects. To investigate the usefulness of LeakChaser in helping programmers unfamiliar with the code, we attempt to simulate what these programmers would do. First, we need to understand the basic modules and functions of the program so that we can identify regularly occurring events. This is not hard at all, as SPECjbb is a transaction-based system where a `TransactionManager` class runs different transactions types, and the transaction-creating method is only a few calls away from method `main`. This method contains a loop that retrieves a command from an input map per iteration, and creates and runs a transaction whose type corresponds to the command received. This was the knowledge we obtained quickly before trying the tier H approach.

Problem 1: unused objects We added a transaction that encloses the main Jbb transaction-creating method. Each Jbb transaction object is used as the transaction identifier object of its corresponding transaction. We ran the program on our modified VM and let LeakChaser infer unnecessary references. The tool reports 14 violations (detailed statistics are shown in Table 1). Most of the violating objects are `String` and `History` objects cached in orders, and the rest are `Order` objects transitively referenced by `District` objects. We inspected the source code and found that these `String` objects are created to represent district information or names of order lines, and the `History` objects are used to represent histories of orders made by each company. These objects are indeed never used in the program. We modified the program to eliminate these unused strings and `History` objects. The throughput improvements are shown in Figure 7(a). We did not expect to find this problem, which had not been reported before.

Problem 2: mutual references It was unclear to us what to do about the `Order` objects reported above: while many are not used again, some are retrieved by subsequent transactions. We further inspect the code in order to run a more focused diagnosis. The reference paths in our tier H report show that the unused `Order` objects are referenced by `Customer` objects and then by `Company` objects. Following this clue, we inspect all classes related to `Company` and `Customer`. One clear piece of information that we can take advantage of is the ownership relationships among `Company` and `Customer` objects and objects referenced by them. For example, each customer has an order array that stores orders made by that customer. It is clearly problematic if a customer object dies while an order made from this customer is still alive. Using this information, we wrote 72 `diesBefore` assertions to assert such relationships.

We easily added these assertions in constructors, wherever an owned object is assigned to an owner object. Running this version of the program resulted in 4 violations, all of which are related to orders. By inspecting reference paths associated with these viola-

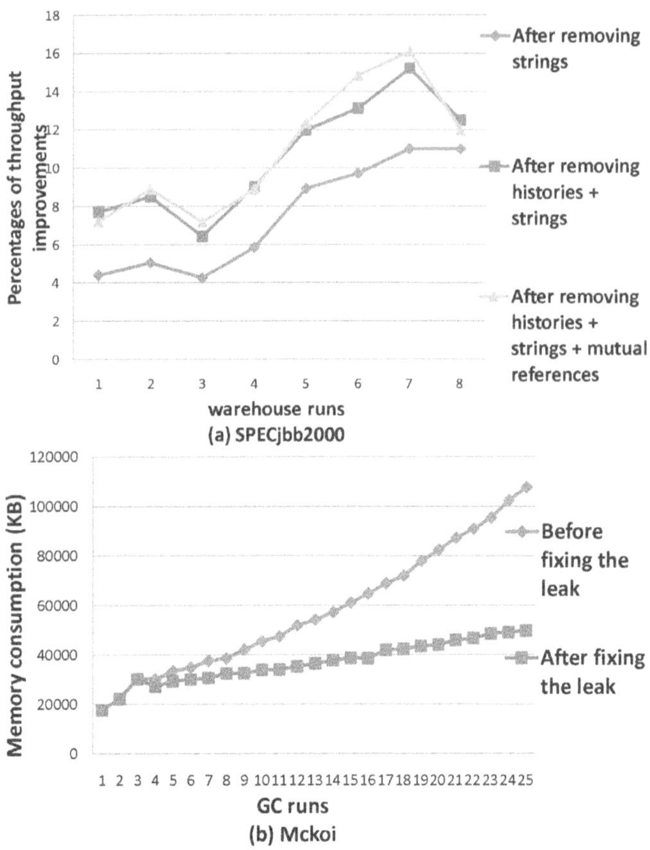

Figure 7. (a) Throughput improvements after fixing the memory problems detected in SPECjbb; (b) Comparison between the memory footprints of Mckoi before and after fixing the leak.

tions, we found the following three important problems. (1) `Order` and `Customer` are mutually referenced, which explains the persistent increase in `Order` objects, even though customers frequently drop orders. (2) `Customer` objects are not released even after their container arrays in `Company` die. They are not released because `Company` holds unnecessary references to these objects. (3) `Order` and `Heap` are mutually referenced, which prevents `Heap` objects from being garbage collected. Fixing all of these problems (including the unused `String` and `History` objects) led to both the elimination of the quick growth of memory consumption and an overall 12.7% throughput improvement (from 13,644 to 15,372 ops/sec). Previous work has not reported all of these problems that we found using LeakChaser.

An important last-use site reported by Sleigh is in method `getObject` of a BTree data structure that is used to retrieve `Order` objects from customers. The associated calling contexts tell us that this call is made transitively by `processLine`. While this is indeed a method that needs to be fixed, the key to understanding the problem is learning about the mutual references among `Order` and other classes. Without such reference information, it remains a daunting task to identify the root cause and develop a fix.

Editor *(Eclipse bug #139465)* This reported memory leak in Eclipse 3.2 occurs when opening a `.outline` file using a customized editor and making selections on the "outline" page. Objects created while displaying the file keep accumulating, and Eclipse eventually crashes. This bug is still open because users can rarely reproduce the leak. While we could not observe the reported symptoms, we still ran the test case with LeakChaser. We wrote a plugin that repeats multiple times the process of opening the editor, making selections, and closing the editor. We added a transaction in this plugin that crosses each such process (which manipulates the editor), and used the editor object as the transaction identifier.

The tier H approach reported only two violations even when we set a very small number (2) as the staleness threshold (see T in Figure 5). For each violation, we could not find any object on its associated reference paths that is related to the editor of interest. Hence, we quickly concluded that there were no unnecessary references for this case in Eclipse 3.2 on the Linux platform where we ran the experiment: had there existed a problem with respect to a transaction, it should have been reported by the tier H approach, as the approach captures references to all objects that are shared but not used. For this case, Sleigh reported four last-use sites, and we found it difficult to verify whether or not these sites are relevant. The key is to understand how these objects are reachable in the heap, instead of where they are used in the program.

WTP *(Eclipse bug #155898)* According to the bug report for this memory leak in the Eclipse Web Tool Platform (WTP), the memory footprint grows quickly when copying and pasting large text blocks in the JSP editor associated with the WTP framework. This bug is still open because it cannot always be reproduced. One developer suspected that "the bug might have already been fixed by the addition of other features in a later version of WTP" one year after it was reported. We reproduced the problem and saw the memory footprint growth by writing a plugin that automatically copies and pastes texts several times. Similarly to the previous case, we added a transaction in the plugin and let it cross each iteration that involves a pair of copy-and-paste operations. Our tier H approach reported a total of 26 violations, among which 11 seemed clearly irrelevant to the problem (e.g., regarding Eclipse's Java Development Tools and other plugins).

To confirm this observation, we use this plugin to perform the same copy-and-paste operations in a regular text editor in Eclipse, which does not have memory problems. These 11 violations also appeared in the generated report. Thus, they were safely discarded. As this bug is caused by copying and pasting text, we focus on string-related violations. Only one violation among the remaining 15 is about `String` objects, shown as follows:

```
Transaction specified at:
  Quick_copy_pastePlugin:mouseUp(MouseEvent), ln 258
Violating objects created at:
  StructuredTextUndoManager:createNewTextCommand(String, String),
                                                          ln 302
Violation type:
  objects shared among transactions are not used
Frequency: 28
Reference paths:
    Type: StructuredTextViewerUndoManager, created at:
              StructuredTextViewerConfiguration
              : getUndoManager(ISourceViewer), ln 469
--> Type: StructuredTextUndoManager, created at:
     BasicStructuredDocument: getUndoManager(), ln 1823
--> Type: BasicCommandStack, created at:
        StructuredTextUndoManager : <init>(), ln 160
--> Type: ArrayList, created at: BasicCommandStack: <init>(),
                                                        ln 67
--> Type: Object[], created at: ArrayList: ensureCapacity(I),
                                                       ln 176
```

This violation clearly shows that the strings are (transitively) referenced by a text undo manager. This information quickly directed us to classes responsible for undo operations. The cause of the problem was clear to us almost immediately after inspecting how an undo operation is performed. In this JSP editor, all commands (and their related data) are cached in a command stack, in case an undo is requested in the future. There is a tradeoff between "undoability" (i.e., how many commands are cached) and performance, especially when there is a large amount of data being cached with each command. In this version of WTP (WTP 1.5 with Eclipse 3.2.0), this command stack can grow to be very deep (it is not cleared even when a save operation is performed), and thus, many strings can be cached, leading to significant performance degradation. A later version has limited the depth of this stack (for other purposes), implicitly fixing this bug. For this case, we understood the problem even without moving to tier M. We did not manage to run Sleigh for this case, as Sleigh was developed on top of an older version of Jikes RVM (2.4.2), which cannot run Eclipse 3.2.

MySQL leak This case is a simplified version of a JDBC application that exhausts memory if the application keeps using the same connection but different SQL statements to access the database. Prior work reproduced this leak to evaluate tolerating leaks [9], but no prior work reports the leak cause. The leak occurs because the JDBC library caches already-executed SQL statements in a container unless the statements are explicitly closed. We create a transaction that crosses the creation and execution of each `PreparedStatement` (in a loop). We executed 100 iterations, and the tier H approach reported 10 violations, all of which were related to `PreparedStatement` (i.e., regarding either the statement object itself, or objects reachable from the statement).

From the associated reference paths, it took only a few minutes for us to identify the container that caches the statements: a `HashMap` created at line 1486 (in the constructor) of class `com.mysql.jdbc.Connection`. For this case, Sleigh reported warnings after the program ran for 303 iterations, significantly longer than for LeakChaser. Sleigh reported a few last-use sites where `PrepareStatement` objects are last touched. We did not find the `HashMap` information in Sleigh's report, which is the key to tracking down this leak bug.

Mckoi leak Mckoi is an open-source SQL database system written in Java (`http://www.mckoi.com`). It contains a leak that previous work reproduced to evaluate leak survival techniques [9, 10]. However, none of the existing work has investigated the root cause of the leak. We reproduced the leak by writing a client that repeatedly (100 times) establishes a connection, executes a few SQL queries, and closes the connection. We started with our tier H approach and created a transaction that crosses each iteration of this process in the client. Our tool reported 10 warnings, all regarding objects that are reachable from a thread object of type `DatabaseDispatcher`. In all the warnings reported, this thread object references a `DatabaseSystem` object, which transitively caches many other never-used objects. By inspecting only the constructors of `DatabaseSystem` and `DatabaseDispatcher`, we found that they are mutually referenced. The creation of each `DatabaseSystem` object explicitly creates a `DatabaseDispatcher` object and runs this thread in the background. There are two major problems:

(1) `DatabaseDispatcher` runs in a `while(true)` loop, which means no `DatabaseSystem` object can ever be garbage collected even though its `dispose` method is invoked. To address this problem, we broke this reference cycle when `dispose` is invoked on `DatabaseSystem`. Next, in `DatabaseDispatcher`, we modified the `while(true)` loop to terminate if its referenced `DatabaseSystem` object becomes null. This modification resulted in a very slight improvement in performance, leading us to believe there must be a bigger problem.

(2) A `DatabaseSystem` object can be created in two situations. (a) A new database needs to be started (e.g., a connection is established); (b) a method `dbExists` (that checks whether a database instance has already been there) is called. In every iteration, two `DatabaseSystem` objects are created but only one of them gets disposed. The one created by `dbExists` is never reclaimed, because `dispose` is not explicitly invoked on this object, which we quickly discovered by using a call graph generated by an IDE tool. The developer took it for granted that this object would be garbage collected, but it is referenced by a live thread. We added a call that invokes `dispose` at the end of method `dbExists`.

For this case, all warnings generated by Sleigh are about objects cached (transitively) by `DatabaseSystem`, and they are far away from the leaking thread. It would be difficult to understand why these objects are not garbage collected without appropriate reference paths, as reported by LeakChaser. The memory footprint of the database before and after the leak is fixed is shown in Figure 7(b). The original version of the program ran out of memory at the 106th iteration, while the modified version ran indefinitely (as far as we could tell).

These six case studies demonstrate that developers do not need to have much implementation knowledge in order to diagnose leaks with LeakChaser. LeakChaser generates more relevant reports than Sleigh: it is easier to find the root cause from reference chains that cache a violating object, than from the allocation or last-use site of the object.

6. Overhead

We evaluated the performance of our technique using 19 programs from the SPECjvm98 [34] and DaCapo [7] benchmarks, on a dual-core machine with an Intel Xeon 2.83GHZ processor, running Linux 2.6.18. We ran each program using the large workload.

Table 2 reports the time and space overheads that our tracking infrastructure incurs on normal executions (without assertions or transactions written). The overhead measurements that we show in this section are obtained based on a (high-performance) FastAdaptiveImmix configuration that uses the optimizing compiler and the state-of-the-art Immix garbage collection algorithm [6].

The LeakChaser infrastructure slows programs by less than 10% on average using the optimizing compiler and an advanced garbage collector. Much of the overhead comes from extra operations during GC and the barrier inserted at each object reference read to check the use of the object. Column (b) of Table 2 reports the detailed GC slowdown caused by our tool, which is 2.3×, averaged across the 19 programs. The space overheads, reported in column (c) of Table 2, are less than 10%, primarily due to the extra word added to the header of each object. In some cases, the peak memory consumption for LeakChaser is even lower than that for the original run (i.e., *OS* is smaller than 1), presumably because GC is triggered at a different set of program points that happens to have a lower maximum reachable memory size.

The overhead of assertion checking and inference is reported in Table 3. The overall running time measurements are available only for *Jbb*, *MySQL*, and *Mckoi*, as the other three cases are all based on Eclipse IDE operations. Note that in a run with 4,346 transactions and 442,988 objects (shown in Table 1), our tool slows the program 6.6× and 5.5× overall for the two configurations. Similarly to Table 2, the overhead can be larger if we consider only GC time. For example, for *Diff*, a 2.8× slowdown can be seen for GC time for FastAdaptiveImmix. Note that these overheads have not prevented us from collecting data from any real-world application. In a production setting, run-time overhead can be effectively reduced by sampling (i.e., the current sampling rate is 100%). Future work could also define a tradeoff framework between the quality of the reported information and the frequency of assertion table scanning (similar to QVM [5]), and find an appropriate sampling rate that can enable the reporting of sufficient information at acceptably low cost.

7. Related Work

While there exists a large body of work on detecting Java memory leaks, ours is the first semantics-aware approach that uses multiple

Bench	(a) Overall time			(b) GC time			(c) Space		
	T_1	T_2	*OT*	G_1	G_2	*OG*	S_1	S_2	*OS*
check	0.033	0.068	2.1	0.016	0.033	2.0	11.4	10.3	0.9
compr	9.4	9.5	1.0	0.016	0.033	2.0	17.9	18.0	1.0
jess	2.2	2.4	1.1	0.022	0.049	2.2	48.9	58.4	1.2
db	4.9	5.0	1.0	0.024	0.062	2.6	22.2	24.9	1.1
javac	2.1	2.4	1.1	0.030	0.064	2.1	98.1	99.0	1.0
mpeg	6.2	6.2	1.0	0.020	0.039	2.0	19.4	19.8	1.0
mtrt	1.6	1.6	1.0	0.031	0.081	2.6	46.5	43.6	0.9
jack	1.7	1.8	1.0	0.025	0.050	2.0	79.6	76.8	1.0
antlr	38.7	43.2	1.1	0.032	0.074	2.3	53.5	57.3	1.1
bloat	98.3	105.9	1.1	0.073	0.169	2.3	515.1	520.0	1.0
chart	19.7	21.4	1.1	0.084	0.232	2.8	367.4	479.4	1.3
eclipse	150.8	157.5	1.0	0.207	0.465	2.2	512.4	532.7	1.0
fop	1.4	1.8	1.3	0.064	0.15	2.3	107.6	102.2	0.9
hsqldb	9.3	16.4	1.8	0.331	1.21	3.7	420.5	432.6	1.0
jython	45.6	48.6	1.1	0.077	0.172	2.2	119.7	137.8	1.2
luindex	35.3	37.7	1.1	0.031	0.070	2.3	45.5	49.8	1.1
lusearch	7.8	8.1	1.0	0.038	0.088	2.3	105.0	129.5	1.2
pmd	22.9	23.6	1.0	0.055	0.127	2.3	115.3	157.5	1.4
xalan	32.3	39.5	1.2	0.066	0.145	2.2	214.2	209.0	1.0
GeoMean	-	-	1.1	-	-	2.3	-	-	1.1

Table 2. Time and space overheads incurred by our infrastructure for the FastAdaptiveImmix configuration. Shown in column (a) are the original overall execution times (T_1) in seconds, the execution times for our modified JVM (T_2), and the overheads (*OT*) in times ($\times$). Column (b) reports the GC times and overheads: G_1 and G_2 show the average times for each GC run in the original RVM and our modified RVM, respectively. *OG* reports the GC overheads as G_2/G_1. Memory consumption and overheads are shown in column (c): S_1 and S_2 are the maximum amounts of memory used during the executions in the original RVM and our RVM, respectively. *OS* reports the space overheads as S_1/S_2.

Bench	(a) Overall time			(b) GC time			(c) Space		
	T_1	T_2	*OT*	G_1	G_2	*OG*	S_1	S_2	*OS*
Diff	-	-	-	0.27	0.75	2.8	534.2	534.4	1.0
Jbb	50.7*	9.2*	5.5	0.008	0.056	7.0	313.7	315.3	1.0
Editor	-	-	-	0.15	0.41	2.7	300.5	367.2	1.2
WTP	-	-	-	0.22	0.58	2.6	52.7	52.9	1.0
MySQL	6.8	14.0	2.1	0.045	0.108	2.4	17.1	17.7	1.0
Mckoi	165.6	172.2	1.0	0.046	0.154	3.3	129.2	144.2	1.1
GeoMean	-	-	2.3	-	-	3.2	-	-	1.0

Table 3. Overheads for the cases that we have studied under FastAdaptiveImmix. * indicates that we measure throughput (#operations per second) instead of running time. For both MySQL and Mckoi, a fixed number of iterations (100) was run for this measurement.

layers to help programmers at different levels of code familiarities to specify, check, and infer unnecessary references. Related work falls into four major categories: leak detection, bloat analysis, checking of unconventional properties, and GC assertions.

Dynamic analysis for memory leak detection Dynamic analysis [8, 13, 14, 16, 17, 18, 20, 23, 28, 29] has typically been used to detect memory problems. As described in Sections 1 and 5, existing techniques have a number of deficiencies. Commercial leak detectors such as [16, 28] enable visualization of heap objects of different types, but do not provide the ability to pinpoint the cause of a memory leak. Existing research detectors use growing types [20, 23] (i.e., types whose number of instances continues to grow) or object staleness [8, 18] to identify suspicious data structures that may contribute to a memory leak. However, in general, a memory leak caused by redundant references is due to a complex interplay of memory growth and staleness and possibly other factors. In addition, these techniques are often unaware of high-level semantics, and perform whole-program profiling; this leads to less relevant information in the generated reports. Xu and Rountev [36] introduce a technique that profiles container behaviors to detect containers that cache large numbers of unused objects. Novark *et al.*. [27] find memory leaks and bloat in C/C++ programs by segregating objects based on their allocation contexts and staleness. Recent work [14] uses a tainting framework to propagate relevant information in order to identify leaking objects for C/C++ programs.

Fundamentally different from these techniques, our work presents an assertion framework that allows programmers to explicitly express their interests (i.e., related to high-level semantics), based on the insight that developers' knowledge is essential for a leak detector to produce highly relevant reports.

Software bloat analysis As a more general problem [26, 40], software bloat analysis [4, 21, 22, 25, 32, 36, 37, 38, 39] attempts to find, remove, and prevent performance problems due to inefficiencies in the code execution and the use of memory. Prior work [22, 24] proposes metrics to provide performance assessment of use of data structures. Mitchell *et al.* [24] propose a manual approach that detects bloat by structuring behavior according to the flow of information, and their later work [22] introduces a way to find data structures that consume excessive amounts of memory. Work by Dufour *et al.* [15] uses a blended escape analysis to characterize and find excessive use of temporary data structures. By approximating object lifetimes, the analysis has been shown to be useful in classifying the usage of newly created objects in the problematic areas. Shankar *et al.* propose Jolt [32], an approach that makes aggressive method inlining decisions based on the identification of regions that make extensive use of temporary objects. Work by Xu *et al.* [38] detects memory bloat by profiling copy chains and copy graphs. Other work [31] dynamically identifies inappropriately used Java collections and recommends to the user those that should really be used. The technique presented in our work can also be considered as a bloat analysis, and it can be used to find a specific type of bloat caused by unnecessary references.

Asserting and inferring unconventional properties The Java Modeling Language [2] contains a few expressions (such as `\duration` and `\space`) that allow programmers to specify performance-related properties of a program. Burnim and Sen propose an assertion framework [11] to specify that regions of a parallel program behave deterministically despite non-deterministic thread interleavings. They later propose to dynamically infer deterministic specifications for parallel programs from the execution, given a set of inputs and schedules [12].

GC Assertions, QVM, and Merlin Closest to our work are heap property assertion frameworks such as GC Assertions [3, 30] and QVM [5, 35]. For example, one can explicitly specify at a certain program point that an object should be dead soon (i.e, *assertDead*), or that an object must be owned by another object in the object graph (i.e., *assertOwns*). While such assertions can be quite useful in helping diagnosis, they are limited in the following three important aspects related to leak detection.

First, reachability information is used to approximate the liveness of objects, which may result in false positives. For example, *assertOwns* (a, b) asserts a reachability relationship between objects a and b, and it fails when b can be reached in a path that does not contain a in a certain GC run. However, it is possible that object b becomes unreachable from object b in one GC, while later b is owned by a again. Second, because a GC assertion predicts a future heap state (i.e., the state at the closest GC run) and the global reachability information evolves all the time, whether or not this assertion will fail depends significantly on when and where the next GC occurs, which may in turn be affected by many factors, such as the initial and maximum heap sizes and specific GC implementation strategies. Third, these approaches are intended for programmers who have sufficiently deep program knowledge and insights. In real-world software development, only a handful of programmers can have such knowledge, especially when a performance problem occurs in program code that is not written by themselves.

Our work solves the first and second problems by allowing programmers to specify objects' lifetime relationships instead of reachability properties. In order to tackle the third problem, we use a combination of assertion checking and transaction property inference to allow programmers with little application-specific knowledge to quickly identify the cause of the problem.

The GC Assertions [3] framework includes a block-structured *assert-alldead* assertion, which asserts that all objects allocated in the block must be dead by the end of the block. While it is related to the transaction abstractions proposed in this paper, there are two important distinctions between them. First, *assert-alldead* does not allow objects in the specified structure to escape the structure, while our approach allows checking and inferring shared objects, providing more flexibility for diagnosing problems. Second, our transaction abstraction separates temporal and spatial scopes of the structure, while these scopes are combined in this earlier work.

Merlin [19] is an efficient algorithm that can provide precise time-of-death statistics for heap objects by computing when objects die using collected timestamps. LeakChaser could potentially exploit this technique in the future to capture assertion failures between GCs, as we currently report an assertion failure only when it is actually witnessed during a GC run.

8. Conclusions and Future Work

This paper presents the first framework that allows programmers with little program knowledge to quickly find the root cause of a memory leak, by bringing high-level program semantics into low-level leak detection. The most significant advantages of this work over existing Java leak detection tools are that (1) the approach uses lightweight user annotations to improve the relevance of the generated reports, and can provide semantics-related diagnostic information (e.g., which object escapes which transaction), and (2) it is designed in a multi-tier way so that programmers at different levels of skill and code familiarity can use it to identify performance problems. Our experience shows that the three-tier technique is quite effective: the tool can help a programmer identify the root cause of a leak after an iterative process of specifying, inferring, and checking object lifetime properties. For the case studies we conducted, the tool provided more relevant information than an existing memory leak detector Sleigh. For example, using the tool, we quickly found the root causes of memory issues in the analyzed programs, including both known memory leaks and problems that have not been reported before. While LeakChaser incurs relatively large overhead (2.9$\times$ on average), we found it acceptable for debugging and performance tuning.

The assertions and transaction constructs may be easily incorporated into the Java language so that they can be used in a production JVM to help detect memory problems. Similarly to functional specifications that are used widely in program testing and debugging, writing performance specifications can have significant advantages. For example, it could enable *unit performance testing* that can identify performance violations even before degradation is observed. In addition, performance specifications (similar to the ones described in this paper) may help bridge the gap between performance analysis and the large body of work on model checking and verification, so that one may be able to prove (statically) a program is "bloat-free" or "bloat-bounded" with respect to the performance specifications provided.

A possible direction of future work would be to investigate such relationships in order to prevent small performance issues in the early stage of software development, before they pile up and become significant.

Acknowledgments

We thank the PLDI reviewers for their valuable and thorough comments. The initial idea for this work was inspired by a conversation that Guoqing Xu had with Nick Mitchell during an internship with IBM T. J. Watson Research Center. This material is based upon work supported by the National Science Foundation under CAREER grants CCF-0546040 and CCF-0953759, grant CCF-1017204, and by an IBM Software Quality Innovation Faculty Award. Guoqing Xu was supported in part by an IBM Ph.D. Fellowship Award.

References

[1] *The Jikes Research Virtual Machine*, 2011. `http://jikesrvm.org`.

[2] *JML Reference Manual*, 2010. `http://www.jmlspecs.org`.

[3] E. E. Aftandilian and S. Z. Guyer. GC Assertions: Using the garbage collector to check heap properties. In *ACM SIGPLAN Conference on Programming Language Design and Implementation (PLDI)*, pages 235–244, 2009.

[4] E. Altman, M. Arnold, S. Fink, and N. Mitchell. Performance analysis of idle programs. In *ACM SIGPLAN International Conference on Object-Oriented Programming, Systems, Languages, and Applications (OOPSLA)*, pages 739–753, 2010.

[5] M. Arnold, M. Vechev, and E. Yahav. QVM: An efficient runtime for detecting defects in deployed systems. In *ACM SIGPLAN International Conference on Object-Oriented Programming, Systems, Languages, and Applications (OOPSLA)*, pages 143–162, 2008.

[6] S. M. Blackburn and K. S. McKinley. Immix: a mark-region garbage collector with space efficiency, fast collection, and mutator performance. In *ACM SIGPLAN Conference on Programming Language Design and Implementation (PLDI)*, pages 22–32, 2008.

[7] S. M. Blackburn, R. Garner, C. Hoffman, A. M. Khan, K. S. McKinley, R. Bentzur, A. Diwan, D. Feinberg, D. Frampton, S. Z. Guyer, M. Hirzel, A. Hosking, M. Jump, H. Lee, J. E. B. Moss, A. Phansalkar, D. Stefanović, T. VanDrunen, D. von Dincklage, and B. Wiedermann. The DaCapo benchmarks: Java benchmarking development and analysis. In *ACM SIGPLAN International Conference on Object-Oriented Programming, Systems, Languages, and Applications (OOPSLA)*, pages 169–190, 2006.

[8] M. D. Bond and K. S. McKinley. Bell: Bit-encoding online memory leak detection. In *International Conference on Architectural Support for Programming Languages and Operating Systems (ASPLOS)*, pages 61–72, 2006.

[9] M. D. Bond and K. S. McKinley. Leak pruning. In *International Conference on Architectural Support for Programming Languages and Operating Systems (ASPLOS)*, pages 277–288, 2009.

[10] M. D. Bond and K. S. McKinley. Tolerating memory leaks. In *ACM SIGPLAN International Conference on Object-Oriented Programming, Systems, Languages, and Applications (OOPSLA)*, pages 109–126, 2008.

[11] J. Burnim and K. Sen. Asserting and checking determinism for multithreaded programs. In *ACM SIGSOFT International Symposium on the Foundations of Software Engineering (FSE)*, pages 3–12, 2009.

[12] J. Burnim and K. Sen. Determin: Inferring likely deterministic specifications of multithreaded programs. In *International Conference on Software Engineering (ICSE)*, pages 415–424, 2010.

[13] CA Technologies. CA Wily Introscope LeakHunter. `www.ca.com/us/application-management.aspx`.

[14] J. Clause and A. Orso. Leakpoint: pinpointing the causes of memory leaks. In *International Conference on Software Engineering (ICSE)*, pages 515–224, 2010.

[15] B. Dufour, B. G. Ryder, and G. Sevitsky. A scalable technique for characterizing the usage of temporaries in framework-intensive Java applications. In *ACM SIGSOFT International Symposium on the Foundations of Software Engineering (FSE)*, pages 59–70, 2008.

[16] ej-technologies GmbH. JProfiler. `www.ej-technologies.com`.

[17] R. Hastings and B. Joyce. Purify: A tool for detecting memory leaks and access errors in C and C++ programs. In *Winter 1992 USENIX Conference*, pages 125–138, 1992.

[18] M. Hauswirth and T. M. Chilimbi. Low-overhead memory leak detection using adaptive statistical profiling. In *International Conference on Architectural Support for Programming Languages and Operating Systems (ASPLOS)*, pages 156–164, 2004.

[19] M. Hertz, S. M. Blackburn, J. E. B. Moss, K. S. McKinley, and D. Stefanović. Generating object lifetime traces with Merlin. *ACM Transactions on Programming Languages and Systems (TOPLAS)*, 28 (3):476–516, 2006.

[20] M. Jump and K. S. McKinley. Cork: Dynamic memory leak detection for garbage-collected languages. In *ACM SIGPLAN-SIGACT Symposium on Principles of Programming Languages (POPL)*, pages 31–38, 2007.

[21] N. Mitchell. The runtime structure of object ownership. In *European Conference on Object-Oriented Programming (ECOOP)*, pages 74–98, 2006.

[22] N. Mitchell and G. Sevitsky. The causes of bloat, the limits of health. In *ACM SIGPLAN International Conference on Object-Oriented Programming, Systems, Languages, and Applications (OOPSLA)*, pages 245–260, 2007.

[23] N. Mitchell and G. Sevitsky. Leakbot: An automated and lightweight tool for diagnosing memory leaks in large Java applications. In *European Conference on Object-Oriented Programming (ECOOP)*, pages 351–377, 2003.

[24] N. Mitchell, G. Sevitsky, and H. Srinivasan. Modeling runtime behavior in framework-based applications. In *European Conference on Object-Oriented Programming (ECOOP)*, pages 429–451, 2006.

[25] N. Mitchell, E. Schonberg, and G. Sevitsky. Making sense of large heaps. In *European Conference on Object-Oriented Programming (ECOOP)*, pages 77–97, 2009.

[26] N. Mitchell, E. Schonberg, and G. Sevitsky. Four trends leading to Java runtime bloat. *IEEE Software*, 27(1):56–63, 2010.

[27] G. Novark, E. D. Berger, and B. G. Zorn. Efficiently and precisely locating memory leaks and bloat. In *ACM SIGPLAN Conference on Programming Language Design and Implementation (PLDI)*, pages 397–407, 2009.

[28] Quest Software. JProbe. `www.quest.com/jprobe`.

[29] D. Rayside and L. Mendel. Object ownership profiling: A technique for finding and fixing memory leaks. In *International Conference on Automated Software Engineering (ASE)*, pages 194–203, 2007.

[30] C. Reichenbach, N. Immerman, Y. Smaragdakis, E. Aftandilian, and S. Z. Guyer. What can the GC compute efficiently? A language for heap assertions at GC time. In *ACM SIGPLAN International Conference on Object-Oriented Programming, Systems, Languages, and Applications (OOPSLA)*, pages 256–269, 2010.

[31] O. Shacham, M. Vechev, and E. Yahav. Chameleon: Adaptive selection of collections. In *ACM SIGPLAN Conference on Programming Language Design and Implementation (PLDI)*, pages 408–418, 2009.

[32] A. Shankar, M. Arnold, and R. Bodik. Jolt: Lightweight dynamic analysis and removal of object churn. In *ACM SIGPLAN International Conference on Object-Oriented Programming, Systems, Languages, and Applications (OOPSLA)*, pages 127–142, 2008.

[33] Y. Tang, Q. Gao, and F. Qin. LeakSurvivor: Towards safely tolerating memory leaks for garbage-collected languages. In *The USENIX Anual Technical Conference (USENIX)*, pages 307–320, 2008.

[34] The Standard Performance Evaluation Corporation. SPECjvm98 Benchmark Set. http://www.spec.org/jvm98/.

[35] M. Vechev, E. Yahav, and G. Yorsh. PHALANX: Parallel checking of expressive heap assertions. In *International Symposium on Memory Management (ISMM)*, pages 41–50, 2010.

[36] G. Xu and A. Rountev. Precise memory leak detection for Java software using container profiling. In *International Conference on Software Engineering (ICSE)*, pages 151–160, 2008.

[37] G. Xu and A. Rountev. Detecting inefficiently-used containers to avoid bloat. In *ACM SIGPLAN Conference on Programming Language Design and Implementation (PLDI)*, pages 160–173, 2010.

[38] G. Xu, M. Arnold, N. Mitchell, A. Rountev, and G. Sevitsky. Go with the flow: Profiling copies to find runtime bloat. In *ACM SIGPLAN Conference on Programming Language Design and Implementation (PLDI)*, pages 419–430, 2009.

[39] G. Xu, N. Mitchell, M. Arnold, A. Rountev, E. Schonberg, and G. Sevitsky. Finding low-utility data structures. In *ACM SIGPLAN Conference on Programming Language Design and Implementation (PLDI)*, pages 174–186, 2010.

[40] G. Xu, N. Mitchell, M. Arnold, A. Rountev, and G. Sevitsky. Software bloat analysis: Finding, removing, and preventing performance problems in modern large-scale object-oriented applications. In *ACM SIGSOFT FSE/SDP Workshop on the Future of Software Engineering Research*, 2010.

Finding and Understanding Bugs in C Compilers

Xuejun Yang Yang Chen Eric Eide John Regehr
University of Utah, School of Computing
{jxyang, chenyang, eeide, regehr}@cs.utah.edu

Abstract

Compilers should be correct. To improve the quality of C compilers, we created Csmith, a randomized test-case generation tool, and spent three years using it to find compiler bugs. During this period we reported more than 325 previously unknown bugs to compiler developers. Every compiler we tested was found to crash and also to silently generate wrong code when presented with valid input. In this paper we present our compiler-testing tool and the results of our bug-hunting study. Our first contribution is to advance the state of the art in compiler testing. Unlike previous tools, Csmith generates programs that cover a large subset of C while avoiding the undefined and unspecified behaviors that would destroy its ability to automatically find wrong-code bugs. Our second contribution is a collection of qualitative and quantitative results about the bugs we have found in open-source C compilers.

Categories and Subject Descriptors D.2.5 [*Software Engineering*]: Testing and Debugging—testing tools; D.3.2 [*Programming Languages*]: Language Classifications—C; D.3.4 [*Programming Languages*]: Processors—compilers

General Terms Languages, Reliability

Keywords compiler testing, compiler defect, automated testing, random testing, random program generation

1. Introduction

The theory of compilation is well developed, and there are compiler frameworks in which many optimizations have been proved correct. Nevertheless, the practical art of compiler construction involves a morass of trade-offs between compilation speed, code quality, code debuggability, compiler modularity, compiler retargetability, and other goals. It should be no surprise that optimizing compilers—like all complex software systems—contain bugs.

Miscompilations often happen because optimization safety checks are inadequate, static analyses are unsound, or transformations are flawed. These bugs are out of reach for current and future automated program-verification tools because the specifications that need to be checked were never written down in a precise way, if they were written down at all. Where verification is impractical, however, other methods for improving compiler quality can succeed. This paper reports our experience in using testing to make C compilers better.

PLDI'11, June 4–8, 2011, San Jose, California, USA.


```
int foo (void) {
  signed char x = 1;
  unsigned char y = 255;
  return x > y;
}
```

Figure 1. We found a bug in the version of GCC that shipped with Ubuntu Linux 8.04.1 for x86. At all optimization levels it compiles this function to return 1; the correct result is 0. The Ubuntu compiler was heavily patched; the base version of GCC did not have this bug.

We created Csmith, a randomized test-case generator that supports compiler bug-hunting using differential testing. Csmith generates a C program; a test harness then compiles the program using several compilers, runs the executables, and compares the outputs. Although this compiler-testing approach has been used before [6, 16, 23], Csmith's test-generation techniques substantially advance the state of the art by generating random programs that are expressive—containing complex code using many C language features—while also ensuring that every generated program has a single interpretation. To have a unique interpretation, a program must not execute any of the 191 kinds of undefined behavior, nor depend on any of the 52 kinds of unspecified behavior, that are described in the C99 standard.

For the past three years, we have used Csmith to discover bugs in C compilers. Our results are perhaps surprising in their extent: to date, we have found and reported more than 325 bugs in mainstream C compilers including GCC, LLVM, and commercial tools. Figure 1 shows a representative example. Every compiler that we have tested, including several that are routinely used to compile safety-critical embedded systems, has been crashed and also shown to silently miscompile valid inputs. As measured by the responses to our bug reports, the defects discovered by Csmith are important. Most of the bugs we have reported against GCC and LLVM have been fixed. Twenty-five of our reported GCC bugs have been classified as P1, the maximum, release-blocking priority for GCC defects. Our results suggest that fixed test suites—the main way that compilers are tested—are an inadequate mechanism for quality control.

We claim that Csmith is an effective bug-finding tool in part because it generates tests that explore atypical combinations of C language features. Atypical code is *not* unimportant code, however; it is simply underrepresented in fixed compiler test suites. Developers who stray outside the well-tested paths that represent a compiler's "comfort zone"—for example by writing kernel code or embedded systems code, using esoteric compiler options, or automatically generating code—can encounter bugs quite frequently. This is a significant problem for complex systems. Wolfe [30], talking about independent software vendors (ISVs) says: "An ISV with a complex code can work around correctness, turn off the optimizer in one or two files, *and usually they have to do that for any of the compilers they use*" (emphasis ours). As another example, the front page of the Web site for GMP, the GNU Multiple Precision Arithmetic Library, states, "Most problems with compiling GMP these days are due to problems not in GMP, but with the compiler."

Improving the correctness of C compilers is a worthy goal: C code is part of the trusted computing base for almost every modern computer system including mission-critical financial servers and life-critical pacemaker firmware. Large-scale source-code verification efforts such as the seL4 OS kernel [12] and Airbus's verification of fly-by-wire software [24] can be undermined by an incorrect C compiler. The need for correct compilers is amplified because operating systems are almost always written in C and because C is used as a portable assembly language. It is targeted by code generators from a wide variety of high-level languages including Matlab/Simulink, which is used to generate code for industrial control systems.

Despite recent advances in compiler verification, testing is still needed. First, a verified compiler is only as good as its specification of the source and target language semantics, and these specifications are themselves complex and error-prone. Second, formal verification seldom provides end-to-end guarantees: "details" such as parsers, libraries, and file I/O usually remain in the trusted computing base. This second point is illustrated by our experience in testing CompCert [14], a verified C compiler. Using Csmith, we found previously unknown bugs in unproved parts of CompCert—bugs that cause this compiler to silently produce incorrect code.

Our goal was to discover serious, previously unknown bugs:

- in mainstream C compilers like GCC and LLVM;
- that manifest when compiling core language constructs such as arithmetic, arrays, loops, and function calls;
- targeting ubiquitous architectures such as x86 and x86-64; and
- using mundane optimization flags such as –O and –O2.

This paper reports our experience in achieving this goal. Our first contribution is to advance the state of the art in compiler test-case generation, finding—as far as we know—many more previously unknown compiler bugs than any similar effort has found. Our second contribution is to qualitatively and quantitatively characterize the bugs found by Csmith: What do they look like? In what parts of the compilers are they primarily found? How are they distributed across a range of compiler versions?

2. Csmith

Csmith began as a fork of Randprog [27], an existing random C program generator about 1,600 lines long. In earlier work, we extended and adapted Randprog to find bugs in C compilers' translation of accesses to volatile-qualified objects [6], resulting in a 7,000-line program. Our previous paper showed that in many cases, these bugs could be worked around by turning volatile-object accesses into calls to helper functions. The key observation was this: while the rules regarding the addition, elimination, and reordering of accesses to volatile objects are not at all like the rules governing ordinary variable accesses in C, they are almost identical to the rules governing function calls.

For some test programs generated by Randprog, our rewriting procedure was insufficient to correct a defect that we had found in the C compiler. Our hypothesis was that this was always due to "regular" compiler bugs not related to the volatile qualifier. To investigate these compiler defects, we shifted our research emphasis toward looking for generic wrong-code bugs. We turned Randprog into Csmith, a 40,000-line C++ program for randomly generating C programs. Compared to Randprog, Csmith can generate C programs that utilize a much wider range of C features including complex control flow and data structures such as pointers, arrays, and structs. Most of Csmith's complexity arises from the requirement that it

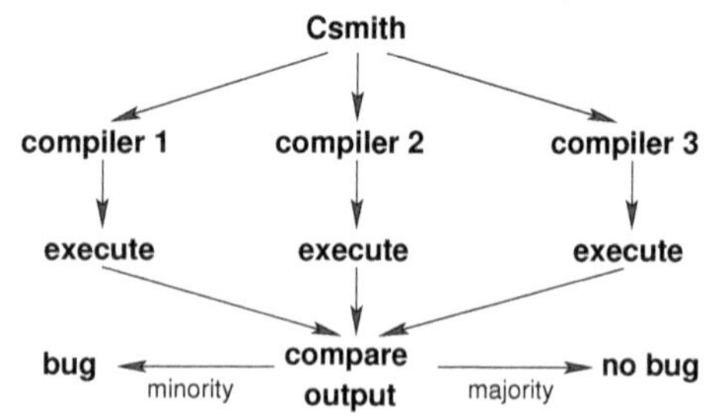

Figure 2. Finding bugs in three compilers using randomized differential testing

interleave static analysis with code generation in order to produce meaningful test cases, as described below.

2.1 Randomized Differential Testing using Csmith

Random testing [9], also called fuzzing [17], is a black-box testing method in which test inputs are generated randomly. Randomized differential testing [16] has the advantage that no oracle for test results is needed. It exploits the idea that if one has multiple, deterministic implementations of the same specification, all implementations must produce the same result from the same valid input. When two implementations produce different outputs, one of them must be faulty. Given three or more implementations, a tester can use voting to heuristically determine which implementations are wrong. Figure 2 shows how we use these ideas to find compiler bugs.

2.2 Design Goals

Csmith has two main design goals. First and most important, every generated program must be well formed and have a single meaning according to the C standard. The meaning of a C program is the sequence of side effects it performs. The principal side effect of a Csmith-generated program is to print a value summarizing the computation performed by the program.[1] This value is a checksum of the program's non-pointer global variables at the end of the program's execution. Thus, if changing the compiler or compiler options causes the checksum emitted by a Csmith-generated program to change, a compiler bug has been found.

The C99 language [11] has 191 *undefined behaviors*—e.g., dereferencing a null pointer or overflowing a signed integer—that destroy the meaning of a program. It also has 52 *unspecified behaviors*—e.g., the order of evaluation of arguments to a function—where a compiler may choose from a set of options with no requirement that the choice be made consistently. Programs emitted by Csmith must avoid all of these behaviors or, in certain cases such as argument-evaluation order, be independent of the choices that will be made by the compiler. Many undefined and unspecified behaviors can be avoided structurally by generating programs in such a way that problems never arise. However, a number of important undefined and unspecified behaviors are not easy to avoid in a structural fashion. In these cases, Csmith solves the problem using static analysis and by adding run-time checks to the generated code. Section 2.4 describes the hazards that Csmith must avoid and its strategies for avoiding them.

Csmith's second design goal is to maximize expressiveness subject to constraints imposed by the first goal. An "expressive" generator supports many language features and combinations of features. Our hypothesis is that expressiveness is correlated with bug-finding power.

[1] Accesses to volatile objects are also side effects as described in the C standard. We do not discuss these "secondary" side effects of Csmith-generated programs further in this paper.

Csmith creates programs with the following features:

- function definitions, and global and local variable definitions
- most kinds of C expressions and statements
- control flow: `if/else`, function calls, `for` loops, `return`, `break`, `continue`, `goto`
- signed and unsigned integers of all standard widths
- arithmetic, logical, and bitwise operations on integers
- structs: nested, and with bit-fields
- arrays of and pointers to all supported types, including pointers and arrays
- the `const` and `volatile` type qualifiers, including at different levels of indirection for pointer-typed variables

The most important language features not currently supported by Csmith are strings, dynamic memory allocation, floating-point types, unions, recursion, and function pointers. We plan to add some of these features to future versions of our tool.

2.3 Randomly Generating Programs

The shape of a program generated by Csmith is governed by a grammar for a subset of C. A program is a collection of type, variable, and function definitions; a function body is a block; a block contains a list of declarations and a list of statements; and a statement is an expression, control-flow construct (e.g., `if`, `return`, `goto`, or `for`), assignment, or block. Assignments are modeled as statements—not expressions—which reflects the most common idiom for assignments in C code. We leverage our grammar to produce other idiomatic code as well: in particular, we include a statement kind that represents a loop iterating over an array. The grammar is implemented by a collection of hand-coded C++ classes.

Csmith maintains a *global environment* that holds top-level definitions: i.e., types, global variables, and functions. The global environment is extended as new entities are defined during program generation. To hold information relevant to the current program-generation point, Csmith also maintains a *local environment* with three primary kinds of information. First, the local environment describes the current call chain, supporting context-sensitive pointer analysis. Second, it contains effect information describing objects that may have been read or written since (1) the start of the current function, (2) the start of the current statement, and (3) the previous sequence point.[2] Third, the local environment carries points-to facts about all in-scope pointers. These elements and their roles in program generation are further described in Section 2.4.

Csmith begins by randomly creating a collection of struct type declarations. For each, it randomly decides on a number of members and the type of each member. The type of a member may be a (possibly qualified) integral type, a bit-field, or a previously generated struct type.

After the preliminary step of producing type definitions, Csmith begins to generate C program code. Csmith generates a program top-down, starting from a single function called by `main`. Each step of the program generator involves the following sub-steps:

1. Csmith randomly selects an allowable production from its grammar for the current program point. To make the choice, it consults a probability table and a filter function specific to the current point: there is a table/filter pair for statements, another for expressions, and so on. The table assigns a probability to each of the alternatives, where the sum of the probabilities is one. After choosing a production from the table, Csmith executes the filter, which decides if the choice is acceptable in the current context. Filters enforce basic semantic restrictions (e.g., `continue` can only appear within a loop), user-controllable limits (e.g., maximum statement depth and number of functions), and other user-controllable options. If the filter rejects the selected production, Csmith simply loops back, making selections from the table until the filter succeeds.
2. If the selected production requires a target—e.g., a variable or function—then the generator randomly selects an appropriate target or defines a new one. In essence, Csmith dynamically constructs a probability table for the potential targets and includes an option to create a new target. Function and variable definitions are thus created "on demand" at the time that Csmith decides to refer to them.
3. If the selected production allows the generator to select a type, Csmith randomly chooses one. Depending on the current context, the choice may be restricted (e.g., while generating the operands of an integral-typed expression) or unrestricted (e.g., while generating the types of parameters to a new function). Random choices are guided by the grammar, probability tables, and filters as already described.
4. If the selected production is nonterminal, the generator recurses. It calls a function to generate the program fragment that corresponds to the nonterminal production. More generally, Csmith recurses for each nonterminal element of the current production: e.g., for each subcomponent of a compound statement, or for each parameter in a function call.
5. Csmith executes a collection of dataflow transfer functions. It passes the points-to facts from the local environment to the transfer functions, which produce a new set of points-to facts. Csmith updates the local environment with these facts.
6. Csmith executes a collection of safety checks. If the checks succeed, the new code fragment is committed to the generated program. Otherwise, the fragment is dropped and any changes to the local environment are rolled back.

When Csmith creates a call to a new function—one whose body does not yet exist—generation of the current function is suspended until the new function is finished. Thus, when the top-level function has been completely generated, Csmith is finished. At that point it pretty-prints all of the randomly generated definitions in an appropriate order: types, globals, prototypes, and functions. Finally, Csmith outputs a `main` function. The `main` function calls the top-level randomly generated function, computes a checksum of the non-pointer global variables, prints the checksum, and exits.

2.4 Safety Mechanisms

Table 1 lists the mechanisms that Csmith uses to avoid generating C programs that execute undefined behaviors or depend on unspecified behaviors. This section provides additional detail about the hazards that Csmith must avoid and its strategies for avoiding them.

Integer safety More and more, compilers are aggressively exploiting the undefined nature of integer behaviors such as signed overflow and shift-past-bitwidth. For example, recent versions of Intel CC, GCC, and LLVM evaluate `(x+1)>x` to 1 while also evaluating `(INT_MAX+1)` to `INT_MIN`. In another example, discovered by the authors of Google's Native Client software [3], routine refactoring of C code caused the expression `1<<32` to be evaluated on a

[2] As explained in Section 3.8 of the C FAQ [25], "A sequence point is a point in time at which the dust has settled and all side effects which have been seen so far are guaranteed to be complete. The sequence points listed in the C standard are at the end of the evaluation of a full expression (a full expression is an expression statement, or any other expression which is not a subexpression within any larger expression); at the `||`, `&&`, `?:`, and comma operators; and at a function call (after the evaluation of all the arguments, and just before the actual call)."

Problem	Code-Generation-Time Solution	Code-Execution-Time Solution
use without initialization	explicit initializers, avoid jumping over initializers	—
qualifier mismatch	static analysis	—
infinite recursion	disallow recursion	—
signed integer overflow	bounded loop vars	safe math wrappers
OOB array access	bounded loop vars	force index in bounds
unspecified eval. order of function arguments	effect analysis	—
R/W and W/W conflicts betw. sequence points	effect analysis	—
access to out-of-scope stack variable	pointer analysis	—
null pointer dereference	pointer analysis	null pointer checks

Table 1. Summary of Csmith's strategies for avoiding undefined and unspecified behaviors. When both a code-generation-time and code-execution-time solution are listed, Csmith uses both.

platform with 32-bit integers. The compiler exploited this undefined behavior to turn a sandboxing safety check into a nop.

To keep Csmith-generated programs from executing integer undefined behaviors, we implemented a family of wrapper functions for arithmetic operators whose (promoted) operands might overflow. This was not difficult, but had a few tricky aspects. For example, the C99 standard does not explicitly identify the evaluation of `INT_MIN%-1` as being an undefined behavior, but most compilers treat it as such. The C99 standard also has very restrictive semantics for signed left-shift: it is illegal (for implementations using 2's complement integers) to shift a 1-bit into or past the sign bit. Thus, evaluating `1<<31` destroys the meaning of a C99 program on a platform with 32-bit ints.

Several safe math libraries for C that we examined themselves execute operations with undefined behavior while performing checks. Apparently, avoiding such behavior is indeed a tricky business.

Type safety The aspect of C's type system that required the most care was *qualifier safety*: ensuring that `const` and `volatile` qualifiers attached to pointers at various levels of indirection are not removed by implicit casts. Accessing a const- or volatile-qualified object through a non-qualified pointer results in undefined behavior.

Pointer safety Null-pointer dereferences are easy to avoid using dynamic checks. There is, on the other hand, no portable run-time method for detecting references to a function-scoped variable whose lifetime has ended. (Hacks involving the stack pointer are not robust under inlining.) Although there are obvious ways to structurally avoid this problem, such as using a type system to ensure that a pointer to a function-scoped variable never outlives the function, we judged this kind of strategy to be too restrictive. Instead, Csmith freely permits pointers to local variables to escape (e.g., into global variables) but uses a whole-program pointer analysis to ensure that such pointers are not dereferenced or used in comparisons once they become invalid.

Csmith's pointer analysis is flow sensitive, field sensitive, context sensitive, path insensitive, and array-element insensitive. A points-to fact is an explicit set of locations that may be referenced, and may include two special elements: the null pointer and the invalid (out-of-scope) pointer. Points-to sets containing a single element serve as must-alias facts unless the pointed-to object is an array element. Because Csmith does not generate programs that use the heap, assigning names to storage locations is trivial.

Effect safety The C99 standard states that "[t]he order of evaluation of the function designator, the actual arguments, and subexpressions within the actual arguments is unspecified." Also, undefined behavior occurs if "[b]etween two sequence points, an object is modified more than once, or is modified and the prior value is read other than to determine the value to be stored."

To avoid these problems, Csmith uses its pointer analysis to perform a conservative interprocedural analysis and determine the *effect* of every expression, statement, and function that it generates. An effect consists of two sets: locations that may be read and locations that may be written. Csmith ensures that no location is both read and written, or written more than once, between any pair of sequence points. As a special case, in an assignment, a location can be read on the RHS and also written on the LHS.

Effects are computed, and effect safety guaranteed, incrementally. At each sequence point, Csmith resets the current effect (i.e., may-read and may-write sets). As fragments of code are generated, Csmith tests if the new code has a read/write or write/write conflict with the current effect. If a conflict is detected, the new code is thrown away and the process restarts. For example, if Csmith is generating an expression `p + func()` and it happens that `func` may modify `p`, the call to `func` is discarded and a new subexpression is generated. If there is no conflict, the read and write sets are updated and the process continues. Probabilistic progress is guaranteed: by design, Csmith always has a non-zero chance of generating code that introduces no new conflicts, such as a constant expression.

Array safety Csmith uses several methods to ensure that array indices are in bounds. First, it generates index variables that are modified only in the "increment" parts of `for` loops and whose values never exceed the bounds of the arrays being indexed. Second, variables with arbitrary value are forced to be in bounds using the modulo operator. Finally, as needed, Csmith emits explicit checks against array lengths.

Initializer safety A C program must not use an uninitialized function-scoped variable. For the most part, initializer safety is easy to ensure structurally by initializing variables close to where they are declared. Gotos introduce the possibility that initializers may be jumped over; Csmith solves this by forbidding gotos from spanning initialization code.

2.5 Efficient Global Safety

Csmith never commits to a code fragment unless it has been shown to be safe. However, loops and function calls threaten to invalidate previously validated code. For example, consider the following code, in which Csmith has just added the loop back-edge at line 7.

```
1  int i;
2  int *p = &i;
3  while (...) {
4    *p = 3;
5    ...
6    p = 0;
7  }
```

The assignment through `p` at line 4 was safe when it was generated. However, the newly added line 7 makes line 4 unsafe, due to the back-edge carrying a null-valued `p`.

One solution to this problem is to be conservative: run the whole-program dataflow analysis before committing any new statement to the program. This is not efficient. We therefore restrict the analysis to local scope except when function calls and loops are involved. For a function call, the callee is re-analyzed at each call site immediately.

Csmith uses a different strategy for loops. This is because so many statements are inside loops, and the extra calls to the dataflow analysis add substantial overhead to the code generator. Csmith's strategy is to optimistically generate code that is *locally safe*. Local safety includes running a single step of the dataflow engine (which reaches a sound result when generating code not inside any loop).

The global fixpoint analysis is run when a loop is closed by adding its back-edge. If Csmith finds that the program contains unsafe statements, it deletes code starting from the tail of the loop until the program becomes globally safe. This strategy is about three times faster than pessimistically running the global dataflow analysis before adding every piece of code.

2.6 Design Trade-offs

Allow implementation-defined behavior An ideally portable test program would be "strictly conforming" to the C language standard. This means that the program's output would be independent of all unspecified and unspecified behaviors and, in addition, be independent of any *implementation-defined behavior*. C99 has 114 kinds of implementation-defined behavior, and they have pervasive impact on the behavior of real C programs. For example, the result of performing a bitwise operation on a signed integer is implementation-defined, and operands to arithmetic operations are implicitly cast to `int` (which has implementation-defined width) before performing the operation. We believe it is impossible to generate realistically expressive C code that retains a single interpretation across all possible choices of implementation-defined behaviors.

Programs generated by Csmith do not generate the same output across compilers that differ in (1) the width and representation of integers, (2) behavior when casting to a signed integer type when the value cannot be represented in an object of the target type, and (3) the results of bitwise operations on signed integers. In practice there is not much diversity in how C implementations define these behaviors. For mainstream desktop and embedded targets, there are roughly three equivalence classes of compiler targets: those where `int` is 32 bits and `long` is 64 bits (e.g., x86-64), those where `int` and `long` are 32 bits (e.g., x86, ARM, and PowerPC), and those where `int` is 16 bits and `long` is 32 bits (e.g., MSP430 and AVR). Using Csmith, we can perform differential testing within an equivalence class but not across classes.

No ground truth Csmith's programs are not self-checking: we are unable to predict their outputs without running them. This is not a problem when we use Csmith for randomized differential testing.

We have never seen an "interesting" split vote where randomized differential testing of a collection of C compilers fails to produce a clear consensus answer, nor have we seen any cases in which a majority of tested compilers produces the same incorrect result. (We would catch the problem by hand as part of verifying the failure-inducing program.) In fact, we have not seen even two unrelated compilers produce the same incorrect output for a Csmith-generated test case. It therefore seems unlikely that all compilers under test would produce the same incorrect output for a test case. Of course, if that did happen we would not detect that problem; this is an inherent limitation of differential testing without an oracle. In summary, despite the fact that Knight and Leveson [13] found a substantial number of correlated errors in an experiment on N-version programming, Csmith has yielded no evidence of correlated failures among unrelated C compilers. Our hypothesis is that the observed lack of correlation stems from the fact that most compiler bugs are in passes that operate on an intermediate representation and there is substantial diversity among IRs.

No guarantee of termination It is not difficult to generate random programs that always terminate. However, we judged that this would limit Csmith's expressiveness too much: for example, it would force loops to be highly structured. Additionally, always-terminating tests cannot find compiler bugs that wrongfully terminate a non-terminating program. (We have found bugs of this kind.) About 10% of the programs generated by Csmith are (apparently) non-terminating. In practice, during testing, they are easy to deal with using timeouts.

Target middle-end bugs Commercial test suites for C compilers [1, 19, 20] are primarily aimed at checking standards conformance. Csmith, on the other hand, is mainly intended to find bugs in the parts of a compiler that perform transformations on an intermediate representation—the so-called "middle end" of a compiler. As a result, we have found large numbers of middle-end bugs missed by existing testing techniques (Section 3.6). At the same time, Csmith is rather poor at finding gaps in standards conformance. For example, it makes no attempt to test a compiler's handling of trigraphs, long identifier names, or variadic functions.

Targeting the middle end has several aspects. First, all generated programs pass the lexer, parser, and typechecker. Second, we performed substantial manual tuning of the 80 probabilities that govern Csmith's random choices. Our goal was to make the generated programs "look right"—to contain a balanced mix of arithmetic and bitwise operations, of references to scalars and aggregates, of loops and straight-line code, of single-level and multi-level indirections, and so on. Third, Csmith specifically generates idiomatic code (e.g., loops that access all elements of an array) to stress-test parts of the compiler we believe to be error-prone. Fourth, we designed Csmith with an eye toward generating programs that exercise the constructs of a compiler's intermediate representation, and we decided to avoid generating source-level diversity that is unlikely to improve the "coverage" of a compiler's intermediate representations. For example, since additional levels of parentheses around expressions are stripped away early in the compilation process, we do not generate them, nor do we generate all of C's syntactic loop forms since they are typically all lowered to the same IR constructs. Finally, Csmith was designed to be fast enough that it can generate programs that are a few tens of thousands of lines long in a few seconds. Large programs are preferred because (empirically—see Section 3.3) they find more bugs. In summary, many aspects of Csmith's design and implementation were informed by our understanding of how modern compilers work and how they break.

3. Results

We conducted five experiments using Csmith, our random program generator. This section summarizes our findings.

Our first experiment was uncontrolled and unstructured: over a three-year period, we opportunistically found and reported bugs in a variety of C compilers. We found bugs in all the compilers we tested—hundreds of defects, many classified as high-priority bugs. (§3.1)

In the second experiment, we compiled and ran one million random programs using several years' worth of versions of GCC and LLVM, to understand how their robustness is evolving over time. As measured by our tests over the programs that Csmith produces, the quality of both compilers is generally improving. (§3.2)

Third, we evaluated Csmith's bug-finding power as a function of the size of the generated C programs. The largest number of bugs is found at a surprisingly large program size: about 81 KB. (§3.3)

Fourth, we compared Csmith's bug-finding power to that of four previous random C program generators. Over a week, Csmith was able to find significantly more distinct compiler crash errors than previous program generators could. (§3.4)

Finally, we investigated the effect of testing random programs on branch, function, and line coverage of the GCC and LLVM source code. We found that these metrics did not significantly improve when we added randomly generated programs to the compilers' existing test suites. Nevertheless, as shown by our other results, Csmith-generated programs allowed us to discover bugs that are missed by the compilers' standard test suites. (§3.5)

We conclude the presentation of results by analyzing some of the bugs we found in GCC and LLVM. (§3.6, §3.7)

	GCC	LLVM
Crash	2	10
Wrong code	2	9
Total	4	19

Table 2. Crash and wrong-code bugs found by Csmith that manifest when compiler optimizations are disabled (i.e., when the –O0 command-line option is used)

3.1 Opportunistic Bug Finding

We reported bugs to 11 different C compiler development teams. Five of these compilers (GCC, LLVM, CIL, TCC, and Open64) were open source and five were commercial products. The eleventh, CompCert, is publicly available but not open source.

What kinds of bugs are there? It is useful to distinguish between errors whose symptoms manifest at compile time and those that only manifest when the compiler's output is executed. Compile-time bugs that we see include assertion violations or other internal compiler errors; involuntary compiler termination due to memory-safety problems; and cases in which the compiler exhausts the RAM or CPU time allocated to it. We say that a compile-time *crash error* has occurred whenever the compiler process exits with a status other than zero or fails to produce executable output. Errors that manifest at run time include the computation of a wrong result; a crash or other abnormal termination of the generated code; termination of a program that should have executed forever; and non-termination of a program that should have terminated. We refer to these run-time problems as *wrong-code errors*. A *silent wrong-code error* is one that occurs in a program that was produced without any sort of warning from the compiler; i.e., the compiler silently miscompiled the test program.

Experience with commercial compilers There exist many more commercial C compilers than we could easily test. The ones we chose to study are fairly popular and were produced by what we believe are some of the strongest C compiler development teams. Csmith found wrong-code errors and crash errors in each of these tools within a few hours of testing.

Because we are not paying customers, and because our findings represent potential bad publicity, we did not receive a warm response from any commercial compiler vendor. Thus, for the most part, we simply tested these compilers until we found a few crash errors and a few wrong-code errors, reported them, and moved on.

Experience with open-source compilers For several reasons, the bulk of our testing effort went towards GCC and LLVM. First and most important, compiler testing is inherently interactive: we require feedback from the development team in the form of bug fixes. Bugs that occur with high probability can mask tricky, one-in-a-million bugs; thus, testing proceeds most smoothly when we can help developers rapidly destroy the easy bugs. Both the GCC and LLVM teams were responsive to our bug reports. The LLVM team in particular fixed bugs quickly, often within a few hours and usually within a week. The second reason we prefer dealing with open-source compilers is that their development process is transparent: we can watch the mailing lists, participate in discussions, and see fixes as they are committed. Third, we want to help harden the open-source development tools that we and many others use daily.

So far we have reported 79 GCC bugs and 202 LLVM bugs—the latter figure represents about 2% of all LLVM bug reports. Most of our reported bugs have been fixed, and twenty-five of the GCC bugs were marked by developers as P1: the maximum, release-blocking priority for a bug. To date, we have reported 325 in total across all tested compilers (GCC, LLVM, and others).

An error that occurs at the lowest level of optimization is pernicious because it defeats the conventional wisdom that compiler bugs can be avoided by turning off the optimizer. Table 2 counts these kinds of bugs, causing both crash and wrong-code errors, that we found using Csmith.

Testing CompCert CompCert [14] is a verified, optimizing compiler for a large subset of C; it targets PowerPC, ARM, and x86. We put significant effort into testing this compiler.

The first silent wrong-code error that we found in CompCert was due to a miscompilation of this function:

```
int bar (unsigned x) {
  return -1 <= (1 && x);
}
```

CompCert 1.6 for PowerPC generates code returning 0, but the proper result is 1 because the comparison is signed. This bug and five others like it were in CompCert's unverified front-end code. Partly in response to these bug reports, the main CompCert developer expanded the verified portion of CompCert to include C's integer promotions and other tricky implicit casts.

The second CompCert problem we found was illustrated by two bugs that resulted in generation of code like this:

```
stwu r1, -44432(r1)
```

Here, a large PowerPC stack frame is being allocated. The problem is that the 16-bit displacement field is overflowed. CompCert's PPC semantics failed to specify a constraint on the width of this immediate value, on the assumption that the assembler would catch out-of-range values. In fact, this is what happened. We also found a handful of crash errors in CompCert.

The striking thing about our CompCert results is that the middle-end bugs we found in all other compilers are absent. As of early 2011, the under-development version of CompCert is the only compiler we have tested for which Csmith cannot find wrong-code errors. This is not for lack of trying: we have devoted about six CPU-years to the task. The apparent unbreakability of CompCert supports a strong argument that developing compiler optimizations within a proof framework, where safety checks are explicit and machine-checked, has tangible benefits for compiler users.

3.2 Quantitative Comparison of GCC and LLVM Versions

Figure 3 shows the results of an experiment in which we compiled and ran 1,000,000 randomly generated programs using LLVM 1.9–2.8, GCC 3.[0–4].0, and GCC 4.[0–5].0. Every program was compiled at –O0, –O1, –O2, –Os, and –O3. A test case was considered valid if every compiler terminated (successfully or otherwise) within five minutes and if every compiled random program terminated (correctly or otherwise) within five seconds. All compilers targeted x86. Running these tests took about 1.5 weeks on 20 machines in the Utah Emulab testbed [28]. Each machine had one quad-core Intel Xeon E5530 processor running at 2.4 GHz.

Compile-time failures The top row of graphs in Figure 3 shows the observed rate of crash errors. (Note that the y-axes of these graphs are logarithmic.) These graphs also indicate the number of crash bugs that were fixed in response to our bug reports. Both compilers became at least three orders of magnitude less "crashy" over the range of versions covered in this experiment. The GCC results appear to tell a nice story: the 3.x release series increases in quality, the 4.0.0 release regresses because it represents a major change to GCC's internals, and then quality again starts to improve.

The middle row of graphs in Figure 3 shows the number of *distinct assertion failures* in LLVM and the number of *distinct internal compiler errors* in GCC induced by our tests. These are the numbers of code locations in LLVM and GCC at which an internal

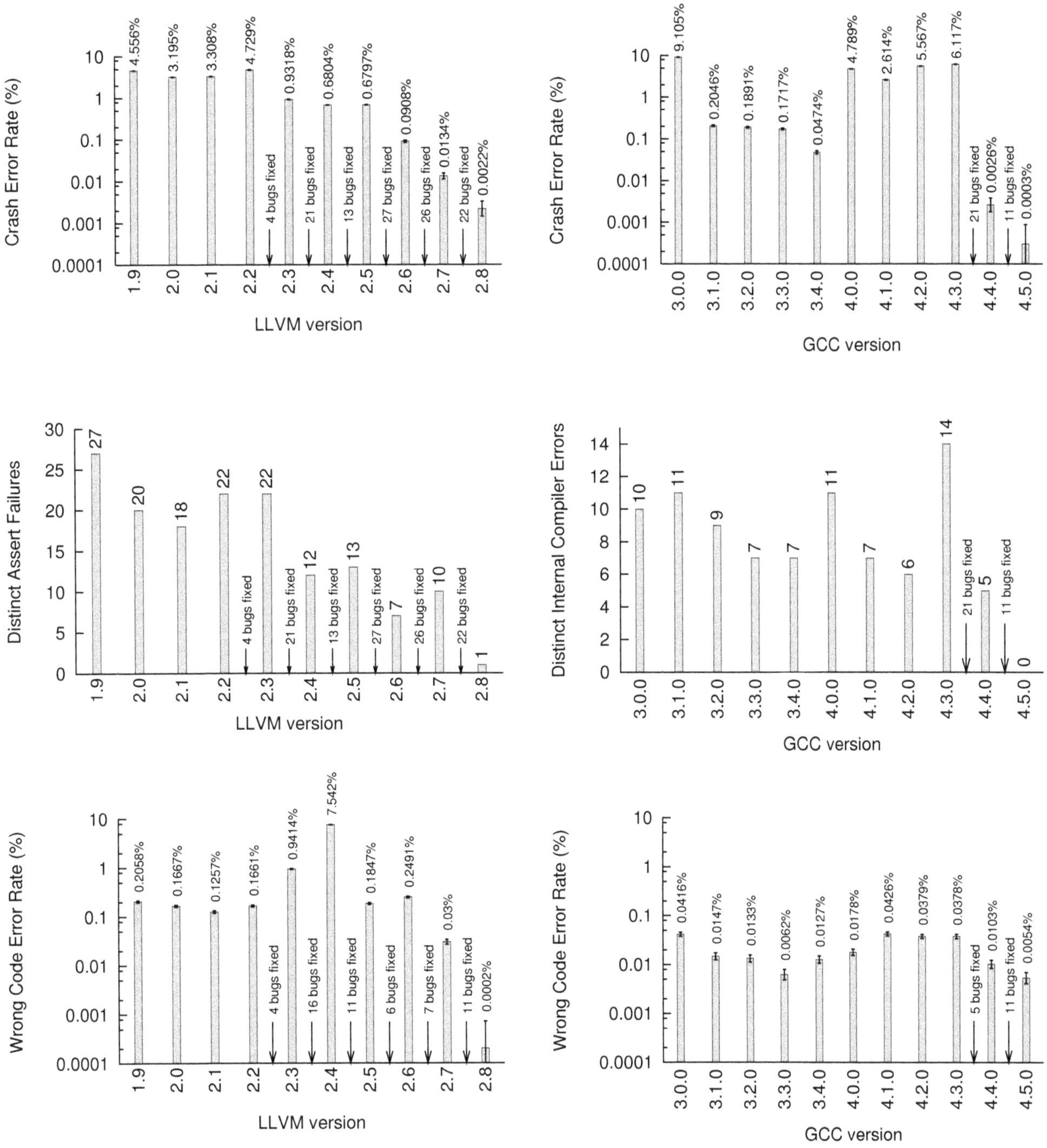

Figure 3. Distinct crash errors found, and rates of crash and wrong-code errors, from recent LLVM and GCC versions

consistency check failed. These graphs conservatively estimate the number of distinct failures in these compilers, since we encountered many segmentation faults caused by use of free memory, null-pointer dereferences, and similar problems. We did not include these faults in our graphed results due to the difficulty of mapping crashes back to distinct causes.

It is not clear which of these two metrics of crashiness is preferable. The rate of crashes is easy to game: we can make it arbitrarily high by biasing Csmith to generate code triggering known bugs, and compiler writers can reduce it to zero by eliminating error messages and always returning a "success" status code to the operating system. The number of distinct crashes, on the other hand, suffers from the drawback that it depends on the quantity and style of assertions in the compiler under test. Although GCC has more total assertions than LLVM, LLVM has a higher density: about one assertion per 100 lines of code, compared to one in 250 for GCC.

Run-time failures The bottom pair of graphs in Figure 3 shows the rate of wrong-code errors in our experiment. Unfortunately, we

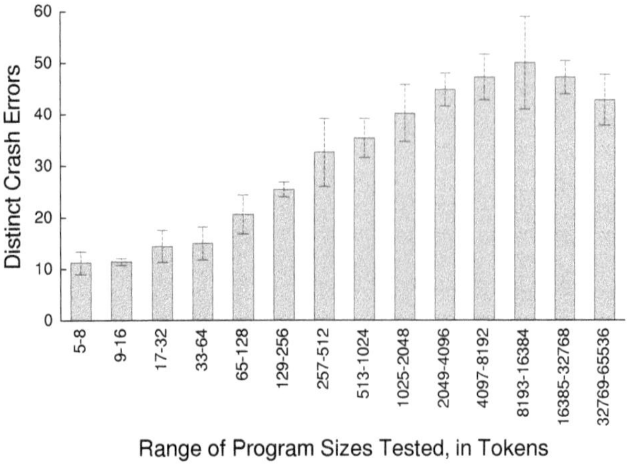

Figure 4. Number of distinct crash errors found in 24 hours of testing with Csmith-generated programs in a given size range

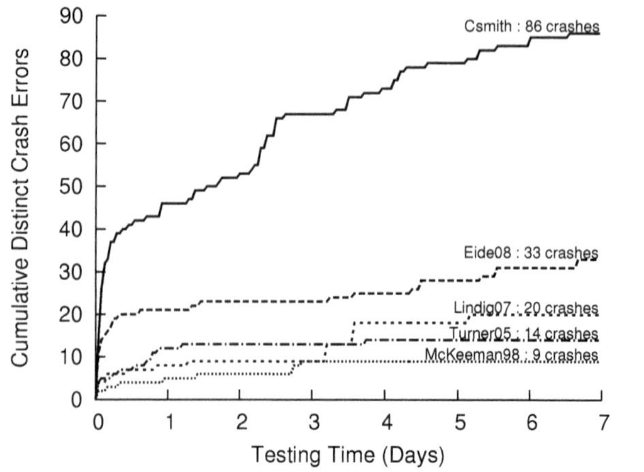

Figure 5. Comparison of the ability of five random program generators to find distinct crash errors

can only report the rate of errors, and not the number of bugs causing them, because we do not know how to automatically map failing tests back to the bugs that cause them. These graphs also indicate the number of wrong-code bugs that were fixed in response to our bug reports.

3.3 Bug-Finding Performance as a Function of Test-Case Size

There are many ways in which a random test-case generator might be "tuned" for particular goals, e.g., to focus on certain kinds of compiler defects. We performed an experiment to answer this question: given the goal of finding many defects quickly, should one configure Csmith to generate small programs or large ones? Other factors being equal, small test cases are preferable because they are closer to being reportable to compiler developers.

Using the same compilers and optimization options that we used for the experiments in Section 3.2, we ran our testing process multiple times. For each run we selected a size range for test inputs, configured Csmith to generate programs in that range,[3] executed the test process for 24 hours, and counted the distinct crash errors found. We repeated this for various ranges of test-input sizes.

Figure 4 shows that the rate of crash-error detection varies significantly as a function of the sizes of the test programs produced by Csmith. The greatest number of distinct crash errors is found by programs containing 8 K–16 K tokens: these programs averaged 81 KB before preprocessing. The confidence intervals are at 95% and were computed based on five repetitions.

We hypothesize that larger test cases expose more compiler errors for two reasons. First, throughput is increased because compiler startup costs are better amortized. Second, the combinatorial explosion of feature interactions within a single large test case works in Csmith's favor. The decrease in bug-finding power at the largest sizes appears to come from algorithms—in Csmith and in the compilers—that have superlinear running time.

3.4 Bug-Finding Performance Compared to Other Tools

To evaluate Csmith's ability to find bugs, we compared it to four other random program generators: the two versions of Randprog described in Section 2 and two others described in Section 5. We ran each generator in its default configuration on one of five identical and otherwise-idle machines, using one CPU on each host. Each generator repeatedly produced programs that we compiled and tested using the same compilers and optimization options that were used for the experiments in Section 3.2. Figure 5 plots the cumulative number of distinct crash errors found by these program generators during the one-week test. Csmith significantly outperforms the other tools.

[3] Although we can tune Csmith to prefer generating larger or smaller output, it lacks the ability to construct a test case of a specific size on demand. We ran this experiment by precomputing seeds to Csmith's random-number generator that cause it to generate programs of the sizes we desired.

		Line Coverage	Function Coverage	Branch Coverage
GCC	make check-c	75.13%	82.23%	46.26%
	make check-c & random	75.58%	82.41%	47.11%
	% change	+0.45%	+0.13%	+0.85%
	absolute change	+1,482	+33	+4,471
Clang	make test	74.54%	72.90%	59.22%
	make test & random	74.69%	72.95%	59.48%
	% change	+0.15%	+0.05%	+0.26%
	absolute change	+655	+74	+926

Table 3. Augmenting the GCC and LLVM test suites with 10,000 randomly generated programs did not improve code coverage much

3.5 Code Coverage

Because we find many bugs, we hypothesized that randomly generated programs exercise large parts of the compilers that were not covered by existing test suites. To test this, we enabled code-coverage monitoring in GCC and LLVM. We then used each compiler to build its own test suite, and also to build its test suite plus 10,000 Csmith-generated programs. Table 3 shows that the incremental coverage due to Csmith is so small as to be a negative result. Our best guess is that these metrics are too shallow to capture Csmith's effects, and that we would generate useful additional coverage in terms of deeper metrics such as path or value coverage.

3.6 Where Are the Bugs?

Table 4 characterizes the GCC and LLVM bugs we found by compiler part. Tables 5 and 6 show the ten buggiest files in LLVM and GCC as measured by our experiment in Section 3.1. Most of the bugs we found in GCC were in the middle end: the machine-independent optimizers. LLVM is a younger compiler and our testing shook out some front-end and back-end bugs that would probably not be present in a more mature software base.

	GCC	LLVM
Front end	0	10
Middle end	49	75
Back end	17	74
Unclassified	13	43
Total	79	202

Table 4. Distribution of bugs across compiler stages. A bug is unclassified either because it has not yet been fixed or the developer who fixed the bug did not indicate what files were changed.

C File Name	Purpose	Wrong-Code Bugs	Crash Bugs
fold-const	constant folding	3	6
combine	instruction combining	1	5
tree-ssa-pre	partial redundancy elim.	0	4
tree-vrp	variable range propagation	0	4
tree-ssa-dce	dead code elimination	0	3
tree-ssa-reassoc	arithmetic expr. reassociation	0	2
reload1	register reloading	1	1
tree-ssa-loop-niter	loop iteration counting	1	1
dse	dead store elimination	2	0
tree-scalar-evolution	scalar evolution	2	0
Other (15 files)	n/a	19	24
Total (25 files)	n/a	29	50

Table 5. Top ten buggy files in GCC

C++ File Name	Purpose	Wrong-Code Bugs	Crash Bugs
Instruction-Combining	mid-level instruction combining	9	6
SimpleRegister-Coalescing	register coalescing	1	10
DAGCombiner	instruction combining	5	3
LoopUnswitch	loop unswitching	1	4
LICM	loop invariant code motion	0	5
LoopStrength-Reduce	loop strength reduction	1	3
FastISel	fast instruction selection	1	3
llvm-convert	GCC-LLVM IR conversion	0	4
ExprConstant	constant folding	2	2
JumpThreading	jump threading	0	4
Other (72 files)	n/a	46	92
Total (82 files)	n/a	66	136

Table 6. Top ten buggy files in LLVM

3.7 Examples of Wrong-Code Bugs

This section characterizes a few of the bugs that were revealed by miscompilation of programs generated by Csmith. These bugs fit into a simple model in which optimizations are structured like this:

```
analysis
if (safety check) {
  transformation
}
```

An optimization can fail to be semantics-preserving if the analysis is wrong, if the safety check is insufficiently conservative, or if the transformation is incorrect. The most common root cause for bugs that we found was an incorrect safety check.

GCC Bug #1: wrong safety check[4] If `x` is variable and `c1` and `c2` are constants, the expression `(x/c1)!=c2` can be profitably rewritten as `(x-(c1*c2))>(c1-1)`, using unsigned arithmetic to avoid problems with negative values. Prior to performing the transformation, expressions such as `c1*c2` and `(c1*c2)+(c1-1)` are checked for overflow. If overflow occurs, further simplifications can be made; for example, `(x/1000000000)!=10` always evaluates to 0 when `x` is a 32-bit integer. GCC falsely detected overflow for some choices of constants. In the failure-inducing test case that we discovered, `(x/-1)!=1` was folded to 0. This expression should evaluate to 1 for many values of `x`, such as 0.

GCC Bug #2: wrong transformation[5] In C, if an argument of type `unsigned char` is passed to a function with a parameter of type `int`, the values seen inside the function should be in the range 0..255. We found a case in which a version of GCC inlined this kind of function call and then sign-extended the argument rather than zero-extending it, causing the function to see negative values of the parameter when the function was called with arguments in the range 128..255.

GCC Bug #3: wrong analysis[6] We found a bug that caused GCC to miscompile this code:

```
1 static int g[1];
2 static int *p = &g[0];
3 static int *q = &g[0];
4
5 int foo (void) {
6   g[0] = 1;
7   *p = 0;
8   *p = *q;
9   return g[0];
10 }
```

The generated code returned 1 instead of 0. The problem occurred when the compiler failed to recognize that p and q are aliases; this happened because q was mistakenly identified as a read-only memory location, which is defined not to alias a mutable location. The wrong not-alias fact caused the store in line 7 to be marked as dead so that a subsequent dead-store elimination pass removed it.

GCC Bug #4: wrong analysis[7] A version of GCC miscompiled this function:

```
int x = 4;
int y;

void foo (void) {
  for (y = 1; y < 8; y += 7) {
    int *p = &y;
    *p = x;
  }
}
```

When `foo` returns, `y` should be 11. A loop-optimization pass determined that a temporary variable representing `*p` was invariant with value `x+7` and hoisted it in front of the loop, while retaining a dataflow fact indicating that `x+7` == `y+7`, a relationship that no longer held after code motion. This incorrect fact lead GCC to generate code leaving 8 in `y`, instead of 11.

[4] `http://gcc.gnu.org/bugzilla/show_bug.cgi?id=42721`
[5] `http://gcc.gnu.org/bugzilla/show_bug.cgi?id=43438`
[6] `http://gcc.gnu.org/bugzilla/show_bug.cgi?id=42952`
[7] `http://gcc.gnu.org/bugzilla/show_bug.cgi?id=43360`

LLVM Bug #1: wrong safety check[8] `(x==c1)||(x<c2)` can be simplified to `x < c2` when `c1` and `c2` are constants and `c1<c2`. An LLVM version incorrectly transformed `(x==0)||(x<-3)` to `x < -3`. LLVM did a comparison between 0 and −3 in the safety check for this optimization, but performed an unsigned comparison rather than a signed one, leading it to incorrectly determine that the transformation was safe.

LLVM Bug #2: wrong safety check[9] `(x|c1)==c2` evaluates to 0 if `c1` and `c2` are constants and `(c1&~c2)!=0`. In other words, if any bit that is set in `c1` is unset in `c2`, the original expression cannot be true. A version of LLVM contained a logic error in the safety check for this optimization, wrongly replacing this kind of expression with 0 even when `c1` was not a constant.

LLVM Bug #3: wrong safety check[10] "Narrowing" is a strength-reduction optimization that can be applied to loads when only part of an object is needed, or to stores where only part of an object is modified. For example, at the level of the abstract machine this code loads and stores an `unsigned int`:

```
unsigned y;

void bar (void) {
  y |= 255;
}
```

Optimizing compilers for x86 may translate `bar` into the following code, which loads nothing and stores a single byte:

```
bar:
  movb $-1, y
  ret
```

We found a case in which LLVM attempted to perform an analogous narrowing operation, but a logic error caused the safety check to succeed even when a different store modified the object prior to the store that was the target of the narrowing transformation.

LLVM Bug #4: wrong analysis[11] This code should print "5":

```
1 void foo (void) {
2   int x;
3   for (x = 0; x < 5; x++) {
4       if (x) continue;
5       if (x) break;
6   }
7   printf("%d", x);
8 }
```

LLVM's scalar evolution analysis computes properties of loop induction variables, including the maximum number of iterations. Line 5 of the program above caused this analysis to mistakenly conclude that `x` was 1 after the loop executed.

4. Discussion

Are we finding bugs that matter? One might suspect that random testing finds bugs that do not matter in practice. Undoubtedly this happens sometimes, but in a number of instances we have direct confirmation that Csmith is finding bugs that matter, because bugs that we have found and reported have been independently rediscovered and re-reported by application developers. By a very conservative estimate—counting only the times that a compiler developer explicitly labeled a wrong-code bug report as a duplicate of one of ours—this has happened eight times: four times for GCC and four for LLVM. We also have indirect confirmation that our bugs matter. The developers of open-source compilers fixed almost all of the bugs that we reported, and the GCC development team marked 25 of our bugs as P1: the maximum, release-blocking priority.

Creating reportable bugs Reporting compiler crash bugs is easy, but reporting wrong-code bugs is harder. Compiler developers will (rightfully) ignore a wrong-code bug report that is based on a large random program. Rather, a bug report must be accompanied by compelling evidence that a bug exists; in most cases the best evidence is a small test case that is obviously miscompiled. Delta debugging [31] automates test-case reduction, but all existing variants that are intended for reducing C programs—such as hierarchical delta debugging [18] and Wilkerson's implementation [29]—introduce undefined behavior. The resulting programs are small but useless. To avoid undefined behavior during reduction, we rely on compiler warnings, dynamic checkers, and manual test-case reduction. There is substantial room for improvement.

The relationship between testing and verification As our CompCert results make plain, verification does not obviate testing, but rather complements it. Testing can provide end-to-end evidence that numerous paths through a system work properly. Verification, on the other hand, typically focuses on a narrow slice of a stack of tools, and the parts outside the slice remain in the trusted computing base. There does not yet appear to be a nuanced understanding of the kinds of testing, and the amount of testing effort, that are rendered unnecessary by artifacts like CompCert [14] and seL4 [12].

Toward realistic, correct compilers Compilers must support rapid development to cope with new optimizations, new source languages, and new target architectures. Generated code often needs to be resource-efficient to support application developers' goals. Finally, compilers should generate correct code. Meeting even two of these goals is challenging, and it is not clear how to meet all three in a single tool. There seem to be four paths forward.

Compiler verification. Although it is difficult to imagine a verified compiler for C++0x, due to the immense complexity of the draft standard, CompCert is an existence proof that a verified, optimizing C compiler is within reach. However, the burden of verification is significant. CompCert still lacks a number of useful C features and few mainstream compiler developers have the formal verification skills that are needed to add new language features and optimization passes. On the other hand, projects such as XCERT [26] may dramatically lower the bar for working on verified compilation.

Compiler simplicity. For non-bottleneck applications, compiler optimization adds little end-user value. It would seem possible to take a simple compiler such as TCC [2], which does not optimize across statement boundaries, and validate it through code inspections, heavy use, and other techniques. At present, however, TCC is much buggier than more heavily-used compilers such as GCC and LLVM.

Compiler testing. We hypothesize that it is possible to gain high confidence in a complex compiler like GCC by choosing a fixed configuration, disabling optimization passes whose effects are significantly non-local, and performing "just enough testing." A test plan would be sufficient if all code paths through the compiler that are used to compile an application of interest had been tested. Clearly, a sophisticated way to abstract over paths is needed.

Equivalence checking. If equivalence checkers for machine code [7] could scale to large programs, verified compilers would be largely unnecessary because one compiler's output could be proved equivalent to another's. Although these tools are not likely to scale up to multi-megabyte applications anytime soon, it should

[8] `http://llvm.org/bugs/show_bug.cgi?id=2844`

[9] `http://llvm.org/bugs/show_bug.cgi?id=7750`

[10] `http://llvm.org/bugs/show_bug.cgi?id=7833`

[11] `http://llvm.org/bugs/show_bug.cgi?id=7845`

be possible to automatically partition applications into smaller parts so that equivalence checking can be done piecewise.

Future work Augmenting Csmith with white-box testing techniques, where the structure of the tested system is taken into account in a first-class way, would be productive. This will be difficult for several reasons. First, we anticipate substantial challenges in integrating the necessary constraint-solving machinery with Csmith's existing logic for generating valid C programs. It is possible that we will need to start over, next time engineering a version of Csmith in which all constraints are explicit and declarative, rather than being buried in a small mountain of C++. Second, the inverse problems that must be solved to generate an input become prohibitively difficult when inputs pass through a parser, particularly if the parser contains hash tables. Godefroid et al. [8] showed a way to solve this problem by integrating a constraint solver with a grammar for the language being generated. However, due to its non-local pointer and effect analyses, the validity decision problem for programs in the subset of C that Csmith generates is far harder than the question of whether a program can be generated by the JavaScript grammar used by Godefroid et al.

5. Related Work

Compilers have been tested using randomized methods for nearly 50 years. Boujarwah and Saleh [4] gave a good survey in 1997. In 1962, Sauder [22] tested the correctness of COBOL compilers by placing random variables in programs' data sections. In 1970, Hanford [10] used a PL/1 grammar to drive the generation of random programs. The grammar was extensible and was augmented by "syntax generators" that could be used, for example, to ensure that variables were declared before being used. In 1972, Purdom [21] used a syntax-directed method to generate test sentences for a parser. He gave an efficient algorithm for generating short sentences from a context-free grammar such that each production of the grammar was used at least once, and he tested LR(1) parsers using this technique.

Burgess and Saidi [5] designed an automatic generator of test cases for FORTRAN compilers. The tests were designed to be self-checking and to contain features that optimizing compilers were known to exploit. In order to predict test cases' results, the code generator restricted assignment statements to be executed only once during the execution of the sub-program or main program. These tests found four bugs in two FORTRAN 77 compilers.

In 1998, McKeeman [16] coined the term "differential testing." His work resulted in DDT, a family of program generators that conform to the C standard at various levels, from level 1 (random characters) to level 7 (generated code is "model conforming," incorporating some high-level structure). DDT is more expressive than Csmith (DDT is capable of generating all legal C programs) and it was used to find numerous bugs in C compilers. To our knowledge, McKeeman's paper contains the first acknowledgment that it is important to avoid undefined behavior in generated C programs used for compiler testing. However, DDT avoided only a small subset of all undefined behaviors, and only then during test-case reduction, not during normal testing. Thus, it is not a suitable basis for automatic bug-finding.

Lindig [15] used randomly generated C programs to find several compiler bugs related to calling conventions. His tool, called Quest, was specially targeted: rather than generating code with control flow and arithmetic, Quest generates code that creates complex data structures, loads them with constant values, and passes them to a function where assertions check the received values. Because its tests are self-checking, Quest is not based on differential testing. Self-checking tests are convenient, but the drawback is that Quest is far less expressive than Csmith. Lindig used Quest to test GCC, LCC, ICC, and a few other compilers and found 13 bugs.

Sheridan [23] also used a random generator to find bugs in C compilers. A script rotated through a list of constants of the principal arithmetic types, producing a source file that applied various operators to pairs of constants. This tool found two bugs in GCC, one bug in SUSE Linux's version of GCC, and five bugs in CodeSourcery's version of GCC for ARM. Sheridan's tool produces self-checking tests. However, it is less expressive than Csmith and it fails to avoid undefined behavior such as signed overflow.

Zhao et al. [32] created an automated program generator for testing an embedded C++ compiler. Their tool allows a general test requirement, such as which optimization to test, to be specified in a script. The generator constructs a program template based on the test requirement and uses it to drive further code generation. Zhao et al. used GCC as the reference to check the compiler under test. They reported greatly improved statement coverage in the tested modules and found several new compiler bugs.

6. Conclusion

Using randomized differential testing, we found and reported hundreds of previously unknown bugs in widely used C compilers, both commercial and open source. Many of the bugs we found cause a compiler to emit incorrect code without any warning. Most of our reported defects have been fixed, meaning that compiler implementers found them important enough to track down, and 25 of the bugs we reported against GCC were classified as release-blocking. All of this evidence suggests that there is substantial room for improvement in the state of the art for compiler quality assurance.

To create a random program generator with high bug-finding power, the key problem we solved was the expressive generation of C programs that are free of undefined behavior and independent of unspecified behavior. Csmith, our program generator, uses both static analysis and dynamic checks to avoid these hazards.

The return on investment from random testing is good. Our rough estimate—including faculty, staff, and student salaries, machines purchased, and university overhead—is that each of the more than 325 bugs we reported cost less than $1,000 to find. The incremental cost of a new bug that we find today is much lower.

Software Csmith is open source and available for download at `http://embed.cs.utah.edu/csmith/`.

Acknowledgments

The authors would like to thank Bruce Childers, David Coppit, Chucky Ellison, Robby Findler, David Gay, Casey Klein, Gerwin Klein, Chris Lattner, Sorin Lerner, Xavier Leroy, Bill McKeeman, Diego Novillo, Alastair Reid, Julian Seward, Zach Tatlock, our shepherd Atanas Rountev, and the anonymous reviewers for their invaluable feedback on drafts of this paper. We also thank Hans Boehm, Xavier Leroy, Michael Norrish, Bryan Turner, and the GCC and LLVM development teams for their technical assistance in various aspects of our work.

This research was primarily supported by an award from DARPA's Computer Science Study Group.

References

[1] ACE Associated Computer Experts. SuperTest C/C++ compiler test and validation suite. `http://www.ace.nl/compiler/supertest.html`.

[2] F. Bellard. TCC: Tiny C compiler, ver. 0.9.25, May 2009. `http://bellard.org/tcc/`.

[3] C. L. Biffle. Undefined behavior in Google NaCl, Jan. 2010. `http://code.google.com/p/nativeclient/issues/detail?id=245`.

[4] A. S. Boujarwah and K. Saleh. Compiler test case generation methods: a survey and assessment. *Information and Software Technology*, 39(9):617–625, 1997.

[5] C. J. Burgess and M. Saidi. The automatic generation of test cases for optimizing Fortran compilers. *Information and Software Technology*, 38(2):111–119, 1996.

[6] E. Eide and J. Regehr. Volatiles are miscompiled, and what to do about it. In *Proc. EMSOFT*, pages 255–264, Oct. 2008.

[7] X. Feng and A. J. Hu. Cutpoints for formal equivalence verification of embedded software. In *Proc. EMSOFT*, pages 307–316, Sept. 2005.

[8] P. Godefroid, A. Kieżun, and M. Y. Levin. Grammar-based whitebox fuzzing. In *Proc. PLDI*, pages 206–215, June 2008.

[9] R. Hamlet. Random testing. In J. Marciniak, editor, *Encyclopedia of Software Engineering*. Wiley, second edition, 2001.

[10] K. V. Hanford. Automatic generation of test cases. *IBM Systems Journal*, 9(4):242–257, Dec. 1970.

[11] International Organization for Standardization. *ISO/IEC 9899:TC2: Programming Languages—C*, May 2005. `http://www.open-std.org/jtc1/sc22/wg14/www/docs/n1124.pdf`.

[12] G. Klein et al. seL4: Formal verification of an OS kernel. In *Proc. SOSP*, pages 207–220, Oct. 2009.

[13] J. C. Knight and N. G. Leveson. An experimental evaluation of the assumption of independence in multiversion programming. *IEEE Trans. Software Eng.*, 12(1):96–109, Jan. 1986.

[14] X. Leroy. Formal verification of a realistic compiler. *Commun. ACM*, 52(7):107–115, July 2009.

[15] C. Lindig. Random testing of C calling conventions. In *Proc. AADEBUG*, pages 3–12, Sept. 2005.

[16] W. M. McKeeman. Differential testing for software. *Digital Technical Journal*, 10(1):100–107, Dec. 1998.

[17] B. P. Miller, L. Fredriksen, and B. So. An empirical study of the reliability of UNIX utilities. *Commun. ACM*, 33(12):32–44, Dec. 1990.

[18] G. Misherghi and Z. Su. HDD: Hierarchical delta debugging. In *Proc. ICSE*, pages 142–151, May 2006.

[19] Perennial, Inc. ACVS ANSI/ISO/FIPS-160 C validation suite, ver. 4.5, Jan. 1998. `http://www.peren.com/pages/acvs_set.htm`.

[20] Plum Hall, Inc. The Plum Hall validation suite for C. `http://www.plumhall.com/stec.html`.

[21] P. Purdom. A sentence generator for testing parsers. *BIT Numerical Mathematics*, 12(3):366–375, 1972.

[22] R. L. Sauder. A general test data generator for COBOL. In *AFIPS Joint Computer Conferences*, pages 317–323, May 1962.

[23] F. Sheridan. Practical testing of a C99 compiler using output comparison. *Software—Practice and Experience*, 37(14):1475–1488, Nov. 2007.

[24] J. Souyris, V. Wiels, D. Delmas, and H. Delseny. Formal verification of avionics software products. In *Proc. FM*, pages 532–546, Nov. 2009.

[25] S. Summit. comp.lang.c frequently asked questions. `http://c-faq.com/`.

[26] Z. Tatlock and S. Lerner. Bringing extensibility to verified compilers. In *Proc. PLDI*, pages 111–121, June 2010.

[27] B. Turner. Random Program Generator, Jan. 2007. `http://sites.google.com/site/brturn2/randomcprogramgenerator`.

[28] B. White et al. An integrated experimental environment for distributed systems and networks. In *Proc. OSDI*, pages 255–270, Dec. 2002.

[29] D. S. Wilkerson. Delta ver. 2006.08.03, Aug. 2006. `http://delta.tigris.org/`.

[30] M. Wolfe. How compilers and tools differ for embedded systems. In *Proc. CASES*, Sept. 2005. Keynote address. `http://www.pgroup.com/lit/articles/pgi_article_cases.pdf`.

[31] A. Zeller and R. Hildebrandt. Simplifying and isolating failure-inducing input. *IEEE Trans. Software Eng.*, 28(2):183–200, Feb. 2002.

[32] C. Zhao et al. Automated test program generation for an industrial optimizing compiler. In *Proc. ICSE Workshop on Automation of Software Test*, pages 36–43, May 2009.

Evaluating Value-Graph Translation Validation for LLVM

Jean-Baptiste Tristan Paul Govereau Greg Morrisett
Harvard University
{tristan,govereau,greg}@seas.harvard.edu

Abstract

Translation validators are static analyzers that attempt to verify that program transformations preserve semantics. Normalizing translation validators do so by trying to match the value-graphs of an original function and its transformed counterpart. In this paper, we present the design of such a validator for LLVM's intra-procedural optimizations, a design that does not require any instrumentation of the optimizer, nor any rewriting of the source code to compile, and needs to run only once to validate a pipeline of optimizations. We present the results of our preliminary experiments on a set of benchmarks that include GCC, a perl interpreter, SQLite3, and other C programs.

Categories and Subject Descriptors F.3.2 [*Logics and Meanings of Programs*]: Semantics of Programming Languages - Algebraic approaches to semantics; F.3.1 [*Logics and Meanings of Programs*]: Specifying and Verifying and Reasoning about Programs - Mechanical Verification; F.3.3 [*Logics and Meanings of Programs*]: Studies of Program Constructs - Program and recursion schemes

General Terms Algorithms, languages, reliability, theory, verification

Keywords Translation validation, symbolic evaluation, LLVM, optimization

1. Introduction

Translation validation is a static analysis that, given two programs, tries to verify that they have the same semantics [13]. It can be used to ensure that program transformations do not introduce semantic discrepancies, or to improve testing and debugging. Previous experiments have successfully applied a range of translation validation techniques to a variety of real-world compilers. Necula [11] experimented on GCC 2.7; Zuck *et al.* [4] experimented on the Tru64 compiler; Rival [14] experimented on unoptimized GCC 3.0; and Kanade *et al.* [8] experimented on GCC 4.

Given all these results, can we effectively validate a production optimizer? For a production optimizer, we chose LLVM. To be effective, we believe our validator must satisfy the following criteria. First, we do not want to instrument the optimizer. LLVM has a large collection of program transformations that are updated and improved at a frantic pace. To be effective, we want to treat the optimizer as a "black box". Second, we do not want to modify the source code of the input programs. This means that we handle the output of the optimizer when run on the input C programs "as is." Third, we want to run only one pass of validation for the whole optimization pipeline. This is important for efficiency, and also because the boundaries between different optimizations are not always firm. Finally, it is crucial that the validator can scale to large functions. The experiments of Kanade *et al.* are the most impressive of all, with an exceptionally low rate of false alarms (note the validator requires heavy instrumentation of the compiler). However the authors admit that their approach does not scale beyond a few hundred instructions. In our experiments, we routinely have to deal with functions having several thousand instructions.

The most important issue is the instrumentation. To our knowledge, two previous works have proposed solutions that do not require instrumentation of the optimizer. Necula evaluated the effectiveness of a translation validator for GCC 2.7 with common-subexpression elimination, register allocation, scheduling, and loop inversion. The validator is simulation-based: it verifies that a simulation-relation holds between the two programs. Since the compiler is not instrumented, this simulation relation is inferred by collecting constraints. The experimental validation shows that this approach scales, as the validator handles the compilation of programs such as GCC or Linux. However, adding other optimizations such as loop-unswitch or loop-deletion is likely to break the collection of constraints.

On the other hand, Tate *et al.* [16] recently proposed a system for translation validation. They compute a value-graph for an input function and its optimized counterpart. They then augment the terms of the graphs by adding equivalent terms through a process known as *equality saturation*, resulting in a data structure similar to the E-graphs of congruence closure. If, after saturation, the two graphs are the same, they can safely conclude that the two programs they represent are equivalent. However, equality saturation was originally designed for other purposes, namely the search for better optimizations. For translation validation, it is unnecessary to saturate the value-graph, and generally more efficient and scalable to simply normalize the graph by picking an orientation to the equations that agrees with what a typical compiler will do (e.g. $1 + 1$ is replaced by 2). Their preliminary experimental evaluation for the Soot optimizer on the JVM shows that the approach is effective and can lead to an acceptable rate of false alarms. However, it is unclear how well this approach would work for the more challenging optimizations available in LLVM, such as global-value-numbering with alias analysis or sparse-conditional constant propagation.

We believe that a *normalizing* value-graph translation validator would have both the simplicity of the *saturation* validator proposed by Tate *et al.*, and the scalability of Necula's constraint-based approach. In this paper we set out to evaluate how well such a design works. We therefore present the design and implementation of such a validator along with experimental results for a number of benchmarks including SQLite [2] and programs drawn from

PLDI'11, June 4–8, 2011, San Jose, California, USA.

spec marks [5], including GCC and a perl interpreter. The optimizations we consider include global-value numbering with alias analysis, sparse-conditional constant propagation, aggressive dead-code elimination, loop invariant code motion, loop unswitching, loop deletion, instruction combining, and dead-store elimination. We have also experimented, on a smaller suite of hand-written programs and optimizations, that our tool could handle without further modification various flavors of scheduling (list, trace, etc.) and loop fusion and fission.

While Tate *et al.* tried a saturation approach on JVM code and found the approach to be effective, we consider here a normalization approach in the context of C code. C code is challenging to validate because of the lack of strong typing and the relatively low-level nature of the code when compared to the JVM. However, our results show that a normalizing value-graph translation validator can effectively validate the most challenging intra-procedural optimizations of the LLVM compiler. Another significant contribution of our work is that we provide a detailed analysis of the effectiveness of the validator with respect to the different optimizations. Finally, we discuss a number of more complicated approaches that we tried but ultimately found less successful than our relatively simple architecture.

The remainder of the paper is organized as follows. Section 2 presents the design of our tool. Section 3 details the construction of the value-graph using examples. Section 4 reviews the normalization rules that we use and addresses their effectiveness through examples. Section 5 presents the results of our experiments. We discuss related work in Section 6 and conclude in Section 7.

2. Normalizing translation validation

Our validation tool is called *LLVM-MD*. At a high-level, LLVM-MD is an optimizer: it takes as input an LLVM assembly file and outputs an LLVM assembly file. The difference between our tool and the usual LLVM optimizer is that our tool certifies that the semantics of the program is preserved. LLVM-MD has two components, the usual off-the-shelf LLVM optimizer, and a translation validator. The validator takes two inputs: the assembly code of a function before and after it has been transformed by the optimizer. The validator outputs a boolean: *true* if it can prove the assembly codes have the same semantics, and *false* otherwise. Assuming the correctness of our validator, a semantics-preserving LLVM optimizer can be constructed as follows (`opt` is the command-line LLVM optimizer, `validate` is our translation validator):

```
function llvm-md(var input) {
  output = opt -options input
  for each function f in input {
    extract f from input as fi and output as fo
    if (!validate fi fo) {
      replace fo by fi in output
    }
  }
  return output
}
```

For now, our validator works on each function independently, hence the limitation to intra-procedural optimizations. We believe that standard techniques can be used to validate programs in the presence of function inlining, but have not yet implemented these. Rather, we concentrate on the workhorse intra-procedural optimizations of LLVM.

At a high level, our tool works as follows. First, it "compiles" each of the two functions into a value-graph that represents the data dependencies of the functions. Such a value-graph can be thought of as a dataflow program, or as a generalization of the result of symbolic evaluation. Then, each graph is normalized by rewriting using rules that mirror the rewritings that may be applied by the off-the-shelf optimizer. For instance, it will rewrite the 3-node sub-graph representing the expression $2+3$ into a single node representing the value 5, as this corresponds to constant folding. Finally, we compare the resulting value-graphs. If they are *syntactically* equivalent, the validator returns *true*. To make comparison efficient, the value-graphs are hash-consed (from now on, we will say "reduced"). In addition, we construct a single graph for both functions to allow sharing between the two (conceptually distinct) graphs. Therefore, in the best case—when semantics has been preserved—the comparison of the two functions has complexity $\mathcal{O}(1)$. The best-case complexity is important because we expect most optimizations to be semantics-preserving.

The LLVM-MD validation process is depicted in figure 1. First, each function is converted into Monadic Gated SSA form [6, 10, 18]. The goal of this representation is to make the assembly instructions *referentially transparent*: all of the information required to compute the value of an instruction is contained within the instruction. More importantly, referential transparency allows us to substitute sub-graphs with equivalent sub-graphs without worrying about computational effects. Computing Monadic Gated SSA form is done in two steps:

1. Make side-effects explicit in the syntax by interpreting assembly instructions as monadic commands. For example, a `load` instruction will have a extra parameter representing the memory state.
2. Compute Gated SSA form, which extends ϕ-nodes with conditions, insert μ-nodes at loop headers, and η-nodes at loop exits[18].

Once we have the Monadic Gated SSA form, we compute a shared value-graph by replacing each variable with its definition, being careful to maximize sharing within the graph. Finally, we apply normalization rules and maximize sharing until the value of the two functions merge into a single node, or we cannot perform any more normalization.

It is important to note that the precision of the semantics-preservation property depends on the precision of the monadic form. If the monadic representation does not model arithmetic overflow or exceptions, then a successful validation does not guarantee anything about those effects. At present, we model memory state, including the local stack frame and the heap. We do not model runtime errors or non-termination, although our approach can be extended to include them. Hence, a successful run of our validator implies that if the input function terminates and does not produce a runtime error, then the output function has the same semantics. Our tool does not yet offer *formal* guarantees for non-terminating or semantically undefined programs.

3. Validation by Example

3.1 Basic Blocks

We begin by explaining how the validation process works for basic blocks. Considering basic blocks is interesting because it allows us to focus on the monadic representation and the construction of the value-graph, leaving for later the tricky problem of placing gates in ϕ- and η-nodes.

Our validator uses LLVM assembly language as input. LLVM is a portable SSA-form assembly language with an infinite number of registers. Because we start with SSA-form, producing the value-graph consists of replacing variables by their definitions while maximizing sharing among graph nodes. For example, consider the

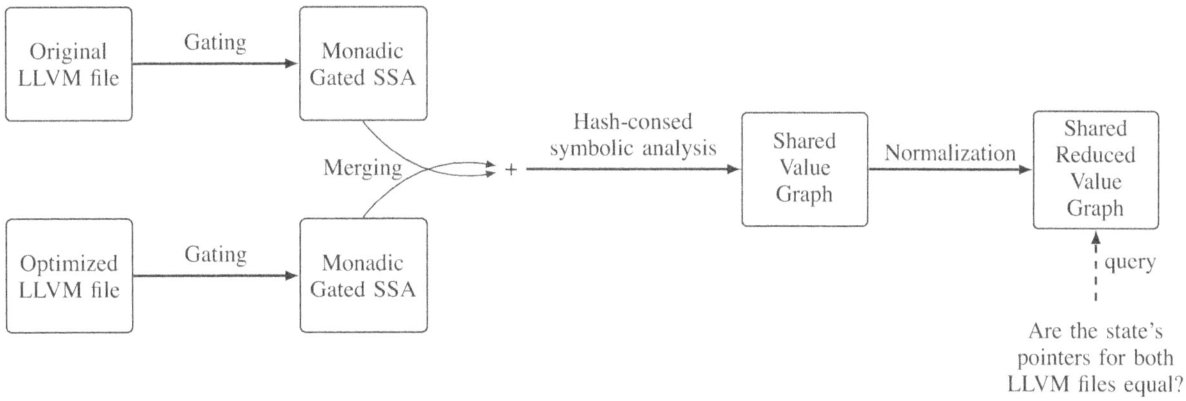

Figure 1: LLVM M.D. from a bird's eye view

following basic block, B1:

$$\begin{aligned} \text{B1:}\quad x_1 &= 3+3 \\ x_2 &= a * x_1 \\ x_3 &= x_2 + x_2 \end{aligned}$$

and its optimized counterpart, B2:

$$\begin{aligned} \text{B2:}\quad y_1 &= a * 6 \\ y_2 &= y_1 << 1 \end{aligned}$$

Replacing variables x_1, x_2, and y_1 by their definition, we obtain the value-graph presented below. The dashed arrows are not part of the value graph, they are only meant to point out which parts of the graph correspond to which program variables. Note that both blocks have been represented within one value graph, and the node for the variable a has been shared.

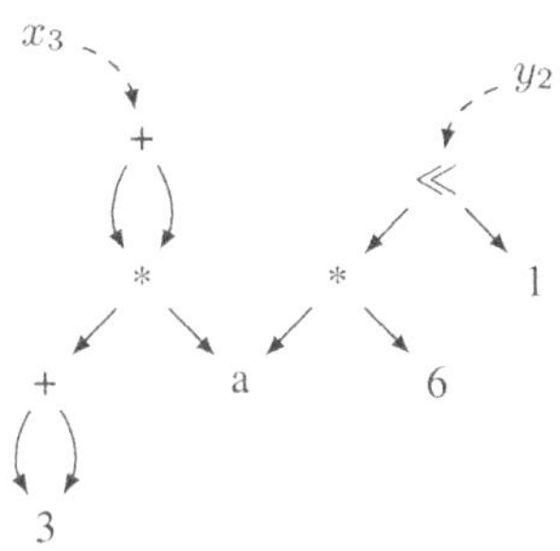

Suppose that we want to show that the variables x_3 and y_2 will hold the same value. Once we have the shared value graph in hand, we simply need to check if x_3 and y_2 are represented by subgraphs rooted at the same graph node. In the value graph above, x_3 and y_2 are not represented by the same subgraph, so we cannot conclude they are equivalent. However, we can now apply normalization rules to the graph. First, we can apply a constant folding rule to reduce the subgraph $3+3$ to a single node 6. The resulting graph is shown below (we have maximized sharing in the graph).

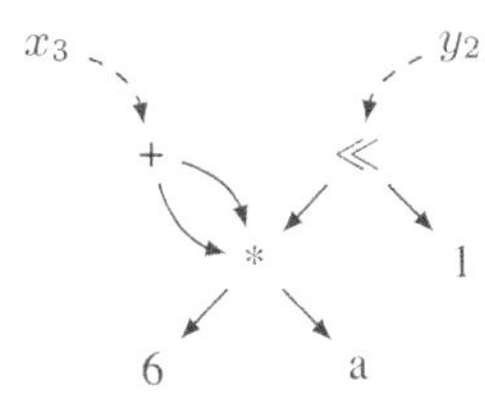

We have managed to make the value graph smaller, but we still cannot conclude that the two variables are equivalent. So, we continue to normalize the graph. A second rewrite rule allows us to replace $x+x$ with $x \ll 1$ for any x. In our setting, this rule is only appropriate if the optimizer would prefer the shift instruction to addition (which LLVM does). After replacing addition with left shift, and maximizing sharing, x_3 and y_2 point to the same node and we can conclude that the two blocks are equivalent.

Side Effects. The translation we have described up to this point would not be correct in the presence of side effects. Consider the following basic block.

$$\begin{aligned} &p_1 = \texttt{alloc}\ 1 \\ &p_2 = \texttt{alloc}\ 1 \\ &\texttt{store}\ x, p_1 \\ &\texttt{store}\ y, p_2 \\ &z = \texttt{load}\ p_1 \end{aligned}$$

If we naively apply our translation, then the graph corresponding to z would be: $z \mapsto$ `load (alloc` 1`)`, which does not capture the complete computation for register z. In order to make sure that we do not lose track of side effects, we use abstract state variables to capture the dependencies between instructions. A simple translation gives the following sequence of instructions for this block:

$$\begin{aligned} p_1, m_1 &= \texttt{alloc}\ 1, m_0 \\ p_2, m_2 &= \texttt{alloc}\ 1, m_1 \\ m_3 &= \texttt{store}\ x, p_1, m_2 \\ m_4 &= \texttt{store}\ y, p_2, m_3 \\ z, m_5 &= \texttt{load}\ p_1, m_4 \end{aligned}$$

Here, the current memory state is represented by the m registers. Each instruction requires and produces a memory register in addition to its usual parameters. This extra register enforces a dependency between, for instance, the `load` instruction and the preceding `store` instructions. This translation is the same as we would get if we interpreted the assembly instructions as a sequence of monadic commands in a simple state monad[10]. Using these "monadic" instructions, we can apply our transformation and produce a value graph that captures all of the relevant information for each register.

The rewriting rules in our system are able to take into account aliasing information to relax the strict ordering of instructions imposed by the monadic transformation. In our setting (LLVM), we know that pointers returned by `alloc` never alias with each other.

Using this information, we are able to replace m_4 with m_3 in the `load` instruction for z. Then, because we have a `load` from a memory consisting of a `store` to the same pointer, we can simplify the `load` to x.

Using the state variables, we can validate that a function not only computes the same value as another function, but also affects the heap in the same way. The same technique can be applied to different kinds of side effects, such as arithmetic overflow, division by zero, and non-termination. Thus far we have only modeled memory side-effects in our implementation. Hence, we only prove semantics preservation for terminating programs that do not raise runtime errors. However, our structure allows us to easily extend our implementation to a more accurate model, though doing so may make it harder to validate optimizations.

3.2 Extended Basic Blocks

These ideas can be generalized to extended basic blocks as long as ϕ-nodes are referentially transparent. We ensure this through the use of *gated* ϕ-nodes. Consider the following program, which uses a normal ϕ-node as you would find in an SSA-form assembly program.

$$
\begin{array}{lll}
\textbf{entry}: & c = a < b & \\
& \texttt{cbr}\ c, \textbf{true}, \textbf{false} & \\
\\
\textbf{true}: & x_1 = x_0 + x_0 & \text{(True branch)} \\
& \texttt{br}\ \textbf{join} & \\
\\
\textbf{false}: & x_2 = x_0 * x_0 & \text{(False branch)} \\
& \texttt{br}\ \textbf{join} & \\
\\
\textbf{join}: & x_3 = \phi(x_1, x_2) & \text{(Join point)}
\end{array}
$$

Rewriting these instructions as is would not be correct. For instance, replacing the condition $a < b$ by $a \geq b$ would result in the same value-graph, and we could not distinguish these two different programs. However, if the ϕ-node is extended to include the conditions for taking each branch, then we can distinguish the two programs. In our example, the last instruction would become $x_3 = \phi(b, x_1, x_2)$, which means x_3 is x_1 if b is *true*, and x_2 otherwise.

In order to handle real C programs, the actual syntax of ϕ-nodes has to be a bit more complex. In general, a ϕ-node is composed of a set of possible branches, one for each control-flow edge that enters the ϕ-node. Each branch has a set of conditions, all of which must be true for the branch to be taken.[1]

$$
\phi \left\{ \begin{array}{c} c_{11} \ldots c_{1n} \rightarrow v_1 \\ \ldots \\ c_{k1} \ldots c_{km} \rightarrow v_k \end{array} \right\}
$$

Given this more general syntax, the notation $\phi(c, x, y)$ is simply shorthand for $\phi(c \rightarrow x, !c \rightarrow y)$.

Gated ϕ nodes come along with a set of normalization rules that we present in the next section. When generating gated ϕ-nodes, it is important that the conditions for each branch are mutually exclusive with the other branches. This way, we are free to apply normalization rules to ϕ-nodes (such as reordering conditions and branches) without worrying about changing the semantics.

It is also worth noting that if the values coming from various paths are equivalent, then they will be shared in the value graph. This makes it possible to validate optimizations based on global-value numbering that is aware of equivalences between definitions from distinct paths.

[1] ϕ-nodes with several branches and many conditions are very common in C programs. For example, an if-statement with a condition that uses short-cut boolean operators, can produce complex ϕ-nodes.

3.3 Loops

In order to generalize our technique to loops, we must come up with a way to place gates within looping control flow (including breaks, continues, and returns from within a loop). Also, we need a way to represent values constructed within loops in a referentially transparent way. Happily, Gated SSA form is ideally suited to our purpose.

Gated SSA uses two constructs to represent loops in a referentially transparent fashion. The first, μ, is used to define variables that are modified within a loop. Each μ is placed at a loop header and holds the initial value of the variable on entry to the loop and a value for successive iterations. The μ-node is equivalent to a non-gated ϕ node from classical SSA. The second, η, is used to refer to loop-defined variables from outside their defining loops. The η-node carries the variable being referred to along with the condition required to reach the η from the variable definition.

Figure 2a shows a simple while loop in SSA form. The Gated SSA form of the same loop is shown in figure 2b. The ϕ-nodes in the loop header have been replaced with μ-nodes, and the access to the x_p register from outside to loop is transformed into an η-node that carries the condition required to exit the loop and arrive at this definition.

With Gated SSA form, recursively defined variables must contain a μ-node. The recursion can be thought of as a cycle in the value graph, and all cycles are dominated by a μ-node. The value graph corresponding to our previous example is presented in figure 2c. Intuitively, the cycle in the value-graph can be thought of as generating a stream of values. The μ-nodes start by selecting the initial value from the arrow marked with an "i". Successive values are generated from the cyclic graph structure attached to the other arrow. This μ-node "produces" the values c, $c+1$, $c+2$,... The η receives a stream of values and a stream of conditions. When the stream of conditions goes from *true* to *false*, the η selects the corresponding value in the value stream.

Generally, we can think of μ and η behaving according to the following formulas:

$$
\begin{aligned}
\mu(a, n) &= a : \mu(n[a/x], n) \\
\eta(0 : \bar{b}, x : \bar{v}) &= \eta(\bar{b}, \bar{v}) \\
\eta(1 : \bar{b}, x : \bar{v}) &= x
\end{aligned}
$$

Of course, for our purposes, we do not need to evaluate these formulas, we simply need an adequate, symbolic representation for the registers x, x_p and b_p. A more formal semantics should probably borrow ideas from dataflow programming languages such as those studied by Tate *et. al.*[16].

4. Normalization

Once a graph is constructed for two functions, if the functions' values are not already equivalent, we begin to normalize the graph. We normalize value graphs using a set of rewrite rules. We apply the rules to each graph node individually. When no more rules can be applied, we maximize sharing within the graph and then reapply our rules. When no more sharing or rules can be applied, the process terminates.

Our rewrite rules come in two basic types: general simplification rules and optimization-specific rules. The general simplification rules reduce the number of graph nodes by removing unnecessary structure. We say *general* because these rules only depend on the graph representation, replacing graph structures with smaller, simpler graph structures. The optimization-specific rules rewrite graphs in a way that mirrors the effects of specific optimizations.

loop :

$x_0 = c$

$x_p = \phi(x_0, x_k)$
$b = x_p < n$
cbr b, **loop1**, **exit**

loop1 :

$x_k = x_p + 1$
br **loop**

exit :

$x = x_p$

(a) SSA while loop

$x_0 = c$

loop :

$x_p = \mu(x_0, x_k)$
$b = x_p < n$
cbr b, **loop1**, **exit**

loop1 :

$x_k = x_p + 1$
br **loop**

exit :

$x = \eta(b, x_p)$

(b) GSSA while loop

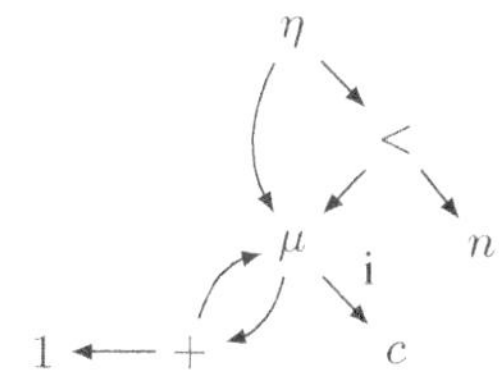

(c) Value graph representation

Figure 2: Representation of while loops

These rules do not always make the graph smaller or simpler, and one often needs to have specific optimizations in mind when adding them to the system.

General Simplification Rules. The notation $a \downarrow b$ means that we match graphs with structure a and replace them with b. The first four general ruless simplify boolean expressions:

$$a = a \downarrow \texttt{true} \tag{1}$$

$$a \neq a \downarrow \texttt{false} \tag{2}$$

$$a = \texttt{true} \downarrow a \tag{3}$$

$$a \neq \texttt{false} \downarrow a \tag{4}$$

These last two rules only apply if the comparison is performed at the boolean type. In fact, all LLVM operations, and hence our graph nodes, are typed. The types of operators are important and uninteresting: we do not discuss types in this paper.

There are two general rules for removing unnecessary ϕ-nodes.

$$\phi\{\ldots, \overline{\texttt{true}_i} \rightarrow t, \ldots\} \downarrow t \tag{5}$$

$$\phi\left\{\overline{c_i \rightarrow t}\right\} \downarrow t \tag{6}$$

The first rule replaces a ϕ-node with one of its branches if all of its conditions are satisfied for that branch. We write $\overline{x_i}$ for a set of terms indexed by i. In the first rule, we have a set of true values. Note that the conditions for each branch are mutually exclusive with the other branches, so only one branch can have conditions which are all true. The second rule removes the ϕ-node if all of the branches contain the same value. A special case of this rule is a ϕ-node with only one branch indicating that there is only one possible path to the ϕ-node, as happens with branch elimination.

The ϕ rules are required to validate sparse conditional constant propagation (SCCP) and global value numbering (GVN). The following example can be optimized by both:

```
if (c) {a = 1; b = 1; d = a;}
  else {a = 2; b = 2; d = 1;}
if (a == b) {x = d;} else {x = 0;}
return x;
```

Applying global-value numbering followed by sparse conditional constant propagation transforms this program to `return 1`. Indeed, in each of the branches of the first if-statement, a is equal to b. Since $a == b$ is always true, the condition of the second if-statement is constant, and sparse conditional constant propagation can propagate the left definition of x. The above program and `return 1` have the same normalized value graph, computed as follows:

$$
\begin{aligned}
x \mapsto & \phi(\phi(c, 1, 2) == \phi(c, 1, 2), \phi(c, 1, 1), 0) & \\
& \downarrow \phi(\texttt{true}, \phi(c, 1, 1), 0) & \text{by (1)} \\
& \downarrow \phi(c, 1, 1) & \text{by (5)} \\
& \downarrow 1 & \text{by (6)}
\end{aligned}
$$

There are also general rules for simplifying η- and μ-nodes. The first rule allows us to remove loops that never execute.

$$\eta(\texttt{false}, \mu(x, y)) \downarrow x \tag{7}$$

This rule rewrites to the initial value of the μ-node before the loop is entered, namely x. This rule is needed to validate loop-deletion, a form of dead code elimination. In addition, there are two rules for loop invariants. The first says that if we have a constant μ-node, then the corresponding η-node can be removed:

$$\eta(c, \mu(x, x)) \downarrow x \tag{8}$$

$$\eta(c, y \mapsto \mu(x, y)) \downarrow x \tag{9}$$

In rule (8), the μ-node has an initial value of x, which must be defined outside of the loop, and therefore cannot vary within the loop. Since, x does not vary within the loop the μ-node does not vary, and the loop structure can be removed. Rule (9), expresses the same condition, but the second term in the μ-node is again the same μ-node (we use the notation $y \mapsto \mu(x, y)$ to represent this self-reference).

These rules are necessary to validate loop invariant code motion. As an example, consider the following program:

```
x = a + 3; c = 3;
for (i = 0; i < n; i++) {x = a + c;}
return x;
```

In this program, variable x is defined within a loop, but it is invariant. Moreover, variable c is a constant. Applying global constant propagation, followed by loop-invariant code motion and loop deletion transforms the program to `return (a + 3)`. The value graph for x is computed as follows:

$$
\begin{aligned}
i_n &\mapsto \mu(0, i_n + 1) & \\
x &\mapsto \eta(i_n < n, \mu(a + 3, a + 3)) & \\
&\downarrow a + c & \text{(by 8)}
\end{aligned}
$$

Note that the global copy propagation is taken care of "automatically" by our representation, and we can apply our rule (8) immediately. The other nodes of the graph (i_n) are eliminated since they are no longer needed.

Optimization-specific Rules. In addition to the general rules, we also have a number of rewrite rules that are derived from the semantics of LLVM. For example, we have a family of laws for simplifying constant expressions, such as:

$$\texttt{add}\ 3\ 2 \downarrow 5$$
$$\texttt{mul}\ 3\ 2 \downarrow 6$$
$$\texttt{sub}\ 3\ 2 \downarrow 1$$

Currently we have rules for simplifying constant expressions over integers, but not floating point or vector types. There are also rules for rewriting instructions such as:

$$\texttt{add}\ a\ a \downarrow \texttt{shl}\ a\ 1$$
$$\texttt{mul}\ a\ 4 \downarrow \texttt{shl}\ a\ 2$$

These last two rules are included in our validator because we know the LLVM's optimizer prefers the shift left instruction. While preferring shift left may be obvious, there are some less obvious rules such as:

$$\texttt{add}\ x\ (-k) \downarrow \texttt{sub}\ x\ k$$
$$\texttt{gt}\ 10\ a \downarrow \texttt{lt}\ a\ 10$$
$$\texttt{lt}\ a\ b \downarrow \texttt{le}\ a\ (\texttt{sub}\ b\ 1)$$

While these transformations may not be optimizations, we believe LLVM makes them to give the instructions a more regular structure.

Finally, we also have rules that make use of aliasing information to simplify memory accesses. For example, we have the following two rules for simplifying loads from memory:

$$\texttt{load}(p, \texttt{store}(x, q, m)) \downarrow \texttt{load}(p, m) \tag{10}$$
$$\texttt{load}(p, \texttt{store}(x, p, m)) \downarrow x \tag{11}$$

when p and q do not alias. Our validator can use the result of a may alias analysis. For now, we only use simple non-aliasing rules: two pointers that originate from two distinct stack allocations may not alias; two pointers forged using `getelemptr` with different parameters may not alias, etc.

4.1 Efficiency

At this point is natural to wonder why we did not simply define a normal form for expressions and rewrite our graphs to this normal form. This is a good option, and we have experimented with this strategy using external SMT provers to find equivalences between expressions. However, one of our goals is to build a practical tool which optimizes the best case performance of the validator (we expect most optimizations to be correct). Using our strategy of performing rewrites motivated by the optimizer, we are often able to validate functions with tens of thousands of instructions (resulting in value graphs with hundreds of thousands of nodes) with only a few dozen rewritings. That is, we strive to make the amount of work done by the validator proportional to the number of transformations performed by the optimizer.

To this end, the rewrite rules derived from LLVM semantics are designed to mirror the kinds of rewritings that are done by the LLVM optimization pipeline. In practice, it is *much* more efficient to transform the value graphs in the same way the optimizer transforms the assembly code: if we know that LLVM will prefer `shl` a 1 to $a + a$, then we will rewrite $a + a$ but not the other way around.

As another, more extreme, example, consider the following C code, and two possible optimizations: SCCP and GVN.

```
a = x < y;
b = x < y;
if (a) {
   if (a == b) {c = 1;} else {c = 2;}
} else {c = 1;}
return c;
```

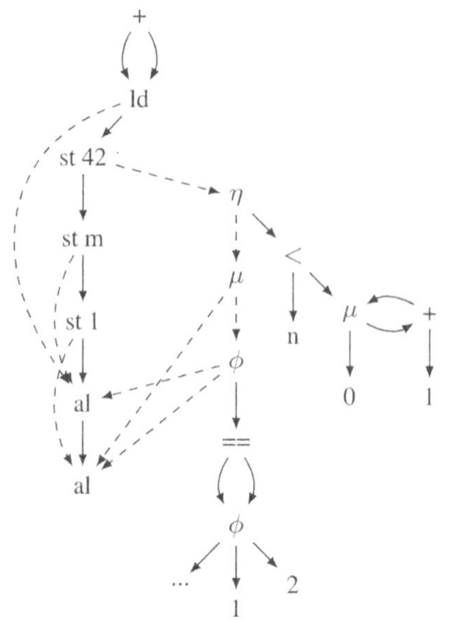

Figure 3: A shared value-graph

If the optimization pipeline is setup to apply SCCP first, then a may be replaced by `true`. In this case, GVN can not recognize that a and b are equal, and the inner condition will not be simplified. However, if GVN is applied first, then the inner condition can be simplified, and SCCP will propagate the value of c, leading to the program that simply returns 1. The problem of how to order optimizations is well-known, and an optimization pipeline may be reordered to achieve better results. If the optimization pipeline is configured to use GVN before SCCP, then, for efficiency, our simplification should be setup to simplify at join points before we substitute the value of a.

4.2 Extended Example

We now present an example where all these laws interplay to produce the normalized value-graph. Consider the C code below:

```
int f(int n, int m) {
  int * t = NULL;
  int * t1 = alloca(sizeof(int));
  int * t2 = alloca(sizeof(int));
  int x, y, z = 0;
  *t1 = 1; *t2 = m;
  t = t1;
  for (int i = 0; i < n; ++i) {
    if (i % 3) {
      x = 1; z = x << y; y = x;
    } else {
      x = 2; y = 2;
    }
    if (x == y)  t = t1;
    else t = t2;
  }
  *t = 42;
  return *t2 + *t2;
}
```

First, note that this function returns $m + m$. Indeed, x is always equal to y after the execution of the first conditional statement in the for loop. Therefore, the second conditional statement always executes the left branch and assigns t_1 to t. This is actually a loop invariant, and, since t_1 is assigned to t before the loop, t_1 is always equal to t. t_1 and t_2 are pointers to two distinct regions of memory and cannot alias. Writing through t_1 does not affect what is pointed to by t_2, namely m. The function therefore returns $m + m$. Since the loop terminates, an optimizer may replace the body of this function with $m \ll 1$, using a blend of global-value numbering with alias analysis, sparse-conditional constant propagation and loop deletion.

Our value-graph construction and normalization produces the value-graph corresponding to $m \ll 1$ for this example. The initial value-graph is presented in figure 3. Some details of the graph have been elided for clarity. We represent `load`, `store`, and `alloca` nodes with `ld`, `st`, and `al` respectively. To make the graph easier to read, we also used dashed lines for edges that go to pointer values. Below is a potential normalization scenario.

- The arguments of the $==$ node are shared; it is rewritten to *true*.
- The gate of the ϕ node is *true*; its predecessor, μ, is modified to point to the target of the true branch of the ϕ node rather than to ϕ itself.
- The arguments of this μ node are shared; its predecessor, η, is modified to point to the target of μ instead of μ itself.
- The condition of the η node is terminating, and its value acyclic; Its predecessor, `st42`, is modified to point to the target of η instead of η itself.
- It is now obvious that the load and its following store use distinct memory regions; the load can "jump over the store."
- The load and its new store use the same memory region; the load is therefore replaced by the stored value, m.
- The arguments of the $+$ node are shared; The $+$ node is rewritten into a left shift.

5. Experimental evaluation

In our experimental evaluation, we aim to answer three different questions.

1. How effective is the tool for a decent pipeline of optimization?
2. How effective is the tool optimization-by-optimization?
3. What is the effect of normalization?

Our measure of effectiveness is simple: the fewer false alarms our tool produces, the more optimized the code will be. Put another way, assuming the optimizer is always correct, what is the cost of validation? In our experiments, we consider any alarm to be a false alarm.

5.1 The big picture

We have tested our prototype validator on the pure C programs of the SPECCPU 2006[5] benchmark (The xalancbmk benchmark is missing because the LLVM bitcode linker fails on this large program). In addition, we also tested our validator on the SQLite embedded database[2]. Each program was first compiled with clang version 2.8[1], and then processed with the mem2reg pass of the LLVM compiler to place ϕ-nodes. These assembly files make up the unoptimized inputs to our validation tool. Each unoptimized input was optimized with LLVM, and the result compared to the unoptimized input by our validation tool.

Test suite information. Table 1 lists the benchmark programs with the size of the LLVM-assembly code file, number of lines of assembly, and the number of functions in the program. Our research prototype does not analyze functions with irreducible control flow graphs. This restriction comes from the front-end's computation of Gated SSA form. It is well known how to compute Gated SSA form for any control-flow graph[18]. However, we have not extended our front-end to handle irreducible control flow graphs. We do not believe the few irreducible functions in our benchmarks will pose any new problems, since neither the Gated SSA form nor our graph representation would need to be modified.

	size	LOC	functions
SQLite	5.6M	136K	1363
bzip2	904K	23K	104
gcc	63M	1.48M	5745
h264ref	7.3M	190K	610
hmmer	3.3M	90K	644
lbm	161K	5K	19
libquantum	337K	9K	115
mcf	149K	3K	24
milc	1.2M	32K	237
perlbench	15M	399K	1998
sjeng	1.5M	39K	166
sphinx	1.7M	44K	391

Table 1: Test suite information

Pipeline information. For our experiment, we used a pipeline consisting of:

- ADCE (advanced dead code elimination), followed by
- GVN (global value numbering),
- SCCP (sparse-condition constant propagation),
- LICM (loop invariant code motion),
- LD (loop deletion),
- LU (loop unswitching),
- DSE (dead store elimination).

The optimizations we chose are meant to cover, as much as possible, the intra-procedural optimizations available in LLVM. We do not include constant propagation and constant folding because both of these are subsumed by sparse-conditional constant propagation (SCCP). Similarly, dead-code and dead-instruction elimination are subsumed by aggressive dead-code elimination (ADCE). We did not include reassociate and instcombine because we haven't addressed those yet. One reason these haven't been our priority is that they are conceptually simple to validate but require many rules.

For each benchmark, we ran all of the optimizations, and then attempted to validate the final result. Since we used the SQLite benchmark to engineer our rules, it is not surprising that, overall, that benchmark is very close to 90%. The rules chosen by studying SQLite are also very effective across the other benchmarks. We do not do quite as well for the perlbench and gcc benchmarks. Currently, our tool only uses the basic rewrite rules we have described here. Also we do not handle global constants or floating point expressions.

Pipeline Results. Overall, with the small number of rules we have described in this paper, we can validate 80% of the per-function optimizations. The results per-benchmark are shown in figure 4. For our measurements, we counted the number of functions for which we could validate all of the optimizations performed on the function: even though we may validate many optimizations, if even one optimization fails to validate we count the entire function as failed. We found that this conservative approach, while rejecting

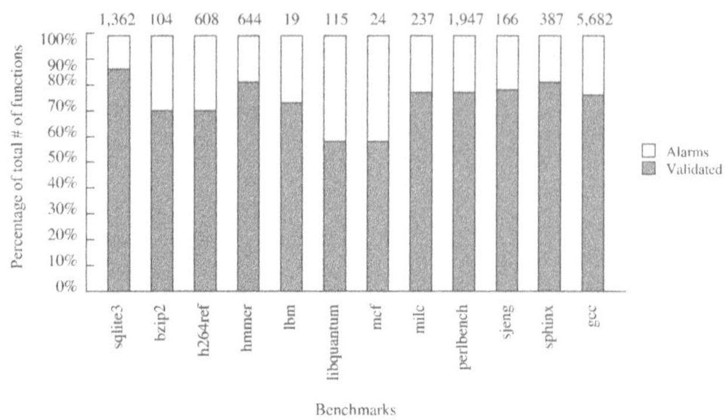

Figure 4: Validation results for optimization pipeline

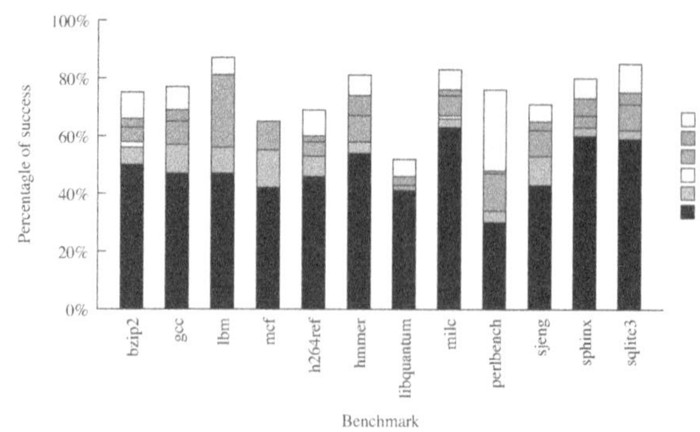

Figure 6: GVN

more optimizations, leads to a simpler design for our validated optimizer which rejects or accepts whole functions at a time. The validation time for GCC is 19m19s, perl 2m56s, and SQLite 55s.

5.2 Testing Individual Optimizations

The charts in Figure 5 summarize the results of validating functions for different, single optimizations. The height of each bar indicates the total number of functions transformed for a given benchmark and optimization. The bar is split showing the number of validated (below) and unvalidated (above) functions. The total number of functions is lower in these charts because we do not count functions that are not transformed by the optimization.

It is clear from the charts that GVN with alias analysis is the most challenging optimization for our tool. It is also the most important as it performs many more transformations than the other optimizations. In the next section we will study the effectiveness of rewrite rules on our system.

5.3 Rewrite Rules

Figure 6 shows the effect of different rewrite rules for the GVN optimization with our benchmarks. The total height of each bar shows the percentage of functions we validated for each benchmark after the GVN optimization. The bars are divided to show how the results improve as we add rewrite rules to the system. We start with no rewrite rules, then we add rules and measure the improvement. The bars correspond to adding rules as follows:

1. no rules
2. ϕ simplification
3. constant folding
4. load/store simplification
5. η simplification
6. commuting rules

We have already described the first five rules. The last set of rules tries to rearrange the graph nodes to enable the former rules. For example, we have a rule that tries to "push down" η-nodes to get them close to the matching μ-nodes.

We can see from this chart that different benchmarks are effected differently by the different rules. For example, SQLite is not improved by adding rules for constant folding or ϕ simplification. However, load/store simplification has an effect. This is probably because SQLite has been carefully tuned by hand and does not have many opportunities for constant folding or branch elimination. The lbm benchmark, on the other hand, benefits quite a lot from ϕ simplification.

From the data we have, it seems that our technique is able to successfully validate approximately 50% of GVN optimizations with no rewrite rules at all. This makes intuitive sense because our symbolic evaluation hides many of the syntactic details of the programs, and the transformations performed by many optimizations are, in the end, minor syntactic changes. By adding rewrite rules we can dramatically improve our results.

Up to this point, we have avoided adding "special purpose" rules. For instance, we could improve our results by adding rules that allow us to reason about specific C library functions. For example, the rule:

$$\begin{array}{l} x = atoi(p); \\ y = atoi(q); \end{array} \quad \Longrightarrow \quad \begin{array}{l} y = atoi(q); \\ x = atoi(p); \end{array}$$

can be added because `atoi` does not modify memory. Another example is:

$$\begin{array}{c} memset(p, x, l_1); \\ y = load(getelemptr(p, l_2)) \end{array} \quad \underset{l_2 < l_1}{\Longrightarrow} \quad y = x$$

which enables more aggressive constant propagation. Both of these rules seem to be used by the LLVM optimizer, but we have not added them to our validator at this time. However, adding these sorts of rules is fairly easy, and in a realistic setting many such rules would likely be desired.

Figure 7 shows similar results for loop-invariant code motion (LICM). The baseline LICM, with no rewrite rules, is approximately 75-80%. If we add in all of our rewrite rules, we only improve very slightly. In theory, we should be able to completely validate LICM with no rules. However, again, LLVM uses specific knowledge of certain C library functions. For example, in the following loop:

```
for (int i = 0; i < strlen(p); i++) f(p[i]);
```

the call to `strlen` is known (by LLVM) to be constant. Therefore, LLVM will lift the call to `strlen` out of the loop:

```
int tmp = strlen(p);
for (int i = 0; i < tmp; i++) f(p[i]);
```

Our tool does not have any rules for specific functions, and therefore we do not validate this transformation. The reason why we sometimes get a small improvement in LICM is because very occasionally a rewriting like the one above corresponds to one of our general rules.

Finally, figure 8 shows the effect of rewrite rules on sparse-conditional constant propagation. For this optimization, we used four configurations:

1. no rules

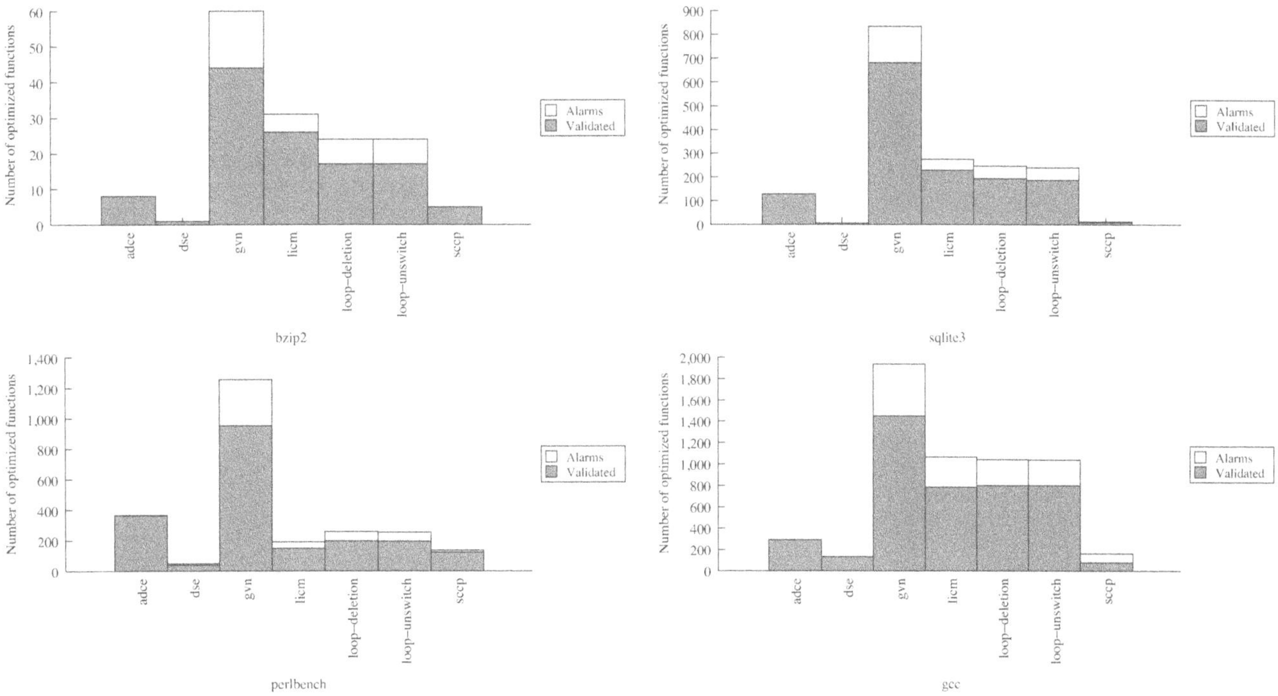

Figure 5: Validator results for individual optimizations

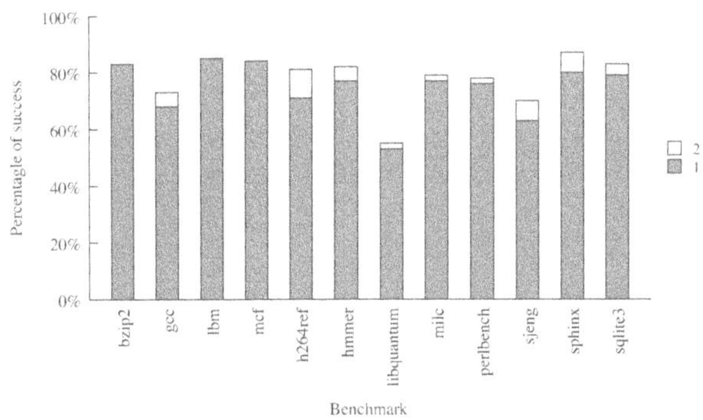

Figure 7: LICM

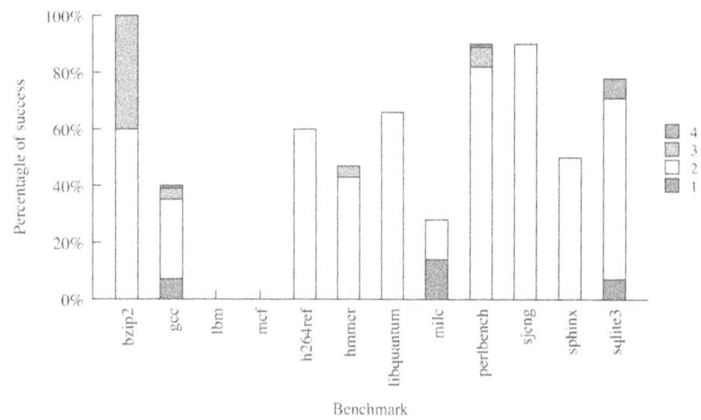

Figure 8: SCCP

2. constant folding
3. ϕ simplification
4. all rules

As expected, with no rules the results are very poor. However, if we add rules for constant folding, we see an immediate improvement, as expected. If we also add rules for reducing ϕ-nodes, bzip2 immediately goes to 100%, even though these rules ave no effect on SQLite. However, additional rules do improve SQLite, but not the other benchmarks.

5.4 Discussion

While implementing our prototype, we were surprised to find that essentially all of the technical difficulties lie in the complex ϕ-nodes. In an earlier version of this work we focused on structured code, and the (binary) ϕ-nodes did not present any real difficulties. However, once we moved away from the structured-code restriction we encountered more problems. First, although the algorithms are known, computing the gates for arbitrary control flow is a fairly involved task. Also, since the gates are dependent on the paths in the CFG, and general C code does not have a simple structured control flow, optimizations will often change the gating conditions even if the control flow is not changed.

Another important aspect of the implementation is the technique for maximizing sharing within the graph. The rewrite rules do a good job of exposing equivalent leaf nodes in the graphs. However, in order to achieve good results, it is important to find equivalent cycles in the graphs and merge them. Again, matching complex ϕ-nodes seems to be the difficult part. To match cycles, we find pairs of μ-nodes in the graph, and trace along their paths in parallel trying to build up a unifying substitution for the graph nodes involved. For ϕ-nodes we sort the branches and conditions and perform a syntactic equality check. This technique is very simple, and efficient because it only needs to query and update a small portion of the graph.

We also experimented with a Hopcroft partitioning algorithm[7]. Rather than a simple syntactic matching, our partitioning algorithm uses a prolog-style backtracking unification algorithm to find congruences between ϕ-nodes. Surprisingly, the partitioning algorithm with backtracking does not perform better than the simple unification algorithm. Both algorithms give us roughly the same percentage of validation. Our implementation uses the simple algorithm by default, and when this fails it falls back to the slower, partitioning algorithm. Interestingly, this strategy performs slightly better than either technique alone, but not significantly better.

Matching expressions with complex ϕ-nodes seems well within the reach of any SMT prover. Our preliminary experiments with Z3 suggest that it can easily handle the sort of equivalences we need to show. However, this seems like a very heavy-weight tool. One question in our minds is whether or not there is an effective technique somewhere in the middle: more sophisticated than syntactic matching, but short of a full SMT prover.

6. Related work

How do those results compare with the work of Necula and Tate *et al.*? The validator of Necula validates part of GCC 2.7 and the experiments show the results of compiling, and validating, GCC 2.91. It is important to note that the experiments were run on a Pentium Pro machine running at 400 MHz. Four optimizations were considered. Common-subexpression elimination, with a rate of false alarms of roughly 5% and roughly 7 minutes running time. Loop unrolling with a rate of false alarms of 6.3% and roughly 17 minutes running time. Register allocation with a rate of false alarms of 0.1% and around 10 minutes running time. Finally, instruction scheduling with a rate of false alarms of 0.01% and around 9 minutes running time. Unfortunately, the only optimization that we can compare to is CSE as we do not handle loop unrolling, and register allocation is part of the LLVM backend. In theory, we could handle scheduling (with as good results) but LLVM does not have this optimization. For CSE, our results are not as good as Necula's. However, we are dealing with a more complex optimization: global value numbering with partial redundancy elimination and alias information, libc knowledge, and some constant folding. The running times are also similar, but on different hardware. It is therefore unclear whether our validator does better or worse.

The validator of Tate *et al.* validates the Soot research compiler which compiles Java code to the JVM. On SpecJVM they report an impressive rate of alarms of only 2%. However, the version of the Soot optimizer they validate uses more basic optimizations than LLVM, and does not include, for instance, GVN. Given that our results are mostly directed by GVN with alias analysis, it makes comparisons difficult. Moreover, they do not explain whether the number they report takes into account all the functions or only the ones that were actually optimized.

The validator of Kanade *et al.*, even though heavily instrumented, is also interesting. They validate GCC 4.1.0 and report no false alarms for CSE, LICM, and copy propagation. To our knowledge, this experiment has the best results. However, it is unclear whether their approach can scale. The authors say that their approach is limited to functions with several hundred RTL instructions and a few hundred transformations. As explained in the introduction, functions with more than a thousand instructions are common in our setting.

There is a wide array of choices for value-graph representations of programs. Weise *et al.* [19] have a nice summary of the various value-graphs. Ours is close to the representation that results from the hash-consed symbolic analysis of a gated SSA graph [6, 18].

7. Conclusion

In conclusion, we believe that normalizing value-graph translation validation of industrial-strengh compilers without instrumentation is feasible. The design relies on well established algorithms and is simple enough to implement. We have been able, in roughly 3 man-months, to build a tool that can validate the optimizations of a decent LLVM pipeline on challenging benchmarks, with a reasonable rate of false alarms. Better yet, we know that many of the false alarms that we witness now require the addition of normalization rules but no significant changes in the design. For instance, insider knowledge of libc functions, floating-points constant folding and folding of global variables are sources of false alarms that can be dealt with by adding normalization rules. There is also room for improvement of the runtime performance of the tool.

There are still a few difficult challenges ahead of us, the most important of which is inter-procedural optimizations. With LLVM, even -O1 makes use of such optimizations and, even though it is clear that simulation-based translation validation can handle inter-procedural optimizations [12], we do not yet know how to precisely generalize normalizing translation. We remark that, in the case of safety-critical code that respects standard code practices [3], as can be produced by tools like Simulink [15], the absence of recursive functions allows us to inline every function (which is reasonable with hash-consing). Preliminary experiments indicate that we are able to validate very effectively inter-procedural optimizations in such a restricted case. Advanced loop transformations are also important, and we believe that this problem may not be as hard as it may seem at first. Previous work [9, 17] has shown that it can be surprisingly easy to validate advanced loop optimizations such as software pipelining with modulo variable expansion if we reason at the value-graph level.

Acknowledgments

We would like to thank Vikram Adve for his early interest and enthusiasm, and Sorin Lerner for discussing this project and exchanging ideas.

References

[1] LLVM 2.8. http://llvm.org.

[2] SQLite 3. http://www.sqlite.org.

[3] The Motor Industry Software Reliability Association. Guidelines for the use of the c language in critical systems. http://www.misra.org.uk, 2004.

[4] Clark W. Barrett, Yi Fang, Benjamin Goldberg, Ying Hu, Amir Pnueli, and Lenore Zuck. TVOC: A translation validator for optimizing compilers. In *Computer Aided Verification*, volume 3576 of *Lecture Notes in Computer Science*, pages 291–295. Springer, 2005.

[5] SPEC CPU2006. http://www.spec.org/cpu2006/.

[6] Paul Havlak. Construction of thinned gated single-assignment form. In *Proc. 6rd Workshop on Programming Languages and Compilers for Parallel Computing*, pages 477–499. Springer Verlag, 1993.

[7] John Hopcroft. An n log n algorithm for minimizing states of a finite automaton. In *The Theory of Machines and Computations*, 1971.

[8] Aditya Kanade, Amitabha Sanyal, and Uday Khedker. A PVS based framework for validating compiler optimizations. In *4th Software Engineering and Formal Methods*, pages 108–117. IEEE Computer Society, 2006.

[9] Xavier Leroy. Formal certification of a compiler back-end, or: programming a compiler with a proof assistant. In *33rd symposium Principles of Programming Languages*, pages 42–54. ACM Press, 2006.

[10] E. Moggi. Computational lambda-calculus and monads. In *4th Logic in computer science*, pages 14–23. IEEE, 1989.

[11] George C. Necula. Translation validation for an optimizing compiler. In *Programming Language Design and Implementation 2000*, pages 83–95. ACM Press, 2000.

[12] Amir Pnueli and Anna Zaks. Validation of interprocedural optimization. In *Proc. Workshop Compiler Optimization Meets Compiler Verification (COCV 2008)*, Electronic Notes in Theoretical Computer Science. Elsevier, 2008.

[13] Amir Pnueli, Michael Siegel, and Eli Singerman. Translation validation. In *Tools and Algorithms for Construction and Analysis of Systems, TACAS '98*, volume 1384 of *Lecture Notes in Computer Science*, pages 151–166. Springer, 1998.

[14] Xavier Rival. Symbolic transfer function-based approaches to certified compilation. In *31st symposium Principles of Programming Languages*, pages 1–13. ACM Press, 2004.

[15] Simulink. http://mathworks.com.

[16] Ross Tate, Michael Stepp, Zachary Tatlock, and Sorin Lerner. Equality saturation: A new approach to optimization. In *36th Principles of Programming Languages*, pages 264–276. ACM, 2009.

[17] Jean-Baptiste Tristan and Xavier Leroy. A simple, verified validator for software pipelining. In *37th Principles of Programming Languages*, pages 83–92. ACM Press, 2010.

[18] Peng Tu and David Padua. Efficient building and placing of gating functions. In *Programming Language Design and Implementation*, pages 47–55, 1995.

[19] Daniel Weise, Roger F. Crew, Michael D. Ernst, and Bjarne Steensgaard. Value dependence graphs: Representation without taxation. In *21st Principles of Programming Languages*, pages 297–310, 1994.

Safe Optimisations for Shared-Memory Concurrent Programs

Jaroslav Ševčík
University of Cambridge, The MathWorks
jarin.sevcik@gmail.com

Abstract

Current proposals for concurrent shared-memory languages, including C++ and C, provide sequential consistency only for programs without data races (the DRF guarantee). While the implications of such a contract for hardware optimisations are relatively well-understood, the correctness of compiler optimisations under the DRF guarantee is less clear, and experience with Java shows that this area is error-prone.

In this paper we give a rigorous study of optimisations that involve both reordering and elimination of memory reads and writes, covering many practically important optimisations. We first define powerful classes of transformations semantically, in a language-independent trace semantics. We prove that any composition of these transformations is sound with respect to the DRF guarantee, and moreover that they provide basic security guarantees (no thin-air reads) even for programs with data races. To give a concrete example, we apply our semantic results to a simple imperative language and prove that several syntactic transformations are safe for that language. We also discuss some surprising limitations of the DRF guarantee.

Categories and Subject Descriptors D.3.3 [*Language Constructs and Features*]: Concurrent programming structures; D.3.4 [*Processors*]: Optimization; F.3.2 [*Semantics of Programming Languages*]

General Terms Languages, Reliability, Theory, Verification

Keywords Relaxed Memory Models, Semantics, Compiler Optimizations

1. Introduction

Standard compiler optimisation, such as common expression elimination, violate sequentially consistent semantics for multi-threaded programs. For example, observe that the following program cannot print value 1 in any of its interleavings.

initially `requestReady = responseReady = data = 0`

Thread 1	Thread 2

`data := 1`
`requestReady := 1`
`if (responseReady==1)`
`  print data`
	`if (requestReady==1) {`
	`  data := 2`
	`  responseReady := 1`
	`}`

However, an optimising compiler propagates the constant 1 from the `data:=1` statement and replaces[1] `print data` with `print 1`. While such an optimisation would be correct for sequential programs, it is not safe for this program in the sequentially consistent semantics because unlike the original program, the optimised program can output 1.

Such a result is worrisome because most theoreticians and practitioners assume a sequentially consistent semantics. Indeed, some researchers believe that compilers should perform only those optimisations that do not break the sequentially consistent semantics (see §7 for more details). In contrast, designers of common languages and hardware do permit and implement aggressive optimisations that can exhibit surprising behaviours for multi-threaded programs, but they provide mechanisms for recovering a sequentially consistent semantics. On multi-processors, programmers can constrain optimisations using memory fence instructions, which often have intricate semantics [3, 11, 20] and high run-time costs, usually in the order of tens to hundreds of cycles.

In higher-level programming languages, the recent trend is to guarantee interleaved semantics for programs without data races [6, 16]; we will call such a specification the *DRF guarantee* [1]. As programming without data races is considered good practice, the DRF guarantee is safe for well-engineered programs while validating most compilers because the possibly unintended effects of common optimisations cannot be observed without data races. However, to our knowledge, there is little rigorous evidence for this claim. We emphasise that the DRF guarantee leaves the behaviours of programs with races unspecified, possibly leading to executions where values appear "out-of-thin-air" [16]. This is unacceptable for languages that aim to give basic security guarantees for arbitrary programs, e.g., Java applets.

Contribution. We prove the DRF guarantee and the absence of out-of-thin-air values for a large class of compiler optimisations. In more detail, we design a novel trace-semantic characterisation of thread-local program transformations that is suitable for reasoning about validity of common optimisations of concurrent data race free programs. Using the characterisation, we establish that the transformations cannot introduce behaviours for race free programs and prevent out-of-thin-air values for arbitrary programs. We demonstrate the power of the semantic technique by applying it on several syntactic transformations, such as reorderings of independent statements, and eliminations of redundant memory accesses in the same block. The main advantage of the semantic approach is its independence from syntax: it allows using the same proof techniques for different languages, such as intermediate languages in compilers. We believe that our semantic transformations are general enough to capture most thread-local optimisations performed by realistic compilers. We also show that, perhaps surprisingly, re-

[1] For example, the gcc compiler version 4.1.2 on the x86 architecture performs this optimisation.

PLDI'11, June 4–8, 2011, San Jose, California, USA.

dundant read introduction invalidates some optimisations that are otherwise safe for the DRF-guarantee.

Approach. We view programs as sets of traces of its individual threads (§3); optimisations are modelled as relations on these tracesets (§4). Our main result shows that given a finite chain of programs, where the first program is data race free and the optimisation relation relates adjacent programs in the chain, the set of behaviours of the last program is a subset of the set of behaviours of the first program (§5), where the behaviours are sequences of externally observable actions (input or output) of all interleavings of the program.

To show the absence of out-of-thin-air values we observe that all our semantic transformations preserve an important property: if a thread writes or outputs a value then it must have read the value before. Using this property, we prove our out-of-thin-air guarantee: if a program does not contain constant c explicitly and there is no way to build c (for example because c is an integer and the program does not contain any arithmetic), then no transformation of the program can read, write or output value c (§5).

We have carried most of our work on semantic level, but we show how to apply our work by defining a simple imperative language with synchronisation primitives together with several simple syntactic transformations, and proving them safe (§6).

2. Traces, DRF and Transformations

In our examples, we use a simple C-like language. By convention, variables with the name beginning with `r` are local (registers), the remaining variables reside in distinct shared-memory locations. Similarly to Java [10, 16] or C++0x [4–6], some locations can be designated by the programmer as *volatile* (atomics in C++0x). We make the syntax and semantics formal in §6. Intuitively, volatile locations are intended for synchronisation between threads and for the purposes of the DRF guarantee, data races on volatile locations do not count as data races, i.e., a program is data race free if it cannot perform two conflicting accesses to the same non-volatile location at the same time. We give a formal definition of data race freedom in §3. Technically, the set of volatile locations should be part of a program. In our examples, all locations are non-volatile, unless stated otherwise. We assume that all locations are zero-initialised.

We represent programs as sets of memory action traces where the trace is a sequence of memory actions of a single thread. We have the following memory actions: $R[l{=}v]$ is a read from location l with value v; $W[l{=}v]$ a write to l with value v, $L[m]$ lock of monitor m; $U[m]$ an unlock of m; $X(v)$ an external action (input or output) with value v; $S(e)$ is a thread start action with entry point e, where the entry point is a thread identifier.

2.1 Transformations by Example

We consider four classes of program transformations and illustrate them on simple examples. We emphasise that the syntactic examples cover only small range of all the transformations allowed by the semantics.

Trace preserving transformations. Since our trace semantics only includes *shared-memory optimisations*, many otherwise non-trivial optimisations, such as loop unrolling or inlining, are identity optimisations in the trace semantics because they do not affect memory accesses. Interestingly, the trace semantics does not directly capture syntactic dependencies. For example, the code snippets `r:=x; if (r==0) y:=1 else y:=1` and `r:=x; y:=1` have the same sets of traces—the set of all sequences of a read of `x` followed by a write of 1 to `y`.

Thread 0	Thread 1
	`r1:=y`
`x:=2`	`print r1`
`y:=1`	`r1:=x`
`x:=1`	`r2:=x`
	`print r2`

(original)

Thread 0	Thread 1
	`r1:=y`
	`print r1`
`y:=1` `x:=1`	`r1:=x`
	`r2:=r1`
	`print r2`

(transformed)

Figure 1. Elimination example.

Elimination. The example in Fig. 1 shows an elimination of an overwritten write to `x` in the first thread and an elimination of a redundant read from `x` in the second thread. Note that such a transformation is not safe in a sequentially consistent semantics: unlike the original program, the transformed program can output 1 followed by 0, assuming that all memory locations are zero-initialised. This does not violate the DRF guarantee since the program contains data races on `x` and `y`. In the absence of data races, we show that eliminations cannot introduce new behaviours (§5).

Eliminations are easy to describe on traces: intuitively, a program is an elimination of another program if for each trace of the transformed program there is a trace in the original program such that we can obtain the transformed trace by eliminating some redundant actions from the original trace. For example, consider the trace $t = [S(1), R[y{=}1], X(1), R[x{=}0], X(0)]$ of Thread 1 of the transformed program from Fig. 1 and observe that we can obtain t from trace $[S(1), R[y{=}1], X(1), R[x{=}0], R[x{=}0], X(0)]$ of the original program by removing the redundant read of `x`. We consider the read redundant because there is an earlier read from the same location of the same value. We give the precise definition of various kinds of redundant actions and of the semantic elimination in §4. The semantic elimination transformation is general enough to cover optimisations that eliminate memory accesses based on data-flow analyses, i.e., common subexpression elimination, constant propagation, or even loop-invariant hoisting if combined with loop unrolling.

Reordering. In the example in Fig. 2, we show a reordering of a read from `y` with a later write to `x`. Again, this transformation is not safe in the interleaved semantics because the original program cannot print 1, as opposed to the transformed program (assuming zero-initialised memory). For semantic reordering we only require each trace of the transformed program to be a permutation of some trace of the original program with certain restrictions, such as preventing reordering of two conflicting accesses to the same memory location. Note that this definition can allow reordering of actions that are control dependent or falsely data dependent. Using our notion of reordering, the code snippet `r:=x; if (r==1) {y:=1;z:=1}else {z:=1;y:=1}` is a reordering of `y:=1;z:=1;r:=x` because any trace of the latter is a permutation of a trace of the former. We give a precise definition of the semantic reordering in §4 and show its safety for DRF programs in §5. The semantic reordering transformation covers code motion transformations, which are typically employed in loop optimisations.

Introduction. It is known that write introduction (sometimes called write speculation) generally violates the DRF guarantee because the introduced write might be seen by a different thread even though there was no data race in the original program [6]. It is less clear whether a redundant read introduction can violate the DRF guarantee in practice, especially in the seemingly harmless case where the program never uses the value obtained from the introduced read. Unsurprisingly, if we introduce irrelevant reads and execute on a sequentially consistent architecture, the reads cannot

Thread 0	Thread 1
r1:=x y:=r1	r2:=y x:=1 print r2

(original)

Thread 0	Thread 1
r1:=x y:=r1	x:=1 r2:=y print r2

(transformed)

Figure 2. Reordering example.

lock m x := 1 print y unlock m	lock m y := 1 print x unlock m

(a) original

r1 := y lock m x := 1 print y unlock m	r2 := x lock m y := 1 print x unlock m

(b) with introduced reads

r1 := y lock m x := 1 print r1 unlock m	r2 := x lock m y := 1 print r2 unlock m

(c) after read elimination

Can the program print two zeros?

Figure 3. Irrelevant read introduction.

change the behaviours. However, if combined with otherwise DRF-friendly optimisations, we can obtain non-sequentially consistent behaviour from programs that are data race free. For example, note that the first program from Fig. 3 cannot print two zeros, but if an optimiser inserts irrelevant reads and then reuses the introduced reads to eliminate other reads, as illustrated by the programs (b) and (c) in the figure, the resulting program can print two zeros even on a sequentially consistent architecture.

One might find both the optimisations from Fig. 3 dubious, but compilers (including `gcc`) do introduce reads when hoisting reads from a loop. Although we have not seen the redundant read elimination across synchronisation in any compiler yet, this optimisation has been proposed and implemented in `gcc` for the upcoming C++0x implementation [12]. In any case, this case of redundant read elimination is safe in the DRF guarantee (§4).

3. Trace Semantics

We begin the technical development with setting up our intuitive trace semantics rigorously.

Actions, Traces and Interleavings. Our traces are sequences of memory operations. In addition to the standard read, write, thread start and synchronisation operations, the traces also include external I/O operations, such as printing, because ultimately we wish to reason about observable I/O behaviours.

The thread start action is always the first action of a thread. Its purpose is to provide a connection between the identity of a thread and its entry point. To simplify the discussion, we create threads statically and we use thread identifiers as entry points.

We will use the following terminology to refer to classes of actions: a *memory access* to location l is a read or a write to l; a *volatile memory access* (resp. *read, write*) is a memory access (resp. read, write) to a volatile location; a *normal memory access* (resp. *read, write*) is an access (resp. read, write) to a non-volatile location; an *acquire* action is either a lock or a volatile read; a *release* action is an unlock or a volatile write; a *synchronisation* action is an acquire or release action.

To work with sequences of actions we use the following notation: $t +\!\!+ t'$ is a *concatenation* of lists t and t'; we write $t \leq t'$ if t is prefix of t', i.e., if there is s such that $t +\!\!+ s = t'$. Trace t is a *strict prefix* of t' ($t < t'$), if $t \leq t'$ and $t \neq t'$; $|t|$ denotes the length of the sequence t; t_i is i-th element of the list t, indices are 0-based; $[a \leftarrow t.\ P(a)]$ stands for the list of all actions in list t that satisfy condition P, in functional languages, this is often written as **filter** $P\ t$; we generalise the filter notation to a *map-filter* notation; the expression $[f(a) \mid a \leftarrow t.\ P(a)]$ denotes the list $[a \leftarrow t.\ P(a)]$ with each element transformed by function f, in functional languages, one would write this as `map` f (**filter** $P\ t$); $t|_S$ is a *sublist* of t that contains all elements with indices from S; for example, $[a, b, c, d]|_{\{1,3\}}$ is $[b, d]$; $\mathrm{dom}(t)$ is the set of all indices to t: $\mathrm{dom}(t) = \{0, \ldots, |t| - 1\}$; $\mathrm{ldom}(t)$ is the list of all indices to t in the increasing order: $\mathrm{ldom}(t) = [0, \ldots, |t| - 1]$.

Programs are represented as sets of traces, called tracesets. The traces in a traceset do not have to be complete; their execution can finish at any point. We model this by assuming that the set of traces of a program is prefix-closed, i.e., for traceset T, $t \leq t'$ and $t' \in T$ implies $t \in T$. We also require the tracesets to be *well locked*, i.e., for each $t \in T$ and monitor m, the number of unlocks of m in t is not greater than the number of locks of m in t. All traces in a traceset must be *properly started* meaning that if a trace is not empty its first action must be a start action.

For example, the traceset of the first program in Fig. 2 is the prefix closure of the following set (V is the set of values):

$$\{[\mathrm{S}(0), \mathrm{R}[\mathtt{x}{=}v], \mathrm{W}[\mathtt{y}{=}v]] \mid v \in V\}$$
$$\cup\ \{[\mathrm{S}(1), \mathrm{R}[\mathtt{y}{=}v], \mathrm{W}[\mathtt{x}{=}1], \mathrm{X}(v)] \mid v \in V\}.$$

We should note that this notion of traceset is rather weak as it does not enforce determinism or receptiveness. For instance, the set of traces $\{[\mathrm{S}(0)], [\mathrm{S}(0), \mathrm{R}[\mathtt{x}{=}1]], [\mathrm{S}(0), \mathrm{W}[\mathtt{y}{=}1]]\}$ is a valid traceset. Having non-determinism is useful to model underspecified features of languages, such as the loose evaluation order in C/C++.

Interleavings and Executions. Interleavings are sequences of thread-identifier–action pairs. For a pair $p = \langle \theta, a \rangle$, we write $\mathcal{A}(p)$ to refer to the action a, and $\mathcal{T}(p)$ for θ. A sequence of such pairs is an *interleaving*. Given an interleaving I, the *trace of θ in I* is the sequence of actions of thread θ in I, i.e., $[\mathcal{A}(p) \mid p \leftarrow I.\ \mathcal{T}(p) = \theta]$. In the text, we often omit the projection $\mathcal{A}(-)$ and write "I_i is a read" instead of "$\mathcal{A}(I_i)$ is a read". We may also omit the interleaving I and write "i is a read" if I is obvious from the context.

Interleaving is an execution of traceset T that respects mutual exclusion, its reads see the values of most recent writes and the traces of its thread are in T. Formally, interleaving I is an *interleaving of traceset* T if for all thread identifiers θ, the trace of θ is in T, thread identifiers correspond to entry-points, i.e., $\mathcal{A}(I_i) = \mathrm{S}(\theta)$ implies $\mathcal{T}(I_i) = \theta$ for all i and θ, and $\mathcal{A}(I_i) = \mathrm{L}[\mathtt{m}]$ implies that for each thread $\theta \neq \mathcal{T}(I_i)$ we have

$$|\{j \mid j < i \wedge \mathcal{T}(I_j) = \theta \wedge \mathcal{A}(I_j) = \mathrm{L}[\mathtt{m}]\}| =$$
$$|\{j \mid j < i \wedge \mathcal{T}(I_j) = \theta \wedge \mathcal{A}(I_j) = \mathrm{U}[\mathtt{m}]\}|.$$

We say that $r \in \mathrm{dom}(I)$ (i) *sees* write w if $\mathcal{A}(I_r) = \mathrm{R}[\mathtt{x}{=}v]$, $\mathcal{A}(I_w) = \mathrm{W}[\mathtt{x}{=}v]$ for some $\mathtt{x}$, v and $w < r$, and for all i such that $w < i < r$ the action I_i is not a write to l, (ii) *sees default value* if I_r is a read of the default value from l (typically 0) and there is no write $i < r$ to location l in I, (iii) *sees the most recent write* if r sees the default value or it sees some write w or r is not a read. Interleaving I is *sequentially consistent* if all $j \in \mathrm{dom}(I)$ see the most recent write in I. Sequentially consistent interleavings of T are called *executions* of T.

Orders on Actions. The sequencing of actions in interleavings imposes a total order on the execution of actions. In reality, actions are often performed concurrently. We will model this by constructing a partial happens-before order [13], which relates actions only if they are ordered by the program code or by synchronisation.

First, we define the program order to relate actions of the same thread in interleaving I, i.e., $\leq_{po}^{I} = \{(i,j) \mid 0 \leq i \leq j < |I| \wedge \mathcal{T}(I_i) = \mathcal{T}(I_j)\}$. We say that i *synchronises-with* j, written $i <_{sw}^{I} j$, if $i < j < |I|$ and $\mathcal{A}(I_i), \mathcal{A}(I_j)$ are a release-acquire pair, where actions a and b are a *release-acquire* pair if a is an unlock of monitor m and b is a lock of m, or a is a write to a volatile location l and b is a read of l. The *happens-before order* of I is the transitive closure of program order and synchronizes-with.

Note that $i \leq_{po}^{I} j$ implies $i \leq j$, and i synchronises-with j implies $i < j$. Hence, $i \leq_{hb}^{I} j$ implies $i \leq j$. As any subset of a total order is antisymmetric and $\leq_{hb}^{I}$ is transitive and reflexive by construction, the happens-before order is a partial order.

A matching is a function that relates the actions in two traces or interleavings. Formally, *matching* between lists I and I' is a partial injective function f from $\mathrm{dom}(I)$ to $\mathrm{dom}(I')$ such that $I_i = I'_{f(i)}$ for all $i \in \mathrm{dom}(f)$. The matching f is *complete* if $\mathrm{dom}(f) = \mathrm{dom}(I)$. We use matchings to relate actions in a trace (resp. interleaving) of a transformed program to a trace (resp. interleaving) of the original program.

Data Race Freedom. Two actions are *conflicting* if they access the same non-volatile location and at least one of them is a write. An interleaving *has a data race* if it contains two adjacent conflicting actions from different threads. A traceset is *data race free* if none of its executions has a data race. Equivalently, one could define data race freedom using the happens-before relation: a program is data race free if in all its executions, all the pairs of conflicting actions are ordered by the happens-before order of the execution [6, 21].

The common way of ensuring data race freedom is protecting every shared-memory location with a lock. Then there cannot be a data race because there must be an unlock-lock pair of actions on the same monitor between any two accesses to the same location in any execution. Alternatively, we can use volatile locations to make a program data race free. For example, if we mark the locations `requestReady` and `responseReady` in the first program in §1 as volatile, the program becomes data race free.

4. Semantic Transformations

We now define eliminations and reorderings semantically.

Eliminations. To define semantic read eliminations, we introduce *wildcard traces*. The wildcard traces are generalisations of ordinary traces, where each each element of a wildcard trace is either an action or a wildcard read R[x=$*$]. We use the wildcards to express independence of the trace's validity on the value that the wildcard reads might read. We say that a (normal) trace t is an *instance* of a wildcard trace t', if we can obtain t by replacing all wildcards in t' with some concrete values. A wildcard trace *belongs-to* traceset T if T contains all instances of the trace.

Similarly, we define wildcard interleavings to be interleavings with some ordinary actions replaced by wildcard reads. We obtain an *instance of a wildcard interleaving* by replacing each wildcard read by a read of the same location with the value of the most recent write to the same location, or with the default value if there is no earlier write to the same location. As opposed to trace instances, the instance of an interleaving is unique. We say that a wildcard interleaving *belongs-to* T if for each thread θ, the (wildcard) trace of θ belongs-to T.

For example, let T be the traceset of the following program

```
y:=1;          ||  r2:=y;
r1:=x;         ||  x:=1;
print r1;      ||
```

and observe that the wildcard traces [S(0), W[y=1], R[x=$*$]] and [S(1), R[y=$*$], W[x=1]] belong-to T. In contrast, the wildcard trace [S(0), W[y=1], R[x=$*$], X(1)] does not belong-to T because some of its instances, e.g., [S(0), W[y=1], R[x=2], X(1)], are not in T.

Our definition of eliminations on traces considers pairs of possibly non-adjacent memory accesses and identifies the conditions on the intervening actions that enable elimination of one of the accesses. Moreover, the definition allows removal of irrelevant (wildcard) reads and certain actions from the end of the trace. The "last-action" eliminations are useful for reordering.

Definition 1. *We say that there is a* release-acquire pair between i *and* j *in trace* t *if there are* r *and* a *such that* $i < r < a < j$, t_r *is a release and* t_a *is an acquire. Given trace* t, *we say that* $i \in \mathrm{dom}(t)$ *is*

1. redundant read after read *if* $t_i = t_j =$ R[l=v] *for some* v, *non-volatile* l *and* $j < i$, *and there is no release-acquire pair or write to* l *between* j *and* i,
2. redundant read after write *if* $t_i =$ R[l=v], $t_j =$ W[l=v] *for some* v, *non-volatile* l *and* $j < i$, *and there is no release-acquire pair or write to* l *between* j *and* i,
3. irrelevant read *if* t_i *is a wildcard non-volatile read,*
4. redundant write after read *if* $t_i =$ W[l=v], $t_j =$ R[l=v] *for some* v, *non-volatile* l *and* $j < i$, *and there is no release-acquire pair or other access to* l *between* j *and* i,
5. overwritten write *if* $t_i =$ W[l=v], $t_j =$ W[l=v'] *for some* v, v', *non-volatile* l *and* $j < i$, *and there is no release-acquire pair or other access to* l *between* j *and* i,
6. redundant last write *if* t_i *is a normal write and there is no later release action and no later memory access to the same location,*
7. redundant release *if* t_i *is a release and there are no later synchronisation or external actions,*
8. redundant external action *if* t_i *is an external action and there are no later synchronisation or external actions.*

An index i *is* eliminable *in* t *if* i *satisfies one of the conditions above. Given traces* t *and* t', *the trace* t' *is an* elimination *of* t *if there is* $S \subseteq \mathrm{dom}(t)$ *such that* $t' = t|_S$ *and all* $i \in \mathrm{dom}(t) \setminus S$ *are eliminable in* t. *A traceset* T' *is an* elimination of a set of traces T *if each trace* $t' \in T'$ *is an elimination of some wildcard trace that belongs-to* T.

For example, in the wildcard trace

$$[\mathrm{S}(0), \mathrm{W}[\mathtt{x}{=}1], \mathrm{R}[\mathtt{y}{=}*], \mathrm{R}[\mathtt{x}{=}1],$$
$$\mathrm{X}(1), \mathrm{L}[\mathtt{m}], \mathrm{W}[\mathtt{x}{=}2], \mathrm{W}[\mathtt{x}{=}1], \mathrm{U}[\mathtt{m}]],$$

the indices 2, 3, and 6 are eliminable; so its elimination could be the trace [S(0), W[x=1], X(1), L[m], W[x=1], U[m]]. For an example of eliminations on tracesets, observe that all traces of the traceset of the program

```
x:=1; print 1; lock m; x:=1; unlock m;
```

are eliminations of some traces belonging-to the traceset of

```
x:=1; r1:=y; r2:=x; print r2;
if (r2!=0) {lock m; x:=2; x:= r2; unlock m;}
```

so the former traceset is an elimination of the latter.

Reordering. The reordering transformation allows changing order of execution of memory actions. However, not all permutations of actions preserve behaviours. We say that a is *reorderable* with b if either (i) a is a non-volatile memory access, and b is a non-conflicting non-volatile memory access, or an acquire action, or an external action; or (ii) b is a non-volatile memory access, and a is a non-conflicting non-volatile memory access, or a release, or an external action. The following table summarises the permissible reordering in a more readable form (cf. Doug Lea's cookbook [14]).

	$b =$				
$a =$	W[x=v_x][1]	R[x=v_y][1]	Acq	Rel	Ext
W[y=v_y][1]	$x \neq y$	$x \neq y$	✓	×	✓
R[y=v_y][1]	$x \neq y$	✓	✓	×	✓
Acquire	×	×	×	×	×
Release	✓	✓	×	×	×
External	✓	✓	×	×	×

Note that reorderability is not symmetric as we can reorder a write with a later acquire, but not the opposite. The only reason for the asymmetry is the so-called roach motel reordering [16], i.e., moving non-volatile memory accesses into synchronized blocks (for example, see rules R-RL, R-UW in Fig. 11).

A traceset T' is a reordering of a traceset T if each trace t' in T' is a permutation of some trace t from T. Moreover, the permutation has to satisfy two conditions: (i) it may only swap reorderable actions, (ii) if we apply the permutation to any prefix of t', i.e., if we leave out from t all the actions that are not in the prefix, then the resulting trace belongs to T.

In the rest of this section we will make this definition precise and then we apply the definition to a simple example. Given trace t, a bijection $f : \mathrm{dom}(t) \to \mathrm{dom}(t)$ is a *reordering function* for t if for all $i < j$ we have that $f(j) < f(i)$ implies that t_j is reorderable with t_i. It might seem that t_i should reorderable with t_j and not the opposite, but reordering function transforms traces in the opposite way: from traces of the transformed program to traces of the original program.

Before lifting the notion of reordering to traces and tracesets, we define a *de-permutation of a prefix* of a given trace t using function f. Formally, for $n \leq |t|$ and bijection f on $\mathrm{dom}(t)$, the *de-permutation of t of length n*, denoted by $f^{\rightarrow}_{<n}(t)$, is the trace

$$[t_{f^{-1}(i)} \mid i \leftarrow \mathrm{ldom}(t).\ f^{-1}(i) < n] .$$

The *de-permutation* of t, written $f^{\rightarrow}(t)$, is the de-permutation of t of length $|t|$.

Note f is a complete matching between t and $f^{\rightarrow}(t)$. Now we lift the notion of reordering to tracesets: Given a set of traces T and trace t', function $f : \mathrm{dom}(t') \to \mathrm{dom}(t')$ *de-permutes* t' to T if f is a reordering function for t' and for any $n \leq |t'|$ we have $f^{\rightarrow}_{<n}(t) \in T$. A set of traces T' is a *reordering of* a set of traces T if for each $t' \in T'$ there is a function that de-permutes t' into T.

We will demonstrate the application of the reordering definition on the example from Fig. 2. The tracesets of the program on the left is the prefix closure of the set

$$\begin{aligned} T =&\{[\mathrm{S}(0), \mathrm{R}[\mathtt{x}{=}v], \mathrm{W}[\mathtt{y}{=}v]] \mid v \in \mathbb{N}\} \cup \\ &\{[\mathrm{S}(1), \mathrm{R}[\mathtt{y}{=}v], \mathrm{W}[\mathtt{x}{=}1], \mathrm{X}(v)] \mid v \in \mathbb{N}\}. \end{aligned}$$

The traceset of the transformed program is the prefix closure of

$$\begin{aligned} T' =&\{[\mathrm{S}(0), \mathrm{R}[\mathtt{x}{=}v], \mathrm{W}[\mathtt{y}{=}v]] \mid v \in \mathbb{N}\} \cup \\ &\{[\mathrm{S}(1), \mathrm{W}[\mathtt{x}{=}1], \mathrm{R}[\mathtt{y}{=}v], \mathrm{X}(v)] \mid v \in \mathbb{N}\}. \end{aligned}$$

Ideally, we would like to show that T' is a reordering of T, i.e., that for any trace $t' \in T'$ there is permutation function de-permuting t' to T. However, this is not the case, because none of the two permutations of the trace $[\mathrm{S}(0), \mathrm{W}[\mathtt{x}{=}1]]$ belongs to T. Therefore, traceset T' cannot be a reordering of T.

This is where the eliminations become useful: we can obtain the trace $[\mathrm{S}(0), \mathrm{W}[\mathtt{x}{=}1]]$ by eliminating the irrelevant read from y from the wildcard trace $[\mathrm{S}(0), \mathrm{R}[\mathtt{y}{=}*], \mathrm{W}[\mathtt{x}{=}1]]$, which belongs to T. More precisely, let $\hat{T} = T \cup [\mathrm{S}(0), \mathrm{W}[\mathtt{x}{=}1]]$ and note that $\hat{T}$ is an elimination of T. It remains to check that T' is a reordering of $\hat{T}$. Let us illustrate this on $t' = [\mathrm{S}(0), \mathrm{W}[\mathtt{x}{=}1], \mathrm{R}[\mathtt{y}{=}1], \mathrm{X}(1)]$. Let

$$f = \{\langle 0, 0\rangle, \langle 1, 2\rangle, \langle 2, 1\rangle, \langle 3, 3\rangle\} \qquad t^n = f^{\rightarrow}_{<n}(t')$$

The meaning of t^n is the following: for $n = |t'|$, t^n is obtained from t' by applying the function f so that $t'_i = t^n_{f(i)}$ or, equivalently, $t'_{f^{-1}(i)} = t^n_i$ for all $i \in \mathrm{dom}(t')$. If $n < |t'|$, then we use the transformation only on the prefix of t' of length n. For illustration, see Figure 4. Since $t^n \in \hat{T}$ for any $n \leq |t'| = 4$, we satisfy the definition of reordering and f reorders $\hat{T}$ to t'. Similarly, for all other traces t' from T' there is a function that de-permutes t' to $\hat{T}$.

We should note that most of the complexity here is required only to cover the roach-motel reorderings, i.e., reordering with synchronisation. In the absence of roach-motel reordering, we could dispense with the de-permutations of prefixes.

5. Safety of Transformations

Here we sketch the main idea of our safety proof. The full details can be found in the author's PhD thesis [21]. We establish that both the elimination and reordering transformations have the following properties: (i) any execution of the transformed traceset has the same behaviour as some execution of the original traceset, provided that the original program was data race free; (ii) the transformations preserve data race freedom; (iii) the transformations cannot introduce values out-of-thin-air.

To prove (i) and (ii), we take an arbitrary execution of the transformed program and construct an execution of the original program that has the same behaviour. For both the elimination and the reordering transformations, we decompose the execution of the transformed program into traces for each thread, use the definitions of transformed tracesets from the previous section to obtain untransformed traces of the original traceset and then we compose the untransformed traces back into an untransformed interleaving so that the order of the external and synchronisation actions is preserved. Then we prove that either the constructed interleaving is an execution of the original traceset or there must have been a data race. Moreover, we show that the transformed program is data race free as the happens-before order of the constructed execution between two actions on the same variable implies happens-before ordering in the execution of the transformed program. We establish (iii) by showing that the transformations cannot introduce origins of values in tracesets, where a trace is an origin for v if there is a trace that contains a write of v or an output of v without any preceding read of v. The rest of this section describes the main proof ideas in more detail.

Elimination. We can prove sequential consistency for untransformed execution of an eliminated traceset directly because the untransformation of elimination embeds the happens-before order on each location. The main technical difficulty in the proof lies in showing that the extra actions introduced by the untransformation of elimination do not break sequential consistency.

Here we show that given a data race free traceset T, its elimination T', and an execution of T', we can untransform the execution so that the untransformation is an execution of T with the same behaviour as the execution of T'. The first step is the definition of the untransformation by lifting the definition of eliminations (Defi-

[1] Locations x and y are not volatile.

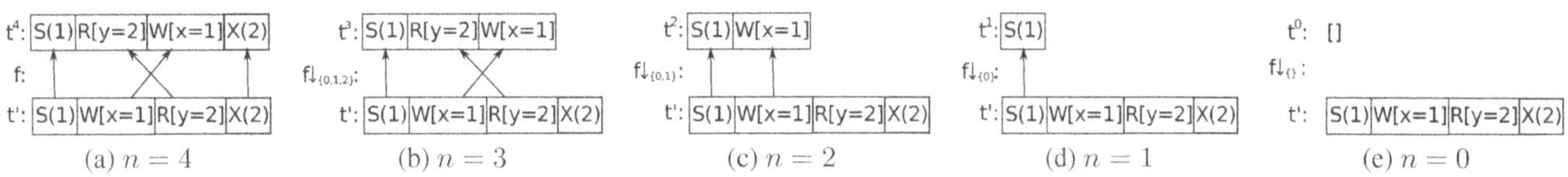

Figure 4. Example of reordering traces.

nition 1) to interleavings. A naïve definition would require that the eliminated interleaving is just a sublist with some eliminable actions left out. However, this does not guarantee sequential consistency for volatile locations in the untransformed interleaving, because the untransformation might introduce a volatile write action. Instead we will allow the untransformation to swap some actions while preserving the program order and the order of synchronisation and external actions. Moreover, all the release and external actions introduced by the untransformation must be ordered after the release and external actions from the interleaving of the transformed program.

The precise definition follows. An *index* i *is eliminable in an interleaving* I if the corresponding index in the trace of $\mathcal{T}(I_i)$, i.e., the index $|\{j \mid j < i \wedge \mathcal{T}(I_i) = \mathcal{T}(I_j)\}|$, is eliminable in the trace of $\mathcal{T}(I_i)$ in I. Function f is an *unelimination* function from interleaving I' to wildcard interleaving I if f is a complete matching between I' and I such that (i) if $i < j \in \mathrm{dom}(I')$ and $\mathcal{T}(I'_i) = \mathcal{T}(I'_j)$ then $f(i) < f(j)$, (ii) if $i < j \in \mathrm{dom}(I')$ and $\mathcal{A}(I'_i)$, $\mathcal{A}(I'_j)$ are synchronisation or external actions then $f(i) < f(j)$, (iii) if $i \in \mathrm{rng}(f)$, $j \in \mathrm{dom}(I) \setminus \mathrm{rng}(f)$ and $\mathcal{A}(I_i)$, $\mathcal{A}(I_j)$ are synchronisation or external actions, then $i < j$, (iv) if $i \in \mathrm{dom}(I) \setminus \mathrm{rng}(f)$, then i is eliminable in I.

Lemma 1. *Let traceset* T' *be an elimination of traceset* T *and* I' *an interleaving of* T'. *Then there is a wildcard interleaving* I *belonging-to* T *and an unelimination function* f *from* I' *to* I.

We construct the function f and the uneliminated interleaving in three steps: we decompose the interleaving I' into individual threads, then we obtain 'uneliminated' traces for each thread, and finally we interleave the 'uneliminated' traces of the threads so that we preserve the order of synchronisation and external actions from I' while ordering all introduced synchronisation and external actions after the synchronisation and external actions from I'.

For example, consider the program (v is volatile)

```
v:=1;   ||  r1:=x;
y:=1;   ||  r2:=v;print r2;
```

By our definition of elimination on tracesets, we can eliminate the last release `v:=1` in the first thread and the irrelevant read `r1:=x` in the second thread:

```
y:=1;   ||  r2:=v;print r2;
```

Consider the following execution of the program:

$$I' = [\langle 0, \mathrm{S}(0)\rangle, \langle 1, \mathrm{S}(1)\rangle, \langle 0, \mathrm{W}[\mathtt{y}{=}1]\rangle, \langle 1, \mathrm{R}[\mathtt{v}{=}0]\rangle, \langle 1, \mathrm{X}(0)\rangle]$$

Figure 5 shows one possible construction of unelimination I of I'. The unelimination function is a composition of the functions $f_{I'}$, f_e and f_I. For example, the unelimination function maps 2 to 6, i.e., it moves the second action of I' to the last position in I. Note that we cannot just insert the eliminated actions back into I' to get the unelimination because we would have to insert the write W[v=1] between the start of thread 0 and the write to y and this would break sequential consistency for the read of v.

Uneliminations have an important property: any unelimination of an execution is also an execution if the eliminated execution contained at most one data race. More precisely, let us have a data race free traceset T, its elimination T', an execution I' of T', a wildcard interleaving I belonging-to T and an unelimination function from I' to I, and let all strict prefixes of I' be data race free. Then the instance of I is an execution of T. Moreover, uneliminations preserve data races. These properties are not obvious. We refer the reader to [21] for a full proof. Consequently, elimination preserves data race freedom: suppose that an elimination of a data race free traceset was not data race free. Then we take the shortest execution I of the eliminated traceset with a data race. By the properties of unelimination, the uneliminated interleaving of I is an execution with a data race. This contradicts data race freedom of the original traceset. Thus, we conclude:

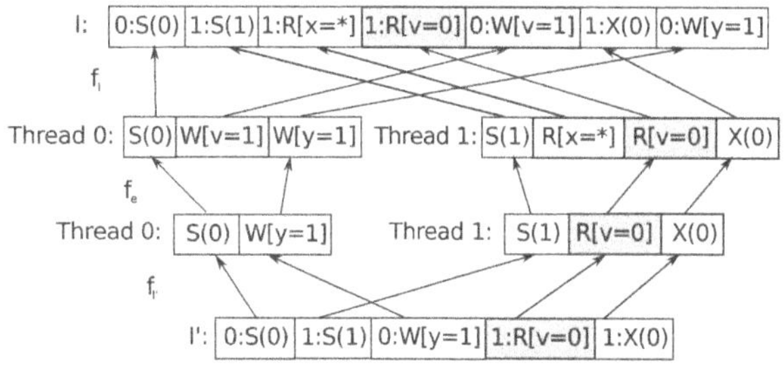

Figure 5. Unelimination construction.

Theorem 1. *Let traceset* T' *be an elimination of a data free traceset* T. *Then* T' *is data race free and any execution of* T' *has the same behaviour as some execution of* T.

Reordering. Since the reordering untransformation does not preserve happens-before order in general, we cannot use the same direct proof we used for elimination. Instead, we prove the safety by induction on the size of the interleaving of the transformed program.

Just like with eliminations, we lift the notion of reordering to interleavings—we define an unordering function describing how to permute the actions in the transformed interleaving to get an interleaving of the original program. We require that whenever restricting an unordering on an interleaving to actions of one thread yields a reordering function on traces, as defined in §4.

Given traceset T and interleaving I', we say that complete matching $f : \mathrm{dom}(I') \to \mathrm{dom}(I')$ is an *unordering* from I' to T if we have: (i) if $i < j \in \mathrm{dom}(I')$, $\mathcal{T}(I'_i) = \mathcal{T}(I'_j)$ and $\mathcal{A}(I'_j), \mathcal{A}(I'_i)$ are not reorderable, then $f(i) < f(j)$, (ii) if $i < j \in \mathrm{dom}(I')$ and $\mathcal{A}(I'_i), \mathcal{A}(I'_j)$ are synchronisation or external actions, then $f(i) < f(j)$, (iii) for each thread θ, the permutation f restricted to actions of θ de-permutes the trace of θ in I' into T.

Using a similar construction to unelimination, unordering always exists. Unlike in the elimination safety proof, we establish the safety by induction on the size of the execution of the reordered traceset. To do that, we observe that restricting a reordering function for an execution to the prefix of the execution without the last element yields a valid reordering function. This allows us to prove by induction on the size of I' that for any unordering function f from an execution I' to a data race free traceset T, the interleaving $I = f^{\to}(I')$ is an execution of T. The technical details of this proof can be found in [21]. The DRF guarantee directly follows.

Theorem 2. *Suppose that traceset T' is a reordering of a data race free traceset T. Then any execution of T' has the same behaviour as some execution of T. Moreover, T' is data race free.*

The data race freedom of T' follows from reordering function being order-reflecting for happens-before order restricted to any individual memory location.

Out-of-thin-air. So far we have seen that the transformations provide an intuitive semantics for programs without data races. But what happens if there are data races in a program? Is anything possible? This would be unacceptable for languages that aim to give security guarantees for arbitrary programs, such as Java with sand-boxing. For an illustration of undesirable behaviours, consider the program

Initially, x = y = 0.

r1:=x;	r2:=y;
y:=r1;	x:=r2;
	print r2;

Since the program does not contain value 42 nor any arithmetic that could create it, no transformation of the program should output 42.

Although our transformations do not give sequential consistency for programs with data races, we can show that out-of-thin-air behaviours, such as the one above, are impossible. More specifically, we will establish that for each output action of some value from an execution of a transformed program there is a statement in the original program that must have created that value. In a language without arithmetic, such as the one introduced in §6, this might mean that if a transformed program outputs value v, then v must be a default value, or the original program must have contained v in its program text as a constant. In a language with dynamic object allocation, we might use similar technique to show that if a program cannot allocate objects of a certain class in any thread, then in no transformed program the reference to such an object appears out-of-thin-air.

The guarantee is based on a simple observation: Let v be a value that is different from the default values. If a program without arithmetic does not contain v as a constant in the source code then in each trace, each write of the value v and each external action with the value v must be preceded by a read of the value v.

Formally, we say that trace t *is an origin* for value v if there is $i \in \mathrm{dom}(t)$ such that t_i is a write of v or an external action with the value v, and there is no $j < i$ such that t_j is a read of the value v. Later, in §6.1, we show an application of this semantic property for a simple language.

Lemma 2. *Let traceset T' be a reordering or an elimination of traceset T and suppose that no trace in T is an origin for v. Let us assume that no location has a singleton type with value v. Then no trace in T' is an origin for v.*

Finally, observe that if T does not contain an origin for a value, no execution of T can output that value:

Lemma 3. *Suppose that v is a value, that is not a default value for any type, T is a traceset, and no t in T is an origin for v. Then there is no execution of T that contains a read, write or external action with the value v.*

6. Connecting Syntax and Semantics

So far we have referred to an intuitive understanding of the relationship between programs and traces. To illustrate the transformations on a concrete syntax, we define a simple concurrent language and several simple but illustrative syntactic program transformations. Then we show that the syntactic transformations correspond to the semantic transformations and thus satisfy the DRF and out-of-thin-air guarantees. It is easy to add more language features, such as pointers, rich expression language and functions, without fundamental changes to the proofs because these features do not have any memory side-effects.

The syntax of our language is given in Fig. 6. The grammar uses distinct identifiers for thread-local register names, ranged over by r or `r1`, `r2` in examples, natural numbers ranged over by i, location names (also called variables) ranged over by l, in examples `x`, `y`, `z`, monitor names ranged over by m, in examples `m1`, `m2`.

We use a labellised small-step semantics to define the meaning of programs in the language introduced. A thread-local configuration is a triple $\langle \Lambda, \sigma, C\rangle$, where monitor state Λ is a function that maps monitor names to the nesting level of locks, local state σ maps register names to values, i.e., natural numbers, and C is a code fragment, which is either S or L or P from the syntax in Fig. 6. The only purpose of the monitor state is to prevent threads from issuing more unlocks than locks on each monitor.

The small-step relation $\langle \Lambda, \sigma, C\rangle \xrightarrow{a} \langle \Lambda', \sigma', C'\rangle$ takes a code fragment C in state Λ, σ to a code fragment C' and states Λ', σ' while issuing shared-memory action a. The action a may be empty, denoted by τ. Fig. 7 contains an inductive definition of the small step relation. We use the term $\mathrm{Val}(\sigma, E)$ for the value of the expression E in the environment σ, i.e., $\mathrm{Val}(\sigma, i) = i$ for any value $i \in \mathbb{N}$, $\mathrm{Val}(\sigma, r) = \sigma(r)$ for register name r, $\mathrm{Val}(\sigma, r_1 \texttt{==} r_2)$ (resp. $\mathrm{Val}(\sigma, r_1 \texttt{!=} r_2)$) is **tt** if $\mathrm{Val}(\sigma, r_1) = \mathrm{Val}(\sigma, r_2)$ (resp. $\mathrm{Val}(\sigma, r_1) = \mathrm{Val}(\sigma, r_2)$) or **ff** otherwise. We write $f[a \mapsto b]$ for a function update, i.e., $f[a \mapsto b](a) = b$ and $f[a \mapsto b](x) = f(x)$ for $x \neq a$.

We will write $\langle \Lambda, \sigma, C\rangle \overset{t}{\underset{n}{\Longrightarrow}} \langle \Lambda', \sigma', C'\rangle$ for a sequence of n transitions, as defined in Fig. 8; notation $\langle \Lambda, \sigma, C\rangle \overset{t}{\Longrightarrow} \langle \Lambda', \sigma', C'\rangle$ stands for a finite number of transition, i.e., it is a shorthand for $\exists n.\ \langle \Lambda, \sigma, C\rangle \overset{t}{\underset{n}{\Longrightarrow}} \langle \Lambda', \sigma', C'\rangle$. A configuration $\langle \Lambda, \sigma, C\rangle$ *may issue trace* t, written $\langle \Lambda, \sigma, C\rangle \Downarrow t$, if there are Λ', σ' and C' such that $\langle \Lambda, \sigma, C\rangle \overset{t}{\Longrightarrow} \langle \Lambda', \sigma', C'\rangle$. The meaning of a code fragment C in thread-local state Λ, σ is the set of all traces that it may issue, i.e., $[\![C]\!]_{\Lambda,\sigma} = \{t \mid \langle \Lambda, \sigma, C\rangle \Downarrow t\}$ The meaning of program P, written $[\![P]\!]$, is the set of traces $[\![P]\!]_{\Lambda_0,\sigma_0}$ where Λ_0 maps all monitor names to 0 and σ maps all locations to 0. Observe that $[\![P]\!]$ is a traceset.

6.1 Transformations: From Syntax to Semantics

Our basic template for local transformation t is given in Fig. 9. Observe that the rules for t cannot perform any transformations yet, i.e., for any P, we have $P \overset{t}{\leadsto} P$ (by induction on the structure of P) and if $P \overset{t}{\leadsto} P'$ then $P = P'$ (by induction on the derivation of $P \overset{t}{\leadsto} P'$). To allow some interesting transformations, we need to add some additional base rules.

Elimination. In Fig. 10, we give the additional base rules for our elimination transformation. Technically, the $\overset{e}{\leadsto}$ relation is defined inductively using the rules from Fig. 10 in addition to the rules from Fig. 9 with $\overset{t}{\leadsto}$ replaced by $\overset{e}{\leadsto}$. The elimination transformation removes redundant (shared-memory) reads and writes. The term $\mathrm{fv}(S)$ stands for all shared-memory locations contained in S. Statement S is sync-free if it does not contain any `lock` or `unlock` statements or accesses to volatile locations. Rule E-RAR (resp. E-RAW) removes redundant read if the value of the location is known from a previous read (resp. write). Rule E-WAR removes a write that follows a read of the same value in the same location. Overwritten writes can be eliminated by rule E-WBW. Rule E-IR removes irrelevant reads which cannot affect the rest of the program because their value is thrown away.

$$
\begin{aligned}
ri &::= r \mid i \\
T &::= ri \;\texttt{==}\; ri \mid ri \;\texttt{!=}\; ri \\
S &::= l \;\texttt{:=}\; r\texttt{;} \mid r \;\texttt{:=}\; l\texttt{;} \mid r \;\texttt{:=}\; ri\texttt{;} \mid \texttt{lock}\; m\texttt{;} \mid \texttt{unlock}\; m\texttt{;} \mid \texttt{skip;} \\
&\quad \mid \texttt{print}\; r\texttt{;} \mid \texttt{\{}L\texttt{\}} \mid \texttt{if}\;(T)\; S \;\texttt{else}\; S \mid \texttt{while}\;(T)\; S \\
L &::= S \mid S\,L \\
P &::= L \,||\, L \,||\, \ldots \,||\, L
\end{aligned}
$$

Figure 6. A simple concurrent language – syntax.

$$
\begin{array}{llll}
\langle \Lambda, \sigma, r\texttt{:=}ri\texttt{;}\rangle & \xrightarrow{\tau} \langle \Lambda, \sigma[r \mapsto \mathrm{Val}(\sigma, ri)], \texttt{skip;}\rangle & & (\textsc{Regs}) \\
\langle \Lambda, \sigma, x\texttt{:=}r\texttt{;}\rangle & \xrightarrow{\mathrm{W}[x=\sigma(r)]} \langle \Lambda, \sigma, \texttt{skip;}\rangle & & (\textsc{Write}) \\
\langle \Lambda, \sigma, r\texttt{:=}x\texttt{;}\rangle & \xrightarrow{\mathrm{R}[x=v]} \langle \Lambda, \sigma[r \mapsto v], \texttt{skip;}\rangle & \text{where } v \in \tau(x) & (\textsc{Read}) \\
\langle \Lambda, \sigma, \texttt{lock}\; m\texttt{;}\rangle & \xrightarrow{\mathrm{L}[m]} \langle \Lambda[m \mapsto \Lambda(m)+1], \sigma, \texttt{skip;}\rangle & & (\textsc{Lock}) \\
\langle \Lambda, \sigma, \texttt{unlock}\; m\texttt{;}\rangle & \xrightarrow{\mathrm{U}[m]} \langle \Lambda[m \mapsto \Lambda(m)-1], \sigma, \texttt{skip;}\rangle & \text{where } \Lambda(m) > 0 & (\textsc{Ulk}) \\
\langle \Lambda, \sigma, \texttt{unlock}\; m\texttt{;}\rangle & \xrightarrow{\tau} \langle \Lambda, \sigma, \texttt{skip;}\rangle & \text{where } \Lambda(m) = 0 & (\textsc{E-Ulk}) \\
\langle \Lambda, \sigma, \texttt{print}\; r\texttt{;}\rangle & \xrightarrow{\mathrm{X}(\sigma(r))} \langle \Lambda, \sigma, \texttt{skip;}\rangle & & (\textsc{Ext}) \\
\langle \Lambda, \sigma, \texttt{if}\;(T)\; S_1 \;\texttt{else}\; S_2\rangle & \xrightarrow{\tau} \langle \Lambda, \sigma, S_1\rangle & \text{if } \mathrm{Val}(\sigma, T) = \mathbf{tt} & (\textsc{Cond-T}) \\
\langle \Lambda, \sigma, \texttt{if}\;(T)\; S_1 \;\texttt{else}\; S_2\rangle & \xrightarrow{\tau} \langle \Lambda, \sigma, S_2\rangle & \text{if } \mathrm{Val}(\sigma, T) = \mathbf{ff} & (\textsc{Cond-F}) \\
\langle \Lambda, \sigma, \texttt{while}\;(T)\; S\rangle & \xrightarrow{\tau} \langle \Lambda, \sigma, S\texttt{;while}\;(T)\; S\rangle & \text{if } \mathrm{Val}(\sigma, T) = \mathbf{tt} & (\textsc{Loop-T}) \\
\langle \Lambda, \sigma, \texttt{while}\;(T)\; S\rangle & \xrightarrow{\tau} \langle \Lambda, \sigma, \texttt{skip;}\rangle & \text{if } \mathrm{Val}(\sigma, T) = \mathbf{ff} & (\textsc{Loop-F}) \\
\langle \Lambda, \sigma, \texttt{skip;}L\rangle & \xrightarrow{\tau} \langle \Lambda, \sigma, L\rangle & & (\textsc{Seq}) \\
\langle \Lambda, \sigma, \texttt{\{skip;\}}\rangle & \xrightarrow{\tau} \langle \Lambda, \sigma, \texttt{skip;}\rangle & & (\textsc{Block}) \\
\langle \Lambda, \sigma, L_0 \,||\, \ldots \,||\, L_n\rangle & \xrightarrow{\mathrm{S}(i)} \langle \Lambda, \sigma, L_i\rangle & \text{where } 0 \le i \le n & (\textsc{Par})
\end{array}
$$

$$
\frac{\langle \Lambda, \sigma, S\rangle \xrightarrow{a} \langle \Lambda', \sigma', S'\rangle}{\langle \Lambda, \sigma, S\; L\rangle \xrightarrow{a} \langle \Lambda', \sigma', S'L\rangle}(\textsc{Ev-Seq}) \qquad \frac{\Lambda, \sigma, L \xrightarrow{a} \Lambda', \sigma', L'}{\langle \Lambda, \sigma, \texttt{\{}L\texttt{\}}\rangle \xrightarrow{a} \langle \Lambda', \sigma', \texttt{\{}L'\texttt{\}}\rangle}(\textsc{Ev-Block})
$$

Figure 7. Small-step Trace Semantics.

$$
\frac{}{\langle \Lambda, \sigma, C\rangle \overset{[]}{\underset{0}{\Longrightarrow}} \langle \Lambda, \sigma, C\rangle}(\textsc{Tr-Id}) \qquad \frac{\langle \Lambda, \sigma, C\rangle \xrightarrow{\tau} \langle \Lambda'', \sigma'', C''\rangle \quad \langle \Lambda'', \sigma'', C''\rangle \overset{\alpha}{\underset{n}{\Longrightarrow}} \langle \Lambda', \sigma', C'\rangle}{\langle \Lambda, \sigma, C\rangle \overset{\alpha}{\underset{n+1}{\Longrightarrow}} \langle \Lambda', \sigma', C'\rangle}(\textsc{Tr-SeqT})
$$

$$
\frac{\langle \Lambda, \sigma, C\rangle \xrightarrow{a} \langle \Lambda'', \sigma'', C''\rangle \quad a \neq \tau \quad \langle \Lambda'', \sigma'', C''\rangle \overset{\alpha}{\underset{n}{\Longrightarrow}} \langle \Lambda', \sigma', C'\rangle}{\langle \Lambda, \sigma, C\rangle \overset{a::\alpha}{\underset{n+1}{\Longrightarrow}} \langle \Lambda', \sigma', C'\rangle}(\textsc{Tr-SeqA})
$$

Figure 8. Multi-step Trace Semantics.

$$
\frac{}{S \overset{t}{\leadsto} S}(\text{T-Id}) \qquad \frac{L \overset{t}{\leadsto} L'}{\texttt{\{}L\texttt{\}} \overset{t}{\leadsto} \texttt{\{}L'\texttt{\}}}(\text{T-Block}) \qquad \frac{S_1 \overset{t}{\leadsto} S_1' \quad L_2 \overset{t}{\leadsto} L_2'}{S_1\, L_2 \overset{t}{\leadsto} S_1'\, L_2'}(\text{T-Seq})
$$

$$
\frac{S_1 \overset{t}{\leadsto} S_1' \quad S_2 \overset{t}{\leadsto} S_2'}{\texttt{if}\;(T)\;\texttt{then}\; S_1 \;\texttt{else}\; S_2 \overset{t}{\leadsto} \texttt{if}\;(T)\;\texttt{then}\; S_1' \;\texttt{else}\; S_2'}(\text{T-If})
$$

$$
\frac{S \overset{t}{\leadsto} S'}{\texttt{while}\;(T)\; S \overset{t}{\leadsto} \texttt{while}\;(T)\; S'}(\text{T-While}) \qquad \frac{\forall i \in \{0, \ldots, n\}.\; S_i \overset{t}{\leadsto} S_i'}{S_0 \,||\, \ldots \,||\, S_n \overset{t}{\leadsto} S_0' \,||\, \ldots \,||\, S_n'}(\text{T-Par})
$$

Figure 9. Transformation template.

$$\frac{x \text{ not volatile} \quad r_1, r_2, x \notin \text{fv}(S) \quad S \text{ sync-free}}{r_1\texttt{:=}x\texttt{;}\ S\texttt{;}\ r_2\texttt{:=}x \overset{e}{\rightsquigarrow} r_1\texttt{:=}x\texttt{;}\ S\texttt{;}\ r_2\texttt{:=}r_1}\ (\text{E-RAR}) \qquad \frac{x \text{ not volatile} \quad r_1, r_2, x \notin \text{fv}(S) \quad S \text{ sync-free}}{x\texttt{:=}r_1\texttt{;}\ S\texttt{;}\ r_2\texttt{:=}x \overset{e}{\rightsquigarrow} x\texttt{:=}r_1\texttt{;}\ S\texttt{;}\ r_2\texttt{:=}r_1}\ (\text{E-RAW})$$

$$\frac{x \text{ not volatile} \quad r, x \notin \text{fv}(S) \quad S \text{ sync-free}}{r\texttt{:=}x\texttt{;}\ S\texttt{;}\ x\texttt{:=}r \overset{e}{\rightsquigarrow} r\texttt{:=}x\texttt{;}\ S\texttt{;}}\ (\text{E-WAR}) \qquad \frac{x \text{ not volatile} \quad r_1, r_2, x \notin \text{fv}(S) \quad S \text{ sync-free}}{x\texttt{:=}r_1\texttt{;}\ S\texttt{;}\ x\texttt{:=}r_2 \overset{e}{\rightsquigarrow} S\texttt{;}\ x\texttt{:=}r_2}\ (\text{E-WBW})$$

$$\frac{x \text{ not volatile}}{r\texttt{:=}x\texttt{;}\ r\texttt{:=}i \overset{e}{\rightsquigarrow} r\texttt{:=}i}\ (\text{E-IR})$$

Figure 10. Additional rules for syntactic elimination.

Our definition of syntactic eliminations (Figure 10) does not include last action eliminations because they are not composable in the sense that trace t_1' being a (last action) elimination of t_1 and t_2' being an elimination of t_2 does not necessarily imply that $t_1' + t_2'$ is an elimination of $t_1 + t_2$. To recover compositionality, we will call index i *properly eliminable* in a wildcard trace t if i is a redundant read after read, or a redundant read after write, or an irrelevant read, or a redundant write after read or an overwritten write. Given traces t and t', the trace t' is a *proper elimination* of t if there is S such that $t' = t|_S$ and all $i \in \text{dom}(t) \setminus S$ are properly eliminable in t. We denote the proper elimination by $t \rightarrow_e t'$.

The following lemma clarifies the relationship between the syntactic elimination and the semantic elimination from §4.

Lemma 4. *Let C be a code fragment and $C \overset{e}{\rightsquigarrow} C'$. Then for any monitor states Λ, Λ', register states σ, σ' and trace t' we have:*

- *If $\langle \Lambda, \sigma, C' \rangle \Downarrow t'$ then there is a wildcard trace t such that $t \rightarrow_e t'$ and for any instance $\hat{t}$ of t we have $\langle \Lambda, \sigma, C \rangle \Downarrow \hat{t}$.*
- *If $\langle \Lambda, \sigma, C' \rangle \overset{t'}{\Longrightarrow} \langle \Lambda', \sigma', \texttt{skip;} \rangle$ then there is a wildcard trace t such that $t \rightarrow_e t'$ and for any instance $\hat{t}$ of t we have $\langle \Lambda, \sigma, C \rangle \overset{\hat{t}}{\Longrightarrow} \langle \Lambda', \sigma', \texttt{skip;} \rangle$.*

As a consequence, if $P \overset{e}{\rightsquigarrow} P'$ for some programs P and P', then $[\![P']\!]$ is an elimination of $[\![P]\!]$. Combining this observation with the results for the semantic elimination (Theorem 1) gives us a compositional DRF guarantee for syntactic elimination:

Theorem 3. *Suppose that $P \overset{e}{\rightsquigarrow} P'$ and $[\![P]\!]$ is data race free. Then $[\![P']\!]$ is data race free, and any execution of $[\![P']\!]$ has the same behaviour as some execution of $[\![P]\!]$.*

Reordering. Fig. 11 shows additional rules for reordering. Similarly to the elimination transformations, the relation $\overset{r}{\rightsquigarrow}$ is defined inductively using the rules from Fig. 11 and relabelled rules from Fig. 9. We capture reordering of independent non-volatile memory accesses in rules R-RW, R-RR, R-WR and R-WW. Rules R-WL, R-RL, R-UW and R-UR allow moving non-volatile memory accesses inside synchronised blocks. Note that the R-RR, R-WR and R-WW rules allow limited reordering of accesses to volatile locations with non-volatile accesses.

The relationship between the syntactic and semantic reordering is more involved in our framework because syntactic reordering corresponds to semantic elimination followed by semantic reordering; for an illustration, see the example in §4. The following lemma formalises the relationship between the syntactic reordering and the trace semantics.

Lemma 5. *Assume that $C \overset{r}{\rightsquigarrow} C'$. Then for each Λ and σ there is a prefix closed set of traces T satisfying these conditions: (i) the set of traces $[\![C]\!]_{\Lambda,\sigma}$ is a subset of T, (ii) each trace from T is an elimination of some wildcard trace that belongs-to $[\![C]\!]_{\Lambda,\sigma}$, (iii) for each trace t', if $\langle \Lambda, \sigma, C' \rangle \Downarrow t'$ holds then there is a function that de-permutes t' into T, (iv) for each trace t', if there are Λ' and σ' such that $\langle \Lambda, \sigma, C' \rangle \overset{t'}{\Longrightarrow} \langle \Lambda', \sigma', \texttt{skip;} \rangle$ then there is a function f that de-permutes t' into T and $\langle \Lambda, \sigma, C \rangle \overset{f^{\rightarrow}(t')}{\Longrightarrow} \langle \Lambda', \sigma', \texttt{skip;} \rangle$.*

Together with the semantic DRF guarantees from §5, we obtain the compositional DRF guarantee for syntactic reordering.

Theorem 4. *Suppose that $P \overset{r}{\rightsquigarrow} P'$ and $[\![P]\!]$ is data race free. Then $[\![P']\!]$ is data race free, and any execution of $[\![P']\!]$ has the same behaviour as some execution of $[\![P]\!]$.*

Out-of-thin-air. To establish the out-of-thin-air-guarantee for our simple language, we first observe that if a program does not contain constant c then the program is not an origin for c:

Lemma 6. *Let v be a value such that v is not a default value for any location, i.e., $v \neq 0$. Let P be a program without any statement of the form $r\texttt{:=}v$, where r is a register name. Then no trace in the traceset of P is an origin for the value v.*

This observation allows us to use our semantic observations from §5 and state the syntactic counterpart of the out-of-thin-air guarantee.

Theorem 5. *Suppose that c is a constant different from 0, and P a program that does not contain a statement of the form $r := c$, where r is a register. Let P' be a program obtained from P by any composition of syntactic reorderings or eliminations. Then P' cannot output c.*

7. Related Work

The existing research on compiler optimisations for shared-memory concurrency concentrates mainly on maintaining sequential consistency for all programs, starting with the foundational work of Shasha and Snir [24], where they take a sequentially consistent execution of a straight line program and describe a set of reordering constraints that preserve sequential consistency. Building on these foundations, papers [15, 17, 26] describe whole program analyses that determine allowable reorderings in multi-threaded programs and compilers that preserve behaviours of arbitrary programs. The emphasis of that line of work is different from ours: while they design a restricted compiler that guarantees (an illusion of) sequential consistency for all programs, we show that commonly used program transformations maintain an illusion of sequential consistency for correctly synchronised programs. We are not aware of any such work in the context of compilers.

Correctness of optimisations is closely related to weak memory models for programming languages and hardware. In fact, validity of common optimisations was the main motivation for designing the Java Memory Model [16]. Despite this, Java does not allow several common optimisations [9, 23], and even the reference implementation of Java Virtual Machine does not conform with the specification [22]. The situation does not seem to be much better

$$\frac{r_1 \neq r_2 \quad x \text{ not volatile}}{r_1\texttt{:=}x\texttt{;}\ r_2\texttt{:=}y\texttt{;}\ \overset{r}{\rightsquigarrow}\ r_2\texttt{:=}y\texttt{;}\ r_1\texttt{:=}x\texttt{;}}\ (\text{R-RR})$$

$$\frac{x \neq y \quad y \text{ not volatile}}{x\texttt{:=}r_1\texttt{;}\ y\texttt{:=}r_2\texttt{;}\ \overset{r}{\rightsquigarrow}\ y\texttt{:=}r_2\texttt{;}\ x\texttt{:=}r_1\texttt{;}}\ (\text{R-WW})$$

$$\frac{r_1 \neq r_2 \quad x \neq y \quad x \text{ or } y \text{ not volatile}}{x\texttt{:=}r_1\texttt{;}\ r_2\texttt{:=}y\texttt{;}\ \overset{r}{\rightsquigarrow}\ r_2\texttt{:=}y\texttt{;}\ x\texttt{:=}r_1\texttt{;}}\ (\text{R-WR})$$

$$\frac{r_1 \neq r_2 \quad x \neq y \quad x, y \text{ not volatile}}{r_1\texttt{:=}x\texttt{;}\ y\texttt{:=}r_2\texttt{;}\ \overset{r}{\rightsquigarrow}\ y\texttt{:=}r_2\texttt{;}\ r_1\texttt{:=}x\texttt{;;}}\ (\text{R-RW})$$

$$\frac{x \text{ not volatile}}{x\texttt{:=}r\texttt{;}\ \texttt{lock}\ m\texttt{;}\ \overset{r}{\rightsquigarrow}\ \texttt{lock}\ m\texttt{;}\ x\texttt{:=}r\texttt{;}}\ (\text{R-WL})$$

$$\frac{x \text{ not volatile}}{r\texttt{:=}x\texttt{;}\ \texttt{lock}\ m\texttt{;}\ \overset{r}{\rightsquigarrow}\ \texttt{lock}\ m\texttt{;}\ r\texttt{:=}x\texttt{;}}\ (\text{R-RL})$$

$$\frac{x \text{ not volatile}}{\texttt{unlock}\ m\texttt{;}x\texttt{:=}r\texttt{;}\ \overset{r}{\rightsquigarrow}\ x\texttt{:=}r\texttt{;unlock}\ m\texttt{;}}\ (\text{R-UW})$$

$$\frac{x \text{ not volatile}}{\texttt{unlock}\ m\texttt{;}r\texttt{:=}x\texttt{;}\ \overset{r}{\rightsquigarrow}\ r\texttt{:=}x\texttt{;unlock}\ m\texttt{;}}\ (\text{R-UR})$$

$$\frac{r_1 \neq r_2 \quad x \text{ not volatile}}{\texttt{print}\ r_1\texttt{;}r_2\texttt{:=}x\texttt{;}\ \overset{r}{\leftrightsquigarrow}\ r_2\texttt{:=}x\texttt{;print}\ r_1\texttt{;}}\ (\text{R-XR})$$

$$\frac{x \text{ not volatile}}{\texttt{print}\ r_1\texttt{;}x\texttt{:=}r_2\texttt{;}\ \overset{r}{\leftrightsquigarrow}\ x\texttt{:=}r_2\texttt{;print}\ r_1\texttt{;}}\ (\text{R-XW})$$

Figure 11. Additional rules for syntactic reordering.

in Microsoft Common Language Infrastructure (CLI): the official specification is in informal prose without any clear guarantees for programmers. In practice, the CLI virtual machine seems to be very conservative, and it appears that it conforms to a much stronger unofficial model [18]. There have been several other suggestions for weak memory models for high-level languages, but none of these addressed validity of compiler transformations [9, 19]. Hardware memory models or hardware-inspired memory models, such as [2, 7, 8], do not seem to be suitable for higher languages because they are either too prohibitive and do not allow reordering of reads with later independent writes/reads at all, or they rely on syntactic notions of dependency for reordering, which can be often removed by optimising compilers. We hope that our work will serve as a basis for a formal weak memory model defined in terms of permissible transformations.

8. Conclusion

We have proved that two large classes of compiler optimisations, elimination and reordering, are safe in the DRF guarantee, i.e., they cannot introduce new behaviours for data race free programs. Since our transformations preserve data race freedom, arbitrary composition of the transformations is also safe.

As reasoning about multi-threading is notoriously error-prone, we mechanised the definitions and difficult parts of the semantic elimination safety proof (such as Lemma 1) in the Isabelle/HOL proof assistant. The mechanisation has about ten thousand lines of proof script. The current development snapshot is available at `http://www.cl.cam.ac.uk/~js861/transafety/mm-traces`.

In our work, we assume that the transformed program always runs sequentially consistently. This might seem to be a severe limitation because few modern processors guarantee sequential consistency. However, it is well-understood how to ensure the DRF guarantee on hardware and all our transformations preserve data race freedom, so we can safely assume sequential consistency in hardware. Unfortunately, we cannot easily recover the out-of-thin-air guarantee without deeper understanding of the processor memory models. Therefore, we started investigating extensions of our techniques to cover hardware memory models. Our first results are encouraging—we can explain the Sun TSO memory model [25], used by most SPARC processors with our semantic transformations. We believe that there similar results can be achieved for other processor memory models.

Acknowledgments

I would like to thank David Aspinall for his guidance and Peter Sewell for many useful comments on earlier drafts of the paper. I acknowledge funding from EPSRC grants EP/F036345, EP/H005633.

References

[1] S. V. Adve and M. D. Hill. Weak ordering — a new definition. In *ISCA'90*, pages 2–14, 1990.

[2] Sarita V. Adve and Kourosh Gharachorloo. Shared memory consistency models: A tutorial. *Computer*, 29(12):66–76, 1996.

[3] J. Alglave, A. Fox, S. Ishtiaq, M. O. Myreen, S. Sarkar, P. Sewell, and F. Zappa Nardelli. The semantics of Power and ARM multiprocessor machine code. In *Proc. DAMP 2009*, January 2009.

[4] M. Batty, S. Owens, S. Sarkar, P. Sewell, and T. Weber. Mathematizing C++ concurrency. In *Proc. POPL*, 2011.

[5] P. Becker, editor. *Programming Languages — C++. Final Committee Draft*. 2010. ISO/IEC JTC1 SC22 WG21 N3092.

[6] Hans-J. Boehm and Sarita V. Adve. Foundations of the C++ concurrency memory model. In *PLDI '08*, pages 68–78, New York, NY, USA, 2008. ACM.

[7] Gérard Boudol and Gustavo Petri. Relaxed memory models: an operational approach. In *POPL '09*, pages 392–403, 2009.

[8] S. Burckhardt, M. Musuvathi, and V. Singh. Verifying local transformations on relaxed memory models. In *CC '10*, pages 104–123, 2010.

[9] P. Cenciarelli, A. Knapp, and E. Sibilio. The Java memory model: Operationally, denotationally, axiomatically. In *16th ESOP*, 2007.

[10] J. Gosling, B. Joy, G. Steele, and G. Bracha. *Java(TM) Language Specification, The (3rd Edition) (Java Series)*. Addison-Wesley Professional, July 2005.

[11] Intel. A formal specification of Intel Itanium processor family memory ordering, 2002. Available from `http://www.intel.com/design/itanium/downloads/251429.htm`.

[12] P. Joisha, R. Schreiber, P. Banerjee, H.-J. Boehm, and D. Chakrabarti. A technique for the effective and automatic reuse of classical compiler optimizations on multithreaded code. Technical Report HPL-2010-81, HP Laboratories, 2010. To appear in POPL 2011.

[13] Leslie Lamport. Time, clocks, and the ordering of events in a distributed system. *Commun. ACM*, 21(7):558–565, 1978.

[14] Doug Lea. The JSR-133 cookbook for compiler writers, 2008. `http://g.oswego.edu/dl/jmm/cookbook.html`.

[15] Jaejin Lee, David A. Padua, and Samuel P. Midkiff. Basic compiler algorithms for parallel programs. In *PPOPP*, pages 1–12. ACM, 1999.

[16] J. Manson, W. Pugh, and S. Adve. The Java memory model. In *POPL '05*, pages 378–391, New York, NY, USA, 2005. ACM Press.

[17] Samuel P. Midkiff and David A. Padua. Issues in the optimization of parallel programs. In *ICPP (2)*, pages 105–113. Pennsylvania State University Press, 1990.

[18] Vance Morrison. Understand the impact of low-lock techniques in multithreaded apps. *MSDN Magazine*, Oct 2005.

[19] V. Saraswat, R. Jagadeesan, M. Michael, and C. von Praun. A theory of memory models. In *PPoPP '07*. ACM, Mar 2007.

[20] S. Sarkar, P. Sewell, F. Zappa Nardelli, S. Owens, T. Ridge, T. Braibant, M. Myreen, and J. Alglave. The semantics of x86-CC multiprocessor machine code. In *POPL'09*, January 2009.

[21] J. Ševčík. *Program Transformations in Weak Memory Models*. PhD thesis, University of Edinburgh, Laboratory for Foundations of Computer Science, 2008.

[22] J. Ševčík. The Sun Hotspot JVM does not conform with the Java memory model. Technical Report EDI-INF-RR-1252, School of Informatics, University of Edinburgh, 2008.

[23] J. Ševčík and D. Aspinall. On validity of program transformations in the Java memory model. In *ECOOP '08*, pages 27–51, 2008.

[24] Dennis Shasha and Marc Snir. Efficient and correct execution of parallel programs that share memory. *ACM Trans. Program. Lang. Syst.*, 10(2):282–312, 1988.

[25] Sparc International. Sparc architecture manual, version 9, 2000. Available from `http://developers.sun.com/solaris/articles/sparcv9.html`.

[26] Z. Sura, X. Fang, C. Wong, S. Midkiff, J. Lee, and D. Padua. Compiler techniques for high performance sequentially consistent Java programs. In *PPoPP '05*, pages 2–13, New York, NY, USA, 2005. ACM.

Spreadsheet Table Transformations from Examples

William R. Harris *
Dept. of Computer Sciences
University of Wisconsin, Madison
Madison, WI, USA
wrharris@cs.wisc.edu

Sumit Gulwani
Microsoft Research
Redmond, WA, USA
sumitg@microsoft.com

Abstract

Every day, millions of computer end-users need to perform tasks over large, tabular data, yet lack the programming knowledge to do such tasks automatically. In this work, we present an automatic technique that takes from a user an example of how the user needs to transform a table of data, and provides to the user a program that implements the transformation described by the example. In particular, we present a language of programs TableProg that can describe transformations that real users require. We then present an algorithm ProgFromEx that takes an example input and output table, and infers a program in TableProg that implements the transformation described by the example. When the program is applied to the example input, it reproduces the example output. When the program is applied to another, potentially larger, table with a "similar" layout as the example input table, then the program produces a corresponding table with a layout that is similar to the example output table. A user can apply ProgFromEx interactively, providing multiple small examples to obtain a program that implements the transformation that the user desires. Moreover, ProgFromEx can help identify "noisy" examples that contain errors.

To evaluate the practicality of TableProg and ProgFromEx, we implemented ProgFromEx as a module for the Microsoft Excel spreadsheet program. We applied the module to automatically implement over 50 table transformations specified by end-users through examples on online Excel help forums. In seconds, ProgFromEx found programs that satisfied the examples and could be applied to larger input tables. This experience demonstrates that TableProg and ProgFromEx can significantly automate the tasks over tabular data that users need to perform.

Categories and Subject Descriptors D.1.2 [*Programming Techniques*]: Automatic Programming; I.2.2 [*Artificial Intelligence*]: Program Synthesis

General Terms Languages, Algorithms, Human Factors

Keywords Program Synthesis, End-user Programming, Programming by Example, Spreadsheet Programming, Table Manipulation, User Intent

* This work was performed during an internship at Microsoft Research, Redmond.

PLDI'11, June 4–8, 2011, San Jose, California, USA.

1. Introduction

More and more end users now apply computers to perform complex and critical tasks on digital data. While users often clearly understand the task that they need a computer to perform, the tools that users may apply to communicate their task to a computer remain limited. At one extreme, graphical user interfaces (GUI's) are highly accessible. However, GUI's typically do not allow users to customize or personalize their program such that the user can fully automate their task. Furthermore, as programs with GUI's support more and more features, users often struggle to discover the features. On the other extreme, general programming languages serve as a fully expressive medium for communicating a task to a computer. However, even the most accessible scripting language requires an amount of time and energy that a typical user is not prepared, and should not be expected, to invest.

Unlike traditional programming, the techniques of *end-user programming* by demonstration or by example [3, 17] allow users to describe a computation via partial execution traces or final outputs resulting from a small set of inputs, without requiring the user to describe how to perform the computation in general. A tool based on such techniques then produces for the user a general program that, given the example inputs, produces the corresponding outputs. Moreover, the program is defined for many more inputs than the examples, so users can apply the program to other inputs to automatically obtain the outputs that they require. Programming by example is an attractive approach, as users often naturally use examples to express the tasks that they need to perform. On help forums that we studied, novice users express tasks through examples so frequently that it is practically a forum convention.

Previous work in programming by example has focused primarily on inferring programs that transform strings of text [9, 15]. However, techniques based on this work cannot yet be used directly by real end users, as in practice, users need to transform rich, semi-structured data. In particular, millions of users every day need to transform tabular data stored in spreadsheets using office programs such as Microsoft Excel [5] or OpenOffice [19]. Often, such transformations do not change the textual content of any cell, or only change the content in a simple way. However, the transformation rearranges the layout of the table, i.e. the manner in which cells are spatially arranged or grouped. Existing techniques for programming by example cannot be applied to infer programs that implement such transformations.

Inferring transformations over spreadsheet tables presents unique challenges compared to the problem of inferring views over relational tables [4]. In particular, a spreadsheet table is in general only a two-dimensional array of cells, where each cell contains a string. Unlike relational tables, rows of a spreadsheet tables are ordered, different rows may contain data with different semantic relationships, and the spreadsheet table may not provide names of column fields. Spreadsheet tables also often have special layout or format-

Example input table:

	Qual 1	Qual 2	Qual 3
Andrew	01.02.2003	27.06.2008	06.04.2007
Ben	31.08.2001		05.07.2004
Carl		18.04.2003	09.12.2009

Example output table:

Andrew	Qual 1	01.02.2003
Andrew	Qual 2	27.06.2008
Andrew	Qual 3	06.04.2007
Ben	Qual 1	31.08.2001
Ben	Qual 3	05.07.2004
Carl	Qual 2	18.04.2003
Carl	Qual 3	09.12.2009

Figure 1. Example input and output tables from an online Excel help forum thread "Using a macro to extract and rearrange data."

ting attributes, such as sub-headers, footers, filler cells (blank cells or cells with some special characters to aid visual readability of table content) [1]. In this paper, we only consider the problem of inferring transformations over spreadsheet tables. All references to "tables" refer to spreadsheet tables, unless otherwise noted.

Example 1. *The tables in Fig. 1 are an example of a common table transformation that a user would like to perform automatically. The tables are from a real Excel help forum thread.* [1] *The thread was started by a novice user, who needed to transform a large table in a given layout into a table in a different layout. To express their transformation, the user provided a small, representative input table, along with the output table that should result from applying the transformation to the input table. Both tables are in Fig. 1. The example input table contains a set of dates on which tests where given, where each date is in a row corresponding to the name of the test taker, and in a column corresponding to the name of the test. For every date, the user needs to produce a row in the output table containing the name of the test taker, the name of the test, and the date on which the test was taken. If a date cell in the input table is empty, then no corresponding row should be produced in the output table. The rows should be produced in the order that the dates are ordered in the input table by row-major order.*

In the help thread, the novice user described their required transformation in a few paragraphs of English, but the novice also included the example input and output tables in Fig. 1 (the output table has been simplified slightly for illustrative purposes; the full implementation of our technique can infer a program for the original example). In about half an hour, an expert user responded with a link to an Excel macro that the expert suspected would be useful for the novice. Twenty minutes after the expert responded, the novice confirmed that the macro implemented the transformation that he or she required.

In this paper, we describe a method for inferring table transformations from examples by applying a general research methodology for designing systems that support programming by example [8]. The steps of this general methodology are:

1. Identify a domain of data on which a large class of users struggle to perform repetitive operations that they can clearly describe with examples.
2. Design a programming language that describes a large proportion of operations that users need to perform on the data domain in practice.
3. Design an algorithm that efficiently infers programs in the language from example inputs and outputs.

In previous work, we applied the above methodology to infer programs that transform strings of text [9]. In this work, we apply the methodology to infer programs that transform tables.

In this paper, we first present a language of programs that implement transformations over tables. While the language cannot describe all transformations over tables, we designed it by studying the transformations that users require in practice, and defining a language that can describe combinations of the most common transformations.

We then present an algorithm that takes an example input and output table and automatically infers in seconds a program in the language that implements a transformation that satisfies the example. If the program is applied to the example input, then the program produces the example output, and if the program is applied to another table with a layout similar to that of the example input, then the program produces a corresponding table with a layout similar to the example output table. End users can apply our language and algorithm to automatically obtain programs that transform multiple, huge tables. To do so, they construct small, representative input and output example tables, and give the example tables to our inference algorithm. The inference algorithm then infers a program which the user can apply to their large input tables. The user in Ex. 1 can apply our algorithm to the example tables in Fig. 1 and in seconds obtain a program that implements their desired table transformation.

The algorithm is highly scalable because it divides the problem of inferring a program that transforms an entire table into subproblems of inferring programs that transform subtables of the original table. It then infers simple programs that transform the subtables, and efficiently combines the simple programs to construct a program that transforms the original table.

On some examples, our algorithm may infer a program that satisfies the input and output pair given by the user, but does not implement the general transformation that the user requires. In this case, the user can refine the inferred program by providing a larger, more descriptive input-output example that demonstrates the behavior on which the original program behaves incorrectly, or by providing multiple input and output examples that together describe the required behavior.

In this paper, we make the following contributions:

1. We present a language of programs, TableProg, that can express a rich set of practical transformations over tabular data. TableProg is designed to express table transformations required by real users, but is conceptually simple and is described by a small semantics.
2. We present a novel algorithm, ProgFromEx, for inferring TableProg programs from example input and output tables. We show the correctness of ProgFromEx, and analyze its complexity.
3. We report our experience using ProgFromEx. We implemented ProgFromEx as a plug-in module for the Microsoft Excel spreadsheet program, and applied the module to automatically infer TableProg programs that implement over 50 transformations specified by examples in online Excel help forums.

The rest of this paper is organized as follows. In §2, we use the example in Fig. 1 to illustrate the challenges of inferring table transformations, the structure of programs in TableProg, and how ProgFromEx infers a program that satisfies the example. In §3, we present TableProg in detail, and in §4, we present ProgFromEx in detail. In §5, we report our experience applying ProgFromEx

[1] http://www.excelforum.com/excel-programming/698490-using-a-macro-to-extract-and-rearrange-data.html

to infer table programs from real-world examples. In §6 we discuss related work, and in §7, we conclude.

2. Overview

Users often need to transform the layout of tables in non-trivial ways. In this section, we use the running example in Fig. 1 to observe in more detail the challenges in inferring a transformation from an example input and output. From these observations, we motivate the design of our language TableProg of table programs and our algorithm for inferring TableProg programs.

2.1 An Example Table Program

Consider a program that, given the example input table from Fig. 1, produces the example output table (i.e. a program that *satisfies* the examples). One insight into a possible structure of such a program is guided by the following property of example tables, which we have observed to hold over almost all example tables given by real users.

Remark 1. Often, a subset of the cells in an output table (i.e. a *substructure* of the output table) can be produced by treating the cells in the input table as a sequence ordered by row-major order, selecting some cells in the sequence, and spatially rearranging the selected cells while preserving their row-major order.

Guided by Remark 1, we initially suppose that a table program makes a series of passes over the input table in row-major order. In each pass, the program selects a subset of cells in the input table, and produces cells in the output table that hold the same text as the selected cells, though they may be produced in a different spatial arrangement. We call each pass a *filter program*, and say that a filter program reads the cells of the input table in row-major order, and checks if each cell satisfies a *mapping condition*. If an input cell satisfies the mapping condition, then the filter program produces a new cell in the output table that contains the same text as the input. The new cell is produced at the bottom of a column determined by an *output sequencer*.

Example 2. *Remark 1 can be applied to the tables in Fig. 1 to derive a filter program* F *that produces column 3 (we adopt the convention of most spreadsheet programs and describe tables using 1-based indexing). To produce column 3, a filter program passes over the cells in the input table in row-major order, and checks each cell against the mapping condition that the cell is not in row 1, not in column 1, and is non-empty. If the input cell satisfies the mapping condition, then the filter program's output sequencer determines that filter program should add the new cell to column 3.*

Ex. 2 illustrates that filter programs are often powerful enough to produce substructures of an output table. However, Fig. 1 demonstrates that filter programs on their own are often insufficient or impractical for producing an entire output table. First, to produce column 1 of the output table, a filter program would need to perform complex reasoning. When the filter program would check the input cell containing "Andrew," it would add cells holding this text to column 1 of the output three times in sequence. However, when the filter program would check the cells with texts "Ben" and "Carl", it would only add cells to column 1 of the output two times each. To produce column 2 of the output table, a filter program would need to apply different complex reasoning. Such a program would check the input cells containing the texts "Qual k," and would produce column 2 of the output table by interleaving multiple cells with these texts. Intuitively, it seems difficult to derive a language of filter programs that can perform such reasoning in a single pass over the input table. To derive programs that can produce such substructures of the output, we apply a new observation.

Remark 2. Two cells in an output table that are in the same row or column often hold the same text as two cells in the input table that are in the same row or the same column.

Example 3. *For Fig. 1, let cell c be any cell in column 1 of the output table, and let cell d be in column 3 of the same row as c. Then c and d hold the same text as cells in columns 1 and 3 of some row of the input table.*

To apply Remark 2, we first enrich our notion of a filter program. Above, we described a filter program as taking a table as input and producing a substructure of a table as output. We now describe a filter program as taking a table as input, and computing a *map* from coordinates of cells in the input table to the coordinates of cells that will be in the output table. In general, a map may be an arbitrary binary relation pairing input and output coordinates; it need not be a function. A table program applies a coordinate map to an input table to produce a substructure of the output table; for every entry (c, d) in the map, the table program produces a new cell in the output table at coordinate d, and fills the cell with the text in the input table at c. If a coordinate map maps every cell that will be in a column k of an output table, then we say that the map *maps to column k*.

Example 4. *In Ex. 2, we described a filter program* F *as producing column 3 of the output table. If we redefine* F *as computing a map m_{F} from coordinates of cells in the input table to coordinates of cells that will be in column 3 of the output table, then m_{F} for the example tables in Fig. 1 is the following set of pairs of input and output coordinates:*

$$m_{\mathsf{F}} = \left\{ \begin{array}{l} ((2,2),(1,3)), ((2,3),(2,3)), ((2,4),(3,3)), \\ ((3,2),(4,3)), ((3,4),(5,3)), \\ ((4,3),(6,3)), ((4,4),(7,3)) \end{array} \right\}$$

By defining filter programs to compute maps between coordinates, we can build *associative programs* from filter programs. Like a filter program, an associative program computes a map from coordinates of cells in the input table to coordinates of cells to be in the output table. However, to do so, an associative program uses a filter program F to compute an initial map between coordinates, and then alters each pair of coordinates in the map to produce its own map. The associative program alters the map computed by F by applying a *relative function* R_1 to each input coordinate to obtain a new input coordinates, and applying another relative function R_2 to each output coordinate to obtain new output coordinates. We denote such an associative program as $(\mathsf{F}, \mathsf{R}_1, \mathsf{R}_2)$.

Example 5. *For Fig. 1, an associative program A_1 maps to column 1 of the output table. A_1 first uses* F *to compute the map m_{F} from Ex. 4. A_1 alters the input coordinates of m_{F} by applying to each input coordinate a relative function $\mathtt{RELCOL}_1$ that computes the coordinate in the same row and in column 1. A_1 alters the output coordinates of m_{F} by applying $\mathtt{RELCOL}_1$ to each output coordinate. The resulting map m_{A_1} maps coordinates in column 1 of the input table to coordinates of cells to be produced in column 1 of the output table:*

$$m_{\mathsf{A}_1} = \left\{ \begin{array}{l} ((2,1),(1,1)), ((2,1),(2,1)), ((2,1),(3,1)), \\ ((3,1),(4,1)), ((3,1),(5,1)), \\ ((4,1),(6,1)), ((4,1),(7,1)) \end{array} \right\}$$

A second associative program A_2 maps to column 2 of the output table. Like A_1, A_2 first uses F *to compute m_{F}. A_2 alters each input coordinate in m_{F} by applying a relative function $\mathtt{RELROW}_1$ that computes the coordinate in the same column but in row 1. A_2 alters each output coordinate in m_{F} by applying a relative function $\mathtt{RELCOL}_2$, where $\mathtt{RELCOL}_2$ is defined analogously to $\mathtt{RELCOL}_1$. The resulting map m_{A_2} maps coordinates in row 1 of the input to* *coordinates of cells to be produced in column 2 of the output:*

$$m_{\mathsf{A}_2} = \left\{ \begin{array}{l} ((1,2),(1,2)),((1,3),(2,2)),((1,4),(3,2)), \\ ((1,2),(4,2)),((1,4),(5,2)), \\ ((1,3),(6,2)),((1,4),(7,2)) \end{array} \right\}$$

An associative program may use a map computed by a filter program, but may in general also use a map computed by another associative program. This is because an associative program only uses a filter program to compute a map over table coordinates, but associative programs themselves compute maps over table coordinates. We thus refer to both filter programs and associative programs as *component programs*, and say that in general, an associative program can be built from a component program.

A table program P built from filter and associative programs can take the example input table from Fig. 1 and produce the example output table. P computes the coordinate map of the filter program F described in Ex. 4, the map of the associative program A_1, and the map of A_2 described in Ex. 5, and then applies the coordinate maps to produce a table. When P is applied to the example input from Fig. 1, it produces the example output. P is a program in the language TableProg, which is presented formally in §3.

2.2 Inferring the Example Table Program

The table program P described in §2.1 satisfies the example tables from Fig. 1. The algorithm ProgFromEx, when given the example tables from Fig. 1, automatically infers P. Like P, each table program is a set of two different types of component programs: filter programs and associative programs. Thus ProgFromEx infers a table program in two steps, building component programs of a particular type in each step. In step 1), ProgFromEx builds a set of filter programs. In step 2), ProgFromEx iteratively builds associative programs from component programs that it has already built until it finds a set of component programs that map to all cells in the example output table.

In step 1), ProgFromEx infers a set of filter programs from a fixed set of *candidate-map rules*. Each candidate-map rule, given example input and output tables, produces a set of *consistent* maps between coordinates in the example tables. A map is consistent for an example input and output if, when applied to the example input, the map produces a substructure of the example output. Unlike a filter program, candidate-map rules cannot compute a map from only an input table. They are applied to an example input and output to suggest a map that a filter program may compute when the program is applied to the example input. Thus we call such a map a *candidate map*. From a candidate map, ProgFromEx infers a general filter program that computes the candidate map when applied to the example input, but also computes analogous maps when applied to other input tables.

Example 6. ProgFromEx *uses a candidate-map rule to suggest the coordinate map m_{F} from Ex. 4.* ProgFromEx *is given candidate-map rules that specify: "map a coordinate in the input table to a coordinate in column k of the output table if and only if the values at those coordinates are equal," with one such rule for each column k in the example output table. The rule for $k = 3$ generates a candidate map from each coordinate holding a date in the input table to the coordinate in the output table holding the same date. This map is m_{F}.*

Given a candidate map, ProgFromEx attempts to infer a filter program that computes the map when the program is applied to the example input. To infer a filter program, ProgFromEx must first infer the filter program's mapping condition. For a filter program to compute the candidate map, the program's mapping condition must be satisfied by every input cell mapped by the candidate map, and must not satisfied by any input cell that is not mapped by the candidate map. ProgFromEx infers the mapping condition as a conjunction over a fixed set of atomic predicates and their negations using a greedy algorithm, discussed in §4.1. Each atomic predicate describes some feature of a cell.

Example 7. ProgFromEx *infers a filter program to implement the candidate map m_{F} suggested by a candidate-map rule in Ex. 6. To infer a filter program,* ProgFromEx *first infers the filter program's mapping condition. The mapping condition must be satisfied by all of the cells in the example input that are mapped by m_{F}, and must not be satisfied by any of the cells in the example input that are not mapped by m_{F}. Suppose that* ProgFromEx *is given a predicate that decides if a cell is in row 1, a predicate that decides if a cell is empty, and for each column k in the example input table, a predicate that decides if a cell is in column k. Given these predicates,* ProgFromEx *infers the conjunctive mapping condition stated informally in Ex. 2.*

To infer a filter program that computes a candidate map, ProgFromEx must also infer an output sequencer for the filter program. To infer an output sequencer, ProgFromEx orders the output coordinates in the candidate map by the order in which the filter program must map them; i.e., ProgFromEx orders the output coordinates by the row-major ordering of the input cells that map to them. ProgFromEx then checks if the ordered sequence of output coordinates matches the output coordinates described by some output sequencer in a fixed set of sequencers. If so, then ProgFromEx builds a filter program by pairing the matching sequencer with the corresponding mapping condition.

Example 8. *For* ProgFromEx *to infer a filter program that computes the candidate map m_{F} from Ex. 6, it must infer an output sequencer that describes the output coordinates mapped to by m_{F}. To infer a sequencer,* ProgFromEx *orders the output coordinates mapped to by m_{F} by the row-major order of the input cells that map to them under m_{F}. The output coordinates ordered in this way form column 3 of the example output table.* ProgFromEx *thus builds a filter program that computes m_{F} from a sequencer that maps to coordinates in column 3, as opposed to a sequencer that maps to coordinates in column 1 or 2.*

In step 1), ProgFromEx generates a set of candidate maps, and infers filter programs that implement the candidate maps; the inferred filter programs serve as an initial set of component programs for step 2) In step 2), ProgFromEx iteratively builds associative programs from the component programs that it has already built. As described in §2.1, an associative program is built from a component program and two relative functions. ProgFromEx thus builds associative programs by combining component programs that it has already built with relative functions drawn from a fixed set. If the resulting associative program computes a map that is consistent for the example tables, then ProgFromEx retains the associative program as a component program from which to build more associative programs.

Example 9. ProgFromEx *builds the associative programs A_1 and A_2 described in Ex. 5 from the filter program* F *described in Ex. 2.* ProgFromEx *finds A_1 by combining filter program* F *and relative functions $\mathtt{RELCOL}_1$ to build the associative program $A_1 = (\mathsf{F}, \mathtt{RELCOL}_1, \mathtt{RELCOL}_1)$. A_1 is consistent with the example input and output table, so* ProgFromEx *retains it as a component program. Similarly,* ProgFromEx *finds A_2 from Ex. 5 by combining* F *and the relative functions $\mathtt{RELROW}_1$ and $\mathtt{RELCOL}_1$ to build the associative program $A_2 = (\mathsf{F}, \mathtt{RELROW}_1, \mathtt{RELCOL}_1)$. A_2 is also consistent with the example tables, so* ProgFromEx *retains it as a component program.*

ProgFromEx *may also build other associative programs, such as $(\mathsf{F}, \mathtt{RELCOL}_1, \mathtt{RELCOL}_2)$ and $(\mathsf{F}, \mathtt{RELROW}_1, \mathtt{RELCOL}_1)$. However,*

$$
\begin{aligned}
\text{TableProg} &:= \texttt{TABPROG}(\text{CompProg}_1, \ldots, \text{CompProg}_n)\\
\text{CompProg} &:= \text{FilterProg} \mid \text{AssocProg}\\
\text{FilterProg} &:= \texttt{FILTER}(\text{MapCond}, \texttt{SEQ}_{i,j,k})\\
\text{MapCond} &:= \texttt{AND}(\text{MapPred}_1, \text{MapPred}_2, \ldots, \text{MapPred}_n)\\
\text{MapPred} &:= \texttt{ROWEQ}(\texttt{TERM}_1, \texttt{TERM}_2) \mid \texttt{COLEQ}(\texttt{TERM}_1, \texttt{TERM}_2)\\
&\quad \mid \texttt{DATAEQ}(\texttt{TERM}_1, \texttt{TERM}_2) \mid \texttt{NOT}(\text{MapPred})\\
\text{AssocProg} &:= \texttt{ASSOC}(\text{CompProg}, \text{RelFunc}_1, \text{RelFunc}_2)\\
\text{RelFunc} &:= \texttt{RELCOL}_i \mid \texttt{RELROW}_i
\end{aligned}
$$

Figure 2. The syntax of TableProg.

ProgFromEx *determines that these associative programs are not consistent with the example input and output, and thus does not retain them as component programs.*

In steps 1) and 2) described above, ProgFromEx infers component programs that map from coordinates of an example input to coordinates of an example output. ProgFromEx must determine when it has inferred enough component programs to produce a table program that satisfies the example. A table program is a set of component programs that map to coordinates of cells to be produced in the output table. A set of component programs forms a table program that satisfies an example if every component program in the set is consistent with the example, and for every coordinate in the example output table, some component program in the set maps to the coordinate.

Example 10. ProgFromEx *finds a set of component programs that map to all coordinates in the output table after executing step 1) and one iteration of step 2). In step 1),* ProgFromEx *finds the filter program* F *described in Ex. 2, which maps to column 3 of the example output table. In one iteration of step 2),* ProgFromEx *finds the associative program* $A_1 = (F, \texttt{RELCOL}_1, \texttt{RELCOL}_1)$, *which maps to column 1 of the example output, and the associative program* $A_2 = (F, \texttt{RELROW}_1, \texttt{RELCOL}_2)$, *which maps to column 2 of the example output.* ProgFromEx *combines* F, A_1, *and* A_2 *to build a table program that maps to all cells of the example output, and thus satisfies the example.*

3. A Language of Table Programs

We now present a language of table programs, TableProg, that can express table transformations required by real users. We first present the syntax of TableProg, and then define the semantics of a program in TableProg as a function from an input table to an output table.

3.1 Syntax of Table Programs

By the formal syntax for TableProg given in Fig. 2, a table program (TableProg) is a set of component programs (CompProg). A component program is either a filter program (FilterProg) or an associative program (AssocProg). A filter program makes a single pass over an input table. During the pass, the filter selects certain cells from the input table and maps them to a substructure of the output table. This is reflected in the syntax of a FilterProg as follows. A FilterProg consists of a mapping condition over states of a filter program (MapCond) and an output coordinate sequencer ($\texttt{SEQ}_{i,j,k}$). The MapCond selects which input coordinates are mapped to the output table, and the $\texttt{SEQ}_{i,j,k}$ for natural numbers i, j, and k defines the output coordinate to which the selected input cell maps. A MapCond is a conjunction of cell predicates (MapPred). Each MapPred is an equality (or disequality) predicate over cell terms. Specifically, a MapPred is an equality predicate either over the row, column, or data in cell TERM's. A cell TERM is either a variable bound to a particular cell (such as the input cell being checked by the filter program) or a constant cell value.

An associative program AssocProg is built from a component program CompProg and two relative functions RelFunc_1, RelFunc_2. A relative function can be $\texttt{RELCOL}_i$ or $\texttt{RELROW}_i$, where i is a fixed natural number.

$$
\begin{aligned}
[\![\texttt{TABPROG}(\{\mathsf{C}_i\})]\!] &= \lambda T_I.\ \left\{ \begin{array}{l} (c_2, d) \mid (c_1, d) \in T_I, \\ \qquad (c_1, c_2) \in \bigcup_i \{[\![\mathsf{C}_i]\!](T_I)\} \end{array} \right\}\\
[\![\texttt{FILTER}(\mathsf{G},\mathsf{S})]\!] &= \lambda T_I.\ \text{FilterIter}_{\mathsf{G},\mathsf{S}}(\text{InitState})\\
[\![\texttt{AND}(\{\mathsf{L}_i\})]\!] &= \lambda\sigma.\ \bigwedge_{i=1}^{n} [\![\mathsf{P}_i]\!](\sigma)\\
[\![\texttt{ROWEQ}(\mathsf{T}_1,\mathsf{T}_2)]\!] &= \lambda\sigma.\ \left(\left(\begin{array}{l} \lambda((r_1,c_2),d_1),((r_2,c_2),d_2). \\ \quad r_1 = r_2 \end{array} \right) (\sigma(\mathsf{T}_1), \sigma(\mathsf{T}_2)) \right)\\
[\![\texttt{SEQ}_{i,j,k}]\!] &= \lambda(\mathrm{r},\mathrm{c}).\ \left(\begin{array}{l} \text{if r} < i \text{ then } (i,j) \\ \text{else if c} < j \text{ then } (r, c+1) \\ \text{else } (r+1, j) \end{array} \right)\\
[\![\texttt{ASSOC}(\mathsf{C},\mathsf{R}_1,\mathsf{R}_2)]\!] &= \lambda T_I.\ \left\{ \begin{array}{l} ([\![\mathsf{R}_1]\!](r_1,c_1), [\![\mathsf{R}_2]\!](r_2,c_2)) \mid \\ ((r_1,c_1),(r_2,c_2)) \in [\![\mathsf{C}]\!](T_I) \end{array} \right\}\\
[\![\texttt{RELCOL}_i]\!] &= \lambda(\mathrm{r},\mathrm{c}).(\mathrm{r}, i)\\
[\![\texttt{RELROW}_i]\!] &= \lambda(\mathrm{r},\mathrm{c}).(i, \mathrm{c})\\
\text{FilterIter}_{\mathsf{G},\mathsf{S}}(\sigma) &= \left(\begin{array}{l} \text{if } [\![\mathsf{G}]\!](\sigma) \\ \text{then } \{(\sigma(\text{CurIn}), \sigma(\text{CurOut}))\} \text{ else } \emptyset \end{array} \right) \\
&\quad \cup \left(\begin{array}{l} \text{if IsLastCell}(\sigma(\text{CurIn})) \text{ then } \emptyset \\ \text{else FilterIter}_{\mathsf{G},\mathsf{S}}(\text{IterUpdate}_{\mathsf{S}}(\sigma)) \end{array} \right)\\
\text{IterUpdate}_{\mathsf{S}}(\sigma) &= \sigma \left[\begin{array}{l} \text{CurIn} \leftarrow \text{NextInCoord}(\sigma), \\ \text{CurOut} \leftarrow [\![\mathsf{S}]\!](\sigma) \end{array} \right]
\end{aligned}
$$

Figure 3. The semantics of TableProg.

3.2 Semantics of Table Programs

We now present the semantics of TableProg. The semantics of TableProg is defined formally in Fig. 3 by the semantic function $[\![\cdot]\!]$ that interprets syntactic forms of TableProg as semantic values. The domain of semantic values is defined as follows. Let a *coordinate* (r, c) with $r, c \in \mathbb{N}$ be an ordered pair built from a row and column number, and let a *cell* $((r, c), d)$ be an ordered pair built from a coordinate (r, c) and data string d. A table T is a set of cells. A table program $\mathsf{P} = \texttt{TABPROG}(\ \{\mathsf{C}_i\}_i)$ is a function from a table to a table. Each component program C_i is interpreted as a partial map from coordinates of cells in the input table to coordinates of cells that will be produced in the output table. For each cell $((r, c), d)$ in the input table with (r, c) a coordinate in the domain of some map $[\![\mathsf{C}_i]\!]$, P produces a cell $([\![\mathsf{C}_i]\!](r, c), d)$ in the output table.

Every component program is either a filter program or an associative program. A filter program $\texttt{FILTER}(\mathsf{G},\mathsf{S})$ maps coordinates of cells in the input table to output coordinates by checking each cell in the input table in a fixed order, such as row-major order. In Fig. 3, this order is defined by a constant InitState that defines the coordinate of the first input cell (e.g. $(0, 0)$ in row-major order), a predicate IsLastCell that decides if a coordinate is the last in the order, and a function NextInCoord from input coordinates to input coordinates that takes an input coordinate and computes the next coordinate in the order. As the filter program checks input cells, it maintains a state σ, which distinguishes certain key cells, such as the current input cell (CurIn) and the current output cell (CurOut), by binding the cells to corresponding variables. When the filter program checks each cell of the input table, it updates σ so that the variable CurIn points to the cell to be checked. The filter program then checks if σ satisfies the filter's mapping condition, $\mathsf{G} = \mathtt{AND}(\{\mathsf{L}_i\}_i)$. A state σ satisfies G if and only if σ satisfies every literal L_i. The semantics of each literal is standard; Fig. 3 gives the semantics of the predicate $\mathtt{ROWEQ}(\mathtt{TERM}_1, \mathtt{TERM}_2)$ as an example. Whether or not σ satisfies a predicate is decided by the values in σ of cell terms, such as the variables CurIn and CurOut. If σ satisfies the mapping condition G, then the filter program maps the current input coordinate, which is bound to CurIn, to the current output coordinate, which is bound to CurOut.

If the filter program maps the current input coordinate, it updates the coordinate of the current output cell according to the filter program's output sequencer S. Whenever an output sequencer $\mathsf{S} = \mathtt{SEQ}_{i,j,k}$ is applied, it updates the current output coordinate to be the next coordinate in the output table by row major order that is at or below row i and between columns j and k. Because j and k are fixed, such a sequencer can be applied by a filter program to produce columns with an unbounded number of rows, but it cannot be applied to produce an unbounded number of columns. In this paper, we assume that an example output table has the same, fixed number of columns as all tables that the user expects the table program to produce. However, we can extend TableProg to infer programs that produce an unbounded number of columns by extending the set of output sequencers.

Like a filter program, an associative program $\mathsf{A} = \mathtt{ASSOC}(\mathsf{C}, \mathsf{R}_1, \mathsf{R}_2)$ maps coordinates in the input table to coordinates of cells to be produced in the output table. A maps coordinates by first computing the map m_C of its component program C. From m_C, A computes its own map by applying the relative function R_1 to each input coordinate in m_C, and by applying the relative function R_2 to each output coordinate in m_C. A relative function $\mathtt{RELCOL}_i$ takes a coordinate and computes the coordinate in the same row, but in column i, where i is a fixed constant. A relative function $\mathtt{RELROW}_i$ takes a coordinate and computes the coordinate in the same column, but in row i. In this way, an associative program A computes a coordinate map by altering the coordinate map of a component program C.

Example 11. *The table program* P *from Ex. 10 is represented formally as follows. Let* $\mathtt{CONSTCELLCOL}(n)$ *be a cell at column* n, *let* $\mathtt{CONSTCELLROW}(n)$ *be a cell at row* n, *and let* $\mathtt{CONSTCELLDATA}(d)$ *be a cell with data* d. *Let*

$$\mathsf{G} = \mathtt{AND}\begin{pmatrix} \mathtt{NOT(ROWEQ(CURCELL, CONSTCELLCOL(1)))}, \\ \mathtt{NOT(COLEQ(CURCELL, CONSTCELLROW(1)))}, \\ \mathtt{NOT(DATAEQ(CURCELL, CONSTCELLDATA(``")))} \end{pmatrix}$$

$$\mathsf{F} = \mathtt{FILTER}(\mathsf{G}, \mathtt{SEQ}_{1,3,3})$$

The table program is then

$$\mathtt{TABPROG}\begin{pmatrix} \mathsf{F}, \mathtt{ASSOC}(\mathsf{F}, \mathtt{RELCOL}_1, \mathtt{RELCOL}_1), \\ \mathtt{ASSOC}(\mathsf{F}, \mathtt{RELROW}_0, \mathtt{RELCOL}_2) \end{pmatrix}$$

4. Inferring Table Programs from Examples

We now give an algorithm ProgFromEx that, given example input and output tables, infers a TableProg program that satisfies the examples. We then claim that ProgFromEx is correct, and analyze its performance.

```
   Input: example input table T_I, example output table T_O,
   Output: TableProg program InferredProg, where
           InferredProg(T_I) = T_O, or unmapped output table.
   /* Step 1): collect filter programs.                    */
1  for CandMap ∈ EnumCandMaps(T_I, T_O, CandRules) do
2      MapCond ← CondFromMap(CandMap, StatePreds) ;
3      OutCoordSeq ← SeqFromMap(CandMap, Seqs) ;
4      FilterProgram ← FILTER(MapCond, OutCoordSeq) ;
5      FilterPrograms ← AddDistMap(FilterPrograms,
       FilterProgram) ;
6  end
   /* Step 2): collect associative programs.               */
7  Comps ← ∅ ;
8  Worklist ← FilterPrograms ;
9  while NewComps ≠ ∅ do
10     CompProg ← Choose( Worklist) ;
11     Worklist ← Worklist \{CompProg} ;
12     for Rel_1, Rel_2 ∈ RelFuncs do
13         AssocPrg ← ASSOC(CompProg, Rel_1, Rel_2) ;
14         if IsConsistent(AssocPrg, T_I, T_O) and
           Map(AssocPrg) ∉ Maps( Comps ∪ Worklist) then
15             Worklist ← AddDistMap(Comps, AssocPrg) ;
16         end
17     end
18 end
19 if IsOnto(Maps(Comps)) then
20     return TABPROG(Comps) ;
21 else
22     return UnmappedOutput(Comps) ;
23 end
```

Figure 4. The inference algorithm ProgFromEx.

4.1 An Inference Algorithm for TableProg

ProgFromEx, given example input and output tables, infers a table program in TableProg that satisfies the example. ProgFromEx infers programs "bottom-up," in that it iteratively collects a set of component programs that may be combined to form a table program. If ProgFromEx finds a set of component programs that form a table program that satisfies the example, then ProgFromEx returns the table program. If ProgFromEx cannot find such a table program, then ProgFromEx provides to the user the substructure of the output table to which no component program maps.

ProgFromEx, given in Fig. 4, takes from the user an example input table T_I and example output table T_O. ProgFromEx also is defined over four fixed sets of objects: a set CandRules of candidate-map rules, a set StatePreds of predicates for mapping conditions, a set Sequencers of output sequencers, and a set RelativeFuncs of relative functions. These sets are fixed, perhaps configured by an expert user or administrator.

ProgFromEx finds a table program to satisfy the example in two steps. In step 1), ProgFromEx collects a set of filter programs that map to substructures of T_O (Fig. 4, lines [4.1]–[4.1]). To find a set of such filter programs, ProgFromEx applies CollectFilters (line [4.1]), which first collects a set of *candidate maps* over the example tables by applying the candidate-map rules CandRules.

Definition 1. A *candidate map* is a map from coordinates of cells in T_I to coordinates of cells in T_O. Each candidate map satisfies the following conditions:

1. The candidate map maps input coordinates to output coordinates with equal data (i.e. the candidate map is consistent). For-

mally, if the candidate map contains an entry $((r_1, c_1), (r_2, c_2))$ with $((r_1, c_1), d_1) \in T_I$ and $((r_2, c_2), d_2) \in T_O$, then $d_1 = d_2$.

2. The candidate map maps to coordinates described by an output sequencer. Formally, the candidate map maps to every coordinate in T_O at or below row i between columns j and k of the output table for some i, j, and k.
3. The candidate map preserves row-major order. The sequence of pairs in the candidate map ordered by the row-major ordering of the input coordinates is equal to the sequence of entries ordered by the row-major ordering of the output coordinates.

For each candidate map CandMap generated by CandRules, ProgFromEx attempts to infer a filter program that computes CandMap (lines [4.1]–[4.1]). To infer such a filter program, it must infer a mapping condition (line [4.1]) and an output sequencer (line [4.1]). To infer a mapping condition, ProgFromEx applies CondFromMap, which computes the states of a hypothetical filter program as it reads, and potentially maps, each cell in the example input table. If in a given state, a filter program reads a cell that is mapped by the candidate map, then let this state be a *read state* of the filter program. For a set of read states RS, CondFromMap constructs the following MapCond, which is the strongest condition that is satisfied by all read states:

$$\mathtt{AND}\left(\bigcap_{\sigma \in \mathsf{RS}} \{l \mid p \in \mathsf{StatePreds}, l \in \{p, \mathtt{NOT}(p)\}, \sigma(l)\}\right)$$

Where $\sigma(l)$ denotes that the literal l is satisfied in σ. CondFromMap then checks if any non-read state satisfies MapCond. If so, then no conjunction of literals from StatePreds may act as a mapping condition for CandMap. If not, then MapCond acts as a mapping condition for CandMap. For G, ProgFromEx can immediately infer an output coordinate sequencer OutCoordSeq (line [4.1]) using conditions (2) and (3) from Defn. 1. ProgFromEx then pairs condition MapCond and sequencer OutCoordSeq to build a filter program that computes CandMap (line [4.1]).

In step 2) (lines [4.1]–[4.1]), ProgFromEx uses the filter programs found in step 1) to build associative programs until it can use the set of filter and associative programs to build a table program that satisfies T_I and T_O, or it determines that no such table program exists. ProgFromEx iteratively builds associative programs as follows. Over each iteration of the loop at line [4.1], ProgFromEx maintains a worklist (Worklist) of component programs that it will use to build more associative programs, and a set of component programs (Comps) from which it has already built associative programs. At the beginning of the first iteration, Worklist is initialized to all of the filter programs found in step 1) (line [4.1]), and Comps is initialized to be empty (line [4.1]).

ProgFromEx executes an iteration of step 2) as follows. First, ProgFromEx chooses an element CompProg from its worklist (line [4.1]). ProgFromEx then builds associative programs from CompProg. An associative program consists of a component program and a pair of relative functions. Thus to build associative programs from a component program CompProg, ProgFromEx enumerates over all pairs of relative functions (line [4.1]). For relative functions $\mathsf{RelFunc}_1$ and $\mathsf{RelFunc}_2$, ProgFromEx builds the corresponding associative program AssocProg (line [4.1]). ProgFromEx then decides if AssocProg computes a map that is consistent for T_I and T_O (line [4.1]). If so, and if the map computed by AssocProg is not computed by any component program in Comps or Worklist, then ProgFromEx adds AssocProg to Worklist (line [4.1]).

ProgFromEx iteratively builds associative programs until it determines either that it has found a set of component programs that map to all cells in T_O (i.e. a set that *covers* T_O), or determines that it can find no such set of component programs (line [4.1]). To check if a set of component programs covers T_O, ProgFromEx checks if every coordinate c in T_O is mapped to by some component program in the set. If ProgFromEx finds such a set, then it builds a table program from the set and returns the table program (line [4.1]). Otherwise, it returns the set of output cells to which no component program maps (line [4.1]). The user can examine the output cells to understand why ProgFromEx could not infer a program to satisfy the examples, perhaps finding errors or noise in the example.

4.2 Correctness of ProgFromEx

We now present fundamental correctness properties of ProgFromEx. In particular, we define notions of soundness and completeness for inferring programs in TableProg, and claim that ProgFromEx is both sound and complete.

Theorem 1. *An table program inference algorithm is* sound *if whenever it infers a table program for an example input and output, then the program satisfies the examples. Formally, a table inference algorithm A is* sound *if for each input table T_I and output table T_O, if $A(T_I, T_O) = P$, then $P(T_I) = T_O$.* ProgFromEx *is sound.*

Proof. See [11]. □

We now define completeness for a table inference algorithm, and argue that ProgFromEx is complete.

Theorem 2. *A table inference algorithm A is* defined *for an example input T_I and example output T_O only if when given the example, it infers a table program. A is* complete *for a language of table programs if whenever some table program P in the language satisfies T_I and T_O, then A is defined on T_I and T_O.* ProgFromEx *is complete for* TableProg.

Proof. See [11]. □

ProgFromEx is complete for inferring programs in TableProg. However, ProgFromEx cannot, in general, infer a table program for an arbitrary example input and output. Instead, TableProg and ProgFromEx can serve as a framework for table program languages and inference algorithms. To obtain a more expressive language of table programs, one can define more expressive sets of candidate-map rules, predicates, output sequencers, and relative functions. We have extended TableProg in this way in our implementation, and the resulting language is expressive enough to implement many transformations required by real users.

4.2.1 Correct for Examples vs. Correct for Expectations

ProgFromEx is effective for finding a table program that satisfies a given example. However, multiple programs in TableProg may satisfy an example, yet in general, implement different table transformations. Thus a user may provide to ProgFromEx an example, ProgFromEx may provide to the user a program that satisfies the example, and the user may then apply the inferred program to other tables only to find that the program does not behave as expected. Yet there may be a different program in TableProg that also satisfies the user's examples and also behaves as the user expects when it is applied to other inputs.

An inference algorithm can apply a variety of approaches to provide to the user the program that the user requires. First, an inference algorithm can *actively* query the user about the program they require until the algorithm finds a unique program that satisfies the user's requirements. This approach is analogous to the one described in [13], and has several nice properties. In particular, if the approach produces a program, then the program is unambiguously correct for all inputs. However, such an approach may need to query the user a prohibitively large number of times. We leave as future work the problem of developing an inference algorithm that follows this approach, yet queries a user a small number of times.

We instead developed ProgFromEx to apply a *lazy* approach. In a lazy approach, the inference algorithm takes an example from the user, and infers some program that satisfies the example. The user applies the inferred program to other inputs; if on another input, the program produces an output that the user does not expect, then the user provides the input and unexpected output to the inference algorithm as an example, and the algorithm infers a new program that satisfies both the original and new example. The user repeats this process until the inference algorithm provides a program that behaves as the user expects for the inputs on which they apply it. Unlike an approach based on active querying, the lazy approach does not guarantee that if the inference algorithm infers a program, then the program is correct for all inputs. However, we have observed that in practice, users do not need to apply table programs to arbitrary input tables. Instead, users apply a table program to a set of tables that all satisfy a strong condition. Requiring users to specify a program's behavior for tables that do not satisfy this condition is unnecessary, and often causes users to refuse to use such a technology. We now describe two extensions of ProgFromEx that allow users to apply it using a lazy approach to quickly infer the program that they require.

If a user applies ProgFromEx to a given example, obtains a program, and finds that the program behaves incorrectly on a different input, then the user can provide the second, different input, along with a corresponding correct output, as another example for ProgFromEx, and obtain a new program that better satisfies their requirements. If the second input extends the first input, then the user may apply ProgFromEx solely to the second input. However, even if the example inputs are incomparable, ProgFromEx can be extended to take multiple examples from a user simultaneously. To take multiple examples, ProgFromEx as presented in Fig. 4 is extended to find filter programs and associative programs that are consistent for a set of multiple examples. To find filter programs that are consistent for all examples, the loop at lines [4.1]–[4.1] is changed to enumerate over the space of all tuples containing a candidate map for each example. For each tuple of candidate maps, ProgFromEx attempts to infer a map condition that classifies exactly the cells mapped by each candidate map, and attempts to infer an output coordinate sequencer that describes the sequence of output cells that are mapped to in each candidate map. To find an associative program that is consistent for all examples, the check at line [4.1] is extended to determine if the associative program AssocProg is consistent with each example. Finally, the checks at lines [4.1] and [4.1] are extended so that ProgFromEx determines that it has found a satisfying table program only when it finds a collection of component programs that map to every cell in all output example tables.

ProgFromEx can also be extended so that it infers a program from a single example that is, in practice, more likely to behave as expected when applied to other tables. Step 2) of ProgFromEx halts when ProgFromEx finds a set of component programs that map to every cell in the example output table. However, the resulting set may include multiple component programs that are redundant, as a smaller set of programs would still map to the same cells. In practice, the more component programs that form a table program, the more likely the table program is to behave incorrectly when applied to other tables. This satisfies an informal notion of Occam's Razor: the simplest table program is often the best. We have thus extended ProgFromEx so that at Fig. 4 line [4.1], it does not necessarily build a table program from all component programs that it finds. Instead, ProgFromEx first applies a greedy algorithm to prune the set of all component programs found to a set that still maps to all cells in the example output, but is locally minimal. The resulting program is intuitively "simpler" than the original program, and in practice more often behaves as expected on larger examples.

4.3 Performance of ProgFromEx

In principle, ProgFromEx does not scale well with the size of the tables given as examples. In the worst case, ProgFromEx may execute in time exponential in the size of the example tables given. This is because the time that ProgFromEx takes to execute is proportional to the number of component programs that it collects with distinct maps, and the number of distinct maps between example tables is exponential in the number of cells in the example tables. For a detailed analysis of the complexity of ProgFromEx, see [11].

If ProgFromEx performed close to its worst-case bound, then it would be highly impractical. Fortunately, real-world input and output examples have properties that allow ProgFromEx to execute quickly, or that allow for heuristics that greatly improve its performance. In particular, the dominating factor in the high complexity of ProgFromEx is the set of component programs with distinct maps that ProgFromEx may collect. In practice, this set is quite small. This is because while many component programs may implement a large set of distinct maps according to the combinatorial bound, in practice only a small set of these maps are consistent for the example tables. Thus candidate-map rules find few candidate maps that are consistent with the examples, and when ProgFromEx checks if an associative program is consistent (Fig. 4 line [4.1]), the check rules out many potential associative programs immediately.

ProgFromEx as given in Fig. 4 can also be optimized by biasing the order in which it picks component programs to build new associative programs. In line [4.1] of Fig. 4, ProgFromEx nondeterministically chooses a component program from its worklist, and builds new associative programs from the chosen component program. The chosen component program may mostly map to output cells that are already mapped to by other component programs in Comps, as may the associative programs built from the chosen component program. However, ProgFromEx can instead prioritize the elements in its worklist so that ProgFromEx first chooses component programs from the worklist that map to many cells not mapped to by any component program in Comps. This may allow ProgFromEx to more quickly find a set of component programs that cover the example output table.

5. Experiments

We implemented an interpreter for TableProg, implemented ProgFromEx, and experimented with the implementations to determine if TableProg and ProgFromEx are useful in practice. The experiments were designed to determine the following:

1. Is TableProg expressive enough to describe table transformations that real end-users require?
2. When a program in TableProg implements the table transformation that a user requires, could ProgFromEx find the program quickly?
3. If ProgFromEx finds a program that satisfies a user's initial examples, and the program is applied to other similar inputs, does the program produce the expected outputs? If not, how many additional examples does a user need to provide before ProgFromEx infers a program that behaves as expected?

We performed the experiments as follows. We searched two online help forums[2] for the Excel spreadsheet program to find table

[2] http://www.excelforum.com and http://www.ozgrid.com/forum/

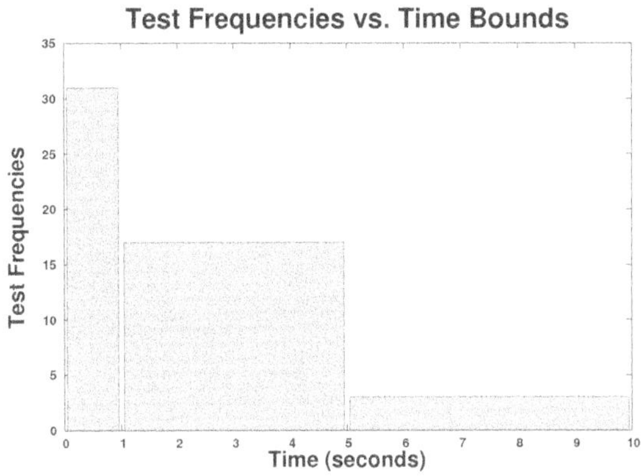

Figure 5. Time for ProgFromEx to infer table transformation programs.

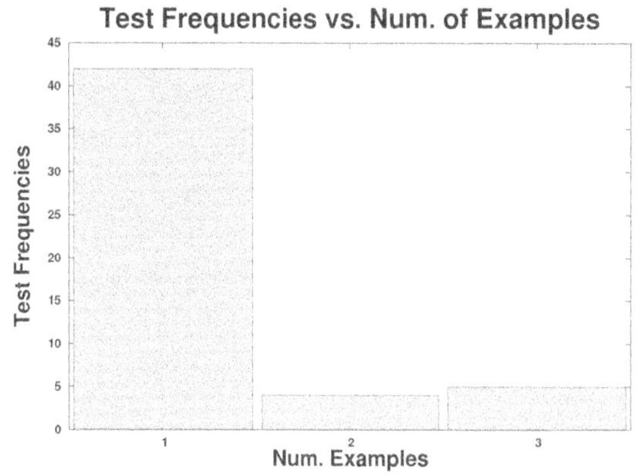

Figure 6. Number of examples required by ProgFromEx to infer programs.

transformations that real users needed to perform, but could not accomplish using the built-in GUI features of Excel. Among the transformations, we picked 51 for which the user provided an example input and output. We gave the input and output examples to ProgFromEx, which inferred a table program for each example. We used the provided examples and the English description of the transformation to manually create a larger input example, applied the inferred program to the larger input, and checked that the program produced the output that we expected. If the program did not produce the expected output, then from the unexpected output, we manually derived a more descriptive example, and applied ProgFromEx to the more descriptive example. We repeated this process until ProgFromEx found a program that behaved as expected for successively larger, different inputs.

The experiments indicate that TableProg describes practical programs, and that ProgFromEx finds practical programs in TableProg efficiently. The times spent by ProgFromEx to infer programs for the 51 tests are presented in Fig. 5. For each of the 51 tests, ProgFromEx found in less than 10 seconds a program in TableProg that satisfied the example. For a majority (31) of the tests, ProgFromEx found a program in less than a second. For a vast majority (48) of the tests, ProgFromEx found a program in less than 5 seconds.

If for a given test, ProgFromEx inferred a program that did not behave as we expected when applied to other inputs, we manually found an input on which ProgFromEx misbehaved and reapplied ProgFromEx to the new input. We repeated this process until ProgFromEx inferred a program that behaved as expected. The numbers of times that we needed to refine examples for the tests are presented in Fig. 6. Observe that for a vast majority (42) of the tests, ProgFromEx inferred the expected program from one example. For the four of the tests, ProgFromEx required two examples, and for five of the tests, it required three examples.

The large number of different help-thread requests that were satisfied by programs in TableProg indicates that TableProg is expressive enough to describe transformations required by real end-users. Moreover, the transformations requested on the help threads are diverse. To illustrate their diversity, we discuss a selection of examples that are satisfied by programs in TableProg. The examples are slightly simplified from their original forms to ease presentation. For a complete list of help threads containing the original examples on which we experimented, see [6]. For detailed descriptions of the tests, see [11].

Example input table:

55660	x1		$530.00		
55660	x3	11/5/2007	$10.00	5	$2,130.00
90210	y1		$25.00		
90210	y2		$25.00		
90210	y3	11/18/2007	$25.00	13	$325.00

Example output table:

55660	11/5/2007	$10.00	$2,130.00
90210	11/18/2007	$25.00	$325.00

Figure 7. Example reproduced from an Excel help thread "Copy Rows Where Column Cell Is Not Blank"

Filtering Key Information In many help requests, users need to transform a table to retain a subset of the table's original information. This subset is defined by key cells in the table, along with cells that are spatially related to the key cell. In a help thread titled "Copy Rows Where Column Cell Is Not Blank," a novice user specified a table transformation using an example reproduced in Fig. 7. The user wanted to transform their input table into a new table that only contains the cells in columns 1, 3, 4, and 6 of each *summary row* of the input table. According to the user's English description, a summary row is any row in which column 6 is not empty. An expert user replied that a GUI feature partially automates this transformation, but the novice replied that they would like to fully automate the transformation. The expert replied with an Excel macro, which presumably satisfied the novice. When we applied ProgFromEx to the example given by the novice, ProgFromEx automatically found a TableProg program that satisfies the example in 0.5 seconds. However, when we reapplied the program to other input tables, we found that it placed cells from a row of the input table in the output table if and only if column 5 was empty. To resolve this, we extended the input to have a row in which the column 5 was empty but column 6 was non-empty, and extended the output to contain cells from the row. Using this example, ProgFromEx inferred a program, again in 0.5 seconds, that behaved as expected when reapplied to other tables. The program consists of a filter program which maps the non-empty cells in column 6 of the input to column 4 of the output. For each of the other three columns in the output, an associative program built from the filter program maps the column.

Splitting and Partially Replicating Rows In many help requests, users need to split cells in a row into different rows, while replicat-

Example input table:

Name	Colour	Price
Toyota	White	2000
Nissan	Red	4000

Example output table:

Toyota	White
Toyota	2000
Nissan	Red
Nissan	4000

Figure 8. Example reproduced from Excel help thread "arranging data using VBA."

Example input table:

3099	905	A4CA				
NO.14	NO.14	Full Copies	6.78	2	* *	0
3200	906	AHG				
9-Jun	9-Jun	Covers Only	4.74	1	* *	0

Example output table:

3099	905	A4CA	NO.14	Full Copies	6.78	2
3200	906	AHG	9-Jun	Covers Only	4.74	1

Figure 9. Example reproduced from an Excel help thread "arrange data."

ing other cells in the original row. In a help forum post titled "Arranging Data Using VBA," a novice user requested a table transformation by providing only the example reproduced in Fig. 8. The user added that though they had provided a small example, they needed to apply a transformation to a table that had thousands of rows. After more than four hours, an expert user provided an Excel macro that presumably satisfied the novice's request. We applied ProgFromEx to the example from the help forum, and ProgFromEx automatically found in 2.3 seconds a table program that satisfies the example. When we reapplied the program to larger, similar examples, it behaved as expected. The table program consists of a filter program that maps cells in columns 2 and 3 of the input to column 2 of the output, and a single associative program built from the filter program that maps to column 1 of the output.

Combining and Filtering Rows In many requests, users need to remove some cells from rows while combining adjacent rows. In a help thread titled "arrange data," a novice user requested a table transformation by providing only the example reproduced in Fig. 9. The transformation concatenates adjacent pairs of rows, filtering out the cell in column 1 in the second row of each pair. In twenty minutes, an expert user provided to the novice a macro that satisfied the example, and the novice reported that they were satisfied, although they did not understand the mechanics of the macro. When we applied ProgFromEx to the example in Fig. 9, it automatically found in 1.2 seconds a TableProg program that implements the transformation requested by the user. When we reapplied the same program to larger, similar examples, it behaved as expected. The program is built from two filter programs that map onto columns 6 and 7 of the output table, two associative programs built from the filter programs that map onto columns 3 and 4 of the output table, a third associative program, built from the associative program that maps onto column 4, that maps onto column 2, and finally a fourth associative program built from the third associative program, that maps onto column 1. This example demonstrates the benefit to the iterative approach applied by ProgFromEx to find associative programs.

Rearranging Groups In many requests, a user has data organized in nested groups, and needs to preserve the grouping of the data while rearranging the layout of the groups. In a help thread titled "Transposing 3 columns into multiple columns," a novice user requested a transformation by providing the example reproduced in Fig. 10. In the novice's input table, grades are arranged vertically, grouped by student and then by subject. In the novice's output table,

Example input table:

Alice	Art&Des	B
	CreatArt	A
	D&T	A
	English	A
	Geo.	A*
Bob	Art&Des	C
	CreatArt	B
	D&T	C
	English	C
	Geo.	C

Example output table:

	Art&Des	CreatArt	D&T	English	Geo.
Alice	B	A	A	A	A*
Bob	C	B	C	C	C

Figure 10. Example reproduced from an Excel help thread "Transposing 3 columns into multiple columns."

Example input table:

PROJ	CAT	SPONSOR	DEPT	ELTS	DUE
SPEC	OOH	Infiniti	Design	elt 1	11/10
SPEC	OOH	Infiniti	Desing	elt 2	
SPEC	Print		Design	elt 3	11/30
SPEC	Print		Design	elt 4	11/30
SPEC	Print	Infiniti	Design	elt 5	11/30

Example output table:

		SPEC	
		OOH	
Infiniti	Design	elt 1	11/10
Infiniti	Desing	elt 2	
		Print	
	Design	elt 3	11/30
	Design	elt 4	11/30
Infiniti	Design	elt 5	11/30

Figure 11. Example reproduced from Excel help thread "printed sheet in different format than worksheet."

grades are arranged horizontally, grouped in a row per student, and a column per subject. After the novice posted their request, one expert user replied with a macro about 40 minutes later, and another expert replied with a macro nearly six hours after the request was posted.

When we applied ProgFromEx to the example in Fig. 10, it automatically found a TableProg program in 1.4 seconds that implements the requested transformation. When we reapplied the same program to larger, similar tables, the program behaved as expected. The table program includes a single filter program that maps to all cells at or below row 2 between columns 2 and 5. One associative program built from this filter program maps onto all cells in column 1 of the output table. A second associative program built from the filter program maps onto all cells in row 1 of the output table.

In a help thread titled "printed sheet in different format than worksheet," a novice user provided the example reproduced in Fig. 11. In the novice's input table, each row of the table is a complete entry for an element of a project. The novice needed to group the elements so that the project and category (columns 1 and 2, respectively) of the element appear as headings and subheadings, followed by the elements that are under the heading and subheading. Although the novice suspected that elements could be grouped semi-automatically using built-in features of Excel, they did not know how to do so. No expert user helped the novice with their request.

When we applied ProgFromEx to the example in Fig. 11, it automatically found a TableProg program in 4.4 seconds that implements the required transformation. In the TableProg program, a filter program maps to column 3 of the output. A set of three associative programs built from the filter program map to columns 1, 2, and 4, with one associative program mapping to each column.

We implemented the interpreter for TableProg and the inference algorithm ProgFromEx as an Excel plug-in module. To use the module, a user selects in the Excel GUI a range of cells to act as the example input, selects a range of cells to act as the example output, selects a range of cells to act as a "full input," selects a location in the spreadsheet where they would like to place the output corresponding to the full input, and pushes a button. The module then automatically infers a program that satisfies the examples, applies the program to the full input, and places the resulting output at the location specified by the user. We plan to extend the interface so that a user may supply only examples, and the module will provide a program that the user can add to a library. The user could then reapply programs in the library whenever they wish.

6. Related Work

The area of program synthesis is gaining renewed interest [8], and this paper is a work in this direction. Program synthesis has traditionally been motivated by the need to synthesize non-trivial algorithms [12, 22, 23] or to discover tricky code-snippets [10, 24]. In this paper, we apply program synthesis to discovering relatively simpler programs, but those that are cared about by a much larger class of spreadsheet end-users, who often struggle with manipulating tabular data in spreadsheets.

There has been some work in the programming languages and the HCI community related to inferring table transformations. PADS [7] takes a large sample of unstructured data and infers a format that describes the data. Users then manually define tools for data in the format. Lenses [2] are a language of combinators that can be applied to solve the *view update problem*, which is related to but distinct from the problem of inferring a transformation over tables from examples. The Wrangler tool, developed in the HCI community, provides a nice visual programming-by-demonstration interface to table transformations for data cleaning [14]. In contrast, we provide an interface based on examples, which is more friendly to end users.

Program sketching [21] may be applied to synthesize programs from examples. In program sketching, a programmer supplies to a sketcher an incomplete version of a program (a *sketch*) and a specification of correct behavior for the program, possibly as a set of input-output examples. The sketcher then completes the program so that the program satisfies the specification. We attempted to apply the SKETCH [20] program sketcher to a sketch of a table program and example tables. However, because SKETCH is a tool for synthesizing general programs, it could not take full advantage of the particular structure of table programs. As a result, when we applied it to infer programs in TableProg, it typically timed out after an hour.

The problem of inferring transformations over tables is related to inferring queries over relations from instances of the relations. These techniques cannot be directly applied to infer transformations over tables, as users treat tables differently from relations; e.g., tables have a notion of order over rows that does not hold by default for relations. In particular, in the *view synthesis problem* [4], one takes a database relation and a view over the database and infers the general query that produces the view. The technique presented in [4] only considers views that are a subset of the original database. Thus the technique cannot be applied to any of the examples given in this paper, or many of the other real-world cases that we studied. The problem of *query by output* [25] is similar to the view synthesis problem, but the technique presented in [25] infers select-project-join queries. Of the examples presented in this paper, such queries can only be applied to satisfy the example in Fig. 7, and such queries cannot be applied to many of the other real-world cases that we studied. We leave as future work the problem of applying our techniques to learn richer queries from instances of databases and views.

The work in [9, 15, 16, 18, 26] gives techniques that take textual input-output examples and infer programs that transform text. However, these techniques only infer transformations over plain text, or strings. Thus they cannot be directly applied to infer transformations over tables. While the techniques can, in principle, be applied by representing tables in plain text, it is then difficult to reason about the spatial relationships between cells in the original table. TableProg represents spatial relationships directly, and the relationships are critical to TableProg's ability to express practical table transformations. Furthermore, the techniques for textual transformations assume that it is easy to find a set of programs that satisfy an individual example of a transformation, and focus on combining sets of programs that satisfy different examples. However, when searching for programs that transform tables, it is non-trivial in general to find a set of programs that satisfy even a single example of a transformation.

7. Conclusion

End users often need to transform semi-structured, tabular data in non-trivial ways. We have presented a language TableProg of programs that implement table transformations that real users require, and an algorithm ProgFromEx that from an example input and output, infers a TableProg program that implements the transformation specified by the example. To demonstrate that TableProg and ProgFromEx are practical, we applied them to infer programs for over 50 table transformations specified as input-output examples by real end users.

References

[1] R. Abraham and M. Erwig. Header and unit inference for spreadsheets through spatial analyses. In *Proceedings of the 2004 IEEE Symposium on Visual Languages - Human Centric Computing (VLHCC)*, pages 165–172, 2004.

[2] D. M. Barbosa, J. Cretin, N. Foster, M. Greenberg, and B. C. Pierce. Matching lenses: alignment and view update. In *ICFP '10*, 2010.

[3] A. Cypher, editor. *Watch What I Do – Programming by Demonstration*. MIT Press, Cambridge, MA, USA, 1993. Full text available at web.media.mit.edu/ lieber/PBE/.

[4] A. Das Sarma, A. Parameswaran, H. Garcia-Molina, and J. Widom. Synthesizing view definitions from data. In *ICDT '10*, 2010.

[5] Excel. Microsoft Excel, 2010. URL `http://office.microsoft.com/en-us/excel`.

[6] Excel Help Forums. Excel help forum threads, 2010. URL `http://cs.wisc.edu/~wrharris/pldi2011/tests.html`.

[7] K. Fisher, D. Walker, K. Q. Zhu, and P. White. From dirt to shovels: fully automatic tool generation from ad hoc data. In *POPL '08*, 2008.

[8] S. Gulwani. Dimensions in program synthesis (invited talk paper). In *ACM Symposium on PPDP*, 2010.

[9] S. Gulwani. Automating string processing in spreadsheets using input-output examples. In *POPL*, pages 317–330, 2011.

[10] S. Gulwani, S. K. Jha, A. Tiwari, and R. Venkatesan. Synthesis of loop-free programs. In *PLDI*, 2011.

[11] W. R. Harris and S. Gulwani. Table Transformations from Examples. Technical Report MSR-TR-2011-34, Microsoft Research, Redmond, March 2011.

[12] S. Itzhaky, S. Gulwani, N. Immerman, and M. Sagiv. A simple inductive synthesis methodology and its applications. In *OOPSLA*, pages 36–46, 2010.

[13] S. Jha, S. Gulwani, S. A. Seshia, and A. Tiwari. Oracle-guided component-based program synthesis. In *ICSE '10*, 2010.

[14] S. Kandel, A. Paepcke, J. Hellerstein, and J. Heer. Wrangler: Interactive visual specification of data transformation scripts. In *ACM Human Factors in Computing Systems (CHI)*, 2011.

[15] T. Lau, S. A. Wolfman, P. Domingos, and D. S. Weld. Programming by demonstration using version space algebra. *Mach. Learn.*, 53(1-2): 111–156, 2003. ISSN 0885-6125.

[16] T. A. Lau, P. Domingos, and D. S. Weld. Version space algebra and its application to programming by demonstration. In *ICML '00*, 2000.

[17] H. Lieberman, editor. *Your wish is my command: programming by example*. Morgan Kaufmann Publishers Inc., San Francisco, CA, USA, 2001. ISBN 1-55860-688-2.

[18] R. Nix. Editing by example. In *POPL '84*, 1984.

[19] OpenOffice. Openoffice.org, 2010. URL `http://www.openoffice.org/`.

[20] SKETCH. Sketch, 2010. URL `https://bitbucket.org/gatoatigrado/sketch-frontend/wiki/Home`.

[21] A. Solar-Lezama, G. Arnold, L. Tancau, R. Bodik, V. Saraswat, and S. Seshia. Sketching stencils. In *PLDI '07*, 2007.

[22] S. Srivastava, S. Gulwani, and J. S. Foster. From program verification to program synthesis. In *POPL*, pages 313–326, 2010.

[23] S. Srivastava, S. Gulwani, S. Chaudhuri, and J. Foster. Path-based inductive synthesis for program inversion. In *PLDI*, 2011.

[24] A. Taly, S. Gulwani, and A. Tiwari. Synthesizing switching logic using constraint solving. In *VMCAI*, pages 305–319, 2009.

[25] Q. T. Tran, C.-Y. Chan, and S. Parthasarathy. Query by output. In *SIGMOD '09*, 2009.

[26] I. H. Witten and D. Mo. *TELS: learning text editing tasks from examples*, pages 183–203. MIT Press, 1993.

Systematic Editing: Generating Program Transformations from an Example

Na Meng Miryung Kim Kathryn S. McKinley
The University of Texas at Austin
mengna152173@gmail.com, miryung@ece.utexas.edu, mckinley@cs.utexas.edu

Abstract

Software modifications are often *systematic*—they consist of similar, but not identical, program changes to multiple contexts. Existing tools for systematic program transformation are limited because they require programmers to manually prescribe edits or only suggest a location to edit with a related example. This paper presents the design and implementation of a program transformation tool called SYDIT. Given an example edit, SYDIT generates a *context-aware, abstract edit script*, and then applies the edit script to new program locations. To correctly encode a relative position of the edits in a new location, the derived edit script includes unchanged statements on which the edits are control and data dependent. Furthermore, to make the edit script applicable to a new context using different identifier names, the derived edit script abstracts variable, method, and type names. The evaluation uses 56 systematic edit pairs from five large software projects as an oracle. SYDIT has high coverage and accuracy. For 82% of the edits (46/56), SYDIT matches the context and applies an edit, producing code that is 96% similar to the oracle. Overall, SYDIT mimics human programmers correctly on 70% (39/56) of the edits. Generation of edit scripts seeks to improve programmer productivity by relieving developers from tedious, error-prone, manual code updates. It also has the potential to guide automated program repair by creating program transformations applicable to similar contexts.

Categories and Subject Descriptors D.2.7 [*Software Engineering*]: Distribution, Maintenance, and Enhancement—restructuring

General Terms Algorithm, Measurement, Experimentation

Keywords Software evolution, program transformation, program differencing, empirical study

1. Introduction

A typical software life-cycle begins with design, prototyping, and new code development. After deployment, software enters a phase where developers spend time fixing bugs, refactoring, and adding functionality to existing code. Recent work observes that many changes are *systematic*—programmers add, delete, and modify code in numerous classes in similar, but not identical ways [15, 16, 25]. For example, Kim et al. find that on average, 75% of structural changes to mature software are systematic. They find that these changes are not identical, but that their contexts have similar characteristics, such as calling the same method or accessing the same field. Nguyen et al. find that 17% to 45% of bug fixes are recurring fixes that involve similar edits to numerous methods [25]. Another class of systematic changes occur when API changes require all the API clients to update their code [12]. Performing systematic edits is currently tedious and error prone.

Existing tools offer limited support for systematic edits. The search and replace feature in a text editor is the most popular approach, but it supports only simple text replacements and cannot handle non-contiguous edits, nor edits that require customization for different contexts. Integrated Development Environments (IDEs), such as Eclipse, help with refactorings, but are confined to a predefined set of semantics-preserving transformations. Recent work proposes approaches for systematic editing, but none derive and apply context-aware edit scripts that use different variable, method, and type names in a new context. Nguyen et al. suggest new locations to edit based on changes to similar code fragments with an example, but require programmers to edit the code manually [23, 25]. With *simultaneous editing*, programmers edit pre-specified clones in parallel, naïvely propagating exactly the same edit to all clones without regard to context, which leads to errors [7, 22, 29]. Programmers can also encode systematic edits in a formal syntax using a source transformation language, but this approach forces programmers to plan edit operations in advance [4, 5]. Andersen and Lawall's patch inference derives a more general edit from *diff* output, but its expressiveness is confined to term-replacements [1, 2]. Furthermore, it does not model the control and data dependence context of edits, and it does not encode the edit positions with respect to relevant context nodes.

This paper describes the design and implementation of an automated program transformation tool called SYDIT. SYDIT generates edit scripts from program differences and their context, and then applies scripts to similar code fragments. SYDIT characterizes edits as Abstract Syntax Tree (AST) node additions, deletions, updates, and moves. It uses control and data dependence analysis to capture the AST *change context*, i.e., relevant unchanged program fragments that depend on the edits or on which edits depend. It abstracts edit positions and the names of variables, methods, and types to create a generalized program transformation that does not depend on exact locations nor concrete identifiers. We call these transformations, *abstract, context-aware edit scripts*. Given a new target location, SYDIT generates concrete AST transformations customized to the new context. SYDIT then transforms the code accordingly.

To evaluate SYDIT, we create an oracle test suite of 56 systematic edit pairs—where two method locations are at least 40% similar in terms of their syntactic contents, and experience at least one common edit between two program versions. We draw this test suite directly from systematic updates performed by pro-

PLDI'11, June 4–8, 2011, San Jose, California, USA.

grammers in jEdit, Eclipse JDT core, Eclipse debug, Eclipse core.runtime and Eclipse compare plug-ins. SYDIT takes as input a source exemplar edit, which consists of an old and a new program fragment, and generates an edit script. In this study, the programmer selects the target, and SYDIT generates concrete edits and applies them to the target. SYDIT produces syntactically valid transformations for 82% of the target methods (46/56). It perfectly mimics developer edits on 70% (39/56) of the targets. Syntactic program differencing considers the human generated version and the SYDIT generated version 96% similar. Therefore, it would likely require only modest manual effort to correct SYDIT's version. SYDIT achieves similar results on a suite of six systematic edits applied to five or more method locations from open-source projects. The key contributions of this paper are: (1) how to generalize a program transformation from an example to make it applicable to similar but not identical contexts, and (2) a rigorous empirical validation of SYDIT.

Our systematic editing approach seeks to improve programmer productivity when developers fix similar bugs, refactor multiple methods similarly, migrate code when APIs change [12, 23, 27], and add similar features to multiple related code locations. This approach is very flexible since developers can first develop and test a modification in a single context and then apply it to multiple contexts. Although in this paper, the programmer is required to select the target edit location and then examine the results, we envision more automated use cases as well. Given an example transformation, additional analysis could automate finding potential edit locations based on code similarity. By integrating SYDIT with automated compilation and testing, developers can have more confidence about the correctness of generated edits before reviewing them. Furthermore, this functionality could help guide automatic program repair by creating transformations applicable to similar contexts, applying them, and running regression tests on the SYDIT generated program version.

The rest of the paper is organized as follows. Section 2 illustrates SYDIT's edit script generation and application on a motivating example from the Eclipse debug plug-in. Section 3 presents our algorithms for edit script generalization and application. Section 4 shows the effectiveness of SYDIT using a test suite of independently developed systematic changes gathered from open-source projects. Section 5 compares our approach to related work and Section 6 discusses the limitations of our approach and ways to improve SYDIT's precision.

2. Motivating Example

This section overviews our approach with a running example drawn from revisions to org.eclipse.debug.core on 2006-10-05 and 2006-11-06. Figure 1 shows the original code in black, additions in **bold blue** with a '+', and deletions in red with a '-'. Consider methods mA and mB: getLaunchConfigurations-(ILaunchConfigurationType type) and getLaunchConfigurations(IProject project). These methods iterate over elements received by calling getAllLaunchConexfigurations(), process the elements one by one, and when an element meets a certain condition, add it to a predefined list.

Suppose that Pat intends to apply similar changes to mA and mB. In mA, Pat wants to move the declaration of variable config out of the while loop and add code to process config as shown in lines 4, and 6-10 in mA. Pat wants to perform a similar edit to mB, but on the cfg variable instead of config. This example typifies *systematic edits*. Such similar yet not identical edits to multiple methods cannot be applied using the search and replace feature or existing refactoring engines in IDE, because they change the semantics of a program. Even though these two program changes are similar,

A_{old} to A_{new}

```
1. public ILaunchConfiguration[] getLaunchConfigurations
   (ILaunchConfigurationType type) throws CoreException {
2.     Iterator iter = getAllLaunchConfigurations().iterator();
3.     List configs = new ArrayList();
4.   + ILaunchConfiguration config = null;
5.     while (iter.hasNext()) {
6.       - ILaunchConfiguration config =
                 (ILaunchConfiguration)iter.next();
7.       + config = (ILaunchConfiguration)iter.next();
8.       + if (!config.inValid()) {
9.       +   config.reset();
10.      + }
11.        if (config.getType().equals(type)) {
12.          configs.add(config);
13.        }
14.    }
15.    return (ILaunchConfiguration[])configs.toArray
                 (new ILaunchConfiguration[configs.size()]);
17.}
```

SYDIT's replication of relevant edits on B_{old}, resulting in B_{new}

```
1. protected List getLaunchConfigurations(IProject project) {
2.     Iterator iter = getAllLaunchConfigurations().iterator();
3.   + ILaunchConfiguration cfg = null;
4.     List cfgs = new ArrayList();
5.     while (iter.hasNext()) {
6.       - ILaunchConfiguration cfg =
                 (ILaunchConfiguration)iter.next();
7.       + cfg = (ILaunchConfiguration)iter.next();
8.       + if (!cfg.inValid()) {
9.       +   cfg.reset();
10.      + }
11.        IFile file = cfg.getFile();
12.        if (file != null && file.getProject().equals(project)) {
13.          cfgs.add(cfg);
14.        }
15.    }
16.    return cfgs;
17.}
```

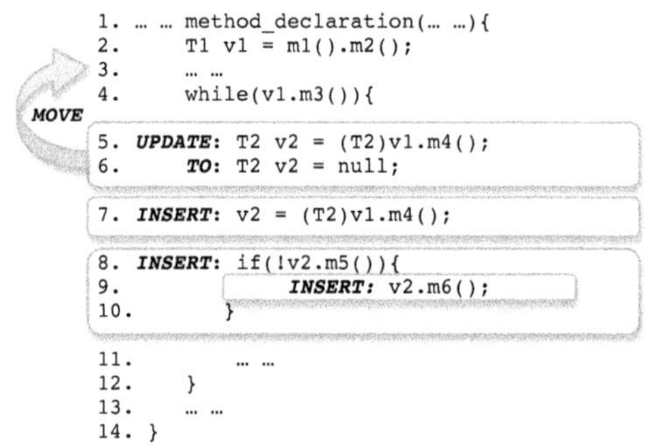

Abstract edit script

Figure 1. Systematic edit from revisions of org.eclipse.debug.core

without assistance, Pat must manually edit both methods, which is tedious and error-prone.

Using SYDIT, Pat applies the change only to mA and then SYDIT creates an edit script and applies it to mB. SYDIT applies a syntactic program differencing algorithm to mA_{old} and mA_{new} and then characterizes the exemplar edit (lines 4, and 6-10) in terms of a sequence of inserts, deletes, moves, and updates. For each edit, it performs data and control dependence analysis to determine the edit's corresponding context. It then abstracts variable, method, and type names and encodes edit positions relative to the extracted context. This identifier and edit position abstraction makes the edits applicable to similar yet not identical contexts.

Pat next identifies mB as a target for this edit script. Based on the extracted context and the abstract names in the edit script, SYDIT matches the extracted context against the mB target and identifies relevant code fragments that the edits are applicable to (i.e., lines 2, 5, and 6 in mB). It then creates *concrete* edits customized to mB, and applies them to mB.

The bottom of Figure 1 illustrates the content of the abstract edit script derived from the two versions of mA. Currently, SYDIT does not guarantee to generate an edit script containing the fewest edits.

Context extraction. SYDIT extracts the context of edits through data and control dependence analysis, which makes it possible to apply the edit script to code fragments that share similar data and control flows but are not identical to mA. For example, the location of the updated `ILaunchConfiguration` declaration is the child position 0 inside the `while` loop. Position 0 means the first AST child node of the while loop. The updated statement is control dependent on the `while` (line 5), and data dependent on the iterator declaration (line 2). We therefore include both lines 2 and 5 in the abstract context of this update.

Identifier abstraction. SYDIT abstracts all variable, method, and type names to make the edits applicable to contexts that use different identifier names. For instance, in the example, it abstracts the `config` variable in mA to v2.

Edit position abstraction. SYDIT encodes the syntactic position of each edit with respect to the extracted context nodes. For example, the source of the moved `ILaunchConfiguration` declaration is child position 0 of the `while` (i.e., its first AST child node), and the target is child position 1 of the method declaration node (i.e., its second AST child node).

Edit script application. To apply an abstract edit script to a target context, SYDIT matches the abstracted context against the target method and concretizes the abstract identifier names and edit positions with respect to the target method. For example, it concretizes `v2` to `cfg`, and encodes the target move position as the child position 1 of mB's method declaration node.

This automatic program transformation approach offers a flexible mechanism for improving programmer productivity. Systematic editing simplifies the tedious task of applying similar changes to multiple locations. Context abstraction and concretization increases the chance to apply systematic edits correctly and consistently. In this paper, the programmer selects both the source and target method and audits the result. With integration with automated compilation and testing, examining the correctness of SYDIT generated edits could be further automated. In all cases, the programmer should audit SYDIT generated versions through testing, inspection, or both. The coverage and accuracy of the edit scripts depend on the choice of the source exemplar edit, how context and abstract names are represented, and the algorithm that matches the extracted edit context to a target.

3. Approach

This section describes the two phases of SYDIT. Phase I takes as input an old and new version of method mA as its exemplar edit, and creates an edit script from mA_o and mA_n. Phase II applies the edit script to a new context, mB, producing a modified method mB_s. We first summarize the steps in each phase and then describe each step in detail.

Phase I: Creating Edit Scripts

- SYDIT compares an exemplar edit, mA_o and mA_n, and describes the differences as a sequence of insertions, deletions, updates, and moves: $\Delta_A = \{e_o, e_1, \ldots, e_n\}$.
- SYDIT identifies the context of the edit Δ_A based on data, control, and containment dependences between each e_i and other statements in mA_o and mA_n.
- SYDIT abstracts the edit, Δ, by encoding each e_i position with respect to its extracted context and by replacing all concrete variable, method, and type names with abstract identifier names.

Phase II: Applying Edit Scripts

- SYDIT matches the abstract context for Δ to mB's syntax tree.
- If they match, SYDIT generates a concrete edit Δ_B by translating abstract edit positions in Δ into concrete positions in mB and abstract identifiers in Δ into concrete identifiers in mB.
- SYDIT then applies Δ_B to mB, producing mB_s.

3.1 Phase I: Creating Abstract Edit Scripts

This section explains how SYDIT create an abstract edit script.

3.1.1 Syntactic Program Differencing

SYDIT compares the syntax trees of an exemplar edit, mA_o and mA_n, using a modified version of ChangeDistiller [9]. ChangeDistiller generates deletes, inserts, moves, and updates. We chose ChangeDistiller in part because it produces concise AST edit operations by (1) representing related node insertions and deletions as moves and updates and (2) aggregating multiple fine-grained expression edits into a single statement edit.

ChangeDistiller computes one-to-one node mappings from the original and new AST trees for all updated, moved, and unchanged nodes. If a node is not in the mappings, ChangeDistiller generates deletes or inserts as appropriate. It creates the mappings bottom-up using: *bigram string similarity* for leaf nodes (e.g., statements and method invocations), and *subtree similarity* for inner nodes (e.g., `while` and `if` statements). It first converts each leaf node to a string and computes its bigram—the set of all adjacent character pairs. The bigram similarity of two strings is the size of their bigram set intersection divided by the average of their sizes. If the similarity is above an input threshold, σ, ChangeDistiller includes the two leafs in its pair-wise mappings. It then computes subtree similarity based on the number of leaf node matches in each subtree, and establishes inner node mappings bottom up.

We modify ChangeDistiller's matching algorithms in two ways. First, we require inner nodes to perform equivalent control-flow functions. For instance, the original algorithm sometimes mapped a `while` to an `if` node. We instead enforce a structural match, i.e., `while` nodes only map to `while` or `for` nodes. Second, we match leaf nodes to inner nodes using bigram string similarity. This change overcomes inconsistent treatment of blocks. For example, ChangeDistiller treats a `catch` clause with an empty body as a leaf node, but a `catch` clause with a non-empty body is an inner node.

Given a resulting set of AST node mappings, SYDIT describes edit operations with respect to the original method mA_o as follows:

delete (Node u): delete node u from mA_o.

insert (Node u, Node v, int k): insert node u and position it as the $(k+1)^{th}$ child of node v.

move (Node u, Node v, int k): delete u from its current position in mA_o and insert u as the $(k+1)^{th}$ child of v.

update (Node u, Node v): replace u in mA_o with v. This step includes changing the AST type in the resulting tree to v's type and maintaining any of u's AST parent and children relationships in v.

The resulting sequence of syntactic edits is $\Delta_A = \{e_i | e_i \in \{$delete (u), insert (u,v,k), move (u,v,k), update (u,v)$\}\}$. We use a total order for e_i to ease relative positioning of edits.

Figure 2 presents the mapping for our example, where 'O' is a node in the old version $\texttt{mA}_o$ and 'N' is a node in the new version $\texttt{mA}_n$. Below we show the concrete edit script Δ_A that transforms $\texttt{mA}_o$ into $\texttt{mA}_n$ for our example:

1. update (O6, N4)
   O6 = `'ILaunchConfiguration config = (ILaunchConfiguration) iter.next();'`
   N4 = `'ILaunchConfiguration config = null;'`
2. move (O6, N1, 2)
3. insert (N7, N5, 0)
   N7 = `'config = (ILaunchConfiguration) iter.next();'`
4. insert (N8, N5, 1) N8 = `'if (!config.inValid())'`
5. insert (N9, N8, 0) N9 = 'then'
6. insert (N10, N9, 0) N10 = `'config.reset();'`

3.1.2 Extracting Edit Contexts

SYDIT extracts relevant context from both the old and new versions. For each edit $e_i \in \Delta_A$, SYDIT analyzes $\texttt{mA}_o$ and $\texttt{mA}_n$ to find the unchanged nodes on which changed nodes in e_i depend. These dependences include containment dependences and the source and sink of control and data dependences. We call these nodes *context*.

Context information increases the chance of generating syntactically valid edits and also serves as anchors to position edits correctly in a new target location. First, in order to respect the syntax rules of the underlying programming language, we include AST nodes that the edits require. For example, insertion of a `return` statement must occur inside a method declaration subtree. This context increases the probability of producing a syntactically valid, compilable program. Second, we use control dependences to describe the position to apply an edit, such as inserting a statement at the first child position of `while` loop. While the edit may be valid outside the `while`, positioning the edit within the `while` increases the probability that the edit will be correctly replicated. Third, context helps preserve data dependences. For example, consider an edit that inserts statement `S2: foo++;` after `S1: int foo = bar;`. If we require `S1` to precede `S2` by including `S1` in the context of `S2`, the resulting edit will guarantee that `foo` is defined before it is incremented. However, including and enforcing more dependence requirements in the edit context may decrease the number of target methods that will match and thus may sacrifice coverage.

Formally, node y is *context dependent* on x if one of the following relationships holds:

- *Data dependence*: node x uses or defines a variable whose value is defined in node y. For example, N10 uses variable `config`, whose value is defined in N7. Therefore, N10 is data dependent on N7.
- *Control dependence*: node y is control dependent on x if y may or may not execute depending on a decision made by x. Formally, given a control-flow graph, node y is control dependent on x, if: (1) y post-dominates every vertex p in $x \rightsquigarrow y, p \neq x$, and (2) y does not strictly post-dominate x [6].
- *Containment dependence*: node y is containment dependent on x if y is a child of x in the AST. For instance, N4 is containment dependent on N1.

To extract the context for an edit script, we compute control, data, and containment dependences on the old and new versions. The context of an edit script Δ_A is the union of these dependences. The containment dependence is usually redundant with immediate control dependence of x, except when loops contain early returns. To combine dependences, SYDIT *projects* nodes found in the new version $\texttt{mA}_n$ onto corresponding nodes in the old version $\texttt{mA}_o$ based on the mappings generated by the modified version of ChangeDistiller. For each $e_i \in \Delta_A$, we determine relevant context nodes as follows.

delete (u)**:** The algorithm computes nodes in $\texttt{mA}_o$ that depend on the deleted node, u.

insert (u, p, k)**:** Since u does not exist in $\texttt{mA}_o$, the algorithm first computes nodes in $\texttt{mA}_n$ on which u depends and then projects them into corresponding nodes in $\texttt{mA}_o$.

move (u, v, k)**:** The algorithm finds the dependent nodes in both $\texttt{mA}_o$ and $\texttt{mA}_n$ related to u. The nodes in the new version help guarantee dependence relationships after the update. It projects the nodes from $\texttt{mA}_n$ into corresponding nodes in $\texttt{mA}_o$ and then unions the two sets.

update (u, v)**:** The algorithm finds the dependent nodes in $\texttt{mA}_o$ related to the updated node, u. It also finds dependent nodes in $\texttt{mA}_n$ related to the node v. It projects the nodes from $\texttt{mA}_n$ into corresponding nodes in $\texttt{mA}_o$ and then unions the two sets.

Consider insert (N7, N5, 0) from Figure 2. The inserted node N7 is control dependent on N5, and data dependent on N2 and N4. Mapping these nodes to the old version yields the context node set {O2, O4, O6}. The move (O6, N1, 2) operation is more complicated because O6 depends on the node set C1 = {O4, O2} in the old version, while N4, N1's child at position 2, depends on the node set C2 = {N1} in the new version. After deriving the two sets, we project C2 onto nodes in $\texttt{mA}_o$, which yields C3 = {O1}. Finally, we union C1 and C3 to get the context node set {O1, O2, O4} for the move operation. Figure 2 illustrates the result, marking irrelevant nodes with dotted lines and context nodes in gray.

SYDIT allows the user to configure the amount of context. For example, the number of dependence hops, k, controls how many surrounding, unchanged nodes to include in the context. Setting $k = 1$ selects just the immediate control and data dependent nodes. Setting $k = \infty$ selects all control and data dependent nodes. We can restrict dependences to reaching definitions or include the nodes in a chain of definitions and uses depending on k. SYDIT differentiates *upstream* and *downstream* dependences. Upstream dependences precede the edit in the text, whereas downstream dependences follow the edit. The default setting of SYDIT is $k = 1$ with control, data, and containment upstream dependences, which was best in practice. Section 4 shows how varying context affects SYDIT's coverage and accuracy.

3.1.3 Abstracting Identifiers and Edit Positions

At this point, the edit script and its context use concrete identifier names and edit positions from the exemplar edit. To make the edit script more applicable, we abstract identifier names and edit positions in the edit script.

To abstract identifiers, we replace all concrete variable, method, and type names with equivalent abstract representations: `T$x`, `m$x`, and `v$x` respectively. Each unique concrete identifier corresponds to a unique abstract one. For example, we convert the concrete expression `!config.inValid()` in Figure 2 to `!v2.m5()` in Figure 3.

We abstract the position of edits to make them applicable to code that differs structurally from the original source example. We encode an edit position as a relative position with respect to all the context nodes, instead of all nodes in the original syntax tree. For example, we convert the concrete edit move (O6, N1, 2) to an abstract edit move (AO4, AN1, 1). In this case, the abstract edit position is child position 1 of the `while` because the context of the edit includes the definition of `ILaunchConfiguration` at abstract child position 0 and no other dependences. This relative position ensures that `ILaunchConfiguration` is defined by some

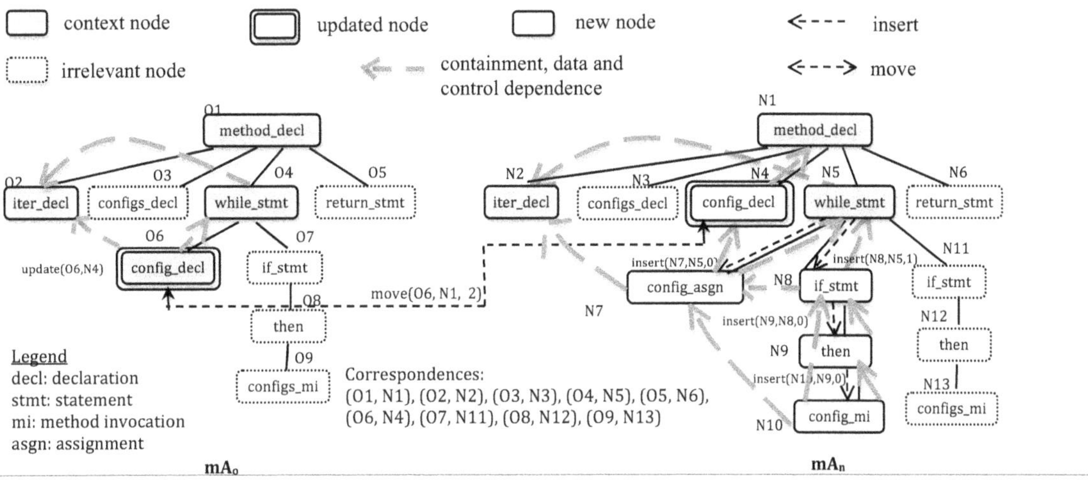

Figure 2. Syntactic edit extraction for mA

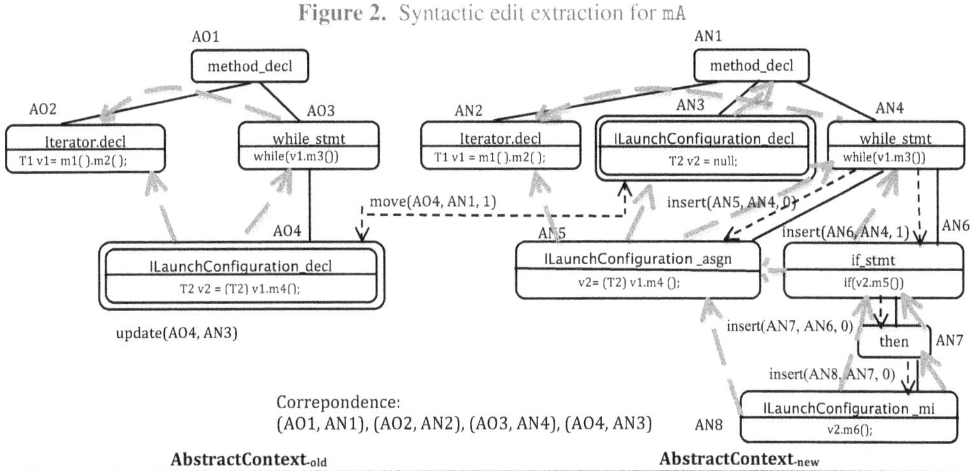

Figure 3. Abstract edit script

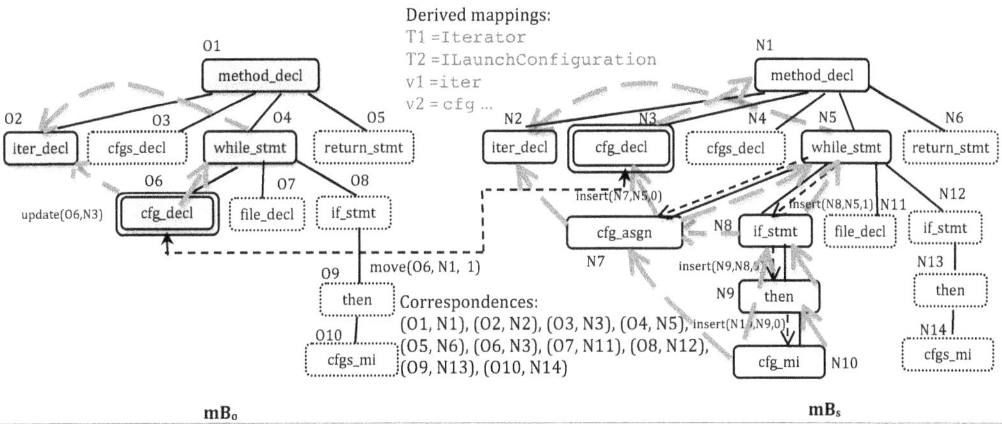

Figure 4. Syntactic edit suggestion for mB

statement before it is used, but requires no other statements in the `while`. When we apply the edit, we require the context to match and apply edits relative to the context position in the target, not the concrete positions in the original method. Abstracting edit positions is essential for applying an edit when the target method satisfies the context dependences, regardless of the exact positions of the statements in the code.

3.2 Phase II: Applying Abstract Edits

This section describes how SYDIT applies an edit script Δ to a method mB, producing a modified method mB_s.

3.2.1 Matching Abstract Contexts

The goal of our matching algorithm is to find nodes in the target method that match the context nodes in Δ and that induce one-to-one mappings between abstract and concrete identifier names. To simplify this process, we first abstract the identifiers in mB. We use the procedure as described in Section 3.1.3 to create $\texttt{mB}_{Abstract}$ from mB. For concision in this section, we simply use mB instead of $\texttt{mB}_{Abstract}$.

This problem can be posed as the labeled subgraph isomorphism problem. Although we experimented with an off-the-shelf implementation [20], adapting it to match nodes while simultaneously requiring one-to-one symbolic identifier mappings is difficult. Yet these two features are essential requirements for applying edits to new contexts. See Section 3.2.2 for more details. The algorithm we propose below tolerates inexact label matches for unchanged context nodes while enforcing one-to-one symbolic identifier mappings.

The intuition behind our algorithm is to first find candidate leaf matches and then use them to match inner nodes. We find as many candidate matches as possible between leaf nodes in the abstract context and leaf nodes in the target tree, $x \in$ AC, $y \in$ mB, where x and y form *an exact match*, i.e., the equivalent AST node types and node labels (see below). Based on these exact matches (x, y), we add node matches (u, v), where u and v are on paths from the respective root nodes, $u \in (root_{AC} \rightsquigarrow x)$ and $v \in (root_{mB} \rightsquigarrow y)$. We add (u, v) type matches bottom-up, requiring only their node types to be equivalent. Finally for each unmatched leaf in the abstract context, we find additional *type matches* based on the established set of matches. We repeat these steps until the set of candidate leaf matches, CL, does not increase any more. We define two types of node matches and one type of path matches:

Type match: Given two nodes u and v, (u,v) is a type match if their AST node types match. For example, both are `if`s or one is a `while` and the other is a `for`. The conditions need not match.

Exact match: Given two nodes u and v, (u,v) is an exact match if it is a type match *and* their AST *labels* are equivalent. We define the label as the abstract strings in the statements and ignore numerics in abstract identifiers. For example, '`T1 v1 = null;`' and '`T2 v2 = null;`' are equivalent since we ignore the numeric and convert them both to '`T v = null;`'.

Path match: Given two paths $p1$ and $p2$, $(p1, p2)$ is a path match if for every node u on $p1$, there exists node v on $p2$ where (u, v) is a type match. For example, given two leaf nodes x and y, the paths match if parent(x) and parent(y) type match, parent(parent(x)) and parent(parent(y)) type match, and so on.

We use these definitions to map the nodes in the abstract context AC in Δ to mB in the following four steps, which Algorithm 1 describes procedurally.

1. SYDIT finds all exact leaf matches between AC and mB and adds each (x, y) pair to a set of candidate leaf matches, CL.
2. Based on CL, SYDIT then tries to find the best path match for each leaf node x where $(x, y) \in CL$ and finds node matches based on the best path match. Let $p1 = root_{AC} \rightsquigarrow x$ and $p2 = root_{mB} \rightsquigarrow y$. This step is broken into three cases, for each node match (x, y) in CL,
   (a) If there exists one path match $(p1, p2)$ between AC and mB, we add all its constituent node matches (u, v) on these paths to M.
   (b) If there exists multiple path matches, e.g., $(p1, (root_{mB} \rightsquigarrow y_1))$ and $(p1, (root_{mB} \rightsquigarrow y_2))$, and one of these path matches contains more constituent nodes already in the set established matches M, we select the best of these path matches and add constituent (u, v) matches to M.
   (c) If there exists multiple path matches with the same number of constituent node matches in M, SYDIT leverages sibling ordering relationships among the leaf nodes to disambiguate the best path match. Given a leaf node $x \in$ AC, suppose that path $p1$ matches with multiple paths, e.g., $(p2 = root_{mB} \rightsquigarrow y_2)$, $(p3 = root_{mB} \rightsquigarrow y_3)$, with the same score and assume that y_2 precedes y_3 in sibling order. If a node match (u, v) exists in M in which u precedes x in terms of sibling order, and v is a sibling between y_2 and y_3, SYDIT prefers a path match $((root_{AC} \rightsquigarrow x), (root_{mB} \rightsquigarrow y_3))$, since this choice is consistent with an already estab-

Algorithm 1: Matching Abstract Context to Target Tree

```
Input: AC, mB /* abstract context and abstract target
    tree                                              */
Output: M /* a set of node matches from AC to mB      */
/* 1. create candidate leaf exact matches             */
CL := ∅;
M := ∅;
foreach leaf node x ∈ AC do
    foreach leaf node y ∈ mB do
        if exactMatch(x, y) then
            CL:= CL ∪ {(x, y)};
        end
    end
end
repeat
    /* 2(a). create matches based on path matches     */
    foreach (x, y) ∈ CL such that ∄ (x, z) ∈ CL ∧ y ≠ z do
        p1 = (root_AC ⇝ x);
        p2 = (root_mB ⇝ y);
        if pathMatch(p1, p2) then
            M:= M ∪ {(u, v) | u ∈ p1 , where (u,v) is a type
            match and v ∈ p2 and u and v appear in the same
            position on paths p1 and p2};
        end
    end
    /* 2(b). select the best path match and add new
       node matches it induces                        */
    foreach (leaf node x ∈ AC such that (x, y) ∈ CL ∧ (x,y) ∉ M)
    do
        p1 = (root_AC ⇝ x);
        p2 = (root_mB ⇝ y);
        select y with the maximum pathMatchScore(p1, p2,
        M);
        M:= M ∪{(u, v) | u ∈ p1 and v ∈ p2, where (u,v) is a
        type match and u and v appear in the same position on
        paths p1 and p2};
    end
    /* 2(c). disambiguate path matches based on the
       sibling order of matched leaf nodes in M       */
    foreach (leaf node x ∈ AC such that (x, y) ∈ CL ∧ (x,y) ∉ M)
    do
        select y with the maximum LCSMatchScore(x,y,M);
        M:= M ∪{(u, v) | u ∈ p1 and v ∈ p2, where (u,v) is a
        type match and u and v appear in the same position on
        paths (root_AC ⇝ x) and (root_mB ⇝ y};
    end
    /* 3. establish symbolic identifier mappings      */
    S:= ∅;
    foreach (u, v) ∈ M do
        S:= S ∪ {(T$n, T$m), (v$i, v$j), and/or (m$k, m$l)
          that are supported by (u, v)};
    end
    removeConflicts(S, M);
    /* 4. relax constraints to add leaf candidates
       */
    CL:= CL ∪ relaxConstraints(AC, M);
until CL reaches its fix point ;
```

lished match (u, v). Similarly, based on this path match, we add constituent node matches on the matched paths to M. While this approach is similar to how the longest common subsequence (LCS) algorithm align nodes [14], our approach matches leaf nodes based on established matches in M.

3. SYDIT establishes mappings between symbolic identifiers in AC and mB by enumerating all node matches in M. For example, if the label of matched nodes are `'T1 v1 = null;'` and `'T2 v2 = null;'`, we add the symbolic identifier mappings `(T1, T2)` and `(v1, v2)` to S. While collecting identifier mappings, the algorithm may encounter inconsistencies, such as `(T1, T3)`, which violates an already established mapping from T1 to T2. To remove the conflict between `(T1, T2)` and `(T1, T3)`, SYDIT counts the number of node matches that support each mapping. It keeps the mapping with the most support, and removes other mappings from S and all their supporting node matches from M.
4. SYDIT leverages the parent-child relationship of matched nodes in M to introduce type matches for unmatched leaf(s) in AC. For each unmatched leaf z in AC, SYDIT traverses bottom-up along its path to root in order to find the first ancestor u which has a match $(u, v) \in M$. Next, if it finds an unmatched node w in the subtree rooted at v and if (z, w) is a type match, SYDIT adds it into CL. We repeat steps 2 to 4 until step 4 does not add any to CL.

At any point in this process, if every node in the abstract context AC has a match in M, then we proceed to derive concrete edits customized to mB, described in Section 3.2.3. If we fail to find a match for each node, SYDIT reports to the user that the edit context does not match and it cannot replicate the edit on the target context.

3.2.2 Alternative matching algorithms

Standard labeled subgraph isomorphism is a promising alternative approach for matching abstract context in Δ to a new target method mB that we also explored. We formulated both the abstract content and target method as graphs in which nodes are labeled with their AST node types, and edges are labeled with constraint relationships between nodes, such as containment, data, and control dependences. To preserve a one-to-one mapping between abstract and concrete identifiers, we included additional labeled nodes to represent the sequence of symbols appearing in the statement. We included variable names, method names, type names, as well as constants like `null` and operators like `=` as node labels. Next, we connected all the identifiers with the same name with edges labeled "same name." We thus converted our problem to finding an isomorphic labeled subgraph in the target method's graph for the abstract context's graph.

Function `pathMatch`(*path p1, path p2*)

```
t1 := p1's bottom-up iterator;
t2 := p2's bottom-up iterator;
while t1.hasPrev() ∧ t2.hasPrev() do
    u := t1.prev();
    v := t2.prev();
    if !EquivalentNodeType(u, v) then
        return false;
    end
end
if t1.hasPrev() then
    return false;
end
return true;
```

Function `pathMatchScore`(*path p1, path p2, matches M*)

```
counter := 0;
t1 := p1's bottom-up iterator;
t2 := p2's bottom-up iterator;
while t1.hasPrev() ∧ t2.hasPrev() do
    u := t1.prev();
    v := t2.prev();
    if (u, v) ∈ M then
        counter + +;
    end
end
return counter;
```

Function `LCSMatchScore`(*node x, node y, matches M*)

```
score := 0;
/* identify left siblings of x and y                          */
l1 := left_children(parent(x), x);
l2 := left_children(parent(y), y);
/* identify right siblings of x and y                         */
r1 := right_children(parent(x), x);
r2 := right_children(parent(y), y);
/* compute the size of longest common sequences of
   l1 and l2 and r1 and r2 respectively with respect
   to M.                                                       */
score := LCS(l1, l2, M) + LCS(r1, r2, M);
return score;
```

Function `removeConflicts`(*mappings S, matches M*)

```
foreach (s1, s2) ∈ S do
    T = {t | (s1, t) ∈ S };
    if |T| > 1 then
        select t with the most supporting matches;
        T = T - (s1, t);
        foreach s2 ∈ T do
            S := S − {(s1, s2)};
            M := M − {(u, v)|(u, v) supports (s1, s2)};
        end
    end
end
```

Function `relaxConstraints`(*context AC, matches M*)

```
CL := ∅
foreach leaf node z ∈ AC such that ∄(z, w) ∈ M do
    u := z;
    repeat
        u := parent(u);
    until u=null ∨∃(u, v) ∈ M ;
    if u ≠null then
        CL := CL ∪{(z, w)|w is a node in the subtree rooted at v,
        where (z, w) is a type match and w is not matched};
    end
end
return CL;
```

A problem with this direct conversion is that it requires each symbol in the abstract context must match a symbol in the target method. This requirement is needlessly strict for the unchanged context nodes. For instance, consider inserting a child of an `if` in the target. When the guard condition of the target `if` is a little different from the known `if`, i.e., `field != null` vs. `this.getField() != null`, exact graph isomorphism fails in this case. Although our algorithm is a little messy compared with an off-the-shelf labeled subgraph isomorphism algorithm [20], the heuristics for identifier replacements and siblings alignment work well in practice. Specifying which node matches to relax, and when and how to relax them is the key contribution of the algorithm we present above.

3.2.3 Generating Concrete Edits

To generate the concrete edit script Δ_B for `mB`, SYDIT substitutes symbolic names used in Δ and recalculates edit positions with respect to the concrete nodes in `mB`. This process reverses the abstraction performed in Section 3.1.3.

The substitution is based on the symbolic identifier mappings established in Section 3.2.1, e.g., `(T1, T2)`, and the abstract-concrete identifier mappings established in Section 3.1.3, e.g., `(T1, int)`, `(T2, int)`. For this specific case, each time `T1` occurs in Δ, SYDIT uses `int` in Δ_B.

Some edits in Δ use symbolic identifiers that only exist in the new version, thus the name does not exist in the original code of $\mathtt{mA}_o$ or $\mathtt{mB}_o$ and this name thus has no match. In this case, we borrow the identifier name from $\mathtt{mA}_n$. For example, the identifier `inValid` used in Figure 1 only exists in $\mathtt{mA}_n$, and is not in $\mathtt{mB}_o$, nor should we ever expect it to appear in $\mathtt{mA}_o$. We thus just use the name from $\mathtt{mA}_n$, stored in Δ for Δ_B.

We make edit positions concrete with respect to the concrete nodes in `mB`. For instance, with the node match (u, v), an abstract edit which inserts a node after u is translated to a concrete edit which inserts a node after v. Using the above algorithms, SYDIT produces the following concrete edits for `mB` (see Figure 4).

1. update (O6, N3), N3 = '`ILaunchConfiguration cfg = null;`'
2. move (O6, N1, 1)
3. insert (N7, N5, 0),
   N7 = '`cfg = (ILaunchConfiguration) iter.next();`'
4. insert (N8, N5, 1), N8 = '`if (!cfg.inValid())`'
5. insert (N9, N8, 0), N9 = `then`
6. insert (N10, N9, 0), N10 = '`cfg.reset();`'

This edit script shows that `mB` is changed similarly to `mA`. It differs because of the move (O6, N1, 1), which puts the designated node in a different location compared to `mA`. This difference does not compromise the edit's correctness since it respects the relevant data dependence constraints encoded in Δ. SYDIT then converts Δ_B to Eclipse AST manipulations to produce $\mathtt{mB}_s$.

4. Evaluation

To assess the coverage and accuracy of SYDIT, we create an oracle data set of 56 pairs of example edits from open source projects, which we refer to simply as the *examples*. To examine the capabilities of SYDIT, we select a range of simple to complex examples, and show that SYDIT produces accurate edits across the examples. We compare SYDIT to common *search and replace* text editor functionality and demonstrate that SYDIT is much more effective. We evaluate the sensitivity of SYDIT to the source and target method. Most correct edits are insensitive to this choice, but when there is a difference, choosing a simpler edit as the source method typically leads to higher coverage. We also study the best way to characterize edit context. We find that more context does not always yield more accurate edits. In fact, minimal, but non-zero context seems to be the sweet spot that leads to higher coverage and accuracy. Configuring SYDIT to use an *upstream* context with $k = 1$ yields the highest coverage and accuracy on our examples.

For the evaluation data set, we collected 56 method pairs that experienced similar edits. We included 8 examples from a prior study of systematic changes to code clones from the Eclipse `jdt.core` plug-in and from `jEdit` [16]. We collected the remaining 48 examples from 42 releases of the Eclipse `compare` plug-in, 37 releases of the Eclipse `core.runtime` plug-in, and 50 releases of the Eclipse `debug` plug-in. For each pair, we computed the syntactic differences with Change Distiller. We identified method pairs `mA` and `mB` that share at least one common syntactic edit between the old and new version and their content is at least 40% similar. We use the following similarity metric:

$$\mathtt{similarity(mA,\ mB)} = \frac{|matchingNodes(mA, mB)|}{size(mA) + size(mB)} \quad (1)$$

where matchingNodes(`mA`, `mB`) is the number of matching AST node pairs computed by ChangeDistiller, and size(`mA`) is the number of AST nodes in method `mA`.

We manually inspected and categorized these examples based on (1) whether the edits involve changing a *single* AST node vs. *multiple* nodes, (2) whether the edits are *contiguous* vs. *non-contiguous*, and (3) whether the edits' content is *identical* vs. *abstract*. An abstract context requires type, method, or variable name abstraction. To test this range of functionality in SYDIT, we chose at least 7 examples in each category. Table 1 shows the number of examples in each of these six categories. The systematic change examples in the data set are non-trivial syntactic edits that include on average 1.66 inserts, 1.54 deletes, 1.46 moves, and 0.70 updates.

	Single node	**Multiple nodes**	
		Contiguous	**Non-contiguous**
Identical	SI	CI	NI
examples	7	7	11
matched	5	7	8
compilable	5	7	8
correct	5	7	8
coverage	71%	100%	73%
accuracy	71%	100%	73%
similarity	100%	100%	100%
Abstract	SA	CA	NA
examples	7	12	12
matched	7	9	10
compilable	6	8	9
correct	6	6	7
coverage	100%	75%	83%
accuracy	86%	50%	58%
similarity	86%	95%	95%
Total coverage	82%	(46/56)	
Total accuracy	70%	(39/56)	
Total similarity	96%	(46)	

Table 1. SYDIT's capabilities, coverage, and accuracy for k=1, upstream control and data dependences

Coverage and accuracy. For each method pair ($\mathtt{mA}_o$, $\mathtt{mB}_o$) in the old version that changed similarly to become ($\mathtt{mA}_n$, $\mathtt{mB}_n$) in the new version, SYDIT generates an abstract, context-aware edit script from $\mathtt{mA}_o$ and $\mathtt{mA}_n$ and tries to apply the learned edits to the target method $\mathtt{mB}_o$, producing $\mathtt{mB}_s$. In Table 1, *matched* is the number of examples for which SYDIT matches the learned context to the target method $\mathtt{mB}_o$. The *compilable* row is the number of examples for which SYDIT produces a syntactically-valid program, and *correct* is the number of examples for which SYDIT replicates edits that are semantically identical to what the programmer actually did. *Coverage* is $\frac{matched}{examples}$, and *accuracy* is $\frac{correct}{examples}$. We also measure syntactic *similarity* between SYDIT's output and the expected output according to the above similarity formula (1).

This table uses our best configuration of k=1, upstream context only, i.e., one source node for each control and data dependence edge in the context, in addition to including a parent node of each edit. For this configuration, SYDIT matches the derived abstract

A_{old} to A_{new}

```
private void paintSides(GC g, MergeSourceViewer tp,
  Canvas canvas, boolean right) {
  ...
- g.setLineWidth(LW);
+ g.setLineWidth(0 /* LW */);
  ...
}
```

B_{old} to B_{new}

```
private void paintCenter(Canvas canvas, GC g) {
  ...
  if (fUseSingleLine) {
    ...
  - g.setLineWidth(LW);
  + g.setLineWidth(0 /* LW */);
  ...
  } else {
    if(fUseSplines){
      ...
    - g.setLineWidth(LW);
    + g.setLineWidth(0 /* LW */);
      ...
      } else {
        ...
      - g.setLineWidth(LW);
      + g.setLineWidth(0 /* LW */);
      }
    } ...
}
```

Figure 5. A non-contiguous identical edit script (NI) for which SYDIT cannot match the change context (org.eclipse.compare: v20060714 vs. v20060917)

A_{old} to A_{new}

```
public IActionBars getActionBars() {
  + IActionBars actionBars = fContainer.getActionBars();
  - if (fContainer == null) {
  + if (actionBars == null && !fContainerProvided) {
      return Utilities.findActionBars(fComposite);
    }
    - return fContainer.getActionBars();
    + return actionBars;
}
```

B_{old} to B_{new}

```
public IServiceLocator getServiceLocator() {
  + IServiceLocator serviceLocator
      = fContainer.getServiceLocator();
  - if (fContainer == null) {
  + if (serviceLocator == null && !fContainerProvided) {
      return Utilities.findSite(fComposite);
    }
    - return fContainer.getServiceLocator();
    + return serviceLocator;
}
```

B_{old} to $B_{suggested}$

```
public IServiceLocator getServiceLocator() {
  + IServiceLocator actionBars
      = fContainer.getServiceLocator();
  - if (fContainer == null) {
  + if (actionBars == null && !fContainerProvided) {
      return Utilities.findSite(fComposite);
    }
    - return fContainer.getServiceLocator();
    + return actionBars;
}
```

Figure 6. A non-contiguous, abstract edit script for which SYDIT produces edits equivalent to the developer's (org.eclipse.compare: v20061120 vs. v20061218)

SI: single, identical edit		
8 targets	8 matched	8 correct
100% coverage (8/8)	100% accuracy (8/8)	100% similarity
CI: contiguous, identical edits		
5 targets	4 matched	4 correct
80% coverage (4/5)	80% accuracy (4/5)	100% similarity
NI: non-contiguous, identical edits		
6 targets	4 matched	0 correct
67% coverage (4/6)	0% accuracy (0/6)	67% similarity
SA: single, abstract edit		
5 targets	5 matched	5 correct
100% coverage (5/5)	100% accuracy (5/5)	100% similarity
CA: contiguous, abstract edits		
4 targets	4 matched	4 correct
100% coverage (4/4)	100% accuracy (4/4)	100% similarity
NA: non-contiguous, abstract edits		
4 targets	4 matched	4 correct
100% coverage (4/4)	100% accuracy (4/4)	100% similarity

Table 2. Replicating similar edits to multiple contexts

context for 46 of 56 examples, achieving 82% coverage. In 39 of 46 cases, the edits are semantically equivalent to the programmer's hand editing. Even for those cases in which SYDIT produces a different edit, the output and the expected output are often similar. For the examples SYDIT produces edits, on average, its output is 96% similar to the version created by a human developer.

In the examples where SYDIT cannot match the abstract context, the target method was usually very different from the source method, or the edit script needs to be applied multiple times in the target method. In Figure 5 (from `org.eclipse.compare`: v20060714 vs. v20060917), `g.setLineWidth(LW)` was replaced with `g.setLineWidth(0)` once in the source method. The same edit needs to be replicated in three different control-flow contexts in the target. Additional user assistance would solve this problem.

Figure 6 shows a complex example (from org.eclipse.compare v20061120 vs. v20061218) that SYDIT handles well. Although the methods $\texttt{mA}_o$ and $\texttt{mB}_o$ use different identifiers, SYDIT successfully matches $\texttt{mB}_o$ to the abstract context AC derived from `mA`, creating a version $\texttt{mB}_s$, which is semantically equivalent to the manually crafted version $\texttt{mB}_n$.

In addition to these 56 pairs, we collected six examples that perform similar edits on multiple contexts—on at least 5 different methods. Table 2 shows the results. In four out of six categories, SYDIT correctly replicates similar edits to all target contexts. In the CI category, SYDIT misses one of five target methods because the target does not fully contain the inferred abstract context. In the NI category, SYDIT produces incorrect edits in two out of six targets because it inserts statements before the statements that define variables used by the inserts, causing a compilation error. To prevent undefined uses, SYDIT should, and in the future will, adjust its insertion point based on data dependences.

Comparison with search and replace. The *search and replace* (S&R) feature is the most widely used approach to systematic editing. Though SYDIT's goal is not to replace S&R but to complement it, we nevertheless compare them to assess how much additional capability SYDIT provides for automating repetitive edits. 32 of the 56 examples in our test suite require non-contiguous and abstract edit scripts. S&R cannot perform them in a straightforward manner because even after a developer applies one or more S&R actions, he or she would have to customize either the type, method, and/or variable names. For those 32 examples, SYDIT produces correct edits in 20 cases. For the remaining 24 examples, we categorize typical user-specified S&R sophistication into three levels:

- Level 1: Search for a single line and replace it.
- Level 2: Search for several contiguous lines and replace them.
- Level 3: Perform multiple S&R operations to modify several non-contiguous lines.

On the remaining 24 examples, SYDIT handles 7 of 11 Level 1 examples, 5 of 5 in Level 2, 7 of 8 in Level 3. Even though Level 1 examples are straightforward with S&R, SYDIT misses cases like the one in Figure 5. Overall, SYDIT is much more effective and accurate than S&R.

Self application of a derived edit script. To assess whether SYDIT generates correct program transformations from an example, we derive an edit script from $\texttt{mA}_o$ and $\texttt{mA}_n$ and then apply it back to $\texttt{mA}_o$. We then compare the SYDIT generated version with $\texttt{mA}_n$. Similarly, we derive an edit script from $\texttt{mB}_o$ and $\texttt{mB}_n$ and compare the application of the script to $\texttt{mB}_o$ with $\texttt{mB}_n$. In our experiments, SYDIT replicated edits correctly in *all* 112 cases.

Selection of source and target method. SYDIT currently requires the user to select a source and target method. To explore how robust SYDIT is to which method the user selects, we switched the source and target methods for each example. In 35 of 56 examples (63%), SYDIT replicates edit scripts in both directions correctly. In 9 of 56 examples (16%), SYDIT could not match the context in either direction. In 7 out of 56 examples (13%), SYDIT replicates edit scripts in only one direction. In the failed cases, the source method experiences a super set of the edits needed in the target. Additional user guidance to select only a subset of edits in the source would solve this problem.

Context characterization. Table 3 characterizes the number of AST nodes and dependence edges in each edit script with the best configuration of $k = 1$ upstream only dependences. On average, an edit script involves 7.66 nodes, 2.77 data dependence edges, 5.63 control dependence edges, 5.04 distinct type names, 4.07 distinct method names, and 7.16 distinct variable names. These results show that SYDIT creates and uses complex abstract contexts.

Table 4 explores how different context characterization strategies affect SYDIT's coverage, accuracy, and similarity for the 56 examples. These experiments vary the amount of control and data dependence context, but always include the containment context (see Section 3.1.2).

The first part of the table shows that SYDIT's results degrade slightly as the number of hops of control and data dependence chains in the context increases. $k = 1$ selects context nodes with one direct upstream or downstream control or data dependence on any edited node. We hypothesized that the inclusion of more contextual nodes would help SYDIT produce more accurate edits without sacrificing coverage. Instead, we found the opposite.

The second part of Table 4 reports on the effectiveness of identifier abstraction for variable (V), method (M), and type (T) names. As expected, abstracting all three leads to the highest coverage, while no abstraction leads to the lowest coverage.

The third part of the same table shows results when varying the setting of upstream and downstream dependence relations for $k = 1$. All uses both upstream and downstream dependence relations to characterize the context, containment only neither uses upstream nor downstream data or control dependences, and upstream only uses only upstream dependence relations. Surprisingly, upstream only—which has neither the most nor fewest contextual nodes—gains the best coverage and accuracy.

ChangeDistiller similarity threshold. SYDIT uses ChangeDistiller to compute AST-level edits between two program versions. When comparing the labels of AST nodes, ChangeDistiller uses a bigram similarity threshold and if the similarity between two node

Size	Min	Max	Median	Average
nodes	1	56	3.5	7.66
data dependences	0	34	0.5	2.77
control dependences	1	38	3	5.63
Abstraction				
types	0	17	4	5.04
methods	0	17	2	4.07
variable	0	26	4.5	7.16

Table 3. SYDIT's context characterization

	matched	correct	% coverage	% accuracy	% similarity
Varying the number of dependence hops					
k=1	44	37	79%	66%	95%
k=2	42	35	75%	63%	95%
k=3	42	35	75%	63%	95%
Varying the abstraction settings					
abstract V T M	46	39	82%	70%	96%
abstract V	37	31	66%	55%	55%
abstract T	37	31	66%	55%	55%
abstract M	45	38	80%	68%	96%
no abstraction	37	31	66%	55%	55%
Control, data, and containment vs. containment only vs. upstream only					
all (k=1)	44	37	79%	66%	95%
containment only	47	38	84%	68%	90%
upstream only (k=1)	46	39	82%	70%	96%

Table 4. SYDIT's sensitivity to context characterization

σ	matched	correct	% coverage	% accuracy	% similarity
0.6	46	39	82%	70%	96%
0.5	46	39	82%	70%	96%
0.4	46	39	82%	70%	96%
0.3	46	39	82%	70%	96%
0.2	45	33	80%	59%	86%

Table 5. SYDIT's sensitivity to input threshold σ used in ChangeDistiller

labels is greater than σ, it matches the nodes. Our experiments use a default setting of 0.5 for σ. Since our edit script generation capability depends heavily on ChangeDistiller's ability to compute syntactic edits accurately in the source example, we experimented with different settings of σ. Table 5 shows that when σ is in the range of 0.3 to 0.6, SYDIT's accuracy does not change. When σ is 0.2, the relaxed similarity criterion leads AST node mismatches, which produce incorrect updates or moves, and consequently SYDIT's coverage, accuracy and similarity decrease.

In summary, SYDIT has high coverage and accuracy, and is relatively insensitive to the thresholds in ChangeDistiller and the number of dependences in the context. The best configuration is upstream with $k = 1$ for SYDIT and $\sigma = 0.5$ for ChangeDistiller, which together achieve 82% coverage, 70% accuracy, and 96% similarity.

5. Related Work

The related work includes program differencing, source transformation languages, simultaneous text editing, and example-based program correction.

Program differencing. Program differencing takes two program versions and matches names and structure at various granularities, e.g., lines [14], abstract syntax tree nodes [9, 32], control-flow graph nodes [3], and program dependence graph nodes [13]. For example, the ubiquitous tool *diff* computes line-level differences per file using the longest common subsequence algorithm [14]. JDiff computes CFG-node level matches between two program versions based on similarity in node labels and nested hammock structures [3]. ChangeDistiller computes syntactic differences using a hierarchical comparison algorithm [9]. It matches statements, such as method invocations, using *bigram string similarity*, and control structures using *subtree similarity*. It outputs tree edit operations—*insert, delete, move,* and *update*. More advanced tools group sets of related differences with similar structural characteristics and find exceptions to identify potentially inconsistent updates [15, 17]. SYDIT extends ChangeDistiller and goes beyond these approaches by deriving an edit script from program differences, abstracting the script, and then applying it elsewhere.

Refactoring. Refactoring is the process of changing a software system that does not alter the external behavior of the code, yet improves the internal structure [21]. Refactorings often require applying one or more elementary transformations to multiple code locations, and refactoring engines in IDEs automate many common types of refactorings such as *replace a magic number with a constant* [10, 26]. While refactoring engines are confined to predefined, semantic-preserving transformations, SYDIT can automate semantic-modifying transformations.

Source transformation languages. Source transformation tools reduce programmer burden by exhaustively applying repetitive, error-prone updates. Programmers use special syntax to specify the code location and transformation [8, 11, 18, 27, 30]. The most ubiquitous approach is simple text substitution, e.g., find-and-replace in Emacs. More sophisticated systems use program structure information. For example, A* and TAWK expose syntax trees and primitive data structures, and Stratego/XT uses algebraic data types and term pattern matching [11, 18, 30]. TXL borrows syntax from the underlying programming language to express systematic tree edits [5]. These tools require programmers to understand low-level program representations. To make this approach easier for programmers, Boshernitsan et al. provide a visual language and an interactive source transformation tool [4]. All these tools require programmers to plan and create edit scripts, whereas SYDIT generates an abstract program transformation from an example edit.

Simultaneous editing. Simultaneous text editing automates repetitive editing [7, 22, 29]. Users interactively demonstrate their edit in one context and the tool replicates *identical lexical* edits on the pre-selected code fragments. In contrast, SYDIT learns an edit script from program differences and performs *similar yet different* edits by instantiating a *syntactic*, context-aware, abstract transformation. The Clever version control system detects inconsistent changes in clones and propagates *identical* edits to inconsistent clones [24]. While Clever and SYDIT both replicate similar edits, SYDIT exploits program structure and generates abstracts edits applicable to contexts using different identifiers.

Suggesting edit locations. LibSync helps client applications migrate library API usages by learning migration patterns [23] with respect to a partial AST with containment and data dependences. Though it suggests what code locations to examine and shows example API updates, it is *unable* to transform code. Furthermore, its flexibility is limited by its inability to abstract variable, method, and type names.

FixWizard identifies code clones based on object usage and interactions, recognizes recurring bug-fixes to the clones, and suggests a location and example edit [25]. FixWizard identifies edit locations automatically only in pre-identified clones. It does *not generate syntactic edits*, nor does it support abstraction of variables, methods, and types. These limitations leave programmers with the burden of manually editing the suggested fix-location, which is error-prone and tedious.

Example based program migration and correction. Programming-by-example [19] (PBD) is a software agent-based approach that infers a generalized action script that corresponds to user's recorded actions. SMARTedit [19] instantiates this PBD approach to automate repetitive text edits by learning a series of functions such as *'move a cursor to the end of a line.'* However, this approach is not suitable for editing a program as it does not consider a program's syntax, control, or data dependences.

The most closely related work focuses on API migration [2, 23]. Andersen and Lawall find differences in the API usage of client code, create an edit script, and transform programs to use updated APIs [1, 2, 27]. Compared to SYDIT, their approach is limited in two respects: the edit scripts are confined to term-replacements and they only apply to API usage changes. Similar to our approach, Andersen and Lawall use control and data dependence analysis to model the context of edits [1]. However, the context includes only inserted and deleted API method invocations and control and data dependences among them. Their context does not include unchanged code on which the edits depend. Thus, when there is no deleted API method invocation, the extracted context cannot be used to position edits in a target method. SYDIT is more flexible because it computes edit context that is not limited to API method invocations and it can include unchanged statements related to edits. Therefore, even if the edits include only insertions, SYDIT can correctly position edits by finding corresponding context nodes in a target method. Furthermore, Andersen and Lawall only evaluate their approach on a few examples, whereas we perform a comprehensive evaluation on open-source applications.

Automatic program repair generates candidate patches and checks correctness using compilation and testing [28, 31]. For example, it generates patches that enforce invariants observed in correct executions but are violated in erroneous executions [28]. It tests patched executions and selects the most successful patch. Weimer et al. [31] generate their candidate patches by replicating, mutating, or deleting code *randomly* from the existing program and thus far have focused on single line edits. SYDIT automates sophisticated multi-line edits that can add functionality or fix bugs. Integrating SYDIT into a testing framework to automate validation is a promising future direction.

6. Discussions and Conclusions

SYDIT is the first tool to perform non-contiguous, abstract edits to different contexts, significantly improving the capabilities of the state-of-the-practice developer tools such as line-based GNU patch or the search and replace feature in text editors. This approach is however amenable to additional user guidance and automation.

To learn and apply a systematic edit, users must provide a source and target method. It would be relatively straight-forward to extend SYDIT to help programmers select a subset of edits to be replicated. Users may also want to configure SYDIT to update multiple locations within a target method, or to select a specific location to perform learned edits.

SYDIT does not recognize naming patterns between related types and variables such as `IServiceLocator` and `serviceLocator`, as shown in Figure 6. Thus, developers may not easily understand the output, even when SYDIT produces semantically equivalent code. By leveraging systematic naming patterns in program differences [17], it should be possible to produce edits that better mimic human developers.

SYDIT relies on ChangeDistiller to detect syntactic differences between two versions. In some cases, ChangeDistiller fails to report a minimal concrete edit and thus SYDIT's derived edit script may include superfluous contextual nodes. For example, instead of selecting one contextual node relevant to an update, it may select multiple contextual nodes relevant to an insert and a corresponding delete. We leave to future work how the choice of program differencing algorithm affects the flexibility of the learned edit scripts.

This paper focuses on single method updates, but it may be possible to generalize the approach for higher-level changes. For example, Kim et al. show that a large percentage of API-level refactorings and class hierarchy changes consist of similar edits to different class and method contexts [15, 17]. For instance, the *extract super class* refactoring moves a set of related fields and methods from subclasses to a super class. This type of functionality will require more sophisticated context representations and matching algorithms.

Another area for future work is automated target selection. For example, exhaustively examining every method in the program may prove useful. When a programmer fixes a bug, SYDIT could generate an edit, then apply it to all applicable code regions, and test the SYDIT generated version. While prior work suggests edit locations for recurring bug-fixes [25], SYDIT could actually apply the edit, automating some program repair and modification tasks. Furthermore, library component developers could use SYDIT to automate API usage updates in client applications by shipping an edit script together with changed library components.

In summary, SYDIT provides needed functionality that helps developers make simple and complex changes that span large programs. By using context extraction, identifier abstraction, and edit position abstraction, SYDIT learns and applies edits with high coverage and accuracy. This approach for program evolution opens a new way of providing higher confidence to developers when they add features and fix bugs.

A. Appendix

We include example edits to show the limitations and power of the current implementation of SYDIT.

Figure 7 shows one of the reasons that prevent SYDIT from mapping an abstract context with a target method. Both source and target share all changes except deletion of line 14 and insertion of line 19. In `mA`, line 14 is a `return` statement, while in `mB`, line 14 is an expression statement. The two statements have different AST node types. As a result, they cannot be matched by SYDIT.

Figure 10 shows an example in which SYDIT establishes matches successfully but produces incorrect edits. In this case, both `mA` and `mB` have a method invocation replaced with the other method invocation. However, when calling the new method, `mA` and `mB` pass different input arguments: `monitor` object in the source vs. `null` in the target. The target method does not provide enough clues on why `null` must be passed as an argument.

Figure 8 shows an example that SYDIT produces edits that are not entirely identical to the programmer's actual edits, because the context and the edit content are slightly different between the source and the target. In both methods, the programmer updates some statements, moves some statements out of the `for` loop, and inserts and deletes some statements within the loop to make programs more concise. However, the task involves different number of edits in the two methods. When SYDIT replicates learned edits to the target, three lines in $\texttt{mB}_{suggested}$ diverge from $\texttt{mB}_{new}$ (see Figure 9): (1) line 19 is incorrectly inserted with `LIST_ENTRY`; (2) line 22 is not deleted since it does not have a counterpart in the abstract context and there is no edit dealing with it; (3) line 25 is incorrectly inserted since `map.put(...)` is not mapped correctly to `list.add(...)`. Despite the three incorrect edits, SYDIT still makes the rest of the edits correctly in `mB`, alleviating part of this programming task.

A_{old} to A_{new}

```
1. public boolean isMigrationCandidate
     (ILaunchConfiguration candidate) throws CoreException {
2. - if(getAttribute(MIGRATION_DELEGATE) != null) {
3.     - if(fDelegates == null) {
4.       - fDelegates = new Hashtable();
5.     - }
6.     - Object delegate = fDelegates.get(MIGRATION_DELEGATE);
7.     - if(delegate == null) {
8.       - delegate = getConfigurationElement()
9.         .createExecutableExtension(MIGRATION_DELEGATE);
10.      - fDelegates.put(MIGRATION_DELEGATE, delegate);
11.    - }
12.    - if(delegate instanceof
13.        ILaunchConfigurationMigrationDelegate) {
14.      - return ((ILaunchConfigurationMigrationDelegate)
15.        delegate).isCandidate(candidate);
16.    - }
17.    + initializeMigrationDelegate();
18.    + if(fMigrationDelegate != null) {
19.      + return fMigrationDelegate.isCandidate(candidate);
20.    }
21.    return false;
22.}
```

B_{old} to B_{new}

```
1. public void migrate(ILaunchConfiguration candidate)
     throws CoreException {
2. - if(getAttribute(MIGRATION_DELEGATE) != null) {
3.      - if(fDelegates == null) {
4.        - fDelegates = new Hashtable();
5.      - }
6.      - Object delegate = fDelegates.get(MIGRATION_DELEGATE);
7.      - if(delegate == null) {
8.        - delegate = getConfigurationElement()
9.          .createExecutableExtension(MIGRATION_DELEGATE);
10.       - fDelegates.put(MIGRATION_DELEGATE, delegate);
11.     - }
12.     - if(delegate instanceof
13.       ILaunchConfigurationMigrationDelegate) {
14.     - ((ILaunchConfigurationMigrationDelegate)
15.       delegate).migrate(candidate);
16.    - }
17.    + initializeMigrationDelegate();
18.    + if(fMigrationDelegate != null) {
19.      + fMigrationDelegate.migrate(candidate);
20.    }
21.    return false;
22.}
```

Figure 7. A contigous, abstract edit script (CA) for which SYDIT cannot match the change context

Acknowledgments

This work was supported in part by the National Science Foundation under grants CCF-1043810, SHF-0910818, and CCF-0811524. We thank anonymous reviewers for their thorough comments on our earlier version of the paper.

References

[1] J. Andersen. *Semantic Patch Inference*. Ph.D. Dissertation, University of Copenhagen, Copenhagen, Nov. 2009. Adviser-Julia L. Lawall.

[2] J. Andersen and J. L. Lawall. Generic patch inference. In *ASE '08: Proceedings of the 2008 23rd IEEE/ACM International Conference on Automated Software Engineering*, pages 337–346, Washington, DC, USA, 2008. IEEE Computer Society. ISBN 978-1-4244-2187-9.

[3] T. Apiwattanapong, A. Orso, and M. J. Harrold. A differencing algorithm for object-oriented programs. In *ASE '04: Proceedings of the 19th IEEE International Conference on Automated Software Engineering*, pages 2–13, Washington, DC, USA, 2004. IEEE Computer Society. ISBN 0-7695-2131-2.

A_{old} to A_{new}

```
protected void setMapAttribute(Element element)
    throws CoreException {
- String listKey = element.getAttribute("key");
+ String listKey = element.getAttribute(KEY);
    NodeList nodeList = element.getChildNodes();
    int entryCount = nodeList.getLength();
    List list = new ArrayList(entryCount);
+ Node node = null;
+ Element selement = null;
    for (int i = 0; i < entryCount; i++) {
    - Node node = nodeList.item(i);
    + node = nodeList.item(i);
    - short type = node.getNodeType();
    - if (type == Node.ELEMENT_NODE) {
      - Element subElement = (Element) node;
      - String nodeName = subElement.getNodeName();
      - if (!nodeName.equalsIgnoreCase("listEntry")) {
    + if (node.getNodeType() == Node.ELEMENT_NODE) {
      + selement = (Element) node;
      + if (!selement.getNodeName().
          equalsIgnoreCase(LIST_ENTRY)) {
          throw getInvalidFormatDebugException();
        }
        - String value = getValueAttribute(subElement);
        - list.add(value);
        + list.add(getValueAttribute(selement));
    }
  }
  setAttribute(listKey, list);
}
```

B_{old} to B_{new}

```
protected void setMapAttribute(Element element)
    throws CoreException {
- String mapKey = element.getAttribute("key");
+ String mapKey = element.getAttribute(KEY);
    NodeList nodeList = element.getChildNodes();
    int entryCount = nodeList.getLength();
    Map map = new HashMap(entryCount);
  + Node node = null;
  + Element selement = null;
    for (int i = 0; i < entryCount; i++) {
    - Node node = nodeList.item(i);
    + node = nodeList.item(i);
    - short type = node.getNodeType();
    - if (type == Node.ELEMENT_NODE) {
      - Element subElement = (Element) node;
      - String nodeName = subElement.getNodeName();
      - if (!nodeName.equalsIgnoreCase("mapEntry")) {
    + if (node.getNodeType() == Node.ELEMENT_NODE) {
      + selement = (Element) node;
      + if (!selement.getNodeName().
          equalsIgnoreCase(MAP_ENTRY)) {
              throw getInvalidFormatDebugException();
      }
        - String key = getKeyAttribute(subElement);
        - String value = getValueAttribute(subElement);
        - map.put(key, value);
        + map.put(getKeyAttribute(selement),
            getValueAttribute(selement));
    }
  }
  setAttribute(mapKey, map);
}
```

Figure 8. A non-contiguous, abstract edit script example

B_{old} to $B_{suggested}$

```
protected void setMapAttribute(Element element)
    throws CoreException {
- String mapKey = element.getAttribute("key");
+ String mapKey = element.getAttribute(KEY);
    NodeList nodeList = element.getChildNodes();
    int entryCount = nodeList.getLength();
    Map map = new HashMap(entryCount);
+ Node node = null;
+ Element selement = null;
    for (int i = 0; i < entryCount; i++) {
    - Node node = nodeList.item(i);
    + node = nodeList.item(i);
    - short type = node.getNodeType();
    - if (type == Node.ELEMENT_NODE) {
      - Element subElement = (Element) node;
      - String nodeName = subElement.getNodeName();
      - if (!nodeName.equalsIgnoreCase("mapEntry")) {
    + if (node.getNodeType() == Node.ELEMENT_NODE) {
      + selement = (Element) node;
      + if (!selement.getNodeName()
          .equalsIgnoreCase(LIST_ENTRY)) {
          throw getInvalidFormatDebugException();
        }
        String key = getKeyAttribute(subElement);
        - String value = getValueAttribute(subElement);
        - map.put(key, value);
        + map.add(getValueAttribute(selement));
    }
  }
  setAttribute(mapKey, map);
}
```

Figure 9. A non-contiguous, abstract edit script for which SYDIT produces output different from the developer's version

A_{old} to A_{new}

```
public void flush(IProgressMonitor monitor){
  - saveContent(getInput());
  + flushContent(getInput(), monitor);
}
```

B_{old} to B_{new}

```
public void run() {
  - saveContent(getInput());
  + flushContent(getInput(), null);
}
```

Figure 10. A single, abstract edit script (SA) for which SYDIT cannot produce correct edits

[4] M. Boshernitsan, S. L. Graham, and M. A. Hearst. Aligning development tools with the way programmers think about code changes. In *CHI '07: Proceedings of the SIGCHI conference on Human factors in computing systems*, pages 567–576, New York, NY, USA, 2007. ACM. ISBN 978-1-59593-593-9.

[5] J. R. Cordy. The txl source transformation language. *Science of Computer Programming*, 61(3):190–210, 2006. ISSN 0167-6423.

[6] R. Cytron, J. Ferrante, B. Rosen, M. Wegman, and K. Zadeck. Efficiently computing static single assignment form and the control dependence graph. *ACM Transactions on Programming Languages and Systems*, 13(4):451–490, Oct. 1991.

[7] E. Duala-Ekoko and M. P. Robillard. Tracking code clones in evolving software. In *ICSE '07: Proceedings of the 29th International Conference on Software Engineering*, pages 158–167, Washington, DC, USA, 2007. IEEE Computer Society. ISBN 0-7695-2828-7.

[8] M. Erwig and D. Ren. A rule-based language for programming software updates. In *RULE '02: Proceedings of the 2002 ACM SIGPLAN workshop on Rule-based programming*, pages 67–78, New York, NY, USA, 2002. ACM. ISBN 1-58113-606-4.

[9] B. Fluri, M. Würsch, M. Pinzger, and H. C. Gall. Change distilling—tree differencing for fine-grained source code change extraction. *IEEE Transactions on Software Engineering*, 33(11):18, November 2007.

[10] W. G. Griswold. *Program Restructuring as an Aid to Software Maintenance*. PhD thesis, University of Washington, 1991.

[11] W. G. Griswold, D. C. Atkinson, and C. McCurdy. Fast, flexible syntactic pattern matching and processing. In *WPC '96: Proceedings of the 4th International Workshop on Program Comprehension*, page 144, Washington, DC, USA, 1996. IEEE Computer Society. ISBN 0-8186-7283-8.

[12] J. Henkel and A. Diwan. Catchup!: Capturing and replaying refactorings to support api evolution. In *ICSE '05: Proceedings of the 27th International Conference on Software Engineering*, pages 274–283, New York, NY, USA, 2005. ACM. ISBN 1-59593-963-2.

[13] S. Horwitz. Identifying the semantic and textual differences between two versions of a program. In *PLDI '90: Proceedings of the ACM SIGPLAN 1990 conference on Programming language design and implementation*, pages 234–245, New York, NY, USA, 1990. ACM. ISBN 0-89791-364-7.

[14] J. W. Hunt and T. G. Szymanski. A fast algorithm for computing longest common subsequences. *Communications of the ACM*, 20(5): 350–353, 1977. ISSN 0001-0782.

[15] M. Kim and D. Notkin. Discovering and representing systematic code changes. In *ICSE '09: Proceedings of the 2009 IEEE 31st International Conference on Software Engineering*, pages 309–319, Washington, DC, USA, 2009. IEEE Computer Society. ISBN 978-1-4244-3453-4.

[16] M. Kim, V. Sazawal, D. Notkin, and G. Murphy. An empirical study of code clone genealogies. In *ESEC/FSE-13: Proceedings of the 10th European Software Engineering Conference held jointly with 13th ACM SIGSOFT International Symposium on Foundations of Software Engineering*, pages 187–196, New York, NY, USA, 2005. ACM. ISBN 1-59593-014-0.

[17] M. Kim, D. Notkin, and D. Grossman. Automatic inference of structural changes for matching across program versions. In *ICSE '07: Proceedings of the 29th International Conference on Software Engineering*, pages 333–343, Washington, DC, USA, 2007. IEEE Computer Society. ISBN 0-7695-2828-7.

[18] D. A. Ladd and J. C. Ramming. A*: A language for implementing language processors. *IEEE Transactions on Software Engineering*, 21 (11):894–901, 1995. ISSN 0098-5589.

[19] H. Lieberman, editor. *Your Wish is My Command: Programming by Example*. Morgan Kaufmann Publishers, 2001.

[20] A. Matzner, M. Minas, and A. Schulte. Efficient graph matching with application to cognitive automation. In A. Schrr, M. Nagl, and A. Zndorf, editors, *Applications of Graph Transformations with Industrial Relevance*, volume 5088 of *Lecture Notes in Computer Science*, pages 297–312. Springer Berlin / Heidelberg, 2008.

[21] T. Mens and T. Tourwe. A survey of software refactoring. *IEEE Transactions on Software Engineering*, 30(2):126–139, 2004. ISSN 0098-5589.

[22] R. C. Miller and B. A. Myers. Interactive simultaneous editing of multiple text regions. In *Proceedings of the General Track: 2002 USENIX Annual Technical Conference*, pages 161–174, Berkeley, CA, USA, 2001. USENIX Association. ISBN 1-880446-09-X.

[23] H. A. Nguyen, T. T. Nguyen, G. W. Jr., A. T. Nguyen, M. Kim, and T. Nguyen. A graph-based approach to api usage adaptation. In *OOPSLA '10: Proceedings of the 2010 ACM SIGPLAN International Conference on Systems, Programming, Languages and Applications*, page 10 pages, New York, NY, USA, 2010. ACM.

[24] T. T. Nguyen, H. A. Nguyen, N. H. Pham, J. M. Al-Kofahi, and T. N. Nguyen. Clone-aware configuration management. In *ASE '09: Proceedings of the 2009 IEEE/ACM International Conference on Automated Software Engineering*, pages 123–134, Washington, DC, USA, 2009. IEEE Computer Society. ISBN 978-0-7695-3891-4. doi: http://dx.doi.org/10.1109/ASE.2009.90.

[25] T. T. Nguyen, H. A. Nguyen, N. H. Pham, J. Al-Kofahi, and T. N. Nguyen. Recurring bug fixes in object-oriented programs. In *ICSE '10: Proceedings of the 32nd ACM/IEEE International Conference on Software Engineering*, pages 315–324, New York, NY, USA, 2010. ACM. ISBN 978-1-60558-719-6.

[26] W. F. Opdyke and R. E. Johnson. Refactoring: An aid in designing application frameworks and evolving object-oriented systems. In *Proceedings of the Symposium on Object Oriented Programming Emphasizing Practical Applications (SOOPPA)*, 1990.

[27] Y. Padioleau, J. Lawall, R. R. Hansen, and G. Muller. Documenting and automating collateral evolutions in linux device drivers. In *Eurosys '08: Proceedings of the 3rd ACM SIGOPS/EuroSys European Conference on Computer Systems 2008*, pages 247–260, New York, NY, USA, 2008. ACM. ISBN 978-1-60558-013-5.

[28] J. H. Perkins, S. Kim, S. Larsen, S. Amarasinghe, J. Bachrach, M. Carbin, C. Pacheco, F. Sherwood, S. Sidiroglou, G. Sullivan, W.-F. Wong, Y. Zibin, M. D. Ernst, and M. Rinard. Automatically patching errors in deployed software. In *SOSP '09: Proceedings of the ACM SIGOPS 22nd symposium on Operating systems principles*, pages 87–102, New York, NY, USA, 2009. ACM. ISBN 978-1-60558-752-3.

[29] M. Toomim, A. Begel, and S. L. Graham. Managing duplicated code with linked editing. In *VLHCC '04: Proceedings of the 2004 IEEE Symposium on Visual Languages - Human Centric Computing*, pages 173–180, Washington, DC, USA, 2004. IEEE Computer Society. ISBN 0-7803-8696-5.

[30] E. Visser. Program transformation with Stratego/XT: Rules, strategies, tools, and systems in StrategoXT-0.9. *Domain-Specific Program Generation*, 3016:216–238, 2004.

[31] W. Weimer, T. Nguyen, C. Le Goues, and S. Forrest. Automatically finding patches using genetic programming. In *ICSE '09: Proceedings of the 31st International Conference on Software Engineering*, pages 364–374, Washington, DC, USA, 2009. IEEE Computer Society. ISBN 978-1-4244-3453-4.

[32] W. Yang. Identifying syntactic differences between two programs. *Software – Practice & Experience*, 21(7):739–755, 1991.

A Security Policy Oracle: Detecting Security Holes Using Multiple API Implementations

Varun Srivastava
Yahoo!
varun_iiit@yahoo.co.in

Michael D. Bond
The Ohio State University
mikebond@cse.ohio-state.edu

Kathryn S. McKinley Vitaly Shmatikov
The University of Texas at Austin
{mckinley,shmat}@cs.utexas.edu

Abstract

Even experienced developers struggle to implement security policies correctly. For example, despite 15 years of development, standard Java libraries still suffer from missing and incorrectly applied permission checks, which enable untrusted applications to execute native calls or modify private class variables without authorization. Previous techniques for static verification of authorization enforcement rely on manually specified policies or attempt to infer the policy by code-mining. Neither approach guarantees that the policy used for verification is correct.

In this paper, we exploit the fact that many modern APIs have *multiple, independent* implementations. Our flow- and context-sensitive analysis takes as input an API, multiple implementations thereof, and the definitions of security checks and security-sensitive events. For each API entry point, the analysis computes the security policies enforced by the checks before security-sensitive events such as native method calls and API returns, compares these policies across implementations, and reports the differences. Unlike code-mining, this technique finds missing checks even if they are part of a rare pattern. Security-policy differencing has no intrinsic false positives: implementations of the same API *must* enforce the same policy, or at least one of them is wrong!

Our analysis finds 20 new, confirmed security vulnerabilities and 11 interoperability bugs in the Sun, Harmony, and Classpath implementations of the Java Class Library, many of which were missed by prior analyses. These problems manifest in 499 entry points in these mature, well-studied libraries. Multiple API implementations are proliferating due to cloud-based software services and standardization of library interfaces. Comparing software implementations for consistency is a new approach to discovering "deep" bugs in them.

Categories and Subject Descriptors D. Software [*D.2 Software Engineering*]: D.2.4 Software/Program Verification; K. Computing Milieux [*K.6 Management of Computing and Information Systems*]: K.6.5 Security and Protection

General Terms Languages, Security, Verification

Keywords Security, Authorization, Access Control, Static Analysis, Java Class Libraries

PLDI'11, June 4–8, 2011, San Jose, California, USA.

1. Introduction

Demand for secure software is increasing, but ensuring that software is secure remains a challenge. Developers are choosing memory-safe systems [9, 39] and languages such as Java and C# in part because they improve security by reducing memory-corruption attacks. Even memory-safe systems, however, rely on the *access-rights model* to ensure that the program has the appropriate permissions before performing sensitive actions. Unfortunately, even experienced developers find it difficult to specify and implement access-rights policies correctly. Consequently, semantic mistakes—such as missing permission checks which enable malicious code to bypass protection—have become a significant cause of security vulnerabilities [26].

This paper presents a new approach to finding security vulnerabilities in software libraries, also known as Application Programming Interfaces (APIs). We leverage the increasing availability of multiple, independent implementations of the same API. By design, these implementations must be interoperable and must implement semantically consistent security policies. A security policy in the access-rights model consists of a mapping between *security checks*, such as verifying permissions of the calling code, and *security-sensitive events*, such as writing to a file or the network. We exploit this consistency requirement to build a *security policy oracle,* which accurately (i) derives security policies realized by each implementation and (ii) finds incorrect policies.

Previous static analysis techniques for finding security vulnerabilities either rely on manual policy specification and/or verification, or infer frequently occurring policies by code-mining. For example, Koved et al. derive a policy and then require programmers to check by hand that permissions held at all sensitive points in the program are sufficient [22, 28]. Sistla et al. take as input manually specified check-event pairs and verify that all occurrences of the event are dominated by the corresponding check [30]. These approaches are error-prone and limited in expressiveness. There are hundreds of potential security-sensitive events and 31 potential checks in the Java Class Library; some policies involve multiple checks and some checks do not always dominate the event. It is easy to overlook a security-sensitive event or omit a rare check-event pair in a manual policy. Koved et al. and Sistla et al. reported no bugs for the Sun Java Development Kit (JDK) and Apache Harmony implementations of the Java Class Library. By contrast, our analysis uncovered multiple, exploitable security vulnerabilities in the same code.

Another approach is code-mining, which infers policies from frequently occurring patterns and flags deviations as potential bugs [10, 14, 35]. These techniques fundamentally assume that the same pattern of security checks and security-sensitive operations occurs in many places in the code, and they are thus likely to miss vulnerabilities that violate a unique policy—such as the Harmony bug described in Section 2. Frequent patterns may or may not represent actual policies, resulting in false positives and negatives. Code-mining techniques face an inherent tradeoff between coverage and the number of false positives. As the statistical threshold is lowered to include more patterns, they may find more bugs, but the number of false positives increases since deviations from rare patterns can be mistakenly flagged as bugs.

Cross-implementation consistency as a "security policy oracle." Our key idea is to use any inconsistency in security semantics between implementations of the same API as an oracle for detecting incorrect policies. Unlike approaches that rely on explicit policies or frequent patterns, this technique completely avoids the need to determine whether the policy is *correct*, replacing it by a much easier task of determining whether two policies are *consistent*.

Our use of consistency checking is very different from the code-mining approaches. In our case, *there are no benign inconsistencies*! Any semantic inconsistency between two implementations of the same API is, at the very least, an interoperability bug or, in the worst case, a security hole. In theory, policy differencing has no intrinsic false positives. In practice, imprecision in conservative static analysis results in a very small number of false positives. Furthermore, our technique can discover a missing permissions check *even if this type of check occurs in a single place in the code*. It may produce false negatives if exactly the same semantic bug occurs in all implementations of a given library routine. This case is unlikely if the implementations are developed independently, as is the case for our main test subject, the Java Class Library.

Finding semantic inconsistencies with static analysis. Our analysis takes as input two or more Java API implementations, security-sensitive events, and security checks. Our definitions of security-sensitive events and checks directly reflect the Java security model. Security-sensitive events include calls to the Java Native Interface (JNI), which is the only mechanism by which Java code communicates to the network, file system, or other external devices. Since user code may change the internal state of the Java Virtual Machine (JVM) using the Java Class Library, we include API returns in the set of security-sensitive events. Application code should not be able to reach security-sensitive events without proper permissions. In the Java security model, security checks verify permissions held by user code by calling methods in the `SecurityManager` class.

For every API entry point, we take all implementations and, for each one, produce context-sensitive policies using flow- and context-sensitive interprocedural analysis together with interprocedural constant propagation. The policies specify which checks *may* and *must* precede each security-sensitive event. We compare the policies for all events relevant to this entry point and report any differences.

Case study: The Java Class Library. We demonstrate the effectiveness of our approach by applying it to the Java Class Library. This prominent, large, widely used API has multiple, independent implementations: Sun JDK, GNU Classpath, Apache Harmony, and several others. For example, JDK was announced in 1996 and is very broadly deployed. It is the product of hundreds of programmers and its source code has been actively studied since Sun published it in 2007. Different implementations of the Java Class Library API are intended to be fully interoperable.

Together, these implementations comprise over 1.7 million lines of code. Any context-sensitive analysis must be concerned with efficiency. Ours uses context memoization [38]. Analyzing each library takes 20 minutes or less, which is likely to be acceptable as part of testing. The three pairings share approximately 4,100 entry points, and over 230 of these methods perform security checks. Our analysis derives between 8,000 and 16,000 *may* and *must* security policies per API.

Our analysis is very precise. It produces only 3 false positives, while finding 20 new security vulnerabilities (6 in JDK, 6 in Harmony, 8 in Classpath) and 11 interoperability bugs that manifest in 499 API entry points. Example vulnerabilities include opening network connections and loading libraries without properly checking permissions of the calling code. We reported all vulnerabilities found by our analysis to the developers of the respective libraries, who accepted and immediately fixed many of them [31–33].

In summary, our analysis uncovered multiple security vulnerabilities in three mature implementations of the Java Class Library, with a minimal number of false positives. This paper demonstrates that our approach (i) scales to industrial implementations of real-world software libraries and (ii) is capable of discovering "deep" bugs even in well-studied, tested, widely used code. Although we describe our design and implementation with respect to the Java programming language, our approach is applicable to other languages, such as C#, that use a similar access-rights model.

Current software engineering trends are likely to increase the applicability of comparative API analysis. For example, the proliferation of distributed, multi-layer software services encourages separation of APIs from their implementations, and thus multiple implementations of the same API. Many platforms are adopting the Software-As-A-Service (SaaS) model [1, 16, 20, 29], which encourages multiple implementations of the same functionality and thus provides the input material for our "security policy oracle." Widely used APIs sometimes have an open-source version, which programmers can use as a reference policy oracle even when their own code is proprietary. Even if all implementations of the same API are proprietary, developers may be willing to share security policies with each other without sharing the actual code.

2. Motivating Example

Figure 1 motivates our approach with an example from the JDK and Harmony implementations of the Java Class Library. In Figure 1(a), the JDK implementation of `DatagramSocket.connect` calls either `checkMulticast`, or `checkConnect` and `checkAccept` before connecting to the network with a JNI call inside the method invocation at line 16. For clarity of presentation, this and all other examples elide unrelated code and the test for a non-null security manager required by all security checks. In Figure 1(b), the Harmony implementation calls either `checkMulticast`, or `checkConnect` before the equivalent method invocation at line 11.

Figure 2 illustrates some of the security policies inferred for this code. Each policy includes a security-sensitive event and a (possibly empty) set of security checks. Consider the API-return event for JDK. There is a *must* and a *may* policy for this event. The *must* check is the empty set and the *may* checks are {{`checkMulticast`} or {`checkConnect, checkAccept`}}. The call to `checkAccept` before the API return and, more importantly, before using JNI to make a network connection as a result of invoking `impl.connect`, are missing in the Harmony *may* policy, introducing a vulnerability.

The security-checking pattern in `connect` is unique. The `checkMulticast` call is very rare and there is no other place in the JDK library where it occurs together with `checkAccept` and `checkConnect`. The "bugs as inconsistencies" methods [14, 35] are not only likely to miss this bug, but may even wrongly flag the JDK implementation because the pattern incorrectly used by Harmony is more common than the correct pattern used by JDK. The rarity of this pattern and the fact that it involves multiple checks mean that a manual policy is likely to miss it, too.

Both Harmony and JDK implement a *may* policy: there is no single check that dominates all paths to the security-sensitive event. Even if the manual policy happens to include all the right event-check pairs, analyses that require the same check(s) on every

```java
// JDK
public void connect(InetAddress address,
                    int port) {
  ... connectInternal(address, port); ...
}
private synchronized void connectInternal(
    InetAddress address, int port) {
  ...
  if (address.isMulticastAddress()) {
    securityManager.checkMulticast(address);
  } else {
    securityManager.checkConnect(address.
        getHostAddress(), port);
    securityManager.checkAccept(address.
        getHostAddress(), port);
  }
  if (oldImpl) {
    connectState = ST_CONNECTED_NO_IMPL;
  } else {
    ... getImpl().connect(address, port); ...
  }
  connectedAddress = address;
  connectedPort = port;
  ...
}
```

(a) JDK implementation of `DatagramSocket.connect`

```java
// Harmony
public void connect(InetAddress anAddr,
                    int aPort) {
  synchronized (lock) {
    ...
    if (anAddr.isMulticastAddress()) {
      securityManager.checkMulticast(anAddr);
    } else {
      securityManager.checkConnect(anAddr.
          getHostName(), aPort);
    }
    ...
    impl.connect(anAddr, aPort);
    ...
    address = anAddr;
    port = aPort;
    ...
  }
}
```

(b) Harmony implementation of `DatagramSocket.connect`

Figure 1: Security vulnerability in Harmony: `checkAccept` is missing. The correct security policy is unique to this method.

```
MUST check:  {}
Event: API return from DatagramSocket.connect

MAY check: {{checkMulticast},{checkConnect, checkAccept}}
Event: API return from DatagramSocket.connect
```

(b) JDK `DatagramSocket.connect` security policies

```
MUST check:  {}
Event: API return from DatagramSocket.connect

MAY check: {{checkMulticast},{checkConnect}}
Event: API return from DatagramSocket.connect
```

(b) Harmony `DatagramSocket.connect` security policies

Figure 2: Example security policies

path [7, 22, 28, 30] will produce a warning for both implementations, which is a false positive for the correct JDK implementation.

Our analysis finds this vulnerability using (1) precise, flow- and context-sensitive interprocedural analysis that computes both *may* and *must* policies, and (2) differencing of policies from multiple implementations.

3. Security Policies

This section explains security policies in the access-rights model in more detail. Section 4 explains how we compute the policies implemented by a given API entry point and Section 5 describes our algorithm for comparing policies.

A *security policy* in the access-rights model is a mapping from *security-sensitive events* to one or more *security checks* for each event. Our analysis takes events and checks as input. A security-sensitive event is a program event, such as a write to a file, that the application should not be able to execute unless it holds certain rights or privileges. A security check verifies that the application holds a particular right. The access-rights model is the cornerstone of Java security. For example, unchecked native method calls can give user applications unauthorized network access, while unchecked returns of internal JVM state, *i.e.*, the value of a private variable, can leak data. The definitions of security checks and events that we use in this paper directly reflect Java's security model.

A security policy "maps" an event to a check if the check occurs before the event. Our analysis computes both *must* and *may* policies. A *must* policy means that the check in question must occur on every execution path leading to the event. A *may* policy means that the check is predicated on some condition. At first glance, *may* policies may appear insecure, but they are often needed to implement the correct security logic. For example, Figure 2(a) shows a policy that always performs one or more checks, but the particular check differs depending on control flow.

Security checks. The `SecurityManager` class in Java provides 31 methods that perform security checks for user code and libraries. For example, `checkPermission()` verifies that the calling context holds a particular permission and throws an exception otherwise. We restrict our analysis to these methods, although programmers can define their own, additional security checks. Our analysis keeps track of *which* of the 31 security checks is invoked at any given point. For example, it differentiates between `checkPermission()` and `checkConnect()`.

Our analysis does not ensure that the parameters to security checks are the same as the ones used by the security event. This imprecision could be a source of false negatives.

Security-sensitive events. The Java Native Interface (JNI) defines all interactions with the outside environment for Java programs, *e.g.*, opening files, connecting to the network, and writing to the console. We therefore define all calls to native methods as security-sensitive events.

In addition, we consider all API returns to be security-sensitive events. If a method performs security checks but does not use the JNI, these checks are thus included in its security policy. Such checks are used in API implementations that give user code access to internal JVM state or private variables, or store parameter values for later use. These accesses should be secured consistently in all implementations of an API because they reveal internal JVM or library state to untrusted applications and/or enable applications to modify this private state. By including API returns, we broaden the definition of security-sensitive events as compared to prior work [22, 28, 30]. This broader definition helps us find more vulnerabilities. For example, Figure 6 shows and Section 6.2

```
// Implementation 1
public Obj A(Obj obj) {
  if (condition) {
    checkRead();
    obj.add(data1);
    return obj;
  } else {
    return null;
  }
  checkRead();
  obj.add(data2);
  // Private data1 and data2 returned in obj
  return obj;
}

// Implementation 2
public Obj A(Obj obj, Data data1, Data data2) {
  if (condition) {
    obj.add(data1);
    return obj;
  } else {
    return null;
  }
  checkRead();
  obj.add(data2);
  // Private data1 and data2 returned in obj
  return obj;
}
```

Figure 3: Hypothetical bug showing the need for a broad definition of security-sensitive events.

describes a vulnerability that we detect because our definition of security-sensitive events is not limited to JNI calls only.

Broader definition of security-sensitive events. Our analysis can further broaden the definition of security-sensitive events. In addition to JNI calls and API returns, we experimented with including individual accesses to private variables, JVM state, and API parameters. In particular, security-sensitive events could include all reads, writes, and method invocations on API parameters and private variables, as well as reads, writes, and method invocations on variables that are data-dependent on API parameters and private variables.

For this definition of security-sensitive events, we computed data dependencies using a simple interprocedural dataflow analysis that propagated an event tag. It marked all statements in the definition-use chains involving private variables and API parameters, and propagated the mark interprocedurally through parameter binding in method invocations. If there were multiple instances of the same event type, *e.g.*, two returns or two accesses to the same parameter, we combined the corresponding policies. This definition of security-sensitive events is very liberal and marks many more events as sensitive. It generates over 90,000 security policies for each Java Library implementation, whereas restricting security-sensitive events to JNI calls and API returns results in 16,700 or fewer policies for each implementation.

This broad definition of security-sensitive events did not result in finding more bugs, nor generating more false positives during our analysis of the Java Class Library, but it helped us diagnose the cause of differences in the implementations' respective security policies. For other APIs, this broad definition may more accurately capture the semantics of library implementations and thus find errors missed with a narrower definition of security-sensitive events.

For example, this broad definition is needed to detect the inconsistency between implementations in the hypothetical example shown in Figure 3. Restricting security-sensitive events to JNI calls and API returns results in a {`checkRead`} *may* policy for the API-return event in both implementations. If we instead consider the reads of private variables `data1` and `data2` as distinct security-sensitive events, the analysis infers (1) a {`checkRead`} *must* policy for the read of `data1` in the first implementation and (2) an empty *must* policy for the same event in the second implementation. The analysis will thus report an inconsistency.

4. Computing Security Policies

Given an API and multiple implementations thereof, our approach extracts and compares *security policies* realized by the implementations. The analysis computes the security checks that each API always performs (*must* analysis) or may perform (*may* analysis) before each security-sensitive event. The analysis uses a flow- and context-sensitive interprocedural algorithm enhanced with flow- and context-sensitive forward constant propagation [17, 36]. Any context-sensitive analysis must be concerned with scalability. To reduce analysis time and guarantee convergence, we do not iterate over recursive call paths. We further eliminate useless re-analysis with a form of memoization [38] that records security policies and relevant parameters at each method invocation.

We implement the analysis in the Soot static analysis framework[1] [25] and use Soot's method resolution analysis, alias analysis, and intraprocedural constant propagation.

Call graph. The analysis starts by building call graphs rooted at all public and protected API entry points, and derives separate policies for each API entry point. Protected methods are included because API clients can potentially call them by overriding the corresponding class. These methods thus represent unintended paths into the API and are important to analyze. In theory, any static analysis is incomplete in the presence of dynamic class loading since the code is not available until run time. In practice, the Java Class Library and many other APIs are closed-world and do not depend on dynamic class loading.

Soot computes application call graphs, but its analysis is engineered for applications with a single entry point. Because APIs have many entry points, we build the call graph on the fly, using Soot's method resolution analysis which resolves 97% of method calls in the Java libraries. If Soot does not resolve a method invocation, our implementation does not analyze it. This inaccuracy could be a source of false negatives or positives, but did not produce false positives in our evaluation. As shown in prior work, type-resolving events, such as allocation, make simple type hierarchy analysis very effective at resolving method invocations [11, 34]. The Java libraries' coding conventions—for example, the use of final methods—further improve the precision of method resolution.

Analysis overview. Computing security policies is essentially a reaching definitions analysis where the *definitions* are security checks and the *uses* are security-sensitive events. The dataflow lattice is the power set of the 31 security-checking methods. The analysis propagates checks (definitions) to events (uses). After converging, the resulting security policy is a mapping from event statements to the checks that reach them.

We perform *interprocedural* and *context-sensitive* analysis, propagate constants across method calls, and eliminate the resulting dead code, for the following reasons. It is typical for an API method to first call a method that performs a security check and then call another method that contains a security-sensitive event. It is also common to perform the security check(s) conditionally, based on the value of a parameter (see Section 4.2 for an example).

[1] `http://www.sable.mcgill.ca/soot/`

Algorithm 1 Intraprocedural Security Policy Dataflow Analysis

procedure *SPDA*
{Initialize dataflow values}
for all $v \epsilon AllStatements$ **do**
  if MUST **then**
    $OUT(v) \leftarrow \bot$
  else {MAY}
    $OUT(v) \leftarrow \top$
  end if
  $NOTVISITED \leftarrow NOTVISITED \cup v$
end for
{Propagate dataflow values}
$worklist \leftarrow EntryPoint$
while $worklist \neq \phi$ **do**
  $v \leftarrow getNode(worklist)$
  if MUST **then**
    $IN(v) \leftarrow \bigcap_{p \in PRED(v)} OUT(p)$
  else {MAY}
    $IN(v) \leftarrow \bigcup_{p \in PRED(v)} OUT(p)$
  end if
  $OUT(v) \leftarrow IN(v) \cup SP(v)$
  if $OUT(v)$ $changed \wedge v \in NOTVISITED$ **then**
    $worklist \leftarrow worklist \cup SUCC(v)$
    $NOTVISITED \leftarrow NOTVISITED - v$
  end if
end while

Algorithm 2 Interprocedural Security Policy Analysis

procedure $ISPA(m, SP, paramConsts)$
if $hashTable.hasKey(\langle m, SP, paramConsts\rangle)$ **then**
  {Same analysis state, so return hashed result}
  return $hashTable.lookup(\langle m, SP, paramConsts\rangle)$
else
  {Compute result for this analysis state}
  $newSP \leftarrow SPDA(m, SP, paramConsts)$
  $hashTable.put(\langle m, SP, paramConsts\rangle, newSP)$
  return $newSP$
end if

4.1 Intraprocedural analysis

For ease of presentation, we first describe the intraprocedural component of the analysis. Algorithm 1 shows our intraprocedural security policy dataflow analysis (SPDA), which propagates security checks. The MUST and MAY analyses differ in (i) the meet function, performing *intersection* for MUST and *union* for MAY, and (ii) the initial flow values, which are $\bot$ for MUST and $\top$ for MAY. SPDA assigns a unique identifier to each of the 31 security-checking methods. It initializes $OUT(v)$ of each statement that performs a check to the corresponding identifier, *i.e.*, $OUT(v) = SP = \{check\}$. For all other statements, it initializes $SP = \emptyset$.

Because SPDA is a reaching definition analysis and uses a lattice that is a powerset, it is *rapid*, converging in two passes with structured control flow [27].

4.2 Interprocedural, context-sensitive analysis

This section explains how we extend the intraprocedural dataflow analysis to make it interprocedural and context sensitive. ISPA, our interprocedural security policy analysis, is shown in Algorithm 2. When ISPA encounters a statement v that contains a method invocation, it invokes the analysis recursively on the target method. As mentioned above, our implementation ignores method invocations that Soot cannot resolve to a unique target, which may lead to false negatives and positives. ISPA performs interprocedural constant propagation together with the security analysis, tracking constant parameter values (described below). The analysis binds any current constant dataflow values to the parameters and uses them together with the current policy as the initial state to analyze the target method.

This analysis does not scale because it analyzes every statically possible calling context separately. In practice, however, many of the method's calling contexts have the same dataflow values. We eliminate redundant work via the following memoization scheme. The first time our analysis encounters a call to some method, it analyzes the method, passing in the initial policy and any constant parameters. If analyzing the method changes the policy, we store the policy and the constant parameters. Otherwise, we simply store the initial policy. When the analysis encounters the same method in a different calling context but with the same policy flow values, it reuses the stored policy and avoids re-analyzing the method.

We use ISPA to analyze each API entry point. The algorithm takes as input a method m and the current analysis state, which consists of the current security policy *SP* and any known constant parameters *paramConsts* to m. The algorithm is mutually recursive with SPDA (Algorithm 1), which invokes ISPA at method invocations with the current values of *SP* and *paramConsts*. Thus, the computation of *OUT(v)* in the while loop requires a change—a recursive call to gather *SP(v)*, if v is a resolved method invocation. SPDA uses *IN(v)* as the initial flow value of the method's entry basic block and seeds constant propagation with the incoming constant parameters (both not shown).

Constant propagation. For better precision, our analysis propagates constants intraprocedurally and interprocedurally. The security policy from Harmony in Figure 4 motivates this analysis. It shows a common pattern in which a parameter determines whether a security check is performed. This code uses two `URL` constructors. The first constructor always passes `null` as the `handler` parameter to the second constructor, which—correctly—performs no security checks. In other contexts, however, the second constructor performs one security check (line 7). Interprocedural constant propagation is required to accurately differentiate these two contexts and prevent false positives.

Soot supports Wegman-Zadeck intraprocedural constant propagation [36]. Soot's algorithm propagates integer and boolean constants and null reference assignments into conditional statements and eliminates unexecutable statements. We extend the analysis at method invocations to pass constant parameters to the target method. Because constant parameters are an essential part of the analysis state, our memoization scheme includes them as dataflow values: both the policy *SP* and the constant parameters *paramConsts* must match in order to reuse previous results.

Convergence. SPDA and ISPA are guaranteed to converge because they are monotone and distributive. Constant propagation is a monotone forward analysis. Intraprocedural constant propagation is guaranteed to converge on the structured control-flow graphs in Java, but because the call graph is recursive and not structured, context-sensitive interprocedural constant propagation is not guaranteed to converge. For example, if a call passes in a constant parameter that the callee increments until it reaches some limit, each context would be considered unique. In a context-sensitive analysis, constant propagation can produce an unbounded number of unique constant parameters due to method recursion. We prevent this case by terminating early on recursive methods. In our implementation, if the analysis encounters a recursive call, *i.e.*, a call to a method that is already on the call stack, it does not re-analyze the method. An alternative implementation could instead bound the number of traversals of a recursive subgraph.

```
// Harmony
public URL(String spec) {
  this((URL) null, spec,
       (URLStreamHandler) null);
}
public URL(URL context, String spec
           URLStreamHandler handler) {
  if (handler != null) {
    securityManager.checkPermission(
        specifyStreamHandlerPermission);
    strmHandler = handler;
  }
  ... protocol = newProtocol; ...
}
```

Figure 4: **A context-sensitive *may* policy.** Note that deriving the precise policy associated with the first entry point requires propagating the `null` constant into the `handler` parameter.

Scalability. Making context-sensitive analysis efficient is difficult in general [18]. Our memoization is similar to Wilson and Lam [38], who record context-sensitive alias sets to avoid redundant analysis. As described above, we memoize context-sensitive security policies and any relevant constant parameters. Unlike context-sensitive, whole-program pointer analyses that must store large sets, our analysis deals with a relatively small number of security checks which must or may precede security-sensitive events.

Even though our analysis essentially explores every call path, it performs well in practice. Section 6 shows that reusing dataflow analysis values for identical incoming flow values improves performance significantly. Other properties of our analysis, such as not analyzing recursive calls and ignoring method invocations that Soot cannot resolve to a unique target, improve scalability as well. We find that calls to a method in the same or other contexts often have the same incoming flow values. Nonetheless, context sensitivity, which differentiates contexts that have different flow values, is key to the precision of our approach.

5. Comparing Security Policies

Given two implementations of the same API entry point, we compute the policies realized by each implementation using the analysis described in the previous section. Our analysis combines distinct occurrences of calls to the same JNI routine and API returns. For example, if a method calls the same JNI routine three times with different policies, we combine all three *must* and *may* policies. We perform intersection to combine *must* policies and union to combine *may* policies. Although this step causes a loss of precision for *must* policies in particular and thus may lead to false positives, we did not find it to be a problem in practice. This step does not introduce false negatives when distinct instances of the same JNI call use different *must* policies, but may introduce false negatives when combining *may* policies. A more precise analysis could try to order and align each instance of a security-sensitive event, but we did not find this necessary.

After combining security-sensitive events in each API, the analysis then compares two policies as follows:

1. If neither implementation has any security policies, or both implementations have identical security policies, the comparison analysis reports no error.
2. If one implementation has no security policy, but the other implementation has one or more security policies, the comparison analysis reports an error.
3. Otherwise, the comparison analysis matches events that occur in both implementations. We ignore events unique to one implementation. Matched events are compared as follows:
   (a) If the two implementations have different sets of security checks for the same event, the comparison analysis reports an error.
   (b) If the two implementations have the same security checks, but at least one check is *may* in one implementation and *must* in the other, the comparison analysis reports an error.

Case 2 is responsible for most of the security vulnerabilities and interoperability bugs we found. Case 3(a) produced one vulnerability, one interoperability bug, and one false positive. Case 3(b) produced one interoperability bug.

6. Evaluation

We evaluate our approach by applying it to recent versions of three mature implementations of the standard Java Class Library. The libraries perform two critical functions in Java. First, they make Java portable by providing an abstract interface to I/O, user interfaces, file systems, the network, operating system, and all other machine-dependent functionality. Second, they provide standard, optimized implementations of widely used data structures and abstractions, such as sets and queues. All Java programs rely on the security and correctness of these libraries.

We analyze three implementations of the Java Class Library, listed below. For each implementation, we analyze the main packages: java.io, java.lang, java.nio, java.security, java.text, java.util, javax.crypto, javax.net, javax.security, and java.net.

1. *JDK:* Sun JDK, version 1.6.0_07, first released in 1996.
2. *Classpath:* GNU Classpath, version 0.97.2, started in 1998.
3. *Harmony:* Apache Harmony libraries, version 1.5.0, svn revision r761593, started in 2005.

Note that two of the implementations are well over 10 years old, yet our approach still found security errors in them. Together, these libraries total about 2.5M lines of code.

Table 1 summarizes the non-comment lines of code, API entry points, and characteristics of security policies for each library. We analyze all public and protected methods because applications can invoke them either directly or via a derived class. Because of this, the number of API entry points varies from implementation to implementation.

We analyze the entire call graph rooted at each of these API entry points. The third row in Table 1 shows that only a small subset of methods performs security checks. The analysis computes between 4,208 and 9,580 *must* and *may* security policies for each implementation. We only compare policies for the API entry points that are identical in two implementations—over 4,100 entry points for each pair—shown in the first row of Table 3. The sheer volume of policies demonstrates that any approach that relies on developers to manually examine inferred policies to detect errors is unlikely to succeed.

Analysis time. Table 2 shows the time in minutes to compute *must* and *may* policies for each of the three libraries. For both *may* and *must* policies, the first row shows the analysis time without memoization of method summaries (Section 4). The second and third rows show time with memoization. In the second row, method summaries are reused only within the same API entry point. In the third row, they are reused across the entire library.

Reuse of summaries within the same entry point yields a factor of 1.5 to 13 improvement and reuse across the entire library yields an additional factor of 3 to 18, resulting in the overall factor of 15 to

	JDK	Harmony	Classpath
Non-comment lines of code	632K	572K	563K
Entry points	6,008	5,835	4,563
Entry points w/ security checks	239	262	250
may security policies	9,580	7,126	4,652
must security policies	7,181	6,757	4,208

Table 1: Library characteristics

		JDK	Harmony	Classpath
MAY	No summaries	300	190	340
	Summaries (per entry point)	180	130	190
	Summaries (global)	10	13	20
MUST	No summaries	560	290	650
	Summaries (per entry point)	50	40	50
	Summaries (global)	10	12	10

Table 2: Analysis time in minutes

	Classpath v Harmony		JDK v Harmony		JDK v Classpath	
Matching APIs		4,161		4,449		4,758
False positives eliminated by ICP		4 (63)		4 (35)		4 (74)
False positives		3 (3)		3 (3)		0 (0)
Root cause of policy difference						
Intraprocedural		1 (1)		5 (6)		2 (3)
Interprocedural		14 (140)		13 (43)		16 (300)
MUST/MAY difference		0 (0)		1 (5)		0 (0)
Total differences		15 (142)		19 (54)		18 (303)
Total interoperability bugs		3 (115)		9 (39)		5 (222)
	Classpath	Harmony	JDK	Harmony	JDK	Classpath
Security vulnerabilities in	5 (12)	4 (11)	1 (2)	6 (10)	5 (21)	8 (60)
		JDK		**Harmony**		**Classpath**
Total security vulnerabilities		6 (23)		6 (11)		8 (61)

The table reports distinct errors with manifestations in parentheses: *distinct (manifestations)*.

Table 3: Security vulnerabilities and interoperability errors detected by security policy differencing analysis

65 improvement in performance due to memoization. Although our analysis is still not blazingly fast, it is intended to be used relatively infrequently, as part of correctness and interoperability testing.

6.1 Analysis results

We categorize the results of our analysis as follows:

Vulnerability: A semantic difference that can be exploited to perform some security-sensitive action without permission.

Interoperability bug: A semantic difference that causes interoperability problems. These differences do not, on the surface, enable applications to perform security-sensitive actions without permission, but could be part of a multi-stage attack.

False positive: Policies are identical, but a difference is mistakenly reported due to imprecision of our analysis.

False negative: A security vulnerability *not* reported by our analysis. False negatives may arise if identical *may* policies apply under different conditions, or if two policies are identical but incorrect. Although these cases seem unlikely, their frequency is hard to quantify.

The remainder of this section surveys the results of security-policy differencing and how different algorithmic features of our analysis contribute to the results. Sections 6.2 and 6.3 discuss the security vulnerabilities and interoperability errors in detail and include examples of each. Section 6.4 explains in more detail why our analysis can have false positives and false negatives.

Table 3 shows the results of our analysis. We compare each implementation to the other two. The analysis finds most errors in both comparisons, but because some entry points differ between implementations, each pairwise comparison finds a few unique errors.

To reduce the number of reports the developer must read, our analysis automatically combines reports when the error stems from the same *root cause*, *i.e.*, when the method containing the error is called from multiple API entry points. The number of entry points (*manifestations*) that can exploit the error is shown in parentheses. We manually examined all root causes to determine the responsible library implementation and classify the bug.

The *ICP* row shows that interprocedural constant propagation eliminates 4 false positives that have over 70 manifestations, resulting in the overall false-positive rate of less than 1%: 3 of 499 manifestations. The *Intraprocedural*, *Interprocedural*, and *MUST/MAY* rows show that every component of our analysis contributes to finding errors. Intraprocedural analysis, which only computes policies local to a method, would miss the majority of the errors. Differences due to a *must* policy in one implementation and a *may* policy in the other revealed one bug. Not shown in a dedicated row in the table is the small number of vulnerabilities revealed by differences between two *may* policies, including the one in Figure 1. Finding most errors requires context-sensitive interprocedural analysis.

Overall, our analysis found 20 security vulnerabilities and 11 interoperability bugs across *all three library implementations*, not just in the least mature one. These errors witness how difficult it is for programmers to get access-rights policies correct. For example, even though more than a hundred developers worked on the JDK implementation for over 15 years, it is still not error-free. We reported all vulnerabilities to the respective implementors, who recognized all of them as bugs and fixed some of them [31–33].

6.2 Security vulnerabilities

This section explains a few of the security vulnerabilities uncovered by our analysis. To demonstrate the power of implementation

```
// JDK
class Runtime {
  public void loadLibrary(String libname) {
    loadLibrary0(System.getCallerClass(),
                 libname);
    return;
  }
  synchronized void loadLibrary0(
      Class fromClass, String libname) {
    ... securityManager.checkLink(libname); ...
    ClassLoader.loadLibrary(fromClass, libname,
                            false);
  }
}

class ClassLoader {
  static void loadLibrary(Class fromClass,
      String name, boolean isAbsolute) {
    ... loadLibrary0(fromClass, libfile); ...
  }
  private static boolean loadLibrary0(
      Class fromClass, final File file) {
    ...
    NativeLibrary lib =
      new NativeLibrary(fromClass, name);
    lib.load(name);
    ...
  }
}
```

(a) JDK implementation of `Runtime.loadLibrary`

```
// Classpath
class Runtime {
  public void loadLibrary(String libname) {
    loadLibrary(libname, VMStackWalker.
        getCallingClassLoader());
    return;
  }
  void loadLibrary(String libname, ClassLoader
      loader) {
    ... securityManager.checkLink(libname); ...
    ... loadLib(filename, loader); ...
  }
  private static int loadLib(String filename,
      ClassLoader loader) {
    ...
    securityManager.checkRead(filename);
    ...
    return VMRuntime.nativeLoad(filename,
        loader);
  }
}
```

(b) Classpath implementation of `Runtime.loadLibrary`

Figure 5: **Security vulnerability:** JDK is missing `checkRead` that Classpath performs before loading a library at run time.

differencing, each vulnerability is accompanied by a correct implementation from another library.

Figure 5 shows one of the six vulnerabilities in JDK. The JDK code returns from `Runtime.loadLibrary` having called only `checkLink` on a dynamically loaded library. By contrast, the Classpath implementation calls both `checkLink` and `checkRead`. Detecting this vulnerability requires interprocedural analysis.

The other five JDK vulnerabilities are detected when our analysis compares JDK with Classpath. They arise because JDK performs some security checks inside a privileged block. Security checks inside a privileged block always succeed. Therefore, they are semantic no-ops and our analysis correctly ignores them. It seems especially difficult for developers to detect this kind of error through manual inspection because a call to the security-checking method is actually present in the source code.

```
// Harmony
public URLConnection openConnection(
    Proxy proxy) throws IOException {
  ...
  return
    strmHandler.openConnection(this, proxy);
}
```

(a) Harmony implementation of `URLConnection.openConnection`

```
// JDK
public URLConnection openConnection(
    Proxy proxy) {
  ...
  if (proxy.type() != Proxy.Type.DIRECT) {
    InetSocketAddress epoint =
      (InetSocketAddress) proxy.address();
    if (epoint.isUnresolved()) {
      securityManager.checkConnect(epoint.
          getHostName(), epoint.getPort());
    } else {
      securityManager.checkConnect(
          epoint.getAddress().getHostAddress(),
          epoint.getPort());
    }
  }
  return handler.openConnection(this, proxy);
}
```

(b) JDK implementation of `URLConnection.openConnection`

Figure 6: **Security vulnerability:** Harmony is missing `checkConnect` that JDK performs before opening a network connection.

Figure 6 shows one of the six vulnerabilities in Harmony, detected when our analysis compared it to JDK. Finding the vulnerability in `OpenConnection` requires using API returns as security-sensitive events because `OpenConnection` does not actually perform network reads and writes with JNI calls. The user must subsequently call `getInputStream()` or `getOutputStream()` to read or write to the network. In Harmony, `OpenConnection` calls a method on the private `strmHandler` variable and returns internal API state to the application without any checks. By contrast, the JDK implementation has a *may* policy that calls `checkConnect` before returning internal API state to the application.

Figure 7 shows one of the eight vulnerabilities in Classpath. Classpath omits all security checks in the `Socket.connect` method, whereas JDK always calls `checkConnect`. This error seems simple to spot, but the method is called in many contexts, some of which do perform checks. Since this method is directly accessible by an application, this vulnerability is easy to exploit and has now been fixed.

6.3 Interoperability bugs

Some interoperability problems arise because Classpath performs much more dynamic class loading than the other implementations. For example, it dynamically loads the `CharsetProvider` class, whereas JDK statically loads it at boot time. The reason may be that Classpath is trying to reduce the size of its JVM when running on an embedded platform. Because of this difference, Classpath contains code that performs `checkPermission(new RuntimePermission("charsetProvider"))`, whereas JDK and Harmony do not.

```
// JDK
class Socket {
  public void connect(SocketAddress, int) {
    ...
    securityManager.checkConnect(...);
    ...
    impl.connect(...);
  }
}
```

(a) JDK implementation of `Socket.connect`

```
// Classpath
class Socket {
  public void connect(SocketAddress, int) {
    ...
    getImpl().connect(endpoint, timeout);
  }
}
```

(b) Classpath implementation of `Socket.connect`

Figure 7: **Security vulnerability:** Classpath is missing `checkConnect` that JDK performs before opening a network connection.

```
// JDK
class String {
 public byte[] getBytes() {
   return
     StringCoding.encode(value, offset, count);
 }
}

class StringCoding {
 static byte[] encode(...) {
   try {
     return encode("ISO-8859-1", ca, off, len);
   } catch (UnsupportedEncodingException x) {
     System.exit(1);
     return null;
   }
 }
}
```

(a) JDK implementation of `String.getBytes`

```
//Harmony
class String {
 public byte[] getBytes() {
   ByteBuffer buffer =
     defaultCharset().encode(...);
   ...
 }
 private Charset defaultCharset() {
   if (DefaultCharset == null) {
     DefaultCharset =
       Charset.forName("ISO-8859-1");
   }
   ...
 }
}
```

(b) Harmony implementation of `String.getBytes`

Figure 8: **Interoperability bug:** JDK requires `checkExit` permission to call `System.exit()`, whereas Harmony throws an exception.

Interoperability problems also arise due to additional functionality in one of the implementations. Figure 8 shows an example from `String.getBytes`. If the default "ISO-8859-1" character set decoder is not present, JDK terminates the application by calling `System.exit()`, whereas `forName` in Harmony throws `UnsupportedEncodingException`. To perform `System.exit()`, the application needs `checkExit` permission which is not needed in the Harmony implementation.

6.4 False positives and negatives

The main reason for false positives is inherent to any static analysis—it is conservative because it includes all possible program paths and not just the actual paths taken during code execution. In practice, our analysis produced only three false positives when analyzing the three implementations of the Java Class Library, all of them due to questionable coding practices in the Harmony implementation. For example, in `java.security.Security.getProperty(String)`, JDK uses `checkPermission()`, whereas Harmony uses `checkSecurityAccess()`. There is a mismatch between required permissions, but both checks achieve the same goal. In this example, both implementations should have used `checkPropertyAccess()`. Similarly, Harmony unnecessarily uses `checkConnect()` to check address reachability inside the `getInetAddresses()` method, whereas JDK simply returns the result of `InetAddrImpl.isReachable()`.

There are two causes of false negatives. First, two libraries may both implement the security policy incorrectly and in the same way. The second cause is imprecision of our analysis. For example, our analysis is not field or variable sensitive. If the library sends the wrong parameter to the security-checking method, or if it checks one variable and then makes a JNI call on another, our analysis will not report an error. Furthermore, our analysis does not determine the potential targets of unresolved method invocations for incomplete call graphs. Since 97% of method invocations were resolved, we did not perform additional analysis, and this inaccuracy may result in false negatives. Finally, our comparison of *may* policies does not consider the conditions under which the checks are executed. Changing our analysis to report these conditions is easy, but would result in an overwhelming number of reports. Verifying whether the conditions for two *may* policies are equivalent is difficult. We examined some of the reports by hand and did not find any false negatives. A quantitative evaluation of false negatives would require an enormous amount of time and expertise from the developers.

7. Related Work

This section describes the closest related work on static analysis for finding security errors and other bugs, as well as program differencing. None of the prior work exploits multiple API implementations to automatically derive correctness criteria for security policies.

7.1 Static analysis and model checking

The closest related static analysis techniques for verifying security mediation in Java code are by Koved et al. [22, 28] and Sistla et al. [30]. Koved et al. take security checks as inputs and use a flow- and context-sensitive interprocedural *must* analysis to compute, for each point in the program, the set of checks performed prior to reaching it. The programmer must manually identify all security-sensitive operations and verify whether the computed checks are sufficient. Our *must* polices are similar, but our policy differencing eliminates the error-prone, manual verification.

Sistla et al. take as input a manual policy specified as pairs of security checks (calls to the security manager) and security events (only JNI calls in their model). They use flow- and context-sensitive interprocedural *must* analysis to find "bad" paths that reach a security event without performing the corresponding check. The MOPS project [7] applied a similar, but flow-insensitive, approach to C programs.

As our analysis shows, correct security enforcement sometimes requires multiple checks. Furthermore, the check(s) may not dominate the event (*e.g.*, see Figure 1), necessitating *may* analysis. In addition to native calls, the set of security events should also include at least API returns. The final and most significant deficiency of these prior approaches is that they provide no mechanism for determining whether the policy used for verification is correct and complete.

These deficiencies are significant in practice. Sistla et al. analyzed the JDK and Harmony libraries, while Koved et al. analyzed JDK—but *neither paper reports any actual bugs.* By using differences between API implementations as an oracle for detecting incorrect policies, we found multiple, confirmed security vulnerabilities in JDK, Harmony, and Classpath, many of which were missed by prior analyses. Furthermore, our analysis produces precise security policies specific to concrete security-sensitive events.

There is an enormous amount of research on model checking that aims to prove programs correct using precise specifications [4–6, 8, 13]. In general, model checking does not yet scale to interprocedural security analysis of large programs, and rigorous specification of security policies and vulnerability patterns has proven elusive so far.

Whaley et al. extract finite-state models of the interface of a class and its accesses to common data structures [37]. Security policies do not always follow their model. For instance, consider the following simple example:

```
securityManager.checkPermission();
doSensitiveOperation();
```

Their analysis cannot detect that `doSensitiveOperation()` should be dominated by `checkPermission()` because there is no data structure shared between the two methods. Furthermore, their analysis is not context sensitive. Our approach could be configured to use arbitrary data structure accesses as security-sensitive events, but we did not find it necessary.

Ganapathy et al. use concept analysis to extract security-sensitive events [15]. Their approach is complementary to ours, since our analysis could take as input the security-sensitive events they generate.

7.2 "Bugs as inconsistencies"

Mining programs for static and dynamic models of correct behavior has become a popular approach for finding bugs [2, 10, 14, 35]. In general, this approach finds bugs that reveal themselves as anomalies in common patterns of correct behavior. The fundamental assumption is that correct patterns occur many times in the program and are thus easy to recognize. Mining algorithms must be tuned to ignore unique or rarely observed behavior, or else they produce an overwhelming number of false positives. Because security policies are often unique to a particular API, the "bugs as inconsistencies" approach is likely to miss many vulnerabilities (*e.g.*, see Section 2).

AutoISES statically mines security patterns in C code and flags deviations from frequent patterns as vulnerabilities [35]. Its analysis targets security checks performed prior to security-sensitive operations in SELinux kernel routines. The AutoISES paper claims that the analysis is context sensitive and flow *insensitive*, but does not describe the actual algorithm or convergence criteria. It does mention that the analysis partitions the call graph into modules for scalability, thus missing security patterns and bugs on cross-module call paths, although the authors argue that maintainable security policies should not cross modules—at least in C programs. In our experience with the Java libraries, both flow and context sensitivity are essential for precision.

Engler et al. statically extract *intraprocedural* patterns of correct behavior, including some security policies, and use them to detect anomalies [14]. Their policy descriptions include "a call to A always or sometimes dominates a call to B" and are thus similar to ours. However, these local patterns are not *interprocedural*—they do not include flow- and context-sensitive policies in which the security check occurs in a different method than the operation it protects. Furthermore, the approach of Engler et al. ignores rare patterns. Dillig et al. find bugs by detecting static inconsistencies in the program [10]. For example, they detect if the program contains both "`if (x==NULL) foo.m();`" and "`*x=y;`" which indicate both that `x` may be null and that `x` is definitely non-null. This analysis finds local contradictions rather than semantic differences. It captures neither rare events, nor interprocedural patterns. Both approaches will miss many vulnerabilities in Java code, where security-sensitive events and the corresponding checks often occur in different methods.

Another approach to mining specification is to observe policies at run time. For example, Ammons et al. observe dynamic traces of method call sequences and use machine learning to create API usage specifications in the form of finite-state machines [2]. Dynamic mining approaches are at a disadvantage when policies are unique and/or rarely or never exercised by the test inputs.

Kim et al. use a database of previously fixed bugs to find their recurrences in new code [21]. Hovemeyer and Pugh use programmer-defined bug patterns to find their occurrences [19]. To avoid false positives, these tools require well-defined bug patterns that apply to all contexts. These types of patterns are useful for describing coding conventions, but generally do not capture context-specific semantics. Because many security policies are context dependent and unique, these techniques cannot classify them as correct or incorrect.

Our work is also distantly related to program differencing. We find inconsistencies between implementations of the same API using identical API entry points, but do not assume that the implementations are identical or even very similar. In our experience, different implementations often choose different algorithms and data structures. Techniques for finding *method clones*—methods that implement semantically similar functionality within the same program [3, 12, 23, 24]—are thus unlikely to classify two methods that implement the same API as clones. However, it might be possible to leverage clone detection by first finding clones, then extracting and comparing their security policies. We leave this exploration to future work.

In summary, our interprocedural, flow-sensitive and context-sensitive analysis is more precise than prior approaches. It does not require multiple instances of correct behavior within the same program and can thus find bugs in very rare patterns, such as the missing `checkAccept` in the example of Section 2. It does, however, require at least two independent implementations of the same API.

8. Discussion and Conclusions

This paper shows how to use precise, flow- and context-sensitive security policy analysis to infer thousands of relationships between security checks and security-sensitive events in Java code, and how to use this information to compare implementations of the same library API. The number of check-event relationships in these implementations is so large that it is clearly impractical for developers to analyze them manually. In fact, prior techniques that produced similar policies for each implementation in isolation did not find any errors. By comparing precise policies from multiple implementations, we create a *security policy oracle*: any policy difference between two implementations of the same functionality indicates an error! Our approach uncovered many security vulnerabilities and interoperability bugs in three large, mature, widely used implementations of the Java Class Library.

Of course, security-policy differencing requires multiple, independent implementations and thus limits the applicability of our approach. However, many critical APIs, such as the Java, C#, and C libraries, have multiple implementations. Furthermore, they are an essential component of virtually every substantial application written in these languages. At least one open-source version of widely used APIs is often available and can be used as a reference. In this use case, programmers of proprietary versions may not even need to read the open-source code, but only study any reported differences in security policies. If all API implementations are proprietary, developers could use this approach to make their respective implementations more secure if one or more of them are willing to share extracted policies.

Security vulnerabilities and other semantic errors in popular libraries open the door to attacks that can compromise many systems, not just a single application. With the advent of cloud computing and increasing demand for portability and architecture-specific optimizations, the prevalence of multiple implementations of the same API is likely to grow. This work shows for the first time *how to leverage multiple implementations to improve the interoperability and security of each.*

Our approach may be applicable to other types of interoperability bugs. As Figure 8 shows, semantic differences sometimes accidentally show up as security-policy differences. A generalization of our analysis that extracts and compares more general semantics of API implementations seems promising. For example, differences in how implementations access parameters, private variables, return values, and flow values from parameters to private variables and return values may reveal interoperability bugs. Similar analysis could detect differences in exceptions that may get thrown by each implementation and in the semantic information carried by return values.

Acknowledgments

Thanks to Andrew John Hughes for his generous help with verifying Classpath bugs and for feedback on the paper text; Sam Guyer for useful discussions about static analysis; and the anonymous reviewers for helpful feedback on the text.

The research described in this paper was partially supported by the NSF grants CNS-0746888, CCF-0811523, CNS-0905602, SHF-0910818, and CCF-1018721, Google research award, and the MURI program under AFOSR Grant No. FA9550-08-1-0352.

References

[1] Amazon. Amazon Web Services. `http://aws.amazon.com/`.

[2] G. Ammons, R. Bodík, and J. R. Larus. Mining specifications. In *ACM Symposium on the Principles of Programming Languages*, pages 4–16, 2002.

[3] B. S. Baker. On finding duplication and near-duplication in large software systems. In *IEEE Working Conference on Reverse Engineering*, pages 86–95, 1995.

[4] T. Ball and S. K. Rajamani. The SLAM project: Debugging system software via static analysis. In *ACM Symposium on the Principles of Programming Languages*, pages 1–3, 2002.

[5] T. Ball, E. Bounimova, B. Cook, V. Levin, J. Lichtenberg, C. McGarvey, B. Ondrusek, S. K. Rajamani, and A. Ustuner. Thorough static analysis of device drivers. In *ACM European Conference on Computer Systems*, pages 73–85, 2006.

[6] D. Beyer, T. A. Henzinger, R. Jhala, and R. Majumdar. The software model checker BLAST. *International Journal on Software Tools for Technology Transfer*, 9(5-6):505–525, 2007.

[7] H. Chen and D. Wagner. MOPS: An infrastructure for examining security properties of software. In *ACM Conference on Computer and Communications Security*, pages 235–244, 2002.

[8] E. M. Clarke, E. A. Emerson, and A. P. Sistla. Automatic verification of finite-state concurrent systems using temporal logic specifications. *ACM Transactions on Programming Languages and Systems*, 8(2): 244–263, 1986.

[9] C. Cowan, P. Wagle, C. Pu, S. Beattie, and J. Walpole. Buffer overflows: Attacks and defenses for the vulnerability of the decade. In *DARPA Information Survivability Conference and Exposition*, pages 119–129, 2000.

[10] I. Dillig, T. Dillig, and A. Aiken. Static error detection using semantic inconsistency inference. In *ACM Conference on Programming Language Design and Implementation*, pages 435–445, 2007.

[11] A. Diwan, K. S. McKinley, and J. E. B. Moss. Using types to analyze and optimize object-oriented programs. *ACM Transactions on Programming Languages and Systems*, 23(1):30–72, 2001.

[12] S. Ducasse, M. Rieger, and S. Demeyer. A language independent approach for detecting duplicated code. In *IEEE International Conference on Software Maintenance*, pages 109–118, 1999.

[13] E. A. Emerson and E. M. Clarke. Characterizing correctness properties of parallel programs using fixpoints. In *Colloquium on Automata, Languages and Programming*, pages 169–181, 1980.

[14] D. Engler, D. Y. Chen, S. Hallem, A. Chou, and B. Chelf. Bugs as deviant behavior: A general approach to inferring errors in systems code. In *ACM Symposium on Operating Systems Principles*, pages 57–72, 2001.

[15] V. Ganapathy, D. King, T. Jaeger, and S. Jha. Mining security-sensitive operations in legacy code using concept analysis. In *ACM International Conference on Software Engineering*, pages 458–467, 2007.

[16] Google. Google Apps. `http://www.google.com/apps/`.

[17] D. Grove and L. Torczon. Interprocedural constant propagation: A study of jump function implementations. In *ACM Conference on Programming Language Design and Implementation*, pages 90–99, 1993.

[18] S. Z. Guyer and C. Lin. Error checking with client-driven pointer analysis. *Science of Computer Programming*, 58(1-2):83–114, 2005.

[19] D. Hovemeyer and W. Pugh. Finding bugs is easy. In *ACM OOPSLA Onward!*, pages 92–106, 2004.

[20] IBM. Cloud Computing. `http://ibm.com/developerworks/cloud/`.

[21] S. Kim, K. Pan, and E. E. J. Whitehead, Jr. Memories of bug fixes. In *ACM Symposium on the Foundations of Software Engineering*, pages 35–45, 2006.

[22] L. Koved, M. Pistoia, and A. Kershenbaum. Access rights analysis for Java. In *ACM Conference on Object-Oriented Programming, Systems, Languages, and Applications*, pages 359–372, 2002.

[23] J. Krinke. Identifying similar code with program dependence graphs. In *IEEE Working Conference on Reverse Engineering*, pages 301–309, 2001.

[24] A. M. Leitao. Detection of redundant code using R^2D^2. *Software Quality Control*, 12(4):361–382, 2004.

[25] O. Lhoták and L. Hendren. Context-sensitive points-to analysis: Is it worth it? In *International Conference on Compiler Construction*, pages 47–64, 2006.

[26] Z. Li, L. Tan, X. Wang, S. Lu, Y. Zhou, and C. Zhai. Have things changed now? An empirical study of bug characteristics in modern open source software. In *Workshop on Architectural and System Support for Improving Software Dependability (ASID)*, pages 25–33, 2006.

[27] T. J. Marlowe and B. G. Ryder. Properties of data flow frameworks. *Acta Informatics (ACTA)*, 28(2):121–163, 1990.

[28] M. Pistoia, R. J. Flynn, L. Koved, and V. C. Sreedhar. Interprocedural analysis for privileged code placement and tainted variable detection. In *European Conference on Object-Oriented Programming*, pages 362–386, 2005.

[29] Salesforce. Salesforce Platform. `http://www.salesforce.com/platform/`.

[30] A. P. Sistla, V. N. Venkatakrishnan, M. Zhou, and H. Branske. CMV: Automatic verification of complete mediation for Java Virtual Machines. In *ACM Symposium on Information, Computer and Communications Security*, pages 100–111, 2008.

[31] V. Srivastava. Vulnerabilities submitted to Classpath, Dec 2009–Jan 2010. `http://gcc.gnu.org/bugzilla/show_bug.cgi?id=42390`.

[32] V. Srivastava. Vulnerabilities submitted to Harmony, Nov 2009. `https://issues.apache.org/jira/browse/HARMONY-6367`.

[33] V. Srivastava. Vulnerabilities submitted to Sun JDK, Jan–Oct 2010. `http://bugs.sun.com/bugdatabase/view_bug.do?bug_id=6914460`.

[34] V. Sundaresan, L. Hendren, C. Razafimahefa, R. Vallée-Rai, P. Lam, E. Gagnon, and C. Godin. Practical virtual method call resolution for Java. In *ACM Conference on Object–Oriented Programming, Systems, Languages, and Applications*, pages 264–280, 2000.

[35] L. Tan, X. Zhang, X. Ma, W. Xiong, and Y. Zhou. AutoISES: Automatically inferring security specifications and detecting violations. In *USENIX Security Symposium*, pages 379–394, 2008.

[36] M. N. Wegman and F. K. Zadeck. Constant propagation with conditional branches. *ACM Transactions on Programming Languages and Systems*, 13(2):181–210, 1991.

[37] J. Whaley, M. C. Martin, and M. S. Lam. Automatic extraction of object-oriented component interfaces. In *ACM International Symposium on Software Testing and Analysis*, pages 218–228, July 2002.

[38] R. P. Wilson and M. S. Lam. Efficient context-sensitive pointer analysis for C programs. In *ACM Conference on Programming Language Design and Implementation*, pages 1–12, 1995.

[39] B. Yee, D. Sehr, G. Dardyk, J. B. Chen, R. Muth, T. Ormandy, S. Okasaka, N. Narula, and N. Fullagar. Native Client: A sandbox for portable, untrusted x86 native code. *Communications of the ACM*, 53(1):91–99, 2010.

Language-Independent Sandboxing of Just-In-Time Compilation and Self-Modifying Code

Jason Ansel
Computer Science and Artificial Intelligence Laboratory
Massachusetts Institute of Technology
jansel@csail.mit.edu

Petr Marchenko
University College London
p.marchenko@cs.ucl.ac.uk

Úlfar Erlingsson, Elijah Taylor, Brad Chen, Derek L. Schuff, David Sehr, Cliff L. Biffle, Bennet Yee
Google Inc.
{ulfar, elijahtaylor, bradchen, dschuff, sehr, cbiffle, bsy}@google.com

Abstract

When dealing with dynamic, untrusted content, such as on the Web, software behavior must be sandboxed, typically through use of a language like JavaScript. However, even for such specially-designed languages, it is difficult to ensure the safety of highly-optimized, dynamic language runtimes which, for efficiency, rely on advanced techniques such as Just-In-Time (JIT) compilation, large libraries of native-code support routines, and intricate mechanisms for multi-threading and garbage collection. Each new runtime provides a new potential attack surface and this security risk raises a barrier to the adoption of new languages for creating untrusted content.

Removing this limitation, this paper introduces general mechanisms for safely and efficiently sandboxing software, such as dynamic language runtimes, that make use of advanced, low-level techniques like runtime code modification. Our *language-independent sandboxing* builds on Software-based Fault Isolation (SFI), a traditionally static technique. We provide a more flexible form of SFI by adding new constraints and mechanisms that allow safety to be guaranteed despite runtime code modifications.

We have added our extensions to both the x86-32 and x86-64 variants of a production-quality, SFI-based sandboxing platform; on those two architectures SFI mechanisms face different challenges. We have also ported two representative language platforms to our extended sandbox: the Mono common language runtime and the V8 JavaScript engine. In detailed evaluations, we find that sandboxing slowdown varies between different benchmarks, languages, and hardware platforms. Overheads are generally moderate and they are close to zero for some important benchmark/platform combinations.

Categories and Subject Descriptors D.4.6 [*Operating Systems*]: Security and Protection

General Terms Languages, Security

PLDI'11, June 4–8, 2011, San Jose, California, USA.

Keywords Sandboxing, Security, Software Fault Isolation, Self-Modifying Code, Just-In-Time Compilation

1. Introduction

The safe confinement of software behavior, or *sandboxing*, is a key requirement in many contexts. On the Web, sandboxing is especially important since Web applications are a form of highly-dynamic, untrusted software, and non-isolated Web software, such as browser plugins and ActiveX controls, have been, and remain, a leading source of security vulnerabilities [6, 17]. As a result, Web applications are mostly written in one of a handful of high-level, dynamic programming languages specifically designed for untrusted content—most commonly JavaScript [16].

Software safety is in tension with efficiency: even languages like Java and JavaScript are executed not through simple interpretation, but on top of highly-efficient runtime platforms. The safety of those language platforms depends on large amounts of trusted (possibly flawed) native code—implementing extensive libraries, as well as advanced mechanisms like runtime code generation and garbage collection [3, 33]. Thus, each such language adds new potential means of attack, as evidenced by the frequent exploits of Web-based languages [13, 55].

Fortunately, as we show in this paper, sandboxing can be *language independent*, provide strong safety guarantees, low overhead, and do this without restricting language choice or language implementation options. The entirety of dynamic software execution can be sandboxed, including the language platform, even if it uses just-in-time compilation, runtime code modification, or large bodies of legacy code. Despite being comprehensive, such sandboxing need induce only moderate slowdowns. As shown by our experimental results, in many important cases sandboxing may incur no overhead. Such language-independent sandboxing promises more technology options for untrusted content development—in particular, on the Web.

Our language-independent sandboxing is not based on hardware protection domains, such as the common process abstraction. These offer neither high assurance nor universal applicability, particularly in cases where a fine granularity of protection domains is desired. Their use is intricate and error-prone, leading to non-portable implementations and partial protection [4, 20, 54]. Also, the performance impact of hardware context switching can severely limit applicability [19].

Instead, our work is based on Software-based Fault Isolation

(SFI) [53], which provides high-assurance safety guarantees and is largely independent of the operating system and other system-level details. SFI relies on machine code verification through static analysis and, to date, has not been applicable to sandboxing software that modify machine code at runtime. Removing this obstacle, we present extensions to SFI techniques that allow efficient, safe sandboxing of mechanisms such as just-in-time code generation and runtime code modification. Key to our extensions are new safety constraints on the structure of machine code that apply, inductively, even across code modification.

We have implemented our extensions in the context of the Native Client open-source project: a production-quality SFI-based sandbox [44, 56]. Our extended sandbox provides efficient ways to add, modify, and delete code. It transparently allows safe reuse of code memory without race conditions and without suspending threads, even on hardware-threaded, concurrent systems. Our extensions add little overhead, partly because our new safety constraints are not onerous, but also because they are verified only when code is modified, not when code is used.

We have ported two popular, representative JIT-compiled language systems to our sandbox: the Mono CLR runtime [41], which supports C#, and the V8 JavaScript engine [27]. V8 motivated our work. Its speed compared to previous JavaScript engines clearly demonstrates the advantages of runtime code generation over even highly-optimized interpretation. Our design was further influenced by V8's use of code rewriting for inline *code caches*—and the 12x slowdown that we saw V8 incur when we disabled its code cache mechanisms.

Porting Mono and V8 consisted primarily of changing them to output verifiably-safe code, and inductively maintaining safety across modifications to that code. We targeted two commodity hardware platforms: the x86-32 and x86-64 instruction set architectures (ISAs) [25, 28]. These two ISAs have significantly different characteristics for the purposes of Native Client sandboxing. On x86-32, hardware segments allow low runtime overheads and simplified implementation of our extensions. On x86-64, extensive use is made of inline code that performs runtime sandboxing, and this both reduces performance and complicates porting efforts.

We found that the Mono and V8 platforms, and their x86-32 and x86-64 variants, spanned a wide range in terms of the porting effort required and the sandboxing slowdown incurred. At one end, Mono-32, porting effort was low and the measured overhead is near negligible. At the other extreme, V8-64, porting took a few weeks and sandboxing slowdown is between 51% and 60% on average, but 196% in one benchmark (due to a porting shortcut, as explained in Section 4). Notably, in all cases sandboxing overhead was much lower than what might be expected of a highly-efficient interpreter, where even favorable workloads incur factors of overhead [21, 43].

1.1 Contributions

This paper makes the following contributions:

- A set of locally-verifiable machine code constraints that allow safe, SFI-based sandboxing even of runtime code modification.
- A technique for safe runtime modification of machine code on commodity hardware, despite the simultaneous execution of that code on other processors by untrusted user threads.
- A technique for the safe deletion of code memory, and its reuse for new instructions, despite potentially concurrent execution of untrusted user threads in that code memory.
- Implementation of our language-independent sandbox for x86-32 and x86-64, as well as ports of the V8 and Mono runtimes, allowing software to embed languages like JavaScript and C# as untrusted components.
- Experience showing that it can be straightforward to port modern, advanced language runtimes to execute within language-independent sandboxing.
- Experimental results showing that, while overhead varies between platforms, sandboxing overhead is generally modest, and that a sandboxed advanced language runtime incurs far less overhead than the published slowdown of using interpretation.
- A somewhat surprising optimization technique relying on careful selection of even unexecuted NOP instructions.

To create safe, low-overhead runtime code-modification mechanisms that were easy to use, we had to simultaneously satisfy a great number of constraints. These include the constraints imposed by the NaCl SFI sandbox, the concrete properties of the NaCl runtime system and the operating systems and hardware CPUs it runs upon, as well as the practical characteristics of language platform implementations. While the primitives introduced are straightforward, the intricacy of the underlying mechanisms—and the lack of similar mechanisms in previous SFI systems—is evidence of the difficulty in creating their implementation.

1.2 Motivating Application

Our work has been motivated by the tantalizing possibility of language-independent software development of safe, untrusted Web applications. The foundation for our implementation, Native Client has been integrated with the Chrome Web browser, where it provides access to JavaScript Web interfaces [44, 56]. Our extended sandboxing allows safe execution of ported language runtimes, and their native libraries, even when they make use of advanced code modification techniques for efficiency. Contrast this with today's reality, where rich, interactive Web clients must be written in JavaScript, either from scratch, or via source-to-source translation, with resulting difficulties and inefficiencies [9, 26]. (The alternatives are neither practical nor appealing: asking users to install Web browser plugins for new languages, or using partially-deployed languages like Java.) Adding our extended sandbox to a Web browser could enable writing a Web page in any language, as long as that language runtime is downloaded as part of the page.

1.3 Outline

The remainder of this paper is organized as follows. Section 2 provides background on SFI and the Native Client sandbox. Section 3 covers the design and implementation of our sandboxing extensions. Section 4 describes our experience porting language runtimes to our extended sandbox. Section 5 shows experimental results, examines the sources of overhead, and explains optimization via NOP instruction selection. Finally, Sections 6 and 7 describe related work and draw conclusions.

2. Background

This work builds on the Native Client open-source project [44, 56] commonly abbreviated "NaCl" when used as an adjective. The NaCl sandbox uses Software-based Fault Isolation (SFI) [32, 53] to restrict what instructions can be executed, in what sequence, and constrain the memory addresses used by instructions. SFI provides high-assurance safety guarantees by combining static analysis with *software guards*: short, inline instruction sequences that perform runtime safety checks or sandboxing operations. In this, SFI is similar to language-runtime mechanisms ranging from dynamic array-bounds checks [39] to concurrency controls such as software-transactional memory [48].

SFI allows the creation of *statically verifiable* machine code: code that, through static analysis, can be independently verified to permit only constrained executions, irrespective of how it was

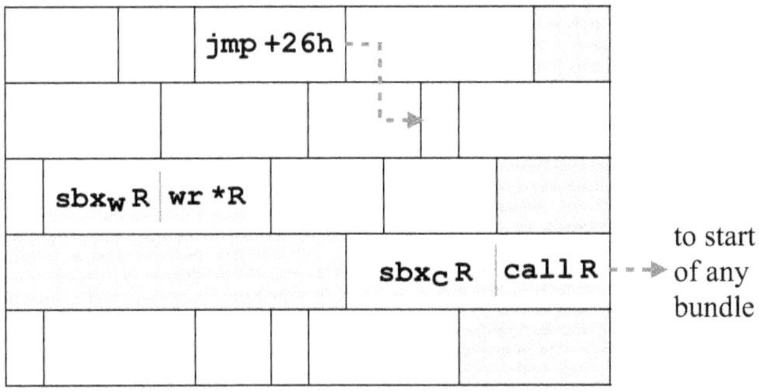

Figure 1. Overview of abstract NaCl machine code, with each fixed-width (32 byte) row denoting a NaCl instruction bundle starting at an aligned address. Vertical lines show instruction boundaries, while shaded regions show NOP padding; dashed arrows indicate permitted direct and indirect control flow. Two NaCl pseudo instructions are shown as gradient-shaded boxes.

created (e.g., through compilation from a high-level language). As with Java bytecode verification [30], SFI establishes safety primarily by checking simple, local properties of code, where those properties, in aggregate, imply global execution invariants. To ensure that safety holds for all possible execution paths, SFI restricts both direct and indirect control transfers, implementing a form of control-flow integrity [1]. SFI must, in particular, prevent control flow from circumventing inline software guards—as this would allow unconstrained execution, including control transfers to disallowed instructions.

On top of its SFI sandboxing, Native Client provides a production-quality, fully-functional platform for the safe execution of untrusted, multi-threaded user-level machine code. Native Client is designed to minimize the overhead of safety: even untrusted, hand-optimized media codecs can be executed at near full speed, since SFI allows safe use of hand-written assembly and model-specific instructions, such as the MMX and SSE extensions on x86. The NaCl platform also provides a programming model for high-level languages using ILP32 (32-bit Integers, Longs and Pointers) primitive types and a portable subset of POSIX-like system calls.

Native Client implements a relatively simple variant of SFI, fundamentally based on *reliable disassembly*: the use of alignment and other machine-code constraints to ensure runtime-reachable instructions can be statically identified. Unlike in more complex SFI implementations [20], each NaCl software guard is combined into a *pseudo instruction* with an adjacent, potentially-unsafe instruction, making each guard constrain the behavior of only a single instruction. As in PittSFIeld [32], NaCl machine code is structured as aligned *instruction bundles* of fixed size (32 bytes). NOP padding is used to ensure that no instruction overlaps the boundary of such an aligned instruction bundle. Control-flow instructions must target valid code, and all computed control transfers must target the start of a instruction bundle. Indirect jumps are allowed only via a pseudo-instruction that aligns the target address, and NOP padding is used to ensure CALL instructions appear only at the end of instruction bundles, so that return addresses are always aligned. In addition, NaCl execution is constrained to a single, contiguous code region, with access to a restricted set of NaCl platform support routines, and memory access is limited to a single, contiguous region of untrusted data memory, which also contains the stacks for threads.

Figure 1 gives an overview of the structure of NaCl machine code for an abstract ISA, showing the details of one NaCl *code region*, comprising five NaCl instruction bundles. Native Client independently verifies the safety of each such code region, one at a time; in our extended sandboxing, this is the region being added or modified. For the first instruction, a direct jump forward by 38 bytes (or 0x26), NaCl verification establishes that the target is a valid instruction boundary within the code region. The two remaining instructions are NaCl pseudo instructions that use the register R to write to memory at address R and call the function at address R. For these pseudo instructions, NaCl verification establishes the correctness of the software guards used to sandbox the register R. For CALL instructions, both their target address and the pushed return address must be the start of an aligned instruction bundle. NaCl verification also imposes many structural constraints on machine code; for instance, direct jumps may not target the inner boundaries of pseudo instructions. NOP padding may need to be used to ensure proper alignment and, as clearly shown in Figure 1, large amounts of such padding may be required, especially around CALL instructions.

Native Client additionally prohibits use of the x86 RET opcode. Returns should be implemented with a POP/JMP sequence. Checking the return address in a register avoids a potential time-of-check/time-of-use race if it were checked on the stack.

Native Client supports three architectures, x86-32, x86-64, and ARM. Like other SFI systems, Native Client also makes use of operating-system and hardware support where appropriate, e.g., to ensure that data is not executable, and that code is not writable and is loaded at the correct address. In particular, on the 32-bit x86 platform, Native Client relies on hardware segments, not software guards, to constrain reads and writes to data memory, as well as code execution. However, the baseline overhead of Native Client will vary with each platform: on ARM and 64-bit x86, bounded segments aren't available, and software guards must be used for each computed access to memory.

Our work in this paper extends SFI techniques to be applicable to runtime code generation and modification through the addition of new, inductively-maintained safety constraints on the structure of machine code. Our motivation is primarily performance: compared to a JIT-compiled runtime, even the most highly-optimized interpreter on its most favorable workload is likely to be twice as slow [21, 43]. Optimized JIT compilation also makes use of runtime code modification—for instance, to allow machine-code constants to be modified to point to new code emitted by the JIT compiler, or to make more extensive updates, such as to the V8 code caches. Instead of modifying immediate constants in machine code, JIT compilers can emit code based on additional levels of indirection; however, such indirection comes at significant performance cost, by pulling in additional cache lines and increasing the rate of memory accesses. Furthermore, language runtimes often make use of runtime code generation or modification for various purposes other than performance, ranging from debugging and profiling, through various instrumentation, to specific mechanisms such as runtime barriers [2, 10, 23, 29, 38]. Even though this paper focuses on JIT compilation, flexibility is another motivation for our work.

3. Core Mechanisms: Design and Implementation

This section describes the design and implementation of our extensions to Native Client to support runtime code modification. After outlining our extensions to the Native Client system call interface, we then describe the implementation in detail, and how it supports dynamic code creation, modification, and deletion.

3.1 Programming Interface

Table 1 lists the interfaces added to the trusted runtime of Native Client to support dynamic code manipulation. NaCl machine code comprises one or more code regions. Our extensions allow the addition and deletion of code regions, as well as the modification

```
int nacl_dyncode_create(void* target,
                        void* src,
                        size_t size);

int nacl_dyncode_modify(void* target,
                        void* src,
                        size_t size);

int nacl_dyncode_delete(void* target,
                        size_t size);
```

Table 1. The interfaces to our NaCl extensions for dynamically adding and deleting code regions, and modifying the instructions within a code region.

of code within a region. All code regions reside within the same single, contiguous address range of executable memory, whose size is set at link time. Executable memory can be modified only through the trusted interfaces, not directly from NaCl code.

As an example of using our interfaces, consider the JIT compilation of a single function. The JIT compiler, running as untrusted NaCl code, generates machine-code in a temporary buffer in data memory. To install the code, the JIT invokes `nacl_dyncode_create`, transferring control into the NaCl trusted runtime. This runtime validates the code and installs it in executable memory, described in detail below.

After creation, the JIT may wish to modify the code, for example, to update a pointer address stored in an immediate pointer. The trusted `nacl_dyncode_modify` interface supports these modifications.

If at some point the code is no longer needed, it can be deleted and the memory reused using `nacl_dyncode_delete`. As Native Client supports concurrent untrusted user threads, the runtime must verify that no threads are executing in the code before it can be safely reused. As `nacl_dyncode_delete` does not block, it will return an error code if it cannot verify that all threads have left the deleted region. Section 3.5 describes the implementation in detail.

3.2 Dynamic Code Creation

Supporting dynamic creation of code required only simple extensions to Native Client. Our implementation leverages existing NaCl verification outlined in Section 2. Code creation involves the following operations:

1. The target code address is verified to be in NaCl executable memory, and aligned to an instruction bundle boundary.
2. To avoid a time-of-test/time-of-use race condition, the code is copied to the private memory of the trusted NaCl runtime.
3. The code is verified using the standard NaCl validator.
4. The target address range in NaCl executable memory is checked to be unused and also reserved, in one atomic operation.
5. The code is safely copied to the target address.

Each NaCl code region is verified independently, and all control flow between code regions, whether direct or computed, must target the start of a NaCl instruction bundle. For this, NaCl verification relies on a property of HLT instructions: in Native Client, executing a HLT (the "halt" instruction) results in the immediate, permanent termination of all NaCl execution threads. To ensure safety, unused executable NaCl memory is filled with HLT instructions. For safe copying of verified code regions, the first byte of each instruction bundle is written as a HLT instruction until all other code bytes have been copied. Then the first byte of each instruction bundle is written with the intended value.

3.3 NaCl Verification of Runtime Code Modifications

Practical sandboxing of dynamic language runtimes requires our extended Native Client platform to support runtime code modification. With our design, verification overhead is proportional to the number of changed instructions. Verification requires inspection only of modified instruction bundles and of instruction bundles targeted by direct control-flow transfers from modified instructions. Table 2 lists the complete set of code safety constraints necessary for NaCl verification of dynamically-modified code. These constraints imply immutability of the instruction boundaries and the NaCl guard instructions in the modified code. They maintain the NaCl safety guarantees across code modification, since they preserve all properties established by runtime guards, as well as the structural properties of NaCl machine code.

These immutability properties restrict the set of allowed code modifications, notably on platforms with variable-length instructions like x86-32. For example, the constraints would prevent two short, adjacent instructions from being overwritten with a single larger instruction, unless the entire code region is deleted first. In practice we have not found these restrictions to be onerous, as demonstrated by our porting work described in Section 4. Immutability also helps prevent race conditions: our safety guarantees hold even in the presence of concurrent, untrusted threads that are executing the code under modification, as long as individual instructions are updated atomically.

3.4 Atomic Modification of Machine-Code Instructions

If a thread uses `nacl_dyncode_modify` to modify an instruction, then concurrent threads should execute either the old or new instructions, but no other instructions.

It is difficult to provide atomicity without a cost to efficiency, especially on multi-core or otherwise hardware-threaded systems. Runtime code modification is relatively uncommon; when used, it is usually performed in a synchronous fashion, via the operating system or a trusted language runtime. Therefore, CPU designers have had few incentives to provide reliable, simple primitives that allow code modification to appear atomic across concurrently-executing hardware threads. Indeed, in order to support mechanisms such as instruction prefetch buffers, AMD and Intel processor documentation outlines a special memory model for updates to concurrently-executing machine-code memory [25, 28].

On multicore and multiprocessor systems, a naive implementation of runtime code modification can lead to the execution of corrupted instructions. To understand the possibility of such instruction stream corruption, we ran highly-concurrent code modification experiments, using straightforward code modification. We found that corruption was indeed possible on all processors that we tested; Sundaresan et al. made similar observations in their development of a Java JIT compiler [49].

Fortunately, with careful implementation, both AMD and Intel processors can support safe "cross-modification" of hardware-threaded machine code from user mode. On Intel processors, regular atomic writes to memory can be used to reliably modify machine-code instructions that fall entirely within a 16-byte aligned region of code memory—although instructions that span two such aligned memory regions cannot be updated atomically. The same holds true for AMD processors, except that only smaller, 8-byte code memory regions are supported. We confirmed these properties through both our experiments and also through a conservative reading of the relevant documentation [25, 28].

When instructions span these code memory alignment boundaries, they can still be modified without instruction-stream corruption, through a careful implementation and use of memory synchronization barriers. We crafted such a code-modification mechanism, and conservatively chose to always apply AMD's

- NEW must satisfy all NaCl safety verification constraints, as outlined in Section 2.
- Both NEW and OLD must start at the same address, be of equal size, and lie within a single code region.
- Any direct control-transfer instructions in NEW must target valid instruction boundaries in the same code region.
- NEW and OLD must start and end at instruction boundaries, and all instruction boundaries between must be identical.
- No pseudo instructions are added or removed. NEW may not introduce new pseudo instructions. All pseudo-instructions in OLD must occur in NEW and have identical guard instructions.

Table 2. Constraints imposed on runtime code modifications by our extended NaCl sandboxing, when machine code OLD is replaced with machine code NEW.

8-byte alignment constraints, which ensures our implementation executes correctly on both AMD and Intel processors.

The pseudo code in Figure 2 shows our mechanism for safe, atomic instruction replacement. One instruction is copied at a time. When possible, we copy an entire instruction with a single 8-byte, aligned write to memory, using a "fast path" modification sequence. This fast path performs a read-modify-write update of the 8-byte, aligned block of of memory around the old instruction. This block of code memory is read into a temporary variable, and the old instruction bytes within it are replaced with those of the new instruction; then the temporary variable is written using a single aligned 8-byte store to code memory.

The above fast path mechanism cannot be used if the old instruction straddles an 8-byte alignment boundary. In this case, our implementation works as shown in Figure 2: we modify the target instruction bytes in three steps, keeping a one-byte HLT as the first byte of the instruction while the instruction is being modified. We use serialization barriers to synchronize the instruction stream and view of code memory for all hardware threads, including other cores or processors [25, 28].

Considering all possible interleavings, it is easy to see why the above code allows a series of machine-code instructions to be atomically replaced with new, equal-size instructions:

- Before the first serialization barrier: The one-byte write will be atomic; a concurrent thread will execute either the original instruction or the HLT instruction.
- Between the serialization barriers: No threads can execute the target instruction without executing the HLT instruction encoded in its first byte.
- After the second serialization barrier: As the one-byte write will be atomic, other threads will execute either the new instruction or the HLT instruction.

Our technique relies on a serialization barrier primitive. The common approach on x86 processors is to use a serializing kernel-mode instruction (such as `cpuid`) on all hardware threads [25, 28], requiring execution of kernel-mode code. As NaCl sandboxing is user-mode only, we require a serialization barrier that can be triggered from user-mode. Conveniently, certain system calls serialize all processors as a side-effect. We used the `mprotect` system call, triggering inter-processor interrupts of remote hardware threads for a "TLB shoot-down", serializing all processors.

Finally, as mentioned previously, any execution of a HLT instruction will result in complete termination of all Native Client threads. Therefore, no thread may ever attempt to execute NaCl code memory while it is being updated: doing so may cause

```
// For an instruction pair OLDI and NEWI,
// with both instructions of size N-1 bytes.
//
if (diff of (OLDI, NEWI) lies in aligned qword)
{
  // Fast path: Read the aligned, 8-byte region
  // around OLDI, then update with NEWI bytes.
  //
  atomic aligned qword write to update OLDI;
}
else
{
  // Slow path: Three-part update sequence,
  // with two memory serialization barriers.
  //
  OLDI[0] = 0xf4;             /* HLT instruction */

  serialize();                /* barrier */

  OLDI[1:N] = NEWI[1:N];

  serialize();                /* barrier */

  OLDI[0] = NEWI[0];
}
```

Figure 2. Pseudo code for instruction replacement in the presence of untrusted concurrent hardware threads.

the thread to execute a HLT. Preventing concurrent execution and modification of the same code is the responsibility of the systems using our NaCl code-modification primitives. This is not an onerous duty: language runtimes should already be taking such measures to prevent instruction-stream corruption like that we have seen in our experiments.

3.5 Dynamic Code Deletion

NaCl executable memory comprises a set of code regions, and a dynamically-generated code region can be deleted to reclaim its executable memory. Thereby, executable memory can be reused for new machine code without the `nacl_dyncode_modify` constraint of preserving instruction boundaries.

Safety dictates that it must not be possible for a sleeping thread to wake up and find that it is executing in the middle of an instruction, because the executable memory at the thread's instruction-pointer address has been reused for a new NaCl code region. To prevent this, we utilize a thread "wind down" mechanism: we note all running threads, mark the code region for deletion, and do not allow the executable memory to be reused until we've confirmed that no thread is executing in the code region to be deleted. To confirm this is the case, we wait for each thread to invoke the trusted Native Client runtime. Being in the trusted runtime, we know a thread is not in the deleted region, and further, that any attempt to resume execution in the deleted region, while obviously incorrect, will also be safe with respect to instruction boundaries as it will target the aligned start of an instruction bundle.

Concretely, our code deletion mechanism will:

1. Ensure that the code region was created dynamically.
2. To ensure that no new threads enter the code region, write a HLT instruction at the start of each instruction bundle. Recall that NaCl computed control flow and returns always target the start of an instruction bundle.
3. Increment the *global generation number*, and record it in the *deletion generation* for the code region to be deleted.
4. As each thread makes a call to the trusted NaCl service runtime,

	LoC total	LoC added/changed
V8-32	190526	1972 (1.04%)
V8-64	189969	5005 (2.63%)
Mono-32	386300	2469 (0.64%)
Mono-64	388123	3240 (0.83%)

Table 3. Changed lines of code for NaCl ports of V8 and Mono.

update that thread's *thread generation number*.

5. The executable memory can be reused when all threads have a generation number greater than or equal to that of the deleted code region.

If only one thread is executing, then invoking our code deletion mechanism will immediately perform all of the above. With multiple threads, the first call to `nacl_dyncode_delete` will return an error code `EAGAIN`. Re-invoking the interface with the same arguments and seeing a success return code indicates deletion is complete. The non-blocking property of the `nacl_dyncode_delete` interface allows user threads to perform useful work, while waiting for executable memory to become reusable.

4. Experience Porting Language Runtimes

This section describes our experience porting both the V8 JavaScript engine [27] and the Mono Common Language Runtime [41] to run inside our extended NaCl sandbox. Each language platform makes use of JIT compilation and also makes use of dynamic code modification techniques. After providing background on each platform, we describe our porting experiences. Because the x86-32 and x86-64 JIT compilers are substantially different on both platforms, our work comprised porting and debugging four distinct JIT implementations.

Table 3 provides data about code modifications required for our sandboxed versions of V8 and Mono. Only about 1% or less of code required changes, evidence of the relative simplicity of adapting a JIT to support our language-independent sandboxing.

4.1 V8 JavaScript Engine

The V8 JavaScript engine [27] is used in the Chromium/Google Chrome Web browser, in the Web browser on Android phones, and in Palm WebOS. In addition to being JIT compiled, V8 achieves a large performance benefit from *inline caching*, a technique first introduced in an implementation of Smalltalk 80 [15]. Inline caches store object properties such as member offsets directly in the machine code of functions. The optimized machine code of each inline cache first checks that object properties haven't changed, invalidating the cache; then, in the common case, object members are accessed directly. Inline caches in V8 rely heavily on runtime machine-code modification, making V8 a good stress test for our language-independent sandboxing.

Inline caches are vital to the efficiency of the V8 engine, a motivation for our support of runtime code modification. Disabling V8 inline caches in an otherwise unmodified V8 x86-32 system induces a 12.22x slowdown on the V8 Benchmark Suite. With our sandboxing enabled, the slowdown is 14.08x. In both cases the positive impact of inline caching is an order of magnitude higher, on all platforms, than the slowdown induced by our language-independent sandboxing.

4.2 Mono Common Language Runtime

Mono [41] is an open source, cross-platform implementation of Microsoft's .NET Framework. Mono provides both an offline compiler that translates C# to Common Intermediate Language (CIL) bytecode and a JIT compiler that reduces CIL bytecode to a number of native targets including x86-32 and x86-64. Many languages, including Microsoft Managed C++ and VB.NET have CIL bytecode compilers. Mono also supports "Ahead-Of-Time" (AOT) compilation of CIL bytecode, a useful facility when JIT compilation is either not possible or not permitted.

4.3 Porting Experiences

A primary task in each of our four porting efforts was modifying the JIT compiler to emit code that would satisfy NaCl code safety verification. For this, only minimal, isolated modifications were required, because NaCl verification is based on checking local machine-code properties. We modified the instruction emission phase of each JIT to satisfy the NaCl alignment constraints and to emit NaCl pseudo instructions for memory references and indirect control flow, as required.

Another task arose from a fundamental constraint imposed by the Native Client platform: only machine-code instructions—and no data—may reside in the NaCl executable memory address range. We modified each of the four JITs to allocate their code, and only their code, in NaCl code regions. For V8, this required moving relocation records and other meta-data from executable memory into appropriate data segments. We implemented similar modifications for Mono, although in a few cases we worked around the constraint by embedding data as immediate constants in a non-executed, legal instruction. Such "data instructions" allow for the creation of code that uses instruction-relative positioning for data constants and still passes NaCl code safety verification. We constructed these data instructions by prefixing a push immediate opcode to the data that needed to be embedded in the code segment; the resulting push instruction is never executed at runtime.

A number of implementation challenges were specific to x86-64. The x86-64 implementation of Native Client uses the ILP32 data model, to facilitate source code portability between x86-32 and x86-64 sandboxes. This tends to conflict with the LP64 or LLP64 data models assumed by the x86-64 implementations of V8 and Mono. In particular, the language implementations assume that a pointer and a register are the same size, which is false in the x86-64 NaCl model. Our Mono and V8 ports took different approaches to resolving these issues. For Mono we introduced an explicit distinction between the register size and pointer size. This approach supports the Mono requirement for C-style structures that are accessed both from managed and unmanaged code. For V8, pointers occupy four bytes on the heap, as per the ILP32 model, but eight bytes on the stack. While this representation accommodates the fact that x86-64 does not support four-byte push or pop operations, it also requires numerous changes to code generation, resulting in a significant, albeit straightforward, engineering effort.

The ILP32 data model also interferes with the optimized representation of 32-bit integers in x86-64 V8. On x86-64, V8 encodes type information in the low-order bits of 64-bit registers to differentiate between immediate 32-bit integer values and pointers to boxed integer objects on the heap. For implementation expediency, we modified the x86-64 version of V8 to use the same integer representation as the x86-32 version. V8-32 uses the least-significant bit of a 32-bit word to differentiate immediate and pointers, storing integers larger than 31-bits as objects. This change also required us to reimplement some arithmetic operations. The difference in integer representations has performance implications for code that operates with large integer values, since they are stored as objects on the heap. This had a large impact on single benchmarks in the SunSpider100 benchmarks, as discussed in Section 5.

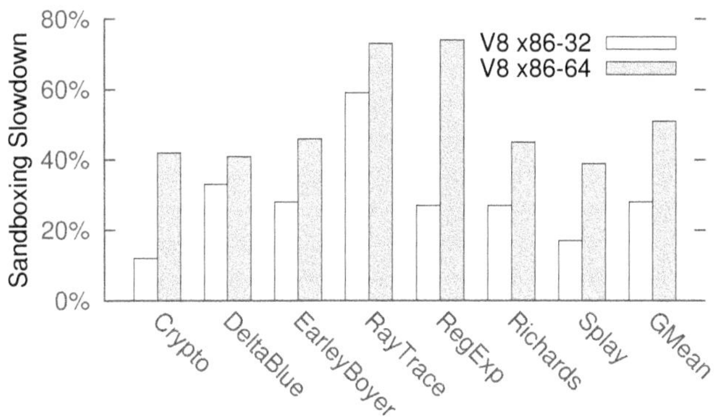

	x86-32	x86-64	x86-32	x86-64
Crypto	4380	4511	3910 (12%)	3176 (42%)
DeltaBlue	6555	5380	4921 (33%)	3825 (41%)
EarleyBoyer	20332	19370	15827 (28%)	13247 (46%)
RayTrace	9277	7979	5849 (59%)	4615 (73%)
RegExp	3367	3534	2660 (27%)	2035 (74%)
Richards	4911	4659	3864 (27%)	3217 (45%)
Splay	15305	14160	13098 (17%)	10188 (39%)
GMean	7528	7059	5868 (28%)	4683 (51%)

(a) Unsafe **(b)** Sandboxed

Figure 3. A chart of NaCl sandboxing slowdown (lower is better) for the V8 JavaScript Benchmark Suite, relative to unmodified V8. GMean is the geometric mean of the overheads of all benchmarks in the suite. Also shown is a table of the chart's underlying data: raw benchmark scores (where higher is better) for native and sandboxed execution, with sandboxing slowdown in parentheses.

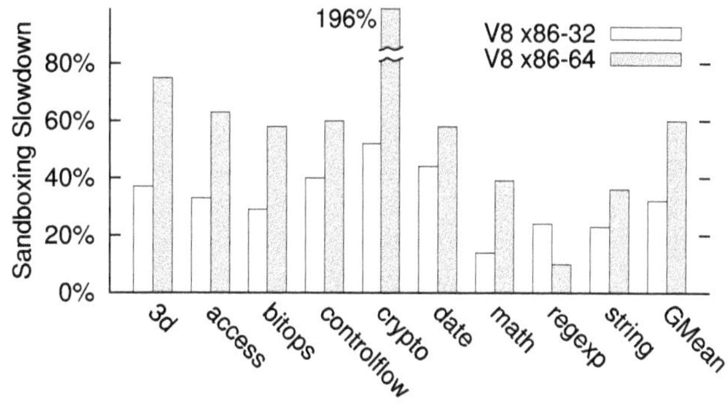

	x86-32	x86-64	x86-32	x86-64
3D	3097	3434	4230 (37%)	5996 (75%)
Access	2867	3248	3815 (33%)	5296 (63%)
BitOps	2240	2047	2892 (29%)	3235 (58%)
ControlFlow	179	199	250 (40%)	318 (60%)
Crypto	1193	857	1812 (52%)	2538 (196%)
Date	2060	2236	2970 (44%)	3541 (58%)
Math	2310	2374	2639 (14%)	3295 (39%)
RegExp	1097	957	1359 (24%)	1057 (10%)
String	5147	5269	6325 (23%)	7186 (36%)
GMean	1693	1676	2241 (32%)	2689 (60%)

(a) Unsafe **(b)** Sandboxed

Figure 4. A chart of NaCl sandboxing slowdown (lower is better) for the SunSpider100 JavaScript benchmarks, relative to unmodified V8. Each bar represents a group of up to four benchmarks. GMean is the geometric mean of all benchmark overheads. Also shown is a table of the chart's underlying data: raw benchmark scores (here, lower scores are better) for native and sandboxed execution, with sandboxing slowdown in parentheses.

5. Experimental Results and Optimizations

Results in this section are from a quad-core Intel Xeon X5550 Nehalem 2.67 GHz processor, except Table 6 as noted. Our test system ran Ubuntu 10.04, kernel version 2.6.32. Performance results are an average of 10 runs. The observed standard deviation ranged from 0 to 2.32%. We summarize performance measurements using the geometric mean [22].

Our implementation extends the latest, up-to-date version of Native Client, which, on x86-64, has added sandboxing of indirect memory reads, as well as writes. Therefore, it is not surprising that our extended NaCl sandboxing for x86-64 has higher measured overheads than those reported in [44].

5.1 Sandboxing Overhead for V8 JavaScript and Mono C#

Figures 3 and 4 show the overheads for our sandboxed version of V8 when running the V8 Benchmark Suite [27], version 6, and the SunSpider Benchmark Suite [50], version 0.9.1. The V8 Benchmark Suite is distributed with V8 and the SunSpider Benchmark Suite is distributed with WebKit. The SunSpider suite consists of very small microbenchmarks; therefore, we created and used a variant, SunSpider100, where each benchmark is run 100 times, instead of once, to facilitate more accurate timing and to emphasize steady state execution over startup delays. We measure overhead relative to the V8 2.2.19 development version that we forked to make our changes on June 21st, 2010.

In the V8 Benchmark Suite, RayTrace showed some of the largest overheads. We investigated the cause of this slowdown on V8-64 using PIN [31], a binary instrumentation tool, and pfmon [52], a performance monitoring tool based on hardware performance counters. Using PIN, we counted executed instructions for RayTrace, both with and without the sandbox. With NaCl sandboxing, RayTrace instruction counts on V8-64 grew to a factor of 1.8x. The largest contributor is NOP padding to align instruction bundles and CALL instructions, adding 39% of the new instructions. The second largest source of additional instructions is software guards for memory references, 38% of the total new instruction. The remaining new instructions came from other software guards and the Native Client runtime. To understand the impact of branch and cache behavior, we used pfmon to measure related hardware events during the RayTrace benchmark. NaCl sandboxing requires the use of a software-guarded indirect jump, instead of a RET instruction for function returns, which we thought would likely increase branch mispredictions. Indeed, we observed a 4x increase in the branch misprediction rate. Sandboxing also increased V8-64 instruction cache pressure, with 2x change in L1 instruction cache misses and 2x change in instruction TLB misses.

The SunSpider100 suite showed similar average performance overhead as the V8 Benchmark Suite, with 32% slowdown for sandboxed V8-32 and 60% for V8-64, as compared to unmodified V8. On x86-64, the crypto benchmarks were an outlier, with over twice the overhead of any other benchmark. The crypto benchmarks are composed of 3 smaller benchmarks: crypto-aes, with 1.8x slowdown; crypto-md5, with 5.0x slowdown; and crypto-sha1, with 3.9x slowdown. The second and third benchmarks depend heavily on 32-bit integer arithmetic operations, and implement these operations through nested use of very small functions, resulting in multiple function invocations per arithmetic operation. Therefore, for these benchmarks, branch misprediction on function returns must be a large source of overhead.

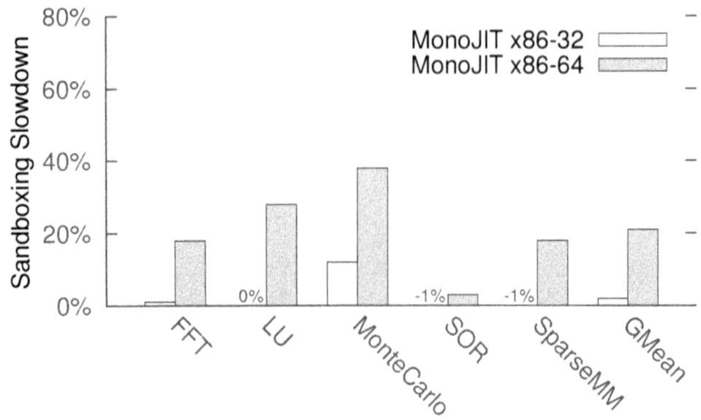

	x86-32	x86-64	x86-32		x86-64	
FFT	323	332	321	(1%)	281	(18%)
LU	668	763	665	(0%)	595	(28%)
MonteCarlo	109	126	97	(12%)	91	(38%)
SOR	886	892	893	(−1%)	863	(3%)
SparseMM	450	507	452	(−1%)	429	(18%)
GMean	393	429	384	(2%)	355	(21%)

(a) Unsafe **(b)** Sandboxed

Figure 5. A chart of NaCl sandboxing slowdown (lower is better) for the SciMark C# Benchmark Suite, relative to unmodified Mono JIT. GMean is a geometric mean of overheads of all benchmarks in the suite. Also shown is a table of the chart's underlying data: raw benchmark scores (where higher is better) for native and sandboxed execution, with sandboxing slowdown in parentheses.

However, the main source of overhead results from the change in representation described in Section 4.3: our V8-64 port uses the representation of small integers from V8-32, and therefore stores integers larger than 2^{31} as heap objects. We chose this implementation for expediency, without realizing its effects. As a result of our porting shortcut, half of the 32-bit arithmetic in the crypto benchmarks will involve boxed heap objects, instead of register values, and, compounding this overhead, NaCl sandboxing on x86-64 requires use of a software guard for each indirect access to heap memory. We could have supported the 64-bit integer representation used in V8-64, since Native Client allows safe use of handwritten machine code or assembly modules; we plan to do so in a future version of our V8-64 port.

Turning to Mono, Figure 5 shows our NaCl sandbox overhead for the SciMark C# Benchmark Suite. For x86-32 the mean overhead was only 2%, while for x86-64 the overhead was 21%. Overheads were higher on x86-64 because of the additional software guards required for NaCl sandboxing of loads and stores. The largest overheads were for the MonteCarlo benchmark, whose kernel uses a tight inner loop that calls two small functions, resulting in NOP padding and branch misprediction overheads. While we haven't yet studied all original causes of this slowdown, we note it is consistent with measured performance of the x86-64 NaCl sandbox for C and C++ benchmarks [44].

5.2 Analysis of the Sources of Sandboxing Overhead

Table 4 shows the estimated breakdown of sandboxing overhead for the V8 Benchmark Suite. This table was generated by disabling NaCl sandboxing features one at a time. Since the performance impact of these different changes may not be independent, this breakdown serves only as an estimate. The largest estimated slowdown is from NOPs inserted for `CALL` and instruction bundle alignment. We estimate that fetch and execution penalties from

Source of overhead	V8-32	V8-64
NOP padding to align bundles	4%	16%
NOP padding to align calls	19%	21%
Software guards for function returns	25%	22%
Software guards for indirect jumps and indirect memory accesses[1]	17%	24%
Runtime validation of code modifications	2%	5%

[1] Indirect memory accesses require software guards only on x86-64.

Table 4. Analysis of the sources of NaCl sandboxing slowdown, measured using the V8 Benchmark Suite (Figure 3). These measurements were generated by disabling NaCl sandboxing features one at a time. Since the performance impact of these features is not independent, these overheads are not additive.

these NOPs cause about half of the total slowdown. Return address masking is the next largest source of slowdown. NaCl sandboxing requires replacing `RET` instructions with a `POP/JMP` sequence. This interferes with the return address prediction hardware in modern processors. Other overheads (not listed) include invocations of the trusted Native Client runtime, slower dynamic code generation, copies required to modify code, and object layout changes required to separate code and code-meta-data. These overheads are small compared to those listed in Table 4.

5.3 Comparing Sandboxing and Language Overheads

Past, published measurements of SFI-based sandboxing slowdown have considered only fully-optimized, ahead-of-time compiled versions of C and C++ benchmarks like SPEC [20, 44, 46, 56]. However, the SciMark Benchmark Suite includes C as well as C# implementations of its benchmarks. This allows us to examine one data point for the relative cost of sandboxing native code vs. JIT compiled code in a modern language runtime. To facilitate this examination, we measured single-threaded SciMark execution, since its C variant runs only single threaded.

Table 5 examines the performance of three variations of SciMark, for both x86-32 and x86-64, executing both with and without NaCl sandboxing. Native is the original C implementation of SciMark; Mono AOT is the C# port, compiled ahead of time and without dynamic code modification; last, Mono JIT is the C# port, executed using JIT compilation. For x86-32, the NaCl sandboxing slowdown ranges from 0 to 5%, for all implementations. For x86-64, the slowdown ranges from 13% to 48%, and is lower for the C# implementations than for C. Despite the higher relative sandboxing overhead, the absolute performance is significantly better for the C implementation. On x86-32, our language-independent sandboxing of Mono has comparable relative overhead to that of conventionally compiled C and C++ under Native Client [56]. For NaCl sandboxed Mono-64, performance of benchmarks such as `LU` and `SparseMM` is also consistent with NaCl overheads for other benchmarks whose execution time is sensitive to path length and branch prediction effects [44].

Notably, the JIT version of the C# port is actually faster than the AOT version, especially on 64-bit platforms. The JIT compiler has knowledge of the locations of most of the data and code in the program when it compiles a method. This allows it to embed direct calls and data references to these locations in the emitted code. It can further optimize the code by backpatching existing calls to new code as it is generated. By contrast the AOT compiler uses indirection techniques such as tables of pointers, resulting in slower execution. This JIT advantage still holds in the sandboxed environment, even if offset slightly by the extra cost of NaCl safety

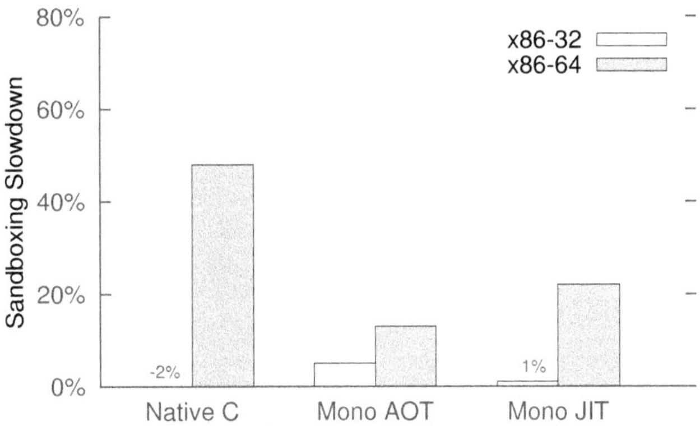

	x86-32	x86-64	x86-32	x86-64
Native (C)	717	868	729 (-2%)	586 (48%)
Mono AOT	383	360	365 (5%)	318 (13%)
Mono JIT	388	426	383 (1%)	350 (22%)

(a) Unsafe **(b)** Sandboxed

Table 5. Performance of SciMark C/C# Benchmark Suite compiled from native C code, with gcc 4.4.3, or with the Mono AOT and JIT compilers for C#. Benchmarks were executed natively and on the unmodified Mono CLR (Unsafe), as well as with NaCl sandboxing. Numbers show benchmark scores, in megaflops (higher is better), and also the NaCl sandboxing slowdown, as a percentage (in parentheses).

constraints.

Overall, these measurements suggest that the relative cost of language-independent NaCl sandboxing can be small compared to the overhead of a dynamic language runtime. The performance difference between the C and Mono benchmarks can be seen as the cost of using a managed-language framework. For the native, unsafe benchmark executions, the cost of executing with Mono ranges from 84% to 141% overhead, while that overhead ranges from 67% to 99% under sandboxed execution.

5.4 NOP Optimizations

We were motivated to optimize the execution of NOP padding, because it is the single largest contributor to overall NaCl sandboxing overhead. To our surprise, we found that choice of NOP padding sequences had a large impact on performance, even when the chosen NOPs were never executed at runtime. For the V8 Benchmark Suite on x86-32, different NOP padding choices reduced sandboxing overheads from a factor of 1.62x to 1.28x.

Figure 6 shows a sampling of the search space of possible NOP paddings and the resulting performance on the V8 benchmark suite. It shows three different strategies for generating NOPs:

- *Shortest NOPs* generates long sequences of the single-byte NOP instruction (`0x90`).
- *Longest NOPs* uses a greedy algorithm to generate the longest NOP instructions allowed. (Using the prefix/addressing mode variations of the `0x0f1f` multi-byte NOP opcode listed in the AMD64 Optimization Guide [24].)
- *Optimized NOPs* uses a lookup table containing optimized NOP sequences from 1 to 31 bytes in length. The table was generated automatically, in about one minute, using a microbenchmark that exhaustively searches the space of different combinations of instructions that have no effect. The individual NOP instructions are drawn from the many different inert variations of the NOP, XCHG, MOV, and LEA opcodes, using different registers and addressing modes.

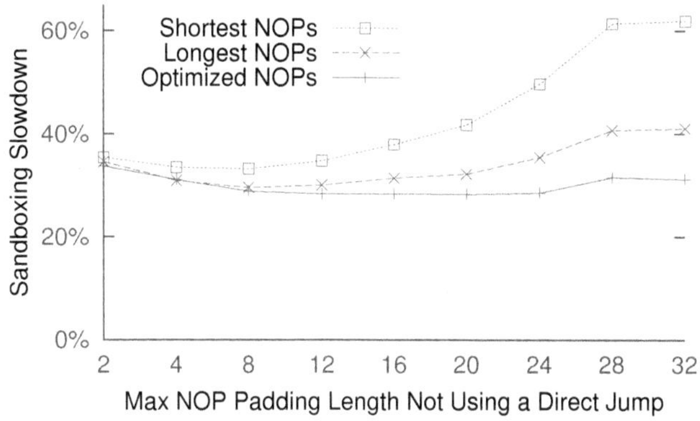

Figure 6. Sandboxing slowdown (lower is better) for different strategies of generating NOP padding for NaCl instruction alignment. The slowdown is measured from the overall GMean of the V8 Benchmark Suite executing on x86-32.

Looking at the tables generated for optimized NOPs, the trend is that variety improves performance: NOP padding sequences that vary the opcodes and registers between all the different NOPs execute much faster than NOP padding sequences that are more homogeneous, e.g., repeating the same instruction over and over. The fastest measured NOP sequences tend to contain one NOP of each possible type. This is possibly a result of more possibilities for instruction level parallelism when a mix of different NOP types is issued on modern microarchitectures.

For long NOP padding, the fastest NOP sequences contain a direct jump instruction that jumps to the end of the padding. Somewhat surprisingly, the choice of the unexecuted NOP instructions immediately after the direct jump has an effect on performance, despite being unreachable. We observed, on different architectures, between a 1.5% and a 1.8% slowdown when we changed these unreachable NOP instructions from optimized sequences of NOPs to sequences of the shortest, single-byte NOPs. We assume that those unexecuted NOP instructions impact some microarchitectural bottleneck in instruction fetching and decoding.

NOP padding performance will vary with microarchitecture, but optimized tables can be generated on each platform. Figure 6 shows the performance effects of different choices for directly jumping to the end of NOP padding sequences on the overall score of the V8 benchmark suite. The left side of the graph ("2" on the x-axis) shows V8-32 performance measured when all NOP padding sequences start with a direct jump (that jump occupies two bytes). The right side of the graph ("32" on the x-axis) shows performance when NOP padding never starts with a direct jump. Notably, starting with a direct jump is not the fastest strategy for all NOP padding lengths. For the optimized NOP selection strategy, a direct jump is faster only when NOP padding is longer than about 24 bytes.

A related optimization is to avoid execution of padding before a CALL instruction by using an explicit PUSH of the would-be return address followed by a JMP to the function entrypoint address. This optimization replaces a call of the form

```
...padding...
call FOO
```

with the sequence

	x86-32	x86-64	x86-32	x86-64
Intel Xeon X5550 Nehalem 2.7GHz	7528	7059	5869 (28%)	4683 (51%)
Intel Core2 Quad Q6600 2.4GHz	5612	5128	4535 (24%)	3296 (56%)
AMD Phenom II X4 905E 2.5GHz	5030	4793	4026 (25%)	3390 (41%)
AMD Athlon 4450E 2.3GHz	3853	3447	2856 (35%)	2385 (45%)
AMD Opteron 8214 HE 2.2GHz	3633	3224	2701 (35%)	2226 (45%)
Intel Atom N450 1.7GHz	1395	1176	1041 (34%)	589 (100%)
	(a) Unsafe		(b) Sandboxed	

Table 6. Performance scores (higher is better) on different microarchitectures for the V8 Benchmark Suite running natively (Unsafe) and in our language-independent sandbox. Sandboxing slowdown is shown in in parentheses.

```
push retloc
jmp FOO
...padding...
retloc:
```

avoiding the need to execute the padding NOPs. This optimization provides modest performance gains, of about 3 percent, and is included in the measurements of Figure 6. Similar to direct jumps over padding, this technique provides largest benefit when only applied when skipping NOP padding sequences of length 20 bytes or more.

5.5 Overhead Variability between CPU Architectures

Table 6 compares the overhead of our language-independent sandboxing when running V8 benchmarks on several modern processors, implementing different microarchitectures. For V8 on x86-32 overheads are consistent, ranging from 28% to 34%. For x86-64 overheads range from 41% to 56%, and the numbers seem to suggest consistently less relative overhead on AMD processors than on the fast Intel processors. The Intel Atom is a notable outlier, with 100% sandboxing slowdown measured for V8-64. While we haven't yet fully explored the Atom's outlier performance, we note that these results match those previously reported for the x86-64 NaCl sandbox [44]. Interestingly, raw performance is better on x86-32 for both the unsafe and sandboxed versions, most likely because V8 has been more heavily optimized for x86-32.

5.6 Application to the new Crankshaft V8

Concurrently to our efforts described so far in porting a fork of the V8 code base to Native Client, the developers of V8 substantially extended the V8 JavaScript platform to use highly-dynamic, profile-driven optimizations. This "Crankshaft" version of V8 has since been released as part of the Chrome Web browser for the x86-32 architecture [34]. Crankshaft greatly improves the performance of V8, through use of SSA-based optimizations, loop-invariant code motion, better register allocation, and function inlining. Also, Crankshaft allows fast, unboxed use of all small integers less than 2^{32} (cf. the old V8, as discussed on page 6).

To gain further insights into the applicability of our work, we ported the x86-32 Crankshaft V8 (version 3.1.4) to use our code-modification primitives. We were pleased to see that our existing NaCl sandboxing port was insensitive to the higher-level changes to V8, such as the mechanisms for SSA-based optimizations. Also, the low-level x86-32 code-emission in the V8 backend remained mostly unchanged, allowing us to reuse a majority of our earlier porting work. All in all, we modified 3,483 lines in the x86-32 Crankshaft V8 codebase (cf. Table 3).

We also made two small tweaks to our port, to tune Crankshaft's mechanisms to the characteristics of the NaCl sandbox. First, we increased the threshold for the function-invocation count at which Crankshaft will specialize a function to its arguments and modify the function's code. Thus, we reduced code modification rates to account for the increased cost of code modification (V8 is tuned for faster, single threaded code modification). Second, we saw that a lot of NOP padding was needed to align indirect jump targets in the middle of the code for general-purpose functions; specialized functions jump to this code if they detect that their specialization does not apply. To avoid the NOP overhead, we used a small table of direct-jump trampolines, placed after the general-purpose function code, to implement these calls.

We re-ran the benchmarking experiments on both versions of our NaCl port of the Crankshaft V8 platform. The results can be seen in Figure 7. After tuning, the absolute performance of the NaCl sandboxed Crankshaft language runtime beats that of the *unmodified, unsafe* x86-32 V8 version we used previously (see Figure 3). It is particularly gratifying that in a span of a few months, the original overhead of our language-independent sandboxing has been more than offset by the independent optimization of the language runtime.

As Figure 7 shows, the relative overhead of NaCl sandboxing is also reduced by almost a third, going from 28% to 19% for the tuned Crankshaft benchmarks. We believe this decrease in relative overhead is primarily due to Crankshaft's function inlining, which reduces both NaCl NOP padding as well as function-return branch mispredictions. The SunSpider100 benchmarks exhibited a similar absolute performance improvement, and also saw sandboxing slowdown fall from 32% to 24%.

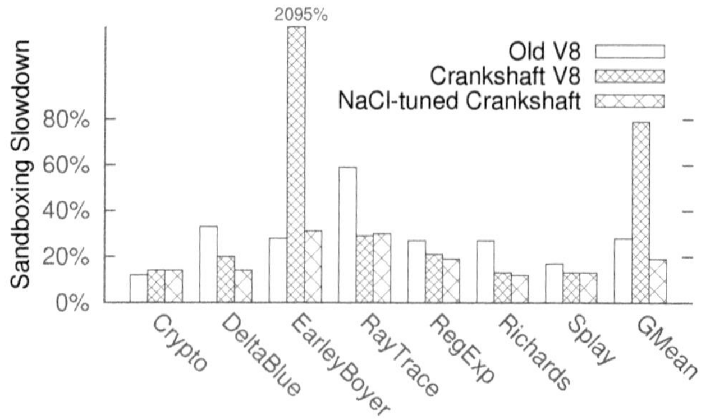

	Old V8	Crankshaft	Crankshaft′
Crypto	3910 (12%)	12521 (14%)	12583 (14%)
DeltaBlue	4921 (33%)	13718 (20%)	14413 (14%)
EarleyBoyer	15827 (28%)	1030 (2095%)	17294 (31%)
RayTrace	5849 (59%)	8923 (29%)	8908 (30%)
RegExp	2660 (27%)	2274 (21%)	2298 (19%)
Richards	3864 (27%)	10862 (13%)	10955 (12%)
Splay	13098 (17%)	3704 (13%)	3699 (13%)
GMean	5868 (28%)	5459 (79%)	8250 (19%)

Figure 7. A chart showing NaCl sandboxing slowdown (lower is better) for the old V8 and Crankshaft V8 platforms running the V8 JavaScript Benchmark Suite. A table of the chart's underlying raw benchmark scores (where higher is better) for NaCl sandboxed execution, with sandboxing slowdown in parentheses. Crankshaft′ denotes the NaCl-tuned version of Crankshaft.

6. Discussion and Related Work

In this paper, we have presented our techniques for safe runtime code generation and modification using the terminology of the Native Client platform upon which our implementation is based. Even so, we are confident that our techniques apply more widely. In particular, we believe that the safety constraints of Table 2 could be easily reformulated for other SFI-based platforms (e.g., XFI [20]), and still provide the immutability guarantees necessary for safe runtime code modification. Our confidence derives from the fundamental basis of our work, which lies not in NaCl-specific properties, but in the use of local code inspection to inductively establish global execution invariants—a common characteristic of many execution monitoring mechanisms.

Our experience porting JIT-based runtime platforms to our language-independent sandbox suggest that it is possible to combine SFI-based sandboxing with dynamic code generation, yielding a system that combines benefits from both techniques. Although the performance impact of sandboxing is not negligible, we believe the resulting system is still viable for a large set of practical use cases, especially considering that some of the relevant languages are still commonly implemented with interpreters. Some will argue that a JIT-based language runtime is safe enough without an SFI sandbox. We note that the verity of this statement relies on the quality of the language implementation, including the language runtime and any extensions.

In all cases, it can be expected that a fully-featured, advanced language runtime will comprise a significant amount of complex, trusted code—even when legacy libraries are *not* considered. Note the total line counts for V8 and Mono in Table 3. Furthermore, in cases where a language implementation is used as a scripting engine for a larger system, such as a Web browser, it is often desirable to sandbox the entire composed system [4, 42].

Like Native Client and other SFI-based mechanisms, our language-independent sandboxing is designed to provide high-assurance guarantees of clearly-defined safety properties, even in the face of malicious software crafted by an adaptive attacker. In comparison, many other software protection systems—such as Nooks [51], to name just one—provide a weaker form of safety by making only a best-effort attempt at containing faults.

Many software protection systems have been implemented using a combination of static analysis of machine code and inline, machine-code software guards that perform runtime checks or sandboxing operations. The first use of these techniques may have been in the late 60's, to allow the kernel execution of untrusted code in a profiling system for the SDS-940 [14]. Since then, these techniques have been used in the original work on SFI [53], subsequent SFI implementations such as MiSFIT [46], SASI x86 [18], XFI [20], and PittSFIeld [32], and in a number of other systems. Compared to Native Client, some of these systems offer finer-granularity safety guarantees for certain aspects of software execution—albeit typically at the cost of higher enforcement overhead. For example, CFI [1] can guarantee that machine-code execution follows a permitted control-flow graph, XFI [20] can enforce integrity properties for the runtime stack, and DFI [11] and its successors like BGI [12] can maintain data-flow integrity properties for even values in heap memory. However, it remains unclear if the techniques of these systems can be used to implement a production-quality, practical execution platform like Native Client, that is portable across both operating systems and hardware architectures with good performance. Furthermore, we know of no such system that provides safety guarantees in the face of runtime code generation and modification.

Programming languages and runtime software mechanisms are recognized as an effective approach to providing safety guarantees and enforcing security policies. Software isolation on the Burroughs B-5000 system depended on applications being written in the Algol high-level language [5] and a similar approach has been taken in later, experimental operating systems such as SPIN [7].

Commonly, language-based isolation is enforced through execution on top of a virtual machine, which is implemented using a trusted compiler or interpreter, and typically makes use of extensive libraries of trusted support routines based on (legacy) native code [45]. In comparison, approaches like Typed Assembly Language (TAL) [35] and Proof-Carrying Code (PCC) [37] provide guarantees about the machine code that is executed on actual hardware machines. SFI, like TAL and PCC, has the attractive characteristic of allowing independent, static safety verification of the machine code to be executed; this not only decouples the execution platform from the language toolchain, but also reduces the size of the trusted computing base [40].

A long line of research aims to preserve the semantic properties of high-level programming languages through translation to lower-level languages. Typed assembly language derives from this field and, in that context, Smith et al. have considered restricted forms of runtime code generation [47]. Recently, this field has seen great progress, starting with Xavier Leroy's work on certifying compilation from C-like languages to PowerPC machine code with full, formal proofs of semantic preservation. This work has been extended to handle incremental runtime code generation, and even self-modifying code, first by Cai et al. [8] and then, most recently, by Magnus O. Myrren [36]—in this later work formally certifying the correctness of a JIT compiler from a small bytecode language to x86 machine code. Our mechanisms also give strong safety guarantees and use techniques amenable to formal verification [32]. However, our language-independent sandboxing does not aim to preserve high-level language semantics, and the implementation of our mechanisms is unencumbered by those semantics.

7. Conclusions

Through use of language-independent, software-based fault isolation, it is possible to safely and efficiently sandbox programs that make use of self-modifying machine code. It suffices to extend traditional SFI techniques with a few new features, including new safety constraints that apply inductively on the structure of machine code, even across code modification. These new safety features are not difficult to implement in practice, e.g., as part of Native Client, an existing, production-quality SFI-based sandboxing platform. It is also rather straightforward to port V8 and Mono, two disparate, modern JIT-compiled languages, to run within a thus extended sandboxing platform. Such language-independent sandboxing holds the promise of facilitating the deployment of new language and technology options for the development of untrusted software, in particular, on the Web.

Acknowledgments

We thank Seth Abraham and Richard Winterton at Intel for their helpful discussions about Intel processor behavior in the presence of cross modifying code.

References

[1] Martín Abadi, Mihai Budiu, Úlfar Erlingsson, and Jay Ligatti. Control-Flow Integrity: Principles, implementations, and applications. *TISSEC*, 2009.

[2] Matthew Arnold and Barbara G. Ryder. A framework for reducing the cost of instrumented code. In *PLDI*, 2001.

[3] John Aycock. A brief history of just-in-time. *CSUR*, 2003.

[4] A. Barth, C. Jackson, C. Reis, and Google Chrome Team. The security architecture of the chromium browser. Technical report, Stanford

University, 2008. URL http://crypto.stanford.edu/websec/chromium/chromium-security-architecture.pdf.

[5] R. S. Barton. A new approach to the functional design of a digital computer. In *IRE-AIEE-ACM (Western)*, 1961.

[6] Mark Barwinski, Cynthia Irvine, and Tim Levin. Empirical study of drive-by-download spyware. Technical report, Naval Postgraduate School, 2006.

[7] B. N. Bershad, S. Savage, P. Pardyak, E. G. Sirer, M. E. Fiuczynski, D. Becker, C. Chambers, and S. Eggers. Extensibility safety and performance in the spin operating system. In *SOSP*, 1995.

[8] Hongxu Cai, Zhong Shao, and Alexander Vaynberg. Certified self-modifying code. In *Proc. PLDI '07*, 2007.

[9] Benjamin Canou, Vincent Balat, and Emmanuel Chailloux. O'Browser: Objective Caml on browsers. In *Workshop on ML*, 2008.

[10] Bryan M. Cantrill, Michael W. Shapiro, and Adam H. Leventhal. Dynamic instrumentation of production systems. In *ATC*, 2004.

[11] Miguel Castro, Manuel Costa, and Tim Harris. Securing software by enforcing data-flow integrity. In *OSDI*, 2006.

[12] Miguel Castro, Manuel Costa, Jean-Philippe Martin, Marcus Peinado, Periklis Akritidis, Austin Donnelly, Paul Barham, and Richard Black. Fast byte-granularity software fault isolation. In *SOSP*, 2009.

[13] Blazakis D. Interpreter exploitation: Pointer inference and JIT spraying. In *Black Hat DC*, 2010.

[14] P. Deutsch and C. A. Grant. A flexible measurement tool for software systems. In *IFIP*, 1971.

[15] Peter Deutsch and Allan Schiffman. Efficient implementation of the Smalltalk-80 system. In *POPL*, 1984.

[16] ECMA, 2001. URL http://www.ecma-international.org/publications/files/ECMA-ST/Ecma-327.pdf.

[17] Manuel Egele, Engin Kirda, and Christopher Kruegel. Mitigating drive-by download attacks: Challenges and open problems. In *iNetSec 2009 Open Research Problems in Network Security*, 2009.

[18] Ú. Erlingsson and Fred B. Schneider. SASI enforcement of security policies: A retrospective. In *NSPW*, 1999.

[19] Úlfar Erlingsson. High-performance binary applets, 1997. URL http://www.cs.cornell.edu/home/ulfar/cuba/paper.

[20] Úlfar Erlingsson, Martín Abadi, Michael Vrable, Mihai Budiu, and George C. Necula. Xfi: software guards for system address spaces. In *OSDI*, 2006.

[21] M. Anton Ertl, David Gregg, Andreas Krall, and Bernd Paysan. Vmgen: a generator of efficient virtual machine interpreters. *Software: Practice and Experience*, 2002.

[22] Philip J. Fleming and John J. Wallace. How not to lie with statistics: the correct way to summarize benchmark results. *CACM*, 1986.

[23] Jonathon T. Giffin, Mihai Christodorescu, and Louis Kruger. Strengthening software self-checksumming via self-modifying code. In *ACSAC*, 2005.

[24] Advance Micro Devices Inc. *Software Optimization Guide for AMD64 Processors*, 2005.

[25] Advance Micro Devices Inc. *AMD64 Architecture Programmers Manual Volume 1: Application Programming*, 2009.

[26] Google Inc. Google web toolkit, . URL http://code.google.com/webtoolkit.

[27] Google Inc. The V8 JavaScript engine, . URL http://code.google.com/p/v8.

[28] Intel Inc. *Intel 64 and IA-32 Architectures Software Developers Manual Volume 3A: System Programming Guide, Part 1*, 2010.

[29] Yuichiro Kanzaki, Akito Monden, Masahide Nakamura, and Ken-ichi Matsumoto. Exploiting self-modification mechanism for program protection. In *COMPSAC*, 2003.

[30] T. Lindholm and F Yellin. *The Java Virtual Machine Specification*. Addison-Wesley, 1996.

[31] Chi-Keung Luk, Robert Cohn, Robert Muth, Harish Patil, Artur Klauser, Geoff Lowney, Steven Wallace, Vijay Janapa Reddi, and Kim Hazelwood. Pin: building customized program analysis tools with dynamic instrumentation. In *PLDI*, 2005.

[32] S. McCamant and G. Morrisett. Evaluating SFI for a CISC architecture. In *Usenix Security*, 2006.

[33] John McCarthy. Recursive functions of symbolic expressions and their computation by machine, part i. *CACM*, 1960.

[34] Kevin Millikin and Florian Schneider, 2010. URL http://blog.chromium.org/2010/12/new-crankshaft-for-v8.html.

[35] G. Morrisett, D. Walker, K. Crary, and N. Glew. From System F to typed assembly language. In *POPL*, 1998.

[36] Magnus O. Myreen. Verified just-in-time compiler on x86. In *Proc. of POPL'10*, 2010.

[37] George C. Necula. Proof-carrying code. In *Proc. of POPL'97*, 1997.

[38] James Newsome and Dawn Song. Dynamic taint analysis for automatic detection, analysis, and signature generation of exploits on commodity software. In *NDSS*, 2005.

[39] Thi Viet Nga Nguyen and François Irigoin. Efficient and effective array bound checking. *TOPLAS*, 2005.

[40] Department of Defense. Trusted computer system evaluation criteria (orange book), 1985.

[41] The Mono Project. The Mono language runtime. URL http://www.mono-project.com.

[42] Charles Reis and Steven D. Gribble. Isolating web programs in modern browser architectures. In *Proc. 4th ACM European conf. on Computer systems*, EuroSys '09, pages 219–232, New York, NY, USA, 2009. ACM. doi: http://doi.acm.org/10.1145/1519065.1519090.

[43] Theodore H. Romer, Dennis Lee, Geoffrey M. Voelker, Alec Wolman, Wayne A. Wong, Jean-Loup Baer, Brian N. Bershad, and Henry M. Levy. The structure and performance of interpreters. In *ASPLOS*, 1996.

[44] David Sehr, Robert Muth, Cliff Biffle, Victor Khimenko, Egor Pasko, Karl Schimpf, Bennet Yee, and Brad Chen. Adapting software fault isolation to contemporary cpu architectures. In *USENIX Security*, 2010.

[45] Joseph Siefers, Gang Tan, and Greg Morrisett. Robusta: taming the native beast of the jvm. In *CCS*, 2010.

[46] C. Small and M. I. Seltzer. MiSFIT: Constructing safe extensible systems. *IEEE Concurrency: Parallel, Distributed and Mobile Computing*, 1998.

[47] Fred Smith, Dan Grossman, Greg Morrisett, Luke Hornoff, and Trevor Jim. Compiling for template-based runtime code generation. *J. of Functional Programming*, 13(3), 2003.

[48] Michael F. Spear. Lightweight, robust adaptivity for software transactional memory. In *SPAA*, 2010.

[49] Vijay Sundaresan, Daryl Maier, Pramod Ramarao, and Mark Stoodley. Experiences with multi-threading and dynamic class loading in a java just-in-time compiler. In *CGO*, 2006.

[50] SunSpider Benchmark Suite. URL http://www2.webkit.org/perf/sunspider/sunspider.html.

[51] Michael M. Swift, Brian N. Bershad, and Henry M. Levy. Improving the reliability of commodity operating systems. *TOCS*, 2005.

[52] The perfmon2 hardware-based performance monitoring interface for Linux. URL http://perfmon2.sourceforge.net.

[53] Robert Wahbe, Steven Lucco, Thomas E. Anderson, and Susan L. Graham. Efficient software-based fault isolation. In *SOSP*, 1993.

[54] Robert Watson, Jonathan Anderson, Ben Laurie, and Kris Kennaway. Capsicum: practical capabilities for unix. In *USENIX Security*, 2010.

[55] Tao Wei, Tielei Wang, Lei Duan, and Jing Luo. Secure dynamic code generation against spraying. In *CCS*, 2010.

[56] Bennet Yee, David Sehr, Gregory Dardyk, J. Bradley Chen, Robert Muth, Tavis Orm, Shiki Okasaka, Neha Narula, and Nicholas Fullagar. Native Client: A sandbox for portable, untrusted x86 native code. In *IEEE Symposium on Security and Privacy*, 2009.

Cruiser: Concurrent Heap Buffer Overflow Monitoring Using Lock-free Data Structures

Qiang Zeng
Department of Computer Science & Engineering, Pennsylvania State University, University Park, PA 16802
quz105@cse.psu.edu

Dinghao Wu
College of Information Sciences & Technology, Pennsylvania State University, University Park, PA 16802
dwu@ist.psu.edu

Peng Liu
College of Information Sciences & Technology, Pennsylvania State University, University Park, PA 16802
pliu@ist.psu.edu

Abstract

Security enforcement inlined into user threads often delays the protected programs; inlined resource reclamation may interrupt program execution and defer resource release. We propose *software cruising*, a novel technique that migrates security enforcement and resource reclamation from user threads to a concurrent monitor thread. The technique leverages the increasingly popular multicore and multiprocessor architectures and uses *lock-free* data structures to achieve *non-blocking* and efficient synchronization between the monitor and user threads. As a case study, software cruising is applied to the heap buffer overflow problem. Previous mitigation and detection techniques for this problem suffer from high performance overhead, legacy code compatibility, semantics loyalty, or tedious manual program transformation. We present a concurrent heap buffer overflow detector, CRUISER, in which a concurrent thread is added to the user program to monitor heap integrity, and custom lock-free data structures and algorithms are designed to achieve high efficiency and scalability. The experiments show that our approach is practical: it imposes an average of 5% performance overhead on SPEC CPU2006, and the throughput slowdown on Apache is negligible on average.

Categories and Subject Descriptors D.2.4 [*Software Engineering*]: Software/Program Verification; D.2.5 [*Software Engineering*]: Testing and Debugging; D.1.3 [*Programming Techniques*]: Concurrent Programming

General Terms Security, Verification, Languages, Algorithms

Keywords Software cruising, buffer overflow, program monitor, multicore, concurrency, lock-free, non-blocking algorithms

1. Introduction

Despite extensive research over the past few decades, buffer overflow remains as one of the top software vulnerabilities. In 2009, 39% of the security vulnerabilities published by US-CERT [67] were related to buffer overflows. As of September 2010, 12 of the 20 most severe vulnerabilities ranked by US-CERT were buffer overflow related. Vulnerabilities listed by security websites such as SecurityFocus [60] and Securiteam [54] manifest a similar pattern. The related exploits, such as CodeRed [10] and SQLSlammer [12], have inflicted billions of dollars worth of damages [38].

A buffer overflow occurs when a program, while writing data to a buffer, overruns the buffer's boundary and overwrites adjacent memory. There are mainly two types of buffer overflows according to the overflowed buffer's memory region, namely stack-based buffer overflows and heap-based buffer overflows.

Stack-based buffer overflows are the most exploited vulnerability, as the return addresses for function calls are stored together with buffers on stack. By overflowing a local buffer, the return address can be overwritten so that, when the function returns, the control flow is redirected to execute malicious code, which is called "stack smashing" [3]. Other forms of stack-based buffer overflow attacks overwrite frame pointers and local variables, e.g. function pointers, to affect program behaviors [8, 50]. Many countermeasures against stack-based buffer overflow attacks have been devised, such as StackGuard [17], StackShield [64], Non-executable stack [63] and Libsafe [66], some of which have been widely deployed.

Exploitation of a heap-based buffer overflow is similar to that of a stack-based buffer overflow, except for that there are no return addresses or frame pointers on heap. For some widely deployed memory allocators, such as Doug Lea's malloc [36] for the glibc library, altering memory management information to achieve arbitrary memory overwrites is a general way to exploit a heap-based buffer overflow [11, 33]. More recently non-control data based exploits [12, 13, 15], by means of tampering the content of a memory block adjacent to the overflowed buffer, have been increasing.

As stack-based buffer overflow attacks are better understood and defended, heap-based buffer overflows have gained growing attention of attackers. According to the National Vulnerability Database [43], 177 heap-based buffer overflow vulnerabilities were published in 2009. As of September 2010, 287 heap-based buffer overflow vulnerabilities had been published in that year. Related exploits have affected widely deployed programs [11, 12].

Current buffer overflow detectors can be roughly classified into two categories: static and dynamic approaches. Static analysis tools usually have high false alarm rates; dynamic buffer overflow detectors can provide precise detection and generally there can be no false alarms [71]. However few dynamic heap buffer overflow detectors are widely deployed due to one or more of the following reasons: (1) Most countermeasures result in high performance overhead [1, 5, 9, 22, 27, 34, 52, 68]; (2) Some only protect specific libc functions [5, 19]; (3) A few of them only work with specific memory allocators [2, 19]; (4) Many require source code for recompilation [1, 4, 9, 31, 34, 42, 52]; (5) Some are incompatible with legacy code [4, 31, 42]; and (6) Some require special platforms or hardware supports that are rarely available [1, 34].

PLDI'11, June 4–8, 2011, San Jose, California, USA.

In this paper, we present Cruiser—a novel dynamic heap buffer overflow detector which does not have those limitations. The key ideas are (1) to create a dedicated monitor thread, which runs concurrently with user threads to *cruise* over, or keep checking, dynamically allocated buffers against buffer overflows; and (2) to utilize lock-free data structures and non-blocking algorithms, through which user threads communicate with the monitor thread with minimum overhead and without being blocked. Buffer addresses are collected in a lock-free data structure efficiently without blocking user threads. By traversing the data structure, buffers on heap are under constant surveillance of the concurrent monitor thread. Each dynamically allocated buffer is surrounded by two canary words; as long as a canary is found corrupted, a buffer overflow is detected.

Different from conventional methods that detect buffer overflows inside user threads, which evidently delays protected programs, we propose to move the detection work out of user threads and enforce it in a separate thread, which we call *software cruising*. The approach leverages the hardware evolution trend that multicore processors and multiprocessor machines are more and more popular, which allows us to deploy dedicated monitor threads running concurrently with user threads to enhance application security. However applications may be significantly slowed down due to the overhead of communication and synchronization between the monitor threads and user threads. We address this problem by designing highly efficient lock-free data structures and non-blocking algorithms; their scalability implies the approach can be applied to not only single-threaded programs but also large-scale multithreaded applications. Our experiments show that the software cruising approach is practical—it only imposes an average of 5% performance overhead on SPEC CPU2006, and the throughput slowdown on Apache is negligible on average.

Our contributions include:

- To the best of our knowledge, this is the first work reported in the open literature that utilizes concurrent threads to detect buffer overflows.
- Among existing buffer overflow detectors, this is the first work that utilizes and designs lock-free data structures to support large-scale applications.
- Cruiser can detect buffer overflows that occur in any function, rather than specific libc functions. In addition, Cruiser can detect buffer underflows, duplicate frees, and memory leakage.
- Cruiser is legacy code compatible and can be applied to protect binary executables transparently, thus no source code or binary rewriting is needed. In addition, Cruiser does not rely on specific memory allocation algorithms; it can work with any memory allocator. Hence, Cruiser can be directly applied to shrink-wrapped software, and can be deployed easily to large-scale systems such as data centers and server farms in an automated manner.
- We propose a novel concurrent program monitoring methodology called *software cruising*, which leverages multicore architectures and utilizes non-blocking data structures and algorithms to achieve good efficiency and scalability; it can be applied to background security enforcement, as demonstrated in this paper, and concurrent resource reclamation (Section 7).

The remainder of the paper is organized as follows. In Section 2 we briefly discuss lock-free synchronization and review related work. We discuss our motivations in Section 3 and present the design overview in Section 4. In Section 5 we describe the design and implementation. In Section 6 we present the evaluation results. We discuss applications of software cruising beyond buffer overflows in Section 7 and conclude with Section 8.

2. Background

2.1 Lock-free Synchronization

A conventional approach to multithreaded programming is to use locks to synchronize access to shared resources. However, the lock-based approach causes many problems, one of which is lock contention. No matter whether the thread holding a lock is running or descheduled, other threads waiting for the lock are blocked, which limits concurrency and scalability. Another problem is priority inversion, i.e. a low priority thread holding the lock cannot get scheduled while high priority threads are waiting for the lock. Although fine-grained locking reduces lock contention, it introduces more lock overhead and increases the risk of deadlock.

In contrast to the lock-based approach, lock-free and wait-free algorithms allow high concurrency and scalability. An algorithm is lock-free if in a finite number of execution steps, at least one of the program threads makes progress, while an algorithm is wait-free if in a finite number of steps, every thread makes progress [28]. All wait-free algorithms are lock-free but the reverse is not necessarily true. Both are non-blocking and, by definition, they are immune to deadlock and priority inversion.

Lock-free algorithms commonly rely on hardware synchronization primitives. A typical primitive is Compare-And-Swap (CAS) [30]; it takes three arguments (addr, expval, newval) and performs the following *atomically*:

```
if (*addr != expval)
    return false;
*addr = newval;
return true;
```

Specifically, if the memory location addr does not hold the expected value expval, the Boolean false is returned; otherwise the new value newval is written to it and the Boolean true is returned, atomically.

2.2 Related Work

We divide the existing countermeasures against buffer overflow attacks into the following seven categories. Given extensive research in this area, this is not intended to be exhaustive.

Bounds checking: Many static analysis tools fall under this category [20, 69], which detect buffer overflows by examining source code statically and automatically. This approach usually suffers from high false positive or negative rate [71]. Some dynamic approaches [4, 31, 42] change the C pointer representation to carry buffer size information with pointers to enable bounds checking, i.e. "fat pointer," which is incompatible with legacy library code. CRED [52], built on the work of Jones and Kelly [32], does not change pointer representations but associates a buffer bound lookup with each pointer reference. However, the performance overhead is more than 2X. A recent work, baggy bounds checking [2], reduces the cost of bounds lookups by relaxing bounds checking precision, which however may lead to false negative, and it relies on specific memory allocators. Some library-based countermeasures [5, 19, 66] provide bounds checking only for specific functions in the C standard library.

Canary checking: Canary was firstly proposed in StackGuard [17], which tackles stack smashing attacks by placing a canary word before the return address on stack. Attempts to overwrite the return address would corrupt the canary value first. Although there are arguments that canary-based countermeasures can be bypassed [8, 50], the wide deployment and successes of StackGuard and its derivation ProPolice [29] have manifested their effectiveness. Robertson et al. [51] first proposed to use canary to protect heap chunk metadata. A canary is placed at the beginning of each chunk, thus when a buffer on heap is overflowed, the canary of the adjacent chunk is corrupted, which, however, is not detected until the adjacent chunk is coalesced, allocated or deallocated; therefore the detection relies on program execution.

Return address (RA) shadow stack or stack split: StackShield [64], RAD [14] and their derivations [23, 49] maintain an RA shadow stack, i.e. a copy of the RA is saved on the shadow stack at the prologue of a function call and is compared against the RA on the conventional stack at the epilogue. If the two RAs diverge, a buffer overflow is detected. In [70], the stack is split into an RA stack and a data stack, such that return addresses are protected from buffer overflows.

Non-executable (NX) memory: By setting the memory pages as non-executable, NX memory [63, 65] prevents code injected onto stack and heap from being executed. However it can be bypassed by a return-to-libc attack, which overwrites function pointers or return addresses with function addresses in libc, e.g. system().

Non-accessible memory: Both Purify [27] and Valgrind [68] insert guard zones, which are marked as inaccessible, surrounding dynamically allocated buffers, and track all memory references. When a guard zone access is detected, e.g. due to buffer overflows, an error is reported. Eletric Fence [22] places an inaccessible memory page immediately after (or before) each dynamically allocated buffer. If a buffer is overflowed (or underflowed), a segmentation fault is signaled. Tools in this category result in significant memory and performance overhead.

Randomization and obfuscation: Address Space Layout Randomization (ASLR) [7, 65] randomizes the locations of stack, heap and/or variable locations for each execution, such that a buffer overflow attack, such as return-to-libc, cannot be achieved reliably; that is, probabilistic protection is provided. However as it requires programs to be compiled into position-independent executables, it is incompatible with legacy code. In addition, it may be defeated by brute-force attacks or bypassed by partial overwrite attacks on the least significant bytes of a pointer [21]. PointGuard [16] encrypts pointers stored in memory and decrypts them before loading them into registers, such that pointers corrupted by attackers will not be decrypted to intended values. This countermeasure is incompatible with legacy code and cannot protect non-pointer data. Instead of randomizing pointers, instruction set randomization [6] keeps instructions encrypted, and decrypts them only before they are fetched into processors, which, however, results in substantial performance overhead. It can be bypassed by return-to-libc attacks.

Execution monitoring: Program shepherding [34] monitors control flow transfer in order to enforce a security policy. Buffer overflow attacks that lead to deviant control flow transfer are prevented. Control-flow integrity [1] determines a program's control flow graph beforehand and ensures that the control flow adheres to it. Castro et al. [9] proposed to compute a data-flow graph using static analysis and monitor whether the program data flow adheres to the graph. Like Cruiser, n-variant execution [18, 53] also takes advantage of multicore and multiprocessor architectures to enhance security. It runs a few variants of a single program simultaneously; behavioral divergences among the variants raise alarms. Execution monitoring usually imposes high performance overhead.

Despite so many countermeasures, only a few of them, such as StackGuard, ASLR, and NX memory, are widely deployed in production systems. Table 1 summarizes the properties of these three approaches and compares them with Cruiser. The common properties of these approaches include *low performance overhead, easiness to deploy and apply, no false alarms,*[1] *compatibility with mainstream platforms* and *program semantics loyalty*. In addition to having all the advantages, Cruiser have three other important properties: *compatibility with legacy code, no need for recompilation*, i.e. working with binary executables, and *ability to precisely locate corrupted buffers*, which is critical for testing, debugging, and security monitoring.

	StackGuard	ASLR	NX	Cruiser
Low performance overhead	√	√	√	√
Easy to deploy and apply	√	√	√	√
No false alarms	√	√	√	√
Mainstream platform compatible	√	√	√	√
Program semantics loyalty	√	√	√	√
Legacy code compatible	√		√	√
No need for recompilation			√	√
Able to locate corrupted buffers				√

Table 1. Comparison of some widely deployed countermeasures and Cruiser.

3. Motivations

3.1 Why Concurrent Detection and Challenges

There are mainly two categories of dynamic heap-based buffer overflow detectors. One category [51] detects buffer overflows inside memory allocation functions such as malloc and free, while the other [5, 19] enforces detection inside specific libc functions such as strcpy and gets. Both execute detection code inside user threads, which inevitably affects application performance, and the performance overhead is proportionally correlated with the invoke density of related functions. In addition, because detection is enforced in specific functions, they suffer from either severe temporal limitations, i.e. buffer overflows are not detected until one of the malloc function family is called, or spatial limitations, i.e. only a few libc functions are protected. Approaches that enforce bounds checking for each buffer reference do not have such limitations; however, they usually incur high performance overhead [32, 52] or false negative rate [2].

We propose to move detection code out of user threads and execute it in a separate monitor thread, which constantly *cruises* over buffers on heap, such that user threads are not delayed. Rich computational resources on modern machines, especially widely available multicore and multiprocessor architectures, enable us to run a dedicated monitor thread without competing too much resources with user threads, in other words, applications can potentially gain enhanced security with no pain.

However, synchronization is one of the major challenges. In Cruiser, a collection of heap buffer addresses needs to be maintained, so that the monitor thread surveils live buffers, and in the meanwhile avoids checking deallocated buffers, which would otherwise incur false alarms or segfaults. Therefore, the user threads and monitor thread have to be synchronized when buffers are allocated or deallocated. A conventional approach to achieving synchronization is to use locks; however, it has various limitations, such as severe performance degradation due to lock contention and low scalability, which is manifested by our first attempt.

In our first attempt, a lock-based red-black tree was used to collect buffer addresses. Inside a malloc call, the address of the newly allocated buffer is inserted into the tree with $O(\log n)$ time complexity where n is the number of collected addresses. Similarly inside a free call, the address of the released buffer is removed from the tree with $O(\log n)$ complexity also. Meanwhile a monitor thread traverses the tree to check the buffers. All the buffer address insert, delete and traverse operations are synchronized using locks. Our experiments showed that user threads were significantly

[1] As described in Section 5.2, one variant of Cruiser does incur false alarms, however, at an extremely low probability ($1/2^{64}$ in 64-bit OS) and can be safely ignored in practice.

delayed. The problem becomes more severe as more user threads contend locks and the tree grows.

3.2 Why Lock-free and Challenges

The limitations of lock-based approach pushed us towards lock-free synchronization in order to avoid lock contention and improve scalability. However, the difficulty of designing non-blocking algorithms is well recognized, which often thwarts the application of this approach.

We escaped the problems in our second attempt by utilizing the state-of-the-art extensible lock-free hash table algorithm proposed by Shalev and Shavit [62], such that the user threads and monitor thread can operate on the hash table concurrently, and each buffer address can be inserted into or removed from the hash table in $O(1)$ time. Although good scalability is achieved, the operation time is significant compared to malloc and free calls. Specifically, the slowdown of each pair of malloc and free calls observed in our experiment is more than 5X on average. The overhead is unacceptable for many applications with massive dynamic memory allocation.

To address these challenges, we have designed our own lock-free data structures and non-blocking algorithms to achieve concurrent detection with low overhead and high scalability, which will be presented in Section 4 and 5.

4. Design Overview

In addition to custom lock-free data structures, two design choices were made. First, as presented above, removing buffer addresses inside free calls may significantly delay user threads. In Cruiser the free function marks the buffer with a tombstone flag; when the monitor thread checks the buffer and finds it no longer alive, the monitor thread removes the buffer address from the collection of heap buffer addresses, such that the concern of delaying frees is resolved and the data structure representing the buffer address collection can be simplified. The details are covered in Section 5.2. Second, instead of modifying a specific memory allocator, Cruiser is implemented as a dynamic shared library to interpose the malloc function family and it passes the allocation requests to the corresponding memory allocator functions, therefore Cruiser can work with any memory allocator and it can be applied to protecting binary executables without instrumenting them.

4.1 Buffer Structure

Our method inserts two canary words around each buffer, namely *head canary* and *tail canary*, as shown in Figure 1, so that whenever a buffer is overflowed (underflowed), the tail (head) canary is corrupted. The *size* field, which is the encryption (XOR) result of the buffer size and a secret key, is used to locate the tail canary given a buffer address. As buffer size information is encrypted, it is not leaked to attackers, and it is more difficult for attackers to counterfeit. The head canary is the encryption result of another secret key, the buffer size and the buffer address. If the head canary and the size field cannot be decrypted to consistent size values, a buffer overflow is detected. As the buffer address is used to generate the canary, each buffer has a unique head canary, thus even if the canary of a buffer is leaked, it is difficult for attackers to forge the canary of another buffer without knowing the buffer sizes and addresses. The tail canary is encrypted and verified the same way using a different secret key. All the keys are initialized as random numbers when the monitored program is started.

4.2 Cruiser

Our previous attempts maintain a collection of buffer addresses but lead to high overhead. To efficiently collect memory allocation information, we design the *cruiser information collection* (CIC) architecture which is composed of (1) a lock-free *express* data structure onto which user threads put information, (2) a lock-free *warehouse* data structure that supports multiple threads to concurrently insert, delete and access information, and (3) a non-blocking *deliver* thread to copy the information from the express to the warehouse data structure. Instead of inserting information into the warehouse directly, user threads put the information onto the express data structure highly efficiently, and the deliver thread takes care of the rest of the information collection work, thus performance impact on user threads is minimized. In addition, as the warehouse structure supports concurrent operations, CIC scales well.

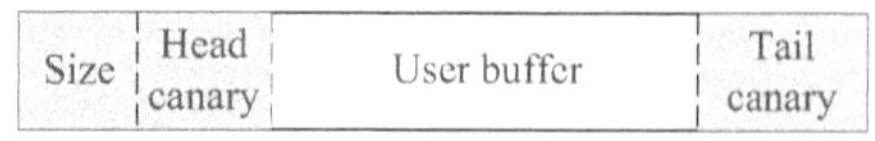

Figure 1. Buffer structure.

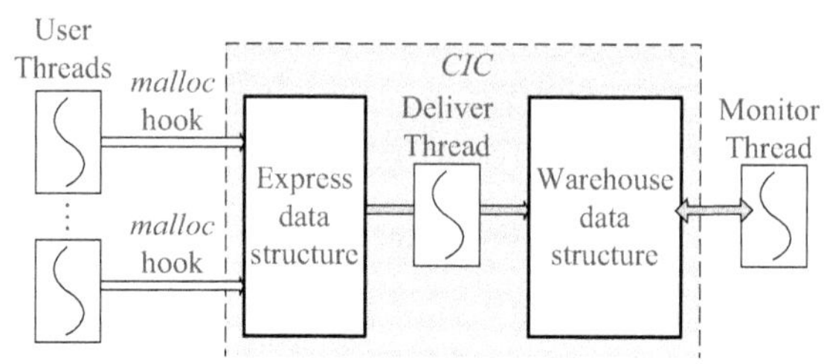

Figure 2. Cruiser architecture.

Based on CIC, we present a dynamic heap-based buffer overflow detector—Cruiser, which uses CIC to collect memory allocation information, e.g. buffer addresses and sizes. As shown in Figure 2, the malloc calls are hooked to place the buffer allocation information onto the express data structure and return promptly; the deliver thread then finishes the information collection.

From the perspective of Cruiser, the life cycle of a dynamically allocated buffer can be divided into three phases: **Pre-checking**: Inside a malloc call, a buffer that is three words larger than what the user thread requests is allocated. The buffer is filled as specified in Section 4.1, and the buffer allocation information used for overflow detection, such as the buffer address, is put onto the express data structure. Then the malloc call returns the address of the *user buffer* (see Figure 1). **Checking**: The pre-checking phase ends when the deliver thread moves the address from the express to the warehouse data structure, which is traversed by the monitor thread to detect buffer overflows. **Post-checking**: Inside the free call, the buffer is marked with a tombstone flag by encrypting the head canary once again using another key; later when the monitor thread checks the buffer and finds it no longer alive, the dated buffer information is removed from the warehouse by the monitor thread, so it is the monitor thread rather than user threads that tides up dated metadata information.

5. Design and Implementation

This section describes the design and implementation of Cruiser. Section 5.1 describes the data structures in CIC and how CIC is used in Cruiser to maintain buffer information. Section 5.2 presents the algorithms to release buffers and delete dated metadata information. We elaborate special issues on extensions and optimizations in Section 5.3.

5.1 Collection of Buffer Information

5.1.1 Express data structure

We implement the express data structure based on the single-producer single-consumer FIFO wait-free ring buffer proposed by Lamport [35]. Lamport's algorithm allows a producer thread and a consumer thread to operate concurrently on a ring. The synchronization overhead between the producer and the consumer is low, as two threads are synchronized via read/write instructions on the two control variables *head* and *tail*. Because of its high efficiency, the data structure has been applied to Gigabit network packet processing systems [24, 37].

To avoid the failure of Enqueue operation when the ring is full, we extend the basic ring to a linked list of rings, called *CruiserRing*, as shown in Figure 3. Whenever the ring is full and a new element is produced, instead of returning failure in Enqueue as in Lamport's algorithm, the producer creates a new ring with doubled capacity and links it after the full ring; the producer proceeds to insert elements into the new ring. Accordingly, in Dequeue when the ring is consumed up and another ring is linked after it, the consumer destroys the empty ring and proceeds to work on the next one. Because the ring size grows exponentially, as long as the speed of the consumer matches that of the producer, CruiserRing will converge to a stable state quickly. (The speed mismatch problem is addressed in Section 5.3.) Unless the new ring creation fails, CruiserRing ensures the success of the producer, which implies that the producer always moves on without dropping data.

As each CruiserRing supports one producer thread, a CruiserRing is needed for each producer thread. The method AddCruiserRing (see Figure 3) shows how to construct a list of CruiserRings in a lock-free manner, such that a single consumer thread can walk along the list to access all CruiserRings.

5.1.2 Warehouse data structure

We implement the warehouse data structure as a custom lock-free list, called *CruiserList*. CruiserList is a linked list of *segments*, each of which is a linked list itself with a never-removed dummy node as the segment head, as shown in Figure 4 and 5.

The basic form of CruiserList contains one segment, which supports a single *insert* thread to insert nodes and a single *traverse* thread to traverse the list concurrently. The method CheckNode is invoked in Traverse to check each node and returns whether the node should be deleted.

New nodes are always inserted between the dummy node and the first genuine node (the node linked immediately after the dummy node). If the first genuine node is determined to be deleted (Line 63), it should not be removed directly, as it may otherwise lead to list corruption or node loss. Specifically, if the first genuine node is removed between the execution of Line 51 and Line 52 when a new node is being inserted, the list is corrupted, because the newly inserted node has been linked to a deleted node. Another situation is when the first genuine node M is determined to be deleted, a new node N is inserted, which is not known by the traverse thread. Consequently, by removing node M, the dummy node is linked to the node after node M, such that node N is lost. The contention between node insertion and deletion is a common problem in lock-free data structures.

A conventional method to resolve the contention problems in non-blocking algorithms is to use CAS in a loop to insert or delete a node, as in the CruiserRing method AddCruiserRing (see Figure 3). However, CAS is relatively expensive and due to contention concurrent operations may experience frequent failure and retry of CAS instructions, which delays the progress of concurrent threads.

In CruiserList, we essentially eliminate the contention and thus CAS is not needed, as shown in the method Traverse. In our algorithm, the first genuine node is never removed until new nodes have been inserted, thus new nodes can always be inserted between the dummy node and the first genuine node safely by the insert thread, while the traverse thread never touches the link between the dummy node and the first genuine node. Therefore, the node insertion and deletion operations essentially play in different arenas, and thus have no contention.

Specifically, when the first genuine node is determined to be deleted, it is marked as to-be-deleted by calling the method MarkDelete, which fills a special *null* value in the data field of the node, or sets the least significant bit (LSB) of the *next* pointer of the node, as the node address is usually word-aligned and the LSB of

```
struct Ring {
    Element *buffer;
    unsigned int size;
    unsigned int head, tail;
    Ring *next; // next Ring
};

struct CruiserRing {
    Ring *pr, *cr; // producer ring and consumer ring
    CruiserRing *next; // next CruiserRing
};

CruiserRing *Head; // head of CruiserRing list

NEXT(index, size) { return (index + 1) % size; }

Enqueue(pr, data) {
    if (NEXT(pr->head, pr->size) == pr->tail) {
        newRing = createRing(2 * (pr->size));
        if (null == newRing)
            return failure;
        pr->next = newRing;
        pr = newRing;
    }
    pr->buffer[pr->head] = data;
    pr->head = NEXT(pr->head, pr->size);
    return success;
}

Dequeue(cr, data) {
    if (cr->head == cr->tail) {
        if (null == cr->next)
            return failure;
        temp = cr; cr = cr->next;
        destroy(temp);
        return Dequeue(cr, data);
    }
    data = cr->buffer[cr->tail];
    cr->tail = NEXT(cr->tail, cr->size);
    return success;
}

AddCruiserRing(cruiserRing) {
    do {
        cruiserRing->next = oldValue = Head;
    } while (!CAS(&Head, oldValue, cruiserRing));
}
```

Figure 3. CruiserRing (Express data structure).

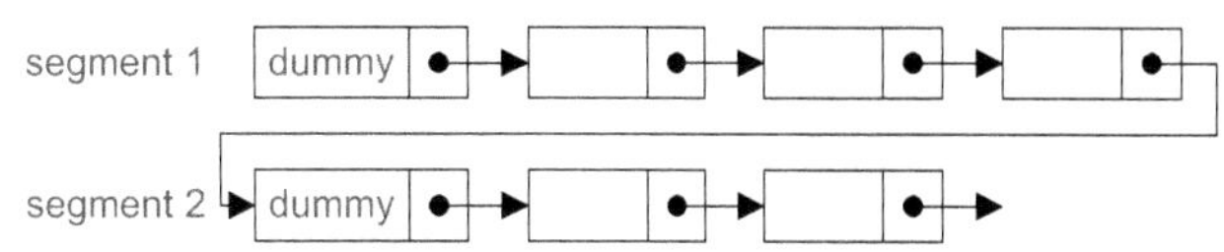

Figure 4. CruiserList.

```
48 Node *head; // head of CruiserList
49
50 Insert(dummy, node) {
51     node->next = dummy->next;
52     dummy->next = node;
53 }
54
55 Traverse() {
56     Node *prev, *cur, *next;
57     cur = leftBoundary->next;
58     if (cur == null)
59         return;
60
61     /*Process the first genuine node*/
62     if (!IsMarkedDelete(cur))
63         if (CheckNode(cur) returns PLEASE_DELETE_ME)
64             /*Node removal is deferred to avoid contention*/
65             MarkDelete(cur);
66
67     /* Process the rest genuine nodes */
68     prev = cur; cur = cur->next;
69     while (cur != rightBoundary) {
70         next = cur->next;
71         if (IsMarkedDelete(cur) ||
72         CheckNode(cur) returns PLEASE_DELETE_ME) {
73             prev->next = next;
74             DeleteNode(cur);
75         }
76         else
77             prev = cur;
78         cur = next;
79     }
80 }
81
82 AddSegment() {
83     Node *newDummy = AllocateDummyNode();
84     do {
85         newDummy->next = oldValue = head;
86     } while (!CAS(&head, oldValue, newDummy));
87     return newDummy;
88 }
```

Figure 5. CruiserList (Warehouse data structure).

the *next* pointer is thus not used. Then the marked node is removed in a future round of traverse when it is no longer the first genuine node. Figure 6 shows the process of removing the first genuine node A. It is first marked, but not deleted. After a new node C is inserted, it will be deleted shortly. It is possible that no more new nodes are inserted and the marked node sticks in the list; however, there is only one such node in a segment and normally this occurs only in the residual period of program execution. Note that the user buffer is freed; only the first metadata node may stay alive after the corresponding buffer is released. We can resolve this using CAS if it becomes a serious issue. The Insert method inserts a node, just as in a single-threaded list, between the never-removed dummy node and the first genuine node which is never removed directly.

The technique of marking a node as to-be-deleted was first used in the lock-free FIFO queue algorithm [48] proposed by Prakash et al., then used in Harris's [26] and Michael's [40] lock-free lists, respectively. All of them use this technique to prevent new nodes from being linked to a marked node. As insertion and deletion may operate on the same node, contention still exists; and they rely on CAS. Our algorithm allows new nodes to be linked to a marked node. Only simple reads and writes are needed.

The basic CruiserList can be easily extended to multiple segments using the method AddSegment, so that it can support multiple insert and traverse threads. Each insert thread has a thread-private variable pointing to the dummy node of a different segment,

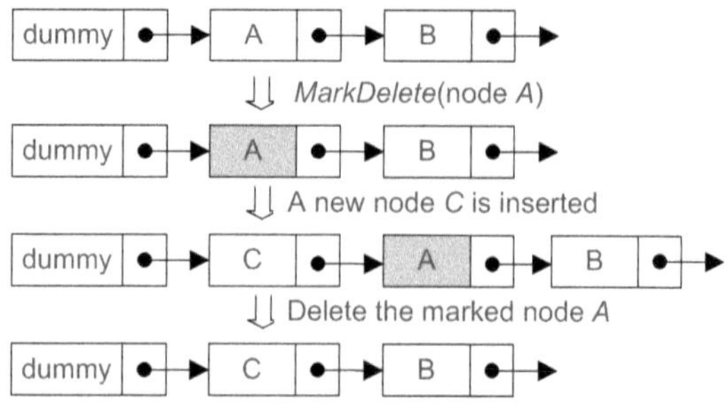

Figure 6. Deletion of the first genuine node.

into which this thread inserts nodes. On the other hand, the segments can be partitioned into multiple disjoint groups; each traverse thread walks on a different group denoted by two thread-private variables *leftBoundary* and *rightBoundary*, which point to the dummy nodes of segments. If there is only one traverse thread, its segment group consists of the whole CruiserList. For the sake of simplicity, the Traverse method in Figure 5 is only for one-segment groups. The time for a traverse thread to cruise through its segment group once is called a *cruise cycle*.

Compared to general-purpose lock-free lists, CruiserList is highly efficient and has the following advantages: (1) *Wait-free access and zero-contention*: Both insert and traverse threads keep making progress, and node insertion and deletion are executed in different arenas; (2) *No ABA problem*: The ABA problem [30] is historically associated with CAS. It happens if in a thread a shared location with a value A was read, then CAS comparing the current value of the shared location against A succeeds though it should not, as between the read and the CAS other threads change the value of the shared location from A to B and back to A again. The only CAS in Line 86 has no ABA problem, because it is impossible for *head*, which was changed from the address of the dummy node A to that of the dummy node B, to change back to A without removing any dummy nodes; and (3) *No special memory reclamation needed*: For a typical lock-free data structure, when a node is removed by a thread, its memory cannot be released immediately because other threads may be accessing it. So special memory reclamation mechanisms are needed, such as reference counters and hazard pointers [39]. On a given segment of the CruiserList, the traverse thread is the only thread that deletes nodes, so it is not concerned with accessing nodes being released by other threads. It is not a problem for the insert thread either, as it only accesses the content of the dummy node, which is never removed.

5.1.3 Applying CIC in Cruiser

Cruiser uses the CIC mechanism to collect memory allocation information (see Figure 2). The malloc calls of user threads are hooked and memory allocation information is put on the CruiserRings. The deliver thread moves the information from CruiserRings to CruiserList, while the *monitor* thread calling Traverse of CruiserList cruises over buffers to detect overflow according to the collected information in CruiserList. The buffer overflow detection code is executed in CheckNode (see Figure 5), which returns PLEASE_DELETE_ME if the buffer is found no longer alive. More details about CheckNode are described in Section 5.2.

Cruiser is implemented as a dynamic shared library to interpose the malloc function family. It contains a constructor (initialization) function, which gets executed when the monitored program is started. Inside the constructor function, the keys are initialized with random numbers in /dev/urandom, the CruiserList is created and initialized, and the deliver thread and the monitor thread are created, which share the same address space as user threads. Each user thread creates its CruiserRing when it invokes its first malloc call. All the memory blocks used by Cruiser (the data structures and keys) are allocated using mmap with two inaccessible guard pages [22] surrounding each of them, such that they cannot be overflowed.

5.2 Buffer Release and Node Removal

Once a buffer is freed, the node in the CruiserList containing the corresponding buffer information becomes dated and should be removed; otherwise, buffer overflow checks over the buffer may incur false alarms or segmentation faults, as the buffer memory may have been reused or unmapped. Removing dated nodes inside free calls may significantly delay user threads. We address the problem with the following two approaches; both enable the monitor thread to tidy-up CruiserList.

The first approach is a lazy two-step memory reclamation algorithm. First, when a free call is intercepted, the target buffer is marked with a tombstone flag by encrypting the head canary with another key, called the *release key*; the free call returns without releasing the buffer, which becomes a *zombie buffer*. Second, when the monitor thread checks the buffer and finds it marked with a tombstone, the method CheckNode in Figure 5 releases the buffer and returns PLEASE_DELETE_ME. This approach removes dated information effectively without incurring false alarms or segfaults. The drawback is that buffer release is delayed; however, since all zombie buffers are bound to be released no later than the next cruise cycle, the delay should be reasonably short.

The second approach does not delay memory reclamation; however, it requires some changes about the head and tail canaries and needs the assistance of recovery techniques. The head canary field is filled with a random number (rather than the encrypted size value), while the tail canary is the encryption (XOR) result of the head canary value and a key. The random number along with the buffer address is collected in CruiserList. Inside the free call, the target buffer is checked against buffer overflow by decrypting the tail canary and comparing with the head canary.[2] If they are different, a buffer overflow is detected; otherwise the head canary is set as zero, after which the buffer is released and the free call returns. When the monitor thread checks a buffer and finds the number stored in the head canary is not the same as that stored in the CruiserList, it assumes the buffer has been released and then the corresponding dated node is removed from the CruiserList. After a buffer is released and reused, the memory location of the original head canary may happen to be written with the same value as that before the buffer was released, so that when the monitor thread checks the node using the dated buffer information, it would incorrectly determine this buffer is still alive and thus false alarms are possible; however, the probability is extremely low (in 64-bit OS, it is $1/2^{64}$), which can be safely ignored in practice.

Three scenarios need to be considered for the second approach. First, when a buffer is tampered due to an overflow occurred in its preceding adjacent buffer, it would be incorrectly determined as a released buffer by the monitor thread; however, this does no harm and as the adjacent buffer is under surveillance, the overflow can still be detected. Second, when a buffer is underflowed, the monitor thread would also treat it as a released buffer. Underflows are rare compared to overflows; moreover we can address the problem by saving the buffer size in the CruiserList node, against which the size field of each buffer is checked by the monitor thread in CheckNode to detect underflows.

[2] If the size field has been corrupted, the tail canary cannot be located correctly. As a result, the read of the tail canary may incur segfault, which, however, essentially exposes buffer overflows. If necessary, the same recovery technique described here can be used to deal with segfault.

Third, when the monitor thread checks a buffer that has been released and the corresponding memory page(s) has been unmapped, a segfault is triggered. The problem can be addressed using some recovery techniques [47]. In Linux, a SIGSEGV signal handler can be installed firstly. Each time before the monitor thread accesses a buffer, it calls sigsetjmp to save the calling environment. Once a SIGSEGV signal is triggered due to an invalid access, the monitor thread is trapped to the SIGSEGV handler, and the calling environment can be recovered by calling siglongjmp. Windows also has similar recovery mechanism called Structured Exception Handling [41].

Cruisers with the two approaches are called *Lazy* Cruiser and *Eager* Cruiser, respectively. We have implemented both in Linux.

5.3 Extensions and Optimizations

5.3.1 Extensions

Flexible deployment options: The deployment of Cruiser is flexible. One method is to implement Cruiser as a dynamic shared library. By setting the LD_PRELOAD environment variable to the path of the Cruiser library, an administrator can selectively enable Cruiser for certain applications. With this method the malloc function family are interposed by Cruiser, which invokes the memory allocation functions in the system library to enforce dynamic memory allocation, thus no system library is altered. This is the deploying method we adopt in the experiments.

A second method is to integrate Cruiser with the system dynamic library for dynamic memory allocation. The advantage is that memory and performance overhead can be reduced. For example, the overhead due to malloc function family interposition can be avoided; some memory allocators, such as dlmalloc [36], place the buffer size information in the beginning of each chunk, so Cruiser does not need to maintain that information additionally.

A third method is to implement Cruiser as a static library and integrate it into the compiler. Considering the two methods above cannot be applied to statically linked applications, the third method is complementary to them. Regardless of the deploying method, Cruiser has no effect on applications that perform their own memory management, neither can it detect buffer overflows inside a structure currently, which is a limitation shared by other techniques that detect buffer overflows at the level of memory blocks [2, 5, 19, 22, 27, 51, 68]. However, Cruiser can be extended to monitor buffers inside a struct by inserting canary words.

More Cruiser threads: Although our experiments show that the Cruiser configuration with one deliver thread and one monitor thread is sufficient for common applications, it may be desirable to extend Cruiser with multiple deliver and monitor threads. For example, there may be many user threads requesting dynamic memory intensively that a single deliver thread cannot match the speed of buffer allocation; or the CruiserList is so long that it takes much time for a monitor thread to traverse through the CruiserList once. As both CruiserList and the list of CruiserRings support multiple threads, Cruiser can be easily extended with more cruiser threads to protect various applications.

5.3.2 Optimizations

Memory reuse: To mitigate memory allocation intensity and speed up node insert and delete in CruiserList, a ring buffer is adopted to store the addresses of removed nodes with the monitor thread as the producer and the deliver thread as the consumer. Nodes removed from CruiserList are not deleted but stored in the ring unless it is full. Accordingly when the deliver thread needs a node, it first tries to retrieve a node from the ring; only when the ring is empty, a new node is allocated. The simple ring buffer can be replaced with other advanced wait-free queues, such as a CruiserRing, to support more efficient nodes buffering strategy.

On the other hand, each user thread requesting dynamic memory owns a CruiserRing. Considering some applications fork and kill threads frequently, instead of allocating and releasing CruiserRings intensively, we reuse CruiserRings. A Boolean flag indicating whether the CruiserRing is available for reuse is added into the CruiserRing structure. As the deliver thread traverses along the list of CruiserRings, if it detects a user thread has exited, it marks the related CruiserRing as available for reuse. When a user thread needs a CruiserRing, it will try to reuse an available CruiserRing before allocating a new one.

Backoff strategies: Although our experiments show that Cruiser imposes low overhead, the performance can be further improved with backoff strategies, for example, by inserting *NOP* instructions or sleep calls inside the monitor thread. Reduced monitor intensity leads to less memory access interference, thus decreases performance impact. Cruiser can also switch to monitor buffers selectively, for example, buffers involved in data flows stemming from networks or user inputs. For Lazy Cruiser, it is a good choice to ignore large buffers and hence release them inside free calls directly under intense memory pressure. More advanced monitor strategies based on computational resource dynamics can be adopted as well.

Variants of the deliver thread: In Cruiser, the deliver thread is busy polling CruiserRings. Actually it can go to sleep when there is no information to deliver and be waken up by user threads via signals. To avoid sending a signal per malloc call, a global status flag indicating whether the deliver thread is asleep can be used. The flag is set as awake or asleep by the deliver thread; a wake-up signal is sent to the deliver thread only when it is asleep.

Another variant is to combine the deliver thread and the monitor thread; we can have the hybrid thread delivering information and monitoring nodes alternatively, such that only one busy thread is needed and the data structures can be further simplified. The drawback is that the monitoring may be interrupted frequently.

Better ring algorithms: Based on Lamport's ring [35], some other ring algorithms have been proposed [24, 37]. We used the ring algorithm proposed by Lee et al. [37] in our experiments to mitigate the false sharing problem in Lamport's ring.

6. Evaluation

We evaluated the effectiveness of Cruiser, its performance and memory overhead, and analyzed the detection latency issue. This section presents our results.

6.1 Effectiveness

We evaluated the effectiveness of Cruiser with two experiments. Our first experiment was carried out using the SAMATE Reference Dataset (SRD) [44] maintained by NIST. The dataset contains 12 test cases on heap-based buffer overflows due to contiguous writes, which are caused by assignments, memcpy, strcpy, snprintf, etc., and another 10 test cases that fix the overflows. Cruiser detects all the overflows in the 12 test cases and there is no false positive for the 10 sound test cases.

The second experiment tested the effectiveness against both well-known historic exploits (wu-ftpd [57], Sudo [61], CVS [55]) and recently published vulnerabilities (libHX [58], Lynx [59], Firefox [56]), shown in Table 2. Each vulnerable program was run with Cruiser and attacks were launched on them. Each attack was executed 50 times and Cruiser detected all the overflows, duplicate and invalid frees.

These experiments demonstrate that our technique is effective in detecting not only heap-based buffer overflows but also memory leakage and heap corruption including duplicate frees and frees on invalid pointers. Therefore, Cruiser is a good candidate for finding heap corruption and memory leakage defects during development as well as monitoring production systems.

Program	Vulnerability
wu-ftpd 2.6.1	Free calls on uninitialized pointers
Sudo 1.6.4	Heap-based buffer overflow
CVS 1.11.4	Duplicate free calls
libHX 3.5	Heap-based buffer overflow
Lynx 2.8.8 dev.1	Heap-based buffer overflow
Firefox 3.0.1	Heap-based buffer overflow

Table 2. The effectiveness experiment against real-world vulnerabilities.

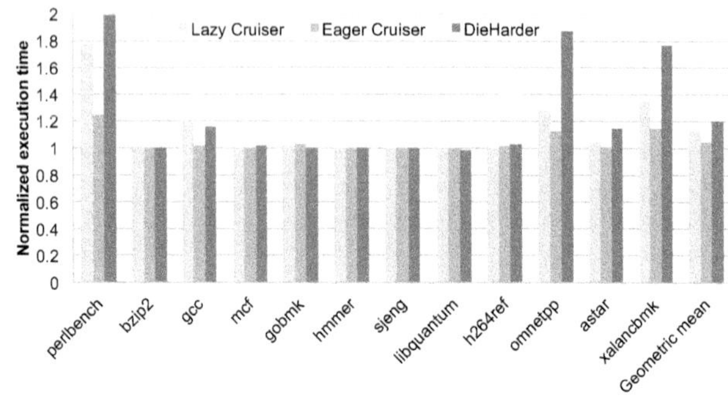

Figure 7. Execution time with Cruiser (normalized by the execution time without Cruiser), compared with DieHarder. The last set of bars is the geometric mean of the execution time of all benchmarks.

6.2 Performance and Memory Overhead

We evaluated the performance and memory overhead of Cruiser using the SPEC CPU2006 Integer benchmark suite. The experiments were performed on a Dell Precision Workstation T5500 with two 2.26GHz Intel Xeon E5507 quad-core processors and 4GB of RAM running 32-bit Linux 2.6.24. Cruiser was implemented as a dynamically linked library and loaded by setting the LD_PRELOAD environment variable. In all the experiments, Cruiser created one deliver thread and one monitor thread with the optimizations *memory reuse* and *better ring algorithms* enabled. We ran each experiment three times and present the average result. The variance was negligible.

We evaluated both Lazy Cruiser and Eager Cruiser, and compared with DieHarder [45], which also provides probabilistic heap safety. Figure 7 shows the execution time of the two implementations normalized by the execution time of original programs. The average performance overhead is 12.5% for Lazy Cruiser and 5% for Eager Cruiser, while DieHarder imposes 20% penalty on average. For the majority of the benchmark programs, the overhead imposed by Cruiser is negligible. The perlbench has the highest overhead due to its significantly dense dynamic memory allocation. Eager Cruiser performs generally better than the lazy version, mainly because the former allows immediate memory reclamation and reuse. The experiments show that Cruiser can be deployed in field practically.

In addition to the three-word tag associated with each buffer, the memory overhead of Cruiser is mainly due to its data structures CruiserRings and CruiserList. For Lazy Cruiser, zombie buffers are another source. To precisely analyze the memory overhead, as shown in Table 3, we measured the maximum size of CruiserRing and the maximum and average lengths of CruiserList normalized by the live buffer counts at sample time (we sampled at the end of each cruise cycle), respectively, from which we can get the percentage of dated nodes and zombie buffers. As the CruiserList length is normalized, the maximum length can be less than the average

Benchmark	Maximum CruiserRing size	Maximum CruiserList length	Average CruiserList length	Average cruise cycle (μs)
perlbench	8192 (1024)	1.06 (1.16)	1.02 (1.06)	4.3e4 (1.2e5)
bzip2	1024 (1024)	1.00 (1.00)	1.00 (1.00)	.43 (1.2)
gcc	2048 (2048)	1.02 (1.05)	1.00 (1.01)	1.3e3 (3.5e3)
mcf	1024 (1024)	1.00 (1.00)	1.00 (1.00)	.35 (.59)
gobmk	1024 (1024)	1.00 (1.00)	1.00 (1.00)	.37 (1.6)
hmmer	1024 (1024)	1.11 (1.29)	1.00 (1.00)	26 (1.6e2)
sjeng	1024 (1024)	1.11 (1.00)	1.00 (1.00)	.36 (0.82)
libquantum	1024 (1024)	1.00 (1.00)	1.00 (1.00)	.16 (0.49)
h264ref	1024 (1024)	1.00 (1.00)	1.00 (1.00)	3.3e2 (1.7e3)
omnetpp	2048 (1024)	1.08 (1.08)	1.02 (1.08)	9.8e4 (3.2e5)
astar	4096 (2048)	1.04 (1.06)	1.00 (1.00)	19 (88)
xalancbmk	2048 (1024)	1.00 (1.00)	1.02 (1.07)	7.3e4 (1.5e5)

Table 3. Memory overhead and cruise cycle (Results of Eager Cruiser are enclosed in parentheses; the maximum/average CruiserList lengths are normalized by the maximum/average heap buffer counts, respectively).

one, as in the case of xalancbmk. The initial CruiserRing has 1024 elements; the size of each element is one word in Lazy Cruiser and two words in Eager Cruiser, respectively. For the majority of benchmarks, the CruiserRing does not grow, while the maximum CruiserRing in perlbench test with Lazy Cruiser experienced 3 times of growth (recall that the ring grows exponentially). The length of CruiserList is close to the count of live buffers on heap. In other words, the percentage of dated nodes and zombie buffers is low, and on average it is negligible.

6.3 Scalability

To evaluate the scalability of our approach on multithreaded programs, we compared the throughputs of the Apache web server with and without Cruiser. We ran Apache 2.2.8 on the same workstation specified in Section 6.2, and used ApacheBench 2.3, which ran on a machine with a 2.4GHz Intel Core 2 Duo processor, 4GB of RAM, and Mac OS X 10.6.4, to measure the Apache throughput over a Gbit LAN network. We issued repeated requests for a 5KB HTML page with various numbers of concurrent clients. We observed that Apache allocated two heap buffers per request; ApacheBench issued one million requests for each concurrency number. Figure 8 shows the throughputs of Apache (labeled as baseline) and Apache with Lazy Cruiser and Eager Cruiser, respectively. The throughputs of Apache with the two versions of Cruiser are almost the same. The maximum 3% slowdown appears around concurrency number 7, while the average slowdown is negligible. For concurrency numbers greater than 11, the throughputs with and without Cruiser are almost identical. We measured until concurrency number 110 when the client's CPU was saturated, and the throughput slowdown remained negligible. The machine running Apache has 8 cores in processors, thus the Cruiser threads compete processor time since concurrency number 6; however as the working threads in Apache increase, the percentage of processor time used by the Cruiser threads decreases, and thus the slowdown declines.

6.4 Detection Latency

Heap-based buffer overflows can be divided into two classes [51]. One class of attacks alter memory allocators' metadata. Exploits in this class are often achieved by releasing a corrupted buffer [33]. Cruiser defeats this kind of exploits completely, as all buffers are checked before release.

The other class comprises attacks that overflow a buffer to alter the content of its adjacent memory block. This kind of exploits

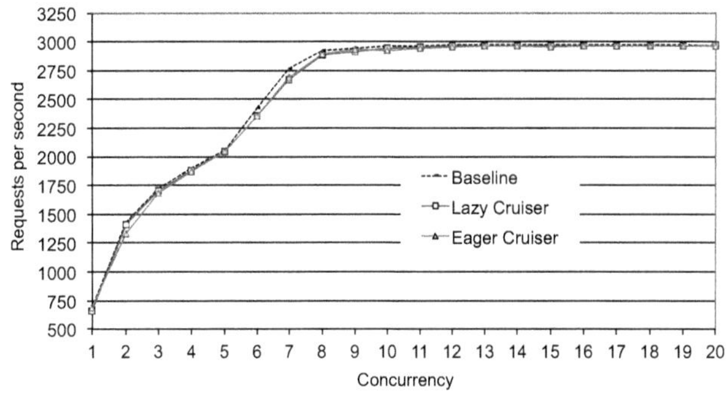

Figure 8. Throughtputs of the Apache web server for varying numbers of concurrent requests.

are not achieved until the corrupted content is used; the attacks are not detected until corrupted buffers are checked by a monitor thread. Like DieHarder, Cruiser provides probabilistic heap safety for this kind of attacks. Assume an attack takes time E to achieve the exploit after canary smashing and a cruise cycle takes time C, if $E \geq C$, Cruiser can detect the overflow before the exploit is achieved; otherwise, assume the detection latency (elapsed time since the overflow until detection) is uniformly distributed on the interval $(0, C]$, the probability P for Cruiser to detect an exploit before it completes is E/C. As shown in Table 3, with Lazy Cruiser, 5 of the 12 benchmarks' average cruise cycles are shorter than 0.5μs, and 8 of them are not longer than 0.5ms; with Eager Cruiser, 5 benchmarks' average cruise cycles are not longer than 1.6μs, and 7 of them are shorter than 0.2ms. The average cruise cycles for Apache test are 16μs and 78μs for Lazy and Eager Cruisers, respectively. Considering $C = NT$, where N is the number of nodes in the CruiserList and T is the average time for a monitor thread to check a node, we can expect a high prevention probability by keeping N small. One way is to divide the CruiserList into several segment groups and create the same number of monitor threads, each of which cruises over a shorter part of CruiserList. For example, by dividing the CruiserList into two parts and running one more monitor thread on either part in omnetpp test, the average cruise cycle decreased by 42% and 47% for Lazy Cruiser and Eager Cruiser, respectively. Another way is to only monitor suspicious buffers, for example, those buffers involved in data flows that stem from networks or user inputs.

Considering Cruiser shares the same address space as user programs, an attacker with arbitrary memory access privileges of the compromised program can bypass Cruiser theoretically. Otherwise a reliable and precise attack against Cruiser is hard to build. In Cruiser, the canaries of a buffer are the XOR result of the buffer's address, size and the keys which were initialized using random numbers, so it is difficult to predict or restore a canary. For example, an elaborate attack that exploits other vulnerabilities, such as format string [50], to obtain the keys still needs the target buffer size and address information to calculate its canaries. Blind access for Cruiser's data structures will normally incur segfault, as they are surrounded by inaccessible guard pages. The function pthread_kill can be interposed by Cruiser to prevent Cruiser threads from being killed, and Cruiser threads can detect the liveness of each other when running, thus it is very unlikely to subvert Cruiser. Detection can be evaded by terminating the process, which, however, explicitly exposes the attack and is not a usual way of real attacks.

7. Software Cruising

We have applied the software cruising technique to efficient heap overflow detection by moving the detection work out of user threads. Potentially all the *inlined* verification, monitoring and resource reclamation work can be migrated from user threads to one or more monitor threads for concurrent execution in *background*. This section discusses other applications of software cruising, some of which we are currently working on as an extension of this work.

Background Software Monitoring: Depending on the security policies enforced, inlined security enforcement may incur high performance overhead. Software cruising takes a very different way by moving inlined security enforcement out of user threads and executing them in concurrent monitor threads, which can reduce considerable performance overhead. Although synchronization and race conditions between user and monitor threads are potential challenges, they can be solved using lock-free data structures as in Cruiser. For example, we can implement a call trace collector by instrumenting the call instruction in the binary and placing the target address in a CruiserRing. A concurrent monitor thread analyzes the call trace to evaluate whether specific control-flow policies are followed. As simple examples, some control transfers are suspicious; or a control-flow policy may require that a certain function is called no more often than another function (such restrictions may be desirable to prevent some "confused deputy" attacks [25]). The monitor thread can detect abnormalities based on the call trace and a finite automaton or simple counting. Other straightforward applications include integrity-checking of important program structures such as the Global Offset Table.

OS Kernel Cruising: It is desirable to adopt software cruising to monitor OS kernel memory integrity and other safety and liveness properties. We plan to develop a prototype that can monitor integrity of OS kernel memory. One of the challenges of cruising OS kernels is how to minimize the impact on the kernel memory layout since kernel code contains many low-level programming idioms that rely on certain memory layouts. One way to solve this problem is to selectively monitor some buffers and make manual transformation.

Concurrent Resource Reclamation: Software Cruising can also be applied to implement efficient resource reclamation, for example safe memory reclamation for lock-free data structures. For lock-free dynamic objects, when a thread removes a node, it is possible that some other thread has earlier read a reference to that node, and is about to access its contents, therefore the memory occupied by the node should not be released or reused directly. When designing lock-free data structures, safe memory reclamation is a major concern. Recent progress was made by Michael [39]. The core idea is to associate a number of pointers, called *hazard pointers*, with each thread. A hazard pointer points to a node that may be accessed later by that thread; whenever a thread frees a retired node, it has to scan hazard pointers of other threads to make sure the node is not pointed to by any of the hazard pointers. To achieve a low amortized overhead, a thread does not free retired nodes until it accumulates a certain number of retired nodes. The inlined batch processing of retired nodes inevitably delays user threads and memory reclamation. The problem can be solved elegantly by deploying a concurrent thread, which takes over the work of memory reclamation by scanning hazard pointers to determine which retired nodes can be released safely. The original methodology is complementary to this solution in case too many retired nodes are accumulated.

8. Conclusion

We have introduced a novel technique, *software cruising*. The core idea is to mitigate inlined verification, monitoring and resource reclamation work from user threads to a concurrent monitor thread. Through lock-free data structures and non-blocking algorithms the monitor thread and user threads can be synchronized with low overhead and high scalability.

We have applied this technique to Cruiser, a dynamic heap-based buffer overflow detector on the Linux platform. It is straightforward to adapt Cruiser to other platforms such as Windows and Mac. We have evaluated Cruiser on a variety of programs to show its effectiveness. The performance overhead of monitoring SPEC CPU2006 benchmark is about 5% on average, and negligible in the majority of cases. Cruiser also scales well on multithreaded programs; the slowdown on the Apache throughput with different numbers of concurrency is negligible on average and 3% maximal. The experiments show that Cruiser is feasible to be applied.

Acknowledgments

The authors would like to thank Ori Shalev and Nir Shavit for sharing the non-blocking hash table code [62], Maged M. Michael for pointing to us the open source project "Amino Concurrent Building Blocks" [46], Andrew Appel and Xi Xiong for their valuable comments, and the anonymous reviewers for their comments that helped shape the final version of this paper.

This work was partially supported by AFOSR FA9550-07-1-0527 (MURI), ARO W911NF-09-1-0525 (MURI), NSF CNS-0905131, and AFRL FA8750-08-C-0137.

References

[1] M. Abadi, M. Budiu, U. Erlingsson, and J. Ligatti. Control-flow integrity. In *CCS '05*, pages 340–353.

[2] P. Akritidis, M. Costa, M. Castro, and S. Hand. Baggy bounds checking: an efficient and backwards-compatible defense against out-of-bounds errors. In *Usenix Security '09*, pages 51–66.

[3] AlephOne. Smashing the stack for fun and profit. *Phrack*, 7(49), 1996.

[4] T. M. Austin, S. E. Breach, and G. S. Sohi. Efficient detection of all pointer and array access errors. In *PLDI '04*, pages 290–301.

[5] K. Avijit and P. Gupta. Tied, libsafeplus, tools for runtime buffer overflow protection. In *Usenix Security '04*, pages 4–4.

[6] E. G. Barrantes, D. H. Ackley, T. S. Palmer, D. Stefanovic, and D. D. Zovi. Randomized instruction set emulation to disrupt binary code injection attacks. In *CCS '03*, pages 281–289.

[7] E. Bhatkar, D. C. Duvarney, and R. Sekar. Address obfuscation: an efficient approach to combat a broad range of memory error exploits. In *Usenix Security '03*, pages 105–120.

[8] Bulba and Kil3r. Bypassing StackGuard and StackShield. *Phrack*, 10 (56), May 2000.

[9] M. Castro, M. Costa, and T. Harris. Securing software by enforcing data-flow integrity. In *OSDI '06*, pages 147–160.

[10] CERT Advisory, CA-2001-19 CodeRed worm.

[11] CERT Advisory, CA-2002-33 Heap Overflow Vulnerability in Microsoft Data Access Components.

[12] CERT Advisory, CA-2003-20 SQLSlammer worm.

[13] S. Chen, J. Xu, E. C. Sezer, P. Gauriar, and R. K. Iyer. Non-control-data attacks are realistic threats. In *Usenix Security '05*, pages 177–192, 2005.

[14] T. Chiueh and F. Hsu. RAD: A compile-time solution to buffer overflow attacks. In *ICDCS '01*, pages 409–417.

[15] M. Conover. w00w00 on heap overflows, 1999. www.w00w00.org/files/articles/heaptut.txt.

[16] C. Cowan and S. Beattie. PointGuard: protecting pointers from buffer overflow vulnerabilities. In *Usenix Security '03*, pages 91–104.

[17] C. Cowan and C. Pu. StackGuard: automatic adaptive detection and prevention of buffer-overflow attacks. In *Usenix Security '98*, pages 63–78, January 1998.

[18] B. Cox, D. Evans, A. Filipi, J. Rowanhill, W. Hu, J. Davidson, J. Knight, A. Nguyen-Tuong, and J. Hiser. N-variant systems: a secretless framework for security through diversity. In *Usenix Security '06*, pages 105–120.

[19] E. D.Berger. HeapShield: Library-based heap overflow protection for free. Tech. report, Univ. of Massachusetts Amherst, 2006.

[20] N. Dor, M. Rodeh, and M. Sagiv. CSSV: towards a realistic tool for statically detecting all buffer overflows in C. In *PLDI '03*, pages 155–167, June 2003.

[21] T. Durden. Bypassing PaX ASLR protection. *Phrack*, 2002.

[22] E. Fence. Malloc debugger. http://directory.fsf.org/project/ElectricFence/.

[23] M. Frantzen and M. Shuey. Stackghost: Hardware facilitated stack protection. In *Usenix Security '01*, pages 55–66.

[24] J. Giacomoni, T. Moseley, and M. Vachharajani. Fastforward for efficient pipeline parallelism: a cache-optimized concurrent lock-free queue. In *PPoPP '08*, pages 43–52.

[25] N. Hardy. The confused deputy. *ACM Oper. Syst. Rev.*, 22(4):36–38.

[26] T. L. Harris. A pragmatic implementation of non-blocking linked lists. In *DISC '01*, pages 300–314.

[27] R. Hastings and B. Joyce. Purify: Fast detection of memory leaks and access errors. In *the Winter 1992 Usenix Conference*, pages 125–136.

[28] M. Herlihy. A methodology for implementing highly concurrent data structures. In *PPoPP '90*, pages 197–206.

[29] IBM. ProPolice detector. www.trl.ibm.com/projects/security/ssp/.

[30] IBM System/370 Extended Architecture, Principles of Operations. IBM Publication No. SA22-7085, 1983.

[31] T. Jim, J. G. Morrisett, D. Grossman, M. W. Hicks, J. Cheney, and Y. Wang. Cyclone: A safe dialect of C. In *Usenix ATC '02*, pages 275–288, June 2002.

[32] R. W. M. Jones and P. H. J. Kelly. Backwards-compatible bounds checking for arrays and pointers in C programs. In *the International Workshop on Automatic Debugging*, 1997.

[33] M. Kaempf. Vudo malloc tricks. *Phrack*, 11(57), 2001.

[34] V. Kiriansky, D. Bruening, and S. P. Amarasinghe. Secure execution via program shepherding. In *Usenix Security '02*, pages 191–206.

[35] L. Lamport. Proving the correctness of multiprocess programs. *IEEE Trans. Softw. Eng.*, 3(2):125–143, 1977.

[36] D. Lea. dlmalloc. http://g.oswego.edu/.

[37] P. Lee, T. Bu, and G. Chandranmenon. A lock-free, cache-efficient multi-core synchronization mechanism for line-rate network traffic monitoring. In *IPDPS '10*, pages 1–12.

[38] R. Lemos. Counting the cost of Slammer, 2003. http://news.cnet.com/Counting-the-cost-of-Slammer/2100-1002_3-982955.html.

[39] M. M. Michael. Hazard pointers: Safe memory reclamation for lock-free objects. *IEEE Trans. Parallel Distrib. Syst.*, 15(6):491–504, 2004.

[40] M. M. Michael. High performance dynamic lock-free hash tables and list-based sets. In *SPAA '02*, pages 73–82.

[41] MSDN. Structured exception handling. http://msdn.microsoft.com/en-us/library/ms680657(VS.85).aspx.

[42] G. C. Necula, J. Condit, M. Harren, S. McPeak, and W. Weimer. CCured: type-safe retrofitting of legacy software. *ACM Trans. Program. Lang. Syst.*, 27(3):477–526, 2005.

[43] NIST. National Vulnerability Database. http://nvd.nist.gov/.

[44] NIST. SAMATE Reference Dataset. http://samate.nist.gov/SRD.

[45] G. Novark and E. D. Berger. Dieharder: securing the heap. In *CCS '10*, pages 573–584.

[46] Open Source project. Amino concurrent building blocks. http://amino-cbbs.sourceforge.net/.

[47] Open Source Project. libsigsegv. http://libsigsegv.sourceforge.net/.

[48] S. Prakash, Y.-H. Lee, and T. Johnson. A nonblocking algorithm for shared queues using compare-and-swap. *IEEE Trans. Comput.*, 43(5): 548–559, 1994.

[49] M. Prasad and T. Chiueh. A binary rewriting defense against stack based buffer overflow attacks. In *Usenix ATC '03*, pages 211–224.

[50] G. Richarte. Four different tricks to bypass StackShield and Stack-Guard protection. Tech. report, Core Security Tech., 2002.

[51] W. Robertson, C. Kruegel, D. Mutz, and F. Valeur. Run-time detection of heap-based overflows. In *LISA '03*, pages 51–60.

[52] O. Ruwase and M. S. Lam. A practical dynamic buffer overflow detector. In *NDSS '04*, pages 159–169.

[53] B. Salamat, T. Jackson, A. Gal, and M. Franz. Orchestra: intrusion detection using parallel execution and monitoring of program variants in user-space. In *EuroSys '09*, pages 33–46.

[54] SecuriTeam. http://www.securiteam.com/.

[55] SecurityFocus. CVS directory request double free heap corruption, 2003.

[56] SecurityFocus. Mozilla Firefox and Seamonkey regular expression parsing heap buffer overflow, 2009.

[57] SecurityFocus. Wu-ftpd file globbing heap corruption, 2001.

[58] SecurityFocus. libHX 'HX_split()' remote heap-based buffer overflow, 2010.

[59] SecurityFocus. Lynx browser 'convert_to_idna()' function remote heap based buffer overflow, 2010.

[60] SecurityFocus. http://www.securityfocus.com/.

[61] SecurityFocus. Sudo password prompt heap overflow, 2002.

[62] O. Shalev and N. Shavit. Split-ordered lists: Lock-free extensible hash tables. *J. ACM*, 53(3):379–405, 2006.

[63] Solar Designer. Non-executable user stack, 1997. http://www.openwall.com/linux/.

[64] StackShield. http://www.angelfire.com/sk/stackshield/, January 2000.

[65] The PaX project. http://pax.grsecurity.net/.

[66] T. K. Tsai and N. Singh. Libsafe: Transparent system-wide protection against buffer overflow attacks. In *DSN '02*, pages 541–541.

[67] US-CERT. Vulnerability notes database. www.kb.cert.org/vuls.

[68] Valgrind. http://valgrind.org/.

[69] D. Wagner, J. S. Foster, E. A. Brewer, and A. Aiken. A first step towards automated detection of buffer overrun vulnerabilities. In *NDSS'00*, pages 3–17.

[70] J. Xu, Z. Kalbarczyk, S. Patel, and R. Iyer. Architecture support for defending against buffer overflow attacks. In *Workshop Evaluating & Architecting Sys. Depend.*, 2002.

[71] M. Zhivich, T. Leek, and R. Lippmann. Dynamic buffer overflow detection. In *Workshop on the Evaluation of Software Defect Detection Tools*, 2005.

Isolating and Understanding Concurrency Errors Using Reconstructed Execution Fragments

Brandon Lucia Benjamin P. Wood Luis Ceze

University of Washington, Department of Computer Science and Engineering

{blucia0a,bpw,luisceze}@cs.washington.edu

http://sampa.cs.washington.edu

Abstract

In this paper we propose *Recon*, a new general approach to concurrency debugging. Recon goes beyond just detecting bugs, it also presents to the programmer short fragments of buggy execution schedules that illustrate how and why bugs happened. These fragments, called *reconstructions*, are inferred from inter-thread communication surrounding the root cause of a bug and significantly simplify the process of *understanding* bugs.

The key idea in Recon is to monitor executions and build graphs that encode inter-thread communication with enough context information to build reconstructions. Recon leverages reconstructions built from multiple application executions and uses machine learning to identify which ones illustrate the root cause of a bug. Recon's approach is *general* because it does not rely on heuristics specific to any type of bug, application, or programming model. Therefore, it is able to deal with single- and multiple-variable concurrency bugs regardless of their type (*e.g.*, atomicity violation, ordering, etc). To make graph collection efficient, Recon employs selective monitoring and allows metadata information to be imprecise without compromising accuracy. With these optimizations, Recon's graph collection imposes overheads typically between 5x and 20x for both C/C++ and Java programs, with overheads as low as 13% in our experiments. We evaluate Recon with buggy applications, and show it produces reconstructions that include all code points involved in bugs' causes, and presents them in an accurate order. We include a case study of understanding and fixing a previously unresolved bug to showcase Recon's effectiveness.

Categories and Subject Descriptors D.1.3 [*Programming Techniques*]: Concurrent Programming; D.2.5 [*Software Engineering*]: Debugging Aids

General Terms Algorithms, Reliability

Keywords concurrency, statistical debugging, multithreading

1. Introduction

Concurrency bugs are a major stumbling block to writing multithreaded programs. Even expert programmers puzzle over complicated behaviors resulting from the unexpected interaction of operations in different threads. Developers face errors such as data races, atomicity violations, deadlocks, and ordering errors.

Concurrency bugs are particularly difficult to diagnose and fix for two main reasons. First, developers must reason about the interactions of many pieces of code executing in multiple threads. Observing one thread's buggy behavior is often insufficient for understanding the cause of the bug, which may lie in another thread. Second, non-determinism in multi-threaded execution complicates the process of interpreting buggy executions. The exact behavior of the application may vary, even from one buggy run to the next, making it very difficult to pin-point the root cause of the bug. Prior work [16] showed that the challenges of concurrency have led developers to give up on some bugs entirely, or to apply incorrect or incomplete stop-gap solutions. As a result, errors remain in the wild, potentially leading to surprising software failures.

There is a large body of work addressing concurrency bugs. A significant fraction of prior work focuses on dynamically detecting data races [6, 25], atomicity violations [8, 17], and locking or sharing discipline violations [1, 26, 33]. Some recent work on testing investigated new ways of systematically exploring executions [5, 21] and replaying buggy executions [24, 31]. Prior work has had considerable success, but there still remains much to be addressed.

First, many prior approaches to *detect* bugs report *too little* information to understand bugs: a single communication event [18, 27, 32] or the thread preemptions from buggy runs [5, 21]. However, concurrency bugs are complex and involve code points distributed over a code base and in multiple threads, requiring more information to be fully understood. To *understand* such bugs, developers benefit from seeing a portion of the execution illustrating the actual code interleaving that led to buggy behavior. Second, replay-based approaches [24, 31] often report *too much* information — effectively, the entire execution schedule. Replay makes bugs reproducible, but programmers must sift through an entire execution trace to comprehend bugs. Finally, many techniques are tailored to a specific class of concurrency errors [17, 23], limiting their applicability. It is infeasible to anticipate every possible error scenario, and design a tool targeting each. Hence, *generality* is crucial.

We propose Recon, a new approach to concurrency debugging based on *reconstructions* of buggy executions. Reconstructions are short, focused fragments of the interleaving schedule surrounding a program event, such as shared-memory communication. Figure 1 illustrates what a reconstruction is and how a reconstruction relates to an execution. Observe that not all program events are included in the reconstruction. Instead, a reconstruction contains a concise summary of program behavior surrounding an event that is likely to be related to a concurrency error. Reconstructions are based on communication graphs that encode information about the ordering of communication events. Based on this ordering, reconstructions show the interleaving that caused buggy behavior, rather than just

PLDI'11, June 4–8, 2011, San Jose, California, USA.

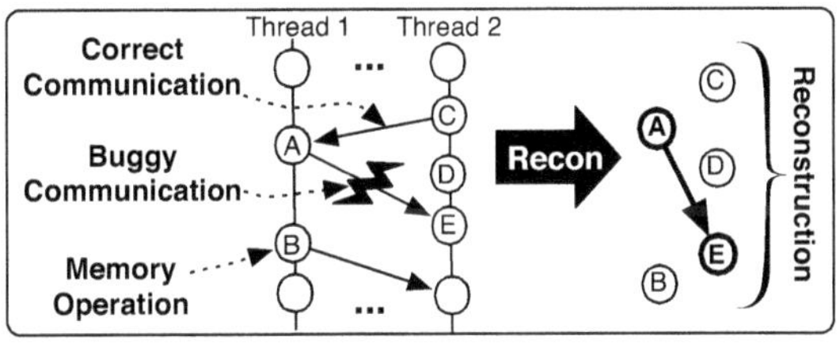

Figure 1. Recon reconstructs fragments of program execution.

some of the code points involved. Reconstructions are *general*, as they make no assumptions about the nature of bugs — *i.e.*, Recon does not look for specific patterns.

Figure 2 shows an overview of Recon's basic operation. The process begins when a programmer observes a bug or receives a bug report. The programmer then derives a test case designed to trigger the bug, and runs the test multiple times under Recon. Recon collects a communication graph from each execution, and the programmer or test environment labels each graph as buggy or nonbuggy, depending on the outcome of the test. Recon then builds reconstructions from edges in buggy graphs; for each one, Recon computes statistical features to quantify the likelihood that they are related to the bug. Recon uses the features to compute a rank for each reconstruction, and presents them to the user in rank order.

With Recon, we make several contributions:

- We propose the concept of reconstructing fragments of multi-threaded executions and develop an algorithm that builds reconstructions from communication graphs.
- We propose a set of features to describe reconstructions and use statistical techniques to identify reconstructions that illustrate the root cause of bugs.
- We develop optimization techniques to build communication graphs efficiently.
- We implement Recon for both C/C++ and Java. Our evaluation uses bugs from the literature, including several large applications, and shows that Recon precisely identifies bugs and their corresponding reconstructions. We include a case study of using Recon to understand and fix an unresolved bug.

The rest of this paper is organized as follows. Section 2 discusses concurrency bugs in general and provides an overview of the role of communication graphs for debugging. Section 3 discusses our approach to reconstructing execution fragments. Section 4 describes how we use machine learning techniques to identify bugs. Section 5 describes our implementation of Recon for C/C++ and Java, and several enabling optimizations. Section 6 describes our experiments, which show that Recon reconstructs buggy executions precisely and efficiently. Section 7 discusses related work and Section 8 concludes.

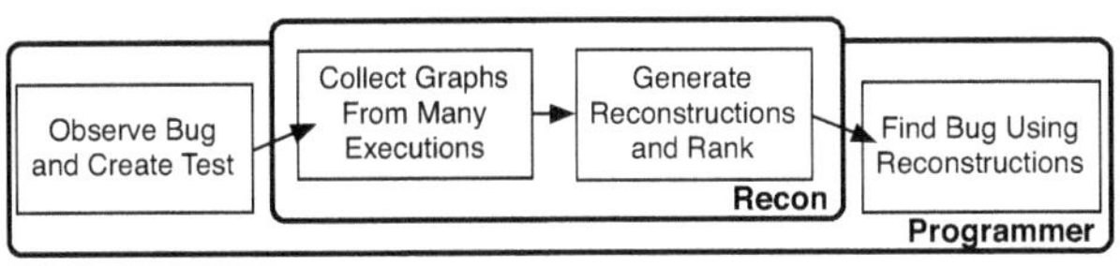

Figure 2. Overview of Recon's operation.

2. Background

2.1 Concurrency Bugs

Data races occur when two different threads access the same memory location, at least one access is a write, and the accesses are not ordered by synchronization. *Ordering violations* involve two or more memory accesses from multiple threads that happen in an unexpected order, due to absent or incorrect synchronization.

Atomicity violations result from a lack of constraints on the interleaving of operations in a program. Figure 3(a) illustrates an atomicity violation bug that was found in `weblech`, a multi-threaded web crawler. The program uses a shared queue that was implemented incorrectly. The check of the queue's size on line 168 should be atomic with the dequeue operation performed on line 189 to ensure that there is always an item to dequeue, but the programmer has not implemented this atomicity constraint.

Figure 3(b) shows an execution trace manifesting the bug. In this trace, the `size()` and `dequeue()` calls in Thread 2 interleave between the `size()` and `dequeue()` calls in Thread 1. Since the queue is emptied by Thread 2, Thread 1's call to `dequeue()` returns `null`, which is stored in the local variable `item`. Thread 1 later crashes with a `NullPointerException` when trying to invoke the `getD()` method on this null `item`.

2.2 Communication Graph Debugging

Prior work [18, 27, 32] has observed that *communication graphs* are useful for detecting concurrency errors. A communication graph is a representation of a program execution that captures inter-thread data-flow. A node in a communication graph represents a memory instruction at some program point. An edge between two nodes, the *source* and *sink*, indicates that the sink instruction read or overwrote data written by the source instruction. Furthermore, the source and sink instructions executed in different threads.

The main idea behind concurrency debugging with communication graphs is that a problematic communication event characterizes the error's behavior, and is represented by an edge in the graph. Identifying the problematic communication event illustrates the bug's behavior to a developer, aiding in debugging. An approach used in prior work for identifying problematic communication is to focus on communication events that tend to occur often in buggy program runs, and infrequently or never in correct program runs [17, 32]. This technique is often useful, but insufficient in general.

To understand why, refer back to the example in Figure 3(b). The problematic communication event is Thread 1's read of the queue's `qsize` field on line 115; it reads a value written by Thread 2 at line 117 rather than the same value Thread 1 read from `qsize`, at line 133. Looking at this communication alone is insufficient to find the bug; the involved instructions communicate in both buggy *and* nonbuggy executions. This difficulty in identifying problematic communication graph edges was the motivation for developing *context-aware communication graphs* in Bugaboo [18].

Context-Aware Communication Graphs. Bugaboo first demonstrated that communication graphs are insufficient for general concurrency bug detection. Bugaboo addresses this inadequacy by adding *communication context* to communication graphs. Communication context is a short (*e.g.*, 5 entries) history of *context events* that is maintained by each thread in an execution. Context events are *Local Reads*, *Local Writes*, *Remote Reads*, and *Remote Writes*. A thread records a "Local" event in its context when it executes a sharing read or write operation. A thread records a "Remote" event in its context when another thread reads or writes a memory location that it has accessed recently. Note that context events record only the type of a memory operation (*e.g.*,"Remote Read"), not the code or data involved.

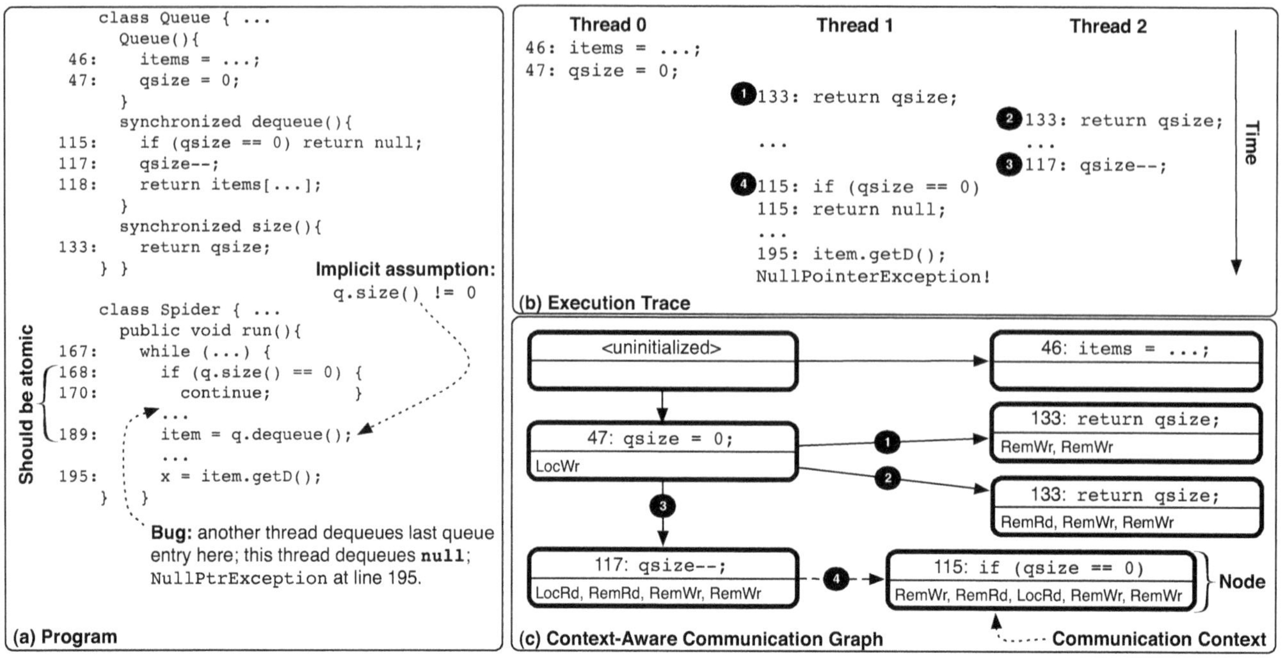

Figure 3. Example showing (a) a buggy program, (b) a bug-triggering execution trace, and (c) the context-aware communication graph produced by the trace. Nodes represent the execution of operations in a specific context. Edges represent communication between nodes. Note that we only include events in nodes' contexts that appear in our abbreviated trace for presentation purposes.

Communication context is the basis for context-aware communication graphs. In a context-aware graph a node is a pair (I, C) representing the execution of a static instruction, I, in communication context, C, instead of just an instruction. Edges in a context-aware graph represent communication between dynamic instruction *instances*. In a context-aware graph, there may be more than one node per static instruction, but the size of the graph is bounded by a function of the context size, as described in prior work [18].

Figure 3(c) shows a context-aware communication graph produced by the execution trace in Figure 3(b). The numbered circles map events in the trace to their corresponding edge in the graph. In the context-aware graph, the sink node of edge 4 occurs only in buggy executions. The most recent (left-most) two events in this node's context are the Remote Write that corresponds to Thread 2's write at line 117, and the Remote Read that corresponds to Thread 2's read at line 133. This context reflects the buggy interleaving of Thread 1's read of `qsize` at line 133, and its read of `qsize` at line 115. Hence, edge 4, which includes this unique context-aware node, occurs in buggy executions' graphs, and not correct executions' graphs. Context-aware graphs provide a way to identify buggy communication in such complex bugs.

Debugging with communication graphs is one of the key motivating ideas behind Recon. However, rather than just isolating graph edges likely to represent problematic communication, as most prior work has done, Recon reconstructs *temporal sequences* of communication events and, using machine learning, infers which sequences most likely illustrate a bug's cause.

3. Reconstructing Execution Fragments

The goal of Recon is to simplify debugging by presenting the programmer with a short, focused, temporally ordered reconstruction of the events that were responsible for buggy behavior. Our technique for reconstructing execution fragments is based on a specialized version of context-aware communication graphs [18].

3.1 Timestamped Communication Graphs

We specialize the context-aware communication graph abstraction to encode ordering between non-communicating nodes. We do so by adding a timestamp to each node, indicating when the node's instruction executed in the node's context. We call this new graph abstraction the *timestamped communication graph*; referring to them as just "graphs" hereafter. To summarize the structure of the graphs used by Recon:

- A node is a pair (I, C) representing the execution of static instruction I in communication context C. Each node is labeled with a timestamp, T, representing the global time when instruction I last executed in context C.
- An edge is a pair of nodes (u, v) representing communication from the instruction instance represented by u to the instruction instance represented by v.

Graph Construction. We collect graphs by keeping a *last-writer record* for each memory location, storing: (1) the thread that last wrote the location; (2) the instruction address and context of that write; and (3) a timestamp for the access. When a memory location is accessed by a different thread than the thread that last wrote the location, an edge is added to the graph. The edge's source node is populated with the instruction address, context, and timestamp from the location's last-writer record. The edge's sink node is populated with the instruction address, context, and timestamp of the operation being performed.

To limit the size of the graph, we record only the most recent pair of timestamps for an edge, *i.e.*, the timestamp is not used to identify a node, only the instruction and context are. When adding a communication edge to the graph, if the edge already exists, only the timestamps are updated. By overwriting timestamps, we lose some ordering information, so we call our extension a *lossy timestamp*. Figure 4(a) shows an example of a timestamped communica-

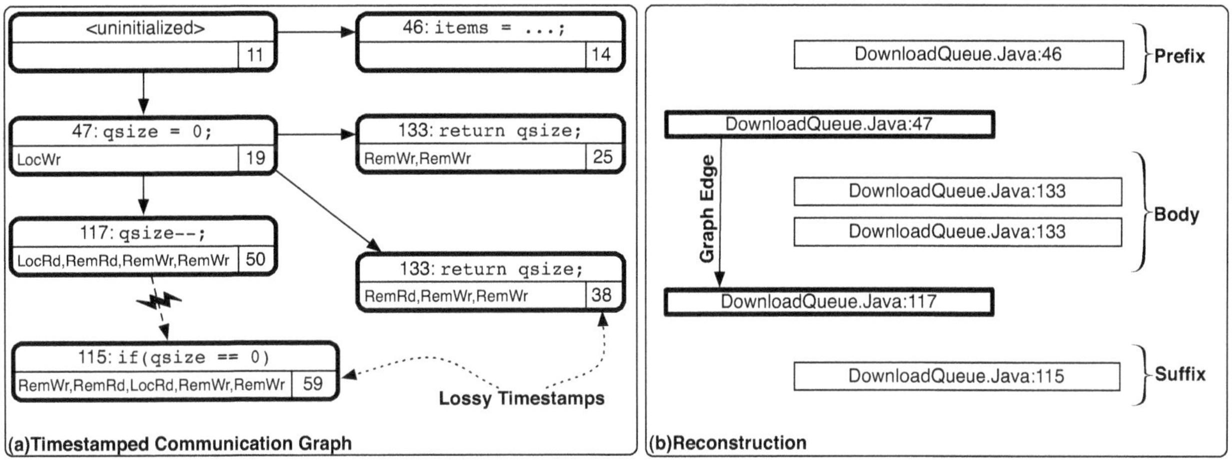

Figure 4. A timestamped communication graph (a) and reconstruction (b). The graph corresponds to Figure 3(c).

tion graph. The graph is similar to the one in Figure 3, except that each node now has a timestamp indicating when it last occurred.

3.2 Reconstructions

A *reconstruction* is a schedule of communicating memory operations that occurred during a short fragment of an execution. In this section, we describe the process of building a reconstruction around a single, arbitrary communication event (*i.e.*, graph edge). Section 4 describes how we identify the reconstructions most likely related to bugs, and Section 5.3 details the entire debugging process.

3.2.1 Building Reconstructions from Graphs

Recon builds reconstructions starting from an edge in a graph. In addition to the instructions represented by the source and sink nodes of the edge, a reconstruction should include the memory operations that executed in a short window prior to the source node, in the time between the source and the sink nodes, and in a short window following the sink. These *regions* of the execution are called the *prefix*, *body*, and *suffix* of the reconstruction, respectively, and are selected from the graph for a single execution according to nodes' timestamps.

The size of the window of nodes considered in computing the prefix and suffix is arbitrary. With a larger window, there is a greater chance that unrelated nodes are included in a reconstruction. With a smaller window, fewer unrelated nodes are likely to end up in a reconstruction, but we risk excluding events related to the bug that occur far away from the communication event. A reasonable window size heuristic is to use the length of the communication context of a node. Using the context length, we include nodes that were influenced by, or influenced the context of the sink or source.

Formal Definition of Reconstruction A reconstruction is a tuple (e, p, b, s). The reconstruction is built around an edge, e, with source node, e_{src} and sink node, e_{sink}. The prefix, p, is a set of consecutive nodes immediately preceding e_{src} in timestamp order. The body, b, is the set of all nodes between e_{src} and e_{sink} in timestamp order. The suffix s is a set of consecutive nodes immediately following e_{sink} in timestamp order. The cardinalities of the prefix and suffix are bounded by fixed constants. The cardinality of the body is bounded by a threshold function described in Section 5.3.

3.2.2 Simpler Debugging Using Reconstructions

Figure 4(b) shows the reconstruction Recon produces from one of the edges in the graph in Figure 4(a). This reconstruction illustrates the buggy interleaving of queue operations shown in Figure 3(b). It includes all the code points involved in the bug, and presents them in the order that leads to buggy behavior. In buggy runs, the read of the queue's size on line 133 and the dequeue on line 115 are interleaved by the dequeuing decrement of `qsize` at line 117. This buggy interleaving is clear in the reconstruction: line 133's node is in the body and line 115's node is in the suffix. The interleaving dequeue operation at line 117 is the sink node, ordered between the body and the suffix.

This example illustrates a key contribution of reconstructions. Looking at the buggy edge between line 117's node and line 115's node does not explicitly indicate the bug — it suggests the involvement of the queue, but not the atomicity violation involving line 133. Instead, the reconstruction built around the *nonbuggy* edge from line 47's node and line 117's node illustrates the bug, showing all three involved code points *and* the buggy execution order.

3.3 Aggregate Reconstructions

We have described how to build a reconstruction for a single edge from a single execution. We can aggregate reconstructions from a *set* of runs to see how frequently code points occur in a region of a reconstruction *across* executions. This information allows us to define our confidence that a code point belongs in a region.

Starting from a set of graphs, we compute a reconstruction for each edge in each execution's graph individually. We then aggregate the reconstructions of each edge across the executions by computing the union of each of their prefixes, the union of each of their bodies, and the union of each of their suffixes, producing the aggregate prefix, body, and suffix. A node may occur in multiple different regions in an aggregate reconstruction, if, for instance, in half of executions it appeared in the prefix, and in half it appeared in the body. Nodes in the same region in an aggregate reconstruction are unordered with one another, but are ordered with the source and the sink of the edge in the reconstruction, and with nodes in other regions. Nodes within a region are unordered because timestamps are not comparable across executions.

When aggregating reconstructions, we associate a confidence value with each node in a region. The confidence value is equal to the fraction of executions in which that node appeared in that region. The confidence value of a node in a region represents the likelihood that a node occurs in that region. In Section 4, we discuss using confidence values to identify reconstructions likely related to buggy behavior.

Figure 5 shows an example of the aggregation process. Part (a) shows reconstructions produced from 4 different executions, and

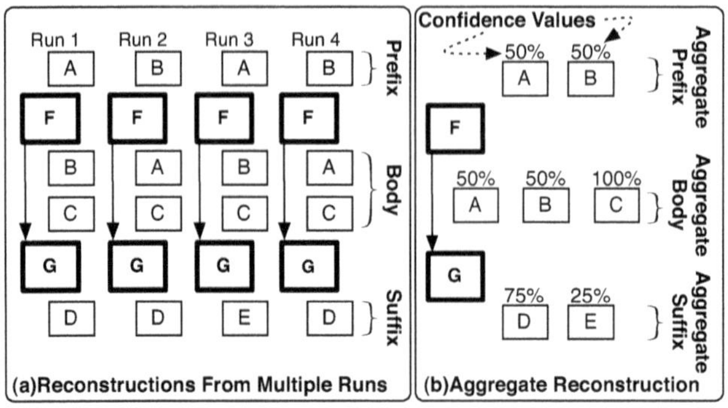

Figure 5. (a) Reconstructions of many runs and (b) the resulting aggregate reconstruction with confidence values.

part (b) shows the aggregate reconstruction produced from these 4 reconstructions. In this example, node A appears in the prefix of half of the reconstructions, and appears in the body in half of the reconstructions. The prefix and body of the aggregate reconstruction therefore both include node A, and assign it a confidence value of 50%. Node C appears in the body of all of the individual reconstructions, so it appears in the body of the aggregate reconstruction with a confidence value of 100%.

4. Debugging with Reconstructions

There are four steps to debugging a program with Recon:

1. The program is run under Recon several times, yielding a set of timestamped communication graphs labeled buggy or nonbuggy (Section 2.1).
2. Next, Recon must decide which edges are worth using as the basis for a reconstruction. Recon selects edges from each buggy graph based on how strongly correlated they are with the occurrence of buggy behavior. Section 4.1.1 describes this correlation.
3. For each selected edge, Recon builds and aggregates reconstructions (Sections 3.2 and 3.3).
4. Finally, Recon ranks the reconstructions by how likely they are to illustrate the bug, as determined by a set of *features* computed from the aggregated reconstructions and the nonbuggy graphs.

We now discuss the features we developed, and how we use them to produce a reconstruction's rank.

4.1 Features of Reconstructions

A key design concern is that features are *general*. A feature that targets one bug type or pattern is not as useful. If we choose features that are not general, we bias our search toward some bugs and miss others entirely. For example, serializability analysis of memory access interleavings has been used to detect atomicity violations [17, 23]. However, it does not detect ordering bugs or any multi-variable bugs.

Our features should capture as much information as necessary to discriminate between reconstructions of buggy fragments of an execution and reconstructions of nonbuggy fragments. We use three features: *Buggy Frequency Ratio* focuses on the correlation between communication events and buggy behavior; *Context Variation Ratio* focuses on variations in communication context that correlate with buggy behavior; and *Reconstruction Consistency* focuses on the consistency with which sequences of code points occur in reconstructions from buggy executions. The rest of this section describes these features in detail and verifies their efficacy empirically using a feature importance metric from machine learning [14].

4.1.1 Buggy Frequency Ratio (B)

Intuition. A reconstruction's Buggy Frequency Ratio, or B value, describes the correlation between the frequency of the communication event from which the reconstruction was built, and the occurrence of buggy behavior. The motivation for this feature is that we are interested in events in an execution that occur often in buggy program runs, but rarely, or never, in nonbuggy runs.

Definition. For each aggregate reconstruction, assume $\#Runs_b$ buggy runs and $\#Runs_n$ nonbuggy runs. Assume the reconstruction's edge occurred in $EdgeFreq_b$ buggy runs and in $EdgeFreq_n$ nonbuggy runs. The fraction of buggy runs in which the edge occurred is:

$$Frac_b = \frac{EdgeFreq_b}{\#Runs_b}$$

The fraction of nonbuggy runs in which the edge occurred is:

$$Frac_n = \frac{EdgeFreq_n}{\#Runs_n}$$

We define B as follows:

$$B = \frac{Frac_b}{Frac_n}$$

If a reconstruction's edge occurs in many buggy runs and few nonbuggy runs, B is large. Conversely, if the edge occurs often in nonbuggy runs and rarely in buggy runs, B is small.

If the edge never occurs in a nonbuggy run, but occurs in buggy runs, then it is very likely related to the bug. However, in such a case, $Frac_n$ is 0, and unless we handle this case specially, B is undefined. In this corner case, we give $Frac_n$ a value that is smaller than the value produced if the edge occurs in one nonbuggy run (by assigning $Frac_n = \frac{1}{\#Runs_n+1}$). This yields large B values for these important edges.

4.1.2 Context Variation Ratio (C)

Intuition. The Context Variation Ratio (C) quantifies how variation of contexts of communicating code points correlates with buggy execution. We can determine the pair of communicating code points in the edge around which a reconstruction is built, since a node is identified by an instruction and context. From that, we can determine all edges involving that pair of code points, regardless of context; we then compute the set of all contexts in which the pair communicated. In a program that has frequent, varied communication, there are many contexts in this set; in a program with little — or less-varied — communication, the set is small. We consider a reconstruction suspicious if the pair of code points forming the edge around which the reconstruction was built execute in a substantially different number of contexts in buggy runs than in correct runs.

Definition. For a reconstruction built around an edge between two code points, we define $\#Ctx_b$ to be the number of contexts in which the code points communicated in buggy runs, and $\#Ctx_n$ to be the number in nonbuggy runs. C is the ratio of the absolute difference of $\#Ctx_b$ and $\#Ctx_n$ to the total number of contexts for the pair of code points in nonbuggy and buggy runs. We define C as follows:

$$C = \frac{|\#Ctx_b - \#Ctx_n|}{\#Ctx_b + \#Ctx_n}$$

Large C values indicate a disparity in communication behavior between buggy and nonbuggy runs. Hence, a reconstruction with a large C value more likely illustrates the communication pattern that led to buggy behavior.

4.1.3 Reconstruction Consistency (R)

Intuition. Reconstruction Consistency (R) is the average confidence value over all code points in an aggregate reconstruction. R is useful because code points that consistently occur in reconstructions of buggy executions are likely related to the cause of the bug. As described in Section 3.2, each node in an aggregate reconstruction has an associated confidence value that represents the frequency with which it occurs at a certain point in that reconstruction. In an aggregate reconstruction produced from a set of buggy runs, a node with a high confidence value occurs consistently in the same region of reconstructions from those buggy runs. Such nodes' operations are therefore likely to be related to the buggy behavior in those runs. Reconstructions containing many high confidence nodes reflect a correlation between the *co-occurrence* of those nodes' code points in the order shown by the reconstruction, and the occurrence of buggy behavior.

Definition. We compute R for a reconstruction as the average confidence value over all its nodes. Formally, for a reconstruction with prefix region P, body B, and suffix S and where $V(n,r)$ is the confidence value of node n in region r, we define R as follows:

$$R = \frac{\sum_{p \in P} V(p,P) + \sum_{b \in B} V(b,B) + \sum_{s \in S} V(s,S)}{|P| + |B| + |S|}$$

Nodes in a reconstruction with a large R value tend to occur in the reconstructed order when buggy behavior occurs. Such reconstructions are therefore more likely to represent problematic interleavings, and to be useful for debugging.

4.2 Using Features to Find Bugs

By construction, large values for B, C, or R indicate that a reconstruction is likely to be buggy. Therefore, we give each reconstruction a score equal to the product of all non-zero features' values. We rank reconstructions, with highest scoring reconstruction first.

Empirical validation of B, C, and R. We now quantitatively justify our features using real buggy code (we describe our experimental setup in Section 6). We assessed the discriminatory power of our features using Weka's [9] ReliefF [14] feature selection function. The magnitude of a feature's ReliefF value is greater if the distance between points of different classes (*e.g.*buggy or non-buggy) is greater along that feature's dimension, on average. The magnitude of a feature's ReliefF value corresponds to how well it discriminates between classes.

Table 1 shows ReliefF values for bugs in several C/C++ applications. All features' ReliefF values are non-zero, meaning they are useful for classification, and many have ReliefF values close to 1.0. The relative importance of features varies by program.

For `apache`, B and R are the most useful. C is less important, indicating there is a similar amount of context variation in buggy and nonbuggy runs. Figure 6 illustrates the relative importance of the features graphically, with pair-wise feature plots. Figure 6(a) shows that when viewed along the axes of highest ReliefF, there is clear segregation of buggy and nonbuggy reconstructions. In the plot, buggy points tend to the upper right, meaning they have larger feature values than nonbuggy points. Figures 6(b) and (c) reiterate the class segregation along the B and R axes, and illustrate the less clear division along the C axis.

`pbzip2`'s ReliefF values are smaller than other applications' values. The disparity indicates that in each dimension, `pbzip2`'s buggy and nonbuggy points tend to be nearer to one another than in other applications. Hence, ranking by a single feature is inadequate to isolate bugs precisely. However, in the three-dimensional space of all features, buggy and nonbuggy reconstructions are far apart. As our results in Section 6.2 confirm, ranking using all three features isolates the reconstruction of the bug in `pbzip2`.

	ReliefF Rank		
Program	B	R	C
apache	0.99	0.91	0.16
mysql	0.20	0.59	0.76
pbzip2	0.26	0.28	0.28
aget	0.84	0.91	0.16

Table 1. ReliefF rank of features for C/C++ programs.

Our ReliefF feature analysis emphasizes two properties of our technique: (1) our features precisely classify buggy reconstructions to identify bugs; and (2) considered together, our features are more powerful than each individually.

5. Implementation

We implemented two versions of Recon: one for C/C++, using Pin [19], and one for Java, using RoadRunner [7]. The implementation has three parts: (1) tracking communication; (2) collecting graphs; and (3) generating and ranking reconstructions.

5.1 Tracking Communication

To track communication we maintain a *metadata table*. This table maps each memory location to an entry containing its last-writer record, and a list of threads that have read from the location since its last write that we call the *sharers list*. Each thread has a communication context. A thread's context is a shift register of events, as described in Section 3. We use a 5-entry context.

When a thread writes to a memory location, it updates the location's last-writer record with its thread ID, the instruction address of the write, its current context, and the current timestamp. If the writing thread is different from the last writer, it does three things: (1) update its context with a local write event; (2) update the context of each thread in the sharers list with a remote write event; and (3) clear the sharers list.

When a thread reads a location, it looks up the last writer thread in the last-writer record. If the reading thread is different from the last writer, it does three things: (1) update its context with a local read; (2) update the last writer thread's context with a remote read; and (3) add the reading thread to the memory location's sharers list.

For C/C++, we implement the metadata table as a fixed size hash table of 32 million entries. To find a memory location's metadata, we index with the address modulo the table size. We use a lossy collision resolution policy: on a hash collision, an access may read or overwrite another colliding location's metadata. We ignore stack accesses, as they are rarely involved in communication. For Java, we use RoadRunner's shadow memory to implement a distributed metadata table. Its size scales with allocated memory and it does not suffer from collisions. Unique identifiers of memory access instructions in the bytecode replace instruction addresses. Contexts are stored as integers, using bit fields. We instrument accesses to fields and arrays, but not local variables.

5.2 Timestamped Communication Graphs

Each thread maintains its own partial communication graph. Partitioning the communication graph over all threads makes adding an edge a thread-local operation, which is critical for performance. When a thread tries to add an edge, it first searches the graph for the edge. If the edge is already in the graph, the thread overwrites the existing timestamps with the timestamps of the edge being added. If not, a new edge is created. When a thread ends, it merges its partial graph into a global graph. Once all partial graphs are merged into the global graph, it is written to a file.

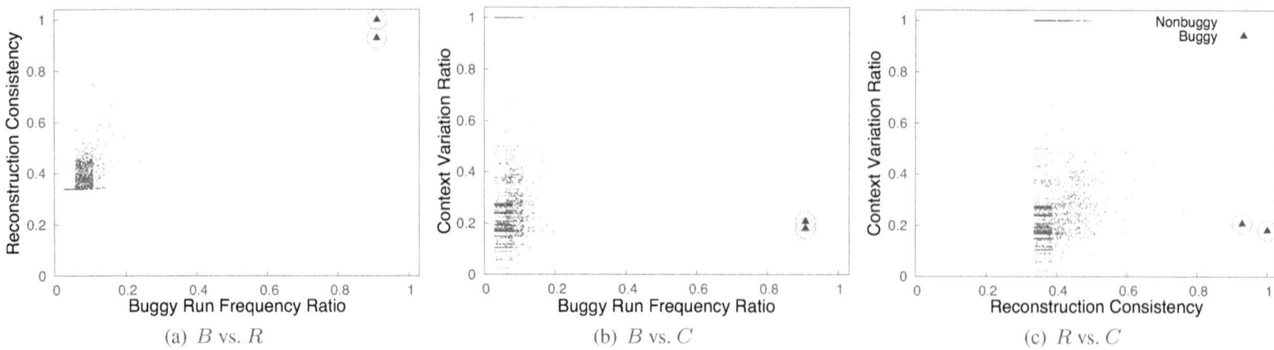

Figure 6. Pair-wise plots of features for `apache` showing the top 2000 ranked reconstructions. Buggy reconstructions' points are circled.

For C/C++, we use the `RDTSC` x86 instruction to track timestamps. We maintain communication graphs as a chaining hash table. Separately for the source and sink node, the hash function sums the entries in each node's context. Each node's sum is then XORed with the node's instruction address. The result of the computation for the source node is then XORed with the result of the computation for the sink, producing the hash key. For Java, we generate timestamps from the system time and implement communication graphs as adjacency lists.

5.3 Generating and Ranking Reconstructions

We generate and rank reconstructions with the following process. We separately load sets of buggy and nonbuggy graphs into memory and create a list of nodes ordered by timestamp for each buggy run. At this point, we compute C and B for each edge in the set of buggy graphs. We then rank these edges by their B values. Next, we generate reconstructions for the top 2000 edges ranked by B, using the algorithm described in Section 3.2. To limit the size of the reconstructions produced, we limit the number of code points in each region. To do so, we threshold by confidence value, excluding from a reconstruction any node that has a confidence value less than half the region's maximum confidence value. After computing reconstructions, we compute their R values and their ranks, and output them in rank order.

5.4 Optimizing Graph Collection

We use two optimizations to reduce overheads: (1) we reduce the number of instructions for which analysis is required and (2) we permit an instrumentation data race to avoid locking overheads.

5.4.1 Selectively Tracking Memory Operations

The simplest way of reducing graph collection overhead is monitoring fewer memory operations. We develop two optimizations to do so. They can lead to lost or spurious edges, but our results (Section 6) show that Recon's accuracy is unaffected.

First Read Only. Repeated reads to a memory location by the same thread are likely redundant. We therefore develop the *first-read* optimization: threads perform analysis only on their first read to each location after a remote write to that location. Skipping updates on subsequent reads is analogous to performing analysis only on cache read misses. Due to the frequency and temporal locality of reads, this optimization eliminates many updates.

This optimization is *lossy*. If a thread repeatedly reads the result of a write, only its first read is reported. If subsequent reads are performed by different code or in different contexts they will not cause edges to be added to the graph. Additionally, context events corresponding to ignored reads are not published to threads' contexts, which may result in fewer distinct contexts and edges.

First Write Only. Repeated writes by the same thread are often redundant or non-communicating. Under the *first-write* optimization, a thread only updates the last-writer table and sharers list on a write to a memory location x when it is not the last thread to write x. This optimization is *noisy*. If a thread that is not the last writer of x writes to x and does not update x's metadata on subsequent writes, another thread's read of x may see outdated metadata and add a spurious edge with incorrect context information to the graph.

5.4.2 Intentional Instrumentation Races

On every memory access, threads check the last writer of the location they are accessing to determine what analysis operations must be performed, as described in Section 5.1. To ensure threads observe consistent metadata, they acquire a lock on each access.

We observe, however, that due to temporal locality these checks are often performed by the location's last writer. In such situations, reading all metadata is unnecessary. The cost of acquiring the lock just to check the last writer outweighs the cost of the check itself. To mitigate this cost, we can perform the check without holding the lock, which we call the *racy-lookups* optimization. If, based on the check, a thread determines it must perform further analysis or update the metadata, it acquires the lock. Only the check to determine the location's last writer races.

In principle, data races can lead to undefined behavior [4] or memory inconsistency [20]. In practice, there are only two inconsistent outcomes of this optimization. The first is that the last writer performs a check that indicates it is not the last writer. In this case, the checking thread last wrote the metadata. On x86 the thread will correctly read its own write, making this situation impossible. In Java, our metadata writes are well ordered, and the read involved in the check is ordered with its metadata update. As a result, the checking thread can only ever correctly read that it was the last writer. The other inconsistency is when a check indicates to a thread that it is the last writer when it is not. This situation is possible in x86 and Java. On x86, the check reports that the checking thread is the last writer, so it does no analysis. Because the check was not synchronized, however, another thread's update to the last-writer field may have been performed, but not yet made visible to all threads. In this case, the checking thread should have seen the update, and added an edge, but did not. This situation can also arise because our instrumentation is not atomic with program accesses. In practice, it has little impact on our analysis. Furthermore, the statistical nature of Recon is robust to noise, so such omissions do not impact Recon's bug detection capability.

	Category	Program	Version	Bug Type
C/C++	Bug Kernel	logandswp	n/a	Atomicity Violation
		circlist	n/a	Atomicity Violation
		textreflow	Mozilla 0.9	Multi-Variable Atomicity Violation
		jsstrlen	Mozilla 0.9	Multi-Variable Atomicity Violation
	Full App.	apache	httpd 2.0.48	Atomicity Violation
		mysql	mysqld 4.0.12	Atomicity Violation
		pbzip2	pbzip2 0.9.1	Ordering Violation
		aget	aget 0.4	Multi-Variable Atomicity Violation
Java	Bug Kernel	stringbuffer	JDK 1.6	Multi-Variable Atomicity Violation
		vector	JDK 1.4	Multi-Variable Atomicity Violation
	Full App.	weblech	weblech 0.0.3	Atomicity Violation

Table 2. The buggy programs we used to evaluate Recon

6. Evaluation

There are several components to our evaluation. We show that our ranking technique is effective at finding bugs and that the reconstructions Recon produces are useful and precise. We show that Recon requires few program runs in order to be effective. We describe a case study of our experience fixing a previously unresolved bug. Finally, we show that with our optimizations Recon's overheads are similar to other analysis tools, and overall data collection time is short.

6.1 Experimental Setup

We evaluated Recon's ability to detect concurrency bugs using the buggy programs described in Table 2. We used a set of full applications, as well as several bug kernels. Our bug kernels are shorter programs with bugs extracted from the literature (`stringbuffer`, `vector`, `circlist`, `logandswp`), and buggy sections of code extracted from full versions of the Mozilla project (`textreflow`, `jsstrlen`). Our benchmarks encompass many bug types observed in the wild [16] including ordering bugs and single- and multiple-variable atomicity bugs. We ran each application in Recon with all optimizations. Our test script used external symptoms such as crashes or corrupt output to label graphs.

We evaluated Recon's runtime and memory overhead, compared to uninstrumented execution. We used the PARSEC benchmark suite [2] with its `simlarge` input for our C/C++ implementation, and for Java we used 6 applications from the DaCapo benchmark suite [3], with default inputs, and all the Java Grande benchmarks [28], with size A inputs. We ran PARSEC and Java Grande with 8 threads; we let the DaCapo benchmarks self-configure based on the number of processors and did not instrument the DaCapo harness. We also ran 4 additional full applications, each with 8 threads: `mysql`, a database server, tested using the sysbench OLTP benchmark with the default table size (10,000) for the performance measurements and table size 100 for debugging; `apache`, a web server, tested using ApacheBench; `aget`, a download accelerator, tested fetching a large web file; and `pbzip2`, a compression tool, tested compressing a 100MB text file. For performance measurements, we ran the uninstrumented version and Recon, with the *first-read*, *first-write*, and *racy-lookups* optimizations. We also ran three less-optimized configurations to understand the impact of each optimization: "Base" analyzes all memory accesses; "FR" uses just the *first-read* optimization; "FR/W" adds the *first-write* optimization. We ran all experiments on an 8-core 2.8GHz Intel Xeon with 16GB of memory and Linux 2.6.24. The Java tool used the OpenJDK 64-bit Server VM 1.6.0 with a 16GB max heap. We report results averaged over 10 runs of each experiment.

6.2 How Effectively Does Recon Find Bugs?

We produced reconstructions using graphs collected from 25 buggy runs and 25 non-buggy runs. We ranked the reconstructions as described in Section 4.2. We examined the highest-ranked reconstruction that illustrated the bug and analyzed the key properties of that reconstruction. Table 3 summarizes our findings.

False Positives. The most important result in Table 3 is that for all applications, *the top-ranked reconstruction revealed the bug*, as shown in Column 2. This result demonstrates that our ranking technique effectively directs programmer attention to buggy code with no distracting false positives. This result also corroborates the results from Section 4.2, showing that our features precisely isolate buggy reconstructions.

Unrelated Code in Reconstructions. Columns 3 and 4 in Table 3 show the number of relevant and irrelevant code points that were included in the bug's reconstruction. We consider a code point related if it performs a memory access that reads or writes a corrupt or inconsistent value, or if it is control- or data-dependent on the buggy code. In most cases, virtually all code in the reconstruction is relevant to the bug. However, some reconstructions include code points unrelated to their bug. In `aget`, the two irrelevant code points are in straight-line code sequences with related code points, at a distance of less than five lines. Such nearby but irrelevant code is not likely to confuse a programmer.

In `mysql`'s case, five out of seven unrelated code points are in straight-line sequences with relevant code. The remaining two in `mysql`'s reconstruction, and all five in `apache`'s reconstruction, were not in straight-line code with relevant points. Instead, they were in another function that was the caller or a callee of a function containing relevant code. Developers debugging programs are likely to understand such caller-callee relationships, suggesting that these code points will not be too problematic.

`weblech` had several irrelevant code points in its reconstruction (28). The reason for their inclusion is that the bug usually occurs at the start of the execution. At this point, constructors have only just initialized data at a variety of code points in the program, resulting in many edges being added between initialization code and other code. The initialization code is easy to identify, especially with program knowledge. These code points clutter the reconstruction, but the bug is reported accurately.

Reconstruction Order Accuracy. Column 5 shows whether or not the code points in the reconstruction were shown in the order leading to buggy behavior. Code points appear in an order that leads to buggy behavior in all cases. In `logandswp`, the last code point in the buggy execution order appears in both the prefix and suffix of the reconstruction, because the code point is in a loop, however, the buggy interleaving is clear.

Program	Rank of Bug	# Code Pts. Rel.	# Code Pts. Irr.	In Order?	Code Pts Missing	Sensitivity To # Buggy w/ 5	Sensitivity To # Buggy w/ 15	Collect Time (h:m:s)
logandswp	1	6	1	Yes	0	1	1	—
circlist	1	3	3	Yes	0	1	1	—
textreflow	1	8	0	Yes	0	1	1	—
jsstrlen	1	7	0	Yes	0	1	1	—
apache	1	5	5	Yes	0	1	1	0:27:32
mysql	1	8	7	Yes	0	34	9	0:07:08
pbzip2	1	11	0	Yes	1	2	1	1:51:56
aget	1	4	2	Yes	0	8	1	0:59:41
stringbuffer	1	6	0	Yes	0	1	1	—
vector	1	6	0	Yes	0	1	1	—
weblech	1	6	28	Yes	0	4	1	0:13:36

Table 3. Properties of reconstructions. Column 1 is the rank of the bug's reconstruction. Columns 2 and 3 show the number of relevant and irrelevant code points in the bug's reconstruction. Column 4 shows whether the bug's reconstruction was in order. Column 5 shows the number of relevant code points missing from the reconstruction. Columns 6 and 7 show the rank of the bug's reconstructions using only 5 and 15 buggy graphs. Column 8 shows the graph collection time.

Missing Code Points. Column 6 shows the number of code points directly involved in the bug that were omitted from the reconstruction. Only one case lacked any involved code points: the code points in `pbzip2`'s reconstruction all relate to establishing the corrupted state condition required for a crash to occur. The actual crashing access is not included.

Sensitivity to Number of Buggy Runs. Columns 7 and 8 illustrate Recon's sensitivity to the number of buggy runs used. Column 7 shows the rank of the bug's reconstruction using 25 nonbuggy runs and 5 buggy runs. Column 8 shows the rank using 25 nonbuggy and 15 buggy runs. Even with very few buggy runs, Recon gives a high rank to reconstructions of the bug. Using fewer buggy runs does not impact precision substantially, except for `mysql`. Excluding `mysql`, Recon ranked the bug's reconstruction 8th or better with just 5 buggy runs, and first with 15 buggy runs. For `mysql`, using fewer runs caused Recon to rank some nonbuggy reconstructions above the bug's — 33 with 5 buggy runs, and 8 with 15 buggy runs. As shown in Column 2, Recon *always* ranked the bug's reconstruction first with 25 buggy runs. These results show that with very few buggy runs, Recon can find bugs with high precision. In cases where a small number of buggy runs is insufficient, adding more runs increases Recon's precision.

Graph Collection Time. Column 9 shows that the total time required to collect 25 buggy and 25 nonbuggy graphs is not prohibitively long. In our experiments, all applications took under two hours; `apache`, `mysql`, and `weblech` all took under 30 minutes. These data show that Recon is not only effective at detecting real bugs in these full applications, but also reasonably fast. In Section 6.4 we characterize the overheads our technique imposes over uninstrumented execution.

6.3 Case Study: Debugging an Unresolved Bug

The `weblech` bug is open and unresolved in the program's bug repository. While the bug has been discussed previously [12], we were unaware of any details of the bug prior to this case study. We used Recon to find the problem, and we were able to write a fix using Recon's output and our limited program knowledge.

We began with a bug report describing intermittent non-termination. Using the input from the report, we were able to reproduce the bug in about 1 in 15 runs. We then ran the application repeatedly and watched the output to identify the hang. We noticed that, consistently, at least one thread crashed on a null pointer dereference during hanging runs. We collected 25 buggy and 25 nonbuggy runs, identifying bugginess by watching for unhandled exceptions. We then produced reconstructions from these runs.

The first reconstruction reported was related mostly to object constructors, but also included evidence of several accesses to a shared queue data structure, as well as a suspicious `while` loop termination condition involving the queue's size. The body of the reconstruction contained the initialization of and accesses to the size of the queue. The sink of the reconstruction's edge was an access to the queue data structure in the dequeue method. In the suffix of the reconstruction was another call to the queue's dequeue method. As we described in Section 2.1, such an interleaving of a dequeue call between an access to the queue's size and a subsequent dequeue call violates the atomicity of the pair of operations. The atomicity violation leads to a thread crashing early due to the `NullPointerException` we observed. Crashing prevents the thread from correctly updating the variable for the `while` loop to read. The crash is therefore also responsible for the program's non-termination, as described in the bug report. We fixed the bug by extending a `synchronized` block including the queue size check and the dequeue. With our fix, we didn't see the buggy behavior in several hundred runs — we conclude that we fixed the bug based on the information provided by Recon.

6.4 Performance

In Table 4, we report runtimes relative to uninstrumented execution for Recon and the three less-optimized configurations. In the best case, Recon imposes slowdowns as low as 34% for C/C++ (`pbzip2`) and 13% for Java (`weblech`).

Slowdown for full applications never exceeds 24x, even during an industrial strength test of a commercial database (`mysql`). For PARSEC, we saw slowdowns ranging from 5.5x to 28x, showing that Recon performs well on applications with a variety of sharing patterns. We saw comparable results for DaCapo: overheads of Recon ranged from 5.6x to 17.3x.

Interestingly, overheads tended to be more severe for applications that perform *infrequent sharing*, than those that share often. For example, `dedup`, which uses shared queues, and `avrora`, which exhibits a high-degree of fine-grained sharing [3], both had fairly low overheads, around 6x. In contrast, `swaptions` has infrequent synchronization [2] and threads in `lusearch` interact very little [3] — both suffered higher overheads, around 18x. This trend is further illuminated by the Java Grande benchmarks; these are primarily data-parallel scientific computations that perform little sharing [28]; their average overhead is 75x. Nonetheless, Recon

	Name	Recon	Slowdown (x) FR/W	FR	Base		Name	Recon	Slowdown (x) FR/W	FR	Base
Apps.	weblech	1.1	1.2	1.2	1.1	PARSEC	dedup	5.5	5.8	5.8	13.8
	pbzip2	1.3	1.3	1.3	1.5		canneal	6.8	6.8	6.5	14.9
	aget	1.9	1.9	1.9	1.9		freqmine	8.8	52.6	56.6	223.8
	apache	5.4	31.7	31.7	177.1		fluidanimate	9.8	9.9	10.1	9.8
	mysql	23.9	102.1	127.2	129.9		streamcluster	10.1	10.1	10.3	10.1
DaCapo	pmd	5.6	5.8	6.0	6.3		blackscholes	14.4	17.8	18.0	40.9
	avrora	5.6	7.9	10.3	27.8		ferret	14.6	70.9	73.1	537.3
	tomcat	6.9	6.2	6.7	9.1		bodytrack	14.9	116.2	120.8	595.5
	xalan	7.1	7.0	7.5	10.8		facesim	15.8	18.8	19.2	29.2
	luindex	8.2	9.1	14.3	20.6		swaption	17.9	96.0	100.6	383.7
	lusearch	17.3	18.1	22.7	22.6		x264	18.9	218.4	236.8	697.4
Java Grande		74.9	85.1	88.4	563.7		vips	28.8	230.6	257.6	996.8

Table 4. Performance of Recon and less-optimized configurations relative to uninstrumented execution.

is efficient in applications with high-frequency sharing and for all the mainstream applications we tested.

Effectiveness of Optimizations. Comparing "FR" with "Base" and "Recon" with "FR/W" in Table 4, we see that the first-read and racy-lookup optimizations, respectively, significantly improve performance. Comparing "FR/W" and "FR", we see that the first-write optimization has less significant effect in general — likely because writes are less common than reads — but for `mysql` and `lusearch`, the first-write optimization is clearly important.

The data show that our optimizations are essential to Recon's efficiency. For many applications, our optimizations reduce Recon's slowdown by orders of magnitude. `apache` is one such application: without optimizations, `apache`'s slowdown is 177x, making full-scale tests nearly impossible due to timeouts and unhandled delay conditions in the code. Optimizations reduce this to just 5.4x, enabling Recon to be used with real bug-triggering inputs.

In our experiments, we used PARSEC's `simlarge` inputs to make experimenting with unoptimized configurations feasible, but there is no need to scale inputs for use with Recon. We also experimented with PARSEC's `native` input, using Recon with all optimizations. Experiments finished quickly, and we saw slowdowns nearly identical to the `simlarge` input.

The optimizations have less impact on our Java implementation, but still account for significant speedups (*e.g.*, `avrora`, `luindex`). For most Java benchmarks, the racy-lookup optimization had little effect. Java uses several techniques that significantly reduce the cost of acquiring locks [13]. It is likely that the racy-lookup optimization is less beneficial than in C/C++ because the cost of locking is lower in Java to begin with.

Memory Overhead. The C/C++ Recon implementation uses a fixed-size 4GB metadata table, dominating memory overheads in our experiments. Graphs are small in comparison. The table is large enough that the impact of hash collisions was negligible. In a memory-constrained setting, a smaller table could be used at the expense of decreased precision due to hash collisions. In Java, each field and array element is shadowed by a metadata location: memory overhead scales roughly linearly with the program's footprint. Peak overheads in the optimized version ranged from 2.5x to 16x.

7. Related Work

Prior work has explored a variety of atomicity violation detection approaches. AVIO [17] is an invariant-based approach that infers from a set of training runs which unserializable interleavings are allowed in correct executions. In subsequent runs, AVIO reports any unserializable interleavings not present in the invariant set as possible atomicity violations. AVIO focuses on single-variable atomicity violations. SVD [30] attempts to infer atomic sections based on data and control flow and determines whether an execution is serializable with respect to those sections. Velodrome [8] is a sound, precise atomicity checker that reports an error if an program execution with explicit atomic blocks is not conflict-serializable.

Recent work introduced general approaches to detecting concurrency errors. Bugaboo [18] first proposed the use of context-aware communication graphs for debugging general concurrency errors. DefUse [27] employs a similar communication-based strategy, by finding communication invariant violations related to errors. Neither approach provides programmers with information about the actual interleaving schedule at the root cause of the bug. Context-aware graphs, and DefUse invariants only isolate a single communication event related to a bug. One of Recon's main contributions is that it provides information about the execution schedule encoded in a reconstruction. Additionally, Bugaboo and DefUse rank anomalies along a single axis of suspiciousness. In contrast, Recon ranks reconstructions along several axes, using the features described in Section 4. Finally, Recon's performance is orders of magnitude better than the performance of Bugaboo's software implementation. DefUse does not show overheads for a standard benchmark suite, so direct comparison is impossible, but Recon's performance on reactive applications is comparable.

Interleaving Constrained MultiProcessor [32] (PSets) proposes architecture support for dynamic bug avoidance. PSets uses test runs to determine happens-before invariants on memory operations and tries to enforce them by manipulating the schedule. This technique handles several types of single-variable bugs. Falcon [23], uses a library of bug patterns to identify potential concurrency bugs; it watches a stream of memory operations to single addresses and searches for a matching pattern. Falcon's technique is mostly applicable to single-variable concurrency bugs. Hammer, *et al.* propose pattern-based dynamic analysis for detecting bugs related to atomicity properties of accesses to sets of variables [10].

Recon is set apart from prior work by the fact that reconstructions are general, handling a variety of single- and multi-variable errors without relying on characteristics of specific bug types. Furthermore, reconstructions illustrate bugs more clearly, showing a focused portion of the interleaving schedule near the bug's cause.

Inter-thread communication invariants have also been used to specify correct communication behavior at the function level and check that a program execution conforms to this specification [29]. In contrast, Recon focuses on communication at the instruction granularity and helps programmers understand unexpected behavior, rather than helping them enforce expected invariants.

Another way of dealing with concurrency bugs is explorative testing to expose buggy executions. CHESS [21] explores executions by interposing on synchronization operations; its goal is to expose buggy executions during testing. Burckhardt *et al.* propose a scheduling technique that probabilistically exposes bugs [5]. CTrigger [22] is a heuristic to expose atomicity bugs. The goal of these techniques is not to detect or explain bugs but to expose buggy executions. In contrast, Recon helps programmers understand bugs by reconstructing the interleavings that likely led to bugs' symptoms. Explorative testing is complementary to our approach.

Liblit *et al.*'s Cooperative Bug Isolation (CBI) [15] uses sampling techniques to collect information from deployed applications. Based on sets of labeled passing or failing runs, CBI finds code points related to failures. CCI [11] extends these sampling techniques to concurrency bug patterns. In contrast, Recon does not require deployment-scale data to detect bugs efficiently. It provides more information about buggy interleavings, and doesn't rely on bug-specific patterns.

8. Conclusion

In this paper we introduced Recon, a *general* approach to isolating and understanding concurrency bugs. Recon works by reconstructing fragments of buggy executions that are likely related to a bug. Recon provides sufficient, yet succinct information to help programmers understand the causes of their bugs.

Reconstructions show the schedule of execution that led to the bug, clearly exposing its root cause. Reconstructions are built by observing multiple executions of a program and collecting timestamped communication graphs that encode information about the ordering of inter-thread communication events. We developed a simple machine-learning approach to identify buggy reconstructions. We proposed three bug-independent features of reconstructions that together precisely isolate reconstructions of buggy executions. In order to provide efficient collection of timestamped graphs, we used several techniques that significantly reduce runtime overheads. We implemented Recon for C/C++ and Java and evaluated it using large software. Our results show Recon reconstructs buggy executions with virtually no false positives, and that collecting the data comprising reconstructions takes just minutes.

Acknowledgments

We thank the anonymous reviewers and the Sampa group for their helpful feedback. Thanks to Joseph Devietti, Laura Effinger-Dean, Colin Gordon, Dan Grossman, and Karin Strauss for their invaluable feedback on the manuscript. Special thanks go to Zachary Rait and Julian Knutsen for early work on the Recon infrastructure. This work was supported in part by an IBM PhD fellowship, an ARCS Foundation Fellowship, a Microsoft Research Faculty Fellowship, NSF grant CCF-0811405, and gifts from Intel.

References

[1] Z. Anderson, D. Gay, R. Ennals, and E. Brewer. SharC: Checking Data Sharing Strategies for Multithreaded C. In *PLDI*, 2008.

[2] C. Bienia, S. Kumar, J. P. Singh, and K. Li. The parsec benchmark suite: Characterization and architectural implications. In *Proceedings of the 17th International Conference on Parallel Architectures and Compilation Techniques*, October 2008.

[3] S. M. Blackburn et al. The DaCapo Benchmarks: Java Benchmarking Development and Analysis. In *OOPSLA*, 2006.

[4] H.-J. Boehm and S. V. Adve. Foundations of the C++ Concurrency Memory Model. In *PLDI*, 2008.

[5] S. Burckhardt, P. Kothari, M. Musuvathi, and S. Nagarakatte. A Randomized Scheduler with Probabilistic Guarantees of Finding Bugs. In *ASPLOS*, 2010.

[6] C. Flanagan and S. N. Freund. FastTrack: Efficient and Precise Dynamic Race Detection. In *PLDI*, 2009.

[7] C. Flanagan and S. N. Freund. The RoadRunner Dynamic Analysis Framework for Concurrent Programs. In *PASTE*, 2010.

[8] C. Flanagan, S. N. Freund, and J. Yi. Velodrome: A Sound and Complete Dynamic Atomicity Checker for Multithreaded Programs. In *PLDI*, 2008.

[9] M. Hall, E. Frank, G. Holmes, B. Pfahringer, P. Reutemann, and I. H. Witten. The WEKA Data Mining Software: An Update. *SIGKDD Explorations*, 2009.

[10] C. Hammer, J. Dolby, M. Vaziri, and F. Tip. Dynamic Detection of Atomic-Set-Serializability Violations. In *ICSE*, 2008.

[11] G. Jin, A. Thakur, B. Liblit, and S. Lu. Instrumentation and Sampling Strategies for Cooperative Concurrency Bug Isolation. In *OOPSLA*, 2010.

[12] P. Joshi and K. Sen. Predictive Typestate Checking of Multithreaded Java Programs. In *ASE*, 2008.

[13] K. Kawachiya, A. Koseki, and T. Onodera. Lock Reservation: Java Locks Can Mostly Do Without Atomic Operations. In *OOPSLA*, 2002.

[14] I. Kononenko. Estimating Attributes: Analysis and Extensions of RELIEF. In *European Conference on Machine Learning*, 1994.

[15] B. Liblit. *Cooperative Bug Isolation*, volume 4440 of *Lecture Notes in Computer Science*. Springer, 2007.

[16] S. Lu, S. Park, E. Seo, and Y. Zhou. Learning from Mistakes - A Comprehensive Study on Real World Concurrency Bug Characteristics. In *ASPLOS*, 2008.

[17] S. Lu, J. Tucek, F. Qin, and Y. Zhou. AVIO: Detecting Atomicity Violations via Access Interleaving Invariants. In *ASPLOS*, 2006.

[18] B. Lucia and L. Ceze. Finding Concurrency Bugs with Context-Aware Communication Graphs. In *MICRO*, 2009.

[19] C.-K. Luk et al. Pin: Building Customized Program Analysis Tools with Dynamic Instrumentation. In *PLDI*, 2005.

[20] J. Manson, W. Pugh, and S. V. Adve. The Java Memory Model. In *POPL*, 2005.

[21] M. Musuvathi, S. Qadeer, T. Ball, G. Basler, P. A. Nainar, and I. Neamtiu. Finding and Reproducing Heisenbugs in Concurrent Programs. In *OSDI*, 2008.

[22] S. Park, S. Lu, and Y. Zhou. CTrigger: Exposing Atomicity Violation Bugs from Their Hiding Places. In *ASPLOS*, 2009.

[23] S. Park, R. W. Vuduc, and M. J. Harrold. Falcon: Fault Localization in Concurrent Programs. In *ICSE*, 2010.

[24] S. Park, Y. Zhou, W. Xiong, Z. Yin, R. Kaushik, K. H. Lee, and S. Lu. PRES: Probabilistic Replay with Execution Sketching on Multiprocessors. In *SOSP*, 2009.

[25] M. Ronsee and K. D. Bosschere. RecPlay: A Fully Integrated Practical Record/Replay System. *ToCS*, 1999.

[26] S. Savage, M. Burrows, G. Nelson, P. Sobalvarro, and T. Anderson. Eraser: A Dynamic Data Race Detector for Multi-Threaded Programs. *ToCS*, 1997.

[27] Y. Shi, S. Park, Z. Yin, S. Lu, Y. Zhou, W. Chen, and W. Zheng. Do I Use the Wrong Definition?: DeFuse: Definition-Use Invariants for Detecting Concurrency and Sequential Bugs. In *OOPSLA*, 2010.

[28] L. A. Smith, J. M. Bull, and J. Obdrzálek. A parallel Java Grande benchmark suite. In *Supercomputing*, 2001.

[29] B. P. Wood, A. Sampson, L. Ceze, and D. Grossman. Composable Specifications for Structured Shared-Memory Communication. In *OOPSLA*, 2010.

[30] M. Xu, R. Bodík, and M. D. Hill. A Serializability Violation Detector for Shared-Memory Server Programs. In *PLDI*, June 2005.

[31] M. Xu, M. D. Hill, and R. Bodik. A Regulated Transitive Reduction (RTR) for Longer Memory Race Recording. In *ASPLOS*, 2006.

[32] J. Yu and S. Narayanasamy. A Case for an Interleaving Constrained Shared-Memory Multi-Processor. In *ISCA*, 2009.

[33] P. Zhou, R. Teodorescu, and Y. Zhou. HARD: Hardware-Assisted Lockset-based Race Detection. In *HPCA*, 2007.

Automated Atomicity-Violation Fixing *

Guoliang Jin Linhai Song Wei Zhang Shan Lu Ben Liblit
University of Wisconsin–Madison
{aliang,songlh,wzh,shanlu,liblit}@cs.wisc.edu

Abstract

Fixing software bugs has always been an important and time-consuming process in software development. Fixing concurrency bugs has become especially critical in the multicore era. However, fixing concurrency bugs is challenging, in part due to non-deterministic failures and tricky parallel reasoning. Beyond correctly fixing the original problem in the software, a good patch should also avoid introducing new bugs, degrading performance unnecessarily, or damaging software readability. Existing tools cannot automate the whole fixing process and provide good-quality patches.

We present AFix, a tool that automates the whole process of fixing one common type of concurrency bug: single-variable atomicity violations. AFix starts from the bug reports of existing bug-detection tools. It augments these with static analysis to construct a suitable patch for each bug report. It further tries to combine the patches of multiple bugs for better performance and code readability. Finally, AFix's run-time component provides testing customized for each patch. Our evaluation shows that patches automatically generated by AFix correctly eliminate six out of eight real-world bugs and significantly decrease the failure probability in the other two cases. AFix patches never introduce new bugs and usually have similar performance to manually-designed patches.

Categories and Subject Descriptors D.1.3 [*Programming Techniques*]: Concurrent Programming; D.2.5 [*Software Engineering*]: Testing and Debugging; D.4.1 [*Operating Systems*]: Process Management

General Terms Algorithms, Experimentation, Languages, Measurement, Performance, Reliability, Verification

Keywords atomicity violations, automated debugging, concurrency, critical regions, deadlock, mutex locks, mutual exclusion, patching, static analysis

* Supported in part by AFOSR grants FA9550-07-1-0210 and FA9550-09-1-0279; DoE contract DE-SC0002153; LLNL contract B580360; NSF grants CCF-0621487, CCF-0701957, CCF-0953478, CCF-1018180, and CNS-0720565; and a Claire Boothe Luce faculty fellowship. Any opinions, findings, and conclusions or recommendations expressed in this material are those of the authors and do not necessarily reflect the views of NSF or other institutions.

PLDI'11, June 4–8, 2011, San Jose, California, USA.


```
          Thread 1                            Thread 2
1 void buf_write(...) {               void buf_write(...) {               1
2   int tmp = buf_len + str_len;        int tmp = buf_len + str_len;      2
3   if (tmp > MAX)                      if (tmp > MAX)                    3
4     return;                             return;                         4
5                                                                         5
6   memcpy(buf[buf_len],                memcpy(buf[buf_len],              6
7          str, str_len);                      str, str_len);             7
8   buf_len = tmp;                      buf_len = tmp;                    8
9 }                                   }                                   9
```

Figure 1. Real-world concurrency bug from Apache. Interleaving "⟶" could cause crash. Interleaving "⇢" could corrupt the log.

1. Introduction

1.1 Motivation

Bug fixing is an indispensable part of software development. It requires developers to understand a bug's root cause, design a patch, implement the patch, and finally validate the patch. This process consumes a huge amount of resources, especially manual effort, during software development. Krebs [15] finds that it frequently takes more than one month to finish the fixing process for one bug. Meanwhile, there are endless bugs waiting to be fixed. Software companies such as Microsoft face pressure to release patches monthly or even more frequently [24]. Furthermore, patches are error-prone. Even after consuming so many development resources, nearly 70% of patches are buggy in their first release [7, 31, 33], often at great financial cost [27]. Self-healing software that fixes its own bugs has long been desired but is yet unrealized [11]. The need for automatic repair techniques remains for concurrency bugs.

Concurrency bugs are synchronization mistakes in multithreaded programs. They are widespread due to software developers' sequential thinking habits. Concurrency bugs have already caused real-world disasters [29]. In the current multi-core era, with multithreaded software becoming pervasive, concurrency bugs are a growing threat to software reliability.

Many advanced techniques have been proposed for bug detection, software testing, and verification to help identify concurrency bugs [9, 25, 37]. However, software reliability does not improve until detected bugs are actually fixed. Unfortunately, fixing concurrency bugs is not trivial and developers are left to themselves to face the enormous pressure of fixing ever-so-many concurrency bugs.

Figure 1 shows an example of a real-world concurrency bug. Existing bug detectors [5, 25, 37] can accurately report two problematic atomicity violations: (1) when lines 2 and 6 are interleaved (⟶) by line 8, Apache could crash; and (2) when lines 6 and 8 are interleaved (⇢) by line 8, Apache could corrupt its log. Unfortunately, even with accurate bug detection, bug fixing is nontrivial:

- To fix the first report, if we simply lock before line 2 and unlock after line 6, the program could deadlock after buf_write exits at line 4.
- To fix the second report, we should not simply put lines 6–8 and line 8 each into one critical region. As line 8 is part of the critical region for lines 6–8, this would lead to deadlock again.
- Two patches that separately fix the above two atomicity violations could deadlock with each other: one thread acquires the first patch's lock at line 2 and waits for the second patch's lock before line 6; a different thread acquires the second patch's lock at line 6 and waits for the first patch's lock before line 8.

Generally speaking, developers face several unique challenges to generate good patches for concurrency bugs. First, concurrency bugs pose unique challenges in understanding their root causes. Their non-determinism makes manual inspection difficult. In addition, understanding their root causes demands non-local and parallel thinking. Even with the help of tools for bug detection [4, 12], failure diagnosis [26], and failure replay [39, 42], it is still non-trivial to understand how to fix a bug's root cause. As a result, it is common that patches released by developers fail to (completely) fix the original concurrency bug. This happened for two of the eight real-world concurrency bugs used in our experimental evaluation.

Second, patches to concurrency bugs often involve synchronization operations that have non-local impact. As a result, these patches can easily introduce additional bugs, such as deadlocks and data races. As a notorious example, the patch to Mozilla concurrency bug #54743 led to new concurrency bugs in the field. Patches for the latter caused further problems, which took more than one year to finally fix [14].

Third, patches to concurrency bugs often constrain program interleavings or introduce serialization bottlenecks, which could cause unexpected and unnecessary performance degradation.

Because of these challenges, long repair times and wrong patches are common for concurrency bugs [20]. Future programming languages may eventually help developers avoid some of these concurrency bugs. For now, though, software developers are in great need of immediate support for automatic repair of concurrency bugs.

1.2 Contributions

In this paper, we build a system, AFix, that automates the *whole* process of fixing one common type of concurrency bug: single-variable atomicity violations [9, 19, 20, 25, 37]. AFix leverages existing techniques for bug detection and interleaving testing to bootstrap its fixing process. It uses static analysis and static code transformation to automatically design and implement code patches. It further incorporates run-time monitoring to help developers validate and evaluate each patch it generates.

The design of AFix focuses on the challenges encountered by developers in their manual patching process. Specifically, AFix tries to fix the original bug without introducing new functionality problems, degrading performance excessively, or harming code readability.

Guided by these goals, AFix automates a developer's typical bug fixing process. The first step is *bug understanding*. AFix discovers single-variable atomicity violations using CTrigger [25], an existing bug-detection and testing tool which we review further in Section 2.

The second step is *patching one bug*. AFix maps the dynamically-based bug report to static code structures. It conducts static analysis and static code transformation to fix one problem. Correctness issues are thoroughly analyzed in this step, which we discuss in Section 3.

The third step is *patch merging and optimization* for a set of bugs. AFix collects the patches for each bug report together and statically identifies patches that can be merged or optimized for better performance or readability. This step is addressed in Section 4.

The fourth step is *patch testing*. AFix conducts testing and run-time analysis customized for each patch. Testing checks whether the original problem has been fixed and looks for new problems. The low-overhead run-time analysis targets correctness and performance properties that cannot be statically guaranteed or optimized in preceding steps. It provides the developers an option to compare and refine patches. We discuss this step in detail in Section 5.

Overall, this paper makes the following contributions:

- AFix makes a first step in automating the *whole* process of fixing one common type of concurrency bug. AFix can save developers' manual bug fixing effort by automatically generating patches or patch candidates for concurrency bugs detected during in-house testing or for concurrency failures discovered during production runs. AFix can also help address some tough challenges that usually bother developers. For example, AFix can avoid generating buggy patches. AFix's run-time analysis also helps developers conduct customized patch testing and evaluation.
- Our experience of applying AFix discovers several limitations of state-of-art bug detectors regarding helping bug diagnosis and bug fixing, such as not grouping bugs with the same root cause together and reporting incorrect root causes. We expect this experience to help guide future research in bug detection.
- We evaluate AFix on eight real-world concurrency bugs, with promising results. AFix correctly fixes six out of eight reported bugs. For the remaining two bugs, where the root causes were incorrectly reported by CTrigger, AFix patches significantly decrease failure rates. AFix patches also have good readability based on our manual inspection and do not introduce any new bugs. In comparison, naïve patches cannot fix any of these bugs, and cause deadlocks in seven out of eight cases. Even the original developers made mistakes in fixing two of these eight bugs. AFix patches also show good performance. Software patched by AFix is less than 1% slower than the original buggy software for all but one case.

2. Background: Bug Detection Using CTrigger

AFix is a bug fixer, not a bug finder. It depends on problem reports from existing bug-detection tools to guide its repairs. The high-level ideas in AFix are general to all atomicity-violation detectors, but the lower-level details are tuned to the specific bug finder used. This section briefly describes CTrigger: the specific concurrency-bug detector and tester used by our current AFix implementation.

2.1 CTrigger General Operation

CTrigger is an in-house concurrency-bug detection and testing framework [25] that targets single-variable atomicity-violation bugs. As shown in Figure 2, when two consecutive accesses that read or write the same shared variable from the same thread are interleaved by another access from a different thread, their execution effect may be different from any serial execution, in which case a single-variable atomicity-violation bug has occurred. An empirical study by Lu et al. [20] finds that single-variable atomicity-violation bugs are one of the most common types of concurrency bug in real code.

CTrigger includes a detection phase and a testing phase. During its detection phase, CTrigger monitors a few executions of the concurrent program, predicts what single-variable atomicity violations could happen in the future under the same input, and outputs the instruction counters for the three instructions involved in each atomicity violation. These three instructions are referred to as p (preceding), c (current), and r (remote), as shown in Figure 2. In its testing phase, CTrigger tries to force each atomicity violation identified above by injecting delays at selected points. If an atomicity

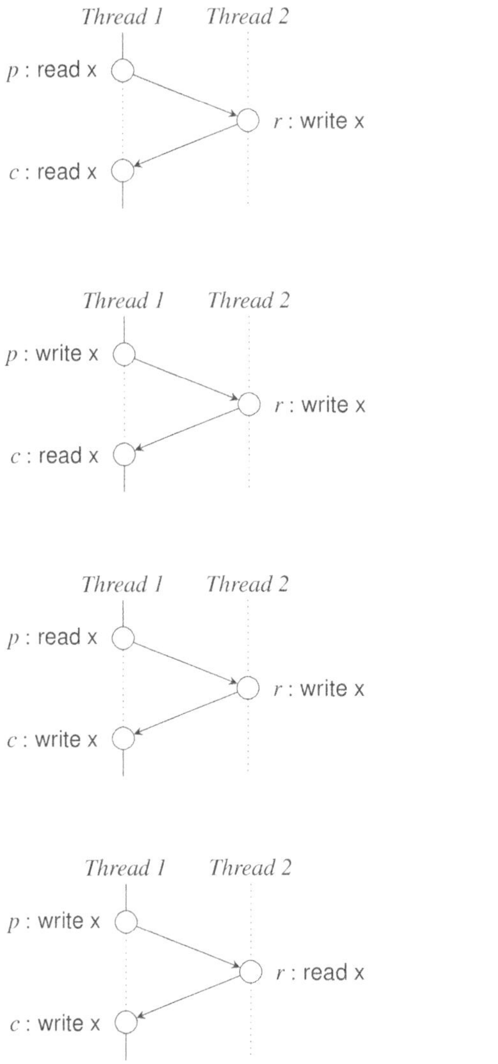

Figure 2. Types of atomicity violations that CTrigger detects. "⟶" shows execution order. "x" is a shared memory location.

violation occurs and the program execution fails, CTrigger reports the involved (p,c,r) triple. At the end, a list of atomicity violations that can truly harm the software are reported.

In this project, we use CTrigger bug reports to drive AFix. We will discuss how to extend AFix for general atomicity-violation bugs in Section 3.7. In remainder of this paper, when we talk about atomicity violations, by default, we mean the type of single-variable bugs reported by CTrigger. We continue to use p, c, and r to represent the three instructions involved in each atomicity violation, as shown in Figure 2.

2.2 CTrigger Modifications and Limitations

During the design and evaluation of AFix, we modified two aspects of CTrigger to better drive automated bug fixing. First, the original CTrigger only reports one (p,c,r) triple for each distinct c instruction, to simplify its design. This is probably a good decision for bug detection, but not a good one for bug fixing, because it leads to incomplete patches. We modified CTrigger to output all possible combinations. Second, the original CTrigger only reports instruction counters for (p,c,r), which again is problematic in bug fixing, especially when p and c are inside different functions (discussed in Section 3). Therefore, we modified CTrigger to report the complete call stack for each p, c, or r.

AFix can be no wiser than the bug detector which drives its fixes. Our CTrigger-based implementation of AFix, then, is affected by a few other features of CTrigger. For the most part these are not peculiar to CTrigger, though, but rather are shared with other concurrency-bug detection and testing tools.

First, separate CTrigger bugs sometimes should not be fixed by separate patches. We discuss this further in Section 4.

Second, CTrigger might detect an atomicity violation that is a side effect of another non-atomicity-violation bug. As a result, no matter how well AFix fixes the reported CTrigger bug, the software failure may still occur. We discuss this further in Section 6.

2.3 A Naïve Fixing Scheme

Given one CTrigger bug report, a naïve patch is to acquire some lock before p and r, then release the same lock after c and r. As shown in Figure 1, for many real-world bugs, this naïve patch would cause problems, such as introducing new bugs, introducing significant and unnecessary performance degradation, and hurting code readability. We have implemented this naïve fixing scheme and compare it with AFix using real-world bugs in Section 6.

3. Fixing One Bug Report

This section describes how AFix fixes a single atomicity violation detected by CTrigger. The next section will discuss how to fix multiple violations together.

3.1 Overview

As discussed in Section 2.1, a single CTrigger bug report identifies an instruction r that may non-serializably interleave two other instructions p and c, thereby causing failure. Fixing this bug requires changing the code to ensure that the code region from p to c is mutually exclusive with r. AFix performs this change in four steps:

1. Put p and c into a critical region. The challenge here is to guarantee that p and c are inside one critical region under all possible control flows, without introducing new bugs. Potential new bugs to avoid include double lock, double unlock, unlock without lock, deadlocks, and others shown in Figure 3. We describe how AFix handles this step in Sections 3.2 to 3.4.
2. Put r into another critical region. This step can be easily done by adding a lock-acquisition operation before r and a lock-release operation after r.
3. Make the above two regions mutually exclusive with respect to each other. This step involves more than just assigning the same lock to both critical sections. We discuss hidden traps and how to avoid them in Section 3.5.
4. Select or introduce a lock to protect the two critical regions. Section 3.6 discusses how a lock is chosen.

3.2 Single-Function Operation

We start with an algorithm that decides where to acquire and release locks when p and c reside in the same function. We further assume that this function is not recursive. Under these restrictions, the algorithm follows a natural strategy: find all nodes that are on any path from p to c, and make sure a lock is held at exactly these nodes.

To implement this strategy, AFix first analyzes the control-flow graph to get the set of CFG nodes that are on any intraprocedural path that starts from p and ends at c without touching p or c in

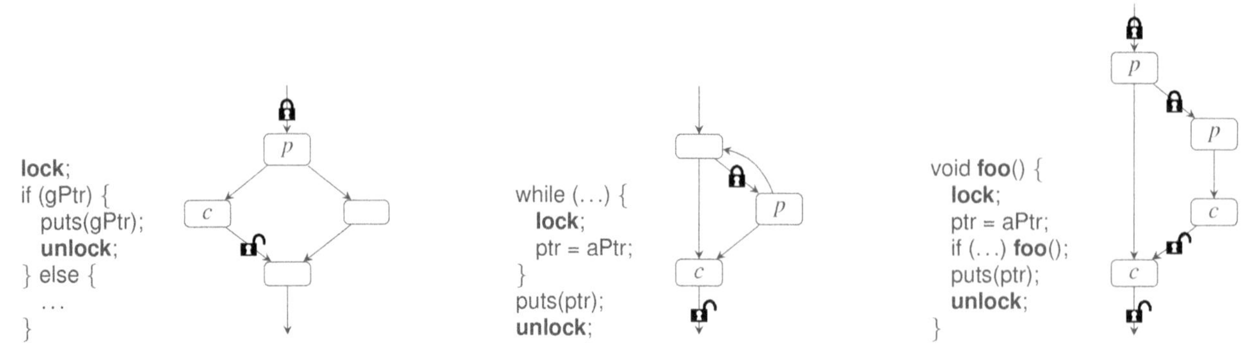

(a) Unreleased lock; potential deadlock later

(b) Potential double lock or unlock without lock

(c) Potential double lock

Figure 3. Traps in bug fixing. Lock and unlock operations have been placed before and after each p and c node, respectively.

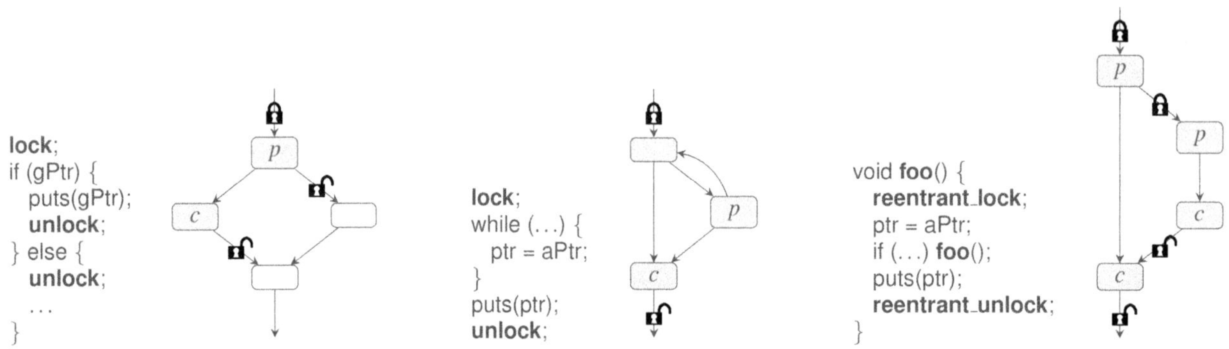

(a) Added unlock avoids unreleased lock

(b) Moved lock avoids double lock or unlock without lock

(c) Reentrant lock avoids double lock

Figure 4. AFix's handling of traps from Figure 3. Shaded nodes comprise the p–c critical region.

between.[1] We refer to this set of nodes as the *protected nodes*: these are the nodes which will be included in the critical region. The protected nodes may be computed as follows:

1. Search forward from p (either depth- or breadth-first) without ever crossing beyond c. That is, temporarily treat c as having no successors for purposes of this search. Call this set of all forward-reachable nodes P.
2. Search backward from c (either depth- or breadth-first) without ever crossing beyond p. That is, temporarily treat p as having no predecessors for purposes of this search. Call this set of all backward-reachable nodes C.
3. The protected nodes are $P \cap C$. This is the set of nodes that are reachable from p, and from which c can be reached, without additional crossings through p or c along the way.

It is not difficult to prove that this algorithm correctly identifies the protected nodes which must form a critical region. Any node in P must be reachable from p without crossing any successor edge of c. Conversely, any node in C must be able to reach c without crossing any predecessor edge of p. Therefore, any node in $P \cap C$ must be along a p–c path in which p and c respectively appear only first and last, never as intermediate nodes.

Each depth- or breadth-first search requires time at most linear in the number of nodes and edges. Computing the intersection is likewise at most linear in the number of nodes. Therefore the entire algorithm to identify protected nodes is at most linear in the number of nodes and edges in the CFG for the function containing p and c.

Next, AFix inserts lock-acquisition operations on each edge that crosses from an unprotected node to a protected node, and inserts lock-release operations on each edge that crosses from a protected node to an unprotected one.[2]

Figure 4 shows the result of applying this approach to the traps from Figure 3. AFix avoids the first trap by inserting a lock release operation for the else clause, and avoids the second one by moving the lock acquisition operation out of the loop. Handling the third trap requires additional analysis (Section 3.3).

AFix patches thus guarantee two important properties. First, the lock is not held at any unprotected nodes, because it is released whenever execution crosses from protected nodes to unprotected nodes. Second, the lock is held at every protected node, including p and c, because it is acquired whenever execution crosses from unprotected nodes to protected nodes. These two properties help us answer the following questions regarding the suitability of the above critical region as part of a bug fix:

Are p ***and*** c ***inside the critical region on all paths?*** Yes, they are. Given any path that goes from p to c, every node on that path must be in the protected node set. The lock is always held throughout any execution along any such path.

[1] No p or c in between is because CTrigger is designed to report atomicity violations between two *consecutive* memory accesses to the same variable.

[2] In practice, to place code "on" an edge from x to y, create a new node n and replace the $x \rightarrow y$ edge with two edges: $x \rightarrow n$ and $n \rightarrow y$. Code intended to appear on the original $x \rightarrow y$ edge is placed in the newly-created node n.

Can the added code introduce double-lock bugs? No, it cannot. AFix only acquires locks on an edge that crosses from an unprotected node to a protected node. Since the lock is not held at unprotected nodes, double-lock bugs never occur in AFix patches. By contrast, the naïve fix suggested in Section 2.3 would easily lead to double-lock problems, as shown in Figure 3b.

Can the added code introduce double-unlock or unlock-before-lock bugs? No, it cannot. AFix only releases locks on an edge that crosses from a protected node to an unprotected node. Since the lock is held at protected nodes, double-unlock or unlock-before-lock bugs never occur in AFix patches. By contrast, the naïve fix suggested in Section 2.3 would easily lead to problems in scenarios like Figure 3b when the while-loop condition is initially false.

Can the added code introduce new data races? No, it cannot. The patch does not introduce any new interleavings into the program. Possible thread schedules in the patched program must be a subset of those that were already possible in the original program.

Can the added code introduce new deadlocks? This is a much tougher question to answer. In general, it is impractical to prove a C/C++ programs deadlock-free. We address this risk using a mixture of static analysis (Section 3.3) and dynamic monitoring (Section 5.1).

Is this the best policy? There could be other policies to decide where to add locks and unlocks in order to protect p and c. We have designed and implemented several other schemes. Some of them generate smaller critical regions than the current AFix does for some special control flow structures. We prefer to use the current AFix algorithm presented above, because it has a huge advantage in simplicity. It is far easier to reason about and has better composability in the interprocedural case than other schemes. The patches generated by it also always have good readability. Furthermore, our experiments never observe any excessive performance degradation caused by the current AFix algorithm.

3.3 Deadlock Analysis and Avoidance

AFix statically analyzes each critical region to determine whether it includes any potentially-blocking operations. These operations include lock-acquisitions, condition-wait operations, barriers, thread join operations, and some ad-hoc synchronizations like spin loops. The first few of these are easy to identify. To identify ad-hoc spin loops, AFix checks whether there is loop inside the critical region, and whether heap or global variables are accessed inside the loop. If any such loop exists, we conservatively assume that it might constitute an ad-hoc spin loop. This could be made more precise in the future [35, 41], but is sufficient for AFix's current needs.

If this analysis finds no potentially-blocking operations within the critical region, then there is no risk of deadlock and AFix uses standard pthread_mutex_lock calls to acquire locks. This is the case for AFix's handling of the first two traps as shown in Figures 4a and 4b. If potentially-blocking operations are found, then deadlock is a real risk. In this case, AFix instead acquires locks using pthread_mutex_timedlock: this will time out if it is unable to acquire the lock after some maximum delay. AFix's run-time system monitors each timed lock in the patch to identify when our attempted fix has actually introduced a circular wait. This information can help developers refine AFix patches. We discuss this further in Section 5.

Currently, we set the time-out delay to a relatively large value: ten seconds by default. The only disadvantage of long time-out limits is longer latency in discovering any deadlocks that do arise.

One subtle issue that is not covered above is recursion. As shown in Figure 3c, double lock/unlock and deadlocks could arise in the case of recursive calls. AFix identifies all such cases using a simple reachability analysis of the static call graph. When recursion is possible, we use reentrant (a.k.a. counted or nested) locks. In all other cases, we use non-reentrant locks as these can be faster. AFix implements reentrant locks by associating a mutex.count counter and a mutex.owner thread-ID with each reentrant lock mutex. mutex.owner records the thread-ID of the lock's current owner, and mutex.count records the current nesting level in the owner thread. AFix uses reentrant locks in all scenarios when an AFix-added critical region could be called by another AFix-added critical region using the same lock. Figure 4c shows how AFix handles the third trap using a reentrant lock.

```
void newlog()     void close() {         void insert() {
{                   ...                    ...
  ...             p: log = CLOSE;        r: if (log == OPEN)
  close();        }                           logwrite(...);
  open();                                  ...
  ...             void open() {          }
}                   ...
                  c: log = OPEN;
                  }
```

Figure 5. Atomicity violation in MySQL. When r executes between p and c, the database log drops an "insert" log entry.

3.4 Multiple-Function Operation

AFix's task is more complicated when p and c come from different functions. This is not unusual; Figure 5 shows one example taken from MySQL.

We could use interprocedural analysis in computing the protected node set. For example, context-free language reachability can describe the interprocedurally-valid paths from p to c with only non–p-or-c nodes in between. However, it is generally considered taboo to put matched lock and unlock operations in distinct functions due to the poor composability of locks. Examination of manually-designed patches shows that programmers usually add each atomic region's lock acquire and release statements inside the same function. We comply with this practice by adopting an intraprocedural approach that starts and ends each newly-added atomic region inside one function.

The extention to the basic algorithm is inspired by the manual approach a developer might take: study the calling contexts of p and c, find a single common function through which both p and c are reached, and add the critical region to this function. For example, for the bug shown in Figure 5, function newlog is a suitable home for the p–c critical region.

To carry out the above design, we modify the original CTrigger bug detection tool to output the complete call stack for each atomicity violation. AFix compares the call stacks of p and c, and identifies the last (innermost) function f on the common prefix of the two call-stack chains. If p is not already directly in f, then we find the call node in f that eventually leads to p in the CTrigger bug report. We treat this call node as the p node to be protected. Similarly, we replace c with the call node in f that eventually reaches c. After performing these substitutions, the new p and c must both be contained within f, and AFix proceeds as described in Section 3.2.

3.5 Harmonizing Two Critical Regions

The process described above yields a critical region protecting all paths from p to c, guarded by some lock. A second critical region is created by acquiring and releasing the same lock immediately before and after r. However, this alone is not enough: some additional analysis is needed to harmonize these two critical regions so that they cooperate without introducing new bugs.

AFix first checks whether these two critical regions overlap. Let f be the function containing both p and c, possibly after performing the substitutions in Section 3.4. If f does not appear on CTrigger's call stack for r, then the two regions do not overlap and no additional work is needed. If r appears directly within f, then the two regions overlap if r is actually in the set of protected nodes computed earlier. If r is not directly in f but f does appear in the call stack leading to r, then identify the specific call node in f that leads to r, and check whether this call node is in the protected set. Recursion can lead to multiple f on the call chain. Handling this requires a minor extension that if any of the calls in f which lead to r are themselves inside the p–c critical region, then the lock operations protecting r are redundant and may be removed. Recall that AFix is working with each specific dynamic stack trace reported by AFix's front-end bug detector. Therefore, AFix knows the exact call instructions along the call chain, which makes the identification easy.

In all cases, the effect is to determine whether reaching r in the stack configuration reported by CTrigger necessarily implies already being inside the p–c critical region. If it does, then the lock operations around r are redundant, and may simply be removed. Otherwise, the lock operations around r are retained.

For example, consider the (line 6, line 8, line 8) atomicity violation depicted in Figure 1. A naïve patch will put lines 6–8 inside one critical region and line 8 inside another. AFix removes the redundant critical region around line 8.

Note that we do not guarantee that there is no other way to reach r; we only promise to protect r when reached in the specific stack configuration reported by CTrigger. If other routes to r avoid the p–c critical region and thereby cause additional failures, we assume that additional bug reports from CTrigger will eventually mark these as needing fixes as well.

3.6 Lock Selection and Reuse

Lastly, AFix decides which lock to use. In our current implementation, when we only face one bug report, AFix simply creates a new global lock to use at the boundaries of the p–c and r critical regions.

One might consider reusing an existing lock. This is especially appealing if p and c are already inside a critical region in the original program. Doing this requires identifying some lock that is live and reachable at r and at every edge entering or leaving the p–c critical region. This is quite challenging in the general case of heap-allocated locks reached by traversing complex, linked data structures. If r is not even in the same function as p and c, and therefore has access to different local variables, the challenge is even greater.

Global locks, however, have fixed names. This makes them inviting targets for reuse. We have implemented a simple scheme that identifies global locks that protect the intended p–c critical region in the same function. If some such global lock is identified, AFix uses it instead of creating a new lock, and elides inserting additional lock acquire/release statements. For example, when one p–c critical region is already protected by a global lock, AFix does not insert additional lock acquire/release statements to protect it. In practice, though, we never find any reusable global locks for the bugs used in our experimental evaluation.

3.7 Implementation Details and Discussion

Implementation Details AFix implements these static analyses in LLVM [17]. After analysis, AFix changes the target software's LLVM byte-code to apply the patch. In our current implementation, AFix uses locks provided by the POSIX threads (pthread) library to enforce mutual exclusion. A subtle implementation issue is that CTrigger describes (p,c,r) triples in terms of executable instruction addresses. To aid patch readability, AFix maps each instruction back to source code lines. We never insert lock or unlock operations in the middle of a source code line, even if this requires slight expansion of critical regions.

```
p: array[1] = 2;
   for (i = 0; i < 2; i++) {
     ...
c:   array[i] = i;
     ...
   }
```

(a) Original code

```
   lock(L);
p: array[1] = 2;
   for (i = 0; i < 2; i++) {
     ...
c:   array[i] = i;
     unlock(L);
     ...
     lock(L);
   }
   unlock(L);
```

(b) AFix patched

Figure 6. Made-up example for the rare case when AFix may fail

Assessing patch quality In terms of correctness, AFix guarantees not to introduce new bugs. In particular, AFix restricts possible interleavings, but never allows any interleaving that was not already possible before patching. Note that AFix patches could cause temporary circular wait, but thanks to timed locks these do not become deadlocks.

AFix can successfully fix bugs reported by CTrigger in all but two scenarios. One is that a lock inside an AFix patch may time out if AFix cannot statically prove deadlock-freedom, and atomicity is no longer guaranteed when the lock does time out. This case is captured by the AFix run time and feedback will be provided for further patch refinement. The other case is very rare. It occurs when p or c has more than one dynamic instance and may access different memory locations. In this situation, the p–c pair that requires protection may not be the consecutive ones protected by AFix. This case is theoretically possible, but very rare in reality. Figure 6 shows one made-up example. In this example, p is followed by two dynamic instances of c. The first instance accesses a different variable from p, while the second instance accesses the same variable as p. AFix puts p and the first dynamic instance of c into the critical region, as shown in Figure 6b, and the control flow could leave the protected region between the two instances of c. However, what should be in the critical region is p and the second dynamic instance of c. In this extremely rare example, AFix patch will mistakenly end the critical region before the second instance of c.

In terms of performance, AFix patch strives to avoid introducing unnecessary performance degradation. AFix always ends a critical region immediately when there is no hope to reach c. Of course, for specific bugs, there could be faster patches by using lock-free data structures, reader-writer locks, etc. Crafting a general algorithm for using these special tricks is left for future work.

Extending AFix AFix focuses on locks, because they are the most commonly supported and used synchronization primitives in multithreaded programs. AFix could be easily extended to other primitives that support atomicity. For example, if we use transactional memory, then the analysis to determine where to lock and unlock is suitable for deciding where to begin and end transactions. Of course, some detailed concerns will be different. For example, concerns over deadlocks and lock selection go away, while new concerns arise over live-lock and I/O inside transactions.

Although our algorithm description and current AFix implementation is for CTrigger, the AFix algorithm can be easily extended to work with other atomicity-violation bug detectors including those for multi-variable atomicity-violation bugs. Bug reports from many atomicity-violation detectors can be generalized as "code region X needs to be mutually exclusive with code region Y." With this knowledge, a patch can be generated using the AFix algorithms

```
lock(L1)
  p1
lock(L2)
  p2
  c2
unlock(L2)
  c1
unlock(L1)
```

(a) Eliminating redundant locks

```
lock(L1)
  p1
lock(L2)
  p2
  c1
unlock(L1)
  c2
unlock(L2)
```

(b) Improving readability and performance

```
lock(L1)
  p1
lock(L2)
  p2
  c1
unlock(L1)
lock(L1)
  r1
unlock(L1)
  c2
unlock(L2)
```

(c) Avoiding deadlock

Figure 7. Scenarios where patches should or must be merged

discussed above: select one function to add lock/unlock operations, determine where inside that function to add lock/unlock operations, analyze the necessity of reentrant and timed locks, harmonize two critical regions, etc.

4. Fixing Multiple Bug Reports

Bug detectors often report multiple bugs that should be fixed by one patch, such as the two atomicity violations in Figure 1 and the scenarios depicted in Figure 7. This section describes how AFix coordinates multiple fixes in order to improve patch quality.

Provided with a set of bug reports, AFix first designs patches for each bug independently. Before applying these patches to the software, AFix considers all patches together. If one patch subsumes another, as shown in Figure 7a, the redundant patch is discarded. If two patches have overlapping critical regions, as shown in Figures 7b and 7c, AFix will further analyze how to merge the patches.

4.1 Removing Redundant Patches

AFix creates two critical regions for each bug triple (p,c,r): one containing p and c, and one containing r alone. Strictly speaking, a patch is completely redundant if both of its critical regions can be subsumed by another patch. Sometimes, a patch's p–c region is subsumed by another patch, but its r region is not. Since the r region is extremely short, AFix still chooses to discard the subsumed p–c critical region in this situation. The lock used to protect r will be changed to the lock used in the subsuming patch.

Under AFix's locking policy, a critical region p–c is subsumed by another critical region p'–c' if and only if the set of CFG nodes in p–c critical region is a subset of those in p'–c'. The reasoning is clear. The lock for p'–c' is held at every node inside its critical region. If all p–c nodes are contained within p'–c', then the p–c lock is redundant.

The above conditions are straightforward to check for two critical regions in the same function intraprocedurally. For two regions in different functions, AFix extends the above subsuming conditions interprocedurally as follows. First, let f denote the function containing critical region p–c, and let f' denote the function containing critical region p'–c'. Let n be the call node inside f' that eventually leads to f (and therefore to p–c), if such a node exists. Then p'–c' subsumes p–c if and only if

1. f' is in the common prefix of p and c's call stacks, and
2. n is inside the p'–c' critical region.

Notice that both f and f' are in the common prefix of p and c's call stacks, and f is chosen by our critical region identification algorithm, so we know that f is closer to p and c than f' on the common prefix of p and c's call stacks.

Since we have modified CTrigger to provide the complete call-stack information, the above analysis is not difficult. Note that the simplicity of our interprocedural subsumption analysis benefits from AFix's policy requiring that each critical region's locks and unlocks appear within the same function.

Overall, AFix compares each pair of patches and deletes the redundant ones.

4.2 Merging Related Patches

The general problem of patch merging can be described as follows. Given a set of critical regions, some guarded by the same lock and some by different locks, how can we adjust the lock variables and the critical-region boundaries to achieve the best balance of performance, readability, and correctness?

This question rarely has a provably-optimal answer, because performance is affected by many factors. These include but are not limited to the length of each critical region, the cost of acquiring and releasing a lock, how many threads will execute each critical region, and how much contention each lock-acquisition will face. Much of this cannot be decided statically.

Facing this challenge, AFix uses a simple heuristic to decide when and how to merge critical regions. We should note that although we believe this scheme can achieve a good balance between performance, readability, correctness, and analysis simplicity, there is no firm guarantee of performance improvement going from non-merged to merged patches. Developers can make informed decisions based on AFix's run-time performance profiling results. Different merging policies can also be plugged into AFix in the future.

4.2.1 When to Merge

AFix merges patches when one patch's lock-protected critical regions include the p, c, or r nodes of another patch. More formally, consider two sets of nodes for any given patch i. Let $Anchors_i$ represent the set of all nodes "anchoring" this patch. Initially this consists of just $\{p_i, c_i, r_i\}$: the set of nodes representing the original bug for which this patch was created. Let $Critical_i$ represent the set of all nodes contained in critical regions guarded by patch i's lock. Initially this will consist of r_i (as a single-node critical region) along with p_i, c_i, and any other protected nodes along p_i–c_i paths as computed in Section 3.2.

For any two patches i, j, if $Anchors_i \cap Critical_j \neq \emptyset$, then patches i and j should be merged. In other words, if the critical regions of one patch include any of the anchor nodes of another, then the two patches should be combined into one. Let the *Anchors* and *Critical* sets of this merged patch be the unions of the corresponding sets for the patches being merged. A single lock will guard all nodes in the combined *Critical* set. This merged patch is available for further merging; the process continues until the original patch collection has been collapsed into a (possibly) smaller one in which no patch's p, c, or r nodes are contained in the lock-guarded critical regions of any other.

4.2.2 Merging Two Critical Regions

Once AFix decides to merge, it enacts the merge in two steps:

1. Update the positions of lock and unlock operations. AFix puts an unlock operation on every edge that exits the merged *Critical* set, and a lock operation at every edge that enters the *Critical* set. This has the effect of removing all redundant lock and unlock operations among merged patches.
2. Unite lock variables. AFix arbitrarily chooses one lock variable to use and puts this variable into every lock and unlock operation performed by the merged patch.

For example, AFix merges the two critical regions in Figure 7b, and deletes **unlock**(L1) and **lock**(L2). Similarly, AFix also merges the three critical regions in Figure 7c, and discards all but the first **lock**(L1) and the last **unlock**(L2), thereby eliminating the potential deadlock. For the bug shown in Figure 1, the final merged patch has just one lock operation inserted before line 2, and two unlock operations inserted before line 4 and after line 8.

The above merging process is only used for critical regions inside the same function. Actually, it covers the intraprocedural case of redundant patch removal from Section 4.1: if a patch is subsumed by another patch in the same function, they will be merged based on AFix's merging policy. Currently, AFix first conducts interprocedural redundant-patch removal and then conducts intraprocedural patch merging. If some other merging policy is adopted in the future, intraprocedural redundant-patch removal may still be needed.

4.2.3 Benefits of Merging

Merging patches as described above has several beneficial effects on patch quality:

- Code readability is improved. In practice, it is common that many atomicity violations are reported within few lines of code, such as the Apache case shown in Figure 1. Using many different locks severely hurts code maintenance and readability.
- Performance can usually improve due to fewer lock and unlock operations without enlarging the critical region too much, such as in Figure 7. Of course, there is no guarantee of performance improvement, because merging can also reduce potential concurrency in certain scenarios.
- Correctness is either the same or improved, because we have larger critical regions now. In fact, Section 6 reports that this helps AFix lower the failure rates of some real-world software bugs that were inaccurately reported by CTrigger.
- Deadlock risk is reduced. It is easy to have one patch deadlock with another patch, as shown in Figure 7c. Merging solves this problem. Under AFix's merging policy, holding one AFix lock and trying to acquire another AFix lock is impossible, because these two locks would have been merged.

5. Run-Time Monitoring and Feedback

Not all properties can be guaranteed statically. AFix collects additional information at run time to help developers refine patches.

5.1 Deadlock and Performance Monitoring

AFix uses time-outs for lock acquisitions that cannot be guaranteed to be deadlock-free as discussed in Section 3.3. Therefore, deadlocks caused by AFix patches manifest as lock time-outs. Of course, a time-out could also occur without deadlock: a lock may simply encounter too much contention and require a longer waiting period.

AFix implements two run-time deadlock-detection algorithms, through LLVM byte-code rewriting, suitable for different usage scenarios. The first, suitable for in-house patch testing, reports whether a deadlock has occurred immediately after a time-out. It has small overhead at each lock/unlock operation. The second deadlock detector, suitable for production-run deployment, has nearly zero overhead if there is no AFix lock time-out. It takes a little bit longer to complete deadlock diagnosis.

In the first scheme, AFix follows the traditional deadlock-detection algorithm: it maintains a resource graph and looks for cycles when an AFix-added lock times out. To maintain a resource graph, AFix monitors every lock acquisition, lock release, and condition-variable signal and wait, all from the beginning of execution. Its overhead, then, depends on the density of these operations.

In the second scheme, AFix starts its monitoring and analysis only after an AFix lock times out, a moment that we will refer to as T. AFix uses information collected after T to recover the resource graph at the moment of T, as follows. When some thread t releases a lock l, AFix checks whether it also saw t return from a **lock**(l) call. If not, then l must have been acquired by t sometime before T, and therefore was held by t at the moment of T. Right after a lock l is acquired by thread t, AFix checks whether it has observed t begin a **lock**(l) call. If not, then t must already have been waiting for l at the moment of T. Eventually, AFix will recover the whole resource graph and report whether there was a deadlock. This post–time-out monitoring ends when either a deadlock is identified or the program exits. If the program encounters another AFix lock time-out, AFix will work on recovering multiple resource graphs at the same time. Since AFix lock time-outs are rare after in-house patch testing, this scheme is well-suited to monitoring production runs.

Of course, AFix's run-time system could miss a deadlock if the deadlock involves ad-hoc synchronization, such as spin loops. This is an open problem for all deadlock detection tools.

Currently, AFix relies on developers to refine the patch using its deadlock-detection results. When a time-out is diagnosed as a non-deadlock, developers may want to extend the time-out threshold in related AFix locks. When the time-out is caused by deadlock, developers could discard this patch and choose another, such as a patch that has some critical regions merged. AFix's run-time can also be combined with previous deadlock-prevention systems [13] to automatically fix patch-induced deadlocks in the future.

Other than deadlock monitoring, AFix also supports performance profiling during in-house testing. In profiling mode, AFix measures the waiting time and the number of time-outs for each lock acquisition inside an AFix patch. If excessive waiting time or time-outs are observed at a critical region that merges multiple bug reports' patches, developers may want to split this big critical region to reduce lock contention and improve performance.

5.2 Patch Testing

Each patch generated by AFix undergoes two testing phases. The first phase uses the existing CTrigger testing. CTrigger provides a noise injection scheme for each bug it reports. Through a binary instrumentation framework [22], CTrigger deterministically calls sleep before or after specific instructions: before c, after p, etc. We apply CTrigger testing to AFix-patched software and see whether software failures could still occur.

The second patch testing phase is a more general interleaving test implemented by us. Before executing every instruction inside an AFix critical region, a random number generator decides whether to sleep or not. Similar random delays are also inserted right before the locks and right after the unlocks added by AFix. The sleep probability and the length of the sleep are tunable knobs. This phase can help identify patches that fail to completely fix the bug due to bug-detection limitations of CTrigger.

6. Experimental Results

AFix is implemented using LLVM version 2.7. Experiments are performed on an eight-core Intel Xeon machine running Red Hat Linux 5 with kernel version 2.6.18.

We evaluated AFix on eight real-world bugs from six open-source applications. These bugs were all initially reported by software users to each application's bug database or mailing list. We apply CTrigger to these applications using the bug-triggering inputs described in the user bug reports. In each case, CTrigger detects one or more (p, c, r) triples. We have confirmed that atomicity violations described by each triple lead to failure symptoms matching users' descriptions. Table 1 gives additional information about these bugs, applications, and CTrigger detection results.

For each bug listed in Table 1, AFix generates two versions of patched software: one with the patch-merging technique presented in Section 4 applied and one without. We refer to the former as

Bug ID	Application	LoC	Developer Fix Time	# CTrigger Reports
FFT	FFT	1.2K	N/A	5
PBZIP2	PBZIP2	2.0K	N/A	4
Apache	Apache	333K	30 days	2
MySQL1	MySQL v4.0.12	681K	10 days	1
MySQL2	MySQL v4.0.19	693K	13 days*	2
Mozilla1	Mozilla-JS v1.4.2	87K	12 days*	2
Mozilla2	Mozilla-JS v1.5	108K	> 3 days♯	1
Cherokee	Cherokee v0.9.2	83K	> 1 day♯	4

Table 1. Bugs used in experimental evaluation. Developer fix time is the time between developers' first response to a bug report and a correct patch checked in, if known. Mozilla-JS is the JavaScript Engine of Mozilla. *: incorrect patches were submitted during this period. ♯: the bug was reported by developers who suggested a fixing strategy in the initial bug report.

Bug ID	naïve	unmerged	merged	manual
FFT	-	-	?	✓
PBZIP2	-	-	-	✓
Apache	-	-	✓	✓
MySQL1	-	✓	✓	✓
MySQL2	-	✓	✓	?
Mozilla1	-	✓	✓	?
Mozilla2	-	✓	✓	✓
Cherokee	-	✓	✓	✓

Table 2. Overall patch quality

the *merged* version and the latter as the *unmerged* version. We also compare AFix with two other versions of patched software: (1) the patch manually generated by developers, referred to as *manual*, and (2) the naïve patch described in Section 2.3, referred to as *naïve*. Our experiments also compare the above patched versions with the original buggy software, referred to as *original*.

Our evaluation considers three aspects of patch quality:

Correctness. We use CTrigger testing and intensive random noise injection to check whether the bug has been fixed and whether new bugs are introduced. We report and compare the failure rates of different versions of software. We also use the AFix run time to check whether timed-out locks actually represent deadlocks.

Performance. We measure the performance of different versions of patched or unpatched software. We also measure how long it takes AFix to perform its static analysis and patch insertion.

Code readability. We manually compare AFix patches with the *manual* patch. We present results through case studies.

6.1 Overall Results

Table 2 presents a compact summary of patch quality. "✓" indicates that the original bug is fixed, no new bug is observed, and performance degradation is negligible. "?" indicates that the patch is incomplete, but decreases the failure rate without hurting performance. "-" marks cases where the fix introduces new bugs, does not significantly reduce the failure rate, or imposes an intolerable performance deficiency. For manual patches, "?" means developers submitted intermediate patches that are later determined to be incomplete by developers or testing groups (i.e., the original software failure can still occur with the patch applied). "✓" means that the first developer-submitted patch is complete. For the bugs in our study, developers submitted no patch that could introduce new bugs or intolerable performance deficiencies. We obtained the above information from corresponding Bugzilla records.

Patches generated with merging are highly competitive with manually-generated patches. AFix successfully fixes six out of eight bugs. In two cases, MySQL2 and Mozilla1, merged patches are even better than the first few patches generated by developers. For FFT and PBZIP2, AFix is limited by CTrigger's inaccurate root-cause identification. Even here, the merged patches reduce (but cannot entirely eliminate) failures.

Unmerged patches fix five out of eight bugs. Deadlock prevents this from fixing the Apache bug that merging does correctly fix. The naïve approach fixes no bug. It causes deadlock in all but FFT, and fails to fix FFT due to CTrigger inaccuracy.

Bug ID	original	naïve	unmerged	merged
FFT	74%	73%	87%	30%
PBZIP2	94%	100%*	66%	20%
Apache	85%	100%*	83%	0%
MySQL1	41%	100%*	0%	0%
MySQL2	53%	100%*	0%	0%
Mozilla1	41%	100%*	0%	0%
Mozilla2	48%	100%*	0%	0%
Cherokee	81%	100%*	0%	0%

Table 3. Failure rates under interleaving testing. "100%*" marks cases where the test input deterministically causes deadlock.

6.2 Correctness Results

Table 3 shows the failure rates of different versions of software under random noise-injection testing (Section 5.2). We set up exactly the same noise injection environment for all versions of software for each bug: the same program region to inject random noise, which is around the buggy code region; the same sleep probability; and the same sleep length. We use slightly different sleep probabilities and sleep lengths for different bugs, because we want to make sure the testing is intensive enough to make the original unpatched software fail frequently. This lets us effectively evaluate whether the patches are useful. We execute each version of software 100 times.

Merged patches eliminate software failures for six out of eight bugs in our testing. Merging provides incomplete patches for FFT and PBZIP2, but drops failure rates from 74% to 30% in FFT and from 94% to 20% in PBZIP2. The failure rates do not drop to 0% because CTrigger's bug detection is inaccurate: atomicity violation is a side effect but not the root-cause of these two bugs. Specifically, following a CTrigger report (p, c, r), merging correctly ensures that r does not execute between p and c. However, the real problem in FFT is that r should not execute after either p or c, while the problem in PBZIP2 is that r should execute after both p and c. Merging can only partially fix these two problems.

Unmerged patching behaves slightly worse than merged, eliminating failures for five out of eight bugs. It leads to non-deterministic deadlocks in Apache and PBZIP2 due to the reason depicted in Figure 7c. Once the lock times out after a deadlock, atomicity violation and subsequent failure can still occur. For FFT, unmerged patching has a much larger failure rate than merged due to its smaller critical-region size. In FFT, the bug occurs when an instruction r executes after any one of a set of six instructions. Merging puts all six into one critical region, making the bug less likely to occur.

Naïve patching is clearly a very bad choice, leading to deadlock in seven out of eight bugs. There are several different reasons for these deadlocks. For MySQL2 and PBZIP2, deadlocks are caused due to intraprocedural control flows, as depicted in Figure 3. For MySQL1 and Mozilla1, p and c are inside different functions. Locking in one function and unlocking in another easily causes

Bug ID	naïve	unmerged	merged	manual
FFT	-0.02%	-0.07%	-0.02%	0.19%
PBZIP2	N/A	89,132%	181.82%	0.20%
Apache	N/A	0.45%	-0.97%	-0.26%
MySQL1	N/A	0.48%	0.48%	0.45%
MySQL2	N/A	-0.09%	-0.09%	1.02%
Mozilla1	N/A	0.49%	0.55%	0.12%
Mozilla2	N/A	-0.40%	-0.40%	-0.20%
Cherokee	N/A	-1.02%	-1.04%	0.39%

Table 4. Performance overheads relative to original

deadlocks when the first function is called twice without the second function in between. In Apache, Cherokee, and Mozilla2, naïve double-lock bugs arise because *r* is inside a *p–c* region. Apache and PBZIP2 also deadlock among different locks added by the patch.

We also reapplied CTrigger to the patched code. According to CTrigger's definitions, both merged and unmerged patches successfully fix all eight bugs. We also manually checked all these patches. Our findings are consistent with the random testing results. In those cases with 0% failure rates, the bugs are all truly fixed.

Overall, merging generates correct patches that not only fix the original bugs but also introduce no new bugs, as long as its front-end bug detector provides a reasonably-accurate bug report. Unmerged patching is also good, but is vulnerable to deadlock.

6.3 Performance Results

Patched application performance Table 4 shows that merged and unmerged AFix fixes provide good run-time performance, with negligible difference between them. Note that overheads cannot be measured for most naïve patches as these lead to deterministic deadlocks. In most cases, AFix patches impose no perceivable performance degradation compared with correct manual patches or even the original buggy software. This is because the relevant critical regions are usually small and off performance-critical paths.

Only PBZIP2 suffers from significant performance degradation under AFix. The PBZIP2 bug is caused by a parent thread occasionally destroying shared objects before worker threads finish. The manual patch makes the main thread wait until all worker threads are done, which is correct and lightweight. Due to CTrigger inaccuracy, AFix mistakenly treats this bug as an atomicity-violation bug, and fixes it by putting almost the whole worker thread into a critical region, which causes huge overhead. The unmerged AFix patch is much slower than the merged patch for PBZIP2, because the former suffers from deadlock time-outs. Deadlock time-outs can also occur in the unmerged patch of Apache, but this never happens during performance evaluation without noise injection.

AFix patch generation performance All of AFix's static analyses have been designed with scalability in mind. On every benchmark, AFix takes no more than one second to analyze the program, develop its patches, and inject them into the code. Clearly, AFix has the potential to significantly speed up the bug-fixing process.

6.4 Readability Case Studies

AFix's patch merging technique improves patch readability and maintainability. For six out of eight bugs, CTrigger reports two to five atomicity violations related to each bug. The unmerged fix therefore adds two to five new locks and up to ten new critical regions into the software. Merging simplifies this to use just one lock in five out of six cases. Manual inspection shows that all merging decisions made by AFix improve readability.

Taking the Cherokee bug as an example, CTrigger reports four atomicity violations in three different functions. The unmerged fix therefore adds four global lock variables, six lock operations, and seven unlock operations into the software. AFix finds some of these critical regions to be redundant and some to be mergeable. The final patch requires only one lock, one lock operation, and one unlock operation, for excellent code readability and maintainability. In fact, the merged patch closely resembles the manual patch.

6.5 Other Results

AFix's run-time deadlock detection gives accurate results for both merged and unmerged patches. For example, in PBZIP2, both merged and unmerged strategies encounter lock time-outs. The AFix run-time system correctly determines that the time-outs in the unmerged patch are caused by deadlocks among patches, but that the time-outs in the merged patch are not. Rather, merging simply has produced large critical regions with much lock contention, and therefore requires longer time-outs.

AFix's post–time-out deadlock-detection algorithm exhibits excellent performance on all bugs. Its overhead is already included in the performance numbers measured in Table 4. AFix's always-on deadlock detection has less than 5% overhead for all bugs except for Mozilla1 and Mozilla2, where the always-on monitoring causes 300% and 97% overhead respectively. This is due to the frequent lock/unlock operations in Mozilla's JavaScript Engine.

7. Related Work

7.1 Concurrency Bug Detection

Many detection tools have been built to identify interleaving problems in multithreaded programs, such as races [4, 6, 10, 12, 32] and atomicity violations [9, 12, 19, 37]. These tools provide good starting points for automated bug fixing.

Of course, since these tools are designed to identify problems, not to fix problems, they still leave many challenges for bug fixing. For example, many bug detection tools have false positives. "Fixing" false positives leads to over-synchronization and unnecessary performance degradation. Many bug reports do not include complete run-time information, which could cause wrong or incomplete patches. Bug detectors seldom put bug reports that can be fixed by one patch together, which can cause too many locks to be added, harming code maintainability. Furthermore, naïve patches for accurately-described bug reports can easily introduce new bugs.

AFix has considered and addressed the challenges above. In the future, AFix can be extended to work with more concurrency-bug detectors to fix more bugs, which will also help bug-detection tools to get more usage during software development.

7.2 Concurrent Program Synthesis

Existing tools that automatically add synchronizations to software mostly have different goals from AFix, and hence different foci. Program synthesis and sketching [8, 34, 38] use smart state-space search and verification techniques to infer synchronization and make concurrent programs satisfy certain specifications. They are powerful in the sense that the specification can be flexible. Unfortunately, the nature of the problem makes them hard to scale to large real-world C/C++ applications such as the ones fixed by AFix.

Some tools [23, 37] encourage programmers to represent their synchronization intentions in non-lock language constructs, such as atomic sets and atomic blocks, and transparently translate these non-lock constructs to lock/unlock operations. In these cases, the critical region boundaries are either directly specified by developers or fixed at the entrances and exits of certain functions; the major challenge is lock assignment. AFix, by contrast, derives critical region boundaries with limited or no human intervention.

TraceFinder [36] performs whole-program synchronization analysis and pointer-alias analysis to identify atomic-block boundaries that can guarantee conflict-serializability for the whole software. TraceFinder has a different goal from AFix. It cannot scale to large applications. It uses atomic blocks for synchronization, and does not worry about lock assignment or deadlocks.

AFix is unique in fixing bugs reported by automatic bug-detectors. AFix does not face the scalability problems encountered by TraceFinder, because it does not try to figure out all the synchronizations a program needs to use. Rather, AFix faces different challenges.

7.3 Hot-Patching Concurrency Bugs at Run Time

Some proposed strategies for hot-patching software at run time are not suitable for concurrency bugs [28]. Recent work by Wu et al. [40] provides a framework to deploy hot patches manually designed by developers. AFix can complement this framework by generating patches automatically, instead of completely relying on developers.

Some run-time tools do not try to permanently fix concurrency bugs in the software. Rather, they steer the execution to make failure less likely. Some pay the cost of performance degradation or require non-existing hardware support [21]. Others assume that critical-region boundaries are known [16, 30]. Deterministic execution systems [1–3] can make some concurrency bugs deterministically happen and some other bugs never occur. This promising approach still faces many challenges, such as run-time overhead, integration with system non-determinism, language design, etc. Even for software executed inside a deterministic run-time, fixing bugs still requires manual intervention. In general, these tools look at different problems from AFix. AFix generates patches that can completely fix bugs without unnecessary performance degradation. AFix and these tools can complement each other.

Kivati [5] combines run-time bug detection with temporary patch generation based on hardware watch-points. Its focus is to lower bug detection overheads. However, the limited watch-point resource (four per machine) prevents Kivati from managing many different critical regions at the same time. Kivati does not handle cases where p and c are inside different functions, such as the Cherokee and MySQL1 bugs in Section 6. It causes unnecessarily long critical regions when there are branches between p and c, as shown in Figure 3a. It also does not handle critical-region merging or deadlocks. Overall, Kivati lacks the off-line static analyses needed to generate high-quality, permanent fixes.

AtomRace [16, 18] combines run-time bug detection with run-time healing, with emphasis on bug detection. Its healer component assumes that critical-region entrances and exits are all provided as inputs. They do not address those challenges faced by the naïve patches discussed in our paper, and do not consider patch merging.

8. Conclusion

We have described AFix, a framework for automatically fixing a common type of concurrency bugs. We have implemented the system and shown AFix to be effective at generating high-quality patches for atomicity-violation bugs detected by an automated bug finder in several large, real-world applications. AFix conducts thorough static analysis to reach a good balance among correctness, performance, and code readability in its automatically generated patches. AFix's testing and monitoring run-time system also provide useful feedback for further patch refinement. In the future we plan to extend AFix to work with more general synchronization primitives and more types of concurrency bug detectors.

References

[1] A. Aviram, S.-C. Weng, S. Hu, and B. Ford. Efficient system-enforced deterministic parallelism. In *OSDI*, 2010.

[2] T. Bergan, N. Hunt, L. Ceze, and S. D. Gribble. Deterministic process groups in dOS. In *OSDI*, 2010.

[3] E. D. Berger, T. Yang, T. Liu, and G. Novark. Grace: safe multithreaded programming for C/C++. In *OOPSLA*, 2009.

[4] M. D. Bond, K. E. Coons, and K. S. McKinley. Pacer: Proportional detection of data races. In *PLDI*, 2010.

[5] L. Chew and D. Lie. Kivati: fast detection and prevention of atomicity violations. In *EuroSys*, 2010.

[6] J.-D. Choi, K. Lee, A. Loginov, R. O'Callahan, V. Sarkar, and M. Sridharan. Efficient and precise datarace detection for multithreaded object-oriented programs. In *PLDI*, 2002.

[7] C. Cowan, H. Hinton, C. Pu, and J. Walpole. The cracker patch choice: An analysis of post hoc security techniques. In *In Proceedings of the National Information Systems Security Conference (NISSC)*, 2000.

[8] J. Deshmukh, G. Ramalingam, V. P. Ranganath, and K. Vaswani. Logical concurrency control from sequential proofs. In *European Symposium on Programming*, 2010.

[9] C. Flanagan and S. N. Freund. Atomizer: a dynamic atomicity checker for multithreaded programs. In *POPL*, 2004.

[10] C. Flanagan and S. N. Freund. FastTrack: efficient and precise dynamic race detection. In *PLDI*, 2009.

[11] M. Harman. Automated patching techniques: the fix is in: technical perspective. *Commun. ACM*, 53(5):108–108, 2010. ISSN 0001-0782. doi: http://doi.acm.org/10.1145/1735223.1735248.

[12] G. Jin, A. Thakur, B. Liblit, and S. Lu. Instrumentation and sampling strategies for Cooperative Concurrency Bug Isolation. In *OOPSLA*, 2010.

[13] H. Jula, D. Tralamazza, C. Zamfir, and G. Candea. Deadlock immunity: Enabling systems to defend against deadlocks. In *OSDI*, 2008.

[14] E. Kandrot and B. Eich. Our JavaScript is 3x slower than IE's, Sept. 2000. URL https://bugzilla.mozilla.org/show_bug.cgi?id=54743.

[15] B. Krebs. A time to patch II: Mozilla. *The Washington Post* Security Fix blog, Feb. 2006. URL http://voices.washingtonpost.com/securityfix/2006/02/a_time_to_patch_ii_mozilla.html.

[16] B. Krena, Z. Letko, R. Tzoref, S. Ur, and T. Vojnar. Healing data races on-the-fly. In *PADTAD*, 2007.

[17] C. Lattner and V. Adve. LLVM: A compilation framework for lifelong program analysis & transformation. In *CGO*, 2004.

[18] Z. Letko, T. Vojnar, and B. Křena. AtomRace: data race and atomicity violation detector and healer. In *PADTAD*, 2008.

[19] S. Lu, J. Tucek, F. Qin, and Y. Zhou. AVIO: Detecting atomicity violations via access-interleaving invariants. In *ASPLOS*, 2006.

[20] S. Lu, S. Park, E. Seo, and Y. Zhou. Learning from mistakes – a comprehensive study of real world concurrency bug characteristics. In *ASPLOS*, Mar. 2008.

[21] B. Lucia, J. Devietti, L. Ceze, and K. Strauss. Atom-Aid: Detecting and surviving atomicity violations. *IEEE Micro*, 29(1), 2009.

[22] C.-K. Luk, R. Cohn, R. Muth, H. Patil, A. Klauser, G. Lowney, S. Wallace, V. J. Reddi, and K. Hazelwood. Pin: building customized program analysis tools with dynamic instrumentation. In *PLDI*, 2005.

[23] B. McCloskey, F. Zhou, D. Gay, and E. Brewer. Autolocker: synchronization inference for atomic sections. In *POPL*, 2006.

[24] Microsoft. Revamping the microsoft security bulletin release process, Feb. 2005. URL http://www.microsoft.com/technet/security/bulletin/revsbwp.mspx.

[25] S. Park, S. Lu, and Y. Zhou. CTrigger: exposing atomicity violation bugs from their hiding places. In *ASPLOS*, 2009.

[26] S. Park, R. W. Vuduc, and M. J. Harrold. Falcon: fault localization in concurrent programs. In *ICSE*, 2010.

[27] R. Pegoraro. Apple updates Leopard–again. Washington Post, Feb. 2008.

[28] J. H. Perkins, S. Kim, S. Larsen, S. P. Amarasinghe, J. Bachrach, M. Carbin, C. Pacheco, F. Sherwood, S. Sidiroglou, G. Sullivan, W.-F. Wong, Y. Zibin, M. D. Ernst, and M. C. Rinard. Automatically patching errors in deployed software. In *SOSP*, 2009.

[29] K. Poulsen. Software bug contributed to blackout. SecurityFocus, Feb. 2004. URL http://www.securityfocus.com/news/8016.

[30] P. Ratanaworabhan, M. Burtscher, D. Kirovski, B. Zorn, R. Nagpal, and K. Pattabiraman. Detecting and tolerating asymmetric races. In *PPoPP*, 2009.

[31] E. Rescorla. Security holes ... who cares? In *USENIX Security Conference*, 2003.

[32] S. Savage, M. Burrows, G. Nelson, P. Sobalvarro, and T. Anderson. Eraser: A dynamic data race detector for multithreaded programs. *ACM Transactions on Computer Systems*, 15, 1997.

[33] S. Sidiroglou, S. Ioannidis, and A. D. Keromytis. Band-aid patching. In *HotDep*, 2007.

[34] A. Solar-Lezama, C. G. Jones, and R. Bodik. Sketching concurrent data structures. In *PLDI*, 2008.

[35] C. Tian, V. Nagarajan, R. Gupta, and S. Tallam. Dynamic recognition of synchronization operations for improved data race detection. In *ISSTA*, 2008.

[36] G. Upadhyaya, S. P. Midkiff, and V. S. Pai. Automatic atomic region identification in shared memory spmd programs. In *OOPSLA*, 2010.

[37] M. Vaziri, F. Tip, and J. Dolby. Associating synchronization constraints with data in an object-oriented language. In *POPL*, 2006.

[38] M. T. Vechev, E. Yahav, and G. Yorsh. Abstraction-guided synthesis of synchronization. In *POPL*, 2010.

[39] D. Weeratunge, X. Zhang, and S. Jagannathan. Analyzing multicore dumps to facilitate concurrency bug reproduction. In *ASPLOS*, 2010.

[40] J. Wu, H. Cui, and J. Yang. Bypassing races in live applications with execution filters. In *OSDI*, 2010.

[41] W. Xiong, S. Park, J. Zhang, Y. Zhou, and Z. Ma. Ad hoc synchronization considered harmful. In *OSDI*, 2010.

[42] C. Zamfir and G. Candea. Execution synthesis: A technique for automated software debugging. In *EuroSys*, 2010.

NDSeq: Runtime Checking for Nondeterministic Sequential Specifications of Parallel Correctness

Jacob Burnim Tayfun Elmas George Necula Koushik Sen

Department of Electrical Engineering and Computer Sciences, University of California, Berkeley

{jburnim,elmas,necula,ksen}@cs.berkeley.edu

Abstract

We propose to specify the correctness of a program's parallelism using a sequential version of the program with controlled nondeterminism. Such a *nondeterministic sequential specification* allows (1) the correctness of parallel interference to be verified independently of the program's functional correctness, and (2) the functional correctness of a program to be understood and verified on a sequential version of the program, one with controlled nondeterminism but no interleaving of parallel threads.

We identify a number of common patterns for writing nondeterministic sequential specifications. We apply these patterns to specify the parallelism correctness for a variety of parallel Java benchmarks, even in cases when the functional correctness is far too complex to feasibly specify.

We describe a sound runtime checking technique to validate that an execution of a parallel program conforms to its nondeterministic sequential specification. The technique uses a novel form of conflict-serializability checking to identify, for a given interleaved execution of a parallel program, an equivalent nondeterministic sequential execution. Our experiments show a significant reduction in the number of false positives versus traditional conflict-serializability in checking for parallelization bugs.

Categories and Subject Descriptors D.2.4 [*Software Engineering*]: Software/Program Verification; D.2.5 [*Software Engineering*]: Testing and Debugging; F.3.1 [*Logics and Meanings of Programs*]: Specifying and Verifying and Reasoning about Programs

General Terms Algorithms, Reliability, Verification

1. Introduction

The spread of multicore processors and the end of rapidly growing single-core performance is increasing the need for programmers to write parallel software. Yet writing correct parallel programs with explicit multithreading remains a difficult undertaking. A programmer must ensure not only that each part of his or her program computes the correct results in isolation, but also that the uncontrolled and nondeterministic interleaving of the program's parallel threads cannot cause harmful interference, leading to incorrect final results. This need to simultaneously reason about sequential functional correctness and the correctness of parallel interleavings poses a great challenge both for programmers writing, understanding, and testing their software and for tools analyzing and verifying such software.

We previously proposed *nondeterministic sequential (NDSeq) specifications* [9] as a means to separate the correctness of the parallelism of a program from its sequential functional correctness. The key idea is for a programmer to specify the *intended* or *algorithmic* nondeterminism in a program using annotations, and then the NDSeq specification is a version of the program that is sequential but includes the annotated nondeterministic behavior. The only valid parallel behaviors are those allowed by the NDSeq specification—any *additional* nondeterminism is an error, due to unintended interference between interleaved parallel threads, such as data races or atomicity violations. Thus, a program with such annotated nondeterminism serves as its own NDSeq specification for the correctness of its parallelism.

Showing that a parallel program conforms to its NDSeq specification is a strong statement that the program's use of parallelism is correct. The behavior of the program can be understood by considering only the NDSeq version of the program, as executing the program in parallel cannot produce any different results. Testing, debugging, and verification of functional correctness can be performed on this sequential version, with no need to deal with the uncontrolled interleaving and interference of parallel threads. We show in this work that NDSeq specifications for parallel applications can be both written and checked in a simple manner, independent of an application's complex functional correctness.

In this paper, we propose several patterns for writing NDSeq specifications, and we apply these patterns to specify the parallelism correctness of a number of Java benchmarks. We find that, with a few simple constructs for specifying intended nondeterministic behavior, adding such specifications to the program text was straightforward for a variety of applications. This is despite the fact that, for many of these applications, writing a traditional functional correctness specification would be extremely difficult. (Imagine, for example, specifying the correct output of an application to render a fractal, or to compute a likely phylogenetic tree given genetic sequence data.) For many of our benchmarks, verifying that the final output is correct even for a single known input is challenging.

We propose a novel sound runtime technique for checking that a structured parallel program conforms to its NDSeq specification. Given a parallel execution of such a program, we perform a conflict-serializability check to verify that the same behavior could have been produced by the NDSeq version of the program. But first, our technique combines a dynamic dependence analysis with a program's specified nondeterminism to show that conflicts involving certain operations in the trace can be soundly ignored when performing the conflict-serializability check. Our experimental results show that our runtime checking technique significantly reduces the number of false positives versus traditional conflict-serializability in checking parallel correctness.

PLDI'11, June 4–8, 2011, San Jose, California, USA.

```
1:  coforeach (i in 1,...,N) {
2:    b = lower_bound_cost(i);
3:    t = lowest_cost;
4:    if (b >= t)
5:        continue;
6:    c = expensive_compute_cost(i);
7:    atomic {
8:        t = lowest_cost
9:        if (c < t) {
10:           lowest_cost = c;
11:           best_soln = i;
12: } } }
```

(a) An example parallel search procedure.

```
1:  nd-foreach (i in 1,...,N) {
2:    b = lower_bound_cost(i);
3:    t = lowest_cost;
4:    if (* && (b >= t))
5:        continue;
6:    c = expensive_compute_cost(i);
7:    atomic {
8:        t = lowest_cost
9:        if (c < t) {
10:           lowest_cost = c;
11:           best_soln = i;
12: } } }
```

(b) Nondeterministic sequential specification for parallel search procedure.

```
1:  coforeach (i in 1,...,N) {
2:    b = lower_bound_cost(i);
3:    t = lowest_cost;
4:    if (true* && (b >= t))
5:        continue;
6:    c = expensive_compute_cost(i);
7:    atomic {
8:        t = lowest_cost
9:        if (c < t) {
10:           lowest_cost = c;
11:           best_soln = i;
12: } } }
```

(c) Parallel search with embedded nondeterministic sequential specification.

Figure 1. An example parallel search procedure (Figure 1(a)) and a nondeterministic sequential specification (NDSeq) for its parallel correctness (Figure 1(b)). Since a parallel program and its NDSeq specification look very similar, in practice, we do not write the NDSeq specification of a parallel program separately, but embed it in the parallel program itself. Figure 1(c) shows the parallel search procedure with its NDSeq specification embedded in the parallel code. The boxed constructs have different semantics when viewed as parallel code or as nondeterministic sequential specification.

2. Overview

In this section, we discuss an example program in detail to motivate NDSeq specifications and to informally describe our runtime checking that a parallel program is parallelized correctly with respect to its NDSeq specification. In Section 3, we then give a formal definition of parallelization correctness. In Section 4, we illustrate the generality of these specifications and of our checking approach on several examples highlighting different parallelization patterns. Section 5 describes the details of the runtime checking algorithm. We discuss the experimental results in Section 6 and conclude in Section 8 by pointing out significance and possible future applications of NDSeq specifications.

2.1 Motivating Example

Consider the simplified version of a generic branch-and-bound procedure given in Figure 1(a). This program takes as input a list of N possible solutions and computes `lowest_cost`, the minimum cost among the possible solutions, and `best_soln`, the index of a solution with minimum cost. Function `expensive_compute_cost(i)` computes the cost of solution `i`. Because this computation is expensive, the program first computes a lower bound for the cost of solution `i` with `lower_bound_cost(i)`. If this lower bound is no smaller than the lowest cost found so far (i.e. `lowest_cost`), then the program skips computing the exact cost for solution `i`.

The program is a *parallel* search—the **coforeach** loop allows different iterations to examine different potential solutions in parallel. Thus, updates to `lowest_cost` and `best_soln` at Lines 8–11 are enclosed in an **atomic** block, a synchronization mechanism that enforces that these lines be executed atomically—that is, all-at-once and without interruption by any other thread. Functions `expensive_compute_cost` and `lower_bound_cost` have no side-effects and do not read any mutable shared data (i.e., `lowest_cost` or `best_soln`), and thus require no synchronization.

2.2 Nondeterministic Sequential Specifications

We would like to formalize and specify that the search procedure in Figure 1(a) is *parallelized correctly*, and we would like some way to verify or test this parallel correctness.

If we could specify the full functional correctness of our example program—i.e. specify precisely which outputs are correct for each input—then this specification would clearly imply that the parallelization of the program was correct. But writing a full functional correctness specification is often a very difficult task. For our example search procedure, the cost of a possible solution may be a complex function whose behavior we are unable to specify, short of reimplementing the entire `expensive_compute_cost` in a specification/assertion language. Even if we could write such a specification, verifying the full functional correctness could similarly require very complex reasoning about the internals of the cost and lower bound computations.

We argue that we should seek to specify the correctness of the parallelism in our example program independently of the program's functional correctness. More generally, we aim to decompose our effort of verifying or checking the correctness of the program into two parts: (1) addressing the correctness of the parallelism, independent of the complex functional correctness and (2) addressing the functional correctness independent of any reasoning about the interleaving of parallel threads.

A natural approach to specifying parallel correctness would be to specify that the program in Figure 1(a) must produce the same results—i.e. compute the same `lowest_cost` and `best_soln`—as a version of the program with all parallelism removed. But if we simply replace the **coforeach** with a traditional **foreach**-loop that iterates `i` sequentially from 1 to `N`, we do not get an equivalent program. Rather, the parallel program has two "freedoms" the sequential program does not:

ND1 First, the parallel search procedure is free to execute the parallel loop iterations in any *nondeterministic* order. If there are multiple solutions of minimum cost, then different runs of the procedure may return different values for `best_soln`, depending on the order in which the loop iterations are scheduled.

The hypothetical sequential version, on the other hand, would be deterministic—it would always first consider solution 1, then solution 2, ..., up to solution `N`.

ND2 Second, the parallel program is free, in a sense, to not perform the optimization in Lines 2–5, in which the rest of an iteration is skipped because the lower bound on the solution cost is larger than the minimum cost found so far.

Consider two iterations with the same cost and with lower bounds equal to their costs. In the hypothetical sequential version, only one of the iterations would proceed to compute its cost. In the parallel code in Figure 1(a), however, both iterations may proceed past the check in Line 3 (as `lowest_cost` is initially ∞).

We propose to specify the correctness of the parallelism by comparing our example parallel program to a version that is sequential but contains the nondeterministic behaviors ND1 and ND2. Such

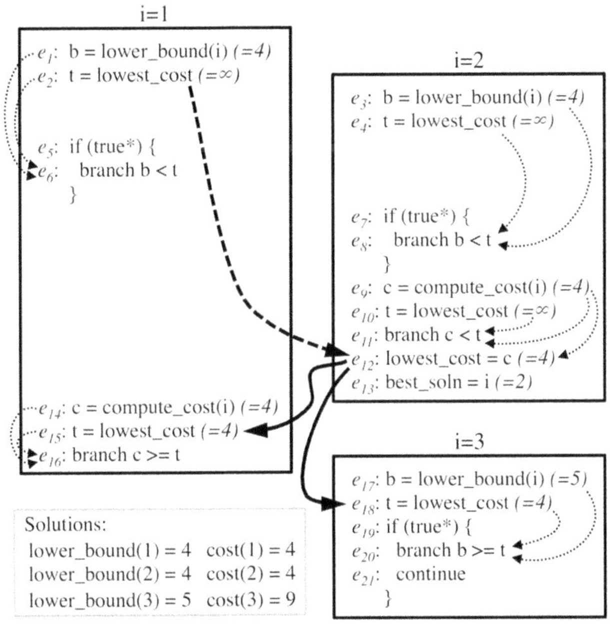

Figure 2. A parallel execution of three iterations (i=1,2,3) of the parallel search procedure. The vertical order of events shows the interleaving. Each assignment shows in parentheses the value being assigned. The thin dotted arrows denote data dependencies. The thick solid and thick dashed arrows denote transactional conflicts. Our analysis proves that the transactional conflict $e_2 \dashrightarrow e_{12}$ can be safely ignored for the serializability check.

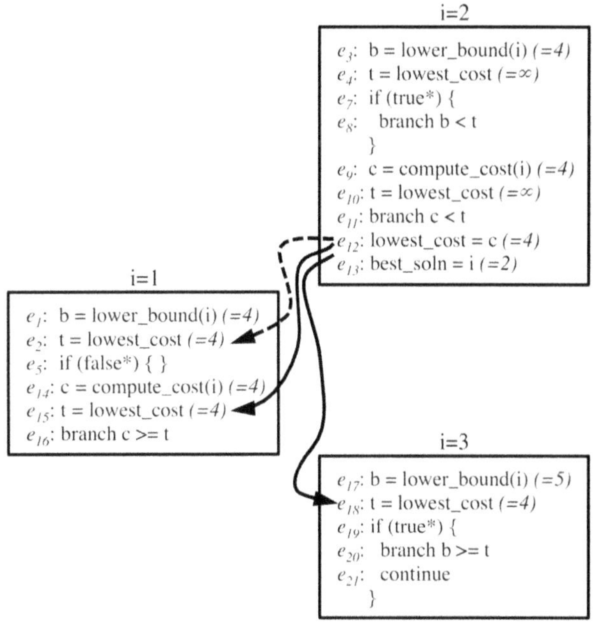

Figure 3. An execution of the nondeterministic sequential version of the search procedure. This execution is a serialization of the parallel execution in Figure 2, producing the same final result. The thick solid and thick dashed arrows denote transactional conflicts. Note that the order of conflicts $e_{12} \rightarrow e_{15}$ and $e_{12} \rightarrow e_{18}$ is the same as in Figure 2, while conflict $e_{12} \dashrightarrow e_2$, involving irrelevant event e_2, has been flipped.

a version of the program is a *nondeterministic sequential (ND-Seq) specification* for the program's parallel correctness. For the program in Figure 1(a), our NDSeq specification is listed in Figure 1(b). The NDSeq specification differs from the parallel program in two ways:

1. The parallel **coforeach** loop at Line 1 is replaced with a sequential but nondeterministic **nd-foreach** loop, which can run its iterations in any order.
2. The "* &&" is added to the condition at Line 4. This expression "*" can nondeterministically evaluate to `true` or `false`, allowing the sequential specification to run the rest of a loop iteration even when `lower_bound_cost(i)` $\geq$ `lowest_cost`.

This specification is a completely sequential version of the program, executing its loop iterations one-at-a-time with no interleaving of different iterations. It contains only the controlled nondeterminism added at the two above points. We say that a parallel program *conforms* to its NDSeq specification when every final result of the parallel program can also be produced by an execution of the NDSeq specification. Section 3 elaborates the semantics of NDSeq specifications and our precise definition of parallelism correctness.

Note the close similarity between the parallel program in Figure 1(a) and its NDSeq specification in Figure 1(b). Rather than maintaining our parallel search procedure and its NDSeq specifications as separate artifacts, we embed the NDSeq specifications into the parallel code, as shown in Figure 1(c). Here we show in boxes the **coforeach** and "*true** &&" to indicate that these two constructs are interpreted differently when we consider Figure 1(c) as a parallel program or as nondeterministic sequential one. That is, in the parallel interpretation, **coforeach** is a standard parallel for-loop and "*true**" always evaluates to *true*, yielding the exact behavior of Figure 1(a). But when interpreted as nondeterministic sequential constructs, **coforeach** is treated as a **nd-foreach** and "*true**" can nondeterministically evaluate to *true* or *false*, yielding exactly the behavior of Figure 1(b). With these annotations, the example program in Figure 1(c) embeds its own NDSeq specification for the correctness of its parallelism.

2.3 Runtime Checking of Parallel Correctness

We now give an overview of our proposed algorithm for the runtime checking that a parallel program conforms to its NDSeq specification. We will present the algorithm in full formal detail in Section 5.

Figure 2 illustrates a possible parallel execution of our example program in Figure 1(c) on $\texttt{N} = 3$ possible solutions. The three iterations of the parallel for-loop are shown in separate boxes, with the $i = 1$ iteration running in parallel with the $i = 2$ iteration, followed by the $i = 3$ iteration. Although the $i = 1$ compute a lower bound and compare it against `lowest_cost`, iteration $i = 2$ is first to compute the full cost of its solution and to update `lowest_cost` $= 4$ and `best_soln` $= 2$.

We would like to verify that the parallelism in this execution is correct. That is, the final result produced is also possible in an execution of the NDSeq specification. The key will be to show that parallel loop iterations together are *serializable* [29]—i.e. there exist some order such that, if the iterations are executed sequentially in that order, then the same final result will be produced.

A common restriction of serializability that can be efficiently checked and is thus often used in practice is *conflict-serializability* [29]. Given a collection of transactions—in this case, we think of each parallel loop iteration as a transaction—we form the *conflict graph* whose vertices are the transactions and with a *conflict edge* from transaction tr to tr' if tr and tr' contain conflicting operations op and op' with op happening before op'. (Two operations from different threads are conflicting if they operate on the same shared global and at least one of them is a write; in our example the conflicts are shown with thick solid or thick dashed arrows.) It is a well-known result [29] that if there are no cycles in the conflict graph, then the transactions are serializable.

But conflict-serializability is too strict for our example in Figure 2. There are three pairs of conflicting operations in this execution: a read-write conflict between e_2 and e_{12}, a write-read conflict between e_{12} and e_{15}, and a write-read conflict between e_{12} and e_{18}. In particular, the $i = 1$ and $i = 2$ transactions are not conflict-serializable because the $i = 2$ transaction's write of `lowest_cost` at e_{12} comes after the read of `lowest_cost` at e_2 but before the read at e_{15}.

In this paper, we generalize conflict-serializability by determining, using a dynamic data dependence analysis, that the only use of the value read for `lowest_cost` at e_2 is in the branch condition at e_6. (The data dependence edges in each thread are shown in Figure 2 with the thin dashed arrows.) But because of our added nondeterminism at Line 4 of our example program, this branch condition is gated by the nondeterministic condition at e_5. Our data dependence analysis tells us that no operation performed inside the `if (true*)` opened at e_5 has any local or global side-effects—thus, in the equivalent sequential execution whose existence we are trying to show, we can choose this nondeterministic condition to be `false`, in which case the read of `lowest_cost` at e_2 will never be used. This shows that the read-write conflict involving e_2 and e_{12} is *irrelevant*, because, once we choose the nondeterministic condition to be false, the value read at e_2 has no effect on the execution.

With only the remaining two *relevant* conflicts, the conflict graph has no cycles, and thus we will conclude that the loop iterations are serializable. Figure 3 shows a serial execution whose existence we have inferred by verifying that there are no conflict cycles. Note that the two *relevant* conflicts, $e_{12} \rightarrow e_{15}$ and $e_{12} \rightarrow e_{18}$, are preserved—they both appear in the serial execution in the same order. But the irrelevant conflict has been flipped. The write of `lowest_cost` at e_{12} now happens before the read at e_2, but this change does not affect the final result of the execution, because the value read for `lowest_cost` does not affect the control-flow or any writes to global variables.

Now suppose that the execution in Figure 2 produces an incorrect result, i.e., violates a functional specification of the parallel program. Because we showed above that this execution is equivalent (with respect to the final relevant state) to the computed serial execution in Figure 3, then the nondeterministic sequential execution exhibits the same functional bugs as the parallel execution. Thus, we can simply debug the serial execution without worrying about thread interleavings.

3. Parallelism Correctness with Nondeterministic Sequential Specifications

In this section, we formally define our programming model, our nondeterministic sequential (NDSeq) specifications, and our notion of parallel correctness. As discussed in Section 2.2, we embed the NDSeq specifications for a parallel program in the program itself. We achieve this both by overloading parallel language constructs and by adding a couple of new constructs. The syntax for the language is shown in Figure 4.

To simplify the presentation we consider a program $\mathcal{P}$ to consist of a single procedure. We omit discussion of multiple procedures and object-oriented concepts, and we assume that each global variable refers to a distinct location on the shared heap and that each local variable refers to a distinct location on the stack of a thread. Handling these details in our dynamic analysis is straightforward.

For each program $\mathcal{P}$, we define two sets of executions *ParExecs*($\mathcal{P}$) and *NdSeqExecs*($\mathcal{P}$), described below. The correctness of a parallel program is then given by relating *ParExecs*($\mathcal{P}$) and *NdSeqExecs*($\mathcal{P}$).

$$
\begin{array}{rl}
g \in \mathit{Global} \quad l \in \mathit{Local} & \mathit{Var} = \mathit{Global} \cup \mathit{Local} \\
x \in \mathit{Var} ::= & l \mid g \\
b ::= & l \mid \boxed{\mathit{true}*} \mid \boxed{\mathit{false}*} \\
s \in \mathit{Stmt} ::= & l = l \ \mathit{op}\ l \mid l = \text{constant} \mid l = l \mid g = l \mid l = g \\
& \mid s; s \mid \textbf{if}(b)\ s \mid \textbf{if}(l)\ s\ \textbf{else}\ s \\
& \mid \textbf{while}(l)\ s \mid \textbf{for}\ (l\ \textbf{in}\ l)\ s \\
& \mid \textbf{continue} \mid \textbf{break} \mid \textbf{return} \mid \cdots \\
& \mid \textbf{atomic}\ s \\
& \mid \boxed{\textbf{coforeach}}\ (l\ \textbf{in}\ l)\ s \mid \boxed{\textbf{cobegin}}\ s; \ldots; s
\end{array}
$$

Figure 4. Selected statements of our language. The constructs with a different semantics in the parallel program and the sequential specification are shown in boxes.

Parallel executions: *ParExecs*($\mathcal{P}$) contains the parallel executions of $\mathcal{P}$ where each **cobegin** and **coforeach** statement creates implicitly new threads to execute its body. **cobegin** $s_1; \ldots; s_n$ is evaluated by executing each of $s_1, \ldots, s_n$ on a separate, newly created thread. **coforeach** is evaluated by executing each iteration of the loop on a separate, newly created thread. Following structured fork/join parallelism, a parallel execution of a **cobegin** and **coforeach** statement terminates only after all the threads created on behalf of the statement terminate. Assignments, the evaluation of conditionals, and entire **atomic** statements, are executed as atomic steps without interruption by other threads. In the parallel semantics, *true*∗ and *false*∗ always evaluate to *true* and *false*, respectively.

Sequential executions: *NdSeqExecs*($\mathcal{P}$) contains the (nondeterministic) sequential executions of $\mathcal{P}$ where all statements are evaluated sequentially by a single thread. Under the sequential semantics, the statements other than **if** with ∗, **cobegin**, and **coforeach** are interpreted in the standard way. Each evaluation of **cobegin** $s_1; \ldots; s_n$ is equivalent to running a nondeterministic permutation of statements $s_1, \ldots, s_n$, where each $s_{i \in [1..n]}$ executes sequentially. A statement **coforeach** is evaluated similarly to its deterministic version (**for**) except that the elements of the collection being iterated over are processed in a nondeterministic order. This, in essence, abstracts the semantics of the collection to an unordered set. Keyword **atomic** has no effect in the sequential case, so **atomic** s is simply equivalent to s. Finally, *true*∗ or *false*∗ yield nondeterministic boolean values each time they are evaluated.

Parallelism Correctness. We describe executions of $\mathcal{P}$ using a standard notion of small-step operational semantics extended with nondeterministic evaluation of **cobegin** and **coforeach**, and nondeterministic branches (*true*∗ and *false*∗).

The parallelism correctness for $\mathcal{P}$ means that every final state reachable by a parallel execution of the program from a given initial state is also reachable by an NDSeq execution from the same initial state. Therefore, parallel executions have no unintended nondeterminism caused by thread interleavings: either the nondeterminism is prevented using synchronization, or it is expressed by the nondeterministic control flow in the sequential specification.

While defining parallel correctness, we distinguish a set of global variables as *focus* variables, which contain the final results of a program. Then, we reason about the equivalence of executions on the final values of the focus variables.

Definition 1 (Parallelism correctness) *A program $\mathcal{P}$ conforms to its NDSeq specification with respect to a set Focus $\subseteq$ Global iff for every parallel execution $E \in$ ParExecs($\mathcal{P}$), there exists a nondeterministic sequential execution $E' \in$ NdSeqExecs($\mathcal{P}$), such that the initial states of E and E' are the same and the final states agree on the values of all variables in Focus.*

4. Nondeterministic Specification Patterns

The use of nondeterministic sequential specifications is an attractive way to specify parallel correctness, yet it is not immediately clear where to introduce the nondeterministic constructs into the specification (1) without breaking the functional correctness while (2) capturing the nondeterminism due to thread interleavings.

Figure 5 shows the pseudo-code for three common patterns that we encountered repeatedly in our experiments. Each of these patterns considers parallel worker tasks where there is a potential for conflicting accesses to shared data. In contrast, applications where shared data is distributed strictly disjointly between tasks do not require use of `if(`*true*∗`)` specifications. Next, we discuss these patterns in detail.

4.1 Optimistic Concurrent Computation

This pattern is a manually implemented analogue of software transactional memory (STM) [37]. A parallel task performs its work optimistically in order to reduce the synchronization with other threads. It reads the shared data (`shared`) required for its work to a local variable (`local`) and performs the computation (`do_work`) without further access to shared data. Before committing the result of the computation back to the shared space, it checks if the input it read previously has been modified by another thread (`is_conflict`). In that case it retries the work. This pattern is used when the time spent for the local computation dominates the time for checking conflict and committing, and the contention on the same regions of shared memory is low.

Such fail-retry behaviors are not normally conflict-serializable when another thread updates `shared` during `do_work`. The update conflicts with the read of `shared` before and after `do_work`. However, in those situations we expect `is_conflict` to return true and the commit to be skipped. The *true*∗ && allows the NDSeq program to nondeterministically skip the conflict checking and the commit. This captures that (1) it is acceptable from a partial-correctness point of view to skip the commit nondeterministically even without checking `is_conflict`, and (2) if the commit is skipped then the read of shared data before and after `do_work` are irrelevant and can be ignored for conflict serializability purposes.

Examples: This pattern is used in non-blocking data structures, e.g., stacks and queues, to implement optimistic concurrent access to the data structure without locks. These data structures implement the atomic block in the pseudo code using a compare-and-swap (CAS) operation [18]. We have also encountered this pattern when parallelizing a mesh refinement program from the Lonestar benchmark suite (see Section 6). Our parallelization instantiates the pattern in Figure 5 as follows:

```
// Processing cavity of a node N:
while (true) {
  local_cavity = read cavity of N from shared mesh;
  refined_cavity = refine the cavity locally;
  atomic {
    if ( true* && mesh still contains all nodes in local_cavity) {
      replace old cavity in mesh with refined_cavity;
      break;
} } }
```

Appendix A gives more examples of NDSeq specifications for non-blocking implementations following the same pattern.

4.2 Redundant Computation Optimization

In contrast with optimistic computation where each parallel task must complete its work, in the redundant computation pattern, each thread may choose to skip its work when it detects that the work is no longer necessary (`is_work_redundant`). Here synchronizing the check for redundancy and the actual work may not be practical when the latter is a long running operation.

```
Optimistic Concurrent Computation Pattern
while (true) {
  local = shared;
  local' = do_work(local);
  atomic {
    if ( true* && !is_conflict(local,shared)) {
      shared = local';  // commit result
      break;
} } }

Redundant Computation Optimization Pattern
if ( true* && is_work_redundant(shared)) {
  // work is unnecessary; skip the work
} else {
  do_work(); // accesses shared
}

Irrelevant Computation Pattern
do_work(local, shared);
if ( true* ) {
  do_irrelevant_work();
}
```

Figure 5. Common concurrency patterns and use of *true*∗ and *false*∗ to express the nondeterminism.

Threads operating under this pattern are not conflict serializable if another thread updates the shared state while our thread calls `is_work_redundant` and finds that it returns false. Those updates conflict with the `shared` read before calling `is_work_redundant` and while executing `do_work`.

The *true*∗ && allows the NDSeq program to nondeterministically skip the call to `is_work_redundant` and do the work anyway. This expresses that (1) it is acceptable from a partial-correctness point of view to skip the redundancy check and to do the actual work, and also that (2) if we skip the redundancy check, then the initial read of shared state is not relevant to the computation and can be ignored for conflict-serializability purposes.

Examples: This pattern is often used when a solution space is examined by multiple threads to improve convergence to an optimal solution. Our running example in Section 2.1 follows this pattern: Lines 2–5 in Figure 1 test the lower bound of the current solution to decide if the computation at Line 6 can produce a better solution. The `phylogeny` benchmark from the Parallel Java Library follows a similar bound check to prune the search space for optimal phylogenetic trees. Programs using caches to avoid multiple computations of a function for the same input also use this pattern.

4.3 Irrelevant Computation

This pattern generalizes tasks that perform some computation (shown in the `if(`*true*∗`)` branch) that does not affect the rest of the execution path and does not produce a result that flows into shared state that is relevant to core functional correctness. One can ignore the irrelevant part of the program when reasoning about the program in the sequential semantics, since either (1) it does not affect the focus state, or (2) it is only necessary for the parallel executions of the program.

Examples: A prevalent instance of case (1) is when updating a statistic counter to profile the procedures of a program. For example, in the following we use `if(`*true*∗`)` to mark the increment of a statistic counter as an irrelevant operation. Updates to `counter` do not affect the final result (with respect to focus variables) of the program. However, without using the `if(`*true*∗`)`, conflicts due to `counter` will not be ignored by our analysis. By surrounding the `if` statement with `if(`*true*∗`)`, the programmer indicates that the `if` branch is not relevant for the final result, and conflicts due to the accesses to counter when executing the branch should not affect the parallel correctness of the program. In fact, one can easily prove statically that, given counter is not a focus variable, skipping the conditional at all is safe for the functionality.

```
do_work(shared, local); // access shared variables exclusively
 if ( true* ) {
   if (counter < MAX_INT) {
      counter = counter + 1;
   }
}
```

Moreover, rebalancing a tree, garbage collection and compaction, maintaining a cache, and load balancing are operations that are performed to improve the performance of a parallel program, but –when implemented correctly– do not affect the core functionality of the program and thus are considered irrelevant.

An instance of (2) is when using a locking library to ensure atomicity of the relevant computation. In contrast with the statistics counters, locks are essential for the correctness of the parallelism, though the locking-state is often irrelevant for reasoning about the core functionality of the program in a sequential run.

5. Runtime Checking of Parallel Correctness

Among the various possible techniques for checking parallelization correctness, we describe here a runtime checking algorithm. We use dynamic data-flow analysis to determine parts of the executions that are not relevant to the final valuation of the focus variables. At the same time the analysis determines appropriate assignments of boolean values to the **if**(*true*∗) nondeterministic branches in the NDSeq execution, in order to eliminate as many serialization conflicts as possible. Therefore, data flow analysis and NDSeq specifications play key roles in improving the applicability of conflict serializability for reasoning about parallelism in real programs. In the rest of this section, we describe the details of the checking algorithm and we sketch its correctness.

In order to simplify the presentation of the runtime checking algorithm for parallelism correctness we make the following assumptions about the parallel program being checked:

A1. Branch predicates are either *true*∗ or a local variable.

A2. The body of an **if**(*true*∗) does not contain unstructured control flow (e.g., **continue**, **break**, **return**), and there is no **else** clause.

These assumptions can be established using standard program refactoring. For example, Lines 4–5 from Figure 1(c) can be translated to:

```
bool cond = false;
if( true* ){ l = (b >= t); if(l){ cond = true; } }
if(cond) continue;
```

where cond and l are new local variables.

Our checking algorithm operates on an execution trace described as a sequence of execution *events*. Let τ denote a trace and e an event. For each event e we have the following information:

- *Type*(e) is the type of the event, defined as follows:

$$T \quad ::= \quad x = x' \mid branch(l) \mid branch(true*)$$

The "$x = x'$" event type corresponds to the assignment and binary operation statements in our language (shown in Figure 4; recall that metavariable x stands for both locals and globals). We use a simple assignment in our formal description to simplify the presentation; unary and binary operators do not pose notable difficulties. We assume that an event can read a global, or write a global, but not both. The "*branch*(l)" event marks the execution of a branch operation when the boolean condition denoted by local l evaluates to true. The case of a branch when the negation of a local is true is similar. Finally, the "*branch*(*true*∗)" marks the execution of an **if**(*true*∗) branch, which in the parallel execution is always taken. Our algorithm does not require specific events to mark the start and end of procedures or atomic blocks.

We write $e : T$ when e has type T.

- *Thread*(e) denotes the thread that generates the event e. Recall that new threads are created when executing **cobegin** and **coforeach** statements.
- *Guard*(e) denotes the event of type *branch*(*true*∗) that corresponds to the most recent invocation of the innermost **if**(*true*∗) that encloses the statement generating e. For events outside any **if**(*true*∗) this value is nil.

  For example, in the trace shown in Figure 2, $Guard(e_6) = e_5$, $Guard(e_8) = e_7$, $Guard(e_{20}) = Guard(e_{21}) = e_{19}$, and $Guard(e) = nil$ for all other events e.

The checking algorithm operates in two stages, shown in Figure 6. The first stage computes a subset of the events in the trace that are relevant (Section 5.1), and the second stage determines whether the relevant part of the trace is conflict serializable (Section 5.2).

5.1 Selecting Relevant Events

A standard conflict-serializability algorithm [29] considers all events in a trace. We observed that in many concurrent programs it is common for partial work to be discarded when a conflict is later detected. In such cases, some of the computations based on previously read values of shared variables are discarded and are not relevant to the rest of the execution. If we can ignore such irrelevant reads of shared variables we can prove that more paths are conflict serializable. Similarly, we can ignore writes that do not affect a relevant control flow and do not flow into the final state of the focus variables. Our experiments show that this makes a difference for most benchmarks where traditional conflict serializability reports false alarms.

Informally, an assignment event is *relevant* if it targets a location that is eventually used in the computation of a final value of a focus variable, or in the computation of a *deterministic* branch. To track this relevance aspect we compute a dynamic data-dependence relation between events. For trace τ, we define the dependence relation $\dashrightarrow$ as follows:

D1. **(Intra-Thread Data Dependence).** For each local variable read $e_j : x = l$ or branch $e_j : branch(l)$, we add a dependence ($e_i \dashrightarrow e_j$) on the last $e_i : l = x'$ that comes before e_j in τ. This dependence represents an actual data flow through local l from e_i to e_j in the current trace. Both of these events are in the same thread (since they operate on the same local) and their order and dependence will be the same in any serialization of the trace. These dependence edges are shown as thin dashed arrows in Figure 2.

D2. **(Inter-Thread Dependence).** For each global variable read $e_j : l = g$ we add dependencies ($e_i \dashrightarrow e_j$) on events $e_i : g = l'$ as follows. From each thread we pick the last write to g that comes before e_j in τ, and the first write to g that comes after e_j in τ. This conservative dependence is necessary because the relative order of reads and writes to the global from different threads may change in a serialization of the trace. Section 5.3 explains the importance of this detail for correctness. In the example shown in Figure 2, we have such dependence edges from e_{12} to all events that read lowest_cost: e_2, e_4, e_{10}, e_{18}.

Let $\dashrightarrow^*$ denote the transitive closure of $\dashrightarrow$.

Algorithm **ComputeRelevant**(τ, *Focus*)
// Collecting relevant events for the serializability check
// Add all writes to focus globals
1 $Relevant = \{e : g = l \in \tau \mid g \in Focus$
$\wedge$ e is last write to g in *Thread* (e)$\}$
// Start with all top-level deterministic branches
2 $Relevant = Relevant \cup \{e : branch(l) \in \tau \mid Guard(e) = nil\}$
3 Compute data dependency relation $\dashrightarrow$ from τ
4 **repeat**
// Add events that some relevant events data-depend on
5 $Relevant = Relevant \cup \{e \in \tau \mid \exists e' \in Relevant.\ e \dashrightarrow^* e'\}$
// Add nondeterministic branches containing relevant events
6 $Relevant = Relevant \cup$
$\{e : branch(true*) \in \tau \mid \exists e' \in Relevant.\ Guard(e') = e\}$
// Add deterministic branches nested inside relevant `if` *(true*)'s*
7 $Relevant = Relevant \cup$
$\{e : branch(l) \in \tau \mid Guard(e) \in Relevant\}$
8 **until** *Relevant* does not change
9 **return** *Relevant*

Algorithm **CheckCycle**(τ, *Focus*)
// Check serializability of trace
10 $Relevant =$ **ComputeRelevant**(τ, *Focus*)
11 Compute conflict relation $\rightsquigarrow$ between threads
12 **if** exists a cycle $t \rightsquigarrow t' \rightsquigarrow^* t$
13 Report unserializable thread t
14 **else**
15 Declare the execution serializable
16 **end if**

Figure 6. The algorithm for checking parallelism correctness.

Figure 6 lists the algorithm **ComputeRelevant** to compute the set of relevant events. We seed the set of relevant events with all the events that assign to the global focus variables (Line 1) and the deterministic branches outside any nondeterministic blocks (Line 2). In Line 5 we add the assignment events on which existing relevant events have data dependence on.

The crucial factor that allows us to find a significant number of irrelevant events is that we can choose to skip the events (assignments and branches) corresponding to nondeterministic `if(`*true**`)` blocks, as long as those blocks are irrelevant in the trace. We extend the relevance notion from assignment events to branches as follows. A *branch*(*true**) event is relevant if and only if it corresponds to the execution of an `if(`*true**`)` block with at least one relevant assignment event (Line 6). For this step we use the previously introduced *Guard* function to relate events inside `if(`*true**`)` blocks with the corresponding *branch*(*true**) event. We also say that a *branch*(l) event is relevant if it represents control flow that must be preserved (it is not nested inside an irrelevant `if(`*true**`)` block). This is enforced in Lines 2 and 7. The computation in Lines 5–7 must be repeated to a fixed point since the additional relevant deterministic branches added in Line 7 can lead to new relevant assignments due to data dependencies.

For example, in the trace in Figure 2, relevant events are e_{9-13} from thread with $i = 2$, e_{14-16} from thread with $i = 1$, and e_{17-21} from thread with $i = 3$. Since the nondeterministic branch events e_5 and e_7 are irrelevant (no events in the rest of the trace data-depend on their bodies), the branch events e_6 and e_8 are not marked as relevant. Thus, events e_{1-2} from thread with $i = 1$ and e_{3-4} from thread with $i = 2$ have no data-dependents in *Relevant* and they remain as irrelevant.

5.2 Checking Serializability of Transactions

The final stage in our runtime checking algorithm is a conflict serializability check implemented as a cycle detection problem similar to [12, 16]. The added element here is that we ignore the conflicts induced by irrelevant events, and we have the flexibility to alter the nondeterministic control flow in order to remove conflicts.

First we define the conflict relation between individual events.

Definition 2 (Conflicting events) *Two events* $e, e' \in \tau$ *are conflicting (written* $e \rightsquigarrow e'$*) iff (a)* e *occurs before* e' *in* τ*, and (b) both events operate on the same shared global variable, and at least one of them represents a write, and (c) both events are* *Relevant* *in trace* τ*.*

Next we lift the conflict relation from events to threads. When comparing two threads for conflicts we need to consider their events and all the events of their descendant threads. Thus, for a thread t we define its *transaction* as the set of events *Trans* (t) that includes all the events of t and of the descendant threads of t.

Definition 3 (Conflicting threads) *Two threads* t, t' *are conflicting in trace* τ *(written* $t \rightsquigarrow t'$*) iff (a) their transaction sets are disjoint (i.e., one is not a descendant of the other), and (b) there exist two events* $e \in$ *Trans* (t) *and* $e' \in$ *Trans* (t') *that are conflicting (*$e \rightsquigarrow e'$*). The relation* $t \rightsquigarrow^* t'$ *is the transitive and reflexive closure of the thread conflict relation.*

The main runtime checking algorithm for parallelism correctness is shown in Lines 10–16 in Figure 6.

For the example trace shown in Figure 2 the event e_2 is not relevant, which allows the algorithm **CheckCycle** to ignore the conflict between e_2 and e_{12} (shown with thick dashed arrow in Figure 2). Without the dependence analysis we could not show that the trace is serializable.

5.3 Algorithm Correctness

The correctness of our runtime checking algorithm can be argued by showing that when the **CheckCycle** algorithm succeeds, the input trace $\tau \in$ *ParExecs*($\mathcal{P}$) can be transformed incrementally into a trace $\tau' \in$ *NdSeqExecs*($\mathcal{P}$) such that the final states in both traces agree on the values of the focus variables. Each incremental transformation preserves the validity of the trace and the final condition on focus variables. Some of the intermediate traces in this process will belong to the larger space of nondeterministic parallel executions *NdParExecs*($\mathcal{P}$), which allow both interleavings (as in *ParExecs*($\mathcal{P}$)) and nondeterministic branches (as in *NdSeqExecs*($\mathcal{P}$)). For these executions the nondeterministic branches *true** and *false** are resolved at runtime nondeterministically to true or false.

The first trace transformation that we perform is to eliminate the events corresponding to `if(`*true**`)` blocks that were found irrelevant by **ComputeRelevant**. The second transformation is to commute adjacent events from different threads that are not in conflict, either because they do not operate on a shared global, or because one of them is irrelevant. The correctness of these steps, i.e., they preserve the validity of the trace and the final values of focus variables, is established by Lemma 1 and Lemma 2.

The rest of the correctness algorithm builds on a standard result from database theory: a trace is conflict serializable if it can be transformed into an equivalent serial trace by commuting adjacent, non-conflicting operations of different threads. This is possible if and only if the transactional conflict graph is acyclic [29].

Lemma 1 (Skip irrelevant nondeterministic blocks)
If $\tau \in$ *ParExecs*($\mathcal{P}$)*, let* τ' *be the subtrace of* τ *obtained by eliminating all events* e *such that* *Guard*(e) $\notin$ **ComputeRelevant**(τ, *Focus*)*. Then* τ' *is a valid trace in* *NdParExecs*($\mathcal{P}$)*, meaning that* τ' *reflects the correct control flow of the program* $\mathcal{P}$ *with the corresponding irrelevant true* resolved to false, and* τ' *agrees with* τ *on the final values of* *Focus* *variables. Furthermore,* **ComputeRelevant**(τ', *Focus*) *returns the same answer as for trace* τ*.*

The proof of this lemma relies first on the assumption (A2) stated earlier that the body of any **if**(*true*∗) has only normal exits and no **else** clause. This means that by removing all the events in any such body results in a trace where control flows properly to the statement after the skipped **if**(*true*∗). All assignment events eliminated in this step are irrelevant since their guard is irrelevant (Line 6 in Figure 6). Therefore subsequent control flow and the final value of focus variables are preserved. The set of relevant events does not change through this transformation because its computation does not depend on irrelevant events.

Lemma 2 (Commutativity of irrelevant events) *Consider a trace $\tau \in$ NdParExecs($\mathcal{P}$) and two adjacent events e_1 and e_2 in τ, such that the events are from different threads, they operate on a shared global g, at least one is a write event, and at least one is irrelevant (not in* **ComputeRelevant**$(\tau, Focus)$*). Then the trace obtained by commuting e_1 and e_2 is still a valid trace in NdParExecs($\mathcal{P}$) and it agrees with τ on the final value of $Focus$ variables.*

Proof Sketch: Considering the types of events we can have in the trace and the conditions of the Lemma, we have three possible cases:

- Read-after-write: $e_1 : g = l$ and $e_2 : l' = g$. If e_2 were relevant then e_1 would also be relevant (Line 5 in the algorithm, with data-dependence rule D2). Thus it must be that e_2 is irrelevant, hence the value of l' does not affect the subsequent control flow or final values of $Focus$ variables. Therefore we can commute the events and the trace remains in *NdParExecs*($\mathcal{P}$). The relevant events computation does not change, since $l \neq l'$ (different threads), and the relative order of *relevant* reads and writes to global does not change.
- Write-after-read: $e_1 : l = g$ and $e_2 : g = l'$. If e_1 were relevant then e_2 would also be relevant (Line 5 in the algorithm, with data-dependence rule D2; this is a crucial part of the correctness argument that depends on the conservative form of the data-dependence rule D2). Thus, e_1 is irrelevant, and the rest of this case follows the same arguments as in the read-after-write case.
- Write-after-write: $e_1 : g = l$ and $e_2 : g = l'$. It must be that there is no nearby relevant read of the global g in the trace, or else both events would be relevant (again due to data-dependence rule D2). This means that it does not matter what we write to g. The relevant set does not change after the swap because we do not change the dependence relation $\dashrightarrow$. It is for this reason that we require the dependence rule D2 to consider the nearest write to a global from each thread.

□

With these results it is straightforward to prove our main correctness result given below using standard conflict-serializability results using our relaxed notion of conflicts, as proved adequate in Lemma 2.

Theorem 1 (Correctness) *Let τ be the trace generated by a parallel execution of $E \in$ ParExecs($\mathcal{P}$) of a program $\mathcal{P}$. If* **CheckCycle**$(\tau, Focus)$ *does not report any unserializable transaction, then there exists a nondeterministic sequential execution $E' \in$ NdSeqExecs($\mathcal{P}$), such that the initial states of E and E' are the same and the final states agree on the value of all variables in $Focus$.*

The theorem implies that if we explore, using a model checker, all parallel executions of the program and show that all these executions are serializable, then we can conclude that the parallel program conforms to its NDSeq specification.

6. Experimental Evaluation

In this section, we describe our efforts to experimentally evaluate our approach to specifying and checking parallel correctness using NDSeq specifications. We aim to evaluate two claims:

(1) That it is feasible to write NDSeq specifications for the parallel correctness of real Java benchmarks,

(2) Our runtime checking algorithm produces significantly fewer false positives than a traditional conflict-serializability analysis in checking parallel correctness of these benchmarks.

To evaluate these claims, we wrote NDSeq specifications for the parallel correctness of a number of Java benchmarks and then used our runtime checking technique on these specifications.

6.1 Benchmarks

We evaluate our technique on a number of benchmarks that have been used in previous research [8, 12, 16] on parallel correctness tools. Note that we focus on *parallel* applications, which use multithreading for performance but fundamentally are performing a single computation that can be understood sequentially. We do not consider *concurrent* benchmarks, such as reactive systems and stream-based systems, because it is not clear whether or not such programs can be understood sequentially.

The names, sizes, and brief descriptions of the benchmarks we used are listed in Table 1. Several benchmarks are from the Java Grande Forum (JGF) benchmark suite [38], the Parallel Java (PJ) Library [20]. We report on all benchmarks that we looked at except `tsp` [46], for which we have not yet found an easy way to write the NDSeq specification (see Section 6.5). We also applied our tool to two large benchmarks in the DaCapo benchmark suite [4]. Benchmark `meshrefine` is a sequential application from the Lonestar benchmark suite [22] that we have parallelized (by converting the application's main loop into a parallel loop). Benchmarks `stack` [39] and `queue` are non-blocking concurrent data structures. For each data structure, we construct a test harness that performs several insertions and removals in parallel (i.e., in a **cobegin**). The `queue` is similar to the Michael and Scott queue [26], but eagerly updates the queue's tail with a 4-word compare-and-swap. This change simplified significantly the NDSeq specification.

6.2 Implementation

Although these benchmarks are written in a structured parallel style, Java does not provide structured parallelism constructs such as **coforeach** or **cobegin**. Thus, we must annotate in these benchmarks the regions of code corresponding to the bodies of parallel loops and **cobegin**'s. Typically, these regions are the bodies of `run` methods of subclasses of `java.lang.Thread`. Similarly, some of these benchmarks use *barrier synchronization*. As barriers have no sequential equivalent, we treat these programs as if they used a series of parallel **coforeach** constructs, ending one parallel loop and beginning another at each barrier. (This is a standard transformation [45] for such code.) We similarly treat each PJ benchmark, which employ sequential loops inside each of a fixed number of worker threads, as instead consisting of structured parallel loops.

In order to write NDSeq specifications, we implemented a simple library for annotating in Java programs the beginning and end of the bodies of **if**(∗), **coforeach**, and **cobegin** constructs, as well as which locations (fields, array elements, etc.) are *focus variables*. Columns 4, 5, and 6 of Table 1 list, for each benchmark, the number of such annotated parallel constructs, annotated **if**(∗), and statements added to mark focus variables.

We implemented our checking technique in a prototype tool for Java, which uses bytecode instrumentation via Soot [42]. In addition to the details described in Section 5, for Java it is necessary

Benchmark		Benchmark Description	Approximate Lines of Code (App + Library)	# of Parallel Constructs	Size of Spec		Size of Trace		Distinct Serializability Warnings	
					# of `if(*)`	# of focus stmts	All Events	Irrelevant Events	Conflict-Serializability	Our Technique
JGF	`sor`	successive over-relaxation	300	1	0	1	1,600k	112	0	0
	`matmult`	sparse matrix-vector multiplication	700	1	0	1	962k	8k	0	0
	`series`	coefficients of Fourier series	800	1	0	5	11k	140	0	0
	`crypt`	encryption and decryption	1100	2	0	3	504k	236	0	0
	`moldyn`	molecular dynamics simulation	1300	4	0	1	4,131k	79k	0	0
	`lufact`	LU factorization	1500	1	0	1	1,778k	6k	0	0
	`raytracer`	ray tracing	1900	1	0	1	6,170k	44k	1	1 **(bug)**
	`montecarlo`	Monte Carlo derivative pricing	3600	1	0	1	1,897k	534k	2	0
PJ	`pi3`	Monte Carlo approximation of π	150 + 15k	1	0	1	1,062k	141	0	0
	`keysearch3`	cryptographic key cracking	200 + 15k	2	0	4	2,059k	91k	0	0
	`mandelbrot`	fractal (Mandelbrot set) rendering	250 + 15k	1	0	6	1,707k	954	0	0
	`phylogeny`	branch-and-bound search	4400 + 15k	2	3	8	470k	5k	6	6 **(bug)**
DaCapo	`sunflow`	image rendering using ray tracing	24k	4	4	3	24,250k	2,264k	28	3 **(no bugs)**
	`xalan`	XML to HTML transformation	302k	1	3	4	16,540k	887k	6	2 **(no bugs)**
`stack`		Treiber non-blocking stack [39]	40	1	2	8	1,744	536	5	0
`queue`		non-blocking queue [26]	60	1	2	8	846	229	9	0
`meshrefine`		Delaunay mesh refinement	1000	1	2	50	747k	302k	30	0

Table 1. Experimental results. Note that the six warnings reported for `phylogeny` are all true violations caused by a single bug.

to handle language features such as objects, exceptions, casts, etc. Any Java bytecode instruction that can throw an exception—e.g., a field dereference, an array look-up, a cast, or a division—must be treated as an implicit branch instruction. That is, changing the values flowing into such an instruction can change the control-flow by causing or preventing an exception from being thrown.

Limitations. While our implementation supports many intricacies of the Java language, it has a couple of limitations:

First, our implementation tracks neither the shared reads and writes nor the flow of data dependence through uninstrumented native code. Thus, we may report an execution as having correct parallelism despite unserializable conflicts in calls to native code.

Second, our tool does not instrument all of the Java standard libraries. This may cause our tool to miss data dependencies carried through the data structures in these libraries, as well as shared reads and writes inside such data structures. To address this limitation, for certain shared data structure objects we introduced fake shared variables and inserted reads or writes of those variables whenever their corresponding objects were accessed. This allows us to conservatively approximate the conflicts and data dependencies for certain critical standard Java data structures.

6.3 Results: Feasibility of Writing Specifications

Writing an NDSeq specification for each benchmark program consisted of two steps: (1) adding code to mark which parts of the program's memory were *in focus*—i.e. storage locations whose values are relevant in the final program state, and (2) adding **if**($*$) constructs to specify intended or expected nondeterminism.

For all of our benchmarks besides `tsp`, it was possible to write an NDSeq specification for the benchmark's parallel correctness. The "Size of Spec" columns of Table 1 lists the number of **if**($*$) constructs added to each benchmark and the number of statements added to mark storage locations as in focus. These numbers show that, overall, the size of the specification written for each benchmark was reasonably small. We further found adding nondeterminism via **if**($*$) to be fairly straightforward, as all necessary nondeterminism fell under one of the NDSeq specification patterns discussed in Section 4. Identifying which storage locations were relevant to the final program result was similarly straightforward. As an example, we show in Appendix A.2 the complete NDSeq specification for the `stack` benchmark.

Though further work is needed to evaluate the general applicability of NDSeq specifications for parallel correctness, we believe it is promising preliminary evidence that we were able to easily write such specifications for a range of parallel applications.

6.4 Results: Runtime Checking

For each benchmark, we generated five parallel executions on a single test input using a simple form of race-directed parallel fuzzing [36]. On each such execution, we checked our NDSeq specification both using our technique and using a traditional, strict conflict-serializability analysis [16].

We report in Column "Size of Trace; All Events" of Table 1 the size of a representative execution trace of each benchmark. The size is the number of reads and writes of shared variables and the number of branches executed during the run. Note that most of our benchmarks generate a few hundred thousand or a few million events during a typical execution on a small test input. For a dynamic analysis, this is a more relevant measure of benchmark size than static lines of code. Column "Size of Trace; Irrelevant Events" reports the number of these events found to be *irrelevant* by our algorithm **ComputeRelevant** in Figure 6. The fraction of events found to be irrelevant, and therefore not considered during our algorithm's serializability checking, range from 0-40%.

The "Distinct Serializability Warnings" columns of Table 1 report the number of serializability warnings produced by a traditional conflict-serializability check and by our technique. Note that, in a trace of a benchmark, a conflict involving a few particular lines of code may generate many cycles among the dynamic events of the trace. We report only the number of *distinct* cycles corresponding to different sets of lines of code.

Both techniques find the two real parallelism bugs—a data race in `raytracer` due to the use of the wrong lock to protect a shared checksum, and an atomicity violation in the `phylogeny` branch-and-bound search involving the global list of min-cost solutions found. (The six warnings for `phylogeny` are all real violations caused by this single bug.) Because of these bugs, neither `raytracer` nor `phylogeny` is equivalent to its NDSeq spec.

A traditional conflict-serializability analysis also gives *false warnings* for six benchmarks—incidents where there are cycles of conflicting reads and writes, but the parallel code is still equivalent to its NDSeq specification. In four of these cases, our algorithm leverages its dynamic dependence analysis and specified nondeterminism and focus variables to verify that these conflicts involve reads and writes *irrelevant* to the final program result. In this way, our algorithm eliminates all false warnings for benchmarks `montecarlo`, `stack`, `queue`, and `meshrefine`.

For benchmarks `sunflow` and `xalan`, our checking algorithm eliminates 25 and 4 false warnings, respectively, produced by strict conflict-serializability checking, but generates 3 of the same false warnings for `sunflow` and 2 for `xalan`. We discuss in greater detail below these false warnings that our analysis was and was not able to eliminate.

Note that previous work on atomicity checking, such as [16], typically evaluate on such benchmarks by checking whether or not each individual method is atomic. Thus, a single cycle of conflicting reads and writes may lead to multiple warnings, as every method containing the cycle is reported to be non-atomic. (Conversely, multiple cycles may be reported as a single warning if they all occur inside a single method.) Our numbers of reported violations are not directly comparable, as we are interested only in whether each execution of an entire parallel construct is serializable and thus equivalent to an execution of its sequential counterpart.

`montecarlo` *Benchmark.* Each parallel loop iteration of the `montecarlo` benchmark contains several conflicting reads and writes on shared static fields. (The reads and writes occur inside the constructor of a temporary object created in each iteration.) To a naïve, traditional conflict-serializability analysis, these reads and writes make it appear that no equivalent serial execution exists. However, it turns out that the values written to and read from these static fields are never used—they affect neither the control flow nor the final program result. Thus, our analysis determines that these events are irrelevant and need not be considered during serializability checking. The remaining, relevant events *are* serializable, and thus our technique reports that the observed executions of `montecarlo` conform to its nondeterministic sequential specification.

`stack`*,* `queue`*, and* `meshrefine` *Benchmarks.* Benchmark `meshrefine` employs the Optimistic Concurrent Computation pattern described in Section 4. Each parallel iteration reads from the shared triangular mesh that is being refined, and then optimistically computes a re-triangulation of a region of the mesh. It then atomically checks that no conflicting modifications have been made to the mesh during its computation and either: (1) commits its changes to the mesh if there are no conflicts, or (2) discards its optimistic computation and tries again. When conflicting modifications occur, an execution of `meshrefine` is clearly not strictly conflict-serializable. However, when we specify with an **if**$(*)$ that the sequential execution is free to nondeterministically discard its optimistic computation and retry, even when there are no conflicts, our analysis can verify that conflicts involving these shared reads and optimistic computation are not relevant when the optimistic work is discarded. And the remaining relevant events are serializable, so our analysis reports no false warnings in this case.

The `stack` and `queue` benchmarks are also instances of the Optimistic Concurrent Computation pattern, where shared reads are performed, but these reads are only relevant when a later compare-and-swap operation succeeds. Conflicts leading to failing CAS operations in these benchmarks lead to false positives for a strict conflict-serializability analysis, but our technique determines that these conflicts are not relevant to the final program result.

`sunflow` *and* `xalan` *Benchmarks.* Benchmarks `sunflow` and `xalan` cause false alarms due to the following lazy initialization pattern:

```
1: if ( true* && flag == true) {
2:   // skip initialization
3: } else {
4:   atomic {
5:     if (flag == false) {
6:       initialize shared object
7:       flag = true;
   } } }
```

In the above pattern, each thread checks if some shared object has been initialized and, if not, initializes the object itself. The `flag` variable, which is initially `false`, indicates whether the object has been initialized.

This pattern has two potential sources of false alarms:

1. One thread may read that `flag` is `false` at Line 1, and then another thread may initialize the object and set `flag` to `true`, so that the first thread then reads that `flag` is `true` at Line 5. This is a violation of conflict-serializability.

   This is an instance of the Redundant Computation Optimization Pattern described in Section 4, as a thread can always choose to skip the check at Line 1, since `flag` will be checked again at Line 5. By annotating the first check with *true∗* &&, our analysis ignores irrelevant conflicts involving threads reading that `flag` is `false` at Line 1 and eliminates this kind of false warning.

2. When one thread initializes the shared object and sets `flag` to `true`, and then other threads read both `flag` and the shared object, our analysis sees conflict edges from the initializing thread to the other threads. These can lead to conflict cycles if the initializing thread later performs any relevant reads of data written by other threads. Our technique will report these cycles as violations.

   But such reports are false warnings, because it does not matter which thread performs this kind of lazy initialization, and it is possible to serialize such executions despite outgoing conflicts from the initialization code. Future work is needed to handle this pattern in our NDSeq specifications and dynamic checking.

6.5 Caveats

While we could easily write the specifications for our benchmarks, NDSeq specifications must be used with care. First, one must be careful to not introduce so much nondeterminism that the resulting NDSeq program exhibits undesired behavior. A catalog of specification patterns, along the lines of those presented in Section 4 can guide programmers to use this technique without breaking functional correctness. Second, we note that when introducing **if**(*true∗*) one can easily introduce nontermination (as shown in several examples in this paper). This is safe as long as we consider only the partial correctness properties of the NDSeq specification.

Our runtime algorithm reduces the number of false positives compared to a standard notion of conflict serializability. However, it can still give false positives for the following reasons:

- We do not apply semantic-level analyses, such as commutativity analysis [33]. However, there are parallel patterns that rely on commutativity, in which it is necessary to ignore low-level conflicts that are part of larger, commutative operations (such as reductions). Two commutative updates on a focus variable (e.g., addition) can have conflicts yet still be serializable when the updates are considered at a semantic level. We are exploring ways to address this limitation.
- We only search for NDSeq executions for which the control-flow path outside **if**(*true∗*) branches is the same as in the parallel execution. Thus, we might miss an equivalent NDSeq path, and falsely report lack of conflict-serializability. One can eliminate this source of imprecision by exploring executions of the program with different control flows.

`tsp` *Benchmark.* For reasons stemming from the limitations given above, we have not found an easy way to write and check the NDSeq specification for the `tsp` [46] benchmark. Figure 7(a) gives the original form of the main search routine. Each thread is implemented as a loop (Lines 2–10): At each iteration it obtains a work `w` from the shared queue `Q` (Line 4), searches the region represented by `w` (Line 6) and updates the shared variable `MinTourLen`

```
1: cobegin <1,...,N> {
2:  while (!isEmpty(Q)) {
3:    atomic {
4:      w = get_work(Q);
5:    }
6:    s = recursive_solve(w);
7:    atomic {
8:      if (s < MinTourLen)
9:         MinTourLen = s;
10:} } }
```

(a) Original search routine

```
1: cowhile (!isEmpty(Q)) {
2:   atomic {
3:     w = get_work(Q);
4:   }
5:   s = recursive_solve(w);
6:   atomic {
7:     if (s < MinTourLen)
8:        MinTourLen = s;
9:} } }
```

(b) Rewritten form of the search

Figure 7. TSP benchmark.

(Lines 8–9). In order to show that each thread as implemented in Figure 7(a) is serializable, one needs to prove that executions of `get_work` are commutative. This requires a nontrivial reasoning because procedure `get_work` may split the work items in `Q` and submit new work items to `Q`, which creates a dependency from a thread processing a work item created by a call to `get_work` by another thread. We found that Figure 7(a) has the equivalent functionality to the rewritten form of the search in Figure 7(b), where each thread performs only one iteration of the `while` loop. In this case, one can show that each iteration at Lines 2–9 in Figure 7(b) is serializable, as procedure `recursive_solve` is a thread-local operation and the (atomic) update of `MinTourLen` at Lines 7–8 is commutative.

7. Related Work

Several generic parallel correctness criteria have been studied for shared memory parallel programs that separates the concerns about functionality and parallelism at different granularities of execution. These criteria include data-race freedom [27, 46], atomicity [14], linearizability [19]. All these criteria provides the separation between parallel and functional correctness partially, as the restriction on thread interleavings is limited, for example, to atomic block boundaries. NDSeq develops this idea up to a complete separation between parallelism and functionality so that the programmer can reason about the intended functionality by examining a sequential or nearly sequential program. NDSeq specification differs from determinism specification and checking [5, 8, 34] in that NDSeq not only allows to specify that some part of the final state is independent of the thread schedule, but also allows to specify that the part of the final state that depends on thread schedule is equivalent to the state arising due to nondeterministic choices in the NDSeq.

We formulate the checking of parallelism correctness to a general notion of atomicity. Various static [10, 14, 40, 41] and dynamic [7, 12, 16, 25, 44, 48, 49] techniques for checking atomicity and linearizability has been investigated in the literature. The main challenge in these techniques is to reason about conflicting accesses that are simultaneously enabled but ineffective on the rest of the execution. In the Purity work [15] Flanagan et al. provide a static analysis to rule out spurious warnings due to such conflicts by abstracting these operations to no-op's. Elmas et al. generalize this idea in a static proof system called QED [11]. They progressively transform a parallel program to an equivalent sequential program with respect to functional specifications expressed using assertions. They abstract reads and writes of shared variables; however, they need to consider functional specification when applying the abstractions to guarantee that the abstraction does not introduce functional bug in the new program. In addition, both Purity and QED are based on Lipton's reduction theory [24], whereas we apply the idea to relax the checking of conflict serializability [2] for nondeterministic specifications.

Atomic-set serializability [43] is an weaker notion of atomicity, which groups storage locations into *atomic sets* and requires, for each atomic set, all atomic blocks are conflict-serializable with respect to the locations in the set. Dynamic techniques for detecting violations of atomic-set serializability has been proposed [17, 23].

Recently, several platforms and languages have been developed to guarantee that parallel programs give deterministic results, i.e. there is no bug due to parallelization. Kendo [28] enforces a deterministic interleaving of parallel tasks by controlling synchronization operations (particularly locks) in the meantime targeting to achieve a load-balancing of parallel tasks close to the nondeterministic case. In Deterministic Parallel Java (DPJ) [5] Bocchino et al. allow programmers to write parallel programs that are deterministic by design (ensured at compile time). DPJ also allows programmers to explicitly mark parallel constructs with nondeterministic sequential semantics and compose them safely with other deterministic constructs without breaking the determinism-by-default guarantees [6]. On the other hand the Galois project [21], Praun et al. [47], and Prabhu et al. [30] aim to exploit the opportunities in parallelizing irregular, inherently sequential programs. The sequential model ensured by these systems allows nondeterministic ordering of parallel loops and pipelines. Praun et al. [47] propose the programming model IPOT that allows programmers to explicitly mark portions of the program for speculative multithreaded and transactional execution. Its `tryasync` construct resembles our `cobegin` construct. IPOT allows internal nondeterminism in that intermediate states may differ from the corresponding sequential execution, but guarantees external determinism where the final state only depends on the inputs, not the thread interleavings. Their runtime technique aims to preserve, rather than checking, sequential semantics. Prabhu et al. [30] propose speculative composition and iteration as programming constructs to parallelize parts of the program with explicit dependencies. They guarantee the obedience to sequential semantics by running a sequential version of the program that verifies the speculated values of each parallel part. Saltz et al. [35], and Rauchwerger et al. [32] present runtime checks for parallelizing executions of loops. Their runtime techniques complement static transformations by tracking at runtime data dependencies across parallel loop iterations similarly to our runtime algorithm does to identify true conflicts between threads.

8. Conclusion

We proposed the use of nondeterministic sequential specifications to separate functional correctness from parallelism correctness of parallel programs. Our proposal has several advantages.

First, NDSeq specifications are lightweight. Unlike traditional mechanisms for functional specification, e.g., invariants and pre/post-conditions, NDSeq specifications do not require one to learn a complex logic or language. The original parallel program along with a few **if**(*true*∗) serves as the specification and can be used alone to detect various parallelism-related bugs.

Second, once we verify parallelism correctness, proving the functional partial correctness of the parallel program amounts to checking the functional correctness of the NDSeq program. Threads being absent, this can be done using well-developed techniques for verifying sequential programs. Note that verification of sequential programs (even with nondeterminism) is much simpler than verification of parallel programs. For example, model checking of Boolean multithreaded programs is undecidable [31], whereas model checking of Boolean nondeterministic sequential programs is decidable [13]. The latter fact has been exploited by several well-known model checkers for nondeterministic sequential programs [1, 3]. Similarly, NDSeq specifications also simplify the reasoning about other concurrency-related properties such as determinism and linearizability.

Third, NDSeq specifications can simplify debugging of functional correctness bugs. When investigating a parallel execution that exhibits a bug, the programmer can be presented with the equivalent, hence similarly buggy, NDSeq execution. This allows the programmer to analyze the bug by examining a sequential behavior of the program, which is much easier to debug than its parallel counterpart.

We proposed a runtime checking algorithm for parallelism correctness. Our algorithm is based on a combination of simple dynamic dataflow analysis and conflict serializability checking. The NDSeq specification is the key factor that improves the precision of conflict serializability by indicating the conflicts that can be safely be ignored by the analysis. We believe that a similar verification can be done statically; such an extension remains a future work. A key aspect of our checking algorithm (unlike static proof systems [11] and type systems [14]) is that it does not need to refer to functional invariants which often complicates the verification process.

Acknowledgments

We would like to Nicholas Jalbert, Pallavi Joshi, and our anonymous reviewers for their valuable comments on this paper. This research supported in part by Microsoft (Award #024263) and Intel (Award #024894) funding and by matching funding by U.C. Discovery (Award #DIG07-10227), by NSF Grants CNS-0720906, CCF-101781, CCF-0747390, CCF-1018729, and CCF-1018730, and by a DoD NDSEG Graduate Fellowship. The last author is supported in part by a Sloan Foundation Fellowship. Additional support comes from Oracle (formerly Sun Microsystems), from a gift from Intel, and from Par Lab affiliates National Instruments, NEC, Nokia, NVIDIA, and Samsung.

References

[1] T. Ball, A. Podelski, and S. K. Rajamani. Boolean and cartesian abstraction for model checking C programs. In *Tools and Algorithms for the Construction and Analysis of Systems (TACAS)*, pages 268–283, 2001.

[2] P. A. Bernstein, V. Hadzilacos, and N. Goodman. *Concurrency Control and Recovery in Database Systems*. Addison-Wesley, 1987.

[3] D. Beyer, T. A. Henzinger, R. Jhala, and R. Majumdar. The software model checker Blast: Applications to software engineering. *Int. J. Softw. Tools Technol. Transf.*, 9:505–525, October 2007.

[4] S. M. Blackburn, R. Garner, C. Hoffmann, A. M. Khang, K. S. McKinley, R. Bentzur, A. Diwan, D. Feinberg, D. Frampton, S. Z. Guyer, M. Hirzel, A. Hosking, M. Jump, H. Lee, J. E. B. Moss, A. Phansalkar, D. Stefanović, T. VanDrunen, D. von Dincklage, and B. Wiedermann. The DaCapo benchmarks: Java benchmarking development and analysis. In *Object-oriented Programming Systems, Languages, and Applications (OOPSLA)*, pages 169–190, 2006.

[5] R. L. Bocchino, Jr., V. S. Adve, D. Dig, S. V. Adve, S. Heumann, R. Komuravelli, J. Overbey, P. Simmons, H. Sung, and M. Vakilian. A type and effect system for Deterministic Parallel Java. In *Object-Oriented Programming, Systems, Languages, and Applications (OOPSLA)*, pages 97–116, 2009.

[6] R. L. Bocchino, Jr., S. Heumann, N. Honarmand, S. V. Adve, V. S. Adve, A. Welc, and T. Shpeisman. Safe nondeterminism in a deterministic-by-default parallel language. In *Principles of Programming Languages (POPL)*, pages 535–548, 2011.

[7] S. Burckhardt, C. Dern, M. Musuvathi, and R. Tan. Line-up: A complete and automatic linearizability checker. In *Programming Language Design and Implementation (PLDI)*, pages 330–340, 2010.

[8] J. Burnim and K. Sen. Asserting and checking determinism for multithreaded programs. In *Foundations of Software Engineering (FSE)*, 2009.

[9] J. Burnim, G. Necula, and K. Sen. Separating functional and parallel correctness using nondeterministic sequential specifications. In *Hot Topics in Parallelism (HOTPAR)*, 2010. *Position paper*.

[10] R. Colvin, L. Groves, V. Luchangco, and M. Moir. Formal verification of a lazy concurrent list-based set algorithm. In *Computer Aided Verification (CAV)*, 2006.

[11] T. Elmas, S. Qadeer, and S. Tasiran. A calculus of atomic actions. In *Principles of Programming Languages (POPL)*, pages 2–15, 2009.

[12] A. Farzan and P. Madhusudan. Monitoring atomicity in concurrent programs. In *Computer Aided Verification (CAV)*, pages 52–65, 2008.

[13] A. Finkel, B. Willems, and P. Wolper. A direct symbolic approach to model checking pushdown systems. In *Workshop on Verification of Infinite State Systems (INFINITY)*, 1997.

[14] C. Flanagan and S. Qadeer. A type and effect system for atomicity. In *Programming Language Design and Implementation (PLDI)*, 2003.

[15] C. Flanagan, S. N. Freund, and S. Qadeer. Exploiting purity for atomicity. In *International Symposium on Software Testing and Analysis (ISSTA)*, pages 221–231, 2004.

[16] C. Flanagan, S. N. Freund, and J. Yi. Velodrome: A sound and complete dynamic atomicity checker for multithreaded programs. In *Programming Language Design and Implementation (PLDI)*, pages 293–303, 2008.

[17] C. Hammer, J. Dolby, M. Vaziri, and F. Tip. Dynamic detection of atomic-set-serializability violations. In *International Conference on Software Engineering (ICSE)*, pages 231–240, 2008.

[18] M. Herlihy and N. Shavit. *The Art of Multiprocessor Programming*. Morgan Kaufmann, March 2008.

[19] M. P. Herlihy and J. M. Wing. Linearizability: A correctness condition for concurrent objects. *ACM Trans. Prog. Lang. Syst.*, 12:463–492, July 1990.

[20] A. Kaminsky. Parallel Java: A Unified API for Shared Memory and Cluster Parallel Programming in 100% Java. In *Parallel and Distributed Processing Symposium (IPDPS)*, March 2007.

[21] M. Kulkarni, K. Pingali, B. Walter, G. Ramanarayanan, K. Bala, and L. P. Chew. Optimistic parallelism requires abstractions. In *Programming Language Design and Implementation (PLDI)*, 2007.

[22] M. Kulkarni, M. Burtscher, C. Cascaval, and K. Pingali. Lonestar: A suite of parallel irregular programs. In *International Symposium on Performance Analysis of Systems and Software, (ISPASS)*, April 2009.

[23] Z. Lai, S. C. Cheung, and W. K. Chan. Detecting atomic-set serializability violations in multithreaded programs through active randomized testing. In *International Conference on Software Engineering (ICSE)*, pages 235–244, 2010.

[24] R. J. Lipton. Reduction: A method of proving properties of parallel programs. *Communications of the ACM*, 18(12):717–721, 1975.

[25] S. Lu, J. Tucek, F. Qin, and Y. Zhou. AVIO: Detecting atomicity violations via access interleaving invariants. In *Architectural Support for Programming Languages and Operating Systems (ASPLOS)*, 2006.

[26] M. M. Michael and M. L. Scott. Simple, fast, and practical non-blocking and blocking concurrent queue algorithms. In *Principles of Distributed Computing (PDOC)*, 1996.

[27] R. H. B. Netzer and B. P. Miller. What are race conditions?: Some issues and formalizations. *ACM Lett. Prog. Lang. Syst.*, 1(1):74–88, 1992.

[28] M. Olszewski, J. Ansel, and S. Amarasinghe. Kendo: Efficient deterministic multithreading in software. In *Architectural Support for Programming Languages and Operating Systems (ASPLOS)*, pages 97–108, 2009.

[29] C. Papadimitriou. *The theory of database concurrency control*. Computer Science Press, Inc., 1986.

[30] P. Prabhu, G. Ramalingam, and K. Vaswani. Safe programmable speculative parallelism. In *Programming Language Design and Implementation (PLDI)*, pages 50–61, 2010.

[31] G. Ramalingam. Context-sensitive synchronization-sensitive analysis is undecidable. *ACM Trans. Prog. Lang. Syst.*, 22(2):416–430, 2000.

```
class Stack :
  class Node {int value; Node next;}
  Node TOP;  int TOP_version;

  void push(int x) {
    Node local_top, new_top;
    int local_version;
    boolean done = false;

    new_top = new Node();
    new_top.value = x;
    while (!done) {
      atomic {
        local_top = TOP;
        local_version = TOP_version;
      }
      new_top.next = local_top;
      if ( true* ) {
        if (CAS2(TOP, TOP_version,
                 local_top, local_version,
                 new_top, local_version+1))
          done = true;
  } } }
```

```
int pop() {
  Node local_top, new_top;
  int local_version;
  boolean done = false;
  int value = EMPTY;

  while (!done) {
    atomic {
      local_top = TOP;
      local_version = TOP_version;
    }
    if ( true* ) {
      if (local_top == null) {
        done = true;
      } else {
        new_top = local_top.next;
        if (CAS2(TOP, TOP_version,
                 local_top, local_version,
                 new_top, local_version+1)) {
          done = true;
          value = local_top.value;
  } } } }
  return value; }
```

```
void harness() {
  Stack stack = new Stack();
  coforeach (i = 1 .. 30) {
    // make a call to stack
    if(randomBoolean()) {
      stack.push(randomInt());
    } else {
      int t = stack.pop();
      mark_focus(t) ;
  } }

  // traverse the stack and mark
  // the final contents relevant
  mark_focus(stack.TOP) ;
  Node node = stack.TOP;
  while(node != null) {
    mark_focus(node.next) ;
    mark_focus(node.value) ;
    node = node.next;
} }
```

Figure 8. A non-blocking stack implementation with its nondeterministic sequential specification embedded.

[32] L. Rauchwerger and D. Padua. The lrpd test: speculative run-time parallelization of loops with privatization and reduction parallelization. In *Programming Language Design and Implementation (PLDI)*, pages 218–232, 1995.

[33] M. C. Rinard and P. C. Diniz. Commutativity analysis: A new analysis framework for parallelizing compilers. In *Programming Language Design and Implementation (PLDI)*, pages 54–67, 1996.

[34] C. Sadowski, S. Freund, and C. Flanagan. SingleTrack: A Dynamic Determinism Checker for Multithreaded Programs. In *European Symposium on Programming (ESOP)*, 2009.

[35] J. Saltz, R. Mirchandaney, and K. Crowley. Run-time parallelization and scheduling of loops. *Computers, IEEE Transactions on*, 40(5):603 –612, 1991.

[36] K. Sen. Race directed random testing of concurrent programs. In *ACM SIGPLAN Conference on Programming Language Design and Implementation (PLDI'08)*, 2008.

[37] N. Shavit and D. Touitou. Software transactional memory. In *Principles of Distributed Computing (PODC)*, pages 204–213, 1995.

[38] L. A. Smith, J. M. Bull, and J. Obdrzálek. A parallel Java Grande benchmark suite. In *Supercomputing (SC)*, 2001.

[39] R. K. Treiber. Systems programming: Coping with parallelism. Technical Report RJ 5118, IBM Almaden Research Center, Apr. 1986.

[40] V. Vafeiadis. Shape-value abstraction for verifying linearizability. In *Verification, Model Checking, and Abstract Interpretation (VMCAI)*, pages 335–348, 2009.

[41] V. Vafeiadis, M. Herlihy, T. Hoare, and M. Shapiro. Proving correctness of highly-concurrent linearisable objects. In *Principles and Practice of Parallel Programming (PPOPP)*, 2006.

[42] R. Vallée-Rai, P. Co, E. Gagnon, L. Hendren, P. Lam, and V. Sundaresan. Soot - a Java bytecode optimization framework. In *Centre for Advanced Studies on Collaborative Research (CASCON)*, pages 125–135, 1999.

[43] M. Vaziri, F. Tip, and J. Dolby. Associating synchronization constraints with data in an object-oriented language. In *Principles of Programming Languages (POPL)*, pages 334–345, 2006.

[44] M. Vechev, E. Yahav, and G. Yorsh. Experience with model checking linearizability. In *SPIN Workshop on Model Checking Software*, pages 261–278, 2009.

[45] M. Vechev, E. Yahav, R. Raman, and V. Sarkar. Verifying determinism of structured parallel programs. In *Static Analysis Symposium (SAS)*, 2010.

[46] C. von Praun and T. R. Gross. Object race detection. In *Object Oriented Programming, Systems, Languages, and Applications (OOPSLA)*, pages 70–82, 2001.

[47] C. von Praun, L. Ceze, and C. Caşcaval. Implicit parallelism with ordered transactions. In *Principles and Practice of Parallel Programming (PPoPP)*, pages 79–89, 2007.

[48] L. Wang and S. D. Stoller. Runtime analysis of atomicity for multithreaded programs. *IEEE Trans. Softw. Eng.*, 32:93–110, 2006.

[49] J. M. Wing and C. Gong. Testing and verifying concurrent objects. *J. Parallel Distrib. Comput.*, 17(1-2):164–182, 1993.

A. NDSeq Specification Examples

A.1 Non-blocking Concurrent Reduction

Consider the simple parallel program in Figure 9. The program consists of a parallel for-loop, denoted `coforeach`—each iteration of this loop attempts to perform a computation (Line 6) based on the shared variable `x`, which is initially 0. In particular, each iteration uses an atomic compare-and-swap (`CAS`) operation to update the shared variable `x`. If multiple iterations try to concurrently update `x`, some of these `CAS`'s will fail and those parallel loop iterations will recompute their updates to `x` and then will try again.

The NDSeq specification of the program, which is embedded in the parallel program in Figure 9, indicates two nondeterministic aspects. First, the box around the **coforeach** construct in Line 1 specifies that the loop iterations can run in any permutation of the set `1,...,N`. This part of the specification captures the intended nondeterministic behavior of the parallel program: `x` can be updated by threads in an arbitrary order due to nondeterministic scheduling of threads. Second, the `if(`*true**`)` annotation in Line 4 specifies that

```
 1:  coforeach (i in 1,...,N) {
 2:    bool done = false;
 3:    while (!done) {
 4:        if ( true* ) {
 5:            int prev = x;
 6:            int curr = i*prev + i;
 7:            bool c = CAS(x,prev,curr);
 8:            if (c) {
 9:                done = true;
10:            }
11:  } }   }
12:  mark_focus(x) ;
```

Figure 9. Simple parallel program to perform the reduction in Line 6 for the integers $\{1,\ldots,N\}$, in some arbitrary order.

the iteration body may be skipped nondeterministically, at least from a partial correctness point of view; this is acceptable, since the while loop in this program fragment is already prepared to deal with the case when the effects of an iteration are ignored following a failed CAS statement.

The **mark_focus** annotation in Line 12 indicates that x is the only focus variable. That is, the functional correctness of the program depends only on the final value of x after all the threads created by coforeach terminate.

A.2 Non-blocking Concurrent Stack

In Figure 8, we give the Java-like code for the NDSeq specification of our non-blocking **stack** benchmark. The stack is represented as a null-terminating, singly-linked list of Node objects. The head of the list is pointed by the TOP field of the stack. In order avoid the ABA problem, we use a version number (TOP_version), which is increased whenever TOP is updated.

The push and pop methods implement the Optimistic Concurrent Computation pattern in Section 4 using a loop that iterates until the operation succeeds. Each method first reads the TOP of the stack without any synchronization and then uses an atomic CAS2 (double compare-and-swap) operation to check for conflicts by comparing TOP and TOP_version with local_top and local_version. If TOP=local_top and TOP_version=local_version then CAS2 commits the operation by writing new_top to TOP and incrementing TOP_version and returns *true*. Otherwise, CAS2 returns *false* and the operation retries.

In the specification, an **if**(*true*∗) statement is placed around the critical CAS2 in push, and around the check whether or not local_top is null in pop. These **if**(*true*∗)'s indicate that the sequential version of the program is free to nondeterministically retry as if there had been a conflict. This added nondeterminism enables our dynamic analysis to mark as irrelevant the reads of TOP and TOP_version by loop iterations in which the CAS2 fails.

The harness method creates a number of threads, each of which calls push with a random input or calls pop. In the code, we mark the focus variables using **mark_focus**. The focus variables are: (1) the values popped by the harness threads (marked after each call to pop), and (2) the last contents of the stack (marked at the end of the harness).

Garbage Collection for Monitoring Parametric Properties *

Dongyun Jin Patrick O'Neil Meredith Dennis Griffith Grigore Roşu
Department of Computer Science, University of Illinois at Urbana-Champaign
{djin3, pmeredit, dgriffi3, grosu}@cs.illinois.edu

Abstract

Parametric properties are behavioral properties over program events that depend on one or more parameters. Parameters are bound to concrete data or objects at runtime, which makes parametric properties particularly suitable for stating multi-object relationships or protocols. Monitoring parametric properties independently of the employed formalism involves *slicing* traces with respect to *parameter instances* and sending these slices to appropriate non-parametric *monitor instances*. The number of such instances is theoretically unbounded and tends to be enormous in practice, to an extent that how to efficiently manage monitor instances has become one of the most challenging problems in runtime verification. The previous formalism-independent approach was only able to do the obvious, namely to garbage collect monitor instances when all bound parameter objects were garbage collected. This led to pathological behaviors where unnecessary monitor instances were kept for the entire length of a program. This paper proposes a new approach to garbage collecting monitor instances. Unnecessary monitor instances are collected lazily to avoid creating undue overhead. This lazy collection, along with some careful engineering, has resulted in RV, the most efficient parametric monitoring system to date. Our evaluation shows that the average overhead of RV in the DaCapo benchmark is 15%, which is two times lower than that of JavaMOP and orders of magnitude lower than that of Tracematches.

Categories and Subject Descriptors D.2.4 [*Software Engineering*]: Assertion checkers, Class invariants, Formal methods, Reliability; D.2.5 [*Software Engineering*]: Debugging aids, Error handling and recovery, Monitors; D.3.2 [*Programming Languages*]: Object-oriented languages; D.3.4 [*Programming Languages*]: Code generation, Memory management

General Terms Languages, Performance, Reliability, Verification

Keywords runtime verification, runtime monitoring, testing, debugging, aspect-oriented programming, garbage collection

* Supported in part by NSF grants CCF-0916893, CNS-0720512, and CCF-0448501, by NASA contract NNL08AA23C, and by an NSA grant, a UIUC Campus Research Board Award, and a Samsung SAIT grant.

PLDI'11, June 4–8, 2011, San Jose, California, USA.

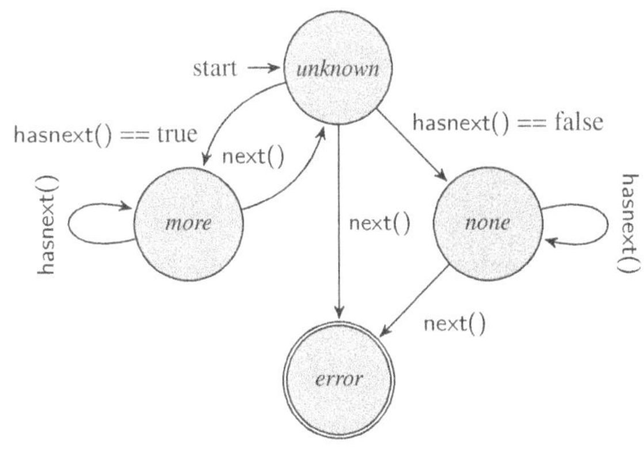

Figure 1. Typestate description for HASNEXT

1. Introduction

Monitoring is an effective technique for ensuring software reliability. The well known concept of *typestate* [31] property can be enforced by using monitoring techniques. Typestates refine the notion of type by stating not only what operations are allowed by a particular object, but also what operations are allowed in what contexts.

Figure 1 shows the typestate description for HASNEXT. The HASNEXT typestate says that it is invalid to call the next() method on an `Iterator` object when there are no more elements in the underlying `Collection`, i.e., when hasnext() returns false, or when it is unknown if there are more elements in the `Collection`, i.e., hasnext() is not called. From the *unknown* state, it is always an error to call the next() method because such an operation could be unsafe. If hasnext() is called and returns true, it is safe to call next(), so the typestate enters the *more* state. If, however, the hasnext() method returns false, there are no more elements, and the typestate enters the *none* state. In the *more* and *none* states, calling the hasnext() method provides no new information. It is safe to call next() from the *more* state, but it becomes unknown if more elements exist, so the typestate reenters the initial *unknown* state. Finally, calling next() from the *none* state results in an error.

Typestate Property Example- It is straightforward to encode this, and all typestate properties, as particular (one-parameter) *parametric* properties. Figure 2 shows this property using the RV system presented in this paper. For demonstration purposes, we specify the same property using two different formalisms. The first formalism is a direct translation of the typestate diagram using the finite state machine (FSM) capabilities of RV, and is denoted by the fsm keyword. Each state in the typestate is written as a name followed by its transitions (i.e., monitored events) in brackets. The first state in the FSM description (unknown) is always considered to be the initial state of a finite state machine in the RV system. The second formalism is linear temporal logic (LTL), prefixed by the keyword ltl. The

```
HasNext(Iterator i) {
  event hasnexttrue after(Iterator i) returning(boolean b) :
    call(* Iterator.hasNext()) && target(i) && condition(b) {}
  event hasnextfalse after(Iterator i) returning(boolean b) :
    call(* Iterator.hasNext()) && target(i) && condition(!b) {}
  event next before(Iterator i) :
    call(* Iterator.next()) && target(i) {}

  fsm :
    unknown [
      hasnexttrue -> more
      hasnextfalse -> none
      next -> error
    ]
    more [
      hasnexttrue -> more
      next -> unknown
    ]
    none [
      hasnextfalse -> none
      next -> error
    ]
    error [  ]
  @error {
    System.out.println("improper Iterator use found!");
  }

  ltl: [](next => (*)hasnexttrue)
  @violation {
    System.out.println("improper Iterator use found!");
  }
}
```

Figure 2. HASNEXT property in RV using FSM and LTL

```
UnsafeIter(Collection c, Iterator i) {
  event create after(Collection c) returning(Iterator i) :
    call(Iterator Collection.iterator()) && target(c) {}
  event update after(Collection c) :
    (call(* Collection.remove*(..))
    || call(* Collection.add*(..))
    || call(* Collection.clear(..))) && target(c){}
  event next before(Iterator i) :
    call(* Iterator.next()) && target(i){}

  ere : update* create next* update+ next
  @match {
    System.out.println("improper Concurrent Modification found!");
  }
}
```

Figure 3. UNSAFEITER property in RV using the ERE plugin

```
SafeLock(Lock l, Thread t){
  event acquire before(Lock l, Thread t):
    call(* Lock.acquire()) && target(l) && thread(t) {}
  event release before(Lock l, Thread t):
    call(* Lock.release()) && target(l) && thread(t) {}
  event begin before(Thread t) :
    execution(* *.*(..)) && thread(t) && !within(Lock+) {}
  event end after(Thread t) :
    execution(* *.*(..)) && thread(t) && !within(Lock+) {}

  cfg : S -> S begin S end | S acquire S release | epsilon
  @fail {    System.out.println("improper Lock use found!");  }
}
```

Figure 4. SAFELOCK property in RV using the CFG plugin

LTL formula here states that any call to next() must *always* ([]) be immediately preceded ((*)) by a call to hasnext() that returned true. The RV system supports multiple logical formalisms, and as this example demonstrates, some formalisms can lead to much more succinct and easy to understand specifications.

The monitored events are prefixed by the keyword event and are encoded using slightly extended AspectJ [26] pointcuts. One such extension is the condition pointcut, which is similar to the if pointcut: it ensures that the given pointcut is only applied if its condition is true, but unlike the if pointcut, it is able to refer to variables bound by returning advice. Thus, the hasnexttrue event is only generated if hasnext() returns true, and the hasnextfalse is only generated if hasnext returns false. The per `Iterator` nature of the HASNEXT typestate is encoded by using *one* `Iterator` parameter.

For each property, the code block following it is referred to as a *handler*. The handler is executed when a condition of its corresponding specification is met. For instance, the FSM handler in Figure 2 is executed when the machine enters the *error* state, while the LTL handler is executed when the LTL formula is violated. Handlers may contain any arbitrary Java code, but here they simply print messages. Such behavior is useful for debugging and testing purposes.

Parametric properties properly *generalize* typestates, as we shall see, by allowing more parameters. This allows us to specify not only properties about a given object such as the HASNEXT example, but also properties that specify *relationships between objects*.

General Parametric Property Examples- Figure 3 shows a property for the unsafe use of `Collection` and `Iterator`. The property flags it as an error if an `Iterator` is created, its underlying `Collection` is modified, and then the `Iterator` is used again. Here we use the extended regular expression (ERE) capabilities of the RV system, as specified by the ere keyword. The occurrence of update* at the beginning of the pattern allows any number of updates before the first create event, in which the `Iterator` is first created. We wish to catch this behavior because Java `Collections` do not allow concurrent modification. The JVM usually throws a runtime exception when this occurs, but the exception is not guaranteed to be thrown in a multi-threaded environment.

Figure 4 shows a specification for the safe use of reentrant locks, called SAFELOCK, stating that the number of calls of an acquire() in a given method is balanced with the number of calls to release(). This property is parametric both in the `Lock` in question and in the `Thread`, and is specified using the context-free grammar (CFG) plugin of the RV system. The events begin and end refer to the beginning and end of *every* method. The thread pointcut is also an RV extension of standard AspectJ pointcuts that allows for binding the current `Thread` of execution in the monitored program. The pattern for the specification, prefixed by the keyword cfg, has S for its start symbol. The first symbol seen is always assumed the start symbol. The CFG pattern requires that begin and end events are matched and properly nested with acquire and release events, which must also be matched.

Monitoring parametric properties in their full generality is a complex task. Several parametric monitoring systems such as Eagle [20], J-Lo [11, 12, 30], Tracematches [4, 8], JavaMOP [16, 17], PTQL [23], PQL [27], QVM [5], SpoX [24], PoET [22], and RuleR [9] have been proposed in recent years. In parametric monitoring systems, the parameters are dynamically bound to objects at runtime, thus resulting in a potentially unlimited number of monitor instances, one per combination of parameter bindings. The main challenge underlying the monitoring of parametric properties is therefore how to effectively manage these monitor instances, in particular how to efficiently retrieve all the monitor instances interested in an event when it takes place, and how to efficiently garbage collect monitor instances which have become unnecessary.

Earlier attempts such as Tracematches [4, 8] are careful to manage their memory, but hardwire their property specification formalism (regular expression only). JavaMOP [16, 17] is generic in specification formalisms, but, however, it has memory leaks. Due to JavaMOP's creation of separate monitor instances in order to handle each separate parameters instantiation, recognizing and removing unnecessary monitor instances is quite challenging. JavaMOP is only able to collect a monitor instance when all the bound parameters are garbage collected, which ensures that no event can happen to the corresponding monitor instance. The problem with this method of garbage collection can be clearly seen in the UNSAFEITER property from Figure 3. Because it is the next event at the end of the pattern that actually causes the error, there is no way to ever match the pattern if the `Iterator` bound to a given monitor instance is garbage collected. However, JavaMOP is only able to collect the associated monitor instance if *both* the `Collection` and the `Iterator` are garbage collected. Unfortunately, in most realistic programs, `Collections` have much longer lifetimes than the `Iterators` created from them. Because of this, JavaMOP would have large numbers of monitor instances–when monitoring most programs–that could never possibly match the pattern because their bound `Iterators` had been collected. The RV system, which is presented in this paper, is a commercial grade system developed by Runtime Verification, Inc. RV is able to collect these monitor instances, as well as many others that JavaMOP does not collect.

To collect monitor instances that JavaMOP is unable to collect, we implement, in RV, a means to prune unnecessary monitor instances based on a static analysis of the monitored property. The results of the static analysis, which we refer to as coenable sets, are used at runtime to determine when a monitor instance can no longer reach a triggering state, and can thus be garbage collected. For example, in UNSAFEITER (Figure 3), the coenable sets associated to event update consist of all those subsets of events which can potentially make update a relevant event for a monitor for UNSAFEITER, that is, {next}, {next, update}, and {next, create, update}. Indeed, in any matching trace containing update, the event update is followed by precisely all the events in one of these subsets. Consider now a monitor M for UNSAFEITER corresponding to a particular parameters instance, say $c \mapsto c_1$ and $i \mapsto i_1$, and suppose that an event update is just being dispatched to M. At this moment, M knows that it has a future only if all the events in at least one of the coenable sets of update are possible. In particular, if the `Iterator` i_1 has already been garbage collected, then M will never match, since each of the coenable sets of update contains a next, which can only be generated by i_1. Thus, M can safely terminate itself and be garbage collected in this situation. Removing unnecessary monitors is still an expensive task, and in the interest of making it as efficient as possible, a lazy collection method is used. This technique makes RV the most efficient parametric monitoring system to date, by a large margin (see Section 5).

Our monitor garbage collection technique is orthogonal to other optimization techniques for parametric monitoring. More precisely, our technique is aimed at improving the base performance of parametric monitoring by means of keeping the number of monitor instances low *without* relying on (expensive) knowledge about the source program or on minimizing the distance between events and their monitors. Other optimizations can be applied on top of our garbage collection technique and thus start from this base performance and improve it. For example, staged indexing (or decentralized indexing), which has been proposed and implemented in [6, 8, 17], piggy-backs indexing trees onto parameter instances. This reduces the cost of lookup due to better cache locality and fewer hash lookups. Also, significant runtime overhead reductions have been achieved using program static analysis [14, 15, 21, 27], by removing unnecessary instrumentation. RV supports both staged indexing and program static analysis via the Clara approach [15]. Nevertheless, *we deliberately disabled these orthogonal optimizations in our evaluation, to properly measure the effectiveness of the proposed garbage collection technique*. Enabling these orthogonal optimizations would only hide the inefficiency of base monitoring.

We evaluate our RV garbage collection technique and compare it to those in JavaMOP and Tracematches in Section 5. We picked these two systems for comparison because they are known for their efficiency (the best so far). The average overhead of RV in version 9.12 of the DaCapo [10] benchmark suite is 15%, even with no static or decentralized indexing optimizations, which is two times lower than 33% of JavaMOP and nine times lower than the 142% of Tracematches *disregarding* those cases where Tracematches *failed to terminate*. Even the largest overhead of RV in two versions of DaCapo, from UNSAFEITER-bloat, is only 251%, while in JavaMOP, 7 cases show overhead higher than 251%, and in Tracematches, 20 cases show higher overhead and 9 cases do not terminate.

Outline The rest of this paper is as follows: Section 2 provides a brief overview of parametric monitoring; Section 3 explains the theory of the coenables sets used for pruning unnecessary monitor instances, and shows some examples; Section 4 discusses our data structures to efficiently garbage collect monitors by using coenables sets, as well as how the coenable sets are actually used during the monitoring process; Section 5 presents our experimental data; and Section 6 provides some concluding remarks.

2. Parametric Properties and Monitoring

To explain the garbage collection of unnecessary monitor instances, we first introduce some background theory on parametric monitoring. For consistency, we follow the notation and terminology recently proposed by the JavaMOP authors in [18]. We begin by introducing the notions of event, trace, and property, first non-parametric and then parametric. Trace slicing is then defined as a reduct operation that forgets events that are unrelated to the given parameter instance.

Definition 1. *Let $\mathcal{E}$ be a finite set of (non-parametric) events, called* ***base events*** *or simply* ***events****. An $\mathcal{E}$*-***trace****, or simply a (non-parametric)* ***trace*** *when $\mathcal{E}$ is understood or not important, is any finite sequence of events in $\mathcal{E}$, that is, an element in $\mathcal{E}^*$. If event $e \in \mathcal{E}$ appears in trace $w \in \mathcal{E}^*$ then we write $e \in w$. ϵ is the empty trace.*

For UNSAFEITER in Section 1, the set of events $\mathcal{E}$ is {create, update, next}, and a possible trace is "create next update next".

Definition 2. *An $\mathcal{E}$*-***property*** *P, or simply a (base or non-parametric)* ***property****, is a function $P\colon \mathcal{E}^* \to \mathcal{C}$ partitioning the set of traces into* ***(verdict) categories*** *$\mathcal{C}$. In general, $\mathcal{C}$ may be any set.*

Consider again UNSAFEITER. The match traces are those matching the pattern, e.g., "create next update next". There are also traces that have not matched yet, but may still match in the future, such as "update create", which we call ? (unknown) traces. Lastly, there are traces that may never match again, such as "create update next next", which we refer to as fail traces. Thus we pick $\mathcal{C}$ to be the set {match, fail, ?}, and define its property $P_{\text{UNSAFEITER}}\colon \mathcal{E}^* \to \mathcal{C}$ as follows: $P_{\text{UNSAFEITER}}(w) =$ match if w is in the language of the UNSAFEITER ere, $P_{\text{UNSAFEITER}}(w) =$? if w is a prefix of a string in the language of the ere, and $P_{\text{UNSAFEITER}}(w) =$ fail otherwise.

We next extend the above definitions to the parametric case. Let $[A \to B]$ be the set of total functions, and let $[A \rightharpoonup B]$ be the set of partial functions from A to B.

Definition 3. ***(Parametric events and traces).*** *Let X be a finite set of* ***parameters*** *and let V be a set of corresponding* ***parameter values****. If $\mathcal{E}$ is a set of base events like in Definition 1, then let $\mathcal{E}\langle X\rangle$ be the set of corresponding* ***parametric events*** *$e\langle\theta\rangle$, where e is a base event in $\mathcal{E}$ and θ is a partial function in $[X \rightharpoonup V]$. Partial functions θ in $[X \rightharpoonup V]$ are called* ***parameter instances****. A* ***parametric trace*** *is a trace with events in $\mathcal{E}\langle X\rangle$, that is, a word in $\mathcal{E}\langle X\rangle^*$.*

A parametric trace for UNSAFEITER could be "update$\langle c \mapsto c_1\rangle$ update$\langle c \mapsto c_2\rangle$ create$\langle c \mapsto c_1, i \mapsto i_1\rangle$ next$\langle i \mapsto i_1\rangle$". To simplify writing we often assume the parameter set implicit, as in the following, which is the same trace: "update$\langle c_1\rangle$ update$\langle c_2\rangle$ create$\langle c_1, i_1\rangle$ next$\langle i_1\rangle$".

Definition 4. *Let X be a finite set of parameters. If $\mathcal{E}$ is a set of base events like in Definition 1, we define a* ***parametric event definition****, or* ***event definition*** *for short, as a function $\mathcal{D}\colon \mathcal{E} \to \mathcal{P}(X)$, where*

$\mathcal{P}$ is the power set, that maps each event e to a set of parameters $\mathcal{D}(e)$ that will be instantiated by e at runtime. $\mathcal{D}$ is extended to $\mathcal{E}^*$ as $\mathcal{D}(\epsilon) = \emptyset$ and $\mathcal{D}(ew) = \mathcal{D}(e) \cup \mathcal{D}(w)$, and to $\mathcal{P}(\mathcal{E})$ as $\mathcal{D}(\emptyset) = \emptyset$ and $\mathcal{D}(\{e\} \cup E) = \mathcal{D}(e) \cup \mathcal{D}(E)$. Parametric event $e\langle\theta\rangle$ is ***$\mathcal{D}$-consistent*** *if $dom(\theta) = \mathcal{D}(e)$. Parametric trace τ is* ***$\mathcal{D}$-consistent*** *if $e\langle\theta\rangle$ is $\mathcal{D}$-consistent for each $e\langle\theta\rangle \in \tau$.*

The UNSAFEITER property contains the parametric event definition $\mathcal{D}(\text{create}) = \{c, i\}$, $\mathcal{D}(\text{update}) = \{c\}$, $\mathcal{D}(\text{next}) = \{i\}$. It states that, for example, parameters c and i will be instantiated at runtime when a parametric event create$\langle\theta\rangle$ is received. For a trace "create update", $\mathcal{D}$(create update) is $\{c, i\}$.

Definition 5. *$\theta, \theta' \in [A \rightharpoonup B]$ are* ***compatible*** *if for any $x \in dom(\theta) \cap dom(\theta')$, $\theta(x) = \theta'(x)$. We can* ***combine*** *compatible instances θ and θ', written $\theta \sqcup \theta'$, as follows:*

$$(\theta \sqcup \theta')(x) = \begin{cases} \theta(x) & \text{if } \theta(x) \text{ is defined} \\ \theta'(x) & \text{if } \theta'(x) \text{ is defined} \\ \text{undefined} & \text{otherwise} \end{cases}$$

$\theta \sqcup \theta'$ is also called the ***least upper bound (lub)*** *of θ and θ'. θ is* ***less informative*** *than θ', written $\theta \sqsubseteq \theta'$, if for any $x \in X$, if $\theta(x)$ is defined then $\theta'(x)$ is also defined and $\theta(x) = \theta'(x)$. $\sqcup$ is extended to $\mathcal{P}_f([X \rightharpoonup V])$ in the natural way. Here $\mathcal{P}_f$ is the finite power set.*

Definition 6. ***(Trace slicing)*** *Given parametric trace $\tau \in \mathcal{E}\langle X\rangle^*$ and θ in $[X \rightharpoonup V]$, let the* ***θ-trace slice*** *$\tau\restriction_\theta \in \mathcal{E}^*$ be the non-parametric trace defined as:*

- *$\epsilon\restriction_\theta = \epsilon$ (recall that ϵ is the empty trace)*
- $(\tau\, e\langle\theta'\rangle)\restriction_\theta = \begin{cases} (\tau\restriction_\theta)\, e & \text{if } \theta' \sqsubseteq \theta \\ \tau\restriction_\theta & \text{otherwise} \end{cases}$

The trace slice $\tau\restriction_\theta$ first filters out all the parametric events that are not relevant for the instance θ, i.e., which contain instances of parameters that θ does not care about, and then, for the remaining events relevant to θ, it forgets the parameters so that the trace can be checked against base, non-parametric properties. It is crucial to discard events from parameter instances that are not relevant to θ during the slicing, including those more informative than θ. Referring back to our parametric trace from above, the non-parametric trace slice for parameter instance $\langle c_2\rangle$ is "update", that for $\langle c_1\rangle$ is "update", the slice for $\langle c_1, i_1\rangle$ is "update next", and the slice for $\langle i_1\rangle$ is "next".

Definition 7. *Let X be a finite set of parameters together with their corresponding parameter values V, like in Definition 3, and let $P\colon \mathcal{E}^* \to \mathcal{C}$ be a non-parametric property like in Definition 2. Then we define the* ***parametric property*** *$\Lambda X.P$ as the property (over traces $\mathcal{E}\langle X\rangle^*$ and verdict categories $[[X \rightharpoonup V] \to \mathcal{C}]$)*

$$\Lambda X.P\colon \mathcal{E}\langle X\rangle^* \to [[X \rightharpoonup V] \to \mathcal{C}]$$

as $(\Lambda X.P)(\tau)(\theta) = P(\tau\restriction_\theta)$ for each $\tau \in \mathcal{E}\langle X\rangle^*$, $\theta \in [X \rightharpoonup V]$.

A parametric property is therefore similar to a normal property, but one partitioning parametric traces in $\mathcal{E}\langle X\rangle^*$ into verdict categories in $[[X \rightharpoonup V] \to \mathcal{C}]$, that is, original (as in the non-parametric property) verdict categories indexed by parameter instances. This allows the parametric property to associate an original category for each parameter instance from $[X \rightharpoonup V]$.

Next we define monitors and parametric monitors. Like for parametric properties, which are just properties over parametric traces, parametric monitors are also just monitors, but for parametric events and with instance-indexed states and verdict categories.

Definition 8. *A* ***monitor*** *M is a tuple $(S, \mathcal{E}, \mathcal{C}, \imath, \sigma, \gamma)$, where S is the set of states, $\mathcal{E}$ is the set of input events, $\mathcal{C}$ is the set of verdict categories, $\imath \in S$ is the initial state, $\sigma\colon S \times \mathcal{E} \to S$ is the transition function, and $\gamma\colon S \to \mathcal{C}$ is the verdict function. The transition function is extended to handle traces, i.e., $\sigma\colon S \times \mathcal{E}^* \to S$ where $\sigma(s, \epsilon) = s$ and $\sigma(s, ew) = \sigma(\sigma(s, e), w)$. $M = (S, \mathcal{E}, \mathcal{C}, \imath, \sigma, \gamma)$ is a* ***monitor for property*** *$P\colon \mathcal{E}^* \to \mathcal{C}$ if $\gamma(\sigma(\imath, w)) = P(w)$ for each $w \in \mathcal{E}^*$. Monitor M defines the property $P_M\colon \mathcal{E}^* \to \mathcal{C}$ with $P_M(w) = \gamma(\sigma(\imath, w))$. Monitors M and M' are equivalent iff $P_M = P_{M'}$.*

```
Algorithm MONITOR(M = (S, E, C, ı, σ, γ))
function main(τ)
  Δ ← ⊥; Δ(⊥) ← ı; Θ ← {⊥}
  foreach e⟨θ⟩ in order in τ do
  : foreach θ' ∈ {θ} ⊔ Θ do
  : : Δ(θ') ← σ(Δ(max{θ'' ∈ Θ | θ'' ⊑ θ'}), e)
  : : Γ(θ') ← γ(Δ(θ'))
  : endfor
  : Θ ← {⊥, θ} ⊔ Θ
  endfor
```

Figure 5. Monitoring Algorithm

We next define parametric monitors starting with a base monitor and a set of parameters: the corresponding parametric monitor can be thought of as a set of base monitors running in parallel, one for each parameter instance.

Definition 9. *Given parameters X with corresponding values V and monitor $M = (S, \mathcal{E}, \mathcal{C}, \imath, \sigma, \gamma)$, the* ***parametric monitor*** *$\Lambda X.M$ is the monitor $([[X \rightharpoonup V] \to S], \mathcal{E}\langle X\rangle, [[X \rightharpoonup V] \to \mathcal{C}], \lambda\theta.\imath, \Lambda X.\sigma, \Lambda X.\gamma)$, with*

- $\Lambda X.\sigma\colon [[X \rightharpoonup V] \to S] \times \mathcal{E}\langle X\rangle \to [[X \rightharpoonup V] \to S]$
- $\Lambda X.\gamma\colon [[X \rightharpoonup V] \to S] \to [[X \rightharpoonup V] \to \mathcal{C}]$

defined as

$$(\Lambda X.\sigma)(\delta, e\langle\theta'\rangle)(\theta) = \begin{cases} \sigma(\delta(\theta), e) & \text{if } \theta' \sqsubseteq \theta \\ \delta(\theta) & \text{otherwise} \end{cases}$$

$$(\Lambda X.\gamma)(\delta)(\theta) = \gamma(\delta(\theta))$$

for each $\delta \in [[X \rightharpoonup V] \to S]$ and each $\theta, \theta' \in [X \rightharpoonup V]$.

Therefore, a parametric monitor $\Lambda X.M$ maintains a state $\delta(\theta)$ of M for each parameter instance θ, takes parametric events as input, and outputs categories indexed by parameter instances (one category of M per instance). Intuitively, one can think of a parametric monitor as a collection of *"monitor instances"*. Each monitor instance, which is indexed by a parameter instance, keeps track of the state of one trace slice. The rule for $\Lambda X.\sigma$ can be read as stating that when an event with parameter instance θ' is evaluated, it updates the state for all monitor instances more informative than the instance for θ', and the instance for θ' itself, leaving all other monitor instances untouched. The rule for $\Lambda X.\gamma$ simply states that γ is applied to a state, as normal, but the state is found by looking up the state of the monitor instance for θ. One of the major results in [18] states that if M is a monitor for P, parametric monitor $\Lambda X.M$ is a monitor for the parametric property $\Lambda X.P$.

Figure 5 shows the basic abstract monitoring algorithm for parametric properties from [18]. Given parametric property $\Lambda X.P$ and M a monitor for P, MONITOR(M) yields a monitor that is equivalent to $\Lambda X.M$, that is, a monitor for $\Lambda X.P$. The functions $[[X \rightharpoonup V] \to S]$ and $[[X \rightharpoonup V] \to \mathcal{C}]$ of $\Lambda X.M$ are encoded by MONITOR(M) as tables Δ and Γ with entries indexed by parameter instances in $[X \rightharpoonup V]$ and with contents states in S and verdict categories in $\mathcal{C}$, respectively. Such tables will have finite entries because each event e binds only a finite number of parameters defined by $\mathcal{D}(e)$.

The monitoring algorithm first clears Δ, which contains the monitor state for each parameter instance, then assigns $\imath$, the initial state, to $\Delta(\perp)$. Θ, which contains all known parameter instances, is initialized to contain only the empty partial function $\perp$. For each event $e\langle\theta\rangle$ that arrives during program execution (line 2), MONITOR(M) generates every compatible parameter instance by combining θ with all the previously known compatible parameter instances (line 3). It then updates the state of every one of these compatible parameter instances (θ') with the state, transitioned by event e, of the "monitor instance" corresponding to the "largest" parameter instance less than or equal to θ' (line 4). At the same time we also calculate the verdict category corresponding to that monitor instance and store it in table Γ (line 5). Rather than storing a whole slice as in Definition 6, the knowledge of the slice is encoded in the state of the monitor instance for θ'. After the algorithm completes, Γ contains the verdict category for each possible trace slice. An actual implementation is free to report a verdict category of interest (e.g., match or fail) as soon as it is discovered.

3. Coenable Sets

When monitoring parametric properties, it is easy to generate a large number of monitor instances. For example, as seen in Section 5, the program bloat generates 1.9 million monitor instances when monitored for the UNSAFEITER property. After some time, some of these monitor instances may become unnecessary, e.g., because they have no hope of reaching a verdict category in $\mathcal{G}$. Indeed, as seen in Section 5, the RV garbage collection technique flags 1.8 million of these monitor instances as unnecessary. Chen et al. [19] proposed a formalism-independent method, called "ENABLE sets", to avoid needlessly *creating* monitors that will never trigger. Here we show how a dual method can be derived to avoid needlessly *retaining* monitors that will never trigger. Computing the coenable sets is expected to be a quick static operation in practice, because they are a function of the specification to monitor (which is expected to be small) and not of the program (which is expected to be large).

Definition 10. *Given $w \in \mathcal{E}^*$ and $e, e' \in w$, we let $e \rightsquigarrow_w e'$ denote that e' occurs after e in w. Let $\text{COENABLE}_w(e) = \{e' \mid e \rightsquigarrow_w e'\}$ be the* ***trace coenable set*** *of e. Given property $P\colon \mathcal{E}^* \to \mathcal{C}$ and a subset of verdict categories of interest (or goal) $\mathcal{G} \subseteq \mathcal{C}$, the* ***property coenable set*** *is defined as the map $\text{COENABLE}_{P,\mathcal{G}}\colon \mathcal{E} \to \mathcal{P}(\mathcal{P}(\mathcal{E}))$ where $\text{COENABLE}_{P,\mathcal{G}}(e) = \{\text{COENABLE}_w(e) \mid w \in \mathcal{E}^* \text{ s.t. } P(w) \in \mathcal{G}, e \in w,\ \text{COENABLE}_w(e) \neq \emptyset\}$ for each $e \in \mathcal{E}$.*

Intuitively, if event e is encountered during monitoring, but none of the event sets of $\text{COENABLE}_{P,\mathcal{G}}(e)$ are possible in the future, it is impossible to reach any verdict category in $\mathcal{G}$, so a monitor for P observing e will never trigger. We drop all $\emptyset$s from $\text{COENABLE}_{P,\mathcal{G}}$ because they can cause monitor instances to be retained that are unnecessary. An $\emptyset$ in $\text{COENABLE}_{P,\mathcal{G}}(e)$ means that the trace suffix consisting of only the event e can lead to a category in $\mathcal{G}$ for some trace prefix. However, our interest is in the ability to reach $\mathcal{G}$ again in the future. If there is a trace suffix that can lead to a state in $\mathcal{G}$ from e, then its events will be added to $\text{COENABLE}_{P,\mathcal{G}}(e)$. If there is no trace suffix that can lead back to a state in $\mathcal{G}$, there is no reason to maintain the monitor instance after it has executed the proper handler due to the occurrence of e.

FSM Example We define finite state machines in the spirit of Definition 8. A finite state machine is a tuple $(S, \mathcal{E}, \mathcal{C}, \imath, \sigma, \gamma)$ where $\mathcal{E}$ is a finite alphabet, S is a finite set of states, $\imath \in S$ is the initial state, $\sigma\colon S \times \mathcal{E} \rightharpoonup S$ a partial transition function, $\mathcal{C}$ a set of verdict categories, and $\gamma\colon S \to \mathcal{C}$ the verdict function. The property monitored by an FSM classifies a trace w into $\gamma(\sigma(\imath, w))$, where σ is extended to strings in the natural way, and fail if $\sigma(\imath, w)$ is undefined.

We can find $\text{COENABLE}_{P,\mathcal{G}}$, for the property monitored by an FSM, by the least fixed point of the following equations. Recall that $\mathcal{G} \subseteq \mathcal{C}$ is the set of verdict categories of interest:

$$\text{SEEABLE}(s) = \bigcup_{\sigma(s,e)=s'} \{\{e\} \cup T \mid T \in \text{SEEABLE}(s')\}$$

$$\text{COENABLE}_{P,\mathcal{G}}(e) = \bigcup_{\sigma(s,e)=s'} \text{SEEABLE}(s')$$

We can use the equations above to generate coenable sets for our example from Figure 3, one need simply generate a finite state machine from the property's ERE. For P = UNSAFEITER and $\mathcal{G} = \{\text{match}\}$, the $\text{COENABLE}_{P,\mathcal{G}}$ sets are:

$$\text{COENABLE}_{P,\mathcal{G}}(\text{create}) = \{\{\text{next}, \text{update}\}\}$$

$$\text{COENABLE}_{P,\mathcal{G}}(\text{update}) = \left\{\begin{matrix}\{\text{next}\}, \{\text{next}, \text{update}\}, \\ \{\text{next}, \text{create}, \text{update}\}\end{matrix}\right\}$$

$$\text{COENABLE}_{P,\mathcal{G}}(\text{next}) = \{\{\text{next}, \text{update}\}\}$$

Note that if we did not remove $\emptyset$s, $\text{COENABLE}_{P,\mathcal{G}}(\text{next})$ would contain $\emptyset$. Each inner set can be thought of as a conjunction of events that must occur at least once for a verdict category in $\mathcal{G}$ to still be reachable, while the outer sets are a disjunction (see Section 4.2.2). For example, if the event seen by monitor instance M is update and next can still be seen at some future point, then M is still necessary. Likewise, if the event seen by M is next, then both next *and* update must be possible for M to ever match. In particular, if the corresponding Collection object instance is already dead then we know that the event update will never be possible, so we can safely garbage collect M. Definition 11 formalizes this notion.

CFG Example A CFG is a tuple $(N, \mathcal{E}, \mathtt{S}, \Pi)$ where N is a finite set of nonterminals, $\mathcal{E}$ is a finite set of terminals, $\mathtt{S} \in N$ is the initial nonterminal, and Π is a set of productions of the form $\mathtt{A} \to \beta$ where $\mathtt{A} \in N$ and $\beta \in (N \cup \mathcal{E})^*$. The monitor for a CFG classifies traces that are in the language of the grammar into the verdict category match.

For a CFG, to compute $\text{COENABLE}_{P,\{\text{match}\}}$ we find the least fixed point of the following equations:

$$\mathrm{G}(\epsilon) = \{\emptyset\} \quad \mathrm{G}(e) = \{\{e\}\} \quad \mathrm{G}(\mathtt{A}) = \textstyle\bigcup_{\mathtt{A}\to\beta} \mathrm{G}(\beta)$$

$$\mathrm{G}(\beta_1\beta_2) = \{T_1 \cup T_2 \mid T_1 \in \mathrm{G}(\beta_1), T_2 \in \mathrm{G}(\beta_2)\}$$

$$C(x) = \left\{T_1 \cup T_2 \;\middle|\; \begin{matrix}\mathtt{A} \to \beta_1 x \beta_2, \\ T_1 \in C(\mathtt{A}), T_2 \in \mathrm{G}(\beta_2)\end{matrix}\right\}$$

$$\text{COENABLE}_{P,\{\text{match}\}}(e) = C(e)$$

Informally, $\mathrm{G}(\mathtt{A})$ is the set of events generated by the CFG, if the symbol $\mathtt{A}$ were used as the initial nonterminal of the CFG. The equation $\mathrm{G}(\beta_1\beta_2) = \{T_1 \cup T_2 \mid T_1 \in \mathrm{G}(\beta_1), T_2 \in \mathrm{G}(\beta_2)\}$ generalizes this notion to entire traces of symbols (where symbols are either events or non-terminals). C is the coenable sets function generalized to traces that include both non-terminals and events. For a production, $\mathtt{A} \to \beta_1\mathtt{B}\beta_2$, $C(\mathtt{B})$ needs to cope with the fact that $\mathtt{A}$ has its own coenable sets. Thus its definition unions possible coenable sets of $\mathtt{A}$ with the sets of symbols that are generated by β_2. The rest of RV only needs to know coenable sets for events so coenables is just the restriction of C to events.

Definition 11. *Given property $P\colon \mathcal{E}^* \to \mathcal{C}$, goal $\mathcal{G} \subseteq \mathcal{C}$, set of parameters X and event definition $\mathcal{D}\colon \mathcal{E} \to \mathcal{P}(X)$ (see Definition 4), the* ***property parameter coenable set*** *is defined as the map $\text{COENABLE}^X_{P,\mathcal{G}}\colon \mathcal{E} \to \mathcal{P}(\mathcal{P}(X))$ where $\text{COENABLE}^X_{P,\mathcal{G}}(e) = \{\mathcal{D}(E) \mid E \in \text{COENABLE}_{P,\mathcal{G}}(e)\}$ for each $e \in \mathcal{E}$.*

The $\text{COENABLE}^X_{P,\mathcal{G}}$ sets tell us which parameter objects must be alive for a verdict category in $\mathcal{G}$ to be reachable. For P = UNSAFEITER, $\mathcal{G} = \{\text{match}\}$, and $X = \{c, i\}$, the $\text{COENABLE}^X_{P,\mathcal{G}}$

sets are:

$$\text{COENABLE}^X_{P,\mathcal{G}}(\mathsf{create}) = \{\{c, i\}\}$$
$$\text{COENABLE}^X_{P,\mathcal{G}}(\mathsf{update}) = \{\{i\}, \{c, i\}\}$$
$$\text{COENABLE}^X_{P,\mathcal{G}}(\mathsf{next}) = \{\{c, i\}\}$$

Now with the $\text{COENABLE}^X_{P,\mathcal{G}}$ sets we can explicitly decide when a monitor instance may be collected. For example, in UNSAFEITER we know that if, at *any time*, the `Iterator` bound to i is garbage collected, then a match can never occur because i occurs in every one of the inner sets. This makes sense because the event that causes a match in the UNSAFEITER pattern is use of the `Iterator`. As mentioned in Section 1, this situation could produce a very large memory leak in JavaMOP [17] where long living `Collections` would cause monitor instances for dead `Iterators` to be retained because it could not remove a monitor instance unless all bound parameter objects were collected. We prove this concept by showing that certain parameters specified by $\text{COENABLE}^X_{P,\mathcal{G}}(e)$ for a trace wew' must be able to occur in w' for a verdict category to be reached.

Theorem 1. *Consider the same assumptions as in Definition 11, and a trace slice $wew' \in \mathcal{E}^*$. If for each $Y \in \text{COENABLE}^X_{P,\mathcal{G}}(e)$ there exists some $y \in Y$ such that $y \notin \mathcal{D}(w')$ then $P(wew') \notin \mathcal{G}$.*

Proof. Suppose, for the sake of contradiction, that $P(wew') \in \mathcal{G}$ and that each $Y \in \text{COENABLE}^X_{P,\mathcal{G}}(e)$ contains a y such that $y \notin \mathcal{D}(w')$. By Definition 10, because $P(wew') \in \mathcal{G}$ there must be some $E \in \text{COENABLE}_{P,\mathcal{G}}(e)$ that contains exactly those events in w'. Then, by Definition 11, there must be $Y \in \text{COENABLE}^X_{P,\mathcal{G}}(e)$ containing exactly the parameters in $\mathcal{D}(w')$. Contradiction. □

Discussion The $\text{COENABLE}^X_{P,\mathcal{G}}$ sets are a conservative approximation of the situations in which a monitor instance may be collected. From Definition 6 we know that an event e where $x \in \mathcal{D}(e)$ can only occur in a trace-slice $\tau\restriction_\theta$ if $\theta(x)$ is still alive in the system. If $\theta(x)$ has been garbage collected, there is no way for any e with $x \in \mathcal{D}(e)$ to occur in trace slice for θ. This is precisely how monitoring arrives in the situation presented in Theorem 1, where all possible suffixes w' of the trace slice wew' do not contain at least one parameter in each set of the $\text{COENABLE}^X_{P,\mathcal{G}}(e)$, and it becomes impossible to reach a verdict category in $\mathcal{G}$. Clearly, if it is impossible for the θ trace slice to ever reach a verdict category in $\mathcal{G}$, there is no reason to keep the monitor instance for θ.

The Tracematches system uses a more precise formulation, which is similar, but based on the *state* of the monitor. Intuitively, the Tracematches garbage collection technique can be thought of as coenables sets indexed by state rather than events, but the formulation as presented in [8] is considerably different. While theirs is more precise, our empirical results, presented in Section 5, show that the coenable set technique is able to reduce memory usage in the RV system to comparable levels with Tracematches, while the RV system has considerably lower runtime overhead. More importantly, the Tracematches garbage collection technique is limited to finite logics, such as the regular expressions of Tracematches. However, our coenable approach is extensible to any underlying monitor implementation. We have a coenables sets generation algorithm for the context-free grammar plugin. A static state-based technique, such as the one used by Tracematches, could not be used for context-free properties because the state space is unbounded.

The coenables technique reclaims much more memory than JavaMOP's garbage collection, which, as already explained, has to wait for all bound parameter objects to be collected (see Section 5).

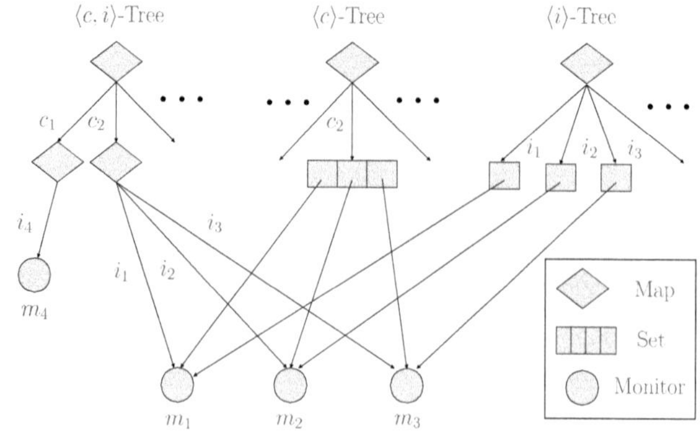

Figure 6. Indexing trees for UNSAFEITER

4. Implementation

The data structures used by previous runtime monitoring systems [4, 17, 20] are not sufficient for efficient garbage collection of monitor instances. The challenge is how to efficiently garbage collect unnecessary monitor instances that are contained in the data structures. Using the standard data structures of previous systems, the overhead of instance removal easily overwhelms the benefit of having fewer instances. Our specialized data structures, introduced here, track the garbage collection of parameter objects and remove unnecessary monitor instances when discovered using coenable sets (Section 3). In this section, we present the modified indexing trees used by RV as well as the mechanism by which unnecessary monitors are garbage collected.

4.1 Indexing Trees

The RV system builds upon the Indexing Tree technique of the JavaMOP system presented in [17]. The indexing trees are an efficient means to represent the tables Δ and Γ from the monitoring algorithm in Figure 5. Locating the correct monitor instances to update for each received event is one of the most important and expensive tasks of a runtime monitoring system that supports formalism-independent parametric properties like JavaMOP and RV. Whenever a parametric event $e\langle\theta\rangle$ is processed, all monitor instances corresponding to parameter instances more informative than θ must be updated. Thus we need a mapping from parameter instances to sets of monitor instances more informative than that instance. Each value in the map is either the next level of the tree or, at the leaves, the appropriate set of monitor instances. Once we have this set we update all the contained monitor instances.

For example, processing $\mathsf{update}\langle c_2\rangle$ for UNSAFEITER (Figure 3) requires that we update the monitor instances that are more informative than $\langle c_2\rangle$. Thus we lookup $\langle c_2\rangle$ in the $\langle c\rangle$-tree of Figure 6 to find the set of monitor instances more informative than $\langle c_2\rangle$ and update each instance. Multiple indexing trees can exist since each event may contain a different subset of parameters; each subset of possible parameters receives its own tree. As an example, for UNSAFEITER we have a $\langle c\rangle$-tree, an $\langle i\rangle$-tree, and a $\langle c, i\rangle$-tree.

4.2 Collecting Unnecessary Monitors

There are two performance benefits to garbage collecting unnecessary monitors: reduced memory usage, and reduction in the time needed to update monitor instances because many of the monitor instances that would be updated are no longer necessary. As an example of the latter, consider UNSAFEITER again. If we have a monitor instance for $\langle c_1, i_1\rangle$ and i_1 is garbage collected, even

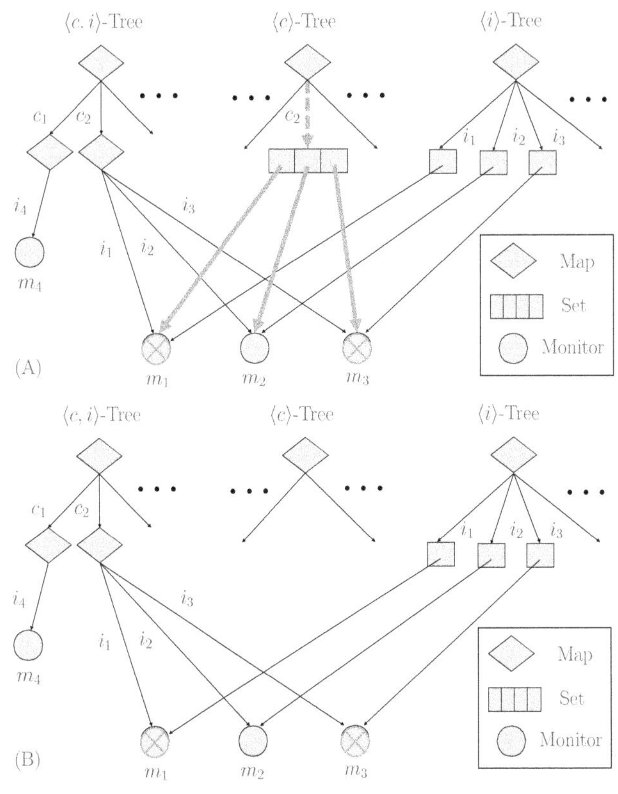

Figure 7. (A) Notifying monitors for garbage collected $\langle c_2 \rangle$ in the $\langle c \rangle$-tree. (B) Cleaning up the broken mapping in the $\langle c \rangle$-tree

though it is impossible to match the UNSAFEITER pattern, all future `update` events are sent to $\langle c_1, i_1 \rangle$. Unfortunately, collecting monitor instances introduces overhead; we must keep this overhead low so that it does not outweigh the benefits of garbage collection.

Eager garbage collection of unnecessary monitors introduces a very large amount of runtime overhead, which almost always overwhelms any benefits. This is because eager collection requires propagating the information regarding liveness of parameter objects to monitor instances far too frequently. Additionally, eager collection can result in removing instances from some data structures that will never be used again.

Therefore, we use a lazy garbage collection scheme. We iterate monitor instances and propagate the information of garbage collections of parameter objects *lazily*, and we remove unnecessary monitors *lazily*. When an indexing tree containing a garbage collected parameter object is accessed and the tree detects this, it informs all the relevant monitor instances contained within itself. Then, the monitor instance decides if it can still possibly reach a verdict category in $\mathcal{G}$ in the absence of the parameter object that has been garbage collected. Later when more space is needed in the data structure or when monitor instances are updated, we remove monitor instances from the accessed data structure but not from other data structures. A monitor instance is garbage collected when it is removed from all data structures. This is similar to mark-and-sweep garbage collection. If a data structure itself is garbage collected, any contained monitor instances never need to be garbage collected separately. The next sections explain this process in detail.

4.2.1 Parameter Object Garbage Collection Notification

Propagation of parameter object garbage collection information starts from the mappings in the indexing tree. The mappings used

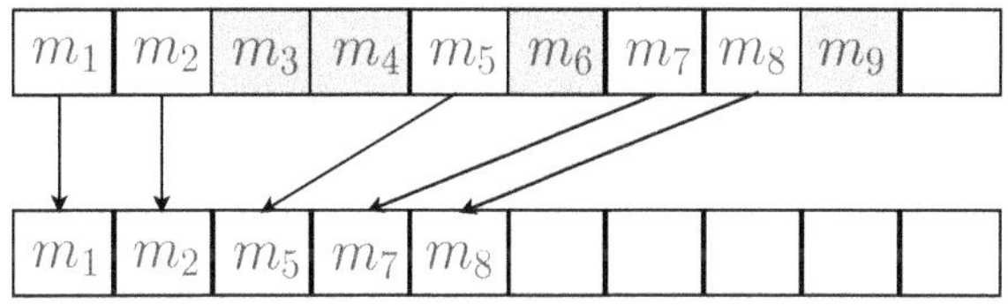

Figure 8. A compaction in `RVSet` when some monitor instances are collectable

in the RV are implemented as a class called `RVMap`. `RVMap` uses `WeakReferences` for its keys. A `WeakReference` in Java does not stop the garbage collector from collecting its referent; when the referent is garbage collected, the `WeakReference` points to `null`. Whenever an operation (`put` or `get`) is performed on an `RVMap`–or the hash table underlying the map needs to be expanded to store more entries–it looks through a subset of its entries for keys with `null` referents. When there is a key with a `null` referent due to a garbage collection, `RVMap` notifies all of the monitor instances below itself in the indexing tree. For example, Figure 7 (A) shows a possible scenario where $\langle c_2 \rangle$ is garbage collected and the $\langle c \rangle$-tree is accessed. The $\langle c \rangle$-tree notifies all of the monitor instances below $\langle c_2 \rangle$.

4.2.2 Determining When Monitor Instances are Unnecessary

When a monitor is notified of a newly garbage collected parameter object, it decides whether it can still reach a verdict category of interest in the absence of garbage collected parameter objects by using the coenable sets introduced in Section 3. Each monitor instance stores the last event it receives, e, so that it may check $\text{COENABLE}^X_{P,\mathcal{G}}(e)$, when this notification takes place. The monitor instance need simply check if all the parameter objects of any set in $\text{COENABLE}^X_{P,\mathcal{G}}(e)$ are alive. RV statically translates $\text{COENABLE}^X_{P,\mathcal{G}}(e)$ to a minimized boolean formula to make this check as efficient as possible:

$$\text{ALIVENESS}(e) = \bigvee_{S \,\in\, \text{COENABLE}^X_{P,\mathcal{G}}(e)} \left(\bigwedge_{x \,\in\, S} live_x \right)$$

where $live_x$ is a boolean that is true only if the parameter object of parameter x has not been garbage collected. Then, $\text{ALIVENESS}(e)$ is true only if the monitor is necessary. Maintaining $live_x$ variables in a given monitor instance for each parameter and checking the generated boolean expression at runtime is sufficient for determining when said instance becomes unnecessary.

Continuing our example from the last section, the monitor instances notified of garbage collected parameters in Figure 7 (A) check their ALIVENESS to determine if they are unnecessary. Here, m_1 and m_3 are unnecessary and therefore marked. Note that the set under $\langle c_2 \rangle$ is not altered because other `RVMaps` in the index tree still point to it. In Figure 7 (B), the `RVMap` removed the broken map entry index by c_2. m_1 and m_3 will be removed at some future time when the $\langle c, i \rangle$-tree or $\langle i \rangle$-tree are accessed or expanded, as we explain in the next section.

5. Evaluation of the RV System

We evaluate our formalism-independent garbage collection for parametric monitoring implemented into RV. Also, we compare the performance of RV to JavaMOP and Tracematches, two of the most optimized monitoring systems in runtime and memory, respectively.

5.1 Experimental Settings

For our experiments, we used a Pentium 4 2.66GHz / 2GB RAM / Ubuntu 9.10 machine and version 9.12 of the DaCapo (DaCapo 9.12)

		HasNext			UnsafeIter			UnsafeMapIter			UnsafeSyncColl			UnsafeSyncMap			All
(A)	Orig (sec)	TM	MOP	RV	TM	MOP	RV	TM	MOP	RV	TM	MOP	RV	TM	MOP	RV	RV
bloat	3.6	2119	448	116	19194	569	251	∞	1203	178	1359	746	212	1942	716	130	982
jython	8.9	13	0	0	11	0	1	150	18	3	11	1	1	10	0	0	4
avrora	13.6	45	54	55	637	311	118	∞	113	42	75	144	80	54	74	16	275
batik	3.5	3	2	3	355	9	8	∞	8	5	208	9	9	5	3	0	28
eclipse	79.0	-2	4	-1	0	-1	-1	5	-3	0	-4	2	1	∞	-1	-1	0
fop	2.0	200	49	48	350	21	13	∞	58	14	∞	78	25	∞	71	19	133
h2	18.7	89	17	13	128	9	4	1350	21	6	868	21	4	83	20	5	23
luindex	2.9	0	0	1	0	0	1	1	4	1	1	1	1	2	0	0	1
lusearch	25.3	-1	1	0	1	2	2	2	2	0	4	0	1	3	1	1	3
pmd	8.3	176	84	59	1423	162	123	∞	571	188	1818	192	76	∞	144	26	620
sunflow	32.7	47	5	3	7	2	0	9	4	1	13	6	5	17	6	6	6
tomcat	13.8	8	1	1	37	1	1	3	1	1	2	0	1	2	1	3	1
tradebeans	45.5	0	-1	1	1	1	2	5	3	-1	-1	1	2	3	1	5	2
tradesoap	94.4	1	3	0	2	1	1	2	0	1	0	0	1	2	2	5	1
xalan	20.3	4	2	2	27	7	2	10	5	2	3	2	3	4	4	3	4
(B)	Orig (MB)	TM	MOP	RV	TM	MOP	RV	TM	MOP	RV	TM	MOP	RV	TM	MOP	RV	RV
bloat	4.9	56.8	19.3	13.2	7.7	146.8	79.0	∞	173.4	56.1	6.8	127.9	48.3	6.9	55.4	12.7	340.9
jython	5.3	5.7	4.6	4.8	4.9	4.6	4.8	6.0	19.5	4.7	5.3	4.5	4.4	5.9	4.8	5.1	4.7
avrora	4.7	4.6	12.4	9.1	4.4	136.2	15.8	∞	14.7	8.5	4.3	28.0	12.6	4.4	13.0	4.9	22.3
batik	79.1	79.2	78.7	79.3	75.2	93.6	86.6	∞	91.2	79.6	78.2	93.2	85.1	79.9	86.9	76.7	104.3
eclipse	95.9	100.8	107.6	97.1	98.3	100.0	110.3	106.9	93.8	101.1	100.4	109.2	90.1	∞	98.6	98.7	98.9
fop	20.7	97.4	47.1	52.5	24.3	24.2	29.4	∞	69.2	28.1	∞	54.8	24.8	∞	55.9	25.2	47.5
h2	265.0	267.8	598.5	565.2	267.2	266.2	262.4	312.4	688.3	268.2	271.4	690.3	265.5	271.0	718.3	270.0	283.7
luindex	6.8	5.6	5.5	5.6	6.3	6.9	6.8	7.4	8.2	6.9	7.4	7.4	7.5	7.1	7.4	11.0	11.8
lusearch	4.6	4.7	4.4	4.8	4.6	4.8	4.2	4.0	4.3	4.8	4.5	4.5	4.6	4.6	4.8	4.7	4.7
pmd	18.0	56.9	59.8	48.5	17.2	146.3	86.4	∞	212.7	93.6	20.3	238.4	84.6	∞	117.1	32.9	420.0
sunflow	4.4	4.5	4.8	4.9	4.8	4.3	4.7	4.7	4.4	4.4	5.1	4.3	4.9	4.5	4.7	4.5	4.6
tomcat	11.6	11.4	12.3	11.4	12.5	11.0	11.5	11.9	11.4	11.0	11.3	11.3	11.3	11.4	11.4	11.8	11.8
tradebeans	63.2	62.9	62.7	62.1	63.7	63.9	64.1	63.3	62.5	62.7	63.2	62.8	62.0	64.0	62.8	64.0	62.5
tradesoap	64.1	61.8	62.3	63.3	63.4	63.1	64.4	64.1	63.5	62.0	60.7	65.0	65.9	65.5	64.5	65.6	64.5
xalan	4.9	4.9	5.0	5.1	4.9	4.9	4.9	4.9	4.5	4.9	5.0	4.8	5.0	5.1	4.9	4.9	5.0

Figure 9. Comparison of Tracematches (TM), JavaMOP (MOP), and RV: (A) average *percent* runtime overhead; (B) total peak memory usage in MB. (convergence within 3%, ∞: not terminated after 1 hour)

benchmark suite [10], the most up-to-date version. We also present the result from the previous version, 2006-10 MR2 of DaCapo (DaCapo 2006-10), but only for the bloat and jython benchmarks. DaCapo 9.12 does not provide the bloat benchmark from the DaCapo 2006-10, which we favor because it generates large overheads when monitoring `Iterator`-based properties. The bloat benchmark with the UnsafeIter specification causes 19194% runtime overhead (i.e., 192 times slower) and uses 7.7MB of heap memory in Tracematches, and causes 569% runtime overhead and uses 147MB in JavaMOP, while the original program uses only 4.9MB. Also, although the DaCapo 9.12 provides jython, Tracematches cannot instrument jython due to an error. Thus, we present the result of jython from the DaCapo 2006-10. The default data input for DaCapo was used and the -converge option to obtain the numbers after convergence within $\pm 3\%$. We also looked into other benchmarks including Java Grande [29] and SPECjvm 2008 [2], and saw little to no overhead even with our `Iterator`-based properties. Instrumentation introduces a different garbage collection behavior in the monitored program, sometimes causing the program to slightly outperform the original program; this accounts for the negative overheads seen in both runtime and memory.

We used the Sun JVM 1.6.0 for the entire evaluation. The AspectJ compiler (ajc) version 1.6.4 is used for weaving the aspects generated by JavaMOP and RV into the target benchmarks. Another AspectJ compiler, abc [7] 1.3.0, is used for weaving Tracematches properties because Tracematches is part of abc and does not work with ajc. For JavaMOP, we used the most recent release version, 2.1.2, from the JavaMOP website [1]. For Tracematches, we used the most recent release version, 1.3.0, from [3], which is included in the abc compiler as an extension. To figure out the reason that some examples do not terminate when using Tracematches, we also used the abc compiler for weaving aspects generated from RV properties. Note that RV is AspectJ compiler independent. RV shows similar overheads and terminates on all examples when using the abc compiler for weaving as when ajc is used. Because the overheads are similar, we do not present the results of using abc to weave RV generated aspects in this paper. However, using abc to weave RV properties confirms that the high overhead and non-termination come from Tracematches itself, not from the abc compiler.

The following properties are used in our experiments. They were borrowed from [13, 14, 19, 28].

- HasNext: Do not use the next element in an Iterator without checking for the existence of it (see Figure 2);
- UnsafeIter: Do not update a Collection when using the Iterator interface to iterate its elements (see Figure 3);
- UnsafeMapIter: Do not update a Map when using the Iterator interface to iterate its values or its keys;
- UnsafeSyncColl: If a Collection is synchronized, then its iterator also should be accessed synchronously;
- UnsafeSyncMap: If a Collection is synchronized, then its iterators on values and keys also should be accessed in a synchronized manner.

All of them are tested on Tracematches, JavaMOP, and RV for comparison. We also monitored all five properties at the same time in RV, which was not possible in other monitoring systems for performance reasons or structural limitations. We have tested several non-`Iterator` based properties: HashSet, SafeEnum, SafeFile, and SafeFileWriter [13, 14, 19, 28]. None of these properties produce overheads above 5% in any of the DaCapo benchmarks, thus their results are not presented in this paper in detail. Complete results for non-`Iterator` based properties, as well

	HasNext				UnsafeIter				UnsafeMapIter				UnsafeSyncColl				UnsafeSyncMap			
	E	M	FM	CM	E	M	FM	CM	E	M	FM	CM	E	M	FM	CM	E	M	FM	CM
bloat	156M	1.9M	1.9M	1.8M	81M	1.9M	1.8M	1.6M	73M	3.6M	44K	3.5M	143M	4.1M	0	3.7M	161M	3.4M	0	3.4M
jython	106	50	47	26	179K	50	38	38	179K	101K	94	101K	156	100	0	83	256	150	0	122
avrora	1.5M	909K	850K	765K	1.4M	909K	860K	808K	1.3M	1.2M	18	1.2M	2.4M	1.8M	0	1.7M	1.5M	909K	0	904K
batik	49K	24K	21K	21K	125K	24K	21K	10K	55K	33K	140	27K	73K	50K	0	34K	50K	26K	0	26K
eclipse	226K	7.6K	5.3K	2.9K	119K	6.6K	5.1K	2.6K	113K	22K	2.2K	7.8K	233K	15K	0	7.5K	241K	18K	0	9.2K
fop	1.0M	184K	74K	151K	709K	7.7K	7.2K	1.8K	499K	177K	67	160K	1.2M	239K	0	217K	1.2M	231K	0	213K
h2	27M	6.5M	6.0M	5.6M	12M	3.7K	3.3K	1.3K	12M	6.6M	9	6.5M	27M	6.5M	0	6.5M	27M	6.5M	0	6.5M
luindex	371	66	40	2	4.4K	65	39	0	378	183	2	59	436	132	0	30	472	125	0	25
lusearch	1.4K	131	196	114	748K	130	210	18	20K	944	338	1.4K	1.7K	262	0	402	1.8K	263	0	158
pmd	8.3M	789K	694K	571K	6.4M	551K	473K	382K	4.3M	1.3M	110K	1.1M	8.8M	1.5M	0	1.3M	8.6M	1.1M	0	999K
sunflow	2.7M	101K	101K	100K	1.3M	2	0	0	1.3M	83K	0	83K	2.7M	101K	0	101K	2.7M	101K	0	101K
tomcat	25	6	0	0	132	4	0	0	68	26	0	0	29	10	0	0	33	12	0	0
tradebeans	11	3	0	0	31	2	0	0	29	13	0	0	13	5	0	0	15	6	0	0
tradesoap	11	3	0	0	31	2	0	0	29	13	0	0	13	5	0	0	15	6	0	0
xalan	11	3	0	0	8.9K	2	0	0	119K	20K	0	20K	13	5	0	0	15	6	0	0

Figure 10. Monitoring statistics: number of events (E), number of created monitors (M), number of flagged monitors (FM), number of collected monitors (CM).

as performance improvements for RV when combined with Clara can be found in [25].

5.1.1 Removing Unnecessary Monitor Instances

Monitor instances are removed lazily because in many cases the maps and sets containing monitor instances flagged for removal may be garbage collected themselves. Eager removal would result in unnecessary work in such cases. For example, in Figure 7 (B), if the $\langle c_2 \rangle$-subtree in the $\langle c, i \rangle$-tree is going to be garbage collected, there is no reason to remove flagged monitor instances from it.

Unnecessary monitor instances are only removed when an indexing tree is accessed. Whenever an `RVMap` looks for keys with `null` referents it also checks the values of mappings which do not have `null` referents. The value can be either a monitor instance, a set, or a lower level map. If the value is a flagged monitor instance or an empty data structure, it removes the mapping. If it is a set, it must be checked for internal monitor instances that have been flagged for removal. When a set is checked for unnecessary monitor instances, all of the instances are collected, and the remaining necessary monitor instances are compacted in one pass, as can be seen in Figure 8.

5.2 Results and Discussions

Figures 9 and 10 summarize the results of the evaluation. Note that the structure of the DaCapo 9.12 allows us to instrument all of the benchmarks plus all supplementary libraries that the benchmarks use, which was not possible for DaCapo 2006-10. Therefore, fop and pmd show higher overheads than the benchmarks using DaCapo 2006-10 from [19]. While other benchmarks show overheads less than 80% in JavaMOP, bloat, avrora, and pmd show prohibitive overhead in both runtime and memory performance. This is because they generate many iterators and all properties in this evaluation are intended to monitor iterators. For example, bloat creates 1,625,770 collections and 941,466 iterators in total while 19,605 iterators coexist at the same time at peak, in an execution. avrora and pmd also create many collections and iterators. Also, they call hasNext() 78,451,585 times, 1,158,152 times and 4,670,555 times and next() 77,666,243 times, 352,697 times and 3,607,164 times, respectively. Therefore, we mainly discuss those three examples in this section, although RV shows improvements for other examples as well.

Figure 9 (A) shows the percent runtime overhead of Tracematches, JavaMOP, and RV. Overall, RV averages two times less runtime overhead than JavaMOP and orders of magnitude less runtime overhead than Tracematches (recall that these are the most optimized runtime verification systems). With bloat, RV shows less than 260% runtime overhead for each property, while JavaMOP always shows over 440% runtime overhead and Tracematches always shows over 1350% for completed runs and *crashed* for UnsafeMapIter. With avrora, on average, RV shows 62% runtime overhead, while JavaMOP shows 139% runtime overhead and Tracematches shows 203% and hangs for UnsafeMapIter. With pmd, on average, RV shows 94% runtime overhead, while JavaMOP shows 231% runtime overhead and Tracematches shows 1139% and hangs for UnsafeMapIter and UnsafeSyncMap.

Also, RV was tested with all five properties together and showed 982%, 275%, and 620% overhead, respectively, which are still faster or comparable to monitoring one of many properties alone in JavaMOP or Tracematches. The overhead for monitoring all the properties simultaneously can be slightly larger than the sum of their individual overheads since the additional memory pressure makes the JVM's garbage collection behave differently.

Figure 9 (B) shows the peak memory usage of the three systems. RV has lower peak memory usage than JavaMOP in most cases. The cases where RV does not show lower peak memory usage are within the limits of expected memory jitter. However, memory usage of RV is still higher than the memory usage of Tracematches in some cases. Tracematches has several finite automata specific memory optimizations [8], which cannot be implemented in a formalism-independent system like RV. Although Tracematches is sometimes more memory efficient, it shows prohibitive runtime overhead monitoring bloat and pmd. There is a trade-off between memory usage and runtime overhead. If RV more actively removes terminated monitors, memory usage will be lower, at the cost of runtime performance. Overall, our monitor termination optimization achieves the most efficient parametric monitoring system with reasonable memory performance.

Figure 10 shows the number of triggered events, of created monitors, of monitors flagged as unnecessary by the coenable set technique, and of monitors collected by the JVM. Among the DaCapo examples, bloat, avrora, h2, pmd and sunflow generated a very large number of events (more than a million) in all properties, resulting in millions of monitors created in most cases. h2 does not exhibit large overhead because monitor instances in h2 have shorter lifetimes, therefore the created monitor instances are not used heavily like in bloat. sunflow has millions of events but does not create as many monitor instances as as other benchmarks. When monitoring the HasNext and UnsafeIter properties, the coenable sets technique effectively flagged monitors as unnecessary and most were collected by the JVM.

6. Conclusion

We presented an effective novel garbage collection technique for monitoring parametric properties. Previous techniques were either completely agnostic to the property to monitor, thus incurring prohibitive runtime overheads due to memory leaks, or were intrinsically dependent on particular specification formalisms, thus being hard or impossible to use in other contexts. Our technique is the first which is both formalism-generic and efficient. As extensive evaluation shows, it is in fact significantly more efficient than the existing techniques, both formalism-generic and formalism-specific.

Our results have at least two implications. On the one hand, they show that runtime monitoring of complex specifications can be used not only for testing, but also as an integral part of the deployed system in many cases. Indeed, in most practical cases the runtime overhead is negligible, so a well-designed recovery schema implemented by means of specification handlers can ensure highly dependable systems by simply not letting them go wrong at runtime. Note that the combinations program/property selected for evaluation in this paper were specifically chosen to be bad. On the other hand, our results set a solid ground for further optimizations. For example, static analyses of the program to monitor, like those in [14, 15, 21, 27], can be used to remove unnecessary instrumentation and thus not even generate many of the monitors. Similarly, staged/decentralized indexing techniques, like those in [6, 8, 17], can reduce the distance between events and their monitors and thus reduce the overhead taken to dispatch events to monitors.

References

[1] JavaMOP. http://javamop.com.

[2] SPECjvm 2008. http://www.spec.org/jvm2008/.

[3] Tracematches Benchmarks. http://abc.comlab.ox.ac.uk/tmahead.

[4] C. Allan, P. Avgustinov, A. S. Christensen, L. J. Hendren, S. Kuzins, O. Lhoták, O. de Moor, D. Sereni, G. Sittampalam, and J. Tibble. Adding trace matching with free variables to AspectJ. In *Object-Oriented Programming, Systems, Languages and Applications (OOPSLA'05)*, pages 345–364. ACM, 2005.

[5] M. Arnold, M. Vechev, and E. Yahav. Qvm: an efficient runtime for detecting defects in deployed systems. In *Object-Oriented Programming Systems, Languages, and Applications (OOPSLA'08)*, pages 143–162. ACM, 2008.

[6] P. Avgustinov and C. Church. *Trace Monitoring with Free Variables*. PhD thesis, Oxford University, 2009.

[7] P. Avgustinov, A. S. Christensen, L. Hendren, S. Kuzins, J. Lhotak, O. Lhotak, O. de Moor, D. Sereni, G. Sittampalam, and J. Tibble. ABC: an extensible AspectJ compiler. In *Aspect-Oriented Software Development (AOSD'05)*, pages 87–98. ACM, 2005.

[8] P. Avgustinov, J. Tibble, and O. de Moor. Making trace monitors feasible. In *Object Oriented Programming, Systems, Languages and Applications (OOPSLA'07)*, pages 589–608. ACM, 2007.

[9] H. Barringer, D. Rydeheard, and K. Havelund. Rule systems for runtime monitoring: from EAGLE to RULER. *J. Logic Computation*, November 2008.

[10] S. M. Blackburn, R. Garner, C. Hoffman, A. M. Khan, K. S. McKinley, R. Bentzur, A. Diwan, D. Feinberg, D. Frampton, S. Z. Guyer, M. Hirzel, A. Hosking, M. Jump, H. Lee, J. E. B. Moss, A. Phansalkar, D. Stefanović, T. VanDrunen, D. von Dincklage, and B. Wiedermann. The DaCapo benchmarks: Java benchmarking development and analysis. In *Object-Oriented Programming, Systems, Languages and Applications (OOPSLA'06)*, pages 169–190. ACM, 2006.

[11] E. Bodden. J-LO, a tool for runtime-checking temporal assertions. Master's thesis, RWTH Aachen University, 2005.

[12] E. Bodden and V. Stolz. Tracechecks: Defining semantic interfaces with temporal logic. In *Software Composition*, pages 147–162, 2006.

[13] E. Bodden, L. Hendren, and O. Lhoták. A staged static program analysis to improve the performance of runtime monitoring. In *European Conference on Object Oriented Programming (ECOOP'07)*, volume 4609 of *LNCS*, pages 525–549. Springer, 2007.

[14] E. Bodden, F. Chen, and G. Roşu. Dependent advice: A general approach to optimizing history-based aspects. In *Aspect-Oriented Software Development (AOSD'09)*, pages 3–14. ACM, 2009.

[15] E. Bodden, P. Lam, and L. Hendren. Clara: A framework for partially evaluating finite-state runtime monitors ahead of time. In *Runtime Verification (RV'10)*, volume 6418 of *LNCS*, pages 183–197. Springer, 2010.

[16] F. Chen and G. Roşu. Java-MOP: A monitoring oriented programming environment for Java. In *Tools and Algorithms for the Construction and Analysis of Systems (TACAS'05)*, volume 3440 of *LNCS*, pages 546–550. Springer, 2005.

[17] F. Chen and G. Roşu. MOP: An efficient and generic runtime verification framework. In *Object-Oriented Programming, Systems, Languages and Applications (OOPSLA'07)*, pages 569–588. ACM, 2007.

[18] F. Chen and G. Roşu. Parametric trace slicing and monitoring. In *Tools and Algorithms for the Construction and Analysis of Systems (TACAS'09)*, volume 5505 of *LNCS*, pages 246–261. Springer, 2009.

[19] F. Chen, P. Meredith, D. Jin, and G. Roşu. Efficient formalism-independent monitoring of parametric properties. In *Automated Software Engineering (ASE'09)*, pages 383–394. IEEE, 2009.

[20] M. d'Amorim and K. Havelund. Event-based runtime verification of Java programs. *ACM SIGSOFT Software Engineering Notes*, 30(4): 1–7, 2005.

[21] M. Dwyer, R. Purandare, and S. Person. Runtime verification in context: Can optimizing error detection improve fault diagnosis. In *Runtime Verification (RV'10)*, volume 6418 of *LNCS*, pages 36–50. Springer, 2010.

[22] U. Erlingsson and F. B. Schneider. Irm enforcement of java stack inspection. In *Symposium on Security and Privacy (SP'00)*, pages 246–. IEEE, 2000.

[23] S. Goldsmith, R. O'Callahan, and A. Aiken. Relational queries over program traces. In *Object-Oriented Programming, Systems, Languages and Applications (OOPSLA'05)*, pages 385–402. ACM, 2005.

[24] K. W. Hamlen and M. Jones. Aspect-oriented in-lined reference monitors. In *Programming languages and analysis for security (PLAS'08)*, pages 11–20. ACM, 2008.

[25] D. Jin, P. O. Meredith, D. Griffith, and G. Roşu. Garbage collection for monitoring parametric properties. Technical Report `http://hdl.handle.net/2142/18751`, Department of Computer Science, University of Illinois at Urbana-Champaign, 2011.

[26] G. Kiczales, E. Hilsdale, J. Hugunin, M. Kersten, J. Palm, and W. G. Griswold. An overview of AspectJ. In *European Conference on Object Oriented Programming (ECOOP'01)*, volume 2072 of *LNCS*, pages 327–353. Springer, 2001.

[27] M. Martin, V. B. Livshits, and M. S. Lam. Finding application errors and security flaws using PQL: a program query language. In *Object Oriented Programming, Systems, Languages and Applications (OOPSLA'07)*, pages 365–383. ACM, 2005.

[28] P. Meredith, D. Jin, F. Chen, and G. Roşu. Efficient monitoring of parametric context-free patterns. *J. Automated Software Engineering*, 17(2):149–180, June 2010.

[29] L. A. Smith, J. M. Bull, and J. Obdrzálek. A parallel java grande benchmark suite. In *Supercomputing (SC'01)*, pages 8–8. ACM, 2001.

[30] V. Stolz and E. Bodden. Temporal Assertions using AspectJ. In *Runtime Verification (RV'05)*, volume 144 of *ENTCS*, pages 109–124. Elsevier, 2005.

[31] R. E. Strom and S. Yemeni. Typestate: A programming language concept for enhancing software reliability. *IEEE Transactions on Software Engineering*, 12:157–171, January 1986.

LL(*): The Foundation of the ANTLR Parser Generator

Terence Parr
University of San Francisco
parrt@cs.usfca.edu

Kathleen Fisher *
Tufts University
kfisher@eecs.tufts.edu

Abstract

Despite the power of Parser Expression Grammars (PEGs) and GLR, parsing is not a solved problem. Adding nondeterminism (parser speculation) to traditional LL and LR parsers can lead to unexpected parse-time behavior and introduces practical issues with error handling, single-step debugging, and side-effecting embedded grammar actions. This paper introduces the *LL(*)* parsing strategy and an associated grammar analysis algorithm that constructs *LL(*)* parsing decisions from ANTLR grammars. At parse-time, decisions gracefully throttle up from conventional fixed $k \geq 1$ lookahead to arbitrary lookahead and, finally, fail over to backtracking depending on the complexity of the parsing decision and the input symbols. *LL(*)* parsing strength reaches into the context-sensitive languages, in some cases beyond what GLR and PEGs can express. By statically removing as much speculation as possible, *LL(*)* provides the expressivity of PEGs while retaining LL's good error handling and unrestricted grammar actions. Widespread use of ANTLR (over 70,000 downloads/year) shows that it is effective for a wide variety of applications.

Categories and Subject Descriptors F.4.2 Grammars and Other Rewriting Systems [*Parsing*]; D.3.1 Formal Languages [*syntax*]; D.3.4 Processors [*Parsing*]

General Terms Algorithms, Languages, Theory

Keywords nondeterministic parsing, backtracking, context-sensitive parsing, semantic predicates, syntactic predicates, deterministic finite automata, augmented transition networks, subset construction, memoization, PEG, GLR

1. Introduction

Parsing is not a solved problem, despite its importance and long history of academic study. Because it is tedious and error-prone to write parsers by hand, researchers have spent decades studying how to generate efficient parsers from high-level grammars. Despite this effort, parser generators still suffer from problems of expressiveness and usability.

When parsing theory was originally developed, machine resources were scarce, and so parser efficiency was the paramount concern. In that era, it made sense to force programmers to contort their grammars to fit the constraints of $LALR(1)$ or $LL(1)$ parser generators. In contrast, modern computers are so fast that programmer efficiency is now more important. In response to this development, researchers have developed more powerful, but more costly, nondeterministic parsing strategies following both the "bottom-up" approach (LR-style parsing) and the "top-down" approach (LL-style parsing).

In the "bottom-up" world, *Generalized LR* (GLR) [19] parsers parse in linear to cubic time, depending on how closely the grammar conforms to classic LR. GLR essentially "forks" new subparsers to pursue all possible actions emanating from nondeterministic LR states, terminating any subparsers that lead to invalid parses. The result is a parse forest with all possible interpretations of the input. *Elkhound* [12] is a very efficient GLR implementation that achieves *yacc*-like parsing speeds when grammars are $LALR(1)$. Programmers unfamiliar with $LALR$ parsing theory, though, can easily get nonlinear GLR parsers. Since GLR parser generators do not issue LR conflict warnings, programmers can unwittingly specify non-$LALR$ grammars that lead to parsers with poor performance.

In the "top-down" world, Ford introduced *Packrat* parsers and the associated *Parser Expression Grammars* (PEGs) [6, 7]. PEGs preclude only the use of left-recursive grammar rules. Packrat parsers are backtracking parsers that attempt the alternative productions in the order specified. The first production that matches at an input position wins. Packrat parsers are linear rather than exponential because they memoize partial results, ensuring input states will never be parsed by the same production more than once. The *Rats!* [8] PEG-based tool vigorously optimizes away memoization events to improve speed and reduce the memory footprint.

A significant advantage of both GLR and PEG parser generators is that they accept any grammar that conforms to their meta-language (with the exception that PEGs cannot be left-recursive). Programmers no longer have to wade through reams of conflict messages. Despite this advantage, neither GLR nor PEG parsers are completely satisfactory, for a number of reasons.

First, GLR and PEG parsers do not always do what was intended. GLR silently accepts *ambiguous grammars*, those that match the same input in multiple ways, forcing programmers to detect ambiguities dynamically. PEGs have no concept of a grammar conflict because they always choose the "first" interpretation, which can lead to unexpected or inconvenient behavior. For example, the second production of PEG rule $A \rightarrow a|ab$ (meaning "A matches either a or ab") will never be used. Input ab never matches the second alternative since the first symbol, a, matches the first alternative. In a large grammar, such hazards are not always obvious and even experienced developers can miss them without exhaustive testing.

Second, debugging nondeterministic parsers can be very difficult. With bottom-up parsing, the state usually represents multiple locations within the grammar, making it difficult for programmers to predict what will happen next. Top-down parsers are easier to understand because there is

* Author worked at AT&T Labs Research when work was done.

PLDI'11, June 4–8, 2011, San Jose, California, USA.

a one-to-one mapping from *LL* grammar elements to parser operations. Further, recursive-descent *LL* implementations allow programmers to use standard source-level debuggers to step through parsers and embedded actions, facilitating understanding. In contrast, there is no easy-to-read counterpart for the state machines derived from *LR* grammars. This advantage is weakened significantly, however, for backtracking recursive-descent packrat parsers. Nested backtracking is very difficult to follow!

Third, generating high-quality error messages in nondeterministic parsers is difficult but very important to commercial developers. GLR parsers pursue all possible paths emanating from *LR* states with conflicts. If no parse attempt succeeds, the parser has to figure out or guess the parse intended by the user to emit a meaningful message. (One way is to pick the failed parse that shifted the most tokens.) Packrat parsers have the same issue since they are always speculating. In fact, they cannot recover from syntax errors because they cannot detect errors until they have seen the entire input. Reducing uncertainty during the parse is the key to recovering well from erroneous input. Deterministic *LL* and *LR* parsers handle erroneous input much better than packrat and GLR parsers.

Finally, nondeterministic parsing strategies cannot easily support arbitrary, embedded grammar actions, which are useful for manipulating symbol tables, constructing data structures, *etc.* Speculating parsers cannot execute side-effecting actions like print statements, since the speculated action may never really take place. Even side-effect free actions such as those that compute rule return values can be awkward in GLR parsers [12]. For example, since the parser can match the same rule in multiple ways, it might have to execute multiple competing actions. (Should it merge all results somehow or just pick one?) GLR and PEG tools address this issue by either disallowing actions, disallowing arbitrary actions, or relying on the programmer to avoid side-effects in actions that could be executed speculatively.

1.1 ANTLR

This paper describes version 3.3 of the ANTLR parser generator and its underlying top-down parsing strategy, called *LL(*)*, that address these deficiencies. The input to ANTLR is a context-free grammar augmented with *syntactic* [17] and *semantic* predicates and embedded actions. Syntactic predicates allow arbitrary lookahead, while semantic predicates allow the state constructed up to the point of a predicate to direct the parse. Syntactic predicates are given as a grammar fragment that must match the following input. Semantic predicates are given as arbitrary Boolean-valued code in the host language of the parser. Actions are written in the host-language of the parser and have access to the current state. As with PEGs, ANTLR requires programmers to avoid left-recursive grammar rules.

The contributions of this paper are 1) the top-down parsing strategy *LL(*)* and 2) the associated static grammar analysis algorithm that constructs *LL(*)* parsing decisions from ANTLR grammars. The key idea behind *LL(*)* parsers is to use regular-expressions rather than a fixed constant or backtracking with a full parser to do lookahead. The analysis tries to construct a deterministic finite automaton (DFA) *for each nonterminal in the grammar* to distinguish between alternative productions. If the analysis cannot find a suitable DFA for a nonterminal, it fails over to backtracking. As a result, *LL(*)* parsers gracefully throttle up from conventional fixed $k \geq 1$ lookahead to arbitrary lookahead and, finally, fail over to backtracking depending on the complexity of the parsing decision. Even within the same parsing decision, the parser decides on a strategy dynamically according to the input sequence. Just because a decision *might* have to scan arbitrarily far ahead or backtrack does not mean that it *will* at parse-time for every input sequence. In practice, *LL(*)* parsers only look one or two tokens ahead on average despite needing to backtrack occasionally (Section 6). *LL(*)* parsers are *LL* parsers with supercharged decision engines.

This design gives ANTLR the advantages of deterministic top-down parsing without the downsides of frequent speculation. In particular, ANTLR accepts all but left-recursive context-free grammars so, as with PEG parsing, programmers do not have to spend a lot of time contorting their grammars to fit the parsing strategy. The lack of left recursion is a disadvantage, though, because some very common constructs, such as arithmetic expressions, are awkward without left recursion.

The next major release of ANTLR will allow rules with immediate left-recursion (self-referential rules) while still supporting the usual tree construction operators and arbitrary actions. Following a technique similar to Hansen [9], our prototype replaces left-recursion with a predicated loop that compares the precedence of the previous and the next operator. For example, here is an expression rule that is *LR* but not *LL* because of the left recursion:

```
e : e '*' e
  | e '+' e
  | INT
  ;
```

Supporting such a grammar is a matter of identifying the operators and rewriting it to the equivalent predicated *LL(*)* grammar:

```
e : e_[0] ;
e_[int p] // pass in precedence of operator(s) to match
  : INT
    ( {p <= 2}? '*' e_[3]
    | {p <= 1}? '+' e_[2]
    )*
  ;
```

The mechanism is sufficiently general to support suffix, prefix, binary, and ternary operators. Operator precedence follows the order of the alternatives, highest to lowest.

Unlike GLR or PEGs, ANTLR can statically identify some grammar ambiguities and dead productions. ANTLR generates top-down, recursive-descent, mostly non-speculating parsers, which means it supports source-level debugging, produces high-quality error messages, and allows programmers to embed arbitrary actions. A survey of 89 ANTLR grammars [1] available from `sourceforge.net` and `code.google.com` reveals that 75% of them had embedded actions, counting conservatively, which reveals that such actions are a useful feature in the ANTLR community.

Widespread use shows that *LL(*)* fits within the programmer comfort zone and is effective for a wide variety of language applications. ANTLR 3.x has been downloaded 41,364 (binary jar file) + 62,086 (integrated into ANTLRworks) + 31,126 (source code) = 134,576 times according to Google Analytics (unique downloads January 9, 2008 - October 28, 2010). Projects using ANTLR include Google App Engine (Python), IBM Tivoli Identity Manager, BEA/Oracle WebLogic, Yahoo! Query Language, Apple XCode IDE, Apple Keynote, Oracle SQL Developer IDE, Sun/Oracle JavaFX language, and NetBeans IDE.

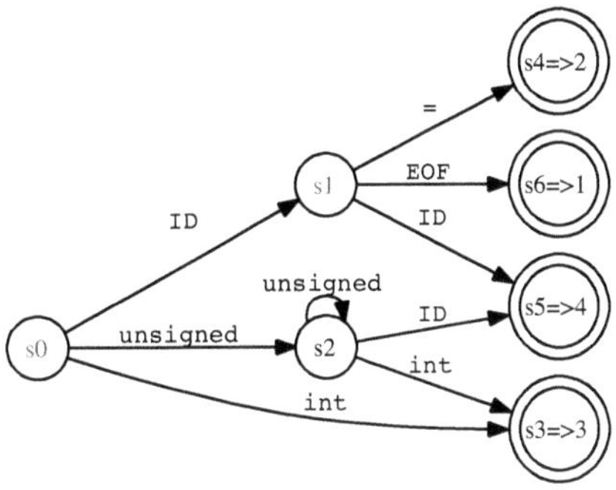

Figure 1. *LL(*)* lookahead DFA for rule `s`. Notation `sn =>` i means "predict the ith alternative."

This paper is organized as follows. We first introduce ANTLR grammars by example (Section 2). Next we formally define *predicated grammars* and a special subclass called *predicated* LL-*regular* grammars (Section 3). We then describe *LL(*)* parsers (Section 4), which implement parsing decisions for predicated *LL*-regular grammars. Next, we give an algorithm that builds lookahead DFA from ANTLR grammars (Section 5). Finally, we support our claims regarding *LL(*)* efficiency and reduced speculation (Section 6).

2. Introduction to *LL(*)*

In this section, we give an intuition for *LL(*)* parsing by explaining how it works for two ANTLR grammar fragments constructed to illustrate the algorithm. Consider nonterminal `s`, which uses the (omitted) nonterminal `expr` to match arithmetic expressions.

```
s : ID
  | ID '=' expr
  | 'unsigned'* 'int' ID
  | 'unsigned'* ID ID
  ;
```

Nonterminal `s` matches an identifier (`ID`), an `ID` followed by an equal sign and then an expression, zero or more occurrences of the literal `unsigned` followed by the literal `int` followed by an `ID`, or zero or more occurrences of `unsigned` followed by two `ID`s. ANTLR grammars use *yacc*-like syntax with extended BNF (EBNF) operators such as Kleene star (`*`) and token literals in single quotes.

When applied to this grammar fragment, ANTLR's grammar analysis yields the *LL(*)* lookahead DFA in Figure 1. At the decision point for `s`, ANTLR runs this DFA on the input until it reaches an accepting state, where it selects the alternative for `s` predicted by the accepting state.

Even though we need arbitrary lookahead to distinguish between the 3rd and 4th alternatives, the lookahead DFA uses the minimum lookahead *per input sequence*. Upon `int` from input `int x`, the DFA immediately predicts the third alternative ($k = 1$). Upon `T` (an `ID`) from `T x`, the DFA needs to see the $k = 2$ token to distinguish alternatives 1, 2, and 4. It is only upon `unsigned` that the DFA needs to scan arbitrarily ahead, looking for a symbol (`int` or `ID`) that distinguishes between alternatives 3 and 4.

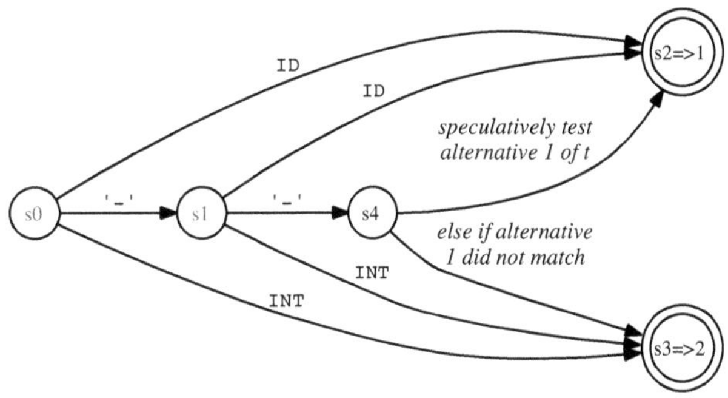

Figure 2. *LL(*)* parsing decision DFA for rule `t` using mixed $k \leq 3$ lookahead and backtracking

The lookahead language for `s` is regular, so we can match it with a DFA. With recursive rules, however, we usually find that the lookahead language is context-free rather than regular. In this case, ANTLR fails over to backtracking if the programmer has requested this feature by adding syntactic predicates. As a convenience, option `backtrack=true` automatically inserts syntactic predicates into every production, which we call *"PEG mode"* because it mimics the behavior of PEG parsers. However, before resorting to backtracking, ANTLR's analysis algorithm builds a DFA that adds a few extra states that allow it avoid backtracking for many input cases. In the following rule `t`, both alternatives can start with an arbitrary number of `-` negation symbols; the second alternative does so using recursive rule `expr`.

```
options {backtrack=true;} // auto-insert syntactic preds
t   : '-'* ID | expr ';' ;
expr: INT     | '-' expr ;
```

Figure 2 shows the lookahead DFA that ANTLR constructs for this input. For clarity, syntactic predicate edges are written in English. This DFA can immediately choose the appropriate alternative upon either input `x` or `1;` by looking at just the first symbol. Upon `-` symbols, the DFA matches a few `-` before failing over to backtracking. The number of times ANTLR unwinds the recursive rule before backtracking is controlled by an internal constant m, which we set to 1 for this example. Despite the possibility of backtracking, the decision will not backtrack in practice unless the input starts with "`--`", an unlikely expression prefix.

LL parsers need more lookahead in general than *LR* parsers do because *LL* parsers must predict which production will succeed whereas *LR* parsers make decisions after examining entire productions. For example, both grammars shown so far are $LR(1)$ but not $LL(k)$ for any fixed k, demonstrating that *LL(*)*'s arbitrary lookahead significantly increases *LL*'s recognition strength. In fact, there is no strict ordering between *LR(k)* and *LL(*)*. Nonterminal `a` in the following grammar is *LL(*)* but not *LR(k)* for any k.

```
a : b A+ X             // token vocabulary = {A, X, Y}
  | c A+ Y
  ;
b : ;
c : ;
```

The LPG (2.0.20) *LALR(k)* parser generator [3] demonstrates this by reporting a conflict even at $k = 10000$:

```
t.g:8:1:8:1:51:51: Warning: Grammar is not LALR(10000) -
it contains 1 reduce/reduce conflicts.
```

Lookahead depth $k = 100000$ exposes the exponential space requirements, forcing LPG to core dump after 1.2 minutes on the OS X box used in Section 6. In contrast, ANTLR quickly creates the following cyclic DFA that distinguishes between a's productions. (0.7 seconds to analyze and generate the *LL(*)* parser and DFA.)

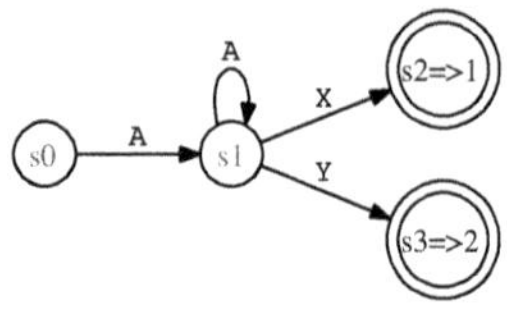

3. Predicated Grammars

To describe *LL(*)* parsing precisely, we need to first formally define the predicated grammars from which they are derived. A predicated grammar $G = (N, T, P, S, \Pi, \mathcal{M})$ has elements:

- N is the set of nonterminals (rule names)
- T is the set of terminals (tokens)
- P is the set of productions
- $S \in N$ is the start symbol
- Π is a set of side-effect-free semantic predicates
- $\mathcal{M}$ is a set of actions (mutators)

Predicated grammars are written using the notation shown in Figure 3. Productions are numbered to express precedence as a means to resolve ambiguities. The first production form represents a standard context-free grammar rule. The second denotes a production gated by a *syntactic predicate*: symbol A expands to α_i only if the current input also matches the syntax described by A'_i. Syntactic predicates enable arbitrary, programmer-specified, context-free lookahead. The third form denotes a production gated by a *semantic predicate*: symbol A expands to α_i only if the predicate π_i holds for the state constructed so far. The final form denotes an action: applying such a rule updates the state according to mutator μ_i.

The derivation rules in Figure 4 define the meaning of a predicated grammar. To support semantic predicates and mutators, the rules reference state $\mathbb{S}$, which abstracts user state during parsing. To support syntactic predicates, the rules reference w_r, which denotes the input remaining to be matched. The judgment form $(\mathbb{S}, \alpha) \overset{\lambda}{\Rightarrow} (\mathbb{S}', \beta)$, may be read: "In machine state $\mathbb{S}$, grammar sequence α reduces in one step to modified state $\mathbb{S}'$ and grammar sequence β while emitting trace λ." The judgment $(\mathbb{S}, \alpha) \overset{\vec{\lambda}}{\Longrightarrow}{}^*(\mathbb{S}', \beta)$ denotes repeated applications of the one-step reduction rule, accumulating all actions in the process. We omit λ when it is irrelevant to the discussion. These reduction rules specify a leftmost derivation. A production with a semantic predicate π_i can fire only if π_i is true of the current state $\mathbb{S}$. A production with syntactic predicate A'_i can fire only if the string derived from A'_i in the current state is a prefix of the remaining input, written $w \preceq w_r$. Actions that occur during the attempt to parse A'_i are executed *speculatively*. They are undone whether or not A'_i matches. Finally, an action production uses the specified mutator μ_i to update the state.

Formally, the language generated by grammar sequence α is $L(\mathbb{S}, \alpha) = \{w \mid (\mathbb{S}, \alpha) \Rightarrow^* (\mathbb{S}', w)\}$ and the language of

$A \in N$	Nonterminal
$a \in T$	Terminal
$X \in (N \cup T)$	Grammar symbol
$\alpha, \beta, \delta \in X^*$	Sequence of grammar symbols
$u, x, y, w \in T^*$	Sequence of terminals
$w_r \in T^*$	Remaining input terminals
ϵ	Empty string
$\pi \in \Pi$	Predicate in host language
$\mu \in \mathcal{M}$	Action in host language
$\lambda \in (N \cup \Pi \cup \mathcal{M})$	Reduction label
$\vec{\lambda} = \lambda_1..\lambda_n$	Sequence of reduction labels
Production Rules:	
$A \to \alpha_i$	i^{th} context-free production of A
$A \to (A'_i)\texttt{=>}\ \alpha_i$	i^{th} production predicated on syntax A'_i
$A \to \{\pi_i\}?\ \alpha_i$	i^{th} production predicated on semantics
$A \to \{\mu_i\}$	i^{th} production with mutator

Figure 3. Predicated Grammar Notation

$$\textit{Prod}\ \frac{A \to \alpha}{(\mathbb{S}, uA\delta) \Rightarrow (\mathbb{S}, u\alpha\delta)} \qquad \textit{Action}\ \frac{A \to \{\mu\}}{(\mathbb{S}, uA\delta) \overset{\mu}{\Rightarrow} (\mu(\mathbb{S}), u\delta)}$$

$$\textit{Sem}\ \frac{\begin{array}{c}\pi_i(\mathbb{S}) \\ A \to \{\pi_i\}?\,\alpha_i\end{array}}{(\mathbb{S}, uA\delta) \overset{\pi_i}{\Longrightarrow} (\mathbb{S}, u\alpha_i\delta)} \qquad \textit{Syn}\ \frac{\begin{array}{c}(\mathbb{S}, A'_i) \Rightarrow^* (\mathbb{S}', w) \\ w \preceq w_r \\ A \to (A'_i)\texttt{=>}\alpha_i\end{array}}{(\mathbb{S}, uA\delta) \overset{A'_i}{\Longrightarrow} (\mathbb{S}, u\alpha_i\delta)}$$

$$\textit{Closure}\ \frac{(\mathbb{S}, \alpha) \overset{\lambda}{\Longrightarrow} (\mathbb{S}, \alpha'),\ (\mathbb{S}, \alpha') \overset{\vec{\lambda}}{\Longrightarrow}{}^*(\mathbb{S}, \beta)}{(\mathbb{S}, \alpha) \overset{\lambda\vec{\lambda}}{\Longrightarrow}{}^*(\mathbb{S}, \beta)}$$

Figure 4. Predicated Grammar Leftmost Derivation Rules

grammar G is $L(G) = \{w \mid (\epsilon, S) \Rightarrow^* (\mathbb{S}, w)\}$. Theoretically, the language class of $L(G)$ is recursively enumerable because each mutator could be a Turing machine. In practice, grammar writers do not use this generality, and so we consider the language class to be the context-sensitive languages instead. The class is context-sensitive rather than context-free because predicates can check both the left and right context.

This formalism has various syntactic restrictions not present in actual ANTLR input, for example, forcing predicates to the left-edge of rules and forcing mutators into their own rules. We can make these restrictions without loss of generality because any grammar in the general form can be translated into this more restricted form [1].

One of the key concepts behind parsing is the language matched by a production at a particular point in the parse.

Definition 1. $\mathcal{C}(\alpha) = \{w \mid (\epsilon, S) \Rightarrow^* (\mathbb{S}, u\alpha\delta) \Rightarrow^* (\mathbb{S}', uw)\}$ *is the* continuation language *for production* α.

Finally, grammar position $\alpha \cdot \beta$ means "*after* α *but before* β *during generation or parsing.*"

3.1 Resolving ambiguity

An ambiguous grammar is one in which the same string may be recognized in multiple ways. The rules in Figure 4 do not preclude ambiguity. However, for a practical parser, we want each input to correspond to a unique parse. To that end, ANTLR uses the order of the productions in the grammar to resolve ambiguities, with conflicts resolved in favor of the rule with the lowest production number. Programmers are instructed to make semantic predicates mutually exclusive for all potentially ambiguous input sequences, making such productions unambiguous. However, that condition cannot be enforced because predicates are written in a Turing-complete language. If the programmer fails to satisfy this condition, ANTLR uses production order to resolve the ambiguity. This policy matches what is done in PEGs [6, 8] and is useful for concisely representing precedence.

3.2 Predicated *LL*-regular grammars

There is one final concept that is helpful in understanding the *LL(*)* parsing framework, namely, the notion of a *predicated* LL*-regular grammar*. In previous work, Jarzabek and Krawczyk [10] and Nijholt [15] define *LL*-regular grammars to be a particular subset of the non-left-recursive, unambiguous CFGs. In this work, we extend the notion of *LL*-regular grammars to predicated *LL*-regular grammars for which we will construct efficient *LL(*)* parsers. We require that the input grammar be non-left-recursive; we use rule ordering to ensure that the grammar is unambiguous.

LL-regular grammars differ from *LL(k)* grammars in that, for any given nonterminal, parsers can use the entire remaining input to differentiate the alternative productions rather than just k symbols. *LL*-regular grammars require the existence of a regular partition of the set of all terminal sequences for *each nonterminal A*. Each block of the partition corresponds to exactly one possible production for A. An *LL*-regular parser determines to which regular set the remaining input belongs and selects the corresponding production. Formally,

DEFINITION 2. *Let* $R = (R_1, R_2, \ldots, R_n)$ *be a partition of* T^* *into n nonempty, disjoint sets* R_i. *If each block* R_i *is regular,* R *is a* regular partition. *If* $x, y \in R_i$, *we write* $x \equiv y\,(mod\ R)$.

DEFINITION 3. *G is predicated* LL*-regular if, for any two alternative productions of every nonterminal A expanding to* α_i *and* α_j, *there exists regular partition R such that*

$$(\epsilon, S) \Rightarrow^* (\mathbb{S}, w_i A \delta_i) \Rightarrow (\mathbb{S}, w_i \alpha_i \delta_i) \Rightarrow^* (\mathbb{S}_i, w_i x) \qquad (1)$$

$$(\epsilon, S) \Rightarrow^* (\mathbb{S}, w_j A \delta_j) \Rightarrow (\mathbb{S}, w_j \alpha_j \delta_j) \Rightarrow^* (\mathbb{S}_j, w_j y) \qquad (2)$$

$$x \equiv y\,(mod\ R) \qquad (3)$$

always imply that $\alpha_i = \alpha_j$ *and* $\mathbb{S}_i = \mathbb{S}_j$.[1]

4. *LL(*)* Parsers

Existing parsers for *LL*-regular grammars, proposed by Nijholt [15] and Poplawski [18], are linear but often impractical because they cannot parse infinite streams such as socket protocols and interactive interpreters. In the first of two passes, these parsers must read the input from right to left.

Instead, we propose a simpler left-to-right, one-pass strategy called *LL(*)* that grafts *lookahead DFA* onto *LL* parsers. A lookahead DFA matches regular partition R associated with a specific nonterminal and has an accept state for each R_i. At a decision point, *LL(*)* parsers expand production i if R_i matches the remaining input. In the worst case, an *LL(*)* parser examines the remaining input at each symbol as it consumes the input. As a result, *LL(*)* parsers are $O(n^2)$, but in practice, they typically examine one or two tokens (Section 6). As with previous parsing strategies, an *LL(*)* parser exists for every *LL*-regular grammar. Unlike previous work, *LL(*)* parsers can take as input a *predicated LL*-regular grammar; they handle predicates by inserting special edges into the *lookahead DFA* that correspond to the predicates.

[1] To be strictly correct, this definition technically corresponds to *Strong LL*-regular, rather than *LL*-regular as Nijholt [15] points out. *Strong LL* parsers ignore left context when making decisions.

$$\frac{p \xrightarrow{a} q}{(\mathbb{S}, p, aw) \mapsto (\mathbb{S}, q, w)} \qquad \frac{\pi_i(\mathbb{S}) \quad p \xrightarrow{\pi_i} f_i}{(\mathbb{S}, p, w) \overset{\pi_i}{\mapsto} (\mathbb{S}, f_i, w)}$$

$$\frac{(\mathbb{S}, f_i, w)}{\text{Accept, predict production } i}$$

Figure 5. Lookahead DFA Configuration Change Rules

DEFINITION 4. Lookahead DFA *are DFA augmented with predicates and accept states that yield predicted production numbers. Formally, given predicated grammar* $G = (N, T, P, S, \Pi, \mathcal{M})$, *DFA* $M = (\mathbb{S}, Q, \Sigma, \Delta, D_0, F)$ *where:*

- $\mathbb{S}$ is the system state inherited from surrounding parser
- Q is the set of states
- $\Sigma = T \cup \Pi$ is the edge alphabet
- Δ is the transition function mapping $Q \times \Sigma \to Q$
- $D_0 \in Q$ is the start state
- $F = \{f_1, f_2, \ldots, f_n\}$ is the set of final states, with one $f_i \in Q$ per regular partition block R_i (production i)

A transition in Δ from state p to state q on symbol $a \in \Sigma$ has the form $p \xrightarrow{a} q$. There can be at most one such transition. Predicate transitions, written $p \xrightarrow{\pi} f_i$, must target a final state. There can be multiple predicate transitions emanating from p but each must have a unique predicate π. The instantaneous configuration c of the DFA is $(\mathbb{S}, p, w_r)$ where $\mathbb{S}$ is the system state and p is the current state; the initial configuration is $(\mathbb{S}, D_0, w_r)$. The notation $c \mapsto c'$ means the DFA changes from configuration c to c' using the rules in Figure 5. As with predicated grammars, the rules do not forbid ambiguous DFA paths arising from predicated transitions. In practice, ANTLR tests edges in order to resolve ambiguities.

For efficiency, lookahead DFA match *lookahead sets* rather than continuation languages. Given $R = (\{ac^*\}, \{bd^*\})$, for example, there is no point in looking beyond the first symbol. The lookahead sets are $(\{a\}, \{b\})$.

DEFINITION 5. *Given partition R distinguishing n alternative productions, the* lookahead set *for production i is the minimal-prefix set of* R_i *that still uniquely predicts i:*

$$LA_i = \{\, w \mid ww' \in R_i, w \notin LA_j \text{ for } j \neq i \text{ and no strict prefix of } w \text{ has the same property}\}$$

4.1 Erasing syntactic predicates

To avoid a separate recognition mechanism for syntactic predicates, we reduce syntactic predicates to semantic predicates that launch speculative parses. To "erase" syntactic predicate (A'_i)`=>`, we replace it with semantic predicate `{synpred(`A'_i`)}?`. Function `synpred` returns true if A'_i matches the current input; otherwise it returns false. To support PEG "not predicates," we can flip the result of calling function `synpred`, as suggested by Ford [7].

4.2 Programmer-specified semantic predicates

Most grammars do not need semantic predicates, but when they do, the predicates are usually small expressions that query a symbol table, check context (e.g., "does this token start in column 1?"), or turn on language constructs (e.g., "should the language allow GCC C extensions?"). They do not represent a significant cost to the programmer. For example, the ANTLR C grammar has just one predicate that tests whether or not an identifier is a type name:

```
type_id : {isTypeName(next input symbol)}? ID ;
```

4.3 Arbitrary actions in predicate grammars

Formal predicated grammars fork new states $\mathbb{S}$ during speculation. In practice, duplicating system state is not feasible. Consequently, ANTLR deactivates mutators during speculation by default, preventing actions from "launching missiles" speculatively. However, some semantic predicates rely on changes made by mutators, such as the symbol table manipulations required to parse C. Avoiding speculation whenever possible attenuates this issue, but still leaves a semantic hazard. To address this issue, ANTLR supports a special kind of action, enclosed in double brackets {{...}}, that executes even during speculation. ANTLR requires the programmer to verify that these actions are either side-effect free or undoable. It is also the responsibility of the programmer to insert actions that undo side-effects. Luckily, symbol table manipulation actions, the most common {{...}} actions, usually get undone automatically. For example, a rule for a `code_block` typically pushes a symbol scope but then pops it on exit. The pop effectively undoes the side-effects that occur during `code_block`.

4.4 Error reporting and arbitrary lookahead

LL(k) parsers report prediction errors by indicating the k-sequence that failed to predict a production of the current nonterminal. For example, given $A \rightarrow ab \,|\, ac$ and input ae, an *LL(k)* parser might report "no viable production upon ae." Because *LL(*)* prediction DFA can scan arbitrarily far ahead, printing the entire erroneous lookahead sequence is impractical. Instead, *LL(*)* parsers should report an error at the specific token that led to a lookahead DFA error state. Given $A \rightarrow a^+b \,|\, a^+c$ and input $aaaaad$, the parser should report that it could not predict a production due to d. Reporting an error at the current symbol (the first a) would be confusing. For prediction errors when backtracking across multiple productions, the parser should report errors at the deepest symbol reached by a failed speculative parse. ANTLR 3.3 does not always conform to this ideal; we plan to address this in a future version.

5. *LL(*)* Grammar Analysis

For *LL(*)*, analyzing a grammar means finding a lookahead DFA for each parsing decision, *i.e.*, for each nonterminal in the grammar with multiple productions. In our discussions, we use A as the nonterminal in question and α_i for $i \in 1..n$ as the corresponding collection of right-hand sides. Our goal is to find for each A a regular partition R, represented by a DFA, that distinguishes between productions. To succeed, A must be *LL*-regular: partition block R_i must contain every sentence in $\mathcal{C}(\alpha_i)$, the continuation language of α_i, and the R_i must be disjoint. The DFA tests the remaining input for membership in each R_i; matching R_i predicts alternative i. For efficiency, the DFA matches lookahead sets instead of partition blocks.

It is important to point out that we are not parsing with the DFA, only predicting which production the parser should expand. The continuation language $\mathcal{C}(\alpha_i)$ is often context-

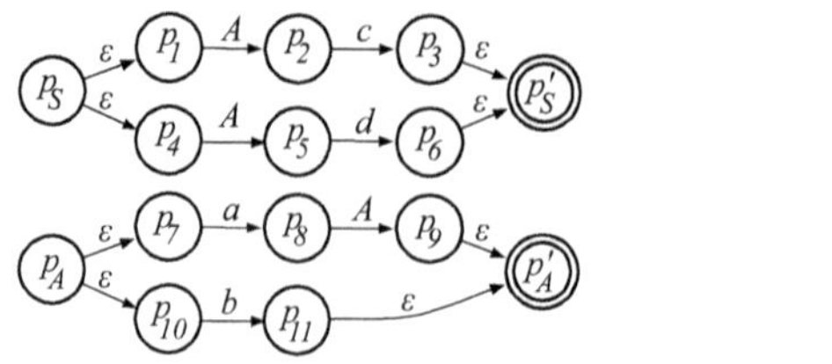

Figure 6. ATN for G with P=$\{S \rightarrow Ac \,|\, Ad, A \rightarrow aA \,|\, b\}$

free, not regular, but experience shows there is usually an approximating regular language that distinguishes between the α_i. For example, consider rule $A \rightarrow [\,A\,] \,|\, \textbf{id}$ that matches balanced brackets around an identifier, *i.e.*, the context-free language $\{[^n\textbf{id}\,]^n\}$. Approximating the $\mathcal{C}(\alpha_i)$ sets with regular expressions gives a partition that satisfies the *LL*-regular condition: $R = \{\{[^*\textbf{id}\,]^*\}, \{\textbf{id}\}\}$. In fact, the first input symbol is sufficient to predict alternatives: $LA = \{\{[\}, \{\textbf{id}\}\}$. The decision is $LL(1)$.

Not all grammars are *LL*-regular and so our algorithm may fail to find a partition for A. Worse, Poplawski [18] showed that the *LL*-regular condition is undecidable so we must use heuristics to prevent nontermination, sometimes forcing the algorithm to give up before finding R even when A is *LL*-regular. In such cases, we fall back on other strategies, discussed in Sections 5.3 and 5.4, rather than failing to create a DFA.

The *LL(*)* analysis algorithm starts by converting the input grammar to an equivalent *augmented transition network* (ATN) [20]. It then computes lookahead DFA by simulating the actions of the ATN in a process that mimics how the well-known *subset construction* algorithm computes a DFA that simulates the actions of an NFA.

5.1 Augmented transition networks

Given predicated grammar $G = (N, T, P, S, \Pi, \mathcal{M})$, the corresponding ATN $M_G = (Q, \Sigma, \Delta, E, F)$ has elements:

- Q is the set of states
- Σ is the edge alphabet $N \cup T \cup \Pi \cup \mathcal{M}$
- Δ is the transition relation mapping $Q \times (\Sigma \cup \epsilon) \rightarrow Q$
- $E = \{p_A \mid A \in N\}$ is the set of submachine entry states
- $F = \{p'_A \mid A \in N\}$ is the set of submachine final states

We describe how to compute Q and Δ shortly.

ATNs resemble the syntax diagrams used to document programming languages, with an ATN submachine for each nonterminal. For example, Figure 6 gives the ATN for a simple grammar. Nonterminal edges $p \xrightarrow{A} p'$ are like function calls. They transfer control of the ATN to A's submachine, pushing return state p' onto a state stack so it can continue from p' after reaching the stop state for A's submachine.

To get an ATN from a grammar, we create a submachine for each nonterminal A as shown in Figure 7. Start state p_A targets $p_{A,i}$ created from the left edge of α_i. The last state created from α_i targets p'_A. The language matched by the ATN is the same as the language of the original grammar.

Grammar analysis is like an inter-procedural flow analysis that statically traces an ATN-like graph representation of a program, discovering all nodes reachable from a top-level call site. The unique configuration of a program for flow purposes is a graph node and the call stack used to reach

Input Grammar Element	Resulting ATN Transitions
$A \to \alpha_i$	$p_A \xrightarrow{\epsilon} p_{A,i} \xrightarrow{\epsilon} \boxed{\alpha_i} \xrightarrow{\epsilon} p'_A$
$A \to \{\pi_i\}?\,\alpha_i$	$p_A \xrightarrow{\epsilon} p_{A,i} \xrightarrow{\pi_i} \boxed{\alpha_i} \xrightarrow{\epsilon} p'_A$
$A \to \{\mu_i\}$	$p_A \xrightarrow{\epsilon} p_{A,i} \xrightarrow{\mu_i} p'_A$
$A \to \epsilon$	$p_A \xrightarrow{\epsilon} p_{A,i} \xrightarrow{\epsilon} p'_A$
$\boxed{\alpha_i} = X_1 X_2 \ldots X_m$ for $X_j \in N \cup T$, $j = 1..m$	$p_0 \xrightarrow{X_1} p_1 \xrightarrow{X_2} \ldots \xrightarrow{X_m} p_m$

Figure 7. Predicated Grammar to ATN transformation

that node. Depending on the type of analysis, it might also track some semantic context such as the parameters from the top-level call site.

Similarly, grammar analysis statically traces paths through the ATN reachable from the "call site" of production α_i, which is the left edge state $p_{A,i}$. The terminal edges collected along a path emanating from $p_{A,i}$ represent a lookahead sequence. Analysis continues until each lookahead sequence is unique to a particular alternative. Analysis also needs to track any semantic predicate π_i from the left edge of α_i in case it is needed to resolve ambiguities. Consequently, an *ATN configuration* is a tuple (p, i, γ, π) with ATN state p, predicted production i, ATN call stack γ, and optional predicate π. We will use the notation $c.p, c.i, c.\gamma$, and $c.\pi$ to denote projecting the state, alternative, stack, and predicate from configuration c, respectively. Analysis ignores machine storage $\mathbb{S}$ because it is unknown at analysis time.

5.2 Modified subset construction algorithm

For grammar analysis purposes, we modify subset construction to process ATN not NFA configurations. Each DFA state D represents the set of possible configurations the ATN could be in after matching a prefix of the remaining input starting from state $p_{A,i}$. Key modifications include:

- The *closure* operation simulates the push and pop of ATN nonterminal invocations.
- If all the configurations in a newly discovered state predict the same alternative, the analysis does not add the state to the work list; no more lookahead is necessary.
- To resolve ambiguities, the algorithm adds predicate transitions to final states if appropriate predicates exist.

The structure of the algorithm mirrors that of subset construction. It begins by creating DFA start state D_0 and adding it to a work list. Until no work remains, the algorithm adds new DFA states computed by the *move* and *closure* functions, which simulate the transitions of the ATN. We assume that the ATN corresponding to our input grammar G, $M_G = (Q_M, N \cup T \cup \Pi \cup \mathcal{M}, \Delta_M, E_M, F_M)$, and the nonterminal A that we are analyzing are in scope for all the operations of the algorithm.

Function *createDFA*, shown in Algorithm 8, is the entry point: calling *createDFA*(p_A) constructs the lookahead DFA for A. To create start state D_0, the algorithm adds configuration $(p_{A,i}, i, [], \pi_i)$ for each production $A \to \pi_i\,\alpha_i$ and configuration $(p_{A,i}, i, [], -)$ for each production $A \to \alpha_i$; the symbol "$-$" denotes the absence of a predicate. The core of

Alg. 8: *createDFA*(ATN State p_A) **returns** DFA

$work := []$; $\Delta := \{\}$; $D_0 := \{\}$;
$F := \{f_i \mid f_i :=$ new DFA state, $1 \ldots numAlts(A)\}$;
$Q := F$;
foreach $p_A \xrightarrow{\epsilon} p_{A,i} \in \Delta_M$ **do**
  if $p_A \xrightarrow{\epsilon} p_{A,i} \xrightarrow{\pi_i} p$ **then** $\pi := \pi_i$ **else** $\pi := -$;
  D_0 += $closure(D_0, (p_{A,i}, i, [], \pi))$;
end
$work$ += D_0; Q += D_0;
$DFA := DFA(-, Q, T \cup \Pi, \Delta, D_0, F)$;
foreach $D \in work$ **do**
  $T_D := \{a \mid p_1 \xrightarrow{a} p_2 \in \Delta_M$ and $(p_1, -, -, -) \in D\}$;
  foreach $a \in T_D$ **do**
    $mv := move(D, a)$;
    $D' := \bigcup_{c \in mv} closure(D, c)$;
    if $D' \notin Q$ **then**
      $resolve(D')$;
      switch $findPredictedAlts(D')$ **do**
        case *Singleton list of j*: $f_j := D'$;
        otherwise $work$ += D';
      endsw
      Q += D';
    end
    Δ += $D \xrightarrow{a} D'$;
  end
  foreach $c \in D$ *such that wasResolved(c)* **do**
    Δ += $D \xrightarrow{c.\pi} f_{c.i}$;
  end
  $work$ -= D;
end
return *DFA*;

createDFA is a combined *move-closure* operation that creates new DFA states by finding the set of ATN states directly reachable upon each input terminal symbol $a \in T$:

$$move(D, a) = \{(q, i, \gamma, \pi) \mid p \xrightarrow{a} q,\ (p, i, \gamma, \pi) \in D\}$$

and then adding the closure of those configurations. Once the algorithm identifies a new state D', it invokes *resolve* to check for and resolve ambiguities. If all of the configurations in D' predict the same alternative j, then D' is marked as f_j, the accept state for alternative j, and D' is not added to the work list: once the algorithm can uniquely identify which production to predict, there is no point in examining more of the input. This optimization is how the algorithm constructs DFA that match the minimum lookahead sets LA_j instead of the entire remaining input. Next, the algorithm adds an edge from D to D' on terminal a. Finally, for each configuration $c \in D$ with a predicate that resolves an ambiguity, *createDFA* adds a transition predicated on $c.\pi$ from D to the final state for alternative $c.i$. The test *wasResolved* checks whether the *resolve* step marked configuration c as having been resolved by a predicate.

Closure The *LL(*) closure* operation, shown in Algorithm 9, is more complex than the *closure* function from NFA subset construction because of the ATN stack. Nevertheless, the intuition is the same. When called on a configuration c, *closure* recursively finds all ATN states reachable from c's state by traversing all ATN edges that are not terminals, *i.e.*, predicates, nonterminals, and mutators.

Alg. 9: *closure*(DFA State D, $c = (p, i, \gamma, \pi)$) **returns** set *closure*

if $c \in D.busy$ **then return** $\{\}$; **else** $D.busy$ += c;
closure := $\{c\}$;
if $p = p'_A$ *(i.e., p is stop state)* **then**
  if $\gamma = p'\gamma'$ **then** *closure* += *closure*$(D, (p', i, \gamma', \pi))$;
  else *closure* += $\bigcup_{\forall p_2 : p_1 \xrightarrow{A} p_2 \in \Delta_M}$ *closure*$(D, (p_2, i, [], \pi))$;
end
foreach *transition t emanating from ATN state p* **do**
  switch t **do**
    case $p \xrightarrow{A} p'$:
      depth := number of occurrences of p' in γ;
      if *depth* = 1 **then**
        $D.recursiveAlts$ += i;
        if $|D.recursiveAlts| > 1$ **then**
          throw *LikelyNonLLRegularException*;
      end
      if *depth* $\geq m$, *(i.e., the max recursion depth)* **then**
        mark D to have recursion overflow;
        return *closure*;
      end
      closure += *closure*$(D, (p_A, i, p'\gamma, \pi))$;
    case $p \xrightarrow{\pi'} q$, $p \xrightarrow{\mu} q$, *or* $p \xrightarrow{\epsilon} q$ *transition:*
      closure += *closure*$(D, (q, i, \gamma, \pi))$;
  endsw
end
return *closure*;

The call *closure*(D, c) takes the DFA state D to which c belongs as an additional argument. The function starts by adding the argument configuration to a *busy* list to avoid redundant computation and infinite loops. To simulate ATN nonterminal transition $p \xrightarrow{A} p'$, *closure* duplicates configuration c, pushing return state p' onto its stack. At submachine stop state p'_A, *closure* duplicates c, popping p' from its stack. If *closure* reaches p_A with an empty stack, we have no information statically about which rule invoked A. (This situation only happens when there is a path from $p_{A,i}$ to p'_A with no terminal edges.) In this case we have to assume any production $p_1 \xrightarrow{A} p_2$ in the input grammar might have invoked A, and so *closure* must chase all such states p_2.

If *closure* detects recursive nonterminal invocations (submachines directly or indirectly invoking themselves) in more than one alternative, it terminates DFA construction for A by throwing an exception; Section 5.4 describes our fall back strategy. If *closure* detects recursion deeper than internal constant m, *closure* marks the state parameter D as having *overflowed*. In this case, DFA construction for A continues but *closure* no longer pursues paths derived from c's state and stack. We discuss this situation more in Section 5.3.

DFA State Equivalence The analysis algorithm relies on the notion of equivalence for DFA states:

DEFINITION 6. *Two DFA states are equivalent, $D \equiv D'$, if their configuration sets are equivalent. Two ATN configurations are equivalent, $c \equiv c'$, if the p, i, and π components are equal and their stacks are equivalent. Two stacks are equivalent, $\gamma_1 \equiv \gamma_2$, if they are equal, if at least one is empty, or if one is a suffix of the other.*

This definition of stack equivalence reflects ATN context information when *closure* encounters a submachine stop state. Because analysis searches the ATN for all possible lookahead sequences, an empty stack is like a wildcard. Any transition $p_1 \xrightarrow{A} p_2$ could have invoked A, so analysis must include the *closure* of every such p_2. Consequently, a *closure* set can have two configurations c and c' with the same ATN state but with $c.\gamma = \epsilon$ and $c'.\gamma \neq \epsilon$. This can only happen when *closure* reaches a nonterminal's submachine stop state with an empty stack and by chasing states following references to that nonterminal, *closure* reenters that submachine. For example, consider the DFA for S in grammar $S \rightarrow a|\epsilon, A \rightarrow SS$. Start state construction computes *closure* at positions $S \rightarrow \cdot a$ and $S \rightarrow \cdot \epsilon$ then $S \rightarrow \epsilon \cdot$, S's stop state. The state stack is empty so *closure* chases states following references to S, such as position $A \rightarrow S \cdot S$. Finally, *closure* reenters S, this time with a nonempty stack.

Equivalence of $\gamma_1 \equiv \gamma_1\gamma_2$ where $\gamma_1, \gamma_2 \neq \epsilon$ degenerates to the previous case of $\gamma_1 = \epsilon$. Given configurations $(p, \_, \gamma_1, \_)$ and $(p, \_, \gamma_1\gamma_2, \_)$ in D, *closure* reaches p following the same sequence of most recent submachine invocations, γ_1. Once γ_1 pops off, *closure* has configurations $(p, \_, [], \_)$ and $(p, \_, \gamma_2, \_)$.

Resolve One of benefits of static analysis is that it can sometimes detect and warn users about ambiguous nonterminals. After *closure* finishes, the *resolve* function (Algorithm 10) looks for *conflicting configurations* in its argument state D. Such configurations indicate that the ATN can match the same input with more than one production.

DEFINITION 7. *If DFA state D contains configurations $c = (p, i, \gamma_i, \pi_i)$ and $c' = (p, j, \gamma_j, \pi_j)$ such that $i \neq j$ and $\gamma_i \equiv \gamma_j$, then D is an* ambiguous DFA state *and c and c' are* conflicting configurations. *The set of all alternative numbers that belong to a conflicting configuration of D is the* conflict set *of D.*

For example, the ATN for subrule $(a|a)$ in $A \rightarrow (a|a)\,b$ merges back together and so analysis reaches the same state from both alternatives with the same (empty) stack context:

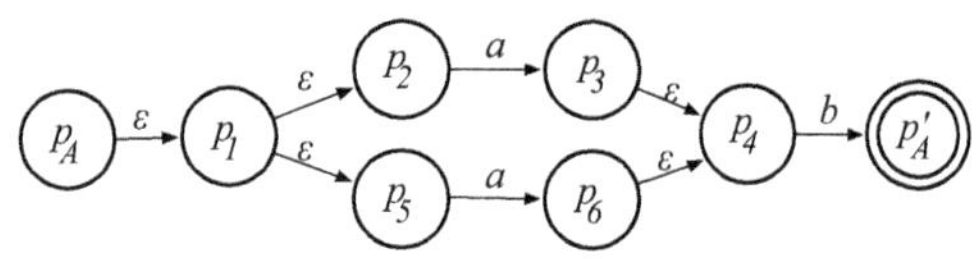

$D_0 = \{(p_2, 1), (p_5, 2)\}$, where we abbreviate $(p_2, 1, [], -)$ as $(p_2, 1)$ for clarity. $D_1 = \{(p_3, 1), (p_4, 1), (p_6, 2), (p_4, 2)\}$, reachable with symbol a, has conflicting configurations $(p_4, 1)$ and $(p_4, 2)$. No further lookahead will resolve the ambiguity because ab is in the continuation language of both alternatives.

If *resolve* detects an ambiguity, it calls *resolveWithPredicate* (Algorithm 11) to see if the conflicting configurations have predicates that can resolve the ambiguity. For example, a predicated version of the previous grammar, $A \rightarrow (\{\pi_1\}?\,a\,|\,\{\pi_2\}?\,a)\,b$, yields ATN:

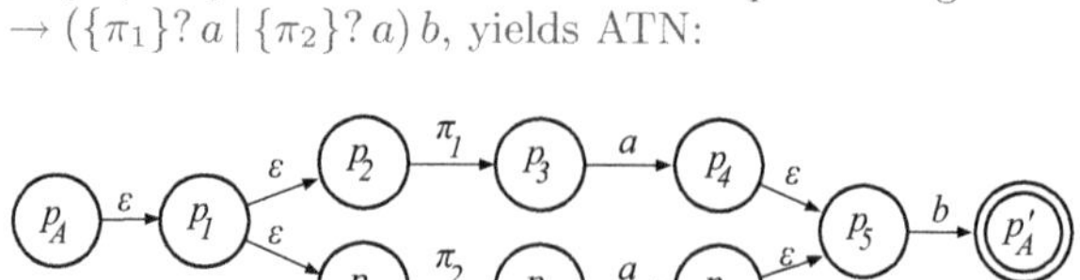

D_0 for decision state p_1 starts with $\{(p_2, 1, [], \pi_1), (p_6, 2, [], \pi_2)\}$ to which we add $\{(p_3, 1, [], \pi_1), (p_7, 2, [], \pi_2)\}$ for *closure*.

Alg. 10: *resolve*(DFA State D)
$conflicts$:= the conflict set of D;
if $|conflicts| = 0$ *and not overflowed(D)* **then return**;
if $resolveWithPreds(D, conflicts)$ **then return**;
resolve by removing all c from D such that $c.i \in conflicts$ and $c.i \neq min(conflicts)$;
if *overflowed(D)* **then** report recursion overflow;
else report grammar ambiguity;

Alg. 11: *resolveWithPreds*(DFA State D, set $conflicts$) **returns** boolean
$pconfigs$:= []; // config with predicate for alt i
foreach $i \in conflicts$ **do**
$pconfigs[i]$:= pick any representative $(\_, i, \_, \pi) \in D$;
end
if $|pconfigs| < |conflicts|$ **then return false**;
foreach $c \in pconfigs$ **do** mark c as *wasResolved*;
return true;

D_1 has conflicting configurations as before, but now predicates can resolve the issue at runtime with DFA $D_0 \xrightarrow{a} D_1$, $D_1 \xrightarrow{\pi_1} f_1$, $D_1 \xrightarrow{\pi_2} f_2$.

If *resolve* found predicates, it returns without emitting a warning, leaving *createDFA* to incorporate the predicates into the DFA. Without predicates, there is no way to resolve the issue at runtime, so *resolve* statically removes the ambiguity by giving precedence to A's lowest conflicting alternative by removing configurations associated with higher-numbered conflicting alternatives. For example, in the unpredicated grammar for A above, the resulting DFA is $D_0 \xrightarrow{a} f_1$ because the analysis resolves conflicts by removing configurations not associated with highest precedence production 1, leaving $\{(p_3, 1), (p_4, 1)\}$.

If *closure* tripped the recursion overflow alarm, *resolve* may not see conflicting configurations in D, but D might still predict more than one alternative because the analysis terminated early to avoid nontermination. The algorithm can use predicates to resolve the potential ambiguity at runtime, if they exist. If not, the algorithm again resolves in favor of the lowest alternative number and issues a warning to the user.

5.3 Avoiding analysis intractability

Because the *LL*-regular condition is undecidable, we expect a potential infinite loop somewhere in any lookahead DFA construction algorithm. Recursive rules are the source of nontermination. Given configuration $c = (p, i, \gamma)$ (we omit π from configurations for brevity in the following) the *closure* of c at transition $p \xrightarrow{A} p'$ includes $(p_A, i, p'\gamma)$. If *closure* reaches p again, it will include $(p_A, i, p'p'\gamma)$. Ultimately, *closure* will "pump" the recursive rule forever, leading to stack explosion. For example, for the ATN with recursive nonterminal A given in Figure 6, the DFA start state D_0 for $S \rightarrow Ac \mid Ad$ is:

$$D_0 = \{(p_1, 1, []), (p_A, 1, p_2), (p_7, 1, p_2), (p_{10}, 1, p_2), (p_4, 2, []), (p_A, 2, p_5), (p_7, 2, p_5), (p_{10}, 2, p_5)\}$$

Function $move(D_0, a)$ reaches $(p_8, 1, p_2)$ to create D_1 via $(p_7, 1, p_2)$ in D_0. The *closure* of $(p_8, 1, p_2)$ traverses the implied ϵ edge to p_A, adding three new configurations: $(p_A, 1, p_9p_2)$, $(p_7, 1, p_9p_2)$, $(p_{10}, 1, p_9p_2)$. D_1 has the same configuration as D_0 for p_7 but with a larger stack. The configuration stacks grow forever as $p_9^m p_2$ for recursion depth m, yielding an ever larger DFA path: $D_0 \xrightarrow{a} D_1 \xrightarrow{a} \ldots \xrightarrow{a} D_m$.

There are two solutions to this problem. Either we forget all but the top m states on the stack (as Bermudez and Schimpf [2] do with $LAR(m)$) or simply avoid computing *closure* on configurations with m recursive invocations to any particular submachine start state. We choose the latter because it guarantees a strict superset of *LL(k)* (when $m \geq k$). We do not have to worry about an approximation introducing invalid sequences in common between the alternatives. In contrast, Bermudez and Schimpf give a family of $LALR(1)$ grammars for which there is no fixed m that gives a valid $LAR(m)$ parser for every grammar in the family. Hard-limiting recursion depth is not a serious restriction in practice. Programmers are likely to use (regular) grammar $S \rightarrow a^*bc \mid a^*bd$ instead of the version in Figure 6.

5.4 Aborting DFA construction

As a heuristic, we terminate DFA construction for nonterminal A upon discovering recursion in more than one alternative. (Analysis for S in Figure 6 would actually terminate before triggering recursion overflow.) Such decisions are extremely unlikely to have exact regular partitions and, since our algorithm does not approximate lookahead, there is no point in pursuing the DFA in vain. ANTLR's implementation falls back on $LL(1)$ lookahead for A, with backtracking or other predicates if *resolve* detects recursion in more than one alternative.

5.5 Hoisting Predicates

This algorithm and the formal predicated grammar semantics in Section 3 require that predicates appear at production left edges. This restriction is cumbersome in practice and can force users to duplicate predicates. The full algorithm in ANTLR automatically discovers and *hoists* all predicates visible to a decision even from productions further down the derivation chain. (See [1] for full algorithm and discussion.) ANTLR's analysis also handles EBNF operators in the right-hand side of productions, *e.g.* $A \rightarrow a^*b$ by adding cycles to the ATN.

6. Empirical Results

This paper makes a number of claims about the suitability and efficiency of our analysis algorithm and the *LL(*)* parsing strategy. In this section, we support these claims with measurements obtained by running ANTLR 3.3 on six large, real-world grammars, described in Figure 12, and profiling the resulting parsers on large sample input sentences, described in Figure 13. We include two PEG-derived grammars to show ANTLR can generate valid parsers from PEGs. (Readers can examine the non-commercial grammars, sample input, test methodology, and raw analysis results [1].)

6.1 Static grammar analysis

We claim that our grammar analysis algorithm statically optimizes away backtracking from the vast majority of parsing decisions and does so in a reasonable amount of time. Table 1 summarizes ANTLR's analysis of the six grammars. ANTLR processes each of them in a few seconds except for the 8,231 line-SQL grammar, which takes 13.1 seconds. Analysis times include input grammar parsing, analysis (with EBNF construct processing and predicate hoisting [1]), and parser generation. (As with the exponentially-complex classic subset construction algorithm, ANTLR's analysis can hit

Java1.5: Native ANTLR grammar, uses PEG mode.

RatsC, RatsJava: *Rats!* grammars, manually converted to ANTLR syntax using PEG mode while preserving the essential structure. We removed left-recursion, which *Rats!* supports but ANTLR does not.

VB.NET, TSQL, C#: Commercial grammars for Microsoft languages provided by *Temporal Wave, LLC*.

Figure 12. Benchmark ANTLR grammars

RatsJavaParser.java: Parser generated by ANTLR for RatsJava grammar; tests both Java parsers.

pre_javaParser.c: Preprocessed ANTLR-generated parser for Java1.5 grammar; tests RatsC parser.

LinqToSqlSamples.cs: Microsoft sample code; tests C#;

big.sql: Collected Microsoft SQL samples; tests TSQL.

Northwind.vb: Microsoft sample code; tests VB.NET.

Figure 13. Benchmark input sentence

Grammar	Lines	n	Fixed	Cyclic	Backtrack	Runtime
Java1.5	1,022	170	150	1	20 (11.8%)	3.1s
RatsC	1,174	143	111	0	32 (22.4%)	2.8s
RatsJava	763	87	73	6	8 (9.2%)	3s
VB.NET	3,505	348	332	0	16 (4.6%)	6.75s
TSQL	8,241	1,120	1,053	10	57 (5.1%)	13.1s
C#	3,476	217	189	2	26 (12%)	6.3s

Table 1. Grammar decision characteristics. "Lines" is the size of the grammar, n is the number of parsing decisions in the grammar, "Fixed" is the number of pure *LL(k)* decisions, "Cyclic" is the number of cyclic DFA falling between LL(k)'s acyclic DFA and DFA with syntactic predicate edges, "Backtrack" is the number of decisions that potentially backtrack, and the "runtime" is the time to process a grammar and generate an *LL(*)* parser. Tests performed under OS X with 2x3.2Ghz Quad-Core Intel Xeon with 14G RAM.

a "land-mine" in rare cases; ANTLR provides a means to isolate the offending decisions and manually set their lookahead parameters. None of these grammars hits land-mines.)

All the grammars use backtracking to some extent, providing evidence that it is not worth contorting a large grammar to make it *LL(k)*. The first three grammars use PEG mode, in which ANTLR automatically puts a syntactic predicate on the left edge of every production. Unlike a PEG parser, however, ANTLR can statically avoid backtracking in many cases. For example, ANTLR strips away syntactic predicates from all but 11.8% of the decisions in Java1.5. As expected, the RatsC grammar has the highest ratio of backtracking decisions at 22.4% because C variable and function declarations and definitions look the same from the left edge. The author of the three commercial grammars manually-specified syntactic predicates, which reduced lookahead requirements. In 4 out of 6 grammars, ANTLR was able to construct cyclic DFA to avoid backtracking.

Table 1 shows that the vast majority of decisions in the sample grammars are fixed *LL(k)* for some k. Table 2 reports the number of decisions per lookahead depth, showing that most decisions are in fact $LL(1)$. The table also shows that

Grammar	*LL(k)*	$LL(1)$	Lookahead depth k					
			1	2	3	4	5	6
Java1.5	88.24%	74.71%	127	20	2	1		
RatsC	77.62%	72.03%	103	7	1			
RatsJava	83.91%	73.56%	64	8	1			
VB.NET	95.40%	88.79%	309	18	4	1		
TSQL	94.02%	83.48%	935	78	11	14	9	6
C#	87.10%	78.34%	170	19				

Table 2. Fixed lookahead decision characteristics

Grammar	Input lines	parse-time	n	avg k	back. k	max k
Java1.5	12,416	78ms	111	1.09	3.95	114
RatsC	37,019	771ms	131	1.88	5.87	7,968
RatsJava	12,416	412ms	78	1.85	5.95	1,313
VB.NET	4,649	351ms	166	1.07	3.25	12
TSQL	794	13ms	309	1.08	2.63	20
C#	3,807	524ms	146	1.04	1.60	9

Table 3. Parser decision lookahead depth. n is the number of decision points covered while parsing. "avg k" is the sum of all decision event lookahead depths divided by the number of decision events. "back. k" is the average speculation depth for backtracking decision events only. "max k" is the deepest lookahead depth encountered during the parse. *LL(*)* parsers were run with Java 1.6.0 under OS X with 2x3.2Ghz Quad-Core Intel Xeon with 14G RAM. VB.NET time includes preprocessing. All times include lexing. Times reflect prior on-the-fly compiler warm-up. Parse times for last 3 include tree construction.

ANTLR is able to statically determine k almost all the time, even though this problem is undecidable in general.

6.2 Parser runtime profiling

At runtime, we claim that *LL(*)* parsing decisions use only a few tokens of lookahead on average and parse with reasonable speed. Table 3 shows that for each sample input file, the average lookahead depth per decision event is roughly one token, with PEG-mode parsers requiring almost two. The average parsing speed is 71,035 lines / second for the first three grammars and 27,196 for the other grammars, which have tree-building overhead.

The average lookahead depth for just the backtracking decisions is less than six tokens, highlighting the fact that although backtracking can scan far ahead, usually it does not. For example, a parser might need to backtrack to match a C type specifier, but most of the time such specifiers look like `int` or `int *` and so they can be identified quickly. The grammars not derived from PEGs have much smaller maximum lookahead depths, indicating the authors did some restructuring to take advantage of *LL(k)* efficiency. The RatsC grammar, in contrast, backtracks across an entire function (looking ahead 7,968 tokens in one decision event) instead of looking ahead just enough to distinguish declarations from definitions, *i.e.*, between `int f();` and `int f() {...}`.

Although we derived two sample grammars from *Rats!*, we did not compare parser execution times nor memory utilization as one might expect. Both ANTLR and *Rats!* are practical parser generators with parsing speed and memory footprints suitable to most applications. *Rats!* is also scannerless, unlike ANTLR, which makes memoization caches hard to compare.

Grammar	Can back.	Did back.	decision events	Back-track	Back. rate
Java1.5	19	16	462,975	2.36%	45.22%
RatsC	30	24	1,343,176	16.85%	65.27%
RatsJava	8	7	628,340	14.07%	74.68%
VB.NET	6	3	109,257	0.46%	20.84%
TSQL	29	19	17,394	3.38%	27.01%
C#	24	19	141,055	3.68%	40.22%

Table 4. Parser decision backtracking behavior. "Can back." is the number of decisions that potentially backtrack. "Did back." is the number of those that did for the sample input. "Backtrack" is the percentage of decision events that backtracked. "Back. rate" is the likelihood that a potentially backtracking decision actually backtracks when triggered.

ANTLR statically removes backtracking from most parser decisions as shown in Table 1. At runtime, ANTLR backtracks even less than predicted by static analysis. For example, statically we find an average of 10.9% of the decisions backtrack for our sample grammars but Table 4 shows that the generated parsers backtrack in only 6.8% of the decision events on average. The non-PEG-derived grammars backtrack only about 2.5% of the time. This is partly because some of the backtracking decisions manage uncommon grammar constructs. For example, there are 1,120 decisions of any kind in the TSQL grammar but the sample input exercises only 309 of them.

Most importantly, just because a decision *can* backtrack, does not mean it will. The last column in Table 4 shows that the potentially backtracking decisions (PBDs) only backtrack about half the time on average across the sample grammars. The commercial VB.NET and TSQL grammars yield PBDs that backtrack in only about 30% of the decision events. Some PBDs never trigger backtracking events. Subtracting the first two columns in Table 4 gives the number of PBDs that avoid backtracking altogether.

We should point out that without memoization, backtracking parsers are exponentially complex in the worst case. This matters for grammars that do a lot of nested backtracking. For example, the RatsC grammar appears not to terminate if we turn off ANTLR memoization support. In constrast, the VB.NET and C# parsers are fine without it. Packrat parsing [6] achieve linear parsing results at the cost of the increased memory for the memoization cache. In the worst case, we need to squirrel away $O(|N| * n)$ decision event results (one for each nonterminal decision at each input position). The less we backtrack, the smaller the cache since ANTLR only memoizes while speculating.

We did not specifically measure the performance of the lookahead DFA portion of ANTLR parsers because the overall performance of such parsers is more than adequate, a claim supported by the performance numbers provided in this section and the experience of developers in the real world. For example, Twitter parses 1 billion queries/day with an ANTLR-generated parser. The speed of the lookahead DFA likely does not contribute significantly to the overall parse time because the average lookahead depth for any decision, backtracking or not, is only one or two tokens (column "avg k" in Table 3).

ANTLR v3's *LL(*)* parsers are about 2.5x faster than ANTLR v2 parsers for the same grammar. For example, parsing the 565k lines of the Java 1.3 library takes 4.9 seconds with ANTLR v2's Java grammar. The same grammar converted to v3 syntax takes only 1.9 seconds. (Neither test warmed up the on-the-fly compiler.) The v2 version needed to backtrack but v3's more powerful *LL(*)* made it unnecessary to backtrack. The Java1.5 grammar from this section, written specifically for v3 and a larger language than Java 1.3, backtracks occasionally and took 3 seconds. Unfortunately, it is difficult to draw conclusions from this specifically about *LL(*)* parsing. The runtime and lexer capabilities of v3 and v2 are so different that we cannot be sure where the speed increase lies.

7. Related work

Many parsing techniques exist, but currently the two dominant strategies are Tomita's bottom-up GLR [19] and Ford's top-down packrat parsing [6], commonly referred to by its associated meta-language PEG [7]. Both are nondeterministic in that parsers can use some form of speculation to make decisions. *LL(*)* is an optimization of packrat parsing just as GLR is an optimization of Earley's algorithm [5]. The closer a grammar conforms to the underlying *LL* or *LR* strategy, the more efficient the parser in time and space. *LL(*)* ranges from $O(n)$ to $O(n^2)$ whereas GLR ranges from $O(n)$ to $O(n^3)$. Surprisingly, the $O(n^2)$ potential comes from cyclic lookahead DFA not backtracking (assuming we memoize). ANTLR generates *LL(*)* parsers that are linear in practice and that greatly reduce speculation, reducing memoization overhead over pure packrat parsers.

GLR and PEG tend be scannerless, which is necessary if a tool needs to support *grammar composition*. Composition means that programmers can easily integrate one language into another or create new grammars by modifying and composing pieces from existing grammars. For example, the *Rats!* Jeannie grammar elegantly composes all of C and Java.

The ideas behind *LL(*)* are rooted in the 1970s. *LL(*)* parsers without predicated lookahead DFA edges implement *LL*-regular grammars, which were introduced by Jarzabek and Krawczyk [10] and Nijholt [15]. Nijholt [15] and Poplawski [18] gave linear two-pass *LL*-regular parsing strategies that had to parse from right-to-left in their first pass, requiring finite input streams (*i.e.*, not sockets or interactive streams). They did not consider semantic predicates.

Milton and Fischer [13] introduced semantic predicates to $LL(1)$ grammars but only allowed one semantic predicate per production to direct the parse and required the user to specify the lookahead set under which the predicates should be evaluated. Parr and Quong [17] introduced syntactic predicates and semantic predicate hoisting, the notion of incorporating semantic predicates from other nonterminals into parsing decisions. They did not provide a formal predicated grammar specification or an algorithm to discover visible predicates. In this paper, we give a formal specification and demonstrate limited predicate discovery during DFA construction. Grimm supports restricted semantic predicates in his PEG-based *Rats!* [8] and arbitrary actions but relies on programmers to avoid side-effects that cannot be undone. Recently, Jim *et al* added semantic predicates to transducers capable of handling all CFGs with Yakker [11].

ANTLR 1.x introduced syntactic predicates as a manually-controlled backtracking mechanism. The ability to specify production precedence came as a welcome, but unanticipated side-effect of the implementation. Ford formalized the notion of ordered alternatives with PEGs. Backtracking in versions of ANTLR prior to 3.x suffered from exponential time complexity without memoization. Ford also solved this problem by introducing packrat parsers. ANTLR 3.x users can turn on memoization with an option.

Previous attempts to extend parsing strength added fixed $k > 1$ lookahead to LL and $LALR$ parsers. Since k-lookahead sets have space $O(|T|^k)$, the challenge was to compress sets to a practical size. Charles [3] represented *LALR(k)* lookahead sets as minimal acyclic DFA with practical space costs on average. Parr [16] used a lossy compression called *linear approximate lookahead* that reduced space to $O(|T| \times k)$ and, in practice, worked for almost all decisions. (ANTLR 2.x used this compression.) The key difference between these techniques and *LL(*)* is that *LL(*)* lookahead DFA can be cyclic, thus, significantly extending parsing strength with arbitrary lookahead.

LL-regular grammars are the analog of LR-regular grammars [4]. Bermudez and Schimpf [2] provided a parsing strategy for LR-regular grammars called $LAR(m)$. Parameter m is a stack governor, similar to ours, that prevents analysis algorithm nontermination. $LAR(m)$ builds an $LR(0)$ machine and grafts on lookahead DFA to handle nondeterministic states. Finding a regular partition for every LL-regular or LR-regular parsing decision is undecidable. Analysis algorithms for *LL(*)* and $LAR(m)$ that terminate construct a valid DFA for a subset of the LL-regular or LR-regular grammar decisions, respectively. In the natural language community, Nederhof [14] uses DFA to approximate entire CFGs, presumably to get quicker but less accurate language membership checks. Nederhof inlines rule invocations to a specific depth, m, effectively mimicking the constant from $LAR(m)$.

8. Conclusion

LL(*) parsers are as expressive as PEGs and beyond because of semantic predicates. While GLR accepts left-recursive grammars, it cannot recognize context-sensitive languages as *LL(*)* and other predicated parsers can. Unlike PEGs or GLR, *LL(*)* parsers enable arbitrary action execution and provide good support for debugging and error handling. The *LL(*)* analysis algorithm constructs cyclic lookahead DFA to handle non-*LL(k)* constructs and then fails over to backtracking via syntactic predicates when it fails to find a suitable DFA. Experiments reveal that ANTLR generates efficient parsers, eliminating almost all backtracking. ANTLR is widely used in practice, indicating *LL(*)* hits a sweet spot in the parsing spectrum.

9. Acknowledgements

We would like to thank the anonymous reviewers for their detailed comments and to thank Sriram Srinivasan for discussing *LL(*)* parsing and grammar analysis at length.

References

[1] Appendix. `http://antlr.org/papers/LL-star/index.html`.

[2] Bermudez, M. E., and Schimpf, K. M. Practical arbitrary lookahead LR parsing. *Journal of Computer and System Sciences 41*, 2 (1990), 230–250.

[3] Charles, P. *A Practical Method for Constructing Efficient LALR(K) Parsers with Automatic Error Recovery.* PhD thesis, New York University, New York, NY, USA, 1991.

[4] Cohen, R., and Culik, K. LR-Regular grammars an extension of LR(k) grammars. In *SWAT '71: Proceedings of the 12th Annual Symposium on Switching and Automata Theory (swat 1971)* (Washington, DC, USA, 1971), IEEE Computer Society, pp. 153–165.

[5] Earley, J. An efficient context-free parsing algorithm. *Communications of the ACM 13*, 2 (1970), 94–102.

[6] Ford, B. Packrat Parsing: Simple, powerful, lazy, linear time. In *Proceedings of annual ACM SIGPLAN International Conference on Functional Programming* (2002), ACM Press, pp. 36–47.

[7] Ford, B. Parsing Expression Grammars: A recognition-based syntactic foundation. In *POPL '04: Proceedings of the 37th annual ACM SIGPLAN-SIGACT symposium on Principles of Programming Languages* (2004), ACM Press, pp. 111–122.

[8] Grimm, R. Better extensibility through modular syntax. In *PLDI'06: Proceedings of annual ACM SIGPLAN Conference on Programming Language Design and Implementation* (2006), ACM Press, pp. 38–51.

[9] Hanson, D. R. Compact recursive-descent parsing of expressions. *Software Practice and Experience 15* (December 1985), 1205–1212.

[10] Jarzabek, S., and Krawczyk, T. LL-Regular grammars. *Information Processing Letters 4*, 2 (1975), 31 – 37.

[11] Jim, T., Mandelbaum, Y., and Walker, D. Semantics and algorithms for data-dependent grammars. In *POPL '10: Proceedings of the 37th annual ACM SIGPLAN-SIGACT symposium on Principles of Programming Languages* (New York, NY, USA, 2010), ACM, pp. 417–430.

[12] McPeak, S., and Necula, G. C. Elkhound: A fast, practical GLR parser generator. In *Compiler Construction* (2004), pp. 73–88.

[13] Milton, D. R., and Fischer, C. N. LL(k) parsing for attributed grammars. In *International Conference on Automata, Languages, and Programming* (1979), pp. 422–430.

[14] Nederhof, M.-J. Practical experiments with regular approximation of context-free languages. *Computational Linguistics 26*, 1 (2000), 17–44.

[15] Nijholt, A. On the parsing of LL-Regular grammars. In *Mathematical Foundations of Computer Science 1976* (Heidelberg, 1976), A. Mazurkiewicz, Ed., vol. 45 of *Lecture Notes in Computer Science*, Springer Verlag, pp. 446–452.

[16] Parr, T. J. *Obtaining practical variants of LL(k) and LR(k) for k > 1 by splitting the atomic k-tuple.* PhD thesis, Purdue University, West Lafayette, IN, USA, 1993.

[17] Parr, T. J., and Quong, R. W. Adding Semantic and Syntactic Predicates to $LL(k)$—*pred-LL(k)*. In *Proceedings of the International Conference on Compiler Construction; Edinburgh, Scotland* (April 1994).

[18] Poplawski, D. A. On LL-Regular grammars. *Journal of Computer and System Sciences 18*, 3 (1979), 218 – 227.

[19] Tomita, M. *Efficient Parsing for Natural Language.* Kluwer Academic Publishers, 1986.

[20] Woods, W. A. Transition network grammars for natural language analysis. *Communications of the ACM 13*, 10 (1970), 591–606.

Cause Clue Clauses: Error Localization using Maximum Satisfiability *

Manu Jose
University of California, Los Angeles
mjose@cs.ucla.edu

Rupak Majumdar
MPI-SWS, Kaiserslautern &
University of California, Los Angeles
rupak@mpi-sws.org

Abstract

Much effort is spent by programmers everyday in trying to reduce long, failing execution traces to the *cause* of the error. We present an algorithm for error cause localization based on a reduction to the maximal satisfiability problem (MAX-SAT), which asks what is the maximum number of clauses of a Boolean formula that can be simultaneously satisfied by an assignment. At an intuitive level, our algorithm takes as input a program and a failing test, and comprises the following three steps. First, using bounded model checking, and a bound obtained from the execution of the test, we encode the semantics of a bounded unrolling of the program as a Boolean *trace formula*. Second, for a failing program execution (e.g., one that violates an assertion or a post-condition), we construct an *unsatisfiable* formula by taking the formula and additionally asserting that the input is the failing test and that the assertion condition does hold at the end. Third, using MAX-SAT, we find a maximal set of clauses in this formula that can be satisfied together, and output the complement set as a potential cause of the error.

We have implemented our algorithm in a tool called BugAssist that performs error localization for C programs. We demonstrate the effectiveness of BugAssist on a set of benchmark examples with injected faults, and show that in most cases, BugAssist can quickly and precisely isolate a few lines of code whose change eliminates the error. We also demonstrate how our algorithm can be modified to automatically suggest fixes for common classes of errors such as off-by-one.

Categories and Subject Descriptors D.2.5 [*Software Engineering*]: Testing and Debugging—Fault-localization; F.3.2 [*Logics and Meaning of Programs*]: Semantics of Programming Languages—Program Analysis

General Terms Verification,Reliability

Keywords Debugging, Fault localization, Maximum Satisfiability

* This research was sponsored in part by the NSF grant CCF-0546170 and the DARPA grant HR0011-09-1-0037.

PLDI'11, June 4–8, 2011, San Jose, California, USA.

1. Introduction

A large part of the development cycle is spent in debugging, where the programmer looks at a long, failing, trace and tries to localize the problem to a few lines of source code that elucidate the cause of the problem. We describe an algorithm for fault localization for software that automates this process. The input to our algorithm is a program, a correctness specification (either a post-condition, an assertion, or a "golden output"), and a program input and corresponding execution (called the *failing execution*) that demonstrates the violation of the specification. The output is a minimal set of program statements such that there exists a way to replace these statements such that the failing execution is no longer valid.

Internally, our algorithm uses symbolic analysis of software based on Boolean satisfiability, and reduces the problem to *maximum Boolean satisfiability*. It takes as input a program and a failing test case and performs the following three steps. First, it constructs a symbolic *trace formula* for the input program. This is a Boolean formula in conjunctive normal form such that the formula is satisfiable iff the program execution is feasible (and every satisfiable assignment to the formula corresponds to the sequence of states in a program execution). The trace formula construction proceeds identically to symbolic execution or bounded model checking algorithms [2, 6, 15].

Second, it extends the trace formula by conjoining it with constraints that ensure the initial state satisfies the values of the failing test and the final states satisfy the program post-condition that was failed by the test. The extended trace formula essentially states that starting from the test input and executing the program trace leads to a state satisfying the specification. Obviously, the extended trace formula for a failing execution must be unsatisfiable.

Third, it feeds the extended trace formula to a *maximum satisfiability solver*. Maximum satisfiability (MAX-SAT) is the problem of determining the maximum number of clauses of a given Boolean formula that can be satisfied by any given assignment. Our tool computes a maximal set of clauses of the extended trace formula that can be simultaneously satisfied, and takes the complement of this set as a candidate set of clauses that can be changed to make the entire formula satisfiable. Since each clause in the extended trace formula can be mapped back to a statement in the code, this process identifies a candidate localization of the error in terms of program statements. Note that there may be several minimal sets of clauses that can be found in this way, and we enumerate each minimal set as candidate localizations for the user. In our experiments, we have found that the number of minimal sets enumerated in this way remains small.

More precisely, our algorithm uses a solver for *partial* MAX-SAT. In partial MAX-SAT, the input clauses can be marked *hard* or *soft*, and the MAX-SAT instance finds the maximum number of soft clauses that can be satisfied by an assignment which satisfies every hard clause. In our algorithm, we mark the input constraints (that ensure that the input is a failing test) as well as constraints arising from the specification are hard. This is necessary: otherwise, the MAX-SAT algorithm can trivially return that changing an input or changing the specification can eliminate the failing execution. In addition, in our implementation, we group clauses arising out of the same program statement together, thus keeping the resulting MAX-SAT instance small.

We have implemented our algorithm in a tool called BugAssist for fault localization of C programs.[1] BugAssist takes as input a C program with an assertion, and a set of failing test cases, and returns a set of program instructions whose replacement can remove the failures. It builds on the CBMC bounded model checker for construction of the trace formula and an off-the-shelf MAX-SAT solver [20] to compute the maximal set of satisfied clauses. We demonstrate the effectiveness of BugAssist on 5 programs from the Siemens set of benchmarks with injected faults [8]. The TCAS program in the test suite is run with all the faulty versions in detail to illustrate the completeness of the tool. In each case, we show that BugAssist can efficiently and precisely determine the exact (to the human) lines of code that form the "bug". The other 4 programs are used to show the scalability of the tool when used in conjunction with orthogonal error trace reduction methods.

We can extend our algorithm to suggest *fixes* for bugs automatically, by noticing that the MAX-SAT instance can be used not only to localize problems, but also to suggest alternate inputs that will eliminate the current failure. In general, this is an instance of Boolean program synthesis, and the cost of the search can be prohibitive. However, we have experimentally validated that automatic suggestions for fixes is efficient when we additionally restrict the search to common classes of programmer errors, such as replacement of comparison operators (e.g., $<$ by $\leq$) or off-by-one arithmetic errors. For these classes of systems, BugAssist can automatically create suggestions for program changes that eliminate the current failure.

Error localization is an important step in debugging, and improved automation for error localization can speed-up manual debugging and improve the usability of automatic error-detection tools (such as model checkers and concolic testers). Based on our implementation and experimental results, we feel BugAssist is a simple yet precise technique for error localization.

Related Work. Fault localization for counterexample traces has been an active area of research in recent years [1, 12, 13, 22, 23]. Most papers perform localization based on multiple program runs, both successful and failing, and defining a heuristic metric on program traces to identify locations which separate failing runs from successful ones.

Griesmayer et al. [12] gives a fault localization algorithm for C programs that constructs a modified system that allows a given number of expressions to be changed arbitrarily and uses the counter example trace from a model checker. This requires instrumenting each expression e_i in the program with (`diag` $==$ i?`nondet()` : e_i), where `diag` is a non deterministic variable and `nondet()` is a new variable with the size equal to that of e_i. The number of diagnosis variables is equal to the number of components that are faulty in the program and need to be analyzed before creating the modified system. So each expression in the program requires a new variable in the modified system along with the diagnosis variables which could blow up the size of the instrumented program under consideration. In this work we avoid these drawbacks using selector variables and efficient MAX-SAT instance formulation using clause grouping technique.

Many existing algorithms for fault localization [1, 13, 23, 33] use the difference between the faulty trace and a number of successful traces. For example, Ball, Naik, and Rajamani [1] use multiple calls to a model checker and compare the counterexamples to a successful trace. The faults are those transitions that does not appear in a correct trace. Our approach does not require comparing the traces or a successful run of the program as benchmark. We report the exact locations where the bug could be corrected instead of a minimal code fragment or a fault neighbor location.

Alternate approaches to reducing the cognitive load of debugging are *delta debugging* [33], where multiple runs of the program are used to minimize the "relevant" portion of the input, and *dynamic slicing* [30], where data and control dependence information is used to remove statements irrelevant to the cause of failure. Our technique is orthogonal to delta-debugging and dynamic slicing, and can be composed profitably. In fact, we demonstrate in our experiments how a combination of dynamic slicing and delta debugging, followed by our technique, can allow us to localize faults in long executions.

While we describe our algorithm in pure symbolic execution terms, our algorithm fits in very well with concolic execution [3, 11, 25], where symbolic constraints are generated while the concrete test case is run. Our motivation for using CBMC was the easy integration with MAX-SAT solvers, but in our implementation, we performed some optimizations (such as using concrete values for external library calls in the trace formula and constant-folding input-independent parts of the constraints) similar to concolic execution.

Unsatisfiability cores and MAX-SAT have been used successfully for design debugging of gate-level hardware circuits [5, 24]. Unsatisfiability cores have also been used to localize over-constrains in declarative models [26].

2. Motivating Example

Program 1 A simple example.

```
int Array[3];
int testme(int index)
  {
  .   ..................
  1   if ( index != 1) /* Potential Bug 2 */
  2      index = 2;
  3   else
  4      index = index + 2; /* Potential Bug 1 */
  .   ..................
  .   ..................
  .
  5   i = index;
  6   return Array[i]; //assert(i >= 0 && i < 3)
  }
```

We start with an informal description of BugAssist. Consider the function `testme` in Program 1 which returns a value at a new location from an array of size 3. The global array `Array` has 3 elements. The function takes in the current index value, does computation on this value (shown in lines 1–4) to find a new index and returns the value in the array at the new index (line 6). The array dereference on line 5 generates implicit assertions about the array bounds shown in line 6.

The program has a bug. If the input `index` is equal to 1, then the else-branch sets `index` to 3, and the subsequent array dereference

[1] The tool, Eclipse plugin, and test cases can be downloaded from our web page http://bugassist.mpi-sws.org.

on line 6 is out of bounds. Testing the program with this input will find the bug, and return a program trace that shows the array bounds violation at the end. But testing or model checking returns a *full execution* path, including details irrelevant to the specific bug, and do not give the reason for failure, or the cause of the bug. The localization algorithm in BugAssist helps to nail down the issue to a few potential bug locations in the program where the correction has to be made.

BugAssist works as follows. Starting with the test input `index` $= 1$ and the program, it first constructs a symbolic *trace formula* TF encoding the program semantics:

$$\mathsf{TF} \equiv \texttt{guard}_1 = (\texttt{index}_1 \neq 1) \wedge$$
$$\texttt{index}_2 = 2 \wedge \texttt{index}_3 = \texttt{index}_1 + 2 \wedge$$
$$\texttt{i} = \texttt{guard}_1 ? \texttt{index}_2 : \texttt{index}_3$$

Every satisfying assignment to the trace formula gives a possible execution of the program, and conversely. We assume that integers and integer operations are encoded in a bit-precise way, and without loss of generality, the trace formula is a Boolean formula in conjunctive normal form. In case there are loops in the program, we unroll loops up to a bound computed from the execution of the test input on the program (roughly, we take the bound as the maximum number of times any loop gets executed along the execution, taking nesting into account). We omit the details of the standard encoding from imperative programs to Boolean formulas (see, e.g., [6]).

Clearly, at the end of the trace, the assertion

$$\texttt{i} < 3$$

does not hold for all inputs to the program. Consider now the formula

$$\Phi \equiv \underbrace{\texttt{index}_1 = 1}_{\text{test input}} \wedge \underbrace{\mathsf{TF}}_{\text{trace formula}} \wedge \underbrace{\texttt{i} < 3}_{\text{assertion}}$$

which is unsatisfiable. Intuitively, the formula captures the execution of the program starting with the error-inducing test input, and asserts that the assertion holds at the end (a contradiction, by choice of the input).

We convert Φ to conjunctive normal form (CNF) and feed it to a partial MAX-SAT solver [20]. A partial MAX-SAT solver takes as input a Boolean formula in CNF where each clause is marked "hard" or "soft," and returns the maximum number of soft clauses (as well as a subset of clauses of maximum cardinality) that can be simultaneously satisfied by an assignment satisfying all the hard clauses. In case of Φ, we make the constraints coming from the test input ($\texttt{index}_1 = 1$) and the assertion ($\texttt{i} < 3$) as hard, and leave the clauses in the trace formula soft. Intuitively, we ask, given that the input and the assertion are fixed, which parts of the trace formula are consistent with the input and the assertion? The partial MAX-SAT solver then tries to find a set of soft clauses of maximum cardinality which can be simultaneously satisfied while satisfying all the hard clauses. The complement of a set of maximally satisfiable clauses (CoMSS) gives a set of soft clauses of minimum cardinality whose removal would make Φ satisfiable, i.e., consistent with the view that the test input does not break the assertion. By tracing the origins of the clauses in this set to the program, we get a set of program locations that are potential indicators of the error. Using clause grouping, described in Section 3, each line in the program is mapped to a bunch of its soft clauses which are enabled and disabled simultaneously.

In our example, the hard and soft clauses are:

$$\text{Hard} : \texttt{index}_1 = 1 \wedge \texttt{i} < 3$$
$$\text{Soft} : \mathsf{TF}$$

MAX-SAT returns that a possible CoMSS maps to the line 4 in the program. This is the unsatisfiable core whose removal or correction can satisfy the formula Φ. We claim that is a potential error location for the program and a fix would be to change the constant to any integer less than 2 and greater than -2.

If the programmer decides this is not a correct localization, we can generate additional localization candidates as follows. We iterate by making another call to MAX-SAT, but this time make clauses arising out of line 4 hard, i.e., asking the MAX-SAT for possible CoMSS where line 4 is kept unchanged. This reveals another potential bug location in the code. We repeat this process until MAX-SAT finds the formula to be unsatisfiable and such that no clauses can be removed to make the instance satisfiable. The error locations reported by BugAssist are underlined in Program 1. On a closer look, these are all the places where the correction can be made. Either changing the constant value at line 4 or the conditional statement at line 1 can fix the program. Our method is limited by the existing code: we cannot "localize" errors that can only be fixed by adding additional code.

Notice that our technique is stronger than simply taking the backward slice of the program trace, and gives fine-grained information about potential error locations. The backward slice for this trace contains all the lines 1, 4, and 5. Our algorithm returns lines 1 and 4 separately as potential error locations. However, slicing is an orthogonal optimization which can be applied before applying our technique.

So far we have focused on error localization. The methodology can be modified to suggest program repairs as well. Intuitively, the fault localization returns a set of program commands that are likely to be wrong. One can then ask, what are potential replacements to these commands that fixes the error? In general, the space of potential replacements is large, and searching this space efficiently is a difficult problem of program synthesis [27, 29]. Instead, we take a pragmatic approach and look for possible fixes for common programmer errors.

Specifically, we demonstrate our idea by fixing "*off by one*" errors. In this example, the error occurs due to accessing an out of bound array element by one. When BugAssist comes back with line 4 as a potential bug location, we try to "fix" the bug by changing the constant whose new value is one off its current value. So we change the value 2 in this line to 3 or 1 and check if either of these values satisfy the properties. This involves modifying the trace formula appropriately and checking if the failing program execution becomes infeasible with either change. So in this case we create two programs with new constants at line 4 as follows.

$$Program1: \ index = index + 3 \ \times$$
$$Program2: \ index = index + 1 \ \surd$$

The new value 1 ensures that the error path is infeasible, and this can be used as a suggestion for repair for the program. The same procedure can be used to check for operator errors like use of plus instead of minus, division instead of multiplication, performing assignment instead of equality test, etc., which are common programmer error patterns.

3. Preliminaries

3.1 Programs: Syntax and Semantics

We describe our algorithm on a simple imperative language based on control-flow graphs. For simplicity of description, we omit features such as function calls or pointers. These are handled by our implementation.

A *program* $G = (X, \mathcal{L}, \ell_0, \mathcal{T})$ consists of a set X of Boolean-valued variables, a set $\mathcal{L}$ of *control locations*, an initial location $\ell_0 \in \mathcal{L}$ and a set $\mathcal{T}$ of *transitions*. Each transition $\tau \in \mathcal{T}$ is a tuple

(ℓ, ρ, ℓ') where ℓ and ℓ' are control locations and ρ is a constraint over free variables from $X \cup X'$, where the variables from X' denote the values of the variables from X in the next state.

For a constraint ρ, we sometimes write $\rho(X, X')$ to denote that the free variables in ρ come from the set $X \cup X'$.

Our notation is sufficient to express common imperative programs (without function calls): the control flow structure of the program is captured by the graph of control locations, and operations such as assignments $x := e$ and assumes $\mathsf{assume}(p)$ captured by constraints $x' = e \wedge \bigwedge\{y' = y \mid y \in X \setminus \{x\}\}$ and $p \wedge \bigwedge\{x' = x \mid x \in X\}$ respectively. A program is *loop-free* if there is no syntactic loop in the graph of control locations.

A *state* of the program $\mathcal{P}$ is a mapping from variables in X to Booleans. We denote the set of all program states by $v.X$. A *computation* of the program is a sequence $\langle m_0, s_0\rangle\langle m_1, s_1\rangle \ldots \in (\mathcal{L} \times v.X)^*$, where $m_0 = \ell_0$ is the initial location, and for each $i \in \{0, \ldots, k-1\}$, there is a transition $(m_i, \rho_i, m_{i+1}) \in \mathcal{T}$ such that (s_i, s_{i+1}) satisfies the constraint ρ_i.

An *assertion* p is a set of program states. A program *violates* an assertion p if there is some computation $\langle m_0, s_0\rangle \ldots \langle m_k, s_k\rangle$ such that s_k is not in p. Typically, assertions can be given as language-level correctness requirements (e.g., "no null pointer dereference"), as programmer-specified asserts in the code, or as post-conditions.

3.2 Trace Formulas

Given a program and a bound $k > 0$, we can unwind the graph of control locations to get a simplified program without loops whose computations all have length at most k and such that each computation of the simplified program is also a computation of the original program. From such a loop-free program, we can derive a (quantifier-free) Boolean formula, called the *trace formula*, such that the set of satisfying assignments to the formula correspond exactly to computations of the program. We briefly describe the construction; see [6] for details.

The construction of the trace formula takes a loop-free program $\mathcal{P}$, all of whose computations have length at most k, and recursively constructs a Boolean formula as follows. Let $X_0, \ldots, X_k$ be independent copies of the set of variables X. For each $\ell \in \mathcal{L}$ and $i \in \{0, \ldots, k-1\}$, let z_i^ℓ be a Boolean variable, and define a constraint $\phi(\ell, i)$ as follows:

$$z_i^\ell \leftrightarrow \bigvee_{(\ell,\rho,\ell')\in\mathcal{T}} \rho(X_i, X_{i+1}) \wedge z_{i+1}^{\ell'} \qquad (1)$$

The trace formula is then defined to be the conjunction over $\ell \in \mathcal{L}$ and $i \in \{0, \ldots, k-1\}$ of the constraints in Equation (1), together with the conjunct $z_0^{\ell_0}$:

$$z_0^{\ell_0} \wedge \bigwedge_{\ell\in\mathcal{L}, i\in\{0,\ldots,k-1\}} \phi(\ell, i) \qquad (2)$$

The construction is well-defined because $\mathcal{P}$ is loop-free.

While we have described trace formulas for our simple programs, a C program with finite bit width data, e.g., 32-bit integers, can be converted into an equivalent Boolean program by separately tracking each bit of the state, and by interpreting fixed-width arithmetic and comparison operators as corresponding Boolean operations on each individual bit. In particular, our implementation handles all features of ANSI-C, including function calls and pointers. We omit the (standard) details, see e.g., [6, 32].

3.3 Partial Maximum Satisfiability

Given a Boolean formula in conjunctive normal form, the *maximum satisfiability* (MAX-SAT) problem asks what is the maximum number of clauses that can be satisfied by any assignment [16]. The MAX-SAT decision problem is NP-complete; note that a formula is satisfiable iff all its clauses can be satisfied by some assignment.

The *partial maximum satisfiability* (pMAX-SAT) problem takes as input a Boolean formula Φ in conjunctive normal form, and a marking of each clause of Φ as *hard* or *soft*, and asks what is the maximum number of soft clauses which can be satisfied by an assignment to the variables which satisfies all hard clauses. Intuitively, each hard clause must be satisfied, and we look for the maximum number of soft clauses which may be satisfied under this constraint.

Recent years have seen a tremendous improvement in engineering efficient solvers for MAX-SAT and pMAX-SAT. The widely used algorithm for MaxSAT is based on branch-and-bound search [17], supported by effective lower bounding and dedicated inference techniques. Recently, unsatisfiability based MaxSAT solvers by iterated identification of unsatisfiable sub-formulas was proposed in [10]. This approach consist of identifying unsatisfiable sub-formulas and relaxing clauses in each unsatisfiable sub-formulas by associating a relaxation variable with each such clause. Cardinality constraints are used to constrain the number of relaxed clauses [19, 20].

In addition to solving the decision problem, MAX-SAT solvers also give a set of clauses of maximum cardinality that can be simultaneously satisfied. The complement of these maximum satisfiable subsets (MSS) are a set of clauses whose removal makes the instance satisfiable (CoMSS). Since the maximum satisfiability subset is maximal, the complement of this set is minimal [18].

In this work we make use of these CoMSS which refers to the clauses whose removal can make the system satisfiable. Since we represent a C program as a boolean satisfiability problem with constraints and properties, the CoMSS are oracles for potential bug locations.

3.4 Efficient Compilation to MAX-SAT

A single transition can lead to multiple clauses in the conjunctive normal form of the trace formula. In this section we provide a method to simplify the MAX-SAT problem by grouping together clauses arising out of a single transition in the program.

For each transition $\tau = (m, \rho, m') \in \mathcal{T}$, we introduce a new Boolean variable λ_τ. Let $\Lambda = \{\lambda_\tau \mid \tau \in \mathcal{T}\}$. Let $\mathsf{CNF}(\rho)$ be a conjunctive normal form representation of ρ. We augment each clause in $\mathsf{CNF}(\rho)$ with λ_τ. For example, suppose $(c_1^1 \vee \ldots) \wedge (c_1^2 \vee \ldots)$ is a conjunctive normal form representation of ρ, then the augmented representation is $(\neg\lambda_\tau \vee c_1^1 \vee \ldots) \wedge (\neg\lambda_\tau \vee c_1^2 \vee \ldots)$.

The augmentation with λ_τ has the following effect. When λ_τ is assigned `true`, the original clauses in the CNF representation of ρ must be satisfied, while when λ_ρ is assigned `false`, each augmented clause is already satisfied. This helps to enable and disable the clauses corresponding to each transition by setting and unsetting the λ_τ variable respectively. The λ-variables are called *selector variables*.

We now augment trace formulas with selector variables. Let $\phi'(\ell, i, \Lambda)$ be the formula in which each clause arising out of $\tau = (\cdot, \rho, \cdot)$ is augmented with λ_τ. Instead of Equation (2) for the trace formula, we use the form:

$$\underbrace{z_0^{\ell_0} \wedge \bigwedge_{\ell\in\mathcal{L}, i\in\{0,\ldots,k-1\}} \phi'(\ell, i, \Lambda)}_{\mathsf{TF}_1} \wedge \underbrace{\bigwedge_{\tau\in\mathcal{T}} \lambda_\tau}_{\mathsf{TF}_2} \qquad (3)$$

where we label the two parts of the formula TF_1 and TF_2 for later reference. Intuitively, clauses from TF_1 will be marked as hard clauses to the MAX-SAT solver, and clauses from TF_2 will be marked soft. Thus, the MAX-SAT solver will explore the space of possible program statements whose replacement will cause the error to go away.

Algorithm 1 Localization Algorithm

Input: Program $\mathcal{P}$ and assertion p
Output: Either p holds for all executions or potential bug locations

```
1: (test, σ) = GenerateCounterexample(P, p)
2: if σ is "None" then
3:    return "No counterexample to p found"
4: else
5:    Φ_H = [[test]] ∧ p ∧ TF_1(σ)
6:    Φ_S = TF_2(σ)
7:    while true do
8:       BugLoc = CoMSS(Φ_H, Φ_S)
9:       if BugLoc = ∅ then
10:         return "No more suspects"
11:      else
12:         output "Potential bug at CoMSS BugLoc"
13:         β = ⋁ {λ_i | λ_i ∈ BugLoc}
14:         Φ_S = Φ_S \ β and Φ_H = Φ_H ∪ β
```

Notice that we allocate a selector variable for each transition of the program, so the number of selector variables is bounded by the size of the program. However, in a trace, the same program transition may occur multiple times (e.g., on unrolling a loop), and there is a distinct clause for each of these occurrences all tagged with the same selector variable.

We use the abstraction technique on transitions, which correspond to line numbers of code in our implementation, but it is also possible to group the clauses from modules and recursively narrow down the problem to a module, and then to a line.

4. Algorithm

We now describe the algorithm for BugAssist. There are two phases of the algorithm: first, generate a failing execution (and a test demonstrating a failing execution), and second, find a minimal set of transitions that can render the failing execution infeasible.

4.1 Generating Failing Tests

In our implementation, we use either failing test cases from a test suite as a starting point. If there are no available tests, we use *bounded model checking* [2, 6] to systematically explore program executions and look for potential assertion violations. Once a failing execution is found, the bounded model checking procedure can generate a concrete initial state that leads to the assertion violation as well as the trace formula.

4.2 The Localization Algorithm

Algorithm 1 shows the BugAssist localization algorithm. Line 1 calls the procedure to generate failing executions for the assertion. If no failing executions are found, the procedure returns. Otherwise, we get a concrete test case test as well as a trace σ demonstrating the failure of the assertion.

Using the test, the failing execution, and the assertion, we construct two formulas (lines 5,6). The formula Φ_H consists of three parts. The first part, $[\![\mathsf{test}]\!]$, is a formula asserting that the initial state coincides with the test case that caused the failure. Formally, for a program state s, the constraint $[\![s]\!]$ is defined as $\bigwedge\{x = s(x) \mid x \in X\}$. The second part is the assertion p. The third part is the first part $\mathsf{TF}_1(\sigma)$ of the trace formula from Equation (3). The formula Φ_S is the second part $\mathsf{TF}_2(\sigma)$ of the trace formula from Equation (3).

Notice that $\Phi_H \wedge \Phi_S$ is unsatisfiable. (Intuitively, it says that if the program is run with the test input test, then at the end of the execution trace σ, the assertion p holds.)

In subsequent calls to pMAX-SAT, clauses in Φ_H are treated as hard clauses, and clauses in Φ_S are treated as soft clauses. Intuitively, treating Φ_S as soft clauses enables us to explore the effect of changing each subset of transitions to see if the failing transition can be made infeasible.

The search for localizations is performed in the **while** loop of lines 7–14. During each iteration of the while loop, we call the pMAX-SAT solver and get a CoMSS for the current (Φ_H, Φ_S) pair. Each of these clauses returned by CoMSS gives potential bug locations in the code, and is output to the programmer.

Whenever we report a potential bug, we add a hard blocking clause for the corresponding CoMSS, so that in subsequent iterations, this CoMSS is not explored again as a potential cause of error. In many of our experiments, the CoMSS returns a single λ_ρ clause as the indicator of error. In general, it returns more than one selector variable which indicates that the program cannot be fixed by changing any one line but must be changed at multiple locations. (This does happen in experiments.) Adding each of these λ_ρ variables as a new hard clause blocks the occurrence of these clauses in a different clause combination. To avoid this problem, we compute a blocking clause β (lines 13) and make the blocking clause hard. For example, suppose the coMSS returned is, $BugLoc = \{\lambda_1, \lambda_2, \ldots, \lambda_k\}$. This means that the bug can be fixed by making simultaneous changes to these k locations. In the next iteration, we add a new hard clause $(\lambda_1 \vee \ldots \vee \lambda_k)$ which ensures that this particular CoMSS is not encountered again, but other combinations of these locations are still allowed.

4.3 Dealing with Multiple Locations

BugAssist may return multiple locations where a correction is possible. The experimental results in section 6.1 shows that the number of potential error locations returned is quite small and, in most cases, the exact bug location is reported using a single failing execution. However, for reliability and further refinement of bug locations, we use a ranking mechanism for bug locations by running the localization algorithm repeatedly with different failing program traces and ranking the bug locations based on their frequency of appearance in each of these runs. For test cases, this requires access to a set of tests that all fail the assertion. For counterexample generation using bounded model checking, we take the Boolean formula constructed by the bounded model checker and generate multiple satisfying assignments by changing the order of variables in the SAT algorithm [7] or by doing a random restart of the solver. Running BugAssist with these new values gives a another set of potential bug locations. Repeating this process and ranking the bug locations can narrow down the search to a few lines in the program.

5. Extensions

We now describe two extensions to the basic algorithm.

5.1 Extension 1: Automated Repair

BugAssist can be extended to suggest potential repairs automatically. In general, program repair reduces to program synthesis. We sacrifice generality for practicality by focusing on specific program repairs inspired by program mutation testing and checking if there is a possible repair from this class that can remove the current test failures. For example, if there is a constant used in a potential error location, we try to synthesize a new constant which can fix the code [12], or if there is an operator used in a potential error location, we try to generate a repair by mutating the operator to a different one. We demonstrate this capability by generating suggestions for fixing *off-by-one errors* [31] in the program. These are a common class of logical errors in programs arising when programmers use an expression e in the program when they should be using $e \pm 1$. For example, this can happen if programmers forget that a sequence starts at zero rather than one (e.g. array indices in many languages like C, C++). It is also caused during boundary check conditions by using a $<$ instead of $\leq$ or vice versa.

During the code parsing phase, we mark lines which have constants in them. After running BugAssist on the code, we look at potential error locations, and for each constant c in this set, we introduce an indicator variable i_c that takes values in the set $\{-1, 0, 1\}$. We replace the constant c with the expression $c + i_c$ in the code. Now, we ask if there exist values to the indicator variables that ensures that the new trace is infeasible. This is a Σ_2 query (does there exist values of i_c such that for all inputs the trace formula is infeasible), and cannot be directly solved by a SAT solver (see [28, 29] for extensions to SAT solvers to solve this problem). In our implementation, we restrict the number of non-zero indicator variables and iteratively call a SAT solver for each assignment of the indicator variables.

5.2 Extension 2: Debugging Loops

Bugs within loop bodies can be particularly hard to debug as they might be hidden in initial iterations and only visible afterwards. The usual bounded model checking methodology to verify properties is by unwinding loops by duplicating the loop body K times for a limit K on the number of unwindings. The programmer would be interested in knowing the iteration at which the assertion is violated to get a better idea about the cause of the error. We suggest a method to catch the potential iteration of the loop where the bug appeared first.

We can do this by grouping clauses and assigning weights to the soft clauses in the pMAX-SAT instance, and using a *weighted* version of the pMAX-SAT algorithm. Each time a loop body is duplicated (till the bound K), we create a new selector variable. For example, for a transition $\tau = (m, \rho, m') \in \mathcal{T}$ in the loop body, during the ith unwinding, we augment each clause arising out of ρ with λ^i_τ. We add these selector variables as soft clauses to the pMAX-SAT instance as before, but additionally assign a weight as follows:

$$Weight(\lambda^i_\tau) = \alpha + K - i \qquad (4)$$

for each $i = 1, \ldots, K$, where α is some default weight for soft clauses. This makes sure that the clauses corresponding to the initial iterations of the loop gets a higher weightage. The weights assigned to the soft clauses in the pMAX-SAT can be thought of as the penalty that has to be paid to falsify the clauses. The solver extracts the CoMSS in such a way that clauses from initial iterations are preferred over clauses from later iterations, since the former have higher weights. This helps to localize the first iteration of the loop which can reproduce the failure.

6. Experimental Results

We now demonstrate the capability of the tool by showing the results from running programs from the Siemens test suite [8]. The Siemens test suite is widely used in the literature for bug localization studies [12, 23]. In Section 6.1, we analyze a simple TCAS program from the Siemens suite [14] in depth and in Section 6.2 we illustrate the scalability of our method using more complex examples.

In our implementation, we used the bounded model checker CBMC [6] to generate failing test inputs as well as to construct the trace formula for an unrolling of the program. For solving the pMAX-SAT instances, we used the *Maximum Satisfiability with UNsatisfiable COREs* (MSUnCORE) tool [20], which can handle large and complex weighted partial MAX-SAT problems. Fixes for off-by-one errors were synthesized using the MiniSAT2 [9] SAT

```
1 int Inhibit_Climb () {
2   return (Climb_Inhibit?Up_Sep+300:Up_Sep);
3   /*return (Climb_Inhibit?Up_Sep+100:Up_Sep);*/
4 }
5 int Non_Crossing_Climb() {
6    upward_preferred=Inhibit_Climb()>Down_Sep;
7    if (upward_preferred) {
8         result = !(Own_Below_Threat()) ||
                   (!(Down_Sep >= ALIM()));  }
9      else{
10       result =  (Cur_Vertical_Sep >= 100)
                  && (Up_Sep >= ALIM());  }
11     return result;
12 }
13 int Non_Crossing_Descend() {
14    upward_preferred=Inhibit_Climb()>Down_Sep;
15    if (upward_preferred) {
16      result = Own_Below_Threat() &&
               (Cur_Vertical_Sep >= 100) &&
                      (Down_Sep >= ALIM());}
17     else{
18       result = !(Own_Above_Threat()) ||
               ((Own_Above_Threat()) &&
               (Up_Sep >= ALIM())); }
19     return result;
20 }
21  int alt_sep_test() {
22      enabled = true; /*conditions omitted*/
23      alt_sep = UNRESOLVED;
24      if (enabled) {
25         need_upward_RA=Non_Crossing_Climb()&&
                                 Own_Below_Threat();
26         need_downward_RA=Non_Crossing_Descend()
                                 && Own_Above_Threat();
27         if (need_upward_RA && need_downward_RA)
28             alt_sep = UNRESOLVED;
29         else if (need_upward_RA)
30             alt_sep = UPWARD_RA;
31         else if (need_downward_RA)
32             alt_sep = DOWNWARD_RA;
33      }
34      return alt_sep;
35 }
36 int main() {/*inputs omitted*/
37    assert(alt_sep_test() == DOWNWARD_RA);
38 }
```

Figure 1. Sample TCAS code. Potential bug locations identified by BugAssist are underlined. Original code on line *3*; mutation on line *2*

engine. All our experiments are preformed on an 3.16 GHz Intel Core 2 Duo CPU with 7.6 GB RAM.

6.1 TCAS Experiments

The TCAS task of the Siemens test suite implements an aircraft collision avoidance system. It consists of 173 lines of code. The authors have created 41 versions of the program by injecting one or more faults. Their goal was to introduce faults that were as realistic as possible, based on their experience with real programs. We refer to the versions as "v1" to "v41". The Siemens test suite also contains 1600 test cases which are valid inputs for the program.

We created the golden outputs for these 1600 test cases by running the original version of the program. Then for each of the faulty versions, we ran those 1600 test vectors and matched with the golden outputs to segregate the failing test cases. Since the program does not contain a specification, we use the failing test cases as counterexamples and the correct value as its specification.

Table 1 shows the result of running BugAssist on the TCAS test suite. BugAssist ran 1440 times over all versions and 1367 of these runs pin-pointed the exact bug location, i.e., in 95% of the total runs. The "$TC\#$" in the table is the number of failed test cases

Version	TC#	Error#	Detect#	Size Reduc%	Run Time	Error Type	–	Version	TC#	Error#	Detect#	Size Reduc%	Run Time	Error Type
v1	132	1	132	8.6	0.016	op		v21	16	1	16	8.6	0.108	op
v2	69	1	69	4.6	0.068	const		v22	11	1	11	5.7	0.056	code
v3	23	1	13	9.8	0.096	op		v23	42	1	41	6.3	0.100	code
v4	26	1	26	9.2	0.104	op		v24	7	1	7	8.6	0.092	op
v5	10	1	10	8.6	0.120	assign		v25	3	1	3	6.9	0.068	code
v6	12	1	12	8.6	0.108	op		v26	11	1	11	9.2	0.108	addcode
v7	36	1	36	9.2	0.072	const		v27	10	1	10	10.9	0.108	addcode
v8	1	1	1	8.6	0.112	const		v28	76	1	58	5.7	0.080	Branch
v9	9	1	9	5.2	0.092	op		v29	18	1	14	5.7	0.092	code
v10	14	2	14	9.2	0.136	op		v30	58	1	58	5.7	0.064	code
v11	14	2	14	6.3	0.080	op		v31	14	2	14	10.9	0.008	addcode
v12	70	1	48	9.2	0.164	op		v32	2	2	2	10.9	0.004	addcode
v13	4	1	4	9.2	0.080	const		v34	77	1	77	8.6	0.100	op
v14	50	1	50	8.1	0.028	const		v35	76	1	58	5.7	0.060	code
v15	10	3	10	7.5	0.104	const		v36	126	1	126	2.9	0.024	op
v16	70	1	70	9.2	0.104	init		v37	93	1	93	8.6	0.040	index
v17	35	1	35	9.2	0.096	init		v39	3	1	3	6.9	0.088	op
v18	29	1	29	6.9	0.124	init		v40	126	2	126	6.3	0.088	assign
v19	19	1	19	9.2	0.112	init		v41	20	1	20	8.6	0.120	assign
v20	18	1	18	9.2	0.120	op		–	–	–	–	–	–	

Table 1. Results of running BugAssist on the TCAS task of the Siemens Test Suite

Error Type	Explanation for the error
op	Wrong operator usage e.g.: <= instead of <
code	Logical coding bug
assign	Wrong assignment expression
addcode	Error due to extra code fragments
const	Wrong constant value supplied e.g.: off-by-one error
init	Wrong value initialization of a variable
index	Use of wrong array index
branch	Error in branching due to negation of branching condition

Table 2. Type of error

for each version. We ran BugAssist with each of these failing test cases as failing program executions and the golden output as the assertion to be satisfied. The column "$Error\#$" shows the number of errors injected in to each version. Most versions have only 1 error but some have 2 and 3 errors. "$Detect\#$" is the number of runs of BugAssist which detected the correct (human-verified) bug location. "$SizeReduc\%$" is the percentage reduction in the code size given by the tool to locate the bug, the ratio of bug locations returned by the tool to the total number of lines in the code. The "$RunTime$" shows the run time for each run of BugAssist in seconds and they are negligible. The last column is the type of bug which is explained in Table 2. For example, the version v2 has one error injected and has 69 failing test cases. We collected the bug locations reported during these 69 runs of the tool which gave 8 potential bug locations, which is 4.6% of the total line number's in the program. The exact location of the fault is contained in the localizations obtained from all the 69 runs.

Except for a few versions like v12, v28 and v35, BugAssist detected the correct bug location for all the runs. For the remaining ones, when we rank locations based on frequency of being reported as bugs, exact bug locations had a count more than half of the total number of runs. The runs in which exact location was not reported did give clues about the real bug. For example, some test cases had wrong constant value assignment to an array element, for which the tool reported the fault at places where that array is accessed rather than the line at which the bad assignment occurred. By analyzing the error locations it is quite evident that the error is due to a wrong value in that array location. On average the number of lines to check for potential bug is reduced to 8% of the total code. It should be noted that most of the single runs of the faulty version have captured the exact bug location.

Figure 1 gives an overview of a version of tcas (v2). The bug is in line 2 (and the original code is shown commented out in line 3). The bug is injected in function *Inhibit_Biased_Climb* at line 2 by changing the constant value. The declaration and initialization of variables, functions, and conditional statements that are not relevant to this bug are omitted in the figure. The program needs to satisfy the safety property *alt_sep_test()* should return *DOWNWARD_RA* and is given as assertion at line 37. There were 69 failing test cases for this version. We ran all these test cases and the tool returned 8 potential bug locations which are shown underlined in Figure 1.

There is no error reported in function *Non_Crossing_Climb()* because the call for that function at line 25 needs the function *Own_Below_Threat()* to be true, but that is false based on a comparison on the input parameters which are made hard clauses. Now lets take a closer look at the reported errors.

1. Line 34 is too weak for a fix because changing the return value can make the assertion always true and that does not serve as a suitable fix.
2. In line 26, setting the *need_downward_RA* variable to true can pick the right value for *alt_sep*. This decision is made by an evaluation of the two functions in that statement. The function *Own_Above_Treat()* returns true based on the input and it is clear that the correction needs to be done to the function call *Non_Crossing_Decend()*.
3. The function *Non_Crossing_Decend()* has a call for the actual faulty function at line 14. It also shows that the repair could be done by changing the return value of this function at line 19 (which we ignore as in case 1 above), or where the wrong evaluation happens (lines 15,16).

4. The actual bug at line 2 is reported as a potential bug location in all the runs.

6.2 Larger Examples

To show the performance and applicability of our approach for larger programs and in the presence of complex pointers and loops, we chose a set of other test cases with function calls, recursion, dynamic memory allocation, loops, and complex programming constructs.

The TCAS test cases were small enough to allow the MAX-SAT solver to deal with the Boolean trace formula without additional optimizations. However, for larger programs, the trace formula obtained by unrolling a program, and the corresponding MAX-SAT instance, was beyond the capacity of the MAX-SAT solver. Therefore, we combine our technique with existing trace reduction techniques like program slicing (S) [30], concolic execution (C) [11], and isolating failure-inducing input using delta debugging (D) [34].

Table 3 shows the result of running BugAssist on 4 other programs from the Siemens suite, each with one injected fault. "*Program*" shows the name of the program from the Siemens testsuite. "*LOC#*" is the total lines of code in the program and "*Proc#*", the number of procedure calls. The kind of reduction technique is specified in "*Reduc*" and "*assign#*" shows the size of the dynamic error trace as the number of assignment expressions before and after performing the reduction technique. The "*var#*" and "*clause#*" is the number of boolean variables and clauses in the MAX-SAT representation of the error trace both before and after the reduction step (the unit "m" denotes million). The number of potential fault locations returned by the tool is given under "*Fault#*". The column "*Time*" shows the runtime in seconds (s) or (in one case) hours (h).

We picked a faulty version of the program and one test input that reveals the bug. The golden output from the non-faulty program with the same input is given as a post condition on the return value of the faulty version. Trace reduction techniques are applied to the program execution with this input to generate a smaller trace formula and given as input to BugAssist. The tool reported the exact bug location in all programs except one (Program 2: `print_token`). Trace reduction techniques significantly reduced the resulting trace and the size of the MAX-SAT instance, as shown in "Before" and "After" sizes in Table 3. The cardinality of the potential fault location set for each of these programs turns out to be small. In all cases, the run time of the tool was smaller than our human effort required to isolate the fault on the original trace. This shows the applicability of the approach.

- The error inducing input to Program `totinfo` was the rows and columns of a matrix. The bug was in the constant value of a conditional operator on checking the product of rows and columns after a few other operations. A simple program slicing removed the assignments irrelevant to the assertion being checked and reduced the number of assignments to 21 and the run time to less than a second.
- Program `print_token` contained a recursive function "next_token" and the input to the program required the loops to be unrolled 8 times in the symbolic trace formula generation. This made the recursive function to have 64 instances in the symbolic trace and the number of assignments went up to 65K without concolic execution. Using concrete execution for the recursive function and variables, the number of assignment statements was bought down to 239. It should be noted that the limitation in using a concrete execution would be to assume that the bug is not present in the functions and loops which are concretized. However, this methodology fits well in programs using functions from a reliable library or for functions which are already verified to be bug free. This program did not show error at the exact location, which was a comparison on a variable which got the value from the concrete execution. This was because the constant propagation used by the symbolic trace generator abstracted away the variable since its value was a constant. Instead, the error was shown in the assignment of the variable to the constant.
- The priority scheduler program 3 and 4, contained a large error inducing input which called a number of procedures before deviating from the golden output of the original program. The trace size was significantly reduced after isolating the error inducing input using delta debugging, but was still quite big (about 400 and 5400 assignment operations respectively). In program 3, the off-by-one error on flushing the number of processes was detected by the presence of a single process creation (leading to a trace of about 400 assignments). However, program 4 required a much larger input and more procedures to expose the failure, resulting in a longer trace. It took BugAssist almost 11 hours to find the exact location (excluding the time taken for input minimization using delta debugging). Each execution of MAX-SAT took around 30 minutes to identify one potential fault location.

Program 2 The strncpy program with an off-by-one error

```
1   #define SIZE 15
2   void MyFunCopy (char *s)
3   {
4       char buf[SIZE];
5       memset(buf, 0, SIZE);
6       strncat(buf, s, SIZE);
7      /*Last argument should be: SIZE-1 */
8       return;
9   }

/*Standard C implementation of strncat*/
10   char *strncat(char *dest, const char *src,
                                   size_t n)
11   {
12        char *ret = dest;
13         while (*dest)
14            dest++;
15         while (n--)
16             if (!(*dest++ = *src++))
17                return ret;
18         *dest = 0; /*Problem cause*/
19         return ret;
20   }
```

6.3 Fixing Off-By-One Errors

We demonstrate the repair capability of BugAssist by synthesizing fixes for off-by-one errors in the use of standard C library routines. We focus on off-by-one errors arising out of the misuse of the C `strncat` string manipulation function [21]. A common misconception with `strncat` is that the guaranteed null termination will not write beyond the maximum length. In reality, `strncat` can write a terminating null character one byte beyond the maximum length specified.

The Program 2 shows an instance of the bug in the function `MyFunCopy`, which takes a string `s` and uses the `strncat` routine to copy the contents to a string `buf` of length `SIZE`. The lines 10–20 shows a standard C implementation of `strncat`. Note that after

	Program	LOC#	Proc#	Reduc	assign#		var#		clause#		Fault#	time
					Before	After	Before	After	Before	After		
1	totinfo	565	7	S	734	21	0.797m	400	1.822m	1225	2	0.19s
2	print_tokens	726	18	C	65698	239	5.507m	7439	53.483m	22634	13	25s
3	schedule	564	21	DS	5914	391	5.173m	0.053m	15.379m	0.142m	13	28s
4	schedule	564	21	DS	41942	5412	78.982m	4.517m	239.385m	13.788m	25	11h
5	totinfo	565	7	CS	865	454	0.862m	0.734m	4.156m	3.728m	3	225s
6	schedule2	374	16	S	398	275	0.021m	0.015m	0.062m	0.048m	9	20s

Table 3. Running BugAssist on larger benchmark programs from the Siemens Test Suite

copying the n characters at line 17, the implementation writes to the $(n+1)$st location of the string `dest` on line 18. This implies that the function `MyFunCopy` should be using `SIZE` $- 1$ as the last argument to `strncat`.

We ran BugAssist on this function, checking whether array accesses are within bounds. We made the assumption that library functions cannot be modified, and the error lies in the client code. That is, in the pMAX-SAT problem formulation, we made constraints arising out of library functions (`strncat` in this case) hard clauses. BugAssist located line 6 as a potential bug location in the code. This location is marked during preprocessing as a statement with a constant; so BugAssist now tries to fix it by changing the value to `SIZE` $- 1$ and `SIZE` $+ 1$ as explained before. This creates two SAT instances with the new constant values, and we use a SAT solver to check if the error is still feasible. In this example, the change to `SIZE` $- 1$ eliminated the bug.

Program 3 The nearest integer square root function with a bug at line 12

```
1     int squareroot()
2     {
3         int val = 50;
4         int i =1;
5         int v =0;
6         int res =0;
7         while(v < val)
8         {
9             v = v + 2*i +1;
10            i = i+1;
11        }
12        res = i;
13        /* res = i - 1; */
14        assert( (res*res <= val) &&
                   ((res+1)*(res+1) > val);
15          return res;
      }
```

6.4 Finding Faulty Loop Iterations

Program 3 contains a function to find the nearest integer square root of a value. The post condition is specified as an assertion, and states that the result `res` should be the closest square root for `val`. The bug locations reported by BugAssist are underlined. The correct code is given as a comment on line 13. Even though the actual bug is not in the loop body, it requires an analysis of the loop body to conclude that the right fix is at line 12. We gave the unwinding limit 50 to CBMC and BugAssist reports a potential repair at line 10 in the 8th iteration of the loop. This gives clue to the programmer that the error occurs if the loop is iterated atleast 8 times.

7. Discussions

Program analysis based on Boolean satisfiability has been extremely successful in detecting subtle errors in large software programs [4, 6, 32]. We show that techniques based on Boolean MAX-SAT can be similarly effective in *localizing* program errors (as well as in identifying potential fixes).

Our fault localization algorithm depends on the underlying Boolean transform of the program to clauses, and is limited by the scalability of bounded model checking tools. In most cases, a single failing input was sufficient to locate the exact error location. Each of the potential error locations are the unsatisfied clauses in each iteration of the MAX-SAT solver. Our fault correction algorithm works by changing existing clauses. We cannot detect or correct code omission faults.

Our experimental results show that trace reduction techniques are crucial in making our implementation scale to reasonably large examples. Trace reduction techniques, such as delta-debugging or slicing, are orthogonal to our approach, and we can build on the extensive literature in these fields. Additionally, the performance can be improved by using an incremental SAT solver for iterative applications of MAX-SAT. While we have described error localization at the line-number (or program statement) level, our reduction to pMAX-SAT is general, and can be used at different levels of granularity. For example, to localize bugs at the function or module level, we can group clauses coming from the same function or module in the pMAX-SAT instance.

To improve the usability of our tool, we have built an Eclipse plugin to use BugAssist interactively during the development process. The plugin marks potential bugs in the code under development and assists in analyzing the right fix.

References

[1] Thomas Ball, Mayur Naik, and Sriram K. Rajamani. From symptom to cause: localizing errors in counterexample traces. In *POPL '03: Principles of Programming Languages*, pages 97–105, 2003. ACM.

[2] A. Biere, A. Cimatti, E. M. Clarke, M. Fujita, and Y. Zhu. Symbolic model checking using sat procedures instead of bdds. In *DAC '09: Design Automation Conference*, pages 317–320, 1999. ACM.

[3] Cristian Cadar, Daniel Dunbar, and Dawson Engler. Klee: unassisted and automatic generation of high-coverage tests for complex systems programs. In *OSDI '08: Operating Systems Design and Implementation*, pages 209–224, 2008. USENIX Association.

[4] Cristian Cadar, Vijay Ganesh, Peter M. Pawlowski, David L. Dill, and Dawson R. Engler. Exe: automatically generating inputs of death. In *CCS '06: Computer and Communications security*, pages 322–335, 2006. ACM.

[5] Yibin Chen, Sean Safarpour, Andreas Veneris, and Joao Marques-Silva. Spatial and temporal design debug using partial maxsat. In *GLSVLSI '09: Great Lakes Symposium on VLSI*, pages 345–350, 2009. ACM.

[6] Edmund Clarke, Daniel Kroening, and Flavio Lerda. A tool for checking ANSI-C programs. In *TACAS '04: Tools and Algorithms*

for the Construction and Analysis of Systems, volume 2988 of *Lecture Notes in Computer Science*, pages 168–176, 2004. Springer.

[7] Martin Davis and Hilary Putnam. A computing procedure for quantification theory. *J. ACM*, 7:201–215, July 1960.

[8] Hyunsook Do, Sebastian Elbaum, and Gregg Rothermel. Supporting controlled experimentation with testing techniques: An infrastructure and its potential impact. *Empirical Softw. Engg.*, 10(4):405–435, 2005.

[9] Niklas Eén and Niklas Sörensson. Minisat v2.0 (beta). In *SAT-Race*, 2006. http://fmv.jku.at/sat-race-2006/.

[10] Zhaohui Fu and Sharad Malik. On solving the partial MAX-SAT problem. In *SAT '06: Theory and Applications of Satisfiability Testing*, volume 4121 of *Lecture Notes in Computer Science*, pages 252–265, 2006. Springer.

[11] Patrice Godefroid, Nils Klarlund, and Koushik Sen. Dart: directed automated random testing. In *PLDI '05: Programming Language Design and Implementation*, pages 213–223, 2005. ACM.

[12] Andreas Griesmayer, Stefan Staber, and Roderick Bloem. Automated fault localization for C programs. *ENTCS*, 174:95–111, 2007.

[13] Alex Groce, Sagar Chaki, Daniel Kroening, and Ofer Strichman. Error explanation with distance metrics. *Int. J. Softw. Tools Technol. Transf.*, 8:229–247, 2006.

[14] Monica Hutchins, Herb Foster, Tarak Goradia, and Thomas Ostrand. Experiments of the effectiveness of dataflow- and controlflow-based test adequacy criteria. In *ICSE '94: International Conference on Software Engineering*, pages 191–200, 1994. IEEE Computer Society.

[15] James C. King. Symbolic execution and program testing. *Commun. ACM*, 19:385–394, July 1976.

[16] Chu Min Li and Felip Manyà. MaxSAT, hard and soft constraints. In *Handbook of Satisfiability*, volume 185 of *Frontiers in Artificial Intelligence and Applications*, chapter 19, pages 613–631. IOS Press, 2009.

[17] Chu Min Li, Felip Manyà, and Jordi Planes. New inference rules for MAX-SAT. *J. Artif. Int. Res.*, 30:321–359, October 2007.

[18] Mark H. Liffiton and Karem A. Sakallah. On finding all minimally unsatisfiable subformulas. In *SAT '05: Theory and Applications of Satisfiability Testing*, volume 3569 of *Lecture Notes in Computer Science*, pages 173–186, 2005. Springer.

[19] Joao Marques-Silva. Minimal unsatisfiability: Models, algorithms and applications (invited paper). In *ISMVL '10: International Symposium on Multiple-Valued Logic*, pages 9–14, 2010. IEEE Computer Society.

[20] Joao Marques-Silva and Jordi Planes. Algorithms for maximum satisfiability using unsatisfiable cores. In *DATE '08: Design, Automation and Test in Europe*, pages 408–413, 2008. ACM.

[21] Todd C. Miller and Theo de Raadt. strlcpy and strlcat: consistent, safe, string copy and concatenation. In *USENIX Annual Technical Conference*, pages 175–178, 1999. USENIX Association.

[22] Dawei Qi, Abhik Roychoudhury, Zhenkai Liang, and Kapil Vaswani. Darwin: an approach for debugging evolving programs. In *ESEC/FSE '09: European Software Engineering Conference and Foundations of Software Engineering*, pages 33–42, 2009. ACM.

[23] Manos Renieres and Steven P. Reiss. Fault localization with nearest neighbor queries. In *ASE '03: Automated Software Engineering*, pages 30 – 39, 2003. IEEE Computer Society.

[24] Sean Safarpour, Hratch Mangassarian, Andreas Veneris, Mark H. Liffiton, and Karem A. Sakallah. Improved design debugging using maximum satisfiability. In *FMCAD '07: Formal Methods in Computer-Aided Design*, pages 13–19, 2007. IEEE Computer Society.

[25] Koushik Sen, Darko Marinov, and Gul Agha. CUTE: a concolic unit testing engine for C. In *ESEC/FSE '05: European Software Engineering Conference and Foundations of Software Engineering*, pages 263–272, 2005. ACM.

[26] Ilya Shlyakhter, Robert Seater, Daniel Jackson, Manu Sridharan, and Mana Taghdiri. Debugging overconstrained declarative models using unsatisfiable cores. *ASE '03: Automated Software Engineering*, pages 94–105, 2003. IEEE Computer Society.

[27] Armando Solar-Lezama, Rodric Rabbah, Rastislav Bodík, and Kemal Ebcioğlu. Programming by sketching for bit-streaming programs. *PLDI '05: Programming Languages Design and Implementation*, pages 281–294, 2005. ACM.

[28] Armando Solar-Lezama, Liviu Tancau, Rastislav Bodík, Sanjit A. Seshia, and Vijay A. Saraswat. Combinatorial sketching for finite programs. In *ASPLOS '06: Architectural Support for Programming Languages and Operating Systems*, pages 404–415, 2006. ACM.

[29] Saurabh Srivastava, Sumit Gulwani, and Jeffrey S. Foster. VS3: SMT solvers for program verification. In *CAV '09: Computer-Aided Verification*, volume 5643 of *Lecture Notes in Computer Science*, pages 702–708, 2009. Springer.

[30] F. Tip. A survey of program slicing techniques. *Journal of Programming Languages*, 3:121–189, 1995.

[31] Wikipedia. Off-by-one error, the free encyclopedia, 2004. [Online; accessed 28-March-2010].

[32] Yichen Xie and Alex Aiken. Scalable error detection using boolean satisfiability. In *POPL '05: Principles of Programming Languages*, pages 351–363, 2005. ACM.

[33] Andreas Zeller. Isolating cause-effect chains from computer programs. In *FSE '10: Foundations of Software Engineering*, pages 1–10, 2002. ACM.

[34] Andreas Zeller and Ralf Hildebrandt. Simplifying and isolating failure-inducing input. *IEEE Trans. Softw. Eng.*, 28:183–200, 2002.

kb-Anonymity: A Model for Anonymized Behavior-Preserving Test and Debugging Data

Aditya Budi, David Lo, Lingxiao Jiang, and Lucia

School of Information Systems, Singapore Management University

{adityabudi, davidlo, lxjiang, lucia.2009}@smu.edu.sg

Abstract

It is often very expensive and practically infeasible to generate test cases that can exercise all possible program states in a program. This is especially true for a medium or large industrial system. In practice, industrial clients of the system often have a set of input data collected either before the system is built or after the deployment of a previous version of the system. Such data are highly valuable as they represent the operations that matter in a client's daily business and may be used to extensively test the system. However, such data often carries sensitive information and cannot be released to third-party development houses. For example, a healthcare provider may have a set of patient records that are strictly confidential and cannot be used by any third party. Simply masking sensitive values alone may not be sufficient, as the correlation among fields in the data can reveal the masked information. Also, masked data may exhibit different behavior in the system and become less useful than the original data for testing and debugging.

For the purpose of releasing private data for testing and debugging, this paper proposes the kb-anonymity model, which combines the k-anonymity model commonly used in the data mining and database areas with the concept of program behavior preservation. Like k-anonymity, kb-anonymity replaces some information in the original data to ensure privacy preservation so that the replaced data can be released to third-party developers. Unlike k-anonymity, kb-anonymity ensures that the replaced data exhibits the same kind of program behavior exhibited by the original data so that the replaced data may still be useful for the purposes of testing and debugging. We also provide a concrete version of the model under three particular configurations and have successfully applied our prototype implementation to three open source programs, demonstrating the utility and scalability of our prototype.

Categories and Subject Descriptors D.2.5 [*Testing and Debugging*]: Symbolic Execution/Testing tools; H.2.8 [*Database Applications*]: Data Mining; K.4.1 [*Public Policy Issues*]: Privacy

General Terms Algorithms, Experimentation, Reliability, Security

Keywords k-anonymity, behavior preservation, privacy preservation, third-party testing and debugging, symbolic execution

PLDI'11, June 4–8, 2011, San Jose, California, USA.

1. Introduction

It is common for companies in healthcare, banking, and other industries to employ third-party software houses to develop software systems for their day-to-day business. These software systems are used to manage and process various datasets containing person-specific information. Building perfect software for these industries in the first attempt is hard; extensive testing and debugging are needed to detect and fix bugs.

From a software developer's point of view, real data that would be processed by the software system in the field may contain more *relevant* test cases and *rare* cases that are bug-revealing. Being able to use such real data can be very helpful for testing and debugging.

A data owner, on the other hand, wants high-quality software systems for their daily business, and helping developers (*e.g.*, providing real data for testing) aligns with their interest. However, much of the data is sensitive or confidential. Such data cannot be released to third parties without proper *anonymization* or *desensitization*. For example, data in a hospital could contain the list of diseases each patient has; data in a bank could contain all transaction records of a client. Sending these datasets directly to third-party software developers could pose security risks and privacy concerns. Even though legal mechanisms, such as non-disclosure agreements (NDAs), can be applied to protect the data from leaking further, it can be very costly for the data owners to recover from any damage caused by violations of NDAs. It would be much safer to avoid unnecessary releases of sensitive or confidential data in the first place.

One solution for protecting privacy is to mask away (*i.e.*, replace, or remove) *identifiers* in all data points that can be used to (uniquely) identify an individual, such as *names* and *full addresses*, before releasing the data to a third party. However, due to data sparsity, a *quasi-identifier*, which is *a set* of fields that can uniquely identify a data point, may still exist in the dataset. For example, Golle and Sweeney found that about 63%-87% of the U.S. population can be uniquely identified by gender, 5-digit US ZIP code, and full date of birth [17, 37]. Simply masking away all possible quasi-identifiers would result in much less useful data, and thus a more sophisticated masking scheme is needed.

Another solution is to mask away sensitive or confidential information in all data points so that no actual private information is seen even though each data point uniquely identifies an individual. The main issue of this solution for the purposes of testing and debugging is that particular sensitive information can be important for triggering and thus testing a particular functionality in a software system. For example, in a healthcare application, there might be code implementing a special process for patients with lung cancer. Thus, we cannot simply mask away all possible sensitive information; a more sophisticated masking scheme is needed.

In this work, we propose a model for anonymizing privacy data that addresses the following challenges:

- The resulting dataset *should not leak individual-identifying* information.
- The resulting dataset should still *preserve the utility* of the original dataset for the purposes of *testing and debugging*.

We address these challenges by performing selective data value replacement in the original dataset at a data owner's site. The value replacement will generate a new dataset satisfying the following requirements. Each data point in the new dataset can still be used as a test case but cannot identify any individual in the original dataset. Also, the behavior of a program on a new data point should be the same as the behavior of the program on some original data point. This would allow failures exhibited by the original dataset to be exhibited by the new dataset, or the test coverage achieved by the original dataset to be achieved by the new dataset.

More specifically, our model and its implementation are mainly a combination and extension of two ideas: the *k-anonymity* model from the data mining and database research communities [7, 32, 38] that can provide guidance on choosing data fields to mask, and *concolic execution* [16, 36] that can guide the generation of new test cases based on known ones and make sure the new test cases satisfy certain properties. Merging the two ideas in various configurations enables us to achieve both privacy and program behavior preservation in various degrees. We call our model *kb-anonymity*[1] to highlight that it can preserve *behavior* and satisfy requirements similar to k-anonymity.

Note that another important difference between k-anonymity and kb-anonymity is that the new data points generated by kb-anonymity may not correctly reflect the original data points, as fake values may be introduced and some original data points may be lost. Certain statistics of the original data (*e.g.*, the geographical distribution of all persons contained in the original dataset or the percentage of persons having cancer) can thus be distorted, rendering the new dataset unsuitable for purposes (*e.g.*, data mining and epidemiological studies) other than testing and debugging. However, we believe that maintaining statistics of the original dataset is not necessary for testing and debugging, as long as the new dataset can exhibit the same kinds of behavior as the original dataset.

We present our privacy and program behavior preservation model in Section 3 and 4. We have built a prototype of the model on top of Java Pathfinder (JPF) [39], JFuzz (an extension of JPF) [18], and an approximation algorithm for creating k-anonymized datasets [7]. The main contributions of this work are as follows:

1. We propose a new problem of privacy preservation for testing and debugging.
2. We propose a new model for preserving both privacy and behavior when generating and releasing data for testing and debugging, and analyze various configurations of the model.
3. We propose several algorithms to implement various configurations of the model.
4. We empirically evaluate our solution on several sliced real programs and show the feasibility of our model and implementation in generating useful anonymized test and debugging data.

The outline of this paper is as follows. Section 2 summarizes necessary concepts and definitions related to k-anonymity and program behavior. We present our model and its privacy and behavior preservation properties in Section 3, and describe various configurations of our model in Section 4. Section 5 elaborates our empirical evaluation. We discuss some further considerations and threats to validity in Section 6. Section 7 describes related work. Finally, we conclude with future work in Section 8.

[1] b stands for *behavior*

2. Preliminaries

In this section, we introduce some concepts and definitions relevant to our work.

2.1 On Privacy Preservation

DEFINITION 2.1 (**Data**). *Each* dataset *is a set of* data points*; each data point in a dataset is a tuple t of the same number of fields: $t = \langle f_1, f_2, \ldots, f_n \rangle$. The value of each field is from a domain specific to the field. We use $t[i]$ to denote the value of the ith field in a tuple t, and $t[i_1, \ldots, i_j]$ to denote the sequence of values from the $i_1^{th}, \ldots, i_j^{th}$ fields.*

Given a dataset D, $D[i]$ denotes the set of values from the ith field of all tuples in D, which can also be viewed as a tuple when the values are arranged in an arbitrary order.

DEFINITION 2.2 (**Raw Data**). *A* raw dataset *is a set of* raw tuples*; each raw tuple is a tuple whose fields may contain person-specific values. Releasing raw tuples to any third party may violate the privacy requirements of the data owner.*

EXAMPLE 1. *Consider a raw dataset containing four patient records, each of which has seven fields (`NID` means national identification number which is abbreviated to 3 digits here):*

Name	NID	Age	Gender	Address	Doctor	Disease
Bob	254	53	Male	Clementi	Dr. Joe	Cancer
Tom	284	53	Male	Clementi	Dr. Joe	Cancer
Bob	893	37	Male	Jurong	Dr. Anne	Hypertension
Sue	283	34	Female	Jurong	Dr. Jill	Flu

Some fields in the raw dataset (*e.g.*, `NID`) uniquely identify an individual, and thus are referred to as *identifiers*. Some sets of fields can also uniquely identify an individual when used together (*e.g.*, the set of fields {`name`, `age`, `gender`, and `address`} in this example); they are referred to as *quasi-identifiers*. Some other fields are usually not used to identify an individual, but provide information about an individual (*e.g.*, `Disease`); they are referred to as *sensitive fields*.

DEFINITION 2.3 (**(In-)distinguishable Tuples**). *For two tuples t_1 and t_2, t_1 is indistinguishable from t_2 if for every identifier or quasi-identifier field f, $t_1[f] = t_2[f]$.*

We cannot release the raw dataset as it is, since each tuple can uniquely identify an individual through either the identifiers or the quasi-identifiers, leaking the patient's privacy. We transform the raw dataset into an *anonymized dataset* by replacing the values of some fields in the raw tuples with some generic values or masking them away with asterisks. Here is an anonymized dataset for Example 1, with which it is impossible to pinpoint a person having a particular disease when the receivers of the anonymized dataset have no other knowledge about the raw dataset. Notice that the values of the identifier field (`NID`) and the quasi-identifier fields (`name`, `age`, `gender`, and `address`) of each patient are equal to those of some other patient.

Name	NID	Age	Gender	Address	Doctor	Disease
Patient	*	53	Male	Clementi	Dr. Joe	Cancer
Patient	*	53	Male	Clementi	Dr. Joe	Cancer
Patient	*	30–39	*	Jurong	Dr. Anne	Hypertension
Patient	*	30–39	*	Jurong	Dr. Jill	Flu

A well-known privacy protection model, k-anonymity [32, 38], provides guidance on choosing data fields to mask:

DEFINITION 2.4 (k**-Anonymity**). *A dataset K is said to satisfy k-anonymity if each tuple in K is indistinguishable from at least k–1 other tuples in K.*

```
void processAPatient (int patient_id, int disease_id, int age) {
  switch ( disease_id ) {
    case 1: // Cancer
      if (age >= 60) {
        if (patient_id <= 1000) // VIP
           treatment("Premium intensive cancer");
        else
           treatment("Intensive cancer");
      } else {
        if (patient_id <= 1000)
           treatment("Premium standard cancer");
        else
           treatment("Standard cancer");
      }
    ...
```

Figure 1. An example to illustrate path conditions

The above example dataset is obviously 2-anonymized with respect to the first five fields. If we also consider `Doctor` as part of the quasi-identifier, only the first two anonymized tuples satisfy 2-anonymity. Without loss of generality, this paper considers the set of *all* fields in a dataset as one quasi-identifier for simpler exposition, unless some fields are explicitly identified as sensitive. Thus, we can simply denote two indistinguishable tuples t_1 and t_2 as $t_1 = t_2$.

DEFINITION 2.5 (**Value Replacement Function).** *Given a dataset R with tuples having n fields, a function $F : R \rightarrow R_U$, where R_U denotes the set of all possible tuples with n fields, is a value replacement function for R, if $\forall t \in R, \forall i \in \{1, \ldots, n\}$, $F(t)[i]$ is defined or equals* $*$.

The number of value replacements induced by F for R is $\sum_{t \in R} \sum_{i=1}^{n} I(\, F(t)[i] \neq t[i] \,)$, where $I(\cdot)$ is an indicator function, which returns 1 if its parameter is true, and 0 otherwise.

DEFINITION 2.6 (**Minimal k-Anonymity).** *Given a raw dataset R and a k-anonymized dataset K, K is said to be* minimal k-anonymized *if there exists a value replacement function from R to K that requires the fewest number of value replacements among all possible replacement functions from R to any k-anonymized dataset.*

Constructing minimal k-anonymized datasets for a given raw dataset has been proved to be NP-complete [7], but there exist algorithms that can approximate minimal solutions in quadratic time [7].

2.2 On Program Behavior

For software testing and debugging, we are also concerned with concepts related to program states, program execution paths, program inputs and outputs, etc.

DEFINITION 2.7 (**Program State).** *A program state corresponds to the complete status of a program at a point at runtime, which can include the values of all program variables, the location of the program counter, the environment on which the program relies (e.g., the file system status), etc. An execution of a program can be viewed as a sequence of program state transitions.*

DEFINITION 2.8 (**Path Condition).** *A path condition for an execution through a control flow path in a program is the conjunction of all the conditionals along the path.*

Example. Consider the program shown in Figure 1. For the input arguments: `patient_id==10`, `disease_id==1`, and `age==65`, the path condition is: $\texttt{disease\_id==1} \wedge \texttt{age} \geqslant \texttt{60} \wedge \texttt{patient\_id} \leqslant \texttt{1000}$.

PROPERTY 1. *For each program execution, there is only one path condition. Two executions following the same control flow paths have equivalent path conditions, although the executions may follow different sequences of program state transitions.*

Last but not least, software testing and debugging is often concerned with reproducible bug reports and test cases, which requires the concept of *equivalent program behavior*. There exist various definitions for this concept. In this paper, we define equivalence based mainly on path conditions:

DEFINITION 2.9 (**Behavior Equivalence).** *Two program executions are said to have equivalent behavior if their corresponding path conditions are equivalent (i.e., they follow the same control flow paths).*

3. Privacy and Behavior Preservation Model

In this section, we aim to establish a formal privacy preservation model, kb-anonymity, that can guide the construction and evaluation of algorithms and tools that generate datasets suitable to be released to third parties for testing and debugging purposes.

3.1 Objectives

There are two dimensions that we need to consider in this work:

Privacy Preservation. We assume that the raw data points contain person-specific information, and the objective of our model is to ensure that the identity of every person whose information is contained in the raw dataset cannot be revealed in the released dataset.

Behavior Preservation. The other objective of our model is to ensure that the program behavior exhibited by the raw dataset can be reproduced by the released dataset to a certain extent without compromising privacy. How program behavior is defined can vary in different configurations of the model.

The above two goals are inversely related. The more privacy is desired, the more values in the raw dataset may need replacement, and the harder it is to preserve program behavior. Similarly, the more behavior preservation is desired, the harder it is to preserve privacy. In the worst case, for a particular level of behavior preservation, it may not be possible to preserve any privacy. We elaborate on our privacy and behavior model in the following subsections.

3.2 Privacy Preservation

k-anonymity [32, 38], summarized in Section 2, is a well-known privacy protection model that requires every released data point to be indistinguishable from at least k–1 other released data points with respect to all identifier and quasi-identifier fields.

Simply conforming to the k-anonymity model does not fit our needs because of the following issues:

- The k-anonymity model allows duplicated data points in the dataset to be released, which may not be meaningful for testing and debugging due to redundant test cases;
- The k-anonymity model often implies that certain values in raw tuples would be replaced with a more generic value (e.g., replacing `California, USA` with `USA`) or an asterisk (`*`, which means "Don't tell"). This may lead to unusable test cases since testing and debugging often require concrete data values.[2]

[2] A "concrete data value" refers to any value in the domain of program inputs. In the above example, if the program accepts any location as an input, then both `California, USA` and `USA` are concrete, but `*` is not; if the program requires a state name as part of its inputs, then only `California, USA` is concrete.

Our kb-anonymity model addresses the issues by requiring a value replacement function to satisfy the following requirements:

R1: All values in a released dataset are concrete so that each data point can be directly used to execute programs;

R2: All released tuples are distinguishable from each other so as to reduce redundant test cases;

R3: For each raw tuple and its corresponding released tuple generated by applying the value replacement function on the raw tuple, there exist at least k–1 other raw tuples that are mapped by the same function to a tuple indistinguishable from this released tuple.

Intuitively, kb-anonymity aims to provide a similar guarantee as k-anonymity (R3), but avoid generic values (R1) and duplicate data points (R2). However, note that kb-anonymity is different from k-anonymity. k-anonymity considers k indistinguishable tuples *within the released dataset* while kb-anonymity considers k indistinguishable tuples *with respect to replacements of the raw dataset*. If the number of raw tuples is m, the number of the released tuples will be at most $\lfloor m/k \rfloor$, while k-anonymity will still have m tuples. The following Theorem 1 states that the R2 and R3 requirements can be easily achieved by applying k-anonymity and suppressing indistinguishable tuples.

3.2.1 $R2 + R3 \equiv k$-Anonymity Modulo Uniqueness

LEMMA 1. *Given a raw dataset R and its k-anonymized version K, K satisfies R3.*

PROOF. Let the value replacement function used to generate the tuples in K from the tuples in R be $F : R \to K$. According to the definition of k-anonymity, for each t'_1 in K, there exist at least k–1 tuples in K, $t'_2, \ldots, t'_k$, such that $\forall i \in \{2, \ldots, k\}$, $t'_1 = t'_i$. Since F maps each raw tuple in R to at most one tuple in K, there must exist at least k raw tuples $t_1, \ldots, t_k$ such that $\forall i \in \{1, \ldots, k\}$, $F(t_i) = t'_i$. By transitivity of indistinguishability, $\forall i \in \{1, \ldots, k\}$, $F(t_i) = t'_1$. □

THEOREM 1. *Given a raw dataset R and its k-anonymized version K, construct a new dataset K' as follows: for each group of indistinguishable tuples in K, add exactly one tuple from the group into K'. Then, K' satisfies R2 and R3.*

PROOF. *i)* K' trivially satisfies R2 due to the removal of indistinguishable tuples. *ii)* For each tuple t' in K', there must exist at least k tuples in K that are indistinguishable from t' (otherwise, t' would not appear in K'); thus R3 is true based on the same reasoning as Lemma 1. □

Theorem 1 provides us a base to build a dataset satisfying R2–R3. The other issue is to replace certain values and asterisks in K' to satisfy R1 while maintaining R2 and R3. Depending on which values to replace and how to perform replacement, we have various choices corresponding to various levels of privacy preservation. The following subsections introduce two options in our model.

3.2.2 No Field Repeat

This subsection proposes the `no field repeat` option for replacing values from raw data points. Its intuition is to ensure every value in the released dataset has not appeared in any raw data point. For example, if `age==30` appears in the raw dataset, `30` would not be used for the `age` field in the released dataset.

DEFINITION 3.1 (**No Field Repeat Option**). *Given a raw dataset R, a released version X of R satisfies* the `no field repeat` option *if X satisfies the following: i) X satisfies R1–R3; ii)* $\forall i \in \{1, \ldots, n\}, \forall t \in R, \forall t' \in X, t[i] \neq t'[i]$.

In some cases, `no field repeat` is impossible. For example, when both `male` and `female` have appeared in the `gender` field in the raw dataset, we may have to use one of two values (unless the program could handle a more generic gender value, such as `unknown`). Thus, we also need a less restrictive option.

3.2.3 No Tuple Repeat

This subsection proposes the `no tuple repeat` option. This option ensures that every released tuple is distinguishable from every raw tuple, but allows them to share some field values.

DEFINITION 3.2 (**No Tuple Repeat Option**). *Given a raw dataset R, a released version X of R satisfies* the `no tuple repeat` option *if X satisfies the following: i) X satisfies R1–R3; ii)* $\forall t \in R, \forall t' \in X, t \neq t'$.

Note that the `no field repeat` option subsumes the `no tuple repeat` option, meaning that a released dataset satisfying `no field repeat` also satisfies `no tuple repeat`.

In summary, we have the following four levels of privacy preservation: *(i)* `None` which imposes no restriction on released tuples, *(ii)* `Standard k-Anonymity` modulo uniqueness, *(iii)* `No Tuple Repeat`, and *(iv)* `No Field Repeat`.

3.3 Behavior Preservation

The second objective of our kb-anonymity model is to ensure the following:

R4: For each released tuple b and each raw tuple t that is mapped to b, b and t must exhibit the same behavior when run on the subject program.

As mentioned in Section 2, various definitions of program behavior and equivalence exist and affect our model that is mainly for the purposes of software testing and debugging. The personnel and tools performing testing and debugging often consider program runs with reusable or reconstructible program execution paths, program inputs and outputs, and program states. Thus, we consider the following four levels of behavior equivalence in this paper: `None`, `Same Path`, `Same Path with Input Restrictions`, and `Same Program States`.

The lowest level, `none`, is used as a baseline that allows arbitrary program behavior to be exhibited by the released dataset and provides no guarantee on behavior preservation.

The second level, `same path`, requires each released data point to follow the same execution path as the path followed by the raw data point mapped to it:

R4-1: A released tuple b is *path preserving* for a raw tuple t mapped to it if b and t follow *the same execution path* in subject programs.

If every raw data point could be mapped to a released data point, the resulting dataset would have the same path coverage (which is a commonly used test sufficiency criterion) as the raw dataset.

The third level, `same path with input restrictions`, aims to consider more program behaviors beyond execution paths, such as particular input values. This is useful for cases when two program runs have different observable effects even if they follow the same path. For example, the following Java function, which accepts the original bank account balance (`orig`) and the withdrawal (`amt`), and returns the final balance, has a functional error when a negative `amt` is fed to it:

```
double reduceBalance(double orig, double amt) {
   return orig - amt;
}
```

The error can be observed (*e.g.*, by an auditor) if the raw dataset contains the input $\langle 5.0, -2.0\rangle$. If the released dataset only contains $\langle 5.0, 2.0\rangle$, the error cannot be observed even though the same path is executed.

Thus, the third level introduces additional restrictions on program inputs, aiming to preserve more program behaviors. The restrictions may be expressed in terms of various constraints (*e.g.*, `amt==-2.0` for the above example). In this paper, we consider only one type of input restrictions: some (arbitrary) fields of the released data points shall preserve their original values. We refer to this as *input preservation*. The framework allows future extensions including the consideration of constraints provided by users and expressed as general first-order predicates. However, this paper utilizes a minimal k-anonymization algorithm to decide the input preservation constraints (*cf.* Section 4.4) without the need for user-specified constraints. Even though the minimal k-anonymization algorithm cannot guarantee to retain all desired values (*e.g.*, –2.0 in the above example), we still have the following benefits: (1) the total number of replaced values in the released dataset can be minimized so that more program behaviors may hopefully be preserved; (2) the need for user-specified constraints is avoided so that there is no risk of leaking privacy data by incorrectly specified constraints.

R4-2: A released tuple b is *path and input preserving* for a raw tuple t if b is path preserving for t and it satisfies the given input constraints.

The fourth level, `same program states`, is an extreme level used as a reference point where the sequence of program states exhibited by each release tuple and the raw tuple mapped to it should be the same.

The following subsection discusses the various combinations of privacy and behavior preservation levels in our model.

3.4 Combining Privacy and Behavior Preservation

Since we have four levels of privacy preservation and four levels of behavior preservation, privacy and behavior presevation could be combined in 16 possible ways, as shown in Figure 2.

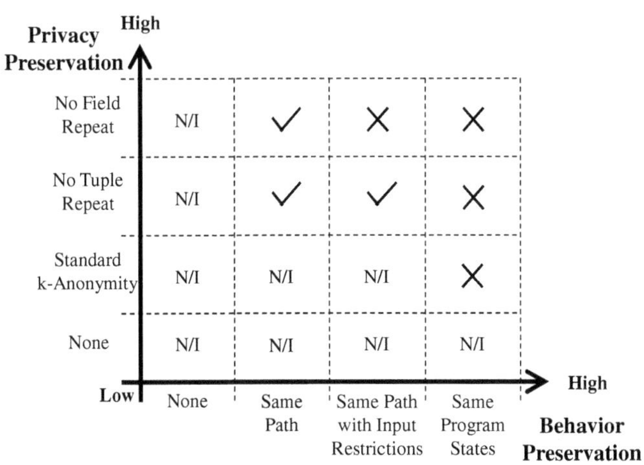

Figure 2. Privacy vs. behavior preservation

Some combinations marked with "X" are impossible to achieve. Many others marked with "N/I" are not interesting for the purpose of preserving privacy and behavior. Those marked with a tick are of interest and possible to achieve. The following paragraphs describe the combinations in more details.[3]

PROPERTY 2. *The privacy preservation level* `none` *is not interesting.*

PROPERTY 3. `Standard k-anonymity` *alone is not interesting since it cannot satisfy R1 required by our kb-anonymity model.*

PROPERTY 4. *The behavior preservation level* `none` *is not interesting for the purposes of software testing and debugging.*

PROPERTY 5. *It is impossible to pair* `same program states` *with any privacy preservation level (except* `none`*).*

EXPLANATION: Since program states include input values to a program, `same program states` implies the same input values. Thus, the released tuple must be the same as a raw tuple, which is only allowed when the raw dataset is already k-anonymized or when there is no desire for privacy. □

PROPERTY 6. *It is impossible to pair* `same path with input restrictions` *with* `no field repeat`.

EXPLANATION: In this paper, we consider input restrictions to be constraints that require some (arbitrary) input fields to have the same values as found in raw tuples. Thus, by definition, datasets complying with `same path with input restrictions` cannot also conform to `no field repeat`. □

With the combination of k-anonymity and behavior preservation, we have the following property stated in Theorem 2. This property can be used to efficiently check whether a dataset can be kb-anonymized (*cf.* Section 4.1).

THEOREM 2. *For each behavior exhibited by a released tuple satisfying R1–R4, there must exist at least k raw tuples that exhibit the same behavior.*

PROOF. *The requirement R1 ensures that a released tuple can be used to run a program, as all raw tuples can. R3 ensures that at least k raw tuples map to each released tuple. R4 ensures that a raw tuple only maps to a released tuple with the same behavior. Thus, it must be the case that for each released tuple, there are at least k raw tuples that map to it and they all have the same behavior.*[4] □

In a nutshell, our kb-anonymity model requires R1–R4 altogether, and there are three interesting configurations:

- (`same path`, `no field repeat`)
- (`same path`, `no tuple repeat`)
- (`same path with input restriction`, `no tuple-repeat`)

As shorthand notations, we refer to these as `P-F`, `P-T`, and `I-T`, respectively. The next section presents our realization of these configurations. In cases when some raw data points cannot be mapped to a released tuple, we simply output error messages.

4. Model Realization

In this section, we describe the algorithms and tools used to realized the three configurations of our kb-anonymity model: `P-T`, `P-F`, and `I-T`. The overall framework of our realization is illustrated in Figure 3.

[3] We do not consider cases where the raw dataset satisfies k-anonymity. These uninteresting cases happen in situations, such as when k=1, or when there is no identifier or quasi-identifier.

[4] R2 is unnecessary for proving Theorem 2, but it eliminates indistinguishable tuples and thus may help to save the cost of testing and debugging.

4.1 Overall Framework

All three configurations require path preservation, which means we need to collect the execution paths of all raw tuples. The *Program Execution* module takes raw tuples and executes a program with each of the tuples, then it collects the path conditions exercised by each execution. We assume that each tuple is processed by the program independently; we do not consider any dependency among program states or path conditions that may be introduced by multiple runs of the program with different tuples. Theoretically, two executions having the same path condition follow the same execution path. Thus, this module can group raw tuples based on the equivalence of their path conditions. At the end of this step, groups of size less than k are discarded due to Theorem 2.

For each of the groups left, the *k-Anonymization* module may replace some field values with asterisks and make sure that each tuple is indistinguishable from at least k–1 other tuples in the group. Then, it outputs a set of unique tuples a la Theorem 1.

Next, the *Constraint Generation* module takes the set of unique tuples from the *k-Anonymization* module and the path conditions for every tuple associated with the unique tuple. Various constraints are then generated for each of the unique tuple according to each of the three configurations.

Last, the *Constraint Solver* takes the constraints for each of the unique tuple and tries to generate one new tuple satisfying the constraints. If the solver finds a satisfying tuple, this tuple will be part of the released dataset. When the solver cannot find a satisfying tuple, our framework simply outputs error messages.

Theorems 3, 4, and 5 state that the datesets outputted by the algorithms satisfy kb-anonymity (R1–R4) and can be released for software testing and debugging.

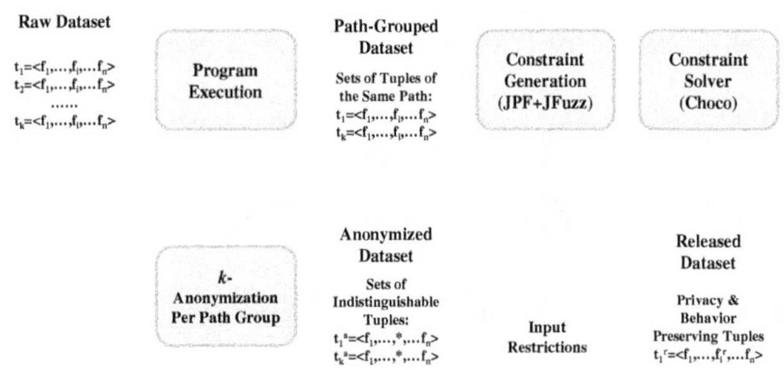

Figure 3. Overall framework of our model realization

The overall parameterized Algorithm 1 realizes the three configurations. At Lines 3–4, we obtain the path condition for every raw tuple. At Lines 2–7, we group the raw tuples into different buckets based on their path conditions. At Lines 8–11, we remove buckets of size less than k because of Theorem 2. In an extreme case when all buckets are of size less than k, the released dataset will be empty. The remaining buckets are those that require value replacement satisfying the given configuration. Then, Lines 14 and 15 run a k-anonymization algorithm for every bucket and generate the anonymized version a la Theorem 1, and Lines 16–21 store the k-anonymized buckets that satisfy certain conditions. Note that for configuration `I-T`, we require Line 13 to invoke the approximate minimal k-anonymization, and only store an anonymized tuple if it contains some concrete values. We can simply discard a tuple if it contains no concrete value (Lines 17–20) since it means no values in the corresponding raw tuples can remain and the `I-T` configuration cannot be satisfied for these tuples. Then, for each bucket that can be k-anonymized (Line 22), Lines 23–29 construct sufficiently strong constraints for the given configuration, feed the conjunction

Algorithm 1 A Realization of kb-Anonymity

Input: R: Raw dataset
k: Level of anonymization
P: A subject program
O: Configuration option: `P-T`, `P-F`, or `I-T`.
Output: R': Anonymized dataset for release

1: $R' \leftarrow \emptyset$
// The *Program Execution* module
2: $PCBuckets \leftarrow \emptyset$, which groups tuples based on path conditions
3: For each t in R
4: Execute P with t and collect the path condition pc
5: If $PCBuckets$ does not contains pc
6: $PCBuckets \leftarrow PCBuckets \cup \{\langle pc, \emptyset\rangle\}$
7: $PCBuckets[pc] \leftarrow PCBuckets[pc] \cup t$
8: For each $Bucket = \langle pc, B\rangle \in PCBuckets$
9: If $|B| < k$
10: $PCBuckets \leftarrow PCBuckets - \{Bucket\}$
11: Output "Error: `unsatisfiable case`" and **continue**
// The *k-Anonymization* module
12: $A \leftarrow \emptyset$, holding intermediate k-anonymized datasets
13: For each $\langle pc, B\rangle \in PCBuckets$
14: Invoke a k-anonymization algorithm on B,
15: and get its result B' with no duplicates a la Theorem 1
16: For each tuple $b' \in B'$
17: If O = `I-T`
18: If $|b'| <= 1$ or no field in b' contain concrete values
19: Output "`Error: unsatisfiable case`"
20: **continue**
21: $A \leftarrow A \cup \{\langle b', pc, B\rangle\}$
// The *Constraint Generation* module
22: For each $\langle b', pc, B\rangle \in A$
// Construct constraints for various configurations
23: If O = `P-F`
24: $S \leftarrow$ Invoke Algorithm 2 on R
25: Else If O = `P-T`
26: $S \leftarrow$ Invoke Algorithm 3 on B
27: Else If O = `I-T`
28: $S \leftarrow$ Invoke Algorithm 4 on $\langle B, b'\rangle$
29: Else Output "`Error: unimplemented option`" and **continue**
30: $S \leftarrow$ Conjunction of S and pc
// The *Constraint Solver* module
31: Invoke a constraint solver on S, and get its result r
32: If r is not an error
33: $R' \leftarrow R' \cup \{r\}$
34: **Return** R'

of the constructed constraints and the path condition for this bucket (Line 30) into a constraint solver (Line 31), and add a valid solution from the solver into the resulting dataset (Lines 32–33). We finally output the dataset for release (Line 34).

We have implemented a prototype of this framework. This prototype uses Java PathFinder (JPF) [39] and jFuzz [18], one of JPF's extensions that supports the combination of concrete and symbolic executions of Java programs, to emulate executions of our subject programs and collect path conditions. We rely on JPF's internal canonical representation of path conditions and use string comparison to check for equivalent path conditions. At the same time, we have implemented an approximate algorithm that can construct k-anonymized datasets [7]. Also, we have extended JPF to allow manipulation of the collected path conditions and generation of the desired constraints. Finally, we utilize the constraint solver used in JPF—Choco [1]—to generate new tuples from the constraints. For now, we only handle constraints with integers and real numbers. In the future, with the coming support for string constraints in JPF [2], we hope our framework can handle programs with strings easily.

The following subsections describe more details and properties for each of the three configurations in our model.

4.2 Same Path, No Field Repeat (P-F)

To realize this configuration option, we perform Algorithm 2 within Algorithm 1 at Line 24.

Algorithm 2 Generation of Constraints for P-F

Input: T: A set of (raw) tuples
Output: S: A (conjunctive) set of constraints for P-F

```
For each field i
  Construct its constraint variable v_i
  For each t ∈ T
    S ← S ∪ {v_i ≠ t[i]}
Return S
```

The realization of this configuration basically generates new data values different from all of the original ones (via Line 24 in Algorithm 1) to ensure no violation of privacy, and ensure preservation of program behavior (via Line 30 in Algorithm 1). Algorithm 2 is invoked on the whole raw dataset to ensure `no field repeat` for all tuples, which of course imposes more constraints and makes it harder for the constraint solver to find a tuple. Alternatively, we could relax the `no field repeat` requirement and invoke Algorithm 2 on B instead (Line 24) without compromising privacy.

Note that there is no particular input restrictions or minimal anonymization requirements in this configuration. It is not necessary to run minimal k-anonymization algorithms (Line 14). We just need to ensure that there are at least k tuples in a bucket B having the same path (Lines 8–11) via Theorem 2 and simply treat all tuples in B as one equivalence partition in its anonymized version. Doing so may only produce one new tuple for each B, but help to speed up the anonymization process. Also, it is not necessary to remove duplicated, intermediate tuples (Line 15), although doing so may help to prevent redundant operations at Lines 22–33 and make the control flows for different configuration options simpler.

THEOREM 3. *An output dataset from Algorithm 1 along with Algorithm 2 satisfies kb-anonymity (R1–R4).*

Proof Sketch: Each dataset generated at Line 14 satisfies R2 and R3 according to Theorem 1; Each tuple generated at Line 31 is obviously path-preserving (via Line 30) and satisfies R4 and R1 (all values concrete). Also, the constraints imposed by P-F, P-T, or I-T ensure no tuples from the raw dataset will appear at Line 31. Thus, the resulting dataset R' at Line 34 satisfies kb-anonymity. □

4.3 Same Path, No Tuple Repeat (P-T)

To realize this configuration, we perform Algorithm 3 within Algorithm 1. Similar to the realization for P-F, P-T generates new data values and tuples to ensure privacy, although its privacy requirement is weaker than that of P-F. Some data values from the raw dataset may remain even though there are no tuples in the intersection between the raw and the released datasets. In particular, Algorithm 3 in this paper only considers changing the first field of all tuples to satisfy `no tuple repeat`. Alternatively, we could choose a random field of all tuples or some random fields from each tuple to strengthen privacy protection.

Also similar to P-F, it is not necessary to run minimal k-anonymization algorithms (Line 14), as there is no need to satisfy any input constraint or maximize the number of released tuples.

THEOREM 4. *An output dataset from Algorithm 1 along with Algorithm 3 satisfies kb-anonymity.*

Proof Sketch: Similar to that of Theorem 3. □

Algorithm 3 Generation of Constraints for P-T

Input: T: A set of (raw) tuples
Output: S: A (conjunctive) set of constraints for P-T

```
For the first field in T
  Construct its constraint variable v_1
For first field in each t in T
  S ← S ∪ {v_1 ≠ t[1]}
Return S
```

4.4 Same Path & Some Input, No Tuple Repeat (I-T)

To realize this configuration, we perform Algorithm 4 within Algorithm 1. Different from the previous realizations, we need to ensure that some—arbitrary one or a few—raw input values are preserved. To do this, we need to run a minimal k-anonymization algorithm at Line 14 in Algorithm 1 to decide the minimal number of field values that need to be masked away to realize k-anonymity. By doing this, we can retain the maximal number of raw concrete values in released tuples (*i.e.*, input preservation) so as to preserve more program behaviors. The process has been proven to be NP-complete, thus we run a variant of k-anonymization [7] to achieve approximate results. After applying the k-anonymization algorithm, we could simply output an error message (Lines 17–20) for tuples for which all fields need to be masked away (*i.e.*, no concrete values can be preserved).

Algorithm 4 Generation of Constraints for I-T

Input: T: A set of (raw) tuples
b: A tuple with generic values or '*'
Output: S: A (conjunctive) set of constraints for I-T

```
// The If-Else ensures No Tuple Repeat
If b contains no generic values or '*'
  S ← Invoke Algorithm 3 on T
  i ← 1
Else
  For the first field i in b containing a generic value or '*'
    Construct its constraint variable v_i
  For each t in T
    S ← S ∪ {v_i ≠ t[i]}
// The following helps to ensure some fields maintain their values
For each field j in b containing a concrete value c and j ≠ i
  Construct its constraint variable v_j
  S ← S ∪ {v_j = b[j]}
Return S
```

THEOREM 5. *An output dataset from Algorithm 1 along with Algorithm 4 satisfies kb-anonymity.*

Proof Sketch: Similar to that of Theorem 3. □

5. Empirical Evaluation

We evaluate the capability and scalability of the realization of our kb-anonymity model with three sample programs: OpenHospital [4], iTrust [3], and PDManager [5]. All experiments are performed on an Intel Xeon server with a 2.53GHz quad-core E5540 CPU and 24 GiB of RAM running 64-bit Windows Server 2008 R2 Standard. Algorithm 1 is implemented in Visual C#.Net, while Algorithms 2, 3 and 4 are implemented in Java within jFuzz [18].

5.1 OpenHospital

OpenHospital is an open source hospital management system. It provides various functionalities including managing patient records, pregnancy management, disease information, drug control, pharmacy management, etc. All patient records are stored in a backend database. We convert a part of the program into an integer program that reads inputs from a file, as our current implementation based on jFuzz does not handle string constraints or database queries.

The part that we convert, denoted as OH_c, is comprised of three Java classes which validate a patient record before storing to database. It validates private information of a patient, including first name, last name, age, gender, address, city, number of siblings, telephone number, birth date, blood type, mother's name, mother's deceased status, father's name, father's deceased status, insurance status, and whether parents live together. Many of the input fields are of string type. We then manually convert them into integers based on their value domains and change corresponding string operations into integer operations.

Even though the program is not big, it demonstrates that our prototype implementation is capable of anonymizing data for testing and debugging, for a large set of inputs. The following example shows sample output for a given set of raw tuples under the `P-T` configuration.

Example. We randomly create synthetic tuples as a raw dataset and run our tool on OH_c with this set. Table 1 shows the raw tuples as well as the results of our tool using `P-T` configuration for $k = 2$. There is an error message for the fifth tuple as it could not satisfy our kb-anonymity requirements. This tuple should not then be released to third-party developers.

No	Raw Data Point	Released Tuple
1	⟨90207, 10125, 2, -1, 16261, 22549, 69883, 914, 8201, -2, 68353, -1, -53, -1, -1, -2⟩	⟨-9999, 10000, 0, -10000, 16261, 22549, 69883, 914, 8201, -2, 68353, -1, -53, -1, -1, -2⟩
2	⟨19892, 16536, 78, 1, 36688, 88797, 172, 7519, 50896, -1, 44500, 1, 7452, -2, -1, 1⟩	
3	⟨35778, 21908, 89, -1, 89965, 41493, 35861, 50182, 79181, 1, 30668, -1, 34926, -2, -1, 1 ⟩	
4	⟨9543, 23693, 48, 1, 18133, 75043, -173, 38100, 14912, 1, 69504, 0, 14969, -1, -2, 1⟩	
5	⟨42164, 40607, -6, 1, 46920, 21328, 15089, 42147, 81975, 1, 24382, -2, -252, -2, -1, -1⟩	Error Message

Table 1. Sample raw tuples and the output tuples after anonymization for OpenHospital. The integers could be mapped to real values. For example, the 3rd field directly maps to age; The 10th field in the tuples corresponds to blood types: 0 means type O, 1 means A, 2 means B, 3 means AB, and negative numbers mean unknown.

Scalability Evaluation. The computational complexities of k-anonymization algorithms and constraint generation and solving are potentially exponential to the number of raw tuples. To investigate the scalability of our proposed approach, we stress test our tool by increasing the number of raw tuples to be anonymized. We experiment with 2,000, 4,000, 6,000, 8,000, and 10,000 tuples, and evaluate the runtime of our tool using the `P-T` and `P-F` configurations for k set to 2, and `I-T` configurations for k set to 2 and 5. We plot the results in Figure 4. Figure 4(a) shows that the runtime per tuple remains practically constant when we increase the number of tuples from 2,000 to 10,000 for all configurations. This implies that in practice the runtime increases linearly with the number of tuples to be processed. Figures 4(a) & (b) show that the `I-T` configuration is slower than the `P-T` and `P-F` configurations. This is because we run a *minimal* k-anonymization algorithm *o*nly for `I-T` configuration (see Section 4) which can take quadratic time. Furthermore, almost all raw tuples were successfully anonymized. In our experiments, at most two tuples out of the thousands of raw tuples failed to be anonymized. This occurred when using `I-T` configuration with k set to 5, while the other configurations were only unable to anonymize at most one tuple.

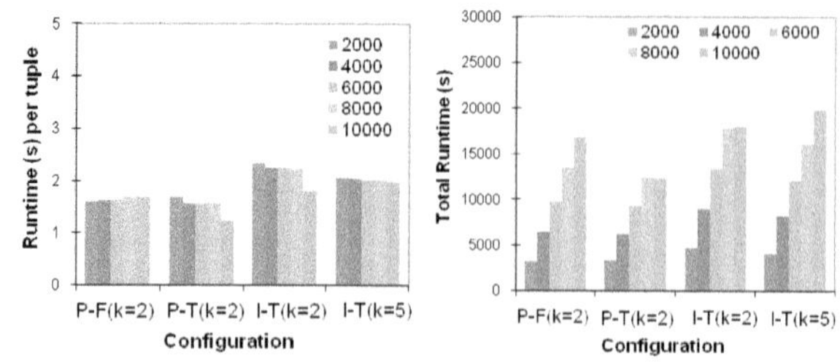

Figure 4. OH_c runtime: per tuple (left) & all tuples (right)

5.2 iTrust

iTrust is an open source medical application that enables patients to maintain their medical history, records, and communications with their doctors. All patient records are also stored in a backend database. Similar to OpenHospital, we convert a part of the program into an integer program that reads input from a file.

The part that we convert, denoted as $iTrust_c$, is comprised of ten Java classes that validate the insurance record of a patient. It involves private and sensitive information including: 1) first name, last name, email, address, city, state, postal code, insurance number, credit card type, credit card number, and telephone number of the patient, 2) name, address, city, state, and postal code of the insurance company, and 3) name and telephone number of an emergency contact person.

Example. Table 2 shows a sample output from our tool for a set of synthetic integer tuples under the `P-F` configuration and $k = 2$.

No	Raw Data Point	Released Tuple
1	⟨70, 549, 288, 499, 490, 246, 15, 110, 137, 519, 840, 91, 128, 31, 3, 28, 466, 113⟩	⟨ 0, 200, 100, 200, 200, 201, 10, 40, 40, 200, 200, 0, 6, 10, 0, 10, 200, 40⟩
2	⟨508, 147, 195, 491, 277, 224, 32, 48, 210, 275, 147, 97, 119, 11, 3, 36, 314, 160 ⟩	
3	⟨754, 418, 72, 779, 437, 69, 13, 91, 94, 567, 710, 203, 104, 34, 1, 20, 848, 79⟩	
4	⟨585, 727, 295, 662, 304, 125, 26, 49, 83, 398, 313, 10, 77, 26, 4, 50, 338, 62⟩	
5	⟨141, 280, 68, 249, 267, 149, 11, 67, 139, 748, 669, 173, 105, 14, 2, 24, 739, 146⟩	

Table 2. Sample raw tuples and the corresponding output after anonymization for iTrust

Scalability Evaluation. Similar to OH_c, we stress test our tool with various numbers of raw tuples, *i.e.*, 2,000, 4,000, 6,000, 8,000 and 10,000, and evaluate the runtime for `P-T` and `P-F` configurations for k set to 2, and `I-T` configurations for k set to 2 and 5. The performance results shown in Figure 5 are similar to those of OH_c. For iTrust, for each configuration and number of raw tuples, all raw tuples were successfully anonymized.

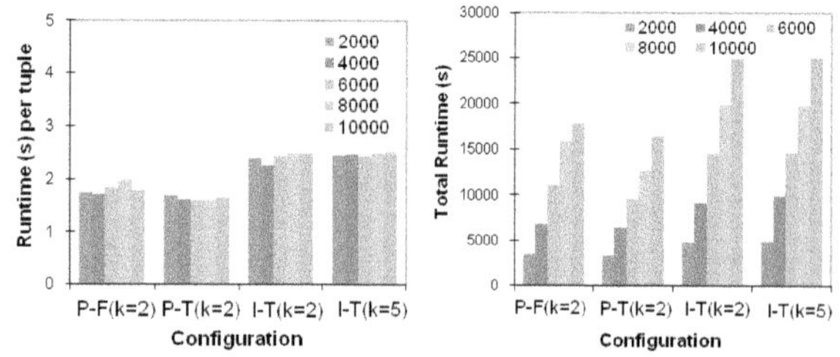

Figure 5. IT_c runtime: per tuple (left) & all tuples (right)

5.3 PDManager

PDManager is an open source insurance agent management system that provides features to manage clients, contracts, and commissions. Similar to OpenHospital and iTrust, we also convert a part of the program into an integer program that reads input from a file.

The part that we convert, denoted as PDM_c, is comprised of eight Java classes that validate the record of an insurance client of an agent. PDM_c takes in 13 input fields representing insurance's name, agent's name, as well as the first name, surname, gender, address, city, state, postal code, telephone number, fax, mobile number, and email of each client.

Example. Table 3 shows sample output of our tool for a set of synthetic integer tuples under the `I-T` configuration with $k = 2$. Note that the 8th fields of the tuples are unchanged.

No	Raw Data Point	Released Tuple
1	⟨1003, 7865, 9479, 1956, 8223, 203, 53, 2, 133, 4707, 1124, 37, 1570 ⟩	⟨ -9999, 10000, 1, -10000, 1, -59, -38, 2, 97, 3505, 600, 289, 809 ⟩
2	⟨1461, 9877, 1786, 4948, 5486, -59, -38, 2, 97, 3505, 600, 289, 809 ⟩	
3	⟨1305, 4352, 994, 6664, 2163, -97, 129, 2, 130, 7458, 9671, -51, 288 ⟩	
4	⟨4629, 1672, 8447, 586, 1072, 112, -42, 1, 93, 3426, 8158, 74, 6900 ⟩	⟨ -9999, 10000, 1, -10000, 1, 112, -42, 1, 93, 3426, 8158, 74, 6900 ⟩
5	⟨7274, 5952, 3798, 3813, 8113, 488, 104, 1, 107, 6176, 7896, -62, 6186 ⟩	

Table 3. Sample raw tuples and the output tuples for PDManager

Scalability Evaluation. Similar to OH_c and $iTrust_c$, we stress test our tool with various numbers of raw tuples and evaluate the runtime for `P-T` and `P-F` configurations for k set to 2, and `I-T` configurations for k set to 2 and 5. The results plotted in Figure 6 are similar to those of OH_c and $iTrust_c$. In our experiments, at most 8 tuples failed to be anonymized for `I-T` and $k = 5$, at most 4 for other configurations, and only 1 failure for all configurations with 2,000 raw tuples.

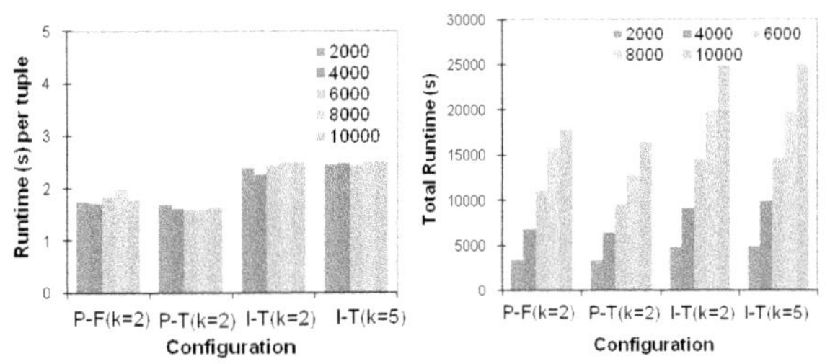

Figure 6. PDM_c runtime: per tuple (left) & all tuples (right)

6. Discussion

Other privacy preservation models. In this paper, we build our kb-anonymity model mainly on top of k-anonymity. There are various other models proposed in the literature, such as l-diversity [25], m-invariance [41], and t-closeness [22]. We leave the possible extensions to cover other privacy preservation models as future work.

Handling more complex programs. In this work, our implementation only handles programs involving integers and real numbers, and cannot solve non-linear or string constraints. In the future, with the advances of symbolic execution, in particular JPF [2], we hope to be able to handle programs with strings and evaluate our prototype implementation on larger, more complex programs.

Also, this paper assumes that each tuple is processed independently. Privacy-related programs, such as healthcare management systems, often deal with individuals and thus only take one tuple as its input, and program states or path conditions for one tuple are not dependent on others. However, there are indeed real-world applications that use multiple individuals' records together (*e.g.*, when analyzing a patient's family medical history), and our current approach will treat those records as one combined tuple. If a piece of code involves multiple tuples in a "batch mode" (*e.g.*, when iterating over a set of patients and printing out each record), it is possible and interesting future work to explore automated program slicing techniques to extract the essential code that deals with one patient only, and then investigate the applicability of our model.

Attacks. We have not considered attack models beyond the natural mappings that come with value replacement functions. We have assumed attackers can only link a released tuple back to a raw tuple through the inverse of a value replacement function. Based on Theorem 2, reversing the function would give no less than k raw tuples and would not breach kb-anonymity. However, it is worthwhile to discuss other kinds of attacks.

k-anonymity is proposed to address the *linking attack* [32, 38] against released datasets that only remove identifier fields. The linking attack works as follows: Some publicly available data (*e.g.*, the voter list of a particular state) contains real values for the identifiers (*e.g.*, a person's name) and the quasi-identifiers that are also contained in a released dataset; then, the values of the quasi-identifiers in the released dataset and the publicly available data may be uniquely matched to recover the values of the identifiers and the sensitive fields of each person. k-anonymity addresses this attack by ensuring that at least k released tuples are indistinguishable from each other. kb-anonymity also addresses the attack by ensuring that each released tuple is mapped to at least k raw tuples. Other attacks against k-anonymity, such as *unsorted matching attack*, *complementary release attack*, and *temporal attack*, can also be addressed by minor modifications of how k-anonymity is applied [32, 38]. kb-anonymity can address these attacks in a similar way by treating all fields *together as one* quasi-identifier.

k-anonymity, however, cannot address other attacks, such as *homogeneity attack* due to the lack of diversity among the values of sensitive fields [25]. Consider the example 2-anonymized dataset in Section 2. One can identify that both Bob and Tom have cancer just by knowing that their age is 53 and their records are in the dataset. As an advantage, our model can address this issue when applied with the `no field repeat` configuration. In this configuration, the disease would be replaced by another value that does not exist in the dataset. There are also other attacks against k-anonymity discussed in the literature [22, 41]. We will investigate the susceptibility of our model to those attacks in future work.

In addition, program versioning may also lead to a privacy concern: our current kb-anonymity model may generate different released datasets for various versions of the same program and attackers may link these versions together to increase the probability of identifying an individual in the raw dataset. Similarly, program back doors may even be a bigger concern. Also, data owners may be tricked into applying our model to programs that violate our assumptions (*e.g.*, a hacker may construct a program whose execution is dependent on not only the current input tuple, but also previous executions with different tuples), then the released data may be used to infer original data. These potential attacks mean that kb-anonymity model needs to be enhanced or applied with appropriate policies to disable undesirable information linkage among various data sources. We leave this as future work.

Data Distortion. As noted in Section 1, kb-anonymity may generate values that do not correctly reflect raw data values. Also, many raw tuples may be suppressed into one released tuple (a la Algorithm 1), causing loss of information. For example, there may be only two released tuples for the example in Section 2, as shown in Table 4, and some sensitive but useful information (*e.g.*, the existence of hypertension) is lost.

Name	NID	Age	Gender	Address	Doctor	Disease
Joel	999	54	Female	Bishan	Dr. Joe	Cancer
Bar	888	32	Female	Changi	Dr. Anne	Flu

Table 4. Sample kb-anonymized tuples that lose information.

Our algorithms may be adapted to remedy the issues for certain cases: Change Line 31 in Algorithm 1 to produce more than one tuple for each path condition so that the values in the released tuples may contain any desired information. However, whether generating additional released tuples is cost-effective or robust against known or unknown attacks is still a question for future investigation. As a result, kb-anonymized datasets are only suitable for the purposes of testing and debugging, where preserving statistics of raw datasets is not a concern.

Threats to Validity. To address threats to construct validity, we have evaluated our model and its realization both qualitatively (by some examples) and quantitatively (by the stress tests for scalability). To reduce threats to external validity on the generalizability of our results, we have evaluated our approach on three different programs. There may still be threats to internal validity (*e.g.*, selection bias) as we choose and slice the three sample programs by ourselves in a similar way. To reduce the threats further, it is possible to include more subject programs and realistic datasets into our evaluations, which we leave as future work. In particular, we plan to employ our model to help a partner in the healthcare industry to anonymize their data and obtain their feedback. In the future, we hope that there will be more interest in this area and a comprehensive benchmark could be built to evaluate similar methodologies and tools.

7. Related Work

In this section, we describe some related threads of work on privacy preservation, symbolic execution, testing & debugging, and legal issues in software engineering.

Privacy Preservation. Motivated by many threats to privacy and issues raised from identity thefts, there have been various studies on privacy preservation. Samarati and Sweeney propose the concept of k-anonymity [32,38]. There have been various studies on applying and extending their work [6, 7, 10]. Aggarwal *et al.* [7] prove that finding the minimum number of value substitutions to ensure k-anonymity is an NP-complete problem; they thus propose an approximation algorithm to ensure approximate k-anonymity in a dataset. We leverage their algorithm in the realization of our kb-anonymity model (*cf.* Section 4).

There are also other models for privacy preservation, including l-diversity by Machanavajjhala *et al.* [25], m-invariance by Xiao and Tao [41], and t-closeness by Li *et al.* [22]. In this study, we only focus on k-anonymity as the model for privacy preservation.

Information Flow Security. In the areas of programming language and security research, many studies use variants of taint analysis and information flow for protecting sensitive information [24, 26, 31]. There are also studies on removing sensitive information from program execution records, such as core dumps, stack frames, and profiles [11, 40]. Some recent studies focus on monitoring the flow of sensitive information in and across applications, such as TaintDroid [14] and TaintEraser [45], so as to prevent misuse of users' private information.

Our approach is different from all these techniques that we do not allow sensitive information going into a program in the first place, while they detect, block, and remove sensitive information from within programs. However, information flow and taint analysis may be helpful to scale up our approach to identify parts of program and program inputs that involve sensitive information.

Symbolic Execution. Symbolic execution [21] is a program analysis technique that tracks variable values symbolically. A common use of symbolic execution is to compute and manipulate path conditions associated with an execution, and when combined with constraint solvers, to guide program analysis, testing, etc. It has been widely used for various software engineering tasks, including testing, debugging, program analysis, and model checking [9, 20, 29, 34, 42]. Recent studies combine symbolic execution with concrete execution to improve its utility and scalability [12, 16, 36].

For Java PathFinder (JPF) [39], there is also a symbolic execution extension [8]. Jayaraman *et al.* [18] provide a concolic whitebox fuzzer, jFuzz, on top of JPF that allows both symbolic and concrete executions. We use jFuzz to collect the path condition corresponding to each test case, which is similar to many existing studies. However, we utilize path conditions for a quite different purpose, which is to guide test data anonymization.

Testing & Debugging. There are numerous studies on testing and debugging. Many test case generation techniques are based on symbolic and concrete executions [12, 15, 36]. Test case prioritization and selection have received much research interest [30, 33]. This is also the case with automated fault localization [19, 23, 35, 43, 44].

In this work we propose a new line of research on data anonymization for testing and debugging. This complements the other research directions on testing and debugging, although it shares some fundamental techniques with them. There might be further interesting research issues raised by combining anonymization problems with test case prioritization, selection, and even fault localization. We leave this research direction as future work.

Legal Issues in Software Engineering. Recently, there have been studies investigating legal issues in software engineering [13, 27, 28]. Metayer *et al.* [27] propose a set of methods and tools to define and establish software liability. Di Penta *et al.* [28] investigate the evolution of software licensing. Cleland-Huang *et al.* [13] propose a machine learning approach for tracing regulatory code to requirements. Technically, these studies are all concerned with software itself, while our study is concerned more about the data that software executes with. However, our study on privacy issues could potentially impact legal aspects in software engineering.

8. Conclusion and Future Work

In this paper, we propose a new problem of privacy preserving testing and debugging. We address the problem of lack of test cases on a developer's side by allowing sensitive yet available test cases to be shipped from software users and data owners to third-party software vendors through anonymization. Anonymization by naively masking away identifiers and sensitive information would not work well due to the issues with quasi-identifiers and ineffectiveness of masked data for testing and debugging. Our approach combines the concept of privacy preservation and program behavior preservation in some interesting ways, and provides guidance on replacing private data values. We build a framework on the top of k-anonymity and concolic execution and implement several configurations. Our empirical evaluations on three sliced real programs show the utility of our prototype on providing effective anonymization for testing and debugging purposes. Our approach would help users to convey more testing and debugging information to software vendors without disclosing private information.

In the future, we plan to address other privacy preservation criteria aside from k-anonymity, incorporate further progress on symbolic execution that is able to handle strings and more complex data structures in programs, and carry out larger case studies.

Acknowledgements

We would like to thank for valuable feedback from the anonymous reviewers and our shepherd Michael Burke. We also thank Julia Lawall and Zhendong Su for their useful comments. Their insightful advice helped to improve our paper.

References

[1] Choco solver. http://www.emn.fr/z-info/choco-solver/.

[2] Fujitsu develops technology to enhance comprehensive testing of java programs. http://www.fujitsu.com/global/news/pr/archives/month/2010/20100112-02.html.

[3] iTrust. http://sourceforge.net/projects/itrust/.

[4] Open hospital. http://sourceforge.net/projects/angal/.

[5] PDmanager. http://sourceforge.net/projects/pdmanager/.

[6] G. Aggarwal, T. Feder, K. Kenthapadi, S. Khuller, R. Panigrahy, D. Thomas, and A. Zhu. Achieving anonymity via clustering. In *PODS*, pages 153–162, 2006.

[7] G. Aggarwal, T. Feder, K. Kenthapadi, R. Motwani, R. Panigrahy, D. Thomas, and A. Zhu. Approximation algorithms for k-anonymity. In *Int. Conf. on Data Theory*, 2005.

[8] S. Anand, C. Pasareanu, and W. Visser. JPF-SE: A symbolic execution extenion to Java PathFinder. In *TACAS*, 2007.

[9] S. Artzi, J. Dolby, F. Tip, and M. Pistoia. Directed test generation for effective fault localization. In *ISSTA*, pages 49–60, 2010.

[10] L. Backstrom, C. Dwork, and J. Kleinberg. Wherefore art thou r3579x? Anonymized social networks, hidden patterns, and structural steganography. In *WWW*, pages 181–190, 2007.

[11] P. Broadwell, M. Harren, and N. Sastry. Scrash: A system for generating secure crash information. In *12th USENIX Security Symposium*, pages 273–284, 2003.

[12] C. Cadar, D. Dunbar, and D. R. Engler. KLEE: Unassisted and automatic generation of high-coverage tests for complex systems programs. In *OSDI*, pages 209–224, 2008.

[13] J. Cleland-Huang, A. Czauderna, M. Gibiec, and J. Emenecker. A machine learning approach for tracing regulatory codes to product specific requirements. In *ICSE*, pages 155–164, 2010.

[14] W. Enck, P. Gilbert, B. gon Chun, L. P. Cox, J. Jung, P. McDaniel, and A. N. Sheth. TaintDroid: An information-flow tracking system for realtime privacy monitoring on smartphones. In *OSDI*, 2010.

[15] P. Godefroid, N. Klarlund, and K. Sen. DART: Directed automated random testing. In *PLDI*, pages 213–223. ACM, 2005.

[16] P. Godefroid, M. Y. Levin, and D. A. Molnar. Automated whitebox fuzz testing. In *NDSS*, 2008.

[17] P. Golle. Revisiting the uniqueness of simple demographics in the US population. In *5th ACM Workshop on Privacy in Electronic Society (WPES)*, pages 77–80, 2006.

[18] K. Jayaraman, D. Harvison, V. Ganesh, and A. Kiezun. jFuzz: A concolic tester for NASA Java. In *NASA Formal Methods Workshop*, 2009.

[19] D. Jeffrey, N. Gupta, and R. Gupta. Fault localization using value replacement. In *ISSTA*, pages 167–178, 2008.

[20] S. Khurshid, C. S. Păsăreanu, and W. Visser. Generalized symbolic execution for model checking and testing. In *TACAS*, pages 553–568, 2003.

[21] J. C. King. Symbolic execution and program testing. *Commun. ACM*, 19(7):385–394, 1976.

[22] N. Li, T. Li, and S. Venkatasubramanian. t-closeness: Privacy beyond k-anonymity and l-diversity. In *Int. Conf. Data Eng.*, 2007.

[23] B. Liblit, A. Aiken, A. X. Zheng, and M. I. Jordan. Bug isolation via remote program sampling. In *PLDI*, pages 141–154, June 2003.

[24] V. B. Livshits, A. V. Nori, S. K. Rajamani, and A. Banerjee. Merlin: Specification inference for explicit information flow problems. In *PLDI*, pages 75–86, 2009.

[25] A. Machanavajjhala, D. Kifer, J. Gehrke, and M. Venkitasubramaniam. l-diversity: Privacy beyond k-anonymity. *ACM Trans. Knowl. Discov. Data*, 1(1), 2007.

[26] S. McCamant and M. D. Ernst. Quantitative information flow as network flow capacity. In *PLDI*, pages 193–205, 2008.

[27] D. L. Métayer, M. Maarek, V. V. T. Tong, E. Mazza, M.-L. Potet, N. Craipeau, S. Frénot, and R. Hardouin. Liability in software engineering: Overview of the LISE approach and illustration on a case study. In *ICSE*, pages 135–144, 2010.

[28] M. D. Penta, D. M. German, Y.-G. Guéhéneuc, and G. Antoniol. An exploratory study of the evolution of software licensing. In *ICSE*, pages 145–154, 2010.

[29] S. Person, M. B. Dwyer, S. G. Elbaum, and C. S. Pasareanu. Differential symbolic execution. In *FSE*, pages 226–237, 2008.

[30] G. Rothermel, R. H. Untch, C. Chu, and M. J. Harrold. Prioritizing test cases for regression testing. In *IEEE Trans. Software Eng.*, pages 929–948, 2001.

[31] A. Sabelfeld and A. C. Myers. Language-based information-flow security. *IEEE Journal on Selected Areas in Communications*, 21(1):5–19, 2003.

[32] P. Samarati. Protecting respondents' identities in microdata release. In *IEEE Transactions on Knowledge and Data Engineering*, 2001.

[33] R. A. Santelices, P. K. Chittimalli, T. Apiwattanapong, A. Orso, and M. J. Harrold. Test-suite augmentation for evolving software. In *ASE*, pages 218–227, 2008.

[34] R. A. Santelices and M. Harrold. Exploiting program dependencies for scalable multiple-path symbolic execution. In *ISSTA*, pages 195–206, 2010.

[35] R. A. Santelices, J. A. Jones, Y. Yu, and M. J. Harrold. Lightweight fault-localization using multiple coverage types. In *ICSE*, pages 56–66, 2009.

[36] K. Sen, D. Marinov, and G. Agha. CUTE: A concolic unit testing engine for C. In *FSE*, pages 263–272, 2005.

[37] L. Sweeney. Uniqueness of simple demographics in the U.S. population. Technical Report LIDAP-WP4, Carnegie Mellon University, School of Computer Science, Data Privacy Laboratory, 2000.

[38] L. Sweeney. k-anonymity: A model for protecting privacy. *International Journal of Uncertainty, Fuzziness and Knowledge-Based Systems*, 10:557–570, 2002.

[39] W. Visser and P. Mehlitz. Model checking programs with Java PathFinder. In *SPIN*, http://babelfish.arc.nasa.gov/trac/jpf, 2005.

[40] R. Wang, X. Wang, and Z. Li. Panalyst: Privacy-aware remote error analysis on commodity software. In *17th USENIX Security Symposium*, pages 291–306, 2008.

[41] X. Xiao and Y. Tao. m-invariance: Towards privacy preserving re-publication of dynamic datasets. In *SIGMOD*, pages 689–700, 2007.

[42] T. Xie, D. Marinov, W. Schulte, and D. Notkin. Symstra: A framework for generating object-oriented unit tests using symbolic execution. In *TACAS*, pages 365–381, 2005.

[43] A. Zeller. Isolating cause-effect chains from computer programs. In *FSE*, pages 1–10, 2002.

[44] X. Zhang, N. Gupta, and R. Gupta. Locating faults through automated predicate switching. In *ICSE*, pages 272–281, 2006.

[45] D. Zhu, J. Jungy, D. Song, T. Kohnoz, and D. Wetherall. TaintEraser: Protecting sensitive data leaks using application-level taint tracking. *ACM SIGOPS Operating Systems Review*, 45(1), 2011.

Kremlin: Rethinking and Rebooting `gprof` for the Multicore Age

Saturnino Garcia, Donghwan Jeon, Chris Louie, and Michael Bedford Taylor
Department of Computer Science & Engineering
University of California, San Diego
La Jolla, CA, USA
{sat,djeon,cmlouie,mbtaylor}@cs.ucsd.edu

Abstract

Many recent parallelization tools lower the barrier for parallelizing a program, but overlook one of the first questions that a programmer needs to answer: *which parts of the program should I spend time parallelizing?*

This paper examines Kremlin, an automatic tool that, given a serial version of a program, will make recommendations to the user as to what regions (e.g. loops or functions) of the program to attack first. Kremlin introduces a novel *hierarchical critical path analysis* and develops a new metric for estimating the potential of parallelizing a region: *self-parallelism*. We further introduce the concept of a *parallelism planner*, which provides a ranked order of specific regions to the programmer that are likely to have the largest performance impact when parallelized. Kremlin supports multiple *planner personalities*, which allow the planner to more effectively target a particular programming environment or class of machine.

We demonstrate the effectiveness of one such personality, an OpenMP planner, by comparing versions of programs that are parallelized according to Kremlin's plan against third-party manually parallelized versions. The results show that Kremlin's OpenMP planner is highly effective, producing plans whose performance is typically comparable to, and sometimes much better than, manual parallelization. At the same time, these plans would require that the user parallelize significantly fewer regions of the program.

Categories and Subject Descriptors D.2.2 [*Software Engineering*]: Design Tools and Techniques; D.1.3 [*Programming Techniques*]: Concurrent Programming—Parallel Programming

General Terms Measurement, Performance

Keywords Hierarchical Critical Path Analysis, Self-Parallelism, Parallelism Planner, Parallel Software Engineering

1. Introduction

The emergence of multicore processors has profoundly impacted the way in which future software performance gains will be achieved. In order to take advantage of the resources available in multicore processors, existing sequential software will need to be refactored for parallel execution.

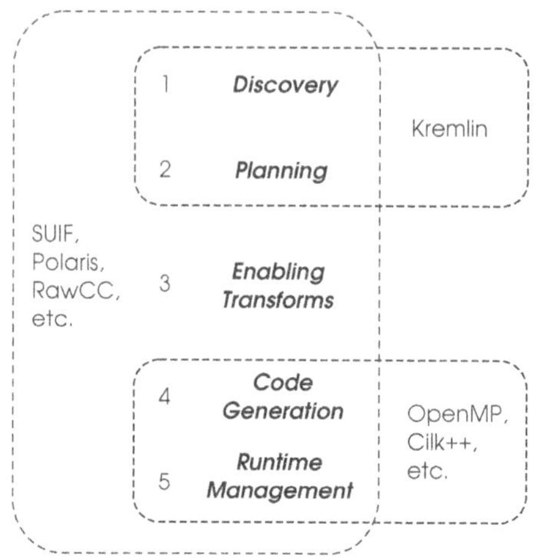

Figure 1. A Taxonomy of Parallelization Tools. The taxonomy categorizes parallelization tools based on which of five fundamental parallelization stages they assist with. Automatically parallelizing compilers like Polaris [7] and SUIF [12] attempt to perform all five without programmer assistance, while tools like OpenMP, Cilk++ [27], and X10 [33] focus on the last two. The paper's tool, Kremlin, targets the first two stages.

The task of parallelizing software has proved to be extremely difficult. To address this difficulty, recent mainstream tools have largely emphasized the ease of expressing parallelism; language extensions such as OpenMP and Cilk++ [27] have greatly reduced the effort involved in expressing opportunities for parallel execution in a program. Other tools guide the programmer in debugging performance or correctness problems in their parallelized code [4, 14, 35]. While these tools increase the efficiency of parallel programmers, there is still a need to assist the earlier stages of parallelization, where programmers must decide how to transform a serial program. The programmer requires new tools for these earlier stages of parallelization that will complement existing tools and form a complete toolflow for parallelization.

This paper examines Kremlin, a new tool that, given a serial version of a program, answers the question: *which parts of the program should I parallelize first?*

This question is not altogether unlike the question that `gprof` attempts to answer for serial programs: which parts of the program should I try to optimize first? In this paper, we rethink the design of a `gprof`-like tool that applies to the parallelization of serial pro-

PLDI'11, June 4–8, 2011, San Jose, California, USA.

grams rather than their serial optimization. Although the motivation, goals, and user interface are quite similar to `gprof`, we find that pursuing parallelism requires a new approach that is quite different, and leads to a tool whose underlying architecture is a total *reboot*, as it were, of the underlying architecture of a serial performance profiler like `gprof`.

A Taxonomy of Parallelization Stages To explain Kremlin's role in the spectrum of parallelization tools, we introduce a taxonomy that describes the basic stages involved in parallelizing a program. Figure 1 shows this taxonomy. Parallelization begins with *Parallelism Discovery*, which is the process of identifying regions of a program that have exploitable parallelism. Locating these regions of the program is especially onerous for large, complex programs or when—as is often the case—the parallel programmer is not the original author of the program. The next stage, *Parallelism Planning*, determines which subset of these regions should be parallelized. Ideally, this plan would factor in important constraints such as the number of cores available and the system's ability to support different types of parallelism. The third step is *Enabling Transforms*. These are source-level transformations that the user performs in order to enhance the parallelizability of the code used in subsequent stages. The parallelization process concludes with the final two steps of *Parallel Code Generation*, where parallel or threaded code is generated, and *Runtime Management*, where a runtime system tries to optimize the efficiency of parallel execution.

As shown in Figure 1, automatic parallelizing compilers such as Polaris [7], RawCC [26], and SUIF [12] seek to automate all of the stages in the parallelization taxonomy. Although they eliminate the need for manual intervention, the performance of code generated by these compilers often pales in comparison with code generated manually. This lack of performance stems from the difficulty of many of these steps; in many cases, the compiler cannot effectively perform them without the benefit of runtime information or without otherwise unsound semantic changes by the user. While additional information could potentially improve performance, accomplishing this integration has proven a difficult problem. Without this additional input, parallelizing compilers have an all-or-nothing feel: the compiler either does all of the work or none of it.

An alternative to the fully-automated approach is to separate the parallelization process into the stages shown in Figure 1 and make use of parallel programming tools to automate as much of the work as possible. These tools would relieve most of the burden on the programmer and allow them to focus on the Enabling Transforms stage where automated tools are most limited[1]. Recent tools such as OpenMP, Cilk++ [27], X10 [33], and Fast Track [17] exemplify how user-centered tools can improve the productivity of parallel programmers. These tools provide extensions to standardized languages that allow a programmer to explicitly specify parallel regions and synchronization points, automatically handling the final two stages of parallelization. However, by the time a programmer can utilize these tools, they must have already performed the initial stages of parallelization without assistance.

Kremlin We have developed Kremlin to aid programmers in both the parallelism discovery and parallelism planning stages of parallelization. Kremlin's parallelism discovery phase utilizes critical path analysis [23], or *CPA*, to quantify the amount of innate parallelism that exists in a piece of code. Kremlin extends traditional critical path analysis by automatically incorporating the nested structure of the program's regions (e.g. loops and functions) into its analysis. Kremlin's *hierarchical critical path analysis*, or *HCPA*, performs critical path analysis across many nested regions in a program. By comparing the amount of parallelism that exists in each parent region to the amount that exists in its children, we are able to localize parallelism to specific regions of the program, revealing the amount of parallelism in each code region.

To accomplish this, Kremlin introduces a new metric, *self-parallelism*, which given a parent region, can factor out the parallelism of subregions, much like `gprof`'s *self-time* metric factors out the time spent in subregions. Our results show that HCPA is highly effective in identifying those code regions that are prime candidates for parallelization.

In addition to its support for parallelism discovery, Kremlin performs parallelism planning by incorporating hierarchical data from parallelism discovery as well as additional constraints. The planner supports the concept of *planning personalities*, which incorporates the impact of parallelization system (e.g. OpenMP) and machine properties. As an example of one such personality, Kremlin includes an OpenMP planner which has been validated on a multicore system with 32 cores.

Our results, acquired by applying Kremlin to serial versions of the NAS Parallel Benchmark Suite [6], and all of the C-language Spec OMP2001 [2] benchmarks, show that our approach is quite effective. Kremlin's recommendations, which required no manual intervention, and relied only on information extracted from the serial version of the program, comprise only 3.0% of the original programs' region count. Comparing to a 3rd-party parallelized version, Kremlin required 1.57× fewer regions to be parallelized. In cases where the recommended parallelization plan was similar, Kremlin's performance averaged within 3.8% of manual parallelization, close enough that applying the saved time to serial optimization would likely produce a better outcome. In cases where Kremlin's plan was significantly different, Kremlin's plan exceeded the manual plan's performance by 85%.

To summarize, this paper makes the following contributions:

- We introduce the technique of hierarchical critical path analysis. Traditional critical path analysis techniques are unable to localize parallelism to specific code regions, which is a fundamental limitation that prevents its widespread use in practical end-programmer tools. Unlike dependence-testing approaches that focus on loop bodies, HCPA allows parallelism in serial program regions to be identified even if the program's current form (e.g. loop nesting structure) does not expose it, which can reveal opportunities where non-intuitive code restructuring can yield large benefits.
- We introduce a new metric, self-parallelism, which is the critical step in extending CPA to HCPA. Self-parallelism is able to quantify the parallelism of a parent region independent of its children. We show that high self-parallelism is well-correlated with achieving real parallel speedup. This metric is analogous to *self-time* in the `gprof` profiling tool.
- We develop the concept of a parallelism planner as a key step in the manual parallelization process; that is to say, because of the complexity of the task, we believe profilers for parallel programming should not only provide self-parallelism, work, and other information about program regions but also combine these factors with Amdahl's Law and target system properties to estimate which regions are worth pursuing.
- We introduce the concept of planning personalities that tailor the planning process based on the target system and language. We describe in detail one such personality, a planner for a multicore processor using OpenMP. Combined with parallelism planners, this is a practical way of bridging the gap between abstract CPA analysis and realistic constraints of today's execution environments.

[1] Nonetheless, some researchers have developed tools which help perform specific refactoring tasks in the Enabling Transforms stage [10, 40].

- We demonstrate Kremlin's OpenMP planner's ability to produce concise plans whose performance is typically comparable to—and sometimes far exceeds—manual parallelization that required many trial-and-error iterations and was able to take advantage of post-parallelization measurements. At the same time, these plans would require that the user parallelize significantly fewer regions of the program.

The rest of this paper is organized as follows. Section 2 motivates the need for improved parallelism discovery and planning tools, and formalizes these concepts. Section 3 presents a high-level overview of Kremlin. Sections 4 and 5 describe the implementation of the profiling and planning aspects of Kremlin. Section 6 demonstrates the capabilities of Kremlin in identifying parallelism as well as creating an effective parallelization plan. Related work is detailed in Section 7, and Section 8 concludes.

2. Examining Parallelism Discovery and Planning

In this section we will first motivate the need for tools that discover and plan for parallelism. We then discuss the challenge of quantifying parallelism in specific parts of a program. Finally, we define the problem of parallelism planning informally and then formally.

2.1 Motivation

Despite recent research into parallel programming tools, many programmers still rely on a relatively painful methodology that employs serial profiling tools such as `gprof` in order to direct their parallelization activities. The process starts with a serial hotspot list, which ranks regions by the amount of time spent inside them. This list effectively becomes the order that they examine the functions to improve their performance.

It is at this point that the process gets especially onerous. The programmer starts leafing through the code trying to puzzle through the dependencies in the code, and the granularity at which to try to exploit it. Since the programmer has no indication of whether a hotspot is parallelizable, they frequently give up before they are able to recognize subtle but large parallelism opportunities, or they spend excessive amounts of time fruitlessly modifying serial parts of the code. Alternatively, even if parallelism does exist, it may not be large enough to yield speedup, or when combined with lower coverage, the overall speedup may not justify the effort. Finally, interference between nested parallel regions may prevent speedup.

Our experience watching graduate students struggle to parallelize serial code led us to realize that the inability to quantify parallelism in these program regions was indirectly responsible for large amounts of wasted time. To our surprise, providing them with a tool that quantifies parallelism was not quite enough. Rather, parallelization also requires planning tools that help process this information and apply both parallel programming system and machine constraints. With the ability to positively identify the existence of parallelism, and also to prioritize regions, users can invest their time more productively, attacking the correct portions of the program.

2.2 Quantifying Parallelism

Amdahl's Law provides guidance to the programmer by defining the basic relationship between parallelizability and speedup. According to this law, two factors directly impact speedup: the percentage of time spent in a section of code and the amount of parallelism within that code. While `gprof` and similar tools offer ready-made solutions for determining the work coverage, quantifying parallelism requires additional tools and techniques.

Promise of Critical Path Analysis Approaches One promising approach for quantifying parallelism is to use a *critical path analysis* [23], or *CPA*. CPA is a dynamic analysis that finds the string of dependencies that forms a lower bound on the execution time (the critical path) of a piece of code. The critical path in turn creates an approximate upper bound on the parallelism available, with the ideal parallel implementation performing all non-critical operations in parallel with the critical path operations. The work and critical path define the average amount of parallelism available according to the equation $p = work/length_{cp}$. We refer to parallelism calculated with this equation as the *total-parallelism*.

```
for(i=win..rows-win) {
  for(j=win..cols-win) {
    currLambda = lambda[i][j];
    ...
    for(k=0..nFeatures) {
      if(features[2][k] < currLambda) {
        ...
        features[0][k] = j;
        features[1][k] = i;
        features[2][k] = currLambda;
      }
} } }
```

Figure 2. Localizing Parallelism. In this nested loop from the fillFeatures function in feature_tracking, only the innermost loop (over k) is parallel. Traditional CPA would erroneously report parallelism in the outer loops because they contain the innermost.

The basic premise behind Kremlin and other parallelism discovery tools that employ critical path analysis [5, 21–23] is to evaluate the application's potential for parallelization under relatively optimistic assumptions based on observation of the program's dynamic execution. Most parallelizing compilers, in contrast, must take relatively pessimistic views because they are responsible for guaranteeing correctness. For example, parallelizing compilers may not be able to prove that two pointers do not alias, while a critical path analysis will at least report that it did not observe such dependencies in the actual execution of the program. The basic idea is to elevate to the user awareness of the at least circumstantial evidence of parallelism in the program, so that users can apply their understanding of the real application constraints (as opposed to what is encoded in program source) and refactor to exploit the parallelism.

Critical Path Analysis's Inability to Localize Parallelism Unfortunately, traditional critical path analysis has not found widespread use as a parallelism quantification tool for parallel programmers because it has one important limitation: it cannot localize the parallelism to a particular level of the nested hierarchy of a program's regions. This limitation is illustrated by a code snippet from the feature_tracking benchmark from the San Diego Vision Benchmark Suite [20], shown in Figure 2. In this example, only the innermost loop is parallel. Traditional CPA would only detect that parallelism exists somewhere among the three loops, not just the innermost.

Localizing Parallelism to Specific Regions Kremlin avoids the aforementioned limitation through two novel contributions: *hierarchical critical path analysis* and a new metric, *self-parallelism*. Hierarchical critical path analysis calculates the amount of parallelism within every nested region in a program. Self-parallelism uses this hierarchical data to factor out the parallelism contributed by a region's subregions, much like `gprof`'s self-time metric factors out the time spent in a region's subregions. These two features combine to help Kremlin localize parallelism to specific regions of a program. Section 4 will define and explore them more formally.

What Is a Region? Kremlin uses the concept of a region to denote a region of code whose parallelism is to be measured from the time that region is entered until the time it is exited. In order for the self-parallelism metric to work, regions must obey a proper nesting structure: regions must not partially overlap, but they may nest or be siblings with the same parent region. Based on this nesting structure, we can define a dynamic region graph which shows the relationship between parent and children regions in the dynamic execution of the program.

Although more arbitrary delineations of regions are possible, Kremlin places regions around all loops and functions, since they tend to correspond well to constructs that users understand well and relate more directly to the process of parallelization.

2.3 Creating a Parallelism Plan

Informally, parallelism planning is the problem of producing a sequence of program regions for the programmer to parallelize, ordered according to their expected impact on program execution. While the self-parallelism and self-time metrics improve our ability to create an effective parallelism plan, factors outside of work coverage and parallelism will also impact planning. One such constraint is the risk of over-parallelizing the program: since parallel execution often incurs some overhead in terms of work and/or resource contention, expressing more parallelism than there are cores available to exploit can result in slowdown. For instance, we found that in OpenMP, on our experimental setup, it was seldom profitable to parallelize a child region of a region that had already been parallelized. Another constraint is that synchronization and data movement costs in the system often affect the smallest parallel region that can attain speedup.

We now formally define the problem of parallelism planning so that we may later solve it algorithmically. Let R_P be the set of parallelizable regions in a program P. A parallelism plan creates an ordering on this set such that the relation defining the ordering, $<$, is true for $A < B$ if A should be parallelized before B.

A set of constraints, C, will help to define the ordering on R_P. Examples of these constraints range from architecture-specific constraints (e.g. the number of cores available), to language-specific constraints (e.g. inability to express pipeline parallelism in OpenMP), and even human factors (e.g. the desire to achieve large speedups as soon as possible). These constraints are combined to form a personality for the planner. A planner personality may range from detailed (e.g. fine-grained parallelism on a 100-core Tilera machine) to general (e.g. coarse-grained parallelism), depending on the goal of the user; detailed planners will have better performance on targeted systems while broader personalities will have more robust performance across a broader range of machines.

2.4 Limitations of Kremlin and Other Profile-Based Tools

Needless to say, Kremlin is naturally affected by the same limitations that apply to other profiling tools, like `gprof`, that make use of dynamic information that is input-dependent and does not necessarily predict the program's execution with other inputs. Our experience in varying inputs suggests that in many cases, the additional information gained by dynamic analysis outweighs the drawbacks. Further, Kremlin supports aggregation of data from multiple runs, which reduces these risks. Another limitation is that Kremlin cannot predict the enhanced parallelism that might be attained by changing algorithms, although a report of low parallelism may surprise the user into realizing they need a more parallel algorithm.

CPA-based tools can also be limited by unnecessary dependencies that are still true dependencies. Although no tool can handle all such cases, Kremlin handles many common cases by breaking such dependencies via induction and reduction variable analysis.

3. Kremlin Overview

In this section, we overview Kremlin's user interface and its high-level system architecture. As shown in Figures 3 and 4, Kremlin takes in unmodified source code and produces an instrumented binary. The user executes this binary as they would the uninstrumented program. This binary produces a parallelism profile that

```
$> make CC=kremlin-cc
$> ./tracking data
$> kremlin tracking --personality=openmp

      File (lines)                 Self-P    Cov.(%)
1     imageBlur.c (49-58)          145.3     9.7
2     imageBlur.c (37-45)          145.3     8.7
3     getInterpPatch.c (26-35)     25.3      8.86
4     calcSobel_dX.c (59-68)       126.2     8.1
5     calcSobel_dX.c (46-55)       126.2     8.1
...   ...                          ...       ...
```

Figure 3. Kremlin's User Interface. After compiling and executing the program, Kremlin produces an ordered parallelism plan based on the selected planner personality. Regions are ordered by their estimated program speedup. In addition to location, Kremlin displays the average amount of region-specific parallelism (self-parallelism) and the execution coverage. Results shown are for the feature_tracking benchmark [20].

Kremlin's parallelism planner uses, along with the specified planner personality, to produce a parallelism plan.

Figure 3 also shows the parallelism plan for the feature_tracking benchmark as it would be displayed to the user. The plan presents an ordered list of regions for the programmer to parallelize along with the self-parallelism and work coverage of those regions. Kremlin sorts the list according to decreasing whole-program potential speedup. The list contains only those regions that are expected to meet a minimum speedup threshold; the programmer can expect to obtain nearly all the performance benefits possible if they parallelize all the regions in the list.

Once the programmer has the plan, the basic usage model is that they visit these regions of code in the specified order and determine how to expose the underlying parallelism that was detected by Kremlin. In the event that the user is unable or unwilling to exploit the parallelism in a region, they can rerun the planner with a list of excluded regions and receive an updated plan. The results in this paper were generated without using the exclusion list feature.

Having explained the user's view of the tool, we now examine the Kremlin System Architecture, shown in Figure 4.

Static Instrumentation Kremlin's discovery components are split into two instrumentation steps: critical path instrumentation and region instrumentation. The first step helps quantify parallelism via critical path analysis while the second step helps uncover the program's structure and localize parallelism to specific regions.

Both stages of the discovery phase utilize LLVM's [25] static instrumentation infrastructure. Static instrumentation has two important benefits over dynamic instrumentation. First, it allows for a deeper analysis of the program since the full program source is available. In our experience, tasks such as identifying induction variables, reduction variables, and region boundaries are challenging in dynamic infrastructures such as Valgrind [30] but are easy when performed statically. Second, by statically inserting instrumentation, Kremlin can heavily optimize the code to produce a more efficient instrumented binary. This helps to lower the overhead associated with the heavyweight analysis infrastructure required for hierarchical critical path analysis. Kremlin performs this optimization after instrumentation occurs so that it does not taint the analysis.

During the critical path and region instrumentation stages, Kremlin inserts calls to instrumentation functions that calculate the critical paths of the program and track region entries and exits. These instrumentation functions are implemented inside the

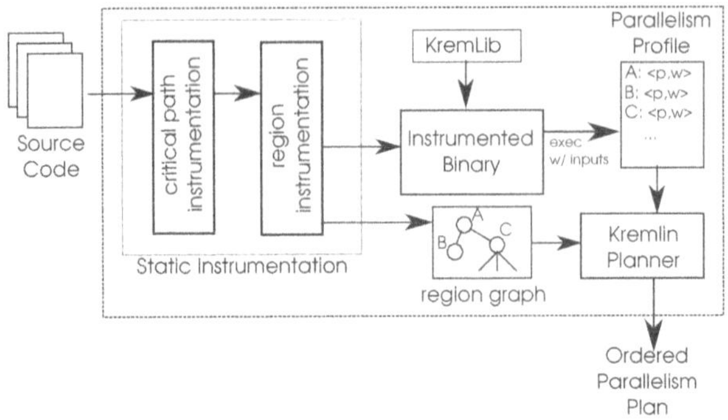

Figure 4. Overview of Kremlin System Architecture. Starting with a program's source code, Kremlin statically instruments the code to insert the proper profiling code and extract the region structure (i.e. region graph) from the program. Running the instrumented binary produces a parallelism profile for each of the program regions. Combined with the region graph, the parallelism profile is used by the parallelism planner to provide the user with a specific list of regions to parallelize (the parallelism plan).

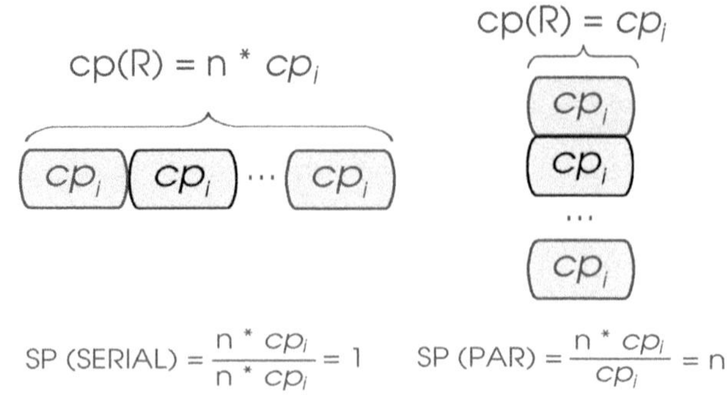

Figure 5. Examples Demonstrating Self-Parallelism (SP) Metric. SP identifies the parallelism local to a region by relating its critical path to the sum of its children's critical paths and its self-work. Shown in the example are SP calculations for two regions; one whose children must execute serially, and one whose children can execute in parallel.

KremLib library. Section 4 provides more details on Kremlin's hierarchical critical path analysis.

Linking and Execution Kremlin next links in the KremLib instrumentation library to produce the instrumented binary. When run, the instrumented binary also produces a parallelism profile output file in addition to its normal outputs that contains parallelism information for each dynamic instance of a program region. Since regions in a program may be executed many times, Kremlin performs an online, dictionary-based compression to greatly reduce the size of the parallelism profile.

Kremlin Planner With the parallelism profile and region graph produced by the discovery phase, Kremlin can begin to create an effective plan to utilize the parallelism in the program. To begin, Kremlin combines the profile data with the region graph information to calculate, among other things, the self-parallelism and work metrics for regions in the program, as described in Section 4.3.

After calculating the self-parallelism for each region, Kremlin designs an ordered plan for the programmer that describes which regions should be parallelized. Kremlin uses both coverage and self-parallelism to estimate the speedup associated with parallelizing specific regions, using this speedup information to order the regions. Kremlin uses planning personalities that incorporate both target- (e.g. OpenMP) and machine-specific parameters in order to improve accuracy; detailed discussion resides in Section 5.

4. Parallelism Discovery

As we discussed earlier, traditional critical path analysis is poor at localizing parallelism to specific code regions. The following subsections describe how Kremlin performs an enhanced form of analysis, hierarchical critical path analysis, and how our new self-parallelism metric is calculated. They also describe a compression technique that reduces the resource requirements of the system.

4.1 Critical Path Analysis

This section describes aspects of hierarchical critical path analysis, including how Kremlin calculates critical path lengths using shadow memory and how it handles both false dependencies and control dependencies.

Calculating Critical Path Length With Shadow Memory Critical path analysis calculates parallelism by quantifying both the amount of work done and the minimum time needed to do that work (i.e. the length of the critical path). The ratio of work to critical path length indicates the average number of instructions that can be executed in parallel in the ideal case. Kremlin efficiently determines both of these values through the use of shadow memory [30, 45].

Kremlin's shadow memory infrastructure works by tracking the earliest possible time that a value stored in a memory location can be calculated. This "availability time" is a function of the longest string of operations required to calculate that value. Kremlin calculates the availability time of each operation by looking up the times of all instructions it depends upon, finding the maximum value, and then adding the operation's latency. Kremlin tracks true data and control dependencies but factors out false dependencies such as anti and output dependencies.

Kremlin utilizes two techniques to limit the overhead associated with shadow memory: dynamic allocation of shadow memory and shadow register tables for local variables. Dynamic shadow memory allocation is enabled by the use of a two-level table that equally splits the whole address space. Kremlin allocates table entries only when they are needed, utilizing calls to `malloc` and `free` as signals of the need to allocate or deallocate. Kremlin uses directly addressable shadow register tables for all local variables. This reduces access time for the common case of reading from local rather than global variables.

Resolving False and Easy-to-Break Dependencies A major challenge for any critical path analysis infrastructure is to mitigate the effects of false and easy-to-break dependencies. Many of these false dependencies, such as unnecessary reuse of a variable, are eliminated by the use of SSA form in LLVM's IR. However, the easy-to-break dependencies associated with induction and reduction variables are more challenging. These types of dependencies can create the false impression of seriality in an otherwise parallel region. Kremlin statically identifies these dependencies and breaks them by using a special shadow memory update rule that ignores the dependency on their old value.

Managing Control Dependencies Kremlin performs static control dependence analysis to identify which values a basic block is control dependent upon. Unfortunately, static analysis cannot fully resolve all control dependencies. Kremlin handles control dependencies through the use of a control dependence stack similar to one proposed in [42]. Kremlin pushes a dependency onto the control stack at the beginning of a control dependent region, popping it off when exiting that region. Availability times in the control stack can only increase. Therefore, Kremlin incorporates control dependencies by checking only the top of the stack.

4.2 Hierarchical Shadow Memory

Hierarchical analysis introduces a new requirement to the shadow memory infrastructure described earlier: we must run separate critical path analyses across each nested dynamic region, and thus must effectively maintain many versions of the shadow memory. When we enter a new region, for the purposes of that region, we start at $time = 0$, $work = 0$, ignoring any dependencies that the parent region is aware of and is tracking. As we execute instructions in the program, we update the dependency times in the shadow memory and the work count for each active region. When we exit a new region, we record a summery of a dynamic region. This summary contains the static region ID, the total work in the region, and the critical path length.

To implement shadow memory for the evolving set of dynamically nested regions as the program runs, each location in the shadow memory and register tables is associated with a set of availability times rather than just one. This set expands when a region is entered and shrinks when a region is exited.

Kremlin optimizes hierarchical shadow memory performance by maintaining a fixed-sized array of shadow data for every memory location. Kremlin assigns a region to a slot based on its depth in the region graph. For instance, the `main` function (the root in the graph) might occupy slot 0, while its children will use slot 1, and so on. A command line flag can vary the range of region depths that are collected, facilitating parallel data collection for the HCPA.

This assignment method leads to multiple regions at the same depth being mapped to the same slot—although they will never use it at the same time—and therefore Kremlin must provide a mechanism to avoid data reuse across region boundaries. Kremlin solves this problem by assigning a unique ID to every region instance and tagging every shadow memory write with the ID of the writer. Kremlin compares the tag with the ID of readers, discarding the data if there is a mismatch and assuming time 0 instead.

4.3 Self-Parallelism

Kremlin incorporates both the parallelism information and the program's structure to calculate a region's self-parallelism. Self-parallelism factors out the parallelism that comes from subregions to determine the amount of parallelism specific to a region.

Kremlin uses the following equation to determine $SP(R)$, the self-parallelism of a region R:

$$SP(R) = \frac{\sum_{k=1}^{n} cp(child(R,k)) + SW(R)}{cp(R)} \quad (1)$$

where n is the number of children of R, $child(R, k)$ is the kth child of R, and $cp()$ is the critical path length of the region. $SW(R)$ represents the amount of work that is performed exclusively in region R (i.e. self-work) and is calculated by the equation:

$$SW(R) = work(R) - \sum_{k=1}^{n} work(child(R,k)) \quad (2)$$

Self-parallelism factors out the children's parallelism by summing the critical path lengths of the children rather than their work, thereby eliminating the parallelism that would otherwise come from the children. Self-parallelism adds work exclusive to the region to capture any remaining parallelism outside of the children.

The self-parallelism metric also allows Kremlin to estimate the speedup from parallelizing a region, R. If the execution time of a R is $ET(R)$, then the execution time after the region is parallelized will be bounded by $ET(R)/SP(R)$. This lower bound on execution time of a parallelized region is used by the planner when determining which regions will bring the largest speedup.

To illuminate the effectiveness of self-parallelism, we will examine the self-parallelism in two cases, shown in Figure 5: a region with n children that can execute in parallel, and a region where all n children must execute serially due to dependencies. For simplicity, we assume that parent regions have no self work and that all children have the same measured critical path length, cp_i.

For the parallel region, its measured critical path will be equal to a single child (i.e. $cp(R) = cp_i$). Thus, the computed self-parallelism, will be $\frac{n*cp_i}{cp_i} = n$; this is as expected because its parallelism is equal to the number of children. Now consider a parent whose child regions must be executed completely serially. In this case, the measured $cp(R)$ will be equal to $n * cp_i$ and therefore the computed self-parallelism will be $\frac{n*cp_{avg}}{n*cp_{avg}} = 1$; again, this is expected because it cannot overlap execution of the regions.

In addition to resolving simple cases like these, the SP heuristic also computes reasonable upper-bounds estimates on self-parallelism for cases where there is self-work in the parent node, and where there are dependencies between child regions that allow partial overlap in execution.

4.4 Compressed Representation

Performing whole-program shadow memory tracing and region analysis is nominally a compute- and memory- intensive endeavor. In order to manage both execution time and storage requirements, Kremlin employs a novel compressed trace representation that enables the planning algorithm to operate on the data without actually decompressing it (analogous to [36] but in a different domain). In this subsection, we describe our implementation and quantify its benefits.

Runtime Compression Technique Kremlin produces a parallelism profile for each dynamic region that is executed. The number of regions is based on the program structure – deeply nested loops can lead to a large number of regions – and the input to the instrumented program and can quickly grow to multiple gigabytes for some programs. Kremlin takes advantage of the fact that many of the region summaries are identical and therefore compression can be used. This reduces not only the amount of data that needs to be written to disk during the instrumented program's execution but also the amount of data that needs to be processed by the planner.

Kremlin utilizes a dictionary-based compression algorithm. When the flow of execution exits a region, Kremlin checks the tuple of ⟨`static region, critical path, work, children`⟩ for the region against the current alphabet of unique regions. If there is no match, a new character is added to the alphabet. If there is a match, the associated character is used. The alphabet necessarily starts with leaf regions. For `children`, Kremlin summarizes child regions via a sorted list of characters, representing compressed regions, and their frequencies. Thus, the children used in the tuple are defined in terms of the existing alphabet rather than the raw region info. Starting from the leaves, the alphabet expands to regions that contain only leaves for children and so on to the root (i.e. `main`).

When the Kremlin planner makes use of the trace files to calculate self-parallelism, it does not need to decompress the data; instead, it operates on each character in the dictionary's alphabet directly. Kremlin exploits the dictionary representation's ability to summarize the critical path and work across recursively nested regions. This can accelerate the calculation of self-parallelism because each dictionary entry essentially summarizes repetitive sequences of large numbers of dynamic regions; processing each character therefore corresponds to processing thousands of dynamic regions.

Benefits We have found that this approach is quite effective. Our original log sizes for the NPB benchmarks [6], using the W inputs, ranged from 750 MB to 54 GB, and averaged 17.9 GB. After compression, they were reduced to between 5 KB and 774 KB, with an average of 150 KB. This was a net average reduction of ~119,000x for log size, and a typically proportional factor for planning time – from minutes to small fractions of a second. Code instrumented with our infrastructure, which is not heavily optimized, is currently about 50× slower than `gprof`-instrumented code; however the parallelism discovery process can be sped up by running instrumentation of disjoint code regions in parallel.

5. Parallelism Planning

In this section we will discuss Kremlin's OpenMP planning personality, and briefly overview a Cilk++ planning personality.

5.1 OpenMP Planner

OpenMP is a popular parallel programming environment with a strong focus on parallelization of loops. Programmers insert pragma statements into their source code and the OpenMP compiler generates the necessary threaded code for them to run. While it does support nested parallelism, the overhead is often too high for it to be effective: the number of execution contexts available is often not enough to handle the extra threads that are spawned and thus the cost of spawning new threads is never amortized. Furthermore, OpenMP requires the programmer to transform loops into parallel (i.e. DOALL) loops in order to achieve good performance.

Kremlin contains a planner that takes into account the major constraints associated with OpenMP. The planner disallows nested parallel regions to avoid the performance penalty we observed on our experimental setup. OpenMP supports reduction variables in parallel loops, but they have significant overheads [8]. We found that the amount of work in a region should be large enough to amortize these costs. For instance, reduction-based loops in the SPEC OMP2001 [2] benchmarks art and ammp have too little work to overcome overheads. On the other hand, ep, from the NAS Parallel Benchmarks [6] ("NPB"), has a reduction-based main function that should be parallelized because it has ample work.

Based on these constraints for OpenMP planning, we can formulate the problem as follows. Given a region graph G, select a set of regions to parallelize, R, such that in any multi-node path, P, in G there is at most one node in R (i.e. $|P \cap R| \leq 1$). The optimal solution will minimize the time required to execute the program.

OpenMP Planning Algorithm A naive algorithm for determining which regions to parallelize would be to repeatedly select the region with the largest potential speedup among all regions considered for parallelization. When a region is selected by the planner, any region that can reach or can be reached from a selected region would then be excluded from consideration to avoid nested parallelization. In some cases, this algorithm may lead to optimal results but in many cases it is suboptimal. For example, a parent region might have the highest single potential speedup, but collectively, a set of its child regions could offer a higher combined speedup. A greedy algorithm would select the parent, precluding the more optimal solution of selecting the set of child regions. Specifically, this problem was observed in two of the NPB benchmarks: ft and lu.

Kremlin's OpenMP planner employs a bottom-up dynamic-programming algorithm. At each level, if we have an optimal plan for parallelizing all of the children, we can make an optimal plan for parallelizing the current node by comparing the expected speedup of the parent versus the cumulative expected speedup of parallelizing the children according to their optimal plan. At the leaves, we select the node by default if it has expected positive speedup.

Additional Constraints for OpenMP and Machine Overheads As part of Kremlin's support for planner personalities, Kremlin can be configured with a few parameters that attempt to capture the system's ability to exploit parallelism. In shared memory and large-scale NUMA machines using runtime schedulers, the cost of data movement and synchronization can be relatively high compared to finer-grained research machines, which impairs their ability to exploit regions with fine-grained parallelism or synchronization.

Clearly many parameters could be incorporated to try to more accurately model the underlying system. However, we would generally prefer to have relatively simple parameters that are useful across a range of systems. As a result, we strove for parameters that are expressed in a relatively architecture-independent fashion.

For the OpenMP planner personality, we found that it was effective to use a set of three threshold parameters. The first is a threshold that determines a minimum level of self-parallelism for a region to be exploited. This mechanism indirectly accounts for the overhead of the the OpenMP scheduler and also the cost of migration between nodes. The second and third thresholds are the minimum required ideal whole-program speedup due to a DOALL region and due to a DOACROSS region. We differentiate between these two kinds of regions because DOACROSS regions are much more synchronization intense (and thus less likely to pay off), and require more programmer effort, and so require a higher ideal whole-program speedup to be justified. As discussed in Section 4.3, Kremlin identifies DOALL loops by checking for equivalence between self-parallelism and iteration count. In this paper, we employ 5.0 as the cutoff for self-parallelism, 0.1% speedup for DOALL loops and 3% speedup for DOACROSS loops. Our sensitivity analysis suggests that Kremlin is not particularly sensitive to minor variations in the settings of these parameters.

Our initial prototype of the OpenMP planner also included the number of cores as a constraint. This initial version capped the speedup of any region at the number of cores available. However, we found that including this constraint had a negative impact on plan quality. With this cap in place, the planner could not differentiate between regions with self-parallelism of N (the number of cores) and those which much higher self-parallelism. Our results suggest that high self-parallelism is correlated with large speedup: a region with much higher self-parallelism likely has more opportunities to amortize parallelization overhead and more flexibility in restructuring to improve memory locality.

5.2 Cilk++ Planning Personality

Kremlin also contains a Cilk++ [27] planner that accounts for Cilk++'s support for nested- and finer-grained parallelism. It employs the same self-parallelism metric as the OpenMP planner but with lower thresholds for self-parallelism and ideal speedup, accounting for Cilk++'s lower underlying costs; it also uses a nesting-aware planning algorithm.

Kremlin was originally developed with a Cilk++ planner, which was used by a group of graduate students in a recent parallel architecture class. Although students found the tool useful, the relative lack of a large, established Cilk++ benchmark suite (and Intel's acquisition of CilkArts) barred us from performing a quantitative evaluation for publication, motivating the development of the OpenMP planner.

5.3 Developing Planning Personalities

Planning personalities provide an avenue for the user to tailor planning recommendations to different systems. Underlying the development of new planning personalities is a fundamental tension between accuracy and portability. The designer of a planning personality must decide the level of architectural independence that is part of the personality. Architectural independence is a desirable property for portability, allowing the planning results to be useful over a wide range of systems, but may need to be sacrificed in order to attain sufficient accuracy.

The development of the OpenMP and Cilk++ personalities provided some insight into the portability-accuracy trade-off. These

Benchmark	MANUAL	Kremlin	Overlap	**Reduction**
ammp	6	3	2	**2.00x**
art	3	4	1	**0.75x**
equake	10	6	6	**1.67x**
bt	54	27	27	**2.00x**
cg	22	9	9	**2.44x**
ep	1	1	1	**1.00x**
ft	6	6	5	**1.00x**
is	1	1	0	**1.00x**
lu	28	11	11	**2.55x**
mg	10	8	7	**1.25x**
sp	70	58	47	**1.21x**
Overall	211	134	116	**1.57x**

(a) Plan Size Comparison

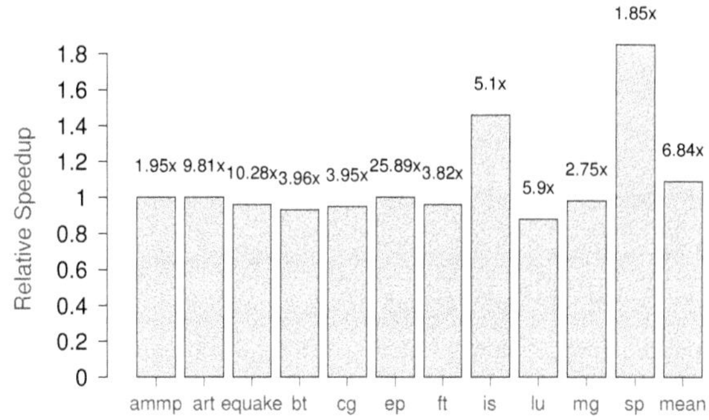

(b) Relative Speedup of Kremlin Compared to MANUAL with Absolute Speedup

Figure 6. Evaluation of Kremlin-Based Parallelization. Table (a) shows MANUAL plan sizes are significantly larger (1.57× on average) than Kremlin plan sizes. Surprisingly, the majority of regions in Kremlin plans are overlapping with MANUAL. Even though Kremlin proposes substantially smaller number of regions to a user, (b) demonstrates that the resulting performance is generally quite close to the manually-parallelized versions, ranging from 12% slower to 85% faster. Note that Kremlin formulated its plans solely by examining the execution of the unmodified serial code. In order to reduce the experimental effects of different effort levels and different programmers for hand tuning, we evaluated the plans for Kremlin by using the parallelized code regions in the manually-parallelized version. In the case of SP and IS, Kremlin's recommendations were significantly different, so we had to manually apply those optimizations.

personalities required that we model only fundamental parameters of the parallel machines: synchronization costs, loop type, and region granularity. These parameters are likely to port well to other parallelization systems, reducing the work necessary to develop new planners for these other systems. We found that while machine-specific parameters such as cache size, page size, and memory bandwidth do influence parallel performance, and influence how code should be transformed, they have limited impact on the set of regions that should be parallelized. These machine-specific parameters therefore are of greater import during the *Enabling Transform* stage in Figure 1 than during the *Planning* stage.

6. Experimental Evaluation

We evaluated Kremlin using all 8 programs in the NAS Parallel Benchmarks (NPB) [6] and all 3 C-language programs in the SPEC OMP2001 [2] benchmark suite. For NPB, we used the third-party OpenMP manually-parallelized version of these programs [1] as a point of comparison for Kremlin's ability to create an effective parallelization plan. For SPEC OMP2001, we ran our tool on the corresponding serial versions of the programs in the SPEC 2000 benchmark suite, and then compared Kremlin's plans against those parallelized by humans in the SPEC OMP2001 versions. For art and ammp, SPEC OMP versions benefit from serial optimizations compared to their SPEC 2000 counterparts [38]. To exclude the effect of serial optimizations, we applied those optimizations on the SPEC 2000 code before running Kremlin. Our evaluation included only third-party benchmarks that have preexisting parallel versions to facilitate comparison and to make our results more credible. The programs vary greatly in terms of speedup (1.5x to 25.89x, Figure 6(b)), but low coverage, low parallelism, parallelization overhead, and other factors significantly reduce the percentage of regions that are good candidates for parallelization (Figure 9).

One might expect that iterative, trial-and-error manual parallelization would do significantly better than Kremlin, because the user has the benefit of performing iterative runtime measurements as they incrementally parallelize the program. We found that parallelization with Kremlin came surprisingly close in terms of performance on all but two benchmarks, and in those cases, it did much better. At the same time, it achieved these results with substantially smaller numbers of regions that needed to be parallelized.

6.1 Methodology

We first ran Kremlin on the unmodified, serial versions of the benchmarks to generate a parallelism plan for each program. The resulting plan was used to create a parallelized version of the serial program. In cases where Kremlin's parallelism plans recommended regions that had also been parallelized in the third-party, manually-parallelized version of the benchmark ("MANUAL"), we reused the parallelized regions from the MANUAL version. This allowed us to control for variances in performance that could result from slightly different parallel implementations of the same region.

To generate and evaluate parallelism plans, the 'W' input set was used for NPB benchmarks while the 'train' input was used for SPEC OMP. Kremlin relies on dynamic analysis and therefore may be affected by varying inputs. To test for input-related sensitivities, we reused the parallelized program based on the 'train' input parallelism plan to measure the speedup numbers for SPEC OMP benchmarks with the larger 'ref' input. We found that Kremlin-based parallelization remained equally competitive on both input sizes, despite requiring a much smaller set of parallelized regions.

Program performance was tested on 32-core system (8 × AMD 8380 Quad-core processors) with 256GB of memory running on the Linux 2.6.18 Kernel. Programs were compiled with gcc version 4.1 with OpenMP and -O3 flags specified. We executed the programs using configurations of 1, 2, 4, 8, 16, and 32 cores. As is typical for these kinds of systems, performance can decline as locality effects start to trump the benefits due to parallelization. For each parallel version, we determined the configuration with the best performance and report that number.

6.2 Evaluation of Parallelism Planning

Kinds of Parallelism Found and Transformations Implied Kremlin detects parallelism of all forms: nested-loop-parallelism including DOACROSS and DOALL, pipelined parallelism between loops and functions, ILP, and thread and task-level-parallelism. All of these exist in our benchmark suite, although Kremlin only recommends regions that are predicted profitable to parallelize according to the planner and personality in use.

Exposing the parallelism detected by Kremlin required user transformations such as: privatization; loop restructuring, fusion and interchange; insertion of OpenMP constructs; and refactoring of code and data structures to eliminate false sharing and contention. These transformations range in difficulty from trivial to difficult, that is, from requiring less than an hour of work to requiring several hours. As we will show in the following sections, Kremlin is able to significantly reduce the number of regions that must be parallelized, thereby significantly reducing the total effort needed to parallelize the program. Kremlin also provides a mechanism whereby the user can specify a set of regions that are too difficult to parallelize and rerun the planner, which recomputes the optimal plan excluding that region.

Plan size comparison Kremlin seeks to focus the programmer's efforts on a small subset of regions that have the most potential for speedup from parallelization. To test Kremlin's effectiveness in this regard, we compared Kremlin's recommended regions ("plans") to the set of regions that were parallelized in the third party-parallelized version of the benchmark suite, referred to as MANUAL. Figure 6(a) provides this plan size comparison.

Across all of the regions in the benchmarks, the MANUAL version included 1.57× more regions than the plan provided by Kremlin. For small benchmarks (e.g. ep, ft, and is) there was little room for improvement, but larger, more complex benchmarks showed larger savings compared to the average. At the extreme end, lu's manually-parallelized plan size was 2.55× the size of Kremlin. The programmer using Kremlin would have had far fewer regions to parallelize than the original third party parallelizers[2].

Performance comparison with MANUAL Next, we evaluated the speedup of parallelized versions based on Kremlin's parallelism plan against the MANUAL version. Figure 6(b) shows the results of this comparison. The Kremlin version of sp and is performed significantly better (1.85×, 1.46×) than MANUAL as Kremlin was able to identify parallelism that was missed in the MANUAL version. In this case, Kremlin recommended a coarse-grained parallelization, requiring privatization and refactoring. Other benchmarks saw a slight degradation in performance, averaging about 3.8%. Kremlin generally selected the same regions as MANUAL, but decided to stop earlier because of the diminishing returns.

To gain additional insight, Figure 7 shows the marginal benefit attained by applying each of the recommendations, in order, from Kremlin's plans. Also shown in the graphs are the marginal benefits of regions parallelized in MANUAL but *not* recommended by Kremlin (regions to the right of the dotted line).

In a large majority of cases, regions not recommended by Kremlin but parallelized by MANUAL provide negligible benefit. Additionally, we can see that, although Kremlin's plans are well-prioritized overall, the incremental contribution of a parallelizing a region can be somewhat noisy. For instance, in several cases, the second recommended region attains a much higher incremental speedup than the first recommended region—this is because as more of the program is parallelized, less data migration happens in the NUMA machine. Often it is groups of regions that must be parallelized before any speedup is observed.

Overall, Kremlin does an excellent job of eliminating regions that offer little benefit. Even for those few regions that were eliminated by Kremlin but had some marginal benefit, the benefits are slight. Given the savings in the number of regions parallelized by Kremlin, we suspect that the programmer could easily make up the difference by applying serial optimizations rather than attempting to parallelize the additional regions.

[2] Programmer effort metrics for the *Enabling Transforms* part of parallelization is clearly a hard problem. We have also explored other metrics, like lines of code, as proxies for programmer effort in Kremlin, since it could perhaps be a better proxy for parallelization complexity. However, our impression from the benchmarks is that, at least, for OpenMP, region count is a better, albeit imperfect, approximation of programmer effort.

	Fraction of Kremlin Plan Applied			
Benchmark	**First 25%**	**First 50%**	**First 75%**	**All 100%**
ammp	74.7 %	100.0 %	100.0 %	100.0 %
art	100.0 %	100.0 %	100.0 %	100.0 %
equake	82.5 %	89.2 %	99.0 %	100.0 %
bt	48.9 %	85.8 %	92.2 %	100.0 %
cg	84.9 %	86.7 %	93.5 %	100.0 %
ep	100.0 %	100.0 %	100.0 %	100.0 %
ft	44.7 %	78.9 %	100.0 %	100.0 %
is	100.0 %	100.0 %	100.0 %	100.0 %
lu	45.8 %	84.0 %	95.4 %	100.0 %
mg	35.6 %	73.0 %	79.5 %	100.0 %
sp	9.6 %	62.1 %	94.5 %	100.0 %
average benefit	56.2 %	86.4 %	95.6 %	100.0 %
marginal average benefit	**56.2 %**	**30.2 %**	**9.2 %**	**4.4 %**

Figure 8. Marginal Benefit of Region Parallelization. A well-prioritized parallelism plan will show decreasing marginal benefits as more of the recommended regions are parallelized. This table shows the average marginal benefit of 25% increments in the fraction of regions parallelized. The final row shows that a majority (56.2%) of benefit comes from the first 25% of regions with the following intervals showing decreasing average marginal benefits. This suggests that Kremlin's parallelism planner is effective at region prioritization.

Effectiveness of Region Prioritization An important aspect of planning is to ensure not only that the regions with the most benefit are selected but also that they are prioritized correctly. The planner attempts to place regions with the largest benefit at the beginning of the plan. Meeting this goal maximizes the productivity of the programmer by focusing their efforts where they are most valuable. To evaluate the effectiveness of the ordering produced by Kremlin, we measured the fraction of total realized execute time reduction attained by following increasing portions of Kremlin's plans, including the first 25%, first 50%, first 75%, and all 100% of the plan. We would expect well-prioritized plans to generally produce monotonically decreasing benefits for each additional fraction that is added. As shown in Figure 8, Kremlin's plans are well-prioritized. The first 25% of the plans average 56.2% of the benefit, the next 25% averages 30.2% of the benefit, while the following 25% yields 9.2%, and the last 25% yields 4.4% of the benefit.

Influences on Plan Size Next, we evaluated how plan size is reduced as additional information is taken into account. The factors that we looked at were work coverage, self-parallelism, and usage of the full OpenMP planner personality. Figure 9 illustrates the impact of each of these factors on the programs. Programmers that take into account only work information (e.g. a `gprof`-based approach) would be left with an average of approximately 59% of the total regions to analyze and attempt to parallelize. With the addition of self-parallelism information for each region, the average plan size is cut to 25.4% of all regions. Finally, when using the full planner an average of only 3.0% of the regions are included in the plan. As we have shown in Figure 6, despite only parallelizing

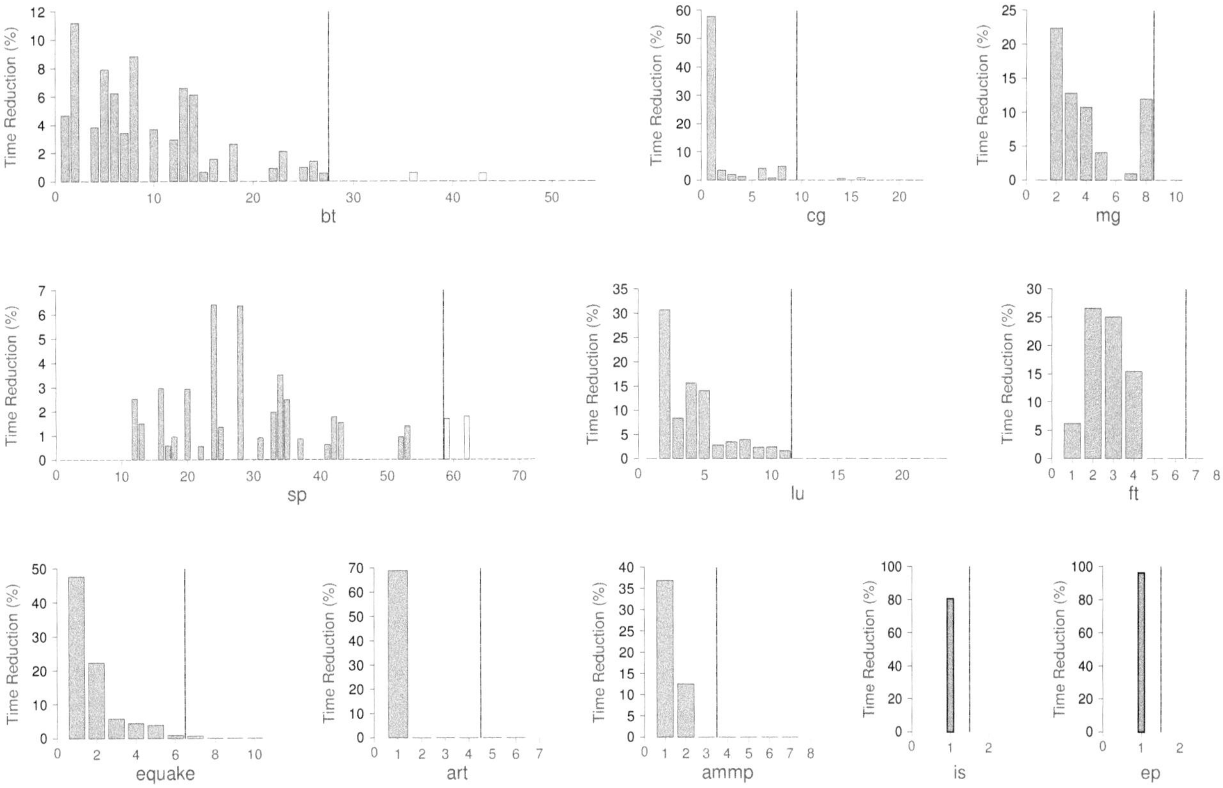

Figure 7. Effectiveness of Region Prioritization. Kremlin provides a list of regions prioritized by their estimated speedup so that users can maximize their productivity. The graphs above show the marginal decrease in execution time, relative to the original program run time, as each region in Kremlin plan is parallelized. We also included regions that were filtered out in the Kremlin plan but were chosen to be parallelized by the expert third party (MANUAL). These regions are shown to the right of the dotted line. As the graphs illustrate, little benefit came from regions that were parallelized by the third-party but that were not suggested by Kremlin.

a fraction of the regions, Kremlin achieves performance that is comparable to the highly-tuned MANUAL version.

Effectiveness of Self-Parallelism Metric To determine the ability of self-parallelism's ability to reduce the number of parallelism false positives (i.e. serial regions that are reported as being parallel), we calculated the self-parallelism and total-parallelism numbers for all 2535 regions that appear in the benchmarks, and classified them according to whether their parallelism is greater than or less than ("high" or "low") a threshold value of 5.0.

The total-parallelism metric identified 25.8% of regions as having low parallelism, while the self-parallelism metric identified 58.9% of regions as having low parallelism, a reduction of 2.28×.

7. Related Work

Parallelism Discovery and Dependence Testing Approaches for parallelism-related profiling have generally fallen into two categories: critical path analysis (CPA) and dependence testing. Critical path analysis dates back several decades, with early important works including [5, 23]. These approaches measured the number of concurrent operations at each time step along the critical path of the program. More recent work includes application of CPA to Java [13] as well as a modified CPA for the purpose of function-level parallelism in Java programs [32]. Unlike these approaches, Kremlin's hierarchical critical path analysis is able to localize parallelism within nested program regions, and provide concrete guidance on which program regions to parallelize.

Allen et al. [3] performed static analysis of Fortran programs in an attempt to automatically identify the correct granularity of parallelism for a target architecture. Kremlin is also able to identify the proper granularity of parallelism through the use of self-parallelism and planning personalities. However, the work in [3] was limited to structured, Fortran code; Kremlin is able to work with unstructured code that contains pointers which cannot be analyzed statically. Furthermore, Kremlin focuses on enabling the user to parallelize complicated code with which automatic parallelizing compilers have traditionally struggled.

Kulkarni et al. [22] used a critical path based analysis to bring insight into the parallelism inherent in the execution of irregular algorithms. In contrast to Kremlin's focus on localizing parallelism to concrete code regions via HCPA, Kulkarni's approach attempts to transcend the details of the implementation and to quantify the amount of latent parallelism in irregular programs that exhibit amorphous data parallelism.

Cilkview [14] is a recent tool that takes an already-parallelized Cilk++ program and estimates how that program's performance will change as the number of cores is increased. Similar to Kremlin, Cilkview leverages runtime information, and analyzes runtime dependencies in the program. However, Cilkview examines dependencies between pre-parallelized threads in a work-queuing runtime system rather than between instructions.

Another approach to parallelism-related profiling has been to use dependence testing to uncover the dependencies between different regions in the program. pp [24] is an early important work that proposed hierarchical dependence testing to estimate the parallelism in loop nests. Notable recent works include Alchemist [43] and SD3 [19], which reduces runtime and memory overhead of dependence testing through the use of parallelization and compression. Although dependence testing and Kremlin's HCPA share similar goals, Kremlin focuses on localizing and quantifying parallelism across many different, nested program regions rather than establishing independence of pre-existing regions. As a result, it can identify more nuanced forms of parallelism even though significant transformation is required to expose it. Dependence testing is generally more pessimistic and sensitive to existing program structure.

A number of works have used dependence testing to determine the probability that specific dependencies will occur [39, 41]. DProf [41] uses a compiler to identify may dependencies and then determine the probability that these dependencies will occur. von Praun et al. [39] introduced the *dependence density* metric to describe the probability that two random tasks would have a dependency. Both of these approaches target optimistic concurrency such as TLS or transactional memory.

The main difference between Kremlin's parallelism discovery and dependence testing frameworks is in the stage of parallelization (Figure 1) that profiling targets. Kremlin's parallelism discovery is meant to quantify the parallelism in a fashion that is not as strongly tied to the program's current structure, exposing hidden sources of parallelism. In contrast, dependence testing-based approaches are more aligned with the enabling transforms stage of parallelization as they enable identifying specific changes that need to be made to enable parallelism. In the absence of discovery and planning tools, [43] orders regions by total execution time. An interesting possibility would be to augment [43]'s approach with the improved analysis provided by Kremlin. ParaScope [18] used static analysis to expose difficult-to-analyze dependencies to the user so that they could circumvent them via refactoring.

The discovery phase takes advantage of a compression scheme that resembles whole-program path compression schemes [44]. We achieve much higher compression levels because we do not need to store information about the relative ordering of child subregions.

Parallelism Planning The task of parallelism planning has been mostly overlooked in the context of manual parallelization. Outside of manual parallelization, automatic parallelizing compilers such as SUIF [12] and Polaris [7] implicitly perform planning. Because these tools do not target user-assisted parallelization, their planning phases focus on finding thresholds for profitable exploitation.

Speculative parallelization systems [31, 34] have created new opportunities for compilers to exploit parallelism even in the face of difficult-to-analyze code, or infrequent dependencies that result in overly conservative execution. These systems typically have a memory speculation system, often in special hardware but sometimes in software, which removes the burden of proving the correctness of potential parallelizations, allowing the compiler to focus on selecting the parallelizations that maximize performance. TLS compilers [9, 11, 29, 31, 37, 46] also benefit from detecting parallelism and often use dynamic critical path or dependence testing analyses in order to establish regions which are likely to be profitable for TLS-style execution. Kremlin's HCPA can be used in a complementary manner by providing a way to guide programmers in restructuring their code to improve parallelism for execution on TLS. This can enable an even larger class of transformations than these systems natively support.

Recent work by Tournavitis et al. [38] provides a semi-automated approach to parallelization. This approach automates parallelism discovery using a form of dependence testing and uses machine learning to pick a set of regions to be parallelized. The selected regions are automatically annotated with OpenMP pragmas. The presumption is that the user will verify the correctness of the parallelization. While this approach has promise, it is limited by the compiler's ability to perform the *Enabling Transforms* phase of parallelization. In contrast, Kremlin has a more optimistic view of parallelism and is able to report regions with parallelism even if the compiler is not up to the task of exploiting it automatically.

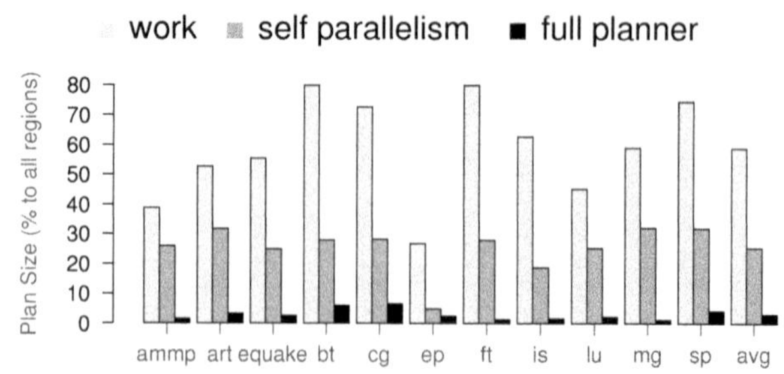

Figure 9. Evaluating Plan Size Reduction Due to Each of Kremlin's Planning Components. Plans based only on work coverage comprised 58.9% of all regions on average. Using self-parallelism to eliminate low parallelism regions cut this more than half (25.4%, on average). Finally, using the full OpenMP planner personality, the plan size was reduced to only 3.0% of the total regions.

Systems such as SUIF Explorer [28] and CAPO-Paraver [16] share Kremlin's focus on empowering the user during parallelization. SUIF Explorer's novelty focuses around its use of static interprocedural program analysis including pointer analysis and slicing; its use of dynamic analysis is very briefly described but appears to detect the absence or presence of memory dependencies within loops, and to provide time profiles for regions. CAPO-Paraver extends the CAPO parallelizing compiler to allow it to insert instrumentation that helps the user understand the load balancing properties of parallelized code. A short paper on Kremlin appeared in PPoPP [15].

8. Conclusion

Kremlin strives to simplify the task of parallelization by addressing the question: *what parts of the program should I spend time parallelizing?* Beginning with unmodified serial source code and sample inputs, Kremlin produces a list of regions in the order that they should be parallelized.

At the heart of Kremlin is an extension of the critical path analysis technique. Critical path analysis, which was invented in 1988, is rarely used in current-day performance profiling tools. In this paper, we extend that work by proposing the hierarchical critical path analysis (HCPA) technique, the self-parallelism metric, and the idea of using a planner algorithm that models the execution of the program on the machine. Given how conceptually straightforward HCPA appears to be, it seems surprising that it has not been proposed earlier, closer to the inception of CPA in the 80's. Although HCPA appears in retrospect to be straightforward, the "hard part" of the research is making the jump from the output of the HCPA algorithm to the creation of an effective parallel plan. The self-parallelism metric and planner concept are the key steps in doing this, and took many people-years of iteration for us to arrive at. One of the challenges with this research is figuring out exactly what information is needed to make meaningful recommendations, and how to decimate the information at each stage of the process. A valid approach must work without the collection of traces that are proportional to the execution time of the program, which can easily amount to terabytes. Further optimization detail is required for creating the multi-versioned shadow memory data-structures and rules that enable HCPA to run quickly and with low overhead.

Kremlin's results are very strong. Typically, by examining only the original serial code, the tool beats iterative parallelization by experts. It reduces the number of unnecessarily parallelized regions by 1.57x, attains better average performance, and in two out of the eleven benchmarks, improves speedups substantially by factors of 1.86x and 1.46x. Our results also show that Kremlin is effective at prioritizing regions: 56.2% of the benefit is captured in the first quarter of recommendations, and 86.4% comes from the first half of recommendations. All of these results suggest that Kremlin is likely to be highly effective at reducing programmer effort.

Acknowledgement

This research was funded by the US National Science Foundation under CAREER Award 0846152, and under Awards 0725357 and 1018850.

References

[1] "NAS Parallel Benchmarks 2.3; OpenMP C." `www.hpcc.jp/Omni/`.

[2] "Spec OMP2001 Benchmarks." `http://www.spec.org/omp`.

[3] F. Allen, M. Burke, R. Cytron, J. Ferrante, W. Hsieh, and V. Sarkar. "A framework for determining useful parallelism." In *Proceedings of the 2nd international conference on Supercomputing*, ICS '88, 1988.

[4] T. E. Anderson, and E. D. Lazowska. "Quartz: A tool for tuning parallel program performance." In *SIGMETRICS*, vol. 18, 1990.

[5] T. Austin, and G. S. Sohi. "Dynamic dependency analysis of ordinary programs." In *ISCA*, 1992.

[6] Bailey et al. "The NAS parallel benchmarks." In *SC*, 1991.

[7] W. Blume, R. Doallo, R. Eigenmann, J. Grout, J. Hoeflinger, T. Lawrence, J. Lee, D. Padua, W. Paek, Y. Pottenger, L. Rauchwerger, and P. Tu. "Parallel programming with Polaris." *IEEE Computer*, Aug 2002.

[8] J. M. Bull, and D. O'Neill. "A microbenchmark suite for openmp 2.0." *SIGARCH Comput. Archit. News*, December 2001.

[9] M. K. Chen, and K. Olukotun. "The Jrpm system for dynamically parallelizing Java programs." In *ISCA*, 2003.

[10] D. Dig, J. Marrero, and M. D. Ernst. "Refactoring sequential java code for concurrency via concurrent libraries." In *ICSE*, 2009.

[11] Z. H. Du, C. C. Lim, X. F. Li, C. Yang, Q. Zhao, and T. F. Ngai. "A cost-driven compilation framework for speculative parallelization of sequential programs." In *PLDI*, 2004.

[12] M. W. Hall, J. M. Anderson, S. P. Amarasinghe, B. R. Murphy, S.-W. Liao, and E. Bu. "Maximizing multiprocessor performance with the SUIF compiler." *IEEE Computer*, Aug 1996.

[13] C. Hammacher, K. Streit, S. Hack, and A. Zeller. "Profiling java programs for parallelism." In *Proceedings of the 2009 ICSE Workshop on Multicore Software Engineering*, IWMSE '09, 2009.

[14] Y. He, C. Leiserson, and W. Leiserson. "The Cilkview Scalability Analyzer." In *SPAA*, 2010.

[15] D. Jeon, S. Garcia, C. Louie, S. Kota Venkata, and M. Taylor. "Kremlin: Like gprof, but for Parallelization." In *Principles and Practice of Parallel Programming*, 2011.

[16] G. Jost, H. Jin, J. Labarta, and J. Gimenez. "Interfacing computer aided parallelization and performance analysis." In *Computational Science ICCS 2003*, vol. 2660 of *Lecture Notes in Computer Science*, 715–715. 2003.

[17] K. Kelsey, T. Bai, C. Ding, and C. Zhang. "Fast track: A software system for speculative program optimization." In *CGO*, 2009.

[18] K. Kennedy, K. S. McKinley, and C. W. Tseng. "Interactive parallel programming using the parascope editor." *IEEE TPDS*, 1991.

[19] M. Kim, H. Kim, and C.-K. Luk. "SD3: A scalable approach to dynamic data-dependence profiling." *Microarchitecture, IEEE/ACM International Symposium on*, 2010.

[20] S. Kota Venkata, I. Ahn, D. Jeon, A. Gupta, C. Louie, S. Garcia, S. Belongie, and M. Taylor. "SD-VBS: The San Diego Vision Benchmark Suite." In *IISWC*, 2009.

[21] D. Kuck, Y. Muraoka, and S.-C. Chen. "On the number of operations simultaneously executable in fortran-like programs and their resulting speedup." *IEEE Transactions on Computers*, Dec. 1972.

[22] M. Kulkarni, M. Burtscher, R. Inkulu, K. Pingali, and C. Casçaval. "How much parallelism is there in irregular applications?" In *PPoPP*, 2009.

[23] M. Kumar. "Measuring parallelism in computation-intensive scientific/engineering applications." *IEEE TOC*, Sep 1988.

[24] J. R. Larus. "Loop-level parallelism in numeric and symbolic programs." *IEEE Trans. Parallel Distrib. Syst.*, 1993.

[25] C. Lattner, and V. Adve. "LLVM: A compilation framework for lifelong program analysis & transformation." In *CGO*, Mar 2004.

[26] W. Lee, R. Barua, M. Frank, D. Srikrishna, J. Babb, V. Sarkar, and S. Amarasinghe. "Space-time scheduling of instruction-level parallelism on a Raw machine." In *ASPLOS*, October 1998.

[27] C. E. Leiserson. "The Cilk++ concurrency platform." In *DAC*, 2009.

[28] S.-W. Liao, A. Diwan, R. P. Bosch, Jr., A. Ghuloum, and M. S. Lam. "Suif explorer: an interactive and interprocedural parallelizer." In *Proceedings of the ACM SIGPLAN symposium on Principles and practice of parallel programming*, 1999.

[29] W. Liu, J. Tuck, L. Ceze, W. Ahn, K. Strauss, J. Renau, and J. Torrellas. "POSH: a TLS compiler that exploits program structure." In *PPoPP*, 2006.

[30] N. Nethercote, and J. Seward. "Valgrind: A framework for heavyweight dynamic binary instrumentation." In *PLDI*, 2007.

[31] L. Rauchwerger, and D. Padua. "The LRPD test: speculative run-time parallelization of loops with privatization and reduction parallelization." In *PLDI*, 1995.

[32] A. Rountev, K. Van Valkenburgh, D. Yan, and P. Sadayappan. "Understanding parallelism-inhibiting dependences in sequential java programs." In *Software Maintenance (ICSM), 2010 IEEE International Conference on*, Sept 2010.

[33] V. A. Saraswat, V. Sarkar, and C. von Praun. "X10: concurrent programming for modern architectures." In *PPoPP*, 2007.

[34] G. Sohi, S. Breach, and T. Vijaykumar. "Multiscalar processors." In *ISCA*, 1995.

[35] N. R. Tallent, and J. M. Mellor Crummey. "Effective performance measurement and analysis of multithreaded applications." In *PPoPP*, 2009.

[36] W. Thies, S. Hall, and S. Amarasinghe. "Manipulating lossless video in the compressed domain." In *ACM Multimedia*, 2009.

[37] C. Tian, M. Feng, V. Nagarajan, and R. Gupta. "Copy or discard execution model for speculative parallelization on multicores." In *MICRO*, 2008.

[38] G. Tournavitis, Z. Wang, B. Franke, and M. F. P. O'Boyle. "Towards a holistic approach to auto-parallelization: integrating profile-driven parallelism detection and machine-learning based mapping." In *PLDI*, 2009.

[39] C. von Praun, R. Bordawekar, and C. Cascaval. "Modeling optimistic concurrency using quantitative dependence analysis." In *PPoPP*, 2008.

[40] J. Wloka, M. Sridharan, and F. Tip. "Refactoring for reentrancy." In *FSE*, 2009.

[41] P. Wu, A. Kejariwal, and C. Caşcaval. "Compiler-driven dependence profiling to guide program parallelization." In *LCPC*, 232–248. 2008.

[42] B. Xin, and X. Zhang. "Efficient online detection of dynamic control dependence." In *ISSTA*, 2007.

[43] X. Zhang, A. Navabi, and S. Jagannathan. "Alchemist: A transparent dependence distance profiling infrastructure." In *CGO*, 2009.

[44] Y. Zhang, and R. Gupta. "Timestamped whole program path representation and its applications." In *PLDI*, 2001.

[45] Q. Zhao, D. Bruening, and S. Amarasinghe. "Umbra: Efficient and scalable memory shadowing." In *CGO*, 2010.

[46] H. Zhong, M. Mehrara, S. Lieberman, and S. Mahlke. "Uncovering hidden loop level parallelism in sequential applications." In *HPCA*, 2008.

Automatic Parallelization via Matrix Multiplication

Shigeyuki Sato Hideya Iwasaki

The University of Electro-Communications, Tokyo, Japan

sato@ipl.cs.uec.ac.jp iwasaki@cs.uec.ac.jp

Abstract

Existing work that deals with parallelization of complicated reductions and scans focuses only on formalism and hardly dealt with implementation. To bridge the gap between formalism and implementation, we have integrated parallelization via matrix multiplication into compiler construction. Our framework can deal with complicated loops that existing techniques in compilers cannot parallelize. Moreover, we have sophisticated our framework by developing two sets of techniques. One enhances its capability for parallelization by extracting max-operators automatically, and the other improves the performance of parallelized programs by eliminating redundancy. We have also implemented our framework and techniques as a parallelizer in a compiler. Experiments on examples that existing compilers cannot parallelize have demonstrated the scalability of programs parallelized by our implementation.

Categories and Subject Descriptors D.3.4 [*Programming Language*]: Processors—Compilers, Optimization; D.1.2 [*Programming Techniques*]: Automatic Programming

General Terms Experimentation, Languages, Design, Algorithms

Keywords automatic parallelization, loop, reduction, scan, matrix multiplication, semiring, linear recurrence equation

1. Introduction

Since 2005, processor vendors have generally adopted multi-core architectures instead of boosting the clock rate of processors. This means that sequential programs cannot be made run faster without parallelization. Thus, we cannot avoid parallel programming in striving for higher performance. However, parallel programming is a challenge for most programmers. The easiest way for programmers to make programs parallel is to use automatic parallelization.

The most commonly used methodology for automatic parallelization of loops is *doall parallelization* [1, 2], whose core is to guarantee the independence of each iteration, i.e., the parallelism among iterations, by analyzing *loop-carried data dependence*. This framework suffices for simple data parallelism, but does not suffice for *reduction*, which is a generalization of summation.

Standard doall parallelizers can recognize simple reductions, e.g., one that just computes the sum of an array:

$$x \leftarrow 0;\ \textbf{for}\ i = 1\ \textbf{to}\ n\ \textbf{do}\ x \leftarrow x + a[i]\ \textbf{done}.$$

PLDI'11, June 4–8, 2011, San Jose, California, USA.

This loop is equivalent to $x \leftarrow 0+\sum_{i=1}^{n} a[i]$. As is well known, the summation can be computed in parallel owing to the *associativity* of the addition; the parallel summation is computed in $O(n/p + \log p)$ time, where p is the number of threads. Although this loop has a loop-carried data dependence with respect to x (i.e., writing x after reading x over an iteration), its doall parallelization succeeds because the definition and use of x are recognized as a reduction.

The summation is a trivial reduction. There are, however, more unobvious and non-trivial reductions. For example, the following loop evaluates a polynomial expression through the Horner scheme, i.e., $\sum_{i=0}^{n} a[n-i]c^i = a[n] + c(a[n-1] + c(a[n-2] + \cdots + c(a[1] + c(a[0] + c \cdot 0)) \cdots))$.

$$x \leftarrow 0;\ \textbf{for}\ i = 0\ \textbf{to}\ n\ \textbf{do}\ x \leftarrow c \cdot x + a[i]\ \textbf{done}.$$

Doall parallelizers cannot recognize this loop as a reduction. As a result, this loop-carried data dependence with respect to x makes its doall parallelization impossible. However, we can rewrite this loop into

$$\boldsymbol{x} \leftarrow \boldsymbol{x}_0;\ \textbf{for}\ i = 0\ \textbf{to}\ n\ \textbf{do}\ \boldsymbol{x} \leftarrow A_i \times \boldsymbol{x}\ \textbf{done},$$

$$\textbf{where}\ \boldsymbol{x} = \begin{pmatrix} x \\ 1 \end{pmatrix},\ \boldsymbol{x}_0 = \begin{pmatrix} 0 \\ 1 \end{pmatrix},\ A_i = \begin{pmatrix} c & a[i] \\ 0 & 1 \end{pmatrix}.$$

This loop is equivalent to $\boldsymbol{x} \leftarrow \left(\prod_{i=0}^{n} A_{n-i}\right) \times \boldsymbol{x}_0$. It is the same as the summation except for changing the addition into the matrix multiplication. Since the matrix multiplication is an associative operation, we can also compute the product of matrices in $O(n/p+\log p)$ time. Thus, this loop can be parallelized.

As shown above, if we can transform a loop body into a matrix multiplication form, we can obtain an efficient parallel version of its loop. This technique is known as a parallel algorithm for solving linear recurrence equations [10]. There is work that applies a generalization of this idea to automatic parallelization [6, 8, 13, 14, 21]. Although the formalism developed in such work is promising for parallelizing complicated loops, no one connects the formalism with the implementation aspect. We have resolved this problem by integrating the formalism into doall parallelization.

Our work to bridge the gap between formalism and practical implementation includes a solution to an important problem concerning the max-operator, which plays a key role in parallelizing dynamic programming. In prior work on algebra-based parallelization [13, 21], this operator is assumed to be given, even though in realistic programs the max-operation is usually described by means of if-statements. We have developed a technique for extracting max-operators automatically from if-statements.

Our work has resulted in the following important contributions.

- We have developed a novel framework for loop parallelization (Sections 3 and 4). The formalization of a loop body by using matrix multiplication over a semiring enables parallelization of various loops, especially one with a complicated body that contains loop-carried data dependence and if-statements. This parallelization is more powerful than the standard doall parallelization. Our framework is an integration of doall parallelization and the existing formalism [6, 8, 13, 14, 21]. To the best of our knowledge, our work is the first to deal seriously with the implementation aspect of deriving associative operators for automatic parallelization.

- We have developed a technique for extracting max-operators automatically and semantically from if-statements by using an off-the-shelf Satisfiability Modulo Theories (SMT) solver (Section 5). This technique plays an important role in our framework for parallelizing various loops whose bodies contain if-statements. Automatic extraction of max-operators has not been addressed in algebra-based parallelization [13, 21]. To the best of our knowledge, our work is the first to deal seriously with the max-plus semiring in the practical context of automatic parallelization.
- We have developed optimization techniques for loops that are parallelized by our framework (Section 6). Because these techniques reduce the intrinsic overhead caused by our parallelization, they are essential in practical situations. One of these techniques is also helpful for doall parallelization (Section 6.4).
- We have implemented our framework and techniques as a parallelizer in a realistic compiler. We have then conducted experiments on examples whose doall parallelization fails and have confirmed the scalability of these versions parallelized by our implementation (Section 7).

2. Preliminaries

2.1 Notations

For program description in this paper, we use a mixture of mathematical operators and syntax constructs of standard procedural languages like Fortran and C.

The two sides of an assignment are connected by $\leftarrow$. If each side is a vector, it is a vectorized assignment, which denotes simultaneous assignment of every entry on the right side to the corresponding entry on the left side. Note that vector and matrix in this paper are virtual, i.e., not an actual data structure. They are simply syntax constructs for expressing vectorized assignment and matrix multiplication. Operators $\cdot$ and $\times$ denote scalar and matrix multiplication, respectively. We omit $\cdot$ when it is obvious. A sequence enclosed by brackets, e.g., $[a_1, \ldots, a_n]$, is an extensible notation of an array, i.e., enumerated values are stored in the array in order. Statement are separated by a semicolon.

for $i = 1$ **to** n **do** b **done** is a for-loop with a control variable of i and a body of b. Unless otherwise noted, n denotes the number of iterations. **if** e **then** b_1 **else** b_2 **endif** is an if-statement. (e_1) ? e_2 : e_3 is a conditional expression using the syntax of C. **parallel** $k \in \{1, \ldots, p\}$ **do** b **done** is a parallel block in which b is executed by p threads in parallel, where k denotes thread ID. Unless otherwise noted, p denotes the number of threads. Here, the shared memory model, i.e., EREW PRAM, and $p \ll n$ are assumed.

2.2 Terminologies

Techniques for identification and parallelization of the *doall loop*, which is a loop whose all iterations can be executed in parallel, have been well studied [1, 2]. In this paper, we use the term *doall parallelization* for these techniques.

To identify a loop as a doall loop, a doall parallelizer analyzes the *loop-carried data dependence*. There is a loop-carried (true) data dependence with respect to a variable (or array element) x iff x is defined in an iteration and x is used in the succeeding iterations where its definition reaches. If there is no loop-carried data dependence in a loop, the loop is identified as a doall loop.

Consider **for** $i = 1$ **to** n **do** $x \leftarrow a_i$ **done**. Because there is no loop-carried data (true) dependence, we can transform this loop into its doall version. However, in its parallelized version, the result of x is nondeterministic. In this case, at the end of the loop, x must be a_n, which is called the *final value* of x, due to its sequential semantics. A guarantee that the final values of variables defined in a parallelized loop coincide with those in its sequential version is called the *final value guarantee*.

We define several terms here.

Definition 1 (Accumulator)**.** A scalar variable x is an accumulator iff there is loop-carried data dependence with respect to x. Unless otherwise noted, x is an accumulator.

Definition 2 (Recurring expression and symbolically constant expression)**.** An expression e in a loop is a recurring expression iff e is computed from some loop-carried value. If e is not a recurring expression, we call e a symbolically constant expression. $\mathcal{C}$ denotes the set of symbolically constant expressions in a given program.

2.3 Target Loops

The target of the proposed parallelization is a non-nested loop the body of which contains neither jumps (e.g., goto, break, and continue), labels, pointers, indirect access to arrays, nor function calls; i.e., a target loop body contains only assignments, if-statements, and side-effect-free expressions. We call a sequence of assignments and if-statements a *block*.

For convenience, the start value of the control variable of each target loop is normalized to 1 using induction variable transformation [1, 2]. There are two characteristic restrictions on target loops:

- There is no loop-carried data dependence with respect to any array element.
- If an accumulator occurs in the condition-part of an if-statement, there is no assignment to the accumulator in either the then-part or else-part.

We can overcome the first restriction by using scalar replacement [5]. A technique for overcoming the second restriction is presented in Section 5, but the explanation in Sections 3 and 4 supposes this restriction. This paper does not deal with programs that cause runtime errors, and ignores arithmetic overflow and round-off errors.

2.4 Parallel Primitives

We introduce parallel primitives, which are generic patterns of parallel computation. The definitions of primitives used are:

$$\mathsf{reduce}(\odot, [x_1, \ldots, x_n]) = x_n \odot \cdots \odot x_1$$
$$\mathsf{scan}(\odot, e, [x_1, \ldots, x_n]) = [e, x_1 \odot e, \ldots, x_{n-1} \odot \cdots \odot x_1 \odot e],$$

where $\odot$ is an associative operator. Although the definitions of reduce and scan above are a bit different from these traditional definitions for convenience, it does not matter essentially.

The reduce algorithm consists of two phases: *local reduction* and *global reduction*. In the local reduction, p threads reduce n elements into p elements independently. In the global reduction, p threads reduce the result of the local reduction into the final result cooperatively. For example, consider $\mathsf{reduce}(+, [a_1, \ldots, a_n])$. In the local reduction, the k-th thread computes $r_k \leftarrow \sum_{(k-1)n/p+1}^{kn/p} a_i$. In the global reduction, p threads compute $\sum_1^n a_i$ through $\sum_1^p r_i$. The time complexity of the local reduction is $O(n/p)$ and that of the global reduction is $O(\log p)$. $O(p)$ space is used.

The scan algorithm consists of three phases: *local reduction*, *global scan*, and *local scan*. The local reduction is the same as that of reduce. In the global scan, p threads produce new p elements from the result of the local reduction cooperatively. In the local scan, p threads compute the final result from the result of the global scan and the input sequence. For example, consider $\text{scan}(+, e, [a_1, \ldots, a_n])$. In the local reduction, the k-th thread computes $r_k \leftarrow \sum_{(k-1)n/p+1}^{kn/p} a_i$. In the global scan, p threads compute $r' \leftarrow \left[e, e + \sum_1^1 r_i, \ldots, e + \sum_1^{p-1} r_i\right]$. In the local scan, the k-th thread computes $\left[e + \sum_1^{(k-1)n/p} a_i, \ldots, e + \sum_1^{kn/p-1} a_i\right]$ from $r'[k-1]$ and the subarray of a. The time complexity of the global scan is $O(\log p)$ and that of the local scan is $O(n/p)$. $O(p)$ space is used for intermediate data.

In the shared memory model, we can simply describe each of the local reduction and local scan as a parallel loop with an iteration space that is block-partitioned. We can merge a doall loop followed by a scan or reduce into the local reduction of the reduce or the local scan of the scan if the number of iterations in the doall loop is the same as the length of an array that the scan or reduce computes. The global reduction and global scan are described in detail elsewhere [18].

3. Formalization based on Matrix Multiplication

Before describing our framework for parallelization, we present examples that are used in this section.

Example 1. Although the following loop contains a simple assignment other than a reduction, doall parallelizers can also handle it.

$x \leftarrow 0;$ **for** $i = 1$ **to** n **do** $x \leftarrow x + a[i];\ a[i] \leftarrow a[i] + 1$ **done**.

Doall parallelizers deal with the above loop by recognizing part of a trivial reduction in an ad hoc way. Thus, they cannot parallelize non-trivial reductions that they cannot recognize as reduction. An example of non-trivial reductions is the polynomial evaluation shown in Section 1. Another example is as follows.

Example 2. The following loop computes the *maximum tail-segment sum* (mts) of a given array, i.e., the maximum sum of a contiguous segment that contains the last element of a given array; e.g., the mts of $[2, -1, -3, 5, 0, -4, 6]$ is $5 + 0 + (-4) + 6 = 7$.

$x \leftarrow 0;$
for $i = 1$ **to** n **do**
if $x + a[i] \geq 0$ **then** $x \leftarrow x + a[i]$ **else** $x \leftarrow 0$ **endif done**.

This is a non-trivial reduction because its loop body contains an if-statement whose condition-part contains an accumulator.

In addition, doall parallelization cannot support using the intermediate results of reduction for other computations.

Example 3. The following loop computes the prefix sum of an array, i.e., $\left[\sum_{i=1}^{1} a[i], \cdots, \sum_{i=1}^{n} a[i]\right]$. Although it resembles summation, its doall parallelization fails due to $a[i] \leftarrow x$.

$x \leftarrow 0;$ **for** $i = 1$ **to** n **do** $x \leftarrow x + a[i];\ a[i] \leftarrow x$ **done**.

Example 4. The following loop resembles Example 2; it computes the start position of the mts of an array. For example, the start position of the mts of $[2, -1, -3, 5, 0, -4, 6]$ is 4.

$x_1 \leftarrow 0;\ x_2 \leftarrow 1;$
for $i = 1$ **to** n **do**
if $x_1 + a[i] \geq 0$ **then** $x_1 \leftarrow x_1 + a[i]$
else $x_1 \leftarrow 0;\ x_2 \leftarrow i + 1$ **endif done**,

where x_1 is the mts and x_2 is its start position. Note that $x_2 \leftarrow i+1$ implicitly uses the intermediate result of x_1 since it is in an if-statement whose condition-part uses x_1. Here, we assume that x_1 is not used after this loop for convenience. The start position of the mts is important for application; e.g., if $a[i]$ be the price of a stock at time i, x_2 is the time when the price of the stock began to rise.

3.1 Matrix Multiplication Form

Recall the example of polynomial evaluation shown in Section 1; its loop has a loop-carried data dependence with respect to x, which makes doall parallelization impossible. However, we can transform its loop body into the following form:

$$\boldsymbol{x} \leftarrow A_i \times \boldsymbol{x}, \quad \textbf{where } \boldsymbol{x} = \begin{pmatrix} x \\ 1 \end{pmatrix},\ A_i = \begin{pmatrix} c & a[i] \\ 0 & 1 \end{pmatrix}.$$

Note that the second entry of the result of $A_i \times \boldsymbol{x}$ is always 1. We permit a constant to be in the left side of an assignment if both sides are always the same. From the above transformation, the loop turns out to be equivalent to $\boldsymbol{x} \leftarrow A_n \times \cdots \times A_0 \times \boldsymbol{x}$. Owing to the associativity of $\times$, we obtain the following assignment:

$$\boldsymbol{x} \leftarrow \text{reduce}\,(\times, [A_0, \ldots, A_n]) \times \boldsymbol{x}.$$

Since we can transform this loop into a reduce, we can compute it in $O(n/p + \log p)$ time. Note that we can combine the generation of A_i from array element $a[i]$ with the local reduction of reduce. The key point of this parallelization is to transform the loop body into matrix-vector multiplication by introducing $\boldsymbol{x}$ and A_i. Then, by unfolding all iterations, we can obtain a chain of matrix multiplications, i.e., a reduction.

We can generalize the above idea over a semiring[1]. We use $(R, \oplus, \otimes)$ to denote a semiring, and $\mathbf{0}$ and $\mathbf{1}$ to denote identity elements regarding $\oplus$ and $\otimes$, respectively. An operator $\times_{\{\oplus,\otimes\}}$ denotes matrix multiplication over $(R, \oplus, \otimes)$, i.e., $\oplus$ and $\otimes$ of $\times_{\{\oplus,\otimes\}}$ correspond to $+$ and $\cdot$ of $\times$, respectively. $(\mathbb{R}, +, \cdot)$, $(\mathbb{R} \cup \{-\infty\}, \uparrow, +)$, and $(\{0,1\}, \vee, \wedge)$, where $\uparrow$ is the max-operator defined as $x \uparrow y = (x < y)\ ?\ y : x$, are useful instances of semirings.

Definition 3 (Matrix multiplication form)**.** A block is in matrix multiplication form iff it is structured as follows:

$$\begin{pmatrix} x_1 \\ \vdots \\ x_m \\ \mathbf{1} \end{pmatrix} \leftarrow \begin{pmatrix} e_{11} & \cdots & e_{1m} & e_{10} \\ \vdots & \ddots & \vdots & \vdots \\ e_{m1} & \cdots & e_{lm} & e_{m0} \\ \mathbf{0} & \cdots & \mathbf{0} & \mathbf{1} \end{pmatrix} \times_{\{\oplus,\otimes\}} \begin{pmatrix} x_1 \\ \vdots \\ x_m \\ \mathbf{1} \end{pmatrix},$$

where $e_{jk} \in \mathcal{C}$.

Theorem 1. *If a loop body is in matrix multiplication form, the loop can be computed in* $O(n/p + \log p)$ *time through* reduce.

As an example, consider Example 2, which has a body of

if $x + a[i] \geq 0$ **then** $x \leftarrow x + a[i]$ **else** $x \leftarrow 0$ **endif**.

If this if-statement is equivalent to an assignment $x \leftarrow (x + a[i]) \uparrow 0$, it can be transformed into the following matrix multiplication form over $(\mathbb{R} \cup \{-\infty\}, \uparrow, +)$.

$$\boldsymbol{x} \leftarrow A_i \times_{\{\uparrow,+\}} \boldsymbol{x}, \quad \textbf{where } \boldsymbol{x} = \begin{pmatrix} x \\ 0 \end{pmatrix},\ A_i = \begin{pmatrix} a[i] & 0 \\ -\infty & 0 \end{pmatrix}.$$

Thus, this loop becomes a parallel reduction: $\boldsymbol{x} \leftarrow \text{reduce}(\times_{\{\uparrow,+\}}, [A_1, \ldots, A_n]) \times_{\{\uparrow,+\}} \boldsymbol{x}$. The success of this parallelization owes much to the transformation of the original if-statement into an expression by means of the max-operator. Thus, in our parallelization, it is quite important to extract the max-operator from the original loop body, which contains (possibly nested) if-statements. Section 5 shows our solution to the problem of max-operator extraction.

[1] A semiring is an algebraic structure similar to a ring, but without the requirement that each element must have an additive inverse.

Of course, we can also transform a simple reduction that doall parallelizers can recognize into a matrix multiplication form. For instance, the loop body of the summation loop in Section 1 is:

$$\boldsymbol{x} \leftarrow A_i \times_{\{+,\cdot\}} \boldsymbol{x}, \quad \textbf{where } \boldsymbol{x} = \begin{pmatrix} x \\ 1 \end{pmatrix},\ A_i = \begin{pmatrix} 1 & a[i] \\ 0 & 1 \end{pmatrix}.$$

3.2 Normal Form

Although the matrix multiplication form covers non-trivial reductions, it is not satisfactory because it cannot express either doall computation, e.g., Example 1, or use of the intermediate results of reduction for other computations, e.g., Examples 3 and 4. Therefore, we need a more general way of parallelization based on matrix multiplication to enhance its applicability in practical situations.

To understand this generalization, recall the loop of Example 1:

$$\textbf{for } i = 1 \textbf{ to } n \textbf{ do } x \leftarrow x + a[i];\ a[i] \leftarrow a[i] + 1 \textbf{ done}.$$

Its loop body consists of a reduction part ($x \leftarrow x + a[i]$) and an increment part ($a[i] \leftarrow a[i] + 1$). We cannot transform this body into a matrix multiplication form. However, observing that the reduction and increment parts are independent computations, we find that this example's loop can be divided into two loops:

$$\textbf{for } i = 1 \textbf{ to } n \textbf{ do } x \leftarrow x + a[i] \textbf{ done};$$
$$\textbf{for } i = 1 \textbf{ to } n \textbf{ do } a[i] \leftarrow a[i] + 1 \textbf{ done}.$$

Both of these two loops are parallelizable; the first is a summation loop shown in Section 1 and the second is a simple doall loop. In this way, we parallelize the loop of Example 1.

Next, recall the loop of Example 3:

$$\textbf{for } i = 1 \textbf{ to } n \textbf{ do } x \leftarrow x + a[i];\ a[i] \leftarrow x \textbf{ done}.$$

Again, it is impossible to transform this loop body into a matrix multiplication form. However, by computing and storing all intermediate values of x into a temporary array in advance, we can divide this loop into the following two loops:

$$\textbf{for } i = 1 \textbf{ to } n \textbf{ do } t[i] \leftarrow x;\ x \leftarrow x + a[i] \textbf{ done};$$
$$\textbf{for } i = 1 \textbf{ to } n \textbf{ do } a[i] \leftarrow a[i] + t[i] \textbf{ done}.$$

These two loops are parallelizable because the first is equivalent to $t \leftarrow \mathsf{scan}(+, x, a);\ x \leftarrow x + t[n]$ and the second is a doall loop. Here, we can eliminate t completely by fusing the local scan of $\mathsf{scan}(+, x, a)$ and the doall version of the second loop.

We can use the above techniques to generalize the matrix multiplication form to the following *normal form*.

Definition 4 (Normal form)**.** A block is in the normal form iff it is structured as follows:

$$\boldsymbol{t} \leftarrow A \times_{\{\oplus,\otimes\}} \boldsymbol{x};\ b;\ \boldsymbol{x} \leftarrow \boldsymbol{t},$$

where $\boldsymbol{t}$ is a vector of temporary variables, $A \times_{\{\oplus,\otimes\}} \boldsymbol{x}$ is the same as the right hand side of the matrix multiplication form, and b is a block of computations that contain no assignment to any accumulator. We call b the *auxiliary part*. Note that a matrix multiplication form can be transformed into a normal form the auxiliary part of which is empty.

The normal form is used to easily distinguish the reduce or scan computation that can be expressed by means of matrix multiplication from other computations. After obtaining a body in the normal form, we can straightforwardly parallelize a loop that has the body by dividing it into two parallel computations: 1) reduce or scan with $\times_{\{\oplus,\otimes\}}$ and 2) a doall computation for the auxiliary part. Note that the latter can be efficiently embedded into the former.

Theorem 2. *If a loop body is in the normal form, the loop can be computed in* $O(n/p + \log p)$ *time with* $O(p)$ *space for intermediate data, by using the* reduce *algorithm or the* scan *algorithm.*

3.3 Separable Normal Form

Sometimes, a single loop contains two (or more) reduction/scan computations. In such cases, although it is impossible to transform the loop body into a single normal form, we can extract a normal form from the body and thereby obtain a sequence of loops, each of which has a normal form.

For example, recall the loop body of Example 4:

$$\textbf{if } x_1 + a[i] \geq 0 \textbf{ then } x_1 \leftarrow x_1 + a[i]$$
$$\textbf{else } x_1 \leftarrow 0;\ x_2 \leftarrow i + 1 \textbf{ endif}.$$

This loop body has two reduction computations for x_1 and x_2. The first is $x_1 \leftarrow (x_1 + a[i] \geq 0)\ ?\ x_1 + a[i] : 0$. The second is $x_2 \leftarrow (x_1 + a[i] \geq 0)\ ?\ x_2 : i + 1$. We can transform the first into the following normal form:

$$\boldsymbol{t} \leftarrow A_i \times_{\{\uparrow,+\}} \boldsymbol{x};\ \boldsymbol{x} \leftarrow \boldsymbol{t},$$
$$\textbf{where } \boldsymbol{t} = \begin{pmatrix} t \\ 0 \end{pmatrix},\ A_i = \begin{pmatrix} a[i] & 0 \\ -\infty & 0 \end{pmatrix},\ \boldsymbol{x} = \begin{pmatrix} x_1 \\ 0 \end{pmatrix}.$$

Now, we expand t to an array and define $\boldsymbol{t}_i = \begin{pmatrix} t[i] & 1 \end{pmatrix}^T$. Because $t[i]$ contains the value of x_1 used in the second statement at the i-th iteration of the loop, we can transform the original loop as follows:

$$\textbf{for } i = 1 \textbf{ to } n \textbf{ do } \boldsymbol{t}_i \leftarrow A_i \times_{\{+,\cdot\}} \boldsymbol{x};\ \boldsymbol{x} \leftarrow \boldsymbol{t}_i \textbf{ done};$$
$$\textbf{for } i = 1 \textbf{ to } n \textbf{ do } x_2 \leftarrow (t[i] + a[i] \geq 0)\ ?\ x_2 : i + 1 \textbf{ done}.$$

Next, we can transform this second loop's body:

$$\boldsymbol{t}' \leftarrow A'_i \times_{\{+,\cdot\}} \boldsymbol{x}';\ \boldsymbol{x}' \leftarrow \boldsymbol{t}',$$
$$\textbf{where } \boldsymbol{t}' = \begin{pmatrix} t' \\ 0 \end{pmatrix},\ \boldsymbol{x}' = \begin{pmatrix} x_2 \\ 0 \end{pmatrix},\ c = (t[i] + a[i] \geq 0),$$
$$A' = \begin{pmatrix} c\ ?\ 1 : 0 & c\ ?\ 0 : i + 1 \\ 0 & 1 \end{pmatrix}.$$

We can parallelize both loops on the basis of Theorem 2. Thus, we have obtained a sequence of parallelizable loops:

$$\textbf{for } i = 1 \textbf{ to } n \textbf{ do } \boldsymbol{t}_i \leftarrow A_i \times_{\{\uparrow,+\}} \boldsymbol{x};\ \boldsymbol{x} \leftarrow \boldsymbol{t}_i \textbf{ done};$$
$$\textbf{for } i = 1 \textbf{ to } n \textbf{ do } \boldsymbol{t}' \leftarrow A'_i \times_{\{+,\cdot\}} \boldsymbol{x}';\ \boldsymbol{x}' \leftarrow \boldsymbol{t}' \textbf{ done}.$$

In this case, the second loop encodes the final value guarantee for x_2. We can implement the final value guarantee more efficiently (see Section 6.4).

Definition 5 (Separable normal form)**.** Let $b_1;\ b_2$ be a sequence of two blocks. b_1 is a separable normal form iff b_1 is in the normal form and no accumulator updated in b_1 is updated in b_2. In addition, if b_2 is also a separable normal form, we call $b_1;\ b_2$ a sequence of separable normal forms.

Corollary 1. *If a loop body is a sequence of separable normal forms, the loop can be computed in* $O(n/p + \log p)$ *time.*

4. Parallelization Algorithm

As shown in Section 3, once we have obtained a normal form (or a sequence of separable normal forms) of a given loop body, we can parallelize the loop straightforwardly in a divide-and-conquer manner: reduce or scan. Therefore, the core of parallelization algorithms of our framework is to extract a normal form from a given loop body. In this section, we describe algorithms for extracting it.

4.1 Extracting a Normal Form

We describe an algorithm for transforming a loop body into a normal form. It consists of two phases: separation and extraction.

In the separation phase, a given block b is split into blocks b_1 and b_2 such that b_1 contains only the updating of accumulators found in b, and b_2 corresponds to the residual computation. We call b_1 the *reduction part* and b_2 the *residual part*. For example, consider the following loop body:

$$\textbf{if } a[i] < 0 \textbf{ then } x \leftarrow x + a[i] \textbf{ else } x \leftarrow 2x \textbf{ endif } a[i] \leftarrow x + 1.$$

We can split this loop body into a reduction part,

$$\textbf{if } a[i] < 0 \textbf{ then } x \leftarrow x + a[i] \textbf{ else } x \leftarrow 2x \textbf{ endif},$$

and a residual part,

$$\textbf{if } a[i] < 0 \textbf{ then } t_x \leftarrow x + a[i] \textbf{ else } t_x \leftarrow 2x \textbf{ endif};\ a[i] \leftarrow t_x + 1,$$

where t_x is a temporary variable. The residual part directly corresponds to the auxiliary part in the normal form.

In the extraction phase, a matrix multiplication form is extracted from the reduction part. First, all if-statements are converted into assignments with conditional expressions, by inserting self-assignments of accumulators as needed. For example,

$$\textbf{if } a[i] < 0 \textbf{ then } x \leftarrow x + a[i] \textbf{ else } \textbf{ endif},$$

can be converted into

$$x \leftarrow (a[i] < 0)\ ?\ x + a[i] : x.$$

Next, the reduction part, which is a sequence of assignments, is converted into a single vectorized assignment by using symbolic substitution of definitions of accumulators to uses of accumulators as needed. For example,

$$x_1 \leftarrow x_1 + x_2 + a[i];\ x_2 \leftarrow a[i] \cdot x_1 + x_2,$$

can be converted into

$$\begin{pmatrix} x_1 \\ x_2 \end{pmatrix} \leftarrow \begin{pmatrix} x_1 + x_2 + a[i] \\ a[i] \cdot (x_1 + x_2 + a[i]) + x_2 \end{pmatrix}.$$

Finally, each entry on the right side of the vectorized assignment is transformed into a matrix multiplication form, by expanding and simplifying each expression on the basis of the axioms of a semiring. For example, the vectorized assignment above can be transformed into

$$\begin{pmatrix} x_1 \\ x_2 \\ 1 \end{pmatrix} \leftarrow \begin{pmatrix} 1 & 1 & a[i] \\ a[i] & a[i]+1 & a[i] \cdot a[i] \\ 0 & 0 & 1 \end{pmatrix} \times_{\{+,\cdot\}} \begin{pmatrix} x_1 \\ x_2 \\ 1 \end{pmatrix}.$$

We intuitively and informally sketches how to extract a coefficient matrix as follows (see [19] for the details of its formal algorithm).

Algorithm 1 (Extraction of coefficient matrix)**.** Let $j, k \in \{1, \ldots, m\}$. Let $\begin{pmatrix} x_1 & \cdots & x_m \end{pmatrix}^T \leftarrow \begin{pmatrix} e_1 & \cdots & e_m \end{pmatrix}^T$ be a given vectorized assignment. Here, we regard e_j as a function over a given semiring whose parameters are $x_1, \ldots, x_m$. An expression e' denotes an entry of an extracted coefficient matrix; e.g., e'_{jk} is the (j,k)-th entry. A coefficient matrix is extracted as follows:

- e'_{jk} is obtained by differentiating e_j with respect to x_k. Then, the linearity of e_j is also checked.
- $e'_{j(m+1)}$ is obtained by substituting $\mathbf{0}$ to all accumulators in e_j.
- $e'_{(m+1)k} = \mathbf{0}$, and $e'_{(m+1)(m+1)} = \mathbf{1}$.

After these two phases, the normal form is immediately obtained. We summarize the overall algorithm as follows.

Algorithm 2 (Extraction of normal form)**.** Let b be a loop body. Semirings are given.

1. Split b into b_1 and b_2, where b_1 contains only updating of each accumulator and b_2 corresponds to a residual computation, Note that b_1 is a sequence of assignments.
2. Convert b_1 into a vectorized assignment.
3. Extract a coefficient matrix from the right side of b_1 by using Algorithm 1; Try it for all semirings until it succeeds.
4. Transform b_1, which is in matrix multiplication form, into a normal form and insert b_2 into its auxiliary part.

Due to space limitations, we omit the algorithm used to transform a loop body into a sequence of separable normal forms. The main difference from Algorithm 2 is to analyze the dependence among accumulators. See [19] for the details.

4.2 Heuristic for Division

When an accumulator in a loop body occurs in an expression of divisors or dividends, the body cannot be transformed into a normal form by using only the axioms of a semiring. However, the axioms of another algebra can be used to transform such a loop body into a normal form. For example, consider the following loop:

$$\textbf{for } i = 1 \textbf{ to } n \textbf{ do}$$
$$x \leftarrow (a[i] \cdot x + b[i])/(c[i] \cdot x + d[i]);\ y[i] \leftarrow x \textbf{ done}.$$

In this body, a Möbius transformation is recurrently applied to x. Let f_i be this Möbius transformation. By means of the projective matrix representation of f_i, we obtain

$$(f_n \circ \cdots \circ f_1)(z) = (d \circ f'_n \circ \cdots \circ f'_1)\left(\begin{pmatrix} z & 1 \end{pmatrix}^T\right),$$

$$\textbf{where } f_i(z) = \frac{a[i] \cdot z + b[i]}{c[i] \cdot z + d[i]},\ f'_i(\boldsymbol{z}) = \mathfrak{H}_i \times \boldsymbol{z},$$

$$\mathfrak{H}_i = \begin{pmatrix} a[i] & b[i] \\ c[i] & d[i] \end{pmatrix},\ d\left(\begin{pmatrix} w_1 \\ w_2 \end{pmatrix}\right) = \frac{w_1}{w_2}.$$

By using this relation, we can transform the above loop into the following loop with a body in normal form:

$$x_1 \leftarrow x;\ x_2 \leftarrow 1;$$
$$\textbf{for } i = 1 \textbf{ to } n \textbf{ do}$$
$$\boldsymbol{t} \leftarrow A \times_{\{+,\cdot\}} \boldsymbol{x};\ y[i] \leftarrow t_1/t_2;\ \boldsymbol{x} \leftarrow \boldsymbol{t} \textbf{ done},$$

$$\textbf{where } \boldsymbol{t} = \begin{pmatrix} t_1 \\ t_2 \\ 1 \end{pmatrix},\ A = \begin{pmatrix} a[i] & b[i] & 0 \\ c[i] & d[i] & 0 \\ 0 & 0 & 1 \end{pmatrix},\ \boldsymbol{x} = \begin{pmatrix} x_1 \\ x_2 \\ 1 \end{pmatrix}.$$

We can generalize this transformation over a division semiring[2]. $(\mathbb{R}, +, \cdot)$ and $(\mathbb{R} \cup \{-\infty\}, \uparrow, +)$ are useful instances of division semirings. Note that the division over $(\mathbb{R}, +, \cdot)$ is $/$, that over $(\mathbb{R} \cup \{-\infty\}, \uparrow, +)$ is $-$.

Theorem 3. *A recurrence equation that applies a Möbius transformation over a division semiring to an accumulator can be transformed into a normal form.*

We use Theorem 3 as a heuristic for divisions in extracting normal forms. We omit the details of its transformation algorithm due to space limitations. See [19] for the details.

5. Max-operator Extraction

The max-operator $\uparrow$ is not a built-in operator in most languages, but, as shown in the parallelization of Example 2, it is quite helpful for parallelization. In this section, we describe a technique for extracting max-operators from if-statements by exploiting an SMT solver, which is, informally, a SAT solver extended to handle numbers, arrays, conditional expressions, etc.

First, we convert a loop body into a conditional vectorized assignment (CVA), whose right side is a conditional expression

[2] A division semiring is similar to a semiring, but with requirement that each element must have a multiplicative inverse.

returning a vector. For example, consider the following loop body[3]:

if $x_1 + a[i] > 0$ **then** $x_1 \leftarrow x_1 + a[i]$ **else** $x_1 \leftarrow 0$ **endif**;

if $x_1 > x_2$ **then** $x_2 \leftarrow x_1$ **else** **endif**.

By iterating symbolic substitution, we convert this body into an equivalent CVA:

$$\begin{aligned} \boldsymbol{x} \leftarrow\ & (x_1 + a[i] > 0)\ ?\ (x_1 + a[i] > x_2)\ ?\ \boldsymbol{x}'_1 : \boldsymbol{x}'_2 \\ & : (0 > x_2)\ ?\ \boldsymbol{x}'_3 : \boldsymbol{x}'_4, \\ \textbf{where } \boldsymbol{x}'_1 &= \begin{pmatrix} x_1 + a[i] \\ x_1 + a[i] \end{pmatrix},\ \boldsymbol{x}'_2 = \begin{pmatrix} x_1 + a[i] \\ x_2 \end{pmatrix}, \\ \boldsymbol{x}'_3 &= \begin{pmatrix} 0 \\ 0 \end{pmatrix},\ \boldsymbol{x}'_4 = \begin{pmatrix} 0 \\ x_2 \end{pmatrix},\ \boldsymbol{x} = \begin{pmatrix} x_1 \\ x_2 \end{pmatrix}. \end{aligned}$$

Next, we eliminate infeasible subexpressions from the right side of the CVA. We can use an SMT solver to detect them. In the above CVA, the right side has no infeasible subexpression. Now observe that $\boldsymbol{x}'_1$, $\boldsymbol{x}'_2$, $\boldsymbol{x}'_3$, and $\boldsymbol{x}'_4$ can be assigned to $\boldsymbol{x}$. If it is possible to convert the conditional expressions into max-expressions, we obtain a vectorized assignment:

$$\begin{pmatrix} x_1 \\ x_2 \end{pmatrix} \leftarrow \begin{pmatrix} (x_1 + a[i]) \uparrow 0 \\ (x_1 + a[i]) \uparrow x_2 \uparrow 0 \end{pmatrix}. \tag{1}$$

This is only an assumption. Then, we confirm this assumption by checking that each assigned value is larger than or equal to other candidate values under the precondition for assigning the value. In the above example, for $x_1 \leftarrow (x_1 + a[i]) \uparrow 0$, we check

$$\begin{aligned} &\forall x_1, x_2, a[i](x_1 + a[i] > 0 \wedge x_1 + a[i] > x_2 \rightarrow x_1 + a[i] \geq 0), \\ &\forall x_1, x_2, a[i](x_1 + a[i] > 0 \wedge x_1 + a[i] \leq x_2 \rightarrow x_1 + a[i] \geq 0), \\ &\forall x_1, x_2, a[i](x_1 + a[i] \leq 0 \wedge x_1 + a[i] > x_2 \rightarrow 0 \geq x_1 + a[i]), \\ &\forall x_1, x_2, a[i](x_1 + a[i] \leq 0 \wedge x_1 + a[i] \leq x_2 \rightarrow 0 \geq x_1 + a[i]). \end{aligned}$$

To encode this problem into satisfiability problems, we convert $\forall$ into $\exists$ by negating each formula. Then, by using an SMT solver, we test the satisfiability of

$$\begin{aligned} &x_1 + a[i] > 0 \wedge x_1 + a[i] > x_2 \wedge x_1 + a[i] < 0, \\ &x_1 + a[i] > 0 \wedge x_1 + a[i] \leq x_2 \wedge x_1 + a[i] < 0, \\ &x_1 + a[i] \leq 0 \wedge x_1 + a[i] > x_2 \wedge 0 < x_1 + a[i], \\ &x_1 + a[i] \leq 0 \wedge x_1 + a[i] \leq x_2 \wedge 0 \geq x_1 + a[i]. \end{aligned}$$

If all these formulae are unsatisfiable, we obtain $x_1 \leftarrow (x_1 + a[i]) \uparrow 0$. We similarly obtain $x_2 \leftarrow (x_1 + a[i]) \uparrow x_2 \uparrow 0$. Finally, we obtain (1), a set of linear recurrence equations over $(\mathbb{R} \cup \{-\infty\}, \uparrow, +)$, which we can parallelize on the basis of Theorem 2.

The steps above are the key to extracting max-operators. If they are applied naïvely, however, max-operators may not be extracted from a CVA that has a symbolically constant condition-part on the right side. For example, consider the loop body

if $x + a[i] \geq 0$ **then** $x \leftarrow (a[i] > 0)\ ?\ x + a[i] : x + a[i] + 1$

else $x \leftarrow 0$ **endif**.

One set of candidate values assigned to x is $\{x + a[i], x + a[i] + 1, 0\}$, and the assumption from this set is $x \leftarrow (x + a[i]) \uparrow (x + a[i] + 1) \uparrow 0$. Because $x + a[i] < x + a[i] + 1$, this assumption is incorrect. However, another set is $\{(a[i] > 0)\ ?\ x + a[i] : x + a[i] + 1, 0\}$, and the assumption from this set is $x \leftarrow ((a[i] > 0)\ ?\ x + a[i] : x + a[i] + 1) \uparrow 0$. This assumption is correct. A conditional expression whose condition-part is a symbolically constant expression is *unharmful* for parallelization. Therefore, before extraction of max-operators, we make an unharmful conditional expression coalesce into a vector. For example, we make the following conditional expression:

$$c\ ?\ \begin{pmatrix} e_{11} \\ e_{12} \end{pmatrix} : \begin{pmatrix} e_{21} \\ e_{22} \end{pmatrix}, \quad \textbf{where } c \in \mathcal{C},$$

coalesce into the following vector:

$$\begin{pmatrix} c\ ?\ e_{11} : e_{21} \\ c\ ?\ e_{21} : e_{22} \end{pmatrix}.$$

We summarize these techniques as follows.

Algorithm 3 (Extraction of max-operators). A CVA whose right side, e, has no infeasible subexpression is given. Iterate Steps 1–4 until e becomes a vector.

1. Make all unharmful conditional expressions in e coalesce into vectors.
2. Extract the most deeply nested conditional subexpression whose all condition-parts are recurring expressions from e.
3. Test the extracted one on the basis of its precondition (using an SMT solver) and obtain its equivalent max-expression.
4. Replace the extracted conditional expression in e with its equivalent max-expression.

We can simply incorporate Algorithm 3 into Algorithm 2. After Step 1, we convert a reduction part (b_1) into a singly nested if-statement, and then convert it into an equivalent CVA, by inserting self-assignments as needed. Next, we eliminate its infeasible subexpressions (possibly by using an SMT solver). Then, we apply Algorithm 3 to this CVA and obtain a vectorized assignment. The rest of the process follows Steps 3 and 4 of Algorithm 2.

6. Optimizations for Our Framework

Unfortunately, our parallelization imposes intrinsic overhead on parallelized programs. Consider a sequential loop whose body is in matrix multiplication form and its parallelized version. The original sequential version iterates matrix-vector multiplication, while the parallelized version iterates matrix-matrix multiplication. Hence, overhead in proportion to the size of a coefficient matrix is imposed on the parallelized version. To obtain good performance in practice, optimizations to minimize intrinsic overhead are important. In this section, we describe several optimizations for parallelized programs. Due to space limitations, we do not explain all optimizations. See [19] for the details.

6.1 Accurate Method of Abstract Matrix Multiplication

Matsuzaki et al. [13] presented an optimization on the basis of abstract matrix multiplication[4] for parallelized reductions on trees. It eliminates redundancy in matrix multiplication. Their original method is a *conservative* one. We have developed an *accurate* method for loops parallelized by our framework.

We describe how to optimize a loop whose body is a matrix multiplication form with a coefficient matrix A. First, we abstract the values of the entries of A to four values Z, I, C, and V. Z and I denote $\mathbf{0}$ and $\mathbf{1}$, respectively. C denotes any constant value other than $\mathbf{0}$ and $\mathbf{1}$. V denotes any non-constant value, i.e., the value of a variable. Then, we simulate runtime matrix multiplication over abstract matrices. Let A_0^* be the abstract matrix of A. Updating of abstract matrices is defined as $A_i^* = A_0^* \times_{\{\oplus^*, \otimes^*\}} A_{i-1}^*$, where $i \geq 1$ and the semantics of $\oplus^*$ and $\otimes^*$ is defined in Figure 1. Here, an updating series of abstract matrices (i.e., $A_0^*, \ldots, A_i^*, \ldots$) reaches a stationary state (constant or periodic) since the size of each matrix is fixed and the domain of each entry is finite.

[3] A loop that has this body is part of mss described in Section 7.

[4] Note that [13] contains incorrect descriptions concerning abstract matrix multiplication, which were fixed in [11].

$\oplus^*$	Z	I	C	V
Z	Z	I	C	V
I	I	V	V	V
C	C	V	V	V
V	V	V	V	V

$\otimes^*$	Z	I	C	V
Z	Z	Z	Z	Z
I	Z	I	C	V
C	Z	C	V	V
V	Z	V	V	V

Figure 1. Semantics of two operators over the four abstract values.

Intuitively, A_i^* indicates how many variables we require for accumulating exponentiation of A and how we update these variables with compile-time constants. For example, the updating series of abstract matrices defined as follows converges at a constant state:

$$A_0^* = \begin{pmatrix} I & V \\ Z & I \end{pmatrix}, \quad A_i^* = \begin{pmatrix} V & V \\ Z & I \end{pmatrix} \quad (i \geq 1).$$

This indicates that, once we have computed a square of A, we require always only two loop-carried scalar variables for exponentiating A. Concretely, A^n over $(R, \oplus, \otimes)$ can be implemented as follows:

$$i \leftarrow 0;\ A' \leftarrow A;\ i \leftarrow 1;\ A'' \leftarrow A \times_{\{\oplus,\otimes\}} A';$$
$$\textbf{for } i = 2 \textbf{ to } n \textbf{ do } A'' \leftarrow A \times_{\{\oplus,\otimes\}} A'' \textbf{ done},$$
$$\textbf{where } A' = \begin{pmatrix} \mathbf{1} & v_2 \\ \mathbf{0} & \mathbf{1} \end{pmatrix}, \quad A'' = \begin{pmatrix} v_1 & v_2 \\ \mathbf{0} & \mathbf{1} \end{pmatrix}.$$

For convergence at a finite set of periodic states, we convert it into a constant state by loop unwinding. Due to space limitations, we omit the details. See [19] for the details.

The primary effect of this technique is, of course, elimination of non-trivial redundancy; i.e., it realizes non-trivial copy propagation and constant folding. In addition, this technique has an important secondary effect: elimination of storing **0** into variables. **0** over $(\mathbb{R} \cup \{-\infty\}, \uparrow, +)$ is $-\infty$. This is a troublesome value because its annihilation property (i.e., $-\infty + a = a + (-\infty) = -\infty$) is difficult to efficiently implement. This technique enables us to identify and eliminate **0** in compile-time.

The main difference between our method and Matsuzaki et al.'s [13] is the semantics of updating of abstract matrices. Their method is conservative with respect to convergence, i.e., over-approximates the stationary state of an updating series of abstract matrices. As a result, their method cannot deal with periodic states effectively and avoid storing **0** into variables, whereas our method can do these successfully by using loop unwinding together.

6.2 Splitting up shift

Sometimes, reduce and scan computations include a kind of doall computation. Such computation appears in a coefficient matrix as its row whose entries are **0** except for the rightmost entry. For example, consider the following loop:

$$\textbf{for } i = 1 \textbf{ to } n \textbf{ do } \boldsymbol{x} \leftarrow A \times_{\{+,\cdot\}} \boldsymbol{x} \textbf{ done},$$
$$\textbf{where } A = \begin{pmatrix} a[i] & 1 & 0 \\ 0 & 0 & a[i] \\ 0 & 0 & 1 \end{pmatrix}, \ \boldsymbol{x} = \begin{pmatrix} x_1 \\ x_2 \\ 1 \end{pmatrix}.$$

The second row, i.e., $x_2 \leftarrow a[i]$, represents doall computation. We can split up the row by introducing a temporary array t as follows:

$$\textbf{for } i = 1 \textbf{ to } n-1 \textbf{ do } t[i] \leftarrow a[i] \textbf{ done};\ t[0] \leftarrow x_2;$$
$$\textbf{for } i = 1 \textbf{ to } n \textbf{ do } \boldsymbol{x}' \leftarrow A' \times_{\{+,\cdot\}} \boldsymbol{x}' \textbf{ done},$$
$$\textbf{where } A' = \begin{pmatrix} a[i] & t[i-1] \\ 0 & 1 \end{pmatrix}, \ \boldsymbol{x}' = \begin{pmatrix} x_1 \\ 1 \end{pmatrix}.$$

The first loop is obviously a doall loop. The second loop, whose body is in the matrix multiplication form, is more efficient than the original loop because the size of A' is smaller than that of A. This efficiency make an effect on matrix-matrix multiplication of the parallelized version. Although this transformation causes $O(n)$ space overhead due to the introduction of t, this space overhead is completely eliminated by *fusion* as mentioned later.

This split up doall computation corresponds to shift [7], a pattern of parallel computation, and this transformation corresponds to the combination of scalar expansion and loop fission in doall parallelization.

6.3 Fusion

Consider a scan followed by a reduce. We can compute both the local scan of the preceding scan and the local reduction of the succeeding reduce simultaneously. If the result of the preceding scan is used only by the succeeding reduce, we can eliminate $O(n)$ space for the intermediate data that the scan produces and that the reduce consumes. Such kind of transformation is called *fusion*. The transformation described above is the fusion of scan and reduce [12]. It is, of course, applicable to ones extracted by our framework. Furthermore, the fusion of shift with scan or reduce [7] is also applicable. We omit the details of these fusion methods.

6.4 Specialization of Final Value Guarantee

Sometimes, a loop body contains the following assignment:

$$x \leftarrow c_1\ ?\ x : c_2, \quad \textbf{where } c_1, c_2 \in \mathcal{C}.$$

We observe that this updating of x does not use the current value of x because self-assignment means no updating. Based on this observation, we can compute the result of x in parallel by using a parallel loop and a reduce. For example, consider the following loop derived from parallelization process of Example 4:

$$\textbf{for } i = 1 \textbf{ to } n \textbf{ do } x_2 \leftarrow (t[i] + a[i] \geq 0)\ ?\ x_2 : i + 1 \textbf{ done}.$$

Its parallelized version is:

$$\textbf{parallel } k \in \{1, \ldots, p\} \textbf{ do}$$
$$v[k] \leftarrow x_2;\ b[k] \leftarrow \text{False};$$
$$\textbf{for } i = 1 + (k-1)n/p \textbf{ to } kn/p \textbf{ do if } t[i] + a[i] \geq 0 \textbf{ then}$$
$$\textbf{else } v[k] \leftarrow i + 1;\ b[k] \leftarrow \text{True} \textbf{ endif done}$$
$$\textbf{done};\ \boldsymbol{x} \leftarrow \mathsf{reduce}(\triangleright, [\boldsymbol{v}_1, \ldots, \boldsymbol{v}_p]),$$
$$\textbf{where } \boldsymbol{x} = \begin{pmatrix} x_2 \\ b[0] \end{pmatrix}, \ \boldsymbol{v}_i = \begin{pmatrix} v[i] \\ b[i] \end{pmatrix}, \ \boldsymbol{v}_i \triangleright \boldsymbol{v}_j = (b[j])\ ?\ \boldsymbol{v}_j : \boldsymbol{v}_i.$$

In this program, v is an array whose k-th element is the partial result computed by the k-th thread and b is an array whose k-th element is the flag to denote that the k-th thread update its partial result. Because this parallelized program does not use matrix multiplication, it is more efficient than one shown in Section 3.3.

From the viewpoint of doall parallelization, this computation corresponds to a final value guarantee for a conditional assignment. In doall parallelization, this kind of guarantee has not been dealt seriously with. In fact, ICC 11.1 with `-parallel -par-threshold0` options did not parallelize a loop that contains this assignment because ICC cannot deal with it. Therefore, the presented technique here is also helpful for doall parallelization.

7. Experiments

We have implemented our framework and techniques as a parallelizer in a compiler infrastructure, COINS[5], which includes a C frontend, a doall analyzer, and a C code generator. Our implementation employs an SMT solver, Yices[6]. Figure 2 shows the entire

[5] `http://coins-compiler.sourceforge.jp/international/`

[6] `http://yices.csl.sri.com/`

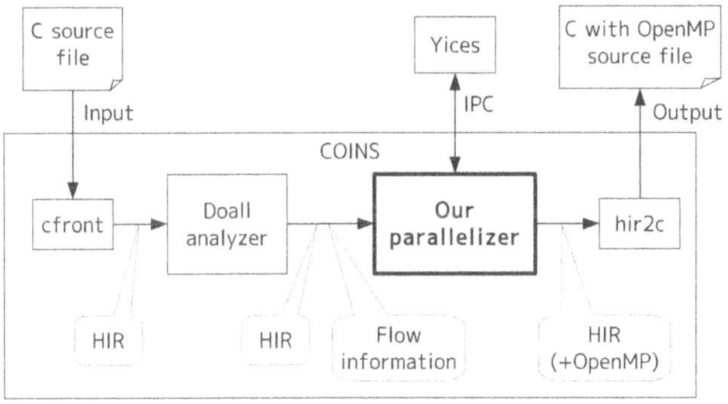

Figure 2. The entire structure of our implementation. HIR is the high-level intermediate representation of COINS. Our parallelizer communicates with Yices through inter-process communication.

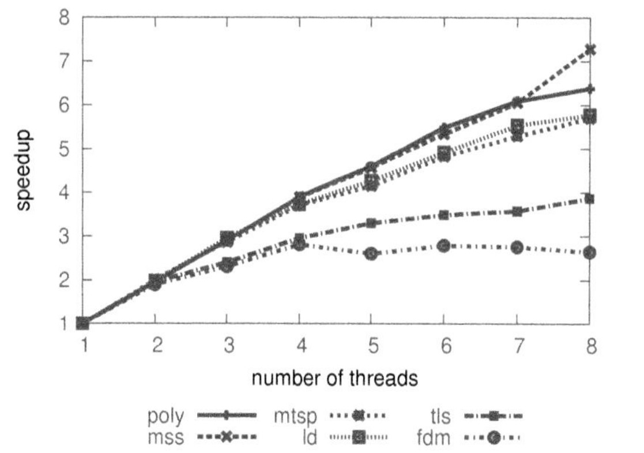

Figure 3. Scalability of parallelized versions of six examples.

structure of our implementation. Our implementation produces parallelized C programs that employ OpenMP constructs.

To confirm the scalability of programs parallelized by our implementation, we conducted experiments on the following example programs, each of whose doall parallelization fails.

poly It computes polynomial evaluation through the Horner scheme. Its parallelized version executes `reduce` with $\times_{\{+,\cdot\}}$ of 2-by-2 matrices. The order of a given polynomial was 2^{27} and it was evaluated with `double` arithmetic.

mss It solves the maximum segment sum problem, which is to compute the maximum sum of a contiguous segment of a given array. It is known as a programming pearl. Its parallelized version executes `reduce` with $\times_{\{\uparrow,+\}}$ of 3-by-3 matrices. The length of a given array was 2^{27} and its each element was `int`.

mtsp It is equivalent to Example 4; it computes the mts of a given array and its start position. Its parallelized version executes `scan` with $\times_{\{\uparrow,+\}}$ of 2-by-2 matrices and executes the final value guarantee for a conditional assignment. The length of a given array was 2^{27} and its each element was `int`.

ld It computes the Levenshtein distance between two given strings through dynamic programming. Our parallelization worked to divide the longer sides of the memo table whose element was `int`. Its parallelized version executes `scan` with $\times_{\{\uparrow,+\}}$ of 2-by-2 matrices. The length of one given string of `char` was 2^{27} and that of the other was 6.

tls It is a solver for tridiagonal linear systems. It consists of three parallelizable loops. The first executes LU decomposition, i.e., obtains $LU\boldsymbol{x} = \boldsymbol{b}$. It was parallelized by using Theorem 3. Its parallelized version executes `scan` $\times_{\{+,\cdot\}}$ of 3-by-3 matrices. The second solves $L\boldsymbol{y} = \boldsymbol{b}$, and the third solves $U\boldsymbol{x} = \boldsymbol{y}$. The parallelized versions of the second and third execute `scan` with $\times_{\{+,\cdot\}}$ of 2-by-2 matrices. The parallelized solver is equivalent to [20]. The dimension of a given system was 2^{26} and it was solved with `double` arithmetic.

fdm It solves a one-dimensional heat equation through an *in-place* finite difference method (FDM). The parallelization of standard implementations of FDM to use a buffer where values in the next time-step are stored is trivial, but that of in-place ones is non-trivial. Its parallelized version does not compute matrix multiplication because its coefficient matrix can shrink completely through splitting up `shift` and its fusion. Its parallel computation is thus done only through the local reduction. The number of space cells was 2^{27}, that of time steps was 10, and the values of temperature were `double`.

	poly	mss	mtsp	ld	tls	fdm
seq. (ms)	360	522	351	1807	487	2483
par. (ms)	578	265	633	2383	1083	3261
seq. / par. (%)	62.2	197	55.4	75.8	45.1	76.1

Table 1. Execution time of original sequential versions and parallelized single-threaded versions of six examples.

p	1	2	3	4	5	6	7	8
r	1.73	1.80	2.41	2.22	2.56	2.63	3.02	3.44

Table 2. Ratio of speed of our parallelized mss to that of Fisher and Ghuloum [8]'s mss; r and p denote ratio of speed (higher is better) and number of threads, respectively.

We used a server equipped with dual Xeon X5550 (4 cores; 3.06 GHz; HT disabled) and 12 GB of memory (DDR3-1333) running Ubuntu 10.04 (64-bit), and we compiled each program to its executable by employing ICC 11.1 with the `O3` optimization.

As shown in Figure 3, the parallelized versions of poly, mtsp, mss, and ld achieved near-linear scalability and nearly 6 or more times speeds with 8 threads. These results reflected the theoretical scalability (shown in Theorem 2). In contrast, the speed of parallelized fdm peaked out on 4 threads and the speedup of parallelized tls degraded. Because these do relatively much memory access, memory bandwidth bound their performance. As mentioned in Section 6, our parallelization causes intrinsic runtime overhead. Table 1 shows the execution time of the original sequential version and parallelized single-threaded version for each program. Each example had expected performance, except for mss. This is because the original sequential version of mss was abnormally slow for unknown reasons. However, this aberration is independent of the correctness and utility of our parallelization. Overall, without memory bandwidth issues, our parallelization achieved good scalability.

Fisher and Ghuloum [8]'s method parallelizes mss automatically into the composition of a scan and reduction, unlike ours. We tested the version parallelized by using their method. Table 2 shows the ratio of the speed of our parallelized mss to that of their parallelized mss. Our framework and techniques enabled the compiler to produce the more efficient parallel mss than theirs.

The SMT problem is not easier than the SAT problem, which is NP-complete. Therefore, to exploit an SMT solver requires high costs potentially. Our implementation exploits Yices to extract max-operators. Our implementation can dump each query for Yices as a file. We measured the execution time of Yices for queries.

example	mss	mtsp	ld
number of queries	8	2	2
total time (ms)	11	4	4

Table 3. Execution time for Yices to extract max-operators.

Yices's version was 1.0.27. Table 3 shows the results. The execution time for each program was short enough for practical use. Moreover, because we can test each query independently, we can obtain better performance by exploiting process-level parallelism. Therefore, our approach based on an SMT solver is very practical.

8. Discussion

8.1 Prior Work and Our Improvement

The most significant prior work is one by Fisher and Ghuloum [8]. They pioneered in automatic parallelization of loops by extracting associative operators. We briefly describe their formalization and technique, and compare ours with theirs.

Their key observation is that, owing to the associativity of the function composition, application of a composite function can compute in parallel by computing the function composition per se. Their key idea is that, if a function is closed under composition, its composition can be computed efficiently. For example, $f_i(x) = a_i x + b_i$, f_i is closed under composition: $(f_1 \circ f_2)(x) = (a_1 a_2)x + (a_1 b_2 + b_1)$. The computation of $\circ$ in $f_1 \circ f_1$ corresponds to that of $a_1 a_2$ and $a_1 b_2 + b_1$. Concretely, they formalized a loop that computes reduction or scan as an application of a composite function consisting of its *modeling function*, which represents its loop body, and then parallelized the loop into a version that computes the composition of the modeling function in parallel.

Obviously, their formalization is more general and powerful than ours. The modeling function of the matrix multiplication form is the affine function over a semiring, which is closed under composition. Hence, our formalization is only a special case of theirs. However, our framework is *more practical* because it is easier to implement in compilers and to derive efficient parallel programs.

The test of closure under composition is potentially very difficult and costly because it necessitates searching in enormous space. This difficulty derives from a fact that proof of disclosure by counterexample is almost impossible because the closure property is too abstract. In contrast, to derive matrix multiplication, we have only to check the linearity of recurrence equations. The linearity is easier to check, and moreover we can find a counterexample of the linearity immediately.

Of course, they had noticed this difficulty. They developed a heuristic to test the closure by checking structural isomorphism of simplified nested conditional expressions. However, this approximation has several problems. First, the generality of this heuristic is such a little that it managed to enable us to extract a single max-operator. Second, to avoid a complicated conditional expression, they split a loop body into as small ones as possible. Then, they parallelized computations for dependent accumulators as independently as possible. As a result, they transform a loop potentially parallelized as a single reduction into a composition of a reduction and scans. In fact, they parallelized mss as a composition of a scan and reduction, whose performance is worse than its single-reduction version (see Table 2).

In contrast, we extract max-operators before trying parallelization. We can then easily parallelize recurrence equations over $(\mathbb{R} \cup \{-\infty\}, \uparrow, +)$. Matrix multiplication can deal with dependent (as well as independent) accumulators as a vector. Therefore, our framework can derive a single reduction from computations for dependent accumulators, e.g., mss. In addition, they did not perform exhaustive search for its complexity, but we easily do it by exploiting an SMT solver. Focusing on max-operators significantly simplifies analysis for parallelization and affords optimizations.

Overall, our framework focuses on techniques rather than formalism and on practicality rather than generality. In spite of the less generality, our framework can deal with all their examples, and furthermore, derive more efficient programs than theirs did. It demonstrates that the power of our framework is empirically no less than that of theirs, and that our framework is more practical.

8.2 Parallelization of Recursive Functions

Matsuzaki et al. [13] dealt with parallelization of a reduction of trees and presented a model of matrix multiplication over a semiring. Hence, our formalization per se is not so novel and is a variation specialized for loops. Their framework does not deal with accumulation and assumes the max-operator to be given. Although their semi-automated code generator is equipped with an optimization mechanism (see also Section 6.1), they did not show any experimental result on the performance of parallelized programs. Therefore, we do not consider their work as fully automatic parallelization in practical situations.

Chin et al. [6] presented the *context preservation* theorem that formalizes the idea of [8] in a functional language, and an algorithm for parallelizing a linear self-recursive function into a list homomorphism [4], which is a naturally parallelizable recursive form.

Xu et al. [21] presented a type-based approach to parallelization on the basis of the context preservation theorem. Their focus was on the analysis that uses an algebra similar to a semiring even though their implementation can generate list homomorphisms. They hardly dealt with higher-order linear recurrences, whereas we have dealt seriously with them. Since they assumed the max-operator to be given, did not deal with optimization, and conducted no experiment on programs parallelized by their implementation, we therefore judge that their work is not one for fully automatic parallelization in practical situations.

Morihata and Matsuzaki [14] presented that quantifier elimination by virtual substitution (QEVS) enables us to directly extract associative operators based on the context preservation theorem from recursive functions, and demonstrated that their QEVS-based implementation with simple heuristics can parallelize non-linear, non-self-recursive, and accumulative functions. Although QEVS is modular, however, QEVS is too costly to implement in compilers, and their technique has less scalability to the number of variables.

Morita et al. [15] presented an algorithm to extract associative operators based on inversion of functions and the third homomorphism theorem. Their work is very interesting, but their parallelization is impractical because the third homomorphism theorem necessitates two equivalent functions for one target problem.

8.3 Linear Recurrence Equation and Scan

Apart from work on automatic parallelization, Kogge and Stone [10] presented a parallel algorithm, which is now an algorithm of scan, for solving a general class of linear recurrence equations by formalizing the class with matrix operations. Stone [20] presented a parallel algorithm for solving a tridiagonal linear system on the basis of scan and a projective matrix of Möbius transformation. Cyclic reduction [9] is another parallel algorithm for solving it.

From this historical background, it is quite natural to parallelize computation of linear recurrence equations through scan with matrix multiplication. Although generalization over an algebra (e.g., a semiring) is not explicitly mentioned in [10, 20], these algorithms are sufficiently generic. Therefore, there is no difficulty in dealing with computation of linear recurrence equations. From the perspective of automatic parallelization, the difficulty is to discover this computation from a given loop *automatically*.

Redon and Feaurier [17] presented methods to detect *sequential* scans in the polytope model. With respect to parallelization, their methods fundamentally depend on the detection of trivial built-in associative operators by pattern matching. Although they mentioned derivation of matrix multiplication from a first-order linear recurrence equation and Möbius transformation, they considered each of these as a special case and did not generalize these at all. They did not deal with parallelization of a loop that has a complicated body such as one containing if-statements and one containing computations other than linear recurrence equations.

Nistor et al. [16] presented optimization techniques for matrix multiplication derived from parallelized linear recurrence equations. Their techniques reduce the space used in matrix multiplication by recovering an expression of one entry from an expression of another entry on the basis of linear relations between these expressions. Because their techniques are independent of ours, we can apply them to our framework.

8.4 Standard Approach in Doall Parallelization

Doall parallelization (and also vectorization [3]) fundamentally necessitates eliminating every loop-carried data dependence in target loops by employing loop transformation. For example, loop skewing [2] eliminates loop-carried data dependence and exposes wavefront parallelism in a nested loop such as ld. Whereas our framework incorporates reduction as a fundamental part, doall parallelization handles reduction as a special case of eliminating loop-carried data dependence.

The book on the standard doall parallelization [2] tells reductions have three essential properties: 1) *"they reduce the elements of some vectors or array dimension down to one element"*, 2) *"only the final result of the reduction is used later; use of an intermediate result voids the reduction"*, and 3) *"there is no variation inside the intermediate accumulation; that is, the reduction operates on the vector and nothing else."* Besides, reduction operators are almost always assumed as built-in associative commutative ones.

Our framework relaxes these properties that are regarded as essential ones. Because our framework can parallelize computation for mutually dependent accumulators, our framework relaxes the first. The use of `scan` overcomes the second and third. Therefore, our framework is a natural generalization of doall parallelization.

9. Conclusion

We have presented novel techniques to parallelize various loops. Our techniques extend doall parallelization.

We think that there is room for future work regarding dealing with nested loops. The most popular framework for optimizing nested loops is the polyhedral model, which often accompanies parallelization. The tie-up between our techniques and the polyhedral model is an innovative work. In addition, we think that our technique to extract max-operators is helpful for vectorization. Therefore, the exploitation of fine-grained data parallelism by using our techniques is another innovative work.

Acknowledgments

We would like to thank Masato Takeichi and Zhenjiang Hu for encouraging our research. We are grateful to Akimasa Morihata, Kento Emoto, and Kiminori Matsuzaki for technical discussions with the first author.

References

[1] A. V. Aho, M. S. Lam, R. Sethi, and J. D. Ullman. *Compilers: Principles, Techniques, and Tools.* Addison Wesley, second edition, 2006.

[2] R. Allen and K. Kennedy. *Optimizing Compilers for Modern Architectures: A Dependence-Based Approach.* Morgan Kaufmann, 2001.

[3] A. J. C. Bik, M. Girkar, P. M. Grey, and X. Tian. Automatic Intra-Register Vectorization for the Intel®Architecture. *Int. J. Parallel Program.*, 30(2):65–98, 2002.

[4] R. S. Bird. An Introduction to the Theory of Lists. In *Logic of Programming and Calculi of Discrete Design*, volume 36 of *NATO ASI Series F*, pages 3–42. Springer-Verlag, 1987.

[5] D. Callahan, S. Carr, and K. Kennedy. Improving Register Allocation for Subscripted Variables. In *Proceedings of the ACM SIGPLAN 1990 Conference on Programming Language Design and Implementation (PLDI '90)*, pages 177–187. ACM, 1990.

[6] W.-N. Chin, A. Takano, and Z. Hu. Parallelization via Context Preservation. In *Proceedings of IEEE International Conference on Computer Languages (ICCL '98)*, pages 153–162. IEEE CS Press, 1998.

[7] K. Emoto, K. Matsuzaki, Z. Hu, and M. Takeichi. Domain-Specific Optimization Strategy for Skeleton Programs. In *Euro-Par 2007 Parallel Processing*, volume 4641 of *Lecture Notes in Computer Science*, pages 705–714. Springer, 2007.

[8] A. L. Fisher and A. M. Ghuloum. Parallelizing Complex Scans and Reductions. In *Proceedings of the ACM SIGPLAN 1994 Conference on Programming Language Design and Implementation (PLDI '94)*, pages 135–146. ACM, 1994.

[9] W. Gander and G. H. Golub. Cyclic Reduction – History and Applications. In *Proceedings of the Workshop on Scientific Computing*, 1997.

[10] P. M. Kogge and H. S. Stone. A Parallel Algorithm for the Efficient Solution of a General Class of Recurrence Equations. *IEEE Trans. Comput.*, 22(8):786–793, 1973.

[11] K. Matsuzaki. *Parallel Programming with Tree Skeletons.* PhD thesis, Graduate School of Information Science and Technology, The University of Tokyo, 2007.

[12] K. Matsuzaki and K. Emoto. Implementing Fusion-Equipped Parallel Skeletons by Expression Templates. In *Implementation and Application of Functional Languages (IFL '09)*, volume 6041 of *Lecture Notes in Computer Science*, pages 72–89. Springer, 2010.

[13] K. Matsuzaki, Z. Hu, and M. Takeichi. Towards Automatic Parallelization of Tree Reductions in Dynamic Programming. In *Proceedings of the 18th Annual ACM Symposium on Parallelism in Algorithms and Architectures (SPAA '06)*, pages 39–48. ACM, 2006.

[14] A. Morihata and K. Matsuzaki. Automatic Parallelization of Recursive Functions using Quantifier Elimination. In *Functional and Logic Programming (FLOPS '10)*, volume 6009 of *Lecture Notes in Computer Science*, pages 321–336. Springer, 2010.

[15] K. Morita, A. Morihata, K. Matsuzaki, Z. Hu, and M. Takeichi. Automatic Inversion Generates Divide-and-Conquer Parallel Programs. In *Proceedings of the 2007 ACM SIGPLAN Conference on Programming Language Design and Implementation (PLDI '07)*, pages 146–155, 2007.

[16] A. Nistor, W.-N. Chin, T.-S. Tan, and N. Tapus. Optimizing the parallel computation of linear recurrences using compact matrix representations. *J. Parallel Distrib. Comput.*, 69(4):373–381, 2009.

[17] X. Redon and P. Feautrier. Detection of Scans in the Polytope Model. *Parallel Algorithms Appl.*, 15(3–4):229–263, 2000.

[18] J. H. Reif, editor. *Synthesis of Parallel Algorithms.* Morgan Kaufmann Pub, 1993.

[19] S. Sato. Automatic Parallelization via Matrix Multiplication. Master's thesis, The University of Electro-Communications, 2011.

[20] H. S. Stone. An Efficient Parallel Algorithm for the Solution of a Tridiagonal Linear System of Equations. *J. ACM*, 20(1):27–38, 1973.

[21] D. N. Xu, S.-C. Khoo, and Z. Hu. PType System: A Featherweight Parallelizability Detector. In *Programming Languages and Systems (APLAS '04)*, volume 3302 of *Lecture Notes in Computer Science*, pages 197–212. Springer, 2004.

ALTER: Exploiting Breakable Dependences for Parallelization

Abhishek Udupa
University of Pennsylvania
audupa@seas.upenn.edu

Kaushik Rajan
Microsoft Research India
krajan@microsoft.com

William Thies
Microsoft Research India
thies@microsoft.com

Abstract

For decades, compilers have relied on dependence analysis to determine the legality of their transformations. While this conservative approach has enabled many robust optimizations, when it comes to parallelization there are many opportunities that can only be exploited by changing or re-ordering the dependences in the program.

This paper presents ALTER: a system for identifying and enforcing parallelism that violates certain dependences while preserving overall program functionality. Based on programmer annotations, ALTER exploits new parallelism in loops by reordering iterations or allowing stale reads. ALTER can also infer which annotations are likely to benefit the program by using a test-driven framework.

Our evaluation of ALTER demonstrates that it uncovers parallelism that is beyond the reach of existing static and dynamic tools. Across a selection of 12 performance-intensive loops, 9 of which have loop-carried dependences, ALTER obtains an average speedup of 2.0x on 4 cores.

Categories and Subject Descriptors D.3.3 [*Programming Languages*]: Language Constructs and Features—Concurrent programming structures; D.3.4 [*Programming Languages*]: Processors—Compilers, Optimization, Run-time environments

General Terms Performance, Languages, Experimentation

1. Introduction

Throughout the long history of research on automatic parallelization, much of the progress has been driven by the compiler's ability to accurately detect the dependences between different parts of the program. Such *dependence analysis* has evolved greatly over the years, encompassing representations such as direction vectors, distance vectors, and affine dependences [12] as well as techniques such as array dataflow analysis [26], interprocedural dependence analysis [9] and constraint-based dependence analysis [32]. The precision of dependence analysis has also depended on improvements in alias analysis, shape analysis, and escape analysis, which each have their own rich history.

Despite the tremendous progress in dependence analysis, in practice it remains commonplace for an incomplete understanding of the program's dependences to prohibit seemingly simple transformations, such as parallelization of DOALL loops. There are three fundamental limitations that prevent any dependence analysis from fully solving the problem of automatic parallelization. First, as the general case of dependence analysis is undecidable [36], any static analysis must be conservative in over-approximating the program dependences, thereby under-approximating the opportunities for parallelization. A related problem is that of induction variable analysis: certain dependences can be soundly eliminated via conversion to a closed-form function of the loop index, but complex induction variables (such as iterators through a linked list) are difficult to detect automatically.

Second, even if dependences are precisely identified (e.g., using dynamic dependence analysis [43], program annotations [45], or speculative parallelization [11, 15, 21, 27, 33, 39, 44]), there remain many programs in which memory dependences are accidental artifacts of the implementation and should not inhibit parallelization. For example, it has been shown that in many performance-intensive loops, the only serializing dependences are due to calls to the memory allocator, which can be freely reordered without impacting correctness [7, 41]. Similar dependences are due to benign references to uninitialized data structures, maintenance or output of unordered debugging information, and other patterns [41]. Only by allowing the compiler to reorder or ignore such dependences is it possible to extract parallelism from many programs.

Third, there are many cases in which broken data dependences do change the course of a program's execution, but the algorithm employed is robust to the changes and arrives at an acceptable output anyway. A simple example is the chain of dependences implied by successive calls to a random number generator, which has the potential to serialize many loops. However, in algorithms such as simulated annealing or monte-carlo simulation, any ordering of the calls is permissible so long as each result is random [7, 41]. A more subtle example is that of successive relaxation algorithms, in which the solution is iteratively improved in a monotonic fashion and broken dependences (such as stale reads) may enable parallelism at the expense of a slight increase in convergence time.

In this paper, we make three contributions towards enabling parallelization of programs that are beyond the reach of dependence analysis. First, we propose a new execution model, `StaleReads`, which enables iterations of a loop to execute in parallel by allowing stale reads from a consistent snapshot of the global memory. This model enforces a well-known guarantee called *snapshot isolation* that is frequently employed in the database community as a permissive and high-performance policy for transactional commit. However, while other concepts from databases have impacted programming languages via transactional memory, we are unaware of any exploration or implementation of snapshot isolation as a general-purpose mechanism for loop parallelization. In addition to the basic model, we also offer support for reductions, in which commutative and associative updates to specific variables are merged upon completion of each iteration. We demonstrate that snapshot isolation exposes useful parallelism in several algorithms, in particular for convergence algorithms that are robust to stale reads (as described in the previous paragraph).

PLDI'11, June 4–8, 2011, San Jose, California, USA.

```
while (CheckConvergence(AMatrix, XVector,
                        BVector, dimA) == 0) {
  tripCount++;
  [StaleReads]
  for (int i = 0; i < dimA; i++) {
    sum = 0;
    // scalarProduct reads all of XVector
    sum = scalarProduct(AMatrix[i], XVector);
    sum -= AMatrix[i][i] * XVector[i];
    // write to XVector[i]
    XVector[i] = (BVector[i] - sum) /
                              AMatrix[i][i];
  }
}
```

Figure 1. Iterative algorithm to solve a system of linear equations of the form Ax=b. The for loop is annotated by ALTER to indicate that the iterations are likely to tolerate stale reads. Parallelization using the ALTER compiler and runtime system gives a speedup of 1.70x on 4 cores (for a sparse matrix A with 40,000 elements).

Our second contribution is a general framework, ALTER, for specifying dependences that do not matter and leveraging that information in a parallel runtime system. Using ALTER, the programmer annotates each loop with one of two permissive execution policies. In addition to `StaleReads`, ALTER supports `OutOfOrder` execution of the loop iterations; this corresponds to the database notion of *conflict serializability* and may break the original dependences so long as execution is consistent with some serial ordering of the iterations. Annotations are also used to declare reduction variables, as described above. Given the annotations, ALTER implements the desired parallelism using a deterministic fork-join model. Each loop iteration (or chunk of iterations) is treated as a transaction, executing in an isolated process and committing with a different policy depending on the model of parallelism. The implementation of ALTER relies on a novel multi-process memory allocator as well as custom collections classes that enable iterators over linked data structures to be recognized as induction variables.

Our third contribution is a practical methodology that leverages ALTER to discover and exploit parallelism. As the ALTER annotations may change the local behavior of a program, it is intractable to infer or verify them using a sound static analysis. However, to assist programmers in exploring the space of potential parallelizations, we propose a test-driven framework that evaluates each possible annotation on each loop in the program and conveys to the programmer the set of annotations that preserve the program output across a test suite. This dynamic analysis, while unsound, can be used to infer likely annotations that are subsequently validated by the programmer. The test-driven framework benefits greatly from ALTER's deterministic execution model, as each test needs to be executed only once. Using this end-to-end methodology, we apply ALTER to assist with parallelization of a set of loops, drawn from Berkeley's parallel dwarfs as well as the STAMP suite. ALTER finds parallelism that is undiscoverable by prior techniques and accelerates performance-intensive loops by an average of 2.0x on four cores.

The rest of this paper is organized as follows. We start with a motivating example for the violation of program dependences during loop parallelization (Section 2). We proceed to describe the ALTER annotation language (Section 3), the implementation of the ALTER compiler and runtime system (Section 4), the annotation inference algorithm (Section 5) and the usage scenarios in which ALTER could be applied (Section 6). We then present our experimental evaluation (Section 7) before wrapping up with related work (Section 8) and conclusions (Section 9).

```
// convergence check simplified for presentation
while (delta > threshold) {
  delta = 0.0;
  [OutOfOrder + Reduction(delta, +)] or
  [StaleReads + Reduction(delta, +)]
  for (i = 0; i < npoints; i++) {
    index = common_findNearestPoint(feature[i],
                nfeatures, clusters, nclusters);
    // If membership changes, increase delta
    // by 1.  membership[i] cannot be
    // changed in other iterations
    if (membership[i] != index) {
      delta += 1.0;
    }
    // Assign the membership to object i
    membership[i] = index;
    // Update new cluster centers :
    // sum of objects located within
    *new_centers_len[index] =
       *new_centers_len[index]) + 1;
    for (j = 0; j < nfeatures; j++) {
      new_centers[index][j] =
          new_centers[index][j] + feature[i][j];
    }
  }
}
```

Figure 2. K-means clustering algorithm from STAMP. ALTER suggests the `OutOfOrder` and `StaleReads` annotations along the for loop, in combination with an additive reduction on the variable *delta* (which is used to determine the termination of the overall algorithm). Parallelizing this algorithm using `StaleReads` gives a speedup of 1.71x on 4 cores.

2. Motivating Examples

This section illustrates two examples where breaking dependences enables parallel execution while preserving the high-level functionality.

The first example (see Figure 1) is a numerical algorithm to solve a system of linear equations of the form $Ax = b$, where A is an $n \times n$ input matrix, b is an input vector of n elements and x is the solution vector of n unknown elements. This algorithm often forms the kernel for solving partial differential equations. The algorithm has two loops, an outer while loop that checks for convergence and an inner for loop that re-calculates each element of *XVector* based on the values of the other elements. The inner loop has a tight dependence chain as the *XVector* element written to in one iteration is read in every subsequent iteration. Thus, the only possible way to parallelize this loop is to violate sequential semantics by not enforcing some of the true dependences.

Based on the results of test cases, ALTER suggests that the inner loop can be parallelized under the `StaleReads` model. While some of the values read from *XVector* will be stale, the algorithm has an outer while loop which checks for convergence and prevents these broken dependences from affecting the overall correctness. This alternate version of the algorithm has been shown in the literature to have the same convergence properties as the sequential version [31]. In fact, this algorithm belongs to a class of algorithms, commonly referred to as algebraic path problems [40], that can tolerate some stale reads. This class includes many popular algorithms such as the Bellman Ford shortest path algorithm, iterative monotonic data-flow analyses, Kleene's algorithm (for deciding whether a regular language is accepted by a finite state automaton) and stencil computations.

Note that it is possible that embracing stale reads can increase the number of (outer loop) iterations needed to converge. For this benchmark, we observe that this increase is quite small in practice.

This is expected as typically the size of *XVector* is large (tens of thousands of elements) while an iteration will read a small number of stale values (at most $(N-1) \times$ *chunkFactor* values on an N-way multicore, where *chunkFactor* is the number of iterations executed per transaction as detailed later). Using ALTER, this parallelization gives a speedup of 1.70x with 4 cores for a problem size of 40,000.

The second example (see Figure 2) shows the main loop of the K-means clustering algorithm. ALTER suggests that the loop can be parallelized with either `OutOfOrder` or `StaleReads` in combination with an additive reduction on the variable *delta*. In this case, `OutOfOrder` and `StaleReads` are equivalent with respect to the program's execution, because every read of a shared variable (*new_centers* and *new_centers_len*) is followed by a write to the same location. Thus, even under the `StaleReads` model there will not be any stale reads in the execution trace, because conflicts in the write sets would cause such concurrent iterations to conflict (this is clarified in the next section). Nonetheless, annotating the loop with `StaleReads` can lead to higher performance than `OutOfOrder`, as it is not necessary to track or compare the read sets within ALTER.

3. Alter Annotation Language

ALTER provides an annotation language for specifying the parallelism in loops (see Figure 3). For all annotated loops, ALTER treats each iteration as a transaction that executes atomically and in isolation. The conditions under which an iteration commits its results are governed by the annotation A, which contains two components: a parallelism policy P and, optionally, a set of reductions R.

The parallelism policy can be one of two types:

1. `OutOfOrder` specifies that ALTER may reorder the loop iterations, so long as the execution is equivalent to some serial ordering of the iterations. This corresponds to the database notion of *conflict serializability*. `OutOfOrder` preserves the semantics of the original program if the iterations are commutative.
2. `StaleReads` is more permissive than `OutOfOrder`: in addition to reordering iterations, the values read in a given iteration may be stale. All stale reads are drawn from a consistent but possibly obsolete snapshot of the global memory. The degree of staleness is bounded: the memory state seen by iteration i, which writes to locations W, is no older than the state committed by the last iteration to write to any location in W. (The only exception is that of reduction variables, which do not count as part of W.)

   This model corresponds to the database notion of *snapshot isolation*; two concurrent iterations can commit so long as their write sets do not overlap. Snapshot isolation is a popular alternative to conflict serializability in the database community, as it leads to better performance. It is adopted by several major database management systems, including InterBase, Oracle, PostgreSQL and Microsoft SQL Server (2005 onward). However, to date there has been no programming language or runtime support for snapshot isolation as a mechanism for loop parallelization.

The second part of an ALTER annotation is an optional set of reductions. Each reduction is specified by the name of a program variable, as well as an operation that is commutative and associative. The annotation asserts that every access to the variable within the loop represents an update using the corresponding operation. For example, if the operation is +, then the variable may appear only in statements of the form *var+=value*. Note that this also prohibits any reads of *var* elsewhere in the loop.

ALTER guarantees that upon completion of the loop, each reduction variable has the value corresponding to a serial execution of the operations that updated it. Note that under the `OutOfOrder` execution model, annotating reductions will not impact the final values assigned to reduction variables, as `OutOfOrder` guarantees that all variables (not just reduction variables) are updated in a manner that is consistent with a serial execution. However, annotating reductions can nonetheless improve the performance under `OutOfOrder`, as iterations that were previously serialized by a dependence on a reduction variable can now execute in parallel. In the case of `StaleReads` execution, annotating reduction variables can impact the final values of those variables (but not any other variables) as well as impacting performance.

$$
\begin{array}{lcl}
A & := & (P, R) \\
P & := & \texttt{OutOfOrder} \mid \texttt{StaleReads} \\
R & := & \epsilon \mid R; R \mid (var, O) \\
O & := & + \mid \times \mid \texttt{max} \mid \texttt{min} \mid \vee \mid \wedge
\end{array}
$$

Figure 3. ALTER annotation language

In addition to the parameters specified in the annotation language, ALTER also allows the user to specify a *chunk factor (cf)*, which dictates the granularity of the execution. While our description above deals in terms of individual iterations, in practice it is beneficial to group multiple iterations together for improving the efficiency of `OutOfOrder` and `StaleReads` execution. The semantics can be understood in terms of chunking: the original loop L is refactored into a nested loop L' in which each iteration of L' represents *cf* iterations of L. The chunk factor can be designated on a per-loop basis, or globally for the entire program.

4. Alter Compiler and Runtime

Given a sequential program and a loop to parallelize, the ALTER compiler produces a concurrent program with embedded calls to the ALTER runtime library. The concurrent program is parameterized by some additional inputs that indicate the semantics to be enforced for each loop. If the user provides annotations for a loop, then these are used to generate the parameters. Otherwise, likely annotations can be inferred by testing their conformance to a test suite (see Section 5). Section 4.2 describes the parameters governing the execution and the assignments needed to exploit the parallelism allowed by the annotations. A salient feature of the ALTER framework is that the output of the compilation process is a deterministic parallel program. Details of how this is achieved are provided in Section 4.3.

4.1 Program Transformation

Program transformations are implemented as phases in the Microsoft Phoenix compiler.

Deterministic Fork Join Model

The ALTER compiler transforms the program to use a process-based fork-join model of computation. The model provides efficient isolation between concurrently executing loop iterations through copy-on-write page protection. Figure 4 shows what the transformed program looks like. The shaded vertices and edges in the figure represent the original sequential control flow.

The high-level functionality of the transformation is to:

1. Create N processes that have identical stack and heap states (apart from ALTER's internal variables), corresponding to the program state on entry to the loop. These N private memories are copy-on-write (COW) mappings of a committed memory state. Thus, just before the loop, there are $N+1$ versions of memory. In the figure, ❶ and ❷ describe the implementation of this functionality using Win32 system calls.

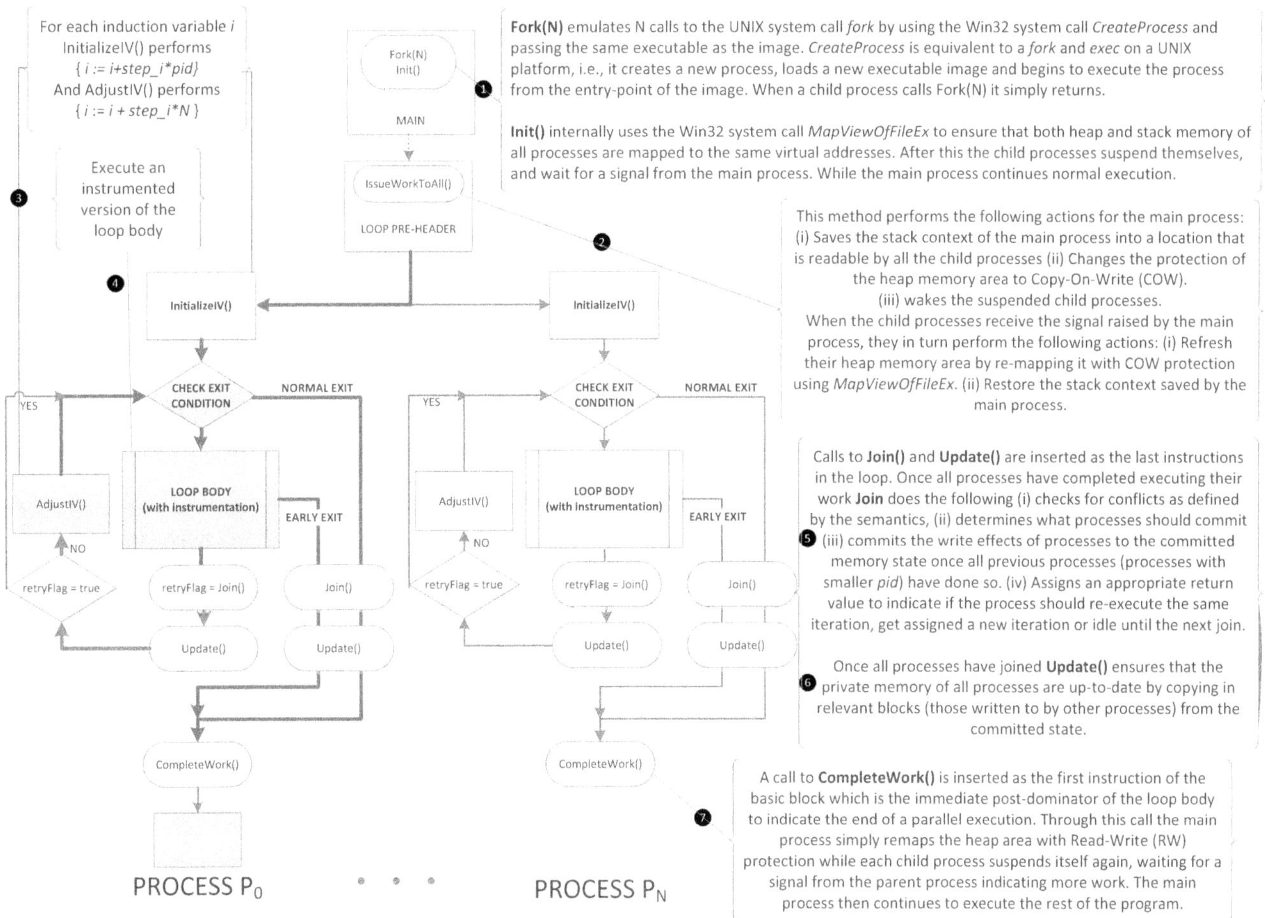

Figure 4. ALTER's fork-join model for executing loop iterations concurrently and in isolation.

2. Distribute iterations to processes and orchestrate a lock-step execution where processes repeatedly: ❸ pickup iterations to execute. ❹ execute them concurrently in isolation on their own private memory while tracking read and write sets (details on instrumentation below). ❺ wait for all processes to complete execution and then depending on validation against execution policy either commit writes to committed memory state or mark the iteration for re-execution next time. Runtime barriers are used to ensure that processes commit changes one after another in deterministic order (ascending order of child pid's). ❻ re-synchronize process private memory with the committed memory state once all processes have committed.

   These steps are repeated until the loop execution is complete.

To keep things simple, Figure 4 depicts the program transformation without chunking. The actual transformation introduces an additional inner loop such that each process executes a consecutive chunk of iterations between joins.

Memory Management

In addition to the above transformation, all calls to memory allocator methods are replaced with calls to the ALTER-allocator. This transformation is essential to ensure that in a multi-process setting, objects can be directly copied between processes without overwriting live values. The ALTER-allocator is designed to be safe and efficient under a multi-process execution environment. It ensures safety by guaranteeing that no two concurrent processes are allocated the same virtual address. We do not describe the design in detail here except to say that it uses techniques similar to ones used by HOARD [5]. Where HOARD is optimized to be efficient in a multi-threaded environment, the ALTER-allocator is designed to be efficient in a multi-process environment. For example, the allocator is optimized to minimally use inter-process semaphores and mutual exclusion primitives. Such inter-process communication primitives are typically much more expensive than locking primitives that can be used in a multi-threaded setting.

ALTER Collection Classes

While simple induction variables can be identified via static analysis, induction variables of loops that iterate over elements of a heap data structure will not be detected by most compilers. To enable parallelization of such loops ALTER exposes a library of standard data structures that are commonly iterated over. When a user wants to parallelize a loop that iterates over such a data structure, she could replace the data-structure with an equivalent ALTER collection class and then use any of the ALTER annotations. ALTER internally manages the state associated with collection classes in a process-safe manner. Note that ALTER collections can also safely be used in a sequential program.

Instrumenting Reads and Writes

The read-write instrumentation performed by the compiler is fairly standard; we briefly describe it here for the sake of completeness. Accesses to both heap memory locations as well as to local stack variables are instrumented by the compiler by adding calls to runtime methods `InstrumentRead` and `InstrumentWrite`. Heap accesses are instrumented at *allocation* granularity. For instance if a statement of the form `ObjPtr->Field = Value;` is encountered, then the object referenced by `ObjPtr` as a whole is instrumented, assuming that the `ObjPtr` refers to an allocation. The compiler performs the following optimizations to avoid unnecessary instrumentation calls:

- No instrumentation is inserted for a memory access if the object to be instrumented already has a dominating instrumentation.
- If a local variable is defined before its first use, i.e., it is defined afresh in each iteration of the loop, then it is not instrumented, unless it is also *live-out* on loop exit.
- If the loop to be parallelized contains function calls, then accesses to local variables in the function are not instrumented.
- If the memory access to be instrumented matches a pattern of an array indexed by an induction variable, i.e., a loop invariant base pointer indexed by an induction variable, then we instrument the *entire range* once rather than instrumenting each individual array access.

At runtime, the library stores the addresses of the instrumented blocks in a (local) hash set as well as a (global) array. The hash set allows quick elimination of duplicates, while the global array allows other processes to check for conflicts against their respective read- and write-sets.

4.2 Runtime Parameters

As mentioned previously the ALTER compiler translates the sequential program into a concurrent program with some additional configuration parameters. Four different parameters are exposed, combinations of which can be used to enforce various formal guarantees for the loop.

1. The `ConflictPolicy` configuration parameter selects one among four different definitions of conflict, which are applied to all memory locations not corresponding to reduction variables. These four policies, `FULL`, `WAW`, `RAW` and `NONE` form a partial order with respect to the conditions under which they allow processes to commit. These terms have the natural intuitive meaning. `FULL` allows a process to commit only if neither its read nor its write set overlaps with the write set of any of the concurrent processes that committed before it. `WAW` allows a process to commit only if its write set does not overlap with the write set of any of the concurrent processes committed before it. `RAW` allows a process to commit only if its read set does not overlap with the write set of any of the concurrent processes committed before it. `NONE` does not check for any conflicts and allows all processes to commit.
2. The `CommitOrderPolicy` defines whether the iterations of the loop should commit in program order (`InOrder`) or are allowed to commit `OutOfOrder`. Note that even under `OutOfOrder`, iterations commit out of program order only if there are conflicts.
3. `ReductionPolicy` takes a set of $\langle var, op\rangle$ pairs and applies reduction as follows. Let $S_c(x)$ denote the latest value of x in the committed memory. Let $oldS_t(x)$ and $newS_t(x)$ denote the values of x in the private memory of transaction t, at the start and end of its execution. ALTER modifies the state depending on the operation in consideration as follows. (1) if op is idempotent, that is $op \in (\vee, \wedge, \mathtt{max}, \mathtt{min})$, then the committed memory state is updated as $S_c(x) := S_c(x)\ op\ newS_t(x)$. (2) if $op = +$ then the committed state is updated as $S_c(x) := S_c(x) + newS_t(x) - oldS_t(x)$. $\times$ is handled similarly. Our framework currently only supports these 6 operations. The library also has partial support for programmer-defined reduction operations but this is not fully tested and is not exposed as yet.
4. Finally, `ChunkFactor` takes a integer that defines the chunk factor to be used. We omit this parameter in discussions below and refer to it only when relevant.

Parameters Respecting ALTER Annotations

The following theorems assert that the ALTER annotations, which represent constraints on the parallelism in loops, can be enforced via certain selections of the runtime parameters.

Theorem 4.1. *Executing a loop under* ALTER *with:*

$\mathtt{ConflictPolicy} = \mathtt{RAW}$,
$\mathtt{CommitOrderPolicy} = \mathtt{OutOfOrder}$,
$\mathtt{ReductionPolicy} = R$

respects the annotation (`OutOfOrder`, *R*).

Proof Sketch The `OutOfOrder` annotation specifies that loop iterations are treated as transactions that commit subject to conflict serializability. ALTER starts concurrent iterations on a consistent memory snapshot and provides isolation for iterations by executing each in its own address space. The `RAW` conflict policy guarantees that a transaction t with location L in its read set will not commit if a concurrent transaction that committed before t has L in its write set, which is the criterion required for conflict serializability. Reordering of iterations is enabled by the `OutOfOrder` ordering policy. □

Theorem 4.2. *Executing a loop under* ALTER *with:*

$\mathtt{ConflictPolicy} = \mathtt{WAW}$,
$\mathtt{CommitOrderPolicy} = \mathtt{OutOfOrder}$,
$\mathtt{ReductionPolicy} = R$

respects the annotation (`StaleReads`, *R*).

Proof Sketch The `StaleReads` annotation specifies that loop iterations are treated as transactions that commit subject to snapshot isolation. ALTER starts concurrent iterations on a consistent memory state and provides isolation for iterations by executing each in its own address space. The `WAW` conflict policy guarantees that a transaction t with location L in its write set will not commit if a concurrent transaction that committed before t has L in its write set, which is the criterion required for snapshot isolation. □

Parameters Respecting Other Semantics

While our focus in this paper is to explore loop semantics that depart from ordinary execution models, ALTER can also be used to implement well-known models such as safe speculative parallelism and DOALL parallelism. This is asserted by the following theorems:

Theorem 4.3. *Executing a loop under* ALTER *with:*

$\mathtt{ConflictPolicy} = \mathtt{RAW}$,
$\mathtt{CommitOrderPolicy} = \mathtt{InOrder}$,
$\mathtt{ReductionPolicy} = \mathtt{NONE}$

offers safe speculative parallelism (equivalent to sequential semantics).

Proof Sketch The iterations commit `InOrder` while respecting all `RAW` dependences, which implies that none of the dependences in the original program are broken. □

Theorem 4.4. *Executing a loop under* ALTER *with:*

$$\texttt{ConflictPolicy} = *,$$
$$\texttt{CommitOrderPolicy} = *,$$
$$\texttt{ReductionPolicy} = R$$

offers DOALL parallelism with a reduction R.

Proof Sketch As DOALL parallelism applies when there are no dependences between iterations, the `ConflictPolicy` and `CommitOrderPolicy` are not relevant. Nonetheless, reductions can be supported using the ALTER framework. □

While other combinations of the ALTER parameters also lead to sensible execution models, we did not find an analogue for them in practice or application for them in example programs. We leave potential investigation of these models for future work.

4.3 Determinism

A salient feature of ALTER is that given a deterministic sequential program as input ALTER produces a deterministic parallel program. That is, every time the generated executable is run with the same program input and the same values for number of processes N, the chunk factor cf and configuration parameters (`ConflictPolicy`, `CommitOrderPolicy`, `ReductionPolicy`) it produces the same output so long as the program terminates. If the program crashes or does not terminate this also happens deterministically. The runtime avoids races by enforcing runtime barriers.

Determinism follows from the following facts: (1) all concurrent processes have independent memory spaces, (2) no process is allowed to execute `join()` until all processes have completed their work, (3) processes commit their changes to the committed memory state one after another in deterministic order, (4) updates from the committed memory state to private memory spaces occur only after all processes have committed, and (5) the same conflicts are detected for every execution with the same inputs. Determinism is a desirable property for a framework like ALTER that uses a dynamic annotation inference engine with test suite conformance as the validation criterion. Determinism is desirable because the correctness of each test can be determined in a single execution.

5. Annotation Inference

In addition to implementing parallelism consistent with the programmer's annotations, ALTER can also be used to infer a set of annotations that are likely valid for a given loop. Because this inference algorithm is unsound, it is important to use it carefully. We discuss specific application scenarios in the next section.

The annotation inference works via a simple test-driven framework. Given a program, ALTER creates many different versions, each containing a single annotation on a single loop. Together, these versions exhaustively enumerate the ways in which one could add a single annotation to the program (details below). Then, ALTER runs each of these programs on every input in the test suite. Because the ALTER runtime is deterministic, only one execution of each test is needed. Those versions matching the output of the unmodified sequential version (according to a program-specific correctness criterion) are presented to the user as annotations that are likely valid.

To enumerate the candidate annotations, our current implementation works as follows. ALTER systematically explores values for P and R (see Figure 3) by fixing the chunk factor at 16 and evaluating all valid candidates for the other runtime parameters. For each reduction R, a bounded search over reduction variables and operators is performed. The search is restricted to (i) apply one of six reduction operators $\langle +, \times, \texttt{max}, \texttt{min}, \wedge, \vee \rangle$, and (ii) apply the same reduction operator (or lack thereof) to all stack variables[1]. Also a search for a valid reduction is performed only if none of the annotations of the form (P, ϵ) are valid.

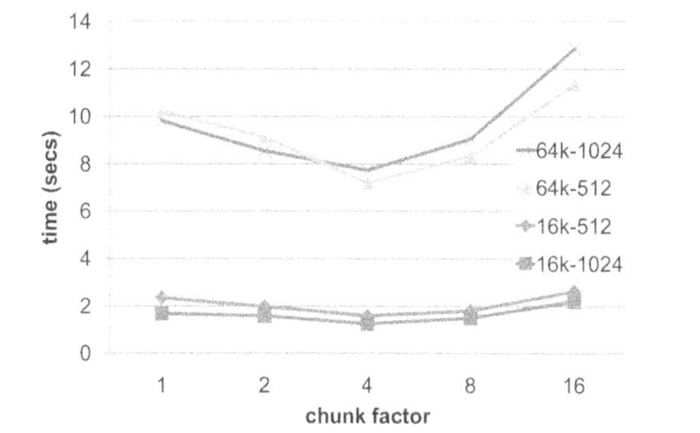

Figure 5. Performance impact of the chunk factor, for various input sizes (numbers of points and clusters) on the K-means benchmark.

After ascertaining valid annotations, an iterative doubling algorithm is used to the find an appropriate chunk factor. Starting from a candidate value of 1 the chunk factor is iteratively doubled until a performance degradation is seen over two successive increments. The candidate that led to the best performance is then chosen as the chunk factor. Our results indicate that the chunk factor is dependent only on the loop structure and not on the inputs. Figure 5 shows how performance varies with increasing chunk factors for different inputs of *K-means*. As can be seen the best performing chunk factor for all 4 inputs remains the same. Similar behavior is observed for other benchmarks.

In addition to reporting the set of annotations that lead to valid executions, ALTER also gives hints as to the cause of failure for annotations that are unsuccessful. For each annotation, the reported outcome is one of the following: *success, failure* $\in$ *(crash, timeout, high conflicts, output mismatch)*. *Success* represents the case where the execution produces a valid output. Failure cases can be classified into cases where no output is produced (*crash, timeout*) and cases where an output is produced but it is either incorrect (*output mismatch*) or is unlikely to lead to performance improvements (*high conflicts*). A *timeout* is flagged if the execution takes more than 10 times the sequential execution time. An execution is flagged as having high conflicts if more than 50% of the attempted commits fail. Both of these behaviors are correlated with performance degradation and hence we deem them as failures.

6. Usage Scenarios

To explore concrete applications of ALTER in real-world contexts, we consider three scenarios – manual parallelization, assisted parallelization, and automatic parallelization. While our primary target is assisted parallelization, under certain circumstances ALTER can also make sense for purely manual or automatic parallelization. We summarize these scenarios in Table 1 and expand on them below.

Assisted parallelization In this scenario, a user is attempting to parallelize a code base for which she has partial but incomplete knowledge. For example, perhaps the user has authored part of the system, but relies on third-party libraries as well. In such a situation, ALTER serves a natural role in assisting the user to parallelize

[1] This is sufficient for our current benchmarks. It should be fairly straightforward to extend the search strategy to explore different reductions for different variables. Because reduction variables are not allowed to interact, either with each other or with the program variables, each variable can be tested independently without leading to a combinatorial explosion.

	Manual Parallelization	Assisted Parallelization	Automatic Parallelization
User has:	deep understanding of code	some familiarity with code	little or no familiarity with code
Annotations are:	written by hand	inferred but checked by hand	inferred and used as-is
ALTER **serves as:**	1) high-level parallelism library 2) tool for rapid prototyping	1) set of hints to investigate further 2) upper bound for discoverable parallelism	1) temporary substitute for human parallelizer 2) unsound parallelizer for tolerant environments

Table 1. Usage scenarios for ALTER. While ALTER is intended primarily for assisted parallelization, it could also find application in purely manual or automatic parallelization.

the code. By evaluating various loop annotations via executions on test suites, ALTER can suggest which models of parallelism are likely to be valid and beneficial for each loop in the program. The user can investigate these suggestions to determine whether or not they are sound before integrating them into source base. In addition, ALTER's suggestions could serve as a useful upper bound for certain kinds of parallelism in the program. If ALTER does not find likely parallelism in any loop, then perhaps a new algorithm will be needed to leverage multicore hardware.

Manual parallelization This scenario applies to cases in which the user of ALTER is authoring a new parallel program or is already equipped with a deep understanding of an existing code base. In this case, the user can think of ALTER as providing an API for exploiting known parallelism in the program. All of the annotations are written by the user herself. The ALTER runtime system could be shipped as part of a product, or applied only for internal prototyping in order to quickly explore the speedups offered by various transformations. In the latter case, the most beneficial transformations may be re-written manually (without the ALTER runtime system) to further customize and optimize the performance.

Automatic parallelization In the final scenario (which remains largely hypothetical), ALTER is applied as an autonomous parallelization engine. Perhaps this could make sense for obscure legacy codes, in which it is unduly expensive for new developers to fully understand the intricacies of the implementation. ALTER could be used to infer parallel annotations by evaluating them for correctness across a large and rigorous test suite. In the case of legacy codes, test suites often provide the only arbiter as to whether changes in the environment have violated implicit assumptions of the code. Just as many human intuitions about very complex systems can only be verified via testing, there might be cases where it is not unreasonable to utilize testing as the sole correctness criterion for a compiler-directed transformation.

Nonetheless, to make sense in a production environment, additional flexibility is likely needed to embrace ALTER as an automatic parallelization engine. For example, if parallel speedups are urgently needed to proceed with whole-system prototyping (e.g., to evaluate the user experience of a new gaming engine), then perhaps ALTER could be applied temporarily until a human developer has a chance to step in and laboriously verify the changes. Alternately, there may be end-user applications where speed is more important than correctness. For example, one may desire a low-latency preview of multimedia content before the official decoder has finished rendering it, even if the preview has a chance of being wrong. Or, on a mobile platform, if the battery is low one may want to quickly execute some application (with some chance of failure) rather than initiating a slower execution that is guaranteed to timeout due to a dead battery.

7. Experimental Evaluation

We evaluate ALTER with algorithms from Berkeley's dwarfs [4] and sequential versions of the STAMP [28] benchmarks (see Table 2). A dwarf represents an algorithmic method that captures a commonly used pattern of computation. We utilize all dwarfs for which we could find a good representative algorithm and all STAMP benchmarks that we could get to compile on Windows[2].

Table 2 describes the benchmarks used. Our transformations target a single loop in each benchmark. For many benchmarks the main computation happens in a single loop nest; we report results for the nesting level that leads to the most parallelism. For benchmarks containing multiple important loops, the targeted loop is indicated in the *description* column of the table. For each benchmark, we use test inputs to infer the annotations and then use a larger input (shown in bold) to measure performance. All performance measurements are conducted on an 8-core Intel Xeon machine ($2 \times quad$ core at 2.4GHz) with a 64-bit Windows Server 2008 operating system.

7.1 Results of Annotation Inference

We utilized the annotation inference algorithm to infer all annotations used in our evaluation. Correctness of the program output was evaluated on a case-by-case basis. For 4 of the benchmarks (*Labyrinth, Genome, GSdense, GSsparse*) assertions in the code validate the output. For the remaining programs, we utilized a program-specific output validation script, which often made approximate comparisons between floating-point values.

The results from the inference algorithm are reported in Table 3. In addition to the models exposed by our language we also check if the program can be parallelized by some existing auto-parallelization techniques. We add a check in `join()` to see if the loop has any loop-carried dependences. The results of this check are shown in column *dep*. We also check to see if the loop is amenable to thread level speculation (`TLS`). The outcome of this check could be one among (*success, failure* $\in$ *(crash, timeout, high conflicts)*).

Interestingly, we find that in all cases a single test is sufficient to identify incorrect annotations. We find that when `TLS`, `OutOfOrder` or `StaleReads` fail, they fail either due to timeouts or due to a large number of conflicts. The only exception is *AggloClust*, where the application crashes under `OutOfOrder` and `TLS`. In these two cases the machine runs out of memory (due to very large read sets). We find that an incorrect reduction leads either to an invalid output or a timeout. An interesting case is the + reduction for *SG3D*. The convergence check in this algorithm looks for $max_{\forall i}(error_i) < threshold$ so a `max` reduction works. A + leads to a check of the form $\sum_{\forall i}(error_i) < threshold$, which also produces a valid output but convergence takes much longer. Other reductions lead to a deviation of $\pm 0.01\%$ from sequential output in some entries.

Overall we find that all but one benchmark (*Labyrinth*) can be parallelized with ALTER. Both *SSCA2* and *Genome*, which are known to be amenable to `OutOfOrder` [28], also lead to a correct execution under `StaleReads`. This is because all variables that are read in the loop are also written to. Hence it is sufficient to check for WAW conflicts alone and no read instrumentation is required. Though it is known that *K-means* can be parallelized with `OutOfOrder` we find that it leads to a very slow execution. We find that the only practical execution model for *K-means* is to use a combination of `StaleReads` and + reduction.

[2] Compiling STAMP benchmarks on Windows requires a substantial manual effort. We succeeded in compiling 4 benchmarks out of the 8 benchmarks in the suite; we present full results for these 4 cases.

BENCHMARK	DESCRIPTION	LOOP WGT	INPUT SIZE (inference; **benchmarking**)
Genome (STAMP)	The genome sequencing algorithm from STAMP is described in detail in [28]. We parallelize the first step (remove duplicate sequences).	89%	4M segments; **16M segments**
SSCA2 (STAMP)	This benchmark includes a set of graph kernels (details in STAMP [28]). We focus on the second loop in kernel 1.	76%*	18; 19; **20 (problem scale)**
K-means (STAMP)	The K-means algorithm is a popular clustering algorithm (we use the implementation from STAMP [28]). The main loop in the algorithm recomputes the association of points to clusters until convergence (see Figure 2).	89%	16K pts, 512 clusts; 16K pts, 1024 clusts; **64K pts, 512 clusts; 64K pts, 1024 clusts**
Labyrinth (STAMP) *uses* ALTER*Vector*	This algorithm does an efficient routing through a mesh (details in STAMP [28]). An ALTERVector is used here.	99%	$128 \times 128 \times 3$ grid, 128 paths; $\mathbf{256 \times 256 \times 5}$ **grid, 256 paths**
AggloClust (Branch and bound) *uses* ALTER*List*	The agglomerative clustering algorithm utilizes a special tree (k-d tree) to efficiently bound *nearest neighbor* searches in a multi-dimensional space. Our implementation is adapted (C++ instead of Java) from Lonestar [22]. We simplify the original implementation by not updating the bounding boxes on k-d tree node deletions. We focus on the main loop of the program ([22] has the pseudo-code). As the loop iterates over a list we replace the sequential list with an ALTERList.	89%	100K pts; **1M pts**
GSdense (Dense linear algebra)	We use the Gauss-Seidel iterative method [31] for solving a system of equations (refer Figure 1). Depending on whether the A matrix is sparse or dense it uses two different representations of the matrix. As noted before, violating some true dependences still preserves the overall functionality and provides the same convergence guarantees.	100%	10000×10000; $\mathbf{20000 \times 20000}$
GSsparse (Sparse linear algebra)		100%	20000×20000; $\mathbf{40000 \times 40000}$
Floyd (Dynamic programming)	The Floyd-Warshall algorithm uses a triply nested loop (on k, i, and j) within which it repeatedly applies the relaxation $path[i][j] := min(path[i][j], path[i][k] + path[k][j])$. Though the loop has a tight dependence chain, it turns out that even if some true dependences are violated, all possible paths between each pair of vertices are still evaluated [40].	100%	1000 nodes; **2000 nodes**
SG3D (Structured grids)	The algorithm uses a 27-point three-dimensional stencil computation to solve a partial differential equation [13]. A triply-nested inner loop iterates over points in 3D space, updating their value and tracking the maximum change (*error*) that occurs at any point. An outer loop tests for convergence by checking if the *error* is less than a given threshold. While the stencil computations can tolerate stale reads, the update of the *error* value must not violate any dependences, or the execution could terminate incorrectly.	96%	$64 \times 64 \times 64$; $\mathbf{128 \times 128 \times 128}$
BarnesHut (N-body methods) *uses* ALTER*List*	The Barnes-Hut algorithm uses a quad-tree data structure to solve the N-body problem. We use the implementation from Olden [10]. We parallelize the main loop that iterates over a list by transforming it to use an ALTERList.	99.6%	4096 particles; **8192 particles**
FFT (Spectral methods)	We utilize the two-dimensional iterative FFT solver from [1].	100%*	1024, **2048**
HMM (Graphical models)	We use the Hidden Markov Model solver from [1].	100%	512, **1024**

** FFT has two identical loops each taking 50% of the execution time. The annotations inferred and speedups obtained apply to both these loops. SSCA2 has an initial random input generation step. We do not include the time taken for random input generation.*

Table 2. Benchmarks used for evaluation. Eight benchmarks are drawn from Berkeley's dwarfs; the algorithm name is subtitled with the dwarf that it represents. Four benchmarks are drawn from STAMP. The "LOOP WGT" (loop weight) column indicates the fraction of the program's runtime that is spent in the loop targeted by ALTER.

Benchmark	Dep	TLS	OutOrd	Stale	Reduction
Genome	Yes	success	success	success	N/A
SSCA2	Yes	timeout	success	success	N/A
K-means	Yes	h.c.	h.c.	h.c.	+
Labyrinth	Yes	h.c.	h.c.	h.c.	N/A
AggloClust	Yes	crash	crash	success	N/A
GSdense	Yes	timeout	timeout	success	N/A
GSsparse	Yes	timeout	timeout	success	N/A
Floyd	Yes	timeout	timeout	success	N/A
SG3D	Yes	h.c.	h.c.	h.c.	max/+
BarnesHut	No	success	success	success	N/A
FFT	No	success	success	success	N/A
HMM	No	success	success	success	N/A

Table 3. Results of annotation inference. The table shows whether there is a dependence carried by the loop (**Dep**) as well as the results for thread-level speculation (**TLS**), `OutOfOrder` execution (**OutOrd**), and `StaleReads` (**Stale**). High conflict results are abbreviated as h.c. Reductions are shown where applicable.

Benchmark	cf	Transaction Count	RW Set / Trans.	Retry Rate
Genome-StaleReads	4096	32768	16	0.2%
Genome-OutOfOrder	4096	32768	89	0.2%
Genome-TLS	4096	32768	90	0.16%
SSCA2-StaleReads	64	16384	277	3.5%
SSCA2-OutOfOrder	64	16384	6340	3.5%
K-means-1024	4	65552	136	3.4%
K-means-512	4	81940	136	6.3%
AggloClust	64	46608	28	3.6%
GSdense	32	2720	62	0
GSsparse	32	12580	32	0
Floyd	256	24576	428	0
SG3D	4	23560	208	0

Table 4. Instrumentation details for representative benchmarks. The columns show the chunk factor (**cf**), the number of chunks (transactions) executed (**Transaction Count**), the average size of the read and write set, in words, per transaction (**RW Set / Trans.**), and the average rate at which iterations fail to commit (**Retry rate**).

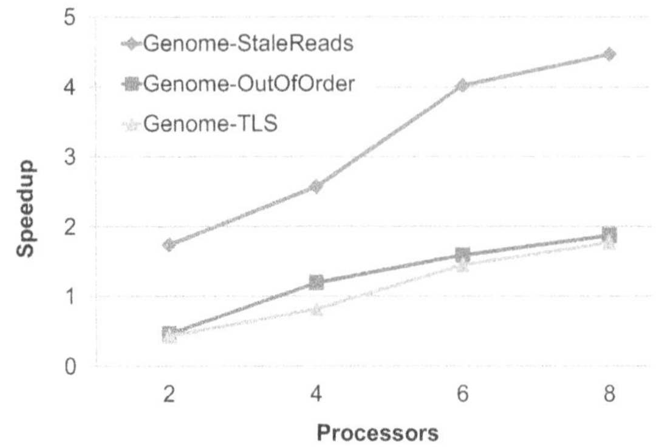

Figure 6. Genome.

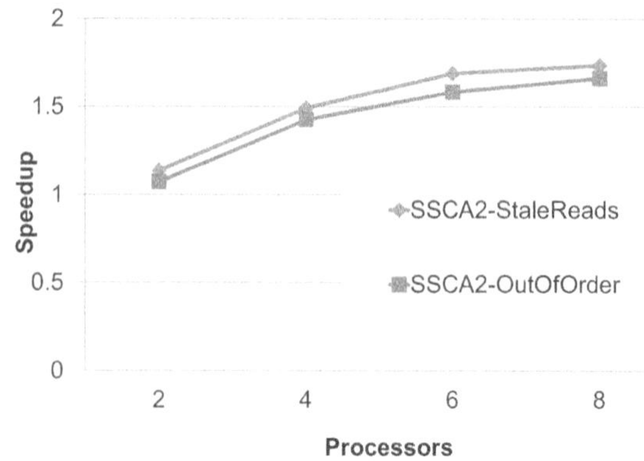

Figure 7. SSCA2.

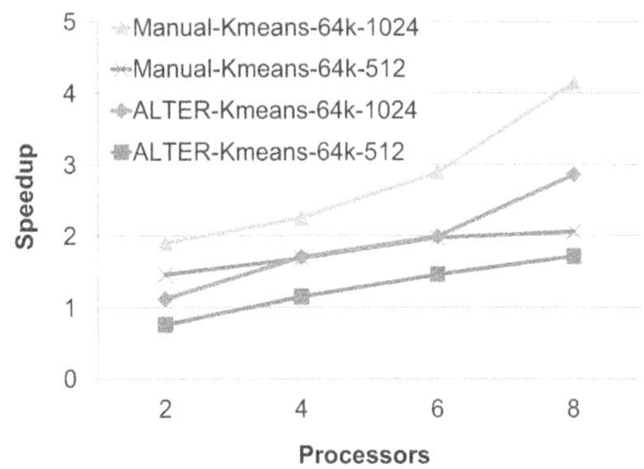

Figure 8. K-means. The plot compares results with manual parallelization on two different inputs.

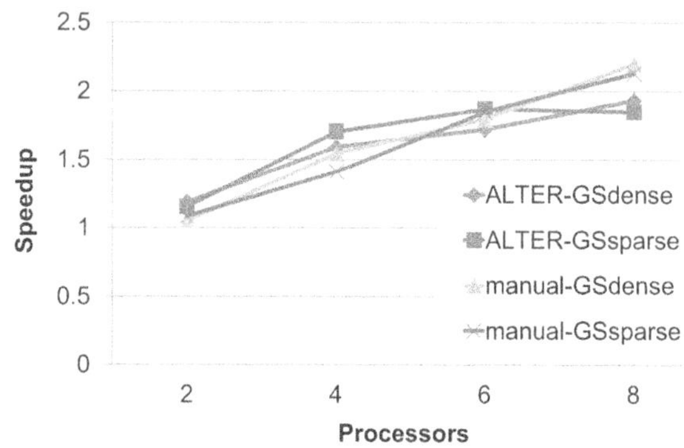

Figure 9. Dense and sparse linear algebra. The plot compares results with manual parallelization for both dense and sparse cases.

Four other benchmarks (*GSdense*, *GSsparse*, *Floyd* and *SG3D*) are tolerant to stale reads. Among these, SSG3D needs a combination of `StaleReads` and reduction for parallelization while the other three do not need reduction. Only three benchmarks have no loop carried dependences and (of those with dependences) only one is amenable to efficient speculation.

7.2 Performance Results

The results for all annotations that lead to a valid execution during testing are shown in Figures 6 through 13. Each figure shows the speedup over the original sequential execution (without ALTER) for the loop nest being parallelized.

A maximum speedup of up to 4.5X is observed (ignoring "trivial" benchmarks with no loop carried dependences) with 8 cores. For the two benchmarks (*Genome* and *SSCA2*) that are amenable to multiple annotations, we find that `StaleReads` leads to much better performance than `OutOfOrder`. This is because enforcing `StaleReads` does not need read instrumentation. We report the size of the read and write sets per transaction as well as retry rates in Table 4. As can be seen by comparing the amount of instrumentation for `OutOfOrder` and `StaleReads` for a given benchmark, there is a much larger number of reads (instrumented by `OutOfOrder`) than writes (instrumented by both `OutOfOrder` and `StaleReads`) within a transaction[3]. Further, we find that for *Genome* TLS performs nearly as well as `OutOfOrder` but not as well as `StaleReads`.

We find that the speedup obtained for *K-means* depends on the number of clusters to be formed. The larger the number of clusters to be formed, the fewer the conflicts. As can be seen from Figure 8, when the number of clusters decreases from 1024 to 512 the speedup comes down from 2.8X to 1.7X. So long as the probability that two points map to the same cluster is low, the algorithm should see a speedup. Further note that while the speedup varies, the best parallelism policy or chunk factor does not change with input. As seen before, both inference and evaluation inputs perform best at the same chunk factor.

Benchmarks *GSdense*, *GSsparse*, and *Floyd* when executed under `StaleReads` lead to no conflicts. This is because while these loops have many RAW dependences there are no loop-carried WAW dependences. We also find that breaking RAW dependences hardly increases the number of iterations needed to converge (GSdense increases from 16 to 17, while GSsparse increases from 20 to 21). Unfortunately, both *GSdense* and *GSsparse* are memory bound and hence do not scale well beyond 4 cores. Like the above bench-

[3] Though STAMP benchmarks come along with instrumentation hints, we ignore them and use our own static analysis to embed instrumentation in the program. Because this analysis is automatic and does not depend on any special knowledge of the program, the overheads observed are likely to generalize to other programs.

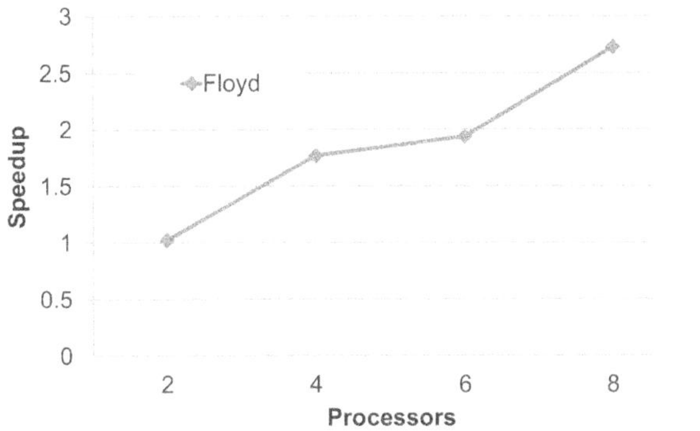

Figure 10. Floyd Warshall algorithm.

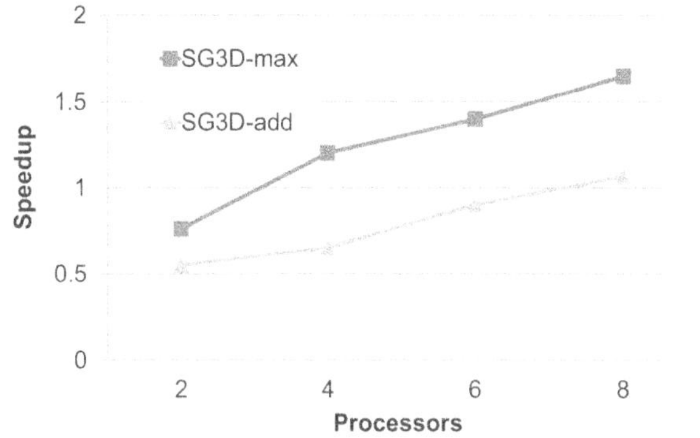

Figure 11. SG3D: 27 point 3D stencil, with alternate reductions.

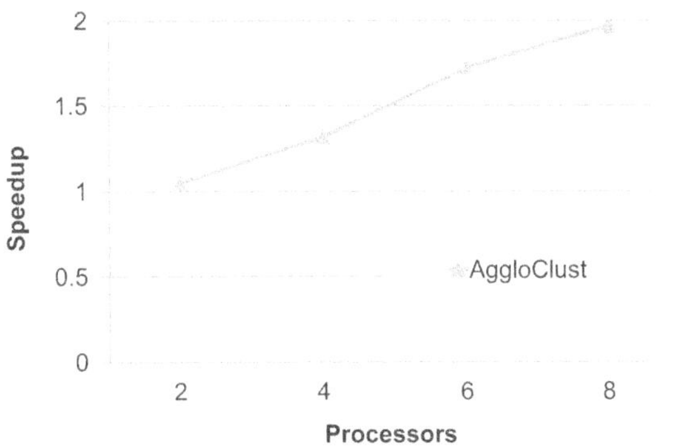

Figure 12. Agglomerative Clustering.

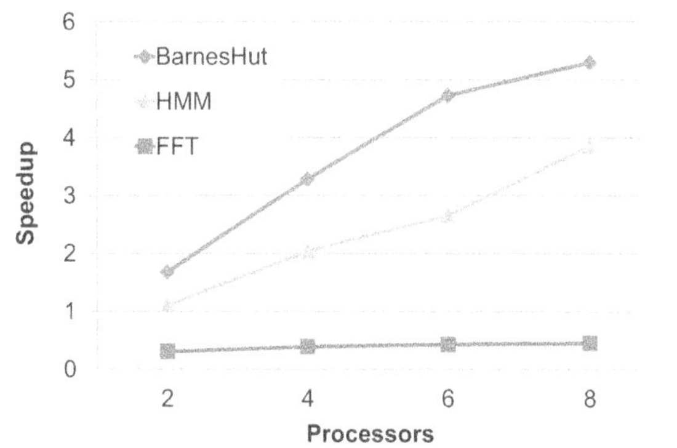

Figure 13. BarnesHut, FFT, and HMM.

marks *SG3D* leads to no conflicts under `StaleReads` with reduction. Among `max` and + reduction we find that using + degrades performance as it leads to a significant increase in the number of iterations to converge (1670 to 2752).

Among the three benchmarks that have no loop carried dependences, ALTER provides reasonable speedups for *HMM* and *barnesHut* but slows down *FFT*. The slowdown on FFT is due to high instrumentation overhead. FFT uses a `complex` data type, which results in many copy constructors that are instrumented by ALTER. This effect could be avoided by a more precise alias analysis or via conversion of complex types to primitive types.

7.3 Comparison with Manual Parallelization

Finally, we manually parallelize two of the benchmarks in order to provide a realistic parallel baseline for ALTER. We manually implement a multi-threaded version of Gauss-Seidel that mimics the runtime behavior of `StaleReads` by maintaining multiple copies of *XVector* that are synchronized in exactly the same way as a chunked execution under ALTER. We also parallelize *K-means* using threads and fine-grained locking.

As shown in Figure 9, ALTER performs comparably to manual parallelization on Gauss-Seidel. However, on *K-means*, it performs 20-47% slower than manual parallelization (considering all tests between 4 and 8 cores) as shown in Figure 8. This slowdown is due to the overhead of the ALTER runtime system as it explores parallelism via optimistic, coarse-grained execution rather than pessimistic fine-grained locking.

8. Related Work

Parallelizing compilers Compilers rely on static analysis to identify parts of the program that can be parallelized. Often they target simple forms of loop parallelism like DOALL and pipeline parallel loops or loops with simple reductions [17]. Parallelizing compilers are typically restricted by the accuracy of static analyses such as data dependence analysis and alias analysis [20]. Richer forms of parallelism can be identified via commutativity analysis [2, 38] that detects if two program tasks commute with each other or not. The analysis needs to be able to prove the equivalence of the final memory state with either order of execution of the tasks before applying a parallelizing transformation. One of the contributions of ALTER is to provide a test-driven framework to identify whether iterations of a loop are likely to commute with each other.

The classic compiler transformation of *privatization* is similar to `StaleReads` in that it enables loop iterations to operate on local copies of global variables [26, 34]. However, there is a key difference between privatization and `StaleReads`: privatization does not allow loop iterations to communicate via the privatized variables. The key aspect of `StaleReads` is that loop iterations *do* communicate, but the values read might be stale, reflecting the update of an earlier iteration rather than the most recent one.

Implicitly parallel programming Rather than providing explicit directives as to the allowable parallelism, as in OpenMP or ALTER, an alternative approach is to utilize an implicitly parallel programming model that enables the compiler to automatically identify and exploit the parallelism [19]. Of the many efforts in this space, some have also proposed an annotation language to prevent spurious dependences from inhibiting parallelization. Bridges et al. advocate using annotations for commutative functions and non-deterministic branches to enable parallelization of legacy code [7]; their "commutative" annotation plays a similar role to our `OutOfOrder` annotation in allowing certain dependences to be reordered. In the Paralax infrastructure [45], the programmer annotates functions, function arguments, and variables with extra information regarding dependences; for example, a "kill" annotation indicates that a given variable is no longer live. The system can infer likely annotations using a dynamic analysis. However, there is a key difference between this inference algorithm and ours: the Paralax system aims to infer annotations that precisely describe the sequential execution, but could not be identified without testing. In contrast, our testing procedure identifies opportunities to *violate* the sequential semantics while maintaining end-to-end functionality.

Parallel runtime systems Systems such as OpenMP allow the programmer to indicate parallelism via a set of annotations, in a manner analogous to ALTER. However, the parallelism offered by ALTER can not be implemented using OpenMP directives. While OpenMP supports DOALL loops and privatized variables, ALTER provides isolated and potentially stale reads of state that is communicated between loop iterations. ALTER is also very different from OpenMP in that (i) ALTER supports various notions of conflicts and provides runtime support to roll back and retry iterations, (ii) it efficiently and automatically handles full state replication without requiring annotations for shared and private variables, and (iii) ALTER is deterministic: for a given thread count and chunk factor, ALTER always produces the same output for a given input, while parallelization with OpenMP may admit non-deterministic data races.

STAPL [3] is a runtime library that provides parallel algorithms and containers for collection classes; it is a superset of the standard template library (STL) in C++. STAPL overlaps our goal of providing customized collection classes that are suitable for parallelization. However, this is only a small piece of our overall system. We utilize the custom collection classes to enable a new execution model and a deterministic parallel runtime for discovering hidden parallelism via testing.

We note that there are other parallelization frameworks that use a process-based model to ensure isolation. These include (1) the behavior oriented parallelization framework [15] that uses process-based isolation for speculative parallelization, and (2) the Grace runtime system [6] that forks off threads as processes in an attempt to avoid common atomicity related concurrency errors.

Test-driven parallelization Closely related to our work is the QuickStep system for parallelizing programs with statistical accuracy tests [29]. QuickStep searches for DOALL parallelism by annotating loops with OpenMP directives and evaluating if the resulting parallelization is acceptably accurate for the inputs in the test suite. Quickstep also explores synchronization, replication, and caching transformations that could improve accuracy or performance, and provides metrics and tools to help programmers find an acceptable parallelization. Both systems share the philosophy of violating dependences to enable new parallelism detection. One difference is in the run-time system: while QuickStep utilizes OpenMP, we propose a new runtime system that enables the `StaleReads` execution model and other benefits (see above). A second difference is that ALTER is designed to provide deterministic execution and freedom from data races, while QuickStep is designed to generate potentially nondeterministic parallel programs that may contain data races. As a consequence, ALTER uses a single execution to verify correctness on a given input, while QuickStep performs multiple test executions on the same input to determine if a candidate parallelization respects the accuracy bounds with acceptable probability.

Profile-driven and speculative parallelization Profile driven parallelization tools augment compiler driven transformations by using profile inputs to identify `DoAll` and pipeline parallelism in programs [30, 41, 43]. Speculative parallelization [11, 15, 27, 33, 35, 44] is a related form of parallelization that can be enabled by profile-driven tools. Execution of speculatively parallelized programs typically requires support for thread level speculation either in hardware [21, 39] or in software [11, 15, 27, 35, 42]. To the best of our knowledge, all existing speculative and profile-driven tools that exploit inter-iteration parallelism in loops are restricted to guarantee sequential semantics for the loop. By contrast, ALTER exposes and exploits alternative semantics, including the ability to permit (bounded) stale reads for certain values while nonetheless preserving overall functionality. In this way, the `StaleReads` execution model is fundamentally different from speculation. While frameworks such as behavior oriented parallelism [15] may have similar goals at the abstract level, thus far (in their concrete form) they have utilized speculation that respects program dependences.

Transactional memory systems Software transactions have been proposed as an alternative to traditional lock-based programming. A transactional memory system [18, 25] is needed to support concurrent execution of software transactions. Transactional memory systems try to provide conflict serializability as the correctness criterion, however the exact semantics provided by most STMs is captured better by a correctness guarantee referred to as `opacity` [16]. Recently, researchers have also explored snapshot isolation as a correctness criterion in STMs [14, 37]; however, the experiments to date have utilized a transactional programming model where the programmer thinks in terms of explicit transactions. ALTER targets existing software and helps to identify whether loops can tolerate stale reads and reordering of iterations.

Language constructs for expressing parallelism Many researchers have investigated new programming language constructs for expressing parallelism. Most of these constructs introduce richer semantics that cannot be detected by existing parallelization tools. The Galois programming system introduces constructs to iterate over sets (optimistic iterators) and allows programmers to specify conditions under which methods commute [23, 24]. With these constructs a programmer can write loops whose iterations can execute optimistically in parallel and commit out of order as long as there are no commutativity violations. The revisions programming model [8] exposes language constructs through which a programmer can assign special isolation types to variables and specify merge functions for them. These merge functions are applied at the end of a parallel section of computation. ALTER's contribution is in determining if existing sequential programs are amenable to richer forms of parallelism, without intervention on the part of the programmer. It also proposes the `StaleReads` execution model, which to our knowledge has not been used as a general approach for loop parallelization.

9. Conclusions

Despite decades of research on automatic parallelization, the results achievable by a compiler are rarely comparable to that of a human. We believe that one of the primary limitations holding compilers back is their conservative treatment of memory dependences. Though humans can and do re-arrange dependences – which are often artifacts of the implementation, or non-essential elements of the algorithm – compilers, for the most part, do not.

In this paper, we take a first step towards bridging this gap by proposing ALTER: a system that violates certain memory dependences in order to expose and exploit parallelism in loops. We emphasize that ALTER is not intended to completely replace a human; as its inferences are unsound, we still rely on human judgement to drive the parallelization process. However, ALTER could greatly assist the developer by providing a new set of parallelism primitives as well as suggestions regarding their most effective use.

Our evaluation indicates that the parallelism exploited by ALTER is beyond the reach of existing static and dynamic tools. In particular, for one third of our benchmarks, the use of snapshot isolation – allowing stale reads within loops – enables parallel execution even when prior techniques such as speculative parallelism and out-of-order commit do not.

Acknowledgments

We are very grateful to Sriram Rajamani, R. Govindarajan, Mahmut Kandemir, and the reviewers for their thoughtful feedback.

References

[1] The Parallel Dwarfs Project. `http://paralleldwarfs.codeplex.com`.

[2] F. Aleen and N. Clark. Commutativity Analysis for Software Parallelization: Letting Program Transformations See the Big Picture. In *ASPLOS*, 2009.

[3] P. An, A. Jula, S. Rus, S. Saunders, T. Smith, G. Tanase, N. Thomas, N. Amato, and L. Rauchwerger. STAPL: An Adaptive, Generic Parallel C++ Library. *LNCS*, 2624:195–210, 2003.

[4] K. Asanovic, R. Bodik, J. Demmel, T. Keaveny, K. Keutzer, J. Kubiatowicz, N. Morgan, D. Patterson, K. Sen, J. Wawrzynek, D. Wessel, and K. Yelick. A view of the parallel computing landscape. *CACM*, 52(10), 2009.

[5] E. Berger, K. McKinley, R. Blumofe, and P. Wilson. Hoard: A Scalable Memory Allocator for Multithreaded Applications. In *ASPLOS*, 2000.

[6] E. Berger, T. Yang, T. Liu, and G. Novark. Grace: Safe Multithreaded Programming for C/C++. In *OOPSLA*, 2009.

[7] M. Bridges, N. Vachharajani, Y. Zhang, T. Jablin, and D. August. Revisiting the sequential programming model for multi-core. In *MICRO*, 2007.

[8] S. Burckhardt, A. Baldassion, and D. Leijen. Concurrent Programming with Revisions and Isolation Types. In *OOPSLA*, 2010.

[9] M. Burke and R. Cytron. Interprocedural dependence analysis and parallelization. *SIGPLAN Notices*, 2004.

[10] M. Carlisle. *Olden: Parallelizing Programs with Dynamic Data Structures on Distributed-Memory Machines*. PhD thesis, Princeton University, June 1996.

[11] T. Chen, F. Min, V. Nagarajan, and R. Gupta. Copy or Discard Execution Model for Speculative Parallelization on Multicores. In *MICRO*, 2008.

[12] A. Darte, Y. Robert, and F. Vivien. *Scheduling and Automatic Parallelization*. Birkhauser Boston, 1st edition, 2000.

[13] K. Datta. *Auto-tuning Stencil Codes for Cache-Based Multicore Platforms*. PhD thesis, UC Berkeley, December 2009.

[14] R. Dias, J. Seco, and J. Lourenco. Snapshot isolation anomalies detection in software transactional memory. In *INForum*, 2010.

[15] C. Ding, X. Shen, K. Kelsey, C. Tice, R. Huang, and C. Zhang. Software Behavior Oriented Parallelization. In *PLDI*, 2007.

[16] R. Guerraoui and M. Kapalka. On the Correctness of Transactional Memory. In *PPoPP*, 2008.

[17] M. Hall, J. Anderson, S. Amarasinghe, B. Murphy, S. Liao, E. Bugnion, and M. Lam. Maximizing Multiprocessor Performance with the SUIF Compiler. *IEEE Computer*, 29:84–89, 1996.

[18] M. Herlihy and J. E. B. Moss. Transactional Memory: Architectural Support for Lock-free Data Structures. In *ISCA*, 1993.

[19] W. Hwu, S. Ryoo, S. Ueng, J. Kelm, I. Gelado, S. Stone, R. Kidd, S. Baghsorkhi, A. Mahesri, S. Tsao, N. Navarro, S. Lumetta, M. Frank, and S. Patel. Implicitly parallel programming models for thousand-core microprocessors. In *DAC*, 2007.

[20] K. Kennedy and J. Allen. *Optimizing Compilers for Modern Architectures: A Dependence-Based Approach*. Morgan Kaufmann Publishers Inc., 2002.

[21] V. Krishnan and J. Torrellas. A Chip-Multiprocessor Architecture with Speculative Multithreading. *IEEE Trans. on Computers*, 48(9), 1999.

[22] M. Kulkarni, M. Burtscher, C. Cascaval, and K. Pingali. Lonestar: A Suite of Parallel Irregular Programs. In *ISPASS*, 2009.

[23] M. Kulkarni, K. Pingali, G. Ramanarayanan, B. Walter, K. Bala, and L. P. Chew. Optimistic Parallelism Benefits from Data Partitioning. In *ASPLOS*, 2008.

[24] M. Kulkarni, K. Pingali, B. Walter, G. Ramanarayanan, K. Bala, and L. P. Chew. Optimistic Parallelism Requires Abstractions. In *PLDI*, 2007.

[25] J. Larus and R. Rajwar. *Transactional Memory (Synthesis Lectures on Computer Architecture)*. Morgan & Claypool Publishers, 2007.

[26] D. Maydan, S. Amarasinghe, and M. Lam. Array data-flow analysis and its use in array privatization. In *POPL*, 1993.

[27] M. Mehrara, J. Hao, P. Hsu, and S. Mahlke. Parallelizing Sequential applications on Commodity Hardware using a Low-cost Software Transactional Memory. In *PLDI*, 2009.

[28] C. Minh, J. Chung, C. Kozyrakis, and K. Olukotun. STAMP: Stanford Transactional Applications for Multi-Processing. In *IISWC*, 2008.

[29] S. Misailovic, D. Kim, and M. Rinard. Parallelizing Sequential Programs With Statistical Accuracy Tests. Technical Report MIT-CSAIL-TR-2010-038, MIT, Aug 2010.

[30] S. Moon and M. W. Hall. Evaluation of Predicated Array Data-flow Analysis for Automatic Parallelization. In *PPoPP*, 1999.

[31] W. Press, S. Teukolsky, W. Vetterling, and B. Flannery. *Numerical Recipes in C*. Cambridge University Press, 2nd edition, 1992.

[32] W. Pugh and D. Wonnacott. Constraint-based array dependence analysis. *ACM TOPLAS.*, 1998.

[33] E. Raman, N. Vachharajani, R. Rangan, and D. August. SPICE: Speculative Parallel Iteration Chunk Execution. In *CGO*, 2008.

[34] L. Rauchwerger and D. Padua. The Privatizing DOALL Test: A Run-Time Technique for DOALL Loop Identification and Array Privatization. In *ICS*, 1994.

[35] L. Rauchwerger and D. Padua. The LRPD Test: Speculative Run-Time Parallelization of Loops with Privatization and Reduction Parallelization. In *PLDI*, 1995.

[36] T. Reps. Undecidability of context-sensitive data-independence analysis. *ACM TOPLAS*, 2000.

[37] T. Riegel, C. Fetzer, and P. Felber. Snapshot isolation for software transactional memory. In *TRANSACT*, 2006.

[38] M. Rinard and P. Diniz. Commutativity Analysis: A New Analysis Technique for Parallelizing Compilers. *ACM TOPLAS*, 19(6), 1997.

[39] G. Sohi, S. Breach, and T. N. Vijaykumar. Multiscalar Processors. In *ISCA*, 1995.

[40] R. Tarjan. A Unified Approach to Path Problems. *J. ACM*, 28(3), 1981.

[41] W. Thies, V. Chandrasekhar, and S. Amarasinghe. A Practical Approach to Exploiting Coarse-Grained Pipeline Parallelism in C Programs. In *MICRO*, 2007.

[42] C. Tian, M. Feng, and R. Gupta. Supporting Speculative Parallelization in the Presence of Dynamic Data Structures. In *PLDI*, 2010.

[43] G. Tournavitis, Z. Wang, B. Franke, and M. O'Boyle. Towards a Holistic Approach to Auto-parallelization: Integrating Profile-driven Parallelism Detection and Machine-learning Based Mapping. *PLDI*, 2009.

[44] N. Vachharajani, R. Rangan, E. Raman, M. Bridges, G. Ottoni, and D. August. Speculative Decoupled Software Pipelining. In *PACT*, 2007.

[45] H. Vandierendonck, S. Rul, and K. Bosschere. The Paralax infrastructure: automatic parallelization with a helping hand. In *PACT*, 2010.

Path-based Inductive Synthesis for Program Inversion

Saurabh Srivastava
University of California, Berkeley
saurabhs@cs.berkeley.edu

Sumit Gulwani
Microsoft Research, Redmond
sumitg@microsoft.com

Swarat Chaudhuri
Pennsylvania State University
swarat@cse.psu.edu

Jeffrey S. Foster
University of Maryland, College Park
jfoster@cs.umd.edu

Abstract

In this paper, we investigate the problem of semi-automated inversion of imperative programs, which has the potential to make it much easier and less error prone to write programs that naturally pair as inverses, such as insert/delete operations, compressors/decompressors, and so on. Viewing inversion as a subproblem of program synthesis, we propose a novel synthesis technique called Path-based Inductive Synthesis (PINS) and apply it to inversion. PINS starts from a program P and a template T for its inverse. PINS then iteratively refines the space of template instantiations by exploring paths in the composition of P and T with symbolic execution. PINS uses an SMT solver to intelligently guide the refinement process, based on the paths explored so far. The key idea motivating this approach is the *small path-bound hypothesis*: that the behavior of a program can be summarized with a small, carefully chosen set of its program paths.

We evaluated PINS by using it to invert 14 programs such as compressors (e.g., Lempel-Ziv-Welch), encoders (e.g., UUEncode), and arithmetic operations (e.g., vector rotation). Most of these examples are difficult or impossible to invert using prior techniques, but PINS was able to invert all of them. We also found that a semi-automated technique we developed to *mine* a template from the program to be inverted worked well. In our experiments, PINS takes between one second to thirty minutes to synthesize inverses. We believe this proof-of-concept implementation demonstrates the viability of the PINS approach to program synthesis.

Categories and Subject Descriptors I.2.2 [*Automatic Programming*]: Program Synthesis; D.2.5 [*Testing and Debugging*]: Symbolic Execution

General Terms Languages, Algorithms, Theory

Keywords PINS, Program Inversion, Inductive Synthesis, Symbolic execution, Testing-inspired Synthesis

1. Introduction

Recently, there has been significant interest in *program synthesis*, in which an automated tool helps the programmer derive program source code from its specification [28, 27, 38, 33, 26, 13]. One particularly interesting synthesis subproblem is *program inversion*, which is the task of constructing a P^{-1} given a program P such that executing P followed by P^{-1} is the identity function. Pairs of inverses are quite common in software, e.g., insert/delete operations on data structures, encryption/decryption, compression/decompression, rollback in transactions, etc.. Automatic program inversion could potentially allow programmers to write only one of each inverse pair, halving the time required to write and maintain such code and eliminating bugs due to inconsistencies between the inverses.

However, existing program synthesis techniques are not well-suited to the inversion task. Proof-theoretic synthesis [38] requires inferring loop invariants, which are unrealistic for programs such as compressors or encoders. Counterexample-guided inductive synthesis [33] requires finitizing the domain (e.g., specifying a bound on loop unrollings and lengths of arrays), and we have found this is a significant burden. Other approaches that are specifically for inversion, rather than general program synthesis, are either hard to implement [8, 12] or are quite restricted in the programs that can be inverted [11, 24, 41, 11].

In this paper, we present a new program synthesis algorithm, *Path-based inductive synthesis (PINS)*, that takes a major step in addressing these challenges. At a high level, the PINS algorithm is straightforward. It iteratively uses symbolic execution to simulate paths through a known program P concatenated with a *template* of an unknown program P^{-1}. The template contains an ordinary program, except it can contain unknown expressions and predicates, i.e., "holes" that need to be filled in. The template also includes sets Π_e of candidate expressions and Π_p of candidate predicates that can instantiate unknowns. PINS uses the *path conditions* generated from symbolic execution to create a query for an SMT solver, and the solution of the query assigns elements of Π_e and Π_p to the unknowns such that P followed by P^{-1} is an inverse along the corresponding paths.

The key idea that underlies PINS is what we call the *small path-bound hypothesis*: for many programs, all behavior can be summarized by examining a small, carefully chosen set of its program paths. This same hypothesis underlies program testing, and just as in testing, it is critical that PINS picks the right set of paths to explore—and this is potentially quite challenging in synthesis, in which we are trying to find useful paths through a program with unknowns. Thus, PINS includes a heuristic technique that tries to guide symbolic execution down program paths likely to reinforce correct solutions and eliminate incorrect solutions. This heuristic helps ensure that when PINS finishes, its output is highly likely (though not guaranteed) to be correct. To further validate correctness, the programmer can use a range of techniques. In our experiments, we used manual code inspection, testing with concrete instantiations of the paths explored by PINS, and bounded model checking [1] to validate PINS's output.

PINS has a number of attractive features compared to other synthesis approaches. First, by using symbolic execution, PINS is able to reason about program paths precisely, but without needing

PLDI'11, June 4–8, 2011, San Jose, California, USA.

strong loop invariants that prove functional correctness. Second, PINS need not finitize the problem domain, since it relies on SMT solving. Finally, SMT solving has another benefit: it allows PINS to model external library functions with axioms, rather than needing source code. For example, we can add axioms about string library functions such as $\forall s, c : \texttt{strlen}(\texttt{append}(s, c)) = \texttt{strlen}(s) + 1$, where s and c are string and character types, respectively. This makes the synthesis task smaller and more modular.

One challenge in using PINS, or any other template-based synthesis approach (e.g., proof-theoretic synthesis [38], invariant-based synthesis for hybrid systems [39] or Sketching [33]), is determining what template to use. For program inversion, we have developed a semi-automated technique for *mining* the template from the program to be inverted. In our approach, an automated tool generates initial guesses for Π_p and Π_e based on the original program text, and the programmer similarly constructs a template program based on the control flow of the original program. The user then runs PINS, using its output to further guide manual refinement of the template. We have found that this approach is much easier than other synthesis techniques that require constructing a template from scratch [38, 39, 33].

We implemented PINS and used it to invert 14 small but complex programs ranging in size from 5 to 25 lines of code. Our benchmarks include several compressors (e.g., Lempel-Ziv-Welch), encoders (e.g., UUEncode), and arithmetic operations (e.g., rotation of a vector). For these benchmarks, PINS worked well in reducing the huge space of possible template instantiations to only a few final candidates. In 11 cases, PINS produced 1 candidate inverse, which was correct. In the remaining 3 cases, PINS produced at most 4 candidates, at least one of which was correct.

For these benchmarks, we found that our semi-automated template mining strategy worked well; we needed only a few changes from the initial template for synthesis to succeed. We also found that the ability to add axioms was critical for our benchmarks, 8 of which called external libraries.

Our results also support the small path-bound hypothesis. Synthesizing inverses for our benchmarks required exploring between 1 and 14 paths, with a median of 5 paths. The running time of PINS varied significantly, ranging from 1 second to 30 minutes. The high variability is due to the large semantic differences between programs and the unpredictable nature of SMT/SAT solving. More engineering may reduce these times much further, but we think that for a prototype, these times are still encouraging, especially as programmer time is far more expensive than processing time.

We believe that PINS takes an important step forward in program synthesis, and presents a promising new approach to the program inversion program.

2. Path-based Inductive Synthesis

We begin our presentation by describing the PINS algorithm. As a running example, we will consider synthesizing an inverse to the function shown in Figure 1, which performs in-place run-length encoding of an input array A of length n. The function imperatively updates the arrays A (destructively) and N to hold the compressed output and the count of how often each compressed element appeared in the input, respectively. The output variable m gives the length of the compressed output. Our aim is to invert this function, i.e., to produce code that generates a new A' to contain the original contents that were in A, using the counts in N.

2.1 Synthesis templates

To constrain the search space for synthesis, PINS uses a *synthesis template* supplied by the programmer. In PINS, a template is a triple (P, Π_e, Π_p), where P is a program that may contain *unknown expressions* ε and *unknown predicates* ρ, and Π_e and Π_p are sets

```
runlength(inout datatype *A, in int n,
          out int *N, out int m)
{
   int i,r;
   assume(n ≥ 0);
   i:=0;
   m:=0;
   while (i < n)
      r := 1;
      while (i + 1 < n ∧ A[i] = A[i + 1])
         r := r + 1; i := i + 1;
      A[m] := A[i];
      N[m] := r;
      m := m + 1;
      i := i + 1;
}
```

Figure 1. In-place run length encoding of an array A of n data elements, where the encoded output is of length m. Another output array N holds the counts.

of expressions and predicates (without unknowns) that ε and ρ, respectively, may range over. Formally, template programs P are defined by the following language:

$$\begin{array}{rcl} P, s & ::= & x, \ldots, x := e, \ldots, e \mid s; s \mid \texttt{if}(*)\ s\ \texttt{else}\ s \\ & & \mid \texttt{while}(*)\ s \mid \texttt{assume}(p) \mid \texttt{exit} \mid \texttt{in}(x, ..) \mid \texttt{out}(x, ..) \\ e & ::= & \varepsilon \mid x \mid e\ op_a\ e \mid \texttt{sel}(e, e) \mid \texttt{upd}(e, e, e) \mid \mathbf{f}(\vec{e}) \\ p & ::= & \rho \mid * \mid e\ op_r\ e \end{array}$$

Program statements consist of parallel assignments to variables, sequencing, conditionals, while loops, and assume statements. We also add a form exit, to mark the exit of the program, and in and out, which indicate which program variables are inputs and outputs, respectively. These last two forms are used to help construct the synthesis template (Section 3).

Note that conditionals and loops are non-deterministic in our language. As is standard, we can encode $\texttt{if}(p)\ s_1\ \texttt{else}\ s_2$ in our language as $\texttt{if}(*)\ (\texttt{assume}(p); s_1)\ \texttt{else}\ (\texttt{assume}(\neg p); s_2)$, and $\texttt{while}(p)\ s$ as $(\texttt{while}(*)\ (\texttt{assume}(p); s)); \texttt{assume}(\neg p)$. For notational convenience, we may use the skip statement as well, which can be modeled in the language as assume(true).

Expressions may either be unknown expressions ε, variables x, arithmetic operations $e\ op_a\ e$, array reads $\texttt{sel}(e_1, e_2)$ (read element e_2 from array e_1), non-destructive array writes $\texttt{upd}(e_1, e_2, e_3)$ (return a new array that is the same as e_1, except element e_2 has value e_3), and uninterpreted function symbols $\mathbf{f}$ (used to model external library calls). Similarly, predicates used in assume expressions may be unknown ρ or known predicates p, which are known expressions compared with relational operators op_r. Then Π_e is a set of expressions that do not contain occurrences of ε, and analogously for Π_p.

As mentioned in the introduction, for program inversion we construct a template for the inverse and then concatenate that to the original program to produce the synthesis template for PINS. We defer discussion of exactly how the inverse template is constructed until Section 3. For our running example, the input to PINS is shown in Figure 2. For clarity, we have written while loops with guards, though as mentioned above we actually encode these with non-deterministic choice and assume. Lines 1–11 are the same as in Figure 1, except they have been translated into our formal language. Lines 12–18 contain the inverse template. Notice that in this particular example, the inverse template has essentially the same shape as the original program, and that the primed variables used by the inverse arise from (unprimed) variables used in the original program. The sets Π_e and Π_p range over expressions extracted from the original program, but translated to work over both primed and selected unprimed variable names.

```
in(A,n);
assume(n ≥ 0);
i,m:=0,0;
while (i < n)
    r := 1;
    while (i+1 < n ∧ sel(A,i) = sel(A,i+1))
        r,i := r+1,i+1;
    A := upd(A,m,sel(A,i));
    N := upd(N,m,r);
    m,i := m+1, i+1;
out(A,N,m);
i',m' := ε1,ε2;
while (ρ1)
    r' := ε3;
    while (ρ2)
        r',i',A' := ε4,ε5,ε6;
    m' := ε7;
out(A',i'); exit;
```

$$\Pi_e = \left\{ \begin{array}{c} 0, 1, m'+1, m'-1, r'+1, r'-1, i'+1, i'-1, \\ upd(A', m', sel(A, i')), upd(A', i', sel(A, m')), sel(N, m') \end{array} \right\}$$

$$\Pi_p = \{\ m' < m, r' > 0, sel(A', i') = sel(A', i'+1)\ \}$$

Figure 2. Program from Figure 1 composed with the template.

ASSN
$$\frac{v_i = V(x_i)+1 \quad V' = V[x_i \mapsto v_i] \quad \forall i \in 1..n \qquad \phi' = \phi \wedge \bigwedge_{j \in 1..n} (x_j^{v_j} = e_j^V)}{S;\Phi \vdash \langle (x_1, \ldots x_n := e_1, \ldots, e_n); \phi; V\rangle \rightarrow \langle \phi'; V'\rangle}$$

ASSUME
$$\frac{\phi \wedge (S(p))^V \not\Rightarrow \texttt{false} \qquad \phi' = \phi \wedge p^V}{S;\Phi \vdash \langle \texttt{assume}(p); \phi; V\rangle \rightarrow \langle \phi'; V\rangle}$$

SEQ
$$\frac{S;\Phi \vdash \langle s_1; \phi; V\rangle \rightarrow \langle \phi_1; V_1\rangle \qquad S;\Phi \vdash \langle s_2; \phi_1; V_1\rangle \rightarrow \langle \phi_2; V_2\rangle}{S;\Phi \vdash \langle (s_1; s_2); \phi; V\rangle \rightarrow \langle \phi_2; V_2\rangle}$$

EXIT
$$\frac{\phi \notin \Phi}{S;\Phi \vdash \langle \texttt{exit}; \phi; V\rangle \rightarrow \langle \phi; V\rangle}$$

COND
$$\frac{S;\Phi \vdash \langle s_i; \phi; V\rangle \rightarrow \langle \phi'; V'\rangle \qquad i = 1 \text{ or } 2}{S;\Phi \vdash \langle (\texttt{if}(*)\ s_1 \texttt{ else } s_2); \phi; V\rangle \rightarrow \langle \phi'; V'\rangle}$$

LOOP
$$\frac{S;\Phi \vdash \langle \texttt{if}(*)\ (s; \texttt{while}(*)\ s) \texttt{ else skip}; \phi; V\rangle \rightarrow \langle \phi'; V'\rangle}{S;\Phi \vdash \langle \texttt{while}(*)\ s; \phi; V\rangle \rightarrow \langle \phi'; V'\rangle}$$

INOUT
$$\frac{io \in \texttt{in}, \texttt{out}}{S;\Phi \vdash \langle io(x, ..); \phi; V\rangle \rightarrow \langle \phi; V\rangle}$$

Figure 3. Symbolic execution with unknowns.

2.2 Symbolic execution of templates

As discussed in the introduction, PINS iteratively uses *symbolic execution* to simulate chosen paths through a template. Symbolic execution has been studied extensively in the literature [25], but our use of symbolic execution has an interesting twist: we need to simulate programs containing unknowns. What makes this possible is that the only unknowns we permit are expressions and predicates, both of which are pure, and thus their evaluation does not affect the program state.

At each step of symbolic execution, we maintain a *path condition* ϕ that describes the path taken and the current and past state of all program variables. To distinguish different definitions of the same variable, we maintain a *version map* V that assigns a version number to each variable. As variables are reassigned, their version numbers monotonically increase, similarly to variable renaming in static single assignment form. As a slight abuse of notation, we will use the version map 0 to denote assigning all variables the version number 0. When an unknown expression ε or predicate ρ is evaluated, we simply pair it with the version map V at that program point, which we write as ε^V or ρ^V. Then at the end of symbolic execution, since the path condition contains the history of all variables, it gives us sufficient information to interpret uses of ε and ρ at any point during the prior execution. For notational convenience, we use the same evaluation strategy for known expressions and predicates, and we write e^V or p^V for the (known or unknown) expression or predicate evaluated under version map V.

As symbolic execution is a subroutine in PINS, it takes two auxiliary inputs. First, our symbolic executor is given a *solution* S, which is an assignment from unknown expressions and predicates to known expressions and predicates, respectively. The solution arises from a previous iteration of PINS, and is used to guide symbolic execution down paths that tend to more quickly refine the solution space; we discuss this further in Section 2.3. Second, our symbolic executor is given a *path condition set* Φ, which is the set of path conditions that have been previously explored and hence should not be simulated again.

Figure 3 formalizes our symbolic executor as a judgment of the form $S;\Phi \vdash \langle s; \phi; V\rangle \rightarrow \langle \phi'; V'\rangle$, which says that, using solution S and avoiding path condition set Φ, evaluating statement s beginning with path condition ϕ and version map V yields a new path condition ϕ' and version map V'.

We discuss the rules briefly. In Rule ASSN, we increment the version numbers of all assigned variables to yield a new version map V', and we create a new path condition ϕ' containing equalities for the newly assigned variables. Notice here we pair the expressions e_j with the old version map V, since the e_j are evaluated at the start of the assignment.

In Rule ASSUME, we write $S(p)$ to mean the predicate p with unknowns replaced according to S. Note that S may be a partial map, and if S does not provide a mapping for p then $S(p)$ equals p. Thus, this rule requires that the conjunction of the current path condition and the assumed predicate is satisfiable according to the solution. In our implementation, we use an SMT query to determine the satisfiability of this constraint.

Rule SEQ is standard. Rule EXIT ensures that the path has not previously been explored. Rule COND non-deterministically executes one of its branches. Rule LOOP unrolls a loop one time. Finally, Rule INOUT ignores in and out expressions, which are only used for constructing the synthesis template and the specification formula for inversion.

2.3 Synthesis algorithm

Given a synthesis template P, the goal of PINS is to find a *solution* S that assigns known expressions and predicates to unknown expressions and predicates, such that $S(P)$ satisfies a given specification. For program inversion, the specification is particularly simple—at a high level, the program should be the identity function. In our running example, at the end of execution, the array A should contain the same elements as at the beginning. While in this paper our focus is on program inversion, PINS is a general algorithm, and we believe it can also be used for other synthesis problems.

The PINS algorithm is shown as Algorithm 1. The input to the algorithm is a synthesis template (P, Π_e, Π_p), a specification *spec*, and a bound m on the number of solutions to request from

Input: Synthesis template (P, Π_e, Π_p), specification *spec*, bound m on number of solutions from solver.
Output: Solution S or *"No Solution."*

```
1  begin
2      Φ := ∅;
3      C := terminate(P);
4      while (true) do
5          sols := solve(C, Π_p, Π_e, m);
6          if sols = ∅ then
7              return "No Solution"; /* Refine abstraction */
8          if stabilized(sols, m) then
9              return sols;
10         S := pickOne(sols);
11         S; Φ ⊢ ⟨P; true; 0⟩ → ⟨φ; V'⟩;
12         Φ := Φ ∪ {φ};
13         C := C ∧ safepath(φ, V', spec);
14 end
```

Algorithm 1: The `PINS` algorithm.

the solver (discussed below). We next give an overview of the algorithm, deferring details of the subroutines `terminate`, `solve`, `stabilized`, `pickOne`, and `safepath` until after the overview.

Throughout its execution, `PINS` maintains a set Φ of program paths that have been symbolically executed so far, and a constraint C that includes constraints gathered from prior symbolic executions. As the algorithm progresses, Φ increases and C accumulates additional constraints. Φ is initially empty, and C is initially set to `terminate`(P), which constrains loops in P to terminate.

The main loop of `PINS` iteratively refines the space of solutions as follows. On line 5, we compute (at most) m solutions to the constraints C, using Π_p and Π_e for the possible values of unknown predicates and expressions in C. If the resulting set of solutions *sols* is empty, then there is no valid template instantiation that satisfies *spec*. Typically this means the template needs to be refined; we describe this process in Section 3.

If *sols* has `stabilized`, meaning it did not change from the last iteration, then we exit and return *sols*. Otherwise, we refine the solution space. On line 10, we set S to be one of the computed solutions, chosen by the heuristic `pickOne`. Then we symbolically execute P, using the solution S to guide the execution, and beginning with the path condition `true` and the version map that assigns version 0 to all variables, which we write simply as 0. Recall that in Rule ASSUME of Figure 3, we require that the guard p is satisfiable according to S—thus, the path taken in the symbolic execution on line 11 is a feasible path in the program $S(P)$. As we will discuss below, this means that the path taken will tend to generate constraints that either reinforce S if it is a valid solution, or contradict S if it is an invalid solution.

Finally, we add the path condition ϕ from the symbolic execution to Φ, and we add to C the constraint `safepath`$(\phi, V', spec)$, which specifies that the path taken meets the specification *spec*. We then repeat this process until no solutions are possible, or the set of solutions has stabilized.

Next, we discuss the subroutines used by `PINS` in more detail and how `PINS` handles uninterpreted functions.

Safety constraints The constraint generated by `safepath` on Line 13 specifies that the symbolic execution, which generated path condition ϕ and final version map V', satisfies *spec*:

$$\texttt{safepath}(\phi, V', spec) \doteq \forall X : \phi \Rightarrow spec^{V'}$$

where X is the set of all program variables at all versions. Notice that in $spec^{V'}$, program variables in *spec* will be interpreted in terms of V', i.e., at their final values at the end of execution.

EXAMPLE 1. *Suppose in Figure 2 we take a path that immediately exits the loop on line 4, enters the loop on line 13, exits the loop on line 15, exits the loop on line 13, and then exits the program. The safety constraint (left) generated for this path (right) is:*

$$\begin{array}{ll}
n^0 \geq 0 \wedge i^1 = 0 \wedge m^1 = 0 \wedge & \ldots n \geq 0; i, m := 0, 0; \\
i^1 \geq n^0 \wedge i'^1 = \varepsilon_1^{V_1} \wedge m'^1 = \varepsilon_2^{V_1} \wedge & \ldots i \geq n; i', m' := \varepsilon_1, \varepsilon_2; \\
\rho_1^{V_2} \wedge r'^1 = \varepsilon_3^{V_2} \wedge & \ldots \rho_1; r' := \varepsilon_3; \\
\neg\rho_2^{V_3} \wedge m'^2 = \varepsilon_7^{V_3} \wedge & \ldots \neg\rho_2; m' := \varepsilon_7; \\
\neg\rho_1^{V_4} & \ldots \neg\rho_1 \\
\Rightarrow spec^{V_4} &
\end{array}$$

where we abbreviate the version maps as $V_1 = \{n \mapsto 0, m \mapsto 1, i \mapsto 1\} \cup 0$, $V_2 = V_1 \cup \{m' \mapsto 1, i' \mapsto 1\}$, $V_3 = V_2 \cup \{r' \mapsto 1\}$, *and* V_4 *is* V_3 *but with* $m' \mapsto 2$. *The identity specification spec is derived syntactically from* `in`(A, n) *and* `out`(A', i')) *as* $n^0 = i'^{V_4} \wedge \forall k : 0 \leq k < n^0 \Rightarrow A^0[k] = A'^{V_4}[k]$. *This path turns out to be infeasible for the actual synthesized inverse (shown in Section 3), but this does not mean that the path is redundant during synthesis. To the contrary, the path imposes constraints on the unknown expressions and predicates that eliminate any candidate for which this path is feasible, thereby pruning the search space.*

Termination constraints The termination constraints generated on Line 3 serve two important purposes. First, they prevent synthesis of programs that diverge, since such programs trivially satisfy any partial specification but are uninteresting in this domain. Second, they ensure that the symbolic execution runs on Line 11 themselves terminate, since those runs are guided by a solution to the constraints.

We generate termination constraints by reasoning about each loop separately. Consider a loop $l = $ `while`$(*)\{$`assume`$(\rho_l); B_l\}$, where the guard ρ_l is an unknown and the body is B_l. We assume there is a corresponding ranking function η_l that is an unknown, ranging over a set of expressions Π_r (discussed below). We impose two kinds of constraints on η_l to ensure the loop terminates.

First, we assume the ranking function is related to the loop guard ρ_l, and generate a constraint

$$\texttt{bounded}(l) \doteq \forall X.\ \rho_l^0 \Rightarrow ({\eta_l}^0 \geq 0)$$

that the guard implies a lower bound on the ranking function. Notice that this constraint does not involve any path condition, and hence the relationship it implies must hold across all possible values of the program variables.

Next, we need to generate a constraint that the ranking function decreases on every iteration through the loop. We introduce an *unknown* loop invariant ${\rho'}_l$, and generate the following constraints:

$$\begin{array}{l}
\texttt{decrease}(l) \doteq \\
\quad \bigwedge_{\langle \phi, V \rangle \in init} \forall X.\ \phi \Rightarrow {\rho'}_l^V \quad \wedge \\
\quad \bigwedge_{\langle \phi, V \rangle \in body} \forall X.\ \phi \wedge {\rho'}_l^0 \Rightarrow {\rho'}_l^V \quad \wedge \\
\quad \bigwedge_{\langle \phi, V \rangle \in body} \forall X.\ \phi \wedge \rho_l^0 \wedge {\rho'}_l^0 \Rightarrow {\eta_l}^V < {\eta_l}^0
\end{array}$$

where *body* is a set of tuples $\langle \phi; V \rangle$ from symbolic executions of the loop body, and *init* is a set of tuples from symbolic executions that start at the program entry and end at the loop entry. From top to bottom, these constraints specify that the invariant holds at the beginning of the loop; that it is maintained during an execution of the loop body; and that the invariant and the loop guard imply that the ranking function decreases on each iteration. Note that although these constraints look complex, in fact the loop invariant required for termination is often far simpler than a loop invariant required for functional correctness. For example, typically we only required an invariant that is a linear relation (real programs shown terminating by others [5, 6] illustrate that linear relations typically suffice), and we never required a quantified invariant.

To compute $body$ and $init$, we use two heuristics. First, to compute $body$ we symbolically execute all possible paths through the loop body (starting with the empty path conditions and empty version map 0), always taking the exit branch of any inner loop to keep the set of paths finite. Thus, we are assuming that inner loops do not affect the termination of outer loops. Second, we initialize $init$ to be empty, and each time PINS symbolically executes some path on Line 11, we take the prefix of that path up to the start of the loop, and add the corresponding $init$-related constraint to C. Thus, we are only constraining the invariant to hold on a finite number of paths, rather than on every path, similar to dynamic approaches that infer likely invariants [10].

Other than the (transition) invariant involving `decrease` and `bounded`, in our experiments, additional inductive safety invariants are typically not required to prove termination. (An example of where we might need an inductive invariant, e.g., $C > 0$, might be when $x := x + C$ is the iteration counter increment.) Other work also shows that termination for typical programs can be proven without inductive reasoning [19].In this simpler case, the SMT/SAT solver discovers it can set the invariant to simply be `true`, in which case $\texttt{decrease}(l)$ simplifies to $\bigwedge_{\langle\phi,V\rangle\in body} \forall X : \phi \wedge \rho_l^0 \Rightarrow {\eta_l}^V < {\eta_l}^0$.

Putting `bounded` and `decrease` together, we have

$$\texttt{terminate}(P) \doteq \bigwedge_{l\in\texttt{loops}(P)} \texttt{decrease}(l) \wedge \texttt{bounded}(l)$$

where $\texttt{loops}(P)$ is the set of all loops in P.

EXAMPLE 2. *Consider the loop, let us call it l_1, on Line 13 in Figure 2. The loop guard is ρ_1, and we assume an unknown ranking function η_{l_1}. For clarity we show the simplified version of* `decrease` *(assuming a loop invariant is not required) as above. Then the termination constraint for the loop is:*

$$\rho_1^0 \wedge r'^1 = \varepsilon_3^0 \wedge \neg\rho_2^{V_1} \wedge m'^1 = \varepsilon_7^{V_1} \Rightarrow ({\eta_{l_1}}^{V_2} < {\eta_{l_1}}^0) \quad ..\texttt{decrease}(l_1)$$
$$\rho_1^0 \Rightarrow ({\eta_{l_1}}^0 \geq 0) \quad ..\texttt{bounded}(l_1)$$

where $V_1 = \{r' \mapsto 1\} \cup 0$ and $V_2 = \{m' \mapsto 1\} \cup V_1$. We will show later that the valid inverse to this program instantiates the unknowns as $\{\rho_1 \mapsto (m' < m), \rho_2 \mapsto (r' > 0), \varepsilon_3 \mapsto (\texttt{sel}(N, m')), \varepsilon_7 \mapsto (m' + 1), \eta_l \mapsto (m - m' - 1)\}$ in which case each conjunct reduces as follows. `bounded`*(l) reduces to the following trivial constraint:*

$$(m' < m)^0 \Rightarrow ((m - m' - 1)^0 \geq 0)$$

Also, $\texttt{decrease}(l)$ *reduces to*

$$(m' < m)^0 \wedge r'^1 = (sel(N, m'))^0 \wedge \neg(r' > 0)^{V_1} \wedge m'^1 = (m' + 1)^{V_1}$$
$$\Rightarrow ((m - m' - 1)^{V_2} < (m - m' - 1)^0)$$

which if we keep the relevant conjuncts simplifies to $m'^0 < m^0 \wedge m'^1 = m'^0 + 1 \Rightarrow (m^0 - m'^1 < m^0 - m'^0)$, which holds.

One issue we have not yet discussed is how to determine Π_r, the expressions η_l may range over. We could ask the user to supply Π_r as part of the synthesis template, but we have found that we can derive Π_r as follows: For each inequality in Π_p, we convert it into an equivalent relation of the form $e \geq 0$ using simple symbolic manipulation, and add e to Π_r. For example, if $(n > s) \in \Pi_p$, we convert it to $n - s - 1 \geq 0$ and thus add $n - s - 1$ to Π_r. We found this simple approach to be effective in practice.

Solving for and enumerating m solutions As we can see from the definitions of `safepath` and `terminate`, the constraint C maintained by PINS has the form $\forall X.C'$, where X is the set of program variables (note that we have lifted the quantification over X to the top level). We wish to solve for the unknown predicates and expressions, and thus the `solve` procedure tries to find m solutions for a constraint $\exists \rho_i \varepsilon_j \eta_l \rho_l.\forall X.C'$ where the unknown predicates, expressions, ranking functions, and dynamic invariants can range over Π_p, Π_e, Π_r, and Π_p, respectively.

Our implementation of `solve` builds upon our earlier work, which uses *constraint-based invariant inference* [36, 38, 17, 18]. The invariant inference problem is to solve a constraint of the form $\exists I_k \forall X.vc$, where the I_k are unknowns in a template assumed for the invariant, X is the set of program variables, and vc is a verification condition. Notice that this constraint is similar in shape to the constraints generated by PINS, and thus we can adapt the solving strategy from this prior work to solve our constraints.

Very briefly, constraint-based invariant inference works by calling an SMT solver a polynomial number of times to extract information from each constraint in vc. It then uses that information to construct a SAT formula that contains boolean indicator variables, whose solution maps back to an assignment of each I_k to one of the possible predicates it may range over [36].

During invariant inference using a program's vc (which is a conjunction of implications, each constructed from some fragment of the program), the unknowns I_k in the invariant templates appear at most twice in each vc implication: at the beginning of the loop, and at the end. However, the constraints generated in PINS can include unknown predicates and expressions that are paired with many different version maps. We therefore needed to extend the earlier work to handle version maps. It turns out that the core theory and algorithm we previously developed [36] holds under multiple versions, and so we only need to make the following implementation changes to build `solve`: (a) we added version maps to track states of variables, (b) we incorporated a stack depth parameter so we can distinguish variable versions across recursive calls, and (c) we replaced the verification condition generator with the symbolic executor from Figure 3.

One nice property of using an SMT/SAT-based reduction for `solve` is that we can easily ask for m different solutions from the solver: Given one solution S for C, we can then pass the constraint $C \wedge \bigvee(\alpha_i \neq S(\alpha_i))$ to the solver to get a different solution, where $\alpha_i \in dom(S)$. As we discuss next, we use this enumeration of possible solutions to determine when to halt iteration of PINS.

Stabilization of solutions PINS stops iteration and returns the current set of solutions when that set is the same as in the last iteration and its size is less than m (Line 8). We actually perform this check by comparing the sizes of the current and last value of *sols*—since the set of constraints C is only added to, if the size of *sols* is the same from one iteration to the next, the solutions themselves must also be the same.

When PINS exits, it is not guaranteed that the returned solutions are correct; this should be clear, because PINS typically only explores a subset of the possible paths through the template program. In our experiments, stabilization happened when only one to four solutions remained, and thus PINS winnowed down a very large space of solutions to only a small set of possibilities. Given this set, the programmer can validate the solutions using other approaches, such as as manual inspection, test case generation, or model checking. We discuss these approaches more in Section 2.5.

Picking one solution On Line 10 of the PINS algorithm, we pick one solution out of *sols* for subsequent symbolic execution. Ideally, we will choose an incorrect solution $S_{bad} \in sols$. Since incorrect solutions are usually incorrect on many paths, we expect that if we explore a path that is feasible in S_{bad}, the constraints generated will show that S_{bad} violates *spec*, and thus S_{bad} will be pruned from the search space (as will many more incorrect solutions, most likely). We found that a good heuristic for picking such a solution is to find one that contradicts many constraints in Φ. More precisely, we define

$$\texttt{infeasible}(S) = |\{\phi \in \Phi \mid S(\phi) \Rightarrow \texttt{false}\}|$$

and then pick a solution $S \in sols$ with the highest $\texttt{infeasible}(S)$. We break ties randomly.

To understand why this heuristic works, consider an incorrect solution $S_{bad} \in sols$. Since S_{bad} has survived previous iterations of PINS, it must agree with C, which was generated from many paths. But as the number of paths represented by C increases, the chance that S_{bad} survived because it satisfies *spec* along paths in Φ diminishes. Instead, it is much more likely that S_{bad} survived because the paths in Φ are infeasible in S_{bad}, i.e., $S_{bad}(\phi)$ is false for $\phi \in \Phi$. (Notice this makes the left-hand side of the implication in safepath false, and hence safepath is trivially satisfied.) Thus, if we pick a solution S with a high $\texttt{infeasible}(S)$, there is a good chance it is an incorrect solution.

Note that even if pickOne selects a solution S that is valid, it will still tend to help PINS converge: Since S is valid, it will survive the next round of iteration, but the additional constraints it imposes on the symbolically executed path should help prune out invalid solutions.

We experimentally compared using infeasible to implement pickOne versus random selection, and we found that random selection yields runtimes that are 20% longer than with infeasible.

Axiomatization for modular synthesis Our language for template programs includes calls of the form $\mathbf{f}(\vec{e})$, where $\mathbf{f}$ is an uninterpreted function. In PINS, these are used to model calls to external libraries. Not surprisingly, library calls are common in practice—in our experiments, 8 of 14 benchmarks use library calls.

Because PINS uses SMT/SAT solving over symbolic constraints, we can readily model the behavior of these library calls as additional axioms over the uninterpreted functions, which are passed directly through to the solver. For example, in our experiments we model strings as an abstract data type with three functions append, strlen, and empty that satisfy axioms such as:

$$\texttt{strlen}(\texttt{empty}()) = 0$$
$$\forall x, y.\ \texttt{strlen}(\texttt{append}(x, y)) = \texttt{strlen}(x) + \texttt{strlen}(y)$$
$$\forall x, c.\ \texttt{strlen}(\texttt{append}(x, `c')) = \texttt{strlen}(x) + 1$$

In another instance, we treat an angle as an abstract data type, with trigonometric interface functions cos and sin. We also use such abstract reasoning for operations that are difficult for SMT solvers, e.g, we can add an axiom $\forall x \neq 0.\texttt{mul}(x, \texttt{div}(1, x)) = 1$ to allow enhanced reasoning about multiplication and division.

Overall, we found the ability to axiomitize library calls to be extremely useful, and as a general technique it helps split the synthesis problem into more modular pieces.

2.4 Discussion

Now that we have presented the PINS algorithm, we can revisit the *small path-bound hypothesis* described in the introduction: That for many programs, all behavior can be summarized by examining a small, carefully chosen set of paths.

PINS is designed around this hypothesis. In each iteration, it explores one path, and then uses the constraints $\texttt{safepath}(\phi, V', spec)$ from that exploration to further restrict the solution space. Specifically, PINS finds a solution S to constraints C and uses S to guide symbolic execution on the next iteration. As discussed earlier, if S is incorrect, it will likely be eliminated, and if S is correct, it will be reinforced and will likely eliminate other, incorrect solutions.

Contrast this with, for example, random path exploration. Suppose a template program contains two nested loops in sequence, as does the run-length example in Figure 2. For this example, a single element array results in the identity compression. For a two element array, the elements can be identical or different. Interesting compression happens only in an array of length three or more. So, we would want to explore the program's behavior on such nontrivial cases. But even if we only consider paths that traverse each loop at most three times, there are still 7,225 unique paths. We tried random path exploration, but we found it did not work even for the simplest examples.

The path-bound hypothesis underlies the idea of software testing as well, and we think it holds for synthesis for the same reasons: a small set of carefully chosen paths can cover both the main behavior and the corner cases of a program because that is typically how programs and algorithms are designed. While the set is small, it needs to be carefully constructed. In the case of software testing, these paths are either provided by a human, or possibly through symbolic execution. For synthesis, we propose PINS's mechanism of directing path exploration using candidate solutions.

2.5 Validating solutions

When PINS terminates, it outputs a set of solutions that satisfy all of the program paths explored during iteration. As discussed earlier, this does not guarantee that the synthesized output is correct over all possible paths, and so to gain further confidence in the output solutions, developers can take several additional steps.

First, developers can manually inspect the solutions for correctness. In our experience, this was fairly easy. For 11 out of 14 of our benchmarks, there was a single solution to inspect, and in all 11 cases it was correct. For the other three benchmarks, there were at most 4 remaining solutions. In one benchmark, we found that the remaining two solutions were indeed both valid, while in the other two benchmarks, we found that only one solution was valid. In each of the three cases, the solutions differed in at most one assignment, so it was no harder to understand the set of solutions than a single solution. We believe that PINS helps the programmer because it can be easier to check a program for correctness than create it.

Second, developers can examine the set of paths explored by PINS. For each path condition ϕ, our implementation uses the SMT solver to output a concrete input that will take that path (by solving $(\exists X.\phi)$ restricted to input variables at version 0). These inputs are concrete test cases that necessarily meet the specification, and we found them very helpful in understanding the generated solution. More particularly, the concrete tests helped us intuitively understand the solution's behavior, without needing to trace through long symbolic paths.

Finally, the programmer can use formal verification techniques to validate the solution. For example, in our experiments we tried using the bounded model checker CBMC [1] to check the synthesized inverses, and we succeeded in doing so for 6 of the 14 benchmarks (more details in Section 4). One limitation of CBMC is that it cannot incorporate new axioms (which we use to model library functions); other formal reasoning techniques that can support axioms may be able to verify the remaining cases.

3. Semi-automated template mining

In this section, we discuss how we construct a synthesis template (P, Π_e, Π_p) for a program inverse. Our approach is inspired by an insight from Dijkstra, who observed that in some cases, a program can be inverted by reversing its control flow edges and assignment statements [8]. Based on this observation, we help the programmer derive the template components from the text of the program to be inverted. We should emphasize that our approach is meant to assist the programmer in constructing a template, but it is still up to a human to identify the final template to use.

We begin by automatically *mining* candidate sets for Π_p and Π_e, in three steps. First, we traverse the original program text and return all expressions e that appear in assignments $x := e$, and all predicates p that appear in assumptions $\texttt{assume}(p)$. (Recall this is the only place predicates can appear, since we have transformed conditionals and while loops to use non-deterministic choice and assume.) We also record which variables are used with `in` and `out`. Next, to these sets we apply *projections* that, given an input expression or predicate, return a set of candidate expressions and predicates. For inversion some of the projections we use are the identity $\lambda x.\{x\}$; subtraction inversion $\lambda(e_1 - e_2).\{e_1 + e_2\}$; addition inversion $\lambda(e_1 + e_2).\{e_1 - e_2\}$; copy inversion $\lambda\texttt{upd}(A, i, \texttt{sel}(B, j)).\{\texttt{upd}(B, j, sel(A, i))\}$; and array read $\lambda(\texttt{sel}(A, i)\ op_r\ X).\{\texttt{sel}(A, i)\}$. We also have a projection that uses the `out` call over `ints` to construct a predicate as $\lambda\texttt{out}(m).\{m' < m\}$, for integer m. In essence, these projections capture specific domain knowledge—in this case, that program inversion often requires inverting operations. In total, we use eight projections, including the ones above, for inversion, and we apply all projections to all possible inputs. For example, since identity is one of our projections, all of the expressions and predicates in the original program are included in the output of the projection phase. Finally, we rename the variables after projection to fresh names.

We leave it up to the programmer to choose the structure of the template program P. For inversion, we found that a good starting place is to make a template program with the same control flow structure the original program text, but replacing guards with unknowns. For each assignment statement, we either simply replace its right-hand side with an unknown, or we opt to invert it, replacing an assignment $x := e$ with a parallel assignment of unknowns to all program variables in e. We also decide whether to keep sequences as-is or reverse them. In general, we found it was not hard to use this heuristic to come up with the inversion template. For instance, the inverse template in our running examples (Lines 12–18 in Figure 2) corresponds to the original program, with the control flow as-is in the outer loop and reversed in the inner loop, intuitively because the inverse needs to traverse the array in order, but then undo the run-length encoding (flipping the direction of the inner loop).

The output of the mining procedure is candidates for Π_p and Π_e. In practice, the automatically mined sets are typically too large for synthesis to succeed if we use them directly, as the space of candidate programs is exponentially related to the number of unknowns and the number of predicate and expression options. However, they give the programmer an excellent starting place for developing the final candidate sets for the template. Making some guesses, we pick a subset of the mined sets and a template program, and then attempt synthesis. If `PINS` succeeds, we are done. If `PINS` times out, we choose a smaller or different subset. If `PINS` eliminates all solutions, then we examine the paths explored by `PINS` (see Section 2.5), which typically provide enough information to determine how to change Π_p and Π_e—either by modifying some element in the chosen subset, or by adding some new predicates and expressions that were not mined. In rare cases, these paths also indicate missing assignments, which leads us to add those to the program template. In our experiments, we found that once we identified the correct subset of Π_p and Π_e, we only needed to manually modify at most a few predicates and expressions, which we easily inferred from the paths explored by `PINS`.

Debugging templates using `PINS` The `PINS` approach is also a significant step forward from previous template-based approaches, e.g., Sketch and proof-theoretic synthesis [38], in providing user guidance when synthesis fails. Both these previous systems simply fail with UNSAT when the template is not expressive enough, with little further assistance. In contrast, if PINS terminates without finding an inverse, the paths explored by PINS provide a witness to the non-invertibility using the template—there is no instantiation of the template that makes all of those paths valid inverses. In our experience, by inspecting those paths we can understand why PINS failed, and distinguish cases in which the template needs to be extended from cases in which inversion is impossible. In fact, our initial implementation of LZ77 (see Section 4 and Appendix A) had an off-by-one bug in it, and inspection of the paths generated by PINS led us to find the bug.

Inverting a run-length encoder To give more insight into the process of inverting a program with `PINS`, we describe how to invert the running example from Figure 2. Running the first step of template mining yields the following predicates and expressions:

$$\left\{\begin{array}{c} 0, 1, m+1, r+1, i+1, upd(A, m, sel(A, i)), upd(N, m, r) \\ sel(A, i) = sel(A, i+1), n \geq 0, i+1 < n, i < n \end{array}\right\}$$

Then applying the projections and renaming variables yields:

$$\left\{\begin{array}{c} 0, 1, m'+1, m'-1, r'+1, r'-1, i'+1, i'-1, \\ upd(A', m', sel(A', i')), upd(A', i', sel(A', m')), \\ upd(N, m', r'), sel(N, m') \\ sel(A', i') = sel(A', i'+1), sel(A', i'), \\ m' < m, r' > 0 \end{array}\right\}$$

Notice that since n does not have a corresponding variable in the decoder, all expressions and predicates referring to it are automatically deleted. The last two predicates come from an inversion projector that scans loop iterators and `out` statements. Now we want to remove elements of this set that are unneeded, since they will slow down the synthesis process. We can see right away that we can remove $upd(N, m', r')$, because the decoder will have no need to modify the array of counts N, and $sel(A', i')$, since A' holds the compressed data, which the decoder should only write to and not read from.

Next we select a template program P. Since we expect the decoder to scan its input starting at the beginning, we choose an outer loop that has assignments to the same variables in the same order. Since we expect the decoder to be reversing the compression process for each element, we choose an inner loop where the body is reversed, i.e., for the variables read from $A, r, i,$ and n (A and n are read in the loop guard) their renamed versions A', r' and i' are written to. We then try running `PINS`, and discover that constraint solving has bogged down. With a little more experimentation, we remove the assignment to i', A' and N that corresponds to assignments between lines 8–10 in Figure 2, yielding the template program at the bottom of that figure.

We run `PINS` again, and this time it terminates but claims no solution exists. It provides the three paths that were used to eliminate all solutions. We examine the paths, and notice that the third one enters the inner loop of the template program and assigns to A'. We examine of current Π_e, and we notice that it contains no expressions that read from A, the array containing the compressed data—thus clearly there is a problem, since A' should contain data expanded from A.

As a fix, we opt to change occurrences of $sel(A', x)$ to $sel(A, x)$ within the upd expressions in Π_e, yielding a $\Pi_p \cup \Pi_e$ of

$$\left\{\begin{array}{c} 0, 1, m'+1, m'-1, r'+1, r'-1, i'+1, i'-1, \\ upd(A', m', sel(A, i')), upd(A', i', sel(A, m')), \\ sel(N, m'), sel(A', i') = sel(A', i'+1), m' < m, r' > 0 \end{array}\right\}$$

Using the current template, `PINS` then takes 7 iterations and 36 seconds total to prune the search space down to one candidate:

```
i', m' := 0, 0;
while (m' < m)
    r' := sel(N, m');
    while (r' > 0)
        r', i', A' := r' - 1, i' + 1, upd(A', i', sel(A, m'));
    m' := m' + 1;
```

This is a dramatic reduction in the search space; for this particular example, there were $11^7 \times (2^3)^2 \approx 2^{30}$ possible inverses given the synthesis template. (Note that each unknown predicate can be instantiated with a subset, denoting conjunction, from Π_p.)

We then manually inspected the inverse to ensure it was correct, and we also verified it using CBMC with bounds of 10 loop unrollings and at an array A of length at most 4 ($n \leq 4$). We also attempted to synthesize the inverse using the Sketch tool [33]. We rewrote our template as a sketch (it takes 53 lines of code in that format), and Sketch was able to synthesize the solution in 156 seconds, using the same bounds of 10 unrollings and $n \leq 4$. (See Section 4.3 for more discussion.)

4. Experiments

We implemented a symbolic executor based directly on rules in Figure 3, and used it to implement PINS.[1] As discussed earlier, our implementation of `solve` is an extension of our prior work [36, 37]. We use Z3 [7] as an SMT solver.

Recall that PINS is parameterized by the number of solutions m to request from the solver. In our experiments, we chose $m = 10$, which we found worked well—it provided enough solutions so that our `pickOne` heuristic could work effectively, while not requiring too much solver time.

Benchmarks We used PINS to synthesize inverses for the 14 programs listed in the leftmost column of Table 1. All of these programs are small, but they are also complex. PINS succeeded in inverting all of these programs, and we should emphasize that, to our knowledge, no other automated technique is able to do so given the same information.

The first group of programs is compressors. We have already discussed the run-length encoder, and we include two variants, one that compresses and decompresses in place, as in Figure 1, and one that uses a separate array for the compressed data. We also invert two well-known compression algorithms, Lempel-Ziv 77 (*LZ77*) and Lempel-Ziv-Welch (*LZW*) [42, 40]. We coded the compressors in C from a description of the algorithm [2].

The second group of programs convert among different formats. The *Base64* program converts binary input to printable ASCII characters. *UUEncode* outputs four printable characters for every three bytes of binary input, plus adds a header and a footer to the output. Again, we coded the compressors in C from their standard descriptions. *Pkt wrapper* wraps a data object (with a set of fields inside) into a variable length packet format by traversing the fields and adding a preamble (the length of the field) to the data bytes for the field. *Serialize* is a toy data structure serialization program that recursively walks over data objects (recursing into any non-primitive types) and writes out a flattened representation. Our serializer is small because it relies on external functions to check whether a field is primitive, get the next field, etc.. We encode the behavior of these external functions using axioms.

The last group of programs perform arithmetic computations. $\sum i$ is a simple iterative computation that adds i to a running sum in the ith iteration. (Our inverse works by iteratively subtracting i from the sum, rather than trying to solve the quadratic $n(n+1)/2$.) *Vector shift*, *Vector scale*, and *Vector rotate* perform the named operation on a set of points on the Euclidean plane, represented as a pair of arrays X and Y. In practice, a programmer would realize that these computations can be reversed by negating the inputs to the program, but that is domain-specific knowledge the synthesizer does not have. Instead, the synthesizer discovers a specialized un-shifter, -scaler, and -rotater that iterate through the vectors, *semantically* negating the operation performed. This is non-trivial for scaling, where the synthesizer needs to be able to reason about $1/x$, and for rotation, where the inverse of $(x', y' := x\texttt{cos}(t) - y\texttt{sin}(t), x\texttt{sin}(t) + y\texttt{cos}(t))$ is $(x'', y'' := x'cos(t) + y'sin(t), y'cos(t) - x'\texttt{sin}(t))$.

[1] Our implementation of PINS is available on the web [3]

Benchmark	LoC	$\Pi_p \cup \Pi_e$			Inv. LoC	Num. Axms
		Mined	Subset	Mod		
In-place RL	12	16	14	1	10	0
Run length	12	16	10	0	10	0
LZ77	22	16	10	3	13	0
LZW	25	20	15	4	20	15
Base64	22	13	10	2	16	3
UUEncode	12	8	7	4	11	3
Pkt wrapper	10	12	8	1	16	2
Serialize	8	7	7	1	8	6
$\sum i$	5	8	6	2	5	0
Vector shift	8	11	7	0	7	0
Vector scale	8	9	7	2	7	1
Vector rotate	8	13	7	0	7	1
Permute count	11	12	7	2	10	0
LU decomp	11	14	9	0	12	2

Table 1. Template mining characteristics.

The *Permute count* program is *Dijkstra's permutation* program from his original note on program inversion [8]. He considered a program that, given a permutation π, computes for the ith element of π the number of elements between $0 \,..\, i$ that are less that $\pi(i)$. The inverse program computes the permutation from an array of these counts. Dijkstra manually derived it from the original program, while PINS synthesizes the inverse from the template.

Finally, *LU-decomposition* performs that operation in-place on a matrix using the Doolittle algorithm [30]. The inverse, which has been manually derived before [4] and which we synthesize using the synthesis template, is a program that multiplies the lower triangular and upper triangular matrices in-place.

4.1 Template construction

Table 1 summarizes the results of the template mining process on our benchmarks. For each benchmark, we first list its size in terms of lines of code, followed by three columns that measure the size of $\Pi_p \cup \Pi_e$. First, we list the size of the candidate sets mined from the original program; then, we give the size of the subset we guessed initially; and lastly, we list the number of modifications we needed to make to elements within the chosen subset for successful synthesis. The second-to-last column lists the size of the portion of the template program containing the inverse (e.g., Lines 12 and below in Figure 1). In this measure, we count loop guards as being on their own line, and we count a parallel assignment to k variables as k lines (since that is what it will ultimately be expanded to).

We found that picking the subset of $\Pi_p \cup \Pi_e$ was fairly straightforward, as we could easily eliminate obviously redundant or useless elements. Then an initial run of PINS gave us enough information to infer the few changes to $\Pi_p \cup \Pi_e$ we needed to make. Overall, the template mining process proved tremendously helpful in coming up with a synthesis template. Although it was still non-trivial to find the correct final template, we found it was much easier to tweak a candidate template than come up with one from scratch.

The rightmost column in Table 1 reports the number of axioms we used during synthesis, as discussed in Section 2.3. These axioms are quite generic over the uninterpreted functions we were abstracting, e.g., the axioms over strings from Section 2.3, and can be reused across many different program synthesis problems that use the same ADTs. In the current implementation, we select axioms for each benchmark because of current limitation of SMT solvers—specifically, quantifier instantiation is expensive, and so we limit how often it occurs by limiting the number of axioms. However, SMT solvers are evolving rapidly, and we expect in the future to write standard libraries of axioms once and use the same libraries across many different synthesis problems.

Benchmark	Srch. Sp. Redn	Num. Iter.	Total Time (s)	|SAT|
In-place RL	$2^{30} \rightarrow 1$	7	36.16	837
Run length	$2^{25} \rightarrow 1$	7	26.19	668
LZ77	$2^{25} \rightarrow 2$	6	1810.31	330
LZW	$2^{31} \rightarrow 2$	4	150.42	373
Base64	$2^{37} \rightarrow 4$	12	1376.82	598
UUEncode	$2^{20} \rightarrow 1$	7	34.00	177
Pkt wrapper	$2^{20} \rightarrow 1$	6	132.32	2161
Serialize	$2^{11} \rightarrow 1$	14	55.33	69
$\sum i$	$2^{15} \rightarrow 1$	4	1.07	51
Vector shift	$2^{16} \rightarrow 1$	3	4.20	187
Vector scale	$2^{16} \rightarrow 1$	3	4.41	191
Vector rotate	$2^{16} \rightarrow 1$	3	39.51	327
Permute count	$2^{3} \rightarrow 1$	1	8.44	4
LU decomp	$2^{5} \rightarrow 1$	1	160.24	10

Table 2. Performance of PINS

Benchmark	Validation			Sketch
	Manual	Tests	CBMC	
In-place RL	ok	2	34.59s	157s
Run length	ok	2	0.62s	30s
LZ77	1 of 2 ok	5	1.93s	29s
LZW	2 of 2 ok	3	—	—
Base64	1 of 4 ok	4	—	—
UUEncode	ok	6	—	—
Pkt wrapper	ok	1	—	—
Serialize	ok	5	—	—
$\sum i$	ok	2	1.15s	fail
Vector shift	ok	1	113.74s	2s
Vector scale	ok	1	—	—
Vector rotate	ok	1	—	—
Permute count	ok	1	1.06s	172s
LU decomp	ok	1	—	—

Table 3. Validating the solutions generated by PINS.

4.2 Performance

Table 2 shows the performance for PINS on our benchmarks. The second column reports the approximate size of the search space and the number of solutions returned when PINS terminates. For example, for the in-place run-length encoder, the synthesis template has roughly 2^{30} possible instantiations, and PINS eliminates all but one of them. PINS returned one solution for 11 of the 14 benchmarks, and only a few solutions in other cases. Thus, we can see that PINS is highly effective in refining the set of possible inverses. For all programs PINS found at least one correct solution; we defer a more detailed discussion of correctness to Section 4.3.

The next column in Table 2 reports the number of full loop iterations until PINS converges. Since PINS calls `solve` at the top of the loop before deciding whether to exit, i full loop iterations corresponds to $i+1$ solver calls (see Algorithm 1). On each full iteration, we explore one program path, so these numbers support our path-bound hypothesis: for these programs, indeed only a small number of paths were required to characterize the programs' behavior.

The third column in the table lists the running times for PINS. We can see that the time varies widely, from one second for $\sum i$ up to 30 minutes for *LZ77*. Even so, these times may be shorter than the time required for a programmer to manually write the inverses. The variability of the times arises from the large semantic differences between these programs and the vagaries of SMT/SAT solvers. We also separately measured how much of the running time was due to each of the various steps within PINS, and we found that symbolic execution (which makes SMT queries) and SMT reduction to SAT take more than 90% of the running time. The actual SAT formulas produced are quite small, as shown in the last column of the table, and solving those and computing our `pickOne` heuristic take little of the running time. (The detailed distribution for individual benchmarks is available in Appendix B.)

4.3 Validation

After PINS terminates, we need to validate the inverses, since PINS does not guarantee their correctness. Table 3 shows the results of validation following the methodology outlined in Section 2.5. The second column counts how many solutions were correct according to manual inspection. We can see that most of the solutions returned by PINS were in fact correct. For the three benchmarks that yielded multiple solutions, *LZ77*, *LZW*, and *Base64*, the solutions were very similar, differing by a single assignment in most cases. Thus, after inspecting one solution, it was easy to understand the others.

When PINS exits, it also outputs concrete test cases, which are concrete assignments to the inputs that will cause the final solutions to take the paths PINS explored. The third column of the table lists the number of such test cases; note that it might be smaller than the number of iterations, since some of the previously explored paths may be infeasible in the final solutions. We found these tests helpful when doing our manual inspection.

The fourth column reports the time for running the bounded model checker CMBC [1] to verify the final solutions. Note that to run CBMC, we needed to bound the number of loop unrollings and, in many cases, the sizes of arrays. Using CMBC gives us further confidence that the synthesized programs are correct. However, most of the benchmarks needed axioms for library functions, and we found no easy way to apply CBMC to those programs—we would instead need to write implementations of the library functions. For some axioms, such as $\forall x \neq 0.\mathtt{mul}(x, \mathtt{div}(1, x)) = 1$, even an implementation would be insufficient, as this particular axiom essentially adds a capability to the solver.

Sketch For comparison, we tried running Sketch [33] on the same synthesis templates we used in our experiments. As with CBMC, Sketch does not have a way to include axioms to model library functions, and so we could only run Sketch on 6 of our benchmarks; we felt that writing the library functions would significantly change the input to the synthesizer, and thus would not be a meaningful comparison. For instance, it dramatically changes the synthesis problem to have an implementation for $\mathtt{inv}(x) = 1/x$ as opposed to the axiom $\forall x \neq 0.\mathtt{mul}(x, \mathtt{div}(1, x)) = 1$, or to have implementations for $\mathtt{cos}(t)$ and $\mathtt{sin}(t)$ as opposed to the axiom $\forall t.\mathtt{cos}^2(t) + \mathtt{sin}^2(t) = 1$. Sketch also requires that the user specify bounds on array sizes.

Sketch was able to synthesize an inverse for 5 out of the 6 benchmarks that did not make external calls; the running times are reported in the rightmost column of Table 3. Sketch only failed on one benchmark—we let it run for an hour, and even after we eliminated all unknown predicates from the template, Sketch still did not terminate. In this case, the program forces Sketch to unroll a loop maxint times, which by default is 32 in Sketch (which sets integers to be 5 bits), and this large number of unrollings seems to cause the timeout. It may be possible to synthesize this example by reducing the number of bits in integers below 5.

For LZ77, Sketch resolves the template an order of magnitude faster than PINS, but note that this is only after we spent considerable effort getting it to terminate, which happened only when we reduced the bound on the array size to 4.

In general, we found that using Sketch was more challenging than we expected, as it took us a significant amount of experimentation to come up with the right bounds. This bounds requirement also highlights a key difference between PINS and Sketch: PINS solves for *all possible input values* along a small set of paths, but Sketch ensures correct synthesis on *all paths within the finitized space*. The details of the parameters we found through experimentation are available in Appendix B.

4.4 Limitations and future work

Our results show that PINS is promising, but it still has several limitations. Scalability is clearly a challenge, both for PINS and for other program synthesis tools. It would be interesting future work to investigate when synthesizing small components of larger applications would be useful, and to improve the scalability of PINS itself. Another challenge is the need to discover templates. We think that templates are a useful tool—they give the developer a way to narrow the search space for synthesis, but, at least in our experience, they are much easier to develop than the programs to be synthesized. For inversion in particular, our template mining approach proved very helpful. It would be worthwhile to study whether similar mining approaches could be used for other domains, and user studies of synthesis could shed light on how much input a human is willing to provide to a synthesis tool. Finally, PINS relies on SMT solving, and more scalable and powerful SMT solvers would enable larger, less-constrained search spaces and faster synthesis.

An interesting direction for future work is to automatically refine templates, rather than requiring the user to do so. One logical starting place is CEGAR, as the paths explored by PINS are analogous to the counterexamples used by CEGAR (although we have observed that CEGAR's refinement cannot be used directly). Inverting many-to-one programs is another interesting question. There are two formulations of the problem we could consider. First, we could try to find an inverse that returns *some*, instead of all, elements of the original program's input. We believe it is possible to handle this formulation with PINS directly, with just a different template. Second, we could try to find an inverse that generates all of the original inputs. This is more difficult; we believe it requires that we specify a different specification than identity, but that the core of PINS should still be applicable.

5. Related Work

Deriving program inverses A range of techniques for program inversion have been previously proposed. Dijkstra [8] and Gries [12] suggest using a set of proof rules to derive an inverse. Our template mining approach is inspired by this idea, but it is hard to envision this approach succeeding in an automated way on many examples. A related proposal uses local inversion plus proof rules that compose the locally inverted fragments into a complete program [4, 9, 31]. These techniques work if all values in the reversed computation can be obtained analytically, which can be a challenge. To our knowledge, these systems have not been automated.

One very interesting inversion technique consists of approximating the behavior of the program with a grammar. If the output of the original program can be parsed using a deterministic grammar, then the inverse of the grammar (written using local inversion, i.e., reading the grammar backwards) corresponds to the program inverse [11, 24, 41]. Grammar-based inversion only works when the input to the program to be inverted has the right (context-free) form—grammar-based approaches can invert run-length encoding, but not the dictionary-constructing compressors LZW and LZ77. Also, grammar-based inversion has been applied to functional programs, where there are no destructive state updates and thus inversion is arguably simpler. Additionally, it is also not clear to us if grammar-based inversion works on any of the arithmetic examples.

Program inverses for restricted cases have been considered in the context of some larger problems. As part of an approach to generate divide-and-conquer parallel functional programs, Morita et al show how to compute a weak right inverse to a program fragment [29]. It is unclear whether this approach can handle loops. Kanade et al propose a simple inversion subroutine to aid representation dependence testing [23]. This latter approach is based on proof rules, and seems hard to use in the general case.

Inductive and deductive program synthesis Inductive synthesis generalizes from finite instances to yield an infinite state program [21]. Deductive synthesis, in contrast, refines a specification to derive the program [28, 32]. Our approach is mostly inductive synthesis since we generalize from a finite set, but it has elements of deductive synthesis because we use paths and symbolic reasoning. Since we use symbolic paths and not concrete traces, each additional path captures the behavior of multiple concrete runs, and more of the space is explored in each iteration. Additionally, while inductive synthesis cannot provide the full formal guarantees of deductive synthesis, symbolic paths provide a close approximation. Lastly, while previous inductive synthesizers refine using either only positive reinforcing examples or only negative counterexamples, we refine using both positive and negative example paths.

Proof-theoretic synthesis [38] and similar approaches for hybrid systems [39] are deductive synthesis techniques, which encode the synthesis problem as a search for invariants, and therefore needs to infer complicated invariants (and requires a formal verifier with support for such reasoning). In contrast, PINS relies on directed path exploration and symbolic execution-based reasoning, and does not reason about invariants. Thus, PINS allows us to synthesize inverses that are infeasible using proof-theoretic synthesis.

As discussed earlier, Sketching [33] is an inductive synthesis technique that uses a model checker to refine the space of candidates. PINS differs from Sketch in several ways. First, Sketch uses domain specific reductions to finitize loops for stencil [33], concurrent [34], and bit-streaming [35] programs, and is engineered to solve the resulting loop-finitized problem. In contrast, PINS finitizes the solution space using templates, but does not finitize loops or the input. We found that this is an important consideration, because in our experiments it was tricky to choose the right finitization for Sketch; smaller sizes lead to faster solving, but may restrict the space such that the synthesized candidates are correct only on the bounded values but not for arbitrary inputs. It took us several hours to get the finitization right for our experiments. Second, PINS prunes using symbolic paths, while Sketch prunes using concrete executions; since multiple concrete executions may follow a single path, a few iterations of PINS suffice for the synthesis. Lastly, PINS uses SMT reasoning to generate concise SAT instances that are easily solved; Sketch uses bit-blasting, which generates large formulas that may be hard to solve [15].

Some previous synthesis techniques can successful synthesize acyclic programs. Gulwani et al have developed SMT-based techniques for synthesizing acyclic programs over a user-specified set of components, which they apply to the synthesis of bit-vector programs [15, 22]. Gulwani et al have also shown that exhaustive search pruned by heuristics, inspired by techniques from the artifical intelligence community, can synthesize ruler and compass-based macros for geometrical drawings [16]. Kuncak et al have developed decision procedures for synthesis of functions specified within a decidable logic [26]. While these techniques do not rely on templates, they are restricted to loop-free programs, in contrast to PINS, which synthesizes programs with loops.

Gulwani et al have developed synthesis techniques based on divide-and-conquer paradigm that can synthesize loopy programs for string [14] and table manipulation [20]. However, these techniques are based primarily on inductive synthesis, and are well-suited for *end-users*, who find it easy to provide examples, but would find the task of providing a formal specification quite daunting. In contrast, the technique presented in this paper can leverage formal logical specifications.

6. Conclusion

We have presented a program synthesis approach called PINS that synthesizes programs by exploring relevant paths in a template program and ensuring that the program meets the specification over those paths. PINS leverages symbolic execution and SMT solving to synthesize programs that take unbounded inputs and may have unbounded loops. An important consideration is finding the right set of paths to efficiently prune the space of possible candidates, for which PINS includes a directed path exploration strategy that is parameterized by a remaining candidate solution. We apply PINS to the task of semi-automated program inversion. We show that it is possible to mine the synthesis template using domain-specific projection operators, which significantly reduces the burden on the user. Our results on inverting 14 small benchmarks suggest that PINS is a promising new approach to inversion in particular, and, we believe, to program synthesis in general.

Acknowledgments

This work was supported in part by NSF grant 1019343 to the Computing Research Association for the CIFellows Project, and by NSF grants CCF-0346982 and CCF-0953507.

References

[1] CBMC. `http://www.cprover.org/cbmc/`.

[2] LZW and LZ77. `http://en.wikipedia.org/wiki/Lempel-Ziv-Welch` and `http://en.wikipedia.org/wiki/LZ77_and_LZ78`.

[3] PINS. `http://www.cs.umd.edu/~saurabhs/vs3/PINS/`.

[4] Wei Chen. A formal approach to program inversion. In *CSC: Proc. of the ACM conference on Cooperation*, pages 398–403, 1990.

[5] Byron Cook, Sumit Gulwani, Tal Lev-Ami, Andrey Rybalchenko, and Mooly Sagiv. Proving conditional termination. In *CAV'08*.

[6] Byron Cook, Andreas Podelski, and Andrey Rybalchenko. Termination proofs for systems code. In *PLDI*, pages 415–426, 2006.

[7] Leonardo de Moura and Nikolaj Bjørner. Z3, 2008. `http://research.microsoft.com/projects/Z3/`.

[8] Edsger W. Dijkstra. Program inversion. In *Program Construction*, `http://www.cs.utexas.edu/~EWD/ewd06xx/EWD671.PDF`, pages 54–57, London, UK, 1979. Springer-Verlag.

[9] David Eppstein. A heuristic approach to program inversion. In *IJCAI*, pages 219–221, 1985.

[10] Michael D. Ernst, Jeff H. Perkins, Philip J. Guo, Stephen McCamant, Carlos Pacheco, Matthew S. Tschantz, and Chen Xiao. The Daikon system for dynamic detection of likely invariants. *Science of Computer Programming*, 69(1–3):35–45, December 2007.

[11] Robert Glück and Masahiko Kawabe. A method for automatic program inversion based on LR(0) parsing. *Fundam. Inf.*, 66(4):367–395, 2005.

[12] David Gries. *The Science of Programming*. Springer-Verlag New York, Inc., 1987.

[13] Sumit Gulwani. Dimensions in program synthesis (invited talk paper). In *ACM Symposium on PPDP*, 2010.

[14] Sumit Gulwani. Automating string processing in spreadsheets using input-output examples. In *POPL*, pages 317–330, 2011.

[15] Sumit Gulwani, Susmit Kumar Jha, Ashish Tiwari, and Ramarathnam Venkatesan. Synthesis of loop-free programs. In *PLDI*, 2011.

[16] Sumit Gulwani, Vijay Korthikanti, and Ashish Tiwari. Synthesizing geometry constructions. In *PLDI*, 2011.

[17] Sumit Gulwani, Saurabh Srivastava, and Ramarathnam Venkatesan. Program analysis as constraint solving. In *PLDI*, 2008.

[18] Sumit Gulwani and Ashish Tiwari. Constraint-based approach for analysis of hybrid systems. In *CAV*, pages 190–203, 2008.

[19] Sumit Gulwani and Florian Zuleger. The reachability-bound problem. In *PLDI'10*, pages 292–304, 2010.

[20] William R. Harris and Sumit Gulwani. Spreadsheet table transformations from examples. In *PLDI*, 2011.

[21] Shachar Itzhaky, Sumit Gulwani, Neil Immerman, and Mooly Sagiv. A simple inductive synthesis methodology and its applications. In *OOPSLA*, pages 36–46, 2010.

[22] Susmit Jha, Sumit Gulwani, Sanjit Seshia, and Ashish Tiwari. Oracle-guided component-based program synthesis. In *ICSE*, 2010.

[23] Aditya Kanade, Rajeev Alur, Sriram Rajamani, and G Ramalingam. Representation dependence testing using program inversion. In *FSE*, 2010.

[24] Masahiko Kawabe and Robert Glück. The program inverter lrinv and its structure. In *PADL*, pages 219–234, 2005.

[25] James C. King. Symbolic execution and program testing. *Communications of the ACM*, 19(7):385–394, 1976.

[26] Viktor Kuncak, Mikael Mayer, Ruzica Piskac, and Philippe Suter. Complete functional synthesis. In *PLDI*, 2010.

[27] Zohar Manna and Richard Waldinger. A deductive approach to program synthesis. *ACM Trans. Program. Lang. Syst.*, 2(1), 1980.

[28] Zohar Manna and Richard J. Waldinger. Toward automatic program synthesis. *Communications of the ACM*, 14(3):151–165, 1971.

[29] Kazutaka Morita, Akimasa Morihata, Kiminori Matsuzaki, Zhenjiang Hu, and Masato Takeichi. Automatic inversion generates divide-and-conquer parallel programs. In *PLDI'07*.

[30] William H. Press, Saul A. Teukolsky, William T. Vetterling, and Brian P. Flannery. *LU Decomposition and Its Applications*, chapter 2.3, pages 34–42. 1993.

[31] Brian J. Ross. Running programs backwards: The logical inversion of imperative computation. *Formal Asp. Comput.*, 9(3):331–348, 1997.

[32] D. R. Smith. Kids: A semiautomatic program development system. *IEEE Trans. Softw. Eng.*, 16:1024–1043, 1990.

[33] Armando Solar-Lezama, Gilad Arnold, Liviu Tancau, Rastislav Bodik, Vijay Saraswat, and Sanjit Seshia. Sketching stencils. In *PLDI*, pages 167–178, 2007.

[34] Armando Solar-Lezama, Christopher Grant Jones, and Rastislav Bodik. Sketching concurrent data structures. In *PLDI*, 2008.

[35] Armando Solar-Lezama, Rodric Rabbah, Rastislav Bodík, and Kemal Ebcioğlu. Prog. by sketching for bit-stream. prgs. In *PLDI*, pages 281–294, 2005.

[36] Saurabh Srivastava and Sumit Gulwani. Program verification using templates over predicate abstraction. In *PLDI*, 2009.

[37] Saurabh Srivastava, Sumit Gulwani, and Jeffrey S. Foster. VS3: SMT solvers for program verification. In *CAV*, 2009.

[38] Saurabh Srivastava, Sumit Gulwani, and Jeffrey S. Foster. From program verification to program synthesis. In *POPL*, 2010.

[39] Ankur Taly, Sumit Gulwani, and Ashish Tiwari. Synthesizing switching logic using constraint solving. In *VMCAI*, pages 305–319, 2009.

[40] T. A. Welch. A technique for high-performance data compression. *Computer*, 17(6):8–19, 1984.

[41] Daniel M. Yellin. *Attribute grammar inversion and source-to-source translation*. Springer-Verlag New York, Inc., 1988.

[42] J. Ziv and A. Lempel. A universal algorithm for sequential data compression. *IEEE Transactions on Information Theory*, IT-23(5):337–343, 1977.

A. Code examples: LZ77 and LZW

To illustrate concretely the difficulty in inverting these benchmarks, Figure 4 shows the code for LZ77 and LZW compressors that we invert. This code and the code for the other benchmarks is available

```
void main(int *A, int n) {
    int *P, *N, *C;
    int i, j, k, c, p, r;
    in(A, n);
    assume(n ≥ 0);
    i := 0; k := 0;
    while (i < n) {
      c := 0; p := 0; j := 0;
      while (j < i) {
        r := 0;
        while (i + r < n − 1 ∧ A[j + r] = A[i + r])
          r := r + 1;
        if (c < r)
          c := r; p := i − j;
        j := j + 1;
      }
      P[k] := p; N[k] := c; C[k] := A[i + c];
      i := i + 1 + c; k := k + 1;
    }
    out(P, N, C, k);
}
```

(a)

```
void main(int n, BitString A) {
    BitString *D;
    int *B, i, p, k, j, r, size, x, go;
    in(A,n);
    assume(n ≥ 1);
    D[0] = "0"; D[1] = "1";
    i := 0; p := 2; k := 0;
    while (i < n) {
      j := i; r := 0; size := −1;
      while (j < n ∧ r ≠ −1) {
        x := 0; r := −1;
        while (x < p) {
          if (D[x] =substr(A, i, j))
            r := x;
          x := x + 1;
        }
        if (r ≠ −1)
          { go := r; size := j − i + 1; }
        j := j + 1;
      }
      B[k] := go; k := k + 1;
      D[p] := substr(A, i, j − 1); p := p + 1;
      i := i + size;
    }
    out(B, D, k);
}
```

(b)

Figure 4. The compressors for (a) LZ77, and (b) LZW, inverted by PINS.

	Percentage of total time				
Benchmark	Sym. Exe.	SMT Red.	SAT Sol.	pickOne	Total Time (s)
In-place RL	41%	51%	6%	2%	36.16
Run length	45%	45%	7%	3%	26.19
LZ77	98%	1%	<0.1%	<0.1%	1810.31
LZW	68%	29%	<1%	3%	150.42
Base64	42%	57%	<1%	<1%	1376.82
UUEncode	84%	12%	1%	3%	34.00
Pkt wrapper	1%	96%	3%	<1%	132.32
Serialize	92%	7%	<1%	<1%	55.33
$\sum i$	50%	38%	4%	8%	1.07
Vector shift	21%	73%	2%	4%	4.20
Vector scale	21%	73%	2%	4%	4.41
Vector rotate	6%	93%	<1%	<1%	39.51
Permute count	96%	2%	<1%	2%	8.44
LU decomp	88%	11%	<0.1%	1%	160.24

Table 4. Breakdown of PINS running time.

on the web [3]. Note that for both programs, none of the dictionary construction has been abstracted away. The only abstraction used is in LZW to model strings, e.g., the call to `substr` extracts a substring between two indices from the given string. (Also note that we assume all pointers point to valid memory.)

B. Experimental parameters and details

This appendix contains some additional details on the reported experimental results.

Table 4 breaks down the time taken by PINS into the four steps of the algorithm that involve constraint solving. The second column gives the time spent in the symbolic executor (which needs to perform SMT queries to determine which branches are feasible; see ASSUME in Figure 3). The third column gives the time spent in SMT reduction in `solve`, which transforms the constraints into a SAT formula, using SMT queries in the process. The fourth column gives the time spent in SAT solving, and the fifth column gives the

	CBMC		Sketch		
Benchmark	Unroll	Size	Unroll	Size	|SAT|
In-place RL	10	4	10	5	2,183k
Run length	10	∞	10	8	718k
LZ77	5	4	8	4	12,456k
$\sum i$	10	∞	fail	fail	fail
Vector shift	5	∞	10	5	35k
Permute count	10	5	8	8	1.76k

Table 5. Parameters required and running times for CBMC and Sketch.

time spent in `pickOne`. Clearly the vast majority of the time is spent in the first two steps.

Table 5 lists the bounds we chose in running CBMC and Sketch, discussed in Section 2.5. We only list the programs that did not need axioms for library functions. For both tools we give the bound on loop unrollings and the bound on sizes of input arrays. For Sketch, we also list the average size of the SAT formula it produces (these are averages of the "find" values, as opposed to the "check" values, across the algorithm).

We arbitrarily started with 10 as the number of unrollings, and then reduced that sufficiently to ensure termination. For CBMC, in half of the benchmarks we had to specify a bound on the size of the input arrays, to get it to terminate. We experimentally found a low enough size for verification, which was 5 in one case and 4 in two others. Sketch *always* requires the input arrays be bounded. We arbitrarily tried a value of 8, which worked for two programs, but had to come down to 5 and 4 for others. Note these bounds are on the sizes of the input arrays. Sketch internally also bounds the bit-widths of all primitive types, e.g., integers are 5 bit wide. Because these systems bit-blast the formula, they are also susceptible to the types of the variables used. For instance, loops can be unrolled much more if instead of `int`s we use `char`s. PINS explores the right set of paths that allow it to effectively search as vast a space as explored through bit-blasting over a small finitized space.

Directed Incremental Symbolic Execution

Suzette Person
NASA Langley Research Center
suzette.person@nasa.gov

Guowei Yang
University of Texas at Austin
gyang@ece.utexas.edu

Neha Rungta
NASA Ames Research Center
neha.s.rungta@nasa.gov

Sarfraz Khurshid
University of Texas at Austin
khurshid@ece.utexas.edu

Abstract

The last few years have seen a resurgence of interest in the use of symbolic execution – a program analysis technique developed more than three decades ago to analyze program execution paths. Scaling symbolic execution and other path-sensitive analysis techniques to large systems remains challenging despite recent algorithmic and technological advances. An alternative to solving the problem of scalability is to *reduce* the scope of the analysis. One approach that is widely studied in the context of regression analysis is to analyze the *differences* between two related program versions. While such an approach is intuitive in theory, finding efficient and precise ways to identify program differences, and characterize their effects on how the program executes has proved challenging in practice.

In this paper, we present *Directed Incremental Symbolic Execution* (DiSE), a novel technique for detecting and characterizing the effects of program changes. The novelty of DiSE is to combine the *efficiencies* of static analysis techniques to compute program difference information with the *precision* of symbolic execution to explore program execution paths and generate path conditions affected by the differences. DiSE is a complementary technique to other reduction or bounding techniques developed to improve symbolic execution. Furthermore, DiSE does not require analysis results to be carried forward as the software evolves—only the source code for two related program versions is required. A case-study of our implementation of DiSE illustrates its effectiveness at detecting and characterizing the effects of program changes.

Categories and Subject Descriptors D.2.5 [*Software Engineering*]: Testing and Debugging—Symbolic execution

General Terms Verification, Algorithms

Keywords Program Differencing, Symbolic Execution, Software Evolution

PLDI '11 June 4–8, San Jose, California, USA
Copyright © 2011 ACM 978-1-4503-0663-8/11/06...$10.00

1. Introduction

Over the last three decades, *symbolic execution* [7, 22]—a program analysis technique for systematic exploration of program execution paths using symbolic input values—has provided a basis for various software testing and verification techniques. For each path it explores, symbolic execution builds a *path condition*, i.e., constraints on the symbolic inputs, that characterizes the program execution path. During symbolic execution, satisfiability checks are performed each time a constraint is added to the path condition to determine the feasibility of the path; if a path condition becomes unsatisfiable, it represents an infeasible path and symbolic execution does not consider any other paths that contain the known infeasible path as its prefix. The set of path conditions computed by symbolic execution can be used to perform various analyses of program behavior, for example, to check conformance of code to rich behavioral specifications using automated test input generation [10, 19].

Initial work on symbolic execution largely focused on checking properties of programs with primitive types, such as integers and booleans [7, 22]. Several recent projects generalized the core ideas of symbolic execution which enabled it to be applied to programs with more general types, including references and arrays [4, 10, 12, 19, 32]. These generalizations have been complimented by recent advances in constraint solving, which is the key supporting technology that affects the effectiveness of symbolic execution—checking path conditions for satisfiability relies heavily on the capabilities of the underlying constraint solvers. During the last few years, not only has raw computing power increased, enabling more efficient constraint solving, but basic constraint solving technology has also advanced considerably, specifically in leveraging multiple decision procedures in synergy, for example, as in Satisfiability Modulo Theory (SMT) solvers [9].

Scaling symbolic execution, as with other path-sensitive analyses, remains challenging because of the large number of execution paths generated during the symbolic analysis. This is known as the *path explosion problem*, and despite recent advances in reduction and abstraction techniques, remains a fundamental challenge to path-sensitive analysis techniques. A large body of work has been dedicated to developing techniques that try to achieve better scalability [1, 3, 11, 20]. One alternative approach to solving the problem of scalability is to reduce the scope of the analysis to only certain parts of the program.

Regression analysis is a well known example where the *differences* between program versions serve as the basis to reduce the scope of the analysis [14, 35, 38]. Analyses based on program *differences* are attractive and have considerable potential benefits since most software is developed following an evolutionary process. And, with the recent push toward agile development, differences between two program versions tend to be small and localized. The challenge, however, lies in determining precisely which program execution behaviors are *affected* by the program changes. Techniques to identify modified parts of the program can be broadly classified into two categories: *syntactic* and *semantic*. Syntactic techniques consider differences in the program source code or some other static representation of the source and can be computed efficiently. Semantic techniques are typically more expensive, but also compute generally more precise differences by considering the differences in the execution behaviors of the program.

In *Directed Incremental Symbolic Execution* (DiSE), our insight is to combine the *efficiencies* of static analysis techniques that compute program difference information with the *precision* of symbolic execution. The path conditions computed by DiSE then characterize the differences between two related program versions. The essence of symbolic execution is that it abstracts the semantics of program behaviors by generating constraints on the program inputs. The constraints for a given program execution behavior (path), referred to as a *path condition*, encode the input values that will cause execution to follow that path. The goal of this work is to direct symbolic execution on a modified program version to explore path conditions that may be *affected* by the changes. Consider a set of concrete (actual) input values that generate paths p and p' in the original and modified versions of the program respectively. If symbolic execution of p and p' result in different path conditions, then the path condition generated along p' is termed as affected.

Affected path conditions can be solved to generate values for the variables which, when used to execute the program, exhibit the *affected* program behaviors. The results of DiSE can then be used by subsequent program analysis techniques to focus on only the program behaviors that are affected by the changes to the program. DiSE enables other program analysis techniques to efficiently perform software evolution tasks such as program documentation, regression testing, fault localization and program summarization.

The novelty of DiSE is to leverage the state-of-the-art in symbolic execution and apply static analyses in synergy to enable more efficient symbolic execution of programs as they evolve. Static analysis and symbolic execution form the two phases in DiSE. Program instructions whose execution may lead to the generation of affected path conditions are termed as affected locations or affected instructions. The goal of the first phase is to generate the set of affected program instructions. The static analysis techniques in the first phase are based on intra-procedural data and control flow dependences. The dependence analyses are used to identify instructions in the source code that define program variables relevant to *changes* in the program. Conditional branch instructions that use those variables, or are themselves affected by the changes, are also identified as affected. In the second phase, the information generated by the static analysis is used to *direct* symbolic execution to explore only the parts of the programs affected by the changes, potentially avoiding a large number of unaffected execution paths. DiSE generates, as output, path conditions only on conditional branch instructions that use variables affected by the change or are otherwise affected by the changes.

In this work, we develop a conceptual framework for DiSE, implement a prototype of our framework in the Java PathFinder symbolic execution framework [26, 28, 36], present a case-study to demonstrate the effectiveness of our approach, and demonstrate, as a proof of concept, how the framework enables incremental program analysis to perform software evolution related tasks. For the examples used in our case-study, DiSE consistently explores fewer states and takes less time to generate fewer path conditions compared to standard symbolic execution when the changes affect only a subset of the program execution paths. This demonstrates the effectiveness of DiSE in terms of reducing the cost of symbolic execution of evolving software. Furthermore, we apply the results of our analysis to test case selection and augmentation to demonstrate the utility of such an analysis.

We make the following contributions:

- *A novel incremental analysis* that leverages the state-of-the-art in symbolic execution and applies a static analysis in synergy to enable efficient symbolic execution of programs as they undergo changes.
- A technique for *characterizing* program differences by generating path conditions affected by the changes.
- *A case-study* that demonstrates the effectiveness of DiSE in reducing the cost of performing symbolic execution and illustrates how DiSE results can be used to support software evolution tasks.

2. Background and Motivation

We begin with a brief explanation of symbolic execution, the underlying algorithm used in DiSE. Next, we present an example to demonstrate the motivation for the development of DiSE.

2.1 Symbolic Execution

Symbolic execution is a program analysis technique for systematically exploring a large number of program execution paths [7, 22]. It uses symbolic values in place of concrete (actual) values as program inputs. The resulting output values are computed as expressions defined over constants and symbolic input values, using a specified set of operators.

A symbolic execution tree characterizes all execution paths explored during symbolic execution. Each node in the tree represents a symbolic program state, and each edge represents a transition between two states. A symbolic program state contains a unique program location identifier (`Loc`), symbolic expressions for the symbolic input variables, and a path condition (`PC`). During symbolic execution, the path condition is used to collect constraints on the program expressions, and describes the current path through the symbolic execution tree. Path conditions are checked for satisfiability during symbolic execution; when a path condition is infeasible, symbolic execution stops exploration of that path and backtracks. In programs with loops and recursion, infinitely long execution paths may be generated. In order to guarantee termination of the execution in such cases, a user-specified depth bound is provided as input to symbolic execution.

We illustrate symbolic execution with the following example:

```
int y;
...
  int testX(int x){
1:  if (x > 0)
2:     y = y + x;
3:  else
4:     y = y - x;
5:  }
```

This code fragment introduces two symbolic variables: Y, the symbolic representation of the integer field `y`, and X, the symbolic representation of the integer argument `x` to procedure `testX`. For this example, symbolic execution explores the two feasible behaviors shown in the symbolic execution tree in Figure 1. When program execution begins, the path condition is set to `true`. When $X > 0$ evaluates to `TRUE` at line 1 in the source code, the expression $Y + X$

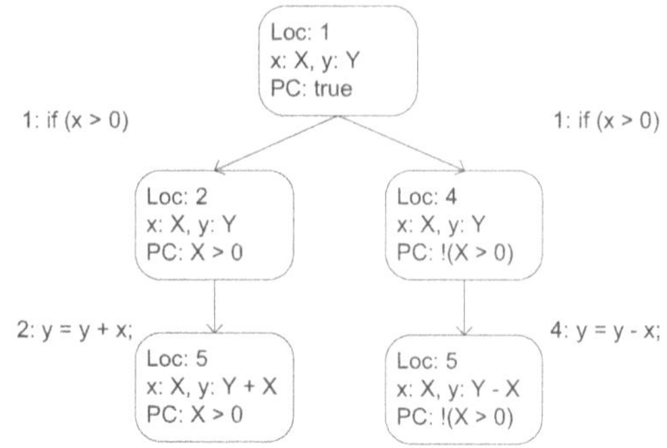

Figure 1. Symbolic execution tree for `testX()`

is computed and stored as the value of y. When $!(X > 0)$, the expression $Y - X$ is computed and stored as the value of y. A *symbolic summary* for procedure `testX` is made up of path conditions that represent the feasible execution paths in `testX`. The path conditions in the symbolic summary can be used as input to a subsequent analysis, e.g., the *solved* path conditions can be used as regression test case inputs.

2.2 Motivating Example

We use the example in Fig. 2 to illustrate how DiSE leverages information about program changes to direct symbolic execution and generate path conditions affected by the changes. Consider the source code for method `update(int PedalPos, int BSwitch, int PedalCmd)` shown in Fig. 2(a). The `update` procedure sets the value of two global variables, `AltPress` and `Meter`, based on the input values of its arguments. Assume a change was made to the `update` method at line 2 in Fig. 2(a) where the comparison operator is changed from $==$ to $<=$, as shown in the modified version of `update` presented in Fig. 2(a). Using full symbolic execution to validate this change results in 21 path conditions, each of which represents a program execution path of the modified version of `update`. As expected, the results of full symbolic execution include *all* execution paths for `update`, and no distinction is made between *affected* and *unaffected* program paths. And, as a result, any validation technique which uses these results may unnecessarily analyze unaffected program behaviors. For a small example such as this, a full analysis may be feasible; however, for larger methods or when complex constraints are involved, a full analysis may be infeasible.

To characterize the effects of the change to `update` using DiSE, we first compute the set of affected program locations. Consider the CFG computed for the modified version of `update` shown in Fig. 2(b). Each node corresponds to a program location in the source code; we use the node label to identify the corresponding code statement(s), and a node identifier appears in *italics* just outside the node, e.g., n_1, n_2, etc. Edges between the nodes represent possible flow of execution between the nodes. Nodes in the CFG that correspond to affected and changed program instructions are termed as affected and changed nodes respectively.

DiSE uses the results of a lightweight source file differential analysis to identify n_0 as having a direct correspondence to the change at line 2. The results of the static analysis computing affected locations indicate that nodes n_1, n_3, n_4, n_5, n_{11}, n_{13}, and n_{14} are *affected* write nodes–nodes that because of the change at line 2, may affect subsequent execution of a control node. Nodes n_0, n_2, n_{10}, and n_{12} are *affected* control nodes–nodes that may be affected by the change and that may affect the path condition. The information about affected locations is used to direct symbolic

```
1: int AltPress := 0; int Meter := 2 /* Global Vars */
procedure update(int PedalPos, int BSwitch, int PedalCmd)
2: if PedalPos <= 0/* changed conditional */ then
3:    PedalCmd = PedalCmd + 1
4: else if PedalPos == 1 then
5:    PedalCmd = PedalCmd + 2
6: else PedalCmd = PedalPos
7:
8: PedalCmd = PedalCmd + 1
9:
10: if BSwitch == 0 then
11:    Meter = 1
12: else if BSwitch == 1 then
13:    Meter = 2
14:
15: if PedalCmd == 2 then
16:    AltPress = 0
17: else if PedalCmd == 3 then
18:    AltPress = 1/4
19: else AltPress = 1/2
```

(a)

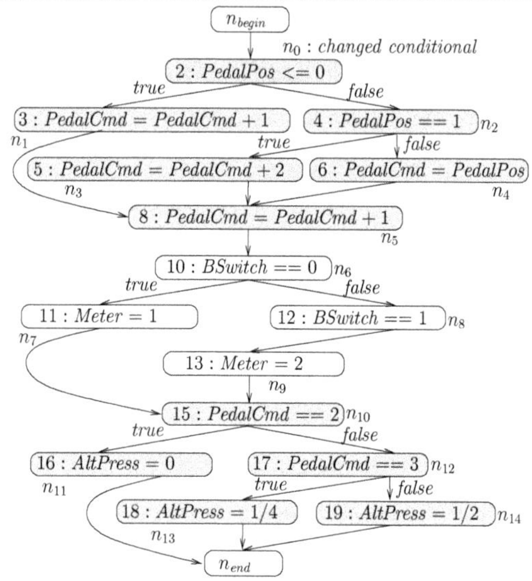

(b)

Figure 2. A simplified version of a Wheel Brake System. (a) Example program. (b) Control flow graph.

execution of the modified version of `update` to explore only the program behaviors affected by the change.

Pruning. To illustrate how DiSE prunes symbolic execution using the set of affected locations, consider a feasible execution path, $p_0 := \langle n_0, n_1, n_5, n_6, n_7, n_{10}, n_{11} \rangle$, generated during directed symbolic execution. The path p_0 contains the sequence of affected nodes, $\langle n_0, n_1, n_5, n_{10}, n_{11} \rangle$, and the sequence of unaffected nodes, $\langle n_6, n_7 \rangle$. However, another feasible path, $p_1 := \langle n_0, n_1, n_5, n_6, n_8, n_9, n_{10}, n_{11} \rangle$, is *pruned* during symbolic execution because the sequence of *affected* nodes is already covered by p_0. The only difference between p_0 and p_1 is the sequence of *unaffected* nodes—p_1 contains $\langle n_6, n_8, n_9 \rangle$ as the sequence of unaffected nodes. DiSE applies the same pruning technique throughout symbolic execution to generate a total of seven path conditions for `update`, versus the 21 path conditions generated by full symbolic execution. Each path condition generated by DiSE characterizes a program execution path that is affected by the change to `update`.

3. Directed Incremental Symbolic Execution

In this section we first provide a high level overview of our DiSE technique. We then present the two main algorithms of DiSE that compute the set of affected path conditions.

3.1 Overview

Inputs to DiSE. The inputs to DiSE are the control flow graphs (CFGs) for two versions of a procedure, *base* and *mod*, and the results of a lightweight differential (*diff*) analysis (e.g., source line or abstract syntax tree *diff*) comparing the two versions of the procedure. The results of the *diff* analysis identify the locations of the differences in the source code between *base* and *mod*. During a pre-processing step, DiSE maps the change information to the corresponding nodes in each CFG. The CFG for the base version, CFG_{base}, has nodes marked as *removed*, *changed*, or *unchanged* with respect to the CFG of the modified version, CFG_{mod}. The nodes in CFG_{mod} are marked as *added*, *changed*, or *unchanged* with respect to CFG_{base}. The results of the *diff* analysis are also used to compute a map ($diffMap$) that stores information relating nodes in CFG_{base} to their corresponding nodes in CFG_{mod}.

Computing Affected Locations. DiSE begins by performing a conservative, intra-procedural analysis to compute the set of nodes in CFG_{mod} that may be affected by the *removed* nodes in CFG_{base} or by the *changed* and *added* nodes in CFG_{mod}. This static analysis uses control dependence and data flow information to generate the set of affected CFG nodes in CFG_{mod}. These nodes correspond to conditional branch statements and to write statements in the modified version of the program that either influence, or may be influenced by the modifications made to the procedure, and as a result, may affect the path conditions computed by symbolic execution. Affected conditional branch nodes directly lead to the generation of affected path conditions. Affected write nodes indirectly lead to the generation of affected path condition–they either define a variable that may be subsequently read at an affected branch node, or the reachability of the affected write nodes is control dependent on an affected conditional branch node.

Directed Symbolic Execution. During this step, DiSE performs a form of *incremental* symbolic execution on the modified version of the procedure, leveraging the information computed during the previous step to explore only the parts of the program that are changed with respect to the base version of the procedure. The affected nodes information *directs* DiSE to explore only (feasible) paths where one or more *affected* nodes in CFG_{mod} are reachable on that path, and that sequence of affected nodes has not yet been explored. If either of these conditions is not met, then symbolic execution backtracks. By effectively "pruning" paths that generate unaffected path conditions, DiSE avoids the cost of exploring execution paths in the modified program version that are not affected by the change(s) to the program. The resulting set of path conditions computed by DiSE then characterizes the set of program execution behaviors in the modified version of the procedure that are affected by the change(s). Each (directly or indirectly) affected conditional branch node on the path is represented by a constraint in the path condition; conditional branch nodes that are not affected by the changes are represented by a constraint that represents a feasible path through the unaffected parts of the program.

3.2 Computing Affected Locations

The set of affected program locations is computed using conservative static analyses based on control and data dependences. The analysis is performed at an intra-procedural (per-method) level. The corresponding ramification is that DiSE does not generate affected path conditions arising from changes at the inter-procedural (sequence of methods) level. Extending the technique for inter-procedural system level analysis is part of our future work. We first present background definitions related to control flow graphs, control dependence, and data flow in order to define the rules DiSE uses to generate the affected locations sets.

Definition 3.1. *A* Control flow graph *(CFG) of a procedure in the program is a directed-graph represented formally by a tuple* $\langle N, E\rangle$. *N is the set of nodes, where each node is labeled with a unique program location identifier. The edges, $E \subseteq N \times N$, represent possible flow of execution between the nodes in the CFG. Each CFG has a single* begin, n_{begin}, *and* end, n_{end}, *node. All the nodes in the CFG are reachable from the n_{begin} and the n_{end} node is reachable from all nodes in the CFG.*

Definition 3.2. *(**Check for a CFG Path**) is a map* `IsCFGPath` : $N \times N \mapsto \{T, F\}$ *that returns true for a pair of nodes (n_i, n_j) if there exists a sequence of nodes $\pi := \langle n_0, n_1, \ldots\rangle$ such that $(n_k, n_{k+1}) \in E$ for $0 \leq k \leq |\pi| - 1$ and $n_0 = n_i$, $n_{|\pi|-1} = n_j$; otherwise it returns false.*

Definition 3.3. ***Vars*** *is the set of variable names that are either read or written to in a procedure.*

Definition 3.4. ***Cond*** *is the set of nodes $Cond \subseteq N$ where $n \in Cond$ is a conditional branch instruction.*

Definition 3.5. ***Write*** *is the set of nodes $Write \subseteq N$ where $n \in Write$ is a write instruction.*

Definition 3.6. *(**Variable Definitions**) is a map* `Def` : $N \mapsto Vars \cup \{\perp\}$ *that returns a variable $v \in Vars$ if the variable, v, is defined at node $n \in N$; otherwise returns $\perp$.*

Definition 3.7. *(**Variable Uses**) is a map* `Use` : $N \mapsto 2^{Vars} \cup \{\perp\}$ *that returns a set of variables $V \subseteq Vars$ where $v \in V$ is a variable being read at node n; otherwise returns $\perp$.*

Definition 3.8. *(**Post Dominance**) is a map* `postDom` : $N \times N \mapsto \{T, F\}$ *that returns true for an input pair of nodes (n_i, n_j) if, for each CFG path from n_i to n_{end}, $\pi := \langle n_i, \ldots, n_{end}\rangle$, there exists a k such that $n_j = n_k$ where $i \leq k \leq |\pi| - 1$ (n_j post dominates n_i); otherwise it returns false.*

Definition 3.9. *(**Control Dependence**) is a map* `controlD` : $N \times N \mapsto \{T, F\}$ *that returns true for an input pair of nodes (n_i, n_j) if node n_i has two successors n_k and n_l such that $(n_i, n_k), (n_i, n_l) \in E$, $n_k \neq n_l$,* `postDom`$(n_k, n_j) == T$, *and* `postDom`$(n_l, n_j) == F$; *otherwise it returns false.*

We provide intuitive descriptions for some definitions above using the example in Fig. 2. The set of $Vars$ contains variables $AltPress$, $PedalPos$, $PedalCmd$, $BSwitch$, and $Meter$. `Def`(n_9) returns the variable $Meter$ which is defined at line 13. Similarly the map `Uses`(n_{10}) returns $PedalCmd$, the variable being used at line 15. The map `postDom`(n_0, n_5) returns true because all paths from node n_0 to n_{end} have to go through n_5; an example path is $\langle n_0, n_1, n_3, n_5, \ldots, n_{end}\rangle$. Finally, node n_1 is control dependent n_0. The node n_0 has two successors n_1 and n_2, where `postDom`(n_1, n_1) is true and `postDom`(n_1, n_2) is false.

Approach. Two sets of affected nodes are computed and used by DiSE– the set of affected conditional (branch) nodes, ACN, and the set of affected write nodes, AWN. These sets contain nodes in CFG_{mod} that are marked as *changed* or *added* by the source line *diff* analysis. (Handling changes arising from remove nodes in CFG_{base} is described later in this section.) The ACN and AWN sets are updated by applying the rules specified in Fig. 3 until the sets reach a fixed-point. The analysis is guaranteed to terminate since the ACN and AWN sets contain nodes in a CFG – even nodes that are part of a loop are added at most once to these sets.

The rules in Fig. 3 specify the conditions under which DiSE adds nodes from CFG_{mod} to the affected sets based on the con-

$$\textbf{if } n_i \in ACN \wedge n_j \in Cond \wedge \texttt{controlD}(n_i, n_j) \quad \textbf{then } ACN := ACN \cup \{n_j\} \tag{1}$$

$$\textbf{if } n_i \in ACN \wedge n_j \in Write \wedge \texttt{controlD}(n_i, n_j) \quad \textbf{then } AWN := AWN \cup \{n_j\} \tag{2}$$

$$\textbf{if } n_i \in AWN \wedge n_j \in Cond \wedge \texttt{Def}(n_i) \in \texttt{Use}(n_j) \wedge \texttt{Def}(n_i) \neq \perp \wedge \texttt{IsCFGPath}(n_i, n_j) \quad \textbf{then } ACN := ACN \cup \{n_j\} \tag{3}$$

Figure 3. Updating affected sets based on control and data flow dependence.

$$\textbf{if } n_i \in Write \wedge (n_j \in AWN \vee n_j \in ACN) \wedge \texttt{Def}(n_i) \in \texttt{Use}(n_j) \wedge \texttt{Def}(n_i) \neq \perp \wedge \texttt{IsCFGPath}(n_i, n_j) \textbf{ then } AWN := AWN \cup \{n_i\} \tag{4}$$

Figure 4. Updating AWN set based on reaching definitions.

procedure `removeNodes`(CFG_{base}, *diffMap*)
1: ACN := `getRemovedConditionalNodes`(CFG_{base})
2: AWN := `getRemovedWriteNodes`(CFG_{base})
3: Apply rules in Fig. 3 and Fig. 4
4: ACN := `updateSets`(ACN, *diffMap*)
5: AWN := `updateSets`(AWN, *diffMap*)
procedure `updateSets`(AN, *diffMap*)
6: $ModN := \{\}$
7: **for each** $n \in AN$ **do**
8: $ModN := ModN \cup \{diffMap.\text{get}(n)\}$
9: **return** $ModN$

(a)

ACN	AWN	n_i	n_j	Rule
$\{n_0\}$	$\{\}$			
$\{n_0, n_2\}$	$\{\}$	n_0	n_2	Eq. (1)
$\{n_0, n_2\}$	$\{n_1\}$	n_0	n_1	Eq. (2)
$\{n_0, n_2\}$	$\{n_1, n_3\}$	n_2	n_3	Eq. (2)
$\{n_0, n_2\}$	$\{n_1, n_3, n_4\}$	n_2	n_4	Eq. (2)
$\{n_0, n_2, n_{10}\}$	$\{n_1, n_3, n_4\}$	n_1	n_{10}	Eq. (3)
$\{n_0, n_2, n_{10}\}$	$\{n_1, n_3, n_4, n_{11}\}$	n_{10}	n_{11}	Eq. (2)
$\{n_0, n_2, n_{10}, n_{12}\}$	$\{n_1, n_3, n_4, n_{11}\}$	n_1	n_{12}	Eq. (3)
$\{n_0, n_2, n_{10}, n_{12}\}$	$\{n_1, n_3, n_4, n_{11}, n_{13}\}$	n_{12}	n_{13}	Eq. (2)
$\{n_0, n_2, n_{10}, n_{12}\}$	$\{n_1, n_3, n_4, n_{11}, n_{13}, n_{14}\}$	n_{12}	n_{14}	Eq. (2)
$\{n_0, n_2, n_{10}, n_{12}\}$	$\{n_1, n_3, n_4, n_5, n_{11}, n_{13}, n_{14}\}$	n_5	n_{10}	Eq. (4)

(b)

Figure 5. Computing affected nodes. (a) Algorithm to compute affected nodes resulting from removing certain program instructions. (b) Demonstration of the computation of affected node set for the example in Fig. 2.

trol dependence relation and the resulting data flow information. The first two rules Eq. (1) and Eq. (2) in Fig. 3 specify that conditional branches and write statements that are control dependent on a *changed* or *added* node in the CFG_{mod}, are added to the affected set. Other nodes are added to the affected sets by repeatedly applying the rules that, in essence compute the transitive closure on the control dependences between the nodes. Eq. (1) states that if there exists a node n_i in ACN, and a conditional node n_j such that n_j is control dependent on n_i, then n_j is added to the set ACN. Similarly in Eq. (2) if n_j is a write statement that is control dependent on n_i, an element in ACN, then n_j is added to AWN. Eq. (3) intuitively specifies that conditional branches that use variables defined in the affected write set are added to the affected conditional set. If the definition of a variable in a write statement, n_i, in AWN is used in a conditional branch statement, n_j, and there is a path in the CFG from n_i to n_j, then n_j is added to ACN. The rules are iteratively applied until the sizes of ACN and AWN do not change.

Eq. (4) in Fig. 4 is applied to update AWN based on the definitions of variables that reach the nodes in the affected sets, after the analysis in Fig. 3 reaches a fixed-point. Eq. (4) specifies that if a variable is defined at a write statement n_i that is used at node n_j such that n_j is in one of the affected sets, and there exists a CFG path from n_i to n_j then n_i is added to the AWN set. The rule specified in Eq. (4) is also guaranteed to reach a fixed-point and terminate since the rule is applied to the nodes in the CFG.

Handling Removed Instructions. When there are nodes marked as *removed* in CFG_{base}, it indicates that the corresponding node does not exist in CFG_{mod}. The removed node may, however, affect the execution of other nodes in CFG_{mod}. The algorithm to compute the effects of the removed nodes is shown in Fig. 5(a).

The `removeNodes` algorithm in Fig. 5 computes the control and data dependence flow information on CFG_{base}. The affected sets are initialized to *removed* nodes, and after applying the rules in Fig. 3 and Fig. 4, the affected sets contain all the nodes in CFG_{base} that are influenced by the remove nodes (lines 1-3 in Fig. 5(a)). Next, for each of the CFG_{base} nodes in the affected sets the corresponding node mapping to CFG_{mod} found in the *diffMap* is used to replace the elements in the affected sets (lines 4-9 in Fig. 5(a)). Recall that the source line differential analysis provides *diffMap* that maps *unchanged* and *changed* nodes corresponding from CFG_{base} to CFG_{mod}. For the nodes marked as *removed* in CFG_{base} the get method on *diffMap* returns the empty set.

The `removeNodes` algorithm in Fig. 5(a) generates all nodes affected by program instructions *removed* from the base version. Finally, the affected set is updated with any other *changed* or *added* nodes present in CFG_{mod} and the computing affected set algorithm as presented earlier is applied to generate the final affected sets.

Example. To illustrate how affected sets are generated, consider the example in Fig. 2. Suppose, the conditional branch at line 2 has the predicate $PedalPos == 0$ in the base program version that is modified to $PedalPos <= 0$ as shown in Fig. 2. The CFG node corresponding to line 2 in Fig. 2(a) is n_0 in Fig. 2(b). The ACN set is initialized to the lone element n_0 (a *changed* node) and the AWN set is initialized as empty. The sets are updated based on the rules in Fig. 3 as shown in Fig. 5(b).

Node n_2 in Fig. 2(b) is a conditional branch statement that is control dependent on n_0 causing n_2 to be added to ACN. The write statements at nodes n_1, n_3, and n_4 are added since they are control dependent on nodes n_0 or n_2. Nodes n_{10} and n_{12} are added to ACN since they use the variable $PedalCmd$ that is defined in nodes n_1, n_3, and n_4 contained in AWN. The write statement at node n_{11} is control dependent on n_{10}, while the write statements at nodes n_{13} and n_{14} are control dependent on n_{12}; hence nodes n_{11}, n_{13}, and n_{14} are added to AWN. Finally, when the sets ACN and AWN reach a fixed-point after applying the rules in Fig. 3, the Eq. (4) in Fig. 4 is applied. Applying the Eq. (4) rule adds the write statement at node n_5 that defines the variable $PedalCmd$ and is also used at nodes n_{10} and n_{12}.

The affected sets are used to direct the symbolic execution in the next phase of DiSE.

3.3 Directed Symbolic Execution

The directed symbolic execution technique executes the feasible paths that contain sequences of affected nodes generated in the static analysis. The analysis generates path conditions that contain constraints related to the modifications in the program. All feasible path conditions related to the affected nodes are generated during the analysis. Each path condition contains a feasible instance of the conditions generated from the unchanged parts of the code. As a result, the directed symbolic execution process generates fully formed path conditions, while at the same time avoids generating many path conditions arising from sequences of unaffected nodes in the program. This enables directed symbolic execution to not only explore all branches in the symbolic execution tree influenced by the affected nodes but, also to prune the paths related to the unaffected parts of the code.

The algorithm for directed symbolic execution is shown in Fig. 6. The inputs to the algorithm are the affected sets ACN and AWN, and a user-specified depth *bound* for the symbolic execution. The `DiSE` procedure is invoked with the initial symbolic state of the program. Recall that the symbolic state contains a current program location, a symbolic representation of the variables, and a path condition. There are four global sets initialized on lines 3 and 4 in Fig. 6. The sets $ExCond$ and $ExWrite$ track which of the affected nodes have been "explored" during symbolic execution while the sets $UnExCond$ and $UnExWrite$ track those nodes that are "unexplored" and still need to be explored. Hence, $ExCond$ and $ExWrite$ are initialized as empty whereas $UnExCond$ and $UnExWrite$ are initialized to the ACN and AWN sets respectively.

The `DiSE` procedure in Fig. 6 provides the basic search strategy. At line 5, if the current state is at a depth bound greater than the user-specified depth *bound* or the state is an error, then the search returns to explore an alternate path; otherwise exploration continues along the same path. The `getCFGNode` method on line 6 takes as input the symbolic state, s, and returns the corresponding CFG node, n. Note that the current program location of the symbolic state is used to map a symbolic state to its CFG node. The procedure `UpdateExploredSet` is invoked with CFG node n. For each successor state of s that the procedure `AffectedLocIsReachable` returns true the `DiSE` procedure is invoked with the corresponding successor state, exploring the relevant states in a depth-first manner.

The procedure `UpdateExploredSet` checks whether the input node n is contained in one of the unexplored sets ($UnExWrite$ or $UnExCond$) in order to track the affected nodes explored during symbolic execution (lines 30–35). If the node n is contained in the unexplored write set, $UnExWrite$, then n is removed from $UnExWrite$ and added to the explored write set, $ExWrite$. Similarly, a corresponding update is performed on $UnExCond$ and $ExCond$ when n is contained within $UnExCond$. The procedure `ResetUnExploredSet`, shown at lines 37–42, does the reverse; removes the input node from the explored sets and adds it to the respective unexplored set.

The `AffectedLocIsReachable` returns true if the CFG node, n_i, corresponding to the input symbolic state, s_i, can reach a node in the set of unexplored affected nodes to indicate that exploration should continue along the path that contains s_i; else, it returns false indicating that the path containing s_i is not influenced by the modifications to the program and should be pruned. The `CheckLoops` procedure is invoked to handle generating sequences of affected nodes through loops at line 15. A temporary set $UnExplored$ is initialized with the nodes in $UnExWrite$ and $UnExCond$, while $Explored$ is initialized with nodes from $ExWrite$ and $ExCond$ at lines 16 and 17. Next, when an affected node in $UnExplored$, n_j, is reachable from n_i; first, the variable *isReachable* is set to true, and

```
procedure init()/* Input := ACN; AWN; bound */
 1: DiSE(getInitState())
 2:
 3: /* ExCond := ∅; ExWrite := ∅ */
 4: /* UnExCond := ACN; UnExWrite := AWN */
procedure DiSE(s)
 5: if GetDepth(s) > bound ∨ error(s) then return
 6: n := GetCFGNode(s)
 7: UpdateExploredSet(n)
 8: for each s_i ∈ GetSuccessors(s) do
 9:    if AffectedLocIsReachable(s_i) then
10:       DiSE(s_i)
11: return
12:
procedure AffectedLocIsReachable(s_i)
13: IsReachable := false
14: n_i := getCFGNode(s_i)
15: CheckLoops(n_i)
16: UnExplored := UnExWrite ∪ UnExCond
17: Explored := ExWrite ∪ ExCond
18: for each n_j ∈ UnExplored do
19:    if ¬IsCFGPath(n_i, n_j) then continue
20:    IsReachable := true
21:    for each n_k ∈ Explored do
22:       if ¬IsCFGPath(n_j, n_k) then continue
23:       ResetUnExploredSet(n_k)
24: return IsReachable
25:
procedure CheckLoops(n)
26: if IsLoopEntryNode(n_i) then
27:    for each n' ∈ GetSCC(n) do
28:       ResetUnExploredSet(n')
29:
procedure UpdateExploredSet(n)
30: if n ∈ UnExWrite then
31:    ExWrite := ExWrite ∪ {n}
32:    UnExWrite := UnExWrite \ {n}
33: if n ∈ UnExCond then
34:    ExCond := ExCond ∪ {n}
35:    UnExCond := UnExCond \ {n}
36:
procedure ResetUnExploredSet(n)
37: if n ∈ ExWrite then
38:    UnExWrite := UnExWrite ∪ {n}
39:    ExWrite := ExWrite \ {n}
40: if n ∈ ExCond then
41:    UnExCond := UnExCond ∪ {n}
42:    ExCond := ExCond \ {n}
```

Figure 6. Pseudocode for the directed symbolic execution algorithm using affected sets.

second the nodes in the explored sets that are reachable from unexplored sets along the execution path containing n_i are moved back to the unexplored set (by invoking the `ResetUnExploredSet` procedure). Resetting the unexplored sets enables directed symbolic execution to explore all sequences of affected nodes that lie along feasible execution paths.

The `CheckLoops` procedure allows DiSE to explore sequences of affected nodes that are contained within loops. If the input node, n to `CheckLoops` is the entry node to a loop (line 26), then for all the nodes that are part of loop (strongly connected component containing n—`GetSCC(n)`) are added to the unexplored set if they have been previously explored by invoking the `ResetUnExploredSet`. A strongly connected component is a set of nodes where each node can be reached from all of the other nodes, and a strongly connected component has a single entry and a single exit point.

Example. In Table 1 we show part of the directed symbolic execution performed for the example in Fig. 2. For brevity, we refer to

	CFG Node for symbolic states	*ExWrite*	*ExCond*	*UnExWrite*	*UnExCond*
1	$\langle\rangle$	$\{\}$	$\{\}$	$\{n_1, n_3, n_4, n_5, n_{11}, n_{13}, n_{14}\}$	$\{n_0, n_2, n_{10}, n_{12}\}$
2	$\langle n_0\rangle$	$\{\}$	$\{n_0\}$	$\{n_1, n_3, n_4, n_5, n_{11}, n_{13}, n_{14}\}$	$\{n_2, n_{10}, n_{12}\}$
3	$\langle n_0, n_1\rangle$	$\{n_1\}$	$\{n_0\}$	$\{n_3, n_4, n_5, n_{11}, n_{13}, n_{14}\}$	$\{n_2, n_{10}, n_{12}\}$
4	$\langle n_0, n_1, n_5\rangle$	$\{n_1, n_5\}$	$\{n_0\}$	$\{n_3, n_4, , n_{11}, n_{13}, n_{14}\}$	$\{n_2, n_{10}, n_{12}\}$
5	$\langle n_0, n_1, n_5, n_6, n_7, n_{10}\rangle$	$\{n_1, n_5\}$	$\{n_0, n_{10}\}$	$\{n_3, n_4, n_{11}, n_{13}, n_{14}\}$	$\{n_2, n_{12}\}$
6	$\langle n_0, n_1, n_5, n_6, n_7, n_{10}, n_{11}\rangle$	$\{n_1, n_5, n_{11}\}$	$\{n_0, n_{10}\}$	$\{n_3, n_4, n_{13}, n_{14}\}$	$\{n_2, n_{12}\}$
7	$\langle n_0, n_1, n_5, n_6, n_7, n_{10}, n_{12}\rangle$	$\{n_1, n_5, n_{11}\}$	$\{n_0, n_{10}, n_{12}\}$	$\{n_3, n_4\}$	$\{n_2\}$
8	$\langle n_0, n_1, n_5, n_6, n_7, n_{10}, n_{12}, n_{13}\rangle$	$\{n_1, n_5, n_{11}, n_{13}\}$	$\{n_0, n_{10}, n_{12}\}$	$\{n_3, n_4, n_{14}\}$	$\{n_2\}$
9	$\langle n_0, n_1, n_5, n_6, n_7, n_{10}, n_{12}, n_{14}\rangle$	$\{n_1, n_5, n_{11}, n_{13}, n_{14}\}$	$\{n_0, n_{10}, n_{12}\}$	$\{n_3, n_4\}$	$\{n_2\}$
10	$\langle n_0, n_1, n_5, n_6, n_8(\textit{no path})\rangle$	$\{n_1, n_5, n_{11}, n_{13}, n_{14}\}$	$\{n_0, n_{10}, n_{12}\}$	$\{n_3, n_4\}$	$\{n_2\}$
11	$\langle n_0, n_2\rangle$	$\{n_1\}$	$\{n_0, n_2\}$	$\{n_3, n_4, n_5, n_{11}, n_{13}, n_{14}\}$	$\{n_{10}, n_{12}\}$

Table 1. Part of the directed symbolic execution performed on the example in Fig. 2.

CFG nodes corresponding to symbolic states when describing the execution and sequence of states. For example the second column in Table 1 shows a sequence of CFG nodes corresponding to the sequence of symbolic states generated during symbolic execution. The *ExWrite* and *ExCond* are initialized to the empty set, while the *UnExWrite* and *UnExCond* are initialized to the respective affected sets. At n_0, an affected conditional node is moved from *UnExCond* to *ExCond* at line 2 in Table 1; similar updates occur at lines 3, 4, 5, and 7. At lines 4 and 5 in Table 1, execution continues along the successor states since a node in an unexplored set is reachable from the last node in the sequence. For example, at line 4, node n_{10} in *UnExCond* is reachable from n_5 at the end of the sequence $\langle n_0, n_1, n_5\rangle$. There is no path to any nodes in the unexplored sets at line 10 in Table 1 from n_8.

In Table 1, at line 11, nodes are moved from explored to the unexplored set. The explored conditional branches n_{10} and n_{12} are reachable from node n_2, and the explored write instructions n_5, n_{11}, n_{13}, and n_{14} are reachable from n_2 as seen in Fig. 2(b); as node n_2 is added to explored set, nodes n_5, n_{10}, n_{11}, n_{12}, n_{13}, and n_{14} are added back to the unexplored sets in order for DiSE to explore different sequences of affected nodes and generate corresponding feasible execution paths (if possible).

Theorem 3.10. *For any sequence of affected nodes that lie on some feasible execution path within the specified depth bound, DiSE explores one execution path containing that sequence of nodes.*

Proof Sketch. By contradiction. There are two cases to consider: I) There exists a feasible path (within the specified depth bound) that contains a sequence of affected nodes, which DiSE does not explore and II) DiSE explores more than one feasible execution path for some sequence of affected nodes (within the specified depth bound).

Case I Let $q := \langle n_1, \ldots, n_k\rangle$ be a sequence of affected nodes, which is not explored by DiSE but is contained in a feasible execution path. By construction, DiSE must explore n_1, since it is an affected node that is added to *UnExWrite* or *UnExCond* during initialization. Assume n_i is the first node in q such that DiSE explores a feasible path, p, that contains the sub-sequence $\langle n_1, \ldots, n_{i-1}\rangle$ but does not explore an execution path that contains the sub-sequence $\langle n_1, \ldots, n_i\rangle$. Consider DiSE's exploration of p when it processes node n_{i-1}. Since n_i is reachable from n_{i-1} and is an affected node, n_i must be contained in *UnExWrite* or *UnExCond* (line 23). Hence DiSE will explore a path that contains the sub-sequence $\langle n_1, \ldots, n_i\rangle$. Contradiction.

Case II Assume for a sequence of affected nodes that lie on path p explored by DiSE, it explores another path p' containing the same sequence of affected nodes. Let n be the last affected node on path p such that the p and p' have the exact same sub-sequence of affected and unaffected nodes up to and including n. Let $q := \langle n, n_1 \ldots n_k, m\rangle$ be the sub-sequence of nodes on p such that each n_i is an unaffected node and m is an affected node. Let $q' := \langle n, n'_1 \ldots n'_j, m\rangle$ be the corresponding sub-sequence of nodes on p'. By the construction of the algorithm in Fig. 6, when DiSE considers the affected node n, it only explores one path and prunes the others by controlling the unexplored and unexplored sets in the `UpdateExploredSets` and `ResetUnExploredSet` until the next affected node, which in this case is m. Hence, q and q' are identical. Contradiction.

4. Evaluation

In this section we evaluate the effectiveness of DiSE at generating affected path conditions relative to the path conditions generated by full symbolic execution of the changed methods in evolving software. To perform our evaluation, we implemented DiSE and performed a case-study on three Java applications, comparing the results of DiSE with full, traditional symbolic execution of the changed versions of the method. We begin this section with a description of our implementation of DiSE.

4.1 Tool Support

We implemented DiSE in Symbolic PathFinder (SPF) [26, 28], a symbolic execution extension to the Java PathFinder model checker–a Java bytecode analysis framework [36]. SPF is an open source execution engine that symbolically executes Java bytecode. SPF supports a variety of constraint solvers/decision procedures for solving path conditions; in this work we use the Choco constraint solver [6]. In general, state matching is undecidable when states represent path conditions on unbounded input data. Hence, SPF does not perform any state matching and explores the symbolic execution tree using a stateless search. Furthermore, if the solver is unable to determine the satisfiability of the path condition within a certain time bound, SPF treats the path condition as unsatisfiable. While this situation does not occur for any of the artifacts in our study, this limitation of constraint solvers could affect DiSE, causing it to miss generating affected path conditions in the modified program. Loops and recursion can be bounded by placing a depth limit on the search depth in SPF or by limiting the number of constraints encoded for any given path; SPF indicates when one of these bounds has been reached during symbolic execution. There are no loops or recursive calls in the artifacts used in our empirical study, hence, we do not specify a depth bound.

DiSE extends SPF by implementing custom data and control dependence analyses that compute a conservative approximation of the the affected locations for a changed method. DiSE performs these analyses when the the modified method is invoked during symbolic execution, and then uses the information about the affected locations to direct symbolic execution within SPF.

4.2 Case-Study

The goal of our technique is to direct symbolic execution on a modified program version to explore only program conditions that are *affected* by the changes to the source code. We evaluate the cost and effectiveness of DiSE relative to full symbolic execution on the changed methods by considering the following research questions:

RQ1: How does the cost of applying DiSE compare to full symbolic execution on the changed method?

RQ2: How does the number of affected path conditions generated by DiSE compare with the number of path conditions generated by full symbolic execution?

4.2.1 Artifacts

To evaluate DiSE we compared method versions from three Java artifacts. The first program, the Wheel Brake System (WBS), is a synchronous reactive component from the automotive domain. The Java model is based on a Simulink model derived from the WBS case example found in ARP 4761 [17, 30]. We use the `update(int PedalPos, boolean AutoBrake, boolean Skid)` method in WBS to evaluate DiSE. This method determines how much braking pressure to apply based on the environment. The Simulink model was translated to C using tools developed at Rockwell Collins and manually translated to Java. It consists of one class and 231 source lines of code.

Our second artifact is a version of the Java program used to model NASA's On-board Abort Executive (OAE) . The OAE models the Crew Exploration Vehicle's prototype ascent abort handling software, receiving its inputs from sensors and other software components. The inputs are analyzed to determine the status of the ascent flight rules and to evaluate which ascent abort modes are feasible. Once a flight rule is broken and an abort mode is selected, it is relayed to the rest of the system for initiation. The version of OAE evaluated for this work consists of five classes. The method under analysis consists of approximately 150 source lines of code.

The third artifact we used to evaluate DiSE is the Altitude Switch (ASW) application. This program is a synchronous reactive component from the avionics domain. It turns power on to a Device Of Interest (DOI) when the aircraft descends below a threshold altitude above ground level (AGL). It was developed as a Simulink model, and was automatically translated to Java using tools developed at Vanderbilt University [34].

To evaluate DiSE in an empirical study we required multiple versions of each method being analyzed. Because multiple versions of these artifacts were not available, we generated versions by manually creating mutants of the base version (v0) of the method under analysis. When creating mutants, we considered a broad range of changes that can be applied to the code: change location, change type and number of changes. We introduced changes at the beginning, middle and end of each method. We also considered the control structures in the code, and make changes at various depths in nested control structures. Each mutant has one, two or three changed Java statements, resulting in up to nine changed nodes in the CFG for the changed version of a method as shown in Table 4.2.1.

In the WBS example, versions 1–6 contain a single changed Java source statement, versions 7–11 contain two changed statements and versions 12–16 contain three changed statements. For the ASW example, we made a single change to versions 1–11, and two changes to versions 12–15. For the OAE example, a single change was made to versions 1–6, two changes are made to versions 7 and 8, and version 9 contains three changed Java source statements. The versions that contain multiple changes were created by combining the individual mutations made to versions with a single change. For example, version 12 of the WBS example contains the same individual changes as versions 1, 4, and 5. Each change involved the addition, removal or modification of a statement. Control statements were modified by mutating the comparison operator, e.g., from $<$ to $<=$, or the operand, e.g., mutating the program variables involved in the comparison. Non-control statements were modified by changing the value assigned to a program variable.

4.2.2 Variables and Measures

The *independent* variable in our study is the symbolic execution algorithm used in our empirical study. We use the DiSE algorithm, and as a control, we use full (traditional) symbolic execution as implemented in the SPF framework. For our study, we selected three dependent variables and measures: 1) *time*, 2) *states explored*, and 3) *number of path conditions generated*. *Time* is measured as the total elapsed time reported by SPF. It includes the time spent computing the affected program locations and the time spent performing symbolic execution. *States explored* provides a count of the number of symbolic states generated during symbolic execution. *Number of path conditions generated* provides a count of the number of program execution paths generated by a given technique. *Time* and *states explored* are used to relate the cost of DiSE to the cost of full symbolic execution of the changed method (RQ1), while *number of path conditions generated* is used to judge the effectiveness of DiSE relative to full symbolic execution (RQ2).

4.2.3 Experiment Setup

To perform our study, we compiled all of our artifacts using Java version 1.6.0_22. We used a custom Java application to perform a lightweight *diff* analysis comparing the abstract syntax tree (AST) for each mutant with the AST for the base version of the program. We then analyzed each mutant version with DiSE, using the results of the AST diff. We also performed symbolic execution on each mutant using standard symbolic execution in SPF (JPF v6). The study was performed on a MacBook Pro running at 2.26 GHz with 2 GB of memory and running Mac OS X version 10.5.8.

4.2.4 Threats to Validity

The primary threats to *external validity* for our study are (1) the use of SPF within which we implemented our technique, (2) the use of Choco as the underlying constraint solver, (3) the selection of artifacts used to evaluate DiSE, and (4) the changes applied to create the mutants. Implementing DiSE in another framework or using another constraint solver/decision procedure could produce different results; however, replicated studies with other tool frameworks would address this threat. The artifacts selected for our study are control applications that are amenable to symbolic execution. The artifacts are comparable in structure and complexity to other artifacts that we are aware of that are used to evaluate symbolic execution techniques. The mutant versions we used to perform our study were created manually, and may or may not reflect actual program changes; however, the mutations were developed in a systematic way that considered program location, change type, and number of changes. Further evaluation of DiSE on a broader range of program types and on programs with actual version histories would address this threat.

The primary threats to *internal validity* are the potential faults in the implementation of our algorithms and in SPF. We controlled for this threat by testing our algorithms on examples that we can manually verify. With respect to threats to *construct validity*, the metrics we selected to evaluate the cost of DiSE are commonly used to measure the cost of symbolic execution.

Version	CFG Nodes		Time (mm:ss)		States Explored		Path Conditions	
	Changed	Affected	DiSE	Full Symbc	DiSE	Full Symbc	DiSE	Full Symbc
v1	0	0	00:19	17:19	23	3,948,476	0	1,728
v2	1	1	00:22	16:49	564	3,948,476	0	1,728
v3	1	16	00:21	17:03	30	3,948,476	1	1,728
v4	4	18	00:20	18:07	34	3,948,476	1	1,728
v5	4	18	00:20	17:56	34	3,948,476	1	1,728
v6	1	26	00:32	16:49	24,036	3,948,476	381	1,728
v7	5	12	00:29	16:37	37	3,957,692	2	1,728
v8	4	12	00:30	16:33	44	3,948,476	3	1,728
v9	4	3	00:32	16:22	23	3,948,476	0	1,728
v10	1	13	00:28	20:15	38	3,948,476	3	1,728
v11	1	0	00:31	22:14	23	3,948,476	0	1,728
v12	4	3	00:32	20:21	23	3,948,476	0	1,728
v13	1	0	00:31	17:13	23	3,948,476	0	1,728
v14	9	18	00:30	18:50	41	3,957,692	2	1,728
v15	5	30	00:47	18:36	24,148	3,948,476	383	1,728

(a) ASW Example

Version	CFG Nodes		Time (mm:ss)		States Explored		Path Conditions	
	Changed	Affected	DiSE	Full Symbc	DiSE	Full Symbc	DiSE	Full Symbc
v1	1	39	03:19	02:30	677,976	677,976	24	24
v2	1	7	00:08	02:22	93	677,976	17	24
v3	1	3	00:27	02:41	65,976	677,976	12	24
v4	1	0	00:08	02:44	17	677,976	1	24
v5	7	56	00:23	03:44	59,610	1,317,048	14	24
v6	1	1	00:08	02:44	17	677,976	1	24
v7	1	39	03:07	02:51	677,976	677,976	24	24
v8	8	57	00:29	03:45	59,610	1,317,048	14	24
v9	2	4	00:33	02:41	65,976	677,976	12	24
v10	2	39	03:40	02:51	677,976	677,976	24	24
v11	7	56	00:28	03:43	59,610	1,317,048	14	24
v12	8	65	00:31	03:54	70,129	1,317,048	6	24
v13	9	57	00:29	03:44	59,610	1,317,048	14	24
v14	3	39	03:39	02:51	677,976	677,976	24	24
v15	3	42	03:37	02:51	677,976	677,976	24	24
v16	8	56	00:28	03:43	59,610	1,317,048	14	24

(b) WBS Example

Version	CFG Nodes		Time (mm:ss)		States Explored		Path Conditions	
	Changed	Affected	DiSE	Full Symbc	DiSE	Full Symbc	DiSE	Full Symbc
v1	1	41	00:30	08:34	81,737	264,885	13,082	130,820
v2	1	2	00:04	08:34	23	264,885	2	130,820
v3	2	2	00:15	08:41	33,341	264,885	3,926	130,820
v4	2	2	00:04	08:39	56	264,882	3	130,820
v5	2	2	00:03	08:41	36	264,885	2	130,820
v6	3	7	00:57	10:27	134,065	264,885	26,164	130,820
v7	2	43	00:53	09:32	107,901	264,885	26,164	130,820
v8	3	4	00:17	10:32	41,193	264,885	7,852	130,820
v9	4	43	00:53	10:31	107,901	264,885	26,164	130,820

(c) OAE Example

Table 2. DiSE and Symbolic Execution Results

4.2.5 Results and Analysis

In this section, we present the results of our case-study, and analyze the results with respect to our two research questions. In Tables 4.2.1(a)–(c) we list the results of running DiSE and full symbolic execution on each version of each Java artifact. For each mutant version of the method, we list the number of CFG nodes changed (*Changed*), the number of CFG nodes affected by the changes (*Affected*), and the metrics described in Section 4.2.2 – the time to perform DiSE and the time to perform traditional symbolic execution of the mutant version as reported by SPF, the number of states explored during execution of each technique, and the number of path conditions generated by each technique in the resulting method summary. The results for DiSE are listed under the subheading *DiSE* and the results for traditional symbolic execution are listed under the subheading *Full Symbc*.

RQ1 (Cost). In Tables 4.2.1(a)–(c), we can see that for all versions of the ASW and OAE examples, and for the majority of versions in the WBS example, DiSE takes considerably less time than full symbolic execution. In many cases, the differences in time is several orders of magnitude. For all of the examples, when the changes to the program do not affect all path conditions (program paths), DiSE takes at most 20% of the time taken by full symbolic execution. For the five versions of the WBS example (v1, v7, v10, v14, and v15) where DiSE explores the same number of states as full symbolic execution, the time taken by DiSE is 9%–30% longer than symbolic execution. This extra execution time accounts for the overhead of computing the affected locations and supporting data structures.

For all of our examples, there is considerable variation in the number of states explored by DiSE; our intuition is that other factors beyond the number of changes, e.g., location and nature

Version	v1	v2	v3	v4	v5	v6	v7	v8	v9	v10	v11	v12	v13	v14	v15
# Changes	1	1	1	1	1	1	1	1	1	1	1	2	2	2	2
Selected	0	0	0	1	0	59	2	2	0	3	0	0	0	2	60
Added	0	0	1	0	1	0	0	0	0	0	0	0	0	0	0
Total Tests	0	0	1	1	1	59	2	2	0	3	0	0	0	2	60

(a) ASW Example

Version	v1	v2	v3	v4	v5	v6	v7	v8	v9	v10	v11	v12	v13	v14	v15	v16
# Changes	1	1	1	1	1	1	2	2	2	2	2	3	3	3	3	3
Selected	20	17	12	1	14	1	20	14	12	20	14	5	14	20	20	14
Added	4	0	0	0	0	0	4	0	0	4	0	1	0	4	4	0
Total Tests	24	17	12	1	14	1	24	14	12	24	14	6	14	24	24	14

(b) WBS Example

Version	v1	v2	v3	v4	v5	v6	v7	v8	v9
# Changes	1	1	1	1	1	1	2	2	3
Selected	1	0	89	2	2	2	178	2	584
Added	291	2	0	0	0	582	0	582	0
Total Tests	292	2	89	2	2	584	178	584	584

(c) OAE Example

Table 3. Regression Testing Results

of the change, also have a considerable effect on the reductions that can be achieved by DiSE (or any other technique that can characterize the effects of program changes). We also conjecture that program structure, particularly with regard to the number and complexity of the constraints generated during symbolic execution contributes to the differences in execution time for each technique.

RQ2 (Effectiveness). The number of path conditions computed by DiSE varies greatly between versions for all three examples as shown in Tables 4.2.1(a)–(c). For the 15 versions analyzed in the ASW example, DiSE computes between zero and three path conditions for 13 versions. For the other two versions, DiSE computes approximately 22% of the path conditions generated by full symbolic execution (381 and 383 path conditions). In v1 of the ASW example, no CFG nodes are changed due to a compiler optimization that effectively masks the change, and for the remaining versions where no path conditions are generated, one or more CFG nodes was affected, however, the changes do not affect the path conditions generated by DiSE.

While none of the changes require DiSE to explore all paths in the ASW or OAE examples, in five of the 16 versions of the WBS example, DiSE generate the same number of path conditions as full symbolic execution. For these five versions, the number of *changed* CFG nodes ranges from one to three (out of 100 CFG nodes), and the number of *affected* CFG nodes ranges from 39 to 42. On the other hand, in v12 of the WBS example where only six path conditions are generated by DiSE (compared with 24 by full symbolic execution), eight CFG nodes are changed and 65 nodes are affected. In the OAE example, the change made to v6 affects seven CFG nodes (10%) and generates 26,164 path conditions – 20% of the path conditions computed by full symbolic execution. In v7, the changes affect 43 CFG nodes (62%) and yet the same number of of path conditions is generated. Based on our analysis of the mutants created for these examples, there does not appear to be any correlation between the number or percentage of affected nodes and the number of affected path conditions.

Overall, our study demonstrates that for the examples used in this study, DiSE has potential application for detecting and characterizing affected program behaviors in evolving software. In the artifacts used in our evaluation, DiSE was able to correctly identify and characterize the subset of path conditions computed by full symbolic execution as *affected*. In some instances, the change affected only a small percentage of path conditions, and in others, the change(s) had a much greater impact. When only a subset of the path conditions were affected by the changes, DiSE was able to consistently compute the affected path conditions in less time – often several orders of magnitude – than full symbolic execution; when all of the path conditions were affected by the changes, the overhead incurred by DiSE was between nine and 30% for these examples.

5. Discussion

The goal of DiSE is to enable more efficient symbolic execution by focusing it on generating affected path conditions. DiSE uses a conservative analysis to identify affected program locations. Thus, in principle, DiSE may generate some path conditions that represent unchanged paths. However, as experimental results demonstrate, DiSE is effective at focusing symbolic execution on affected program behaviors and enables efficient incremental symbolic execution.

5.1 Bug finding using DiSE

DiSE can handle programs with assertions when the "assert" statements are de-sugared into "if" and "throw" statements. In Java programs, this de-sugaring takes place when assert statements in Java source are compiled into Java byte code. Since DiSE performs symbolic execution on Java byte code, DiSE will not miss detecting a failed assertion violation caused by a program change. Thus, DiSE supports finding bugs when assertions are present and assertion failures characterize bugs. If the assertions were written in a language other than the underlying programming language (e.g., Alloy [16] assertions in Java programs), our technique would work with the assertions translated to Java (e.g., from Alloy).

5.2 Software evolution

The results of DiSE can be used to support various software evolution tasks. We present one such application—regression testing as it relates to test case selection and augmentation. We note that our goal is not to demonstrate the effectiveness of test case selection and augmentation, but, rather to demonstrate one application of DiSE results to support software evolution tasks.

SPF outputs values that can be used for the method arguments (test inputs) based on the generated path conditions. The test inputs are produced by solving the constraints in the path condition and using the resulting values to generate a call to the method under analysis. The results are output in string format. Our implementation of test case selection and augmentation is trivial in its approach – it simply performs a string comparison of the test cases generated for the original version (by full symbolic execution) with the tests generated by DiSE. Tests generated for the original version of the method represent an existing test suite. Tests generated by DiSE that are also found in the tests generated for the original version are marked as *selected*, while the other tests are considered tests to be *added* to augment the test suite.

The results of using DiSE to perform test case selection and test case augmentation for our three examples are shown in Tables 3(a)–(c). The combination of *selected* and *added* tests execute all of the branches in the program that are in some way affected by the changes made to the method under analysis. Full symbolic execution on the original version of ASW generates 256 tests, while full symbolic execution on the WBS and OAE examples generates 24 tests and 2,920 tests respectively. Note that the number of test cases generated by symbolic execution and by DiSE differs from the number of path conditions generated by each technique; this is due to the fact that the current implementation of the test generation tool computes input values only for the method arguments, i.e., a partial state. As a result, when fields are represented by symbolic values, multiple path conditions generated by a given technique may map to a single set of concrete inputs to the method under analysis.

For all of the artifacts in our study, the results of DiSE can be used to identify test cases that can be re-used, and the test cases that exercise affected path conditions for which test cases must be generated. For the ASW and WBS examples, DiSE results show that only a small number of test cases is necessary to augment the test suite for the new version of the program. For the OAE example, the results of DiSE indicate that for some changes, e.g., v3, it is unnecessary to generate any new test cases. For versions v6 and v8, however, only two of the existing test cases are valid for the new version of the program and 584 test cases are necessary to test the program behaviors identified as affected by DiSE. When only a subset of the path conditions is affected by the changes to a program, using DiSE results for test case selection and augmentation of the artifacts in our study would result in executing between 20% and 70% of the test cases that would be run in a re-test all approach, reducing the time necessary for regression testing of the new version of the program.

The requirements for soundness and completeness of an analysis are driven by the needs of the specific evolution task that uses the results of the analysis. For example, the test selection and augmentation application considered here covers all the branches in the method that are affected by the change. However, it does not necessarily provide full (bounded) path coverage. To achieve full path coverage, additional information could potentially be recorded from a previous run, and combined with DiSE results. As future work, we plan to investigate the use of DiSE for other software evolution tasks.

6. Related Work

Recent years have seen a significant growth in research projects based on symbolic execution, first introduced in the 1970's by Clarke [7] and King [22]. These projects have pursued three primary research directions to enhance traditional symbolic execution: (1) to improve its effectiveness [4, 10, 12, 19, 32]; (2) to improve its efficiency [1, 3, 5, 11, 20, 31, 37]; and (3) to improve its applicability [8, 18, 27, 33]. The novelty of DiSE is to leverage state-of-the-art symbolic execution techniques and apply a static analysis in synergy to enable symbolic execution to perform more efficiently as a program undergoes changes.

The projects to enhance the effectiveness of symbolic execution have focused on two areas. First, is to enable symbolic execution to handle programs written in commonly used languages, such as Java and C/C++, by providing support for symbolic execution over the core types used in these languages [4, 10, 12, 19, 32]. The second area of focus is to enable symbolic execution to work around the traditional limitation of undecidability of path conditions through the use of mixed symbolic/concrete execution to attempt to prevent the path conditions from becoming too complex [12, 32].

Research to enhance the efficiency of symbolic execution has followed three basic directions. One, to use abstraction with symbolic execution to reduce the space of exploration [1, 20]. Two, to perform *compositional* symbolic execution, where summaries of parts of code are used in place of an actual implementation to enable the underlying constraint solvers to perform more efficiently [3, 11]. Three, to enable symbolic execution to find bugs faster through the use of heuristics, e.g., genetic algorithms [37], that directly control the symbolic exploration and focus it on parts that are more likely to contain bugs.

Static analysis has also been used effectively for guiding symbolic execution. Chang's recent doctoral dissertation [5] uses a def-use analysis based on user-provided control points of interest, and applies a program transformation that incorporates boundary conditions on program inputs into the program logic to enable more efficient bug finding. Santelices and Harrold [31] use control and data dependencies to symbolically execute groups of paths, rather than individual paths to enable scalability. The key difference between DiSE and previous work is the ability of DiSE to utilize information about program differences for efficient symbolic execution as code undergoes changes.

While several projects have made significant advances in applying symbolic execution to test input generation and program verification – two traditional applications of symbolic execution – recent projects have used it as an enabling technology for various novel applications, including program differencing [27], data structure repair [18], dynamic discovery of invariants [8], as well as estimation of energy consumption on hardware devices with limited battery capacity [33].

An application of symbolic execution with a focus on program differences is regression testing [14, 15, 25]. Several recent projects use symbolic execution as a basis of test case selection and augmentation [29, 35, 38]. DiSE differs from these projects in its focus on the core symbolic execution technique to enable a variety of software evolution tasks – not only regression testing.

Program differencing, in general, is a well-studied research area with several techniques for computing differences [2, 21, 27] as well as leveraging them to enable various software evolution tasks [23]. Research in utilizing differences to speed-up symbolic execution by focusing it on code changes has only recently begun. Godefroid et al. [13] consider the problem of statically validating symbolic test summaries against changes, specifically for compositional dynamic test generation. Our approach is complementary since it uses change impact information to explore only the paths of the symbolic execution tree that are affected by the change, thereby reducing the cost of recomputing symbolic summaries.

The Java PathFinder model checker [36] has previously been used for incremental checking of programs that undergo changes [24, 39]. Incremental state-space exploration (ISSE) [24] focuses on evolving programs and stores the explored state space graph to use it for checking a subsequent version of the program, and reduces the time necessary for state-space exploration by avoiding the execution of some transitions and related computations that are not necessary. Regression model checking (RMC) [39] presents a complementary approach to ISSE and uses the difference between two versions to drive the pruning of the state space when model checking the new version. RMC computes reachable program coverage elements, e.g., basic blocks, for each program state during a recording mode run of RMC on the original version. Impact analysis is then used to calculate dangerous elements whose behavior may now differ because of changes. This is done by comparing the bytecodes and control-flow graphs for the two program versions. The dangerous elements information is then combined with the reachable elements information to prune safe sub-state spaces during a pruning mode run of RMC on the modified version of the program. DiSE takes inspiration from RMC and supports incremental symbolic execution, which is not addressed by RMC and ISSE. Moreover, a key difference between DiSE and previous work is that to analyze the current program version DiSE does not require the availability of the internal states of the previous analysis run – ISSE requires the state-space graph and RMC requires the dynamic reachability information for program coverage elements.

7. Conclusions and Future Work

In this paper, we introduced Directed Incremental Symbolic Execution (DiSE), a novel technique that leverages program differences to guide symbolic execution to explore and characterize the effects of program changes. We implemented DiSE in the symbolic execution extension of the Java PathFinder verification framework, and evaluated its cost and effectiveness on methods from three Java applications. The results of our case-study demonstrate that DiSE efficiently generates the set of path conditions affected by the change(s) to a program. We demonstrate the utility of our technique by using DiSE results to perform test case selection and test input generation for the examples in our study.

DiSE is an intra-procedural, incremental analysis technique that generates and characterizes method-level differences. DiSE does not generate affected path conditions arising from the control and data flow between various methods. As a result, DiSE does not consider the effects of the return value of a changed method flowing back to its calling context, nor does DiSE capture the effects of changes to the global state if whatever change is causing the effect does not also affect the path condition. We plan to extend DiSE to use an inter-procedural analysis to generate affected path conditions over the entire system as part of our future work.

We observed from our study that the number of changes is only one factor affecting which (and how many) path conditions are changed; program structure and the nature of the change also appear to have a considerable effect. We expect these factors to also affect the number of path conditions that are changed when we evaluate DiSE on a more diverse set of programs. In future work, we plan to conduct a more comprehensive evaluation of our DiSE technique.

Acknowledgments

The authors gratefully acknowledge the contributions of Matt Dwyer and Gregg Rothermel to early work on DiSE. The authors also thank Eric Mercer for the helpful comments to improve the paper. The work of Yang and Khurshid was supported in part by the NSF under Grant Nos. IIS-0438967 and CCF-0845628, and AFOSR grant FA9550-09-1-0351.

References

[1] S. Anand, C. S. Pasareanu, and W. Visser. Symbolic execution with abstraction. *International Journal on Software Tools for Technology Transfer (STTT)*, 11:53–67, January 2009.

[2] T. Apiwattanapong, A. Orso, and M. J. Harrold. Jdiff: A differencing technique and tool for object-oriented programs. *Automated Software Engineering*, 14(1):3–36, 2007.

[3] W. R. Bush, J. D. Pincus, and D. J. Sielaff. A static analyzer for finding dynamic programming errors. *Software: Practice and Experience*, 30(7):775–802, 2000.

[4] C. Cadar and D. R. Engler. Execution generated test cases: How to make systems code crash itself. In *SPIN*, pages 2–23, 2005.

[5] W. C. Chang. *Improving Dynamic Analysis with Data Flow Analysis*. PhD thesis, University of Texas at Austin, 2010.

[6] Choco. Main-page Choco. `http://www.emn.fr/z-info/choco-solver/`, 2010.

[7] L. A. Clarke. A program testing system. In *Proceedings of the 1976 annual conference*, ACM '76, pages 488–491, 1976.

[8] C. Csallner, N. Tillmann, and Y. Smaragdakis. Dysy: Dynamic symbolic execution for invariant inference. In *ICSE*, pages 281–290, 2008.

[9] L. de Moura and N. Bjørner. Z3: An efficient SMT solver. In *TACAS*, pages 337–340, 2008.

[10] X. Deng, Robby, and J. Hatcliff. Kiasan/KUnit: Automatic test case generation and analysis feedback for open object-oriented systems. In *TAICPART-MUTATION*, pages 3–12, 2007.

[11] P. Godefroid. Compositional dynamic test generation. In *POPL*, pages 47–54, 2007.

[12] P. Godefroid, N. Klarlund, and K. Sen. DART: Directed automated random testing. In *PLDI*, pages 213–223, 2005.

[13] P. Godefroid, S. K. Lahiri, and C. Rubio-Gonzalez. Incremental compositional dynamic test generation. Technical Report MSR-TR-2010-11, Microsoft Research, 2010.

[14] T. L. Graves, M. J. Harrold, J.-M. Kim, A. Porter, and G. Rothermel. An empirical study of regression test selection techniques. *ACM Transactions Software Engineering and Methodology*, 10(2):184–208, 2001.

[15] M. J. Harrold, J. A. Jones, T. Li, D. Liang, A. Orso, M. Pennings, S. Sinha, S. A. Spoon, and A. Gujarathi. Regression test selection for java software. In *OOPSLA*, pages 312–326, 2001.

[16] D. Jackson. *Software Abstractions: Logic, Language, and Analysis*. The MIT Press, Cambridge, MA, 2006.

[17] A. Joshi and M. Heimdahl. Model-Based Safety Analysis of Simulink Models Using SCADE Design Verifier. In *SAFECOMP*, volume 3688 of *LNCS*, pages 122–135, September 2005.

[18] S. Khurshid, I. García, and Y. L. Suen. Repairing structurally complex data. In *SPIN*, pages 123–138, 2005.

[19] S. Khurshid, C. S. Păsăreanu, and W. Visser. Generalized symbolic execution for model checking and testing. In *TACAS*, pages 553–568, 2003.

[20] S. Khurshid and Y. L. Suen. Generalizing symbolic execution to library classes. In *PASTE*, pages 103–110, 2005.

[21] M. Kim, D. Notkin, and D. Grossman. Automatic inference of structural changes for matching across program versions. In *ICSE*, pages 333–343, 2007.

[22] J. C. King. Symbolic execution and program testing. *Communications of the ACM*, 19(7):385–394, 1976.

[23] S. K. Lahiri, K. Vaswani, and T. Hoare. Differential static analysis: Opportunities, applications, and challenges. In *FoSER*, pages 201–204, 2010.

[24] S. Lauterburg, A. Sobeih, D. Marinov, and M. Viswanathan. Incremental state-space exploration for programs with dynamically allocated data. In *ICSE*, pages 291–300, 2008.

[25] H. Leung and L. White. Insights into regression testing. In *ICSM*, pages 60–69, 1989.

[26] C. Păsăreanu and N. Rungta. Symbolic PathFinder: symbolic execution of Java bytecode. In *ASE*, pages 179–180, 2010.

[27] S. Person, M. B. Dwyer, S. Elbaum, and C. S. Păsăreanu. Differential symbolic execution. In *FSE*, pages 226–237, 2008.

[28] C. S. Păsăreanu, P. C. Mehlitz, D. H. Bushnell, K. Gundy-Burlet, M. Lowry, S. Person, and M. Pape. Combining unit-level symbolic execution and system-level concrete execution for testing NASA software. In *ISSTA*, pages 15–25, 2008.

[29] D. Qi, A. Roychoudhury, and Z. Liang. Test generation to expose changes in evolving programs. In *ASE*, pages 397–406, 2010.

[30] SAE-ARP4761. *Guidelines and Methods for Conducting the Safety Assessment Process on Civil Airborne Systems and Equipment*. SAE International, December 1996.

[31] R. Santelices and M. J. Harrold. Exploiting program dependencies for scalable multiple-path symbolic execution. In *ISSTA*, pages 195–206, 2010.

[32] K. Sen, D. Marinov, and G. Agha. CUTE: a concolic unit testing engine for c. In *ESEC/FSE*, pages 263–272, 2005.

[33] C. Seo, S. Malek, and N. Medvidovic. An energy consumption framework for distributed Java-based software systems. Technical Report USC-CSE-2006-604, University of Southern California, 2006.

[34] J. Sztipanovits and G. Karsai. Generative programming for embedded systems. In *GPCE*, pages 32–49, 2002.

[35] K. Taneja, T. Xie, N. Tillmann, J. de Halleux, and W. Schulte. Guided path exploration for regression test generation. In *ICSE, New Ideas and Emerging Results*, pages 311–314, 2009.

[36] W. Visser, K. Havelund, G. P. Brat, S. Park, and F. Lerda. Model checking programs. *Automated Software Engineering*, 10(2):203–232, 2003.

[37] Z. Xu, M. B. Cohen, and G. Rothermel. Factors affecting the use of genetic algorithms in test suite augmentation. In *GECCO*, pages 1365–1372, 2010.

[38] Z. Xu and G. Rothermel. Directed test suite augmentation. In *APSEC*, pages 406–413, 2009.

[39] G. Yang, M. B. Dwyer, and G. Rothermel. Regression model checking. In *ICSM*, pages 115–124, 2009.

Mining Hot Calling Contexts in Small Space

Daniele Cono D'Elia
Dept. of Computer and System Sciences
Sapienza University of Rome
danielecono.delia@gmail.com

Camil Demetrescu
Dept. of Computer and System Sciences
Sapienza University of Rome
demetres@dis.uniroma1.it

Irene Finocchi
Dept. of Computer Science
Sapienza University of Rome
finocchi@di.uniroma1.it

Abstract

Calling context trees (CCTs) associate performance metrics with paths through a program's call graph, providing valuable information for program understanding and performance analysis. Although CCTs are typically much smaller than call trees, in real applications they might easily consist of tens of millions of distinct calling contexts: this sheer size makes them difficult to analyze and might hurt execution times due to poor access locality. For performance analysis, accurately collecting information about hot calling contexts may be more useful than constructing an entire CCT that includes millions of uninteresting paths. As we show for a variety of prominent Linux applications, the distribution of calling context frequencies is typically very skewed. In this paper we show how to exploit this property to reduce the CCT size considerably.

We introduce a novel run-time data structure, called *Hot Calling Context Tree (HCCT)*, that offers an additional intermediate point in the spectrum of data structures for representing interprocedural control flow. The HCCT is a subtree of the CCT that includes only hot nodes and their ancestors. We show how to compute the HCCT without storing the exact frequency of all calling contexts, by using fast and space-efficient algorithms for mining frequent items in data streams. With this approach, we can distinguish between hot and cold contexts on the fly, while obtaining very accurate frequency counts. We show both theoretically and experimentally that the HCCT achieves a similar precision as the CCT in a much smaller space, roughly proportional to the number of distinct hot contexts: this is typically several orders of magnitude smaller than the total number of calling contexts encountered during a program's execution. Our space-efficient approach can be effectively combined with previous context-sensitive profiling techniques, such as sampling and bursting.

Categories and Subject Descriptors C.4 [*Performance of Systems*]: Measurement Techniques; D.2.2 [*Software Engineering*]: Tools and Techniques—programmer workbench; D.2.5 [*Software Engineering*]: Testing and Debugging—diagnostics, tracing

General Terms Algorithms, Measurement, Performance.

Keywords Performance profiling, dynamic program analysis, data streaming algorithms, frequent items, program instrumentation.

PLDI'11, June 4–8, 2011, San Jose, California, USA.

1. Introduction

Context sensitive profiling provides valuable information for program understanding, performance analysis, and runtime optimizations. Previous works have demonstrated its effectiveness for tasks such as residual testing [30, 35], function inlining [12], statistical bug isolation [15, 23], object allocation analysis [29], or anomaly-based intrusion detection [11]. A *calling context* is a sequence of routine calls that are concurrently active on the run-time stack and that lead to a program location. Collecting context information in modern object-oriented software is very challenging: application functionalities are divided into a large number of small routines, and the high frequency of function calls and returns might result in considerable profiling overhead, Heisenberg effects, and huge amounts of contexts to be analyzed by the programmer.

Several data structures have long been used to maintain information about interprocedural control flow. In a *call graph*, nodes represent routines and arcs caller-callee relationships. The use of call graph profiles was pioneered by gprof [17], that attributes the time for each routine to its callers by propagating times along edges of the call graph. Although very space- and time-efficient, this approach can lead to misleading results, as pointed out in [31, 34]. On the other side, each node of a *call tree* represents a different routine invocation. This yields very accurate context information, but requires extremely large (possibly unbounded) space. The inaccuracy of call graphs and the huge size of call trees have motivated the introduction of *calling context trees (CCT)* [2]: differently from call trees, CCTs do not distinguish between different invocations of the same routine within the same context. While maintaining good accuracy, typically CCTs are several orders of magnitude smaller than call trees: the number of nodes may be large in the presence of recursion, but this is seldom the case in practice. The exhaustive approach to constructing a CCT is based on the instrumentation of each routine call and return, incurring considerable slowdown even using efficient instrumentation mechanisms [2, 37]. Sampled stack-walking reduces slowdown, but at the price of accuracy. The adaptive bursting mechanism proposed in [37] selectively inhibits redundant profiling, dramatically reducing the overhead over the exhaustive approach while preserving good profile accuracy.

As noticed in previous works [11, 37], even calling context trees may be very large and difficult to analyze in several applications. Moreover, their sheer size might hurt execution time due to poor access locality during construction and query. As an example, in Table 1 we report the number of nodes of the call graph, call tree, and calling context tree for a variety of off-the-shelf applications in a typical Linux distribution. These numbers have been obtained from short runs of each application, which yield millions of calling contexts. The optimistic assumption that each CCT node requires 20 bytes (previous works use larger nodes [2, 34]) already results in almost 1GB needed just to store a CCT with 48 million nodes for an application such as Open Office – calc. To face this space issue, the

Table 1. Number of nodes of call graph, call tree, calling context tree, and number of distinct call sites for different applications.

Application	|Call graph|	Call sites	|CCT|	|Call tree|
amarok	13 754	113 362	13 794 470	991 112 563
ark	9 933	76 547	8 171 612	216 881 324
audacity	6 895	79 656	13 131 115	924 534 168
bluefish	5 211	64 239	7 274 132	248 162 281
dolphin	10 744	84 152	11 667 974	390 134 028
firefox	6 756	145 883	30 294 063	625 133 218
gedit	5 063	57 774	4 183 946	407 906 721
ghex2	3 816	39 714	1 868 555	80 988 952
gimp	5 146	93 372	26 107 261	805 947 134
gwenview	11 436	86 609	9 987 922	494 753 038
inkscape	6 454	89 590	13 896 175	675 915 815
oocalc	30 807	394 913	48 310 585	551 472 065
ooimpress	16 980	256 848	43 068 214	730 115 446
oowriter	17 012	253 713	41 395 182	563 763 684
pidgin	7 195	80 028	10 743 073	404 787 763
quanta	13 263	113 850	27 426 654	602 409 403
sudoku	5 340	49 885	2 794 177	325 944 813
vlc	5 692	47 481	3 295 907	125 436 877

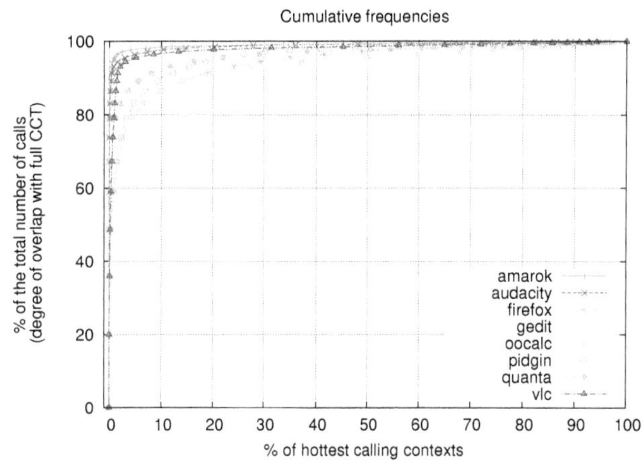

Figure 1. Skewness of calling contexts distribution on a representative subset of benchmarks.

approach proposed in [11] maintains a one-word probabilistically unique value per context, achieving minimal space overhead when all contexts have to be stored, but specific information about them is unnecessary. As noted in [11], even this approach, however, can run out of memory on large traces with tens of millions of contexts.

Although very useful, e.g., in bug or intrusion detection applications, probabilistic calling context was not designed for profiling with the purpose of understanding and improving application performance, where it is crucial to maintain for each context the sequence of active routine calls along with performance metrics. In this scenario, only the most frequent contexts are of interest, since they represent the hot spots to which optimizations must be directed. As observed in [37]: "Accurately collecting information about hot edges may be more useful than accurately constructing an entire CCT that includes rarely called paths." Figure 1 shows that, for different applications, only a small fraction of contexts are hot: in accordance with the well-known Pareto principle, more than 90% of routine calls take place in only 10% of contexts. The skewness of context distribution suggests that space could be greatly reduced by keeping information about hot contexts only and discarding on the fly contexts that are likely to be cold, i.e., to have low frequency or to require small time throughout the entire execution.

Our Contributions. In this paper we introduce a novel run-time data structure, called *Hot Calling Context Tree (HCCT)*, that compactly represents all the hot calling contexts encountered during a program's execution, offering an additional intermediate point in the spectrum of data structures for representing interprocedural control flow. The HCCT is a subtree of the CCT that includes only hot nodes and their ancestors. For each hot calling context, it also maintains an estimate of its performance metrics (for simplicity, we focus on frequency counts throughout the paper, but our approach can be easily extended to arbitrary metrics such as execution time, cache misses, or instruction stalls). Our main contributions can be summarized as follows:

- We formalize the concept of Hot Calling Context Tree and we cast the problem of identifying the most frequent contexts into a data streaming setting: we show that the HCCT can be computed without storing the exact frequency of all calling contexts, by using fast and space-efficient algorithms for mining frequent items in data streams. With this approach, we can distinguish between hot and cold contexts on the fly, while obtaining very accurate frequency counts.
- We implement three variants of space-efficient context-sensitive profilers based on three different streaming algorithms. For one of the algorithms, we devise a highly tuned implementation that is more efficient in practice than the one proposed by the authors and that might be of independent interest.
- We integrate our space-efficient approach with previous techniques aimed at reducing time overhead: we focus in particular on static bursting and adaptive bursting with re-enablement [37], which offer very good time-accuracy tradeoffs.
- We perform an extensive experimental analysis of performances and accuracy on a variety of prominent Linux applications. We test many different parameter settings and consider several metrics, including degree of overlap and hot edge coverage used in previous works. The experiments not only confirm, but reinforce the theoretical prediction, showing that the HCCT represents the hot portions of the full CCT very well using only an extremely small percentage of the space required by the entire CCT. Even when the peak memory usage of our profilers is only 1% of standard context-sensitive profilers, we can show the following:
  - all the hottest calling contexts are always identified correctly (no false negatives);
  - frequency counters are very close to the true values;
  - the number of false positives (cold contexts that are considered as hot) is very small;
  - using bursting, the running time overhead can be kept under control without affecting accuracy in a substantial way.

The rest of this paper is organized as follows. Section 2 gives preliminary definitions about calling contexts and data stream algorithmics. Section 3 introduces the HCCT and describes our approach. Section 4 focuses on implementation and engineering aspects, and Section 5 presents the outcome of our experimental study. Relations with related work are discussed in Section 6.

2. Background

2.1 Calling Context Tree

The dynamic calling context of a routine invocation is the sequence of un-returned calls from the program's root function to the routine invocation. The calling context tree (CCT) compactly represents all calling contexts encountered during the execution of a program. CCT nodes correspond to routines and a path from a node v to the tree root represents the calling context of v. A routine with multiple contexts will appear more than once in a CCT, but each calling context is represented just once and metrics for identical contexts are aggregated, trading precision for space. Slightly extended definitions can be given to bound the depth of a CCT in the presence of recursion and to distinguish calls that take place at different call sites of the same calling procedure [2].

A CCT can be constructed on-the-fly during the execution of a program. Let v be a cursor pointer that points to the current routine context, i.e., to the CCT node corresponding to the calling context of the currently active routine (v is initialized to the CCT root node). At each routine invocation, the algorithm checks whether v has a child associated with the called routine. If this is the case, the existing child is used and its metrics are updated, if necessary. Otherwise, a new child of v is added to the CCT. In both cases, the cursor is moved to the callee. Upon routine termination, the cursor is moved back to the parent node in the CCT. This approach can be implemented either by instrumenting every routine call and return or by performing stack-walking if sampling is used to inhibit redundant profiling [5, 36, 37].

2.2 Frequent Items in Data Streams

In recent years there has been much interest in the design of algorithms able to perform near-real time analyses on massive data streams, where input data come at a very high rate and cannot be stored entirely due to their huge, possibly unbounded size [14, 28]. This line of research has been mainly motivated by networking and database applications: for instance, a relevant IP traffic analysis task consists of monitoring the packet log over a given link in order to estimate how many distinct IP addresses used that link in a given period of time. Since the stream may be very long and stream items may also be drawn from a very large universe (e.g., the set of source-destination IP address pairs), space-efficient data streaming algorithms can maintain a compact data structure that is dynamically updated upon arrival of new input data, supporting a variety of application-dependent queries. Approximate answers are allowed when it is impossible to obtain an exact solution using only limited space. Streaming algorithms are therefore designed to optimize four main performance measures: space required to store the data structure, update time (i.e., per-item processing time), query time, and guaranteed solution quality.

The *frequent items* (a.k.a. heavy hitters) problem has been extensively studied in data streaming computational models. Given a frequency threshold $\phi \in [0,1]$ and a stream of lenght N, the problem (in its simplest formulation) is to find all items that appear in the stream at least $\lfloor \phi N \rfloor$ times, i.e., having frequency $\geq \lfloor \phi N \rfloor$. For instance, for $\phi = 0.1$ the problems seeks all items that appear in the stream at least 10% of the times. At most $1/\phi$ items can have frequency larger than $\lfloor \phi N \rfloor$. It can be proved that any algorithm that outputs an exact solution requires $\Omega(N)$ bits, even using randomization [28]. Hence, research focused on solving an approximate version of the problem:

DEFINITION 1. (ϕ, ε)*-heavy hitters problem. Given two parameters* $\phi, \varepsilon \in [0,1]$, *with* $\varepsilon < \phi$, *return all items with frequency* $\geq \lfloor \phi N \rfloor$ *and no item with frequency* $\leq \lfloor (\phi - \varepsilon) N \rfloor$.

In the approximate solution, false negatives cannot exist, i.e., all frequent items must be returned. Instead, some good false positives are allowed, but their actual frequency is guaranteed to be at most εN-far from the threshold $\lfloor \phi N \rfloor$. Variations of the problem arise when, besides returning the heavy hitters, it is necessary to estimate

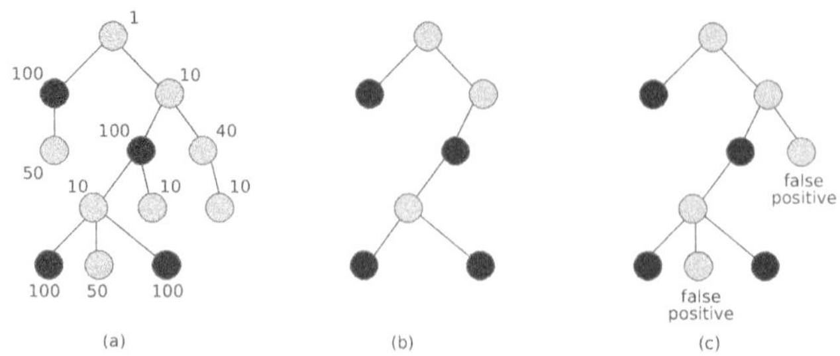

Figure 2. (a) CCT; (b) HCCT; and (c) (ϕ, ε)-HCCT. Hot nodes are darker. The number close to each node is the frequency count of the corresponding calling context. In this example $N = 581$, $\phi = 1/10$, and $\varepsilon = 1/30$: the approximate HCCT includes all contexts with frequency $\geq \lfloor \phi N \rfloor = 58$ and no context with frequency $\leq \lfloor (\phi - \varepsilon) N \rfloor = 38$.

accurately their true frequencies, when the stream length N is not known in advance, and when the items are given weights.

Many different algorithms for computing (ϕ, ε)-heavy hitters have been proposed in the literature in the last ten years. In this paper we focus on counter-based algorithms that, according to extensive experimental studies [13], have superior performance with respect to space, running time, and accuracy. Counter-based algorithms track a subset of items from the input and monitor counts associated with them. For each new arrival, the algorithms decide whether to store the item or not, and, if so, what counts to associate with it. There are three main embodiments of this approach: *Space Saving*, *Sticky Sampling*, and *Lossy Counting*. Sticky Sampling [25] is probabilistic: it fails to produce the correct answer with a minuscole probability, say δ, and uses at most $\frac{2}{\varepsilon} \log(\phi^{-1}\delta^{-1})$ entries in its data structure. Space Saving [27] and Lossy Counting [25] are deterministic and use $\frac{1}{\varepsilon}$ and $\frac{1}{\varepsilon} \log(\varepsilon N)$ entries, respectively. The theoretical results are even better when stream items have a skewed distribution (e.g., Zipfian). In a general-purpose implementation of counter-based algorithms, the update times are dominated by a small (constant) number of dictionary or heap operations.

3. HCCT: Hot Calling Context Tree

The execution trace of routine invocations and terminations can be naturally regarded as a stream of items. Each item is a triple containing routine name, call site, and event type. As shown in Table 1, the number of distinct routines (i.e., the number of nodes of the call graph) is small compared to the stream length (i.e., to the number of nodes of the call tree), even for complex applications. Hence, non-contextual profilers – such as vertex profilers – can maintain a hash table of size proportional to the number of routines, using routine names as hash keys in order to update the corresponding metrics. This may be difficult in the case of contextual profiling, when the number of distinct calling contexts (i.e., the number of CCT nodes) is too large and hashing would be inefficient. Motivated by the fact that execution traces are typically very long and their items (calling contexts) are taken from a large universe, we cast the problem of identifying the most frequent contexts into a data streaming setting.

3.1 Approach

Let N be the number of calling contexts encountered during a program's execution: N equals the number of nodes of the call tree, the sum of the frequency counts of CCT nodes, as well as the number routine invocations in the execution trace. Given a frequency threshold $\phi \in [0,1]$, we will regard a calling context as *hot* if the frequency count of the corresponding CCT node is larger than $\lfloor \phi N \rfloor$. All the other contexts are considered *cold*. We define

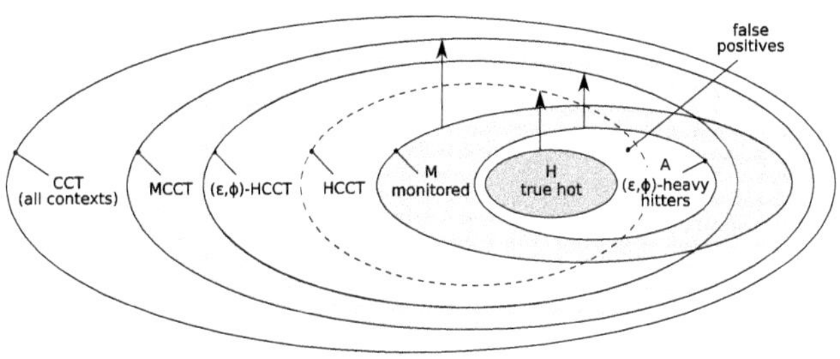

Figure 3. Tree data structures and calling contexts classification. We use graphical notation S $\uparrow$ T to indicate that T is the minimal subtree of the CCT spanning all nodes in S.

the *Hot Calling Context Tree (HCCT)* as the (unique) subtree of the CCT obtained by pruning all cold nodes that are not ancestors of a hot node. In graph theory, the HCCT corresponds to the Steiner tree of the CCT with hot nodes used as terminals, i.e., to the minimal connected subtree of the CCT spanning hot nodes. An example of HCCT is given in Figure 2(b). It is worth noticing that all hot nodes are included in the HCCT and that all its leaves are necessarily hot (the converse, however, is not true).

The HCCT is the most compact data structure representing information about hot calling contexts. The space lower bound for the heavy hitters problem (see Section 2.2) extends to the problem of computing the HCCT, that cannot be calculated exactly in small space (in particular, using a space asymptotically smaller than the entire CCT). Hence, we relax the problem and compute an *Approximate Hot Calling Context Tree*, which we denote by *(ϕ,ε)-HCCT*, where $\varepsilon < \phi$ controls the degree of approximation. The (ϕ,ε)-HCCT contains all hot nodes (true positives), but may possibly contain some cold nodes without hot descendants (false positives). The true frequency of these false positives, however, is guaranteed to be at least $\lfloor(\phi-\varepsilon)N\rfloor$. Similarly to the HCCT, the (ϕ,ε)-HCCT can be thought of as a minimal subtree of the CCT spanning a set of (ϕ,ε)-heavy hitters. Differently from the HCCT, a (ϕ,ε)-HCCT is not uniquely defined, since the set of (ϕ,ε)-heavy hitters is not unique: in particular, nodes with frequencies smaller than $\lfloor\phi N\rfloor$ and larger than $\lfloor(\phi-\varepsilon)N\rfloor$ may be either included in such a set or not.

The Venn diagram in Figure 3 summarizes some important relations:

- H $\subseteq$ A, where H is the set of hot contexts and A is a set of (ϕ,ε)-heavy hitters. Nodes in A $\setminus$ H are false positives.
- H $\subseteq$ HCCT. Nodes in HCCT $\setminus$ H are cold nodes that have a descendant in H.
- A $\subseteq(\phi,\varepsilon)$-HCCT. Nodes in (ϕ,ε)-HCCT $\setminus$ A are cold nodes that have a descendant in A.
- HCCT $\subseteq(\phi,\varepsilon)$-HCCT, as implied by the previous inclusions. Both of them are connected subtrees of the full CCT.

Figure 3 also introduces two additional sets: the set M of monitored nodes and the subtree MCCT spanning all nodes in M. To compute the set A of (ϕ,ε)-heavy hitters, we use as subroutines counter-based streaming algorithms that monitor a slightly larger set M $\supseteq$ A. When a user query asks for the most frequent contexts, these algorithms prune M and return A. In addition to M, our algorithm maintains the subtree MCCT of the CCT consisting of the nodes in M and of all their ancestors. At query time, the MCCT is appropriately pruned and the (ϕ,ε)-HCCT $\subseteq$ MCCT is returned.

Discussion and Example. To understand why the heavy hitters and the approximate HCCT are not maintained directly, but derived

```
   prune(x, MCCT):
1.     V ← update(x, M)
2.     for each context v ∈ V \ {x}
3.         while (v is a leaf in MCCT ∧ v ∉ M) do
4.             remove v from MCCT
5.             v ← parent(v)
```

Figure 4. On-line pruning algorithm.

by pruning M and MCCT, respectively, consider the following example: the execution trace contains the initial invocation of the `main` function, which in turn invokes once a routine p and $N-2$ times a different routine q. Assume that $N \geq 8$, $\varepsilon = 1/4$, $\phi = 1/2$, and that the counter-based streaming subroutine can maintain at least three counters. Then only node q has frequency larger than $\lfloor(\phi-\varepsilon)N\rfloor$ and is a (ϕ,ε)-heavy hitter, but the algorithm will maintain in M both p and q together with their exact frequencies. Since p has frequency 1, it would be an error returning it as a heavy hitter. For this reason, M needs to be post-processed in order to eliminate low-frequency items that may be included when there are more available counters than heavy hitters. Details on updating and querying M and MCCT are given in Section 3.2.

3.2 Data Structures Update and Query

At each function call, the set M of monitored contexts is updated by a counter-based streaming algorithm (see Section 2.2). When M is changed, the subtree MCCT spanning nodes in M needs to be brought up to date as well. To describe how this happens, we assume that the interface of the streaming algorithm provides two main functions:

`update(x,M)` → `V`: given a calling context x, update M to reflect the new occurrence of x in the stream (e.g., if x was already monitored in M, its frequency count may be increased by one). The `update` function might return a set V of *victim* contexts that were previously monitored in M and are evicted during the update (as a special case, x itself may be considered as a victim if the algorithm decides not to monitor it).

`query(M)` → `A`: remove low-frequency items from M and return the subset A of (ϕ,ε)-heavy hitters (see Figure 3).

Details on the implementation of `update` and `query` depend on the specific streaming algorithm.

Similarly to the CCT, during the construction of the MCCT we maintain a cursor pointer that points to the current calling context, creating a new node if the current context x is encountered for the first time (see Section 2.1). Additionally, we prune the MCCT according to the victim contexts returned by the streaming `update` operation (these contexts are no longer monitored in M). The pseudocode of the pruning algorithm is given in Figure 4. Since the tree must remain connected, victims can be removed from the MCCT only if they are leaves. Moreover, removing a victim might expose a path of unmonitored ancestors that no longer have descendants in M: these nodes are pruned as well. The current context x is never removed from the MCCT, even if it is not necessarily monitored in M. This guarantees that no node in the path from the tree root to x will be removed: these nodes have at least x as a descendant and the leaf test (line 3 in Figure 4) will always fail.

A similar pruning strategy can be used to compute the (ϕ,ε)-HCCT from the MCCT. The streaming `query` operation is first invoked on M, returning the support A of the (ϕ,ε)-HCCT. All MCCT nodes that have no descendant in A are then removed, following bottom up path traversals as in the prune operation.

3.3 Discussion

Compared to the standard approach of maintaining the entire CCT, our solution requires to store the heavy hitters data structure M and the subtree MCCT spanning nodes in M. The space required by M depends on the specific streaming algorithm that is used as a subroutine, and is roughly proportional to $1/\varepsilon$ (see Section 2.2 for the exact bounds). This space can be customized by appropriately choosing ε, e.g., according to the amount of available memory. An appropriate choice of ε appears to be crucial for the effectiveness of our approach: smaller values of ε guarantee more accurate results (less false positives and more precise counters), but imply a larger memory footprint. As we will see experimentally in Section 5, the high skewness of context frequency distribution guarantees the existence of very convenient tradeoffs between accuracy and space.

The MCCT consists of nodes corresponding to contexts monitored in M and of all their ancestors, which may be cold contexts without a corresponding entry in M. Hence, the space required by the MCCT dominates the space required by M. The number of cold ancestors cannot be analyzed theoretically: it depends on properties of the execution trace and on the structure of the calling context tree. In Section 5 we will show that in practice this amount is negligible with respect to the number of entries in M.

Updates of the MCCT can be performed very quickly. As we will see in Section 4, the streaming `update` operation requires constant time. Moreover, our implementation hinges upon very simple and cache-efficient data structures, with no need for time-consuming hashing. Simple amortized analysis arguments also show that the amortized running time of tree pruning is constant.

Differently from previous approaches such as, e.g., adaptive bursting [37], the MCCT adapts automatically to the case where the hot calling contexts vary over time, and new calling patterns are not likely to be lost. Contexts that are growing more popular are added to the tree as they become more frequent, while contexts that lose their popularity are gradually replaced by hotter contexts and are finally discarded. This guarantees that heavy hitters queries can be issued at any point in time, and will always be able to return the set of hot contexts up to that time.

Our data-streaming based approach is orthogonal to previous techniques and can be integrated, e.g., with sampled stack-walking [5, 36] or with more recent techniques such as static and adaptive bursting [37]. In addition to frequency counts, it can be extended to support arbitrary performance metrics, exploiting the ability of some streaming algorithms to compute the heavy hitters in weighted item sets.

4. Implementation and Engineering

We implemented in C three variants of the HCCT construction algorithm described in Section 3, based on three different streaming algorithms for the computation of frequent items: Space Saving [27], Sticky Sampling [25], and Lossy Counting [25]. In our experiments, Sticky Sampling consistently proved itself to be less efficient and accurate than its competitors, so we will not mention it any further. All our implementations (including the construction of the entire CCT) are cast in a common framework in which different streaming algorithms can be plugged in.

We use a first-child, next-sibling representation for calling context trees. Each MCCT node also contains a pointer to its parent, the routine ID, the call site, and the performance metrics. The first-child, next-sibling representation is very space-efficient and still guarantees that the children of each node can be explored in time proportional to their number. According to our experiments with several benchmarks, the average number of scanned children is a small constant around 2-3, so this representation turns out to be convenient also for checking whether a routine ID already appears among the children of a node. The parent field, which is needed to perform tree pruning efficiently (see Figure 4), is not required in CCT nodes. As routine ID, we use the routine address. Overall, CCT and MCCT nodes require 20 and 24 bytes, respectively, on 32 bit architectures. Using the bit stealing technique, we also encode in one of the pointer fields a Boolean flag that tells if the calling context associated with the node is monitored in the streaming data structure M, without increasing the number of bytes per node.

To improve time and space efficiency, we allocate nodes through a custom, page-based allocator, which maintains blocks of fixed size. Any additional algorithm-specific information needed to maintain the heavy hitters is stored as trailing fields within fat MCCT nodes.

We now describe our implementation of the streaming algorithms, focusing on Space Saving (SS) and Lossy Counting (LC).

4.1 Space Saving

Space Saving [27] monitors a set of $1/\varepsilon = |M|$ pairs of the form $(item, count)$, initialized by the first $1/\varepsilon$ distinct items and their exact counts. After the init phase, when a calling context c is observed in the stream the `update` operation (see Section 3.2) works as follows:

1. if c is monitored, the corresponding counter is incremented;
2. if c is not monitored, the $(item, count)$ pair with the smallest count is chosen as a victim and has its item replaced with c and its count incremented. Heavy hitters queries are answered by returning entries in M such that count $\geq \lfloor \phi N \rfloor$.

The update time is bounded by the dictionary operation of checking whether an item is monitored, and by the priority queue operations of finding and maintaining the item with minimum count. In our setting, we can avoid the dictionary operation using the cursor pointer to the MCCT: using this pointer, we can directly access the `monitored` flag of the MCCT node associated with the current context. The priority queue must support two operations, `find-min` and `increment`, which return the item with minimum count and increment a counter, respectively. In [27], it is suggested to use an ordered bucket list, where each bucket points to a list of items (MCCT nodes) with the same count, and buckets are ordered by increasing count values.

In addition to the implementation realized by the Space Saving authors [27], we devised a more efficient variant based on a lazy priority queue. We will refer to our implementation as *Lazy Space Saving* (LSS). We use an unordered array M of size $1/\varepsilon$, where each array entry points to an MCCT node. We also (lazily) maintain the value `min` of the minimum counter and the smallest index `min-idx` of an array entry that points to a monitored node with counter equal to `min`. The `increment` operation does not change M, since counters are stored directly inside MCCT nodes. However, `min` and `min-idx` may become temporarily out of date after an `increment`: this is why we call the approach lazy. The `find-min` operation described in Figure 5 restores the invariant property on `min` and `min-idx`: it finds the next index in M with counter equal to `min`. If such an index does not exist, it completely rescans M in order to find a new `min` value and its corresponding `min-idx`.

LEMMA 1. *After a* `find-min` *query, the lazy priority queue correctly returns the minimum counter value in O(1) amortized time.*

PROOF. Counters are never decremented. Hence, at any time, if a monitored item with counter equal to `min` exists, it must be found in a position larger than or equal to `min-idx`. This yields correctness.

To analyze the running time, let Δ be the value of `min` after k `find-min` and `increment` operations. Since there are $|M|$ counters $\geq \Delta$, counters are initialized to 0, and each `increment` operation adds 1 to the value of a single counter, it must be $k \geq |M|\Delta$.

```
find-min():
    while (M[min-idx] ≠ min ∧ min-idx ≤ M) do
        min-idx ← min-idx +1
    if (min-idx > M) then
        min ← minimum in M
        min-idx ← smallest index j such that M[j] = min
    return min
```

Figure 5. `find-min` operation used in Lazy Space Saving.

For each distinct value assumed by `min`, the array is scanned twice. We therefore have at most 2Δ array scans each of length $|M|$, and the total cost of `find-min` operations throughout the whole sequence of operations is upper bounded by $2|M|\Delta$. It follows that the amortized cost is $(2|M|\Delta)/k \leq 2$. □

4.2 Lossy Counting

Lossy Counting [25] maintains a set M of triples of the form (item, count, Δ), where count represents the exact frequency of the item since it was last inserted in M and Δ is the maximum possible underestimation of count: the algorithm guarantees that at any time the true frequency of a monitored item is $\leq$ count $+ \Delta$. The incoming stream is conceptually divided into bursts of width $\lceil 1/\varepsilon \rceil$. During burst i, if an item x arrives that already exists in M, the corresponding count is incremented. Otherwise:

- if x corresponds to a node v with count c that is an ancestor of another node in M, we increment c by 1, leave Δ untouched, and then add (x, c, Δ) to M;
- otherwise, we add $(x, 1, i-1)$ to M.

We slightly modified the insertion algorithm of [25] to achieve better precision by exploiting the advantages of the MCCT data structure.

At the end of burst i, M is pruned by deleting entries such that (count $+ \Delta$) $\leq i$: the set V of victims returned by the `update` operation (see Section 3.2) is therefore always empty, except at burst boundaries. Heavy hitters queries are answered by returning entries in M such that count $+ \Delta \geq \lfloor \phi N \rfloor$; again, we modified the original algorithm to reduce – sometimes considerably – the number of false positives returned in the answer.

Since triples are dynamically added to and deleted from M, it is convenient to maintain M using an unordered linked list. For the sake of efficiency, in our implementation we superimpose M on the MCCT by allocating fat MCCT nodes containing Δ and the pointer to the next element of M in addition to the standard fields. Hence, Lossy Counting uses 28 bytes per node. Checking whether an item is monitored can be done quickly as described in Section 4.1. Every $\lceil 1/\varepsilon \rceil$ operations M is scanned and removed items are marked `unmonitored` and pruned from the MCCT as described in Figure 4.

5. Experimental Evaluation

In this section, we present an extensive experimental study of our data-streaming based profiling mechanism. We implemented several variants of space-efficient context-sensitive profilers and we analyzed their performances and the accuracy of the produced (ϕ, ε)-HCCT with respect to several metrics and using many different parameter settings. Our test suite includes profilers based on the three different streaming algorithms discussed in Section 4: Lazy Space Saving (LSS), Bucket Space Saving (BSS), and Lossy Counting (LC). Besides the exahustive approach, where each routine call and return is instrumented, we integrate our implementations with previous techniques aimed at reducing time overhead: we focus in particular on static bursting and adaptive bursting with re-enablement [37], which offer very convenient time-accuracy trade-offs. The experimental analysis not only confirms, but reinforces the theoretical prediction: the (ϕ, ε)-HCCT represents the hot portions of the full CCT very well using only an extremely small percentage of the space required by the entire CCT: all the hottest calling contexts are always identified correctly, their counters are very accurate, and the number of false positives is rather small. Using the bursting technique, the running time overhead can be kept under control without affecting accuracy in a substantial way. Before discussing the results, we present the details of our experimental methodology, focusing on benchmarks and accuracy metrics, and we describe how the parameters of the streaming algorithms can be tuned.

5.1 Methodology and Experimental Setup

Benchmarks. Tests were performed on a variety of large-scale Linux applications, including graphics programs (`inkscape` and `gimp`), an hexadecimal file viewer (`ghex2`), audio players/editors (`amarok` and `audacity`), an archiver (`ark`), an Internet browser (`firefox`), an HTML editor (`quanta`), a chat program (`pidgin`), the Open Office suite for word processing (`oowriter`), spreadsheets (`oocalc`), and drawing (`ooimpress`). To ensure deterministic replay of the execution of the interactive applications in out test suite, we used the PIN dynamic instrumentation framework [24] to record timestamped execution traces for typical usage sessions. After the startup, in each session we interactively used the application for approximately ten up to twenty minutes: e.g., we created a 420×300 pixel image with `gimp` applying a variety of graphic filters and color effects, we reproduced fifty images in slideshow mode with `gwenview`, we played a ten minutes audio file with `amarok`, and we wrote a two pages formatted text, including tables, with `oowriter`. Statistical information about test sets is shown in Table 1: even short sessions of a few minutes result in CCTs consisting of tens of millions of calling contexts, whereas the call graph has only a few thousands nodes. The number of distinct call sites is roughly one order of magnitude larger than the call graph.

Metrics. We test the accuracy of the (ϕ, ε)-HCCT produced by our profilers according to a variety of metrics:

1. Degree of overlap, considered in [4, 5, 37], is used to measure the completeness of the (ϕ, ε)-HCCT with respect to the full CCT and defined as follows:

$$overlap((\phi,\varepsilon)\text{-HCCT,CCT}) = \frac{1}{N} \sum_{\text{arcs } e \in (\phi,\varepsilon)\text{-HCCT}} w(e)$$

where N is the total number of routine activations (corresponding to the CCT total weight) and $w(e)$ is the true frequency of the target node of arc e in the CCT.

2. Hot edge coverage, introduced in [37], measures the percentage of hot edges of the CCT that are covered by the (ϕ, ε)-HCCT, using an edge-weight threshold $\tau \in [0, 1]$ to determine hotness. Since (ϕ, ε)-HCCT$\subseteq$CCT, hot edge coverage can be defined as follows:

$$cover((\phi,\varepsilon)\text{-HCCT,CCT}, \tau) = \frac{|\{e \in (\phi,\varepsilon)\text{-HCCT}: w(e) \geq \tau H\}|}{|\{e \in \text{CCT}: w(e) \geq \tau H\}|}$$

where H is the weight of the hottest CCT arc.

3. Maximum frequency of uncovered calling contexts, where a context is uncovered if is not included in the (ϕ, ε)-HCCT:

$$maxUncov((\phi,\varepsilon)\text{-HCCT,CCT}) = \max_{e \in \text{CCT} \setminus (\phi,\varepsilon)\text{-HCCT}} \frac{w(e)}{H_1} \times 100$$

Average frequency of uncovered contexts is defined similarly.

Table 2. Typical thresholds

Benchmark	HCCT nodes $\phi = 10^{-3}$	HCCT nodes $\phi = 10^{-5}$	HCCT nodes $\phi = 10^{-7}$
audacity	112	9 181	233 362
dolphin	97	14 563	978 544
gimp	96	15 330	963 708
inkscape	80	16 713	830 191
oocalc	136	13 414	1 339 752
quanta	94	13 881	812 098

4. Number of false positives, i.e., $|A \setminus H|$: the smaller this number, the better the (ϕ, ε)-HCCT approximates the exact HCCT obtained from CCT pruning.
5. Counter accuracy, i.e., maximum error in the frequency counters of (ϕ, ε)-HCCT nodes with respect to their true value in the full CCT:

$$maxError((\phi,\varepsilon)\text{-HCCT}) = \max_{e \in (\phi,\varepsilon)\text{-HCCT}} \frac{|w(e) - \widetilde{w}(e)|}{w(e)} \times 100$$

where $w(e)$ and $\widetilde{w}(e)$ are the true and the estimated frequency of context e, respectively. Average counter error is defined similarly.

An accurate solution should maximize degree of overlap and hot edge coverage, and minimize the remaining metrics.

Platform. Our experiments were performed on a 2.53GHz Intel Core2 Duo T9400 with 128KB of L1 data cache, 6MB of L2 cache, and 4 GB of main memory DDR3 1066, running Ubuntu 8.04, Linux Kernel 2.6.24, 32 bit.

5.2 Parameter Tuning

Before describing our experimental findings, we discuss how to choose parameters ϕ and ε to be provided as input to the streaming algorithms. According to the theoretical analysis, an accurate choice of ϕ and ε might greatly affect the space used by the algorithms and the accuracy of the solution. In our study we considered many different choices of ϕ and ε across rather heterogeneous sets of benchmarks and execution traces, always obtaining similar results that we summarize below.

A rule of thumb about ϕ and ε validated by previous experimental studies [13] suggests that it is sufficient to choose $\varepsilon = \phi/10$ in order to obtain high counter accuracy and a small number of false positives. We found this choice overly pessimistic in our scenario: the extremely skewed cumulative distribution of calling context frequencies shown in Figure 1 makes it possible to use much larger values of ε without sacrificing accuracy. This yields substantial benefits on the space usage, which is roughly proportional to $1/\varepsilon$. Unless otherwise stated, in all our experiments we used $\varepsilon = \phi/5$.

Let us now consider the choice of ϕ: ϕ is the hotness threshold with respect to the stream length N, i.e., to the number of routine enter events. However, N is unknown *a priori* during profiling, and thus choosing ϕ appropriately may appear to be difficult: too large values might result in returning very few hot calling contexts (even no context at all in some extreme cases), while too small values might result in using too much space and returning too many contexts without being able to discriminate accurately which of them are actually hot. Our experiments suggest that an appropriate choice of ϕ is mostly independent of the specific benchmark and of the stream length: as shown in Table 2, different benchmarks have HCCT sizes of the same order of magnitude when using the same ϕ threshold (results for omitted benchmarks are similar). This is a consequence of the skewness of context frequency distribution, and greatly simplifies the choice of ϕ in practice. Unless otherwise stated, in our experiments we used $\phi = 10^{-4}$, which corresponds to mining roughly the hottest 1 000 calling contexts.

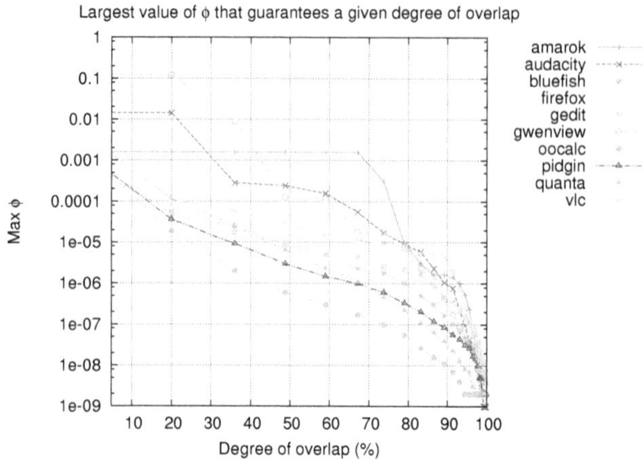

Figure 6. Relation between ϕ and degree of overlap between the exact HCCT and the full CCT on a representative subset of benchmarks.

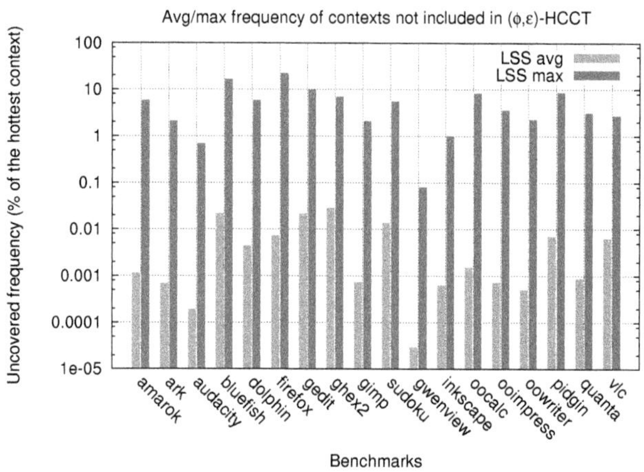

Figure 7. Maximum and average frequency of calling contexts not included in the (ϕ, ε)-HCCT generated by LSS. Results for LC are almost identical and are not shown in the chart.

5.3 Accuracy: exact HCCT

We first discuss the accuracy of the exact HCCT with respect to the full CCT. Since the HCCT is a subtree of the (ϕ, ε)-HCCT computed by our algorithms, the results described in this section apply to the (ϕ, ε)-HCCT, as well. In particular, the values of degree of overlap and hot edge coverage on the HCCT are a lower bound to the corresponding values in the (ϕ, ε)-HCCT, while the frequency of uncovered contexts is an upper bound.

It is not difficult to see that the cumulative distribution of calling context frequencies shown in Figure 1 corresponds exactly to the degree of overlap with the full CCT. This distribution roughly satisfies the 10% - 90% rule: hence, with only 10% of hot contexts, we have a degree of overlap around 90% on all benchmarks. Figure 6 illustrates the relationship between degree of overlap and hotness threshold, plotting the value $\widetilde{\phi}$ of the largest hotness threshold for which a given degree of overlap d can be achieved: using any $\phi \leq \widetilde{\phi}$, the achieved degree of overlap will be larger than or equal to d. The value of $\widetilde{\phi}$ decreases as d increases: if we want to achieve a larger degree of overlap, we must include in the HCCT a larger number of nodes, which corresponds to choosing a smaller hotness

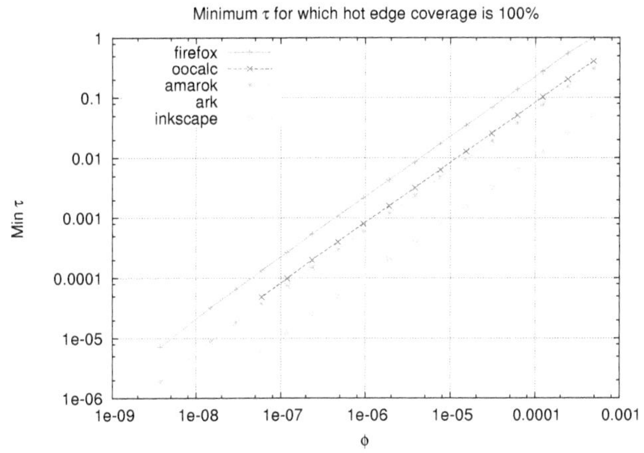

Figure 8. Hot edge coverage of the exact HCCT: relation between ϕ and edge-weight threshold τ.

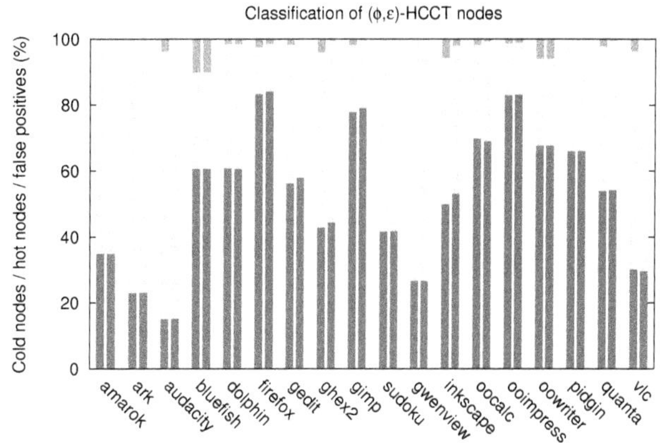

Figure 9. Partition of (ϕ, ε)-HCCT nodes into: cold (bottom bar), hot (middle bar), and false positives (top bar) for LSS and LC. The two bars for each benchmark are related to LC (left) and LSS (right), respectively.

threshold. However, when computing the (ϕ, ε)-HCCT, the value of ϕ indirectly affects the space used by the algorithm and in practice cannot be too small (see Section 5.2). By analyzing hot edge coverage and uncovered frequency, we will show below that even when the degree of overlap is not particularly large, the HCCT and the (ϕ, ε)-HCCT are nevertheless good approximations of the full CCT: values of $\phi \in [10^{-4}, 10^{-6}]$ represent on all our benchmarks a good tradeoff between accuracy and space reduction.

Consider, as an example, $\phi = 10^{-4}$, which yields degree of overlap as small as 10% on two of the less skewed benchmarks (`oocalc` and `firefox`). In this apparently bad scenario, Figure 7 analyzes how the remaining 90% of the total CCT weight is distributed among uncovered contexts: the average frequency of uncovered contexts is about 0.01% of the frequency of the hottest context, and the maximum frequency is typically less than 10%. This suggests that uncovered contexts are likely to be uninteresting with respect to the hottest contexts, and that the distribution of calling context frequencies obeys a "long-tail, heavy-tail" phenomenon: the CCT contains a huge number of calling contexts that rarely get executed, but overall these low-frequency contexts account for a significant fraction of the total CCT weight.

Figure 8 confirms this intuition, showing that the HCCT represents the hot portions of the full CCT remarkably well even for values of ϕ for which the degree of overlap may be small. The figure plots, as a function of ϕ, the smallest value $\widetilde{\tau}$ of the hotness threshold τ for which hot edge coverage of the HCCT is 100%. Results are shown only on some of the less skewed, and thus more difficult, benchmarks. Note that $\widetilde{\tau}$ is directly proportional to and roughly one order of magnitude larger than ϕ. This is because the HCCT contains all contexts with frequency $\geq \lfloor \phi N \rfloor$, and always contains the hottest context (which implies $H_1 = H_2$ in the definition of hot edge coverage in Section 5.1). Hence, the hot edge coverage is 100% as long as $\lfloor \phi N \rfloor \geq \tau H_1$, which yields $\widetilde{\tau} = \lfloor \phi N \rfloor / H_1$. The experiment shows that 100% hot edge coverage is always obtained for $\tau \geq 0.01$. As a frame of comparison, notice that the τ thresholds used in [37] to analyze hot edge coverage are always larger than 0.05, and for those values we always guarantee total coverage.

5.4 Accuracy: (ϕ, ε)-HCCT

We now discuss the accuracy of the (ϕ, ε)-HCCT computed by our algorithms compared to the exact HCCT. Figure 9 shows the percentages of cold nodes, true hots, and false positives in the (ϕ, ε)-HCCT using $\phi = 10^{-4}$ and $\varepsilon = \phi/5$. Both algorithms include in the tree only very few false positives (less than 10%

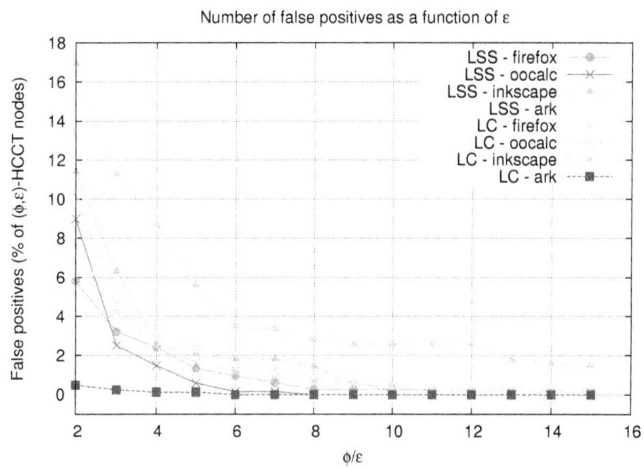

Figure 10. False positives in the (ϕ, ε)-HCCT as a function of ε on a representative subset of benchmarks. The value of ϕ is fixed to 10^{-4}.

of the total number of tree nodes in the worst case), and Lazy Space Saving consistently proved to be better than Lossy Counting. Figure 10 also shows that the number of false positives decreases considerably as we decrease ε, getting very close to 0% on most benchmarks when the ratio ϕ/ε is larger than 10.

A very interesting feature of our approach is that counter estimates are very close to the true frequencies, as shown in Figure 11. Lossy Counting on average achieves almost exact counters for the hot contexts (0.057% average difference from the true frequency), and even the maximum error in the worst case is smaller than 8%. Lazy Space Saving as described in this paper computes less accurate counters. The error, however, can be considerably reduced and made comparable to Lossy Counting by maintaining, for each monitored context, the maximum possible overestimation resulting from the initialization of the counter when the context was last inserted in the data structure [27]. Due to the lack of space, we defer the details of this improvement to the full version of this paper.

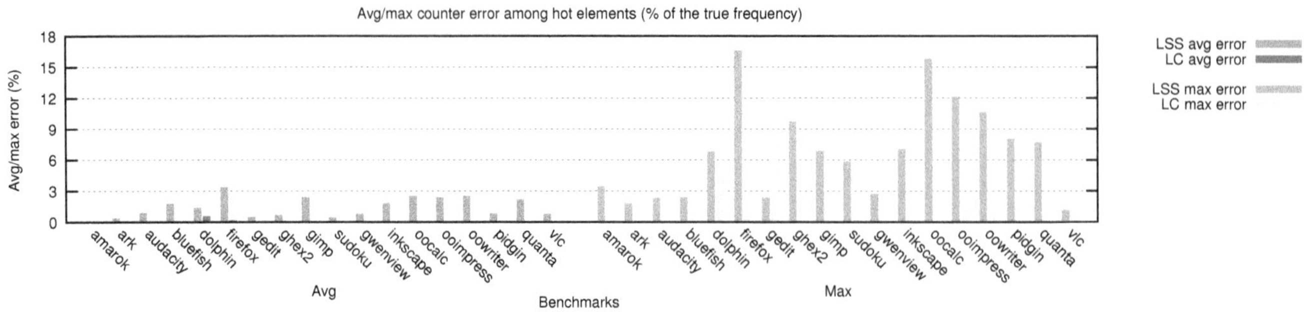

Figure 11. Accuracy of context frequencies computed by LSS and LC, measured on hot contexts included in the (ϕ, ε)-HCCT.

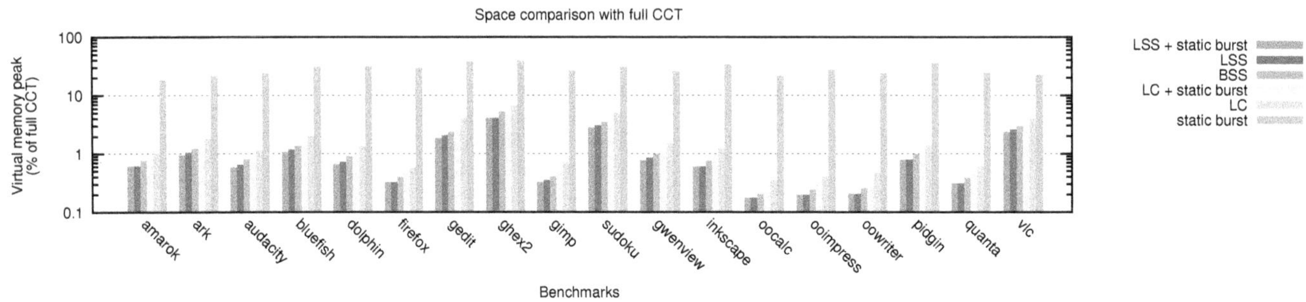

Figure 12. Space analysis on several benchmarks of LSS/LC, static and adaptive bursting [37], and LSS/LC combined with static and adaptive bursting with sampling interval 2 msec, and burst length 0.2 msec.

5.5 Performance

To analyze time and space performances of our profilers we consider LSS, LC, BSS (omitted from the previous discussions as it computes exactly the same (ϕ, ε)-HCCT as LSS), and the combination of these algorithms with static and adaptive bursting.

Memory Usage. We first evaluate how much space can be saved by our approach. Figure 12 plots the peak memory usage of our profilers as a percentage of the full CCT. We recall that during the computation we store the minimal subtree MCCT of the CCT spanning all monitored contexts. This subtree is eventually pruned to obtain the (ϕ, ε)-HCCT (see Section 3.1). The peak memory usage is proportional to the number of MCCT nodes, which is typically much larger than the actual number of hot contexts obtained after pruning. In spite of this, a considerable amount of space is saved by all algorithms. On many benchmarks, our profilers use less than 1% of the space required by the full CCT, and even in the worst case the space usage is about 6.5%. Space Saving is always more efficient than Lossy Counting, and the lazy approach is preferable to the bucket-based implementation. It should be noted, however, that the space used in practice by Lossy Counting is much smaller than the theoretical prediction. Quite surprisingly, static bursting also improves space usage (results for adaptive bursting are similar and are not reported in the chart). This depends on the fact that sampling reduces the variance of calling context frequencies: MCCT cold nodes that have a hot descendant are more likely to become hot when sampling is active, and monitoring these nodes reduces the total MCCT size. The histogram also shows that static bursting alone (i.e., without streaming) is not sufficient to reduce the space substantially: in addition to hot contexts, a large fraction of cold contexts is also sampled and included in the CCT. On the `oocalc` benchmark, even adaptive bursting without re-enablement requires 127 times more space than LSS. We also observed that the larger the applications, the larger the space reduction of our approach over bursting alone.

Since the average node degree is a small constant, cold HCCT nodes are typically a fraction of the total number of nodes, as shown in Figure 9 for $\phi = 10^{-4}$. In our experiments we observed that this fraction strongly depends on the hotness threshold ϕ, and in particular decreases with ϕ: cold nodes that have a hot descendant are indeed more likely to become hot when ϕ is smaller.

Time Overhead. We conclude by analyzing running times. Since our approach is independent of any specific instrumentation mechanisms, and different techniques for tracing routine enter and exit events might incur rather different overheads in practice, we focus on the time required by the analysis routines only, omitting instrumentation times. Compared to the the standard construction of the CCT, streaming algorithms incur a small overhead, which can be considerably reduced by exploiting sampling and bursting techniques: in Figure 13, we plot the speedup that can be obtained by combining our approach with static bursting and with adaptive bursting. We compared the performance of six variants (from slowest to fastest) for both LSS and LC: full (ϕ, ε)-HCCT construction (on the entire routine enter/exit stream), static bursting, adaptive bursting with re-enable ratio equal to 20%, 10%, and 5%, and adaptive bursting without re-enablement (for a description of the adaptive bursting technique, we refer the interested reader to [37]). We also considered bursting alone (both static and adaptive), while we omitted sample-driven stack walking, which has been shown to be largely inferior to bursting with respect to the accuracy [37]. The construction of the HCCT greatly benefits from bursting, achieving speedups up to $35\times$. LSS is always faster than LC, but both of them are slower than bursting without streaming: the speedup difference, however, is moderate and for LSS is typically smaller than 2.

As shown in Figure 14, the accuracy of the HCCT (and in particular the hot edge coverage) is not affected substantially by the combination of streaming and bursting (except for adaptive sampling without re-enablement). We take as an example the `vlc` benchmark considered in Figure 13 for $\tau = 0.025$: the HCCT computed

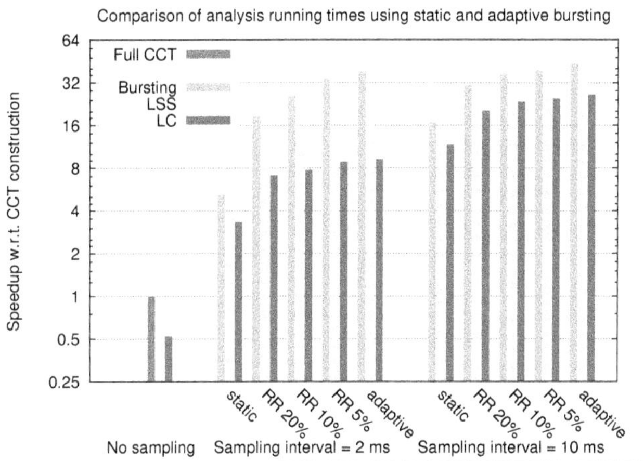

Figure 13. Speedup analysis relative to full CCT construction on the `vlc` benchmark for LSS/LC, static and adaptive bursting [37], and LSS/LC combined with static and adaptive bursting: (1) no sampling (left histogram); (2) sampling interval 2 msec and burst length 0.2 msec (middle histogram); (3) sampling interval 10 msec and burst length 0.2 msec (right histogram). The CCT construction baseline is about 1.5 seconds for $2.5 \cdot 10^8$ routine enter/exit events.

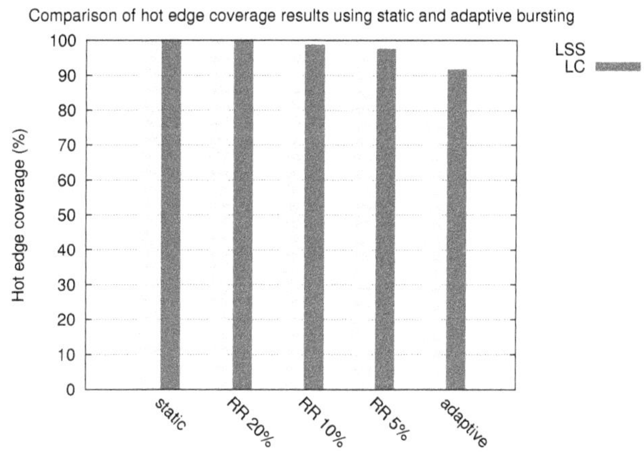

Figure 14. Hot edge coverage analysis on the `vlc` benchmark for LSS/LC combined with static and adaptive bursting [37] for $\tau = 0.025$, with $\phi = 4 \cdot 10^{-5}$, $\epsilon = \phi/2$, sampling interval 2 msec, and burst length 0.2 msec. Static and adaptive bursting alone always achieve 100% hot edge coverage in this experiment and are not reported.

without bursting has coverage 100%, which is also achieved using static busting and adaptive bursting with re-enable ratio 20%. The hot edge coverage decreases as sampling becomes more aggressive, but in this experiment is always larger than 78% and 91% for LSS and LC, respectively.

6. Related Work

This section describes research on context sensitive profiling: it focuses on calling context trees and briefly considers other forms of contextual profiling at both inter and intraprocedural level.

Early approaches. The utility of calling context information was already clear in the 80s: gprof [17] approximates context sensitive profiles by associating procedure timing with caller-callee pairs rather than with single procedures. This single level of context sensitivity, however, may yield to several inaccuracies [31, 34]. Goldberg and Hall [19] introduce call path profiles of monotonic program resources and show how they can be computed in Unix processes using interval-based sampling: a call path is a sequence of function pairs in a caller-callee relationship, and the profile is a sorted list of call paths and of their performance metrics. The space usage with this approach can be prohibitive, since at each sample point metrics are recorded along with the entire call stack.

Calling context trees. Calling context trees have been introduced in [2] as a practical data structure to associate performance metrics with paths through a program's call graph: Ammons, Ball, and Larus suggest to build a CCT by instrumenting procedure code and to compute metrics by exploiting hardware counters available in modern processors. It has been later observed, however, that exhaustive instrumentation can lead to large slowdown.

Time-efficiency vs. profile accuracy. To reduce overhead, Bernat and Miller [8] generate path profiles including only methods of interest, while statistical profilers [5, 16, 19, 36] attribute metrics to calling contexts through periodic sampling of the call stack. For call-intensive programs, sample-driven stack-walking can be orders of magnitude faster than exhaustive instrumentation, but may incur significant loss of accuracy with respect to the complete CCT: sampling guarantees neither high coverage [11] nor accuracy of performance metrics [37], and its results may be highly inconsistent in different executions.

A variety of works explores the combination of sampling with bursting [4, 20, 37]. Most recently, Zhuang *et al.* suggest to perform stack-walking followed by a burst during which the profiler traces every routine call and return [37]: experiments show that adaptive bursting can yield very accurate results. In [33], the profiler infrequently collects small call traces that are merged afterwards to build large calling context trees: ambiguities might emerge during this process, and the lack of information about where the partial CCTs should be merged to does not allow it to reconstruct the entire CCT univocally. The main goal of all these works is to reduce profiling overhead without incurring significant loss of accuracy. Our approach is orthogonal to this line of research and regards space efficiency as an additional resource optimization criterion besides profile accuracy and time efficiency. When the purpose of profiling is to identify hot contexts, exhaustive instrumentation, sampling, and bursting might all be combined with our approach and benefit of our space reduction technique.

Reducing space. A few previous works have addressed techniques to reduce profile data (or at least the amount of data presented to the user) in context sensitive profiling. Incremental call-path profiling lets the user choose a subset of routines to be analyzed [8]. Call path refinement helps users focus the attention on performance bottlenecks by limiting and aggregating the information revealed to the user [18]. These works are quite different in spirit from our approach, where only hot contexts are profiled and identified automatically during program's execution. Quite recently, probabilistic calling contexts have been introduced as an extremely compact representation (just a 32-bit value per context), especially useful for tasks such as residual testing, statistical bug isolation, and anomaly-based intrusion detection [11]. Bond and McKinley target applications where coverage of both hot and cold contexts is necessary. This is not the case in performance analysis, where identifying a few hot contexts is typically sufficient to guide code optimization. Hence, although sharing with [11] the common goal of space reduction, our approach targets a rather different application context.

Path profiling. At the intraprocedural level, the seminal work of Ball and Larus [6] has spawned much research on flow sensitive profiling [1–3, 7, 9, 10, 21, 22, 35]. Ball-Larus path profiling computes a unique number through each possible path in the control flow graph [6]: a path profile determines how many times each acyclic path in a routine executes, extending the more common basic block and edge profiling. Melski and Reps have proposed interprocedural path profiling in order to capture both inter- and intraprocedural control flow [26]. However, their approach does not scale due to the large number of statically possible paths existing across procedure boundaries.

7. Conclusions

Calling context trees offer a compact representation of all calling contexts encountered during a program's execution. Even for short runs of medium-sized applications, CCTs can be rather large and difficult to analyze. Motivated by the observation that only a very small fraction of calling contexts are hot, in this paper we have presented a novel technique for improving the space efficiency of the full calling context tree without sacrificing accuracy. By adapting modern data mining techniques, we have devised an algorithm for interprocedural contextual profiling that can discard on the fly cold contexts and appears to be extremely practical. We have evaluated our approach on several large-scale Linux applications, showing significant space saving with respect to the full CCT.

We believe that a careful use of data mining techniques has the potential benefit of enabling some previously impossible dynamic program analysis tasks, which would otherwise be too costly. In particular, our techniques could be applied to certain forms of path profiling: e.g., they could help leverage the scalability problems encountered when collecting performance metrics about interprocedural paths (i.e., acyclic paths that may cross procedure boundaries) [26] or k-iteration paths (i.e., intraprocedural cyclic paths spanning up to k loop iterations) for large values of k [32]. We plan to investigate these applications in future work.

Acknowledgments

We thank the anonymous reviewers for their valuable comments. This work is supported in part by the Italian Ministry for Education, University, and Research (MIUR) under the PRIN national research project "AlgoDEEP: Algorithmic challenges for data-intensive processing on emerging computing platforms".

References

[1] G. Ammons and J. R. Larus. Improving data-flow analysis with path profiles. *SIGPLAN Not.*, 39(4):568–582, 2004.

[2] G. Ammons, T. Ball, and J. R. Larus. Exploiting hardware performance counters with flow and context sensitive profiling. *SIGPLAN Not.*, 32(5):85–96, 1997. ISSN 0362-1340.

[3] T. Apiwattanapong and M. J. Harrold. Selective path profiling. In *Proc. ACM SIGPLAN-SIGSOFT workshop on Program analysis for software tools and engineering*, pages 35–42. ACM, 2002.

[4] M. Arnold and B. Ryder. A framework for reducing the cost of instrumented code. In *PLDI*, pages 168–179. ACM, 2001.

[5] M. Arnold and P. Sweeney. Approximating the calling context tree via sampling. Technical Report RC 21789, IBM Research, 2000.

[6] T. Ball and J. R. Larus. Efficient path profiling. In *MICRO 29: Proceedings of the 29th annual ACM/IEEE international symposium on Microarchitecture*, pages 46–57, 1996.

[7] T. Ball, P. Mataga, and M. Sagiv. Edge profiling versus path profiling: the showdown. In *POPL*, pages 134–148. ACM, 1998.

[8] A. R. Bernat and B. P. Miller. Incremental call-path profiling. Technical report, University of Wisconsin, 2004.

[9] M. D. Bond and K. S. McKinley. Continuous path and edge profiling. In *Proc. 38th annual IEEE/ACM International Symposium on Microarchitecture*, pages 130–140. IEEE Computer Society, 2005.

[10] M. D. Bond and K. S. McKinley. Practical path profiling for dynamic optimizers. In *CGO*, pages 205–216. IEEE Computer Society, 2005.

[11] M. D. Bond and K. S. McKinley. Probabilistic calling context. *SIGPLAN Not. (proceedings of the 2007 OOPSLA conference)*, 42(10): 97–112, 2007.

[12] P. P. Chang, S. A. Mahlke, W. Y. Chen, and W. mei W. Hwu. Profile-guided automatic inline expansion for c programs. *Softw., Pract. Exper.*, 22(5):349–369, 1992.

[13] G. Cormode and M. Hadjieleftheriou. Finding frequent items in data streams. *Proceedings of the VLDB Endowment*, 1(2):1530–1541, 2008.

[14] C. Demetrescu and I. Finocchi. Algorithms for data streams. In *Handbook of Applied Algorithms: Solving Scientific, Engineering, and Practical Problems*. John Wiley and Sons, 2007.

[15] H. H. Feng, O. M. Kolesnikov, P. Fogla, W. Lee, and W. Gong. Anomaly detection using call stack information. In *Proc. 2003 IEEE Symposium on Security and Privacy*, SP '03, pages 62–. IEEE Computer Society, 2003. ISBN 0-7695-1940-7.

[16] N. Froyd, J. Mellor-Crummey, and R. Fowler. Low-overhead call path profiling of unmodified, optimized code. In *Proc. 19th Annual International Conf. on Supercomputing*, pages 81–90. ACM, 2005.

[17] S. L. Graham, P. B. Kessler, and M. K. McKusick. gprof: a call graph execution profiler (with retrospective). In K. S. McKinley, editor, *Best of PLDI*, pages 49–57. ACM, 1982. ISBN 1-58113-623-4.

[18] R. J. Hall. Call path refinement profiles. *IEEE Trans. Softw. Eng.*, 21 (6):481–496, 1995.

[19] R. J. Hall and A. J. Goldberg. Call path profiling of monotonic program resources in UNIX. In *Proc. Summer 1993 USENIX Technical Conference*, pages 1–19. USENIX Association, 1993.

[20] M. Hirzel and T. Chilimbi. Bursty tracing: A framework for low-overhead temporal profiling. In *Proc. 4th ACM Workshop on Feedback-Directed and Dynamic Optimization*, 2001.

[21] R. Joshi, M. D. Bond, and C. Zilles. Targeted path profiling: Lower overhead path profiling for staged dynamic optimization systems. In *CGO*, page 239. IEEE Computer Society, 2004.

[22] J. R. Larus. Whole program paths. *SIGPLAN Not.*, 34(5):259–269, 1999.

[23] B. Liblit, A. Aiken, A. X. Zheng, and M. I. Jordan. Bug isolation via remote program sampling. In *PLDI*, pages 141–154. ACM, 2003.

[24] C.-K. Luk, R. Cohn, R. Muth, H. Patil, A. Klauser, G. Lowney, S. Wallace, V. J. Reddi, and K. Hazelwood. Pin: building customized program analysis tools with dynamic instrumentation. In *PLDI*, pages 190–200, 2005.

[25] G. S. Manku and R. Motwani. Approximate frequency counts over data streams. In *VLDB*, pages 346–357. Morgan Kaufmann, 2002.

[26] D. Melski and T. W. Reps. Interprocedural path profiling. In S. Jähnichen, editor, *CC*, volume 1575 of *Lecture Notes in Computer Science*, pages 47–62. Springer, 1999. ISBN 3-540-65717-7.

[27] A. Metwally, D. Agrawal, and A. E. Abbadi. An integrated efficient solution for computing frequent and top-k elements in data streams. *ACM Trans. Database Syst.*, 31(3):1095–1133, 2006.

[28] S. Muthukrishnan. Data streams: Algorithms and applications. *Foundations and Trends in Theoretical Computer Science*, 1(2), 2005.

[29] N. Nethercote and J. Seward. Valgrind: a framework for heavyweight dynamic binary instrumentation. In *PLDI*, pages 89–100, 2007.

[30] C. Pavlopoulou and M. Young. Residual test coverage monitoring. In *ICSE*, pages 277–284, 1999.

[31] C. Ponder and R. J. Fateman. Inaccuracies in program profilers. *Softw., Pract. Exper.*, 18(5):459–467, 1988.

[32] S. Roy and Y. N. Srikant. Profiling k-iteration paths: A generalization of the ball-larus profiling algorithm. In *CGO*, pages 70–80, 2009.

[33] M. Serrano and X. Zhuang. Building approximate calling context from partial call traces. In *CGO*, pages 221–230, 2009.

[34] J. M. Spivey. Fast, accurate call graph profiling. *Softw., Pract. Exper.*, 34(3):249–264, 2004.

[35] K. Vaswani, A. V. Nori, and T. M. Chilimbi. Preferential path profiling: compactly numbering interesting paths. In *POPL*, pages 351–362. ACM, 2007.

[36] J. Whaley. A portable sampling-based profiler for Java virtual machines. In *Proceedings of the ACM 2000 Conference on Java Grande*, pages 78–87. ACM Press, 2000.

[37] X. Zhuang, M. J. Serrano, H. W. Cain, and J.-D. Choi. Accurate, efficient, and adaptive calling context profiling. In *PLDI*, pages 263–271, 2006.

Verification of Semantic Commutativity Conditions and Inverse Operations on Linked Data Structures

Deokhwan Kim Martin C. Rinard

Massachusetts Institute of Technology

{dkim,rinard}@csail.mit.edu

Abstract

We present a new technique for verifying *commutativity conditions*, which are logical formulas that characterize when operations commute. Because our technique reasons with the abstract state of verified linked data structure implementations, it can verify commuting operations that produce semantically equivalent (but not necessarily identical) data structure states in different execution orders. We have used this technique to verify sound and complete commutativity conditions for all pairs of operations on a collection of linked data structure implementations, including data structures that export a set interface (ListSet and HashSet) as well as data structures that export a map interface (AssociationList, HashTable, and ArrayList). This effort involved the specification and verification of 765 commutativity conditions.

Many speculative parallel systems need to undo the effects of speculatively executed operations. *Inverse operations*, which undo these effects, are often more efficient than alternate approaches (such as saving and restoring data structure state). We present a new technique for verifying such inverse operations. We have specified and verified, for all of our linked data structure implementations, an inverse operation for every operation that changes the data structure state.

Together, the commutativity conditions and inverse operations provide a key resource that language designers, developers of program analysis systems, and implementors of software systems can draw on to build languages, program analyses, and systems with strong correctness guarantees.

Categories and Subject Descriptors D.1.3 [*Programming Techniques*]: Concurrent Programming; D.2.4 [*Software Engineering*]: Software/Program Verification; F.3.1 [*Logics and Meanings of Programs*]: Specifying and Verifying and Reasoning about Programs

General Terms Languages, Reliability, Verification

Keywords Commutativity Condition, Data Structure, Inverse Operation, Verification

1. Introduction

Commuting operations on shared data structures (operations that produce the same result regardless of the order in which they execute) play a central role in many parallel computing systems:

- **Parallelizing Compilers:** If a compiler can statically detect that all operations in a given computation commute, it can generate parallel code for that computation [41].
- **Deterministic Parallel Languages:** Including support for commuting operations in deterministic parallel languages increases the expressive power of the language while preserving guaranteed deterministic parallel execution [5, 42].
- **Transaction Monitors:** If a transaction monitor can detect that operations within parallel transactions commute, it can use efficient locking algorithms that allow commuting operations from different transactions to interleave [17, 49]. Because such locking algorithms place fewer constraints on the execution order, they increase the amount of exploitable parallelism.
- **Irregular Parallel Computations:** Exploiting commuting operations has been shown to be critical for obtaining good parallel performance in irregular parallel computations that manipulate linked data structures [28–30]. The reason is essentially the same as for efficient transaction monitors — it enables the use of efficient synchronization algorithms for atomic transactions that execute multiple (potentially commuting) operations on shared objects. For similar reasons, exploiting commuting operations has also been shown to be essential for obtaining good parallel performance for the SPEC benchmarks [7].

Despite the importance of commuting operations, there has been relatively little research in automatically analyzing or verifying the conditions under which operations commute. Indeed, the deterministic parallel language, transaction monitor, and irregular parallel computation systems cited above all rely on the developer to identify commuting operations, with no way to determine whether the operations do, in fact, commute or not. A mistake in identifying commuting operations invalidates both the principles upon which the systems operate and the correctness guarantees that they claim to provide.

1.1 Previous Research

Commutativity analysis [41] uses static program analysis to find operations that produce identical concrete object states in all execution orders. But this approach is inadequate for linked data structures — consider, for example, a linked list that implements a set interface. Operations that insert elements into this data structure commute at the semantic level — all insertion orders produce the same abstract set of elements. But they do not commute at the concrete implementation level — different insertion orders (even though they produce the same set) produce different linked lists. Any commutativity analysis that reasons at the concrete implementation level (as opposed to the abstract semantic level) would therefore conservatively conclude that such operations do not commute.

Another approach uses *random interpretation* [22] to detect commuting operations [1]. This technique explores control flow paths from different execution orders, with affine join operations combining states from different control flow paths to avoid exponential blowup in the number of analyzed states. Instead of directly comparing states from different execution orders, the technique reasons about the return values of the functions that the program uses to observe the different states. Because effective affine join operations do not currently exist for linked data structures, this approach does not detect commuting operations on linked data structures.

PLDI'11, June 4–8, 2011, San Jose, California, USA.

Both of these approaches are designed only to find operations that commute in all possible object states and for all possible parameter values. But some operations commute only under certain conditions. Consider, for example, an operation that removes a key, value pair from a hash table and an operation that looks up a given key in the hash table. These operations commute only if the two keys are different. Recognizing and exploiting such *commutativity conditions* is essential to obtaining good parallel performance for many irregular computations [28–30] — these computations use the commutativity conditions to dynamically recognize and exploit commuting operations whose commutativity properties they cannot statically resolve.

1.2 Semantic Commutativity Analysis

This paper presents a new approach for verifying the specific conditions under which operations on linked data structures semantically commute. Instead of reasoning directly about the concrete data structure state, this approach builds on the availability of fully verified linked data structure implementations [51, 52] to reason at the higher semantic level of the (verified) abstract data structure state. The approach is therefore able to detect operations that commute at the semantic level even though they may produce different concrete data structure states. We have used this approach to verify both *soundness* (conceptually, if the conditions hold, the operations produce the same abstract data structure state regardless of the order in which they execute, see Section 4) and *completeness* (conceptually, if the conditions do not hold, then different execution orders produce different abstract data structure states, see Section 4) of commutativity conditions.

We have specified and verified sound and complete commutativity conditions for all pairs of operations from a variety of linked data structure implementations:

- **Sets:** ListSet and HashSet both implement a set interface. ListSet uses a singly-linked list; HashSet uses a hash table.
- **Maps:** AssociationList, HashTable, and ArrayList all implement a map interface. AssociationList uses a singly-linked list of key, value pairs; HashTable implements a separately-chained hash table — an array contains linked lists of key, value pairs with a hash function mapping keys to linked lists via the array. ArrayList maps integers to objects and is optimized for storing maps from a dense subset of the integers starting at 0.
- **Accumulator:** Accumulator maintains a value that clients can increase and read.

Altogether, we specified and verified 765 commutativity conditions (216 from ListSet and HashSet, 294 from AssociationList and HashTable, 243 from ArrayList, and 12 from Accumulator).

Because the implementations of all of these data structures have been verified to correctly implement their specifications, the semantic commutativity conditions and inverses are guaranteed to be valid for the concrete data structure implementations that execute when the program runs. We emphasize, however, that our technique works with data structure specifications, not data structure implementations. In particular, it is capable of verifying semantic commutativity conditions and inverses even in the absence of any implementation at all (in this case, of course, the commutativity conditions and inverses are sound only to the extent that the actual data structure implementation, when provided, correctly implements its specification).

We note that the well-known difficulty of reasoning about semantic properties of linked data structures [43] has limited the range of available results in this area. These verified commutativity conditions therefore provide a solid foundation for the use of these linked data structures in a range of parallel programs and systems.

1.3 Inverse Operations

In one of our usage scenarios, the system uses the commutativity conditions to dynamically detect speculatively executed operations that do not commute with previously executed operations [28–30]. In this case, the system must roll the data structure back to the abstract semantic state before the operations executed, then continue from this restored state.

Executing *inverse operations* that undo the effect of executed operations can be substantially more efficient than alternate approaches (such as pessimistically saving the data structure state before operations execute, then restoring the state to roll back the effect of the operations). Note that even though the restored abstract semantic state is the same, the underlying concrete states may differ. For example, the inverse of an operation that removes an element from a set implemented as a linked list inserts the removed element back into the list. Even though the reinserted element may appear in a different position in the list, the restored abstract set is the same as the original set.

We have developed an approach that is capable of verifying semantic inverse operations. We have specified inverses for all of the operations on our set of data structures that update the data structure state. We have used our approach to verify that all of these inverses undo the effect of the corresponding operation to correctly restore the initial abstract state of the linked data structure.

We note that the need to undo the effects of executed operations occurs pervasively throughout computer systems, from classical database transaction processing systems [21] to systems that recover from security breaches [20, 27, 38, 45]. In addition to the specific motivating use described above, the verified inverse operations may therefore find broader applicability in a variety of contexts in which it is desirable to efficiently undo data structure state changes.

1.4 Jahob

We use the Jahob program specification and verification system to specify and verify the data structure implementations, commutativity conditions, and inverse operations. Jahob enables developers to write higher-order logic specifications for Java programs [51, 52]. It also enables developers to guide proofs of complex program properties by using the Jahob integrated proof language to resolve key choice points in these proofs [52]. Once these choice points have been resolved, Jahob uses *integrated reasoning* to invoke a variety of powerful reasoning systems (such as first-order provers [44, 48], SMT provers [10, 19], MONA [24], and the BAPA [31, 34] decision procedure) to discharge the resulting automatically generated verification conditions [51, 52].

In our approach, a data structure implementor specifies commutativity conditions for pairs of data structure operations and/or inverses for individual operations that update the data structure state. Our commutativity condition and inverse operation verification system generates stylized Jahob methods whose verification establishes the validity of the corresponding commutativity conditions and inverse operations. In our experience, Jahob is often able to verify these methods without further intervention from the data structure implementor. Specifically, for our set of linked data structure implementations, all but 57 of the 1530 automatically generated commutativity testing methods and all of the eight automatically generated inverse testing methods verify as generated. If a method does not verify, the data structure implementor uses the Jahob proof language [52] to appropriately guide the verification of the method. For our set of linked data structure implementations, Jahob was able to verify the remaining 57 commutativity testing methods after we augmented the methods with a total of 201 Jahob proof language commands (see Section 5).

1.5 Contributions

This paper makes the following contributions:

- **Semantic Commutativity Analysis:** It presents a new commutativity analysis technique that verifies the soundness and completeness of semantic commutativity conditions for linked data structures. Because this analysis reasons about the abstract semantic state of the data structure (as opposed to the concrete implementation state), it can verify semantic commutativity conditions that are inherently beyond the reach of previously proposed approaches.

  To the best of our knowledge, this analysis is the first to verify semantic commutativity conditions for linked data structures.
- **Semantic Commutativity Conditions:** It presents verified sound and complete commutativity conditions for a variety of linked data structures. In this paper all of these commutativity conditions are provided by the developer and verified by our implemented system.

  To the best of our knowledge, these are the first fully verified semantic commutativity conditions for linked data structures.
- **Semantic Inverse Analysis:** It presents a new analysis for verifying inverse operations that undo the effect of previously executed operations on linked data structures. Because the analysis reasons about the abstract data structure state, it can verify semantic inverses that correctly restore the abstract data structure state even though they may produce different concrete states.

  To the best of our knowledge, this analysis is the first to verify semantic inverse operations for linked data structures.
- **Semantic Inverse Operations:** It presents verified inverses for operations that update the data structure state. Systems can use these operations to efficiently roll back speculatively executed data structure operations.

  To the best of our knowledge, these are the first fully verified semantic inverse operations for linked data structures.
- **Experience:** It discusses our experience using the Jahob [6, 51, 52] program specification and verification system to specify and verify commutativity conditions and inverse operations for a group of data structures including a ListSet and HashSet that implement a set interface, an AssociationList, HashTable, and ArrayList that implement a map interface, and an Accumulator.

We emphasize that in this paper, we focus on the specification and verification of the commutativity conditions and inverse operations. We assume that any parallel system that uses these conditions will implement some synchronization mechanism that ensures that the operations execute atomically. Such mechanisms are already implemented and available in many of the systems which we expect to be of interest [5, 7, 17, 28, 29, 41, 42, 49].

2. Example

Figure 1 presents the Jahob interface for the HashSet class, which uses a separately-chained hash table [9] to implement a set interface. The HashSet class, like all of our data structures, is written in Java augmented with specifications written in the Jahob higher-order logic specification language. The interface exports a collection of specified operations. Each operation specification consists of a precondition (the `requires` clause), a postcondition (the `ensures` clause), and a `modifies` clause. These specifications completely capture the desired behavior of the data structure (with the exception of properties involving execution time and/or memory consumption) [51, 52].

2.1 Abstract State

The interface uses the *abstract state* of the HashSet to specify the behavior of HashSet operations. This state consists of the set `contents` of objects in the HashSet, the `size` of this set, and the flag `init`, which is true if the HashSet has been initialized (see lines 2, 3, and 4 of Figure 1). The specification for the `add(v)` operation, for example, uses this abstract state to specify that, if the HashSet is initialized and the parameter `v` is not null, it adds `v` to the set of objects in the HashSet (see lines 11-14 of Figure 1).

2.2 Concrete State and Abstraction Function

When the program runs, the HashSet operations manipulate the *concrete state* of the HashSet. The concrete state consists of the array `table`, which contains pointers to linked lists of elements in the HashSet, and the `int _size`, which stores the size of the hash table (see lines 5 and 6 of Figure 1).

An *abstraction function* in the form of Jahob invariants (not shown, but see the complete data structure specifications and implementations available in the technical report version of the paper [26]) specifies the relationship between the concrete and abstract states [51, 52]. Like all of the data structures in this paper, we have used the Jahob system to verify that the HashSet correctly implements its interface [51, 52]. This verification, of course, includes the verification of the abstraction function.

2.3 Commuting Operations

Consider the `add(v1)` and `contains(v2)` operations on a HashSet `s`. These operations commute if and only if `v1` does not equal `v2` or `v1` is already in `s`. Figure 2 presents the two methods that our system automatically generates to verify the soundness and completeness of this commutativity condition. The first method (`contains_add_between_s_40`, line 1 of Figure 2) verifies soundness. The second method (`contains_add_between_c_40`, line 14 of Figure 2) verifies completeness. The methods are written in a subset of Java with Jahob annotations [52].

2.4 Verifying Commutativity Condition Soundness

The generated soundness testing method executes the `add(v1)` and `contains(v2)` operations in both execution orders on equivalent HashSets (HashSets with the same abstract state). The method specification checks that, if the commutativity condition is true, then both execution orders produce the same return values and final abstract HashSet states. If Jahob verifies the method (which it does in this case without developer assistance), it has verified that if the commutativity condition holds, then the operations commute.

The `requires` clause (lines 2 and 3 of Figure 2) ensures that the method starts with two HashSets (`sa` and `sb`) that have identical abstract states. The method first applies the `sa.contains(v1)` and `sa.add(v2)` operations to one of the HashSets (`sa`). A Jahob `assume` command (line 8 of Figure 2) instructs Jahob to assume the commutativity condition (`v1 ~= v2 | r1a`). The method next executes the two operations in the reverse order on the second HashSet `sb` (lines 10 and 11 of Figure 2). The `assert` command at the end of the method (line 12 of Figure 2) checks that the return values are the same in both execution orders and that the two HashSets have the same abstract states at the end of the method.

In this example the commutativity condition works with the *between state* that is available after the first operation executes but before the second operation executes. A system would use such a *between condition* just before executing the `add(v2)` operation to dynamically check if this operation commutes with a previously executed `contains(v1)` operation. We also verify *before conditions* (which may be used to determine if two operations that have yet to execute will commute when they execute) and *after conditions* (which may be used to trigger rollbacks when already executed operations do not commute [28, 29]).

```
public class HashSet {
    /*: public ghost specvar init :: "bool" = "False"; */

    /*: public ghost specvar contents :: "obj set" = "{}"; */
    /*: public specvar size :: "int"; */

    private Node[] table;
    private int _size;

    public HashSet()
    /*: modifies "init", "contents", "size"
        ensures "init & contents = {} & size = 0" */ { ... }

    public boolean add(Object v)
    /*: requires "init & v ~= null"
        modifies "contents", "size"
        ensures "(v ~: old contents --> contents = old contents Un {v} & size = old size + 1 & result) &
                 (v : old contents --> contents = old contents & size = old size & ~result)" */ { ... }

    public boolean contains(Object v)
    /*: requires "init & v ~= null"
        ensures "result = (v : contents)" */ { ... }

    public boolean remove(Object v)
    /*: requires "init & v ~= null"
        modifies "contents", "size"
        ensures "(v : old contents --> contents = old contents - {v} & size = old size - 1 & result) &
                 (v ~: old contents --> contents = old contents & size = old size & ~result)" */ { ... }

    public int size()
    /*: requires "init"
        ensures "result = size" */ { ... }
}
```

Figure 1. The Jahob HashSet Specification

```
static void contains_add_between_s_40(HashSet sa, HashSet sb, Object v1, Object v2)
/*: requires "sa ~= null & sb ~= null & sa ~= sb & sa..init & sb..init & v1 ~= null & v2 ~= null &
              sa..contents = sb..contents & sa..size = sb..size"
    modifies "sa..contents", "sb..contents", "sa..size", "sb..size"
    ensures "True" */
{
    boolean r1a = sa.contains(v1);
    /*: assume "v1 ~= v2 | r1a" */
    sa.add(v2);

    sb.add(v2);
    boolean r1b = sb.contains(v1);

    /*: assert "r1a = r1b & sa..contents = sb..contents & sa..size = sb..size" */
}

static void contains_add_between_c_40(HashSet sa, HashSet sb, Object v1, Object v2)
/*: requires "sa ~= null & sb ~= null & sa ~= sb & sa..init & sb..init & v1 ~= null & v2 ~= null &
              sa..contents = sb..contents & sa..size = sb..size"
    modifies "sa..contents", "sb..contents", "sa..size", "sb..size"
    ensures "True" */
{
    boolean r1a = sa.contains(v1);
    /*: assume "~(v1 ~= v2 | r1a)" */
    sa.add(v2);

    sb.add(v2);
    boolean r1b = sb.contains(v1);

    /*: assert "~(r1a = r1b & sa..contents = sb..contents & sa..size = sb..size)" */
}
```

Figure 2. HashSet Commutativity Testing Methods for Between Commutativity Condition for `contains(v1)` and `add(v2)`

```
static void add_0(HashSet s, Object v)
/*: requires "s ~= null & s..init & v ~= null"
    modifies "s..contents ", "s..size"
    ensures "True" */
{
    boolean r = s.add(v);
    if (r) { s.remove(v); }

    /*: assert "s..contents = s..(old contents) & s..size = s..(old size)" */
}
```

Figure 3. HashSet Inverse Operation Testing Method for `add(v)`

```
static void put_0(HashTable s, Object k, Object v)
/*: requires "s ~= null & s..init & k ~= null & v ~= null"
    modifies "s..contents ", "s..size"
    ensures "True" */
{
    Object r = s.put(k, v);
    if (r != null) { s.put(k, r); } else { s.remove(k); }

    /*: assert "s..contents = s..(old contents) & s..size = s..(old size)" */
}
```

Figure 4. HashTable Inverse Operation Testing Method for `put(k, v)`

2.5 Verifying Commutativity Condition Completeness

The `contains_add_between_c_40` method, which checks completeness, uses a similar pattern except it negates both the commutativity condition and the assertion at the end of the generated method. If Jahob verifies the method (which it does in this case without developer assistance), it has verified that if the commutativity condition does not hold, then the operations produce different return values or different abstract data structure states when they execute in different orders.

2.6 Verifying Inverse Operations

Figure 3 presents the generated inverse testing method for the HashSet `add(v)` operation. This method first executes the `add(v)` operation, then the inverse `if (r) { s.remove(v); }`. The inverse must consider two cases: when `v` was in the set before the execution of `add(v)` (in which case the inverse must not remove `v`) and when `v` was not in the set before the execution of `add(v)` (in which case the inverse must remove `v`). Note that the inverse uses the return value `r` to distinguish these two cases. The final `assert` command forces Jahob to prove that the final abstract state is the same as the initial abstract state. Note that there is no requirement that the final concrete state must be the same as the initial concrete state.

Figure 4 presents the inverse testing method for a more complex operation, the HashTable `put(k, v)` operation. If the initial state of the HashTable mapped `k` to a value, the inverse reinserts the mapping (the value to which the HashTable mapped `k` is available as the return value `r` from the `put(k, v)` operation). If the initial state did not map `k` to a value, the inverse removes the mapping that the `add(k,v)` inserted, leaving `k` unmapped as in the initial state.

Both of the inverses in our example use the return value from the operation to carry information from the initial state that the inverse can then use to undo the effect of the operation. This approach works for all of our linked data structures. We note that it is, in general, possible for operations to destroy information from the initial state that the inverse needs to restore this initial state. In this case the operation needs to save information from the initial state so that the inverse can later use this saved information to restore the initial state.

3. Commutativity and Inverse Testing Methods

The commutativity testing method generator takes as input the data structure interface and, for each pair of data structure operations, developer-specified before, between, and after commutativity conditions. It produces as output the commutativity testing methods. It then presents each method to the Jahob program verification system [51, 52]. If the method verifies, the system has verified the corresponding commutativity condition. If it does not verify, either the commutativity condition is not sound or complete or Jahob is not capable of verifying the soundness and completeness without additional developer assistance. The developer then, as appropriate, either modifies the commutativity condition or augments the generated commutativity testing methods with additional proof commands written in the Jahob proof language [52].

3.1 Completeness Commutativity Testing Template

Figure 5 presents the template that the generator uses to produce the completeness commutativity testing method. The generation process simply iterates over all commutativity testing conditions (and corresponding pairs of operations in the data structure interface), filling in the template parameters as appropriate. In Figure 5 all template parameters appear in *italic font*.

The name of the commutativity testing method contains the names of the two operations, a field that specifies whether the method tests a before, between, or after commutativity condition, the tag `c` (which identifies the method as a completeness testing method), and a numerical identifier *id*. The method takes as parameters two data structures (*sa* and *sb*) and the parameters of the two data structure operations. The `requires` clause ensures the data structures are distinct but have identical abstract states.

The generated method uses Jahob `assume` commands to instruct Jahob to assume that the preconditions of the operations hold in the first execution order. If the preconditions do not involve the state of the data structure (as in our example in Figure 2), the generator moves the preconditions up into the `requires` clause.

The generator also uses an `assume` command to insert the negation of the commutativity condition (recall that the template is a completeness template and therefore includes the negation of the condition) in the appropriate place in the generated method. The template identifies the insertion points for all three kinds of commutativity conditions (before, between, and after). A generated method, of course, contains a commutativity condition at only one of these points.

The method next contains the operations in the reverse order, with `assume` commands instructing Jahob to assume that the preconditions of the operations hold. Once again, if the preconditions do not depend on the data structure state, the generator places them in the `requires` clause of the method, not before the operation invocations as in the template.

The method ends with the final assertion (which Jahob must prove) that either one of the corresponding return values or the final abstract states are different in the two different execution orders.

As is appropriate for a completeness testing method, this structure forces Jahob to prove that if the operation preconditions and the negation of the commutativity condition holds in the first execution order, then either one of the operation preconditions is violated in the reverse execution order or the final assertion holds.

3.2 Soundness Commutativity Testing Template

The soundness commutativity testing template has the same basic structure as the completeness template, with the exception that 1) it inserts the commutativity testing condition (not its negation), 2) it omits the `assume` command for the operation preconditions in the second execution order, and 3) the final assertion forces Jahob to prove that the return values and final abstract states are the same in both execution orders.

As is appropriate for a soundness testing method, this structure forces Jahob to prove that if the operation preconditions and commutativity condition holds in the first execution order, then the operation preconditions hold in the reverse execution order and the return values and final abstract states are the same.

3.3 Inverse Testing Methods

The inverse testing method generator takes as input the data structure interface and a developer-specified set of inverse operation pairs. It produces as output the inverse testing methods and feeds each method to the Jahob program verification system [52]. As for the commutativity testing methods, the developer may, if necessary, augment the inverse testing methods with additional Jahob proof commands.

Figure 6 presents the template that the generator uses to produce the inverse testing methods. The generation process simply iterates over all of the specified inverses, filling in the template parameters (in *italic font*) as appropriate. The final Jahob `assert` command requires Jahob to prove that the final abstract state (after the application of the inverse operation) is the same as the initial abstract state from the start of the method. Jahob must also prove the precondition of the inverse operation.

```
static void method1_method2_(before | between | after)_c_id
                (sa_decl, sb_decl, argv1_decls, argv2_decls)
/*: requires "sa ~= null & sb ~= null & sa ~= sb &
              sa_abstract_state = sb_abstract_state"
    modifies "sa_frame_condition", "sb_frame_condition"
    ensures "True" */
{
    [/*: assume "~(before_commutativity_condition)" */]
    /*: assume "method1_precondition" */
    r1a_type r1a = sa.method1(argv1);
    [/*: assume "~(between_commutativity_condition)" */]
    /*: assume "method2_precondition" */
    r2a_type r2a = sa.method2(argv2);
    [/*: assume "~(after_commutativity_condition)" */]

    /*: assume "method2_precondition" */
    r2b_type r2b = sb.method2(argv2);
    /*: assume "method1_precondition" */
    r1b_type r1b = sb.method1(argv1);

    /*: assert "~(r1a = r1b & r2a = r2b &
                 sa_abstract_state = sb_abstract_state)" */
}
```

Figure 5. Template for Completeness Commutativity Testing Methods

```
static void method_id(s_decl, argv_decls)
/*: requires "s ~= null & method_precondition"
    modifies "s_frame_condition"
    ensures "True" */
{
    r_type r = s.method(argv);
    execute_inverse_operation();

    /*: assert "s_abstract_state = s_initial_abstract_state" */
}
```

Figure 6. Template for Inverse Testing Methods

4. Formal Treatment

We assume a set $s \in S$ of concrete states and a corresponding set $\widehat{s} \in \widehat{S}$ of abstract states. We also assume that the data structure defines an abstraction function $\alpha : S \to \widehat{S}$.

The commutativity and inverse testing methods work with logical formulas written in the higher-order logic Jahob specification language [52]. For our data structures, the specifications, commutativity conditions, commutativity testing methods, and inverse testing methods require only first-order logic.

Given an operation $m(v)$ on a given data structure, $\mathrm{pre}(m(v))$ denotes the precondition of the method m from the data structure specification. The precondition is a logical formula written in the Jahob specification language [52]. It is expressed in the name space of the caller (i.e., with the formal parameter from the definition of m replaced by the actual parameter v from the caller). We write $\alpha(s) \models \mathrm{pre}(m(v))$ if the precondition is true in the abstract state $\alpha(s)$.

We write $\langle s', r\rangle = s.m(v)$ if executing the operation $m(v)$ in state s produces return value r and new state s'. Given a starting state s and two operations $m_1(v_1)$ and $m_2(v_2)$, we are interested in the following states and return values (see Figure 7):

- $\langle s_{\textcircled{1};2}, r_{\textcircled{1};2}\rangle = s.m_1(v_1)$: the intermediate state $s_{\textcircled{1};2}$ and return value $r_{\textcircled{1};2}$ that results from executing $m_1(v_1)$ in the original state s.
- $\langle s_{1;\textcircled{2}}, r_{1;\textcircled{2}}\rangle = s_{\textcircled{1};2}.m_2(v_2)$: the final state $s_{1;\textcircled{2}}$ and return value $r_{1;\textcircled{2}}$ that results from executing $m_2(v_2)$ in the intermediate state $s_{\textcircled{1};2}$.
- $\langle s_{\textcircled{2};1}, r_{\textcircled{2};1}\rangle = s.m_2(v_2)$: the intermediate state $s_{\textcircled{2};1}$ and return value $r_{\textcircled{2};1}$ that results from executing $m_2(v_2)$ in the original state s.
- $\langle s_{2;\textcircled{1}}, r_{2;\textcircled{1}}\rangle = s_{\textcircled{2};1}.m_1(v_1)$: the final state $s_{2;\textcircled{1}}$ and return value $r_{2;\textcircled{1}}$ that results from executing $m_1(v_1)$ in the intermediate state $s_{\textcircled{2};1}$.

We are interested in states and return values for the two operations $m_1(v_1)$ and $m_2(v_2)$ executing in both execution orders ($m_1(v_1)$ followed by $m_2(v_2)$ and $m_2(v_2)$ followed by $m_1(v_1)$). The subscripts in our notation are designed to identify both the execution order and (with a circle) the most recent operation that has executed. So, for example, $s_{\textcircled{1};2}$ denotes the state after the opera-

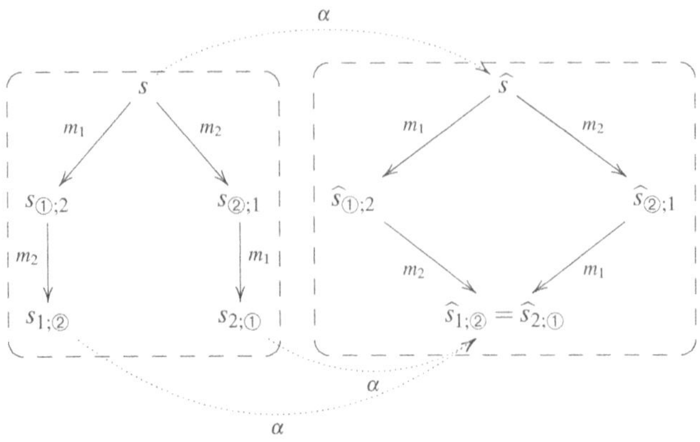

Figure 7. Execution on Concrete States and Abstract States

tion $m_1(v_1)$ executes when the operation $m_1(v_1)$ executes first and then $m_2(v_2)$ executes. Similarly, $r_{2;①}$ denotes the value that the operation $m_1(v_1)$ returns when the operation $m_2(v_2)$ executes first and then the operation $m_1(v_1)$ executes and returns $r_{2;①}$.

4.1 Commutativity Conditions

A commutativity condition ϕ is a logical formula written in the Jahob specification language [52]. In general, the free variables of ϕ can include the arguments v_1 and v_2, the return values $r_{①;2}$ and $r_{1;②}$, and abstract specification variables that denote various elements of the three abstract states $\alpha(s)$, $\alpha(s_{①;2})$, and $\alpha(s_{1;②})$. We write $(\langle s_{①;2}, r_{①;2}\rangle = s.m_1(v_1); \langle s_{1;②}, r_{1;②}\rangle = s_{①;2}.m_2(v_2)) \models \phi$ if the commutativity condition ϕ is satisfied when the operations execute in the order $m_1(v_1)$; $m_2(v_2)$ (first $m_1(v_1)$, then $m_2(v_2)$).

We anticipate that static analyses will work with commutativity conditions that involve the abstract state. Systems that dynamically evaluate commutativity conditions, of course, must work with the concrete data structure state, not the abstract data structure state. We therefore use the abstraction function to translate commutativity conditions over the abstract states into commutativity conditions over the concrete states. Section 5 presents examples that illustrate this translation.

4.1.1 Soundness and Completeness

Conceptually, a commutativity condition is *sound* if, whenever the commutativity condition and the preconditions of the two operations are satisfied in the first execution order, then 1) the preconditions of the operations are satisfied in the second execution order, 2) the operations return the same return values in both execution orders, and 3) the abstract final states are the same in both execution orders. We formalize this concept as follows.

Given a commutativity condition ϕ for two operations $m_1(v_1)$ and $m_2(v_2)$, the verification of the soundness commutativity testing method for these two operations establishes (by the construction of this method) the following property:

Property 1 (soundness)**.**
If $\alpha(s) \models \text{pre}(m_1(v_1))$ *and* $\alpha(s_{①;2}) \models \text{pre}(m_2(v_2))$ *and*
$(\langle s_{①;2}, r_{①;2}\rangle = s.m_1(v_1); \langle s_{1;②}, r_{1;②}\rangle = s_{①;2}.m_2(v_2)) \models \phi$
then $\alpha(s) \models \text{pre}(m_2(v_2))$ *and* $\alpha(s_{②;1}) \models \text{pre}(m_1(v_1))$ *and*
$r_{①;2} = r_{2;①}$ *and* $r_{1;②} = r_{②;1}$ *and* $\alpha(s_{1;②}) = \alpha(s_{2;①})$.

Conceptually, a commutativity condition is *complete* if, whenever the preconditions of the two operations are satisfied in the first execution order but the commutativity condition is not satisfied, then either 1) the preconditions of the operations are not satisfied in the second execution order, 2) the return values are different in the second execution order, or 3) the abstract final states are different in the two execution orders. We formalize this concept as follows.

Given a commutativity condition ϕ for two operations $m_1(v_1)$ and $m_2(v_2)$, the verification of the completeness commutativity testing method for these two operations establishes (by the construction of this method) the following property:

Property 2 (completeness)**.**
If $\alpha(s) \models \text{pre}(m_1(v_1))$ *and* $\alpha(s_{①;2}) \models \text{pre}(m_2(v_2))$ *and*
$(\langle s_{①;2}, r_{①;2}\rangle = s.m_1(v_1); \langle s_{1;②}, r_{1;②}\rangle = s_{①;2}.m_2(v_2)) \models \tilde{}\phi$
then $\alpha(s) \models \tilde{}\text{pre}(m_2(v_2))$ *or* $\alpha(s_{②;1}) \models \tilde{}\text{pre}(m_1(v_1))$ *or*
$r_{①;2} \neq r_{2;①}$ *or* $r_{1;②} \neq r_{②;1}$ *or* $\alpha(s_{1;②}) \neq \alpha(s_{2;①})$.

4.1.2 Kinds of Commutativity Conditions

In general, a system or analysis may wish to test if a commutativity condition is satisfied either 1) before either operation executes, 2) after the first operation executes but before the second operation executes, and/or 3) after both operations execute. We therefore identify the following kinds of commutativity conditions:

- **Before Condition:** A commutativity condition ϕ is a *before condition* if its free variables include at most the arguments v_1 and v_2 and elements of the initial abstract state $\alpha(s)$. Because a before condition does not involve the return values $r_{①;2}$ and $r_{1;②}$, the intermediate state $\alpha(s_{①;2})$, or the final state $\alpha(s_{1;②})$, it is possible to evaluate the condition before either of the operations executes.
- **Between Condition:** A commutativity condition ϕ is a *between condition* if its free variables include at most the arguments v_1 and v_2, the initial abstract state $\alpha(s)$, the first return value $r_{①;2}$, and elements of the intermediate abstract state $\alpha(s_{①;2})$. Because the between condition does not involve the second return value $r_{1;②}$ or the final abstract state $\alpha(s_{1;②})$, it is possible to evaluate the condition after the first operation $m_1(v_1)$ executes but before the second operation $m_2(v_2)$ executes. Note that if the between condition references elements of the initial abstract state $\alpha(s)$, the system may need to save corresponding values from this state before the first operation $m_1(v_1)$ executes so that it can subsequently use the saved values to evaluate the between condition after the first operation executes.
- **After Condition:** All commutativity conditions are *after conditions*. Note that if an after condition references the first return value $r_{①;2}$ or elements of the initial or intermediate abstract states $\alpha(s)$ or $\alpha(s_{①;2})$, the system may need to save referenced elements of these states so that it can evaluate the after condition after both operations execute.

In practice we expect developers to minimize references to elements of previously computed initial or intermediate abstract states when they specify between and after conditions. One strategy replaces clauses in commutativity conditions that reference elements of the initial or intermediate abstract states with equivalent clauses that reference return values from executed operations. Before conditions for our set-based data structures, for example, often test whether a parameter v of one of the operations is an element of the set in the initial state s. The return value of the operation often indicates whether the element was, in fact, an element of this initial set. The corresponding between and after conditions can then replace the clause that tests membership in the initial set with an equivalent clause that tests the return value. See Section 5 for specific occurrences of this pattern in the commutativity conditions for our set of data structures.

For completeness, some of the between conditions cannot help querying the initial state (the state before the first operation executes). For the same reason, some of the after conditions query the initial and/or between states. In practice, there are two ways to dynamically check such commutativity conditions: 1) perform the query before the operation executes and record the result for the commutativity condition to check after the operation executes, or 2) drop the clause containing the query from the commutativity condition and use the resulting simpler, conservative, but not complete commutativity condition that does not reference the initial and/or between states.

Because the commutativity conditions for our set of data structures are both sound and complete, the before, between, and after conditions are equivalent even if they reference different return values or elements of different abstract states.

4.2 Inverse Operations

Conceptually, an operation is an *inverse* of an initial operation if whenever the precondition of the initial operation is satisfied, then 1) the precondition of the inverse is satisfied after the initial operation executes and 2) executing the inverse after the initial operation executes restores the abstract state (but not necessarily the concrete state) back to what it was before the initial operation executed. We formalize this concept as follows.

Given an operation $m_1(v_1)$ with inverse operation $m_2(v_2)$, the verification of the inverse testing method for these two operations establishes (by the construction of this method) the following property:

Property 3 (inverse).
If $\alpha(s) \models \mathrm{pre}(m_1(v_1))$
then $\alpha(s_{①;2}) \models \mathrm{pre}(m_2(v_2))$ *and* $\alpha(s) = \alpha(s_{1;②})$.

5. Experimental Results

We next discuss the commutativity conditions, inverse operations, and verification process for our set of data structures. We first discuss the operations that each data structure exports. The source code for all of the data structures (including both specification and implementation) as well as the commutativity and inverse testing methods (which contain all of the commutativity conditions and Jahob proof constructs required to enable Jahob to verify the methods) is available in the technical report version of the paper [26].

The Accumulator implements a counter with two operations:

- `increase(v)`: Adds the number `v` to the counter.
- `read()`: Returns the value in the counter.

HashSet and ListSet implement a set of elements with the following operations. Because they implement the same specification, they have the same commutativity conditions.

- `add(v)`: Adds the element `v` to the set of elements in the data structure. Returns false if the element was already present and true otherwise.
- `contains(v)`: Returns true if the element `v` is in the set and false otherwise.
- `remove(v)`: Removes the element `v` from the set. Returns true if `v` was included in the set and false otherwise.
- `size()`: Returns the number of elements in the set.

HashTable and AssociationList implement a map from keys to values with the following operations. Because they implement the same specification, they have the same commutativity conditions.

- `containsKey(k)`: Returns true if there exists a value `v` for the key `k` in the map.
- `get(k)`: Returns the value `v` for the key `k`, or `null` if `k` is not mapped.
- `put(k, v)`: Maps the key `k` to the value `v`. Returns the previous value for the key `k`, or `null` if `k` was not mapped.
- `remove(k)`: Removes the mapping for the key `k`. Returns the value that the key `k` was mapped to, or `null` if the data structure did not have a mapping for the key `k`.
- `size()`: Returns the number of key, value pairs in the data structure.

ArrayList implements a map from the integers to objects with the following operations:

- `add_at(i, v)`: Pushes all objects with indices greater than or equal to `i` up one position to create an empty position at index `i`, then inserts the object `v` into that position.
- `get(i)`: Returns the object at index `i`.
- `indexOf(v)`: Returns the index of the first occurrence of the object `v` or -1 if the object `v` is not in the map.
- `lastIndexOf(v)`: Returns the index of the last occurrence of the object `v` or -1 if the object `v` is not in the map.
- `remove_at(i)`: Removes the element at the specified index `i`, then slides all objects above `i` down one position to fill the newly empty position at index `i`.
- `set(i, v)`: Replaces the object at the index `i` with the object `v`. Returns the replaced object previously at index `i`.
- `size()`: Returns the number of elements in the map.

5.1 Commutativity Conditions

Tables 1 through 7 present the commutativity conditions for selected illustrative pairs of operations from our set of linked data structures. For space reasons, we do not present all 765 commutativity conditions (the complete set of conditions is available in the technical report version of the paper [26]).

The first and second columns in each table identify the pair of operations. The third column presents the commutativity conditions in terms of the arguments, return values, and abstract data structure states. These commutativity conditions are suitable for static analyses that reason about the commutativity conditions at the level of the abstract states. The fourth column translates any abstract state queries (typically set membership operations) into operations that can be invoked on the concrete data structure. These commutativity conditions are suitable for dynamically checking the commutativity conditions when the program runs.

The commutativity conditions assume the operations operate on the same data structure (operations on different data structures trivially commute). s_1 denotes the data structure state before the first operation executes; s_2 denotes the state of the same data structure after the first operation executes but before the second operation executes. Each commutativity condition in the table corresponds to the execution order in which the operation in the first column executes first followed by the operation in the second column.

The before condition tables are symmetric (for a given pair of operations, the commutativity conditions are the same for both execution orders). The between condition tables may be asymmetric if the commutativity condition references either the return value from the first operation (which is not available in the other execution order) or depends on the intermediate data structure state (which may be different in the other execution order). Similarly, the after tables may be asymmetric if the commutativity condition depends on the intermediate or final data structure states.

In general, the commutativity conditions take the form of a disjunction of clauses. Dropping clauses produces conservative sound commutativity conditions that may be easier (for static analyses) or more efficient (for dynamic checkers) to work with. Such com-

Methods		Before / Between / After Commutativity Condition
s_1.increase(v_1)	s_2.increase(v_2)	*true*
	$r_2 = s_2$.read()	$v_1 = 0$
$r_1 = s_1$.read()	s_2.increase(v_2)	$v_2 = 0$
	$r_2 = s_2$.read()	*true*

Table 1. Before / Between / After Commutativity Conditions on Accumulator

Methods		Before Commutativity Condition	
s_1.add(v_1)	s_2.add(v_2)	*true*	*true*
	$r_2 = s_2$.contains(v_2)	$v_1 \neq v_2 \vee v_1 \in s_1$	$v_1 \neq v_2 \vee s_1$.contains(v_1) $=$ *true*
	s_2.remove(v_2)	$v_1 \neq v_2$	$v_1 \neq v_2$
$r_1 = s_1$.contains(v_1)	s_2.add(v_2)	$v_1 \neq v_2 \vee v_1 \in s_1$	$v_1 \neq v_2 \vee s_1$.contains(v_1) $=$ *true*
	$r_2 = s_2$.contains(v_2)	*true*	*true*
	s_2.remove(v_2)	$v_1 \neq v_2 \vee v_1 \notin s_1$	$v_1 \neq v_2 \vee s_1$.contains(v_1) $=$ *false*
s_1.remove(v_1)	s_2.add(v_2)	$v_1 \neq v_2$	$v_1 \neq v_2$
	$r_2 = s_2$.contains(v_2)	$v_1 \neq v_2 \vee v_1 \notin s_1$	$v_1 \neq v_2 \vee s_1$.contains(v_1) $=$ *false*
	s_2.remove(v_2)	*true*	*true*

Table 2. Before Commutativity Conditions on ListSet and HashSet

Methods		Between Commutativity Condition	
s_1.add(v_1)	s_2.add(v_2)	*true*	*true*
	$r_2 = s_2$.contains(v_2)	$v_1 \neq v_2 \vee v_1 \in s_1$	$v_1 \neq v_2 \vee s_1$.contains(v_1) $=$ *true*
	s_2.remove(v_2)	$v_1 \neq v_2$	$v_1 \neq v_2$
$r_1 = s_1$.contains(v_1)	s_2.add(v_2)	$v_1 \neq v_2 \vee r_1 =$ *true*	$v_1 \neq v_2 \vee r_1 =$ *true*
	$r_2 = s_2$.contains(v_2)	*true*	*true*
	s_2.remove(v_2)	$v_1 \neq v_2 \vee r_1 =$ *false*	$v_1 \neq v_2 \vee r_1 =$ *false*
s_1.remove(v_1)	s_2.add(v_2)	$v_1 \neq v_2$	$v_1 \neq v_2$
	$r_2 = s_2$.contains(v_2)	$v_1 \neq v_2 \vee v_1 \notin s_1$	$v_1 \neq v_2 \vee s_1$.contains(v_1) $=$ *false*
	s_2.remove(v_2)	*true*	*true*

Table 3. Between Commutativity Conditions on ListSet and HashSet

Methods		Before Commutativity Condition	
$r_1 = s_1$.get(k_1)	$r_2 = s_2$.get(k_2)	*true*	*true*
	s_2.put(k_2, v_2)	$k_1 \neq k_2 \vee \langle k_1, v_2 \rangle \in s_1$	$k_1 \neq k_2 \vee s_1$.get(k_1) $= v_2$
	s_2.remove(k_2)	$k_1 \neq k_2 \vee \langle k_1, \_ \rangle \notin s_1$	$k_1 \neq k_2 \vee s_1$.containsKey(k_1) $=$ *false*
s_1.put(k_1, v_1)	$r_2 = s_2$.get(k_2)	$k_1 \neq k_2 \vee \langle k_1, v_1 \rangle \in s_1$	$k_1 \neq k_2 \vee s_1$.get(k_1) $= v_1$
	s_2.put(k_2, v_2)	$k_1 \neq k_2 \vee v_1 = v_2$	$k_1 \neq k_2 \vee v_1 = v_2$
	s_2.remove(k_2)	$k_1 \neq k_2$	$k_1 \neq k_2$
s_1.remove(k_1)	$r_2 = s_2$.get(k_2)	$k_1 \neq k_2 \vee \langle k_1, \_ \rangle \notin s_1$	$k_1 \neq k_2 \vee s_1$.containsKey(k_1) $=$ *false*
	s_2.put(k_2, v_2)	$k_1 \neq k_2$	$k_1 \neq k_2$
	s_2.remove(k_2)	*true*	*true*

Table 4. Before Commutativity Conditions on AssociationList and HashTable

Methods		After Commutativity Condition	
$r_1 = s_1$.get(k_1)	$r_2 = s_2$.get(k_2)	*true*	*true*
	s_2.put(k_2, v_2)	$k_1 \neq k_2 \vee r_1 = v_2$	$k_1 \neq k_2 \vee r_1 = v_2$
	s_2.remove(k_2)	$k_1 \neq k_2 \vee r_1 =$ *null*	$k_1 \neq k_2 \vee r_1 =$ *null*
s_1.put(k_1, v_1)	$r_2 = s_2$.get(k_2)	$k_1 \neq k_2 \vee \langle k_1, v_1 \rangle \in s_1$	$k_1 \neq k_2 \vee s_1$.get(k_1) $= v_1$
	s_2.put(k_2, v_2)	$k_1 \neq k_2 \vee v_1 = v_2$	$k_1 \neq k_2 \vee v_1 = v_2$
	s_2.remove(k_2)	$k_1 \neq k_2$	$k_1 \neq k_2$
s_1.remove(k_1)	$r_2 = s_2$.get(k_2)	$k_1 \neq k_2 \vee \langle k_1, \_ \rangle \notin s_1$	$k_1 \neq k_2 \vee s_1$.containsKey(k_1) $=$ *false*
	s_2.put(k_2, v_2)	$k_1 \neq k_2$	$k_1 \neq k_2$
	s_2.remove(k_2)	*true*	*true*

Table 5. After Commutativity Conditions on AssociationList and HashTable

Methods		Between Commutativity Condition	
$s_1.\texttt{add\_at}(i_1, v_1)$	$s_2.\texttt{add\_at}(i_2, v_2)$	$(i_1 < i_2 \leq \lvert s_2\rvert - 1 \wedge s_2[i_2] = v_2) \vee$ $(i_1 = i_2 \wedge v_1 = v_2) \vee$ $(i_1 > i_2 \wedge s_2[i_1 - 1] = v_1)$	$(i_1 < i_2 \leq s_2.\texttt{size}() - 1 \wedge s_2.\texttt{get}(i_2) = v_2) \vee$ $(i_1 = i_2 \wedge v_1 = v_2) \vee$ $(i_1 > i_2 \wedge s_2.\texttt{get}(i_1 - 1) = v_1)$
	$r_2 = s_2.\texttt{indexOf}(v_2)$	$\neg(\exists i : s_2[i] = v_2) \vee$ $(\exists i < i_1 : s_2[i] = v_2) \vee$ $(\neg(\exists i < i_1 : s_2[i] = v_2) \wedge s_2[i_1] = v_2 \wedge$ $s_2[i_1 + 1] = v_2)$	$s_2.\texttt{indexOf}(v_2) < 0 \vee$ $0 \leq s_2.\texttt{indexOf}(v_2) < i_1 \vee$ $(s_2.\texttt{indexOf}(v_2) = i_1 \wedge$ $s_2.\texttt{get}(i_1 + 1) = v_2)$
	$s_2.\texttt{remove\_at}(i_2)$	$(i_1 < i_2 < \lvert s_2\rvert - 1 \wedge$ $s_2[i_2] = s_2[i_2 + 1]) \vee$ $(\lvert s_2\rvert - 2 \geq i_1 = i_2 \wedge s_2[i_1 + 1] = v_1) \vee$ $(\lvert s_2\rvert - 2 \geq i_1 > i_2 \wedge s_2[i_1 + 1] = v_1)$	$(i_1 < i_2 < s_2.\texttt{size}() - 1 \wedge$ $s_2.\texttt{get}(i_2) = s_2.\texttt{get}(i_2 + 1)) \vee$ $(s_2.\texttt{size}() - 2 \geq i_1 = i_2 \wedge s_2.\texttt{get}(i_1 + 1) = v_1) \vee$ $(s_2.\texttt{size}() - 2 \geq i_1 > i_2 \wedge s_2.\texttt{get}(i_1 + 1) = v_1)$
$r_1 = s_1.\texttt{indexOf}(v_1)$	$s_2.\texttt{add\_at}(i_2, v_2)$	$(r_1 < 0 \wedge v_1 \neq v_2) \vee$ $0 \leq r_1 < i_2 \vee$ $(r_1 = i_2 \wedge v_1 = v_2)$	$(r_1 < 0 \wedge v_1 \neq v_2) \vee$ $0 \leq r_1 < i_2 \vee$ $(r_1 = i_2 \wedge v_1 = v_2)$
	$r_2 = s_2.\texttt{indexOf}(v_2)$	*true*	*true*
	$s_2.\texttt{remove\_at}(i_2)$	$r_1 < 0 \vee$ $0 \leq r_1 < i_2 \vee$ $(r_1 = i_2 \wedge i_2 < \lvert s_2\rvert - 1 \wedge s_2[i_2 + 1] = v_1)$	$r_1 < 0 \vee$ $0 \leq r_1 < i_2 \vee$ $(r_1 = i_2 \wedge i_2 < s_2.\texttt{size}() - 1 \wedge s_2.\texttt{get}(i_2 + 1) = v_1)$
$s_1.\texttt{remove\_at}(i_1)$	$s_2.\texttt{add\_at}(i_2, v_2)$	$(i_1 < i_2 \wedge s_2[i_2 - 1] = v_2) \vee$ $(i_1 = i_2 \wedge s_1[i_1] = v_2) \vee$ $(i_1 > i_2 \wedge s_2[i_1 - 1] = s_1[i_1])$	$(i_1 < i_2 \wedge s_2.\texttt{get}(i_2 - 1) = v_2) \vee$ $(i_1 = i_2 \wedge s_1.\texttt{get}(i_1) = v_2) \vee$ $(i_1 > i_2 \wedge s_2.\texttt{get}(i_1 - 1) = s_1.\texttt{get}(i_1))$
	$r_2 = s_2.\texttt{indexOf}(v_2)$	$(\neg(\exists i : s_2[i] = v_2) \wedge s_1[i_1] \neq v_2) \vee$ $(\exists i < i_1 : s_2[i] = v_2) \vee$ $(\neg(\exists i < i_1 : s_2[i] = v_2) \wedge s_2[i_1] = v_2 \wedge$ $s_1[i_1] = v_2 \wedge i_1 < \lvert s_2\rvert)$	$(s_2.\texttt{indexOf}(v_2) < 0 \wedge s_1.\texttt{get}(i_1) \neq v_2) \vee$ $0 \leq s_2.\texttt{indexOf}(v_2) < i_1 \vee$ $(s_2.\texttt{indexOf}(v_2) = i_1 \wedge$ $s_1.\texttt{get}(i_1) = v_2 \wedge i_1 < s_2.\texttt{size}())$
	$s_2.\texttt{remove\_at}(i_2)$	$(i_1 < i_2 \wedge s_2[i_2 - 1] = s_2[i_2]) \vee$ $i_1 = i_2 \vee$ $(\lvert s_2\rvert > i_1 > i_2 \wedge s_1[i_1] = s_2[i_1])$	$(i_1 < i_2 \wedge s_2.\texttt{get}(i_2 - 1) = s_2.\texttt{get}(i_2)) \vee$ $i_1 = i_2 \vee$ $(s_2.\texttt{size}() > i_1 > i_2 \wedge s_1.\texttt{get}(i_1) = s_2.\texttt{get}(i_1))$

Table 6. Between Commutativity Conditions on ArrayList

Methods		After Commutativity Condition	
$s_1.\texttt{add\_at}(i_1, v_1)$	$s_2.\texttt{add\_at}(i_2, v_2)$	$(i_1 < i_2 \leq \lvert s_3\rvert - 2 \wedge s_3[i_2 + 1] = v_2) \vee$ $(i_1 = i_2 \wedge v_1 = v_2) \vee$ $(i_1 > i_2 \wedge s_3[i_1] = v_1)$	$(i_1 < i_2 \leq s_3.\texttt{size}() - 2 \wedge s_3.\texttt{get}(i_2 + 1) = v_2) \vee$ $(i_1 = i_2 \wedge v_1 = v_2) \vee$ $(i_1 > i_2 \wedge s_3.\texttt{get}(i_1) = v_1)$
	$r_2 = s_2.\texttt{indexOf}(v_2)$	$r_2 < 0 \vee$ $0 \leq r_2 < i_1 \vee$ $(r_2 = i_1 \wedge s_3[i + 1] = v_2)$	$r_2 < 0 \vee$ $0 \leq r_2 < i_1 \vee$ $(r_2 = i_1 \wedge s_3.\texttt{get}(i_1 + 1) = v_2)$
	$s_2.\texttt{remove\_at}(i_2)$	$(i_1 < i_2 < \lvert s_3\rvert \wedge s_2[i_2] = s_3[i_2]) \vee$ $(\lvert s_3\rvert - 1 \geq i_1 = i_2 \wedge s_3[i_1] = v_1) \vee$ $(\lvert s_3\rvert - 1 \geq i_1 > i_2 \wedge s_3[i_1] = v_1)$	$(i_1 < i_2 < s_3.\texttt{size}() \wedge s_2.\texttt{get}(i_2) = s_3.\texttt{get}(i_2)) \vee$ $(s_3.\texttt{size}() - 1 \geq i_1 = i_2 \wedge s_3.\texttt{get}(i_1) = v_1) \vee$ $(s_3.\texttt{size}() - 1 \geq i_1 > i_2 \wedge s_3.\texttt{get}(i_1) = v_1)$
$r_1 = s_1.\texttt{indexOf}(v_1)$	$s_2.\texttt{add\_at}(i_2, v_2)$	$(r_1 < 0 \wedge v_1 \neq v_2) \vee$ $0 \leq r_1 < i_2 \vee$ $(r_1 = i_2 \wedge v_1 = v_2)$	$(r_1 < 0 \wedge v_1 \neq v_2) \vee$ $0 \leq r_1 < i_2 \vee$ $(r_1 = i_2 \wedge v_1 = v_2)$
	$r_2 = s_2.\texttt{indexOf}(v_2)$	*true*	*true*
	$s_2.\texttt{remove\_at}(i_2)$	$r_1 < 0 \vee$ $0 \leq r_1 < i_2 \vee$ $(r_1 = i_2 \wedge i_2 < \lvert s_3\rvert \wedge s_3[i_2] = v_1)$	$r_1 < 0 \vee$ $0 \leq r_1 < i_2 \vee$ $(r_1 = i_2 \wedge i_2 < s_3.\texttt{size}() \wedge s_3.\texttt{get}(i_2) = v_1)$
$s_1.\texttt{remove\_at}(i_1)$	$s_2.\texttt{add\_at}(i_2, v_2)$	$(i_1 < i_2 \wedge s_3[i_2 - 1] = v_2) \vee$ $(i_1 = i_2 \wedge s_1[i_1] = v_2) \vee$ $(i_1 > i_2 \wedge s_3[i_1] = s_1[i_1])$	$(i_1 < i_2 \wedge s_3.\texttt{get}(i_2 - 1) = v_2) \vee$ $(i_1 = i_2 \wedge s_1.\texttt{get}(i_1) = v_2) \vee$ $(i_1 > i_2 \wedge s_3.\texttt{get}(i_1) = s_1.\texttt{get}(i_1))$
	$r_2 = s_2.\texttt{indexOf}(v_2)$	$(r_2 < 0 \wedge s_1[i_1] \neq v_2) \vee$ $0 \leq r_2 < i_1 \vee$ $(r_2 = i_1 \wedge s_1[i_1] = v_2 \wedge i_1 < \lvert s_3\rvert)$	$(r_2 < 0 \wedge s_1.\texttt{get}(i_1) \neq v_2) \vee$ $0 \leq r_2 < i_1 \vee$ $(r_2 = i_1 \wedge s_1.\texttt{get}(i_1) = v_2 \wedge i_1 < s_3.\texttt{size}())$
	$s_2.\texttt{remove\_at}(i_2)$	$(i_1 < i_2 \wedge s_3[i_2 - 1] = s_2[i_2]) \vee$ $i_1 = i_2 \vee$ $(\lvert s_3\rvert + 1 > i_1 > i_2 \wedge s_1[i_1] = s_3[i_1 - 1])$	$(i_1 < i_2 \wedge s_3.\texttt{get}(i_2 - 1) = s_2.\texttt{get}(i_2)) \vee$ $i_1 = i_2 \vee$ $(s_3.\texttt{size}() + 1 > i_1 > i_2 \wedge s_1.\texttt{get}(i_1) = s_3.\texttt{get}(i_1 - 1))$

Table 7. After Commutativity Conditions on ArrayList

mutativity conditions are, of course, no longer complete. If the dropped clauses usually have no effect on the value of the commutativity condition, the gain in ease of reasoning or efficiency may be worth the loss of completeness.

One particularly useful special case is when the commutativity condition is `true` — i.e., the operations commute regardless of the data structure state. For example, `add` operations typically commute with other `add` operations, `contains` operations typically commute with other `contains` operations, and `remove` operations typically commute with other `remove` operations. Such commutativity conditions are particularly easy to reason about at compile time since the compiler does not need to reason about the parameter values or state to find commuting operations.

In general, our data structures implement the update operations that return values (`add(v)`, `remove(v)`, `put(k, v)`, `remove(k)`, `remove_at(i)`, and `set(i, v)`). For example, the `add(v)` operation from the ListSet and HashSet data structures returns true if the elememt `v` was not already present in the abstract set, while the `remove(v)` operation returns true if the element `v` was in the abstract set.

We have verified commutativity conditions for two variants of these operations — one in which the client records the return value (typically by assigning the return value to a variable) and another in which the client discards the return value. The tables in this paper present the commutativity conditions only for the variants that discard the return value; the complete tables available in the technical report version of the paper [26] present commutativity conditions for both variants. Because clients that record the return values observe more information about the data structure, the commutativity conditions for these variants can be more complex. For example, the between commutativity condition for the `r1a = sa.add(v1)`, `r2a = sa.add(v2)` pair is `(v1 ~= v2 | ~r1a)` (i.e., either `v1` and `v2` are different or `v1` was already in the set before the first operation executed), while the commutativity condition for the `s.add(v1)`, `s.add(v2)` pair is simply `true`.

For a data structure with n operations, there are $3n^2$ commutativity conditions — a before, between, and after condition for each pair of operations. For our data structures we consider two versions of operations that update the data structure — one with a return value and one that discards the return value. So there are 2 operations for Accumulator, 6 for HashSet and ListSet, 7 for HashTable and AssociationList, and 9 for ArrayList, for a total of $(3*2^2)+2*(3*6^2)+2*(3*7^2)+(3*9^2) = 765$ commutativity conditions and 1530 generated commutativity testing methods — a soundness testing method and a completeness testing method for each commutativity condition.

5.2 Verification of the Commutativity Conditions

For HashSet, ListSet, AssociationList, HashTable, and Accumulator, all of the automatically generated commutativity testing methods verify as generated. Table 8 presents the time required to verify all of these automatically generated methods. The verification times are all quite reasonable — less than four minutes for all data structures except ArrayList.

For ArrayList, 429 of the 486 methods verify as generated. The entry for ArrayList in Table 8 indicates that Jahob spent 12m 18s attempting to verify all 486 automatically generated methods (with the majority of this time spent waiting for the Jahob integrated reasoning systems to time out as they try, but fail, to verify the 57 methods that require additional proof commands), 3m 04s verifying the 429 methods that verify as generated, and 27s verifying the remaining 57 methods after the addition of the required Jahob proof commands.

In general, the commutativity conditions for ArrayList are substantially more complicated than for other the data structures. We attribute this complexity in part to the use of integer indexing and in part to the presence of operations (such as `add_at` and `remove_at`) that shift the indexing relationships across large regions of the data structure.

Data Structure	Verification Time
Accumulator	0.8s
AssociationList	1m 35s
HashSet	44s
HashTable	3m 20s
ListSet	40s
ArrayList	12m 18s† (3m 04s, 27s)

Table 8. Commutativity Testing Method Verification Times

Proof Language Command	Count
`note`	128
`assuming`	51
`pickWitness`	22
Total	201

Table 9. Additional Jahob Proof Language Commands for Remaining 57 ArrayList Commutativity Testing Methods

The verification of the remaining 57 ArrayList commutativity testing methods required the addition of 128 `note` commands, 51 `assuming` commands, and 22 `pickWitness` commands (see Table 9).

In general, the `note` command allows the developer to specify an intermediate formula for Jahob to prove. Jahob can then use this formula in subsequent proofs. In this way, the developer can identify a lemma structure that helps Jahob find the proof.

The `assuming` command allows the developer to prove formulas of the form $A \implies B$ (by assuming A, then using A to prove B). We typically use the `assuming` command when Jahob is unable to prove a goal B in one case A of the cases of the commutativity condition (or, when proving completeness, the negation of the commutativity condition). Providing a proof of $A \implies B$ enables Jahob to verify the commutativity condition.

The `pickWitness` command allows the developer to start with an existentially quantified formula, name an element for which the formula holds, then remove the quantifier and use the resulting formula in a subsequent proof. We typically use this command when the commutativity condition (or its negation) contains an existential quantifier and we need to use the commutativity condition to prove a goal.

5.3 Verifying the Remaining 57 Methods

The 57 remaining methods fall naturally into four categories. Each requires the proof language commands to manipulate either an existentially quantified formula or the negation of such a formula.

12 of the 57 methods are a soundness testing method for a combination of either `add_at(i,v1)` or `remove_at(i)` with either `indexOf(v2)` or `lastIndexOf(v2)`. The commutativity condition is either a between or after condition. We discuss the between condition for `add_at(i,v1)` with `indexOf(v2)`. The other combinations are similar. One of the cases of the commutativity condition states that `v2` is not present in the intermediate state of the map (so that `indexOf(v2)` returns -1). In this case Jahob must prove that the element is also not present in the initial state before `add_at(i,v1)` executes (so that the return value of `indexOf(v2)` is -1 in both execution orders). In effect, Jahob must prove that if the element is not present in the intermediate state, it is also not present in the initial state — in other words, Jahob must prove that the

† The Z3 [10] and CVC3 [19] decision procedures were each given a 20-second timeout.

negation of one existentially quantified formula implies the negation of another existentially quantified formula. To enable Jahob to prove this fact, we use an `assuming` command, a `pickWitness` command, and several `note` commands to prove the contraposition (i.e., that if the element is present in the initial state, then it is also present in the intermediate state). A key step in the proof of the contraposition involves the identification of the new position of `v2` in the array after the `add_at(i,v1)` shifts it over (Jahob can automatically prove the cases when it is not shifted).

8 of the 57 methods are a soundness testing method for combinations of `remove_at(i)` with `indexOf(v)`. In these methods Jahob must prove that the return value of `indexOf(v)` is the same in both execution orders. The proof involves a case analysis of the initial state of the ArrayList. In one of the cases, the initial state contains two adjacent copies of `v`: one at location `i` and the other at location `i+1`. In this case, `remove_at(i)` removes the first occurrence of `v`, leaving the second occurrence of `v` in location `i`. In both execution orders `indexOf(v)` returns `i` (but `i` references conceptually different versions of `v` in the two execution orders). Jahob is unable to prove this fact without help. The addition of a `note` command that identifies the case and the new position of the second `v` after the `remove_at(v)` operation executes enables Jahob to complete the proof. The formula that identifies the case is the negation of a complex existentially quantified formula.

20 of the 57 methods are a completeness testing method for various combinations of `add_at(i,v)`, `remove_at(i,v)`, and `set(i,v)`. In these methods Jahob must prove that the two final abstract states are different. In general, Jahob accomplishes such a proof by finding an element that is present in one abstract state but not the other. In some cases, however, Jahob is unable to find such an element. The addition of an `assuming` command (which identifies the case) and `note` commands that identify the element and help Jahob prove which abstract state contains the element and which does not enables Jahob to complete the case analysis. The relevant formula identifying the case is existentially quantified.

17 of the 57 methods are a completeness testing method for combinations of either `add_at(i,v1)` or `remove_at(i)` with either `indexOf(v2)` or `lastIndexOf(v2)`. Recall that the operation `add_at(i,v1)` shifts the region of the map above `i` up to make space for `v1` at index `i`. Similarly, `remove_at(i)` shifts the region of the map above `i` down to fill the hole left by the removed element. The verification of the completeness testing method involves a case analysis of the relative positions of the inserted or removed element and the element `v2` (whose index is returned by `indexOf(v2)` or `lastIndexOf(v2)`). In one of the cases Jahob is unable to reason successfully about these relative positions. The addition of an `assuming` command (which identifies the case) and a `note` command that identifies the precise position of `v2` (this `note` command follows from the formula which identifies the case) enables Jahob to complete the case analysis. Once again, the formula identifying the relevant case is existentially quantified.

5.4 Inverse Operations

Table 10 presents, for every operation that changes the data structure's abstract state, the corresponding inverse operation that rolls back the effect of the first operation to restore the original abstract state. s_1 and s_2 denote the data structure states before and after the first operation executes, respectively. Note that some of the inverse operations use the return value from the first operation. Any system that applies such inverse operations must therefore store the return value from the first operation so that it can provide the return value to the corresponding inverse operation. All of the eight inverse testing methods verified as generated without the need for additional Jahob proof commands.

Operation		Inverse Operation
Accumulator	s_1.increase(v)	s_2.increase($-v$)
ListSet HashSet	$r = s_1$.add(v)	if $r = true$ then s_2.remove(v)
	$r = s_1$.remove(v)	if $r = true$ then s_2.add(v)
AssociationList HashTable	$r = s_1$.put(k, v)	if $r \neq null$ then s_2.put(k, r) else s_2.remove(k)
	$r = s_1$.remove(k)	if $r \neq null$ then s_2.put(k, r)
ArrayList	s_1.add_at(i, v)	s_2.remove_at(i)
	$r = s_1$.remove_at(i)	s_2.add_at(i, r)
	$r = s_1$.set(i, v)	s_2.set(i, r)

Table 10. Inverse Operations

6. Related Work

A general theme in this research is decoupling the verification of data structure implementations from the analysis of data structure clients. The immediate goal of the research presented in this paper is to verify commutativity conditions and inverses for sophisticated linked data structures. Other systems can then build on the availability of these verified conditions and inverses to more effectively analyze and transform clients that use the data structures.

This approach is designed to encapsulate the complex reasoning required to verify sophisticated data structure properties (such as commutativity and inverses) within a specialized analysis and verification framework. This encapsulation then enables the development of simpler but more scalable client analyses that can work at the higher level of the verified properties rather than attempting to directly analyze the data structure implementations along with the client together in the same analysis framework.

Decoupling data structure and client analyses is appropriate because data structure implementations and clients have different analysis/verification needs. With current technology, the verification of linked data structure implementations requires the use of sophisticated but unscalable techniques. Such techniques are appropriate in this context because of the tractable size of data structure implementations, the abstraction boundary between data structure implementations and clients, and because the cost of the resulting ambitious data structure verification efforts can be effectively amortized across many uses of the verified properties. Client analyses, in contrast, face significant scalability requirements. Working with verified data structure properties (instead of directly with data structure implementations) can enable the development of simpler but still precise client analyses that can acceptably scale to analyze large client code bases.

In previous research we have found that aspect-oriented techniques can help developers productively factor and modularize the desired client correctness properties, enabling client analyses to work within an appropriately focused analysis scope [35]. In particular, this approach supports the expression and verification of client correctness properties that involve interactions among multiple data structures and invariants over them. Other examples of projects that are designed to exploit or enable decoupled data structure implementation and client analyses include the Hob project [33, 35–37, 50], the Jahob project [6, 51, 52], research on efficient implementations of multiple relations over objects [23], and research on verifying properties of programs that use containers [13]. Typestate analyses are designed to scalably verify simpler properties involving abstract object state changes [3, 11, 15, 16, 18, 32, 37, 47].

We recently became aware of a project that reduces the verification of commutativity conditions and inverses to solving automatically generated SAT problems [40]. The specification language is an abstract imperative language (as opposed to logic specifications as in our research). To enable the reduction to SAT, the specification language does not include loops and recursion. It instead adds additional constructs to provide an acceptably expressive specification language.

We have already surveyed related work in detecting and exploiting commuting operations (see Section 1). To use the commutativity conditions in practice, systems must typically deploy some synchronization mechanism to ensure that operations execute atomically. The specific synchronization mechanisms are orthogonal to the issues we address in this paper (our goal is to verify the correctness of commutativity conditions and inverses, not to design mechanisms that ensure that operations execute atomically).

One synchronization approach is to simply use standard pessimistic (such as mutual exclusion locks [2, 4, 21] or their extension to views of objects [12]) or optimistic (such as optimistic locks [21] or software transactional memory [46]) concurrency control mechanisms. It is also possible to deploy customized nonblocking synchronization algorithms that are tailored for the specific data structure at hand [25, 39].

It is often possible to exploit the structure of the commutativity conditions to develop optimized synchronization mechanisms. For example, *abstract locks*, *forward gatekeepers*, and *general gatekeepers* are successively more general synchronization mechanisms, each of which is appropriate for a successively larger class of commutativity conditions [30]. Our sound and complete commutativity conditions typically take the form of a disjunction of clauses. Dropping clauses produces sound, simpler, but in general incomplete commutativity conditions. Simpler commutativity conditions are typically more efficient to check but expose less concurrency. It is possible to start with a sound and complete commutativity condition and generate a lattice of sound commutativity conditions by dropping clauses (here the least upper bound is disjunction [30]). Which commutativity condition is most appropriate for a given context depends on the interaction between the commutativity condition checking overhead and the amount of concurrency that the commutativity condition exposes in that context.

Commuting operations can also be used to simplify correctness proofs of parallel programs [14]. The basic idea is to use commutativity information to enable *reduction* — obtaining larger-grained atomic blocks by showing that finer-grain statements adjacent in one thread commute with statements in other threads. The specific method uses a form of computation abstraction (replacing statements with statements that have more behaviors) to enhance their ability to obtain statements that commute with other statements. While this may increase the possible behaviors of the program, the idea is to prove assertions at the end of the program. If these assertions are valid under the extended set of behaviors of the abstracted program, they are also valid for the original program.

The research presented in this paper uses a different form of abstraction (data abstraction as opposed to computation abstraction) for a different purpose (reasoning about the semantic equivalence of commuting and inverse operations on linked data structures). Our results may, however, enhance the effectiveness of techniques that reason about explicitly parallel programs — they provide such reasoning techniques with useful commutativity and inverse information about operations that manipulate linked data structures.

Bridge predicates enable developers to specify equivalent states in parallel programs with operations that are intended to execute atomically but whose execution is, in practice, interleaved [8]. These predicates can then be used to recognize and discard false positives in the interleaved execution. In the absence of bridge predicates, such false positives occur when the interleaved execution produces a concrete state that is unrealizable in the atomic execution but nevertheless semantically equivalent to some state that an atomic execution produces. Bridge predicates enable the testing system to recognize the state equivalence and therefore the acceptability of the interleaved execution.

7. Conclusion

Commuting operations, commutativity conditions, and inverse operations play an important role in a broad range of current and envisioned static reasoning systems and parallel programs, languages, and systems. We have presented new techniques for verifying semantic commutativity conditions and inverse operations for linked data structures. Our results show that these techniques can effectively verify inverse operations and sound and complete commutativity conditions for a collection of challenging linked data structures. Our results therefore provide a useful foundation that others can build on as they develop static reasoning systems and parallel programs, languages, and systems.

In the longer term we envision the integration of the commutativity condition and inverse verification techniques presented in this paper into mature software development kits. Deploying these techniques in this way would promote their wider use by developers within a familiar environment as well as their productive integration with other software development tools.

Acknowledgments

We would like to thank Karen Zee for explaining various aspects of Jahob in detail. We also acknowledge an earlier technical report version of this paper [26].

This work was supported in part by the National Science Foundation (Grants CCF-0811397, CCF-0905244, CCF-1036241 and IIS-0835652), the United States Department of Energy (Grant DE-SC0005288), and the Engineering Research Center of Excellence Program of Korea Ministry of Education, Science and Technology / National Research Foundation of Korea (Grant 2010-0001717).

References

[1] F. Aleen and N. Clark. Commutativity analysis for software parallelization: Letting program transformations see the big picture. In *Proc. of the International Conference on Architectural Support for Programming Languages and Operating Systems (ASPLOS)*, 2009.

[2] T. E. Anderson. The performance of spin lock alternatives for shared-memory multiprocessors. *IEEE Trans. Parall. Distrib. Syst.*, 1(1), 1990.

[3] H. Attiya, R. Guerraoui, D. Hendler, P. Kuznetsov, M. M. Michael, and M. Vechev. Laws of order: Expensive synchronization in concurrent algorithms cannot be eliminated. In *Proc. of the ACM SIGACT-SIGPLAN Symposium on Principles of Programming Languages (POPL)*, 2011.

[4] D. F. Bacon, R. Konuru, C. Murthy, and M. Serrano. Thin locks: Featherweight synchronization for Java. In *Proc. of the ACM SIGPLAN Conference on Programming Language Design and Implementation (PLDI)*, 1998.

[5] R. L. Bocchino Jr., V. S. Adve, D. Dig, S. V. Adve, S. Heumann, R. Komuravelli, J. Overbey, P. Simmons, H. Sung, and M. Vakilian. A type and effect system for Deterministic Parallel Java. In *Proc. of the ACM SIGPLAN Conference on Object-Oriented Programming, Systems, Languages and Applications (OOPSLA)*, 2009.

[6] C. Bouillaguet, V. Kuncak, T. Wies, K. Zee, and M. C. Rinard. Using first-order theorem provers in the Jahob data structure verification system. In *Proc. of the International Conference on Verification, Model Checking, and Abstract Interpretation (VMCAI)*, 2007.

[7] M. J. Bridges, N. Vachharajani, Y. Zhang, T. B. Jablin, and D. I. August. Revisiting the sequential programming model for the multicore era. *IEEE Micro*, 28(1), 2008.

[8] J. Burnim, G. Necula, and K. Sen. Specifying and checking semantic atomicity for multithreaded programs. In *Proc. of the International Conference on Architectural Support for Programming Languages and Operating Systems (ASPLOS)*, 2011.

[9] T. H. Cormen, C. E. Leiserson, and R. L. Rivest. *Introduction to Algorithms*. The MIT Press and McGraw-Hill Book Company, 1989.

[10] L. de Moura and N. Bjørner. Efficient E-matching for SMT solvers. In *Proc. of the International Conference on Automated Deduction (CADE)*, 2007.

[11] R. DeLine and M. Fähndrich. Enforcing high-level protocols in low-level software. In *Proc. of the ACM SIGPLAN Conference on Programming Language Design and Implementation (PLDI)*, 2001.

[12] B. Demsky and P. Lam. Views: Object-inspired concurrency control. In *Proc. of the ACM/IEEE International Conference on Software Engineering (ICSE)*, 2010.

[13] I. Dillig, T. Dillig, and A. Aiken. Precise reasoning for programs using containers. In *Proc. of the ACM SIGACT-SIGPLAN Symposium on Principles of Programming Languages (POPL)*, 2011.

[14] T. Elmas, S. Qadeer, and S. Tasiran. A calculus of atomic actions. In *Proc. of the ACM SIGACT-SIGPLAN Symposium on Principles of Programming Languages (POPL)*, 2009.

[15] M. Fähndrich and R. DeLine. Adoption and focus: Practical linear types for imperative programming. In *Proc. of the ACM SIGPLAN Conference on Programming Language Design and Implementation (PLDI)*, 2002.

[16] M. Fähndrich and K. R. M. Leino. Heap monotonic typestates. In *Proc. of the International Workshop on Aliasing, Confinement and Ownership in Object-Oriented Programming (IWACO)*, 2003.

[17] A. Fekete, N. A. Lynch, M. Merritt, and W. E. Weihl. Commutativity-based locking for nested transactions. In *Proc. of the International Workshop on Persistent Object Systems (POS)*, 1989.

[18] J. Field, D. Goyal, G. Ramalingam, and E. Yahav. Typestate verification: Abstraction techniques and complexity results. In *Proc. of the International Static Analysis Symposium (SAS)*, 2003.

[19] Y. Ge, C. Barrett, and C. Tinelli. Solving quantified verification conditions using satisfiability modulo theories. In *Proc. of the International Conference on Automated Deduction (CADE)*, 2007.

[20] A. Goel, K. Po, K. Farhadi, Z. Li, and E. de Lara. The Taser intrusion recovery system. In *Proc. of the ACM Symposium on Operating Systems Principles (SOSP)*, 2005.

[21] J. Gray and A. Reuter. *Transaction Processing: Concepts and Techniques*. Morgan Kaufmann, 1993.

[22] S. Gulwani and G. C. Necula. Precise interprocedural analysis using random interpretation. In *Proc. of the ACM SIGACT-SIGPLAN Symposium on Principles of Programming Languages (POPL)*, 2005.

[23] P. Hawkins, A. Aiken, K. Fisher, M. Rinard, and M. Sagiv. Data representation synthesis. In *Proc. of the ACM SIGPLAN conference on Programming Language Design and Implementation (PLDI)*, 2011.

[24] J. G. Henriksen, J. Jensen, M. Jørgensen, N. Klarlund, R. Paige, T. Rauhe, and A. Sandholm. Mona: Monadic second-order logic in practice. In *Proc. of the International Conference on Tools and Algorithms for the Construction and Analysis of Systems (TACAS)*, 1995.

[25] M. Herlihy, V. Luchangco, and M. Moir. Obstruction-free synchronization: Double-ended queue as an example. In *Proc. of the International Conference on Distributed Computing Systems (ICDCS)*, 2003.

[26] D. Kim and M. C. Rinard. Verification of semantic commutativity conditions and inverse operations on linked data structures. Technical Report MIT-CSAIL-TR-2010-056, Computer Science and Artificial Intelligence Laboratory, Massachusetts Institute of Technology, Dec. 2010.

[27] T. Kim, X. Wang, N. Zeldovich, and M. F. Kaashoek. Intrusion recovery using selective re-execution. In *Proc. of the Symposium on Operating Systems Design and Implementation (OSDI)*, 2010.

[28] M. Kulkarni, K. Pingali, B. Walter, G. Ramanarayanan, K. Bala, and L. P. Chew. Optimistic parallelism requires abstractions. In *Proc. of the ACM SIGPLAN conference on Programming Language Design and Implementation (PLDI)*, 2007.

[29] M. Kulkarni, D. Prountzos, D. Nguyen, and K. Pingali. Defining and implementing commutativity conditions for parallel execution. Technical Report TR-ECE-09-11, School of Electrical and Computer Engineering, Purdue University, Aug. 2009.

[30] M. Kulkarni, D. Nguyen, D. Prountzos, X. Sui, and K. Pingali. Exploiting the commutativity lattice. In *Proc. of the ACM SIGPLAN Conference on Programming Language Design and Implementation (PLDI)*, 2011.

[31] V. Kuncak and M. Rinard. Towards efficient satisfiability checking for Boolean algebra with Presburger arithmetic. In *Proc. of the International Conference on Automated Deduction (CADE)*, 2007.

[32] V. Kuncak, P. Lam, and M. Rinard. Role analysis. In *Proc. of the ACM SIGACT-SIGPLAN Symposium on Principles of Programming Languages (POPL)*, 2002.

[33] V. Kuncak, P. Lam, K. Zee, and M. C. Rinard. Modular pluggable analyses for data structure consistency. *IEEE Trans. Softw. Eng.*, 32 (12), 2006.

[34] V. Kuncak, H. H. Nguyen, and M. Rinard. Deciding Boolean algebra with Presburger arithmetic. *Journal of Automated Reasoning*, 36(3), 2006.

[35] P. Lam, V. Kuncak, and M. Rinard. Crosscutting techniques in program specification and analysis. In *Proc. of the International Conference on Aspect-Oriented Software Development (AOSD)*, 2005.

[36] P. Lam, V. Kuncak, and M. Rinard. Hob: A tool for verifying data structure consistency. In *Proc. of the International Conference on Compiler Construction (CC)*, 2005.

[37] P. Lam, V. Kuncak, and M. Rinard. Generalized typestate checking for data structure consistency. In *Proc. of the International Conference on Verification, Model Checking, and Abstract Interpretation (VMCAI)*, 2005.

[38] P. Mahajan, R. Kotla, C. C. Marshall, V. Ramasubramanian, T. L. Rodeheffer, D. B. Terry, and T. Wobber. Effective and efficient compromise recovery for weakly consistent replication. In *Proc. of the ACM European Conference on Computer Systems (EuroSys)*, 2009.

[39] M. M. Michael and M. L. Scott. Simple, fast, and practical non-blocking and blocking concurrent queue algorithms. In *Proc. of the ACM Symposium on Principles of Distributed Computing (PODC)*, 1996.

[40] E. Moss. Personal communication, 2011.

[41] M. C. Rinard and P. C. Diniz. Commutativity analysis: a new analysis technique for parallelizing compilers. *ACM Trans. Prog. Lang. Syst.*, 19(6), 1997.

[42] M. C. Rinard and M. S. Lam. The design, implementation, and evaluation of Jade. *ACM Trans. Prog. Lang. Syst.*, 20(3), 1998.

[43] S. Sagiv, T. W. Reps, and R. Wilhelm. Parametric shape analysis via 3-valued logic. *ACM Trans. Prog. Lang. Syst.*, 24(3), 2002.

[44] S. Schulz. E — a brainiac theorem prover. *AI Commun.*, 15(2–3), 2002.

[45] F. Shafique, K. Po, and A. Goel. Correlating multi-session attacks via replay. In *Proc. of the Workshop on Hot Topics in System Dependability (HotDep)*, 2006.

[46] N. Shavit and D. Touitou. Software transactional memory. *Distributed Computing*, 10(2), 1997.

[47] R. E. Strom and S. Yemini. Typestate: A programming language concept for enhancing software reliability. *IEEE Trans. Softw. Eng.*, 12(1), 1986.

[48] C. Weidenbach. Combining superposition, sorts and splitting. In A. Robinson and A. Voronkov, editors, *Handbook of Automated Reasoning*, volume 2, chapter 27, pages 1965–2013. The MIT Press, 2001.

[49] W. E. Weihl. Commutativity-based concurrency control for abstract data types. *IEEE Trans. Comput.*, 37(12), 1988.

[50] T. Wies, V. Kuncak, P. Lam, A. Podelski, and M. Rinard. Field constraint analysis. In *Proc. of the International Conference on Verification, Model Checking, and Abstract Interpretation (VMCAI)*, 2006.

[51] K. Zee, V. Kuncak, and M. C. Rinard. Full functional verification of linked data structures. In *Proc. of the ACM SIGPLAN Conference on Programming Language Design and Implementation (PLDI)*, 2008.

[52] K. Zee, V. Kuncak, and M. C. Rinard. An integrated proof language for imperative programs. In *Proc. of the ACM SIGPLAN Conference on Programming Language Design and Implementation (PLDI)*, 2009.

Exploiting the Commutativity Lattice *

Milind Kulkarni
School of Electrical and Computer Engineering
Purdue University
milind@purdue.edu

Donald Nguyen[1], Dimitrios Prountzos[1], Xin Sui[1], Keshav Pingali[1,2]
[1]Department of Computer Science, [2]Institute for Computational Engineering and Sciences
The University of Texas at Austin
{ddn, dprountz, xinsui, pingali}@cs.utexas.edu

Abstract

Speculative execution is a promising approach for exploiting parallelism in many programs, but it requires efficient schemes for detecting conflicts between concurrently executing threads. Prior work has argued that checking semantic commutativity of method invocations is the right way to detect conflicts for complex data structures such as kd-trees. Several ad hoc ways of checking commutativity have been proposed in the literature, but there is no systematic approach for producing implementations.

In this paper, we describe a novel framework for reasoning about commutativity conditions: the *commutativity lattice*. We show how commutativity specifications from this lattice can be systematically implemented in one of three different schemes: abstract locking, forward gatekeeping and general gatekeeping. We also discuss a disciplined approach to exploiting the lattice to find different implementations that trade off precision in conflict detection for performance. Finally, we show that our novel conflict detection schemes are practical and can deliver speedup on three real-world applications.

Categories and Subject Descriptors D.1.3 [*Programming Techniques*]: Concurrent Programming—Parallel Programming; D.3.3 [*Programming Languages*]: Language Constructs and Features—Concurrent Programming Structures

General Terms Languages

Keywords Commutativity lattice, transactions, optimistic parallelism

1. Introduction

Speculative execution of high-level language programs has emerged as an important concept in multicore programming [12, 19, 22]. A central concern in implementing such systems is detecting conflicts accurately and with low overhead. These two goals are usually contradictory. For example, a single global lock on all of shared-memory will detect conflicts with low overhead, but it prevents parallel execution of speculative computations. Transactional memory (TM) is a better approach that tracks the set of locations (or objects) read and written by each transaction and reports conflicts if a location written by one transaction is read or written by another concurrently executing transaction [12]. This results in more fine-grained conflict detection than the first scheme and permits much more concurrency but at the expense of potentially higher overhead, especially if the TM is implemented in software.

Though the TM approach works well for many programs, it has been pointed out in the literature [10, 18, 25] that conflict detection at the memory level can be overly conservative for programs that use complex abstract data types (ADTs). Consider the disjoint-set union-find data structure. Two transactions might both invoke the find method, and these invocations may result in modifications to the concrete (internal) representation of the data structure because of path compression, causing memory-level conflicts[1]. However, from the ADT perspective, find operations do not modify the disjoint sets; they are read-only operations that commute with each other and do not conflict. Intuitively, there may be several *concrete states* of the data structure that represent the same *abstract state*; if the client of the ADT only cares about the abstract state, memory-level conflict detection can be overly conservative, reducing concurrency. This problem can also arise with other ADTs such as sets and kd-trees, as we discuss later in the paper.

Although issues surrounding the behavior of commutativity based conflict detection have been explored in prior work [10, 15, 25], no work has discussed how such semantic conflict checks should be *implemented*. It is straightforward to see how memory-level conflict checking can be performed for a complex data structure, but it is far less apparent how to implement a correct and efficient conflict detection scheme based on the semantics of union-find. Worse, every abstract data type potentially requires a different conflict-detection scheme. Prior work has relied on *ad hoc* implementations for the specific data structures they focus on [4, 10, 18, 20], but what is missing is a *systematic* way of generating correct conflict detectors.

Complicating matters further is that for a given abstract data type, there may be multiple correct conflict detection schemes that nevertheless provide different amount of parallelism at different overheads. For example, Ni *et al.* present a conflict checker for sets based on read/write locks on keys inserted into the set [20]. In contrast, Herlihy and Koskinen propose a conflict checker for sets based on exclusive locks on keys [10]. Given two conflict checkers, how do we know which one to use? Which one will expose more parallelism? Which one will have higher overhead? Intuitively, a more complex scheme may be able to expose more parallelism at

* This work is supported in part by NSF grants 0923907, 0833162, 0719966, and 0702353 and by grants from IBM, NEC and Intel.

[1] Ironically, a simpler ADT implementation for union-find that does not perform path compression would let the two invocations proceed concurrently!

PLDI'11, June 4–8, 2011, San Jose, California, USA.

the cost of additional run-time overhead; is this always the case? Can we produce multiple conflict checkers for a data structure in a disciplined way?

This paper addresses these issues through a novel way of reasoning about commutativity in abstract data types: a lattice of *commutativity specifications*. A commutativity specification is a set of predicates associated with pairs of methods in a data structure; a pair of methods commute if the predicate associated with them evaluates to **true**. There are many possible commutativity specifications for a data structure, and Section 2 shows that they can be arranged into a *commutativity lattice*, ordered by the amount of parallelism they permit.

Section 3 shows how commutativity specifications can be systematically turned into commutativity checking implementations. We present three novel constructions: one that generates abstract lock-based schemes and two that generate novel conflict detection schemes called *gatekeepers*. Section 4 shows that different commutativity checking implementations for a data structure are actually implementations of different specifications from the commutativity lattice, and describes a disciplined way of producing different implementations for a given data structure. Section 5 explores the tradeoff between performance and precision, and shows that our systematically constructed conflict detectors can deliver scalable performance. Section 6 concludes and presents related work.

Contributions This paper makes the following contributions:

1. We give a definition of commutativity conditions and specifications, and describe a lattice-theoretic approach to reasoning about various commutativity specifications for a data structure.
2. We present three approaches for implementing commutativity specifications, *abstract locking*, *forward gatekeeping* and *general gatekeeping*. We develop algorithms for systematically constructing commutativity checkers of each type given a specification. We discuss the expressivity of each scheme, and their overheads.
3. We show for three real-world applications that our commutativity schemes are practical. We quantify the potential tradeoffs between the parallelism exposed and the overhead incurred by different schemes. We also show, paradoxically, that for some benchmarks the higher-parallelism scheme in fact has lower overhead.

2. Commutativity

We begin in Section 2.1 by briefly explaining how commutativity of method invocations can be used to check serializability. Section 2.2 next defines commutativity conditions, which are predicates a run-time system can use to guarantee serializability. Section 2.3 describes the language used to specify commutativity conditions. We then present a lattice-theoretic view of commutativity specifications in Section 2.4. Section 2.5 provides example specifications for a few data structures, illustrating the potential complexity of commutativity properties.

2.1 Serializability through commutativity

Our goal is to ensure that two transactions, A and B, that execute concurrently maintain transactional semantics. In particular, we want to ensure that A and B are serializable: that the parallel execution of A and B produce the same results as if A and B were executed sequentially in some order[2].

We consider data structures that provide a set of methods $m \in \mathcal{M}$. The data structure's state, σ, consists of any information needed to capture the *abstract* behavior of the structure. For example, a set data structure's abstract state is the set of elements contained in the data structure. In general, many concrete representations of a data structure have the same abstract state. For example, a set represented as a linked list and one represented as a hash set will have different concrete states, but, if they contain the same elements, would have the same abstract state.

The program consists of a series of method invocations performed by transactions on the data structure. Transaction T invoking a method m with argument v in state σ will be written $\langle m^T(v)\rangle_\sigma$. We will omit arguments, states and transaction labels unless necessary for clarity.

Each of these method invocations is atomic: when a method m is invoked, it appears to execute instantaneously at some point between when m was invoked and when it returned. More formally, we consider *linearizable* data structures [13]. Note that this means we need only consider interleavings of transactions at the granularity of method invocations [15].

A *history* is a series of method invocations performed by one or more transactions, starting from a particular state. The history records method invocations as well as their return values[3]. Note that because the invocations are atomic, the return values are available immediately after the method is invoked. Histories will be written as: $\langle m_1(v_1), m_2(v_2), \ldots, m_k(v_k)\rangle_\sigma$, indicating a series of method invocations starting from state σ. We can also discuss sub-histories, which are subsequences of larger histories; as these sub-histories also have some initial state, they can be considered histories in their own right.

Two histories H and H' are equivalent, denoted $H \equiv H'$, if their initial states are the same, they contain of the same method invocations (albeit potentially in a different order), each invocation returns the same result, and the states at the end of the histories are the same. Note that if we consider two equivalent sub-histories h and h', where h is a sub-history of some larger history H, replacing h with h' in H produces an equivalent history H'.

We can define *commutativity* in terms of history equivalence:

Definition 1. *Two invocations* $m_1(v_1)$ *and* $m_2(v_2)$ *commute with respect to a state* σ *if and only if* $\langle m_1(v_1), m_2(v_2)\rangle_\sigma \equiv \langle m_2(v_2), m_1(v_1)\rangle_\sigma$.

In other words, two method invocations commute with respect to a given state if they are invoked consecutively starting in that state, and interchanging them produces an equivalent history[4].

We can use the commutativity of method invocations performed by A and B to check if their execution is serializable. Intuitively, if every method invocation in A commutes with every method invocation in B, then A and B are serializable, and B can be seen as executing before A. This type of serializability can be thought of as an extension of *d-serializability* [21] from non-interfering method invocations to commuting method invocations. As this approach has been used by several prior works ([10, 15, 18]), we present only an informal inductive argument here.

Assume that the first invocation performed by transaction A is $\langle m_1(v_1)^A\rangle_{\sigma_1}$, producing some new state σ'. When transaction B later performs its *last* invocation $\langle m_2(v_2)^B\rangle_{\sigma_2}$, a run-time check must be performed. If σ_2 is σ' (meaning each transaction has invoked one method), it suffices to show that $m_1(v_1)^A$ and $m_2(v_2)^B$ commute with respect to σ_1. This check allows the methods to be

[2] The following discussion will assume that there are only two transactions executing, and that the transactions access a single data structure; the approach to guaranteeing serializability generalizes straightforwardly.

[3] Because return values are determined by method arguments and state, we do not explicitly represent the return values in the history.

[4] Prior work has distinguished between left-moving and right-moving commutativity, which constrain in which directions method invocations can be moved [15]. In this paper, we consider *both-moving* commutativity, where invocations can be moved in either direction.

"interchanged" in the history, producing a history where $m_2^B(v_2)$ executes before $m_1^A(v_1)$.

In most cases, however, σ_2 will be separated from σ_1 by some intervening invocations by both A and B. It is apparent that we can move $m_1^A(v_1)$ and $m_2^B(v_2)$ towards each other by proving that the invocations commute with the intervening methods and swapping their positions in the history (hence pushing all later invocations from A after $m_2^B(v_2)$, and all earlier invocations from B before $m_1^A(v_1)$). At this point, let σ_1' be the state $m_1^A(v_1)$ in which is actually invoked, while $m_2^B(v_2)$ is invoked in the next state, σ_2'. If we can then prove that $m_1^A(v_1)$ and $m_2^B(v_2)$ commute with respect to σ_1', we can swap the two invocations and produce a serial history where all invocations from B occur before any invocations from A.

2.2 Commutativity conditions

It is apparent from the previous discussion that, if we could find predicates $\psi_{m_1;m_2}(\sigma, v_1, v_2)$, for all pairs of methods m_1 and m_2, that were true for histories $\langle m_1(v_1), m_2(v_2)\rangle_\sigma$ if and only if the two method invocations commuted in that history, we could check this formula as part of a run-time system that verified that two concurrently executing transactions were serializable. Furthermore, such predicates clearly exist (even if they are not easily expressible in a particular logic, or, for method invocations that don't commute, they are merely **false**).

Unfortunately, in a realistic run-time system, method invocations from two transactions will not appear back to back in a program's execution history. Instead, transaction A might invoke $\langle m_1(v_1)\rangle_{\sigma_1}$ and, much later, transaction B might invoke $\langle m_2(v_2)\rangle_{\sigma_2}$. What we desire is a *commutativity condition*: a predicate over method invocations that could occur in *any* two states that nevertheless lets us prove the commutativity of method invocations when they appear back-to-back and must be swapped. To make the definition of commutativity conditions more clear, we first define a more refined equivalence properties for histories:

Definition 2. *Two histories H and H' are* C-EQUIVALENT, *denoted $H \equiv_C H'$, iff H can be transformed into H' by replacing sub-histories of the form $\langle m_1(v_1), m_2(v_2)\rangle_\sigma$ with equivalent sub-histories of the form $\langle m_2(v_2), m_1(v_1)\rangle_\sigma$.*

In other words, two histories are C-EQUIVALENT if one can be transformed into the other by swapping commuting method invocations.

We can now define commutativity conditions, which are over two method invocations that occur in two non-consecutive states in some history H:

Definition 3. *A* commutativity condition, *ϕ, is a predicate on two method invocations $\langle m_1(v_1)\rangle_{\sigma_1}$ and $\langle m_2(v_2)\rangle_{\sigma_2}$ in an execution history H that is* **true** *only if, for all histories $H' \equiv_C H$ that contain a sub-history $h = \langle m_1(v_1), m_2(v_2)\rangle_{\sigma'}$, $m_1(v_1)$ and $m_2(v_2)$ commute with respect to σ'.*

In other words, a commutativity condition is a predicate ϕ that, when true in one history, means that in any C-EQUIVALENT history where the two method invocations happen back to back, the invocations commute. We say that a predicate is a *valid* commutativity condition if it satisfies the requirements of Definition 3.

In practice, these conditions can be expressed as a particular formula for a pair of methods, parameterized on the arguments, return value and states of the method invocations. Such commutativity formulae are thus written $\phi_{m_1;m_2}(\sigma_1, v_1, r_1, \sigma_2, v_2, r_2)$ (where r_1 and r_2 are the return values of $\langle m_1(v_1)\rangle_{\sigma_1}$ and $\langle m_2(v_2)\rangle_{\sigma_2}$, respectively, and can be read informally as:

$$\langle m_1(v_1)\rangle_{\sigma_1}/r_1 \text{ commutes with } \langle m_2(v_2)\rangle_{\sigma_2}/r_2 \text{ if } \phi$$

If, for each pair of method invocations $\langle m_1(v_1)\rangle_{\sigma_1}$ and $\langle m_2(v_2)\rangle_{\sigma_2}$ invoked by concurrently executing transactions, the run-time system ensures that $\phi_{m_1;m_2}(\sigma_1, v_1, r_1, \sigma_2, v_2, r_2)$ is **true**, then the current execution is serializable (a proof of this claim is given in Appendix A).

If one of these *commutativity checks* does not succeed, then the run-time can preserve serializability by undoing one transaction and re-executing it later when it will not be concurrent with the conflicting transaction. The implementation of commutativity checks is the subject of Section 3.

Discussion

Commutativity conditions are somewhat complex, and producing a valid commutativity condition for a pair of methods may seem daunting. While this paper does not address the construction and correctness of commutativity conditions (the verification problem, though not the construction problem, is addressed by techniques such as [14]), we discuss some interesting properties of commutativity conditions that can inform their specification and verification.

First, most commutativity conditions are expressible solely in terms of the arguments and return values of an invocation. While the return values are dependent on the states the invocations occur in, return values have a distinguished place in the definition of commutativity (specifically, return values must remain the same when two commuting method invocations are swapped). This means that such a predicate on method invocations in one history is true if and only if it is true in all C-EQUIVALENT histories, as the arguments and return values are invariant up to commutative swaps. Thus it suffices to consider the effects of two method invocations appearing back-to-back when creating such commutativity conditions.

As we will see in Section 2.5, some commutativity conditions are based on more than just arguments and return values. Instead, they also make use of relations over the abstract state of the data structure. It is less obvious how to reason about valid commutativity conditions in such cases. One approach is to consider the relations over abstract state to be merely auxiliary, "hidden," return values of the method invocations. As such, commuting methods must preserve these hidden return values as well as the actual return values. This is complicated by the complex conditions we see in some data structures, where the state relations are over abstract state as well as information from *future* method invocations. In such cases, determining that a commutativity condition is valid requires a more substantial proof; we leave this investigation to future work.

Note that a particular commutativity condition need not allow the run-time to detect that two transactions can execute in parallel, even if a different commutativity condition would. If the commutativity condition for two method invocations is simply **false**, the run-time system will determine that the two transactions cannot execute concurrently and will delay the execution of one transaction until the other completes. This reduces parallelism by preventing concurrent execution, but preserves serializability. The implications of the mismatch between schedules that can be proved serializable given certain commutativity conditions and those that could be proved serializable given better commutativity conditions is explored in Section 2.4.

2.3 Commutativity specifications

A *commutativity specification* is a set of logical formulae that represent commutativity conditions for each pair of methods in a data structure. The logic, L_1, of these formulae is given in Figure 1. The vocabulary of the logic includes the arguments and return values of method invocations. The specification can also use arbitrary functions over the arguments as well as the abstract states in which the methods are invoked. The logic allows boolean connectives, equality and arithmetic, but no quantifiers. In Section 3, we present some

S	:=	$\sigma_1 \mid \sigma_2$	*Abstract states*
V	:=	$v_1 \mid v_2 \mid r_1 \mid r_2$	*Arguments, return values,*
	|	$\mathbf{Z} \mid \mathbf{B}$	*constants*
F	:=	$f(S, V, V, \ldots)$	$(S \times V \times V \times \cdots) \rightarrow \mathbf{Z} \cup \mathbf{B}$
O	:=	$+ \mid - \mid * \mid / \mid < \mid >$	*Arithmetic connectives*
	|	$\wedge \mid \vee$	*Boolean connectives*
	|	$=$	*Equality*
P	:=	$V \mid F$	*Primitive formula*
C	:=	$P\ O\ P \mid (C) \mid \neg C \mid C\ O\ C$	*Formula*

$$\phi_{m_1;m_2}(\sigma_1, v_1, r_1, \sigma_2, v_2, r_2) = C$$

Figure 1. L_1: Logic to express commutativity conditions

(1)	$\langle \mathsf{add}(a) \rangle_{\sigma_1} / r_1$	commutes with if	$\langle \mathsf{add}(b) \rangle_{\sigma_2} / r_2$ $a \neq b \vee (r_1 = \textbf{false} \wedge r_2 = \textbf{false})$
(2)	$\langle \mathsf{add}(a) \rangle_{\sigma_1} / r_1$	commutes with if	$\langle \mathsf{remove}(b) \rangle_{\sigma_2} / r_2$ $a \neq b \vee (r_1 = \textbf{false} \wedge r_2 = \textbf{false})$
(3)	$\langle \mathsf{add}(a) \rangle_{\sigma_1} / r_1$	commutes with if	$\langle \mathsf{contains}(b) \rangle_{\sigma_2} / r_2$ $a \neq b \vee r_1 = \textbf{false}$
(4)	$\langle \mathsf{remove}(a) \rangle_{\sigma_1} / r_1$	commutes with if	$\langle \mathsf{remove}(b) \rangle_{\sigma_2} / r_2$ $a \neq b \vee (r_1 = \textbf{false} \wedge r_2 = \textbf{false})$
(5)	$\langle \mathsf{remove}(a) \rangle_{\sigma_1} / r_1$	commutes with if	$\langle \mathsf{contains}(b) \rangle_{\sigma_2} / r_2$ $a \neq b \vee r_1 = \textbf{false}$
(6)	$\langle \mathsf{contains}(a) \rangle_{\sigma_1} / r_1$	commutes with	$\langle \mathsf{contains}(b) \rangle_{\sigma_2} / r_2$

Figure 2. Commutativity specification for sets.

restricted logics that are subsets of L_1, and show that if a specification is expressible in those restricted logics we can derive efficient commutativity checking implementations.

An example commutativity specification for a set is given in Figure 2[5]. Note that add and remove return a boolean that indicates whether the invocation modified the set. Each condition is relatively straightforward: methods commute with each other if (i) neither modifies the set or (ii) their arguments are different. For example, condition (1) states that $\mathsf{add}(x)$ commutes with $\mathsf{add}(y)$ if $x \neq y$ or neither invocation of add modified the set (as indicated by their returning false).

For linearizable data structures, the relevant state of the data structure is the *abstract* state; the *concrete* implementation of the data structure is not relevant to commutativity. For example, a set data structure implemented concretely using a linked list has the same commutativity properties as a set data structure implemented using a red-black tree. If a commutativity specification *does* refer to the concrete (*i.e.*, memory-level) state of a data structure, then it will only be valid for particular implementations of the ADT.

2.4 A Commutativity Lattice

While Figure 2 presents a single commutativity specification for sets, it is by no means the only one. Recall that a commutativity condition is a predicate that satisfies Definition 3. However, as discussed in Section 2.2, for each pair of methods in an ADT, there may be multiple valid commutativity conditions (for example, **false** is always a valid commutativity condition).

Despite there being multiple valid conditions for a pair of methods, there is only one *precise* condition, ϕ^*, which is true if and only if the conditions of Definition 3 hold. Note that this means that all commutativity conditions $\phi_{m_1;m_2} \Rightarrow \phi^*_{m_1;m_2}$. The commutativity specification given in Figure 2 is precise, meaning that all the formulae capture precise commutativity conditions.

[5] The commutativity formulae presented in this paper are symmetric: $\phi_{m_1;m_2}$ is the same as $\phi_{m_2;m_1}$. A full specification also includes these symmetric conditions, which have been excluded for brevity.

(1)	$\langle \mathsf{add}(a) \rangle_{\sigma_1} / r_1$	commutes with if	$\langle \mathsf{add}(b) \rangle_{\sigma_2} / r_2$ $a \neq b$
(2)	$\langle \mathsf{add}(a) \rangle_{\sigma_1} / r_1$	commutes with if	$\langle \mathsf{remove}(b) \rangle_{\sigma_2} / r_2$ $a \neq b$
(3)	$\langle \mathsf{add}(a) \rangle_{\sigma_1} / r_1$	commutes with if	$\langle \mathsf{contains}(b) \rangle_{\sigma_2} / r_2$ $a \neq b$
(4)	$\langle \mathsf{remove}(a) \rangle_{\sigma_1} / r_1$	commutes with if	$\langle \mathsf{remove}(b) \rangle_{\sigma_2} / r_2$ $a \neq b$
(5)	$\langle \mathsf{remove}(a) \rangle_{\sigma_1} / r_1$	commutes with if	$\langle \mathsf{contains}(b) \rangle_{\sigma_2} / r_2$ $a \neq b$
(6)	$\langle \mathsf{contains}(a) \rangle_{\sigma_1} / r_1$	commutes with	$\langle \mathsf{contains}(b) \rangle_{\sigma_2} / r_2$

Figure 3. A strengthened commutativity specification for sets.

If we consider the set of all valid commutativity conditions for a pair of methods, S, we can build a partially ordered set (poset), $P = (S, \prec)$ based on logical implication, such that $\phi_1 \preceq \phi_2$ iff $\phi_1 \Rightarrow \phi_2$. This poset has a natural least element, $\bot = \textbf{false}$, which is obviously less than all the other elements and is also trivially a valid commutativity condition. More interestingly, ϕ^* is the greatest element ($\top$) of the poset. This follows directly from the definitions of commutativity conditions and ϕ^*.

We can then define two binary operators, $\sqcup$ (least upper bound, or join) and $\sqcap$ (greatest lower bound, or meet) for every pair of conditions in S, as follows:

$$a \sqcap b \Leftrightarrow a \wedge b$$
$$a \sqcup b \Leftrightarrow a \vee b$$

The structure $(S, \sqcup, \sqcap, \top, \bot)$ forms a *bounded lattice*. Note that $a \preceq b \Leftrightarrow (a \sqcup b = b) \Leftrightarrow (a \sqcap b = a)$.

Note that a particular commutativity condition (in particular, ϕ^*) may not be expressible in a given logic L. We can create a restriction of the set of valid commutativity conditions to those expressible in L, S_L. Provided that L is closed under disjunction (as L_1 is), we can build a lattice over S_L with its $\top$ as the *weakest* commutativity condition expressible in L.

While the lattice has been defined only for a pair of methods of an ADT, it can be readily extended to create a bounded lattice of commutativity specifications, with elements of the lattice representing specifications that are distinct up to logical equivalence. For two commutativity specifications Φ_1 and Φ_2, $\Phi_1 \preceq \Phi_2$ if and only if, for each pair of methods m_1, m_2, where ϕ_1 is the commutativity condition for m_1 and m_2 from Φ_1 and ϕ_2 is the corresponding condition from Φ_2, $\phi_1 \preceq \phi_2$. We can define $\sqcup$ and $\sqcap$ in a similar manner (joining or meeting corresponding pairs of commutativity conditions from the two specifications). $\bot$ is the specification where all conditions are **false**, and $\top$ is the specification where all conditions are precise: Φ^*.

Moving up and down the commutativity lattice

Different points in the commutativity specification lattice have different properties; as you move down in the lattice, the commutativity conditions become *stronger*, and hence less likely to prove that two methods commute (and $\bot$ does not allow any methods to commute). Recall that two transactions are allowed to proceed in parallel if we can prove that the method invocations from those transactions commute. As a consequence, *stronger commutativity conditions permit fewer transactions to proceed in parallel, potentially reducing the amount of parallelism an application exhibits.*

For example, consider the specification for sets, Φ', given in Figure 3, which is derived by dropping some of the clauses from Φ^*, the precise specification of Figure 2. It is obvious that the new specification is lower in the commutativity lattice than the precise specification. If two transactions A and B, each execute $\mathsf{add}(x)$ on a set that already contains x, the adds commute according to Φ^*, but not according to Φ'. A conflict detection scheme based on the former specification will allow A and B to execute in parallel, while one based on the latter will not, reducing parallelism.

Definitions:
$\mathsf{dist}(a, b)$ is an algorithm defined-distance metric such that $\mathbf{nearest}(a)$ returns the nearest point according to dist.

(1)	$\langle\mathsf{nearest}(a)\rangle_{\sigma_1}/r_1$	commutes with	$\langle\mathsf{nearest}(b)\rangle_{\sigma_2}/r_2$
(2)	$\langle\mathsf{nearest}(a)\rangle_{\sigma_1}/r_1$	commutes with if	$\langle\mathsf{add}(b)\rangle_{\sigma_2}/r_2$ $r_2 = \mathbf{false} \vee$ $\mathsf{dist}(a, b) > \mathsf{dist}(a, r_1)$
(3)	$\langle\mathsf{nearest}(a)\rangle_{\sigma_1}/r_1$	commutes with if	$\langle\mathsf{remove}(b)\rangle_{\sigma_2}/r_2$ $(a \neq b \wedge r_1 \neq b) \vee$ $r_2 = \mathbf{false}$
(4)	$\langle\mathsf{remove}(a)\rangle_{\sigma_1}/r_1$	commutes with if	$\langle\mathsf{remove}(b)\rangle_{\sigma_2}/r_2$ $a \neq b \vee$ $(r_1 = \mathbf{false} \wedge r_2 = \mathbf{false})$
(5)	$\langle\mathsf{remove}(a)\rangle_{\sigma_1}/r_1$	commutes with if	$\langle\mathsf{add}(b)\rangle_{\sigma_2}/r_2$ $a \neq b \vee$ $(r_1 = \mathbf{false} \wedge r_2 = \mathbf{false})$
(6)	$\langle\mathsf{add}(a)\rangle_{\sigma_1}/r_1$	commutes with if	$\langle\mathsf{add}(b)\rangle_{\sigma_2}/r_2$ $a \neq b \vee$ $(r_1 = \mathbf{false} \wedge r_2 = \mathbf{false})$

Figure 4. Commutativity specification for kd-trees.

The choice of which commutativity specification from the lattice to use as the basis for a conflict detector clearly has implications for parallelism. However, as we will see in Section 3, different commutativity specifications have properties that allow them to be implemented using different approaches. Hence, different choices of specifications also affect the *overhead* of a conflict detector. In fact, it may be worth accepting less parallelism in exchange for lower overhead. Although the precise commutativity specification will expose the most parallelism, conflict detectors based on less precise schemes may achieve low enough overhead to deliver superior performance. Sections 4 and 5 investigate this tradeoff.

2.5 Example specifications

In this section, we provide the commutativity specifications for two complex data structures, the kd-tree and the union-find structure, that have particularly interesting commutativity properties. As we will see in the next section, the complexity of these specifications constrains their implementation choices.

Kd-tree Kd-trees are used to find the nearest point to a given point among a set of points in space. They operate by recursively partitioning a high-dimensional space along one dimension at a time. The abstract state of a kd-tree is the set of points in the tree (in this respect, kd-trees are similar to sets) as well as a relation dist over pairs of points that captures the distance (usually Euclidean) between two points. The basic operations of a kd-tree are $\mathsf{add}(a)$, which adds point a to the kd-tree, and $\mathsf{remove}(a)$, which removes point a from the kd-tree. The query $\mathsf{nearest}(a)$ returns the nearest point to a.

One implementation of a kd-tree is as follows. Points are stored only in the leaf nodes, and each interior node records the location of its splitting plane. To accelerate nearest calls, each node also stores the bounding box of all the points contained in the subtree below it. When a node is added, the tree is walked to find the appropriate leaf node and the point is added there. The bounding box of each node from the root to this leaf node is then updated to account for the new point. Removing a node functions similarly. When nearest is invoked, we use the splitting planes and the bounding boxes to determine which subtrees could potentially contain a nearby point. These bounding boxes allow us to avoid traversing some subtrees of the kd-tree, allowing nearest queries to be executed in expected time that is logarithmic in the number of points.

The commutativity conditions for kd-trees are given in Figure 4. The commutativity conditions (4–6), are similar to those for sets. The conditions dealing with nearest however are more complex. Recall that the $\mathsf{nearest}(a)$ returns the point closest to a according to a distance metric dist. As nearest is a read-only operation, it clearly commutes with itself, as stated in condition (1). Condition (3) states that nearest commutes with remove as long as remove does not remove either the argument or return value of nearest. Condition (2) states that $\mathsf{nearest}(a)$ commutes with $\mathsf{add}(b)$ as long as $\mathsf{add}(b)$ does not modify state, or b is not closer to the a than the return value of $\mathsf{nearest}(a)$ is.

Definitions:

$$\mathsf{rep}(\sigma, x) = \text{return value of } \mathsf{find}(x) \text{ invoked in state } \sigma$$

$$\mathsf{rank}(\sigma, x) = \text{the ``rank'' of } x \text{ in state } \sigma \text{ (as defined in union-by-rank).}$$

$$\mathsf{loser}(\sigma, x, y) = \begin{cases} \mathsf{rep}(\sigma, x) & \text{if } \mathsf{rank}(\mathsf{rep}(\sigma, x)) < \mathsf{rank}(\mathsf{rep}(\sigma, y)) \\ \mathsf{rep}(\sigma, y) & \text{otherwise} \end{cases}$$

(1)	$\langle\mathsf{union}(a, b)\rangle_{\sigma_1}$	commutes with if	$\langle\mathsf{union}(c, d)\rangle_{\sigma_2}$ $\mathsf{rep}(\sigma_1, c) \neq \mathsf{loser}(\sigma_1, a, b) \wedge$ $\mathsf{rep}(\sigma_1, d) \neq \mathsf{loser}(\sigma_1, a, b)$
(2)	$\langle\mathsf{union}(a, b)\rangle_{\sigma_1}$	commutes with if	$\langle\mathsf{find}(c)\rangle_{\sigma_2}/r_2$ $\mathsf{rep}(\sigma_1, c) \neq \mathsf{loser}(\sigma_1, a, b)$
(3)	$\langle\mathsf{union}(a, b)\rangle_{\sigma_1}$	commutes with if	$\langle\mathsf{create}(c)\rangle_{\sigma_2}/r_2$ $\mathbf{false}$
(4)	$\langle\mathsf{find}(a)\rangle_{\sigma_1}/r_1$	commutes with	$\langle\mathsf{find}(b)\rangle_{\sigma_2}/r_2$
(5)	$\langle\mathsf{find}(a)\rangle_{\sigma_1}/r_1$	commutes with if	$\langle\mathsf{create}(b)\rangle_{\sigma_2}/r_2$ $\mathbf{false}$
(6)	$\langle\mathsf{create}(a)\rangle_{\sigma_1}/r_1$	commutes with if	$\langle\mathsf{create}(b)\rangle_{\sigma_2}/r_2$ $\mathbf{false}$

Figure 5. Commutativity specification for union-find structures.

Union-find The abstract state of a union-find data structure is the set of disjoint sets. Each set also has an associated *representative* element, and a *rank* that determines how two sets should be merged. Union-find data structures support two operations on disjoint sets: $\mathsf{union}(a, b)$, which merges the subset containing a with that of b, and $\mathsf{find}(a)$, which determines which subset a belongs to, returning its representative element. The most efficient union-find implementation is a disjoint-set forest. Each subset is represented as a tree rooted at the set's representative element, which is used to identify the entire subset. Each element in the subset points to some other element as its parent. To find which subset an element belongs to, we start at the element and traverse parent pointers until we reach the root, and then return the representative element. To merge two subsets, the representative element of the set with larger rank is made the parent of the representative element of the other.

For asymptotic efficiency, it is necessary to use path compression. When invoking find, the parent pointer of every element traversed to find the representative element is updated to point to that representative element, "flattening" that portion of the tree. An interesting side effect of path compression is that find operations update the data structure. While the *semantic* state of the data structure does not change (invoking find on an element does not change the membership of any subset), the *concrete* state of the data structure can change due to path compression.

The union-find data structure has the most complex commutativity conditions. As expected, find operations commute with each other (see condition (4)). More complex are the conditions dealing with union. We use three helper functions that return properties of the abstract state: $\mathsf{rep}(\sigma, a)$, which returns a's representative node; $\mathsf{rank}(\sigma, x)$, which returns the rank of the subset containing x and $\mathsf{loser}(\sigma, a, b)$ which finds the representative nodes of a and b in state σ and returns the one with lowest rank or $\mathsf{rep}(\sigma, b)$ if the ranks are equal. Condition (1) states that two unions commute as long as the second doesn't operate on the loser from the first. Note that this is defined by evaluating rep on the arguments to the second union *in the state that the first union executed in.* Similarly, condition (2) states that union commutes with find provided that find *would not have returned the loser of the union had it executed in* σ_1. The dependence of commutativity on evaluating functions in an earlier state using information from a later method invocation introduces subtle difficulties, as we discuss in the following section.

For simplicity, conditions (3), (5) and (6) state that create does not commute with anything (more precise conditions are possible, but they are quite complex).

3. Implementing commutativity specifications

As discussed in the previous section, for a given ADT there is a range of commutativity specifications to choose from, and different choices can expose different amounts of parallelism. However, what is not clear is *which* specification to choose. This choice is influenced by the *implementation* of the commutativity specification: the code that actually detect conflicts between concurrently executing transactions according to the commutativity specifications of the data structures they access.

Most prior work that has discussed using high-level conflict detection has provided *ad hoc* conflict detection schemes for a few chosen data structures [10, 18, 20]. However, previous work has left unanswered whether there are *systematic* approaches to building efficient, correct conflict detectors. In this section, we show that conflict detectors can be built systematically (albeit not automatically) given a commutativity specification. We present three such techniques, one based on abstract locks and two based on logging, that we call *gatekeepers*. We also discuss how the properties of a commutativity specification constrain its implementation and relate these constraints to the lattice-theoretic view of commutativity.

3.1 Soundness and Completeness

In general, there are many ways to implement a commutativity specification. For simple data structures like sets, abstract locks are one popular approach [10, 20], but it is not clear that they can implement the commutativity specifications for more complex data structures like kd-trees and union-find data structures. In fact, we show in Section 3.2 that abstract locks are too "coarse" to implement commutativity conditions for these data structures. To formalize the notions of correctness and coarseness, we introduce the following definitions.

Definition 4. *A commutativity checker is* SOUND *with respect to a commutativity specification* Φ *if it allows two concurrent method invocations,* m_1 *and* m_2*, to execute without detecting a conflict only if the methods commute according to the* Φ.

Definition 5. *A commutativity checker is* COMPLETE *with respect to a commutativity specifcation* Φ *if it permits every pair of methods invocations* m_1 *and* m_2 *that commute according to the* Φ *to execute without conflict.*

A sound and complete implementation of a commutativity specification therefore guarantees safe parallel execution and will permit the maximum amount of parallelism allowed by the specification. It is interesting to note that if a commutativity checker is sound but not complete with respect to a specification Φ, it *must* be sound and complete with respect to some specification Φ' such that $\Phi' \Rightarrow \Phi$ (in other words, the checker is sound and complete with respect to some specification lower in the commutativity lattice). Similarly, if a commutativity checker is sound with respect to a specification Φ, it is sound with respect to all other specifications Φ' such that $\Phi \Rightarrow \Phi'$.

3.2 Abstract Locking Schemes

The first commutativity checking scheme we discuss is *abstract locking*. An abstract lock is a lock with a number of *modes*. When attempting to acquire a lock in a particular mode, the acquisition succeeds if no other entity holds the lock in an incompatible mode. The compatibility of modes is determined by a lock's *compatibility matrix*. These abstract locks are a generalization of database mode locks [8] and subsume the abstract locks used in [20].

V_1	$:=$	$v_1 \mid r_1$	*Arguments, return values of* m_1
V_2	$:=$	$v_2 \mid r_2$	*Arguments, return values of* m_2
P	$:=$	$(V_1 \neq V_2) \mid P \wedge P$	*Conjunctive formula*
C	$:=$	$P \mid \textbf{true} \mid \textbf{false}$	*Formula*

$$\phi_{m_1;m_2}(\sigma_1, v_1, r_1, \sigma_2, v_2, r_2) = C$$

Figure 6. L_2: Logic for SIMPLE commutativity conditions

(1)	$\langle \text{increment}(a) \rangle_{\sigma_1}$	commutes with	$\langle \text{increment}(b) \rangle_{\sigma_2}$
(2)	$\langle \text{increment}(a) \rangle_{\sigma_1}$	commutes with if	$\langle \text{read}() \rangle_{\sigma_2} / r_2$ **false**
(3)	$\langle \text{read}() \rangle_{\sigma_1} / r_1$	commutes with	$\langle \text{read}() \rangle_{\sigma_2} / r_2$

Figure 7. Commutativity specification for accumulators.

An *abstract locking scheme* for a data structure operates as follows: the data structure associates an abstract lock with each of its data members (defined as any arguments or return values to methods of the data structure). The data structure also has an abstract lock which represents whole data structure. When a transaction invokes a method, the abstract locks on its arguments and on the data structure *may* be acquired in some mode, and when the method returns, the abstract lock on the return value may be acquired in some mode. If an abstract lock cannot be acquired, it must be held in a conflicting mode by another transaction. The abstract locking scheme triggers a conflict, and a compensating action must be taken (either the current transaction or the conflicting transaction must be aborted). All abstract locks are released when a transaction ends[6].

To create a locking scheme for a particular data structure, we must choose which locks are acquired, in which modes, and the particular mode compatibility matrix for the abstract locks.

Abstract locks are well-suited for providing conflict checking for collections [4, 20] and other basic data structures [10]. However, in prior work, programmers had to carefully consider the semantics of a data structure to build ad hoc abstract locking schemes. Two key questions were left unanswered: (i) *can abstract locks provide a sound and complete implementation of a commutativity specification?* and (ii) *can an abstract lock-based conflict detector be systematically constructed?*

Constructing abstract locking schemes

We now present an algorithm for constructing sound and complete abstract locking schemes for commutativity specifications whose conditions satisfy the following property:

Definition 6. *A commutativity condition* $\phi_{m_1;m_2}$ *is* SIMPLE *if one of three conditions holds: (i)* $\phi_{m_1;m_2} = \textbf{false}$ *(the methods do not commute); (ii)* $\phi_{m_1;m_2} = \textbf{true}$ *(the methods always commute); or (iii)* $\phi_{m_1;m_2}$ *is a conjunction of clauses of the form* $a \neq b$ *where every* a *is an argument or return value of* m_1 *and every* b *is an argument or return value of* m_2.

More formally, a commutativity specification is SIMPLE if all of its conditions are expressed in the language L_2, given in Figure 6.

To produce an abstract locking scheme, we must (i) define the abstract locks, and their modes; (ii) determine which abstract locks should be acquired when a method is invoked, and in which mode; and (iii) construct the compatibility matrix between the various abstract lock modes. We provide a systematic procedure for accomplishing these steps. As a running example, we will explain how the procedure applies to an accumulator data structure, using the commutativity specification given in Figure 7.

[6] One can imagine a more liberal abstract locking scheme that allows simple predicates to be evaluated before acquiring a lock. We leave the precise definition and investigation of such schemes to future work.

	inc:ds	*inc:x*	*read:ds*	*read:ret*
inc:ds	√	√	×	√
inc:x	√	√	√	√
read:ds	×	√	√	√
read:ret	√	√	√	√

(a) Compatibility matrix for accumulator abstract locks

	inc:ds	*read:ds*
inc:ds	√	×
read:ds	×	√

(b) Reduced compatibility matrix

Figure 8. Compatibility matrices for accumulator abstract locks

1. **Define the abstract locks and their modes:** An abstract lock is associated with each data member and with the data structure itself. Each lock supports several modes: one mode per method to represent the method's access to the data structure as a whole, and one mode for each argument and return value of a method.

   For example, the accumulator data structure associates abstract locks with the data structure as a whole, as well as every object that can be passed as an argument or returned by a method (these object locks can be allocated as needed, rather than being created ahead of time). Each lock supports four modes: increment(x) requires two modes, one for its argument (called *inc:x*) and one for the data structure (called *inc:ds*); $\langle \text{read}() \rangle_{\sigma_\sigma} / r_\sigma$ requires two modes, one for its return value (called *read:ret*) and one for the data structure (called *read:ds*).

2. **Define which abstract locks should be acquired when a method is invoked:** Any time a method is invoked it acquires the data structure lock in its mode, as well as locks on all its arguments in their appropriate modes.

   For example, when increment is invoked, it acquires the data structure lock in *inc:ds* mode and the lock on its argument in *inc:x* mode. Similarly, when read is invoked, it acquires the data structure lock in *read:ds* mode and the lock on its return value in *read:ret* mode.

3. **Construct the compatibility matrix:** To this point, our definitions of abstract locks and modes did not refer to the commutativity specification. The specification is used to determine the compatibility between various abstract lock modes.

   To derive the mode compatibility matrix, we consider each pair of methods m_1 and m_2 and their commutativity condition, $\phi_{m_1;m_2}$, and applying the following three rules to determine the compatibility of the methods' modes:

   1. If $\phi_{m_1;m_2}$ = **false**, modes m_1:*ds* and m_2:*ds* are incompatible, but all other modes are left undefined. Hence, *inc:ds* is incompatible with *read:ds*.
   2. For each conjunct $x \neq y$ in $\phi_{m_1;m_2}$, where x is an argument or return value of m_1 and y is an argument or return value of m_2, mode $m_1{:}x$ is incompatible with mode $m_2{:}y$.
   3. Any pair of lock modes whose compatibility is left undefined by rules 1 and 2 are assumed to be compatible.

   The compatibility matrix thus generated for the accumulator is shown in Figure 8(a). Note that this compatibility matrix, as well as the rules of abstract locks acquisition, prevents reads from being executed if another transaction has executed increment, while transactions can simultaneously execute read.

Given the full compatibility matrix, we note that if a lock mode is compatible with all other lock modes, acquiring it is superfluous. We can eliminate any such lock modes and remove the corresponding lock acquisitions from the relevant methods. This optimization yields the reduced compatibility matrix in Figure 8(b). The reduced abstract locking scheme acquires the data structure lock in *inc:ds* mode whenever increment is called, allowing other calls to increment to proceed without conflict, and read equivalently acquires the lock in *read:ds* mode.

While it is possible to produce a sound abstract locking scheme for any commutativity specification (a single, global exclusive lock constitutes a sound abstract locking scheme), not all specifications have a complete abstract locking implementation. For example, the kd-tree specification in Figure 4 relies on evaluating a function (to find the distance between two points) to determine whether nearest commutes with add, which cannot be captured by abstract locks. In fact, we can show the following:

Theorem 1. *Given a commutativity specification* Φ, *a sound and complete abstract locking scheme exists iff* Φ *is* SIMPLE. □

The proof of Theorem 1 is given in Appendix B. This theorem means that while the strengthened commutativity specification for sets in Figure 3 can be implemented using an abstract locking scheme, the precise specification of Figure 2 cannot.

3.3 Gatekeeping

In this section, we present a new conflict detection paradigm called *gatekeeping*. A *gatekeeper* is a special object associated with a particular data structure whose role is to ensure that methods invoked by concurrently executing transactions on a data structure respect the specified commutativity conditions. At a high level, gatekeepers operate as follows. When an transaction A invokes a method m on a data structure, the gatekeeper "intercepts" the invocation and determines if the method invocation commutes with all other active method invocations (*i.e.*, methods invoked by all transactions B which have not yet ended). If the invocation commutes with all active method invocations, it is allowed to proceed and the transaction receives the result. If the invocation does not commute, then the gatekeeper triggers a conflict.

To determine if a method m_1 commutes with an active method m_2, the gatekeeper is allowed to evaluate predicates on the arguments and return values of m_1 and m_2. Additionally, the gatekeeper can invoke methods on the data structure it protects. The ability to evaluate arbitrary predicates and methods makes the gatekeeping approach strictly more expressive than abstract locking.

Because a gatekeeper interacts with a data structure only by invoking methods on it, the data structure is effectively a "black box." This means that the gatekeeper is agnostic to the actual implementation details of the data structure, and a gatekeeper constructed to protect one abstract data type (*e.g.*, a gatekeeper which protects sets) can protect *all* implementations of that abstract data type. However, the gatekeeper's behavior must appear atomic. In other words, the entire sequence of events: (i) intercepting a method invocation, (ii) checking commutativity; (iii) executing the method on the data structure, and (iv) returning the result to the invoking transaction, should appear atomic. There are two types of gate-keepers. The first type, *forward* gatekeepers, can only implement a restricted set of commutativity specifications, while the second, *general* gatekeepers, can implement more general commutativity conditions.

3.3.1 Forward gatekeepers

A forward gatekeeper operates by building up information about method invocations as they are invoked, storing that information in logs associated with the invocation, and using those logs to verify that every invocation commutes with all preceding invocations from other transactions. Consider the operation of a forward gatekeeper for kd-trees:

Whenever nearest(x) is invoked, returning r, the gatekeeper must both ensure that nearest commutes with preceding invocations and also record enough information to ensure that later method invocations can check their commutativity with nearest(x). It does this by storing the tuple $\langle x, \text{dist}(x, r) \rangle$ in a log associated

S	$:=$	$\sigma_1 \mid \sigma_2$	*Abstract states*
V	$:=$	$v_1 \mid v_2 \mid r_1 \mid r_2$	*Arguments, return values,*
	$\mid$	$\mathbf{Z} \mid \mathbf{B}$	*constants*
V_1	$:=$	$v_1 \mid r_1$	Arguments, return values of m_1
F_1	$:=$	$f(\sigma_1, V_1, V_1, ...)$	Function of σ_1 and m_1 information
F_2	$:=$	$f(\sigma_2, V, V, ...)$	Function of σ_2 and any value
O	$:=$	$+ \mid - \mid * \mid / \mid < \mid >$	*Arithmetic connectives*
	$\mid$	$\wedge \mid \vee$	*Boolean connectives*
	$\mid$	$=$	*Equality*
P	$:=$	$V \mid F_1 \mid F_2$	*Primitive formula*
C	$:=$	$P\ O\ P \mid (C) \mid \neg C \mid C\ O\ C$	*Formula*

$$\phi_{m_1;m_2}(\sigma_1, v_1, r_1, \sigma_2, v_2, r_2) = C$$

Figure 9. L_3: Logic for ONLINE-CHECKABLE conditions

with the invocation. When a transaction later invokes $\mathsf{add}(y)$, the information from this log is used to evaluate $\mathsf{dist}(x, r) < \mathsf{dist}(x, y)$ to check commutativity. The point y is then stored in a log associated with the invocation $\mathsf{add}(y)$ to facilitate later commutativity checks. As transactions commit or abort, the logs associated with their invocations are cleared.

Constructing forward gatekeepers

Forward gatekeepers can be constructed for commutativity specifications whose conditions are ONLINE-CHECKABLE:

Definition 7. $\phi_{m_1;m_2}(v_1, \sigma_1, r_1, v_2, \sigma_2, r_2)$ *is* ONLINE-CHECKABLE *if any function of v_2, σ_2 or r_2 in $\phi_{m_1;m_2}$ is* not *a function of σ_1.*

In other words, a condition is ONLINE-CHECKABLE if there is no function that must be invoked in the state of the first method invocation using information from the second method invocation. More formally, an ONLINE-CHECKABLE condition is one that can be expressed using the logic L_3, given in Figure 9. Note that L_3 is very similar to L_1 (Figure 1), with the exception that functions that deal with abstract state σ_1 cannot also use v_2 or r_2 as arguments. This restriction means that conditions (1–2) of the union-find specification in Figure 5 are not ONLINE-CHECKABLE.

Before describing forward gatekeepers, let us define the set C_m of primitive functions associated with each method, m. For each commutativity condition $\phi_{m_1;m_2}$, collect any functions from F_1 (which only operate over the arguments, return value and abstract state of m_1) that appear in the formula. Place these into C_{m_1}. Note that in general, for a given method m its associated set C_m will have functions from *every* commutativity condition that m participates in.

Given the function sets constructed as above, the operation of a forward gatekeeper proceeds as follows:

1. When a gatekeeper sees a method invocation $m(v)$, it evaluates every function in C_m and records the result in a result log $L_{m(v)}$. It also records the return value of $m(v)$ in $L_{m(v)}$. Note that this result log is keyed by both the method and its arguments.
2. The gatekeeper records $m(v)$ as an *active* invocation (*i.e.*, a method invoked by a currently executing transaction).
3. The gatekeeper checks the commutativity of $m(v)$ by evaluating, for every active method invocation $m_a(v_a)$ made by other transactions, the predicate $\phi_{m_a;m}$. This can be done efficiently using results stored in $L_{m_a(v_a)}$ as well as the arguments and return values of $m(v)$. If any such commutativity condition evaluates to **false**, $m(v)$ cannot proceed, and one of the conflicting transactions must be aborted.

   Crucially, because all the commutativity conditions are ONLINE-CHECKABLE, $L_{m_a(v_a)}$ contains all the information necessary from $m_a(v_a)$ for evaluating $\phi_{m_a;m}$. Thus, the gatekeeper can determine commutativity simply by recording information about method invocations *as they happen*, rather than well after they execute.
4. When a transaction completes, the gatekeeper removes the result sets L associated with the methods invoked by that transaction, and removes the methods from the active invocation list.

Because the forward gatekeeper explicitly evaluates $\phi_{m_1;m_2}$ when determining the commutativity of m_1 and m_2, it is obviously sound and complete. Furthermore, it is apparent that if the online-checkability condition is violated, there will be a function f that uses σ_1 as well as arguments or return values from m_2. This function cannot be evaluated when m_1 is executed, and hence the forward gatekeeper will be unable to record information in its logs to evaluate $\phi_{m_1;m_2}$.

3.3.2 General gatekeepers

General gatekeepers are conflict detection schemes that can capture any commutativity specification expressible in L_1 (Figure 1). For conditions which are not ONLINE-CHECKABLE, the gatekeeper will perform a rollback by executing undo methods to evaluate the commutativity condition in the appropriate state and then restore the data structure state by re-executing the forward actions. This means that the gatekeeper must keep a log of all actions in case they need to be rolled back to check commutativity. Note that this entire process must appear atomic. General gatekeepers can be thought of as forward gatekeepers that perform state rollback to evaluate any commutativity conditions that are *not* ONLINE-CHECKABLE.

A general gatekeeper for union-find: We now describe the design of a general gatekeeper that fully captures the commutativity conditions of Figure 5 for the operations union and find. The union-find gatekeeper maintains two logs: *find-reps* which stores all the active elements that have been returned by a call to find as representatives of some set and *loser-rep*, which records the result of evaluating $\mathsf{loser}(a, b)$ whenever $\mathsf{union}(a, b)$ is invoked.

For each invocation, $\mathsf{union}(a, b)$, the gatekeeper first computes $\mathsf{loser}(a, b)$. If the loser has been recorded in the *find-reps* log as the return value of an active find, then a conflict is detected. Additionally, if either of these representatives has been recorded in the *loser-rep* log as the loser representative involved in a previous union, then a conflict is detected. The gatekeeper subsequently performs the call to union and updates *loser-rep* appropriately.

In the case of an invocation $\mathsf{find}(a)$, the gatekeeper first executes the actual call on the data structure, getting the result r_a. A subtle, but important point is that if $\mathsf{find}(a)$ had executed earlier, before some active invocation of union, it may have returned a different result. This is captured in condition (2) of Figure 5 as commutativity dependent on the results of calling find in a different state. To ensure that commutativity holds, the gatekeeper undoes the effects of all potentially interfering calls to union, and re-executes $\mathsf{find}(a)$ to ensure it still returns r_a. If so, invoking $\mathsf{find}(a)$ does not violate commutativity. If not, a conflict is detected. The gatekeeper then restores the state of the data structure by re-invoking the unions. Finally, r_a is stored in *find-reps* to aid in conflict checking.

3.4 Discussion of expressivity and overheads

The three conflict detection schemes we present, abstract locking, forward gatekeeping and general gatekeeping, form a hierarchy, ranked by expressivity and overhead. The lowest-overhead scheme is abstract locking, as it merely requires acquiring a small number of locks per method invocation. Forward gatekeeping incurs more overhead as it can require a substantial amount of logging. General gatekeepers have the highest overhead, as they may perform rollbacks to evaluate complex commutativity conditions. The hierarchy of expressivity is identical: abstract locking schemes can be generated for SIMPLE specifications, while forward gatekeepers can be generated for more complex ONLINE-CHECKABLE specifications and general gatekeepers can be generated for all specifications.

Given this hierarchy of performance and precision, a natural question becomes: which scheme should we use for a particular data structure? A particular specification can be implemented using one particular scheme; can we produce different conflict detectors that use different schemes? The next section discusses how to leverage the commutativity lattice to create different commutativity implementations in a disciplined manner.

4. Exploiting the commutativity lattice

4.1 The precision/performance tradeoff

Up to this point, we have focused on producing sound and complete implementations of commutativity specifications using a variety of conflict detection schemes. However, for a given application, a given conflict detection scheme for a data structure may have unacceptably high overheads or enable too little parallelism.

Prior work on high-level conflict detection has implicitly accepted this point. For example, in [10] the conflict detection scheme for a set explicitly does not permit concurrent adds when the arguments are identical, even though, as discussed in Section 2, doing so may allow more parallelism. Similar tradeoffs are made in [4, 18, 20]. In other words, incomplete conflict detection schemes are used in order to sacrifice parallelism for overhead. Unfortunately, it is difficult to directly produce incomplete yet sound commutativity implementations or to safely modify existing sound implementations to create other implementations.

To tackle this problem, we turn to the commutativity lattice of Section 2.4. Rather than change the conflict detection implementation directly, we can choose a less precise specification from the commutativity lattice that can be implemented in a more efficient manner. Recall that if a commutativity checker is sound with respect to this less precise specification, it must be sound with respect to the original specification.

As a simple example of this, consider using the specification $\bot$ to build a commutativity checker for any data structure. This specification is SIMPLE and trivially correct. The abstract locking synthesis algorithm will produce the correct implementation: a single, global lock that prevents transactions from accessing the data structure concurrently. This example also illustrates the precision/performance tradeoff, as the conflict checker has very low overhead but admits no parallelism.

A more compelling example is to consider the set specifications from Figures 2 and 3. While the former specification is not SIMPLE and must therefore be implemented using a forward gatekeeper, the latter *is*, and can be implemented using the abstract locking construction algorithm (which will use read/write locks on the method arguments). We can move still further down the commutativity lattice by allowing contains to commute with contains only if the arguments differ; this new SIMPLE specification will induce an abstract locking scheme that uses cheaper exclusive locks on method arguments. Crucially, *it is far easier to reason about the relationships between specifications in the commutativity lattice than it is to determine whether an abstract locking scheme constitutes a sound but incomplete refinement of a forward gatekeeper.*

While we can generate different conflict detection schemes for a given data structure in a disciplined manner using the commutativity lattice, it is unclear how to *select* the appropriate scheme. This is because the overhead and parallelism of a particular scheme is dependent on application characteristics. In fact, as we demonstrate in Section 5, in certain cases the higher parallelism schemes based on gatekeeping have lower overhead than less precise schemes!

4.2 Disciplined lock coarsening

The commutativity lattice approach also allows us to reason in a systematic way about other conflict detection optimizations. One such optimization is *lock coarsening* [17], where a data structure such as a graph is partitioned, and locks are acquired on entire partitions when any object in the partition is accessed. While this optimization seems complex, it can be formulated in a straightforward manner in terms of the commutativity lattice.

We begin with a set data structure that has been *logically partitioned*: every element that may appear in the set is assigned a partition. A helper method, part, returns the partition an object is assigned to. We can then produce a stronger commutativity specification where every clause in the specification of Figure 3 of the form $a \neq b$ is replaced by $\mathsf{part}(a) \neq \mathsf{part}(b)$. This new specification is very similar to a SIMPLE specification, except that it deals in partitions rather than individual data elements. The commutativity lattice lets us immediately see that this partition-based scheme is stronger than the original scheme, as $\mathsf{part}(a) \neq \mathsf{part}(b) \Rightarrow a \neq b$. It can be implemented in an analogous manner. Rather than acquiring locks on arguments and return values, an implementation of this new specification will acquire locks on partitions.

Partition-based specifications can be created from *any* SIMPLE specification, allowing us to automatically derive partition-based conflict checkers for many data structures. Note that these conflict checkers again trade off parallelism for overhead (intuitively, the parallelism becomes bounded by the number of partitions). Section 5 discusses this issue in more detail and quantifies the tradeoff.

4.3 Reasoning about transactional memory

The precision of transactional memory [9, 12, 19] can be reasoned about in terms of the commutativity lattice. For a particular concrete instantiation of an ADT, we can define a commutativity specification, Φ_C, that refers to the memory-level state of the data structure. By referencing memory, Φ_C can be based on establishing *concrete commutativity* rather than semantic commutativity. Two methods will commute according to this specification if executing them in either order produces the same *concrete* state. Because concrete commutativity implies semantic commutativity, it is apparent that Φ_C can be found in the commutativity lattice, but that $\Phi_C \preceq \Phi^*$.

If two transactions can execute in parallel according to a TM, they must leave the data structure in the same concrete state regardless of the order in which they execute, effectively enforcing concrete commutativity. As TM constitutes a sound (though not necessarily complete) implementation of Φ_C, we can see that a sound and complete implementation of the precise specification will always expose at least as much parallelism as TM (although potentially with higher overhead).

5. Experimental Evaluation

In this section, we present several experiments. First, we discuss a microbenchmark based on sets that allows us to explore the effects of moving between the various set commutativity specifications (and hence implementations) discussed in this paper. Then we present three case studies of real-world applications. The first, preflow push, shows the effects of switching between systematically constructed conflict detection schemes in a realistic application. The second, agglomerative clustering, shows that forward gatekeepers can deliver scalable performance. The third, Boruvka's algorithm, shows the same for general gatekeepers.

For each case study, we estimate the two parameters: the average parallelism and the overhead of conflict detection. This allows us to study the potential tradeoff between parallelism and overhead demonstrated by implementations based on different points in the commutativity lattice. These results are shown in Table 1.

Application	Variant	Path length	Parallelism	Overhead
Preflow-push	part	2789217	25.69	1.14
	ex	51978	1894.88	1.80
	ml	47558	2072.52	5.62
Boruvka	uf-ml	3678	271.89	2.5
	uf-gk	3681	271.67	1.31
Clustering	kd-ml	2209	115.88	58.76
	kd-gk	123	2018.15	2.32

Table 1. Critical path lengths, average parallelism and overheads for different applications and conflict detection schemes.

We used ParaMeter [16] to estimate the average amount of parallelism in an application when using a particular conflict detection scheme. We parallelized our benchmarks using the Galois system [18][7]. We estimate the overhead of conflict detection to be the ratio between the run time of the parallelized application running on a single thread and the runtime of the original sequential version.

As a baseline, we also implemented our benchmarks using a software transactional memory, DSTM2 (version 2.1b) [11]. For each benchmark we used boosted objects [10] wherever possible (for example, the worklist), except for our target data structures, which used object-based conflict detection. Boosting allowed us to isolate any performance or parallelism differences to only the data structures under study. Each benchmark also used the best available contention manager (determined empirically). Parallelism metrics were estimated by tracking memory-level read/write conflicts in ParaMeter.

Our performance evaluations were performed on a Nehalem server running Ubuntu Linux version 8.06. The system consists of two 2.93 GHz quad-core processors. Each core has two 32KB L1 caches and a unified 256 KB L2 cache. Each processor has a shared 8 MB L3 cache, and the system contains 24 GB of main memory. The applications and the Galois system are written in Java and run on the Sun HotSpot 64-bit virtual machine, version 1.6.0.

Set microbenchmark To study the effects of using different conflict detection schemes of varying overheads and permittivity, we built a microbenchmark based on a set. In the microbenchmark, a number of threads concurrently query and update a global set. Each thread picks an arbitrary object from a shared pool and, at random, inserts it to the set (with add) or checks if it is already there (with contains). The benchmark performs 1 million operations, using one of two inputs: in the first, all examined objects are distinct, and in the second, objects are in 10 equivalence classes.

We consider four conflict detection schemes generated from specifications drawn from the set's commutativity lattice: (i) a global lock generated from the $\perp$ specification; (ii) exclusive abstract locks placed on set elements generated from the specification discussed in Section 4; (iii) r/w abstract locks generated from the specification in Figure 3; and (iv) a forward gatekeeper generated from the precise specification of Figure 2.

Table 2 shows the results of running the microbenchmark on 4 threads. For both inputs, the global lock provides poor performance: the low single thread overhead is outweighed by the non-existent parallelism (and resulting high abort rate). We note that the advantage of the gatekeeping and read/write lock schemes over exclusive locks arises when multiple transactions access the same key in the set. As this does not occur in the distinct-element input, all variants have no aborts and the low-overhead exclusive lock solution performs best. In contrast, in the repeated-element input, the advantage of allowing multiple threads to access the same element (when invoking contains, or add on an element already in the set) manifests, and gatekeeping performs the best, followed by

[7] While our evaluation uses the Galois system, the techniques given for constructing conflict detectors and using the commutativity lattice are general.

Program	(a) Distinct		(b) Repeats	
	Abort Ratio %	Time (sec)	Abort Ratio %	Time (sec)
Global Lock	48.68	4.644	44.07	3.935
Abs. Lock (Ex.)	0	1.097	1.53	1.538
Abs. Lock (RW)	0	1.365	0.09	0.818
Gatekeeper	0	1.191	0	0.697

Table 2. 4-thread results for set microbenchmark. (a) 1 million distinct elements. (b) 1 million elements in 10 equivalence classes.

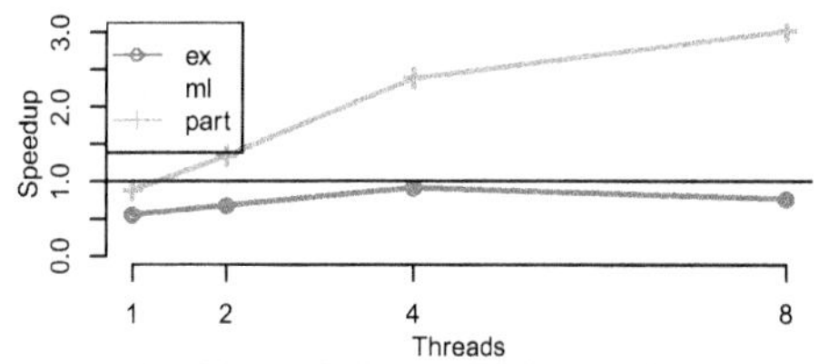

Figure 10. Preflow-push speedup (serial time 53 sec.)

the read/write scheme. Gatekeeping has a lower abort ratio because non-mutating adds can proceed in parallel.

Preflow-push We used preflow-push [7] to investigate the performance of different conflict detection schemes for a single benchmark. Preflow push finds the maximum flow of a network by pushing excess flow from the source towards the A worklist is initialized with the source node. In each iteration, a node with excess flow is removed from the worklist. It is *relabeled* and flow is *pushed* to neighboring nodes along edges that have remaining capacity. This increases the excess flow at the destination node, decreases the excess flow at the source, and decrements the capacity of the edge. Any nodes that gained excess flow are added back to the worklist. The algorithm terminates when no more flow can be pushed.

This algorithm is implemented in terms of a graph-like ADT, which supports relabel, pushFlow and getNeighbors. The methods relabel and pushFlow do not commute with other methods that access the same nodes, while getNeighbors commutes with itself. All the conditions in this specification are SIMPLE, and can be implemented with read/write abstract locks on nodes and edges. Note that this conflict detection strategy is identical to the conflict detection performed by a transactional memory.

We also investigate two schemes based on strengthened specifications from lower in the commutativity lattice. The first does not allow getNeighbors to commute with methods that access the same nodes; in effect, this converts read/write locks on nodes to exclusive locks. The second uses the partition-based scheme derived in Section 4.2, using 32 partitions. Table 1 shows parallelism and overhead data for the three versions of preflow push: memory level locking (*ml*), exclusive locking (*ex*) and partition-locking (*part*). As input, we use a GENRMF "challenge" input from [1].

We see the expected behavior: implementations based on specifications from higher in the commutativity lattice expose more parallelism. However, the performance results in Figure 10 show that run-time is inversely correlated with the amount of parallelism: in this application, moving down in the commutativity lattice produces lower parallelism, but lower overhead conflict checkers. This is especially interesting in the case of the partition-based conflict detector, as the critical-path length is a factor of 50 longer than the precise scheme. However, parallelism beyond the number of processors available for execution is superfluous. Since the average parallelism of partition-based conflict detection is well above the number of processors, trading parallelism for overhead is effective.

Agglomerative Clustering To study the behavior of forward gatekeeping, we implement an algorithm called *agglomerative clustering* that uses the kd-tree data structure (described in Section 2.5). The input to agglomerative clustering is (i) a set of points and (ii)

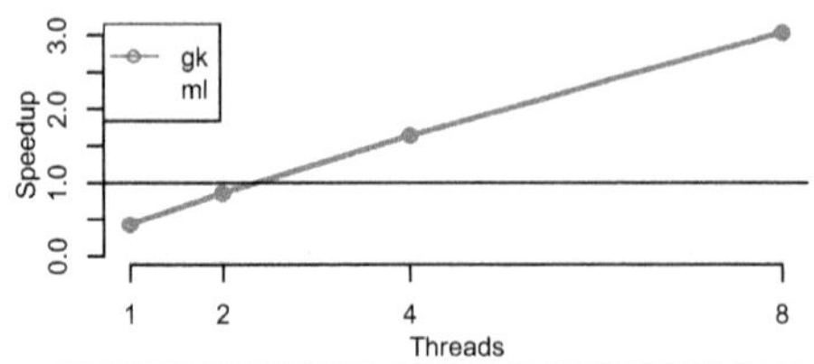

Figure 11. Agglomerative clustering speedup (serial time 7.8 sec.)

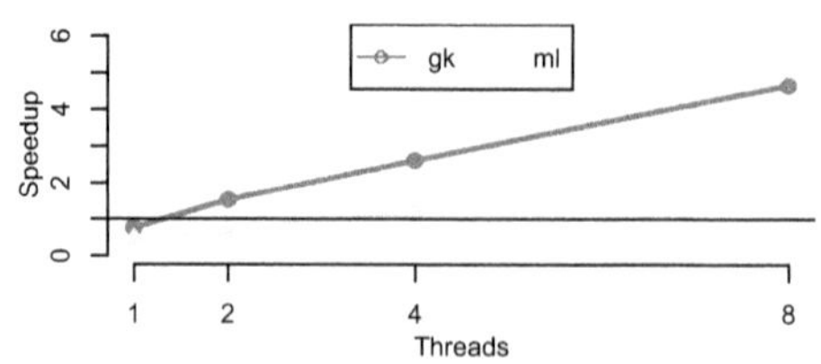

Figure 12. Boruvka's algorithm speedup (serial time 3.7 sec.)

a metric which measures the distance between two points. The algorithm builds a hierarchical clustering of points, called a *dendrogram*, in a bottom-up manner. The structure of the dendrogram exposes the similarity between points.

One approach to building the dendrogram was proposed by Walter *et al.* [24]. We first build a kd-tree that contains all the points. At each step of the algorithm, an arbitrary point p is chosen, and its nearest neighbor n is determined by querying the kd-tree. We then find the nearest neighbor of n; if that is p, the two points are clustered together by removing them from the kd-tree and inserting a new point representing that cluster. The algorithm terminates when there is a single cluster; by convention, the point at infinity is the closest point if the data set contains a single point.

Table 1 shows the critical path length and average parallelism on an input of 100,000 randomly generated points for a forward-gatekeeping implementation (*kd-gk*) and the baseline implementation (*kd-ml*). The gatekeeping implementation exposes significantly more parallelism than the baseline; although the same amount of work is done, the critical path of *kd-ml* is an order of magnitude larger than that of *kd-gk*. This is because the operations on the kd-tree manipulate the bounding boxes of interior kd-tree nodes, resulting in memory-level conflicts even when the operations commute. We do not investigate an abstract locking implementation because there is no straightforward SIMPLE specification that does not merely prevent add and nearest from executing concurrently.

Figure 11 shows the performance of the gatekeeping version of agglomerative clustering as well as the transactional memory baseline, using an input of 500,000 randomly generated points. The gatekeeping conflict detector is built using the construction procedure of Section 3.3.1. Interestingly, despite the precision of the commutativity specification implemented by the forward gatekeeper (and the resulting high parallelism), it has lower overhead and better scalability than the memory-level conflict checker. This is because the gatekeeper need only track semantic information about the data structure, rather than each memory access. Clearly, forward gatekeeping, despite its complexity, is a viable approach to conflict detection for complex commutativity specifications.

Boruvka's algorithm Finally, to study the behavior of general gatekeeping, we evaluated an algorithm built around the union-find data structure (see Section 2.5), Boruvka's algorithm. Boruvka's algorithm builds minimal spanning trees (MST's) of undirected graphs. Initially, each node of the graph is in a component by itself. At each step, the algorithm (i) picks an arbitrary component, (ii) determines the lightest weight edge e connecting that component to another component, (iii) merges the two components, and (iv) adds e to the MST. The algorithm terminates when the entire graph is in one component.

At each point during the execution of the algorithm, nodes in different components are in disjoint sets. When two components are merged, the corresponding sets of nodes are as well. Therefore, a union-find data structure can be used in step (ii) to find whether or not the end points of an edge are in the same component.

Table 1 shows the parallelism and overhead of Boruvka's algorithm when run on a randomly generated 1000×1000 mesh using both a general gatekeeper (*uf-gk*), built using our construction, and our baseline TM (*uf-ml*). Curiously, we see that general gatekeeping does not offer a parallelism benefit over memory level locking. Recall that although stronger commutativity specifications will typically permit less parallelism than specifications from higher in the lattice, this is entirely dependent on application behavior. In the case of union-find, additional parallelism is exposed by a gatekeeper if multiple interfering finds are performed (as path compression prevents a memory-level approach from performing them concurrently). However, Boruvka's does not perform such finds, obviating the gatekeeper's parallelism advantage.

Interestingly, however, the general gatekeeper, despite its complexity, has fairly low overhead ($\sim 31\%$), and far less than a TM, because it need only track semantic changes to the data structure (an especially large advantage considering all of the reads and writes involved in path compression). This advantage is further pressed when scaling up, as Figure 12 shows that the general gatekeeper provides better performance than the baseline. It is apparent that, for some applications, even a conflict detection scheme as involved as general gatekeeping can provide acceptable performance.

Putting it all together

The results for our example applications demonstrate that different conflict detection schemes can provide vastly different performance. To understand the tradeoffs between different schemes, consider a simple model in terms of the following three factors:

- T = sequential runtime of algorithm,
- o_d = overhead of conflict detection scheme d, and
- α_d = average parallelism enabled by d.

$T * o_d$ is the single-threaded runtime while performing conflict detection, and $T * o_d/\alpha_d$ is the best-case parallel runtime, assuming perfect load-balance. Note that α_d and o_d correspond to the "parallelism" and "overhead" columns, respectively, in Table 1.

Both α and o are application specific. However, this model can help illuminate the choice of conflict detection. Consider two conflict detection schemes l and h for which $o_l < o_h$ and $\alpha_l < \alpha_h$ (*i.e.*, scheme l has less overhead but also permits less parallelism).

- The lower overhead, lower parallelism conflict detection scheme l offers better performance if $o_l/\alpha_l < o_h/\alpha_h$ (*i.e.*, lower overhead makes up for lower parallelism). This explains why exclusive locking outperforms read/write locking in preflow push.
- Most current systems have only a small number of processors, so the actual runtime of an algorithm on a machine with p processors may be bounded above by $T * o_d/p$. If $\alpha_l \gg p$, we should use the lower overhead, lower parallelism scheme l, since the relative amount of parallelism exposed by different conflict detection schemes ceases to be the dominant factor in performance. This explains why partition locking for preflow push is the best-performing conflict detection scheme.
- If $\alpha_h > \alpha_l$ but $o_h < o_l$ then the higher parallelism scheme actually has lower overhead. Our model suggests that in such situations, we should prefer the higher parallelism scheme. This situation arises when considering the gatekeeping implementations of kd-trees and union-find.

In short, the best conflict checker for an ADT can depend on the characteristics of both the application and the parallel machine;

a single choice of conflict detector is likely not ideal for every application. However, measuring simple parameters can guide the selection of conflict checker.

While the construction techniques of Section 3 are intended to permit library writers to develop commutativity checkers for their ADTs, the commutativity lattice provides a useful interface between the library writer and the programmers who use the ADTs. The library writer can produce a range of sound checkers for a given ADT, using the construction techniques of Section 3 and the strengthening techniques of Section 4. The lattice then allows the library writer to rank the checkers according to expressiveness. The user can then make an informed decision to move between implementations if his/her application demands more parallelism or less overhead. Alluringly, the ability to rank checkers by permittivity can allow an automated system to adaptively and dynamically select from these implementations as run-time needs change, given observations of parallelism and overhead, though we leave the design and development of such a system to future work.

6. Related work and conclusions

Related work Commutativity conditions can be seen as a highly generalized form of predicate locks as used in databases [6], where locks on arbitrary predicates are used to determine when transactions can successfully execute in parallel. Database research has been the source of a considerable number of techniques to exploit the high level properties of abstract data types, including commutativity, for concurrency control [2, 23, 25]. That work laid the foundation for subsequent work that focused on exploiting data structure semantics in speculative parallelization and synchronization systems on shared memory systems [5, 10, 18, 20].

Ni *et al.* addressed the shortcomings of memory-level locking in transactional memory systems by introducing *open nesting*, which uses abstract locks to synchronize access to data structures by exploiting their semantics [20]. However, the work focuses mainly on the mechanism of integrating abstract locking with a transactional memory, rather than on how to use abstract locks in data structures in a disciplined manner. In fact, the authors note that improper use of open nesting could lead to deadlock situations.

Kulkarni *et al.* described an approach to checking commutativity [18]. This technique applies to ONLINE-CHECKABLE specifications, but requires logging entire method invocations, and hence is not as efficient as forward gatekeeping, which can benefit from common sub-clauses in commutativity conditions.

Herlihy and Koskinen proved that commutativity information informs a disciplined, safe approach for implementing open nesting [10]. The key difference between their work and our work is that the former focused on how commuting methods could be used to enforce serializability, while we focus on implementation approaches for conflict detection. Rather than using *ad hoc* conflict detectors, we provide systematic approaches for constructing commutativity checkers, each with well-defined expressive power. Furthermore, we provide a disciplined approach to systematically generating the simpler abstract locking implementations used in prior work.

Recently, Demsky and Lam proposed using object-level *views* to synthesize high-level concurrency control [5]. Views are similar in spirit to our SIMPLE specifications, but allow for more complex interactions. As a result, their lock-generation algorithm is greedy, rather than precise. An interesting avenue of future research is to determine how a view specification is related to a commutativity specification, and whether the former can be derived from the latter.

Other recent work from Burnim *et al.* discusses verifying that method invocations on a data structure that are meant to be atomic indeed are [3]. Their notion of atomicity is semantic: two methods are atomic if they preserve certain semantic *bridge predicates* that refer to the data structure's semantic state, rather than its concrete state. This results in a notion of atomicity that is similar to semantic commutativity. Their atomicity checks are performed at compile time by performing a limited search through a space of possible parallel executions. Unlike in our work, their aim is to show that a particular pair of method invocations (with particular arguments) are atomic; they do not consider commutativity conditions, which constrain the kinds of method invocations that will appear atomic.

Kim and Rinard look at *verifying* commutativity conditions [14]. Given a definition of the abstract state of a data structure, how methods use that abstract state, and commutativity conditions between methods, Kim and Rinard's technique can verify that the commutativity conditions are, indeed, correct. This technique is complementary to the goals of our paper: we have not considered the correctness of commutativity conditions, instead relying on external techniques such as theirs to ensure that they are valid.

Future work and conclusions There are a number of promising directions for future research. First, for data structures such as union-find, determining appropriate commutativity conditions is difficult; can we *generate* commutativity conditions given a data structure specification? Second, there are interesting avenues of implementation research: although gatekeepers are expressive, they can be quite inefficient. Are there more efficient conflict detection schemes that do not overly sacrifice expressibility?

In Section 1, we posed three questions: (i) how should semantic conflict checks be implemented? (ii) can we trade off conflict checking precision for performance? and (iii) which conflict detection scheme should be used? Through our commutativity lattice framework, we showed that conflict detectors can be reasoned about in terms of a lattice of commutativity specifications. We showed how different points in the lattice can be implemented systematically by three different conflict detection schemes. We also showed how the lattice can be exploited to derive lower parallelism/lower overhead detectors by strengthening commutativity specifications. Finally we studied the tradeoffs between precision and performance and showed that our systematically generated conflict detectors can provide acceptable performance.

Acknowledgements

We would like to thank Roman Manevich for his insights and comments regarding the presentation of this paper. We would also like to thank the anonymous reviewers for their helpful feedback.

References

[1] Synthetic maximum flow families. `http://www.avglab.com/andrew/CATS/maxflow_synthetic.htm`.

[2] A. Bondavalli, N. De Francesco, D. Latella, and G. Vaglini. Shared abstract data type: an algebraic methodology for their specification. In *MFDBS 89*, 1989.

[3] J. Burnim, G. Necula, and K. Sen. Specifying and checking semantic atomicity for multithreaded programs. In *ASPLOS'11: Proceedings of the 16th International Conference on Architectural Support for Programming Languages and Operating Systems*, 2011.

[4] B. D. Carlstrom, A. McDonald, C. Kozyrakis, and K. Olukotun. Transactional collection classes. In *PPoPP*, 2007.

[5] B. Demsky and P. Lam. Views: object-inspired concurrency control. In *ICSE*, 2010.

[6] K. P. Eswaran, J. N. Gray, R. A. Lorie, and I. L. Traiger. The notions of consistency and predicate locks in a database system. *Commun. ACM*, 19(11):624–633, 1976.

[7] A. V. Goldberg and R. E. Tarjan. A new approach to the maximum-flow problem. *J. ACM*, 35(4):921–940, 1988.

[8] J. Gray and A. Reuter. *Transaction Processing: Concepts and Techniques*. Morgan Kaufmann Publishers Inc., 1992.

[9] T. Harris and K. Fraser. Language support for lightweight transactions. In *OOPSLA*. Oct 2003.

[10] M. Herlihy and E. Koskinen. Transactional boosting: a methodology for highly-concurrent transactional objects. In *PPoPP*, 2008.

[11] M. Herlihy, V. Luchangco, and M. Moir. A flexible framework for implementing software transactional memory. In *OOPSLA*, 2006.

[12] M. Herlihy and J. E. B. Moss. Transactional memory: architectural support for lock-free data structures. In *ISCA*, 1993.

[13] M. P. Herlihy and J. M. Wing. Linearizability: a correctness condition for concurrent objects. *TOPLAS*, 12(3):463–492, 1990.

[14] D. Kim and M. Rinard. Verification of semantic commutativity conditions and inverse operations on linked data structures. In *PLDI*, 2011.

[15] E. Koskinen, M. Parkinson, and M. Herlihy. Coarse-grained transactions. In *POPL*, 2010.

[16] M. Kulkarni, M. Burtscher, R. Inkulu, K. Pingali, and C. Casçaval. How much parallelism is there in irregular applications? In *PPoPP*, 2009.

[17] M. Kulkarni, K. Pingali, G. Ramanarayanan, B. Walter, K. Bala, and L. P. Chew. Optimistic parallelism benefits from data partitioning. In *ASPLOS*, 2008.

[18] M. Kulkarni, K. Pingali, B. Walter, G. Ramanarayanan, K. Bala, and L. P. Chew. Optimistic parallelism requires abstractions. In *PLDI*, 2007.

[19] J. Larus and R. Rajwar. *Transactional Memory (Synthesis Lectures on Computer Architecture)*. Morgan & Claypool Publishers, 2007.

[20] Y. Ni, V. Menon, A.-R. Adl-Tabatabai, A. L. Hosking, R. Hudson, J. E. B. Moss, B. Saha, and T. Shpeisman. Open nesting in software transactional memory. In *PPoPP*, 2007.

[21] C. H. Papadimitriou. The serializability of concurrent database updates. *J. ACM*, 26(4):631–653, 1979.

[22] L. Rauchwerger and D. Padua. The LRPD test: Speculative run-time parallelization of loops with privatization and reduction parallelization. In *PLDI*, 1995.

[23] P. M. Schwarz and A. Z. Spector. Synchronizing shared abstract types. *ACM Trans. Comput. Syst.*, 2(3):223–250, 1984.

[24] B. Walter, K. Bala, M. Kulkarni, and K. Pingali. Fast agglomerative clustering for rendering. In *Interactive Ray Tracing*, 2008.

[25] W. Weihl. Commutativity-based concurrency control for abstract data types. *IEEE Transactions on Computers*, 37(12), 1988.

A. Proof of serializability

Here we prove the serializability claim made in Section 2.1. The theorem is stated in terms of an execution history consisting of two transactions A and B, which each start at the beginning of the history and finish at the end of the history (*i.e.*, the transactions fully overlap and are coextensive with the history itself). The theorem can easily be extended to longer histories, with multiple transactions that only partially overlap. The theorem proceeds by showing how to construct a serial schedule when commutativity conditions have been shown true for all pairs of method invocations.

We begin by showing that if we can show a commutativity condition to be true in one history H, then in any C-EQUIVALENT history H' there exists some commutativity condition over the same method invocations that is true. This allows us to claim that even as we rearrange invocations while constructing a serial schedule, we can assume that the commutativity conditions are true.

Lemma 1. *If the following three conditions hold:*

- *History H contains the invocations $\langle m_1(v_1)\rangle_{\sigma_1}$ and $\langle m_2(v_2)\rangle_{\sigma_2}$*
- *There exists a C-EQUIVALENT history H' with invocations $\langle m_1(v_1)\rangle_{\sigma_3}$ and $\langle m_2(v_2)\rangle_{\sigma_4}$*
- *$\phi_{m_1;m_2}(\sigma_1, v_1, r_1, \sigma_2, v_2, r_2)$ is a commutativity condition in H*

then there exists a commutativity condition $\phi'_{m_1;m_2}(\sigma_3, v_1, r_1, \sigma_4, v_2, r_2)$ in H' such that $\phi_{m_1;m_2}(\sigma_1, v_1, r_1, \sigma_2, v_2, r_2) \Leftrightarrow \phi'_{m_1;m_2}(\sigma_3, v_1, r_1, \sigma_4, v_2, r_2)$.

Proof. We begin by assuming that H and H' exist according to the conditions of the lemma, and that $\phi_{m_1;m_2}(\sigma_1, v_1, r_1, \sigma_2, v_2, r_2)$ is a commutativity condition. There clearly exists a predicate $\phi'_{m_1;m_2}(\sigma_3, v_1, r_1, \sigma_4, v_2, r_2)$ that is true if and only if $\phi_{m_1;m_2}$ is true (though it may not be expressible in a logic such as L_1). All that remains is to show that this predicate is, indeed, a commutativity condition (in other words, that when it is **true**, the conditions of Definition 3 are satisfied).

We begin by constructing the set of histories that are C-EQUIVALENT to H and in which $m_1(v_1)$ and $m_2(v_2)$ appear consecutively:

$$S(H) = \{H'' | H'' \equiv_C H \land \exists \text{ sub-history } h \text{ of } H'' = \langle m_1(v_1), m_2(v_2)\rangle_\sigma\}$$

We have assumed that $\phi'_{m_1;m_2}$ is **true**, and hence so is $\phi_{m_1;m_2}$. It follows from the definition of commutativity conditions that if $\phi_{m_1;m_2}(\sigma_1, v_1, r_1, \sigma_2, v_2, r_2)$ holds, then all sub-histories of the form $\langle m_1(v_1), m_2(v_2)\rangle_\sigma$ found in the histories of $S(H)$ are equivalent to their swapped sub-histories, $\langle m_2(v_2), m_1(v_1)\rangle_\sigma$. Because the C-EQUIVALENCE relation forms an equivalence class, the set $S(H') = S(H)$. Thus, $\phi'_{m_1;m_2}$ is a valid commutativity condition in H'. □

We can now prove the following theorem:

Theorem 2. *If, in an execution history H, consisting of method invocations from two transactions A and B, for each pair of method invocations $\langle m_a^A(v_a)\rangle_{\sigma_a}$ (returning r_a) and $\langle m_b^B(v_b)\rangle_{\sigma_b}$ (returning r_b), the commutativity condition $\phi_{m_a;m_b}(\sigma_a, v_a, r_a, \sigma_b, v_b, r_b)$ holds, then there is an equivalent history H' where all the invocations of B appear before all the invocations of A.*

Proof. The proof proceeds by induction on the length of the sub-history, h, starting with the first method invoked by A in H, $m_1^A(v_1)$, and ending with the last method invoked by B in H, $m_2^B(v_2)$. We can disregard invocations from B that occur before $m_1^A(v_1)$, as they already appear before all invocations from A, and likewise for invocations from A that occur after $m_2^B(v_2)$. If there is no such sub-history, then H is already serialized.

Base case: When a sub-history $h = \langle m_1^A(v_1), m_2^B(v_2)\rangle_\sigma$, we can directly apply the commutativity condition $\phi_{m_1;m_2}$ to produce a C-EQUIVALENT history $h' = \langle m_2^B(v_2), m_1^A(v_1)\rangle_\sigma$.

Inductive hypothesis: When a sub-history h contains n or fewer invocations from A and m or fewer invocations from B, we can construct a sub-history $h' \equiv_C h$ that has all invocations from B before all invocations from A.

Inductive step: We will look at two cases: one where there are $n+1$ invocations from A and m invocations from B in h, and a second where there are n invocations from A and $m+1$ invocations from B in h.

Case 1: Consider the sub-history of h, i, that is the suffix of h starting with the last invocation from A in h:

$$i = \langle m_{n+1}^A(v_{n+1}), m_k^B(v_k), \ldots, m_m^B(v_m)\rangle_\sigma$$

i has at most m invocations from B and 1 invocation from A, and hence the inductive hypothesis applies. We can construct $i' \equiv_C i$ where all the invocations from B appear first. Substituting i' for i in h gives us a C-EQUIVALENT history h'.

The commutativity conditions provided by the conditions of the theorem only apply to h, not to h'. By appealing to Lemma 1, we know there are commutativity conditions between the pairs of methods in h' that are all **true**. Note that h' has at least one method invocation from A at the very end. We can now consider the sub-history j of h' that excludes that last method invocation. This new sub-history has n invocations from A and m invocations from B, allowing us to apply the inductive hypothesis again, constructing an equivalent j' in which all the invocations from A are at the end.

Substituting j' for j in h' gives us a new sub-history h'' that is equivalent to h but has all the invocations from B occurring before any invocations from A, proving this case.

Case 2: This case proceeds analogously to Case 1.

We have thus shown that there exists a sub-history h' that is C-EQUIVALENT to sub-history h for sub-histories of any length. Substituting h' for h in the complete history H produces a C-EQUIVALENT history H' that has all invocations from A after all invocations from B, and hence is serialized. □

B. Proof of Theorem 1

In this section, we provide the proof of Theorem 1 (that a sound a complete abstract locking scheme exists for a specification iff that specification is SIMPLE). The proof proceeds in two parts. First, we show that the construction algorithm presented in Section 3.2 produces a sound and complete implementation of a SIMPLE commutativity specification. Then, we show that if a specification is not SIMPLE, there does not exist a sound and complete abstract locking scheme for it.

B.1 Soundness and completeness

Lemma 2. *The abstract locking construction presented in the paper produces an abstract locking scheme that is sound and complete with respect to a* SIMPLE *commutativity specification.*

Proof. We will use the contrapositive definitions of soundness and completeness in this lemma, as described below.

- *Soundness.* For an abstract locking scheme to be a sound implementation of a commutativity specification, if two method invocations are allowed to proceed by the scheme (*i.e.*, both can successfully acquire their abstract locks), then the methods must commute according to the specification. By contrapositive, if two method invocations *conflict* according to the specification, then one or more abstract lock acquires performed by the scheme must fail, triggering a conflict.
- *Completeness.* For an abstract locking scheme to be complete, we must show that if two method invocations commute according to the specification, the abstract locking scheme will not detect a conflict. By contrapositive, if the abstract locking scheme detects a conflict between two method invocations (because one cannot acquire its abstract locks), then the methods must conflict according to the specification.

Because each method acquires its abstract locks in separate modes, it suffices to address the soundness and completeness of each commutativity predicate in isolation. For a commutativity specification to be SIMPLE, all commutativity predicates must satisfy one of three conditions. We address the three cases separately.

Case 1: $\phi_{m_1;m_2}$ = **false**. In this case, the m_1 and m_2 always conflict. We see that our lock compatibility table requires that the lock modes on the data structure lock used by the two methods interfere, hence preventing the second method from successfully acquiring the data structure lock. Thus the implementation is sound. Completeness is trivial, as the methods always conflict.

Case 2: $\phi_{m_1;m_2}$ = **true**. In this case, m_1 and m_2 *never* conflict. For soundness, this case is uninteresting; regardless of the behavior of the abstract locking scheme, the implementation will be sound. Completeness requires that the abstract locking scheme allow m_1 and m_2 to be successfully invoked by concurrently executing transactions. Because every method acquires locks in its own modes, and lock modes are compatible by default, we see that our abstract locking scheme lets m_1 and m_2 proceed.

Case 3: $\phi_{m_1;m_2} = ...\wedge(x \neq y)\wedge....$ To show soundness, consider the negation of this condition: a disjunction of equalities of the form $x = y$. If any of the equality clauses are true, our abstract locking scheme triggers a conflict. The equality of arguments means that the two method invocations will attempt to acquire locks on the same data item, and our compatibility matrix construction guarantees that the modes in which that lock will be acquired are incompatible.

To show completeness, we note that if our scheme detects a conflict, then two method invocations must have acquired the same argument lock in conflicting modes. By our construction, this can only happen if the commutativity condition contains a clause of the form $x \neq y$. Hence, the *conflict* condition contains the clause $x = y$, and the two methods conflict according to the specification.

Because the abstract locking scheme instantiated by our algorithm for a SIMPLE commutativity specification is sound and complete with respect to each commutativity predicate, the overall scheme is sound and complete. □

B.2 Expressivity of abstract locking schemes

Lemma 2 shows that if a commutativity specification is SIMPLE, we can produce a sound and complete abstract locking scheme for it by applying our construction algorithm. However, it is unclear whether sound and complete abstract locking schemes exist for non-SIMPLE commutativity specifications. The following lemma shows that they do not.

Lemma 3. *If a commutativity specification is* not SIMPLE, *then there does not exist a sound and complete abstract locking scheme that implements it.*

Proof. We proceed by contradiction. Assume that there is a non-SIMPLE commutativity specification, Φ, with a sound and complete abstract locking implementation. From this abstract locking scheme, construct Φ' as follows: For each pair of methods m_1 and m_2, consider at the compatibility sub-matrix induced by the locks acquired when invoking each method. If two argument locks, a and b are incompatible, the commutativity condition $\phi_{m_1;m_2}$ contains the conjunct $a \neq b$. If data structure locks acquired by the methods are incompatible, $\phi_{m_1;m_2}$ is simply **false**.

Note that Φ' is clearly SIMPLE, and the abstract locking scheme is a sound and complete implementation of Φ' by construction (specifically, applying the abstract locking construction algorithm to Φ' will produce the original abstract locking scheme). As the locking scheme is also sound and complete with respect to Φ, Φ and Φ' must be logically equivalent, contradicting the assumption that Φ is non-SIMPLE. □

Theorem 1 follows directly from Lemmas 2 and 3.

Separation Logic + Superposition Calculus = Heap Theorem Prover

Juan Antonio Navarro Pérez
Technische Universität München
navarrop@in.tum.de

Andrey Rybalchenko
Technische Universität München
rybal@in.tum.de

Abstract

Program analysis and verification tools crucially depend on the ability to symbolically describe and reason about sets of program behaviors. Separation logic provides a promising foundation for dealing with heap manipulating programs, while the development of practical automated deduction/satisfiability checking tools for separation logic is a challenging problem. In this paper, we present an efficient, sound and complete automated theorem prover for checking validity of entailments between separation logic formulas with list segment predicates. Our theorem prover integrates separation logic inference rules that deal with list segments and a superposition calculus to deal with equality/aliasing between memory locations. The integration follows a modular combination approach that allows one to directly incorporate existing advanced techniques for first-order reasoning with equality, as well as account for additional theories, e.g., linear arithmetic, using extensions of superposition. An experimental evaluation of our entailment prover indicates speedups of several orders of magnitude with respect to the available state-of-the-art tools.

Categories and Subject Descriptors D.2.4 [*Software Engineering*]: Software/Program Verification—Formal methods; F.3.1 [*Logics and Meanings of Programs*]: Specifying and Verifying and Reasoning about Programs—Mechanical verification; F.4.1 [*Mathematical Logic and Formal Languages*]: Mathematical Logic—Mechanical theorem proving

General Terms Verification, Logic, Reasoning

Keywords Separation Logic, Superposition

1. Introduction

Program analysis and verification tools crucially depend on the ability to symbolically describe and reason about program behaviors, e.g., using constraints [21], logical formulas/predicates [1, 9, 20, 22, 34], types [25, 28], and abstract domains [8, 26]. Automated deduction techniques can deliver automation support for such reasoning tasks. Today, propositional and Satisfiability Modulo Theory (SMT) solvers are ubiquitous components of software analysis, verification, and debugging tools. These solvers can efficiently deal with practically relevant logical theories of various scalar data types, e.g., fixed length bit-vectors and numbers, as well as uninterpreted functions and arrays [2, 10, 14, 19].

Dealing with programs that manipulate heap-allocated data structures using pointers imposes additional challenges on symbolic reasoning tools. Existing formalisms for tracking the shape of heap graphs, e.g., three valued structures, separation logic, Boolean heaps, and monadic second-order logic of graph types [27, 31–33, 35], demonstrate the feasibility of automated reasoning about heap manipulating programs while providing a wide spectrum of trade-offs w.r.t. automation, precision, efficiency, and applicability.

Separation logic provides a promising foundation for dealing with programs that manipulate the heap following a certain discipline [33]. This discipline can be effectively exploited for manual/tool assisted proof development [18, 28, 37], extended static checking [6, 16], and automatic inference of heap shapes [7, 12, 17, 38]. All these approaches depend on the ability to check logical entailment between separation logic formulas, e.g., for validation of loop invariant candidates or fixpoint detection.

Automation of separation logic—usually extended with recursively defined shape predicates such as lists, trees, or nested containers—relies on decidable sub-classes together with the corresponding proof systems or heuristic approaches based on folding/unfolding strategies for recursive shape definitions [6, 7, 11, 13, 23, 29, 36, 38]. Development of practical entailment checking tools for separation logic is a challenging problem. Since the existing proof systems pursue an intricate interplay between aliasing of memory locations and their occurrence in scope of the shape predicates, the proof search becomes a complex procedure exposed to the non-determinism of the inference rule applications. Heuristic approaches require sophisticated (un)folding strategies, which are difficult to get right in a predictable and robust way. As a result, entailment checkers for separation logic have not reached yet the level of applicability on par with state-of-the-art SAT and SMT solvers.

In this paper, we present an efficient, sound and complete automated theorem prover for checking validity of entailments between separation logic formulas with list segment predicates. In contrast to the existing tools, our approach puts to work the framework of paramodulation-based theorem proving [30]. Instead of representing proof rules as an axiom schema and performing a generic inference-based proof search, by applying the framework we obtain specialized inference rules together with an adequate, optimized rule application strategy, without compromising either soundness or completeness.

Our theorem prover relies on a combination of separation logic inference rules that deal with list segments and a superposition calculus to deal with equality/aliasing between memory locations. Our separation logic inference rules are obtained from an existing proof system for separation logic with list segments [4], which is a basis for various separation logic based tools [6, 11, 16, 36], by factoring out its built-in equality reasoning. We use a standard superposition

PLDI'11, June 4–8, 2011, San Jose, California, USA.

calculus for equality, and rely on its ability to generate (partial) models. The model generation ties together the equality and list segment reasoning. Given an entailment to check, our prover first constructs a model for the equality predicates and then uses this model to disambiguate the heap shape for the subsequent treatment of the list segments. Since the reasoning about the list segments can produce additional equalities, the entire process is repeated with the updated model.

By explicating the connection between the equality and separation logic inferences through the equality models, our theorem prover becomes more efficient than the original proof system. Since the equality model excludes certain heap shapes from consideration, several non-deterministic proof search steps in the original proof system turn into deterministic ones and can be efficiently implemented using a rewriting process.

An experimental evaluation of our entailment prover indicates speedups of several orders of magnitude with respect to the available state-of-the-art tools. Our implementation, which is written in Prolog to allow a declarative specification of the inference rules of the proof system, is able to check thousands of entailments of increasing complexity in seconds rather than minutes.

This paper makes the following contributions:

1. An effective factorization an important existing proof system for separation logic into equality and separation reasoning;
2. An algorithm for proving entailments that exploits this factorization;
3. Application of equality models for disambiguating heap shapes and thus eliminating the corresponding non-determinism from the proof search;
4. An efficient implementation of the theorem prover and its evaluation.

In summary, to the best of our knowledge we present to the first paramodulation-based automated theorem prover for separation logic with list segments.

Our ultimate goal is a theorem prover for an expressive fragment that combines separation logic with other theories useful for program reasoning, including arithmetic and various data structure shapes (such as trees). We believe that building upon a well-understood calculus, such as superposition, offers a viable starting point. Existing extensions of superposition with linear arithmetic [24] and SMT theories [3, 15] suggest immediate steps for extending expressiveness of our current fragment. The increasing extensibility and programmability of state-of-the-art theorem provers, where Z3 is a prominent example, suggest that the presented approach could be implemented within the existing tools.

2. Illustration

We illustrate our theorem proving algorithm using the following example. Assume we want to establish the validity of an entailment E given by

$$c \not\simeq e \wedge \mathsf{lseg}(a,b) * \mathsf{lseg}(a,c) * \mathsf{next}(c,d) * \mathsf{lseg}(d,e) \\ \rightarrow \mathsf{lseg}(b,c) * \mathsf{lseg}(c,e) ,$$

where $\simeq$ is equality among program expressions, $\mathsf{next}(x,y)$ is a portion of the heap in the program state where x 'points to' y; $\mathsf{lseg}(x,y)$ is a portion of the heap (possibly empty if $x = y$) containing an acyclic path from x to y following the 'points to' relation; and '$*$' is the union of disjoint portions of the heap. The entailment itself states that any program state, composed of a stack and a heap, which satisfies the conditions on the left-hand side of the formula, should also satisfy the right-hand side.

The first step of our approach is to build a clausal representation of the *negation* of the entailment, i.e. $\neg E$. This set, denoted $\mathrm{cnf}(E)$, has the tree clauses:

$$c \simeq e \rightarrow \emptyset \tag{1}$$

$$\emptyset \rightarrow \mathsf{lseg}(a,b) * \mathsf{lseg}(a,c) * \mathsf{next}(c,d) * \mathsf{lseg}(d,e) \tag{2}$$

$$\mathsf{lseg}(b,c) * \mathsf{lseg}(c,e) \rightarrow \emptyset \tag{3}$$

where $\emptyset \rightarrow F$ asserts a formula to be *true*, while $F \rightarrow \emptyset$ asserts a formula as *false*. More generally, a clause such as $A, B \rightarrow C, D$ asserts that if *all* the facts on the left-hand side are true, then *at least one of* the facts on the right should be true.

From the clause (2), since $\mathsf{lseg}(a,b) * \mathsf{lseg}(a,c)$ represents two disjoint portions of the heap, we know that either $a \simeq b$ or $a \simeq c$, i.e. one of these two segments should be empty. Thus we derive a new clause

$$\emptyset \rightarrow a \simeq b, a \simeq c\,. \tag{4}$$

Now we ask a superposition-based theorem prover to find for us a model for the pure clauses, those which *only* contain equalities, that have been computed so far, i.e. (1) and (4). Such a prover could tell us that assuming $a \simeq c$, and the rest of the variables distinct from each other, would do. In particular $a \simeq c$ satisfies the clause (4).

We apply this information and derive a new clause by 'superposition' of (4) into (2) to obtain

$$\emptyset \rightarrow a \simeq b, \mathsf{lseg}(a,b) * \mathsf{next}(a,d) * \mathsf{lseg}(d,e)\,, \tag{5}$$

where c is replaced with a and a resulting empty list segment is removed. Note that $a \simeq b$ also appears in the clause, intuitively as a reminder that 'we have yet to try' the other alternative. But let us continue by analyzing the heap described in clause (5). Now, from $\mathsf{next}(a,d)$, we know that a is definitely pointing to something in the heap; and thus the disjoint $\mathsf{lseg}(a,b)$ should be empty. So, in either case, $a \simeq b$ and we derive a new pure clause

$$\emptyset \rightarrow a \simeq b\,. \tag{6}$$

We ask our superposition-based prover to find us a new model, and this time it tells us that, in fact, just setting $a \simeq b$ would do. This is enough to satisfy the clause (6), as well as the previous two pure clauses. So we now try a superposition of (6) into (2) to obtain

$$\emptyset \rightarrow \mathsf{lseg}(a,c) * \mathsf{next}(c,d) * \mathsf{lseg}(d,e)\,, \tag{7}$$

this time replacing b with a and removing the empty list segment. This description of a heap now looks all fine, so let us apply a superposition of (6) into clause (3), which comes from the left-hand side of the entailment, to produce

$$\mathsf{lseg}(a,c) * \mathsf{lseg}(c,e) \rightarrow \emptyset\,. \tag{8}$$

Now we see that it is possible to match and 'resolve away' these two complementary heap formulas by 'unfolding' the list segment $\mathsf{lseg}(c,e)$ into the disjoint union of $\mathsf{next}(c,d) * \mathsf{lseg}(d,e)$. This is in fact possible if $c \not\simeq e$; but if otherwise $c \simeq e$ then $\mathsf{lseg}(c,e)$ would be empty while $\mathsf{next}(c,d) * \mathsf{lseg}(d,e)$ is definitely not (at least c is pointing to something). So we have to continue and consider the alternative when

$$\emptyset \rightarrow c \simeq e\,. \tag{9}$$

But this time when we ask our superposition-based prover to find us a model for the pure clauses, we are told that there are no models anymore! In fact the clauses (1) and (9) are contradictory and derive the empty clause. This exercise proves that the set of clauses $\mathrm{cnf}(E)$, equivalent to $\neg E$, is not satisfiable and thus the original entailment *must* be valid. More than this, these inference steps actually constitute a proof of the validity of the entailment (c.f. Figure 4) which we describe later in detail in Section 5.

3. Preliminaries

This section presents preliminary definitions. We introduce notation for dealing with relations and functions, separation logic, as well as equality reasoning using superposition.

Relations We write $x \Rightarrow y$ to denote the ordered pair (x, y) and, for a binary relation R, $x \Rightarrow_R y$ to denote $x \Rightarrow y \in R$. The *domain* $\operatorname{dom} R$ of a relation is the projection of R on its first component, i.e. $\operatorname{dom} R = \{x \mid \exists y : x \Rightarrow_R y\}$. We write $\Rightarrow_R^*$ to denote the reflexive and transitive closure of R; and $\Leftrightarrow_R^*$ for the symmetric, reflexive, and transitive closure of R. An element y is *irreducible* by R if $y \notin \operatorname{dom} R$. Furthermore, y is a *normal form* of x with respect to R if $x \Rightarrow_R^* y$ and y is irreducible.

A binary relation R is *well-founded* if there is no infinite sequence $x_1 \Rightarrow_R x_2 \Rightarrow_R \cdots$; and *confluent* if having $x \Rightarrow_R^* y$ and $x \Rightarrow_R^* y'$ implies that there is a z such that $y \Rightarrow_R^* z$ and $y' \Rightarrow_R^* z$. A well-founded and confluent relation is called *convergent*. Given a convergent relation R, every x has a unique normal form denoted by x_R. Furthermore, we have that $x \Leftrightarrow_R^* y$ if and only if $x_R \equiv y_R$, i.e. two elements are equivalent with respect to R whenever their normal forms are identical.

Functions A *function* f is a relation where $x \Rightarrow_f y$ and $x \Rightarrow_f y'$ implies $y \equiv y'$. If $x \in \operatorname{dom} f$ we write $f(x)$ to denote the (unique) element y such that $x \Rightarrow_f y$. We say that f *is a function from* X *to* Y, denoted $f\colon X \to Y$, if $\operatorname{dom} f = X$ and $f(x) \in Y$ for each $x \in X$. In contrast, f *is a* partial function *form* X *to* Y, denoted $f\colon X \rightharpoonup Y$, if $\operatorname{dom} f \subseteq X$ and $f\colon \operatorname{dom} f \to Y$. We write $f[a \Rightarrow b]$ for a *function update* such that $(f[a \Rightarrow b])(x) = b$ if $x \equiv a$ and $(f[a \Rightarrow b])(x) = f(x)$ otherwise. Semicolons are used to compose function updates, i.e., $f[a \Rightarrow b; c \Rightarrow d] = (f[a \Rightarrow b])[c \Rightarrow d]$. Given a pair of functions f and g, we write $h = f * g$ when $h = f \cup g$ and $\operatorname{dom} f \cap \operatorname{dom} g = \emptyset$, i.e. h is the union of two functions f and g with disjoint domains.

Edges and paths A relation R is an *edge from* x *to* y, denoted $R\colon x \Rightarrow y$, if $R = \{x \Rightarrow y\}$; and a relation R is a *simple path from* x *to* y, denoted $R\colon x \Rightarrow^* y$, if $R = \{x_1 \Rightarrow x_2, \ldots, x_{n-1} \Rightarrow x_n\}$ where $x_1 = x$, $x_n = y$, and $x_i \neq x_j$ if $i \neq j$. Each simple path from x to y is acyclic, and $y \notin \operatorname{dom} R$. Edges and simple paths are functions. For example, $R = \{a \Rightarrow b, b \Rightarrow c, c \Rightarrow d\}$ is a simple path and a function with $\operatorname{dom} R = \{a, b, c\}$; and applying an update $R[b \Rightarrow d; d \Rightarrow c] = \{a \Rightarrow b, b \Rightarrow d, d \Rightarrow c, c \Rightarrow d\}$, the simple path property is invalidated.

3.1 Separation logic

Separation logic is used to reason about programs that manipulate pointer data structures [33]. The following is an abridged presentation of the considered fragment from Berdine et al. [5].

Syntax Let Var be a set of constant symbols together with a distinguished constant symbol nil such that $\mathsf{nil} \notin \mathsf{Var}$. We use Var to represent program variables, and nil represents the null pointer. Let x and y be constant symbols. We say that $x \simeq y$ is a *pure* atom, while $\mathsf{next}(x, y)$ and $\mathsf{lseg}(x, y)$ are *basic spatial* atoms. Then, we write $\mathsf{f}(x, y)$ for a basic spatial atom, where f is either next or f is lseg, and refer to x as the *address* of the atom. Given a multiset of basic spatial atoms that contains elements $S_1, \ldots, S_n$, we say that $S_1 * \cdots * S_n$ is a *spatial atom*; and emp denotes the empty multiset. A spatial atom Σ is *well-formed* if (1) no basic atom in Σ has a nil address, and (2) no two basic atoms in Σ share the same address.

The set of separation logic *formulas* consists of pure atoms, spacial atoms, and their boolean combinations obtained using conjunction $\wedge$, disjunction $\vee$, and negation $\neg$. A *literal* is either an atom A or its negation $\neg A$; an *entailment* $F \to G$ is a shorthand for $\neg F \vee G$; and a *logic equivalence* $F \leftrightarrow G$ abbreviates the formula $F \to G \wedge G \to F$. For a formula F, constant symbols x and y, the substitution $F[y/x]$ replaces all occurrences of x in F with y.

Semantics Let Loc be a set of *memory locations* and nil a special location such that $nil \notin \mathsf{Loc}$. We define $\mathsf{Loc}^+ = \mathsf{Loc} \cup \{nil\}$. An *interpretation* (s, h) for a separation logic formula consists of a function *stack* $s\colon \mathsf{Var} \to \mathsf{Loc}^+$ and a partial function *heap* $h\colon \mathsf{Loc} \rightharpoonup \mathsf{Loc}^+$. Given a stack s, we define the *evaluation* function $\hat{s}\colon \mathsf{Var} \cup \{\mathsf{nil}\} \to \mathsf{Loc}^+$ as $\hat{s} = s[\mathsf{nil} \Rightarrow nil]$.

Given an interpretation (s, h) and an atom A, we define the *satisfaction* relation $s, h \models A$ as follows:

$$
\begin{array}{lll}
s, h \models x \simeq y & \text{if} & \hat{s}(x) = \hat{s}(y)\,, \\
s, h \models \mathsf{next}(x, y) & \text{if} & h\colon \hat{s}(x) \Rightarrow \hat{s}(y)\,, \\
s, h \models \mathsf{lseg}(x, y) & \text{if} & h\colon \hat{s}(x) \Rightarrow^* \hat{s}(y)\,, \\
s, h \models S_1 * \cdots * S_n & \text{if} & \text{exist } h_1, \ldots, h_n \text{ such that} \\
 & & \quad h = h_1 * \cdots * h_n \text{ and} \\
 & & \quad s, h_i \models S_i \text{ for each } 1 \leq i \leq n.
\end{array}
$$

From the above definition follows that the empty spatial atom emp can only be satisfied by an interpretation $(s, \emptyset)$. We extend the satisfaction relation $\models$ to deal with logical connectives in a canonical way, i.e. $s, h \models \neg F$ if (s, h) does not satisfy F, while $s, h \models F_1 \wedge \cdots \wedge F_n$ if (s, h) satisfies every conjunct F_i, and $s, h \models F_1 \vee \cdots \vee F_n$ if (s, h) satisfies some disjunct F_i. We also write $s \models F$ when, for all heaps h, the pair (s, h) is a model of F.

An interpretation that satisfies a formula is called a *model*; a formula is *satisfiable* if it has a model; and a *valid* formula is satisfied by every interpretation. Note that an entailment $F \to G$ is valid if every model of F satisfies G or, equivalently, if $F \wedge \neg G$ is not satisfiable. Program analysis and verification tools often require checking the validity of entailments of the form

$$\Pi \wedge \Sigma \to \Pi' \wedge \Sigma'$$

where Π and Π' are conjunctions of pure literals, while Σ and Σ' are spatial atoms.

3.2 Clausal normal form

We use a clausal form to represent logic formulas. A *clause* is a disjunction of the form

$$\neg A_1 \vee \cdots \vee \neg A_n \vee A_{n+1} \vee \cdots \vee A_{n+m}$$

where each A_i is an atom and at most one of them is a spatial atom. A set of clauses $\mathcal{S}$ represents the conjunction of its elements. Thus, an interpretation satisfies the set of clauses $\mathcal{S}$ if the interpretation satisfies every clause in $\mathcal{S}$. For brevity, we write clauses in the form

$$\Gamma \to \Delta\,,$$

where the sets $\Gamma = \{A_1, \ldots, A_n\}$ and $\Delta = \{A_{n+1}, \ldots, A_{n+m}\}$ are, respectively, the sets of negative and positive atoms in the clause. Commas are used in clauses to denote union and element inclusion, e.g. $\Gamma, \Gamma', A \to \Delta$ stands for $\Gamma \cup \Gamma' \cup \{A\} \to \Delta$. The symbol $\Box$ denotes the *empty clause*, i.e. the clause $\Gamma \to \Delta$ where both $\Gamma = \Delta = \emptyset$. A clause is *pure* if it contains only pure atoms, and is *spatial* otherwise. Given a set of clauses $\mathcal{S}$ we write $\mathrm{Pure}(\mathcal{S})$ to denote the subset of pure clauses contained in $\mathcal{S}$.

Let E be an entailment $\Pi \wedge \Sigma \to \Pi' \wedge \Sigma'$ such that

$$
\begin{aligned}
\Pi &= P_1 \wedge \cdots \wedge P_n \wedge \neg N_1 \wedge \cdots \wedge \neg N_m\,, \\
\Pi' &= P_1' \wedge \cdots \wedge P_{n'}' \wedge \neg N_1' \wedge \cdots \wedge \neg N_{m'}'\,.
\end{aligned}
$$

We define a *clausal embedding* function cnf (stands for *clausal normal form*) that takes an entailment E and returns a representation of its negation $\neg E$ given by the set of clauses:

$$
\begin{aligned}
\mathrm{cnf}(E) = \{\emptyset \to P_1, \quad \ldots, \quad \emptyset \to P_n, \quad \emptyset \to \Sigma \\
N_1 \to \emptyset, \quad \ldots, \quad N_m \to \emptyset, \quad \Pi'_+, \Sigma' \to \Pi'_-\}\,,
\end{aligned}
$$

where the sets $\Pi'_+ = \{P'_1, \ldots, P'_{n'}\}$ and $\Pi'_- = \{N'_1, \ldots, N'_{m'}\}$ are, respectively, the sets of atoms occurring positively and negatively in Π'. Because the conjunction of clauses $\text{cnf}(E)$ is logically equivalent to $\neg E$, the entailment E is valid if and only if its clausal embedding $\text{cnf}(E)$ is not satisfiable.

Since it is enough for our purposes, we assume that clauses have at most one spatial atom. Furthermore, in the following we assume that the symbols Γ and Δ represent sets of *pure* atoms, and a spatial atom occurring in a clause (if any) is written explicitly. Therefore a clause can either be a *pure clause*, $\Gamma \to \Delta$, a *positive spatial clause*, $\Gamma \to \Sigma, \Delta$, or a *negative spatial clause*, $\Gamma, \Sigma \to \Delta$.

3.3 Superposition calculus for equality reasoning

A key point of our approach is that it allows the use of existing and well established techniques in automated deduction in order to reason about equality in the context of separation logic. A proof system which fits our needs is that of the *superposition calculus* as presented, for example, by Nieuwenhuis and Rubio [30] (specifically the system $\mathcal{I}$ defined for general clauses in their Section 3.5). This is a proof system with inference rules such as

$$\frac{\Gamma \to x \simeq y, \Delta \qquad \Gamma' \to x \simeq y', \Delta'}{\Gamma, \Gamma' \to y \simeq y', \Delta, \Delta'}$$

where the clauses above the line are the *premises* of the rule and the clause below is its *conclusion*.

Given a set of clauses $\mathcal{S}$, if clauses matching the premises of an inference rule are found in $\mathcal{S}$, then we say that $\mathcal{S}$ *derives* the conclusion of the inference rule. In general we write $\mathcal{S} \vdash_{\mathcal{X}} C$ if it is possible to derive a clause C from a set $\mathcal{S}$ by a successive application of inference rules in $\mathcal{X}$; and write $\text{Cns}_{\mathcal{X}}(\mathcal{S}) = \{C \mid \mathcal{S} \vdash_{\mathcal{X}} C\}$ to denote the set of all *consequences* derived from $\mathcal{S}$ by inferences in the set $\mathcal{X}$. A set of clauses $\mathcal{S}^*$ is *saturated*, with respect to the inferences $\mathcal{X}$, if $\mathcal{S}^* = \text{Cns}_{\mathcal{X}}(\mathcal{S}^*)$.

In the particular case of the proof system $\mathcal{I}$, a number of *superposition* inference rules are defined which derive clauses that logically follow from $\mathcal{S}$ by interpreting '$\simeq$' as an equality relation. To make the system useful in practice, inferences are constrained with respect to an appropriate order $\succ$ over the terms of the language, and only 'maximal' atoms are allowed to participate in inferences. For further details we refer the reader to [30]; in the following we only give a brief summary of the concepts and definitions that are required to develop the work in this paper.

The proof system $\mathcal{I}$ is refutation complete for pure clauses. This means that if $\mathcal{S}^* = \text{Cns}_{\mathcal{I}}(\mathcal{S})$ is the saturation of a set $\mathcal{S}$ of pure clauses, then the empty clause $\square \in \mathcal{S}^*$ if, and only if, the set $\mathcal{S}$ is not satisfiable. Completeness of the proof system is proved showing that if $\square \notin \mathcal{S}^*$ then it is possible to build a model, given by a relation R, as a witness of the satisfiability of $\mathcal{S}$. In this case R satisfies a pure atom $x \simeq y$, denoted $R^* \mathrel{|\!\!\simeq} x \simeq y$, if $x \Leftrightarrow^*_R y$. Moreover, if R is a convergent relation, then R satisfies an atom $x \simeq y$ if, and only if, their normal forms $x_R \equiv y_R$ are identical.

The relation $R = \text{Gen}(\mathcal{S}^*)$ is defined in terms of a *generating* function Gen (see Definition 3.8 in [30]) which selects some clauses $C \in \mathcal{S}^*$ and *generates* edges $x \Rightarrow_R y$. For our purposes it is not important exactly how are clauses are selected from $\mathcal{S}^*$; as we only rely on the following properties of such relation R.

Lemma 3.1. *Let $\mathcal{S}^*$ be a set of pure clauses saturated with respect to $\mathcal{I}$, and let $R = \text{Gen}(\mathcal{S}^*)$. The relation R is (1) convergent; and (2) if there is an edge $x \Rightarrow_R y$ then $x \succ y$, there is a clause $\Gamma \to x \simeq y, \Delta \in \mathcal{S}^*$—which generated the edge—and $R^* \not\mathrel{|\!\!\simeq} \Gamma \to \Delta$ (c.f. Lemma 3.9 in [30]).*

We will sometimes write $\langle R, g\rangle = \text{Gen}(\mathcal{S}^*)$ to denote the fact that the generating function provides both the relation R and a mapping g from each edge in R to its corresponding *generating* clause in $\mathcal{S}^*$ satisfying the conditions of item 2 in previous lemma.

Completeness is established showing that, if the proof system $\mathcal{I}$ is unable to derive the empty clause, then R is indeed a model of the set of pure clauses.

Theorem 3.1. *Let $\mathcal{S}$ be a set of pure clauses, let $\mathcal{S}^* = \text{Cns}_{\mathcal{I}}(\mathcal{S})$ and let $R = \text{Gen}(\mathcal{S}^*)$. If $\square \notin \mathcal{S}^*$ then $R^* \mathrel{|\!\!\simeq} \mathcal{S}$.*

Observe that, in this context, models and interpretations for pure clauses are defined in terms of a relation (w.r.t. $\mathrel{|\!\!\simeq}$) while, in the previous section, we used a stack and a heap (w.r.t. $\models$). A simple result shows that, in fact, for a pure formula there is a one to one correspondence between its relation and stack models. For this we only need to make the assumption that nil is a minimal element with respect to the order $\succ$ used to generate the relation, i.e. $x \succ \mathsf{nil}$ for every other constant symbol x in the logic.

Definition 3.1. Given a convergent relation R, the induced stack $s_R \colon \mathsf{Var} \to \mathsf{Loc}^+$ is defined as $s_R(x) = \mathit{nil}$ if $x_R \equiv \mathsf{nil}$, and $s_R(x) = \iota(x_R)$ otherwise; where $\iota \colon \mathsf{Var} \to \mathsf{Loc}$ is an arbitrary, but fixed, injection that maps different program variables into different non-nil memory locations.

The condition asking nil to be a minimal element makes sure that if $x \Leftrightarrow^*_R \mathsf{nil}$, then $x_R \equiv \mathsf{nil}$ and s_R maps x to nil. Moreover, by definition $\hat{s}_R(x) = \hat{s}_R(x_R)$. In the following, to ease the notation and if a suitable relation R clear by context, we simply write $\hat{x}$ as a shorthand for the memory location $\hat{s}_R(x)$.

Theorem 3.2. *Let R be a convergent relation and let F be a pure formula. $R^* \mathrel{|\!\!\simeq} F$ if, and only if, $s_R \models F$.*

Proof. Since the formula F is pure it is enough to consider the case of a pure atom $x \simeq y$ and an arbitrary heap h. The result follows since, from the definition of s_R, the normal forms are identical, i.e. $x_R \equiv y_R$, if and only if the two symbols evaluate to the same memory location, i.e. $\hat{x} = \hat{y}$. □

4. Proof system for separation logic entailments

In the previous section we described the superposition calculus, the proof system $\mathcal{I}$, which allows us to reason about equalities in the pure fragment of the logic. We now focus on introducing the necessary inference rules to reason about the spatial component of our separation logic formulas.

4.1 Spatial reasoning

The proof system $\mathcal{SI}$ is obtained by augmenting $\mathcal{I}$ with a number of additional inference rules shown in Figure 1. These rules are grouped into three main groups of normalization, well-formedness, and unfolding inferences.

- $\mathcal{N}$: The normalization inference N1 allows to use the information in a pure clause to 'rewrite' the spatial atom occurring on a positive spatial clause; while the rule N2 discards trivial basic atoms of the form $\mathsf{lseg}(x, x)$. Rules N3 and N4 are their respective counterparts for negative spatial clauses.
- $\mathcal{W}$: The second group of well-formedness rules, W1 to W5, check for possible inconsistencies that could occur in positive spatial clauses. In particular they make sure that nil is not used as an address in the heap, and that two disjoint parts of the heap do not share a common address.
- $\mathcal{U}$: Finally the unfolding inferences include the rules U1 to U5, which perform a one-step 'unfold' of a basic atom $\mathsf{lseg}(x, z)$ in a negative spatial clause by using the information contained in a positive spatial clause; and the rule SR of *spatial resolu-*

Normalization ($\mathcal{N}$):

$$\text{N1}\ \frac{\Gamma \to x \simeq y, \Delta \qquad \Gamma' \to \Delta', \Sigma}{\Gamma, \Gamma' \to \Delta, \Delta', \Sigma[y/x]} \qquad \text{N2}\ \frac{\Gamma \to \Delta, \mathsf{lseg}(x,x) * \Sigma}{\Gamma \to \Delta, \Sigma}$$

$$\text{N3}\ \frac{\Gamma \to x \simeq y, \Delta \qquad \Gamma', \Sigma \to \Delta'}{\Gamma, \Gamma', \Sigma[y/x] \to \Delta, \Delta'} \qquad \text{N4}\ \frac{\Gamma, \mathsf{lseg}(x,x) * \Sigma \to \Delta}{\Gamma, \Sigma \to \Delta}$$

Well-formedness ($\mathcal{W}$):

$$\text{W1}\ \frac{\Gamma \to \Delta, \mathsf{next}(\mathsf{nil}, y) * \Sigma}{\Gamma \to \Delta} \qquad \text{W2}\ \frac{\Gamma \to \Delta, \mathsf{lseg}(\mathsf{nil}, y) * \Sigma}{\Gamma \to y \simeq \mathsf{nil}, \Delta} \qquad \text{W3}\ \frac{\Gamma \to \Delta, \mathsf{next}(x,y) * \mathsf{next}(x,z) * \Sigma}{\Gamma \to \Delta}$$

$$\text{W4}\ \frac{\Gamma \to \Delta, \mathsf{next}(x,y) * \mathsf{lseg}(x,z) * \Sigma}{\Gamma \to x \simeq z, \Delta} \qquad \text{W5}\ \frac{\Gamma \to \Delta, \mathsf{lseg}(x,y) * \mathsf{lseg}(x,z) * \Sigma}{\Gamma \to x \simeq y, x \simeq z, \Delta}$$

Unfolding ($\mathcal{U}$):

$$\text{U1}\ \frac{\Gamma \to \Delta, \mathsf{next}(x,z) * \Sigma \qquad \Gamma', \mathsf{lseg}(x,z) * \Sigma' \to \Delta'}{\Gamma', \mathsf{next}(x,z) * \Sigma' \to x \simeq z, \Delta'} \qquad \text{U2}\ \frac{\Gamma \to \Delta, \mathsf{next}(x,y) * \Sigma \qquad \Gamma', \mathsf{lseg}(x,z) * \Sigma' \to \Delta'}{\Gamma', \mathsf{next}(x,y) * \mathsf{lseg}(y,z) * \Sigma' \to x \simeq z, \Delta'}\ y \not\equiv z$$

$$\text{U3}\ \frac{\Gamma \to \Delta, \mathsf{lseg}(x,y) * \Sigma \qquad \Gamma', \mathsf{lseg}(x,\mathsf{nil}) * \Sigma' \to \Delta'}{\Gamma', \mathsf{lseg}(x,y) * \mathsf{lseg}(y,\mathsf{nil}) * \Sigma' \to \Delta'}\ y \not\equiv \mathsf{nil}$$

$$\text{U4}\ \frac{\Gamma \to \Delta, \mathsf{lseg}(x,y) * \mathsf{next}(z,w) * \Sigma \qquad \Gamma', \mathsf{lseg}(x,z) * \Sigma' \to \Delta'}{\Gamma', \mathsf{lseg}(x,y) * \mathsf{lseg}(y,z) * \Sigma' \to \Delta'}\ y \not\equiv z$$

$$\text{U5}\ \frac{\Gamma \to \Delta, \mathsf{lseg}(x,y) * \mathsf{lseg}(z,w) * \Sigma \qquad \Gamma', \mathsf{lseg}(x,z) * \Sigma' \to \Delta'}{\Gamma', \mathsf{lseg}(x,y) * \mathsf{lseg}(y,z) * \Sigma' \to z \simeq w, \Delta'}\ y \not\equiv z \qquad \text{SR}\ \frac{\Gamma, \Sigma \to \Delta \qquad \Gamma' \to \Delta', \Sigma}{\Gamma, \Gamma' \to \Delta, \Delta'}$$

Figure 1. Spatial inference rules of the $\mathcal{SI}$ proof system

Well-formedness	*Unfolding*
W1: $\mathsf{next}(\mathsf{nil}, y) * \Sigma \to \emptyset$	U1: $\mathsf{next}(x,z) * \Sigma \to x \simeq z, \mathsf{lseg}(x,z) * \Sigma$
W2: $\mathsf{lseg}(\mathsf{nil}, y) * \Sigma \to y \simeq \mathsf{nil}$	U2: $\mathsf{next}(x,y) * \mathsf{lseg}(y,z) * \Sigma \to x \simeq z, \mathsf{lseg}(x,z) * \Sigma$
W3: $\mathsf{next}(x,y) * \mathsf{next}(x,z) * \Sigma \to \emptyset$	U3: $\mathsf{lseg}(x,y) * \mathsf{lseg}(y,\mathsf{nil}) * \Sigma \to \mathsf{lseg}(x,\mathsf{nil}) * \Sigma$
W4: $\mathsf{next}(x,y) * \mathsf{lseg}(x,z) * \Sigma \to x \simeq z$	U4: $\mathsf{lseg}(x,y) * \mathsf{lseg}(y,z) * \mathsf{next}(z,w) * \Sigma \to \mathsf{lseg}(x,z) * \mathsf{next}(z,w) * \Sigma$
W5: $\mathsf{lseg}(x,y) * \mathsf{lseg}(x,z) * \Sigma \to x \simeq y, x \simeq z$	U5: $\mathsf{lseg}(x,y) * \mathsf{lseg}(y,z) * \mathsf{lseg}(z,w) * \Sigma \to z \simeq w, \mathsf{lseg}(x,z) * \mathsf{lseg}(z,w) * \Sigma$

Figure 2. Separation logic axiom schemas

tion, which resolves away a common spatial atom occurring in complementary spatial clauses.

These inference rules, which can be thought of as coming from the separation logic axiom schemas in Figure 2, are a variation of the proof system for separation logic entailments originally proposed by Berdine et al. [5]. The main difference between the two systems is that, while the proof system from Berdine et al. operates at the level of entailments; our inferences have been rearranged in the form of clauses. This is key to the results presented in this paper, since it allows us to clearly separate the stages of pure equality and spatial reasoning, thus enabling the direct application of a wide array of techniques from the theorem proving community into the context of separation logic.

4.2 Soundness

It is easy to check that all inferences of the $\mathcal{SI}$ proof system are sound; namely if a pair (s, h) of a stack and a heap is a model of the premises of an inference rule, then (s, h) is also a model of the conclusion of the rule.

Theorem 4.1. *Let $E \equiv \Pi \wedge \Sigma \to \Pi' \wedge \Sigma'$ be an entailment, and let $\mathcal{S}^* = \mathrm{Cns}_{\mathcal{SI}}(\mathrm{cnf}(E))$. If $\Box \in \mathcal{S}^*$ then the entailment is valid.*

Proof. As all inferences in $\mathcal{SI}$ preserve models, any model of the clausal embedding $\mathrm{cnf}(E)$ would also be a model of the empty clause $\Box$. However, since the empty clause doesn't have any models, the set of clauses $\mathrm{cnf}(E)$ is unsatisfiable and, by construction of the embedding, E is valid. $\Box$

4.3 Completeness by model generation

The completeness of the $\mathcal{SI}$ proof system is proved by showing that, if the system is unable to derive the empty clause from the clausal embedding of an entailment, then it is possible to build a counterexample for the entailment.

The sketch of the proof is as follows: In section 3.3 we described a construction that generates a convergent relation R as a model of a satisfiable set of pure clauses and, furthermore, how this relation induces a corresponding stack s_R. What remains to be done is, after a suitable relation R is fixed, to build a corresponding heap that is used to refute a given entailment. For this we introduce the notion of the *graph* of a spatial atom Σ; in particular we show that if Σ is well-formed, then its graph $\mathrm{gr}_R\,\Sigma$ is actually a heap.

Given a spatial atom Σ, we also define its normalization with respect to the relation R and prove that normalization inferences are able to 'normalize' the spatial atom. Then we prove that well-formedness inferences make sure that the normalized Σ_R is indeed well-formed. Finally we show that if unfolding inferences are able to successfully rewrite a spatial atom Σ'_R into another Σ_R, then $s_R \models \Sigma \to \Sigma'$. Otherwise, if the unfolding fails, then it is possible to tweak the graph $\mathrm{gr}_R\,\Sigma$ into a counterexample showing that $s_R, h \not\models \Sigma \to \Sigma'$; and thus allows us to refute entailments.

Now that we have sketched the main idea of the proof, we are ready to delve into its details. We start by defining, as promised, the graph and the normalization of a spatial atom with respect to a given relation R.

Definition 4.1. The *graph* of a basic spatial atom S with respect to a convergent relation R is $\mathrm{gr}_R\,S = \{\hat{x} \Rightarrow \hat{y}\}$ if either

- $S \equiv \mathsf{next}(x, y)$, or
- $S \equiv \mathsf{lseg}(x, y)$ and $\hat{x} \neq \hat{y}$;

and $\mathrm{gr}_R\,S = \emptyset$ otherwise. The *graph* of $\Sigma \equiv S_1 * \cdots * S_n$ is defined as $\mathrm{gr}_R\,\Sigma = \mathrm{gr}_R\,S_1 \cup \cdots \cup \mathrm{gr}_R\,S_n$.

Definition 4.2. Given a spatial atom Σ and a convergent relation R, the *normal form* of Σ with respect to R is the atom Σ_R obtained by (1) replacing each constant symbol x occurring in Σ with its normal form x_R, and then (2) removing any trivial basic atoms of the form $\mathsf{lseg}(x, x)$.

For example, given a relation $R = \{w \Rightarrow y\}$ and an spatial atom $\Sigma \equiv \mathsf{lseg}(x, y) * \mathsf{lseg}(y, w) * \mathsf{lseg}(y, z) * \mathsf{next}(w, y)$, the normalized $\Sigma_R \equiv \mathsf{lseg}(x, y) * \mathsf{lseg}(y, z) * \mathsf{next}(y, y)$, and its graph is given by $\mathrm{gr}_R\,\Sigma = \{\hat{x} \Rightarrow \hat{y}, \hat{y} \Rightarrow \hat{z}, \hat{y} \Rightarrow \hat{y}\}$. As the following lemma shows, this normal form is useful since it allows to quickly determine the relationships between an atom Σ, a relation R and its graph $\mathrm{gr}_R\,\Sigma$.

Lemma 4.1. *Given a spatial atom Σ and a convergent relation R:*

1. $\mathrm{gr}_R\,\Sigma = \mathrm{gr}_R\,\Sigma_R$ *and* $s_R \models \Sigma \leftrightarrow \Sigma_R$*;*
2. *if two constants $x \not\equiv y$ occur in Σ_R, then $R^* \not\models x \simeq y$;*
3. *if Σ_R is well-formed, then $h = \mathrm{gr}_R\,\Sigma$ is a heap and $s_R, h \models \Sigma$;*

Proof. Both claims in the first item follow from the observation that the evaluation $\hat{x} = \hat{s}_R(x) = \hat{s}_R(x_R)$ or, in other words, the stack s_R cannot distinguish between a constant x and its normal form x_R. Furthermore, since trivial atoms the form $\mathsf{lseg}(x, x)$ have an empty graph and are only satisfied by the empty heap, they can be safely removed from Σ_R.

The second item trivially holds since the constants x, y in Σ_R are already in their normal forms and, if $x \not\equiv y$, then $R^* \not\models x \simeq y$.

For the last item let $\Sigma_R \equiv S_1 * \cdots * S_n$, and take $h_i = \mathrm{gr}_R\,S_i$ for each basic spatial atom in Σ_R. Note that if x_i is the address of the basic atom S_i, and since there are no trivial atoms in Σ_R, then necessarily $\mathrm{dom}\,h_i = \{\hat{x}_i\}$. Because Σ_R is well-formed it follows that $h = h_1 * \cdots * h_n$ is indeed a heap (i.e. $\mathsf{nil} \notin \mathrm{dom}\,h$ and any two heaps h_i, h_j with $i \neq j$ have disjoint domains). Moreover, by construction $s_R, h_i \models S_i$ and, therefore, $s_R, h \models \Sigma_R$. But, by definition, $h = \mathrm{gr}_R\,\Sigma_R$ and, from the first item, it follows that both $h = \mathrm{gr}_R\,\Sigma$ and $s_R, h \models \Sigma$ as well. □

Definition 4.3. Given a spatial clause $C \equiv \Gamma \to \Delta, \Sigma$, a relation R is said to *force* the spatial atom Σ, denoted $R, C \rightsquigarrow \Sigma$, if R is not a model of the pure part of the clause, i.e. $R^* \not\models \Gamma \to \Delta$. Similarly, for a clause $C \equiv \Gamma, \Sigma \to \Delta$, we write $R, C \rightsquigarrow \neg\Sigma$ if $R^* \not\models \Gamma \to \Delta$.

Intuitively, if $R, C \rightsquigarrow \Sigma$ (resp. $\neg\Sigma$) then the model induced by R forces the spatial atom Σ to be *true* (resp. *false*) in order to satisfy the clause C. The following three lemmas are at the core of our main result, as they explicate the role of normalization, well-formedness and unfolding inference rules in the $\mathcal{SI}$ proof system.

Lemma 4.2 (Normalization)**.** *Let $\mathcal{S}^*$ be a set of pure clauses saturated with respect to $\mathcal{I}$, let $R = \mathrm{Gen}(\mathcal{S}^*)$, and let C be a spatial clause. If $R, C \rightsquigarrow \Sigma$ (resp. $\neg\Sigma$) then there is a clause C' such that $\mathcal{S}^*, C \vdash_{\mathcal{N}} C'$ and $R, C' \rightsquigarrow \Sigma_R$ (resp. $\neg\Sigma_R$).*

Proof. More generally let $\langle R, g\rangle = \mathrm{Gen}(\mathcal{S}^*)$ be the generated relation and its selection function. By definition, if $R, C \rightsquigarrow \Sigma$ for a clause $C \equiv \Gamma \to \Delta, \Sigma$, then the relation $R \not\models \Gamma \to \Delta$. Now, if there is a constant symbol x occurring in Σ such that $x \not\equiv x_R$, there should be a rule $x \Rightarrow_R y$ for some y and, from Lemma 3.1, a clause $D \equiv g(x \Rightarrow_R y) = \Gamma' \to x \simeq y, \Delta' \in \mathcal{S}^*$ such that $R^* \not\models \Gamma' \to \Delta'$. An application of the normalization rule N1 between C and D yields a clause C_1 such that $\mathcal{S}^*, C \vdash_{\mathcal{N}} C_1$, also $R, C_1 \rightsquigarrow \Sigma[y/x]$ and the spatial atom is *closer* to its normal form. Iterating this process all constant symbols are rewritten to their normal form. Finally, trivial atoms are removed with the rule N2 to yield a clause C' such that $S, C \vdash_{\mathcal{N}} C'$ and $R, C' \rightsquigarrow \Sigma_R$.

An analogous argument using normalization rules N3 and N4 shows that if $R, C \rightsquigarrow \neg\Sigma$ then a clause C' is derived such that $S, C \vdash_{\mathcal{N}} C'$ and $R, C' \rightsquigarrow \neg\Sigma_R$. □

As a result of this lemma, for a spatial clause C we allow ourselves to write $\mathit{Norm}(\langle R, g\rangle; C)$ to denote any such clause C' where the spatial atom Σ has been normalized to Σ_R. Furthermore, from the proof it follows that given the relation R and the clause selection function g, it is possible to compute a normalized C' in a straightforward way without requiring any search.

The following lemma deals with rules for well-formedness, and shows how they ensure that a normalized atom Σ_R is indeed well-formed. To simplify the notation, we use $\mathrm{PCns}_{\mathcal{X}}(\mathcal{S})$ as a shorthand for the set $\mathrm{Pure}(\mathrm{Cns}_{\mathcal{X}}(\mathcal{S}))$ of *pure* clauses that are derived from $\mathcal{S}$ with inferences in $\mathcal{X}$.

Lemma 4.3 (Well-formedness)**.** *Let $\mathcal{S}^*$ be a set of pure clauses saturated with respect to $\mathcal{I}$, let $R = \mathrm{Gen}(\mathcal{S}^*)$, and let C be a spatial clause such that $R, C \rightsquigarrow \Sigma_R$. If $\mathrm{PCns}_{\mathcal{W}}(\{C\}) \subseteq \mathcal{S}^*$ and $\square \notin \mathcal{S}^*$ then Σ_R is well-formed.*

Proof. Since $R, C \rightsquigarrow \Sigma_R$, the clause C is of the form $\Gamma \to \Delta, \Sigma_R$ and $R^* \not\models \Gamma \to \Delta$. Moreover, since $\square \notin \mathcal{S}^*$, by Theorem 3.1 the relation $R^* \models \mathcal{S}^*$ and, by hypothesis, $R^* \models \mathrm{PCns}_{\mathcal{W}}(\{C\})$.

Now, if Σ_R were not well-formed then one of the inference rules in $\mathcal{W}$ would apply—either W1 or W2 if there is a nil address in Σ_R, or one of W3, W4 or W5 if there are two basic spatial atoms with the same address—to derive a pure clause D such that $C \vdash_{\mathcal{W}} D$ but $R^* \not\models D$, and thus contradicting the fact that the relation $R^* \models \mathrm{PCns}_{\mathcal{W}}(\{C\})$.

For example, if there is a basic atom $\mathsf{lseg}(\mathsf{nil}, y)$ occurring in Σ_R then $\mathsf{nil} \not\equiv y$, because the atom is not trivial, and by Lemma 4.1 it follows that $R^* \not\models \mathsf{nil} \simeq y$. Applying the rule W2 to C, a pure clause is derived such that $R^* \not\models \Gamma \to \mathsf{nil} \simeq y, \Delta$. □

Observe that there is no search involved in the computation of $\mathrm{PCns}_{\mathcal{W}}(\{C\})$, as it is enough to match C against the premises of rules in $\mathcal{W}$ to immediately compute its consequences. Finally, the last of these lemmas formalzes the application of unfolding inferences in the proof system $\mathcal{SI}$.

Lemma 4.4 (Unfolding). *Let $\mathcal{S}^*$ be a set of pure clauses saturated with respect to $\mathcal{I}$, let $R = \mathrm{Gen}(\mathcal{S}^*)$, and let C, C' be spatial clauses such that $R, C \rightsquigarrow \Sigma_R$ and $R, C' \rightsquigarrow \neg\Sigma'_R$. If the set $\mathrm{PCns}_{\mathcal{U}}(\{C, C'\}) \subseteq \mathcal{S}^*$, $\Box \notin \mathcal{S}^*$, and Σ_R is well-formed, then there is an h such that $s_R, h \not\models \Sigma \to \Sigma'$.*

Proof. Since the atom Σ_R is well-formed, from Lemma 4.1, it follows that $s_R, h \models \Sigma_R$ where $h = \mathrm{gr}_R\, \Sigma_R$. Now, if $s_R, h \not\models \Sigma'_R$ we are done, as our h satisfies the conditions of the lemma.

Assume that otherwise, $s_R, h \models \Sigma'_R$. Now, take the normalized atom $\Sigma'_R \equiv S'_1 * \cdots * S'_n$ with no trivial basic atoms, it follows that the graph $h = \mathrm{gr}_R\, \Sigma_R = h'_1 * \cdots * h'_n$ for some non-empty heaps h'_i such that $s_R, h'_i \models S'_i$. In particular, since $\mathrm{gr}_R\, \Sigma_R$ is the separated union of graphs for basic atoms in Σ_R, for each h'_i there is an atom T_i occurring in Σ_R for which $h'_i = \mathrm{gr}_R\, T_i$ and, moreover, the spatial atom $\Sigma_R \equiv T_1 * \cdots * T_n$.

We now show that either: (a) unfolding inference rules are able to derive from $\{C, C'\}$ a clause C'' such that $R, C'' \rightsquigarrow \neg\Sigma_R$ by 'rewriting'each atom S'_i in Σ'_R into the corresponding T_i in Σ_R or (b) h can be fixed to satisfy the statement of the theorem. Proceed for each S'_i as follows:

- $S'_i \equiv \mathsf{next}(x, y)$. Then the graph $\mathrm{gr}_R\, T_i\colon \hat{x} \Rightarrow \hat{y}$ is an edge and the spatial atom $T_i \equiv \mathsf{f}(x, y)$. If the symbol $\mathsf{f} \equiv \mathsf{next}$ then, since $S'_i \equiv T_i$, the atom S_i has been rewritten into T_i. For the alternative, $\mathsf{f} \equiv \mathsf{lseg}$, the case (b) holds since then the pair $(s_R, h[\hat{x} \Rightarrow w; w \Rightarrow \hat{y}])$, where $w \notin \mathrm{dom}\, h$, would be a model of Σ but not of Σ'.
- $S'_i \equiv \mathsf{lseg}(x, z)$. Then the graph $\mathrm{gr}_R\, T_i\colon \hat{x} \Rightarrow^* \hat{z}$ is a simple path and the spatial atom $T_i \equiv \mathsf{f}_1(x_1, x_2) * \cdots * \mathsf{f}_k(x_k, z)$ where $x_1 \equiv x$. For each $1 \leq j \leq k$, let

  $$T_{i,j} = \mathsf{f}_1(x_1, x_2) * \cdots * \mathsf{f}_{j-1}(x_{j-1}, x_j) * \mathsf{lseg}(x_j, z)\ ,$$

  i.e. the first $j - 1$ basic spatial atoms from T_i followed by the atom $\mathsf{lseg}(x_j, z)$. Note that $T_{i,1} \equiv S'_i$, while $T_{i,k}$ is identical to T_i except possibly for f_k. For each $1 \leq j < k$ we will prove that if $\{C, C'\} \vdash_{\mathcal{U}} C_j$ for a clause such that $R, C_j \rightsquigarrow \neg\Sigma_R[T_{i,j}/S'_i]$; then a clause C_{j+1} such that $R, C_{j+1} \rightsquigarrow \neg\Sigma_R[T_{i,j+1}/S'_i]$ can be derived by unfolding S'_i and 'walking' over T_i according to the following two cases:
  - $\mathsf{f}_j \equiv \mathsf{next}$. Since $x_j \not\equiv z$ because the graph of T_i is a simple path, $R^* \not\models x_j \simeq z$ and the rule U2 rewrites $T_{i,j}$ into $T_{i,j+1}$.
  - $\mathsf{f}_j \equiv \mathsf{lseg}$. If $z \not\equiv \mathsf{nil}$ then the inference rule U3 does the rewrite, and if z is the address of an atom in Σ_R then either U4 or U5 should apply. In the remaining case—when the symbol $y \not\equiv \mathsf{nil}$, z is not the address of any basic atom in Σ_R and therefore $\hat{z} \notin \mathrm{dom}\, h$—again (b) holds since then the interpretation $(s_R, h[\hat{y}_{k_1} \Rightarrow \hat{z}; \hat{z} \Rightarrow \hat{y}_k])$ is a model of Σ and not of Σ'.

  So we have shown that it is possible to rewrite S'_i into $T_{i,k}$, which is identical to T_i except if $\mathsf{f}_k \equiv \mathsf{next}$. But in such case, since $x_k \not\equiv z$, the unfolding rule U1 rewrites $T_{i,k}$ into T_i.

From the previous argument if (b) is proved then again we are done, otherwise the rewrite in (a) is successful and we derive a clause C'' such that $R, C'' \rightsquigarrow \neg\Sigma_R$. But from hypothesis we also had $R, C \rightsquigarrow \Sigma_R$ and an application of the spatial resolution rule SR derives a pure clause D such that $R^* \not\models D$. However this is a contradiction, since by construction $D \in \mathrm{PCns}_{\mathcal{U}}(\{C, C'\}) \subseteq \mathcal{S}^*$, and the relation R was supposed to be a model of D. $\Box$

One more time, from the argument of the proof it follows that there is no search required in order to compute the clauses, if any, in the set $\mathrm{PCns}_{\mathcal{U}}(\{C, C'\})$. This is a key property of our proof system: since $R, C \rightsquigarrow \Sigma_R$ and Σ_R is normalized, the basic atoms in Σ_R guide the application of unfolding inferences in a deterministic manner; *thus eliminating the nondeterminism due to the associativity-commutativity of the separating conjunction.* After having finished the proofs of these lemmas, we are ready to show the completeness of our proof system $\mathcal{SI}$.

```
 1: function prove(Π ∧ Σ → Π' ∧ Σ')
 2:   S := Pure(cnf(Π ∧ Σ → Π' ∧ Σ'))
 3:   do
 4:     repeat
 5:       S* := Cns_I(S)
 6:       if □ ∈ S* return valid
 7:       ⟨R, g⟩ := Gen(S*)
 8:       C := Norm(⟨R, g⟩; ∅ → Σ)
 9:       S := S* ∪ PCns_W({C})
10:     until S = S*
11:     if R ⊭ Π' return c-example(S*, C)
12:     C' := Norm(⟨R, g⟩; Π'+, Σ' → Π'−)
13:     S := S* ∪ PCns_U({C, C'})
14:     if S = S* return c-example(S*, C, C')
15:   loop
```

Figure 3. Algorithm for entailment checking

Theorem 4.2 (Completeness). *Let $E \equiv \Pi \wedge \Sigma \to \Pi' \wedge \Sigma'$ be an entailment, and let $\mathcal{S}^* = \mathrm{Cns}_{\mathcal{SI}}(\mathrm{cnf}(E))$. If $\Box \notin \mathcal{S}^*$ then the entailment is not valid (i.e. there is a counterexample).*

Proof. Let $\mathcal{S}^*_{\simeq} = \mathrm{Pure}(\mathcal{S}^*)$ be the subset of the pure clauses in the saturated set $\mathcal{S}^*$. Since $\Box \notin \mathcal{S}^*$ then neither $\Box \notin \mathcal{S}^*_{\simeq}$ and, by Theorem 3.1, the relation R is a model of $\mathcal{S}^*_{\simeq}$. Moreover, from the definition of $\mathrm{cnf}(E)$, the relation $R^* \models \Pi$.

Since the clause $C \equiv \emptyset \to \Sigma \in \mathrm{cnf}(E)$, and $R^* \not\models \Box$ we have that $R, C \rightsquigarrow \Sigma$. From Lemma 4.2, it follows that there is a spatial clause C_{n}, derived by normalization inferences, such that $R, C_{\mathsf{n}} \rightsquigarrow \Sigma_R$. Furthermore, since $\Box \notin \mathcal{S}^*_{\simeq}$ and $\mathcal{S}^*$ is already saturated with respect to $\mathcal{W}$ rules, by Lemma 4.3 it follows that the spatial atom Σ_R is well-formed. Then, from Lemma 4.1, there is a heap h such that $s_R, h \models \Sigma$. Also, since $R^* \models \Pi$, from Theorem 3.2 we get that $s_R, h \models \Pi$. Indeed the pair (s_R, h) is a model of $\Pi \wedge \Sigma$.

Now, if $R^* \not\models \Pi'$ we are done since, also from Theorem 3.2, $s_R, h \not\models \Pi'$ and we have found a counterexample. Otherwise, if $R^* \models \Pi'$ then, equivalently, $R^* \not\models \Pi'{+} \to \Pi'{-}$ and, since the clause $C' \equiv \Pi'{+}, \Sigma \to \Pi'{-} \in \mathrm{cnf}(E)$, we have that $R, C' \rightsquigarrow \neg\Sigma$. Again by Lemma 4.2 there is a clause C'_{n} derived from C' by normalization rules such that $R, C'_{\mathsf{n}} \rightsquigarrow \neg\Sigma'_R$. In this case all the assumptions of Lemma 4.4 are satisfied and a suitable h' such that the pair (s_R, h') invalidates the entailment should therefore exist. $\Box$

5. Algorithm for entailment checking

In the previous section we established the soundness and completeness of our proof system for the fragment of separation logic under consideration. We now turn our attention to use the insight gained in the construction of such a proof, in order to build an efficient algorithm for proving the validity of entailments.

Along the lines of the proof of completeness, the algorithm for checking an entailment $E \equiv \Pi \wedge \Sigma \to \Pi' \wedge \Sigma'$, which is given as pseudocode in Figure 3, emerges from a careful interleaving of inferences using: superposition reasoning for pure clauses (line 5), normalization inferences (lines 8 and 12), well-formedness inferences (line 9), and unfolding inferences (line 13).

The algorithm works by incrementally building a set $\mathcal{S}$ with all the *pure* clauses that are derived from $\mathrm{cnf}(E)$. Initially $\mathcal{S}$ is set

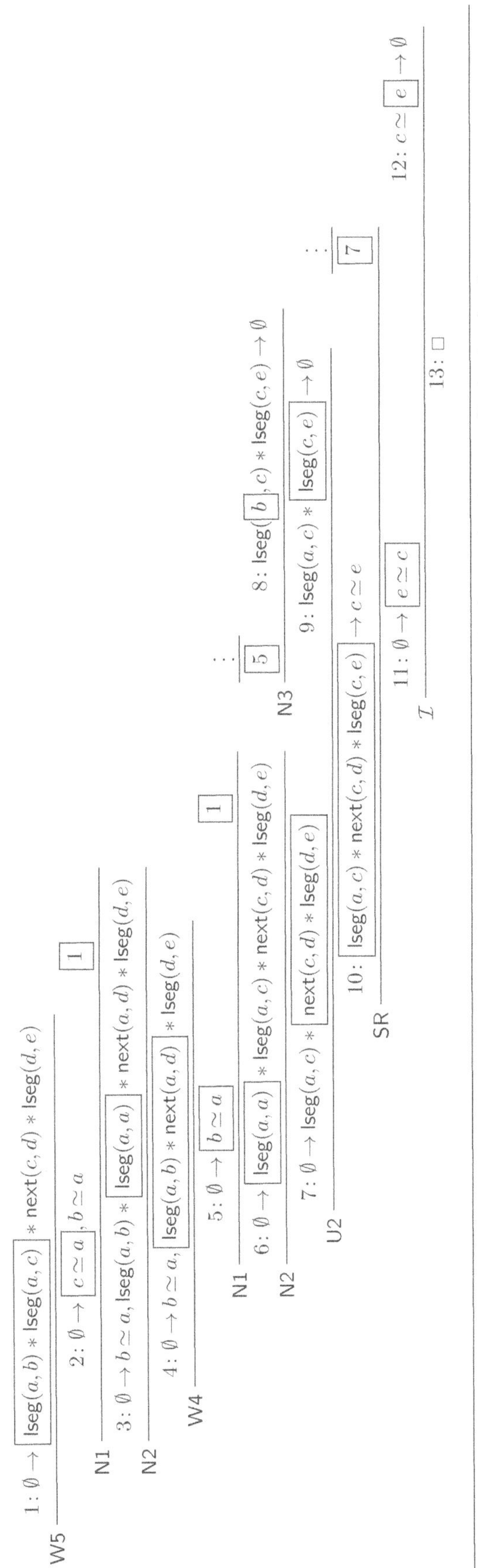

Figure 4. Proof tree for the entailment: $c \not\simeq e \wedge \mathsf{lseg}(a,b) * \mathsf{lseg}(a,c) * \mathsf{next}(c,d) * \mathsf{lseg}(d,e) \to \mathsf{lseg}(b,c) * \mathsf{lseg}(c,e)$

to the subset of pure clauses in the clausal embedding of E, i.e. $\mathcal{S} := \{\emptyset \to A \mid A \in \Pi+\} \cup \{A \to \emptyset \mid A \in \Pi-\}$.

The inner loop in lines 4–10 will first saturate the set $\mathcal{S}$ with superposition inferences using the proof system $\mathcal{I}$ and, if the empty clause is derived in such process, the entailment is proved as valid. Otherwise the algorithm continues using the pair $\langle R, g\rangle$ generated from the saturated set $\mathcal{S}^*$ to normalize the clause $\emptyset \to \Sigma \in \mathrm{cnf}(E)$ into a clause of the form $C := \Gamma \to \Sigma_R, \Delta$. Finally $\mathcal{S}$ is updated with the set of pure clauses that are derived from C using well-formedness inference rules in $\mathcal{W}$. The loop repeats until either the entailment is proved valid, or a fixpoint is reached when $\mathcal{S} = \mathcal{S}^*$. Moreover, in the later case, we know that the spatial atom Σ_R in C must be well-formed.

If we exit the inner loop, the clause $\Pi'_+, \Sigma' \to \Pi'_- \in \mathrm{cnf}(E)$ is then normalized to a clause of the form $C' := \Gamma', \Sigma'_R \to \Delta'$, and pure clauses derived from $\{C, C'\}$ using unfolding inference rules in $\mathcal{U}$ are added to $\mathcal{S}$. If no new clauses are derived, then from Lemma 4.4 it is possible to build a counterexample for the entailment. Otherwise a new pure clause has been discovered and the main loop of the function iterates.

Theorem 5.1. *The function* prove(E) *in Figure 3 terminates, is sound and complete.*

Proof. Soundness of the algorithm immediately follows from the soundness of the $\mathcal{SI}$ proof system. And the algorithm terminates since the growing set $\mathcal{S}$ is bounded by $\mathrm{PCns}_{\mathcal{SI}}(E)$, which is itself bounded by the finite number of distinct pure clauses which can be written with the constant symbols occurring in E.

Completeness follows from the following invariants: The normalized clause C computed in line 8 satisfies $R, C \rightsquigarrow \Sigma_R$ (c.f. Lemma 4.2); after exiting the inner loop in line 10 also $R, C \rightsquigarrow \Sigma_R$ and Σ_R is well-formed (c.f. Lemma 4.3). In particular, upon exiting the loop, it is proved that $\Pi \wedge \Sigma$ is satisfiable by a model (s_R, h); if at this point $R^* \not\models \Pi'$ we have found a counterexample. Otherwise the C' computed in line 12 satisfies $R, C \rightsquigarrow \Sigma'_R$ (c.f. Lemma 4.2); and if after line 13 a fix-point is detected, we have also found a counterexample (c.f. Lemma 4.4). □

In order to get a more concrete feeling of how the algorithm works, let us run again through the example from Section 2 to establish the validity of the entailment E given by

$$c \not\simeq e \wedge \mathsf{lseg}(a,b) * \mathsf{lseg}(a,c) * \mathsf{next}(c,d) * \mathsf{lseg}(d,e) \to \mathsf{lseg}(b,c) * \mathsf{lseg}(c,e)\ .$$

The algorithm begins with $\mathcal{S} = \{D_1\}$, where $D_1 \equiv c \simeq e \to \emptyset$ is the only pure clause in $\mathrm{cnf}(E)$. Then $\mathcal{S}^* = \mathrm{Cns}_{\mathcal{I}}(\mathcal{S}) = \mathcal{S}$ is trivially computed. No clauses are selected since $R = \mathrm{Gen}(\mathcal{S}^*) = \emptyset$ is a model of $\mathcal{S}^*$; and normalization leaves the clause $C := \emptyset \to \Sigma$, where $\Sigma \equiv \mathsf{lseg}(a,b) * \mathsf{lseg}(a,c) * \mathsf{next}(c,d) * \mathsf{lseg}(d,e)$, intact.

Now the well-formedness rule W5 derives from C a new pure clause $D_2 \equiv \emptyset \to a \simeq b, a \simeq c$. The inner loop iterates and the saturated set $\mathcal{S}^* := \mathrm{Cns}_{\mathcal{I}}(\{D_1, D_2\})$ is computed. Assume an order $a \prec b \prec c$ and thus, D_2 is selected to generate the relation $R = \mathrm{Gen}(\mathcal{S}^*) = \{c \Rightarrow a\}$. Now normalization rewrites the input clause $\emptyset \to \Sigma$ into $C := \emptyset \to a \simeq b, \Sigma_R$, where the spatial atom $\Sigma_R \equiv \mathsf{lseg}(a,b) * \mathsf{next}(a,d) * \mathsf{lseg}(d,e)$.

This time, the inference rule W4 derives from C a third pure clause $D_3 \equiv \emptyset \to a \simeq b$. Another iteration of the inner loop now updates $\mathcal{S}^* := \mathrm{Cns}_{\mathcal{I}}(\{D_1, D_2, D_3\})$, which are satisfied by selecting D_3 and producing $R = \mathrm{Gen}(\mathcal{S}^*) = \{b \Rightarrow a\}$; while normalization rewrites the input clause $\emptyset \to \Sigma$ into $C := \emptyset \to \Sigma_R$ where $\Sigma_R \equiv \mathsf{lseg}(a,c) * \mathsf{next}(c,d) * \mathsf{lseg}(d,e)$.

At this point no more well-formedness rules in $\mathcal{W}$ apply, we have reached a fixpoint. Note that, indeed, Σ_R is finally a well-formed atom. We exit the inner loop and proceed to normalize the

				Time (secs.)		
Vars.	P_{lseg}	$P_{\not\simeq}$	% Valid	jStar	Smallfoot	SLP
10	0.10	0.20	54	300.08	13.46	1.02
11	0.09	0.15	50	(16%)	27.02	1.06
12	0.09	0.11	54	(3%)	86.75	1.46
13	0.08	0.11	55	(1%)	119.66	1.48
14	0.07	0.11	53	(10%)	153.93	1.74
15	0.06	0.12	52	(8%)	155.72	1.73
16	0.05	0.17	50	(9%)	140.95	1.59
17	0.05	0.13	54	(3%)	258.31	2.15
18	0.04	0.20	49	(11%)	176.46	1.88
19	0.04	0.15	50	(5%)	383.26	2.15
20	0.04	0.11	52	(0%)	(90%)	2.65

Table 1. Benchmarking 1000 random instances of $F \to \bot$.

				Time (secs.)	
Vars.	P_{next}	% Valid	jStar	Smallfoot	SLP
10	0.70	53	(10%)	28.50	1.29
11	0.69	53	(3%)	56.72	1.24
12	0.69	53	(1%)	106.69	1.49
13	0.70	53	(1%)	166.53	1.82
14	0.69	53	(0%)	271.48	2.19
15	0.69	52	(0%)	404.61	2.49
16	0.69	49	(0%)	(80%)	2.68
17	0.71	53	(0%)	(79%)	3.06
18	0.70	49	(0%)	(49%)	3.60
19	0.70	53	(0%)	(30%)	3.65
20	0.70	49	(0%)	(19%)	3.87

Table 2. Benchmarking 1000 random instances of $F \to G$.

clause $\mathsf{lseg}(b, c) * \mathsf{lseg}(c, e) \to \emptyset \in \mathrm{cnf}(E)$ into the corresponding clause $C' := \Sigma'_R \to \emptyset$ where $\Sigma'_R \equiv \mathsf{lseg}(a, c) * \mathsf{lseg}(c, e)$. Then the application of unfolding is successful since, from C and C', we derive the new pure clause $D_4 \equiv \emptyset \to e \simeq c$, add it to $\mathcal{S}$, and start a new iteration of the main loop.

However now the set $\mathcal{S}^* = \mathrm{Cns}_{\mathcal{I}}(\mathcal{S})$ is inconsistent, since the clauses $D_1, D_4 \in \mathcal{S}$ are contradictory and therefore $\square \in \mathcal{S}^*$. This proves that the original entailment E is indeed valid. Furthermore, from the run of this algorithm it is possible to reconstruct a proof for the unsatisfiability of $\mathrm{cnf}(E)$, which is shown in Figure 4. The figure shows how the empty clause $\square$ is derived from the set of input clauses $\mathrm{cnf}(E)$ using the appropriate inference rules from the $\mathcal{SI}$ proof system. Each derived clause is numbered, and vertical dots are used to denote the reuse of a clause previously derived in the tree. The 'active' part of each clause, on which the respective inference operates, is also highlighted with a frame box.

6. Experimental evaluation

In order to empirically evaluate of the algorithm that we described in the previous section, we implemented a theorem proving tool for separation logic entailments that we call SLP. The tool is implemented in Prolog and consists of about a hundred lines of code to encode the logic of the algorithm in Figure 3 together with a declarative specification of the inference rules of the $\mathcal{SI}$ proof system. The pure model finder is implemented in about fifty lines of code, and an additional four hundred lines are for reading the program input, encoding into and manipulating internal data structures, as well as pretty printing.

	Time (secs.)		
Copies	jStar	Smallfoot	SLP
1	0.30	0.01	0.11
2	0.37	0.07	0.06
3	0.89	1.03	0.08
4	2.65	9.53	0.13
5	9.44	55.85	0.38
6	38.09	245.69	2.37
7	166.86	(64%)	20.83
8	(30%)	(15%)	212.17

Table 3. Benchmarking 'clones' of Smallfoot examples.

In a series of benchmarks, we compare the performance of our tool with two other available state-of-the-art verification tools: Smallfoot [6], and jStar [16]. Both of these tools take as input annotated functions with pre- and post-conditions (respectively in C or in Java) and, through a process of symbolic execution, generate a number of verification conditions that have to be discharged in order to prove the validity of the program specifications.

Each of this verifications conditions corresponds to an entailment check which could be alternatively discharged by our tool. Note that, currently, SLP does not perform verification or symbolic execution or programs. Indeed, what we want to compare is only the performance of SLP against the entailment checkers implemented in Smallfoot and jStar. This is easily done with jStar, which provides a command `run_logic` with direct access to the prover; while, in the case of Smallfoot, queries to the entailment checker can be faked with minimal overhead by asking it to verify no-op functions of the form

`fun(`*vars*`) [`F`] { } [`G`]`

which are valid if, and only if, the entailment $F \to G$ holds.

In order to benchmark these separation logic provers on a wide class of formulas with increasing complexity, we first generated some synthetic entailments according to two different random distributions. The first of these distributions generates entailment checks of the form $\Pi \wedge \Sigma \to \bot$, with n program variables from the set $\mathsf{Var} = \{x_1, \ldots, x_n\}$, as follows:

- if $i \neq j$, with probability P_{lseg} include $\mathsf{lseg}(x_i, x_j)$ in Σ;
- if $i < j$, with probability $P_{\not\simeq}$ include $x_i \not\simeq x_j$ in Π.

Note that lseg edges, as well as pure inequalities, are chosen at random independently of each other. Furthermore, this kind of entailments can be proved (or refuted) by superposition, normalization and well-formedness rules only (i.e. the inner loop in the algorithm of Figure 3). Specifically: if these rules are able to prove that $\Pi \wedge \Sigma$ is inconsistent, then the entailment is valid; conversely if these rules are enough to build a model for $\Pi \wedge \Sigma$, then the entailment has a counterexample.

Moreover, note that for fixed values of n and P_{lseg}, we can use the parameter $P_{\not\simeq}$ to tune the proportion of generated entailments that turn out to be valid. When $P_{\not\simeq} = 0$, then Π is empty, there is a trivial model for Σ—the one which makes all variables equal to nil—and the entailment is invalid. Conversely, if $P_{\not\simeq}$ is high enough, adding inequalities between pairs of variables constrains the space of models for $\Pi \wedge \Sigma$ to the point where, with high probability, it becomes empty and renders the entailment valid. We use this feature to calibrate the model so that, roughly, about half of the generated entailments are valid.

Each row in Table 1 shows the time spent by each of the provers—jStar, Smallfoot, and SLP—to check 1000 randomly generated entailments with parameters ranging from 10 to 20 variables. Each time the provers were run with a single input file containing all the entailments to check, so that we don't have to pay the time of starting up the process a thousand times. When a prover timed out after 10 minutes of execution, we show in parenthesis the percentage of the instances that were successfully solved before hitting the time limit. SLP outperforms the other proves by several orders of magnitude, solving thousands of instances not in minutes but in a few seconds.

Our second random distribution stresses the role of unfolding inferences in the entailment checks. Again we assume a fixed set of n program variables $\mathsf{Var} = \{x_1, \ldots, x_n\}$, and we let π be a random permutation of the indices of these variables such that $\pi(i) \neq i$. Then the spatial atom

$$\Sigma = \mathsf{f}(x_1, x_{\pi(1)}) * \cdots * \mathsf{f}(x_n, x_{\pi(n)})$$

where each f is randomly selected as either next, with probability p_{next}, or lseg, with probability $1 - p_{\mathsf{next}}$. Note that in this case, by construction, Σ is already well-formed. Now Σ' starts as a copy of Σ, and then we randomly 'fold' some paths in Σ'. For this we randomly pick a variable x_i and, if it appears as the address of a basic atom that has not been folded yet, the longest path stating from x_i by yet unfolded atoms is completely folded into an atom $\mathsf{lseg}(x_i, x_i^*)$, where x_i^* is the last variable reached through this path. This operation is repeated until all basic atoms have been folded. Finally we ask to provers to check the validity of $\Sigma \to \Sigma'$.

In this case the parameter p_{next} can be used to tune the proportion of valid and invalid entailments. Table 2 shows the time spent by the provers checking 1000 randomly generated entailments with parameters ranging from 10 to 20 variables. Again SLP outperforms the other provers, which have trouble figuring out the correct unfolding required to prove/disprove each of these entailments.

Our last set of benchmarks comes from the examples included in the Smallfoot distribution. This includes some 18 'real-life' list manipulating programs, along with some specifications to prove. Note that these also include some examples with arbitrary data fields (other than a next pointer) which our implementation can already handle. This involves slight modifications to the $\mathcal{SI}$ rules, not shown for brevity. For the verification of all of these programs, Smallfoot generates about 209 verification conditions that have to be discharged. These are actually some rather simple entailments to check, as all the three separation logic provers are able to tackle them all in under a second.[1] In order to create more challenging benchmarks, which still have some resemblance with those arising from real-life applications, we make use of a simple 'cloning' technique. For each verification condition $\Pi \wedge \Sigma \to \Pi' \wedge \Sigma'$ generated by Smallfoot, we generate the equivalent but more challenging

$$\Pi_1 \wedge \cdots \wedge \Pi_n \wedge \Sigma_1 * \cdots * \Sigma_n \\ \to \Pi'_1 \wedge \cdots \wedge \Pi'_n \wedge \Sigma'_1 * \cdots * \Sigma'_n$$

where each Π_i, Σ_i, Π'_i, and Σ'_i, is a copy of the formulas in the original entailment with their variables renamed appart.

Table 3 shows the running time spent by the provers trying to prove or refute these 209 entailments. In this case, jStar seems to fare better than Smallfoot, however recall that jStar is incomplete and fails to prove 59 of the entailments which are actually valid. Nevertheless, SLP, which is both sound and complete, outperforms the other two provers in all of the cases.

[1] With the caveat that the logic rules provided with jStar are incomplete for the fragment of separation logic under consideration (personal communication with D. Distefano) and, therefore, unable to prove the validity of 59 of these entailments.

7. Conclusions

In this paper we developed a proof system $\mathcal{SI}$ for proving the validity of separation logic entailments with list predicates. A key result from this development is a separation from the reasoning required to deal with pure equality predicates, and the reasoning required to manipulate the spatial information of such formulas. This enabled the design of an efficient, sound, and complete algorithm for this kind of entailments, which leverages techniques that have been developed in the theorem proving community from the past three to four decades. The effectiveness of our proposed algorithm is demonstrated by the implementation of a tool, SLP, which indicates speedups of orders of magnitudes with respect to the available state-of-the-art. We expect these ideas to prove fruitful in the further development and automation of program analysis and verification techniques for heap manipulating programs.

References

[1] T. Ball, R. Majumdar, T. D. Millstein, and S. K. Rajamani. Automatic predicate abstraction of c programs. In *PLDI*, pages 203–213, 2001.

[2] C. Barrett and C. Tinelli. CVC3. In *CAV*, pages 298–302, 2007.

[3] P. Baumgartner and U. Waldmann. Superposition and model evolution combined. In *CADE*, pages 17–34, 2009.

[4] J. Berdine, C. Calcagno, and P. W. O'Hearn. A decidable fragment of separation logic. In *FSTTCS*, number 3328 in LNCS, pages 97–109, 2004.

[5] J. Berdine, C. Calcagno, and P. W. O'Hearn. Symbolic execution with separation logic. In *APLAS*, pages 52–68, 2005.

[6] J. Berdine, C. Calcagno, and P. W. O'Hearn. Smallfoot: Modular automatic assertion checking with separation logic. In *FMCO*, 2006.

[7] J. Berdine, C. Calcagno, B. Cook, D. Distefano, P. W. O'Hearn, T. Wies, and H. Yang. Shape analysis for composite data structures. In *CAV*, pages 178–192, 2007.

[8] B. Blanchet, P. Cousot, R. Cousot, J. Feret, L. Mauborgne, A. Miné, D. Monniaux, and X. Rival. A static analyzer for large safety-critical software. In *PLDI*, pages 196–207, 2003.

[9] C. Bouillaguet, V. Kuncak, T. Wies, K. Zee, and M. C. Rinard. Using first-order theorem provers in the Jahob data structure verification system. In *VMCAI*, pages 74–88, 2007.

[10] R. Bruttomesso, A. Cimatti, A. Franzén, A. Griggio, and R. Sebastiani. The MathSAT 4SMT solver. In *CAV*, pages 299–303, 2008.

[11] C. Calcagno, M. Parkinson, and V. Vafeiadis. SmallfootRG. In *SAS*, pages 233–238, 2007.

[12] C. Calcagno, D. Distefano, P. O'Hearn, and H. Yang. Compositional shape analysis by means of bi-abduction. In *POPL*, pages 289–300, 2009.

[13] B.-Y. E. Chang and X. Rival. Relational inductive shape analysis. In *POPL*, pages 247–260, 2008.

[14] L. M. de Moura and N. Bjørner. Z3: An efficient SMT solver. In *TACAS*, 2008.

[15] L. M. de Moura and N. Bjørner. Tapas theory combinations and practical applications. In *FORMATS*, 2009.

[16] D. Distefano and M. Parkinson. jStar: Towards practical verification for Java. In *OOPSLA*, pages 213–226, 2008.

[17] D. Distefano, P. W. O'Hearn, and H. Yang. A local shape analysis based on separation logic. In *TACAS*, pages 287–302, 2006.

[18] R. Dockins, A. Hobor, and A. W. Appel. A fresh look at separation algebras and share accounting. In *APLAS*, pages 161–177, 2009.

[19] B. Dutertre and L. D. Moura. The Yices SMT solver. Technical report, Computer Science Laboratory, SRI International, 2006.

[20] C. Flanagan, K. R. M. Leino, M. Lillibridge, G. Nelson, J. B. Saxe, and R. Stata. Extended static checking for Java. In *PLDI*, pages 234–245, 2002.

[21] D. Gay and A. Aiken. Memory management with explicit regions. In *PLDI*, pages 313–323, 1998.

[22] T. A. Henzinger, R. Jhala, R. Majumdar, and G. Sutre. Lazy abstraction. In *POPL*, pages 58–70, 2002.

[23] B. Jacobs and F. Piessens. The VeriFast program verifier. Technical Report CW-520, Katholieke Universiteit Leuven, Belgium, 2008.

[24] K. Korovin and A. Voronkov. Integrating linear arithmetic into superposition calculus. In *Computer Science Logic (CSL'07)*, volume 4646 of *Lecture Notes in Computer Science*, pages 223–237. Springer, 2007.

[25] N. Marti and R. Affeldt. A certified verifier for a fragment of separation logic. *Computer Software*, 25(3):135–147, 2008.

[26] M. Méndez-Lojo and M. V. Hermenegildo. Precise set sharing analysis for Java-style programs. In *VMCAI*, pages 172–187, 2008.

[27] A. Møller and M. I. Schwartzbach. The pointer assertion logic engine. In *PLDI*, pages 221–231, 2001.

[28] A. Nanevski, G. Morrisett, A. Shinnar, P. Govereau, and L. Birkedal. Ynot: Dependent types for imperative programs. In *ICFP*, pages 229–240, 2008.

[29] H. H. Nguyen, V. Kuncak, and W.-N. Chin. Runtime checking for separation logic. In *VMCAI*, pages 203–217, 2008.

[30] R. Nieuwenhuis and A. Rubio. Paramodulation-based theorem proving. In J. A. Robinson and A. Voronkov, editors, *Handbook of Automated Reasoning*, volume I, chapter 7, pages 371–443. Elsevier, 2001.

[31] A. Podelski and T. Wies. Boolean heaps. In *SAS*, pages 268–283, 2005.

[32] A. Podelski and T. Wies. Counterexample-guided focus. In *POPL*, pages 249–260, 2010.

[33] J. Reynolds. Separation logic: A logic for shared mutable data structures. In *LICS*, pages 55–74, 2002.

[34] M. C. Rinard. Integrated reasoning and proof choice point selection in the Jahob system — mechanisms for program survival. In *CADE*, pages 1–16, 2009.

[35] S. Sagiv, T. W. Reps, and R. Wilhelm. Parametric shape analysis via 3-valued logic. *ACM Trans. Program. Lang. Syst.*, 24(3):217–298, 2002.

[36] J. Villard, É. Lozes, and C. Calcagno. Tracking heaps that hop with Heap-Hop. In *TACAS*, pages 275–279, 2010.

[37] H. Yang. An example of local reasoning in bi pointer logic: the schorr-waite graph marking algorithm. In *SPACE workshop*, 2001.

[38] H. Yang, O. Lee, J. Berdine, C. Calcagno, B. Cook, D. Distefano, and P. W. O'Hearn. Scalable shape analysis for systems code. In *CAV*, pages 385–398, 2008.

Precise and Compact Modular Procedure Summaries for Heap Manipulating Programs *

Isil Dillig
Department of Computer Science
Stanford University
isil@cs.stanford.edu

Thomas Dillig
Department of Computer Science
Stanford University
tdillig@cs.stanford.edu

Alex Aiken
Department of Computer Science
Stanford University
aiken@cs.stanford.edu

Mooly Sagiv
Department of Computer Science
Tel Aviv University
msagiv@post.tau.ac.il

Abstract

We present a strictly bottom-up, summary-based, and precise heap analysis targeted for program verification that performs strong updates to heap locations at call sites. We first present a theory of heap decompositions that forms the basis of our approach; we then describe a full analysis algorithm that is fully symbolic and efficient. We demonstrate the precision and scalability of our approach for verification of real C and C++ programs.

Categories and Subject Descriptors D.2.4 [*Software Engineering*]: Software/Program Verification

General Terms Languages, Verification, Experimentation

1. Introduction

It is well-known that precise static reasoning about the heap is a key requirement for successful verification of real-world software. In standard imperative languages, such as Java, C, and C++, much of the interesting computation happens as values flow in and out of the heap, making it crucial to use a precise, context- and flow-sensitive heap analysis in program verification tools. Flow-sensitivity, in particular, enables *strong updates*. Informally, when analyzing an assignment `a := b`, a strong update replaces the analysis information for `a` with the analysis information for `b`. This natural rule is unsound if `a` is a *summary location*, meaning `a` may represent more than one concrete location. In previous work there is an apparent tension between scalability and precision in heap analysis:

- For scalability, it is desirable to analyze the program in pieces, for example, one function at a time. Many of the most scalable analyses in the literature are modular [1, 2].
- For precision, a large body of empirical evidence shows it is necessary to perform strong updates wherever possible [3, 4].

It is not obvious, however, how to perform strong updates in a modular heap analysis. Consider a function $\mathtt{h}(\mathtt{x}, \mathtt{y})\{\mathtt{e}\}$. When analyzing `h` in isolation, we do not know how many, or which, locations `x` and `y` may point to at a call site of `h`—it may be many (if either `x` or `y` is a summary location), two, or even one (if `x` and `y` are aliases). Without this information, we cannot safely apply strong updates to `x` and `y` in `e`. Thus, while there is a large body of existing work on flow- and context-sensitive heap analysis, most algorithms for this purpose either perform a whole-program analysis or perform strong updates under very restrictive conditions.

In this paper, we present a modular, strictly bottom-up, flow- and context-sensitive heap analysis that uses summaries to apply strong updates to heap locations at call sites. As corraborated by our experiments, strong updates are crucial for the level of precision required for successful verification. Furthermore, we are interested in a modular, summary-based analysis because it offers the following key advantages over a whole program analysis:

- *Reuse of analysis results:* A major problem with whole-program analysis is that results for a particular program component cannot be reused, since functions are analyzed in a particular context. For instance, adding a single caller to a library may require complete re-analysis of the entire library. In contrast, modular analyses allow complete reuse of analysis results because procedure summaries are valid in any context.
- *Analysis scalability:* Function summaries express a function's behavior in terms of its input/output interface, abstracting away its internal details. We show experimentally that our function summaries do not grow with program size; thus, an implementation strategy that analyzes a single function at a time, requiring only one function and its callee's summaries to be in memory, should scale to arbitrarily large programs.
- *Parallelizability:* In modular analysis, any two functions that do not have a caller/callee relationship can be analyzed in parallel. Thus, such analyses naturally exploit multi-core machines.

* This work was supported by grants from NSF and DARPA (CCF-0430378, CCF-0702681).

PLDI'11, June 4–8, 2011, San Jose, California, USA.

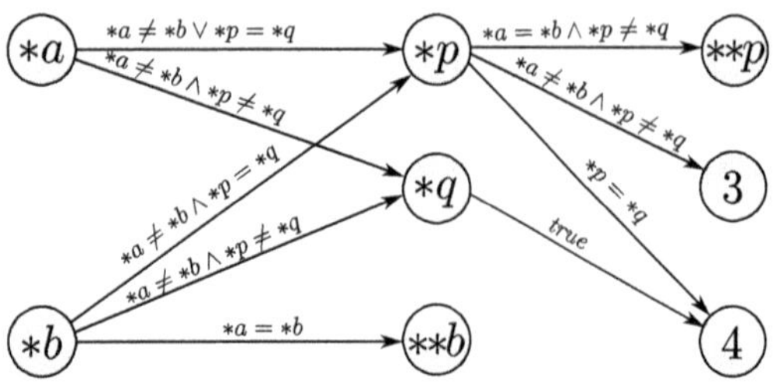

Figure 1. Summary associated with function `f`

To illustrate our approach, consider the following simple function `f` along with its three callers `g1`, `g2`, and `g3`:

```
void f(int** a, int** b, int* p, int* q) {
  *a = p; *b = q; **a = 3; **b = 4; }
```

```
void g1() {
  int** a, int** b;
  a = new int*;
  b = new int*;
  int p = 0, q=0;
  f(a, b, &p, &q);
  assert(p == 3); }
```

```
void g2() {
  int** a, int** b;
  a = new int*;
  b = new int*;
  int p = 0;
  f(a, b, &p, &p);
  assert(p == 4); }
```

```
void g3() {
  int** a, int** b;
  a = new int*;
  b = a;
  int p = 0, q=0;
  f(a, b, &p, &q);
  assert(p == 0); }
```

Here, although the body of `f` is conditional- and loop-free, the value of `*p` after the call to `f` may be either 3, 4, or remain its initial value. In particular, in contexts where `p` and `q` are aliases (e.g., `g2`), `*p` is set to 4; in contexts where neither `a` and `b` nor `p` and `q` are aliases (e.g., `g1`), `*p` is set to 3, and in contexts where `a` and `b` are aliases but `p` and `q` are not (e.g., `g3`), the value of `*p` is unchanged after a call to `f`. Furthermore, to discharge the assertions in `g1`, `g2`, and `g3`, we need to perform strong updates to all the memory locations.

To give the reader a flavor of our technique, the function summary of `f` computed by our analysis is shown in Figure 1, which shows the points-to graph on exit from `f` (i.e., the heap when `f` returns). Here, points-to edges between locations are qualified by constraints, indicating the condition under which this points-to relation holds. The meaning of a constraint such as $*p = *q$ is that the location pointed to by `p` and the location pointed to by `q` are the same, i.e., `p` and `q` are aliases. Observe that Figure 1 encodes all possible updates to `*p` precisely: In particular, this summary indicates that `*p` has value 3 under constraint $*a \neq *b \wedge *p \neq *q$ (i.e., neither `a` and `b` nor `p` and `q` are aliases); `*p` has value 4 if `p` and `q` are aliases, and `*p` retains its initial value (`**p`) otherwise.

There are three main insights underlying our approach:

- First, we observe that a heap abstraction H at any call site of `f` can be overapproximated as the finite union of some structurally distinct *skeletal points-to graphs* $\hat{H}_1, \ldots \hat{H}_m$ where each abstract location points-to *at most one* location. This observation yields a naive, but sound, way of performing summary-based analysis where the heap state after a call to function `f` is conditioned upon the skeletal graph at the call site.
- Second, we symbolically encode all possible skeletal heaps on entry to `f` in a *single* symbolic heap where points-to edges are qualified by constraints. This insight allows us to obtain a single, *polymorphic* heap summary valid at any call site.
- Third, we observe that using summaries to apply strong updates at call sites requires a negation operation on constraints. Since these constraints may be approximations, simultaneous reasoning about may and must information on points-to relations is necessary for applying strong updates when safe. To solve this difficulty, we use *bracketing constraints* [4].

The first insight, developed in Section 2, forms the basic framework for reasoning about the correctness and precision of our approach. The second and third insights, exploited in Section 4, yield a symbolic and efficient encoding of the basic approach. To summarize, this paper makes the following contributions:

- We develop a theory of abstract heap decompositions that elucidates the basic principle underlying modular heap analyses. This theory shows that a summary-based analysis must lose extra precision over a non-summary based analysis in some circumstances and also sheds light on the correctness of earlier work on modular alias analyses, such as [5–7].
- We present a full algorithm for performing modular heap analysis in a symbolic and efficient way. While our algorithm builds on the work of [7] in predicating summaries on aliasing patterns, our approach is much more precise and is capable of performing strong updates to heap locations at call sites.
- We demonstrate experimentally that our approach is both scalable and precise for verifying properties about real C and C++ applications up to 100,000 lines of code.

2. Foundations of Modular Heap Analysis

As mentioned in Section 1, our goal is to analyze a function f independently of its callers and generate a summary valid in any context. The main difficulty for such an analysis is that f's *heap fragment* (the portion of the program's heap reachable through f's arguments and global variables on entry to f) is unknown and may be arbitrarily complex, but a modular analysis must model this unknown heap fragment in a conservative way.

Our technique models f's heap fragment using abstractions $H_1, \ldots, H_k$ such that (i) in each H_i, every location points to *exactly one location variable* representing the unknown points-to targets of that location on function entry, (ii) each H_i represents a distinct aliasing pattern that may arise in some calling context, and (iii) the heap fragment reachable in f at any call site is overapproximated by combining a subset of the heaps in $H_1, \ldots, H_k$.

As the above discussion illustrates, our approach requires representing the heap abstraction at any call site as the finite union of heap abstractions where each pointer location has exactly one target. We observe that every known modular heap analysis, including ours, has this this *one-target* property. In principle, one could allow the unknown locations in a function's initial heap fragment to point to 2, 3, or any number of other unknown heap locations, but it is unclear how to pick the number or take advantage of the potential extra precision.

In this section, we present *canonical decompositions*, through which the heap is decomposed into a set of heaps with the one-target property, and *structural decompositions*, which coalesce isomorphic canonical heaps. We then show how these decompositions can be used for summary-based heap analysis.

2.1 Preliminaries

We describe the basic ideas on a standard *may points-to* graph, which we usually call a *heap* for brevity. A labeled node A represents one or more concrete memory locations $\zeta(A)$.

DEFINITION 1. **(Summary Location)** *An abstract location that may represent multiple concrete locations is a* summary location *(e.g., modeling elements in an array/list). An abstract location representing exactly one concrete location is a* non-summary location.

For any two distinct abstract locations A and A', we require $\zeta(A) \cap \zeta(A') = \emptyset$, and that $|\zeta(A)| = 1$ if A is a non-summary node. An edge (A, B) in the points-to graph denotes a partial function $\zeta_{(A,B)}$ from pointer locations in $\zeta(A)$ to locations in

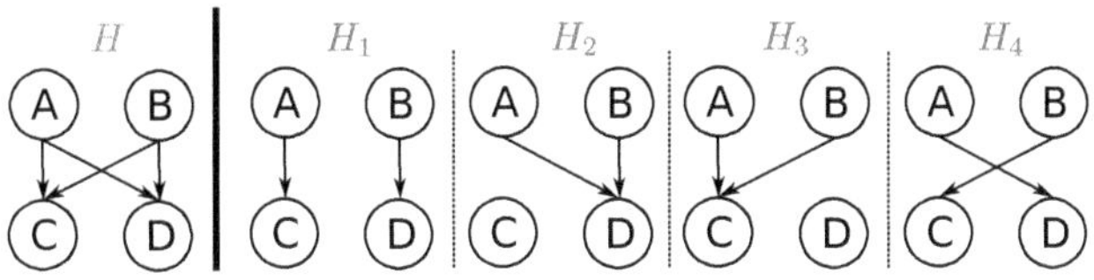

Figure 2. A heap H and its canonical decomposition $H_1, \ldots, H_4$

$\zeta(B)$, with the requirement that for every pointer location $l \in \zeta(A)$ there is exactly one node B such that $\zeta_{(A,B)}(l)$ is defined (i.e., each pointer location has a unique target in a concrete heap). Finally, each possible choice of ζ and compatible edge functions $\zeta_{(A,B)}$ for each edge (A, B) maps a points-to graph H to one concrete heap. We write $\gamma(H)$ for the set of all such possible concrete heaps for the points-to graph H. We also write $H_1 \sqsupseteq H_2$ if $\gamma(H_1) \supseteq \gamma(H_2)$, and $H_1 \sqcup H_2$ for the heap that is the union of all nodes and edges in H_1 and H_2. We define a semantic judgment $H \models S : H'$ as:

$$H \models S : H' \Leftrightarrow \forall h \in \gamma(H).\ \exists h' \in \gamma(H').\ eval(h, S) = h'$$

where $eval(h, S)$ is the result of executing code fragment S starting with concrete heap h. Now, we write $H \vdash_a S : H'$ to indicate that, given a points-to graph H and a program fragment S, H' is the new heap obtained after analyzing S using pointer analysis a. The pointer analysis a is sound if for all program fragments S:

$$H \vdash_a S : H' \ \Rightarrow\ H \models S : H'$$

2.2 Canonical Decomposition

In this section, we describe how to express a points-to graph H as the union of a set of points-to graphs $H_1, \ldots, H_k$ where in each H_i, every abstract location points to *at most one* location.

DEFINITION 2. **(Canonical points-to graph)** *We say a points-to graph is* canonical *if every abstract memory location has an edge to at most one abstract memory location.*

DEFINITION 3. **(Canonical decomposition)** *The canonical decomposition of heap H is obtained by applying these steps in order:*

1. *If a summary node A points to multiple locations $T_1, \ldots, T_k$, replace $T_1, \ldots, T_k$ with a single summary node T such that any edge to/from any T_i is replaced with an edge to/from T.*
2. *Let B be a location with multiple edges to $T_1, \ldots, T_k$. Split the heap into $H_1, \ldots, H_k$ where in each H_i, B has exactly one edge to T_i, and recursively apply this rule to each H_i.*

LEMMA 1. *Let $H_1, \ldots, H_k$ be the canonical decomposition of H. Then $(H_1 \sqcup \ldots \sqcup H_k) \sqsupseteq H$.*

PROOF 1. *Let H' be the heap obtained from step 1 of Definition 3. To show $H' \sqsupseteq H$ we must show $\gamma(H') \supseteq \gamma(H)$. Let $h \in \gamma(H)$ and let ζ_H by the corresponding mapping. We choose $\zeta^{H'}(T) = \zeta^H(T_1) \cup \ldots \cup \zeta^H(T_k)$ and $\zeta^{H'}(X) = \zeta^H(X)$ otherwise, and construct the edge mappings $\zeta^H_{(A,B)}$ from $\zeta^{H'}_{(A,B)}$ analogously. Thus, $h \in \gamma(H')$ and we have $\gamma(H') \supseteq \gamma(H)$. In step 2, observe that any location B with multiple edges to $T_1, \ldots, T_k$ must be a non-summary location. Hence, the only concrete location represented by B must point to exactly one T_i in any execution. Thus, in this step, $(H_1 \sqcup \ldots \sqcup H_k) = H' \sqsupseteq H$.* □

EXAMPLE 1. *Figure 2 shows a heap H with only non-summary locations. The canonical decomposition of H is H_1, H_2, H_3, H_4, representing four different concrete heaps encoded by H.*

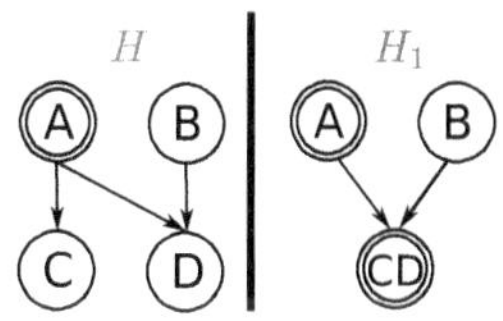

Figure 3. A heap H and its canonical decomposition H_1

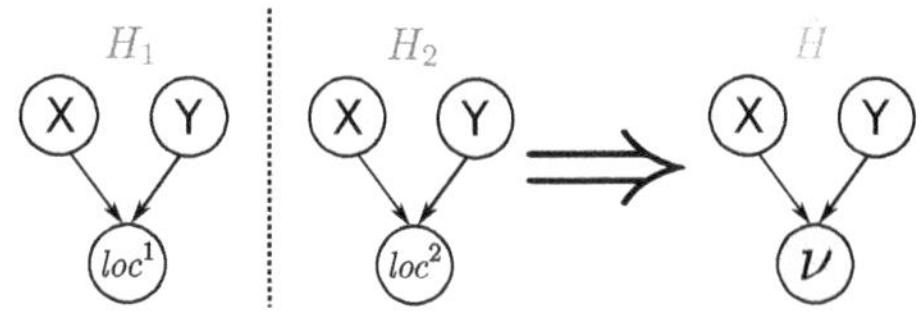

Figure 4. Two isomorphic canonical heaps and their skeleton

EXAMPLE 2. *Figure 3 shows another heap H with summary node A (indicated by double circles) and its canonical decomposition H_1. Heap H_1 is obtained from H by collapsing locations C and D into a summary location CD. Observe that we cannot split H into two heaps H_1 and H_2 where A points to C in H_1 and to D in H_2: Such a decomposition would incorrectly state that all elements in A must point to the same location, whereas H allows distinct concrete elements in A to point to distinct locations.*

COROLLARY 1. *If H has no summary nodes with multiple edges, then its canonical decomposition is exact, i.e., $\bigsqcup_{1 \leq i \leq k} H_i = H$.*

PROOF 2. *This follows immediately from the proof of Lemma 1.* □

LEMMA 2. *Consider a sound pointer analysis "a" and a heap H with canonical decomposition $H_1, \ldots, H_k$ such that:*

$$H_1 \vdash_a S : H'_1 \quad \ldots \quad H_k \vdash_a S : H'_k$$

Then, $H \models S : H'_1 \sqcup \ldots \sqcup H'_k$.

PROOF 3. *This follows directly from Lemma 1.* □

According to this lemma, we can conservatively analyze a program fragment S by first decomposing a heap H into canonical heaps $H_1, \ldots, H_k$, then analyzing S using each initial heap H_i, and finally combining the resulting heaps $H'_1, \ldots, H'_k$.

Recall that in a modular heap analysis, we require each node in a function f's initial heap abstraction to have the single-target property. Corollary 1 implies that if a call site of f has no summary nodes with multiple targets, then this assumption results in no loss of information, because we can use multiple distinct heaps for f that, in combination, are an exact representation of the call site's heap. However, if a summary location has multiple targets and there is aliasing involving that summary node, as illustrated in Figure 3, the modular analysis may strictly overapproximate the heap after a call to f. In this case, the requirement that f's initial heap have the single-target property means that f can only represent the call-site's heap (shown on the left of Figure 3) by an overapproximating heap that merges the target nodes (shown on the right of Figure 3).

2.3 Structural Decomposition

Consider the result of analyzing a program fragment S starting with initial canonical heaps H_1 and H_2 shown in Figure 4. Here, nodes labeled X and Y represent memory locations of x and y, which are the only variables in scope in S. Since the only difference between H_1 and H_2 is the label of the node pointed to by x and y, the heaps H'_1 and H'_2 obtained after analyzing S will be identical except

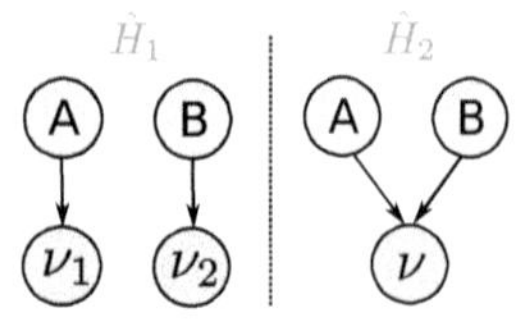

Figure 5. Structural decomposition of heap H from Figure 2

for the label of a single node. Thus, S can be analyzed only once starting with heap $\hat{H}$ in Figure 4, and H_1' and H_2' can be obtained from the resulting heap by renaming ν to loc^1 and loc^2 respectively. The rest of this section makes this discussion precise.

DEFINITION 4. **(Skeleton)** *Given a set of nodes N, let $\xi_N(H)$ be the heap obtained by erasing the labels of all nodes in H except for those in N. Now ξ_N defines an equivalence relation $H \equiv_N H'$ if $\xi_N(H) = \xi_N(H')$. We select one heap in each equivalence class of $\equiv_N$ as the class' unique* skeleton.

Note that nodes of skeletons are labeled—label erasure is only used to determine equivalence class membership.

EXAMPLE 3. *In Figure 4, H_1 and H_2 have the same skeleton $\hat{H}$.*

In other words, if heaps $H_1, \ldots, H_k$ have the same aliasing patterns with respect to a set of root locations N, then $\hat{H}$ is a unique points-to graph which represents their common aliasing structure. Skeletons are useful because, if N represents formals and globals in a function f, all possible aliasing patterns at call sites of f can be expressed using a finite number of skeletons.

DEFINITION 5. **(Π)** *Let H be a heap and let $\hat{H}$ be its skeleton w.r.t. nodes N. The mapping $\Pi_{H,\hat{H}}$ maps every node label in $\hat{H}$ to the label of the corresponding node in H and any other node to itself.*

DEFINITION 6. **(Structural Decomposition)** *Given heap H and nodes N, the* structural decomposition *of H w.r.t. N is a set of heaps D such that for every H_i in the canonical decomposition of H, the sketelon $\hat{H}$ of H_i w.r.t. N is in D.*

Observe that the cardinality of the structural decomposition of H is never larger than the cardinality of H's canonical decomposition.

DEFINITION 7. **(Instances of skeleton)** *Let $\hat{H}$ be a skeleton in the structural decomposition of H. The* instances *of $\hat{H}$, written $\mathcal{I}_H(\hat{H})$, are the canonical heaps of H with skeleton $\hat{H}$.*

EXAMPLE 4. *Consider heap H from Figure 2 and the root set $\{A, B\}$. The structural decomposition $\hat{H}_1, \hat{H}_2$ of H is shown in Figure 5. Observe that canonical heaps H_1 and H_4 from Figure 2 have the same skeleton $\hat{H}_1$, and H_2 and H_3 have skeleton $\hat{H}_2$. Thus, $\mathcal{I}_H(\hat{H}_1) = \{H_1, H_4\}$ and $\mathcal{I}_H(\hat{H}_2) = \{H_2, H_3\}$. Also:*

$$\Pi_{H_1,\hat{H}_1} = [\nu_1 \mapsto C, \nu_2 \mapsto D] \quad \Pi_{H_4,\hat{H}_1} = [\nu_1 \mapsto D, \nu_2, \mapsto C]$$
$$\Pi_{H_2,\hat{H}_2} = [\nu \mapsto D] \quad \Pi_{H_3,\hat{H}_2} = [\nu \mapsto C]$$

LEMMA 3. *Consider program fragment S and nodes N representing variables in scope at S. Let H_N be the heap fragment reachable through N before analyzing S and let $\hat{H}_1, \ldots, \hat{H}_m$ be the structural decomposition of H_N w.r.t. N. If*

$$\hat{H}_1 \vdash_a S : \hat{H}_1' \quad \ldots \quad \hat{H}_m \vdash_a S : \hat{H}_m'$$

and if $\hat{H}_N'$ is the heap defined as:

$$\hat{H}_N' = \bigsqcup_{1 \le i \le m} \left(\bigsqcup_{H_{ij} \in \mathcal{I}_{H_N}(\hat{H}_i)} \Pi_{H_{ij},\hat{H}_i}(\hat{H}_i') \right)$$

then $H_N \models S : \hat{H}_N'$.

PROOF 4. *First, by Definitions 4 and 2, we have:*

$$\bigsqcup_{1 \le i \le m} \left(\bigsqcup_{H_{ij} \in \mathcal{I}_{H_N}(\hat{H}_i)} H_{ij} \right) \sqsupseteq H_N$$

Second, using Lemma 2, this implies:

$$H_N \models S : \bigsqcup_{1 \le i \le m} \left(\bigsqcup_{H_{ij} \in \mathcal{I}_{H_N}(\hat{H}_i)} H_{ij}' \right) \quad (*)$$

where $H_{ij} \vdash_a S : H_{ij}'$. From Definition 7, since H_{ij} and $\hat{H}_i$ are equivalent up to renaming, then H_{ij}' and $\hat{H}_i'$ are also equivalent up to this renaming, given by $\Pi_{H_{ij},\hat{H}_i}$. Together with (*), this implies $H_N \models S : \bigsqcup_{1 \le i \le m} \left(\bigsqcup_{H_{ij} \in \mathcal{I}_{H_N}(\hat{H}_i)} \Pi_{H_{ij},\hat{H}_i}(\hat{H}_i') \right)$. □

In other words, the heap defined as $\hat{H}_N'$ in Lemma 3 gives us a sound abstraction of the heap after analyzing program fragment S. Furthermore, $\hat{H}_N'$ is precise in the sense defined below:

LEMMA 4. *Let $\hat{H}_N'$ be the heap defined in Lemma 3, and let $H_1, \ldots, H_k$ be the canonical decomposition of the heap fragment reachable from N before analyzing S. If $H_j \vdash_a H_j'$, then:*

$$\hat{H}_N' = \bigsqcup_{1 \le j \le k} H_j'$$

PROOF 5. *This follows from Corollary 1 and Definition 6.* □

The following corollary states a stronger precision result:

COROLLARY 2. *Let H_N and $\hat{H}_N'$ be the heap abstractions from Lemma 3, and let $H_N \vdash_a S : H_N'$. If H_N does not contain summary locations with multiple points-to targets, then*

$$\hat{H}_N' \sqsubseteq H_N'$$

PROOF 6. *This follows from Lemma 4 and Corollary 1.*

2.4 From Decompositions to Modular Heap Analysis

We now show how the ideas described so far yield a basic modular heap analysis. In the remainder of this section, we assume there is a fixed bound on the total number of memory locations used by a program analysis. (In practice, this is achieved by, e.g., collapsing recursive fields of data structures to a single summary location.)

LEMMA 5. *Consider a function f, and let N denote the abstract memory locations associated with the formals and globals of f. Then, there is a finite set Q of skeletons such that the structural decomposition D w.r.t. N of the heap fragment reachable from N in any of f's call sites satisfies $D \subseteq Q$.*

PROOF 7. *Recall that in any canonical heap, every location has exactly one target. Second, observe that when there is bound b on the total number of locations in any heap, any canonical heap must have at most b locations. Thus, using a fixed set of nodes, we can only construct a finite set Q of structurally distinct graphs.* □

Since there are a bounded number of skeletons that can arise in any context, this suggests the following strategy for computing a complete summary of function f: Let N be the set of root locations (i.e., formals and globals) on entry to f, and let $\hat{H}_1, \ldots, \hat{H}_k$ be the set of all skeletons that can be constructed from root set N. We analyze f's body for each initial skeleton $\hat{H}_i$, obtaining a new heap $\hat{H}_i'$. Now, let C be a call site of f and let R be the subset of the skeletons $\hat{H}_1, \ldots, \hat{H}_k$ that occur in the structural decomposition of heap H in context C. Then, following Lemma 3, the heap fragment after the call to f can be obtained as:

$$\bigsqcup_{\hat{H}_i \in R} \left(\bigsqcup_{H_{ij} \in \mathcal{I}_H(\hat{H}_i))} \Pi_{H_{ij}, \hat{H}_i}(\hat{H}_i') \right)$$

This strategy yields a fully context-sensitive analysis because f's body is analyzed for any possible entry aliasing pattern $\hat{H}_i$, and at a given call site C, we only use the resulting heap $\hat{H}_i$ if $\hat{H}_i$ is part of the structural decomposition of the heap at C.

Furthermore, as indicated by Corollary 2, this strategy is as precise as analyzing the inlined body of the function if there are no summary locations with multiple points-to targets at this call site; otherwise, the precision guarantee is stated in Lemma 4.

2.5 Discussion

While the decompositions described here are useful for understanding the principle underlying modular heap analyses, the naive algorithm sketched in Section 2.4 is completely impractical for two reasons: First, since the number of skeletons may be exponential in the number of abstract locations reachable through arguments, such an algorithm requires analyzing a function body exponentially many times. Second, although two initial skeletons may be different, the resulting heaps after analyzing the function body may still be identical. In the rest of this paper, we describe a symbolic encoding of the basic algorithm that does not analyze a function more than once unless cycles are present in the callgraph (see Section 4). Then, in Section 5, we show how to identify only those initial skeletons that may affect the heap abstraction after the function call.

3. Language

To formalize our symbolic algorithm for modular heap analysis, we use the following typed, call-by-value imperative language:

$$\begin{array}{lll}
\textit{Program } P & := & F^+ \\
\textit{Function } F & := & \textit{define } f(a_1 : \tau_1, \ldots, a_n : \tau_n) = S; \\
\textit{Statement } S & := & v_1 \leftarrow *v_2 \mid *v_1 \leftarrow v_2 \mid v \leftarrow \textit{alloc}^\rho(\tau) \\
& & \mid f^\rho(v_1, \ldots, v_k) \mid \textit{assert}(v_1 = v_2) \\
& & \mid \textit{let}^\rho\ v : \tau \textit{ in } S \textit{ end} \mid S_1; S_2 \mid \textit{choose}(S_1, S_2) \\
\textit{Type } \tau & := & \textit{int} \mid \textit{ptr}(\tau)
\end{array}$$

A program P consists of one or more (possibly recursive) functions F. Statements in this language are loads, stores, memory allocations, function calls, assertions, let bindings, sequencing, and the *choose* statement, which non-deterministically executes either S_1 or S_2 (i.e., a simplified conditional). Allocations, function calls, and let bindings are labeled with globally unique program points ρ.

Since this language is standard, we omit its operational semantics and highlight a few important assumptions: Execution starts at the first function defined, and an assertion failure aborts execution. Also, all bindings in the concrete store have initial value *nil*.

4. Modular & Symbolic Heap Analysis

In this section, we formally describe our symbolic algorithm for modular heap analysis. In Section 4.1, we first decribe the abstract domain used in our analysis. Section 4.2 formally defines *function summaries*, and Section 4.3 presents a full algorithm for summary-based heap analysis for the language defined in Section 3.

4.1 Abstract Domain

Abstract locations π represent a set of concrete locations:

$$\begin{array}{lll}
\textit{Abstract Locations } \pi & := & \alpha \mid l \\
\textit{Location Variables } \alpha & := & \nu_i \mid * \alpha \\
\textit{Location Constants } l & := & loc^{\vec{\rho}} \mid nil
\end{array}$$

An abstract location π in function f is either a *location variable* α or a *location constant* l. Location constants represent stack or heap allocations in f and its transitive callees as well as *nil*. In contrast, location variables represent the unknown memory locations reachable from f's arguments at call sites, similar to access paths in [5]. Informally, location variables correspond to the node labels of a skeleton from Section 2.3. Recall from Section 2 that, in any canonical points-to graph, every abstract memory location points to at most one other abstract memory location; hence, location variable $*\nu_i$ describes the unknown, but unique, points-to target of f's i'th argument in some canonical heap at a call site of f.

Abstract environment $\mathbb{E}$ maps program variables v to abstract locations π, and abstract store $\mathbb{S}$ maps each abstract location π to an *abstract value set* θ of (abstract location, constraint) pairs:

$$\textit{Abstract value set } \theta := 2^{(\pi, \phi)}$$

The abstract store defines the edges of the points-to graph from Section 2. A mapping from abstract location π to abstract value set $\{(\pi_1, \phi_1), \ldots, (\pi_k, \phi_k)\}$ in $\mathbb{S}$ indicates that the heap abstraction contains a points-to edge from node labeled π to nodes labeled $\pi_1, \ldots, \pi_k$. Observe that, unlike the simple may points-to graph we considered in Section 2, points-to edges in the abstract store are qualified by constraints, which we utilize to symbolically encode all possible skeletons in one symbolic heap (see Section 4.3).

Constraints in our abstract domain are defined as follows:

$$\begin{array}{lll}
\phi & := & \langle \varphi_{may}, \varphi_{must} \rangle \\
\varphi & := & T \mid F \mid \varphi_1 \wedge \varphi_2 \mid \varphi_1 \vee \varphi_2 \mid \neg\varphi \mid t_1 = t_2
\end{array}$$

Here, ϕ is a *bracketing constraint* $\langle \varphi_{may}, \varphi_{must} \rangle$ as in [4], representing the condition under which a property may and must hold. Recall from Section 1 that the simultaneous use of may and must information is necessary for applying strong updates whenever safe. In particular, updates to heap locations require negation (see Section 4.3). Since the negation of an overapproximation is an underapproximation, the use of bracketing constraints allows a sound negation operation, defined as $\neg\langle \varphi_{may}, \varphi_{must} \rangle = \langle \neg\varphi_{must}, \neg\varphi_{may} \rangle$. Conjunction and disjunction are defined on these constraints as expected:

$$\langle \varphi_{may}, \varphi_{must} \rangle \star \langle \varphi'_{may}, \varphi'_{must} \rangle = \langle \varphi_{may} \star \varphi'_{may}, \varphi_{must} \star \varphi'_{must} \rangle$$

where $\star \in \{\wedge, \vee\}$. In this paper, any constraint ϕ is a bracketing constraint unless stated otherwise. To make this clear, any time we do not use a bracketing constraint, we use the letter φ instead of ϕ. Furthermore, if the may and must conditions of a bracketing constraint are the same, we write a single constraint instead of a pair. Finally, for a bracketing constraint $\phi = \langle \varphi_{may}, \varphi_{must} \rangle$, we define $\lceil \phi \rceil = \varphi_{may}$ and $\lfloor \phi \rfloor = \varphi_{must}$.

In the definition of constraint φ, T and F represent the boolean constants true and false, and a term t is defined as:

$$\textit{Term } t := v \mid \textit{drf}(t) \mid \textit{alloc}(\vec{\rho}) \mid nil$$

Here, v represents a variable, *drf* is an uninterpreted function, and *alloc* is an *invertible* uninterpreted function applied to a vector of constants $\vec{\rho}$. Thus, constraints φ belong to the theory of equality with uninterpreted functions. Our analysis requires converting between abstract locations and terms in the constraint language; we therefore define a *lift* operation, written $\overline{\pi}$, for this purpose:

$$\overline{\nu_i} = \nu_i \quad \overline{*\alpha} = \textit{drf}(\overline{\alpha}) \quad \overline{nil} = nil \quad \overline{loc^{\vec{\rho}}} = \textit{alloc}(\vec{\rho})$$

Observe that a location constant loc^{ρ} is converted to a term $\textit{alloc}(\vec{\rho})$, which effectively behaves as a constant in the constraint language: Since *alloc* is an invertible function, $\textit{alloc}(\vec{\rho}) = \textit{alloc}(\vec{\rho'})$ exactly when $\rho = \rho'$. A location variable ν is converted to a constraint variable of the same name, and the location variable $*\nu$ is represented by the term $\textit{drf}(\nu)$ which represents the unknown points-to target

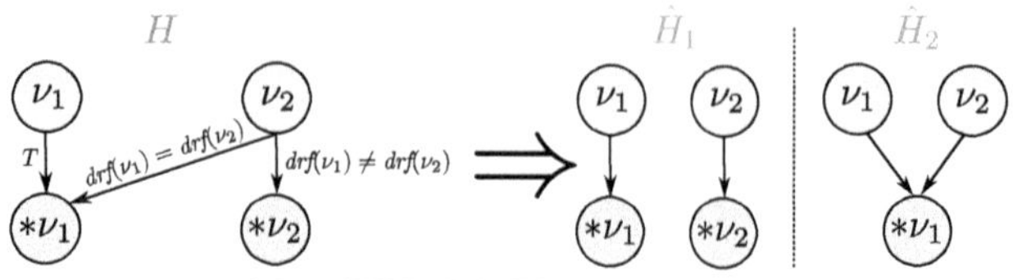

Figure 6. A symbolic heap representing two skeletons

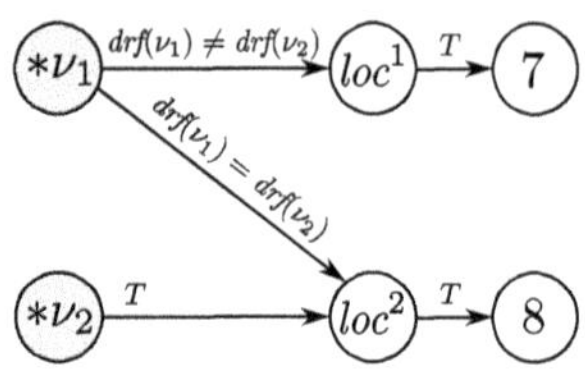

Figure 7. The abstract store in f's summary

of ν on function entry. We write $lift^{-1}(t)$ to denote the conversion of a term to an abstract location.

EXAMPLE 5. *In Figure 6, a symbolic heap H represents two skeletons $\hat{H}_1$ and $\hat{H}_2$. In H, the constraint* $\mathrm{drf}(\nu_1) = \mathrm{drf}(\nu_2)$ *describes contexts where the first and second arguments are aliases. Observe that, at call sites where the first and second arguments alias,* $\mathrm{drf}(\nu_1) = \mathrm{drf}(\nu_2)$ *instantiates to* true *and* $\mathrm{drf}(\nu_1) \neq \mathrm{drf}(\nu_2)$ *is* false*; thus at this call site, H instantiates exactly to $\hat{H}_2$. Similarly, if the first and second arguments do not alias, H instantiates to $\hat{H}_1$.*

4.2 Function Summaries

A *summary* Δ for a function f is a pair $\Delta = \langle \phi, \mathbb{S} \rangle$ where ϕ is a constraint describing the precondition for f to succeed (i.e., not abort), and $\mathbb{S}$ is a symbolic heap representing the heap abstraction after f returns. More specifically, let $\hat{H}_1, \ldots, \hat{H}_k$ be the set of all skeletons for any possible call site of f, and let $\hat{H}_i \vdash S : \hat{H}'_i$ where S is the body of f. Then, the abstract store $\mathbb{S}$ symbolically encodes that in contexts where the constraints in $\mathbb{S}$ are satisfied by initial heap $\hat{H}_i$, the resulting heap is $\hat{H}'_i$.

Observe that a summary can also be viewed as the Hoare triple $\{\phi\} f \{\mathbb{S}\}$. Thus, the computation of a summary for f is equivalent to the inference of sound pre- and post-conditions for f.

EXAMPLE 6. *Consider the function:*

```
define f(a1 : ptr(ptr(int)), a2 : ptr(ptr(int))) =
1 :  *a1 ← alloc¹(int);
2 :  *a2 ← alloc²(int);
3 :  let t1 : ptr(int) in t1 ← *a1; *t1 ← 7 end;
4 :  let t2 : ptr(int) in t2 ← *a2; *t2 ← 8 end;
5 :  let t3 : ptr(int) in t3 ← *a1;
6 :      let t4 : int in t4 ← *t3; assert(t4 == 7) end;
7 :  end
```

The summary for f *is* $\langle\, \mathrm{drf}(\nu_1) \neq \mathrm{drf}(\nu_2),\ \mathbb{S}\,\rangle$ *where $\mathbb{S}$ is shown in Figure 7. The pre-condition* $\mathrm{drf}(\nu_1) \neq \mathrm{drf}(\nu_2)$ *indicates that the assertion fails in those contexts where arguments of f are aliases. Also, in symbolic heap $\mathbb{S}$, the abstract location reached by dereferencing a_1 (whose location is ν_1) is either* loc_1*, corresponding to the allocation at line 1, or* loc_2*, associated with the allocation at line 2, depending on whether a_1 and a_2 are aliases.*

A *global summary environment* $\mathbb{G}$ is a mapping from each function f in the program to a summary Δ_f.

$$\frac{\begin{array}{l}\mathbb{E} = [a_1 \leftarrow \nu_1, \ldots, a_k \leftarrow \nu_k] \\ \forall\ \alpha_i \in dom(\mathbb{A}). \\ \quad \mathbb{S}(\alpha_i) \leftarrow \cup_{k \leq i}(*\alpha_k, (\bigwedge_{j<k} \overline{*\alpha_i} \neq \overline{*\alpha_j}) \wedge \overline{*\alpha_i} = \overline{*\alpha_k})\end{array}}{\mathbb{A} \vdash init\_heap(a_1, \ldots, a_k) : \mathbb{E}, \mathbb{S}}$$

Figure 8. Local Heap Initialization

4.3 The Analysis

We now present the full algorithm for the language of Section 3. Section 4.3.1 describes the symbolic initialization of the local heap to account for all possible aliasing relations on function entry. Section 4.3.2 gives abstract transformers for all statements except function calls, which is described in Section 4.3.3. Finally, Section 4.3.4 describes the generation of function summaries.

4.3.1 Local Heap Initialization

To analyze a function f independent of its callers, we initialize f's abstract store to account for all possible relevant aliasing relationships at function entry. To perform this local heap initialization, we utilize an *alias partition environment* $\mathbb{A}$ with the signature $\alpha \rightarrow 2^{\alpha}$. This environment maps each location variable α to an *ordered* set of location variables, called α's *alias partition set*. If $\alpha' \in \mathbb{A}(\alpha)$, then f's summary may differ in contexts where α and α' are aliases. Since aliasing is a symmetric property, any alias partition environment $\mathbb{A}$ has the property $\alpha' \in \mathbb{A}(\alpha) \Leftrightarrow \alpha \in \mathbb{A}(\alpha')$. Any location aliases itself, and so $\mathbb{A}$ is also reflexive: $\alpha \in \mathbb{A}(\alpha)$. A correct alias partition environment $\mathbb{A}$ can be trivially computed by stipulating that $\alpha' \in \mathbb{A}(\alpha)$ if α and α' have the same type. We discuss how to compute a more precise alias partition environment $\mathbb{A}$ in Section 5.

A key component of the modular analysis is the *init_heap* rule in Figure 8. Given formal parameters $a_1, \ldots, a_k$ to function f, this rule initializes the abstract environment and store on entry to f. The environment $\mathbb{E}$ is initialized by binding a location variable ν_i to each argument a_i. The initialization of the abstract store $\mathbb{S}$, however, is more involved because we need to account for all possible entry aliasing relationships permitted by $\mathbb{A}$.

Intuitively, if $\mathbb{A}$ indicates that α_1 and α_2 may alias on function entry, we need to analyze f's body with two skeletal heaps, one where α_1 and α_2 point to the same location, and one where α_1 and α_2 point to different locations. To encode this symbolically, one obvious solution is to introduce three location variables, $*\alpha_1$, $*\alpha_2$, and $*\alpha_{12}$ such that α_1 (resp. α_2) points to $*\alpha_1$ (resp. $*\alpha_2$) if they do not alias (i.e., under constraint $drf(\alpha_1) \neq drf(\alpha_2)$) and point to a common location named $*\alpha_{12}$ if they alias (i.e., under $drf(\alpha_1) = drf(\alpha_2)$). While this encoding correctly describes both skeletal heaps, it unfortunately introduces an exponential number of locations, one for each subset of entry alias relations in $\mathbb{A}$.

To avoid this exponential blow-up, we impose a total order on abstract locations such that if α_i and α_j are aliases, they both point to a common location $*\alpha_k$ such that α_k is the least element in the alias partition class of α_i and α_j. Thus, in the *init_heap* rule of Figure 8, α_i points to $*\alpha_k$ where $k \leq i$ under constraint:

$$(\bigwedge_{j<k} \overline{*\alpha_i} \neq \overline{*\alpha_j}) \ \wedge\ \overline{*\alpha_i} = \overline{*\alpha_k}$$

This condition ensures that α_i points to a location named $*\alpha_k$ only if it does not alias any other location $\alpha_j \in \mathbb{A}(\alpha_i)$ with $j < k$.

EXAMPLE 7. *Consider the function defined in Example 6. Suppose the alias partition environment $\mathbb{A}$ contains the following mappings:*

$$\nu_1 \mapsto \{\nu_1, \nu_2\}, \nu_2 \mapsto \{\nu_1, \nu_2\}, *\nu_1 \mapsto \{*\nu_1\}, *\nu_2 \mapsto \{*\nu_2\},$$
$$** \nu_1 \mapsto \{** \nu_1\}, ** \nu_2 \mapsto \{** \nu_2\}$$

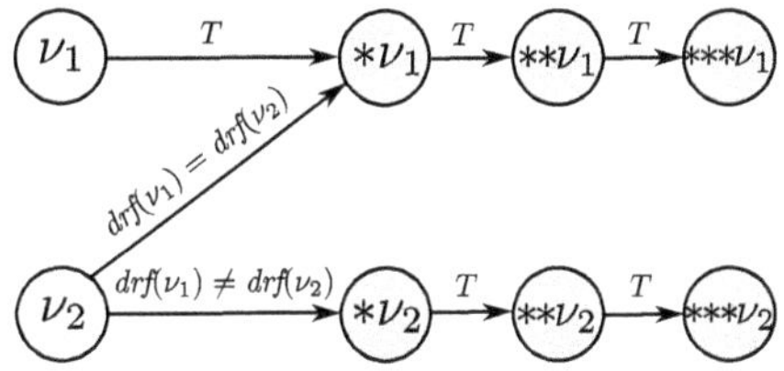

Figure 9. The initial heap abstraction for function from Example 6

Figure 9 shows the initial heap abstraction using $\mathbb{A}$ and the ordering $\nu_1 < \nu_2$. Since $\mathbb{A}$ includes ν_1 and ν_2 in the same alias partition set, ν_2 points to $*\nu_1$ under $\mathrm{drf}(\nu_1) = \mathrm{drf}(\nu_2)$ *and to $*\nu_2$ under its negation. But ν_1 only points to $*\nu_1$ since $\nu_2 \not< \nu_1$.*

The following lemma states that the initial heap abstraction correctly accounts for all entry aliasing relations permitted by $\mathbb{A}$:

LEMMA 6. *Let α_i and α_j be two abstract locations such that $\alpha_j \in \mathbb{A}(\alpha_i)$. The initial local heap abstraction $\mathbb{S}$ constructed in Figure 8 encodes that α_i and α_j point to distinct locations* exactly *in those contexts where they do not alias.*

PROOF 8. *Without loss of generality, assume $i < j$.*
$\Rightarrow$ Suppose α_i and α_j are not aliases in a context C, but $\mathbb{S}$ encodes they may point to the same location $*\alpha_k$ in context C. Let ϕ and ϕ' be the constraints under which α_i and α_j point to α_k respectively. By construction, $k \leq i$, and ϕ implies $\mathrm{drf}(\alpha_i) = \mathrm{drf}(\alpha_k)$ *and ϕ' implies* $\mathrm{drf}(\alpha_j) = \mathrm{drf}(\alpha_k)$. *Thus, we have* $\mathrm{drf}(\alpha_i) = \mathrm{drf}(\alpha_j)$, *contradicting the fact that α_i and α_j do not alias in C.*
$\Leftarrow$ Suppose α_i and α_j are aliases in context C, but $\mathbb{S}$ allows α_i and α_j to point to distinct locations $*\alpha_k$ and $*\alpha_m$. Let ϕ and ϕ' be the constraints under which α_i points to $*\alpha_k$ and α_j points to $*\alpha_m$ respectively. Case (i): Suppose $k < m$. Then, by construction, ϕ implies $\mathrm{drf}(\alpha_i) = \mathrm{drf}(\alpha_k)$, *and ϕ' implies* $\mathrm{drf}(\alpha_j) \neq \mathrm{drf}(\alpha_k)$. *Hence, we have* $\mathrm{drf}(\alpha_j) \neq \mathrm{drf}(\alpha_i)$, *contradicting the assumption that α_i and α_j are aliases in C. Case (ii): $k > m$. Then, ϕ' implies* $\mathrm{drf}(\alpha_j) = \mathrm{drf}(\alpha_m)$, *and ϕ implies* $\mathrm{drf}(\alpha_i) \neq \mathrm{drf}(\alpha_m)$, *again contradicting the fact that α_i and α_j are aliases in C.* □

LEMMA 7. *For each alias partition set of size n, the init_heap rule adds $n(n+1)/2$ points-to edges.*

As Lemma 7 states, this construction introduces a quadratic number of edges in the size of each alias partition set to represent all possible skeletal heaps. Furthermore, the number of abstract locations in the initial symbolic heap is no larger than the maximum number of abstract locations in any individual skeleton.

4.3.2 Abstract Transformers for Basic Statements

In this section, we describe the abstract transformers for all statements except function calls, which is the topic of Section 4.3.3. Statement transformers are given as inference rules of the form

$$\mathbb{E}, \mathbb{S}, \mathbb{G}, \phi \vdash S : \mathbb{S}', \phi'$$

which states that under abstract environment $\mathbb{E}$, store $\mathbb{S}$, summary environment $\mathbb{G}$, and precondition ϕ, statement S produces a new abstract store $\mathbb{S}'$ and a new precondition ϕ' of the current function. The operation $\mathbb{S}(\theta)$ looks up the value of each π_i in θ:

$$S(\{(\pi_1, \phi_1), \ldots, (\pi_k, \phi_k)\}) = \bigcup_{1 \leq i \leq k} \mathbb{S}(\pi_i) \wedge \phi_i$$

where $\mathbb{S}(\pi_i) \wedge \phi_i$ is a shorthand defined as follows:

$$\theta \wedge \phi = \{(\pi_j, \phi_j \wedge \phi) | (\pi_j, \phi_j) \in \theta\}$$

(1)
$$\frac{\begin{array}{c}\mathbb{E}(v_1) = \pi_1 \;\; \mathbb{E}(v_2) = \pi_2 \\ \mathbb{S}(\pi_2) = \theta \;\; \mathbb{S}' = \mathbb{S}[\pi_1 \leftarrow \mathbb{S}(\theta)]\end{array}}{\mathbb{E}, \mathbb{S}, \mathbb{G}, \phi \vdash v_1 \leftarrow *v_2 : \mathbb{S}', \phi}$$

(2)
$$\frac{\begin{array}{c}\mathbb{E}(v_1) = \pi_1 \;\; \mathbb{E}(v_2) = \pi_2 \\ \mathbb{S}(\pi_1) = \theta_1 \;\; \mathbb{S}(\pi_2) = \theta_2 \\ \mathbb{S}' = \mathbb{S}[\pi_i \leftarrow ((\theta_2 \wedge \phi_i) \cup (\mathbb{S}(\pi_i) \wedge \neg\phi_i)) \mid (\pi_i, \phi_i) \in \theta_1]\end{array}}{\mathbb{E}, \mathbb{S}, \mathbb{G}, \phi \vdash *v_1 \leftarrow v_2 : \mathbb{S}', \phi}$$

(3)
$$\frac{\begin{array}{c}\mathbb{E}(v) = \pi \\ \mathbb{S}' = \mathbb{S}[\pi \leftarrow \{(loc^\rho, T)\},\ loc^\rho \leftarrow \{(nil, T)\}]\end{array}}{\mathbb{E}, \mathbb{S}, \mathbb{G}, \phi \vdash v \leftarrow alloc^\rho(\tau) : \mathbb{S}', \phi}$$

(4)
$$\frac{\begin{array}{c}\mathbb{E}(v_1) = \pi \;\; \mathbb{E}(v_2) = \pi' \\ \mathbb{S}(\pi) = \{\ldots, (\pi_i, \phi_i), \ldots\} \\ \mathbb{S}(\pi') = \{\ldots, (\pi'_j, \phi'_j), \ldots\} \\ \phi' = \bigvee_{i,j}(\pi_i = \pi'_j \wedge \phi_i \wedge \phi'_j)\end{array}}{\mathbb{E}, \mathbb{S}, \mathbb{G}, \phi \vdash assert(v_1 = v_2) : \mathbb{S}, \phi \wedge \phi'}$$

(5)
$$\frac{\begin{array}{c}\mathbb{E}' = \mathbb{E}[v \leftarrow loc^\rho] \\ \mathbb{S}' = \mathbb{S}[*loc^\rho \leftarrow \{(nil, T)\}] \\ \mathbb{E}', \mathbb{S}', \mathbb{G}, \phi \vdash S : \mathbb{S}'', \phi'\end{array}}{\mathbb{E}, \mathbb{S}, \mathbb{G}, \phi \vdash let^\rho\ v : \tau\ in\ S\ end\ : \mathbb{S}'' \backslash loc^\rho, \phi'}$$

(6)
$$\frac{\begin{array}{c}\mathbb{E}, \mathbb{S}, \mathbb{G}, \phi \vdash S_1 : \mathbb{S}', \phi' \\ \mathbb{E}, \mathbb{S}', \mathbb{G}, \phi' \vdash S_2 : \mathbb{S}'', \phi''\end{array}}{\mathbb{E}, \mathbb{S}, \mathbb{G}, \phi \vdash S_1; S_2 : \mathbb{S}'', \phi''}$$

(7)
$$\frac{\begin{array}{c}\mathbb{E}, \mathbb{S}, \mathbb{G}, \phi \vdash S_1 : \mathbb{S}_1, \phi_1 \\ \mathbb{E}, \mathbb{S}, \mathbb{G}, \phi \vdash S_2 : \mathbb{S}_2, \phi_2\end{array}}{\mathbb{E}, \mathbb{S}, \mathbb{G}, \phi \vdash\ choose\ (S_1, S_2) : \mathbb{S}_1 \sqcup \mathbb{S}_2, \phi_1 \wedge \phi_2}$$

Figure 10. Abstract Transformers for Basic Statements

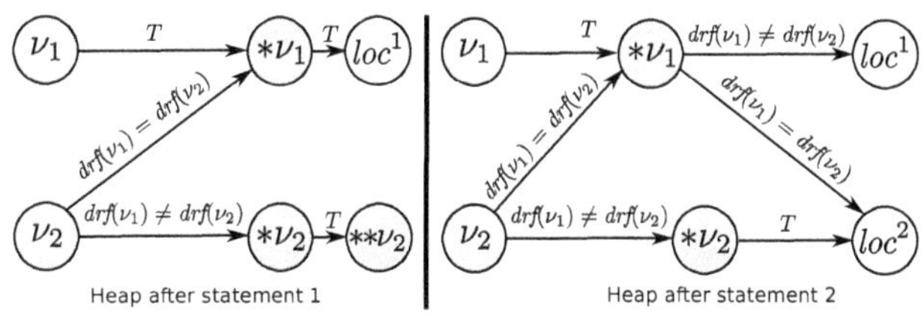

Figure 11. The symbolic heap before and after line 2 in Example 6

In Figure 10, rules (1) and (2) give the transformers for loads and stores respectively. The rule for loads is self-explanatory; thus, we focus on the store rule. In the third hypothesis of rule (2), each π_i represents a location that v_1 points to under constraint ϕ_i, and θ_2 is the value set for v_2. Since the write to π_i happens under constraint ϕ_i, the new value of π_i in $\mathbb{S}'$ is θ_2 under constraint ϕ_i and retains its old value set $\mathbb{S}(\pi_i)$ under $\neg\phi_i$. Observe that if ϕ_i is *true*, this rule performs a standard strong update to π_i. On the other hand, if v_1 points to π_i under some entry alias assumption, then there is a strong update to π_i exactly in those calling contexts where this alias assumption holds.

EXAMPLE 8. *Figure 11 shows the relevant portion of the heap abstraction before and after the store at line 2 in Example 6.*

Rule (3) processes allocations by introducing a new location loc^ρ and initializing its value in the store to *nil*. Rule (4) analyzes an assertion by computing the condition ϕ' for the assertion to hold such that if ϕ' can be proven valid in a calling context, then this assertion must hold at that call site. In rule (4), ϕ' is computed as

$$\frac{}{\mathbb{S}, \mathbb{I} \vdash \mathit{map\_loc}(\nu : \mathit{int}) : \mathbb{I}} \qquad \frac{\mathbb{S}, \mathbb{I} \vdash \mathit{map\_loc}(*\nu : \tau) : \mathbb{I}'}{\mathbb{S}, \mathbb{I} \vdash \mathit{map\_loc}(\nu : \mathit{ptr}(\tau)) : \mathbb{I}'}$$

$$\frac{\mathbb{I}' = \mathbb{I}[*\alpha \leftarrow \mathbb{S}(\mathbb{I}(\alpha))]}{\mathbb{S}, \mathbb{I} \vdash \mathit{map\_loc}(*\alpha : \mathit{int}) : \mathbb{I}'} \qquad \frac{\begin{array}{c}\mathbb{I}' = \mathbb{I}[*\alpha \leftarrow \mathbb{S}(\mathbb{I}(\alpha))] \\ \mathbb{I}' \vdash \mathit{map\_loc}(**\,\alpha : \tau) : \mathbb{I}''\end{array}}{\mathbb{S}, \mathbb{I} \vdash \mathit{map\_loc}(*\alpha : \mathit{ptr}(\tau)) : \mathbb{I}''}$$

$$\frac{\begin{array}{c}\mathbb{S}, [\nu_1 \leftarrow \{(\mathbb{E}(v_1), T)\}] \vdash \mathit{map\_loc}(\nu_1) : \mathbb{I}_1 \\ \cdots \\ \mathbb{S}, \mathbb{I}_{k-1}[\nu_k \leftarrow \{(\mathbb{E}(v_k), T)\}] \vdash \mathit{map\_loc}(\nu_k) : \mathbb{I}_k\end{array}}{\mathbb{E}, \mathbb{S} \vdash \mathit{map\_args}(v_1 : \tau_1, \ldots, v_k : \tau_k) : \mathbb{I}_k}$$

Figure 12. Rules for computing instantiation environment $\mathbb{I}$

$$\frac{}{\mathbb{I}, \rho \vdash \mathit{inst\_loc}(\mathit{nil}) : \{(\mathit{nil}, T)\}} \qquad \frac{\theta = \{(\mathit{loc}^{\rho::\vec{\rho'}}, T)\}}{\mathbb{I}, \rho \vdash \mathit{inst\_loc}(\mathit{loc}^{\vec{\rho'}}) : \theta}\ (\rho \notin \vec{\rho'})$$

$$\frac{}{\mathbb{I}, \rho \vdash \mathit{inst\_loc}(\alpha) : \mathbb{I}(\alpha)} \qquad \frac{\theta = \{(\mathit{loc}^{\vec{\rho'}}, \langle T, F \rangle)\}}{\mathbb{I}, \rho \vdash \mathit{inst\_loc}(\mathit{loc}^{\vec{\rho'}}) : \theta}\ (\rho \in \vec{\rho'})$$

Figure 13. Rules for instantiating locations

the disjunction of all pairwise equalities of the elements in the two abstract value sets associated with v_1 and v_2, i.e., a case analysis of their possible values. Rule (5) describes the abstract semantics of let statements by binding variable v to a new location loc^ρ in $\mathbb{E}$. Rule (6) for sequencing is standard, and rule (7) gives the semantics of the *choose* construct, which computes the join of two abstract stores $\mathbb{S}_1$ and $\mathbb{S}_2$. To define a join operation on abstract stores, we first define *domain extension*:

DEFINITION 8. **(Domain Extension)** *Let π be any binding in abstract store $\mathbb{S}'$ and let (π_i, ϕ_i) be any element of $\mathbb{S}'(\pi)$. We say an abstract store $S'' = \mathbb{S}_{\mapsto \mathbb{S}'}$ is a domain extention of $\mathbb{S}$ with respect to $\mathbb{S}'$ if the following condition holds:*

1. If $\pi \in \mathrm{dom}(\mathbb{S}) \wedge (\pi_i, \phi_i') \in \mathbb{S}(\pi)$, then $(\pi_i, \phi_i') \in \mathbb{S}_{\mapsto \mathbb{S}'}(\pi)$.
2. Otherwise, $(\pi_i, \mathrm{false}) \in \mathbb{S}_{\mapsto \mathbb{S}'}(\pi)$

DEFINITION 9. **(Join)** *Let $\mathbb{S}_1' = \mathbb{S}_{1 \mapsto \mathbb{S}_2}$ and let $\mathbb{S}_2' = \mathbb{S}_{2 \mapsto \mathbb{S}_1}$. If $(\pi', \langle \varphi^1_{\mathrm{may}}, \varphi^1_{\mathrm{must}} \rangle) \in \mathbb{S}_1'(\pi)$ and $(\pi', \langle \varphi^2_{\mathrm{may}}, \varphi^2_{\mathrm{must}} \rangle) \in \mathbb{S}_2'(\pi)$, then:*

$$(\pi', \langle \varphi^1_{\mathrm{may}} \vee \varphi^2_{\mathrm{may}}, \varphi^1_{\mathrm{must}} \wedge \varphi^2_{\mathrm{must}} \rangle) \in (\mathbb{S}_1 \sqcup \mathbb{S}_2)(\pi)$$

4.3.3 Instantiation of Summaries

The most involved statement transformer is the one for function calls, which we describe in this subsection. Figure 15 gives the complete transformer for function calls, making use of the helper rules defined in Figures 12- 14, which we discuss in order.

Given the actuals $v_1, \ldots, v_k$ for a call to function f, Figure 12 computes the *instantiation environment* $\mathbb{I}$ with signature $\alpha \rightarrow \theta$ for this call site. This environment $\mathbb{I}$, which serves as the symbolic equivalent of the mapping Π from Section 2, maps location variables used in f to their corresponding locations in the current (calling) function. However, since $\mathbb{I}$ is symbolic, it produces an abstract value set $\{(\pi_1, \phi_1), \ldots, (\pi_k, \phi_k)\}$ for each α such that α instantiates to π_i in some canonical heap under constraint ϕ_i.

Figure 13 describes the rules for instantiating any location π used in the summary. If π is a location variable, we use environment $\mathbb{I}$ to look up its instantiation. On the other hand, if π is a location constant allocated in callee f, we need to rename this constant to distinguish allocations made at different call sites for full context-sensitivity. In general, we rename the location constant $loc^{\vec{\rho'}}$ by prepending to $\vec{\rho'}$ the program point ρ associated with the call site.

$$\frac{\begin{array}{l}\mathbb{I}, \rho \vdash \mathit{inst\_loc}(\mathit{lift}^{-1}(t_1)) : \{(\pi_1, \phi_1), \ldots, (\pi_k, \phi_k)\} \\ \mathbb{I}, \rho \vdash \mathit{inst\_loc}(\mathit{lift}^{-1}(t_2)) : \{(\pi_1', \phi_1'), \ldots, (\pi_m', \phi_m')\} \\ \phi = \bigvee_i (k = \pi_i \wedge \phi_i) \quad \phi' = \bigvee_j (k' = \pi_j' \wedge \phi_j') \ \ (k, k' \ \mathit{fresh})\end{array}}{\mathbb{I}, \rho \vdash \mathit{inst}_\varphi(t_1 = t_2) : k = k', \phi \wedge \phi'}$$

$$\frac{b \in \{T, F\}}{\mathbb{I}, \rho \vdash \mathit{inst}_\varphi(b) : b, T} \qquad \frac{\mathbb{I}, \rho \vdash \mathit{inst}_\varphi(\varphi) : \varphi_1, \phi_2}{\mathbb{I}, \rho \vdash \mathit{inst}_\varphi(\neg\varphi) : \neg\varphi_1, \phi_2}$$

$$\frac{\mathbb{I}, \rho \vdash \mathit{inst}_\varphi(\varphi_1) : \varphi, \phi \quad \mathbb{I}, \rho \vdash \mathit{inst}_\varphi(\varphi_2) : \varphi', \phi'}{\mathbb{I}, \rho \vdash \mathit{inst}_\varphi(\varphi_1 \star \varphi_2) : \varphi \star \varphi', \phi \wedge \phi'} (\star \in \{\wedge, \vee\})$$

$$\frac{\begin{array}{l}\mathbb{I}, \rho \vdash \mathit{inst}_\varphi(\varphi_{may}) : \varphi'_{may}, \phi'_{may} \quad \mathbb{I}, \rho \vdash \mathit{inst}_\varphi(\varphi_{must}) : \varphi'_{must}, \phi'_{must} \\ \varphi''_{may} = \lceil QE(\exists \vec{k}.\ (\varphi'_{may} \wedge \phi'_{may})) \rceil \quad \varphi''_{must} = \lfloor QE(\exists \vec{k}.\ (\varphi'_{must} \wedge \phi'_{must})) \rfloor\end{array}}{\mathbb{I}, \rho \vdash \mathit{inst}_\phi(\langle \varphi_{may}, \varphi_{must} \rangle) : \langle \phi''_{may}, \phi''_{must} \rangle}$$

Figure 14. Rules for instantiating constraints

However, in the presence of recursion, we need to avoid creating an unbounded number of location constants; thus, in Figure 13, we check if this allocation is created on a cyclic path in the callgraph by testing whether the current program point ρ is already in $\vec{\rho'}$. In the latter case, we do not create a new location constant but weaken the bracketing constraint associated with $loc^{\vec{\rho'}}$ to $\langle T, F \rangle$, which has the effect of ensuring that stores into this location only apply weak updates [4], meaning that $loc^{\vec{\rho'}}$ behaves as a summary location.

In addition to instantiating locations, we must also instantiate the associated constraints, which is described in Figure 14. In the last rule of this figure, $inst_\phi$ instantiates a bracketing constraint, making use of $inst_\varphi$ to map the constituent may and must conditions. The $inst_\varphi$ rule derives judgments of the form $\mathbb{I}, \rho \vdash inst_\varphi(\varphi) : \varphi', \phi$, where φ' preserves the structure of φ by substituting each term t in φ with a temporary variable k and ϕ constrains the values of k.

The first rule in Figure 14 for instantiating a leaf $t_1 = t_2$ is the most interesting one: Here, we convert t_1 and t_2 to their corresponding memory locations using the $lift^{-1}$ operation from Section 4.1 and instantiate the corresponding locations using *inst_loc* to obtain abstract value sets θ_1 and θ_2. We then introduce two temporary variables k and k' representing θ_1 and θ_2 respectively, and introduce constraints ϕ and ϕ', stipulating the equality between k and θ_1 and between k' and θ_2. Observe that in the last rule of Figure 14, these temporary variables k and k' are removed using a *QE* procedure to eliminate existentially quantified variables.

Figure 15 makes use of all the afore-mentioned rules to instantiate the summary of function f at a given call site ρ. In the last rule of this figure, we first look up f's summary $\langle \phi_f, \mathbb{S}_f \rangle$ in the global summary environment $\mathbb{G}$. The precondition ϕ_f is instantiated to ϕ_f' using $inst_\phi$. Observe that if ϕ_f' is valid, then the potential assertion failure in f is discharged at this call site; otherwise, ϕ_f' is conjoined with the precondition ϕ of the current function.

Next, we compose the partial heap $\mathbb{S}_f$, representing the heap fragment reachable in f after the call, with the existing heap $\mathbb{S}$ before the function call. The *compose_partial_heap* rule used in *compose_heap* instantiates an entry $\pi \mapsto \theta$ in f's summary. Observe that if location π in f's summary instantiates to location π_i in the current function under ϕ_i, existing values of π_i are only preserved under $\neg\phi_i$. Hence, if ϕ_i is *true*, this rule applies a strong update to π_i. On the other hand, if π instantiates to π_i under some entry alias condition, then this rule represents a strong update to π_i only in those contexts where the entry aliasing condition holds.

EXAMPLE 9. *Consider a call to function f of Example 6:*

```
define g(a1 : ptr(ptr(int))) = f3(a1, a1)
```

$$\frac{\mathbb{I},\rho \vdash \mathit{inst\_loc}(\pi_1)=\theta_1,\ldots \mathit{inst\_loc}(\pi_k)=\theta_k}{\mathbb{I},\rho\vdash \mathit{inst\_theta}(\{(\pi_1,\phi_1),\ldots,(\pi_k,\phi_k)\}) : \bigcup_{1\le i\le k}(\theta_i\wedge\phi_i)}$$

$$\frac{\begin{array}{c}\mathbb{I},\rho \vdash \mathit{inst\_loc}(\pi)=\theta_s\\ \mathbb{I},\rho \vdash \mathit{inst\_theta}(\theta)=\theta_t\\ \mathbb{S}'=\mathbb{S}[\pi_i \leftarrow (\theta_t\wedge\phi_i)\cup(\mathbb{S}(\pi_i)\wedge\neg\phi_i)\mid(\pi_i,\phi_i)\in\theta_s]\end{array}}{\mathbb{S},\mathbb{I},\rho\vdash \mathit{compose\_partial\_heap}(\pi,\theta):\mathbb{S}'}$$

$$\frac{\begin{array}{c}\mathbb{S}_f=[(\pi_1\mapsto\theta_1),\ldots,(\pi_k\mapsto\theta_k)]\\ \mathbb{S},\mathbb{I},\rho\vdash \mathit{compose\_partial\_heap}(\pi_1,\theta_1):\mathbb{S}_1\\ \ldots\\ \mathbb{S}_{k-1},\mathbb{I},\rho\vdash \mathit{compose\_partial\_heap}(\pi_k,\theta_k):\mathbb{S}_k\end{array}}{\mathbb{S},\mathbb{I},\rho\vdash \mathit{compose\_heap}(\mathbb{S}_f):\mathbb{S}_k}$$

$$\frac{\begin{array}{c}\mathbb{G}(f)=\langle\phi_f,\mathbb{S}_f\rangle\\ \mathbb{E},\mathbb{S}\vdash \mathit{map\_args}(v_1,\ldots,v_k):\mathbb{I}\\ \mathbb{I},\rho\vdash \mathit{inst}_\phi(\phi_f):\phi'_f\\ \mathbb{S},\mathbb{I},\rho\vdash \mathit{compose\_heap}(\mathbb{S}_f):\mathbb{S}'\end{array}}{\mathbb{E},\mathbb{S},\mathbb{G},\phi\vdash f^\rho(v_1,\ldots,v_k):\mathbb{S}',\phi\wedge\phi'_f}$$

Figure 15. Summary Instantiation rules

Before the call to f, g's local heap is depicted as:

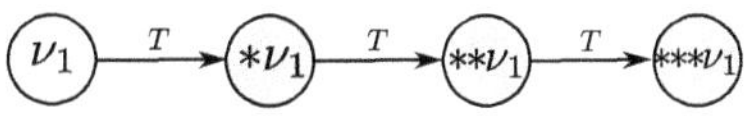

Recall from Example 6 that f's precondition is $\mathrm{drf}(\nu_1)\neq\mathrm{drf}(\nu_2)$, which instantiates to $\mathrm{drf}(\nu_1)\neq\mathrm{drf}(\nu_1)\Leftrightarrow$ false at this call site, indicating that the assertion is guaranteed to fail. The store in f's summary from Figure 7 is instantiated at the call site to:

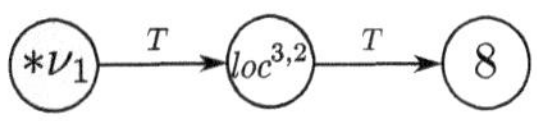

Composing initial heap (*) with the instantiated heap (**), we obtain the final heap after the function call:

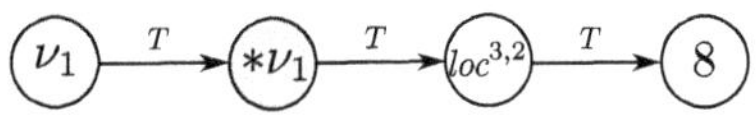

Observe that the resulting abstract heap is as precise as analyzing the inlined body of f.

4.3.4 Summary Generation and Fixed-point Computation

We now conclude this section by describing function summary generation, given in Figure 16. Before analyzing the body of f, the local abstract heap $\mathbb{S}$ is initialized as described in Section 4.3.1. Next, f's body is analyzed using the abstract transformers from Section 4.3.2 and 4.3.3, which yields a store $\mathbb{S}'$ and a precondition ϕ'. According to the last hypothesis in Figure 16, the summary $\langle\phi_f,\mathbb{S}_f\rangle$ is sound if $\mathbb{S}_f$ overapproximates $\mathbb{S}\backslash\{\nu_1,\ldots,\nu_k\}$ and ϕ_f implies ϕ'. Here, $\mathbb{S}_1\sqsubseteq\mathbb{S}_2$ is defined as:

DEFINITION 10. *($\sqsubseteq$) Let $\mathbb{S}'_1=\mathbb{S}_{1\mapsto\mathbb{S}_2}$ and $\mathbb{S}'_2=\mathbb{S}_{2\mapsto\mathbb{S}_1}$. We say $\mathbb{S}_1\sqsubseteq\mathbb{S}_2$ if for every $\pi\in\mathrm{dom}(\mathbb{S}'_1)$ and for every π' such that $(\pi',\langle\varphi^1_{\mathrm{may}},\varphi^1_{\mathrm{must}}\rangle)\in\mathbb{S}'_1(\pi)$, $(\pi',\langle\varphi^2_{\mathrm{may}},\varphi^2_{\mathrm{must}}\rangle)\in\mathbb{S}'_2(\pi)$, we have:*

$$\varphi^1_{\mathrm{may}}\Rightarrow\varphi^2_{\mathrm{may}}\wedge\varphi^2_{\mathrm{must}}\Rightarrow\varphi^1_{\mathrm{must}}$$

While the rule in Figure 16 verifies that $\langle\phi_f,\mathbb{S}_f\rangle$ is a sound summary, it does not give an algorithmic way of computing it. In the presence of recursion, we perform a least fixed-point computation where all entries in $\mathbb{G}$ are initially $\bot$ (i.e., any location points to any other location under *false*), and a new summary for f is obtained by computing the join of f's new and old summaries:

$$\langle\mathbb{S}_1,\phi_1\rangle\sqcup\langle\mathbb{S}_2,\phi_2\rangle=\langle\mathbb{S}_1\sqcup\mathbb{S}_2,\phi_1\wedge\phi_2\rangle$$

$$\frac{\begin{array}{c}\mathbb{A}\vdash \mathit{init\_heap}(a_1,\ldots,a_k):\mathbb{E},\mathbb{S}\\ \mathbb{E},\mathbb{S},\mathbb{G},\mathit{true}\vdash S:\phi',\mathbb{S}'\\ \mathbb{G}\vdash f:\langle\phi_f,\mathbb{S}_f\rangle\\ \phi_f\Rightarrow\phi'\quad \mathbb{S}_f\sqsupseteq(\mathbb{S}'\backslash\{\nu_1,\ldots,\nu_k\})\end{array}}{\mathbb{G},\mathbb{A}\vdash \mathit{define}\ f(a_1:\tau_1,\ldots,a_k:\tau_k)=S:\langle\phi_f,\mathbb{S}_f\rangle}$$

Figure 16. Summary generation rule

$\Pi_{H_2,H_1}(E)=C$

$\Pi_{H_2,H_1}(G)=C$

$\Pi_{H_2,H_1}(F)=D$

$\Pi_{H_2,H_1}(H)=D$

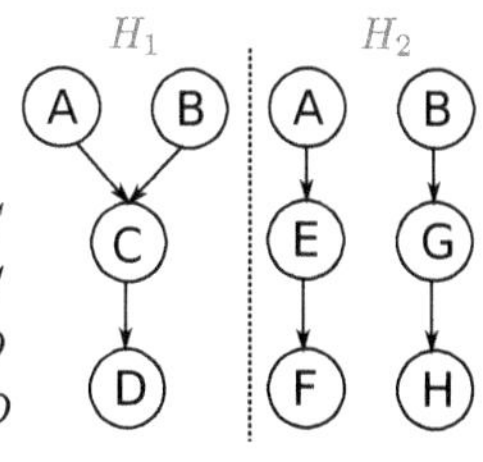

Figure 17. Heaps from Lemma 8

This strategy ensures that the analysis is monotonic by construction. Furthermore, since the analysis creates a finite number of abstract locations and the constraints are over a finite vocabulary of predicates, this fixed-point computation is guaranteed to converge. In fact, for an acyclic callgraph, each function is analyzed only once if a reverse topological order is used.

5. Computing Alias Partition Sets

In the previous section, we assumed the existence of an alias partition environment $\mathbb{A}$ that is used to query whether aliasing between locations α and α' may affect analysis results. One simple way to compute such an environment is to require that $\alpha'\in\mathbb{A}(\alpha)$ if α and α' have the same type (at least in a type-safe language). Fortunately, it is possible to compute a much more precise alias partition environment because many aliasing relations at a call site of f do not affect the state of the heap after a call to f. The following lemma elucidates when we can safely ignore potential aliasing between two locations in a code fragment S.

LEMMA 8. *Let H_1 and H_2 be the canonical heap fragments shown in Figure 17, and let S be a program fragment such that:*

- *There is either no store to A and no store to B, or*
- *There is a store to only A that is not followed by a load from B, or*
- *There are only stores to both A and B, but the store to A must happen after the store to B*

Let $H_1\vdash S:H'_1$ and $H_2\vdash S:H'_2$, and let O be a partial order such that $O(B)\prec O(A)$ if there must be a write to A after a write to B in S. Let H''_2 be the graph obtained by replacing G's targets with E's targets in H'_2 if $\Pi_{H_2,H_1}(A)=\Pi_{H_2,H_1}(B)$ and $O(B)\prec O(A)$. Then, $H'_1=\Pi_{H_2,H_1}(H''_2)$.

PROOF 9. *(sketch) There are three cases: (i) If there is no store to A or B, then in H'_2, E and G still point to F and H, both of which are equivalent to D in H'_1. Thus, $H'_1=\Pi_{H_2,H_1}(H'_2)$. (ii) There is only a store to A, not followed by a load from B: In H'_1, C will point to some set of new locations $T_1,\ldots,T_k$. In H'_2, E must also point to $T'_1,\ldots,T'_k$ such that $T_i=\Pi_{H_2,H_1}(T'_i)$ and G must point to H. First, the result of any load from B (i.e., H) can be correctly renamed to D, as the read happens before the store to A. Second,*

	LiteSQL	OpenSSH	Inkscape widget lib.	Digikam
Lines	16,030	22,615	37,211	128,318
Strong updates at instantiation				
Running time (1 CPU)	4.5 min	3.9 min	7.2 min	45.1 min
Running time (8 CPUs)	1.6 min	1.8 min	2.3 min	8.7 min
Memory use	430 MB	230 MB	195 MB	400 MB
Error reports	7	6	7	37
False positives	2	1	3	9
Weak updates at instantiation				
Running time (1 CPU)	7.1 min	4.8 min	8.1 min	60.0 min
Running time (8 CPUs)	4 min	3.6 min	2.5 min	10.1 min
Memory use	410 MB	250 MB	200 MB	355 MB
Error reports	312	209	730	1140
False positives	307	204	726	1112

Figure 18. Comparison of strong/weak updates at call sites

H_2'' is obtained by removing the edge from G to H and adding edges from G to each T_i'. Thus, $\Pi_{H_2,H_1}(G) = \Pi_{H_2,H_1}(E) = C$ and G and E's targets are renamed to $T_1, \ldots, T_k$. (iii) Similar to (ii).

This lemma shows the principle that can be used to reduce the number of entries in $\mathbb{A}$: Assuming we can impose an order on the sequence of updates to memory locations and assuming we instantiate summary edges in this order, then the initial heap abstraction only needs to account for aliasing between α_1 and α_2 if there is a store to α_1 followed by a load from α_2, which is necessary because updates through α_1 to a location may now affect locations that are reachable through α_2. On the other hand, if there is no load after a store and the updates to memory locations can be ordered, it is possible to "fix up" the summary at the call site by respecting the order of updates during instantiation.

To allow such an optimization in the analysis described in Section 4, we impose a partial order $\prec$ on points-to relations such that $(\pi_1 \mapsto \theta_1) \prec (\pi_2 \mapsto \theta_2)$ indicates that π_1 must be assigned to θ_1 before π_2 is assigned to θ_2. Then, to respect the order of updates in the callee when instantiating the summary, we ensure that if $\pi_i \mapsto \theta_i \prec \pi_j \mapsto \theta_j$, the *compose_partial_heap* rule is invoked on $\pi_i \mapsto \theta_i$ before $\pi_j \mapsto \theta_j$ in the *compose_heap* rule of Figure 15.

Thus, assuming we modify the analysis from Section 4 as described above, we can compute a better alias partition environment $\mathbb{A}$ by performing a least fixed-point computation over the current function f. In particular, $\mathbb{A}(\alpha)$ is initialized to $\{\alpha\}$ for each location variable α. Then, if the analysis detects a store to α followed by a load from α' of the same type, then $\alpha' \in \mathbb{A}(\alpha)$ and $\alpha \in \mathbb{A}(\alpha')$. Similarly, if there is a store s_1 to α and a store s_2 to α' (of the same type) such that there is no happens-before relation between s_1 and s_2, then $\alpha' \in \mathbb{A}(\alpha)$ and $\alpha \in \mathbb{A}(\alpha')$.

6. Experiments

We have implemented the technique described in this paper in our COMPASS program verification framework for analyzing C and C++ applications. Our implementation extends the algorithm described in this paper in two ways: First, our analysis is fully (i.e., interprocedurally) path-sensitive and uses the algorithm of [8] for this purpose. Second, our implementation improves over the analysis presented here by employing the technique described in [4], which uses *indexed locations* to reason precisely about contents of arrays and containers. Hence, the algorithm we implemented is significantly more precise than a standard may points-to analysis.

Figure 18 summarizes the results of our first experiment, which involves verifying memory safety properties (buffer overruns, null dereferences, casting errors, and access to deleted memory) in four real C and C++ applications ranging from 16,030 to 128,318 lines. The first part of the table, labeled "Strong Updates at Instantiation", reports the results obtained by using the modular heap analysis described in this paper. Observe that the proposed technique is both scalable, memory-efficient, and precise. First, the running times on 8 CPU's range from 1.6 minutes to 8.7 minutes, and increase roughly linearly with the size of the application. Furthermore, observe that the modular analysis takes advantage of multiple CPUs to significantly reduce its wall-clock running time. Second, the maximum memory used by any process does not exceed 430 MB, and, most importantly, the memory usage is not correlated with the application size. Figure 19 sheds some light on the scalability of the analysis: This figure plots the maximum call stack depth against summary size, computed as the number of points-to edges weighted according to the size of the edge constraints plus the size of the precondition. In this figure, observe that summary size does not increase with depth of the callstack, confirming our hypothesis that summaries are useful for exploiting information locality and therefore enable analyses to scale.

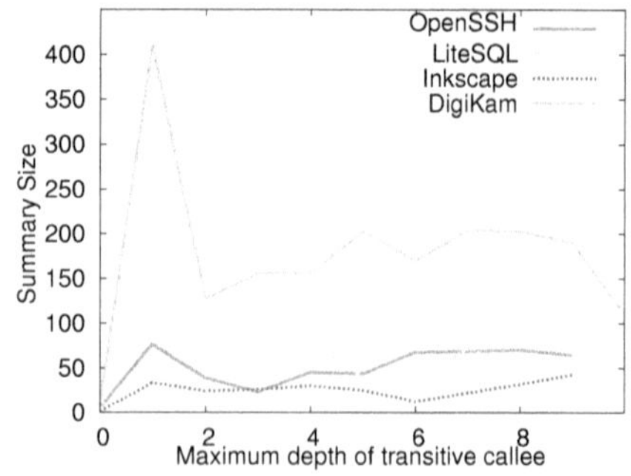

Figure 19. Callstack depth vs. summary size

	hostname	chroot	rmdir	su	mv
Lines	304	371	483	1047	1151
Modular analysis running time	0.53s	0.75s	1.54s	2.3s	2.55s
Whole program running time	3.1s	6.3s	21.6s	45.9s	30.7s

Figure 20. Comparison of modular and whole program analysis

Figure 18 also illustrates that performing strong updates at call sites is crucial for the precision required by verification tools. Observe that the analysis using strong updates at instantiation sites is very precise, reporting only a handful of false positives on all the applications. In contrast, if we use only weak updates when applying summaries, the number of false positives ranges from 200 to 1000, confirming that the application of strong updates interprocedurally is a key requirement for successful verification.

In a second set of experiments on smaller benchmarks, we compare the running times of our verification tool using the modular analysis described here with the running times of the same tool using a whole-program analysis. Figure 20 shows a comparison of the analysis running times of the modular and whole program analysis on five Unix Coreutils applications. As shown in this figure, the whole program analysis, which did not report any errors, takes $\sim$50 seconds on a program with only 1000 lines, whereas the modular analysis, which also did not report any errors, analyzes the same program in 2.3 seconds. Furthermore, observe that the running time of the whole program analysis increases much more quickly in the size of the application than that of the modular analysis.

In a final set of experiments, we plot the size of the alias partition set vs. the frequency of this set size for the benchmarks from Figure 18. The solid (red) line shows the size of the alias partition sets obtained by assuming $\alpha' \in \mathbb{A}(\alpha)$ if α and α' have compati-

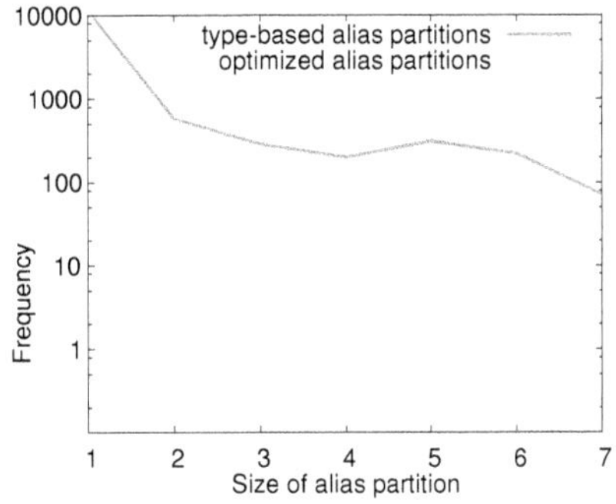

Figure 21. Size of alias partition set vs. Frequency

ble types. In contrast, the dashed (green) line shows the size of the alias partition sets obtained as described in Section 5. Observe that these optimizations significantly reduce the size of alias partition sets and substantially improve running time. In particular, without these optimizations, the benchmarks take an average of 2.7 times longer.

7. Related Work

Compositional Alias Analysis Modular alias analysis of a procedure performed by starting with unknown values to all parameters was also explored in [6] and then in Relevant Context Inference (RCI) [7]. The technique presented in [6] computes a new *partial transfer function* as new aliasing patterns are encountered at call sites and requires reanalysis of functions. In contrast, the technique in [7] is purely bottom-up, and uses equality and disequality queries to generate *summary transfer functions*. Our approach is similar to [7] in that we perform a strictly bottom-up analysis where the unknown points-to target of an argument is represented using one location variable and summary facts are predicated upon possible aliasing patterns at function entry. In contrast to our technique, RCI is only able to perform strong updates in very special cases intraprocedurally, and cannot perform strong updates at call sites. In fact, the summary computation described in [7] is only sound under the assumption that no points-to relations are killed by summary application. In contrast, summaries generated by our analysis are used to perform strong updates at call sites, and for the recursion-free fragment of the language from Section 3, applying a summary is as precise as analyzing the inlined body of the function.

The compositional pointer analysis algorithms given in [9, 10] assume there is no aliasing on function entry and analyze the function body under this assumption. However, since summaries computed in this way may be unsound, the summary is "corrected" using a fairly involved fixed-point computation at call sites. This approach is also much less precise than our technique because it only performs strong updates in a very limited number of situations.

Compositional Shape Analysis Recently, there has also been interest in compositional shape analysis using separation logic [11, 12]. Both of these works use *bi-abduction* to compute pre- and post-conditions on the shapes of recursive data structures. However, neither of these works guarantee precision. While this paper does not address computing summaries about shapes of recursive data structures, our technique can handle deep sharing and allows disjunctive facts.

General Modular Analysis Frameworks Theoretical foundations for modular program analysis are explored in [13], [14], and [15]. The work in [16] provides a framework for computing precise and concise summaries for IFDS [17] and IDE [18] dataflow problems. This framework is mainly specialized for typestate properties and relies on global points-to information. While it may be possible to apply this framework to obtain some form of modular heap analysis in principle, it is unclear how to do so, and the authors of [16] list this application as a future research direction.

References

[1] Aiken, A., Bugrara, S., Dillig, I., Dillig, T., Hackett, B., Hawkins, P.: An overview of the saturn project. In: PASTE, ACM (2007) 43–48

[2] Bush, W., Pincus, J., Sielaff, D.: A static analyzer for finding dynamic programming errors. Software: Practice and Experience **30**(7) (2000) 775–802

[3] Reps, T.W., Sagiv, S., Wilhelm, R.: Static program analysis via 3-valued logic. In: CAV. Volume 3114., Springer (2004) 15–30

[4] Dillig, I., Dillig, T., Aiken, A.: Fluid updates: Beyond strong vs. weak updates. In: ESOP. (2010)

[5] Landi, W., Ryder, B.G.: A safe approximate algorithm for interprocedural aliasing. SIGPLAN Not. **27**(7) (1992) 235–248

[6] Wilson, R.P., Lam, M.S.: Efficient context-sensitive pointer analysis for c programs. In: PLDI. (1995)

[7] Chatterjee, R., Ryder, B., Landi, W.: Relevant context inference. In: POPL, ACM (1999) 133–146

[8] Dillig, I., Dillig, T., Aiken, A.: Sound, complete and scalable path-sensitive analysis. In: PLDI, ACM (2008) 270–280

[9] Whaley, J., Rinard, M.: Compositional pointer and escape analysis for Java programs. In: OOPSLA, ACM (1999) 187–206

[10] Salcinau, A.: Pointer Analysis for Java Programs: Novel Techniques and Applications. PhD thesis, MIT (2006)

[11] Calcagno, C., Distefano, D., O'Hearn, P., Yang, H.: Compositional shape analysis by means of bi-abduction. POPL (2009) 289–300

[12] Gulavani, B., Chakraborty, S., Ramalingam, G., Nori, A.: Bottom-up shape analysis. SAS (2009) 188–204

[13] Cousot, P., Cousot, R.: Modular static program analysis. In: CC. (2002) 159–178

[14] Gulwani, S., Tiwari, A.: Computing procedure summaries for interprocedural analysis. ESOP (2007) 253–267

[15] Pnueli, M.: Two approaches to interprocedural data flow analysis. Program Flow Analysis: Theory and Applications (1981) 189–234

[16] Yorsh, G., Yahav, E., Chandra, S.: Generating precise and concise procedure summaries. POPL **43**(1) (2008) 221–234

[17] Reps, T.W., Horwitz, S., Sagiv, S.: Precise interprocedural dataflow analysis via graph reachability. In: POPL. (1995) 49–61

[18] Sagiv, S., Reps, T.W., Horwitz, S.: Precise interprocedural dataflow analysis with applications to constant propagation. Theor. Comput. Sci. **167**(1&2) (1996) 131–170

On Inter-Procedural Analysis of Programs with Lists and Data *

Ahmed Bouajjani Cezara Drăgoi Constantin Enea Mihaela Sighireanu

LIAFA, University Paris Diderot & CNRS

{abou,cezarad,cenea,sighirea}@liafa.jussieu.fr

Abstract

We address the problem of automatic synthesis of assertions on sequential programs with singly-linked lists containing data over infinite domains such as integers or reals. Our approach is based on an accurate abstract inter-procedural analysis. Program configurations are represented by graphs where nodes represent list segments without sharing. The data in these list segments are characterized by constraints in abstract domains. We consider a domain where constraints are in a universally quantified fragment of the first-order logic over sequences, as well as a domain constraining the multisets of data in sequences.

Our analysis computes the effect of each procedure in a local manner, by considering only the reachable part of the heap from its actual parameters. In order to avoid losses of information, we introduce a mechanism based on unfolding/folding operations allowing to strengthen the analysis in the domain of first-order formulas by the analysis in the multisets domain.

The same mechanism is used for strengthening the sound (but incomplete) entailment operator of the domain of first-order formulas. We have implemented our techniques in a prototype tool and we have shown that our approach is powerful enough for automatic (1) generation of non-trivial procedure summaries, (2) pre/post-condition reasoning, and (3) procedure equivalence checking.

Categories and Subject Descriptors F.3.2. [*Logics and Meanings of Programs*]: Specifying and Verifying and Reasoning about Programs—Program analysis; F.3.1. [*Logics and Meanings of Programs*]: Specifying and Verifying and Reasoning about Programs—Invariants, Assertions; D.2.5. [*Software Engineering*]: Testing and Debugging—Symbolic execution; E.2 [*Data*]: Data Storage Representations—Linked representations

General Terms Algorithms, Languages, Theory, Verification

Keywords interprocedural analysis, abstract interpretation, pointer analysis, shape analysis, data constraints

* This work has been supported by the French ANR project Veridyc.

PLDI'11, June 4–8, 2011, San Jose, California, USA.


```
typedef struct list {
  int data;
  struct list *next;
 } list;
list * quicksort(list *a){
  list *left,*right,*pivot,*res,*start;
  int d;
  if (a == NULL || a->next == NULL)
    res = clone(a);
  else {
    d = a->data;
    pivot = create(1); // list of length 1
    pivot->data = d;
    start = a->next;
    split(start,d,&left,&right);
    left = quicksort(left);
    right = quicksort(right);
    res = concat(left,pivot,right); }
  return res; }
```

Figure 1. The `quicksort` algorithm on singly-linked lists.

1. Introduction

Automatic synthesis of valid assertions about programs, such as loop invariants or procedure summaries, is an important and highly challenging problem. In this paper, we address this problem for sequential programs manipulating singly-linked lists with unbounded data such as integers or reals. These programs may contain procedure calls, and actually they are in many cases naturally written using recursive procedures.

Assertions about these programs typically involve constraints on the shape of the structures, their sizes, the data values contained in the memory cells, the multisets of their data, etc. Consider for instance the algorithm `quicksort` in Figure 1 that sorts the input list pointed to by the variable `a` (and where the call `split(start,d,&left,&right)` copies all the cells of the list pointed to by `start` which have data larger than `d` in the list `right`, and all the other ones in the list `left`). The specification of `quicksort` includes (1) the sortedness of the output list pointed to by `res`, expressed by the formula:

$$\forall y_1, y_2.\ 0 \leq y_1 \leq y_2 < \mathbf{len}(\mathtt{res}) \Rightarrow \mathtt{data}(y_1) \leq \mathtt{data}(y_2) \quad \text{(A)}$$

where y_1 and y_2 are interpreted as integers and used to refer to positions in the list pointed to by `res`, $\mathbf{len}(\mathtt{res})$ denotes the length of this list, and $\mathtt{data}(y_1)$ denotes the integer stored in the element of `res` at position y_1, and (2) the preservation property saying that the multiset of data of the input list `a` is equal to the multiset of data of the output list `res`. This property is expressed by

$$\mathtt{ms}(\mathtt{a}^0) = \mathtt{ms}(\mathtt{res}) \quad \text{(B)}$$

where $\mathtt{ms}(\mathtt{a}^0)$ (resp. $\mathtt{ms}(\mathtt{res})$) denotes the multiset of integers stored in the list pointed to by `a` at the beginning of the procedure (resp. `res` at the end of the procedure).

We propose an approach for automatic assertion synthesis based on inter-procedural analysis within the framework of abstract interpretation [7], that is, we consider abstract domains for expressing constraints on relations between program configurations, and we define compositional techniques for computing procedure summaries concerning various aspects such as shapes, sizes, and data.

We build on the work by Bouajjani et al. in [2] where they define an accurate *intra*-procedural abstract analysis for synthesizing invariants of programs with lists and without procedure calls. In their approach, abstract domains are defined where elements are pairs composed of a heap backbone and an abstract data constraint. The heap backbone is an abstraction of the *heap graph* (the graph representing the allocated memory) where only a bounded number of nodes are kept, including all sharing nodes and all the nodes pointed to by program variables. An edge in the backbone represents a path (without sharing nodes) relating the source and target nodes in the original heap. The data constraint is given as an element of some abstract domain and allows to specify properties of the data sequences represented by the edges of the heap backbone. The provided analysis in that paper is based on (a) unfolding the structures in order to reveal the properties of some internal nodes in the lists, which makes necessary to introduce in the structures some nodes, called simple nodes, others than the sharing nodes or those pointed to by variables, and then (b) folding the structures by eliminating the simple nodes and in the same time collecting the informations on these nodes using a formula that speaks about sequences of data. The analysis is iterated several times, which may lead to additional unfoldings and foldings. Then, widening techniques on numerical domains are used in order to force termination. Several abstract domains are defined for the analysis, and in particular, domains where elements are (1) formulas in a universally quantified fragment of the first-order logic over data words, or (2) conjunctions of equality constraints between unions of multisets of data in words. The formulas in the first abstract domain contain a (quantified) universal part which is a conjunction of formulas $\forall \mathbf{y}.\ (P \Rightarrow U)$, where $\mathbf{y}$ is a vector of variables interpreted as positions in the words, P is a constraint on the positions (seen as integers) associated with the $\mathbf{y}$'s, and U is a constraint on the data values at these positions. It is assumed that P is obtained from a finite set of fixed *patterns* corresponding to, e.g., order constraints or difference constraints. While the techniques presented in [2] are strong enough to generate complex invariants for iterative programs, they cannot be applied for compositional computation of procedure summaries.

In this paper, we propose an extension of the approach in [2] by defining new techniques for accurate *inter*-procedural abstract analysis. This extension is not trivial due to many delicate problems that appear when addressing the compositionality issue. Indeed, in the spirit of [23], at each procedure call, the callee has only access to the part of the heap that is reachable from its actual parameters. The use of such local heaps is delicate due to the fact that there are relations between the elements of the local heap of the callee, and of the heaps of the procedures that are in the call stack. If these relations are lost during the analysis, this one can be unsound in some cases, or very imprecise in others. However, it is not feasible to maintain explicitly these relations during the analysis. Let us examine this crucial problem.

This problem has been addressed in [23] in a framework where data are not considered. In this case, the relations inter-local heaps are due to reachability: nodes in the local heap of the callee can be reachable from the other heaps through paths that do not contain nodes pointed to by the parameters of the procedure (the entry points of the local heap). If during the call these nodes become locally unreachable and deleted, the analysis becomes unsound. The solution to this proposed in [23] consists in maintaining along the calls the points, called cutpoints, where these (inter-local heap)

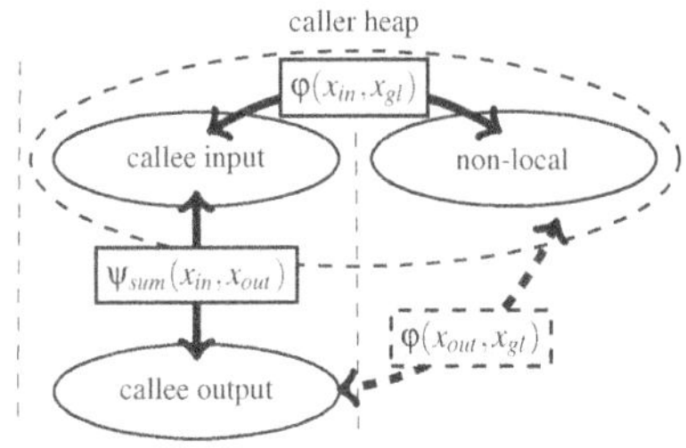

Figure 2. Relation between caller and callee local heaps.

paths enter local heaps. This is a tricky problem since in general the number of cutpoints may be unbounded. However, there is a significant class of programs for which cutpoints are never generated during the analysis. The class of such cutpoint free programs [24] includes programs such as sorting algorithms, traversal of lists, insertion, deletion, etc. In this paper, we consider cutpoint free programs and focus on the problems induced by data manipulation.

Indeed, even for cutpoint free programs, the problem above persists when data constraints are considered as we do in our framework. The reason is that elements in the local heap of a procedure can be related to elements in the rest of the heap with data constraints such as equality, ordering, etc. This situation is depicted in Figure 2. Elements in the local heap of the callee are linked at the call point to external elements by some data relation, φ, and the analysis generates a summary ψ_{sum} of the procedure relating the input heap with the output heap. Then, the problem is whether there is a link φ between the elements in the callee output heap and the external elements in the caller heap. This problem depends on the accuracy of the used summarization technique. Consider for instance the `quicksort` procedure that takes the first element `d` of the input list `a` as the pivot, splits the tail of the list `a` into two lists `left` and `right` where all the elements of `left` resp. `right` are smaller resp. greater than `d`, and then performs two recursive calls on the lists `left` and `right`, before composing the results, together with `d`, into a sorted list. After the recursive call at line 16 on `left`, the information we obtain from the analysis with the domain of first-order formulas is that the output list `left'` is sorted. Since we had already the information that the elements of the input list `left` were all less than `d`, we must infer after the return from that call that the elements of `left'` are also less than `d`. But, since the link between `d` and the elements of `left` has not been passed to the recursive call, this information cannot be computed. This is because the used abstract domain cannot express the fact that a list is a permutation of another list (which requires formulas beyond the universally quantified fragment). Again, maintaining all the relations between the elements of the local heaps and the external elements is not feasible. Our solution to this problem is based on strengthening the analysis in the domain of first-order formulas with the analysis in the domain of multiset constraints. Indeed, for the `quicksort` example, knowing that `left` and `left'` have the same multisets of elements should allow to infer from the fact that all elements of `left` are less than `d`, that the same fact also holds about the elements of `left'`.

Another problem that must be addressed for the design of compositional analysis is due to the use of patterns P for left-hand sides of implications in the first-order formulas. Indeed, the analysis of different procedures may need the use of different sets of patterns, and therefore it is important to be able to localize the choice of these patterns to each procedure. Otherwise, it would be necessary to use a set of patterns including the union of all the sets that are used during the whole analysis, and this would obviously make the analysis inefficient. For instance, the computation of the for-

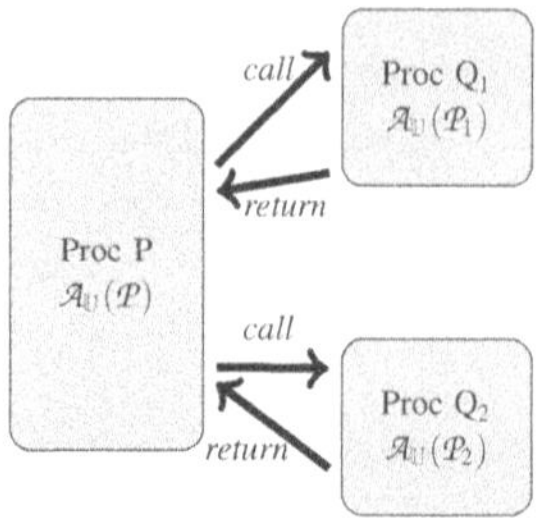

Figure 3. Compositional analysis with patterns.

mula $(\forall y.\ 0 \leq y < \mathtt{len}(\mathtt{left}) \Rightarrow \mathtt{data}(y) \leq d) \wedge (\forall y.\ 0 \leq y < \mathtt{len}(\mathtt{right}) \Rightarrow \mathtt{data}(y) > d)$ describing the effect of the procedure `split` called by `quicksort` does not need the use of the pattern $0 \leq y_1 \leq y_2 < \mathtt{len}(\mathtt{res})$ that is used for the generation of the sortedness property. Consequently, during the analysis, at procedure calls and returns, we need to switch from an abstract domain of formulas parametrized by some set of patterns, say $\mathcal{P}$, to an abstract domain parametrized by another set of patterns $\mathcal{P}_1$ or $\mathcal{P}_2$ as shown in Figure 3 ($\mathcal{A}_{\mathbb{U}}(\mathcal{P})$ denotes the domain of first-order formulas parametrized by the set of patterns $\mathcal{P}$).

The two problems exposed above show that in order to define a compositional and accurate inter-procedural analysis, we need to define an operation for composing abstract domains (e.g., first-order formulas with multiset constraints, or first-order formulas of different types). We propose in this paper a mechanism which allows to solve these problems. This mechanism is based on unfolding/folding operations which can be used, at procedure calls and returns, to (1) compute an over-approximation of the intersection between a first-order formula and a multiset constraint and (2) to convert universal formulas defined over a set of patterns $\mathcal{P}_1$ to formulas defined over a set of patterns $\mathcal{P}_2$.

Beyond compositional summary computation, the operation we define for combining abstract domains allows to tackle two other interesting problems. First, it allows to define an entailment operation on combined constraints of the form $\phi \wedge \psi \Rightarrow \phi'$ where ϕ and ϕ' are two universal first-order formulas (potentially over different sets of patterns), and ψ is a multiset constraint. This provides a lightweight sound (but not complete) decision procedure for such kind of formulas, which is useful for carrying out pre-post condition reasoning. Furthermore, our techniques are accurate enough to be used for automatic procedure equivalence checking. It is easy to see that this problem can be reduced to inter-procedural analysis, provided that it is possible to express equality between structures, and derive such properties. This is not trivial in general since reasoning about combined abstract domains is needed. For instance, to check that two sorting procedures P_1 and P_2 are equivalent, it is possible to call each of them on two identical input lists I_1 and I_2, and then assert that the two outputs O_1 and O_2 are equal. Assuming that the summary of P_i is $sorted(O_i) \wedge \mathtt{ms}(I_i) = \mathtt{ms}(O_i)$, for $i \in \{1,2\}$, this amounts to check the validity of the formula:

$$\begin{aligned}\big(equal(I_1,I_2) \wedge sorted(O_1) \wedge \mathtt{ms}(I_1) = \mathtt{ms}(O_1)\\ \wedge\, sorted(O_2) \wedge \mathtt{ms}(I_2) = \mathtt{ms}(O_2)\big)\\ \Rightarrow equal(O_1,O_2),\end{aligned} \quad \text{(C)}$$

where the predicates *equal* and *sorted* are expressed by first-order formulas. Our techniques are able to find that this formula is indeed valid.

We have implemented our techniques and carried out several experiments showing the strength of our approach.

2. Programs

Let *PVar* be a set of variables of type reference to a record type called `list` defined by a single reference field `next` and one data field `data` of integer type. We consider that *PVar* includes the constant NULL. Also, let *DVar* be a set of variables interpreted as integers. The generalization to record types with several data fields and data fields of different basic types is straightforward.

Syntax: A *program* is defined by a set of procedures, each of them represented by its *intra-procedural control flow graph* (CFG, for short). Formally, a procedure P is a tuple $(\mathbf{fpi}, \mathbf{fpo}, \mathbf{loc}, G)$, where $\mathbf{loc} \subseteq PVar \cup DVar$ is the vector of local variables, $\mathbf{fpi} \subseteq \mathbf{loc}$ and $\mathbf{fpo} \subseteq \mathbf{loc}$ are the vectors of formal input, resp. output, parameters, and G is its CFG. W.l.o.g., we suppose that the CFG of P contains a unique *entry point* s_P and a unique *exit point* e_P. Its edges are labeled by (1) statements of the form p=`new`, p=q, p->`next`=q, p->`data`=dt, and $\mathbf{y}$=$Q(\mathbf{x})$, where $p,q \in PVar$, dt is a term representing an integer (built over terms of the form $d \in DVar$ and p->`data` using operations over $\mathbb{Z}$), and $\mathbf{y},\mathbf{x} \subseteq PVar \cup DVar$, (2) boolean conditions on data built using predicates over $\mathbb{Z}$, (3) boolean conditions on pointers of the form p==q where $p,q \in PVar$, or (4) statements of the form `assert` φ and `assume` φ, where φ is a formula (see Section 4 for more details concerning the syntax of φ). The semantics assumes a garbage collector and consequently, the statement `free` is useless. We assume a call-by-value semantics for the procedure parameters and that each procedure has its own set of local variables. We forbid pointers to procedures and pointer arithmetic.

The *inter-procedural control flow graph* (ICFG, for short) of a program is defined as usual by replacing edges labeled by procedure calls with (1) a *call to start* edge labeled by $\langle \mathbf{call}\ \mathbf{y}$=$Q(\mathbf{x})\rangle$, and (2) an *exit to return* edge labeled by $\langle \mathbf{ret}\ \mathbf{y}$=$Q(\mathbf{x})\rangle$.

Semantics: A program configuration is a valuation of the variables interpreted as integers together with a configuration of the allocated memory. The latter is represented by a labeled directed graph where nodes correspond to objects of type `list` and edges correspond to values of the reference field `next`. The nodes are labeled by the values of the field `data` and by the program pointer variables which are pointing to the corresponding objects. The constant NULL is represented by a distinguished node $\sharp$. Such a representation for a program configuration is called a *heap*.

DEFINITION 2.1 **(Heap).** *A* heap over *PVar* and *DVar is a tuple* $H = (N,S,V,L,D)$ *where:*

1. *N is a finite set of nodes which contains a distinguished node $\sharp$,*
2. *$S : N \times N$ is a set of edges such that S contains at most one edge (n,n'), for any $n \in N$, and S does not contain an edge $(\sharp,n)$ with $n \in N$,*
3. *$V : PVar \rightarrow N$ is a function associating nodes to pointer variables s.t. $V(\mathtt{NULL}) = \sharp$,*
4. *$L : N \rightharpoonup \mathbb{Z}$ is a partial function associating nodes to integers s.t. only $L(\sharp)$ is undefined, and*
5. *$D : DVar \rightarrow \mathbb{Z}$ is a valuation for the data variables.*

DEFINITION 2.2 **(Simple/crucial node).** *A node which is labeled by a pointer variable or which has at least two predecessors is called a* crucial node. *Otherwise, it is called a* simple node.

For any procedure $P = (\mathbf{fpi}, \mathbf{fpo}, \mathbf{loc}, G)$ and any control point c in P, we consider relations between program configurations at the entry point of P and program configurations at c. These relations can be represented using a double vocabulary $\mathbf{loc} \cup \mathbf{loc}^0$, where $\mathbf{loc}^0 = \{v^0 \mid v \in \mathbf{loc}\}$ denote the values of the variables in $\mathbf{loc}$ at the entry point of P. A relation associated to P at c is represented by a heap over $\mathbf{loc} \cup \mathbf{loc}^0$ containing a valuation for the integer variables in $(\mathbf{loc} \cap DVar) \cup (\mathbf{loc} \cap DVar)^0$ together with a graph which is the union of two sub-graphs: G^0 represents the heap at the entry point of P and G represents the heap at the control point c. For example, a relation associated to `quicksort` at line 16 is represented by the valuation $[d^0 = 0, d = 6]$ and the labeled graph in Figure 4(a) (we suppose that local integer variables are initialized to 0). The nodes which correspond to objects pointed to by program variables are circled. The subgraph containing only nodes reachable from the node labeled by a^0 represents the input configuration while the rest of the graph represents the heap configuration at line 16.

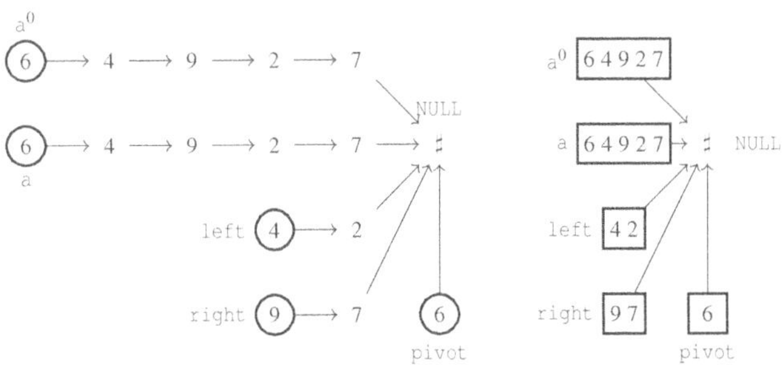

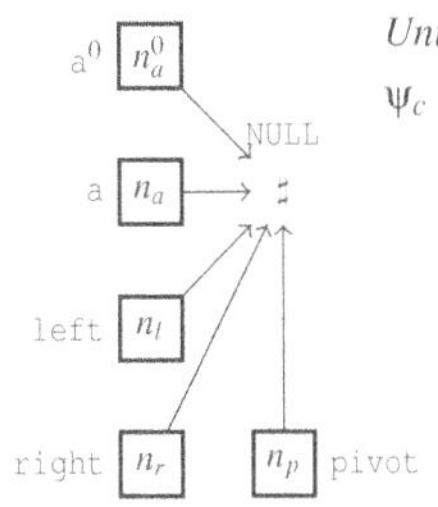

Universally quantified formula:

$$\begin{aligned}\psi_c : &\ \mathtt{hd}(n_l) \leq \mathtt{hd}(n_p) \wedge \mathtt{hd}(n_r) > \mathtt{hd}(n_p)\\ &\wedge \mathtt{len}(n_a) = \mathtt{len}(n_l) + \mathtt{len}(n_r) + \mathtt{len}(n_p)\\ &\wedge \forall y.\, y \in \mathtt{tl}(n_l) \Rightarrow n_l[y] \leq \mathtt{hd}(n_p)\\ &\wedge \forall y.\, y \in \mathtt{tl}(n_r) \Rightarrow n_r[y] > \mathtt{hd}(n_p)\\ &\wedge d = \mathtt{hd}(n_p) \wedge eq_\forall(n_a, n_a^0) \wedge \mathtt{len}(n_p) = 1,\end{aligned}$$

Multiset formula:

$$\begin{aligned}\psi'_c : &\ \mathtt{ms}(n_a) = \mathtt{ms}(n_l) \cup \mathtt{ms}(n_r) \cup \mathtt{ms}(n_p)\\ &\wedge \mathtt{ms}(n_a^0) = \mathtt{ms}(n_a)\end{aligned}$$

(c)

Figure 4. Relations between program configurations.

The concrete semantics defines a mapping ρ which associates to each control point c in the CFG of a procedure P a set of heaps over $\mathbf{loc} \cup \mathbf{loc}^0$. As usual, the mapping ρ is defined by a system of recursive equations [8, 28] of the form:

$$R_{init} \in \rho(s_P) \text{ and } \rho(c) = \rho(c) \cup \bigcup_{c' \xrightarrow{St} c} \mathtt{post}(St, \rho(c')), \qquad \text{(D)}$$

where (1) R_{init} is a heap containing two copies of the initial configuration of some procedure $P = (\mathbf{fpi}, \mathbf{fpo}, \mathbf{loc}, G)$, one copy over $\mathbf{loc}^0$, and one copy over $\mathbf{loc}$, (2) $c' \xrightarrow{St} c$ is an edge from the ICFG labeled by St, and (3) `post` is the postcondition operator.

For any statement, except for procedure calls and returns, `post` affects only the part of the heap reachable from nodes labeled by variables in **loc**. For simplicity, we assume that (1) heaps don't contain garbage, i.e., all the nodes are reachable from nodes labeled by pointer variables, and (2) each pointer assignment `p->next=q`, resp. `p=q`, is preceded by `p->next=NULL`, resp. `p=NULL`. The semantics of the procedure calls and returns is based on *local heaps* [23], i.e. heaps containing only objects reachable from the actual parameters. For example, in Figure 4(a), the local heap for the procedure call `quicksort(left)` contains only the nodes reachable from the node labeled by `left`. As we consider only cutpoint-free programs [24], the definition of this semantics is straightforward.

3. Abstractions of program relations

In this section, we recall the abstract domains defined in [2].

Preliminaries on abstract interpretation: Let $\mathcal{C} = (C, \subseteq)$ and $\mathcal{A} = (A, \sqsubseteq)$ be two lattices ($\subseteq$, resp. $\sqsubseteq$, are order relations on C, resp. A). The lattice $\mathcal{A}$ is an *abstract domain* for $\mathcal{C}$ [7, 10] if there exists a monotonic function $\gamma : A \to C$. In the following, an abstract domain $\mathcal{A}$ is denoted by $\mathcal{A} = (A, \sqsubseteq, \sqcap, \sqcup, \top, \bot)$, where $\sqcap$ denotes its greatest lower bound (meet) operator, $\sqcup$ denotes its lowest greater bound (join) operator, $\top$ its top element and $\bot$ its bottom element. Moreover, as usual in the abstract interpretation framework, ∇ represents the widening operator. Let $\mathcal{F}_C$ be a set of concrete transformers, that is, of functions from C into C. If $\mathcal{A}$ is an abstract domain for $\mathcal{C}$, the set of its abstract transformers, denoted $\mathcal{F}^\#_{\mathcal{A}}$, contains a function $f^\# : A \to A$ for each $f \in \mathcal{F}_C$. The transformer $f^\#$ is *sound* if $f(\gamma(a)) \subseteq \gamma(f^\#(a))$, for any $a \in A$.

3.1 Abstract domains for heaps

The abstraction of a labeled graph H representing (relations between) program configurations is defined starting from a *decomposition* obtained by (1) keeping only some nodes from H but at least all the crucial nodes (2) adding an edge between any two nodes which are reachable in the initial graph, and (3) labeling every node n with a word over $\mathbb{Z}$ which contains the integers on the path from H between n and its successor in the new graph. For example, Figure 4(b) gives a decomposition for the graph in Figure 4(a).

Abstractions of program relations can be defined by representing the values of the integer program variables and the words over $\mathbb{Z}$ as formulas in some logic. The logics we use capture various aspects such as constraints on the sizes, the multisets of their letters, or the data at different positions of the words. For example, the graph and the formula ψ_c in Figure 4(c) represent an abstraction of the program relation in Figure 4(a) obtained starting from the decomposition in Figure 4(b). The same holds for the graph and the multiset formula ψ'_c in Figure 4(c). Such a pair between a graph and a formula is called *abstract heap*. In the formula ψ_c, n_a^0, n_a, n_l, n_r, and n_p are variables interpreted as words over $\mathbb{Z}$, $\mathtt{hd}(n_l)$ denotes the first letter of the word denoted by n_l, $\mathtt{len}(n_a)$ denotes the length of the word denoted by n_a, y is a variable interpreted as a position in some word (as usual, the positions of a word $a_0 a_1 \ldots a_n$ are the integers from 0 to n), $y \in \mathtt{tl}(n_l)$ means that y belongs to the *tail* of n_l (i.e., the suffix starting with the second letter), and $n_l[y]$ is a term interpreted as the letter at the position y of n_l. The formula $eq_\forall(n_a, n_a^0)$ states that the words denoted by n_a and n_a^0 are identical. We distinguish the first letter of a word from its tail because programs assignments can update only this first letter (the statement `p->data=...` updates the first letter of the word associated to the node labeled by p). In the multiset formula, $\mathtt{ms}(n_a)$ denotes the multiset containing all the letters of n_a.

Let $\mathbb{Z}^+$ denote the set of non-empty sequences over $\mathbb{Z}$ and let *DWVar* be a set of *data word variables* interpreted as elements of $\mathbb{Z}^+$. A *data words logic* is a (possibly infinite) set of formulas from a first order logic $\mathsf{FO}(DWVar, DVar, \mathbb{O}, \mathbb{P})$ over the variables $DWVar \cup DVar$, where $\mathbb{O}$ is a set of operation symbols and $\mathbb{P}$ is a set of predicate symbols. In order to express program transformations we suppose that $\mathbb{O}$ contains at least the concatenation operator $\cdot$, a function symbol $\mathtt{len} : \mathbb{Z}^+ \to \mathbb{Z}$ which returns the length of the input sequence and the equality predicate between words eq. However, we do not require that these symbols are used in the set of formulas belonging to some data words logic.

DEFINITION 3.1 (**$\mathbb{LDW}$-domain).** *A logical data words abstract domain over DWVar and DVar ($\mathbb{LDW}$-domain, for short) is a lattice $\mathcal{A}_{\mathbb{W}} = (A^{\mathbb{W}}, \sqsubseteq^{\mathbb{W}}, \sqcap^{\mathbb{W}}, \sqcup^{\mathbb{W}}, \top^{\mathbb{W}}, \bot^{\mathbb{W}})$, where $A^{\mathbb{W}}$ is a data words logic, which is an abstract domain for the lattice of sets of pairs (L, D) with $L : DWVar \to \mathbb{Z}^+$ and $D : DVar \to \mathbb{Z}$.*

Notice that $\sqsubseteq^{\mathbb{W}}$ is a sound approximation of the logical implication $\Rightarrow$ between formulas (i.e., if $\varphi_1 \sqsubseteq^{\mathbb{W}} \varphi_2$ then $\varphi_1 \Rightarrow \varphi_2$).

DEFINITION 3.2 (**Abstract heap).** *An* abstract heap over *PVar, DVar*, and an $\mathbb{LDW}$-domain $\mathcal{A}_{\mathbb{W}}$ *is a tuple* $\widetilde{H} = (N, S, V, \widetilde{W})$ *where* N, S, V *are as in the definition of heaps, and* $\widetilde{W}$ *is a formula in* $\mathcal{A}_{\mathbb{W}}$ *over the data word variables* $N \setminus \{\sharp\}$ *(we assume that for each node in N there exists a data word variable with the same name) and the data variables DVar. A k-*abstract heap *is an abstract heap with at most k simple nodes.*

Two abstract heaps are *isomorphic* if their underlying graphs are isomorphic. Let $\mathcal{C}_{\mathbb{H}}$ denote the lattice of sets of heaps. We define $\mathcal{A}_{\mathbb{H}}(k, \mathcal{A}_{\mathbb{W}})$ an abstract domain for $\mathcal{C}_{\mathbb{H}}$ whose elements are k-abstract heaps over $\mathcal{A}_{\mathbb{W}}$ s.t. (1) for any two isomorphic abstract heaps, the lattice operators are obtained by applying the corresponding operators between the values from $\mathcal{A}_{\mathbb{W}}$, and (2) the join and the widening (resp. meet) of two non-isomorphic abstract heaps is $\top^{\mathbb{H}}$ (resp. $\bot^{\mathbb{H}}$). Notice that $\nabla^{\mathbb{H}}$ is a widening operator because the heaps generated by the programs which manipulate only singly-linked lists contain a bounded number of crucial nodes [19].

The domains used in the analysis are finite powerset domains over $\mathcal{A}_{\mathbb{H}}(k, \mathcal{A}_{\mathbb{W}})$. Their elements are called *k-abstract heap sets*.

DEFINITION 3.3 (**Abstract heap set).** *A k-*abstract heap set over *PVar, DVar*, and an $\mathbb{LDW}$-domain $\mathcal{A}_{\mathbb{W}}$ *is a finite set of non-isomorphic k-abstract heaps over PVar, DVar, and* $\mathcal{A}_{\mathbb{W}}$. *The abstract domain of k-abstract heap sets is denoted by* $\mathcal{A}_{\mathbb{HS}}(k, \mathcal{A}_{\mathbb{W}}) = (A^{\mathbb{HS}}(k, \mathcal{A}_{\mathbb{W}}), \sqsubseteq^{\mathbb{HS}}, \sqcap^{\mathbb{HS}}, \sqcup^{\mathbb{HS}}, \top^{\mathbb{HS}}, \bot^{\mathbb{HS}})$, *where* $A^{\mathbb{HS}}(k, \mathcal{A}_{\mathbb{W}})$ *is the set of all k-abstract heap sets over PVar, DVar, and* $\mathcal{A}_{\mathbb{W}}$.

The operators from $\mathcal{A}_{\mathbb{HS}}(k, \mathcal{A}_{\mathbb{W}})$ and the widening operator are obtained from those of $\mathcal{A}_{\mathbb{H}}(k, \mathcal{A}_{\mathbb{W}})$ as usual [9]. For example, the join of two abstract heap sets is computed by taking the union of these sets and by applying the join operator between any two isomorphic abstract heaps.

3.2 An $\mathbb{LDW}$-domain with universally quantified formulas

We present the abstract domain $\mathcal{A}_{\mathbb{U}} = (A^{\mathbb{U}}, \sqsubseteq^{\mathbb{U}}, \sqcap^{\mathbb{U}}, \sqcup^{\mathbb{U}}, \top^{\mathbb{U}}, \bot^{\mathbb{U}})$ whose elements are first-order formulas with free variables in $DWVar \cup DVar$. This domain is parametrized by a set of constraints on position variables (which are interpreted as positions in the words), called *guard patterns*. Guard patterns are conjunctions of:

- formulas that associate vectors of position variables with data word variables ($\mathbf{y} \in \mathtt{tl}(\omega)$ means that the position variables from the vector $\mathbf{y}$ are interpreted as positions in the tail of ω),
- formulas that impose a total order between the values of the position variables associated with the same data word variable ($y^1 \prec_1 y^2 \prec_2 \ldots \prec_m y^m$, where $\prec_i \in \{\leq, <, <_1\}$ with $y <_1 y'$ iff $y' = y + 1$), and
- a linear constraint on the values of the position variables which are the first in the order constraints considered above.

Let $\mathcal{V} \subseteq DWVar$ and let $\mathcal{P}$ be a set of guard patterns. Also, let $\mathcal{P}(\mathcal{V})$ be a set of formulas obtained from guard patterns in $\mathcal{P}$ by substituting all data word variables with variables from $\mathcal{V}$. An element of $A_{\mathbb{U}}$ is a formula of the form:

$$\widetilde{W}(\mathcal{V}) ::= E(\mathcal{V}) \wedge \bigwedge_{g(\mathbf{y}) \in \mathcal{P}(\mathcal{V})} \forall \mathbf{y}.\, g(\mathbf{y}) \Rightarrow U_g \qquad \text{(E)}$$

where $E(\mathcal{V})$ is a quantifier-free arithmetical formula over *DVar* and terms $\mathtt{hd}(w)$, $\mathtt{len}(w)$ with $w \in \mathcal{V}$, $g(\mathbf{y})$ is a guard over the vector of position variables $\mathbf{y}$, and U_g is a quantifier-free arithmetical formula over the terms in $E(\mathcal{V})$ together with $w[y]$ and y, for any $w \in \mathcal{V}$ and $y \in \mathbf{y}$. It is assumed that the term $w[y]$ appears in U_g only if $g(\mathbf{y})$ associates y with w. Also, E and U_g represent elements of some numerical abstract domain $\mathcal{A}_{\mathbb{Z}} = (A^{\mathbb{Z}}, \sqsubseteq^{\mathbb{Z}}, \sqcap^{\mathbb{Z}}, \sqcup^{\mathbb{Z}}, \top^{\mathbb{Z}}, \bot^{\mathbb{Z}})$ which is a parameter of $\mathcal{A}_{\mathbb{U}}$.

Lattice operators: The value $\top^{\mathbb{U}}$ (resp. $\bot^{\mathbb{U}}$) is defined by the formula in which E and all U_g are $\top^{\mathbb{Z}}$ (resp. $\bot^{\mathbb{Z}}$). Let

$$\widetilde{W}(\mathcal{V}_1) = E(\mathcal{V}_1) \wedge \textstyle\bigwedge_{g(\mathbf{y}) \in \mathcal{P}(\mathcal{V}_1)} \forall \mathbf{y}.\, (g(\mathbf{y}) \Rightarrow U_g) \text{ and}$$
$$\widetilde{W}'(\mathcal{V}_2) = E'(\mathcal{V}_2) \wedge \textstyle\bigwedge_{g(\mathbf{y}) \in \mathcal{P}(\mathcal{V}_2)} \forall \mathbf{y}.\, (g(\mathbf{y}) \Rightarrow U'_g).$$

Before applying any lattice operator we add to $\widetilde{W}$ (resp. $\widetilde{W}'$) universally quantified formulas $\forall \mathbf{y}.\, g(\mathbf{y}) \Rightarrow \top^{\mathbb{Z}}$, for any $g(\mathbf{y}) \in \mathcal{P}(\mathcal{V}_1) \setminus \mathcal{P}(\mathcal{V}_2)$ (resp. $g(\mathbf{y}) \in \mathcal{P}(\mathcal{V}_2) \setminus \mathcal{P}(\mathcal{V}_1)$).

Then, $\widetilde{W} \sqsubseteq^{\mathbb{U}} \widetilde{W}'$ iff (1) $E \sqsubseteq^{\mathbb{Z}} E'$, and (2) for each guard $g(\mathbf{y}) \in \mathcal{P}(\mathcal{V}_1) \cup \mathcal{P}(\mathcal{V}_2)$ which associates the vector of position variables $\mathbf{y_i}$ with the data word variable w_i, for all $1 \leq i \leq n$, the following holds: if $E \sqsubseteq^{\mathbb{Z}} \mathtt{len}(w_i) \geq |\mathbf{y}_i| + 1$, for all $1 \leq i \leq n$, then $E \sqcap^{\mathbb{Z}} U_g \sqsubseteq^{\mathbb{Z}} U'_g$.

Also, $\widetilde{W} \sqcup^{\mathbb{U}} \widetilde{W}'$ is defined by

$$\left(E \sqcup^{\mathbb{Z}} E'\right) \wedge \bigwedge_{g(\mathbf{y}) \in \mathcal{P}(\mathcal{V}_1) \cup \mathcal{P}(\mathcal{V}_2)} \forall \mathbf{y}.\, g(\mathbf{y}) \Rightarrow \left(U_g \sqcup^{\mathbb{Z}} U'_g\right).$$

The operators $\sqcap^{\mathbb{U}}$ and $\nabla^{\mathbb{U}}$ are defined in a similar way.

3.3 An $\mathbb{LDW}$-domain with multiset formulas

We present the abstract domain $\mathcal{A}_{\mathbb{M}} = (A^{\mathbb{M}}, \sqsubseteq^{\mathbb{M}}, \sqcap^{\mathbb{M}}, \sqcup^{\mathbb{M}}, \top^{\mathbb{M}}, \bot^{\mathbb{M}})$ whose elements are multiset constraints with free variables in $DWVar \cup DVar$. A *basic multiset term* is $u ::= \mathtt{mhd}(n) \mid \mathtt{mtl}(n) \mid d$, where $n \in DWVar$ and $d \in DVar$. The term $\mathtt{mhd}(n)$ (resp. d) represents the singleton containing the first letter of the word associated to n (resp. the value of d). The term $\mathtt{mtl}(n)$ represents the multiset containing all the letters of the word associated to n except for the first one. As a shorthand, $\mathtt{ms}(n)$ denotes the term $\mathtt{mhd}(n) \cup \mathtt{mtl}(n)$.

A *multiset constraint* is a conjunction of formulas of the form $u_1 \cup u_2 \cup \cdots \cup u_s = v_1 \cup v_2 \cup \cdots \cup v_t$, where $s \geq 1$, $t \geq 1$, and for all $1 \leq i \leq s$ and $1 \leq j \leq t$, u_i and v_j are pairwise distinct basic multiset terms, and $\cup$ is the usual union operator between multisets.

Multiset constraints can be represented by a polyhedron with a dimension for any basic term: a formula $u_1 \cup u_2 \cup \cdots \cup u_s = v_1 \cup v_2 \cup \cdots \cup v_t$ is represented by the linear constraint $u_1 + u_2 + \cdots + u_s = v_1 + v_2 + \cdots + v_t$. The entailment relation between the multiset constraints is defined by the entailment relation between the corresponding polyhedra. The lattice of multiset constraints is finite (for finite *DWVar* and *DVar*) and consequently, there is no need for a widening operator.

4. Abstract semantics

The abstract semantics defines a mapping $\rho^{\#}$, which associates to each control point of the program an abstract heap set. It is defined by the system of equations obtained from the one defining the concrete semantics in (D), by replacing `post` with a *sound abstract transformer* $\mathtt{post}^{\#}$ over abstract heap sets. The termination of the fixpoint computation is guaranteed by applying the widening operator at the start of each intra-procedural loop and at the entry and exit point of each recursive procedure.

The analysis that we have implemented tabulates the input configurations of the computed procedure summaries. In this way, we avoid to compute twice the same procedure summary. For any label *St* of some ICFG edge, we define $\mathtt{post}^{\#}$ as follows:

- if *St* is different from `assume`, `assert`, procedure call and procedure return, we first define the abstract transformer $\mathtt{post}^{\#}$ over abstract heaps. Then, $\mathtt{post}^{\#}(St, HS)$, where HS is some abstract heap set, is the join in $\mathcal{A}_{\mathbb{HS}}$ of $\mathtt{post}^{\#}(St, \widetilde{H})$, for each $\widetilde{H} \in HS$;
- otherwise, we define $\mathtt{post}^{\#}$ directly over abstract heap sets.

The statement p=NULL: The abstract transformer corresponding to this statement begins by moving the label p to the node $\sharp$. It may happen that the obtained abstract heap contains more than k simple nodes. If it is the case, the transformer calls a procedure called $\mathtt{fold}^{\#}$ which, for any $\tilde{H} \in \mathcal{A}_{\mathbb{H}}$, returns an abstract heap $\tilde{H}'$ with no simple nodes which over-approximates $\tilde{H}$ (i.e., the concretization of $\tilde{H}'$ includes the concretization of $\tilde{H}$).

Let $\tilde{H} = (N,S,V,\widetilde{W})$ be an abstract heap and let $n_1,\ldots,n_t$ be all its simple nodes. For simplicity, suppose that they are on the same path between two crucial nodes n and m. We define $\mathtt{fold}^{\#}(\tilde{H}) = (N',S',V,\widetilde{W}')$, where (N',S') are obtained by removing the nodes $n_1,\ldots,n_t$ and by adding the edge (n,m) and $\widetilde{W}'$ is a formula in $\mathcal{A}_{\mathbb{W}}$ which is an over-approximation of the following formula

$$\left(\exists n \exists n_1 \ldots \exists n_t.\ \left(\overline{n} = n \cdot n_1 \cdot \ldots \cdot n_t \wedge \widetilde{W}\right)\right)[\overline{n} \leftarrow n]. \qquad \text{(F)}$$

The formula in (F) belongs to $\mathcal{A}_{\mathbb{W}}$ extended with quantification over data word variables, and a concatenation operation symbol "$\cdot$". Intuitively, (F) says that the word associated to n in $\mathtt{fold}^{\#}(\tilde{H})$ (denoted in (F) by $\overline{n}$) is the concatenation of the words associated to $n,n_1,\ldots,n_t$ in $\tilde{H}$.

The transformer $\mathtt{concat}^{\#}$ from [2] computes an over-approximation of (F) in $\mathcal{A}_{\mathbb{U}}$. It is precise for domains $\mathcal{A}_{\mathbb{U}}$ parametrized by *closed sets of patterns*. Roughly, a set of patterns $\mathcal{P}$ is closed if whenever it contains a pattern P over the set of position variables $\mathbf{y}$ it also contains all the projections of P (in Presburger arithmetics) on subsets of $\mathbf{y}$. In $\mathcal{A}_{\mathbb{M}}$, an over-approximation of (F) can be obtained by:

- updating in $\widetilde{W}$, $\mathtt{mtl}(n_1)$ to

  $$\mathtt{mtl}(n_1) \cup \mathtt{mhd}(n_2) \cup \mathtt{mtl}(n_2) \cup \cdots \cup \mathtt{mhd}(n_t) \cup \mathtt{mtl}(n_t)$$

- removing all the constraints on the variables $n_2,\ldots,n_t$.

Statements involving reference fields: For a statement St of the form p->next=NULL (resp. q=p->next), the concrete post modifies the edge (resp. the target of the edge) starting in the node labeled by p. The abstract transformer $\mathtt{post}^{\#}(St,\tilde{H})$, where $\tilde{H} = (N,S,V,\widetilde{W})$, can not directly modify this edge because it may correspond to a path of arbitrary length in the concrete heap. Thus, $\mathtt{post}^{\#}(St,\tilde{H})$ begins by calling a procedure $\mathtt{unfold}^{\#}(\tilde{H},p)$ which returns two abstract heaps $\tilde{H}_1$ and $\tilde{H}_2$ such that the concretization of $\tilde{H}$ is included in the union of the concretizations of $\tilde{H}_1$ and $\tilde{H}_2$. The abstract heap $\tilde{H}_1$ (resp. $\tilde{H}_2$) corresponds to the case when the length of the word associated to the node n labeled by p in $\tilde{H}$ is 1 (resp. strictly greater than 1). Thus, $\tilde{H}_1 = (N,S,V,\widetilde{W}')$ where $\widetilde{W}'$ is a formula in $\mathcal{A}_{\mathbb{W}}$ which over-approximates $\varphi_1 : \widetilde{W} \wedge \mathtt{len}(n) = 1$ (i.e., $\varphi_1 \Rightarrow \widetilde{W}'$). Then, $\tilde{H}_2 = (N',S',V,\widetilde{W}'')$ corresponds to the case $\mathtt{len}(n) > 1$, where (N',S') is obtained by adding a new node n' between n and its successor n'' in $\tilde{H}$ and $\widetilde{W}''$ is a formula in $\mathcal{A}_{\mathbb{W}}$ that over-approximates the following formula (given in an extension of the logic of $\mathcal{A}_{\mathbb{W}}$ with quantification over word variables and with a concatenation operation symbol "$\cdot$"):

$$\left(\exists n.\ \left(n = \overline{n} \cdot n' \wedge \mathtt{len}(\overline{n}) = 1 \wedge \widetilde{W} \wedge \mathtt{len}(n) > 1\right)\right)[\overline{n} \leftarrow n] \qquad \text{(G)}$$

This formula says that the word associated to n in $\tilde{H}_2$ is only the first letter of the word associated to n in $\tilde{H}$ and the word associated to n' in $\tilde{H}_2$ is the tail of the word associated to n in $\tilde{H}$. The abstract transformer $\mathtt{split}^{\#}$ given in [2] computes this over-approximation in the domain of universal formulas. If $\widetilde{W}$ is a multiset constraint in $\mathcal{A}_{\mathbb{M}}$, an over-approximation for (G) can be obtained by substituting $\mathtt{mhd}(n)$ with $\mathtt{mhd}(n) \cup \mathtt{mhd}(n') \cup \mathtt{mtl}(n')$.

The statements **assume** ***and*** **assert:** The assertions φ we consider for these statements are disjunctions of formulas of the form $\varphi_G \wedge \varphi_{\mathbb{W}}$, where φ_G describes a unique graph (N,S,V) as in the definition of heaps and $\varphi_{\mathbb{W}}$ is a formula in the data words logic of $\mathcal{A}_{\mathbb{W}}$ over the data word variables N. For simplicity, we assume that φ_G is a separation logic formula [22] defined as a separating conjunction of atomic formulas of the form $\mathtt{ls}(n,n')$, where n,n' are variables interpreted as distinct nodes in the graph. A formula $\mathtt{ls}(n,n')$ is true in some abstract heap iff there exists an edge between the nodes represented by n and n' (i.e a path connecting them in the concrete heap). We require that φ_G (1) contain at most one atomic formula $\mathtt{ls}(n,n')$, for every n, and (2) induce a graph that does not contain simple nodes. Then, let A_H be an abstract heap set from $\mathcal{A}_{\mathbb{H}}(\mathcal{A}_{\mathbb{W}})$ and let φ be a formula $\varphi_G \wedge \varphi_{\mathbb{W}}$ that describes an element A'_H from the same abstract domain $\mathcal{A}_{\mathbb{H}}(\mathcal{A}_{\mathbb{W}})$. Thus, $\mathtt{post}^{\#}(\mathtt{assume}\ \varphi, A_H) = A_H \sqcap^{\mathbb{HS}} A'_H$. Also, $\mathtt{post}^{\#}(\mathtt{assert}\ \varphi, A_H) = A_H$ if $\mathtt{fold}^{\#}(A_H) \sqsubseteq^{\mathbb{HS}} A'_H$ and $\mathtt{post}^{\#}(\mathtt{assert}\ \varphi, A_H) = \bot^{\mathbb{HS}}$, otherwise. The extension of this definition to disjunctions of such formulas is straightforward.

Procedure calls: The abstract transformer corresponding to a *call to start* edge, **call y** $= P(\mathbf{x})$, where $P = (\mathbf{fpi},\mathbf{fpo},\mathbf{loc},G)$, computes abstract heap sets over $\mathbf{loc}^0 \cup \mathbf{loc}$. For any abstract heap $\tilde{R}^c = (N^c,S^c,V^c,\widetilde{W}^c)$ from the input abstract heap set it returns an abstract heap $\tilde{R}^s = (N^s,S^s,V^s,\widetilde{W}^s)$, where:

- the local heap corresponding to the call $P(\mathbf{x})$, denoted $\mathtt{local}(\tilde{R}^c,P(\mathbf{x})) = (N^{\mathbf{x}},S^{\mathbf{x}},V^{\mathbf{x}},\widetilde{W}^{x})$, is defined by (1) $(N^{\mathbf{x}},S^{\mathbf{x}},V^{\mathbf{x}})$ is the sub-graph of $\tilde{R}^c$ containing only nodes reachable from the nodes labeled by variables in $\mathbf{x}$ in which actual parameters are replaced by the corresponding formal parameters and (2) $\widetilde{W}^{\mathbf{x}}$ is an over-approximation of $\exists(N^c \setminus N^{\mathbf{x}}).\ \widetilde{W}^c$(where $\exists(N^c \setminus N^{\mathbf{x}})$ denotes an existential quantification over all the word variables in $N^c \setminus N^{\mathbf{x}}$).
- the graph (N^s,S^s,V^s) contains two copies of $(N^{\mathbf{x}},S^{\mathbf{x}},V^{\mathbf{x}})$ (the nodes of one copy are labeled by variables in $\mathbf{loc}^0$) and $\widetilde{W}^s$ is an over-approximation in $\mathcal{A}_{\mathbb{W}}$ of the formula:

  $$\widetilde{W}^{\mathbf{x}} \wedge \widetilde{W}^{\mathbf{x}}\left[n \leftarrow n^0 \mid n \in N^{\mathbf{x}}\right] \wedge \bigwedge_{\substack{n^0 \in N^0,\ n \in N \\ n \text{ is a copy of } n^0}} eq(n,n^0),$$

  where $eq(n,n^0)$ is expressing the equality between the data of the words denoted by n and n^0. In $\mathcal{A}_{\mathbb{U}}$, $eq(n,n^0)$ is expressed precisely by

  $$\begin{aligned} eq_{\forall}(n,n^0):\ & \mathtt{hd}(n) = \mathtt{hd}(n^0) \wedge \mathtt{len}(n) = \mathtt{len}(n^0) \\ & \wedge \left(\forall y_1,y_2.\ (y_1 \in \mathtt{tl}(n^0) \wedge y_2 \in \mathtt{tl}(n) \wedge y_1 = y_2)\right. \\ & \qquad \left.\Rightarrow n^0[y_1] = n[y_2]\right). \end{aligned} \qquad \text{(H)}$$

  while $\mathcal{A}_{\mathbb{M}}$ can represent only an over-approximation by

  $$eq_m(n,n^0):\ \mathtt{mhd}(n) = \mathtt{mhd}(n^0) \wedge \mathtt{mtl}(n) = \mathtt{mtl}(n^0). \qquad \text{(I)}$$

Procedure returns: Consider now an *exit to return* edge, labeled by **ret y** $= P(\mathbf{x})$, from the exit point of $P = (\mathbf{fpi},\mathbf{fpo},\mathbf{loc},G)$, denoted e_P, to some control point r in the CFG of a procedure Q. Let c be the call point associated to r and $\tilde{R}^c = (N^c,S^c,V^c,\widetilde{W}^c) \in \rho^{\#}(c)$. The abstract transformer for **ret y** $= P(\mathbf{x})$ computes an abstract heap set whose elements are denoted by $\tilde{R}^r = (N^r,S^r,V^r,\widetilde{W}^r)$. To this, it uses the (pre) computed summary for this call of the procedure P, represented by an abstract heap set whose elements are denoted $\tilde{R}^e = (N^e,S^e,V^e,\widetilde{W}^e)$. The summary must satisfy the property that its input configuration R^e_{in} is implied by the constraints on the actual parameters, i.e. $\mathtt{local}(\tilde{R}^c,P(\mathbf{x})) \sqsubseteq^{\mathbb{H}} \tilde{R}^e_{in}$. To compute $\tilde{R}^r = (N^r,S^r,V^r,\widetilde{W}^r)$:

- we take the union between the call graph (N^e,S^e,V^e) and the exit graph $(N^{out},S^{out},V^{out})$ of the output configuration in the summary R^e,

- we eliminate the input version of the parameters of P,
- we define $\widetilde{W}^r$ by (a) defining $\texttt{Combine}(\widetilde{W}^c, \widetilde{W}^e)$ which applies the conjunction between $\widetilde{W}^c$ and $\widetilde{W}^e$ after it ensures that the nodes in N^c belonging to the local heap of this call have the same name as the corresponding nodes in N^e representing the input configuration and (b) computing an over-approximation of $\exists N^0. \texttt{Combine}(\widetilde{W}^c, \widetilde{W}^e)$, where N^0 is the set of nodes in N^e representing the input configuration.

In $\mathcal{A}_{\mathbb{U}}$ and $\mathcal{A}_{\mathbb{M}}$, over-approximations of existentially quantified formulas can be defined by, roughly, removing sub-formulas containing the existentially quantified data word variables.

5. Combining abstract domains

Let us take a closer look to the analysis of the `quicksort` procedure from Figure 1 with the domain of universally-quantified formulas, $\mathcal{A}_{\mathbb{HS}}(\mathcal{A}_{\mathbb{U}})$, over the set of guard patterns

$$y \in \texttt{tl}(\omega), \qquad y_1, y_2 \in \texttt{tl}(\omega) \wedge y_1 \leq y_2,$$
$$y_1 \in \texttt{tl}(\omega_1) \wedge y_2 \in \texttt{tl}(\omega_2) \wedge y_1 = y_2.$$

The analysis manipulates universally-quantified implications where the left part is one of the formulas above, where the ω's are data word variables. Typically, in the case of recursive procedures, the analysis starts by computing procedure summaries for input lists of length 1 and then, for input lists of length 2, and so on until it reaches a fixpoint (to terminate it applies the widening operator).

The analysis is able to compute a procedure summary $\psi^{\mathbb{U}}_{sum}$: $sorted(n'_o) \wedge \texttt{len}(n_l) \leq 2$ for input lists of length at most 2, where n'_o represents the list pointed to by the output formal parameter `res` of `quicksort`. In the next iteration, the context of the first recursive call "`left=quicksort(left)`" is given by the graph and the formula ψ_c in Figure 4(c). The abstract transformer for procedure return computes $\exists n_l.\ (\psi_c \wedge \psi^{\mathbb{U}}_{sum})$. This projection will remove all the constraints on n_l which is the actual input parameter. The same holds for the list pointed to by `right` and the second recursive call. The relation obtained after the two calls is given in Figure 5. We have lost the property that all the elements of `left` are less than the pivot. Consequently, after calling `concat`, we can't obtain that the list pointed to by `res` is sorted.

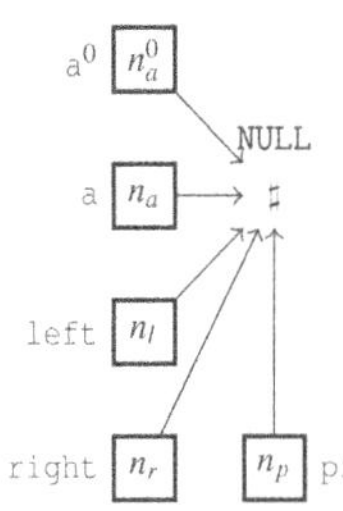

$$\psi : d = \texttt{hd}(n_p) \wedge \texttt{len}(n_p) = 1 \wedge eq_{\mathbb{V}}(n_a, n_a^0)$$
$$\wedge sorted(n_l) \wedge \texttt{len}(n_l) \leq 3$$
$$\wedge sorted(n_r) \wedge \texttt{len}(n_r) \leq 3,$$

$$sorted(n) : \forall y.\ y \in \texttt{tl}(n) \Rightarrow \texttt{hd}(n) \leq n[y]$$
$$\wedge \forall y_1, y_2.\ ((y_1, y_2) \in \texttt{tl}(n) \wedge y_1 \leq y_2)$$
$$\Rightarrow n[y_1] \leq n[y_2]$$

Figure 5. The relation synthesized at line 17 of `quicksort`.

Next, we give a solution for this problem based on a combination of abstract analyses. Thus, at the return from the first recursive call, the abstract transformer computes

$$\exists n_l.\ \left(\texttt{strengthen}_{\mathbb{M}}\left(\psi_c \wedge \psi^{\mathbb{U}}_{sum}, \psi^{\mathbb{M}}_{sum}\right)\right), \tag{J}$$

where $\psi^{\mathbb{M}}_{sum} : \texttt{ms}(n'_o) = \texttt{ms}(n_l)$ is the summary for `quicksort` computed in $\mathcal{A}_{\mathbb{HS}}(\mathcal{A}_{\mathbb{M}})$ and $\texttt{strengthen}_{\mathbb{M}} : \mathcal{A}_{\mathbb{U}} \times \mathcal{A}_{\mathbb{M}} \to \mathcal{A}_{\mathbb{U}}$. The operator $\texttt{strengthen}_{\mathbb{M}}$ returns

$$\psi_c \wedge \psi^{\mathbb{U}}_{sum} \wedge \texttt{hd}(n'_o) \leq \texttt{hd}(n_p) \wedge \forall y.\ y \in \texttt{tl}(n'_o) \Rightarrow n'_o[y] \leq \texttt{hd}(n_p),$$

and consequently, by eliminating the constraints on n_l (due to the existential quantification), we preserve the fact that the elements of the list pointed to by `left` are smaller than the pivot.

The function $\texttt{strengthen}_{\mathbb{M}}$ is an instance of a more general procedure denoted $\texttt{strengthen}_{\mathbb{W}}$.

Given $\mathcal{A}_{\mathbb{W}}$ an $\mathbb{LDW}$-domain, the definition of $\texttt{strengthen}_{\mathbb{W}}$ uses a procedure $\texttt{infer}_{\mathbb{W}}$ which, for any two abstract values $\widetilde{W}_{in} \in \mathcal{A}_{\mathbb{U}}$ and $\widetilde{W}_{aux} \in \mathcal{A}_{\mathbb{W}}$, returns an over-approximation of their conjunction expressed in $\mathcal{A}_{\mathbb{U}}$.

DEFINITION 5.1. *Let $\mathcal{A}_{\mathbb{W}}$ be some $\mathbb{LDW}$-domain and* $\texttt{infer}_{\mathbb{W}} : \mathcal{A}_{\mathbb{U}} \times \mathcal{A}_{\mathbb{W}} \to \mathcal{A}_{\mathbb{U}}$ *such that*

$$\left(\widetilde{W}_{in} \wedge \widetilde{W}_{aux}\right) \Rightarrow \texttt{infer}_{\mathbb{W}}(\widetilde{W}_{in}, \widetilde{W}_{aux}).$$

The function $\texttt{strengthen}_{\mathbb{W}} : \mathcal{A}_{\mathbb{U}} \times \mathcal{A}_{\mathbb{W}} \to \mathcal{A}_{\mathbb{U}}$ *is defined by*

$$\texttt{strengthen}_{\mathbb{W}}(\widetilde{W}_{in}, \widetilde{W}_{aux}) = \widetilde{W}_{in} \sqcap^{\mathbb{U}} \texttt{infer}_{\mathbb{W}}(\widetilde{W}_{in}, \widetilde{W}_{aux}).$$

Before giving the formal definition of $\texttt{infer}_{\mathbb{W}}$ let us consider two examples, one for computing $\texttt{infer}_{\mathbb{M}}$ and one for computing $\texttt{infer}_{\mathbb{U}}$.

Computing $\texttt{infer}_{\mathbb{M}}$***:*** Consider the application of $\texttt{strengthen}_{\mathbb{M}}$ from (J). From its arguments, we should only remember the multiset constraint $\texttt{ms}(n'_o) = \texttt{ms}(n_l)$ and the following formula:

$$\varphi(n_l) : \texttt{hd}(n_l) \leq \texttt{hd}(n_p) \wedge \forall y.\ y \in \texttt{tl}(n_l) \Rightarrow n_l[y] \leq \texttt{hd}(n_p) \tag{K}$$

which says that all the elements of the word n_l are less than $\texttt{hd}(n_p)$.

The result of $\texttt{strengthen}_{\mathbb{M}}$ is computed using $\texttt{infer}_{\mathbb{M}}$ applied on the same inputs. Roughly, to compute $\texttt{infer}_{\mathbb{M}}$ (1) we unfold a bounded length prefix p_1, resp. p_2, of the word n'_o, resp. n_l; thus, $n'_o = p_1 \cdot s_1$ and $n_l = p_2 \cdot s_2$, where $\cdot$ denotes the concatenation of words, (2) we infer the properties of the nodes in p_1 and p_2 implied by the conjunction between the constraint in the domain of universally-quantified formulas and the constraint in the multiset domain and (3) we fold the prefixes p_1 and p_2 and collect the informations on these nodes using a universally-quantified formula. Then, we continue to apply the same transformations on the words s_1 and s_2 until we reach a fixpoint.

This unfolding/folding mechanism reduces the initial problem (of inferring universally-quantified constraints implied by the conjunction of the inputs) to the problem of inferring *quantifier-free* constraints implied by the conjunction of the inputs.

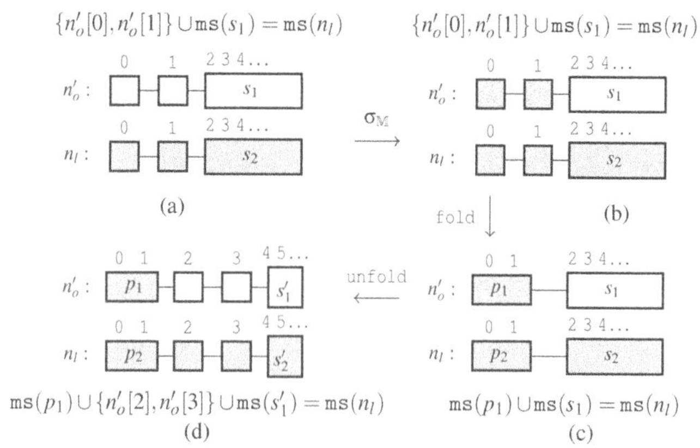

Figure 6. Computing $\texttt{infer}_{\mathbb{M}}$.

Some steps from the computation of $\texttt{infer}_{\mathbb{M}}$ are given in Figure 6. The unfolding of a prefix of length 2 is given in Figure 6(a). Above each sub-word we give the positions from the initial word it contains. The sub-words are colored if their elements satisfy the property from $\varphi(n_l)$. At this step, only the sub-words of n_l are colored. In the multiset constraint, for any $i \geq 0$, $\{n'_o[i]\}$ denotes the singleton multiset containing the element of n'_o at position i. This syntax is not exactly the one used in the formulas manipulated by our analysis but we use it for the sake of simplicity. On this unfolding we apply a *partial reduction operator* [9], denoted $\sigma_{\mathbb{M}}$, which deduces new properties on the unfolded prefix based on the multiset constraints. Here, it deduces that, for any $0 \leq i \leq 1$,

$$n'_o[i] \in \mathtt{ms}(n_l) \wedge \varphi(n_l) \text{ implies } n'_o[i] \leq \mathtt{hd}(n_p).$$

The result of applying $\sigma_{\mathbb{M}}$ is given in Figure 6(b). Now, we can apply a folding operation in the two abstract domains whose result is given in Figure 6(c). Then, we continue by unfolding another prefix of length 2 from the sub-word of n_o that starts with position 2 (this is pictured in Figure 6(d)). We repeat these steps until the fixpoint computation terminates. The result will be:

$$\mathtt{infer}_{\mathbb{M}}\left(\psi_c \wedge \psi^{\mathbb{U}}_{sum}, \psi^{\mathbb{M}}_{sum}\right) = \psi_c \wedge \psi^{\mathbb{U}}_{sum} \wedge \varphi(n'_o).$$

Computing $\mathtt{infer}_{\mathbb{U}}$***:*** Let $\mathcal{A}^1_{\mathbb{U}}$, resp. $\mathcal{A}^2_{\mathbb{U}}$, be a domain with universal formulas parametrized by a set of patterns $\mathcal{P}_1$, resp. $\mathcal{P}_2$. Using a similar mechanism, we compute, for any $\widetilde{W} \in \mathcal{A}^1_{\mathbb{U}}$, an over-approximation of $\widetilde{W}$ in $\mathcal{A}^2_{\mathbb{U}}$, denoted $\mathtt{convert}(\mathcal{P}_1, \mathcal{P}_2)(\widetilde{W})$. For example, let

$$\begin{aligned}
\mathcal{P}_1 &= \{y \in \mathtt{tl}(\omega), \quad y_1, y_2 \in \mathtt{tl}(\omega) \wedge y_1 \leq y_2\} \\
\mathcal{P}_2 &= \{y \in \mathtt{tl}(\omega) \wedge y = 1, \quad y \in \mathtt{tl}(\omega) \wedge y = \mathtt{len}(\omega) - 1, \\
&\quad\; y_1, y_2 \in \mathtt{tl}(\omega) \wedge y_1 <_1 y_2\},
\end{aligned}$$

and let $\widetilde{W}$ be the sortedness property $sorted(n)$ in Figure 5. Computing $\mathtt{convert}(\mathcal{P}_1, \mathcal{P}_2)(\widetilde{W})$ allows us to prove that $\widetilde{W}$ implies

$$\gamma(n) : \forall y_1, y_2.\ (y_1, y_2 \in \mathtt{tl}(n) \wedge y_1 <_1 y_2) \Rightarrow n[y_1] \leq n[y_2]$$

which can not be done using the entailment relation $\sqsubseteq^{\mathbb{U}}$ defined in $\mathcal{A}^1_{\mathbb{U}}$ or $\mathcal{A}^2_{\mathbb{U}}$. We start with the formula $\widetilde{W}' : true$ and we apply a procedure $\mathtt{infer}_{\mathbb{U}}$ to strengthen it using the information from $\widetilde{W}$. Again, we unfold a bounded-length prefix of n. For instance, if we unfold a prefix of length 3, the formula $\widetilde{W}'$ remains unchanged and the formula $\widetilde{W}$ is transformed into a formula $\widetilde{W}_1$ given by:

$$n[0] \leq n[1] \wedge n[1] \leq n[2] \wedge n[2] \leq n[3] \wedge sorted(n[3]),$$

where $sorted(n[3])$ denotes the fact that the formula $sorted$ is true starting from the third position of n. Then, we apply a partial reduction operator, $\sigma_{\mathbb{U}}$, that takes the existential part of $\widetilde{W}_1$ and adds it to $\widetilde{W}'$. Afterwards, we apply a folding operation and the word n is split into a word n' containing only its first 3 elements and a word n'' containing all the other elements. The formula in $\mathcal{A}^2_{\mathbb{U}}$ becomes

$$\begin{aligned}
&\forall y.\ (y \in \mathtt{tl}(n') \wedge y = 1) \Rightarrow \mathtt{hd}(n') \leq y \\
&\wedge \forall y_1, y_2.\ (y_1, y_2 \in \mathtt{tl}(n') \wedge y_1 <_1 y_2) \Rightarrow n'[y_1] \leq n'[y_2] \\
&\wedge \forall y.\ (y \in \mathtt{tl}(n') \wedge y = \mathtt{len}(n') - 1) \Rightarrow y \leq \mathtt{hd}(n'').
\end{aligned}$$

As in the previous case, by iterating these two steps into a fixpoint computation that traverses all the elements of n, we obtain $\mathtt{convert}(\mathcal{P}_1, \mathcal{P}_2)(\widetilde{W})$ which is given by

$$\begin{aligned}
&\forall y.\ (y \in \mathtt{tl}(n) \wedge y = 1) \Rightarrow \mathtt{hd}(n) \leq y \\
&\wedge \forall y_1, y_2.\ (y_1, y_2 \in \mathtt{tl}(n) \wedge y_1 <_1 y_2) \Rightarrow n[y_1] \leq n[y_2].
\end{aligned}$$

Clearly, $\mathtt{convert}(\mathcal{P}_1, \mathcal{P}_2)(\widetilde{W}) \sqsubseteq^{\mathbb{U}} \gamma(n)$ which finishes our proof.

5.1 The procedure $\mathtt{infer}_{\mathbb{W}}$

The output of $\mathtt{infer}_{\mathbb{W}}$ is defined by the analysis of a program without procedures with an abstract domain which is a *partially reduced product* [9] between $\mathcal{A}_{\mathbb{HS}}(\mathcal{A}_{\mathbb{U}})$ and $\mathcal{A}_{\mathbb{HS}}(\mathcal{A}_{\mathbb{W}})$. The elements of this

```
while((zm!=NULL) &&
      (zn!=NULL))
 { zm = zm->next;
   zn = zn->next; }
 while(zm!=NULL)
   zm = zm->next;
 while(zn!=NULL)
   zn = zn->next;
```

Figure 7. A program for computing $\mathtt{infer}_{\mathbb{W}}$.

abstract domain are pairs from $\mathcal{A}_{\mathbb{HS}}(\mathcal{A}_{\mathbb{U}}) \times \mathcal{A}_{\mathbb{HS}}(\mathcal{A}_{\mathbb{W}})$. The analysis computes an invariant for the reachable program configurations at each control point. Almost all the abstract transformers in this analysis are defined by:

$$\mathtt{post}^{\#}(St, (HS_{in}, HS_{aux})) = (\mathtt{post}^{\#}{}_{\mathbb{U}}(St, HS_{in}), \mathtt{post}^{\#}{}_{\mathbb{W}}(St, HS_{aux})),$$

where $\mathtt{post}^{\#}{}_{\mathbb{U}}(St, HS_{in})$ is the abstract transformer in $\mathcal{A}_{\mathbb{HS}}(\mathcal{A}_{\mathbb{U}})$ and $\mathtt{post}^{\#}{}_{\mathbb{W}}(St, HS_{aux})$ is the abstract transformer in $\mathcal{A}_{\mathbb{HS}}(\mathcal{A}_{\mathbb{W}})$. The only exception is the statement p=q->`next` whose abstract transformer calls a *a partial reduction operator* [9] $\sigma_{\mathbb{W}} : \mathcal{A}_{\mathbb{HS}}(\mathcal{A}_{\mathbb{U}}) \times \mathcal{A}_{\mathbb{HS}}(\mathcal{A}_{\mathbb{W}}) \rightarrow \mathcal{A}_{\mathbb{HS}}(\mathcal{A}_{\mathbb{U}}) \times \mathcal{A}_{\mathbb{HS}}(\mathcal{A}_{\mathbb{W}})$. This operator propagates information between the two abstract domains and its output should satisfy the following: for any $A_H \in \mathcal{A}_{\mathbb{HS}}(\mathcal{A}_{\mathbb{U}})$ and $A'_H \in \mathcal{A}_{\mathbb{HS}}(\mathcal{A}_{\mathbb{W}})$,

$$\begin{gathered}
\sigma^1_{\mathbb{W}}(A_H, A'_H) \sqsubseteq^{\mathbb{HS}} A_H,\ \sigma^2_{\mathbb{W}}(A_H, A'_H) \sqsubseteq^{\mathbb{HS}} A'_H, \text{ and} \\
\gamma(\sigma^1_{\mathbb{W}}(A_H, A'_H)) \cup \gamma(\sigma^2_{\mathbb{W}}(A_H, A'_H)) = \gamma(A_H) \cup \gamma(A'_H),
\end{gathered}$$

where $\sigma^i_{\mathbb{W}}(A_H, A'_H)$ is the projection of $\sigma_{\mathbb{W}}(A_H, A'_H)$ on the ith component, for any $1 \leq i \leq 2$. If St': p=q->`next` then

$$\begin{aligned}
&\mathtt{post}^{\#}(St', (HS_{in}, HS_{aux})) = \\
&\qquad \sigma_{\mathbb{W}}(\mathtt{post}^{\#}{}_{\mathbb{U}}(St', HS_{in}), \mathtt{post}^{\#}{}_{\mathbb{W}}(St', HS_{aux})).
\end{aligned} \tag{L}$$

Let M denote the set of data word variables in $\widetilde{W}_{aux}$. The program that computes $\mathtt{infer}_{\mathbb{W}}$ depends on M. In practice, we can heuristically choose to consider only some of the data word variables in $\widetilde{W}_{aux}$. The result of $\mathtt{infer}_{\mathbb{W}}$ is still sound.

For example, let $M = \{m, n\}$. The program used in $\mathtt{infer}_{\mathbb{W}}$ is given in Figure 7 and consists in `while` loops that traverse the lists represented by the nodes in M.

The initial configuration of the program is a pair of abstract heaps $(\tilde{H}_{in}, \tilde{H}_{aux})$ which contain the same graph (N, S, V) such that (1) the graphs contain one node for each data word variable in $\widetilde{W}_{in}$ or $\widetilde{W}_{aux}$ with an edge towards $\sharp$, (2) each node $n \in N$ is labeled by at least two variables, one being `zn`, (3) $\tilde{H}_{in} = (N, S, V, \widetilde{W}_{in})$ and $\tilde{H}_{aux} = (N, S, V, \widetilde{W}_{aux})$. The first loop traverses simultaneously the two list segments. At each iteration, the pointer variables `zm` and `zn` are advanced to the next element. Since the lists may not have the same length, we add another two `while` loops to continue the traversing of the unfinished list starting from where the previous loop stopped.

Let $(A_H, A'_H) \in \mathcal{A}_{\mathbb{HS}}(\mathcal{A}_{\mathbb{U}}) \times \mathcal{A}_{\mathbb{HS}}(\mathcal{A}_{\mathbb{W}})$ be the postcondition of this program (i.e, the pair of abstract heap sets associated to the last control point). Remark that $\mathtt{fold}^{\#}(A_H) = \{\tilde{H}\}$ and $\mathtt{fold}^{\#}(A'_H) = \{\tilde{H}'\}$, where $\tilde{H}$ and $\tilde{H}'$ are abstract heaps that contain exactly the same graph as the abstract heaps from the precondition. We define $\mathtt{infer}_{\mathbb{W}}(\widetilde{W}_{in}, \widetilde{W}_{aux}) = \widetilde{W}$, where $\widetilde{W}$ is the $\mathcal{A}_{\mathbb{U}}$ formula from $\tilde{H}$ projected on the variables from $\widetilde{W}_{in}$.

The partial reduction operator $\sigma_{\mathbb{W}}$***:*** The definition of $\sigma_{\mathbb{W}}$ over abstract heap sets uses a similar operator on abstract heaps which again, uses a similar operator on $\mathbb{LDW}$-domains. The operator $\sigma_{\mathbb{W}}(A_H, A'_H)$ on abstract heap sets takes the join of $\sigma_{\mathbb{W}}(\tilde{H}, \tilde{H}')$, for any two isomorphic abstract heaps $\tilde{H} \in A_H$ and $\tilde{H} \in A'_H$. Then, let

$$\frac{\mathtt{mhd}(n) \subseteq \mathtt{mtl}(n') \text{ and } \widetilde{W} \sqsubseteq^{\mathbb{U}} \forall y.\ y \in n' \Rightarrow \varphi}{\exists y.\ (\varphi[n'[y] \leftarrow \mathtt{hd}(n))]} \qquad \frac{\mathtt{mhd}(n) \subseteq \mathtt{mhd}(n')}{\mathtt{hd}(n) = \mathtt{hd}(n')}$$

Figure 8. Inference rules for $\sigma^1_{\mathbb{M}}$.

$\tilde{H} = (N, S, V, \widetilde{W}) \in \mathcal{A}_{\mathbb{HS}}(\mathcal{A}_{\mathbb{U}})$ and $\tilde{H}' = (N, S, V, \widetilde{W}') \in \mathcal{A}_{\mathbb{HS}}(\mathcal{A}_{\mathbb{W}})$ be two isomorphic abstract heaps (we suppose that the nodes related by the isomorphism have the same name). We define

$$\sigma_{\mathbb{W}}(\tilde{H}, \tilde{H}') = \left(\left(N, S, V, \sigma^1_{\mathbb{W}}(\widetilde{W}, \widetilde{W}')\right), \left(N, S, V, \sigma^2_{\mathbb{W}}(\widetilde{W}, \widetilde{W}')\right)\right).$$

The procedure $\mathtt{infer}_{\mathbb{U}}$**:** When $\mathcal{A}_{\mathbb{W}}$ is some abstract domain $\mathcal{A}'_{\mathbb{U}}$, we obtain an instantiation of $\mathtt{infer}_{\mathbb{W}}$, denoted $\mathtt{infer}_{\mathbb{U}}$. To define $\mathtt{infer}_{\mathbb{U}}$, we have to provide only the definition of the partial reduction operator $\sigma_{\mathbb{U}} : \mathcal{A}_{\mathbb{U}} \times \mathcal{A}'_{\mathbb{U}} \to \mathcal{A}_{\mathbb{U}} \times \mathcal{A}'_{\mathbb{U}}$. Thus, let $\widetilde{W}$, resp. $\widetilde{W}'$, be an abstract value in $\mathcal{A}_{\mathbb{U}}$, resp. $\mathcal{A}'_{\mathbb{U}}$. We define $\sigma^1_{\mathbb{U}}(\widetilde{W}, \widetilde{W}') = \widetilde{W} \wedge E'$, where E' is the quantifier-free part of $\widetilde{W}'$, and $\sigma^2_{\mathbb{U}}(\widetilde{W}, \widetilde{W}') = \widetilde{W}'$.

In the following, we will describe another instantiation of $\mathtt{infer}_{\mathbb{W}}$, when $\mathcal{A}_{\mathbb{W}}$ is the domain of multiset constraints.

5.2 Combining multiset constraints and universal formulas

Let $\widetilde{W} \in \mathcal{A}_{\mathbb{U}}$ and $\widetilde{W}' \in \mathcal{A}_{\mathbb{M}}$ be two formulas over the set of data word variables N. The $\mathcal{A}_{\mathbb{U}}$ formula $\sigma^1_{\mathbb{M}}(\widetilde{W}, \widetilde{W}')$ is obtained from $\widetilde{W}$ by adding new constraints on the values of $\mathtt{hd}(n)$ with $n \in N$ based on the multiset constraint $\widetilde{W}'$. The $\mathcal{A}_{\mathbb{M}}$ formula $\sigma^2_{\mathbb{M}}(\widetilde{W}, \widetilde{W}')$ is obtained by adding to $\widetilde{W}'$ an equality $\mathtt{mhd}(n) = \mathtt{mhd}(n')$ for any equality $\mathtt{hd}(n) = \mathtt{hd}(n')$ implied by the first output. In the following, we describe the computation of $\sigma^1_{\mathbb{M}}(\widetilde{W}, \widetilde{W}')$.

To help the intuition, we start by an example. Let $\widetilde{W}$: $\forall y.\ y \in \mathtt{tl}(n) \Rightarrow n[y] > 5$ and $\widetilde{W}'$: $\mathtt{mhd}(n_1) \cup \mathtt{mtl}(n_2) = \mathtt{mtl}(n)$.

By an abuse of notation we can rewrite $\widetilde{W}$ as $\forall val.\ val \in \mathtt{mtl}(n).\ val < 5$, where val is a variable interpreted as an integer. Notice that $\widetilde{W}'$ implies that $\mathtt{hd}(n_1)$ belongs to $\mathtt{mtl}(n)$ and consequently we obtain that $\widetilde{W} \wedge \widetilde{W}'$ implies $\mathtt{hd}(n_1) < 5$. This deduction can be done using the first inference rule in Figure 8.

In general, a multiset constraint induces multiple choices w.r.t. the multisets to which the singletons belong to. For example if $\widetilde{W}' ::= \mathtt{mhd}(n_1) \cup \mathtt{mtl}(n_2) = \mathtt{mtl}(n) \cup \mathtt{mtl}(m)$ then $\widetilde{W}'$ implies that either $\mathtt{hd}(n_1) \in \mathtt{mtl}(n)$ or $\mathtt{hd}(n_1) \in \mathtt{mtl}(m)$. In each case, the property on $\mathtt{hd}(n_1)$ added to the formula $\widetilde{W}$ might be different. However, there are a finite number of choices. For each of them, we construct a strengthening of $\widetilde{W}$ and then we define $\sigma^1_{\mathbb{M}}(\widetilde{W}, \widetilde{W}')$ as the join of all of these strengthenings.

Formally, the formula $\sigma^1_{\mathbb{M}}(\widetilde{W}, \widetilde{W}')$ is built as follows:

1. we deduce the set of all conjunctions of the form
$$\psi ::= \mathtt{mhd}(n_1) \subseteq bt_1 \wedge \ldots \wedge \mathtt{mhd}(n_k) \subseteq bt_k, \qquad \text{(M)}$$
where bt_i is a basic multiset term, for any $1 \le i \le k$, such that (1) $\widetilde{W}'$ implies the disjunction of all formulas ψ as above (in the logic obtained from $\mathcal{A}_{\mathbb{M}}$ by adding the usual inclusion operator between multisets $\subseteq$) and (2) ψ contains exactly once all the terms of the form $\mathtt{mhd}(n_i)$ from $\widetilde{W}'$. Note that if, for example, $bt_1 = \mathtt{mhd}(n')$ then the conjunction will not contain any other atomic formula over the term $\mathtt{mhd}(n')$.
2. for every such conjunction, we use its atomic formulas to apply the inference rules in Figure 8 and deduce new facts on the values of $\mathtt{hd}(n)$ with $n \in N$. These facts are conjuncted to $\widetilde{W}$.
3. $\sigma^1_{\mathbb{M}}(\widetilde{W}, \widetilde{W}')$ is the join of all abstract values in $\mathcal{A}_{\mathbb{U}}$ obtained in the previous step.

6. Applications

In this section, we describe several applications of the procedure $\mathtt{strengthen}_{\mathbb{W}}$.

6.1 Changing the set of patterns

To obtain a compositional analysis with the abstract domain $\mathcal{A}_{\mathbb{HS}}(\mathcal{A}_{\mathbb{U}})$, we need to transform an abstract value A_1 in a domain $\mathcal{A}_{\mathbb{HS}}(\mathcal{A}^1_{\mathbb{U}})$ over a set of patterns $\mathcal{P}_1$ into an abstract value A_2 in a domain $\mathcal{A}_{\mathbb{HS}}(\mathcal{A}^2_{\mathbb{U}})$ over a set of patterns $\mathcal{P}_2 \neq \mathcal{P}_1$.

Thus, we define an operator $\mathtt{convert}(\mathcal{P}_1, \mathcal{P}_2) : \mathcal{A}^1_{\mathbb{U}} \to \mathcal{A}^2_{\mathbb{U}}$ parameterized by a pair of pattern sets $(\mathcal{P}_1, \mathcal{P}_2)$, such that $\mathtt{convert}(\mathcal{P}_1, \mathcal{P}_2)(\widetilde{W}_1)$ is an over-approximation of $\widetilde{W}_1$ in the domain $\mathcal{A}^2_{\mathbb{U}}$. Intuitively, $\mathtt{convert}(\mathcal{P}_1, \mathcal{P}_2)(\widetilde{W}_1)$ returns a formula $\widetilde{W}_2$ which contains (1) constraints from $\widetilde{W}_1$ using the patterns in $\mathcal{P}_1 \cap \mathcal{P}_2$ and (2) constraints using the patterns in $\mathcal{P}_2 \setminus \mathcal{P}_1$ implied by $\widetilde{W}_1$ (in $\mathsf{FO}(DWVar, DVar, \mathbb{O}, \mathbb{P})$). Thus,

$$\mathtt{convert}(\mathcal{P}_1, \mathcal{P}_2)(\widetilde{W}_1) = \mathtt{strengthen}_{\mathbb{U}^2}(\top^{\mathbb{U}^2}, \widetilde{W}_1),$$

where $\top^{\mathbb{U}^2}$ is the top element in $\mathcal{A}^2_{\mathbb{U}}$.

The extension of $\mathtt{convert}$ to an operator on the $\mathcal{A}_{\mathbb{HS}}(\mathcal{A}_{\mathbb{U}})$ domains is done in a straightforward manner: the graph is kept the same and only constraints associated to the graph are converted. This operator is the base ingredient for the following applications.

6.2 Computing procedure summaries

In order to be able to compute procedure summaries parametrized by different sets of guard patterns, we modify the definition of the abstract transformers corresponding to procedure calls and returns as follows. Let Q_1 be a procedure for which a set of patterns $\mathcal{P}_1$ has been fixed. Suppose that Q_1 calls a procedure Q_2 associated with the set of patterns $\mathcal{P}_2$. The transformer $\mathtt{post}^\#(\mathbf{call\ y} = Q_2(\mathbf{x}), \tilde{R}^c)$, where $\tilde{R}^c$ is over the patterns $\mathcal{P}_1$, computes the local graph $\mathtt{local}(\tilde{R}^c, Q_2(\mathbf{x}))$ (see Section 4) over patterns in $\mathcal{P}_1$ and then applies $\mathtt{convert}(\mathcal{P}_1, \mathcal{P}_2)$ to obtain an over-approximation of the local graph for Q_2. Similarly, the transformer $\mathtt{post}^\#(\mathbf{ret\ y} = Q_2(\mathbf{x}))$ is modified by applying $\mathtt{convert}(\mathcal{P}_2, \mathcal{P}_1)$ to the combination between the context of the call and the summary for Q_2.

As shown for the quicksort example, the $\mathtt{strengthen}_{\mathbb{M}}$ operator allows to increase the precision of the analysis in the $\mathcal{A}_{\mathbb{HS}}(\mathcal{A}_{\mathbb{U}})$ domains. For this, the analysis computes two over-approximations for the mapping ρ defining the semantics of a program: a mapping $\rho^\#_{\mathbb{U}}$ with values in $\mathcal{A}_{\mathbb{HS}}(\mathcal{A}_{\mathbb{U}})$ and a mapping $\rho^\#_{\mathbb{M}}$ with values in $\mathcal{A}_{\mathbb{HS}}(\mathcal{A}_{\mathbb{M}})$. The abstract values at the initial control point of the CFG, c_0, are such that $\rho^\#_{\mathbb{M}}(c_0)$ is an over-approximation in $\mathcal{A}_{\mathbb{HS}}(\mathcal{A}_{\mathbb{M}})$ of $\rho^\#_{\mathbb{U}}(c_0)$. The recursive equations for $\rho^\#_{\mathbb{U}}$ and $\rho^\#_{\mathbb{M}}$ remain unchanged. The only difference is the definition of the abstract transformer in $\mathcal{A}_{\mathbb{HS}}(\mathcal{A}_{\mathbb{U}})$ corresponding to procedure returns.

Consider the edge $e_{Q_2} \xrightarrow{\mathbf{ret\ y}=Q_2(\mathbf{x})} r$ in the CFG of some procedure Q_1. Also, let c be the call point associated to r. The abstract transformer $\mathtt{post}^\#(\mathbf{ret\ y} = Q_2(\mathbf{x}), \tilde{R}^e)$, where $\tilde{R}^e = (N^e, S^e, V^e, \widetilde{W}^e) \in \rho^\#_{\mathbb{U}}(e_{Q_2})$, is an abstract heap set obtained by composing any relation $\tilde{R}^c = (N^c, S^c, V^c, \widetilde{W}^c) \in \rho^\#_{\mathbb{U}}(c)$ with $\tilde{R}^e$ and a relation $\tilde{R}^e_{aux} = (N^e_{aux}, S^e_{aux}, V^e_{aux}, \widetilde{W}^e_{aux}) \in \rho^\#_{\mathbb{M}}(e_{Q_2})$. This composition is applied only if the three relations correspond to the same call. If it is the case, the composition is an abstract heap $\tilde{R}^r = (N^r, S^r, V^r, \widetilde{W}^r)$, where (N^r, S^r, V^r) is built as in Section 4, and $\widetilde{W}^r$ is built by replacing $\mathtt{Combine}(\widetilde{W}^c, \widetilde{W}^e)$ with $\mathtt{strengthen}_{\mathbb{M}}(\mathtt{Combine}(\widetilde{W}^c, \widetilde{W}^e), \widetilde{W}_{aux})$.

6.3 Assertion checking

Let A^1_H be the abstract value in a domain $\mathcal{A}_{\mathbb{HS}}(\mathcal{A}^1_{\mathbb{U}})$ computed at the control point of the statement assert φ, where φ describes an element $A^2_H \in \mathcal{A}_{\mathbb{HS}}(\mathcal{A}^2_{\mathbb{U}})$. If $\mathcal{P}_1 = \mathcal{P}_2$, checking that A^1_H satisfies φ is done using the entailment operator of $\mathcal{A}_{\mathbb{HS}}$, i.e. $\mathtt{fold}^\#(A^1_H) \sqsubseteq^{\mathbb{HS}} A^2_H$. To improve the precision of this entailment checking, we can apply $\mathtt{strengthen}_{\mathbb{M}}(A^1_H, A^{aux}_H)$, where A^{aux}_H is the assertion

```
1  assume(equal(fpi1, fpi2));
2  list *y1, *y2;
3  y1=P1(fpi1);
4  y2=P2(fpi2);
5  assert(equal(y1, y2));
```

Figure 9. Procedure equivalence checking.

synthesized by $\mathcal{A}_{\mathbb{HS}}(\mathcal{A}_{\mathbb{M}})$ at the same control point, to obtain A'_H in $\mathcal{A}_{\mathbb{HS}}(\mathcal{A}^1_{\mathbb{U}})$ and then check that $\mathtt{fold}^{\#}(A'_H) \sqsubseteq^{\mathbb{HS}} A^2_H$ in $\mathcal{A}_{\mathbb{HS}}(\mathcal{A}^1_{\mathbb{U}})$.

When $\mathcal{P}_1 \neq \mathcal{P}_2$, we modify the abstract transformer of `assert` φ such that, for any abstract heap set $A^1_H \in \mathcal{A}_{\mathbb{HS}}(\mathcal{A}^1_{\mathbb{U}})$, $\mathtt{post}^{\#}(\mathtt{assert}\ \varphi, A^1_H) = A^1_H$ if $\mathtt{fold}^{\#}(\mathtt{convert}(\mathcal{P}_1,\mathcal{P}_2)(A^1_H)) \sqsubseteq^{\mathbb{HS}} A^2_H$, i.e., the output of $\mathtt{fold}^{\#}$ for the over-approximation of A^1_H in $\mathcal{A}_{\mathbb{HS}}(\mathcal{A}^2_{\mathbb{U}})$ entails A^2_H.

6.4 Equivalence checking

Let P_1 and P_2 be two procedures having the same input and output formal parameters. Then, P_1 and P_2 are *equivalent* if they return exactly the same heap when they receive the same input. We use the program in Figure 9 to obtain a sound procedure for equivalence checking. In every configuration of this program, the heap contains two disjoint regions, each region representing the heap configuration of one of these procedures. Initially, the program assumes that the heap contains two copies of the same input configuration. For that, we use the predicate $equal(\mathbf{fpi_1}, \mathbf{fpi_2})$ where $\mathbf{fpi_1}$ and $\mathbf{fpi_2}$ are two copies of the input parameters. We consider that $equal(\mathbf{fpi_1}, \mathbf{fpi_2})$ holds for an abstract heap if and only if it is formed of two sub-graphs G_1 and G_2 s.t. (1) G_1, resp. G_2, contains only nodes reachable from pointer variables in $\mathbf{fpi_1}$, resp. $\mathbf{fpi_2}$, (2) G_1 and G_2 are isomorphic, and (3) for any two nodes related by the isomorphism, the integer sequences attached to them are equal. Equality of integer sequences can be expressed using the universally-quantified formula $eq_{\forall}$ given by the equation (H) (page 6). The two procedures are called on this input configuration. Notice that the procedure P_1 (resp. P_2) can modify only the graph G_1 (resp. G_2). The inter-procedural analysis applied to this program computes an invariant I describing the configurations reachable after returning from the two procedures (line 5). This invariant is formed of a set of abstract heaps. The two procedures are equivalent if for any abstract heap in I, the regions reachable from the output parameters of P_1, $\mathbf{y_1}$, and from the output parameters of P_2, $\mathbf{y_2}$, are equal. To express this equality we use the predicate $equal(\mathbf{y_1}, \mathbf{y_2})$.

Notice that the program in Figure 9 can be used in the intra-procedural setting by inlining the procedures. However, the advantage of the compositional inter-procedural analysis is that each procedure is analyzed independently (using the local heap semantics).

7. Experimental results

Implementation details: We have implemented our inter-procedural analysis in a plugin called CELIA [5] of the FRAMA-C platform [4] for C program analysis. CELIA takes as input the ICFG built by FRAMA-C from the C program. The implementation of CELIA invokes/adapts (1) the heap abstract domains $\mathcal{A}_{\mathbb{HS}}(\mathcal{A}_{\mathbb{U}})$ and $\mathcal{A}_{\mathbb{HS}}(\mathcal{A}_{\mathbb{M}})$ provided by the CINV tool [2], (2) the numerical domains of the APRON platform [17], and (3) the generic module of fixpoint computation over control-flow graphs due to B. Jeannet [16]. It has been carried out by implementing in C the abstract transformers including the abstract domain combination/strengthening.

Benchmark: We have applied CELIA to a benchmark of C programs which is available on the web site of CELIA. The benchmark includes all the basic functions that are used in usual libraries on singly-linked lists, for example the GTK `gslist` library which is part of the Linux distribution. Table 1 gives a sample of functions in this benchmark, split in six classes. The class **sll** includes C functions performing elementary operations on list: *add*ing/*del*eting the *f*irst/*l*ast element, *init*ializing a list of some length. The classes **map** and **map2** include C functions performing a traversal of one resp. two lists, without modifying their structures, but modifying their data. The classes **fold** and **fold2** include C functions computing from one resp. two input lists some output parameters of type list or integer. Finally, the **sort** class includes sorting algorithms on lists. The procedures in classes **map*** and **fold*** are tail recursive, thus we consider for them both iterative and recursive versions. The third column of Table 1 specifies the versions considered (iterative/recursive) and the number of nested loops or recursive calls.

The benchmark also contains programs which do several calls of the above functions on lists. For example, we handle some programs manipulating chaining hash tables. For that, we use abstraction techniques (slicing, unfolding fixed-size arrays) available through the Frama-C platform. Also, the benchmark includes programs allowing to test the applications discussed in the previous section and which we detail in the following.

Computing procedure summaries: Table 1 describes some of our experimental results on the synthesis of procedure summaries.

Column 5 indicates the set of patterns used for the analysis with $\mathcal{A}_{\mathbb{HS}}(\mathcal{A}_{\mathbb{U}})$. These patterns are:

$$P_{=}(x,x') \equiv \forall y_1 \in \mathtt{tl}(x), y_2 \in \mathtt{tl}(x').\ y_1 = y_2,$$

$$P_1(x) \equiv \forall y \in \mathtt{tl}(x), \qquad P_2(x) \equiv \forall y_1, y_2 \in \mathtt{tl}(x).\ y_1 \leq y_2$$

The pattern $P_{=}$ is used by default for each analysis since it is needed to capture the relation of equality between actual and formal function parameters. The choice of P_1 and P_2 is made according to a heuristics that is based on syntactical criteria such as the number of nested loops or the number of recursive calls in the body of the program. (These numbers are reported in column 3 of Table 1.) The pattern P_1 is used for programs with at least one loop (resp. recursive call) and one iteration variable over lists. The pattern P_2 is used for nested loops, more than one recursive call, or two iteration variables.

Column 6 of Table 1 shows samples of procedure summaries that CELIA can synthesize. (We use the & sign to denote, like in C, the output parameters.)

Columns 4–5 provide the global running times for the analysis, including calls to the APRON libraries. All experiments have been done on an Intel i3-370M with 2.4 GHz and 2 GB of RAM.

All examples in our benchmark corresponding to common functions for list manipulation (classes **sll–fold2** in Table 1, except the function `merge`) are analyzed in less than 1 second. During the analysis of these programs, the manipulated relations are represented using at most 6 abstract heaps, each of them having at most 16 nodes. For the rest of the examples, these relations have at most 18 abstract heaps. The sorting algorithms are time consuming due to (1) the use of widening operators (we have implemented) that are more accurate than the standard ones available in APRON, and (2) the frequent use of the `strengthen` operation in examples such as `quicksort`.

Besides dealing with recursion, compositional inter-procedural allows to have a much more scalable analysis. For instance, consider a program that calls the *init(v)* function on 10 different lists. Our analysis computes once the summary of this function and reuse it, while the analysis after inlining computes successively the effect of all the calls. Thus, the inter-procedural analysis is ten times faster for this example than the intra-procedural analysis.

Combination of abstract domains: The use of the `strengthen` operation is needed in many examples of programs with procedure calls. For instance, as we have seen throughout the paper, the analysis of the recursive sorting algorithm `quicksort` requires

class	fun	nesting (loop,rec)	$\mathcal{A}_{\mathbb{M}}$ t (s)	$\mathcal{A}_{\mathbb{U}}$ $\mathcal{P}$	$\mathcal{A}_{\mathbb{U}}$ t (s)	Examples of summaries synthesized
sll	*create*	$(0,-)$	0.013	$P_=, P_1$	0.021	
	addfst	–	0.003	$P_=$	0.002	
	addlst	$(0,1)$	0.031	$P_=$	0.033	$\rho^\#_{\mathbb{U}}(create(\&x,\ell)): \ \mathtt{hd}(x)=0 \land \mathtt{len}(x)=\ell \land \forall y \in \mathtt{tl}(x) \Rightarrow x[y]=0$
	delfst	–	0.001	$P_=$	0.001	
	dellst	$(0,1)$	0.034	$P_=$	0.042	
map	*init*(v)	$(0,1)$	0.024	$P_=, P_1$	0.034	$\rho^\#_{\mathbb{U}}(init(v,x)): \ \mathtt{len}(x^0)=\mathtt{len}(x) \land \mathtt{hd}(x)=v \land \forall y \in \mathtt{tl}(x).\ x[y]=v$
	initSeq	$(0,1)$	0.024	$P_=, P_1$	0.034	$\rho^\#_{\mathbb{U}}(add(v,x)): \ \mathtt{len}(x^0)=\mathtt{len}(x) \land \mathtt{hd}(x)=\mathtt{hd}(x^0)+v \land$
	add(v)	$(0,1)$	0.021	$P_=$	0.032	$\forall y_1 \in \mathtt{tl}(x), y_2 \in \mathtt{tl}(x^0).\ y_1=y_2 \Rightarrow x[y_1]=x^0[y_2]+v$
map2	*add*(v)	$(0,1)$	0.089	$P_=$	0.517	$\rho^\#_{\mathbb{U}}(add(v,x,z)): \ \mathtt{len}(x^0)=\mathtt{len}(x) \land \mathtt{len}(z^0)=\mathtt{len}(z) \land eq_\forall(x,x^0) \land$
	copy	$(0,1)$	0.063	$P_=$	0.078	$\forall y_1 \in \mathtt{tl}(x), y_2 \in \mathtt{tl}(z).\ y_1=y_2 \Rightarrow x[y_1]+v=z[y_2]$
fold	*del*Pred	$(0,1)$	0.062	$P_=, P_1$	0.145	$\rho^\#_{\mathbb{M}}(split(v,x,\&l,\&u)): \ \mathtt{ms}(x)=\mathtt{ms}(x^0)=\mathtt{ms}(l)\cup\mathtt{ms}(u)$
	max	$(0,1)$	0.031	$P_=, P_1$	0.048	$\rho^\#_{\mathbb{U}}(split(v,x,\&l,\&u)): \ eq_\forall(x,x^0) \land \mathtt{len}(x)=\mathtt{len}(l)+\mathtt{len}(u) \land$
	clone	$(0,1)$	0.071	$P_=$	0.315	$l[0] \le v \land \forall y \in \mathtt{tl}(l) \Rightarrow l[y] \le v \land$
	split	$(0,1)$	0.245	$P_=, P_1$	0.871	$u[0] > v \land \forall y \in \mathtt{tl}(u) \Rightarrow u[y] > v$
fold2	*equal*	$(0,1)$	0.127	$P_=$	0.261	$\rho^\#_{\mathbb{M}}(merge(x,z,\&r)): \ \mathtt{ms}(x)\cup\mathtt{ms}(z)=\mathtt{ms}(r) \land \mathtt{ms}(x^0)=\mathtt{ms}(x) \land \ldots$
	concat	$(0,1)$	0.217	$P_=, P_1, P_2$	0.806	$\rho^\#_{\mathbb{U}}(merge(x,z,\&r)): \ eq_\forall(x,x^0) \land eq_\forall(z,z^0) \land sorted(x^0) \land sorted(z^0) \land$
	merge	$(0,1)$	1.014	$P_=, P_1, P_2$	2.306	$sorted(r) \land \mathtt{len}(x)+\mathtt{len}(z)=\mathtt{len}(r)$
sort	*bubble*	$(1,-)$	0.387	$P_=, P_1, P_2$	2.190	
	insert	$(1,-)$	0.557	$P_=, P_1, P_2$	3.292	$\rho^\#_{\mathbb{M}}(quicksort(x)): \ \mathtt{ms}(x)=\mathtt{ms}(x^0)=\mathtt{ms}(res)$
	quick	$(-,2)$	1.541	$P_=, P_1, P_2$	121.1	$\rho^\#_{\mathbb{U}}(quicksort(x)): \ eq_\forall(x,x^0) \land sorted(res)$
	merge	$(-,2)$	1.547	$P_=, P_1, P_2$	95.94	

Table 1. Experimental results for functions in our benchmark.

combining universal formulas with multiset constraints. Without this combination, the `quicksort` procedure must be transformed to have two parameters (the first and the last element of the list), like in [24]. Therefore, the pivot is given as a parameter which helps to recover at the return from the recursive calls the property that all elements are less/greater than the pivot. Actually, the techniques of [24] cannot handle the version of `quicksort` given in Figure 1, which is the standard implementation of the `quicksort`.

Non-recursive programs may also need strengthening operations for their analysis due to the fact that different sets of patterns may be used for different procedure calls. To experiment that, we have considered programs performing multiple calls to procedures given in Table 1, taking $\{P_=, P_1, P_2\}$ as set of patterns for the analysis of the main procedure. For example, we have considered a procedure that calls `bubblesort` on a list x, and then copies it in a variable y using the procedure `clone` (the procedure `bubblesort` is analyzed using $\{P_=, P_1, P_2\}$ and the procedure `clone` using $\{P_=\}$). For the call to `clone`, we obtain that the two lists x and y are equal, but the sortedness property of x is not transferred to y. However, this property can be recovered at the return of `clone` (using the `strengthen` operation) from the fact that y is equal to x and that x is sorted.

Equivalence checking: We have experimented this approach for checking equivalence between sorting algorithms. The `strengthen` operation plays an essential role. To explain this, consider the example from introduction which considers the equivalence checking of two sorting procedures P_1 and P_2 working on two input lists I_1 and I_2, and producing two outputs O_1 and O_2. The problem is reduced to checking the validity of the implication (C) (page 3) because, for the template of Figure 9, we have that:

- $equal(I_1, I_2)$ corresponds to the assume statement at line 1,
- $sorted(O_1)$ (resp. $\mathtt{ms}(I_1) = \mathtt{ms}(O_1)$) is the summary of P_1 in the $\mathcal{A}_{\mathbb{U}}$ (resp. $\mathcal{A}_{\mathbb{M}}$) domain,
- $sorted(O_2)$ (resp. $\mathtt{ms}(I_2) = \mathtt{ms}(O_2)$) is the summary of P_2 in the $\mathcal{A}_{\mathbb{U}}$ (resp. $\mathcal{A}_{\mathbb{M}}$) domain,
- $equal(O_1, O_2)$ corresponds to the assert statement at line 5.

As explained in Section 6.4, the $equal(I_1, I_2)$ annotation is translated in the $\mathcal{A}_{\mathbb{U}}$ domain into a $eq_\forall$ formula (equation H) and approximated in the $\mathcal{A}_{\mathbb{M}}$ domain into the eq_m formula (equation I). To check the validity of (C), we call $\mathtt{strengthen}(\psi^{\mathbb{U}}, \psi^{\mathbb{M}})$ where:

$$\psi^{\mathbb{U}} \ : \ eq_\forall(I_1, I_2) \land sorted(O_1) \land sorted(O_2)$$
$$\psi^{\mathbb{M}} \ : \ \mathtt{ms}(I_1) = \mathtt{ms}(I_2) \land \mathtt{ms}(I_1) = \mathtt{ms}(O_1) \land \mathtt{ms}(I_2) = \mathtt{ms}(O_2),$$

and obtain the universally quantified formula $\psi^{\mathbb{U}} \land eq_\forall(O_1, O_2)$.

For all experiments, the time needed to check the validity of (C) is negligible compared with the time to compute the procedure summaries.

8. Related work

Automatic synthesis of assertions about programs with dynamic data structures has been addressed using different approaches including abstract interpretation [2, 3, 6, 8, 11–13, 15, 20, 21, 23–27, 29], constraint solving [1, 14], Craig interpolants [18].

In the intra-procedural case, several works consider invariant synthesis for programs that manipulate dynamic data structures. The generated invariants are either universally-quantified first-order formulas [2, 13, 15, 20] or multiset constraints [2, 21].

Concerning the approaches based on abstract interpretation which can handle procedure calls, most of them [3, 8, 23, 25] focus on shape properties and do not consider constraints on sizes and data. The approach in [24] can synthesize procedure summaries that describe data if the instrumentation predicates which guide the abstraction speak about data. Providing patterns is simpler than providing instrumentation predicates on data because patterns contain only constraints between (universally-quantified) positions (in the left-hand-side of the implication) and no constraints on data. For example, in [24] the predicate $dle(v, u)$ allows to synthesize the summary for a procedure that sorts in ascending order, but cannot be used for a procedure that sorts in descending order. However, using the pattern $y1 \le y2$ allows with our approach to synthesize the summaries for both kind of procedures. The same pattern may also allow to discover other properties than sortedness. Actually, patterns are in many cases simple (ordering/equality constraints) and can be discovered using natural heuristics based on the program syntax or proposed/guessed by the user, whereas constraints on data can be more complex. Our approach allows to discover (maybe unpredictable) data constraints for given guard patterns. To establish the fact that a procedure preserves the data values in the input list, the method used in [24] is based on reachability, that is, every cell in the input list remains reachable in the output list. This method can be applied only for programs that never modify/permute the contents of data fields. In our approach, using the multiset domain, we can handle programs that can permute positions of cells in the list or modify/permute the contents of their data fields.

The approach in [11] considers abstract domains where the elements are pairs formed of a graph and a constraint on data. The inter-procedural analysis based on these domains can not synthesize constraints in form of universally-quantified formulas as our analysis can do. In [26], the authors introduce *trace partitioning abstract domains* which start from a partition of the set of traces and compute an invariant for each class. The partitioning can be static (usually based on the control structure of the program) or dynamic. From this point of view, the approach in [26] considers mainly statically-defined partitions. The abstract domain in our paper, based on the unfolding/folding operations, can be seen as an instance of a trace partitioning abstract domain with a dynamic partitioning. The corresponding partitioning puts in the same class all the traces for which the number of dereferences of the `next` pointer field is the same modulo some fixed constant k (which is a parameter of the analysis). The approach in [26] considers mainly numerical abstract domains and it is not faced to the difficulties raised by a compositional analysis on programs manipulating dynamic data structures. The analysis in [12] combines a numerical abstract domain with a shape analysis. It is not restricted by the class of data structures but it considers only properties related to the shape and to the size of the memory.

9. Conclusion

We have defined an accurate inter-procedural analysis for programs with lists and data. The key contribution of this paper is a technique for combining the analysis in different abstract domains and its use in compositional analysis techniques that are able to infer non trivial procedure summaries.

The combination mechanism we propose, based on an unfolding/folding technique combined with partial reduction operators, could be applied for other abstract domains than those considered in this paper. In particular, other abstract domains based on first-order formulas, e.g., the one defined in [13], can be used to strengthen the analysis in our domain of universal formulas.

Another interesting aspect of our work is that it allows to manipulate constraints without requirement of decidability, contrary to many works based on decision procedures. Our abstract domains allow actually to express verification conditions that appear in pre-post condition reasoning. These conditions are typically implications, and then, our entailment checking can be used to check safely their validity. Therefore our framework allows to combine smoothly pre-post condition reasoning with assertion synthesis.

Future work includes the generalization of our framework to structures such as multi-linked lists, trees, and nested structures.

References

[1] D. Beyer, T.A. Henzinger, R. Majumdar, and A. Rybalchenko. Invariant synthesis for combined theories. In *VMCAI*, volume 4349 of *LNCS*, pages 378–394. Springer, 2007.

[2] A. Bouajjani, C. Drăgoi, C. Enea, A. Rezine, and M. Sighireanu. Invariant synthesis for programs manipulating lists with unbounded data. In *CAV*, volume 6174 of *LNCS*, pages 72–88. Springer, 2010.

[3] C. Calcagno, D. Distefano, P.W. O'Hearn, and H. Yang. Compositional shape analysis by means of bi-abduction. In *POPL*, pages 289–300. ACM, 2009.

[4] CEA. *Frama-C Platform*. `htp://frama-c.com`.

[5] Celia plugin. `http://www.liafa.jussieu.fr/celia`.

[6] B.-Y.E. Chang and X. Rival. Relational inductive shape analysis. In *POPL*, pages 247–260. ACM, 2008.

[7] P. Cousot and R. Cousot. Abstract interpretation: A unified lattice model for static analysis of programs by construction or approximation of fixpoints. In *POPL*, pages 238–252. ACM, 1977.

[8] P. Cousot and R. Cousot. Static determination of dynamic properties of recursive procedures. In *IFIP Conf. on Formal Description of Programming Concepts*, pages 237–277. North-Holland Publishing Company, 1977.

[9] P. Cousot and R. Cousot. Systematic design of program analysis frameworks. In *POPL*, pages 269–282. ACM, 1979.

[10] P. Cousot and R. Cousot. Abstract interpretation frameworks. *Journal of Logic and Computation*, 2(4):511–547, 1992.

[11] A. Deutsch. On determining lifetime and aliasing of dynamically allocated data in higher-order functional specifications. In *POPL*, pages 157–168. ACM, 1990.

[12] S. Gulwani, T. Lev-Ami, and S. Sagiv. A combination framework for tracking partition sizes. In *POPL*, pages 239–251. ACM, 2009.

[13] S. Gulwani, B. McCloskey, and A. Tiwari. Lifting abstract interpreters to quantified logical domains. In *POPL*, pages 235–246. ACM, 2008.

[14] A. Gupta, R. Majumdar, and A. Rybalchenko. From tests to proofs. In *TACAS*, volume 5505 of *LNCS*, pages 262–276. Springer, 2009.

[15] N. Halbwachs and M. Péron. Discovering properties about arrays in simple programs. In *PLDI*, pages 339–348. ACM, 2008.

[16] B. Jeannet. *Fixpoint*. `http://gforge.inria.fr/`.

[17] B. Jeannet and A. Miné. Apron: A library of numerical abstract domains for static analysis. In *CAV*, volume 5643 of *LNCS*, pages 661–667. Springer, 2009.

[18] R. Jhala and K.L. McMillan. Array abstractions from proofs. In *CAV*, volume 4590 of *LNCS*, pages 193–206. Springer, 2007.

[19] R. Manevich, E. Yahav, G. Ramalingam, and S. Sagiv. Predicate abstraction and canonical abstraction for singly-linked lists. In *VMCAI*, volume 3385 of *LNCS*, pages 181–198. Springer, 2005.

[20] B. McCloskey, T.W. Reps, and S. Sagiv. Statically inferring complex heap, array, and numeric invariants. In *SAS*, volume 6337 of *LNCS*, pages 71–99. Springer, 2010.

[21] V. Perrelle and N. Halbwachs. An analysis of permutations in arrays. In *VMCAI*, volume 5944 of *LNCS*, pages 279–294, 2010.

[22] J. C. Reynolds. Separation logic: A logic for shared mutable data structures. In *LICS*, pages 55–74. IEEE Computer Society, 2002.

[23] N. Rinetzky, J. Bauer, T.W. Reps, S. Sagiv, and R. Wilhelm. A semantics for procedure local heaps and its abstractions. In *POPL*, pages 296–309. ACM, 2005.

[24] N. Rinetzky, S. Sagiv, and E. Yahav. Interprocedural shape analysis for cutpoint-free programs. In *SAS*, volume 3672 of *LNCS*, pages 284–302. Springer, 2005.

[25] X. Rival and B.-Y.E. Chang. Calling context abstraction with shapes. In *POPL*, pages 173–186. ACM, 2011.

[26] X. Rival and L. Mauborgne. The trace partitioning abstract domain. *ACM Transactions on Programming Languages and Systems*, 29, 2007.

[27] S. Sagiv, T.W. Reps, and R. Wilhelm. Parametric shape analysis via 3-valued logic. *ACM Transactions on Programming Languages and Systems*, 24(3):217–298, 2002.

[28] M. Sharir and A. Pnueli. Two approaches to interprocedural data flow analysis. In *Program Flow Analysis: Theory and Applications*, pages 189–234. New York University, 1981.

[29] V. Vafeiadis. Shape-value abstraction for verifying linearizability. In *VMCAI*, volume 5403 of *LNCS*, pages 335–348. Springer, 2009.

Scaling Abstraction Refinement via Pruning

Percy Liang
UC Berkeley
pliang@cs.berkeley.edu

Mayur Naik
Intel Labs Berkeley
mayur.naik@intel.com

Abstract

Many static analyses do not scale as they are made more precise. For example, increasing the amount of context sensitivity in a k-limited pointer analysis causes the number of contexts to grow exponentially with k. Iterative refinement techniques can mitigate this growth by starting with a coarse abstraction and only refining parts of the abstraction that are deemed relevant with respect to a given client.

In this paper, we introduce a new technique called *pruning* that uses client feedback in a different way. The basic idea is to use coarse abstractions to prune away parts of the program analysis deemed irrelevant for proving a client query, and then using finer abstractions on the sliced program analysis. For a k-limited pointer analysis, this approach amounts to adaptively refining and pruning a set of prefix patterns representing the contexts relevant for the client. By pruning, we are able to scale up to much more expensive abstractions than before. We also prove that the pruned analysis is both sound and complete, that is, it yields the same results as an analysis that uses a more expensive abstraction directly without pruning.

Categories and Subject Descriptors D.2.4 [*Software Engineering*]: Software/Program Verification

General Terms Algorithms, Experimentation, Theory, Verification

Keywords heap abstraction, static analysis, concurrency, abstraction refinement, pruning, slicing

1. Introduction

Making a static analysis more precise requires increasing the complexity of the underlying abstraction—in pointer analysis, by increasing the amount of context/object sensitivity [7, 8, 12, 13, 16, 22]; or in model checking, by adding more abstraction predicates [1, 3]. However, the complexity of these analyses often grows exponentially as the abstraction is refined. Much work has been done on curbing this exponential growth (e.g., client-driven [4] and demand-driven [5] approaches in pointer analysis; lazy abstraction [6, 11] and other iterative refinement approaches in model checking). We refer to these techniques as *selected refinement*, where the main idea is to only refine an abstraction along components deemed relevant according to client feedback.

In this paper, we introduce *pruning*, a new and orthogonal approach which represents a significant departure from existing selected refinement techniques. Pruning is applicable to static analyses expressed as a set of inference rules where a program property of interest (a client query) is proven by the inability to derive a designated fact using the given rules. For concreteness, assume that the static analysis is expressed as a Datalog program. A Datalog program takes a set of input tuples and derives new tuples via a set of inference rules. These inference rules capture the abstract semantics of the static analysis and the evaluation of the client query using the analysis result; the input tuples encode the program we are analyzing and the abstraction we are using. The program property is proven if a designated query tuple cannot be derived.

The key idea behind pruning is to identify input tuples which are provably irrelevant for deriving the query tuple and remove these tuples completely from analysis. Consequently, when the abstraction is refined, only the relevant tuples are refined, potentially resulting in major computational savings. It is helpful to think of pruning in terms of generalized program slicing, where irrelevant parts of the program (irrelevant input tuples) are removed, resulting in a smaller program that is cheaper to analyze. Existing selected refinement techniques attempt to keep the set of input tuples small by simply not refining some of them; pruning keeps the set small by removing some of them entirely.

Pruning can be a dangerous affair though. With selected refinement, we are always performing a static analysis with respect to an abstraction and therefore inherit the soundness guarantees of abstract interpretation. However, once we start pruning input tuples, we are no longer running a valid static analysis on the original program. Soundness therefore is no longer automatic, though we do prove that our method is sound with respect to a given client.

While soundness is trivial for selected refinement but requires some argument for pruning, the situation is reversed for *completeness*. By completeness, we mean that the analysis is as precise as if we had refined all the components of an abstraction. Selected refinement only refines a subset of an abstraction, so it is unclear that the resulting abstraction is as precise as an abstraction obtained by refining all components. However, with pruning, we conceptually work with the fully-refined abstraction; by removing input tuples, we cannot prove fewer queries; thus, completeness is automatic.

To capitalize on the idea of pruning, we propose an algorithm, which we call the *Prune-Refine algorithm*. The idea is to start with a coarse abstraction and prune the irrelevant input tuples before refining the abstraction; the algorithm iterates until the query is proven or a specified computational budget is reached. We prove that the Prune-Refine algorithm computes the same answers to client queries as directly using a refined abstraction without pruning, which would be precise but possibly infeasible.

We apply pruning to the k-object-sensitivity abstraction [12], where objects in the heap are abstracted using chains of allocation sites; these chains are the input tuples we maintain. To facilitate pruning, we introduce two new heap abstractions: The first abstraction truncates chains to avoid repeating allocation sites; this allows us to increase k without getting bogged down by long chains created due to recursion. The second abstraction replaces allocation sites by types (a generalization of [17]). We show that these abstractions can be composed to further improve the effectiveness of pruning.

PLDI'11, June 4–8, 2011, San Jose, California, USA.

We ran our experiments on five Java benchmarks using three clients that depend heavily on having a precise pointer analysis: downcast safety checking, monomorphic call site inference, and race detection. We show that with pruning, our Prune-Refine algorithm enables us to perform a k-object-sensitive pointer analysis with a substantially much finer abstraction (larger k) compared to a full k-object-sensitive pointer analysis or even using the selected refinement strategy of [10]. In a few cases, the non-pruning approaches hit a wall around $k = 3$ but the Prune-Refine algorithm is able to go well beyond $k = 10$.

2. Preliminaries

Our pruning technique works on Datalog, a general language which can be used to express static analyses declaratively [2, 21]. Normally, these analyses and their underlying abstractions are encoded by one monolithic Datalog program which evaluates a query abstractly. For us, it will be convenient to consider the Datalog program, which evaluates a query concretely,[1] as distinct from the abstraction, which transforms the input to the Datalog program, resulting in an abstract evaluation of the query. This separation allows us to make theoretical statements comparing the behavior of the same Datalog program across different abstractions.

We first define Datalog and the computation of a concrete query (Section 2.1). Then, we focus on the abstraction (Section 2.2), which interacts with the Datalog program by transforming the input tuples. Throughout this section, we will use Figure 1 as a running example.

2.1 Datalog

A *Datalog program* consists of a set of *constants* $\mathcal{C}$ (e.g., $0, [03] \in \mathcal{C}$), a set of *variables* $\mathcal{V}$ (e.g., $i, j \in \mathcal{V}$), and a set of *relations* $\mathcal{R}$ (e.g., $\texttt{edge} \in \mathcal{R}$).

A *term* t consists of a relation $t.r \in \mathcal{R}$ and a list of arguments $t.\mathbf{a}$, where each argument $t.a_i$ is either a variable or a constant, (that is, $t.a_i \in \mathcal{V} \cup \mathcal{C}$) for $i = 1, \dots, |t.\mathbf{a}|$. We will write a term in any of the following three equivalent ways:

$$t \equiv t.r(t.\mathbf{a}) \equiv t.r(t.a_1, \dots, t.a_{|t.\mathbf{a}|}). \quad (1)$$

For example, $\texttt{ext}(j, c, c')$ is a term. We call a term whose arguments are all constants a *tuple* (e.g., $\texttt{ext}(0, [\,], [0])$). Note that the tuple includes the relation as well as the arguments. We let x_Q denote a designated *query tuple* (e.g., $\texttt{common}(\text{G}_1, \text{G}_2, 3)$), whose truth value we want to determine.

Let $\mathcal{Z}$ denote the set of rules, where each *rule* $z \in \mathcal{Z}$ consists of a target term $z.t$ and a set of source terms $z.\mathbf{s}$. We write a rule with $z.t = t$ and $z.\mathbf{s} = \{s_1, \dots, s_k\}$ as

$$t \Leftarrow s_1, \dots, s_k. \quad (2)$$

An *assignment* is a function $f : \mathcal{V} \mapsto \mathcal{C}$ which maps variables to constants. To simplify notation later, we extend an assignment f so that it can be applied (i) to constants ($f(c) = c$ for $c \in \mathcal{C}$), and (ii) to terms by replacing the variables in the term with constants ($f(t) = t.r(f(t.a_1), \dots, f(t.a_{|t.\mathbf{a}|}))$).

Derivations A Datalog program takes a set of input tuples and derives new tuples. To formalize this computation, we define the notation of a derivation.

A *derivation* (of the query x_Q) with respect to a set of input tuples X is a sequence $\mathbf{x} = (x_1, \dots, x_n)$ such that

[1] We refer to this computation as "concrete" to contrast with abstract computation we will consider later, but note that this "concrete" computation could already contain some level of abstraction. For example, the Datalog program might correspond to ∞-object-sensitivity without abstraction and k-object-sensitivity with abstraction.

Graph Example

Input relations:

$\texttt{edge}(g, i, j)$	(edge from node i to node j in graph g)
$\texttt{head}(c, i)$	(first element of array c is i)
$\texttt{ext}(i, c, c')$	(i prepended to c yields c': $c' = [i] + c$)

Rules:

$\texttt{path}(g, [0])$.
$\texttt{path}(g, c') \Leftarrow \texttt{path}(g, c),\ \texttt{head}(c, i),\ \texttt{edge}(g, i, j),\ \texttt{ext}(j, c, c')$.
$\texttt{common}(g_1, g_2, i) \Leftarrow \texttt{path}(g_1, c),\ \texttt{path}(g_2, c),\ \texttt{head}(c, i)$.

Query tuple: $x_Q = \texttt{common}(\text{G}_1, \text{G}_2, 3)$.

Constants: $\mathcal{C} = \{\text{G}_1, \text{G}_2, 0, 1, 2, 3, [0], [01], \dots\}$.

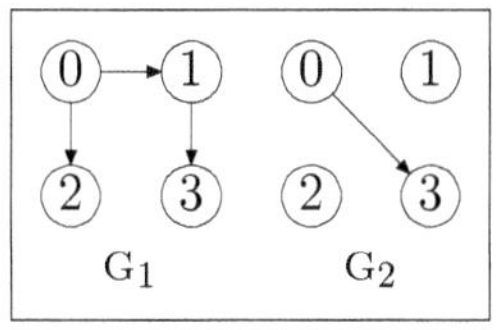

Input tuples:	**Derived tuples:**
$\texttt{edge}(\text{G}_1, 0, 1)$	$\texttt{path}(\text{G}_1, [0])$
$\texttt{edge}(\text{G}_1, 0, 2)$	$\texttt{path}(\text{G}_1, [10])$
$\texttt{edge}(\text{G}_1, 1, 3)$	$\texttt{path}(\text{G}_1, [20])$
$\texttt{edge}(\text{G}_2, 0, 3)$	$\texttt{path}(\text{G}_1, [310])$
$\texttt{head}([0], 0)$	$\texttt{path}(\text{G}_2, [0])$
...	$\texttt{path}(\text{G}_2, [30])$
$\texttt{ext}(1, [0], [10])$	
...	

Figure 1. A simple example illustrating Datalog: Suppose we have two graphs G_1 and G_2 defined on the same set of nodes $\{0, 1, 2, 3\}$, and we want to compute the query tuple $\texttt{common}(\text{G}_1, \text{G}_2, 3)$, asking whether the two graphs have a common path from node 0 to node 3. Given the input tuples encoding the graph, the Datalog program computes a set of derived tuples from the rules. In this case, the absence of $\texttt{common}(\text{G}_1, \text{G}_2, 3)$ from the derived tuples means the query is false (proven).

$\mathcal{C}$	(concrete values)
$\mathcal{P}(\mathcal{C})$	(abstract values)
$\alpha : \mathcal{C} \mapsto \mathcal{P}(\mathcal{C})$	(abstraction, maps to equivalence class)
x_Q	(designated query tuple)
$\mathbf{D}(X)$	(derivations of x_Q using input tuples X)
$\mathbf{E}(X)$	(tuples involved in deriving x_Q)
$\mathbf{P}(X)$	(input tuples relevant to deriving x_Q)
A_k	(abstract input tuples after k iterations)
$\tilde{A}_k$	(relevant abstract input tuples after pruning)

Figure 2. Notation.

(i) for each $i = 1, \dots, n$, we have $x_i \in X$; or there exists a set of indices J such that (J, i) satisfies the following two conditions: $j < i$ for each $j \in J$, and there is a rule $z \in \mathcal{Z}$ and an assignment f such that $f(z.t) = x_i$ and $\{x_j : j \in J\} = \{f(s) : s \in z.\mathbf{s}\}$;

(ii) $x_n = x_Q$; and

(iii) for each $j = 1, \dots, n-1$, there exists J such that $j \in J$ and an index i such that (J, i) satisfies the two conditions in (i).

Define $\mathbf{D}(X)$ to be the set of all derivations with respect to the input tuples X.

Condition (i) says that each tuple in a derivation should either be given as an input tuple ($x_i \in X$) or be the result of some rule $z \in \mathcal{Z}$. Condition (ii) says that the query tuple x_Q is derived at the end. Condition (iii) says that in the derivation of x_Q, every tuple is somehow "relevant" for deriving x_Q.

We say that the query x_Q is false (proven) if and only if $\mathbf{D}(X)$ is empty. Although this answer to the query is the ultimate quantity of interest, the Datalog program can be used to provide more information, which will be useful for pruning. Specifically, we define $\mathbf{E}(X)$ as the set of all tuples used in any derivation (of x_Q) and $\mathbf{P}(X)$ to be the subset of $\mathbf{E}(X)$ which are input tuples:

$$\mathbf{E}(X) \triangleq \bigcup_{\mathbf{x} \in \mathbf{D}(X)} \mathbf{x}, \tag{3}$$

$$\mathbf{P}(X) \triangleq X \cap \mathbf{E}(X). \tag{4}$$

We call $\mathbf{P}(X)$ the set of *relevant input tuples*. As we will see later, any tuple not in this set can be safely pruned. In fact, $\mathbf{P}(X)$ also tells us whether the query is true or false. In particular, $\mathbf{D}(X) = \emptyset$ if and only if $\mathbf{P}(X) = \emptyset$ (assuming x_Q cannot be derived trivially without inputs). This equivalence suggests that proving and pruning are intimately related; in some sense, proving the query is just pruning away the query tuple. In the remainder of the paper, we will make heavy use of $\mathbf{P}$ as the principal proving/pruning operator. In our graph example, $\mathbf{D}(X) = \mathbf{P}(X) = \emptyset$, but as we will see later, this is not true if we apply an abstraction to X.

Computation Given input tuples X, a Datalog solver returns the set of derived tuples Y; the query is proven if $x_Q \notin Y$. Note that Y is a superset of the relevant derived tuples $\mathbf{E}(X)$, which itself is a superset of the relevant input tuples $\mathbf{P}(X)$, which is needed for pruning.

We can compute $\mathbf{P}(X)$ by using the Datalog program transformation technique described in [10]: We augment our existing Datalog program with a set of new relations $\mathcal{R}' = \{r' : r \in \mathcal{R}\}$. For a term $t = t.r(t.\mathbf{a})$ we let $t' = t.r'(t.\mathbf{a})$ be the term that uses the corresponding new relation $t.r'$. We then add the following new Datalog rules:

$$x'_Q \Leftarrow x_Q, \tag{5}$$

$$s' \Leftarrow z.t', z.\mathbf{s} \quad \text{for each } z \in \mathcal{Z} \text{ and } s \in z.\mathbf{s}. \tag{6}$$

For example, the last rule of the original Datalog program in Figure 1 generates the following three new rules:

$$\begin{aligned}
\texttt{path}'(g_1, c) &\Leftarrow \texttt{common}'(g_1, g_2, i), \texttt{path}(g_1, c), \texttt{path}(g_2, c), \texttt{head}(c, i).\\
\texttt{path}'(g_2, c) &\Leftarrow \texttt{common}'(g_1, g_2, i), \texttt{path}(g_1, c), \texttt{path}(g_2, c), \texttt{head}(c, i).\\
\texttt{head}'(c, i) &\Leftarrow \texttt{common}'(g_1, g_2, i), \texttt{path}(g_1, c), \texttt{path}(g_2, c), \texttt{head}(c, i).
\end{aligned}$$

The key is that a tuple x' is derived by the new Datalog program if and only if $x \in \mathbf{E}(X)$. Rules generated by (5) and (6) construct $\mathbf{E}(X)$ recursively: The base case (5) states that the query tuple $x_Q \in \mathbf{E}(X)$. The recursive case (6) states that if $x \in \mathbf{E}(X)$ and a rule z (with some assignment f) was used to produce x, then for every source term $s \in z.\mathbf{s}$ of that rule, we also have $f(s) \in \mathbf{E}(X)$. Having obtained $\mathbf{E}(X)$, we get $\mathbf{P}(X)$ by keeping only tuples in X.

The advantage of this technique is that we can use any Datalog solver as a black-box to compute $\mathbf{P}(X)$. In practice, we will not actually run $\mathbf{P}$ on concrete input tuples X, but on abstract input tuples. From the point of view of the Datalog solver, there is no difference between the two. We consider constructing abstract tuples next.

2.2 Abstractions

Given a Datalog program, an *abstraction* is an equivalence relation over constants $\mathcal{C}$. In particular, we represent the abstraction as the function which maps each constant to its equivalence class.

Definition 1. *An abstraction is a function $\alpha : \mathcal{C} \to \mathcal{P}(\mathcal{C})$ such that for each set $s \in$ range(α), we have $\alpha(c) = s$ for all $c \in s$.*

We will refer to constants $\mathcal{C}$ as the concrete values and range(α) as the abstract values. We assume the natural partial order on abstractions, where $\alpha_1 \preceq \alpha_2$ if and only if $\alpha_1(c) \supseteq \alpha_2(c)$ for all c—that is, α_2 is finer than α_1.

$\{[0]\}$				$\{[1]\}$			
$\{[00]\}$		$\{[01]\}$		$\{[10]\}$		$\{[11]\}$	
$[000]*$	$[001]*$	$[010]*$	$[011]*$	$[100]*$	$[101]*$	$[110]*$	$[111]*$

Figure 3. The 14 abstract values defined by the k-limited abstraction π_k with $\mathbb{H} = \{0, 1\}$ and $k = 3$. Specifically, π_k maps each chain $c \in \mathbb{H}^*$ to one of the values above.

Example: k-limited abstraction The main abstraction we will work with in this paper is the k-limited abstraction [12, 16]. Our general theory does not depend on this particular choice, but we present the abstraction here so we can use it as a running example.

First, we define some notation. Let $\mathbb{H}$ be an arbitrary set; for the graph example of Figure 1, let $\mathbb{H} = \{0, 1, 2, 3\}$ be the nodes of the graph; later, $\mathbb{H}$ will be the set of allocation sites in a program. Define a *chain* $c \in \mathbb{H}^*$ to be a finite sequence of elements from this set. Let $|c|$ denote the length of the chain. Let $c[i]$ be the i-th element of c (starting with index 1) and let $c[i..j]$ be the subchain $[c[i] \cdots c[j]]$ (boundary cases: $c[i..j] = [\,]$ if $i > j$ and $c[i..j] = c[i..|c|]$ if $j > |c|$). For two chains c_1 and c_2, let $c_1 + c_2$ denote their concatenation.

The *k-limited abstraction* partitions chains based on their length k prefix. First, for a chain c, let $c*$ denote the set of all chains with prefix c; formally:

$$c* \triangleq \{c' \in \mathbb{H}^* : c'[1..|c|] = c\}. \tag{7}$$

For an integer truncation level $k \geq 0$, define the k-limited abstraction π_k as follows:

$$\pi_k(c) \triangleq \begin{cases} \{c\} & \text{if } |c| < k \\ c[1..k]* & \text{if } |c| \geq k. \end{cases} \tag{8}$$

If the concrete chain c is shorter than length k, we map it to the singleton set $\{c\}$; otherwise, we map it to the set of chains that share the first k elements. It is easy to verify that π_k is a valid abstraction under Definition 1.

For example, if $c = [01]$, then we have that $\pi_1(c) = [0]* = \{[0], [00], [01], [000], \dots\}$ are the chains that start with $[0]$. As another example, Figure 3 shows the range of π_3.

It is important that we represent $\{c\}$ and $c*$ as distinct abstract values. In contrast, traditional k-limited analyses are parametrized by a set S of abstract values "c", where each abstract "c" represents the set of concrete chains whose longest matching prefix in S is c. With this setup, every concrete chain would map to some abstract value regardless of S (note that we must have "$[\,]$" $\in S$). Therefore, pruning would be impossible using this representation.

Extending the abstraction Given an abstraction α, it will be useful to extend the definition of α to not just concrete values, but also to abstract values, and (sets of) concrete/abstract tuples.

First, we extend α from concrete values c to abstract values s as follows:

$$\alpha(s) \triangleq \{\alpha(c) : c \in s\}, \quad s \in \mathcal{P}(\mathcal{C}). \tag{9}$$

Note that $\alpha(s)$ returns a set of abstract values. This allows us to naturally define the composition of two abstractions. In particular, given two abstractions, α and β, define their composition to be:

$$(\alpha \circ \beta)(c) \triangleq \cup_{s \in \alpha(\beta(c))} s. \tag{10}$$

Note that the composition $\alpha \circ \beta$ need not be an abstraction even if α and β are.[2] Therefore, when we compose abstractions in Section 3.2, it will be important to check that the resulting compositions are valid abstractions.

An important case in which compositions yield valid abstractions is when $\alpha \preceq \beta$ (β is finer than α). In this case, $\alpha \circ \beta = \alpha$, corresponding to the fact that applying a finer abstraction first has no impact.

Next, we extend α to concrete tuples x and sets of concrete tuples X in the natural way:

$$\alpha(x) \triangleq x.r(\alpha(x.a_1), \ldots, \alpha(x.a_{|x.\mathbf{a}|})), \tag{11}$$

$$\alpha(X) \triangleq \{\alpha(x) : x \in X\}. \tag{12}$$

Here, $\alpha(x)$ is an *abstract tuple* (one where the arguments are abstract values) and $\alpha(X)$ is a set of abstract tuples. For example:

$$\pi_1(\mathtt{ext}(1, [0], [10])) = \mathtt{ext}(1, [0]*, [1]*).$$

Finally, we extend α to abstract tuples b and sets of abstract tuples B:

$$\alpha(b) \triangleq \{b.r(s_1, \ldots, s_{|b.\mathbf{a}|}) : \forall i, s_i \in \alpha(b.a_i)\}, \tag{13}$$

$$\alpha(B) \triangleq \cup_{b \in B} \alpha(b). \tag{14}$$

(13) applies the abstraction function to each component of b and takes the cross product over the resulting abstract values; the result is a set of abstract tuples. (14) aggregates these sets of abstract tuples. For example:

$$\pi_1(\mathtt{ext}(1, [00]*, [10]*)) = \{\mathtt{ext}(1, [0]*, [1]*)\}.$$

Using the abstraction Given an abstraction α, we want to run the Datalog program to compute an abstract answer to the query. We do this by applying the abstraction to the concrete input tuples X, producing a set of abstract input tuples $\alpha(X)$. We then feed these tuples into the Datalog program to produce $\mathbf{P}(\alpha(X))$. (Note that the Datalog program is oblivious to whether the tuples are abstract or concrete.) Figure 4 shows an example of performing this computation on the graph example from Figure 1 with the k-limited abstraction π_1.

We say the query is proven by α if $\mathbf{P}(\alpha(X)) = \emptyset$. Because abstraction is sound, this happens only if the query is actually false ($\mathbf{P}(X) = \emptyset$). This fact is stated formally below (see Appendix A for the proof):

Proposition 1 (Abstraction is sound). *Let α be an abstraction and let X be any set of input tuples. If $\mathbf{P}(\alpha(X)) = \emptyset$ (the query is false abstractly), then $\mathbf{P}(X) = \emptyset$ (the query is false concretely).*

If α is coarse, $\mathbf{P}(\alpha(X))$ will be imprecise; but if α is fine, $\mathbf{P}(\alpha(X))$ will be expensive to compute. The next section shows how pruning can allow us to use a fine abstraction α without incurring the full cost of computing $\mathbf{P}(\alpha(X))$.

3. General theory

We first describe the core idea behind pruning (Section 3.1) and then show how it can be used in the Prune-Refine algorithm (Section 3.2).

3.1 Pruning

Recall that the central operation of a static analysis is $\mathbf{P}$, which serves two roles: (i) determining if the query is proven (when $\mathbf{P}$ returns $\emptyset$); and (ii) returning the relevant input tuples. The following theorem provides the key equation that drives everything in this paper (see Appendix A for the proof):

Theorem 1 (Pruning is sound and complete). *Let α and β be two abstractions such that $\beta \preceq \alpha$ (β is coarser than α). Then for any set of concrete input tuples X, we have:*

$$\boxed{\mathbf{P}(\alpha(X)) = \mathbf{P}(\alpha(X) \cap \alpha(\mathbf{P}(\beta(X))))}. \tag{15}$$

The left-hand side of (15) corresponds to running the analysis with respect to α. The right-hand side corresponds to first pruning the input tuples X with β and then running the analysis with α. The theorem states that the two procedures obtain identical results (the right-hand side is sound and complete with respect to the left-hand side). The significance of this is that the right-hand side is often much cheaper to compute than the left-hand side.

Let us decipher (15) a bit more. On the right-hand side, the abstract input tuples $\beta(X)$ are fed into the Datalog solver which computes $\mathbf{P}(\beta(X))$, which is the subset of input tuples, namely those that participate in any derivation of the abstract query tuple $\beta(x_Q)$. These relevant tuples are then refined via α to yield a set of tuples which are used to prune $\alpha(X)$. The resulting subset is fed into the analysis $\mathbf{P}$. On the left-hand side, $\mathbf{P}(\alpha(X))$ is the result of directly running the analysis on the abstract tuples $\alpha(X)$ without pruning.

To obtain some intuition behind pruning, consider the following simpler idea: first run the analysis with β; if the query is proven, stop and declare *proven*; otherwise, run the analysis with α and output that answer. It is easy to see that this two-step procedure returns the same answer as just running α: Because $\beta \preceq \alpha$, if β proves the query, then so does α (Proposition 1). (15) can be thought of as an extension of this basic idea: instead of using β to just determine whether the query tuple is proven, we obtain more information, namely the whole set of input tuples that are relevant.

The complexity of an analysis is largely determined by the number of input tuples. Traditionally, the abstraction alone determines the set of input tuples and thus also the complexity of the analysis. In our case, however, the set of input tuples is pruned along the way, so the abstraction only partially determines the complexity. As we will see later, with sufficient pruning of the input tuples, we can use a very refined abstraction at a low cost.

3.2 The Prune-Refine algorithm

We now turn Theorem 1 into a full algorithm, which we call the Prune-Refine algorithm. Figure 5 shows the pseudocode of the algorithm and a diagram showing the computation of the various abstract input tuples computed.

This algorithm essentially applies (15) repeatedly. We first present a simplified version of the algorithm which ignores the pre-pruning step (we take $A_t = A'_t$). We are given a sequence of successively finer abstractions $\alpha_0, \alpha_1, \ldots$ (e.g., $\alpha_t = \pi_t$ for the k-limited abstractions) and a set of input abstract tuples A_0, which is computed under the initial abstraction α_0. Then the algorithm alternates between a pruning step and a refining step, maintaining only the abstract input tuples that could participate in a derivation of the query tuple x_Q. On iteration t, our current input tuples A_t are first pruned to $\tilde{A}_t$ using $\mathbf{P}$; this is subsequently refined to A_{t+1}. Figure 6 shows an example of running this algorithm on the graph example from Figure 1; the first pruning step is shown in Figure 4.

Now we discuss pre-pruning. Pre-pruning requires the user to provide another sequence of successively finer abstractions $\beta_0, \beta_1, \ldots$ which are coarser than $\alpha_0, \alpha_1, \ldots$, respectively. These abstractions will also be used to prune the input tuples. The idea is that before refining A_t to A_{t+1}, we perform two steps of pruning: (i) first we use β_t in a pre-pruning step; (ii) then we use α_t during the main pruning step.

[2] For example, suppose $\mathcal{C} = \{1, 2, 3\}$; $\alpha(1) = \alpha(2) = \{1, 2\}$, $\alpha(3) = \{3\}$; and $\beta(1) = \beta(3) = \{1, 3\}$, $\beta(2) = \{2\}$. Then $(\alpha \circ \beta)(1) = \{1, 2, 3\}$ but $(\alpha \circ \beta)(2) = \{1, 2\}$. Therefore, $\alpha \circ \beta$ is not a valid abstraction.

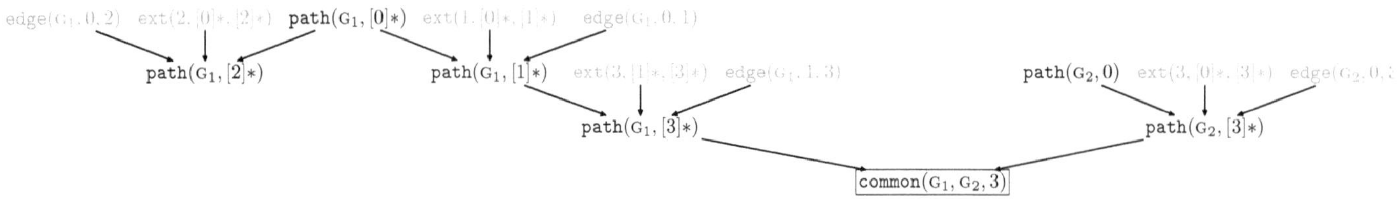

Figure 4. Computation of $\mathbf{P}(\pi_1(X))$ on the graph example from Figure 1, where X is the set of concrete input tuples, and π_1 is the 1-limited abstraction which maps each path onto the set of paths with the same first element. In the figure, each abstract tuple is derived by a rule whose source terms are connected via incoming edges. Relevant input tuples ($\mathbf{P}(\pi_1(X))$, shown in green) are the ones which are reachable by following the edges backwards; ones which are not backwards-reachable are pruned ($\pi_1(X)\backslash\mathbf{P}(\pi_1(X))$, shown in red).

Prune-Refine algorithm

Input:
Sequence of abstractions: $\alpha_0 \preceq \alpha_1 \preceq \alpha_2 \preceq \cdots$
[Auxiliary abstractions: $\beta_t \preceq \alpha_t, t = 0, 1, 2, \ldots$]
$A_0 = \alpha_0(X)$, set of tuples

For $t = 0, 1, 2, \ldots$:
[Pre-prune: $A'_t \leftarrow A_t \cap \alpha_t(\mathbf{P}(\beta_t(A_t)))$]
Prune: $\tilde{A}_t = \mathbf{P}(A'_t)$. If $\tilde{A}_t = \emptyset$: return *proven*.
Refine: $A_{t+1} = \alpha_{t+1}(\tilde{A}_t)$.

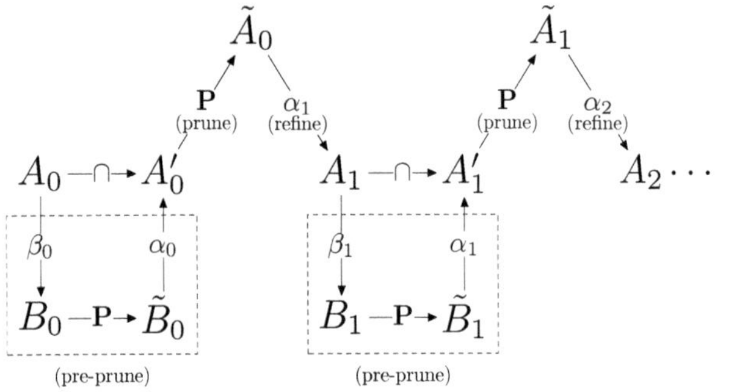

Figure 5. The pseudocode and the schema for the Prune-Refine algorithm. The algorithm maintains a set of (abstract) input tuples which could be involved in some derivation of the query x_Q and attempts to prune down this set. The basic version of the algorithm, which excludes the lines in square brackets and the dotted boxes, simply alternates between pruning and refining. The full version includes a pre-pruning step, which uses auxiliary abstractions to further reduce the number of tuples.

Pre-pruning requires a sequence of auxiliary abstractions (β_t) which are coarser than the main abstractions (α_t). A standard way to obtain auxiliary abstractions is by composing the main abstractions with another abstraction τ; formally, $\beta_t = \alpha_t \circ \tau$. We can use any τ for which $\alpha_t \circ \tau$ yields a valid abstraction, but the speedup we obtain from pre-pruning depends on the relationship between τ and α_t. If τ is the total abstraction ($\tau(c) = C$), then pre-pruning will be fast but nothing will be pre-pruned, so we get no speedup. If τ is no abstraction ($\tau(c) = c$), then pre-pruning is equivalent to just running the pruning step, so we again get no speedup. A good rule of thumb is that τ should be "complementary" to α_t (we will see some examples in Section 5).

Theorem 2 states that the Prune-Refine algorithm is both sound and complete. In other words, pruning has no impact on the answer to a query. The proof is given in Appendix A and uses Theorem 1.

A_0	$\tilde{A}_0$	A_1	$\tilde{A}_1$
ext(1, [0]*, [1]*)	ext(1, [0]*, [1]*)	ext(1, {[0]}, [10]*)	*(none)*
ext(2, [0]*, [2]*)	ext(3, [0]*, [3]*)	ext(3, {[0]}, [30]*)	
ext(3, [0]*, [3]*)	ext(3, [1]*, [3]*)	ext(3, {[1]}, [31]*)	
ext(3, [1]*, [3]*)		ext(3, [10]*, [31]*)	

Figure 6. The abstract input tuples computed by the Prune-Refine algorithm on the graph example from Figure 1 (without pre-pruning). We are using k-limited abstractions ($\alpha_t = \pi_t$). During the first pruning step, ext(2, [0]*, [2]*) is pruned from A_0, yielding $\tilde{A}_0$. In the refinement step, we expand [1]* to {[1]} and [10]*. In the second pruning step, we prove the query (pruning everything).

Theorem 2 (Correctness of the Prune-Refine algorithm). *At iteration t, using the incrementally pruned abstraction A_t is equivalent to using the full abstraction $\alpha_t(X)$ in that $\mathbf{P}(\alpha_t(X)) = \mathbf{P}(A_t)$. Consequently, if the algorithm returns "proven," then $\mathbf{P}(X) = \emptyset$ (the query is actually false).*

4. k-limited Pointer Analysis

We now introduce our k-object-sensitive pointer analysis [12], on which we will apply the Prune-Refine algorithm. Each node in the control-flow graph of each method $m \in \mathbb{M}$ is associated with a simple statement (e.g., $v_2 = v_1$). We omit statements that have no effect on our analysis (e.g., operations on data of primitive type). For simplicity, we assume each method has a single argument and no return value.[3] Figure 7 describes the Datalog program corresponding to this analysis.

The analysis represents both contexts and abstract objects using chains of allocation sites ($\mathbb{C} = \mathbb{H}^*$). Contexts are extended into new contexts via the ext relation, which prepends an allocation site to a chain (e.g., ext(3, [12], [312])). Note that these chains are not truncated in the Datalog program, and therefore, running the Datalog program directly (ignoring the fact that it might not terminate) corresponds to performing an ∞-object-sensitivity analysis.

Although this Datalog program itself is an approximation to the concrete program semantics—it is flow-insensitive, does not handle primitive data, etc., we will informally say that a client query computed with respect to this analysis yields a concrete answer. In contrast, we obtain an abstract answer by computing the client query with respect to a k-limited abstraction, which we will discuss in Section 4.2.

We now briefly describe the Datalog rules in Figure 7. Rule (1) states that the main method m_{main} is reachable in a distinguished context [ ]. Rule (2) states that a target method of a reachable call

[3] Our actual implementation is a straightforward extension of this simplified analysis which handles multiple arguments, return values, class initializers, and objects allocated through reflection.

Domains:

(method)	m	$\in$	$\mathbb{M} = \{m_{\text{main}}, \ldots\}$
(local variable)	v	$\in$	$\mathbb{V}$
(global variable)	g	$\in$	$\mathbb{G}$
(object field)	f	$\in$	$\mathbb{F}$
(method call site)	i	$\in$	$\mathbb{I}$
(allocation site)	h	$\in$	$\mathbb{H}$
(statement)	p	$\in$	$\mathbb{P}$
(method context)	c	$\in$	$\mathbb{C} = \mathbb{H}^*$
(abstract object)	o	$\in$	$\mathbb{O} = \mathbb{H}^*$

$$p ::= v = \texttt{new}\, h \mid v_2 = v_1 \mid g = v \mid v = g \mid v_2.f = v_1 \mid v_2 = v_1.f \mid i(v)$$

Input relations:

body	$\subset$	$\mathbb{M} \times \mathbb{P}$	(method contains statement)
trgt	$\subset$	$\mathbb{I} \times \mathbb{M}$	(call site resolves to method)
argI	$\subset$	$\mathbb{I} \times \mathbb{V}$	(call site's argument variable)
argM	$\subset$	$\mathbb{M} \times \mathbb{V}$	(method's formal argument variable)
ext	$\subset$	$\mathbb{H} \times \mathbb{C} \times \mathbb{C}$	(extend context with site)
	$=$	$\{(h, c, [h] + c) : h \in \mathbb{H}, c \in \mathbb{C}\}$	

Output relations:

reachM	$\subset$	$\mathbb{C} \times \mathbb{M}$	(reachable methods)
reachP	$\subset$	$\mathbb{C} \times \mathbb{P}$	(reachable statements)
ptsV	$\subset$	$\mathbb{C} \times \mathbb{V} \times \mathbb{O}$	(points-to sets of local variables)
ptsG	$\subset$	$\mathbb{G} \times \mathbb{O}$	(points-to sets of static fields)
heap	$\subset$	$\mathbb{O} \times \mathbb{F} \times \mathbb{O}$	(heap graph)
cg	$\subset$	$\mathbb{C} \times \mathbb{I} \times \mathbb{C} \times \mathbb{M}$	(call graph)

Rules:

$$\texttt{reachM}([], m_{\text{main}}). \quad (1)$$
$$\texttt{reachM}(c, m) \Leftarrow \texttt{cg}(*, *, c, m). \quad (2)$$
$$\texttt{reachP}(c, p) \Leftarrow \texttt{reachM}(c, m),\ \texttt{body}(m, p). \quad (3)$$

$$\texttt{ptsV}(c, v, o) \Leftarrow \texttt{reachP}(c, v = \texttt{new}\, h),\ \texttt{ext}(h, c, o). \quad (4)$$
$$\texttt{ptsV}(c, v_2, o) \Leftarrow \texttt{reachP}(c, v_2 = v_1),\ \texttt{ptsV}(c, v_1, o). \quad (5)$$
$$\texttt{ptsG}(g, o) \Leftarrow \texttt{reachP}(c, g = v),\ \texttt{ptsV}(c, v, o). \quad (6)$$
$$\texttt{ptsV}(c, v, o) \Leftarrow \texttt{reachP}(c, v = g),\ \texttt{ptsG}(g, o). \quad (7)$$
$$\texttt{heap}(o_2, f, o_1) \Leftarrow \texttt{reachP}(c, v_2.f = v_1),\ \texttt{ptsV}(c, v_1, o_1),\ \texttt{ptsV}(c, v_2, o_2). \quad (8)$$
$$\texttt{ptsV}(c, v_2, o_2) \Leftarrow \texttt{reachP}(c, v_2 = v_1.f),\ \texttt{ptsV}(c, v_1, o_1),\ \texttt{heap}(o_1, f, o_2). \quad (9)$$

$$\texttt{cg}(c, i, o, m) \Leftarrow \texttt{reachP}(c, i),\ \texttt{trgt}(i, m),\ \texttt{argI}(i, v),\ \texttt{ptsV}(c, v, o). \quad (10)$$
$$\texttt{ptsV}(c, v, c) \Leftarrow \texttt{reachM}(c, m),\ \texttt{argM}(m, v). \quad (11)$$

Figure 7. Datalog implementation of our k-object-sensitivity pointer analysis with call-graph construction. Our abstraction $\mathbf{a}$ affects the analysis solely through ext, which specifies that when we prepend s to c, we truncate the resulting sequence to length $\mathbf{a}_s$.

site is also reachable. Rule (3) states that every statement in a reachable method is also reachable. Rules (4) through (9) implement the transfer function associated with each kind of statement. Rule (10) analyzes the target method m in a separate context o for each abstract object o to which the distinguished `this` argument of method m points, and rule (11) sets the points-to set of the `this` argument of method m in context o to the singleton $\{o\}$.

This pointer analysis computes the reachable methods (reachM), reachable statements (reachP), and points-to sets of local variables (ptsV), each with the associated context; the context-insensitive points-to sets of static fields (ptsG) and heap graph (heap); and a context-sensitive call graph (cg).

4.1 Clients

The core pointer analysis just described is used by three clients, which each defines a set of queries.

Monomorphic call site detection Monomorphic call sites are dynamically dispatched call sites with at most one target method. These can be transformed into statically dispatched ones which are cheaper to execute. For each call site $i \in \mathbb{I}$ whose target is a virtual method, we create a query $\texttt{poly}(i)$ asking whether i is polymorphic. This query can be computed with the following rule:

$$\texttt{poly}(i) \Leftarrow \texttt{cg}(*, i, *, m_1), \texttt{cg}(*, i, *, m_2), m_1 \neq m_2. \quad (16)$$

Downcast safety checking A safe downcast is one that cannot fail because the object to which the downcast is applied is guaranteed to be a subtype of the target type. Therefore, safe downcasts obviate the need for run-time cast checking. We create a query for each downcast—statement of the form $v_1 = v_2$ where the declared type of v_2 is not a subtype of the declared type of v_1. The query can be computed with the following rule:

$$\texttt{unsafe}(v_1, v_2) \Leftarrow \texttt{ptsV}(*, v_2, o), \texttt{typeO}(o, t_2), \texttt{typeV}(v_1, t_1), \neg\texttt{subtype}(t_1, t_2). \quad (17)$$

Here, typeV is a relation on a variable and its declared type and typeO is a relation on an abstract object and its type (computed by inspecting the initial allocation site of o).

Race detection In race detection, each query consists of a pair of heap-accessing statements of the same field in which at least one statement is a write. We implemented the static race detector of [14], which declares a (p_1, p_2) pair as racing if both statements may be reachable, may access thread-escaping data, may point to the same object, and may happen in parallel. All four components rely heavily on the context- and object-sensitive pointer analysis.

4.2 Relationship to general notation

We now describe the k-object-sensitive pointer analysis (Figure 7) in terms of our general notation presented in Section 2. The set of concrete values $\mathcal{C}$ is the union of all the domains (e.g.., allocation sites $\mathbb{H} = \{1, 2, 3, \ldots\}$, abstract objects $\mathbb{C} = \mathbb{H}^*$, etc.). The input tuples X are specified by the input relations (e.g., $X = \{\texttt{body}(m_{\text{main}}, x = \texttt{new}\,3), \texttt{ext}(3, [12], [312])\}$). Each of the three clients defines a set of possible query tuples, for example, $x_Q = \texttt{unsafe}(\texttt{v4}, \texttt{v8})$ for downcast safety checking of an assignment $\texttt{v4} = \texttt{v8}$.

Recall that $\mathbf{P}(X)$ corresponds to obtaining an answer to a client query with respect to ∞-object-sensitivity. To obtain k-object-

```
class A {
  f() {
0:  v = new A
    if (*) return v
    else return v.f()
  }
}
```

```
1:  x1 = new A
2:  x2 = new A
    y1 = x1.f()
    y2 = x2.f()
```

Figure 8. An example illustrating the repetition of allocation sites. The points-to set of `y1` using ∞-object-sensitivity is $\{[01], [001], [0001], \dots\}$ (any positive number of zeros followed by a 1), and the points-to set of `y2` is $\{[02], [002], [0002], \dots\}$. While these two sets are disjoint, if we use a k-limited abstraction for any finite k, we would conclude erroneously that both variables might point to $\mathbf{0}_k*$, where $\mathbf{0}_k$ is a chain of k zeros. Incidentally, this demonstrates an intrinsic limitation of the k-object-sensitivity abstraction. Using the barely-repeating k-limited abstraction, we can increase k while avoiding chains longer than [00] since [00] is barely-repeating. This results in computational savings, and in this case, in no loss in precision.

sensitivity, we first apply the k-limited abstraction π_k to the input tuples and run the Datalog program on these abstract tuples ($\mathbf{P}(\pi_k(X))$). Note that only the `ext` tuples are affected by the abstraction.

5. Abstractions

We have already defined the k-limited abstraction, which corresponds to k-object-sensitivity. We now present two orthogonal variants of this basic abstraction: one that additionally limits the repetition of allocation sites (Section 5.1) and one that further abstracts allocation sites using type information (Section 5.2).

5.1 Barely-repeating k-limited abstraction

When we applied the k-limited abstraction in practice, we noticed empirically that a major reason why it did not scale was the seemingly unnecessary combinatorial explosion associated with chains formed by cycling endlessly through the same allocation sites. For k-CFA, this repetition corresponds to recursion. For k-object-sensitivity, this corresponds to recursive allocation, as illustrated in Figure 8.[4] We therefore wish to define an abstraction that not only truncates chains at length k but also truncates a chain when it starts repeating.

For a sequence c, we say c is *non-repeating* if all its elements are distinct. We say c is *barely-repeating* if (i) c excluding the last element ($c[1..|c|-1]$) is *non-repeating* and (ii) the last element of c is repeated earlier in c. Let $\delta(c)$ be the length of the longest prefix of c that is barely-repeating, if it exists, and ∞ otherwise:

$$\delta(c) \triangleq \begin{cases} \max_{m' : c[1..m'] \text{ is barely-repeating}} m' & \text{if } m' \text{ exists,} \\ \infty & \text{otherwise.} \end{cases} \quad (18)$$

For example, $\delta([10010]) = 3$ because [100] is barely-repeating, but [1001] is not.

We now define the *barely-repeating k-limited abstraction* $\hat{\pi}_k$ as follows:

$$\hat{\pi}_k(c) \triangleq \pi_{\min\{k, \delta(c)\}}(c), \quad (19)$$

Figure 9 shows an example of $\hat{\pi}_k$. We show that $\hat{\pi}_k$ is a valid abstraction:

[4] Incidentally, the example in the figure also gives an interesting example where k-object-sensitivity for any finite k (no matter how large) is less precise than ∞-object-sensitivity.

$\{[0]\}$ $\{[1]\}$
$[00]*$ $\{[01]\}$ $\{[10]\}$ $[11]*$
$[010]*$ $[011]*$ $[100]*$ $[101]*$

Figure 9. For the barely-repeating k-limited abstraction for $\mathbb{H} = \{0, 1\}$ and $k = 3$, we show the equivalence classes under $\hat{\pi}_k$. Compare this with the classes for the k-limited abstraction (Figure 3). Note that, for example, $[000]*$ and $[001]*$ are collapsed into $[00]*$ since [000] and [001] are not barely-repeating, but [00] is.

Proposition 2. *The function $\hat{\pi}_k$ defined in (19) is a valid abstraction (Definition 1).*

Proof. We consider two cases: (i) for $\{c\} \in \text{range}(\hat{\pi}_k)$, we have $\hat{\pi}_k(c) = \{c\}$; and (ii) for any $c* \in \text{range}(\hat{\pi}_k)$, either $|c| = k$ or c is barely-repeating; in either case, it is easy to see that any extension $c' \in c*$ will have $\hat{\pi}_k(c') = c*$. □

Remark: one might wonder why we defined the abstraction using the barely-repeating criterion as opposed to the simpler non-repeating criterion. It turns out that using the latter in (18) would not result in a valid abstraction. If $\hat{\pi}_k$ were defined using the non-repeating criterion, then $\hat{\pi}_3([00]) = [0]*$. But for $[01] \in [0]*$, we have $\hat{\pi}_3([01]) = \{[01]\} \neq [0]*$.

5.2 Type-based abstraction

We now introduce an abstraction that we will use in the pre-pruning step of the Prune-Refine algorithm. We start by defining an equivalence relation over allocation sites $\mathbb{H}$, represented by a function $\tau : \mathbb{H} \mapsto \mathcal{P}(\mathbb{H})$ mapping each allocation site $h \in \mathbb{H}$ to its equivalence class. In the graph example, we might have $\tau(0) = \tau(1) = \{0, 1\}$ and $\tau(2) = \tau(3) = \{2, 3\}$.

Given such a τ, we extend it to sequences by taking the cross product over elementwise applications:

$$\tau(c) = \tau(c[1]) \times \cdots \times \tau(c[|c|]), \quad c \in \mathbb{H}^*. \quad (20)$$

In the running example, $\tau([02]) = \{[02], [03], [12], [13]\}$.

To construct τ for k-limited pointer analysis, we consider using two sources of type information associated with an allocation site, motivated by [17]:

$$\text{I}(h) = \text{declaring type of allocation site } h \quad (21)$$

$$\text{C}(h) = \text{type of class containing allocation site } h \quad (22)$$

Using these two functions, we can construct three equivalence relations, τ_{I}, τ_{C}, and $\tau_{\text{I}\times\text{C}}$ as follows:

$$\tau_f(h) = \{h' : f(h) = f(h')\}, \quad (23)$$

for $f \in \{\text{I}, \text{C}, \text{I} \times \text{C}\}$.

Now we have three choices for τ: one that uses the declaring type (τ_{I}), one that uses the type of the containing class (τ_{C}), and one that uses both ($\tau_{\text{I}\times\text{C}}$). Recall that all three are complementary to the k-limited abstraction π_k: Specifically, τ abstracts a chain by abstracting each site uniformly, whereas π_k performs no abstraction on the first k sites, but performs a total abstraction on the rest of the chain. Recall that this complementarity is desirable for effective pre-pruning.

Since τ is not coarser than π_k, we cannot use it directly in the Prune-Refine algorithm. We must compose τ with π_k or $\hat{\pi}_k$ to yield another abstraction which is coarser than π_k or $\hat{\pi}_k$, respectively. But in what order should we compose? We must be careful because the composition of two abstractions is not necessarily an abstraction. Fortunately, the following proposition shows which compositions are valid:

Proposition 3. *The functions (i) $\pi_k \circ \tau$ and (ii) $\tau \circ \pi_k$ are valid abstractions (see Definition 1) and equivalent; (iii) $\hat{\pi}_k \circ \tau$ is also valid, but (iv) $\tau \circ \hat{\pi}_k$ is not.*

Proof. For each of these four composed functions, each set s in the range of the function must be either of the form $s = w_1 \times \cdots \times w_m$ for $m < k$ (case 1) or $s = w_1 \times \cdots \times w_m \times \mathbb{H}^*$ for some $m \le k$ (case 2), where $w_i \in \text{range}(\tau)$ for each $i = 1, \dots, m$.

For (i) and (ii), it is straightforward to check that $(\pi_k \circ \tau)(c) = (\tau \circ \pi_k)(c) = s$ for each $c \in s$. Intuitively, the truncation (π_k) and coarsening (τ) operate independently and can be interchanged.

For (iii) and (iv), the two dimensions do not act independently; the amount of truncation depends on the amount of coarsening: the coarser τ is, the more truncation one might need to limit repetitions. Showing that $\hat{\pi}_k \circ \tau$ is valid proceeds in a similar manner to Proposition 2. If s falls under case 1, note that no $c \in s$ is repeating because the w_i's must be disjoint; therefore $\hat{\pi}_k(\tau(c)) = s$. If s falls under case 2, note that for any $c[1..m] \in s$ must be barely-repeating but any longer prefix is not, and therefore, $\hat{\pi}_k(\tau(c)) = s$.

To show that (iv) is not an abstraction, consider the following counterexample: let $\mathbb{H} = \{0, 1, 2\}$, and define $\tau(h) = \mathbb{H}$ for all $h \in \mathbb{H}$ (there is one equivalence class). Consider applying $\tau \circ \hat{\pi}_3$ to two elements [01] and [00]: For [01], we have $\hat{\pi}_3([01]) = \{[01]\}$, so $\tau(\hat{\pi}_3([01])) = \mathbb{H}^2$; for [00], we have $\hat{\pi}_3([00]) = [00]*$, so $\tau(\hat{\pi}_3([00])) = \mathbb{H}^2 \times \mathbb{H}^*$. But $\mathbb{H}^2 \subsetneq \mathbb{H}^2 \times \mathbb{H}^*$ (notably, the two sets are neither equal nor disjoint), so $\tau \circ \hat{\pi}_3$ does not define a valid abstraction. □

In light of this result, we will use the valid abstractions $\pi_k \circ \tau$ and $\hat{\pi}_k \circ \tau$, which work by first applying the type-based abstraction τ and then applying π_k or $\hat{\pi}_k$.

6. Experiments

In this section, we apply the Prune-Refine algorithm (Section 3.2) to k-object-sensitivity for our three clients (Section 4.1): downcast safety checking (DOWNCAST), monomorphic call site inference (MONOSITE), and race detection (RACE). Our main empirical result is that across different clients and benchmarks, pruning is effective at curbing the exponential growth, which allows us to run analyses using abstractions finer than what is possible without pruning.

6.1 Setup

Our experiments were performed using IBM J9VM 1.6.0 on 64-bit Linux machines. All analyses were implemented in Chord, an extensible program analysis framework for Java bytecode,[5] which uses the BDD Datalog solver `bddbddb` [21]. We evaluated our analyses on five Java benchmarks shown in Table 1. In each run, we allocated 8GB of memory and terminated the process when it ran out of memory.

We experimented with various combinations of abstractions and refinement algorithms (see Table 2). As a baseline, we consider running an analysis with a full abstraction α (denoted FULL(α)). For α, we can either use k-limited abstractions ($\boldsymbol{\pi} = (\pi_k)_{k=0}^{\infty}$), in which case we recover ordinary k-object-sensitivity, or the barely-repeating variants ($\hat{\boldsymbol{\pi}} = (\hat{\pi}_k)_{k=0}^{\infty}$). We also consider the site-based refinement algorithm of [10], which considers a sequence of abstractions $\boldsymbol{\alpha} = (\alpha_0, \alpha_1, \dots)$ but stops refining sites which have been deemed irrelevant. This algorithm is denoted SITE($\boldsymbol{\alpha}$).

As for the new algorithms that we propose in this paper, we have PR($\boldsymbol{\alpha}$), which corresponds to the Prune-Refine (PR) algorithm using a sequence of abstractions $\boldsymbol{\alpha}$ with no pre-pruning; and PR($\boldsymbol{\alpha}, \tau$), which performs pre-pruning using $\beta_t = \alpha_t \circ \tau$ for $t = 0, 1, 2, \dots$. We consider three choices of τ which use different kinds of type information ($\tau_{\text{I}}, \tau_{\text{C}}, \tau_{\text{I}\times\text{C}}$).

In our implementation of the Prune-Refine algorithm, we depart slightly from our presentation. Instead of maintaining the full set of relevant input tuples, we instead maintain only the set of allocation site chains which exist in some relevant input tuple. This choice results in more conservative pruning, but reduces the amount of information that we have to keep. We can modify the original Datalog program so that the original Prune-Refine algorithm computes this new variant: Specifically, first introduce new input tuples `active`(c) for each $c \in \mathbb{H}^*$. Then encode existing `ext` input tuples as rules with no source terms; `ext` is no longer an input relation. Finally, add `active`(c) to the right-hand side of each existing rule that uses a chain-valued variable. Computing the relevant input tuples in this modified Datalog program corresponds exactly to computing the set of relevant allocation site chains.

Abstractions	
$\boldsymbol{\pi} = (\pi_k)_{k=0}^{\infty}$	(k-limited abstractions (8))
$\hat{\boldsymbol{\pi}} = (\hat{\pi}_k)_{k=0}^{\infty}$	(barely-repeating k-limited abstractions (19))
τ_{I}	(abstraction using type of allocation site)
τ_{C}	(abstraction using type of containing class)
$\tau_{\text{I}\times\text{C}}$	(abstraction using both types)
Algorithms	
FULL(α)	(standard analysis using an abstraction α)
SITE($\boldsymbol{\alpha}$)	(site-based refinement [10] on abstractions $\boldsymbol{\alpha}$)
PR($\boldsymbol{\alpha}$)	(PR algorithm using $\boldsymbol{\alpha}$, no pre-pruning)
PR($\boldsymbol{\alpha}, \tau$)	(PR algorithm using $\boldsymbol{\alpha}$, using $\boldsymbol{\alpha} \circ \tau$ to pre-prune)

Table 2. Shows the abstractions and algorithms that we evaluated empirically. For example, PR($\hat{\boldsymbol{\pi}}, \tau_{\text{I}\times\text{C}}$) means running the Prune-Refine algorithm on the barely-repeating k-limited abstraction ($\alpha_k = \hat{\pi}_k$), using a composed abstraction based on the type of an allocation site (τ_{I}) and the type of the declaring class (τ_{C}) to do pre-pruning (specifically, $\beta_k = \hat{\pi}_k \circ \tau_{\text{I}\times\text{C}}$).

6.2 Results

We ran the four algorithms of Table 2 using k-limited abstractions, seeing how far we could increase k until the analyses ran out of memory. For each analysis, we also measured the number of input tuples given to the Datalog solver; this quantity is denoted as $|A'_t|$ (see Figure 5). In this section, the number of iterations t is the same as the k value.

Figure 10 plots the number of tuples $|A'_t|$ as a function of number of iterations t. We see that the non-pruning algorithms completely hit a wall after a few iterations, with the number of tuples exploding exponentially. On most benchmark-client pairs, the pruning algorithms are able to continue increasing k much further, though on several pairs, pruning only manages to increase k by one beyond the non-pruning algorithms. We also observed that pruning does yield speedups, although these are less pronounced than the differences in the number of tuples. Nonetheless, pruning overcomes the major bottleneck—that standard k-limited analyses run out of memory even for moderate k. By curbing the growth of the number of tuples, pruning makes it possible to run some analyses at all.

However, there are several caveats with pruning: First, we are using BDDs, which can actually handle large numbers of tuples so long as they are structured; pruning destroys some of this structure, yielding less predictable running times. Second, pruning requires solving the transformed Datalog program for computing $\mathbf{P}(X)$, which is more expensive than the original Datalog program. Finally, we must solve the Datalog program several times, not just

[5] `http://code.google.com/p/jchord/`

	description	# classes	# methods	# bytecodes	$\|\mathbb{H}\|$
`elevator`	discrete event simulation program	154	629	39K	637
`hedc`	web crawler	309	1,885	151K	1,494
`weblech`	website downloading and mirroring tool	532	3,130	230K	2,545
`lusearch`	text indexing and search tool	611	3,789	267K	2,822
`avrora`	simulation and analysis framework for AVR microcontrollers	1,498	5,892	312K	4,823

Table 1. Benchmark characteristics: the number of classes, number of methods, total number of bytecodes in these methods, and number of allocation sites ($|\mathbb{H}|$) deemed reachable by 0-CFA.

	$\frac{\|B_t\|}{\|A_t\|}$	$\frac{\|\tilde{B}_t\|}{\|B_t\|}$	$\frac{\|A'_t\|}{\|A_t\|}$	$\frac{\|\tilde{A}_t\|}{\|A_t\|}$	$\frac{\|A_{t+1}\|}{\|A_t\|}$
DOWNCAST/`hedc`	0.28	0.72	0.68	0.65	1.63
DOWNCAST/`weblech`	0.19	0.18	0.26	0.19	3.28
DOWNCAST/`lusearch`	0.17	0.04	0.03	0.02	1.89
DOWNCAST/`avrora`	0.21	0.03	0.05	0.03	1.57
MONOSITE/`elevator`	0.10	0.55	0.21	0.21	1.67
MONOSITE/`hedc`	0.22	0.30	0.36	0.29	3.78
MONOSITE/`weblech`	0.19	0.18	0.25	0.18	3.33
MONOSITE/`lusearch`	0.26	0.10	0.15	0.12	3.39
MONOSITE/`avrora`	0.30	0.05	0.04	0.03	1.85
RACE/`elevator`	0.10	0.57	0.22	0.21	1.58
RACE/`hedc`	0.28	0.28	0.34	0.25	4.01
RACE/`weblech`	0.19	0.18	0.27	0.18	3.43
RACE/`lusearch`	0.30	0.15	0.18	0.14	3.96
RACE/`avrora`	0.38	0.08	0.08	0.06	2.71
Average	0.23	0.24	0.22	0.18	2.72

Table 3. Shows the shrinking and growth of the number of tuples during the various pruning and refinement operations (see Figure 5) for our best algorithm PR($\pi, \tau_{1\times C}$) across all the clients and benchmarks, averaged across iterations. The columns are as follows: First, $\frac{|B_t|}{|A_t|}$ measures the number of tuples after projecting down to the auxiliary abstraction $\beta_t = \pi_t \circ \tau_{1\times C}$ for pre-pruning; note that running the analysis using types instead of allocation sites is much cheaper. Next, $\frac{|\tilde{B}_t|}{|B_t|}$ shows the fraction of abstract values kept during pre-pruning; When we return from types to allocation sites, we see that the effect of pre-pruning carries over ($\frac{|A'_t|}{|A_t|}$). Next, pruning kept $\frac{|\tilde{A}_t|}{|A_t|}$ of the chains. Finally, $\frac{|A_{t+1}|}{|A_t|}$ measures the ratio between iterations, which includes both pruning and refinement. Note that there is still almost a three-fold growth of the number of tuples (on average), but this growth would have been much more unmanageable without the pruning.

client/benchmark \ k	1	2	3	4	5
DOWNCAST/`elevator`	0	-	-	-	-
DOWNCAST/`hedc`	10	8	3	**2**	**2**
DOWNCAST/`weblech`	24	14	6	**6**	-
DOWNCAST/`lusearch`	36	14	6	**5**	**5**
DOWNCAST/`avrora`	12	10	6	**6**	**6**
MONOSITE/`elevator`	1	1	1	1	1
MONOSITE/`hedc`	164	149	149	**149**	-
MONOSITE/`weblech`	273	258	252	**252**	-
MONOSITE/`lusearch`	593	454	447	**447**	-
MONOSITE/`avrora`	288	278	272	-	-
RACE/`elevator`	475	440	437	437	437
RACE/`hedc`	23,033	22,043	21,966	-	-
RACE/`weblech`	7,286	4,742	4,669	-	-
RACE/`lusearch`	33,845	23,509	16,957	-	-
RACE/`avrora`	62,060	61,807	61,734	-	-

Table 4. The number of unproven queries (unsafe downcasts, polymorphic sites, races) for each of the clients and benchmarks over the first five iterations. All analyses obtain the exact results on iterations where they obtain an answer. Bolded numbers refer to k values reached by PR($\pi, \tau_{1\times C}$) but not by any non-pruning algorithm. While pruning enables to increase k more, we get strictly more precise results for only two of the client/benchmark pairs (DOWNCAST/`hedc` and DOWNCAST/`lusearch`). This points out inherent limitations of this family of k-limited abstractions.

once. These three caveats also apply to the site-based refinement algorithm of [10] (SITE), so pruning is at least a strict improvement over that algorithm.

We found that the best instantiation of the Prune-Refine algorithm is PR($\pi, \tau_{1\times C}$), which involves pre-pruning with both kinds of type information ($\tau_{1\times C}$); this works better than both no pre-pruning and pre-pruning with only τ_1 or τ_C alone.

Table 3 provides more details on the quantitative impact of pruning for PR($\pi, \tau_{1\times C}$). We see that pre-pruning has a significant impact: we can eliminate about three-quarters of the tuples by just operating on the coarser level of types rather than allocation sites (see the $\frac{|\tilde{B}_t|}{|B_t|}$ column). Importantly, the effect of this pruning carries over to the original k-limited abstraction (see the $\frac{|A'_t|}{|A_t|}$ column).

So far, we have been using the k-limited abstraction; we now compare this abstraction with the barely-repeating k-limited abstraction introduced in Section 5.1. As Figure 11 shows, for a few cases, the barely-repeating k-limited abstraction requires fewer tuples than the k-limited abstraction; but in most cases, it does not improve scalability. The reason is that the barely-repeating abstraction curbs refinement, but often, somewhat paradoxically, it is exactly the refinement which enables more pruning.

Finally, Table 4 shows the effect on the number of queries proven. While pruning enables us to increase k much more than before, it turns out that our particular analyses for these clients saturate quite quickly, so over all the clients and benchmarks, we were only able to prove two queries more than using the non-pruning techniques. On the surface, these findings seem to contradict [9], which showed a sharp increase in precision around $k = 4$ for k-CFA. However, this discrepancy merely suggests that our flow-insensitive analyses are simply limited: since [9] offers upper bounds on precision, we know for sure that low k values are insufficient; the fact that we don't see an increase in precision for higher k suggests that the non-k-related aspects of our analyses are insufficient. Given that our pruning approach is general, it would be interesting to tackle other aspects of program analysis such as flow-sensitivity.

7. Related Work

There is a wealth of literature which attempts to scale static analyses without sacrificing precision. One general theme is to work with a flexible family of abstractions, which in principle allows us to conform to the needs of the client. Milanova et al. [12, 13] consider abstractions where each local variable can be independently treated context-sensitively or context-insensitively, and different k values can be chosen for different allocation sites. Lhoták and Hendren [7, 8] present Paddle, a parametrized framework for BDD-based, k-limited pointer analyses. [17] scale up k-object-

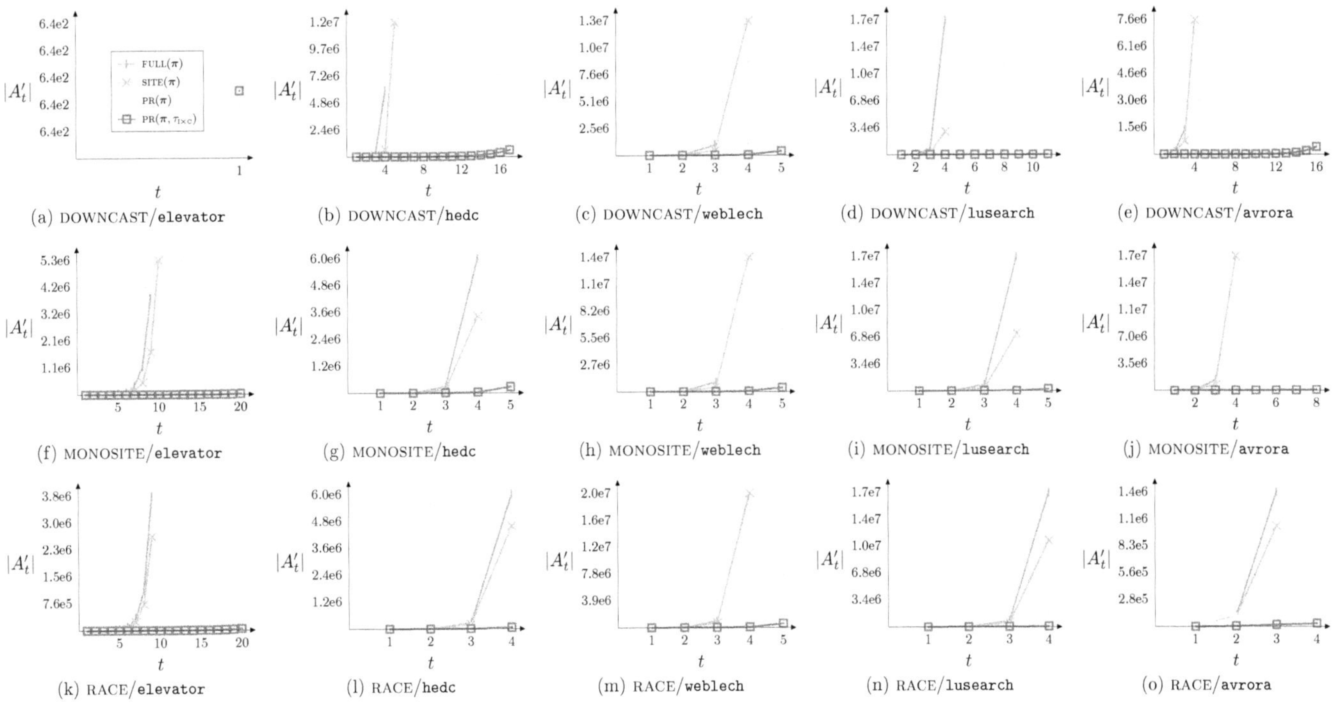

Figure 10. For each client/benchmark pair, we show the growth of the number of input tuples $|A'_t|$ across iterations (recall that A'_t are the tuples fed into the Datalog program). Table 2 describes the four algorithms. We see that the pruning algorithms ($\text{PR}(\pi)$ and $\text{PR}(\pi, \tau_{1\times C})$) drastically cut down the number of input tuples by many orders of magnitude.

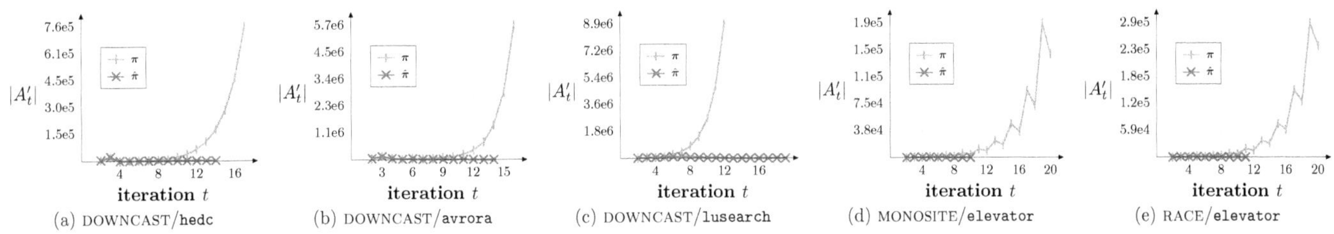

Figure 11. Shows the 5 (out of the 15) client/benchmark pairs for which using the barely-repeating k-limited abstraction ($\hat{\pi}$) allows one to increase k much more than the plain k-limited abstraction (π). On the other 10 client/benchmarks where k cannot get very large, limiting repetitions is actually slightly worse in terms of scalability. Also note that three of the plots for $\hat{\pi}$ stop early, not because the algorithm runs out of memory, but because the algorithm has actually converged and increasing k would have no effect.

sensitivity, increasing k by one using types rather than allocation sites. However, in all of this work, which parts of the abstraction should be more refined is largely left up to the user.

Client-driven approaches use feedback from a client query to determine what parts of an abstraction to refine. Plevyak and Chien [15] use a refinement-based algorithm for type inference, where context-sensitivity is driven by detecting type conflicts. Guyer and Lin [4] present a pointer analysis for C which detects loss of precision (e.g., at merge points) and introduce context-sensitivity. Our method for determining relevant input tuples is similar in spirit but more general.

Section 3.1 of Liang et al. [10] (not the focus of that work) also computes the set of relevant tuples by running a transformed Datalog program. However, what is done with this information is quite different there. [10] merely stops refining the irrelevant sites whereas we actually prune all irrelevant tuples, thereby exploiting this information more fully. As we saw in Section 6, this difference had major ramifications.

Demand-driven analyses [5, 23] do not refine the abstraction but rather try to compute an analysis on an existing abstraction more efficiently. Sridharan et al. [19] presents an algorithm which casts pointer analysis as a CFL-reachability problem and relaxes the problem by introducing additional "match" edges.

Our Prune-Refine algorithm has a client-driven flavor in that we refine our abstraction, but also a demand-driven flavor in that we do not perform a full computation (in particular, ignoring tuples which were pruned). However, there are two important differences between the present work and the work described earlier: First, while most of that work is specific to pointer analysis, our Prune-Refine algorithm is applicable to any Datalog program. Second, past work is based on selected refinement, which is orthogonal to pruning. Selected refinement merely governs the abstractions $(\alpha_t)_{t=0}^{\infty}$ that we use, whereas pruning focuses on removing input tuples. Given that the input tuples encode the program analysis, pruning is analogous to program slicing.

Other forms of pruning have been implemented in various settings. [20] uses dynamic analysis to prune down the set of paths and then focuses a static analysis on these paths. [18] uses pruning for type inference in functional languages, where pruning is simply a heuristic which shortcuts a search algorithm. As a result, pruning can hurt precision. One advantage of our pruning approach is that it comes with strong soundness and completeness guarantees.

8. Conclusion

We have introduced pruning as a general technique for scaling up static analyses written in Datalog. The basic idea is to run an analysis using a coarse abstraction, only keeping input tuples deemed relevant, and then using a finer abstraction on the remaining tuples. Theoretically, we showed that pruning is both sound and complete (our analysis is valid and we lose no precision). Empirically, we showed that pruning enables us to scale up analyses based on k-object-sensitivity much more than previous approaches.

Acknowledgments

We thank Mooly Sagiv and Hongseok Yang for discussion and useful feedback. We also thank the anonymous reviewers for their insightful comments.

References

[1] T. Ball, R. Majumdar, T. Millstein, and S. Rajamani. Automatic predicate abstraction of C programs. In *PLDI*, pages 203–213, 2001.

[2] M. Bravenboer and Y. Smaragdakis. Strictly declarative specification of sophisticated points-to analyses. In *OOPSLA*, pages 243–262, 2009.

[3] S. Graf and H. Saidi. Construction of abstract state graphs with PVS. *Computer Aided Verification*, 1254:72–83, 1997.

[4] S. Guyer and C. Lin. Client-driven pointer analysis. In *SAS*, pages 214–236, 2003.

[5] N. Heintze and O. Tardieu. Demand-driven pointer analysis. In *PLDI*, pages 24–34, 2001.

[6] T. A. Henzinger, R. Jhala, R. Majumdar, and G. Sutre. Lazy abstraction. In *POPL*, 2002.

[7] O. Lhoták and L. Hendren. Context-sensitive points-to analysis: is it worth it? In *CC*, pages 47–64, 2006.

[8] O. Lhoták and L. Hendren. Evaluating the benefits of context-sensitive points-to analysis using a BDD-based implementation. *ACM Transactions on Software Engineering and Methodology*, 18(1):1–53, 2008.

[9] P. Liang, O. Tripp, M. Naik, and M. Sagiv. A dynamic evaluation of static heap abstractions. In *OOPSLA*, pages 411–427, 2010.

[10] P. Liang, O. Tripp, and M. Naik. Learning minimal abstractions. In *POPL*, 2011.

[11] K. McMillan. Lazy abstraction with interpolants. In *CAV*, pages 123–136, 2006.

[12] A. Milanova, A. Rountev, and B. Ryder. Parameterized object sensitivity for points-to and side-effect analyses for Java. In *ISSTA*, pages 1–11, 2002.

[13] A. Milanova, A. Rountev, and B. Ryder. Parameterized object sensitivity for points-to analysis for Java. *ACM Transactions on Software Engineering and Methodology*, 14(1):1–41, 2005.

[14] M. Naik, A. Aiken, and J. Whaley. Effective static race detection for Java. In *PLDI*, pages 308–319, 2006.

[15] J. Plevyak and A. Chien. Precise concrete type inference for object-oriented languages. In *OOPSLA*, pages 324–340.

[16] O. Shivers. Control-flow analysis in Scheme. In *PLDI*, pages 164–174, 1988.

[17] Y. Smaragdakis, M. Bravenboer, and O. Lhotak. Pick your contexts well: Understanding object-sensitivity. In *POPL*, 2011.

[18] S. A. Spoon and O. Shivers. Demand-driven type inference with subgoal pruning: Trading precision for scalability. In *ECOOP*, 2004.

[19] M. Sridharan and R. Bodík. Refinement-based context-sensitive points-to analysis for Java. In *PLDI*, pages 387–400, 2006.

[20] V. Vipindeep and P. Jalote. Efficient static analysis with path pruning using coverage data. In *International Workshop on Dynamic Analysis (WODA)*, 2005.

[21] J. Whaley. *Context-Sensitive Pointer Analysis using Binary Decision Diagrams*. PhD thesis, Stanford University, 2007.

[22] J. Whaley and M. Lam. Cloning-based context-sensitive pointer alias analysis using binary decision diagrams. In *PLDI*, pages 131–144, 2004.

[23] X. Zheng and R. Rugina. Demand-driven alias analysis for C. In *POPL*, pages 197–208, 1998.

A. Proofs

Instead of directly proving Proposition 1, we state a more general theorem which will be useful later:

Theorem 3 (Soundness). *Let α and β be two abstractions with $\beta \preceq \alpha$ (β is coarser), and let X be any set of input tuples. For any derivation $\mathbf{a} \in \mathbf{D}(\alpha(X))$, define $\mathbf{b} = (b_1, \dots, b_{|\mathbf{a}|})$ where each b_i is the unique element in $\beta(a_i)$. Then $\mathbf{b} \in \mathbf{D}(\beta(X))$.*

Proof of Theorem 3. Define $A = \alpha(X)$ and $B = \beta(X)$. Consider $\mathbf{a} \in \mathbf{D}(A)$ and let $\mathbf{b}$ be as defined in the theorem. For each position i, we have two cases. First, if $a_i \in A$, then $b_i \in (\beta \circ \alpha)(X) = \beta(X) = B$. Otherwise, let $z \in \mathcal{Z}$ be the rule and J be the indices of the tuples used to derive a_i. The same rule z and the corresponding tuples $\{b_j : j \in J\}$ can also be used to derive b_i. Therefore, $\mathbf{b} \in \mathbf{D}(B)$. □

Proof of Proposition 1 (abstraction is sound). Apply Theorem 3 with $\beta = \alpha$ and α as the identity function (no abstraction). □

Before we prove Theorem 1, we state a useful lemma.

Lemma 1 (Pruning is idempotent). *For any set of tuples (concrete or abstract) X, $\mathbf{P}(X) = \mathbf{P}(\mathbf{P}(X))$.*

Proof. Since $\mathbf{P}(X) \subset X$ by definition and $\mathbf{P}$ is monotonic, we have $\mathbf{P}(\mathbf{P}(X)) \subset \mathbf{P}(X)$. For the other direction, let $x \in \mathbf{P}(X)$. Then x is part of some derivation ($x \in \mathbf{x} \in \mathbf{D}(X)$). All the input tuples of $\mathbf{x}$ (those in $\mathbf{x} \cap X$) are also in $\mathbf{P}(X)$, so $\mathbf{x} \in \mathbf{D}(\mathbf{P}(X))$. Therefore $x \in \mathbf{P}(\mathbf{P}(X))$. □

Proof of Theorem 1 (pruning is sound and complete). We define variables for the intermediate quantities in (15): $A = \alpha(X)$ and $B = \beta(X)$, $\tilde{B} = \mathbf{P}(B)$, $\tilde{A} = \alpha(\tilde{B})$, and $A' = A \cap \tilde{A}$. We want to show that pruning is sound ($\mathbf{P}(A) \subset \mathbf{P}(A')$) and complete ($\mathbf{P}(A) \supset \mathbf{P}(A')$). Completeness follows directly because $A \supset A'$ and $\mathbf{P}$ is monotonic (increasing the number of input tuples can only increase the number of derived tuples).

Now we show soundness. Let $a \in \mathbf{P}(A)$. By definition of $\mathbf{P}$ ((3)), there is a derivation $\mathbf{a} \in \mathbf{D}(A)$ containing a. For each $a_i \in \mathbf{a}$, let b_i be the unique element in $\beta(a_i)$ (a singleton set because $\beta \preceq \alpha$), and let $\mathbf{b}$ be the corresponding sequence constructed from the b_is. Since $\beta \preceq \alpha$, we have $\mathbf{b} \in \mathbf{D}(B)$ by Theorem 3, and so each input tuple in $\mathbf{b}$ is also in $\mathbf{P}(B) = \tilde{B}$; in particular, $b \in \tilde{B}$ for $\beta(a) = \{b\}$. Since $\beta \preceq \alpha$, $a \in \alpha(b)$, and so $a \in \tilde{A}$. We have thus shown that $\mathbf{P}(A) \subset \tilde{A}$. Finishing up, $\mathbf{P}(A') = \mathbf{P}(A \cap \tilde{A}) \supset \mathbf{P}(A \cap \mathbf{P}(A)) = \mathbf{P}(\mathbf{P}(A)) = \mathbf{P}(A)$, where the last equality follows from idempotence (Lemma 1). □

We now show that the Prune-Refine algorithm is correct, which follows from a straightforward application of Theorem 1.

Proof of Theorem 2 (correctness of the Prune-Refine algorithm). First, we argue that pre-pruning is correct. For each iteration t, we invoke Theorem 1 with $\alpha = \alpha_t, \beta = \beta_t$ and X be such that $\alpha(X) = A_t$. The result is that $\mathbf{P}(A_t) = \mathbf{P}(A_t')$, so without loss of generality, we will assume $A_t = A_t'$ for the rest of the proof.

Now fix an iteration t. We will show that $\mathbf{P}(\alpha_t(X)) = \mathbf{P}(A_t)$ by induction, where the inductive hypothesis is $\mathbf{P}(\alpha_t(X)) = \mathbf{P}(\alpha_t(\tilde{A}_s))$. For the base case ($s = -1$), we define $\tilde{A}_{-1} = \{X\}$, we get a tautology. For the inductive case, apply the theorem with applied to $\beta = \alpha_s, \alpha = \alpha_t$ and X such that $\alpha_s(X) = \alpha_s(\tilde{A}_{s-1})$, we get that

$$\mathbf{P}(\alpha_t(\tilde{A}_{s-1})) = \mathbf{P}(\alpha_t(\mathbf{P}(\alpha_s(\tilde{A}_{s-1})))) = \mathbf{P}(\alpha_t(\tilde{A}_s)).$$

When $s = t - 1$, we have $\mathbf{P}(\alpha_t(X)) = \mathbf{P}(\alpha_t(\tilde{A}_{t-1})) = \mathbf{P}(A_t)$, completing the claim. Finally, if the algorithm returns *proven*, we have

$$\emptyset = \mathbf{P}(A_t) = \mathbf{P}(\alpha_t(X)) \supset \mathbf{P}(X).$$

□

Taming the Wildcards: Combining Definition- and Use-Site Variance

John Altidor
Department of Computer Science
University of Massachusetts, Amherst
Amherst, MA 01003, USA
jaltidor@cs.umass.edu

Shan Shan Huang
LogicBlox Inc.
Two Midtown Plaza
Atlanta, GA 30309, USA
ssh@logicblox.com

Yannis Smaragdakis
Department of Computer Science,
University of Massachusetts,
Amherst, MA 01003, USA
and Department of Informatics,
University of Athens, 15784, Greece
yannis@cs.umass.edu—smaragd@di.uoa.gr

Abstract

Variance allows the safe integration of parametric and subtype polymorphism. Two flavors of variance, definition-site versus use-site variance, have been studied and have had their merits hotly debated. Definition-site variance (as in Scala and C#) offers simple type-instantiation rules, but causes fractured definitions of naturally invariant classes; Use-site variance (as in Java) offers simplicity in class definitions, yet complex type-instantiation rules that elude most programmers.

We present a unifying framework for reasoning about variance. Our framework is quite simple and entirely denotational, that is, it evokes directly the definition of variance with a small core calculus that does not depend on specific type systems. This general framework can have multiple applications to combine the best of both worlds: for instance, it can be used to add use-site variance annotations to the Scala type system. We show one such application in detail: we extend the Java type system with a mechanism that *modularly infers* the definition-site variance of type parameters, while allowing use-site variance annotations on any type-instantiation.

Applying our technique to six Java generic libraries (including the Java core library) shows that 20-58% (depending on the library) of generic definitions are inferred to have single-variance; 8-63% of method signatures can be relaxed through this inference, and up to 91% of existing wildcard annotations are unnecessary and can be elided.

Categories and Subject Descriptors D.3.1 [*Programming Languages*]: Formal Definitions and Theory; D.3.3 [*Programming Languages*]: Language Constructs and Features—Polymorphism,Data types and structures,Classes and objects

General Terms Design, Languages

Keywords variance, definition-site variance, use-site variance, wildcards, language extensions

PLDI'11, June 4–8, 2011, San Jose, California, USA.

1. Introduction

Genericity is one of the most significant programming language advances of the past 40 years. Variance mechanisms are the keystone of safe genericity in modern programming languages, as they attempt to reconcile the two fundamental forms of genericity: parametric and subtype polymorphism. Concretely, variance mechanisms aim to answer the question "under what conditions for type expressions *Exp1* and *Exp2* is `C<`*Exp1*`>` a subtype of `C<`*Exp2*`>`?"

The conventional answer to this question has been *definition-site variance*: the definition of generic class `C<X>` determines its variance [2, 9, 13]. Depending on how the type parameter `X` is used, `C` can have one of four flavors of variance: it can be *covariant*, meaning that `C<S>` is a subtype of `C<T>` if `S` is a subtype of `T`; it can be *contravariant*, meaning that `C<S>` is a subtype of `C<T>` if `T` is a subtype of `S`; it can be *bivariant*, meaning that `C<S>` is always a subtype of `C<T>`; or it can be *invariant*, meaning that `C<S>` and `C<T>` are never subtype-related for different types `T` and `S`.

An alternative approach has been introduced in the past decade: *Use-site variance* [17, 22] interprets the definition of a generic class `C<X>` as the introduction of 4 distinct types in the type system: the covariant, contravariant, bivariant, and invariant part of `C<X>`. Each of these types only supports the methods compatible with each variance designation. For instance, the covariant part of `C<T>` would only support methods that would be safe to call on an object of type `C<S>` when `S` is a subtype of `T`. In this way, the use-site of a generic class declares what it can accept, with a vocabulary such as "C-of-any-subtype-of-T" (concretely written `C<? extends T>` in Java), and the type system checks that the use is indeed valid.

Use-site variance is a truly elegant idea. Producing automatically all different variance flavors from a single class definition is an approach of hard-to-dispute flexibility. The idea was quickly integrated in Java in the form of *wildcards* and it is widely used in standard Java libraries. Despite the conceptual elegance, however, the practical deployment of wildcards has been less than entirely successful. Among opponents, "wildcards" has become a virtual synonym for a language design mess. (E.g., Josh Bloch's presentation at Javapolis 2008 emphasized "We simply cannot afford another wildcards" [4].) The reason is that use-site variance results in conceptual complexity, requires anticipation of generality at all usage points, and postpones the detection of overly restrictive type signatures until their use.

For these pragmatic reasons, newer languages, such as Scala [20] and C# [15], have returned to and refined the tried-and-true approach of definition-site variance. Definition-site variance is hardly free of usability problems, however. For a class that is not purely covariant or contravariant, the only way to achieve full genericity is by introducing specialized interfaces that correspond to the class's co-, contra-, and bivariant parts. Consequently, users have to remember the names of these interfaces, library designers must anticipate genericity, and a combinatorial explosion in the number of introduced interfaces is possible. (E.g., for a type `Triple<X,Y,Z>`, we may need an interface for each of the $3^3 = 27$ possible access combinations, such as "covariant with respect to `X`, contravariant with respect to `Y` and `Z`". The number is 3^3 and not 4^3 only because bivariance is not allowed as an explicit annotation.)

In this paper, we introduce an approach that mitigates the tension between use-site and definition-site variance. We present a core calculus, *VarLang*, for reasoning about definition-site variance in the presence of use-site variance annotations (wildcards). The calculus is very general and its soundness is based *directly on the definition of variance*, and not on any specific type system features. This calculus can be used as the basis for variance reasoning in any type system, for either inference or checking. For instance, our approach can be directly employed for extending Scala with use-site variance annotations, or for extending Java with definition-site variance.

We explore one such application in detail: we define a type system that adds *inference* of definition-site variance to Java. That is, we infer variance automatically for classes that are purely covariant, purely contravariant, or purely bivariant with respect to a type parameter. Our solution is fully compatible with existing Java syntax and only changes the type system to make it more permissive in cases of purely variant types, so that exhaustive use-site annotation is unnecessary. For instance, with our type system, the Apache Commons-Collections programmer would not need to write `Iterator<? extends Map.Entry<? extends K,V>>` because `Iterator` and `Map.Entry` are inferred to be purely covariant with respect to their (first) parameter, hence the type `Iterator<Map.Entry<K,V>>` is exactly as general.

Illustration of approach. The variance of a class with respect to its type parameters is constrained by the variance of the positions these type parameters occur in. For instance, an argument type position is contravariant, while a return type position is covariant. However, in the presence of recursive type constraints and wildcards, no past technique reasons in a general way about the variance of a type expression in a certain position. For instance, past techniques would not infer anything other than *invariance* for classes `C` and `D`:

```
class C<X> {
  X     foo (C<? super X>   csx) { ... }
  void bar (D<? extends X> dsx) { ... }
}
class D<Y> {
  void baz (C<Y> cx) { ... }
}
```

Our approach is based on assigning a variance to every type expression, and defining an operator, $\otimes$ (pronounced "transform"), used to compose variances. In our calculus, inferring the most general variance for the above type definitions reduces to finding the maximal solution for a constraint system over the standard variance lattice ($*$ is top, o is bottom, $+$ and $-$ are unordered, with a join of $*$ and a meet of o). If c stands for the (most general) variance of the definition of `C<X>` with respect to type parameter `X`, and d stands for the variance of `D<Y>` with respect to `Y`, the constraints (simplified) are:

$$c \sqsubseteq +$$

$$c \sqsubseteq - \otimes (- \sqcup c)$$

$$c \sqsubseteq - \otimes (+ \sqcup d)$$

$$d \sqsubseteq - \otimes c$$

Consider the first of these constraints. Its intuitive meaning is that the variance of class `C` (with respect to `X`) has to be at most covariance, $+$, (because `X` occurs as a return type of `foo`). Similarly, for the third constraint, the variance of `C` has to be at most the variance of type expression `D<? extends X>` transformed by the variance, $-$, of the (contravariant) position where the type expression occurs. The variance of type expression `D<? extends X>` itself is the variance of type `D` joined with the variance of the type annotation, $+$.

We will see the full rules and definition of $\otimes$, as well as prove their soundness, later, but for this example it suffices to know that $-\otimes+ = -$, $-\otimes- = +$, $-\otimes* = *$, and $-\otimes o = o$. It is easy to see with mere enumeration of the possibilities that the most general solution has $c = +$ and $d = -$. Thus, by formulating and solving these constraints, we correctly infer the most general variance: class `C` is *covariant* with respect to `X`, and class `D` is *contravariant* with respect to `Y`. We note that the interaction of wildcards and type recursion is non-trivial. For instance, removing the "`? super`" from the type of argument `csx` would make both `C` and `D` be invariant.

Contributions. Our paper makes several contributions:

- We present a general approach for reasoning about variance. The approach consists of a core calculus, whose soundness is proved by direct appeal to the definition of variance, i.e., independently of any specific type system. To our knowledge, this is the first approach to allow general reasoning about definition-site variance in the presence of either use-site variance annotations or type recursion.
- We apply the approach in the context of Java to produce a (conservative) inference algorithm for computing the definition-site variance of classes and interfaces. Unlike past work (e.g., [19]), our inference technique is *modular*: the variance of a generic class is purely determined by its own interface definition (and that of the types it uses), *not* by the code that uses the class. Under our updated type system, many uses of variance annotations become redundant. All previously legal Java programs remain legal, although some newly type-correct programs might have been previously rejected.
- We conduct a large study to show how use-site and definition-site variance coexist fruitfully, even in code that was written with only use-site variance in mind. Past literature [12, 17] has largely assumed that single-variant type parameters are seldom used, thus promoting use-site variance for flexibility. We show that this is not the case—over all libraries (including the standard library: all packages in `java.*`) we find that 32% of the generic classes and interfaces have single-variance type parameters. This is strong evidence for the need to combine definition- and use-site variance, since they both occur commonly. Additionally, 13% of all signatures of methods using generics are found to use too-restricted types. (Importantly, this analysis is without concern for what the method actually does—i.e., treating the body as a black box, which can change in the future.) Furthermore, our inference algorithm obviates the need for many uses of wildcards: 37% of existing wildcard uses in these libraries are rendered unnecessary.

2. Type-Checking Variance

The study of variance has a long history [2, 6–9, 13, 16, 17, 23]. It aims to provide safe conditions for subtyping between different instantiations of the same generic class or interface. Consider the following example:

```
class List<X> {
  void set(int i, X x) { ... }
  X    get(int i)      { ... }
}
```

If we naively assume that List<S> <: List<T> for any S <: T (where <: is the subtyping relation), the following ill-typed code could pass compile-time type-checking, and result in runtime errors:

```
List<Integer> intList = new List<Integer>();
List<Number>  numList = intList;
numList.set(0, new Float(0.0f));
           // Writing Float into intList!
```

The key to safe parametric subtyping lies with the concept of the *variance* of type parameter X in the definition of C<X>. If X only appears *covariantly*, then it is always safe to assume that C<S> <: C<T> if S <: T. If X only appears *contravariantly*, it is always safe to assume that C<S> <: C<T> if T <: S. If X appears both co- and contravariantly, C is invariant: C<S> <: C<T> only if S = T. This notion of variance is called *definition-site variance*.

2.1 Definition-site Variance.

Languages supporting definition-site variance [15, 20] typically require each type parameter to be declared with a variance annotation. For instance, Scala [20] requires the annotation + for covariant type parameters, - for contravariant type parameters, and invariance is the default. A well-established set of rules can then be used to verify that the use of the type parameter in the generic[1] is consistent with the annotation. We provide an overview of these rules here, as they form the basis of both use-site variance and our inference.

Each typing position in a generic's signature has an associated variance. For instance, method return and exception types, supertypes, and upper bounds of type parameters are covariant positions; method argument types and type parameter lower bounds are contravariant positions; field types are both co- and contravariant occurrences, inducing invariance. Type checking the declared variance annotation of a type parameter requires determining the variance of the positions the type parameter occurs in. *The variance of all such positions should be at most the declared variance of the type parameter.* Consider the following templates of Scala classes, where ν_X, ν_Y, and ν_Z stand for variance annotations.

```
abstract class RList[vXX] { def get(i:Int):X }
abstract class WList[vYY] { def set(i:Int, y:Y):Unit }
abstract class IList[vZZ] { def setAndGet(i:Int, z:Z):Z }
```

The variance ν_X is the declared definition-site variance for type variable X of the Scala class RList. If ν_X = +, the RList class type checks because X does not occur in a contravariant position. If ν_Y = +, the WList class does not type check because Y occurs in a contravariant position (second argument type in set method) but ν_Y = + implies Y should only occur in a covariant position. IList type checks only if $\nu_Z = o$ because Z occurs in a covariant and a contravariant position.

Intuitively, RList is a read-only list: it only supports retrieving objects. Retrieving objects of type T can be safely thought of as retrieving objects of any supertype of T. Thus, a read-only list of Ts (RList[T]) can always be safely thought of as a read-only list of some supertype of Ts (RList[S], where T <: S). This is the exact definition of covariant subtyping. Thus, RList is covariant in X.[2] Similarly, WList is a write-only list, and is intuitively contravariant. Its definition supports this intuition: Objects of type T can be written to a write-only list of Ts and to a write-only list of WList[S], where T <: S, because objects of type T are also objects of type S. Hence, a WList[S] can be safely thought of as a WList[T], if T <: S.

The variance of type variables is *transformed* by the variance of the context the variables appear in. Covariant positions *preserve* the variance of types that appear in them, whereas contravariant positions *reverse* the variance of the types that appear in them. The "reverse" of covariance is contravariance, and vice versa. The "reverse" of invariance is itself. Thus, we can consider the occurrence of a type parameter to be initially covariant. For instance, consider again the Scala classes above. In RList, X only appears as the return type of a method, which preserves the initial covariance of X, so RList is covariant in X. In WList, Y appears in a contravariant position, which reverses its initial covariance, to contravariance. Thus, WList is contravariant.

When a type parameter is used to instantiate a generic, its variance is further transformed by the declared definition-site variance of that generic. For example:

```
class SourceList[+Z] { def copyTo(to:WList[Z]):Unit }
```

Suppose the declared definition-site variance of WList (with respect to its single parameter) is contravariance. In WList[Z], the initial covariance of Z is transformed by the definition-site variance of WList (contravariance). It is then transformed again by the contravariant method argument position. As a result, Z appears covariantly in this context, and SourceList is covariant in Z, as declared. Any variance transformed by invariance becomes invariance. Thus, if Z was used to parameterize an invariant generic, its appearance would have been invariant. In Section 3.1 we generalize and formalize this notion of transforming variance.

We have so far neglected to discuss *bivariance*: C<X> is bivariant implies that C<S> <: C<T> for any types S and T. Declaring a bivariant type parameter is not supported by the widely used definition-site variant languages. At first this seems to not be entirely surprising. For a type parameter to be bivariant, it must only appear bivariantly in a generic. This means either it does not appear at all, or it appears only as the type argument to instantiate other bivariant generics. If a type parameter does not appear in a generic's signature at all, then it is useless to parameterize over it; if it is only used to instantiate other bivariant generics, it could just as well be replaced by any arbitrary type, since, by definition, a bivariant generic does not care what type it is instantiated with. Nevertheless, this argument ignores type recursion. As we discuss in Section 3.3 and in our experimental findings, several interesting interface definitions are inherently bivariant.

Finally, instead of declaring the definition-site variance of a type parameter and checking it for consistency, it is tempting to *infer* the most general such variance from the definition of a generic. This becomes hard in the presence of type recursion and supporting it in full generality is one of the contributions of our work.

2.2 Use-site Variance.

An alternative approach to variance is *use-site variance* [7, 17, 23]. Instead of declaring the variance of X at its definition site, generics are assumed to be *invariant* in their type parameters. However, a type-instantiation of C<X> can be made co-, contra-, or bivariant using variance annotations.

For instance, using the Java wildcard syntax, C<? extends T> is a *covariant* instantiation of C, representing a type "C-of-some-subtype-of-T". C<? extends T> is a supertype of all type-instantiations C<S>, or C<? extends S>, where S <: T. In exchange for such liberal subtyping rules, type C<? extends T> can only access those methods and fields of C in which X appears covariantly. In determining this, use-site variance applies the same set of rules used in definition-site variance, with the additional condition that the upper bound of a wildcard is considered a covariant position, and the lower bound of a wildcard a contravariant position.

[1] We refer to all generic types (e.g., classes, traits, interfaces) uniformly as "generics".

[2] We use interchangeably the wordings "C is ν-variant in X", "C is ν-variant/has variance ν with respect to X", and "X's variance in C is ν". For brevity, if it is clear from the context, we do not specify which type parameter a definition-site variance is with respect to.

For example, List<? extends T>, only has access to method "X get(int i)", but not method "void set(int i, X x)". (More precisely, method set can only be called with null for its second argument. We elide such fine distinctions in this section.)

Similarly, C<? super T> is the contravariant version of C, and is a supertype of any C<S> and C<? super S>, where T <: S. Of course, C<? super T> has access only to methods and fields in which X appears contravariantly or not at all.

Use-site variance also allows the representation of the *bivariant* version of a generic. In Java, this is accomplished through the unbounded wildcard: C<?>. Using this notation, C<S> <: C<?>, for any S. The bivariant type, however, only has access to methods and fields in which the type parameter does not appear at all. In definition-site variance, these methods and fields would have to be factored out into a non-generic class.

2.3 A Comparison.

Both approaches to variance have their merits and shortcomings. Definition-site variance enjoys a certain degree of conceptual simplicity: the generic type instantiation rules and subtyping relationships are clear. However, the class or interface designer must pay for such simplicity by splitting the definitions of data types into co-, contra, and bivariant versions. This can be an unnatural exercise. For example, the data structures library for Scala contains immutable (covariant) and mutable (invariant) versions of almost every data type—and this is not even a complete factoring of the variants, since it does not include contravariant (write-only) versions of the data types.

The situation gets even more complex when a generic has more than one type parameter. In general, a generic with n type parameters needs 3^n (or 4^n if bivariance is allowed as an explicit annotation) interfaces to represent a complete variant factoring of its methods. Arguably, in practice, this is often not necessary.

Use-site variance, on the other hand, allows users of a generic to create co-, contra-, and bivariant versions of the generic on the fly. This flexibility allows class or interface designers to implement their data types in whatever way is natural. However, the users of these generics must pay the price, by carefully considering the correct use-site variance annotations, so that the type can be as general as possible. This might not seem very difficult for a simple instantiation such as List<? extends Number>. However, type signatures can very quickly become complicated. For instance, the following method signature is part of the Apache Commons-Collections Library:

```
Iterator<? extends Map.Entry<? extends K,V>>
  createEntrySetIterator(
     Iterator<? extends Map.Entry<? extends K,V>>)
```

2.4 Generalizing the Design Space.

Our goal is to combine the positive aspects of use-site and definition-site variance, while mitigating their shortcomings. The key is to have a uniform and general treatment of definition and use-site variance in the same type system. This creates opportunities for interesting language designs. For instance:

- A language can combine explicit definition- and use-site variance annotations and perform type *checking* to ensure their soundness. For instance, Scala or C# can integrate wildcards in their syntax and type reasoning. This will give programmers the opportunity to choose not to split the definition of a type just to allow more general handling in clients. If, for instance, a List is supposed to support both reading and writing of data, then its interface can be defined to include both kinds of methods, and not split into two types. The methods that use List can still be made fully general, as long as they specify use-site annotations. Generally, allowing both kinds of variance in a single language ensures modularity: parts of the code can be made fully general regardless of how other code is defined. This reduces the need for anticipation and lowers the burden of up-front library design.

  Similarly, Java can integrate explicit definition-site variance annotations for purely variant types. This will reduce the need for use-site annotation and the risk of too-restricted types.

- A language can combine use-site variance annotations with *inference* of definition-site variance (for purely variant types). This is the approach that we implement and explore in later sections. Consider the above example of the long signatures in the two type-instantiations of Iterator. Our approach can infer that Iterator is covariant, and Map.Entry is covariant in its first type parameter—without having to change the definition of either generic. Thus, the following signature in our system has exactly the same generality without any wildcards:

```
Iterator<Map.Entry<K,V>>
  createEntrySetIterator(Iterator<Map.Entry<K,V>>)
```

Furthermore, specifying the most general types proves to be challenging for even the most seasoned Java programmers: (at least) 8% of the types in method signatures of the Java core library (java.*) are overly specific. We will discuss the details of our findings in Section 5.2.

3. Reasoning about Variance

In order to meet our goal of a general, unified framework (for both checking and inference of both use-site and definition-site variance) we need to solve three different problems. The first is that of composing variances, the second deals with the integration of use-site annotations in definition-site reasoning, and the third concerns the handling of recursive types.

3.1 Variance Composition

In earlier variance formalisms, reasoning about nested types, such as A<B<X>>, has been hard. Igarashi and Viroli pioneered the treatment of variant types as unions of sets of instances. Regarding nested types, they note (Section 3.3 of [17]): "We could explain more complicated cases that involve nested types but it would get harder to think of the set of instances denoted by such types." The first observation of our work is that it is quite easy to reason about nested types, not as sets of instances but as variance composition. That is, given two generic types A<X> and B<X>, if the (definition-site) variances of A and B (with respect to their type parameters) are known, then we can compute the variance of type A<B<X>>.[3] This composition property generalizes to arbitrarily complex-nested type expressions. The basis of the computation of composed variances is the *transform* operator, ⊗, defined in Figure 1. The relation $v_1 \otimes v_2 = v_3$ intuitively denotes the following: If the variance of a type variable X in type expression E is v_2 and the definition-site variance of the type parameter of a class C is v_1,[4] then the variance of X in type expression C<E> is v_3.

The behavior of the transform operator is simple: invariance transforms everything into invariance, bivariance transforms everything into bivariance, covariance transforming a variance leaves it

[3] This relies on a natural extension of the definition of variance, to include the concept of a variance of an arbitrary type expression with respect to a type variable. E.g., type expression E is covariant in X iff $T_1 <: T_2 \implies E[T_1/X] <: E[T_2/X]$. (These brackets denote substitution of a type for a type variable and should not be confused with the Scala bracket notation for generics, which we shall avoid except in pure-Scala examples.)

[4] For simplicity, we often refer to generics with a single type parameter. For multiple type parameters the same reasoning applies to the parameter in the appropriate position.

Definition of variance transformation: $\otimes$			
$+ \otimes + = +$	$- \otimes + = -$	$* \otimes + = *$	$o \otimes + = o$
$+ \otimes - = -$	$- \otimes - = +$	$* \otimes - = *$	$o \otimes - = o$
$+ \otimes * = *$	$- \otimes * = *$	$* \otimes * = *$	$o \otimes * = o$
$+ \otimes o = o$	$- \otimes o = o$	$* \otimes o = *$	$o \otimes o = o$

Figure 1. Variance transform operator.

the same, and contravariance reverses it. (The reverse of bivariance is itself, the reverse of invariance is itself.) To sample why the definition of the transform operator makes sense, let us consider some of its cases. (The rest are covered exhaustively in our proof of soundness.)

- Case $+ \otimes - = -$: This means that type expression C<*E*> is contravariant with respect to type variable X when generic C is covariant in its type parameter and type expression E is contravariant in X. This is true because, for any T_1, T_2:

$$\begin{aligned} T_1 <: T_2 &\implies && \text{(by contravariance of } E\text{)} \\ E[T_2/\mathtt{X}] <: E[T_1/\mathtt{X}] &\implies && \text{(by covariance of C)} \\ \mathtt{C<}E[T_2/\mathtt{X}]\mathtt{>} <: \mathtt{C<}E[T_1/\mathtt{X}]\mathtt{>} &\implies && \\ \mathtt{C<}E\mathtt{>}[T_2/\mathtt{X}] <: \mathtt{C<}E\mathtt{>}[T_1/\mathtt{X}] && & \end{aligned}$$

  Hence, C<*E*> is contravariant with respect to X.

- Case $*\otimes v = *$: This means that type expression C<*E*> is bivariant with respect to type variable X when generic C is bivariant in its type parameter, regardless of the variance of type expression E (even invariance). This is true because:

$$\begin{aligned} \text{for any types } S \text{ and } T &\implies && \text{(by bivariance of C)} \\ \mathtt{C<}E[S/\mathtt{X}]\mathtt{>} <: \mathtt{C<}E[T/\mathtt{X}]\mathtt{>} &\implies && \\ \mathtt{C<}E\mathtt{>}[S/\mathtt{X}] <: \mathtt{C<}E\mathtt{>}[T/\mathtt{X}] && & \end{aligned}$$

  Hence, C<*E*> is bivariant with respect to X.

As can be seen by inspection of all cases in Figure 1, operator $\otimes$ is associative. The operator would also be commutative, except for the case $* \otimes o = * \neq o = o \otimes *$. This is a design choice, however. With the types-as-sets approach that we follow in our formalization, operator $\otimes$ would be safe to define as a commutative operator, by changing the case $o \otimes *$ to return $*$. To see this, consider the meaning of $o \otimes *$. When generic C is invariant with respect to its type parameter X and type expression E is bivariant in X, should type expression C<*E*> be bivariant or invariant with respect to X? The answer depends on what we mean by "invariance". We defined invariance earlier as "C<*S*> <: C<*T*> only if $S = T$". Is the type equality "$S = T$" syntactic or semantic? (I.e., does type equality signify type identity or equivalence, as can be established in the type system?) If type equality is taken to be syntactic, then the only sound choice is $o \otimes * = o$:

$$\begin{aligned} \mathtt{C<}E\mathtt{>}[S/\mathtt{X}] <: \mathtt{C<}E\mathtt{>}[T/\mathtt{X}] &\implies && \\ \mathtt{C<}E[S/\mathtt{X}]\mathtt{>} <: \mathtt{C<}E[T/\mathtt{X}]\mathtt{>} &\implies && \text{(by invariance of C)} \\ E[S/\mathtt{X}] = E[T/\mathtt{X}] &\implies && \text{(assuming X occurs in } E\text{)} \\ S = T && & \end{aligned}$$

Hence, C<*E*> is invariant with respect to X. If, however, the definition of invariance allows for type equivalence instead of syntactic equality, then it is safe to have $o \otimes * = *$: By the bivariance of E, $E[S/\mathtt{X}] <: E[T/\mathtt{X}]$ and $E[T/\mathtt{X}] <: E[S/\mathtt{X}]$. Hence, $E[S/\mathtt{X}]$ is equivalent to $E[T/\mathtt{X}]$ and consequently C<*E*>[*S* / X] can be shown equivalent to C<*E*>[*T* / X] (assuming a natural extensionality axiom in the type system).

We chose the conservative definition, $o \otimes * = o$, in Figure 1 to match that used in our implementation of a definition-site variance inference algorithm for Java, discussed later. Since, in our application, bivariance is often inferred (not stated by the programmer) and since Java does not naturally have a notion of semantic type equivalence, we opted to avoid the possible complications both for the user and for interfacing with other parts of the language.

Similar reasoning to the transform operator is performed in Scala to check definition-site variance annotations. Section 4.5 of [20] defines the variance position of a type parameter in a type or template and states "Let the opposite of covariance be contravariance, and the opposite of invariance be itself." It also states a number of rules defining the variance of the various type positions such as "The variance position of a method parameter is the opposite of the variance position of the enclosing parameter clause." The $\otimes$ operator is a generalization of the reasoning stated in that section; it adds the notion of bivariance and how the variance of a context transforms the variance of a type actual in general instead of defining the variance of a position for language specific constructs.

3.2 Integration of Use-Site Variance

The second new element of our work is the integration of use-site annotations in the reasoning about definition-site variance. Earlier work such as [17] showed how to reason about use-site variance for Java. Emir et al [13] formalized definition-site variance as it occurs in of C#.[5] However, no earlier work explained how to formally reason about variance in a context including both definition-site and use-site variance. For example, suppose Scala is extended with support for use-site variance, v is a variance annotation (+, −, or o), and the following are syntactically legal Scala classes.

```
abstract class C[vX] {
 def set(arg1:X):Unit
}
abstract class D[+X] {
 def compare(arg2:C[+X]):Unit
}
```

Section 2.1 gave an overview of how declared definition-site variance annotations are type checked in Scala. Since class C only contains the set method, it type checks with v = - because X only appears contravariantly in the type signature of the set method. However, type checking class D with the compare method requires reasoning about the variance of X in the argument type expression C[+X].

In our unified framework, a use-site annotation corresponds to a join operation in the standard variance lattice (Figure 2). That is, if generic C<X> has definition-site variance v_1 with respect to X, then the type expression C[v_2X] has variance $v_1 \sqcup v_2$ with respect to X.

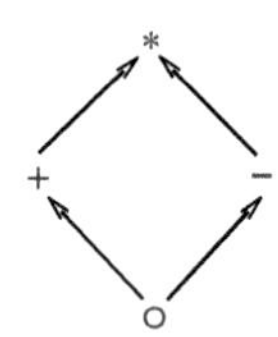

Figure 2. Usual variance lattice.

Intuitively, this rule makes sense: When applying use-site variance annotations, it is as if we are removing from the definition of the generic the elements that are incompatible with the use-site variance. For instance, when taking the covariant version, C[+X], of our Scala class C, above, we can only access the members that

[5] Their calculus is an extension of C# minor [18].

use type parameter X covariantly—e.g., method set would be inaccessible. Hence, if class C is naturally contravariant in X (meaning that X only occurs contravariantly in the body of C), then C[+X] is a type that cannot access any member of C that uses X. Thus, C[+X] is bivariant in X: the value of the type parameter cannot be used. This is precisely what our lattice join approach yields: $+ \sqcup - = *$. As a result, any declared definition-site variance for class D would be legal.

To see more rigorously why the lattice-join approach is correct, let us consider the above case formally. (Other cases are covered exhaustively in our proof of soundness.) Given a contravariant generic C, why is it safe to infer that $C<+X>$ (C[+X] in Scala syntax) is bivariant in X? We start from the Igarashi and Viroli approach to variance: All types are in a lattice with subtyping as its partial order and the meaning of $C<+T>$ is $\bigsqcup_{T' <: T} C<T'>$. This definition yields the standard variance theorems $T <: T' \Rightarrow C<+T> <: C<+T'>$ and $C<T> <: C<+T>$. Consider then the bottom element of the type lattice. (This lattice depends on the type system of the language and is not to be confused with the simple variance lattice of Figure 2.) We have:

$$\begin{array}{ll} \bot <: T \Rightarrow & \text{(by first theorem above)} \\ C<+\bot> <: C<+T> & (1) \end{array}$$

But also, for any type T':

$$\begin{array}{ll} \bot <: T' \Rightarrow & \text{(C contravariant)} \\ C<T'> <: C<\bot> & (2) \end{array}$$

Therefore:

$$\begin{array}{ll} C<+T> = & \text{(by variance def)} \\ \bigsqcup_{T' <: T} C<T'> <: & \text{(by (2), above)} \\ C<\bot> <: & \text{(by second theorem above)} \\ C<+\bot> & (3) \end{array}$$

Hence, from (1) and (3), all $C<+T>$ are always subtype-related, i.e., have type $C<*>$.

A Note on Scala: To enable interoperability between Scala and Java, Scala represents Java wildcard types as existential types. For example, a Java Iterator<?> could be written as Iterator[T] forSome { type T } or more compactly as Iterator[_]. Similarly, the type Java Iterator<? extends Comparator> maps to the Scala type Iterator[_ <: Comparator>], and the type Java Iterator<? super Comparator> maps to the Scala type Iterator[_ >: Comparator>]. However, Scala variance reasoning with existential types is too conservative because it just assumes that the use-site variance annotation overrides the definition-site variance instead of reasoning about how they both interact. For example, consider the Scala traits below.

```
trait GenType[+Y] { def get(i:Int):Y }
trait Wild[-X] {
  def add(elem:X):Unit
  // flagged as error but actually safe
  def compare(w:GenType[_ >: X]):Unit
}
```

The Scala compiler flags an error because it assumes the variance of X in GenType[_ >: X] is contravariance. This contravariance occurrence is then negated (transformed by contravariance) to covariance because it occurs in an argument (contravariant) position. Because the Scala compiler assumes X occurs in a covariant position in compare's argument type but the definition-site of X in trait Wild is contravariance, Scala flags this occurrence as an error. However, it is safe to assume that the variance of X in GenType[_ >: X] is bivariance. Because GenType is covariant in its type parameter, the contravariant version of GenType essentially provides no members of GenType that contain GenType's type parameter in their type signature. Our joining of the definition-site and use-site variances takes advantage of this reasoning enabling more safe code to type check.

3.3 Recursive Variances

The third novel element of our approach consists of reasoning about recursive type definitions. This is particularly important for inferring (instead of just checking) definition-site variance. With type recursion, the unknown variance becomes recursively defined and it is not easy to compute the most general solution. Furthermore, type recursion makes the case of bivariance quite interesting. In contrast to non-recursive types, recursive types can be bivariant even when their type parameter is used. For instance the following type is safely bivariant:

```
interface I<X> {  I<X> foo (I<X> i); }
```

To appreciate the interesting complexities of reasoning about type recursion, we discuss some cases next.

Recursive Variance Type 1: The following interface demonstrates a most simple form of recursive variance:

```
interface C1<X> {  C1<X> foo1 (); }
```

The variance of C1 depends on how X appears in its signature. The only appearance of X is in the return type of foo1, a covariant position, as the argument to C1. Thus, the variance of X in this appearance is its initial covariance, transformed by the variance of C1—the very variance we are trying to infer! This type of recursive variance essentially says that the variance of C1 is the variance of C1, and thus can be satisfied by any of the four variances: covariance, contravariance, invariance, or bivariance. Without any more appearances of X, the most liberal form of variance for C1 is bivariance.

If X does appear in other typing positions, however, the variance of its declaring generic is completely determined by the variance of these appearances:

```
interface C2<X> extends C1<X> {  void  bar2 (X x);  }
interface C3<X> extends C1<X> {  X     bar3 ();     }
```

The definition-site variance of C2 is constrained by the variance of C1, as well as X's appearance as a method argument type—a contravariant appearance. Since C1's variance is completely unconstrained, C2 is simply contravariant. Similarly, C3 is only constrained by X's appearance as a method return type—a covariant appearance—and is thus covariant, as well.

The above pattern will be common in all our recursive variances. Without any constraints other than the recursive one, a generic is most generally bivariant. When other constraints are factored in, however, the real variance of C1 can be understood informally as "can be either co- or contravariant".

Recursive Variance Type 2: The next example shows a similar, but much more restrictive form of recursive variance:

```
interface D1<X> {  void foo1 (D1<X> dx);  }
```

The variance of D1 is again recursively dependent on itself, only this time X appears in D1<X> which is a method argument. If a recursive variance did not impose any restrictions in a covariant position, why would it be any different in a contravariant position? Interestingly, the contravariance means that the variance of D1 is the variance of D1 transformed by the contravariance. This means the variance of D1 must be the *reverse* of itself!

The only two variances that can satisfy such a condition are bi- and invariance. Again, without any other uses of X, D1<X> is most generally bivariant.

However, if X does appear either co- or contravariantly in combination with this type of recursive variance, the resulting variance can only be *invariance*:

```
interface D2<X> extends D1<X> {  void  bar2 (X x); }
interface D3<X> extends D1<X> {  X     bar3 ();    }
```

In the above example, X appears contravariantly in D2, as the argument of bar2. At the same time, the variance of X must be the opposite of itself, as constrained by the recursive variance in supertype D1. This is equivalent to X appearing covariantly, as well. Thus, the only reasonable variance for D2 is invariance. A similar reasoning results in the invariance of D3.

Thus, recursive variance of this type can be understood informally as "cannot be either co- or contravariant" when other constraints are taken into account.

Recursive Variance Type 3: The following example shows yet a third kind of recursive variance:

```
interface E1<X> {  E1<E1<X>> foo1 ();  }
```

The variance of E1 is the same as X's variance in E1<E1<X>>. That is, the initial covariance of X, transformed by the variance of E1—twice. This type of recursive variance can, again, like the previous two, be satisfied by either in- or bivariance. However, the key insight is that, no matter whether E1 is contra- or covariant, any variance transformed by E1 twice (or any even number of times, for that matter) is always preserved. This is obvious if E1 is covariant. If E1 is contravariant, being transformed by E1 twice means a variance is reversed, and then reversed again, which still yields a preserved variance. Thus, unless E1 is bi- or invariant, X in E1<E1<X>> is always a covariant appearance.

Thus, when other appearances of X interact with this form of recursive variance, its informal meaning becomes "cannot be contravariant". In other words, when this recursive variance is part of the constraints of a type, the type can be bivariant, covariant, or invariant. The following examples demonstrate this:

```
interface E2<X> extends E1<X> {  void bar2 (X x); }
interface E3<X> extends E1<X> {  X    bar3 ();    }
```

X appears contravariantly in E2, eliminating bivariance and covariance as an option for E2. However, X also appears in E1<E1<X>> through subtyping, which means it cannot be contravariant. Thus, E2 is invariant.

In E3, X appears covariantly, and X in E1<E1<X>> can still be covariant. Thus, E3 can safely be covariant.

Recursive Variance Type 4: Our last example of recursive variance is also twice constrained by itself. But this time, it is further transformed by a contravariance:

```
interface F1<X> {  int foo1(F1<F1<X>> x); }
```

The variance of F1 is the same as X's variance in F1<F1<X>>, then transformed by the contravariant position of the method argument type. That is, X's initial covariance, transformed twice by the variance of F1, then reversed. Like all the other recursive variances, bi- and invariance are options. However, since the twice-transformation by any variance preserves the initial covariance of X in F1<F1<X>>, the transformation by the contravariance produces a contravariance. Thus, if F1 cannot be bivariant, it must be contravariant (or invariant).

In other words, along with other constraints, F1 has the informal meaning: "cannot be covariant". For instance:

```
interface F2<X> extends F1<X> {  void bar2 (X x); }
interface F3<X> extends F1<X> {  X    bar3 ();    }
```

In F2, X appears contravariantly as a method argument. Combined with the recursive variance through subtyping F1<X>, F2 can be contravariant. In F3, however, X appears covariantly. With bivariance and contravariance no longer an option, the only variance satisfying both this covariant appearance and the recursive variance of F1<F1<X>> is invariance. Thus, F3 is invariant in X.

Handling Recursive Variance. The above list of recursive variances is not exhaustive, although it is representative of most obvious cases. It should be clear that handling recursive variances in their full generality is hard and requires some form of search. The reason our approach can handle recursive variance well is that all reasoning is based on constraint solving over the standard variance lattice. Constraints are simple inequalities ("below" on the lattice) and can capture type recursion by having the same constant or variable (in the case of type inference) multiple times, both on the left and the right hand side of an inequality.

A Note on Scala: Scala's reasoning about recursive variances is limited because it does not have the notion of bivariance; it does not allow the most general types to be specified. Consider the three following traits.

trait C1[v_XX] { def foo:C1[X] }
trait C2[v_YY] extends C1[Y] { def bar(arg:Y):Unit }
trait C3[v_ZZ] extends C1[Z] { def baz:Z }

Because trait C1 has type 1 recursive variance, if Scala supported bivariant annotations, it would be safe to set the definition-site variances as follows: $v_X = *$, $v_Y = -$, and $v_Z = +$. Since Scala does not support bivariant annotations, no assignments allow both trait C2 to be contravariant and trait C3 to be covariant. For example, setting $v_X = +$ implies attempting to compile trait C2 will generate an error because Scala infers Y occurs covariantly in the base type expression occurring in "C2[-Y] extends C1[Y]"; since Y is declared to be contravariant, Y should not occur in a covariant position in the definition of C2. Below are the only three assignments allowed by the Scala compiler.

$v_X = -$	$v_Y = -$	$v_Z = o$
$v_X = +$	$v_Y = o$	$v_Z = +$
$v_X = o$	$v_Y = o$	$v_Z = o$

4. Putting It All Together: A Core Language and Calculus

We combine all the techniques of the previous section into a unified framework for reasoning about variance. We introduce a core language, *VarLang*, for describing the various components of a class that affect its variance. Reasoning is then performed at the level of this core language, by translating it to a set of constraints.

4.1 Syntax

A sentence S in *VarLang* is a sequence (treated as a set) of modules, the syntax of which is given in Figure 3.

$$\texttt{M} \in \textit{Module} ::= \texttt{module C<}\overline{\texttt{X}}\texttt{> \{ }\overline{\texttt{Tv}}\texttt{ \}}$$
$$\texttt{T} \in \textit{Type} ::= \texttt{X} \mid \texttt{C<}\overline{\texttt{vT}}\texttt{>}$$
$$\texttt{v} \in \textit{Variance} ::= + \mid - \mid * \mid o$$
$$\texttt{C} \in \textit{ModuleNames} \text{ is a set of module names}$$
$$\texttt{X} \in \textit{VariableNames} \text{ is a set of variable names}$$

Figure 3. Syntax of *VarLang*

Note that variance annotations, v, (+/-/*/o) can appear in two places: at the top level of a module, as a suffix, and at the type level, as a prefix. Informally, a v at the top level means that the corresponding type appears covariantly/contravariantly/invariantly (i.e., in a covariant/contravariant/invariant position). A v on a type means that the type parameter is qualified with the corresponding use-site variance annotation, or no annotation (for invariance). For instance, consider the *VarLang* sentence:

```
module C<X> { X+, C<-X>-, void+, D<+X>- }
module D<Y> { void+, C<oY>- }
```

This corresponds to the example from the Introduction. That is, the informal meaning of the *VarLang* sentence is that:

- In the definition of class `C<X>`, `X` appears covariantly; `C<? super X>` appears contravariantly; `void` appears covariantly; `D<? extends X>` appears contravariantly.
- In the definition of class `D<Y>`, `void` appears covariantly; `C<Y>` appears contravariantly.

4.2 *VarLang* Translation

Our reasoning approach consists of translating a *VarLang* sentence S into a set of constraints over the standard variance lattice (Figure 2). The constraints are "below"-inequalities and contain variables of the form $var(\texttt{X}, \texttt{T})$ and $var(\texttt{X}, \texttt{C})$, pronounced "variance of type variable `X` in type expression `T`" and "(definition-site) variance of type variable `X` in generic `C`". The constraints are then solved to compute variances, depending on the typing problem at hand (checking or inference). The following rules produce the constraints. (Note that some of the constraints are vacuous, since they establish an upper bound of $*$, but they are included so that the rules cover all syntactic elements of *VarLang* and the translation from a *VarLang* sentence to a set of constraints is obvious.)

$$var(\texttt{X}, \texttt{C}) \sqsubseteq \texttt{v}_i \otimes var(\texttt{X}, \texttt{T}_i), \forall i, \quad \text{where } \texttt{module C<}\overline{\texttt{X}}\texttt{> \{ }\overline{\texttt{Tv}}\texttt{ \}} \in S \tag{1}$$

$$var(\texttt{X}, \texttt{C<>}) \sqsubseteq * \tag{2}$$

$$var(\texttt{X}, \texttt{Y}) \sqsubseteq *, \text{ where } \texttt{X} \neq \texttt{Y} \tag{3}$$

$$var(\texttt{X}, \texttt{X}) \sqsubseteq + \tag{4}$$

$$var(\texttt{X}, \texttt{C<}\overline{\texttt{vT}}\texttt{>}) \sqsubseteq (\texttt{v}_i \sqcup var(\texttt{Y}, \texttt{C})) \otimes var(\texttt{X}, \texttt{T}_i), \forall i, \quad \text{where Y is the } i\text{-th type variable in the definition of C.} \tag{5}$$

Rule 1 specifies that for each type $\texttt{T}_i$ in module `C`, the variance of the type variable `X` in `C` must be below the variance of `X` in $\texttt{T}_i$ transformed by $\texttt{v}_i$, the variance of the position that $\texttt{T}_i$ appears in. This corresponds to the traditional reasoning about definition site variance from Section 2.1.

Rules 2 and 3 specify that the `X` can have any variance in a type expression for which it does not occur in. Rule 4 constrains the initial variance of a type variable to be at most covariance.

Rule 5 is the most interesting. It integrates our reasoning about how to compose variances for complex expressions (using the transform operator, as described in Section 3.1) and how to factor in use-site variance annotations (using a join in the variance lattice, as described in Section 3.2).

Note that the rules use our transform operator in two different ways: to combine the variance of a position with the variance of a type, and to compose variances.

We prove the soundness of the above rules denotationally—that is, by direct appeal to the original definition and axioms of use-site variance [17]. The proof can be found in the extended version of this paper [1, Appendix I].

Example. We can now revisit in more detail the example from the Introduction, containing both recursive variance and wildcards:

```
class C<X> {
  X    foo (C<? super X>   csx) { ... }
  void bar (D<? extends X> dsx) { ... }
}
class D<Y> { void baz (C<Y> cx) { ... }  }
```

As we saw, the corresponding *VarLang* sentence is:

```
module C<X> { X+, C<-X>-, void+, D<+X>- }
module D<Y> { void+, C<oY>- }
```

The generated constraints (without duplicates) are:

$var(\texttt{X}, \texttt{C}) \sqsubseteq + \otimes var(\texttt{X}, \texttt{X})$	(rule 1)
$var(\texttt{X}, \texttt{X}) \sqsubseteq +$	(rule 4)
$var(\texttt{X}, \texttt{C}) \sqsubseteq - \otimes var(\texttt{X}, \texttt{C<-X>})$	(rule 1)
$var(\texttt{X}, \texttt{C<-X>}) \sqsubseteq (- \sqcup var(\texttt{X}, \texttt{C})) \otimes var(\texttt{X}, \texttt{X})$	(rule 5)
$var(\texttt{X}, \texttt{C}) \sqsubseteq + \otimes var(\texttt{X}, \texttt{void})$	(rule 1)
$var(\texttt{X}, \texttt{void}) \sqsubseteq *$	(rule 2)
$var(\texttt{X}, \texttt{C}) \sqsubseteq - \otimes var(\texttt{X}, \texttt{D<+X>})$	(rule 1)
$var(\texttt{X}, \texttt{D<+X>}) \sqsubseteq (+ \sqcup var(\texttt{Y}, \texttt{D})) \otimes var(\texttt{X}, \texttt{X})$	(rule 5)
$var(\texttt{Y}, \texttt{D}) \sqsubseteq + \otimes var(\texttt{Y}, \texttt{void})$	(rule 1)
$var(\texttt{Y}, \texttt{void}) \sqsubseteq *$	(rule 2)
$var(\texttt{Y}, \texttt{D}) \sqsubseteq - \otimes var(\texttt{Y}, \texttt{C<oY>})$	(rule 1)
$var(\texttt{Y}, \texttt{C<oY>}) \sqsubseteq (o \sqcup var(\texttt{X}, \texttt{C})) \otimes var(\texttt{Y}, \texttt{Y})$	(rule 5)
$var(\texttt{Y}, \texttt{Y}) \sqsubseteq +$	(rule 3)

4.3 Revisiting Recursive Type Variances

Armed with our understanding of variance requirements as symbolic constraints on a lattice, it is quite easy to revisit practical examples and understand them quickly. For instance, what we called type 2 recursive variance in Section 3.3 is just an instance of a recursive constraint $c \sqsubseteq - \otimes c$, where c is some variable of the form $var(\texttt{X}, \texttt{C})$. This is a case of a type that recursively (i.e., inside its own definition) occurs in a contravariant position. (Of course, the recursion will not always be that obvious: it may only become apparent after other constraints are simplified and merged.) It is easy to see from the properties of the transform operator that the only solutions of this constraint are o and $*$; i.e., "cannot be either co- or contravariant" as we described in Section 3.3. If $c = +$, then the constraint generated by type 2 recursive variance would be violated, since $c = + \not\sqsubseteq - \otimes c = - \otimes + = -$. Similar reasoning shows c cannot be $-$ and satisfy the constraint.

4.4 Constraint Solving

Checking if a variance satisfies a constraint system (i.e., the constraints generated for a *VarLang* module) corresponds to checking definition-site variance annotations in type definitions that can contain use-site variance annotations. Analogously, inferring the most general definition-site variances allowed by a type definition corresponds to computing the most general variances that satisfy the constraint system representing the type definition. The trivial and least general solution that satisfies a constraint system is assigning the definition-site variance of all type parameters to be invariance. Assigning invariance to all type parameters is guaranteed to be a solution, since invariance is the bottom element, which must be below every upper bound imposed by the constraints. Stopping with this solution would not take advantage of the subtyping relationships allowed by type definitions. Fortunately, the most general solution is always unique and can be computed efficiently by fixed-point computation running in polynomial time of the program size (number of constraints generated).

The only operators in constraint systems are the binary operators $\sqcup$ and $\otimes$. Both of these are monotone, as can be seen with the variance lattice and Figure 1.

Every constraint system has a unique maximal solution because there is guaranteed to be at least one solution (assign every type parameter invariance) and solutions to constraint systems are closed under point-wise $\sqcup$; we get a maximal solution by joining all of the greatest variances that satisfy each constraint. Because operators $\sqcup$ and $\otimes$ are monotone, we can compute the maximal solution efficiently with fixed point iteration halting when the greatest fixed point of the equations has been reached. We demonstrate this algorithm below by applying it to the example Java classes C and D from Section 4.2.

First, because we are only interested in inferring definition-site variance, we only care about computing the most general variances for terms of the form $var(\mathtt{X},\ \mathtt{C})$ but not $var(\mathtt{X},\ \mathtt{T})$. We can expand $var(\mathtt{X},\ \mathtt{T})$ terms with their upper bounds containing only unknowns of the form $var(\mathtt{X},\ \mathtt{C})$ Consider the constraint generated from foo's argument type: $var(\mathtt{X},\ \mathtt{C}) \sqsubseteq - \otimes var(\mathtt{X},\ \mathtt{C<-X>})$. Because we are computing a maximal solution and because of the monotonicity of $\sqcup$ and $\otimes$, we can replace $var(\mathtt{X},\ \mathtt{C<-X>})$ and $var(\mathtt{X},\ \mathtt{X})$ by their upper bounds, rewriting the constraint as:

$$var(\mathtt{X},\ \mathtt{C}) \sqsubseteq - \otimes \underbrace{(- \sqcup var(\mathtt{X},\ \mathtt{C})) \otimes \overbrace{+}^{var(\mathtt{X},\ \mathtt{X})}}_{var(\mathtt{X},\ \mathtt{C<-X>})}$$

Lastly, we can ignore type expressions that do not mention a type parameter because they impose no real upper bound; their upper bound is the top element (e.g. $var(\mathtt{X},\ \mathtt{void}) \sqsubseteq *$). This leads to the following constraints generated for the example two Java classes:

$$\begin{array}{lcl}
\text{foo return type} & \Longrightarrow & var(\mathtt{X},\ \mathtt{C}) \sqsubseteq + \otimes \underbrace{+}_{var(\mathtt{X},\ \mathtt{X})} \\
\text{foo arg type} & \Longrightarrow & var(\mathtt{X},\ \mathtt{C}) \sqsubseteq - \otimes \underbrace{(var(\mathtt{X},\ \mathtt{C}) \sqcup -)}_{var(\mathtt{X},\ \mathtt{C<-X>})} \\
\text{bar arg type} & \Longrightarrow & var(\mathtt{X},\ \mathtt{C}) \sqsubseteq - \otimes \underbrace{(var(\mathtt{Y},\ \mathtt{D}) \sqcup +)}_{var(\mathtt{X},\ \mathtt{D<+X>})} \\
\text{baz arg type} & \Longrightarrow & var(\mathtt{Y},\ \mathtt{D}) \sqsubseteq - \otimes \underbrace{(var(\mathtt{X},\ \mathtt{C}) \sqcup o)}_{var(\mathtt{Y},\ \mathtt{C<oY>})}
\end{array}$$

Letting c denote $var(\mathtt{X},\ \mathtt{C})$ and d denote $var(\mathtt{Y},\ \mathtt{D})$, the above constraints correspond to the four constraints presented in the Introduction.

For each expanded constraint $r \sqsubseteq l$ in a constraint system, r is a $var(\mathtt{X},\ \mathtt{C})$ term and l is an expression where the only unknowns are $var(\mathtt{X},\ \mathtt{C})$ terms. The greatest fixed-point of a constraint system is solved for by, first, assigning every $var(\mathtt{X},\ \mathtt{C})$ term to be $*$ (top). Each constraint $r \sqsubseteq l$ is then transformed to $r \leftarrow l \sqcap r$, since r need not increase from the value it was lowered to by other assignments. The last step is to iterate through the assignments for each constraint until the $var(\mathtt{X},\ \mathtt{C})$ terms no longer change, which results in computing the greatest fixed-point. Finally, computing the greatest fixed-point runs in at most $O(2n)$ iterations, where n is the number of constraint inequalities, since for each $r \leftarrow l \sqcap r$, r can decrease at most 2 times to invariance (bottom) from initially being bivariance (top).

5. An Application: Definition-Site Variance Inference for Java

To showcase the potential of our unified treatment of use-site and definition-site variance, we implemented a mapping from Java to *VarLang*, used it to produce a (definition-site) variance *inference* algorithm, and evaluated its impact on large Java libraries with generics (including the standard library).

5.1 Applications

Our mapping from Java to *VarLang* is straightforward: We produce a *VarLang* module definition for each Java class or interface, and all Java type expressions are mapped one-to-one on *VarLang* type expressions with the same name. The module definitions contain variance constraints that correspond to the well-understood variance of different positions (as discussed in Section 2): return types are a covariant position, argument types are a contravariant position, types of non-final fields are both covariant and contravariant positions, supertypes are a covariant position.

Our mapping is conservative: although we handle the entire Java language, we translate some "tricky" aspects of the language into an invariance constraint, potentially making our algorithm infer less general variances than is occasionally possible. For instance, we do not try to infer the most general variance induced by polymorphic methods: if a class type parameter appears at all in the upper bound of a type parameter of a polymorphic method, we consider this to be an instance of an invariant position. Another source of conservatism is that we ignore the potential for more general typing through reasoning about member visibility (i.e., private/protected access control). Member visibility, in combination with conditions on self-reference in type signatures, can be used to establish that some fields or methods cannot be accessed from outside a class/package. Nevertheless, our mapping does not try to reason about such cases to produce less restrictive variance constraints.

The reason for our conservatism is that we do not want to reason about language specific constructs that are orthogonal to the denotational meaning of variance and would make our soundness proof be of the same complexity as in e.g., TameFJ [7]. We prefer to use only positions of unquestionable variance at the expense of slightly worse numbers (which still fully validate the potential of our approach).

We used this mapping to implement a definition-site variance inference algorithm. That is, we took regular Java code, written with no concept of definition-site variance in mind, and inferred how many generics are purely covariant/contravariant/bivariant. Inferring pure variance for a generic has several practical implications:

- One can use our algorithm to replace the Java type system with a more liberal one that infers definition-site variance and allows subtyping based on the inferred variances. Such a type system would accept all current legal Java programs, yet allow programs that are currently not allowed to type-check, without violating soundness. This would mean that wildcards can be omitted in many cases, freeing the programmer from the burden of always specifying tedious types in order to get generality. For instance, if a generic C is found to be covariant, then any occurrence of C<? extends T> is unnecessary. (We report such instances as "unnecessary wildcards" in our measurements.) Furthermore, any occurrence of C<T> or C<? super T> will be immediately considered equivalent to C<? extends T> or C<?>, respectively, by the type system, resulting in more general code. (We report such instances as "over-specified methods" in our measurements.)
- One can use our algorithm as a programmer's assistant in the context of an IDE or as an off-line tool, to offer suggestions for more general types that are, however, still sound. For instance, for a covariant generic, C, every occurrence of type C<T> can be replaced by C<? extends T> to gain more generality without any potential for more errors. Just running our algorithm once over a code body will reveal multiple points where a programmer missed an opportunity to specify a more general type. The programmer can then determine whether the specificity was intentional (e.g., in anticipation that the referenced generic will later be augmented with more methods) or accidental.

In practice, our implementation (in Scala) of the optimized constraint solving algorithm described in Section 4.4 takes less than 3 minutes (on a 3.2GHz Intel Core i3 machine w/ 4GB RAM) to analyze the generics of the entire Java standard library. Almost all

Library		# Type defs	# Generic defs	Type Definitions					Recursive variances	Unnecess. wildcards	Over-specif. methods
				invar.	variant	cov.	contrav.	biv.			
java.*	classes	5550	99	69%	31%	20%	17%	4%	10%	12%	7%
	interfaces	1710	44	43%	57%	41%	25%	0%	22%	12%	16%
	total	7260	143	61%	39%	27%	20%	3%	14%	12%	8%
JScience	classes	70	25	76%	24%	0%	0%	24%	76%	90%	19%
	interfaces	51	11	55%	45%	0%	9%	36%	7%	100%	11%
	total	121	36	69%	31%	0%	3%	28%	53%	91%	19%
Apache Collec.	classes	226	187	66%	34%	14%	21%	2%	4%	63%	17%
	interfaces	23	22	55%	45%	32%	18%	0%	24%	20%	0%
	total	249	209	65%	35%	16%	21%	1%	6%	62%	17%
Guava	classes	204	101	90%	10%	9%	1%	0%	8%	51%	18%
	interfaces	35	26	46%	54%	38%	19%	4%	18%	38%	5%
	total	239	127	81%	19%	15%	5%	1%	10%	50%	17%
GNU Trove	classes	25	8	62%	38%	12%	25%	0%	33%	0%	62%
	interfaces	8	4	0%	100%	25%	100%	0%	0%	0%	0%
	total	33	12	42%	58%	17%	50%	0%	20%	0%	62%
JPaul	classes	77	65	75%	25%	12%	12%	5%	18%	86%	23%
	interfaces	9	9	67%	33%	11%	33%	0%	9%	0%	0%
	total	86	74	74%	26%	12%	15%	4%	17%	86%	23%
Total	**classes**	**6152**	**485**	**73%**	**27%**	**13%**	**14%**	**3%**	**11%**	**42%**	**13%**
	interfaces	**1836**	**116**	**47%**	**53%**	**32%**	**24%**	**4%**	**18%**	**19%**	**15%**
	total	**7988**	**601**	**68%**	**32%**	**17%**	**16%**	**3%**	**13%**	**39%**	**13%**

Figure 4. Class/Interface Inference Results

Library		# Type Parameters	Type Parameters				
			inv.	variant total	cov.	contrav.	biv.
java.*	classes	128	67%	33%	16%	14%	3%
	interfaces	54	46%	54%	33%	20%	0%
	total	182	61%	39%	21%	16%	2%
JScience	classes	29	79%	21%	0%	0%	21%
	interfaces	14	64%	36%	0%	7%	29%
	total	43	74%	26%	0%	2%	23%
Apache Collec.	classes	254	72%	28%	11%	16%	1%
	interfaces	33	64%	36%	24%	12%	0%
	total	287	71%	29%	13%	15%	1%
Guava	classes	150	93%	7%	7%	1%	0%
	interfaces	39	54%	46%	26%	18%	3%
	total	189	85%	15%	11%	4%	1%
GNU Trove	classes	9	67%	33%	11%	22%	0%
	interfaces	6	0%	100%	17%	83%	0%
	total	15	40%	60%	13%	47%	0%
JPaul	classes	93	76%	24%	10%	9%	5%
	interfaces	11	64%	36%	9%	27%	0%
	total	104	75%	25%	10%	11%	5%
Total	**classes**	**663**	**77%**	**23%**	**10%**	**10%**	**3%**
	interfaces	**157**	**53%**	**47%**	**24%**	**20%**	**3%**
	total	**820**	**72%**	**28%**	**13%**	**12%**	**3%**

Figure 5. Type Parameter Inference Results

of the time is spent on loading, parsing, and processing files, with under 30sec constraint solving time.

Finally, we need to emphasize that our inference algorithm is *modular*. Not only does it reason entirely at the interface level (does not inspect method bodies), but also the variance of a generic depends only on its own definition and the definition of types *it* (transitively) references, and not on types that reference it. This is the same modularity guarantee as with standard separate compilation. If we were to allow our algorithm to generate constraints after inspecting method bodies, we would get improved numbers (since, for instance, an invariant type may be passed as a parameter, but only its covariance-safe methods may be used—e.g., a list argument may only be used for reading). Nevertheless, analyzing the bodies of methods would have a cost in modularity: the analysis would still not depend on clients of a method, but it would need to examine subtypes, to analyze all the possible overriding methods. This is yet another way in which our numbers are conservative and only compute a lower bound of the possible impact of integrating definition-site variance inference in Java.

5.2 Analysis of Impact

To measure the impact of our approach, we ran our inference algorithm over 6 Java libraries, the largest of which is the core Java library from Sun's JDK 1.6, i.e., classes and interfaces in the packages of `java.*`. The other libraries are JScience [10], a Java library for scientific computing; Guava [5], a superset of the Google collections library; GNU Trove [14]; Apache Commons-Collection [3]; and JPaul [21], a library supporting program analysis.

The results of our experiment appear in Figure 4. Together, these libraries define 7,988 classes and interfaces, out of which 601 are generics. The five "invar./variant/cov./contrav./biv/" columns show the percentage of classes and interfaces that are inferred by our algorithm to be invariant versus variant, for all three flavors of variance. The statistics are collapsed per-class: An invariant class is invariant in all of its type parameters, whereas a variant class is variant in at least one of its type parameters. Hence, a class can be counted as, e.g., both covariant and contravariant, if it is covariant in one type parameter and contravariant in another. The "variant" column, however, counts the class only once. Statistics per type parameter are in included in Figure 5.

As can be seen, 32% of classes or interfaces are variant in at least one type parameter. (Our "Total" row treats all libraries as if they were one, i.e., sums individual numbers before averaging. This means that the "Total" is influenced more by larger libraries, especially for metrics that apply to all *uses* of generics, which may also occur in non-generic code.) This means that about 1/3 of the generics defined should be allowed to enjoy general variant subtyping without users having to annotate them with wildcards.

The next column shows how many generics have a recursive variance constraint. One can see that these numbers are usually low, especially considering that they include direct self-recursion (e.g., a trivial constraint $var(\mathtt{X}, \mathtt{C}) \sqsubseteq + \otimes var(\mathtt{X}, \mathtt{C})$).

The last two columns illustrate the burden of default invariant subtyping in Java, and the benefits of our approach. "Unnecessary Wildcards" shows the percentage of wildcards in method signatures that are unnecessary in our system, based on the inferred definition-site variance their generics. For instance, given that our technique infers interface `java.util.Iterator<E>` to be covariant, all instantiations of `Iterator<? extends T>`, for any `T`, are unnecessary. This number shows that, using our technique, 37% of the current wildcard annotations can be eliminated without sacrificing either type safety or the generality of types!

The "Over-specified Method" column lists the percentage of method arguments that are overly specific *in the Java type system*, based on the inferred definition-site variance of their generics. For instance, given that the inferred definition-site variance of `Iterator<E>` is covariant, specifying a method argument with type `Iterator<T>`, instead of `Iterator<? extends T>`, is overly specific, since the Java type system would preclude safe invocations of this method with arguments of type `Iterator`-of-some-subtype-of-`T`. Note again that this percentage is *purely based on the inferred definition-site variance of the arguments' types, not on analysis of the arguments' uses in the bodies of methods.* We find that 13% of methods are over-specified. This means that 13% of the methods could be used in a much more liberal, yet still type-safe fashion. It is also interesting that this number is derived from *libraries* and not from client code. We expect that the number of over-specified methods would be much higher in client code, since programmers would be less familiar with wildcards and less confident about the operations supported by variant versions of a type.

Backward Compatibility and Discussion. As discussed earlier, our variance inference algorithm can be used to replace the Java type system with a more liberal one, or can be used to offer suggestions to programmers in the context of an IDE. Replacing the Java type system with a type system that infers definition-site variance is tempting, but would require a pragmatic language design decision, since there is a cost in backward compatibility: in some cases the programmer may have relied on types being rejected by Java, even though these types can never cause a dynamic type error.

We found one such instance in our experiments. In the reference implementation for JSR 275 (Measures and Units) [11], included with the JScience library [10], a group of 11 classes and interfaces are collectively bivariant in a type parameter, `Q extends Quantity`. In the definition of `Unit<Q extends Quantity>`, for example, the type parameter `Q` appears nowhere other than as the type argument to `Unit<Q>`. Closer inspection of the code shows that `Quantity` is extended by 43 different subinterfaces, such as `Acceleration`, `Mass`, `Torque`, `Volume`, etc. It appears that the authors of the library are actually relying on the invariant subtyping of Java generics, to ensure, e.g., that `Unit<Acceleration>` is never used as `Unit<Mass>`.

Of course, full variance inference is only one option in the design space. Any combination of inference and explicitly stated variance annotations, or just adding explicit definition-site variance to Java, are strictly easier applications from a typing standpoint. The ultimate choice is left with the language designer, yet the potential revealed by our experiments is significant.

6. Conclusions

In this work we showed that the need for the flexibility of use-site variance is somewhat overrated, and the rigidity of definition-site variance is unwarranted. We introduce the first unified framework for reasoning about variance, allowing type system designs that combine the benefits of both definition- and use-site variance. Thus, our approach resolves questions that are central in the design of any language involving parametric polymorphism and subtyping. Our work is the first to fully study how definition-site variance interacts with use-site variance annotations and type recursion. Our calculus allows to reason about complex constraints independently of specific type systems on variances involved in recursive class definitions. As a specific application, we introduce a type system for Java that *modularly infers* definition-site variance, while allowing use-site variance annotations where necessary. We show that combining definition-site and use-site variance allows us to infer more general types than either approach alone. Our Java implementation demonstrates the benefits and practicality of our approach, and our algorithm can also be used in other contexts, such as to aid a programmer via an IDE plugin to choose types that generalize method signatures as much as possible.

Acknowledgments

We would like to thank Jens Palsberg (especially for valuable insights on the constraint solving algorithm) as well as Christoph Reichenbach and several anonymous reviewers for their suggestions that helped improve the paper. This work was funded by the National Science Foundation under grants CCF-0917774, CCF-0934631, and IIP-0838747 to the University of Massachusetts.

References

[1] J. Altidor, S. S. Huang, and Y. Smaragdakis. Taming the wildcards: Combining definition- and use-site variance (extended version). `http://www.cs.umass.edu/~yannis/variance-extended2011.pdf`.

[2] P. America and F. van der Linden. A parallel object-oriented language with inheritance and subtyping. In *OOPSLA/ECOOP '90: Proc. of the European Conf. on object-oriented programming on Object-oriented programming systems, languages, and applications*, 1990.

[3] Apache Software Foundation. Apache commons-collections library. `http://larvalabs.com/collections/`. Version 4.01.

[4] J. Bloch. The closures controversy. http://www.javac.info/bloch-closures-controversy.ppt. Accessed Nov. 2010.

[5] K. Boumillion and J. Levy. Guava: Google core libraries for Java 1.5+. http://code.google.com/p/guava-libraries/. Accessed Nov. 2010.

[6] G. Bracha and D. Griswold. Strongtalk: typechecking smalltalk in a production environment. In *OOPSLA '93: Proc. of the Conf. on Object-oriented programming systems, languages, and applications*, 1993.

[7] N. Cameron, S. Drossopoulou, and E. Ernst. A model for Java with wildcards. In *ECOOP '08: Proc. of the 22nd European Conf. on Object-Oriented Programming*, 2008.

[8] R. Cartwright and J. Guy L. Steele. Compatible genericity with run-time types for the Java programming language. In *OOPSLA '98: Proc. of the 13th ACM SIGPLAN Conf. on Object-oriented programming, systems, languages, and applications*, 1998.

[9] W. Cook. A proposal for making eiffel type-safe. In *ECOOP '89: Proc. of the 3rd European Conf. on Object-Oriented Programming*, 1989.

[10] J.-M. Dautelle et al. Jscience. http://jscience.org/. Accessed Nov. 2010.

[11] J.-M. Dautelle and W. Keil. Jsr-275: Measures and units. http://www.jcp.org/en/jsr/detail?id=275. Accessed Nov. 2010.

[12] M. Day, R. Gruber, B. Liskov, and A. C. Myers. Subtypes vs. where clauses: constraining parametric polymorphism. In *OOPSLA '95: Proc. of the tenth annual Conf. on Object-oriented programming systems, languages, and applications*, 1995.

[13] B. Emir, A. Kennedy, C. Russo, and D. Yu. Variance and generalized constraints for C# generics. In *ECOOP '06: Proc. of the European Conf. on Object-Oriented Programming*, 2006.

[14] E. Friedman and R. Eden. Gnu Trove: High-performance collections library for Java. http://trove4j.sourceforge.net/. Version 2.1.0.

[15] A. Hejlsberg, S. Wiltamuth, and P. Golde. *C# Language Specification*. Addison-Wesley Longman Publishing Co., Inc., Boston, MA, 2003.

[16] S. S. Huang, D. Zook, and Y. Smaragdakis. cJ: Enhancing Java with safe type conditions. In *Proc. of the 6th Intl. Conf. on Aspect-Oriented Software Development*, 2007.

[17] A. Igarashi and M. Viroli. Variant parametric types: A flexible subtyping scheme for generics. *ACM Trans. Program. Lang. Syst.*, 28(5):795–847, 2006.

[18] A. Kennedy and D. Syme. Transposing f to c#: expressivity of parametric polymorphism in an object-oriented language: Research articles. *Concurr. Comput. : Pract. Exper.*, 16:707–733, 2004.

[19] A. Kiezun, M. Ernst, F. Tip, and R. Fuhrer. Refactoring for parameterizing Java classes. In *ICSE '07: Proc. of the 29th Intl. Conf. on Software Engineering*, 2007.

[20] M. Odersky. *The Scala Language Specification v 2.8*. 2010.

[21] A. Salcianu. Java program analysis utilities library. http://jpaul.sourceforge.net/. Version 2.5.1.

[22] K. K. Thorup and M. Torgersen. Unifying genericity: Combining the benefits of virtual types and parameterized classes. In *ECOOP '99: Proc. of the European Conf. on Object-Oriented Programming*, 1999.

[23] M. Torgersen, C. P. Hansen, E. Ernst, P. von der Ahe, G. Bracha, and N. Gafter. Adding wildcards to the Java programming language. In *SAC '04: Proc. of the 2004 Symposium on Applied Computing*, 2004.

Taming Wildcards in Java's Type System *

Ross Tate
University of California, San Diego
rtate@cs.ucsd.edu

Alan Leung
University of California, San Diego
aleung@cs.ucsd.edu

Sorin Lerner
University of California, San Diego
lerner@cs.ucsd.edu

Abstract

Wildcards have become an important part of Java's type system since their introduction 7 years ago. Yet there are still many open problems with Java's wildcards. For example, there are no known sound and complete algorithms for subtyping (and consequently type checking) Java wildcards, and in fact subtyping is suspected to be undecidable because wildcards are a form of bounded existential types. Furthermore, some Java types with wildcards have no joins, making inference of type arguments for generic methods particularly difficult. Although there has been progress on these fronts, we have identified significant shortcomings of the current state of the art, along with new problems that have not been addressed.

In this paper, we illustrate how these shortcomings reflect the subtle complexity of the problem domain, and then present major improvements to the current algorithms for wildcards by making slight restrictions on the usage of wildcards. Our survey of existing Java programs suggests that realistic code should already satisfy our restrictions without any modifications. We present a simple algorithm for subtyping which is both sound and complete with our restrictions, an algorithm for lazily joining types with wildcards which addresses some of the shortcomings of prior work, and techniques for improving the Java type system as a whole. Lastly, we describe various extensions to wildcards that would be compatible with our algorithms.

Categories and Subject Descriptors D.3.1 [*Programming Languages*]: Formal Definitions and Theory; D.3.2 [*Programming Languages*]: Language Classifications—Java; D.3.3 [*Programming Languages*]: Language Constructs and Features—Polymorphism

General Terms Algorithms, Design, Languages, Theory

Keywords Wildcards, Subtyping, Existential types, Parametric types, Joins, Type inference, Single-instantiation inheritance

1. Introduction

Java 5, released in 2004, introduced a variety of features to the Java programming language, most notably a major overhaul of the type system for the purposes of supporting generics. Although Java has undergone several revisions since, Java generics have remained unchanged since they were originally introduced into the language.

Java generics were a long-awaited improvement to Java and have been tremendously useful, leading to a significant reduction in the amount of unsafe type casts found in Java code. However, while Java generics improved the language, they also made type checking extremely complex. In particular, Java generics came with *wildcards*, a sophisticated type feature designed to address the limitations of plain parametric polymorphism [18].

Wildcards are a simple form of existential types. For example, `List<?>` represents a "list of unknowns", namely a list of objects, all of which have the same unknown static type. Similarly, `List<? extends Number>` is a list of objects of some unknown static type, but this unknown static type must be a subtype of `Number`. Wildcards are a very powerful feature that is used pervasively in Java. They can be used to encode use-site variance of parametric types [6, 16–18], and have been used to safely type check large parts of the standard library without using type casts. Unfortunately, the addition of wildcards makes Java's type system extremely complex. In this paper we illustrate and address three issues of wildcards: subtyping, type-argument inference, and inconsistencies in the design of the type system.

Subtyping with wildcards is surprisingly challenging. In fact, there are no known sound and complete subtyping algorithms for Java, soundness meaning the algorithm accepts only subtypings permitted by Java and completeness meaning the algorithm always terminates and accepts all subtypings permitted by Java. Subtyping with wildcards is even suspected to be undecidable, being closely related to the undecidable problem of subtyping with bounded existential types [20]. In Section 3 we will illustrate this challenge, including examples of programs which make `javac`† suffer a stack overflow. In Section 4 we will present our simple subtyping algorithm which is sound and complete given certain restrictions.

Java also includes type-argument inference for generic methods, which again is particularly challenging with wildcards. Without type-argument inference, a programmer would have to provide type arguments each time a generic method is used. Thus, to make generic methods convenient, Java infers type arguments at method-invocation sites. Furthermore, Java can infer types not expressible by users, so that explicit annotation is not always an option. Unfortunately, there is no known sound and complete type-argument inference algorithm. Plus, type-argument inference can even affect the semantics of a program. We illustrate these issues in Section 5 and present our improvements on the state of the art in Section 6.

Wildcards also introduce a variety of complications to Java's type system as a whole. While Java attempts to address these complications, there are yet many to be resolved. In some cases Java is overly restrictive, while in others Java is overly relaxed. In fact, the type-checking algorithm used by `javac` is non-deterministic from the user's perspective due to wildcards. In Section 7 we will illustrate these issues, and in Section 8 we will present our solutions.

A few of our solutions involve imposing restrictions on the Java language. Naturally one wonders whether these restrictions are practical. As such, we have analyzed 9.2 million lines of open-

* This work was supported by NSF grant CCF-0644306 and a Microsoft Research PhD Fellowship.

† When we refer to `javac` we mean version 1.6.0_22.

PLDI'11, June 4–8, 2011, San Jose, California, USA.

source Java code and determined that *none* of our restrictions are violated. We present our findings in Section 9, along with a number of interesting statistics on how wildcards are used in practice.

Java is an evolving language, and ideally our algorithms can evolve with it. In Section 10 we present a variety of extensions to Java which preliminary investigations indicate would be compatible with our algorithms. These extensions also suggest that our algorithms could apply to other languages such as C# and Scala.

Many of the above difficulties of wildcards are by no means new and have been discussed in a variety of papers [2, 8, 13, 20]. In response to these challenges, researchers have explored several ways of fixing wildcards. The work by Smith and Cartwright [13] in particular made significant progress on improving algorithms for type checking Java. Throughout this paper we will identify the many contributions of these works. However, we will also identify their shortcomings, motivating the need for our improvements. Although this paper does not solve all the problems with type checking Java, it does significantly improve the state of the art, providing concrete solutions to many of the open issues with wildcards.

2. Background

In early proposals for adding parametric polymorphism to Java, namely GJ [1], one could operate on `List<String>` or on `List<Number>`, yet operating on arbitrary lists was inconvenient because there was no form of variance. One had to define a method with a polymorphic variable `P` and a parameter of type `List<P>`, which seems natural except that this had to be done even when the type of the list contents did not matter. That is, there was no way no refer to all lists regardless of their elements. This can be especially limiting for parametric classes such as `Class<P>` for which the type parameter is not central to its usage. Thus, Java wanted a type system beyond standard parametric polymorphism to address these limitations.

2.1 Wildcards

Wildcards were introduced as a solution to the above problem among others [18]. `List<?>` stands for a list whose elements have an arbitrary unknown static type. Types such as `List<String>`, `List<Number>`, and `List<List<String>>` can all be used as a `List<?>`. The ? is called a wildcard since it can stand for any type and the user has to handle it regardless of what type it stands for. One can operate on a `List<?>` as they would any list so long as they make no assumptions about the type of its elements. One can get its length, clear its contents, and even get `Object`s from it since in Java all instances belong to `Object`. As such, one might mistake a `List<?>` for a `List<Object>`; however, unlike `List<Object>`, one cannot add arbitrary `Object`s to a `List<?>` since it might represent a `List<String>` which only accepts `String`s or a `List<Number>` which only accepts `Number`s.

Wildcards can also be constrained in order to convey restricted use of the type. For example, the type `List<? extends Number>` is often used to indicate read-only lists of `Number`s. This is because one can get elements of the list and statically know they are `Number`s, but one cannot add `Number`s to the list since the list may actually represent a `List<Integer>` which does not accept arbitrary `Number`s. Similarly, `List<? super Number>` is often used to indicate write-only lists. This time, one cannot get `Number`s from the list since it may actually be a `List<Object>`, but one can add `Number`s to the list. Note, though, that this read-only/write-only usage is only convention and not actually enforced by the type system. One can mutate a `List<? extends Number>` via the `clear` method and one can read a `List<? super Number>` via the `length` method since neither method uses the type parameter for `List`.

Java's subtyping for types with wildcards is very flexible. Not only can a `List<Error>` be used as a `List<? extends Error>`, but a `List<? extends Error>` can even be used as a `List<? extends Throwable>` since `Error` is a subclass of `Throwable`. Similarly, a `List<Throwable>` can be used as a `List<? super Throwable>` which can be used as a `List<? super Error>`. Thus by constraining wildcards above one gets covariant subtyping, and by constraining wildcards below one gets contravariant subtyping. This is known as use-site variance [16] and is one of the basic challenges of subtyping with wildcards. However, it is only the beginning of the difficulties for subtyping, as we will demonstrate in Section 3. Before that, we discuss the connection between wildcards and existential types as it is useful for understanding and formalizing the many subtleties within wildcards.

2.2 Existential Types

Since their inception, wildcards have been recognized as a form of existential types [2, 3, 6, 8, 17, 18, 20]. The wildcard ? represents an existentially quantified type variable, so that `List<?>` is shorthand for the existentially quantified type ∃`X. List<X>`. Existential quantification is dual to universal quantification; a ∀`X. List<X>` can be used as a `List<String>` by instantiating `X` to `String`, and dually a `List<String>` can be used as an ∃`X. List<X>` by instantiating `X` to `String`. In particular, any list can be used as an ∃`X. List<X>`, just like `List<?>`. The conversion from concrete instantiation to existential quantification is often done with an explicit *pack* operation, but in this setting all packs are implicit in the subtype system.

Bounded wildcards are represented using bounded quantification. The wildcard type `List<? extends Number>` is represented by ∃`X extends Number. List<X>`. A list belongs to this existential type if its element type is a subtype of `Number`. Examples are `List<Integer>` and `List<Double>`, which also belong to `List<? extends Number>` as expected. Once again this is dual to bounded universal quantification.

Even subtyping of wildcards can be formalized by existential subsumption (dual to universal subsumption [7, 9, 10]). For example, ∃`X extends Error. List<X>` subsumes ∃`Y extends Throwable. List<Y>` because the type variable `Y` can be instantiated to the type `X` which is a subtype of `Throwable` because `X` is constrained to be a subtype of `Error` which is a subclass of `Throwable`. Often this subsumption relation is accomplished by explicit *open* and *pack* operations. The left side is opened, moving its variables and their constraints into the general context, and then the types in the opened left side are packed into the variables bound in the right side and the constraints are checked to hold for those packed types. In the context of wildcards, the opening process is called wildcard capture [5, 18] and is actually part of the specification for subtyping [5: Chapter 4.10.2].

2.3 Implicit Constraints

While users can explicitly constrain wildcards via the `extends` and `super` clauses, Java also imposes implicit constraints on wildcards to make them more convenient. For example, consider the following interfaces specializing `List` via F-bounded polymorphism [4]:

```
interface Numbers<P extends Number> extends List<P> {}
interface Errors<P extends Error> extends List<P> {}
```

If a user uses the type `Numbers<?>`, Java implicitly constrains the wildcard to be a subtype of `Number` [5: Chapter 5.1.10], saving the user the effort of expressing a constraint that always holds. The same is done for `Errors<?>`, so that `Errors<?>` is a subtype of `List<? extends Error>` [5: Chapter 4.10.2]. (Note that we will reuse these interfaces throughout this paper.)

Implicit constraints on wildcards are more than just a syntactic convenience though; they can express constraints that users cannot express explicitly. Consider the following interface declaration:

```
interface SortedList<P extends Comparable<P>> extends List<P> {}
```

If one uses the type `SortedList<?>`, Java implicitly constrains the wildcard, call it `X`, so that `X` is a subtype of `Comparable<X>` [5: Chapter 5.1.10]. However, it is impossible to state this constraint explicitly on the wildcard argument to `SortedList`. This is because the

```
class C implements List<List<? super C>> {}

Is C a subtype of List<? super C>?

Step 0)    C <: List<? super C>
Step 1)    List<List<? super C>> <: List<? super C> (inheritance)
Step 2)    C <: List<? super C> (checking wildcard ? super C)
Step ...   (cycle forever)
```

Figure 1. Example of cyclic dependency in subtyping [8]

```
class C<P> implements List<List<? super C<C<P>>>> {}

Is C<Byte> a subtype of List<? super C<Byte>>?

Step 0)    C<Byte> <: List<? super C<Byte>>
Step 1)    List<List<? super C<C<Byte>>>> <: List<? super C<Byte>>
Step 2)    C<Byte> <: List<? super C<C<Byte>>>
Step 3)    List<List<? super C<C<Byte>>>> <: List<? super C<C<Byte>>>
Step 4)    C<C<Byte>> <: List<? super C<C<Byte>>>
Step ...   (expand forever)
```

Figure 2. Example of acyclic proofs in subtyping [8]

explicit constraint would need to make a recursive reference to the wildcard, but wildcards are unnamed so there is no way to reference a wildcard in its own constraint. One might be tempted to encode the constraint explicitly as SortedList<? extends Comparable<?>>, but this does not have the intended semantics because Java will not correlate the wildcard for Comparable with the one for SortedList.

This means that implicit constraints offer more than just convenience; they actually increase the expressiveness of wildcards, producing a compromise between the friendly syntax of wildcards and the expressive power of bounded existential types. However, this expressiveness comes at the cost of complexity and is the source of many of the subtleties behind wildcards.

2.4 Notation

For traditional existential types in which all constraints are explicit, we will use the syntax $\exists\Gamma : \Delta.\ \tau$. The set Γ is the set of bound variables, and the set Δ is *all* constraints on those variables. Constraints in Δ have the form v <:: τ' analogous to extends and v ::> τ' analogous to super. Thus we denote the traditional existential type for the wildcard type SortedList<? super Integer> as ∃X:X ::> Integer, X <:: Comparable<X>. SortedList<X>.

For an example with multiple bound variables, consider the following class declaration that we will use throughout this paper:

```
class Super<P, Q extends P> {}
```

We denote the traditional existential type for the wildcard type Super<?,?> as ∃X, Y:Y <:: X. Super<X,Y>.

3. Non-Termination in Subtyping

The major challenge of subtyping wildcards is non-termination. In particular, with wildcards it is possible for a subtyping algorithm to always be making progress and yet still run forever. This is because there are many sources of infinity in Java's type system, none of which are apparent at first glance. These sources arise from the fact that wildcards are, in terms of existential types, impredicative. That is, List<?> is itself a type and can be used in nearly every location a type without wildcards could be used. For example, the type List<List<?>> stands for List<∃X. List<X>>, whereas it would represent simply ∃X. List<List<X>> in a predicative system.

We have identified three sources of infinity due to impredicativity of wildcards, in particular due to wildcards in the inheritance hierarchy and in type-parameter constraints. The first source is infinite proofs of subtyping. The second source is wildcard types that represent infinite traditional existential types. The third source is proofs that are finite when expressed using wildcards but infinite using traditional existential types. Here we illustrate each of these challenges for creating a terminating subtyping algorithm.

3.1 Infinite Proofs

Kennedy and Pierce provide excellent simple examples illustrating some basic difficulties with wildcards [8] caused by the fact that wildcards can be used in the inheritance hierarchy. In particular, their examples demonstrate that with wildcards it is quite possible for the question of whether τ is a subtype of τ' to recursively depend on whether τ is a subtype of τ' in a non-trivial way. Consider the program in Figure 1 and the question "Is C is subtype of List<? super C>?". The bottom part of the figure contains the steps in a potential proof for answering this question. We start with the goal of showing that C is a subtype of List<? super C>. For this goal to hold, C's superclass List<List<? super C>> must be a subtype of List<? super C> (Step 1). For this to hold, List<List<? super C>> must be List of some supertype of C, so C must be a subtype of List<? super C> (Step 2). This was our original question, though, so whether C is a subtype of List<? super C> actually depends on itself non-trivially. This means that we can actually prove C is a subtype of List<? super C> *provided* we use an infinite proof.

The proof for Figure 1 repeats itself, but there are even subtyping proofs that expand forever without ever repeating themselves. For example, consider the program in Figure 2, which is a simple modification of the program in Figure 1. The major difference is that C now has a type parameter P and in the superclass the type argument to C is C<P> (which could just as easily be List<P> or Set<P> without affecting the structure of the proof). This is known as expansive inheritance [8, 19] since the type parameter P expands to the type argument C<P> corresponding to that same type parameter P. Because of this expansion, the proof repeats itself every four steps except with an extra C<-> layer so that the proof is acyclic.

Java rejects all infinite proofs [5: Chapter 4.10], and javac attempts to enforce this decision, rejecting the program in Figure 1 but suffering a stack overflow on the program in Figure 2. Thus, neither of the subtypings in Figures 1 and 2 hold according to Java. Although this seems natural, as induction is generally preferred over coinduction, it seems that for Java this is actually an inconsistent choice for reasons we will illustrate in Section 3.3. In our type system, infinite proofs are not even possible, avoiding the need to choose whether to accept or reject infinite proofs. Our simple recursive subtyping algorithm terminates because of this.

3.2 Implicitly Infinite Types

Wehr and Thiemann proved that subtyping of bounded impredicative existential types is undecidable [20]. Wildcards are a restricted form of existential types though, so their proof does not imply that subtyping of wildcards is undecidable. However, we have determined that there are wildcard types that actually cannot be expressed by Wehr and Thiemann's type system. In particular, Wehr and Thiemann use *finite* existential types in which all constraints are explicit, but making all implicit constraints on wildcards explicit can actually result in an *infinite* traditional existential type.

Consider the following class declaration:

```
class Infinite<P extends Infinite<?>> {}
```

The wildcard type Infinite<?> translates to an infinite traditional existential type because its implicit constraints must be made explicit. In one step it translates to ∃X : X <:: Infinite<?>. Infinite<X>, but then the nested Infinite<?> needs to be recursively translated which

Java Wildcards

`class C extends Super<Super<?,?>,C> {}`

Is `C` a subtype of `Super<?,?>`?

Steps of Proof

`C <: Super<?,?>`
`Super<Super<?,?>,C> <: Super<?,?>` (inheritance)
(completes)

Traditional Existential Types

`class C extends Super<∃X,Y:Y <:: X. Super<X,Y>,C> {}`

Is `C` a subtype of `∃X',Y':Y' <:: X'. Super<X',Y'>`?

Steps of Proof

`C <: ∃X',Y':Y' <:: X'. Super<X',Y'>`
`Super<∃X,Y:Y <:: X. Super<X,Y>,C> <: ∃X',Y':Y' <:: X'. Super<X',Y'>`
`C <: ∃X,Y:Y <:: X. Super<X,Y>`
(repeats forever)

Figure 3. Example of an implicitly infinite subtyping proof

repeats ad infinitum. Thus `Infinite<?>` is implicitly infinite. Interestingly, this type is actually inhabitable by the following class:

```
class Omega extends Infinite<Omega> {}
```

This means that wildcards are even more challenging than had been believed so far. In fact, a modification like the one for Figure 2 can be applied to get a wildcard type which implicitly represents an acyclically infinite type. Because of implicitly infinite types, one cannot expect structural recursion using implicit constraints to terminate, severely limiting techniques for a terminating subtyping algorithm. Our example illustrating this problem is complex, so we leave it until Section 4.4. Nonetheless, we were able to surmount this challenge by extracting implicit constraints lazily and relying only on finiteness of the explicit type.

3.3 Implicitly Infinite Proofs

Possibly the most interesting aspect of Java's wildcards is that finite proofs of subtyping wildcards can actually express infinite proofs of subtyping traditional existential types. This means that subtyping with wildcards is actually more powerful than traditional systems for subtyping with existential types because traditional systems only permit finite proofs. Like before, implicitly infinite proofs can exist because of implicit constraints on wildcards.

To witness how implicitly infinite proofs arise, consider the programs and proofs in Figure 3. On the left, we provide the program and proof in terms of wildcards. On the right, we provide the translation of that program and proof to traditional existential types. The left proof is finite, whereas the right proof is infinite. The key difference stems from the fact that Java does not check implicit constraints on wildcards when they are instantiated, whereas these constraints are made explicit in the translation to traditional existential types and so need to be checked, leading to an infinite proof.

To understand why this happens, we need to discuss implicit constraints more. Unlike explicit constraints, implicit constraints on wildcards do not need to be checked after instantiation in order to ensure soundness because those implicit constraints must already hold *provided* the subtype is a valid type (meaning its type arguments satisfy the criteria for the type parameters). However, while determining whether a type is valid Java uses subtyping which implicitly assumes all types involved are valid, potentially leading to an implicitly infinite proof. In Figure 3, `Super<Super<?,?>,C>` is a valid type provided `C` is a subtype of `Super<?,?>`. By inheritance, this reduces to whether `Super<Super<?,?>,C>` is a subtype of `Super<?,?>`. The implicit constraints on the wildcards in `Super<?,?>` are not checked because Java implicitly assumes `Super<Super<?,?>,C>` is a valid type. Thus the proof that `Super<Super<?,?>,C>` is valid implicitly assumes that `Super<Super<?,?>,C>` is valid, which is the source of infinity after translation. This example can be modified similarly to Figure 2 to produce a proof that is implicitly acyclically infinite.

Implicitly infinite proofs are the reason why Java's rejection of infinite proofs is an inconsistent choice. The programs and proofs

`class C<P extends List<? super C<D>>> implements List<P> {}`
Decl. 1) `class D implements List<C<?>> {}`
Decl. 2) `class D implements List<C<? extends List<? super C<D>>>> {}`

Is `C<D>` a valid type?

Using Declaration 1

`D <: List<? super C<D>>` (check constraint on `P`)
`List<C<?>> <: List<? super C<D>>` (inheritance)
`C<D> <: C<?>` (check wildcard `? super C<D>`)
Accepted (implicitly assumes `C<D>` is valid)

Using Declaration 2

`D <: List<? super C<D>>`
`List<C<? extends List<? super C<D>>>> <: List<? super C<D>>`
`C<D> <: C<? extends List<? super C<D>>>`
`D <: List<? super C<D>>`
Rejected (implicit assumption above is explicit here)

Figure 4. Example of the inconsistency of rejecting infinite proofs

in Figure 4 are a concrete example illustrating the inconsistency. We provide two declarations for class `D` which differ only in that the constraint on the wildcard is implicit in the first declaration and explicit in the second declaration. Thus, one would expect these two programs to be equivalent in that one would be valid if and only if the other is valid. However, this is not the case in Java because Java rejects infinite proofs. The first program is accepted because the proof that `C<D>` is a valid type is finite. However, the second program is rejected because the proof that `C<D>` is a valid type is infinite. In fact, `javac` accepts the first program but suffers a stack overflow on the second program. Thus Java's choice to reject infinite proofs is inconsistent with its use of implicit constraints. Interestingly, when expressed using traditional existential types, the (infinite) proof for the first program is exactly the same as the (infinite) proof for the second program as one would expect given that they only differ syntactically, affirming that existential types are a suitable formalization of wildcards.

Note that none of the wildcard types in Figures 3 and 4 are implicitly infinite. This means that, even if one were to prevent proofs that are infinite using subtyping rules for wildcards and prevent implicitly infinite wildcard types so that one could translate to traditional existential types, a subtyping algorithm can still always make progress and yet run forever. Our algorithm avoids these problems by not translating to traditional or even finite existential types.

4. Improved Subtyping

Now that we have presented the many non-termination challenges in subtyping wildcards, we present our subtyping rules with a simple sound and complete subtyping algorithm which always termi-

```
class C<P extends Number> extends ArrayList<P> {}
List<? extends List<? extends Number>> cast(List<C<?>> list)
  {return list;}
```

Figure 5. Example of subtyping incorrectly rejected by `javac`

$$
\begin{aligned}
\overset{\exists}{\tau} &:= v \mid \exists\Gamma:\Delta(\Delta).\, C\langle\overset{\exists}{\tau},\ \ldots,\ \overset{\exists}{\tau}\rangle \\
\Gamma &:= \varnothing \mid \Gamma, v \\
\Delta &:= \varnothing \mid \Delta, v <:: \overset{\exists}{\tau} \mid \Delta, v ::> \overset{\exists}{\tau}
\end{aligned}
$$

Figure 6. Grammar of our existential types (coinductive)

SUB-EXISTS

$$
\frac{\begin{array}{c}
C\langle P_1,\ \ldots,\ P_m\rangle \text{ is a subclass of } D\langle\bar{\tau}_1,\ \ldots,\ \bar{\tau}_n\rangle \\
\Gamma, \Gamma \xleftarrow{\varnothing} \Gamma' \vdash D\langle\bar{\tau}_1,\ \ldots,\ \bar{\tau}_n\rangle[P_1 \mapsto \overset{\exists}{\tau}_1, \ldots, P_m \mapsto \overset{\exists}{\tau}_m] \approx_\theta D\langle\overset{\exists}{\tau}'_1,\ \ldots,\ \overset{\exists}{\tau}'_n\rangle \\
\text{for all } i \text{ in } 1 \text{ to } n,\ \ \mathbf{\Gamma}, \Gamma : \mathbf{\Delta}, \Delta \vdash \bar{\tau}_i[P_1 \mapsto \overset{\exists}{\tau}_1, \ldots, P_m \mapsto \overset{\exists}{\tau}_m] \cong \overset{\exists}{\tau}'_i[\theta] \\
\text{for all } v <:: \hat{\tau} \text{ in } \Delta',\ \ \mathbf{\Gamma}, \Gamma : \mathbf{\Delta}, \Delta \vdash \theta(v) <: \hat{\tau}[\theta] \\
\text{for all } v ::> \hat{\tau} \text{ in } \Delta',\ \ \mathbf{\Gamma}, \Gamma : \mathbf{\Delta}, \Delta \vdash \hat{\tau}[\theta] <: \theta(v)
\end{array}}{\mathbf{\Gamma} : \mathbf{\Delta} \vdash \exists\Gamma:\Delta(\Delta).\, C\langle\overset{\exists}{\tau}_1,\ \ldots,\ \overset{\exists}{\tau}_m\rangle <: \exists\Gamma':\Delta'(\Delta').\, D\langle\overset{\exists}{\tau}'_1,\ \ldots,\ \overset{\exists}{\tau}'_n\rangle}
$$

SUB-VAR

$$
\frac{}{\mathbf{\Gamma} : \mathbf{\Delta} \vdash v <: v}
$$

$$
\frac{v <:: \overset{\exists}{\tau} \text{ in } \mathbf{\Delta} \qquad \mathbf{\Gamma} : \mathbf{\Delta} \vdash \overset{\exists}{\tau} <: \overset{\exists}{\tau}'}{\mathbf{\Gamma} : \mathbf{\Delta} \vdash v <: \overset{\exists}{\tau}'}
$$

$$
\frac{v ::> \overset{\exists}{\tau}' \text{ in } \mathbf{\Delta} \qquad \mathbf{\Gamma} : \mathbf{\Delta} \vdash \overset{\exists}{\tau} <: \overset{\exists}{\tau}'}{\mathbf{\Gamma} : \mathbf{\Delta} \vdash \overset{\exists}{\tau} <: v}
$$

Figure 7. Subtyping rules for our existential types (inductive and coinductive definitions coincide given restrictions)

nates even when the wildcard types and proofs involved are implicitly infinite. We impose two simple restrictions, which in Section 9 we demonstrate already hold in existing code bases. With these restrictions, our subtype system has the property that all possible proofs are finite, although they may still translate to infinite proofs using subtyping rules for traditional existential types. Even without restrictions, our algorithm improves on the existing subtyping algorithm since `javac` fails to type check the simple program in Figure 5 that our algorithm determines is valid. Here we provide the core aspects of our subtyping rules and algorithms; the full details can be found in our technical report [15].

4.1 Existential Formalization

We formalize wildcards using existential types. However, we do not use traditional existential types. Our insight is to use a variant that bridges the gap between wildcards, where constraints can be implicit, and traditional existential types, where all constraints must be explicit. We provide the grammar for our existential types, represented by $\overset{\exists}{\tau}$, in Figure 6.

Note that there are two sets of constraints so that we denote our existential types as $\exists\Gamma : \Delta(\Delta).\ \overset{\exists}{\tau}$. The constraints Δ are the constraints corresponding to traditional existential types, combining both the implicit and explicit constraints on wildcards. The constraints Δ are those corresponding to explicit constraints on wildcards, with the parenthetical indicating that only those constraints need to be checked during subtyping.

Our types are a mix of inductive and coinductive structures, meaning finite and infinite. Most components are inductive so that we may do structural recursion and still have termination. However, the combined constraints Δ are coinductive. This essentially means that they are constructed on demand rather than all ahead of time. This corresponds to only performing wildcard capture when it is absolutely necessary. In this way we can handle wildcards representing implicitly infinite types as in Section 3.2.

4.2 Existential Subtyping

We provide the subtyping rules for our existential types in Figure 7 (for sake of simplicity, throughout this paper we assume all problems with name hiding are taken care of implicitly). The judgement $\mathbf{\Gamma} : \mathbf{\Delta} \vdash \overset{\exists}{\tau} <: \overset{\exists}{\tau}'$ means that $\overset{\exists}{\tau}$ is a subtype of $\overset{\exists}{\tau}'$ in the context of type variables $\mathbf{\Gamma}$ with constraints $\mathbf{\Delta}$. The subtyping rules are syntax directed and so are easily adapted into an algorithm. Furthermore, given the restrictions we impose in Section 4.4, the inductive and coinductive definitions coincide, meaning there is no distinction between finite and infinite proofs. From this, we deduce that our algorithm terminates since all proofs are finite.

The bulk of our algorithm lies in SUB-EXISTS, since SUB-VAR just applies assumed constraints on the type variable at hand. The first premise of SUB-EXISTS examines the inheritance hierarchy to determine which, if any, invocations of D that C is a subclass or subinterface of (including reflexivity and transitivity). For Java this invocation is always unique, although this is not necessary for our algorithm. The second premise adapts unification to existential types permitting equivalence and including the prevention of escaping type variables. The third premise checks that each pair of corresponding type arguments are equivalent for some chosen definition of equivalence such as simple syntactic equality or more powerful definitions as discussed in Sections 7.3 and 8.3. The fourth and fifth premises recursively check that the explicit constraints in the supertype hold after instantiation. Note that only the explicit constraints Δ' in the supertype are checked, whereas the combined implicit and explicit constraints Δ in the subtype are assumed. This separation is what enables termination and completeness.

We have no rule indicating that all types are subtypes of `Object`. This is because our existential type system is designed so that such a rule arises as a consequence of other properties. In this case, it arises from the fact `Object` is a superclass of all classes and interfaces in Java and the fact that all variables in Java are implicitly constrained above by `Object`. In general, the separation of implicit and explicit constraints enables our existential type system to adapt to new settings, including settings outside of Java. General reflexivity and transitivity are also consequences of our rules. In fact, the omission of transitivity is actually a key reason that the inductive and coinductive definitions coincide.

Although we do not need the full generality of our existential types and proofs to handle wildcards, this generality informs which variations of wildcards and existential types would still ensure our algorithm terminates. In Section 10, we will present a few such extensions compatible with our existential types and proofs.

4.3 Wildcard Subtyping

While the existential formalization is useful for understanding and generalizing wildcards, we can specialize the algorithm to wildcards for a more direct solution. We present this specialization of our algorithm in Figure 8, with τ representing a Java type and $\overset{?}{\tau}$ representing a Java type argument which may be a (constrained) wildcard. The function *explicit* takes a list of type arguments that may be (explicitly bound) wildcards, converts wildcards to type variables, and outputs the list of fresh type variables, explicit bounds on those type variables, and the possibly converted type arguments. For example, *explicit*(`Numbers<? super Integer>`) returns $\langle$`X`; `X` $::>$ `Integer`; `Numbers<X>`$\rangle$. The function *implicit* takes a list

$$\textsc{Sub-Exists}\quad \dfrac{\begin{array}{c} C\langle P_1,\ \ldots,\ P_m\rangle \text{ is a subclass of } D\langle\bar{\tau}_1,\ \ldots,\ \bar{\tau}_n\rangle \\ \mathit{explicit}(\overset{?}{\tau}_1,\ldots,\overset{?}{\tau}_m) = \langle\Gamma;\Delta\!\!\!\cdot\,;\tau_1,\ldots,\tau_m\rangle \\ \mathit{explicit}(\overset{?}{\tau}{}'_1,\ldots,\overset{?}{\tau}{}'_n) = \langle\Gamma';\Delta\!\!\!\cdot\,';\tau'_1,\ldots,\tau'_n\rangle \\ \mathit{implicit}(\Gamma;C;\tau_1,\ldots,\tau_m) = \Delta\!\!\!\circ \\ \text{for all } i \text{ in } 1 \text{ to } n,\ \bar{\tau}_i[P_1\mapsto\tau_1,\ldots,P_m\mapsto\tau_m] = \tau'_i[\theta] \\ \text{for all } v <:: \hat{\tau} \text{ in } \Delta\!\!\!\cdot\,',\ \ \Gamma,\Gamma : \mathbf{\Delta}, \Delta\!\!\!\circ, \Delta\!\!\!\cdot \vdash \theta(v) <: \hat{\tau} \\ \text{for all } v ::> \hat{\tau} \text{ in } \Delta\!\!\!\cdot\,',\ \ \Gamma,\Gamma : \mathbf{\Delta}, \Delta\!\!\!\circ, \Delta\!\!\!\cdot \vdash \hat{\tau} <: \theta(v) \end{array}}{\Gamma : \mathbf{\Delta} \vdash C\langle\overset{?}{\tau}_1,\ \ldots,\ \overset{?}{\tau}_m\rangle <: D\langle\overset{?}{\tau}{}'_1,\ \ldots,\ \overset{?}{\tau}{}'_n\rangle}$$

$$\textsc{Sub-Var}\quad \dfrac{}{\Gamma : \mathbf{\Delta} \vdash v <: v}$$

$$\dfrac{v <:: \tau \text{ in } \mathbf{\Delta}\quad \Gamma{:}\mathbf{\Delta} \vdash \tau <: \tau'}{\Gamma : \mathbf{\Delta} \vdash v <: \tau'} \qquad \dfrac{v ::> \tau' \text{ in } \mathbf{\Delta}\quad \Gamma{:}\mathbf{\Delta} \vdash \tau <: \tau'}{\Gamma : \mathbf{\Delta} \vdash \tau <: v}$$

Figure 8. Subtyping rules specialized for wildcards

of constrainable type variables, a class or interface name C, and a list of type arguments, and outputs the constraints on those type arguments that are constrainable type variables as prescribed by the requirements of the corresponding type parameters of C, constraining a type variable by `Object` if there are no other constraints. For example, *implicit*(`X`; `Numbers`; `X`) returns `X` $<::$ `Number`. Thus, applying *explicit* and then *implicit* accomplishes wildcard capture. Note that for the most part $\Delta\!\!\!\cdot$ and $\Delta\!\!\!\circ$ combined act as Δ does in Figure 7.

4.4 Termination

Unfortunately, our algorithm does not terminate without imposing restrictions on the Java language. Fortunately, the restrictions we impose are simple, as well as practical as we will demonstrate in Section 9. Our first restriction is on the inheritance hierarchy.

Inheritance Restriction

For every declaration of a direct superclass or superinterface τ of a class or interface, the syntax `? super` *must not occur within τ.*

Note that the programs leading to infinite proofs in Section 3.1 (and in the upcoming Section 4.5) violate our inheritance restriction. This restriction is most similar to a significant relaxation of the contravariance restriction that Kennedy and Pierce showed enables decidable subtyping for declaration-site variance [8]. Their restriction prohibits contravariance altogether, whereas we only restrict its usage. Furthermore, as Kennedy and Pierce mention [8], wildcards are a more expressive domain than declaration-site variance. We will discuss these connections more in Section 10.1.

Constraints on type parameters also pose problems for termination. The constraint context can simulate inheritance, so by constraining a type parameter `P` to extend `List<List<? super P>>` we encounter the same problem as in Figure 1 but this time expressed in terms of type-parameter constraints. Constraints can also produce implicitly infinite types that enable infinite proofs even when our inheritance restriction is satisfied, such as in Figure 9 (which again causes `javac` to suffer a stack overflow). To prevent problematic forms of constraint contexts and implicitly infinite types, we restrict the constraints that can be placed on type parameters.

Parameter Restriction

For every parameterization `<`P_1 `extends` τ_1`, ...,` P_n `extends` τ_n`>`, *every syntactic occurrence in τ_i of a type* C`<..., ? super` τ`, ...>` *must be at a covariant location in τ_i.*

Note that our parameter restriction still allows type parameters to be constrained to extend types such as `Comparable<? super P>`, a well known design pattern. Also note that the inheritance restriction

```
class C<P extends List<List<? extends List<? super C<?>>>>>
  implements List<P> {}
```

Is `C<?>` **a subtype of** `List<? extends List<? super C<?>>>`**?**

Steps of Proof

```
C<?> <?: List<? extends List<? super C<?>>>
    C<?> ↦ C<X> with X <:: List<List<? extends List<? super C<?>>>>
C<X> <?: List<? extends List<? super C<?>>>
X <?: List<? super C<?>>
List<List<? extends List<? super C<?>>>> <?: List<? super C<?>>
C<?> <?: List<? extends List<? super C<?>>>
(repeats forever)
```

Figure 9. Example of infinite proof due to implicitly infinite types

is actually the conjunction of the parameter restriction and Java's restriction that no direct superclass or superinterface may have a wildcard as a type argument [5: Chapters 8.1.4 and 8.1.5].

With these restrictions we can finally state our key theorem.

Subtyping Theorem. *Given the inheritance and parameter restrictions, the algorithm prescribed by the rules in Figure 8 always terminates. Furthermore it is a sound and complete implementation of the subtyping rules in the Java language specification [5: Chapter 4.10.2] provided all types are valid according to the Java language specification [5: Chapter 4.5].*‡

Proof. Here we only discuss the reasons for our restrictions; the full proofs can be found in our technical report [15]. The first thing to notice is that, for the most part, the supertype shrinks through the recursive calls. There are only two ways in which it can grow: applying a lower-bound constraint on a type variable via Sub-Var, and checking an explicit lower bound on a wildcard via Sub-Exists. The former does not cause problems because of the limited ways a type variable can get a lower bound. The latter is the key challenge because it essentially swaps the subtype and supertype which, if unrestricted, can cause non-termination. However, we determined that there are only two ways to increase the number of swaps that can happen: inheritance, and constraints on type variables. Our inheritance and parameter restrictions prevent this, capping the number of swaps that can happen from the beginning and guaranteeing termination. □

4.5 Expansive Inheritance

Smith and Cartwright conjectured that prohibiting expansive inheritance as defined by Kennedy and Pierce [8] would provide a sound and complete subtyping algorithm [13]. This is because Kennedy and Pierce built off the work by Viroli [19] to prove that, by prohibiting expansive inheritance, any infinite proof of subtyping in their setting would have to repeat itself; thus a sound and complete algorithm could be defined by detecting repetitions.

Unfortunately, we have determined that prohibiting expansive inheritance as defined by Kennedy and Pierce does not imply that all infinite proofs repeat. Thus, their algorithm adapted to wildcards does not terminate. The problem is that implicit constraints can cause an indirect form of expansion that is unaccounted for.

Consider the class declaration in Figure 10. According to the definition by Kennedy and Pierce [8], this is not expansive inheritance since `List<Q>` is the type argument corresponding to `P` rather than to `Q`. However, the proof in Figure 10 never repeats itself. The key observation to make is that the context, which would be fixed in Kennedy and Pierce's setting, is continually expanding in this

‡ See Section 7.4 for a clarification on type validity.

```
class C<P, Q extends P> implements List<List<? super C<List<Q>,?>>> {}
```

Is `C<?,?>` a subtype of `List<? super C<?,?>>`?

Constraints	Subtyping (wildcard capture done automatically)
$X_1 <:: X_0$	$C<X_0,X_1> \lessdot: List<? super C<?,?>>$
$Y_1 <:: Y_0$	$C<Y_0,Y_1> \lessdot: List<? super C<List<X_1>,?>>$
$X_2 <:: List<X_1>$	$C<List<X_1>,X_2> \lessdot: List<? super C<List<Y_1>,?>>$
$Y_2 <:: List<Y_1>$	$C<List<Y_1>,Y_2> \lessdot: List<? super C<List<X_2>,?>>$
$X_3 <:: List<X_2>$	$C<List<X_2>,X_3> \lessdot: List<? super C<List<Y_2>,?>>$
$Y_3 <:: List<Y_2>$	$C<List<Y_2>,Y_3> \lessdot: List<? super C<List<X_3>,?>>$
$X_4 <:: List<X_3>$	$C<List<X_3>,X_4> \lessdot: List<? super C<List<Y_3>,?>>$
	(continue forever)

Figure 10. Example of expansion through implicit constraints

```
class Var {
  boolean mValue;
  void addTo(List<? super Var> trues, List<? super Var> falses)
    {(mValue ? trues : falses).add(this);}
}
```

Figure 11. Example of valid code erroneously rejected by `javac`

setting. In the last step we display, the second type argument of `C` is a subtype of `List<? extends List<? extends List<?>>>`, which will keep growing as the proof continues. Thus Smith and Cartwright's conjecture for a terminating subtyping algorithm does not hold. In our technical report we identify syntactic restrictions that would be necessary (although possibly still not sufficient) to adapt Kennedy and Pierce's algorithm to wildcards [15]. However, these restrictions are significantly more complex than ours, and the adapted algorithm would be strictly more complex than ours.

5. Challenges of Type-Argument Inference

So far we have discussed only one major challenge of wildcards, subtyping, and our solution to this challenge. Now we present another major challenge of wildcards, inference of type arguments for generic methods, with our techniques to follow in Section 6.

5.1 Joins

Java has the expression `cond ? t : f` which evaluates to `t` if `cond` evaluates to true, and to `f` otherwise. In order to determine the type of this expression, it is useful to be able to combine the types determined for `t` and `f` using a $join(\tau, \tau')$ function which returns the most precise common supertype of τ and τ'. Unfortunately, not all pairs of types with wildcards have a join (even if we allow intersection types). For example, consider the types `List<String>` and `List<Integer>`, where `String` implements `Comparable<String>` and `Integer` implements `Comparable<Integer>`. Both `List<String>` and `List<Integer>` are a `List` of something, call it `X`, and in both cases that `X` is a subtype of `Comparable<X>`. So while both `List<String>` and `List<Integer>` are subtypes of simply `List<?>`, they are also subtypes of `List<? extends Comparable<?>>` and of `List<? extends Comparable<? extends Comparable<?>>>` and so on. Thus their join using only wildcards is the undesirable infinite type `List<? extends Comparable<? extends Comparable<? extends ...>>>`.

`javac` addresses this by using an algorithm for finding *some* common supertype of τ and τ' which is not necessarily the most precise. This strategy is incomplete, as we even saw in the classroom when it failed to type check the code in Figure 11. This simple program fails to type check because `javac` determines that the type of `(mValue ? trues : falses)` is `List<?>` rather than the obvious `List<? super Var>`. In particular, `javac`'s algorithm may even fail to return τ when both arguments are the same type τ.

```
<P> P getFirst(List<P> list) {return list.get(0);}
Number getFirstNumber(List<? extends Number> nums)
  {return getFirst(nums);}
Object getFirstNonEmpty(List<String> strs, List<Object> obs)
  {return getFirst(!strs.isEmpty() ? strs : obs);}
Object getFirstNonEmpty2(List<String> strs, List<Integer> ints)
  {return getFirst(!strs.isEmpty() ? strs : ints);}
```

Figure 12. Examples of capture conversion

Smith and Cartwright take a different approach to joining types. They extend the type system with union types [13]. That is, the join of `List<String>` and `List<Integer>` is just `List<String> | List<Integer>` in their system. $\tau \mid \tau'$ is defined to be a supertype of both τ and τ' and a subtype of all common supertypes of τ and τ'. Thus, it is by definition the join of τ and τ' in their extended type system. This works for the code in Figure 11, but in Section 5.2 we will demonstrate the limitations of this solution.

Another direction would be to find a form of existential types beyond wildcards for which joins always exist. For example, using traditional existential types the join of `List<String>` and `List<Integer>` is just $\exists X : X <:: Comparable<X>. List<X>$. However, our investigations suggest that it may be impossible for an existential type system to have both joins and decidable subtyping while being expressive enough to handle common Java code. Therefore, our solution will differ from all of the above.

5.2 Capture Conversion

Java has generic methods as well as generic classes [5: Chapter 8.4.4]. For example, the method `getFirst` in Figure 12 is generic with respect to `P`. Java attempts to infer type arguments for invocations of generic methods [5: Chapter 15.12.2.7], hence the uses of `getFirst` inside the various methods in Figure 12 do not need to be annotated with the appropriate instantiation of `P`. Interestingly, this enables Java to infer type arguments that cannot be expressed by the user. Consider `getFirstNumber`. This method is accepted by `javac`; `P` is instantiated to the type variable for the wildcard `? extends Number`, an instantiation of `P` that the programmer cannot explicitly annotate because the programmer cannot explicitly name the wildcard. Thus, Java is implicitly opening the existential type `List<? extends Number>` to `List<X>` with $X <:: Number$ and then instantiating `P` as `X` so that the return type is `X` which is a subtype of `Number`. This ability to implicitly capture wildcards, known as capture conversion [5: Chapter 5.1.10], is important to working with wildcards but means type inference has to determine when to open a wildcard type.

Smith and Cartwright developed an algorithm for type-argument inference intended to improve upon `javac` [13]. Before going into their algorithm and showing some of its limitations, let us first go back to Figure 11. Notice that the example there, although originally presented as a join example, can be thought of as an inference example by considering the `? :` operator to be like a generic method. In fact, Smith and Cartwright have already shown that type-argument inference inherently requires finding common supertypes of two types [13], a process that is often performed using joins. Thus the ability to join types is closely intertwined with the ability to do type-argument inference. Smith and Cartwright's approach for type-argument inference is based on their union types, which we explained in Section 5.1. Their approach to type inference would succeed on the example from Figure 11, because they use a union type, whereas `javac` incorrectly rejects that program.

Although Smith and Cartwright's approach to type-argument inference improves on Java's approach, their approach is not strictly

```
<P> List<P> singleton(P elem) {return null;}
<Q extends Comparable<?>> Q foo(List<? super Q> list) {return null;}
String typeName(Comparable<?> c) {return "Comparable";}
String typeName(String s) {return "String";}
String typeName(Integer i) {return "Integer";}
String typeName(Calendar c) {return "Calendar";}
boolean ignore() {...};
String ambiguous() {
  return typeName(foo(singleton(ignore() ? "Blah" : 1)));
}
```

Figure 13. Example of ambiguous typing affecting semantics

better than Java's. Consider the method `getFirstNonEmpty` in Figure 12. `javac` accepts `getFirstNonEmpty`, combining `List<String>` and `List<Object>` into `List<?>` and then instantiating `P` to the captured wildcard. Smith and Cartwright's technique, on the other hand, fails to type check `getFirstNonEmpty`. They combine `List<String>` and `List<Object>` into `List<String> | List<Object>`. However, there is no instantiation of `P` so that `List<P>` is a supertype of the union type `List<String> | List<Object>`, so they reject the code. What their technique fails to incorporate in this situation is the capture conversion permitted by Java. For the same reason, they also fail to accept `getFirstNonEmpty2`, although `javac` also fails on this program for reasons that are unclear given the error message. The approach we will present is able to type check all of these examples.

5.3 Ambiguous Types and Semantics

In Java, the type of an expression can affect the semantics of the program, primarily due to various forms of overloading. This is particularly problematic when combining wildcards and type-argument inference. Consider the program in Figure 13. Notice that the value returned by `ambiguous` depends solely on the type of the argument to `typeName`, which is the return type of `foo` which depends on the inferred type arguments for the generic methods `foo` and `singleton`. Using `javac`'s typing algorithms, `ambiguous` returns `"Comparable"`. Using Smith and Cartwright's typing algorithms [13], `ambiguous` returns either `"String"` or `"Integer"` depending on how the types are (arbitrarily) ordered internally. In fact, the answers provided by `javac` and by Smith and Cartwright are not the only possible answers. One could just as well instantiate `P` to `Object` and `Q` to `Calendar` to get `ambiguous` to return `"Calendar"`, even though a `Calendar` instance is not even present in the method.

The above discussion shows that, in fact, *all four* values are plausible, and which is returned depends on the results of type-argument inference. Unfortunately, the Java specification does not provide clear guidance on what should be done if there are multiple valid type arguments. It does however state the following [5: Chapter 15.12.2.7]: "The type-inference algorithm should be viewed as a heuristic, designed to perform well in practice." This would lead one to believe that, given multiple valid type arguments, an implementation can heuristically pick amongst them, which would actually make any of the four returned values a correct implementation of `ambiguous`. This is not only surprising, but also leads to the unfortunate situation that by providing `javac` with smarter static typing algorithms one may actually change the semantics of existing programs. This in turn makes improving the typing algorithms in existing implementations a risky proposition.

6. Improving Type-Argument Inference

Here we present an algorithm for joining wildcards as existential types which addresses the limitations of union types and which is complete provided the construction is used in restricted settings. We also describe preliminary techniques for preventing ambiguity due to type-argument inference as discussed in Section 5.3.

6.1 Lazily Joining Wildcards

As we mentioned in Section 5.1, it seems unlikely that there is an existential type system for wildcards with both joins and decidable subtyping. Fortunately, we have determined a way to extend our type system with a *lazy* existential type that solves many of our problems. Given a potential constraint on the variables bound in a lazy existential type we can determine whether that constraint holds. However, we cannot enumerate the constraints on the variables bound in a lazy existential type, so lazy existential types must be used in a restricted manner. In particular, for any use of $\tau <: \tau'$, lazy existential types may only be used in covariant locations in τ and contravariant locations in τ'. Maintaining this invariant means that τ' will never be a lazy existential type. This is important because applying SUB-EXISTS requires checking all of the constraints of τ', but we have no means of enumerating these constraints for a lazy existential type. Fortunately, `cond ? t : f` as well as unambiguous type-argument inference only need a join for covariant locations of the return type, satisfying our requirement.

So suppose we want to construct the join ($\sqcup$) of captured wildcard types $\exists\Gamma:\Delta.\ C\langle\tau_1,\ \ldots,\ \tau_m\rangle$ and $\exists\Gamma':\Delta'.\ D\langle\tau'_1,\ \ldots,\ \tau'_n\rangle$. Let $\{E_i\}_{i \text{ in } 1 \text{ to } k}$ be the set of minimal raw superclasses and superinterfaces common to C and D. Let each $E_i\langle\bar{\tau}^i_1,\ \ldots,\ \bar{\tau}^i_{\ell_i}\rangle$ be the superclass of $C\langle P_1,\ \ldots,\ P_m\rangle$, and each $E_i\langle\hat{\tau}^i_1,\ \ldots,\ \hat{\tau}^i_{\ell_i}\rangle$ the superclass of $D\langle P'_1,\ \ldots,\ P'_n\rangle$. Compute the anti-unification [11, 12] of all $\bar{\tau}^i_j[P_1{\mapsto}\tau_1, \ldots, P_m{\mapsto}\tau_m]$ with all $\hat{\tau}^i_j[P'_1{\mapsto}\tau'_1, \ldots, P'_n{\mapsto}\tau'_n]$, resulting in $\overset{\sqcup}{\tau}{}^i_j$ with fresh variables $\Gamma_\sqcup$ and assignments θ and θ' such that each $\overset{\sqcup}{\tau}{}^i_j[\theta]$ equals $\bar{\tau}^i_j[P_1{\mapsto}\tau_1, \ldots, P_m{\mapsto}\tau_m]$ and each $\overset{\sqcup}{\tau}{}^i_j[\theta']$ equals $\hat{\tau}^i_j[P'_1 \mapsto \tau'_1, \ldots, P'_n \mapsto \tau'_n]$. For example, the anti-unification of the types `Map<String,String>` and `Map<Integer,Integer>` is `Map<`v`,`v`>` with assignments $v \mapsto$ `String` and $v \mapsto$ `Integer`. The join, then, is the lazy existential type

$$\begin{array}{l}\exists\Gamma_\sqcup : \langle\theta \mapsto \Gamma : \Delta; \theta' \mapsto \Gamma' : \Delta'\rangle. \\ \quad E_1\langle\overset{\sqcup}{\tau}{}^1_1,\ \ldots,\ \overset{\sqcup}{\tau}{}^1_{\ell_1}\rangle\ \&\ \ldots\ \&\ E_k\langle\overset{\sqcup}{\tau}{}^k_1,\ \ldots,\ \overset{\sqcup}{\tau}{}^k_{\ell_k}\rangle\end{array}$$

The lazy constraint $\langle\theta \mapsto \Gamma : \Delta; \theta' \mapsto \Gamma' : \Delta'\rangle$ indicates that the constraints on $\Gamma_\sqcup$ are the constraints that hold in context $\Gamma : \Delta$ after substituting with θ and in context $\Gamma' : \Delta'$ after substituting with θ'. Thus the total set of constraints is not computed, but there is a way to determine whether a constraint is in this set. Note that this is the join because Java ensures the $\bar{\tau}$ and $\hat{\tau}$ types will be unique.

Capture conversion can be applied to a lazy existential type, addressing the key limitation of union types that we identified in Section 5.2. The lazy constraint $\langle\theta \mapsto \Gamma : \Delta; \theta' \mapsto \Gamma' : \Delta'\rangle$ is simply added to the context. The same is done when SUB-EXISTS applies with a lazy existential type as the subtype. When SUB-VAR applies for $v <: \tau'$ with v constrained by a lazy constraint rather than standard constraints, one checks that both $\theta(v) <: \tau'[\theta]$ holds and $\theta'(v) <: \tau'[\theta']$ holds, applying the substitutions to relevant constraints in the context as well. A similar adaptation is also made for $\tau <: v$. This extended algorithm is still guaranteed to terminate.

With this technique, we can type check the code in Figure 11 that `javac` incorrectly rejects as well as the code in Figure 12 including the methods that Smith and Cartwright's algorithm incorrectly rejects. For example, for `getFirstNonEmpty2` we would first join `List<String>` and `List<Integer>` as the lazy existential type

$$\exists \texttt{X} : \langle\{\texttt{X} \mapsto \texttt{String}\} \mapsto \varnothing : \varnothing; \{\texttt{X} \mapsto \texttt{Integer}\} \mapsto \varnothing : \varnothing\rangle.\ \texttt{List<X>}$$

This type would then be capture converted so that the type parameter `P` of `getFirst` would be instantiated with the lazily constrained type variable `X`. Although not necessary here, we would also be able to determine that the constraint `X` $<::$ `Comparable<X>` holds for the lazily constrained type variable.

Occasionally one has to join a type with a type variable. For this purpose, we introduce a specialization of union types. This specialization looks like $\tau_\sqcup(v_1 \mid \ldots \mid v_n)$ or $\tau_\sqcup(\tau \mid v_1 \mid \ldots \mid v_n)$ where each v_i is not lazily constrained and $\tau_\sqcup$ is a supertype of some wildcard capture of each upper bound of each type variable (and of τ if present) with the property that any other non-variable τ' which is a supertype of each v_i (and τ) is also a supertype of $\tau_\sqcup$. A type τ' is a supertype of this specialized union type if it is a supertype of $\tau_\sqcup$ or of each v_i (and τ). Note that $\tau_\sqcup$ might not be a supertype of any v_i or of τ and may instead be the join of the upper bounds of each v_i (plus τ) *after* opening the lazy existential type. This subtlety enables capture conversion to be applied unambiguously when called for. Unfortunately, we cannot join a type with a type variable that is lazily constrained because we cannot enumerate its upper bounds.

6.2 Inferring Unambiguous Types

We believe that the Java language specification should be changed to prevent type-argument inference from introducing ambiguity into the semantics of programs. Since the inferred return type is what determines the semantics, one way to prevent ambiguity would be to permit type-argument inference only when a most precise return type can be inferred, meaning the inferred return type is a subtype of all other return types that could arise from valid type arguments for the invocation at hand. Here we discuss how such a goal affects the design of type-argument inference. However, we do not present an actual algorithm since the techniques we present need to be built upon further to produce an algorithm which prevents ambiguity but is also powerful enough to be practical.

Typical inference algorithms work by collecting a set of constraints and then attempting to determine a solution to those constraints. If those constraints are not guaranteed to be sufficient, then any solution is verified to be a correct typing of the expression (in this case the generic-method invocation). Both `javac` [5: Chapters 15.12.2.7 and 15.12.2.8] and Smith and Cartwright [5] use this approach. Smith and Cartwright actually collect a set of sets of constraints, with each set of constraints guaranteed to be sufficient.

However, to prevent ambiguity due to type-argument inference, necessity of constraints is important rather than sufficiency. For the ambiguous program in Figure 13, each of the solutions we described in Section 5.3 was sufficient; however, none of them were necessary, which was the source of ambiguity. Unfortunately, Smith and Cartwright's algorithm is specialized to find sufficient rather than necessary sets of constraints. This is why their algorithm results in two separate solutions for Figure 13. However, their algorithm could be altered to sacrifice sufficiency for sake of necessity by producing a less precise but necessary constraint at each point where they would currently introduce a disjunction of constraints, which actually simplifies the algorithm since it no longer has to propagate disjunctions.

After a necessary set of constraints has been determined, one then needs to determine a solution. Some constraints will suggest that it is necessary for a type argument to be a specific type, in which case one just checks that the specific type satisfies the other constraints on that type argument. However, other type arguments will only be constrained above and/or below by other types so that there can be many types satisfying the constraints. In order to prevent ambiguity, one cannot simply choose solutions for these type arguments arbitrarily. For example, if the parameterized return type of the method is covariant (and not bivariant) with respect to a type parameter, then the solution for the corresponding type argument must be the join of all its lower bounds, ensuring the inferred return type is the most precise possible. Fortunately, since such joins would occur covariantly in the return type, it is safe to use the construction described in Section 6.1.

Unfortunately, requiring the inferred return type to be the most precise possible seems too restrictive to be practical. Consider the `singleton` method in Figure 13. Under this restriction, type-argument inference would never be permitted for any invocation of `singleton` (without an expected return type) even though the inferred types of most such invocations would not affect the semantics of the program. In light of this, we believe the unambiguous-inference challenge should be addressed by combining the above techniques with an ability to determine when choices can actually affect the semantics of the program. We have had promising findings on this front, but more thorough proofs and evaluations need to be done, so we leave this to future work.

6.3 Removing Intermediate Types

The processes above introduce new kinds of types, namely lazy existential types. Ideally these types need not be a part of the actual type system but rather just be an algorithmic intermediary. Fortunately this is the case for lazy existential types. By examining how the lazy existential type is used while type checking the rest of the program, one can determine how to replace it with an existential type which may be less precise but with which the program will still type check. This is done by tracking the pairs $v <: \tau'$ and $\tau <: v$, where v is lazily constrained, that are checked and found to hold using the modified SUB-VAR rules. After type checking has completed, the lazy existential type can be replaced by an existential type using only the tracked constraints (or slight variations thereof to prevent escaping variables). Proof-tracking techniques can also be used to eliminate intersection types, important for addressing the non-determinism issues we will discuss in Section 7.2, as well as our specialized union types.

7. Challenges of Type Checking

Wildcards pose difficulties for type checking in addition to the subtyping and inference challenges we have discussed so far. Here we identify undesirable aspects of Java's type system caused by these difficulties, and in Section 8 we present simple changes to create an improved type system.

7.1 Inferring Implicit Constraints

Java ensures that all types use type arguments satisfying the criteria of the corresponding type parameters. Without wildcards, enforcing this requirement on type arguments is fairly straightforward. Wildcards, however, complicate matters significantly because there may be a way to implicitly constrain wildcards so that the type arguments satisfy their requirements. For example, consider the following interface declaration:

```
interface SubList<P extends List<? extends Q>, Q> {}
```

Java accepts the type `SubList<?,Number>` because the wildcard can be implicitly constrained to be a subtype of `List<? extends Number>` with which the requirements of the type parameters are satisfied. However, Java rejects the type `SubList<List<Integer>,?>` even though the wildcard can be implicitly constrained to be a supertype of `Integer` with which the requirements of the type parameters are satisfied (in our technical report we formalize when a wildcard can be implicitly constrained [15]). Thus, Java's implicit-constraint inference is incomplete and as a consequence types that could be valid are nonetheless rejected by Java.

This raises the possibility of extending Java to use complete implicit-constraint inference (assuming the problem is decidable). However, we have determined that this would cause significant algorithmic problems (in addition to making it difficult for users to predict which types will be accepted or rejected as illustrated in our technical report [15]). In particular, complete implicit-constraint inference would enable users to express types that have an implicitly infinite body rather than just implicitly infinite constraints. Consider the following class declaration:

```
class C<P extends List<Q>, Q> extends List<C<C<?,?>,?>> {}
```

For the type C<C<?,?>,?> to be valid, C<?,?> must be a subtype of List<X> where X is the last wildcard of C<C<?,?>,?>. Since C<?,?> is a subtype of List<C<C<?,?>,?>>, this implies X must be equal to C<C<?,?>,?>, and with this implicit constraint the type arguments satisfy the requirements of the corresponding type parameters. Now, if we expand the implicit equality on the last wildcard in C<C<?,?>,?> we get the type C<C<?,?>,C<C<?,?>,?>>, which in turn contains the type C<C<?,?>,?> so that we can continually expand to get the infinite type C<C<?,?>,C<C<?,?>,...>>. As one might suspect, infinite types of this form cause non-termination problems for many algorithms.

In light of these observations, we will propose using implicit-constraint inference slightly stronger than Java's in order to address a slight asymmetry in Java's algorithm while still being user friendly as well as compatible with all algorithms in this paper.

7.2 Non-Deterministic Type Checking

The type checker in javac is currently non-deterministic from the user's perspective. Consider the following interface declaration:

```
interface Maps<P extends Map<?,String>> extends List<P> {}
```

javac allows one to declare a program variable m to have type Maps<? extends Map<String,?>>. The type of m, then, has a wildcard which is constrained to be a subtype of both Map<?,String> and Map<String,?>. This means that m.get(0).entrySet() has two types, essentially ∃X. Set<Entry<X,String>> and ∃Y. Set<Entry<String,Y>>, neither of which is a subtype of the other. However, the type-checking algorithm for javac is designed under the assumption that this will never happen, and as such javac only checks whether one of the two options is sufficient for type checking the rest of the program, which is the source of non-determinism.

javac makes this assumption because Java imposes single-instantiation inheritance, meaning a class (or interface) can extend C<τ_1, ..., τ_n> and C<τ'_1, ..., τ'_n> only if each τ_i equals τ'_i [5: Chapter 8.1.5] (in other words, prohibiting multiple-instantiation inheritance [8]). However, it is not clear what single-instantiation inheritance should mean in the presence of wildcards. The Java language specification is ambiguous in this regard [5: Chapter 4.4], and javac's enforcement is too weak for the assumptions made by its algorithms, as demonstrated above.

Thus, we need to reconsider single-instantiation inheritance in detail with wildcards in mind. There are two ways to address this: restrict types in some way, or infer from two constraints a stronger constraint that is consistent with single-instantiation inheritance. We consider the latter first since it is the more expressive option.

Knowing that the wildcard in m's type above is a subtype of both Map<?,String> and Map<String,?>, single-instantiation inheritance suggests that the wildcard is actually a subtype of Map<String,String>. With this more precise constraint, we can determine that the type of m.get(0).entrySet() is Set<Entry<String,String>>, which is a subtype of the two alternatives mentioned earlier. For this strategy to work, given two upper bounds on a wildcard we have to be able to determine their meet: the most general common subtype consistent with single-instantiation inheritance. Interestingly, the meet of two types may not be expressible by the user. For example, the meet of List<?> and Set<?> is ∃X. List<X> & Set<X>.

Unfortunately, meets encounter many of the same problems of complete implicit-constraint inference that we discussed in Section 7.1. Assuming meets can always be computed, predicting when two types have a meet can be quite challenging. Furthermore, meets pose algorithmic challenges, such as for equivalence checking since with them Maps<? extends Map<String,?>> is equivalent to Maps<? extends Map<String,String>> even though neither explicit constraint is redundant.

```
class C implements List<D<? extends List<D<? extends C>>>> {}
class D<P extends C> {}
```

Is D<? extends List<D<? extends C>>>
equivalent to D<? extends C>?

Key Steps of Proof

D<? extends List<D<? extends C>>> $\stackrel{?}{\cong}$ D<? extends C>
(Checking :>) D<? extends C> $<:$ D<? extends List<D<? extends C>>>
C $<:$ List<D<? extends C>>
List<D<? extends List<D<? extends C>>>> $<:$ List<D<? extends C>>
D<? extends List<D<? extends C>>> $\stackrel{?}{\cong}$ D<? extends C>
(repeat forever)

Figure 14. Example of infinite proofs due to equivalence

This problem is not specific to combining implicit and explicit constraints on wildcards. Java allows type parameters to be constrained by intersections of types: <P extends τ_1 & ... & τ_n>. Although Java imposes restrictions on these intersections [5: Chapter 4.4], when wildcards are involved the same problems arise as with combining implicit and explicit constraints. So, while javac rejects the intersection Map<?,String> & Map<String,?>, javac does permit the intersection Numbers<?> & Errors<?>. Should P be constrained by this intersection, then due to the implicit constraints on the wildcards P is a subtype of both List<? extends Number> and List<? extends Error>, which once again introduces non-determinism into javac's type checking.

As a more severe alternative, one might consider throwing out single-instantiation inheritance altogether and redesigning the type checker for multiple-instantiation inheritance, especially if Java decided to also throw out type erasure. However, multiple-instantiation inheritance in the presence of wildcards can actually lead to ambiguity in program semantics. Suppose an object has an implementation of both List<String> and List<Integer>. That object can be passed as a List<?>, but which List implementation is passed depends on whether the wildcard was instantiated with String or Integer. Thus an invocation of get(0) to get an Object from the List<?> (which is valid since the wildcard implicitly extends Object) would return different results depending on the subtyping proof that was constructed (non-deterministically from the user's perspective). Thus a language with wildcards would either need to use single-instantiation inheritance or statically determine when subtyping can ambiguously affect semantics.

After careful consideration, our solution will be to restrict intersections and explicit constraints on wildcards so that they are consistent with single-instantiation inheritance adapted to wildcards.

7.3 Equivalence

Numbers<?> is equivalent to Numbers<? extends Number> because of the implicit constraint on the wildcard. As such, one would expect List<Numbers<?>> to be equivalent to List<Numbers<? extends Number>>. However, this is not the case according to the Java language specification [5: Chapters 4.5.1.1 and 4.10.2] and the formalization by Torgersen et al. [17] referenced therein (although javac makes some attempts to support this). The reason is that Java uses syntactic equality when comparing type arguments, reflected in our SUB-EXISTS rule by the use of = in the fifth premise.

Ideally equivalent types could be used interchangeably. Thus, during subtyping Java should only require type arguments to be equivalent rather than strictly syntactically identical. The obvious way to implement this is to simply check that the type ar-

$$\frac{\mathit{explicit}(\overset{?}{\tau}_1, \ldots, \overset{?}{\tau}_m) = \langle \Gamma; \Delta; \tau_1, \ldots, \tau_m \rangle \qquad \mathit{explicit}(\overset{?}{\tau}'_1, \ldots, \overset{?}{\tau}'_n) = \langle \Gamma'; \Delta'; \tau'_1, \ldots, \tau'_n \rangle \qquad \text{for all} \left\{ \begin{array}{c} C\texttt{<}P_1, \ldots, P_m\texttt{>} \text{ is a subclass of } E\texttt{<}\bar{\tau}_1, \ldots, \bar{\tau}_k\texttt{>} \\ \text{and} \\ D\texttt{<}P'_1, \ldots, P'_n\texttt{>} \text{ is a subclass of } E\texttt{<}\bar{\tau}'_1, \ldots, \bar{\tau}'_k\texttt{>} \end{array} \right\} \text{ and } i \text{ in 1 to } k,\ \bar{\tau}_i[P_1 \mapsto \tau_1, \ldots, P_m \mapsto \tau_m] = \bar{\tau}'_i[P'_1 \mapsto \tau'_1, \ldots, P'_n \mapsto \tau'_n]}{\mathbb{\Gamma} : \mathbf{\Delta} \vdash C\texttt{<}\overset{?}{\tau}_1, \ \ldots, \ \overset{?}{\tau}_m\texttt{>} \sqcap D\texttt{<}\overset{?}{\tau}'_1, \ \ldots, \ \overset{?}{\tau}'_n\texttt{>}}$$

Figure 15. Definition of when two types intersect monomorphically

guments are subtypes of each other, as proposed by Smith and Cartwright [13]. Yet, to our surprise, this introduces another source of infinite proofs and potential for non-termination. We give one such example in Figure 14, and, as with prior examples, this example can be modified so that the infinite proof is acyclic. This example is particularly problematic since it satisfies both our inheritance and parameter restrictions. We will address this problem by canonicalizing types prior to syntactic comparison.

7.4 Inheritance Consistency

Lastly, for sake of completeness we discuss a problem which, although not officially addressed by the Java language specification, appears to already be addressed by `javac`. In particular, the type `Numbers<? super String>` poses an interesting problem. The wildcard is constrained explicitly below by `String` and implicitly above by `Number`. Should this type be opened, then transitivity would imply that `String` is a subtype of `Number`, which is inconsistent with the inheritance hierarchy. One might argue that this is sound because we are opening an uninhabitable type and so the code is unreachable anyways. However, this type is inhabitable because Java allows `null` to have any type. Fortunately, `javac` appears to already prohibit such types, preventing unsoundness in the language. Completeness of our subtyping algorithm actually assumes such types are rejected; we did not state this as an explicit requirement of our theorem because it already holds for Java as it exists in practice.

8. Improved Type System

Here we present a variety of slight changes to Java's type system regarding wildcards in order to rid it of the undesirable properties discussed in Section 7.

8.1 Implicit Lower Bounds

Although we showed in Section 7.1 that using complete implicit-constraint inference is problematic, we still believe Java should use a slightly stronger algorithm. In particular, consider the types `Super<Number,?>` and `Super<?,Integer>`. The former is accepted by Java whereas the latter is rejected. However, should Java permit type parameters to have lower-bound requirements, then the class `Super` might also be declared as

```
class Super<P super Q, Q> {}
```

Using Java's completely syntactic approach to implicit-constraint inference, under this declaration now `Super<Number,?>` would be rejected and `Super<?,Integer>` would be accepted. This is the opposite of before, even though the two class declarations are conceptually equivalent. In light of this, implicit-constraint inference should also infer implicit lower-bound constraints for any wildcard corresponding to a type parameter P with another type parameter Q constrained to extend P. This slight strengthening addresses the asymmetry in Java's syntactic approach while still having predictable behavior from a user's perspective and also being compatible with our algorithms even with the language extensions in Section 10.

8.2 Single-Instantiation Inheritance

We have determined an adaptation of single-instantiation inheritance to existential types, and consequently wildcards, which addresses the non-determinism issues raised in Section 7.2:

> *For all types τ and class or interface names C, if τ has a supertype of the form $\exists\Gamma:\Delta.\ C\texttt{<}\ldots\texttt{>}$, then τ has a most precise supertype of that form.*

Should this be ensured, whenever a variable of type τ is used as an instance of C the type checker can use the most precise supertype of τ with the appropriate form without having to worry about any alternative supertypes.

Java only ensures single-instantiation inheritance with wildcards when τ is a class or interface type, but not when τ is a type variable. Type variables can either be type parameters or captured wildcards, so we need to ensure single-instantiation inheritance in both cases. In order to do this, we introduce a concept we call monomorphically intersecting types, defined in Figure 15.

Conceptually, two types intersect monomorphically if they have no wildcards in common. More formally, for any common superclass or superinterface C, there is a most precise common supertype of the form $C\texttt{<}\tau_1,\ \ldots,\ \tau_n\texttt{>}$ that is monomorphic, meaning none of τ_i is a wildcard type argument. For Java specifically, we should impose additional requirements in Figure 15: C or D must be an interface to reflect single inheritance of classes [5: Chapter 8.1.4], and C and D cannot have any common methods with the same signature but different return types (after erasure) to reflect the fact that no class would be able to extend or implement both C and D [5: Chapter 8.1.5].

Using this new concept, we say that two types validly intersect each other if either is a subtype of the other or they intersect monomorphically. With this, we can impose our restriction ensuring single-instantiation inheritance for type parameters and captured wildcard type variables so that single-instantiation inheritance holds for the entire type system.

Intersection Restriction

For every syntactically occurring intersection τ_1 `&` … `&` τ_n, every τ_i must validly intersect with every other τ_j. For every explicit upper bound τ on a wildcard, τ must validly intersect with all other upper bounds on that wildcard.

This restriction has an ancillary benefit as well. Monomorphically intersecting types have the property that their meet, as discussed in Section 7.2, is simply the intersection of the types. This is not the case for `List<?>` with `Set<?>`, whose meet is `∃X. List<X> & Set<X>`. Our intersection restriction then implies that all intersections coincide with their meet, and so intersection *types* are actually unnecessary in our system. That is, the syntax `P extends` τ_1 `&` … `&` τ_n can simply be interpreted as `P extends` τ_i for each i in 1 to n without introducing an actual type τ_1 `&` … `&` τ_n. Thus our solution addresses the non-determinism issues discussed in Section 7.2 and simplifies the formal type system.

$$\frac{\vdash \tau \mapsto \bar{\tau} \quad \vdash \tau' \mapsto \bar{\tau}' \quad \bar{\tau} = \bar{\tau}'}{\Gamma : \Delta \vdash \tau \cong \tau'}$$

$$\frac{\begin{array}{c} \mathit{explicit}(\overset{?}{\tau}_1, \ldots, \overset{?}{\tau}_n) = \langle \Gamma; \Delta; \tau_1, \ldots, \tau_n \rangle \\ \mathit{implicit}(\Gamma; C; \tau_1, \ldots, \tau_n) = \dot{\Delta} \\ \{v <:: \hat{\tau} \text{ in } \Delta \mid \text{for no } v <:: \hat{\tau}' \text{ in } \dot{\Delta}, \vdash \hat{\tau}' \lessdot \hat{\tau}\} = \Delta_{<::} \\ \{v ::> \hat{\tau} \text{ in } \Delta \mid \text{for no } v ::> \hat{\tau}' \text{ in } \dot{\Delta}, \vdash \hat{\tau} \lessdot \hat{\tau}'\} = \Delta_{::>} \\ \text{for all } i \text{ in 1 to } n, \vdash \tau_i \mapsto \tau_i' \\ \{v <:: \hat{\tau}' \mid v <:: \hat{\tau} \text{ in } \Delta_{<::} \text{ and } \vdash \hat{\tau} \mapsto \hat{\tau}'\} = \Delta'_{<::} \\ \{v ::> \hat{\tau}' \mid v ::> \hat{\tau} \text{ in } \Delta_{::>} \text{ and } \vdash \hat{\tau} \mapsto \hat{\tau}'\} = \Delta'_{::>} \\ \langle \Gamma; \Delta'_{<::}, \Delta'_{::>}; \tau_1', \ldots, \tau_n' \rangle = \mathit{explicit}(\overset{?}{\tau}{}_1', \ldots, \overset{?}{\tau}{}_n') \end{array}}{\vdash C\langle \overset{?}{\tau}_1, \ldots, \overset{?}{\tau}_n \rangle \mapsto C\langle \overset{?}{\tau}{}_1', \ldots, \overset{?}{\tau}{}_n' \rangle}$$

$$\frac{}{\vdash v \mapsto v}$$

$$\frac{\begin{array}{c} \mathit{explicit}(\overset{?}{\tau}_1, \ldots, \overset{?}{\tau}_n) = \langle \Gamma; \Delta; \tau_1, \ldots, \tau_n \rangle \\ \mathit{explicit}(\overset{?}{\tau}{}_1', \ldots, \overset{?}{\tau}{}_n') = \langle \Gamma'; \Delta'; \tau_1', \ldots, \tau_n' \rangle \\ \text{for all } i \text{ in 1 to } n, \text{ if } \tau_i' \text{ in } \Gamma' \text{ then } \tau_i = \tau_i'[\theta] \text{ else } \tau_i \text{ not in } \Gamma \\ \mathit{implicit}(\Gamma; C; \tau_1, \ldots, \tau_n) = \dot{\Delta} \\ \text{for all } v <:: \hat{\tau} \text{ in } \Delta', \ \theta(v) <:: \hat{\tau}' \text{ in } \dot{\Delta}, \Delta \text{ with } \vdash \hat{\tau}' \lessdot \hat{\tau} \\ \text{for all } v ::> \hat{\tau} \text{ in } \Delta', \ \theta(v) ::> \hat{\tau}' \text{ in } \dot{\Delta}, \Delta \text{ with } \vdash \hat{\tau} \lessdot \hat{\tau}' \end{array}}{\vdash C\langle \overset{?}{\tau}_1, \ldots, \overset{?}{\tau}_n \rangle \lessdot C\langle \overset{?}{\tau}{}_1', \ldots, \overset{?}{\tau}{}_n' \rangle}$$

$$\frac{}{\vdash v \lessdot v}$$

Figure 16. Rules for equivalence via canonicalization

8.3 Canonicalization

In order to support interchangeability of equivalent types we can apply canonicalization prior to all checks for syntactic equality. To enable this approach, we impose one last restriction.

Equivalence Restriction

For every explicit upper bound τ on a wildcard, τ must not be a strict supertype of any other upper bound on that wildcard. For every explicit lower bound τ on a wildcard, τ must be a supertype of every other lower bound on that wildcard.

With this restriction, we can canonicalize wildcard types by removing redundant explicit constraints under the assumption that the type is valid. By assuming type validity, we do not have to check equivalence of type arguments, enabling us to avoid the full challenges that subtyping faces. This means that the type validator must check original types rather than canonicalized types. Subtyping may be used inside these validity checks which may in turn use canonicalization possibly assuming type validity of the type being checked, but such indirect recursive assumptions are acceptable since our formalization permits implicitly infinite proofs.

Our canonicalization algorithm is formalized as the $\mapsto$ operation in Figure 16. Its basic strategy is to identify and remove all redundant constraints. The primary tool is the $\lessdot$ relation, an implementation of subtyping specialized to be sound and complete between class and interface types only if τ is a supertype of τ' or they intersect monomorphically.

Equivalence Theorem. *Given the parameter restriction, the algorithm prescribed by the rules in Figure 16 terminates. Given the intersection and equivalence restrictions, the algorithm is furthermore a sound and nearly complete implementation of type equivalence provided all types are valid according to the Java language specification [5: Chapter 4.5].*

Proof. Here we only discuss how our restrictions enable soundness and completeness; the full proofs can be found in our technical report [15]. The equivalence restriction provides soundness and near completeness by ensuring the assumptions made by the $\lessdot$ relation hold. The intersection restriction provides completeness by ensuring that non-redundant explicit bounds are unique up to equivalence so that syntactic equality after recursively removing all redundant constraints is a complete means for determining equivalence. □

We say our algorithm is nearly complete because it is complete on class and interface types but not on type variables. Our algorithm will only determine that a type variable is equivalent to itself. While type parameters can only be equivalent to themselves, captured wildcard type variables can be equivalent to other types. Consider the type `Numbers<? super Number>` in which the wildcard is constrained explicitly below by `Number` and implicitly above by `Number` so that the wildcard is equivalent to `Number`. Using our algorithm, `Numbers<? super Number>` is not a subtype of `Numbers<Number>`, which would be subtypes should one use a complete equivalence algorithm. While from a theoretical perspective this seems to be a weakness, as Summers et al. have argued [14], from a practical perspective it is a strength since it forces programmers to use the more precise type whenever they actually rely on that extra precision rather than obscure it through implicit equivalences. Plus, our weaker notion of equivalence is still strong enough to achieve our goal of allowing equivalent types to be used interchangeably (provided they satisfy all applicable restrictions). As such, we consider our nearly complete equivalence algorithm to be sufficient and even preferable to a totally complete algorithm.

9. Evaluation of Restrictions

One might consider many of the examples in this paper to be contrived. Indeed, a significant contribution of our work is identifying restrictions that reject such contrived examples but still permit the Java code that actually occurs in practice. Before imposing our restrictions on Java, it is important to ensure that they are actually compatible with existing code bases and design patterns.

To this end, we conducted a large survey of open-source Java code. We examined a total of 10 projects, including NetBeans (3.9 MLOC), Eclipse (2.3 MLOC), OpenJDK 6 (2.1 MLOC), and Google Web Toolkit (0.4 MLOC). As one of these projects we included our own Java code from a prior research project because it made heavy use of generics and rather complex use of wildcards. Altogether the projects totalled 9.2 million lines of Java code with 3,041 generic classes and interfaces out of 94,781 total (ignoring anonymous classes). To examine our benchmark suite, we augmented the OpenJDK 6 compiler to collect statistics on the code it compiled. Here we present our findings.

To evaluate our inheritance restriction, we analyzed all declarations of direct superclasses and superinterfaces that occurred in our suite. In Figure 17, we present in logarithmic scale how many of the 118,918 declared superclasses and superinterfaces had type arguments and used wildcards and with what kind of constraints. If a class or interface declared multiple direct superclasses and superinterfaces, we counted each declaration separately. Out of all these declarations, *none* of them violated our inheritance restriction.

To evaluate our parameter restriction, we analyzed all constraints on type parameters for classes, interfaces, and methods that occurred in our suite. In Figure 18, we break down how the 2,003 parameter constraints used type arguments, wildcards, and constrained wildcards. Only 36 type-parameter constraints contained the syntax `? super`. We manually inspected these 36 cases and determined that out of all type-parameter constraints, *none* of them violated our parameter restriction. Interestingly, we found no case

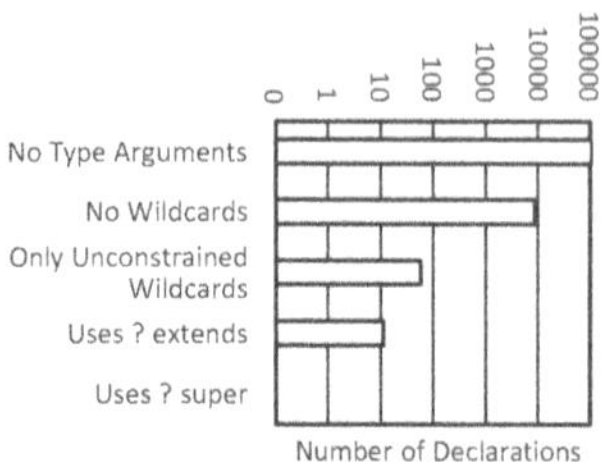

Figure 17. Wildcard usage in inheritance hierarchies

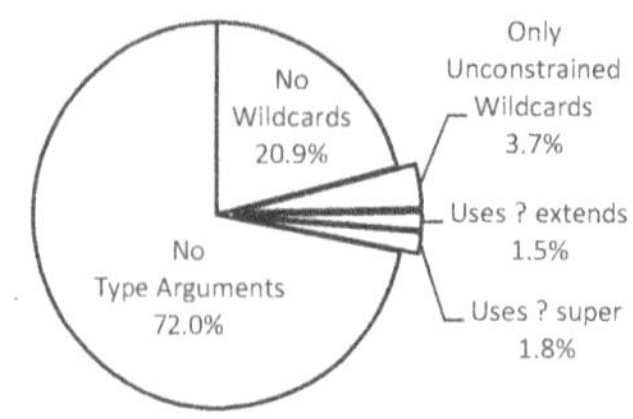

Figure 18. Wildcard usage in type-parameter constraints

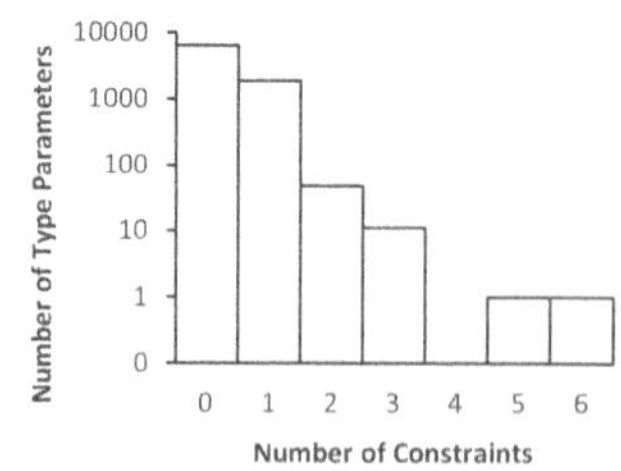

Figure 19. Number of constraints per type parameter

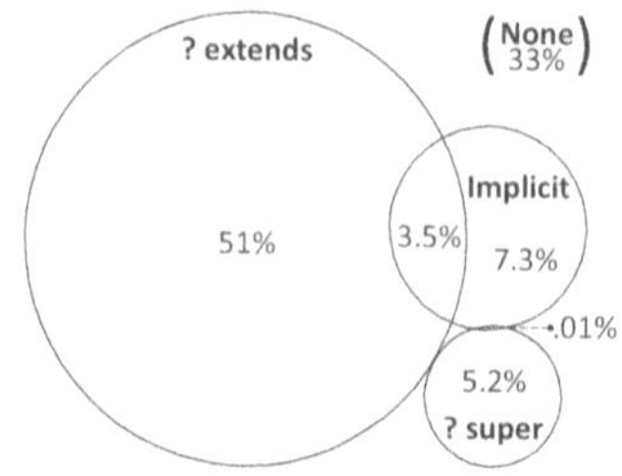

Figure 20. Distribution of constraints on wildcards

where the type with a ? super type argument was nested inside the constraint; only the constraint itself ever had such a type argument.

To evaluate the first half of our intersection restriction, we examined all constraints on type parameters for classes, interfaces, and methods that occurred in our suite. In Figure 19 we indicate in logarithmic scale how many type parameters had no constraints, one constraint, or multiple constraints by using intersections. In our entire suite there were only 61 intersections. We manually inspected these 61 intersections and determined that, out of all these intersections, *none* of them violated our intersection restriction.

To evaluate the second half of our intersection restriction as well as our equivalence restriction, we examined all wildcards that occurred in our suite. In Figure 20 we break down the various ways the 19,018 wildcards were constrained. Only 3.5% of wildcards had both an implicit and an explicit upper bound. In all of those cases, the explicit upper bound was actually a subtype of the implicit upper bound (interestingly, though, for 35% of these cases the two bounds were actually equivalent). Thus out of all explicit bounds, *none* of them violated either our intersection restriction or our equivalence restriction. Also, in the entire suite there were only 2 wildcards that had both an explicit lower bound and an implicit upper bound, and in both cases the explicit lower bound was a strict subtype of the implicit upper bound.

In summary, *none* of our constraints were ever violated in our entire suite. This leads us to believe that the restrictions we impose will most likely have little negative impact on programmers.

We also manually investigated for implicitly infinite types, taking advantage of the syntactic classification of implicitly infinite types described in our technical report [15]. We encountered only one example of an implicitly infinite type. It was actually the same as class `Infinite` in Section 3.2; however, we investigated this further and determined this was actually an error which we easily corrected [15]. We also did a manual investigation for implicitly infinite proofs and found none. These findings are significant because Cameron et al. proved soundness of wildcards assuming all wildcards and subtyping proofs translate to finite traditional existential types and subtyping proofs [3], and Summers et al. gave semantics to wildcards under the same assumptions [14], so although we have determined these assumptions do not hold theoretically our survey demonstrates that they do hold in practice. Nonetheless, we expect that Cameron et al. and Summers et al. would be able to adapt their work to implicitly infinite types and proofs now that the problem has been identified.

10. Extensions

Although in this paper we have focused on wildcards, our formalism and proofs are all phrased in terms of more general existential types [15]. This generality provides opportunity for extensions to the language. Here we offer a few such extensions which preliminary investigations suggest are compatible with our algorithms, although full proofs have not yet been developed.

10.1 Declaration-Site Variance

As Kennedy and Pierce mention [8], there is a simple translation from declaration-site variance to use-site variance which preserves and reflects subtyping. In short, except for a few cases, type arguments τ to covariant type parameters are translated to `? extends` τ, and type arguments τ to contravariant type parameters are translated to `? super` τ. Our restrictions on `? super` then translate to restrictions on contravariant type parameters. For example, our restrictions would require that, in each declared direct superclass and superinterface, only types at covariant locations can use classes or interfaces with contravariant type parameters. Interestingly, this restriction does not coincide with any of the restrictions presented by Kennedy and Pierce. Thus, we have found a new termination result for nominal subtyping with variance. It would be interesting to investigate existing code bases with declaration-site variance to determine if our restrictions might be more practical than prohibiting expansive inheritance.

Because declaration-site variance can be translated to wildcards, Java could use both forms of variance. A wildcard should not be used as a type argument for a variant type parameter since it is unclear what this would mean, although Java might consider interpreting the wildcard syntax slightly differently for variant type parameters for the sake of backwards compatibility.

10.2 Existential Types

The intersection restriction has the unfortunate consequence that constraints such as `List<?> & Set<?>` are not allowed. We can address this by allowing users to use existential types should they wish to. Then the user could express the constraint above using `exists X. List<X> & Set<X>`, which satisfies the intersection restriction. Users could also express potentially useful types such as `exists X. Pair<X,X>` and `exists X. List<List<X>>`.

Besides existentially quantified type variables, we have taken into consideration constraints, both explicit and implicit, and how to restrict them so that termination of subtyping is still guaranteed since the general case is known to be undecidable [20]. While all bound variables must occur somewhere in the body of the existential type, they cannot occur inside an explicit constraint occurring in the body. This both prevents troublesome implicit constraints and permits the join technique in Section 6.1. As for the explicit constraints on the variables, lower bounds cannot reference bound variables and upper bounds cannot have bound variables at covariant locations or in types at contravariant locations. This allows potentially useful types such as `exists X extends Enum<X>. List<X>`. As for implicit constraints, since a bound variable could be used in many locations, the implicit constraints on that variable are the accumulation of the implicit constraints for each location it occurs at. All upper bounds on a bound variable would have to validly intersect with each other, and each bound variable with multiple lower bounds would have to have a most general lower bound.

10.3 Lower-Bounded Type Parameters

Smith and Cartwright propose allowing type parameters to have lower-bound requirements (i.e. super clauses) [13], providing a simple application of this feature which we duplicate here.

```
<P super Integer> List<P> sequence(int n) {
  List<P> res = new LinkedList<P>();
  for (int i = 1; i <= n; i++)
    res.add(i);
  return res;
}
```

Our algorithms can support this feature provided lower-bound requirements do not have explicitly bound wildcard type arguments. Also, they should not be other type parameters in the same parameterization since that is better expressed by upper bounds on those type parameters.

10.4 Universal Types

Another extension that could be compatible with our algorithms is a restricted form of predicative universal types like forall X. List<X>. Although this extension is mostly speculative, we mention it here as a direction for future research since preliminary investigations suggest it is possible. Universal types would fulfill the main role that raw types play in Java besides convenience and backwards compatibility. In particular, for something like an immutable empty list one typically produces one instance of an anonymous class implementing raw List and then uses that instance as a List of any type they want. This way one avoids wastefully allocating a new empty list for each type. Adding universal types would eliminate this need for the back door provided by raw types.

11. Conclusion

Despite their conceptual simplicity, wildcards are formally complex, with impredicativity and implicit constraints being the primary causes. Although most often used in practice for use-site variance [6, 16–18], wildcards are best formalized as existential types [2, 3, 6, 8, 17, 18, 20], and more precisely as coinductive existential types with coinductive subtyping proofs [15], which is a new finding to the best of our knowledge.

In this paper we have addressed the problem of subtyping of wildcards, a problem suspected to be undecidable in its current form [8, 20]. Our solution imposes simple restrictions, which a survey of 9.2 million lines of open-source Java code demonstrates are already compatible with existing code. Furthermore, our restrictions are all local, allowing for informative user-friendly error messages should they ever be violated.

Because our formalization and proofs are in terms of a general-purpose variant of existential types [15], we have identified a number of extensions to Java that should be compatible with our algorithms. Amongst these are declaration-site variance and user-expressible existential types, which suggests that our algorithms and restrictions may be suited for Scala as well, for which subtyping is also suspected to be undecidable [8, 20]. Furthermore, it may be possible to support some form of universal types, which would remove a significant practical application of raw types so that they may be unnecessary should Java ever discard backwards compatibility as forebode in the language specification [5: Chapter 4.8].

While we have addressed subtyping, joins, and a number of other subtleties with wildcards, there is still plenty of opportunity for research to be done on wildcards. In particular, although we have provided techniques for improving type-argument inference, we believe it is important to identify a type-argument inference algorithm which is both complete in practice *and* provides guarantees regarding ambiguity of program semantics. Furthermore, an inference system would ideally inform users at declaration-site how inferable their method signature is, rather than having users find out at each use-site. We hope our explanation of the challenges helps guide future research on wildcards towards solving such problems.

Acknowledgements

We would like to thank Nicholas Cameron, Sophia Drossopoulou, Erik Ernst, Suresh Jagannathan, Andrew Kennedy, Jens Palsberg, Pat Rondon, and the anonymous reviewers for their many insightful suggestions and intriguing discussions.

References

[1] Gilad Bracha, Martin Odersky, David Stoutamire, and Philip Wadler. Making the future safe for the past: Adding genericity to the Java programming language. In *OOPSLA*, 1998.

[2] Nicholas Cameron and Sophia Drossopoulou. On subtyping, wildcards, and existential types. In *FTfJP*, 2009.

[3] Nicholas Cameron, Sophia Drossopoulou, and Erik Ernst. A model for Java with wildcards. In *ECOOP*, 2008.

[4] Peter Canning, William Cook, Walter Hill, Walter Olthoff, and John C. Mitchell. F-bounded polymorphism for object-oriented programming. In *FPCA*, 1989.

[5] James Gosling, Bill Joy, Guy Steel, and Gilad Bracha. *The Java^{TM} Language Specification*. Addison-Wesley Professional, third edition, June 2005.

[6] Atsushi Igarashi and Mirko Viroli. On variance-based subtyping for parametric types. In *ECOOP*, 2002.

[7] Simon Peyton Jones, Dimitrios Vytiniotis, Stephanie Weirich, and Mark Shields. Practical type inference for arbitrary-rank types. *Journal of Functional Programming*, 17:1–82, January 2007.

[8] Andrew Kennedy and Benjamin Pierce. On decidability of nominal subtyping with variance. In *FOOL*, 2007.

[9] Daan Leijen. HMF: Simple type inference for first-class polymorphism. In *ICFP*, 2008.

[10] Martin Odersky and Konstantin Läufer. Putting type annotations to work. In *POPL*, 1996.

[11] Gordon D. Plotkin. A note on inductive generalization. In *Machine Intelligence*, volume 5, pages 153–163. Edinburgh University Press, 1969.

[12] John C. Reynolds. Transformational systems and the algebraic structure of atomic formulas. In *Machine Intelligence*, volume 5, pages 135–151. Edinburgh University Press, 1969.

[13] Daniel Smith and Robert Cartwright. Java type inference is broken: Can we fix it? In *OOPSLA*, 2008.

[14] Alexander J. Summers, Nicholas Cameron, Mariangiola Dezani-Ciancaglini, and Sophia Drossopoulou. Towards a semantic model for Java wildcards. In *FTfJP*, 2010.

[15] Ross Tate, Alan Leung, and Sorin Lerner. Taming wildcards in Java's type system. Technical report, University of California, San Diego, March 2011.

[16] Kresten Krab Thorup and Mads Torgersen. Unifying genericity - combining the benefits of virtual types and parameterized classes. In *ECOOP*, 1999.

[17] Mads Torgersen, Erik Ernst, and Christian Plesner Hansen. Wild FJ. In *FOOL*, 2005.

[18] Mads Torgersen, Christian Plesner Hansen, Erik Ernst, Peter von der Ahé, Gilad Bracha, and Neal Gafter. Adding wildcards to the Java programming language. In *SAC*, 2004.

[19] Mirko Viroli. On the recursive generation of parametric types. Technical Report DEIS-LIA-00-002, Università di Bologna, September 2000.

[20] Stefan Wehr and Peter Thiemann. On the decidability of subtyping with bounded existential types. In *APLAS*, 2009.

Composable Asynchronous Events

Lukasz Ziarek, KC Sivaramakrishnan, Suresh Jagannathan
Purdue University
{lziarek, chandras, suresh}@cs.purdue.edu

Abstract

Although asynchronous communication is an important feature of many concurrent systems, building *composable* abstractions that leverage asynchrony is challenging. This is because an asynchronous operation necessarily involves two distinct threads of control – the thread that initiates the operation, and the thread that discharges it. Existing attempts to marry composability with asynchrony either entail sacrificing performance (by limiting the degree of asynchrony permitted), or modularity (by forcing natural abstraction boundaries to be broken).

In this paper, we present the design and rationale for *asynchronous events*, an abstraction that enables composable construction of complex asynchronous protocols without sacrificing the benefits of abstraction or performance. Asynchronous events are realized in the context of Concurrent ML's first-class event abstraction [16]. We discuss the definition of a number of useful asynchronous abstractions that can be built on top of asynchronous events (e.g., composable callbacks) and provide a detailed case study of how asynchronous events can be used to substantially improve the modularity and performance of an I/O-intensive highly concurrent server application.

Categories and Subject Descriptors: D.1.1 [Programming Techniques] Applicative (functional) programming; D.3.1 [*Programming Languages*]: Formal Definitions and Theory; D.3.2 [*Programming Languages*]: Language Classifications - Concurrent, distributed, and parallel languages, ML; D.3.3 [*Programming Languages*]: Language Constructs and Features - Concurrent programming structures

General Terms: Design, Languages, Theory

Keywords: Asynchrony, Concurrent ML, First-Class Events, Composability, Message-Passing

1. Introduction

Software complexity is typically managed using programming abstractions that encapsulate behaviors within modules. A module's internal implementation can be changed without requiring changes to clients that use it, provided that these changes do not entail modifying its signature. For concurrent programs, the specifications that can be described by an interface are often too weak to enforce this kind of strong encapsulation, especially in the presence of communication that spans abstraction boundaries. Consequently, changing the implementation of a concurrency abstraction by adding, modifying, or removing behaviors often requires pervasive change to the users of the abstraction. Modularity is thus compromised.

PLDI'11, June 4–8, 2011, San Jose, California, USA.

This is particularly true for asynchronous behavior generated internally within a module. An asynchronous operation initiates two temporally distinct sets of actions, neither of which are exposed in its enclosing module's interface. The first set defines *post-creation* actions – these are actions that must be executed after an asynchronous operation has been initiated, without taking into account whether the effects of the operation have been witnessed by its recipients. For example, a post-creation action of an asynchronous send on a channel might initiate another operation on that same channel; the second action should take place with the guarantee that the first has already deposited its data on the channel. The second are *post-consumption* actions – these define actions that must be executed only after the effect of an asynchronous operation has been witnessed. For example, a post-consumption action might be a callback that is triggered when the client retrieves data from a channel sent asynchronously.

In this paper, we describe how to build and maintain asynchronous concurrency abstractions that give programmers the ability to express *composable* and *extensible* asynchronous protocols. By weaving protocols through the use of post-creation and post-consumption computations, we achieve composability without sacrificing modularity, enabling reasoning about loosely coupled communication partners that span logical abstraction boundaries. To do so, we enable the construction of signatures and interfaces that specify asynchronous behavior via abstract post-creation and post-consumption actions. We present our extensions in the context of the Concurrent ML's (CML) first-class communication events [16]. Just as CML's synchronous events provide a solution to composable, synchronous message-passing that could not be easily accommodated using λ-abstraction and application, the asynchronous events defined here offer a solution for composable asynchronous message-passing not easily expressible using synchronous communication and explicit threading abstractions. There are three overarching goals of our design:

1. Asynchronous combinators should permit uniform composition of pre/post-creation and consumption actions. This means that protocols should be allowed to extend the behavior of an asynchronous action both with respect to the computation performed before and after it is created and consumed.
2. Asynchronous actions should provide sensible visibility and ordering guarantees. A post-creation computation should execute with the guarantee that the asynchronous action it follows has been created, even if that action has not been fully discharged. The effects of consumed asynchronous actions should be consistent with the order in which they were created.

```
spawn      : (unit -> 'a) -> threadID
sendEvt    : 'a chan * 'a -> unit Event
recvEvt    : 'a chan -> 'a Event
alwaysEvt  : 'a -> 'a Event
never      : 'a Event
sync       : 'a Event -> 'a
wrap       : 'a Event * ('a -> 'b) -> 'b Event
guard      : (unit -> 'a Event) -> 'a Event
choose     : 'a Event list -> 'a Event
```

Figure 1: CML event operators.

3. Communication protocols should be agnostic with respect to the kinds of actions they handle. Thus, both synchronous and asynchronous actions should be permitted to operate over the same set of abstractions (e.g., communication channels).

Contributions.

1. We present a comprehensive design for asynchronous events, and describe a family of combinators analogous to their synchronous variants available in CML. To the best of our knowledge, this is the first treatment to consider the meaningful integration of composable CML-style event abstractions with asynchronous functionality.
2. We provide implementations of useful asynchronous abstractions such as callbacks and mailboxes (buffered channels), along with a number of case studies extracted from realistic concurrent applications (e.g., a concurrent I/O library, concurrent file processing, etc.). Our abstractions operate over ordinary CML channels, enabling interoperability between synchronous and asynchronous protocols.
3. We discuss an implementation of asynchronous events that has been incorporated into Multi-MLton, a parallel extension of MLton [14], a whole-program optimizing compiler for Standard ML, and present a detailed case study that shows how asynchronous events can help improve the expression and performance of highly concurrent server application.

The paper is organized as follows. Sec. 2 provides a brief introduction to Concurrent ML. Additional motivation for asynchronous events is given in Sec. 3. Sec. 4 describes the asynchronous combinators and abstractions we support. Sec. 5 gives a formal operational semantics for asynchronous events. A detailed case study is presented in Sec. 6. Related work and conclusions are provided in Sec. 7 and Sec. 8.

2. Background: Concurrent ML

Context: We explore the design of asynchronous events in the context of Concurrent ML [16] (CML). CML is a concurrent extension of Standard ML that utilizes synchronous message passing to enable the construction of synchronous communication protocols. Threads perform `send` and `recv` operations on typed channels; these operations block until a matching action on the same channel is performed by another thread.

CML also provides first-class synchronous *events* that abstract synchronous message-passing operations. An event value of type `'a event` when synchronized on yields a value of type `'a`. An event value represents a potential computation, with latent effect until a thread synchronizes upon it by calling `sync`. The following equivalences thus therefore hold: `send(c, v)` $\equiv$ `sync(sendEvt(c,v))` and `recv(c)` $\equiv$ `sync(recvEvt(c))`.

Notably, thread creation is *not* encoded as an event – the thread `spawn` primitive simply takes a thunk to evaluate as a separate thread, and returns a thread identifier that allows access to the newly created thread's state.

Besides `sendEvt` and `recvEvt`, there are other base events provided by CML. The `never` event, as its name suggests, is never available for synchronization; in contrast, `alwaysEvt` is always available for synchronization. These events are typically generated based on the (un)satisfiability of conditions or invariants that can be subsequently used to influence the behavior of more complex events built from the event combinators described below.

Much of CML's expressive power derives from event combinators that construct complex event values from other events. We list some of these combinators in Fig. 1. The expression `wrap (ev, f)` creates an event that, when synchronized, applies the result of synchronizing on event `ev` to function `f`. Conversely, `guard(f)` creates an event that, when synchronized, evaluates `f()` to yield event `ev` and then synchronizes on `ev`. The `choose` event combinator takes a list of events and constructs an event value that represents the non-deterministic choice of the events in the list; for example, `sync(choose[recvEvt(a),sendEvt(b,v)])` will either receive a unit value from channel `a`, or send value `v` on channel `b`. Selective communication provided by choice motivates the need for first-class events. We cannot, for example, simply build complex event combinators using function abstraction and composition because function closures do not allow inspection of the computations they encapsulates, a necessary requirement for combinators like `choice`.

3. Motivation

Given CML synchronous events, we can envision a simple way to express asynchrony in terms of lightweight threads that encapsulate synchronous operations:

```
fun asyncEvt (evt) = wrap(alwaysEvt(),
                          fn() => spawn(sync(evt)))
```

Evaluating `asyncEvt(evt)` yields an event that, when synchronized, spawns a new thread to perform the actions defined by `evt`. (The use of `alwaysEvt` ensures that the event is always available for synchronization.) Thus,

```
fun asend(c,v) = sync(asyncEvt(sendEvt(c,v)))
```

defines a function that asynchronously sends value `v` on channel `c`, when applied. The use of explicit user-defined threads to express asynchrony in this way, however, fails to provide sensible ordering guarantees. For example, in the expression:

```
let val evt1 = asend(c,v)
    val evt2 = asend(c,v')
in recvEvt(c) end
```

the value returned when this expression is synchronized may be either `v` or `v'` (depending on the implementation of the underlying thread scheduler), even though `evt1` is synchronized before `evt2`.

Besides not preserving desired ordering, there are more fundamental issues at play here. Suppose we wish to add post-creation and post-consumption actions to an asynchronous event; post-creation actions are to be performed once the thread is spawned, and post-consumptions actions must be performed once the communication action is complete. We could modify the definition of `asyncEvt` so that post-creation and post-consumption actions are supplied when the event is constructed:

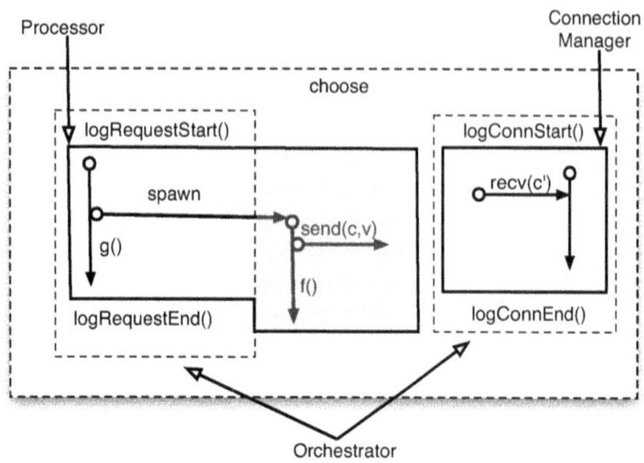

Figure 2: The figure shows the events built up by the three modules that comprise our abstract server. The events created by the processor and connection manager, depicted with thick squares, are opaque to the orchestrator and cannot be deconstructed. Notably, this means the orchestrator does not have the ability to modify or extend the behavior of the thread created by `processorEvt` (shown in grey) using only synchronous event combinators.

```
fun asyncEvt(f,g,evt) =
    wrap(alwaysEvt(),
         fn() => (spawn(fn() => sync(wrap(evt, f))); g()))
```

Given this definition, an asynchronous send event might be defined to perform a post-consumption action, here `f` (e.g., an action that waits for an acknowledgment indicating the sent data was received with no errors). Similarly, the event may be equipped with a post-creation action, here `g` (e.g., an operation that performs local clean-up or finalization).

To illustrate the composability and modularity issues that arise in using `asyncEvt` defined in this way, consider the definition of a simple resource manager (like a web-server) that consists of three modules: (1) a *connection manager* that listens for and accepts new connections, (2) a *processor* that processes and sends data based on input requests, and (3) an *orchestrator* that enables different kinds of interactions and protocols among clients, the processor, and the connection manager. If each established connection represents an independent group of actions (e.g., requests), we can leverage asynchrony to allow multiple requests to be serviced concurrently. We discuss this design in more detail in Sec. 6.

One simple definition of an orchestrator is a procedure that chooses between the communication event defined by the processor (call it `processorEvt`) and the connection manager (call it `managerEvt`). Suppose `processorEvt` internally leveraged our definition of `asyncEvt` to perform a send asynchronously and then executed some post-creation action `g` and post-consumption action `f`. Even if the details of the communication protocol used by the connection manager and processor were visible to the orchestrator, the orchestrator would not be able to change their internal functionality since they are encapsulated within events, which abstract the computation actions and effects they perform. Nonetheless, the orchestrator is still free to *augment* these protocols to yield additional behavior. For example, the following definition:

```
fun orchestrate(processorEvt, managerEvt) =
  sync(choose([processorEvt, managerEvt]))
```

uses choice to non-deterministically select whichever event is available to be synchronized against. This definition allows the execution of the `managerEvt` if a new connection is available, or the `processorEvt` if the current input request has been satisfied, or a non-deterministic choice among the two if both can execute.

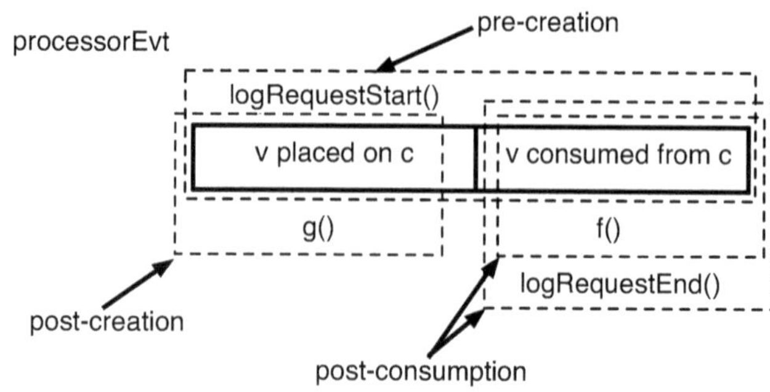

Figure 3: The figure shows how asynchronous events can alleviate the problems illustrated in Fig. 2. By making creation and consumption actions explicit in `processorEvt`'s definition, we are able to specify `logRequestEnd` as a post consumption action correctly extending the protocol in the orchestrator.

Unfortunately, composing more expressive asynchronous protocols in this way is difficult. To see why, consider a further modification to the orchestrator that incorporates logging information. We can wrap our processor event with a function that logs requests and our connection manager with one that logs connection details. The `guard` event combinator can be used to specify pre-synchronization actions. In this example, these actions would be logging functions that record the start of a connection or request. [1]

```
fun orchestrate(processorEvt, managerEvt) =
  sync(choose([guard(fn () => logRequestStart();
                     wrap(processorEvt, logRequestEnd)),
               guard(fn () => logConnStart();
                     wrap(managerEvt, logConnEnd))]))
```

This code does not provide the functionality we desire, however. Since the processor handles its internal protocols asynchronously, wrapping *logRequestEnd* around `processorEvt` specifies an action that will occur in the main thread of control after the execution of `g`, the post-creation action defined when the event was created (see Fig. 2). However, the request should only be completed after the post-consumption action `f`, which is executed by the thread created internally by the event. Since this thread is *hidden* by the event, there is no way to extend it. Moreover, there is no guarantee that the request has been successfully serviced even after `g` completes. We could recover composability by either (a) not spawning an internal thread in `asyncEvt`, (b) weaving a protocol that required `g` to *wait* for the completion of `f`, effectively yielding synchronous behavior, or (c) modifying `procesorEvt` and `managerEvt` to handle the post-consumption action explicitly. The first two approaches force `f` and `g` to be executed prior to *logRequestEnd*, but a synchronous solution of this kind would not allow multiple requests to be processed concurrently; approach (c) retains asynchrony, but at the cost of modularity, requiring server functionality to be modified anytime clients wish to express additional behaviors.

The heart of the problem is a dichotomy in language abstractions; asynchrony is fundamentally expressed using distinct threads of control, yet composablity is achieved through event abstractions that are thread-unaware. The result is that CML events cannot be directly applied to build post-consumption actions for realizing composable asynchronous communication protocols.

Fig. 3 diagrammatically shows how extensible post-creation and post-consumption actions can be leveraged to achieve our desired

[1] In CML, we could also use the `withNack` combinator to avoid firing both the `logRequestStart` and `logConnStart` during the choice [16].

behavior. In Section 4.1, we show a modified implementation of the orchestrator using the asynchronous event primitives and combinators we define in the following section that captures the behavior shown in the figure.

Putting it All Together. Although synchronous first-class events alleviate the complexity of reasoning about arbitrary thread interleavings, and enable composable synchronous communication protocols, using threads to encode asynchrony unfortunately re-introduces these complexities. Our design introduces first-class *asynchronous* events with the following properties to alleviate this drawback: *(i)* they are extensible both with respect to pre- and post-creation as well as pre- and post-consumption actions; *(ii)* they can operate over the same channels that synchronous events operate over, allowing both kinds of events to seamlessly co-exist; and, *(iii)* their visibility, ordering, and semantics is independent of the underlying runtime and scheduling infrastructure.

4. Asynchronous Events

In order to provide primitives that adhere to the desired properties outlined above, we extend CML with the following two base events: `aSendEvt` and `aRecvEvt`, to create an asynchronous send event and an asynchronous receive event, resp. The differences in their type signature from their synchronous counterparts reflect the split in the creation and consumption of the communication action they define:

```
 sendEvt  : 'a chan * 'a -> unit Event
aSendEvt  : 'a chan * 'a -> (unit, unit) AEvent

 recvEvt  : 'a chan -> 'a Event
aRecvEvt  : 'a chan -> (unit, 'a) AEvent
```

An `AEvent` value is parametrized with respect to the type of the event's post-creation and post-consumption actions. In the case of `aSendEvt`, both actions are of type `unit`: when synchronized on, the event immediately returns a `unit` value and places its `'a` argument value on the supplied channel. The post-consumption action also yields `unit`. When synchronized on, an `aRecvEvt` returns `unit`; the type of its post-consumption action is `'a` reflecting the type of value read from the channel when it is paired with a send.

As an example, consider Fig 3, where the `processorEvt` event upon synchronization initiates an asynchronous action to place the value `v` on channel `c` and then executes `g`. When the send is paired with a receive, `f` is first executed, and then *logRequestEnd*. In this case, the type of the computation would be:

(*return-type-of* `g`, *return-type-of* `logRequestEnd`) `AEvent`

The semantics of both asynchronous send and receive guarantees that successive communication operations performed by the same thread get witnessed in the order in which they were issued. In this respect, an asynchronous send event shares functionality with a typical non-blocking send of the kind found in languages like Erlang [1] or libraries like MPI. However, an asynchronous receive does not exhibit the same behavior as a typical non-blocking receive. Indeed, CML already provides polling methods that can be used to implement polling loops found in most non-blocking receive implementations. The primary difference between the two is that an asynchronous receive places itself on the channel at the point where it is synchronized (regardless of the availability of a matching send), while a non-blocking receive typically only queries for the existence of a value to match against, but does not alter the underlying channel structure. By actually depositing itself on the channel, an asynchronous receive thus provides a convenient mechanism to implement *ordered* asynchronous buffers or streams – successive asynchronous receives are guaranteed to receive data from a matching send in the order in which they were synchronized.

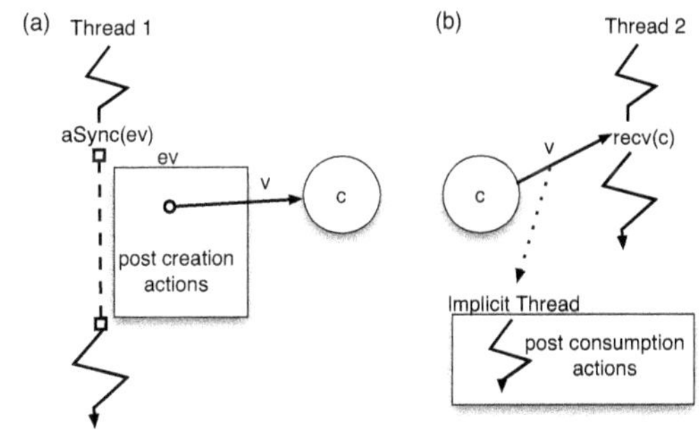

Figure 4: The figure shows a complex asynchronous event `ev`, built from a base `aSendEvt`, being executed by Thread 1. When the event is synchronized via. `aSync`, the value `v` is placed on channel `c` and post-creation actions are executed (see (a)). Afterwards, control returns to Thread 1. When Thread 2 consumes the value `v` from channel `c`, an implicit thread of control is created to execute any post-consumption actions (see (b)).

In addition to these new base events, we also introduce a new synchronization primitive: `aSync`, to synchronize asynchronous events. The `aSync` operation fires the computation encapsulated by the asynchronous event of type `('a, 'b) AEvent` and returns a value of type `'a`, corresponding to the return type of the event's post-*creation* action (see Fig. 4).

```
sync    : 'a Event -> 'a
aSync   : ('a, 'b) AEvent -> 'a
```

Unlike their synchronous variants, asynchronous events do *not* block if no matching communication is present. For example, executing an asynchronous send event on an empty channel places the value being sent on the channel and then returns control to the executing thread (see Fig. 4(a)). In order to allow this non-blocking behavior, an *implicit* thread of control is created for the asynchronous event when the event is paired, or *consumed* as shown in Fig. 4(b). If a receiver is present on the channel, the asynchronous send event behaves similarly to a synchronous event; it passes the value to the receiver. However, it still creates a new implicit thread of control if there are any post-consumption actions to be executed.

Similarly, the synchronization of an asynchronous receive event does not yield the value received (see Fig. 5); instead, it simply enqueues the receiving action on the channel. Therefore, the thread which synchronizes on an asynchronous receive always gets the value `unit`, even if a matching send exists. The actual value consumed by the asynchronous receive can be passed back to the thread which synchronized on the event through the use of combinators that process post-consumption actions. This is particularly well suited to encode reactive programming idioms: the post-consumption actions encapsulate a reactive computation.

To illustrate the differences between synchronous and asynchronous primitive events, consider the two functions `f` and `af` shown below:

```
fun  f () =
    (spawn (fn () => sync (sendEvt(c, v)));
     sync (sendEvt(c, v'));
     sync (recvEvt(c)))

fun af () =
    (spawn (fn () => sync (sendEvt(c, v)));
     aSync (aSendEvt(c, v'));
     sync (recvEvt(c)))
```

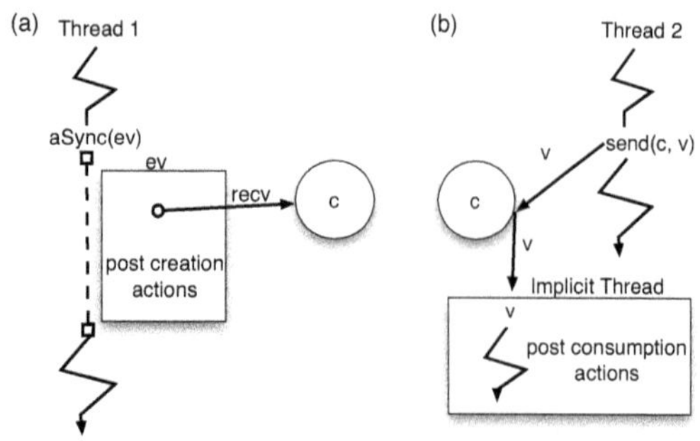

Figure 5: The figure shows a complex asynchronous event `ev`, built from a base `aRecvEvt`, being executed by Thread 1. When the event is synchronized via `aSync`, the receive action is placed on channel `c` and post-creation actions are executed (see (a)). Afterwards, control returns to Thread 1. When Thread 2 sends the value `v` to channel `c`, an implicit thread of control is created to execute any post-consumption actions passing `v` as the argument (see (b)).

The function `f`, if executed in a system with no other threads will always block because there is no recipient available for the send of `v'` on channel `c`. On the other hand, suppose there was another thread willing to accept communication on channel `c`. In this case, the only possible value that `f` could receive from `c` is `v`. This occurs because the receive will only happen after the value `v'` is consumed from the channel. Notice that if the spawned thread enqueues `v` on the channel before `v'`, the function `f` will block even if another thread is willing to receive a value from the channel, since a function cannot synchronize with itself. The function `af` will never block. The receive may see either the value `v` or `v'` since the asynchronous send event *only* asserts that the value `v'` has been placed on the channel and *not* that it has been consumed. If we swapped lines 6 and 7, the receive operation on line 8 is guaranteed to read `v'`. While asynchronous events do not block, they still enforce *ordering* constraints that reflect the order in which they were synchronized.

4.1 Combinators

In CML, the `wrap` combinator allows for the specification of a post-synchronization action. Once the event is completed the function wrapping the event is evaluated. For asynchronous events, this means the wrapped function is executed after the action the event encodes is *placed* on the channel and not necessarily after that action is consumed.

```
sWrap : ('a, 'b) AEvent * ('a -> 'c) ->  ('c, 'b) AEvent
aWrap : ('a, 'b) AEvent * ('b -> 'c) ->  ('a, 'c) AEvent
```

To allow for the specification of both post-creation and post-consumption actions for asynchronous events, we introduce two new combinators: `sWrap` and `aWrap`. `sWrap` is used to specify post-creation actions. The combinator `aWrap`, on the other hand, is used to express post-consumption actions. We can apply `sWrap` and `aWrap` to an asynchronous event in any order.

```
sWrap(aWrap(e, f) g) ≡ aWrap(sWrap(e, g), f)
```

We can use `sWrap` and `aWrap` to encode a composable variant of `asyncEvt` (presented in the motivation) which is also parameterized by a channel `c` and value `v`. We create a base asynchronous send event to send `v` on `c` and use `sWrap` and `aWrap` to specify `g` and `f` as a post-creation action and a post-consumption action, resp.:

```
fun asyncEvt(f,g,c,v) = aWrap(sWrap(aSendEvt(c,v),g), f)
```

Since post-creation actions have been studied in CML extensively (they act as post-synchronization actions in a synchronous context), we focus our discussion on `aWrap` and the specification of post-consumption actions. Consider the following program fragment:

```
fun f() =
  let val c_local = channel()
  in aSync (aWrap(aSendEvt(c, v),fn () => send(c_local, ())));
     g();
     recv(c_local);
     h()
  end
```

The function `f` first allocates a local channel c_{local} and then executes an asynchronous send `aWrap`-ed with a function that sends on the local channel. The function `f` then proceeds to execute functions `g` and `h` with a receive on the local channel between the two function calls. We use the `aWrap` primitive to encode a simple *barrier* based on the consumption of `v`. We are guaranteed that `h` executes in a context in which `v` has been consumed. The function `g`, on the other hand, can make no assumptions on the consumption of `v`. However, `g` is guaranteed that `v` is on the channel. Therefore, if `g` consumes values from `c`, it can witness `v` and, similarly, if it places values on the channel, it is guaranteed that `v` will be consumed *prior* to the values it produces. Of course, `v` could always have been consumed *prior* to `g`'s evaluation. If the same code was written with a synchronous wrap, we would have no guarantee about the consumption of `v`. In fact, the code would block, as the send encapsulated by the wrap would be executed by the *same* thread of control executing `f`. Thus, the asynchronous event implicitly creates a new evaluation context and a new thread of control; the wrapping function is evaluated in this context, not in the context associated with thread that performed the synchronization.

This simple example illustrates the essential ingredients of a basic callback mechanism. The code shown below performs an asynchronous receive and passes the result of the receive to its wrapped function. The value received asynchronously is passed as an argument to `h` by sending on the channel c_{local}.

```
let val c_local = channel()
in aSync (aWrap(aRecvEvt(c), fn x => send(c_local, x)));
   ... h(recv(c_local)) ...
end
```

Although this implementation suffices as a basic callback, it is not particularly abstract and cannot be composed with other asynchronous events. We can create an abstract callback mechanism using both `sWrap` and `aWrap` around an input event.

```
callbackEvt : ('a, 'c) AEvent * ('c -> 'b) ->
              ('b Event, 'c) AEvent
```

```
fun callbackEvt(ev, f) =
  let val c_local = channel()
  in sWrap(aWrap(ev,
                 fn x => (aSync(aSendEvt(c_local, x)); x)),
           fn _ => wrap(recvEvt(c_local), f))
  end
```

If `ev` contains post-creation actions when the callback event is synchronized on, they are executed, followed by execution of the `sWrap` as shown in Fig. 6(a). The event returned by the `sWrap` (call it `ev'`), which when synchronized on will first receive a value on the local channel (c_{local}) and then apply the function `f` to this value. Synchronizing on this event (which need not happen at the point where the callback event itself is synchronized) will subsequently block until the event `ev` is discharged. Once `ev` completes, its post-consumption actions are executed in a new thread of control since `ev` is asynchronous (see Fig. 6(b)). The body of

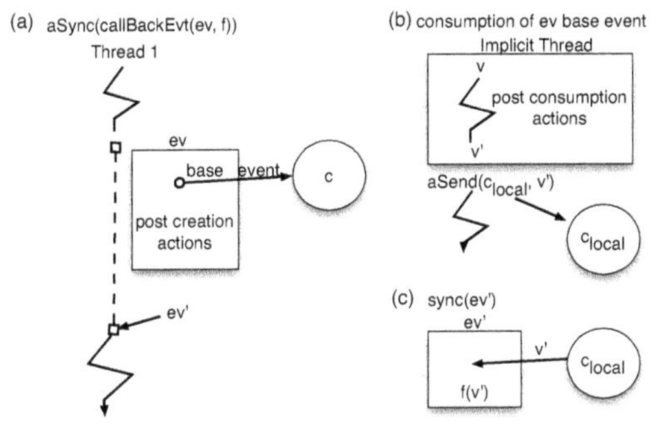

Figure 6: The figure shows a callback event constructed from a complex asynchronous event `ev` and a callback function `f`. When the callback event is synchronized via `aSync`, the action associated with the event `ev` is placed on channel `c` and post-creation actions are executed. A new event `ev'` is created and passed to Thread 1 (see (a)). An implicit thread of control is created after the base event of `ev` is consumed. Post-consumption actions are executed passing `v`, the result of consuming the base event for `ev`, as an argument (see (b)). The result of the post-consumption actions, `v'` is sent on c_{local}. When `ev'` is synchronized upon, `f` is called with `v'` (see (c)).

the `aWrap`-ed function simply sends the result of synchronizing on `ev` (call it `v'`) on c_{local} and then passes the value `v'` to any further post-consumption actions. This is done asynchronously because the complex event returned by `callbackEvt` can be further extended with additional post consumption actions. Those actions should not be blocked if there is no thread willing to synchronize on `ev'`. Thus, synchronizing on a callback event executes the base event associated with `ev` *and* creates a new event as a post-creation action, which when synchronized on, executes the callback function synchronously.

We can think of the difference between a callback and an `aWrap` of an asynchronous event in terms of the thread of control which executes them. Both specify a *post*-consumption action for the asynchronous event, but the callback, when synchronized upon, is executed potentially by an *arbitrary thread* whereas the `aWrap` is *always* executed in the implicit thread created when the asynchronous event is consumed. Another difference is that the callback can be *postponed* and only executes when two conditions are satisfied: *(i)* the asynchronous event has completed and *(ii)* the callback is synchronized on. An `aWrap` returns once it has been synchronized on, and does not need to wait for other asynchronous events or post-consumption actions it encapsulates to complete.

A guard of an asynchronous event behaves much the same as a guard of a synchronous event does; it specifies pre-synchronization actions (i.e. pre-creation computation):

```
aGuard : (unit -> ('a, 'b) AEvent) -> ('a, 'b) AEvent
```

To see how we might use asynchronous guards, notice that our definition of `callbackEvt` has the drawback that it allocates a new local channel regardless of whether or not the event is ever synchronized upon. The code below uses an `aGuard` to specify the allocation of the local channel only when the event is synchronized on:

```
fun callbackEvt(ev, f) =
  aGuard(fn () =>
    let val c_local = channel()
    in sWrap(aWrap(ev,
                 fn x => (aSync(aSendEvt(c_local, x));x)),
           fn _ => wrap(recvEvt(c_local), f))
    end)
```

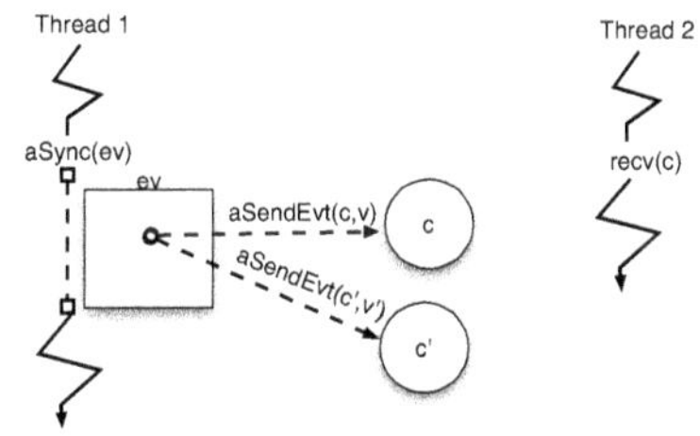

Figure 7: The figure shows Thread 1 synchronizing on a complex asynchronous event `ev`, built from a choice between two base asynchronous send events; one sending `v` on channel `c` and the other `v'` on `c'`. Thread 2 is willing to receive from channel `c`.

One of the most powerful combinators provided by CML is a non-deterministic choice over events. The combinator `choose` picks an *active* event from a list of events. If no events are active, it waits until one becomes active. An active event is an event which is available for synchronization. We define an asynchronous version of the choice combinator, `aChoose`, that operates over asynchronous events. Since asynchronous events are non-blocking, all events in the list are considered *active*. Therefore, the asynchronous choice always non-deterministically chooses from the list of available asynchronous events. We also provide a synchronous version of the asynchronous choice, `sChoose`, which blocks until one of the asynchronous base events has been consumed. Post-creation actions are not executed until the choice has been made. [2]

```
 choose : 'a Event list -> 'a Event
aChoose : ('a, 'b) AEvent list -> ('a, 'b) AEvent
sChoose : ('a, 'b) AEvent list -> ('a, 'b) AEvent
```

To illustrate the difference between `aChoose` and `sChoose`, consider a complex event `ev` defined as follows:

```
val ev = aChoose[aSendEvt(c, v), aSendEvt(c',v')]
```

If there exists a thread only willing to receive from channel `c`, `aChoose` will, with equal probability, execute the asynchronous send on `c` and `c'` (see Fig. 7). However, if we redefined `ev` to utilize `sChoose` instead, the behavior of the choice changes:

```
val ev = sChoose[aSendEvt(c, v), aSendEvt(c',v')]
```

Since `sChoose` blocks until one of the base asynchronous events is satisfiable, if there is only a thread willing to accept communication on `c` (see Fig. 7), the choice will only select the event encoding the asynchronous send on `c`.

We have thus far provided a mechanism to choose between sets of synchronous events and sets of asynchronous events. However, we would like to allow programmers to choose between both synchronous and asynchronous events. Currently, their different type structure would prevent such a formulation. Notice, however, that an asynchronous event with type `('a, 'b) AEvent` and a synchronous event with type `'a Event` both yield `'a` in the thread which synchronizes on them. Therefore, it is sensible to allow choice to operate over *both* asynchronous and synchronous events provided the type of the asynchronous event's post-creation action is the same as the type encapsulated by the synchronous event. To facilitate this interoperability, we provide combinators to transform asynchronous event types to synchronous event types and *vice-versa*:

```
aTrans : ('a, 'b) AEvent -> 'a Event
sTrans : 'a Event -> (unit, 'a) AEvent
```

[2] This behavior is equivalent to a scheduler not executing the thread which created the asynchronous action until it has been consumed.

The `aTrans` combinator takes an asynchronous event and creates a synchronous version by *dropping* the asynchronous portion of the event from the type (i.e. encapsulating it). As a result, we can no longer specify post-consumption actions for the event. However, we can still apply `wrap` to specify post-creation actions to the resulting synchronous portion exposed by the `'a Event`. Asynchronous events that have been transformed and are part of a larger `choose` event are only selected if their base event is satisfiable. Therefore, the following equivalence holds for two asynchronous events, `aEvt1` and `aEvt2`:

```
choose[aTrans(aEvt1), aTrans(aEvt2)] ≡
aChoose[aEvt1, aEvt2]
```

The `sTrans` combinator takes a synchronous event and changes it into an asynchronous event with no post-creation actions. The wrapped computation of the original event occurs now as a post-consumption action. We can encode an asynchronous version of `alwaysEvt` from its synchronous counterpart. Similarly, we can encode an asynchronous variant of `never`.

```
aAlwaysEvt : 'a -> (unit, 'a) AEvent
aNever   : (unit, 'a) AEvent
aAlwaysEvt(v) =  sTrans alwaysEvt(v)
aNever = sTrans never
```

Orchestrator revisited: Armed with asynchronous events and the combinators discussed above, we can now implement a composable orchestrator module from our simple abstract server example given in Sec. 3. We use `aGuard` to specify pre-creation actions and `aWrap` for asynchronous post-consumption actions. If `managerEvt` defines a synchronous protocol (since it merely listens for and accepts new connects), and `processorEvt` defines an asynchronous one (since it can process and communicate data concurrently with other ongoing requests), we can use `aTrans` to hide its post-consumption actions from the orchestrator. This allows us to freely choose between the asynchronous `processorEvt` and the synchronous `managerEvt`.

```
fun orchestrate(processorEvt, managerEvt) =
 sync(choose([aTrans
              aGuard(fn () => logRequestStart();
                     aWrap(processorEvt, logRequestEnd)),
              guard(fn () => logConnStart();
                    wrap(managerEvt, logConnEnd))]))
```

Mailboxes and Multicast: Using asynchronous events we can encode other CML structures such as mailboxes (i.e., buffered channels with asynchronous send and synchronous receive semantics) and multicasts channels, reducing code size and complexity. Asynchronous events provide the components from which a mailbox structure can be defined, allowing the construction of mailboxes from regular CML channels (a facility not available in CML), and providing a mechanism to define *asynchronous* send events on the mailbox trivially using the base asynchronous send event. Having an asynchronous send event operation defined for mailboxes allows for their use in selective communication. Additionally, asynchronous events now provide the ability for programmers to specify post-creation *and* post-consumption actions. Using asynchronous events, we reduced the original CML mailbox implementation from 240 LOC to 70 LOC, with a corresponding 52% improvement in performance on synthetic stress tests exercising various producer/-consumer configurations. Similarly, we were able to express multicast channels in 60 LOC, compared to 87 LOC in CML, with a roughly 19% improvement in performance.

5. Semantics

Our semantics (see Fig. 8) is defined in terms of a core call-by-value functional language with threading and communication primitives. Communication between threads is achieved using synchronous channels and events. Our language extends a synchronous-event core language with asynchronous constructs. For perspicuity, the language omits many useful event combinators such as `choose` (and its variants); a semantics formalizing the full set of combinators discussed in this paper is available in an accompanying technical report [19].

In our syntax, v ranges over values, p over primitive event constructors, and e over expressions. Besides abstractions, a value can be a message identifier, used to track communication actions, a channel identifier, or an event context. An event context ($\varepsilon[]$) demarcates event expressions that are built from asynchronous events and their combinators [3] that are eventually supplied as an argument to a synchronization action. The rules use function composition $f \circ g \equiv \lambda x. f(g(x))$ to sequence event actions and computations.

The semantics also includes a new expression form, $\{e_1, e_2\}$ to denote asynchronous communication actions; the expression e_1 corresponds to the creation (and post-creation) of an asynchronous event, while e_2 corresponds to the consumption (and post-consumption) of an asynchronous event. For convenience, both synchronous and asynchronous events are expressed in this form. For a synchronous event, e_2 simply corresponds to an uninteresting action. We refer to e_1 as the synchronous portion of the event, the expression which is executed by the current thread, and e_2 as the asynchronous portion of the event, the expression which is executed by a newly created thread (see rule SYNCEVENT).

A program state consists of a set of threads ($\overline{T}$), a communication map (Δ), and a channel map ($\mathcal{C}$). The communication map is used to track the state of an asynchronous action, while the channel map records the state of channels with respect to waiting (blocked) actions. Evaluation is specified via a relation ($\rightarrow$) that maps one program state to another. Evaluation rules are applied up to commutativity of parallel composition ($\|$).

Encoding Communication: A communication action is split into two message parts: one corresponding to a sender and the other to a receiver. A send message part is, in turn, composed of two conceptual primitive actions: a *send act* (`sendAct`(c, v)) and a *send wait* (`sendWait`):

`sendAct`: $(\mathit{ChannelId} \times \mathit{Val}) \rightarrow \mathit{MessageId} \rightarrow \mathit{MessageId}$
`sendWait`: $\mathit{MessageId} \rightarrow \mathit{Val}$

The *send act* primitive, when applied to a message identifier, places the value (v) on the channel (c), while the *send wait*, when applied to a message identifier, blocks until the value has been consumed off of the channel, returning `unit` when the message has been consumed.

The message identifier m, generated for each base event (see rule `SyncEvent`) is used to correctly pair the "act" and "wait". Similarly, a receive message part is composed of *receive act* (`recvAct`(c)) and a *receive wait* (`recvWait`) primitives:

`recvAct`: $\mathit{ChannelId} \rightarrow \mathit{MessageId} \rightarrow \mathit{MessageId}$
`recvWait`: $\mathit{MessageId} \rightarrow \mathit{Val}$

A *receive wait* behaves as its send counterpart. A *receive act* removes a value from the channel if a matching send action exists;

[3] We describe the necessity of a guarded event context when we introduce the combinators later in this section.

$$
\begin{array}{rcl}
e \in \mathit{Exp} & := & v \mid x \mid p\ e \mid e\ e \\
& \mid & \{e, e'\} \mid \texttt{spawn}\ e \mid \texttt{sync}\ e \mid \texttt{ch}() \\
& \mid & \texttt{sendEvt}(e, e) \mid \texttt{recvEvt}(e) \\
& \mid & \texttt{aSendEvt}(e, e) \mid \texttt{aRecvEvt}(e) \\
& \mid & \texttt{aWrap}(e, e) \mid \texttt{sWrap}(e, e) \mid \texttt{aGuard}(e) \\
v \in \mathit{Val} & := & \texttt{unit} \mid c \mid m \mid \lambda x.e \mid \varepsilon[e] \\
p \in \mathit{Prim} & := & \texttt{sendAct}(c, v) \mid \texttt{sendWait} \mid \texttt{recvAct}(c) \mid \texttt{recvWait}
\end{array}
$$

$$
\begin{array}{rcl}
E & := & \bullet \mid E\ e \mid v\ E \mid p\ E \mid \texttt{sync}\ E \\
& \mid & \texttt{sendEvt}(E, e) \mid \texttt{sendEvt}(c, E) \\
& \mid & \texttt{aSendEvt}(E, e) \mid \texttt{aSendEvt}(c, E) \\
& \mid & \texttt{recvEvt}(E) \mid \texttt{aRecvEvt}(E) \\
& \mid & \texttt{aWrap}(E, e) \mid \texttt{sWrap}(E, e) \mid \texttt{aWrap}(v, E) \mid \texttt{sWrap}(v, E) \\
& \mid & \texttt{aGuard}(E)
\end{array}
$$

$$
\begin{array}{rcll}
m & \in & \mathit{MessageId} & \\
c & \in & \mathit{ChannelId} & \\
\varepsilon[e], \varepsilon[e]^g & \in & \mathit{Event} & \\
\mathcal{A} & \in & \mathit{Action} & := \mathcal{A}_r \mid \mathcal{A}_s \\
\mathcal{A}_r & \in & \mathit{ReceiveAct} & := \mathcal{R}_\varepsilon^m \\
\mathcal{A}_s & \in & \mathit{SendAct} & := \mathcal{S}_{c,v}^m
\end{array}
$$

$$
\begin{array}{rclcl}
T & \in & \mathit{Thread} & := & (\texttt{t}, e) \\
\overline{T} & \in & \mathit{ThreadCollection} & := & \emptyset \mid T \mid T \mid\mid \overline{T} \\
\Delta & \in & \mathit{CommMap} & := & \mathit{MessageId} \rightarrow \mathit{Val} \\
\mathcal{C} & \in & \mathit{ChanMap} & := & \mathit{ChannelId} \rightarrow \overline{\mathit{Action}} \\
\langle \overline{T} \rangle_{\Delta,\mathcal{C}} & \in & \mathit{State} & := & \langle \overline{T}, \mathit{CommMap}, \mathit{ChanMap} \rangle
\end{array}
$$

App

$$\frac{}{\langle (\texttt{t}, E[(\lambda x.e)\ v]) \mid\mid \overline{T} \rangle_{\Delta,\mathcal{C}} \rightarrow \langle (\texttt{t}, E[e[v/x]]) \mid\mid \overline{T} \rangle_{\Delta,\mathcal{C}}}$$

Channel

$$\frac{c\ \mathit{fresh}}{\langle (\texttt{t}, E[\texttt{ch}()]) \mid\mid \overline{T} \rangle_{\Delta,\mathcal{C}} \rightarrow \langle (\texttt{t}, E[c]) \mid\mid \overline{T} \rangle_{\Delta,\mathcal{C}[c \mapsto \emptyset]}}$$

Spawn

$$\frac{\texttt{t}'\ \mathit{fresh}}{\langle (\texttt{t}, E[\texttt{spawn}\ e]) \mid\mid \overline{T} \rangle_{\Delta,\mathcal{C}} \rightarrow \langle (\texttt{t}', e) \mid\mid (\texttt{t}, E[\texttt{unit}]) \mid\mid \overline{T} \rangle_{\Delta,\mathcal{C}}}$$

SendEvent

$$\frac{}{\langle (\texttt{t}, E[\texttt{sendEvt}(c, v)]) \mid\mid \overline{T} \rangle_{\Delta,\mathcal{C}} \rightarrow \langle (\texttt{t}, E[\varepsilon[\{\texttt{sendWait} \circ \texttt{sendAct}(c, v), \lambda x.\texttt{unit}\}]]) \mid\mid \overline{T} \rangle_{\Delta,\mathcal{C}}}$$

ASendEvent

$$\frac{}{\langle (\texttt{t}, E[\texttt{aSendEvt}(c, v)]) \mid\mid \overline{T} \rangle_{\Delta} \rightarrow \langle (\texttt{t}, E[\varepsilon[\{\texttt{sendAct}(c, v), \texttt{sendWait}\}]]) \mid\mid \overline{T} \rangle_{\Delta,\mathcal{C}}}$$

RecvEvent

$$\frac{}{\langle (\texttt{t}, E[\texttt{recvEvt}(c)]) \mid\mid \overline{T} \rangle_{\Delta,\mathcal{C}} \rightarrow \langle (\texttt{t}, E[\varepsilon[\{\texttt{recvWait} \circ \texttt{recvAct}(c), \lambda x.\texttt{unit}\}]]) \mid\mid \overline{T} \rangle_{\Delta,\mathcal{C}}}$$

ARecvEvent

$$\frac{}{\langle (\texttt{t}, E[\texttt{aRecvEvt}(c)]) \mid\mid \overline{T} \rangle_{\Delta,\mathcal{C}} \rightarrow \langle (\texttt{t}, E[\varepsilon[\{\texttt{recvAct}(c), \texttt{recvWait}\}]]) \mid\mid \overline{T} \rangle_{\Delta,\mathcal{C}}}$$

SyncEvent

$$\frac{m\ \mathit{fresh} \quad \texttt{t}'\ \mathit{fresh}}{\langle (\texttt{t}, E[\texttt{sync}\ \varepsilon[\{e, e'\}]]) \mid\mid \overline{T} \rangle_{\Delta,\mathcal{C}} \rightarrow \langle (\texttt{t}, E[e\ m]) \mid\mid (\texttt{t}', e'\ m) \mid\mid \overline{T} \rangle_{\Delta,\mathcal{C}}}$$

Message

$$\frac{}{\Delta, \mathcal{S}_{c,v}^m \Rightarrow \Delta[m \mapsto \texttt{unit}]} \qquad \frac{}{\Delta, \mathcal{R}_\varepsilon^m, v \Rightarrow \Delta[m \mapsto v]}$$

SendMatch

$$\frac{\mathcal{C}(c) = \mathcal{R}_\varepsilon^{m'} : \overline{\mathcal{A}_r} \qquad \Delta, \mathcal{S}_{c,v}^m \Rightarrow \Delta' \quad \Delta', \mathcal{R}_\varepsilon^{m'}, v \Rightarrow \Delta''}{\langle (\texttt{t}, E[(\texttt{sendAct}(c, v))\ m]) \mid\mid \overline{T} \rangle_{\Delta,\mathcal{C}} \rightarrow \langle (\texttt{t}, E[m]) \mid\mid \overline{T} \rangle_{\Delta'',\mathcal{C}[c \mapsto \overline{\mathcal{A}_r}]}}$$

RecvMatch

$$\frac{\mathcal{C}(c) = \mathcal{S}_{c,v}^{m'} : \overline{\mathcal{A}_s} \qquad \Delta, \mathcal{S}_{c,v}^{m'} \Rightarrow \Delta' \quad \Delta', \mathcal{R}_\varepsilon^{m}, v \Rightarrow \Delta''}{\langle (\texttt{t}, E[(\texttt{recvAct}(c))\ m]) \mid\mid \overline{T} \rangle_{\Delta,\mathcal{C}} \rightarrow \langle (\texttt{t}, E[m]) \mid\mid \overline{T} \rangle_{\Delta'',\mathcal{C}[c \mapsto \overline{\mathcal{A}_s}]}}$$

SendBlock

$$\frac{\mathcal{C}(c) = \overline{\mathcal{A}_s} \quad \mathcal{C}' = \mathcal{C}[c \mapsto \overline{\mathcal{A}_s} : \mathcal{S}_{c,v}^m]}{\langle (\texttt{t}, E[(\texttt{sendAct}(c, v))\ m]) \mid\mid \overline{T} \rangle_{\Delta,\mathcal{C}} \rightarrow \langle (\texttt{t}, E[m]) \mid\mid \overline{T} \rangle_{\Delta,\mathcal{C}'}}$$

RecvBlock

$$\frac{\mathcal{C}(c) = \overline{\mathcal{A}_r} \quad \mathcal{C}' = \mathcal{C}[c \mapsto \overline{\mathcal{A}_r} : \mathcal{R}_\varepsilon^m]}{\langle (\texttt{t}, E[(\texttt{recvAct}(c))\ m]) \mid\mid \overline{T} \rangle_{\Delta,\mathcal{C}} \rightarrow \langle (\texttt{t}, E[m]) \mid\mid \overline{T} \rangle_{\Delta,\mathcal{C}'}}$$

SendWait

$$\frac{\Delta(m) = \texttt{unit}}{\langle (\texttt{t}, E[\texttt{sendWait}\ m]) \mid\mid \overline{T} \rangle_{\Delta,\mathcal{C}} \rightarrow \langle (\texttt{t}, E[\texttt{unit}]) \mid\mid \overline{T} \rangle_{\Delta,\mathcal{C}}}$$

ReceiveWait

$$\frac{\Delta(m) = v}{\langle (\texttt{t}, E[\texttt{recvWait}\ m]) \mid\mid \overline{T} \rangle_{\Delta,\mathcal{C}} \rightarrow \langle (\texttt{t}, E[v]) \mid\mid \overline{T} \rangle_{\Delta,\mathcal{C}}}$$

Figure 8: A core language for asynchronous events.

if none exists, it simply records the *intention* of performing the receive on the channel queue. We can think of computations occurring after an act as post-creation actions and those occurring after a wait as post-consumption actions. Splitting a communication message part into an "act" and a "wait" primitive functions allows for the expression of many types of message passing. For instance, a traditional synchronous send is simply the sequencing of a *send act* followed by a *send wait*: $\texttt{sendWait} \circ \texttt{sendAct}(c, v)$. This encoding immediately causes the thread executing the operation to block after the value has been deposited on a channel, unless there is a matching *receive act* currently available. A synchronous receive is encoded in much the same manner.

We use the global communication map (Δ) to track act and wait actions for a given message identifier. A message id is created at a synchronization point, ensuring a unique message identifier for each synchronized event. Once a send or receive act occurs, Δ is updated to reflect the value yielded by the act (see Rule MESSAGE) through an auxiliary relation ($\Rightarrow$). When a send act occurs the communication map will hold a binding to `unit` for the corresponding message, but when a receive act occurs the communication map binds the corresponding message to the value received. The values stored in the communication map are passed to the wait actions corresponding to the message (Rules SEND WAIT and RECV WAIT).

Base Events: There are four rules for creating base events, (SENDEVENT) and (RECVEVENT) for synchronous events, and (ASENDEVENT) and (ARECVEVENT) for their asynchronous counterparts. From base act and wait actions, we define asynchronous events ($\varepsilon[\{\texttt{sendAct}(c, v), \texttt{sendWait}\}]$). The first component of an asynchronous event is executed in the thread in which the expression evaluates, and is the target of synchronization (`sync`), while the second component defines the actual asynchronous computation. For asynchronous events we split the act from the wait. Synchronous events can also be encoded using this notation: $\varepsilon[\{\texttt{sendWait} \circ \texttt{sendAct}(c, v), \lambda x.\texttt{unit}\}]$. In a synchronous event both the act and its corresponding wait occur in the synchronous portion of the event. The base asynchronous portion is simply a lambda that yields a unit value.

Event Evaluation: As mentioned above, events are deconstructed by the `sync` operator in rule (SYNCEVENT). It strips the event context ($\varepsilon[]$), generates a new message identifier for the base event, creates a new thread of control, and triggers the evaluation of the internal expressions. The asynchronous portion of the event is wrapped in a new thread of control and placed in the regular pool of threads. If the event abstraction being synchronized was generated by a base synchronous event, the asynchronous portion is an uninteresting value (e.g. , $\lambda x.\texttt{unit}$). The newly created thread, in the case of an asynchronous event, will not be able to be evaluated further as it blocks until the corresponding act for the base event comprising the complex asynchronous event is discharged.

Communication and Ordering: There are four rules for communicating over channels (SENDMATCH, RECVMATCH, SENDBLOCK, and RECVBLOCK. The channel map ($\mathcal{C}$) encodes abstract channel states mapping a channel to a sequence of actions ($\overline{\mathcal{A}}$). This sequence encodes a FIFO queue and provides ordering between actions on the channel. The channel will have either a sequence of send acts ($\mathcal{A}_s$) or receive acts ($\mathcal{A}_r$), but never both at the same time. This is because if there are, for example, send acts enqueued on it, a receive action will immediately match the send, instead of needing to be enqueued and *vice versa* (rules SENDMATCH and RECVMATCH). If a channel already has send acts enqueued on it, any thread wishing to send on the channel will enqueue its act and *vice versa* (rules SENDBLOCK) and (RECVBLOCK). After enqueueing its action, a thread can proceed with its evaluation.

Ordering for asynchronous acts and their post consumption actions as well as blocking of synchronous events is achieved by rules (SENDWAIT) and (RECVWAIT). Both rules block the evaluation of a thread until the corresponding act has been evaluated. In the case of synchronous events, this thread is the one that initiated the act; in the case of an asynchronous event, the thread that creates the act is different from the one that waits on it, and the blocking rules only block the implicitly created thread. For example, the condition $\Delta(m) = unit$ in rule SENDWAIT is established either by rule SENDMATCH, in the case of a synchronous action (created by SENDEVENT), or rules SENDBLOCK and RECVMATCH for an asynchronous one (created by ASENDEVENT).

Combinators: Complex events are built from the combinators described earlier; their definitions are shown in Figure 9. We define two variants of wrap, SWRAP for specifying extensions to the *synchronous* portion of the event and AWRAP for specifying extension to the *asynchronous* portion of the event. In the case of a synchronous event, we have SWRAP extend the event with post-consumption actions as the base event will perform both the *act* and *wait* in the synchronous portion of the event. Similarly, leveraging AWRAP on a synchronous event allows for the specification of general asynchronous actions. If the base event is asynchronous, SWRAP expresses post creation actions and AWRAP post consumption actions.

The specification of the guard combinator is a bit more complex. Since a guard builds an event expression out of a function, that when executed yields an event, the concrete event is only generated at the synchronization point. This occurs because the guard is only executed when synchronized upon. The rule GUARD simply places the function applied to a unit value (the function is really a thunk) in a specialized guarded event context ($\varepsilon[(\lambda x.e)\texttt{unit}]^g$). The rule SYNC GUARDED EVENT simply strips the guarded event context and synchronizes on the encapsulated expression. This expression, when evaluated, will yield an event. Guarded events cannot be immediately extended with an SWRAP or AWRAP as the expression contained within a guarded event context is a function. Instead, wrapping an event in a guarded context simply moves the wrap expression into the event context.

6. Case Study: A Parallel Web-server

We have implemented asynchronous events in Multi-MLton, an open source, multi-core aware implementation of MLton [14]. Our implementation closely follows the semantics given in Section 5, and comprises roughly 4K LOC wholly written in ML.

`Swerve` [14] is an open-source, third-party, multithreaded webserver wholly written in CML and is roughly 16K lines of CML code. We briefly touch upon three aspects of Swerve's design that were amenable to using asynchronous events, and show how these changes lead to substantial improvement in throughput and performance.

To better understand the utility of asynchronous events, we consider the interactions of four of `Swerve`'s modules: the `Listener`, the `File Processor`, the `Network Processor`, and the `Timeout Manager`. The `Listener` module receives incoming HTTP requests and delegates file serving requirements to concurrently executing processing threads. For each new connection, a new listener is spawned; thus, each connection has one main governing entity. The `File Processor` module handles access to the underlying file system. Each file that will be hosted is read by a file processor thread that chunks the file and sends it via message-sWRAP

$$\frac{}{\langle(\texttt{t}, E[\texttt{sWrap}(\varepsilon[\{e, e'\}], \lambda x.e'')]) \,||\, \overline{T}\rangle_{\Delta,C} \rightarrow \langle(\texttt{t}, E[\varepsilon[\{\lambda x.e'' \circ e, e'\}]]) \,||\, \overline{T}\rangle_{\Delta,C}}$$

AWRAP

$$\frac{}{\langle(\texttt{t}, E[\texttt{aWrap}(\varepsilon[\{e, e'\}], \lambda x.e'')]) \,||\, \overline{T}\rangle_{\Delta,C} \rightarrow \langle(\texttt{t}, E[\varepsilon[\{e, \lambda x.e'' \circ e'\}]]) \,||\, \overline{T}\rangle_{\Delta,C}}$$

GUARD

$$\frac{}{\langle(\texttt{t}, E[\texttt{aGuard}(\lambda x.e)]) \,||\, \overline{T}\rangle_{\Delta,C} \rightarrow \langle(\texttt{t}, E[\varepsilon[(\lambda x.e)\ \texttt{unit}]^{g}]) \,||\, \overline{T}\rangle_{\Delta,C}}$$

SYNC GUARDED EVENT

$$\frac{}{\langle(\texttt{t}, E[\texttt{sync}\ \varepsilon[e]^{g}]) \,||\, \overline{T}\rangle_{\Delta,C} \rightarrow \langle(\texttt{t}, E[\texttt{sync}\ e]) \,||\, \overline{T}\rangle_{\Delta,C}}$$

sWRAP GUARDED EVENT

$$\frac{}{\langle(\texttt{t}, E[\texttt{sWrap}(\varepsilon[e]^{g}, \lambda x.e')]) \,||\, \overline{T}\rangle_{\Delta,C} \rightarrow \langle(\texttt{t}, E[\varepsilon[\texttt{sWrap}(e, \lambda x.e')]^{g}]) \,||\, \overline{T}\rangle_{\Delta,C}}$$

AWRAP GUARDED EVENT

$$\frac{}{\langle(\texttt{t}, E[\texttt{aWrap}(\varepsilon[e]^{g}, \lambda x.e')]) \,||\, \overline{T}\rangle_{\Delta,C} \rightarrow \langle(\texttt{t}, E[\varepsilon[\texttt{aWrap}(e, \lambda x.e')]^{g}]) \,||\, \overline{T}\rangle_{\Delta,C}}$$

Figure 9: Combinator extension for a core language for asynchronous events.

passing to the `Network Processor`. The `Network Processor`, like the `File Processor`, handles access to the network. The `File Processor` and `Network Processor` execute in lock-step, requiring the `Network Processor` to have completed sending a chunk before the next one is read from disk. Timeouts are processed by the `Timeout Manager` through the use of timed events.

Lock-step File and Network I/O: Swerve was engineered assuming lock-step file and network I/O. While adequate under low request loads, this design has poor scalability characteristics. This is because (a) file descriptors, a bounded resource, can remain open for potentially long periods of time, as many different requests are multiplexed among a set of compute threads, and (b) for a given request, a file chunk is read only after the network processor has sent the previous chunk. Asynchronous events can be used to alleviate both bottlenecks.

To solve the problem of lockstep transfer of file chunks, we might consider using simple asynchronous sends. However, Swerve was engineered to require the file processor to be responsible for detecting timeouts. If a timeout occurs, the file processor sends a notification to the network processor on the same channel used to send file chunks. Therefore, if asynchrony was used to simply buffer the file chunks, a timeout would not be detected by the network processor until *all* the chunks were processed. Changing the communication structure to send timeout notifications on a separate channel would entail substantial structural modifications to the code base.

The code shown in Fig. 10 is a simplified version of the file processing module modified to use asynchronous events. It uses an arbitrator defined within the file processor to manage the file chunks produced by the `fileReader`. Now, the `fileReader` sends file chunks asynchronously to the arbitrator on the channel `arIn` (line 12) as a post-consumption action. Each such asynchronous send acts as an arbitrator for the next asynchronous send (lines 18-20). The `arbitrator` accepts file chunks from the `fileReader` on this channel and synchronously sends the file chunks to the consumer as long as a timeout has not been detected. This is accomplished by choosing between an `abortEvt` (used by the `Timeout` manager to signal a timeout) and receiving a chunk from file processing loop (lines 13-20). When a timeout is detected, an asynchronous message is sent on channel `arOut` to notify the file processing loop of this fact (line 9); subsequent file processing then stops. This loop synchronously chooses between accepting a timeout notification (line 17), or asynchronously processing the next chunk (lines 11 - 12).

```
datatype Xfr = TIMEOUT | DONE | X of chunk
1. fun fileReader name abortEvt consumer =
2. let
3.   val (arIn, arOut) = (channel(), channel())
4.   fun arbitrator() = sync
5.       (choose [
6.         wrap (recvEvt arIn,
7.               fn chunk => send (consumer, chunk)),
8.         wrap (abortEvt, fn () =>
9.               (aSync(aSendEvt(arOut, ()));
10.              send(consumer, TIMEOUT)))])
11. fun sendChunk(chunk) =
12.       aSync(aWrap(aSendEvt(arIn, X(chunk)),arbitrator))
13. fun loop strm =
14.       case BinIO.read (strm, size)
15.       of SOME chunk => sync
16.             (choose [
17.               recvEvt arOut,
18.               wrap(alwaysEvt,
19.                     fn () => (sendChunk(chunk);
20.                                loop strm))])
21.       | NONE => aSync(aSendEvt(arIn, DONE))
22. in
23. case BinIO.openIt name of
24.       NONE => ()
25.     | SOME strm => (loop strm; BinIO.closeIt strm)
26. end
```

Figure 10: A simplified version of the file processing module in Swerve.

Since asynchronous events operate over regular CML channels, we were able to modify the file processor to utilize asynchrony without having to change any of the other modules or the communication patterns and protocols they expect. Being able to choose between synchronous and asynchronous events in the `fileReader` function also allowed us to create a buffer of file chunks, but stop file processing file if a timeout was detected by the `arbitrator`.

Parallel Packetizing: In CML, channels are often used to implement shared input/output buffered streams. For example, in Swerve, the network processor uses a buffered stream to collect concurrently-processed data chunks generated by the file processor. These chunks are subsequently transformed into packets amenable for transmission back to the client. Asynchronous receives allow parallel processing of these chunks that *automatically* preserves the order in which these chunks were generated. Associated with each element in the buffered stream is a thread that asynchronously waits for the element to be deposited, processes the chunk into a packet, and sends it on a dedicated local channel. This functionality is encapsulated within an event (that leverages an asynchronous receive) that is eventually synchronized by a collator thread which waits for packets to be generated before sending the result back to the client:

```
fun packetEvt(is) =
  aGuard(fn () =>
    let val c = channel()
    in sWrap(aWrap(aRecvEvt(is),
             fn x => send(c, packetize(parse(x))),
       fn () => recvEvt(c)))
    end)
```

When the event returned by `packetEvt` is synchronized, an asynchronous receive event is deposited on the input stream (`is`), and a new event is returned, which, when synchronized in turn, will yield the final packet to be sent on the network.

Given a parameter, `bufferSize`, of how many packets we wish to processes in parallel, we can express the `collate` function as follows:

```
fun collate(bufferSize) =
  let fun createEvents(0, evts) = evts
        | createEvents(x, evts) =
          createEvents(x-1, evts@[sync(packetEvt(is))])
      fun sendPackets([]) = ()
        | sendPackets(e::evts) =
            (networkIO.send(socket,sync(e));
             sendPackets(evts))
  in sendPackets(createEvents(bufferSize, []))
  end
```

The auxiliary function `createEvents` synchronizes on `bufferSize` number of `parseAndPacketEvts`. This results in a list of events which, when synchronized, will yield the final packets. This list of events consists of the synchronous receive events over local channels returned by `parseAndPacketEvts`.

Without asynchronous events, the concurrency afforded by this implementation could be realized by having a collection of explicit packet-izing threads all contending on the stream, waiting for a new element to be deposited. However, because these threads can process the chunks out-of-order, additional metadata such as a sequence number must be provided in the deposited chunks. This requires modifying the module which is responsible for the input stream to embed relevant metadata, as well as augmenting the collator to make sure to stitch things back into correct order using these sequence numbers. Asynchronous receives *implicitly* provide these ordering guarantees, alleviating the burden of weaving this metadata management in the protocol, resulting in cleaner, more modular, code.

Underlying I/O and Logging: To improve scalability and responsiveness, we also implemented a non-blocking I/O library composed of a language-level interface and associated runtime support. The library implements all MLton I/O interfaces, but internally utilizes asynchronous events. The library is structured around callback events as defined in Sec. 4.1 operating over I/O resource servers. Internally, all I/O requests are translated into a potential series of callback events.

Web-servers utilize logging for administrative purposes. For long running servers, logs tend to grow quickly. Some web-servers (like Apache) solve this problem by using a *rolling log*, which automatically opens a new log file after a set time period (usually a day). In Swerve, all logging functions were done asynchronously. Using asynchronous events, we were able to easily change the logging infrastructure to use rolling logs. Post consumption actions were utilized to implement the rolling log functionality, by closing old logs and opening new logs after the appropriate time quantum.

In addition, Swerve's logging infrastructure is tasked with exiting the system if a fatal error is detected. The log notates that the occurrence of the error, flushes the log to disk, and then exits the system. This ensure that the log contains a record of the error prior to the system's exit. Unfortunately, for the modules that utilize logging, this poses additional complexity and breaks modularity. Instead of logging the error at the point which it occurred, the error must be logged *after* the module has performed any clean up actions because of the synchronous communication protocol between the module and the log. Thus, if the module logs any actions during the clean up phase, they will appear in the log *prior* to the error. We can leverage asynchronous callback events to extend the module without changing the communication protocol to the log.

```
let val logEvt = aSendEvt(log, fatalErr)
    val logEvt' = callbackEvt(logEvt,
                    fn () => (Log.flush();
                              System.exit()))
    val exitEvt = aSync(logEvt')
in ( clean up; sync(exitEvt))
end
```

In the code above, `logEvt` corresponds to an event that encapsulates the communication protocol the log expects: a simple asynchronous send on the log's input channel `log`. The event `logEvt'` defines a callback. This event, when synchronized, will execute an asynchronous send to the log and will create a new event that becomes bound to `exitEvt`. When `exitEvt` is synchronized upon, we are guaranteed that the log has received the notification of the fatal error. With this simplification we can also simplify the log by removing checks to see if a logged message corresponds to a fatal error and the exit mechanism; logging and system exit are now no longer conflated.

6.1 Results

To measure the efficiency of our changes in Swerve, we leveraged the server's internal timing and profiling output for per-module accounting. The benchmarks were run on an AMD Opteron 865 server with 8 processors, each containing two symmetric cores, and 32 GB of total memory, with each CPU having its own local memory of 4 GB. The results as well as the changes to the largest modules are summarized in Table 1. Translating the implementation to use asynchronous events leads to a 4.7X performance improvement as well as a 15X reduction in client-side observed latency over the original, with only 103 lines of code changed out of 16KLOC.

Not surprisingly, the results show that asynchronous communication, when carefully applied, can yield substantial performance gains. More significantly, however, is that these gains were achieved with only small changes to the overall structure of the application. These changes were almost always mechanical, often just involving the replacement of a synchronous event combinator with an asynchronous one. No changes were required to module interfaces or the program's overall logical structure.

To put the performance gains in perspective, our modified version of Swerve with asynchronous events has a throughput within 10% of Apache 2.2.15 on workloads that establish up to 1000 concurrent connections and process small/medium files at a total rate of 2000 requests per second. For server performance measurements and workload generation we used httperf – a tool for measuring web-server performance.

Module	LOC	LOC modified	improvement
Listener	1188	11	2.15 X
File Processor	2519	35	19.23 X
Network Processor	2456	25	24.8 X
Timeout Manager	360	15	4.25 X
Swerve	16,000	103	4.7 X

Table 1: Per module performance numbers for Swerve.

7. Related Work

Many functional programming languages such as Erlang [1], JoCaml [10], and F# [18] provide intrinsic support for asynchronous programming. In Erlang, message sends are inherently asynchronous. In JoCaml, complex asynchronous protocols are defined using join patterns [2, 11] that define synchronization protocols over asynchronous and synchronous channels. In F#, asynchronous behavior is defined using asynchronous work flows that permit asynchronous objects to be created and synchronized. Convenient monadic-style `let!` -syntax permits callbacks, represented as continuations, to be created within an asynchronous computation. While these different techniques provide expressive ways to define asynchronous computations, they do not focus on issues of composability (our primary interest in this paper), especially with respect to asynchronous post-consumption actions. There have also been efforts to simplify asynchronous programming in imperative languages [3] by providing new primitives that are amenable to compiler analysis; here again, the primary focus is not on composability or modularity of asynchronous event-based protocols.

Reactive programming [12] is an important programing style often found in systems programming that uses event loops to react to outside events (typically related to I/O). In this context, events do not define abstract communication protocols (as they do in CML), but typically represent I/O actions delivered asynchronously by the underlying operating system. While understanding how reactive events and threads can co-exist is an important one, we believe such efforts are orthogonal to the focus of this work.Indeed we can encode reactive style programming idioms in ACML through the use of asynchronous receive events and/or lightweight servers.

Asynchronous exceptions as discussed in [13] provide abstractions that concurrent applications can use to allow one thread to seamlessly and asynchronously signal another. Kill-safe abstractions [8] provide a related solution to safely terminate a cooperative user-level thread without violating sensible invariants on shared objects. While asynchronous events are a general mechanism for composable and modular asynchronous programming, and thus were not designed specifically with these purposes in mind, we believe they can be used to serve such roles effectively as well, as described in the logging infrastructure example given in Sec. 6.

There have been incarnations of CML in languages and systems other than ML (e.g., Haskell [4, 17], Scheme [8], and MPI [5]). There has also been much recent interest in extending CML with transactional support [6, 7] and other flavors of parallelism [9]. We believe transactional events [6, 7] provide an interesting platform upon which to implement a non-blocking version of `sChoose` that retains the same semantics. Additionally, we expect that previous work on specialization of CML primitives [15] can be applied to improve the performance of asynchronous primitives.

8. Concluding Remarks

This paper presents the design, rationale, and implementation for asynchronous events, a concurrency abstraction that generalizes the behavior of CML-based synchronous events to enable composable construction of asynchronous computations. Our experiments indicate that asynchronous events can seamlessly co-exist with other CML primitives, and can be effectively leveraged to improve performance of realistic highly-concurrent applications.

Acknowledgements. This work is supported by the National Science Foundation under grants CCF-0701832 and CCF-0811631, and a gift from Samsung Corporation.

References

[1] Joe Armstrong, Robert Virding, Claes Wikstrom, and Mike Williams. *Concurrent Programming in Erlang*. Prentice-Hall, 2nd edition, 1996.

[2] Jean-Pierre Banâtre and Daniel Le Métayer. Programming by Multiset Transformation. *Commun. ACM*, 36(1), 1993.

[3] Prakash Chandrasekaran, Christopher L. Conway, Joseph M. Joy, and Sriram K. Rajamani. Programming asynchronous layers with clarity. In *FSE*, pages 65–74, 2007.

[4] Avik Chaudhuri. A Concurrent Ml Library in Concurrent Haskell. In *ICFP*, pages 269–280, 2009.

[5] Erik Demaine. First-Class Communication in MPI. In *MPIDC '96: Proceedings of the Second MPI Developers Conference*, 1996.

[6] Kevin Donnelly and Matthew Fluet. Transactional Events. *The Journal of Functional Programming*, pages 649–706, 2008.

[7] Laura Effinger-Dean, Matthew Kehrt, and Dan Grossman. Transactional Events for ML. In *ICFP*, pages 103–114, 2008.

[8] Matthew Flatt and Robert Bruse Findler. Kill-safe Synchronization Abstractions. In *PLDI*, pages 47–58, 2004.

[9] Matthew Fluet, Mike Rainey, John Reppy, and Adam Shaw. Implicitly-Threaded Parallelism in Manticore. In *ICFP*, pages 119–130, 2008.

[10] Cédric Fournet, Fabrice Le Fessant, Luc Maranget, and Alan Schmidt. JoCaml: A Language for Concurrent Distributed and Mobile Programming. In *Advanced Functional Programming*, pages 129–158. 2002.

[11] Cédric Fournet and Georges Gonthier. The reflexive cham and the join-calculus. In *POPL*, pages 372–385, 1996.

[12] Peng Li and Steve Zdancewic. Combining Events and Threads for Scalable Network Services, and Evaluation of Monadic, Application-Level Concurrency Primitives. In *PLDI*, pages 189–199, 2007.

[13] Simon Marlow, Simon Peyton Jones, Andrew Moran, and John Reppy. Asynchronous Exceptions in Haskell. In *PLDI*, pages 274–285, 2001.

[14] MLton. http://www.mlton.org.

[15] John Reppy and Yingqi Xiao. Specialization of CML Message-Passing Primitives. In *POPL*, pages 315–326, 2007.

[16] John H. Reppy. *Concurrent Programming in ML*. Cambridge University Press, 1999.

[17] George Russell. Events in Haskell, and How to Implement Them. In *ICFP*, pages 157–168, 2001.

[18] Don Syme, Adam Granicz, and Antonio Cisternino. *Expert F#*. Apress, 2007.

[19] Lukasz Ziarek, K.C. Sivaramakrishnan, and Suresh Jagannathan. Composable Asynchronous Events. Technical Report TR-11-09, Dept. of Computer Science, Purdue University, 2011.

Synchronization via Scheduling

Techniques For Efficiently Managing Shared State

Micah J Best
University of British Columbia
mjbest@cs.ubc.ca

Shane Mottishaw *
Craig Mustard Mark Roth
Alexandra Fedorova
Simon Fraser University
{smottish, cam14, mroth, fedorova}@cs.sfu.ca

Andrew Brownsword
Electronic Arts, Inc
brownsword@ea.com

Abstract

Shared state access conflicts are one of the greatest sources of error for fine grained parallelism in any domain. Notoriously hard to debug, these conflicts reduce reliability and increase development time. The standard task graph model dictates that tasks with potential conflicting accesses to shared state must be linked by a dependency, even if there is no explicit logical ordering on their execution. In cases where it is difficult to understand if such *implicit* dependencies exist, the programmer often creates more dependencies than needed, which results in constrained graphs with large monolithic tasks and limited parallelism.

We propose a new technique, Synchronization via Scheduling (SvS), that uses the results of static and dynamic code analysis to manage potential shared state conflicts by exposing the data accesses of each task to the scheduler. We present an in-depth performance analysis of SvS via examples from video games, our target domain, and show that SvS performs well in comparison to software transactional memory (TM) and fine grained mutexes.

Categories and Subject Descriptors D.1.3 [*Concurrent Programming*]: Parallel programming; D.3.4 [*Processors*]: Compilers; D.3.4 [*Processors*]: Run-time environments

General Terms Design, Languages, Measurement, Performance, Reliability

Keywords parallel programming, shared state management, Synchronization via Scheduling, Dynamic Reachability Analysis

1. Introduction

Shared state access conflicts are the cause of majority of errors in parallel programming. Race conditions and corruption of shared data are common. These bugs can be notoriously difficult to track down as they often manifest rarely, depending on the state of not just one, but several threads of execution. Unfortunately most existing frameworks don't provide mechanisms to automatically protect shared state. Runtime systems such as the one driving Cilk [12], OpenMP [4] and the venerable pthreads are largely concerned with dispatching code for execution. Systems such as Intel's TBB [6] do provide a vast array of synchronization primitives, including a number of distinct types of mutexes, for the programmer to construct their own state protection. Unfortunately, they contain very little in the way of support for orchestrating these schemes. Software Transactional Memory(STM) [25] does address this problem and as STM is the closest in effect to our proposed technique, we will discuss it further in the context of our experiments in Section 3.

Very few domains have been as profoundly affected by the multicore revolution as video games. The complexity and high level of interaction of the systems which often rivals operating systems, a nearly inexhaustible demand for better performance, large programming teams and tight deadlines makes it an ideal testbed for parallel techniques. The volume of this software and its commercial appeal would make the problems worth solving even if they were unique to the domain, but any technique developed have application in many other domains. For these reasons we have chosen to let the needs of this domain drive our research. Our assumptions and choice of experiments reflect this.

Programmers faced with the difficulties in managing the data accesses of a large collection of tasks tend to leave many tasks monolithic, comprised sometimes of thousands of lines of codes. The embarrassingly parallel kernels, those without complex state interaction, will generally be dispatched in patterns similar to `parallel_for`. This has lead to the structure of the current generation of video games. Often the work of an entire subsystem or one its major components will be assigned to a single processing context, co-scheduled with other components that are guaranteed to be conflict free. Interspersed between the execution of these groups will be the execution of the embarrassingly parallel sections and a number of explicit synchronization points. This structure is common in the industry [1]. The lack of parallel width in many phases of execution leaves resources idle and this approach will not scale as the number of cores increase.

The parallel structure of the program is often represented in the standard task graph model where tasks that have not had a dependency declared between them can be scheduled concurrently. There are cases where ensuring ordering of tasks with dependencies is necessary for correctness. However, there remain many cases where there is not an explicit logical ordering between the tasks and a dependency is declared to prevent two tasks that touch the

* Partially supported by the Natural Sciences and Engineering Research Council of Canada (NSERC)

PLDI'11, June 4–8, 2011, San Jose, California, USA.

same data from running concurrently. This serializing of tasks is necessary even if the two tasks touch the same data rarely.

When a program is executed and tasks are serialized unnecessarily because of unneeded dependencies, parallelism is reduced and performance can suffer. This work proposes a mechanism to correct this deficiency. Our model only requires that the programmer state *explicit* inter-task dependencies, i.e., those that are required by the program logic. In cases where tasks that are not explicitly dependent on each other *may* touch the same data, our system automatically inserts a new *implicit* dependency between them, which will prevent these tasks from running concurrently and corrupting shared state. We use conventional static analysis to determine when implicit dependencies are necessary. During runtime, when we can determine more precisely what data the task will actually access, we detect and remove any overly constraining implicit dependencies – to accomplish this we propose new dynamic analysis techniques. Making the shared state access patterns of each applicable task available to the scheduler we are able to safely schedule tasks with potential conflicts. We call this technique *Synchronization via Scheduling*(SvS).

The general concept of SvS is not overly complicated. The chief difficulty lies in utilizing the information provided by the static analysis and refinement without adding much overhead. To achieve the highly desirable performance of 60 frame-per-second (FPS), a frame must be constructed in just over $16ms$. For optimal parallelization many tasks will have runtimes in the tens or hundreds of microseconds. This strict time budget does not allow for much extra computation. One of the major contributions of this work is the description of algorithms to achieve this high speed organization and to demonstrate that they work in practical contexts.

SvS differs from optimistic techniques such as STM in that the work of evaluating the admissibility of a task is done prior to its execution. Though some of the mechanisms used to realize SvS are similar to those in some STM implementations this difference means that there are no expensive rollbacks and there is a much smaller requirement for extra bookkeeping during state access. Additionally, STM requires programmers to define atomic transactions while SvS is an automatic technique completely handled by the compiler and runtime components. We will show a comparison between SvS and STM in section 3.

The rest of the paper is organized as follows. In Section 2 we discuss the model, algorithms and implementation of SvS. Experimental results, drawn from several applications in our domain, are presented in Section 3. In section 4 we will discuss related work and in Section 5 we will conclude and give a short discussion of our future work.

2. SvS Model and Implementation

2.1 Motivation and Overview

Task graph models are a standard pattern for structuring parallelism in programs [20]. A prevailing problem with this model is the lack of automatic shared state management between tasks. Consider an example of skeletal character animation. Typically, multiple animations are applied to the bones of a single character to produce realistic looking motion [2]. For example, to produce a character that is walking and limping we may blend the "walking" and "limping" animations. The mathematical operations performed by these two routines are commutative, so there is no explicit ordering between them. However, it is unsafe to execute these animation routines in concurrent tasks, because they *may* touch the same bones of the same character. In this case there exists a special type of dependency between tasks, which we term *implicit*. An implicit dependency exists when there is no logical ordering between the tasks imposed by data or control dependencies, but the tasks may access the same shared state and so it is unsafe to run them concurrently.

Without automatic shared state management, programmers must manage shared state by inserting explicit dependencies where implicit dependences exist. Protecting shared state via explicit dependencies has two problems. First, this is prone to programmer error, especially when considering dynamic, pointer-based memory accesses. Second, this unnecessarily constrains parallelism in cases where the tasks *may* incur conflicting accesses of the shared state, but do not *actually* perform them at runtime.

We address the issue of shared state management in task graph models by introducing a new technique called Synchronization via Scheduling (SvS). SvS provides *automatic* shared state management by combining static and dynamic analysis to determine if two tasks can potentially access shared state. The result of static analysis is a task graph with dependencies that guarantee the protection of shared state. Dynamic analysis then utilizes run-time information to potentially remove unnecessary dependencies between tasks, allowing for increased parallelism. In this way, SvS determines the set of *possible* memory accesses a task makes *before* it is executed and schedules tasks such that no two tasks concurrently access the same memory. In this section, we will provide the details behind the model and implementation of SvS. In section 2.2 we outline the framework for SvS, followed by a brief discussion of relevant background information in sections 2.3 and 2.4. Starting in section 2.5, we will go into detail on the model and implementation of SvS.

2.2 Framework

Figure 1 shows the four main components that comprise the SvS framework: an SvS compatible language, static analysis, dynamic analysis, and the task scheduler. An SvS compatible language allows a programmer to group blocks of code into units called tasks. Programmers can provide a logical ordering between tasks but do not need to manage shared state between them. Beyond providing a task-graph abstraction, an SvS compatible language must be type safe and disallow pointer arithmetic. We describe our prototypical implementation of an SvS compatible language in section 2.4.

At compile time, a program written in an SvS compatible language is passed through a static analysis phase that generates information pertaining to symbols (linguistic abstractions for memory accesses) and task dependencies. This information defines a static task graph which provides an initial scheduling of tasks that ensures the protection of shared state. Information from static analysis is stored for use during dynamic analysis.

We purposely visualize the static analysis in figure 1 as a "black box" because SvS is indifferent to the implementation of static analysis. Static analysis techniques that produce a correct list of task dependencies and a list of all symbols that a task may access are suitable for use within the SvS framework. Static analysis in SvS is formally defined as *task dependency analysis* in section 2.5; this section also explains how task dependency analysis can be implemented using existing techniques. The classic limiting factor of static analysis when applied to parallelization is that it is limited to compile time information. As a result, it often is forced to create dependencies that are potentially unnecessary, thus restricting parallelism. This problem can be alleviated using dynamic analysis.

Throughout the execution of an SvS program, dynamic analysis maintains dynamic reachability information (i.e. potential memory accesses) for symbols accessed by tasks. As tasks are considered for scheduling, this information is used to generate and compare read/write sets of tasks in order to remove any implicit dependencies that were deemed necessary by the static analysis, but were found to be non-existent when dynamic reachability information became available at runtime. We call this process of removing unnecessary static dependencies *refinement*.

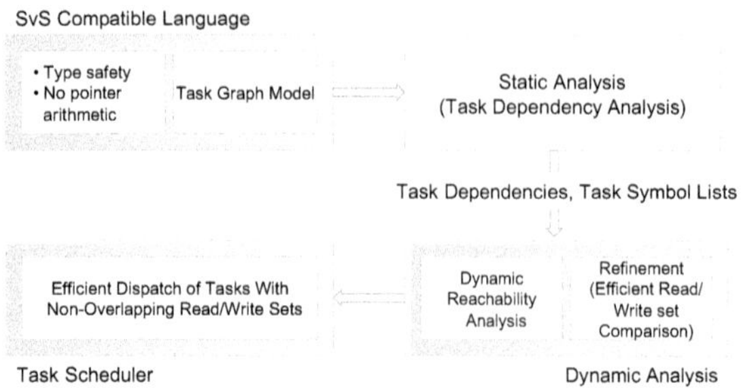

Figure 1. SvS Framework

Finally, the scheduler respects the set of refined dependencies by ensuring that all concurrently executing tasks have distinct read-/write sets (i.e. no implicit dependencies), in effect, performing synchronization via scheduling.

While the SvS framework is the new contribution of this work, its implementation relies on both new and existing techniques. In particular, our framework allows for the use of existing well-established static analysis techniques, but the algorithms used in dynamic analysis and in scheduling are new to this work.

2.3 Task Graph Model

In this section, we define the task-graph model that is assumed by the current implementation of SvS. In task-graph based execution, code is divided into discrete units called *tasks* and a *task graph* defines a static scheduling of these tasks through directed edges. If there is an edge (A, B) then the task A, the parent, must complete before B, the child, can be executed. These edges are referred to as *dependencies* and a dependency is *satisfied* when the parent completes execution. Our task-graph model also includes explicit dataflow where one task, a *producer*, 'sends' data to another task, a *consumer*. Two tasks involved in dataflow have a *dataflow dependency*. Currently, our task graph model does not allow the programmer to specify cyclic dependencies.

A task that has no parents or has all dependencies satisfied is considered runnable. Additionally, a consumer task must also have been sent data to be runnable. A task *instance* is a task running on a processor. When a task is runnable, we say that an *instance* of it can be scheduled. Task instances are generated in one of two ways. If the task is a consumer task, then a copy (i.e. instance) is executed for each data item received, and the collection of all instances define a data-parallel operation. We describe these instances as being part of a single data-parallel task. For all other tasks, an instance is generated "statically" at the beginning of the program.

Besides dependencies, there is also an implicit temporal ordering between executions of a task graph in that we execute all tasks in the graph and wait for them to finish before executing the graph again. More formally, if we define the execution of all tasks in a task-graph to be an *iteration*, then iteration i must complete before $i + 1$ begins.

The dependencies and constructs described in this section support the task-graph requirements of an SvS compatible language, which we describe in the next section.

2.4 CDML

To facilitate writing programs based on the task-graph model outlined in section 2.3 and enable the static analysis required for SvS, we have developed the Cascade Data Management Language (CDML). Because C++ is the standard language for game development, CDML is similar to C++ with a few added annotations and restrictions. Note that CDML is not a requirement for SvS; as described in section 2.2, essentially any language that includes the following features is suitable for SvS: (1) syntax for articulating the task graph model described in section 2.3, (2) type safety, (3) no pointer arithmetic.

Additionally, because the current specification for CDML does not yet support object-oriented programming, we assume no inheritance or polymorphism in our current implementation of SvS, but this is not a requirement. We plan to address inheritance and polymorphism in future work. Because we are not presenting CDML as a contribution of this work, the full syntax and features of CDML will not be discussed here.

The grammar for CDML tasks is shown in figure 2. There are two task types in our current language specification: *transform* and *itemizer*. A transform is just a (static) single instance task. An itemizer is used to implement data-parallel tasks, where multiple instances of the task's body are executed to process items received at run-time. An instance is created for each item received.

Our system assumes that there is no specific ordering between tasks, unless the programmer explicitly specifies a dependency. *Explicit* (i.e. "ordering") constraints are expressed in a tasks *constraints*. At run-time, explicit constraints specified by the programmer are never broken. In many cases, a programmer would not need to specify an explicit ordering between tasks, because the same outcome will be achieved regardless of the ordering. This is especially the case for video game engines and scientific computing applications where many computations are commutative. The programmer can also specify data-flow dependencies using the *send* constraint.

Programmers do not have to manage shared memory accesses between tasks. Static and dynamic analysis are used to automatically detect when two tasks can access the same memory. In the case where tasks may perform conflicting accesses to the same data, SvS chooses an arbitrary ordering for the tasks and runs them sequentially. Otherwise, tasks can be run concurrently.

We implemented a translator that converts CDML code into C++. The translator also performs the static analysis to detect implicit dependencies, as described in the next section.

```
task := task_type task_name ':' constraints? body
task_type := 'itemizer' | 'transform'
constraints := ( send | receive | explicit )+
body := '{' statements '}'
```

Figure 2. CDML task syntax

2.5 Static Analysis

We term the static analysis performed in SvS as *task dependency analysis*. The goal of task dependency analysis is to statically find implicit dependencies between tasks – that is, determine whether two tasks (or task-instances) can potentially access the same memory location. The collection of implicit and explicit dependencies define a task graph that ensures the protection of shared state. Because task dependency analysis is essentially a form of dependency analysis, we will present the definition of dependency analysis and derive from it a formal definition for task dependency analysis.

In traditional dependency analysis [9], the fundamental goal is to determine whether a statement T depends on a statement S. T depends on S if there exists an instance S' of S, an instance T' of T, and a memory location M such that:

1. Both S' and T' reference M, and at least one reference is a write
2. In the serial execution of the program, S' is executed before T'
3. In the serial execution, M is not written between the time that S' finishes and the time T' starts

As mentioned in the previous section, the ordering between tasks in SvS, and thus their accesses, are assumed to be commutative unless the programmer enforces an ordering between tasks by inserting explicit dependencies. For the remaining pairs of tasks, we are not concerned with the order in which they execute. Because of this, conditions number 2 and 3 are not applicable to SvS. It follows from this that task dependency analysis is not concerned with whether the dependency is flow-dependent, anti-dependent, or output-dependent. Therefore, task dependence analysis in SvS can be restated as follows: A dependency exists between task T and a task S if there exists an instance S' of S, an instance T' of T, and a memory location M such that:

> Both S' and T' reference M, and at least one reference is a write. A task references M if there exists a statement X in the body of the task that references M.

In modern programming languages, a reference to a memory location M might be represented as a scalar variable, array, or pointer. In SvS, we refer to these abstractions for memory locations as *symbols*. The syntax for a symbol in CDML is provided in figure 3 and mirrors the syntax of C/C++ expressions for array, variable, and member access. Since symbols abstract references to memory, task dependency analysis becomes collecting the symbols in the body of a task and determining if a symbol x in task S can reference the same memory location M as symbol y in task T where at least one of the references is a write. The problem of determining if two symbols can reference the same memory has been thoroughly explored by research in static analysis including pointer analysis [8], array dependence analysis [21], shape analysis [19], and disjoint heap analysis [15].

Because it is not our goal to expand upon work that has already been done in static analysis, our current implementation is very conservative. As a result, our current approach performs the necessary symbol collection and produces a set of dependencies that generally result in a dependency being placed between each pair of tasks. In this case, dynamic analysis is exclusively responsible for uncovering parallelism. As it will be discussed in sections 2.6.4 and 2.7, this is achieved by collecting run-time information describing the potential memory accesses of the symbols extracted during static analysis in order to "recalculate" (i.e. refine) dependencies. We will show in section 3 that SvS is feasible even with dynamic analysis performing most of the work. However, we hypothesize that using more sophisticated static analysis could only reduce the amount of dynamic checks (i.e. dependency refinement), thus decreasing run-time overhead. Expanding the role of static analysis and implementing more sophisticated static analysis is a definite part of future work for SvS.

SvS is indifferent to what techniques are used to solve task dependency analysis as long as the output is a set of symbols for each task, and a set of dependencies between tasks that guarantees no two task instances can concurrently access the same memory location (which will be the case if the techniques correctly solve the task dependency analysis problem). Therefore it is not a goal of SvS to expand upon the work that has already been done in static analysis, but rather to address the deficiencies associated with static analysis.

2.6 Dynamic Analysis

Due to the limitations of compile time information, static analysis is often forced to make conservative assumptions. This may result in unnecessary dependencies, thus hindering parallelism. The goal of dynamic analysis is to potentially remove such dependencies at run-time. To achieve this, we use information available at run-time to generate more precise read/write sets for tasks. Then, as task instances are considered for scheduling, we efficiently compare their read/write sets to see if a dependency actually exists (a process we call refinement) and subsequently scheduling non-dependent tasks to execute concurrently.

```
symbol := identifier acessor*
identifier := [a-zA-Z_][a-ZA-Z0-9_]*
accessor :=
     '->'  identifier
   | '.' identifier
   | ('[' expression ']')+
```

Figure 3. CDML symbol syntax

To calculate read/write sets, we monitor the connectivity and reachability properties of memory objects, our online abstraction for memory accesses, to determine the set of all addresses that can possibly be *reached* by a memory object. We call this set of accesses the *reachability* of a memory object and its connectivity properties are represented as a *reachability graph* (section 2.6.1). We use *dynamic reachability analysis* (sections 2.6.4 and 2.6.3) to maintain dynamic changes to reachability graphs as memory objects are created and linked together. Since symbols reference memory objects at run-time, this enables us to determine the reachability of symbols accessed by tasks and therefore more precise sets of potential reads and writes.

We will also introduce *signatures* (section 2.6.2), which are used to compactly represent read/write sets and efficiently determine which tasks have non-overlapping memory accesses. Tasks with non-overlapping read/write sets can then be scheduled concurrently. Two new scheduling algorithms that efficiently accomplish this goal will be presented in section 2.7.

2.6.1 Memory Objects, Links, Reachability and Reachability Graphs

We use the notion of a *memory object* to abstract memory accesses in SvS. In the simplest case, a memory object is a single primitive (e.g. `int`) and provides a direct access to memory. In general, memory objects may contain one or more primitives or other memory objects. Primitives and/or other memory objects that compose it are called its *members*. Memory objects may also contain *links*. A link 'points-to' a child memory object, which allows the parent memory object that contains the link to access all the memory addressable by the child memory object. The difference between members and links is that members are *static* – they cannot be removed from the object and their memory addresses within the enclosing object cannot be modified, whereas links are dynamic. The child that a link points to can be changed at any time, thus changing the set of memory addresses that a memory object can access. Links can also exist on their own, in that they do not need to be declared as a member of a memory object. Therefore, SvS tries to solve the problem of determining what memory objects a task can possibly access before the task runs, where memory objects can be accessed directly through members and indirectly through links.

We formalize these definitions by representing the problem as a graph. Memory objects represent nodes in the graph. A *member* edge is a directed edge defined as (X, Y) where memory object Y is a Member of X. A 'link' edge is a directed edge defined as (A, B) where A is a memory object that contains a link L that points to memory object B. We say that A is the parent of L and B is its child. If a link does not have a parent, it is essentially just an alias for the memory object it points to. Changing L to point to a different memory object C effectively removes the edge (A, B) and adds the edge (A, C). This graph represents the *dynamic reachability* of the memory object and is called the *reachability graph*.

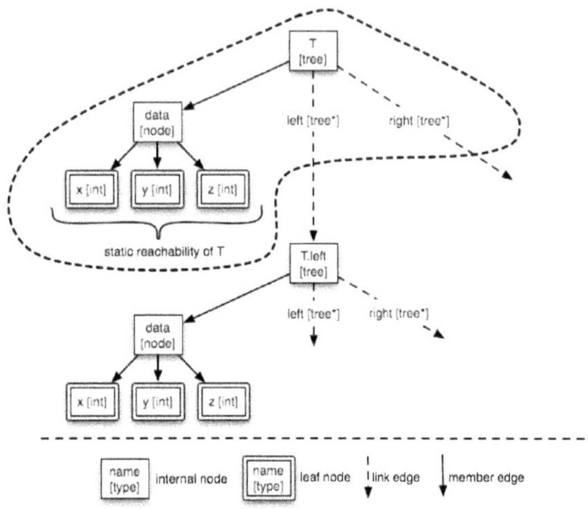


```
struct node {          struct tree {
    int x;                 node data;
    int y;                 tree* left;
    int z;                 tree* right;
};                     };
```

Figure 4. The graph for a memory object representing a binary tree. The sub-graph inside of the dashed boundary represents the result of a breadth-first search that only follows member edges. The leaf nodes in the area are the containment of the memory object T. Related C++ definitions are provided on the bottom.

Given any node, (i.e. memory object), in the graph, the set of memory addresses that can be reached (i.e. accessed) by the node is called its *reachability* and is defined as the set of all leaf-nodes reachable by performing a breadth (or depth) first search starting at the given node. Because leaf nodes are primitives, they directly correspond to an addresses in memory, and thus define a set of memory addresses. Figure 4 provides an example of a graph that would be defined by a typical binary tree. The leaf-nodes inside of the dashed boundary represent the static reachability (unique, static set of memory accesses) of the root node of the tree.

By keeping track of the structure of the reachability graph for each memory object (a process we call *dynamic reachability analysis*), we are able to dynamically monitor reachability information providing significant insight into the potential memory accesses of tasks. This is particularly useful when dealing with dynamic data structures that allow for ambiguous accesses to memory. Implementation of reachability graphs and pertinent algorithms are described in the next sections.

2.6.2 Signatures: Representing Memory Accesses

Sets of memory accesses in SvS are represented as *signatures*: constant length bitstrings. When two signatures have the same bit set, it means they represent access to the same memory location (or memory object) and are said to overlap. To build a signature, id's (i.e. memory object id's) representing reads or writes are passed to a hash function to determine the bit to set in the signature. Signature overlap is checked using simple and efficient bit-wise operations.

Note that signatures are effectively Bloom filters [11] using a single hash function. Also, because signatures are constant in length and use hashing, there is the opportunity that false positives occur when comparing signatures. This does not affect correctness and its impact to performance can be greatly reduced by using large signature sizes with negligible impact to performance, which will be discussed in section 3.1.

2.6.3 Implementing Reachability Graphs and Dynamic Reachability Analysis

As discussed in the previous section, there are two main components to a reachability graph: memory objects and links. The goal of the implementation for these structures is to provide the metadata and meta-functions necessary to efficiently maintain reachability graphs and extract the reachability of a memory object.

Memory Objects Memory objects are implemented as classes that inherit from a MemoryObject class template. The MemoryObject class stores the id of a memory object that is generated inside the class's constructor.

The **getSignature** function of the MemoryObject class returns a signature representing the reachability of a memory object. A straightforward way to implement this function is to simply perform a breadth first search by calling the **getSignature** function of each member, or the **getSignature** function of the memory object a link points to, and combine the returned signatures using a bitwise-or operation. For large reachability graphs, a breadth first search will be too expensive. Instead, we have implemented a more efficient method that utilizes the implementation of links as described in the next section.

Links Links are implemented in SvS as a smart pointer template class. Since a link is just an edge in the reachability graph, the smart pointer representing the link stores pointers to a parent and child memory object. The child pointer represents the memory object that a link "points-to" whereas the parent pointer denotes the memory object that the link is a member of. A null parent represents the case where a link is just a reference or alias to the memory object it points to and is not considered to be an edge in the reachability graph.

We now discuss how smart pointers are used to calculate and maintain the reachability of a memory object. The reachability of a memory object is changed when we change the child node of a link edge. This is equivalent to link assignment, and thus by overloading the assignment operator for the smart pointer class, we can detect a change in reachability and perform the necessary updates. The algorithm that performs these updates is called *dynamic reachability analysis*. First, consider the situation where each memory object stores a signature that accurately represents its reachability. Initially, the reachability of a memory object is just the signature created from its object id (i.e. the signature representing its static reachability). When a link L is changed to point to a memory object B, it means that the memory object $A = parent(L)$ can now access all memory objects reachable by B. It also means that all memory objects that can reach A can also reach memory objects reachable by B. Therefore, during link assignment, we could perform a reverse breadth first search starting at A, recursively updating the signature of each node to include the signature for the reachability of B. However, we want to reduce the cost of this breadth first search. To do this, we introduce the concept of *master* nodes.

A master node M represents a bounded set of reachable nodes, i.e. a set of nodes X such that a path $M \rightsquigarrow X$ exists. We call the set of nodes X the *domain* of M. A master M maintains a signature that accurately represents its reachability; this signature is shared by all nodes in the domain of M. M is also responsible for propagating changes in the reachability of nodes in its domain to all other masters that can reach M.

All other nodes are called internal nodes. An internal node X can belong to multiple domains and keeps track of which masters (i.e. domains) it belongs to. X is responsible for notifying each of its masters when its reachability changes. We call the first domain an internal node is assigned to its *primary master*. An internal node belonging to multiple domains has multiple signatures that conservatively (but correctly) represent its reachability, so we arbitrarily choose the signature of the primary master to represent its reachability.

By introducing master and internal nodes, we essentially establish a tree of masters that is smaller than the original reachability graph and only maintain precise reachability information for masters. This decreases the cost of the reverse breadth first search required to monitor reachability. Under this implementation, the **getSignature** function of a memory object just returns the signature of its primary master. We are currently investigating more efficient methods for maintaining dynamic reachability information, but algorithm 1 provides our current implementation of dynamic reachability analysis, including how masters are created. In this algorithm, the list `Node.owningMasters` are the masters to whose domain `Node` belongs. `Master.notifyMasters` is the list of masters that the `Master` must notify on when its reachability changes, because these masters can reach the nodes in Master's reachability. Note that our algorithm also performs cycle detection in the reachability graph, but we omit the pseudo-code due to space limitations.

2.6.4 Implementation of Dynamic Refinement

The goal of dynamic refinement is to remove unnecessary implicit dependencies created by static analysis. To this end, the dynamic refinement process determines which memory objects the task may *actually* access by using the reachability of the referenced symbols and retrieving the corresponding signatures. The implementation of generating signatures for tasks during refinement is shown in algorithm 2.

Our algorithm is only concerned with the reachability of global symbols or received symbols (those that were received as an argument) (see line 4). Symbols that are local to the task are not of concern since they are invisible outside of task boundaries, unless they alias global or received symbols. Our implementation of static analysis keeps track of aliasing, so the potential shared accesses of local symbols would be represented as the reachability of the corresponding global or received objects.

Note that the signature generated by our algorithm is guaranteed to represent all possible memory accesses that a task will make during execution, even if the task performs link assignment, i.e. changes the reachability of a memory object. This is because we account for the reachability of *all* memory objects a task can access, and link assignment just changes the reachability of one memory object to include the reachability of another memory object, and thus does not change the cumulative reachability of all the memory objects in the task.

Each task in SvS has a **makeSignature** function that implements algorithm 2; the code for **makeSignature** is generated by the translator using symbols collected during static analysis. As link assignments occur during program execution, dynamic reachability analysis maintains signatures representing reachability (possible memory accesses) of memory objects. Because **makeSignature** builds a composite signature of symbols (which reference specific memory objects at run-time), the signature returned represents a description of memory objects that a task can access at that time. Therefore, the process of refining a dependency between two tasks is basically just calling **makeSignature** for each task and comparing the resulting signatures to see if a dependency in fact exists. By performing this check, we can dynamically re-calculate dependencies between tasks. This process is only performed for implicit dependencies. If an explicit dependency was specified by a programmer, then this dependency will not be removed.

Also note that false positives can occur during signature comparison. Besides the false positives caused by using signatures, there are two additional causes for false positives. The first is due to the conservative assumption that a task accesses the entire reachability of a memory object. The second is due to multiple memory objects sharing the signature of a master node, as described in section 2.6.3.

While refinement is conceptually a separate component in the SvS framework, its implementation is integrated with scheduling, as described in the next section.

Algorithm 1: Link Assignment

```
Input: A link lhs with parent memory object A, and a link
       rhs whose child is B
Output: New edge (A, B)
begin
    if A.owningMasters = ∅ then
        /* A is its own master                         */
        A.owningMasterList.add( A )
        A.domainSize = 0
    end
    if (A.primaryMaster.domainSize < K) or
    not(B.owningMasters = ∅) then
        if B.owningMasters = ∅ then
            A.primaryMaster.domainSize++
        end
        foreach a ∈ A.owningMasters do
            foreach b ∈ B.owningMasters do
                b.notifyMasters.add( a )
            end
            a.updateReachability( getSignature(B) )
        end
    else
        B.owningMasters.add( B )
        foreach a ∈ A.owningMasters do
            B.notifyMasters.add( a )
        end
    end
end
```

Algorithm 2: run-time calculation of a signature to represent all possible memory accesses that a task will make

```
  Input: Task T
  Output: Signature S
1 begin
2     Let L_T = symbols(T)
3     foreach symbol ∈ L_T do
4         if symbol is not local then
5             S += getSignature(symbol)
6         end
7     end
8     return S
9 end
```

2.7 Scheduling Tasks

The key job of the task scheduler is to efficiently dispatch tasks with non-overlapping signatures to be executed concurrently. This effectively insures that each task's set of refined dependencies are respected.

Note that up to this point, we have discussed the process of refinement as comparing signatures between tasks in order to potentially remove dependencies. However, in cases where static analysis generates "many" dependencies (which is currently the case in our system), then performing pair-wise comparisons between tasks for each dependency as described in section 2.6.4 may not be very efficient. As mentioned in section 2.5, our current static analysis is extremely conservative and essentially ends up placing a dependency between each pair of tasks/task instances. In this case, refinement would be faced with approximately $\binom{T}{2}$ comparisons where T is the number of task *instances*, which can be large when dealing with data-parallel tasks. Therefore, instead of removing static dependencies, the scheduler essentially ignores this information and uses tasks' signatures (algorithm 2) to efficiently determine which task instances can be executed together concurrently. This is particularly useful for data-parallel tasks in general; data-parallel task instances are generated dynamically, making it difficult for static analysis to generate "meaningful" or "efficient" dependencies (e.g. if the operation is not obviously embarrassingly parallel, static analysis may just end up serializing all potential instances of the data-parallel task). In future work, we intend to incorporate dependency information in order to reduce the number of dynamic checks required to perform dynamic refinement and scheduling of tasks.

We designed and implemented two scheduling algorithms, which we present next. Due to space constraints we omit the pseudo-code for these algorithms and provide only textual descriptions.

2.7.1 Generations

The goal of generations scheduling is to create groups of task-instances such that no two instances have overlapping signatures; we call these groups generations. A single thread is elected to build generations. This thread tries to add a task to a generation in $delayList$, where each generation has a signature representing all tasks currently in the generation. A task can be added to a generation if the task's signature does not overlap with the generation's signature. If a task cannot be added to any of the generations in $delayList$, a generation from $delayList$ is released for processing and a new generation is added to $delayList$. The task is then added to this new generation and the signature of the new generation is initialized. Worker threads concurrently process tasks in a generation and ensure that tasks from different generations are never run concurrently by waiting for all threads to complete before advancing to the next generation in $scheduleList$.

2.7.2 Progressive

Progressive scheduling, attempts to execute tasks/task-instances as soon as possible, without violating dependencies. To do this, we maintain a signature, $workingSig$, that represents all tasks/task-instances currently running. For each task, a signature is created ($currentSig$) and we atomically compare $currentSig$ to $workingSig$, and if there is no conflict (i.e. no overlap between signatures), we atomically update $workingSig$ to include $currentSig$. If there is a conflict, $workingSig$ is not updated and the task is put back onto the queue for later execution. Otherwise, no dependencies exist between the current task and any tasks being executed, so the current task can be dispatched.

Because it is not possible to "subtract" from signatures when a task is completed, $workingSig$ will eventually become stale. This does not affect correctness, but it can affect performance in the form of false positives. To address this issue, we also keep track of the total number of signature updates and consecutive conflicts. If either of these values reach a threshold, we wait for all worker threads to finish executing tasks and then reset $workingSig$ and all flags.

2.8 Ensuring Correctness

It is important to underscore that SvS always generates a correct parallelization of the code written in CDML. The first step of this is the static task dependency analysis of the code, which builds a task graph that may contain unnecessary dependencies, but guarantees that shared memory accesses are protected. At run-time, SvS will dynamically recalculate dependencies and schedule tasks to prevent conflicting memory accesses between task-instances at run-time, enabling a greater degree of parallelism while still ensuring correctness.

3. Evaluation

Video games are a collection of tightly integrated systems (rendering, gameplay, physics, simulation, AI, animation, audio, user input, networking, GUI, etc) [1] that operate in concert on a rapid and repetitive timeline. Given the significant amount of code involved in a full game engine, studying one in its entirety is a difficult proposition. The complexity of commercial game engines and their attendant tool chains and development environments means that even building the project can be a daunting task. Thus converting an engine from the traditional sequential model into a modern task-based model is almost insurmountable and is not often attempted, not even in industry where it is usually preferable to instead re-implement from the ground up. So it necessary to isolate a particular facet or subset of features in order to study the effects of a particular technique. Therefore, we evaluate SvS using a collection of existing benchmarks and real applications.

We present two game based experiments. Firstly, Cal3D [2] is a third-party open-source skeletal animation engine used in several video games. Chosen because it has a relatively compact and clean code base, Cal3d represents typical computations performed in modern game engines. Secondly, QuakeSquad, our own video game benchmark, focuses on spatial partitioning, entity management, AI and managing numerous agents.

While not strictly game related, we also present three benchmarks from the PARSEC suite [10]: Canneal, Fluidanimate and Blackscholes. We chose these because PARSEC is a well known and respected benchmark suite and will help put our results in context.

To provide an evaluation of the primary parameters and costs associated with SvS, we developed micro-benchmarks and several experiments which are presented in the next section.

All SvS tests were written in CDML and executed using the Generational scheduling algorithm which our initial testing shows performs slightly better than Progressive. Further optimization of these algorithms is future work. For the sake of comparison we also parallelized Cal3D and QuakeSquad using Intel TBB 3.0 [6] and software transactional memory (STM) using the Dresden TM Compiler [14] and TinySTM++ library. In each case we found that the encounter time locking (ETL) algorithm performed the best for STM. The PARSEC benchmarks we used were available already parallelized with pthreads and in some cases TBB. Our experiments were run on a machine with two Intel Xeon E5405 chips with four cores each. Each two cores share a 6MB L2 cache for a total of 12MB per chip.

3.1 SvS Overhead

In this section, we provide an evaluation of the primary parameters and costs associated with SvS. SvS has two main run-time costs: false positives and the absolute cost of performing dynamic reachability analysis during link assignment. The key parameters governing these associated costs are signature and master domain sizes. In the following sections, we break down our analysis into two categories: signatures and dynamic reachability analysis.

3.1.1 Signatures

As mentioned in section 2.6.2, false positives can occur during signature comparison, potentially limiting parallelism. We define parallel width to be the number of tasks that are able to execute concurrently at a given time. In the the simplest case where a task accesses a single memory object, using signatures limits the theoretical maximum parallel width to the size (in bits) of the signature.

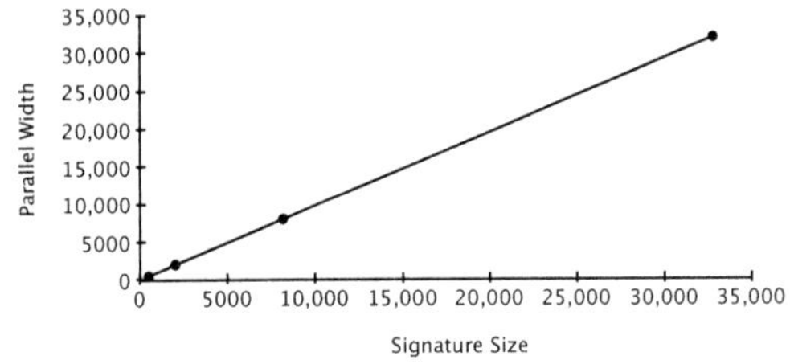

Figure 5. Parallel width for 128,000 task-instances under varying signature sizes

To demonstrate how signature size affects parallel width, we have designed an experiment consisting of a single producer task that sends unique memory objects to a data-parallel consumer task. The consumer task simply writes to a field of a received object. Note that the objects sent by the producer are single memory objects with no links as members (i.e. its reachability is static). Therefore, when an object is queried for its reachability, it just returns a signature representing its static reachability: a signature with a single bit set by hashing the id of the memory object. This means that there will be no false positives due to master nodes or conservative assumptions during refinement. Therefore, since all objects are unique, any detected conflicts are strictly due to false positives caused by signature size.

Figure 5 provides the average parallel width (y-axis) for varying signature sizes (x-axis) when the producer sends 128,000 objects. (This number was chosen to reflect the number of particles involved in modern fluid dynamics simulations). Note that because we use the generations algorithm, the parallel width at any given time is the size of the currently executing generation. Therefore to measure parallel width, we just record the sizes of each generation. The average parallel width was calculated over 100 executions of the producer and consumer.

Note that for all signature sizes, we (approximately) achieve the theoretical maximum parallel width and therefore the graph shows a linear increase in parallel width as signature size increases. This demonstrates that when conflicts occur, the generations algorithm is often successful in finding a generation in $delayList$ with a signature that does not conflict with the current object.

It is also important to note that the computational cost of increasing signature size is negligible. We have experimentally determined the cost of setting a bit to be about 10 cycles, and the cost of checking overlap on a 64-bit machine to be about $\frac{n}{64} * 10$ cycles, where n is the number of bits in the signature. This cost is further minimized by the fact that some signature operations can happen concurrently with executing tasks. Finally, the bitwise operations used when comparing/calculating signatures are prime candidates for vectorization.

Because parallel width increases linearly with signature size and the computational cost of increasing signatures is small, the overall cost of using signatures does not have a significant impact on the performance of SvS.

3.1.2 Dynamic Reachability Analysis

Dynamic reachability analysis has two primary costs associated with it that contribute to the overhead of SvS. The first cost is the absolute cost of performing dynamic reachability analysis, i.e. performing a link assignment. The second cost is false positives that occur due to memory objects in a domain sharing the same reachability signature: the signature of the master node representing that domain. Any false positives will in turn affect parallel width.

In general, absolute cost and parallel width are affected by the size (number of memory objects and links) and *shape* (i.e. layout/connectivity) of reachability graphs. In the case of absolute cost, larger reachability graphs potentially (although not necessarily) lead to more expensive reverse breadth first searches during link assignment. Also, since memory objects share the signature of a master and the reachability of a master is greater than the reachability of its successors, the larger the graph, the larger the potential for false positives due to sharing master-node signatures. The effective size of reachability graphs is regulated by the size of a master node's domain: the larger the domain, the fewer the master nodes in a reachability graph.

The following experiments demonstrate how absolute cost and parallel width are affected by the size of a reachability graph and the size of master domains. Because dynamic reachability analysis is also affected by the shape of reachability graphs, it is important to give consideration to the data-structures that we used for these experiments. The micro-benchmark that we implemented builds a binary space partitioning (BSP) tree of depth d. BSP trees are commonly used data-structures in computer graphics algorithms and are generated by continuously bisecting a space and creating nodes to represent each resulting bisection. It is also common for the leafs of a BSP tree to store pointers to all the objects (e.g. game entities or polygons) that are located in the space represented by each leaf. Therefore each leaf also contains a linked list of objects (in our case game entities). If the spaces represented by leafs are small enough, each leaf will likely point to one or zero objects. The entities pointed to by leafs are also stored in a global linked list and each entity contains a list of "items".

To simulate the assignment of entities to partitions represented by the leafs of a BSP tree, the producer sends out $(leaf, entity)$ pairs and the consumer performs the associated link assignment, along with synthetic work. The $(leaf, entity)$ pairs sent by the producer ensure that each entity is assigned to a unique leaf. In this case, no synchronization is actually required to protect the assignment of the entity to the leaf.

Using this micro-benchmark, we perform three experiments, which respectively demonstrate how absolute cost, parallel width, and overall overhead varies as the number of memory objects, and the size of domains change. In all experiments, we demonstrate results for approximately 20,000 ($d = 10$, $entities = 1000$) and 40,000 ($d = 11$, $entities = 2000$) total memory objects.

Absolute Cost For absolute cost, we measured the time it takes a consumer to perform a link assignment under varying domain sizes. The results are shown in figure 6, with the cost in microseconds on the y-axis and domain sizes (maximum number of objects per domain) on the x-axis. Figure 6 demonstrates that as domain sizes increase, the cost decreases from about 7.8-4.7μs and 8.5-4.9μs for 20,000 and 40,000 objects respectively. There is also a slight overall increase (4%-7%) in cost going from 20,000 objects to 40,000 objects. Therefore, domain size appears to have a more significant affect on cost than the size of reachability graphs.

Note that it is important to put the absolute cost of dynamic reachability analysis into perspective. For example, acquiring a mutex lock (that does not actually protect any code) can take anywhere from a hundred cycles to as much as 20 microseconds, depending on the level of contention. The cost of dynamic reachability analysis (and SvS in general) is not affected by the amount of contention/sharing in an application. Also, although way are paying a cost during link assignment, SvS does not pay the cost of conflict resolution paid by other techniques such as TM. In the following sections we demonstrate, with real applications, that the benefits produced by SvS are outweighed by its costs.

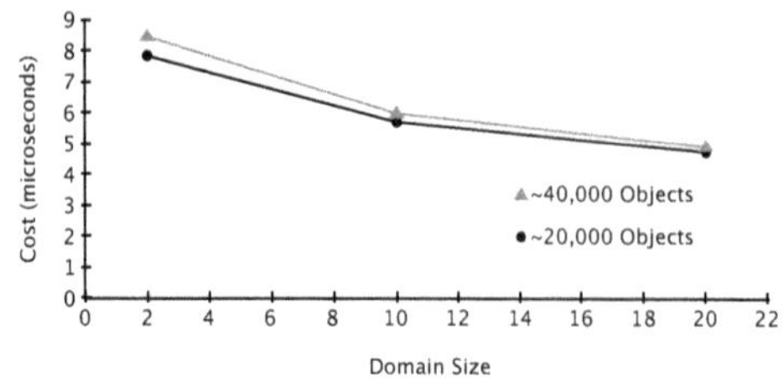

Figure 6. Cost of link assignment under varying domain and reachability graph sizes

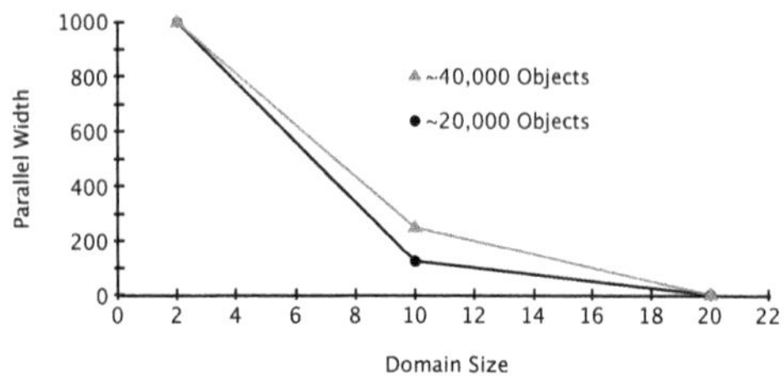

Figure 7. Parallel width under varying domain and reachability graph sizes

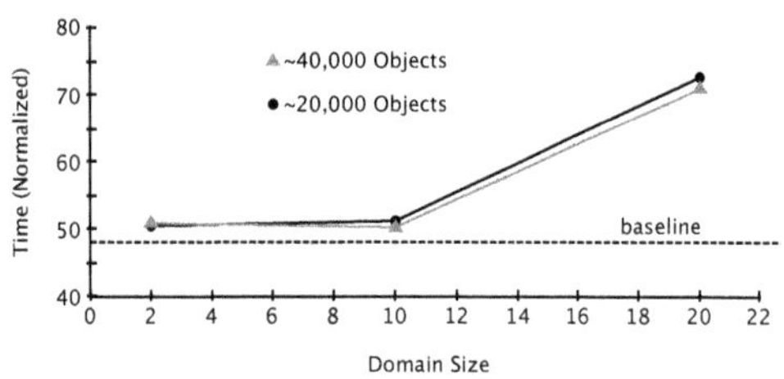

Figure 8. Overall run-time overhead (normalized) of the consumer for varying domain and reachability graph sizes

Parallel Width Figure 7 demonstrates the change in parallel width (y-axis) as we increase domain sizes (x-axis). We used a signature size of 8192 and measured the parallel width as described in section 3.1.1. Here we see that parallel width is dramatically affected by the size of master domains. As master domains increase, more memory objects share the same signature and master nodes decrease. As the number of master nodes decrease, their respective reachability increases, thus increasing the chances of conflict between the reachability of master nodes. This accounts for the dramatic decreases in parallel width demonstrated by both curves in figure 7. As in the previous section, the size of the reachability graph does not appear to have a significant affect on parallel width.

Overall Overhead For this experiment, we again used a signature size of 8192. Also, because no sharing actually occurs, we can compare the run-times of our system with SvS enabled and disabled in order to get a worst case scenario overhead for SvS. This overhead not only includes the cost of false positives and link assignment, but also any costs associated with refinement and scheduling, thus providing an overall worst-case cost of dynamic analysis performed at run-time.

Figure 8 demonstrates the overall run-time (y-axis, normalized to the number of $(leaf, entity)$ pairs sent by the producer) for different domain sizes (x-axis). We see that there is essentially no change between domain sizes 2 and 10, since the decrease in absolute cost is negated by the decrease in parallelism when domain sizes increase. After a domain size of 10, we see a sharp increase due to the sharp decrease in parallelism that figure 7 demonstrated. The dotted-line labeled "baseline" is the run-time of the benchmark when SvS is disabled. This means that the overall overhead of SvS, for a domain size of 2, is about 5% for 20,000 objects and about 6% for 40,000 objects.

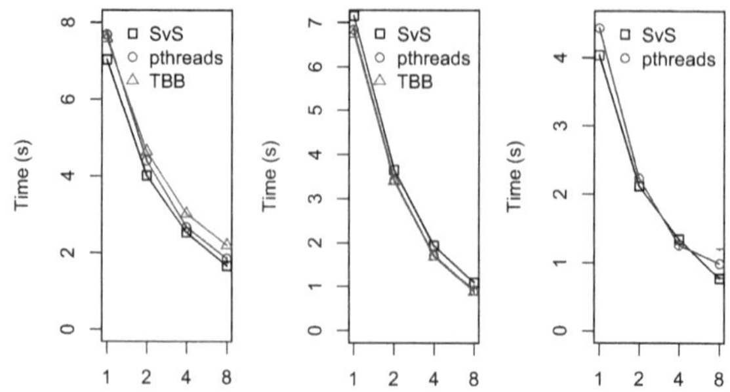

(a) Fluidanimate (b) Blackscholes (c) Canneal

Figure 9. Performance and scalability of the PARSEC benchmarks.

3.1.3 Discussion

One crucial characteristic of SvS is that its overhead is not dependent on the amount of sharing in the system. Rather, it depends on a few internal parameters and, more predominantly, the size and shape of data-structures and their resulting reachability graphs. This is fundamentally different from existing techniques where performance decreases as the amount of sharing increases (e.g. contention over shared locks, cost of transaction aborts). This is not the case for SvS. In fact, since SvS knows the memory accesses of tasks before they execute, in can mitigate sharing conflicts by grouping together non-conflicting tasks. This is what generations accomplishes by using look-ahead. This is an important distinction between SvS and existing techniques. We demonstrate in the next sections that this distinction leads to SvS being able to perform as well as, or better than several existing techniques, with the added benefit that it performs shared state protection *automatically*.

3.2 PARSEC

PARSEC is a parallel benchmark suite designed to represent state-of-the-art parallel workloads [10]. While the majority of these benchmarks do not need SvS, we converted Fluidanimate and Canneal which do have shared state conflicts. We also converted Blackscholes, which has no conflicts, in order to show the performance of SvS even when not required.

Blackscholes is a benchmark from the financial domain which calculates prices for stock options. Option prices can be calculated independently from one another and the results are stored in an array. SvS is used to protect the array from having the same array slot written to simultaneously.

Fluidanimate, as the name implies, performs simulation of fluid. The existing parallel implementation divides the 3D space of fluid cells into partitions. During an update, a cell only needs to modify the values of adjacent cells. Therefore the internal nodes of a partition can be processed without any synchronization. Cells on a common border, ghost cells, require locking before being modified. In the SvS implementation, ghost cells are protected from race conditions automatically. For the SvS version we used the number of partitions that is much larger than the number of cores and SvS is then able to process partitions that do not share ghost cells in parallel.

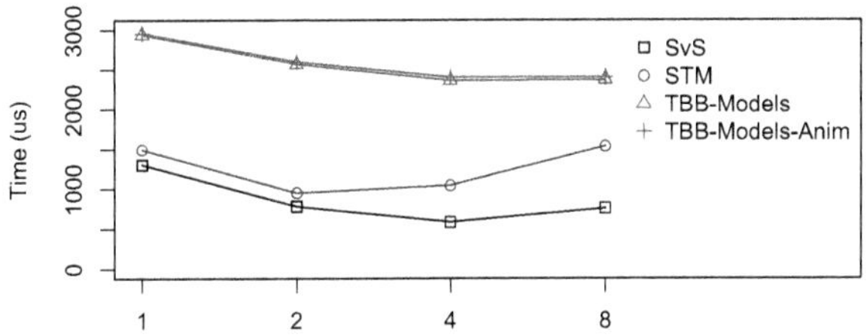

Figure 10. Scalability comparison between SvS, TBB and STM implementations of character animation.

The Canneal benchmark is a place-and-route simulation that uses simulated annealing to minimize the routing cost on the chip. The algorithm iteratively finds a better routing by picking two elements at random and then swapping them if this is determined to be beneficial. The third-party TBB implementation for this benchmark was not available. The pthread implementation uses a construct called an *atomic pointer* in order to swap two elements, relying on compare-and-swap (CAS) operations to ensure atomicity. The implementation purposefully allows for data races to occur [10]. However, the algorithm is designed to recover from those race conditions. We replace the use of atomic pointers with SvS in order to provide a safe way of swapping the elements in parallel. To accomplish this SvS applied to pairs of elements is used to automatically determine which swaps can safely execute.

We report runtimes calculated over an average of five runs using the *simlarge* dataset. Times reported for Canneal and Blackscholes are from the parallel section of the code. Fluidanimate has parallel sections throughout and so the total execution time is reported. Standard error was negligible in all cases except the Canneal pthread version with eight threads where it was 22%, which we believe to be caused by unpredictable latency of CAS's.

In Figure 9 we show the performance with different number of threads for SvS and the third-party pthreads and TBB implementations. In the pthreads and TBB implementation fine-grained mutexes are used to provide synchronization unless otherwise noted earlier. The results demonstrate that SvS is able to match performance of the pthreads[1] and TBB even though it does not require the programmer to explicitly protect access to shared state. This suggests that SvS may accomplish similar performance as other models with less programming effort although user studies would be needed to confirm this statement.

3.3 Cal3D

The Cal3D library implements a typical character animation algorithm. Shown in Figure 11, the algorithm iterates through all character models, blending several animations on each. Animations are blended by iterating through a model's bones and modifying a bone's position and rotation according to the current state of the animation. Animations typically modify some bones of a model, but not all of them. For example, an animation of a running motion updates the positions and rotations of bones of the legs and the arms, but not the chest bones. A waving animation updates the bones of one arm.

In order to correctly parallelize animation, two animations must not update the same bone concurrently. Different models do not share bones, so the iterations of the first loop in Figure 11 can run in parallel. However, because different animations may touch

[1] SvS performs *better* than pthreads in Canneal, because the pthreads implementation of Canneal is limited by the heavy use of CAS's. SvS avoids this bottleneck by only allowing the elements that can be swapped safely without synchronization to be processed in parallel.

```
foreach(model in modelList){
  foreach(animation in model.animList){
    animation->calculateBonePositions(timeDelta);
    foreach(bone in animation.bones){
      skeleton.bones[bone.ID].blend(bone)
    }
  }
}
```

Figure 11. The character animation algorithm using a conventional loop notation.

the same bone, the second loop cannot be parallelized without protecting against concurrent accesses. Thus, there are four ways to parallelize character animation: restrict parallelism to models, or process models and animations in parallel and protect accesses to bones with locks, transactional memory or SvS.

Figure 10 compares performance and scalability of four parallel implementations of the main animation loop in Cal3D. To drive the loop we use the Cally animation example included in the Cal3D distribution, and we use 4 models and 8 animations per model. These numbers reveal several interesting facts.

TBB-Models processes models in parallel, and since we are processing 4 models, reaches maximum performance at 4 threads. TBB-ModelsAnims parallelizes processing models and animations, protecting accesses to bones with locks. Despite extra parallelism, TBB-ModelsAnims performs similarly to TBB-Models due to high lock contention over shared bones.

For the STM version, we used our parallel runtime system to create a transactional task for each model, animation and bone combination. We present the best performing STM algorithm. Since each transaction is a guaranteed write, it seems that STM performance suffers due to a high conflict rate between transactions writing to the same bone.

To use SvS, we created tasks as in STM, but each task is scheduled using SvS. SvS achieves better performance than other implementations due to the greater parallelism uncovered. Despite many potential conflicts, demonstrated in TBB and STM, the large number of runnable items available to be scheduled allows SvS to achieve good parallelism and performance.

Performance for SvS and STM stops improving when we have more than four threads. The reason has nothing to do with the method of synchronization, but is rooted in the very fine-granular nature of tasks in this example. Each task only takes 3500 cycles to complete, and the overhead of work-stealing dominates the computation. We found that if we implement a semi-static version of the scheduling algorithm that places tasks into thread-local queues and restricts work-stealing we are able to achieve scaling beyond four threads and improve performance in the eight-threaded case by more than a factor of three (these results are not shown).

This suggests an important direction for future research: investigation of semi-static scheduling techniques (in contrast to traditional work-stealing) in order to accomplish good performance for systems with very fine-granular parallelism, or automatically determining the right task granularity in order to minimize the overhead of handling fine-grained tasks. Although there are hardware proposals aiming to reduce the overhead of task scheduling [24], we believe that maximum efficiency can be obtained when software is also structured to avoid the overhead.

3.4 QuakeSquad

Artificial Intelligence (AI), determining the actions of game entities, and Entity Management, managing the movements and interactions of game objects, together make up one common game subsystem and are notoriously difficult to parallelize [5]. This difficulty has two main sources. First, AI logic tends to be arbitrary and complex being defined by game programmers to fit the circumstances instead of fitting some mathematical formalism. Secondly, the large number of interactions involved in Entity Management mean that several modifications may be made to a single object in one frame. These interactions can often set off chains of interactions that cluster in unforeseen ways. These two complicating factors, and the large amount of shared state that can potentially affected, make this system a primary concern for parallelization.

We took the approach of Lupei et al [18] with their SynQuake benchmark and created an application, QuakeSquad, that captures the essential computational patterns and data structures of video games while remaining simple enough for meaningful testing.

QuakeSquad, consists of a two dimensional world with four types of entities: bombs, walls, citizens and techs. These are governed by a few simple rules:

- bombs explode reducing the health of citizens and techs within a set radius and not obstructed by a wall.
- bombs 'project' fear onto citizens and technicians who are within a set distance and in the line of sight of the bomb.
- fearful citizens will move away from the closest source of fear while a calm citizen will move randomly.
- calm citizens will not move into an area where it would be subject to fear.
- techs will move toward the closet source of fear and if the tech touches a bomb it is disarmed.

With a large number of entities in the system, the 'line-of-sight' tests for occlusion are by far the most expensive. Without further optimization each test would have to consider every entity in the world. To reduce these tests, the world is divided into a grid where each cell is associated with an unordered list of every entity in that area. When an entity moves from one cell to another it will remove itself from its current list and add itself to the new one. The cell size is set such that when making a line-of-sight calculation only the current cell and adjacent cells need be considered. This division of entities, analogous to the spatial partitioning structures used in 3D environments, reduces the number of tests by at least two orders of magnitude. However, even with this optimization, occlusion testing still dominates the computation and so would benefit most from parallelization. These tests occur most frequently when citizens move and when bombs project fear onto citizens and technicians. The same tests also occur when a bomb explodes, but bombs explode infrequently and so we focus on parallelizaton of citizen movement and fear projection.

When these aspects are transformed into data parallel operations where entities are concurrently updated, potential shared state conflicts are exposed. During bomb updates it is common for bomb radii to overlap and they may modify the same entity simultaneously. During citizen movement a large number of citizens cross grid boundaries and thus expose the associated entity lists to potential concurrent modifications. In both cases SvS can be used to ensure that no race conditions occur, which we detail below. We perform each test with 35 bombs, 100 citizens, 40 techs and 120 walls. 2048 bit signatures are used for SvS.

3.4.1 Sending lists (Updating Bombs)

First, we focus on updating the bomb entities and determining which human entities are affected. The runtime of this operation is completely dominated by line-of-sight checks. First a task determines the entities in each bomb's radius and builds temporary linked lists of potential techs and citizens to scare. These lists of potential candidates are then sent to a data-parallel consumer which perform line-of-sight testing. If an entity is not occluded, the entity become fearful. The reachability of the underlying list is queried to

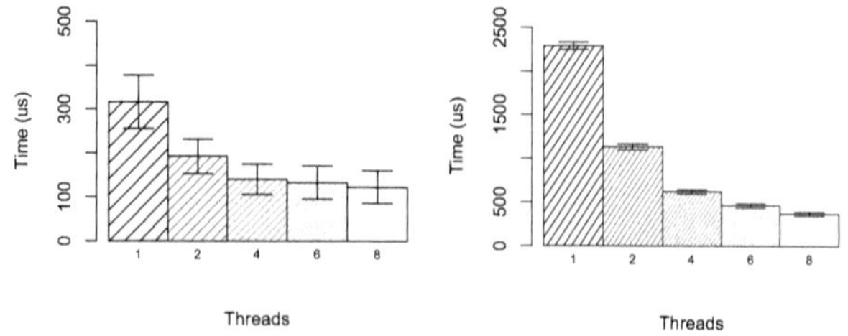

(a) Bomb Update (b) Citizen Movement

Figure 12. Scalability of the two QuakeSquad phases.

return a signature representing its contents, which is passed to the scheduler. Figure 12(a) shows the execution times averaged over 100 frames. With one thread, the processing takes 1944 μs. At 8 threads the execution time drops to 675 μs. The standard deviation in all cases is bellow 100 μs

3.4.2 Modifying lists (Updating Citizens)

When a citizen moves, it will avoid moving into areas with bombs. This update is also dominated by line of sight checks. A producer task determines the potential new location for each citizen and then sends this to a data-parallel consumer which will perform a line of sight check and move the entity if no bomb is visible. This case is complicated by the grid of entity lists. When an entity moves from one grid to another, a reference is removed from one list and added to another. If two entities move into the same grid simultaneously the linked lists will be subject to concurrent modification. Additionally, the line of sight checks require reading the eight adjacent cells around current location cell and the eight cells adjacent to the prospective destination. Errors will occur if the structure of one of these lists is modified while it is being read. We use SvS to prevent these potential state access conflicts. Again, the reachability of the list queried to produce a signature for the scheduler. Figure 12(b) shows the execution times of this phase averaged over 100 frames. Executions times go from 4617 μs with one thread to 866 μs with eight. The standard deviation in all cases is bellow 90 μs.

3.4.3 Putting it together

The previous discussion has shown that both of these major tasks scale well in isolation. We now consider results for entire frames of QuakeSquad, which combines modifying lists and sending lists. For comparison we created a version using TBB with mutexes and another using STM. The results, averaged over 100 frames, are shown in figure 13. Scaling from one to eight threads in the SvS version reduces the frame execution time from 7633 μs to 1442 μs. Shared state accesses conflict approximately 10% of the time on average, meaning SvS detects and manages a conflict 1 in every 10 accesses. While the TBB version performs similarly to the SvS version, the STM version fails to benefit from extra threads. A closer examination showed that roll-backs were causing the data-parallel instances to lengthen and increase total runtime.

QuakeSquad is a comprehensive example representing a previously difficult to parallelize subsystem of modern game engines. The performance and scalability achieved by SvS in the results demonstrate its ability to utilize reachability graphs and dynamic reachability analysis to efficiently determine the reads/writes of tasks that access linked data structures and subsequently concurrently schedule tasks with non-overlapping read/write sets.

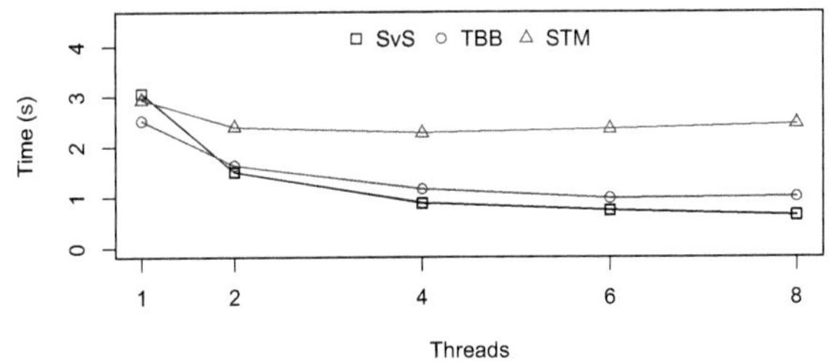

Figure 13. Scalability comparison between SvS, TBB and STM versions of QuakeSquad.

4. Related Work

SvS was previously introduced by us in a short workshop paper, which gave only a high-level overview of the idea, but the system was not fully specified or implemented at that time. This paper contains the first, self-contained, presentation of the model and implementation of SvS as well as detailed specification of algorithms, and evaluation with multiple benchmarks.

There is a great need in the video game industry for domain appropriate parallelization techniques. Developers for major games studios such as EA [1], Epic [5] and Valve [26] have expressed the need for comprehensive and efficient parallelism and have cited shared state management as a major roadblock.

There are an ever increasing number of parallel environments and language/runtime combinations such as Chapel [13], Cilk [12], OpenMP [4], Gossamer [23] and Intel's TBB [6] and Ct\RapidMind [3]. However, they don't provide automatic mechanisms for shared state protection, generally focusing instead on providing tools for the programmer to manually manage state. SvS or an SvS-like technique could be implemented in a number of these systems.

The Jade [22] language and the Prometheus [7] package both address shared state protection. Jade proposes a set of parallel extensions to C where a programmer denotes blocks of code as tasks and specifies their data constraints. Although Jade also schedules tasks based on their constraints there are fundamental differences. Jade is based around task-parallelism and constraints must be specified by the programmer whereas in SvS they are derived automatically, thus freeing the programmer from the need to concentrate on implicit and hard to spot data dependencies. A task's scheduling is based entirely on the information available *before* the task runs. Prometheus' Serialization Sets work similarly to Jade, but they are applied to an object-oriented language and protect from races within an object. Shared state protection using SvS is more general.

While there is a large body of existing work on static dependency analysis, OoOJava [16] represents recent work in this field that similar to SvS attempts to combine static and dynamic analysis. OoOJava abstracts collections of objects as heap region nodes and uses disjoint reachability analysis [15] to statically infer connectivity between objects. The result is a set of reachability states that are used to determine if two objects x and y are disjoint i.e. cannot reference the same heap node. If it is determined that they might reach the same heap node, in very specific cases they are able to check at run-time if $x = y$ in order to test for disjointness. Otherwise, they are forced to conservatively assume a dependency between x and y since they do not have full reachability information at compile time. SvS addresses this issue by introducing the concepts of reachability and reachability graphs and using dynamic reachability analysis to provide an efficient way to maintain and extract complete reachability information.

Many techniques that address shared state are optimistic in that they attempt to do computations without explicit synchronization and 'roll-back' or undo conflicting operations. Software transactional memory (STM) is the most prominent of these techniques and provides database-like transactional atomicity. A programmer wraps code that requires protection in an atomic block and the STM system automatically handles conflicts. The key difference between TM and SvS is that SvS determines whether or not two tasks might conflict before they are executed, whereas TM detects conflicts during execution. This means that TM is less conservative but may be subject to expensive rollbacks. Since rollback cost are high, STM performs well when most transactions are able to complete successfully. So STM may be advantageous to SvS in cases where actual conflicts between tasks are extremely rare, but SvS would serialize them to avoid potential races. This suggests an interesting opportunity for *combining* STM and SvS: using STM when actual conflicts are rare and using SvS when the conflicts are frequent. Such adaptive use of synchronization primitives may enable to exploit the best of both models and is an interesting direction for future work.

There has also been some work in the STM community on deliberately co-scheduling transactions that appear (based on static or dynamic information) to be unlikely to conflict with one another [27]. However, this work uses the history of previous conflicts, and perform co-scheduling for performance. SvS performs scheduling for correctness. SvS also relies on static and dynamic analysis to determine the potential memory accesses of a task before it executes, rather than conflict history recorded after the fact.

Galois [17] is an optimistic framework, focusing on data-parallelism, that falls outside of STM. Galois focuses on the parallelization of 'irregular applications', those with interdependent loop iterations. This framework differs from SvS in that it focusses on commutativity analysis as opposed to dependency analysis and is optimistic and must contend with overhead created by roll-backs.

5. Conclusion and Future Work

We presented SvS – a new framework for automatic protection of shared state in task graph models. We demonstrated that SvS performs comparably to other synchronization techniques, without requiring the programmer to explicitly manage shared state.

While this work demonstrates the feasibility of SvS, there are many opportunities for further research. First of all, there is an opportunity to incorporate more powerful static analysis, including disjoint reachability analysis [15]. In doing so, we may be able to extract greater parallelism statically, which will reduce the complexity and overhead of the algorithms that we use at runtime. Second, as we discovered in the character animation example, there are opportunities for investigating better software techniques for handling fine-grained tasks, including scheduling and determining the optimal task size. Finally, we are interested in expanding the scope of SvS codebase and performing user studies in order to fully understand the impact of SvS on programmer productivity.

References

[1] Parallel futures of a game engine `http://publications.dice.se/attachments/Sthlm10_ParallelFutures_Final.ppt`.

[2] Cal3d character animation library `http://home.gna.org/cal3d/`.

[3] Intel ct `http://software.intel.com/en-us/data-parallel/`.

[4] The openmp specification for parallel programming `http://www.openmp.org`.

[5] The quest for more processing power:part two: Multi-core and multi-threaded gaming `http://www.anandtech.com/show/1645/3`.

[6] Thread building blocks `www.threadingbuildingblocks.org`.

[7] M. D. Allen et al. Serialization sets: a dynamic dependence-based parallel execution model. In *PPoPP '09*, pages 85–96. ACM, 2009. ISBN 978-1-60558-397-6. doi: http://doi.acm.org/10.1145/1504176.1504190.

[8] L. O. Andersen. Program analysis and specialization for the c programming language. Technical report, 1994.

[9] U. K. Banerjee. *Dependence Analysis for Supercomputing*. Kluwer Academic Publishers, Norwell, MA, USA, 1988. ISBN 0898382890.

[10] C. Bienia et al. The parsec benchmark suite: characterization and architectural implications. PACT '08, 2008.

[11] B. H. Bloom. Space/time trade-offs in hash coding with allowable errors. *Commun. ACM*, 13(7):422–426, 1970. ISSN 0001-0782. doi: http://doi.acm.org/10.1145/362686.362692.

[12] R. D. Blumofe et al. Cilk: An efficient multithreaded runtime system. In *J. of Parallel and Dist. Comp.*, pages 207–216, 1995. doi: http://citeseerx.ist.psu.edu/viewdoc/summary?doi=10.1.1.18.3175.

[13] B. L. Chamberlain et al. Parallel programmability and the chapel language. *Intl. J. of High Perf. Computing Applications*, 21:291–312, 2007.

[14] P. Felber et al. Transactifying applications using an open compiler framework. In *TRANSACT*, August 2007.

[15] J. Jenista et al. Disjointness analysis for java-like languages. *Technical Report UCI- ISR-09-1*, 2009.

[16] J. C. Jenista et al. Ooojava: An out-of-order approach to parallel programming. In *HotPar '10*, 2010.

[17] M. Kulkarni et al. Scheduling strategies for optimistic parallel execution of irregular programs. In *SPAA '08*, pages 217–228. ACM, 2008. ISBN 978-1-59593-973-9. doi: http://doi.acm.org/10.1145/1378533.1378575.

[18] D. Lupei et al. Transactional memory support for scalable and transparent parallelization of multiplayer games. EuroSys '10, 2010.

[19] M. Marron et al. Sharing analysis of arrays, collections, and recursive structures. In *PASTE '08*, pages 43–49. ACM, 2008. ISBN 978-1-60558-382-2. doi: http://doi.acm.org/10.1145/1512475.1512485.

[20] M. D. McCool. Structured parallel programming with deterministic patterns. In *Proceedings of the 2nd USENIX conference on Hot topics in parallelism*, HotPar'10, pages 5–5, Berkeley, CA, USA, 2010. USENIX Association. URL `http://portal.acm.org/citation.cfm?id=1863086.1863091`.

[21] W. Pugh et al. Constraint-based array dependence analysis. *ACM Trans. Program. Lang. Syst.*, pages 635–678, 1998. ISSN 0164-0925.

[22] M. C. Rinard and M. S. Lam. The design, implementation, and evaluation of jade. *ACM Trans. Program. Lang. Syst.*, 20(3):483–545, 1998. ISSN 0164-0925. doi: http://doi.acm.org/10.1145/291889.291893.

[23] Roback et al. Gossamer: A lightweight programming framework for multicore machines. In *HotPar '10*, 2010. URL `http://www.usenix.org/event/hotpar10/tech/full_papers/Roback.pdf`.

[24] D. Sanchez et al. Flexible architectural support for fine-grain scheduling. *SIGARCH Comput. Archit. News*, 38(1):311–322, 2010. ISSN 0163-5964. doi: http://doi.acm.org/10.1145/1735970.1736055.

[25] N. Shavit et al. Software transactional memory. In *PODC '95*, pages 204–213. ACM, 1995. ISBN 0-89791-710-3. doi: http://doi.acm.org/10.1145/224964.224987.

[26] Valve. Dragged kicking and screaming: Source multicore. In *Game Developers Conference*, 2007. URL `http://www.valvesoftware.com/publications/2007/GDC2007_SourceMulticore.pdf`.

[27] R. M. Yoo and H. S. Lee. Adaptive transaction scheduling for transactional memory systems. In *Proceedings of the twentieth annual symposium on Parallelism in algorithms and architectures*, SPAA '08, pages 169–178, New York, NY, USA, 2008. ACM. ISBN 978-1-59593-973-9. doi: http://doi.acm.org/10.1145/1378533.1378564. URL `http://doi.acm.org/10.1145/1378533.1378564`.

Author Index

www.ingramcontent.com/pod-product-compliance
Ingram Content Group UK Ltd.
Pitfield, Milton Keynes, MK11 3LW, UK
UKHW051418290926
15471UKWH00009B/1670

9 781450 306638